HANDBOOK
OF
FEDERAL INDIAN LAW

HANDBOOK
OF
FEDERAL INDIAN LAW

FELIX S. COHEN

GYAN

Published by

Gyan Publishing House
5, Ansari Road
Daryaganj, New Delhi-110002
Phone: 011-47034999, 9811692060
E-mail: books@gyanbooks.com

Distribution Network
gyanbooks.com
India, USA, Canada, UK, Australia

ISBN: 978-93-6433-033-6 (HB)

First Published, 1941

2nd Impression 2024

Printed at: Gyan Press, Delhi.

HANDBOOK OF FEDERAL INDIAN LAW
Author: FELIX S. COHEN

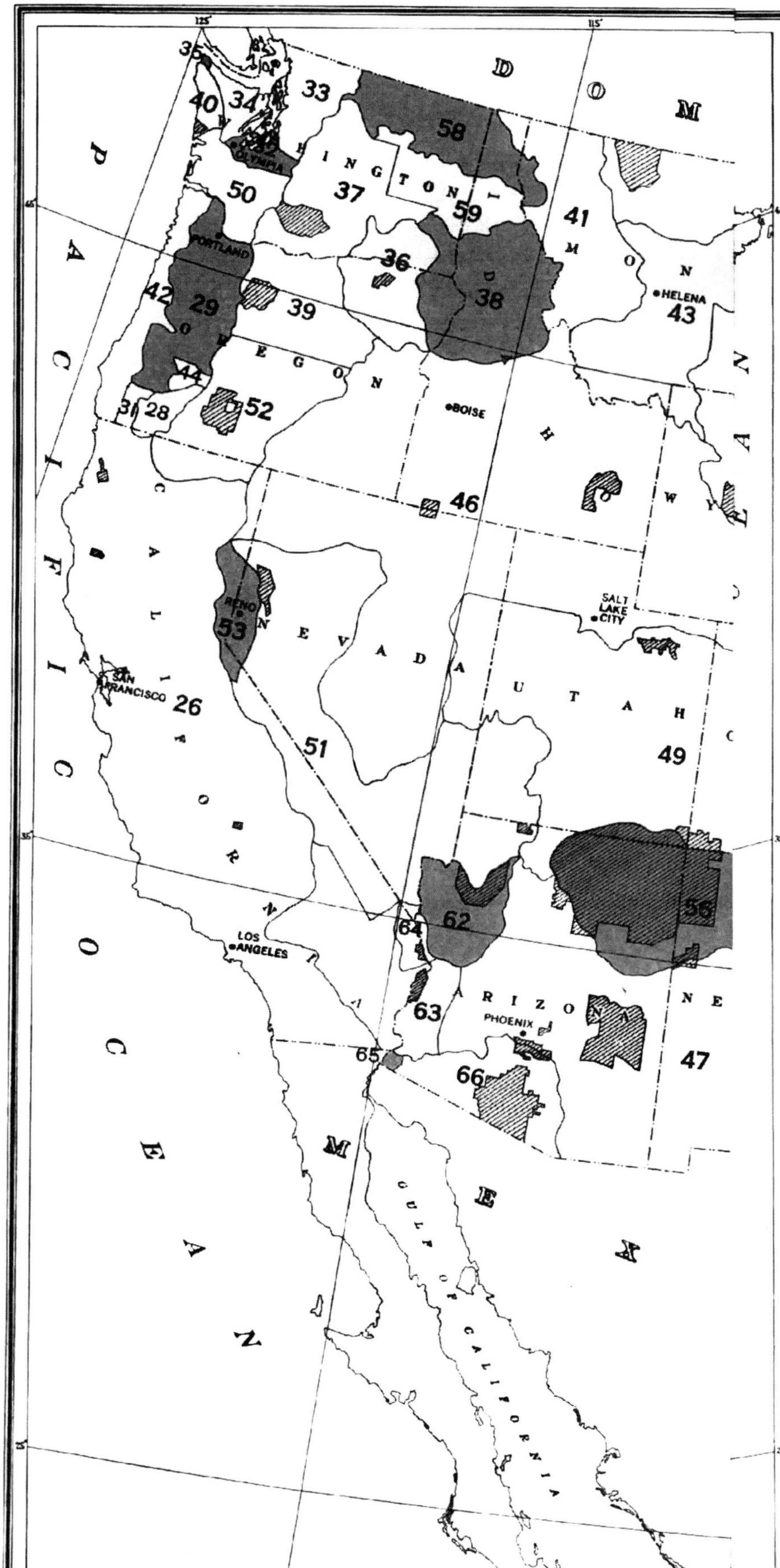

LIST OF TRIBES

1 - Iroquois
2 - Cherokee
3 - Creek
4 - Wyandotte, Delaware, Chippewa and allied tribes
5 - Choctaw and Chickasaw
6 - Kaskaskia
7 - Delaware
8 - Sac and Fox
9 - Piankeshaw
10 - Osage
11 - Ottawa, Chippewa and Potawatomie
12 - Quapaw
13 - Potawatomie
14 - Miami
15 - Chippewa
16 - Ottawa and Chippewa
17 - Seminole
18 - Kansas
19 - Winnebago
20 - Sac and Fox, Sioux, Omaha, Iowa, Otoe and Missouri
21 - Menominee
22 - Otoe and Missouri
23 - Pawnee
24 - Caddo
25 - Sioux
26 - California Indians
27 - Sioux, Cheyenne, Arapahoe, Crow, Assiniboine, Gros Ventre, Mandan and Arikara
28 - Rogue River
29 - Umpqua and Calapooia
30 - Omaha
31 - Chasta et al.
32 - Nisqually, Puyallup et al.
33 - Dwamish, Suquamish et al.
34 - Sklallam
35 - Makah
36 - Walla Walla, Cayuse, and Umatilla
37 - Yakima
38 - Nez Perce
39 - Confederated Tribes of Middle Oregon
40 - Quinaielt and Quileute
41 - Flathead et al.
42 - Coast Tribes of Oregon
43 - Blackfoot, Flathead and Nez Perce
44 - Molala
45 - Ponca
46 - Shoshone
47 - Apache
48 - Arapahoe and Cheyenne
49 - Ute
50 - Chehalis, Chinook et al
51 - Paiute
52 - Klamath et al.
53 - Washoe
54 - Comanche and Kiowa
55 - Crow
56 - Navajo
57 - Arikara, Gros Ventre and Mandan
58 - Methow, Okanagan et al
59 - Coeur d' Alene et al
60 - Gros Ventre, Blackfoot and River Crow
61 - Sioux, Northern Cheyenne and Arapahoe
62 - Walapai
63 - Yuma
64 - Mohave
65 - Cocopah
66 - Papago, Pima and Maricopa

The foregoing tribes are listed in the order in which land cessions were effected. Tribes which made no cessions to the Federal Government are not included. The principal areas reserved from cession or receded to Indian tribes and commonly referred to as Indian reservations are shown thus

UNITED STATES DEPARTMENT OF THE INTERIOR
OFFICE OF THE SOLICITOR

HANDBOOK
of
FEDERAL INDIAN LAW

WITH REFERENCE TABLES AND INDEX

By

FELIX S. COHEN
Chairman, Board of Appeals
Department of the Interior

Foreword by

HAROLD L. ICKES
Secretary of the Interior

Introduction by

NATHAN R. MARGOLD
Solicitor for the Department
of the Interior

First Printing 1941
Second Printing 1942
Third Printing 1942
Fourth Printing 1945

UNITED STATES GOVERNMENT PRINTING OFFICE
WASHINGTON : 1945

CONTENTS

FOREWORD

There are few subjects in the history and law of the United States on which public views are more dramatically and flagrantly erroneous than on the subject of Indian affairs. According to the popular view, the Indian is a vanishing race; his lands are steadily dwindling; restricted as to the hunt and denied the warpath, he has nothing to live for and nothing to contribute to our civilization; he is not entitled to the rights of citizenship; he subsists on "rations"; and he cannot sign his name without the approval of a reservation superintendent.

The facts are very different. Indians today are probably the most rapidly increasing racial group in our population; the total area of Indian lands has been increasing slowly but steadily for nearly 5 years; the Indian today is making significant and vital contributions to American art and craftsmanship, and to our knowledge and enjoyment of the resources of forests, plains, streams, and trails that were here long before white immigrants came; all native Indians today are citizens, entitled to all of the rights and bound by all of the obligations of citizenship; if some of them still have equitable interests in property which they cannot alienate, they share this disability, or advantage, with a large number of their non-Indian fellow citizens.

That Indians have legal rights is a matter of little practical consequence unless the Indians themselves and those who deal with them are aware of those rights. Such, however, is the complexity of the body of Indian law, based upon more than 4,000 treaties and statutes and upon thousands of judicial decisions and administrative rulings, rendered during a century and a half, that one can well understand the vast ignorance of the subject that prevails even in ordinarily well informed quarters. For more than a century, commissioners of Indian affairs have appealed for aid in reducing this unmanageable mass of materials to some orderly form. Yet during that period none of the attempts to compile a simple manual of the subject was carried to completion.

Ignorance of one's legal rights is always the handmaid of despotism. This Handbook of Federal Indian Law should give to Indians useful weapons in the continual struggle that every minority must wage to maintain its liberties, and at the same time it should give to those who deal with Indians, whether on behalf of the federal or state governments or as private individuals, the understanding which may prevent oppression.

It is entirely fitting that this contribution to the enlightenment of administrators and Indians should have been made under the leadership of one who has striven valiantly to free our national relations with the Indian tribes from the despotic traces of less tolerant epochs. On April 28, 1934, President Franklin D. Roosevelt, in urging the passage of the Wheeler-Howard Act, which, with its recent extensions to Oklahoma and Alaska, stands today as the most important segment of our Indian law, declared:

> The Wheeler-Howard bill embodies the basic and broad principles of the administration for a new standard of dealing between the Federal Government and its Indian wards.
>
> It is, in the main, a measure of justice that is long overdue.
>
> We can and should, without further delay, extend to the Indian the fundamental rights of political liberty and local self-government and the opportunities of education and economic assistance that they require in order to attain a wholesome American life. This is but the obligation of honor of a powerful nation toward a people living among us and dependent upon our protection.
>
> Certainly the continuance of autocratic rule, by a Federal department, over the lives of more than 200,000 citizens of this Nation is incompatible with American ideals of liberty. It also is destructive of the character and self-respect of a great race.
>
> The continued application of the allotment laws, under which Indian wards have lost more than two-thirds of their reservation lands, while the costs of Federal administration of these lands have steadily mounted, must be terminated.
>
> Indians throughout the country have been stirred to a new hope. They say they stand at the end of the old trail. Certainly, the figures of impoverishment and disease point to their impending extinction, as a race, unless basic changes in their conditions of life are effected.
>
> I do not think such changes can be devised and carried out without the active cooperation of the Indians themselves.
>
> The Wheeler-Howard bill offers the basis for such cooperation. It allows the Indian people to take an active and responsible part in the solution of their own problems.

This Handbook of Federal Indian Law will constitute, I believe, a lasting contribution towards the ideals thus enunciated.

This work cannot have the legal force of an act of Congress or the decision of a court. Whatever legal force it will have must be derived from the original authorities which have been assiduously gathered and patiently analyzed. In publishing this work the Department of the Interior does not assume responsibility for every generalization, prediction, or inference that may be found in the volume. What is implicit, however, in the fact of publication is a considered judgment that this volume will prove a valuable aid in fulfilling the obligation which Congress has laid upon the Department of the Interior to protect and safeguard the rights of our oldest national minority.

The labors which Solicitor Nathan R. Margold, Assistant Solicitor Felix S. Cohen, and their aides and collaborators have devoted to this pioneer work will be appreciated, not only by those Indians and Indian Service administrators whose needs it most directly serves, but by all of us who hold dear the civilized ideals of liberty and tolerance.

(Signed) Harold L. Ickes.

July 9, 1940.

INTRODUCTION

1. THE BACKGROUND OF FEDERAL INDIAN LAW

We in this country are slowly learning to appreciate the significance of the problem of Indian rights for the cause of democracy here in the United States and throughout the Western Hemisphere. Over the radio, a few months ago, came the words of a man who knows more than any one else in the world about Indians as human beings. His words are a better introduction to the Indian problem than I can write.

> What sort of treatment dominant groups give to subject groups—how governments treat minorities—and how big countries treat little countries: This is a subject that comes down the centuries, and never was it a more burning subject than in this year 1939—even in this month, December 1939.
>
> So the question: How has our own country treated its oldest and most persisting minority, the Indians; how has it treated them, and how is it treating them now? This is an important question. I believe that nearly all Americans realize the importance of this question. Many millions of our citizens feel an interest. curious and sympathetic and sometimes enthusiastic, in our Indian minority.
>
> What I shall describe will be a bad beginning which lasted a long time, which broke Indian hearts for generation after generation, which inflicted destructions that no future time can wholly repair. Then I shall describe how the long-lasting bad record was changed to something good; how, although the change came so late, it did not come too late; how when the change came, it still found hundreds of Indian tribes ready to respond to the opportunity which at last had been given them. I shall describe how the good change has developed across three Presidencies, so that it is not an achievement or program of a single political party. But I shall describe, too, the decisive and immense good change which has come under President Franklin D. Roosevelt and Secretary of the Interior, Harold L. Ickes.[1]

I shall not quote the main body of Commissioner Collier's speech, for that reappears, amplified and developed somewhat, in the pages that follow. I quote, again, only his final words:

> No, the task is not finished. It is only well begun. But one part of the task is finished, and it marks and makes an epoch. The repressions which crushed the Indian spirit have been lifted away. From out of an ancient and dark prison house the living Indian has burst into the light, into the living sunlight and the future. All of his age-tempered powers and his age-tried discipline are still there. He knows that the future is his; and that the century of dishonor, for him, is ended.
>
> But he needs our continuing help, and our nation's debt to him is not yet paid.
>
> The thing we have started to do, and with your help, you citizens of our country, will continue to do, is to aid the Indian work out his own destiny. We have helped him to retain and to rebuild the richness of his own national life, and in doing this we think we have enriched the national life, the national heritage and the national honor of 130,000,000 Americans. This is the way the democracy of the United States is solving the minority problem of its first Americans.
>
> Let me carry your thought beyond our own national borders. Our Indians are a tiny, though now a growing minority. But south of the Rio Grande, the Indians number not hundreds of thousands, but millions. Pure-blooded Indians are the major population in Mexico, in Guatemala, Honduras, Peru, Ecuador. There are thirty million Indians—one growing race, and one of the world's great races. And that race is marching toward power. It may be that the most dependable guarantee of the survival and triumph of real democracy in our hemisphere, south of the Rio Grande, is this advance toward power of the Indians, who from most ancient times, and now, are believers in, and practicers of local democracy.
>
> What we are doing—what with your help we shall do—to meet our own Indian minority problem has a deep significance to these 30,000,000 other Indians, and to all the countries where they are located. Here we enter within the battleground and effort-ground of our Western Hemisphere destiny. It is upon this scale of two continents, and of a democracy defended and increased through at least one-half of our globe. that world-history will view our own record with our Indian minority.

---

[1] "America's Handling of its Indigenous Indian Minority," an address by John Collier, December 4, 1939, 7 Indians at Work, No. 5, January, 1940, pp. 11, 16.

Against this background of history and of struggle and hope, the federal law governing Indian affairs may be viewed not, as it has too often been viewed, as a curious collection of anachronisms and mysteries, but rather as a revealing record in the development of our American constitutional democracy. The decline of dictatorship in the Indian country is fresh enough in our national memory so that we may perhaps profit from an analysis of weaknesses that dictatorial bluster ever seeks to conceal, and from an understanding of the ways in which the forms and forces of democracy have, in this small sector of an endless battle line, won victory.

2. THE BASIS OF FEDERAL INDIAN LAW

For more than a century, Supreme Court Justices, Attorneys General, and Commissioners of Indian Affairs have commented on the intricate complexity and peculiarity of federal Indian law. Yet until now no writer has attempted to gather into a single work these intricacies. The reason may perhaps best be appreciated by those who have attempted that task. The federal law governing Indians is a mass of statutes, treaties, and judicial and administrative rulings, that includes practically all the fields of law known to textbook writers—the law of real property, contracts, corporations, torts, domestic relations, procedure, criminal law, federal jurisdiction, constitutional law, conflict of laws, and international law. And in each of these fields the fact that Indians are involved gives the basic doctrines and concepts of the field a new quirk which sometimes carries unpredictable consequences.

To survey a field which includes, for instance, more than four thousand distinct statutory enactments, one must generalize. And generalization on the subject of Indian law is peculiarly dangerous.

For about a century the United States dealt separately with the various Indian tribes and the legal rights of the members of each tribe were fixed by treaty.[2] These treaties are for the most part still in force and of recognized validity. In them one finds reflected the very wide pre-Columbian divergencies that existed, for instance, between the great agricultural towns and confederacies of the Southeast and the loosely organized nomadic hunters of the Plains area, or between the small fish-eating, slave-owning bands of the Northwest Coast and the great constitutional democracy that was the League of the Iroquois.

When Congress in 1871 enacted a law[3] prohibiting further treaty making with the Indian tribes, the form of governmental dealing with the Indians was changed, but the essential character of those dealings was not modified. Congress continued to deal with the Indian tribes, in large measure, through "agreements," ratified by both Houses of Congress, which do not differ from treaties in legal effect. The only substantial change accomplished by the law of 1871 was that whereas Indian treaties were submitted for the ratification of the Senate alone, as the Constitution of the United States provides,[4] agreements are ratified by the action of both Houses, and thus the House of Representatives, which had long been excluded from equal participation in Indian affairs, has achieved an equal status with the Senate in that field. Apart from treaties and agreements with particular tribes, the dealings of the Federal Government with the Indians have been predominantly by way of special statutes applying to named tribes, and, most recently, by way of tribal constitutions and tribal charters, all varying very considerably among the different tribes. Until the last years of the nineteenth century there was very little general legislation applying a uniform pattern to all tribes, and what little there was usually turns out, on analysis, to be in the nature of generalization from provisions that had appeared in several treaties.

During what may be roughly defined as the allotment period—from 1887, when the General Allotment law[5] was passed, to 1933, when the process of allotment came to an end—there developed a tendency to impose upon all Indian tribes a uniform pattern of general laws and general regulations. This tendency was commonly justified in terms of administrative efficiency and economy, and to this justification there was sometimes added the thought that Indian treaties, special statutes, and regional differences were all outworn relics which had to be sacrificed in the march of national progress. The effect, however, of this policy of ignoring the special rights conferred on individual tribes by treaty and statute and ignoring the political autonomy and cultural diversity of the tribes was to cause tremendous and widespread resentment among the Indians. The Indians found Indian and white champions. Protest against mistreatment of the Indian led to many investigations. A survey was conducted by the Institute for Government Research at the request of Secretary of Interior Work. The results of this study, published in 1928 under the title: "The Problem of Indian Administration," gave direction

[2] See Chapter 3, for an analysis of these treaties.

[3] Act of March 3, 1871, 16 Stat. 544, 566, R. S. § 2079, 25 U. S. C. 71.

[4] Article II, sec. 2.

[5] Act of February 8, 1887, 24 Stat. 388, 25 U. S. C. 331 *et sec*,

for more than a decade to Indian reform. On February 1, 1928, the Senate authorized its Committee on Indian Affairs to carry out an intensive survey of the condition of the Indians in the United States.[6]

These investigations have brought to light many of the evils resulting from attempts to impose a uniform pattern of treatment upon groups with different wants, and thus have strengthened the tendency towards special consideration of the legal problems of particular tribes. The policy of superseding the old pattern of uniformity and absolutism found expression in the Wheeler-Howard (Indian Reorganization) Act. Pursuant to this law, approved on June 18, 1934,[7] more than a hundred tribes in the United States adopted their own constitutions for self-government.[8] Practically all the regulations of the Indian Service have now been made subject to modifications for particular tribes through the provisions of these tribal constitutions and tribal ordinances.

These considerations indicate that a work on federal Indian law must deal with law made for, and in large part by, diverse groups with divergent economic interests, political institutions, and levels of cultural attainment.

Anyone who has worked in the field of Indian litigation is frequently asked by otherwise well informed people whether he understands "the Indian language." There are, in fact, more than 200 different Indian languages, some of them as distinct from each other as English and Chinese. This linguistic diversity is paralleled by diversities in the conditions and legal problems of more than 200 different Indian reservations.

Common opinion pictures the original American dressed in feathers and wampum, his belt adorned with scalps, mounted on a horse, gazing after buffalo. This picture blurs over the fact that many Indians, before white contact, were farmers and fishermen who had never seen feather head-dresses, wampum, scalps, or buffalo, that no Indian ever rode a horse before the Spaniards brought horses into North America, and that the special combination of striking Indian peculiarities which the modern "circus Indian" embodies did not exist before the rise of modern American showmanship.

Just as the popular picture of the Indian embodies a false juxtaposition of traits, so the popular view of Indian law embodies a false juxtaposition of ideas.

The popular view of the Indian's legal status proceeds from the assumption that the Indian is a ward of the Government, and not a citizen, that therefore he cannot make contracts without Indian Bureau approval, that he holds land in common under "Indian title," that he is entitled to education in federal schools when he is young, to rations when he is hungry, and to the rights of American citizenship when he abandons his tribal relations.

This is, on the whole, a thoroughly false picture, although historical exemplification may be found for each feature.

It would be absurd to set up in place of this false and oversimplified picture of federal Indian law any other equally simple picture. It may be worth while, however, to set forth certain hypotheses concerning the recurrent patterns of federal Indian law, which will be tested against decisions, statutes, and treaties in the pages that follow. These hypotheses may be conveniently grouped under four leading principles: (1) The principle of the political equality of races; (2) the principle of tribal self-government; (3) the principle of federal sovereignty in Indian affairs; and (4) the principle of governmental protection of Indians.

---

[6] Whereas there are two hundred and twenty-five thousand Indians presently under the control of the Bureau of Indian Affairs, who are, in contemplation of law, citizens of the United States but who are in fact treated as wards of the Government and are prevented from the enjoyment of the free and independent use of property and of liberty of contract with respect thereto; and

Whereas the Bureau of Indian Affairs handles, leases, and sells Indian property of great value, and disposes of funds which amount to many millions of dollars annually without responsibility to civil courts and without effective responsibility to Congress; and

Whereas it is claimed that the control by the Bureau of Indian Affairs of the persons and property of Indians is preventing them from accommodating themselves to the conditions and requirements of modern life and from exercising that liberty with respect to their own affairs without which they can not develop into self-reliant, free, and independent citizens and have the rights which belong generally to citizens of the United States; and

Whereas numerous complaints have been made by responsible persons and organizations charging improper and improvident administration of Indian property by the Bureau of Indian Affairs; and

Whereas it is claimed that preventable diseases are widespread among the Indian population, that the death rate among them is not only unreasonably high but is increasing, and that the Indians in many localities are becoming pauperized; and

Whereas the acts of Congress passed in the last hundred years having as their objective the civilization of the Indian tribes seem to have failed to accomplish the results anticipated; and

Whereas it is expedient that said acts of Congress and the Indian policy incorporated in said acts be examined and the administration and operation of the same as affecting the condition of the Indian population be surveyed and appraised: Now, therefore, be it

Resolved, That the Committee on Indian Affairs of the Senate is authorized and directed to make a general survey of the conditions of the Indians and of the operation and effect of the laws which Congress has passed for the civilization and protection of the Indian tribes; to investigate the relation of the Bureau of Indian Affairs to the persons and property of Indians and the effect of the acts, regulations, and administration of said bureau upon the health, improvement, and welfare of the Indians; and to report its findings in the premises, together with recommendations for the correction of abuses that may be found to exist, and for such changes in the law as will promote the security, economic competence, and progress of the Indians.

Said committee is authorized to send for persons, books, and papers, to administer oaths, to employ such clerical assistance as is necessary, to sit during any recess of the Senate, and at such places as it may deem advisable. Any subcommittee, duly authorized thereto, shall have the powers conferred upon the committee by this resolution.

The expenses of said investigation shall be paid out by the contingent fund of the Senate and shall not exceed $30,000. (S. Res. 79, 70th Cong., 1st sess.)

[7] 48 Stat. 984, 25 U. S. C. 461 *et seq.* For subsequent amendments and extensions, see Chapter 7.

[8] See Chapter 7.

A. POLITICAL EQUALITY

The right to be immune from racial discrimination by governmental agencies is an essential part of the fabric of democratic government in the United States. In part, this right is constitutionally affirmed by the fifth, fourteenth, and fifteenth amendments to the Federal Constitution; in part, the right is embodied in statutes providing penalties for racial discrimination by agencies of Federal and State Government; and, in part, the right is no more than a moral right implicit in the character of democratic government but not always protected by adequate legal machinery.

Despite a widely prevalent impression to the contrary, all Indians born in the United States are citizens of the United States and of the state in which they reside.[9] As citizens they are entitled to the rights of suffrage guaranteed by the fifteenth amendment,[10] and they are likewise entitled to hold public office,[11] to sue,[12] to make contracts,[13] and to enjoy all the civil liberties guaranteed to their fellow citizens.[14] These rights take on a special significance against the background of highly organized administrative control. They indicate that a body of federal Indian law, considered as "racial law," would be as much an anomaly as a body of federal law for persons of Teutonic descent, and that the existence of federal Indian law can be neither justified nor understood except in terms of the existence of Indian *tribes*.

B. TRIBAL SELF-GOVERNMENT

The principle that an Indian tribe is a political body with powers of self-government was first clearly enunciated by Chief Justice Marshall in the case of *Worcester* v. *Georgia*.[15] Indian tribes or nations, he declared,

> * * * had always been considered as distinct, independent, political communities, retaining their original natural rights, * * *. (P. 559.)

To this situation was applied the accepted rule of international law:

> * * * the settled doctrine of the law of nations is, that a weaker power does not surrender its independence—its right to self-government—by associating with a stronger, and taking its protection. (P. 560.)

From these premises the courts have concluded that Indian tribes have all the powers of self-government of any sovereignty except insofar as those powers have been modified or repealed by act of Congress or treaty. Hence over large fields of criminal and civil law, and particularly over questions of tribal membership, inheritance, tribal taxation, tribal property, domestic relations, and the form of tribal government, the laws, customs, and decisions of the proper tribal governing authorities have, to this day, the force of law.[16]

C. FEDERAL SOVEREIGNTY

The doctrine that Indian affairs are subject to the control of the Federal Government, rather than that of the states, derives from two legal sources.[17] In the first place, the Federal Constitution expressly conferred upon the Congress of the United States the power "to regulate commerce with the Indian tribes." [18] Matters internal to the tribe itself even to this day have been left largely in the hands of tribal governments. Federal power has generally been invoked in matters arising out of commerce with the Indian tribes, in the broad sense in which that phrase has been used to include all transactions by which Indians sought to dispose of land or other property in exchange for money, liquor, munitions or other products of the white man's civilization. The growth of the commerce clause has meant the expansion of federal power in Indian affairs, at the expense of state power.

Supplementary to the express constitutional power over commerce with the Indian tribes which was conferred upon Congress, the Federal Government was constitutionally endowed with plenary power over the making of treaties. Since the Federal Government had made several treaties with Indian tribes prior to the adoption of the Constitution in 1787, and continued to make such treaties for more than eight decades thereafter, the growth of federal power over Indian relations, at the expense of all claims of state power, was continuous and unchecked during the period in which the outlines of our present law of Indian affairs were established.

[9] See Chapter 8, sec. 2.
[10] See Chapter 8, sec. 3.
[11] See Chapter 8, sec. 4.
[12] See Chapter 8, sec. 6.
[13] See Chapter 8, sec. 7.
[14] See Chapter 8, sec. 10
[15] 6 Pet. 515 (1832).
[16] See Chapter 7.
[17] See Chapter 5.
[18] Art. I, sec. 8.

At the present time it may be laid down as a rough general rule that Indians on an Indian reservation are not subject to state law. This exemption is of particular importance in the fields of criminal law and taxation. The general rule has been modified in a few particulars by congressional action conferring upon the state specific power over certain subjects. Perhaps the most important of these laws delegating power to the states is the General Allotment Act,[19] which provides that, when tribal lands have been individualized, the individual parcels shall be inherited in accordance with the laws of the state. Another important exception to the general rule of federal sovereignty exists in the case of Oklahoma, where very extensive powers over Indians have been conferred upon the government of the state.[20] In both of these cases, as well as in various other matters, the power of the state is defined by federal legislation.[21]

D. GOVERNMENTAL PROTECTION OF INDIANS

Most of the legislation of the United States with respect to Indian affairs is subject to a dual interpretation. To the cynic such legislation may frequently appear as a mechanism for the orderly plundering of the Indian. To those more charitably inclined, the Government has appeared as the protector of the Indians against individuals who wished to separate the Indian from his possessions. Without attempting to anticipate the judgment that history will render on this conflict of doctrine, it may be said that at least the theory of American law governing Indian affairs has always been that the Government owed a duty of protection to the Indian in his relations with non-Indians. As was said by the Supreme Court of the United States in the case of *United States* v. *Kagama*:[22]

> Because of the local ill feeling, the people of the States where they [the Indian tribes] are found are often their deadliest enemies. From their very weakness and helplessness, so largely due to the course of dealing of the Federal Government with them, and the treaties in which it has been promised, there arises the duty of protection, and with it the power. This has always been recognized by the Executive and by Congress, and by this court, whenever the question has arisen. (P. 384.)

As a practical matter the individuals against whom the Indian needed the most vigorous kind of protection were the trader and the settler. Both wanted Indian land. The trader also wanted furs. The trader offered directly or indirectly, in exchange for land or furs, kettles, knives, clothing, liquor, firearms, ammunition, and other commodities. Some of these commodities were unknown in the pre-Columbian cultures, and the tribes had developed no adequate social controls over their use; the byproducts of this trade were disease, violence and, in many cases, the destruction of the game on which the Indians had subsisted. The settler wanted Indian land. Often he offered, in exchange for the land, the trader's goods; often he took the land without offering any *quid pro quo*. This intercourse between Indians and whites threatened the decimation of Indians through violence, disease, and starvation and imposed upon the Federal Government a tremendous cost for military protection of the white frontier families against the not always discriminating retaliation of the despoiled natives. The effort to control this intercourse was the guiding motif of federal Indian legislation down to our own generation.

Thus the problems of federal Indian law have been primarily the problems of (1) the regulation of Indian traders, (2) controlling the disposition of Indian land, (3) the protection of that land against trespass, and (4) the control of the liquor traffic. A few words on each of these four points may suggest the general contours of our federal law on Indian affairs.

(1) In 1790 the Federal Congress adopted the policy of regulating trade with the Indians through a system of licensing traders.[23] Except for a brief period, from 1796 to 1822, when a system of Government trading houses was maintained, the principle of control of Indian trade through licenses has been in force. Under this system federal supervision of the character and quality of goods sold and prices charged has been possible. Sales of liquor, and of firearms and ammunition not needed for useful purposes, have been banned. The system depended very largely for its effectiveness upon the isolation of the Indian groups affected, and in recent years the growth of towns and cities upon or near various Indian reservations and the development of mail-order trade have introduced elements of uncertainty into the question of the present efficacy and future development of our federal control over Indian trade.

[19] Act of February 8, 1887, 24 Stat. 388, 25 U. S. C. 331 *et seq.* See Chapter 11.

[20] See Chapter 23.

[21] See Chapter 6.

[22] 118 U. S. 375, 384 (1886). The comma after "them" in the third line of the quotation appears in the Supreme Court Reporter edition but not in the U. S. Reports edition. It is essential to the sense of the passage. The Supreme Court itself corrected this error the first time it had occasion to quote this passage (*Choctaw Nation* v. *United States*, 119 U. S. 1, 27 (1886)), but in recent years the error has generally gone unnoticed and the direct dependence of federal power over Indians upon treaties has often been overlooked.

[23] See Chapter 16.

(2) The problem of federal control over the disposition of Indian lands becomes a very esoteric legal problem if pursued into the mysteries which have been created by those who sought to deduce specific limitations upon Indian land sales from the inherent attributes of the general concept of "Indian title." The notion of "Indian title," as a supposed special form of tenure involving rights of possession but no right of alienation, is a notion that depends upon certain feudal doctrines of sovereignty, dominion, and seizin, on which endless controversy is possible. The subject, however, loses much of its mystery if the sale of land be viewed against the background of federal control over other types of Indian trade. The fact is that, while recognizing that the Indian tribes owned lands in their possession and had the right to dispose of them the Federal Government has always circumscribed such disposition by means of laws prescribing the manner and terms upon which Indian land may be alienated.[24] The economic significance of this control is apparent in the following statement of the United States Supreme Court:[25]

> The Indian right to the lands as property, was not merely of possession; that of alienation was concomitant; both were equally secured, protected and guarantied by Great Britain and Spain, subject only to ratification and confirmation by the license, charter or deed from the governor representing the king. Such purchases enabled the Indians to pay their debts, compensate for their depredations on the traders resident among them, to provide for their wants; while they were available to the purchasers as payment of the considerations which at their expense had been received by the Indians. It would have been a violation of the faith of the government to both, to encourage traders to settle in the province, to put themselves and property in the power of the Indians, to suffer the latter to contract debts, and when willing to pay them by the only means in their power, a cession of their lands, withhold an assent to the purchase, which, by their laws or municipal regulations, was necessary to vest a title. (Pp. 758–759.)

The first Indian Intercourse Act [26] provided that all alienations of Indian land should be made "at some public treaty, held under the authority of the United States." In the land sales that were made by treaty the United States was generally the purchaser, but in a few cases States or private individuals were designated as purchasers of the land sold.

Apart from treaties, a series of special statutes, generally but not always dependent upon the consent of the Indians concerned, provided for the sale of Indian lands. Other statutes, general as well as special, have provided for the leasing, by the Indians or by the Secretary of the Interior on their behalf, of Indian lands and minerals and the sale of Indian-owned timber.[27] Legislation authorizing the allotment of tribal lands, and supplementary laws dealing with such allotments, have provided for the sale or lease of allotted lands, under various degrees of federal administrative supervision.[28]

By maintaining its control over the transactions by which Indians dispose of land, the United States has been able to establish a degree of control over the moneys or other *quid pro quo* received by the Indians in connection with such disposition.[29] Thus various types of tribal and individual funds, generally representing returns from the disposition of Indian land and subject to federal control, have been established, and a good deal of the attention which Congress and the Interior Department have given to the Indian problem has been directed to the proper use of this money. Part of this vast fund, obtained from the disposition of Indian natural resources, has been used for the administration of education, health, and other public services on the Indian reservations; part of it has been distributed to the Indians in per capita payments, and part has been utilized, with or without the consent of the Indians, for expenses of government administration on the reservations. The various service functions of the Indian Service which have developed out of the administration of these funds must be left for later treatment.[30] It is enough for our present purposes to note that the principle of federal protection of the Indian, applied specifically to Indian lands, continued to exert its force beyond the transaction of Indian land sale, and that by virtue of this principle federal control came to be extended over almost the entire economic life of the Indian.

(3) The protection of Indian land against trespass was one of the first responsibilities assumed by the Federal Government. The promise of such protection for lands retained by the Indian tribes was an important *quid pro quo* in the process of treaty-making by which the United States acquired a vast public domain.[31] This

[24] See Chapter 15.
[25] *Mitchel* v. *United States*, 9 Pet. 711, 758–759 (1835). And see Chapter 15, sec. 18.
[26] Act of July 22, 1790, 1 Stat. 137.
[27] See Chapter 15.
[28] See Chapters 9, 11.
[29] See Chapter 10.
[30] See Chapter 12
[31] See Chapter 3.

promise of protection was sometimes backed up by a treaty provision declaring that trespassers put themselves outside the protection of the Federal Government, and might be dealt with by the tribes themselves according to their own laws and customs.

It is characteristic of the piecemeal approach characterizing federal legislation on Indian affairs that despite the importance of the subject of trespass upon Indian lands no general legislation on the subject has ever been enacted. Apart from the various treaty provisions with particular tribes, there are separate laws dealing with trespass by unlicensed traders, by horse thieves, and other criminals or would-be criminals, by settlers, by persons driving livestock to graze on Indian lands, and by hunters and trappers.[32] But there is to this day no general law which can be invoked against those trespassers whose occupation Congress has not foreseen. Ordinary civil actions have been brought by, or on behalf of, Indians and Indian tribes to protect Indian lands against trespass, but Indian unfamiliarity with legal procedure has often rendered this remedy ineffective. In recent years the Federal Government has devoted considerable attention to litigation for the protection of Indian lands against trespass. The right of the Federal Government to bring such suits has been justified either on the theory that title to the lands rested with the Federal Government or on the more general theory that the Federal Government has a special obligation, as guardian of the Indians, to protect their lands against trespass even where full title in fee simple is held by the Indian tribe.[33] It is pertinent to note, finally, that the federal protection of Indian lands against trespass by State authorities has given rise to the established doctrine that such lands are not subject to State land taxes.[34] This doctrine has been invoked, in turn, by state authorities as a reason for not rendering to reservation Indians various public services that are rendered to other citizens of the state, *e. g.* public education.[35]

(4) In the belief that a great deal of Indian disorder was the result of traffic in intoxicants, Congress early established a total prohibition law for the Indian country.[36] This law has been maintained in force continuously for more than a century. The breaking down of early conditions of isolation has made the enforcement of this legislation an increasingly difficult problem.

E. SUMMARY

In each of the foregoing four fields of legislation the principle of federal protection of the Indians has been carried into effect by means of some type of federal control over transactions between Indians and non-Indians, whether through complete prohibition, licensing, or the prescribing of conditions governing particular transactions. It is fair to say that historically and logically federal control over transactions of these four types is at the root of the entire body of federal legislation on Indian affairs. Thus this tremendous and unwieldy mass of legislation, comprising more than 4,300 distinct enactments, may be viewed in its entirety as the concrete content of the abstract principle of federal protection of the Indian.

In terms, this principle, an offspring of the more general one of federal sovereignty over Indian affairs, is entirely consistent with the principles of racial equality and of tribal self-government in matters internal to the tribe. In practice, however, the unsolved problems of our federal law in the field of Indian affairs all deal fundamentally with the demarcation of domain among these independent competing principles.

3. METHOD OF TREATMENT

This handbook does not purport to be a cyclopedia. It does not attempt to say the last word on the varied legal problems which it treats. If one who seeks to track down a point of federal Indian law finds in this volume relevant background, general perspective, and useful leads to the authorities, the handbook will have served the purpose for which it was written. More than this might have been done if it had been possible to carry through the work on the scale in which it was originally planned by Assistant Attorney General McFarland.

The method of this handbook is dictated by its subject matter. Federal Indian law is a subject that cannot be understood if the historical dimension of existing law is ignored. As I have elsewhere observed,[37] the groups of human beings with whom Federal Indian law is immediately concerned have undergone, in the century and a half of our national existence, changes in living habits, institutions, needs and aspirations far greater than the changes that separate from our own age the ages for which Hammurabi, Moses, Lycurgus, or Justinian legislated.

[32] See Act of July 22, 1790, 1 Stat. 137; Act of March 1, 1793, 1 Stat. 329; Act of May 19, 1796, 1 Stat. 469; Act of March 3, 1799, 1 Stat. 743; Act of March 30, 1802, 2 Stat. 139; Act of June 30, 1834, 4 Stat. 729.

[33] See Chapter 15, sec. 10D.

[34] *The New York Indians*, 5 Wall. 761 (1866). And see Chapter 13.

[35] See Chapter 6.

[36] See Chapter 17.

[37] U. S. Department of the Interior, Office of the Solicitor, Statutory Compilation of the Indian Law Survey: A Compendium of Federal Laws and Treaties Relating to Indians, edited by Felix S. Cohen, Chief, Indian Law Survey, with a Foreword by Nathan R. Margold, Solicitor, Department of the Interior (1940, 46 vols.) vol. 1, pp. ii–iii.

Telescoped into a century and a half, one may find changes in social, political, and property relations which stretch over more than 30 centuries of European civilization. The toughness of law which keeps it from changing as rapidly as social conditions change in our national life is, of course, much more serious where the rate of social change is 20 times as rapid. Thus, if the laws governing Indian affairs are viewed as lawyers generally view existing law, without reference to the varying times in which particular provisions were enacted, the body of the law thus viewed is a mystifying collection of inconsistencies and anachronisms. To recognize the different dates at which various provisions were enacted is the first step towards order and sanity in this field.

Not only is it important to recognize the temporal "depth" of existing legislation, it is also important to appreciate the past existence of legislation which has, technically, ceased to exist. For there is a very real sense in which it can be said that no provision of law is ever completely wiped out. This is particularly true in the field of Indian law. At every session of the Supreme Court, there arise cases in which the validity of a present claim depends upon the question: "What was the law on such and such a point in some earlier period?" Laws long repealed have served to create legal rights which endure and which can be understood only by reference to the repealed legislation. Thus, in seeking a complete answer to various questions of Indian law, one finds that he cannot rest with a collection of laws "still in force," but must constantly recur to legislation that has been repealed, amended, or superseded.

Important, however, as is the historical factor in the understanding of federal Indian law, a mere chronology of laws and decisions would be of little value. Systematic analysis is needed, the more so because no treatise has ever been written on the subject of federal Indian law. Indeed the subject hardly exists, as yet, except as a mass of rules and laws relating to a single subject matter. Unfortunately relation to a single subject matter is not enough to establish systematic interconnections among the rules and statutes so related. This any lawyer can see for himself by referring to treatises on "the law of horses" or "the law of fire engines." Federal Indian law does exhibit a systematic interconnectedness of parts, but to discover and define the common standards, principles, concepts, and modes of analysis that run through this massive body of statutes and decisions is an analytical task of the first order.

History and analysis need to be supplemented by an understanding of the actual functioning of legal rules and concepts, the actual consequences of statutes and decisions. Language on statute books, in the field of Indian law as in other fields, frequently has only a tenuous relation to the law-in-action which courts and administrators and the process of government have derived from the words of Congress. The words of court opinions frequently have as tenuous a relation to the actual holdings. Magic "solving words" like "Indian title," "wardship," and "competency," are often used to establish connections, between a case under consideration and some precedent, that turn out on reflection to be purely verbal. Functional study of the federal Indian law in action is essential to a work that may serve the practical purposes of administrators.

While it has been fashionable in some circles to consider historical, analytical, and functional approaches to legal problems as mutually exclusive and antagonistic, a more tolerant and useful viewpoint is expressed in the keynote article of one of the most promising of the newer legal periodicals:

> Precisely because it is a very different question from these questions that have occupied so large a part of traditional jurisprudence, the question of the human significance of law must be posed as a supplement to established lines of inquiry in legal science rather than as a substitute for them. Indeed, there is an intimate and mutual interdependence among these lines of inquiry, historical, analytical, ethical, and functional.
>
> The law of the present is a tenuous abstraction hovering between legal history and legal prophecy. The functionalist cannot describe the present significance of any rule of law without reference to historical elements. It is equally true that the historical jurist cannot reconstruct the past unless he grasps the meaning of the present.
>
> The functionalist must have recourse to the logical instruments that analytical jurisprudence furnishes. Analytical jurisprudence, in turn, may develop more fruitful modes of analysis with a better understanding of the law-in-action.
>
> Functional description of the workings of a legal rule will be indispensable to one who seeks to pass ethical judgments on law. The functionalist, however, is likely to be lost in an infinite maze of trivialities unless he is able to concentrate on the *important* consequences of a legal rule and ignore the *unimportant* consequences, a distinction which can be made only in terms of an ethical theory.[38]

[38] F. S. Cohen, The Problems of a Functional Jurisprudence, 1 Modern Law Review (London) (1937) 5, 7.

When I assigned to the writer of these words the task of applying to the field of Indian law the standards of scholarship which he had written about and demonstrated in several other fields,[30] I did so with the conviction that the resulting work would be a contribution to legal scholarship and legal method as well as to the immediate field of Indian law. Assistant Solicitor Felix S. Cohen has brought to bear in the writing of this work not only an unusual equipment in fields of research but seven years of practical experience in handling on the various Indian reservations the most difficult controversies that have arisen during that period and in drafting a significant part of the legislation about which he writes.

(Signed) Nathan R. Margold,
Solicitor.

Department of the Interior, *July 3, 1940.*

---

[30] The Ethical Basis of Legal Criticism (1931), 41 Yale Law Jour. 201; Ethical Systems and Legal Ideals (1933); (In collaboration with Mr. Justice Shientag) Summary Judgments in the Supreme Court of New York (1932), 32 Col. Law Rev. 825; The Subject Matter of Ethical Science (1932), 42 Int. Jour. of Ethics 397; Modern Ethics and the Law (1934), 4 Brooklyn Law Rev. 33; Transcendental Nonsense and the Functional Approach (1935), 35 Col. Law Rev. 809; Anthropology and the Problems of Indian Administration (1937), 18 Southwestern Social Science Quarterly No. 2; The Relativity of Philosophical Systems and the Method of Systematic Relativism (1939), 36 Journal of Philosophy 57; The Social and Economic Consequences of Exclusionary Immigration Laws (1939), 2 Nat. Lawyers Guild Quart. 171; Indian Rights and the Federal Courts (1940), 24 Minn. Law Rev. 145.

AUTHOR'S ACKNOWLEDGMENTS

It is a pleasant duty to acknowledge the aid of the many individuals who have cooperated in the preparation of this work.

In the first place, it must be said that this work would not have been completed but for the strong belief of my two chiefs, Secretary Harold L. Ickes and Solicitor Nathan R. Margold, and of Commissioner of Indian Affairs John Collier in the importance of the work and their inspiring confidence in the ability of our tiny staff to carry it to completion.

Secondly, I must acknowledge the aid and encouragement that were given in the early stages of the work by Carl A. McFarland, then Assistant Attorney General, and his able assistant, Charles E. Collett, then Chief of the Trial Section in the Lands Division of the Department of Justice. Theirs was the vision that those who have worked in the preparation of this Handbook have tried to carry out, and their cooperation in this work, so long as they were able to give it, was unstinted.

Of those who aided in the actual preparation of this Handbook I owe a special debt to my chief collaborator, Theodore H. Haas, but for whose indefatigable energies a large part of this work must have remained unwritten. I am happy also to acknowledge the loyal aid given by two others who were with the work "for the duration," Mrs. Mima Pollitt and Miss Bettie Renner, both of the Department of Justice.

Because of unfortunate exigencies over which none of us had any control, the aid rendered by other attorneys collaborating in the project was limited in each case to a few weeks or months. I am nonetheless aware of the vital contributions that were made to the writing of this Handbook by Pedro Capo-Rodriguez, whose many years of experience representing the United States in Indian litigation have been of the greatest value in the preparation of this work, and by attorneys Fred G. Folsom, Jr., Abraham Glasser, Mrs. Pauline B. Heller, Thomas L. Karsten, Samuel Miller, Clifford Stearns, and Miss Doris Williamson. Valuable aid in the historical research involved in various portions of this work was given by Miss Mary K. Morris and Miss Lucy M. Kramer. Finally, I should like to acknowledge the part played in the preparation of this work by Mrs. Griselda G. Lobell and Mr. Joseph Watson, who checked and filed thousands of items of source material upon which the writing of this work was based.

Those of us who did the actual writing of this Handbook constitute only a small part in the stream of human energies that have influenced the form and content of this work. My associates in the Department of the Interior, particularly Ebert K. Burlew, First Assistant Secretary; Oscar L. Chapman, Assistant Secretary; William Zimmerman, Jr., Assistant Commissioner of Indian Affairs; Frederic L. Kirgis, First Assistant Solicitor; William H. Flanery, Charlotte T. Lloyd, Kenneth Meiklejohn, H. Byron Mock, Phineas Indritz, Marie Berger, and Frances Lavender, Assistant Solicitors; William A. Brophy, Special Attorney for the Pueblo Indians; John R. T. Reeves, General Counsel of the Indian Office; Samuel J. Flickinger, Assistant General Counsel; E. S. McMahon, Attorney; Fred H. Daiker, Assistant to the Commissioner of Indian Affairs; Allan G. Harper, Field Representative; George A. Hossick, Chief of the Alaska Unit of the Division of Game Management, and Seton H. Thompson, Assistant Chief of the Division of Alaska Fisheries, both of the Fish and Wildlife Service; and David E. Thomas, Chief of the Alaska Section of the Office of Indian Affairs, have all contributed in different ways to this work.

Finally I should like to make grateful acknowledgment of the aid given along the many vital steps that lie between writing and publication, by Dr. W. C. Mendenhall, Director of the Geological Survey; William Barton Greenwood, Finance Officer for the Bureau of Indian Affairs; Fred W. Johnson, Commissioner of the General Land Office; Floyd E. Dotson, Chief Clerk of the Interior Department; Frank C. Updike, Chief of the Miscellaneous Service Division; Miss Helen Logan and John H. Ady, in charge of the printing work of the Department; and Miss Marie J. Turinsky and Mrs. Grace L. Dent, to whom the task of proof-reading was entrusted.

Even this lengthy roster, sufficient as it is to dispel any illusory author's pride, is far from representing a complete sum of the human efforts that move through the pages of this volume. To do justice to these efforts one would have to mention the writers of books, articles and briefs, which are quoted at length in these chapters, the judges whose opinions form the backbone of the volume, the administrative officials whose reports and legal memoranda have proved so valuable in fields not yet covered by the decided cases, the statesmen in the White House, in Congress, and among the Indian tribes whose thoughts have taken form in the language of statute, treaty, and tribal law, which makes up so large a portion of this study, the many critics outside of Government circles who have brought to light defects in Indian law and administration, the critics of preliminary drafts of these chapters who have aided in many successive revisions, and the score or more of clerical and stenographic assistants who have performed many tasks incidental to the preparation of this work. But any such attempt to place on a written page all the names of those on whom one has depended would be inevitably vain. For each of us in his appointed work, in Government service as elsewhere, is the instrument of forces that run through an entire generation. What has made this work possible, in the final analysis, is a set of beliefs that form the intellectual equipment of a generation—a belief that our treatment of the Indian in the past is not something of which a democracy can be proud, a belief that the protection of minority rights and the substitution of reason and agreement for force and dictation represent a contribution to civilization, a belief that confusion and ignorance in fields of law are allies of despotism, a belief that it is the duty of the Government to aid oppressed groups in the understanding and appreciation of their legal rights, a belief that understanding of the law, in Indian fields as elsewhere, requires more than textual exegesis, requires appreciation of history and understanding of economic, political, social, and moral problems. These beliefs represent, I think, the American mind in our generation as it impinges upon one tiny segment of the many problems which modern democracy faces. It is fundamentally to these beliefs and to this mind that an author's acknowledgments, gratitude, and loyalty are due.

(Signed) FELIX S. COHEN.

JULY 1, 1940.

ANALYSIS OF CHAPTERS

CHAPTER 6

THE SCOPE OF STATE POWER OVER INDIAN AFFAIRS

CHAPTER 7

THE SCOPE OF TRIBAL SELF-GOVERNMENT

CHAPTER 8

PERSONAL RIGHTS AND LIBERTIES OF INDIANS

Chapter 9

INDIVIDUAL RIGHTS IN TRIBAL PROPERTY

Chapter 10

THE RIGHTS OF THE INDIAN IN HIS PERSONALTY

Chapter 11

INDIVIDUAL RIGHTS IN REAL PROPERTY

Chapter 12

FEDERAL SERVICES FOR INDIANS

CHAPTER 13

TAXATION

CHAPTER 14

THE LEGAL STATUS OF INDIAN TRIBES

CHAPTER 15

TRIBAL PROPERTY

CHAPTER 16

INDIAN TRADE

CHAPTER 17

INDIAN LIQUOR LAWS

CHAPTER 18

CRIMINAL JURISDICTION

CHAPTER 19

CIVIL JURISDICTION

CHAPTER 20

PUEBLOS OF NEW MEXICO

CHAPTER 21

ALASKAN NATIVES

CHAPTER 22

NEW YORK INDIANS

CHAPTER 23

SPECIAL LAWS RELATING TO OKLAHOMA

HANDBOOK OF FEDERAL INDIAN LAW

CHAPTER 1

THE FIELD OF INDIAN LAW: INDIANS AND THE INDIAN COUNTRY

TABLE OF CONTENTS

SECTION 1. THE FIELD OF INDIAN LAW

Indians are human beings, and like other human beings become involved in lawsuits. Nearly all of these lawsuits involve problems in the law of contracts, torts, and other recognized fields which have no particular relevance to Indian affairs. In many cases the only legal problems presented are of this character. Not every lawsuit, therefore, which involves Indians can be considered a part of our Indian law. Conversely, not every case that presents a problem of Indian law involves Indians as litigants. Most of the land in the United States, for example, was purchased from Indians, and therefore almost any title must depend for its ultimate validity upon issues of Indian law even though the last Indian owners and all their descendants be long forgotten.

Our subject, therefore, cannot be defined in terms of the parties litigant appearing in any case. It must be defined rather in terms of the legal questions which are involved in a case. Where such questions turn upon rights, privileges, powers, or immunities of an Indian or an Indian tribe or an administrative agency set up to deal with Indian affairs, or where governing rules of law are affected by the fact that a place is under Indian ownership or devoted to Indian use, the case that presents such questions belongs within the confines of this study.

Further, we shall use the term "federal Indian law" to cover not only decisions of courts, strictly so-called, but also decisions of administrative agencies and such materials, contained in statute, treaty, Executive order, or governmental regulation custom and practice, as are accorded, by courts and administrators, "the force of law."

This subject matter is treated, in the course of this volume from several distinct perspectives.

In the present chapter the scope of federal Indian law is considered, particularly in terms of the class of persons and places with which this branch of law deals.

The following three chapters treat, from an historical perspective, the three basic strands of development which make up the federal Indian law—administration (Chapter 2), treaty-making (Chapter 3), and legislation (Chapter 4).

The following three chapters deal with the problems of federal Indian law in terms of the question, "From what governmental source do legal relations flow?" These chapters deal, respectively, with the powers of federal (Chapter 5), state (Chapter 6), and tribal (Chapter 7) governments.

Chapters 8 to 17 treat the substantive law of the field from the standpoint of the generic question: What are the rights, powers, privileges, and immunities of the parties?

Of these chapters, the first four deal with the legal status of individual Indians, treating personal rights and liberties (Chapter 8), rights of participation in tribal property (Chapter 9), individual rights in personal property (Chapter 10), and individual rights in real property (Chapter 11).

The following two chapters deal with rights, vested both in tribes and in individuals, which are subsumed under the headings "Federal Services for Indians" (Chapter 12) and "Taxation" (Chapter 13).

The substantive rights, powers, privileges, and immunities of Indian tribes form the subject of Chapters 14 and 15, the former dealing generally with "The Status of Indian Tribes," the latter with "Tribal Property."

The final two chapters of this substantive law section of the Handbook deal with matters involving primarily the legal position of two classes of non-Indians who have a special relation to Indian affairs, to wit: traders (Chapter 16) and purveyors of liquor (Chapter 17).

Chapters 18 and 19 deal with problems of court jurisdiction, the former in the field of criminal law, the latter in the field of civil law.

The last four chapters of this Handbook treat of four groups of Indians occupying peculiar positions in the law. Chapter 20 deals with the Pueblos of New Mexico; Chapter 21 analyzes the peculiar problems of the Natives of Alaska; Chapter 22 comments briefly on the New York Indians; and Chapter 23 offers a sketch of "Special Laws Relating to Oklahoma."

With these comments on the substance and structure of the volume, we turn to a more explicit delimitation of the persons and places that are the primary subjects of our federal Indian law.

In this demarcation of domains we may properly begin by considering the various definitions that have been offered of the terms "Indian" and "Indian country."

SECTION 2. DEFINITIONS OF "INDIAN"

The term "Indian" may be used in an ethnological or in a legal sense. Ethnologically, the Indian race may be distinguished from the Caucasian, Negro, Mongolian, and other races. If a person is three-fourths Caucasian and one-fourth Indian, it is absurd, from the ethnological standpoint, to assign him to the Indian race. Yet legally such a person may be an Indian. From a legal standpoint, then, the biological question of race is generally pertinent, but not conclusive. Legal status depends not only upon biological, but also upon social factors, such as the relation of the individual concerned to a white or Indian community. This relationship, in turn, has two ends—an individual and a community. The individual may withdraw from a tribe or be expelled from a tribe; or he may be adopted by a tribe. He may or may not reside on an Indian reservation. He may or may not be subject to the control of the Federal Government with respect to various transactions. All these social or political factors may affect the classification of an individual as an "Indian" or a "non-Indian" for legal purposes, or for certain legal purposes. Indeed, in accordance with a statute reserving jurisdiction over offenses between tribal members to a tribal court, a white man adopted into an Indian tribe has been held to be an Indian,[1] and the decided cases do not foreclose the argument that a person of entirely Indian ancestry who has never had any relations with any Indian tribe or reservation may be considered a non-Indian for most legal purposes.

What must be remembered is that legislators, when they use the term "Indian" to establish special rules of law applicable to "Indians," are generally trying to deal with a group distinguished from "non-Indian" groups by public opinion,[2] and this public opinion varies so widely that on certain reservations it is common to refer to a person as an Indian although 15 of his 16 ancestors, 4 generations back, were white persons; while in other parts of the country, as in the Southwest, a person may be considered a Spanish-American rather than an Indian although his blood is predominantly Indian.

The lack of unanimity which exists among those who would attempt a definition of Indians is reflected in the difference in instructions to the enumerators of the 1930 and 1940 censuses. In the 1930 census enumerators were instructed to return as Indians not only those of full Indian blood, but also those of mixed white and Indian blood, "except where the percentage of Indian blood is very small" or where the individual was "regarded as a white person in the community where he lives." The instructions further specified that "a person of mixed Indian and Negro blood shall be returned as a Negro unless the Indian blood predominates and the status as an Indian is generally accepted in the community."[3]

In the 1940 census on the other hand, enumerators were directed that "a person of mixed white and Indian blood should be returned as Indian, if enrolled on an Indian agency or reservation roll; or if not so enrolled, if the proportion of Indian blood is one-fourth or more, or if the person is regarded as an Indian in the community where he lives." The provision concerning persons of mixed Indian and Negro blood was changed to provide for the return of such an individual as Negro, unless the Indian blood *very definitely* predominates and he is *universally* accepted in the community as an Indian.[4]

Recognizing the possible diversity of definitions of "Indianhood," we may nevertheless find some practical value in a definition of "Indian" as a person meeting two qualifications: (*a*) That some of his ancestors lived in America before its discovery by the white race, and (*b*) that the individual is considered an "Indian" by the community in which he lives.

The function of a definition of "Indian" is to establish a test whereby it may be determined whether a given individual is to be excluded from the scope of legislation dealing with Indians.

A typical statute dealing with Indians is the Trade and Intercourse Act of 1834,[5] which in section 25 provides:

> * * * That so much of the laws of the United States as provides for the punishment of crimes committed within any place within the sole and exclusive jurisdiction of the

[1] *Nofire* v. *United States*, 164 U. S. 657 (1897).

[2] A graphic example of the borrowing by courts of uncritical impressions of what constitutes an Indian is found in a series of cases on the question whether the natives of the Pueblos are "Indians." In 1869, the Supreme Court of the Territory decided that they could not be considered Indians because they were "honest, industrious, and law abiding citizens" and "a people living for three centuries in fenced abodes and cultivating the soil for the maintenance of themselves and families, and giving an example of virtue, honesty, and industry to their more civilized neighbors." *United States* v. *Lucero*, 1 N. M. 422, 438, 442 (1869). In 1876, the Supreme Court, likewise, held that these people could not be considered Indians because they were "a peaceable, industrious, intelligent, honest, and virtuous people * * * Indians only in feature, complexion, and a few of their habits * * *." *United States* v. *Joseph*, 94 U. S. 614 616 (1876). So long as these impressions continued to prevail, efforts of the Indian Bureau to assert full powers of "guardianship" over the Pueblos were unsuccessful. See Chapter 20, sec. 3, *infra*. In 1913 however, the Indian Bureau compiled enough reports of immorality among the Pueblos to convince the Supreme Court that its earlier observations on Pueblo character had been based upon erroneous information and that these people were really Indians needing Indian Bureau supervision. The Court, *per* Van Devanter, *J.*, quoted at length from agents' reports of drunkenness, debauchery, dancing, and communal life in support of the conclusion that they were Indians, being a "simple, uninformed and inferior people." *United States* v. *Sandoval*, 231 U. S. 28, 39–47 (1913). It may be doubted whether the conception of what makes a man an Indian, implicit in all these opinions, would be accepted today.

The test of "common understanding" is advanced by Cardozo, *J.*, in *Morrison* v. *California*, 291 U. S. 82, 86 (1934), in support of the view that "not improbably" a person with Indian blood of less than one-fourth degree is to be regarded as an Indian.

[3] The Indian population of the United States and Alaska, 1930, U. S. Department of Commerce, Bureau of the Census, Washington, D. C. For a discussion of statutes distinguishing between Indians and freedmen see Chapter 8, sec. 11.

[4] The results of the 1940 census are not available at the time of publication of this book so that it is not possible to compare the possible differences in results occasioned by the difference of instructions to enumerators. In the census of 1910, though the question of who should be returned as Indian was left to the discretion of the enumerator, he was obliged, once he had decided an individual was an Indian, to obtain information concerning tribe and blood. According to the census of 1930 there were 332,393 Indians in continental United States and 29,983 in Alaska, while in 1910 there were 265,683 Indians in continental United States and 25,331 in Alaska. In commenting on the results of these two censuses, Dr. George B. L. Arner, in The Indian Population of the United States and Alaska, 1930—U. S. Department of Commerce, Bureau of the Census, stated:

> In the case of the Indian population, rates of increase or decrease are of little significance, as the size of the Indian population depends entirely upon the attention paid to the enumeration of mixed bloods, and the interpretation of the term "Indian" in the instructions to enumerators. It is not without significance that at the two censuses in which specific questions were asked as to tribe and blood, the number of Indians should have been much larger than at censuses in which these questions were not asked. If the definition of the Indian population were limited to Indians maintaining tribal relations, the enumeration of the Bureau of Indian Affairs is probably more nearly accurate than that of the census. This enumeration in 1932, showed a total of 228,381. On the other hand, if all persons having even a trace of Indian blood were returned as Indians, the number would far exceed even the total returned at the census of 1930. (P. 2.)

As of January 1, 1939, the Bureau of Indian Affairs estimated that there were under its jurisdiction 351,878 Indians in continental United States and 29,983 in Alaska, or a total of 381,861. This number includes individuals of as little as 1/64 Indian blood entitled to certain rights or benefits as Indians, as well as white persons adopted into an Indian tribe. Statistical Supplement to the Annual Report of the Commissioner of Indian Affairs, 1939.

[5] Act of June 30, 1834, sec. 25, 4 Stat. 729, R. S. § 2145, 25 U. S. C. 217.

United States, shall be in force in the Indian country: *Provided*, The same shall not extend to crimes committed by one Indian against the person or property of another Indian. (P. 733.)

Lacking other criteria than the words of the statute, the courts have, reasonably enough, taken the position that the term "Indian" is one descriptive of an individual who has Indian blood in his veins and who is regarded as an Indian by the society of Indians among whom he lives. Thus, in holding that a white man who is adopted into an Indian tribe does not thereby become an Indian within the meaning of the foregoing statute,[6] the Court, in *United States* v. *Rogers*,[7] said:

> * * * And we think it very clear, that a white man who at mature age is adopted in an Indian tribe does not thereby become an Indian, and was not intended to be embraced in the exception above mentioned. He may by such adoption become entitled to certain privileges in the tribe, and make himself amenable to their laws and usages. Yet he is not an Indian; and the exception is confined to those who by the usages and customs of the Indians are regarded as belonging to their race. It does not speak of members of a tribe, but of the race generally,—of the family of Indians; and it intended to leave them both, as regarded their own tribe, and other tribes also, to be governed by Indian usages and customs. (Pp. 572–573.)

Though a white man cannot by association become an Indian, within the application of the foregoing statute, an Indian may, nevertheless, under some circumstances, lose his identity as an Indian. It has been held that the General Allotment Act[8] operates to make Indians who are descendants of aboriginal tribes, but who have taken up residence apart from any tribe and adopted habits of civilization, non-Indians, within the meaning of an Alaska statute defining Indians for the purpose of liquor regulation as "aboriginal races inhabiting Alaska when annexed to the United States, and their descendants of the whole or half blood who have not become citizens of the United States."[9]

In upholding the constitutionality of the federal statute making murder of an Indian by another Indian on an Indian reservation a federal crime, the Supreme Court declared:

> the fair inference is that the offending Indian shall belong to that or some other tribe.[10]

On the other hand, an Indian does not lose his identity as such within the meaning of federal criminal jurisdictional acts, even though he has received an allotment of land, is not under the control or immediate supervision of an Indian agent, and has become a citizen of the United States and of the state in which he resides.[11]

[6] Act of June 30, 1834, 4 Stat. 729.

[7] 4 How. 567 (1846). Accord: *United States* v. *Ragsdale*, 27 Fed. Cas. No. 16113 (C. C. Ark., 1847); *Ex Parte Morgan*, 20 Fed. 298 (D. C. W. D. Ark., 1883); *Westmoreland* v. *United States*, 155 U. S. 545 (1895); *Alberty* v. *United States*, 162 U. S. 499 (1896) (holding that a Negro does not by adoption into a tribe become an Indian).

The same rule would seem to apply to a white man married to an Indian woman and residing on a reservation. At least, it has been held that a white man, married to an Indian woman, residing on a reservation, and made a member of the tribe or nation, is not an Indian entitled to share in tribal funds or in the allotment of Indian lands. *Red Bird* v. *United States*, 203 U. S. 76 (1906).

[8] Act of February 8, 1887, 24 Stat. 388, 25 U. S. C. 331, *et seq.*

[9] *Nagle* v. *United States*, 191 Fed. 141 (C. C. A. 9, 1911).

[10] *United States* v. *Kagama*, 118 U. S. 375, 383 (1886). And see Chapter 14, fn. 9.

[11] *United States* v. *Flynn*, 25 Fed. Cas. No. 15124 (C. C. Minn. 1870); *Hallowell* v. *United States*, 221 U. S. 317 (1911); *United States* v. *Kiya*, 126 Fed. 879 (D. C. N. D. 1903); *United States* v. *Celestine*, 215 U. S. 278 (1909); *United States* v. *Sutton*, 215 U. S. 291 (1909). Also see Chapter 8, sec. 2C.

Within the meaning of those various statutes which though applicable to Indians do not define them, the courts, in defining the status of Indians of mixed Indian and other blood,[12] have largely followed the test laid down in *United States* v. *Rogers*,[13] to the effect that an individual to be considered an Indian must not only have some degree of Indian blood but must in addition be recognized as an Indian. In determining such recognition the courts have heeded both recognition by the tribe or society of Indians and recognition by the Federal Government as expressed in treaty and statute.[14]

Thus in *United States* v. *Higgins*[15] it was said:

> In determining as to what class half-breeds belong, we may refer, then, to the treatment and recognition the executive and political departments of the government have accorded them. * * * (P. 350.)
>
> Considering the treaties and statutes in regard to half-breeds, I may say that they never have been treated as white people entitled to rights of American citizenship. Special provision has been made for them,—special reservations of land, special appropriations of money. No such provision has been made for any other class. It is well known to those who have lived upon the frontier in America that, as a rule, half-breeds or mixed-blood Indians have resided with the tribes to which their mothers belonged; that they have, as a rule, never found a welcome home with their white relatives, but with their Indian kindred. It is but just, then, that they should be classed as Indians, and have all of the rights of the Indian. In 7 Op. Attys. Gen. 746, it is said, "Half-breed Indians are to be treated as Indians, in all respects, so long as they retain their tribal relations." (P. 352.)

[12] The term "mixed blood Indian" has been held to include not only those of half white or more than half white blood, but every Indian having an identifiable admixture of white blood, however small. *United States* v. *Detroit First Nat. Bank*, 234 U. S. 245 (1914); *State* v. *Nicolls*, 61 Wash. 142, 112 Pac. 269 (1910). For a discussion of distinctions based on degrees of Indian blood, see Chapter 8, sec. 8B(1)(a).

[13] *Supra*, fn. 7.

[14] Numerous treaties, as well as statutes, have recognized individuals of mixed blood as Indians. Treaty of September 29, 1817, with the Wyandot and other tribes, 7 Stat. 163; Treaty of October 6, 1818, with the Miami Indians, 7 Stat. 191; Treaty of August 4, 1824, with the Sac and Fox Indians, 7 Stat. 229; Treaty of November 15, 1824, with the Quapaw Indians, 7 Stat. 233; Treaty of June 2, 1825, with the Osage Indians, 7 Stat. 240; Treaty of June 3, 1825, with the Kansas Indians, 7 Stat. 245; Treaty of August 5, 1826, with the Chippewas, 7 Stat. 291; Treaty of October 16, 1826, with the Pottawatomie Indians, 7 Stat. 298, 299; Treaty of October 23, 1826, with the Miami Indians, 7 Stat. 302; Treaty of August 1, 1829, with the Winnebago Indians, 7 Stat. 324; Treaty of July 15, 1830, with the Sioux Indians, 7 Stat. 330; Treaty of August 30, 1831, with the Ottawa Indians, 7 Stat. 362; Treaty of September 15, 1832, with the Winnebago Indians, 7 Stat. 372; Treaty of September 21, 1832, with the Sac and Fox Indians, 7 Stat. 374; Treaty of October 27, 1832, with the Pottawatomie Indians, 7 Stat. 400; Treaty of March 28, 1836, with the Ottawa and other Indians, 7 Stat. 493; Treaty of July 29, 1837, with the Chippewa Indians, 7 Stat. 537; Treaty of September 29, 1837, with the Sioux Indians, 7 Stat. 539; Treaty of November 1, 1837, with the Winnebago Indians, 7 Stat. 545; Treaty of October 4, 1842, with the Chippewa Indians, 7 Stat. 592; Treaty of October 18, 1848, with the Menominee Indians, 9 Stat. 952; Treaty of March 15, 1854, with the Ottoe and Missouria Indians, 10 Stat. 1038; Treaty of February 22, 1855, with the Chippewa Indians, 10 Stat. 1169; Treaty of February 27, 1855, with the Winnebago Indians, 10 Stat. 1174; Treaty of September 24, 1857, with the Pawnee Indians, 11 Stat. 731; Treaty of March 12, 1858, with the Ponca Indians, 12 Stat. 999; Treaty of September 29, 1865, with the Osage Indians, 14 Stat. 689; Treaty of October 14, 1865, with the Cheyenne Indians, 14 Stat. 705; Treaty of March 21, 1866, with the Seminole Indians, 14 Stat. 756; Act of April 27, 1816, 6 Stat. 171; Act of June 30, 1834, 4 Stat. 740; Act of March 2, 1887, 6 Stat. 689; Act of June 5, 1872, 17 Stat. 226; 25 U. S. C. 479, 25 U. S. C. 163; Act of May 27, 1908, 35 Stat. 312, 25 U. S. C. 184, 28 U. S. C. 41(24).

In at least one treaty, children are described as quarter-blood Indians. Treaty of September 29, 1817, with the Wyandot and other tribes, 7 Stat. 163.

[15] 103 Fed. 348 (C. C. Mont. 1900).

Presumptively, a person of mixed blood residing upon a reservation, and enrolled in a tribe, is an Indian for purposes of legislation on federal criminal jurisdiction.[16] It has been held[17] that an individual of less than one-half Indian blood enrolled in a tribe and recognized as an Indian by the tribe is an Indian within the Act of March 4, 1909,[18] extending federal jurisdiction to rape committed by one Indian against another within the limits of an Indian reservation. Likewise, it has been held[19] that mixed bloods who are recognized by the tribe as members thereof may properly receive allotments of lands as Indians. In *Sully v. United States*,[20] where one-eighth bloods were involved, the court stated that the persons were "of sufficient Indian blood to substantially handicap them in the struggle for existence," and held that they were Indians and were entitled to be enrolled as such.

Citizenship has been denied a person of half white and half Indian blood on the ground that such an individual is not a "white person" within the meaning of that phrase as used in the statute.[21]

On the question of the status of offspring of white and Indian or Negro and Indian parents, there are conflicting lines of authority. One holds to the common law doctrine that the offspring of free parents assumes the status of the father; the other to the general tribal custom that the offspring assumes the status of the mother.[22]

In the first category are decisions to the effect that the offspring of the union between a white man[23] and an Indian woman or between a Negro[24] and an Indian woman assume the status of the father and are therefore not Indians within the meaning of statutes extending or denying federal jurisdiction over crimes committed by an Indian against another Indian. And there are holdings that where a child is born off the reservation of a white father and an Indian mother, he will not, by returning to the reservation, and receiving an allotment of land as an Indian, be classed as an Indian so as either to exempt his property from state taxation[25] or to bring himself within the criminal jurisdictional statutes relating to Indians.[26]

In the second category we find many cases which follow the usual tribal custom wherein it is held that the offspring of an Indian mother and a white or Negro father assumes the status of the mother.[27] Here again the ultimate question of the status of the individual will depend on his or his mother's recognition as an Indian by the tribe. In this connection the language of the court in *Waldron v. United States*[28] may be noted:

> * * * In this proceeding the court has been informed as to the usages and customs of the different tribes of the Sioux Nation, and has found as a fact that the common law does not obtain among said tribes, as to determining the race to which the children of a white man, married to an Indian woman, belong; but that, according to the usages and customs of said tribes, the children of a white man married to an Indian woman take the race or nationality of the mother.
>
> * * * * *
>
> * * * The United States have never, so far as legislation is concerned, recognized the technical rule of the common law in reference to the children born of a white father and an Indian mother. In 1897, Congress in the Indian appropriation act of that year (Act June 7, 1897, c. 3, 30 Stat. 90), declared:
>
> > "That all children, born of a marriage heretofore solemnized between a white man and an Indian woman by blood and not by adoption, where said Indian woman is at this time, or was at the time of her death, recognized by the tribe, shall have the same rights and privileges to the property of the tribe to which the mother belongs or belonged at the time of her death by blood, as any other member of the tribe, and no prior act of Congress shall be construed as to debar such child of such rights."
>
> * * * * *
>
> In *Davison v. Gibson*, 56 Fed. 445, 5 C. C. A. 545, the Circuit Court of Appeals of this circuit said:
>
> > "It is common knowledge, of which the court should take judicial knowledge, that the domestic relations of the Indians of this country have never been regulated by the common law of England, and that that law is not adapted to the habits, customs, and manners of the Indians."
>
> The court has considered the cases cited by counsel for defendants wherein, upon certain facts, persons were held not to be Indians; but these cases either seek to invoke what they say was the common law, or are in criminal proceedings. These cases, so far as they seek to invoke the common law to the Indians, are not followed, for reasons herein stated, and, so far as they seek to construe criminal statutes, are inapplicable as there is a wide distinction to be made between the construction of a criminal statute and a contract between a tribe of Indians and the United States. (Pp. 419–420.)

That, however, even with reference to statutes on federal criminal jurisdiction, the child of an Indian mother may assume her status is borne out by the decision of the court in *United States v. Sanders*.[29]

Likewise, it has been held[30] that the child of a white father and an Indian mother, abandoned by the father and residing in tribal relationship with the mother, is an Indian within the meaning of a statute defining the offense of selling liquor to Indians.

In the foregoing discussion notice has been taken with but a single exception only of those statutes wherein no definition of the word "Indian" was attempted.

Although Congress has classified Indians for various particular purposes, it has never laid down a classification and either specified or implied that individuals not falling within the classification were not Indians. In various enactments classification has

---

[16] *Famous Smith v. United States*, 151 U. S. 50 (1894).

[17] *United States v. Gardner*, 189 Fed. 690 (D. C. E. D. Wis. 1911). Accord: *State v. Campbell*, 53 Minn. 354, 55 N. W. 553 (1893).

[18] 35 Stat. 1088, 1151.

[19] *Sloan v. United States*, 118 Fed. 283 (C. C. Neb. 1902).

[20] 195 Fed. 113 (C. C. S. D. 1912).

[21] *In re Camille*, 6 Fed. 256 (C. C. Ore. 1880) (Construing R. S. § 671.)

[22] On tribal power over determination of membership see Chapter 7, sec. 4.

[23] *Ex Parte Reynolds*, 20 Fed. Cas. No. 11719 (D. C. W. D. Ark., 1879).

[24] *United States v. Ward*, 42 Fed. 320 (C. C. S. D. Cal. 1890).

[25] *United States v. Higgins*, 110 Fed. 609 (C. C. Mont. 1901). See Chapter 13, sec. 4.

[26] *United States v. Hadley*, 99 Fed. 437 (C. C. Wash. 1900). See Chapter 18.

[27] In *United States v. Higgins*, 103 Fed. 348, 352 (C. C. Mont. 1900), it was held that one born of a white father and an Indian mother, and who was a recognized member of the tribe of Indians in which his mother belonged, was not subject to taxation under the laws of the state in which he resided. In *Vezina v. United States*, 245 Fed. 411 (C. C. A. 8, 1917) the daughter of a half- to three-fourths blood Chippewa woman and a white man was held to be by blood a member of the Fond du Lac Band of Chippewas of Lake Superior, the court thereby overruling the action of the Department of Indian Affairs in refusing enrollment and allotment to the daughter. And in *Alberty v. United States*, 162 U. S. 499 (1896), the court held that an illegitimate child, born of an Indian man and a colored woman, takes the status of its mother and is therefore not an Indian.

[28] 143 Fed. 413 (C. C. S. D. 1905); see also *Sioux Mixed Blood*, 20 Op. A. G. 711 (1894).

[29] 27 Fed. Cas. No. 16220 (C. C. Ark. 1847). *Cf. Ex Parte Pero*, 99 F. 2d 28 (C. C. A. 7, 1938) (holding that the child of an Indian mother and a half-blood father who lives on the reservation and is recognized as an Indian, is an Indian within federal criminal jurisdictional statutes).

[30] *Farrell v. United States*, 110 Fed. 942 (C. C. A. 8, 1901). Accord: *Halbert v. United States*, 283 U. S. 753 (1931).

been based primarily upon the presence of some quantum of Indian blood. Thus, the Indian Appropriation Act of May 25, 1918,[31] provides:

> No appropriation, except appropriations made pursuant to treaties, shall be used to educate children of less than one-fourth Indian blood * * *

For the purpose of controlling the traffic in liquor with the Indians Congress has classified Indians under the "charge of any Indian superintendent or agent."[32] By a later act[33] the classification was changed to include "any Indian to whom allotment of land has been made while the title to the same shall be held in trust by the Government" or "any Indian a ward of the Government under charge of any Indian superintendent or agent" or "any Indian, including mixed bloods, over whom the Government, through its departments, exercises guardianship." This classification is perhaps as broad as any that may be found in congressional enactment, extending as it does to all mixed bloods providing only that they be considered as wards of the government.[34]

Various special acts relating to certain tribes have provided for the removal of restrictions on alienation from lands of the members of the tribe of less than one-half Indian blood.[35] Other acts have used the term "mixed blood."[36]

In the Act of March 4, 1931,[37] relating to the Eastern Band of Cherokees of North Carolina, Congress states:

> * * * That thereafter no person of less than one-sixteenth degree of said Eastern Cherokee Indian blood shall be recognized as entitled to any rights with the Eastern Band of Cherokee Indians except by inheritance from a deceased member or members: * * * (P. 1518.)

Congress had previously recognized Indians of less than this degree of blood for in the Act of June 4, 1924,[38] it provided:

> That any member of said band whose degree of Indian blood is less than one-sixteenth may, in the discretion of the Secretary of Interior, be paid a cash equivalent in lieu of an allotment of land. (P. 379.)

[31] 40 Stat. 564, 25 U. S. C. 297.

[32] Act of July 23, 1892, 27 Stat. 260, 261.

[33] Act of January 30, 1897, 29 Stat. 506. See Chapter 17.

[34] For a discussion of wardship see Chapter 8, sec. 9.

[35] Act of May 27, 1908, 35 Stat. 312 (Five Civilized Tribes); Act of March 3, 1921, 41 Stat. 1249 (Osage).

[36] Act of June 21, 1906, 34 Stat. 353; Act of March 1, 1907, 34 Stat. 1034.

[37] 46 Stat. 1518.

[38] 43 Stat. 366.

A recent statutory definition of an Indian is that contained in the Indian Reorganization Act,[39] which in section 19 provides:

> The term "Indian" as used in this Act shall include all persons of Indian descent who are members of any recognized Indian tribe now under Federal jurisdiction, and all persons who are descendants of such members who were, on June 1, 1934, residing within the present boundaries of any Indian reservation, and shall further include all other persons of one-half or more Indian blood. For the purposes of this Act, Eskimos and other aboriginal peoples of Alaska shall be considered Indians.[40] (P. 988.)

In this act as in the foregoing acts, the definition of "Indian" is limited in its connotation to the purposes of the legislation.

Apart from statute, the administrative agencies of the Federal Government dealing with Indian affairs commonly consider a person who is of Indian blood and a member of a tribe, regardless of degree of blood, an Indian.[41]

Thus the Indian Law and Order Regulations approved by the Secretary of the Interior on November 27, 1935,[42] contain the provision:

> For the purpose of the enforcement of the regulations in this part, an Indian shall be deemed to be any person of Indian descent who is a member of any recognized Indian tribe now under Federal jurisdiction * * *.

This definition exemplifies the idea that in dealing with Indians the Federal Government is dealing primarily not with a particular race as such but with members of certain social-political groups towards which the Federal Government has assumed special responsibilities.

[39] Act of June 18, 1934, 48 Stat. 984, 25 U. S. C. 461, *et seq.*

[40] For further definitions of Alaskan natives as Indians see Chapter 21, sec. 1.

[41] Here, too, however, one finds administrative regulations which classify Indians according to blood quantum for particular purposes. Thus by Executive order of January 31, 1939, Indians of one-fourth or more Indian blood were exempted insofar as positions in the Bureau of Indian Affairs were concerned, from Civil Service examination. See Chapter 8, sec. 4B(2). On the other hand regulations concerning the admission of Indians into Indian hospitals and sanitoria provide that:

> 85.2. Persons who are in need of hospitalization and who are enrolled Indians, recognized members of a tribe, and who are unable to provide such hospitalization from their own funds, may be admitted to such institutions.
>
> * * * * *
>
> 85.4. Preference should be given to those of a higher degree of Indian blood. * * *

(25 C. F. R. 85.2 and 85.4)

[42] 25 C. F. R. 161.2.

SECTION 3. INDIAN COUNTRY

Although the term "Indian country" has been used in many senses, it may perhaps be most usefully defined as country within which Indian laws and customs and federal laws relating to Indians are generally applicable. The phrase "generally applicable" is used because for certain purposes tribal law and custom and federal law relating to Indians have a validity regardless of locality. Thus, for example, Congress has made it a crime to sell liquor to Indians anywhere in the United States,[43] and the status which an Indian acquires by tribal custom marriage will generally be recognized in all parts of the United States.[44]

The greater part, however, of the body of federal Indian law and tribal law applies only to certain areas which have a peculiar relation to the Indians and which in their totality comprise the Indian country.

The Indian country at any particular time must be viewed with reference to the existing body of federal and tribal law. Until 1817 it is country within which the criminal laws of the United States are not generally applicable, so that crimes in Indian country by whites against whites, or by Indians, are not cognizable in state or federal courts,[45] any more than crimes committed on the soil of Canada or Mexico. Treaties defined the boundaries between the United States, or the separate states.

[43] Act of July 23, 1892, 27 Stat. 260, as amended by Act of June 15, 1938, 52 Stat. 696, 25 U. S. C. 241. And see Chapter 17, sec. 3.

[44] 54 I. D. 39 (1932); and see R. A. Brown, The Indian Problem and the Law (1930) 39 Yale L. J. 307, 315. See also Chapter 7, sec. 5.

[45] Under the Act of July 22, 1790, 1 Stat. 137, federal jurisdiction was extended over any crime committed by a citizen or inhabitant of the United States against the person or property of any friendly Indian in any town, settlement, or territory belonging to any nation or tribe of Indians. Since the act specified that it was to be in force only for 2 years, it was superseded by the Act of March 1, 1793, 1 Stat. 329, which extended federal jurisdiction as before. On criminal jurisdiction see Chapter 18.

and the territories of the various Indian tribes or nations.[46] Within these territories the Indian tribes or nations had not only full jurisdiction over their own citizens, but the same jurisdiction over citizens of the United States that any other power might lawfully exercise over emigrants from the United States.[47] Treaties between the United States and various tribes commonly stipulated that citizens of the United States within the territory of the Indian nations were to be subject to the laws of those nations.[48]

It is against this legal background that the first legislative definitions must be understood. As early as July 22, 1790,[49] Congress used the expression "Indian country" in the first trade and intercourse act, apparently with the meaning of country belonging to the Indians, occupied by them, and to which the Government recognized them as having some kind of right and title. In the Act of March 1, 1793,[50] Indian country and Indian territory were used synonymously.

The Act of May 19, 1796,[51] contained the first statutory delimitation of Indian country, fixing, according to the then existing treaties, the boundary line between Indian country and the United States. In this act, as in those which followed it, the term "Indian country" is used as descriptive of the country within the boundary lines of the Indian tribes. In 1799,[52] and again in 1802,[53] the boundary of Indian country was redefined by Congress to conform with new treaties. In each instance it was provided that a citizen or inhabitant of the United States committing a crime against a friendly Indian, or Indians within Indian country should be subject to the jurisdiction of the federal courts. In both of these acts the words "Indian country" and "Indian territory" are used synonymously.[54]

The inconvenience of a territory in which white desperados could escape the force of state and federal law made itself felt in the Act of March 3, 1817,[55] which extended federal law to cover crimes committed by an Indian or white person within any town, district, or territory belonging to any nation or tribe of Indians, subject, however, to the limitation that the act should not be construed to extend to an offense by one Indian against another Indian within any Indian boundary.

Indian country in all these statutes is territory, wherever situated, within which tribal law is generally applicable, federal law is applicable only in special cases designated by statute, and state law is not applicable at all. This conception of the Indian country reflects a situation which finds its counterpart in international law in the case of newly acquired territories, where the laws of those territories continue in force until repealed or modified by the new sovereign. We find that Congress, when called upon to define Indian country in the Act of June 30, 1834,[56] said:

> * * * That all that part of the United States west of the Mississippi, and not within the states of Missouri and Louisiana, or the territory of Arkansas, and, also, that part of the United States east of the Mississippi river, and not within any state to which the Indian title has not been extinguished, for the purposes of this act, be taken and deemed to be the Indian country.

Whether Indian reservations within the exterior boundaries of a state but exempted by treaty or statute from state jurisdiction were included within the foregoing distinction is a question not free from doubt.[57] Such doubts, however, were resolved by a series of judicial decisions and by the failure to include section 1 of the Act of 1834[58] in the Revised Statutes, thereby repealing it.[59]

No subsequent statutory definition of Indian country appears, though for purposes of defining federal criminal jurisdiction reference is made in numerous acts[60] to "Indian country."

---

[46] Treaty of January 21, 1785, with the Wiandot, Delaware, Chippawa, and Ottawa Nations, 7 Stat. 16; Treaty of November 28, 1785, with the Cherokees, 7 Stat. 18; Treaty of January 3, 1786, with the Choctaw Nation, 7 Stat. 21; Treaty of January 10, 1786, with the Chickasaw Nation, 7 Stat. 24; Treaty of January 9, 1789, with the Wyandot, Delaware, Ottawa, Chippawa, Pattawattima, and Sac Nations, 7 Stat. 28; Treaty of August 7, 1790, with the Creek Nation, 7 Stat. 35; Treaty of July 2, 1791, with the Cherokee Nation, 7 Stat. 39; Treaty of August 3, 1795, with the Wyandots, Delawares, Shawanoes, Ottawas, Chipewas, Putawatimes, Miamis, Eel River, Weea's, Kickapoos, Piankashaws, and Kaskaskias, 7 Stat. 49; Treaty of October 2, 1798, with the Cherokee Nation, 7 Stat. 62; Treaty of December 17, 1801, with the Chactaw Nation, 7 Stat. 66; Treaty of October 17, 1802, with the Choctaw Nation, 7 Stat. 73; Treaty of November 3, 1804, with the Sac and Fox, 7 Stat. 84; Treaty of July 4, 1805, with the Wyandot, Ottawa, Chippawa, Munsee and Delaware, Shawanee, and Pottawatima Nations, 7 Stat. 87. See also Chapter 3, secs. 3A(2), 3A(3).

[47] It is interesting to note in this connection that some of the early Trade and Intercourse Acts contained a provision requiring a citizen or inhabitant of the United States to acquire a passport before going into the country secured by treaty to the Indians. Act of May 19, 1796, 1 Stat. 469; Act of March 3, 1799, 1 Stat. 743; Act of March 30, 1802, 2 Stat. 139. The provision was modified in the Act of June 30, 1834, 4 Stat. 729 so as not to apply to citizens of the United States. See Chapter 3, sec. 3A(3); Chapter 4, sec. 6.

[48] Treaty of January 21, 1785, with the Wiandot, Delaware, Chippawa, and Ottawa Nations, 7 Stat. 16; Treaty of November 28, 1785, with the Cherokees, 7 Stat. 18; Treaty of January 3, 1786, with the Choctaw Nation, 7 Stat. 21; Treaty of January 10, 1786, with the Chickasaw Nation, 7 Stat. 24; Treaty of January 31, 1786, with the Shawanoe Nation, 7 Stat. 26; Treaty of January 9, 1789, with the Wyandot, Delaware, Ottawa, Chippawa, Pattawattima, and Sac Nations, 7 Stat. 28; Treaty of August 7, 1790, with the Creek Nation, 7 Stat. 35; Treaty of July 2 1791, with the Cherokee Nation, 7 Stat. 39; Treaty of August 3, 1795, with the Wyandots, Delawares, Shawanoes, Ottawas, Chipewas, Putawatimes, Miamis, Eel River, Weea's, Kickapoos, Piankashaws, and Kaskaskias, 7 Stat. 49.

[49] 1 Stat. 137.

[50] 1 Stat. 329, similarly in the Act of March 3, 1799, 1 Stat. 743, and in Act of March 30, 1802, 2 Stat. 139.

[51] 1 Stat. 469.

[52] Act of March 3, 1799, 1 Stat. 743.

[53] Act of March 30, 1802, 2 Stat. 139.

[54] For a later meaning of the term "Indian territory" see Chapter 23.

[55] 3 Stat. 383.

[56] 4 Stat. 729. In the report of the Committee of Indian Affairs to the House of Representatives concerning, among others, this act we find the following interesting commentary suggesting a basis for the definition of Indian country as therein contained.

> The *Indian country* * * * will include all the territory of the United States west of the Mississippi, not within Louisiana, Missouri, and Arkansas, and those portions east of that river, and not within the limits of any State, to which the Indian title is not extinguished. The Southern Indians are not embraced within it. Most of them have agreed to emigrate. To all their lands, with the exception of those of a part of a single tribe, the Indian title has been extinguished; and the States in which the Indians of that excepted tribe remain, have extended their laws over them.
>
> * * * * *
>
> This act is intended to apply to the whole Indian country, as defined in the first section. On the west side of the Mississippi its limits can only be changed by a legislative act; on the east side of that river it will continue to embrace only those sections of country not within any State to which the Indian title shall not be extinguished. The effect of the extinguishment of the Indian title to any portion of it, will be the exclusion of such portion from the Indian country. The limits of the Indian country will thus be rendered at all times obvious and certain. By the intercourse act of 1802, the boundary of the Indian country was a line of metes and bounds, variable from time to time by treaties. And, from the multiplicity of those treaties, it is now somewhat difficult to ascertain what, at any given period, was the boundary or extent of the Indian country. (P. 10.)

H. Rept. No. 474, 23d Cong., 1st sess., vol. 4, May 20, 1834.

[57] It was early held that lands in territorial status to which Indian title had not been extinguished and which were exempted by treaty or statute from state jurisdiction remain Indian country within the meaning of the 1834 Act, notwithstanding the admission of the state into the Union. *United States* v. *Bridleman*, 7 Fed. 894 (D. C. Ore. 1881).

[58] 4 Stat. 729.

[59] R. S. § 5596; *Donnelly* v. *United States*, 228 U. S. 243, 268 (1913).

[60] Act of March 27, 1854, 10 Stat. 269, 270; Act of February 18, 1875, 18 Stat. 316, 318, R. S. § 2146, 25 U. S. C. 218. For statutes making it a criminal offense to introduce liquor into "Indian country" see Chapter 17, sec. 3.

Notwithstanding the repeal of section 1 of the Act of 1834,[61] the Supreme Court, when called upon to determine whether certain land was Indian country, applied in a number of instances the definition contained therein.[62]

The first case[63] to reach the Supreme Court after the repeal of section 1 of the 1834 act involved the legality of the seizure of liquor by a military officer under the authority contained in the Act of 1834, as amended by the Act of 1864. The legality of the seizure depended on whether or not it was made in Indian country, the locus being at a point within the territory of Dakota. In an unusual opinion the Court, *per* Mr. Justice Miller, made the following observations:

> Notwithstanding the immense changes which have since taken place in the vast region covered by the act of 1834, by the extinguishment of Indian titles, the creation of States and the formation of territorial governments, Congress has not thought it necessary to make any new definition of Indian country. Yet during all this time a large body of laws has been in existence, whose operation was confined to the Indian country, whatever that may be. And men have been punished by death, by fine, and by imprisonment, of which the courts who so punished them had no jurisdiction, if the offences were not committed in the Indian country as established by law. These facts afford the strongest presumption that the Congress of the United States, and the judges who administered those laws, must have found in the definition of Indian country, in the act of 1834, such an adaptability to the altered circumstances of what was then Indian country as to enable them to ascertain what it was at any time since then. (P. 207.)

After analyzing the definition as contained in section 1 of the 1834 Act the Court further said:

> * * * if the section be read as describing lands west of the Mississippi, outside of the States of Louisiana and Missouri, and of the Territory of Arkansas, and lands east of the Mississippi not included in any State, but lands alone to which the Indian title has not been extinguished, we have a description of the Indian country which was good then, and which is good now, and which is capable of easy application at any time.
>
> * * * * *
>
> It follows from this that all the country described by the act of 1834 as Indian country remains Indian country so long as the Indians retain their original title to the soil, and ceases to be Indian country whenever they lose that title, in the absence of any different provision by treaty or by act of Congress. (Pp. 208–209.)

In following the Bates decision, the courts have held that reservation lands to which Indian title has not been extinguished come within the definition of Indian country as contained in the 1834 Act, whether situated within a territory[64] or state.[65]

Ordinarily, Indian title is extinguished by cession under treaty or act of Congress, and the land ceases to be Indian country when the cession becomes effective.[66] Where the land, however, is held by the United States in trust, to be sold for the benefit of the Indian tribe, the courts have held that it remains "Indian land" until actually sold.[67]

The first important extension of the rule laid down in the Bates case occurred in 1913 in the case of *Donnelly* v. *United States,*[68] which involved the question of whether the jurisdiction of the United States extended to the crime of murder committed on an executive-order Indian reservation. In holding that federal criminal law was applicable, the Court said:

> It is contended for plaintiff in error that the term "Indian country" is confined to lands to which the Indians retain their original right of possession, and is not applicable to those set apart as an Indian reservation out of the public domain, and not previously occupied by the Indians. * * * In the Indian Intercourse Act of June 30, 1834, 4 Stat. 729, c. 161, the first section defined the "Indian country" for the purposes of that act. But this section was not reenacted in the Revised Statutes, and it was therefore repealed by § 5596, Rev. Stat. *Ex parte Crow Dog,* 109 U. S. 556, 561; *United States* v. *Le Bris,* 121 U. S. 278, 280; *Clairmont* v. *United States,* 225 U. S. 551, 557. Under these decisions the definition as contained in the act of 1834 may still "be referred to in connection with the provisions of its original context that remain in force, and may be considered in connection with the changes which have taken place in our situation, with a view of determining from time to time what must be regarded as Indian country where it is spoken of in the statutes." With reference to country that was formerly subject to the Indian occupancy, the cases cited furnish a criterion for determining what is "Indian country." But "the changes which have taken place in our situation" are so numerous and so material, that the term cannot now be confined to land formerly held by the Indians, and to which their title remains unextinguished. And, in our judgment, nothing can more appropriately be deemed "Indian country," within the meaning of those provisions of the Revised Statutes that relate to the regulation of the Indians and the government of the Indian country, than a tract of land that, being a part of the public domain, is lawfully set apart as an Indian reservation. (P. 268–269.)

In the same year, the Supreme Court in the case of *United States* v. *Sandoval*[69] held that the lands of the Pueblo Indians come within the definition of Indian country for the purpose of federal liquor regulation. The Pueblo lands were not, strictly speaking, a reservation, but were lands held by communal ownership in fee simple. It would seem that the term Indian country as applied to the Pueblos means any lands occupied by "distinctly Indian communities" recognized and treated by the Government as "dependent communities" entitled to its protection.[70]

The foregoing decisions are concerned with lands in tribal tenure. While the Supreme Court in the Donnelly case eliminated the necessity for original tribal title as a condition to the application of federal criminal law, it failed to consider the applicability of the category of Indian country to the individual Indian holdings.

Under the practice of allotting lands in severalty to individual Indians, title to the allotted land was held in trust by the Government for the benefit of the allottee, or vested in the

[61] 4 Stat. 729, 733.

[62] *Bates* v. *Clark,* 95 U. S. 204 (1877); *Ex Parte Crow Dog,* 109 U. S. 556 (1883); *United States* v. *LeBris,* 121 U. S. 278 (1887); *Clairmont* v. *United States,* 225 U. S. 551 (1912).

[63] *Bates* v. *Clark,* 95 U. S. 204 (1887).

[64] *Ex Parte Crow Dog,* 109 U. S. 556 (1883).

[65] *United States* v. *LeBris,* 121 U. S. 278 (1887). *Cf. United States* v. *Forty-Three Gallons of Whiskey,* 108 U. S. 491 (1883) (holding that, by statute, ceded Indian lands may remain Indian country for the purpose of enforcing federal liquor laws); *Clairmont* v. *United States,* 225 U. S. 551 (1912); *Dick* v. *United States,* 208 U. S. 340 (1908).

[66] *United States* v. *La Plant,* 200 Fed. 92 (D. C. S. D. 1911) (holding that land held under "mere occupancy" ceased to be Indian reservation land when ceded, even before sale to private parties); *United States* v. *Myers,* 206 Fed. 387 (C. C. A. 8, 1913).

[67] *Ash Sheep Co.* v. *United States,* 252 U. S. 159 (1920), aff'g 250 Fed. 591 (C. C. A. 9, 1918), and 254 Fed. 59 (C. C. A. 9, 1918). And see Chapter 15, sec. 21.

[68] 228 U. S. 243 (1913). Accord: *Pronovost* v. *United States,* 232 U. S. 487 (1914). ("An Indian reservation is Indian country.")

[69] 231 U. S. 28 (1913).

[70] For a fuller discussion of this case see Chapter 20, sec. 4. In holding that jurisdiction to punish the offense of larceny committed within a Pueblo resided in the Federal Government, the Court defined Indian country as "any unceded lands owned or occupied by an Indian nation or tribe of Indians." *United States* v. *Chaves,* 290 U. S. 357 (1933).

allottee subject to a restraint against alienation. Obviously, in either case tribal title is not involved.

By virtue of a series of murders committed on allotted lands, the Supreme Court was called upon to decide whether such lands were Indian country for the purpose of federal criminal jurisdiction. In the case of *United States* v. *Pelican*,[71] a case involving the murder of an Indian upon a trust allotment, the court held that trust allotments retain, during the trust period, a distinctive Indian character, being devoted to "Indian occupancy under the limitations imposed by Federal legislation," and that they were embraced within the term "Indian country."

Thereafter in *United States* v. *Ramsey*[72] Indian country was held to include a restricted allotment as well, the court saying:

> The sole question for our determination, therefore, is whether the place of the crime is Indian country within the meaning of § 2145. The place is a tract of land constituting an Indian allotment, carved out of the Osage Indian reservation and conveyed in fee to the allottee named in the indictment, subject to a restriction against alienation for a period of 25 years. That period has not elapsed, nor has the allottee ever received a certificate of competency authorizing her to sell. (P. 470.)
>
> * * * * *
>
> * * * it would be quite unreasonable to attribute to Congress an intention to extend the protection of the criminal law to an Indian upon a trust allotment and withhold it from one upon a restricted allotment; and we find nothing in the nature of the subject matter or in the words of the statute which would justify us in applying the term Indian country to one and not to the other. (Pp. 471–472.)

Thus, the application of Federal criminal law is extended to cover lands to which the tribal title has been extinguished and title has been vested in an individual.

The last important step in the application of Federal criminal law to lands in tribal tenure has been to extend it to lands, wherever situated, which have been purchased by the Federal Government and set apart for Indian occupancy.

In this connection it is well to note the illuminating opinion of Mr. Justice Black in the case of *United States* v. *McGowan*,[73] holding that Indian country comprises lands wherever situated, which have been validly set apart for the use and occupancy of Indians. The Court declared:

> The Reno Indian Colony is composed of several hundred Indians residing on a tract of 28.38 acres of land owned by the United States and purchased out of funds appropriated by Congress in 1917 and in 1926. The purpose of Congress in creating this colony was to provide lands for needy Indians scattered over the State of Nevada, and to equip and supervise these Indians in establishing a permanent settlement.
>
> The words "Indian country" have appeared in the statutes relating to Indians for more than a century. We must consider "the changes which have taken place in our situation, with a view of determining from time to time what must be regarded as Indian country where it is spoken of in the statutes." Also, due regard must be given to the fact that from an early period of our history, the Government has prescribed severe penalties to enforce laws regulating the sale of liquor on lands occupied by Indians under government supervision. Indians of the Reno Colony have been established in homes under the supervision and guardianship of the United States. The policy of Congress, uniformly enforced through the decisions of this Court, has been to regulate the liquor traffic with Indians occupying such a settlement. This protection is extended by the United States "over all *dependent Indian communities within its borders*, whether within its original territory or territory subsequently acquired, and *whether within or without the limits of a State*."
>
> The fundamental consideration of both Congress and the Department of the Interior in establishing this colony has been the protection of a dependent people. Indians in this colony have been afforded the same protection by the government as that given Indians in other settlements known as "reservations." Congress alone has the right to determine the manner in which this country's guardianship over the Indians shall be carried out, and it is immaterial whether Congress designates a settlement as a "reservation" or "colony."
>
> * * * * *
>
> The Reno Colony has been validly set apart for the use of the Indians. It is under the superintendence of the Government. The Government retains title to the lands which it permits the Indians to occupy. * * *
>
> When we view the facts of this case in the light of the relationship which has long existed between the Government and the Indians—and which continues to date—it is not reasonably possible to draw any distinction between this Indian "colony" and "Indian country." We conclude that § 247 of Title 25, *supra*, does apply to the Reno Colony. (Pp. 537–539.)[74]

The foregoing decisions leave open the question of whether an allotment within the exterior boundaries of an Indian reservation which is held by the allottee in fee simple may be subject to the application of federal criminal law and tribal law, or whether such land is subject to the exclusive jurisdiction of the state.[75]

Whether land acquired by the United States and used for Indian purposes which do not involve Indian occupancy right, *e. g.*, school, hospital, or agency sites not within a reservation, are "Indian country" is a queston which has not been definitely settled by any court decision. Administrative practices and rulings, however, indicate that such lands are not considered "Indian country."[76]

---

[71] 232 U. S. 442 (1914). *Cf. United States* v. *Sutton*, 215 U. S. 291 (1909); *Hallowell* v. *United States*, 221 U. S. 317 (1911); *Ex Parte Van Moore*, 221 Fed. 954 (D. C. S. D. 1915).

[72] 271 U. S. 467 (1926).

[73] 302 U. S. 535 (1938).

[74] It has been indicated that in the light of the *McGowan* case lands purchased under the Indian Reorganization Act (Act of June 18, 1934, 48 Stat. 984) not yet proclaimed a reservation or added to an existing reservation, are purchased for the purpose of being Indian reservations and that therefore the Federal Government has law and order jurisdiction over the Indians on such purchased lands pending the formal declaration of their reservation status. Memo. Sol. I. D., February 17, 1939.

[75] See Chapter 18.

[76] The Solicitor for the Interior Department, after analyzing the *McGowan* case, commented:

> A legal situation similar to that presented by the Reno Indian colony has occurred in the case of some of the abandoned military reservations which were turned over to this Department for Indian school purposes under the act of July 31, 1882 (22 Stat. 181, 25 U. S. C. A. sec. 276), and which have been accepted as Indian reservations. In these instances title to the land was held by the United States without any formal trust designation, but the land was occupied by Indians whose occupancy rights came to be recognized by Congress and by the Department. Examples are the Fort Bidwell and Fort Mohave reservations, in dealing with which Congress expressly referred to the rights of the Indians in the reservations. (See act of January 27, 1913, 37 Stat. 652, and act of June 25, 1910, 36 Stat. 855, 858.) Another example is the Fort Totten Reservation which was recognized in the act of April 27, 1904 (33 Stat. 319) as part of the Devils Lake Indian Reservation and belonging to the Indians residing on the reservation. In the case of *LaDuke* v. *Melin*, 45 N. D. 349, 177 N. W. 673, the court reviewed the history of this military reservation devoted to Indian school purposes and acknowledged the fact that it might be considered an "Indian reservation."
>
> These examples demonstrate that lands held by the United States without a declaration of trust and used for school or other institutional purposes may be considered Indian reservations where Indian communities have occupancy rights in the land. They point the distinction between this type of land and lands held exclusively by the United States for institutional purposes where there are no Indian residents nor Indian occupancy rights. The latter class of lands is best illustrated by the nonreservation schools and hospitals which the Department has itself not classified as Indian reservations. (*Cf.* Handbook of October 15, 1929. "General Data concerning Indian Reservations.")
>
> Another way of demonstrating this conclusion is by reference to the general proposition that Indian country is country where not only Federal laws but also Indian laws and customs apply. It is apparent that Indian laws apply only in areas occupied by Indian groups and communities and not to lands held for Federal institutions in Pierre, Phoenix, or any other non-Indian community.
>
> In brief, my conclusion is that lands held by the United States and purchased for the purpose of establishing Federal institutions for Indian welfare are not Indian country nor Indian reservations unless an Indian tribe or group has occupancy rights in the land. Such lands may be "reservations of the United States" as, for example, that term is used in right-of-way statutes (Memo. Solicitor, I. D., July 1, 1938), but they would not be "Indian reservations."

Memo. Sol. I. D., July 9, 1940.

CHAPTER 2

THE OFFICE OF INDIAN AFFAIRS

TABLE OF CONTENTS

SECTION 1. THE DEVELOPMENT OF THE INDIAN SERVICE

A. ESTABLISHMENT

The relations of the United States with the Indians generally have been through designated administrative agencies, and it is therefore important to examine the structure, guiding policy, and manner of functioning of these agencies at various periods.

As a general rule, the Crown and the colonies regulated intercourse between their own subjects and the Indians, but made no attempt to govern the internal relations of Indian tribes.[1]

After the French and Indian War, and prior to the adoption of the Constitution, two superintendencies of Indian affairs were created—one for the northern and one for the southern colonies. The superintendents were in effect ambassadors, a role which to a limited extent superintendents fill today. Their duties consisted of observing events, negotiating treaties, and generally keeping peace between Indians and the border settlers.[2]

On July 12, 1775,[3] the Continental Congress, as one of its first acts, and exercising definite governmental power for all the colonies, declared its jurisdiction over Indian tribes by creating three departments of Indian affairs—northern, southern, and middle; at the head of each were placed commissioners, five for the southern, three (later four)[4] for the northern, and three for the middle department. Their duties were "* * * to treat with the Indians * * * in order to preserve peace and friendship with the said Indians and to prevent their taking any part in the present commotions."[5] The duties of the commissioners did not differ from those of the colonial superintendents but their status as official representatives of a new government, not the Crown, did.

The importance of these offices is indicated by the fact that the commissioners of the middle department unanimously elected on July 12, 1775, were Benjamin Franklin, Patrick Henry, and James Wilson.[6]

[1] Schmeckebier, The Office of Indian Affairs, Its History, Activities, and Organization (1927), p. 12.

[2] *Ibid.*

[3] Jour. Cont. Cong. (Library of Congress ed.), vol. II, p. 175.

[4] *Ibid.*, p. 183.

[5] *Ibid.*, p. 175.

[6] *Ibid.*, p. 183.

By a general ordinance for the regulation of Indian affairs of August 7, 1786,[7] the Congress of the Confederation followed the colonial precedent and established two departments—the northern, north of the Ohio River, and west of the Hudson River, and the southern, south of the Ohio River. At the head of each was placed a superintendent under the control of and reporting to the Secretary of War. Each had power to grant licenses to trade and live with the Indians.

This ordinance remained partially in force after the adoption of the Constitution of the United States.[8]

On August 7, 1789,[9] early in the first Congress, the War Department was established, upon whose Secretary devolved all matters relative to Indian affairs as were "* * * entrusted to him by the President of the United States, agreeably to the Constitution * * *."

The first Congress and the first President recognized the need for remedying a problem of conflict of Indian and white interests, serious even then.[10]

On August 20, 1789,[11] 5 months after the first Congress convened, it appropriated $20,000 for "negotiating and treating with the Indian tribes," the first of a long series of appropriations for that purpose.

On September 11, 1789,[12] in an early act establishing the salaries of executive officers of the Government, Congress began the policy of making the governor of a territory superintendent of Indian affairs in that jurisdiction by appropriating $2,000 to "the Governor of the western territory, for his salary as such, and for

[7] Jour. Cont. Cong. (Library of Congress ed.), vol. XXXI, p. 491.

[8] The Act of September 11, 1789, 1 Stat. 67, 68, refers to "* * * superintendent of Indian affairs in the northern department, * * *." The Intercourse Act of July 22, 1790, 1 Stat. 137, mentions "* * * the superintendent of the department * * *."

[9] Act of August 7, 1789, 1 Stat. 49, 50.

[10] See Schmeckebier, *op. cit.*, pp. 18–19 for Washington's statement to the Senate on broken treaties: "* * * the treaty with the Cherokees has been entirely violated by the disorderly white people on the frontiers of North Carolina." (Annals of Congress, 1st Cong., 1st sess., p. 66).

[11] Act of August 20, 1789, 1 Stat. 54.

[12] Act of September 11, 1789, 1 Stat. 67, 68.

discharging the duties of superintendent of Indian affairs in the northern department * * *." [13]

In 1790, Congress, exercising its power under the commerce clause of the Constitution, passed the first act "* * * to regulate trade and intercourse with the Indian tribes" [14] which provided for licensing of Indian traders, and conferred extensive regulatory powers on the President. This temporary act was renewed with modifications until 1802 when the first permanent Intercourse Act was passed.[15]

The first specific appropriation for Indian affairs appears in the Act of December 23, 1791.[16] The sum of $39,424.71 was appropriated "For defraying all expenses incident to the Indian department,[17] authorized by law, * * *."

The Treasury Department was given responsibility for the purchase of Indian goods as well as other War Department supplies by the Act of May 8, 1792.[18]

Trading houses under Government ownership were maintained from 1796 [19] to 1822.[20] Their function was to supply the Indians with necessary goods at a fair price, and offer a fair price for their furs in exchange.[21] The agents were appointed by the President and responsible to him. Their accounts were transmitted to the Secretary of the Treasury.

The office of Superintendent of Indian Trade was set up in 1806.[22] The superintendent, like the agent for each trading house, was appointed by the President. His duties were, among other things, "* * * to purchase and take charge of all goods intended for trade with the Indian nations * * * and to transmit the same to such places as he shall be directed by the President." [23]

After the abolition of the office of Superintendent of Indian Trade in 1822,[24] Secretary of War Calhoun created the Bureau of Indian Affairs by order of March 11, 1824,[25] and placed at its head Thomas L. McKenney who had formerly been superintendent of Indian trade. His duties included the administration of the civilization fund [26] under departmental regulations, the examination of claims arising out of laws regulating intercourse with Indian tribes, and routine office correspondence.[27]

His staff consisted of a chief clerk and one assistant.[28] His representatives in the field included superintendents, agents, and subagents.[29]

B. DEVELOPMENT

The period between 1824 and 1832, when the statutory office of Commissioner of Indian Affairs in the War Department was established, appears to have been one of confusion in the Bureau of Indian Affairs.[30]

By Act of July 9, 1832,[31] Congress authorized the President to appoint, with the consent of the Senate, a Commissioner of Indian Affairs who was to have "* * * the direction and management of all Indian affairs, and of all matters arising out of Indian relations * * *." He was under the direction of the Secretary of War and subject to the regulations prescribed by the President.

The number of clerks was not specified. The Secretary of War was empowered to transfer or appoint the necessary number of clerks "* * * so as not to increase the number now employed * * *" [32] by the department.

Two years later the Act of June 30, 1834,[33] since considered the organic law of the Indian Office,[34] was passed "to provide for the organization of the department of Indian affairs." This statute established certain agencies and abolished others. It provided for the employment of subagents, interpreters, and other employees, the payment of annuities, the purchase and distribution of supplies, etc. It was in effect, a reorganization of the field force of the War Department having charge of Indian affairs,[35] and in no way altered the power of the Secretary of War or the Commissioner,[36] or changed the status of the Bureau of Indian Affairs in the War Department.[37]

Subsequent appropriation acts provided for the hiring of additional personnel.[38]

Under section 5 of the Act of March 3, 1849,[39] by which the Home Department of the Interior was established, the Bureau

[13] As new territories were created, the governor was often made, *ex officio*, superintendent of Indian affairs, a position which he generally held until the territory became a state; in some cases, however, the duties of the superintendent were transferred before statehood, to one of the general superintendencies in the Indian Service or to the Washington Office. (Schmeckebier, *op. cit.*, p. 19.)

In 1867, at the time the Indian Peace Commission was created (Act of July 20, 1867, 15 Stat. 17) there were four territories whose governors were also superintendents of Indian affairs, *ex officio*—Colorado, Dakota, Idaho, Montana (Schmeckebier, *op. cit.*, p. 52). The Peace Commission in its report strongly urged that those governors be divested of their duties as superintendent. (Report of Commissioner of Indian Affairs (1868) p. 48.)

[14] Act of July 22, 1790, 1 Stat. 137, in force for 2 years.

[15] Act of March 30, 1802, 2 Stat. 139. For a summary of these acts, see Chapter 4, secs. 2 and 3. See also Chapter 16.

[16] 1 Stat. 226, 228.

[17] This is the first mention in an appropriation act of the existence of an "Indian department."

[18] 1 Stat. 279.

[19] Act of April 18, 1796, 1 Stat. 452. This act was a temporary measure reenacted every 2 or 3 years up to the abolition of Government trading houses in 1822. See Chapter 16.

[20] Abolished by Act of May 6, 1822, 3 Stat. 679.

[21] "In several of his annual addresses to Congress, Washington had strongly urged the establishment of trading houses by the Government, in order to protect the Indians from the practices of private traders. * * *" (Schmeckebier, *op. cit.*, p. 23. See also pp. 20–22.)

[22] Act of April 21, 1806, 2 Stat. 402.

[23] *Ibid.*, sec. 2. Appropriation acts indicate the expansion of the office of Indian trade by providing for compensation of additional clerks. *E. g.*, Act of March 3, 1809, 2 Stat. 544; Act of February 26, 1810, 2 Stat. 557, 559.

[24] Act of May 6, 1822, 3 Stat. 679.

[25] H. Doc. No. 146, 19th Cong., 1st sess., p. 6.

[26] Act of March 3, 1819, 3 Stat. 516, provided a permanent annual appropriation of $10,000 for "* * * introducing among them [the Indians] the habits and arts of civilization * * *"; repealed by Act of February 14, 1873, c. 138, 17 Stat. 437, 461. For further discussion see Chapter 12, sec. 2A.

[27] Report of the Commissioner of Indian Affairs, 1932, p. 1. Hereafter in this chapter these reports will be referred to as "Rep. Comm. Ind. Aff."

[28] Schmeckebier, *op. cit.*, p. 27. Act of March 2, 1827, 4 Stat. 233, provides for one clerk in the Bureau of Indian Affairs. Act of February 12, 1828, 4 Stat. 247, for one clerk and messengers.

[29] Rep. Comm. Ind. Aff., 1932, p. 1.

[30] Schmeckebier, *op. cit.*, p. 27 quotes Schoolcraft (Personal Memoirs, 1828, p. 319) on the "derangements in the fiscal affairs of the Indian department * * * there is a screw loose in the public machinery somewhere."

[31] 4 Stat. 564, R. S. § 462–463, 25 U. S. C. 1–2.

[32] *Ibid.*, sec. 2.

[33] 4 Stat. 735.

[34] See Rep. Comm. Ind. Aff., 1932, p. 1.

[35] Kinney, A Continent Lost—A Civilization Won (1937), p. 104.

[36] Schmeckebier, *op. cit.*, p. 28.

[37] Congress continued to pass appropriation acts for the "Indian department" as it had since 1791 (Act of December 23, 1791, 1 Stat. 226, 228; see *e. g.* Act of January 27, 1835, 4 Stat. 746), and to allow compensation for the Commissioner of Indian Affairs and his clerks (Act of March 3, 1835, 4 Stat. 760).

[38] See *e. g.* Act of May 9, 1836, 5 Stat. 26; Joint Resolution of May 2, 1840, 5 Stat. 409.

[39] 9 Stat. 395, R. S. § 441, 5 U. S. C. 485.

of Indian Affairs passed from military to civil control. This act provided: "That the Secretary of the Interior shall exercise the supervisory and appellate powers now exercised by the Secretary of the War Department, in relation to all the acts of the Commissioner of Indian Affairs."

The administration of Indian affairs was not markedly affected by this transfer, because as early as 1834 the office was essentially a civilian bureau.[40] Army officers continued to be employed occasionally as agents.[41]

After 1849 Congress debated for years the expediency of transferring the Indian Bureau back to the War Department.[42] Constant fluctuations of responsibility between the two departments ensued.[43]

In 1869,[44] to correct mismanagement in the purchase and handling of Indian supplies, the Board of Indian Commissioners was created, to be appointed by, and report to, the President. It was composed of not more than 10 "men eminent for intelligence and philanthropy, to serve without pecuniary compensation * * *" and exercise joint control with the Secretary of the Interior over the appropriations in that act. By Act of July 15, 1870,[45] the Board was empowered "* * * to supervise all expenditures of money appropriated for the benefit of Indians * * * and to inspect all goods purchased for said Indians * * *." Although the Board was entirely independent of the Bureau of Indian Affairs, it studied and advised on important questions of Indian policy.[46]

This Board was abolished by Executive Order 6145, May 25, 1933,[47] which provided that the Board's affairs be wound up by the Secretary of the Interior, and that its records, property, and personnel be transferred to, or remain under, his supervision.

By title 5, section 485, of the United States Code,[48] the Secretary of the Interior now has supervision over "* * * public business relating to * * * The Indians," and by title 25, section 2, of the United States Code,[49] the Commissioner of Indian affairs over "* * * the management of all Indian affairs and of all matters arising out of Indian relations * * *" under the direction of the Secretary of the Interior and according to regulations prescribed by the President.

C. LIST OF COMMISSIONERS

Prior to 1832, the Secretary of War was chief officer in charge of Indian matters. From 1806 to 1822 he had the advice of the Superintendent of Indian Trade, and from 1824 to 1832 of the three successive heads of the new Bureau of Indian Affairs—Thomas L. McKenney (1824–30); Samuel S. Hamilton (1830–31); Elbert Herring (1831–32). Herring became first Commissioner of Indian Affairs in 1832.[50]

In the 108 years following the establishment of the office of Commissioner of Indian Affairs, that post has been held by some 32 individuals representing a wide range of variation in their outlook upon the responsibilities and opportunities of that office. These individuals have set forth in the Commissioners' Annual Reports[51] and in unofficial writings[52] their views on the Indian question, and these expressions are in many ways the most useful guides to the variations of Government Indian policy.

In tracing prevailing policies for a particular period, the following list[53] of Commissioners of Indian Affairs, with the Secretaries and Presidents under whom they served, may prove useful:

---

[40] Administration of the Indian Office (Bureau of Municipal Research Publication No. 65) (1915), p. 13.

[41] Schmeckebier, *op. cit.*, p. 43. By Act of July 15, 1870, 16 Stat. 315, 319, Congress prohibited the appointment of the military officers to civil posts unless commissions were vacated.

However, the exception later made affecting Indian agencies appears to be a survival of the period of military control. By Act of July 13, 1892, c. 164, sec. 1, 27 Stat. 120; Act of July 1, 1898, c. 545, sec. 1, 30 Stat. 571, 573, R. S. § 2062, 25 U. S. C. 27.

> The President may detail officers of the United States Army to act as Indian agents at such agencies as in the opinion of the President may require the presence of any Army officer, and while acting as Indian agents such officers shall be under the orders and direction of the Secretary of the Interior.

(From 25 U. S. C. 27).

[42] Administration of the Indian Office (Bureau of Municipal Research Publication No. 65) (1915), p. 13; Schmeckebier, *op. cit.*, pp. 50, 51.

In 1867, a commission appointed by Congress (Pub. Res. of March 3 1865, 13 Stat. 572) to inquire into civil and military authority over Indians reported,

> * * * The question whether the Indian bureau should be placed under the War Department or retained in the Department of the Interior is one of considerable importance, and both sides have very warm advocates. * * * (P. 6.)

(Sen. Rept. No. 156, 39th Cong., 2d sess., pp. 3–8.)

Commissioner of Indian Affairs Taylor in his report of 1868 gave 11 reasons for his vigorous opposition to the transfer. He held, among other things, that the professed Indian policy was peace, but transfer was tantamount to perpetual war.

> * * * I cannot for the life of me perceive the propriety or the efficacy of employing the military instead of the civil departments, unless it is intended to adopt the Mohammedan motto, and proclaim to these people "Death or the Koran." (P. 10.)

On January 7, 1868, the Peace Commission (appointed by Act of July 20, 1867, 15 Stat. 17) recommended that "* * * Indian affairs be committed to an independent bureau or department." (Rep. Comm. Ind. Aff., 1868, p. 48.) However, at the end of the same year (October 9, 1868) in a supplementary report to the President it stated,

> * * * in the opinion of this commission the Bureau of Indian Affairs should be transferred from the Department of the Interior to the Department of War.

(Rep. Comm. Ind. Aff., 1868, p. 372).

[43] Administration of the Indian Office (Bureau of Municipal Research Publication (No. 65) (1915), p. 13.

Excerpts from official reports reveal this conflict. *E. g.*, Commissioner Manypenny in his report for 1854 states:

> Occasions frequently arise in our intercourse with the Indians requiring the employment of force. * * *. The Indian Bureau would be relieved from embarrassment, and rendered more efficient, if, in such cases, the department had the direct control of the means necessary to execute its own orders. (P. 17.)

In Secretary of Interior Harlan's introduction to the Report of the Commissioner of Indian Affairs for 1865, he states that:

> On taking charge of this department on the 15th day of May last, the relations of officers respectively engaged in the military and civil departments in the Indian country were in an unsatisfactory condition. A supposed conflict of jurisdiction and a want of confidence in each other led to mutual criminations, whereby the success of military operations against hostile tribes and the execution of the policy of this department were seriously impeded. Upon conferring with the War Department, it was informally agreed that the agents and officers under the control of the Secretary of the Interior should hold no intercourse, except through the military authorities, with tribes of Indians against whom hostile measures were in progress; and that the military authorities should refrain from interference with such agents and officers in their relations with all other tribes, except to afford the necessary aid for the enforcement of the regulations of this department. * * * (P. iv.)

[44] R. S. § 2039, 25 U. S. C. 21, derived from Act of April 10, 1869, 16 Stat. 13, 40, and Act of July 15, 1870, sec. 3, 16 Stat. 335, 360. See *Ryan v. United States*, 8 C. Cls. 265 (1872).

[45] 16 Stat. 335, 360.

[46] Schmeckebier, *op. cit.*, p. 57.

[47] See 25 U. S. C. 21.

[48] R. S. § 441, derived from Act of March 3, 1849, c. 108, 9 Stat. 395.

[49] R. S. § 463, derived from Act of July 9, 1832, c. 174, sec. 1, 4 Stat. 564 and Act of July 27, 1868, c. 259, sec. 1, 15 Stat. 228.

[50] Schmeckebier, *op. cit.*, pp. 26–27; Kinney, *op. cit.*, p. 102.

[51] The heads of the Bureau of Indian Affairs also reported annually to the Secretary of War from 1824 to 1832.

[52] Walker, The Indian Question (1874); Manypenny, Our Indian Wards (1880); Leupp, The Indian and His Problem (1910)

[53] Rep. Comm. Ind. Aff., 1932, pp. 1–2.

Commissioners of Indian Affairs

Commissioner	Date	Secretary	President
Herring, Elbert	July 10, 1832	Cass [1]	Jackson.
Harris, Carey A	July 4, 1836	Cass [1] and Poinsett [1]	Do.
Crawford, T. Hartley	Oct. 22, 1838	Poinsett [1] to Marcy [1]	Van Buren.
Medill, William	Oct. 28, 1845	Marcy [1] and Ewing [2]	Polk.
Brown, Orlando	May 31, 1849	Ewing	Taylor.
Lea, Luke	July 1, 1850	Ewing to Stuart	Taylor and Fillmore.
Manypenny, George W.	Mar. 24, 1853	McClelland and Thompson.	Pierce.
Denver, James W	Apr. 17, 1857	Thompson	Buchanan.
Mix, Charles E	June 14, 1858	do	Do.
Denver, James W	Nov. 8, 1858	do	Do.
Greenwood, Alfred B	May 4, 1859	do	Do.
Dole, William P	Mar. 13, 1861	Smith to Harlan	Lincoln.
Cooley, Dennis N	July 10, 1865	Harlan and Browning	Johnson.
Bogy, Lewis V	Nov. 1, 1866	Browning	Do.
Taylor, Nathaniel G	Mar. 29, 1867	Browning and Cox	Do.
Parker, Ely S	Apr. 21, 1869	Cox and Delano	Grant.

[1] Secretaries of War.
[2] Ewing and all following, Secretaries of the Interior.

Commissioners of Indian Affairs—Continued

Commissioner	Date	Secretary	President
Walker, Francis A	Nov. 21, 1871	Delano	Do.
Smith, Edward P	Mar. 20, 1873	Delano and Chandler	Do.
Smith, John Q	Dec. 11, 1875	Chandler and Schurz	Do.
Hayt, Ezra A	Sept. 27, 1877	Schurz	Hayes.
Trowbridge, R. E	Mar. 15, 1880	do	Do.
Price, Hiram	May 4, 1881	Kirkwood and Teller	Garfield.
Atkins, John D. C	Mar. 21, 1885	Lamar	Cleveland.
Oberly, John H	Oct. 10, 1888	Vilas	Do.
Morgan, Thomas J	June 10, 1889	Noble	Harrison.
Browning, Daniel M	Apr. 17, 1893	Smith and Francis	Cleveland.
Jones, William A	May 3, 1897	Bliss and Hitchcock	McKinley.
Leupp, Francis E	Dec. 7, 1904	Hitchcock, Garfield and Ballinger.	Roosevelt.
Valentine, Robt. G	June 16, 1909	Ballinger, Fisher	Taft.
Sells, Cato	June 2, 1913	Lane and Payne	Wilson.
Burke, Charles H	Apr. 1, 1921	Fall, Work, West, Wilbur.	Harding, Coolidge.
Rhoads, Charles J	July 1, 1929	Wilbur	Hoover.
Collier, John	Apr. 21, 1933	Ickes	Roosevelt.

SECTION 2. THE DEVELOPMENT OF INDIAN SERVICE POLICIES

The history of Indian Service policies is the story of the rise and decline of a system of paternalism for which it is difficult to find a parallel in American history. The Indian Service begins as a diplomatic service handling negotiations between the United States and the Indian nations and tribes, characterized by Chief Justice Marshall as "domestic dependent nations." [54] By a process of jurisdictional aggrandisement, on the one hand, and voluntary surrenders of tribal powers, on the other, the Indian Service reached the point where nearly every aspect of Indian life was subject to the almost uncontrolled discretion of Indian Service officials.[55] In recent years there has been a marked reversal of these tendencies.

The reports of various Commissioners of Indian Affairs give the most graphic chronological insight into changing administrative policies.

A. THE PERIOD FROM 1825 TO 1850

In 1825 Thomas L. McKenney, as head of the new Bureau of Indian Affairs[56] in his first brief report[57] to the Secretary of War, wrote, regarding those Indians whose titles to land had been extinguished and who had elected to remove, that it was "* * * the policy of the Government to guarantee to them lasting and undisturbed possession" of their new land beyond the boundaries of Missouri and Arkansas.

The extent to which this policy was carried into effect is elsewhere discussed.[58]

In his lengthier report for 1826,[59] McKenney, in urging increased appropriations for the support of Indian schools,[60] was firmly convinced of—

> * * * the vast benefits which the Indian children are deriving from these establishments; and which go further, in my opinion, towards securing our borders from bloodshed, and keeping the peace among the Indians themselves, and attaching them to us, than would the physical force of our Army, if employed exclusively towards the accomplishment of those objects.[61]

McKenney early foresaw the problem of the returned student, and recommended that—

> * * * as these youths are qualified to enter upon a course of civilized life, sections of land be given to them, and a suitable present to commence with, of agricultural or other implements suited to the occupations in which they may be disposed, respectively, to engage. They will then have become an "intermediate link between our own citizens, and our wandering neighbors, softening the shades of each, and enjoying the confidence of both." [62]

Samuel S. Hamilton, in his only report[63] as head of the Bureau of Indian Affairs, recommended in 1830 that with "* * * the increase of our population, and the consequent extension of our settlements, * * *" the act to regulate trade and intercourse with the Indian tribes, passed in 1802, be revised, and the line setting the Indian boundary by that act be redefined. This recommendation, repeated in 1831, was finally acted upon in the Intercourse Act of 1834.[64]

Elbert Herring, who headed the Bureau of Indian Affairs for 1 year, and subsequently became its first Commissioner, commended the Government's recent policy of removal as the only means of checking the complete disintegration of the Indian tribes.

> * * * tribes numerous and powerful have disappeared from among us in a ratio of decrease, ominous to the existence of those that still remain, unless counteracted by the substitution of some principle sufficiently potent to check the tendencies to decay and dissolution. This salutary principle exists in the system of removal; of change of residence; of settlement in territories exclusively their own, and under the protection of the United States; connected with the benign influences of education and instruction in agriculture and the several mechanic arts, whereby social is distinguished from savage life.[65]

In his report for 1832 as Commissioner of Indian Affairs, Herring again commends the policy of removal in exalted terms:

> * * * In the consummation of this grand and sacred object rests the sole chance of averting Indian annihilation. Founded in pure and disinterested motives, may it meet the approval of heaven, by the complete attainment of its beneficent ends! [66]

[54] See Chapter 14, sec. 6.

[55] A discussion of the subjects of Indian administrative power will be found in Chapters 5, 8, 11, 12, 15, 16, 17.

[56] The head of the Bureau of Indian Affairs was not denominated Commissioner until 1832.

[57] Annual Report for 1825, Office of Indian Affairs, p. 91.

[58] See Chapter 3, sec. 4E, and Chapter 15, secs. 5, 21.

[59] Annual Report for 1826, Office of Indian Affairs, p. 508.

[60] In the years immediately following, reports devote a section to the increase in school attendance as an indication of civilization.

[61] Annual Report for 1826, Office of Indian Affairs, p. 508. Compare this early attitude regarding the use of the military, with that expressed by Commissioner Walker in 1872, *infra*.

[62] *Ibid.*, p. 508.

[63] Annual Report for 1830, Superintendent of Indian Affairs, p. 163.

[64] Act of June 30, 1834, 4 Stat. 729. See sec. 1A, and fns. 14 and 15, *supra*, and see Chapter 1, sec. 3; Chapter 4, sec. 6.

[65] Annual Report for 1831, Indian Bureau, p. 172.

[66] Annual Report for 1832, Office of Indian Affairs, p. 160.

In this report appears the first mention of vaccination as a health measure for the benefit of the Indians, and the employment of physicians by the Bureau.[67]

In 1833 appears the first mention in Commissioners' reports of the need among Indian tribes for

> * * * something, however simple, in the shape of a code of laws, suited to their wants, * * * devised and submitted for their adoption, to obviate the inconveniences, and secure the benefits incident thereto, in the relations that are springing up under the fostering care of the Government. * * *[68]

Jacksonian policy[69] was reflected in the increasing emphasis in commissioners' reports on the use of the military to effect what began as voluntary removal. In his report for 1834, apropos of the failure of the Cherokee to date to sign a treaty of removal, Commissioner Herring wrote:

> * * * Should occasion call for it, the military will be ordered out for the protection of those who decide on emigration, and of the emigrating officers of Government engaged in this hazardous and responsible service.[70]

In 1835 he wrote:

> There has been no intermission of exertion to induce the removal of the Cherokees to the west of the Mississippi, in conformity with the policy adopted by the Government * * *.[71]

In 1836 the new Commissioner of Indian Affairs, Carey A. Harris, wrote:

> The removal of the Creek Indians, like that of the Seminoles, was made a military operation on the commission by them of hostile acts. * * *[72]

T. Hartley Crawford, in his first report as Commissioner of Indian Affairs for 1838,[73] apropos of removal, states that for the most part it has been peaceful, including that of the Cherokees. However, the "indisposition" of the Pottawatomies "to comply with their engagements" caused the agent

> on the application of the white settlers, to call upon the Governor of Indiana for a military force to repress any outbreak that might occur. The Governor authorized General John Tipton to accept the services of one hundred volunteers; who raised them, and used their services in the collection and removal of the Pottawatomies.[74]

Commissioner Crawford urged that some evidence of title to lands granted to them in the West be given Indians on removal.[75]

In the field of education he reports:

> The principal lever by which Indians are to be lifted out of the mire of folly and vice in which they are sunk, is education. * * * To teach a savage man to read, while he continues a savage in all else, is to throw seed on a rock. * * * Manual-labor schools are what the Indian condition calls for.[76]

The educational policy of civilizing the Indians through manual training in agriculture and the "mechanic arts" became the accepted policy of the Indian office.[77]

The problem of the Indian field agent who becomes too closely identified with a particular tribe attracted concern. "Is there not some hazard of his becoming attached to their particular interests * * *?"[78] "By transferring them from one position to another," Commissioner Crawford wrote, "as frequently as may be regarded proper, they will be cut off from the strong enlistment of their feelings * * *."[79]

Vaccination for smallpox during an epidemic and medical services supplied by the Bureau of Indian Affairs are again mentioned.[80]

Commissioner Crawford, like Commissioner Herring,[81] recommended a code of laws for the government of the Western tribes, but added: "* * * this, as it seems to me, indispensable step to their advancement in civilization cannot be taken without their own consent."[82]

Like many commissioners before and after him, Commissioner Crawford felt that the policy of allotment was the only proper policy for the Government to pursue. "Common property and civilization cannot coexist."[83]

Of a proposed plan, for a confederation of Indian tribes west of the Mississippi, he held that "* * * prudential considerations would seem to require that they should be kept distinct from each other."[84]

For the next few years, commissioners report "progress" in removal, treaty-making and education in the manual arts. They begin to include "accompanying documents" prepared by field personnel.

Commissioner Medill in his report for 1847 told of the need for a "statistical account of the various tribes, including a digest of their industrial means, peculiar habits, resources, and employments of every kind * * *" which would "* * * materially aid the Department in suggesting the most suitable measures for their improvement."[85] This need was reiterated and various attempts were made to fill it.[86]

---

[67] *Ibid.*, p. 162. For a discussion of federal health services, see Chapter 12, sec. 3.

[68] Rep. Comm. Ind. Aff., 1833, p. 186. Some of the tribes, notably the Five Civilized Tribes, early adopted their own code of laws. In 1882, Commissioner Price tells of the preparation and submission by the Pottawatomies of their own code of laws to the department for approval. (Rep. Comm. Ind. Aff., 1882, p. VIII.)

[69] See Chapter 3, sec. 4E. Commenting on the situation that arose with the election of President Jackson, Schmeckebier writes:

> The election of Jackson to the Presidency in 1828 resulted in a definite change in the Indian policy in regard to removal. Both Monroe and Adams had adopted the policy of voluntary emigration, but Jackson was determined to use force if necessary. A mere reading of the statutes and the treaties would indicate no definite change, but when the method of obtaining the treaties is taken into consideration it is easy to see that the government was determined to use any pressure necessary to accomplish its ends.

(Schmeckebier, *op. cit.*, p. 33.)

[70] Rep. Comm. Ind. Aff., 1834, p. 243.

[71] Rep. Comm. Ind. Aff., 1835, p. 262.

[72] Rep. Comm. Ind. Aff., 1836, p. 368.

[73] Rep. Comm. Ind. Aff., 1838.

[74] *Ibid.*, p. 413.

[75] *Ibid.*, p. 414.

[76] *Ibid.*, pp. 420–421. Many later treaties contained a specific provision for the establishment of manual labor schools.

[77] See Chapter 12, sec. 2.

[78] Rep. Comm. Ind. Aff., 1838, p. 422.

[79] *Ibid.*

[80] *Ibid.*, p. 424. Commissioner Crawford states that in the northwest alone, at least 17,200 deaths occurred. Three thousand persons were vaccinated in the Columbia River region.

[81] See *supra*, and Rep. Comm. Ind. Aff., 1833, p. 186.

[82] Rep. Comm. Ind. Aff., 1838, p. 424.

[83] *Ibid.*, p. 425. See Chapter 11, sec. 1.

[84] *Ibid.*, p. 426.

[85] Rep. Comm. Ind. Aff., 1847, pp. 747–748.

[86] *E. g.*, Act of June 27, 1846, 9 Stat. 20, 34, provided for a survey, but failed to provide the necessary means to execute it; Act of March 3, 1847, sec. 5, 9 Stat. 203, 204, likewise provided for a census to illustrate "* * * the history, the present condition, and future prospects of the Indian tribes of the United States." At the time of Commissioner Medill's report, results were being returned by agents and subagents "* * * of most interesting and satisfactory character" (Rep. Comm. Ind. Aff., 1847, p. 748). Some 12 years later, in 1859, Secretary of the Interior Thompson wrote:

> The statistical information in the possession of the Indian office is too meager and vague to enable us to determine with

The role that was played by missionary groups through their teachers and schools was clearly stated by Commissioner Medill:

> In every system which has been adopted for promoting the cause of education among the Indians, the Department has found its most efficient and faithful auxiliaries and laborers in the societies of the several Christian denominations * * *.[87]

Commissioner Orlando Brown, in addition to various reports on the status of removal, including a full report on the proposed removal of the Seminoles to be "* * * conducted by the military alone * * *,"[88] made recommendations for various changes in policy: That (1) "* * * in all treaties hereafter to be made with the Indians, the policy of giving goods, farming utensils, provisions, etc., in lieu of money, be insisted on * * *" as far as practicable;[89] that (2) Congress take steps for the ultimate participation in the national legislation of those Indians qualified or soon to be so;[90] that (3) there be made various changes in personnel: the number of superintendents be increased from 5 to 7,[91] the duties of agent and superintendent. and superintendent and governor of a Territory be separated,[92] the position of subagent (salary $750 per annum, with duties often equal to those of agent) be abolished[93] and that of minor agent, with a salary lower than that of agent ($1,500 per annum) where the responsibilities and Indians are fewer, be established.[94]

B. THE PERIOD FROM 1851 TO 1867

The question of the status of the Indian, and the technique by which he might be civilized, had not been answered satisfactorily in 1851 when Commissioner Luke Lea wrote:

> On the general subject of the civilization of the Indians, many and diversified opinions have been put forth; but, unfortunately, like the race to which they relate, they are too wild to be of much utility. The great question, How shall the Indians be civilized? yet remains without a satisfactory answer. The magnitude of the subject, and the manifold difficulties inseparably connected with it, seem to have bewildered the minds of those who have attempted to give it the most thorough investigation. * * * I therefore leave the subject for the present, remarking only, that any plan for the civilization of our Indians will, in my judgment, be fatally defective, if it do not provide, in the most efficient manner, first, for their concentration; secondly, for their domestication; and, thirdly, for their ultimate incorporation into the great body of our citizen population.[95]

Commissioner Lea's recommendation that the Indians be concentrated was effectuated through the gradual diminution of the size of most Indian reservations. The plea for domestication had appeared in earlier reports, and was, in fact, the accepted practice of the Bureau of Indian Affairs at that time. The recommendation that Indians be ultimately incorporated into the citizenry of the country may mark a new departure from the theory and practice of removal and segregation. It apparently bore fruit in the Allotment Act,[96] with its provisions for citizenship and fee simple tenure of land.

precision the ratio of increase or decrease among the aboriginal population. * * *

(Excerpt. Report of Secretary of the Interior, 1859, p. 4, in Rep. Comm. Ind. Aff., 1859.)

[87] Rep. Comm. Ind. Aff., 1847, p. 749.

[88] Rep. Comm. Ind. Aff., 1849, pp. 939–941.

[89] *Ibid.*, p. 958.

[90] *Ibid.*

[91] *Ibid.*, p. 953.

[92] *Ibid.*, pp. 952, 953.

[93] *Ibid.*, pp. 954, 955.

[94] This would circumvent the limitation to 11, of full agents authorized by law (Rep. Comm. Ind. Aff., 1849, pp. 954, 955).

[95] Rep. Comm. Ind. Aff., 1851; pp. 12–13.

[96] Act of February 8, 1887, 24 Stat. 388. See Chapter 11.

In 1853, Commissioner Manypenny objected to the practice of permitting Indian tribes, engulfed in the stream of western migration, to retain portions of their tribal domains as reservations.

> With but few exceptions, the Indians were opposed to selling any part of their lands, as announced in their replies to the speeches of the commissioner. Finally, however, many tribes expressed their willingness to sell, but on the condition that they could retain tribal reservations on their present tracts of land. * * *[97] The idea of retaining reservations, which seemed to be generally entertained, is not deemed to be consistent with their true interests, and every good influence ought to be exercised to enlighten them on the subject. If they dispose of their lands, no reservations should, if it can be avoided, be granted or allowed. There are some Indians in various tribes who are occupying farms, comfortably situated, and who are in such an advanced state of civilization, that if they desired to remain, the privilege might well, and ought perhaps to be granted, and their farms in each case reserved for their homes. Such Indians would be qualified to enjoy the privileges of citizenship. But to make reservations for an entire tribe on the tract which it now owns, would, it is believed, be injurious to the future peace, prosperity, and advancement of these people. The commissioner, as far as he judged it prudent, endeavored to enlighten them on this point, and labored to convince them that it was not consistent with the true interest of themselves and their posterity that they should have tribal reservations within their present limits.[98]

Commissioner Manypenny further urged the revision of the Intercourse Act of 1834[99] and the regulations promulgated thereunder, to meet changing conditions in Indian relations.

> * * * A new code of regulations is greatly needed for this branch of the public service. That now in force was adopted many years since, and, in many particulars, has become obsolete or inapplicable, especially in our new and distant territories. The regulations now existing are based upon laws in force respecting Indian affairs, and the President has authority, under the act of June 30, 1834,[100] providing for the organization of the department of Indian Affairs, to prescribe such rules as he may think fit for carrying into effect its provisions.[101]

That plea is repeated by succeeding commissioners.

In his second annual report,[102] Commissioner Manypenny foresaw a crisis in the whole removal policy, and urged its abandonment in favor of fixed and permanent settlements "thereafter not to be disturbed."

> * * * By alternate persuasion and force, some of these tribes [in Kansas territory] have been removed, step by step, from mountain to valley, and from river to plain, until they have been pushed half-way across the continent. They can go no further; on the ground they now occupy the crisis must be met, and their future determined.[103]
>
> * * * * *
>
> The wonderful growth of our distant possessions, and the rapid expansion of our population in every direction, will render it necessary, at no distant day, to restrict the limits of all the Indian tribes upon our frontiers, and cause them to be settled in fixed and permanent localities, thereafter not to be disturbed. The policy of removing Indian tribes from time to time, as the settlements approach their habitations and hunting-grounds, must be abandoned. The emigrants and settlers were formerly content to remain in the rear, and thrust the Indians before them into the wilderness; but now the white population overleaps the reservations and homes of the Indians, and is beginning

[97] Rep. Comm. Ind. Aff., 1853, p. 249.

[98] *Ibid.*, p. 250. See Commissioner Denver's report (1857), *infra*, of Indians being permitted to retain such tribal land.

[99] Act of June 30, 1834 4 Stat. 729.

[100] Act of June 30, 1834, 4 Stat. 735.

[101] Rep. Comm. Ind. Aff., 1853, pp. 261–262.

[102] Rep. Comm. Ind. Aff., 1854.

[103] *Ibid.*, p. 10.

to inhabit the valleys and the mountains beyond; hence removal must cease, and the policy abandoned. * * *[104]

To protect Indian funds from fraud, Commissioner Manypenny recommended that—

> * * * All executory contracts of every kind and description, made by Indian tribes or bands with claim agents, attorneys, traders, or other persons, should be declared by law null and void, and an agent, interpreter, or other person, employed in or in any way connected with the Indian service, guilty of participation in transactions of the kind referred to, should be instantly dismissed and expelled from the Indian country; and all such attempts to injure and defraud the Indians, by whomsoever made or participated in, should be penal offences, punishable by fine and imprisonment. We have now penal laws to protect the Indians in the secure and unmolested possession of their lands, and also from demoralization by the introduction of liquor into their country, and the obligation is equally strong to protect them in a similar manner from the wrongs and injuries of such attempts to obtain possession of their funds.[105]

Secretary of the Interior McClelland in 1854, apropos of treaty obligations, reiterates:

> * * * The duty of the government is clear, and justice to the Indians requires that it should be faithfully discharged. Experience shows that much is gained by sacredly observing our plighted faith with these poor creatures, and every principle of justice and humanity prompts to a strict performance of our obligations.[106]

Commissioner Denver, in 1857,[107] tells of the successful extinguishing of title to all lands owned by Indians west of Missouri and Iowa "* * * except such portions as were reserved for their future homes * * *."[108]

Of Indians who have removed to

> * * * large reservations of fertile and desirable land, entirely disproportioned to their wants for occupancy and support, * * *. Their reservations should be restricted so as to contain only sufficient land to afford them a comfortable support by actual cultivation, and should be properly divided and assigned to them, with the obligation to remain upon and cultivate the same.[109]

Commissioner Denver urged discontinuance of the practice of distributing funds due to tribes in per capita payments to individual members. This practice, he thought, tended to break down the authority of the chiefs, and thus

> * * * disorganizes and leaves them without a domestic government * * * The distribution of the money should be left to the chiefs, so far at least as to enable them to punish the lawless and unruly by withholding it from them * * *.[110]

Commissioner Denver tells of the attempt by the Government to suppress the practice in California of kidnapping Indian children and selling them for servants.[111]

[104] *Ibid.*, p. 17.

[105] *Ibid.*, pp. 21–22. See also extract from Report of Secretary of Interior, 1862, p. 13, in Rep. Comm. Ind. Aff., 1862.

> All contracts with them should be prohibited, and all promises or obligations made by them should be declared void.

Legislation along the lines urged was enacted in 1871. See Chapter 14, sec. 5.

[106] Extract from Annual Report of the Secretary of Interior, 1854, p. 41, in Rep. Comm. of Ind. Aff., 1854.

[107] Rep. Comm. of Ind. Aff., 1857.

[108] *Ibid.*, p. 3. See Commissioner Manypenny's Report for 1853, *supra*, pp. 249, 250 for opposition to such a policy.

[109] *Ibid.*, p. 4.

[110] *Ibid.*, p. 7.

[111] *Ibid.*, p. 10.

He concludes his report with a plea for a recodification of Indian law:

> * * * I urgently repeat the recommendation of my immediate predecessor, that there be an early and complete revision and codification of all the laws relating to Indian affairs, which, from lapse of time and material changes in the location, condition, and circumstances of the most of the tribes, have become so insufficient and unsuitable as to occasion the greatest embarrassment and difficulty in conducting the business of this branch of the public service.[112]

In 1858, Commissioner Mix estimated the number of Indians to be about 350,000,[113] approximately the same number as it is estimated exists today.[114] He further estimated that about 393 treaties had been signed since the adoption of the Constitution; and that approximately 581,163,188 acres had been acquired through cession at a cost of $49,816,344.[115]

The principle upon which treaty-making with the Indians for land cessions rested was thus stated:

> that the Indian tribes possessed the occupant or usufruct right to the lands they occupied, and that they were entitled to the peaceful enjoyment of that right until they were fairly and justly divested of it.[116]

However, that principle was apparently not adhered to in the Territories of Oregon and Washington.

> * * * strong inducements were held out to our people to emigrate and settle there, without the usual arrangements being made, in advance, for the extinguishment of the title of the Indians who occupied and claimed the lands.[117]

According to Commissioner Mix, past Government policy had been in error in at least three respects: (1) Removal from place to place prevented the acquiring of "* * * settled habits and a knowledge of and taste for civilized pursuits * * *";[118] (2) assignment of too large a country to be held in common resulted in improper use and failure to acquire "* * * a knowledge of separate and individual property * * *";[119] (3) annuities resulted in indolence among Indians and fraudulent practices by whites.[120]

> The policy of concentrating the Indians on small reservations of land, and of sustaining them there for a limited period, until they can be induced to make the necessary exertions to support themselves, was commenced in 1853, with those in California. It is, in fact, the only course compatible with the obligations of justice and humanity.[121]

The military appears to have been used in the vicinity of reservations "to prevent the intrusion of improper persons upon them [the Indians], to afford protection to the agents, and to aid in controlling the Indians and keeping them within the limits assigned to them."[122]

In 1859, Secretary of the Interior Thompson reports progress in the shift of Government policy from that of removal to that of fixed reservations.[123]

[112] *Ibid.*, p. 12.

[113] Rep. of Comm. of Ind. Aff., 1858, p. 1.

[114] See Chapter 1, sec. 2, fn. 4.

[115] Rep. Comm. of Ind. Aff., 1858, p. 1.

[116] *Ibid.*, p. 6.

[117] *Ibid.*, p. 7.

[118] *Ibid.*, p. 7. He notes the difference in development between the northern tribes and those of the South who were permitted to remain for long periods in their original locations (pp. 6–7).

[119] *Ibid.*, p. 6.

[120] *Ibid.*, p. 6.

[121] *Ibid.*, p. 9.

[122] *Ibid.*, p. 10.

[123] See Commissioner Manypenny's recommendation for such a shift in 1854, *supra*.

The policy heretofore adopted of removing the Indians from time to time, as the necessities of our frontier population demanded a cession of their territory, the usual consideration for which was a large money annuity to be divided among them *per capita* had a deleterious effect upon their morals, and confirmed them in their roving, idle habits. This policy, we are now compelled by the necessity of the case to change. At present, the policy of the government is to gather the Indians upon small tribal reservations, within the well-defined exterior boundaries of which small tracts of land are assigned, in severalty, to the individual members of the tribe, with all the rights incident to an estate in fee-simple, except the power of alienation. This system, wherever it has been tried, has worked well, and the reports of the superintendents and agents give a most gratifying account of the great improvement which it has effected in the character and habits of those tribes which have been brought under its operation.[124]

Alfred B. Greenwood, Commissioner of Indian Affairs, under Secretary Thompson,[125] recommended that the reservation policy, as it had been pursued in California, be abandoned.

> * * * neither the Government nor California recognizes any right in the Indians of that State to one foot of land within her borders. An unnecessary number of reservations and separate farms have been established; the locations of many of them have proved to be unsuitable, and have not been sufficiently isolated; * * *[126]
>
> * * * * *
>
> Under these circumstances, and being desirous to initiate a policy for California which will secure our own citizens from annoyance, and, at the same time, save the Indians from the speedy extinction with which they are threatened, I feel constrained to recommend the repeal of all laws authorizing the appointment of superintendent, agents, and sub-agents for California, and the abandonment of the present, and the substitution of a somewhat different plan of operations. * * * the State should be divided into two districts, and an agent appointed for each * * *. The agents should give the Indians in their respective districts to understand that they are not to be fed and clothed at government expense; but that they must supply all their wants by means of their own labor.[127]
>
> * * * * *
>
> Should Congress authorize a change in the present system, and new reservations be established, great care should be taken so as to isolate the Indians from contact with the whites. Fertile lands should be selected which will repay the efforts to cultivate them * * *.[128]

During the Civil War period, when defections from the Federal Government occurred and tribes were concluding treaties with the Confederate Government,[129] the movement to terminate the practice of dealing with Indian tribes by treaty and to deal with them instead as objects of national charity, lacking legal rights, gained momentum.

Secretary of the Interior Caleb B. Smith clearly stated the new policy.

> It may well be questioned whether the government has not adopted a mistaken policy in regarding the Indian tribes as quasi-independent nations, and making treaties with them for the purchase of the lands they claim to own. They have none of the elements of nationality; they are within the limits of the recognized authority of the United States and must be subject to its control. The rapid progress of civilization upon this continent will not permit the lands which are required for cultivation to be surrendered to savage tribes for hunting grounds. Indeed, whatever may be the theory, the government has always demanded the removal of the Indians when their lands were required for agricultural purposes by advancing settlements. Although the consent of the Indians has been obtained in the form of treaties, it is well known that they have yielded to a necessity which they could not resist.[130]
>
> * * * * *
>
> * * * A radical change in the mode of treatment of the Indians should, in my judgment, be adopted. Instead of being treated as independent nations they should be regarded as wards of the government, entitled to its fostering care and protection. Suitable districts of country should be assigned to them for their homes, and the government should supply them, through its own agents, with such articles as they use, until they can be instructed to earn their subsistence by their labor.[131]

Under the Lincoln administration, Commissioner Dole concerned himself with the legal disadvantage under which Indians labor, in the conflict between state and federal jurisdiction.[132]

> * * * they find themselves amenable to a system of local and federal laws, as well as their treaty stipulations, all of which are to the vast majority of them wholly unintelligible. If a white man does them an injury, redress is often beyond their reach; or, if obtained, is only had after delays and vexations which are themselves cruel injustice. If one of their number commits a crime, punishment is sure and swift, and oftentimes is visited upon the whole tribe. * * *[133]

Better cooperation between the Federal Government and the states was recommended, with state legislation leading to ultimate citizenship the goal to be pursued.

> Very much of the evil attendant upon the location of Indians within the limits of States might be obviated, if some plan could be devised whereby a more hearty co-operation with government on the part of the States might be secured. It being a demonstrated fact that Indians are capable of attaining a high degree of civilization, it follows that the time will arrive, as in the case of some of the tribes it has doubtless now arrived, when the peculiar relations existing between them and the federal government may cease, without detriment to their interests or those of the community or State in which they are located; in other words, that the time will come when, in justice to them and to ourselves, their relations to the general government should be identical with those of the citizens of the various States. In this view, a more generous legislation on the part of most of the States within whose limits Indians are located, looking to a gradual removal of the disabilities under which they labor, and their ultimate admission to all the rights of citizenship, as from time to time the improvement and advancement made by a given tribe may warrant, is earnestly to be desired, and would, I doubt not, prove a powerful incentive to exertion on the part of the Indians themselves.[134]

At the end of the Civil War, Secretary of the Interior Harlan reported the terms of a negotiated peace with those Indians who had joined forces with Confederate soldiers.[135]

> * * * Such preliminary arrangements were made as, it is believed, will result in the abolition of slavery among them, the cession within the Indian territory of lands for the settlement of the civilized Indians now residing on reservations elsewhere, and the ultimate establishment of civil government, subject to the supervision of the United States.[136]

[124] Extract from Report of the Secretary of the Interior, 1859, pp. 4–5 in Rep. Comm. Ind. Aff., 1859.

[125] Rep. Comm. Ind. Aff., 1859.

[126] *Ibid.*, p. 22.

[127] *Ibid.*, p. 23.

[128] *Ibid.*, p. 24.

[129] See Chapter 3, sec. 4H and Chapter 8, sec. 11.

[130] Extract from Report of the Secretary of the Interior, 1862, p. 7, in Rep. Comm. Ind. Aff., 1862.

[131] *Ibid.*, p. 9.

[132] See Chapter 8, sec. 10.

[133] Rep. Comm. Ind. Aff., 1862, p. 12.

[134] *Ibid.*, p. 12.

[135] See Chapter 3, sec. 4I and Chapter 8, sec. 11.

[136] Extract from Report of the Secretary of the Interior, 1865, p. III, in Rep. Comm. Ind. Aff., 1865.

Apparently, even at this late date the policy of complete extermination of the Indian was advocated by "gentlemen of high position, intelligence, and personal character." [137]

> Financial considerations forbid the inauguration of such a policy. * * * It is estimated that the maintenance of each regiment of troops engaged against the Indians of the plains costs the government two million dollars per annum. * * * Such a policy is manifestly as impracticable as it is in violation of every dictate of humanity and Christian duty.[138]

Secretary Harlan, in urging Congressional action for the necessary reforms in the administration of justice on Indian reservations, stated:

> It is earnestly recommended that the superintendents, and also agents of a suitable grade, be empowered to act as civil magistrates within the limits of reservations where the tribal relations are maintained, and also on the plains remote from the jurisdiction of civil authorities. The want of an acceptable and efficient provision for the administration of justice has been sensibly felt in cases arising between members of the tribes, or between Indians and the white men who have been permitted to reside among them.[139]

Commissioner Cooley [140] recommended various radical reforms in Indian Service personnel, particularly with regard to traders and agents. To eliminate collusion between them, he urged Congress to make it a penal offense for

> * * * any agent or other officer in the Indian service to be in any manner, directly or indirectly, interested in the profits of the business of any trader, or in any contract for the purchase of goods, or in any trade with the Indians, at their own or any other agency; the same penalties to apply to the licensing of any relative to trade, or to purchasing goods or provisions for the use of the Indians of any firm in which they or any relative may be partners or in any way interested. * * * [141]

In urging, as commissioners had done before, increase in agents' salary above the $1,500 they had received since 1834,[142] as a means of securing more thoroughly qualified persons, Commissioner Cooley held:

> * * * The fact that innumerable applicants stand ready to take any places which are vacated is not, in my judgment, an argument against an increase of pay; it is simply a proof of the commonly received idea of the outside profit of the business. * * * [143]

He noted progress in the civilization of the Indian:

> Another evidence of progress in the right direction is the request made by several agents, on behalf of the Indians, that the kind of goods furnished to them may be changed from the blankets, bright-colored cloths, and various gewgaws, which have from time immemorial gone to make up invoices of Indian goods, to substantial garments, improved agricultural implements, etc.[144]

[137] *Ibid.*, p. III.

[138] *Ibid.*, pp. III, IV.

[139] *Ibid.*, p. IV. See Chapter 7, sec. 9.

[140] Rep. Comm. Ind. Aff., 1865.

[141] *Ibid.*, p. 2. Legislation along the lines proposed was enacted in 1874. Act of June 22, 1874, sec. 10, 18 Stat. 146, 177, 25 U. S. C. 87. This, in effect, strengthened the restrictions contained in section 14 of the Act of June 30, 1834, 4 Stat. 735, 738, R. S. § 2078, 25 U. S. C. 68. The Act of June 19, 1939, 53 Stat. 840, 25 U. S. C. 87a, modified these two prohibitory statutes to permit purchases for personal use by federal employees.

[142] By Act of April 20, 1818, 3 Stat. 461, agents' salaries varied from $1,200 to $1,800, and subagents' were fixed at $500. By Act of June 30, 1834, 4 Stat. 735, agents' salaries were fixed at $1,500, and subagents' at $750.

[143] Rep. Comm. Ind. Aff., 1865, pp. 2–3.

[144] *Ibid.*, p. 4.

In 1867, Acting Commissioner Mix summarized the obstacles to Indian civilization as he saw them, and the means to overcome them.

> * * * mainly * * * his almost constant contact with the vicious, unscrupulous whites, who not only teach him their base ways, but defraud and rob him, and, often without cause, with as little compunction as they would experience in killing a dog, take even his life.[145]

Further

> * * * the Indian has no certainty as to the permanent possession of the land he occupies and which he is urged to improve, for he knows not how long he may be permitted to enjoy it. * * * [146] Evidently the remedy for these evils lies in securing to the Indians a permanent home in a country exclusively set apart for them, upon which no whites or citizens, except government agents and employes, shall be permitted to reside or intrude; in the granting to them allotments of land as individual property, to cultivate and improve; in the appointment of moral, honest, and efficient agents, with a fair compensation for services; and in the prompt fulfilment by the government of its treaty and other obligations, furnishing the necessary aid required for teaching, and placing them in the way of becoming self-sustaining and eventually independent of the government.[147]

He recommended to the Secretary the repeal of section 4 of the Act of July 26, 1866,[148] allowing any citizen "of proper character" to trade with Indians, since the Department had no authority to restrict the numbers, nor discretion to determine the fitness or ability of a trader.[149]

C. THE PERIOD FROM 1868 TO 1876

For the next few years, with Indians largely in the process of being settled or resettled on western reservations, commissioners concerned themselves primarily with problems of permanent policy and administration. Should treaty-making be abandoned? What was the proper role of the military? Should the Bureau of Indian Affairs be transferred back to the War Department?[150] How should the Indian Service be reorganized so as to overcome charges of dishonesty and inefficiency? What was the best technique for individualizing and controlling the Indian? What were the present rights and future prospects of the Indian?

Although Commissioner Parker in 1869 urged that treaties then in force be "promptly and faithfully executed," nevertheless he recommended, as Secretary Smith had in 1862,[151] that the whole policy of treaty-making be abandoned.

> * * * A treaty involves the idea of a compact between two or more sovereign powers, each possessing sufficient authority and force to compel a compliance with the obligations incurred. The Indian tribes of the United States are not sovereign nations, capable of making treaties, as none of them have an organized government of such inherent strength as would secure a faithful obedience of its people in the observance of compacts of this character. They are held to be the wards of the government, and the only title the law concedes to them to the lands they occupy or claim is a mere possessory one. But, because treaties have been made with them, generally for the extinguishment of their supposed absolute title to land inhabited by them, or over which they roam, they have

[145] Rep. Comm. Ind. Aff., 1867, p. 1.

[146] *Ibid*, p. 1.

[147] *Ibid.*, p. 2.

[148] 14 Stat. 255, 280. R. S. § 2128.

[149] Rep. Comm. Ind. Aff., 1867, pp. 5–6.

[150] See sec. 1B, *supra*, for a discussion of that problem, and the recommendations of various commissioners and the Indian Peace Commission of 1867.

[151] See Rep. Comm. Ind. Aff., 1862, p. 7, and *supra*.

> become falsely impressed with the notion of national independence. It is time that this idea should be dispelled, and the government cease the cruel farce of thus dealing with its helpless and ignorant wards. Many good men, looking at this matter only from a Christian point of view, will perhaps say that the poor Indian has been greatly wronged and ill treated; that this whole country was once his, of which he has been despoiled, and that he has been driven from place to place until he has hardly left to him a spot where to lay his head. This indeed may be philanthropic and humane, but the stern letter of the law admits of no such conclusion, and great injury has been done by the government in deluding this people into the belief of their being independent sovereignties, while they were at the same time recognized only as its dependents and wards. As civilization advances and their possessions of land are required for settlement, such legislation should be granted to them as a wise, liberal, and just government ought to extend to subjects holding their dependent relation. * * * [152]

By the Act of March 3, 1871,[153] treaty-making was abandoned. However, agreements, approved by both Senate and House of Representatives, continued to be made. In 1873 Commissioner Edward P. Smith urged that even agreements cease.

> * * * We have in theory over sixty-five independent nations within our borders, with whom we have entered into treaty relations as being sovereign peoples; and at the same time the white agent is sent to control and supervise these foreign powers, and care for them as wards of the Government. This double condition of sovereignty and wardship involves increasing difficulties and absurdities, as the traditional chieftain, losing his hold upon his tribe, ceases to be distinguished for anything except for the lion's share of goods and moneys which the Government endeavors to send, through him, to his nominal subjects, and as the necessities of the Indians, pressed on every side by civilization, require more help and greater discrimination in the manner of distributing the tribal funds. So far, and as rapidly as possible, all recognition of Indians in any other relation than strictly as subjects of the Government should cease. To provide for this, radical legislation will be required.[154] *

On the use of the military, official opinion varied. Commissioner Taylor (1868)[155] was strongly opposed; Commissioner Parker (1869),[156] himself a general, believed in its use, particularly for those Indians who failed to remove. In his 1870 report [157] he lamented the passage by Congress of an act [158] which "* * * prohibited the employment of army officers in any civil capacity * * *." Commissioner Francis A. Walker (also a general) in 1872 [159] urged the use of the military to effect the "peace policy."[160]

> * * * Such a use of the military constitutes no abandonment of the "peace policy," and involves no disparagement of it. It was not to be expected—it was not in the nature of things—that the entire body of wild Indians should submit to be restrained in their Ishmaelitish proclivities without a struggle on the part of the more audacious to maintain their traditional freedom. * * * [161]

Commissioner Walker complained that his policy had beer widely misunderstood and criticized by the press.

> * * * This misunderstanding in regard to the occasional use of force in making effective and universal the policy of peace, has led no small portion of the press of the country to treat the more vigorous application of the scourge to refractory Indians which has characterized the operations of the last three months as an abandonment of the peace policy itself, whereas it is, in fact, a legitimate and essential part of the original scheme which the Government has been endeavoring to carry out, with prospects of success never more bright and hopeful than to-day.[162]

In 1873, Commissioner Edward P. Smith urged that a military force be set up among the Sioux, notwithstanding treaty assurances to the contrary.

> Hitherto the military have refrained from going on this reservation because of the express terms of the treaty with the Sioux, in which it is agreed that no military force shall be brought over the line. I respectfully recommend that provision be made at once for placing at each of the Sioux reservations a military force sufficient to enable the agents to enforce respect for their authority, and to conduct agency affairs in an orderly manner.[163]

After many years of charges against Indian Service field personnel of dishonesty and inefficiency,[164] a new system of choosing agents was inaugurated in 1869 under President Grant.[165] Their nomination was for the most part delegated to various religious bodies active in missionary work, particularly the Society of Friends. The remaining agencies were filled by Army officers detailed for such duty,[166] until the Appropriation Act of July 15, 1870,[167] caused them to relinquish civil posts.

Commissioner Parker in 1869 and in 1870 reported the plan working well.[168] However, it was gradually abandoned and completely discontinued by the early eighties.[169]

On the question of the techniques for individualizing and controlling the Indians, commissioners differed somewhat, although all agreed basically on allotment of land in severalty as one of the major methods.

> * * * The policy of giving to every Indian a home that he can call his own is a wise one, as it induces a strong incentive to him to labor and make every effort in his power to better his condition. By the adoption, generally, of this plan on the part of the Government, the Indians would be more rapidly advanced in civilization than they would if the policy of allowing them to hold their land in common were continued.[170]
>
> * * * * *
>
> * * * A fundamental difference between barbarians and a civilized people is the difference between a herd and an individual. * * * The starting-point of indi-

[152] Rep. Comm. Ind. Aff., 1869, p. 6.

[153] 16 Stat. 544, 566, R. S. § 2079, 25 U. S. C. 71. See Chapter 8.

[154] Rep. Comm. Ind. Aff., 1873, p. 3.

[155] Rep. Comm. Ind. Aff., 1868, pp. 8–10.

[156] Rep. Comm. Ind. Aff., 1869, p. 5.

[157] Rep. Comm. Ind. Aff., 1870, pp. 9–10.

[158] Act of July 15, 1870, 16 Stat. 315, 319. See fn. 41, *supra*. By Act of July 13, 1892, c. 164, sec. 1, 27 Stat. 120; and Act of July 1, 1898, c. 545, sec. 1, 30 Stat. 571, 573, the President was given the power to detail Army officers for duty to Indian agencies. 25 U. S. C. 27.

[159] Rep. Comm. Ind. Aff., 1872.

[160] In 1867 (Act of July 20, 1867, 15 Stat. 17) the Indian Peace Commission was authorized by Congress to study the cause and cure for Indian wars. Their recommendations in 1868 (Report of January 7, 1868 to the President, in Rep. Comm. Ind. Aff., 1868, pp. 26–50) were the basis for the new "peace policy" of the Government. See discussion sec. 1, *supra*.

[161] Rep. Comm. of Ind. Aff., 1872, p. 5.

[162] *Ibid.*, p. 6.

[163] Rep. Comm. Ind. Aff., 1873, p. 6.

[164] Rep. Comm. Ind. Aff., 1869, p. 5.

[165] 1st Annual Message to Congress, December 6, 1869.

> I have attempted a new policy towards these wards of the nation * * *. The Society of Friends is well known as having succeeded in living in peace with the Indians in the early settlement of Pennsylvania, while their white neighbors of other sects in other sections were constantly embroiled. They are also known for their opposition to all strife, violence, and war, and are generally noted for their strict integrity and fair dealings. These considerations induced me to give the management of a few reservations of Indians to them and to throw the burden of the selection of agents upon the society itself * * *. For superintendents and agents not on the reservations, officers of the Army were selected. (Richardson, Messages and Papers of the Presidents, 1897, Vol. IX, pp. 3992–3993.)

According to Schmeckebier this policy was inaugurated by Grant to insure against opposition to his appointments by the Senate. (Schmeckebier, *op. cit.*, p. 54.)

[166] Rep. Comm. Ind. Aff., 1869, p. 5.

[167] 16 Stat. 315, 319. See fn. 157, *supra*.

[168] Rep. Comm. Ind. Aff., 1869, p. 5; Rep. Comm. Ind. Aff., 1870, pp. 9–10.

[169] Schmeckebier, *op. cit.*, p. 55, fn. 92.

[170] Rep. Comm. Ind. Aff., 1870, p. 9. See Chapter 11, sec. 1.

vidualism for an Indian is the personal possession of his portion of the reservation.[171]

In 1870, Commissioner Parker reported, as an indication of Indian progress, that many were asking to have their land surveyed and allotted.[172]

In 1872, Commissioner Walker defended the "feeding" policy which had been in effect for 3 years.

> The Indian policy, so called, of the Government, is a policy, and it is not a policy, or rather it consists of two policies, entirely distinct, seeming, indeed, to be mutually inconsistent and to reflect each upon the other: the one regulating the treatment of the tribes which are potentially hostile, that is, whose hostility is only repressed just so long as, and so far as, they are supported in idleness by the Government; the other regulating the treatment of those tribes which, from traditional friendship, from numerical weakness, or by the force of their location, are either indisposed toward, or incapable of, resistance to the demands of the Government. * * *[173] It is, of course, hopelessly illogical that the expenditures of the Government should be proportioned not to the good but to the ill desert of the several tribes; that large bodies of Indians should be supported in entire indolence by the bounty of the Government simply because they are audacious and insolent, while well-disposed Indians are only assisted to self-maintenance, since it is known they will not fight. * * * And yet, for all this, the Government is right and its critics wrong; and the "Indian policy" is sound, sensible, and beneficent, because it reduces to the minimum the loss of life and property upon our frontier, and allows the freest development of our settlements and railways possible under the circumstances.[174]
>
> * * * * *
>
> There is no question of national dignity, be it remembered, involved in the treatment of savages by a civilized power. With wild men, as with wild beasts, the question whether in a given situation one shall fight, coax, or run, is a question merely of what is easiest and safest.[175]

Commissioner Walker discussed the function of the reservation as he saw it.

> * * * the Indians should be made as comfortable on, and as uncomfortable off, their reservations as it was in the power of the Government to make them; that such of them as went right should be protected and fed, and such as went wrong should be harassed and scourged without intermission. * * * Such a use of the strong arm of the Government is not war, but discipline.[176]
>
> * * * * *
>
> * * * The reservation system affords the place for thus dealing with tribes and bands, without the access of influences inimical to peace and virtue. It is only necessary that Federal laws, judiciously framed to meet all the facts of the case, and enacted in season, before the Indians begin to scatter, shall place all the members of this race under a strict reformatory control by the agents of the Government. Especially is it essential that the right of the Government to keep Indians upon the reservations assigned to them, and to arrest and return them whenever they wander away, should be placed beyond dispute. * * *[177]

The problem of the consolidation and sale of surplus land on reservations had already appeared in 1872.

> The reservations granted heretofore have generally been proportioned, and rightly so, to the needs of the Indians in a roving state, with hunting and fishing as their chief means of subsistence, which condition implies the occupation of a territory far exceeding what could possibly be cultivated. As they change to agriculture, however rude and primitive at first, they tend to contract the limits of actual occupation. With proper administrative management the portions thus rendered available for cessation or sale can be so thrown together as in no way to impair the integrity of the reservation. Where this change has taken place, there can be no question of the expediency of such sale or cession. The Indian Office has always favored this course, and notwithstanding the somewhat questionable character of some of the resulting transactions, arising especially out of violent or fraudulent combinations to prevent a fair sale, it can be confidently affirmed that the advantage of the Indians has generally been subserved thereby.[178]

The present rights and the future prospects of the Indian appears to have concerned many commissioners.

Commissioner Taylor, in 1868, asked the question:

> Shall our Indians be civilized, and how?
>
> * * * Assuming that the government has a right, and that it is its duty to solve the Indian question definitely and decisively, it becomes necessary that it determine at once the best and speediest method of its solution, and then, armed with right, to act in the interest of both races.
>
> If might makes right, we are the strong and they the weak; and we would do no wrong to proceed by the cheapest and nearest route to the desired end, and could, therefore, justify ourselves in ignoring the natural as well as the conventional rights of the Indians, if they stand in the way, and, as their lawful masters, assign them their status and their tasks, or put them out of their own way and ours by extermination with the sword, starvation, or by any other method.
>
> If, however, they have rights as well as we, then clearly it is our duty as well as sound policy to so solve the question of their future relations to us and each other, as to secure their rights and promote their highest interest, in the simplest, easiest, and most economical way possible.
>
> But to assume they have no rights is to deny the fundamental principles of Christianity, as well as to contradict the whole theory upon which the government has uniformly acted towards them; we are therefore bound to respect their rights, and, if possible, make our interests harmonize with them. * * *[179]

Commissioner Walker, in 1872, answered the question in one way.

> It belongs not to a sanguine, but to a sober view of the situation, that three years will see the alternative of war eliminated from the Indian question, and the most powerful and hostile bands of to-day thrown in entire helplessness on the mercy of the Government. * * *
>
> * * * * *
>
> No one certainly will rejoice more heartily than the present Commissioner when the Indians of this country cease to be in a position to dictate, in any form or degree, to the Government; when, in fact, the last hostile tribe becomes reduced to the condition of suppliants for charity. * * *[180]

Commissioner John Q. Smith in 1876 answered the question in another way.

> * * * No new hunting-grounds remain, and the civilization or the utter destruction of the Indians is inevitable. The next twenty-five years are to determine the fate of a race. If they cannot be taught, and taught very soon, to accept the necessities of their situation and begin in earnest to provide for their own wants by labor in civilized pursuits, they are destined to speedy extinction.[181]
>
> * * * * *
>
> * * * We have despoiled the Indians of their rich hunting-grounds, thereby depriving them of their ancient means of support. Ought we not and shall we not give them at

[171] Rep. Comm. Ind. Aff., 1878, p. 4.
[172] Rep. Comm. Ind. Aff., 1870, p. 9.
[173] Rep. Comm. Ind. Aff., 1872, p. 3.
[174] *Ibid.*, p. 4.
[175] *Ibid.*, p. 5.
[176] *Ibid.*, p. 6.
[177] *Ibid.*, pp. 11–12.
[178] *Ibid.*, p. 18.
[179] Rep. Comm. Ind. Aff., 1868, p. 16.
[180] Rep. Comm. Ind. Aff., 1872, p. 9.
[181] Rep. Comm. Ind. Aff., 1876, p. VI.

least a secure home, and the cheap but priceless benefit of just and equitable laws? [182]

Along with the broad problems of administration and policy, were the problems of specific reform in legislation as inadequacies became apparent in laws governing intercourse and trade with the Indians, and in the extension of United States law and the jurisdiction of the courts over Indians. These specific reforms had been recommended for many years, the revision of the Intercourse Act of 1834 [183] since 1853,[184] and law and order reform since at least 1862.[185]

In 1871 Acting Commissioner Clum wrote that the laws regulating trade

> * * * are so defective as to fail to secure the Indians against the encroachments of the whites * * *. A revision of these laws is very much to be desired to meet the changed circumstances now surrounding the Indians, arising out of the building of railroads through their lands, the rapid advance of white settlements, and the claims and rights of squatters, miners, and prospecting parties.[186]

The request for reform in the administration of justice over the Indians was made in the report of the Board of Indian Commissioners for 1871; [187] it was reiterated in 1873 [188] by Commissioner Edward P. Smith, who urged that agents and superintendents be given magisterial powers, and again in 1875, when he urged that authority be given

> * * * to the Secretary of the Interior to prescribe for all tribes prepared, in his judgment, to adopt the same, an elective government, through which shall be administered all necessary police regulations of the reservation.[189]

Commissioner John Q. Smith recommended the

> * * * Extension over them [the Indians] of United States law and the jurisdiction of United States courts.[190]

D. THE PERIOD FROM 1877 TO 1904

In 1877 Commissioner Hayt made seven specific recommendations for policy, that of a system of compulsory common schools being particularly noteworthy: (1) A code of laws for reservations and means for dispensing justice; (2) Indian police under which shall be vested in individuals and inalienable for twenty of land "* * * into farms of convenient size, the title to which shall be vested in individuals and inalienable for twenty years * * *"; (4) The establishment of a compulsory common school system, including industrial schools; (5) Free access to Indians of missionaries; (6) Insistence on labor in return for food and clothing; and (7) A steady concentration of the smaller bands on larger reservations.[191]

In 1880, Acting Commissioner Marble included statistical tables of population and amount and types of work accomplished during the year.[192] He reported extensively on educational advances, particularly the opening of new boarding schools.[193] "The importance of having at least one good boarding-school at each agency need not be argued." [194]

The system of Indian police, in operation less than 3 years, was reported to be working admirably with a force of 162 officers and 653 privates.[195]

The plea for a "uniform and perfect title to their lands, as a measure conducive in the highest degree to their present and future welfare" was again urged for the Indians.[196]

Commissioner Price, as a business man, was concerned with Indian administration and personnel.

> * * * Within the last year seven entire months were consumed in making such a change at one of the agencies, where any correct business man transacting his own business would have made the change in less than seven days. This is the fault of the law, and ought to be changed.[197]
>
> * * * * *
>
> I give it as my honest conviction as a business man after one year and a half of close observation, in a position where the chances for a correct knowledge of this question are better than in any other, that the true policy of the government is to pay Indian agents such compensation and place them under such regulations of law as will insure the services of first-class men. It is not enough that a man is honest; he must, in addition to this, be capable. He must be up to standard physically as well as morally and mentally. Men of this class are comparatively scarce, and as a rule cannot be had unless the compensation is equal to the service required. Low-priced men are not always the cheapest. A bad article is dear at any price. Paying a man as Indian agent $1,200 or $1,500, and expecting him to perform $3,000 or $4,000 worth of labor, is not economy, and in a large number of cases has proven to be the worst kind of extravagance.[198]

He urged increased appropriations for education, particularly for industrial schools.

> * * * If one million of dollars for educational purposes given *now* will save several millions in the future, it is wise economy to give that million at once, and not dole it out in small sums that do but little good.[199]

Commissioner Price departed from the accepted theory in Indian education of the superiority of boarding over day schools.[200]

> * * * It is as common a belief that the boarding should supersede the day school as it is that training-schools remote from the Indian country ought to be substituted for those located in the midst of the Indians. But I trust that the time is not far distant when a system of district schools will be established in Indian settlements, which will serve not only as centers of enlightenment for those neighborhoods, but will give suitable employment

---

[182] *Ibid.*, p. XI. Commissioner Smith commends, as "* * * The only thing yet done by the Government * * * permanent and far-reaching * * * the dedication of the Indian Territory as the final home for the race." (P. XI.) See Chapter 23, sec. 5, on the throwing open of Indian Territory lands for settlement.

[183] Act of June 30, 1834, 4 Stat. 729. See Chapter 16.

[184] See Rep. Comm. Ind. Affairs, 1853, pp. 261–262, and *supra*.

[185] See Rep. Comm. Ind. Affairs, 1862, p. 12, and *supra*.

[186] Rep. Comm. Ind. Aff., 1871, p. 6.

[187] Third Annual Report of the Board of Indian Commissioners, in Rep. Comm. Ind. Aff., 1871, p. 16.

[188] Rep. Comm. Ind. Aff., 1873, pp. 4–5.

[189] Rep. Comm. Ind. Aff., 1875, p. 16.

[190] Rep. Comm. Ind. Aff., 1876, p. VII. See Chapter 7, sec. 9; Chapters 18 and 19.

[191] Rep. Comm. Ind. Aff., 1877, pp. 1–2.

[192] Rep. Comm. Ind. Aff., 1880, pp. III–IV.

[193] *Ibid.*, pp. V–VI.

[194] *Ibid.*, p. VI.

[195] *Ibid.*, p. IX. Act of May 27, 1878, 20 Stat. 63, 86. Their duties involved discovery and arrest of thieves, action as truant officers, protection of annuities and property, prevention of depredations to timber and of the introduction of liquor, action as messengers and census takers, etc. (p. X).

[196] *Ibid.*, p. XVI.

[197] Rep. Comm. Ind. Aff., 1882, p. V.

[198] *Ibid.*, pp. V, VI. Commissioner E. P. Smith in his report for 1873 (pp. 9–10) had urged that salaries be increased to $2,000 or $2,500, depending on the remoteness of the reservation; Commissioner John Q. Smith in his report for 1876 (pp. III, IV) to $3,000; Commissioner E. A. Hayt in his report for 1877 (pp. 6–7) that salaries be scaled according to the number of Indians under an agent's jurisdiction. Recommendations for increasing agents' salaries appear constantly in Commissioners' reports.

[199] *Ibid.*, p. VII.

[200] See Chapter 12, sec. 2.

to returned students, especially the young women, for whom it is specially difficult to provide.[201]

* * * * * *

The cost of maintaining an Indian pupil in a reservation boarding school may be set down as a little over $150 per annum; in a day school at about $30 per annum.[202]

In the matter of health, also, Commissioner Price had specific recommendations.

When the length of time (three or four years) which is required for the physician to familiarize himself with the language, habits, and mental peculiarities of Indians is taken into consideration, and also the diplomacy which is required to obtain and maintain their confidence, it is obvious that it is specially desirable to procure efficient and, if possible, permanent medical officers of pronounced moral and temperate habits, of great will power, capable of making good and enduring impressions on the Indians. It is detrimental to the service to be continually changing medical officers.

In connection with permament medical officers, a system should be inaugurated of caring for the blind, insane, and destitute aged Indians.[203]

The problem of freedmen in Indian Territory, pressing since the close of the Civil War, had not been solved by 1882.

The rights guaranteed to the freedmen in the Indian Territory by treaty stipulations have been ignored, and so far as their interests are involved the treaties themselves have been virtually set aside, both by the Indians and by the government.[204]

* * * * *

In this report of January 26, 1882, Agent Tufts states that—

It is unpopular in the Cherokee Nation to advocate a measure that provides for placing the colored man on an equality with Cherokees, and the politicians are civilized enough to do nothing that might lessen their chances for political success; hence until the sentiment shall undergo a revolution there will be no favorable action.

From the hesitancy heretofore shown by the nation to carry out in good faith toward the colored people simply what has been granted them by the treaty, I am convinced that the nation will not fix and settle the status of the colored people until a more peremptory demand is made on the nation to execute the conditions of their treaty respecting them.

Many of the colored people speak the Cherokee language, and having been brought up among Cherokees and accustomed to their ways, it would be a hardship to remove them from that country, and remaining in the nation, they should be accorded all their rights. Agent Tufts recommended the appointment of a commission to visit the agency with authority to hear evidence and determine the question whether the claimants were freedmen liberated by voluntary act of owner, or by law, or whether they were free colored persons and in the country at the commencement of the rebellion; and whether they were residents of the nation at the time of the treaty, or returned within six months thereafter—the findings of the commission to be submitted to the department for approval.[205]

With the discovery of valuable coal deposits in an Indian reservation in Arizona Territory, arose the problem of its extraction and removal. Commissioner Price felt that the Indians could not be prevailed upon to remove again, that the Government could not undertake to work the mines, that the Indians themselves were not capable technically of doing so, and even were they, they could not dispose of the coal since

* * * under existing law there is no authority for permitting the severance and removal from an Indian reservation, for purposes of sale or speculation, of any material attached to or forming a part of the realty, such as timber, coal, or other minerals.[206]

Commissioner Price therefore recommended a system of leasing.

After carefully considering the questions involved, this office became convinced that the most practicable solution of the matter would be the adoption of a system of leasing upon a royalty plan; and accordingly a draft of a joint resolution was prepared in this office and submitted to the department in April last with a view to securing the needful legislation therefore. It was believed that by this means a very large part of the annual expenditure for the support and care of the Indians of Arizona and New Mexico might be reimbursed to the government from the profit of the mines without hardship to consumers, and that the Indians themselves would be greatly benefited, not only by the example of industry set, but through the opportunity that would be afforded them to earn wages by their own labor.[207]

According to Commissioner Atkin's report for 1886,[208] the system of leasing grazing land had been tried on the Cheyenne and Arapaho Reservation unsuccessfully. By Presidential proclamation [209] the leases were declared null and void, and the cattle and cattlemen removed, much to the satisfaction of the Indians who

* * * no longer contemplate the monopoly of nine-tenths of their reservation by outsiders, but in place thereof they view with satisfaction their own fields of corn, and farms inclosed with fences, put up by their own labor, * * *.[210]

The system of leasing Indian lands was further complicated by a decision of the Attorney General to the effect that—

* * * the system of leasing Indian lands which has hitherto prevailed is illegal without the consent of Congress * * *.[211]

Commissioner Atkins recommended that the leasing system either be legalized, as his predecessor had recommended before him,[212] or abolished.[213]

If Congress would authorize Indians to dispose of their grass, or would take any definite action as to the policy which this office can legally pursue in regard to Indian grazing lands, it would materially lessen the perplexities and confusion which now pertain to the subject. Moreover, if some way could be adopted by which, under proper restrictions, the surplus grass on the several Indian reservations could be utilized with profit to the Indians, the annual appropriations needed to care for the Indians could be correspondingly and materially reduced.[214]

Of the general allotment bill, which had passed the Senate and was favorably reported in the House, Commissioner Atkins reported:

* * * As there seems to be no substantial opposition to this bill, it is hoped that it will become a law during the coming winter. Its passage will relieve this office of much embarrassment and enable it to make greater progress in

[201] Rep. Comm. Ind. Aff., 1882, p. XXXV.
[202] *Ibid.*, p. XL.
[203] *Ibid.*, p. XLVIII. See Chapter 12, sec. 3.
[204] Rep. Comm. Ind. Aff., 1882, p. LV.
[205] Rep. Comm. Ind. Aff., 1882, p. LVII.
[206] Rep. Comm. Ind. Aff., 1882, p. XLIX. See Chapter 15, sec. 19.
[207] *Ibid.*, p. XLIX.
[208] Rep. Comm. Ind. Aff., 1886.
[209] See Sen. Ex. Doc. 17, 48th Cong., 2d sess., vol. I, pt. I, 1885.
[210] Rep. Comm. Ind. Aff., 1886, p. XVIII.
[211] *Ibid.*, p. XIX. 18 Op. A. G. 235 (1885).
[212] See Rep. Comm. Ind. Aff. (Hiram Price) 1882, p. XLIX, and *supra.*
[213] Rep. Comm. Ind. Aff., 1886, p. XIX.
[214] *Ibid.*, p. XIX.

the important work of assisting the Indians to become individual owners of the soil by an indefeasible title.[215]

Of courts of Indian offenses which had been instituted at various agencies to try minor offenses, Commissioner Atkins wrote:

> These courts are also unquestionably a great assistance to the Indians in learning habits of self-government and in preparing themselves for citizenship. I am of the opinion that they should be placed upon a legal basis by an act of Congress authorizing their establishment, under such rules and regulations as the Secretary of the Interior may prescribe. Their duties and jurisdiction could then be definitely determined and greater good accomplished.[216]

Commissioner Atkins expressed a hope with regard to traders which has not yet been realized.

> But it is earnestly hoped that the necessity for white traders upon the reservations will soon be superseded. Under the law the full-blood Indian is guaranteed the right to trade with the Indians of his tribe, without the restrictions imposed upon half-breeds and white traders. It is the constant aim and effort of the Indian Office to make the Indian self-reliant and self-sustaining, and if this policy is persevered in, with the aid of the educational advantages available at almost every agency, I cannot but believe that the Indians will at an early day acquire sufficient ability to manage the trading posts themselves and supply their people with such goods as they may need.[217]

In the report of the Commissioner of Indian Affairs for 1888 one notes the beginnings of a problem which grew into major proportions in later years—the problem of the annuity roll.

> In this connection, I would suggest that action should be taken by Congress to confine the benefits arising under Indian treaties to those justly entitled thereto, by excluding from participation therein whites hereafter enrolled as Indians by adoption and also the descendants of whites and Indians beyond a certain degree.[218]

Of the application of the Allotment Act,[219] which had been in force for more than a year, Commissioner Oberly reports slow progress,[220] and considerable opposition.

> Considerable opposition to the allotment policy has been developed from two sources. Those who believe in the wisdom of tribal ownership, and in the policy of continuing the Indian in his aboriginal customs, habits, and independence, oppose it because it will eventually dissolve his tribal relations and cause his absorption into the body politic. On the other hand, those who expected that the severalty act would immediately open to public settlement long-coveted Indian lands, oppose it because they have learned that these expectations will not be realized.
>
> There is a third class of persons who are heartily in favor of allotting Indian lands, but who are apprehensive that, under the flexible terms of the allotment act, allotments may be forced upon Indians before they are ready to receive, use, and hold them. * * *[221]

Commissioner Oberly presents a detailed analysis of the status of Indian health[222]—the diseases prevalent among Indians, the scarcity of physicians[223] and nurses, and the need for a hospital at every agency.

In his report on the operation of the contract system of purchasing Indian supplies, whereby numerous contractors submit samples which the Government is forced to examine, he recommends that the Indian Office fix the standard sample on which bids are to be received, thus assuring uniformity of quality, saving time, and eliminating charges of favoritism.[224]

Since Commissioner Oberly had been United States Civil Service Commissioner[225] as well as Superintendent of Indian Schools,[226] he was particularly interested in incorporating school employees under Civil Service, to correct the "party spoils system" method of appointment and dismissal.

> * * * for no matter how desirous the Commissioner of Indian Affairs and the Superintendent of Indian Schools may be to obtain good material for the service, and no matter how conscientiously both may endeavor to improve its condition, they will, so long as this system is endured, be obstructed in all such efforts by clamorous demands that the places on Indian reservations, and in the schools not on reservations, shall be dispensed as rewards for partisan activity. In short, the Commissioner and Superintendent, with 1,200 places (exclusive of Indians) at their disposal, can not give to the agency and the school competent employes until after they shall have secured protection from partisan pressure and personal solicitation; and such protection can be afforded to them only by the provisions of the civil-service act of 1883. As United States Civil Service Commissioner I gave to this subject much consideration, and I have no doubt that the provisions of that act could be applied to the Indian service, and, that by their application thereto, under wise rules promulgated by the President, the cause of Indian civilization would be advanced many years. * * *[227]

Commissioner Thomas J. Morgan entered upon his duties on July 1, 1889, and made his first report in October of that year. He offers, until such time as he may acquaint himself

> * * * by personal observation with the practical workings of the Indian field-service * * * a few simple, well-defined, and strongly cherished convictions:
>
> *First.*—The anomalous position heretofore occupied by the Indians in this country can not much longer be maintained. The reservation system belongs to a "vanishing state of things" and must soon cease to exist.
>
> *Second.*—The logic of events demands the absorption of the Indians into our national life, not as Indians, but as American citizens.
>
> *Third.*—As soon as a wise conservatism will warrant it, the relations of the Indians to the Government must rest solely upon the full recognition of their individuality. Each Indian must be treated as a man, be allowed a man's rights and privileges, and be held to the performance of a man's obligations. Each Indian is entitled to his proper share of the inherited wealth of the tribe, and to the protection of the courts in his "life, liberty, and

---

[215] *Ibid.*, p. XX. In an earlier report (1885) Commissioner Atkins had recommended that "When the Indians have taken their lands in severalty in sufficient quantities * * *," the remainder should be purchased by the Government and thrown open for homesteading.

> The money paid by the Government for their lands should be held in trust in 5 percent bonds, to be invested as Congress may provide for the education, civilization, and material development and advancement of the red race, reserving for each tribe its own money. (Rep. Comm. Ind. Aff., 1885, p IV.)

This became part of the General Allotment Act of February 8, 1887, 24 Stat. 388, 25 U. S. C. 331 *et seq.* and was the basis of trust-fund reports of succeeding commissioners. For a discussion of the background of the allotment system, see Chapter 11, sec. 1.

[216] *Ibid.*, p. XXVII. The courts of Indian offenses were established in 1882 according to the Report of the Commissioner of Indian Affairs for 1889 (p. 26).

[217] *Ibid.*, p. XL. See Chapter 16.

[218] Rep. Comm. Ind. Aff. (John H. Oberly), 1888, p. XXXIII.

[219] Act of February 8, 1887, 24 Stat. 388, 25 U. S. C. 331, *et seq.*

[220] Rep. Comm. Ind. Aff., 1888, p. XXXVII. The necessity for surveying prior to allotment, and the late date at which the appropriation bill passed are the reasons given.

[221] *Ibid.*, pp. XXXVIII–XXXIX. *Cf.* report of the previous commissioner, Atkins, in 1886, *supra*, of "* * * no substantial opposition to this bill * * *." (P. XX.)

[222] Rep. Comm. Ind. Aff., 1888, pp. XXXIV–XXXV.

[223] There were 81 physicians for more than 200,000 Indians—approximately 1 for every 2,500 Indians.

[224] Rep. Comm. Ind. Aff., 1888, pp. LXXXI, LXXXII.

[225] *Ibid.*, p. LXXXV. From April 17, 1886, to October 10, 1888, according to the Civil Service Commission official files.

[226] *Ibid.*, p. LXXXIV. From 1880 to 1886, according to Indian Office Library files.

[227] *Ibid.*, p. LXXXV.

pursuit of happiness." He is not entitled to be supported in idleness.

Fourth.—The Indians must conform to "the white man's ways," peaceably if they will, forcibly if they must. They must adjust themselves to their environment, and conform their mode of living substantially to our civilization. This civilization may not be the best possible, but it is the best the Indians can get. They can not escape it, and must either conform to it or be crushed by it.

Fifth.—The paramount duty of the hour is to prepare the rising generation of Indians for the new order of things thus forced upon them. A comprehensive system of education modeled after the American public-school system, but adapted to the special exigencies of the Indian youth, embracing all persons of school age, compulsory in its demands and uniformly administered, should be developed as rapidly as possible.

Sixth.—The tribal relations should be broken up, socialism destroyed, and the family and the autonomy of the individual substituted. The allotment of lands in severalty, the establishment of local courts and police, the development of a personal sense of independence, and the universal adoption of the English language are means to this end.

Seventh.—In the administration of Indian affairs there is need and opportunity for the exercise of the same qualities demanded in any other great administration—integrity, justice, patience, and good sense. Dishonesty, injustice, favoritism, and incompetency have no place here any more than elsewhere in the Government.

Eighth.—The chief thing to be considered in the administration of this office is the character of the men and women employed to carry out the designs of the Government. The best system may be perverted to bad ends by incompetent or dishonest persons employed to carry it into execution while a very bad system may yield good results if wisely and honestly administered.[228]

In 1890, Commissioner Morgan made a very detailed report (144 pp.) of the duties, difficulties, hopes, and improvements of his administration.[229] One of the chief difficulties was lack of personnel. A chief clerk, solicitor, and medical expert for the office were urged, in addition to other clerical help.[230] Agents' salaries were still too low for adequate performance.[231]

Another difficulty was the whole reservation policy.

> The entire system of dealing with them [the Indians] is vicious, involving, as it does, the installing of agents, with semi-despotic power over ignorant, superstitious, and helpless subjects; the keeping of thousands of them on reservations practically as prisoners, isolated from civilized life and dominated by fear and force; the issue of rations and annuities, which inevitably tends to breed pauperism; the disbursement of millions of dollars worth of supplies by contract, which invites fraud; the maintenance of a system of licensed trade, which stimulates cupidity and extortion, etc.[232]

Commissioner Morgan looked with hope on

> * * * the settled policy of the Government to break up reservations, destroy tribal relations, settle Indians upon their own homesteads, incorporate them into the national life, and deal with them not as nations or tribes or bands, but as individual citizens. The American Indian is to become the Indian American. * * *[233]

The rapid process of individualizing the Indian, Commissioner Morgan felt, was best indicated by the reduction of reservations.[234] More than 17,400,000 acres, or about one-seventh of all Indian land had been acquired by the Government during the year.[235]

Commissioner Morgan reported:

> * * * the growing recognition on the part of Western people that the Indians of their respective States and Territories are to remain permanently and become absorbed into the population as citizens. * * *
>
> * * * * *
>
> There is also a growing popular recognition of the fact that it is the duty of the Government, and of the several States where they are located, to make ample provision for the secular and industrial education of the rising generation, * *.[236]

Commissioner Morgan refused to grant further licenses for Indians to leave the reservation for the purpose of travel with "Wild West" shows on the grounds of the demoralizing influence.[237]

"* * * I consider the payment of cash to Indians," Commissioner Morgan wrote, "except in return for service rendered or labor performed for themselves or their people, as of very little real benefit in a majority of cases * * *."[238]

In the matter of traders, the policy of the office was to permit at least two on every reservation.

> Competition within the reservation, in addition to that growing up outside, is fostered by licensing on each reserve as many traders as practicable.[239]

Commissioner Browning, in 1895, reports progress, particularly in the education and the employment of the Indians.

> * * * a large increase has been made in the number of Indian employees, and in filling positions at agencies and schools Indians have been given the preference for appointment when found competent to do the work required.[240]

In education, opposition from the older Indians appears to have lessened.[241] Enrollment and school attendance increased.

> * * * without resort to coercion even to the extent allowed by law. * * * I have refrained from using such means, preferring the better course of moral suasion and convincing arguments, and finding them ultimately effective. It gives me pleasure to note the success of such methods, * * *.[242]

---

[228] Rep. Comm. Ind. Aff., 1889, pp. 3–4.

[229] Rep. Comm. Ind. Aff., 1890.

[230] *Ibid.*, pp. IV–V. See sec. 3B *infra.*

[231] *Ibid.*, pp. CXVIII–CXIX. Salaries ranged from $800 to $2,200, and averaged $1,533. See fn. 142, *supra.*

[232] *Ibid.*, p. V.

[233] Rep. Comm. Ind. Aff., 1890, p. VI. For an index of prevailing policy on allotment versus tribal ownership, see the Act of March 3, 1893, 27 Stat. 557, 561 (Kickapoo).

[234] *Ibid.*, p. VI.

[235] *Ibid.*, p. XXXIX. Of the reduction of Indian-owned lands Commissioner Morgan felt constrained to say:

> This might seem like a somewhat rapid reduction of the landed estate of the Indians, but when it is considered that for the most part the land relinquished was not being used for any purpose whatever, that scarcely any of it was in cultivation, that the Indians did not need it and would not be likely to need it at any future time, and that they were, as, is believed, reasonably well paid for it, the matter assumes quite a different aspect. The sooner the tribal relations are broken up and the reservation system done away with the better it will be for all concerned. If there were no other reason for this change, the fact that individual ownership of property is the universal custom among the civilized people of this country would be a sufficient reason for urging the handful of Indians to adopt it. (P. XXXIX.)

[236] *Ibid.*, pp. VI–VII.

[237] *Ibid.*, pp. VIII, LVII. By letter of August 4, 1890, the Secretary of the Interior directed that no more licenses be granted. (*Ibid.*, p. LVII.) On the issuance of passes to Indians leaving a reservation, see Chapter 8, sec. 10A(2).

[238] Rep. Comm. Ind. Aff., 1890, p. CXVIII.

[239] *Ibid.*, p. LX. However, Commissioner Morgan felt the whole license system was archaic. "* * * a relic of the old system of considering an Indian as a ward, a reservation as a corral, and a tradership as a golden opportunity for plunder and profit." (*Ibid.*, p. LIX.)

[240] Rep. Comm. Ind. Aff., 1895, p. 1.

[241] *Ibid.*, p. 3.

[242] *Ibid.*, p. 4.

Commissioner Browning reports in detail on the leasing of Indian lands. The Act of February 28, 1891,[243] authorized the leasing of unalloted or tribal lands, and allotted lands where age or disability of allottee warrants it. By Act of August 15, 1894,[244] and later acts these leasing statutes were broadened.

On this point, Commissioner Browning stated:

> * * * the indiscriminate leasing of allotments will not be permitted. * * * the indiscriminate leasing of allotments would defeat the very purpose for which they were made. * * *[245]

Commissioner Jones,[246] like his predecessor, reports progress in all fields, follows a statistical pattern of summarizing, and offers accompanying papers in support. The activity of the Bureau of Indian Affairs centered mainly about education; allotment and the problems arising therefrom—leasing, homesteading, surveying; the sale of liquor; railroads; and disturbances on reservations.

E. THE PERIOD FROM 1905 TO 1928

Commissioner Francis E. Leupp, in his first report in 1905, presents his outlines of an Indian policy as "* * * one of the fruits of my twenty years' study of the Indian face to face and in his home, as well as of his past and present environment * * *."[247]

The Indian, says Commissioner Leupp,

> * * * will never be judged aright till we learn to measure him by his own standards, as we whites would wish to be measured if some more powerful race were to usurp dominion over us.[248]

Commissioner Leupp has various recommendations for a new Indian policy—in education, in individualizing Indian land and money, in weaning the Indian from the licensed trader, in making him a part of his community.[249]

To carry out this policy,

> * * * our main hope lies with the youthful generation * * *. The task we must set ourselves is to win over the Indian children by sympathetic interest and unobtrusive guidance. It is a great mistake to try, as many good persons of bad judgment have tried, to start the little ones in the path of civilization by snapping all the ties of affection between them and their parents, and teaching them to despise the aged and non-progressive members of their families. * * *[250]

Manual training is the basis of Commissioner Leupp's educational policy. He would limit the ordinary Indian boy scholastically to enough of the "3 R's" so that

> * * * he can read the simple English of the local newspaper, can write a short letter which is intelligible though maybe ill-spelled, and knows enough of figures to discover whether the storekeeper is cheating him. * * *[251]

Of the policy of individualizing the Indian through division of tribal lands and tribal funds, Commissioner Leupp says:

> * * * it is our duty to set him upon his feet and sever forever the ties which bind him either to his tribe, in the communal sense, or to the Government. This principle must become operative in respect to both land and money. * * *[252] Thanks to the late Senator Henry L. Dawes of Massachusetts, we have for eighteen years been individualizing the Indian as an owner of real estate by breaking up, one at a time, the reservations set apart for whole tribes and establishing each Indian as a separate landholder on his own account. Thanks to Representative John F. Lacey of Iowa, I hope that we shall soon be making the same sort of division of the tribal funds.[253]

In order that the Indian might rapidly become a member of his community instead of a "necessary nuisance,"[254] Commissioner Leupp would encourage him to trade in local market towns; he would have Indian money deposited in local banks; he would teach him to shop competitively instead of with the obsolescent licensed trader.

In 1908, Commissioner Leupp reports the success of his plan

> * * * for systematic cooperation between various departments and bureaus of the Government, so as to get rid of the "wheels within wheels" which are so grave a source of waste in administration.[255]

The Reclamation Service, Geological Survey, and Forest Service in the Department of the Interior, and the Bureaus of Plant Industry and Animal Industry in the Department of Agriculture cooperated with the Bureau of Indian Affairs on specific projects of common interest.[256]

In 1911, Commissioner Valentine reports individual Indian money as a source of both good and harm. It had been used for houses, farm repairs, etc., helping to quicken industrial development of the Indians.[257] It had also caused traders to inculcate extravagant habits in the possessors of funds, and caused a great increase in indebtedness.[258] He recommends a continuance of the policy of "liberal supervision" over Indian funds by superintendents.[259]

---

[243] Sec. 3, 26 Stat. 794, 795 partly embodied in 25 U. S. C. 397. See Chapter 15, sec. 19, Chapter 11, sec. 5.

[244] 28 Stat. 286, 305. See Chapter 15, sec. 19, Chapter 11, secs. 1C and 5.

[245] Rep. Comm. Ind. Aff., 1895, p. 34.

[246] Rep. Comm. Ind. Aff., 1897.

[247] Rep. Comm. Ind. Aff., 1905, p. 1. Many of Commissioner Leupp's views on Indian affairs are set forth in The Indian and His Problem (1910).

[248] *Ibid.*, p. 1. To illustrate his point, Commissioner Leupp goes on to say:

> Suppose, a few centuries ago, an absolutely alien people like the Chinese had invaded our shores and driven the white colonists before them to districts more and more isolated, destroyed the industries on which they had always subsisted, and crowned all by disarming them and penning them on various tracts of land where they could be fed and clothed and cared for at no cost to themselves, to what condition would the white Americans of today have been reduced? In spite of their vigorous ancestry they would surely have lapsed into barbarism and become pauperized. No race on earth could overcome, with forces evolved from within themselves, the effect of such treatment. That our red brethren have not been wholly ruined by it is the best proof we could ask of the sturdy traits of character inherent in them. (P. 2.)

[249] *Ibid.*, pp. 3–5.

[250] *Ibid.*, p. 2.

[251] *Ibid.*, p. 3. Commissioner Leupp would have a girl trained in the domestic arts necessary for frontier life—cooking, sewing, washing, and ironing (p. 3).

[252] *Ibid.*, p. 3.

[253] *Ibid.*, p. 4. Two years later Congress enacted legislation providing for the breaking up of tribal funds. Act of March 2, 1907, 34 Stat. 1221, 25 U. S. C. 119. See Chapter 15, sec. 23B; Chapter 10, sec. 4; Chapter 9, sec. 6.

[254] *Ibid.*, p. 4.

[255] Rep. Comm. Ind. Aff., 1908, p. 2. See sec. 3, *infra*, for a discussion of the extensive cooperation between bureaus and departments that has been effected.

[256] *Ibid.*, pp. 2–9. The joint projects were the result either of direct approach between departments, or specific legislation. *E. g.*, the Act of May 30, 1908, 35 Stat. 558 directed the Secretary of the Interior to cause an examination of the lands on the Fort Peck Reservation to be made by Reclamation Service and Geological Survey (p. 3). See sec. 3C, *infra*, and Chapter 12, sec. 7.

[257] Rep. Comm. Ind. Aff., 1911, p. 21.

[258] *Ibid.*, p. 22.

[259] *Ibid.*, p. 21.

Various amendments[260] to the Allotment Act permitting alienation had been passed, some causing difficulty. The Act of June 25, 1910,[261] requiring that the Secretary determine the heirs of deceased allottees and issue patents in fee entailed

> * * * a vast amount of work; many allotments are now of 20 years' standing; estates are contested; and the questions of law, and particularly of fact, become extremely difficult, largely through difficulty in obtaining Indian testimony of value. As allotments have been made on 55 reservations, and upon the Winnebago Reservation alone—one of the smaller reservations—there are 600 heirship cases, the work to be done under this act will become one of the greater tasks of the office. * * *[262]

The leasing system, in general operation since 1891 "* * * raises some of the gravest questions of policy with which the Indian Office has to deal."[263] Commissioner Valentine analyzes the cases where leasing has been of real value to the Indian—where the Indian is already farming as much as his capital and help permit; where the Indian has chosen some other industrial pursuit than farming; where he is ill or otherwise incapacitated.[264] For the most part, however, "* * * leasing as it has been practiced is * * * a positive detriment to the Indians. * * * a steady rental from his land is one of the strongest incentives not to begin to work."[265]

Commissioner Valentine reports the result of investigation into the status of "State" Indians—Indians who have long been more or less independent of the Federal Government.[266]

> * * * It is noteworthy that in many cases these Indians have worked out for themselves, with some assistance from their States, problems which the service has still to meet in other parts of the field.[267]

Although, by the Act of May 8, 1906,[268] the Secretary of the Interior was given the power, before the expiration of the 25-year trust period, to issue a patent in fee "whenever he shall be satisfied that any Indian allottee is competent and capable of managing his or her affairs * * *," a conservative policy was followed.[269] Each application had to be considered on its merits, and was accompanied by a report of the superintendent. However, even with this conservative policy, during the first 3 years of the law's operation, 60 percent of the patentees disposed of their land and its proceeds.[270]

Commissioner Valentine, therefore, inaugurated a policy of requiring more rigid proof of competency, and superintendents were required to answer more specific questions.[271] In his report for 1911, he sums up his policy thus:

> *** * * I am opposed to granting patents in fee unless circumstances clearly show that a title in fee will be of undoubted advantage to the applicant. * * * In the face of existing evidences of carelessness and incompetence any liberal policy of giving patents in fee would be utterly at cross-purposes with the other efforts of the Government to encourage industry, thrift, and independence.**[272]

In 1917, under Commissioner Cato Sells,[273] a more drastic policy was inaugurated.

> Broadly speaking, a policy of greater liberalism will henceforth prevail in Indian administration to the end that every Indian, as soon as he has been determined to be as competent to transact his own business as the average white man, shall be given full control of his property and have all his lands and moneys turned over to him, after which he will no longer be a ward of the Government.
>
> Pursuant to this policy, the following rules shall be observed:
>
> 1. *Patents in fee.*—To all able-bodied adult Indians of less than one-half Indian blood, there will be given as far as may be under the law full and complete control of all their property. Patents in fee shall be issued to all adult Indians of one-half or more Indian blood who may, after careful investigation, be found competent, provided, that where deemed advisable patents in fee shall be withheld for not to exceed 40 acres as a home.
>
> Indian students, when they are 21 years of age, or over, who complete the full course of instruction in the Government schools, receive diplomas and have demonstrated competency will be so declared.
>
> 2. *Sale of lands.*—A liberal ruling will be adopted in the matter of passing upon applications for the sale of inherited Indian lands where the applicants retain other lands and the proceeds are to be used to improve the homesteads or for other equally good purposes. A more liberal ruling than has hitherto prevailed will hereafter be followed with regard to the applications of noncompetent Indians for the sale of their lands where they are old and feeble and need the proceeds for their support.
>
> 3. *Certificates of competency.*—The rules which are made to apply in the granting of patents in fee and the sale of lands will be made equally applicable in the matter of issuing certificates of competency.
>
> 4. *Individual Indian moneys.*—Indians will be given unrestricted control of all their individual Indian moneys upon issuance of patents in fee or certificates of competency. Strict limitations will not be placed upon the use of funds of the old, the indigent, and the invalid.
>
> 5. *Pro rata shares—trust funds.*—As speedily as possible their pro rata shares in tribal trust or other funds shall be paid to all Indians who have been declared competent, unless the legal status of such funds prevents. Where practicable the pro rata shares of incompetent Indians will be withdrawn from the Treasury and placed in banks to their individual credit.
>
> * * * * *
>
> This is a new and far-reaching declaration of policy. It means the dawn of a new era in Indian administration. It means that the competent Indian will no longer be treated as half ward and half citizen. It means reduced appropriations by the Government and more self-respect and independence for the Indian. It means the ultimate absorption of the Indian race into the body politic of the Nation. It means, in short, the beginning of the end of the Indian problem.[274]

Competency commissions were set up, and superintendents were requested to furnish—

> * * * a list of all Indians of one-half or less Indian blood, who are able-bodied and mentally competent,

---

[260] See Chapter 5, secs. 11B and 11C. And *cf.* Rep. Comm. Ind. Aff., 1911, p. 26.

[261] 36 Stat. 855. See Chapter 5, sec. 11C.

[262] Rep. Comm. Ind. Aff., 1911, p. 26.

[263] *Ibid.*, p. 26. See Chapter 11, sec. 5 and Chapter 15, sec. 19.

[264] Rep. Comm. Ind. Aff., 1911, pp. 26–27.

[265] *Ibid.*, p. 27.

[266] *E. g.* the Catawba Indians of South Carolina, over whom the State of South Carolina had assumed sovereign rights without federal objection. It had treated with the Indians since 1763, had granted them a reservation and had attempted to extinguish their title in 1840. The Alabama Indians in Texas lived on land granted to them conditionally by the state about 1850. Rep. Comm. Ind. Aff., 1911, pp. 46, 47.

[267] Rep. Comm. Ind. Aff., 1911, p. 46.

[268] 34 Stat. 182, 183, generally known as the Burke Act. See Chapter 5, sec. 11B.

[269] Schmeckebier, *op. cit.*, pp. 150–151.

[270] *Ibid.*, p. 151.

[271] According to Schmeckebier (*op. cit.*, p. 151), between 1909 and 1912, 3,400 applications for patents were approved, and approximately 2,000 denied.

[272] Rep. Comm. Ind. Aff., 1911, pp. 22–23.

[273] Cato Sells was Commissioner of Indian Affairs for 8 years under President Wilson (from 1913 to 1921), the first Commissioner to hold office for that length of time.

[274] Report of the Commissioner of Indian Affairs, 1917, pp. 3–4, declaration of policy of April 17, 1917. (Schmeckebier, *op. cit.*, pp. 152–153.) From 1917 to 1920, 10,956 fee simple patents were issued, as compared with 9,894 from 1906 to 1916. (Schmeckebier, *op. cit.*, p. 154. Also Rep. Comm. Ind. Aff., 1920, p. 8.)

twenty-one years of age or over, together with a description of land allotted to said Indians, and the number of the allotment. It is intended to issue patents in fee simple to such Indians.[275]

The question of Indian citizenship became prominent after Indian participation in the World War.[276] In reply to critics, Commissioner Sells wrote in 1920:

> I have, however, gone further and taken the position that the citizenship of Indians should not be based upon their ownership of lands, tribal or in severalty, in trust or in fee, but upon the fact that they are real Americans, and favorable report has been made on a bill introduced in Congress having for its purpose the conferring of citizenship on all Indians, but retaining control of the estates of incompetents.[277]

Commissioner Sells adopted the policy with respect to individual Indian money of paying it directly to competent adult Indians without deposit, or having it disbursed in large sums by the superintendents from funds deposited under their supervision.[278]

In 1921, with a change in administration, the new commissioner [279] declared:

> This practice, however [of issuing patents in fee to Indians of one-half or less Indian blood without any further proof of competency], has been discontinued, and in all cases involving the issuance of patents to Indians, the practice is now to require a formal application and proof of competency.[280]

The result of the shift in policy is clear from the following tabulation of patents issued from 1921 to 1926:[281]

Fiscal year:	
1921	1,692
1922	911
1923	625
1924	913
1925	451
1926	322

In his brief report for 1922, Commissioner Burke devotes a considerable portion to education.

> In the education of the Indian youth lies the hope of the future generations of the American Indian. In this time, when it is so essential to practice economy in every possible way, it should be realized that the child who is allowed to grow up in this country without being taught English and manual skill in some useful occupation is always in danger of becoming a liability. It is false economy to neglect the education of any children.[282]

An industrial survey of all the reservations, based on a house-to-house canvass of Indian families, was inaugurated

> * * * to ascertain their condition, needs, and resources, with the view to organizing the work of the reservation service so that each family will make the best use of its resources. * * *[283]

The industrial survey was to form the basis of a more comprehensive one for each reservation, embracing the needs—for health, education, housing, sanitation, social welfare on the one hand, and the resources—both tribal and individual on the other. The purpose of such a survey would be "to formulate for each reservation a definite program or policy which may be followed for such term of years as will place the Indians on a self-supporting basis."[284]

Increasing cooperation with Federal health agencies, as well as with state, local, and voluntary agencies, is noted during Commissioner Burke's administration.[285]

> It is hoped that closer cooperation may be established between States having Indian populations and the Federal Government in dealing with questions of education, health, and law enforcement. Probably States should ultimately assume complete responsibility for the Indians within their borders, but pending that time, there is much to be done by the Federal service.[286]

F. THE PERIOD FROM 1929 TO 1939

The survey of the social and economic conditions of the Indians, begun at the invitation of the Interior Department in 1926 by the Institute for Government Research,[287] was completed in 1928.

The publication of this report helped to inaugurate a new era in the Indian Service. The criticisms and recommendations contained in the report commanded the attention of the Bureau,[288] as well as the general public. The report raised serious doubts as to the wisdom of such established Indian policies as that which had developed around the allotment problem. Of the policy of individual allotment, the report declared:

> * * * Not accompanied by adequate instruction in the use of property, it has largely failed in the accomplishment of what was expected of it. It has resulted in much loss of land and an enormous increase in the details of administration without a compensating advance in the economic ability of the Indians. The difficult problem of inheritance is one of its results. * * * (P. 41.)

Even more serious doubts were raised as to the efficiency and adequacy of the public services rendered by the Indian Bureau. On the question of health, the survey reported:

> The health of the Indians as compared with that of the general population is bad. (P. 3.)
> * * * For some years it has been customary to speak of the Indian medical service as being organized for public health work, yet the fundamentals of sound public health work are still lacking. (P. 190.)

[275] Letter of March 7, 1919, to superintendents in Schmeckebier, *op. cit.*, pp. 153–154. This liberal policy of Commissioner Sells under the secretaryship of Franklin K. Lane has resulted in litigation based on forced allotments and sale of land for taxes, which is still one of the chief concerns of the Department of Justice. See Chapter 11.

[276] By Act of November 6, 1919, 41 Stat. 350, 8 U. S. C. 3, citizenship had been made available to Indian participants in the World War, honorably discharged, on declaration of courts of competent jurisdiction. See Chapter 8, sec. 2.

[277] Rep. Comm. Ind. Aff., 1920, p. 8. By Act of June 2, 1924, c. 233, 43 Stat. 253, 8 U. S. C. 3, 173, such general citizenship was granted. See Chapter 8, sec. 2.

[278] Rep. Comm. Ind. Aff., 1920, p. 50.

[279] Charles H. Burke became the new Commissioner of Indian Affairs, and served for more than 8 years under 2 Presidents. The reports again become brief summaries as they were at the beginning of the Bureau of Indian Affairs in 1824.

[280] Rep. Comm. Ind. Aff., 1921, p. 23.

[281] Schmeckebier, *op. cit.*, p. 154.

[282] Rep. Comm. Ind. Aff., 1922, p. 7.

[283] *Ibid.*, p. 11.

[284] *Ibid.*, p. 11. That program was later followed in the establishment of a unit of the Soil Conservation Service, known as Technical Cooperation, Bureau of Indian Affairs (TC-BIA), in November 1935. The purpose of the TC-BIA is to make such surveys and recommendations for each reservation, in collaboration with the Soil Conservation Service.

[285] Rep. Comm. Ind. Aff., 1928, p. 1.

[286] *Ibid.*, 1928, p. 7.

[287] Meriam, Problem of Indian Administration (1928). In a publication of the American Indian Defense Association (American Indian Life, Bulletin No. 12, June 1928, p. 6) the survey was evaluated.

> The report of the Institute for Government Research is the most important single document in Indian Affairs since Helen Hunt Jackson's "The Century of Dishonor" published 45 years ago. It contains three sections which intrinsically are very fine. (Health, Education, and Women and Family and Community Life.) Its 847 pages of text are a result of team-work between ten specialists. The studied moderation of its language; the avoidance of a suggestion even as to where responsibility shall be placed; the omission (save in regard to health and education) of most of the facts which give a quality of sinister deliberateness to the wrongs suffered by Indians; its nearly total avoidance of those skeleton closets, the handling of individual Indian trust moneys and reimbursable indebtedness: these qualities of the report increase its convincingness and usefulness.

[288] Rep. Comm. Ind. Aff., 1928, pp. 4–7.

> Special hospital equipment, such as X-ray, clinical laboratory, and special treatment facilities is generally lacking. (P. 282.)
>
> No sanatorium in the Indian Service meets the minimum requirements of the American Sanatorium Association. (P. 287.)
>
> The hospitals, sanatoria, and sanatorium schools maintained by the Service, despite a few exceptions, must be generally characterized as lacking in personnel, equipment, management, and design. (P. 9.)

On the subject of education, the survey was scarcely less critical.

> The work of the government directed toward the education and advancement of the Indian himself, as distinguished from the control and conservation of his property, is largely ineffective. (P. 8.)
>
> The survey staff finds itself obliged to say frankly and unequivocally that the provisions for the care of Indian children in boarding schools are grossly inadequate. (P. 11.)

On the economic problems of the Indians, the survey did much to overthrow the popular impression, based largely on the publicity given to a few "oil" Indians, that the Indians generally occupied a favored economic position:

> An overwhelming majority of the Indians are poor, even extremely poor, and they are not adjusted to the economic and social system of the dominant white civilization. (P. 3.)
>
> The prevailing living conditions among the great majority of the Indians are conducive to the development and spread of disease. (P. 3.)
>
> Even under the best conditions it is doubtful whether a well rounded program of economic advancement framed with due consideration of the natural resources of the reservation has anywhere been thoroughly tried out. The Indians often say that programs change with superintendents. Under the poorest administration there is little evidence of anything which could be termed an economic program. (P. 14.)

Of the general social objectives of Indian administration, the survey had this to say:

> The Indian Service has not appreciated the fundamental importance of family life and community activities in the social and economic development of a people. The tendency has been rather toward weakening Indian family life and community activities than toward strengthening them. (P. 15.)

On the question of law and order, the survey reported:

> Most notable is the confusion that exists as to legal jurisdiction over the restricted Indians in such important matters as crimes and misdemeanors and domestic relations. The act of Congress providing for the punishment of eight major crimes applies to the restricted Indians on tribal lands and restricted allotments, and cases of this character come under the unquestioned jurisdiction of the United States courts. Laws respecting the sale of liquor to Indians and some other special matters have been passed, and again jurisdiction is clear. For the great body of other crimes and misdemeanors the situation is highly unsatisfactory. (Pp. 16-17.)

The positive recommendations of the survey, which have greatly influenced the policy of the Indian Bureau since 1928,[289] stressed the need for a comprehensive educational program designed to meet the problems of reservation life, the need for sustained and coordinated economic planning and development, the need for a strengthened, more efficient and better paid personnel, the encouragement of Indian use of Indian lands, the strengthening of Indian community life, the clarification of confusions in the Indian law and order situation, and the final settlement of outstanding legal claims.[290]

Commissioner Rhoads,[291] like his predecessor, devotes a good part of his reports to education, particularly to federal-state relations.[292] In 1929 he reports:

> * * * The States and the local public-school districts appear to be generally in sympathy with the plan of education by the States, conditioned, however, upon such financial assistance as they need and as the Federal Government can offer. * * *[293]

In 1931 Commissioner Rhoads reiterates:

> * * * Indian education is in no sense solely a Federal problem, but a State and local problem as well. When Congress in 1924 made all Indian citizens it served notice that Indians could no longer be overlooked in the citizenry of any State.[294]

In 1932, Commissioner Rhoads states:

> The most significant feature of the year in Indian education was the determined effort to make the change from boarding school attendance to local day or public school attendance for Indian children.[295]

This was in keeping with the new educational policy of providing the Indian's education "* * * in his own community setting."[296]

Throughout the reports[297] of recent commissioners appears the title "Additional lands for Indian use," one result of the Allotment Act. In some cases tribal funds are used on a reimbursable plan for such purchases.[298]

Commissioner Collier in his first report in 1933 discusses the four main lines along which his policy is to be directed: Indian lands, Indian education, Indians in Indian Service, and reorganization of the Indian Service.

> (1) *Indian lands.*—The allotment system has enormously cut down the Indian landholdings and has rendered many areas, still owned by Indians, practically unavailable for Indian use. The system must be revised both as a matter of law and of practical effect. Allotted lands must be consolidated into tribal or corporate ownership with individual tenure, and new lands must be acquired for the 90,000 Indians who are landless at the present time. A modern system of financial credit must be instituted to enable the Indians to use their own natural resources. And training in the modern techniques of land use must be supplied Indians. The wastage of Indian lands through erosion must be checked.
>
> (2) *Indian education.*—The redistribution of educational opportunity for Indians, out of the concentrated boarding school, reaching the few, and into the day school, reaching the many, must be continued and accelerated. The boarding schools which remain must be specialized on lines of occupational need for children of the older groups, or of the need of some Indian children for institutional care. The day schools must be worked out on lines of community service, reaching the adult as well as the child, and influencing the health, the recreation, and the economic welfare of their local areas.
>
> (3) *Indians in Indian Service.*—The increasing use of Indians in their own official and unofficial service must

---

[289] For an account of the effect which this report had on Indian education, for instance, see Chapter 12, sec. 2.

[290] It will be noted that most of these recommendations had been made from time to time in commissioners' reports.

[291] Charles J. Rhoads, 1929–33.

[292] See, for example, Rep. Comm. Indian Aff., for 1929, pp. 4–7; for 1930, pp. 7–13; for 1931, pp. 4–13; for 1932, pp. 4–9.

[293] Rep. Comm. Ind. Aff., 1929, p. 5.

[294] *Ibid.* 1931, p. 7.

[295] *Ibid.*, 1932, p. 4.

[296] *Ibid.*, 1932, p. 5.

[297] See *e. g.*, Rep. Comm. Ind. Aff., 1928, p. 23, 1929, p. 10, etc.

[298] See *e. g.*, Rep. Comm. Ind. Aff., 1928, p. 28, 1931, pp. 30–31, etc. See Chapter 15, secs. 6, 8.

> be pressed without wearying. To this end, adjustments of Civil Service arrangements to Indian need must be sought; but in order that standards may not be lowered, opportunities for professional training must be made genuinely accessible to Indians. With respect to unofficial Indian self-service, a steadily widening tribal and local participation by Indians in the management of their own properties and in the administration of their own services must be pursued.
>
> (4) *Reorganization of the Indian Service.*—A decentralizing of administrative routine must be progressively attempted. The special functions of Indian Service must be integrated with one another and with Indian life, in terms of local areas and of local groups of Indians. An enlarged responsibility must be vested in the superintendents of reservations and beyond them, or concurrently, in the Indians themselves. This reorganization is in part dependent on the revision of the land allotment system; and in part it is dependent on the steady development of cooperative relations between the Indian Service as a Federal agency, on the one hand, and the States, counties, school districts, and other local units of government on the other hand.[299]

Commissioner Collier's major policies found statutory expression in the Wheeler-Howard (Indian Reorganization) Act of June 18, 1934.[300] The extent to which they have been embodied in existing law and practice will be one of the principal inquiries of the substantive chapters that follow.

G. HISTORICAL RETROSPECT

Recent trends in our national Indian policy are set forth against the background of history in a statement prepared by the Office of Indian Affairs in 1938, at the request of the Department of State:[301]

> * * * The chief issue around which Indian policy revolved prior to 1933 was whether this transfer of ownership [of land and resources] could best be brought about through peaceful treaty, through force of arms, or through the usual legal forms of patent, deed and mortgage. Indian policy and Indian administration, even today when this motive has been reversed, is underlaid with strata of the earlier policies, and can be understood only as these earlier policies are understood.
>
> During the years when the rivalries of England, France and Spain on the continent gave the various Indian tribes positions of strategic power, negotiations with these tribes were carried on by the Colonies and later by the United States on the basis of international treaties. These treaties acknowledge the sovereignty of Indian tribes and implied the acknowledgement of a possessory right in the soil that the tribes occupied. After the cession of Louisiana by France in 1803, the termination of the war with Great Britain in 1814 and the cession of Florida by Spain in 1819, there developed an increasing tendency to deny the sovereignty of Indian tribes and to deal with them by force of arms.[302]
>
> * * * * *
>
> The use of military force to control Indians was a dominant factor in United States policy from the 1820's until the 1850's and did not wholly disappear with the last of the Indian wars in the 1890's. This warfare materially handicapped the settlement of the West and proved costly to the Federal Government. It was officially estimated with probable correctness about 1870 that Indian wars had cost the Government in excess of $1,000,000 for every dead Indian.[303]
>
> * * * * *
>
> While treaties and wars had failed to break down the internal organization and culture of the Indian tribes, the allotment policy brought with it a growing roster of white superintendents, farm agents, teachers, inspectors and missionaries who superseded Indian leaders and to a large extent succeeded in destroying Indian culture. There was developed a system of closed reservations ruled autocratically by the Indian Bureau, which in 1849 had been transferred from the War Department to the Department of the Interior. This autocratic rule was carried out under an ever-increasing number of uncorrelated statutes; a never codified and vast body of administrative regulations; and the personal government of Indian agents who were politically appointed. Misery became extreme upon the reservations, graft became notorious and led to more Indian outbreaks, and as a measure of relief, President Grant, in his first term, placed Christian mission bodies administratively in charge of Indian affairs in numerous parts of the country. This official identification of missionary bodies with Indians gradually was brought to an end in later years, but the political identification of the mission bodies with the Indian Bureau had not been dissolved until very recent times. * * * It was not acknowledged that Indians were entitled to the constitutional guarantees of liberty of conscience.[304]
>
> The guiding concepts in what may be called the autocratic phase of the Federal policy toward Indians were the destruction of all Indian tribal bonds, the effacing of Indian languages and cultural heritages, the forcing of the Indian as an individual to become identified with and lost in the white life, and the breaking of tribal, communal and even family landholdings into individual allotments of farm, timber and grazing lands.[305]
>
> * * * * *
>
> In the autocratic phase of Indian policy, a uniform pattern of administration and of program was imposed throughout the Indian country.[306]
>
> * * * * *
>
> Against the above background the present phase of governmental Indian policy can be better understood. The present policy continues the Federal guardianship over Indians and trusteeship over Indian property while seeking to establish individual and group liberty within the guardianship.[307] * * * In the new phase, the stress is against uniformity and in the direction of the maximum of local adaptation, both of method and of goal.[308]
>
> In all of these phases of the present-day government policy toward Indians, an underlying factor is the realization that the Indian is no longer the "vanishing American," but is actually increasing in numbers. During the past eight years the growth in population as reported by Indian agencies in the United States has been at the rate of over 1 per cent per annum. As with various other peoples during periods of development, the birth rate has been decreasing, but the decline in the Indian death rate has been even greater.
>
> To help Indians in making adjustments to the drastic changes in their way of life made necessary by the overwhelming invasion of the alien white race, and yet to foster the perpetuation of much of their cultural heritage, to train and stimulate them for complete economic self-sufficiency, looking toward a better standard of living for this vital race, are the ultimate goals of the present Administration.
>
> Although only slightly over a third of a million in population in a nation of approximately 130 million people, the Indians of the United States will become an even greater factor in its cultural, social, and economic life.[309]

---

[299] Annual Report of The Secretary of the Interior, 1933, Rep. Comm. Ind. Aff., pp. 68–69.

[300] 48 Stat. 984, 25 U. S. C. 461 *et seq.* See Chapter 4, sec. 16.

[301] "A Brief Statement on the Background of Present-day Indian Policy" (submitted November 21, 1938).

This statement was for the use of the American delegation at the Eighth International Conference of American States, at Lima, Peru, December 9, 1938.

[302] *Ibid.*, pp. 1–2.

[303] *Ibid.*, p. 2.

[304] *Ibid.*, p. 3.

[305] *Ibid.*, pp. 3–4.

[306] *Ibid.*, p. 8.

[307] *Ibid.*, p. 6.

[308] *Ibid.*, p. 8.

[309] *Ibid.*, p. 9.

SECTION 3. ADMINISTRATION OF THE INDIAN SERVICE TODAY

A. ORGANIZATION AND ACTIVITIES

The organization and functions of the Office of Indian Affairs today are pictured in the accompanying chart.[310]

The Commissioner of Indian Affairs is the titular and functioning head of the entire office, both in Washington and in the field. He has directly under him the Assistant Commissioner, who shares the duties of office and acts in his place. Those duties are: General management of and promulgation of policies covering all matters relating to Indians and to the natives of Alaska, including economic development; organization of tribes; education; health activities; land acquisitions, leases, sales; forest and grazing management; construction, maintenance, and operation of irrigation facilities; construction and upkeep of roads and bridges on Indian reservations; conservation work; and relief activities; and the interpretation of the needs of the Indian Service in legislative and budgetary terms.

[310] Chart on Organization and Functions prepared by the Office of Indian Affairs as of May 1940. All the descriptions of duties contained in this section are based on information supplied by the Indian Office. The chart appears also in Blauch, Educational Service for Indians (President's Advisory Committee on Education, Staff Study No. 18, 1939), p. 28.

The Probate Division and the Legal Division are jointly under the Office of the Commissioner of Indian Affairs and under the Solicitor for the Department.

The Probate Division[311] determines heirs and probates wills of all deceased Indians outside the Five Tribes and Osage Nation; reviews the work of the Probate Attorneys of the Five Tribes, and the probate recommendations of the Osage Tribal Attorney and Superintendent; and handles income and inheritance tax matters of Five Tribes.

The Legal Division reviews matters covering legal and other questions affecting the Indians, including reviewed reports on Congressional bills affecting Indians, and passes on a host of other legal matters involving Indians or their property, rights-of-way, condemnation, taxation, irrigation, determination of heirs, etc.

The Assistants to the Commissioner are the Commissioner's immediate staff officers. They are assigned from time to time numerous duties which devolve upon the Commissioner's Office. In general the Assistants to the Commissioner serve to coordinate the diverse functions of the Service and to stimulate cooperative planning. There are at present three field representatives, four

[311] See Chapter 11, sec. 6.

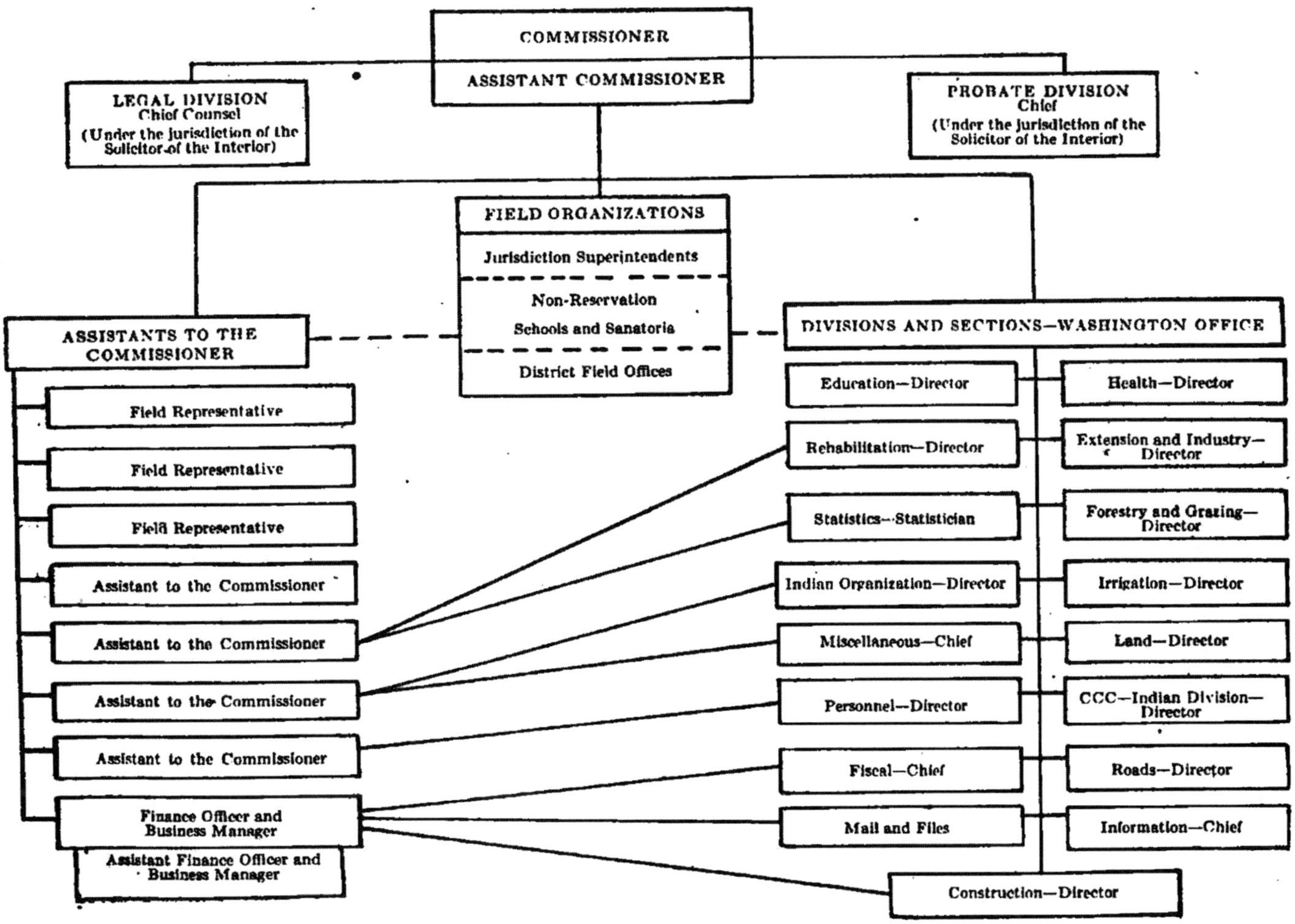

Organization Chart of the Office of Indian Affairs, 1940

special assistants, and two finance officers. One field representative is in charge of contacts with Indian tribes; the second, in charge of conferences and the relating of educational, health, and other facilities to new projects and management problems; the third, in charge of cooperation with other agencies. Of the four special assistants, one is in charge of land use, consolidation, and heirship problems. A second coordinates projects involving land use and resettlement and works chiefly with the Statistics Section and the Rehabilitation Division. A third handles all matters relating to Indian tribal organization, Indian delegations, law and order, individual Indian moneys, field investigations, and works chiefly with the Indian Organization Division and the Miscellaneous Section. A fourth is in charge of personnel policies and works with the Personnel Division. The finance officer and his assistant are in charge of all fiscal matters for the Office of Indian Affairs—its budget, expenditure of funds under appropriation acts, and legislation.

In the Washington office, organizational functions are broken up into 17 divisions and sections directly under the Office of the Commissioner. At the head of each division is a director. The division directors are responsible to the Commissioner for the general development of policies and programs and the professional direction of activities within the spheres of their several interests. They work through the agency superintendents and in cooperation with each other and the assistants to the Commissioner. Each division director collaborating with the finance officer prepares estimates of needed funds, presents these to the Bureau of the Budget and the committees of Congress. They advise the finance officer in the allotment of funds to agencies. They collaborate with the personnel officer in the preparation of civil-service examinations and in the selection, placement, in-service training, transfer, and separation of personnel.

The Education Division has professional direction of the educational program of Indian schools in the United States and of schools for the natives of Alaska; handles all matters relating to the attendance of Indian children in public schools; administers educational loan funds; coordinates social welfare services.

The Civilian Conservation Corps, Indian Division, administers C. C. C. funds allocated to the Indian Service and gives general direction to work projects, safety measures, and the enrollee program of welfare, instruction, and recreation.

The Irrigation Division has general direction of the construction, operation, and maintenance, including power service of irrigation projects, together with the development of subsistence gardens and domestic and stock water supplies on Indian reservations.

The Roads Division develops and directs policies and programs of road and bridge work on Indian reservations, including construction and maintenance, prepares specifications, and purchases all road machinery, equipment, and trucks.

The Health Division develops policies and programs of health conservation and gives professional supervision to all medical, dental, nursing, and sanitation activities.[312]

The Division of Forestry and Grazing encourages conservation practices, exercises professional direction of the general forestry and grazing program.

The Division of Extension and Industry stimulates and aids the development of agricultural and livestock enterprises and home improvement.

The Land Division is responsible for protection and proper handling of all Indian-owned land, and for acquisition of additional lands needed for tribal, individual, school, hospital, or other purposes; and reviews or initiates legislation pertaining to Indian lands, mineral rights, and tribal claims.

[312] See Chapter 12, sec. 3.

The Statistics Section collects, tabulates, and analyses data obtained from the field on population, health, Indian income, land, agricultural, and other activities of Indians needed in dealing with Indian problems and Indian development; and coordinates statistical needs, improves statistical records, and designs forms for use in the field and by divisions of the Washington office.

The Rehabilitation Division applies for allotments of emergency relief funds, and in consultation with other divisions and with field superintendents, allots to agencies these funds for approved rehabilitation projects.

The Indian Organization Division assists Indian tribes and bands to draft constitutions, bylaws, and charters of incorporation under authority of the Act of June 18, 1934,[313] the Oklahoma Indian Welfare Act[314] and the Alaska Reorganization Act;[315] conducts educational work and supervises elections in connection therewith; assists tribes to make intelligent use of the powers acquired through organization and incorporation; reviews ordinances and resolutions adopted by tribes and presented for departmental review or approval; and determines the tribal status of individual Indians or groups of Indians.

The Miscellaneous Section initiates correspondence on the following: maintenance of law and order, individual Indian money, claims for withdrawal of pro-rata shares and Sioux benefits, traders, dance and ceremonies, Indian monuments, delegations to Washington, and a variety of miscellaneous subjects.

The Personnel Division develops personnel policies, stimulates and coordinates in-service training, discovers employment opportunities in private industry for Indians, and provides records and procedures for the orderly and efficient management of personnel.

The Fiscal Division directs and supervises bookkeeping and accounting matters; examination of accounts and claims; requisition of funds for advance to disbursing agents; investment and deposit of Indian funds; and property accounting.

The Service Section provides services such as a stenographic pool, mail room for handling of incoming and outgoing mails, and organized files of all pertinent correspondence for the orderly and efficient handling of the business of the office.

The Construction Division in cooperation with the superintendents and the several division directors, prepares plans and specifications, estimates costs, and supervises the construction of all Indian Service buildings; gathers engineering data and prepares engineering reports on buildings, utility services, and plant maintenance.

The Information Division advises on articles for publication and public speeches by employees of the Office of Indian Affairs; assembles and interprets to the public pertinent facts concerning Indians and the work of the Indian Office; and has editorial supervision over the office publication "Indians at Work."

Directly under the Office of Indian Affairs, and solely responsible to it are field organizations covering 64 superintendents and 25 independent units—6 sanatoria, 10 schools, and 9 district offices.

The superintendent is responsible directly to the Commissioner of Indian Affairs for the orderly and efficient administration of governmental affairs relating to the Indians of his jurisdiction, including moneys, property, and personnel. He coordinates the work of his staff and utilizes all available technical and professional aid from the Washington and district offices in developing and administering a program that serves the needs of the Indians of his jurisdiction.

[313] See Chapter 4, sec. 16.

[314] See Chapter 23, sec. 13.

[315] See Chapter 21, sec. 9.

An examination of the regulations under which the Indian Service operates will illustrate its manifold activities. The codified regulations cover Alaska; antiquities; attorneys and agents; Civilian Conservation Corps, Indian Division; credit to Indians; education of Indians; enrollment and reallotment of Indians; forestry, grazing; heirs and wills; hospital and medical care of Indians; irrigation projects; law and order; leases, permits, and sale of minerals on restricted Indian lands; moneys, tribal and individual; patents in fee, competency certificates, sales, and reinvestment of proceeds; records (Oklahoma Indian tribes); relief of Indians; rights-of-way; roads and highways; trading with Indians; wilderness and roadless areas; wildlife. In addition to the regulations contained in the Code of Federal Regulations there are many special regulations.[316]

B. PERSONNEL

The Act of July 9, 1832,[317] which provided for the appointment of a Commissioner of Indian Affairs at a salary of $3,000, made no provision for specific clerical assistance or contingent expenses of the office. The Appropriation Act of June 18, 1834,[318] provided for the first time, in addition to $3,000 for salary of the Commissioner of Indian Affairs, $5,000 for salary of clerks in the office of the Commissioner, $700 for salary of the messenger, and $800 for contingent expenses.[319]

Provisions for various increases and new offices gradually appeared in the appropriation acts.[320]

The Commissioner of Indian Affairs[321] and the Assistant Commissioner[322] are appointed by the President with the consent of the Senate. All other employees[323] are appointed by the Secretary of the Interior after certification by the Civil Service Commission,[324] with the exception of specified field personnel and certain administrative offices in the Washington office.[325] The salaries are fixed basically by the Classification Act of March 4, 1923.[326] The extent to which Indians themselves are employed is elsewhere discussed.[327]

Up to 1893 officers in immediate control of Indians were known as "agents." They were appointed by the President with the consent of the Senate.[328] To remove this office from politics the Act of March 3, 1893,[329] authorized the Commissioner of Indian Affairs, with the approval of the Secretary of the Interior, to devolve the duties of agent upon the superintendent of the school located at the agency.

With the closing of Government schools many "superintendents" were left without schools. "Agency" has again become the term for units of administration, but officers in charge are still called "superintendents."[330]

The superintendent of an agency is a bonded officer, responsible for all expenditures.[331] The superintendent is authorized to acknowledge deeds, administer various oaths, take depositions.[332] He instructs new employees in their duties and the statutory limitations or prohibitions.[333] He may not serve as a guardian of an Indian under appointment by a local court.[334]

No employee of the United States Government may have any interest or concern in any trade with the Indians, except for and on account of the United States; and any person offending is liable to a penalty of $5,000 and removal from office.[335] The purchase of articles from Indians for home use by Government employees is not held to constitute trade.[336]

According to Commissioner Collier,

> *The major principle of field administration is that the Superintendent of a jurisdiction is the responsible officer in that jurisdiction.* He is responsible directly to the Commissioner of Indian Affairs. There is no intervening administrative authority between him and the Commissioner, nor is there any intervening administrative authority between him and the employees under his jurisdiction. * * *[337]

Commissioner Cato Sells expressed the same idea in 1916:

> Inspecting officers should impress superintendents with the fact that they are held responsible for every activity

---

[316] This list is taken from title 25 of the Code of Federal Regulations (1940) pp. 1–3. The major subjects covered by these regulations are discussed in other chapters of this book.

[317] 4 Stat. 564, 25 U. S. C. 1, R. S. § 462, 25 U. S. C. 2, R. S. § 463.

[318] 4 Stat. 677.

[319] This is the budget for the Office of the Commissioner only, and does not include the field. There were separate appropriations for the "Indian Department."

[320] By the Act of June 15, 1880, 21 Stat. 210, the Commissioner's salary was raised to $3,500 and the budget for the office raised to $77,080. By the Act of August 5, 1882, 22 Stat. 219, the Commissioner's salary was raised to $4,000. By the Act of July 31, 1886, 24 Stat. 172, the Office of Assistant Commissioner was created at a salary of $3,000. The Assistant Commissioner also performed the duties of chief clerk. The Commissioner's salary was raised to $5,000 by the Act of April 28, 1902, 32 Stat. 120, 158. Under the Appropriation Act of June 18, 1940, 76th Cong., 3d sess., Pub., No. 640, the Commissioner's salary is $9,000 annually and the Assistant Commissioner's $7,500. By the Act of February 26, 1907, 34 Stat. 935, 936, the Chief Clerk's Office was separated from that of Assistant Commissioner and by the Act of June 17, 1910, 36 Stat. 468, the Chief Clerk's title was changed to Second Assistant Commissioner. By the Act of May 10, 1916, 39 Stat. 66, 100, the Second Assistant Commissioner's Office was abolished and the title of Chief Clerk reinstated. This act also provided compensation for forester, financial clerk, chiefs of divisions, law clerk, examiner of irrigation accounts, draftsman, etc.

[321] Act of July 9, 1832, 4 Stat. 564, 25 U. S. C. 1, R. S. § 462.

[322] Act of July 31, 1886, 24 Stat. 172.

[323] On June 30, 1926, Schmeckebier reported 5,002 employees in the entire service, 190 in Washington office, with a total salary of $6,198,313. (Schmeckebier, *op. cit.*, p. 293.) There were, according to the 1940 budget, 9,173 employees in the Bureau of Indian Affairs (including emergency and conservation employees), of which 388 were in Washington, with a total salary of $14,781,927. (Figures from Office of Indian Affairs, May, 1940.)

[324] The Civil Service Commission has to some extent recognized the specialized problems that exist in the Indian Service, and has held examinations for the purpose of filling specific positions in the Indian Service, such as those for teachers and nurses. (Annual Report of the Secretary of the Interior (1937), p. 241; *ibid.* (1936), p. 203.) Annual reports of the Secretary of the Interior comment on the extreme diversity in the types of personnel needed, and on the need for persons with ability to handle human relation problems, in addition to their particular training. (Annual Report of the Secretary of the Interior (1937), pp. 240–242; Annual Report of the Secretary of the Interior (1938), p. 256.) The need for such peculiarly equipped employees was voiced by Commissioners for more than 100 years. See sec. 2, *supra*. Also Schmeckebier, *op. cit.*, pp. 296–299.

[325] See Schmeckebier, *op. cit.*, pp. 293, 294, for a list of such exceptions.

[326] 42 Stat. 1488. Amended by the Act of May 28, 1928, 45 Stat. 776 (Welsh Act); Act of July 3, 1930, 46 Stat. 1003 (Brookhart Act); and by Executive Order No. 6746, June 21, 1934.

[327] See Chapter 8, sec. 4B.

[328] Schmeckebier, *op. cit.*, p. 282.

[329] 27 Stat. 612, 614, 25 U. S. C. 66. This provision was carried in later Indian appropriation acts up to March 1, 1907, 34 Stat. 1015, 1020.

[330] Schmeckebier, *op. cit.*, pp. 282–284.

[331] Department of the Interior, U. S. Indian Field Service Regulations (1939), Section A—Administration, p. A–8. The superintendent is bonded in such amount as the President or Secretary of the Interior may require.

[332] *Ibid.*, pp. A–11, A–12.

[333] *Ibid.*, p. A–9.

[334] *Ibid.*, p. A–9. See Chapter 12, sec. 2.

[335] *Ibid.*, p. A–52. Based on R. S. § 2078 (derived from Act of June 30, 1834, 4 Stat. 735, 738), 25 U. S. C. 68; Act of June 22, 1874, 18 Stat. 146, 177, 25 U. S. C. 87. See letter of Attorney General dated February 15, 1940, holding that an employee of the Indian Service may not accept employment after hours as salaried manager of an Indian community store. And see Memo. Sol. I. D., November 7, 1939, holding Indian Service employee may not lease land from Indian for home site.

[336] *Ibid.*, p. A–52. (Order of Secretary of the Interior, September 30, 1912.) See also Act of June 19, 1939, 53 Stat. 840, 25 U. S. C. (Supp.) 87a.

[337] Office of Indian Affairs, Order No. 481, Field District Plan, June 21, 1937, p. 2.

relating to Indians within their jurisdiction, from "saving the babies" to taking care of old Indians. (Department of Interior, Office of Indian Affairs, "Methods and Suggestions for Inspecting Officers of the United States Indian Service," February 23, 1916, p. 7.)

C. COOPERATION WITH OTHER AGENCIES

Some decentralization of administrative control over Indian life[338] has been effected in recent years by the distribution of governmental powers among the federal, state, and tribal governments. In earlier decades, cooperation, where it has existed, has been primarily between the Indian Bureau and other federal agencies,[339] not between the Indians and the agencies. In recent years various federal agencies have been in direct contact with the Indians. They include the Soil Conservation Service, the Farm Security Administration, the Social Security Board, the Civilian Conservation Corps,[340] the National Youth Administration, the Public Works Administration, and the Works Progress Administration.

The General Land Office assists the Indian Office in the sale of land which the Indian tribes cede to the United States.[341] It also adjudicates or administers Indian allotments and Indian homesteads,[342] and issues allotments on certification by the Commissioner of Indian Affairs,[343] who must also consent to the granting of various licenses by the Federal Power Commission[344] and other agencies for irrigation, right-of-way, power development, and other land use.

In the field of conservation the Indian Service often unites for common action with one or more state or federal bureaus. The Interdepartmental Rio Grande Board, composed of representatives of the Indian Service, Grazing Service, and the Bureau of Reclamation of the Department of the Interior, and the Soil Conservation Service, the Forest Service, the Farm Security Administration and the Bureau of Agricultural Economics of the Department of Agriculture,[345] seeks to determine how a native rural population of Indians and Spanish Americans can subsist permanently through the utilization of the Rio Grande watershed in central and northern New Mexico.[346]

A survey and planning unit was created by the Soil Conservation Service to study Indian reservations and prepare plans for proper land use and conservation for the Indian Service.[347] This unit (TC–BIA) has supplied a new type of integrated administrative procedure in which two services are functionally integrated, though preserving technical and organizational distinctions.[348] The TC–BIA works with and through the Indian superintendents, their local staffs, and Indian governing bodies. They are consulted in its surveys, they comment on its findings, and they are expected to carry out its program.[349]

Section 4 of the Act of March 10, 1934,[350] provides:

> The Office of Indian Affairs, the Bureau of Fisheries, and the Bureau of Biological Survey are authorized, jointly, to prepare plans for the better protection of the wild-life resources, including fish, migratory waterfowl and upland game birds, game animals and fur-bearing animals, upon all the Indian reservations and unallotted Indian lands coming under the supervision of the Federal Government.

It also empowers the Secretary of the Interior to promulgate such plans and to make rules for their enforcement.

Because there is danger of depletion of fish and animals, particularly in the case of spawning salmon, where fox or mink farmers may exploit small local runs, the Office cooperates with the Alaska Game Commission and the Division of Alaskan Fisheries, Bureau of Fisheries, in settling problems affecting the rights of Indians.

An interesting cooperative enterprise is the joint operation by the Indian Service and the Bureau of Animal Industry of a sheep genetics laboratory at Fort Wingate, New Mexico.[351]

The Indian Service has always cooperated with the Department of Justice in enforcing prohibition laws and suppressing liquor traffic with the Indians, and generally in litigation affecting Indians.

Other cooperating agencies[352] include the Extension Service of the Department of Agriculture, the Bureaus of Mines, Standards, Animal Industry, and Plant Industry, the Public Health Service,[353] the Children's Bureau of the Department of Labor, state agricultural colleges, and education and welfare bureaus of various states.[354]

Mr. Joseph C. McCaskill, one of Commissioner Collier's four assistants, has summed up the recent trend in Indian administration:

> Thus we see the Indian Office divesting its authority into three directions; first among other agencies of the Federal Government which have specialized services to render; second among the local state and county governments, which are much more closely associated with the problems in some areas than Washington can be; and finally among the tribal governments which have organized governing bodies, and which expect eventually to take over and manage all of the affairs of Indians. Perhaps thus, but not at once, it may be found possible to cease special treatment, special protective and beneficial legislation for the Indians, and they shall become self-supporting, self-managing, and self-directing communities within our national citizenry. (P. 76.)[355]

[338] See Chapter 5. See also sec. 2F, *supra*, for a statement of policy regarding decentralization by Commissioner Collier in 1933.

[339] *E. g.*, the Bureaus of Plant and Animal Industry of Agriculture and the Reclamation Service, Geological Survey and Forest Service of Interior had cooperated with the Indian Bureau under Commissioner Leupp in 1908. (See sec. 2 *supra*. Also see Rep. Comm. Ind. Aff. 1908, pp. 2–9.)

[340] The Indian Office has a special division devoted to the C. C. C. See sec. 3A *supra*.

[341] Conover, The General Land Office (1923), p. 76.

[342] *Ibid.*, p. 88.

[343] *Ibid.*, pp. 61–62.

[344] Since the primary responsibility for administering an Indian reservation is in the Commissioner of Indian Affairs and the Secretary of the Interior, it has been urged that the Federal Power Commission must decline to issue a permit if the Secretary believes that a proposed power development would be inconsistent with the purposes of the reservation. (Letter of Assistant Commissioner of Indian Affairs to Chairman, Federal Power Commission, February 19, 1935.)

[345] National Resources Planning Board, General Land Office, and Reconstruction Finance Corporation are consulting members. (Annual Report of the Secretary of the Interior (1939) p. 64.)

[346] Annual Report of the Secretary of the Interior (1938), p. 253.

[347] Annual Report of the Secretary of the Interior (1936), p. 188. The unit is commonly designated as TC–BIA, Technical Cooperation, Bureau of Indian Affairs.

[348] Annual Report of the Secretary of the Interior (1936), p. 188.

[349] Indian Office Order 483, United States Indian Field Service, Rules and Regulations (1939), section A—Administration, pp. A–5, A–6.

[350] 48 Stat. 401, 402.

[351] See Annual Report of the Secretary of the Interior (1938), p. 253.

[352] Annual Report of the Secretary of the Interior (1936), pp. 169–172, 180–183.

[353] The United States Public Health Service, since 1926, has detailed personnel to the Indian Service, for health and medical work on reservations. *Ibid.*, p. 179.

[354] Under the Johnson-O'Malley Act of April 16, 1934, 48 Stat. 596, amended by Act of June 4, 1936, 49 Stat. 1458, state educational and health services were made available to certain Indian tribes by contract between the State and the Federal Government. As of 1939, California, Washington, and Minnesota have contracted for the education of Indian children, Wisconsin for child-welfare services, and Arizona for limited educational services. (Annual Report of the Secretary of Interior (1939), p. 64.) See Chapter 12, sec. 1.

[355] Joseph C. McCaskill, The Cessation of Monopolistic Control of Indians by the Indian Office, in Indians of the United States, April 1940, pp. 69–76. This paper was prepared for the First Inter-American Conference on Indian Life, held at Patzcuaro, Mexico, in April 1940.

CHAPTER 3

INDIAN TREATIES

TABLE OF CONTENTS

SECTION 1. THE LEGAL FORCE OF INDIAN TREATIES

One who attempts to survey the legal problems raised by Indian treaties must at the outset dispose of the objection that such treaties are somehow of inferior validity or are of purely antiquarian interest. These objections apparently spring from the belief that when the treaty method of dealing with the natives was abandoned in the Indian Appropriation Act of 1871[1] the force of treaties in existence at that time also disappeared.

Such an assumption is unfounded. Although treaty making itself is a thing of the past, treaty enforcement continues.[2] As a matter of fact, the act in question expressly provides that there shall be no lessening of obligations already incurred.

The reciprocal obligations assumed by the Federal Government and by the Indian tribes during a period of almost a hundred years constitute a chief source of present-day Indian law. As one legal commentator has pointed out:

> * * * The chief foundation [of federal power over Indian affairs] appears to have been the treaty-making power of the President and Senate with its corollary of Congressional power to implement by legislation the treaties made.
>
> * * * * *
>
> And by a broad reading of these treaties the national government obtained from the Indians themselves authority to legislate for them to carry out the purpose of the treaties.[3]

That treaties with Indian tribes are of the same dignity as treaties with foreign nations is a view which has been repeat-

[1] Act of March 3, 1871, 16 Stat. 544, 566, R. S. § 2079, 25 U. S. C. 71.

[2] See, for example, Act of June 15, 1935, sec. 4, 49 Stat. 378.

[3] See Rice, The Position of the American Indian in the Law of the United States (1934), 16 J. Comp. Leg. 78, 80–81. See also Chapter 5, sec. 1.

Justice Baldwin, in the case of *Cherokee Nation* v. *Georgia*, 5 Pet. 1 (1831), gives an interesting account of the negotiation of treaties by the Continental Congress with the Indians:

> The proceedings of the old congress will be found in 1 Laws U. S. 597, commencing 1st June 1775, and ending 1st September 1788, of which some extracts will be given. 30th June 1775: "Resolved, that the committee for Indian affairs do prepare proper talks to the several tribes of Indians; as the Indians depend on the colonists for arms, ammunition and clothing which are become necessary for their subsistence." "That the commissioners have power to treat with the Indians;" "to take to their assistance gentlemen of influence among the Indians." "To preserve the confidence and friendship of the Indians, and prevent their suffering for want of the necessaries of life, 40,000*l.* sterling of Indian goods be imported." "No person shall be permitted to trade with the Indians, without a license;" "traders shall sell their goods at reasonable prices; allow them to the Indians for their skins, and take no advantage of their distress and intemperance;" "the trade to be only at posts designated by the commissioners." Specimens of the kind of intercourse between the congress and deputations of Indians may be seen in pages 602 and 603. They need no incorporation into a judicial opinion. (P. 34.)

edly confirmed by the federal courts and never successfully challenged.[4]

As late as 1828 Attorney General William Wirt, in an opinion to the President on Georgia and the Treaty of Indian Spring,[5] found it necessary to answer the contention that treaties with Indians were not effective because they were not treaties with an independent nation, and because, even if independent, the Indians were uncivilized. In discussing the first objection the Attorney General said, in part:

> If it be meant to say that, although capable of treating, their treaties are not to be construed like the treaties of nations absolutely independent, no reason is discerned for this distinction in the circumstance that their independence is of a limited character. If they are independent to the purpose of treating, they have all the independence that is necessary to the argument. * * * The point, then, once conceded, that the Indians are independent to the purpose of treating, their independence is, *to that purpose*, as *absolute* as that of any other nation.
>
> * * * Nor can it be conceded that their independence as a nation is a limited independence. Like all other independent nations, they are governed solely by their own laws. Like all other independent nations, they have the absolute power of war and peace. Like all other independent nations, their territory is inviolable by any other sovereignty. Questions have arisen as to the character of their title to that territory; but these discussions have resulted in this conclusion: that, whether their title be that of sovereignty in the jurisdiction or the soil, or a title by occupancy only, it is such a title as no other nation has a right to interfere with, or to take from them; and which no other nation can rightfully acquire, but by the same means by which the territory of all other nations, however absolute their independence, may be acquired—that is, by cession or conquest. * * * As a nation they are still free and independent. They are entirely self-governed—self-directed. They treat, or refuse to treat, at their pleasure; and there is no human power which can rightfully control them in the exercise of their discretion in this respect. In their treaties, in all their contracts with regard to their property, they are as free, sovereign, and independent as any other nation. And being bound, on their own part, to the full extent of their contracts, they are surely entitled, on every principle of reason, justice, and equity to hold those with whom they thus treat and contract equally bound to them. Nor can I discover the slightest foundation for applying different rules to the construction of their contracts from those which are applied to all other contracts, *because they reside within the local limits of the sovereignty of Georgia.* (Pp. 132–135.)

The Circuit Court for the Michigan District said:[6]

> * * * It is contended that a treaty with Indian tribes, has not the same dignity or effect, as a treaty with a foreign and independent nation. This distinction is not authorized by the constitution. Since the commencement of the government, treaties have been made with the Indians, and the treaty-making power has been exercised in making them. They are treaties, within the meaning of the constitution, and, as such, are the supreme laws of the land. (P. 346.)

It is clear that the Constitution recognized as part of the supreme law of the land treaties made with Indian tribes prior to its ratification.[7] The Supreme Court said with reference to the provisions of an Indian treaty:[8]

> * * * the Constitution declares a treaty to be the supreme law of the land; and Chief Justice Marshall, in *Foster and Elam* v. *Neilson*, 2 Pet. 314, has said, "That a treaty is to be regarded, in courts of justice, as equivalent to an act of the legislature, whenever it operates of itself, without the aid of any legislative provision." No legislation is required to put the seventh article in force; and it must become a rule of action, if the contracting parties had power to incorporate it in the treaty of 1863. About this there would seem to be no doubt. * * * (P. 196.)

Generally speaking, the incidents attaching to a treaty with a foreign power have been held applicable to Indian treaties. Thus, in accordance with the general rule applicable to foreign treaties, the courts will not go behind a treaty which has been ratified to inquire whether or not an Indian tribe was properly represented by its head men, nor determine whether a treaty has been procured by duress or fraud, and declare it inoperative for that reason.[9]

> * * * the treaty, after executed and ratified by the proper authorities of the Government, becomes the supreme law of the land, and the courts can no more go behind it for the purpose of annulling its effect and operation, than they can behind an act of Congress.[10]

An Indian treaty, like a foreign treaty, may be modified by mutual consent.[11]

The fact that Congress has, by legislation, repealed, modified, or disregarded various Indian treaties has been thought by some to show that Indian treaties are of inferior legal validity. The fact is, however, that the power of Congress to enact legislation in conflict with treaties is well established in the field of foreign affairs, as well as in the field of Indian affairs.[12]

In upholding legislation contravening a treaty, the Supreme Court in *Lone Wolf* v. *Hitchcock*[13] said:

> * * * Until the year 1871 the policy was pursued of dealing with the Indian tribes by means of treaties, and, of

[4] *Holden* v. *Joy*, 17 Wall. 211, 242–243 (1872); *Worcester* v. *Georgia*, 6 Pet. 515, 559 (1832); *Turner* v. *American Baptist Missionary Union*, 24 Fed. Cas. No. 14251 (C. C. Mich. 1852).

[5] 2 Op. A. G. 110 (1828).

[6] *Turner* v. *American Baptist Missionary Union*, 24 Fed. Cas. No. 14251 (C. C. Mich. 1852).

[7] *Worcester* v. *Georgia*, 6 Pet. 515, 559 (1832). Examples of such treaties are found in the opinion of the Supreme Court in *Cherokee Nation* v. *Georgia*, 5 Pet. 1, 32–38 (1831).

[8] *United States* v. *Forty-three Gallons of Whiskey*, 93 U. S. 188 (1876).

[9] *United States* v. *New York Indians*, 173 U. S. 464 (1899); *United States* v. *Old Settlers*, 148 U. S. 427, 466 (1893). See fn. 8, *supra*, and on the form of tribal government, see Chapter 7, sec. 3.

[10] *Fellows* v. *Blacksmith*, 60 U. S. 366, 372 (1856).

[11] 14 Pet. 4 (1840). Justice McLean said in the case of *Latimer* v. *Poteet:*

> It is argued that it was not in the power of the United States and the Cherokee nation, by the treaty of Tellico, in 1798, to vary in any degree the treaty line of Holston; so as to affect private rights, or the rights of North Carolina. The answer to this is, that the Tellico treaty does not purport to alter the boundary of the Holston treaty, but by the acts of the parties, this boundary is recognised. Not that a new boundary was substituted, but that the old one was substantially designated. Will any one deny that the parties to the treaty are competent to determine any dispute respecting its limits. In what mode can a controversy of this nature be so satisfactorily determined as by the contracting parties. If their language in the treaty be wholly indefinite, or the natural objects called for are uncertain or contradictory, there is no power but that which formed the treaty which can remedy such defects. And it is a sound principle of national law, and applies to the treaty-making power of this government, whether exercised with a foreign nation or an Indian tribe, that all questions of disputed boundaries may be settled by the parties to the treaty. And to the exercise of these high functions by the government, within its constitutional powers, neither the rights of a state, nor those of an individual, can be interposed. We think it was in the due exercise of the powers of the executive and the Cherokee nation, in concluding the treaty of Tellico, to recognize in terms, or by acts, the boundary of the Holston treaty. (P. 13.)

[12] The Supreme Court in *Ex parte Webb*, 225 U. S. 663 (1912), said:

> Of course, an act of Congress may repeal a prior treaty as well as it may repeal a prior act. *The Cherokee Tobacco*, 11 Wall. 616; *Fong Yue Ting* v. *United States*, 149 U. S. 698, 720; *Ward* v. *Race Horse*, 163 U. S. 504, 511; *Draper* v. *United States*, 164 U. S. 240, 248. (P. 683.)

[13] 187 U. S. 553, 565–566 (1903). Also see *Cherokee Tobacco*, 11 Wall. 616 (1870); *Ward* v. *Race Horse*, 163 U. S. 504 (1896); *Thomas* v. *Gay*, 169 U. S. 264 (1898); 16 Op. A. G. 300 (1879). Accord: 26 Op. A. G. 340, 347 (1907); 54 I. D. 401 (1934).

At one time this principle was not well established. This is shown by the following excerpt from H. Rept. No. 474, Comm. on Indian Affairs, 23d Cong., 1st sess., May 20, 1834:

> It was not competent for an act of Congress to alter the stipulations of the treaty or to change the character of the agents appointed under it. (P. 5.)

course, a moral obligation rested upon Congress to act in good faith in performing the stipulations entered into on its behalf. But, as with treaties made with foreign nations, *Chinese Exclusion Case*, 130 U. S. 581, 600, the legislative power might pass laws in conflict with treaties made with the Indians. *Thomas* v. *Gay*, 169 U. S. 264, 270; *Ward* v. *Race Horse*, 163 U. S. 504, 511; *Spalding* v. *Chandler*, 160 U. S. 394, 405; *Missouri, Kansas & Texas Ry. Co.* v. *Roberts*, 152 U. S. 114, 117; *The Cherokee Tobacco*, 11 Wall. 616.

The power exists to abrogate the provisions of an Indian treaty, though presumably such power will be exercised only when circumstances arise which will not only justify the government in disregarding the stipulations of the treaty, but may demand, in the interest of the country and the Indians themselves, that it should do so. When, therefore, treaties were entered into between the United States and a tribe of Indians it was never doubted that the *power* to abrogate existed in Congress, and that in a contingency such power might be availed of from considerations of governmental policy, particularly if consistent with perfect good faith towards the Indians. * * *

The Attorney General has ruled:[14]

> By the 6th article of the Constitution, treaties as well as statutes are the laws of the land. There is nothing in the Constitution which assigns different ranks to treaties and to statutes. The Constitution itself is of higher rank than either by the very structure of the Government. A statute not inconsistent with it, and a treaty not inconsistent with it, relating to subjects within the scope of the treaty-making power, seem to stand upon the same level, and to be of equal validity; and as in the case of all laws emanating from an equal authority, the earlier in date yields to the later. (P. 357.)

This doctrine has been qualified by some cases. In the case of *Jones* v. *Meehan*[15] it was held that title to land granted to an Indian by treaty cannot be divested by any subsequent action of the lessor, Congress or the Executive department.

> The construction of treaties is the peculiar province of the judiciary; and, except in cases purely political, Congress has no constitutional power to settle the rights under a treaty, or to affect titles already granted by the treaty itself. *Wilson* v. *Wall*, 6 Wall. 83, 89; *Reichart* v. *Felps*, 6 Wall. 160; *Smith* v. *Stevens*, 10 Wall. 321, 327; *Holden* v. *Joy*, 17 Wall. 211, 247 (P. 32).

Thus the issuance of a patent by the General Land Office upon lands reserved by a treaty with Indian tribes is void.[16]

The Supreme Court has often coupled a statement about the absolute power of Congress to supersede a treaty obligation with a discussion of the moral obligation of the Government to redress such a violation. In holding that an act of Congress extended revenue laws over the Indian Territory, despite a prior treaty exempting tobacco raised on Indian reservations, the Court wrote:[17]

> A treaty may supersede a prior act of Congress,* and an act of Congress may supersede a prior treaty.# In the cases referred to these principles were applied to treaties with foreign nations. Treaties with Indian nations within the jurisdiction of the United States, whatever considerations of humanity and good faith may be involved and require their faithful observance, cannot be more obligatory. They have no higher sanctity; and no greater inviolability or immunity from legislative invasion can be claimed for them. The consequences in all such cases give rise to questions which must be met by the political department of the government. They are beyond the sphere of judicial cognizance. In the case under consideration the act of Congress must prevail as if the treaty were not an element to be considered. If a wrong has been done, the power of redress is with Congress, not with the judiciary, and that body, upon being applied to, it is to be presumed, will promptly give the proper relief. (P. 621.)
>
> * *Foster & Elam* v. *Neilson*, 2 Peters, 314.
>
> \# *Taylor* v. *Morton*, 2 Curtis, 454; *The Clinton Bridge*, 1 Walworth, 155.

By many statutes and occasionally by treaties, the Court of Claims has been authorized to determine many claims for treaty violations.[18]

In construing a jurisdictional act,[19] the Supreme Court discussed the liability of the United States for a violation of a treaty with the Creek tribe:

> * * * But we think it plain that that act only gave authority to the Court of Claims to hear and determine claims "for the amount due or claimed to be due said bands from the United States under any treaties or laws of Congress." It does not purport to alter or enlarge any rights conferred on petitioners by the treaties or laws of the United States or authorize any recovery except in accordance with the legal principles applicable in determining those rights under laws and treaties of the United States. See *United States* v. *Old Settlers*, 148 U. S. 427, 468, 469; *United States* v. *Mille Lac Chippewas*, 290 U. S. 498, 500. (P. 436.)

---

[14] 13 Op. A. G. 354 (1870).

> * * * congress has never abrogated treaties promiscuously by legislation, those with Indians, Chinese, and the French treaty of 1778, being the chief ones in point.

Boyd, The Expanding Treaty Power, in Selected Essays on Constitutional Law, vol. 3, The Nation and The States (1938), pp. 410, 414.

The Solicitor of the Department of the Interior has said:

> Congress has paramount authority over such reservations and the Indians occupying them (*Lone Wolf* v. *Hitchcock*, 187 U. S. 553, 565), and may, if it sees fit so to do, provide game laws to restrict the Indians in their natural and immemorial rights of fishing and hunting. *In re Blackbird*, *supra* [100 Fed. 139 (D. C. W. D. Wis. 1901]. And even though such laws should conflict with the provisions of prior treaties with the Indians, there is respectable authority for upholding their validity. Thus in *The Cherokee Tobacco Case* (11 Wall. 616), it was held that a law of Congress imposing a tax on tobacco, if in conflict with a prior treaty with the Cherokees, was paramount to the treaty. And in *Ward* v. *Race Horse* (163 U. S. 504), the court ruled that the provision in treaty of February 24, 1869, with the Bannock Indians, whose reservation was within the limits of what is now the State of Wyoming, that "they shall have the right to hunt upon the unoccupied lands of the United States so long as game may be found thereon", was superseded by the provisions of the Enabling Act admitting Wyoming into the Union, and that the treaty provision did not give the Indians the right to exercise the hunting privilege within the limits of the State in violation of its laws. (54 I. D. 517, 520 (1934).)

[15] 175 U. S. 1 (1899), holding unconstitutional Joint Resolution of August 4, 1894, 28 Stat. 1018, authorizing departmental approval of a lease after the execution of a different lease by the Indian landowner.

[16] *United States* v. *Carpenter*, 111 U. S. 347 (1884). Also see *Spalding* v. *Chandler*, 160 U. S. 394 (1896). It has been held that an Executive order which purports to restore to the public domain land granted by treaty to Indians is inoperative. 18 Op. A. G. 141 (1885).

[17] *Cherokee Tobacco*, 11 Wall. 616 (1870). For an example of the superseding of a treaty by the General Allotment Act see Op. Sol. I. D., M. 25930, June 30, 1930, 53 I. D. 183.

The moral obligation to perform treaties faithfully was recognized in the preamble to the Treaty of August 9, 1814, with the Creek Nation, 7 Stat. 120, which referred to the fulfillment "with punctuality and good faith" by the United States of former treaties with the Creeks up to the time of their waging war against the United States. Also see Chapter 14, sec. 2, fn. 41.

An example of a treaty superseding a statute is noted in Choctaw Indians, 13 Op. A. G. 354 (1870).

[18] See Chapter 14, sec. 6, and Chapter 19, sec. 3; Ray A. Brown, The Indian Problem and the Law (1930), 39 Yale L. J. 307, 323–324, and Meriam, Problem of Indian Administration (1928), pp. 805–811. Treaties are often the foundation for claims. *United States* v. *Old Settlers*, 148 U. S. 427, 467–468 (1893). Congress may waive the benefit of the rule of *res adjudicata* by allowing another trial of a claim against the United States, *Cherokee Nation* v. *United States*, 270 U. S. 476 (1926), or disregarding laches, *United States* v. *Old Settlers*, 148 U. S. 427, 473 (1893).

[19] *Sioux Indians* v. *United States*, 277 U. S. 424 (1928). The Act of April 11, 1916, 39 Stat. 47 (Sisseton and Wahpeton bands of Sioux), authorizes the Court of Claims to hear and determine claims "for the amount due or claimed to be due said bands from the United States under any treaties or laws of Congress."

The Supreme Court in *United States* v. *Blackfeather*, 155 U. S. 180 (1894), held that when the United States undertook by treaty to "expose to sale to the highest bidder" the land ceded to the United States by the Indians, and disposed of a large part of such land at private sale, the Federal Government was guilty of a violation of trust.

In a subsequent case the Court held that provisions granting claims against the United States are strictly construed. *Blackfeather* v. *United States*, 190 U. S. 368, 376 (1903). The Court said:

> * * * The moral obligations of the Government toward the Indians, whatever they may be, are for Congress alone to recognize,

Certain treaties with the Indians were invalidated by hostilities.[20] During the Civil War Congress expressly authorized the President to declare all treaties with a tribe engaged in hostility toward the United States abrogated by such tribe, "if in his opinion the same can be done consistently with good faith and legal and national obligations."[21]

While the United States often abrogated treaty provisions,[22] some treaties contained drastic penalties for Indians who might commit violations. Article 4 of the Treaty of June 19, 1818,[23] required the chiefs and warriors of the tribe to deliver "to the authority of the United States, (to be punished according to law,) each and every individual of the said tribe, who shall, at any time hereafter, violate the stipulations of the treaty * * *." The Treaty of August 9, 1814,[24] after denouncing them as violators or instigators of violation, required the "caption and surrender of all the prophets and instigators of the war, whether foreigners or natives, who have not submitted to the arms of the United States * * *." The Treaty of March 2, 1868,[25] provided that a chief violating an essential part of the treaty shall forfeit his position.

Some treaties provided for the modification[26] or abrogation of previous provisions[27] or declared previous treaties null and void and canceled claims under them,[28] or nullified preemption rights and reservations created under them,[29] or expressly recognized former treaties.[30]

Treaties sometimes provided saving clauses in the event of rejection of some of the articles. For example, article 7 of the Treaty of August 5, 1826, with the Chippewas,[31] provides among other things:

> * * * But it is expressly understood and agreed, that the fourth, fifth, and sixth articles, or either of them, may be rejected by the President and Senate, without affecting the validity of the other articles of the treaty.

Future contingencies sometimes provided for included violation by a chief of an essential part of the treaty[32] or relinquishment by chiefs of land reserved by treaty,[33] nonratification,[34] nonremoval of the Indians,[35] abandonment of land[36] and insufficiency of "good tillable land" ceded to the tribe.[37]

The legal force of Indian treaties did not insure their actual enforcement. Some important treaties were negotiated but never ratified by the Senate,[38] or ratified only after a long delay.[39] Treaties were sometimes consummated by methods amounting to bribery,[40] or signed by representatives of only a small part of the signatory tribes.[41] The Federal Government failed to fulfill the terms of many treaties,[42] and was sometimes unable or unwilling to prevent states,[43] or white people,[44] from violating treaty rights of the Indians.

> and the courts can exercise only such jurisdiction over the subject as Congress may confer upon them. (P. 373.)

[20] See Preamble to Treaty of August 9, 1814 with the Creeks, 7 Stat. 120. Also see *Leighton* v. *United States*, 161 U. S. 291, 296 (1895). On what constitutes war between the United States and a tribe see *Marks* v. *United States*, 161 U. S. 297 (1896); *McCandless* v. *United States* ex rel. *Diabo*, 25 F. 2d 71 (C. C. A. 3, 1928).

[21] Act of July 5, 1862, 12 Stat. 512, 528, R. S. § 2080, 25 U. S. C. 72, discussed in *Holden* v. *Joy*, 17 Wall. 211, 215 (1872).

[22] See fn. 14, *supra*.

[23] With the Pitavirate Noisy Pawnees, 7 Stat. 173, 174. The same provision was contained in other treaties, such as the Treaty of June 18, 1818, with the Grand Pawnee Tribe, Art. 4, 7 Stat. 172; Treaty of June 22, 1818, with the Pawnee Marhar Tribe, Art. 4, 7 Stat. 175.

[24] With the Creeks, Art. 6, 7 Stat. 120.

[25] With the Utes, Art. 17, 15 Stat. 619.

[26] For example, see Treaty of January 20, 1825, with the Choctaws, 7 Stat. 234. Sometimes permanent additions to treaties in force were made (Treaty of September 25, 1818, with the Osages, Art. 3, 7 Stat. 183) and rights under previous treaties were preserved (Treaty of July 15, 1830, with the Sacs and others, Art. 12, 7 Stat. 328).

[27] The Treaty of August 31, 1822, with the Osages, 7 Stat. 222, abrogates the Treaty of November 10, 1808, Art. 2, 7 Stat. 107: the Treaty of September 3, 1822, with the Sac and Fox Tribes, 7 Stat. 223, abrogates the Treaty of November 3, 1804, 7 Stat. 84; the Treaty of February 27, 1867, with the Pottawatomies, Art. 13, 15 Stat. 531, 534, voids all provisions of former treaties inconsistent with the provisions of this treaty

The Treaty of April 1, 1850, with the Wyandots, Art. 11, 9 Stat. 987, abrogated and declared null and void all former treaties between the United States and the Wyandots, except provisions previously made for the benefit of individuals "by grants of reservations of lands, or otherwise, which are considered as *vested* rights, and not to be affected by any thing contained in this treaty."

Article 21 of the Treaty of June 22, 1855, with the Choctaws and Chickasaws, 11 Stat. 611, provided:

> This convention shall supersede and take the place of all former treaties between the United States and the Choctaws, and also of all treaty stipulations between the United States and the Chickasaws, and between the Choctaws and Chickasaws, inconsistent with this agreement, and shall take effect and be obligatory upon the contracting parties, from the date hereof, whenever the same shall be ratified by the respective councils of the Choctaw and Chickasaw tribes, and by the President and Senate of the United States.

Also see Treaty of August 7, 1856, with the Creeks, Art. 26, 11 Stat. 699

[28] Treaty of January 24, 1826, with the Creeks, Art. 1, 7 Stat. 286.

[29] Supplementary articles to the Treaty of December 29, 1835, with the Cherokees, 7 Stat. 488; Treaty of May 18, 1854, with the Sacs and Foxes Art. 1, 10 Stat. 1074; Treaty of May 18, 1854, with the Kickapoos, Art. 8, 10 Stat. 1078; Treaty of July 31, 1855, with the Ottawas and Chippewas, Art. 3, 11 Stat. 621.

[30] Treaty of October 25, 1805, with the Cherokees, Art. 1, 7 Stat. 93; Treaty of July 18, 1815, with the Potawatamies, Art. 4, 7 Stat. 123; Treaty of July 18, 1815, with the Piankishaws, Art. 3, 7 Stat. 124; Treaty of September 25, 1818, with the Illinois Nation, Art. 2, 7 Stat. 181.

[31] 7 Stat. 290.

[32] Treaty of March 2, 1868, with the Utes, Art. 13, 15 Stat. 619.

[33] Treaty of September 18, 1823, with the Florida Indians, Additional Art., 7 Stat. 224, 226.

[34] By Art. 16, the rejection of any article would not affect the other provisions in the Treaty of June 28, 1862, with the Kickapoos, 13 Stat. 623; Art. 6 of the Treaty of November 23, 1838, with the Creeks, 7 Stat. 574, provided that the rejection of a certain article would not affect the other provisions.

[35] For example, see Treaty of November 15, 1854, with the Rogue River Tribe, Art. 4, 10 Stat. 1119.

[36] Treaty of September 21, 1833, with the Otoes and Missourias, Art. 8, 7 Stat. 429.

[37] Treaty of September 18, 1823, with the Florida Tribes, Art. 9, 7 Stat. 224.

[38] Hoopes, Indian Affairs and their Administration, with Special Reference to the Far West (1932), p. 86.

[39] *Ibid.*, p. 115.

[40] Kinney, A Continent Lost—A Civilization Won (1937), pp. 37, 38, 42, 56, 71, 94; Schmeckebier, The Office of Indian Affairs, Its History, Activities, and Organization (1927), p. 31.

[41] Kinney, *op. cit.* pp. 44, 45.

[42] Kinney, *op. cit.* p. 68; Hoopes, *op. cit.* pp. 180, 218, 219; Schmeckebier describes this condition:

> One of the defects of the treaty system was that agreements were continually being made which were not carried into effect. This was due in part to inefficient administration, in part to the failure of Congress to make the necessary appropriations, and in part to the inherent difficulties presented by the nature of the problem.
>
> * * * * *
>
> Some of the stipulations of almost all treaties which it was impossible to carry out were those guaranteeing the Indians against the intrusion of the white settlers and providing for the punishment of white persons committing offenses against the Indians. As the exterior boundaries reserved to the Indians were thousands of miles in extent, it was impossible to police this area in such a way as to prevent trespass or to secure evidence against offenders. (P. 62.)

[43] See Kinney, *op. cit.* p. 71.

[44] *Ibid.*, pp. 148, 149, 174, 184, 208; Hoopes, *op. cit.* pp. 84, 226, 228–32, 236; Schmeckebier, *op. cit.* p. 44.

> Treaty guarantees of land to the Indians were often violated. In 1789 Secretary of War McHenry, in his instructions to the Commissioners for negotiating a treaty with the Cherokees, made the following comment: "The arts and practices to obtain Indian land, in defiance of treaties and the laws, and at the risk of involving the whole country in war, have become so daring, and received such countenance, from persons of prominent influence, as to render it necessary that the means to countervail them shall be augmented." Am. St. Papers, Indian Affairs, vol. 1, p. 639, quoted by Schmeckebier, *ibid.*, pp. 24–25.

SECTION 2. INTERPRETATION OF TREATIES [45]

A cardinal rule in the interpretation of Indian treaties is that ambiguities are resolved in favor of the Indians.[46]

For example, a proviso in an Indian treaty which exempts lands from "levy, sale, and forfeiture" is not, in the absence of expressions so limiting it, confined to the levy and sale under ordinary judicial proceedings, but also includes the levy and sale by county officers for the nonpayment of taxes.[47]

An agreement embodied in an act of Congress which in terms "ceded, granted, and relinquished" to the United States all of their "right, title, and interest," did not make the lands public lands in the sense of being subject to sale or other disposition under the general land laws, but only in the manner provided for in the special agreement with the Indians.[48]

The best interests of the Indians,[49] however, do not necessarily coincide with a grant to them of the broadest power over lands. The Supreme Court has held that the best interests of the Indians do not require that they should be allotted lands in fee rather than lands held in trust by the government for them.[50]

While trying to serve the Indians' best interests, the courts have indicated that they will not dispense with any of the conditions or requirements of the treaties upon any notion of equity or general convenience or substantial justice. Justice Harlan, in the case of *United States* v. *Choctaw Nation*,[51] said:

> But in no case has it been adjudged that the courts could by mere interpretation or in deference to its view as to what was right under all the circumstances, incorporate into an Indian treaty something that was inconsistent with the clear import of its words. It has never been held that the obvious, palpable meaning of the words of an Indian treaty may be disregarded because, in the opinion of the court, that meaning may in a particular transaction work what it would regard as injustice to the Indians. That would be an intrusion upon the domain committed by the Constitution to the political departments of the Government. Congress did not intend, when passing the act under which this litigation was inaugurated, to invest the Court of Claims or this court with authority to determine whether the United States had, in its treaty with the Indians, violated the principles of fair dealing. What was said in *The Amiable Isabella*, 6 Wheat. 1, 71, 72, is evidently applicable to treaties with Indians. Mr. Justice Story, speaking for the court, said: "In the first place, this court does not possess any treaty-making power. That power belongs by the Constitution to another department of the Government, and to alter, amend, or add to any treaty by inserting any clause, whether small or great, important or trivial, would be on our part an usurpation of power and not an exercise of judicial functions. It would be to make, and not to construe a treaty. Neither can this court supply a *casus omissus* in a treaty, any more than in a law. We are to find out the intention of the parties by just rules of interpretation applied to the subject-matter; and, having found that, our duty is to follow it as far as it goes and to stop where that stops—whatever may be the imperfections or difficulties which it leaves behind. * * * In the next place, this court is bound to give effect to the stipulations of the treaty in the manner and to the extent which the parties have declared, and not otherwise. We are not at liberty to dispense with any of the conditions or requirements of the treaty, or to take away any qualification or integral part of any stipulation, upon any notion of equity or general convenience, or substantial justice. The terms which the parties have chosen to fix, the forms which they have prescribed, and the circumstances under which they are to have operation, rest in the exclusive discretion of the contracting parties, and whether they belong to the essence or the modal part of the treaty, equally give the rule to the judicial tribunals." (Pp. 532–533.)

So, too, it has been held that the reservation of a privilege to fish and hunt on lands transferred by a contract ratified by a treaty does not prevent the prosecution of tribal Indians violating a conservation law on such lands, since the transfer does not expressly or impliedly limit the right of the state to enact conservation measures.[52]

A somewhat different, although related, rule of treaty interpretation is to the effect that, since the wording in treaties was designed to be understood by the Indians, who often could not read and were not learned in the technical language, doubtful clauses are resolved in a nontechnical way as the Indians would have understood the language.[53]

---

[45] Also see Chapter 15, sec. 5C. Agreements with Indians are interpreted according to the same principles as treaties. (See sec. 6, *infra.*) *Marlin* v. *Lewallen*, 276 U. S. 58, 64 (1928). Mr. Justice Stone said in the case of *Carpenter* v. *Shaw*, 280 U. S. 363 (1930):

> While in general tax exemptions are not to be presumed and statutes conferring them are to be strictly construed, *Heiner* v. *Colonial Trust Co.*, 275 U. S. 232, the contrary is the rule to be applied to tax exemptions secured to the Indians by agreement between them and the national government. *Choate* v. *Trapp*, *supra*, 675. Such provisions are to be liberally construed. Doubtful expressions are to be resolved in favor of the weak and defenseless people who are the wards of the nation, dependent upon its protection and good faith. Hence, in the words of Chief Justice Marshall, "The language used in treaties with the Indians should never be construed to their prejudice. If words be made use of, which are susceptible of a more extended meaning than their plain import, as connected with the tenor of the treaty, they should be considered as used only in the latter sense." *Worcester* v. *The State of Georgia*, 6 Pet. 515, 582. See *The Kansas Indians*, 5 Wall. 737, 760. And they must be construed not according to their technical meaning but "in the sense in which they would naturally be understood by the Indians." *Jones* v. *Meehan*, 175 U. S. 1, 11. (Pp. 366–367.)

[46] *Winters* v. *United States*, 207 U. S. 564 (1908); 34 Op. A. G. 439 (1925); 6 Op. A. G. 658 (1854); *Worcester* v. *Georgia*, 6 Pet. 515, 582 (1832). And see Art. 11 of Treaty of September 9, 1849, with Navajo, 9 Stat. 974.

[47] *The Kansas Indians*, 5 Wall. 737 (1866).

[48] The Act of April 27, 1904, 33 Stat. 352 (Crow Reservation) interpreted in *Ash Sheep Co.* v. *United States*, 252 U. S. 159 (1920).

[49] See 32 Op. A. G. 586 (1921).

[50] *Starr* v. *Long Jim*, 227 U. S. 613, 623 (1913).

[51] 179 U. S. 494 (1900). Also see *United States* v. *Minnesota*, 270 U. S. 181 (1926).

[52] *Kennedy* v. *Becker*, 241 U. S. 556 (1916). The clause "Also, excepting and reserving to them * * * the privilege of fishing and hunting on the said tract of land hereby intended to be conveyed" (Treaty of September 15, 1797, with the Seneca Nation, 7 Stat. 601, 602) was interpreted as

> * * * reservation of a privilege of fishing and hunting upon the granted lands in common with the grantees, and others to whom the privilege might be extended, but subject nevertheless to that necessary power of appropriate regulation, as to all those privileged, which inhered in the sovereignty of the State over the lands where the privilege was exercised. (Pp. 563–564.)

Interpretations of other clauses are noted in sec. 4 of this Chapter and Chapter 6, sec. 3B, and Chapter 14, sec. 7.

[53] *Fleming* v. *McCurtain*, 214 U. S. 56, 60 (1909); Chapter 8, sec. 9I. See *Worcester* v. *Georgia*, 6 Pet. 515, 551–553 (1832). In commenting on frequent mistakes one writer said:

> * * * As the Indians had no written language and few of the chiefs even had a knowledge of English, the negotiations were carried on generally through interpreters, many of whom were inefficient. The description of the lands ceded was also a source of misunderstanding. In the region east of the Mississippi, the geography was fairly well known, and it was possible to describe areas with a fair degree of accuracy by reference to the streams and ridges; the area west of the Mississippi, however, was little known when many of the treaties were made, and the descriptions were of the most indefinite character.
>
> The method of making the treaties varied according to the character of the commissioners negotiating for them. Some were manifestly fraudulent; notably the treaty with the Creeks made in 1825. Others were signed by the Indians practically under duress. For instance, George C. Sibley, factor at Fort Osage, gives the following account of the negotiations with that tribe in 1808:
>
> "* * * On the 8th of November, 1808, Peter Chouteau, the United States' agent for the Osages, arrived at Fort Clark. On the 10th he assembled the Chiefs and warriors of the Great and Little Osages in council, and proceeded to state to them the substance of a treaty, which, he said, Governor Lewis had deputed him to offer the Osages, and to execute with them. Having briefly explained to them the purport of the treaty, he addressed them to this effect, in my hearing, and very nearly in the following words: 'You have heard this treaty explained to you. Those who now come forward and sign it, shall be considered friends of the United

The Supreme Court in the case of *Jones* v. *Meehan* [54] said:

> In construing any treaty between the United States and an Indian tribe, it must always (as was pointed out by the counsel for the appellees) be borne in mind that the negotiations for the treaty are conducted, on the part of the United States, an enlightened and powerful nation, by representatives skilled in diplomacy, masters of a written language, understanding the modes and forms of creating the various technical estates known to their law, and assisted by an interpreter employed by themselves; that the treaty is drawn up by them and in their own language; that the Indians, on the other hand, are a weak and dependent people, who have no written language and are wholly unfamiliar with all the forms of legal expression, and whose only knowledge of the terms in which the treaty is framed is that imparted to them by the interpreter employed by the United States; and that the treaty must therefore be construed, not according to the technical meaning of its words to learned lawyers, but in the sense in which they would naturally be understood by the Indians. (Pp. 10–11.)

These principles received many applications in decisions interpreting terms derived from private conveyances which were often used in treaties with the Indians.[55] For example, the word "grant" is not construed as an absolute fee simple, unless the treaty by some other words clearly indicates that the tribe so understood the nature of the conveyance.[56]

The United States Supreme Court,[57] interpreting the clause,

> The United States shall cause to be conveyed to the Choctaw Nation a tract of country west of the Mississippi River, in fee simple to them and their descendants, to inure to them while they shall exist as a nation and live on it; * * * (P. 58.)

held that this did not create a trust for the individuals then comprising the nation and their respective descendants.

Although an interpretation of a treaty should be made in the light of conditions existing when the treaty was executed, as often indicated by its history before and after its making,[58] the exact situation which caused the inclusion of a provision is often difficult to ascertain.[59] New conditions may arise which could not be anticipated by the signatories to a treaty. A practical administrative construction of a treaty which has long been acquiesced in by congressional inaction is usually followed by the courts.[60]

> States, and treated accordingly. Those who refuse to come forward and sign it shall be considered enemies of the United States, and treated accordingly.' The Osages replied in substance, 'that if their great American father wanted a part of their land he must have it, that he was strong and powerful, they were poor and pitiful, what could they do? he had demanded their land and had thought proper to offer them something in return for it. They had no choice, they must either sign the treaty or be declared enemies of the United States.'" Schmeckebier, The Office of Indian Affairs, Its History, Activities, and Organization (1927), pp. 59–60.

In discussing the status of Indian tribes during the Civil War, one writer stated:

> * * * Moreover, the Indians fought as solicited allies, some as nations, diplomatically approached. Treaties were made with them as with foreign powers and not in the farcical, fraudulent way that had been customary in times past. Abel, The American Indian as Slaveholder and Secessionist, vol. 1, The Slaveholding Indians (1915), p. 17.

[54] 175 U. S. 1. (1899).

[55] *Fleming* v. *McCurtain*, 215 U. S. 56, 59 (1909). For example, by Art. 4 of the Treaty of September 18, 1823, 7 Stat. 224, the United States promised to guarantee the signatory Florida tribes "the peaceable possession of the district of country" assigned them, and the Treaty of September 26, 1833, with the Chippewas and others, Art. 2, 7 Stat. 431, provides that in consideration of the cession of land, "the United States shall grant to the said United Nation of Indians to be held as other Indian lands are held which have lately been assigned to emigrating Indians, a tract of country west of the Mississippi river, to be assigned to them by the President of the United States * * *."

[56] 3 Op. A. G. 322 (1838). And see Chapter 15, sec. 5C.

[57] *Fleming* v. *McCurtain*, 215 U. S. 56, 58–60 (1909).

[58] *Seminole Nation* v. *United States*, 78 C. Cls. 455, 458 (1933). Also see *Ayres* v. *United States*, 44 C. Cls. 48, 85, 95 (1908).

[59] 32 Op. A. G. 586 (1921). See *Fish* v. *Wise*, 52 F. 2d 544 (C. C. A. 10, 1931), cert. den. 282 U. S. 903 (1931), in which the court declined to permit the testimony of interested witnesses 30 years after its execution to thwart the object of an agreement as interpreted by the courts.

[60] *Hicks* v. *Butrick*, 12 Fed. Cas. No. 6458 (C. C. Kan. 1875). Also see *Ayres* v. *United States*, *supra*, fn. 58, and see Chapter 5, sec. 7.

SECTION 3. THE SCOPE OF TREATIES

In the Constitution [61] the President was given power to make treaties, with the advice and consent of the Senate, provided two-thirds of the Senators present concur.[62] The Supreme Court, in interpreting this provision, said: [63]

> * * * inasmuch as the power is given, in general terms, without any description of the objects intended to be embraced within its scope, it must be assumed that the framers of the Constitution intended that it should extend to all those objects which in the intercourse of nations had usually been regarded as the proper subjects of negotiation and treaty, if not inconsistent with the nature of our government and the relation between the States and the United States. (*Holmes* v. *Jennison et al.*, 14 Peters, 569; 1 Kent, 166; 2 Story on the Constitution, § 1508; 7 Hamilton's Works, 501; Duer's Jurisprudence, 229.)

Again, the scope of this power was described by the Supreme Court in the case of *United States* v. *Forty-three Gallons of Whiskey:* [64]

> Besides, the power to make treaties with the Indian tribes is, as we have seen, coextensive with that to make treaties with foreign nations. In regard to the latter, it is, beyond doubt, ample to cover all the usual subjects of diplomacy. * * * (P. 197.)

During the last period of treaty making, amendments by the Senate were frequent.[65]

A special limitation of the treaty-making power is that it cannot appropriate money.[66] Referring to this fact, the Circuit Court for the District of Michigan [67] said that a treaty

> * * * cannot bind or control the legislative action in this respect, and every foreign government may be presumed to know, that so far as the treaty stipulates to pay money, the legislative sanction is required. (P.346.)

---

[61] Treaties already made were recognized by the Constitution. *Cherokee Nation* v. *Georgia*, 5 Pet. 1 (1831); *Worcester* v. *Georgia*, 6 Pet. 515, 559 (1832).

[62] Art. 2, sec. 2, cl. 2. An amendment to a treaty adopted by the Senate which did not receive Presidential approval and was not embodied in his proclamation cannot be regarded as part of the treaty. *New York Indians* v. *United States*, 170 U. S. 1, 23 (1898). Professor Willoughby writes of the early practice:

> During the first years under the Constitution the relations between the President and the Senate were especially close. In 1789 President Washington notified the Senate that he would confer with them with reference to a treaty with certain of the Indian tribes, and, on the next day, and again two days later, went with General Knox before that body for that purpose. Again, in 1790, President Washington in a written communication asked the advice of the Senate as to a new boundary treaty to be entered into with the Cherokee. Willoughby, The Constitutional Law of the United States, (2d ed. 1929) vol. I, p. 521.

[63] *Holden* v. *Joy*, 17 Wall. 211, 242–243 (1872).

[64] 93 U. S. 188 (1876). Also see *Geofroy* v. *Riggs*, 133 U. S. 258, 266 (1890).

[65] See, for example, Treaty of February 18, 1867, with Sac and Fox Indians, 15 Stat. 495; Treaty of February 23, 1867, with the Senecas, and others, Art. 40, 15 Stat. 513, 523.

[66] 24 Op. A. G. 623 (1903); 25 Op. A. G. 163 (1904).

[67] *Turner* v. *American Baptist Missionary Union*, 24 Fed. Cas. No. 14251 (C. C. Mich. 1852).

However, as Boyd has pointed out:[68]

> Although in regard to treaties calling for appropriations congress has seemed reluctant to act without making it plain that there was a discretionary right vested in congress in the premises, such appropriations have always been forthcoming.

Apart from this limitation, treaties may contain provisions which could not constitutionally be included in acts of Congress.[69]

Within the broad scope of "all the usual subjects of diplomacy," the Federal Government and the Indian tribes adopted treaties covering not only all aspects of intercourse between Indians and whites but also some of the internal affairs of the tribes themselves. Among the most important of the subjects covered were:[70]

- A. The international status of the tribe.
  1. War and peace.
  2. Boundaries.
  3. Passports.
  4. Extradition.
  5. Relations with third powers.
- B. Dependence of tribes on the United States.
  1. Protection.
  2. Exclusive trade relations.
  3. Representation in Congress.
  4. Congressional power.
  5. Administrative power.
  6. Termination of treaty-making.
- C. Commercial relations.
  1. Cessions of land.
  2. Reserved rights in ceded land.
  3. Payments and services to tribes.
- D. Jurisdiction.
  1. Criminal jurisdiction.
  2. Civil jurisdiction.
- E. Control of tribal affairs.

A. THE INTERNATIONAL STATUS OF THE TRIBE

Until the last decade of the treaty-making period, terms familiar to modern international diplomacy were used in the Indian treaties.

The United States sometimes guaranteed the integrity of the territory of a nation;[71] unprovoked war was "* * * repelled, prosecuted and determined * * * in conformity with principles of national justice and honorable warfare";[72] some of the Creek Nation acted "contrary to national faith" and "suffered themselves to be instigated to violations of their national honor";[73] the United States desired that "* * * perfect peace shall exist between the nations or tribes * * *" named and the republic of Mexico.[74]

Many provisions show the international status of the Indian tribes,[75] through clauses relating to war, boundaries, passports, extradition, and foreign relations.

[68] Boyd, The Expanding Treaty Power, in Selected Essays on Constitutional Law, vol. 3. The Nation and the States, (1938), p. 410, 414.

[69] *Missouri* v. *Holland*, 252 U. S. 416 (1920). Also see Selected Essays on Constitutional Law, vol. 3, *op. cit.* fn. 68, pp. 397–435.

[70] For discussion of removal provisions see sec. 4E of this Chapter. Relevant treaty provisions are discussed in other chapters.

[71] Treaty of September 17, 1778, with the Delawares, Art. 6, 7 Stat. 13, 15; Treaty of August 9, 1814, with the Creeks, Art. 2, 7 Stat. 120, 121.

[72] Preamble to Treaty of August 9, 1814, with the Creeks, 7 Stat. 120.

[73] *Ibid.*

[74] Treaty of August 24, 1835, with the Comanche and others, Art. 9, 7 Stat. 474, 475.

[75] Also see Chapter 14, sec. 7.

1. *War and peace.*—The capacity of Indian tribes to make war was frequently recognized.[76] Most of the very early treaties were treaties of peace and friendship,[77] and often provided for the restoration or exchange of prisoners,[78] and sometime for hostages until prisoners were restored.[79]

Indian tribes have also waged wars with states. The state of Georgia and the Creek Nation were engaged in several wars towards the close of the eighteenth century.[80]

The Supreme Court[81] commented on the status of Indian wars in these terms:

> * * * We recall no instance where Congress has made a formal declaration of war against an Indian nation or tribe; but the fact that Indians are engaged in acts of general hostility to settlers, especially if the Government has deemed it necessary to dispatch a military force for their subjugation, is sufficient to constitute a state of war. *Marks* v. *United States*, 161 U. S. 297. (P. 267.)

A few treaties included mutual assistance pacts. By Article 8 of the Treaty of January 9, 1789 with the Wiandot and others,[82] the parties agreed to give notice of war or any harm that might be meditated against the other party, "and do all in their power to hinder and prevent the same * * *." Article 2 of the Treaty of July 22, 1814, with the Wyandots and others[83] provided that:

> The tribes and bands abovementioned, engage to give their aid to the United States in prosecuting the war against Great-Britain, and such of the Indian tribes as still continue hostile; and to make no peace with either without the consent of the United States.

In some treaties the Indians agreed to suppress insurrections and permit the military occupation of their country by the United States,[84] or the establishment of garrisons or forts by the

[76] *E. g.*, Treaty of Dancing Rabbit Creek of September 27, 1830, with the Choctaw Nation, 7 Stat. 333, 334:

> * * * no war shall be undertaken or prosecuted by said Choctaw Nation but by declaration made in full Council, and to be approved by the U. S. unless it be in self-defence * * * (Art. V).

For a discussion see *Fleming* v. *McCurtain*, 215 U. S. 56, 60 (1909).

[77] See Treaty of September 17, 1778, with the Delaware Nation, 7 Stat. 13. "That a perpetual peace and friendship shall from henceforth take place * * *" (Art. 2). Later treaties "gave peace." That this was intended to cover "peace and friendship" is made clear in Treaty of January 9, 1789, with the Wiandots, etc., Art. XIII, 7 Stat. 28, which "renewed and confirmed the peace and friendship" entered into in an earlier treaty. That earlier treaty merely gave peace. Treaty of January 21, 1785, with the Wiandots, etc., Preamble, 7 Stat. 16. See, for example, "A Treaty of Peace and Friendship" with the Sacs, May 13, 1816, 7 Stat. 141, and Treaty of September 20, 1816, with the Chickasaws, Art. 1, 7 Stat. 150.

[78] Treaty of November 28, 1785, with the Cherokees, Arts. 1 and 2, 7 Stat. 18; Treaty of July 2, 1791, with the Cherokees, Art. 3, 7 Stat. 39.

[79] Treaty of October 22, 1784, with the Six Nations, Art. 1, 7 Stat. 15; Treaty of January 21, 1785, with the Wiandots and others, Art. 1, 7 Stat. 16.

[80] See 2 Op. A. G. 110 (1828).

[81] *Montoya* v. *United States*, 180 U. S. 261 (1901). See Chapter 14, sec. 3.

[82] 7 Stat. 28. See also Treaty of August 3, 1795, with the Wyandots, Art. 9, 7 Stat. 49; Treaty of November 28, 1785, with the Cherokees, Art. 11, 7 Stat. 18; Treaty of January 3, 1786, with the Choctaws, Art. 10, 7 Stat. 21; Treaty of January 31, 1786, with the Shawanoe Nation, Art. 4, 7 Stat. 26.

[83] 7 Stat. 118. Article 12 of the Treaty of November 10, 1808, with the Great and Little Osage Nations, 7 Stat. 107, provided:

> And the chiefs and warriors as aforesaid, promise and engage that neither the Great nor Little Osage nation will ever, by sale, exchange or as presents, supply any nation or tribe of Indians, not in amity with the United States, with guns, ammunitions or other implements of war.

Also see Treaty of July 30, 1825, with the Belantse-etoa or Minnetsaree Tribe, Art. 7, 7 Stat. 261.

[84] Treaty of March 21, 1866, with the Seminoles, Art. 1, 14 Stat. 755.

President;[85] or to prevent other tribes from making hostile demonstrations against the United States government or people.[86]

2. *Boundaries.*[87]—Nations are usually separated by frontiers. Many treaties fixed the boundaries between the United States and Indian tribes[88] and between Indian tribes.[89] Old boundaries were sometimes altered,[90] and during the removal period,[91] treaties generally described the new territory granted to the Indians.[92]

Frequently treaties prohibited the trespass[93] or settlement[94] of American citizens on Indian territory, unless licensed to trade.[95]

Such provisions were supplemented by statutes.[96]

3. *Passports.*—Additional evidence of the national character of the Indian tribes appears in the provisions requiring passports for citizens or inhabitants of the United States to enter the domain of an Indian tribe. The Treaty of August 7, 1790,[97] with the Creek Nation provided in part:

> * * * Nor shall any such citizen or inhabitant go into the Creek country, without a passport first obtained from the Governor of some one of the United States, or the officer of the troops of the United States commanding at the nearest military post on the frontiers, or such other person as the President of the United States may, from time to time, authorize to grant the same.

Such provisions were supplemented by statutes which required citizens of the United States, as well as foreigners, to secure passports before entering the Indian country, this statutory requirement being later waived in the case of citizens.[98]

4. *Extradition.*—The surrender of fugitives from justice by one nation to another is usually covered by treaty; similarly with the Indians and the United States.

Some treaties required the Indian tribes to deliver up persons committing crimes who were on their land, to be punished by the United States.[99] A few treaties provided for the extradition of such persons for punishment by the states,[100] or by the "states or territory of the United States northwest of the Ohio."[101] A few early treaties provided for the punishment of United States citizens in the presence of the Indians.[102] A particularly broad provision in regard to extradition was contained in the Treaty of June 19, 1858, with the Sioux,[103] which requires the extradition of violators of treaties, laws, and regulations of the United States, or of the laws of the State of Minnesota. Other treaties provided that the Indians shall prevent fugitive slaves from taking shelter among them and shall deliver such fugitives to the Indian agent.[104]

5. *Relations with third powers.*—During the first few decades of the Republic, the political relations of many of the Indian tribes were not confined to the United States. As late as 1835[105] the "friendly relations" existing between some Indian tribes and the Republic of Mexico,[106] the Republic of Texas,[107] and among the several Indian tribes were formally recognized by the United States.[108]

B. DEPENDENCE OF TRIBES ON THE UNITED STATES

While the national character of Indian tribes has been frequently recognized in treaties[109] and statutes,[110] numerous treaty provisions establish their status as *dependent* nations.[111]

---

[85] Treaty of June 16, 1802, with the Creek Nation, Art. 3, 7 Stat. 68; Treaty of November 10, 1808, with the Osages, Art. 1, 7 Stat. 107.

[86] Treaty of October 20, 1865, with the Dakotas, Art. 1, 14 Stat. 731.

[87] See Chapter 15, sec. 12, and sec. 4C of this Chapter.

[88] See Chapter 1, sec. 3, fn. 46. The primary purpose of some treaties was to establish boundaries, 5 Op. A. G. 31 (1848).

[89] Treaty of August 19, 1825, with the Sioux and others, 7 Stat. 272, Article 1 provided for peace between Sioux and Chippewas, Sacs and Foxes and the Ioways.

[90] Treaty of July 2, 1791, with the Cherokees, Art. 4, 7 Stat. 39; Treaty of October 17, 1802, with the Choctaws, Art. 3, 7 Stat. 73.

[91] See sec. 4E, *infra*. Also see Treaty of December 29, 1835, with the Cherokees, Art. 16, 7 Stat. 478, providing for removal in 2 years. Article 5 of the Treaty of January 19, 1832, with a band of the Wyandots, 7 Stat. 364, provides that the band may

> * * * remove to Canada, or to the river Huron in Michigan, where they own a reservation of land, or to any place they may obtain a right or privilege from other Indians to go.

[92] See sec. 4E, *infra;* and see Chapter 15, sec. 5.

[93] Article 8 of the Treaty of May 24, 1834, with the Chickasaws, 7 Stat. 450, provides that

> * * * the agent of the United States, upon the application of the chiefs of the nation, will resort to every legal civil remedy, (at the expense of the United States,) to prevent intrusions upon the ceded country; * * *.

Article 7 of the Treaty of March 6, 1861, with the Sacs and others, 12 Stat. 1171, provided that no nonmember of a tribe, except Government employees or persons connected with Government services, shall go on the reservation except with the permission of the agent or the Superintendent of Indian Affairs.

[94] Treaty of January 21, 1785, with the Wiandots and others, Art. 5, 7 Stat. 16; Treaty of July 2, 1791, with the Cherokee Nation, Art. 8, 7 Stat. 39. Also see sec. 4C *infra*.

[95] See Chapter 16.

[96] Act of May 19, 1796, 1 Stat. 469; also see Act of March 3, 1799, sec. 2, 1 Stat. 743 and Act of March 30, 1802, sec. 2, 2 Stat. 139. See fn. 47, Chapter 1.

[97] Art. 7, 7 Stat. 35, 37. See also Treaty of July 2, 1791, with the Cherokees, Art. 9, 7 Stat. 39.

[98] See Chapter 4, sec. 6.

[99] Article 9 of the Treaty of January 21, 1785, with the Wiandots and others, 7 Stat. 16, provides:

> If any Indian or Indians shall commit a robbery or murder on any citizen of the United States, the tribe to which such offenders may belong shall be bound to deliver them up at the nearest post, to be punished according to the ordinances of the United States.

Also see Treaty of September 27, 1830, with the Choctaws, Art. 8, 7 Stat. 333.

[100] Treaty of July 2, 1791, with the Cherokee Nation, Art. 11, 7 Stat. 39.

[101] Treaty of January 9, 1789, with the Wiandots and others, Art. 6, 7 Stat. 28.

[102] Treaty of November 28, 1785, with the Cherokees, Art. 7, 7 Stat. 18; Treaty of January 3, 1786, with the Choctaw Nation, Art. 6, 7 Stat. 21. Article 7 of the Treaty of May 15, 1846, with the Comanches and other tribes, 9 Stat. 844, provided that Indians guilty of insurrection shall be delivered up to the United States.

[103] Art. 6, 12 Stat. 1037. Also see Treaty of March 12, 1858, with the Poncas, Art. 7, 12 Stat. 997. For an example of a provision providing for extradition between tribes see Treaty of August 7, 1856, with the Creeks and Seminoles, Art. 14, 11 Stat. 699.

[104] Treaty of September 18, 1823, with the Floridas, Art. 7, 7 Stat. 224.

[105] Treaty of August 24, 1835, with the Comanche and others, 7 Stat. 474.

[106] *Ibid.*, Art. 9.

[107] Treaty of May 26, 1837, with the Kioway and others, 7 Stat. 533.

[108] See fn. 105, Art. 1. Indian tribes also made treaties with the states and with the Confederacy. The Federal Government sometimes supervised state dealings with Indians. While states entered into treaties with Indians prior to the ratification of the Constitution (W. A. Duerr, Course of Lectures on the Constitutional Jurisprudence of the United States, 2d ed. (1856), p. 281), the Constitution forbids a state from entering "into any treaty, alliance, or federation * * *." (Art. 1, sec. 8. See *Coffee* v. *Groover,* 123 U. S. 1, 13–14 (1887).) Many states like New York entered into numerous treaties with Indian tribes subsequent to the Constitution with the consent of the United States. The Supreme Court in *Worcester* v. *Georgia,* 6 Pet. 515, 581, said: "Under the constitution no state can enter into any treaty; and it is believed, that, since its adoption, no state, under its own authority, has held a treaty with the Indians." *Accord: Coffee* v. *Groover,* 123 U. S. 1, 13 (1887). See Chapter 8, sec. 11. On the view of the South that each state succeeded to the property rights of Great Britain and could treat with the Indians as it pleased, see *United States* v. *Swain County, N. C.,* 46 F. 2d 99 (D. C. W. D. N. C. 1930), rev'd sub nom. *United States* v. *Wright, et al.,* 53 F. 2d 300 (C. C. A. 8, 1931), cert. den. 285 U. S. 539.

[109] Treaty of January 21, 1785, with the Wiandots and others, Art. 2, 7 Stat. 16; Treaty of November 28, 1785, with the Cherokees, Art. 3, 7 Stat. 18; Treaty of January 3, 1786, with the Choctaw Nation, Art. 2, 7 Stat. 21.

[110] See Chapter 14, sec. 3.

[111] The relationship of the United States to the Indians has been likened to suzerainty. Wilson and Tucker, International Law (1935), p. 68.

1. *Protection.*—For example, article 2 of the Treaty of August 13, 1803, with the Kaskaskias [112] provides that—

> The United States will take the Kaskaskia tribe under their immediate care and patronage, and will afford them a protection as effectual against the other Indian tribes and against all other persons whatever as is enjoyed by their own citizens. And the said Kaskaskia tribe do hereby engage to refrain from making war or giving any insult or offence to any other Indian tribe or to any foreign nation, without having first obtained the approbation and consent of the United States. (P. 78.)

Similar provisions are contained in other treaties.[113]

In construing a similar provision, the Supreme Court said: [114]

> * * * By this treaty [Treaty of Hopewell] the Cherokees were recognized as one people, composing one tribe or nation, but subject, however, to the jurisdiction and authority of the Government of the United States, which could regulate their trade and manage all their affairs. (P. 295.)

Treaties with many of the other tribes left no doubt of the protectorate of the United States over them.[115]

In many respects this relationship is similar to that established in a great variety of cases between great powers and small, weak or backward states. Thus the limitations upon Indian law making and enforcement which appear in some treaties, may be likened to the limitations imposed upon the jurisdiction of certain oriental states, such as China, over the nationals of western countries residing within their territories.[116]

The practical inequality of the parties must be borne in mind in reading Indian treaties. It explains the presence of many clauses and the frequency with which similar or identical provisions appear in many Indian treaties during certain periods.[117]

2. *Exclusive trade relations.*[118]—The political dependence of the Indian tribes upon the Federal Government implied, and was implied by, their economic dependence. This economic dependence found expression in agreements by the tribes not to sell real or personal property or otherwise have commercial dealings with other sovereignties than the Federal Government or with their citizens or even with citizens of the United States not authorized by the Federal Government to engage in such transactions.

In some cases, these undertakings were explicit, as in Article 10 of the Treaty of November 10, 1808,[119] whereby the Osages disclaimed all right to

> * * * cede, sell or in any manner transfer their lands to any foreign power, or to citizens of the United States or inhabitants of Louisiana, unless duly authorised by the President of the United States to make the said purchase or accept the said cession on behalf of the government.

In other cases, the exclusiveness of economic relations with the Federal Government was implicit in agreements that the United States "shall have the sole and exclusive right of regulating the trade with the Indians." [120]

Occasionally a tribe was given power to regulate trade and intercourse, "so far as may be compatible with the constitution of the United States and the laws made in pursuance thereof regulating trade and intercourse with the Indians," [121] or was empowered to veto the granting of a trading license to trade within certain areas.[122]

Some treaties provided for the appointment of an agent to trade with the Indians,[123] and established trading posts [124] or designated places for trade.[125] Occasionally Indians were prohibited from trading outside the limits of the United States,[126] or were required to apprehend foreigners or other unauthorized persons coming "into their district of country, for the purposes of trade or other views," and to deliver them to federal officials.[127]

---

[112] 7 Stat. 78.

[113] The Treaty of August 7, 1790, with the Creek Nation, Art. 2, 7 Stat. 35, provides that:

> The undersigned Kings, Chiefs, and Warriors, for themselves and all parts of the Creek Nation within the limits of the United States, do acknowledge themselves, and the said parts of the Creek Nation, to be under the protection of the United States of America, and of no other sovereign whosoever; and they also stipulate that the said Creek Nation will not hold any treaty with an individual State, or with individuals of any State. (P. 35.)

The Treaty of November 17, 1807, with the Ottoways and others, Art. 7, 7 Stat. 105, provides that:

> The said nations of Indians acknowledge themselves to be under the protection of the United States, and no other power, and will prove by their conduct that they are worthy of so great a blessing.

Compare the following excerpt from the first section of a law passed by the Georgia legislature on October 31, 1787, quoted in 2 Op. A. G. 110, 124 (1828):

> * * * That from and immediately after the passing of this act, the Creek Indians shall be considered as out of the protection of this State; and it shall be lawful for the government and people of the same to put to death or capture the said Indians, wherever they may be found within the limits of the State * * *. (Pp. 124–125.)

[114] *Eastern Band of Cherokee Indians* v. *United States*, 117 U. S. 288 (1886).

[115] For example, Treaty of December 30, 1849, with the Utah Indians, Arts. 1 and 4, 9 Stat. 984.

[116] E. D. Dickinson, The Equality of States in International Law (1920), p. 224.

[117] For example, Treaty of September 26, 1825, with the Ottoes and Missourias, 7 Stat. 277, and the Treaty of September 30, 1825, with the Pawnees, 7 Stat. 279; Treaty of October 28, 1867, with the Cheyenne-Arapahoe Tribes, Art. 11, 15 Stat. 593, and Treaty of April 29, *et. seq.*, 1868, with the Sioux, Art. 11, 15 Stat. 635. Also see Chapter 8, sec. 11.

[118] *Cf.* Chapter 16.

[119] 7 Stat. 107, 109. Also see Treaty of January 9, 1789, with the Wiandots and others, Art. 3, 7 Stat. 28; Treaty of September 21, 1832, with Sacs and Foxes, Art. 8, 7 Stat. 374. Treaty of May 15, 1846, with the Comanches and others, Art. 2, 9 Stat. 844.

[120] Treaty of November 28, 1785, with the Cherokees, Art. 9, 7 Stat. 18; Treaty of January 10, 1786, with the Chickasaws, Art. 8, 7 Stat. 24.

Article 1 of the Treaty of June 9, 1825, with the Poncar Tribe, 7 Stat. 247, contains another type of trade clause:

> * * * The said tribe also admit the right of the United States to regulate all trade and intercourse with them.

Also see Treaty of January 3, 1786, with the Choctaw Nation, Arts. 8, 9, 7 Stat. 21.

Sometimes this power was granted for mutual considerations. Treaty of July 6, 1825, with the Chayenne Tribe, Art. 4, 7 Stat. 255; Treaty of July 30, 1825, with the Belantse-etoa or Minnetsaree Tribe, Art. 5, 7 Stat. 261.

The Treaty of December 30, 1849, Arts. 1 and 4, 9 Stat. 984, provided for the submission of the Utah Indians to the power and authority of the United States and extended to these Indians the trade and intercourse laws already applicable to other tribes. Also see Treaty of September 9, 1849, with the Navajos, Art. 3, 9 Stat. 974. Some of the treaties did not contain such sweeping provisions, but merely provided that "the United States agree to admit and licence traders to hold intercourse with said tribe [the signatory tribe], under mild and equitable regulations." Treaty of June 9, 1825, with the Poncar Tribe, Art. 4, 7 Stat. 247. For similar provisions see Treaty of June 22, 1825, with the Teton, Yancton, and Yanctonies bands of Sioux, Art. 4, 7 Stat. 250; and Treaty of July 5, 1825, with the Sioune and Ogallala Tribes of Sioux, Art. 4, 7 Stat. 252.

[121] Treaty of August 7, 1856, with the Creeks and Seminoles, Art. 15, 11 Stat. 699. But *cf.* 1 Op. A. G. 645 (1824).

[122] Treaty of July 19, 1866, with the Cherokees, Art. 8, 14 Stat. 799.

[123] *E. g.*, Treaty of September 17, 1778, with the Delawares, Art. 5, 7 Stat. 13.

[124] Treaty of January 9, 1789, with the Wiandots and others, Arts. 10, 11, and 12, 7 Stat. 28; Treaty of June 29, 1796, with the Creeks, Art. 3, 7 Stat. 56. See Chapter 16.

[125] Treaty of July 5, 1825, with the Sioune and Ogallala Tribes, Art. 3, 7 Stat. 252; Treaty of July 6, 1825, with the Chayenne Tribe, Art. 4, 7 Stat. 255; Treaty of January 9, 1789, with the Wiandots and others, Art. 7, 7Stat. 28; Treaty of August 3, 1795, with the Wiandots and others, Art. 8, 7 Stat. 49.

[126] Treaty of December 26, 1854, with the Nisquallys and others, Art 12, 10 Stat. 1132.

[127] Treaty of September 26, 1825, with the Ottoe and Missouri Tribe, Art. 4, 7 Stat. 277; Treaty of September 30, 1825, with the Pawnees, Art. 4, 7 Stat. 279.

3. *Representation in Congress.*—Further light on the relations between the tribes and the Federal Government may be found in treaties which provided for the sending of Indian delegates to Congress.[128] This practice was explained in the report of the House Committee on Indian Affairs on the Trade and Intercourse Act of 1834.[129]

> The proposition for allowing Indians a delegate is not now for the first time brought forward.
>
> It was first suggested in 1778, and in the first treaty ever formed by the United States with any Indian tribe. The treaty with the Delawares of the 17th September, 1778, contains the following article: "And it is further agreed on, by the contracting parties, (should it, for the future, be found conducive for the interests of both parties,) to invite any other tribes who have been friends to the interests of the United States, to join the present confederation, and to form a State, whereof the Delaware nation shall be the head, and have a representative in Congress: *Provided*, Nothing contained in this article is to be considered as conclusive until it meets with the approbation of Congress."
>
> In the treaty of Hopewell, of 1785, is the following article: "Article 12. That the Indians may have full confidence in the justice of the United States, respecting their interests, they shall have the right to send a deputy of their choice, whenever they think fit, to Congress."
>
> In the treaty with the Choctaws, of September, 1830, they requested the privilege of having a delegate in the House of Representatives; and the treaty states that "the commissioners do not feel that they can, under a treaty stipulation, accede to the request, but at their desire present it in the treaty, that Congress may consider of and decide the application."
>
> The proposition is now presented to Congress, with the decided opinion of the committee that it ought to receive a favorable consideration. (Pp. 21–22.)

This recommendation was never effectuated.

4. *Congressional power.*—The extent to which Indian treaties conferred or confirmed congressional power to legislate over Indian affairs is the subject of a separate inquiry.[130] For the present it is sufficient to note that federal statutes have been extended over Indian country by the mere force of a treaty,[131] and that treaties sometimes provided for the creation of United States courts in the Indian country.[132] Thus, for example, Article 2 of the Treaty of October 4, 1842,[133] with the Chippewa Indians provides in part:

> The Indians stipulate * * * that the laws of the United States shall be continued in force, in respect to their trade and intercourse with the whites, until otherwise ordered by Congress.

Article 7 of the Treaty of October 2, 1863,[134] with the Chippewa Indians reads:

> * * * The laws of the United States now in force, or that may hereafter be enacted, prohibiting the introduction and sale of spirituous liquors in the Indian country, shall be in full force and effect throughout the country hereby ceded, until otherwise directed by congress or the President of the United States.

The Treaty of February 27, 1855,[135] with the Winnebago Indians provided:

> The laws which have been or may be enacted by Congress, regulating trade and intercourse with the Indian tribes, shall continue and be in force within the country herein provided to be selected as the future permanent home of the Winnebago Indians, and those portions of said laws which prohibit the introduction, manufacture, use of, and traffic in, ardent spirits, in the Indian country, shall continue and be in force within the country herein ceded to the United States, until otherwise provided by Congress.

5. *Administrative power.*—The President was frequently granted considerable power by treaties. He was authorized to establish trading posts;[136] military posts or garrisons on Indian lands;[137] to designate places for trade;[138] to appoint agents;[139] to arbitrate claims of whites against Indians and Indians against whites;[140] to arbitrate territorial[141] and other difficulties between tribes;[142] to prescribe the time of the removal and settlement of Indians;[143] to determine whether grants of land to certain Indians shall be conveyed;[144] to dispose of certain reserved lands as he sees fit;[145] to give reservations to the headmen of a tribe,[146] or cattle,[147] or agricultural aid;[148] to extend to an Indian tribe "from time to time, such benefits and acts of kindness as may be convenient, and seem just and proper" to him;[149] to decrease the amount of annuities in proportion to any annual decrease of the Poncas, and stop the payment of annuities in the event that satisfactory efforts to advance and improve their condition were not made;[150] to approve attorneys chosen by the chiefs and headmen;[151] to invest tribal money in stocks;[152] to make payments to the relations and friends of Indians;[153] and to receive complaints of injuries done by individuals to the Indians and use such prudent means "as shall be necessary to preserve the said peace and friendship" with an Indian tribe.[154]

Article 7 of the Treaty of September 30, 1809,[155] with the Delawares and others provided in part:

> * * * when any theft or other depredation shall be committed by any individual or individuals of one of the tribes above mentioned, upon the property of any individual or individuals of another tribe, the chiefs of the party injured shall make application to the agent of the

---

[128] See sec. 4B, *infra*.

[129] H. Rept. No. 474, Comm. on Ind. Aff., 23 Cong., 1st sess., May 20, 1834.

[130] See Chapter 5, sec. 2.

[131] *Ex parte Crow Dog*, 109 U. S. 556, 567 (1883).

[132] Treaty of July 19, 1866, with the Cherokees, Art. 7, 14 Stat. 799.

[133] 7 Stat. 591.

[134] 13 Stat. 667. See Chapter 17, sec. 1, fn. 14.

[135] Art. 8, 10 Stat. 1172.

[136] Treaty of June 29, 1796, with the Creek Nation, Art. 3(a), 7 Stat. 56.

[137] Treaty of June 16, 1802, with the Creek Nation, Art. 3, 7 Stat. 68. Other federal officials like the Secretary of the Interior and the Commissioner of Indian Affairs were also granted power by treaty.

[138] Treaty of July 5, 1825, with the Sioune and Ogallala Tribes, Art. 4, 7 Stat. 252; Treaty of July 6, 1825, with the Chayenne Tribe, Art. 3, 7 Stat. 255.

[139] Treaty of October 20, 1832, with the Chickasaw Nation, Art. 9, 7 Stat. 381.

[140] Treaty of January 8, 1821, with the Creek Nation, 7 Stat. 217.

[141] Treaty of August 11, 1827, with the Chippewa and others, Art. 2, 7 Stat. 303.

[142] Treaty of September 21, 1833, with the Otoes and Missourias, Art. 8, 7 Stat. 429.

[143] Treaty of February 8, 1831, with the Menomonies, Art. 1, 7 Stat. 342.

[144] Treaty of September 17, 1818, with the Wyandots and others, Art. 3, 7 Stat. 178; Treaty of October 2, 1818, with the Potawatamie Nation, Art. 4, 7 Stat. 185.

[145] Treaty of June 2, 1825, with the Osages, Art. 10, 7 Stat. 240.

[146] Treaty of October 1, 1863, with the Western Band of Shoshonees, Art. 6, 18 Stat. 689.

[147] *Ibid.*, Art. 7.

[148] Treaty of September 24, 1819, with the Chippewa Nation, Art. 8, 7 Stat. 203.

[149] Treaty of June 6, 1825, with the Chayenne Tribe, Art. 2, 7 Stat. 255.

[150] Treaty of March 12, 1858, with the Poncas, Art. 2, 12 Stat. 997; also see Treaty of February 18, 1861, with the Arapahoe and Cheyenne Indians, Art. 4, 12 Stat. 1163.

[151] Treaty of November 5, 1857, with the Tonawanda Band of Senecas, Art. 5, 12 Stat. 991.

[152] *Ibid.*, Art. 6. Also see Treaty of October 1, 1859, with the Sacs and Foxes of the Mississippi, Art. 11, 15 Stat. 467, giving the Secretary power over tribal money.

[153] Treaty of November 1, 1837, with the Winnebago Nation, Art. 4, 7 Stat. 544, interpreted in 3 Op. A. G. 471 (1839).

[154] Treaty of August 3, 1795, with the Wyandots and others, Art. 9, 7 Stat. 49.

[155] 7 Stat. 113.

> United States, who is charged with the delivery of the annuities of the tribe to which the offending party belongs, whose duty it shall be to hear the proofs and allegations on either side, and determine between them: and the amount of his award shall be immediately deducted from the annuity of the tribe to which the offending party belongs, and given to the person injured, or to the chief of his village for his use.

Treaties provided for the withholding, for a year or for such time as an administrator should determine, of annuities of an Indian drinking intoxicating liquors or providing others with liquor in violation of treaty provisions.[156] Administrative determinations were also authorized for reducing annuities in cases of depredations[157] and horse stealing.[158]

6. *Termination of treaty-making.*—The last stage of dependence is reached when a treaty-making power abandons the right to make further treaties. Such a provision is found in the Treaty of February 18, 1861[159] with the Arapahoe and Cheyenne Indians:

> * * * And, in order to render unnecessary any further treaty engagements or arrangements hereafter with the United States, it is hereby agreed and stipulated that the President, with the assent of Congress, shall have full power to modify or change any of the provisions of former treaties with the Arapahoes and Cheyennes of the Upper Arkansas, in such manner and to whatever extent he may judge to be necessary and expedient for their best interests.

A similar result is achieved by treaties in which a tribe makes provision for the termination of its tribal existence.[160]

C. COMMERCIAL RELATIONS

Commercial dealings generally formed the substance of those treaties which were not specifically treaties of peace.

1. *Cessions of land.*—That which the Indians had which the United States most desired was, until very recently, land. The process of treaty-making was the first method of acquiring lands for, as well as from, the Indians.[161] The United States and the Indians sometimes exchanged land,[162] and land was sometimes ceded to the states.[163]

The right to pass through the Indian territory in certain places was sometimes reserved by the United States,[164] as were rights to build roads and establish inns and ferrys,[165] or to permit telegraph lines or railroads[166] or a named railroad to have a right-of-way (provided just compensation is paid),[167] and options to purchase rights-of-way.[168]

Considerable power was often given to the Federal Government by provisions relating to land. The Treaty of August 5, 1826,[169] granted to the United States the right to search for minerals.

Many treaties empowered the United States to allot land to Indians,[170] which, in a few cases was made "exempt from taxa-

---

[156] Treaty of March 12, 1858, with the Poncas, 12 Stat. 997; Treaty of June 19, 1858, with the Sioux, Art. 7, 12 Stat. 1037. The use of congressional power in conjunction with the treaty-making power to impose prohibitions against the liquor traffic by treaties with the Indians is discussed in Chapter 17, sec. 2. Treaty provisions regarding the enforcement of liquor prohibition laws were common.

Article 12 of the Treaty of October 18, 1820, with the Choctaw Nation, 7 Stat. 210, provided:

> In order to promote industry and sobriety amongst all classes of the Red people, in this nation, but particularly the poor, it is further provided by the parties, that the agent appointed to reside here, shall be, and he is hereby, vested with full power to seize and confiscate all the whiskey which may be introduced into said nation, except that used at public stands, or brought in by the permit of the agent, or the principal Chiefs of the three Districts.

The Indians were sometimes required to aid in the enforcement of these laws. Thus provisions were sometimes made whereby the Indians promised to tell the agent of violations of liquor prohibitions. (Treaty of May 15, 1846, with the Comanche and other tribes, Art. 12, 9 Stat. 844.)

In some of the treaties the Indians promised "to use their best efforts to prevent the introduction and use of ardent spirits in their country." (Treaty of May 18, 1854, with the Sacs and Foxes, Art. 10, 10 Stat. 1074.) The Treaty of February 11, 1856, with the Menomonee Tribe, Art. 3(2), 11 Stat. 679, provided "That the Menomonees will suppress the use of ardent spirits among their people, and resist, by all prudent means, its introduction in their settlements."

The Treaty of February 22, 1855, with the Chippewas, Art. 9, 10 Stat. 1165 provides:

> * * * that they will abstain from the use of intoxicating drinks and other vices to which they have been addicted.

[157] Treaty of September 30, 1809, with the Delawares and others, Art. 7, 7 Stat. 113.

[158] Treaty of June 26, 1794, with the Cherokee Nation, Art. 4, 7 Stat. 43. Article 7 of the Treaty of January 22, 1855, with the Willamette Indians, 10 Stat. 1143, provided that:

> * * * any one of them who shall drink liquor, or procure it for other Indians to drink, may have his or her proportion of the annuities withheld from him or her for such time as the President may determine.

Also see Treaty of December 26, 1854, with the Nisquallys, Art. 9, 10 Stat. 1132.

[159] Art. 7, 12 Stat. 1163.

[160] See Chapter 14, secs. 1–2.

[161] See Chapter 15, sec. 5; Westwood, Legal Aspects of Land Acquisition, p. 2, Indians and the Land, Contributions by the Delegation of the United States, First Inter-American Conference on Indian Life, Patzcuaro, Mexico, published by Office of Indian Affairs, April 1940.

For an example of cession by the United States to Indians see Treaty of September 15, 1832, with the Winnebagoes, Art. 2, 7 Stat. 370. For an example of a reservation for a tribe of land from a cession see Treaty of September 21, 1832, with the Sacs and Fox, Art. 2, 7 Stat. 374. Land was reserved to the Indians, including the right to lease salt lands. The salt was not to be sold at a higher price than $7 per bushel of 50 pounds weight: otherwise the lease would be forfeited. Treaty of October 19, 1818, with the Chickasaws, Art. 4, 7 Stat. 192. It is well settled that good title to lands of an Indian tribe may be granted to Indians by a treaty between the United States and the tribe, without an act of Congress or any patent from the executive authority of the United States. Tribal land can be disposed of by treaty. 9 Op. A. G. 24 (1857).

Examples of treaty provisions on land cessions by the Indians to the United States will be found in the Treaty of August 27, 1804, with the Piankeshaws, Art. 1, 7 Stat. 83; Treaty of September 30, 1809, with the Delawares and others, Art. 1, 7 Stat. 113; Treaty of July 8, 1817, with the Cherokees, Art. 10, 7 Stat. 156.

[162] Treaty of June 30, 1802, with the Senecas, 7 Stat. 70; Treaty of July 8, 1817, with the Cherokees, Arts. 1 and 2, 7 Stat. 156; Treaty of February 12, 1825, with the Creek Nation, Art. 2, 7 Stat. 237.

[163] Treaty of May 31, 1796, with the Seven Nations of Canada, 7 Stat. 55.

[164] Treaty of August 3, 1795, with the Wyandots and others, Art. 3, 7 Stat. 49. On provisions regarding free navigation for all through navigable streams, see Treaty of July 8, 1817, with the Cherokees, Art. 9, 7 Stat. 156.

[165] Treaty of September 29, 1817, with the Wyandots and others, Art. 14, 7 Stat. 160. Also see Treaty of November 11, 1794, with the Six Nations, Art. 5, 7 Stat. 44; Treaty of August 16, 1825, with the Kansas, Arts. 1, 2, and 3, 7 Stat. 270. Art. 5 provided for compensation for this privilege. Treaty of August 7, 1856, with the Creeks and Seminoles, Art. 19, 11 Stat. 699.

[166] Treaty of July 4, 1866, with the Delawares, Art. 13, 14 Stat. 793. Also see Treaty of June 22, 1855, with the Choctaws and Chickasaws, Art. 18, 11 Stat. 611.

[167] Treaty of January 22, 1855, with the Willamettes, Art. 8, 10 Stat. 1143.

[168] Treaty of November 15, 1861, with the Pottawatomies, Art. 5, 12 Stat. 1191. Also see Treaty of May 30, 1860, with the Delawares, Art. 3, 12 Stat. 1129.

[169] With the Chippewas, Art. 3, 7 Stat. 290.

[170] Treaty of July 8, 1817, with the Cherokees, Art. 8, 7 Stat. 156; Treaty of February 27, 1855, with the Winnebagos, Art. 4, 10 Stat. 1172; Treaty of January 31, 1855, with the Wyandots, Arts. 3 and 4, 10 Stat. 1159, construed in *Hicks* v. *Butrick*, 12 Fed. Cas. No. 6,458 (C. C. Kan. 1875). Sometimes a differentiation was made between full-bloods and half-bloods. Treaty of June 3, 1825, with the Kansas Nation, Art. 6, 7 Stat. 244. Treaty stipulations apply to half-bloods as well as full-bloods, unless otherwise specially provided. 20 Op. A. G. 742 (1894).

tion, levy, sale, or forfeiture, until otherwise provided by Congress." [171] There were also many other types of restrictive clauses such as the promise that land "shall be exempt from levy, sale, or forfeiture, until otherwise provided by State legislation, with the assent of Congress," [172] or the granting to the chiefs for the use of a number of tribes tracts of land which "shall not be liable to taxes of any kind so long as such land continues the property of the said Indians." [173]

The extent to which Indian treaties revolved about land cession will form a principal thread of inquiry in section 4 of this chapter.

2. *Reserved rights in ceded lands.*—By way of softening the shock of land cession, the Indian tribes were often guaranteed special rights in ceded lands, such as the exclusive right of taking fish in streams bordering on the reservation,[174] or "the right of hunting on the ceded territory, with the other usual privileges of occupancy, until required to remove by the President of the United States," [175] or to hunt on lands ceded to the United States or "perpetual right of fishing" at a falls [176] "without hindrance or molestation, so long as they demean themselves peaceably, and offer no injury to the people of the United States," [177] or to hunt and make sugar on ceded land.[178]

The nature of these rights forms a part of a later discussion of tribal property.[179]

3. *Payments and services to tribes.*—In payment for lands ceded, and occasionally by way of compensation for other benefits or indemnification for injuries done to Indians, the Federal Government assumed extensive financial obligations to the Indian tribes. These obligations might be discharged either by lump sum or annuity payments of money or by payment in services and commodities. This is the source not only of the intricate legal problems in which tribal funds,[180] per capita payments,[181] and individual Indian moneys [182] are involved, but also of the federal services which today constitute the chief function of the Indian Service.[183]

Frequently services of various kinds were provided for in treaties. Among the articles commonly specified in treaties were those which represented the differences between the white and the Indian civilizations—cattle, hogs, iron, steel, wagons, plows, and other farming tools.[184] The purpose of civilizing the Indians is apparent in the choice of goods and services which the tribe will receive.[185] Such services included the providing of "one grist-mill and one saw-mill * * * one blacksmith and one gunsmith * * * and * * * such implements of agriculture as the proper agent may think necessary" and "one hundred and sixty bushels of salt" annually;[186] farming utensils, cattle, black-

[171] Treaty of October 5, 1859, with the Kansas Indians, Art. 3, 12 Stat. 1111. See Chapter 13, sec. 3A.

[172] Treaty of January 31, 1855, with the Wyandots, Art. 4, 10 Stat. 1159.

[173] Treaty of September 29, 1817, with the Wyandots and others, Art 15, 7 Stat. 160.

[174] Treaty of June 11, 1855, with Nez Perce, Art. 3, 12 Stat. 957.

[175] Treaty of October 4, 1842, with the Chippewas, Art. 2, 7 Stat. 591.

[176] Treaty of June 16, 1820, with Chippeway Tribe, Art. 3, 7 Stat. 206. Also see Treaty of June 9, 1855, with the Walla-Wallas, Cayuses, and Umatilla Tribes, 12 Stat. 945, discussed in Memo. Sol. I. D., June 15, 1937. Also see Chapter 15, sec. 21.

[177] Treaty of August 3, 1795, with the Wyandots and others, Art. 7, 7 Stat. 49.; also see Art 5.

[178] Treaty of September 29, 1817, with the Wyandots and others, Art 11, 7 Stat. 160; Treaty of September 24, 1819, with Chippewa Nation, Art. 5, 7 Stat. 203.

[179] See Chapter 15, sec. 21. See also Chapter 14, sec. 7.

[180] See Chapter 15, secs. 22, 23, 24; Chapter 9, sec. 6.

[181] *Ibid.* And see Chapter 10, secs. 4, 5.

[182] *Ibid.*

[183] See Chapter 12. The unpublished Treaty of April 23, 1792, with the Five Nations (Archives No. 19) provided:

> THE UNITED STATES, in order to promote the happiness of the five nations of Indians, will cause to be expended annually the amount of one thousand five hundred dollars, in purchasing for them clothing, domestic animals and implements of husbandry, and for encouraging useful artificers to reside in their villages.

The Treaty of September 27, 1830, with the Choctaw Nation, 7 Stat. 333, provided:

> * * * The U. S. agree also to erect a Council House for the Nation at some convenient central point, after their people shall be settled; and a House for each Chief, also a Church for each of the three Districts, to be used also as school houses, until the Nation may conclude to build others; and for these purposes ten thousand dollars shall be appropriated; also fifty thousand dollars (viz) twenty-five hundred dollars annually shall be given for the support of three teachers of schools for twenty years. Likewise there shall be furnished to the Nation three Blacksmiths one for each district for sixteen years, and a qualified Mill Wright for five years; Also there shall be furnished the following articles, twenty-one hundred blankets, to each warrior who emigrates a rifle, moulds, wipers and ammunition. One thousand axes, ploughs, hoes, wheels and cards each; and four hundred looms. There shall also be furnished, one ton of iron and two hundred weight of steel annually to each District for sixteen years. (Art. 20.)

Article 4 of the Treaty of February 8, 1831, with the Menomonee Nation, 7 Stat. 342, provides:

> * * * The above reservation being made to the Menomonee Indians for the purpose of weaning them from their wandering habits, by attaching them to comfortable homes, the President of the United States, as a mark of affection for his children of the Menomonee tribe, will cause to be employed five farmers of established character for capacity, industry, and moral habits, for ten successive years, whose duty it shall be to assist the Menomonee Indians in the cultivation of their farms, and to instruct their children in the business and occupation of farming. Also, five females shall be employed, of like good character, for the purpose of teaching young Menomonee women, in the business of useful housewifery, during a period of ten years.—The annual compensation allowed to the farmers shall not exceed five hundred dollars, and that of the females three hundred dollars. And the United States will cause to be erected, houses suited to their condition, on said lands, as soon as the Indians agree to occupy them, for which ten thousand dollars shall be appropriated; also, houses for the farmers, for which three thousand dollars shall be appropriated; to be expended under the direction of the Secretary of War. Whenever the Menomonees thus settle their lands, they shall be supplied with useful household articles, horses, cows, hogs, and sheep, farming utensils, and other articles of husbandry necessary to their comfort, to the value of six thousand dollars; and they desire that some suitable device may be stamped upon such articles, to preserve them from sale or barter, to evil disposed white persons: none of w'ich, nor any other articles with which the United States may at any time furnish them, shall be liable to sale, or be disposed of or bargained, without permission of the agent. The whole to be under the immediate care of the farmers employed to remain among said Indians, but subject to the general controul of the United States' Indian Agent at Green Bay acting under the Secretary of War. The United States will erect a grist and saw mill on Fox river, for the benefit of the Menomonee Indians, and employ a good miller, subject to the direction of the agent, whose business it shall be to grind the grain, required for the use of the Menomonee Indians, and saw the lumber necessary for building on their lands, as also to instruct such young men of the Menomonee nation, as desire to, and conveniently can be instructed in the trade of a miller. The expenses of erecting such mills, and a house for the miller to reside in, shall not exceed six thousand dollars, and the annual compensation of the miller shall be six hundred dollars, to continue for ten years. And if the mills so erected by the United States, can saw more lumber or grind more grain, than is required for the proper use of said Menomonee Indians, the proceeds of such milling shall be applied to the payment of other expenses occurring in the Green bay agency, under the direction of the Secretary of War.

Article 13 of the Treaty of April 29, *et seq.*, 1868, with the Sioux Nation, 15 Stat. 635, provides that:

> The United States hereby agrees to furnish annually to the Indians the physician, teachers, carpenter, miller, engineer, farmer, and blacksmiths, as herein contemplated, and that such appropriations shall be made from time to time, on the estimates of the Secretary of the Interior, as will be sufficient to employ such persons. (P. 640.)

See also Chapter 15, sec. 23A, fn. 608.

[184] Art. 4 of Treaty of October 23, 1826, 7 Stat. 300, 301 (Miami). See also Act of May 1, 1888, Art. 3, 25 Stat. 113, 114 (concerning use of sums due to Indians of the Blackfeet, Fort Peck, and Fort Belknap Reservations). *Cf.* Act of April 30, 1888, sec. 17, 25 Stat. 94, 100 (Sioux). The Southern Utes were entitled to receive annuities in the form of sheep. Act of February 20, 1895, sec. 5, 28 Stat. 677, 678.

[185] *Cf.* Treaty of September 24, 1857, with the Pawnee, Art. 4, 11 Stat. 729.

[186] Treaty of October 6, 1818, with the Miame Nation, Art. 5, 7 Stat. 189; *Cf.* Treaty of June 29, 1796, with the Creeks, Art. 8, 7 Stat. 56; Treaty of June 7, 1803, with the Delawares and others, Art. 3, 7 Stat. 74; Treaty of November 14, 1805, with the Creeks, Art. 4, 7 Stat. 96; Treaty of September 18, 1823, with the Floridas, Art. 6, 7 Stat. 224; Treaty of February 12, 1825, with the Creeks, Art. 7, 7 Stat. 237.

smith and such agricultural assistants as the President may deem expedient;[187] two boats,[188] horses, perogues and provisions;[189] rifles, guns, ammunition, etc., in compensation for homes left by Indians who were removed;[190] to each warrior removing, "a blanket, kettle, rifle gun, bullet moulds and nippers, and ammunition sufficient for hunting and defence, for one year," plus corn;[191] 200 cattle, 200 hogs, plus 2,000 pounds of iron, 1,000 pounds of steel and 1,000 pounds of tobacco annually, and the assistance of laborers;[192] the payment of annuities in the form of money, merchandise, provisions, or domestic animals, at the option of the Indians;[193] the building of houses for chiefs;[194] mills and millers for a period of 3 years;[195] annuities and money for the repair of mill and schoolhouse;[196] the building of a church and an allowance for a Catholic priest.[197]

The United States agreed in treaties with most of the tribes to pay annuities in various forms: for education, blacksmiths, farmers, laborers, millers, millwrights, iron, coal, steel, salt, agricultural implements, tobacco, and transportation.[198]

Many treaties contained clauses providing for additional annuities,[199] or for the commutation of annuities,[200] or for presents and annuities,[201] and goods,[202] rations,[203] and clothing.[204]

By treaties, the United States also agreed to make payments to enable the raising of a tribal corps of light horse;[205] to pay a state for a balance due by a tribe;[206] to provide money for poor Indians;[207] to pay demands for slaves and other property alleged to have been stolen by the Indians;[208] to pay debts or other obligations owed by the nation;[209] to pay the Indians for land ceded to a state;[210] for expenses incurred by the sachem and headmen in attending to tribal business for 5 years;[211] "to indemnify the individuals of the Cherokee nation for losses sustained by them in consequence of the march of the militia and other troops in the service of the United States through that nation * * *."[212]

D. JURISDICTION

1. *Criminal jurisdiction.*—Many treaties deal with the difficult political problems created by offenses of Indians against whites or whites against Indians.

Some of the earliest treaties adopt the rule usual in treaties between equals. Whites committing offenses within the Indian country against Indian laws are subjected to punishment by the Indian tribe, just as Indians committing offenses against state or federal laws outside the Indian country are subjected to punishment by state or federal courts.[213]

A number of treaties adopt a modified rule, similar to that found in treaties between the United States and various Oriental nations,[214] whereby the United States is granted jurisdiction over its citizens in the Indian country, to punish them for offenses they may commit, and the Indian tribe undertakes to deliver such offenders to agents of the Federal Government.[215]

Finally, a number of treaties confer upon the Federal Government authority to punish Indians who commit offenses against non-Indians even within the Indian country.[216]

Not until some time after the end of the treaty-making period did the Federal Government take the ultimate step of asserting jurisdiction over offenses committed by Indians against Indians within the Indian country.[217]

2. *Civil jurisdiction.*—Most treaties contain no express provisions on civil jurisdiction and therefore, by implication, confirm the rule that tribal law governs the members of the tribe within the Indian country, to the exclusion of state law.[218]

A few treaties, however, make explicit and emphatic the assurance that state laws will not be applied to the Indians. These clauses are usually found in treaties with tribes that have had sad experiences with state jurisdiction, and the intensity of Indian feeling on the subject is sometimes reflected in the language of the treaty. Thus the purpose of the Treaty of May 6, 1828, with the Cherokee Nation[219] is stated to be the securing to the Cherokees migrating westward of

> * * * *a permanent* home, and which shall, under the most solemn guarantee of the United States, be, and remain, theirs forever—a home that shall never, in all future time, be embarrassed by having extended around it the

[187] Treaty of September 24, 1819, with the Chippewas, Art. 8, 7 Stat. 203.

[188] Treaty of July 30, 1819, with the Kickapoos, Art. 8, 7 Stat. 200.

[189] Treaty of October 3, 1818, with the Delawares, Art. 3, 7 Stat. 188.

[190] Treaty of July 8, 1817, with the Cherokees, Art. 6, 7 Stat. 156.

[191] Treaty of October 18, 1820, with the Choctaws, Art. 5, 7 Stat. 210

[192] Treaty of October 23, 1826, with the Miamis, Art. 4, 7 Stat. 300.

[193] Treaty of June 2, 1825, with the Osages, Art. 8, 7 Stat. 240.

[194] Treaty of June 2, 1825, with the Osages, Art. 4, 7 Stat. 240. Also see Treaty of November 10, 1808, with the Osages, Art. 3, 7 Stat. 107.

[195] Treaty of December 2, 1794, with the Oneidas and others, Arts. 2 and 3, 7 Stat. 47. *Cf.* Treaty of January 7, 1806, with the Cherokees, Art. 2, 7 Stat. 101.

[196] Treaty of June 5, 1854, with the Miamis, Art. 18, 10 Stat. 1093.

[197] Treaty of August 13, 1803, with the Kaskaskias, Art. 3, 7 Stat. 78.

[198] Repts. of Committees, No. 474, 23d Cong., 1st sess., May 20, 1834, vol. IV (pp. 58–60), lists these as the most important, but contains references to other types. For examples, see Treaty of November 17, 1807, with the Ottoways and others, Art. 2, 7 Stat. 105; Treaty of August 5, 1826, with the Chippewas, Art. 6, 7 Stat. 290; Treaty of June 9, 1855, with the Walla-Wallas and others, Art. 4, 12 Stat. 945; Treaty of April 19, 1858, with the Yancton Sioux, Art. 4, 11 Stat. 743. Some treaties prohibited the use of annuities for the payment of debts of individuals. Treaty of November 18, 1854, with the Chastas and others, Art. 7, 10 Stat. 1122; Treaty of November 29, 1854, with the Umpquas and others, Art. 7, 10 Stat. 1125.

[199] The Treaty of December 30, 1805, with the Piankishaws, Art. 3, 7 Stat. 100, provided for annuities and added that "the United States may, at any time they shall think proper, divide the said annuity amongst the individuals of the said tribe." Also see Treaty of August 13, 1803, with the Kaskaskias, Art. 3, 7 Stat. 78.

[200] Treaty of November 17, 1807, with the Ottoways and others, Art. 3, 7 Stat. 105.

[201] Treaty of November 11, 1794, with the Six Nations, Art. 6, 7 Stat. 44. Also see Treaty of March 24, 1832, with the Creeks, Art. 13, 7 Stat. 366.

[202] Treaty of January 21, 1785, with the Wiandots and others, Art. 10 7 Stat. 16; Treaty of June 26, 1794, with the Cherokees, Art. 3, 7 Stat. 43; Treaty of December 29, 1835, with the Cherokees, Art. 18, 7 Stat. 478.

[203] Treaty of December 21, 1855, with the Molels, Art. 5, 12 Stat. 981.

[204] Treaty of May 7, 1868, with the Crows, Art. 9, 15 Stat. 649. Also see Treaty of May 10, 1868, with the Cheyennes and others, Art. 6, 15 Stat. 655. For some other types of provisions relating to annuities see Treaty of July 1, 1835, with the Caddo Nation and the State of Louisiana, Art. 4, 7 Stat. 470; Treaty of November 23, 1838, with the Creeks, Art. 6, 7 Stat. 574.

[205] Treaty of October 18, 1820, with the Choctaws, Art. 13, 7 Stat. 210.

[206] Treaty of January 8, 1821, with the Creeks, Art. 4, 7 Stat. 215.

[207] Treaty of October 23, 1826, with the Miamis, Art. 6, 7 Stat. 300.

[208] Treaty of May 9, 1832, with the Seminoles, Art. 6, 7 Stat. 368.

[209] Treaty of November 10, 1808, with the Osages, Art. 4, 7 Stat. 107.

[210] Treaty of March 22, 1816, with the Cherokees, Art. 2, 7 Stat. 138.

[211] Treaty of November 24, 1848, with the Stockbridge Indians, Art. 18, 9 Stat. 955.

[212] Treaty of March 22, 1816, with the Cherokees, Art. 5, 7 Stat. 139.

[213] See Chapter 1, sec. 3, fn. 48.

[214] See *e. g.*, Art. 21 of Treaty of July 3, 1844, with China, 8 Stat. 592, 596.

[215] See *e. g.*, Art. 6 of Treaty of August 24, 1818, with the Quapaw Tribe, 7 Stat. 176, 177. *Cf.* Treaty of May 15, 1846, with the Comanches and others, Art. 12, 9 Stat. 844, providing that any person introducing intoxicating liquors among these Indians "shall be punished according to the laws of the United States."

[216] See *e. g.*, Art. 9 of Treaty of January 21, 1785, with the Wiandots and others, 7 Stat. 16, 17; Art. 6 of Treaty of November 28, 1785, with the Cherokee, 7 Stat. 18.

[217] See Chapter 7, sec. 9; Chapter 18.

[218] See Chapter 7, secs. 1, 2.

[219] 7 Stat. 311. *Accord*: Art. 5 of Treaty of New Echota, December 29, 1835, with the Cherokee Tribe, 7 Stat. 478.

> lines, or placed over it the jurisdiction of a Territory or State, nor be pressed upon by the extension, in any way, of any of the limits of any existing Territory or State; * * *

Various other treaties contained similar pledges.[220] Some treaties contained specific guaranties against taxation.[221]

E. CONTROL OF TRIBAL AFFAIRS

From 1776 to 1849 we find no treaty provision which limits the powers of self-government of any tribe with respect to the internal affairs of the tribe. All limitations upon tribal power, during this period, are in some way related to intercourse with non-Indians. Even the sporadic treaty provisions authorizing allotment of tribal land either list, as part of the treaty itself, the individuals, or define the class of individuals, who are to receive allotments,[222] or provide for the issuance of patents by the authorities of the tribe.[223]

In the wake of the War with Mexico, several treaties were imposed upon tribes of the newly acquired territory in which the long-established distinction between internal and external affairs of the tribes was abandoned and the internal affairs of the tribes were declared subject to federal control.

The language contained in the Treaty of September 9, 1849, with the Navajo,[224] whereby that tribe agreed that the United States "shall, at its earliest convenience, designate, settle, and adjust their territorial boundaries, and pass and execute in their territory such laws as may be deemed conducive to the prosperity and happiness of said Indians"[225] is symptomatic rather than legally important. It symbolizes a tendency to disregard the national character of the Indian tribes, a tendency that was perhaps stimulated by the loose organization and backward culture of the Southwestern nomadic tribes.

A year later, in 1850, began a series of treaties by which various tribes undertook to abandon their tribal existence.[226]

In 1851, a new breadth of authority was conferred upon the executive branch of the Federal Government by such clauses as the following:

> Rules and regulations to protect the rights of persons and property among the Indians, parties of this Treaty, and adapted to their condition and wants, may be prescribed and enforced in such manner as the President or the Congress of the United States, from time to time, shall direct.

This provision, taken from the Treaty of July 23, 1851, with the See-see-toan (Sisseton) and Way-pay-toan (Wahpeton) Sioux,[227] was copied bodily in several later treaties.[228]

The most important breach in the scope of tribal self-government made by treaty was made in 1854 and thereafter, by those treaties which conferred upon the President power to allot tribal lands to individual Indians.[229]

Along with this encroachment upon the powers of the tribes to apportion rights in tribal land among the members of the tribe, there came other extensions of federal authority over the handling and distribution of tribal funds and other incidental matters.[230]

The Civil War brought new occasions for the use of federal power in tribal affairs as a result of conflicts between different factions of a tribe. The Treaty of June 14, 1866, provided for "a general amnesty of all past offences against the laws of the United States, committed by any member of the Creek Nation * * *" and "an amnesty for all past offences against their government, * * *."[231]

Thus during the last decade or so of the treaty-making period, the basis upon which treaties had been made was gradually undermined by successive specific encroachments upon the autonomy of various tribes.

[220] See, *e. g.*, Art. 14 of the Treaty of March 24, 1832, with the Creek Tribe, 7 Stat. 366, 368; Art. 11 of the Treaty of July 20, 1831, with the Wyandots, Senecas, and Shawnees, 7 Stat. 351, 353.

[221] For example, Treaty of September 29, 1817, with the Wyandots and others, Art. 15, 7 Stat. 160, 166.

[222] Treaty of August 9, 1814, with Creek Nation, 7 Stat. 120; Treaty of September 29, 1817, with the Wyandot, Seneca, Delaware, and other tribes, 7 Stat. 160.

[223] Treaty of November 6, 1838, with the Miami Tribe, 7 Stat. 569. And *cf.* Act of March 3, 1839, 5 Stat. 349 (Brothertown), providing for allotment by chiefs of tribe, who were to observe "the existing laws, customs, usages, or agreements of said tribe." *Accord:* Act of March 3, 1843, 5 Stat. 645 (Stockbridge).

[224] 9 Stat. 974.

[225] *Ibid.*, Art. 9. *Accord:* Art. 7 of Treaty of December 30, 1849, with the Utah Indians, 9 Stat. 984.

[226] Treaty of April 1, 1850, with the Wyandot Indians, 9 Stat. 987. And see Chapter 14, sec. 2.

[227] 10 Stat. 949, 950.

[228] *E. g.*, Treaty of August 5, 1851, with the Med-ay-wa-kan-toan, etc., Sioux, 10 Stat. 954.

[229] See Treaty of March 15, 1854, with the Ottoe and Missouria Indians, 10 Stat. 1038, and Treaty of March 16, 1854, with the Omaha Tribe, 10 Stat. 1043, discussed in sec. 4G, *infra*.

[230] See sec. 3B(5), *supra*.

[231] Art. 1, 14 Stat. 785. Also see Chapter 8, sec. 11. Also see the pre-Civil War Treaty of August 6, 1846, with the Cherokee Nation, "Treaty Party," and "Old Settlers," Art. 2, 9 Stat. 871, whereby the Cherokee Nation declared a general amnesty for all past offenses after a period of civil strife, and agreed to a bill of rights.

SECTION 4. A HISTORY OF INDIAN TREATIES

A. PRE-REVOLUTIONARY PRECEDENTS: 1532–1776

First mention of the necessity of a civilized nation treating with the Indian tribes to secure Indian consent to cessions of land or changes of political status[232] was made in 1532 by Franciscus de Victoria,[233] who had been invited by the Emperor of Spain to advise on the rights of Spain in the New World.

After considering in detail the argument that barbarians could not own land by reason of the sin of unbelief or other mortal sin, or by reason of "unsoundness of mind," Victoria reached the conclusion that:

> * * * the aborigines in question were true owners, before the Spaniards came among them, both from the public and the private point of view.[234]

Since the Indians were true owners, Victoria held, discovery could convey no title upon the Spaniards, for title by discovery can be justified only where property is ownerless.[235] Nor could Spanish title to Indian lands be validly based upon the divine rights of the Emperor or the Pope,[236] or upon the unbelief or sinfulness of the aborigines.[237] Thus, Victoria concluded, even the Pope had no right to partition the property of the Indians, and in the absence of a just war only the voluntary consent of the aborigines could justify the annexation of their territory.[238] No less than their property, the government of the aborigines was entitled to respect by the Spaniards, according to the view of Victoria. So long as the Indians respected the natural rights of Spaniards, recognized by the law of nations, to travel in their

[232] Victoria, De Indis et De Jure Belli Relectiones (Trans. by John Pawley Bate, 1917), 1557, sec. 2, titles 6, 7.

[233] *Ibid.*, Introduction (Nys), p. 71.

[234] *Ibid.*, sec. 1, title 24, p. 128.

[235] *Ibid.*, sec. 2, p. 139.

[236] *Ibid.*, sec. 2, titles 1–6.

[237] *Ibid.*, sec. 2, titles 8–16.

[238] *Ibid.*

lands and to sojourn, trade, and defend their rights therein, the Spaniards could not wage a just war against the Indians,[239] and therefore could not claim any rights by conquest. In that situation, however, sovereign power over the Indians might be secured through the consent of the Indians themselves.

> Another possible title is by true and voluntary choice, as if the Indians, aware alike of the prudent administration and the humanity of the Spaniards, were of their own motion, both rulers and ruled, to accept the King of Spain as their sovereign. This could be done and would be a lawful title, by the law natural too, seeing that a State can appoint any one it will to be its lord, and herefor the consent of all is not necessary, but the consent of the majority suffices. For, as I have argued elsewhere, in matters touching the good of the State the decisions of the majority bind even when the rest are of a contrary mind; otherwise naught could be done for the welfare of the State, it being difficult to get all of the same way of thinking. Accordingly, if the majority of any city or province were Christians and they, in the interests of the faith and for the common weal, would have a prince who was a Christian, I think that they could elect him even against the wishes of the others and even if it meant the repudiation of other unbelieving rulers, and I assert that they could choose a prince not only for themselves, but for the whole State, just as the Franks for the good of their State changed their sovereigns and, deposing Childeric, put Pepin, the father of Charlemagne, in his place, a change which was approved by Pope Zacharias. This, then, can be put forward as a sixth title.[240]

The Emperors of Spain and their subordinate administrators, like many able administrators since, did not consistently carry out Fra Victoria's legal advice. They did, however, adopt many laws and issue many charters recognizing and guaranteeing the rights of Indian communities,[241] and the theory of Indian title put forward by Victoria came to be generally accepted by writers on international law of the sixteenth, seventeenth, and eighteenth centuries who were cited as authorities in early federal litigation on Indian property rights.[242]

The idea that land should be acquired from Indians by treaty involved three assumptions: (1) That both parties to the treaty are sovereign powers; (2) that the Indian tribe has a transferable title, of some sort, to the land in question; and (3) that the acquisition of Indian lands could not safely be left to individual colonists but must be controlled as a governmental monopoly. These three principles are embodied in the "New Project of Freedoms and Exemptions," drafted about 1630 for the guidance of officials of the Dutch West India Co., which declares:

> The Patroons of New Netherland, shall be bound to purchase from the Lords Sachems in New Netherland, the soil where they propose to plant their Colonies, and shall acquire such right thereunto as they will agree for with the said Sachems.[243]

The Dutch viewpoint was shared by some of the early English settlers. In the spring of 1636, Roger Williams, who insisted that the right of the natives to the soil could not be abrogated by an English patent, founded the Rhode Island Plantations.[244] This was the territory inhabited by the Narragansetts and for which Williams had treated.

From time to time other British colonies became parties to treaties with the Indians.[245] Unauthorized treating for the purchase of Indian land by individual colonists was prohibited in Rhode Island as early as 1651.[246] By the middle of the eighteenth century, eight other colonies had laws forbidding such purchase unless approved by the constituted authorities.[247] The effect of such laws was to eliminate conflicts of land titles that otherwise resulted from overlapping grants by individual Indians or tribes, to protect the Indians, in some measure, against fraud, and to center in the colonial governments a valuable monopoly.

With the outbreak of the French and Indian War the problem of dealing with the natives which had been left largely to the individual colonies was temporarily returned to the control of the mother country.[248] Later, treaties with the Indians were again negotiated by the colonies.[249]

On several occasions the Crown indicated its belief in the sanctity of treaty obligations.[250] Some of the treaties contained definite stipulations regarding land tenure.[251]

B. THE REVOLUTIONARY WAR AND THE PEACE: 1776–83

From the first days of the organization of the Continental Congress great solicitude for the natives was evidenced. The Congress pledged itself to unusual exertions in securing and preserving the friendship of the Indian nations.[252] First fruit of this effort was the treaty of alliance with the Delaware Indians of September 17, 1778.[253] Its provisions are so significant that Chief Justice Marshall's analysis in this respect should be noted:

> The first treaty was made with the Delawares, in September 1778. The language of equality in which it is drawn, evinces the temper with which the negotiation was undertaken, and the opinion which then prevailed in the United States. * * * 6. The sixth article is entitled to peculiar attention, as it contains a disclaimer of designs which were, at that time, ascribed to the United States, by their enemies, and from the imputation of which congress was then peculiarly anxious to free the government. It is in these words: "Whereas, the enemies of the United States have endeavored, by every artifice in their power, to possess the Indians in general with an opinion, that it is the design of the states aforesaid to extirpate the Indians, and take possession of their country; to obviate such false suggestion, the United States do engage to guaranty to the aforesaid nation of Delawares, and their heirs, all their terri-

[239] *Ibid.*, sec. 8, title 1, *et seq.*

[240] *Ibid.*, sec. 3, title 16, p. 159.

[241] See Chapter 20, sec. 1.

[242] Victoria, *supra*, Introduction (Nys). See also Vattel, Le Droit des Gens, vol. 1, bk. 1, c. 18, sec. 209, and other authorities cited by counsel for both parties in *Johnson* v. *McIntosh*, 8 Wheat. 543 (1823). And see Chapter 15, sec. 4.

[243] J. R. Brodhead, Documents Relative to the Colonial History of the State of New York (Holland Documents II, No. 27) (1855, O'Callaghan ed.), vol. 1, p. 99.

[244] Kinney, A Continent Lost—A Civilization Won (1937), pp. 11–12.

[245] In Pennsylvania, in advance of settlement, William Penn sent several commissioners to confer with the Indians and conclude with them a treaty of peace (18th Annual Report, Bureau of Ethnology, 1896–97, pt. II, pp. 591–599). Also see Chapter 15, sec. 4.

[246] Kinney, *op. cit.*, p. 14. As early as 1609 English colonists in Virginia purchased land directly from the Indians in that territory. (P. 12.)

[247] *Ibid.* The colonies were Massachusetts, Virginia, New Jersey, Pennsylvania, Maryland, North Carolina, South Carolina, and Georgia.

[248] Mohr, Federal Indian Relations (1933), pp. 4–9.

[249] See, for example, the Treaty of Hard Labor on October 14, 1768, which defined the boundary of Virginia, and the Treaty of Fort Stanwix, November 5, 1768, defining the boundary of the northern district (Mohr, *op. cit.*, pp. 9–10).

[250] See, *e. g.*, *Worcester* v. *Georgia*, 6 Pet. 515, 546, 548 (1832).

[251] In 1783 Sir John Johnson, prominent representative of the British Government, referring to the boundaries established by the treaty of peace with the United States of that year, told the Six Nations:

> You are not to believe or even think that by the line which has been described it was meant to deprive you of an extent of country of which the right of soil belongs to you and is in yourselves as sole proprietors as far as the boundary line agreed upon [by treaty of 1768] and established in the most solemn and public manner in the presence and with the consent of the governors and commissioners deputed by the different colonies for that purpose * * *. (Mohr, *op. cit.*, p. 118.)

[252] Jour. Cont. Cong. (Library of Congress ed.) 1775, vol. II, p. 174.

[253] Treaty of September 17, 1778, 7 Stat. 13.

torial rights, in the fullest and most ample manner, as it hath been bounded by former treaties, as long as the said Delaware nation shall abide by, and hold fast the chain of friendship now entered into" The parties further agree, that other tribes, friendly to the interest of the United States, may be invited to form a state, whereof the Delaware nation shall be the heads, and have a representation in congress This treaty, in its language, and in its provisions, is formed, as near as may be, on the model of treaties between the crowned heads of Europe. The sixth article shows how congress then treated the injurious calumny of cherishing designs unfriendly to the political and civil rights of the Indians "[254]

Articles 4 and 5 are also noteworthy By Article 4, any offenders of either party against the treaty of peace and friendship were not to be punished, except

> * * * by imprisonment, or any other competent means, till a fair and impartial trial can be had by judges or juries of both parties, as near as can be to the laws, customs and usages of the contracting parties and natural justice * * *

Article 5 [255] provided for a

> * * * well-regulated trade, under the conduct of an intelligent, candid agent, with an adequate sallery, one more influenced by the love of his country, and a constant attention to the duties of his department by promoting the common interest, than the sinister purposes of converting and binding all the duties of his office to his private emolument * * *

C. DEFINING A NATIONAL POLICY: 1783–1800

Following the close of the Revolutionary War the United States entered into a series of treaties with Indian tribes by which the "hatchet" was "forever buried" [256]

In the spring of 1784 Congress appointed commissioners to negotiate with the Indians Full power was given them to draw boundary lines and conclude a peace, with the understanding that they would make clear that the Indian territory was forfeit as a result of the military victory [257] This idea was not novel General Washington, on September 7, 1783, had expressed himself as agreeable to regarding the territory held by the Indians as "conquered provinces," although opposed to driving them from the country altogether [258] The commissioners met at Fort Stanwix and on October 22 concluded a treaty with the hostile tribes of the Six Nations.[259] In the opening paragraph the United States receives the Indians "into their protection." This has been cited as the source of the concept of the Federal Government as the guardian of Indian tribes [260]

Article 2 provides that the "Oneida and Tuscarora Nations shall be secured in the possession of the lands on which they are settled" [261]

Article 4 orders

> * * * goods to be delivered to the said Six Nations for their use and comfort

Thus began a practice which later developed into a comprehensive system of supplying promised goods and services to Indian tribes [262]

Soon afterwards another treaty was agreed upon with the Wiandots, Delawares, Chippawas, and Ottawas at Fort McIntosh on January 21, 1785 [263] The next year the Shawnee chiefs signed a treaty at the mouth of the Miami [264] These three treaties, which are the only ones entered into with the northern tribes before the adoption of the Constitution, are very similar in nature All of them recite the conclusion of hostilities and the extension of the protective influence of the United States [265]

In the Treaty of January 21, 1785, at Fort McIntosh,[266] and the Treaty of January 31, 1786, at the Miami,[267] the boundaries between the Indian nations and the United States are defined and the lands therein are allotted to the said nations to live and hunt on, with the provision that if any citizen of the United States should attempt to settle on their territory, he would forfeit the protection of the United States [268] In addition both treaties [269] provided for the return to the United States of Indian robbers and murderers In the treaty with the Shawnees [270] there is a similar provision with regard to United States offenders against the Indians

Congress was slower in taking action regarding the southern tribes It was not until March 15, 1785,[271] that a resolution was

---

[254] *Worcester* v *Georgia*, 6 Pet 515, 548, 549 (1832) See also Art 12 Treaty with the Cherokees of November 28, 1785, 7 Stat 18, discussed below, which granted to the Cherokees the right to send a deputy of their own choice to Congress whenever they think fit. This, however, was never carried into effect See also sec 3B(3), *supra*

[255] See Chapter 4, sec 2, and Chapter 16

[256] The phrase appears in the Treaties at Hopewell with the Cherokees November 28, 1785, Art 13, 7 Stat. 18, with the Choctaws, January 3 1786, Art 11, 7 Stat 21, and with the Chickasaws, January 10 1786 Art. 11, 7 Stat. 24.

This phrase was later supplanted by the phrase "all animosities for past grievances shall henceforth cease" See fn 288, *infra* As the disturbances caused by the Revolutionary War settled, this phrase disappeared

[257] Mohr, *op cit*, p. 108. In 1786 the Continental Congress, through its chairman, David Ramsay, again tried to make it clear, this time to the Seneca Indian, Cornplanter, that

> * * * the United States alone possess the sovereign power within the limits described at the late Treaty of peace between them and the King of England, * * * You may also assure the Indians that they tell lies, who say that the King of England has not in his late Treaty with the United States given up, to them the lands of the Indians (Jour Cont Cong, Library of Congress ed, 1786, vol XXX, p 286)

[258] 10 Ford, Washington Writings, vol X (1891), pp. 303–312

[259] Treaty of October 22, 1784, 7 Stat 15 The Treaty was construed in *New York Indians*, 5 Wall 761 (1866) and in *Commonwealth* v *Coxe*, 4 Dall 170 (1800)

[260] *United States* v *Douglas*, 190 Fed 482 (C C A 8, 1911)

[261] An illuminating statement regarding title claimed under the Treaty of Fort Stanwix is found in *Deere* v *State of New York*, 22 F 2d 851 (D C N D N. Y 1927):

> * * * The source of title here is not letters patent or other form of grant by the federal government Here the Indians claim immemorial rights, arising prior to white occupation, and recognized and protected by treaties between Great Britain and the United States and between the United States and the Indians By the treaty of 1784 between the United States and the Six Nations of Indians, and the treaty of 1796 between the United States, the state of New York and the Seven Nations of Canada, the right of occupation of the lands in question by the St Regis Indians, was not granted, but recognized and confirmed (P 851)

[262] See, for a similar provision, the Treaty of Fort McIntosh with the Wiandots, Delawares, etc, January 21, 1785, 7 Stat 16

[263] Treaty of January 21, 1785, 7 Stat 16. By this treaty the United States Supreme Court states, in *Jones* v. *Meehan*, 175 U S 1 (1899)

> * * * the United States relinquished and quitclaimed to the said nations respectively all the lands lying within certain limits, to live and hunt upon, and otherwise occupy as they saw fit; but the said nations, or either of them, were not to be at liberty to dispose of those lands, except to the United States * * * (P 9)

See also *Commonwealth* v *Coxe*, 4 Dall 170 (1800)

[264] Treaty of January 31, 1786, 7 Stat 26.

[265] The Fort McIntosh treaty in its 10th article introduces a technique of giving presents upon the signing of the instrument which is soon to become standard practice in negotiating agreements with the Indians Also to be noticed is the reserving for the first time of land within Indian boundaries for establishment of United States trading posts which is provided in Article 4 of the same treaty

[266] Arts. 3, 4, 5, 7 Stat 16

[267] Arts 6, 7, 7 Stat 26.

[268] For a discussion of the significance of this stipulation see Treaty of July 2, 1791, with the Cherokees, 7 Stat 39; and fn. 294 and 295, *infra*.

[269] Art. 9, 7 Stat 16; Art. 3, 7 Stat 26

[270] Art 8, Treaty of January 31, 1786, 7 Stat 26 The Treaties at Hopewell, *infra*, contain a similar provision with the Cherokee, November 28, 1785, Art 7, 7 Stat. 18; the Choctaw, January 3, 1786, Art 6, 7 Stat 21, the Chickasaw, January 10, 1786, Art 6, 7 Stat. 24

[271] Jour Cont. Cong (Library of Congress ed), 1785, vol XXVIII, pp 160–162.

passed for the appointment of commissioners to deal with the Indian nations in the southern part of the country

The federal commissioners met with the Cherokees at Hopewell on the Keowee, and concluded a treaty on November 28 1785,[273] which declared that the United States "* * * give peace to all the Cherokees, and receive them into the favour and protection of the United States of America, on the following conditions" In *Worcester* v *Georgia*,[274] Chief Justice Marshall gave the following answer to the argument that this language put the Indians in an inferior status

> * * * When the United States gave peace, did they not also receive it? Were not both parties desirous of it? If we consult the history of the day, does it not inform us, that the United States were at least as anxious to obtain it as the Cherokees? We may ask further, did the Cherokees come to the seat of the American government to solicit peace, or, did the American commissioners go to them to obtain it? The treaty was made at Hopewell, not at New York The word "give", then, has no real importance attached to it

Marshall, at the same time, also called attention to Article 3 of the Hopewell agreement which acknowledges the Cherokees to be under the protection of no other power but the United States, saying [275]

> The general law of European sovereigns, respecting their claims in America, limited the intercourse of Indians, in a great degree, to the particular potentate whose ultimate right of domain was acknowledged by the others This was the general state of things, in time of peace It was sometimes changed in war The consequence was, that their supplies were derived chiefly from that nation, and their trade confined to it Goods, indispensable to their comfort, in the shape of presents, were received from the same hand What was of still more importance, the strong hand of government was interposed to restrain the disorderly and licentious from intrusions into their country, from encroachments on their lands, and from those acts of violence which were often attended by reciprocal murder The Indians perceived in this protection only what was beneficial to themselves—an engagement to punish aggressions on them It involved, practically, no claim to their lands—no dominion over their persons It merely bound the nation to the British crown, as a dependent ally, claiming the protection of a powerful friend and neighbor, and receiving the advantages of that protection without involving a surrender of their national character This is the true meaning of the stipulation, and is, undoubtedly, the sense in which it was made

Article 9 of the Hopewell treaty with the Cherokees holds that

> * * * the United States in Congress assembled shall have the sole and exclusive right of regulating the trade with the Indians, and managing all their affairs in such manner as they think proper

In *Worcester* v *Georgia* it was argued that in this article the Indians had surrendered control over their internal affairs This interpretation was vigorously rejected by the Supreme Court

> To construe the expression "managing all their affairs," into a surrender of self-government, would be, we think, a perversion of their necessary meaning, and a departure from the construction which has been uniformly put on them The great subject of the article is the Indian trade, the influence it gave, made it desirable that congress should possess it. The commissioners brought forward the claim, with the profession that their motive was "the benefit and comfort of the Indians, and the prevention of injuries or oppressions" This may be true, as respects the regulation of their trade, and as respects the regulation of all affairs connected with their trade, but cannot be true, as respects the management of all their affairs The most important of these are the cession of their lands and security against intruders on them Is it credible, that they should have considered themselves as surrendering to the United States the right to dictate their future cessions, and the terms on which they should be made? or to compel their submission to the violence of disorderly and licentious intruders? It is equally inconceivable that they could have supposed themselves, by a phrase thus slipped into an article, on another and most interesting subject, to have divested themselves of the right of self-government on subjects not connected with trade Such a measure could not be "for their benefit and comfort," or for "the prevention of injuries and oppression" Such a construction would be inconsistent with the spirit of this and of all subsequent treaties, especially of those articles which recognise the right of the Cherokees to declare hostilities, and to make war It would convert a treaty of peace, covertly, into an act annihilating the political existence of one of the parties Had such a result been intended, it would have been openly avowed [276]

Article 12, permitting Cherokee representation in Congress, is of particular interest, although it was never fulfilled [277]

During the last year of the Confederation the dissatisfaction among the Indians resulting from using the "conquered province" concept as the basis for treaty deliberations became apparent The Secretary of War, therefore, on May 2, 1788,[278] recommended a change in policy which would permit the outright purchase of the soil of the western territories described in former treaties with such additions as might be affected by further negotiations [279] Acting on this suggestion, Congress appropriated $20,000 00 on July 2, 1788,[280] which, together with the balance remaining from the sum allocated on October 22, 1787,[281] was earmarked for use in extinguishing Indian claims to land already ceded

The immediate result of this step were the treaties of Fort Harmar with the Wiandot, Delaware, Chippewa, and Ottawa, Indians,[282] and with the Six Nations, entered into early in 1789,[283] which reaffirmed many of the original terms of the Fort Stanwix and Fort McIntosh treaties Both of these agreements provide for the United States relinquishing and quitclaiming certain described territory to the Indian nations However, article 3 of the Fort Harmar treaty with the Wyandots, Delawares, Chippewas, and Ottawas,[284] added that the said nations should not be at liberty

> * * * to sell or dispose of the same, or any part thereof, to any sovereign power, except the United States, nor to the subjects or citizens of any other sovereign power, nor to the subjects or citizens of the United States

Article 7 also provided for the opening up of trade with Indians, establishing a system of licensing with guaranties of protection to certified traders, and a promise by the Indians to apprehend and deliver to the United States those individuals who intrude themselves without such authority Article 6 makes first mention of depredations, and binds both parties to a method of handling claims arising therefrom.

Although the Fort Harmar conferences were held during the life of the Confederation, the report of the results obtained was received in the first months of the new government operating

[273] 7 Stat 18

[274] 6 Pet. 515, 551 (1832)

[275] *Ibid*, p 551

[276] Ibid, pp 553–554

[277] See Art 6, Treaty with the Delawares of September 17, 1778, 7 Stat 13, and fn 254, *supra*

[278] Mohr, *op cit*, p 132

[279] *Ibid*

[280] *Ibid*

[281] *Ibid*

[282] Treaty of January 9, 1789, 7 Stat 28

[283] Treaty of January 9, 1789 (unratified), 7 Stat 33 See also fn 263 *supra*, for interpretation of this treaty in *Jones* v *Meehan*, 175 U S 1, 9 (1899)

[284] Treaty of January 9, 1789, 7 Stat 28.

under the Constitution, and transmitted to the Senate of the United States on May 25, 1789, for its approval.[284]

Puzzled over the proper procedure, George Washington wrote to the Senate asking what it meant by advising him to "execute and enjoin" the observance of the treaties.

> It is said to be the general understanding and practice of nations, as a check on the mistakes and indiscretions of ministers or commissioners, not to consider any treaty negotiated and signed by such officers, as final and conclusive, until ratified by the sovereign or government from whom they derive their powers. This practice has been adopted by the United States respecting their treaties with European nations, and I am inclined to think it would be advisable to observe it in the conduct of our treaties with the Indians. * * *[285]

Not unmindful of the significance of the ratification of Indian treaties, the Senate appointed a special committee to investigate the matter. After several days of debate the Senate advised formal ratification.[286]

On August 22, 1789, George Washington appeared in the Senate Chamber to point out to the assembled group the gravity of the Indian situation in the South. North Carolina and Georgia, the President said, had not only protested against the treaties of Hopewell but had disregarded them. Moreover, open hostilities existed between Georgia and the Creek Nation. All of this, the President continued, involved so many complications that he wished to raise particular issues for the "advice and consent" of the Senate. Accordingly, he put seven questions which resulted in instructions to deal with the Creek situation first and, if need be, to use the whole amount of the current appropriation for Indian treaties for this purpose.[287]

On August 7, 1790, articles of agreement were concluded between the President of the United States and the kings, chiefs, and warriors of the Creek Nation.[288] Article 5 is a solemn guarantee to the Creeks of all their lands within certain described limits. Article 7 stipulated that—

> No citizen or inhabitant of the United States shall attempt to hunt or destroy the game on the Creek lands: Nor shall any such citizen or inhabitant go into the Creek country, without a passport first obtained from the Governor of some one of the United States. * * *

The obligation thus assumed by treaty the United States proceeded to implement in section 2 of the Indian Intercourse Act of May 19, 1796,[289] which made it a criminal offense for strangers to hunt, trap, or drive livestock in the Indian country.

It was found necessary to attach secret articles providing for transportation of merchandise duty free into the Creek Nation by the United States in the event of hostilities between the Creeks and Spaniards.[290]

In Article 5 of the secret treaty, the United States, for the first time,

> * * * agree to educate and clothe such of the Creek youth as shall be agreed upon, not exceeding four in number at any one time.[291]

In the following year, 1791, the commissioners turned their attention to the difficulties between the Cherokees and the State of Georgia. Finally, on July 2, near the junction of the Holston River and the French Broad, the Cherokee Nation abandoned its claims to certain territories in return for $1,000 annuity.[292] The instrument signed on that occasion was well described by the court in *Worcester* v. *Georgia:*

> The third article contains a perfectly equal stipulation for the surrender of prisoners. The fourth article declares, that "the boundary between the United States and the Cherokee nation shall be as follows, beginning," etc. We hear no more of "allotments" or of "hunting-grounds." A boundary is described, between nation and nation, by mutual consent. The national character of each—the ability of each to establish this boundary, is acknowledged by the other. To preclude forever all disputes, it is agreed, that it shall be plainly marked by commissioners, to be appointed by each party; and in order to extinguish forever all claims of the Cherokees to the ceded lands, an additional consideration is to be paid by the United States. For this additional consideration, the Cherokees release all right to the ceded land, forever. By the fifth article, the Cherokees allow the United States a road through their country, and the navigation of the Tennessee river. The acceptance of these cessions is an acknowledgment of the right of the Cherokees to make or withhold them. By the sixth article, it is agreed, on the part of the Cherokees, that the United States shall have the sole and exclusive right of regulating their trade. No claim is made to the management of all their affairs. This stipulation has already been explained. The observation may be repeated, that the stipulation is itself an admission of their right to make or refuse it. By the seventh article, the United States solemnly guaranty to the Cherokee nation all their lands not hereby ceded. The eighth article relinquishes to the Cherokees any citizens of the United States who may settle on their lands; and the ninth forbids any citizen of the United States to hunt on their lands, or to enter their country without a passport. The remaining articles are equal, and contain stipulations which could be made only with a nation admitted to be capable of governing itself.[293]

This treaty of July 2, 1791, again includes a provision (Article 8) noticed before, viz: that any citizen settling on Indian land "* * * shall forfeit the protection of the United States, and the Cherokees may punish him or not, as they please."[294] This

[284] The Debates and Proceedings in the Congress of the United States (1789–90), vol. 1, pp. 40–41. (Hereinafter referred to as Debates and Proceedings.)

[285] *Ibid.*, p. 83.

[286] *Ibid.*, p. 84. It is interesting to note that the committee report (p. 82) which was rejected drew a distinction between treaties with European powers and treaties with the aborigines insisting that solemnities were not necessary in the latter case.

[287] *Ibid.*, pp. 66–71. Washington asked the Senate "* * * if all offers should fail to induce the Creeks to make the desired cessions to Georgia, shall the Commissioners make it an ultimatum." (P. 70.) The Senate answered "No." (P. 71.)

[288] 7 Stat. 35. A recital often found in Indian treaties is the following, which appears in Art. 13: "All animosities for past grievances shall henceforth cease." (See also Treaty of July 2, 1791, Art. 15, 7 Stat. 39; Treaty of June 29, 1796, Art. 9, 7 Stat. 56.) It should be further noted that Art. 2 pledges the Creeks to refrain from treating with any individual State, or the individuals of any State. *Patterson* v. *Jenks*, 2 Pet. 216 (1829), construes provisions of this treaty relative to grants of land within the territorial limits of the State of Georgia.

[289] 1 Stat. 469.

[290] Treaty of August 7, 1790, Archives No. 17, Debates and Proceedings, vol. 1, p. 1029 (*supra*, fn. 284).

The Creek Treaty was amended on June 29, 1796, by a treaty which among other things provided that the United States give to the Creek Nation "goods to the value of six thousand dollars, and * * * send to the Indian nation, two blacksmiths, with strikers, to be employed for the upper and lower Creeks with the necessary tools." Art. 8, Treaty of June 29, 1796, 7 Stat. 56.

[291] See Art. 3, Treaty with the Kaskaskias, August 13, 1803, 7 Stat. 78, *infra*, for the first contribution by the United States for organized education in the support of a priest "* * * to instruct * * * in the rudiments of literature." See also Chapter 12, sec. 2.

[292] Art. 4, Treaty of July 2, 1791, 7 Stat. 39. This sum was increased later to $1,500 by the Treaty at Philadelphia of February 17, 1792, 7 Stat. 42. The Holston Treaty was further amended by the Treaty of Tellico of October 2, 1798, 7 Stat. 62, construed in *Preston* v. *Browder*, 1 Wheat. 115 (1816); *Lattimer* v. *Poteet*, 14 Pet. 4, 13 (1840).

[293] *Worcester* v. *Georgia*, 6 Pet. 515, 555–556 (1832).

[294] See fn. 268 *supra*. A similar provision appears in the Treaties of January 21, 1785, with the Wiandots, Delawares, Chippawas, and Otta-

article, the court in *Raymond* v. *Raymond* [295] cites as the basis for the lack of jurisdiction of the federal judiciary in suits between members of the Cherokee Nation, saying:

> It is not material to the present issue that this provision has been subsequently modified. It shows, as do subsequent treaties, that for more than a century this tribe of Indians had claimed and exercised, and the United States have guarantied and secured to it, the exclusive right to regulate its local affairs, to govern and protect the persons and property of its own people, and of those who join them, and to adjudicate and determine their reciprocal rights and duties. * * * (P. 722.)

Despite efforts at conciliation, dissatisfaction was spreading among the Indian tribes. Word was received that the Indians of the Northwest Territory were preparing to cooperate with the Six Nations in a major war. Washington dispatched instructions to Colonel Pickering to hold a council with the Six Nations. At the same time preparations were made to take military action on the western frontier and General Wayne, a Revolutionary War veteran, was put in charge of the troops, who on August 20, 1794, routed the natives in the battle of Fallen Timbers.

A new treaty was made with the Six Nations on November 11, 1794.[296] In this agreement the lands belonging to the Oneidas, Onondagas, Cayugas, and Senecas were described and acknowledged by the United States as the property of the aforementioned Indian nations and in addition the United States pledged to add the sum of $3,000 to the $1,500 annuity already allowed by the Treaty of April 23, 1792,[297] with the Five Nations.

Shortly thereafter, a treaty [298] was concluded with the nations which had participated in the ill-fated expedition against General Wayne. This agreement provides for the cession of an immensely important area which today comprises most of the State of Ohio and a portion of Indiana. At the same time the United States stipulates (Article 5):

> The Indian tribes who have a right to those lands, are quietly to enjoy them, hunting, planting, and dwelling thereon so long as they please, without any molestation from the United States; but when those tribes, or any of them, shall be disposed to sell their lands, or any part of them, they are to be sold only to the United States; and until such sale, the United States will protect all the said Indian tribes in the quiet enjoyment of their lands against all citizens of the United States, and against all other white persons who intrude upon the same.

The exact meaning of this recital was at issue in *Williams* v. *City of Chicago*. After examining the instrument in detail the court held:

> * * * We think it entirely clear that this treaty did not convey a fee simple title to the Indians; that under it no tribe could claim more than the right of continued occupancy; and that when this was abandoned all legal right or interest which both tribe and its members had in the territory came to an end. * * * [299] (Pp. 437–438.)

The Seven Nations of Canada on May 31, 1796,[300] released all territorial claims within the State of New York, with the exception of a tract of land 6 miles square.[301]

D. EXTENDING THE NATIONAL DOMAIN: 1800–17

By 1800 the rapid growth of the nation had given impetus to the drive to add to the territory under federal ownership. This could be done effectively by extinguishing native title to desired lands. The treaty makers of this period may be said to have had a single objective—the acquisition of more land.

Success in this direction was almost immediate and by 1803 the President of the United States was able to report to Congress:

> The friendly tribe of Kaskaskia Indians * * * has transferred its country to the United States, reserving only for its members what is sufficient to maintain them in an agricultural way. * * * This country, among the most fertile within our limits, extending along the Mississippi from the mouth of the Illinois to and up the Ohio, though not so necessary as a barrier since the acquisition of the other bank, may yet be well worthy of being laid open to immediate settlement, as its inhabitants may descend with rapidity in support of the lower country, should future circumstances expose that to foreign enterprise.[302]

Article 3 of the Kaskaskia treaty [303] contains the first provision for contributions by the United States for organized education,[304] for the erection of a new church,[305] and for the building of a house for the chief as a gift.[306]

The Indians pledge themselves to refrain from waging war or giving any insult or offense to any other Indian tribe or to any foreign nation without first having obtained the approbation and consent of the United States (Art. 2). The United States in turn take the tribe under their immediate care and patronage, and guarantee a protection similar to that enjoyed by their own citizens. The United States also reserve the right to divide the annuity promised to the tribe "* * * amongst the several families thereof, reserving always a suitable sum for the great chief and his family." (Art. 4.)

President Jefferson selected William Henry Harrison, Governor of Indiana Territory, to represent the United States Government in its negotiations with the Indian tribes of the West.[307]

After protracted negotiations at Fort Wayne with the Delawares, Shawnees, and other tribes of the Northwest Territory, a substantial cession of territory was secured by the Treaty of June 7, 1803.[308]

An interesting provision is found in Article 3, whereby the United States guaranteed to deliver to the Indians annually salt

---

was, Art. 5, 7 Stat. 16; November 28, 1785, with the Cherokees, Art. 5, 7 Stat. 18; January 3, 1786, with the Choctaws, Art. 4, 7 Stat. 21; January 10, 1786, with the Chickasaws, Art. 4, 7 Stat. 24; January 31, 1786, with the Shawnees, Art. 7, 7 Stat. 26; January 9, 1789, with the Wiandots, Delawares, Chippewas, and Ottawas, Art. 9, 7 Stat. 28; August 7, 1790, with the Creeks, Art. 6, 7 Stat. 35; August 3, 1795, with the Wyandots, Delawares, Chipewas, Ottawas, etc., Art. 6, 7 Stat. 49. See also Chapter 1, sec. 3.

[295] *Raymond* v. *Raymond*, 83 Fed. 721 (C. C. A. 8, 1897).

[296] 7 Stat. 44. An earlier treaty had been concluded October 22, 1784, 7 Stat. 15.

[297] Unpublished treaty (Archives No. 19).

[298] Treaty with the Wyandots, Delawares, Shawanoes, etc., August 3, 1795, at Greenville, 7 Stat. 49. "The ratification of this treaty is to be considered as the *terminus a quo* a man might safely begin a settlement on the Western frontier of Pennsylvania." *Morris's Lessee* v. *Neighman*, 4 Dall. 209, 210 (1800). For provisions under this treaty relating to disposal of land by Indians see *Patterson* v. *Jenks*, fn. 288, *supra*. Chippewa Indians were treated as a single tribe in this treaty. *Chippewa Indians of Minnesota* v. *United States*, 301 U. S. 358 (1937).

[299] 242 U. S. 434 (1917).

[300] Treaty of May 31, 1796, 7 Stat. 55. "The 7 tribes signified are the Skighquan (Nipissing), Estjage (Saulteurs), Assisagh (Missisauga), Karhadage, Adgenauwe, Karrihaet, and Adirondax (Algonkins). The 4th, 5th, and 6th are unidentified." Bull. No. 30, Bureau of American Ethnology, Handbook of American Indians, pt. 2, p. 515.

[301] This tract was reserved for the Indians of St. Regis village, and is now the St. Regis Reservation. See Chapter 22, sec. 2C.

[302] Message of October 17, 1803, in Debates and Proceedings (1803–4), vol. 13, pp. 12–13.

[303] Treaty of August 13, 1803, 7 Stat. 78.

[304] See Unpublished Treaty of August 7, 1790 (Archives No. 17), fn. 290 *supra*, and Chapter 12, sec. 2.

[305] In 1794 the United States agreed to contribute $1,000 toward rebuilding a church for the Oneidas destroyed by the British in the Revolutionary War. Treaty of December 2, 1794, Art. 4, 7 Stat. 47.

[306] Gifts to the chief were continued in later treaties.

[307] Oskison, Tecumseh, and his Times (1938), p. 96.

[308] 7 Stat. 74. While certain commercial concessions have been noticed before this, for the first time the United States is granted (Art. 4) the

not to exceed 150 bushels from a salt spring which the Indians had ceded.

The next year another large area was secured from the Delawares.[309] In this treaty the United States expressly recognizes the Delaware Indians "as the rightful owners of all the country" specifically bounded (Art. 4).

Since the Piankishaw Tribe refused to recognize the title of the Delawares to the land ceded by this treaty,[310] Harrison negotiated a separate treaty.[311] It provided for land cessions and reserved the right to the United States of apportioning the annuity, "allowing always a due proportion for the chiefs." [312]

Harrison went to St. Louis to meet the chiefs of the Sacs and Foxes, and bargain for their land, which was rich in mineral deposits of copper and lead. There he succeeded in getting, on November 3, 1804,[313] as has been noted by his biographer Dawson, "the largest tract of land ever ceded in one treaty by the Indians since the settlement of North America * * *." [314]

In this agreement it is stipulated (Art. 8) that "the laws of the United States regulating trade and intercourse with the Indian tribes, are already extended to the country inhabited by the Saukes and Foxes." The tribes also promise to put an end (Art. 10) to the war which waged between them and the Great and Little Osages. Article 11 guarantees a safe and free passage through the Sac and Fox country to every person travelling under the authority of the United States.[315]

The conclusion of the treaty at St. Louis brings to an end for several years negotiations with the Indians of the West. However, treaty-making in other quarters continued and Jefferson was able to inform Congress in 1805:

> Since your last session, the northern tribes have sold [316] to us the land between the Connecticut Reserve and the former Indian boundary, and those on the Ohio, from the same boundary to the Rapids, and for a considerable depth inland. The Chickasaws and the Cherokees have sold [317] us the country between and adjacent to the two districts of Tennessee, and the Creeks [318] the residue of their lands in the fork of Ocumlgee up to the Ulcofauhatche. The three former purchases are important, inasmuch as they consolidate disjoined parts of our settled country, and render their intercourse secure; and the second particularly so, as, with the small point on the river, which we expect is by this time ceded by the Piankeshaws,[319] it completes our possession of the whole of both banks of the Ohio, from its source to near its mouth, and the navigation of that river is thereby rendered forever safe to our citizens settled and settling on its extensive waters. The purchase from the Creeks too has been for some time particularly interesting to the State of Georgia.[320]

A treaty negotiated with the Choctaws in November 16, 1805,[321] contained the first reservation of land for the use of individual Indians.[322]

Article 2 carries the significant provision of

> Forty eight thousand dollars to enable the Mingoes to discharge the debt due to their merchants and traders * * *.[323]

The treaty with the Great and Little Osages of November 10, 1808,[324] provided in addition to land cessions,[325] the pledge (Art. 12) that the Osages would not furnish "* * * any nation or tribe of Indians not in amity with the United States, with guns, ammunitions, or other implements of war."

In one of his last official messages to Congress on November 8, 1808, Jefferson observed:

> With our Indian neighbors the public peace has been steadily maintained. Some instances of individual wrong have, as at other times, taken place, but in no wise implicating the will of the nation. Beyond the Mississippi, the Iowas, the Sacs, and the Alabamas, have delivered up for trial and punishment individuals from among themselves, accused of murdering citizens of the United States. On this side of the Mississippi, the Creeks are exerting themselves to arrest offenders of the same kind; and the Choctaws have manifested their readiness and desire for amicable and just arrangements respecting depredations committed by disorderly persons of their tribe. * * * one of the two great divisions of the Cherokee nation have now under consideration to solicit the citizenship of the United States, and to be identified with us in laws and government, in such progressive manner as we shall think best.[326]

During this time there had come into power and influence among a great number of Indian tribes a Shawnee, Tecumseh, and his brother Laulewasikau called "The Prophet." When disturbing reports of the behavior of the two Shawnees reached Harrison, he resolved to press further before all Indian tribes were rendered unwilling to part with their land. Accordingly in September 1809, he convened the head men of the Delawares, Pottawatomies, Miamis, and Eel River Miamis and requested some 2,600,000 acres.[327] This they yielded.[328] A month later

---

right to locate three tracts of land as sites for houses of entertainment. However, if ferries are esablished in connection therewith, the Indians are to cross said ferries toll free.

Six other treaties which need not be examined at length were negotiated during the first years of Jefferson's Administration: Chickasaws, Treaty of October 24, 1801, 7 Stat. 65; Choctaws, Treaty of December 17, 1801, 7 Stat. 66; Creeks, Treaty of June 16, 1802, 7 Stat. 68; Senecas, Treaty of June 30, 1802, 7 Stat. 72; Choctaws, Treaty of October 17, 1802, 7 Stat. 73; Choctaws, Treaty of August 31, 1803, 7 Stat. 80. These included two treaties for the building of roads through Indian territory, two treaties relinquishing areas of land to private individuals under the sanction of the United States, and two treaties for running boundary lines in accordance with previous negotiations, and two treaties providing for cessions of territory to the United States.

[309] Treaty of August 18, 1804, 7 Stat. 81.

[310] See Art. 6, Treaty of August 18, 1804, with the Delawares, 7 Stat. 81.

[311] August 27, 1804, 7 Stat. 83.

[312] *Ibid.*, Art. 4.

[313] Treaty of November 3, 1804, 7 Stat. 84, construed in *Sac and Fox Indians of the Mississippi in Iowa* v. *Sac and Fox Indians of the Mississippi in Oklahoma*, 220 U. S. 481 (1911).

[314] Oskison, *op. cit.* p. 105.

[315] An additional article provided that under certain conditions grants of land from the Spanish Government, not included within the treaty boundaries should not be invalidated. This particular provision was given application in a decision by the Supreme Court of the United States in *Marsh* v. *Brooks*, 14 How. 513 (1852).

[316] Treaty with the Wyandots, Ottawas, etc., of July 4, 1805, 7 Stat. 87; Treaty with the Delawares, Pottawatimies, etc., of August 21, 1805, 7 Stat. 91. In this last-mentioned treaty the United States agreed to consider (Art. 4) the Miamis, Eel River, and Wea Indians as "joint owners" of a certain area of land and for the first time agreed not to purchase said land without the consent of each of said tribes. In early treaties the Chippewas were dealt with as a single tribe. *Chippewa Indians of Minnesota* v. *United States*, 301 U. S. 358 (1937).

[317] Treaty with the Chickasaws of July 23, 1805, 7 Stat. 89; Treaties with the Cherokees of October 25 and 27, 1805, 7 Stat. 93, 95.

[318] Treaty of November 14, 1805, 7 Stat. 96, construed in *Coffee* v. *Groover*, 123 U. S. 1, 14 (1887).

[319] Treaty of December 30, 1805, 7 Stat. 100.

[320] Message of December 3, 1805, in Debates and Proceedings (1805–7), vol. 15, p. 15.

[321] Treaty of November 16, 1805, 7 Stat. 98.

[322] *Ibid.*, Art. 1. A tract of land was reserved for the use of Alzira and Sophia, daughters of a white man and Choctaw woman.

[323] This is not the first time that allusion to the distressed financial situation of the Indians was made in a treaty. Both the Treaty with the Creeks, June 16, 1802, Art. 2, 7 Stat. 68, and the Treaty with the Chickasaws, July 23, 1805, Art. 2, 7 Stat. 89, make mention of debts owed by the natives. Also see Chapter 8, sec. 7C.

[324] Treaty of November 10, 1808, 7 Stat. 107, construed in Hot Springs Cases, 92 U. S. 698, 704 (1875).

[325] Debates and Proceedings (1808–9), vol. 19, p. 13.

[326] *Ibid.* By the Treaty of Detroit, November 17, 1807, 7 Stat. 105, and the Treaty of Brownstown, November 25, 1808, 7 Stat. 112, less important territorial concessions were secured.

[327] Oskison, *op. cit.*, p. 106.

[328] Treaty of September 30, 1809, 7 Stat. 113.

Harrison concluded an agreement with the Weas recognizing their claim to the land just ceded and extinguishing it for an annuity and a cash gift; and promised additional money if the Kickapoos should agree to the cession.[329] Shortly thereafter, December 9, 1809, the Kickapoos capitulated and ceded some 256,000 acres for a $500 annuity plus $1,500 in goods.[330]

These cessions soon occasioned dissatisfaction among the Indians and, in the summer of 1810, with Indian war imminent in the Wabash valley, Harrison summoned Tecumseh and his warriors to a conference at Vincennes.[331] Here the Shawnee Chief delivered his ultimatum. Only with great regret would he consider hostilities against the United States, against whom land purchases were the only complaint. However, unless the treaties of the autumn of 1809 were rescinded, he would be compelled to enter into an English alliance.[332]

Upon being informed by the Governor that such conditions could not be accepted by the Government of the United States, Tecumseh proceeded to merge Indian antagonisms with those of a larger conflict—the War of 1812 with Great Britain. The only treaty of military alliance the United States was able to negotiate was that with the Wyandots, Delawares, Shawanoese, Senecas, and Miamies on July 22, 1814.[333]

In 1813 war broke out among the Upper Creek towns that had been aroused by the eloquence of Tecumseh several years before. Fort Mims near Mobile was burned, and the majority of its inhabitants killed.[334] Andrew Jackson, in charge of military operations in that quarter, launched an obstinate and successful campaign, leveling whole towns in the process.[335]

Since the Creeks were a nation, and the hostile Creeks could not make a separate peace, Jackson met with representatives of the nation, friendly for the most part, and presented his "Articles of Agreement and Capitulation."[336]

The General demanded the surrender of 23,000,000 acres,[337] half or more of the ancient Creek domain,[338] as an indemnity for war expenses. Failure to comply would be considered hostile.[339] A large part of this territory belonged to the loyal Creeks, but Jackson made no distinction. Under protest, the "Articles of Agreement and Capitulation" were signed August 9, 1814.[340]

Certain other provisions indicate the spirit of capitulation in which the treaty was negotiated. For example, Article 3 demands that all communication with the British and the Spanish be abandoned, and Article 6 provides that "all the prophets and instigators of the war * * * who have not submitted to the arms of the United States * * *" be surrendered.

The terms of the peace which brought to an end the War of 1812 provided for a general amnesty for the Indians,[341] and the Federal Government proceeded to come to terms of peace with the various tribes. Twenty treaties were negotiated in 2 years, providing chiefly for mutual forgiveness, perpetual peace, and delivering up of prisoners, the recognition of former treaties, and acknowledgment of the United States as sole protector.[342]

E. INDIAN REMOVAL WESTWARD: 1817–46

With the increasing reluctance of Indians to part with their lands by treaties of cession, the policy of removal westward was accelerated. The United States offered lands in the West for territory possessed by the Indians in the eastern part of the United States. This served the double purpose of making available for white settlement a vast area, and solving the problem of conflict of authority caused by the presence of Indian nations within state boundaries.

Although the program had been considered in certain quarters for some time, it was not until after the close of the War of 1812 that the first exchange treaty was concluded.[343] Then for al-

[329] Treaty of October 26, 1809, 7 Stat. 116.

[330] Treaty of December 9, 1809, 7 Stat. 117. Acreage from Oskison, *op. cit.*, p. 107.

[331] Adams, History of the United States of America During the First Administration of James Madison (1890), vol. VI, p. 85.

[332] *Ibid.*, pp. 87–88.

[333] Treaty of July 22, 1814, 7 Stat. 118.

[334] Adams, *op. cit.*, vol. VII, pp. 228–231.

[335] *Ibid.*, vol. VII, pp. 255–257.

[336] *Ibid.*, vol. VII, pp. 259–260.

[337] James, Andrew Jackson (1933), p. 189.

[338] Adams, *op. cit.* vol. VII, p. 260. Adams estimates that two-thirds of the Creek land was demanded; James estimates one-half (*op. cit.* p. 189).

[339] James, *op. cit.* p. 190; Adams, *op. cit.* p. 260.

[340] 7 Stat. 120. "Title of the Creek Nation" to lands in Georgia "was extinguished throughout most of the southern part of the state by the treaties made with the nation in 1802, 1805, and 1814. 7 Stat. 68, 96, 120." *Coffee* v. *Groover*, 123 U. S. 1, 14 (1887). This land cession was the subject of much controversy for more than a century. After the passage of the so-called jurisdiction act (Act of May 24, 1924, 43 Stat. 139), giving jurisdiction to the Court of Claims to render judgment on claims arising out of Creek treaties, the Creek Nation filed a petition seeking payment for the twenty-three millions and more acres of land with interest, averring that—

> * * * the representatives of the Creek Nation met, all of them, with one exception, being friendly and not hostile to the United States, and protested to General Jackson that the lands were perpetually guaranteed to the Creek Nation by treaty, that the hostile Creeks had no interest in the fee to the lands, and that the treaty as drawn did not provide any compensation for the lands required to be ceded. * * * "that said Jackson represented to said council that he was without power to make any agreement to compensate them for their lands and that unless they signed the treaty as he had drawn it he would furnish the whole tribe with provisions and ammunition and that they could go down to Pensacola and join the Red Sticks and British and that, by the time they got there, he would be on their tracks and whip them and the British and drive them into the sea," and that driven to this extremity they submitted and signed the treaty. (Pp. 271–272.)

This petition was dismissed on March 7, 1927, the Court of Claims holding that the jurisdictional act does not give jurisdiction over a claim, the allowance of which involved the setting aside of a treaty on the ground that it was entered into under fraud. *Creek Nation* v. *United States*, 63 C. Cls. 270 (1927), cert. den. 274 U. S. 751.

[341] Ninth Article, Treaty of Ghent of December 24, 1814, 8 Stat. 218.

[342] Poutawatamie, July 18, 1815, 7 Stat. 123; Piankishaw, July 18, 1815, 7 Stat. 124; Teeton, July 19, 1815, 7 Stat. 125; Sioux of Lake, July 19, 1815, 7 Stat. 126; Sioux of the River of St. Peters, July 19, 1815, 7 Stat. 127; Yankton, July 19, 1815, 7 Stat. 128; Mahas, July 20, 1815, 7 Stat. 129; Kickapoos, September 2, 1815, 7 Stat. 130; Delawares, Wyandots, Senecas, etc., September 8, 1815, 7 Stat. 131; Great and Little Osage, September 12, 1815, 7 Stat. 133. The Supreme Court in construing the treaty with the Great and Little Osages, September 12, 1815, states: "peace was reestablished between the contracting parties, and former treaties were renewed * * *." *State of Missouri* v. *State of Iowa*, 7 How. 559, 668 (1849). Sac, September 13, 1815, 7 Stat. 134; Fox, September 14, 1815, 7 Stat. 135; Iaway, September 16, 1815, 7 Stat. 136; Kanzas, October 28, 1815, 7 Stat. 137; Sacs of Rock River, May 13, 1816, 7 Stat. 141; Sioux of the Leaf, Sioux of the Broad Leaf, and Sioux Who Shoot in the Pine Tops, June 1, 1816, 7 Stat. 143; Winnebago, June 3, 1816, 7 Stat. 144; Menomenee, March 30, 1817, 7 Stat. 153; Ottoes, June 24, 1817, 7 Stat. 154; Poncarar, June 25, 1817, 7 Stat. 155.

Five other treaties negotiated during this period provided for cessions of territory: Cherokees, March 22, 1816, 7 Stat. 138; Ottawas, Chipawas, etc., August 24, 1816, 7 Stat. 146; Cherokee, September 14, 1816, 7 Stat. 148; Chickasaws, September 20, 1816, 7 Stat. 150; Chactaw, October 24, 1816, 7 Stat. 152.

The Treaty of September 20, 1816, 7 Stat. 150, with the Chickasaws, made provision (Art. 6) for liberal presents to specified chiefs and individual Indians. Article 7 provided that no more licenses were to be granted to peddlers to traffic in goods in the Chickasaw Nation.

[343] Treaty of July 8, 1817, 7 Stat. 156. Construed in *Cherokee Nation* v. *Georgia*, 5 Pet. 1, 6 (1831); *Marsh* v. *Brooks*, 8 How. 223, 232 (1850); *Holden* v. *Joy*, 17 Wall. 211, 212 (1872). The Supreme Court again construed this treaty in *Heckman* v. *United States*, 224 U. S. 413, 429 (1912). "In 1817 * * * the Cherokee Nation ceded to the United States certain tracts which they formerly held, and in exchange the United States bound themselves to give to that branch of the Nation on the Arkansas as much land as they had received, or might thereafter

most 30 years thereafter Indian treaty making was concerned almost solely with removing certain tribes of natives to the vacant lands lying to the westward. The first and most significant of these treaties was concluded with the southern tribes later known as the "Five Civilized Tribes."

1. *Cherokees.*—In 1816 Andrew Jackson as Commissioner for the United States met with the Cherokees to discuss the proposition of exchanging lands. Many influential Cherokees were bitterly opposed to it, and the great majority of Indians were extremely dubious of the value of removing elsewhere.

However, the next year a treaty, prepared by Andrew Jackson, was accepted by representatives of the Cherokee Nation.[344] Its recitals include (Art. 5) a cession of the land occupied by the Cherokee Nation in return for a proportionate tract of country elsewhere, a stipulation (Art. 3) for the taking of a census of the Cherokee Nation in order to determine those emigrating and those remaining behind and thus divide the annuities between them; compensation for improvements (Arts. 6 and 7), and (Art. 8) reservations of 640 acres of Cherokee land in life estate with a reversion in fee simple to their children, to "each and every head of any Indian family residing on the east side of the Mississippi River * * * who may wish to become citizens * * *."[345] These "reservations" were the first allotments, and the idea of individual title with restrictions on alienation, as a basis of citizenship, was destined to play a major role in later Indian legislation.

When the attempt to execute the treaty was made, its weaknesses came to light. Removal was voluntary, and the national will to remove was lacking. In 1819 a delegation of Cherokees appeared in Washington and negotiated with Secretary Calhoun a new treaty,[346] which contemplated a cessation of migration.

The Cherokee Nation opposed removal and further cession of land, but once more the Federal Government sought to persuade them to move west. By the treaty of May 6, 1828,[347] made with that portion of the Cherokee Nation which had removed across the Mississippi pursuant to earlier treaties, another offer was made. Article 8 provides:

> * * * that their Brothers yet remaining in the States may be induced to join them * * * it is further agreed, on the part of the United States, that to each Head of a Cherokee family now residing within the chartered limits of Georgia, or of either of the States, East of the Mississippi, who may desire to remove West, shall be given, on enrolling himself for emigration, a good Rifle, a Blanket, and Kettle, and five pounds of Tobacco: (and to each member of his family one Blanket,) also, a just compensation for the property he may abandon, to be assessed by persons to be appointed by the President of the United States.[348]

This treaty was negotiated to define the limits of the Cherokees' new home in the West—limits which were different from those contemplated by the treaty of 1817 and convention of 1819 and included the following promise:

> The United States agree to possess the Cherokee, and to guarantee it to them forever, and that guarantee is hereby solemnly pledged, of seven millions of acres of land, * * *.[349]

Also interesting is the preamble wherein is stated:

> * * * the anxious desire of the Government of the United States to secure to the Cherokee nation of Indians * * * a *permanent* home, and which shall, under the most solemn guarantee of the United States, be, and remain, theirs forever—a home that shall never, in all future time, be embarrassed by having extended around it the lines, or placed over it the jurisdiction of a Territory or State, nor be pressed upon by the extension, in any way, of any of the limits of any existing Territory or State; * * *.[350] (P. 311.)

Article 6 provided that whenever the Cherokees desired it, a set of plain laws suited to their condition would be furnished.[351]

Confidential agents were then sent to the Cherokee Nation to renew efforts to secure immigrants to the west, but these efforts met with little success.[352] Obviously more forceful measures would have to be used, and the expansionists awaited eagerly the replacing of John Quincy Adams with a Chief Executive who would not hesitate to take such action.[353]

The election of 1828 supplied just such a President. Despite a conciliatory inaugural address,[354] Andrew Jackson immediately made it clear that the Indians must go West.[355] In this he was

---

receive, east of the Mississippi. * * *" The tribe (Cherokee) was divided into two bodies, one of which remained where they were, east of the Mississippi, and the other settled themselves upon United States land in the country on the Arkansas and White rivers.

The effect of reserves to individual Indians of a mile square each, secured to heads of families by the Cherokee treaties of 1817 and 1819, is directly decided in the case of *Cornet* v. *Winton's Lessee*, 2 Yergers Ten. Rep. 143 (1826). The division of the Cherokee Nation into two parties is also discussed in *Old Settlers* v. *United States*, 148 U. S. 427. 435–436 (1893).

[344] Treaty of July 8, 1817, 7 Stat. 156. It is to be noted that in the preamble of the treaty the following quotation of President Madison is cited with approval:

> * * * when established in their new settlements, we shall still consider them as our children, give them the benefit of exchanging their peltries for what they will want at our factories, and always hold them firmly by the hand.

[345] For opinions of the Attorney General on compensation provided by the sixth and seventh articles on rights of reservees and on descent of lands, see 3 Op. A. G. 326 (1838); 3 Op. A. G. 367 (1838); 4 Op. A. G. 116 (1842); 4 Op. A. G. 580 (1847).

[346] Treaty of February 27, 1819, 7 Stat. 195.

[347] 7 Stat. 311.

[348] The term "property which he may abandon" is construed as fixed property, "that which he could not take with him; in a word, the land and improvements which he had occupied" in 2 Op. A. G. 321 (1830).

[349] Treaty of May 6, 1828, Art. 2, 7 Stat. 311.

[350] This treaty was ratified with the proviso that it should not interfere with the lands assigned or to be assigned to the Creek Indians nor should it be construed to cede any lands heretofore ceded to any tribe by any treaty now in existence.

On February 14, 1833, a treaty (7 Stat. 414) to settle disputed Creek claims was negotiated with the Cherokee Nation west of the Mississippi. In addition to certain amendments to the preceding agreement, an outlet described as a

> * * * perpetual outlet, West, and a free and unmolested use of all the Country lying West of the Western boundary of the above described limits, and as far West as the sovereignty of the United States, and their right of soil extend.

which had been guaranteed in Treaty of May 6, 1828, Art. 2, 7 Stat. 311, was reaffirmed.

[351] This article was canceled, at Cherokee request, by Treaty of February 14, 1833, Art. 3, 7 Stat. 414.

[352] Foreman, Indian Removal (1932), pp. 21, 231; Abel, Indian Consolidation, in Annual Report, American Historical Association (1906), vol. 1, p. 361.

[353] Abel, *op. cit.*, p. 370.

[354] In his speech of March 4, 1829, Jackson said:

> It will be my sincere and constant desire to observe toward the Indian tribes within our limits a just and liberal policy, and to give that humane and considerate attention to their rights and their wants which is consistent with the habits of our Government and the feelings of our people. (H. Misc. Doc., 53d Cong. 2d sess. (1893–94), vol. 37, pt. 2, p. 438.)

[355] See Abel *op. cit.*, p. 370, 378; Foreman, *op. cit.*, p. 21. In his first message to Congress of December 8, 1829, Jackson urged voluntary removal as a protection to the Indians and the states. (H. Misc. Doc., 53d Cong. 2d sess. (1893–94), vol. 37, pt. 2, p. 458.) On May 28, 1830, the Indian Removal Act (4 Stat. 411, 25 U. S. C. 174, R. S. § 2114) was passed. (Amendments guaranteeing protection to the Indians from the states and respect for treaty rights until removal were defeated (Abel, *op cit.*, p. 380).) It gave to President Jackson power to initiate proceedings for exchange of lands. This was begun, with requests for conferences, in August of 1830 (Foreman, *op. cit.*,

aided by the legislature of Georgia which had enacted laws to harrass and make intolerable the life of the Eastern Cherokee.[356]

When the objectives of the hostile legislation became evident the chief of the Cherokee Nation, John Ross, determined to seek relief and filed a motion in the Supreme Court of the United States to enjoin the execution of certain Georgia laws. The bill reviewed the various guarantees in the treaties between the Cherokee Nation and the United States and complained that the action of the Georgia legislature was in direct violation thereof.

While the jurisdiction of the Supreme Court was denied on the grounds that the Cherokee Nation was not a *foreign* state within the meaning of the Constitution, Chief Justice Marshall nevertheless gave utterance to a highly significant analysis—the first judicial analysis—of the effect of the various treaties upon the status of the Indian nation:

> * * * The numerous treaties made with them by the United States, recognise them as a people capable of maintaining the relations of peace and war, of being responsible in their political character for any violation of their engagements, or for any aggression committed on the citizens of the United States, by any individual of their community. Laws have been enacted in the spirit of these treaties. The acts of our government plainly recognise the Cherokee nation as a state, and the courts are bound by those acts.[357]

Shortly thereafter, two missionaries, Worcester and Butler, were indicted in the Superior Court of Gwinnett County for residing in that part of the Cherokee country attached to Georgia by recent state laws, in violation of a legislative act which forbade the residence of whites in Cherokee country without an oath of allegiance to the state and a license to remain.[358] Mr. Worcester pleaded that the United States had acknowledged in its treaties with the Cherokees the latter's status as a sovereign nation and as a consequence the prosecution of state laws could not be maintained. He was tried, convicted and sentenced to 4 years in the penitentiary.

On a writ of error the case was carried to the Supreme Court of the United States, where the Court asserted its jurisdiction and reversed the judgment of the Superior Court for the County of Gwinnett in the State of Georgia, declaring that it had been pronounced under color of a law which was repugnant to the Constitution, laws and treaties of the United States. Chief Justice Marshall in delivering this opinion examined the recitals of the various treaties with the Cherokees and proceeded to point out:

> * * * They [state laws] interfere forcibly with the relations established between the United States and the Cherokee nation, the regulation of which, according to the settled principles of our constitution, are committed exclusively to the government of the Union. They are in direct hostility with treaties, repeated in a succession of years, which mark out the boundary that separates the Cherokee country from Georgia; guaranty to them all the land within their boundary; solemnly pledge the faith of the United States to restrain their citizens from trespassing on it; and recognise the pre-existing power of the nation to govern itself. They are in hostility with the acts of congress for regulating this intercourse, and giving effect to the treaties. * * *[359]

In September 1831, the President sent Benjamin F. Currey of Tennessee into the Cherokee country to superintend the work of enrolling the natives for the journey to the west.[360] Currey found the task difficult and slow, only 71 families enrolling by December.[361] The Cherokees were divided on removal, one group headed by John Ridge favorable to emigration, another faction remaining loyal to their chief, John Ross, and opposed to the program.[362] In 1834 the Ridge faction negotiated a sweeping treaty for removal which failed of ratification by the Cherokee council.[363]

In 1835, delegates from both factions were sent to Washington. After the Ross group had refused the President's terms, negotiations were opened with the opposing party, and on March 14 an agreement was drawn up which was not to be considered binding until it should receive the approval of the Cherokee people in full council.[364]

At a full council meeting in October 1835, at Red Clay, Tennessee, both factions, temporarily abandoning their quarrels, united in opposition to this treaty and rejected it.[365] Another meeting was then called at New Echota, and a new treaty was negotiated and signed.[366]

By Article 1, the Cherokee Nation ceded all their land east of the Mississippi River to the United States for $5,000,000.

Article 2 of this instrument recites that whereas by treaties with the Cherokees west of the Mississippi, the United States had guaranteed and secured to be conveyed by patent a certain territory as their permanent home, together with "a perpetual outlet west," provided that other tribes shall have access to saline deposits on said territory, it is now agreed "to convey to the said Indians, and their descendants by patent, in fee simple * * *" certain additional territory.

The estate of the Cherokees in their new homeland (by Art. 2, 7,000,000 acres and an additional 800,000 acres) has been variously called a fee simple,[367] an estate in fee upon a condition subsequent,[368] and a base, qualified or determinable fee.[369]

Article 5 provides that the new Cherokee land should not be included within any state or territory without their consent, and

---

pp. 21–22). The Indians were advised that refusal meant end of federal protection and abandonment to state laws (Abel, *op. cit.*, p. 382; Foreman, *op. cit.*, pp. 231–232.)

[356] See *Worcester* v. *Georgia*, 6 Pet. 515 (1832). See also, Foreman, *op. cit.*, pp. 229–230.

[357] *Cherokee Nation* v. *Georgia*, 5 Pet. 1, 16 (1831). See Chapter 14, sec. 3.

[358] Foreman, *op. cit.* p. 235.

[359] *Worcester* v. *Georgia*, 6 Pet. 515, 561, 562, (1832). On the failure of Georgia to abide by the Supreme Court decision, see Chapter 7, sec. 2.

[360] The methods which were employed at this time have been described thus:

> Intrigue was met by intrigue. Currey secretly employed intelligent mixed-breeds for a liberal compensation to circulate among the Indians and advance arguments calculated to break down their resistance. * * * Plied with liquor, the Indians were charged with debts for which their property was taken with or without process of law. (*Foreman, op cit.*, p. 236.)

[361] *Ibid.*, p. 241.

[362] Abel, *op. cit.* fn. 352 p. 403.

[363] Treaty of June 19, 1834 (unratified). This treaty ceded to the United States all the Cherokee land in Georgia, North Carolina, Tennessee, and Alabama, and the Indians agreed to move west. Abel, *op. cit.*, p. 403; Foreman, *op cit.*, pp. 264, 265.

[364] Treaty of March 14, 1835 (unratified). By this treaty the tribe ceded all its eastern territory and agreed to move west for $4,500,000. Foreman, *op cit.*, p. 266; Abel, *op. cit.* pp. 403, 404.

[365] Foreman, *op. cit.*, pp. 266–267.

[366] December 29, 1835, 7 Stat. 478, 488 (Supplement). The events leading to this treaty are analyzed in L. K. Cohen, The Treaty of New Echota (1936), 3 Indians at Work, No. 19.

[367] *Cherokee Nation* v. *Southern Kansas Railway Co.*, 135 U. S. 641 (1890). In *United States* v. *Rogers*, 23 Fed. 658, 664 (D. C. W. D. Ark. 1885), the court insisted:

> * * * By looking at the title of the Cherokees to their lands, we find that they hold them all by substantially the same kind of title, the only difference being that the outlet is incumbered with the stipulation that the United States is to permit other tribes to get salt on the Salt plains. With this exception, the title of the Cherokee Nation to the outlet is just as fixed, certain, extensive, and perpetual as the title to any of their lands.

The President and Senate in concluding a treaty, can lawfully covenant that a patent should issue to convey lands which belong to the United States. *Holden* v. *Joy*, 17 Wall. 211 (1872).

[368] *Holden* v. *Joy*, 17 Wall. 211 (1872).

[369] *United States* v. *Reese*, 27 Fed. Cas. No. 16,137 (D. C. Mass. 1868).

that their right to make laws not inconsistent with the Constitution or intercourse acts should be secured.[370]

The New Echota treaty also provided (Art. 12) under certain conditions, reservations of 160 acres for those who wished to remain east of the Mississippi[371] and for settlement of claims (Art. 13) for former reservations. In addition a commission was established (Art. 17) to adjudicate these claims.[372]

2. *Chickasaws.*—Although the domain of the Chickasaw Nation was considerably restricted by the treaties of 1816[373] and 1818[374] it was not until 1830 that the subject of "removal" was given serious consideration. During the summer of that year, the President met the principal chiefs of the Chickasaw Nation and warned them that they would be compelled either to migrate to the west or to submit to the laws of the state.[375] After several days of conference a provisional treaty[376] was signed. However, performance was conditional upon the Chickasaws being given a home in the West on the lands of the Choctaw Nation, and as the two nations could come to no agreement the treaty remained unfulfilled.[377] Nevertheless, white infiltration into Chickasaw land east of the Mississippi was accelerated, and the problem of removal became a pressing government problem.[378]

On October 20, 1832,[379] another treaty for removal was negotiated in which all of the land of the tribe east of the Mississippi was ceded to the United States[380] to be sold at public auction.[381] Article 4 provides:

> * * * that the Chickasaw people shall not deprive themselves of a comfortable home, in the country where they now are, untill they shall have provided a country in the west to remove to * * *. It is therefore agreed * * * that they will endeavor as soon as it may be in their power, after the ratification of this treaty, to hunt out and procure a home for their people, west of the Mississippi river, * * * they are to select out of the surveys, a comfortable settlement for every family in the Chickasaw nation, to include their present improvements, if the land is good for cultivation, and if not they may take it in any other place in the nation, which is unoccupied by any other person. * * * All of which tracts of land, so selected and retained, shall be held, and occupied by the Chickasaw people, uninterrupted until they shall find and obtain a country suited to their wants and condition. And the United States will guaranty to the Chickasaw nation, the quiet possession and uninterrupted use of the said reserved tracts of land, so long as they may live on and occupy the same. * * *

Despite the guarantee of the United States to the Chickasaws of the "quiet possession and uninterrupted use" of the reserved tracts,[382] white settlers continued to overrun and occupy their country unlawfully.[383] Furthermore, the problem of finding land in the West proved a difficult one. Finally convinced of the need for amending the treaty in certain particulars, the Government consented to the conclusion of another treaty on May 24, 1834.[384] This altered the program of removal, granted in fee certain reservations, while asserting that the Chickasaws "still hope to find a country, adequate to the wants and support of their people, somewhere west of the Mississippi * * *."[385]

By Article 2, the Chickasaws on their removal west were to be protected by the United States from the hostile prairie tribes. They pledged themselves never to make war on another tribe, or on whites, "unless they are so authorized by the United States." Article 4 set up a commission of Chickasaws to pass on the competency of members of the tribe to handle and sell their land. Articles 5 and 6 listed the cases in which reservations could be granted in fee, and determined the amount of land in each case.[386] Article 9 provided that funds from the sale of Chickasaw lands be used for schools, mills, blacksmith shops, etc.[387]

3. *Choctaws.*—By 1820 it was evident that the Choctaws, disturbed by the number of settlers who were pouring into the rich valleys of the Mississippi, would consent to "removal." Ac-

[370] In *Cherokee Nation* v. *Southern Kansas Railway Co.*, 135 U. S. 641 (1890), the Supreme Court commented on this clause:

> * * * By the Treaty of New Echota, 1835, the United States covenanted and agreed that the lands ceded to the Cherokee Nation should at no future time, without their consent, be included within the territorial limits or jurisdiction of any State or Territory, and that the government would secure to that nation "the right by their national councils to make and carry into effect all such laws as they may deem necessary for the government of the persons and property within their own country, belonging to their people, or such persons as have connected themselves with them;" * * *. But neither these nor any previous treaties evinced any intention, upon the part of the government, to discharge them from their condition of pupilage or dependency, and constitute them a separate, independent, sovereign people, with no superior within its limits. * * * (P. 654.)

[371] The Indians who remained behind under this provision dissolved their connection with the Cherokee Nation (*Cherokee Trust Funds*, 117 U. S. 288 (1886)), without becoming citizens either of the United States or North Carolina. *United States* v. *Boyd*, 83 Fed. 547 (C. C. A. 4, 1897).

In later years some of the ceded Cherokee lands were bought back by Cherokees who resisted removal. In 1925 this land was reconveyed to the United States in trust by Indians for disposition under the Act of June 4, 1924, 43 Stat. 376. See Historical Note, 25 U. S. C. A. 331.

[372] That the President has power to appoint new commissioners there being no limitation to this authority, except the fulfillment of its purposes, but that the expenses cannot be defrayed out of the Cherokees' fund is the advice of the Attorney General. 16 Op. A. G. 300 (1879); 4 Op. A. G. 73 (1842). See also 5 Op. A. G. 268 (1850); H. Rept. No. 391, 28th Cong., 1st sess. (1844).

[373] Treaty of September 20, 1816, 7 Stat. 150. For certain ceded lands north and south of the Tennessee River, the Indians received $12,000 per annum for 10 years (Arts. 2 and 3).

Article 7 prohibits the licensing of peddlers to trade within the Chickasaw Nation and describes the activities of the trader as a disadvantage to the nation.

[374] Treaty of October 19, 1818, 7 Stat. 192, construed in *Porterfield* v. *Clark*, 2 How. 76, 83 (1844). All Chickasaw land north of the south boundary of Tennessee was ceded for $300,000—$20,000 annually for 15 years (Arts. 2 and 3).

[375] Foreman, *op. cit.*, p. 193. Each of the Chickasaw chiefs was to receive four sections of land if the treaty were ratified.

[376] Treaty of September 1, 1830 (unratified).

[377] Several official attempts were made by the Government to persuade the Chickasaws of the desirability of amalgamating with the Choctaws. Foreman, *op. cit.*, pp. 193–196.

[378] *Ibid.*, p. 197.

[379] 7 Stat. 381. Supplementary and explanatory articles (7 Stat. 388) adopted October 22, 1832. Art. 9 is of interest. The Chickasaws

> "* * * will always need a friend to advise and direct them. * * * There shall be an agent kept with the Chickasaws as heretofore, so long as they live within the jurisdiction of the United States as a nation * * *. And whenever the office of agent shall be vacant, * * * the President will pay due respect to the wishes of the nation * * *.

[380] *Ibid.*, Art. 1.

[381] *Ibid.*, Art. 2.

[382] *Ibid.* See Arts. 4 and 15.

[383] Foreman, *op. cit.* p. 199.

[384] Treaty of May 24, 1834, 7 Stat. 450. It is of interest that in previous treaties the word "cede" was used. In this the phrase "abandon their homes" is used (Art. 2).

[385] Art. 2. Such land was not found until 1837, when the Chickasaws purchased a large tract of land from the Choctaws. Foreman, *op. cit.* p. 203.

[386] For opinion that a widow keeping house and having children or other persons residing with her, except slaves, is the head of a family unless said children or other persons are provided for under the sixth and eighth articles; that as many Indian wives as were living with their children apart from their husbands (though wives of the same Indian) are "heads of a family" within the meaning of the fifth article of the treaty, see 3 Op. A. G. 34, 41 (1836). And see, on the scope of investments under Art. 11, 3 Op. A. G. 170 (1837).

Title to reservations was complete when the locations were made to identify them. *Best* v. *Polk*, 18 Wall. 112 (1873).

For details concerning the number of claimants for lands; the number approved; and the names of the assignees of those Indians who obtained lands pursuant to the provisions of the Chickasaw treaty made at Washington in 1834, see H. Rept. No. 190, 29th Cong. 1st sess., vol. VI (1846).

[387] Also see sec. 3C3 of this Chapter.

cordingly negotiations were begun and on October 18, 1820,[388] the Indians ceded to the United States the "coveted tract" in western Mississippi[389] for land west of the Mississippi between the Arkansas and Red rivers.[390]

Article 4 of the treaty contains the guarantee that the boundaries established should remain without alteration

> * * * until the period at which said nation shall become so civilized and enlightened as to be made citizens of the United States, and Congress shall lay off a limited parcel of land for the benefit of each family or individual in the nation.

Article 12 gives the agent full power to confiscate all whiskey except that brought under permit into the nation. This appears to be the first attempt by treaty to regulate traffic in liquor.

Shortly after the treaty was signed it was discovered that a part of Choctaw's new country was already occupied by white settlers.[391] The President called to Washington delegates from the Choctaw Nation to reconsider the matter and negotiate another treaty. This was done on January 20, 1825,[392] and the Choctaws for $6,000 a year for 16 years (Art. 3), and a permanent annuity of $6,000 (Art. 2), ceded back all the land lying east of a line which today is the boundary between Arkansas and Oklahoma. By Article 4 of the 1825 treaty it is also agreed that all those who have reservations under the preceding treaty "shall have power, with the consent of the President of the United States, to sell and convey the same in fee simple." Article 7 calls for the modification of Article 4 of the preceding treaty so that the Congress of the United States shall not exercise the power of allotting lands to individuals without the consent of the Choctaw Nation.

A few years later, federal agents, anxious to speed up the migration program under the Removal Act of 1830[393] held another series of conferences in the Choctaw Nation.

At Dancing Rabbit Creek, at a conference characterized by generous present-giving,[394] a treaty was signed on September 27, 1830.[395] By this agreement the Choctaws ceded the remainder of their holdings east of the Mississippi to the United States Government in return for

> * * * a tract of country west of the Mississippi River, in fee simple to them and their descendants, to inure to them while they shall exist as a nation and live on it, * * *.[396]

This tract was the same as that in the Treaty of January 20, 1825.[397]

Provision is also made for reservations of land to individual Indians in Articles 14[398] and 19.[399] In Article 14, it is also stipulated that a grant in fee simple shall issue upon the fulfillment of certain conditions.[400]

Whether a true construction of Article 14 created a trust for the children of each reservee was one of the questions before the United States Supreme Court in *Wilson* v. *Wall*. Said the Court:

> The parties to this contract may justly be presumed to have had in view the previous custom and usages with regard to grants to persons "desirous to become citizens." The treaty suggests that they are "a people in a state of rapid advancement in education and refinement." But it does not follow that they were acquainted with the doctrine of trusts. * * *[401] (P. 87.)

The following provisions of Article 4 of the Treaty of Dancing Rabbit Creek deserve to be noted:

> The Government and people of the United States are hereby obliged to secure to the said Choctaw Nation of Red People the jurisdiction and government of all the persons and property that may be within their limits west, so that no Territory or State shall ever have a right to pass laws for the Government of the Choctaw Nation of Red People and their descendants; and that no part of the land granted them shall ever be embraced in any Territory or State; but the U. S. shall forever secure said Choctaw Nation from and against, all laws except such as from time to time may be enacted in their own National Councils, not inconsistent with the Constitution, Treaties, and Laws of the United States; * * *.[402]

[388] Treaty of Doak's Stand of October 18, 1820, 7 Stat. 210. Construed in *Choctaw Nation* v. *United States*, 119 U. S. 1 (1886); *United States* v. *Choctaw Nation*, 179 U. S. 494, 507 (1900); *Mullen* v. *United States*, 224 U. S. 448, 450 (1912). In *Elk* v. *Wilkins*, 112 U. S. 94, 100 (1884), this treaty was cited in support of the statement that the alien and dependent condition of the members of the Indian tribes could not be put off at their own will without the action or assent of the United States. In *Fleming* v. *McCurtain*, 215 U. S. 56, 59 (1909), the Supreme Court declared that by this treaty the United States ceded certain lands to the Choctaw Nation with "no qualifying words."

[389] Abel, *op cit.* fn. 352, p. 286. The tract was coveted particularly by the state of Mississippi. See Art. 1.

[390] Art. 2.

[391] Abel, *op. cit.*, pp. 286–287.

[392] Treaty of January 20, 1825, 7 Stat. 234, construed in 2 Op. A. G. 465 (1831), and 3 Op. A. G. 48 (1836).

[393] Act of May 28, 1830, 4 Stat. 411, R. S. § 2114, 25 U. S. C. 174.

[394] The expense account for the negotiations of Dancing Rabbit Creek submitted by the federal commissioners included items of $1,409.84 for calicos, quilts, razors, soap, etc. Sen. Doc. No. 512, 23rd Cong. 1st sess., pp. 251–255.

[395] 7 Stat. 333. This was the first treaty made and ratified under the Removal Act of May 28, 1830, 4 Stat. 411.

[396] Art. 2. In 1909 the United States Supreme Court examined this particular provision and ruled that this was a grant to the Choctaw Nation and was not to be held in trust for members of the tribe, which upon dissolution of the tribal relationship would confer upon each individual absolute ownership as tenants in common. *Fleming* v. *McCurtain*, 215 U. S. 56 (1909). See Chapter 15, sec 1A.

[397] 7 Stat. 234.

[398] Article 14 provided reservations of land for those electing to remain and become citizens of the states. Such persons retained their Choctaw citizenship, but lost their annuity if they removed. That in the event of the death of reservees under the fourteenth article of the treaty of 1830, before the fulfillment of the condition precedent to the grant in fee simple of the reserve, the interest thereby acquired passes to those persons who under state laws succeed to the inheritable interest of the individual in question. See 3 Op. A. G. 107 (1836).

If an Indian was prevented by the force or fraud of individuals having no authority from the Government from complying with the conditions of Article 14 of the treaty of Dancing Rabbit Creek, it is considered by the Attorney General that the remedy was against such individuals, although if permanent dispossession was produced by the sale of the land by the Government (even though he might have temporarily lost possession by such tortious acts) his claim is still valid. 4 Op. A. G. 513 (1846). And see, on eligibility to receive reservations, 5 Op. A. G. 251 (1850).

[399] No forfeiture has resulted from the fraudulent acts of the agent of the Government who induced claimants to apply for reserves under the nineteenth article, and which were located for them, but for which patents have not been demanded, nor issued. See 4 Op. A. G. 452 (1845).

To the effect that the essential provisions of the Choctaw treaty of 1830 must take precedence over any rights claimed under the preemption laws, but that regulations to carry treaty into effect need not be inflexible and may be modified in any way not inconsistent with the treaty. See 3 Op. A. G. 365 (1838).

[400] Residence for 5 years after ratification of the treaty with the intention of becoming a citizen, is a condition.

[401] *Wilson* v. *Wall*, 6 Wall. 83, 87–90 (1867).

[402] In a negligence action brought in error to the United States Court in the Indian Territory, the defense advanced was a general denial and a plea of the statute of limitations which, it was claimed, was in force in the Indian Territory when that country was a part of the territory of Missouri, and remained in force notwithstanding the separation of the territory. This Circuit Judge Caldwell denied, calling attention to the treaty with the Choctaw Nation of September 27, 1830, 7 Stat. 333, by which the United States Government "bound itself in the most solemn manner to exclude white people from the territory, and never to permit the laws of any state or territory to be extended over it." *St. Louis & S. F. R. Co.* v. *O'Loughlin*, 49 Fed. 440, 442 (C. C. A. 8, 1892).

That this does not empower the Choctaws to punish by their own laws white men who come into their nation, see 2 Op. A. G. 693 (1834). And see Chapter 7, sec. 9.

The nature and extent of the jurisdiction of the Choctaw Nation were reviewed by Attorney General Caleb Cushing in 1855:

> Now, among the provisions of the treaty of Dancing Rabbit Creek are several of a very significant character having exclusive reference to the question of *criminal* jurisdiction.
>
> In the first place, it provides that any Choctaw, committing acts of violence upon the person or property of "citizens of the United States," shall be delivered up for trial and punishment by the laws of the United States; by which also are to be punished all acts of violence committed upon persons or property of the Choctaw nation by "citizens of the United States." Provision less explicit, but apparently on the same principle, is made for the repression or punishment of theft. General engagement is made by the United States to prevent or punish the *intrusion* of their "citizens" into the territory of the nation. (Arts. 6, 7, 9, 12.)
>
> In the second place, the Choctaws express a wish in the treaty that Congress would grant to the Choctaws the right of punishing, by their own laws, "any white man" who shall come into the nation, and infringe any of their national regulations (art. 4.) But Congress did not accede to this request. On the contrary, it has made provision, by a series of laws, for the punishment of crimes affecting white men, committed by or on them in the Indian country, including that of the Choctaws, by the courts of the United States. (See act of June 30, 1834, iv Stat. at Large, p. 729, and act of June 17, 1844, v Stat. at Large, p. 680.) These acts cover, so far as they go, all crimes except those committed by Indian against Indian.
>
> But there is no provision of treaty, and no statute, which takes away from the Choctaws jurisdiction of a case like this, a question of property strictly internal to the Choctaw nation; nor is there any written law which confers jurisdiction of such a case on any court of United States. * * * [603] (Pp. 174, 178–179.)

Before the Treaty of Dancing Rabbit Creek was proclaimed,[604] whites began to move into Choctaw country illegally,[605] and Indians, "ill-organized and inadequately provisioned" began to move west [606] under the aegis of Greenwood Le Flore, a mixed blood and former Choctaw chief.[607] President Jackson then ordered that removal be supervised by the Army.[608] Removal began on a large scale in the fall of 1831.[609] It had not been entirely completed at the end of the century.[610]

4. *Creeks.*—The cession [611] of land by the Creeks after the uprising of the "hostiles" in 1812 "was the first step in the direction of systematic removal." [612]

The Compact of 1802 [613] became the source of constant agitation in Georgia for change in the Creek boundary line. On January 22, 1818, a redefinition of the boundary of the Creek Nation was secured,[614] but the lands obtained by this agreement were less fertile [615] than had been anticipated and another treaty was negotiated January 8, 1821.[616] Part of the consideration tendered the Creeks on this occasion (Art. 4) was the payment to the State of Georgia of "* * * whatever ballance may be found due by the Creek nation to the citizens of said state * * *." The value of the ceded land was placed at $450,000, of which not more than $250,000 was to be paid to settle the claims of Georgia citizens against the Creek Nation,[617] the exact amount of which is left to the decision of the President of the United States.

After the award had been made, Georgia asked that it be enlarged to cover other claims. The Attorney General, after advising that the award of President Monroe must be considered final and conclusive, reviewed the contents of the treaties between the United States and the Creek Nation and asserted:

> One head of these claims submitted for my opinion is the claim for *property destroyed*, and which the people of Georgia carry back to 1783, the date of the treaty of Augusta. How stands this claim under these treaties? There is not one treaty which contains any stipulation to answer for *property destroyed.* * * * what is the effect, in a *treaty of peace, of express provisions with regard to some past wrongs, and a total silence as to others?* Is it not a virtual extinguishment of all claims for antecedent wrongs with regard to which the treaty is silent?
>
> * * * * *
>
> It is further asked, why the Creek nation did not stipulate for the payment over to themselves of the large surplus that must inevitably remain, upon the supposition that the claim for property destroyed was not to be allowed? * * * They were at the feet of the white people, with whom they were treating. They saw a formidable array of claims, * * * and of the circumstances attending which, the living race of Creeks must have been wholly ignorant—and now dug up from the dead, by the State of Georgia, and presented and pressed as living and valid claims. * * * the alleged debtors were Indians, a conquered and despised race, for whom it was natural for them to suppose that no sympathy was left either by the creditor or the judge. Is it not probable that, under these circumstances, they were ignorant enough to think it probable that no surplus would remain, and that they were willing enough to surrender to the United States the whole $250,000, on the condition of their relieving them from claims to which there seemed to be no end, but which threatened to be immortal? * * * [618]

In 1824 commissioners from the United States Government arrived in the Creek Nation to negotiate for still another session. At Broken Arrow, in Alabama, they met with the Creeks and told them that the President had extensive holdings beyond the Mississippi which he wished to give them in exchange for the land they then occupied.[619]

The Creek chiefs replied:

> * * * ruin is the almost inevitable consequence of a removal beyond the Mississippi, we are convinced. It is true, very true, that "we are surrounded by white people;" that there are encroachments made—what assurances have we that similar ones will not be made on us, should we deem it proper to accept your offer, and remove beyond

[603] 7 Op. A. G. 174, 178–179 (1855). See Chapter 7, sec. 9.

[604] February 24, 1831.

[605] Foreman, *op. cit.* p. 31.

[606] *Ibid.*, p. 33.

[607] *Ibid.*

[608] *Ibid.*, p. 42.

[609] *Ibid.*, pp. 48–49.

[610] *Ibid.*, p. 104.

[611] Treaty of August 9, 1814, 7 Stat. 120.

[612] Abel, *op. cit.* fn. 352, p. 278. See sec. 4D, *supra*.

[613] By that compact, Georgia ceded territory now part of Alabama and Mississippi in consideration of which the United States agreed to extinguish Indian title within the limits of Georgia as soon as it could be done "peaceably and on reasonable terms." Abel, *op cit.*, pp. 322, 324.

Ordinarily lands ceded to the United States became part of the public domain. By the Georgia pact, it became the property of the state. Hence, Georgia felt her failure to share sufficiently in previous land cessions was the result of national selfishness (Abel, *op. cit.*, p. 322).

[614] Treaty of January 22, 1818, 7 Stat. 171.

[615] Indian Office Letter Books, Series I, D., p. 324, cited in Abel, *op. cit.*, pp. 323, 328.

[616] Treaty of January 8, 1821, 7 Stat. 215. Subsequent to this treaty, the question of whether the United States was keeping her part of the Georgia compact arose. A House committee reporting on January 7, 1822 (American State Papers, "Indian Affairs," II, p. 259), held that it was not. According to Abel, (*op. cit.*, p. 328), the constitutional significance of removal dates from that report.

[617] By the Treaty of August 7, 1790, 7 Stat. 35, the Creeks had undertaken responsibility to return prisoners, white or Negro, in any part of the nation (Art. 3). By that article, the Treaty of Indian Springs of January 8, 1821 (Art. 4), 7 Stat. 215, held them responsible for claims not exceeding $250,000 by the citizens of Georgia; for runaway slaves. Foreman, *op. cit.*, p. 317.

[618] 2 Op. A. G. 110, 129, 150–151 (1828).

[619] Talk, December 7, 1824, Journal of Proceedings at Broken Arrow (Indian Office MS. Records) cited in Abel, *op. cit.* fn. 352, p. 337.

the Mississippi, and how do we know that we would not be encroaching on the people of other nations.[420]

Finally after days of unavailing speech-making the conference was adjourned. However, one Commissioner, Duncan G. Campbell, aware that one faction in the Creek Nation headed by William McIntosh[421] favored migration, brought about the resumption of treaty negotiations at Indian Springs, its stronghold in Georgia.[422]

Significantly the Great Chief of the Creeks, Little Prince, and his second in command, Big Warrior, were absent, having dispatched a representative to the treaty council to protest against the lack of authority of those in attendance.[423] Undiscouraged, Campbell continued the negotiations and on February 12, 1825,[424] a treaty was concluded providing for the surrender of certain Creek holdings for $400,000 for lands of "like quantity, acre for acre, westward of the Mississippi."[425]

A year later a new treaty[426] was negotiated and referred to the Senate which refused its "advice and consent."[427] A few days later a supplementary article[428] providing for an additional cession of land was submitted and with this alteration, the treaty received Senate confirmation.[429]

Here, however, the matter did not end. Georgia now denied that treaties with the Indians had the same effect as those with civilized nations and asked that the whole question of claims under the Treaty of 1821 be reconsidered. This was refused by the Attorney General of the United States who declared:

> The matter of this objection requires to be coolly analyzed.
>
> First, they are an *uncivilized nation.* And what then? Are not the treaties which are made with them obligatory on both sides? It was made a question in the age of Grotius, whether treaties made by Christians with heathens were obligatory on the former. "This discussion," says Vattel (book ii, chap. xii, sec. 161), "might be necessary at a time when the madness of party still darkened those principles which it had long caused to be forgotten, but we may venture to believe it would be superfluous in our age. *The law of nature alone regulates the treaties of nations.* The difference of religion is a thing absolutely foreign to them. Different people treat with each other *in quality of men,* and not under the character of *Christians or of Mussulmans.* Their common safety requires that they should treat with each other, and treat with security. * * *
>
> What Vattel says of difference of religion is equally applicable to this objection * * *. And that civilization which should claim an exemption from the full obligations of a treaty, or seek to narrow it by construction, on the ground that the other party to the treaty was uncivilized, would be as little entitled to our respect as the religion which should claim the same consequences on the ground that the other treating party was a heathen.[430]

With the departure from the Presidency of John Quincy Adams the strict observance of treaty obligations with the Indian tribes ceased to be an accepted national policy. Henceforth the emphasis was to be on "removal," and a few days after his inauguration Andrew Jackson insisted that it was necessary for the Creeks to migrate as soon as possible.[431] In vain the Creeks protested.[432] Their delegation to Washington was granted an audience on the condition that they would be fully empowered to negotiate in conformity with the wishes of the Government.[433] Finally, a treaty was concluded March 24, 1832,[434] and all the Creek land east of the Mississippi passed into the possession of the Federal Government.

By article 14 of this agreement, the United States solemnly promised tribal self-government to the Creeks. A number of years later this guarantee figured in a charge to the jury regarding robbery committed in the Indian country. The court in denying that the Indian country was under the sole and exclusive jurisdiction of the United States said:

> * * * A sole and exclusive jurisdiction would exclude all Indian laws and regulations, punish crimes committed by Indian on Indian, and regulate and govern property and contracts and the civil and political relations of the inhabitants, Indians and others, in that country. It would be wholly opposed to a self-government by any Indian tribe or nation. This self-government is expressly recognized and secured by several treaties between the United States and Indian tribes in the Indian country attached by the act of 1834 to Arkansas or Missouri District for certain purposes. This may be seen from the treaty with the Choctaws in 1830, and the treaty with the Creeks in 1832, and other Indian treaties. * * *[435] (P 1004.)

For a number of years it was alleged that the United States had not fulfilled its obligations under this treaty. Suit was brought by the Creek Nation in the Court of Claims under the jurisdictional act of May 24, 1924.[436] The plaintiff sought to recover the 1837 value of the entire reserves except as to those sales for which it had been proved that the owners received the stipulated "fair consideration," alleging that the Government

---

[420] Talk, December 8, 1824, Journal of Proceedings cited in Abel, *op cit*, p 337.

[421] A mixed blood, cousin of Governor Troup of Georgia, and leader of the lower Creek towns (Abel, *op cit*, p 335).

[422] Campbell had suggested various ways of securing the Creek signature to a "removal" treaty. Finally he was informed that the President would not countenance a treaty unless it were made "in the usual form, and upon the ordinary principles with which Treaties, are held with Indian tribes * * *" Indian Office Letter Books, Series II, No. 1, pp. 309-310, cited in Abel, *op cit*, p 339

[423] Abel, *op cit*, p 340

[424] 7 Stat. 237

[425] Art. 2. All Creek holdings within the State of Georgia were included in the cession

[426] Treaty of Washington of January 24, 1826, 7 Stat. 286

[427] Abel, *op cit*, p 352

[428] Supplementary article of March 31, 1826, 7 Stat. 289

[429] In the Committee of the Whole, Berrien of Georgia, asked that the first article be altered so that the Indian Spring Treaty could be abrogated without reflecting upon its negotiation.' This was refused. Berrien and five others were the only members of the Senate who on the final vote refused to consent to ratification. Afterwards, Berrien admitted that he had voted against the treaty because he felt that it did not contain enough of an inducement to migration. American State Papers, Indian Affairs II, pp 748-749, cited in Abel, *op cit*, p. 352.

Before the whole matter was settled to the satisfaction of Georgia, which claimed that more than the described territory should have been relinquished, another treaty of cession was negotiated. Treaty of November 15, 1827, 7 Stat. 307.

[430] 2 Op A. G 110, 135–136 (1828) See also sec 1, *supra*, fn. 5

[431] Indian Office Letter Books, Series II, No 6, pp 373–375, cited in Abel, *op. cit.* fn 352, p 370.

[432] On February 6, 1832, the Head Men and Warriors of the Creek Indians addressed the Congress of the United States entreating them not to insist on the program of removal pointing out "We are assured that, beyond the Mississippi, we shall be exempted from further exaction, * * * Can we obtain * * * assurances more distinct and positive, than those we have already received and trusted? Can their power exempt us from intrusion in our promised borders, if they are incompetent to our protection where we are? * * * H Doc. No 102, 22d Cong, 1st sess (1832), vol. 3, pp. 1, 3.

[433] Indian Office Letter Books, Series II, No 7, p 422, cited in Abel, *op cit*, pp. 337–338

[434] 7 Stat 366 (This was amended in certain particulars by treaties of February 14, 1833, 7 Stat. 417, and November 23, 1838, 7 Stat. 574.) Article IV of the Treaty of February 14, 1833, 7 Stat 417, expressly mentioned the Seminole Indians in Florida and provided for a permanent and comfortable home on the lands of the Creek Nation according to treaty negotiations with the Seminoles May 9, 1832, 7 Stat. 368

[435] Anonymous, 1 Fed. Cas. No. 447 (C. C Missouri 1843) And see *Atlantic and Pacific Railroad Co. v. Mingus,* 165 U S. 413, 435–436 (1897) See Chapter 23.

[436] C. 181, 43 Stat. 139.

failed to remove intruders from the country ceded as guaranteed by Article V of the treaty and that as a result it became impossible to fulfill Articles II and III involving the surveying and selection by the Indians, of reserved lands. While the Court of Claims found that the Creek Nation, with certain exceptions, had waived all claims and demands in a subsequent treaty, its holding on the execution of this treaty is illuminating:

> * * * While the record leaves no room for doubt that most dastardly frauds by impersonation were perpetrated upon the Indians in the sales of a large part of the reserves, the conclusion is justified, and we think inescapable, that because of repeated investigations prosecuted by the Government these frauds were largely eliminated. The investigations were conducted by able and fearless men and were most thorough. Every possible effort was exerted by them to have individual reservees who claimed they had been defrauded to present their claims. Chiefs of the nation were invited to bring to the attention of the investigators all claims of fraudulent practices upon the Indians, and were assured all claims would be considered and justice done. Hundreds of contracts upon investigation were found to have been fraudulently procured and their cancellation recommended by the investigating agents. While the identity of the particular cases investigated and found to have been fraudulent, and the final action of the Government on the agent's reports recommending the reversal of such cases are not disclosed, it is manifest their recommendations were in the main followed and new contracts of sales were made, certified to the President and approved by him. (Pp. 260–261.)[437]

5. *Florida Indians.*[438]—One of the problems arising from the treaty with Spain by which the Floridas[439] were acquired was that of the proper disposition[440] of the Indians who inhabited that region.[441] In some quarters it was insisted that the Indians had been living in the territory by sufferance only and even if this were not true their lands were now forfeit by conquest.[442] General Jackson in particular was outspoken in his opposition to treating with the Indians, asserting that if Congress were ever going to exercise its power over the natives it could not do better than to begin with these "conquered" natives.[443]

After 2 years of considering the various viewpoints, concentration in Florida was decided upon, and President Monroe appointed commissioners to treat with the Florida Indians. The result was the Treaty of Camp Moultrie of September 18, 1823.[444] Article 1 of this instrument recites that—

> The undersigned chiefs and warriors, for themselves and their tribes, have appealed to the humanity, and thrown themselves on, and have promised to continue under, the protection of the United States, and of no other nation, power, or sovereign; and, in consideration of the promises and stipulations hereinafter made, do cede and relinquish all claim or title which they may have to the whole territory of Florida * * *.

In return the United States (Art. 4) "assigned" land with a guarantee of peaceable possession, and gave them (Art. 3) in addition to implements, stock and an annuity, protection against all persons

> * * * provided they conform to the laws of the United States, and refrain from making war, or giving any insult to any foreign nation, without having first obtained the permission and consent of the United States.

An additional article granted to six chiefs permission to remain and large tracts of lands.

Soon it was obvious that the territory assigned was unsatisfactory. Agriculture was impossible in the swamps of the interior. Although as provided by Article 9 the boundary line was to be extended to find "good tillable land," it still failed to afford the tribe adequate means of support.[445]

Friction developed between Indians who remained and white settlers, and between the removed Indians and whites searching for runaway slaves. The plight of those who had removed grew steadily worse.[446]

In 1832 at Payne's Landing, they were persuaded to migrate, although the treaty[447] was not to be considered binding until an initial party explored the west and found a suitable home. However, in 1833 the chiefs who undertook this preliminary search, without authority to do so, signed another treaty[448] which was construed to make removal under the early treaty obligatory instead of conditional. This treaty was never accepted by the tribe, and large scale removal of Seminoles never took place.[449]

6. *Other tribes.*—In the Northwest Territory a treaty of removal was concluded with the Delaware Indians on October 3, 1818.[450] Article 2 of this agreement binds the United States in exchange for land in Indiana "* * * to provide for the Delawares a country to reside in, upon the west side of the Mississippi, and to guaranty to them the peaceable possession of the same."

The next year treaties signed at Edwardsville, Illinois,[451] and at Fort Harrison[452] provided for exchange of Kickapoo lands from Indiana and Illinois to Missouri territory. By the terms of the Edwardsville treaty (Art. 6) the United States ceded to the Indians and their heirs forever a certain tract of land in Missouri territory, provided that "the said tribe shall never sell the said land without the consent of the President of the United States." Article 4 of the Fort Harrison treaty refers to the contemplation by the tribe of Kickapoos of the Vermilion, of "removing from the country they now occupy * * *."

In 1824, a treaty[453] with the Quapaw Nation was concluded, whereby the Quapaws ceded all their land in Arkansas territory and agreed to remove to the land of the Caddo Indians (Art. 4).

These agreements were for a number of years the major attempts made by the United States to persuade the Indians of

---

[437] *Creek Nation v. The United States*, 77 C. Cls. 226, 252, 260 (1933). On alleged diversion of Creek Orphan fund under Article II; distinctions as to issuing of patents on individual reserves under II, III, IV, as to state citizenship and right to patent, Art. 4. See 16 Op. A. G. 31 (1878); 3 Op. A. G. 288 (1837), 585 (1840).

[438] See fn. 417, *supra*.

[439] Treaty of February 22, 1819; October 29, 1820, with Spain, ratified by United States, February 18, 1821, 8 Stat. 252.

[440] In 1821, a subagent, Penieres, was appointed for the Florida Indians by Jackson (then Governor) to explore the country, determine the number of Indians, and prepare them either for concentration in Florida or for removal elsewhere. Abel, *op. cit.*, p. 328.

[441] They were known as Seminoles ("separatist") and consisted of descendants of Creek Tribes, Hitchiti, Yamasee, Yuchi, and a Negro element. Foreman, *op. cit.*, p. 315.

[442] Abel, *op. cit.*, p. 328. The first Seminole War, with General Andrew Jackson in command, had ended in 1818, disastrously for the Indians. Escape by runaway slaves into their territory continued, as did the subsequent white raids. Foreman, *op. cit.*, p. 318.

[443] Abel, *op. cit.*, p. 329.

[444] 7 Stat. 224. For the first time (Art. 7) recognition is taken of the fugitive slave problem and the Indians agree to prevent such individuals from taking refuge, and to apprehend and return them for a compensation. See also Treaty of June 18, 1833, 7 Stat. 427, in which the Appalachicola Band of Indians relinquished all privileges to which they were entitled by this treaty (Art. 1).

[445] Abel, *op. cit.*, pp. 330–334; Foreman, *op. cit.*, pp. 318–319.

[446] Foreman, *op. cit.* pp. 318–320.

[447] Treaty of May 9, 1832, Preamble and Art. 1, 7 Stat. 368.

[448] Treaty of March 28, 1833, 7 Stat. 423. This treaty was the cause of the second Seminole War. Foreman, *op. cit.*, p. 321. Some of the Indians fled to the swamps where desultory fighting went on for years.

[449] Foreman, *op. cit.*, p. 323.

[450] Treaty of October 3, 1818, 7 Stat. 188. And see supplement to this treaty, September 24, 1829, 7 Stat. 327.

[451] Treaty of July 30, 1819, 7 Stat. 200.

[452] Treaty of August 30, 1819, 7 Stat. 202.

[453] Treaty of November 15, 1824, 7 Stat. 232.

that region to exchange their holdings for land lying elsewhere.[454] Then, in the autumn of 1832 four treaties were negotiated at Castor Hill, Missouri, which assured the departure from Missouri of the remnants of the Kickapoos,[455] the Shawanoes and Delawares,[456] the Kaskaskias and Peorias,[457] and the Piankeshaws and Weas.[458] In the meantime other federal commissioners were negotiating with the bands of Pottawatomies, who inhabited Indiana, Illinois, and Michigan. Although a number of treaties [459] providing for cession of their land were concluded with them, it was not until late in 1834 that their signature was secured to the first of a series of "removal" treaties.[460] The treaty of February 11, 1837,[461] provided for final removal within 2 years.

For a number of years the white settlers in the Northwest and the Sacs and Foxes had clashed. In 1804 [462] the United Tribes of Sac and Fox Indians had made a treaty of limits with the United States. The white settlers interpreted that to mean relinquishment of all claims east of the Mississippi. This cession the Sacs and Foxes never recognized.[463] Dissatisfaction was further increased by the treaties of August 4, 1824 [464] August 19, 1825,[465] and July 15, 1830.[466] After the making of the last treaty, the Indians left on their winter hunt and upon returning discovered that their lands north of Rock River, which had been in dispute for some time, had been surveyed and sold during their absence. Hostilities ensued. At the battle of Bad Axe, August 2, 1832, the Winnebagoes and the Sacs and Foxes were defeated.[467] In the treaties of Fort Armstrong which resulted, the United States secured from the Winnebagoes all their claims east of the Mississippi,[468] and from the Sacs and Foxes nearly all of eastern Iowa with the exception of a small reserve on which they were concentrated.[469]

In the following year the Federal Government obtained the consent of the "United Nation of Chippewa, Ottowa and Potawatamie Indians" to a treaty at Chicago, Illinois. In this treaty [470] the United States, in exchange for the land the Indians held—about 5,000,000 acres including the western shore of Lake Michigan—granted to them (Art. 2) approximately the same amount of territory "to be held as other Indian lands are held."

At about the same time, the Quapaws were concentrated in the northeast corner of the Indian territory.[471] This was done because of the failure of the original plan [472] to confine them to lands occupied by the Caddo Indians.[473]

It is not to be assumed that during this period treaty-makers were occupied with "removal" to the exclusion of all else. In fact, until 1828, the number of treaties negotiated solely for the purpose of extinguishing aboriginal title to land predominated.[474] Even during the years 1828–40 when the migration program was at its height, treaties were concluded with the Otoes and Missourias.[475] Pawnees,[476] Menominees,[477] the Miamis,[478] (3 treaties) the Wyandots,[479] the United Nations of Chippewas, Ottawa, and Potawatamie Indians,[480] Ioways,[481] Yankton Sioux,[482] Sioux,[483] and

---

[454] Treaties of cession were common during this period, but outright removal to exchanged lands was not.

[455] Treaty of October 24, 1832, 7 Stat. 391.

[456] Treaty of October 26, 1832, 7 Stat. 397.

[457] Treaty of October 27, 1832, 7 Stat. 403.

[458] Treaty of October 29, 1832, 7 Stat. 410.

[459] Treaty of October 2, 1818, with the Potawatamie, 7 Stat. 185; Treaty of August 29, 1821, with the Ottawa, Chippewa, etc., 7 Stat. 218; Treaty of August 19, 1825, with the Sioux and Chippewa, etc., 7 Stat. 272; Treaty of October 16, 1826, with the Potawatamie, 7 Stat. 295; Treaty of September 19, 1827, with the Potawatamie, 7 Stat. 305; Treaty of August 25, 1828, with the United Tribes of Potawatamie, Chippewa, etc., 7 Stat. 315; Treaty of September 20, 1828, with the Potowatami, 7 Stat. 317; Treaty of July 29, 1829, with the United Nations of Chippewas, Ottawa, etc., 7 Stat. 320; Treaty of October 20, 1832, with the Potawatamie, 7 Stat. 378; Treaty of October 26, 1832, with the Pottawatimie, 7 Stat. 394; Treaty of October 27, 1832, with the Potowatomies, 7 Stat. 399; Treaty of December 4, 1834, with the Potawattimie, 7 Stat. 467; Treaty of December 16, 1834, with the Potawattamie, 7 Stat. 468.

[460] Treaty of December 17, 1834, 7 Stat. 469; Treaty of March 26, 1836, 7 Stat. 490; Treaty of March 29, 1836, 7 Stat. 498; Treaty of April 11, 1836, 7 Stat. 499; Treaty of April 22, 1836, 7 Stat. 500; Treaty of April 22, 1836, 7 Stat. 501; Treaty of August 5, 1836, 7 Stat. 505; Treaty of September 20, 1836, 7 Stat. 513; Treaty of September 22, 1836, 7 Stat. 514; Treaty of September 23, 1836, 7 Stat. 515; Treaty of February 11, 1837, 7. Stat. 532.

[461] 7 Stat. 532.

[462] Treaty of November 3, 1804, 7 Stat. 84.

[463] Abel, *op. cit.*, pp. 388–389.

[464] 7 Stat. 229. Interpreted in *Marsh* v. *Brooks*, 8 How. 223, 231, 232 (1850).

[465] 7 Stat. 272. Construed in *Beecher* v. *Wetherby*, 95 U. S. 517 (1877). To this treaty the Sioux and the Chippewas, Menominie, Ioway, Winnebagoe, and a portion of the Ottawa, Chippewa, and Potawattomie tribes were also parties.

On October 21, 1837, by a treaty with the Sacs and Foxes of Missouri, 7 Stat. 543, the right or interest to the country described in the second article and recognized in the third article of this treaty, was ceded to the United States together with all claims or interests under the treaties of November 3, 1804, 7 Stat. 84; August 4, 1824, 7 Stat. 229; July 15, 1830, 7 Stat. 328; and September 17, 1836, 7 Stat. 511.

[466] 7 Stat. 328.

[467] Abel, *op. cit.*, p. 391.

[468] Treaty of September 15, 1832, 7 Stat. 370.

[469] Treaty of September 21, 1832, 7 Stat. 374.

[470] Treaty of September 26, 1833, 7 Stat. 431.

[471] Treaty of May 13, 1833, 7 Stat. 424.

[472] Treaty of November 15, 1824, 7 Stat. 232.

[473] The lands given them by the Caddoes proved very poor, hence they returned to their old home in Arkansas. (Preamble, Treaty of May 13, 1833, 7 Stat. 424.)

It should be noted that by Treaty of July 1, 1835, the Caddo Indians (7 Stat. 470) agreed to removal in these terms: "* * * promise to remove at their own expense out of the boundaries of the United States * * * and never more return to live settle or establish themselves as a nation tribe or community of people within the same."

[474] There are 21 of these which have not been noted before: Treaty of September 29, 1817, with Wyandot, Seneca, etc., 7 Stat. 160; Treaty of September 17, 1818, with Wyandot, Seneca, etc., 7 Stat. 178; Treaty of September 20, 1818, with Wyandots, 7 Stat. 180; Treaty of October 2, 1818, with Wea Tribe, 7 Stat. 186 ("The United States, by treaty with the Delaware Indians in 1818, agreed to provide a country for them to reside in." *United States* v. *Stone*, 2 Wall. 525 (1864)); Treaty of October 6, 1818, with Miame Nation, 7 Stat. 189; Treaty of September 24, 1819, with Chippewa Nation, 7 Stat. 203; Treaty of June 16, 1820, with Chippeway Tribe, 7 Stat. 206 (7 Stat. 203 and 7 Stat. 206, construed in *Chippewa Indians of Minnesota* v. *United States*, 301 U. S. 358, 360 (1937)); *Spalding* v. *Chandler*, 160 U. S. 394, 403 (1896); Treaty of July 6, 1820, with Ottawa and Chippewa Nations, 7 Stat. 207; Treaty of August 11, 1820, with Wea Tribe, 7 Stat. 209; Treaty of August 5, 1826, with Chippewa Tribe, 7 Stat. 290; Treaty of October 23, 1826, with Miami Tribe, 7 Stat. 300; Treaty of August 11, 1827, with Chippewa, Menomonie, and Winebago Tribes, 7 Stat. 303; Treaty of August 24, 1818, with Quapaw Nation, 7 Stat. 176; Treaty of September 25, 1818, with Great and Little Osage Nation, 7 Stat. 183; Treaty of June 2, 1825, with Great and Little Osage Nation, 7 Stat. 240, construed in *Holden* v. *Joy*, 17 Wall. 211, 245 (1872); Treaty of August 10, 1825, with Great and Little Osage Nations, 7 Stat. 268; Treaty of June 3, 1825, with Kansas Nation, 7 Stat. 244 (construed in *Jones* v. *Meehan*, 175 U. S. 1 (1899); *Smith* v. *Stevens*, 10 Wall. 321, 325 (1870); *State of Missouri* v. *State of Iowa*, 7 How. 660 (1849)); Treaty of November 7, 1825, with Shawonee Nation, 7 Stat. 284; Treaty of September 25, 1818, with Peoria, Kaskaskia, etc., 7 Stat. 181; Treaty of February 11, 1828, with Eel River or Thorntown party of Miami Indians, 7 Stat. 309.

[475] Treaty of September 21, 1833, 7 Stat. 429.

[476] Treaty of October 9, 1833, 7 Stat. 448.

[477] Treaty of October 27, 1832, 7 Stat. 405. This modified the treaty concluded February 8, 1831, 7 Stat. 342, and provided for a grant of land to the Stockbridge, Munsee and Brothertown Indians, and New York Indians. Later the Stockbridge Indians migrated west under the terms of the Treaty of September 3, 1839, 7 Stat. 580.

[478] Treaty of October 23, 1834, 7 Stat. 458; Treaty of November 6, 1838, 7 Stat. 569; Treaty of November 28, 1840, 7 Stat. 582.

[479] Treaty of April 23, 1836, 7 Stat. 502.

[480] Treaty of July 29, 1829, 7 Stat. 320.

[481] Treaty of October 19, 1838, 7 Stat. 568.

[482] Treaty of October 21, 1837, 7 Stat. 542.

[483] Treaty of September 29, 1837, 7 Stat. 538.

Great and Little Osage Indians,[484] providing for a considerable restriction of their ancient domains. A series of treaties were also negotiated about 1825 by Brig. Gen. Henry Atkinson of the United States Army and Benjamin O'Fallon, Indian agent, which dealt only with problems of trade and friendship.[485]

F. TRIBES OF THE FAR WEST: 1846-54

In the late summer of 1846, war having been declared with Mexico,[486] General Philip Kearney in command, the Army of the West advanced into New Mexico.

Without doing battle New Mexico's governor fled, leaving Kearney in control of the province.[487] Following the cession of the province to the United States by the Treaty of Guadalupe Hidalgo, of February 2, 1848,[487a] a treaty of peace with the Navaho Indians who inhabited that region was concluded in 1849.[488]

Two months later, December 30, 1849, another far western tribe, the Utahs, signed a treaty,[489] and the period of negotiating with the Indians who roamed through the area acquired from Mexico and the Oregon Territory may be said to have opened.[490]

To Fort Laramie in the early autumn of 1851 came a great number of Sioux, Cheyenne, Arapaho, Crow, Assiniboine, Gros Ventre, Mandan, and Aricara. After several days of conference, Indian agent Thomas Fitzpatrick secured their signatures to a treaty in which the natives promised peace, acknowledged certain boundaries and agreed to recognize the right of the United States to erect posts and maintain roads within their territory.[491]

This treaty was never formally proclaimed by the President and because of this its validity was challenged in *Roy v. United States and Ogallala Tribe of Sioux Indians.*[492] The Court of Claims examined the circumstances, found that the treaty had been acted upon by Congress, and referred to in subsequent agreements, and held that proclamation was not necessary to give it effect and that both parties were bound by the covenant from the date of its signature.

In the meantime the discovery of gold in California had caused the migration westward to assume the proportions of a stampede. Soon this newly admitted state was faced with the familiar problem of keeping available for preemption purposes an ample supply of public land. An equally familiar solution was quickly decided upon. Congress appropriated $25,000 and dispatched commissioners to treat with the California Indians regarding the territory they occupied.[493]

Some 18 treaties with 18 California tribes were negotiated by these federal agents in 1851. All of them provided for a surrender of native holdings in return for small reservations of land elsewhere. Other stipulations made the Indians subject to state law.[494]

When the terms of these various agreements became known the California State Legislature formally protested the granting of any lands to the Indians. The reasons for this opposition were reviewed by the President and the Secretary of the Interior, and finally a number of months after the agreements had been negotiated they were submitted to the Senate of the United States for ratification. This was refused on July 8, 1852.[495]

The Indians, however, had already begun performance of their part of the agreement. Urged by government officials to anticipate the approval of the treaties they had started on the journey to the proposed reservations. Now they found themselves in the unfortunate position of having surrendered their homes for lands which were already occupied by settlers and regarding which the Federal Government showed no willingness to take action. This situation was never remedied unless the creation in the 1920's of several small reservations for the use of these Indians can be said to have done so.[496]

In 1852 the Apaches, occupying portions of the territory relinquished by Mexico, were invited to a Treaty Council at Santa Fe, New Mexico. They came and duly promised perpetual peace (Art. 2) with the United States.[497] They also engaged (Art. 5) to refrain from warlike incursions into Mexico.

The following year the Comanches, Kiowas, and Apaches met at Fort Atkinson. An agreement very similar in substance to the Santa Fe Treaty was concluded July 27, 1853.[498]

Although the number of families traveling the Oregon trail had increased steadily during the 40's, no agreements were made with the Indians of the territory until 1853. Then, in September of that year, the Rogue River Indians signed a treaty with the United States providing for a substantial cession of land (Art. 1) from which a certain portion was to be reserved for a temporary home until such time as a permanent residence should be designated by the President of the United States (Art. 2).[499] A similar arrangement was made with another Oregon tribe, the Cow Creek Band, on September 19, 1853.[500]

While these first treaties were being signed with the Indian tribes of the Far West, agreements with other tribes were being negotiated. Eight treaties [501] providing for territorial cessions

[484] Treaty of January 11, 1839, 7 Stat. 576.

[485] Treaty of June 9, 1825, with Poncar Tribe, 7 Stat. 247; Treaty of June 22, 1825, with Teton, Yancton, and Yanctonies Bands of Sioux Tribe, 7 Stat. 250; Treaty of July 5, 1825, with Sioune and Ogallala Tribe, 7 Stat. 252; Treaty of July 6, 1825, with Chayenne Tribe, 7 Stat. 255; Treaty of July 16, 1825, with Hunkpapa Band of Sioux, 7 Stat. 257; Treaty of July 18, 1825, with Ricara Tribe, 7 Stat. 259; Treaty of July 30, 1825, with Belantse-etoa or Minnetsaree Tribe, 7 Stat. 261; Treaty of July 30, 1825, with Mandan Tribe, 7 Stat. 264; Treaty of September 26, 1825, with Ottoe and Missouri Tribe, 7 Stat. 277; Treaty of September 30, 1825, with Pawnee Tribe, 7 Stat. 279; Treaty of October 6, 1825, with Maha Tribe, 7 Stat. 282.

[486] Act of May 13, 1846, 9 Stat. 9, and Presidential Proclamation, Appendix No. 2, 9 Stat. 999.

[487] The province was taken in the name of the United States on August 22, 1846, and Kearney was made governor. Wise, The Red Man in the New World Drama (1931), p. 408.

[487a] 9 Stat. 922. See Chapter 20, sec. 3.

[488] Treaty of September 9, 1849, 9 Stat. 974. Article 2 states "That from and after the signing of this treaty, hostilities between the contracting parties shall cease, and perpetual peace and friendship shall exist * * *."

[489] Treaty of December 30, 1849, 9 Stat. 984.

[490] An agreement with the Comanche, Ioni, Anadaca, Caddo, etc., on May 15, 1846, 9 Stat. 844, negotiated in Texas shortly after the Republic had become a member of the Union actually antedates these. The first articles of all three agreements acknowledge the jurisdiction of the United States.

[491] Treaty of September 17, 1851, 11 Stat. 749. Three of these tribes—the Assiniboines, the Arapahoes, and the Gros Ventres—were treating with the United States for the first time. See Rept. Comm. Ind. Aff. (1852), pp. 299-300.

[492] 45 C. Cls. 177 (1910).

[493] Act of September 30, 1850, 9 Stat. 544, 558.

[494] Wise, *op. cit.*, p. 419.

[495] *Ibid.*, pp. 421-425.

[496] *Ibid.*, p. 426. *Cf.* Act of May 18, 1928, 45 Stat. 602, conferring jurisdiction over California Indian claims upon Court of Claims.

[497] Treaty of July 1, 1852, 10 Stat. 979.

[498] Treaty of July 27, 1853, 10 Stat. 1013.

[499] Treaty of September 10, 1853, 10 Stat. 1018. Construed in *Ross, Ex'r v. United States and Rogue River Indians*, 29 C. Cls. 176 (1894). By the treaty of November 15, 1854, 10 Stat. 1119, the Rogue River Indians agreed to permit other tribes and bands, under certain conditions, to reside on their reservation (Art. 1).

[500] Treaty of September 19, 1853, 10 Stat. 1027.

[501] Treaty of January 14, 1846, with Kansas Tribe, 9 Stat. 842; Treaty of August 2, 1847, with Chippewa of the Mississippi and Lake Superior, 9 Stat. 904; Treaty of August 21, 1847, with Pillager Band of Chippewa Indians, 9 Stat. 908; Treaty of August 6, 1848, with Pawnees, 9 Stat. 949; Treaty of April 1, 1850, with Wyandot Nation of Indians, 9 Stat. 987; Treaty of July 23, 1851, with Sioux-Sisseton and Wahpeton Bands, 10 Stat. 949.

and 10 treaties[502] stipulating for removal of the Indians to unoccupied land were signed during these years.

G. EXPERIMENTS IN ALLOTMENT:[503] 1854-61

On March 24, 1853, George W. Manypenny, of Ohio, became Commissioner of Indian Affairs. The new official was designated by the President to enter into negotiations with the tribes west of the states of Missouri and Iowa for white settlement on their land, and extinguishment of their title.[504]

His first success in this connection was with the Ottoes and Missourias on March 15, 1854.[505] Article 6 of the instrument signed on that occasion provides:

> The President may, from time to time, at his discretion, cause the whole of the land herein reserved * * * to be surveyed off into lots, and assign to such Indian or Indians of said confederate tribes, as are willing to avail [themselves] of the privilege, and who will locate on the same as a permanent home, if a single person over twenty-one years of age, one eighth of a section; to each family of two, one quarter section; to each family of three and not exceeding five, one half section; to each family of six and not exceeding ten, one section; and to each family exceeding ten in number, one quarter section for every additional five members. And he may prescribe such rules and regulations as will secure to the family, in case of the death of the head thereof, the possession and enjoyment of such permanent home and the improvements thereon. And the President may, at any time in his discretion, after such person or family has made a location on the land assigned for a permanent home, issue a patent to such person or family for such assigned land, conditioned that the tract shall not be aliened or leased for a longer term than two years; and shall be exempt from levy, sale, or forfeiture, which conditions shall continue in force until a State constitution embracing such land within its boundaries shall have been formed, and the legislature of the State shall remove the restrictions. And if any such person or family shall at any time neglect or refuse to occupy and till a portion of the land assigned, and on which they have located, or shall rove from place to place, the President may, if the patent shall have been issued, revoke the same, or if not issued, cancel the assignment, and may also withhold from such person or family, their proportion of the annuities or other moneys due them, until they shall have returned to such permanent home, and resumed the pursuits of industry; and in default of their return, the tract may be declared abandoned, and thereafter assigned to some other person or family of such confederate tribes, or disposed of as is provided for the disposal of the excess of said land. And the residue of the land hereby reserved, after all the Indian persons or families of such confederate tribes shall have had assigned to them permanent homes, may be sold for their benefit, under such laws, rules, or regulations as may hereafter be prescribed by the Congress or President of the United States. No State legislature shall remove the restriction herein provided for without the consent of Congress.

This treaty, like many other treaties negotiated during the administration of Commissioner Manypenny, included a clause (Art. 3) by which the Indians relinquished all claims to moneys due under earlier treaties. The policy of paying Indians for lands by means of permanent annuities, which had involved the conservation of the Indian estate, was thrown into discard, and there was substituted a policy of quick distribution of tribal funds, parallel to the quick distribution of tribal lands which allotment entailed. Underlying this policy of quick distribution was the assumption that tribal existence was to be brought to an end within a short time.

On March 16, 1854, an agreement similar in its recitals regarding allotments was concluded with the Omahas.[506]

A third treaty providing for the individualization of land holdings was signed by the Shawnee Indians on May 10, 1854.[507] The terminology used in this instrument varies somewhat from that of the preceding treaties. Instead of the provision that—

> "The President may, from time to time * * * cause * * * to be surveyed off into lots, and to assign",

article 2 holds that

> all Shawnees * * * shall be entitled to * * * two hundred acres, and if the head of a family, a quantity equal to two hundred acres for each member of his or her family * * *.

Detailed provisions are also included for the assignment of individual holdings to intermarried persons, minors, orphans, adopted persons and incompetents, the latter to have the selection made by some disinterested person or persons appointed by the Shawnee Council and approved by the United States Commissioner. Further, article 8 provides that "competent" Shawnees shall receive their share of the annuity in money, but that that of the "incompetent" Indians "shall be disposed of by the President" in the manner best calculated to promote their interests, the Shawnee Council being first consulted with respect to such persons.

Six treaties[508] stipulating allotment of land in severalty were

---

[502] Treaty of November 28, 1840, with Miami, 7 Stat. 582; Treaty of March 17, 1842, with Wyandot, 11 Stat. 581; Treaty of October 4, 1842, with Chippewa Indians of the Mississippi and Lake Superior, 7 Stat. 591; Treaty of October 11, 1842, with Sac and Foxes, 7 Stat. 596; Treaty of June 5 and 17, 1846, with Pottowautomie, 9 Stat. 853; Treaty of October 18, 1848, with Menomonee, 9 Stat. 952; Treaty of November 24, 1848, with Stockbridge, 9 Stat. 955; Treaty of March 15, 1854, with Ottoes and Missourias, 10 Stat. 1038.

[503] Prior to 1854, several treaties were signed which provided for the allotment of lands. See Chapter 11, sec. 1A; Chapter 8, sec. 2A1. Several early treaties used the words "allot" and "allotted" but they referred to the assignment of lands to groups of Indians. Kinney, A Continent Lost—A Civilization Won (1937), pp. 82–83.

[504] Rept. of the Comm. of Ind. Aff. (1853), p. 249.

[505] Treaty of March 15, 1854, 10 Stat. 1038.

[506] Treaty of March 16, 1854, 10 Stat. 1043. Construed in *United States* v. *Celestine*, 215 U. S. 278 (1909); *United States* v. *Sutton*, 215 U. S. 291 (1909); *United States* v. *Payne*, 264 U. S. 446 (1924). By the terms of this agreement the United States under certain conditions agreed to pay the Indians $881,000 for land ceded (Arts. 4 and 5). Later it was contended by the Omaha Tribe in a case argued before the Court of Claims in 1918 that although the cession had been made, the Government had failed to pay anything. This the Government admitted but contended that the Omaha Indians did not own and did not have the right to make a cession thereof. In finding for the plaintiff the court said: "At the time the treaty was made the United States recognized the Omahas as having title to this land north of the due-west line, and specifically promised to pay for it. * * * the defendants can not now be heard to say that the Indians did not own the land when the treaty was made and had no right to make a cession of it." *Omaha Tribe* v. *United States*, 53 C. Cls. 549, 560 (1918), mod. 253 U. S. 275, 55 C. Cls. 521.

[507] Treaty of May 10, 1854, 10 Stat. 1053. Construed in *Walker* v. *Henshaw*, 16 Wall. 436 (1872); *United States* v. *Blackfeather*, 155 U. S. 180, 186–187 (1894); *Jones* v. *Meehan*, 175 U. S. 1 (1899); *Blackfeather* v. *United States*, 190 U. S. 368 (1903); and *Dunbar* v. *Greene*, 198 U. S. 166 (1905). Commenting on this treaty, the Supreme Court declared:

> The treaty of 1854 left the Shawnee people a united tribe, with a declaration of their dependence on the National government for protection and the vindication of their rights. Ever since this their tribal organization has remained as it was before. * * * While the general government has a superintending care over their interests, and continues to treat with them as a nation, the State of Kansas is estopped from denying their title to it. She accepted this status when she accepted the act admitting her into the Union. Conferring rights and privileges on these Indians cannot affect their situation, which can only be changed by treaty stipulation, or a voluntary abandonment of their tribal organization. As long as the United States recognizes their national character they are under the protection of treaties and the laws of Congress, and their property is withdrawn from the operation of State laws.

The *Kansas Indians*, 5 Wall. 737, 756–757 (1866).

[508] Delawares, Treaty of May 6, 1854, 10 Stat. 1048; Ioways, Treaty of May 17, 1854, 10 Stat. 1069; Sacs and Fox of the Missouri, Treaty of May 18, 1854, 10 Stat. 1074; Kickapoos, Treaty of May 18, 1854, 10 Stat. 1078; Kaskaskias, Peorias, etc., Treaty of May 30, 1854, 10 Stat. 1082; Miamis, Treaty of June 5, 1854, 10 Stat. 1093.

concluded by Commissioner Manypenny in the next 2 months. In one of these, provision is made for the setting up of a permanent fund with the proceeds from the sale of the lands ceded by the Indians. The United States is charged with the duty of administering this fund. The extent of this obligation was determined by the Court of Claims which held in the *Delaware Tribe* v. *The United States* that the intended trust related to the preservation of the principal received from the sale of the lands and could not be considered, as the Delaware Tribe claimed, an obligation to maintain unimpaired the face value of the securities in which the principal had been first invested.[509]

In the autumn of 1854 the Chippewa of Lake Superior became a party to a treaty providing for the allotment of land to individual Indians by the President at his discretion, and with the power to make

> * * * rules and regulations, respecting the disposition of the lands in case of the death of the head of a family, or single person occupying the same, or in case of its abandonment by them.[510]

Article 2 also provides for the patenting of 80 acres to each mixed blood over 21 years of age.

The Wyandot treaty concluded January 31, 1855[511] is particularly interesting. The first article stipulates that tribal bands are dissolved, declares the Indians to be citizens of the United States and subject to the laws thereof and of the territory of Kansas, although those who wish to be exempted from the immediate operation of such provisions shall have continued to them the assistance and protection of the United States. Article 2 provides for the cession of their holdings to the United States stipulating the "object of which cession is, that the said lands shall be subdivided, assigned, and reconveyed, by patent, in fee simple, in the manner hereinafter provided for, to the individuals and members of the Wyandott nation, in severalty." Articles 4 and 5 provide for the most detailed method of allotment yet encountered, in which three commissioners, one from the United States and two from the Wyandott nation, were to make a distribution of lands to certain specified classes of individuals. Patents are then to issue containing an absolute and unconditional grant of fee simple to those individuals listed as "competent" by the commissioners, but for those not so listed the patents will contain certain restrictions and may be withheld by the Commissioner of Indian Affairs. None of the land thus assigned and patented is subject to taxation for a period of 5 years.

In February of 1855 the Chippewa of Minnesota and the Winnebago signed treaties[512] ceding their territorial holdings but out of which there is "reserved" and "set apart" for the Chippewas and "granted" for the Winnebagos land for a permanent home. Further, the President is authorized whenever he deems it advisable to allot their lands in severalty.

The tribes of the Far West were not overlooked in this burst of treaty-making activity. In the closing months of 1854 and the opening days of the following year six treaties[513] were negotiated with the Indians of Oregon, the various tribes of the Puget Sound region, etc. All of these provided for the allotment of land in severalty and for reservations of territory described by such phrases as "such portions * * * as may be assigned to them," "shall be held * * * as an Indian reservation," and "district which shall be designated for permanent occupancy."

Seven more treaties providing for the assignment of land to individual Indians were negotiated during Commissioner Manypenny's administration, which ended in 1857. All of these feature extensive land cessions with certain areas either "set apart as a residence * * *" or "held and regarded as an Indian reservation" or "reserved * * * for the use and occupation."[514]

James W. Denver, Charles E. Mix, and Alfred B. Greenwood, who successively held the position of Commissioner of Indian Affairs until the outbreak of the Civil War, were likewise committed to a treaty policy providing for allotment in severalty. Under their auspices seven such agreements[515] were negotiated. These instruments in form and substance differ little from those of the Manypenny administration.

H. THE CIVIL WAR: 1861–65

The four years of conflict between the states had its effect on the various Indian tribes. Violence and bloodshed had become commonplace and several Indian tribes seized the occasion to accompany demands upon the Federal Government with a display of force.[516] This was particularly the case in Minnesota.

[509] 72 C. Cls. 483 (1931).

For opinion that a patent under Art. 13 should issue to Christian Indians but it may be restricted by act of Congress after issue unless the effect would be to invalidate title of bona fide purchaser; that title of Christian Indians will not be vested in the Indians comprising the tribe called by that name as tenants in common, but in the tribe itself or the nation; see 9 Op. A. G. 24 (1857). And see Chapter 15, sec. 1A.

[510] Treaty of September 30, 1854, Art. 3, 10 Stat. 1109. Construed in *Fee* v. *Brown*, 162 U. S. 602 (1896); *Wisconsin* v. *Hitchcock*, 201 U. S. 202 (1906); *Chippewa Indians of Minnesota* v. *United States*, 301 U. S. 358 (1937); and *Minnesota* v. *United States*, 305 U. S. 382 (1939).

The President is empowered by Art. 3 to issue patents with "such restrictions of the power of alienation as he may see fit to impose." A stipulation that the patentee and his heirs shall not sell, lease, or in any manner alienate said tract without the consent of the President of the United States is within the meaning of this Article. *United States* v. *Raiche*, 31 F. (2d) 624 (D. C. W. D. Wis., 1928). Moreover such restrictions extend to the timber on the land as well as the land itself. *Starr* v. *Campbell*, 208 U. S. 527 (1908).

The court in holding that state fish and game laws have no application to the Bad River Reservation because federal laws are exclusive also called attention to Art. 11 of the above treaty which gave the right to hunt and fish on lands ceded until otherwise ordered by the President. *In re Blackbird*, 109 Fed. 139 (D. C. W. D. Wis., 1901).

[511] Treaty of January 31, 1855, 10 Stat. 1159. Construed in *Goudy* v. *Meath*, 203 U. S. 146, 149 (1906) (power of voluntary sale granted; land withheld from taxation or forced alienation); *Walker* v. *Henshaw*, 16 Wall. 436, 441 (1872); *Schrimpscher* v. *Stockton*, 183 U. S. 290 (1902); *Conley* v. *Ballinger*, 216 U. S. 84 (1910).

[512] Treaty of February 22, 1855, 10 Stat. 1165. Construed in *United States* v. *Mille Lac Band of Chippewa Indians*, 229 U. S. 498, 500, 501 (1913); *United States* v. *First National Bank*, 234 U. S. 245, 261 (1914) (dealing with rights of mixed blood Chippewas); *Johnson* v. *Gearlds*, 234 U. S. 422, 437 (1914) (discussing liquor provisions); *United States* v. *Minnesota*, 270 U. S. 181 (1926); and *Chippewa Indians of Minnesota* v. *United States*, 301 U. S. 358 (1937). Treaty of February 27, 1855, 10 Stat. 1172.

[513] Treaty with the Umpqua, etc., of November 29, 1854, 10 Stat. 1125; Treaty with the Chasta, etc., of November 18, 1854, 10 Stat. 1122; Treaty with the Willamette, of January 22, 1855, 10 Stat. 1143; Treaty with the Wyandott, January 31, 1855, 10 Stat. 1159; Treaty with the Nisqually, etc., December 26, 1854, 10 Stat. 1132; Treaty with the Mississippi Chippewa, February 22, 1855, 10 Stat. 1165.

[514] Treaty of June 9, 1855, with Walla-Wallas, Cayuses, and Umatilla Tribes, 12 Stat. 945; Treaty of June 25, 1855, with Indians in middle Oregon, 12 Stat. 963; Treaty of June 9, 1855, with Yakamas, 12 Stat. 951; Treaty of June 11, 1855, with Nez Perces, 12 Stat. 957; Treaty of July 16, 1855, with Flatheads, etc., 12 Stat. 975; Treaty of July 31, 1855, with Ottawas and Chippewas, 11 Stat. 621; Treaty of August 2, 1855, with Chippewas, 11 Stat. 633.

[515] Mendawakanton and Wahpakoota Bands of Sioux, Treaty of June 19, 1858, 12 Stat. 1031; Sisseeton and Wahpaton Bands of Sioux, Treaty of June 19, 1858, 12 Stat. 1037; Winnebago, Treaty of April 15, 1859, 12 Stat. 1101; Swan Creek Chippewas and Christian Indians, Treaty of July 16, 1859, 12 Stat. 1105; Sacs and Foxes, Treaty of October 1, 1859, 15 Stat. 467; Kansas Indians, Treaty of October 5, 1859, 12 Stat. 1111; Delawares, Treaty of May 30, 1860, 12 Stat. 1129.

[516] However several treaties of allotment were negotiated during this period. Treaty of March 13, 1862, with Kansas Indians, 12 Stat. 1221; Treaty of June 24, 1862, with Ottawas, 12 Stat. 1237; Treaty of June 28, 1862, with Kickapoos, 13 Stat. 623; Treaty of June 9, 1863, with the Nez Perce, 14 Stat. 647; Treaty of October 14, 1864, with the

where in the summer of 1862, the Sioux of the Mississippi participated in a general unsuccessful uprising against the whites.[517]

While no treaty negotiations were attempted with the Sioux of that state, the Chippewas were called to a series of treaty councils in 1863 and 1864. Here their signatures were secured to treaties providing for removal and allotment of land in severalty.[518]

In the Far West the United States succeeded in making treaties at Fort Bridger,[519] Box Elder[520] and Tuilla Valley[521] in the Utah Territory and at Ruby Valley[522] in the Nevada Territory with the Shoshonees; at Lapwai in the Territory of Washington with the Nez Perce;[523] at Cosnejos in the Colorado Territory with the Utahs;[524] and at Klamath Lake in Oregon with the Klamath Indians.[525] The last mentioned were negotiating with the United States for the first time and Article 9 of the agreement signed by them included the very broad stipulation then being inserted in many treaties that

> * * * They will submit to and obey all laws and regulations which the United States may prescribe for their government and conduct.

I. POST CIVIL WAR TREATIES: 1865–71

The years immediately after the close of the Civil War were filled with Indian councils and conferences. Usually these parleys resulted in the signing of treaties in which mutual pledges of amity and friendship were prominent and frequent.

In October of 1865 the Cheyenne and Arapaho,[526] the Apache, Cheyenne, and Arapaho,[527] the Comanche and Kiowa[528] met with Army officers Sanborn and Harney and signed treaties promising that peace would hereafter be maintained. A few days later eight tribes of Sioux at Fort Sully made the same promise.[529]

Immediately after the close of war, commissioners representing the President of the United States, appeared among the Five Civilized Tribes. Some of these Indians had been openly sympathetic with the rebel cause, even entering into treaties with the Confederacy. This action was seized upon by the commissioners as an indication of disloyalty; and a treaty negotiated in 1865 with the Creeks, Cherokees, Choctaws, Chickasaws, Osage, Seminoles, Senecas, Shawnee, and Quapaw tribes opens with the statement that the Indians by their defection had become liable to a forfeiture of all the guarantees which the United States had previously made to them.[530]

While this treaty was never ratified, the principle announced undoubtedly colored subsequent negotiations and is reflected in the treaties of 1866 with the Seminoles,[531] Choctaws and Chickasaws,[532] Creeks,[533] and Cherokees.[534] These agreements provide, among other things, for the surrender of a considerable portion of the territory occupied by the Indians; they pledge peace, general amnesty, the abolition of slavery, and the assurance of civil and property rights to freedmen, and acknowledge a large measure of control by the Federal Government over the affairs of the tribes.

The summer of 1867 found the Plains still in the grip of the Sioux War. Moreover, the Cheyenne and Arapaho, the Comanche and Kiowa had joined the belligerents, carrying hostilities over a wide area.

The Indian Peace Commission,[535] composed of civilians and Army officers appointed "to investigate the cause of the war and to arrange for peace,"[536] was successful in part. At Medicine Lodge Creek in Kansas, the Kiowa, Comanche, and Apache;[537] and the Arapaho and Cheyenne[538] promised peace, the abandonment of the chase, and the pursuit of the habits of civilized living.

In the summer of 1868, many Sioux, together with a scattering of Cheyenne and Arapaho warriors, renewed hostilities, which were terminated by the treaty of April 29, 1868.[539] A month later the Crows[540] and the Northern Arapaho and Cheyenne[541] put an end to hostilities in two agreements concluded May 7, 1868, and

---

Klamaths, 16 Stat. 707. In addition, an agreement amendatory of the Treaty of October 5, 1859, 12 Stat. 1111 was entered into with the Kansas Indians, Treaty of March 13, 1862, 12 Stat. 1221. Also see Chapter 8, sec. 11.

517 Seymour, Story of the Red Man (1929) 268–287.

518 Treaty of March 11, 1863, with Chippewa of the Mississippi and the Pillager and Lake Winibigoshish Bands, 12 Stat. 1249; Treaty of October 2, 1863, with Red Lake and Pembina Bands of Chippewa, 13 Stat. 667; Treaty of April 12, 1864, with Red Lake and Pembina Bands of Chippewa, 13 Stat. 689; Treaty of May 7, 1864, with Chippewa of the Mississippi and the Pillager and Winnebagoshish Bands, 13 Stat. 693; Treaty of October 18, 1864, with Chippewa of Saginaw, Swan Creek, and Black River, 14 Stat. 657.

519 Treaty of July 2, 1863, with Eastern Bands of Shoshonee Indians, 18 Stat. 685.

520 Treaty of July 30, 1863, with Northwestern Bands of Shoshonee Indians, 13 Stat. 663.

521 Treaty of October 12, 1863, with Shoshone-Goship Bands, 18 Stat. 681.

522 Treaty of October 1, 1863, with Western Bands of Shoshonee Indians, 18 Stat. 689. Art. 6 of the treaty recites:

> The said bands agree that whenever the President of the United States shall deem it expedient for them to abandon the roaming life, which they now lead, and become herdsmen or agriculturists, he is hereby authorized to make such reservations for their use as he may deem necessary within the country above described; and they do also hereby agree to remove their camps to such reservations as he may indicate, and to reside and remain therein.

Art. 6 of the treaty with the Shoshone-Goship Bands (see fn. 521, *supra*) is similar.

523 Treaty of June 9, 1863, with the Nez Perce, 14 Stat. 647.

524 Treaty of October 7, 1863, with Tabeguache Band of Utahs, 13 Stat. 673.

525 Treaty of October 14, 1864, with Klamath and Moadoc tribes and Yahooskin Band of Snake Indians, 16 Stat. 707.

526 Treaty of October 14, 1865, 14 Stat. 703.

527 Treaty of October 17, 1865, 14 Stat. 713.

528 Treaty of October 18, 1865, 14 Stat. 717.

529 Two Kettles Band of Sioux Indians, Treaty of October 19, 1865, 14 Stat. 723; Blackfeet Band of Sioux, Treaty of October 19, 1865, 14 Stat. 727; Sans Arc Band of Sioux, Treaty of October 20, 1865, 14 Stat. 731; Onkpa'pah Band of Sioux, Treaty of October 20, 1865, 14 Stat. 739; Yanktonai Band of Sioux, Treaty of October 20, 1865, 14 Stat. 735; Upper Yanktonai Band of Sioux, Treaty of October 28, 1865, 14 Stat. 743; O'Gallala Band of Sioux, Treaty of October 28, 1865, 14 Stat. 747; Lower Brule Band of Sioux, Treaty of October 14, 1865, 14 Stat. 699.

The peace established by these agreements was a fleeting one. War continued with the Sioux save for a brief interruption for 2 years thereafter.

530 Kinney, *op. cit.*, p. 157.

531 Treaty of March 21, 1866, 14 Stat. 755.

532 Treaty of April 28, 1866, 14 Stat. 769.

533 Treaty of June 14, 1866, 14 Stat. 785.

534 Treaty of July 19, 1866, 14 Stat. 799.

535 Established by Act of July 20, 1867, 15 Stat. 17.

536 Report of the Commissioner of Indian Affairs, 1868, p. 4.

537 Treaty of October 21, 1867, 15 Stat. 581; Treaty of October 21, 1867, 15 Stat. 589.

538 Treaty of October 28, 1867, 15 Stat. 593.

539 Treaty of April 29, 1868, 15 Stat. 635. By the Sioux treaty, the United States agreed that for every 30 children (of the said Sioux tribe who can be induced or compelled to attend school) a house should be provided and a teacher competent to teach the elementary branches of our English education should be furnished. (*Quick Bear* v. *Leupp*, 210 U. S. 50, 80 (1908).)

540 Treaty of May 7, 1868, 15 Stat. 649. Construed in *Draper* v. *United States*, 164 U. S. 240 (1896): *United States* v. *Powers*, 305 U. S. 527, 529 (1939).

541 Treaty of May 10, 1868, 15 Stat. 655.

May 10, 1868. By summer the Navajo,[542] the eastern band of Shoshonee and the Bannock,[543] and the Nez Perce[544] had also become signatories to treaties of peace. These were the last treaties made by the United States with Indian tribes.

[542] Treaty of June 1, 1868, 15 Stat. 667. Provision for allotment of land in severalty to individuals wishing to farm is found in Art. 5 of this treaty. This agreement also contains in Art. 1 this familiar recital:

> If bad men among the Indians shall commit a wrong or depredation upon the person or property of any one, white, black, or Indian, subject to the authority of the United States and at peace therewith, the Navajo tribe agree that they will, on proof made to their agent, and on notice by him, deliver up the wrongdoer to the United States, to be tried and punished according to its laws * * *.

In 1909, the Supreme Court of Arizona in holding the district court in error in denying to several Indians who had been imprisoned by the War Department a writ of habeas corpus called attention to this recital saying:

> * * * This stipulation amounts to a covenant that bad Indians shall not be punished by the United States, except pursuant to laws defining their offenses and prescribing the punishments therefor. While Congress by its legislation may disregard treaties, the executive branch of the government may not do so. The district court was in error in denying the writ of *habeas corpus*.

In re By-A-Lil-Le, 12 Ariz. 150, 155 (1909).

[543] Treaty of July 3, 1868, 15 Stat. 673. Construed in *Harkness* v. *Hyde*, 98 U. S. 476 (1878); *Marks* v. *United States*, 161 U. S. 297 (1896); and *Ward* v. *Race Horse*, 163 U. S. 504 (1896).

In *United States* v. *Shoshone Tribe of Indians*, 304 U. S. 111 (1938), it was held that the right of the Shoshone Tribe in the lands set apart for it, under the treaty of July 3, 1868, with the United States, included the mineral and timber resources of the reservation; and the value of these was properly included in fixing the amount of compensation due for so much of the lands as was taken by the United States.

[544] Treaty of August 13, 1868, 15 Stat. 693.

SECTION 5. THE END OF TREATY-MAKING

The advancing tide of settlement in the years following the close of the Civil War dispelled the belief that it would ever be possible to separate the Indians from the whites and thus give them an opportunity to work out their salvation alone. Assimilation, allotment, and citizenship became the watchwords of Indian administration[545] and attacks on the making of treaties grew in force.[546]

The termination of the treaty-making period was presaged by section 6 of the Act of March 29, 1867,[547] which provided:

> And all laws allowing the President, the Secretary of the Interior, or the commissioner of Indian affairs to enter into treaties with any Indian tribes are hereby repealed, and no expense shall hereafter be incurred in negotiating a treaty with any Indian tribe until an appropriation authorizing such expense shall be first made by law.

This provision marked the growing opposition of the House of Representatives to the practical exclusion of that House from control over Indian affairs. The provision in question was repealed a few months later[548] but the House continued its struggle against the Indian treaty system. Schmeckebier recounts the incidents of that struggle in these terms:

> While the Indian Peace Commission succeeded in ending the Indian wars, the treaties negotiated by it and ratified by the Senate were not acceptable to the House of Representatives. As the Senate alone ratified the treaties, the House had no opportunity of expressing its opinion regarding them until the appropriation bill for the fiscal year 1870, making appropriations for carrying out the treaties, came before it for approval during the third session of the Fortieth Congress. The items providing funds for fulfilling the treaties were inserted by the Senate, but the House refused to agree to them, and the session expired on March 4, 1869, without any appropriations being made for the Indian Office for the fiscal year beginning July 1. When the first session of the Forty-first Congress convened in March, 1869, a bill was passed by the House in the same form as at the previous session. The Senate promptly amended it to include the sums needed to carry out the treaties negotiated by the Peace Commission. The House again refused to agree but a compromise was finally reached by which there was voted in addition to the usual appropriations a lump sum of two million dollars "to enable the President to maintain peace among and with the various tribes, bands, and parties of Indians, and to promote civilization among said Indians, bring them, where practicable, upon reservations, relieve their necessities, and encourage their efforts at self-support" (16 Stat. L., 40).
>
> The House also insisted on the insertion of a section providing "That nothing in this act contained, or in any of the provisions thereof, shall be so construed as to ratify or approve any treaty made with any tribes, bands or parties of Indians since the twentieth day of July, 1867." This was rather a remarkable piece of legislation in that while it did not abrogate the treaties, it withheld its approval although the treaties had already been formally ratified and proclaimed. It had no legal effect, but merely wrote into the act the feeling of the House of Representatives. At the next session of Congress a similar section was added to the Indian appropriation act for the fiscal year 1871, with the additional provision that nothing in the act should ratify, approve, or disaffirm any treaty made since July 20, 1867, "or affirm or disaffirm any of the powers of the Executive and Senate over the subject." The entire section, however, was inadvertently omitted in the enrollment of the bill, and was not formally enacted until the passage of the appropriation act for the fiscal year 1872 (16 Stat. L., 570).
>
> Probably one of the reasons for the refusal of the House to agree to the treaty provisions was its distrust of the administration of the Office of Indian Affairs, for it was during the debate on this bill that General Garfield made his scathing indictment of that Office. * * * (Pp. 55–56.)
>
> * * * * * *
>
> *Discontinuance of treaty making, 1871.*—When the appropriation bill for the fiscal year 1871 came up in the second session of the Forty-first Congress the fight of the previous year was renewed, the Senate insisting on appropriations for carrying out the new treaties and the House refusing to grant any funds for that purpose. As the end of the session approached it appeared as if the bill would fail entirely, but after the President had called the attention of Congress to the necessity of making the appropriations, the two houses finally reconciled their differences.
>
> The strong fight made by the House and expressions of many members of the Senate made it evident that the treaty system had reached its end, and the Indian appropriation act for the fiscal year 1872, approved on March 3, 1871 (16 Stat. L., 566), contained the following clause, tacked on to a sentence making an appropriation for the Yankton Indians: "*Provided*, That hereafter no Indian nation or tribe within the territory of the United States shall be acknowledged or recognized as an independent nation, tribe, or power with whom the United States may contract by treaty: *Provided further*, That nothing herein

[545] See Chapter 2, sec. 2, for excerpts from commissioners' reports advocating termination of the treaty system.

[546] *Ibid.*

[547] 15 Stat. 7, 9. Also see Act of April 10, 1869, sec. 5, 16 Stat. 13, 40. The first annual report of the Board of Indian Commissioners submitted late in 1869, and the annual report of the Commissioner of Indian Affairs for the same year recommended the abolition of the treaty system of dealing with the tribes. Kinney, A Continent Lost—A Civilization Won (1937), pp. 148, 159, 160.

[548] Act of July 20, 1867, 15 Stat. 18.

contained shall be construed to invalidate or impair the obligation of any treaty heretofore lawfully made and ratified with any such Indian nation or tribe." (P. 58.)[549]

[549] Schmeckebier, Office of Indian Affairs, 1927, pp. 56–58, Act of March 3, 1871, 16 Stat. 544, 566, R. S. § 2079, 25 U. S. C. 71. See also the statement of former Commissioner of Indian Affairs, Francis A. Walker, who wrote in 1874:

> In 1871, however, the insolence of conscious strength, and the growing jealousy of the House of Representatives towards the prerogative—arrogated by the Senate—of determining, in connection with the executive, all questions of Indian right and title, and of committing the United States incidentally to pecuniary obligations limited only by its own discretion, for which the House should be bound to make provision without inquiry, led to the adoption, after several severe parliamentary struggles, of the declaration * * * (pp. 11–12), that "hereafter no Indian nation or tribe within the territory of the United States shall be acknowledged or recognized as an independent nation, tribe, or power, with whom the United States may contract by treaty." (P. 5.) (Walker, The Indian Question, 1874.)

Following this enactment, a congressional committee was appointed to prepare a compilation of treaties still in force. Act of March 3, 1873, 17 Stat. 579.

SECTION 6. INDIAN AGREEMENTS

The substance of treaty-making was destined, however, to continue for many decades. For in substance a treaty was an agreement between the Federal Government and an Indian tribe. And so long as the Federal Government and the tribes continue to have common dealings, occasions for agreements are likely to recur. Thus the period of Indian land cessions was marked by the "agreements" through which such cessions were made.[550] These agreements differed from formal treaties only in that they were ratified by both houses of Congress instead of by the Senate alone.[551] Like treaties, these agreements can be modified,[552] except that rights created by carrying the agreement into effect cannot be impaired.[553] In referring to such an agreement, Justice Van Devanter said:[554]

> But it is said that the act of 1902 contemplated that they alone should receive allotments and be the participants in the distribution of the remaining lands, and also of the funds, of the tribe. No doubt such was the purport of the act. But that, in our opinion, did not confer upon them any vested right such as would disable Congress from thereafter making provision for admitting newly born members of the tribe to the allotment and distribution. The difficulty with the appellants' contention is that it treats the act of 1902 as a contract, when "it is only an act of Congress and can have no greater effect." *Cherokee Intermarriage Cases*, 203 U. S. 76, 93. It was but an exertion of the administrative control of the Government over the tribal property of tribal Indians, and was subject to change by Congress at any time before it was carried into effect and while the tribal relations continued. *Stephens* v. *Cherokee Nation*, 174 U. S. 445, 488; *Cherokee Nation* v. *Hitchcock*, 187 U. S. 294; *Wallace* v. *Adams*, 204 U. S. 415, 423. (P. 648.)

Legislation based upon Indian consent does not come to an end with the close of the period of Indian land cessions and the stoppage of Indian land losses in 1934. For in that very year the underlying assumption of the treaty period that the Federal Government's relations with the Indian tribes should rest upon a basis of mutual consent was given new life in the mechanism of federally approved tribal constitutions and tribally approved federal charters established by the Act of June 18, 1934.[555] Thus, while the form of treaty-making no longer obtains, the fact that Indian tribes are governed primarily on a basis established by common agreement remains, and is likely to remain so long as the Indian tribes maintain their existence and the Federal Government maintains the traditional democratic faith that all Government derives its just powers from the consent of the governed.

[550] Such agreements are exemplified by the Act of April 29, 1874, with the Utes, 18 Stat. 36; Act of July 10, 1882, with the Crows, 22 Stat. 157; Act of March 1, 1901, with the Cherokees, 31 Stat. 848. The propriety of legislation dependent upon Indian consent was questioned for a time but apparently doubts were set at rest, and the practice of legislating on the basis of Indian consent became solidly established. See G. F. Canfield, Legal Position of the Indian (1881), 15 Am. L. Rev. 21, 25.

[551] Thus in *Dick* v. *United States*, 208 U. S. 340, 359 (1908), the Supreme Court upheld the constitutionality of a prohibition against introduction of liquor into certain ceded lands, which was contained in an agreement of 1893 with the Nez Perce Tribe, as "a valid regulation based upon the treaty-making power of the United States and upon the power of Congress to regulate commerce with those Indians."

Even the wording of statutes providing for the negotiation of agreements sometimes discloses their kinship with treaties. For example, the Act of May 1, 1876, 19 Stat. 41, 45, provides for the payment of a commission "to treat with the Sioux Indians for the relinquishment of the Black Hills country in Dakota Territory."

[552] The Supreme Court in the case of *United States* v. *Seminole Nation*, 299 U. S. 417, 428 (1937), said:

> * * * "That Congress had the power to change the terms of the agreement and authorize these payments, is well established. * * *" *Lone Wolf* v. *Hitchcock*, 187 U. S. 553, 564–567.

The Attorney General has said, 26 Op. A. G. 340, 347 (1907):

> * * * Certainly if, as has been often adjudged, Congress may abrogate a formal treaty with a sovereign nation (*Chinese Exclusion case*, 130 U. S., 581; *Horner* v. *United States*, 143 U. S., 578; *Fong Yue Ting* v. *United States*, 149 U. S., 706; *La Abra Silver Mining Co.* v. *United States*, 175 U. S., 460), it may alter or repeal an agreement of this kind with an Indian tribe.

In considering whether it has been superseded by a general law, an agreement has been accorded the same status as a special law. *Marlin* v. *Lewallen*, 276 U. S. 58, 67 (1928). Accord: *Longest* v. *Langford*, 276 U. S. 69 (1928).

[553] *Choate* v. *Trapp*, 224 U. S. 665, 671 (1912).

[554] *Gritts* v. *Fisher*, 224 U. S. 640, 648 (1912), quoted with approval in *Sizemore* v. *Brady*, 235 U. S. 441, 450 (1914).

[555] 48 Stat. 984, 25 U. S. C. 461, *et seq.*, discussed in Chapter 4, sec 16.

CHAPTER 4

FEDERAL INDIAN LEGISLATION

TABLE OF CONTENTS

While federal Indian legislation forms the basic material of all the substantive chapters that follow, it may serve a useful purpose to present at this point a brief panorama of the more important general statutes in the field that have been enacted during the century and a half which this book covers. Such a panorama may convey some sense of the dynamic development of Indian legislation, and throw some light upon the basic purposes that have dominated Indian legislation at different periods in our history. Such historical perspective is of particular usefulness in the field of Indian law. Solicitor Margold, in his introduction to the Statutory Compilation of the Indian Law Survey,[1] comments on "the importance of the factor of history in this field of law" in the following terms:

> During the century and a half that this compilation covers, the groups of human beings with whom this law deals have undergone changes in living habits, institutions, needs, and aspirations far greater than the changes that separate from our own age the ages for which Hammurabi, Moses, Lycurgus, or Justinian legislated. Telescoped into a century and a half, one may find changes in social, political, and property relations which stretch over more than thirty centuries of European civilization. The toughness of law which keeps it from changing as rapidly as social conditions change in our national life is, of course, much more serious where the rate of social change is twenty times as rapid. Thus, if the laws governing Indian affairs are viewed as lawyers generally view existing law, without reference to the varying times in which particular provisions were enacted, the body of the law thus viewed is a mystifying collection of inconsistencies and anachronisms. To recognize the different dates at which various provisions were enacted is the first step towards order and sanity in this field.
>
> Not only is it important to recognize the temporal "depth" of existing legislation, it is also important to appreciate the past existence of legislation which has, technically, ceased to exist. For there is a very real sense in which it can be said that no provision of law is ever completely wiped out. This is particularly true in the field of Indian law. At every session of the Supreme Court, there arise cases in which the validity of a present claim depends upon the question: What was the law on such and such a point in some earlier period? Laws long repealed have served to create legal rights which endure and which can be understood only by reference to the repealed legislation. Thus, in seeking a complete answer to various questions of Indian law, one finds that he cannot rest with a collection of laws "still in force," but must constantly recur to legislation that has been repealed, amended, or superseded.

Let this serve at the same time as an apology for including in this work a chronicle of Indian legislation and as an explanation of the rudimentary character of this chronicle. To analyze the legal problems raised by each of the statutes noted is, after all, the main task of the rest of the book. For our present purposes it suffices simply to note what legislative problems in the field of Indian law have been faced in each decade of our national existence.[2]

[1] U. S. Dept. of the Interior, Office of the Solicitor, Statutory Compilation of the Indian Law Survey: A Compendium of Federal Laws and Treaties Relating to Indians, edited by Felix S. Cohen, Chief, Indian Law Survey, with a Foreword by Nathan R. Margold, Solicitor, Department of the Interior (1940), 46 vols.

[2] On the interpretation of Indian statutes, see Chapter 8, sec. 9I.

SECTION 1. THE BEGINNINGS: 1789

During the first year of the first Congress, and indeed in the space of some 5 weeks, there were enacted four statutes which established the outlines of our Indian legislation for many years to come. The first of these was the Act of August 7, 1789,[3] establishing the Department of War, which provided that that Department should handle, in addition to its primary military affairs "such other matters * * * as the President of the United States shall assign to the said department * * * relative to Indian affairs." We have elsewhere noted how the authority thus conferred was later transferred to the Department of the Interior.[4] While the days have long passed when our military relations with the Indian tribes were the most

[3] 1 Stat. 49.

[4] See Chapter 2, sec. 1B, and Chapter 8, sec. 10A(3).

important aspect of Indian affairs to the Federal Government, the types of administrative control established under the Act of August 7, 1789, still play a large part in Indian law.

The second statute[5] referring to Indians enacted by the new Congress provided for the government of the Northwest Territory and in effect reenacted, with minor amendments, the Northwest Ordinance of 1787 containing the following article on Indian affairs:

> ART. 3. * * * The utmost good faith shall always be observed towards the Indians; their land and property shall never be taken from them without their consent; and in their property, rights, and liberty, they never shall be invaded or disturbed, unless in just and lawful wars authorized by Congress; but laws founded in justice and humanity shall from time to time be made, for preventing wrongs being done to them, and for preserving peace and friendship with them.

This represented the first of many measures by which Congress, in administering the government of the territories, legislated over Indian affairs with "plenary" authority. Congress legislated for the territories with the same latitude that the states enacted legislation to govern human conduct within state boundaries.[6]

The statute dealing with the Northwest Territory was followed by statutes establishing territorial or state governments for 35 states admitted to the Union after the adoption of the Constitution. In these 35 states were located nearly all the Indians with whom the federal law on Indian affairs now deals. Here perhaps is one clue to the frequent use of the concept of "plenary power" vested in the Federal Government over Indian affairs.

The third act of Congress dealing with Indian affairs was the Act of August 20, 1789,[7] which appropriated a sum not exceeding $20,000 to defray "the expense of negotiating and treating with the Indian tribes" and provided for the appointment of commissioners to manage such negotiations and treaties. This statute thus marks the beginning of a mode of dealing with Indian affairs that was to remain the primary mode of governmental action in this field for many decades to come.[8]

The fourth and last of the statutes enacted by Congress at its first session which dealt with Indian affairs was the Act of September 11, 1789,[9] which specified salaries to be paid to the "superintendent of Indian affairs in the northern department," a position held *ex officio* by the governor of the western territory.

Noteworthy is the fact that of the first 13 statutes enacted by the first Congress of the United States, four dealt primarily or partially with Indian affairs. In these four statutes we find the essential administrative machinery for dealing with Indian affairs established, and its expenses provided for. And we find four important sources of federal authority in dealing with Indian matters invoked: The power to make war (and, presumably, peace); the power to govern territories; the power to make treaties, and the power to spend money.[10]

[5] Act of August 7, 1789, 1 Stat. 50. For a discussion of colonial dealings with the Indians concerning land, see Chapter 15, sec. 9.

[6] See Chapter 5, sec. 5.

[7] 1 Stat. 54.

[8] See Chapter 3.

[9] 1 Stat. 67.

[10] Also see Chapter 5, sec. 1.

SECTION 2. LEGISLATION FROM 1790 TO 1799

The first act of Congress specifically defining substantive rights and duties in the field of Indian affairs was the Act of July 22, 1790,[11] significantly titled, "An Act to regulate trade and intercourse with the Indian tribes." The significance of the title becomes clear when one notes that the act deals not only with the conduct of licensed traders, but also with the sale of Indian lands, the commission of crimes and trespasses against Indians and the procedure for punishing white men committing offenses against Indians. It seems fair to infer that the legislators who adopted this statute thereby gave a practical and contemporaneous construction to the clause of the Federal Constitution which gives to Congress

> * * * the power to regulate commerce * * * with the Indian tribes * * *.[12]

The Act of July 22, 1790, contained seven sections. The first three provided that trade or intercourse with the Indian tribes should be limited to persons licensed by the Federal Government; that such licenses might be revoked for violations of regulations governing such trade, prescribed by the President, and that persons trading without licenses should forfeit all merchandise in their possession.[13]

Section 4 declared:

> * * * That no sale of lands made by any Indians, or any nation or tribe of Indians within the United States, shall be valid to any person or persons, or to any state, whether having the right of pre-emption to such lands or not, unless the same shall be made and duly executed at some public treaty, held under the authority of the United States.[14]

Sections 5 and 6 dealt with crimes and trespasses committed by non-Indians against Indians within "any town, settlement or territory belonging to any nation or tribe of Indians * * *." Such offenders were to be subject to the same punishment to which they would be subject if the offenses had been committed against a non-Indian within the jurisdiction of the state or district from which the offender came, and the procedure applicable in cases involving crimes against the United States was made applicable to such offenders.[15]

The final section declared that the act should "be in force for the term of two years, and from thence to the end of the next session of Congress, and no longer."

It may be noted that each of the substantive provisions of the first Indian trade and intercourse act fulfilled some obligation assumed by the United States in treaties with various Indian tribes. In its first treaty with an Indian tribe, the Treaty of September 17, 1778, with the Delaware Nation,[16] the United States had undertaken to provide for the accommodation of the Delawares—

> * * * a well-regulated trade, under the conduct of an intelligent, candid agent, with an adequate sallery, one more influenced by the love of his country, and a constant attention to the duties of his department by promoting the common interest, than the sinister purposes of converting and binding all the duties of his office to his private emolument * * *. (Art. 5.)

Similar undertakings, providing for congressional action in the regulation of traders, had been undertaken in various other

[11] C. 33, 1 Stat. 137.

[12] Art. 1, sec. 8, cl. 3. Also see Chapter 5, sec. 3.

[13] See Chapter 16, sec. 1.

[14] See Chapter 15, sec. 18C.

[15] See Chapter 18, sec. 5.

[16] 7 Stat. 13.

treaties which, by 1790, had been concluded with most of the tribes then within the boundaries of the United States.[17]

Section 4, limiting land sales to the United States, also supplemented provisions contained in various treaties.[18]

The provisions with reference to the punishment of non-Indians committing crimes or trespasses within the territory of the Indian tribes likewise carried out obligations which had been assumed as early as September 17, 1778, in the treaty of that date with the Delaware Nation,[19] providing for fair and impartial trials of offenders against Indians,

> * * * The mode of such tryals to be hereafter fixed by the wise men of the United States in Congress assembled, with the assistance of such deputies of the Delaware nation, as may be appointed to act in concert with them in adjusting this matter to their mutual liking.

Similar provisions promising punishment of white offenders as a substitute for other methods of redress employed by Indian tribes had been included in practically all the treaties which were in force when the first Indian trade and intercourse act was adopted.[20]

The foregoing analysis of statutes as fulfillments of treaty obligations would probably apply equally to each of the later Indian trade and intercourse acts, culminating in the permanent Act of June 30, 1834.[21]

Despite the caution of Congress in making the first Indian trade and intercourse act a temporary measure, the substance of each of the provisions contained in this act remains law to this day.

Minor amendments were made in the language of these provisions by the second Indian trade and intercourse act, that of March 1, 1793.[22] This act also introduced a number of new provisions which have for the most part found their way into existing law. A prohibition against settlement on Indian lands and authority to the President to remove such settlers are contained in section 5 of this act. Section 6 deals with horse thieves and horse traders. Section 7 prohibits employees in Indian affairs from having "any interest or concern in any trade with the Indians."[23] Section 9 provides for the furnishing of various goods and services to the Indian tribes. Section 13 specifies that Indians within the jurisdiction of any of the individual states shall not be subject to trade restrictions.

This act, like the preceding act, was declared a temporary measure.[24]

The Act of May 19, 1796[25] constitutes the third in a series of trade and intercourse acts. Generally it follows the 1793 act, with minor modifications. It adds a detailed definition of Indian country.[26] It adds a prohibition against the driving of livestock on Indian lands.[27] It requires passports for persons travelling into the Indian country.[28]

The 1796 act contained, for the first time, a provision (sec. 14) for the punishment of any Indian belonging to a tribe in amity with the United States who shall cross into any state or territory and there commit any one of various listed offenses.[29] In the first instance, application for "satisfaction" was to be made to the nation or tribe to which the Indian offender belonged; if such application proved fruitless, after a reasonable waiting period fixed at 18 months, the President of the United States was authorized to take such measures as might be proper to obtain satisfaction for the injury. In the meantime, the injured party was guaranteed "an eventual indemnification" if he refrained from "attempting to obtain private satisfaction or revenge * * *." The only specific measure of redress which the President was authorized to take under this act was the withholding of annuities due to the tribe in question.

The fourth and last of the temporary Indian trade and intercourse acts was the Act of March 3, 1799.[30] This act made only minor changes in the provisions of the 1796 act.

Apart from the four temporary Indian trade and intercourse acts passed during the decade from 1790 to 1799, the only statute of special importance was the Act of April 18, 1796,[31] which established Government trading houses with the Indians, under the control of the President of the United States. While the institution of the Government trading house was abolished in 1822,[32] some of the provisions designed to assure the honesty of employees of these establishments have been carried over into the law which now governs Indian Service employees.[33] Control of the Government trading houses became the most important administrative function of the Federal Government in the field of Indian affairs, and when the Government trading houses were finally abolished it was only natural that the superintendent of Indian trade in charge of these establishments became the first head of the Bureau of Indian Affairs.[34]

---

[17] *E. g.*, Article 9 of Treaty of November 28, 1785, with the Cherokees, 7 Stat, 18, 20; Art. 8 of Treaty of January 3, 1786, with the Choctaw Nation, 7 Stat. 21, 22; Art. 8 of Treaty of January 10, 1786, with the Chickasaws, 7 Stat. 24, 25; Art. 7 of Treaty of January 9, 1789, with the Wiandot, Delaware, Ottawa, Chippewa, Pattawattima, and Sac Nations, 7 Stat. 28, 30. See Chapter 3, sec. 3B(2).

[18] Art. 3 of Treaty of January 9, 1789, with the Wiandots and others had provided:

> * * * But the said nations, or either of them, shall not be at liberty to sell or dispose of the same, or any part thereof, to any sovereign power, except the United States; nor to the subjects or citizens of any other sovereign power, nor to the subjects or citizens of the United States.

The following treaties contained specific guarantees against settlement on Indian lands by citizens of the United States: Art. 5 of Treaty of January 21, 1785, with the Wiandot, Delaware, Chippawa and Ottawa Nations, 7 Stat. 16, 17; Art. 5 of Treaty of November 28, 1785, with the Cherokees, 7 Stat. 18, 19; Art. 4 of Treaty of January 3, 1786, with the Choctaw Nation, 7 Stat. 21, 22; Art. 4 of Treaty of January 10, 1786, with the Chickasaws, 7 Stat. 24, 25; Art. 7 of Treaty of January 31, 1786, with the Shawanoe Nation, 7 Stat. 26, 27. Other treaties provided generally for the protection of Indian lands.

[19] Art. 4, 7 Stat. 13, 14.

[20] See treaties cited in fns. 17 and 18, *supra*.

[21] 4 Stat. 729. See Chapter 3, sec. 3.

[22] 1 Stat. 329.

[23] See Chapter 2, sec. 3B.

[24] Sec. 15, 1 Stat. 329, 332.

[25] 1 Stat. 469.

[26] Sec. 1. See Chapter 1, sec. 3.

[27] Sec. 2. See Chapter 15, sec. 10.

[28] Sec. 3. See Chapter 3, sec. 3A(5); Chapter 8, sec. 10A(3).

[29] See Chapter 18, sec. 4.

[30] C. 46, 1 Stat. 743.

[31] 1 Stat. 452.

[32] Act of May 6, 1822, 3 Stat. 679.

[33] See Act of April 18, 1796, sec. 3, 1 Stat. 452, followed in Act of June 30, 1834, sec. 14, 4 Stat. 735, 738, R. S. § 2078, 25 U. S. C. 68. And see Chapter 2, sec. 3B.

[34] See Chapter 2, sec. 1A.

SECTION 3. LEGISLATION FROM 1800 TO 1809

The most important legislation enacted by Congress during the first decade of the nineteenth century was the permanent trade and intercourse act of March 30, 1802.[35] The four temporary Indian trade and intercourse acts adopted in 1790, 1793, 1796, and 1799 had, by a process of trial and error, marked out the main outlines of federal Indian law, and the Act of 1802 made few substantial changes in reducing to permanent form the provisions of the Act of March 3, 1799.[36] The only significant addition made by the 1802 act appears in section 21 of that act, which deals with the liquor problem in these terms:

> * * * That the President of the United States be authorized to take such measures, from time to time, as to him may appear expedient to prevent or restrain the vending or distributing of spirituous liquors among all or any of the said Indian tribes, any thing herein contained to the contrary thereof notwithstanding.

The circumstances under which this provision, urged by various Indian chiefs, was recommended by President Jefferson and enacted by Congress are elsewhere noted.[37]

Apart from the permanent Indian trade and intercourse act, two legislative enactments during the decade from 1800 to 1809 deserve notice. Both of them imposed upon the Indian Service marks of its military origin which endured for more than a century.

The first of these statutes was the Act of January 17, 1800,[38] entitled "An Act for the preservation of peace with the Indian tribes." This act was apparently designed to prevent the European belligerents of that time from inciting the Indian tribes on our western frontier to attacks against the United States. The first section of this act provides:

> * * * That if any citizen or other person residing within the United States, or the territory thereof, shall send any talk, speech, message or letter to any Indian nation, tribe, or chief, with an intent to produce a contravention or infraction of any treaty or other law of the United States, or to disturb the peace and tranquillity of the United States, he shall forfeit a sum not exceeding two thousand dollars, and be imprisoned not exceeding two years.

After a long and checkered career, this provision of law[39] was repealed by the Act of May 21, 1934.[40]

[35] 2 Stat. 139.
[36] C. 46, 1 Stat. 743. See sec. 2, *supra*.
[37] See Chapter 17, sec. 1.
[38] 2 Stat. 6.
[39] The provision in question was incorporated in the Act of June 30, 1834, sec. 13, 4 Stat. 729, 731, and became R. S. § 2111 and 25 U. S. C. 171.
[40] 48 Stat. 787. See 25 U. S. C. A. 171 (Supp.).

Section 2 of this act prescribed penalties for the carrying or delivering of messages of the character prescribed by section 1 "to or from any Indian nation, tribe, or chief * * *."[41]

The third section of this act[42] dealt with seditious correspondence with foreign nations respecting Indian affairs, and also contained the following language which, considered apart from the circumstances of its enactment, imposed severe limits upon criticism of the Indian Service:

> * * * or in case any citizen or other person shall alienate, or attempt to alienate the confidence of the Indians from the government of the United States, or from any such person or persons as are, or may be employed and entrusted by the President of the United States, as a commissioner or commissioners, agent or agents, in any capacity whatever, for facilitating or preserving a friendly intercourse with the Indians, or for managing the concerns of the United States with them, he shall forfeit a sum not exceeding one thousand dollars, and be imprisoned not exceeding twelve months.

Another statute enacted by Congress during this decade which left a mark upon the Indian Service for many years was the Act of May 13, 1800,[43] which provided for the issuance of rations out of army provisions to Indians visiting the military posts of the United States. This is the first congressional statute supporting the system of inducing peace by paying tribute which characterized Indian Service policy for many years.[44]

The same statute likewise provided for repaying to Indian delegates the expense of their visits to Washington.[45]

During the decade from 1800 to 1809, there was no further Indian legislation of general and permanent significance. Appropriation acts, acts extending Indian trading house legislation, legislation for the establishing of new states and territories, measures for executing treaty provisions, and laws dealing with the disposition of lands acquired from the Indians by treaty make up the bulk of the legislation enacted during this decade in the field of Indian affairs.

[41] Sec. 2, incorporated in Act of June 30, 1834, sec. 14, 4 Stat. 729, 731, R. S. § 2112, 25 U. S. C. 172; repealed by Act of May 21, 1934, 48 Stat. 787.
[42] Incorporated in Act of June 30, 1834, sec. 15, 4 Stat. 729, 731, R. S. § 2113, 25 U. S. C. 173, repealed by Act of May 21, 1934, 48 Stat. 787. On recent uses of this statute, prior to its repeal, see Chapter 8, sec. 10A(2).
[43] C. 68, 2 Stat. 85; incorporated in Act of June 30, 1934, sec. 16, 4 Stat. 735, 738, R. S. § 2110, 25 U. S. C. 141.
[44] See Chapter 2, sec. 2C; Chapter 12, secs. 1, 4.
[45] Sec. 2.

SECTION 4. LEGISLATION FROM 1810 TO 1819

Congressional legislation on Indian affairs in the decade from 1810 to 1819 continues the trends noted in the preceding decade. Two statutes of special significance deserve to be noted.

The Act of March 3, 1817,[46] established for the first time a system of criminal justice applicable to Indians as well as to non-Indians within the Indian country. The act provided that Indians or other persons committing offenses within the Indian country should be subject to the same punishment that would be applicable if the offense had been committed in any place under the exclusive jurisdiction of the United States. Federal courts were given jurisdiction to try such cases. The statute contained an important proviso (sec. 2), safeguarding the criminal jurisdiction of the Indian tribes:

> * * * nothing in this act shall be so construed as to affect any treaty now in force between the United States and any Indian nation, or to extend to any offence committed by one Indian against another, within any Indian boundary.

The proviso, as well as the main provision of the statute, have found their way, with some modifications, into existing law."[47]

[46] C. 92, 3 Stat. 383.

[47] See 25 U. S. C. 217, 218. Note, however, that the historical notes to these sections in the U. S. Code and the U. S. Code Annotated fail to show their actual origin. For further discussion of the significance of these sections, see Chapter 5, sec. 1; Chapter 7, sec. 9; Chapter 18, secs. 3, 4.

A second important statute adopted during this decade was the Act of March 3, 1819[48] entitled "An Act making provision for the civilization of the Indian tribes adjoining the frontier settlements."

Section 1 of this act, which is law to this day,[49] provides:

> * * * That for the purpose of providing against the further decline and final extinction of the Indian tribes, adjoining the frontier settlements of the United States, and for introducing among them the habits and arts of civilization, the President of the United States shall be, and he is hereby authorized, in every case where he shall judge improvement in the habits and condition of such Indians practicable, and that the means of instruction can be introduced with their own consent, to employ capable persons of good moral character, to instruct them in the mode of agriculture suited to their situation; and for teaching their children in reading, writing, and arithmetic, and performing such other duties as may be enjoined, according to such instructions and rules as the President may give and prescribe for the regulation of their conduct, in the discharge of their duties.

Section 2 of this act established a permanent annual appropriation of $10,000 for carrying out the provisions of section 1.[50]

[48] C. 85, 3 Stat. 516.

[49] R. S. § 2071, 25 U. S. C. 271.

[50] See Chapter 12, sec. 2 for a discussion of the use made of these appropriations.

SECTION 5. LEGISLATION FROM 1820 TO 1829

By the Act of May 6, 1822,[51] the United States trading houses with the Indian tribes were abolished. On the same day a law was enacted specifying the conditions under which licensed Indian traders were to operate.[52] The act imposed various conditions upon the activities of licensed traders and conferred broad authority over such traders upon administrative officials. The act also provided (sec. 3) for the regular settlement of accounts of Indian agents. Section 4 of this act established a rule, which is still law, which in its present code form declares:

> In all trials about the right of property in which an Indian may be a party on one side, and a white person on the other, the burden of proof shall rest upon the white person, whenever the Indian shall make out a presumption of title in himself from the fact of previous possession or ownership.[53]

Apart from the foregoing general acts, treaties and legislation providing for the enforcement of treaty provisions continued to represent the main growing point of Indian law.

[51] 3 Stat. 679.

[52] Act of May 6, 1822, c. 58, 3 Stat. 682.

[53] 25 U. S. C. 194, derived from Act of June 30, 1834, sec. 22, 4 Stat. 729, 733; R. S. § 2126.

SECTION 6. LEGISLATION FROM 1830 TO 1839

The decade of the 1830's is marked by five statutes of great importance, the Act of May 28, 1830, governing Indian removal, the Act of July 9, 1832, establishing the post of Commissioner of Indian Affairs, the Indian Trade and Intercourse Act of June 30, 1834, the act of the same date providing for the organization of the Department of Indian Affairs, and the Act of January 9, 1837, regulating the disposition made of proceeds of ceded Indian lands.

The first of these acts[54] established in general terms the policy, which had theretofore been worked out in several specific cases,[55] of exchanging federal lands west of the Mississippi for other lands then held by Indian tribes. The act provided that such exchanges should be voluntary; that payment should be made to individuals for improvements relinquished, and that suitable guaranties should be given to the Indians as to the permanent character of the new homes to which they were migrating.

Section 3 provided:

> * * * That in the making of any such exchange or exchanges, it shall and may be lawful for the President solemnly to assure the tribe or nation with which the exchange is made, that the United States will forever secure and guaranty to them, and their heirs or successors, the country so exchanged with them; and if they prefer it, that the United States will cause a patent or grant to be made and executed to them for the same: *Provided always*, That such lands shall revert to the United States, if the Indians become extinct, or abandon the same.

Sections 6 and 7 defined the administrative authority of the President and the duty of protection owing to migrating tribes in the following terms:

> SEC. 6. * * * That it shall and may be lawful for the President to cause such tribe or nation to be protected, at their new residence, against all interruption or disturbance from any other tribe or nation of Indians, or from any other person or persons whatever.
>
> SEC. 7. * * * That it shall and may be lawful for the President to have the same superintendence and care over any tribe or nation in the country to which they may remove, as contemplated by this act, that he is now authorized to have over them at their present places of residence: *Provided*, That nothing in this act contained shall be construed as authorizing or directing the violation of any existing treaty between the United States and any of the Indian tribes.[56]

The Act of July 9, 1832,[57] entitled "An Act to provide for the appointment of a commissioner of Indian Affairs, and for other purposes," represents the first legislative authorization for the post of Commissioner of Indian Affairs. Its significance in the development of Indian administration has been discussed elsewhere.[58]

Section 1 of this act[59] which is still invoked as a basis for the administrative authority of the Commissioner of Indian Affairs, declared:

> * * * That the President shall appoint, by and with the advice and consent of the Senate, a commissioner of Indian affairs, who shall, under the direction of the Secretary of War, and agreeably to such regulations as the President may, from time to time, prescribe, have the direction and management of all Indian affairs, and of all matters arising out of Indian relations, and shall receive a salary of three thousand dollars per annum.

Other sections of the act dealt with the appointment of clerks to the office of the Commissioner of Indian Affairs, the supervision of accounts by the Commissioner, and the discontinuance of

[54] Act of May 28, 1830, 4 Stat. 411. Secs. 7 and 8 were later incorporated in R. S. § 2114, 25 U. S. C. 174.

[55] See Chapter 2, sec. 2A; Chapter 3, sec. 4B.

[56] R. S. § 2114, 25 U. S. C. 174.

[57] C. 174, 4 Stat. 564.

[58] See Chapter 2, sec. 1B.

[59] R. S. §§ 462–463, 25 U. S. C. 1–2. See Chapter 5, sec. 8.

"* * * the services of such agents, subagents, interpreters, and mechanics, as may from time to time become unnecessary, in consequence of the emigration of the Indians, or other causes"[60] —an illuminating commentary upon the aura of impermanence which even then surrounded the treatment of the Indian problem.

Included in this act was a general prohibition against the introduction of ardent spirits into the Indian country,[61] which is part of the law to this day.

June 30, 1834, is perhaps the most significant date in the history of Indian legislation. On this day there were enacted two comprehensive statutes which, in large part, form the fabric of our law on Indian affairs to this day. Of these two statutes one stands as the final act in a series of acts "to regulate trade and intercourse with the Indian tribes."[62] The other, approved on the same day, is entitled "An Act to provide for the organization of the department of Indian Affairs."[63] The two statutes[64] were dealt with in a single report of the House Committee on Indian Affairs,[65] which contains an illuminating analysis of the entire legislative situation with respect to Indian affairs.

The difficulties and the general objectives in terms of which this legislation of 1834 was drafted are suggested in the following statements of the Committee report:

> The committee are aware of the intrinsic difficulties of the subject—of providing a system of laws and of administration, simple and economical, and, at the same time, efficient and liberal—that shall be suited to the various conditions and relations of those for whose benefit it is intended; and that shall, with a due regard to the rights of our own citizens, meet the just expectations of the country in the fulfilment of its proper and assumed obligations to the Indian tribes. Yet, so manifestly defective and inadequate is our present system, that an immediate revision seems to be imperiously demanded. What is now proposed is only an approximation to a perfect system. Much is necessarily left for the present to Executive discretion, and still more to future legislation.[66]
>
> The Indians, for whose protection these laws are proposed, consist of numerous tribes, scattered over an immense extent of country, of different languages, and partaking of all the forms of society in the progression from the savage to an approximation to the civilized. With the emigrant tribes we have treaties, imposing duties of a mixed character, recognising them in some sort as dependent tribes, and yet obligating ourselves to protect them, even against domestic strife, and necessarily retaining the power so to do. With other tribes we have general treaties of amity; and with a considerable number we have no treaties whatever. To most of the tribes with whom we have treaties, we have stipulated to pay annuities in various forms. The annexed tables (A, B, I, J, K, L) exhibit a condensed view of these relations, and will assist in determining the nature and extent of the legislation necessary for the Indian Department. These, though a part of the consideration of the cessions of land, are intended to promote their improvement and civilization, and which may now be considered as the leading principle of this branch of our legislation.[67]

The Indian Trade and Intercourse Act of 1834 followed in many respects the similar act of March 30, 1802,[68] and incorporated provisions of other acts which have already been noted.[69]

[60] Sec. 5, R. S. § 2073, 25 U. S. C. 66.

[61] Sec. 4, R. S. § 2139, 25 U. S. C. 241. See Chapter 17, sec. 3, fn. 85.

[62] 4 Stat. 729.

[63] 4 Stat. 735.

[64] This report also dealt with a third proposed bill, relating to the tribes of the proposed "western territory," which was never enacted.

[65] H. Rept. No. 474, 23d Cong., 1st sess. (May 20, 1834).

[66] *Ibid.*, p. 1.

[67] *Ibid.*, p. 2.

[68] 2 Stat. 139. See sec. 3, *supra*.

[69] See fns. 38, 46, 51, *supra*.

By its first section it substituted a general definition of Indian country for the definition by metes and bounds that had been contained in the 1802 act and that had become largely obsolete as a result of treaty cessions.[70]

Sections 2 to 5 of the act deal with licensed traders and impose a more detailed system of control over such traders than had been previously in force. These controls constitute, in large part, the present law on the subject and are elsewhere analyzed.[71] The purpose of the legislation with respect to control of traders is set forth in the following terms in the House Committee report:

> The Indian trade, as heretofore, will continue to be carried on by licensed traders. The Indians do not meet the traders on equal terms, and no doubt have much reason to complain of fraud and imposition. Some further provision seems necessary for their protection. Heretofore, it has been considered that every person (whatever might be his character) was entitled to a license on offering his bond. It has been the source of much complaint with the Indians. Power is now given to refuse licenses to persons of bad character, and for a more general reason, "that it would be improper to permit such persons to reside in the Indian country;" and to revoke licenses for the same reasons. The committee are aware that this is granting an extensive power to the agents, and which may be liable to abuse; yet, when it is recollected that the distance from the Government at which the traders reside, will prevent a previous consultation with the head of the department; that what is necessary to be done should be done promptly; that the agents act under an official responsibility; that they are required to assign the reasons of their conduct to the War Department; that an appeal is given to the party injured; and that the dismissal of the agent would be the consequence of a wanton act of injustice, the rights of the traders will be found as well secured as is compatible with the security of the Indians.
>
> The report of the commissioners, appended to this report, contains a detailed statement of the exorbitant prices demanded by the Indian traders. As a remedy in part, they recommend, first, a substitution of goods for money in the payment of annuities. This suggestion has been adopted so far as to authorize it to be done by the consent of the tribe. In addition to the direct benefit, it will furnish them with something like a standard of the value of goods, and enable them to deal on more equal terms with the Indian traders. * * *[72]

Section 6 of the act relaxes the prior requirement that all persons going into the Indian country must bear a passport, so as to make the requirement applicable only to foreigners.[73]

Sections 7 to 12 of the 1834 Trade and Intercourse Act reenact with minor modifications provisions of the 1802 Trade and Intercourse Act.[74]

Sections 13 to 15 of the act reenact provisions of the Act of January 17, 1800,[75] relating to subversive activities among Indian

[70] Act of June 30, 1834, 4 Stat. 729. For a discussion of the significance of the 1834 definition see Chapter 1, sec. 3.

[71] See Chapter 16.

[72] H. Rept., *op. cit.*, p. 11.

[73] "Other nations have excluded foreigners from trade and intercourse with the Indians within their territories. We have adopted the same policy as the only one safe for us, or beneficial to the Indians. The provision is therefore continued, that no foreigner shall enter the Indian country without a passport. But it is not deemed necessary that all the restrictions of the former laws as to our own citizens should be retained. Of them, as mere travellers in or through the Indian country, we ought not to have the same, or even any jealousy. And so frequent and necessary are the occasions of our citizens to pass into the Indian country, that of them no passports will be required for such objects. Such has been the inconvenience of obtaining passports, that, for years, the provision in the act of 1802, requiring them, has been a dead letter. If, however, our citizens desire *to trade* or *to reside* in the Indian country for any purpose whatever, a license for that particular purpose is required." H. Rept., *op. cit.*, p. 11.

[74] See fn. 85, *supra*.

[75] 2 Stat. 6, discussed in sec. 3, *supra*. See 25 U. S. C. 171, 172, 173.

tribes. On the question of allowing the executive power to remove undesirable non-Indians the Committee declared:

> To facilitate the negotiations of treaties, it is deemed absolutely necessary that the commissioners should have power to control or remove all white persons who may attempt to prevent or impede the negotiations, and that they should have, if necessary, the aid of a military force.[76]

Section 17 reenacts and amplifies provisions of the 1802 act relating to Indian depredations.

The remaining provisions of the statute deal primarily with the prosecution of crimes. Officials of the Indian Department are empowered to make arrests.[77] The liquor prohibition provisions of the 1832 act[78] are reenacted and amplified.[79] The provision in the Act of May 6, 1822[80] relating to Indian witnesses is likewise reenacted (Section 22).[81]

Provisions on criminal jurisdiction are thus summarized in the House Committee report:

> In consequence of the change in our Indian relations, the laws relating to crimes committed in the Indian country, and to the tribunals before whom offenders are to be tried, require revision. By the act of 3d March, 1817, the criminal laws of the United States were extended to *all persons* in the Indian country, without exception, and by that act, as well as that of 30th March, 1802, they might be tried wherever apprehended. It will be seen that we cannot, consistently with the provisions of some of our treaties, and of the territorial act, extend our criminal laws to offences committed by or against Indians, of which the tribes have exclusive jurisdiction; and it is rather of courtesy than of right that we undertake to punish crimes committed in that territory by and against our own citizens. And this provision is retained principally on the ground that it may be unsafe to trust to Indian law in the early stages of their Government. It is not perceived that we can with any justice or propriety extend our laws to offences committed by Indians against Indians, *at any place* within their own limits.
>
> Some doubts have been suggested as to the constitutionality of so much of these acts as provides for the trial of offenders wherever apprehended: without expressing any opinion on that subject, it is thought that provisions more convenient to all parties, and at the same time free from all constitutional doubts, might be adopted. And for this end it is proposed, *for the sole purpose of executing this act*, to annex the Indian country to the judicial districts of the adjoining Territories and States. This is done principally with a view to offences that are to be prosecuted by indictment. In all cases of offences, when the punishment, by former laws, was fine or imprisonment, the imprisonment is now omitted, leaving the penalty to be recovered in an action of debt, prosecuted in any district where the offender may be found.[82]

The second[83] of the basic 1834 acts was intended to deal comprehensively with the organization and functions of the Indian Department. This purpose is developed in the sponsoring House Committee's report in the following terms:

> The present organization of this department is of doubtful origin and authority. Its administration is expensive, inefficient, and irresponsible.
>
> The committee have sought, in vain, for any lawful authority for the appointment of a majority of the agents and subagents of Indian affairs now in office. For years, usage, rendered colorably lawful only by reference to indirect and equivocal legislation, has been the only sanction for their appointment. Our Indian relations commenced at an early period of the revolutionary war. What was necessary to be done, either for defence or conciliation, was done; and being necessary, no inquiry seems to have been made as to the authority under which it was done. This undefined state of things continued for nearly twenty years. Though some general regulations were enacted, the government of the department was chiefly left to Executive discretion. In the subsequent legislation, what was, in fact, mere usage, seems to have been taken as having been established by law. It does not appear that the origin or history of the department has ever attracted the attention of Congress. No report of its investigation is found in its records. In ascertaining the authority of the appointment of the officers in the department, the committee have referred to the acts of the Government, of which they will now present a brief history, and which, it is believed, will fully sustain the position that a majority of the agents and subagents of Indian affairs have been appointed without lawful authority. This position is not taken with a view to put any particular administration in fault, for it applies to every administration for the last thirty years.[84]

The conclusion as to the lack of legal authority for various positions actually maintained in the office of Indian Affairs was borne out by a detailed review of the legislation of Congress beginning with ordinances enacted prior to the Declaration of Independence. The statute substitutes for the patchwork theretofore existing, a comprehensive schedule of departmental officers and makes all such officers responsible to the President of the United States and to regulations promulgated by him.[85]

Other sections of the 1834 act providing for the organization of the department of Indian Affairs seek to restore and guarantee tribal rights upon which administrative encroachments had apparently been made, and to encourage Indians to take over an increased measure of responsibility for the administration of the Indian Service. In matters of annuity payments, the 1834 act establishes the principle that all such payments are to be made to the chiefs of the respective tribes or to such other representatives as the tribes themselves may appoint. In explanation of this provision (sec. 11), the Committee declared:

> In the course of their investigations, the committee have become satisfied that much injustice has been done to the Indians in the payment of their annuities. The payments are required, by the terms of the treaties, to be paid to the tribe as a political body capable of acting as a nation; and it would seem, as a necessary consequence, that the payments should be made to the constituted authorities of the tribe. If those authorities distribute the annuities thus paid with a partial hand, they alone are responsible. If injustice shall be done, we are not the instruments; we have discharged our obligation. With what propriety can our Government undertake to apportion the annuities among the individuals of the tribes? And in what manner can it be done, with safety or convenience? If distributed to heads of families in proportion to the number of each family, it would require an annual enumeration, or a register of the changes. If paid to the individuals at their residences, it would be troublesome and expensive; if the individuals were required to travel to the agency, to receive the pittance of their share, to many it would not be worth going for. What security can be given against the frauds of the agents? What vouchers shall he produce to account for the payments? The payment to the chiefs is a mode simple and certain, and the only mode that will render the annuities beneficial to the tribe, by enabling it to apply them to the expenses of their Government, to the purpose of education, or to some object of general concern. When distributed to individuals, the amount is too small to be relied on as a support, yet sufficiently large to induce them to forego the labor necessary to procure their supplies. And it is found that those are the most industrious and thrifty who have no such aid.
>
> Individual payments were introduced probably with a view to induce emigration, by paying those who choose to

---

[76] H. Rept., *op. cit.*, p. 14.
[77] Sec. 19.
[78] See fn. 61, *supra*.
[79] Secs. 20 and 21.
[80] See fn. 53, *supra*.
[81] 4 Stat. 729, 733.
[82] H. Rept., *op. cit.*, pp. 13, 14.
[83] Act of June 30, 1834, 4 Stat. 735.

[84] H. Rept., *op. cit.*, pp. 2, 3. See Chapter 2, sec. 1B.
[85] Secs. 1, 2, 8.

> emigrate their supposed share of the annuity. Whatever may have been the policy which gave rise to it, neither policy nor justice requires its continuance.
>
> With a view to prevent frauds of another kind, in reference principally to the payment of goods, the President is authorized to appoint an officer of rank to superintend the payment of annuities. This, and the provision relating to the purchase of goods for the Indians, will place sufficient guards to prevent fraudulent payments.
>
> The committee have reason to believe abuses have existed in relation to the supply of goods for presents at the making of treaties, or to fulfil treaty stipulations. Those for presents are at the loss of the Government. Those under treaty stipulations are at the loss of the Indians. The goods for presents have been usually furnished by the Indian traders, and at an advance of from 60 to 100 per cent. This the Government has been obliged to submit to, or the trader will make use of his influence to prevent a treaty. Should this in future be attempted, the Government will now have a sufficient remedy by revoking the license. The goods furnished under treaties have been charged at (what has been represented as a moderate rate) an advance of 50 per cent, and at that rate delivered to the Indians. It is now provided that the goods in both cases are to be purchased by an agent of the Government; and where there is time (as in case of goods purchased under treaties) they are to be purchased on proposals based on previous notice.[56]

The objective of staffing the Indian Service itself with Indians was embodied in a provision of section 9 of this act reading:

> And in all cases of the appointments of interpreters or other persons employed for the benefit of the Indians, a preference shall be given to persons of Indian descent, if such can be found, who are properly qualified for the execution of the duties.[57]

A related objective was to be achieved by the following provision in section 9, which is law to this day (except that the Secretary of the Interior has succeeded to the powers of the Secretary of War):

> And where any of the tribes are, in the opinion of the Secretary of War, competent to direct the employment of their blacksmiths, mechanics, teachers, farmers, or other persons engaged for them, the direction of such persons may be given to the proper authority of the tribe.[58]

The purpose behind these provisions is illuminated by a passage in the Committee report which declares:

> The education of the Indians is a subject of deep interest to them and to us. It is now proposed to allow them some direction in it, with the assent of the President, under the superintendence of the Governor, so far as their annuities (K) are concerned; and that a preference should be given to educated youth, in all the employments of which they are capable, as traders, interpreters, schoolmasters, farmers, mechanics, &c.; and that the course of their education should be so directed as to render them capable of those employments. Why educate the Indians unless their education can be turned to some practical use? and why educate them even for a practical use, and yet refuse to employ them?[59]

Other provisions of the act in question prohibit employees of the Indian Department from having "any interest or concern in any trade with the Indians, except for, and on account of, the United States."[60]

Provisions of earlier acts with respect to supplies and rations are reenacted (secs. 15 and 16). The latter provision is a reenactment of section 2 of the Act of May 13, 1800, authorizing issuance of rations to Indians at military posts.[61]

Section 17 centralizes responsibility for regulations authorized by law in the following terms:

> That the President of the United States shall be, and he is hereby, authorized to prescribe such rules and regulations as he may think fit, for carrying into effect the various provisions of this act, and of any other act relating to Indian affairs, and for the settlement of the accounts of the Indian department.[62]

The purpose of this section is set forth in the following language of the Committee report:

> The President is authorized to make the necessary regulations for carrying into effect the several acts relating to Indian affairs. In 1829, such regulations having reference to the laws then in force, were reported to the House by Messrs. Clark and Cass, commissioners appointed for that purpose. They appear to have been drawn with great care, and, with such alterations as the bills reported require, would, in the opinion of the committee, be proper and efficient; and should the acts reported pass, it would be proper to have the regulations reported to Congress at the next session, when they can be adopted by an act of Congress, or go into operation under the general provision referred to.[63]

The fifth important segment of the existing law on Indian affairs that took shape under legislation of the 1830's is that relating to payments made to tribes, by reason of treaty provisions, by the Federal Government from proceeds derived from the disposition of ceded Indian lands. The Act of January 9, 1837,[64] comprises three sections containing provisions of substantive law. The first section[65] requires the deposit in the United States Treasury of moneys received from the sale of lands ceded to the United States by treaties providing either for the investment or for the payment of such proceeds to the Indians.

Section 2 of the act[66] provides:

> That all sums that are or may be required to be paid, and all moneys that are or may be required to be invested by said treaties, are hereby appropriated in conformity to them, and shall be drawn from the Treasury as other public moneys are drawn therefrom, under such instructions as may from time to time be given by the President.

Section 3[67] declares:

> That all investments of stock, that are or may be required by said treaties, shall be made under the direction of the President; and special accounts of the funds under said treaties shall be kept at the Treasury, and statements thereof be anually laid before Congress.

These provisions of law established what was for a long time the basis of handling Indian tribal funds derived from sales of ceded land. As the sums involved increased year by year the handling of them became more and more important as providing the sustenance upon which the activities of the Indian Service were based.

[56] H. Rept., *op. cit.*, pp. 9, 10.

[57] Sec. 9, 4 Stat. 735, 737, R. S. § 2069, 25 U. S. C. 45. See Chapter 8, sec. 4B.

[58] *Ibid.* See Chapter 7, sec. 10.

[59] H. Rept., *op. cit.*, p. 20.

[60] Sec. 14, 4 Stat. 735, 738. See Chapter 2, sec. 3B, fn. 335.

[61] See fns. 43–45, *supra*.

[62] R. S. § 465, 25 U. S. C. 9. See Chapter 5, sec. 8.

[63] H. Rept., *op. cit.*, pp. 22, 23.

[64] C. 1, 5 Stat. 135.

[65] R. S. § 2093, 25 U. S. C. 152

[66] R. S. § 2094, 25 U. S. C. 153.

[67] R. S. § 2095, 25 U. S. C. 157.

SECTION 7. LEGISLATION FROM 1840 TO 1849

During the decade of the 1840's two statutes were enacted which have impressed a lasting mark upon federal Indian law. The first of these was the Act of March 3, 1847,[98] which amended in various respects the comprehensive legislation of June 30, 1834.[99] These amendments included a broadening of the language of the Indian liquor legislation.[100] Section 3 of the 1847[101] act relaxed the requirement that had been established by the 1834 legislation to the effect that moneys due tribes should be paid to tribal officers, and authorized payment of such moneys "to the heads of families and other individuals entitled to participate therein." This, in effect, substituted the judgment of federal officials for that of tribal governments on the question of tribal membership, so far as the disposition of funds was concerned. This provision was the first in a long series of statutes designed to individualize tribal property.[102]

[98] 9 Stat. 203.

[99] See sec. 6, *supra*.

[100] Sec. 2 of the 1847 act amended sec. 20, Act of June 30, 1834, 4 Stat. 729.

[101] Amending sec. 11, Act of June 30, 1834, 4 Stat. 735.

[102] See Chapter 2, secs. 2C, 2E, for a discussion of official policy on that point.

The same section of the 1847 act contains a prohibition against the payment of annuities to Indians while there is liquor in the vicinity.[103]

A second statute of the 1840's which has had an important bearing upon Indian administration is the Act of March 3, 1849,[104] establishing "a new executive department of the government of the United States, to be called the Department of the Interior; the head of which department shall be called the Secretary of the Interior * * *."[105] Section 5 of this act declared:

> That the Secretary of the Interior shall exercise the supervisory and appellate powers now exercised by the Secretary of the War Department, in relation to all the acts of the Commissioner of Indian Affairs; and shall sign all requisitions for the advance or payment of money out of the treasury, on estimates or accounts, subject to the same adjustment or control now exercised on similar estimates or accounts by the Second Auditor and Second Comptroller of the Treasury.

This marked the termination of direct War Department control over the Indian problem.

[103] See Chapter 15, sec. 23B.

[104] 9 Stat. 395. See Chapter 2, sec. 1B.

[105] Sec. 1.

SECTION 8. LEGISLATION FROM 1850 TO 1859

Throughout the decade of the 1850's treaties rather than legislation formed the growing point of Indian law, and little legislation of a general and permanent character was enacted. Three minor statutory provisions which date from this period deserve note.

Section 3 of the Appropriation Act of March 3, 1853[106] prohibits the payment to attorneys or agents of sums due to Indians or Indian tribes and prohibits the executive branch of the Government from recognizing any contract between Indians and their attorneys or agents for the prosecution of claims against the United States.

The Act of March 27, 1854,[107] contained an important amendment of sections 20 and 25 of the Act of June 30, 1834[108] which had the effect of removing from the jurisdiction of the federal courts Indians committing various offenses against non-Indians in the Indian country who have "been punished by the local law of the tribe * * *."[109]

Sections 4 and 5 of this act mark the beginnings of a rudimentary criminal code for the Indian country. It covered arson[110] and assault by a white man against an Indian or by an Indian against a white man, with a deadly weapon and with intent to kill or maim.[111]

A third statutory provision enacted in this decade was section 2 of the Appropriation Act of June 12, 1858.[112] This section, symbolic of the growing concentration of power in the hands of the Commissioner, declared that that officer might

> * * * remove from any tribal reservation any person found therein without authority of law, or whose presence within the limits of the reservation may, in his judgment, be detrimental to the peace and welfare of the Indians. * * *

That aggrandizement of power by the administrative authorities was feared by Congress even at the time extreme powers were being conferred upon such administrative authorities, is indicated by section 7 of the Act of February 28, 1859[113] authorizing the Commissioner of Indian Affairs, under the direction of the Secretary of the Interior,

> to prepare rules and regulations for the government of the Indian service, and for trade and intercourse with the Indian tribes and the regulations of their affairs; and when approved by the President shall be submitted to the Congress of the United States for its approval: *Provided*, That such laws, rules, and regulations proposed shall not be in force until enacted by Congress.

It does not appear that this mandate was ever executed.

The same statute which carried the foregoing direction also contained a provision repealing prior legislation under which the United States had undertaken to indemnify whites suffering from Indian trespasses.[114]

Important legislation enacted during this decade relating to the pueblos is elsewhere discussed.[115]

[106] 10 Stat. 226, 239.

[107] C. 26, sec. 3, 10 Stat. 269.

[108] 4 Stat. 729. See sec. 6, *supra*.

[109] See Chapter 18, sec. 4.

[110] Sec. 4, 10 Stat. 269, 270, R. S. § 2143, 25 U. S. C. 212.

[111] Sec. 5, R. S. § 2142, 25 U. S. C. 213.

[112] 11 Stat. 329, 332, R. S. § 2149, 25 U. S. C. 222, repealed by Act of May 21, 1934, 42 Stat. 787.

[113] C. 66, 11 Stat. 388, 401.

[114] Sec. 8, R. S. § 2156, 25 U. S. C. 229, repealing sec. 17 of Act of June 30, 1834, 4 Stat. 729, 731–732.

[115] See discussion of Act of December 22, 1858, 11 Stat. 374, in Chapter 20, sec. 3A.

SECTION 9. LEGISLATION FROM 1860 TO 1869

The decade of the 1860's is marked by an increasing volume of general Indian legislation, coincident with a decline in the use of Indian treaties as an instrument of national policy. These statutes for the most part strengthened or modified earlier provisions affecting Indian trade and intercourse. To a certain extent they mark new advances along the path of individualization of Indian property.[116]

The Act of February 13, 1862,[117] contains a comprehensive restatement of the Indian liquor law.

The Act of June 14, 1862,[118] entitled "An act to protect the property of Indians who have adopted the habits of civilized life," included three sections which have remained law to this day. The first section provides that when a member of a tribe has had a portion of tribal land allotted to him in severalty the superintendent "shall take such measures, not inconsistent with law, as may be necessary to protect such Indian in the quiet enjoyment of the land so allotted to him." [119] The second section of the act provides for punishment of any unallotted Indian who trespasses upon an allotment, through a deduction of damages from future annuities and payment thereof to the injured party.[120] The third section provides that if the trespasser is a chief or headman he shall be removed from office for 3 months.[121] This legislation is evidence of the resistance which the new allotment system was already encountering from tribal Indians who did not wish to see tribal lands checker-boarded with private boundary lines.[122]

A proviso in the first section of the Appropriation Act of July 5, 1862,[123] authorizes the President,

> * * * in cases where the tribal organization of any Indian tribe shall be in actual hostility to the United States, * * * to declare all treaties with such tribe to be abrogated by such tribe, if, in his opinion, the same can be done consistently with good faith and legal and national obligations.

Section 6 of the same act deprives guardians appointed by the several Indian tribes of the right to receive "moneys due to incompetent or orphan Indians." [124]

The Appropriation Act of March 3, 1865,[125] contains, as do most of the appropriation acts enacted in this period, a number of provisions of substantive law which have little or no relation to appropriations. Sections 8 and 9, emanating no doubt from the disturbed conditions attending the conclusion of the Civil War and the re-uniting of the sadly divided tribes of the Indian Territory, provide: [126]

> SEC. 8. That any person who may drive or remove, except as hereinafter provided, any cattle, horses, or other stock from the Indian Territory for the purposes of trade or commerce, shall be guilty of a felony, and on conviction be punished by fine not exceeding five thousand dollars, or by imprisonment not exceeding three years, or by both such fine and imprisonment.
>
> SEC. 9. That the agent of each tribe of Indians, lawfully residing in the said Indian Territory, be, and he is hereby authorized to sell for the benefit of said Indians any cattle, horses, or other live stock belonging to said Indians, and not required for their use and subsistence, under such regulations as shall be established by the Secretary of the Interior: *Provided*, That nothing in this and the preceding section shall interfere with the execution of any order lawfully issued by the Secretary of War, connected with the movement or subsistence of the troops of the United States.

Both these provisions are still law.

The Joint Resolution of March 3, 1865,[127] marked a step in the fulfillment of a promise made by President Lincoln that upon the conclusion of the Civil War, if he survived, the Indian system should be reformed.[127a] This resolution directed a thoroughgoing inquiry into the treatment of the Indian tribes by the civil and military authorities. The results of this investigation are elsewhere discussed.[128]

The Act of July 27, 1868,[129] marks a final step in the consolidation of administrative control over Indian affairs in the Department of the Interior. Section 1 of this act [130] transfers to the Secretary of the Interior all "supervisory and appellate powers and duties in regard to Indian affairs, which may now by law be vested in the said Secretary of the Treasury * * *."

[116] For history of allotment policy, see Chapter 11, sec. 1. On treaty provisions on allotments see Chapter 8, sec. 4G.
[117] C. 24, 12 Stat. 338.
[118] 12 Stat. 427.
[119] R. S. § 2119, 25 U. S. C. 185.
[120] R. S. § 2120, 25 U. S. C. 186.
[121] R. S. § 2121, 25 U. S. C. 187.
[122] See Chapter 2, secs. 2 B, C, and D.
[123] 12 Stat. 512, 528, R. S. § 2080, 25 U. S. C. 72.
[124] R. S. § 2108, 25 U. S. C. 159.
[125] 13 Stat. 541, 563.
[126] Sec. 8, R. S. § 2138, amended by Act of June 30, 1919, sec. 1, 41 Stat. 9, 25 U. S. C. 214; sec. 9, R. S. § 2127, 25 U. S. C. 192.
[127] No. 33, 13 Stat. 572.
[127a] See H. B. Whipple, Lights and Shadows of a Long Episcopate (1899), p. 137.
[128] See Chapter 2, sec. 1B, fn. 42 and sec. 2C.
[129] 15 Stat. 228.
[130] Embodied in part in R. S. § 463, 25 U. S. C. 2.

SECTION 10. LEGISLATION FROM 1870 TO 1879

The 1870's marked the first decade in which the growth of federal Indian law was entirely a matter of legislation rather than of treaty. The decade is marked by a steady increase in the statutory powers vested in the officials of the Indian Service and by a steady narrowing of the rights of individual Indians and Indian tribes.[131] Nevertheless, as we have elsewhere noted, the termination of treaty-making did not stop the process of treating with the Indians by agreement.[132]

The Appropriation Act of March 3, 1871, provided not only for the termination of treaty-making with Indian tribes,[133] but also, (sec. 3), for the withdrawal from noncitizen Indians and from Indian tribes of power to make contracts involving the payment of money for services relative to Indian lands or claims against the United States, unless such contracts should be approved by the Commissioner of Indian Affairs and the Secretary of the Interior. Since many of the grievances of the Indians were grievances against these officers, the Indians were effectually deprived by this statute of one of the most basic rights known to the common law, the right to free choice of counsel for the redress of injuries. These prohibitions were amplified by the Act of May 21, 1872.[134]

[131] See Chapter 2, sec. 2C.
[132] Chapter 3, secs. 5 and 6; Chapters 2, sec. 2C.
[133] 16 Stat. 544, 566, R. S. § 2079, 25 U. S. C. 71. See Chapter 3, sec. 5.
[134] 17 Stat. 136, sec. 1, R. S. § 2103, 25 U. S. C. 81; sec. 2, R. S. § 2104, 25 U. S. C. 82, and R. S. § 2106, 25 U. S. C. 84; sec. 3, R. S. § 2105, 25 U. S. C. 83.

The effect of this legislation upon the rights of Indians[135] and Indian tribes[136] is elsewhere discussed.

A remarkable enactment of this period was that requiring Indian creditors of the United States to perform useful labor as a condition of receiving payments of money or goods which the United States was pledged to make. Such a provision, constituting permanent legislation, appears in section 3 of the Appropriation Act of June 22, 1874,[137] and again in section 3 of the Appropriation Act of March 3, 1875.[138]

An appropriation act of the following year consolidates power over Indian traders in the hands of the Commissioner of Indian Affairs, in the following terms:

> And hereafter the Commissioner of Indian Affairs shall have the sole power and authority to appoint Traders to the Indian tribes and to make such rules and regulations as he may deem just and proper specifying the kind and quantity of goods and the prices at which such goods shall be sold to the Indians.[139]

During this period legislation was enacted requiring each agent having supplies to distribute

> to make out, at the commencement of each fiscal year, rolls of the Indians entitled to supplies at the agency, with the names of the Indians and of the heads of families or lodges, with the number in each family or lodge, and to give out supplies to the heads of families, and not to the heads of tribes or bands, and not to give out supplies for a greater length of time than one week in advance.[140]

While these successive grants of power were being made to the administrative officers of the Indian department, a series of complaints against the abuses of power was leading to the multiplication of specific prohibitions against various administrative practices. Most of these prohibitions are comparatively unimportant, but mention should be made of provisions prohibiting Government employees from having any personal interest in various types of Indian trade and commercial activities relating thereto.[141]

[135] See Chapter 8, sec. 7.
[136] See Chapter 14, sec. 5.
[137] 18 Stat. 146, 176. See Chapter 12, sec. 1, Chapter 15, sec. 23A.
[138] 18 Stat. 420, 449.
[139] Sec. 5, Act of August 15, 1866, 19 Stat. 176, 200, 25 U. S. C. 261.
[140] Sec. 4, Act of March 3, 1875, 18 Stat. 420, 449, 25 U. S. C. 133.
[141] Sec. 10, Act of June 22, 1874, 18 Stat. 146, 177, 25 U. S. C. 87. *Cf.* fn. 90, *supra*. And see Chapter 2, sec. 2B, fn. 141 and sec. 3B, fn. 335.

SECTION 11. LEGISLATION FROM 1880 TO 1889

The decade of the 1880's was marked by the rapid settlement and development of the West. As an incident to this process, legislation providing for acquisition of lands and resources from the Indians was demanded. Ethical justification for this was found in the theory of assimilation. If the Indian would only adopt the habits of civilized life he would not need so much land, and the surplus would be available for white settlers. The process of allotment and civilization was deemed as important for Indian welfare as for the welfare of non-Indians.

The first general statutory provision relating to disposition of Indian resources, other than land itself, is found in a paragraph of section 2 of the Act of March 3, 1883,[142] which declares:

> The proceeds of all pasturage and sales of timber, coal, or other product of any Indian reservation, except those of the five civilized tribes, and not the result of the labor of any member of such tribe, shall be covered into the Treasury for the benefit of such tribe under such regulations as the Secretary of the Interior shall prescribe; and the Secretary shall report his action in detail to Congress at its next session.

For some peculiar reason, this fund came to be known as "Indian moneys, proceeds of labor." The present status of funds so classified is dealt with elsewhere.[143]

A few years later this provision was supplemented by the Act of February 16, 1889,[144] authorizing the sale of dead timber on Indian reservations under such regulations as the President might prescribe.

Meanwhile the process of assimilation, on its moral side, was demanding congressional attention. Shocked by the *Crow Dog* case,[145] Congress appended to the Appropriation Act of March 3, 1885, a section[146] specifying seven major crimes over which the federal courts were henceforth to exercise jurisdiction, even though both the offender and the victim were Indians and therefore subject only to tribal jurisdiction in the absence of congressional statute.[147]

The same act that contained the "seven crimes" provision embodied a comprehensive attempt to deal with the problem of Indian depredations by providing for a general investigation by the Secretary of the Interior into depredation claims where treaties with Indian tribes authorized the United States to pay damages out of moneys due to the tribes.[148]

The most important statute of the decade is, of course, the General Allotment Act,[149] frequently referred to as the Dawes Act. The objectives of this legislation and the legal problems which it raised are elsewhere discussed.[150] For the sake of the general historical picture, a brief summary of the provisions of this act may be offered.

The first section authorizes the President to allot tribal lands in designated quantities to reservation Indians.[151] The second section provides that the Indian allottees shall, so far as practicable, make their own selections of land so as to embrace improvements already made.[152] Section 3 provides that allotments shall be made by agents, regular or special.[153] Section 4 allows "any Indian not residing upon a reservation, or for whose tribe no reservation has been provided" to secure an allotment upon the public domain.[154]

Section 5 provides that title in trust to allotments shall be held by the United States for 25 years, or longer if the President deems an extension desirable. During this trust period encumbrances or conveyances are void. In general, the laws of descent and partition in the state or territory where the lands are situate apply after patents have been executed and delivered. If any surplus lands remain after the allotments have been made, the Secretary is authorized to negotiate with the tribe for the purchase of such land by the United States, purchase money to be

[142] 22 Stat. 582, 590, 25 U. S. C. 155.
[143] See Chapter 5, sec. 10; Chapter 15, sec. 23.
[144] 25 Stat. 673, 25 U. S. C. 196. See Chapter 15, sec. 15.
[145] See Chapter 7, sec. 2.
[146] Sec. 9, 23 Stat. 362, 385, later incorporated, with amendments, in 18 U. S. C. 548.
[147] See Chapter 7, sec. 9.
[148] Act of March 3, 1885, 23 Stat. 362, 376. Authorization to continue this investigation is found in the Appropriation Act of May 15, 1886, 24 Stat. 29, 44.
[149] Act of February 8, 1887, 24 Stat. 388.
[150] See Chapter 11, sec. 1, and Chapter 13, sec. 3B.
[151] See 25 U. S. C. 331.
[152] 24 Stat. 388, 25 U. S. C. 332.
[153] 24 Stat. 388, 389. See 25 U. S. C. 333.
[154] 24 Stat. 388, 389, 25 U. S. C. 334.

held in trust for the sole use of the tribes to whom the reservation belonged but subject to appropriation by Congress for the education and civilization of such tribe or its members. This section also contains an important provision for the preference of Indians in employment in the Federal Government.[155]

Section 6 of the act sets forth the nonpecuniary benefits which the Indians are to receive in view of the destruction of tribal property and tribal existence which the act contemplates.[156]

Section 7 of the act provides the basic law upon which water rights to allotments have been measured.[157]

The remainder of the act contains sections which exempt from the allotment legislation various tribes of the Indian Territory, the reservations of the Seneca Nation in New York, and an Executive order reservation in the State of Nebraska, and which authorize appropriations for surveys. In addition, the act contains various saving clauses for the maintenance of then existing congressional and administrative powers.

[155] 24 Stat. 388, 389, 25 U. S. C. 348. See Chapter 6, sec. 2A, and Chapter 8, sec. 4B(3)(b).

[156] 24 Stat. 388, 390. See 25 U. S. C. 349. And see Chapter 8, sec. 2A(3).

[157] 24 Stat. 388, 390, 25 U. S. C. 381. See Chapter 11, sec. 8.

In the following year the process of amending the Allotment Act began. Section 2 of the Act of October 19, 1888,[158] authorizes the Secretary of the Interior to accept surrenders of patents by Indian allottees. A proviso permits the Indian allottee, if he so chooses, to make a lieu selection.

A critical point in the process of assimilation arose in the intermarriage of white men and Indian women. The so-called "squawmen" were in many cases individuals who took unto themselves at least a proportionate share of tribal property and tribal control. Section 1 of the Act of August 9, 1888,[159] provided, that, with the exception of the Five Civilized Tribes, intermarried whites should not by such marriage acquire "any right to any tribal property, privilege, or interest whatever to which any member of such tribe is entitled." Section 2 provided that an Indian woman married to a white man shall by such marriage become a citizen of the United States, without detriment to her rights of participation in tribal property.[160] The third section of the act[161] dealt with evidence required to show marriage.

[158] 25 Stat. 611, 612, 25 U. S. C. 350.

[159] 25 Stat. 392, 25 U. S. C. 181.

[160] 25 U. S. C. 182.

[161] 25 U. S. C. 183.

SECTION 12. LEGISLATION FROM 1890 TO 1899

The decade of the 1890's shows no sweeping legislation comparable in scope to the General Allotment Act, but rather embodies piecemeal development of earlier statutes. This development proceeds along four main lines: (1) Amendments to the Allotment Act, particularly for the purpose of permitting leases of allotments; (2) the development of a body of law governing Indian education; (3) increased protection for individual Indian rights; and (4) the clearing up of Indian depredation claims.

Under the first heading may be listed the Act of February 28, 1891.[162] The first two sections modified those provisions of the General Allotment Act relating to the amounts of land to be allotted. Section 3 of the act[163] permits the leasing of individual allotments, under rules prescribed by the Secretary of the Interior, wherever the Secretary finds that the allottee, "by reason of age or other disability," cannot "personally and with benefit to himself occupy or improve his allotment or any part thereof."

A proviso of this section permits leasing of tribal lands, where such lands are occupied by Indians who have bought and paid for them, "by authority of the Council speaking for such Indians," but "subject to the approval of the Secretary of the Interior."

Section 4 of the act supplements previous legislation on homestead allotments.[164] Section 5 of the act provides that for purposes of descent, cohabitation "according to the custom and manner of Indian life" shall be considered valid marriage.[165]

Further amendments to the allotment system adopted during this decade include provisions extending leasing privileges,[166] conferring jurisdiction upon the federal courts to adjudicate suits for allotments,[167] and authorizing the Secretary of the Interior to correct errors in patents, and particularly in cases of "double allotment."[168]

Of the numerous statutes on Indian education enacted during the decade of the 1890's the earliest confer a large measure of authority upon the administrative officials, and the later statutes proceed to limit that authority. The Appropriation Act of July 13, 1892,[169] includes a provision[170] authorizing the Commissioner of Indian Affairs to make and enforce regulations to secure the attendance of Indian children "at schools established and maintained for their benefit."

The Appropriation Act of March 3, 1893,[171] contains a provision[172] authorizing the Secretary of the Interior to

> * * * prevent the issuing of rations or the furnishing of subsistence either in money or in kind to the head of any Indian family for or on account of any Indian child or children between the ages of eight and twenty-one years who shall not have attended school during the preceding year in accordance with such regulations.

This tactic apparently created considerable Indian and public resentment, as did the parallel practice of taking children from their parents and sending them to distant nonreservation boarding schools.[173] Section 11 of the Appropriation Act of August 15, 1894,[174] prohibits the sending of children to schools outside the state or territory of their residence without the consent of their parents or natural guardians, and forbids the withholding of rations as a technique for securing such consent. This provision is reenacted in the Appropriation Act of March 2, 1895,[175] and, again, the Appropriation Act of June 10, 1896,[176] provides "That hereafter no Indian child shall be taken from any school in any State or Territory to a school in any other State against its will or without the written consent of its parents."[177]

A further limitation upon the broad authority of administrative officers over Indian education is found in a provision of the Appropriation Act of June 7, 1897[178] declaring it to be the

[162] 26 Stat. 794.

[163] See 25 U. S. C. 395.

[164] See 25 U. S. C. 336.

[165] 25 U. S. C. 371.

[166] Act of August 15, 1894, 28 Stat. 286, 305, 25 U. S. C. 402.

[167] Act of August 15, 1894, 28 Stat. 286, 305, 25 U. S. C. 345.

[168] Act of January 26, 1895, 28 Stat. 641, 25 U. S. C. 343.

[169] 27 Stat. 120.

[170] 27 Stat. 120, 143, 25 U. S. C. 284.

[171] 27 Stat. 612.

[172] 27 Stat. 612, 628, 25 U. S. C. 283.

[173] See Tucker, Massacring the Indians, 1927, American Indian Life (October-November 1927 Supplement) 6, 9.

[174] 28 Stat. 286, 313–314.

[175] 28 Stat. 876, 906, 25 U. S. C. 286.

[176] 29 Stat. 321, 348.

[177] 25 U. S. C. 287.

[178] 30 Stat. 62, 79, 25 U. S. C. 278. See Chapter 12, sec. 2D.

policy of Congress to "make no appropriation whatever for education in any sectarian school."

The role which these various statutes on Indian education have had in the development of the present law governing that subject is elsewhere discussed.[179]

Concern for the protection of individual Indian rights was one of the more constructive consequences of the allotment legislation. The Appropriation Act of March 3, 1893,[180] contains a provision, elsewhere discussed,[181] requiring United States district attorneys to render legal services to Indians. Further concern for individual Indian rights is indicated by section 10 of the Appropriation Act of August 15, 1894,[182] requiring the Interior Department to employ Indians in all employments in the Indian Service wherever practicable.

The final subject of importance covered in the legislation of the 1890's is the subject of Indian depredations. The Act of March 3, 1891,[183] established a comprehensive basis upon which all pending depredation claims were, in a comparatively short time, disposed of by the Court of Claims.[184]

[179] See Chapter 12, sec. 2.

[180] 27 Stat. 612, 631, 25 U. S. C. 175.

[181] See Chapter 12, sec. 8.

[182] 28 Stat. 286, 313, 25 U. S. C. 44. See Chapter 8, sec. 4B.

[183] 26 Stat. 851.

[184] See Chapter 14, sec. 1.

SECTION 13. LEGISLATION FROM 1900 TO 1909

Legislation of the decade from 1900 through 1909, like that of the preceding decade, consists almost entirely of piece-meal additions to and modifications of past legislation. The center of gravity is throughout the decade almost entirely in the problem of how Indian lands or interests therein may be transferred from Indian tribe to individual Indian or from individual Indian to individual white man.

Authorization for individual leasing of allotments is contained in the Appropriation Act of May 31, 1900.[185]

The Act of February 6, 1901[186] amplifies prior legislation allowing the Indian a day in court to prove his right to an allotment.

The Appropriation Act of March 3, 1901, contains a provision authorizing the Secretary of the Interior to grant rights-of-way in the nature of easements across tribal and allotted lands for telephone and telegraph lines and offices.[187] The same section contains a provision subjecting allotted lands to condemnation under the laws of the state or territory in which they are located.[188]

The Appropriation Act of May 27, 1902, established a procedure whereby the adult heirs of a deceased allottee may convey lands in heirship status with the approval of the Secretary of the Interior.[189]

The Appropriation Act of June 21, 1906, contains three important provisions of substantive law.[190] In the first place it permits the President to continue the trust period or period of restriction during which allotted land is inalienable.[191] Another provision of this statute provides that:

> No lands acquired under the provisions of this Act shall, in any event, become liable to the satisfaction of any debt contracted prior to the issuing of the final patent in fee therefor.[192]

A third item of general legislation in this appropriation act declares:

> That no money accruing from any lease or sale of lands held in trust by the United States for any Indian shall become liable for the payment of any debt of, or claim against, such Indian contracted or arising during such trust period, or, in case of a minor, during his minority, except with the approval and consent of the Secretary of the Interior.[193]

While a provision in the foregoing act had established an administrative powers to continue restrictions on Indian land beyond the point at which they were to have ceased, a provision in the Appropriation Act of March 1, 1907,[194] extended administrative discretion and flexibility in the opposite direction. Under this legislation sale of restricted land was to be permitted prior to the time when such restriction was to have expired "under such rules and regulations as the Secretary of the Interior may prescribe" and the proceeds might be used for the benefit of the vendor "under the supervision of the Commissioner of Indian Affairs."[195]

The Act of March 2, 1907,[196] entitled "An Act Providing for the allotment and distribution of Indian tribal funds," applies to the realm of funds the principles applied to land in the General Allotment Act. Under section 1 of this act,[197] the Secretary of the Interior was authorized to designate Indians deemed capable of managing their own affairs and to allot to such Indians a pro rata share of tribal funds, upon the application of the Indian. Section 2 of this act,[198] authorized payment, under direction of the Secretary of the Interior, of their pro rata share of tribal funds to Indians mentally or physically disabled.[199]

The Act of May 29, 1908, extended the authority to sell allotted lands, permitting the Secretary to make such sales upon the death of the original allottee and permitting and authorizing the issuance of a patent to the vendee of such Indian heirship lands.[200]

The Appropriation Act of March 3, 1909, authorizes the grant of Indian lands to railroads for various designated purposes.[201] The same statute authorizes leasing of allotted lands for mining purposes[202] under terms approved by the Secretary of the Interior.

A third substantive item contained in this appropriation act authorizes the Secretary of the Interior to make such arrangements as he deems to be "for the best interest of the Indians" in connection with irrigation projects affecting Indian reservation lands.[203]

In general it may be said that these provisions introduce an element of administrative discretion and flexibility into a system which when originally proposed had been considered a means of releasing the Indian from dependence upon administrative authorities.

[185] 31 Stat. 221, 229. See fn. 163, *supra*.

[186] 31 Stat. 760.

[187] Sec. 3, 31 Stat. 1058, 1083, 25 U. S. C. 319.

[188] Sec. 3, 31 Stat. 1058, 1084, 25 U. S. C. 357.

[189] Sec. 7, 32 Stat. 245, 275, 25 U. S. C. 379. And see Chapter 11 sec. 6C.

[190] 34 Stat. 325.

[191] 34 Stat. 325, 326, 25 U. S. C. 391.

[192] 34 Stat. 325, 327, 25 U. S. C. 354.

[193] 34 Stat. 325, 327, 25 U. S. C. 410.

[194] 34 Stat. 1015.

[195] 34 Stat. 1015, 1018, 25 U. S. C. 405.

[196] 34 Stat. 1221.

[197] 25 U. S. C. 119. See Chapter 10, sec. 4.

[198] See 25 U. S. C. 121.

[199] See Chapter 10, sec. 4.

[200] 35 Stat. 444, 25 U. S. C. 404. Also see Chapter 5, sec. 11.

[201] 35 Stat. 781, 25 U. S. C. 320.

[202] 35 Stat. 781, 783, 25 U. S. C. 396. See Chapter 11, sec. 5.

[203] 35 Stat. 781, 798, 25 U. S. C. 382.

SECTION 14. LEGISLATION FROM 1910 TO 1919

During the decade from 1910 through 1919, two trends dominate Indian legislation. In the first place, the allotment system is rendered more flexible and administrative powers in connection with the allotment system are greatly expanded. In the second place, the attempt to wind up tribal existence reaches a new high point and various powers formerly vested in the tribes are transferred by Congress to administrative officials.

Except for the single act of June 25, 1910,[204] which constitutes a comprehensive revision of the allotment law,[205] all the significant general legislation of this period is tucked away in provisions of appropriation acts.

The first such measure is found in a proviso of the Appropriation Act of April 4, 1910,[206] which makes specific the powers conferred upon the Secretary of the Interior the year before[207] with regard to irrigation projects on Indian reservations.[208]

The Act of June 25, 1910,[209] constitutes what is probably the most important revision of the General Allotment Act that has been made. Based on 23 years of experience in the administration of the act, it seeks to fill gaps and deficiencies brought to light in the course of that period. These relate particularly (*a*) to the administration of estates of allottees, (*b*) to the making of leases and timber contracts for allotted lands, and (*c*) to the cancellation or relinquishment of trust patents.

Section 1 of this act[210] sets forth a comprehensive plan for the administration of allottees' estates, conferring plenary authority upon the Secretary of the Interior to administer such estates and to sell heirship lands. Section 2[211] authorizes testamentary disposition of allotments with the approval of the Secretary of the Interior and the Commissioner of Indian Affairs. Section 3[212] permits relinquishment of allotments by allottees in favor of unallotted children, who had been completely ignored in the original scheme of allotment to living Indians, and sale of surplus lands to whites.

Section 4 of the act[213] permits leasing of Indian allotments held by trust patent for periods not to exceed 5 years in accordance with regulations of the Secretary of the Interior, and confers upon the Secretary power to supervise or expend for the Indians' benefit the rentals thereby received. Section 5[214] makes it unlawful to induce an Indian to execute any conveyance of land held in trust, or interests therein, thus taking account of a practice which had resulted in large losses of Indian land through fraudulent or semifraudulent means. Section 6[215] contains various provisions for the protection of Indian timber against trespass and fire. Section 7[216] contains a general authorization for the sale of timber on unallotted lands under regulations prescribed by the Secretary of the Interior. Section 8[217] contains a similar authorization for timber sales on restricted allotted lands.

Section 13 of the act[218] authorizes the Secretary of the Interior to reserve from entry Indian power and reservoir sites, and the following section[219] authorizes the Secretary of the Interior to cancel patents covering such sites upon making allotment of other lands of equal value and reimbursing the Indian for improvements on the cancelled allotment. Other sections contain minor amendments to the General Allotment Act and related legislation.[220]

The provision of this act relating to testamentary disposition of allotments was amended and amplified by the Act of February 14, 1913.[221] As amplified, the privilege of testamentary disposition subject to departmental approval is extended not only to Indians possessed of allotments, but also to Indians having individual Indian moneys or other property held in trust by the United States.[222]

The Appropriation Act of June 30, 1913, declares:[223]

> No contract made with any Indian, where such contract relates to the tribal funds or property in the hands of the United States, shall be valid, nor shall any payment for services rendered in relation thereto be made unless the consent of the United States has previously been given.

The Appropriation Act of August 1, 1914, contains provisions of substantive law authorizing quarantine of Indians afflicted with contagious diseases,[224] and gives recognition to the existence of agency jails by requiring reports of confinements therein.[225]

Contained in the Appropriation Act of May 18, 1916, is a provision authorizing the leasing of allotted lands susceptible of irrigation where the Indian owner, by reason of age or disability, cannot personally occupy or improve the land.[226]

The same appropriation act includes a mandate to the Secretary of the Interior to make a comprehensive report of the use to which tribal funds have been put by administrative authorities. A proviso to this mandate which has become an important part of existing Indian law declares that following the submission of such report, in December 1917—

> no money shall be expended from Indian tribal funds without specific appropriation by Congress except as follows: Equalization of allotments, education of Indian children in accordance with existing law, per capita and other payments, all of which are hereby continued in full force and effect: *Provided further*, That this shall not change existing law with reference to the Five Civilized Tribes.[227]

The Appropriation Act of May 25, 1918, contains a number of "economy" provisions, the most important of which is that prohibiting the use of appropriations, other than those made pursuant to treaties—

> to educate children of less than one-fourth Indian blood whose parents are citizens of the United States and of the State wherein they live and where there are adequate free school facilities provided.[228]

Another provision of this appropriation act contains a reminder of the recent admission of the states of New Mexico and Arizona

---

[204] 36 Stat. 855.

[205] See H. Rept. No. 1, 135, 61st Cong., 2d sess., April 24, 1910, for a comprehensive outline of the purposes of the act (H. R. 24992).

[206] 36 Stat. 269, 270.

[207] Act of March 3, 1909, 35 Stat. 781, 798. See fn. 203, *supra*.

[208] 36 Stat. 269, 270, 271, 25 U. S. C. 383–385. See Chapter 12, sec. 7.

[209] 36 Stat. 855.

[210] 36 Stat. 855, 25 U. S. C. 372.

[211] 36 Stat. 855, 856, 25 U. S. C. 373.

[212] 36 Stat. 855, 856, 25 U. S. C. 408.

[213] 36 Stat. 855, 856, 25 U. S. C. 403.

[214] 36 Stat. 855, 857, 18 U. S. C. 115.

[215] 36 Stat. 855, 857, 18 U. S. C. 104, 107.

[216] 36 Stat. 855, 857, 25 U. S. C. 407.

[217] 36 Stat. 855, 857, 25 U. S. C. 406.

[218] 36 Stat. 855, 858, 43 U. S. C. 148,

[219] 36 Stat. 855, 859, 25 U. S. C. 352.

[220] See sec. 16, 36 Stat. 855, 859 (incorporated in 25 U. S. C. 312) (rights-of-way); sec. 17, 36 Stat. 855, 859 (incorporated in 25 U. S. C. 331) (amending secs. 1 and 4 of the original allotment act); sec. 31, 36 Stat. 855, 863, 25 U. S. C. 337 (allotments within national forests).

[221] 37 Stat. 678. See 25 U. S. C. 373.

[222] See Chapter 10, sec. 10; Chapter 11, sec. 6. See also Sen. Rept. No. 720, 62d Cong. 2d sess., May 9, 1912, on H. R. 1332.

[223] 38 Stat. 77, 97, 25 U. S. C. 85. See Chapter 8, Sec. 7.

[224] 38 Stat. 582, 584, 25 U. S. C. 198.

[225] 38 Stat. 582, 586, 25 U. S. C. 200.

[226] 39 Stat. 123, 128, 25 U. S. C. 394. See Chapter 11, sec. 5.

[227] 39 Stat. 123, 158–159, 25 U. S. C. 123.

[228] 40 Stat. 561, 564, 25 U. S. C. 297.

to the Union, in the form of a prohibition against the executive creation of further Indian reservations in those two states.[229]

Section 28 of this act represents what is perhaps the culmination of the tendency to break up Indian tribes and tribal property. This section[230] authorizes the Secretary of the Interior to withdraw from the United States Treasury and segregate all tribal funds held in trust by the United States, apportioning a pro rata share of such funds to each member of the tribe. This provision for the dividing up of tribal funds required a final roll of persons entitled to participate in the division. Such authorization was conferred by the Appropriation Act of June 30, 1919.[231]

This same act included a comprehensive scheme for the granting of leases and prospecting permits on tribal lands of nine far western states by the Secretary of the Interior, under such regulations as he might prescribe.[232] This statute, probably stimulated by wartime demand for minerals, completely disregards any tribal voice in the disposition of tribal property. It is of a piece with legislation, already noted, looking to the complete dissolution of the Indian tribes and the division of tribal funds, as well as tribal lands, among the members thereof.

[229] 40 Stat. 561. 570, 25 U. S. C. 211.

[230] 40 Stat. 561. 591, 25 U. S. C. 162, repealed by Act of June 24, 1938, sec. 2, 52 Stat. 1037, so far as the former statute authorized distribution of tribal funds. See Chapter 9, sec. 6; Chapter 10, sec. 4; Chapter 15, sec. 23.

[231] 41 Stat. 3. 9, 25 U. S. C. 163.

[232] Sec. 26, 41 Stat. 3, 31, 25 U. S. C. 399, amended by Act of December 16, 1926, 44 Stat. 922, and Act of May 11, 1938, 52 Stat. 347, 25 U. S. C. 396A–396F. See Chapter 15, secs. 14 and 19.

SECTION 15. LEGISLATION FROM 1920 TO 1929

The decade from 1920 through 1929 is singularly devoid of basic Indian legislation. In fact, the decade marks a lull between the legislative activity in which the development of the allotment system was realized and the new trends towards corporate activity and the protection of Indian rights which were to take form in the following decade.

Seven statutes embodying permanent general legislation adopted during this decade deserve notice.

The Appropriation Act of February 14, 1920, contains a direction to the Secretary of the Interior to require owners of irrigable land under Indian irrigation projects to make payments for costs of construction.[233] The same statute contains a proviso authorizing the Secretary of the Interior to make and enforce regulations to secure regular attendance of "eligible Indian children who are wards of the government" in federal or state schools.[234]

The Appropriation Act of March 3, 1921, contains general authorization for the leasing of restricted allotments for farming and grazing purposes, subject to departmental regulations.[235]

By the Act of May 29, 1924,[236] Congress authorized the execution of oil and gas leases "at public auction by the Secretary of the Interior, with the consent of the council speaking for such Indians," wherever such lands were subject to mining leases under the Act of February 28, 1891.[237]

Perhaps the most significant legislation of the decade is the Act of June 2, 1924, which made "all non-citizen Indians born within the territorial limits of the United States" citizens of the United States.[238] The title of this act as given in the Statutes at Large, "An Act To authorize the Secretary of the Interior to issue certificates of citizenship to Indians" is the result of a clerical error which has been a source of considerable misunderstanding. The bill as originally introduced contemplated a procedure whereby the Secretary of the Interior was to issue such certificates. The act as finally passed, however, acted of its own force to confer citizenship upon the Indian and in fact as passed by both houses the title of the bill reads: "A bill granting citizenship to Indians, and for other purposes."[239] This act brought to completion a process whereby various classes of Indians had successively been granted the status of citizenship.[240]

By the Act of May 17, 1926,[241] Congress acted to regularize the handling of "Indian moneys, proceeds of labor," making such moneys

> available for expenditure, in the discretion of the Secretary of the Interior, for the benefit of the Indian tribes, agencies, and schools on whose behalf they are collected, subject, however, to the limitations as to tribal funds, imposed by section 27 of the Act of May 18, 1916 (Thirty-ninth Statutes at Large, page 159).[242]

The status of these funds is elsewhere discussed.[243]

A comprehensive statute on oil and gas mining upon unallotted lands within Executive order reservations is the Act of March 3, 1927.[244] Section 1 of this act[245] extends to Executive order reservations the leasing privileges already applicable to other reservations under the Act of May 29, 1924, noted above.[246]

Section 2 of this act[247] provides for the deposit of rentals, royalties, and bonuses in the Treasury of the United States to the credit of the Indian tribe concerned, such funds to be available for appropriation by Congress. This section contains a significant proviso indicating a new trend in Indian legislation:

> *Provided*, That said Indians, or their tribal council, shall be consulted in regard to the expenditure of such money, but no per capita payment shall be made except by Act of Congress.

Section 3 of the act[248] subjects proceeds and operations under the act to state taxation.[249] Section 4 contains general legislation not restricted to the matter of oil and gas leases:

> * * * hereafter changes in the boundaries of reservations created by Executive order, proclamation, or otherwise for the use and occupation of Indians shall not be

[233] 41 Stat. 408, 409. 25 U. S. C. 386. See Chapter 12, sec. 7.

[234] 41 Stat. 408, 410. See Chapter 12, sec. 2.

[235] 41 Stat. 1225, 1232. 25 U. S. C. 393. See Chapter 11, sec. 5.

[236] 43 Stat. 244. 25 U. S. C. 398.

[237] 26 Stat. 794, 795, 25 U. S. C. 397.

[238] 43 Stat. 253, 8 U. S. C. 3. See Chapter 8, sec. 2.

[239] See H. Rept. No. 222. 68th Cong., 1st sess., February 22, 1924, on H. R. 6355. wherein the Committee on Indian Affairs said:

> At the present time it is very difficult for an Indian to obtain citizenship without either being allotted and getting a patent in fee simple, or leaving the reservation and taking up his residence apart from any tribe of Indians. This legislation will bridge the present gap and provide means whereby an Indian may be given citizenship without reference to the question of land tenure or the place of his residence * * *.

The Senate amended the bill so as to eliminate all departmental discretion in its application. See Sen. Rept. No. 441, 68th Cong., 1st sess., April 21, 1924; and see 65 Cong. Rec. 8621–8622, 9303–9304.

[240] See Chapter 8, sec. 2.

[241] 44 Stat. 560. See 25 U. S. C. 161b.

[242] See H. Rept. No. 897, 69th Cong., 1st sess., April 15, 1926, on H. R. 11171.

[243] Chapter 5, sec. 10.

[244] 44 Stat. 1347.

[245] 44 Stat. 1347, 25 U. S. C. 398a.

[246] 43 Stat. 244. See fn. 236, *supra*.

[247] 44 Stat. 1347, 25 U. S. C. 398b.

[248] 44 Stat. 1347, 25 U. S. C. 398c.

[249] See Chapter 13, sec. 2.

made except by Act of Congress: *Provided*, That this shall not apply to temporary withdrawals by the Secretary of the Interior.[250]

This limitation of a basic executive power in the field of Indian affairs is the precursor of a series of limitations upon executive authority enacted in the following decade.

The unfavorable comparisons drawn by the Meriam report[251] in 1928 between the service standards of the Indian Bureau and those of state agencies[252] led to a series of statutes looking to the transfer of power over Indian affairs from the Interior Department to the states. A first step in this devolution of power was taken by the Act of February 15, 1929,[253] which directs the Secretary of the Interior to permit the agents and employees of any state to enter upon Indian lands[254]

> * * * for the purpose of making inspection of health and educational conditions and enforcing sanitation and quarantine regulations or to enforce compulsory school attendance of Indian pupils, as provided by the law of the State, under such rules, regulations, and conditions as the Secretary of the Interior may prescribe.

[250] 44 Stat. 1347, 25 U. S. C. 398d. See Sen. Rept. No. 1240, 69th Cong., 2d. sess., January 11, 1927, on S. 4893.

[251] Meriam, Problem of Indian Administration (1928).

[252] See Chapter 2, sec. 2F, *supra*.

[253] 45 Stat. 1185, 25 U. S. C. 231.

[254] See H. Rept. 2135, 70th Cong., 2d sess., January 17, 1929, on H. R. 15523.

SECTION 16. LEGISLATION FROM 1930 TO 1939

The decade from 1930 to 1939 is as notable in the history of Indian legislation as that of the 1830's or the 1880's. Through the series of general and permanent laws enacted in the field of Indian affairs during this decade there runs the motive of righting past wrongs inflicted upon a nearly helpless minority. The sense of these wrongs owed much to the labors that went into the Meriam report,[255] much to the investigations conducted by the Senate,[256] and much to the volunteer labors of individuals and organizations willing to assume the thankless task of criticizing the workings of our governmental institutions.[257]

The first of these attempts to remedy past wrongs was the so-called Leavitt Act of July 1, 1932.[258] Both the Meriam report and the special subcommittee of the Senate Committee on Indian Affairs had made it clear that in the development of irrigation projects on Indian reservations, Indians had been charged with tremendous costs for construction work which they had never requested and which brought them little or no benefit. The Leavitt Act authorized the Secretary of the Interior

> to adjust or eliminate reimbursable charges of the Government of the United States existing as debts against individual Indians or tribes of Indians in such a way as shall be equitable and just in consideration of all the circumstances under which such charges were made: * * *.

Such action was to be subject to congressional rescission by concurrent resolution.

A further provision of this act deferred the collection of construction charges against Indian-owned lands until the Indian title thereto should have been extinguished. The place of the Leavitt Act in current Indian irrigation work is elsewhere discussed.[259] Legislation along similar lines was later extended to white users of water on Indian irrigation projects.[260]

The first legislative result of the depression in the field of Indian affairs was an act designed to meet the problem of defaults on timber contracts. The Act of March 4, 1933, permitted the Secretary of the Interior, with the consent of the Indians involved, expressed through a regularly called general council, and of the purchasers, to modify the terms of uncompleted contracts of sale of Indian tribal timber.[261] Similar provision was made with respect to allotted timber.[262] In all such modified contracts Indian labor was to be given preference.[263] The insistence upon Indian consent marks a trend that was to continue through the remainder of the decade.[264]

General emergency legislation, such as the National Industrial Recovery Act,[265] with its public works provisions, and the Emergency Appropriation Act of June 19, 1934,[266] under which the Indian Division of the Civilian Conservation Corps was established, made a very significant impression upon the economic situation of the Indian reservations.

An important item of general and permanent legislation was the so-called Johnson-O'Malley Act[267] of April 16, 1934,[268] authorizing (sec. 1) the Secretary of the Interior to enter into contracts with states or territories—

> * * * for the education, medical attention, agricultural assistance, and social welfare, including relief of distress, of Indians in such State or Territory, through the qualified agencies of such State or Territory.

Federal moneys and federal facilities might be turned over to such state or territorial agencies.[269] This legislation constituted a response to the criticism made by the Meriam report that the standards of social service in the Indian Bureau were in large part inferior to those of parallel state agencies.[270]

Next in the list of Indian grievances to be corrected was the provision in the law governing sales of Indian heirship lands requiring the Indian to refund moneys paid by a defaulting purchaser. Fall of real-estate values and widespread defaults on uncompleted contracts made this provision particularly onerous to the Indians. By the Act of April 30, 1934,[271] the usual rule of law that instalments on a defaulted contract inure to the benefit of the vendor was applied to the Indians.[272]

The next attempt to right old wrongs was embodied in the Act of May 21, 1934,[273] an act which repealed 12 sections of the United States Code that laid peculiar restrictions upon civil liberties in the Indian country.[274] This statute marked the first step in a process of freeing the Indians and the Indian Service from the burden of obsolete laws enacted to fit long-outgrown

[255] See Chapter 2, sec. 2F.

[256] See Chapter 1, sec. 1. See also H. Rept. No. 951, 72d Cong., 1st sess.

[257] See particularly American Indian Life, Bulletins 10 (1927) to 24 (1934).

[258] 47 Stat. 564, 25 U. S. C. 386a.

[259] See Chapter 12, sec. 7.

[260] Act of June 22, 1936, 49 Stat. 1803, 25 U. S. C. 389 *et seq.*

[261] Act of March 4, 1933, sec. 1, 47 Stat. 1568, 25 U. S. C. 407a.

[262] Sec. 2, 47 Stat. 1568, 25 U. S. C. 407b.

[263] Sec. 3, 47 Stat. 1568, 1569, 25 U. S. C. 407c.

[264] See H. Rept. No. 1302, 72d Cong., 1st sess., May 13, 1932; Sen. Rept. No. 1281, 72d Cong., 2d sess., February 21, 1933, on H. R. 6684.

[265] Act of June 16, 1933, 48 Stat. 195.

[266] Act of June 19, 1934, 48 Stat. 1021, 1056. For a continuous account of these activities see the publication of the Office of Indian Affairs, "Indians at Work."

[267] When originally introduced it was known as the Swing-Johnson bill.

[268] 48 Stat. 596. See 25 U. S. C. 452.

[269] See Sen. Rept. No. 511, 73d Cong., 2d sess., March 20, 1934, on S. 2571.

[270] See Chapter 2, sec. 2F, and Chapter 12, secs. 2 and 3.

[271] 48 Stat. 647. See 25 U. S. C. 372 (Supp.).

[272] See H. Rept. No. 825, 73d Cong., 2d sess., February 21, 1934, on H. R. 5075.

[273] 48 Stat. 787.

[274] For a discussion of the sections repealed see Chapter 8, sec. 10A(2).

conditions.[275] The statutes repealed constitute only a small part of the mass of such obsolete laws.

The most comprehensive measure of the decade, probably equaled in scope and significance only by the legislation of June 30, 1834,[276] and the General Allotment Act of February 8, 1887,[277] is the Act of June 18, 1934.[278] Although the various provisions of this act are discussed in other chapters, an outline sketch of the entire act may show the context and perspective in which each of these provisions has to be viewed.

The general purposes of the legislation are set forth at length in Hearings before the House Indian Affairs Committee [279] and in briefer form in Hearings before the Senate Indian Affairs Committee.[280] In a series of conferences held throughout the Indian country the purposes of the proposed legislation as envisioned by officials of the Interior Department and the views voiced by Indians which were embodied in the act as finally passed are set forth in some detail.[281]

More briefly the objectives of the legislation are summed up in the report presented by Senator Wheeler, one of the co-sponsors of the measure, on behalf of the Committee on Indian Affairs, of which he was chairman. The report recommending enactment of the measure [282] declared:

> The purposes of the bill, briefly stated, are as follows:
> (1) To stop the alienation, through action by the Government or the Indian, of such lands, belonging to ward Indians, as are needed for the present and future support of these Indians.
> (2) To provide for the acquisition, through purchase, of land for Indians, now landless, who are anxious and fitted to make a living on such land.
> (3) To stabilize the tribal organization of Indian tribes by vesting such tribal organizations with real, though limited, authority, and by prescribing conditions which must be met by such tribal organizations.
> (4) To permit Indian tribes to equip themselves with the devices of modern business organization, through forming themselves into business corporations.
> (5) To establish a system of financial credit for Indians.
> (6) To supply Indians with means for collegiate and technical training in the best schools.
> (7) To open the way for qualified Indians to hold positions in the Federal Indian Service.

Section 1 [283] prohibits further allotment of Indian lands. This provision embodied a considered judgment that the allotment system was incapable of contributing to the economic advancement of the Indians. As was stated in the House report,[284]

> The bill now under consideration definitely puts an end to the allotment system through the operation of which the Indians have parted with 90,000,000 acres of their land in the last 50 years. (P. 6.)

Section 2 [285] extends, until otherwise directed by Congress, existing periods of trust and restrictions on alienation placed on Indian lands.

Section 3,[286] apart from the lengthy provisos relating to the Papago Reservation,[287] authorized the Secretary of the Interior "to restore to tribal ownership the remaining surplus lands of any Indian reservation heretofore opened, or authorized to be opened, to sale, or any other form of disposal * * *."[288] Commenting on this section, the Senate Committee Report declares:

> When allotment was carried out on various reservations, tracts of surplus or ceded land remained unallotted and were placed with the Land Office of the Department of the Interior for sale, the proceeds to be paid to the Indians. Some of these tracts remain unsold and by section 3 of the bill they are restored to tribal use. (P. 2.)

Section 4 of the act [289] constitutes a rather complicated amalgam of differing Senate and House drafts on the subject of alienation of Indian land. The scope and effect of this section are elsewhere explored.[290] In general, it may be said that the section prohibits *inter vivos* transfers of restricted Indian land except to an Indian tribe and limits testamentary disposition of such land to the heirs of the devisee, to members of the tribe having jurisdiction over the land, or the tribe itself.

Section 5 [291] authorizes the acquisition of lands for Indians [292] and declares that such lands shall be tax exempt.

Section 6 [293] directs the promulgation of various conservation regulations.

Section 7 [294] gives the Secretary authority to add newly acquired land to existing reservations and extends federal jurisdiction over such lands.

Section 8 [295] leaves scattered Indian homesteads on the public domain out of the scope of this measure.

The first eight sections of the law as finally enacted correspond to the provisions of the bills considered and reported by the House and Senate Committees. In the remaining sections of the measure as finally enacted, various combinations and compromises were made between two different drafts which passed the two houses and, therefore, the House and Senate debates and committee reports must be read with caution.

Section 9 [296] authorizes an appropriation for the expenses of organizing Indian chartered corporations and other organizations created under the act.

Section 10 [297] authorizes the establishment of a $10,000,000 revolving credit fund from which loans may be made to incorporated tribes. Loans had been made by the Indian Service for many years to individual Indians but the experience with such loans had not been satisfactory. The individual Indian receiving money or goods from a federal official was apt to place the trans-

[275] See Sen. Rept. No. 634, 73d Cong., 2d sess., March 28, 1934, on S. 2671, wherein it is stated "* * * it appears that the only use now made of these obsolete sections is as an excuse for arbitrary abuses by bureaucratic officials."

[276] See sec. 6, *supra*.

[277] See sec. 11, *supra*.

[278] 48 Stat. 984, 25 U. S. C. 461, *et seq.*

[279] Readjustment of Indian Affairs. Hearings, H. Comm. on Ind. Aff., on H. R. 7902, 73d Cong., 2d sess. (1934).

[280] Hearings, Sen. Comm. on Ind. Aff., on S. 2755 and S. 3645, 73d Cong., 2d sess. (1934).

[281] See, for example, Minutes of the Plains Congress, March 2–5, 1934 (Rapid City Indian School); Minutes of All-Pueblo Council, Santo Domingo Pueblo, March 15, 1934; Report of Southern Arizona Indian Conference, Pheonix, Arizona, March 15–16, 1934 (Phoenix Indian School); Proceedings of the Conference for the Indians of the Five Civilized Tribes of Oklahoma, Muskogee, Oklahoma, March 22, 1934.

[282] Sen. Rept. No. 1080, 73d Cong., 2d sess. (May 10 (calendar day, May 22), 1934).

[283] 48 Stat. 984, 25 U. S. C. 461. See Chapter 11, sec. 1.

[284] H. Rept. No. 1804, 73d Cong., 2d sess., on H. R. 7902 (May 28, 1934).

[285] 48 Stat. 984, 25 U. S. C. 462.

[286] 48 Stat. 984, 25 U. S. C. 463.

[287] Later amended by Act of August 28, 1937, 50 Stat. 862.

[288] See Chapter 15, Secs. 1, 7, 21.

[289] 48 Stat. 984, 985, 25 U. S. C. 464.

[290] See Chapter 11, sec. 4; Chapter 15, sec. 18.

[291] 48 Stat. 984, 985, 25 U. S. C. 465.

[292] "The title to land thus acquired will remain in the United States. The Secretary may permit the use and occupancy of this newly acquired land by landless Indians; he may loan them money for improvements and cultivation, but the continued occupancy of this land will depend on its beneficial use by the Indian occupant and his heirs." (H. Rept. No. 1804, 73d Cong., 2d sess. (May 28, 1934), p. 7.)

[293] 48 Stat. 984, 986, 25 U. S. C. 466.

[294] *Ibid.*, 25 U. S. C. 467.

[295] 48 Stat. 984, 986, 25 U. S. C. 468.

[296] 48 Stat. 984, 986, 25 U. S. C. 469.

[297] 48 Stat. 984, 986, 25 U. S. C. 470.

action in the context of goods received under treaty or agreement or by way of charity, and the urge to repayment was slight. The new legislation precluded loans from the Federal Government to individual Indians. Henceforth the individual Indian was to be responsible in the matter of repayment to his own tribe.[298]

Section 11[299] authorized "loans to Indians for the payment of tuition and other expenses in recognized vocational and trade schools," and "loans to Indian students in high schools and colleges."

Section 12[300] reenacted a promise of Indian employment which had been made in several earlier statutes during the preceding century.[301] Specifically, it directed the Secretary of the Interior to establish standards for appointment "without regard to civil-service laws, to the various positions maintained, now or hereafter, by the Indian Office, in the administration of functions or services affecting any Indian tribe," and provided that Indians meeting such non-civil-service standards "shall hereafter have the preference to appointment to vacancies in any such positions." The administration of this provision is elsewhere discussed.[302]

Sections 13,[303] 14,[304] and 15[305] of the act dealt with the exemption of various tribes from all or some of the provisions of the act, provided for the continuance of "Sioux benefits,"[306] and put forward a promise

> that no expenditures for the benefit of Indians made out of appropriations authorized by this Act shall be considered as offsets in any suit brought to recover upon any claim of such Indians against the United States.

Sections 16[307] and 17[308] deal with the problem of tribal organization and tribal incorporation. Since these sections were the work of a conference committee which took phrases from the bill that had passed the House and other phrases from the bill that had passed the Senate, the House and Senate committee reports and legislative history prior to the conference report must be used with extreme circumspection, in aiding the interpretation of these two sections. The scope of these two sections and the interpretations placed thereon are elsewhere discussed.[309]

Section 18[310] provided that the act as a whole should not apply to any reservation wherein a majority of the Indians voted against its application.[311]

Section 19[312] of the act includes definitions of "Indians," "tribes," and "adult Indians." Of these definitions the definition of the term "Indian" is of particular importance:

> The term "Indian" as used in this Act shall include all persons of Indian descent who are members of any recognized Indian tribe now under Federal jurisdiction, and all persons who are descendants of such members who were, on June 1, 1934, residing within the present boundaries of any Indian reservation, and shall further include all other persons of one-half or more Indian blood.

Although many provisions of the act as originally enacted did not apply to the Territory of Alaska or the State of Oklahoma, which together accounted for approximately one-half of the Indian population of the United States, experience in the administration of the act and intensive discussion of its provisions in the exempted areas led to the adoption of legislation extending the main provisions of the act, with minor modifications, to Alaska[313] and to Oklahoma.[314]

An analysis of the workings of the Act of June 18, 1934, was published in 1938 by a committee of students of Indian affairs.[315] The conclusions reached by this committee after an analysis of concrete experiences on typical reservations are worth quoting:

> * * * these concrete experiences point dramatically to the new world of opportunity that has been opened to all Indian tribes by the development of three cardinal principles of present-day Indian administration: Indian self-government, the conservation of Indian lands and resources, and socially directed credit. On almost every reservation today, even on reservations that voted to reject the Indian Reorganization Act, one finds a deep and growing concern for these basic principles, a conscious striving to secure their application to local problems, the beginnings of constructive achievement, and hope for the future where there was once only hopeless regret for the past.
>
> * * * * *
>
> INDIAN SELF-GOVERNMENT
>
> The first major move of the present administration in the direction of Indian self-government was a provision in the Pueblo Relief Act of May 31, 1933, prohibiting the Secretary of the Interior from spending moneys appropriated under that act for the various Pueblos "without first obtaining the approval of the governing authorities of the Pueblo affected."
>
> The same principle was established on a broader scale by the Indian Reorganization Act of June 18, 1934, which gave to all Indian tribes organizing under its terms the final power of approval or veto over the disposition of all tribal assets.

---

[298] See Chapter 14.

[299] 48 Stat. 984, 986, 25 U. S. C. 471.

[300] 48 Stat. 984, 986, 25 U. S. C. 472.

[301] See Chapter 8, sec. 4B.

[302] See Chapter 8, sec. 4B(3)(b).

[303] 48 Stat. 984, 986, 25 U. S. C. 473.

[304] 48 Stat. 984, 987, 25 U. S. C. 474.

[305] 48 Stat. 984, 987, 25 U. S. C. 475. This provision, insofar as it promised that appropriations authorized by the act should not be considered offsets in Indian claim suits against the United States, was later repudiated in large part, by a rider to the Appropriation Act of August 12, 1935, 49 Stat. 571, 596, 25 U. S. C. 475a.

[306] See Act of March 2, 1889, sec. 17, 25 Stat. 888, 894; Act of June 10, 1896, 29 Stat. 321, 334.

[307] 48 Stat, 984, 987, 25 U. S. C. 476.

[308] 48 Stat. 984, 988, 25 U. S. C. 477.

[309] See Chapter 7, sec. 3; Chapter 14, sec. 4.

[310] 48 Stat. 984, 988, 25 U. S. C. 478.

[311] For a holding that the right to reject the entire act included the right to reject the special provisions dealing with the Papago Reservation, see 38 Op. A. G. 121 (1934). Under the original act, elections had to be called on the act within 1 year after its approval. By the Act of June 15, 1935, 49 Stat. 378, this period was extended another year. Under the original act a majority of all the Indians entitled to vote was required to render the act inapplicable to a particular reservation. Unreported Op. A. G., April 19, 1935. The amendment above referred to modified this rule so as to require only a majority of those voting in an election in which not less than 30 percent of those entitled to vote actually vote.

[312] 48 Stat. 984, 988, 25 U. S. C. 479. For definition of Indians see Chapter 1, sec. 2.

[313] Act of May 1, 1936, 49 Stat. 1250, 48 U. S. C. 362, 358a, discussed in Chapter 21.

[314] Act of June 26, 1936, 49 Stat. 1967, 25 U. S. C. 501–509, discussed in Chapter 23.

[315] The New Day for the Indians: A survey of the Working of the Indian Reorganization Act of 1934 (1938), edited by Jay B. Nash, Oliver LaFarge, and W. Carson Ryan; sponsored by Pablo Abeita, Louis Bartlett, Ruth Benedict, Bruce Bliven, Leonard Bloomfield, Franz Boas, Ray A. Brown, Fay Cooper-Cole, John M. Cooper, George P. Clements, Harold S. Colton, Byron Cummings, William A. Durant, Ben Dwight, Herbert R. Edwards, Haven Emerson, Edwin R. Embree, Howard S. Gans, Robert Gessner, Rev. Philip Gordon, John J. Hannon, John P. Harrington, M. Raymond Harrington, Melville J. Herskovits, Frederick W. Hinrichs, Jr., F. W. Hodges, Edgar Howard, Ales Hrdlicka, Albert Ernest Jenks, A. V. Kidder, Charles IKe, Oliver LaFarge, Robert Lansdale, Ralph T. Linton, Charles T. Loram, John Joseph Mathews, William Gibbs McAdoo, Margaret McKittrick, H. Scudder Mekeel, Jay B. Nash, William F. Ogburn, Father Bona Ventura Oblasser, Robert Redfield, W. Carson Ryan, Lester F. Scott, Elizabeth Sheply Sergeant, Ernest Thompson Seton, Guy Emery Shipler, Frank G. Speck, Vilhjalmur Stefansson, Fred M. Stein, Huston Thompson, George C. Vaillant, Wilson D. Wallis, James P. Warbasse, and B. D. Weeks.

The Indian Reorganization Act further authorized the various Indian tribes to take over positive control of their own resources and to carry on tribal enterprises as membership corporations under a gradually vanishing federal supervision.

The law as finally enacted, left to the future many grants of power included in the original bill, for which it was felt that the Indians were not yet ready. Thus the power to remove undesirable employees from a reservation, the power to appropriate tribal funds held in the United States Treasury, and the power to take over services now rendered by the Interior Department to individual Indians—such services, for instance, as are connected with education, health, the probate and sale of allotments, and the handling of individual Indian moneys—all were deleted from the original bill.

What was perhaps more important than the specific powers which the act, as finally passed, conferred upon organized Indian tribes was the solemn pledge contained in the act that never again would the Federal Government tear down the municipal and economic organizations that should establish themselves under the protection of the act, and that powers vested in the tribes under past laws and treaties would not be diminished without tribal consent.

The principle of Indian self-government was carried to a new phase when the Indians themselves were asked to vote on whether or not the law establishing self-governing powers should apply on the different reservations. The great majority of the Indians voting on the question voted in favor of the Indian Reorganization Act. In accordance with the expressed desires of tribes originally excluded from the act, its essential principles were extended to Alaska by the act of May 1, 1936, and to Oklahoma by the act of June 26, 1936. Indians numbering 252,211 are now under the act. They are grouped into tribes or bands numbering 206. They represent 68.8 percent of the total of Indians in the United States and Alaska.

As of September 1, 1938, 85 tribes, with a population of 99,813, had already adopted constitutions and by-laws under the Indian Reorganization Act. Fifty-nine of these have already received charters of incorporation. No tribe or group which adopted the act, or which was brought within the terms of the act without formal vote, as in Oklahoma and Alaska, has asked by vote or by majority petition to be relieved of the terms of the act. On the other hand, a number of groups in tribes which once rejected the act have petitioned for a second chance to vote on the ground that their original adverse vote was influenced by misinformation. What the adoption of Indian constitutions has meant in the spiritual regeneration of the Indians concerned is illustrated more forcefully by the concrete experiences related in the first part of this report than by any statistical figures.

One significant change in the direction of Indian self-government can best be put in negative terms. During the century from 1833 to 1933 hundreds of laws affecting Indian tribes were enacted and a great part of these laws, perhaps a majority of them, in some way deprived the Indian tribes of rights or possessions they had once enjoyed. Since 1933 no law has been enacted which took from any Indian tribe, against its will, any of its liberties or any of its possessions.

Conservation of Natural Resources

During the years from the passage of the General Allotment Act of 1887 until the beginning of the present administration, Indian land holdings were reduced from approximately 137,000,000 acres to less than 50,000,000 acres. Of the area that remained in Indian ownership a large part was desert or mountainside. The grazing land and farming land still owned by the Indians had seriously deteriorated as a result of overgrazing, the plowing of sod that should never have been broken, reckless timber-cutting and the emigration of the topsoil by various water and aerial routes to points east and west.

These figures represented stark tragedy for a people whose economy was rooted in the soil, whose reverence for the soil was so deep that they never fully grasped the white man's concept of buying and selling land. Little groups of Indians for whom the process of land-loss had gone to its final end, the advance guard of an army moving towards landlessness, could be found in rural slums and town garbage-dumps, living in the depths of squalor and hopelessness.

Against this background the government's present conservation policies stand out in sharp relief. The loss of Indian lands through sales to whites was stopped, except for a few emergency cases, by an order of Commissioner Collier, approved by Secretary Ickes August 14, 1933, and by the general prohibition against further allotments and against sales of restricted land which is contained in the Indian Reorganization Act. Guarantees against alienation of tribal lands have been written into every tribal constitution and charter.

Between March 1933 and December 1937 the total of Indian land holdings increased by approximately 2,780,000 acres. The Indian Reorganization Act authorized an appropriation of $2,000,000 a year for land purchase. In the four years following the passage of the act a total of $2,950,000 was actually appropriated and contracts involving an additional $500,000 were authorized. This money was used to acquire 246,110 acres (as of December 1, 1937) for Indian use. During the same period an additional 349,207 acres was added to Indian reservations, under the authority which the Indian Reorganization Act confers upon the Secretary of the Interior to restore lands which have been taken away from the Indian tribes as "surplus" lands, wherever such lands are still held by the Federal Government. Restitution of a total area of approximately 5,000,000 acres is under consideration. Special legislation enacted under the present administration accounts for the addition of another 1,203,808 acres to the Indian domain. An additional area of approximately a million acres has been included in submarginal land purchases for Indians made by the Resettlement Administration in consultation with the Interior Department.

Meanwhile, vigorous measures were being taken to stop overgrazing. The soil of the Indian country was being rebuilt through an extensive program of water development and flood control, a program which was carried out by the Indians themselves on the basis of financial aid from the Public Works Administration, the Soil Conservation Service, the Civil Works Administration, and the Indian Division of the Civilian Conservation Corps. All timber-cutting on Indian lands (except in a small problem area in Washington State) was being put upon a perpetual yield basis. Oil development on a score of reservations where oil has been found was being strictly controlled in the interests of a national conservation policy. In short, the Indian estate that a few years ago was being dissipated and destroyed is today being conserved, amplified, and improved for the benefit of the Indian people today and for the unborn Indian generations.

Economic Planning

Economic planning is no new thing on Indian reservations. The Blackfeet adopted a five-year development plan in 1921, and it was later copied on many other reservations. What is new in the economic planning under the present administration is that whereas formerly the Indian Service planned *for* Indians and dealt with Indians as individuals, the Indian Service now yields to the tribes that have incorporated under the Indian Reorganization Act a large share of responsibility for developing and administering a reservation economic plan. On several reservations new tribal enterprises, suited to the resources of the reservation and the interests of the Indians, form an integral part of the reservation plan. On several reservations cooperative cattle associations, cooperative stores, and other forms of cooperative enterprise have been developed. On most reservations economic planning is still entirely in terms of individual programs, but even here the control of credit, upon which economic planning depends, has become a collective responsibility of the tribe.

Under the Reorganization Act $4,000,000 has already been appropriated for loans to incorporated Indian tribes. These credit funds are being expended almost entirely for capital investment, in the form of agricultural machinery, farm buildings, and other improvements, livestock, saw mills, and fishing equipment. This credit program, if it is supplemented by a sound land program, and if it does not become too deeply entangled in departmental red tape and remote control, is likely to establish for the first time a stable basis of economic independence for tribes some of which have lived in the depths of poverty, or are kept alive on the edge of starvation by income from annuities, land sales, and leases of land.

* * * * *

WHAT REMAINS TO BE DONE

One who seeks to achieve a just appraisal of the record in the field of Indian affairs must conclude that substantial progress has been made in the removal of injustices and anachronisms that have characterized our national Indian policy. The progress achieved is particularly creditable when one realizes the obstacles that were met: the opposition of vested interests, the well-earned suspicion or hostility among the Indians themselves in the face of new promises of better life, the entrenched habits of a civil service trained in disrespect for Indians and Indian ways, and the tremendous inertia which governmental institutions, financial, legal, and procedural, always offer against fundamental reforms.

Taking account of these obstacles and appreciating at their full value the gains achieved, we must nevertheless recognize that the administration of Indian affairs is not yet something of which white Americans can be proud. The achievements of the present policy represent only the beginning of a liberal Indian program. * * *

* * * * *

Progress in the direction of Indian self-government has been striking. Unfortunately this progress remains for the most part in its promissory stages. The vital question is: "Will the promises of self-government embodied in the Indian Reorganization Act and in the tribal constitutions and charters actually be fulfilled or will these promises be treated like so many earlier promises of the United States embodied in solemn treaties with the Indian tribes?"

Already Congress has cut down the appropriations which the Indian Reorganization Act authorized for land purchase, for credit, for loan funds, and for the expenses of tribal organization. Already Congress has shown a disposition to ignore the veto power which it conferred upon organized tribes in the expenditure of tribal funds.

Finally, it is important that the measures of self-government already achieved be regarded as a beginning and an earnest of good faith rather than as a final goal. The organized Indian tribes, in carrying through the program they have begun, will meet situations in which additional powers, legal and financial, are essential to success. They need sympathy and understanding in their struggle to achieve these further powers of self-government.

The problem of land is still the greatest unsolved problem of Indian administration. The condition of allotted lands in heirship status grows more complicated each year. Commissioner Collier supplied the House Appropriations Committee a year ago with examples showing probate and administrative expenditures upon heirship lands totaling costs seventy times the value of the land; and under existing law these costs are destined to increase indefinitely. Responsibility lies with Congress and the administration to work out a practical solution to this problem, either in terms of corporate ownership of lands, or through some modification of the existing inheritance system. (Pp. 26–34.)

Following the passage of the Wheeler-Howard or Indian Reorganization Act, Congress made another effort to remedy old wrongs in the Act of August 27, 1935,[216] dealing with the problem of Indian arts and crafts. For decades the Indian Bureau had discouraged the practices and conditions out of which Indian arts and crafts had emerged. The substitution of store products for native products, outside of the field of agricultural production, had been a continuing strand of Indian Service policy for more than a century. By the act establishing the Indian Arts and Crafts Board, Congress gave encouragement and protection to a movement already started by traders, artists, and Indians for the revival of native forms of artistic and craft production. The board established by this measure was authorized to engage in research and experimentation, to establish market contacts, to aid in securing financial assistance for the production and sale of Indian products, and to create government trade-marks for Indian products. A full measure of control over the use of such trade-marks was conferred upon the Indian Arts and Crafts Board, and criminal penalties were provided for those imitating or counterfeiting such marks, or advertising products as Indian products without justification.[217]

Another effort by Congress to remedy an established wrong is found in the Act of June 20, 1936.[218] This act exempted from taxation restricted Indian lands which had been purchased out of trust or restricted Indian funds on the understanding that such lands would be nontaxable[219]—an understanding which came to grief when earlier court decisions on the subject were reversed.[220]

The Act of May 11, 1938,[221] superseded earlier legislation which had given the Secretary of the Interior wide powers to dispose of minerals on Indian reservations to prospectors and lessees and established a comprehensive system of mineral leasing on Indian tribal lands, giving primary power to lease to the Indian council or government, subject to departmental approval except where provision has been made, by the terms of tribal charters, for dispensing with requirements of departmental approval.[222]

Finally, the legislation already commented upon[223] looking to the break-up and distribution of tribal funds in the United States Treasury was repealed by section 2 of the Act of June 24, 1938.[224] Section 1 of this act recodified the laws under which tribal funds may be deposited by administrative officials.[225]

The foregoing summary of legislation enacted during the decade from 1930 to 1939 covers, of course, only the more important measures of general and permanent application. It is fair to say, however, that the principles embodied in these measures were at the same time applied in a much larger mass of legislation dealing with particular tribes and areas.

---

[216] 49 Stat. 891, 25 U. S. C. 305, *et seq.*

[217] See Sen. Rept., No. 900, 74th Cong., 1st sess., May 13, 1935, and Rept. Comm. on Indian Arts and Crafts to Hon. Harold L. Ickes on S. 2203, incorporated therein.

[218] 49 Stat. 1542, amended by Act of May 19, 1937, 50 Stat. 188, 25 U. S. C. 412a.

[219] See H. Rept., No. 2398, 74th Cong., 2d sess., April 13, 1936, on H. R. 7764. See also Sen. Rept., No. 332, 75th Cong., 1st sess., April 12, 1937, on S. 150, amending the Act of June 20, 1936, wherein it is said:

> The said act * * * was designed to bring relief and reimbursement to Indians who by failure to pay taxes have lost or now are in danger of losing lands purchased for them under supervision, advice, and guidance of the Federal Government, which losses were not the fault of the Indians, but were purchased with the understanding and belief on their part and induced by representations of the Government that the lands be nontaxable after purchase.

[220] See Chapter 13, sec. 3D.

[221] 52 Stat. 347, 25 U. S. C. 396 *et seq.* See Chapter 15, sec. 19.

[222] See Sen. Rept., No. 985, 75th Cong., 1st sess., July 22, 1937, on S. 2689.

[223] See sec. 14, *supra*.

[224] 52 Stat. 1037, 25 U. S. C. 162a.

[225] See Sen. Rept., No. 531, 75th Cong., 1st sess., May 10, 1937, on S. 2163.

SECTION 17. INDIAN APPROPRIATION ACTS: 1789 TO 1939

Appropriation legislation plays a peculiar role in Indian law. Not only does one find a large part of the substantive law governing Indian affairs hidden away in the interstices of appropriation acts, but frequently the actual appropriations and the conditions prescribed for the expenditure of money are given considerable weight, at least administratively, in determining the rights and powers of administrative officials. Thus, for example, the fact that Congress has for many decades appropriated money for Indian judges and Indian policemen, has commonly been viewed as providing congressional authorization for the activities of these officials, although there is no substantive federal law expressly recognizing or conferring such authority.

We have already noted in the preceding sections of this chapter the more important of the provisions of general and permanent legislation which are found among the sections and provisos of appropriation laws. In other chapters attention is paid to the significance of appropriations in various specific problems of federal Indian law.[326] For the present it will be enough to offer a few suggestions as a guide to those who, in tracking down some problem of federal Indian law, must go through the relevant appropriation acts.

Appropriations affecting Indian affairs are found in appropriation acts for the Interior Department, for the War Department, the Department of Commerce, the Treasury Department, the Department of Agriculture, the Department of State, the Department of Justice, and various other agencies. Among the regular departments, only those of Labor and Navy appear to be immune from provisions affecting Indians. However, the main stream of Indian appropriation legislation has followed a narrower course. It begins with appropriations "for defraying the expenses of the Indian department." The first such general appropriation appears in the Appropriation Act of February 28, 1793,[327] entitled "An Act making appropriations for the support of Government for the year one thousand seven hundred and ninety-three." A year later the item reappears in "An Act making appropriations for the support of the Military establishment of the United States, for the year one thousand seven hundred and ninety-four."[328] Thereafter the annual appropriation act for the military establishment, or in some cases, for the military and naval establishments, contains a regular appropriation, increasing year by year, "for the Indian department."

Apart from these appropriations for the Indian department, separate appropriations were made, from time to time, for the expenses of wars against Indians,[329] the expenses of treaties with Indians[330] (which frequently included considerable gifts), and expenses of carrying into effect treaty provisions.[331]

At first these appropriation acts for the carrying out of treaty promises made permanent appropriations, either for a term of years or "forever."[332] Later, the practice of making annual appropriations to carry out the terms of Indian treaties was substituted.[333]

In 1826 Congress began to enact special appropriation acts for the Indian department.[334] This practice continued until 1909. After 1826 one finds in the appropriations for the military establishment only incidental references to expenses involved in the management of Indian affairs, such as, for example, the expense of maintaining Indian prisoners, the salaries of Indian scouts and other strictly military matters. The last regular appropriation act for the "Indian department" was the act of March 3, 1909.[335] In the following year the appropriation act[336] refers in its title to the "Bureau of Indian Affairs," a name which had indeed been used for nearly a century. Regular appropriation acts for the Bureau of Indian Affairs continued until the Act of March 3, 1921.[337] Since the Appropriation Act of May 24, 1922,[338] appropriations for Indian affairs have been made within the regular Interior Department appropriation act.

Although the practice of inserting the year's crop of Indian legislation at the end of annual Indian appropriation acts was abandoned during the first decade of the century,[339] and parliamentary efforts have been made to bar the inclusion of items of substantive permanent legislation in appropriation acts during recent years, such items continue to crop up from time to time.[340] Even when completely stripped of provisions of general substantive legislation, the Indian provisions of the current Interior Department appropriation acts present so complicated a picture of layer upon layer of residues left by the treaties and laws of the past that it is difficult to read one of these statutes intelligently without a comprehensive historical prospective upon the course of Indian legislation. Efforts in recent years to simplify the form of these appropriation acts have been vigorous but unavailing.[341]

[326] See particularly Chapter 12.

[327] 1 Stat. 325, 326.

[328] Act of March 21, 1794, 1 Stat. 346.

[329] See, for instance, Act of February 11, 1791, 1 Stat. 190.

[330] See, for instance, Act of August 20, 1789, 1 Stat. 54; Act of July 22, 1790, 1 Stat. 136; Act of March 2, 1793, 1 Stat. 333.

[331] See, for example, Act of March 3, 1805, 2 Stat. 338.

[332] See, for example, Act of March 3, 1805, 2 Stat. 338; Act of April 21, 1806, 2 Stat. 407; Act of March 3, 1817, 3 Stat. 393; Act of March 3, 1819, 3 Stat. 517; Act of May 20, 1826, 4 Stat. 181.

[333] See, for example, Act of March 2, 1827, 4 Stat. 232; Act of May 24, 1828, 4 Stat. 300; Act of March 2, 1829, 4 Stat. 361.

[334] See, for example, Act of March 25, 1826, 4 Stat. 150; Act of March 2, 1827, 4 Stat. 217; Act of May 9, 1828, 4 Stat. 267.

[335] 35 Stat. 781.

[336] Act of April 4, 1910, 36 Stat. 269.

[337] 41 Stat. 1225.

[338] 42 Stat. 552.

[339] See, for example, the Act of June 21, 1906, 34 Stat. 325.

[340] See, for example, fn. 305, *supra*.

[341] See the Act of March 2, 1933, 47 Stat. 1422 (providing for "alternate budget").

CHAPTER 5

THE SCOPE OF FEDERAL POWER OVER INDIAN AFFAIRS

TABLE OF CONTENTS

SECTION 1. SOURCES OF FEDERAL POWER

Since the National Government derives its sovereignty from powers delegated to it by the states, the Constitution of the United States forms the basis of federal control of Indian affairs.

The principal sources of congressional authority over Indian affairs are summarised by a leading authority in these terms:[1]

> * * * What is the constitutional basis of the national authority over the Indians? The national government is one of powers delegated by the states; yet Indians are mentioned in the U. S. Constitution only twice—once to exclude "Indians not taxed" (a phrase never more explicity defined, but probably meaning today Indians resident on reservations, that is, on land not taxed by the states) from the count for determining representation in the lower house of Congress; and again to empower Congress to regulate "commerce with foreign nations, among the several states, and with the Indian tribes." This commerce power is an express constitutional basis for Congressional action concerning the Indians, as is also, so far as appropriations for Indians are concerned, the power of Congress to raise and spend money "for the general welfare." But the regulation of Indians from Washington has gone much farther. Much power has been exercised because the whole Indian country, except the few eastern reservations, was formerly part of the national domain, with exclusive title and sovereignty (except to the extent it was recognized to be restricted by Indian occupancy) in the national government. In this respect, the reservations within the bounds of the original thirteen states, having a different history, are probably subject to a different legal regime. * * * The setting up of states in the territory once governed only from Washington has not affected the title of the nation to these lands. This ownership of the land supports a mass of Congressional and departmental regulations of land tenure on the reservations west of the Alleghenies; but even this, added to the express powers of Congress already mentioned, does not sustain the full extent of the national control of Indians wherever they are tribally organized. The chief foundation appears to have been the treaty-making power of the President and Senate with its corollary of Congressional power to implement by legislation the treaties made. The colonies before 1776 (and the original states thereafter) often deal with the Indian tribes through political agreements. When in 1787 the Constitution made exclusive grant of treaty power to the national government, these precedents formed a strong basis for national dealings with Indian tribes, especially those beyond the bounds of any state. Habitually for nearly 100 years the nation treated with the Indians pursuant to the constitutional forms that were used in dealing with foreign states. And by a broad reading of these treaties the national government obtained from the Indians themselves authority to legislate for them to carry out the purpose of the treaties.
>
> In view of the express grants of the commerce power and the expenditure-for-the-general-welfare power, of the fact that the greater Indian tribes lived on the national domain and not within any state (until the west was piece-meal admitted to statehood) and of the custom of dealing with Indian tribes by treaty, the United States Supreme Court has never found, so far as I can learn, that any Congressional regulation of Indians has been beyond the reach of national power. Indeed the net result is the creation of a new power, a power to regulate Indians. * * * (Pp. 80–81.)

In addition to the constitutional sources of authority over commerce[2] with Indian tribes,[3] expenditures for the general

[1] Rice, The Position of the American Indian in the Law of the United States (1934), 16 J. Comp. Leg. 78.

[2] Art. 1, sec. 8, cl. 3.

[3] This limitation upon federal power to situations involving the existence of a tribe is emphasized by the Supreme Court in the case of *United States* v. *Forty-Three Gallons of Whiskey*, 93 U. S. 188 (1876):

> As long as these Indians remain a distinct people, with an existing tribal organization, recognized by the political department

welfare,[4] property of the United States,[5] and treaties,[6] noted by Professor Rice, other constitutional grants of power have played a role in Indian legislation. Most important, perhaps, are the power of Congress to admit new states and (inferentially) to prescribe the terms of such admission,[7] and to make war.[8] Congressional powers of lesser importance involved in Indian legislation include the power to establish post-roads,[9] to establish tribunals inferior to the Supreme Court,[10] and to establish a "uniform rule of naturalization."[11]

While the decisions of the courts may be explained on the basis of express constitutional powers, the language used in some cases seems to indicate that decisions were influenced by a consideration of the peculiar relationship between Indians and the Federal Government.[12]

Thus in *United States* v. *Kagama*[13] the Supreme Court found that the protection of the Indians constituted a national problem and referred to the practical necessity of protecting the Indians and the nonexistence of such a power in the states.

Reference to the so-called "plenary" power of Congress over the Indians, or, more qualifiedly, over "Indian tribes" or "tribal Indians," becomes so frequent in recent cases that it may seem captious to point out that there is excellent authority for the view that Congress has no constitutional power over Indians except what is conferred by the commerce clause and other clauses of the Constitution. The most famous defender of federal power over Indians, Chief Justice Marshall, declared:[14]

> * * * That instrument [the Constitution] confers on congress the powers of war and peace; of making treaties, and of regulating commerce with foreign nations, and among the several states, and with the Indian tribes. These powers comprehend all that is required for the regulation of our intercourse with the Indians. They are not limited by any restrictions on their free actions; the

---

> of the government, Congress has the power to say with whom, and on what terms, they shall deal * * *. (P. 195.)

And see cases cited in Chapter 14, sec. 1, fn. 9. Note, however, that congressional objectives based upon federal power over the tribe may involve an exercise of jurisdiction over individual Indians or individual non-Indians, even outside of Indian lands. *Dick* v. *United States*, 208 U. S. 340 (1908).

In the case of *The Kansas Indians*, 5 Wall. 737 (1866), the Supreme Court said:

> While the general government has a superintending care over their interests, and continues to treat with them as a nation, the State of Kansas is estopped from denying their title to it. She accepted this status when she accepted the act admitting her into the Union. Conferring rights and privileges on these Indians cannot affect their situation, which can only be changed by treaty stipulation, or a voluntary abandonment of their tribal organization. As long as the United States recognizes their national character they are under the protection of treaties and the laws of Congress, and their property is withdrawn from the operation of State laws. (P. 757.)

[4] Art. 1, sec. 8, cl. 1. Art. 1, sec. 9, cl. 7 provides that "No money shall be drawn from the treasury, but in consequence of appropriations made by law * * *." Congress has appropriated money in the nature of a compromise of Indian claims against the Federal Government, and has made this appropriation conditioned on the consent of the tribe concerned. Act of March 3, 1903, 32 Stat. 982, 995 (Creek Nation). The validity of this provision was sustained in 24 Op. A. G. 623 (1903).

[5] Art. 4, sec. 3, cl. 2.

[6] Art. 2, sec. 2, cl. 2.

[7] Art. 4, sec. 3, cl. 1. See *Ex Parte Webb*, 225 U. S. 663 (1912).

The Supreme Court in *Cramer* v. *United States*, 261 U. S. 219 (1923) said:

> Congress itself, in apparent recognition of possible individual Indian possession, has in several of the state enabling acts required the incoming State to disclaim all right and title to lands "owned or *held* by *any Indian* or Indian tribes". (P. 228.)

See Act of February 22, 1889, c. 180, sec. 4, par. 2, 25 Stat. 676, 48 U. S. C. 1460a; Act of July 16, 1894, c. 138, sec. 3, par. 2, 28 Stat. 107. Also see Act of June 16, 1906, 34 Stat. 267.

[8] Art. 1, sec. 8, cl. 11.

[9] Art. 1, sec. 8, cl. 7.

[10] Art. 1, sec. 8, cl. 9; Art. 3, sec. 1. The Supreme Court in the case of *Roff* v. *Burney*, 168 U. S. 218 (1897), said:

> * * * Congress may pass such laws as it sees fit prescribing the rules governing the intercourse of the Indians with one another and with citizens of the United States, and also the courts in which all controversies to which an Indian may be party shall be submitted. (Pp. 221–222.)

By virtue of the power to constitute tribunals inferior to the Supreme Court, Congress has created territorial district courts with jurisdiction over the crime of murder committed by any person other than an Indian upon an Indian reservation. *In re Wilson*, 140 U. S. 575 (1891). The Supreme Court, after alluding to the "power of Congress to provide for the punishment of all offenses committed" on reservations, "by whomsoever committed," said:

> * * * And this power being a general one, Congress may provide for the punishment of one class of offences in one court, and another class in a different court. (Pp. 577–578.)

See Chapter 14, sec. 6A. Also see Chapter 19, sec. 3.

Pursuant to this power, Congress has passed many jurisdictional statutes empowering Indian tribes to sue the Federal Government in the Court of Claims for claims arising out of Indian treaties, agreements, or statutes. Congress may confer jurisdiction upon this court to decide on the proper amount of recovery for property taken by an Indian tribe in amity with the United States. See *Leighton* v. *United States*, 161 U. S. 291 (1896); *United States* v. *Navarre*, 173 U. S. 77 (1899).

While granting statehood to a territory, Congress has also been upheld in transferring the jurisdiction of general crimes committed in districts over which the United States retains exclusive jurisdiction from territorial to federal courts. *Pickett* v. *United States*, 216 U. S. 456 (1910).

[11] Art. 1, sec. 8, cl. 4. See Chapter 8, sec. 2.

[12] See Chapter 8, sec. 9. Also see *Lone Wolf* v. *Hitchcock*, 187 U. S. 553 (1903); *Cherokee Nation* v. *Hitchcock*, 187 U. S. 294 (1902); *Brader* v. *James*, 246 U. S. 88 (1918); N. D. Houghton, The Legal Status of Indian Suffrage in the United States, 19 Cal. L. Rev. (1931) pp. 507, 512; *cf.* Krieger, Principles of Indian Law, 3 Geo. Wash. L. Rev. (1935) pp. 279, 291; 13 Yale L. J. (1904) p. 250. "* * * Congress possesses the broad power of legislating for the protection of the Indians wherever they may be within the territory of the United States, * * *." (*United States* v. *Ramsey*, 271 U. S. 467, 471 (1926).

The Supreme Court said in *Perrin* v. *United States*, 232 U. S. 478, 486 (1914):

> As the power is incident only to the presence of the Indians and their status as wards of the Government, it must be conceded that it does not go beyond what is reasonably essential to their protection, and that, to be effective, its exercise must not be purely arbitrary, but founded upon some reasonable basis. * * * On the other hand, it must also be conceded that, in determining what is reasonably essential to the protection of the Indians, Congress is invested with a wide discretion, and its action, unless purely arbitrary must be accepted and given full effect by the courts.

In *Gritts* v. *Fisher*, 224 U. S. 640 (1912), the Court said:

> * * * As in the instance of other tribal Indians, the members of this tribe were wards of the United States, which was fully empowered, whenever it seemed wise to do so, to assume full control over them and their affairs, to determine who were such members, to allot and distribute the tribal lands and funds among them, and to terminate the tribal government. * * * (Pp. 642–643.)

The Court said in *United States* v. *Thomas*, 151 U. S. 577 (1894):

> * * * The Indians of the country are considered as the wards of the nation, and whenever the United States set apart any land of their own as an Indian reservation, whether within a State or Territory, they have full authority to pass such laws and authorise such measures as may be necessary to give to these people full protection in their persons and property, and to punish all offences committed against them or by them within such reservations. (P. 585.)

The Court said in *United States* v. *McGowan*, 302 U. S. 535 (1938):

> * * * Congress alone has the right to determine the manner in which the country's guardianship * * * shall be carried out * * *. (P. 538.)

Also see *Surplus Trading Co.* v. *Cook*, 281 U. S. 647 (1930); *United States* v. *Nice*, 241 U. S. 591 (1916); *United States* v. *Quiver*, 241 U. S. 602 (1916); *United States* v. *Hamilton*, 233 Fed. 685 (D. C. W. D. N. Y. 1915); *In re Lincoln*, 129 Fed. 247 (D. C. N. D. Calif. 1904); *United States* v. *Rickert*, 188 U. S. 432 (1903); *In re Blackbird*, 109 Fed. 139 (D. C. W. D. Wis. 1901).

[13] 118 U. S. 375 (1886). For a criticism of this decision see Willoughby, The Constitutional Law of the United States (1929), p. 386.

[14] *Worcester* v. *Georgia*, 6 Pet. 515 (1832). And see Willoughby, The Constitutional Law of the United States (1929), pp. 379–402, 1327, 1368.

shackles imposed on this power, in the confederation, are discarded. (P. 559.)

Whatever view be taken of the possibility or danger of federal power arising from "necessity," it is clear that the powers mentioned by Chief Justice Marshall proved to be so extensive that in fact the Federal Government's powers over Indian affairs are as wide as state powers over non-Indians, and therefore one is practically justified in characterizing such federal power as "plenary." This does not mean, however, that congressional power over Indians is not subject to express limitations upon congressional power, such as the Bill of Rights.[15] In the pages that follow we shall attempt to survey the scope and limits of congressional power over Indian affairs. In later portions of this chapter we shall consider the secondary question of how far such power has been, or may be, validly delegated to administrative officials.

[15] Chief Justice Fuller of the Supreme Court in the case of *Stephens v. Cherokee Nation*, 174 U. S. 445, 478 (1899), said that Congress possesses "plenary power of legislation" in regard to Indian tribes, "subject only to the Constitution of the United States."

SECTION 2. CONGRESSIONAL POWER—TREATY-MAKING

The first and chief foundation for the broad powers of the Federal Government over the Indians is the treaty-making provision [16] which received its most extensive early use in the negotiation of treaties with the Indian tribes. Beginning with an Indian treaty submitted to the Senate by President Washington on May 25, 1789, the President and the Senate entered into some treaty relations with nearly every tribe and band within the territorial limits of the United States.[17]

To carry out the obligations and execute the powers derived from these treaties became a principal responsibility of Congress,[18] which enacted many statutes relating to or supplementing treaties.[19]

The scope of the obligations assumed and powers conferred upon Congress by treaties with Indian tribes has been discussed in Chapter 3 of this volume and need not be reexamined at this point.

[16] Earlier treaties under the Articles of Confederation are discussed in Chapter 3, sec. 4B.

[17] See *Marks v. United States*, 161 U. S. 297, 302 (1896).

[18] The United States assumed many obligations towards the Indians, including the following:

> * * * to secure them in the title and possession of their lands, in the exercise of self-government, and to defend them from domestic strife and foreign enemies: and powers adequate to the fulfilment of those obligations are necessarily reserved. (P. 17.) H. Rept. No. 474, Comm. Ind. Aff., 23d Cong., 1st sess., May 20, 1834.

The view that tribal power has been conferred upon the Federal Government by treaty is upheld by *United States v. Forty-Three Gallons of Whiskey*, 93 U.S. 188 (1876).

[19] Act of January 9, 1837, 5 Stat. 135, 25 U. S. C. 152, 153, 157, 158, regulates the disposition of proceeds of lands ceded to the United States by treaty with the Indians. Also see Act of January 17, 1800, 2 Stat. 6; Act of March 30, 1802, 2 Stat. 139; Act of May 28, 1830, 4 Stat. 411; Act of June 30, 1834, 4 Stat. 729. And see Chapter 4, secs. 1, 3. Numerous appropriation acts have been enacted to fulfill treaty stipulations with the various Indian tribes. See Chapter 4, sec. 17.

SECTION 3. CONGRESSIONAL POWER—COMMERCE WITH INDIAN TRIBES

The power of Congress to regulate commerce with Indian tribes has for its field of action the entire nation, not just the Indian country. Commerce with tribal members anywhere, even wholly within a state, may be the subject of congressional regulation. While Congress has not usually exercised such sweeping regulation, its power has been completely demonstrated in the Indian liquor laws, which constituted one of the early examples of federal control over tribal Indians.[20]

The commerce clause [21] is the only grant of power in the Federal Constitution which mentions Indians. The congressional power over commerce with the Indian tribes plus the treaty-making power is much broader than the power over commerce between states.[22]

[20] These laws are discussed in Chapter 17. One of the reasons for the drastic liquor prohibition provisions in sections 20 and 21 of the Trade and Intercourse Act of June 30, 1834, 4 Stat. 729, 732, 733 (R. S. § 2141, 25 U. S. C. 251; R. S. § 2150, 25 U. S. C. 223, amended by Act of May 21, 1934, 48 Stat. 787), was to enable administrative officials to prevent the manufacture of whiskey by Indians, who believed that they had the right to do as they pleased in their own country, and acknowledged no restraint beyond the laws of their own tribe. H. Rept. No. 474, Comm. Ind. Aff., 23d Cong., 1st sess., May 20, 1834. p. 103.

In *United States v. Holliday*, 3 Wall. 407 (1865), the Supreme Court held that Congress could forbid the sale of liquor to an Indian in charge of an agent in a state and outside of an Indian reservation. The Court declared:

> "Commerce," says Chief Justice Marshall, in the opinion in *Gibbons v. Ogden*, to which we so often turn with profit when this clause of the Constitution is under consideration, "commerce undoubtedly is traffic, but is something more; it is intercourse." The law before us professes to regulate traffic and intercourse with the Indian tribes. It manifestly does both. It relates to buying and selling and exchanging commodities, which is the essence of all commerce, and it regulates the intercourse between the citizens of the United States and those tribes, which is another branch of commerce, and a very important one.
>
> If the act under consideration is a regulation of commerce, as it undoubtedly is, does it regulate that kind of commerce which is placed within the control of Congress by the Constitution? The words of that instrument are: "Congress shall have power to regulate commerce with foreign nations, and among the several States, and with the Indian tribes." Commerce with foreign nations, without doubt, means commerce between citizens of the United States and citizens or subjects of foreign governments, as individuals. And so commerce with the Indian tribes, means commerce with the individuals composing those tribes. The act before us describes this precise kind of traffic or commerce, and, therefore, comes within the terms of the constitutional provision.
>
> Is there anything in the fact that this power is to be exercised within the limits of a State, which renders the act regulating it unconstitutional?
>
> In the same opinion to which we have just before referred, Judge Marshall, in speaking of the power to regulate commerce with foreign states, says, "The power does not stop at the jurisdictional limits of the several States. It would be a very useless power if it could not pass those lines." "If Congress has power to regulate it, that power must be exercised wherever the subject exists." It follows from these propositions, which seem to be incontrovertible, that if commerce, or traffic, or intercourse, is carried on with an Indian tribe, or with a member of such tribe, it is subject to be regulated by Congress, although within the limits of a State. The locality of the traffic can have nothing to do with the power. The right to exercise it in reference to any Indian tribe, or any person who is a member of such tribe, is absolute, without reference to the locality of the traffic, or the locality of the tribe, or of the member of the tribe with whom it is carried on. It is not, however, intended by these remarks to imply that this clause of the Constitution authorizes Congress to regulate any other commerce, originated and ended within the limits of a single State, than commerce with the Indian tribes. (Pp. 417–418.)

[21] Article I, sec. 8, cl. 3 of the Constitution empowers Congress "To regulate commerce with foreign nations, and among the several States, and with the Indian tribes." See Chapters 16 and 17.

[22] See 1 Op. A. G. 645 (1824). Prentice and Egan in The Commerce Clause of the Federal Constitution (1898) describe the purpose of this commerce clause as follows:

> * * * The purpose with which this power was given to Congress was not merely to prevent burdensome, conflicting or dis-

Chief Justice Marshall, in the case of *Cherokee Nation* v. *Georgia*,[23] said that it was the intention of the Constitutional Convention

> * * * to give the whole power of managing those affairs to the government about to be instituted, the convention conferred it explicitly; and omitted those qualifications which embarrassed the exercise of it, as granted in the confederation. (P. 13.)

In *United States* v. *Forty-Three Gallons of Whiskey*[24] the Supreme Court declared:

> * * * Under the articles of confederation, the United States had the power of regulating the trade and managing all affairs with the Indians not members of any of the States; provided that the legislative right of a State within its own limits be not infringed or violated. Of necessity, these limitations rendered the power of no practical value. This was seen by the convention which framed the Constitution; and Congress now has the exclusive and absolute power to regulate commerce with the Indian tribes,—a power as broad and as free from restrictions as that to regulate commerce with foreign nations. * * * (P. 194.)

The commerce clause in the field of Indian affairs was for many decades broadly interpreted to include not only transactions by which Indians sought to dispose of land or other property in exchange for money, liquor, munitions, or other goods,[25] but also aspects of intercourse which had little or no relation to commerce, such as travel,[26] crimes by whites against Indians or Indians against whites,[27] survey of land,[28] trespass and settlement by whites in the Indian country,[29] the fixing of boundaries,[30] and the furnishing of articles, services, and money by the Federal Government.[31]

The admission of a new state was held not to affect laws forbidding the sale of liquor to Indians living on the territory from which the state was formed.[32]

The Federal Government may constitutionally forbid the sale of liquor in an area adjoining an Indian reservation in order that Indians will not be tempted by the close proximity of this forbidden beverage.[33]

The Supreme Court, in the case of *Dick* v. *United States*[34] sustained federal liquor statutes protecting against the introduc-

---

> criminating State legislation, but to prevent fraud and injustice upon the frontier, to protect an uncivilised people from wrongs by unscrupulous whites, and to guard the white population from the danger of savage outbreaks.
>
> A grant made with such a purpose must convey a different power from one whose purpose was to insure the freedom of commerce. Congress has, in the case of the Indians, prohibited trade in certain articles, it has limited the right to trade to persons licensed under Federal laws, and in many ways asserted a greater control than would be possible over other branches of commerce. (P. 342.)

[23] 5 Pet. 1 (1831).

[24] 93 U. S. 188 (1876). Also see Article IX of the Articles of Confederation.

[25] See Chapter 17 and Chapter 18, sec. 2. See also *United States* v. *Nice*, 241 U. S. 591 (1916); *Perrin* v. *United States*, 232 U. S. 478 (1914). Mr. Knoepfler has said:

> * * * Commerce with the Indian tribes has been construed to mean practically every sort of intercourse with the Indians either in the tribes or as individuals. (Legal Status of American Indian & His Property (1922), 7 Ia. L. B. 232, 234.)

This regulation included the fixing of the prices of goods sold to the Indians. Act of April 18, 1796, sec. 4, 1 Stat. 452, 453. Licensed traders were prohibited from purchasing from Indians or receiving in barter or trade from them certain articles, such as "a gun, or other article commonly used in hunting, any instrument of husbandry, or cooking utensil, of the kind usually obtained by the Indians, in their intercourse with white people, or any article of clothing, excepting skins or furs, * * *" or "any horse." Act of May 19, 1796, secs. 9, 10, 1 Stat. 469, 471. For similar provisions see Act of April 21, 1806, sec. 7, 2 Stat. 402, 403; Act of March 3, 1799, secs. 9, 10, 1 Stat. 743, 746. Sec. 4 of the Act of July 26, 1866, 14 Stat. 255, 280, which requires traders on Indian reservations to furnish surety bond, is also applicable to Indians. Memo. Sol. I. D., November 20, 1934.

The Act of June 30, 1834, 4 Stat. 729, which forms the basis for the present trade regulations, authorizes the President to prohibit trade with an Indian tribe "whenever in his opinion the public interest may require." Sec. 3, 25 U. S. C. 263, R. S. § 2132. The Circuit Court for the Ohio District, in *United States* v. *Cisna*, 25 Fed. Cas. No. 14,795 (C. C. Ohio, 1835), said:

> * * * The exercise of the power to prohibit any intercourse with the Indians, except under a license, must be considered within the power to regulate commerce with them, if such regulation could not be effectual short of an intercourse thus restricted. (P. 424.)

[26] For example, see Act of May 19, 1796, sec. 3, 1 Stat. 469, 470.

[27] See Act of July 22, 1790, sec. 5, 1 Stat. 137, 138; Act of March 1, 1793, secs. 4, 5, 10, 11, 1 Stat. 329 *et seq.*; Act of May 19, 1796, secs. 4, 6, 1 Stat. 469, 470; Act of March 3, 1799, secs. 2, 4, 5, 7, 8, 1 Stat. 743 *et seq.*; Act of March 30, 1802, sec. 4, 2 Stat. 139, 141; Act of June 30, 1834, sec. 25, 4 Stat. 729, 733. Superintendents, agents, and subagents were empowered to procure the arrest and trial of all Indians accused of committing any crimes and of other persons who may have committed crimes or offenses within a state or territory and fled into the Indian country. Act of June 30, 1834, sec. 19, 4 Stat. 729, 732. The President was authorized to sanction other means of securing the arrest and trial of these Indians, including the employment of the military force of the United States.

[28] The survey of lands belonging to or reserved or granted by the United States to any Indian tribe was made a crime. Act of May 19, 1796, sec. 5, 1 Stat. 469, 470. Also see Act of March 3, 1799, sec. 5, 1 Stat. 743, 745, and Act of March 30, 1802, sec. 5, 2 Stat. 139, 141.

[29] Act of July 22, 1790, sec. 5, 1 Stat. 137, 138; Act of March 3 1799, sec. 4, 1 Stat. 743, 744; Act of March 30, 1802, sec. 4, 2 Stat. 139, 141. The Act of June 30, 1834, sec. 10, 4 Stat. 729, 730, R. S. § 2147, 25 U. S. C. 220, empowered the superintendents of Indian affairs and Indian agents and subagents to remove from the Indian country all persons found therein contrary to law, and authorized the President to direct the military force to be employed in such removal. The President was also authorized (sec. 11) to employ the military force to drive off persons making "settlement on any lands belonging, secured, or granted by treaty with the United States to any Indian tribe." R. S. § 2118, 25 U. S. C. 180. On the issuance of passports to enter the Indian country see Chapter 1, sec. 3, fn. 47; Chapter 4, sec. 5, fn. 73.

[30] The Trade and Intercourse Act of May 19, 1796, secs. 1, 20, 1 Stat. 469, 474 provides for the marking of the boundary lines described in the acts and treaties between the United States and various Indian tribes. Also see Act of March 30, 1802, sec. 1, 2 Stat. 139.

[31] Money was often appropriated for allowances for agents and for the purpose of trading with the Indian nations. Act of April 18, 1796, secs. 5, 6, 1 Stat. 452, 453; also see Act of March 3, 1795, 1 Stat. 443; Act of March 3, 1809, sec. 1, 2 Stat. 544. The President was empowered to furnish animals, implements of husbandry, and goods and moneys to the Indians. Act of March 1, 1793, sec. 9, 1 Stat. 329, 331; Act of March 30, 1802, sec. 13, 2 Stat. 139, 143.

[32] *Ex parte Webb*, 225 U. S. 663 (1912). A cession by Indians may be qualified by a stipulation that the land shall continue to be under the liquor prohibition laws, though within state boundaries. See *Clairmont* v. *United States*, 225 U. S. 551 (1912).

[33] *United States* v. *Forty-Three Gallons of Whiskey*, 93 U. S. 188 (1876). The Supreme Court, in the case of *Johnson* v. *Gearlds*, 234 U. S. 422 (1914), said:

> That it is within the constitutional power of Congress to prohibit the manufacture, introduction, or sale of intoxicants upon Indian lands, including not only lands reserved for their special occupancy, but also lands outside of the reservations to which they may naturally resort; and that this may be done even with respect to lands lying within the bounds of a State, are propositions so thoroughly established, and upon grounds so recently discussed, that we need merely cite the cases. *Perrin* v. *United States*, 232 U. S. 478, 483; *United States* v. *Forty-three Gallons of Whiskey*, 93 U. S. 188, 195, 197; *Dick* v. *United States*, 208 U. S. 340. (Pp. 438–439.)

[34] 208 U. S. 340 (1908). Congress has power to prohibit the sale of liquor to Indians living on land owned in fee by their tribe. (*United States* v. *Sandoval*, 231 U. S. 28 (1913), and the introduction into an Indian reservation from a point within the state in which the reserva-

tion of intoxicants, for 25 years, lands ceded by, as well as lands allotted to, the Nez Perce Indians:

> If Congress has the power, as the case we have last cited decides, to punish the sale of liquor anywhere to an individual member of an Indian tribe, why cannot it also subject to forfeiture liquor introduced for an unlawful purpose into territory in proximity to that where the Indians live? There is no reason for the distinction; and, as there can be no divided authority on the subject, our duty to them, our regard for their material and moral well-being, would require us to impose further legislative restrictions, should country adjacent to their reservations be used to carry on the liquor traffic with them. (P. 357.)

The power over liquor traffic is not unlimited. The Supreme Court in *Perrin v. United States*,[35] said:

> As the power is incident only to the presence of the Indians and their status as wards of the Government, it must be conceded that it does not go beyond what is reasonably essential to their protection, and that, to be effective, its exercise must not be purely arbitrary, but founded upon some reasonable basis. Thus, a prohibition like that now before us, if covering an entire State when there were only a few Indian wards in a single county, undoubtedly would be condemned as arbitrary. And a prohibition valid in the beginning doubtless would become inoperative when in regular course the Indians affected were completely emancipated from Federal guardianship and control. A different view in either case would involve an unjustifiable encroachment upon a power obviously residing in the State. On the other hand, it must also be conceded that, in determining what is reasonably essential to the protection of the Indians, Congress is invested with a wide discretion, and its action, unless purely arbitrary, must be accepted and given full effect by the courts. (P. 486.)

tion is situated, though interstate commerce is not involved (*United States v. Wright*, 229 U. S. 226 (1913)). Also see *United States v. Soldana*, 246 U. S. 530 (1918); Robert C. Brown, The Taxation of Indian Property (1931), 15 Minn. L. Rev. 182.

[35] 232 U. S. 478 (1914).

SECTION 4. CONGRESSIONAL POWER—NATIONAL DEFENSE

Although comparatively little has been written about the war powers of Congress[36] and the Indian, these powers underlay much of the federal power exercised over Indian land and Indians during the early history of the Republic. In international law conquest brings legal power to govern.

At least 1,012 statutes, public and private, have been enacted by Congress to deal with matters arising out of Indian warfare.[37]

When the Constitution was adopted, the chief mode of dealing with Indians was warfare. Accordingly Indian affairs were entrusted to the War Department by the Act of August 7, 1789,[38] the first law of Congress relating to Indians.

The Congressional power "To * * * provide for the common defence * * * of the United States"[39] was again utilized by the Act of September 29, 1789,[40] which authorized the President to call into service from time to time such part of the militia of the states as he may judge necessary "for the purpose of protecting the inhabitants of the frontiers of the United States from the hostile incursions of the Indians." Many other early statutes indicate the seriousness with which Congress considered the danger of Indian invasion. Such laws authorize an appropriation for "preserving peace with the Indian tribes,"[41] the raising of three regiments which "shall be discharged as soon as the United States shall be at peace with the Indian tribes,"[42] and mustering the militia to repel "imminent danger of invasion from any foreign nation or Indian tribe."[43] Some early repressions of civil liberties sprang from attempts to attain peace with the Indians.[44]

The Act of July 20, 1867,[45] authorizes the appointment of a commission composed of three generals and four civilians to conclude peace with hostile Indian tribes in the path of the proposed railroads to the Pacific and secure their consent to remove to reservations. Provision was made in the event of failure of the commission for the services of mounted volunteers, not exceeding 4,000, for the suppression of Indian hostilities.[46] Military campaigns were frequently waged against Indians, ranging from expeditions of detachments of militia[47] to regiments carrying on wars against Indian tribes.[48]

The occupation of Florida by United States troops was justified on the basis of necessity to protect Georgia from hostile Indians from the peninsula.[49] Money[50] and ammunition[51] were supplied to territorial and state officials for defense against the Indians, and as late as August 5, 1876, a joint resolution was passed

[36] Art. 1, sec. 8, cls. 1, 11, 12, 15, 16, 17.

Cf. Duerr, Course of Lectures on the Constitutional Jurisprudence of the United States (1856), pp. 285–286, said:

> The powers to regulate commerce, declare war, make peace, and conclude treaties, comprise all that is required for regulating our intercourse with the Indian tribes.

[37] *Cf.* Chapter 8, sec. 4B(4)(c).

[38] 1 Stat. 49.

[39] U. S. Constitution, Art. 1, sec. 8, cl. 1.

[40] 1 Stat. 95, 96.

[41] Act of July 22, 1790, 1 Stat. 136.

[42] Act of March 5, 1792, 1 Stat. 241, repealed Act of March 3, 1795, 1 Stat. 430.

[43] Act of May 2, 1792, 1 Stat. 264. A similar provision is contained in the Act of February 28, 1795, 1 Stat. 424. Early protective statutes against the Indians include Act of January 2, 1812, 2 Stat. 670; Act of March 3, 1813, 2 Stat. 829. The Act of May 28, 1830, sec. 6, 4 Stat. 411, 412, authorized the President to protect migrating Indians "against all interruption or disturbance from any other tribe or nation of Indians * * *." The Act of July 14, 1832, 4 Stat. 595, authorized the appointment by the President of three commissioners to treat with the Indians in order to insure the protection promised the Indians in this provision. Also see Act of May 23, 1836, 5 Stat. 32.

[44] Act of January 17, 1800, 2 Stat. 6, discussed in Chapter 8, sec. 10A(2) *fn.* 311.

[45] 15 Stat. 17.

[46] For further post-Civil War statutory evidence of hostility with the Indians, see Act of March 3, 1873, 17 Stat. 566; Jt. Res. of July 3, 1876, 19 Stat. 214; Act of August 15, 1876, 19 Stat. 204; Jt. Res. August 5, 1876, 19 Stat. 216; Act of June 7, 1878, 20 Stat. 252. And see Chapter 14, sec. 3.

[47] See Act of May 13, 1800, 2 Stat. 82; Act of April 10, 1812, 2 Stat. 704; Act of July 2, 1836, 5 Stat. 71.

[48] See Act of April 20, 1818, 3 Stat. 459; Act of May 4, 1822, 3 Stat. 676; Act of May 26, 1824, 4 Stat. 70.

[49] Joint Resolution of January 15, 1811, 2 Stat. 666; Joint Resolution of January 15, 1811, 3 Stat. 471; Act of February 12, 1812, 3 Stat. 472; Act of March 30, 1822, 3 Stat. 654. The Joint Resolution of March 3, 1881, 21 Stat. 520, deals with expenditures of the State of Florida in suppressing hostile Indians.

[50] Act of July 27, 1866, 14 Stat. 307. The State of California floated four Indian war bonds. See Act of March 3, 1881, 21 Stat. 510; Act of June 27, 1882, 22 Stat. 111; Act of January 6, 1883, 22 Stat. 399.

[51] Act of April 7, 1866, 14 Stat. 26; Act of May 21, 1872, 17 Stat. 138; Act of January 16, 1889, 25 Stat. 646; Joint Resolution of December 9, 1890, 26 Stat. 1111.

authorizing the President to prohibit the sale of special metallic cartridges to hostile Indians.[52]

There are several statutes in force[53] which illustrate the exercise of the war power in relation to the Indians. The Act of July 5, 1862,[54] authorizes the abrogation of treaties with tribes engaged in hostilities; the Act of March 2, 1867,[55] authorizes the withholding of annuities from hostile Indians; the Act of February 14, 1873,[56] regulates the sale of arms to hostile Indians; and the Act of March 3, 1875,[57] forbids payments to Indian bands at war.

Apart from the specific statutes that mark the heritage of decades of military control, other less tangible relics of this control managed to persist long after the Indian Service was removed from the War Department.[58]

[52] 19 Stat. 216.

[53] See Chapter 14, sec. 3.

[54] 12 Stat. 512, 528, R. S. § 2080, 25 U. S. C. 72.

[55] 14 Stat. 492, 515, R. S. § 2100, 25 U. S. C. 127.

[56] 17 Stat. 437, 457, 459, R. S. § 467, 2136, 25 U. S. C. 266.

[57] 18 Stat. 420, 449, 25 U. S. C. 128.

[58] See Chapter 8, sec. 10A(3). See also Chapter 2, sec. 2.

SECTION 5. CONGRESSIONAL POWER—UNITED STATES TERRITORY AND PROPERTY

The principal Indian tribes lived on the national domain. By virtue of its control over the public domain and the United States' territories, the Federal Government was able to exercise broad dominion and control over the Indians, and to effectuate many Indian policies such as those predicated on westward removal, reservations and allotments.[59] Today the control over the Alaskan natives is partly based on this power.[60]

The control of land, water, and other property belonging to the United States is vested exclusively in Congress by the Constitution.[61] The Supreme Court has upheld a broad exercise of this power.

The power of Congress over a territory and its inhabitants is also exclusive and paramount, except as restricted by the Constitution,[62] and Congress can exercise all the sovereign and reserved powers of state governments subject to the provisions of the Constitution specifically restricting the power of the Federal Government.[63] The extent of this power of Congress over Indians is shown by many decisions of the Supreme Court. The Court in the case of *United States* v. *Kagama*[64] said:

> But these Indians are within the geographical limits of the United States. The soil and the people within these limits are under the political control of the Government of the United States, or of the States of the Union. There exist within the broad domain of sovereignty but these two. There may be cities, counties, and other organized bodies with limited legislative functions, but they are all derived from, or exist in, subordination to one or the other of these. The territorial governments owe all their powers to the statutes of the United States conferring on them the powers which they exercise, and which are liable to be withdrawn, modified, or repealed at any time by Congress. What authority the State governments may have to enact criminal laws for the Indians will be presently considered. But this power of Congress to organize territorial governments, and make laws for their inhabitants, arises not so much from the clause in the Constitution in regard to disposing of and making rules and regulations concerning the Territory and other property of the United States, as from the ownership of the country in which the Territories are, and the right of exclusive sovereignty which must exist in the National Government, and can be found nowhere else. *Murphy* v. *Ramsey*, 114 U. S. 15, 44. (Pp. 379-380.)

The Supreme Court, in the case of *United States* v. *Rogers*,[65] said:

> * * * we think it too firmly and clearly established to admit of dispute, that the Indian tribes residing within the territorial limits of the United States are subject to their authority, and where the country occupied by them is not within the limits of one of the States, Congress may by law punish any offence committed there, no matter whether the offender be a white man or an Indian. (P. 572.)

A. TRIBAL LANDS

The control by Congress of tribal lands has been one of the most fundamental expressions, if not the major expression, of the constitutional power of Congress over Indian affairs,[66] and has provided most frequent occasion for judicial analysis of that power. From the wealth of judicial statement there may be

[59] For example, large areas of the public domain have been withdrawn for Indian reservations.

[60] See Chapter 21, sec. 4. Also see *Nelson* v. *United States*, 30 Fed. 112, 116 (C. C. Ore. 1887) and *Endelman* v. *United States*, 86 Fed. 456 (C. C. A. 9, 1898).

[61] See *Hallowell* v. *United States*, 221 U. S. 317, (1911). Since the time when the necessity for the exercise of the authority arose, there has been almost no question as to the absolute power of Congress to determine the form of political and administrative control to be erected over the territories, and to fix the extent to which their inhabitants shall be admitted to a participation in their own government. Both by legislative practice and by judicial sanction, the principle has from the first been asserted that upon this matter the judgment of Congress is absolute. Willoughby, The Constitution of the United States (1929), p. 439.

> The Congress shall have power to dispose of and make all needful Rules and Regulations respecting the Territory or other property belonging to the United States; and nothing in this Constitution shall be so construed as to Prejudice any Claims of the United States, or of any particular State. (Art. 4, sec. 3, cl. 2.)
>
> Congress can grant to Indians fishing privileges in waters connected with a reservation. (Op. Sol. I. D., M. 28978, April 19, 1937.)

[62] See *Oklahoma* v. *A., T. & Santa Fe Ry. Co.*, 220 U. S. 277, 285 (1911).

[63] *Oklahoma K. & M. I. Ry. Co.* v. *Bowling*, 249 Fed. 592 (C. C. A. 8, 1918).

[64] 118 U. S. 375 (1886).

[65] 4 How. 567 (1846).

[66] The plenary power over tribal relations and tribal property of the Indians has been frequently exercised by Congress. See *Roff* v. *Burney*, 168 U. S. 218 (1897); *Cherokee Nation* v. *Hitchcock*, 187 U. S. 294 (1902); *Blackfeather* v. *United States*, 190 U. S. 368 (1903); *Choate* v. *Trapp*, 224 U. S. 665 (1912); *Ex parte Webb*, 225 U. S. 663 (1912); *United States* v. *Osage County*, 251 U. S. 128 (1919); *Nadeau* v. *Union Pacific R. R. Co.*, 253 U. S. 442 (1920).

The Attorney General said, in 34 Op. A. G. 171 (1924):

> * * * the Indian possession has always been recognized as complete and exclusive until terminated by conquest or treaty, or by the exercise of that plenary power of guardianship to dispose of tribal property of the Nation's wards without their consent. (P. 180.)

The United States has power to legislate concerning the distribution of tribal land. *United States* v. *Boylan*, 265 Fed. 165, 173 (C. C. A. 2, 1920), app. dism. 257 U. S. 614; *Heckman* v. *United States*, 224 U. S. 413 (1912). Also see *United States* v. *Candelaria*, 271 U. S. 432 (1926) and *United States* v. *Sandoval*, 231 U. S. 28, 48 (1913), and Chapter 11, sec. 1.

derived the basic principle that Congress has a very wide power to manage and dispose of tribal lands.

Examples of Supreme Court statements of the principle are the following:

Justice Brandeis, speaking for the United States Supreme Court in the case of *Morrison* v. *Work*,[67] declared:

> It is admitted that, as regards tribal property subject to the control of the United States as guardian of Indians, Congress may make such changes in the management and disposition as it deems necessary to promote their welfare. The United States is now exercising, under the claim that the property is tribal, the powers of a guardian and of a trustee in possession. (P. 485.)

The Supreme Court said in the case of *Nadeau* v. *Union Pacific Railroad Company*:[68]

> It seems plain that, at least, until actually allotted in severalty (1864) the lands were but part of the domain held by the Tribe under the ordinary Indian claim—the right of possession and occupancy—with fee in the United States. *Beecher* v. *Wetherby*, 95 U. S. 517, 525. The power of Congress, as guardian for the Indians, to legislate in respect of such lands is settled. *Cherokee Nation* v. *Southern Kansas Ry. Co.*, 135 U. S. 641, 653; *United States* v. *Rowell*, 243 U. S. 464, 468; *United States* v. *Chase*, 245 U. S. 89. (Pp. 445–446.)

A necessary corrollary to this principle is that control of tribal land is a political function not to be exercised by the courts.[69]

The Supreme Court in the case of *Sioux Indians* v. *United States*[70] said:

> * * * Jurisdiction over them [the Indians] and their tribal lands was pecularly within the legislative power of Congress and may not be exercised by the courts in the absence of legislation conferring rights upon them such as are the subject of judicial cognizance. See *Lone Wolf* v. *Hitchcock*, *supra*, 565; *Cherokee Nation* v. *Hitchcock*, 187 U. S. 294; *Stephens* v. *Cherokee Nation*, 174 U. S. 445, 483. This the jurisdictional Act of April 11, 1916, plainly failed to do. (P. 437.)

In the case of *Cherokee Nation* v. *Hitchcock*,[71] the Supreme court said:

> * * * The power existing in Congress to administer upon and guard the tribal property, and the power being political and administrative in its nature, the manner of its exercise is a question within the province of the legislative branch to determine, and is not one for the courts. (P. 308.)

The power of Congress extends from the control of the use of the lands,[72] through the grant of adverse interests in the lands,[73] to the outright sale and removal of the Indians' interests.[74] And this is true, whether or not the lands are disposed of for public or private purposes.[75]

To illustrate, the power of Congress to grant rights-of-way across tribal land is clearly established.[76] To quote the Supreme Court:[77]

[67] 266 U. S. 481 (1925), aff'g 290 Fed. 306 (App. D. C. 1923).

[68] 253 U. S. 442 (1920). The Attorney General wrote in 26 Op. A. G. 340 (1907):

> It is unnecessary to go into any detailed discussion of the power of Congress to alter, modify, or repeal the provisions of the agreement with the Seminole Nation ratified by the act of July 1, 1898, and otherwise provide for the administration of their property and funds, as provided by the act of April 26, 1906, because the question has been conclusively settled by the decisions of the Supreme Court. (*Stephens* v. *Cherokee Nation*, 174 U. S. 445; *Cherokee Nation* v. *Hitchcock*, 187 U. S. 294; Lone *Wolf* v. *Hitchcock*, 187 U. S. 553; *Morris* v. *Hitchcock*, 194 U. S. 384, 388; *Wallace* v. *Adams*, 204 U. S. 415).
>
> These decisions maintain the plenary authority of Congress to control the affairs and administer the property of the Five Civilized Tribes in the Indian Territory and other Indian tribes. (P. 346.)

[69] The courts have usually denominated this power as political and not subject to the control of the judicial department of the government. See *Lone Wolf* v. *Hitchcock*, 187 U. S. 553, 565 (1903) sustaining the disposal of a reservation of an Indian tribe on the ground that it was a legitimate exercise of congressional power over tribal Indians and their property. This case is discussed in *Oklahoma* v. *Texas*, 258 U. S. 574, 592 (1922). Also see *Cherokee Nation* v. *Hitchcock*, 187 U. S. 294, 308 (1902).

[70] 277 U. S. 424 (1928), aff'g 58 C. Cls. 302 (1923). Also see *Tiger* v. *Western Investment Co.*, 221 U. S. 286, 311–312 (1911).

[71] 187 U. S. 294 (1902).

The court cited with approval the following excerpt from *Stephens* v. *Cherokee Nation*, 174 U. S. 445 (1899):

> It may be remarked that the legislation seems to recognise, especially the act of June 28, 1898, a distinction between admission to citizenship merely and the distribution of property to be subsequently made, as if there might be circumstances under which the right to a share in the latter would not necessarily follow from the concession of the former. But in any aspect, we are of opinion that the constitutionality of these acts in respect of the determination of citizenship cannot be successfully assailed on the ground of the impairment or destruction of vested rights. The lands and moneys of these tribes are public lands and public moneys, and are not held in individual ownership, and the assertion by any particular applicant that his right therein is so vested as to preclude inquiry into his status involves a contradiction in terms.

The court concluded:

> The holding that Congress had power to provide a method for determining membership in the five civilised tribes, and for ascertaining the citizenship thereof preliminary to a division of the property of the tribe among its members, necessarily involved the further holding that Congress was vested with authority to adopt measures to make the tribal property productive, and secure therefrom an income for the benefit of the tribe. (P. 307.)

[72] *E.g.* grazing. See Act of June 18, 1934, sec. 6, 48 Stat. 984, 986, 25 U. S. C. 466.

[73] *E.g.* rights-of-way. See Chapter 4, sec. 18. And see fn. 76, *infra*.

[74] Congress in dissolving a tribe may also provide for the liquidation and distribution of tribal property. *United States* v. *Seminole Nation*, 299 U. S. 417 (1937). See also *United States* v. *Nice*, 241 U. S. 591, 598 (1916); 14 Col. L. Rev. 587–589 (1914). But the court will not assume that Congress abdicated its powers over the tribe or its property, without an unequivocal expression of that intent. *Chippewa Indians* v. *United States*, 307 U. S. 1 (1939); *United States* v. *Boylan*, 265 Fed. 165, 171 (C. C. A. 2, 1920), app. dism. 257 U. S. 614 (1921).

[75] But the land so managed and disposed of must be tribal land. Indians have frequently taken to court the complaint that the tribal property has become vested, by previous act or treaty, in individuals, and is no more subject to congressional control than the private property of other individuals. The courts, however, tend to construe such previous acts and treaties, wherever possible, against the vesting of private rights in tribal property. *Chippewa Indians of Minnesota* v. *United States*, 301 U. S. 358 (1937), aff'g 80 C. Cls. 410 (1935); *United States* v. *Chase*, 245 U. S. 89 (1917), rev'g 222 Fed. 593 (C. C. A. 8, 1915). Until property is allotted, Congress possesses plenary power to deal with tribal lands and funds as tribal property. *Sizemore* v. *Brady*, 235 U. S. 441 (1914). Also see *United States* v. *Mille Lac Chippewas*, 229 U. S. 498 (1913).

[76] *Nadeau* v. *Union Pacific R. R. Co.*, 253 U. S. 442 (1920).

Federal statutes provide for the taking of tribal lands by the United States. For example, the Act of May 23, 1908, 35 Stat. 268, created a national forest upon lands held by the Federal Government as a trustee for the Chippewa Indian Tribe. This law is discussed in *Chippewa Indians* v. *United States*, 305 U. S. 479 (1939). For other cases on eminent domain see *Shoshone Tribe* v. *United States*, 299 U. S. 476 (1937); *United States* v. *Creek Nation*, 295 U. S. 103 (1935), s. c. 302 U. S. 620 (1938). See, for example, Act of March 3, 1901, 31 Stat. 1058, 1084, discussed in 49 L. D. 896 (1923).

The right of eminent domain may be exercised by the Federal Government over land held by an Indian nation in fee simple under patent from the United States, without the consent of the tribe. *Cherokee Nation* v. *Kansas Ry. Co.*, 135 U. S. 641 (1890), which rejected the contention that land was held by the Cherokees as a sovereign nation. Some treaties provided that railroads should have rights-of-way upon payment of just compensation to the Indian tribes. Treaty of June 5, 1854, with the Miamis, Art. 10, 10 Stat. 1093. See Chapter 15, sec. 1B.

The Act of March 2, 1899, 30 Stat. 990, authorised any railroad company or telegraph and telephone company to take and condemn a right-of-way in or through any lands which have been or may hereafter be allotted in severalty, but have not been conveyed to the allottee with full power of alienation. The Act of February 28, 1902, sec. 23, 32 Stat. 43, discussed in *Oklahoma K. & M. I. Ry. Co.* v. *Bowling*, 249 Fed. 592 (C. C. A. 8, 1918), made this statute inapplicable to the Indian Territory and Oklahoma Territory.

[77] *Missouri, Kansas & Texas R'y Co.* v. *Roberts*, 152 U. S. 114 (1894). Even though an Indian tribe has granted a purported exclusive license to a telephone company, Congress may issue a similar license to another

The United States had the right to authorize the construction of the road of the Missouri, Kansas, and Texas Railway Company through the reservation of the Osage Indians, and to grant absolutely the fee of the two hundred feet as a right of way to the ocmpany. Though the lands of the Indians were reserved by treaty for their occupation, the fee was always under the control of the government; and when transferred, without reference to the possession of the lands and without designation of any use of them requiring the delivery of their possession, the transfer was subject to their right of occupancy; and the manner, time, and conditions on which that right should be extinguished were matters for the determination of the government, and not for legal contestation in the courts between private parties. This doctrine is applicable generally to the rights of Indians to lands occupied by them under similar conditions. It was asserted in *Buttz* v. *The Northern Pacific Railroad Company*, 119 U. S. 55, and has never, so far as we are aware, been seriously controverted. * * * Though the law as stated with reference to the power of the government to determine the right of occupancy of the Indians to their lands has always been recognized, it is to be presumed, as stated by this court in the *Buttz case*, that in its exercise the United States will be governed by such considerations of justice as will control a Christian people in their treatment of an ignorant and dependent race, the court observing, however, that the propriety or justice of their action towards the Indians, with respect to their lands, is a question of governmental policy, and is not a matter open to discussion in a controversy between third parties neither of whom derives title from the Indians. The right of the United States to dispose of the fee of land occupied by them, it added, has always been recognized by this court from the foundation of the government. (Pp. 116–118.)

Plenary authority does not mean absolute power, and the exercise of the power must be founded upon some reasonable basis.[78] Thus, plenary power does

> * * * * not enable the United States to give the tribal lands to others, or to appropriate them to its own purposes, without rendering, or assuming an obligation to render, just compensation for them; for that "would not be an exercise of guardianship, but an act of confiscation." [79]

The Supreme Court, *per* Mr. Justice Van Devanter, recently said:[80]

> * * * Our decisions, while recognizing that the government has power to control and manage the property and affairs of its Indian wards in good faith for their welfare, show that this power is subject to constitutional limitations and does not enable the government to give the lands of one tribe or band to another, or to deal with them as its own.[11] * * * (P. 375–376.)
>
> [11] *Lane* v. *Santa Rosa*, 249 U. S. 110, 113: *United States* v. *Creek Nation*, 295 U. S. 103, 109–110; *Shoshone Tribe* v. *United States*, 299 U. S. 476, 497.

Thus, while Congress has broad powers over tribal lands, the United States does not have complete immunity from liability for the actions of Congress. If Congress takes tribal land from the Indians without either their consent or the payment of compensation, the United States is liable under the Fifth Amendment to the United States Constitution for the payment of just compensation,[81] which must include payment for the minerals and timber.[82] But the right of the Indians to just compensation is legally imperfect unless Congress itself passes legislation permitting suit by the Indians against the United States as the United States is not liable to suit without its consent.[83] While there is general legislation permitting suits for just compensation, this does not embrace suits by Indian tribes, and thus far they have been authorized to sue only by jurisdictional acts applying only to individual tribal complaints.[84]

---

company. The Circuit Court of Appeals in the case of *Muskogee Nat. Tel. Co.* v. *Hall*, 118 Fed. 382 (C. C. A. 8, 1902), said:

> * * * It is well settled that, in the exercise of its power to regulate commerce among the several states and with the Indian tribes, Congress has full authority to grant rights of way through the land occupied by the five Indian tribes domiciled in the Indian Territory for the construction of railroads (*Cherokee Nation* v. *Southern Kan. R. Co.*, 135 U. S. 641, 10 Sup. Ct. 965, 34 L. Ed. 295; *Stephens* v. *Cherokee Nation*, 174 U. S. 445, 485, 19 Sup. Ct. 722, 43 L. Ed. 1041); and in the exercise of this power it has recently authorized the secretary of the interior to grant rights of way through the Indian Territory for the construction, operation, and maintenance of telephone and telegraph lines. 31 Stat. 1083, c. 832, § 3. It follows, of course, that none of these tribes had the power to declare that any one telephone company should have the sole right to construct and operate telephone lines within its borders, since the existence of such a monopoly would have a necessary tendency to prevent free communication between those who reside outside of, and those who reside within, the territory. To this extent the grant of such a franchise as the one in question operates to obstruct interstate commerce. (P. 385.)

The Solicitor of the Department of the Interior has said:

> About the plenary power of Congress over *tribal* Indian property there can be no doubt and in the absence of some controlling reason to the contrary Congress undoubtedly has the power to subject such property to taxation either by the State or Federal Government. (Op. Sol. I. D., M. 14237, December 23, 1924.)

[78] Wise, Indian Law and Needed Reforms (1926), 12 A. B. A. Jour. 37, 38–39.

[79] *United States* v. *Creek Nation*, 295 U. S. 103, 110 (1935).

Property rights can be conferred by treaty as well as by formal grant. *United States* v. *Creek Nation*, 295 U. S. 103 (1935); *Morrow* v. *United States*, 243 Fed. 854 (C. C. A. 8, 1917). Government liability on the conduct of Indian affairs arises only from statutes or treaties with the tribe. *McCalib, Adm'r* v. *United States*, 83 C. Cls. 79, 87 (1936). See *Shoshone Tribe* v. *United States*, 299 U. S. 476, 497 (1937), in which the Court said:

> * * * Power to control and manage the property and affairs of Indians in good faith for their betterment and welfare may be exerted in many ways and at times even in derogation of the provisions of a treaty.

Also see Op. Sol. I. D., M. 29616, February 19, 1938.

[80] *Chippewa Indians* v. *United States*, 301 U. S. 358 (1937), aff'g 80 C. Cls. 410 (1935). Also see *Creek Nation* v. *United States*, 302 U. S. 620 (1938).

[81] The portion of this amendment which prohibits confiscation reads: "* * * nor shall private property be taken for public use without just compensation."

"* * * It is fundamental that tribal assets cannot be disposed of by the United States without the consent of the tribe or without compensation." Op. Sol. I. D., M. 29616, February 19, 1938, p. 7.

If vested rights are created in a tribe by a treaty or agreement, the Federal Government becomes liable for its violation by Congress. As the Supreme Court said in the case of *United States* v. *Mille Lac Chippewas*, 229 U. S. 498 (1913):

> * * * That the wrongful disposal was in obedience to directions given in two resolutions of Congress does not make it any the less a violation of the trust. The resolutions, unlike the legislation sustained in *Cherokee Nation* v. *Hitchcock*, 187 U. S. 294, 307, and *Lone Wolf* v. *Hitchcock*, *Id.* 553, 564, 568, were not adopted in the exercise of the administrative power of Congress over the property and affairs of dependent Indian wards, but were intended to assert, and did assert, an unqualified power of disposal over the lands as the absolute property of the Government. Doubtless this was because there was a misapprehension of the true relation of the Government to the lands, but that does not alter the result. (Pp. 509–510.)

Accord: *Blackfeet et al. Nations* v. *United States*, 81 C. Cls. 101 (1935).

Typical jurisdictional acts provide for recovery by a tribe against the United States "if * * * the United States Government has wrongfully appropriated any lands belonging to the said Indians" (Act of May 26, 1920, sec. 3, 41 Stat. 623) (Klamath); or for "misappropriation of any of the * * * lands of said tribe" (Act of June 3, 1920, sec. 1, 41 Stat. 738) (Sioux); or "the loss to said Indians of their right, title, or interest, arising from occupancy and use, in lands or other tribal or community property, without just compensation therefor, shall be held sufficient ground for relief" (Act of June 19, 1935, 49 Stat. 388) (Tlingit and Haida).

[82] *United States* v. *Shoshone Tribe*, 304 U. S. 111 (1938). See Chapter 15, secs. 14, 15. Also see C. T. Westwood, Legal Aspects of Land Acquisition, Indians and the Land, Contributions by the delegation of the United States, First Inter-American Conference on Indian Life, Patzcuaro, Mexico, published by Office of Indian Affairs (April, 1940) p. 4.

[83] However, suits against officers of the United States based on alleged illegal acts require no such statutory authority. *Lane* v. *Pueblo of Santa Rosa*, 249 U. S. 110 (1919), wherein it was held that the Secretary of the Interior could be enjoined from disposing of certain Indian lands as public lands of the United States. See Chapter 20, sec. 7.

[84] See Chapter 14, sec. 6B.

B. TRIBAL FUNDS

The power of Congress over tribal funds is the same as its power over tribal lands, and is, historically speaking, a result of the latter power, since tribal funds arise principally from the use and disposition of tribal lands. The extent of congressional power has been expressed by the Attorney General as follows:[85]

> Now, as these royalties are tribal funds, it can not be seriously contended that Congress had not power to provide for their disbursement for such purposes as it might deem for the best interest of the tribe. That power resides in the Government as the guardian of the Indians, and the authority of the United States as such guardian is not to be narrowly defined, but on the contrary is plenary.
>
> Examples of the exercise of such power over the tribal property of Indians, and decisions sustaining it, are found in many of the adjudicated cases, among them *Cherokee Nation* v. *Hitchcock*, 187 U. S. 294; *Lone Wolf* v. *Hitchcock*, 187 U. S. 553; *Gritts* v. *Fisher*, 224 U. S. 640; *Sizemore* v. *Brady*, 235 U. S. 441; *Chase* v. *United States*, decided April 11, 1921. (P. 63.)

The congressional control over tribal funds was defined by Justice Van Devanter in the case of *Sizemore* v. *Brady*.[86]

As in the case of lands, Congress cannot divert tribal funds from tribal purposes in the absence of Indian consent or corresponding benefit without being liable, when suit is brought, for the amount diverted. Thus, there has been occasion, not infrequently, for judicial analysis of the manner of disposition of tribal funds. On the whole the tendency of the Court of Claims has been to uphold expenditures authorized by Congress as made for tribal purposes.[87]

C. INDIVIDUAL LANDS

The power of Congress over individual lands, while less sweeping than its power over tribal lands, is clearly broad enough to cover supervision of the alienation of individual lands.[88] In fact the exercise of congressional power over individual lands has been largely directed toward the release, extension, or reimposition of restrictions surrounding their alienation, depending on whether the policy of conserving or of opening up Indian lands was dominant in Congress.

As "an incident to guardianship"[89] Congress not only has the power to extend,[90] modify, or remove existing restrictions on the alienation of such lands[91] but while the Indian is still the ward of the nation it may reimpose restrictions on property already freed from restrictions or delegate such power to an executive officer.[92]

This power includes permitting alienation upon such terms as Congress or the federal officer delegated with the power deems advisable from the standpoint of the protection of the Indians.[93] Such restrictions must be expressed and are not implied merely because the owner of land is an Indian,[94] nor can such restrictions be made retroactive so as to invalidate a conveyance made by an Indian before the restriction was imposed.[95]

Congress may lift the restriction on alienation of allotments to mixed-blood Indians and continue the restrictions on full-blood Indians, until the Secretary of the Interior is satisfied that such Indians are competent to handle their own affairs.[96] In deciding this question the Supreme Court said:

> * * * it is necessary to have in mind certain matters which are well settled by the previous decisions of this court. The tribal Indians are wards of the Government, and as such under its guardianship. It rests with Congress to determine the time and extent of emancipation. Conferring citizenship is not inconsistent with the continuation of such guardianship, for it has been held that even after the Indians have been made citizens the relation of guardian and ward for some purposes may continue. On the other hand, Congress may relieve the Indians from such guardianship and control, in whole or in part, and may, if it sees fit, clothe them with full rights and responsibilities concerning their property or give to them a partial emancipation if it thinks that course better for their protection. *United States* v. *Nice*, 241 U. S. 591, 598, and cases cited. (Pp. 459–460.)

The restrictions on alienation of land express a public policy designed to protect improvident people.[97] Hence under the statutes, despite the good faith or motives of a grantee of land conveyed in violation of the restrictions,[98] the conveyance is void.[99]

As in the case of private property generally, Congress cannot deprive an Indian of his land or any interest therein without due process of law or take such property for public purposes without just compensation. An outstanding decision on this subject is

---

[85] 33 Op. A. G. 60 (1921). Also see *Chickasaw Nation* v. *United States*, 87 C. Cls. 91 (1938), cert. den. 307 U. S. 646. Congress may appropriate tribal funds for the civilization and self-support of the Indian tribe, *Lane* v. *Morrison*, 246 U. S. 214 (1918). See Chapter 12, sec. 2.

[86] 235 U. S. 441 (1914). See sec. 6, *infra*.

The power of Congress over Osage tribal funds is upheld in *Ne-kah-wah-she-tun-kah* v. *Fall*, 290 Fed. 303 (App. D. C. 1923), app. dism. 266 U. S. 595 (1925).

[87] See *Gritts* v. *Fisher*, 224 U. S. 640 (1912).

[88] Congress has not exerted authority over individual lands not in a trust or restricted category except in so far as to reimpose restrictions and restore them to the class of lands under its supervision.

[89] *La Motte* v. *United States*, 254 U. S. 570, 575 (1921).

[90] *Tiger* v. *Western Inv. Co.*, 221 U. S. 286 (1911); *Heckman* v. *United States*, 224 U. S. 413 (1912). Also see *United States* v. *Jackson*, 280 U. S. 183, 191 (1930), involving extension of trust period of homestead patent under Act of July 4, 1884, 23 Stat. 76, 96, on the ground that the Indians possessed no vested right until a fee patent was issued; and *United States* v. *Pelican*, 232 U. S. 442, 451 (1914) involving congressional retention of trusteeship of land thrown open to settlement.

For a list of reservations in which the trust or restricted period was extended, see 25 C. F. R., appendix to Chapter 1, pp. 480–483.

[91] *Goat* v. *United States*, 224 U. S. 458 (1912); *Deming Inv. Co.* v. *United States*, 224 U. S. 471 (1912); *Jones* v. *Prairie Oil Co.*, 273 U. S. 195 (1927).

[92] *Brader* v. *James*, 246 U. S. 88 (1918), cited with approval in *McCurdy* v. *United States*, 246 U. S. 263, 273 (1918).

[93] *Mullen* v. *United States*, 224 U. S. 448 (1912). See *United States* v. *Noble*, 237 U. S. 74 (1915); *Sunderland* v. *United States*, 266 U. S. 226 (1924).

[94] *Doe* v. *Wilson*, 23 How. 457 (1859).

[95] *Wilson* v. *Wall*, 6 Wall. 83 (1867).

[96] *United States* v. *Waller*, 243 U. S. 452 (1917). From time to time Congress has by statute empowered the Secretary to remove restrictions or issue certificates of competency to Indians deemed capable of managing their own affairs. See Chapter 11, sec. 4.

[97] * * * In adopting the restrictions, Congress was not imposing restraints on a class of persons who were *sui juris*, but on Indians who were being conducted from a state of dependent wardship to one of full emancipation and needed to be safeguarded against their own improvidence during the period of transition. The purpose of the restrictions was to give the needed protection * * *. (Pp. 464–465.) *Smith* v. *McCullough*, 270 U. S. 456 (1926).

[98] *United States* v. *Brown*, 8 F. 2d 564 (C. C. A. 8, 1925), cert. den., 270 U. S. 644 (1926).

[99] *Heckman* v. *United States*, 224 U. S. 413 (1912); *Goat* v. *United States*, 224 U. S. 458 (1912); *Starr* v. *Long Jim*, 227 U. S. 613 (1913); *Monson* v. *Simonson*, 231 U. S. 341 (1913), holding that a deed by an Indian of an allotment subject to restrictions against alienation was absolutely void if made before final patent, even if made after passage of an act of Congress permitting the Secretary of the Interior to issue such patent; and that the unrestricted title subsequently acquired by the allottee under the patent does not inure to the grantee. Also see *Miller* v. *McClain*, 249 U. S. 308 (1919); *United States* v. *Reynolds*, 250 U. S. 104 (1919); and *Smith* v. *Stevens*, 77 U. S. 321, 326 (1870), discussing the policy behind restrictions on sale of land in Treaty between United States and Kansas Indians of June 3, 1825, 7 Stat. 244, 245, and the Act of May 26, 1860, 12 Stat. 21. Also see Chapter 11, sec. 4H.

Choate v. *Trapp*,[100] which held that exemption from taxation established by Congress created in the Indian landholder a vested right not subject to impairment by later legislative act.[101]

The Supreme Court distinguished between the exemption from taxation and the restriction on alienation:[102]

> But the exemption and non-alienability were two separate and distinct subjects. One conferred a right and the other imposed a limitation. * * * The right to remove the restriction was in pursuance of the power under which Congress could legislate as to the status of the ward and lengthen or shorten the period of disability. But the provision that the land should be non-taxable was a property right, which Congress undoubtedly had the power to grant. That right fully vested in the Indians and was binding upon Oklahoma. *Kansas Indians*, 5 Wall. 737, 756; *United States* v. *Rickert*, 188 U. S. 432. (P. 673.)

As part of its supervision of alienation of individual lands, Congress has provided for the disposition and inheritance, by descent or devise, of trust and restricted lands,[103] and the exercise of this power has been sustained.[104] Congress has also vested jurisdiction in the county courts over probate proceedings of such property.[105]

D. INDIVIDUAL FUNDS

The power of Congress over individual funds is an outgrowth of its control over restricted lands and the same general principles are applicable to both.[106]

---

[100] 224 U. S. 665 (1912). Also see *Morrow* v. *United States*, 243 Fed. 854 (C. C. A. 8, 1917); Chapter 13, secs. 1, 5, 10; 49 L. D. 348, 352 (1922); Op. Sol. I. D., M. 13864, December 24, 1924; Op. Sol. I. D., M. 25737, March 3, 1930.

[101] The Supreme Court said:

> There have been comparatively few cases which discuss the legislative power over private property held by the Indians. But those few all recognize that he is not excepted from the protection guaranteed by the Constitution. His private rights are secured and enforced to the same extent and in the same way as other residents or citizens of the United States. *In re Heff*, 197 U. S. 488, 504; *Cherokee Nation* v. *Hitchcock*, 187 U. S. 294, 307; *Smith* v. *Goodell*, 20 Johns. (N. Y.) 188; *Lowry* v. *Weaver*, 4 McLean, 82; *Whirlwind* v. *Von der Ahe*, 67 Mo. App. 628; *Taylor* v. *Drew*, 21 Arkansas, 485, 487. His right of private property is not subject to impairment by legislative action, even while he is, as a member of a tribe and subject to the guardianship of the United States as to his political and personal status. This was clearly recognized in the leading case of *Jones* v. *Meehan*, 175 U. S. 1. * * *
>
> Nothing that was said in *Tiger* v. *Western Investment Co.*, 221 U. S. 286, is opposed to the same conclusion here. For that case did not involve property rights, but related solely to the power of Congress, to extend the period of the Indian's disability. The statute did not attempt to take his land or any right, member or appurtenance thereunto belonging. It left that as it was. But, having regard to the Indian's inexperience, and desiring to protect him against himself and those who might take advantage of his incapacity, Congress extended the time during which he could not sell. On that subject, after calling attention to the fact that "Tiger was still a ward of the Nation, so far as the alienation of these lands was concerned, and a member of the existing Creek Nation," it was said that "Incompetent persons, though citizens, may not have the full right to control their property," and that there was nothing in citizenship incompatible with guardianship, or with restricting sales by Indians deemed by Congress incapable of managing their estates.
>
> But there was no intimation that the power of wardship conferred authority on Congress to lessen any of the rights of property which had been vested in the individual Indian by prior laws or contracts. Such rights are protected from repeal by the provisions of the Fifth Amendment. (Pp. 677, 678.)

A recognition of this restriction on Federal power appears in Article XI of the Treaty of April 1, 1850, with the Wyandots, 9 Stat. 987, 992, which provided:

> All former treaties between the United States and the Wyandot nation of Indians are abrogated and declared null and void by this treaty—except such provisions as may have been made for the benefit of private individuals of said nation, by grants of reservations of lands, or otherwise, which are considered as *vested* rights, and not to be affected by anything contained in this treaty.

[102] *Choate* v. *Trapp*, 224 U. S. 665, 673 (1912). Apparently the removal of the restriction against alienation does not vest any rights in the Indian landholder. See *Brader* v. *James*, 246 U. S. 88 (1918).

Congress may assent to a state tax levied on the production of oil and gas under a lease of tribal lands. *British-American Co.* v. *Board*, 299 U. S. 159 (1936).

[103] Also see Chapter 11, sec. 6.

[104] *Lone Wolf* v. *Hitchcock*, 187 U. S. 553 (1903); *Brader* v. *James*, 246 U. S. 88 (1918). See Chapter 10, sec. 10; Chapter 11, sec. 6.

[105] On jurisdiction of county courts over the Five Civilized Tribes, see Chapter 23, sec. 11C, and Act of May 27, 1908, 35 Stat. 312, amended by Act of April 10, 1926, 44 Stat. 239.

[106] For a discussion of congressional control of individual funds see Chapter 10, sec. 2.

SECTION 6. CONGRESSIONAL POWER—MEMBERSHIP

The Indian tribes have original power to determine their own membership.[107] Congress has the power, however, to supersede that determination when necessary for the administration of tribal property, particularly its distribution among the members of the tribe[108]

The United States may assume full control over Indian tribes and determine membership in the tribe for the purpose of adjusting rights in tribal property.[109] The assumption of power on the part of the Federal Government to distribute tribal funds and land among the individual members of the tribe required the preparation of payment or census rolls. Several treaties[110] and statutes[111] authorized the establishment of such rolls and the pro rata distribution of tribal or public property among the enrollees. Rarely (considering the multitude of individual grievances presented annually by individual Indians or alleged Indians) has Congress specifically provided for additions to tribal rolls in individual cases.[112]

In addition to its ultimate authority to determine tribal membership, Congress may, as part of its power to administer tribal property, alter the basic rule that tribal property may

---

[107] See Chapter 7, sec. 4.

[108] The Circuit Court of Appeals in the case of *Farrell* v. *United States*, 110 Fed. 942 (C. C. A. 8, 1901), said:

> * * * It is the settled rule of the judicial department of the government, in ascertaining the relations of Indian tribes and their members to the nation, to follow the action of the legislative and executive departments, to which the determination of these questions has been especially intrusted. *U. S.* v. *Holliday*, 3 Wall. 407, 419, 18 L. Ed. 182; *U. S.* v. *Earl* (C. C.) 17 Fed. 75, 78. (P. 951.)

[109] *Stephens* v. *Cherokee Nation*, 174 U. S. 445 (1899). See *Cherokee Nation* v. *Hitchcock*, 187 U. S. 294, 306, 307 (1902).

[110] See, for example, Treaty of July 8, 1817, with the Cherokees, Art. 3, 7 Stat. 156; Treaty of November 24, 1848, with the Stockbridge Tribe, Art. 2, 9 Stat. 955; Treaty of November 15, 1861, with the Pottawatomie Nation, Art. 2, 12 Stat. 1191; Treaty of June 24, 1862, with the Ottawa Indians, Art. 8, 12 Stat. 1237; Treaty of June 28, 1862, with the Kickapoo Indians, Art. 2, 13 Stat. 623; Treaty of October 14, 1865, with the Cheyenne and Arrapahoe Tribes, Art. 7, 14 Stat. 703.

The general rule is that "in the absence of [statutory] provision to the contrary, the right of individual Indians to share in tribal property, whether lands or funds, depends upon tribal membership, is terminated when the membership is ended, and is neither alienable nor descendible." *Wilbur* v. *United States*, 281 U. S. 206, 216 (1930); also see *Halbert* v. *United States*, 283 U. S. 753, 762, 763 (1931). For a fuller discussion, see Chapter 9, sec. 3; Chapter 7, sec. 4.

[111] See, for example, Act of March 3, 1873, sec. 4, 17 Stat. 631 (Miamie); Act of March 3, 1881, sec. 4, 21 Stat. 414, 433 (Miami); Act of July 1, 1902, sec. 1, 32 Stat. 636 (Kansas); Act of June 4, 1920, 41 Stat. 751 (Crow); Act of May 19, 1924, 43 Stat. 132 (Lac du Flambeau band of Chippewas). Also see *Campbell* v. *Wadsworth*, 248 U. S. 169 (1918).

[112] See, for example, Act of May 30, 1896, 29 Stat. 736 (a Sac and Fox woman); Joint Resolution of October 20, 1914, 38 Stat. 780 (Five Civilized Tribes); Act of May 31, 1924, c. 215, 43 Stat. 246 (Flathead), discussed in Op. Sol. I. D., M.14233, April 24, 1925; also see *Gritts* v. *Fisher*, 224 U. S. 640, 648 (1912).

be distributed only to tribal members.[113] It may thus provide that all children born of a marriage between a white man and an Indian woman who was recognized by the tribe at the time of her death shall have the same rights and privileges to the property of the tribe to which the mother belonged as have members of the tribe.[114]

Congress may authorize an administrative body to make a roll descriptive of the persons thereon so that they might be identified, to take a census of the tribes and to adopt any other means deemed necessary by the commission. It may provide that such rolls, when approved by the Secretary, shall be final, and that persons thereon and their descendants born thereafter and such persons as intermarry according to tribal laws should alone constitute the several tribes they represent.[115]

Enrollment does not ordinarily give a vested right in tribal property.[116] Congress may disregard the existing membership rolls of a tribe and direct that the per capita distribution be made upon the basis of a new roll, even though such act may be inconsistent with prior legislation, treaties, or agreements with the tribe.[117] Thus, the Supreme Court in the case of *Sizemore* v. *Brady*,[118] said:

> * * * Like other tribal Indians, the Creeks were wards of the United States, which possessed full power, if it deemed such a course wise, to assume full control over them and their affairs, to ascertain who were members of the tribe, to distribute the lands and funds among them, and to terminate the tribal government. * * * (P. 447.)

The Supreme Court, in holding that Congress may add to a tribal roll even though it purports to be final said:[119]

> It is not proposed to disturb the individual allotments made to members living September 1, 1902, and enrolled under the act of 1902, and therefore we are only concerned with whether children born after September 1, 1902, and living on March 4, 1906, should be excluded from the allotment and distribution. The act of 1902 required that they be excluded, and the legislation in 1906, as we have seen, provides for their inclusion. It is conceded, and properly so, that the later legislation is valid and controlling unless it impairs or destroys rights which the act of 1902 vested in members living September 1, 1902, and enrolled under that act. As has been indicated, their individual allotments are not affected. But it is said that the act of 1902 contemplated that they alone should receive allotments and be the participants in the distribution of the remaining lands, and also of the funds, of the tribe. No doubt such was the purport of the act. But that, in our opinion, did not confer upon them any vested right such as would disable Congress from thereafter making provision for admitting newly born members of the tribe to the allotment and distribution. The difficulty with the appellants' contention is that it treats the act of 1902 as a contract, when "it is only an act of Congress and can have no greater effect." *Cherokee Intermarriage Cases*, 203 U. S. 76, 93. It was but an exertion of the administrative control of the Government over the tribal property of tribal Indians, and was subject to change by Congress at any time before it was carried into effect and while the tribal relations continued. *Stephens* v. *Cherokee Nation*, 174 U. S. 445, 488; *Cherokee Nation* v. *Hitchcock*, 187 U. S. 294; *Wallace* v. *Adams*, 204 U. S. 415, 423. It is not to be overlooked that those for whose benefit the change was made in 1906 were not strangers to the tribe, but were children born into it while it was still in existence and while there was still tribal property whereby they could be put on an equal, or approximately equal, plane with other members. The council of the tribe asked that this be done, and we entertain no doubt that Congress in acceding to the request was well within its power. (Pp. 647–648.)

In the important case of *Wallace* v. *Adams*[120] the Supreme Court held that the Act of July 1, 1902,[121] creating the Choctaw-Chickasaw citizenship court and giving it power to examine the judgments of the Indian territorial courts and determine whether they should be annulled on account of irregularities, was a valid exercise of power. This and other cases in this field are based on the theory of the ultimate power of Congress over matters of membership of the tribes and its power to adopt any reasonable measures to ascertain who are entitled to its prerogatives. If the result of one of the methods which it adopts is unsatisfactory, it may try another.[122]

Congress may make the finding of an administrative commission, approved by the Secretary of the Interior, a final determination of tribal membership.[123] The Supreme Court in the case of *United States* v. *Wildcat*[124] said:

> * * * There was thus constituted a *quasi*-judicial tribunal whose judgments within the limits of its jurisdiction were only subject to attack for fraud or such mistake of law or fact as would justify the holding that its judgments were voidable. Congress by this legislation evidenced an intention to put an end to controversy by providing a tribunal before which those interested could be heard and the rolls authoritatively made up of those who were entitled to participate in the partition of the tribal lands. It was to the interest of all concerned that the beneficiaries of this division should be ascertained. To this end the Commission was established and endowed with authority to hear and determine the matter.
>
> A correct conclusion was not necessary to the finality and binding character of its decisions. It may be that the Commission in acting upon the many cases before it made mistakes which are now impossible of correction. This might easily be so, for the Commission passed upon the rights of thousands claiming membership in the tribe and ascertained the rights of others who did not appear before it, upon the merits of whose standing the Commission had to pass with the best information which it could obtain.
>
> When the Commission proceeded in good faith to determine the matter and to act upon information before it, not arbitrarily, but according to its best judgment, we think it was the intention of the act that the matter, upon the approval of the Secretary, should be finally concluded and the rights of the parties forever settled, subject to such attacks as could successfully be made upon judgments of this character for fraud or mistake.
>
> We cannot agree that the case is within the principles decided in *Scott* v. *McNeal*, 154 U. S. 34, and kindred

[113] See Chapter 9, sec. 3.

[114] *Vezina* v. *United States*, 245 Fed. 411 (C. C. A. 8, 1917). And see Chapter 9, sec. 3.

[115] See *Stephens* v. *Cherokee Nation*, 174 U. S. 445, 490, 491 (1899); Chapter 7, sec. 4.

Congress may also provide that for the purpose of determining the quantum of Indian blood possessed by members of these tribes, and their capacity to alienate allotted lands, the rolls of citizenship approved by the Secretary of the Interior are conclusive.

Act of April 26, 1906, 34 Stat. 137, and Act of May 27, 1908, 35 Stat. 312, interpreted in *United States* v. *Ferguson*, 247 U. S. 175 (1918). Accord: *Cully* v. *Mitchell*, 37 F. 2d 493 (C. C. A. 10, 1930).

It has been held that Congress is not bound by the tribal rule regarding membership and may determine for itself whether a person is an Indian from the standpoint of a federal criminal statute. *United States* v. *Rogers*, 4 How. 567 (1846).

[116] *Wilbur* v. *United States ex rel. Kadrie*, 281 U. S. 206 (1930).

[117] See *Stephens* v. *Cherokee Nation*, 174 U. S. 445, 488 (1899); Op. Sol. I. D., M.27759, January 22, 1935. *Cf. Lone Wolf* v. *Hitchcock*, 187 U. S. 553 (1903).

[118] 235 U. S. 441 (1914).

[119] *Gritts* v. *Fisher*, 224 U. S. 640 (1912), discussed in Chapter 9, sec. 3. An example of "final" pro rata distribution of tribal assets is found in the Appropriation Act of May 31, 1900, 31 Stat. 221, 233 (Siletz Reservation). *Cf.* Act of April 21, 1904, 33 Stat. 189, 201 (Otoe and Missouria, Stockbridge and others).

[120] 204 U. S. 415 (1907).

[121] 32 Stat. 641, 647.

[122] See *Stephens* v. *Cherokee Nation*, 174 U. S. 445 (1899), and *Wallace* v. *Adams*, 204 U. S. 415, 423 (1907). Also see Chapter 19, sec. 4.

[123] *United States* v. *Atkins*, 260 U. S. 220 (1922).

[124] 244 U. S. 111 (1917).

cases, in which it has been held that in the absence of a subject-matter of jurisdiction an adjudication that there was such is not conclusive, and that a judgment based upon action without its proper subject being in existence is void. * * * (Pp. 118–119.)

* * * * *

* * * We think the decision of such tribunal, when not impeached for fraud or mistake, conclusive of the question of membership in the tribe, when followed, as was the case here by the action of the Interior Department confirming the allotment and ordering the patents conveying the lands, which were in fact issued. * * * (P. 120.)

SECTION 7. ADMINISTRATIVE POWER—INTRODUCTION

By necessity Congress has delegated much of its power over the Indians to administrative officials. This power is dependent upon and supplementary to the legislative power. Although rhetorical figures of speech, like "guardianship,"[125] have tended to blur the distinction between administrative and legislative powers, it is important to distinguish between the problem of whether Congress possesses the authority to pass certain legislation and the problem of whether Congress has vested its power in an administrative officer or department.

"We have no officers in this government," the Supreme Court said, in the case of *The Floyd Acceptances*,[126] "from the President down to the most subordinate agent, who does not hold office under the law, with prescribed duties and limited authority." (Pp. 676–677.)

Therefore, in seeking to trace the scope of administrative power in the field of Indian law, our primary concern must be with the statutes and treaties that confer such power.

The interplay of the legislative and administrative branches of Government in Indian affairs has caused the frequent application of two rules of administrative law. The first is that if properly promulgated pursuant to law the rules and regulations of an administrative body have the force and effect of statutes and the courts will take judicial notice of them.[127] The Supreme Court in *Maryland Casualty Co.* v. *United States*,[128] said:

> * * * It is settled by many recent decisions of this court that a regulation by a department of government, addressed to and reasonably adapted to the enforcement of an act of Congress, the administration of which is confided to such department, has the force and effect of law if it be not in conflict with express statutory provision. *United States* v. *Grimaud*, 220 U. S. 506; *United States* v. *Birdsall*, 233 U. S. 223, 231; *United States* v. *Smull*, 236 U. S. 405, 409, 411; *United States* v. *Morehead*, 243 U. S. 607. * * * (P. 349.)

The second principle is that courts and administrative authorities give great weight to a construction of a statute consistently given by an executive department charged with its administration,[129] especially if it is a rule affecting considerable property or a doubtful question.[130]

The Supreme Court has given great weight to an administrative interpretation even if not long continued.[131]

These rules are based on the theory that the failure of Congress by subsequent legislation to change the construction of administrative bodies charged with the administration of a statute constitutes acquiescence in the practical construction of a statute.

[125] See Chapter 8, sec. 9.

[126] 7 Wall. 666 (1868). Also see *United States* v. *MacDaniel*, 7 Pet. 1 (1833); *United States* v. *McMurray*, 181 Fed. 723, 728 (C. C. E. D. Okla., 1910); 34 Op. A. G. 320 (1924). The power of administrative authorities to carry out treaty promises is shown in 23 Op. A. G. 214 (1900). Also see Chapter 3, sec. 3.

[127] The Circuit Court of Appeals in the case of *Bridgeman* v. *United States*, 140 Fed. 577 (C. C. A. 9, 1905) said:

> Counsel are agreed that the rules and regulations of the Indian Department promulgated under the authority of law have the force and effect of statutes, and that the court will take judicial notice of them. * * * (P. 583.)

[128] 251 U. S. 342 (1920). Also see *Montana Eastern Limited* v. *United States*, 95 F. 2d 897 (C. C. A. 9, 1938).

[129] *United States ex rel. West* v. *Hitchcock*, 205 U. S. 80 (1907); 4 Op. A. G. 75 (1842); 38 L. D. 553 (1910); *United States* v. *Jackson*, 280 U. S. 183, 193 (1930).

> When the law has been so construed by Government Departments during a long period as to permit a certain course of action, and Congress has not seen fit to intervene, the interpretation so given is strongly persuasive of the existence of the power. * * * (34 Op. A. G. 320 326 (1924).)

The Supreme Court in *Cramer* v. *United States*, 261 U. S. 219 (1923), said:

> That such individual occupancy [by a non-reservation Indian] is entitled to protection finds strong support in various rulings of the Interior Department, to which in land matters this Court has always given much weight [citing cases]. (P. 227.)

[130] 4 Op. A. G. 75 (1842). Also see *Wisconsin* v. *Hitchcock*, 201 U. S. 202 (1906); *Kindred* v. *Union Pacific R. R. Co.*, 225 U. S. 582, 596 (1912).

[131] The Supreme Court in *United States* v. *First National Bank*, 234 U. S. 245 (1914), said:

> While departmental construction of the Clapp Amendment does not have the weight which such constructions sometimes have in long continued observance, nevertheless it is entitled to consideration, the early administration of that amendment showing the interpretation placed upon it by competent men having to do with its enforcement. * * * (P. 261.)

A recent administrative interpretation will sometimes be given weight, though conflicting with early interpretation. *United States* v. *Reynolds*, 250 U. S. 104, 109 (1919). Departmental sponsorship of legislation is also considered. The Supreme Court in *Blanset* v. *Cardin*, 256 U. S. 319 (1921), said:

> * * * And there can be no doubt that the act was the suggestion of the Interior Department, and its construction is an assistant, if not demonstrative criterion, of the meaning and purpose of the act. *Swigart* v. *Baker*, 229 U. S. 187; *Jacobs* v. *Prichard*, 223 U. S. 200; *United States* v. *Cerecedo Hermanos*, 209 U. S. 337. And the regulations of the Department are administrative of the act and partake of its legal force. (P. 326.)

SECTION 8. THE RANGE OF ADMINISTRATIVE POWERS

The specific functions of officials of the Indian Service and of other federal officials dealing with Indian affairs are necessarily discussed in various parts of this chapter and in other chapters.[132] It may be worth while, however, at this point, to indicate the scheme of authorities which Congress has conferred in this field.

In general, administrative powers in the field of Indian affairs have been conferred upon the President, the Secretary of the Interior, and the Commissioner of Indian Affairs.

Administrative powers of the President include the consolidation of agencies, and, with the consent of the tribes, the consolidation of one or more tribes on reservations created by Executive order;[133] dispensing with unnecessary agents,[134] or transferring

[132] See especially Chapter 2. Chapters 9 to 11 deal largely with administrative powers over property. Chapter 12 discusses administrative duties regarding federal services for the Indians; Chapter 16 deals with licensing of traders; Chapter 17, sec. 5, covers administration of liquor laws.

[133] Act of May 17, 1882, sec. 6, 22 Stat. 68, 88, 25 U. S. C. 63; Act of July 4, 1884, sec. 6, 23 Stat. 76, 97, 25 U. S. C. 63.

[134] Act of June 22, 1874, sec. 1, 18 Stat. 146, 147, 25 U. S. C. 64; Act of March 3, 1875, sec. 1, 18 Stat. 420, 421, 25 U. S. C. 64, interpreted in 15 Op. A. G. 405 (1877).

any agent "from the place or tribe designated by law, to such other place as the public service may require." [135]

The Secretary of the Interior, who has been described by a Solicitor of his Department as "guardian of all Indian interests," [136] acts on behalf of the President in the administration of Indian affairs. His acts are presumed to be the acts of the President. [137]

Administrative powers of the Secretary of the Interior include the establishing of superintendencies, agencies, and subagencies by tribes or by geographical boundaries, [138] the appointment of members of the Indian Arts and Crafts Board, [139] and the appointment of various Indian Bureau employees. [140]

Other duties are expressly delegated to the Commissioner of Indian Affairs, such as issuing trader's licenses [141] and publishing statutory provisions regulating the duties of Indian Bureau employees. [142]

Provisions in many statutes [143] and occasional treaties confer on the President [144] or the Secretary of the Interior [145] or the Commissioner of Indian affairs [146] or all three [147] power to make rules and regulations. [148] The wide range of regulations concerning Indians is shown by title 25 of the Code of Federal Regulations. [149] Important statutes providing for rule-making in relation to the Indian which are included in title 25 of the United States Code are discussed in various parts of this volume. [150] A brief description of the subject matter of some of them will therefore suffice to show the variety of statutes expressly conferring regulatory power on the Secretary of the Interior. He is authorized to make regulations governing the business of the Indian Arts and Crafts Board, [151] concerning the operation of various types of leases affecting restricted Indian lands, [152] concerning service fees from individual Indians, [153] to secure attendance at school, [154] to admit white children to Indian day

---

[135] Act of June 30, 1834, sec. 4, 4 Stat. 729; 735, 25 U. S. C. 62. The power given in this section is not affected by the Senate being in session. 15 Op. A. G. 405 (1877). Also see *Morrison* v. *Fall,* 290 Fed. 306 (App. D. C. 1923), aff'd 266 U. S. 481 (1925), which also discusses the power of the President over agents.

The early tendency to place administrative responsibility on the President is exemplified by the Act of July 22, 1790, 1 Stat. 137, and the Act of March 3, 1795, 1 Stat. 443, which appropriated $50,000 for the purchase of goods for the Indians, and provided "that the sale of such goods be made under the direction of the President of the United States."

The President delegated to Indian superintendents and agents his duty to disburse funds. 15 Op. A. G. 66 (1875).

Other Presidential powers of appointment are conferred by the Act of May 25, 1824, sec. 1, 4 Stat. 35, and the Act of July 20, 1867, 15 Stat. 17.

See Act of May 20, 1826, 4 Stat. 188, providing for commissioners to treat with the Choctaw and Chickasaw Indians; Joint Resolution of May 7, 1872; 17 Stat. 395, to inquire into depredations; Act of January 12, 1891, 26 Stat. 712, to arrange for selection of reservations for Mission Indians in California. Also see Act of March 3, 1797, 1 Stat. 498, 501; Act of February 19, 1799, 1 Stat. 618; Act of May 1, 1876, 19 Stat. 41; Act of September 30, 1890 (Southern Utes), 26 Stat. 504, 524; Act of September 25, 1890, 26 Stat. 468; Act of April 30, 1908, sec. 1, 35 Stat. 70, 73, 25 U. S. C. 12.

Other statutory powers granted to the President regarding the Indians are discussed in later sections of this Chapter. Also see 25 U. S. C. 27, 28, 51, 65, 72, 112, 139, 140, 141, 153, 174, 180, 263, 331–333. For examples of treaty powers see Chapter 3, sec. 3B(5).

[136] 42 L. D. 493, 499 (1913).

[137] *Wolsey* v. *Chapman,* 101 U. S. 755, 769 (1879). The action of the Commissioner of Indian Affairs must be presumed to be the action of the President. *Belt* v. *United States,* 15 C. Cls. 92 (1879). The same rule has been applied for other departments. *Maxwell* v. *United States,* 49 C. Cls. 262, 274 (1914). The direction of the President is generally presumed in instructions and orders issuing from competent federal departments. 7 Op. A. G. 453 (1855).

In the absence of statutory authority subordinate officials have no power with respect to the duties of an office involving the exercise of judgment and discretion. *United States* v. *Watashe,* 102 F. 2d 428 (C. C. A. 10, 1939). See also *Robertson* v. *United States,* 285 Fed. 911 (App. D. C., 1922); *Turner* v. *Seep,* 167 Fed. 646 (C. C. E. D. Okla., 1909), mod. 179 Fed. 74; Memo. Sol. I. D., December 11, 1937.

Administrative or ministerial functions may be delegated without statutory authorisation. The Secretary of the Interior has delegated some of his regulatory power over Indians to other officials or bodies. For instance, he has delegated administrative authority to the judges of the Court of Indian Offenses and to tribal courts.

The Solicitor of the Department of the Interior, in an opinion dated September 29, 1921, 48 L. D. 455 (1921), wrote:

> * * * During earlier times the Indians were practically confined on reservations and controlled by the strong arm of the Military. The President as "The Great White Father" was looked to as the protector of their interests, and was charged with many responsibilities and duties in their behalf. Gradually, by specific statute in some cases, but more rapidly within comparatively recent times by general legislation, that responsibility and duty has been lodged elsewhere, notably in the Secretary of the Interior. * * * (P. 457.)

As late as 1895, the Attorney General was asked whether the President must personally approve depredation claims. 21 Op. A. G. 131 (1895).

Also see Chapter 3, sec. 3; 3 Op. A. G. 367 (1838) and 471 (1839); 6 Op. A. G. 49 (1853) and 462 (1854); 16 Op. A. G. 225 (1878); 17 Op. A. G. 258, 259, (1882), and 265 (1882); and Goodnow, Administrative Law of the United States (1905).

[138] Act of June 30, 1834, 4 Stat. 735, amended by Act of March 3, 1847, 9 Stat. 202, 25 U. S. C. 40.

[139] Act of August 27, 1935, sec. 1, 49 Stat. 891, 25 U. S. C. 305.

[140] Act of March 3, 1819, 3 Stat. 516, 25 U. S. C. 271; Act of March 2, 1889, sec. 10, 25 Stat. 980, 1003, 25 U. S. C. 272; Act of March 3, 1863, sec. 1, 12 Stat. 774, 792, 25 U. S. C. 41. Various special acts provide for agents for particular tribes, Act of May 18, 1824, 4 Stat. 25 (Osage); Act of February 25, 1831, 4 Stat. 445 (Winnebago); Act of July 1, 1862, 12 Stat. 498 (Grand River and Wintah).

The Secretary of the Interior, under the direction of the President, has been authorised to discontinue the services "of such agents, sub-agents, interpreters, and mechanics, as may, from time to time, become unnecessary, in consequence of the emigration of the Indians, or other causes." Act of July 9, 1832, sec. 5, 4 Stat. 564, amended by Act of February 27, 1877, sec. 1, 19 Stat. 240, 244, 25 U. S. C. 65.

[141] See Chapter 16.

[142] Act of May 17, 1882, sec. 7, 22 Stat. 68, 88, 25 U. S. C. 3.

[143] Act of July 31, 1854, 10 Stat. 315; Act of March 3, 1865, 13 Stat. 541; Act of May 8, 1872, 17 Stat. 85; Act of May 23, 1876, 19 Stat. 55; Act of February 28, 1891, sec. 3, 26 Stat. 794, interpreted in 18 L. D. 497 (1894); also see 40 L. D. 211 (1911); Act of August 1, 1914, 38 Stat. 582, 583; Act of February 14, 1920, 41 Stat. 408, 410, 25 U. S. C. 282; Act of May 26, 1928, 45 Stat. 750, 25 U. S. C. 318a; Act of April 16, 1934, sec. 2, 48 Stat. 596, amended June 4, 1936, 49 Stat. 1458, 25 U. S. C. 454; Act of June 7, 1935, 49 Stat. 331; also see special statutes: Act of March 3, 1863, 12 Stat, 819 (Sioux); Act of March 3, 1931, c. 414, 46 Stat. 1495 (Crow); Act of February 14, 1931, 46 Stat. 1107 (Chippewa).

[144] Treaty of October 14, 1864, with the Klamaths, 16 Stat. 707; Treaty of September 30, 1854, with the Chippewas, 10 Stat. 1109, 1110; unpublished treaty with the Creeks, Archives 17, August 7, 1790; Treaty of November 14, 1805, with the Creeks, 7 Stat. 96.

[145] Treaty of February 8, 1831, with the Menominee, 7 Stat. 342; Treaty of March 6, 1865, with the Omaha, 14 Stat. 667.

[146] Treaty of October 21, 1867, with the Kiowas and Comanches, Art. 9, 15 Stat. 581.

[147] Treaty of June 9, 1863, with the Nez Perce, Art. 3, 14 Stat. 647.

[148] The procedure adopted by the Office of Indian Affairs in drafting regulations is discussed in Monograph 20, Attorney General's Committee on Administrative Procedure (1940).

[149] The subjects covered in this Code are noted in Chapter 2, sec. 3A.

[150] Chapters 2, 4, 8, 9, 10, 12, 15, 16.

[151] Act of August 27, 1935, sec. 3, 49 Stat. 891, 892, 25 U. S. 305b.

[152] Act of May 11, 1938, sec. 4, 52 Stat. 347, 348, 25 U. S. C. 396d; see Chapter 15, sec. 19.

[153] Act of May 9, 1938, sec. 1, 52 Stat. 291, 313 as amended by Act of May 10, 1939, sec. 1, 53 Stat. 685, 708, 25 U. S. C. 561.

[154] Act of July 13, 1892, sec. 1, 27 Stat. 120, 143, 25 U. S. C. 284; Act of March 3, 1893, sec. 1, 27 Stat. 612, 628, 25 U. S. C. 288; Act of February 14, 1920, sec. 1, 41 Stat. 408, 410, 25 U. S. C. 282; Chapter 12, sec. 2.

schools [155] and Indian boarding schools,[156] for the conduct of an Indian reform school,[157] for disposal by will of restricted allotments,[158] governing the use of water on irrigation lands [159] and the apportionment of irrigation costs,[160] and covering trading licenses.[161]

In addition to those statutes which confer regulatory power for specific purposes, there are several general statutes which have sometimes been relied upon as the basis for the exercise of administrative power. Section 17 of the Act of June 30, 1834,[162] provides:

> * * * the President of the United States shall be, and he is hereby, authorised to prescribe such rules and regulations as he may think fit, for carrying into effect the various provisions of this act, and of any other act relating to Indian affairs, and for the settlement of the accounts of the Indian department.

This general statute fills the needs of practical administration arising from the fact that many acts of Congress require the issuance of regulations for their proper interpretation and enforcement, although such regulations are not expressly authorized.[163]

Section 1 of the Act of July 9, 1832,[164] as amended by the Act of March 3, 1849,[165] establishing the Department of the Interior, provides that a Commissioner of Indian Affairs shall, under the direction of the Secretary of the Interior, and "agreeably to such regulations as the President may prescribe, have the management of all Indian affairs and of all matters arising out of Indian relations."

This statute, enacted in 1832, was obviously not intended to vest in the newly created office of the Commissioner of Indian Affairs the power to regulate Indian conduct generally. Since the acts of the Commissioner were expressly made subject to regulations prescribed by the President, the limits of which have already been outlined, the phrase "management of all Indian affairs" clearly does not mean "management of the affairs of the Indians," any more than the phrase "management of foreign affairs" means "management of the affairs of foreign nations or of foreigners."[166] The phrases "Indian affairs" and "Indian relations" are intended to cover the relations between the United States and the Indian tribes, which relations are commonly established either by treaty or by statute.[167]

Whether the President, the Secretary of the Interior, or the Commissioner of Indian Affairs has "general supervisory authority" over Indians in the absence of specific legislation has been questioned in several cases.

In the case of *Francis* v. *Francis* [168] the President, pursuant to a treaty reserving land to individual Indians and their heirs, issued a patent conveying a title with restrictions upon conveyance. The Supreme Court held ineffectual the restrictive clause because the "President had no authority, in virtue of his office, to impose any such restriction; certainly not, without the authority of an act of Congress, and no such act was ever passed." (P. 242.)

The question of whether internal affairs of Indian tribes, in the absence of statute, are to be regulated by the tribe itself or by the Interior Department was squarely before the Supreme Court in the case of *Jones* v. *Meehan*.[169] One of the questions presented by that case was whether inheritance of Indian land, in the absence of statute, was governed "by the laws, usages, and customs of the Chippewa Indians" or by the rules and regulations of the Secretary of the Interior.[170] In line with numerous decisions of lower courts, the Supreme Court held that the Secretary of the Interior did not have the power claimed, and that in the absence of statute such power rested with the tribe and not with the Interior Department.

In *Romero* v. *United States*,[171] a regulation of the President regarding the salaries of Indian Service officials was held invalid despite the claim that this might be justified under Revised Stat-

---

[155] Act of March 1, 1907, 34 Stat. 1015, 1018, 25 U. S. C. 288.

[156] Act of March 3, 1909, 35 Stat. 781, 783, 25 U. S. C. 289.

[157] Act of June 21, 1906, 34 Stat. 325, 328, 25 U. S. C. 302.

[158] Act of June 25, 1910, sec. 2, 36 Stat. 855, amended by Act of February 14, 1913, 37 Stat. 678, 25 U. S. C. 373; see Chapter 11, sec. 6B.

[159] Act of February 8, 1887, sec. 7, 24 Stat. 388, 25 U. S. C. 381; see Chapter 12, sec. 7.

[160] Act of April 4, 1910, secs. 1 and 3, 36 Stat. 269; Act of August 1, 1914, sec. 1, 38 Stat. 582, 25 U. S. C. 385; see Chapter 12, sec. 7.

[161] Act of July 31, 1882, 22 Stat. 179, 25 U. S. C. 264; also see Chapter 17; for other examples in 25 U. S. Code see secs. 14 (money accruing to Indians from governmental agencies); 192 (sale by agents of unnecessary cattle and horses); 275 (leaves of absence to certain employees of Indian Service); 292 (suspension of schools); 319 (rights-of-way); 454 (standard of state services). Many of the rules and regulations require the Secretary of the Interior or the Commissioner of Indian Affairs to approve or disapprove specified transactions. See for example 25 Code of Federal Regulations (1940), secs. 21.13, 21.9, 21.46 and 28.35.

[162] 4 Stat. 735, 738, 25 U. S. C. 9.

[163] The Act of February 14, 1903, sec. 12, 32 Stat. 825, 830, as embodied in 5 U. S. C. 485, provides:

> The Secretary of the Interior is charged with the supervision of public business relating to the following subjects:
>
> * * * * *
>
> Second. The Indians.

[164] 4 Stat. 564, 25 U. S. C. 2.

[165] 9 Stat. 395. Also see Act of July 27, 1868, 15 Stat. 228.

[166] See the explanation of a similar phrase in *Worcester* v. *Georgia*, 6 Pet. 515, 558 (1832), discussed in Chapter 3, sec. 4C. And see definition of duties of Commissioners and other department employees in Act of January 17, 1800, 2 Stat. 6, in terms of "facilitating or preserving a friendly intercourse with the Indians, or for managing the concerns of the United States with them, * * *."

[167] 5 U. S. C. 22, R. S. § 161, as derived from the Acts of July 27, 1789, 1 Stat. 28; August 7, 1789, 1 Stat. 49; September 2, 1789, 1 Stat. 65; September 15, 1789, 1 Stat. 68; April 30, 1798, 1 Stat. 553; March 3, 1849, 9 Stat. 393, 395; June 22, 1870, 16 Stat. 163; June 8, 1872, 17 Stat. 283, provides:

> *Departmental regulations.*—The head of each department is authorized to prescribe regulations, not inconsistent with law, for the government of his department, the conduct of its officers and clerks, the distribution and performance of its business, and the custody, use, and preservation of the records, papers, and property appertaining to it.

This statute is obviously directed to the regulation of internal matters within the various departments, such as the allocation of authority to officials, the forms to be used in departmental business, and other matters *ejusdem generis*. It cannot be reasonably construed as a grant of power to any administrative officer to promulgate regulations requiring obedience outside of the federal service.

[168] 203 U. S. 233 (1906).

[169] 175 U. S. 1 (1899). Similarly in other fields: The case of *United States* v. *George*, 228 U. S. 14 (1913) holds that a regulation of the Interior Department relating to public lands is invalid where not authorized by any act of Congress. The argument that general power to prescribe reasonable regulations governing public lands is conferred by Revised Statutes, section 441, and by other similar statutes, was rejected by the Supreme Court in this case with the following comment:

> It will be seen that they confer administrative power only. This is undubitably so as to sections 161, 441, 453, and 2478; and certainly under the guise of regulation legislation cannot be exercised. *United States* v. *United Verde Copper Co.*, 196 U. S. 207. (P. 20.)

Also see *Morrill* v. *Jones*, 106 U. S. 466, 467 (1882).

Unless empowered by statute, the Secretary of the Interior is not authorized to issue regulations granting an extension of time for the payment of certain accrued water right charges, Op. Sol. I. D., M. 26034, July 3, 1930, nor to create a charge against the Indians on their lands, Op. Sol. I. D., M. 27512, February 20, 1935. Also see *Romero* v. *United States*, 24 C. Cls. 331 (1889); *Lecoy* v. *United States*, 190 Fed. 289 (C. C. A. 8, 1911); app. dism. 232 U. S. 731 (1914); *Mason* v. *Sams*, 5 F. 2d, 255 (D. C. W. D. Wash. 1925), and *Hale* v. *Wilder*, 8 Kans. 545 (1871).

[170] 175 U. S. 1, 31.

[171] 24 C. Cls. 331 (1889).

utes, section 465.[172] The court declared that such regulations "must be in execution of, and supplementary to, but not in conflict with the statutes." The actual holding in this case may be explained on the theory that the regulation questioned conflicted with general provisions of law on tenure of office.

In the case of *Leecy* v. *United States* [173] the claim of the Department that Revised Statutes 441 [174] and 463 [175] were a grant of general regulatory powers was again rejected. In this case, as in the *Romero* case, it may be argued that the regulation in question was in derogation of the statutory rights of the Indians. A fair reading of the opinion, however, indicates that the supposed statutory rights invaded were so tenuous that every unauthorized regulation of the conduct of an Indian, or any other citizen, could similarly be regarded as a violation of statutory or constitutional rights. The real force of the decision is the holding that sections 441 and 463 of the Revised Statutes do not create independent powers.[176]

The claim of administrative officers to plenary power to regulate Indian conduct has been rejected in every decided case where such power was not invoked simply to implement the administration of some more specific statutory or treaty provision.

There is sometimes a tendency to regard the scope of administrative authority over Indians as broad enough to encompass almost every form of regulation. This idea, like the view of an omnipotent congressional power,[177] has been nurtured by descriptions of the extent of this power in dicta in decisions involving a specific legislative grant of administrative power.[178] Such language may influence later decisions in doubtful cases involving questions as to whether administrative power was implicit though not clearly delegated by the language of the statute.

The scope of administrative powers raises problems of particular importance in five fields: (*a*) tribal lands;[179] (*b*) tribal funds;[180] (*c*) individual lands;[181] (*d*) individual funds;[182] and (*e*) tribal membership.[183]

[172] Act of June 30, 1834, sec. 17, 4 Stat. 735, 738, 25 U. S. C. 9.

[173] 190 Fed. 289 (C. C. A. 8, 1911), app. dism. *United States* v. *Leecy*, 232 U. S. 781 (1914).

[174] Derived from Act of March 3, 1849, 9 Stat. 395, 5 U. S. C. 485.

[175] Derived from Act of July 9, 1832, 4 Stat. 564, 25 U. S. C. 2.

[176] In *LaMotte* v. *United States*, 254 U. S. 570 (1921), mod'g and aff'g 256 Fed. 5 (C. C. A. 8, 1919), the Supreme Court upheld the validity of regulations covering the leasing of restricted lands which were subject to the approval of the Secretary of the Interior by the Act of June 28, 1906, sec. 7, 34 Stat. 539, on the ground that "The regulations appear to be consistent with the statute, appropriate to its execution, and in themselves reasonable."

In *United States* v. *Birdsall*, 233 U. S. 223 (1914), rev'g 206 Fed. 818 (D. C. N. D. Iowa 1913), the regulation challenged and upheld dealt with the conduct of departmental employees, and was authorized by Revised Statutes § 2058, 25 U. S. C. 31, derived from Act of June 30, 1834, sec. 7, 4 Stat. 736, Act of June 5, 1850, sec. 4, 9 Stat. 437, and Act of February 27, 1851, sec. 5, 9 Stat. 587.

[177] See secs. 1–6, *supra*.

[178] Chief Justice Hughes (then associate justice), in describing the functions of the Office of Indian Affairs, said in *United States* v. *Birdsall*, 233 U. S. 223 (1914), rev'g 206 Fed. 818 (D. C. N. D. Iowa 1913):

> * * * The object of the establishment of the office was to create an administrative agency with broad powers adequate to the execution of the policy of the Government, as determined by the acts of Congress, with respect to the Indians under its guardianship. * * * (P. 232.)
>
> * * * * *
>
> * * * In executing the powers of the Indian Office there is necessarily a wide range for administrative discretion and in determining the scope of official action regard must be had to the authority conferred; and this, as we have seen, embraces every action which may properly constitute an aid in the enforcement of the law. (P. 235.)

In upholding the power of the Commissioner of Indian Affairs to require bill collectors to remain away from the Indian agency on the days when payments were being made, Mr. Justice Van Devanter, then on the Circuit Court of Appeals, wrote in *Rainbow* v. *Young*, 161 Fed. 835 (C. C. A. 8, 1908):

> * * * we turn to the statutes bearing upon the authority of the Commissioner of Indian Affairs, and in considering them it is well to remember, as was said in *United States* v. *Macdaniel*, 7 Pet. 1, 14, 8 L. Ed. 587, that:
>
> "A practical knowledge of the action of any one of the great departments of the government must convince every person that the head of a department, in the distribution of its duties and responsibilities, is often compelled to exercise his discretion. He is limited in the exercise of his powers by the law; but it does not follow that he must show statutory provision for everything he does. No government could be administered on such principles. To attempt to regulate by law the minute movements of every part of the complicated machinery of government would evince a most unpardonable ignorance on the subject. Whilst the great outlines of its movements may be marked out, and limitations imposed on the exercise of its powers there are numberless things which must be done, that can neither be anticipated nor defined, and which are essential to the proper action of the government." (P. 837.)
>
> * * * * *
>
> In our opinion the very general language of the statutes makes it quite plain that the authority conferred upon the Commissioner of Indian Affairs was intended to be sufficiently comprehensive to enable him, agreeably to the laws of Congress and to the supervision of the President and the Secretary of the Interior, to manage all Indian affairs, and all matters arising out of Indian relations, with a just regard, not merely to the rights and welfare of the public, but also to the rights and welfare of the Indians, and to the duty of care and protection owing to them by reason of their state of dependency and tutelage. And, while there is no specific provision relating to the exclusion of collectors from Indian agencies at times when payments are being made to the Indians, it does not follow that the commissioner is without authority to exclude them; for by section 2149 he is both authorized and required, with the approval of the Secretary of the Interior, to remove from any tribal reservation "any person" whose presence therein may, in his judgment, be detrimental to the peace and welfare of the Indians. This applies alike to all persons whose presence may be thus detrimental, and commits the decision of that question to the commissioner. Of course, it is necessary to the adequate protection of the Indians and to the orderly conduct of reservation affairs, that some such authority should be vested in someone, and it is in keeping with other legislation relating to the Indians that it should be vested in the commissioner. *United States ex rel. West* v. *Hitchcock*, 205 U. S. 80, 27 Sup. Ct. 423, 51 L. Ed. 718. There is no provision for a re-examination by the courts of the question of fact so committed to him for decision, and, considering the nature of the question, the plenary power of Congress in the matter, and the obvious difficulties in the way of such a re-examination, we think it is intended that there shall be none. *United States ex rel. West* v. *Hitchcock, supra*; *Stanclift* v. *Fox*, 81 C. C. A. 623, 152 Fed. 697 (pp. 838–839).

See also *United States ex rel. West* v. *Hitchcock*, 205 U. S. 80 (1907); Memo. Sol. I. D., February 28, 1935, which refers to *United States* v. *Clapox*, 35 Fed. 575, 577 (D. C. Ore. 1888); *Adams* v. *Freeman*, 50 Pac. 135, 138 (1897); Memo. Sol. I. D., August 30, 1938; Op. Sol. I. D. M. 27750, July 14, 1934; 32 Op. A. G. 586 (1921).

[179] See sec. 9, *infra*.

[180] See sec. 10, *infra*.

[181] See sec. 11, *infra*.

[182] See sec. 12, *infra*.

[183] See sec. 13, *infra*.

SECTION 9. ADMINISTRATIVE POWER—TRIBAL LANDS

A. ACQUISITION

One of the most important powers granted to the Secretary of the Interior is the power to acquire land for tribes. Apart from the many special statutes in this field,[184] two provisions of general law deserve mention.

Section 3 of the Wheeler-Howard Act [185] provides:

> The Secretary of the Interior, if he shall find it to be in the public interest, is hereby authorized to restore to tribal ownership the remaining surplus lands of any Indian reservation heretofore opened, or authorized to be opened, to sale, or any other form of disposal by Presidential proclamation, or by any of the public-land laws

[184] See Chapter 15, secs. 6–8.

[185] Act of June 18, 1934, 48 Stat. 984, 985, 25 U. S. C. 463.

> of the United States: *Provided, however,* That valid rights or claims of any persons to any lands so withdrawn existing on the date of the withdrawal shall not be affected by this Act: *Provided further,* That this section shall not apply to lands within any reclamation project heretofore authorized in any Indian reservation: * * *

This provision was originally framed in mandatory language, but was amended to make the restoration a discretionary act.[186] The administrative determination of this question may be guided by the fact, among others, that the protection of the property rights of the tribes is a federal function in which the public at large is interested.[187]

A second method by which the Secretary of the Interior is authorized to acquire lands for Indian tribes is set forth in section 5 of the Wheeler-Howard Act.[188] This section authorizes the Secretary:

> * * * in his discretion, to acquire, through purchase, relinquishment, gift, exchange, or assignment, any interest in lands, water rights, or surface right to lands, within or without existing reservations, including trust and otherwise restricted allotments, whether the allottee be living or deceased, for the purpose of providing land for Indians.

The procedure followed under this authority and the status of lands thereby acquired are elsewhere discussed.[189]

B. LEASING

The Secretary of the Interior has no power to enter into or approve a lease without authority from either a treaty[190] or a statute.[191] A few statutes permit the Secretary alone to make tribal leases for land rights,[192] but the law covering the leasing of most tribal land permits the tribal council to lease the lands subject to the approval of the Secretary.[193] Some of these statutes have been recently summarized by the Solicitor of the Department of the Interior.[194] Under existing laws,[195] and under many tribal charters[196] adopted pursuant to the Wheeler-Howard Act,[197] the tribal council has a right to make leases and permits on its own initiative subject to the approval of the Department. Under most of the statutes it is held that the Secretary acts in a quasi-judicial capacity in acting upon the recommendations of the superintendent and the actions of the tribal council regarding these leases, and hence cannot delegate this function to the superintendent.[198] It has been administratively held that the determination of the council should be conclusive upon the Department of the Interior, at least in the absence of evidence of mistake, fraud, or undue influence.[199]

C. ALIENATION

The general prohibition against alienation of tribal lands is elsewhere analyzed.[200] These restraints upon alienation apply to federal administrative officers, as well as to tribal authorities, and to interests less than a fee as well as to conveyances in fee simple.[201] Thus, in the absence of express statutory authorization, the Secretary of the Interior has no power to diminish the tribal estate by withdrawing a right-of-way for the construction of irrigation ditches.[202] Congress, however, has conferred upon administrative authorities various statutory powers to alienate interests in tribal land less than a fee, particularly easements and rights-of-way.[203] Generally these statutes do not make tribal consent a condition to the validity of the alienation, but as a practical administrative matter tribal consent is frequently made a condition of the grant.[204]

---

[186] Memo. Sol. I. D., September 29, 1937; Op. Sol. I. D., M. 29798, June 15, 1938. See also Op. Sol. I. D., M. 29616, February 19, 1938.

Even prior to the passage of this section, the Secretary of the Interior had adequate authority to withdraw lands from the public domain for public purposes.

See Act of June 25, 1910, 36 Stat. 836, 847, relating to "public lands." The authority to make temporary withdrawals was expressly preserved by sec. 4 of the Act of March 3, 1927, 44 Stat. 1347, which provides:

> That hereafter changes in the boundaries of reservations created by Executive order, proclamation, or otherwise for the use and occupation of Indians shall not be made except by Act of Congress: *Provided,* That this shall not apply to temporary withdrawals by the Secretary of the Interior.

Memo. Sol. I. D., September 17, 1934.

[187] For discussion of tribal property see Chapter 15.

[188] 48 Stat. 984, 985, 25 U. S. C. 465.

[189] See Chapter 15, sec. 8. See also Memo. Sol. I. D., August 14, 1937; Memo. Sol. I. D., September 29, 1937.

[190] See 23 Op. A. G. 214, 220 (1900).

[191] 18 Op. A. G. 235 (1885); 18 Op. A. G. 486 (1886). It has been customary to utilise revocable permits on tribal lands which could not be leased under the statutes in order to preserve the value of the lands and to obtain a revenue from them rather than allowing them to lie idle. Memo. Sol. I. D., January 12, 1937.

[192] Act of June 28, 1898, sec. 13, 30 Stat. 495 (Indian Terr.). Statutes of this nature concerning mineral leasing are described in Chapter 15, sec. 19.

[193] Act of February 28, 1891, 26 Stat. 794, sec. 3, 25 U. S. C. 397, extended by Act of August 15, 1894, sec. 1, 28 Stat. 286, 305, 25 U. S. C. 402. Also see Act of May 11, 1938, sec. 1, 52 Stat. 347, 25 U. S. C. 396a. and Chapter 15, sec. 19.

[194] Memo. Sol. I. D., October 21, 1938:

> Leases or permits covering use of tribal lands, entry or residence thereon, or removal of resources therefrom, may be executed through the concurrent action of the tribe and the Secretary of the Interior, or his duly authorised representative, under the following statutes and regulations: United States Code, title 25, sections 179, 397, 398, and 402; regulations governing the leasing of tribal lands for mining purposes, approved May 31, 1889, section 2; general grazing regulations, approved December 23, 1935, section 6; see 55 Decisions, Department of Interior 14, at pages 50–56.
>
> *   *   *   *   *
>
> The tribe may, with departmental approval, assign certain tracts of tribal land to individual members of the tribe or to particular families.
>
> Such assignments may be purely for personal use and occupancy or they may permit leasing to outsiders under departmental supervision. * * *
>
> *   *   *   *   *
>
> * * * The tribe has no right to lease any part of the reservation without departmental approval. So, too, the individual Indian has no right to make a lease covering any part of the reservation without departmental approval.
>
> The Department may withhold its approval from any lease, permit or assignment which does not do substantial justice to the claims of the tribe as a whole and the individual Indians who may have built improvements in particular areas.

Also see Chapter 15, secs. 19 and 20. On the power of the President to authorise the sale or other disposition of dead timber on reservations, see Act of February 16, 1889, 25 Stat. 673, 25 U. S. C. 196.

[195] See Act of June 7, 1924, sec. 17, 43 Stat. 636; Act of May 29, 1924, 43 Stat. 244, 25 U. S. C. 398, interpreted in *British-American Co.* v. *Board,* 299 U. S. 159 (1936).

[196] See Chapter 15, secs. 19 and 20. Some tribal charters require departmental approval of leases but not of permits. *Ibid.* sec. 20.

[197] 48 Stat. 984.

[198] Memo. So. I. D., March 25, 1939. Some permits, like grazing permits for tribal lands, are frequently issued by the superintendent and then approved by the governing body of the tribe.

[199] Memo. Sol. I. D., May 22, 1937, containing a discussion of the principles which should guide administrative practice. Also see *White Bear* v. *Barth,* 61 Mont. 322, 203 Pac. 517 (1921).

Although an original lease of tribal lands was signed by the Secretary and a lessee, it has been administratively held that after the passage of the Wheeler-Howard Act and the adoption of a tribal constitution conferring power to prevent any lease affecting tribal land without the consent of the tribe, the Secretary of the Interior cannot modify such lease without securing the approval of the Indian tribe. Memo. Sol. I. D., July 19, 1937.

[200] See Chapter 15, sec. 18.

[201] See Memo. Sol. I. D., September 2, 1936; Memo. Sol. I. D., September 6, 1934, and Memo. Sol. I. D., March 11, 1935. See also 25 C. F. R. 256.83.

[202] Memo. Sol. I. D., April 12, 1940 (Flathead).

[203] See 25 U. S. C. 311–322.

[204] See 25 C. F. R. 256.24, 256.53, 256.83.

Where statutory authority for the issuance of a right-of-way exists, it has been administratively held that such authority is not repealed by section 4 of the Act of June 18, 1934.[205] In thus construing the Act of June 18, 1934, the Solicitor for the Interior Department declared:[206]

> * * * The only limitations which the Reorganization Act imposes upon the exercise of authority conferred by such specific acts of Congress are: (a) a tribe organized under section 16 may veto the grant under the broad power given it by that section "to prevent the sale, disposition, lease, or encumbrance of tribal lands, interests in lands, or other tribal assets without the consent of the tribe" and (b) a tribe incorporated under section 17 may be given the power to make such grants without restriction.

Although the grant of an easement is held to be outside the prohibition of section 4 of the Act of June 18, 1934, it would appear that section 16 of the act[207] requires the consent of an organized tribe to any grant of right-of-way which the Secretary is authorized to make.[208] Tribal consent is likewise required where the Secretary of the Interior seeks to set aside tribal lands for reservoir purposes for an irrigation project.[209]

> * * * It is true that the United States in its sovereign capacity may condemn tribal land for certain purposes and may even appropriate tribal land by act of Congress subject to constitutional requirements of compensation. But the rights and powers with respect to tribal property granted by the Constitution and Charter of the Confederated Salish and Kootenai Tribes are effective against officers of the United States not acting under direct mandate of Congress. Indeed, unless officers of the Department can be restrained by the Tribe from disposing of tribal property, all meaning has vanished from the provision in section 16 of the Indian Reorganization Act granting to an organized tribe the power "to prevent the sale, disposition, lease, or encumbrance of tribal lands, interests in lands, or other tribal assets without the consent of the tribe." The only persons against whom this provision can be directed are officers of the United States. Private individuals never have had the power to sell tribal land or to dispose of tribal assets. If then * * * the restrictions contained in the above-quoted provision do not run against the United States, they are meaningless and the constitutional provisions enacted in accordance therewith are a false promise.

[205] 48 Stat. 984, 985, 25 U. S. C. 464.

[206] Memo. Sol. I. D., September 2, 1936.

[207] 48 Stat. 986, 25 U. S. C. 476.

[208] See 25 C. F. R. 256.83.

[209] Memo. Sol. I. D., July 8, 1936. And see 25 C. F. R. 256.44.

SECTION 10. ADMINISTRATIVE POWER—TRIBAL FUNDS[210]

In defining the scope of federal administrative power over tribal funds it is important to bear in mind certain distinctions between various classes of funds, all of which are, in some sense of the word, tribal.

Funds which an Indian tribe has derived from its own members or from third parties without the interposition of the Federal Government, as where tribal authorities hold a fair or dance and charge admission, are, in a very real sense, "tribal," yet it has never been held that federal administrative authorities have any control over such funds.[211]

A second class of funds which may be called "tribal" comprises those funds held in the treasury of a tribe which has become incorporated under section 17 of the Act of June 18, 1934,[212] or organized under section 16 of that act.[213] In both cases the scope of departmental power with respect to such funds is marked out by the provisions of tribal constitution or charter. Typically, departmental review is required where the financial transactions exceed a fixed level of magnitude or importance, but not in lesser matters. In the case of incorporated tribes, such departmental supervisory powers are generally temporary.[214]

A third class of funds consists of moneys held in the Treasury of the United States in trust for an Indian tribe. It is this class of funds which is customarily referred to under the phrase "tribal funds." These funds arise from two sources, in general:

1. Payments promised by the Federal Government to the tribe for lands ceded or other valuable consideration,[215] usually arising out of a treaty, and
2. Payments made to federal officials by lessees, land purchasers, or other private parties in exchange for some benefit, generally tribal land or interests therein.[216]

In view of the fact that the land itself was subject to a considerable measure of control, it was natural to find a similar control placed over the funds into which tribal lands were transmuted. Congress has, in general, reserved complete power over the disposition of these funds, requiring that each expenditure of such funds be made pursuant to an appropriation act, although this strict rule has been relaxed for certain favored purposes.[217] Thus it has developed that administrative authority for any disbursement of "tribal funds," in the strict sense, must be derived from the language of some annual appropriation act or from those statutes which are, in effect, permanent appropriations of tribal funds for specified purposes.[218]

[210] The Act of April 1, 1880, c. 41, 21 Stat. 70, provided:

> That the Secretary of the Interior be, and he is hereby, authorized to deposit, in the Treasury of the United States, any and all sums now held by him, or which may hereafter be received by him, as Secretary of the Interior and trustee of various Indian tribes, on account of the redemption of United States bonds, or other stocks and securities belonging to the Indian trust-fund, and all sums received on account of sales of Indian trust lands, and the sales of stocks lately purchased for temporary investment, whenever he is of the opinion that the best interests of the Indians will be promoted by such deposits, in lieu of investments; and the United States shall pay interest semi-annually, from the date of deposit of any and all such sums in the United States Treasury, at the rate per annum stipulated by treaties or prescribed by law, and such payments shall be made in the usual manner, as each may become due, without further appropriation by Congress.

Previous to the enactment of this law, the Secretary of the Interior invested tribal funds in various kinds of bonds, including state bonds, some of which were defaulted.

[211] It has been suggested that the Federal Government might bring suit on behalf of an Indian to insure a fair distribution of such funds, but there are no decisions on this point. See Memo. Sol. I. D., November 18, 1936 (Palm Springs).

[212] See Chapter 15, secs. 23 and 24.

[213] See Chapter 15, sec. 23.

[214] *Ibid.*, secs. 23 and 24.

[215] See Chapter 1, sec. 1; Chapter 2, sec. 2; Chapter 3, sec. 3C(3); Chapter 15, sec. 23. The payment of annuities and distribution of goods is a ministerial duty, enforceable by mandamus, if the Secretary is arbitrary or capricious. *Work* v. *United States*, 18 F. 2d 820 (App. D. C. 1927). *Cf. United States ex rel. Coburn* v. *Work*, 18 F. 2d 822 (App. D. C. 1927); *United States ex rel. Detling* v. *Work*, 18 F. 2d 822 (App. D. C. 1927).

[216] See Chapter 15, sec. 23.

[217] *Ibid.*

[218] The Act of May 18, 1916, sec. 27, 39 Stat. 123, 158, 159, requires specific congressional appropriation for expenditure of tribal funds except as follows:

> * * * Equalization of allotments, education of Indian children in accordance with existing law, per capita and other payments, all of which are hereby continued in full force and effect: * * *

See Chapter 15, sec. 23. Provisions relating to the deposit or investment of funds are numerous. For example, the Secretary of the Interior is authorized to "invest in a manner which shall be in his judgment most safe, and beneficial for the fund, all moneys that may be received under treaties containing stipulations for the payment to the Indians, annually, of interest upon the proceeds of the lands ceded by them; and he shall make no investment of such moneys, or of any portion, at a lower rate

633058—45——9

Among the most important of the permanent authorizations for the disbursement of tribal funds are the various statutes providing for the division and apportionment of tribal funds among the members of the tribe.[219]

While any administrative control over these funds must be based on statutory authority, it is not necessary, nor is it indeed possible, that every detail of the expenditure shall be expressly covered by statute.[220]

The Court of Claims in the case of *Creek Nation* v. *United States* [221] said:

> * * * The Secretary of the Interior has only such authority over the funds of Indian tribes as is confided in him by Congress. He cannot legally disburse and pay out Indian funds for purposes other than those authorized by law. This rule is the test by which the legal right of the Secretary of the Interior to make the disbursements involved must be determined. The contention, however, that the Secretary of the Interior could legally make only such disbursements as were expressly authorized by Congress cannot be conceded. The authorities cited in plaintiff's brief in support of this contention, when considered in the light of the precise questions presented, do not sustain it. The opinion of Attorney General Mitchell of October 5, 1929 (36 Op. Attys. Gen. 98–100), in fact, refutes the contention, and in effect lays down the rule that the authority of the Secretary of the Interior over Indian property may arise from the necessary implication as well as from the express provisions of a statute. We think this is the correct rule and will apply it in determining whether the Secretary of the Interior was authorized to make the payments in question. The authority of the Secretary of the Interior to make the payments, or his lack of authority to make them, must be found in the treaties between the United States and the Creek Nation, and the various acts of Congress dealing with Creek tribal affairs. (P. 485.)

Quite apart from the necessity of finding some statutory source for authority to expend funds held in the United States Treasury in trust for an Indian tribe, there are certain positive statutory limitations upon the ways in which such funds may be disbursed. These statutes, which are elsewhere listed,[222] limit the administrative authority derived from appropriation acts construed in conjunction with section 17 of the Act of June 30, 1834,[223] which gave the President power to "prescribe such rules and regulations as he may think fit, for carrying into effect the various provisions of this act, and of any other act relating to Indian affairs, and for the settlement of the accounts of the Indian department."

Perhaps the most important of these statutory limitations in effect today is that imposed by section 16 of the Act of June 18, 1934,[224] which gives an organized tribe the right to prevent any disposition of its assets without the consent of the proper officers of the tribe. This includes the right to prevent disbursements of tribal funds by departmental officials, where the tribe has not consented to such disbursements. Unless an act of Congress authorizing disbursements of tribal funds expressly repeals relevant provisions of the Indian Reorganization Act, such appropriation legislation does not nullify the power of the tribe to prevent such expenditure.[225]

There is a fourth category of funds which may be called "tribal funds" but which are subject neither to the uncontrolled tribal power pertaining to the first class of funds discussed; to the defined tribal power of the second class, nor to the detailed congressional control pertaining to the third class. This fourth category includes funds which have accrued to administrative officials as a result of various Indian activities not specially recognized or regulated by act of Congress.

The Act of March 3, 1883,[226] as amended, provides:

> The proceeds of all pasturage and sales of timber, coal, or other product of any Indian reservation, except those of the five civilized tribes, and not the result of the labor of any member of such tribe, shall be covered into the Treasury for the benefit of such tribe under such regulations as the Secretary of the Interior shall prescribe; and the Secretary shall report his action in detail to Congress at its next session.

The Comptroller General in a report on Indian funds dated February 28, 1929,[227] stated:

> * * * The absolute control and almost indiscriminate use of these funds, through authority delegated to the several Indian agents by the Commissioner of Indian

---

of interest than 5 per centum per annum." (25 U. S. C. 158, R. S. § 2096, derived from Act of June 14, 1836, 5 Stat. 36, 47, as amended by Act of January 9, 1837, sec. 4, 5 Stat. 135.)

There are many special statutes relating to the disposition of tribal funds. For example, the Act of June 20, 1936, 49 Stat. 1543, provides:

> That tribal funds now on deposit or later placed to the credit of the Crow Tribe of Indians, Montana, may be used for per-capita payments, or such other purposes as may be designated by the tribal council and approved by the Secretary of the Interior. * * *

The Comptroller General has differentiated between two types of tribal funds:

> There are several classes of *trust funds* provided for by law, the moneys in which are held in trust for certain beneficiaries specified therein. The following may serve as examples:
>
> * * * * *
>
> (*b*) Section 7 of the act of January 14, 1889 (25 Stat., 645), provides that the net proceeds of sales of lands ceded to the United States by the Chippewa Indians shall be placed in the Treasury to the credit of said Indians as a permanent fund, which shall draw interest at the rate of 5 per centum per annum, principal and interest to be expended for the benefit of said Indians.
>
> (*c*) Section 5 of the act of June 15, 1880 (21 Stat., 204), in consideration of lands ceded to the United States, provides as follows:
>
> "That the Secretary of the Treasury shall, out of any moneys in the Treasury not otherwise appropriated, set apart, and hold as a perpetual trust-fund for said Ute Indians, an amount of money sufficient at four per centum to produce annually fifty thousand dollars, which interest shall be paid to them per capita in cash, annually. * * *"
>
> The moneys in the *general fund* and also those in *special funds* are available for public expenditures. There is, however, an important distinction in these two classes of funds. Moneys in the *general fund* can only be withdrawn from the Treasury in pursuance of an appropriation made by law; but moneys in *special funds*, having been dedicated by Congress for expenditure for specified objects before they were covered into the Treasury, in which they have been placed for safe-keeping only, are subject to withdrawal from the Treasury for expenditure for these objects without an appropriation (13 Comp. Dec. 219, 700). It is true that in some instances, as in that of the *special fund* called the "reclamation fund" (3, *supra*), Congress has used the term "appropriation" in constituting certain moneys to be collected *special funds*; but as the term is so applied to the moneys before they are collected it is obvious that the term is so used in a general sense only, for which the term "dedicated" appears to be more appropriate.
>
> Moneys in *trust funds* are not properly available for expenditures of the Government. They are payable to or for the use of the beneficiaries only. The beneficiaries may be either a single person or a class of persons. In the three classes of *trust funds* given above, the trust moneys in the first class (*a*) were received directly from the donors; those in the second class (*b*) were collected as revenues of the United States charged with the trust; those in the third class (*c*) were a grant of moneys in the *general fund* of the Treasury in pursuance of a treaty obligation. (14 Decisions Comptroller Treasury, 361, 365–366 (1907).)

[219] These statutes are discussed in Chapter 9, sec. 6; Chapter 10, sec. 5; Chapter 15, sec. 23.

[220] Act of May 18, 1916, sec. 27, 39 Stat. 123, 158, requires with a few exceptions specific congressional appropriation for tribal expenditures of tribal moneys. The Act of May 25, 1918, secs. 27 and 28, 40 Stat. 561, authorizes the Secretary to invest restricted funds, tribal or individual, in United States Government bonds. Also see Chapter 15, sec. 22F.

[221] 78 C. Cls. 474 (1933). On the lack of power of the Secretary to restore to the Creek orphan fund the funds erroneously expended for general benefit of tribe, see 16 Op. A. G. 31 (1878).

[222] See Chapter 9, sec. 6; Chapter 10, sec. 5; Chapter 15, sec. 23.

[223] 4 Stat. 735, 738, 25 U. S. C. 9, construed to cover disbursement of tribal funds in 5 Op. A. G. 36 (1848).

[224] 48 Stat. 984.

[225] Memo. Sol. I. D., October 5, 1936.

[226] 22 Stat. 582, 590; amended Act of March 2, 1887, 24 Stat. 449, 463; Act of May 17, 1926, sec. 2, 44 Stat. 560; Act of May 29, 1928, sec. 68, 45 Stat. 986, 991, 25 U. S. C. 155.

[227] Sen. Doc. 263, 70th Cong., 2d sess., 1928–29. For a discussion see American Indian Life, Bull. No. 14 (May 1929), American Defense Association, Inc., p. 19.

> Affairs pursuant to section 463, Revised Statutes, is apparently causing complaint on the part of groups of Indians. (P. 40.)

The report also contained some evidence justifying the discontent of the Indians.

> * * * "Indian moneys, proceeds of labor," were being used for such purposes as the purchase of adding machines and office equipment, furniture, rugs, draperies, etc., for employees' quarters, papering and painting the superintendent's house, and the purchase of automobiles for the field units. (P. 40.)[228]

The Comptroller General concluded that—

> * * * This condition has through the years of practice brought about a very broad interpretation of what constitutes "the benefit" of the Indian. (P. 39.)[229]

The Act of June 13, 1930,[230] provides:

> SEC. 2. All tribal funds arising under the Act of March 3, 1883 (22 Stat. 590), as amended by the Act of May 17, 1926 (44 Stat. 560), now included in the fund 'Indian Money, Proceeds of Labor,' shall, on and after July 1, 1930, be carried on the books of the Treasury Department in separate accounts for the respective tribes, and all such funds with account balances exceeding $500 shall bear simple interest at the rate of 4 per centum per annum from July 1, 1930.
>
> SEC. 3. The amount held in any tribal fund account which, in the judgment of the Secretary of the Interior, is not required for the purpose for which the fund was created, shall be covered into the surplus fund of the Treasury; and so much thereof as is found to be necessary for such purpose may at any time thereafter be restored to the account on books of the Treasury without appropriation by Congress.

The extent to which funds which are still called "I. M. P. L." are subject to the statutory limitations applicable to tribal funds in the strict sense is an intricate problem upon which no opinion will be here ventured.[231]

[228] Sen. Doc. 263, *op. cit.*

[229] *Ibid.*

[230] C. 483, 46 Stat. 584. There are 300 tribal "funds of principal" held in trust by the United States in the Treasury (Department of the Treasury, Combined Statement of Receipts and Expenditures, Balances, etc., of the United States for Fiscal Year ended June 30, 1939, pp. 417–427), and 266 interest accounts, which are classified by the Treasury as general funds (*Ibid.*, pp. 260–269). The Department of the Interior breaks down many of the principal funds into subordinate classifications.

[231] See Chapter 15, sec. 23A.

SECTION 11. ADMINISTRATIVE POWER—INDIVIDUAL LANDS

Administrative power over individual Indian lands is of particular importance at five points:

(*a*) Approval of allotments,
(*b*) Release of restrictions,
(*c*) Probate of estates,
(*d*) Issuance of rights-of-way,
(*e*) Leasing.

A. APPROVAL OF ALLOTMENTS

The statutes and treaties which confer upon individual Indians rights to allotments are elsewhere discussed,[232] as is the legislation governing jurisdiction over suits for allotments.[233] Within the fabric of rights and remedies thus defined there is a certain scope of administrative discretion[234] which is described in a recent ruling of the Solicitor for the Interior Department in these terms:[235]

> * * * The Secretary may for good reason refuse to approve an allotment selection, but he may not cancel his approval of an allotment except to correct error or to relieve fraud. Cf. *Corneleus* v. *Kessel* (128 U. S. 456) (public land entry). It is very doubtful whether the Secretary would be privileged to return allotment selections to tribal ownership simply on the ground that the Wheeler-Howard Act possibly forbids the trust patenting of such selections.
>
> * * * * *
>
> (2) Where the Secretary has approved an allotment, the ministerial duty arises to issue a patent. With approval his discretion is ended except, of course, for such reconsideration of his approval as he may find necessary (24 L. D. 264). Since only the routine matter of issuing a patent remains, the allottee after his allotment is approved is considered as having a vested right to the allotment as against the Government. Raymond Bear Hill (42 L. D. 689 (1929)). (*Cf.* Where a certificate of approval has issued as in the Five Civilized Tribe cases, *Ballinger* v. *Frost* (216 U. S. 240); and where right to a homestead is involved, *Stark* v. *Starre* (6 Wall. 402).) And then the allottee may bring mandamus to obtain the patent. See *Vachon* v. *Nichols-Chisolm Lumber Co.* (126 Minn. 303, 148 N. W. 288, 290 (1914).) *Cf. Lane* v. *Hoglund* (244 U. S. 174); *Butterworth* v. *United States* (112 U. S. 50); *Barney* v. *Dolph* (97 U. S. 652, 656).
>
> * * * * *
>
> (3) Where an allotment has not been approved, on the other hand, approval and the issuance of a patent cannot be compelled by mandamus. *West* v. *Hitchcock* (205 U. S. 80); *United States* v. *Hitchcock* (190 U. S. 316). But it is recognized that an allottee acquires rights in land with some of the incidents of ownership when the allotting agents have set apart allotments and he has made his selection. Until that time an Indian eligible for allotment has only a floating right which is personal to himself and dies with him. *La Roque* v. *United States* (239 U. S. 62). See Philomme Smith (24 L. D. 323, 327). The owner of an allotment selection, even before its approval, has an inheritable interest (*United States* v. *Chase* (245 U. S. 89); *Smith* v. *Bonifer* (166 Fed. 846) (C. C. A. 9th, 1909)); which will be protected from the outside world (*Smith* v. *Bonifer*, *supra*); and which he can transfer within limits (*Henkel* v. *United States*, *supra*; *United States* v. *Chase*, *supra*); and which is sufficient to confer on him the privileges of State citizenship as granted to all "allottees" by the act of 1887 (*State* v. *Norris*, *supra*). Moreover, where the Government has issued an erroneous patent for the allotment selections, the owner of such selection will be protected in his right against the adverse interests possessing the patent (*Hy-Yu-Tse-Mil-Kin* v. *Smith* (194 U. S. 401); *Smith* v. *Bonifer* (132 Fed. 889 (C. C. Ore. 1904), 166 Fed. 846 (C. C. A. 9th, 1909)), and against the Government itself. *Conway* v.

[232] See Chapter 11, sec. 2.

[233] See Chapter 10, sec. 2.

[234] The Act of March 3, 1885, sec. 6, 23 Stat. 340 (Cayuse and others) which authorizes the Secretary to determine all disputes and questions arising between Indians regarding their allotments, exemplifies one of the many administrative powers over allotments. The Supreme Court in *Hy-Yu-Tse-Mil-Kin* v. *Smith*, 194 U. S. 401 (1904) said that if two Indians claim the same land, the allotment should be "made in favor of the one whose priority of selection and residence and whose improvements on the land equitably entitled such person to the land." (P. 414.)

The Court in the case of *La Roque* v. *United States*, 239 U. S. 62 (1915) said:

> * * * The regulations and decisions of the Secretary of the Interior, under whose supervision the act was to be administered, show that it was construed by that officer as confining the right of selection to living Indians and that he so instructed the allotting officers. While not conclusive, this construction given to the act in the course of its actual execution is entitled to great respect and ought not to be overruled without cogent and persuasive reasons. (P. 64.)

On the scope of discretion of the Secretary of the Interior in allotting lands, see *Chase, Jr.*, v. *United States*, 256 U. S. 1 (1921).

[235] Op. Sol., I. D., M. 28086, July 17, 1935. And see Memo. Sol., I. D., September 17, 1934.

United States (149 Fed. 261) (C. C. Neb. 1907). In these cases the courts lay down the principle that where an Indian has done all that is necessary and that he can do to become entitled to land and fails to attain the right through the neglect or misconduct of public officers, the courts will protect him in such right. Again, where the claimant does all required of him he acquires a right against the Government for the perfection of his title, and the right is to be determined as of the date it should have been perfected. *Payne* v. *New Mexico* (255 U. S. 367); *Raymond Bear Hill*, supra.

Further, where the right to the allotment has failed to become vested through the neglect of public officers to attach approval to the selection, one court has indicated that the right to the allotment would be considered as already vested so as to be beyond the reach of a later act of Congress. *Lemieux* v. *United States* (15 Fed. (2d) 518, 521 (C. C. A. 8th, 1926)). In the Lemieux case the Secretary's approval under the act of 1887 would have had to include determination of the qualifications of the applicants but in the Fort Belknap situation, no question of qualifications arises since previous enrollment on the allotment list is made by statute conclusive evidence of the enrollee's right to allotment. Thus the position of the Fort Belknap allottee compels even more strongly to the conclusion suggested in the Lemieux case. It has also been suggested that where the Indian possesses all the qualifications entitling him to an allotment, the Secretary has no longer any discretion to refuse approval. See *State* v. *Norris*, *supra* (55 N. W. at 1089.)

In ruling that the Secretary of the Interior could disapprove allotment selections on a reservation which had voted to exclude itself from the Wheeler-Howard Act, the Solicitor of the Department of Interior said:[336]

> * * * the owners of allotment selections have certain rights and interests which will be protected against outside interests and errors by Government agents. *United States* v. *Chase* (245 U. S. 89); *Hy-Yu-Tse-Mil-Kin* v. *Smith* (194 U. S. 401); *Smith* v. *Bonifer* (166 Fed. 846, C. C. A. 9th, 1909); *Conway* v. *United States* (149 Fed. 261, C. C. Neb. 1907). But they ordinarily have no vested right to approval or to a patent. In other words, they cannot prevent Congress from annuling their selection (*Lemieux* v. *United States*, 15 Fed. (2d) 518, 521 (C. C. A. 8th, 1926)), nor force the Secretary to grant approval. *West* v. *Hitchcock* (205 U. S. 80).
>
> Decidedly, the conservation of Indian land in tribal ownership when as imperative as in the Ft. Peck situation, if it can be accomplished, would appear to be sufficient justification for the exercise of the discretion of the Secretary to refuse approval to allotment selections. Precedent is not available for guidance here since cases dealing with the discretion of the Secretary to refuse approval to allotments have dealt only with his power as applied to particular applications for allotment and resulting from certain defects in the application. However, in one of these cases, *West* v. *Hitchcock* (205 U. S. 80), the stewardship of the Secretary over tribal property was recognized as a source of power to refuse allotments injurious to the tribe. The power would seem at least as great when applied on a large scale as in a single instance. Accordingly, I conclude that the Secretary is privileged to disapprove the Ft. Peck selections upon the grounds of policy.

The Solicitor of the Department of the Interior has further described the power of the Secretary over allotment selections in a subsequent opinion dealing with the Fort Peck Indian Reservation. He declared:[337]

> Where allotment selections have been duly made under authority of the Department and pursuant to its official instructions and in accordance with a course of allotment on the reservation, in my opinion it is probable that a court would hold that the Secretary cannot decline to approve particular selections because of a subsequent change in land policy. His authority to disapprove such selections would be limited to disapproving particular selections not entitled to approval because of error or the ineligibility of the applicant or other such reason. I base my opinion on the fact that when an official allotment selection has been duly made in accordance with the laws and regulations at the time of the selection, in ordinary circumstances the selector acquires a certain property interest in the land and a right to the perfection of his title which courts will protect.
>
> An Indian eligible for allotment who has not properly selected an allotment under the instructions of the Interior Department has only a floating right to an allotment which is not inheritable and which gives him no vested interest in any land. *La Roque* v. *United States*, 239 U. S. 62; *Woodbury* v. *United States*, 170 Fed. 302, C. C. A. 8th, 1909. After *proper* selection of an allotment, however, an Indian has been held to have an individual interest in the land with many of the incidents of individual ownership. His interest is inheritable, transferable within limits, and deserving of protection against adverse claims by third persons. *United States* v. *Chase*, 245 U. S. 89; *Henkel* v. *United States*, 237 U. S. 43; *Hy-Yu-Tse-Mil-Kin* v. *Smith*, 194 U. S. 401; *Bonifer* v. *Smith*, 166 Fed. 846, C. C. A. 9th, 1909; see 55 I. D. 295, at 303.
>
> The cases before the Interior Department and before the courts which are of most concern in this problem are the cases dealing with the protection of an allotment selection against adverse action by the Government, either by Congress or by the Executive. The Department has taken the view that acts of Congress limiting allotment rights in "undisposed of" tribal lands do not apply to allotment selections even though they have not been approved. *Fort Peck and Uncompahgre Allotments*, 53 I. D. 538; *Raymond Bear Hill*, 52 L. D. 689. In these decisions it was held that the filing and recording of an allotment selection segregates the land from other disposal, withdraws the land from the mass of tribal lands, and creates in the Indian an individual property right.
>
> * * * * *
>
> * * * a judicial determination of whether or not an allotment selection merits protection against adverse governmental action involves a weighing of the equities in the light of the intent of Congress and the history of administrative action. In the Palm Springs case the act contemplated that no allotments should be made until the Secretary of the Interior was satisfied of their advisability. No allotments were in fact made and the Secretary was clearly not satisfied of their advisability. If a court attempted to force the recognition and completion of tentative selections in the field, it would encroach upon executive discretion. In the *Payne* and *Lecey* cases, however, whatever discretion had been given to the Executive as to the advisability of allotments had been exercised and a course of allotment had been established. Thereafter, individual allotment selections were approved or disapproved according to their individual merits. In this situation a court could properly prevent, as an abuse of discretion, the failure to approve an individual allotment selection, not because of its own demerits, but because of extraneous policies.

B. RELEASE OF RESTRICTIONS

Perhaps the most important power vested in administrative officials with respect to allotted land is the power to pass upon the alienation of such lands. We have elsewhere noted the rigid restrictions placed upon the alienation of tribal lands from early times.[338] Allotments carried the obvious risk that the land given to the individual allottee would be speedily alienated.[339] Accordingly restrictions of various kinds were imposed upon allotments for the purpose of controlling alienation. Such restrictions were

[336] Memo. Sol. I. D., July 17, 1935.

[337] Op. Sol. I. D., M. 30256, May 31, 1939. In reaching his conclusion, the Solicitor discussed, among other cases, the following: *United States* v. *Payne*, 264 U. S. 446 (1924); *Lecoy* v. *United States*, 190 Fed. 289 (C. C. A. 8, 1911), app. dism. *United States* v. *Lecoy*, 232 U. S. 731 (1914); and the Palm Springs Reservation case, *St. Marie* v. *United States*, 24 F. Supp. 237 (D. C. S. D. Cal. 1938), aff'd 108 F. 2d 876 (C. C. A. 10, 1940).

[338] See Chapter 15, sec. 18.

[339] See Chapter 11, sec. 1.

embodied in various treaties [240] and statutes [241] that preceded the General Allotment Act.

At the present time restrictions upon alienation of allotments are in general of two kinds: (1) the "trust patent" and (2) the "restricted fee."

(1) Under the General Allotment Act and related legislation,[242] the allottee receives what is called a "trust patent", the theory being that the United States retains legal title to the land. Alienation of the land, therefore, requires either the consent of the United States to the alienation or, as a prerequisite to a valid conveyance, the issuance of a fee patent to the allottee.

Section 5 of the General Allotment Act [243] provided that at the expiration of 25 years the trust should terminate and a fee patent should be issued.[244] The President, however, was given discretionary authority to extend this period,[245] and by the Act of May 8, 1906,[246] the Secretary of the Interior was given power to issue a patent in fee simple "whenever he shall be satisfied that any Indian allottee is competent and capable of managing his or her affairs." Finally, the Act of June 25, 1910,[247] authorized the Secretary to sell trust patented lands in heirship status.

The Act of May 8, 1906, did not in terms require the consent of the Indian allottee as a condition to the issuance of a patent in fee simple by the Secretary of the Interior. Under a deliberate policy of hastening the "emancipation" of the Indian, many fee patents were issued without Indian application and even over Indian protest.[248] Many years later the courts held that the Act of May 8, 1906, had not been properly construed, that no patent could properly issue prior to the expiration of the trust period without the consent of the Indian, and that taxes paid by the Indians upon lands thus patented without Indian consent might be recovered.[249] In the case of *United States* v. *Ferry County, Wash.*,[250] the court declared, after reviewing numerous authorities:

> The United States as trustee may not liquidate the trust without the consent of the allottees and the Act of May 8, 1906, on which defendants rely must have so intended, *U. S.* v. *Benewah County, Idaho*, 9 Cir., 290 F. 628. (P. 400.)

Congress has taken cognizance of the error involved in the assumption by the Interior Department of power to issue fee patents without Indian consent and has authorized appropriations to repay to Indians taxes paid on such lands and to repay to county authorities judgments obtained in favor of Indians paying such taxes.[251]

The Secretary's authority to sell trust patented lands was revoked, except for sales to Indian tribes and exchanges of land of equal value, by section 4 of the Act of June 18, 1934,[252] on those reservations to which that statute applies. The Secretary of the Interior, however, still has power to issue a fee patent to the holder of a trust patent in advance of the expiration of the 25-year period, at least where the allottee makes application therefor. Section 2 of the same act extended the trust period "until otherwise directed by Congress."

(2) A second form of restriction upon the alienability of allotments involves the holding of a legal fee by the allottee under a deed which prevents alienation without the consent of some administrative officer, usually the Secretary of the Interior.[253] Such tenure, for instance, is provided by various statutes dealing with allotments among the Five Civilized Tribes.[254] The acquisition of land by federal authorities for individual Indians has frequently been effected by means of these restricted deeds.[255] Section 2 of the Act of June 18, 1934,[256] extends the period of such restrictions indefinitely until Congress shall otherwise provide, but does not prohibit the termination of such period by mutual agreement between the Indian and the appropriate administrative official. Alienation of allotments held in fee simple subject to restrictions on alienation may be authorized by the Secretary of the Interior, prior to the expiration of the statutory period, under the Act of March 1, 1907.[257] Issuance of a "certificate of competency" prior to the expiration of the statutory period is authorized by the Act of June 25, 1910.[258] As in the case of trust-

[240] Thus, for example, Article 3 of the Treaty of September 30, 1854, with the Chippewas, 10 Stat. 1109, 1110, authorized the President to impose restrictions upon allotted lands. In *Starr* v. *Campbell*, 208 U. S. 527 (1908), it was held that these restrictions covered the disposition of timber.

[241] See Chapter 11, sec. 1.

[242] See Chapter 11, sec. 1. Also see Chapter 4, sec. 11.

[243] Act of February 8, 1887, 24 Stat. 388, 389, amended, Act of March 3, 1901, sec. 9, 31 Stat. 1058, 1085, 25 U. S. C. 348.

[244] To the effect that upon the expiration of the trust period there then remains nothing to be done but the purely ministerial duty of casting the legal title on the person or persons to whom such title belongs, see Op. Sol. I. D. M. 5379, July 14, 1921; Op. Sol. I. D. M. 5702, April 27, 1922. But *cf.* 30 L. D. 258 (1900).

[245] Act of June 21, 1906, 34 Stat. 325, 326, 25 U. S. C. 391. In *United States* v. *Jackson*, 280 U. S. 183 (1930), the Supreme Court held that presidential power under this provision extended to Indian public domain homesteads.

It has been held that when the trust period has expired it cannot be re-imposed in the guise of an "extension" without express statutory authority *Reynolds* v. *United States*, 252 Fed. 65 (C. C. A. 8, 1918), revd. sub nom. *United States* v. *Reynolds*, 250 U. S. 104 (1919), on another ground; Op. Sol. I. D. M. 27930, April 9, 1935. *Cf. McCurdy* v. *United States*, 246 U. S. 263 (1918). For an example of such a statute see Act of February 26, 1927, 44 Stat. 1247, 25 U. S. C. 352.

[246] 34 Stat. 182, 25 U. S. C. 349.

[247] Sec. 1, 36 Stat. 855, amended, Act of March 3, 1928, 45 Stat. 161, amended, Act of April 30, 1934, 48 Stat. 647, 25 U. S. C. 372.

[248] See Chapter 2, sec. 3E.

[249] See Chapter 13, sec. 3B.

[250] 24 F. Supp. 399 (D. C. E. D. Wash. 1938).

[251] Act of June 11, 1940 (Pub. No. 590—76th Cong.). See, for a history of this erroneous departmental interpretation and its consequences in the field of taxation, H. Rept. No. 669, 76th Cong., 1st sess. (1939).

[252] 48 Stat. 984, 25 U. S. C. 464.

[253] The power delegated to the Secretary of the Interior to approve the alienation of restricted property cannot generally be transferred or delegated to any other governmental agency. Op. Sol. I. D. M. 25258, June 26, 1929. *United States* v. *Watashe*, 102 F. 2d 428 (C. C. A. 10, 1939).

[254] See Chapter 23, sec. 8A.

[255] The Secretary of the Interior may impose restrictions on land purchased by him for an Indian from restricted money. *United States* v. *Brown*, 8 F. 2d 564 (C. C. A. 8, 1925), cert. den. 270 U. S. 644 (1926), discussed in 39 Harv. L. R. 780 (1926) (money paid under lease of allotted lands). The underlying theory is that the Secretary's control over the funds embraces the power to invest them in land subject to the condition against alienation. A similar theory is advanced to justify the power of the Secretary to restrict lands purchased with money paid for allotted lands. See *Sunderland* v. *United States*, 266 U. S. 226 (1924) (money paid for allotted lands).

On the problem of taxation raised thereby, see Chapter 13, sec. 3D.

[256] 48 Stat. 984, 25 U. S. C. 462.

[257] 34 Stat. 1015, 1018, 25 U. S. C. 405. On the effective date of Secretarial approval of a deed, see 53 I. D. 412 (1931).

[258] Sec. 1, 36 Stat. 855, 25 U. S. C. 372.

The Circuit Court of Appeals in *Ex parte Pero*, 99 F. 2d 28 (C. C. A. 7, 1938), cert. den. 306 U. S. 643 (1939), in holding that the issuance of a certificate of competency under the Act of June 25, 1910, 36 Stat. 855, does not satisfy the requirement for the issuing of a patent in fee simple, said:

> The scope and expressed purpose of the Act of 1910 is narrow and definitely stated. The Secretary of the Interior is authorized to issue a certificate of competency to any Indian ("or in case of his death to his heirs") to whom a patent in fee containing restrictions on alienation has been, or may be issued. "And such certificate shall have the effect of removing the restrictions on alienation contained in such patent." Since the effect of removing the restrictions on a restricted patent in fee is to put the holder in the condition of one who has received a patent in fee simple "under any law or treaty." * * * Since Congress expressly provided that the Secretary of the Interior should first be satisfied that a trust allottee was competent and capable of managing his own affairs as a condition precedent to the issuance of patent in fee simple, it would seem to be doing violence to legislative intent for this court to substitute a certificate of competency for both

patented lands, however, the power of the Secretary to permit alienation was terminated with respect to tribes covered by section 4 of the Act of June 18, 1934.[279]

We have elsewhere noted how the Federal Government, through the leverage of its veto power over the alienation of tribal land, was able to impose various conditions upon the use of "tribal funds" derived therefrom.[280] In the same way, the power of administrative officials to approve or veto the alienation of allotments has been used to impose various conditions upon the manner and terms of such alienation and upon the disposition of the individual Indian moneys derived therefrom.[281]

C. PROBATE OF ESTATES

(1) *Intestate succession.*—The Secretary of the Interior is vested with statutory power to determine heirs in inheritance proceedings affecting restricted allotted lands and other restricted property[282] of an Indian to whom an allotment of land has been made (except Indians of the Five Civilized Tribes and the Osage Nation). The Secretary may issue patents in fee to heirs whom he deems "competent to manage their own affairs"[283] in cases of allottees dying intestate; may sell land in heirship status; or may partition it, if he finds that partitioning would be for the benefit of the heirs, and sell the portions of the incompetent heirs.[284]

The Secretary is, in general, not bound by decree or decision of any court in inheritance proceedings affecting restricted allotted lands.[285]

The determination by the Secretary of the heirs of Indians is "final and conclusive." In the comparatively few instances in which his decision has been attacked the courts have refused to look behind his determination.[286]

In *Red Hawk* v. *Wilbur*[287] the Court of Appeals of the District of Columbia held that under the provisions of the Act of June 25, 1910, the Secretary's exercise of power is not subject to review by the courts in the absence of fraud or a showing of a want of jurisdiction, and that consequently his decision respecting the distribution of allotted lands of an Indian dying before the issuance of a patent in fee was not reviewable by the court.

In ruling that the power of the Secretary to determine the descent of lands extends to lands purchased with Indian trust funds, even though they were unrestricted prior to the purchase, the Solicitor of the Department of the Interior said:[288]

> It is clearly within the power of the Secretary of the Interior to attach conditions to sales of Indian allotted lands because such power is expressly conferred in acts authorizing such sales; that is, they are to be made subject to his approval and on such terms and conditions and under such regulations as he may prescribe. It was held in the case of *United States* v. *Thurston County, Nebraska, et al.* (143 Fed. 287), that the proceeds of sales of allotted lands are held in trust for the same purposes as were the lands; that no change of form of property divests it of the trust; and that the substitute takes the nature of the original and stands charged with the same trust. From this situation arose the practice of inserting in deeds of conveyance covering property purchased for an Indian with trust funds the nonalienation clause referred to, which is merely a continuation over the new property of the trust declared for the old or original property. For sanction of this practice see 13 Ops. A. A. G., 109; *Jackson* v. *Thompson et al.* (80 Pac., 454); and *Beck* v. *Flournoy Live-Stock and Real-Estate Co.* (65 Fed. 30).
>
> It thus being established that lands purchased with trust funds continue under the trust as originally declared and that power exists to insert in deeds covering such lands a condition against alienation and incumbrance, it follows that upon the death of an Indian for whom the property is held in trust his heirs are to be determined by the Department the same as in the case of the original property from the sale of which the purchase funds are derived. Apparently no question is raised as to the authority of the Department to determine the descent of property purchased with trust funds derived from the sale of lands previously held in trust or restricted. The question submitted has reference to lands that were unrestricted prior to purchase. The theory on which the Department and the courts have proceeded in this matter is that property purchased with trust funds becomes impressed with the trust nature of the purchase money. In this view it can make no difference whether the purchased lands are restricted or unrestricted; the authority to determine heirs is coexistent with the continuation of the trust. By the act of June 25, 1910 (36 Stat. 855), Congress conferred exclusive jurisdiction upon the Secretary of the Interior to determine the heirs of deceased Indian allottees, and this power extends not only to property held in trust but also to property on which restricted fee patents have issued, under legislation providing for "determining the heirs of deceased Indian allottees having any right, title, or interest, in any

---

> the determination of competency and the final and essential act of issuing the patent in fee simple. And special force is added to the foregoing since the issuance of a patent in fee simple by the Secretary is not mandatory upon his being satisfied that a trust allottee is competent and capable of managing his own affairs. (P. 34.)

See also the Act of May 8, 1906, 34 Stat. 182; 38 L. D. 427 (1910). For a discussion of incompetency, see Chapter 8, sec. 8.

[279] 48 Stat. 984, 985, 25 U. S. C. 464.

[280] See Chapter 1, sec. 1D(2); Chapter 3, sec. 3B(2); Chapter 12, sec. 1; Chapter 15, sec. 23A.

[281] *United States* v. *Brown*, 8 F. 2d 564 (C. C. A. 8, 1925), cert. den. 270 U. S. 644 (1926); *Sunderland* v. *United States*, 266 U. S. 226 (1924).

[282] On inheritance of real property see Chapter 11, sec. 6. On inheritance of personal property see Chapter 10, sec. 10.

The power to determine the inheritance of allotted lands was inferred from section 5 of the General Allotment Act of February 8, 1887, 24 Stat. 388, 389, which imposed upon the Secretary the duty to convey a fee patent to the heirs of a deceased allottee.

The Act of August 15, 1894, 28 Stat. 286, was construed as conferring power to determine heirs upon the federal courts. See *Hallowell* v. *Commons*, 239 U. S. 506 (1916); see also *McKay* v. *Kalyton*, 204 U. S. 458. 468 (1907). This act was amended by the Act of February 6, 1901, sec. 2, 31 Stat. 760, 25 U. S. C. 346. Sec. 7 of the Act of May 27, 1902, 32 Stat. 245, 275, authorized the Secretary to approve transfer of restricted allotted lands by the heirs of such lands. This statute was construed in *Hellen* v. *Morgan*, 283 Fed. 433 (D. C. E. D. Wash. 1922) as giving the Secretary of the Interior final authority to determine heirs in such cases. See also *Egan* v. *McDonald*, 246 U. S. 227 (1918).

The Act of May 29, 1908, sec. 1, 35 Stat. 444, expressly authorized the Secretary to determine the heirs of restricted lands, except in Oklahoma, Minnesota, and South Dakota. This was amended by the Act of June 25, 1910, 36 Stat. 855, amended Act of March 3, 1928, 45 Stat. 161; Act of April 30, 1934, 48 Stat. 647, 25 U. S. C. 372, interpreted in 40 L. D. 120 (1910) (upheld as constitutional in *Hallowell* v. *Commons*, 239 U. S. 506 (1916)).

The Act of August 1, 1914, sec. 1, 38 Stat. 582, 586, 25 U. S. C. 374, empowered the Secretary to compel the attendance of witnesses in probate hearings. The Probate Regulations are expressly made inapplicable to tribes organized under the Wheeler-Howard Act insofar as they conflict with tribal constitutions and charters. 25 C. F. R. 81.62.

[283] Act of June 25, 1910, 36 Stat. 855, amended Act of March 3, 1928, 45 Stat. 161; Act of April 30, 1934, 48 Stat. 647, 25 U. S. C. 372, interpreted in 40 L. D. 120 (1910).

[284] The power to effect a partition or sale of inherited Indian land is conferred on the Secretary by the Act of June 25, 1910, sec. 1, 36 Stat. 855, as amended Act of March 3, 1928, 45 Stat. 161; and Act of April 30, 1934, 48 Stat. 647, 25 U. S. C. 372; and Act of May 18, 1916, sec. 1, 39 Stat. 123, 127, 25 U. S. C. 378. The fact that one or more of the heirs is white does not affect the Secretary's power to sell or partition their land for all the heirs. *Reed* v. *Clinton*, 23 Okla. 610, 101 Pac. 1055 (1909).

[285] 42 L. D. 493 (1913).

[286] *First Moon* v. *White Tail*, 270 U. S. 243 (1926); *cf. Nimrod* v. *Jandron*, 24 F. 2d 613 (App. D. C. 1928).

[287] 39 F. 2d 293 (App. D. C. 1930).

Other decisions of the Secretary have also been held outside of the scope of judicial review, such as his determination of whether an Indian and his land were under federal control. *Lane* v. *United States ex rel Mickadiet and Tiebault*, 241 U. S. 201 (1916).

[288] 49 L. D. 414 (1923).

trust or restricted allotment, under regulations prescribed by the Secretary of the Interior." (*United States* v. *Bowling et al.*, 256 U. S. 484.) (Pp. 415–416.)

(2) *Wills.*—Prior to 1910 an Indian allottee could not by will devise his restricted land.

Section 2 of the Act of June 25, 1910,[369] as amended by the Act of February 14, 1913,[370] provides for the bequest of restricted funds by will, in accordance with rules prescribed by the Secretary of the Interior, and the devise of allotments "prior to the expiration of the trust period and before the issue of a fee simple patent;" but in order to be valid, the will must be approved by the Secretary either before or after the testator's death.[371]

If, for some reason, the will should not be approved by the Secretary, the property descends to those who are found by him to be heirs under the laws of the state where it is located.[372] Death of the testator and approval of the will does not release the property from the trust. The Secretary may pay the moneys to the legatees either in whole or in part from time to time as he may deem advisable, or use it for their benefit.[373]

The decision in *Blanset* v. *Cardin* [374] holds that if the will is approved by the Secretary of the Interior and such approval remains uncancelled by him, the state law of descent and distribution does not apply and the state law cannot control as to the portions the will conveys or as to the objects of the testator's bounty.

D. ISSUANCE OF RIGHTS-OF-WAY [375]

Many statutes have granted the Secretary of the Interior various duties and powers in regard to rights-of-way through Indian lands. The Act of March 3, 1901,[376] authorized the Secretary to grant permission to the proper state or local authority for the establishment of public highways through any Indian reservation or through restricted Indian lands which had been allotted in severalty to any individual Indian under any law or treaty. The Act of March 2, 1899,[377] authorized the Secretary to grant rights-of-way for railway, telegraph, and telephone lines, and town-site stations.[378] It was required that the Secretary approve the surveys and maps of the line of route of the railroad and that compensation be made to each occupant or allottee for all property taken or damage done to his land, claim, or improvement, by reason of the construction of such railroad.[379] In the absence of amicable settlement with any such occupant or allottee, the Secretary was empowered to appoint three disinterested referees to determine the compensation.[380] An aggrieved party was permitted judicial review.[381] The Secretary was also authorized to grant a right-of-way in the nature of an easement for the construction of telephone and telegraph lines;[382] to acquire lands for reservoirs or material for railroads [383] and rights-of-way for pipe lines.[384]

The necessity for the consent of the Secretary has occasionally been a major point in judicial decisions. In such a case the Circuit Court of Appeals said: [385]

> The third question can be briefly disposed of. The United States, the holder of the title to the lands in question, was not made a party to the proceedings in the state court, and consequently is not bound by those proceedings had behind its back. *Appalachian Electric Power Co.* v. *Smith* (C. C. A. 4th) 67 F. (2d) 451, 456; *Wood* v. *Phillips* (C. C. A. 4th) 50 F. (2d) 714, 717. If a roadway over the Indian lands was desired, application should have been made to the Secretary of the Interior pursuant to provision of the Act of March 3, 1901, § 4, 31 Stat. 1058, 1084 (25 U. S. C. A. § 311). A right of way could no more be acquired over these lands by proceedings against the Indians than title to lands embraced in a government forest could be tried by suit against the forester, nor than post office property could be condemned for purposes of a street by proceedings against the postmaster. In *Rollins* v. *Eastern Band of Cherokee Indians*, 87 N. C. 229, it was held that the courts of the state of North Carolina, without the consent of Congress, were without jurisdiction to entertain suit on contract against these Indians. A fortiori, the state courts, without such consent, have no jurisdiction of proceedings affecting land held by the United States in trust for the Indians. (Pp. 314, 315.)

E. LEASING

Approval of leases of restricted Indian lands is an important administrative function.[386] The Supreme Court said in *Miller* v. *McClain*: [387]

> By a course of legislation beginning in 1891 and extending to 1900, authority was conferred upon the Secretary of the Interior to sanction, when enumerated and exceptional conditions existed, leases of land allotted under the Act of 1887, and the power was given to the Secretary to adopt rules and regulations governing the exercise of the right

[369] 36 Stat. 855, interpreted in 40 L. D. 120 (1911), 40 L. D. 212 (1911), and 48 L. D. 455 (1922).

[370] 37 Stat. 678.

[371] To facilitate the adjudication of heirship, Indians over the age of 21 may dispose of restricted property by will, but the approval of the Secretary of the will is necessary before it is regarded as a valid testamentary act. The final approval of the will is not given until after the death of the decedent. 25 C. F. R. 81.54, 81.55. Prior to the death of the maker the Secretary only passes on the form of the will. Before and after the death of the testator the authority of the Secretary of the Interior is limited to the approval or disapproval of an Indian will, and he lacks authority to change its provisions. Act of June 25, 1910, 36 Stat. 855, amended Act of February 14, 1913, 37 Stat. 678. On Secretary's power to grant a rehearing, see *Nimrod* v. *Jandron*, 24 F. 2d 613 (App. D. C. 1928).

[372] Act of June 25, 1910, as amended by Act of February 14, 1913, 37 Stat. 678.

[373] See *Blanset* v. *Cardin*, 256 U. S. 319 (1921).

[374] *Ibid.*

[375] On regulations relating to rights-of-way over Indian lands, see 25 C. F. R., pt. 256. On regulations relating to the construction and maintenance of roads on Indian lands, see 25 C. F. R., pt. 261. On regulations relating to establishment of roadless and wild areas on Indian reservations, see 25 C. F. R., pt. 281.

[376] Sec. 4, 31 Stat. 1058, 1084, 25 U. S. C. 311. For a statute requiring state authorities laying out roads across restricted Indian lands to secure consent of superintendent, see Act of March 4, 1915, 38 Stat. 1188.

[377] Sec. 1, 30 Stat. 990, as amended by Act of February 28, 1902, sec. 23, 32 Stat. 43, 50, Act of June 25, 1910, sec. 16, 36 Stat. 855, 859, 25 U. S. C. 312.

[378] The Secretary had also been given many powers and duties by numerous acts granting rights-of-way through Indian territory to specific railways. See *e. g.*, Act of March 2, 1887, 24 Stat. 446.

[379] Act of March 2, 1899, sec. 3, 30 Stat. 990, 991, as amended by Act of February 28, 1902, sec. 23, 32 Stat. 43, 50, 25 U. S. C. 314. The Secretary lacks power to authorize the construction of a railroad across an Indian reservation prior to the ascertainment (and fixing) and payment of compensation as provided by statute. 19 Op. A. G. 199 (1888).

[380] *Ibid.*

[381] *Ibid.* For the power of the Secretary in the event of the failure of the railroad to complete the road on time, see Act of March 2, 1899, sec. 4, 30 Stat. 990, 991, 25 U. S. C. 315.

[382] Act of March 3, 1901, sec. 3, 31 Stat. 1058, 1083, 25 U. S. C. 319, interpreted in *Swendig* v. *Washington Water Power Co.*, 265 U. S. 322 (1924); *City of Tulsa* v. *Southwestern Bell Telephone Co.*, 75 F. 2d 343 (C. C. A. 10, 1935), cert. den. 295 U. S. 744 (1935).

[383] Act of March 3, 1909, 35 Stat. 781, amended by Act May 6, 1910, 36 Stat. 349, 25 U. S. C. 320.

[384] Act of March 11, 1904, sec. 1, 33 Stat. 65, amended by Act of March 2, 1917, sec. 1, 39 Stat. 969, 25 U. S. C. 321.

[385] *United States* v. *Colvard et al.*, 89 F. 2d 312 (C. C. A. 4, 1937). An extended discussion of administrative consent appears in *United States* v. *Minnesota*, 95 F. 2d 468 (C. C. A. 8, 1938) pp. 471–472. The Supreme Court, in affirming the decision, 305 U. S. 382 (1939), did not consider the question of administrative consent and affirmed the case on other grounds.

[386] The congressional delegation of this power to the Secretary of the Interior has been sustained. See *Bunch* v. *Cole*, 263 U. S. 250 (1923).

[387] 249 U. S. 308 (1919).

(Acts of February 28, 1891, c. 383, 26 Stat. 794, 795; August 15, 1894, c. 290, 28 Stat. 286, 305; June 7, 1897, c. 3, 30 Stat. 62, 85; May 31, 1900, c. 598, 31 Stat. 221, 229). The general scope of the legislation is shown by the following provision of the Act of 1900, which does not materially differ from the prior acts.

"That whenever it shall be made to appear to the Secretary of the Interior that, by reason of age, disability, or inability, any allottee of Indian lands cannot personally and with benefit to himself, occupy or improve his allotment or any part thereof, the same may be leased upon such terms, regulations, and conditions as shall be prescribed by the Secretary for a term not exceeding five years, for farming purposes only."

The regulations for the purpose of carrying out the power given prescribed a general form of lease to be used under the exceptional circumstances which the statute contemplated and subjected its execution and the subjects connected with it to the scrutiny of the Indian Bureau and to the express or implied approval of the Secretary. (See "Amended rules and regulations to be observed in the execution of leases of Indian Allotments," approved by the Secretary of the Interior March 16, 1905.)

The foregoing provisions were enlarged by the Act of June 25, 1910, c. 431, 36 Stat. 855, 856, as follows:

"That any Indian allotment held under a trust patent may be leased by the allottee for a period not to exceed five years, subject to and in conformity with such rules and regulations as the Secretary of the Interior may prescribe, and the proceeds of any such lease shall be paid to the allottee or his heirs, or expended for his or their benefit, in the discretion of the Secretary of the Interior."

And the regulations of the Secretary which were adopted under this grant of power in express terms modified the previous regulations on the subject "so far as to permit Indian allottees of land held under a trust patent, or the heirs of such allottees who may be deemed by the superintendent in charge of any competency commission to have the requisite knowledge, experience, and business capacity to negotiate lease contracts, to make their own contracts for leasing their lands." * * * (Pp. 310–311.)

The right of an administrative official to withhold his consent to a contract includes, it has been held, the right to impose conditions on his approval.[288]

In discussing the approval of leases, the Supreme Court said:[289]

> The statute is plain in its provisions—that no lease, of the character here in question, can be valid without the approval of the Secretary. Such approval rests in the exercise of his discretion; unquestionably this authority was given to him for the protection of Indians against their own improvidence and the designs of those who would obtain their property for inadequate compensation. It is also true that the law does not vest arbitrary authority in the Secretary of the Interior. But it does give him power to consider the advantages and disadvantages of the lease presented for his action, and to grant or withhold approval as his judgment may dictate.
>
> * * * * *
>
> We find nothing in this record to indicate that the Secretary of the Interior has exceeded the authority which the law vests in him. The fact that he has given reasons in the discussion of the case, which might not in all respects meet with approval, does not deprive him of authority to exercise the discretionary power with which by statute he is invested. *United States ex rel. West* v. *Hitchcock*, 205 U. S. 80, 85, 86.

Although powers expressly entrusted to the Secretary of the Interior to approve the alienation of restricted property cannot generally be transferred or delegated to any other governmental agency,[290] certain leasing statutes provide that the power of approval may be delegated by the Secretary to superintendents or other officials in the Indian Service,[291] and other statutes permit approval by such officials as may be designated in regulations issued by the Secretary of the Interior.[292]

In general, the consent of the Indian allottees to the leasing of land is necessary.[293] As the Assistant Secretary has said:[294]

> * * * While the powers of the Secretary of the Interior are broad, under the principle of guardianship referred to in the letter, there is no statutory provision which enables the Department to execute leases for the Indian owner of an allotment without his consent. Such consent is required, on the contrary, by statute and by the regulations for the leasing of Indian allotments. (Section 395, title 25 U. S. C.; section 3, Regulations Governing the Leasing of Indian Allotments for Farming, Grazing, and Business Purposes.) This is not a case where the heirs have not been determined, and leasing by the Superintendent is permitted by the regulations due to uncertainty in the ownership of the land, nor is it a case where a minority of the heirs refuses to lease inherited land and the Government is authorized to intervene in order that the land may be of some economic value to the Indians (section 7, Leasing Regulations). * * *

---

[288] *Sunderland* v. *United States*, 266 U. S. 226 (1924); *United States* v. *Brown*, 8 F. 2d 564 (C. C. A. 8, 1925), cert. den. 270 U. S. 644 (1926); *United States* v. *Pumphrey*, 11 App. D. C. 44 (1897); *La Motte* v. *United States*, 254 U. S. 570 (1921).

The consent of the Indian owner is generally required by statute and regulations for the leasing of Indian allotments. 25 U. S. C. 395; 25 C. F. R., subchapter Q. But see Memo. Asst. Sec'y. I. D., August 23, 1938.

[289] *Anicker* v. *Gunsburg*, 246 U. S. 110, 119, 120 (1918).

[290] Op. Sol. I. D., M. 25258, June 26, 1929. Under the Act of April 21, 1904, 33 Stat. 189, 204, a deed executed by an Indian to sell lands which had been purchased for her with restricted funds was ineffectual, and the grantees acquired no estate in the land when the deed was approved only by an assistant superintendent and not by the Secretary. *United States* v. *Watashe*, 102 F. 2d 428 (C. C. A. 10, 1939). On limits upon alienation of property, see Chapters 9, 10, and 11.

[291] Act of May 11, 1938, sec. 5, 52 Stat. 347, 348, 25 U. S. C. 396e. The Circuit Court of Appeals regarded this provision as indicative of congressional belief that his authorization was necessary for the delegation of this authority *United States* v. *Watashe*, 102 F. 2d 428, 431 (C. C. A. 10, 1939).

R. S. § 439 provides:

> The Assistant Secretary of the Interior shall perform such duties in the Department of the Interior as shall be prescribed by the Secretary, or may be required by law.

This provision was declared constitutional in *Robertson* v. *United States*, 285 Fed. 911, 915 (App. D. C. 1922).

The Circuit Court of Appeals, in *Turner* v. *Seep*, 167 Fed. 646 (C. C. E. D. Okla. 1909), in holding that the Secretary may delegate to the Assistant Secretary authority to approve leases of Indian lands and assignments thereof said:

> * * * so long as the powers so delegated to the Assistant Secretary of the Interior by his superior remain unrevoked, the authority of the Assistant Secretary is co-ordinate and concurrent with that of the Secretary. * * * (P. 650.)

In referring to this function of the Assistant Secretary of the Interior, the Supreme Court said, in *Wilbur* v. *United States ex rel. Kadrie*, 281 U. S. 206 (1930):

> The powers and duties of such an office are impersonal and unaffected by a change in the person holding it. (P. 217.)

[292] See *e. g.*, Act of March 3, 1921, sec. 1, 41 Stat. 1225, 1232, 25 U. S. C. 393 (leasing of restricted allotments).

[293] In holding that the superintendent of an agency cannot compel a nonconsenting heir to sign leases, the Solicitor of the Department of the Interior said:

> The letter purports to authorize the Superintendent to sign the name of nonconsenting heirs owning less than a majority in interest of the estate, in two cases: (1) Where the nonconsenting heirs "by reason of their absence from the reservation, or unknown whereabouts, cannot be reached after a reasonable effort has been made"; and (2) where the nonconsenting heirs "refuse to sign without giving good and sufficient reason for refusing."
>
> In the first mentioned case, legal authority for action by the Superintendent can probably be derived from a relation of agency between the absent heir and the Superintendent. No objection is raised to this portion of the letter. In the second case, however, such special legal justification is lacking, and full weight must therefore be given to the governing leasing statute which provides that restricted allotments "may be leased for farming and grazing purposes by the allottee or his heirs, subject only to the approval of the Superintendent * * *." (Act of March 3, 1929, 41 Stat. 1232, 25 U. S. C., sec. 393.) Unless special circumstances exist to provide a legal justification for signature by the Superintendent on behalf of protesting heirs it appears that the statute prohibits such action on his part. (Memo. Sol. I. D., August 10, 1936.)

[294] Memo of Asst. Sec'y. I. D., August 23, 1938.

In some cases Congress has laid down a policy requiring the consent of Indians to modifications of contracts affecting them.[295]

Some statutes [296] empower the Secretary to renew leases "upon such reasonable terms and conditions" as he may prescribe. In construing a provision in such a statute, the Solicitor of the Department of the Interior said: [297]

> * * * Such power obviously cannot be taken away by any act of the lessee through contract or otherwise. The only limitation to which the power is subject is that the conditions of renewal must be reasonable. The authority to determine the reasonableness of the conditions is also committed to the Secretary and in its exercise he is necessarily invested with broad discretion. That this power and authority extend to the imposition as a condition for renewal, a requirement that the operating royalty shall not exceed a figure to be determined by the Secretary to be the maximum economic royalty, I have little doubt.

[295] Timber contracts, Act of March 4, 1933, 47 Stat. 1568; Op. Sol. I. D., M. 27499, August 8, 1933.

[296] See, for example, Act of August 21, 1916, 39 Stat. 519 (Shoshone Indian Reservation).

[297] Memo. Sol. I. D., June 3, 1938.

SECTION 12. ADMINISTRATIVE POWER—INDIVIDUAL FUNDS

Statutes restricting the Indian in the use of his funds may provide for the investment of his funds under the direction of the Secretary of the Interior.[298] The statute may specify certain investments or may be more general, giving the official selective powers. In any case, he is bound strictly by the authority granted in the statute.

If the Secretary of the Interior is empowered to handle the Indian's money, he cannot create trusts transferring such property from his authority to a private agency without the specific authority of Congress.[299]

On this point Attorney General Mitchell ruled: [300]

> * * * while it has been the purpose of Congress to place the supervising control over Indian funds in the Secretary of the Interior, his control is not unlimited, but is based upon directions contained in the various statutes of Congress. I find no provision or implication in any statute to the effect that the Secretary of the Interior may delegate control of these Indian funds, while held under restrictions, to outside agencies.
>
> I regard the control and supervision over Indian funds so committed to the Secretary of the Interior and the Department of the Interior as an imposition of a specific duty by Congress, and am of the opinion that it cannot lawfully be transferred by the Secretary of the Interior to agencies outside of his Department. The suggested creation of a trust, in which the custody and control of the trust funds would be in a private trustee, would be an abdication on the part of the Secretary of the control of restricted Indian funds with which Congress has vested him. I believe that this would be improper in the absence of specific congressional authority to that end, and I do not find that such authority has been given by Congress by existing statutes. (P. 100.)

The Secretary is not authorized to make donations or gifts of Indian property,[301] nor to purchase single premium annuity policies, unless for assenting adult Indians capable of understanding the nature of the investment.[302]

[298] See Chapter 10.

[299] Memo. Sol. I. D., September 19, 1931. See also Op. Sol. I. D., M.25258, June 26, 1929; 55 I. D. 500 (1936). The Act of January 27, 1933, 47 Stat. 777, placed under the jurisdiction of the Secretary of the Interior the funds and securities of Indians of the Five Civilized Tribes of one-half or more Indian blood until April 26, 1956. Sec. 2 authorizes the Secretary to permit,

> * * * in his discretion and subject to his approval, any Indian of the Five Civilized Tribes, over the age of twenty-one years, having restricted funds or other property subject to the supervision of the Secretary of the Interior, to create and establish, out of the restricted funds or other property, trusts for the benefits of such Indian, his heirs, or other beneficiaries designated by him, such trusts to be created by contracts or agreements by and between the Indian and incorporated trust companies or such banks as may be authorized by law to act as fiduciaries or trustees: * * *

For a discussion of this Act see Chapter 23, sec. 10.

[300] 36 Op. A. G. 98 (1929). If the Secretary, in violation of a statute, invests funds due to a certain class of Indians, and a loss occurs, Congress and not the Secretary may provide for a reimbursement. 16 Op. A. G. 31 (1878).

[301] Act of June 25, 1910, 36 Stat. 855. *Mott* v. *United States*, 283 U. S. 747, 751–752 (1931).

[302] 36 Op. A. G. 98 (1929).

The Court of Appeals after quoting with approval from the Sunderland [303] case said: [304]

> If Congress, in the exercise of its guardianship, can go to the extent approved in the Sunderland Case, we find no difficulty in applying the act here in question to the disposition of the funds in the possession of the Secretary. They came into his possession in the lawful course of his supervisory power over the lands in question, and were still in his possession at the time the act of Congress was passed. Assuming, therefore, without deciding, that technically the jurisdiction over this fund passed to the Oklahoma court with the removal of the restrictions upon the land, the court had not acquired such jurisdiction as to place the fund beyond the control and power of Congress to further restrict it in the hands of the Secretary. (P. 982.)

The authority of the Interior Deartment over individual Indian moneys is, generally a derivative authority. By virtue of the control which the Department exercises over the alienation of Indian lands and interests therein, conditions have been imposed upon the manner in which proceeds derived from such lands are to be handled. In some cases the statutes providing for the leasing or alienation of individual lands specify that the proceeds "shall be paid to the allottee or disposed of for his benefit under regulations to be prescribed by the Secretary of the Interior." [305] Other statutes do not refer specifically to the proceeds of transactions subject to the approval of the Interior Department, but contain broad language authorizing regulations covering the transaction which is construed to permit a comprehensive supervision of the proceeds derived therefrom.[306]

Ordinarily the method of disbursement of restricted individual Indian money is governed by the regulations issued by the Department of the Interior.[307] In a few instances Congress prescribes the method and permissible purposes of such disbursement.[308] For example, the Act of March 3, 1933,[309] regulating the disbursement of restricted individual money of members of the Ute Indians of Utah was designed to direct the expenditures of the Indian moneys so as to assure permanent improvements or other expenditures which will enable the Indians to become self-supporting. It also provides:

> That in cases of the aged, infirm, decrepit, or incapacitated members their shares may be used for their proper maintenance and support in the discretion of the Secretary of the Interior.[310]

[303] *Sunderland* v. *United States*, 266 U. S. 226 (1924).

[304] *King* v. *Ickes*, 64 F. 2d 979 (App. D. C. 1933).

[305] Act of June 25, 1910, sec. 8, 36 Stat. 855, 857, 25 U. S. C. 407 (sale of timber on allotments). And see sec. 4, 36 Stat. 855, 856, 25 U. S. C. 403 (leases of trust allotments).

[306] See, for example, Act of March 3, 1909, 35 Stat. 781, 783, 25 U. S. C. 396 (mining leases)

[307] See Chapter 10, sec. 8.

[308] Memo. Sol. I. D., September 12, 1934.

[309] 47 Stat. 1488.

[310] *Ibid.*, p. 1489.

SECTION 13. ADMINISTRATIVE POWER—MEMBERSHIP

A. AUTHORITY OVER ENROLLMENT

At various times Congress has delegated to the Department of the Interior much of its sweeping power over the determination of tribal membership.[211] During the periods when the federal policy was designed to break up the tribal organization, this power was one of the most important administrative powers, since the sharing in tribal property usually depended upon being placed upon a roll prepared by the Department or subject to its approval. At present, under the policy of encouraging tribal organization, membership problems are not usually as crucial as formerly.[212] However, they may be important for other purposes, such as determining the right to vote in a tribal election. The most important limitation on the Secretary's power[213] when the tribe is still in existence is the principle that in the absence of express congressional legislation to the contrary an Indian tribe has complete authority to determine all questions of its own membership.[214]

The power of the Secretary to determine tribal membership[215] for the purpose of segregating the tribal funds was granted by section 163 of title 25 of the United States Code,[216] which reads as follows:

> The Secretary of the Interior is authorized, wherever in his discretion such action would be for the best interest of the Indians, to cause a final roll to be made of the membership of any Indian tribe; such rolls shall contain the ages and quantum of Indian blood, and when approved by the said Secretary are declared to constitute the legal membership of the respective tribes for the purpose of segregating the tribal funds * * *, and shall be conclusive both as to ages and quantum of Indian blood: *Provided*, That the foregoing shall not apply to the Five Civilized Tribes or to the Osage Tribe of Indians, or to the Chippewa Indians of Minnesota, or the Menominee Indians of Wisconsin.

Treaties often provide for the payment of money to an Indian of a tribe whose membership is ascertained by an administrative authority which shall examine and determine questions of fact concerning the identity of the members.[217] Statutes also impose such duty upon the Secretary[218] or a *quasi* judicial tribunal,[219] whose determinations are subject to the approval of the Secretary of the Interior. Such enrollments are presumptively correct,[220] and unless impeached by very clear evidence of fraud, mistake, or arbitrary action they are conclusive upon the courts.[221]

B. REMEDIES

Where the determination of membership in a tribe is left to the Secretary of the Interior, his decision is final and cannot be controlled by mandamus unless his act is arbitrary and in excess of the authority conferred upon him by Congress.[222]

It has also been held that the duty imposed upon him to restore names to the tribal roll is not a mere ministerial act, but calls for the determination of issues of fact and interpretations of law, and that his decisions are not ordinarily subject to review or controlled by mandamus, even though he is wrong or may change his mind within the period allowed.[223]

For example, the Secretary of the Interior was empowered by section 2 of the Act of April 26, 1906,[224] to complete the rolls of the Creek Nation, and his jurisdiction to approve the enrollment ceased on the last day set by the statute. In *United States ex rel. Johnson* v. *Payne*,[225] the Secretary had approved the decision of the Commissioner of the Five Civilized Tribes and then reversed it and ordered the name of the petitioner stricken from the rolls. The Supreme Court said:

> * * * While the case was before him he was free to change his mind, and he might do so none the less that he had stated an opinion in favor of one side or the other. He did not lose his power to do the conclusive act, ordering and approving an enrollment, *Garfield* v. *Goldsby*, 211 U. S. 249, until the act was done. *New Orleans* v. *Paine*, 147 U. S. 261, 266. *Kirk* v. *Olson*, 245 U. S. 225, 228. The petitioners' names never were on the rolls. The Secretary was the final judge whether they should be, and they cannot be ordered to be put on now, upon a suggestion that

---

[211] See Chapter 10, sec. 4.

[212] See Chapter 10, sec. 4.

[213] The limitations on administrative power over membership are indicated by an opinion of the Circuit Court of Appeals in *Ex parte Pero*, 99 F. 2d 28 (C. C. A. 7, 1938):

> * * * Only Indians are entitled to be enrolled for the purpose of receiving allotment and the fact of enrollment would be evidence that the enrollee is an Indian. But the refusal of the Department of Interior to enroll a certain Indian as a member of a certain tribe is not necessarily an administrative determination that the person is not an Indian. Moore's mother failed to be enrolled as a St. Croix Indian because she was too young, not because she was not an Indian. (Pp. 31–32.)

[214] See Chapter 7, sec. 4. In matters affecting the distribution of tribal funds and other property under the supervisory authority of the Secretary, tribal action on membership is subject to the supervisory authority of the Secretary. See Chapter 7, sec. 4; Sol. Memo. October 12, 1937; Sol. Memo. March 24, 1936. According to administrative practice, in doubtful cases the tribal action is regarded as controlling.

The Circuit Court of Appeals in *Vezina* v. *United States*, 245 Fed. 411, 415 (C. C. A. 8, 1917), said

> The law did not call for the consent of the Indians to the making of the list for allotment. That power was solely vested in the commissioners, but they wisely in the main decided to take the advice of an Indian council, * * *.

[215] Citizenship in a tribe and tribal membership are sometimes used synonymously. *Seminole Nation* v. *United States*, 78 C. Cls. 455 (1933).

The agent has the duty of preparing certain statistics concerning Indians under his charge. Sec. 4 of the Act of March 3, 1875, 18 Stat. 420, 449, 25 U. S. C. 133, provides:

> That hereafter, for the purpose of properly distributing the supplies appropriated for the Indian service, it is hereby made the duty of each agent in charge of Indians and having supplies to distribute, to make out, at the commencement of each fiscal year, rolls of the Indians entitled to supplies at the agency, with the names of the Indians and of the heads of families or lodges, with the number in each family or lodge, and to give out supplies to the heads of families, and not to the heads of tribes or bands, and not to give out supplies for a greater length of time than one week in advance.

Sec. 9 of the Act of July 4, 1884, 23 Stat. 76, 98, 25 U. S. C. 298, provides that the Indian agent shall submit in his annual report a census of the Indians at his agency or upon the reservation under his charge, and the number of school children between the ages of 6 and 16, the number of school houses at his agency, and other data concerning the education of the Indians.

[216] Act of June 30, 1919, sec. 1, 41 Stat. 3, 9.

[217] 5 Op. A. G. 320 (1851).

[218] Act of June 4, 1920, 41 Stat. 751 (Crow). See *Cully* v. *Mitchell*, 37 F. 2d 493 (C. C. A. 10, 1930); *United States* v. *Wildcat*, 244 U. S. 111 (1917).

[219] *United States* v. *Wildcat*, 244 U. S. 111 (1917).

[220] Unless Congress confers authority upon the Secretary to inquire into the validity of the enrollment of a person whose name appears on the final rolls, the rolls must be regarded as determinative of legal membership in the tribe at the time the rolls were completed and closed. See Op. Sol. I. D., M.27759, January 22, 1935.

[221] *United States ex rel. West* v. *Hitchcock*, 205 U. S. 80 (1907). The Secretary has been held not to have the power to strike names from the roll without giving notice and an opportunity to be heard. *Garfield* v. *United States ex rel. Goldsby*, 211 U. S. 249 (1908). It has been held that he has power, after such notice and hearing, to strike from the rolls names which have been placed thereon through fraud or mistake. *Lowe* v. *Fisher*, 223 U. S. 95 (1912).

Determinations of the Dawes Commission were subject to attack for extrinsic fraud or mistake. *Tiger* v. *Twin State Oil Co.*, 48 F. 2d 509 (C. C. A. 10, 1931).

[222] *Garfield* v. *United States ex rel. Goldsby*, 211 U. S. 249 (1908). See *United States ex rel. West* v. *Hitchcock*, 205 U. S. 80 (1907).

[223] *Stookey* v. *Wilbur*, 58 F. 2d 522 (App. D. C., 1932).

[224] 34 Stat. 137.

[225] 253 U. S. 209 (1920).

the Secretary made a mistake or that he came very near to giving the petitioners the rights they claim. (P. 211).

In the absence of fraud, or arbitrary action, the courts will not issue a mandamus directed against the Secretary of the Interior if the question involves the exercise of judgment and discretion. The Supreme Court, in the case of *Wilbur* v. *United States ex rel. Kadrie*,[226] decided that the duty of determining to whom payments shall be made of certain interest annuities accruing to the Chippewa Indians rested with the Secretary of the Interior and not with the courts.

Where the Secretary has nothing but a ministerial duty to perform, the court in a proper case will award a writ of mandamus.[227]

---

[226] 281 U. S. 206 (1930). Mr. Justice Van Devanter, speaking for the Supreme Court, said:

> If at the time of the decision in 1927 the Secretary of the Interior was without power to reconsider and revoke the decision of 1919, it well may be that the relators would be entitled to the relief by mandamus which they seek.[5] But there was no such want of power. The decision in 1919 was, not a judgment pronounced in a judicial proceeding, but a ruling made by an executive officer in the exertion of administrative authority. That authority was neither exhausted nor terminated by its exertion on that occasion, but was in its nature continuing. Under it the Secretary who made the decision could reconsider the matter and revoke the decision if found wrong; and so of his successor. The latter was charged, no less than the former had been, with the duty of supervising the payment of the interest annuities and of causing them to be distributed among those entitled to them and no others; and if he found that individuals not so entitled were sharing in the annuities by reason of a mistaken or erroneous ruling of the former his authority to revoke that ruling and stop further payments under it was the same as if it had been his own act.[6] The powers and duties of such an office are impersonal and unaffected by a change in the person holding it. (Pp. 216–217.)
>
> * * * * *
>
> Mandamus is employed to compel the performance, when refused, of a ministerial duty, this being its chief use. It also is employed to compel action, when refused, in matters involving judgment and discretion, but not to direct the exercise of judgment or discretion in a particular way nor to direct the retraction or reversal of action already taken in the exercise of either.[7]
>
> The duties of executive officers, such as the Secretary of the Interior, usually are connected with the administration of statutes which must be read and in a sense construed to ascertain what is required. But it does not follow that these administrative duties all involve judgment or discretion of the character intended by the rule just stated. Where the duty in a particular situation is so plainly prescribed as to be free from doubt and equivalent to a positive command it is regarded as being so far ministerial that its performance may be compelled by mandamus, unless there be provision or implication to the contrary.[8] But where the duty is not thus plainly prescribed but depends upon a statute or statutes the construction or application of which is not free from doubt, it is regarded as involving the character of judgment or discretion which cannot be controlled by mandamus.[9] (Pp. 218–219.)
>
> * * * * *
>
> The questions mooted before the Secretary and decided by him were whether the fund is a tribal fund, whether the tribe is still existing and whether the distribution of the annuities is to be confined to members of the tribe, with exceptions not including the relators. These are all questions of law the solution of which requires a construction of the act of 1889 and other related acts. A reading of these acts shows that they fall short of plainly requiring that any of the questions be answered in the negative and that in some aspects they give color to the affirmative answers of the Secretary. That the construction of the acts insofar as they have a bearing on the first and third questions is sufficiently uncertain to involve the exercise of judgment and discretion is rather plain. The second question is more easily answered, for not only does the act of 1889 show very plainly that the purpose was to accomplish a gradual rather than an immediate transition from the tribal relation and dependent wardship to full emancipation and individual responsibility, but Congress in many later acts—some near the time of the decision in question—has recognized the continued existence of the tribe.[10] This recognition was respected by the Secretary and is not open to question here.[11] With the tribe still existing the criticism by counsel for the relators of the Secretary's decision in other particulars loses much of its force. (Pp. 221–222.)

[5] *United States* v. *Schurz*, 102 U. S. 378, 402–403; *Noble* v. *Union River Logging R. R.*, 147 U. S. 167, 171; *Garfield* v. *Goldsby*, 211 U. S. 249, 261 262.

[6] *West* v. *Standard Oil Co.*, 278 U. S. 200, 210; *Beley* v. *Naphtaly*, 169 U. S. 353, 364; *Knight* v. *U. S. Sand Association*, 142 U. S. 161, 181–182; *New Orleans* v. *Paine*, 147 U. S. 261, 266; *Greenameyer* v. *Coate*, 212 U. S. 434, 442; *Parcher* v. *Gillen*, 26 L. D. 34, 43; *Aspen Consolidated Mining Co.* v. *Williams*, 27 L. D. 1, 10–11. And see *Pearsons* v. *Williams*, 202 U. S. 281, 284–285.

[7] *Commissioner of Patents* v. *Whiteley*, 4 Wall. 522, 534; *United States ex rel.* v. *Black*, 128 U. S. 40, 48; *Riverside Oil Co.* v. *Hitchcock*, 190 U. S. 316, 324–325; *Louisiana* v. *McAdoo*, 234 U. S. 627, 633; *Interstate Commerce Commission* v. *Waste Merchant Ass'n*, 260 U. S. 32, 34.

[8] *Roberts* v. *United States*, 176 U. S. 221, 231; *Lane* v. *Hoglund*, 244 U. S. 174, 181; *Work* v. *McAlester-Edwards Co.*, 262 U. S. 200, 208; *Work* v. *Lynn*, 266 U. S. 161, 168, *et seq.*, *Wilbur* v. *Krushnic*, 280 U. S. 306.

[9] *Riverside Oil Co.* v. *Hitchcock*, 190 U. S. 316, 324–325; *Ness* v. *Fisher*, 223 U. S. 683, 691; *Knight* v. *Lane*, 228 U. S. 6, 13; *Lane* v. *Mickadiet*, 241 U. S 201, 208, 209; *Alaska Smokeless Coal Co.* v. *Lane*, 250 U. S. 549, 555; *Hull* v. *Payne*, 254 U. S. 343, 347; *Work* v. *Rives*, 267 U. S. 175, 183–184. And see *United States ex rel.* v. *Hitchcock*, 205 U. S. 80, 86.

[10] Acts of August 1, 1914, c. 222, 38 Stat. 592; May 18, 1916, c. 125, 39 Stat. 135; March 2, 1917, c. 146, 39 Stat. 979; May 25, 1918, c. 86, 40 Stat. 572; June 30, 1919, c. 4, 41 Stat. 14; February 14, 1920, c. 75, 41 Stat. 419; November 19, 1921, c. 135, 42 Stat. 221; January 30, 1925, c. 114, 43 Stat. 798; February 19, 1926, c. 22, 44 Stat., P. 2, 7; March 4, 1929, c. 705, 45 Stat. 1584.

[11] *United States* v. *Holliday*, 3 Wall. 407, 419; *United States* v. *Rickert*, 188 U. S. 432, 445; *Tiger* v. *Western Investment Co.*, 221 U. S. 286, 315.

The same principle has been applied to many discretionary acts of the Commissioner of Indian Affairs, 24 L. D. 323 (1897). See also *Lane* v. *Morrison*, 246 U. S. 214 (1918); *Quick Bear* v. *Leupp*, 210 U. S. 50 (1908).

Generally a suit will fail if a subordinate officer and not the Secretary of Interior is made defendant. *Moore* v. *Anderson*, 68 F. 2d 191 (C. C. A. 9, 1933). Hence a suit to compel the superintendent of an agency to supplement the tribal rool will be dismissed because the Secretary is a necessary party. *Webster* v. *Fall*, 266 U. S. 507 (1925).

[227] *Garfield* v. *United States ex rel. Goldsby*, 211 U. S. 249 (1908).

CHAPTER 6

THE SCOPE OF STATE POWER OVER INDIAN AFFAIRS

TABLE OF CONTENTS

SECTION 1. INTRODUCTION

That state laws[1] have no force within the territory of an Indian tribe in matters affecting Indians is a general proposition that has not been successfully challenged, at least in the United States Supreme Court, since that Court decided, in *Worcester* v. *Georgia*,[2] that the State of Georgia had no right to imprison a white man residing on an Indian reservation, with the consent of tribal and federal authorities, who refused to conform to state laws governing Indian affairs. In that case the court declared, *per* Marshall, *C. J.:*

> The Cherokee nation, then, is a distinct community, occupying its own territory, with boundaries accurately described, in which the laws of Georgia can have no force, and which the citizens of Georgia have no right to enter, but with the assent of the Cherokees themselves, or in conformity with treaties, and with the acts of congress. (P. 560.)

The State of Georgia never did carry out the mandate of the Supreme Court in this case,[3] and many other state courts and state legislatures since the decision in this case have likewise refused to acknowledge the implications of the decision. Nevertheless, when critical cases have been presented to the United States' Supreme Court, the principles laid down in *Worcester* v. *Georgia* have been repeatedly reaffirmed.[4]

The reasons judicially advanced for this incapacity of the states to legislate on Indian affairs have been variously formulated in different cases, although the actual decisions of the Supreme Court have followed a consistent pattern. One of the most persuasive considerations as to the lack of state power is the inclusion in enabling acts and state constitutions of express disclaimers of state jurisdiction over Indian lands.[5] One of the most famous statements explanatory of the limitations upon state power in this field is the statement in *United States* v. *Kagama*,[6] a case which upheld the constitutionality of congressional legislation on offenses between Indians committed on an Indian reservation:

> It seems to us that this is within the competency of Congress. These Indian tribes *are* the wards of the nation. They are communities *dependent* on the United States. Dependent largely for their daily food. Dependent for their political rights. They owe no allegiance to the States, and receive from them no protection. Because of the local ill feeling, the people of the States where they are found are often their deadliest enemies. From their very weakness and helplessness, so largely due to the course of dealing of the Federal Government with them,[7] and the treaties in which it has been promised, there arises the duty of protection, and with it the power. This has always been recognized by the Executive and by Congress, and by this court, whenever the question has arisen.
>
> * * * * *

[1] Specific bodies of state law are dealt with in other chapters of this work. Thus, state laws involving questions of discrimination against Indians, in the matter of franchise or in other respects, are dealt with in Chapter 8. State laws of inheritance are considered in Chapters 10 and 11. State laws on taxation are analyzed in Chapter 13. Those state laws which deal with Indian hunting and fishing rights are treated in Chapter 14, sec. 7. Chapter 15 touches upon state laws relating to recognition or protection of tribal property. Chapters 18 and 19 deal respectively with criminal and civil jurisdiction of state courts as well as federal and tribal courts.

[2] 6 Pet. 515 (1832).

[3] See Chapter 7, sec. 2. *Cf.* Report and Remonstrance of the Legislature of Georgia, Sen. Doc. No. 98, 21st Cong., 1st sess. (March 8, 1830).

[4] For an analysis of these cases, see F. S. Cohen, Indian Rights and the Federal Courts (1940), 24 Minn. L. Rev. 145.

[5] "* * * said Indian lands shall remain under the absolute jurisdiction and control of the Congress of the United States * * *." Act of July 16, 1894, sec. 3, 28 Stat. 107, 108 (Utah). Accord: Act of June 20, 1910, secs. 2, 20, 36 Stat. 557 (New Mexico and Arizona). And *cf.* Act of June 16, 1906, sec. 28, 34 Stat. 267, 281 (Oklahoma).

[6] 118 U. S. 375 (1886).

[7] The omission of this comma in the official United States Report has created some confusion as to the meaning of this sentence. Without the comma, the sentence seems to suggest that the weakness and helplessness of the Indians is due in part to treaties and that it is because of the weakness and helplessness of the Indians that the Federal Government may exercise the power of protection. With the comma, the sentence suggests rather that the factual situation of weakness and helplessness is only part of the basis of legal power, the other, and legally more important, basis being the obligations assumed by the United States towards Indian tribes by treaty. This comma is found in the Supreme Court Reporter edition of the opinion (6 Sup. Ct. 1109).

> The power of the General Government over these remnants of a race once powerful, now weak and diminished in numbers, is necessary to their protection, as well as to the safety of those among whom they dwell. It must exist in that government, because it never has existed anywhere else, because the theater of its exercise is within the geographical limits of the United States, because it has never been denied, and because it alone can enforce its laws on all the tribes. (Pp. 383–385.)

Insofar as this argument relies upon treaties it is legally unassailable, for the treaties made between the Federal Government and the Indian tribes are part of the supreme law of the land[8] and, as we have already noted, these treaties quite generally promised the tribes, either expressly or by implication, that they would not be subject to the sovereignty of the individual states, but would be subject only to the Federal Government.

On the other hand, insofar as the opinion in the *Kagama* case relies upon the factual helplessness of the Indians, the enmity of the state populations, and the impossibility of state control, serious questions may be raised both as to the validity of the argument and as to its scope and application, when the factual premises noted no longer correspond to the facts. It would, however, be a digression at this point to analyze the various doctrines advanced in support of the conclusion that, within the Indian country in matters affecting Indians, federal law applies to the exclusion of state law.[9]

It is enough for the present to note that the domain of power of the Federal Government over Indian affairs marked out by the federal decisions is so complete that, as a practical matter, the federal courts and federal administrative officials now generally proceed from the assumption that Indian affairs are matters of federal, rather than state, concern, unless the contrary is shown by act of Congress or special circumstance. Thus, without questioning the constitutional doctrine that states possess original and complete sovereignty over their own territories save insofar as such sovereignty is limited by the Federal Constitution, a sense of realism must compel the conclusion that control of Indian affairs has been delegated, under the Constitution, to the Federal Government and that state jurisdiction in any matters affecting Indians can be upheld only if one of two conditions is met: either that Congress has expressly delegated back to the state, or recognized in the state, some power of government respecting Indians; or that a question involving Indians involves non-Indians to a degree which calls into play the jurisdiction of a state government. Of these two situations, the former is undoubtedly more definite and therefore simpler to analyze. Such an analysis requires a listing of the acts of Congress which confer upon the states, or recognize in the states, specific powers of government with respect to Indians.

---

[8] *United States* v. *Forty-Three Gallons of Whiskey*, 93 U. S. 188 (1876); *Worcester* v. *Georgia*, 6 Pet. 515 (1832); *Fellows* v. *Blacksmith*, 19 How. 366 (1856); *United States* v. *New York Indians*, 173 U. S. 464 (1899). See *United States* v. *Winans*, 198 U. S. 371, 379, 384 (1905). *Cf. United States* v. *Rio Grande Dam and Irrigation Co.*, 174 U. S. 690, 703 (1899); *United States* v. *Rickert*, 188 U. S. 432, 437, 438 (1903); *United States* v. *Seminole Nation*, 299 U. S. 417, 428 (1937), cert. granted 299 U. S. 526; *Wallace* v. *Adams*, 204 U. S. 415 (1907). See Chapter 8, sec. 3.

[9] For further discussion of these doctrines see Chapter 4, sec. 2, and Chapter 5.

SECTION 2. FEDERAL STATUTES ON STATE POWER

It will be convenient to group the federal statutes which grant or recognize state power over Indian affairs into two categories: (*a*) Those that apply throughout the United States; and (*b*) those that apply only to particular tribes or areas.

A. GENERAL STATUTES

The most important field in which state laws have been applied to Indians by congressional fiat is the field of inheritance. In the absence of federal legislation, it is established that all questions relating to descent and distribution of the property of individual Indians are governed by the laws and customs of the tribe to which the Indians belong.[10] A given tribe may, of course, adopt such state laws as it considers suitable, and it may do this either by ordinance,[11] or, in conjunction with the Federal Government, by treaty.[12] Without such action of the tribal or the Federal Government, state laws of inheritance have no application to Indians residing on an Indian reservation.

This situation, however, has been greatly changed by congressional legislation affecting Indians to whom reservation lands have been allotted in severalty. The most important portion of this congressional legislation is contained in Section 5 of the General Allotment Act,[13] providing:

> That upon the approval of the allotments provided for in this act by the Secretary of the Interior, he shall cause patents to issue therefor in the name of the allot-

---

[10] See Chapter 7, sec. 6 and Chapter 11, sec. 6.

[11] See 55 I. D. 14, 42 (1934). See also Chapter 7, sec. 6.

[12] Thus, *e. g.*, Article 8 of the Treaty of February 27, 1867, with the Pottawatomie Indians, 15 Stat. 531, 533 provides:

> Where allottees under the treaty of eighteen hundred and sixty-two shall have died, or shall hereafter decease, if any dispute shall arise in regard to heirship to their property, it shall be competent for the business committee to decide such question, taking for their rule of action the laws of inheritance of the State of Kansas * * *

[13] 24 Stat. 388, 389; amended Act of March 3, 1901, sec. 9, 31 Stat. 1058, 1085; 25 U. S. C. 348.

This section as originally enacted, also provided:

> That the law of descent and partition in force in the State or Territory where such lands are situate shall apply thereto after patents therefor have been executed and delivered, except as herein otherwise provided; and the laws of the State of Kansas regulating the descent and partition of real estate shall, so far as practicable, apply to all lands in the Indian Territory which may be allotted in severalty under the provisions of this act.

The General Allotment Act expressly exempted from its operation the territory occupied by the Five Civilized Tribes and the Miamies and Peorias, and Sacs and Foxes in the Indian Territory, now a part of the State of Oklahoma, and also the reservation of the Seneca Nation of New York Indians in the State of New York, as to which see *United States ex rel. Kennedy* v. *Tyler*, 269 U. S. 13 (1925), aff'g. *United States ex rel. Pierce* v. *Waldow*, 294 Fed. 111 (D. C. W. D. N. Y. 1923). See also *New York* v. *Dibble*, 21 How. 366 (1858).

The Confederated Wea, Kaskaskia, Peoria, Piankeshaw, and Western Miamies were allotted under the Act of March 2, 1889, 25 Stat. 1013, but by that Act, the provisions of the General Allotment Act were extended to these tribes. The same is true as to other tribes allotted under special acts of Congress, such for instance as the Chippewas of Minnesota, who were allotted under the Act of January 14, 1889, 25 Stat. 642, in accordance with the provisions of the General Allotment Act. The Quapaw Indians were allotted under the Act of March 2, 1895, 28 Stat. 876, 907, without reference to the General Allotment Act, and would seem to have been excluded from the provisions of that Act, so that the laws of Kansas did not apply to them.

The Sacs and Foxes were allotted under the Act of February 13, 1891, 26 Stat. 749, and under the provisions of that Act they became subject

tees, which patents shall be of the legal effect, and declare that the United States does and will hold the land thus allotted, for the period of twenty-five years, in trust for the sole use and benefit of the Indian to whom allotment shall have been made, *or, in case of his decease, of his heirs according to the laws of the State or Territory where such land is located*, and that at the expiration of said period the United States will convey the same by patent to said Indian, *or his heirs as aforesaid*, in fee, discharged of said trust and free of all charge or incumbrance whatsoever. [Italics supplied.]

As will be readily perceived, these provisions entirely withdraw from the operation of tribal laws and customs all matters of descent and partition concerning allotments made to Indians under the General Allotment Act, and the laws of the state in which the land is situated must govern such matters, except insofar as these matters are otherwise covered by federal statutes.

The scope of state power in the matter of inheritance of allotments has been considerably limited however, by legislation which confers upon the Secretary of the Interior full power to determine heirs and to partition allotments.[14] Thus, for example, the Supreme Court has held [15] that a will made by an Indian woman in accordance with departmental regulations, and approved by the Secretary of the Interior, devising her restricted land to others than her husband, was valid, notwithstanding a provision in the Oklahoma law prohibiting a married woman from bequeathing more than two-thirds of her property away from her husband.

The Court said:

> The Secretary of the Interior made regulations which were proper to the exercise of the power conferred upon him and the execution of the act of Congress, and it would seem that no comment is necessary to show that § 8341 [Oklahoma Code] is excluded from pertinence or operation. (P. 324.)
>
> * * * * *
>
> In a word, the act of Congress is complete in its control and administration of the allotment and of all that is connected with or made necessary by it, and is antagonistic to any right or interest in the husband of an Indian woman in her allotment under the Oklahoma Code. (P. 326.)

In a later case approving this decision,[16] the Court sustained the validity of a lease made by an Indian on his family homestead which violated an Oklahoma statute requiring execution by both spouses. The Court said:

> Nor is the validity of the extension lease affected by the provision in the Oklahoma constitution that nothing in the laws of the United States shall deprive any Indian or other allottee of the benefit of the homestead laws of the State. Whether or not this provision was intended to do more than to protect the allottees from the enforced seizure of their homesteads, it is sufficient to say that, whatever its purpose, it can have no more effect than the Oklahoma statute in giving validity to laws of the State repugnant to the reserved power of the United States in legislating in respect to the lands of Indians. Neither the constitution of a State nor any act of its legislature, whatever rights it may confer on Indians or withhold from them, can withdraw them from the operation of an act which Congress passes concerning them in the exercise of its paramount authority. *United States* v. *Holliday*, 3 Wall. 407, 419. (P. 497.)

A second field in which state law has been extended to Indian reservations by congressional fiat is the realm of laws covering "inspection of health and educational conditions" and the enforcement of "sanitation and quarantine regulations" as well as "compulsory school attendance." By the Act of February 15, 1929,[17] Congress authorized the enforcement of such laws upon Indian reservations by state officials "under such rules, regulations, and conditions as the Secretary of the Interior may prescribe."

A third body of state laws is extended over Indian reservations by section 289 of the Criminal Code [18] which makes offenses by non-Indians against Indians and by Indians against non-Indians punishable in the federal courts in accordance with state laws existing at the time of the federal enactment in question.[19]

It will be noted that the foregoing statute is expressly made inapplicable to any offense committed by and against an Indian, by the terms of section 218 of title 25 of the U. S. Code.[20]

Apart from these three fields there has been no general congressional legislation authorizing the extension of state laws to Indians on Indian reservations.[21]

Within those three fields it is probable that any devolution of authority from Congress to the states may be revoked at such time as Congress sees fit.[22]

B. SPECIAL STATUTES

Apart from the general statutes noted in the preceding section, a number of acts of Congress dealing with particular tribes or areas confer various powers upon state courts, state legislatures, and state administrative officials. These statutes deal most commonly with such subjects as crimes,[23] taxation,[24] pro-

to the laws of the Territory of Oklahoma. And the Osages, were allotted under the Act of June 28, 1906, 34 Stat. 539, and under the provisions of that Act became subject to the laws of that Territory. See, however, sec. 6 of the Act of 1906, *supra*. See also sec. 3 of the Act of April 18, 1912, 37 Stat. 86, subjecting the persons and property of Osage Indians to the jurisdiction of the county courts of Oklahoma in probate matters. As to the Five Civilized Tribes of Oklahoma, see *Stewart* v. *Keyes*, 295 U. S. 403 (1935), pet. for rehearing den., 296 U. S. 661 (1935).

[14] Act of June 25, 1910, 36 Stat. 855, 25 U. S. C. 371; Act of May 18, 1916, 39 Stat. 123, 127, 25 U. S. C. 321. See Chapter 10, sec. 10; Chapter 11, sec. 6; Chapter 5, sec. 10.

[15] *Blanset* v. *Cardin*, 256 U. S. 319 (1921).

[16] *Sperry Oil Co.* v. *Chisholm*, 264 U. S. 488 (1924).

[17] 45 Stat. 1185, 25 U. S. C. 231. And see Taylor Grazing Act of June 28, 1934, 48 Stat. 1269, amended June 26, 1936, 49 Stat. 1976, discussed in 56 I. D. 38 (1936).

[18] 18 U. S. C. 468; derived from: R. S. § 5391; Act of July 7, 1898, sec. 2, 30 Stat. 717; Act of June 15, 1933, 48 Stat. 152.

[19] Congress has not attempted to give force to state laws later enacted, apparently having in mind the possibility that such legislation might be considered an unconstitutional delegation of power or a violation of Constitutional requirements of certainty in penal legislation. *Cf. Wayman* v. *Southard*, 10 Wheat. 1 (1825); *Field* v. *Clark*, 143 U. S. 649 (1891); *Wichita Railroad* v. *Public Utilities Com.*, 260 U. S. 48 (1922); *Hampton & Co.* v. *United States*, 276 U. S. 394 (1928); *Panama Refining Co.* v. *Ryan*, 293 U. S. 388 (1935).

[20] R. S. § 2146, amended by Act of February 18, 1875, 18 Stat. 316, 318. See Chapter 7, sec. 9; Chapter 18, sec. 3.

[21] Note, however, the legalization of state-federal administrative cooperation by the Johnson-O'Malley Act of April 16, 1934, 48 Stat. 596, amended Act of June 4, 1936, 49 Stat. 1458, 25 U. S. C. 452 *et seq.* And see Chapter 4, sec. 15; Chapter 12, sec. 1.

[22] See *Truskett* v. *Closser*, 236 U. S. 223 (1915); *Rice* v. *Maybee*, 2 F. Supp. 669 (D. C. W. D. N. Y. 1933); *People ex rel. Cusick* v. *Daly*, 212 N. Y. 183, 196–197, 105 N. E. 1048 (1914).

[23] Act of February 21, 1863, sec. 5, 12 Stat. 658, 660 (Winnebago); Act of June 8, 1940 (Pub. No. 565, 76th Cong.) (State of Kansas).

[24] Act of March 3, 1921, 41 Stat. 1249, 1251, authorizing State of Oklahoma to tax oil and gas production from Indian lands (upheld in 38 Op. A. G. 60 (1921) discussed in Op. Sol. I. D., M.26672, September 22, 1931); Act of May 10, 1928, 45 Stat. 495, 496 (subjecting mineral production from Five Civilized Tribes' lands in Oklahoma to state taxes). *Cf.* Act of June 26, 1936, sec. 1, 49 Stat. 1967. See Chapter 13, secs 2, 5; Chapter 23, sec. 9.

bate,[25] acquisition of water rights,[26] recording laws,[27] and liens upon cut timber.[28]

In Oklahoma there has been a particularly broad devolution of powers to the state government.[29] The organs of the state government however, in exercising such powers have been considered federal agencies. Thus in *Parker* v. *Richard*[30] the Supreme Court, in referring to the authority of the county courts of Oklahoma under section 9 of the Act of May 27, 1908,[31] said:

> * * * That the agency which is to approve or not is a state court is not material. It is the agency selected by Congress and the authority confided to it is to be exercised in giving effect to the will of Congress in respect of a matter within its control. Thus in a practical sense the court in exercising that authority acts as a federal agency; and this is recognized by the Supreme Court of the State. *Marcy* v. *Board of Commissioners*, 45 Oklahoma 1. (P. 239.)

[25] Act of April 30, 1888, 25 Stat. 94, 98 (Sioux); Act of March 2, 1889, 25 Stat. 888, 891 (Sioux); Act of January 12, 1891, 26 Stat. 712 (Mission); Act of February 13, 1891, 26 Stat. 749, 751 (Sac and Fox); Act of June 28, 1906, 34 Stat. 539 (Osage); Act of April 18, 1912, 37 Stat. 86 (Osage); Act of June 14, 1918, 40 Stat. 606 (Five Civilized Tribes); Act of February 27, 1925, 43 Stat. 1011 (Osage). For a discussion of the provisions of these acts see Op. Sol. I. D., M.18008, December 18, 1925; Op. Sol. I. D., October 4, 1926; Op. Sol. I. D., D-46929, September 30, 1922; Op. Sol. I. D., M.24203, June 19, 1928.

[26] Act of March 3, 1905, 33 Stat. 1016, 1017 (Shoshone) discussed *In re Parkins*, 18 F. 2d. 642, 643 (D. C. D. Wyo. 1926).

[27] Act of February 19, 1875, 18 Stat. 330, 331 (Seneca).

[28] Act of March 31, 1882, 22 Stat. 36, 37 (Wisconsin).

[29] See Chapter 23, secs. 8–10.

[30] 250 U. S. 235 (1919).

[31] 35 Stat. 312, 315.

SECTION 3. RESERVED STATE POWERS OVER INDIAN AFFAIRS

While the general rule, as we have noted, is that plenary authority over Indian affairs rests in the Federal Government to the exclusion of state governments, we have likewise noted two major exceptions to this general rule: First, where Congress has expressly declared that certain powers over Indian affairs shall be exercised by the states, and second, where the matter involves non-Indian questions sufficient to ground state jurisdiction.

In proceeding to analyze this latter exception to the generel rule, we may note that in point of constitutional doctrine, the sovereignty of a state over its own territory[32] is plenary and therefore the fact that Indians are involved in a situation, directly or indirectly, does not *ipso facto* terminate state power. State power is terminated only if the matter is one that falls within the constitutional scope of exclusive federal authority.[33]

A case in which the factors of situs, person and subject matter all point to exclusive federal jurisdiction, as, for example, in a transaction involving a transfer of restricted property between Indians on an Indian reservation, the basis of exclusive federal power is clear. On the other hand, where all three factors point away from federal jurisdiction, the power of the state is clear. There exists, however, a broad twilight zone in which one or two of the three elements noted—situs, person and subject matter—point to federal power and the remainder to state power. These are the situations which require analysis and the various combinations of these factors present six situations for consideration.

(A) Indian outside Indian country engaged in non-federal transaction.

(B) Indian outside Indian country engaged in federal transaction.

(C) Indian within Indian country engaged in non-federal transaction.

(D) Non-Indian outside Indian country engaged in federal transaction.

(E) Non-Indian in Indian country engaged in federal transaction.

(F) Non-Indian in Indian country engaged in non-federal transaction.

A brief discussion of these six type-situations is in order.

A. INDIAN OUTSIDE INDIAN COUNTRY ENGAGED IN NON-FEDERAL TRANSACTION

It is undoubtedly true, as a general rule, that an Indian who is "off the reservation" is subject to the laws of the state or territory in which he finds himself, to the same extent that a non-Indian citizen or alien would be subject to those laws.[34]

B. INDIAN OUTSIDE INDIAN COUNTRY ENGAGED IN FEDERAL TRANSACTION

To the general rule set forth in the preceding paragraph, an exception must be noted. If the subject matter of the transaction is a subject matter over which Congress has asserted its constitutional power, the state must yield to the superior power of the nation.[35] For example, Congress has taken the position that its constitutional concern with Indian tribes requires a prohibition of sales of liquor to all "ward" Indians, even outside of Indian reservations, and the courts have upheld this exercise of power.[36] Under the circumstances, any state interference with this prohibition would undoubtedly be held invalid.

A second example may be found in the realm of restricted personal property of Indians. Where, for example, a herd of cattle is held by an Indian or an Indian tribe subject to federal restrictions upon alienation,[37] it seems clear that the removal of the property from the reservation would not free it from such federal restrictions, and any state laws or proceedings inconsistent with federal control would be clearly unconstitutional.[38]

The line between federal transactions which are of such concern to the Federal Government that the state cannot legislate in the matter and other transactions on which the state is permitted to legislate, is not always easy to draw. Where, for

[32] Ordinarily an Indian reservation is considered part of the territory of the state. *Utah and Northern Railway* v. *Fisher*, 116 U. S. 28 (1885). But in some cases, the enabling act or other congressional legislation, or the state constitution itself, declares that Indian reservations shall not be deemed part of the territory of the state. See, for example, *The Kansas Indians*, 5 Wall. 737 (1866); *Harkness* v. *Hyde*, 98 U. S. 476 (1878), qualified in *Langford* v. *Monteith*, 102 U. S. 145 (1880).

[33] See sec. 1, *supra*; and see Chapter 5.

[34] *Hunt* v. *State*, 4 Kan. 60 (1866) (murder of Indian by Indian); *In re Wolf*, 27 Fed. 606, 610 (D. C. Ark. 1886) (conspiracy by Indians to obtain money by false pretences from Indian nation in D. C.); *State* v. *Williams*, 13 Mont. 335, 43 Pac. 15 (1895) (murder of Indian by Indian); *Pablo* v. *People*, 23 Colo. 134, 46 Pac. 636 (1896) (murder of Indian by Indian); *State* v. *Spotted Hawk*, 22 Mont. 33, 55 Pac. 1026 (1899) (murder of white man by Indian); *State* v. *Little Whirlwind*, 22 Mont. 425, 56 Pac. 820 (1899) (murder of white man by Indian); *Ex parte Moore*, 28 S. D. 339, 133 N. W. 817 (1911) (murder of Indian by Indian on public domain allotment), commented on in Ann. Cas. 1914 B, 648, 652. And see state cases collected in Note 13, Ann. Cas. 192.

[35] See Chapter 7, sec. 9, fn. 213; and see Chapter 18, sec. 2. *Cf. The Kansas Indians*, 5 Wall. 737, 755, 756 (1866), "If under the control of Congress, from necessity there can be no divided authority. * * * There can be no question of State sovereignty in the case, * * *."

[36] See Chapter 17, sec. 8.

[37] See Chapter 10, sec. 12.

[38] *Cf. United States* v. *Cook*, 19 Wall. 591 (1873); *Pine River Logging Co.* v. *United States*, 186 U. S. 279 (1902) (tribal timber illegally alienated); discussed in Chapter 15, sec. 15.

example, hunting or fishing rights off the reservation have been promised to Indians, the question has arisen whether such rights may be controlled by state conservation statutes. In the present state of the law, no simple answer can be given to the question.[39] Likewise, the question of whether taxable land purchased for Indians, outside of a reservation, and held subject to federal restrictions upon alienation, is immune from the tax laws of the state, has given rise to considerable litigation.[40] In this situation it seems that, despite the federal concern in the subject matter, the state may levy property taxes if Congress is silent, but may not do so if Congress prohibits such legislation.[41]

C. INDIAN WITHIN INDIAN COUNTRY ENGAGED IN NON-FEDERAL TRANSACTION

It is well settled that the state has no power over the conduct of Indians within the Indian country, whether or not the conduct is of special concern to the Federal Government.[42] Thus Indian marriage and divorce, offenses between Indians, and sales of personal property between Indians are matters over which the state cannot exercise control, so long as the Indians concerned remain within the reservation.[43] This disability has generally been explained in terms of tribal sovereignty and a federal policy of protecting such tribal sovereignty against state invasion. Thus, in denying state jurisdiction over adultery among Indians on an Indian reservation, the Supreme Court declared in *United States* v. *Quiver*,[44] *per* Van Devanter, *J.*:

> At an early period it became the settled policy of Congress to permit the personal and domestic relations of the Indians with each other to be regulated, and offenses by one Indian against the person or property of another Indian to be dealt with, according to their tribal customs and laws. * * * (Pp. 603–604.)

Whether the local state laws may be applied to the Indians of a tribe with their consent, expressed through agreement or otherwise, is a question which the Supreme Court does not seem to have passed upon squarely.[45] There is no doubt that many tribes in the past have accepted state laws.[46] Indeed, in the early years of the Republic, it appears that various treaties were made between Indian tribes and the various states.[47] The validity, however, of such formal or informal arrangements, has not been definitely established. It would seem that if state laws are adopted by Indian tribes, they have effect as tribal laws and not simply as exercises of state sovereignty.[48]

[39] See Chapter 14, sec. 7; and Chapter 15, sec. 21.

[40] See Chapter 13.

[41] *Ibid.*

[42] See Chapter 7.

[43] *Ibid.*, and see Chapter 13, sec. 5. And see Memo. Sol. I. D., April 26, 1939, holding that the State of California is without jurisdiction to compel Indians residing on rancherias within the state to take out licenses for dogs owned by them.

[44] 241 U. S. 602 (1916).

[45] *Cf. United States ex rel. Kennedy* v. *Tyler*, 269 U. S. 13 (1925).

[46] See, for example, the discussion of New York Indians in Chapter 22, and the comments on the Eastern Cherokee of North Carolina in Chapter 14, sec. 2.

[47] See *Cherokee Nation* v. *Georgia*, 5 Pet. 1, (1831); *Seneca Nation* v. *Christy*, 126 N. Y. 122, 27 N. E. 275 (1891); 2 Op. A. G. 110 (1828); Rice, The Position of the American Indian in the Law of the United States (1934), 16 J. Comp. Leg. 78, 85. While the Constitution forbids a state's entering into any treaty, alliance, or confederation (Art. 1, sec. 10, discussed in *Worcester* v. *Georgia*, 6 Pet. 515, 579 (1832)), the position has been taken by at least one state court that this did not prevent treaties or compacts for the extinguishment of Indian title between states and Indian tribes. *Seneca Nation* v. *Christy*, *supra*.

[48] "An Indian tribe may, if it so chooses, adopt as its own the laws of the State in which it is situated and may make such modifications in these laws as it deems suitable to its peculiar conditions." 55 I. D. 14, 42 (1934).

D. NON-INDIAN OUTSIDE INDIAN COUNTRY ENGAGED IN FEDERAL TRANSACTION

Although ordinarily a non-Indian outside of Indian country is in no way subject to federal law governing Indian affairs, and is wholly subject to state law, there are certain subject matters in which the federal interest is so strong that even with respect to non-Indians outside the Indian country, federal law will supersede state law. Such a matter, for instance, is the transfer from one non-Indian to another of restricted property unlawfully taken from an Indian reservation.[49] Another example may be found in the realm of transactions between an employee of the Indian Bureau and a third party, consummated outside of the Indian country, which involve a personal interest in Indian trade.[50] This class of transactions in which non-Indians outside of the Indian country must take account of federal Indian law, is extremely limited in scope, applying primarily to matters involving property in which the Federal Government has an interest,[51] and to the personnel of the Indian Service itself.[52]

E. NON-INDIAN IN INDIAN COUNTRY ENGAGED IN FEDERAL TRANSACTION

If, where the subject matter is of federal concern, a non-Indian is subject to federal, rather than state jurisdiction, even for acts occurring outside of an Indian reservation, *a fortiori* he is subject to federal jurisdiction for acts of federal concern committed within an Indian reservation. Indeed, there is a very broad realm of conduct in which non-Indians on an Indian reservation are subject to federal rather than state power. With respect to all offenses committed by whites against Indians on an Indian reservation, state jurisdiction yields to federal jurisdiction,[53] although in fact the Federal Government has adopted state laws in providing for the punishment of such offenses by the federal courts.[54] Likewise, there are various reservation offenses for which Congress has prescribed penalties enforceable in federal courts, which are applicable to non-Indians, and in some instances to Indians as well.[55] It has been administratively held that even a state officer cannot claim the protection of state law if he enters an Indian reservation without congressional authorization for the purpose of searching an Indian's home for property thought to be in the unlawful possession of the Indian.[56]

Although the federal constitutional jurisdiction over matters affecting Indian affairs on an Indian reservation has generally been viewed as an exclusive jurisdiction, excluding all state legislation, an exception to the general rule has been recognized where the state legislation supplements the protection of Indians provided by federal law. Such state legislation, which may be termed "ancillary" to federal law, is upheld in *State of*

[49] See fn. 38, *supra*.

[50] See Chapter 2, sec. 3B.

[51] See *Oregon* v. *Hitchcock*, 202 U. S. 60, 68–69 (1906); *Naganab* v. *Hitchcock*, 202 U. S. 473 (1906); *Winters* v. *United States*, 207 U. S. 564 (1908); *United States* v. *Winans*, 198 U. S. 371 (1905); *Morrison* v. *Work*, 266 U. S. 481, 487–488 (1925); *United States* v. *Morrison*, 203 Fed. 364 (C. C. Colo. 1901).

[52] See Chapter 2, sec. 3B, and Chapter 16.

[53] See Chapter 18, sec. 5. There may be situations, however, in which a concurrent jurisdiction may be exercised by the state to protect Indians against non-Indians. *State of New York* v. *Dibble*, 62 U. S. 366 (1858), discussed in Chapter 15, sec. 10C.

[54] See sec. 2A, *supra*.

[55] See Chapter 18, sec. 3.

[56] 56 I. D. 38 (1936).

New York v. *Dibble*,[57] where the Supreme Court, in upholding a state prohibition against trespass upon Indian lands, declared:

> The statute in question is a police regulation for the protection of the Indians from intrusion of the white people, and to preserve the peace. It is the dictate of a prudent and just policy. Notwithstanding the peculiar relation which these Indian nations hold to the Government of the United States, the State of New York had the power of a sovereign over their persons and property, so far as it was necessary to preserve the peace of the Commonwealth, and protect these feeble and helpless bands from imposition and intrusion. The power of a State to make such regulations to preserve the peace of the community is absolute, and has never been surrendered. The act is therefore not contrary to the Constitution of the United States. (P. 370.)

Other cases have applied this rule to state laws forbidding sale of liquor to Indians,[58] and to other protective and ancillary legislation.[59]

F. NON-INDIAN IN INDIAN COUNTRY ENGAGED IN NON-FEDERAL TRANSACTION

The mere fact that the locus of an event is on an Indian reservation does not prevent the exercise of state jurisdiction where the parties involved are not Indians and the subject matter of the transaction is not of federal concern. Thus, it has been held that murder of a non-Indian by a non-Indian on an Indian reservation, in the absence of express federal legislation to the contrary, is a matter of exclusive state jurisdiction.[60] Likewise the validity of state taxation of personalty of a non-Indian within Indian country has been sustained.[61]

G. SUMMARY

The rules applicable to each of the foregoing types of situations are not established beyond the possibility of doubt, and they leave much room for debate in defining the three factors in terms of which these rules have been formulated: "Indian,"[62] "Indian country,"[63] and "transaction of federal concern."[64] But these are questions elsewhere treated,[65] and the views above expressed on the various combinations of factors necessary to support state jurisdiction on Indian matters are probably as close to the actual decisions as any simple scheme can come. The foregoing sections may be summarized in two propositions:

> (1) *In matters involving only Indians on an Indian reservation, the state has no jurisdiction in the absence of specific legislation by Congress.*
>
> (2) *In all other cases, the state has jurisdiction unless there is involved a subject matter of special federal concern.*

---

[57] 21 How. 366 (1858). See Chapter 15, sec. 10C.

[58] *State* v. *Kenney*, 145 Pac. 450 (Wash. 1915); *State* v. *Mamlock*, 58 Wash. 631, 109 Pac. 47 (1910).

[59] See *State* v. *Wolf*, 145 N. C. 440, 59 S. E. 40 (1907) (upholding state law requiring school attendance of Eastern Cherokee Indians), commented on in Note, Ann. Cas. 1915D, 871.

[60] *United States* v. *McBratney*, 104 U. S. 621 (1881); *Draper* v. *United States*, 164 U. S. 240 (1896); and see Chapter 7, sec. 9 and Chapter 18, sec. 6.

[61] *Thomas* v. *Gay*, 169 U. S. 264 (1898). And see Chapter 13, sec. 4.

[62] The definition of "Indian" is considered in Chapter 1, sec. 2. On the question of the applicability of state laws, special importance should be assigned to the cases which suggest that when tribal existence ceases, Indians cease to be under federal jurisdiction and become subject to state control.

See opinion of Mr. Justice Johnson in *Fletcher* v. *Peck*, 6 Cranch. 87, 146 (1810), and opinion of Mr. Justice McLean in *Worcester* v. *Georgia*, 6 Pet. 515, 580 (1832). See also *Scott* v. *Sanford*, 19 How. 393 (1857), where the Supreme Court, with reference to the Indians, said:

> * * * and if an individual should leave his nation or tribe, and take up his abode among the white population, he would be entitled to all the rights and privileges which would belong to an emigrant from any other foreign people. (P. 404.)

See also dicta in *The Cherokee Trust Funds*, 117 U. S. 288, 309 (1886) to the effect that the so-called Eastern Band of Cherokee Indians who separated themselves from the main body of the Cherokee Nation in its migration to the West, became "bound" to the state laws of North Carolina. See also and *cf. United States* v. *Boyd*, 83 Fed. 547 (C. C. A. 4, 1897); *United States* v. *Wright*, 53 F. 2d 300 (C. C. A. 4, 1931); and *United States* v. *Colvard*, 89 F. 2d 312 (C. C. A. 4, 1937), to the effect that these Indians having been recognized and treated by the Federal Government as a tribe must be regarded as such. For a more extended discussion of tribal existence and its termination see Chapter 14, secs. 1 and 2. On the right of expatriation see Chapter 8, sec. 10B(1).

Also see *Ex parte Kenyon*, 14 Fed. Cas. No. 7720 (C. C. W. D. Ark., 1878):

> * * * When the members of a tribe of Indians scatter themselves among the citizens of the United States, and live among the people of the United States, they are merged in the mass of our people, owing complete allegiance to the government of the United States and of the states where they may reside, and, equally with the citizens of the United States and of the several states, subject to the jurisdiction of the courts thereof. *Ex parte Reynolds* [Case No. 11,719]; *United States* v. *Elm* [Id. 15,048] * * * opinion by Wallace, *J.* (Senate Report 268, 41st Cong. 3d sess.) p. 11; 2 Story Const. § 1933, *Dred Scott* v. *Sandford*, 19 How. [60 U. S.] 404.

And see cases collected in Note 13 Ann. Cas. 192,193.

A unique situation exists with respect to the Sac and Fox Indians of Iowa. The State of Iowa, which had exercised jurisdiction over these Indians and which held title to their land in trust for them, transferred to the Federal Government "exclusive jurisdiction of the Sac and Fox Indians residing in Iowa and retaining the tribal relation, and of all other Indians dwelling with them * * *." (Act of February 14, 1896, Acts 26th General Assembly, p. 114.) The state, however, reserved from such transfer jurisdiction of crimes against the state laws committed within the reservation by Indians or others. In *Peters* v. *Malin*, 111 Fed. 244 (C. C. Iowa, 1901) it was held that this reservation of authority in the state did not affect the exclusive jurisdiction of the Federal Government over the relation of the Indians among themselves. See, on this question, Memo. Sol. I. D., June 15, 1940.

Also see *In re Now-ge-shuck*, 69 Kans. 410, 76 Pac. 877 (1904); *State* v. *Big Sheep*, 75 Mont. 219, 243 Pac. 1067 (1926); *State* v. *Williams*, 13 Wash. 335, 43 Pac. 15 (1895); *State* v. *Howard*, 33 Wash. 250, 74 Pac. 382 (1903); *State* v. *Nimrod*, 30 S. D. 239, 138 N. W. 377 (1912).

Indians residing in Maine, while they have a communal organization for tenure of property and local affairs, are deemed by the courts of the state to be without political organization and to be subject, like other individuals, to game laws of the state. *State* v. *Newell*, 84 Maine 465, 24 Atl. 943 (1892).

It was believed at one time that the grant of citizenship to individual Indians, whether by an act of Congress or by the provisions of a treaty, had the effect of terminating tribal relations, placing the Indians beyond the power of Congress, and subjecting them to state jurisdiction. This view was taken by the United States Supreme Court in the famous case, *Matter of Heff*, 197 U. S. 488 (1905). Later, however, this ruling was ignored in *Hallowell* v. *United States*, 221 U. S. 317 (1911) and *United States* v. *Sandoval*, 231 U. S. 28 (1913), and finally expressly overruled in *United States* v. *Nice*, 241 U. S. 591 (1916). See, in this connection, Chapter 8, secs. 2C and 10B(1).

[63] See Chapter 1, sec. 3; Chapter 18, sec. 2.

[64] See Chapter 13, sec. 1A; Chapter 14, sec. 7. As noted in the discussion above, the term "transactions of federal concern" is used to cover matters over which the power of the Federal Government has been exercised, whether through legislation, through authorized administrative action, or in any other valid manner. The content of the term is therefore to be found in the materials discussed in various other chapters, particularly Chapters 5, 9, 10, 11, 12, 13, 14, 15, 16, 17, 18, and 19.

[65] See fns. 62, 63, and 64, *supra*.

CHAPTER 7

THE SCOPE OF TRIBAL SELF-GOVERNMENT[1]

TABLE OF CONTENTS

SECTION 1. INTRODUCTION

The Indian's right of self-government is a right which has been consistently protected by the courts, frequently recognized and intermittently ignored by treaty-makers and legislators, and very widely disregarded by administrative officials. That such rights have been disregarded is perhaps due more to lack of acquaintance with the law of the subject than to any drive for increased power on the part of administrative officials.

The most basic of all Indian rights, the right of self-government, is the Indian's last defense against administrative oppression, for in a realm where the states are powerless to govern and where Congress, occupied with more pressing national affairs, cannot govern wisely and well, there remains a large no-man's-land in which government can emanate only from officials of the Interior Department or from the Indians themselves. Self-government is thus the Indians' only alternative to rule by a government department.

Indian self-government, the decided cases hold, includes the power of an Indian tribe to adopt and operate under a form of government of the Indians' choosing, to define conditions of tribal membership, to regulate domestic relations of members, to prescribe rules of inheritance, to levy taxes, to regulate property within the jurisdiction of the tribe, to control the conduct of members by municipal legislation, and to administer justice.

Perhaps the most basic principle of all Indian law, supported by a host of decisions hereinafter analyzed, is the principle that *those powers which are lawfully vested in an Indian tribe are not, in general, delegated powers granted by express acts of Congress, but rather inherent powers of a limited sovereignty which has never been extinguished.* Each Indian tribe begins its relationship with the Federal Government as a sovereign power, recognized as such in treaty and legislation. The powers of sovereignty have been limited from time to time by special treaties and laws designed to take from the Indian tribes control of matters which, in the judgment of Congress, these tribes could no longer be safely permitted to handle. The statutes of Congress, then, must be examined to determine the limitations of tribal sovereignty rather than to determine its sources or its positive content. What is not expressly limited remains within the domain of tribal sovereignty.

The acts of Congress which appear to limit the powers of an Indian tribe are not to be unduly extended by doubtful inference.[2]

[1] This chapter is so largely based upon the opinion of Solicitor Margold, Powers of Indian Tribes (Op. Sol. I. D., M.27781, October 25, 1934, 55 I. D. 14), and on the article of F. S. Cohen, Indian Rights and the Federal Courts (1940), 24 Minn. L. Rev. 145, that quotation marks have been dispensed with, as superfluous, in incorporating considerable portions of these works in the present chapter.

[2] See *In re Mayfield, Petitioner,* 141 U. S. 107, 115, 116 (1891).

SECTION 2. THE DERIVATION OF TRIBAL POWERS

From the earliest years of the Republic the Indian tribes have been recognized as "distinct, independent, political communities,"[3] and, as such, qualified to exercise powers of self-government, not by virtue of any delegation of powers from the Federal Government, but rather by reason of their original tribal sovereignty. Thus treaties and statutes of Congress have been looked to by the courts as limitations upon original tribal powers, or, at most, evidences of recognition of such powers, rather than as the direct source of tribal powers. This is but an application of the general principle that "It is only by positive enactments, even in the case of conquered and subdued nations, that their laws are changed by the conqueror."[4]

In point of form it is immaterial whether the powers of an Indian tribe are expressed and exercised through customs handed down by word of mouth or through written constitutions and statutes. In either case the laws of the Indian tribe owe their force to the will of the members of the tribe.

[3] *Worcester v. Georgia,* 6 Pet. 515, 559 (1832).

[4] *Wall v. Williamson,* 8 Ala. 48, 51 (1845), upholding tribal law of divorce. And see Wharton, Conflict of Laws (3d ed. 1905), vol. 1, sec. 9; Wheaton, Elements of International Law (5th ed. by Phillipson, 1916) 66–68.

The earliest complete expression of these principles is found in the case of *Worcester* v. *Georgia*.[5] In that case the State of Georgia, in its attempts to destroy the tribal government of the Cherokees, had imprisoned a white man living among the Cherokees with the consent of the tribal authorities. The Supreme Court of the United States held that his imprisonment was in violation of the Constitution, that the state had no right to infringe upon the federal power to regulate intercourse with the Indians, and that the Indian tribes were, in effect, subjects of federal law, to the exclusion of state law, and entitled to exercise their own inherent rights of sovereignty so far as might be consistent with such federal law. The court declared, *per* Marshall, *C. J.*:

> The Indian nations had always been considered as distinct, independent, political communities, * * *. (P. 559.)
>
> * * * * *
>
> * * * and the settled doctrine of the law of nations is, that a weaker power does not surrender its independence—its right to self-government—by associating with a stronger, and taking its protection. A weak state, in order to provide for its safety, may place itself under the protection of one more powerful, without stripping itself of the right of government, and ceasing to be a state. Examples of this kind are not wanting in Europe. "Tributary and feudatory states," says Vattel, "do not therby cease to be sovereign and independent states, so long as self-government, and sovereign and independent authority, are left in the administration of the state." At the present day, more than one state may be considered as holding its right of self-government under the guarantee and protection of one or more allies.
>
> The Cherokee nation, then, is a distinct community, occupying its own territory, with boundaries accurately described, in which the laws of Georgia can have no force, and which the citizens of Georgia have no right to enter, but with the assent of the Cherokees themselves, or in conformity with treaties, and with the acts of congress. The whole intercourse between the United States and this nation, is, by our constitution and laws, vested in the government of the United States. The act of the state of Georgia, under which the plaintiff in error was prosecuted, is, consequently void, and the judgment a nullity. * * * (P. 560.)

John Marshall's analysis of the basis of Indian self-government in the law of nations has been consistently followed by the courts for more than a hundred years. The doctrine set forth in this opinion has been applied to an unfolding series of new problems in scores of cases that have come before the Supreme Court and the inferior federal courts. The doctrine has not always been so highly respected in state courts and by administrative authorities. It was of the decision in *Worcester* v. *Georgia* that President Jackson is reported to have said, "John Marshall has made his decision; now let him enforce it."[6] As a matter of history, the State of Georgia, unsuccessful defendant in the case, never did carry out the Supreme Court's decision, and the "successful" plaintiff, a guest of the Cherokee Nation, continued to languish in a Georgia prison, under a Georgia law which, according to the Supreme Court decision, was unconstitutional.

The case in which the doctrine of Indian self-government was first established has a certain prophetic character. Administrative officials for a century afterwards continued to ignore the broad implications of the judicial doctrine of Indian self-government. But again and again, as cases came before the federal courts, administrative officials, state and federal, were forced to reckon with the doctrine of Indian self-government and to surrender powers of Indian tribes which they sought to usurp. Finally, after 101 years, there appeared an administration that accepted the logical implications of Indian self-government.[7]

The whole course of judicial decision on the nature of Indian tribal powers is marked by adherence to three fundamental principles: (1) An Indian tribe possesses, in the first instance, all the powers of any sovereign state. (2) Conquest renders the tribe subject to the legislative power of the United States and, in substance, terminates the external powers of sovereignty of the tribe,[8] *e. g.*, its power to enter into treaties with foreign nations, but does not by itself affect the internal sovereignty of the tribe, *i. e.*, its powers of local self-government. (3) These powers are subject to qualification by treaties and by express legislation of Congress,[9] but, save as thus expressly qualified, full powers of internal sovereignty are vested in the Indian tribes and in their duly constituted organs of government.

A striking affirmation of these principles is found in the case of *Talton* v. *Mayes*.[10] The question was presented in that case whether the Fifth Amendment of the Federal Constitution operated as a limitation upon the legislation of the Cherokee Nation. A law of the Cherokee Nation authorized a grand jury of five persons to institute criminal proceedings. A person indicted upon this procedure and held for trial in the Cherokee courts sued out a writ of habeas corpus, alleging that the law in question violated the Fifth Amendment to the Constitution of the United States, since a grand jury of five was not a grand jury within the contemplation of the Fifth Amendment. The Supreme Court held that the Fifth Amendment applied only to the acts of the Federal Government; that the sovereign powers of the Cherokee Nation, although *recognized* by the Federal Government, were not *created* by the Federal Government; and that the judicial authority of the Cherokees was, therefore, not subject to the limitations imposed by the Bill of Rights:

> The question, therefore, is, does the Fifth Amendment to the Constitution apply to the local legislation of the Cherokee nation so as to require all prosecutions for offences committed against the laws of that nation to be initiated by a grand jury organized in accordance with the provisions of that amendment. The solution of this question involves an inquiry as to the nature and origin of the power of local government exercised by the Cherokee nation and recognized to exist in it by the treaties and statutes above referred to. Since the case of *Barron* v. *Baltimore*, 7 Pet. 243, it has been settled that the Fifth Amendment to the Constitution of the United States is a limitation only upon the powers of the General Government, that is, that the amendment operates solely on the Constitution itself by qualifying the powers of the National Government which the Constitution called into being. * * *
>
> The case in this regard therefore depends upon whether the powers of local government exercised by the Cherokee

[5] 6 Pet. 515 (1832).

[6] Greeley, American Conflict (1864), vol. 1, p. 106.

[7] The most comprehensive piece of Indian legislation since the Act of June 30, 1834, 4 Stat. 735, is the Act of June 18, 1934, 48 Stat. 984, 25 U. S. C., 461–479, entitled "An Act to conserve and develop Indian lands and resources; to extend to Indians the right to form business and other organizations; to establish a credit system for Indians; to grant certain rights of home rule to Indians; to provide for vocational education for Indians; and for other purposes," and commonly known as the Wheeler-Howard Act or Indian Reorganization Act. Since its enactment, this statute has been amended in minor particulars (Act of June 15, 1935, 49 Stat. 378, 25 U. S. C. 478a, 478b; Act of August 12, 1935, sec. 2, 49 Stat. 571, 596, 25 U. S. C. 475a; Act of August 28, 1937, 50 Stat. 862, 25 U. S. C. 463–463c), and its more important provisions have been extended to Alaska (Act of May 1, 1936, 49 Stat. 1250, 48 U. S. C. 362) and Oklahoma (Act of June 26, 1936, 49 Stat. 1967, 25 U. S. C. 501–509).

[8] Certain external powers of sovereignty, such as the power to make war and the power to make treaties with the United States, have been recognized by the Federal Government. See Chapter 14, sec. 3.

[9] See for example, *Bell* v. *Atlantic & P. R. Co.*, 63 Fed. 417 (C. C. A. 8, 1894). And see Chapter 5, sec. 6.

[10] 163 U. S. 376 (1896).

nation are Federal powers created by and springing from the Constitution of the United States, and hence controlled by the Fifth Amendment to that Constitution, or whether they are local powers not created by the Constitution, although subject to its general provisions and the paramount authority of Congress. The repeated adjudications of this court have long since answered the former question in the negative. * * *

* * * * *

True it is that in many adjudications of this court the fact has been fully recognized, that although possessed of these attributes of local self-government, when exercising their tribal functions, all such rights are subject to the supreme legislative authority of the United States. *Cherokee Nation* v. *Kansas Railway Co.*, 135 U.S. 641, where the cases are fully reviewed. But the existence of the right in Congress to regulate the manner in which the local powers of the Cherokee nation shall be exercised does not render such local powers Federal powers arising from and created by the Constitution of the United States. It follows that as the powers of local self government enjoyed by the Cherokee nation existed prior to the Constitution, they are not operated upon by the Fifth Amendment, which, as we have said, had for its sole object to control the powers conferred by the Constitution on the National Government. * * * (Pp. 382–384.)

The decision in *Talton* v. *Mayes* does not mean that Indian tribes are not subject to the Constitution of the United States. It remains true that an Indian tribe is subject to the Federal Constitution in the same sense that the city of New Orleans, for instance, is subject to the Federal Constitution. The Federal Constitution prohibits slavery absolutely. This absolute prohibition applies to an Indian tribe as well as to a municipal government and it has been held that slave-holding within an Indian tribe became illegal with the passage of the Thirteenth Amendment.[11] It is, therefore, always pertinent to ask whether an ordinance of a tribe conflicts with the Constitution of the United States.[12] Where, however, the United States Constitution levies particular restraints upon federal courts or upon Congress, these restraints do not apply to the courts or legislatures of the Indian tribes.[13] Likewise, particular restraints upon the states are inapplicable to Indian tribes.

It has been held that the guaranty of religious liberty in the First Amendment of the United States Constitution does not protect a resident of New Orleans from religious oppression by municipal authorities.[14] Neither does it protect the Indian against religious oppression on the part of tribal authorities. As the citizen of New Orleans must write guaranties of religious liberty into his city charter or his state constitution, if he desires constitutional protection in this respect, so the members of an Indian tribe must write the guaranties they desire into tribal constitutions. In fact, many tribes have written such guaranties into tribal constitutions that are now in force.[15]

An extreme application of the doctrine of tribal sovereignty is found in the case of *Ex parte Crow Dog*,[16] in which it was held that the murder of one Sioux Indian by another upon an Indian reservation was not within the criminal jurisdiction of any court of the United States, but that only the Indian tribe itself could punish the offense.

The contention that the United States courts had jurisdiction in a case of this sort was based upon the language of a treaty with the Sioux, rather than upon considerations applicable generally to the various Indian tribes. The most important of the treaty clauses upon which the claim of federal jurisdiction was based provided:

> * * * And Congress shall, by appropriate legislation, secure to them an orderly government; they shall be subject to the laws of the United States, and each individual shall be protected in his rights of property, person, and life. (P. 568.)

Commenting upon this clause, the Supreme Court declared:

> It is equally clear, in our opinion, that the words can have no such effect as that claimed for them. The pledge to secure to these people, with whom the United States was contracting as a distinct political body, and orderly government, by appropriate legislation thereafter to be framed and enacted, necessarily implies, having regard to all the circumstances attending the transaction, that among the arts of civilized life, which it was the very purpose of all these arrangements to introduce and naturalize among them, was the highest and best of all, that of self-government, the regulation by themselves of their own domestic affairs, the maintenance of order and peace among their own members by the administration of their own laws and customs. They were nevertheless to be subject to the laws of the United States, not in the sense of citizens, but, as they had always been, as wards subject to a guardian; not as individuals, constituted members of the political community of the United States, with a voice in the selection of representatives and the framing

---

[11] *In re Sah Quah*, 31 Fed. 327 (D. C. Alaska, 1886).

[12] *Cf. Roff* v. *Burney*, 168 U. S. 218 (1897), discussed *infra*, sec. 4.

[13] In *United States* v. *Seneca Nation of New York Indians*, 274 Fed. 946 (D. C. W. D. N. Y. 1921), it was held that federal courts have no power to set aside action of a tribal council allegedly confiscatory of the property rights of a member of the tribe.

That the First Amendment guaranteeing religious liberty does not limit the action of a tribal council is the holding of Memo. Sol. I. D., August 8, 1938 (Lower Brule Sioux).

[14] *Permoli* v. *First Municipality*, 3 How. 589 (1845).

[15] A typical Indian bill of rights is the following, taken from the constitution of the Blackfeet Tribe, approved December 13, 1935, by the Secretary of the Interior, pursuant to sec. 16 of the Act of June 18, 1934 (48 Stat. 984, 987, 25 U. S. C. 476):

ARTICLE VIII—BILL OF RIGHTS

SECTION 1. *Suffrage.*—Any member of the Blackfeet Tribe, twenty-one (21) years of age or over, shall be eligible to vote at any election when he or she presents himself or herself at a polling place within his or her voting district.

SEC. 2. *Economic rights.*—All members of the tribe shall be accorded equal opportunities to participate in the economic resources and activities of the reservation.

SEC. 3. *Civil liberties.*—All members of the tribe may enjoy without hindrance freedom of worship, conscience, speech, press, assembly, and association.

SEC. 4. *Rights of accused.*—Any member of the Blackfeet Tribe accused of any offense shall have the right to a bond, open and public hearing, with due notice of the offense charged, and shall be permitted to summon witnesses on his own behalf. Trial by jury may be demanded by any prisoner accused of any offense punishable by more than thirty days' imprisonment. Excessive bail shall not be required and cruel punishment shall not be imposed.

Twenty-one other tribal constitutions adopted prior to June 1, 1940, contain more or less similar guaranties, as follows: Constitution of the Confederated Salish and Kootenai Tribes of the Flathead Reservation, Article VII; Confederated Tribes of the Grand Ronde Community, Article VIII; Hopi Tribe, Article IX; Lower Brule Sioux Tribe, Article VII; Makah Tribe, Article VII; Muckleshoot Indian Tribe, Article VII; Northern Cheyenne Tribe, Article V; Papago Tribe, Article VI; Puyallup Tribe, Article VII; Quileute Tribe, Article VII; San Carlos Apache Tribe, Article VI; Shoshone-Bannock Tribes of the Fort Hall Reservation, Article VII; Shoshone-Paiute Tribes of the Duck Valley Reservation, Article VII; Swinomish Indians of the Swinomish Reservation, Article VII; Tulalip Tribes, Article VII; Ute Indian Tribe, Article VII; Sac and Fox Tribe of Indians of Oklahoma, Article IX; Pawnee Indians of Oklahoma, Article VII; Caddo Indian Tribe of Oklahoma, Article X; Confederated Tribes of the Warm Springs Reservation of Oregon, Article VII; Tonkawa Tribe of Indians of Oklahoma, Article IX; Skokomish Indian Tribe of the Skokomish Reservation, Article VII. Absentee-Shawnee Tribe of Indians of Oklahoma, Article IX; Alabama-Quassarte Tribal Town, Article IX; Citizen Band of Potawatomi Indians of Oklahoma, Article X; Thlopthlocco Tribal Town of Oklahoma, Article VII; Port Gamble Indian Community of Washington, Article V; Eastern Shawnee Tribe of Oklahoma, Article IX; Shivwits Band of Paiute Indians of Shivwits Reservation, Utah, Article VI.

[16] 109 U. S. 556 (1883). Also see Chapter 18.

> of the laws, but as a dependent community who were in a state of pupilage, advancing from the condition of a savage tribe to that of a people who, through the discipline of labor and by education, it was hoped might become a self-supporting and self-governed society. * * * (Pp. 568–569.)

In finally rejecting the argument for federal jurisdiction the Supreme Court declared:

> * * * It is a case where, against an express exception in the law itself, that law, by argument and inference only, is sought to be extended over aliens and strangers; over the members of a community separated by race, by tradition, by the instincts of a free though savage life, from the authority and power which seeks to impose upon them the restraints of an external and unknown code, and to subject them to the responsibilities of civil conduct, according to rules and penalties of which they could have no previous warning; which judges them by a standard made by others and not for them, which takes no account of the conditions which should except them from its exactions, and makes no allowance for their inability to understand it. * * * (P. 571.)

The force of the decision in *Ex parte Crow Dog* was not weakened, although the scope of the decision was limited, by subsequent legislation which withdrew from the rule of tribal sovereignty a list of 7 major crimes, only recently extended to 10.[17] Over these specified crimes jurisdiction has been vested in the federal courts. Over all other crimes, including such serious crimes as kidnaping, attempted murder, receiving stolen goods, and forgery, jurisdiction resides not in the courts of nation or state but only in the Indian tribe itself.

We shall defer the question of the exact scope of tribal jurisdiction for more detailed consideration at a later point. We are concerned for the present only in analyzing the basic doctrine of tribal sovereignty. To this doctrine the case of *Ex parte Crow Dog* contributes not only an intimation of the vast and important content of criminal jurisdiction inherent in tribal sovereignty, but also an example of the consistent manner in which the United States Supreme Court has opposed the efforts of lower courts and administrative officials to infringe upon tribal sovereignty and to assume tribal prerogatives without statutory justification. The legal powers of an Indian tribe, measured by the decisions of the highest courts, are far more extensive than the powers which most Indian tribes have been actually permitted by energetic officials to exercise in their own right.

The acknowledgment of tribal sovereignty or autonomy by the courts of the United States[18] has not been a matter of lip service to a venerable but outmoded theory. The doctrine has been followed through the most recent cases, and from time to time carried to new implications. Moreover, it has been administered by the courts in a spirit of wholehearted sympathy and respect. The painstaking analysis by the Supreme Court of tribal laws and constitutional provisions in the *Cherokee Intermarriage Cases*,[19] is typical, and exhibits a degree of respect proper to the laws of a sovereign state.[20]

The sympathy of the courts towards the independent efforts of Indian tribes to administer the institutions of self-government has led to the doctrine that Indian laws and statutes are to be interpreted not in accordance with the technical rules of the common law, but in the light of the traditions and circumstances of the Indian people. An attempt in the case of *Ex parte Tiger*[21] to construe the language of the Creek Constitution in a technical sense was met by the appropriate judicial retort:

> * * * If the Creek Nation derived its system of jurisprudence through the common law, there would be much plausibility in this reasoning. But they are strangers to the common law.[22] They derive their jurisprudence from an entirely different source, and they are as unfamiliar with common-law terms and definitions as they are with Sanskrit or Hebrew. With them, "to indict" is to file a written accusation charging a person with crime. * * *

So, too, in the case of *McCurtain v. Grady*,[23] the court had occasion to note that:

> * * * The Choctaw constitution was not drawn by geologists or for geologists, or in the interest of science, or with scientific accuracy. It was framed by plain people, who have agreed among themselves what meaning should be attached to it, and the courts should give effect to that interpretation which its framers intended it should have. * * *

The realm of tribal autonomy which has been so carefully respected by the courts has been implicitly confirmed by Congress in a host of statutes providing that various administrative acts of the President or the Interior Department shall be carried out only with the consent of the Indian tribe or its chiefs or council.[24]

The whole course of congressional legislation with respect to the Indians has been based upon a recognition of tribal autonomy, qualified only where the need for other types of governmental control has become clearly manifest. As was said in a report of the Senate Judiciary Committee in 1870:

> Their right of self-government, and to administer justice among themselves, after their rude fashion, even to the extent of inflicting the death penalty, has never been questioned.[25]

It is a fact that state governments and administrative officials have frequently trespassed upon the realm of tribal autonomy, presuming to govern the Indian tribes through state law or departmental regulation or arbitrary administrative fiat,[26] but these trespasses have not impaired the vested legal powers of local self-government which have been recognized again and again when these trespasses have been challenged by an Indian tribe. "Power and authority rightfully conferred do not nec-

---

[17] See sec. 9, *infra*.

[18] The doctrine of tribal sovereignty is well summarized in the following passage in the case of *In re Sah Quah*, 31 Fed. 327 (D. C. Alaska 1886):

> From the organization of the government to the present time, the various Indian tribes of the United States have been treated as free and independent within their respective territories, governed by their tribal laws and customs, in all matters pertaining to their internal affairs, such as contracts and the manner of their enforcement, marriage, descents, and the punishment for crimes committed against each other. They have been excused from all allegiance to the municipal laws of the whites as precedents or otherwise in relation to tribal affairs, subject, however, to such restraints as were from time to time deemed necessary for their own protection, and for the protection of the whites adjacent to them. *Cherokee Nat.* v. *Georgia*, 5 Pet. 1, 16, 17; *Jackson* v. *Goodell*, 20 Johns. 193. (P. 329.)

And in the case of *Anderson* v. *Mathews*, 174 Cal. 587, 163 Pac. 902, 905 (1917), it was said:

> * * * The Indian tribes recognized by the federal government are not subject to the laws of the state in which they are situated. They are under the control and protection of the United States, but they retain the right of local self-government, and they regulate and control their own local affairs and rights of persons and property, except as Congress has otherwise specially provided by law. * * *

See, also, to the same effect, Story, Commentaries on the Constitution of the United States (1891), sec. 1099; Kent, Commentaries on American Law (14th ed., 1896), 383–386.

[19] 203 U. S. 76 (1906). And see *Famous Smith* v. *United States*, 151 U. S. 50 (1894); 8 Op. A. G. 300 (1857).

[20] And see sec. 8, *infra*.

[21] 2 Ind. T. 41, 47 S. W. 304, 305 (1898).

[22] See *Waldron* v. *United States*, 143 Fed. 413 (C. C. S. D. 1905); *Henson* v. *Johnson*, 246 Pac. 868 (1926).

[23] 1 Ind. T. 107, 38 S. W. 65, 71 (1896).

[24] See sec. 10, *infra*; 25 U. S. C. 130, 132, 159, 162, 184, 218, 225, 229, 371, 397, 398, 402. These provisions are discussed later under relevant headings.

[25] Sen. Rept. No. 268, 41st Cong., 3d sess., p. 10.

[26] See Oskison, In Governing the Indian Use the Indian! (1917), 23 Case & Comment 722.

essarily cease to exist in consequence of long nonuser."[27] The Wheeler-Howard Act,[28] by affording statutory recognition of these powers of local self-government and administrative assistance in developing adequate mechanisms for such government, may reasonably be expected to end the conditions that have in the past led the Interior Department and various state agencies to deal with matters that are properly within the legal competence of the Indian tribes themselves.[29]

Neither the allotting of land in severalty nor the granting of citizenship has destroyed the tribal relationship upon which local autonomy rests.[30] The extent, however, to which the foregoing principles may apply to scattered Indian groups which have never exercised powers of self-government presents questions to which no authoritative answers have yet been given.[31]

[27] *United States ex rel. Standing Bear v. Crook*, 25 Fed. Cas. No. 14891 (C. C. Neb. 1879).

[28] Act of June 18, 1934, 48 Stat. 984, 25 U. S. C. 461 *et seq.* See fn. 7, *supra*.

[29] On the subordination of departmental regulations to the provisions of tribal constitutions, see 25 C. F. R. 71.4, 161.1, 171.13. And see Memo. Sol. I. D., November 11, 1935 (re Grazing Regulations). The Secretarial order approving a tribal constitution regularly contains this statement:

> All rules and regulations heretofore promulgated by the Interior Department or by the Office of Indian Affairs, so far as they may be incompatible with any of the provisions of the said Constitution and Bylaws are hereby declared inapplicable to these Indians.

[30] See Chapter 8, sec. 2C, and Chapter 14, secs. 1, 2.

[31] See Goodrich, The Legal Status of the California Indians (1926), 14 Calif. L. Rev. 83, 157.

SECTION 3. THE FORM OF TRIBAL GOVERNMENT

Since any group of men, in order to act as a group, must act through forms which give the action the character and authority of group action, an Indian tribe must, if it has any power at all, have the power to prescribe the forms through which its will may be registered. The first element of sovereignty, and the last which may survive successive statutory limitations of Indian tribal power, is the power of the tribe to determine and define its own form of government. Such power includes the right to define the powers and duties of its officials, the manner of their appointment or election, the manner of their removal, the rules they are to observe in their capacity as officials, and the forms and procedures which are to attest the authoritative character of acts done in the name of the tribe.[32]

Such power also includes the power to interpret its own laws and ordinances, which interpretations will be followed by the Federal courts.[33]

The question of whether action taken in the name of an Indian tribe is in truth tribal action, has been before state and federal courts on many occasions, and in every case the courts have held that the definition of the form of tribal government is a matter for the decision of the Indians themselves.

Such a decision for example is found in the case of *Pueblo of Santa Rosa v. Fall*.[34] Certain attorneys claimed to represent an Indian pueblo and asserted ownership of a large area which the Federal Government considered public domain. The Indians themselves, apparently, denied the authority of the attorneys in question to put forward such a claim, but the attorneys justified their action on the basis of an alleged agreement with the "captain" of the Pueblo. When the case came before the Supreme Court, that body found that according to the custom of the Pueblo the "captain" would have no authority to act for the Pueblo in a matter of this sort, and that such action without the approval of the Pueblo council would be void. On the issue of fact the court found:

> * * * That Luis was without power to execute the papers in question, for lack of authority from the Indian council, in our opinion is well established. (Pp. 319–320.)

The Supreme Court reversed the decision of the lower court, which had dismissed the suit on the merits, and held:

> * * * the cause must be remanded to the court of first instance with directions to dismiss the bill, on the ground that the suit was brought by counsel without authority, but without prejudice to the bringing of any other suit hereafter by and with the authority of the alleged Pueblo of Santa Rosa. (P. 321.)

Special statutes relating to particular tribes frequently designate the tribal council, committee, or official who is to pass upon

[32] One of the current popular superstitions about Indians is the notion that every Indian male over the age of 30 is either a chief or a "Big Chief." This superstition is of great help to those Indians or pseudo-Indians who seek to earn a respectable living by selling snake oil to the sick, or by selling their fellow-tribesmen's land to land speculators or to the Federal Government, or by lecturing to women's clubs and congressional committees, or by endowing indigent lawyers with tribal business. It is generally very difficult to persuade those who have paid for or profited by such transactions with Indian "chiefs" that the Indian in question was not an officer of his tribe and had no tribal lands, tribal suits, or tribal wisdom to give away. It is, therefore, a matter of some concern to an Indian tribe that it should have the right to define a framework of official action and to insist that acts of individuals and groups that do not fall within that framework are not acts of the tribe. This definition of a framework or government may take the form of a written constitution, or it may take the form of the British Constitution, a disorderly mass of practices shading off into parliamentary procedure and court etiquette but including at its core the essential canons that we invoke, consciously or unconsciously, to decide whether the acts of certain individuals are governmental or nongovernmental or antigovernmental.

On the form of tribal organization, a leading authority has this to say:

> The "tribe" is something we conceive of rather chaotically. Yet these native peoples were as neatly and elaborately organized politically as many civilized peoples. * * * (P. 181.)
>
> * * * * *
>
> * * * The police of the Plains tribes are, one may say, merely one facet of an elaborate and highly complex bureaucratic political organization. (P. 200.) MacLeod, Police and Punishment among Native Americans of the Plains (1937), 28 J. Crim. Law and Criminology 181.

[33] *Talton v. Mayes*, 163 U. S. 376 (1896). This rule has been generally followed by administrative authorities. See for example Memo. Sol. I. D., July 5, 1940, holding that the choice between two reasonable interpretations of a provision of the Constitution of the San Carlos Apache Tribe should be made by the tribe or its tribal council rather than by the Interior Department.

[34] 273 U. S. 315 (1927). To the same effect, see 7 Op. A. G. 142 (1855); Memo. Sol. I. D., March 11, 1935.

In 5 Op. A. G. 79 (1849), the opinion is expressed that a release to be executed by the "Creek Indians" would be valid "provided, that the chiefs and headmen executing it are such chiefs and headmen, and constitute the whole or a majority of the council of the Creek nation."

In *Rollins and Presbrey v. United States*, 23 C. Cls. 106 (1888), the court finds that a chief's authority to act in the name of the tribe has been established by the tacit assent of the tribe and by their acceptance of the benefits of his acts.

On the general question of how a tribe may contract, see Chapter 14, sec. 5.

In the case of *Mt. Pleasant v. Gansworth*, 271 N. Y. Supp. 78 (1934), it is held that the Tuscarora tribal council has never been endowed with probate jurisdiction, that no other body has been set up by the tribe to exercise probate powers, and hence that state courts may step in to remedy the lack. Whether or not the final conclusion is justified, in the light of such cases as *Patterson v. Council of Seneca Nation*, 245 N. Y. 433, 157 N. E. 734 (1927), the opinion of the court indicates at least that the limitations which a tribe may impose upon the jurisdiction of its own governmental bodies and officers will be respected.

matters entrusted to the tribe by Congress [55] Some statutes confer upon the President or the Secretary of the Interior supervisory powers over certain named tribal councils [56] Numerous appropriation acts specify the tribal governing bodies or officers recognized by the Federal Government, in making provisions for tribal approval of various expenditures or in appropriating tribal or federal funds for salaries of Indian councils, courts, or chiefs [57] And treaties with Indian tribes frequently declare in express language, or show by the manner of Indian ratification, the character of tribal government [58] Other treaties guarantee that such tribal governments will not be subjected to state or territorial law [59] Other treaties guarantee to various Indian tribes "the right to establish their own form of government, appoint their own officers, and administer their own laws, subject, however, to the legislation of the Congress of the United States regulating trade and intercourse with the Indians" [60] Various other powers, including the power to pass upon various federal expenditures, the power to manage schools supported by the Federal Government, the power to allot land, and the power to designate missionaries to act in a supervisory capacity with respect to annuity distributions, are conferred or confirmed by special treaty provisions [61]

In accordance with the rule applicable to foreign treaties, the courts have repeatedly indicated that they will not go behind the terms of a treaty to inquire whether the representatives of the tribe accepted as such by the President and the Senate were proper representatives [62]

Treaties must be viewed not only as forms of exercising federal power, but equally as forms of exercising tribal power [63] And from the standpoint of tribal law, a later ordinance may supersede a treaty, just as a later act of Congress may supersede a treaty, although in either case an international liability may result [64]

Recognition of tribal governments and tribal powers may be found not only in acts of Congress and in treaties but also in state statutes, which, when adopted with the advice and consent of the Indians themselves, have been accorded special weight [65]

Not only must officers presuming to act in the name of an Indian tribe show that their acts fall within their allotted function and authority, but likewise the procedural formalities which tradition or ordinance require must be followed in executing an act within the acknowledged jurisdiction of the officer or set of officers [66]

---

[55] Act of March 3, 1839, 5 Stat 349 (Brothertown), R S §§ 1765–1779, Act of March 3, 1843, 5 Stat 645 (Stockbridge), Act of August 6, 1846, 9 Stat 55 (Stockbridge), Act of May 23, 1872, 17 Stat 159 (Pottawatomie and Absentee Shawnee), Act of August 7, 1882, 22 Stat 349 (Indian Territory), Act of March 3, 1885, 23 Stat 340 (Umatilla), Act of October 19, 1888, 25 Stat 608 (Cherokee), Act of February 28, 1889, 25 Stat 687 (Shoshones and Bannocks, etc), Act of July 1, 1898, 30 Stat 567 (Seminole), Act of July 1, 1902 32 Stat 636 (Kansas), Act of June 28, 1906, 34 Stat 539 (Osage), Joint Res of March 2, 1906, 34 Stat 822 (Five Civilized Tribes), Act of February 8, 1918 40 Stat 433 (Choctaw and Chickasaw), Act of May 14, 1926, 44 Stat 555 (Chippewa), Act of July 2, 1926, 44 Stat 801 (Pottawatomie), Act of July 3, 1926, 44 Stat 807 (Crow), Act of May 26, 1928, 45 Stat 787 (Choctaw and Chickasaw), Act of March 1 1929, 45 Stat 1439 (Klamath), Act of March 2, 1929, 45 Stat 1478 (Osage), Joint Res of May 12 1930, 46 Stat 268 (Yankton Sioux Tribe), Act of June 19, 1930, 46 Stat 788 (Choctaw and Chickasaw), Act of February 14, 1931 46 Stat 1105 (Klamath); Act of April 21, 1932, 47 Stat 88 (Choctaw and Chickasaw), Act of April 25, 1932, 47 Stat 137 (Cherokee), Act of April 27, 1932, 47 Stat 140 (Seminole), Act of June 6, 1932, 47 Stat 169, (L'Anse Band of Lake Superior), Act of June 30, 1932, 47 Stat 420 (Crow and Fort Peck), Act of June 6, 1934, 48 Stat 910 (Quinault), Act of June 19, 1935 49 Stat 388 (Tlingit and Haida Indians of Alaska), Act of August 19, 1937, 50 Stat 699 (Cherokee), Act of June 25, 1938, 52 Stat 1207 (Klamath)

[56] See Act of June 7, 1897, 30 Stat 62, 84 (Five Tribes), Act of March 3 1901, 31 Stat 1058, 1077 (Five Tribes), Act of June 28, 1906, 34 Stat 539, 545 (conferring power to remove members of Osage Council), upheld in *United States ex rel Brown v Lane*, 232 U S 598 (1914)

[57] Act of June 30, 1834, 4 Stat 682, 685, Act of July 27, 1868, 15 Stat 198, 210, 211, Act of July 15, 1870, 16 Stat 335, 359, Act of March 3, 1871, 16 Stat 544, 560, Act of May 29, 1872, 17 Stat 165, 189, Act of February 14, 1873, 17 Stat 437, 460, Act of June 22, 1874, 18 Stat 146, 171, Act of March 3, 1875, 18 Stat 420, 434 444, 451, Act of March 3 1877, 19 Stat 271, 280, Act of May 15, 1886, 24 Stat 29, 32, Act of June 7, 1897, 30 Stat 62, 84, 92, Act of March 3, 1901, 31 Stat 1058, 1077, Act of March 3, 1903, 32 Stat 982, 1009, Act of June 21, 1906, 34 Stat 325, 342, Act of March 3, 1909, 35 Stat 781, 805, Act of March 3, 1911, 36 Stat 1058, 1065, Act of June 30, 1913, 38 Stat 77, Act of August 1, 1914, 38 Stat 582, Act of May 18, 1916, 39 Stat 123, Act of March 2, 1917, 39 Stat 969, Act of May 25, 1918, 40 Stat 561, Act of June 30, 1919, 41 Stat 3, Act of February 14, 1920, 41 Stat 408, Act of March 3, 1921, 41 Stat 1225, Act of May 24, 1922, 42 Stat 552, Act of January 24, 1923, 42 Stat 1174, Act of June 5, 1924, 43 Stat 390, Act of March 3, 1925, 43 Stat 1141, Act of May 10, 1926, 44 Stat 453, 458, Act of January 12, 1927, 44 Stat 934, 939, Act of March 4, 1929, 45 Stat 1562, 1566, 1584, Act of April 22, 1932, 47 Stat 91, 94, 112, Act of February 17, 1933, 47 Stat 820, 824, 839, Act of March 2, 1934, 48 Stat 362, 366, Act of May 9, 1935, 49 Stat 176, 182, 195, Act of June 22, 1936, 49 Stat 1757, 1768, Act of May 9, 1938, 52 Stat 291, 314, 315

[58] Treaty of August 7, 1790, with the Creek Nation, 7 Stat 35, Treaty of September 14, 1816, with the Cherokee Nation, 7 Stat 148, Treaty of July 8, 1817, with the Cherokee Nation, 7 Stat 156, Treaty of February 12, 1825, with the Creek Nation, 7 Stat 237, Treaty of September 21, 1832, with the Sac and Fox Indians, 7 Stat 374, Treaty of April 1, 1850, with the Wyandot Tribe, 9 Stat 987, Treaty of May 10, 1854, with the Shawnee Indians, 10 Stat 1053, Treaty of January 17, 1837, with the Choctaws and Chickasaws, 11 Stat 573, Treaty of July 31, 1855, with the Ottowa and Chippewa Indians, 11 Stat 621, Treaty of August 2, 1855, with the Chippewa Indians, 11 Stat 633, Treaty of July 19, 1866, with the Cherokee Nation, 14 Stat 799, Treaty of June 30, 1902, with the Creek Tribe, 32 Stat 500 And see *United States* v *Anderson*, 225 Fed 825 (D C E D Wis 1915)

[59] Art IV of Treaty of September 27, 1830, with the Choctaw Nation, 7 Stat 333, 334, Art XIV of the Treaty of March 24, 1832, with the Creek Tribe, 7 Stat 366 368, Art V of the Treaty of December 29, 1835, with the Cherokee Tribe, 7 Stat 478, 481

[60] Art IV of the Treaty of January 15, 1838, with the New York Indians, 7 Stat 550, 551 Accord Art 7 of the Treaty of June 22, 1855, with the Choctaws and Chickasaws, 11 Stat 611, 612 *Cf* 19 Op A G 342 (1889) (holding establishment of national bank in Creek Nation unlawful) See Chapter 23, sec 3

[61] Treaty of January 31, 1786, with the Shawanoe Nation, 7 Stat 26, Treaty of June 3, 1825, with the Kansas Nation, 7 Stat 244, Treaty of January 24, 1826, with the Creek Nation, 7 Stat 286, Art VIII of Treaty of July 20, 1831, with the Shawnees and Senecas, 7 Stat 351, 353, Art VI of the Treaty of March 28, 1836, with the Ottowas and Chippewas, 7 Stat 491, 493, Art III of the Treaty of April 23, 1836, with the Wyandots, 7 Stat 502, Art I of the Treaty of January 4, 1845, with the Creeks and Seminoles, 9 Stat 821, Art II of the Treaty of August 6, 1846, with the Cherokees, 9 Stat 871, Art VI, of the Treaty of June 22, 1852, with the Chickasaws, 10 Stat 974, 975, Art IV of the Treaty of March 17, 1842, with the Wyandott Nation, 11 Stat 581, 582, Art VI and Art VII of the Treaty of June 22, 1855, with the Choctaw and Chickasaw tribes, 11 Stat 611, 612, 613, Art III of the Treaty of February 5, 1856, with the Stockbridge and Munsee tribes, 11 Stat 663, 665, Art VI of the Treaty of August 7, 1856, with Creek and Seminole Indians, 11 Stat 699, 703–704, Art V of the Treaty of September 24, 1857, with the Pawnee Indians, 11 Stat 729, 731, Art VII of the Treaty of March 12, 1858, with the Ponca Tribe, 12 Stat 997, 1000, Art VII of the Treaty of May 7, 1864, with the Chippewa Indians, 13 Stat 693, 694, Art I of the Treaty of March 21, 1866, with the Seminole Indians, 14 Stat 755, 756, Treaty of April 7, 1866, with the Bois Forte band of Chippewa Indians, 14 Stat 765, Art XXIV of the Treaty of April 28, 1866, with the Choctaw and Chickasaw Nations, 14 Stat 769, 776–777, Treaty of June 14, 1866, with the Creek Nation, 14 Stat 785, Treaty of July 19, 1866, with the Cherokee Nation, 14 Stat 799, Treaty of February 19, 1867, with the Sisseton and Wahpeton bands of Dakota or Sioux Indians, 15 Stat 505, Art VIII of the Treaty of February 23, 1867, with the Shawnees Indians, 15 Stat 513, 515

[62] *United States* v *New York Indians*, 173 U S 464 (1899), *Fellows* v *Blacksmith*, 19 How 366 (1856) See Chapter 8, sec 1

[63] See Chapter 14, sec 3

[64] *The Cherokee Freedmen*, 183 U S 115 (1901) See Chapter 8, sec 1

[65] *United States ex rel Kennedy* v *Tyler*, 269 U S 13 (1925) And see Chapter 8

[66] Thus in *Walker* v *McLoud*, 204 U S 302 (1907), the Supreme Court held invalid a claim of title under a sale by a sheriff of the Choctaw Nation,

The doctrine of *de facto* officers has been applied to an Indian tribe, in accordance with the rule applied to other governmental agencies, so as to safeguard from collateral attack acts and documents signed by officers acting under color of authority, though subject, in proper proceedings, to removal from office.[47]

Based upon the analogy of the constitutional law of the United States, the doctrine has been applied to Indian statutes and constitutional provisions that statutes deemed by the courts to be violative of constitutional limitations are to be regarded as void.[48]

The earlier statutes of Congress frequently recognized the authority of chiefs and headmen to act for a tribe.[49] In conformity with the policy of breaking down such authority, later statutes frequently contemplated action by general councils open to all male adult members of the tribe.[50]

Other congressional legislation has specifically recognized the propriety of paying salaries to tribal officers out of tribal funds.[51]

The power to define a form of government is one which has been exercised to the full, and it would be impossible within the compass of this chapter to analyze the forms of government that different Indian communities have established for themselves. Indeed, it may be said that the constitutional history of the Indian tribes covers a longer period and a wider range of variation than the constitutional history of the colonies, the states, and the United States. It was some time before the immigrant Columbus reached these shores, according to eminent historians, that the first Federal Constitution on the American Continent was drafted, the Gayaneshagowa, or Great Binding Law of the Five (later six) Nations (Iroquois).[52] It was in this constitution that Americans first established the democratic principles of initiative, recall, referendum, and equal suffrage.[53] In this constitution, also, were set forth the ideal of the responsibility of governmental officials to the electorate, and the obligation of the present generation to future generations which we call the principle of conservation.[54]

Between the time of the adoption of the Constitution of the Five Nations and the adoption by more than a hundred Indian tribes of written constitutions pursuant to the Act of June 18, 1934, there is a fascinating history of political development that has never been pieced together.[55] Students of Indian law know of the achievements of the Five Civilized Tribes in constitution making by reason of occasional references in the decided cases

---

for the reason that the sheriff had failed to act in accordance with Choctaw laws governing such sales.

In 19 Op. A. G. 179 (1888), it is held that a decree of divorce which has not been signed by a judge or clerk of court, as required by the laws of the Choctaw Nation, is invalid.

In re Darch, 265 N. Y. Supp. 86 (1933), involves action of a special tribal council meeting to which only a few members of the council were invited. The action was declared invalid on the ground that the council's rules of procedure required due notice of a special meeting to be given to all the members of the council. Based on an analogy taken from corporation law, the rule was laid down that violation of this requirement rendered the acts of the council invalid.

In 25 Op. A. G. 308, 309, 312 (1904), it appeared that certain sums were to be paid to attorneys "only after the tribal authorities, thereunto duly and specifically authorized by the tribe, shall have signed a writing * * *." By resolution of the tribe the business committee had been authorized to sign the writing in question. The signatures of the business committee, in the opinion of the Attorney General, met the statutory requirement:

> The proceedings of the council were regular, and the motions were carried by a sufficient number of voters, though less than a majority of those present. (See *State* v. *Vanosdal*, 131 Ind., 388; *Attorney-General* v. *Shepard*, 62 N. H. 383; and *Mount* v. *Parker*, 32 N. J. Law, 341.)

[47] See *Nofire* v. *United States*, 164 U.S. 657 (1897); *Seneca Nation of Indians* v. *John*, 16 N. Y. Supp. 40 (1891).

[48] See *Whitmire, Trustee* v. *Cherokee Nation, et al.*, 30 C. Cls. 138 (1895); *Delaware Indians* v. *Cherokee Nation*, 38 C. Cls. 234 (1903), aff'd 193 U. S. 127 (1904); 19 Op. A. G. 229 (1889).

[49] 25 U. S. C. 130:

> *Withholding of moneys or goods on account of intoxicating liquors.* No annuities, or moneys, or goods, shall be paid or distributed to Indians * * * until the chiefs and headmen of the tribe shall have pledged themselves to use all their influence and to make all proper exertions to prevent the introduction and sale of such liquor in their country. (R. S. § 2087.)

25 U. S. C. 132:

> *Mode of distribution of goods.*—Whenever goods and merchandise are delivered to the chiefs of a tribe, for the tribe, such goods and merchandise shall be turned over by the agent or superintendent of such tribe to the chiefs in bulk, and in the original package, as nearly as practicable, and in the presence of the headmen of the tribe, if practicable, to be distributed to the tribe by the chiefs in such manner as the chiefs may deem best, in the presence of the agent or superintendent. (R. S. § 2090.)

And cf. Act of June 14, 1862, sec. 3, 12 Stat. 427, 25 U. S. C. 187, R. S. § 2121.

[50] See *Klamath & Modoc Tribes* v. *United States*, 296 U. S. 244, 248 (1935).

[51] 25 U. S. C. 162, after providing generally for the segregation, deposit, and investment of tribal funds, contains the following qualification:

> * * * That any part of tribal funds required for support of schools or pay of tribal officers shall be excepted from segregation or deposit as herein authorized and the same shall be expended for the purposes aforesaid: * * *

[52] A. C. Parker, "The Constitution of the Five Nations" (New York State Museum Bulletin, No. 184).

[53] 93. Whenever a specially important matter or a great emergency is presented before the Confederate Council and the nature of the matter affects the entire body of the Five Nations, threatening their utter ruin, then the Lords of the Confederacy must submit the matter to the decision of their people and the decision of the people shall affect the decision of the Confederate Council. This decision shall be a confirmation of the voice of the people.

> 94. The men of every clan of the Five Nations shall have a Council Fire ever burning in readiness for a council of the clan. When it seems necessary for a council to be held to discuss the welfare of the clans, then the men may gather about the fire. This council shall have the same rights as the council of the women.
>
> 95. The women of every clan of the Five Nations shall have a Council Fire ever burning in readiness for a council of the clan. When in their opinion it seems necessary for the interest of the people they shall hold a council and their decision and recommendation shall be introduced before the Council of Lords by the War Chief for its consideration.
>
> 96. All the Clan council fires of a nation or of the Five Nations may unite into one general council fire, or delegates from all the council fires may be appointed to unite in a general council for discussing the interests of the people. The people shall have the right to make appointments and to delegate their power to others of their number. When their council shall have come to a conclusion on any matter, their decision shall be reported to the Council of the Nation or to the Confederate Council (as the case may require) by the War Chief or the War Chiefs. (The Constitution of the Five Nations, translated and edited by A. C. Parker.)

[54] 28. When a candidate Lord is to be installed he shall furnish four strings of shells (or wampum) one span in length bound together at one end. Such will constitute the evidence of his pledge to the Confederate Lords that he will live according to the constitution of the Great Peace and exercise justice in all affairs.

> When the pledge is furnished the Speaker of the Council must hold the shell strings in his hand and address the opposite side of the Council Fire and he shall commence his address saying: "Now behold him. He has now become a Confederate Lord. See how splendid he looks." An address may then follow. At the end it shall send the bunch of shell strings to the opposite side and they shall be received as evidence of the pledge. Then shall the opposite side say:
>
> "We now do crown you with the sacred emblem of the deer's antlers, the emblem of your Lordship. You shall now become a mentor of the people of the Five Nations. The thickness of your skin shall be seven spans—which is to say that you shall be proof against anger, offensive actions and criticism. Your heart shall be filled with peace and good will and your mind filled with a yearning for the welfare of the people of the Confederacy. With endless patience you shall carry out your duty and your firmness shall be tempered with tenderness for your people. Neither anger nor fury shall find lodgment in your mind and all your words and actions shall be marked with calm deliberation. In all of your deliberations in the Confederate Council, in your efforts at law making, in all your official acts, self interest shall be cast into oblivion. Cast not over your shoulder behind you the warnings of the nephews and nieces should they chide you for any error or wrong you may do, but return to the way of the Great Law which is just and right. Look and listen for the welfare of the whole people and have always in view not only the present but also the coming generations, even those whose faces are yet beneath the surface of the ground—the unborn of the future Nation." (The Constitution of the Five Nations, translated and edited by A. C. Parker.)

[55] Descriptive accounts of various tribal governments will be found in: J. J. Thompson, Law Among the Aborigines (1924), 6 Ill. L. Q. 204; Hagan, Tribal Law of the American Indian (1917), 23 Case & Com. 735; E. L. Watson, The Indian as a Lawyer (1930), 7 Dicta, No. 9, p. 10.

to the Cherokee,[56] Creek,[57] and Choctaw[58] constitutions. What is not generally known is that many other Indian tribes have operated under written constitutions.[59] The writing of Indian constitutions under the Wheeler-Howard Act of June 18, 1934, is therefore no new thing in the legal history of this continent, and it is possible to hope that some of the political wisdom that has already stood the test of centuries of revolutionary change in Indian life has been embodied in the constitutions of the hundred or more tribes which have been organized under that act.[60]

While the Act of June 18, 1934,[61] had little or no effect upon the substantive powers of tribal self-government vested in the

---

[56] The constitution of the Cherokees was a wonderful adapation to the circumstances and conditions of the time, and to a civilization that was yet to come. It was framed and adopted by a people some of whom were still in the savage state, and the better portion of whom had just entered upon that stage of civilization which is characterized by industrial pursuits; and it was framed during a period of extraordinary turmoil and civil discord, when the greater part of the Cherokee people had just been driven by military force from their mountains and valleys in Georgia, and been brought by enforced immigration into the country of the Western Cherokees; when a condition of anarchy and civil war reigned in the territory—a condition which was to continue until the two branches of the nation should be united under the treaty of 1846 (27 C. Cls. R., 1); yet for more than half a century it has met the requirements of a race steadily advancing in prosperity and education and enlightenment so well that it has needed, so far as they are concerned, no material alteration or amendment, and deserves to be classed among the few great works of intelligent statesmanship which outlive their own time and continue through succeeding generations to assure the rights and guide the destinies of men. And it is not the least of the successes of the constitution of the Cherokees that the judiciary of another nation are able, with entire confidence in the clearness and wisdom of its provisions, to administer it for the protection of Cherokee citizens and the maintenance of their personal and political rights. *Journeycake* v. *Cherokee Nation and United States*, 28 C. Cls. 281, 317–318 (1893).

[57] See *Ex parte Tiger*, 2 Ind. T. 41, 47 S. W. 304 (1898).

[58] See *McCurtain* v. *Grady*, 1 Ind. T. 107, 38 S. W. 65 (1896).

[59] As of December 13, 1934, constitutions or documents in the nature of constitutions were recorded in the Interior Department for the following tribes: Absentee Delaware; Absentee Shawnee; Annette Islands Reserve; Blackfeet; Cherokee; Cheyenne and Arapahoe; Cheyenne River; Chickasaw; Chippewas of Michigan; Choctaw; Choctaw (Mississippi); Colorado River; Creek or Muskogee; Crow; Eastern Cherokee; Flathead; For Belknap; Fort Bidwell; Fort Hall; Fort McDowell; Fort Peck; Fort Yuma; Grand Portage; Grand Ronde; Hoopa Valley; Hopi Iroquois Confederacy; Kickapoo; Kiowa; Klamath; Laguna Pueblo; Lovelock; Makah; Menominee; Mescalero; Mohican; Navajo; Osage; Pima; Pine Ridge; Potowatomie (Kansas); Potowatomie (Okla.); Pyramid Lake; Quinaielt; Red Lake; Rocky Boy; Rosebud; San Carlos; Seminole; Seneca (N. Y.); Seneca (Okla.); Shoshone-Arapahoe; Siletz; Sisseton; Standing Rock; Swinomish; Tongue River; Turtle Mountain; Uintah and Ouray; Warm Springs; Western Shoshone; White Earth; Winnebago; Yakima; Yankton.

[60] As of May 15, 1940, the following tribes had adopted constitutions or charters under the Act of June 18, 1934, as amended:

Arizona.—San Carlos Apache Tribe, constitution approved January 17, 1936; Gila River Pima-Maricopa Indian Community, May 14, 1936, charter ratified February 28, 1938; Fort McDowell Mohave-Apache Community, November 24, 1936, charter June 6, 1938; Hopi Tribe, December 19, 1936; Papago Tribe, January 6, 1937; Yavapai-Apache Indian Community, February 12, 1937; Colorado River Indian Tribes of the Colorado River Reservation, Arizona and California, August 13, 1937; White Mountain Apache Tribe, August 26, 1938; Hualapai Tribe of the Hualapai Reservation, December 17, 1938; Havasupai Tribe of the Havasupai Reservation, March 27, 1939.

California.—Big Valley Band of Pomo Indians of the Big Valley Rancheria, January 15, 1936; Upper Lake Band of Pomo Indians of the Upper Lake Rancheria, January 15, 1936; Me-wuk Indian Community of the Wilton Rancheria, January 15, 1936; Tule River Indian Tribe, January 15, 1936; Tuolumne Band of Me-wuk Indians of the Tuolumne Rancheria, January 15, 1936, charter November 12, 1937; Fort Bidwell Indian Community, January 28, 1936; Kashia Band of Pomo Indians of the Stewart's Point Rancheria, March 11, 1936; Manchester Band of Pomo Indians of the Manchester Rancheria, March 11, 1936, charter February 27, 1937; Covelo Indian Community, December 16, 1936, charter November 6, 1937; Quechan Tribe, December 18, 1936; Quartz Valley Indian Community, June 15, 1939, charter March 12, 1940.

Colorado.—Southern Ute Tribe of the Southern Ute Reservation, November 4, 1936, charter November 1, 1938.

Idaho.—Shoshone-Bannock Tribes of the Fort Hall Reservation, April 30, 1936, charter April 17, 1937.

Iowa.—Sac and Fox Tribe of the Mississippi in Iowa, December 20, 1937.

Kansas.—Iowa Tribe in Nebraska and Kansas, February 26, 1937, charter June 19, 1937; Kickapoo Tribe in Kansas, February 26, 1937, charter June 19, 1937; Sac and Fox Tribe of Missouri, March 2, 1937, charter June 19, 1937.

Michigan.—Hannahville Indian Community, July 23, 1936, charter August 21, 1937; Bay Mills Indian Community, November 4, 1936, charter November 27, 1937; Keweenaw Bay Indian Community, December 17, 1936, charter July 17, 1937; Saginaw Chippewa Indian Tribe of Michigan, May 6, 1937, charter August 28, 1937.

Minnesota.—Lower Sioux Indian Community in the State of Minnesota, June 11, 1936, charter July 17, 1937; Prairie Island Indian Community in the State of Minnesota, June 20, 1936, charter July 23, 1937; Minnesota Chippewa Tribe, July 24, 1936, charter November 13, 1937.

Montana.—Confederated Salish and Kootenai Tribes of the Flathead Reservation, October 28, 1935, charter April 25, 1936; Chippewa Cree Tribe of the Rocky Boy's Reservation, November 23, 1935, charter July 25, 1936; Northern Cheyenne Tribe, November 23, 1935, charter November 7, 1936; Blackfeet Tribe of the Blackfeet Indian Reservation, December 13, 1935, charter August 15, 1936; Fort Belknap Indian Community, December 13, 1935, charter August 25, 1937.

Nebraska.—Omaha Tribe of Nebraska, March 30, 1936, charter August 22, 1936; Ponca Tribe of Native Americans, April 3, 1936, charter August 15, 1936; Santee Sioux Tribe of Nebraska, April 3, 1936, charter August 22, 1936; Winnebago Tribe of Nebraska, April 3, 1936, charter August 15, 1936.

Nevada.—Reno-Sparks Indian Colony, January 15, 1936, charter January 7, 1938; Pyramid Lake Paiute Tribe, January 15, 1936, charter November 21, 1936; Washoe Tribe, January 24, 1936, charter February 27, 1937; Shoshone-Paiute Tribes of the Duck Valley Reservation, April 20, 1936, charter August 22, 1936; Fort McDermitt Paiute and Shoshone Tribe, July 2, 1936, charter November 21, 1936; Yerington Paiute Tribe, January 4, 1937, charter April 10, 1937; Walker River Paiute Tribe, March 26, 1937, charter May 8, 1937; Te-Moak Bands of Western Shoshone Indians, August 24, 1938, charter December 12, 1938; Yomba Shoshone Tribe, December 20, 1939, charter December 22, 1939.

New Mexico.—Pueblo of Santa Clara, December 20, 1935; Apache Tribe of the Mescalero Reservation, March 25, 1936, charter August 1, 1936; Jicarilla Apache Tribe of New Mexico, August 4, 1937, charter September 4, 1937.

North Dakota.—Three Affiliated Tribes of the Fort Berthold Reservation, June 29, 1936, charter April 24, 1937.

Oregon.—Confederated Tribes of the Grande Ronde Community, May 13, 1936, charter August 22, 1936; Confederated Tribes of the Warm Springs Reservation, February 14, 1938, charter April 23, 1938.

South Dakota.—Lower Brule Sioux Tribe, November 27, 1935, charter July 11, 1936; Rosebud Sioux Tribe, December 20, 1935, charter March 16, 1937; Cheyenne River Sioux Tribe, December 27, 1935; Oglala Sioux Tribe of the Pine Ridge Reservation, January 15, 1936; Flandreau Santee Sioux Tribe, April 24, 1936, charter October 31, 1936.

Texas.—Alabama-Coushatta Tribes of Texas, August 19, 1938, charter October 17, 1939.

Utah.—Ute Indian Tribe of the Uintah and Ouray Reservation, January 19, 1937, charter August 10, 1938; Shivwits Band of Paiute Indians of the Shivwits Reservation, March 21, 1940.

Washington.—Tulalip Tribes, January 24, 1936, charter October 3, 1936; Swinomish Indian Tribal Community, January 27, 1936, charter July 25, 1936; Puyallup Tribe, May 13, 1936; Muckleshoot Indian Tribe, May 13, 1936, charter October 31, 1936; Makah Indian Tribe, May 16, 1936, charter February 27, 1937; Quileute Tribe of the Quileute Reservation, November 11, 1936, charter August 21, 1937; Skokomish Indian Tribe of the Skokomish Reservation, May 3, 1938, charter July 22, 1939; Kalispel Indian Community of the Kalispel Reservation, March 24, 1938, charter May 28, 1938; Port Gamble Indian Community, September 7, 1939.

Wisconsin.—Red Cliff Band of Lake Superior Chippewa Indians, June 1, 1936, charter October 24, 1936; Bad River Band of the Lake Superior Tribe of Chippewa Indians of the State of Wisconsin, June 20, 1936, charter May 21, 1938; Lac du Flambeau Band of Lake Superior Chippewa Indians of Wisconsin, August 15, 1936, charter May 8, 1937; Oneida Tribe of Indians of Wisconsin, December 21, 1936, charter May 1, 1937; Forest County Potawatomi Community, February 6, 1937, charter October 30, 1937; Stockbridge-Munsee Community, November 18, 1937, charter May 21, 1938; Sokaogon Chippewa Community, November 9, 1938, charter October 7, 1939.

[61] 48 Stat. 984, 25 U. S. C. 461, *et. seq.*

various Indian tribes,[62] it did bring about the regularization of the procedures of tribal government and a modification of the relations of the Interior Department to the activities of tribal government. Section 16 of the Act of June 18, 1934,[63] established a basis for the adoption of tribal constitutions approved by the Secretary of the Interior, which could not thereafter be changed except by mutual agreement or by act of Congress. This section was explained in a circular letter of the Commissioner of Indian Affairs sent out almost immediately after the approval of the Act of June 18, 1934, in the following terms:

> SEC. 16. *Tribal Organization.*—
>
> Under this section, any Indian tribe that so desires may organize and establish a constitution and by-laws for the management of its own local affairs.
>
> Such constitution and by-laws become effective when ratified by a majority of all the adult members of the tribe,[64] or the adult Indians residing on the reservation, at a special election. It will be the duty of the Secretary of the Interior to call such a special election when any responsible group of Indians has prepared and submitted to him a proposed constitution and by-laws which do not violate any Federal Law, and are fair to all the Indians concerned. When such a special election has been called, all Indians who are members of the tribe, or residents on the reservation if the constitution is proposed for the entire reservation, will be entitled to vote upon the acceptance of the constitution. * * * If a tribe or reservation adopts the constitution and by-laws in this manner, such constitution and by-laws may thereafter be amended or entirely revoked only by the same process.
>
> The powers which may be exercised by an Indian tribe or tribal council include all powers which may be exercised by such tribe or tribal council at the present time, and also include the right to employ legal counsel (subject to the approval of the Secretary of the Interior with respect to the choice of counsel and the fixing of fees), the right to exercise a veto power over any disposition of tribal funds or other assets, the right to negotiate with Federal, State and local governments, and the right to be advised of all appropriation estimates affecting the tribe, before such estimates are submitted to the Bureau of the Budget and Congress.
>
> The following Indian groups are entitled to take advantage of this section: Any Indian tribe, band, or pueblo in the United States (outside of Oklahoma) or Alaska, and also any group of Indians who reside on the same reservation, whether they are members of the same tribe or not.

The constitutions adopted pursuant to this section and those adopted pursuant to similar provisions of law applicable to Alaska [65] and Oklahoma [66] vary considerably with respect to the form of tribal government, ranging from ancient and primitive forms in tribes where such forms have been perpetuated, to models based upon progressive white communities.

The powers of self-government vested in these various tribes likewise vary in accordance with the circumstances, experience, and resources of the tribe.[67] The extent to which tribal powers are subject to departmental review is again a matter on which tribal constitutions differ from each other.

The procedure by which tribal ordinances are reviewed, where such review is called for, is a matter which in nearly all tribal constitutions has been covered in substantially identical terms. A typical provision is that of the constitution of the Blackfeet Tribe,[68] which reads as follows:

> ARTICLE VI. POWERS OF THE COUNCIL
>
> * * * * *
>
> SEC. 2. *Manner of review.*—Any resolution or ordinance which, by the terms of this constitution, is subject to review by the Secretary of the Interior, shall be presented to the superintendent of the reservation, who shall, within ten (10) days thereafter, approve or disapprove the same. If the superintendent shall approve any ordinance or resolution, it shall thereupon become effective, but the superintendent shall transmit a copy of the same, bearing his endorsement, to the Secretary of the Interior, who may, within ninety (90) days from the date of enactment, rescind the said ordinance or resolution for any cause, by notifying the tribal council of such decision. If the superintendent shall refuse to approve any resolution or ordinance submitted to him, within ten (10) days after its enactment, he shall advise the Blackfeet Tribal Business Council of his reason thereof. If these reasons appear to the council insufficient, it may, by a majority vote, refer the ordinance or resolution to the Secretary of the Interior, who may, within ninety (90) days from the date of its enactment, approve the same in writing, whereupon the said ordinance or resolution shall become effective.

Under the procedure thus established, positive action is required to validate an ordinance that is subject to departmental review. Failure of the superintendent to act within the prescribed period operates as a veto.[69] Failure of the superintendent or other departmental employees to act promptly in transmitting to the Secretary an ordinance validly submitted and approved does not extend the period allowed for secretarial veto.[70] On the other hand, where a superintendent vetoes an ordinance, failure of the tribe to act in accordance with the prescribed procedure of referring the ordinance, after a new vote, to the Secretary of the Interior, will preclude validation of the ordinance.[71]

Secretarial review of tribal ordinances, like Presidential review of legislation, involves judgments of policy as well as judgments of law and constitutionality. Only a small proportion of such ordinances have been vetoed. The reasons most commonly advanced for such action by the Secretary of the Interior are:

1. That the ordinance violates some provision of the tribal constitution;[72]
2. That the ordinance violates some federal law;
3. That the ordinance is unjust to a minority group within the tribe.

[62] See Memo. Sol. I. D., March 25, 1939. Undoubtedly, the act had some effect upon the attitude of administrative agencies towards powers which had been theoretically vested in Indian tribes but frequently ignored in practice. See, for instance, decision of the Comptroller General A-86599, June 30, 1937, upholding tribal power to collect rentals from tribal land and declaring:

> * * * having in view the broad purposes of the act, as shown by its legislative history, to extend to Indians the fundamental rights of political liberty and local self-government, and there having been shown the fact that some of the power so granted by the new act would require the use of tribal funds for their accomplishment—being necessary incidents of such powers—and the further fact that the act of June 25, 1936, 49 Stat. 1928, provides that section 20 of the Permanent Appropriation Repeal Act, 48 Stat. 1233, shall not apply to funds held in trust for individual Indians, associations of individual Indians, or for Indian corporations chartered under the act of June 18, 1934, this office would not be required to object to the procedures suggested in your memorandum for the handling of tribal funds of Indian tribes organized pursuant to the said act of June 18, 1934.

[63] 48 Stat. 984, 987, 25 U. S. C. 476.

[64] This rule was modified by the Act of June 15, 1935, sec. 1, 49 Stat. 378, 25 U. S. C. 478a, which substituted the requirement of majority vote of those voting in an election where 30 percent of the eligible voters cast ballots.

[65] See Chapter 21, sec. 9.

[66] For a list of Oklahoma constitutions and charters, see Chapter 23, sec. 13.

[67] It has been administratively determined that constitutions of groups not previously recognized as tribes, in the political sense, cannot include powers derived from sovereignty, such as the power to tax, condemn land of members, and regulate inheritance. Memo. Sol. I. D., April 15, 1936. (Lower Sioux Indian Community; Prairie Island Indian Community.)

[68] Approved December 13, 1935.

[69] Memo. Sol. I. D., April 11, 1940 (Walker River Paiute).

[70] Memo. Sol. I. D., October 28, 1936 (San Carlos Apache).

[71] See Memo. Sol. I. D., April 11, 1940 (Walker River Paiute).

[72] See, for example, Memo. Sol. I. D., December 14, 1937 (Hopi).

During the 6 years following the enactment of the Act of June 18, 1934, Congress found no occasion to rescind any tribal constitution or ordinance, although it undoubtedly has power to do so,[73] nor was any tribal constitution adopted by an Indian tribe vetoed by the Secretary of the Interior. During this period, perhaps the chief threat to the integrity of tribal government has been the willingness of certain tribal officers to relinquish responsibilities vested in them by tribal constitutions. This tendency has been somewhat checked by rulings to the effect that the Interior Department will not approve or be party to such relinquishment of responsibility.[74]

An attempt to outline the probable future development of these Indian constitutions is made in a recent article on the subject How Long Will Indian Constitutions Last?[75]

> Any answer to this question that is more than mere guesswork must square with the recorded history of Indian constitutions. Tribal constitutions, after all, are not a radical innovation of the New Deal. The history of Indian constitutions goes back at least to the Gayaneshagowa (Great Binding Law) of the Iroquois Confederacy which probably dates from the 15th century. * * *
>
> So too, we have the written constitutions of the Creek, Cherokee, Choctaw, Chickasaw, and Osage nations, printed usually on tribal printing presses, which were in force during the decades from 1830 to 1900.
>
> These constitutions are merely historical records today. Other Indian constitutions, however, retain their vitality. A good many tribes have had rudimentary written constitutions, which simply recorded the procedure of their general council meetings, the method of electing or removing representatives or "business committees," and perhaps a brief statement of the duties of officers. Other tribes are governed by elaborate constitutions which have never been recorded. The difference between a written and an unwritten constitution should not be exaggerated. The rules concerning council procedure, selection of officers, and official responsibilities, which have been followed by the Creek towns, or by the Rio Grande Pueblos, without substantial alteration across four centuries, certainly deserve to be called constitutions. They do not lose their potency when they are reduced to writing, as the constitution of Laguna Pueblo was reduced to writing thirty years ago.
>
> In all the recorded history of Indian constitutions, two basic facts stand out.
>
> It is a fact of deep significance that no Indian constitution has ever been destroyed except with the consent of the governed. Congress has never legislated a tribal government out of existence except by treaty, agreement or plebiscite. Even the wholesale destruction of the governments of the Five Civilized Tribes in the old Indian Territory was accomplished only when the members of these tribes, by majority vote, had accepted the wishes of Congress. These governments ceased to exist as governments primarily because they had admitted to citizenship, and to rights of occupancy in tribal lands, so many white men that the original Indian communities could no longer maintain a national existence apart from the white settlers. The acts of Congress and the plebiscite votes of the tribes, which were dominated by the "squaw-men" and mixed-bloods, reflected an existing fact. The constitution of the Iroquois Confederacy likewise was broken only by the Indians themselves when the Six Nations could not agree on the question of whether to support the American revolutionaries or the British.
>
> The second basic fact that stands out in a survey of the life span of Indian constitutions is that the Indians themselves cease to want a constitution when their constituted government no longer satisfies important wants. When this happens, a tribal government, like any other government, either dissolves in chaos or yields place to some other governing agency that commands greater power or promises to satisfy in greater measure the significant wants of the governed.
>
> If we are to be realistic in seeking to answer the question, "How long will the new Indian Constitutions last?", we must focus attention on the human wants that tribal governments under these constitutions are able to satisfy rather than on guesses as to what future Congresses and future administrations may think of Indian self-government. * * * It is extremely likely that organized Indian tribes will continue to exist as long as American democracy exists and as long as the American people are unwilling to use the army to carry out Indian policies,—provided that the Indians themselves feel that tribal governments satisfy important human wants.
>
> What are the wants that a tribal government can help to satisfy?
>
> I
>
> The most fundamental of the goods which a tribe may bring to its members is economic security. Few things bind men so closely as a common interest in the means of their livelihood. No tribe will dissolve so long as there are lands or resources that belong to the tribe or economic enterprises in which all members of the tribe may participate. The young man who in the plastic years of adolescence, goes to his tribal government to obtain employment in a tribal lumber mill, cooperative store, hotel, mine, farm, or factory, gives that government the most enduring kind of recognition. The returned student who applies to a committee of his tribal council for permission to build up his herds on tribal grazing land, or for the chance to establish a farm, or to build a home and garden upon tribal lands assigned to his occupancy, cannot ignore this tribal government. * * *
>
> It follows that governmental credit policies in making loans to Indian tribes are of critical importance. If, in such loans, special attention is given to encouraging tribal enterprises, a real basis of social solidarity is provided; all members of the tribe are interested in the success of the enterprise, in the efficiency and honesty of its management; the development of a tribal enterprise becomes a course of adult education in economics and government. On the other hand, if credit operations are entirely confined to individual enterprises, no such common interest is created. The struggle for a lion's share of tribal loan funds may prove, on the contrary, a disintegrating and faction-producing drive. The tribal officials instead of being producers will be bankers. And there is no reason to believe that the bankers of an Indian tribe will be less cordially detested by their debtors than are bankers in any country of the world today.
>
> Second in importance only to the reservation credit program is the reservation land-acquisition program. A landless tribe can evoke no more respect, among farmers, than a landless individual. But more than paper ownership of tribal land is here in question. The issue is whether the tribe that "owns" land will be allowed to exercise the powers of a landowner, to receive rentals and fees, to regulate land use, to withdraw land privileges from those who flout its regulations, or whether the Federal Government will administer "tribal" lands for the benefit of the Indians as it administers National Monuments, for instance, for the benefit of posterity, with the Indians having perhaps as much actual voice in the former case as posterity has in the latter.
>
> The roots of any tribal constitution are likely to be as deep as the tribe's actual control over economic resources.

[73] On federal review of legislation of the Five Civilized Tribes, see Chapter 23, sec. 6.

[74] Memo. Sol. I. D., May 14, 1938 (veto of Oglala Sioux resolution delegating taxation powers to superintendent). See also Memo. Acting Sol. I. D., July 16, 1937 (disapproving proposal for indefinite review of actions of Business Committee of Chippewa-Cree Indians of the Rocky Boy's Reservation, affecting federally financed business but approving contractual provision for review of such ordinances during period of indebtedness); Memo. Sol. I. D., October 16, 1936 (terms of loan to Lower Brule Sioux Tribe); Memo. Sol. I. D., July 12, 1937 (Ft. Belknap; delegation of leasing power to superintendent disapproved); Memo. Sol. I. D., May 28, 1936 (Ft. Hall; same).

[75] F. S. Cohen, How Long Will Indian Constitutions Last (1939), 6 Indians at Work, No. 10. The excerpts here quoted follow the cited publication except with respect to editorial abridgments and corrections made therein.

II

Less tangible than the possession of common property, but perhaps equally important in the continuity of a social group, is the existence of common enjoyments. In community life, as in marriage, community of interest in the useless and enjoyable things of life makes for stability and loyalty.

Any governmental organization must do a good many unpleasant jobs. Arresting law-breakers and collecting taxes are not activities that inspire gratitude and loyalty. Thus government comes to be looked upon as a necessary evil, at best, unless it actively sponsors some of life's every-day enjoyments. An Indian tribe that enriches the recreational life of its members through the development of community recreational facilities is building for itself a solid foundation in human loyalty.

There is no doubt that the remarkable tenacity of traditional government in the Pueblos of New Mexico derives in large part from the role which that government plays in the popular dances, communal hunts, and similar social activities. To relieve the barrenness of life on some of the northern reservations is a task hardly less important than the reestablishment of the economic basis of life. * * *

In this field, much will depend upon the attitude of Indian Service officials, and particularly upon the attitude of teachers, social workers, and extension agents. It will be hard for them to surrender the large measure of control that they now exercise over the recreational and social life of the reservations, but unless they are willing to yield control in this field to the tribal government, that government may find itself barred from the hearts of its people.

III

Outside of Indian reservations, local government finds its chief justification in the performance of municipal services, and particularly the maintenance of law and order, the management of public education, the distribution of water, gas, and electricity, the maintenance of health and sanitation, the relief of the needy, and activities designed to afford citizens protection against fire and other natural calamities. On most Indian reservations all of these functions, if performed at all, are performed not by the tribal councils but by employees of the Indian Service. Thus the usual reason for the maintenance of local government is lacking.

The cure for this situation is, obviously, the progressive transfer of municipal functions to the organized tribe. Already some progress has been made in this direction in the field of law and order. Codes of municipal ordinances are being adopted by several organized tribes; judges are removable, in some cases, by the Indians to whom they are responsible; and the czaristic powers of the Superintendent in this field have been substantially abolished. In the other fields of municipal activity no such change has yet taken place.

Where Indian schools are maintained, the Indians generally have nothing to say about school curricula, the appointment or qualifications of teachers, or even the programs to be followed in the commencement exercises. Many reasons will occur to the Indian Service employee why the tribal government should have nothing to say about Indian education. It will be said that the Federal Government pays for Indian education and should therefore exercise complete control over it—an ironic echo of the familiar argument that real-estate owners pay for public education and should therefore control it. It will be said that Indians are not competent to handle educational problems. It will be said that giving power to tribal councils will contaminate education with "politics."

None of these objections has any particular rational force. In several cases teachers are now being paid not out of Federal funds but out of tribal funds. So far as the law is concerned, an act of Congress that has been on the statute books since June 30, 1834, specifically provides that the direction of teachers, and other employees, even though they be paid out of Federal funds, may be given to the proper tribal authorities wherever the Secretary of the Interior (originally, the Secretary of War) considers the tribe competent to exercise such direction. Indians are considered competent enough to serve on boards of education where public schools have been substituted for Indian Service schools. And there is no good reason why tribal "politics" deserves to be suppressed, any more than national "politics." If these common arguments are without rational force, they are nevertheless significant because they symbolize the unwillingness of those who have power, positions, and salaries, to jeopardize the status quo.

This is true not only in the field of education. It is true in the field of health, community planning, relief, and all other municipal services. It is true of government outside of the Indian Service, and perhaps it is true of all human enterprise. The shift of control from a Federal bureau to the local community is likely to come not through gifts of delegated authority from the Federal bureau, but rather as a result of insistent demands from the local community that it be entrusted with increasing control over its own municipal affairs.

Where this demand for local autonomy is found, there is ground to hope that a tribal constitution will prove to be a relatively permanent institution as human institutions go. Where this demand is not found, there is reason to believe that the tribal government will not be taken very seriously by the governed, that Indian Service control of municipal functions will continue until superseded by state control, and that the tribe will disappear as a political organization.

IV

A fourth source of vitality in any tribal constitution is the community of consciousness which it reflects. Where many people think and feel as one, there is some ground to expect a stable political organization. Where, on the other hand, such unity is threatened either by factionalism within the tribe or by constant assimilation into a surrounding population, continuity of tribal organization cannot be expected.

* * * * *

V

A fifth source of potential strength for any tribal organization lies in the role which it may assume as protector of the rights of its members.

In most parts of the country, Indians are looked down upon and discriminated against by their white fellow-citizens. They are denied ordinary rights of citizenship—in several states even the right to vote—in a few states the right to intermarry with the white race or to attend white schools—in most states the right to use state facilities of relief, institutional care, etc. Discrimination against Indians in private employment is widespread. Social discrimination is almost universal. The story of Federal relations with the Indian tribes is filled with accounts of broken treaties, massacres, land steals, and practical enslavement of independent tribes under dictatorial rule by Indian agents.

It is not to be wondered at that this history of discrimination and oppression has left a bitter, rankling resentment in the hearts of most Indians. A responsible tribal government must express this resentment, and express it in more effective ways than are open to an individual; otherwise it has failed in one of its chief functions. Where there is a popular consciousness of grievances, the governing body of the community must seek their redress, whether against state officials, Indian Service employees, white traders, or any other group. To be in the pay of any such group is, on most reservations, a black mark against a popular representative.

In this field of activity, tribal governments can achieve significant results. A council, for instance, that employs an attorney to enjoin the enforcement of an unconstitutional statute depriving Indians of the right to vote is likely to secure a first lien on the respect of its constituency and materially increase the life expectancy of the tribal constitution. A tribal council that makes a determined fight to secure enforcement of laws—some of them more than a hundred years old—granting Indians preference in Indian Service employment will win Indian support even it it loses its immediate fight. So with many other common grievances on which collective tribal action is possible. A rubber stamp council that simply takes what the Indian Office gives it is not likely to establish permanent foundations for tribal autonomy. Rubber is a peculiarly perishable material, and it gives off a bad smell when it decays.

There is, then, no single answer that can be given to the question, "How long will Indian constitutions last?" We may be sure that different constitutions will perish at different ages. Some, no doubt, have been still-born. Such constitutions may exist in the eyes of the law but not in the hearts of the Indians, and at the first signal of official displeasure, they will disappear. Other constitutions represent realities as stable as the reality that is the United States of America or the City of St. Louis.

One who seeks a mathematical formula can perhaps measure the life expectancy of various tribal constitutions by assigning numbers to the factors we have discussed—the extent to which the organized tribe ministers to the common economic needs of the people, the degree in which the organized tribe satisfies recreational and cultural wants, the extent and efficiency of municipal services which the tribe renders, the general social solidarity of the community, and the vigor with which the tribal government expresses the dissatisfactions of the people and organizes popular resentment along rational lines.

More generally one can say that a constitution is the structure of a reality that exists in human hearts. An Indian constitution will exist as long as there remains in human hearts a community of interdependence, of common interests, aspirations, hopes, and fears, in realms of art and politics, work and play.

SECTION 4. THE POWER TO DETERMINE TRIBAL MEMBERSHIP [76]

The courts have consistently recognized that in the absence of express legislation by Congress [77] to the contrary, an Indian tribe has complete authority to determine all questions of its own membership.[78] It may thus by usage or written law, or by treaty with the United States or intertribal agreement,[79] determine under what conditions persons shall be considered members of the tribe. It may provide for special formalities of recognition, and it may adopt such rules as seem suitable to it, to regulate the abandonment of membership, the adoption of non-Indians or Indians of other tribes, and the types of membership or citizenship which it may choose to recognize. The completeness of this power receives statutory recognition in a provision that the children of a white man and an Indian woman by blood shall be considered members of the tribe if, and only if, "said Indian woman was * * * recognized by the tribe."[80] The power of the Indian tribes in this field is limited only by the various statutes of Congress defining the membership of certain tribes for purposes of allotment or for other purposes,[81] and by the statutory authority given to the Secretary of the Interior to promulgate a final tribal roll for the purpose of dividing and distributing tribal funds.[82]

The power of an Indian tribe to determine questions of its own membership derives from the character of an Indian tribe as a distinct political entity. In the case of *Patterson* v. *Council of Seneca Nation* [83] the Court of Appeals of New York reviewed the many decisions of that court and of the Supreme Court of the United States recognizing the Indian tribe as a "distinct political society, separated from others, capable of managing its own affairs and governing itself"[84] and, in reaching the conclusion that mandamus would not lie to compel the plaintiff's enrollment by the defendant council, declared:

> Unless these expressions, as well as similar expressions many times used by many courts in various jurisdictions, are mere words of flattery designed to soothe Indian sensibilities, unless the last vestige of separate national life has been withdrawn from the Indian tribes by encroaching state legislation, then, surely, it must follow that the Seneca Nation of Indians has retained for itself that prerequisite to their self-preservation and integrity as a nation, the right to determine by whom its membership shall be constituted. (P. 786.)
>
> * * * * *
>
> It must be the law, therefore, that, unless the Seneca Nation of Indians and the state of New York enjoy a relation inter se peculiar to themselves, the right to enrollment of the petitioner, with its attending property rights, depends upon the laws and usages of the Seneca Nation and is to be determined by that Nation for itself, without interference or dictation from the Supreme Court of the state. (P. 736.)

After examining the constitutional position of the Seneca Nation and finding that tribal autonomy has not been impaired by any legislation of the state, the court concludes:

> The conclusion is inescapable that the Seneca Tribe remains a separate nation; that its powers of self-government are retained with the sanction of the state; that the ancient customs and usages of the nation except in a few particulars, remain, unabolished, the law of the Indian land; that in its capacity of a sovereign nation the Seneca Nation is not subservient to the orders and directions of

---

[76] For an analysis of congressional power over tribal membership, see Chapter 5, sec. 6. For an analysis of federal administrative power on the same subject, see chapter 5, sec. 18.

[77] There is no dispute as to the plenary power of Congress over the field of tribal membership. See *Wallace* v. *Adams*, 204 U. S. 415 (1907), and Chapter 5, sec. 6.

[78] It must be noted that property rights attached to membership are largely in the control of the Secretary of the Interior rather than the tribe itself. See, sec. 8, *infra*, and see Chapters 5, 9, and 15.

[79] See *Delaware Indians* v. *Cherokee Nation*, 193 U. S. 127 (1904).

[80] 25 U. S. C. 184 declares:

> * * * all children born of a marriage heretofore solemnized between a white man and an Indian woman by blood and not by adoption, where said Indian woman is at this time, or was at the time of her death, recognized by the tribe shall have the same rights and privileges to the property of the tribe to which the mother belongs, or belonged at the time of her death, by blood, as any other member of the tribe, and no prior Act of Congress shall be construed as to debar such child of such right. (Act of June 7, 1897, c. 3, sec. 1, 30 Stat. 62, 90.)

The phrase "recognized by the tribe" is construed in *Oakes* v. *United States*, 172 Fed. 305 (C. C. A. 8, 1909); *Pape* v. *United States*, 19 F. 2d 219 (C. C. A. 9, 1927); *United States* v. *Rolfson*, 38 F. 2d 896 (C. C. A. 9, 1930), rev'd 283 U. S. 753 (1931); 43 L. D. 149 (1914); 50 L. D. 551 (1924).

[81] Various enrollment statutes provide for enrollment by chiefs, with departmental approval. Act of March 3, 1881, sec. 4, 21 Stat. 414, 433 (Miami); Act of March 2, 1889, 25 Stat. 1013 (United Peorias and Miamies), construed in 12 L. D. 168 (1890); Act of February 13, 1891, 26 Stat. 749, 753 (Sac and Fox and others). *Cf.* Act of June 18, 1926, 44 Stat. 1609 (requiring the Secretary to enroll for allotment a person adopted by the Kiowa tribe); Act of June 28, 1898, sec. 21, 30 Stat. 495, 502 ("Cherokee * * * lawfully admitted to citizenship by the tribal authorities"). Other statutes provide for enrollment by the Secretary of the Interior, with the assistance of chiefs. Act of May 19, 1924, 43 Stat. 132 (Lac du Flambeau) and Act of June 15, 1934, 48 Stat. 965 (Menominee) (action by the Secretary after findings by Menominee Tribal Council).

Another procedure involved a commission including Indian members, acting with the approval of the Secretary of the Interior. See Act of March 3, 1921, 41 Stat. 1355 (Ft. Belknap), construed in *Stoockey* v. *Wilbur*, 58 F. 2d 522 (App. D. C. 1932). Still other statutes provide for enrollment by the Secretary of the Interior. See Chapter 5, sec. 6.

Even in these cases, the Secretary sometimes utilized a roll prepared by officers of the tribe. See *Jump* v. *Ellis*, 100 F. 2d 130 (C. A. A. 10, 1938), cert. den. 306 U. S. 645 (1938).

Occasionally Congress has specifically required that the Interior Department recognize a tribal adoption. See Act of April 4, 1910, sec. 18, 36 Stat. 269, 280 (Kiowa).

[82] 25 U. S. C. 163. (June 30, 1919, c. 4, sec. 1, 41 Stat. 3, 9). See Chapter 5, secs. 12 and 13, Chapter 9, sec. 6, and Chapter 10, sec. 4.

[83] 245 N. Y. 433, 157 N. E. 734 (1927).

[84] Marshall, C. J., in *Cherokee Nation* v. *Georgia*, 5 Pet. 1, 15 (1831).

> the courts of New York state; that, above all, the Seneca Nation retains for itself the power of determining who are Senecas, and in that respect is above interference and dictation. (P. 738.)

In the case of *Waldron* v. *United States*,[85] it appeared that a woman of five-sixteenth Sioux Indian blood on her mother's side, her father being a white man, had been refused recognition as an Indian by the Interior Department although, by tribal custom, since the woman's mother had been recognized as an Indian, the woman herself was so recognized. The court held that the decision of the Interior Department was contrary to law, declaring:

> In this proceeding the court has been informed as to the usages and customs of the different tribes of the Sioux Nation, and has found as a fact that the common law does not obtain among said tribes, as to determining the race to which the children of a white man, married to an Indian woman, belong; but that, according to the usages and customs of said tribes, the children of a white man married to an Indian woman take the race or nationality of the mother.[86] (P. 419.)

In the *Cherokee Intermarriage Cases*,[87] the Supreme Court of the United States considered the claims of certain white men, married to Cherokee Indians, to participate in the common property of the Cherokee Nation. After carefully examining the constitutional articles and the statutes of the Cherokee Nation, the court reached the conclusion that the claims in question were invalid, since, although the claimants had been recognized as citizens for certain purposes, the Cherokee Nation had complete authority to qualify the rights of citizenship which it offered to its "naturalized" citizens, and had, in the exercise of this authority, provided for the revocation or qualification of citizenship rights so as to defeat the claims of the plaintiffs. The Supreme Court declared, *per* Fuller, *C. J.*:

> The distinction between different classes of citizens was recognized by the Cherokees in the differences in their intermarriage law, as applicable to the whites and to the Indians of other tribes; by the provision in the intermarriage law that a white man intermarried with an Indian by blood acquires certain rights as a citizen, but no provision that if he marries a Cherokee citizen not of Indian blood he shall be regarded as a citizen at all; and by the provision that if, once having married an Indian by blood, he marries the second time a citizen not by blood, he loses all of his rights as a citizen. And the same distinction between citizens as such and citizens with property rights has also been recognized by Congress in enactments relating to other Indians that the Five Civilized Tribes. Act August 9, 1888, 25 Stat. 392, c. 818; act May 2, 1890, 26 Stat. 96, c. 182; act June 7, 1897, 30 Stat. 90, c. 3. (P. 88.)
>
> * * * The laws and usages of the Cherokees, their earliest history, the fundamental principles of their national policy, their constitution and statutes, all show that citizenship rested on blood or marriage; that the man who would assert citizenship must establish marriage; that when marriage ceased (with a special reservation in favor of widows or widowers) citizenship ceased; that when an intermarried white married a person having no rights of Cherokee citizenship by blood it was conclusive evidence that the tie which bound him to the Cherokee people was severed and the very basis of his citizenship obliterated. (P. 95.)[88]

An Indian tribe may classify various types of membership and qualify not only the property rights, but the voting rights of certain members.[89] Similarly, an Indian tribe may revoke rights of membership which it has granted. In *Roff* v. *Burney*,[90] the Supreme Court upheld the validity of an act of the Chickasaw legislature depriving a Chickasaw citizen of his citizenship, declaring:

> The citizenship which the Chickasaw legislature could confer it could withdraw. The only restriction on the power of the Chickasaw Nation to legislate in respect to its internal affair is that such legislation shall not conflict with the Constitution or laws of the United States, and we know of no provision of such Constitution or laws which would be set at naught by the action of a political community like this in withdrawing privileges of membership in the community once conferred. (P. 222.)

The right of an Indian tribe to make express rules governing the recognition of members, the adoption of new members, the procedure for abandonment of membership, and the procedure for readoption, is recognized in *Smith* v. *Bonifer*.[91] In that case the plaintiffs' right to allotments depended upon their membership in a particular tribe. The court held that such membership was demonstrated by the fact of tribal recognition, declaring:

> Indian members of one tribe can sever their relations as such, and may form affiliations with another or other tribes. And so they may, after their relation with a tribe has been severed, rejoin the tribe and be again recognized and treated as members thereof, and tribal rights and privileges attach according to the habits and customs of the tribe with which affiliation is presently cast. As to the manner of breaking off and recasting tribal affiliations we are meagerly informed. It was and is a thing, of course, dependent upon the peculiar usages and customs of each particular tribe, and therefore we may assume that no general rule obtains for its regulation.

---

[85] 143 Fed. 413 (C. C. S. D. 1905). Also see Chapter 1, sec. 2.

[86] To the effect that tribal action on recognition of members is conclusive "as there was no treaty, agreement, or statute of the United States imposing upon any officer of the United States the power to make a complete roll, and declaring that the acts of said officer should be conclusive upon the questions involved," see *Sully* v. *United States*, 195 Fed. 113, 125 (C. C. S. D. 1912) (suit for allotment).

The same view is maintained in 19 Op. A. G. 115 (1888), in a case in which exclusive power to determine membership was vested in the tribal authority by treaty:

> * * * It was the Indians, and not the United States, that were interested in the distribution of what was periodically coming to them from the United States. It was proper then that they should determine for themselves, and finally, who were entitled to membership in the confederated tribe and to participate in the emoluments belonging to that relation.
>
> The certificate of the chiefs and councillors referred to is possibly as high a grade of evidence as can be procured of the fact of the determination by the chiefs of the right of membership under the treaty of February 23, 1867, and seems to be such as is warranted by the usage and custom of the Government in its general dealings with these people and other similar tribes. (P. 116.)

See to the same effect: *In re William Banks*, 26 L. D. 71 (1898); *Black Tomahawk* v. *Waldron*, 19 L. D. 311 (1894); 35 L. D. 549 (1907); 43 L. D. 125 (1914); 20 Op. A. G. 711 (1894); *Western Cherokees* v. *United States*, 27 C. Cls. 1, 54 (1891), mod. 148 U. S. 427, 28 C. Cls. 557; *United States* v. *Heyfron* (two cases), 138 Fed. 964, 968 (C. C. Mont. 1905); Memo. Sol. I. D., May 14, 1935 (Red Lake Chippewa) and see Memo Sol. I. D., December 18, 1937 (Kansas and Wisconsin Pottawatomie). As was said in the last cited memorandum:

> * * * However, if the Prairie Band still refuses, in the light of this information, to accept the children into membership, the Department is without power to enroll the children of its own accord, and the Business Committee should be so informed. While the Department may approve or disapprove adoptions into the tribe and expulsions therefrom made by the tribal authorities, no case holds that the Department, in the absence of express statutory authorization, may grant a person tribal membership over the protest of the tribal authorities. Such action would be contrary to the rules ennunciated in the cases and to the position taken by the Department in the drafting of tribal constitutions.

[87] 203 U. S. 76 (1906).

[88] See, to the same effect, 19 Op. A. G. 109 (1888).

[89] Thus in 19 Op. A. G. 389 (1889), the view is expressed that a tribe may by law restrict the rights of tribal suffrage, excluding white citizens from voting, although by treaty they are guaranteed rights of "membership." Accord: 8 Op. A. G. 300 (1857).

[90] 168 U. S. 218 (1897). And see Memo. Sol. I. D., February 18, 1938, to the effect that a tribal roll may be amended pursuant to a tribal constitution.

[91] 154 Fed. 883 (C. C. D. Ore. 1907), aff'd sub. nom. *Bonifer* v. *Smith*, 166 Fed. 846 (C. C. A. 9, 1909), s. c. 132 Fed. 889 (C. C. D. Ore. 1904).

Now, the first condition presented is that the mother of Philomme was a full-blood Walla Walla Indian. She was consequently a member of the tribe of that name. Was her status changed by marriage to Tawakown, an Iroquois Indian? This must depend upon the tribal usage and customs of the Walla Wallas and the Iroquois. It is said by Hon. William A. Little, Assistant Attorney General, in an opinion rendered the Department of the Interior in a matter involving this very controversy:

> "That inheritance among these Indians is through the mother and not through the father, and that the true test in these cases is to ascertain whether parties claiming to be Indians and entitled to allotments have by their conduct expatriated themselves or changed their citizenship."

But we are told that:

> "Among the Iroquoian tribes kinship is traced through the blood of the woman only. Kinship means membership in a family; and this in turn constitutes citizenship in the tribe, conferring certain social, political, and religious privileges, duties, and rights, which are denied to persons of alien blood." Handbook of American Indians, edited by Frederick Webb Hodge, Smithsonian Institute, Government Printing Office, 1907.

Marriage, therefore, with Tawakown would not of itself constitute an affiliation on the part of his wife with the Iroquois tribe, of which he was a member, and a renunciation of membership with her own tribe. * * * (P. 886.)

Considering a second marriage of the plaintiff to a white person, the court went on to declare:

> * * * But notwithstanding the marriage of Philomme to Smith, and her long residence outside of the limits of the reservation, she was acknowledged by the chiefs of the confederated tribes to be a member of the Walla Walla tribe. From the testimony adduced herein, read in connection with that taken in the case of *Hy-yu-tse-mil-kin v. Smith*, supra, it appears that Mrs. Smith was advised by Homily and Show-a-way, chiefs, respectively, of the Walla Walla and Cayuse tribes, to come upon the reservation and make selections for allotments to herself and children, and that thereafter she was recognized by both these chiefs, and by Peo, the chief of the Umatillas, as being a member of the Walla Walla tribe. It is true that she was not so recognized at first, but she was finally, and by a general council of the Indians held for the especial purpose of determining the matter. (P. 888.)

Where tribal laws have not expressly provided for some certificate of membership,[92] the courts, in cases not clearly controlled by recognised tribal custom, have looked to recognition by the tribal chiefs as a test of tribal membership.[93]

The weight given to tribal action in relation to tribal membership is shown by the case of *Nofire v. United States*.[94] In that case the jurisdiction of the Cherokee courts in a murder case, the defendants being Cherokee Indians, depended upon whether the deceased, a white man, had been duly adopted by the Cherokee Tribe. Finding evidence of such adoption in the official records of the tribe, the Supreme Court held that such adoption deprived the federal court of jurisdiction over the murder and vested such jurisdiction in the tribal courts.

A similar decision was reached in the case of *Raymond v. Raymond*[95] in which the jurisdiction of a tribal court over an adopted Cherokee was challenged. The court declared, *per* Sanborn, *J.*:

> * * * It is conceded that under the laws of that nation the appellee became a member of that tribe, by adoption, through her intermarriage with the appellant. It is settled by the decisions of the supreme court that her adoption into that nation ousted the federal court of jurisdiction over any suit between her and any member of that tribe, and vested the tribal courts with exclusive jurisdiction over every such action. *Alberty v. U. S.*, 162 U. S. 499, 16 Sup. Ct. 864; *Nofire v. U. S.*, 164 U. S. 657, 658, 17 Sup. Ct. 212. (P. 723.)

It is of course recognized throughout the cases that tribal membership is a bilateral relation, depending for its existence not only upon the action of the tribe but also upon the action of the individual concerned. Any member of any Indian tribe is at full liberty to terminate his tribal relationship whenever he so chooses,[96] although it has been said that such termination will not be inferred "from light and trifling circumstances."[97]

Apart from the foregoing cases, there are a number of decisions excluding from rights of tribal membership persons claiming to be members who have been recognized *neither* by the tribal *nor* by the federal authorities.[98] Such cases, of course, cast little light on the scope of tribal power.

The tribal power recognized in the foregoing cases is not overthrown by anything said in the case of *United States ex rel. West v. Hitchcock*.[99] In that case, an adopted member of the Wichita tribe was refused an allotment by the Secretary of the Interior because the Department had never approved his adoption. Since the Secretary, according to the Supreme Court, had unreviewable discretionary authority to grant or deny an allotment even to a member of the tribe by blood, it was unnecessary for the Supreme Court to decide whether refusal of the Interior Department to approve the relator's adoption was within the authority of the Department. The court, however, intimated that the general authority of the Interior Department under section 463 of the Revised Statutes[100] was broad enough to justify a regulation requiring departmental approval of adoptions, but added that since the relator would have no legal right of appeal even if his adoption without Department approval were valid, "it hardly is necessary to pass upon that point."[101]

While the actual court decisions in the field of tribal membership are all consistent with the view that complete power over tribal membership rests with the tribe, except where Congress otherwise provides, the opinion in the West case appears to diverge from this view. Several alternative ways of reconciling the apparent conflict of judicial views in this field have been suggested. The Interior Department has expressed its view in these terms:

> The power of an Indian tribe to determine its membership is subject to the qualification, however, that in the distribution of tribal funds and other property under the supervision and control of the Federal Government, the action of the tribe is subject to the supervisory authority of the Secretary of the Interior.[102] The original power to

[92] See 19 Op. A. G. 115 (1888).

[93] *Hy-yu-tse-mil-kin v. Smith*, 194 U. S. 401, 411 (1904); *United States v. Higgins*, 103 Fed. 348 (C. C. D. Mont. 1900).

[94] 164 U. S. 657 (1857).

[95] 83 Fed. 721 (C. C. A. 8, 1897). Accord: 7 Op. A. G. 174 (1855). But *cf.* 2 Op. A. G. 402 (1830).

[96] See Chapter 8, sec. 10B(1). And see Chapter 14, secs. 1 and 2, on termination of tribal relations by groups.

[97] See *Vezina v. United States*, 245 Fed. 411, 420 (C. C. A. 8, 1917) (suit for allotment). Accord: *Wau-pe-man-qua v. Aldrich*, 28 Fed. 489 (C. C. Ind. 1886). But *cf. Sac and Fox Indians v. United States*, 45 C. Cls. 287 (1910), aff'd 220 U. S. 481 (1911).

[98] See, for example, *Reynolds v. United States*, 205 Fed. 685 (D. C. S. D. 1913); *Oakes v. United States*, 172 Fed. 305 (C. C. A. 8, 1909); 20 L. D. 167 (1895); 42 L. D. 489 (1913).

[99] 205 U. S. 80 (1907).

[100] *Duties of Commissioner.*—The Commissioner of Indian Affairs shall, under the direction of the Secretary of the Interior, and agreeably to such regulations as the President may prescribe, have the management of all Indian affairs and of all matters arising out of Indian relations. 25 U. S. C. 2.

[101] Accord: *LaClair v. United States*, 184 Fed. 128 (C. C. E. D. Wash. 1910) (declining to pass on necessity of departmental approval of adoption in allotment case).

[102] Citing: *United States ex rel. West v. Hitchcock*, 205 U. S. 80 (1907); *Mitchell v. United States*, 22 F. 2d 771 (C. C. A. 9, 1927); *United*

> determine membership, including the regulation of membership by adoption, nevertheless remains with the tribe * * *.[102] (pp. 39-40.)

An alternative formula for reconciling the cases in this field is suggested in the case of *Sloan* v. *United States*,[104] in which the distinction was drawn between adoption, which is a tribal matter, and departmental action in recognizing such adoption. The court declared:

> * * * claimants who cannot bring themselves within the provisions of the act of 1882 by showing that when that act took effect, they were residing on the reservation in the tribal relation, but who claim that, as a matter of fact, they were recognized by the tribe to be members thereof, cannot rightfully expect that the courts will refuse to accept and follow the ruling of the department upon the question of such recognition. The agents charged with the duty of making the allotments, who visit the tribe, have a much better knowledge of the action taken by the tribe than can be gained by the court; and their decision upon a fact of this nature, especially when duly affirmed by the officers of the interior department, should ordinarily be accepted as conclusive. In the numerous reports of the alloting agents introduced in evidence in these cases it is reported that none of the several claimants are recognized by the tribe as members entitled to allotments, and these findings of fact have been approved by the secretary of the interior, and they will, for the reasons stated, be accepted as final by this court in the further consideration of these suits. (p. 292.)

Another basis, not radically different from the two views above suggested, that would permit a reconciliation of all the cases and dicta, is the idea of tribal membership as a relative affair, existing in some cases for certain purposes and not for others. Precedent for this idea may be found in *United States* v. *Rogers*,[105] where Chief Justice Taney held that although a white man, by arrangement with an Indian tribe, might become a member thereof, he could not thereby divest the federal courts of jurisdiction over him as a "white man." On this view it might be said that for purposes in which the tribe has the last word, tribal adoption is valid without reference to departmental approval,[106] while for those purposes in which departmental action is authorized, the department may demand the right to approve or disapprove adoption.

Whatever may be the exact extent of departmental power in this field, in view of the broad provisions of the Wheeler-Howard Act it has been administratively held that the Secretary of the Interior may define and confine his power of supervision in accordance with the terms of a constitution adopted by the tribe itself and approved by him.

The written constitutions of tribes which have organized under the Act of June 18, 1934, contain provisions on membership which vary considerably. Generally these constitutions provide that descendants of two parents, both of whom are members of the tribe, shall be deemed members of the tribe. With respect to the offspring of mixed marriages, constitutions differ. Some make the membership of such offspring dependent upon whether his degree of Indian blood is more than one-half or one-quarter. Others make the membership of such offspring depend upon whether its parents maintain a residence on the reservation. Nearly all tribal constitutions provide for adoption through special action by the tribe, subject to review by the Secretary of the Interior. The general trend of the tribal enactments on membership is away from the older notion that rights of tribal membership run with Indian blood, no matter how dilute the stream. Instead it is recognized that membership in a tribe is a political relation rather than a racial attribute. Those who no longer take part in tribal affairs, who do not live upon the reservation, who marry non-Indians, may retain their claims upon tribal property, but most Indian tribes now deny such individuals the opportunity to claim a share of tribal assets for each child produced. The trend is toward making the sharing in tribal property correlative with the obligations that fall upon the members of the Indian community.[107]

One conclusion is clear, from the cases and developments above discussed: that a number of generalities in common currency on the subject of tribal membership must be severely qualified before they can be accepted as sound statements of law. For it is clear that such power as rests in the tribes with respect to membership has been and is being exercised along widely divergent lines.

States v. *Provoe*, 38 F. 2d 799 (C. C. A. 9, 1930), rev'd. on other grounds, 283 U. S. 753 (1931). See also *Wilbur* v. *United States, ex rel. Kadrie*, 281 U. S. 206 (1930).

[103] 55 I. D. 14, 39 (1934).

[104] 118 Fed. 283 (C. C. D. Neb. 1902), app. dism. 193 U. S. 614 (1904).

[105] 4 How. 567 (1846). Accord: *Westmoreland* v. *United States*, 155 U. S. 545 (1895); *United States* v. *Ragsdale*, 27 Fed. Cas. No. 16,113 (C. C. Ark. 1847).

[106] This finds support in such cases as *Katzenmeyer* v. *United States*, 225 Fed. 523 (C. C. A. 7, 1915), holding that for purposes of applying federal liquor laws, application for adoption and approval by the tribe establish tribal membership. And *cf. United States* v. *Higgins*, 110 Fed. 609 (C. C. Mont. 1901).

Theoretical justification for this view is offered by Wharton, A Treatise on the Conflict of Laws or Private International Law (3d ed. 1905), vol. 1, sec. 252.

[107] Typical membership provisions in tribal constitutions are the following:

Article III of the Constitution of the Jicarilla Apache Tribe, approved August 4, 1937

Membership in the Jicarilla Apache Indian Tribe shall extend to all persons of Indian blood whose names appear on the official census roll of the Jicarilla Apache Reservation of 1937; and to all children of one-fourth or more Indian blood, not affiliated with another tribe, born after the completion of the 1937 census roll to any member of the Tribe who is a resident of the Jicarilla Apache Reservation. Membership by adoption may be acquired by a three-fourths majority vote of the tribal council and the approval of the Secretary of the Interior.

Article II of the Constitution of the Hopi Tribe, approved December 19, 1936

SECTION 1. Membership in the Hopi Tribe shall be as follows:

(a) All persons whose names appear on the census roll of the Hopi Tribe as of January 1st, 1936, but within one year from the time that this Constitution takes effect corrections may be made in the roll by the Hopi Tribal Council with the approval of the Secretary of the Interior.

(b) All children born after January 1, 1936, whose father and mother are both members of the Hopi Tribe.

(c) All children born after January 1, 1936, whose mother is a member of the Hopi Tribe, and whose father is a member of some other tribe.

(d) All persons adopted into the Tribe as provided in Section 2.

SEC. 2. Nonmembers of one-fourth degree of Indian blood or more, who are married to members of the Hopi Tribe, and adult persons of one-fourth degree of Indian blood or more whose fathers are members of the Hopi Tribe, may be adopted in the following manner: Such person may apply to the Kikmongwi of the village to which he is to belong, for acceptance. According to the way of doing established in that village, the Kikmongwi may accept him, and shall tell the Tribal Council. The Council may then by a majority vote have that person's name put on the roll of the Tribe, but before he is enrolled he must officially give up membership in any other tribe.

Article III of the Constitution of the Seneca-Cayuga Tribe of Oklahoma, ratified May 15, 1937

The membership of the Seneca-Cayuga Tribe of Oklahoma shall consist of the following persons:

1. All persons of Indian blood whose names appear on the official census roll of the Tribe as of January 1, 1937.
2. All children born since the date of the said roll, both of whose parents are members of the Tribe.
3. Any child born of a marriage between a member of the Seneca-Cayuga Tribe and a member of any other Indian tribe who chooses to affiliate with the Seneca-Cayuga Tribe.
4. Any child born of a marriage between a member of the Seneca-Cayuga Tribe and any other person, if such child is admitted to membership by the Council of the Seneca-Cayuga Tribe.

Tribal constitutional provisions on membership are construed in Memo. Sol. I. D., April 12, 1938 (Rosebud Sioux), and Memo. Sol. I. D., July 12, 1938 (Rosebud Sioux).

Thus, for example, it is frequently said that a person cannot be a member of two tribes at once. This undoubtedly represents a well-established policy with respect to allotment and other distribution of tribal property or federal benefits.[108] It cannot, however, be validly inferred from this that two tribes could not formally recognize the membership of a single individual, for voting or other purposes. So, too, the generalities to be found in several cases as to the tribal membership of offspring of mixed marriages fail to correspond to the realities of tribal action. One may find, in the decided cases, two principles which, between them, cover the field: *partus sequitur ventrem*[109] and *partus sequitur patrem*.[110] This pair of principles is, of course, totally useless when it comes to reaching or predicting particular decisions.

[108] See *Mandler* v. *United States*, 49 F. 2d 201 (C. C. A. 10, 1931), rehearing den., 52 F. 2d 713 (C. C. A. 10, 1931); 19 L. D. 329 (1894).

[109] *United States* v. *Sanders*, 27 Fed. Cas. No. 16220 (C. C. A. Ark. 1847); *Alberty* v. *United States*, 162 U. S. 499 (1896).

[110] *Ex parte Reynolds*, 20 Fed. Cas. No. 11719 (D. C. W. D. Ark. 1879); *United States* v. *Ward*, 42 Fed. 320 (C. C. S. D. Cal. 1890); *United States* v. *Hadley*, 99 Fed. 437 (C. C. Wash. 1900); *United States* v. *Higgins*, 110 Fed. 609 (C. C. Mont. 1901).

SECTION 5. TRIBAL REGULATION OF DOMESTIC RELATIONS

The Indian tribes have been accorded the widest possible latitude in regulating the domestic relations of their members.[111] Indian custom marriage has been specifically recognized by federal statute, so far as such recognition is necessary for purposes of inheritance.[112] Indian custom marriage and divorce has been generally recognized by state and federal courts for all other purposes.[113] Where federal law or written laws of the tribe do not cover the subject, the customs and traditions of the tribe are accorded the force of law, but these customs and traditions may be changed by the statutes of the Indian tribes.[114] In defining and punishing offenses against the marriage relationship, the Indian tribe has complete and exclusive authority in the absence of legislation by Congress upon the subject. No law of the state controls the domestic relations of Indians living in tribal relationship,[115] even though the Indians concerned are citizens of the state.[116] The authority of an Indian tribal council to appoint guardians for incompetents and minors is specifically recognized by statute,[117] although this statute at the same time deprives such guardians of the power to administer federal trust funds. Property relations of husband and wife, or parent and child, are likewise governed by tribal law and custom.[118]

The case of *United States* v. *Quiver*[119] provided a critical test of the doctrine of Indian self-government in the field of domestic relations. The case arose through a prosecution for adultery in the United States District Court for South Dakota. Both of the individuals involved were Sioux Indians and the offense was alleged to have been committed on one of the Sioux reservations. The Department of Justice authorized prosecution on the theory that Congress had, by section 3 of the Act of March 3, 1887,[120] terminated the original tribal control over Indian domestic relations.

The question was: Did this statute, which applied to all areas within the exclusive jurisdiction of Congress, apply to the conduct of Indians on an Indian reservation? The Supreme Court held that it did not. The analysis of the subject by Mr. Justice Van Devanter is illuminating, not only on the immediate question of jurisdiction over adultery, but on the broader question of the civil jurisdiction of an Indian tribe:

> At an early period it became the settled policy of Congress to permit the personal and domestic relations of the Indians with each other to be regulated, and offenses by one Indian against the person or property of another Indian to be dealt with, according to their tribal customs and laws. Thus the Indian Intercourse Acts of May 19, 1796, c. 30, 1 Stat. 469, and of March, 1802, c. 13, 2 Stat. 139, provided for the punishment of various offenses by white persons against Indians and by Indians against white persons, but left untouched those by Indians against each other; and the act of June 30, 1834, c. 161, Sec. 25, 4 Stat. 729, 733, while providing that "so much of the laws of the United States as provides for the punishment of crimes committed within any place within the sole and exclusive jurisdiction of the United States shall be in force in the Indian country," qualified its action by saying, "the same shall not extend to crimes committed by one Indian against the person or property of another Indian." That provision with its qualification was later carried into the Revised Statutes as Secs. 2145 and 2146. This was the situation when this court, in *Ex parte Crow Dog*, 109 U. S. 556, held that the murder of an Indian by another Indian on an Indian reservation was not punishable under the laws of the United States and could be dealt with only according to the laws of the tribe. The first change came when, by the act of March 3, 1885, c. 341, Sec. 9, 23 Stat. 362, 385, now Sec. 328 of the Penal Code, Congress pro-

[111] On the application of tribal custom in domestic relations to the natives of Alaska, see 54 I. D. 39 (1932). And see Chapter 21, sec. 6.

[112] Sec. 5, Act of February 28, 1891, 26 Stat. 794, 795, as embodied in 25 U. S. C. 371, provides:

> *Descent of land*.—For the purpose of determining the descent of land to the heirs of any deceased Indian under the provisions of section 348, of this title, whenever any male and female Indian shall have cohabited together as husband and wife according to the custom and manner of Indian life the issue of such cohabitation shall be, for the purpose aforesaid, taken and deemed to be the legitimate issue of the Indians so living together * * *.

And see Act of March 3, 1873, sec. 11, 17 Stat. 566, 570 (pensions to "widows of colored or Indian soldiers").

[113] See Note (1904) 13 Yale L. J. 250, and cases cited.

[114] It has been held that a tribal ordinance authorizing divorce by tribal action does not by implication abolish tribal custom divorce. *Barnett* v. *Prairie Oil & Gas Co.*, 19 F. 2d 504 (C. C. A. 8, 1927), aff'g sub. nom. *Kunkel* v. *Barnett*, 10 F. 2d 804, cert. den. 275 U. S. 563.

[115] *In re Lelah-puc-ka-chee*, 98 Fed. 429 (D. C. N. D. Iowa, 1899), holding state court without jurisdiction to appoint guardian of tribal Indian. See Chapter 12, sec. 2. *Cf. Davison* v. *Gibson*, 56 Fed. 443 (C. C. A. 8, 1893), holding law of forum applicable to question of married woman's property if tribal law is not shown.

[116] *Yakima Joe* v. *To-is-lap*, 191 Fed. 516 (C. C. D. Ore. 1910).

[117] R. S. § 2108, 25 U. S. C. 159.

Adoption on the Crow Reservation is governed by the Act of March 3, 1931, c. 413, 46 Stat. 1494.

Appointment of guardians among the Pottawatomies was governed by Art. 8 of the Treaty of February 27, 1867, 15 Stat. 531; among the Ottawas by Art. 8 of the Treaty of June 24, 1862, 12 Stat. 1237. And *cf.* Act of February 13, 1891, 26 Stat. 749, 752 (Sacs, Foxes, Iowas); Act of March 2, 1889, 25 Stat. 980, 994 (Peoria, etc.).

To the effect that state court action in the matter of adoptions is not entitled to departmental recognition if the tribe has set up its own procedure for adoption, see Memo. Sol. I. D., December 2, 1937.

The Interior Department has taken the position that guardians appointed by a Court of Indian Offenses are "legal guardians" within the meaning of such legislation as the Act of February 25, 1933, 47 Stat. 907, governing payments of funds by governmental agencies "to incompetent adult Indians or minor Indians, who are recognized wards of the federal government, for whom no legal guardians or other fiduciaries have been appointed." Memo. Sol. I. D., March 25, 1936.

[118] *Hicks* v. *Butrick*. 12 Fed. Cas. No. 6458 (C. C. D. Kan. 1875).

[119] 241 U. S. 602 (1916).

[120] That section provides:

> That whoever commits adultery shall be punished by imprisonment in the penitentiary not exceeding three years; * * * (24 Stat. 635, 18 U. S. C. 516.)

vided for the punishment of murder, manslaughter, rape, assault with intent to kill, assault with a dangerous weapon, arson, burglary and larceny when committed by one Indian against the person or property of another Indian. In other respects the policy remained as before. After South Dakota became a State, Congress, acting upon a partial cession of jurisdiction by that State, c. 106, Laws 1901, provided by the act of February 2, 1903, c. 351, 32 Stat. 793, now Sec. 329 of the Penal Code, for the punishment of the particular offenses named in the act of 1885 when committed on the Indian reservations in that State, even though committed by others than Indians, but this is without bearing here, for it left the situation in respect of offenses by one Indian against the person or property of another Indian as it was after the act of 1885.

> We have now referred to all the statutes. There is none dealing with bigamy, polygamy, incest, adultery or fornication, which in terms refers to Indians, these matters always having been left to the tribal customs and laws and to such preventive and corrective measures as reasonably could be taken by the administrative officers. (Pp. 603–605.)

Recognition of the validity of marriages and divorces consummated in accordance with tribal law or custom is found in numerous cases.[131]

Legal recognition has not been withheld from marriages by Indian custom, even in those cases where Indian custom sanctioned polygamy. As was said in *Kobogum* v. *Jackson Iron Co.*:[132]

> * * * The testimony now in this case shows what, as matter of history, we are probably bound to know judicially, that among these Indians polygamous marriages have always been recognized as valid, and have never been confounded with such promiscuous or informal temporary intercourse as is not reckoned as marriage. While most civilized nations in our day very wisely discard polygamy, and it is not probably lawful anywhere among English speaking nations, yet it is a recognized and valid institution among many nations, and in no way universally unlawful. We must either hold that there can be no valid Indian marriage, or we must hold that all marriages are valid which by Indian usage are so regarded. There is no middle ground which can be taken, so long as our own laws are not binding on the tribes. They did not occupy their territory by our grace and permission, but by a right beyond our control. They were placed by the constitution of the United States beyond our jurisdiction, and we had no more right to control their domestic usages than those of Turkey or India. * * * We have here marriages had between members of an Indian tribe in tribal relations, and unquestionably good by the Indian rules. The parties were not subject in those relations to the laws of Michigan, and there was no other law interfering with the full jurisdiction of the tribe over personal relations. We cannot interfere with the validity of such marriages without subjecting them to rules of law which never bound them. (Pp. 605–606.)

Despite a popular impression to the contrary, marriage in accordance with tribal law or custom has exactly the same validity that marriage by state license has among non-Indians. Many Indian tribes have a clearly defined marriage ritual.[133] Some tribes have provided for regular tribal marriage licenses, the validity of which has been affirmed by the United States Supreme Court.[134]

The jurisdiction of a tribal court over divorce actions has been recognized by federal and state courts.[135]

The basis of tribal jurisdiction over divorce was set forth with lucidity in the case of *Wall* v. *Williamson*:[136]

> It is only by positive enactments, even in the case of conquered and subdued nations, that their laws are changed by the conqueror. (P. 51.)

The fact that Indians may obtain marriage licenses from state officials does not deprive the tribe of jurisdiction to issue a divorce where the parties are properly before tribal court. In this respect Indians are in the same position as persons who, after marrying under the law of one state, may be divorced under the law of another state or of a foreign nation.[137]

---

[131] *Johnson* v. *Johnson*, 30 Mo. 72 (1860); *Boyer* v. *Dively*, 58 Mo. 510 (1875); *Earl* v. *Godley*, 42 Minn. 361, 44 N. W. 254 (1890); *People ex rel. LaForte* v. *Rubin*, 98 N. Y. Supp. 787 (1905); *Ortley* v. *Ross*, 78 Nebr. 339, 110 N. W. 982 (1907); *Yakima Joe* v. *To-is-lap*, 191 Fed. 516 (C. C. Ore. 1910); *Cyr* v. *Walker*, 29 Okla. 281, 116 Pac. 931 (1911); *Buck* v. *Branson*, 34 Okla. 807, 127 Pac. 436 (1912); *Butler* v. *Wilson*. 54 Okla. 229, 153 Pac. 823 (1915); *Carney* v. *Chapman*, 247 U. S. 102 (1918); *Hallowell* v. *Commons*, 210 Fed. 793 (C. C. A. 8, 1914); *Johnson* v. *Dunlap*, 68 Okla. 216, 173 Pac. 359 (1918); *Davis* v. *Reeder*, 102 Okla. 106, 226 Pac. 880 (1924); *Pompey* v. *King*, 101 Okla. 258, 225 Pac. 175 (1924); *Proctor* v. *Foster*, 107 Okla. 95, 230 Pac. 753 (1924); *Unussee v. McKinney*, 133 Okla. 40, 270 Pac. 1096 (1928); and *cf.* *Connolly* v. *Woolrich*. 11 Lower Can. Jur. 197 (1867). See, also, *Parr* v. *Colfax*, 197 Fed. 302 (C. C. A. 9, 1912); *Porter* v. *Wilson*, 239 U. S. 170 (1915); and see Wharton, Conflict of Laws (3d ed. 1905), vol. 1, sec. 128a.

[132] 76 Mich. 498, 43 N. W. 602 (1889).

[133] Under Chapter 3, sec. 2, of the Law and Order Regulations approved by the Secretary of the Interior November 27, 1935, 25 C. F. R. 161.28, it became the duty of each tribal council to determine the procedure to be followed in tribal custom marriage. See fn. 180, *infra*.

[134] *Nofire* v. *United States*, 164 U. S. 657 (1897).

[135] *Raymond* v. *Raymond*, 83 Fed. 721 (C. C. A. 8, 1897); 19 Op. A. G. 109 (1888).

[136] 8 Ala. 48 (1845).

[137] In upholding the power of a tribal court to issue a divorce decree where one of the parties was a non-Indian, the Solicitor for the Interior Department declared (Memo. February 11, 1939):

> A divorce action has been frequently described as an action in rem in which the res is the marital status of the parties. It is necessary for a court to have jurisdiction of the res in order to grant a divorce, although it need not have jurisdiction of both the parties. It is well established that a State court has the necessary jurisdiction of the marital status where the plaintiff is a resident of the State and the State is the location of the marital domicile, even though the State has no jurisdiction of the defendant spouse who is not a resident or a citizen of the State and can be reached only by constructive notice. *Atherton* v. *Atherton*, 181 U. S. 155; *Haddock* v. *Haddock*, 201 U. S. 562; *Delanoy* v. *Delanoy*, 13 Pac. (2d) 719 (Cal. 1932), 86 A. L. R. 1321.
> The foregoing principles are based upon the interest of the State in the marital status of its residents, and this interest is considered sufficiently great to permit a State to act upon the marital status of a resident in certain cases even though the other party was never within the jurisdiction of the State. As said by one court:
>
> > "Every State or sovereignty has the right to determine the domestic relations of all persons having their domiciles within their [sic] territory and where the husband or wife is domiciled within a particular State, the courts of that State can take jurisdiction over the status, and for proper cause act on this rem and dissolve the relation." *Coffey* v. *Coffey*, 71 S. W. (2d) 141, 142 (Mo. 1934).
>
> If the foregoing principles are applied to such a situation as that now presented, a tribal court could exercise jurisdiction to grant a divorce to a tribal member residing on the reservation whose spouse has abandoned the marital domicile on the reservation, regardless of the tribal membership or race or residence of the other spouse.
> Reliance need not be placed entirely upon application of these general principles of jurisdiction, however, in order to sustain the jurisdiction of a tribal court to divorce tribal members from white spouses, since a number of cases have already recognized as valid marriages and divorces under tribal law between tribal members and white persons. *Wall* v. *Williamson*, 8 Ala. 48; *Wall* v. *Williams*, 11 Ala. 826; *Morgan v. McGhee*, 5 Humph. (Tenn.) 14; *Johnson* v. *Johnson's Administrator*, 30 Mo. 72, 77 Am. Dec. 598; *La Riviere* v. *La Riviere*, 77 Mo. 512; *Cyr*. v. *Walker*, 29 Okla. 281, 116 Pac. 931; 35 L. R. A. (n. s.) 795; 14 R. C. L. 122. The foregoing cases determine that a white person who established a residence among an Indian tribe in its territory will be considered married to or divorced from a tribal member according to the law of the tribe. In the leading case of *Cyr*. v. *Walker*, *supra*, an adopted member of the tribe divorced his white wife on the reservation under tribal law and the validity of this divorce was recognized even though the parties had been married under State law. In all of these cases the divorce was an Indian custom divorce through separation by mutual consent or by abandonment by one of the parties. The principle, however, would not be affected because an Indian tribe may now require formal tribal court action in place of the earlier Indian custom.
> The *Cyr* case would seem to go so far as to recognize a tribal divorce by a tribal member against a white person who did not consent to the divorce. However, it is not necessary to decide at this time whether such a principle would now be accepted so that a tribal member could obtain a divorce in a tribal court against a white spouse who objected to the jurisdiction of the

It is, however, a matter of state law whether state courts will recognize the validity of such divorces. In the absence of reported decisions on this point it is not possible to say with any certainty how states are likely to treat such tribal divorces in cases that come up in state courts. So far as the Federal Government is concerned, the validity of such divorces is conceded.[128] The current Law and Order Regulations of the Indian Service, approved by the Secretary of the Interior on November 27, 1935,[129] recognize the validity of Indian custom marriage and divorce and leave it to the governing authorities of each tribe to define what shall constitute such marriage and divorce.[130] These regulations also authorize decrees by Courts of Indian Offenses compelling payment for support,[131] and judgments on the issue of paternity.[132]

The constitutions for tribes organized under the Act of June 18, 1934, generally provide for the exercise by the tribal council and tribal court of general jurisdiction over domestic relations.[133] Generally no departmental review of such tribal action is required.

A few of these tribal constitutions provide that all marriages shall be in conformity with state law.[134] Several tribes have adopted special ordinances governing domestic relations.[135]

> court. All that need be decided at this time is that under the accepted divorce law a tribal member may obtain a tribal divorce from a white spouse who has consented to the jurisdiction of the tribal court or who has abandoned his tribal spouse and his marital domicile on the reservation. It might be pointed out than an unjustified abandonment is itself an implied consent to a divorce action by the abandoned spouse in the court of the latter's domicile. (See *Delanoy* v. *Delanoy*, *supra*, at 723.)

[128] The Comptroller General, however, ruled otherwise in a case where a divorce action was pending in a state court. Settlement Certificate, Claim No. 013388 (25), January 23, 1936.

[129] See 55 I. D. 401 (1935).

[130] Chapter 3, sec. 2.

> *Tribal Custom Marriage and Divorce.*—The Tribal Council shall have authority to determine whether Indian custom marriage and Indian custom divorce for members of the tribe shall be recognized in the future as lawful marriage and divorce upon the reservation, and if it shall be so recognized, to determine what shall constitute such marriage and divorce and whether action by the Court of Indian Offenses shall be required. When so determined in writing, one copy shall be filed with the Court of Indian Offenses, one copy with the Superintendent in charge of the reservation, and one copy with the Commissioner of Indian Affairs. Thereafter, Indians who desire to become married or divorced by the custom of the tribe shall conform to the custom of the tribe as determined. Indians who assume or claim a divorce by Indian custom shall not be entitled to remarry until they have complied with the determined custom of their tribe nor until they have recorded such divorce at the agency office.
>
> Pending any determination by the Tribal Council on these matters, the validity of Indian custom marriage and divorce shall continue to be recognized as heretofore. (55 I. D. 401, 407 (1935).)

[131] C. F. R. 161.30, 161.64. A superintendent may enforce such a judgment against the defendant's restricted funds. Memo. Sol. I. D., September 8, 1938.

[132] 25 C. F. R. 161.30.

[133] Thus, for example, the Constitution of the Fort Belknap Indian Community, Montana, approved on December 13, 1935, provides:

> Article V, Section 1. *Enumerated powers.*—The council of the Fort Belknap Community shall have the following powers, the exercise of which shall be subject to popular referendum as provided hereafter: * * *
>
> (o) To regulate the domestic relations of members of the community.

[134] See, *e. g.*, the Constitution of the San Carlos Apache Tribe, approved January 17, 1936, which provides:

> Article V, Section XII. *Domestic relations.*—The council shall have the power to regulate the domestic relations of members of the tribe, but all marriages in the future shall be in accordance with the State laws * * *"

[135] The Code of Ordinances of the Gila River Pima-Maricopa Indian Community (1936) provides:

> CHAPTER 4. DOMESTIC RELATIONS
>
> SEC. 1. *Marriage.*—The Community Court may issue marriage licenses to proper persons, both of whom are members of the Community. Any tribal custom marriage not so licensed shall not be recognized as valid.
>
> SEC. 2. *Divorce.*—The Community Court may issue decrees of divorce for causes which it deems sufficient, where both parties are members of the Community.
>
> SEC. 3. *Recording of Marriages and Divorces.*—All Indian marriages and divorces, whether consummated in accordance with the State law or in accordance with Community Ordinances, shall be recorded within thirty days at the agency.

SECTION 6. TRIBAL CONTROL OF DESCENT AND DISTRIBUTION

It is well settled that an Indian tribe has the power to prescribe the manner of descent and distribution of the property of its members, in the absence of contrary legislation by Congress.[136] Such power may be exercised through unwritten customs and usages,[137] or through written laws of the tribe. This power extends to personal property as well as to real property. By virtue of this authority an Indian tribe may restrict the descent of property on the basis of Indian blood or tribal membership, and may provide for the escheat of property to the tribe where there are no recognized heirs. An Indian tribe may, if it so chooses, adopt as its own the laws of the state in which it is situated and may make such modifications in these laws as it deems suitable to its peculiar conditions.

The only general statutes of Congress which restrict the power of an Indian tribe to govern the descent and distribution of property of its members are section 5 of the General Allotment Act,[138] which provides that allotments of land shall descend "according to the laws of the State or Territory where such land is located," the Act of June 25, 1910,[139] which provides that the Secretary of the Interior shall have unreviewable discretion to determine the heirs of an Indian in ruling upon the inheritance of individual allotments issued under the authority of the General Allotment Law, and section 2 of the same act, as amended by the Act of February 14, 1913,[140] which gives the Secretary of the Interior final power to approve and disapprove Indian wills devising restricted property.

These statutes abolished the former tribal power over the descent and distribution of property, with respect to allotments of land made under the General Allotment Act, and rendered tribal rules of testamentary disposition subject to the authority of the Secretary of the Interior, when the estate includes restricted property. They do not, however, affect testamentary disposition of unrestricted property or intestate succession to personal property or to interests in land other than allotments (e. g., possessory interests in land to which title is retained by the tribe).[141] With respect to property other than allotments of land made under the General Allotment Act and similar special legislation, the inheritance laws and customs of the Indian tribe are still of supreme authority.[142]

[136] See Chapter 5, sec. 11; Chapter 11, sec. 6.

[137] See Beaglehole, Ownership & Inheritance in an Indian Tribe (1935), 20 Ia. L. Rev. 304; Hagan, Tribal Law of the American Indian (1917), 23 Case & Com. 735; and see authorities cited *supra*, sec. 3, fn. 55.

[138] Act of February 8, 1887, 24 Stat. 388, 389, 25 U. S. C. 348.

Treaties and special statutes occasionally stipulated that state laws were to apply to descent of allotments. See, for example, Article 8 of the Treaty of February 27, 1867, with the Pottawatomies, 15 Stat. 531, 533.

[139] Sec. 1, 36 Stat. 855, 25 U. S. C. 372.

[140] 37 Stat. 678. See 25 U. S. C. 373.

[141] *Gooding* v. *Watkins*, 142 Fed. 112 (C. C. A. 8, 1905). See Chapter 5, sec. 11 and Chapter 11, sec. 6.

[142] The foregoing general analysis is inapplicable to the Five Civilized Tribes, and Osages, Congress having expressly provided that state probate courts shall have jurisdiction over the estates of allotted Indians of the Five Civilized Tribes leaving restricted heirs (Act of June 14, 1918, c. 101, sec. 1, 40 Stat. 606, 25 U. S. C. 375), and over the estates of Osage Indians (Act of April 18, 1912, sec. 3, 37 Stat. 86). See Chapter 23, secs. 9, 12.

The authority of an Indian tribe in the matter of inheritance is clearly recognized by the United States Supreme Court in the case of *Jones* v. *Meehan.*[143] Land had been allotted to Chief Moose Dung. After his death, the Chief's eldest son, Moose Dung the Younger, leased the land in 1891 for 10 years, to two white men, the plaintiffs, on the assumption that he was, by the custom of his tribe, the sole heir to the property and entitled, in his own right, to dispose of it. Thereafter, in 1894, a second lease of the same land was executed in favor of another white man, the defendant. The Secretary of the Interior took the view that the earlier lease was invalid. The Secretary of the Interior approved the second lease, pursuant to a joint resolution of Congress specifically authorizing the approval of the second lease. Under the second lease, the Secretary of the Interior held, the rentals were to be divided among six descendants of the older Chief Moose Dung, and Moose Dung the Younger was to receive only a one-sixth share. Thus the Supreme Court was faced with a clear question: Did Moose Dung the Younger have the right, in 1891, to make a valid lease which neither the Secretary of the Interior nor Congress itself could thereafter annul? Faced with this question, the Court declared, *per* Gray, *J.*:

> The Department of the Interior appears to have assumed that, upon the death of Moose Dung the elder, in 1872, the title in his land descended by law to his heirs general, and not to his eldest son only.
>
> But the elder Chief Moose Dung being a member of an Indian tribe, whose tribal organization was still recognized by the Government of the United States, the right of inheritance in his land, at the time of his death, was controlled by the laws, usages and customs of the tribe, and not by the law of the State of Minnesota, nor by any action of the Secretary of the Interior. (P. 29.)
>
> * * * * *
>
> The title to the strip of land in controversy, having been granted by the United States to the elder Chief Moose Dung by the treaty itself, and having descended, upon his death, by the laws, customs and usages of the tribe, to his eldest son and successor as chief, Moose Dung the younger, passed by the lease executed by the latter in 1891 to the plaintiffs for the term of that lease; and their rights under that lease could not be divested by any subsequent action of the lessor, or of Congress, or of the Executive Departments. (P. 32.)

The opinion of the Supreme Court in *Jones* v. *Meehan* cites a long series of cases in federal and state courts which likewise uphold the validity of tribal laws and customs of inheritance.[144] The upshot of the cases cited is summarized in the words of a New York court:

> When Congress does not act no law runs on an Indian reservation save the Indian tribal law and custom.[145]

The decision of the Supreme Court in *Jones* v. *Meehan* is a clear refutation of the theory that in the absence of law plenary power over Indian affairs rests with the Interior Department.[146] The case holds not only that power over inheritance, in the absence of congressional legislation, rests with the Indian tribe, but that *Congress itself cannot disturb rights which have vested under tribal law and custom.*

Other decisions confirm the rule laid down in the *Moose Dung* case.[147]

[143] 175 U. S. 1 (1899).

[144] *United States* v. *Shanks*, 15 Minn. 369 (1870); *Dole* v. *Irish*, 2 Barb. (N. Y.) 639 (1848); *Hastings* v. *Farmer*, 4 N. Y. 293, 294 (1850); *The Kansas Indians*, 5 Wall. 737 (1866); *Wau-pe-man-qua* v. *Aldrich*, 28 Fed. 489 (C. C. Ind. 1886); *Brown* v. *Steele*, 23 Kans. 672 (1880); *Richardville* v. *Thorp*, 28 Fed. 52 (C. C. Kans. 1886).

[145] *Woodin* v. *Seeley*, 141 Misc. 207, 252 N. Y. Supp. 818 (1931).

[146] See 20 L. D. 157 (1895), mod. 29 L. D. 628 (1900). See Chapter 5, secs. 7, 8.

[147] See Chapter 10, sec. 10. And see Dembitz, Land Titles (1895), vol. 1, p. 498.

In the case of *Gray* v. *Coffman*,[148] the court held that the validity of the will of a member of the Wyandot tribe depended upon its conformity with the written laws of the tribe. The court declared:

> The Wyandot Indians, before their removal from Ohio had adopted a written constitution and laws, and among others, laws relating to descent and wills. These are in the record, and are shown to have been copied from the laws of Ohio, and adopted by the Wyandot tribe, with certain modifications, to adapt them to their customs and usages. One of these modifications was that only living children should inherit, excluding the children of deceased children, or grandchildren. The Wyandot council, which is several times referred to in the treaty of 1855, was an executive and judicial body, and had power, under the laws and usages of the nation, to receive proof of wills, etc.; and this body continued to act, at least to some extent, after the treaty of 1855. * * * under the circumstances, the court must give effect to the well established laws, customs, and usages of the Wyandot tribe of Indians in respect to the disposition of property by descent and will. (Pp. 1005–1006.)

In the case of *O'Brien* v. *Bugbee*,[149] it was held that a plaintiff in ejectment could not recover without positive proof that under tribal custom he was lawful heir to the property in question. In the absence of such proof, it was held that title to the land escheated to the tribe, and that the tribe might dispose of the land as it saw fit.

Tribal autonomy in the regulation of descent and distribution is recognized in the case of *Woodin* v. *Seeley*[150] and in the case of *Patterson* v. *Council of Seneca Nation.*[151]

In the case of *Y-Ta-Tah-Wah* v. *Rebock*,[152] the plaintiff, a medicine-man imprisoned by the federal Indian agent and county sheriff for practicing medicine without a license, brought an action of false imprisonment against these officials, and died during the course of the proceedings. The court held that the action might be continued, not by an administrator of the decedent's estate appointed in accordance with state law, but by the heirs of the decedent by Indian custom.[153] The court declared, *per* Shiras, *J.*:

> If it were true that, upon the death of a tribal Indian, his property, real and personal, became subject to the laws of the state directing the mode of distribution of estates of decedents, it is apparent that irremediable confusion would be caused thereby in the affairs of the Indians * * *. (P. 262.)

In a case[154] involving the right of an illegitimate child to inherit property, the authority of the tribe to pass upon the status of illegitimates was recognized in the following terms:

> The Creek Council, in the exercise of its lawful function of local self-government, saw fit to limit the legal rights of an illegimate child to that of sharing in the estate of his putative father, and not to confer upon such child

[148] 10 Fed. Cas. No. 5,714 (C. C. Kan. 1874). Accord: *Gooding* v. *Watkins*, 142 Fed. 112 (C. C. A. 8, 1905).

[149] 46 Kan. 1, 26 Pac. 428 (1891).

[150] 141 Misc. 207, 252 N. Y. Supp. 818 (1931), discussed in Note (1932) 9 N. Y. U. L. Q. Rev. 498.

[151] 245 N. Y. 433, 157 N. E. 734 (1927).

[152] 105 Fed. 257 (C. C. N. D. Iowa 1900).

[153] Compare, however, the decision of the Supreme Court of New Mexico in *Trujillo* v. *Prince*, 42 N. M. 337, 78 P. 2d 145 (1938), holding that an administrator of a Pueblo Indian appointed by a state court was empowered to sue under a state wrongful death statute. The Solicitor for the Interior Department and the Special Attorney for the Pueblo Indians supported the position which the Supreme Court of New Mexico finally adopted, on the ground that the action was not an action over which the tribal courts would have jurisdiction, but was entirely a creature of state legislation operating on events that occurred outside of any reservation. Memo. Sol. I. D., September 21, 1937.

[154] *Oklahoma Land Co.* v. *Thomas*, 34 Okla. 681, 127 Pac. 8 (1912).

generally the status of a child born in lawful wedlock. (P. 13.) [155]

In the case of *Dole* v. *Irish*,[156] it was held that a surrogate of the State of New York has no power to grant letters of administration to control the disposition of personal property belonging to a deceased member of the Seneca tribe. The court declared:

> I am of the opinion that the private property of the Seneca indians is not within the jurisdiction of our laws respecting administration; and that the letters of administration granted by the surrogate to the plaintiff are void. I am also of the opinion that the distribution of indian property according to their customs passes a good title, which our courts will not disturb; and therefore that the defendant has a good title to the horse in question, and must have judgment on the special verdict. (Pp. 642–643.)

In *United States* v. *Charles*,[157] the distribution of real and personal property of the decedent through the Iroquois custom of the "dead feast" is recognized as controlling all rights of inheritance.

In the case of *Mackey* v. *Cowe*,[158] the Supreme Court held that letters of administration issued by a Cherokee court were entitled to recognition in another jurisdiction, on the ground that the status of an Indian tribe was in fact similar to that of a federal territory.

In the case of *Meeker* v. *Kaelin*,[159] the court recognized the validity of tribal custom in determining the descent of real and personal property and indicated that the tribal custom of the Puyallup band prescribed different rules of descent for real and for personal property.

The applicability of tribal law in matters involving determination of heirs [160] is recognized in the Law and Order Regulations of the Indian Service.[161] These regulations provide that when any member of a tribe dies,

> leaving property other than an allotment or other trust property subject to the jurisdiction of the United States, any member claiming to be an heir of the decedent may bring a suit in the Court of Indian Offenses to have the Court determine the heirs of the decedent and to divide among the heirs such property of the decedent.[162]

In such suits, the regulations provide:

> In the determination of heirs, the Court shall apply the custom of the tribe as to inheritance if such custom is proved. Otherwise the Court shall apply State law in deciding what relatives of the decedent are entitled to be his heirs.[163]

A special provision covers the situation where the statutory jurisdiction of the Department attaches to part of an estate that is otherwise subject to tribal jurisdiction:

> Where the estate of the decedent includes any interest in restricted allotted lands or other property held in trust by the United States, over which the Examiner of Inheritance would have jurisdiction, the Court of Indian Offenses may distribute only such property as does not come under the jurisdiction of the Examiner of Inheritance, and the determination of heirs by the court may be reviewed, on appeal, and the judgment of the court modified or set aside by the said Examiner of Inheritance, with the approval of the Secretary of the Interior, if law and justice so require.[164]

The Law and Order Regulations of the Indian Service further provide that Courts of Indian Offenses shall have jurisdiction to probate wills of tribal Indians,

> disposing only of property other than an allotment or other trust property subject to the jurisdiction of the United States.[165]

Tribal custom is recognized in the provision:

> If the Court determines the will to be validly executed, it shall order the property described in the will to be given to the persons named in the will or to their heirs; but no distribution of property shall be made in violation of a proved tribal custom which restricts the privilege of tribal members to distribute property by will.[166]

Indian Service regulations covering the determination of heirs and approval of wills [167] provide that the activity of examiners of inheritance in cases of intestate succession shall not extend to unallotted reservations.[168]

Tribal constitutions generally provide that the governing body of the tribe shall have power—

> to regulate the inheritance of real and personal property, other than allotted lands, within the Territory of the Community.[169]

A typical tribal inheritance law, adopted by the Gila River Pima-Maricopa Indian Community on June 3, 1936, is set forth in the footnote below.[170]

---

[155] Accord: *Butler* v. *Wilson*, 54 Okla. 229, 153 Pac. 823 (1915).

[156] 2 Barb. (N. Y.) 639 (1848).

[157] 23 F. Supp. 346 (D. C. W. D. N. Y. 1938); accord: *George* v. *Pierce*, 148 N. Y. Supp. 230 (1914).

[158] 18 How. 100 (1855). See Chapter 14, sec. 3.

[159] 173 Fed. 216 (C. C. W. D. Wash. 1909).

[160] Recognition of tribal rules of descent is found in such special legislation as the Act of February 19, 1875, 18 Stat. 330, dealing with leases of Seneca lands, and the Act of March 1, 1901, 31 Stat. 861, dealing with Creek allotments.

To the effect that inheritance of a house on tribal land is governed by tribal rather than state law, see Memo. Sol. I. D., November 18, 1938.

[161] 25 C. F. R. 161.31–161.32.

[162] Law and Order Regulations, approved November 27, 1935, c. 3, sec. 5, 25 C. F. R. 161.31

[163] *Ibid.*

[164] *Ibid.*

[165] 25 C. F. R. 161.32.

[166] 25 C. F. R. 161.32.

[167] Approved by Secretary of the Interior May 31, 1935, 25 C. F. R., Part 81.

[168] 25 C. F. R. 81.18, 81.28.

[169] Constitution of the Fort Belknap Indian Community of the Fort Belknap Reservation, Mont., approved December 13, 1935, Art. V, Sec. 1(m).

[170] Sec. 6. *Approval of Wills.*—When any member of the tribe dies, leaving a will disposing only of property other than an allotment or other trust property subject to the jurisdiction of the United States, the Court shall, at the request of any member of the tribe named in the will or any other interested party, determine the validity of the will after giving notice and full opportunity to appear in court to all persons who might be heirs of the decedent. A will shall be deemed to be valid if the decedent had a sane mind and understood what he was doing when he made the will and was not subject to any undue influence of any kind from another person, and if the will was made in writing and signed by the decedent in the presence of two witnesses who also signed the will. If the Court determines the will to be validly executed, it shall order the property described in the will to be given to the persons named in the will or to their heirs, if they are dead.

Sec. 7. *Determination of Heirs.*—Property of members of the Community, other than allotted lands, if not disposed of by will shall be inherited according to the following rules:

1. The just debts and funeral expenses of the deceased shall be paid before the heirs take any property.
2. If the deceased leaves a surviving spouse, all the property shall go to the surviving spouse, who shall make such disposition as seems proper.
3. If the deceased leaves children or grandchildren, but no spouse, all the property shall go to them.
4. If the deceased leaves no spouse nor descendants, all the property shall go to his or her parents, if either or both is alive.
5. In any other case, the nearest relatives shall inherit.

Where there is more than one heir, all the heirs shall meet and agree among themselves upon the division of the property.

If no agreement can be reached among all the interested parties, any party may, upon depositing a fee of five dollars in the Community Court, require the Court to pass on the distribution of the estate.

Where the interested parties agree among themselves on the disposition of the estate, they shall file a report of such distribution with the Community Court.

SECTION 7. THE TAXING POWER OF AN INDIAN TRIBE

One of the powers essential to the maintenance of any government is the power to levy taxes. That this power is an inherent attribute of tribal sovereignty which continues unless withdrawn or limited by treaty or by act of Congress [171] is a proposition which has never been successfully disputed.

A landmark in this field is the case of *Buster* v. *Wright*.[172] The Creek Nation, one of the Five Civilized Tribes, had imposed a tax or license fee upon all persons, not citizens of the Creek Nation, who traded within the borders of that nation. The Interior Department sought the advice of the Attorney General as to the legality of this tax, and was advised that the tax was legal and that the Interior Department was under an implied duty to assist in its enforcement.[173] Thereupon the Interior Department promulgated appropriate regulations to assist the tribe in making collections of license fees. The plaintiffs in the case of *Buster* v. *Wright* were traders doing business on town sites within the boundaries of the Creek Nation, who sought to enjoin officers of the Creek Nation and of the Interior Department from closing down their business and ousting them for nonpayment of taxes. On demurrer, the plaintiffs' bill was dismissed by the trial court. The decision of the trial court was affirmed by the Court of Appeals of the Indian Territory,[174] again by the Circuit Court of Appeals for the Eighth Circuit,[175] and finally by the United States Supreme Court.[176] The learned opinion of Judge Sanborn in the Circuit Court of Appeals illuminates the entire subject:

> The authority of the Creek Nation to prescribe the terms upon which noncitizens may transact business within its borders did not have its origin in act of Congress, treaty, or agreement of the United States. It was one of the inherent and essential attributes of its original sovereignty It was a natural right of that people, indispensable to its autonomy as a distinct tribe or nation, and it must remain an attribute of its government until by the agreement of the nation itself or by the superior power of the republic it is taken from it. Neither the authority nor the power of the United States to license its citizens to trade in the Creek Nation, with or without the consent of that tribe, is in issue in this case, because the complainants have no such licenses. The plenary power and lawful authority of the government of the United States by license, by treaty, or by act of Congress to take from the Creek Nation every vestige of its original or acquired governmental authority and power may be admitted, and for the purposes of this decision are here conceded. The fact remains nevertheless that every original attribute of the government of the Creek Nation still exists intact which has not been destroyed or limited by act of Congress or by the contracts of the Creek tribe itself.
>
> Originally an independent tribe, the superior power of the republic early reduced this Indian people to a "domestic, dependent nation" (*Cherokee Nation* v. *State of Georgia*, 5 Pet. 1–20, 8 L. Ed. 25), yet left it a distinct political entity, clothed with ample authority to govern its inhabitants and to manage its domestic affairs through officers of its own selection, who under a Constitution modeled after that of the United States, exercised legislative, executive and judicial functions within its territorial jurisdiction for more than half a century. The governmental jurisdiction of this nation was neither conditioned nor limited by the original title by occupancy to the lands within its territory. * * * Founded in its original national sovereignty, and secured by these treaties, the governmental authority of the Creek Nation, subject always to the superior power of the republic, remained practically unimpaired until the year 1889. Between the years 1888 and 1901 the United States by various acts of Congress deprived this tribe of all its judicial power, and curtailed its remaining authority until its powers of government have become the mere shadows of their former selves. Nevertheless its authority to fix the terms upon which noncitizens might conduct business within its territorial boundaries guarantied by the treaties of 1832, 1856, and 1866, and sustained by repeated decisions of the courts and opinions of the Attorneys General of the United States, remained undisturbed.
>
> * * * It is said that the sale of these lots and the incorporation of cities and towns upon the sites in which the lots are found authorized by act of Congress to collect taxes for municipal purposes segregated the town sites and the lots sold from the territory of the Creek Nation, and deprived it of governmental jurisdiction over this property and over its occupants. But the jurisdiction to govern the inhabitants of a country is not conditioned or limited by the title to the land which they occupy in it, or by the existence of municipalities therein endowed with power to collect taxes for city purposes, and to enact and enforce municipal ordinances. Neither the United States, nor a state, nor any other sovereignty loses the power to govern the people within its borders by the existence of towns and cities therein endowed with the usual powers of municipalities, nor by the ownership nor occupancy of the land within its territorial jurisdiction by citizens or foreigners. (Pp. 950–952.)

The case of *Buster* v. *Wright* dealt with what may be called a license or privilege tax, but the principles therein affirmed are equally applicable to a tax on property. Such a tax was upheld in *Morris* v. *Hitchcock*.[177] This case dealt with a tax levied by the Chickasaw Nation on cattle owned by noncitizens of that nation and grazed on private land within the national boundaries. The opinion of the United States Court of Appeals for the District of Columbia declares:

> A government of the kind necessarily has the power to maintain its existence and effectiveness through the exercise of the usual power of taxation upon all property within its limits, save as may be restricted by its organic law. Any restriction in the organic law in respect of this ordinary power of taxation, and the property subject

[171] No treaty provisions or special statutes dealing with tribal taxation have been found. But *cf.* Act of August 2, 1882, 22 Stat. 181, empowering Congress to tax certain railroad rights-of-way for the benefit of tribal grantors.

[172] 135 Fed. 947 (C. C. A. 8. 1905), app. dism. 203 U. S. 599.

[173] * * * the legal right to purchase land within an Indian nation gives to the purchaser no right of exemption from the laws of such nation, nor does it authorize him to do any act in violation of the treaties with such nation. These laws requiring a permit to reside or carry on business in the Indian country existed long before and at the time this act was passed. And if any outsider saw proper to purchase a town lot under this act of Congress, he did so with full knowledge that he could occupy it for residence or business only by permission from the Indians. * * *

> The treaties and laws of the United States make all persons, with a few specified exceptions, who are not citizens of an Indian nation or members of an Indian tribe, and are found within an Indian nation without permission, intruders there, and require their removal by the United States. This closes the whole matter, absolutely excludes all but the excepted classes, and fully authorizes these nations to absolutely exclude outsiders, or to permit their residence or business upon such terms as they may choose to impose, and it must be borne in mind that citizens of the United States have, as such, no more right or business to be there than they have in any foreign nation, and can lawfully be there at all only by Indian permission; and that their right to be or remain or carry on business there depends solely upon whether they have such permission.
>
> As to the power or duty of your Department in the premises there can hardly be a doubt. Under the treaties of the United States with these Indian nations this Government is under the most solemn obligation, and for which it has received ample consideration, to remove and keep removed from the territory of these tribes, all this class of intruders who are there without Indian permission. The performance of this obligation, as in other matters concerning the Indians and their affairs, has long been devolved upon the Department of the Interior. * * *

Trespassers on Indian Lands, 23 Op. A. G. 214, 217–218 (1900).

[174] *Buster* v. *Wright*, 82 S. W. 855 (1904).

[175] 135 Fed. 947 (C. C. A. 8, 1905).

[176] 203 U. S. 599 (1906), app. dism. without opinion.

[177] 21 App. D. C. 565 (1903), aff'd 194 U. S. 384 (1904).

> thereto, ought to appear by express provision or necessary implication. *Board Trustees* v. *Indiana*, 14 How. 268, 272; *Talbott* v. *Silver Bow Co.*, 139 U. S. 438, 448. Where the restriction upon this exercise of power by a recognized government, is claimed under the stipulations of a treaty with another, whether the former be dependent upon the latter or not, it would seem that its existence ought to appear beyond a reasonable doubt. We discover no such restriction in the clause of Article 7 of the Treaty of 1855, which excepts white persons from the recognition therein of the unrestricted right of self-government by the Chickasaw Nation, and its full jurisdiction over persons and property within its limits. The conditions of that exception may be fully met without going to the extreme of saying that it was also intended to prevent the exercise of the power to consent to the entry of non-citizens, or the taxation of property actually within the limits of that government and enjoying its benefits.[178] (P. 593.)

The power to tax does not depend upon the power to remove and has been upheld where there was no power in the tribe to remove the taxpayer from the tribal jurisdiction.[179] Where, however, the tribe does have power to remove a person from its jurisdiction, it may impose conditions upon his remaining within tribal territory, including the condition of paying license fees. An opinion of the Attorney General dated September 17, 1900, quoted with approval in *Morris* v. *Hitchcock*,[180] declares:

> "Under the treaties with the Five Civilized Tribes of Indians, no person not a citizen or member of a tribe, or belonging to the exempted classes, can be lawfully within the limits of the country occupied by these tribes without their permission, and they have the right to impose the terms upon which such permission will be granted." (P. 391.)

It is therefore pertinent, in analyzing the scope of tribal taxing powers, to inquire how far an Indian tribe is empowered to remove nonmembers from its reservation. This question is the more important today because statutes authorizing the Commissioner of Indian Affairs to remove "undesirable" persons from Indian country were repealed, at the urging of the present administration, in the interests of civil liberty.[181] Because of its peculiar jurisdictional status an Indian reservation is sometimes infested with white criminals or simple trespassers, and the problem of what effective legal action can be taken by a tribe to remove such persons from its reservation is a serious one.

The law as to the power of a tribe to exclude nonmembers from its territory is clearly stated in a series of authorities running back to the earliest days of the Republic. We find in the first volume of the Opinions of the Attorney General the following answer to a question raised by the Secretary of War as to the right of the Seneca Nation to exclude trespassers from its lands:

> So long as a tribe exists and remains in possession of its lands, its title and possession are sovereign and exclusive; and there exists no authority to enter upon their lands, for any purpose whatever, without their consent.[182]

The present state of the law on the power to remove nonmembers is thus summarized in the Solicitor's Opinion of October 25, 1934, on "Powers of Indian Tribes":

> Over tribal lands, the tribe has the rights of a landowner as well as the rights of a local government, dominion as well as sovereignty. But over all the lands of the reservation, whether owned by the tribe, by members thereof, or by outsiders, the tribe has the sovereign power of determining the conditions upon which persons shall be permitted to enter its domain, to reside therein, and to do business, provided only such determination is consistent with applicable Federal laws and does not infringe any vested rights of persons now occupying reservation lands under lawful authority.[183]

The power of an Indian tribe to levy taxes upon its own members and upon nonmembers doing business within the reservations has been affirmed in many tribal constitutions approved under the Wheeler-Howard Act, as has the power to remove nonmembers from land over which the tribe exercises jurisdiction. The following clauses are typical statements of these tribal powers:

> (h) To levy taxes upon members of the tribe and to require the performance of reservation labor in lieu thereof, and to levy taxes or license fees, subject to review by the Secretary of the Interior, upon non-members doing business within the reservation.
>
> (i) To exclude from the restricted lands of the reservation persons not legally entitled to reside therein, under ordinances which shall be subject to review by the Secretary of the Interior.[184]

Under such provisions, tribal tax ordinances imposing poll taxes, vehicle and other license taxes on members of the tribe, and permit and license taxes on nonmembers occupying tribal property have been held valid by the Interior Department.[185] And as the payment of a tax or license fee may be made a condition of entry upon tribal land, it may also be made a condition to the grant of other privileges, such as the acquisition of a tribal lease.[186]

It has been held that the Fifth Amendment does not restrict tribal taxation of tribal members,[187] but tribal constitutional requirements were held violated when a tribal council tried to delegate its taxing powers to a reservation superintendent.[188]

[178] Other authorities supporting the power of an Indian tribe to levy taxes or license fees are: *Crabtree* v. *Madden*, 54 Fed. 426 (C. C. A. 8, 1893); *Maxey* v. *Wright*, 3 Ind. T. 243, 54 S. W. 807, aff'd 105 Fed. 1003 (C. C. A. 8, 1900); 18 Op. A. G. 34, 36 (1884); 23 Op. A. G. 214, 219, 220, (1900); *ibid.*, p. 528 (1901).

[179] *Buster* v. *Wright*, *supra*.

[180] 194 U. S. 384 (1904).

[181] Act of May 21, 1934, 48 Stat. 787, repealing 25 U. S. C. 220 *et seq.*

[182] 1 Op. A. G. 465, 466 (1821). Accord: *United States* v. *Rogers*, 23 Fed. 658 (D. C. W. D. Ark. 1885). And see Chapter 15, sec. 10.

[183] 55 I. D. 14, 50, citing *Morris* v. *Hitchcock*, 194 U. S. 384 (1904), and other cases. See also Memo. Sol. I. D., August 7, 1937.

[184] Constitution of the Rosebud Sioux Tribe, approved December 20, 1935, Art. IV, sec. 1.

[185] Memo. Sol. I. D., February 17, 1939 (Rosebud Sioux).

[186] Memo. Sol. I. D., March 28, 1939.

[187] Memo. Sol. I. D., February 17, 1939 (Rosebud Sioux).

[188] Memo. Sol. I. D., May 14, 1938 (Oglala Sioux).

SECTION 8. TRIBAL POWERS OVER PROPERTY

The powers of an Indian tribe with respect to property derive from two sources. In the first place, the tribe has, with respect to tribal property, certain rights and powers commonly incident to property ownership. In the second place, the Indian tribe has, among its powers of sovereignty, the power to regulate the use and disposition of individual property among its members. While the distinction between these two sorts of power must remain largely conventional[189] and, in most concrete situations, even academic, those rights and powers which Indian tribes

[189] M. R. Cohen, Property and Sovereignty, in Law and the Social Order (1934), 41.

share with other property owners are sufficiently distinguishable to deserve treatment in a separate chapter.[190] On this subject it will be sufficient for our present purposes to note that the powers of an Indian tribe with respect to tribal land are not limited by any rights of occupancy which the tribe itself may grant to its members, that occupancy of tribal land does not create any vested rights in the occupant as against the tribe,[191] and that the extent of any individual's interest in tribal property is subject to such limitations as the tribe may see fit to impose.[192]

The power of a tribe over hunting and fishing on tribal territory may be analyzed either in governmental or in proprietary terms.[193]

In holding that a Pueblo is a stockowner, within the Taylor-Grazing Act, the Acting Solicitor for the Interior Department, after citing the foregoing cases, declared:[194]

> It thus is clear that a determination whether a Pueblo is a "stock owner" within the meaning of the Taylor Act and the Federal Range Code must be made by reference to the internal structure of the community and to its laws and customs. In his request for an opinion, the Commissioner states:
>
> > "It is impossible, realistically or pragmatically, to apply either to Pueblo livestock or to Pueblo range or water, concepts of ownership familiar in white life; the only way that realism can be achieved is by a concept treating all of these properties as properties of the community, whose keeping is vested by formal or informal community and/or religious decree in an individual or family."
>
> It appears that the custom is that certain individuals are designated by the governing body of the Pueblo to carry on the function of livestock raising. While in a limited sense and for certain purposes the livestock may be regarded as the personal property of these individuals, the livestock are subject to call by either the secular community, through the Governor and Council, the religious community, or the khiva or secret society organizations, indicating that the ultimate responsibility of the individuals is to the community and that the ultimate interest is that of the community. The individual's rights are basically usufructuary and always subject to the higher demand of the community itself. In these circumstances I am unable to see that any violence is done Anglo-Saxon legal concepts in holding that a Pueblo is an owner of livestock within the meaning of the Taylor Act and the Federal Range Code. (Pp. 13–14.)

The chief limitation upon tribal control of membership rights in tribal property is that found in acts of Congress guaranteeing to those who sever tribal relations to take up homesteads on the public domain,[195] and to children of white men and Indian women, under certain circumstances,[196] a continuing share in the tribal property. Except for these general limitations and other specific statutory limitations found in enrollment acts and other special acts of Congress, the proper authorities of an Indian tribe have full power to regulate the use and disposition of tribal property by the members of the tribe.

The authority of an Indian tribe in matters of property is not restricted to those lands or funds over which it exercises the rights of ownership. The sovereign powers of the tribe extend over the property as well as the person of its members.

Thus, in *Crabtree* v. *Madden*,[197] it is recognized that questions of the validity of contracts among members of the tribe are to be determined according to the laws of the tribe.[198]

In *Jones* v. *Laney*,[199] the question arose whether a deed of manumission freeing a Negro slave, executed by a Chickasaw Indian within the territory of the Chickasaw Nation was valid. The lower court had charged the jury "that their (Chickasaw) laws and customs and usages, within the limits defined to them, governed all property belonging to anyone domesticated and living with them." Approving this charge, upon the basis of

---

[190] See Chapter 15. See also Chapters 9, 10, and 11.

[191] *Sizemore* v. *Brady*, 235 U. S. 441 (1914); *Franklin* v. *Lynch*, 233 U. S. 269 (1914); *Gritts* v. *Fisher*, 224 U. S. 640 (1912); *Journeycake* v. *Cherokee Nation and United States*, 28 C. Cls. 281 (1893); *Sac and Fox Indians of the Mississippi in Iowa* v. *Sac and Fox Indians of the Mississippi in Oklahoma*, 220 U. S. 481 (1911) aff'g 45 C. Cls. 287 (1910); *Hayes* v. *Barringer*, 168 Fed. 221 (C. C. A. 8, 1909); *Whitmire, Trustee* v. *Cherokee Nation et al.*, 30 C. Cls. 138 (1895); *Dukes* v. *Goodall*, 5 Ind. T. 145, 82 S. W. 702 (1904); *In re Narragansett Indians*, 20 R. I. 715, 40 Atl. 347 (1898); *Terrance* v. *Gray*, 156 N. Y. Supp. 916 (1916); *Reservation Gas Co.* v. *Snyder*, 88 Misc. 209; 150 N. Y. Supp. 216 (1914); *Application of Parker*, 237 N. Y. Supp. 134 (1929); *McCurtain* v. *Grady*, 1 Ind. T. 107, 38 S. W. 65 (1896); *Myers* v. *Mathis*, 2 Ind. T. 3, 46 S. W. 178 (1898).

In the case of *Sizemore* v. *Brady*, *supra*, the Supreme Court declared:

> lands and funds belonged to the tribe as a community, and not to the members severally or as tenants in common. (P. 446.)

Similarly, in *Franklin* v. *Lynch*, *supra*, the Supreme Court declared:

> As the tribe could not sell, neither could the individual members, for they had neither an undivided interest in the tribal land nor vendible interest in any particular tract. (P. 271.)

In the case of *Hayes* v. *Barringer*, *supra*, the court declared, in considering the status of Choctaw and Chickasaw tribal lands:

> * * * At that time these were the lands of the Choctaw and Chickasaw Nations, held by them, as they held all their lands, in trust for the individual members of their tribes, in the sense in which the public property of representative governments is held in trust for its people. But those were public lands and, while the enrolled members of these tribes undoubtedly had a vested equitable right to their just shares of them against strangers and fellow members of their tribes, they had no separate or individual right to or equity in any of these lands which they could maintain against the legislation of the United States or of the Indian Nations. *Stephens* v. *Cherokee Nation*, 174 U. S. 445, 488, 19 Sup. Ct. 722, 43 L. Ed. 1041; *Cherokee Nation* v. *Hitchcock*, 187 U. S. 294, 23 Sup. Ct. 115, 47 L. Ed. 183; *Lone Wolf* v. *Hitchcock*, 187 U. S. 553, 23 Sup. Ct. 216, 47 L. Ed. 299; *Wallace* v. *Adams*, 143 Fed. 716, 74 C. C. A. 540; *Ligon* v. *Johnston* (C. C. A.) 164 Fed. 670. (Pp. 222–223.)

So, too, in *United States* v. *Lucero*, 1 N. M. 422, (1869): title to lands within a pueblo is recognized to lie in the pueblo itself, rather than in the individual members thereof.

[192] In *United States* v. *Chase*, 245 U. S. 89 (1917), the Supreme Court held that assignments made pursuant to treaty might be revoked by congressional action taken at the instance of tribal authorities. And *cf. Gritts* v. *Fisher*, 224 U. S. 640 (1912) and Chapter 5, sec. 5, Chapter 23, sec. 3.

In the case of *McCurtain* v. *Grady*, *supra*, a provision of the Choctaw Constitution conferring upon the discoverer of coal the right to mine all coal within a mile radius of the point of discovery was upheld as a valid exercise of tribal power.

In *Whitmire, Trustee* v. *Cherokee Nation*, *supra*, the Court of Claims held that the general property of the Cherokee Nation, under the provisions of the Cherokee Constitution, might be used for public purposes, but could not be diverted to per capita payments to a favored class.

On the power of the tribe with respect to assignments of tribal land to members, see Memo. Sol. I. D., October 20, 1937 (Mdewekanton Sioux); Memo. Sol. I. D., April 14, 1939 (Santa Clara Pueblo). And see Chapter 9, secs. 1, 5; Chapter 15, sec. 20.

[193] See Chapter 14, sec. 7.

[194] Op. Acting Sol. I D., M. 29797, May 14, 1938.

[195] 43 U. S. C. 189 (Act of March 3, 1875, c. 131, sec. 15, 18 Stat. 420) provides that an Indian severing tribal relations to take up a homestead upon the public domain "shall be entitled to his distributive share of all annuities, tribal funds, lands and other property, the same as though he had maintained his tribal relations." For a discussion of this and related statutes, see *Oakes* v. *United States*, 172 Fed. 305 (C. C. A. 8, 1909); *Halbert* v. *United States*, 283 U. S. 753 (1931). And see sec. 4 *supra*, and Chapter 9, sec. 3.

[196] 25 U. S. C. 184.

[197] 54 Fed. 426 (C. C. A. 8, 1893).

[198] See, to the same effect, *In re Sah Quah*, 31 Fed. 327 (D. C. Alaska, 1886). Chattel mortgage forms approved by the Interior Department for use by tribes making loans to members regularly provide:

> This mortgage and all questions and controversies arising thereunder shall be subject to the laws of the United States and of the ———— Tribe. Any question or controversy which cannot be decided under such laws shall be dealt with according to the laws of the State of ————.

See Memo Sol. I. D., December 22, 1938; and see Memo. Asst. Sec. I. D., August 17, 1938.

[199] 2 Tex. 342 (1844).

which the jury had found the deed to be valid, the appellate court declared:

> Their laws and customs, regulating property, contracts, and the relations between husband and wife, have been respected, when drawn into controversy, in the courts of the State and of the United States. (P. 348.)

In the case of *Delaware Indians* v. *Cherokee Nation*,[300] it is said:

> The law of real property is to be found in the law of the situs. The law of real property in the Cherokee country therefore is to be found in the constitution and laws of the Cherokee Nation. (P. 251.)

In the case of *James H. Hamilton* v. *United States*,[301] it appeared that land, buildings, and personal property owned by the claimant, a licensed trader, within the Chickasaw Reservation, had been confiscated by an act of the Chickasaw legislature. The plaintiff brought suit to recover damages on the theory that such confiscation constituted an "Indian depredation." The Court of Claims dismissed the suit, declaring:

> The claimant by applying for and accepting a license to trade with the Chickasaw Indians, and subsequently acquiring property within the limits of their reservation, subjected the same to the jurisdiction of their laws. (P. 287.)

The authority of an Indian tribe to impose license fees upon persons engaged in trade with its members within the boundaries of the reservation is confirmed in *Zevely* v. *Weimer*,[302] as well as in the various cases cited under section 7 of this chapter dealing with "The Taxing Power of an Indian Tribe."

[300] 38 C. Cls. 234 (1903), decree mod. 193 U. S. 127.

[301] 42 C. Cls. 282 (1907). *Cf.* sec. 29 of Act of May 2, 1890, 26 Stat. 81, 93 (tribal law made applicable to contracts between Indian and non-Indian in Indian Territory).

[302] 5 Ind. T. 646, 82 S. W. 941 (1904).

The power of an Indian tribe to regulate the inheritance of individual property owned by members of the tribe likewise has been analyzed under a separate heading.[303]

Within the scope of local self-government, it has been held, fall such powers as the power to charter corporations.[304]

Repeatedly, in the situations above discussed, federal and state courts have declined to interfere with the decisions of tribal authorities on property disputes internal to the tribe.[305]

It clearly appears, from the foregoing cases, that the powers of an Indian tribe are not limited to such powers as it may exercise in its capacity as a landowner. In its capacity as a sovereign, and in the exercise of local self-government, it may exercise powers similar to those exercised by any state or nation in regulating the use and disposition of private property, save insofar as it is restricted by specific statutes of Congress.

The laws and customs of the tribe, in matters of contract and property generally (as well as on questions of membership, domestic relations, inheritance, taxation, and residence), may be lawfully administered in the tribunals of the tribe, and such laws and customs will be recognized by courts of state or nation in cases coming before these courts.[306]

[303] Sec. 6.

[304] See, for example, the Cherokee resolution of March 8, 1813, chartering a corporation, embodied in the Treaty of February 27, 1819, with the Cherokee Nation, 7 Stat. 195. And see Memo. Sol. I. D., May 24, 1937 (Fort Hall); Memo. Sol. I. D., March 14, 1938 (Blackfeet).

[305] *Washburn* v. *Parker*, 7 F. Supp. 120 (D. C. W. D., N. Y., 1934); *Mulkins* v. *Snow*, 175 N. Y. Supp. 41 (1919), affd. 178 N. Y. Supp. 905, discussed in Note (1922) 31 Yale L. J. 331; accord: 7 Op. A. G. 174 (1855).

[306] See Pound, Nationals without a Nation (1922), 22 Col. L. Rev. 97; Rice, The Position of the American Indian in the Law of the United States (1934), 16 J. Comp. Leg. 78.

SECTION 9. TRIBAL POWERS IN THE ADMINISTRATION OF JUSTICE

The powers of an Indian tribe in the administration of justice derive from the substantive powers of self-government which are legally recognized to fall within the domain of tribal sovereignty. If an Indian tribe has power to regulate the marriage relationships of its members, it necessarily has power to adjudicate, through tribunals established by itself, controversies involving such relationships.[307] So, too, with other fields of local government in which our analysis has shown that tribal authority endures. In all these fields the judicial powers of the tribe are coextensive with its legislative or executive powers.[308]

The decisions of Indian tribal courts, rendered within their jurisdiction and according to the forms of law or custom recognized by the tribe, are entitled to full faith and credit in the courts of the several states.

As was said in the case of *Standley* v. *Roberts*:[309]

> * * * the judgments of the courts of these nations, in cases within their jurisdiction, stand on the same footing with those of the courts of the territories of the Union and are entitled to the same faith and credit. (P. 845.)

And in the case of *Raymond* v. *Raymond*, the court declared:

> The Cherokee Nation * * * is a distinct political society, capable of managing its own affairs and governing itself. It may enact its own laws, though they may not be in conflict with the constitution of the United States. It may maintain its own judicial tribunals, and their judgments and decrees upon the rights of the persons and property of members of the Cherokee Nation as against each other are entitled to all the faith and credit accorded to the judgments and decrees of territorial courts. (P. 722.)[310]

The question of the judicial powers of an Indian tribe is particularly significant in the field of law and order. For in the fields of civil controversy the rules and decisions of the tribe and its officers have a force that state courts and federal courts will respect.[311] But in accordance with the well-settled principle that one sovereign will not enforce the criminal laws of another sovereign, state courts and federal courts alike must decline to enforce penal provisions of tribal law. Responsibility for the maintenance of law and order is therefore squarely upon the Indian tribe, unless this field of jurisdiction has been taken over by the states or the Federal Government.

It is illuminating to deal with the question of tribal criminal jurisdiction as we have dealt with other questions of tribal authority, by asking, first, what the original sovereign powers of

[307] The power of an Indian tribe over the administration of justice has been held to include the power to prescribe conditions of practice in the tribal courts. Memo. Sol. I. D., August 7, 1937. And see 25 C. F. R. 161.9.

[308] *Washburn* v. *Parker*, 7 F. Supp. 120 (D. C. W. D. N. Y. 1934); *Raymond* v. *Raymond*, 83 Fed. 721 (C. C. A. 8, 1897); 19 Op. A. G. 109 (1888); 7 Op. A. G. 174 (1855).

[309] 59 Fed. 836 (C. C. A. 8, 1894), app. dism. 17 Sup. Ct. 999 (1896); and see Chapter 14, sec. 3.

[310] 83 Fed. 721 (C. C. A. 8, 1897). Accord: *Nofire* v. *United States*, 164 U. S. 657 (1897); *Mehlin* v. *Ice*, 56 Fed. 12 (C. C. A. 8, 1893).

[311] Note, however, that courts have sometimes taken the position that tribal law or custom must be shown by the party relying thereon, and that otherwise the common law will be applied. See *Hockett* v. *Alston*, 110 Fed. 910 (C. C. A. 8, 1901); *Wilson* v. *Owens*, 86 Fed. 571 (C. C. A. 8, 1898); *Pyeatt* v. *Powell*, 51 Fed. 551 (C. C. A. 8, 1892). And see Chapter 14, sec. 5.

the tribes were, and then, how far and in what respects these powers have been limited.

So long as the complete and independent sovereignty of an Indian tribe was recognized, its criminal jurisdiction, no less than its civil jurisdiction, was that of any sovereign power. It might punish its subjects for offenses against each other or against aliens and for public offenses against the peace and dignity of the tribe. Similarly, it might punish aliens within its jurisdiction according to its own laws and customs.[212] Such jurisdiction continues to this day, save as it has been expressly limited by the acts of a superior government.

It is clear that the original criminal jurisdiction of the Indian tribes has never been transferred to the states. Sporadic attempts of the states to exercise jurisdiction over offenses between Indians, or between Indians and whites, committed on an Indian reservation, have been held invalid usurpation of authority.

The principle that a state has no criminal jurisdiction over offenses involving Indians committed on an Indian reservation is too well established to require argument, attested as it is by a line of cases that reaches back to the earliest years of the Republic.[213]

A state, of course, has jurisdiction over the conduct of an Indian off the reservation.[214] A state also has jurisdiction over some, but not all, acts of non-Indians within a reservation.[215] But the relations between whites and Indians in "Indian country" and the conduct of Indians themselves in Indian country are not subject to the laws or the courts of the several states.

The denial of state jurisdiction, then, is dictated by principles of constitutional law.[216]

In these respects the territories occupy a legal position similar to the states.[217]

On the other hand, the constitutional authority of the Federal Government to prescribe laws and to administer justice upon the Indian reservations is plenary. The question remains how far Congress has exercised its constitutional powers.[218]

The basic provisions of federal law with regard to Indian offenses are found in sections 217 and 218 of U. S. Code, title 25:

> SEC. 217. *General laws as to punishment extended to Indian country.*—Except as to crimes the punishment of which is expressly provided for in this title, the general laws of the United States as to the punishment of crimes committed in any place within the sole and exclusive jurisdiction of the United States, except the District of Columbia, shall extend to the Indian country.
>
> SEC. 218. *Exceptions as to extension of general laws.*—The preceding section shall not be construed to extend to crimes committed by one Indian against the person or property of another Indian, nor to any Indian committing any offense in the Indian country who has been punished by the local law of the tribe, or to any case where, by treaty stipulations, the exclusive jurisdiction over such offenses is or may be secured to the Indian tribes respectively.[219]

These provisions recognize that, with respect to crimes committed by one Indian against the person or property of another Indian, the jurisdiction of the Indian tribe is plenary. These provisions further recognize that, in addition to this general jurisdiction over offenses between Indians, an Indian tribe may possess, by virtue of treaty stipulations, other fields of exclusive jurisdiction (necessarily including jurisdiction over cases involving non-Indians). "The local law of the tribe" is further recognized to the extent that the punishment of an Indian under such law must be deemed a bar to further prosecution under any applicable federal laws, even though the offense be one against a non-Indian.

Such was the law when the case of *Ex parte Crow Dog*,[220] which has been discussed in an earlier connection, arose. The United States Supreme Court there held that federal courts had no jurisdiction to prosecute an Indian for the murder of another Indian committed on an Indian reservation, such jurisdiction never having been withdrawn from the original sovereignty of the Indian tribe.

---

[212] This power is expressly recognized, for instance, in the Treaty of July 2, 1791, with the Cherokees, 7 Stat. 39, providing:

> If any citizen of the United States, or other person not being an Indian, shall settle on any of the Cherokees' lands, such person shall forfeit the protection of the United States, and the Cherokees may punish him or not, as they please. (Sec. 8.)

Other treaties acknowledging tribal jurisdiction over white trespassers on tribal lands are: Treaty of January 21, 1785, with the Delawares, 7 Stat. 16; Treaty of January 10, 1786, with the Chickasaws, 7 Stat. 24; Treaty of January 9, 1789, with the Wiandots, Delawares, and others, 7 Stat. 28; Treaty of August 7, 1790, with the Creeks, 7 Stat. 35; Treaty of July 2, 1791, with the Cherokees, 7 Stat. 39; Treaty of August 3, 1795, with the Wyandots, Delawares, and others, 7 Stat. 49. Later provisions require the tribes to seize and surrender trespassers "without other injury, insult, or molestation" to designated federal officials. Treaty of November 10, 1808, with Osage Nations, 7 Stat. 107. *Cf. Leak Glove Manuf'g Co.* v. *Needles*, 69 Fed. 68 (C. C. A. 8, 1895), and see Chapter 1.

[213] *Worcester* v. *Georgia*, 6 Pet. 515 (1832); *United States* v. *Kagama*, 118 U. S. 375 (1886); *United States* v. *Thomas*, 151 U. S. 577 (1894); *Toy Toy* v. *Hopkins*, 212 U. S. 542 (1909); *United States* v. *Celestine*, 215 U. S. 278 (1909); *Donnelly* v. *United States*, 228 U. S. 243 (1913); *United States* v. *Pelican*, 232 U. S. 442 (1914); *United States* v. *Ramsey*, 271 U. S. 467 (1926); *United States* v. *King*, 81 Fed. 625 (D. C. E. D., Wis., 1897); *In re Blackbird*, 109 Fed. 139 (D. C. W. D., Wis., 1901); *In re Lincoln*, 129 Fed. 247 (D. C. N. D., Cal., 1904); *United States ex rel. Lynn* v. *Hamilton*, 233 Fed. 685 (D. C. W. D., N. Y., 1915); *James H. Hamilton* v. *United States*, 42 C. Cls. 282 (1907); *Yohyowan* v. *Luce*, 291 Fed. 425 (D. C. E. D., Wash., 1923); *State* v. *Campbell*, 53 Minn. 354, 55 N. W. 553 (1893); *State* v. *Big Sheep*, 75 Mont. 219, 243 Pac. 1067 (1926); *Ex parte Cross*, 20 Nebr. 417, 30 N. W. 428 (1886); *People ex rel. Cusick* v. *Daly*, 212 N. Y. 183, 105 N. E. 1048 (1914); *State* v. *Cloud*, 228 N. W. 611 (1930); *State* v. *Rufus*, 205 Wis. 317, 237 N. W. 67 (Wis.) (1931). And see *United States* v. *Sa-coo-da-cot*, 27 Fed. Cas. No. 16212 (C. C. Nebr. 1870). See also Chapter 6.

[214] See *Pablo* v. *People*, 23 Colo. 134, 46 Pac. 636 (1896) (upholding state jurisdiction over murder of Indian by Indian outside of reservation). And see Chapters 6, 18.

[215] See *United States* v. *McBratney*, 104 U. S. 621 (1881) (declining federal jurisdiction over murder of non-Indian by non-Indian on reservation). And see Chapters 6, 18.

[216] See Willoughby, The Constitutional Law of the United States (2d ed. 1929), c. 21.

[217] *United States* v. *Kie*, 26 Fed. Cas. No. 15528a (D. C. D. Alaska 1885). And see Chapter 21.

[218] See Chapter 5.

[219] These provisions are derived from the Act of March 3, 1817, 3 Stat. 383, which, in extending federal criminal laws to territory belonging to any Indian tribe, specifies:

> * * * That nothing in this act shall be so construed as to affect any treaty now in force between the United States and any Indian nation, or to extend to any offence committed by one Indian against another, within any Indian boundary.

Similar provisions were contained in sec. 25 of the Act of June 30, 1834, c. 161, 4 Stat. 729, 733; sec. 3 of the Act of March 27, 1854, 10 Stat. 269, 270; and R. S. §§ 2145–2146, amended by sec. 1 of the Act of February 18, 1875, 18 Stat. 316, 318.

[220] 109 U. S. 556 (1883). Shortly before the decision in this case, an opinion had been rendered by the Attorney General in another Indian murder case holding that where an Indian of one tribe had murdered an Indian of another tribe on the reservation of a third tribe, even though it was not shown that any of the tribes concerned had any machinery for the administration of justice, the federal courts had no right to try the accused. The opinion concluded:

> If no demand for Foster's surrender shall be made by one or other of the tribes concerned, founded fairly upon a violation of some law of one or other of them having jurisdiction of the offense in question according to general principles, and by forms substantially conformable to natural justice, it seems that nothing remains except to discharge him. (17 Op. A. G. 566, 570. (1883).)

A similar decision had been reached in state courts. See *State* v. *McKenney*, 18 Nev. 182, 2 Pac. 171 (1883). See also, *Anonymous*, 1 Fed. Cas. No. 447 (C. C. D. Mo. 1848) (robbery).

Although the right of an Indian tribe to inflict the death penalty had been recognized by Congress,[231] so much consternation was created by the Supreme Court's decision in *Ex parte Crow Dog* that within 2 years Congress had enacted a law making it a federal crime for one Indian to murder another Indian on an Indian reservation.[232] This law also prohibited manslaughter, rape, assault with intent to kill, arson, burglary, and larceny. In later years notorious cases of robbery, incest, and assault with a dangerous weapon resulted in the piece-meal addition of these three offenses to the federal code of Indian crimes.[233] There are thus, at the present time, 10 major offenses for which federal jurisdiction has displaced tribal jurisdiction. Federal courts also have jurisdiction over the ordinary federal crimes applicable throughout the United States (such as counterfeiting, smuggling,[234] and offenses relative to the mails), over violations of special laws for the protection of Indians,[235] and over offenses committed by an Indian against a non-Indian or by a non-Indian against an Indian which fall within the special code of offenses for territory "within the exclusive jurisdiction of the United States." [236] All offenses other than these remain subject to tribal law and custom and to tribal courts.

Although the statute covering the "10 major crimes" does not expressly terminate tribal jurisdiction over the enumerated crimes, and may be interpreted as conferring only a concurrent jurisdiction upon the federal courts, it is arguable that the statute removes all jurisdiction over the enumerated crimes from the Indian tribal authorities.

Some support is given this argument by the decision in *United States* v. *Whaley*.[237] In this case, which arose soon after the passage of the statute in question, it had appeared fitting to the tribal council of the Tule River Reservation that a medicine man who was believed to have poisoned some 21 deceased patients should be executed, and he was so executed. The four tribal executioners were found guilty of manslaughter, in the federal court, on the theory, apparently, that the Act of March 3, 1885, had terminated tribal jurisdiction over murder cases. Whether tribal authorities may still inflict the death penalty for offenses other than the enumerated 10 major crimes is a matter of some doubt.

In opposition to the argument that the 1885 act limits tribal jurisdiction over crimes, it may be said that concurrent jurisdiction of federal and tribal authorities is clearly recognized by section 218 of title 25 of the United States Code, above set forth, which exempts from federal punishment otherwise merited persons who have "been punished by the local law of the tribe," and that the current Indian Law and Order Regulations recognize concurrent federal-tribal jurisdiction over crime.[238]

The lacunae in this brief criminal code of 10 commandments are serious, and indicate the importance of tribal jurisdiction in the field of law and order.

"Assault" cases that do not involve a "dangerous weapon" or where "intent to kill" cannot be proven, cannot be prosecuted in the federal court, no matter how brutal the attack may be, or how near death the victim is placed, if death does not actually ensue; men brutally beating their wives and children are, therefore, exempt from prosecution in the federal courts, and as above shown, the state courts do not have jurisdiction. Even assault with intent to commit rape or great bodily injury is not punishable under any federal statute.[239]

Aside from rape and incest, the various offenses involving the relation of the sexes (*e. g.*, adultery, seduction, bigamy, and solicitation), as well as those involving the responsibility of a man for the support of his wife and children, are not within the cases that can be prosecuted in federal courts.[240]

Other offenses which may be mentioned, to which no state or federal laws now have application, and over which no state or federal court now has any jurisdiction, are: kidnaping, receiving stolen goods, poisoning (if the victim does not die), obtaining money under false pretenses, embezzlement, blackmail, libel, forgery, fraud, trespass, mayhem, bribery, killing of another's livestock, setting fire to prairie or timber, use of false weights and measures, carrying concealed weapons, gambling, disorderly conduct, malicious mischief, pollution of water supplies, and other offenses against public health.[241]

The difficulties of this situation have prompted agitation for the extension of federal or state laws over the Indian country, which has continued for at least five decades, without success.[242] The propriety of the objective sought is not here in question, but the agitation itself is evidence of the large area of human conduct which must be left in anarchy if it be held that tribal authority to deal with such conduct has disappeared.

Fortunately, such tribal authority has been repeatedly recognized by the courts, and although it has not been actually exercised always and in all tribes, it remains a proper legal basis

---

[231] See report cited above, fn. 25.

[232] Act of March 3, 1885, 23 Stat. 362, 385. 18 U. S. C. 548.

Earlier attempts to extend federal criminal laws to crimes by Indians against Indians (*e. g.* Letter from Secretary of the Interior, March 31, 1874, Sen. Misc. Doc., No. 95, 43d Cong., 1st sess.) had failed. On May 20, 1874, the Senate Committee on Indian Affairs, rejecting the proposed bills, declared:

> * * * The Indians, while their tribal relations subsist, generally maintain laws, customs, and usages of their own for the punishment of offenses. They have no knowledge of the laws of the United States, and the attempt to enforce their own ordinances might bring them in direct conflict with existing statutes and subject them to prosecutions for their violation. (Sen. Rept. No. 367, 43d Cong., 1st sess., vol. 2.)

This same report condemned other provisions of the proposed bill as vesting in Indian agents "a very dangerous and formidable discretion." *Cf.* Chapter 2, sec. 2C.

[233] Act of March 4, 1909, sec. 328, 35 Stat. 1088, 1151; Act of June 28, 1932, 47 Stat. 336, 337.

[234] See *Bailey* v. *United States*, 47 F. 2d 702 (C. C. A. 9, 1931), confirming conviction of tribal Indian for offense of smuggling.

[235] See 18 U. S. C. 104 (Timber depredations on Indian lands), 107 (Starting fires on Indian lands), 110 (Breaking fences or driving cattle on inclosed public lands), 115 (Inducing conveyances by Indians of trust interests in lands); 25 U. S. C. 83 (Receipt of money under prohibited contracts), 177 (Purchases or grants of land from Indians), 179 (Driving stock to feed on Indian lands), 180 (Settling on or surveying lands belonging to Indians by treaty), 195 (Sale of cattle purchased by Government to nontribal members), 212 (Arson), 213 (Assault with intent to kill), 214 (Disposing or removing cattle), 216 (Hunting on Indian lands), 241 (Intoxicating liquors; sale to Indians or introducing into Indian country), 241a (Sale, etc., of liquors in former Indian territory), 244 (Possession of intoxicating liquors in Indian country), 251 (Setting up distillery), 264 (Trading without license, 265 (Prohibited purchases and sales), 266 (Sale of arms).

[236] See 18 U. S. C., chaps. 11 and 13.

[237] 37 Fed. 145 (C. C. S. D. Cal. 1888). See also dictum in *United States* v. *Cardish*, 145 Fed. 242 (D. C. E. D. Wis. 1906).

[238] Memo. Sol. I. D., November 17, 1936 (Ft. Hall).

[239] *United States* v. *King*, 81 Fed. 625 (D. C. E. D. Wis. 1897).

[240] See *United States* v. *Quiver*, 241 U. S. 602 (1916), discussed above under sec. 5.

[241] *Cf.* statements of Assistant Commissioner Meritt, before House Committee on Indian Affairs, 69th Cong., on H. R. 7826. Hearings (Reservation Courts of Indian Offenses), p. 91.

[242] See Harsha, Law for the Indians (1882), 134 N. A. Rev. 272; Thayer, A People Without Law (1891), 68 Atl. Month. 540, 676; Austin Abbott, Indians and the Law (1888), 2 Harv. Law Rev. 167; Hornblower, Legal Status of Indians (1891), 14 A. B. A. Rept. 261; Report of Comm. on Law and Courts for Indians (1892), 15 A. B. A. Rept. 423; Pound, Nationals Without a Nation (1922), 22 Col. L. Rev. 97; Meriam and Associates, Problem of Indian Administration (1928), chap. 13; Ray A. Brown, The Indian Problem and the Law (1930), 39 Yale L. J. 307; Report of Brown, Mark, Cloud, and Meriam on "Law and Order on Indian Reservations of the Northwest." Hearings Sen. Subcom. of Comm. on Ind. Aff., 72d Cong., 1st sess., pt. 26, p. 14137, et seq. (1932).

for the tribal administration of justice wherever an Indian tribe desires to make use of its legal powers.

The recognition of tribal jurisdiction over the offenses of tribal Indians accorded by the Supreme Court in *Ex parte Crow Dog*, *supra*, and *United States* v. *Quiver*, *supra*, indicates that the criminal jurisdiction of the Indian tribes has not been curtailed by the failure of certain tribes to exercise such jurisdiction, or by the inefficiency of its attempted exercise, or by any historical changes that have come about in the habits and customs of the Indian tribes. Likewise it has been held that a gap in a tribal criminal code does not confer jurisdiction upon the federal courts.[233] Only specific legislation terminating or transferring such jurisdiction can limit the force of tribal law.

A recent writer,[234] after carefully analyzing the relation between federal and tribal law, concludes:

> This gives to many Indian tribes a large measure of continuing autonomy, for the federal statutes are only a fragment of law, principally providing some educational, hygienic, and economic assistance, regulating land ownership, and punishing certain crimes committed by or upon Indians on a reservation. Where these statutes do not reach, Indian custom is the only law. As a matter of convenience, the regular courts (white men's courts) tacitly assume that the general law of the community is the law in civil cases between Indians; but these courts will apply Indian custom whenever it is proved. (P. 90.)

A careful analysis of the relation between a local tribal government and the United States is found in an early opinion of the Attorney General,[235] in which it is held that a court of the Choctaw Nation has complete jurisdiction over a civil controversy between a Choctaw Indian and an adopted white man, involving rights to property within the Choctaw Nation:

> On the other hand, it is argued by the United States Agent, that the courts of the Choctaws can have no jurisdiction of any case in which a citizen of the United States is a party * * *.
>
> In the first place, it is certain that the Agent errs in assuming the legal impossibility of a citizen of the United States becoming subject, in civil matters, or criminal either, to the jurisdiction of the Choctaws. It is true that no citizen of the United States can, while he remains within the United States, escape their constitutional jurisdiction, either by adoption into a tribe of Indians, or any other way. But the error in all this consists in the idea that any man, citizen or not citizen, becomes divested of his allegiance to the United States, or throws off their jurisdiction or government, in the fact of becoming subject to any local jurisdiction whatever. This idea misconceives entirely the whole theory of the Federal Government, which theory is, that all the inhabitants of the country are, in regard to certain limited matters, subject to the federal jurisdiction, and in all others to the local jurisdiction, whether political or municipal. The citizen of Mississippi is also a citizen of the United States; and he owes allegiance to, and is subject to the laws of, both governments. So also an Indian, whether he be Choctaw or Chickasaw, and while subject to the local jurisdiction of the councils and courts of the nation, yet is not in any possible relation or sense divested of his allegiance and obligations to the Government and the laws of the United States. (Pp. 177–178.)

In effect, then, an Indian tribe bears a relation to the Government of the United States similar to that which a territory bears to such government, and similar again to that relationship which a municipality bears to a state. An Indian tribe may exercise a complete jurisdiction over its members and within the limits of the reservation,[236] subordinate only to the expressed limitations of federal law.

Some tribes have exercised a similar jurisdiction, under express departmental authorization, over Indians of other tribes found on the reservation.[237] This has been justified on the ground that the original tribal sovereignty extends over visiting Indians and also on the ground that the Department of the Interior may transfer the jurisdiction vested in the Courts of Indian Offenses to tribal courts, so far as concerns jurisdiction over members of recognized tribes.[238]

On the other hand, attempts of tribes to exercise jurisdiction over non-Indians, although permitted in certain early treaties,[239] have been generally condemned by the federal courts since the end of the treaty-making period, and the writ of habeas corpus has been used to discharge white defendants from tribal custody.[240]

Recognition of tribal authority in the administration of justice is found in the statutes of Congress, as well as in the decisions of the federal courts.

U. S. Code, title 25, section 229, provides that redress for a civil injury committed by an Indian shall be sought in the first instance from the "Nation or tribe to which such Indian shall belong."[241] This provision for collective responsibility evidently assumes that the Indian tribe or nation has its own resources for exercising disciplinary power over individual wrongdoers within the community.

We have already referred to title 25, section 218, of the United States Code, with its express assurance that persons "punished by the law of the tribe" shall not be tried again before the federal courts.

What is even more important than these statutory recognitions of tribal criminal authority is the persistent silence of Congress on the general problem of Indian criminal jurisdiction. There is nothing to justify an alternative to the conclusion that the Indian tribes retain sovereignty and jurisdictions over a vast area of ordinary offenses over which the Federal Government has never presumed to legislate and over which the state governments have not the authority to legislate.

Attempts to administer a rough-and-ready sort of justice through Indian courts commonly known as Courts of Indian Offenses, or directly through superintendents, cannot be held to have impaired tribal authority in the field of law and order. These agencies have been characterized, in the only reported case squarely upholding their legality, as "mere educational and disciplinary instrumentalities by which the Government

---

[233] *In re Mayfield*, 141 U. S. 107 (1891).

[234] Rice, The Position of the American Indian in the Law of the United States (1934), 16 J. Comp. Leg. (3d series), pt. 1, 78.

[235] 7 Op. A. G. 174 (1855).

[236] The jurisdiction of the Indian tribe ceases at the border of the reservation (see 18 Op. A. G. 440 (1886), holding that the authority of the Indian police is limited to the territory of the reservation), and Congress has never authorized appropriate extradition procedure whereby an Indian tribe may secure jurisdiction over fugitives from its justice. See *Ex parte Morgan*, 20 Fed. 298 (D. C. W. D. Ark., 1883).

[237] See Memo. Sol. I. D., February 17, 1939 (Rocky Boy's Blackfeet). But *cf.* Memo. Sol. I. D., October 15, 1938 (Ft. Berthold). For a fuller discussion of the question of jurisdiction of the person, raised in such cases as *Ex parte Kenyon*, 14 Fed. Cas. No. 7720 (C. C. W. D. Ark., 1878), see Chapter 18.

[238] *Ibid.*

[239] See Chapter 1, sec. 3.

[240] *Ex parte Kenyon*, 14 Fed. Cas. No. 7720 (C. C. W. D. Ark., 1878), and see Chapter 18.

[241] This provision was apparently first enacted as sec. 14 of the Trade and Intercourse Act of May 19, 1796, 1 Stat. 469, 472; reenacted as sec. 14 of the Trade and Intercourse Act of March 3, 1799, 1 Stat. 743, 747; reenacted as sec. 14 of the Trade and Intercourse Act of March 30, 1802, 2 Stat. 139, 143; and finally embodied in sec. 17 of the Trade and Intercourse Act of June 30, 1834, 4 Stat. 729, 731.

Of a similar character are treaty provisions in which tribes undertake to punish certain types of Indian offenders. See, *e. g.*, Art. 7 of Treaty

of the United States is endeavoring to improve and elevate the condition of these dependent tribes to whom it sustains the relation of guardian" [342] Perhaps a more satisfactory defense of their legality is the doctrine put forward by a recent writer that the Courts of Indian Offenses "derive their authority from the tribe, rather than from Washington." [343]

Whichever of these explanations be offered for the existence of the Courts of Indian Offenses, their establishment cannot be held to have destroyed or limited the powers vested by existing law in the Indian tribes over the province of law and order and the administration of civil and criminal justice.

Today the administration of law and order is being taken over as a local responsibility by most of the tribes that since the enactment of the Wheeler-Howard Act of June 18, 1934, have adopted constitutions for self-government.[344]

Faced with a tremendous problem, the Indian tribes have done an admirable job of maintaining law and order, wherever they have been permitted to function.[345] There are some reservations in which the moral sanctions of an integrated community are so strong that apart from occasional drunkenness and accompanying violence, crime is unknown. Crime is more of a problem on reservations where the social sanctions based on tribal control of property have been broken down through the allotment system, and the efforts of these tribes to meet their law and order problem through tribal codes, tribal courts, and tribal police, are worthy of serious attention.

The earliest codes adopted by tribes which have organized under the Act of June 18, 1934, generally differ from comparable state penal codes in the following respects:

1. The number of offenses specified in a tribal code generally runs between 40 and 50, whereas a state code (exclusive of local municipal ordinances) generally specifies between 800 and 2,000 offenses.[346]

2. The maximum punishment specified in the Indian penal codes is generally more humane, seldom exceeding imprisonment for 6 months, even for offenses like kidnapping, for which state penal codes impose imprisonment for 20 years or more, or death.

3. Except for fixing a maximum penalty, the Indian penal codes leave a large discretion to the court in adjusting the penalty to the circumstances of the offense and the offender.

4. The form of punishment is typically forced labor for the benefit of the tribe or of the victim of the offense, rather than imprisonment.

5. The tribal penal codes, for the most part, do not contain the usual catch-all provisions to be found in state penal codes (vagrancy, conspiracy, criminal syndicalism, etc.), under which almost any unpopular individual may be convicted of crime.

6. The tribal penal code is generally put into the hands of every member of the tribe, and widely read and discussed, which is not the case with state penal codes.

On the basis of this comparison it seems fair to say that the confidence which the United States Supreme Court indicated, in the *Crow Dog* case,[347] in the ability of Indian tribes to master "the highest and best of all * * * the arts of civilized life * * * that of self-government * * * the maintenance of order and peace among their own members by the administration of their own laws and customs" has been amply justified in the half century that has passed since that case was heard.

of November 15, 1865, with Confederated Tribes of Middle Oregon, 14 Stat. 751, 752; Art. 12 of Treaty of February 5, 1856, with Stockbridges and Munsees, 11 Stat. 663, 666.

Tribal responsibility for surrender or extradition of Indian horse thieves, murderers, or "bad men" generally was imposed by various treaties: Treaty of January 21, 1785, with Wiandots, Delawares, and others, 7 Stat. 16; Treaty of January 10, 1786, with the Chickasaws, 7 Stat. 24; Treaty of January 9, 1789, with Wiandots, Delawares, and others, 7 Stat. 28; Treaty of August 7, 1790, with the Creek Nation, 7 Stat. 35; Treaty of July 2, 1791, with Cherokee Nation, 7, Stat. 39; Treaty of November 3, 1804, with Sacs and Foxes, 7 Stat. 84; Treaty of November 10, 1808, with Great and Little Osage Nations, 7 Stat. 107; Treaty of September 30, 1809, with Delawares and others, 7 Stat. 113; Treaty of May 15, 1846, with Comanches and others, 9 Stat. 844.

[342] *United States* v. *Clapox*, 35 Fed. 575 (D. C. Ore., 1888); and *cf. Ex parte Bi-a-lil-le*, 12 Ariz. 150, 100 Pac. 450 (1909).

[343] Rice, The Position of the American Indian in the Law of the United States (1934), 16 J. Comp. Leg. (3d Ser.), pt. 1, pp. 78, 93.

[344] See, for example, Code of Ordinances of the Gila River Pima-Maricopa Indian Community, adopted June 3, 1936, and approved by the Secretary of the Interior on August 24, 1936; Rosebud Code of Offenses, adopted April 8, 1937, and approved by the Secretary of the Interior July 7, 1937.

[345] See Meriam, *op. cit.*, p. 17 ("* * * on the whole they work well"). On aboriginal police organizations, see MacLeod, Police and Punishment among Native Americans of the Plains (1937), 28 J. Crim. Law and Criminology 181.

[346] The Penal Code of New York State (39 McKinney's Cons. Laws of N. Y., 1936 supp.) lists 54 offenses under the letter "A." The Penal Code of Montana (Rev. Codes of Montana, 1921) contains 871 sections defining crimes.

[347] *Ex parte Crow Dog*, 109 U. S. 556 (1883).

SECTION 10. STATUTORY POWERS OF TRIBES IN INDIAN ADMINISTRATION

Within the field of Indian Service administration various powers have been conferred on Indian tribes by statute. These powers differ, of course, in derivation from those tribal powers which spring from tribal sovereignty. They are rather of federal origin, and no doubt subject to constitutional doctrines applicable to the exercise or delegation of federal governmental powers.

Potentially the most important of these statutory tribal powers is the power to supervise regular Government employees, subject to the findings of the Secretary of the Interior as to the competency of the tribe to exercise such control. Section 9 of the Act of June 30, 1834,[348] now embodied in U. S. Code, title 25, sec. 48, provides:

> *Right of tribes to direct employment of persons engaged for them.*—Where any of the tribes are, in the opinion of the Secretary of the Interior, competent to direct the employment of their blacksmiths, mechanics, teachers, farmers, or other persons engaged for them, the direction of such persons may be given to the proper authority of the tribe.

Under the terms of this statute it is clearly within the discretionary authority of the Secretary of the Interior to grant to the proper authorities of an Indian tribe all powers of supervision and control over local employees which may now be exercised by the Secretary, *e. g.*, the power to specify the duties, within a general range set by the nature of the employment, which the employee is to perform, the power to prescribe standards for appointment, promotion and continuance in office, and the power to compel reports, from time to time, of work accomplished or begun.

It will be noted that the statute in question is not restricted to the cases in which a federal employee is paid out of tribal funds. Senators are responsible to their constituents regardless of the source of their salaries, and heretofore most Indian Service employees have been responsible only to the Federal

[348] 4 Stat. 735, 737, R. S. § 2072.

Government, though their salaries might be paid from the funds of the tribe.

In directing the employment of Indian Service employees, an Indian tribe may impose upon such employees the duty of enforcing the laws and ordinances of the tribe, and the authority of federal employees so acting has been repeatedly confirmed by the courts.[249]

The section in question has not, apparently, been extensively used by the Interior Department, and that Department at one time recommended its repeal. This recommendation was later withdrawn.[250]

Various other statutes make Indian Service administration dependent, in several respects, upon tribal consent.

Thus, U. S. Code, title 25, section 63,[251] provides that the President may "consolidate one or more tribes, and abolish such agencies as are thereby rendered unnecessary," but that such action may be undertaken only "with the consent of the tribes to be affected thereby, expressed in the usual manner."

Section 111 of the same title[252] provides that payments of moneys and distribution of goods for the benefit of any Indians or Indian tribes shall be made either to the heads of families and individuals directly entitled to such moneys or goods or else to the chiefs of the tribe, for the benefit of the tribe, or to persons appointed by the tribe for the purpose of receiving such moneys or goods. This section finally provides that such moneys or goods "by consent of the tribe" may be applied directly by the Secretary to purposes conducive to the happiness and prosperity of the tribe.

Section 115 of the same title[253] provides:

> The President may, at the request of any Indian tribe, to which an annuity is payable in money, cause the same to be paid in goods, purchased as provided in section 91.

Section 140[254] of the same title provides that specific appropriations for the benefit of Indian tribes may be diverted to other uses "with the consent of said tribes, expressed in the usual manner."

Perhaps the most important provision for tribal participation in federal Indian administration is found in the last sentence of section 16 of the Act of June 18, 1934, which, applying to all tribes adopting constitutions under that act, declares:

> The Secretary of the Interior shall advise such tribe or its tribal council of all appropriation estimates or Federal projects for the benefit of the tribe prior to the submission of such estimates to the Bureau of the Budget and the Congress.[255]

Under this section each organized tribe has the right to present its comments and criticisms on the budgetary plans of the Interior Department covering its own reservation prior to the time when such plans are considered by the Bureau of the Budget or by Congress. This is a power quite distinct from the tribal power to prevent the disposition of tribal funds without tribal consent, a power elsewhere discussed.[256]

While this provision imposes a legal duty upon administrative authorities, it is, of course, purely advisory so far as Congress is concerned.

---

[249] *Morris* v *Hitchcock*, 194 U. S. 384 (1904); *Buster* v. *Wright*, 135 Fed. 947 (C. C. A. 8, 1905), app. dism. 203 U. S. 599; *Maxey* v. *Wright*, 3 Ind. T. 243, 54 S. W. 807 (1900), aff'd 105 Fed. 1003 (1900); *Zevely* v. *Weimer*, 5 Ind. T. 646, 82 S. W. 941 (1904); 23 Op. A. G. 528.

[250] See annotations to 25 U. S. C. 48 in various annual supplements to U. S. C. A.

[251] Act of May 17, 1882, sec. 66, 22 Stat. 68, 88, reenacted Act of July 4, 1884, sec. 6, 23 Stat. 76, 97.

[252] Act of June 30, 1834, sec. 11, 4 Stat. 735, 737; amended Act of March 3, 1847, sec. 3, 9 Stat. 203; amended Act of August 30, 1852, sec. 3, 10 Stat. 41, 56; amended Act of July 15, 1870, secs. 2–3, 16 Stat. 335, 360. See Chapter 15, secs. 22, 23.

[253] Act of June 30, 1834, sec. 12, 4 Stat. 735, 737.

[254] Act of March 1, 1907, 34 Stat. 1015, 1016.

[255] 48 Stat. 984, 987, 25 U. S. C. 476.

[256] See Chapter 5, sec. 5B, and Chapter 15, sec. 24.

CHAPTER 8

PERSONAL RIGHTS AND LIBERTIES OF INDIANS

TABLE OF CONTENTS

SECTION 1. INTRODUCTION

To analyze the personal rights and liberties of Indians is to assume that Indians are persons. This proposition has not always been universally accepted. The first authoritative determination that Indians are human beings is to be found in the Bull *Sublimis Deus* of Pope Paul III, issued June 4, 1537. This Bull declared:

> The enemy of the human race, who opposes all good deeds in order to bring men to destruction, beholding

and envying this, invented a means never before heard of, by which he might hinder the preaching of God's word of Salvation to the people: He inspired his satellites who, to please him, have not hesitated to publish abroad that the Indians of the West and the South, and other people of whom We have recent knowledge should be treated as dumb brutes created for our service, pretending that they are incapable of receiving the catholic faith.

We, who, though unworthy, exercise on earth the power of our Lord and seek with all our might to bring those sheep of His flock who are outside, into the fold committed to our charge, consider, however, that the Indians are truly men and that they are not only capable of understanding the catholic faith but, according to our information, they desire exceedingly to receive it. Desiring to provide ample remedy for these evils, we define and declare by these our letters, or by any translation thereof signed by any notary public and sealed with the seal of any ecclesiastical dignitary, to which the same credit shall be given as to the originals, that, notwithstanding whatever may have been or may be said to the contrary, the said Indians and all other people who may later be discovered by Christians, are by no means to be deprived of their liberty or the possession of their property, even though they be outside the faith of Jesus Christ; and that they may and should, freely and legitimately, enjoy their liberty and the possession of their property; nor should they be in any way enslaved; should the contrary happen, it shall be null and of no effect.[1]

Despite this pronouncement, doubts as to the human character of Indians have persisted until fairly recently, particularly among those charged with the administration of Indian affairs. These doubts are reflected in the statement on "Policy and Administration of Indian Affairs" contained in the "Report on Indians Taxed and Indians Not Taxed, at the Eleventh Census: 1890," which declares:

> An Indian is a person within the meaning of the laws of the United States. This decision of Judge Dundy, of the United States district court for Nebraska, has not been reversed; still, by law and the Interior Department, the Indian is considered a ward of the nation and is so treated.[1a]

The doubts that have existed as to whether an Indian is a person or something less than a person have infected with uncertainty much of the discussion of Indian personal rights and liberties. Clear thinking on the subject has been sacrificed in the effort to find ambiguous terms which will permit us, by appropriate juggling, to maintain three basic propositions:

(1) that Indians are human beings;

(2) that all human beings are created equal, with certain inalienable rights; and

(3) that Indians are an "inferior" class not entitled to these "inalienable rights."

Experience shows that it is possible to pay due deference to these three propositions, inconsistent though they are with each other, by means of a skillful juggling of words of many meanings, such as "wardship" and "incompetency."

[1] Translation from F. A. MacNutt, Bartholomew de Las Casas: His Life, His Apostolate, and His Writings (1909), pp. 429, 431.

[1a] H. R. Misc. Doc. No. 340, 52d Cong., 1st sess., part 15 (1894), p. 64.

In 1842, Attorney General Legare wrote:[1b]

> * * * There is nothing in the whole compass of our laws so anomalous—so hard to bring within any precise definition, or any logical and scientific arrangement of principles, as the relation in which the Indians stand towards this government, and those of the States. (P. 76.)

Eight decades later, when the eminent jurist, Judge Cuthbert Pound, wrote of "Nationals without a Nation,"[2] the anomalies attendant upon the legal status of the Indian had not disappeared.

In part, the difficulties of the subject derive from the unique international relationship existing between the United States and Indian tribes, treated as "domestic, dependent nations" with which we entered into treaties that continue in force to this day.

The complexity of the problem has been very much aggravated by the host of special treaties and special statutes assigning rights and obligations to the members of particular tribes, all of which creates a complex diversity that can be simplified only at the risk of ignoring facts and violating rights. Attempts have been made, of course, in some judicial opinions, as well as in less authoritative writings, to ride roughshod over the facts and to lay down certain simple rules of alleged universal applicability, most of which have turned out to be erroneous.

Whatever the causes of this confusion may be, the fact remains that erroneous notions on the legal status of the Indian are widely prevalent.[3] Large sections of our population still believe that Indians are not citizens, and recent instances have been reported of Indians being denied the right to vote because the electoral officials in charge were under the impression that Indians have never been made citizens. Indeed, some people have persuaded Indians themselves that they are not citizens and can achieve citizenship only by selling their land, by having the Indian Office abolished, or by performing some other act of benefit to those advisors who have volunteered aid in the achievement of American citizenship.

Another prevalent misconception is the notion that "ward Indians," whatever that term may mean, have no capacity at law to make contracts or to bring or defend law suits.

These are but two examples among a host of more or less widespread misconceptions that are woven about such terms as "citizenship," "wardship," and "incompetency."

We shall be concerned in this chapter to analyze the legal position of the Indian with respect to ten matters:

(*a*) Citizenship (sec. 2).
(*b*) Suffrage (sec. 3).
(*c*) Eligibility for public office and employment (sec. 4).
(*d*) Eligibility for state assistance (sec. 5).
(*e*) Right to sue (sec. 6).
(*f*) Right to contract (sec. 7).
(*g*) Incompetency (sec. 8).
(*h*) Wardship (sec. 9).
(*i*) Civil liberties (sec. 10).
(*j*) Status of freedmen and slaves (sec. 11).

[1b] 4 Op. A. G. 75 (1842).

[2] (1922), 22 Col. L. Rev. 97.

[3] Op. Sol., I. D., M.28869, February 13, 1937.

SECTION 2. CITIZENSHIP

Since June 2, 1924, all Indians born within the territorial limits of the United States have been citizens, by virtue of the act of that date.[4] This act provides:

> That all non-citizen Indians born within the territorial limits of the United States be, and they are hereby, declared to be citizens of the United States: *Provided*, That the granting of such citizenship shall not in any manner impair or otherwise affect the right of any Indian to tribal or other property.

The substance of this section was incorporated in the Nationality Act of October 14, 1940.[4a]

Prior to the Citizenship Act of 1924 approximately two-thirds of the Indians of the United States had already acquired citizenship in one or more of the following ways:

(*a*) Treaties with Indian tribes.
(*b*) Special statutes naturalizing named tribes or individuals.
(*c*) General statutes naturalizing Indians who took allotments.
(*d*) General statutes naturalizing other special classes.

A brief analysis of each of these methods of acquiring citizenship may suffice to explain those current misconceptions on the subject of Indian citizenship which are a survival of what was once actual law.

A. METHODS OF ACQUIRING CITIZENSHIP

(1) **Treaties with Indian tribes.**—Some early treaties between the United States and Indian tribes provided for the granting of citizenship.[5] In some cases, citizenship was made dependent upon acceptance of an allotment of land in severalty,[6] and sometimes the alternative to accepting an allotment was removal with the tribe to a new reservation.[7]

Implicit in this arrangement was the thought that citizenship was incompatible with continued participation in tribal government or tribal property. This supposed incompatibility, removed from its specific treaty context and generalized, has become one of the most fruitful sources of contemporary confusion on the question of Indian citizenship.

The later treaties usually require the submission of evidence of fitness for citizenship, and empower an administrative body or official to determine whether the applicant for citizenship conforms to the standards in the treaty. To illustrate, the Treaty of November 15, 1861,[8] with the Pottawatomies, requires the President of the United States to be satisfied that the male heads of families are "sufficiently intelligent and prudent to conduct their affairs and interests," and the Treaty of February 23, 1867,[9] forbids tribal membership to Wyandottes who had consented to become citizens under a prior treaty, unless they were found "unfit for the responsibilities of citizenship." [10]

(2) **Special statutes.**—Before and after the termination of the treaty-making period, the members of several tribes were naturalized collectively by statute.[11] The tribe was in a few cases dissolved at the same time and its land distributed to the members.[12] Sometimes other conditions were embodied in the statute, such as adopting the habits of civilized life, becoming self-supporting, and learning to read and speak the English language.[13]

After the ratification of the Fourteenth Amendment, several acts were passed naturalizing Indians of certain tribes. Most of these statutes were similar to the Act of July 15, 1870.[14] By section 10 of this law a Winnebago Indian in the State of Minnesota could apply to the Federal District Court for citizenship. He was required to prove to the satisfaction of the court that he was sufficiently intelligent and prudent to control his affairs

---

[4] 43 Stat. 253, 8 U. S. C. 3. This act naturalized 125,000 native-born Indians. Rice, The Position of the American Indian in the Law of the United States (1934), 16 J. Comp. Leg. 78, 86; Hon. Hubert Work, Secretary of the Interior, Indian Policies: Comments on Resolutions of the Advisory Council on Indian Affairs (U. S. Govt. Printing Office 1924, p. 6); *cf.* Fifty-fifth Annual Report of Board of Indian Commissioners (1924) pp. 1 and 2. On the legislative history of this act, see Chapter 4, sec. 15.

[4a] Pub. No. 853, 76th Cong., sec. 201 of which declares:

> The following shall be nationals and citizens of the United States at birth:
>
> * * * * *
>
> (b) A person born in the United States to a member of an Indian, Eskimo, Aleutian, or other aboriginal tribe.

[5] Treaty of September 27, 1830, with Choctaws, Art. 14, 7 Stat. 333, 335. For illustrations of treaties conferring citizenship on heads of families, see Treaty of July 8, 1817, with Cherokees, Art. 8, 7 Stat. 156, 159; Treaty of February 27, 1819, with Cherokees, Art. 2, 7 Stat. 195, 196.

[6] Treaty of June 28, 1862, with Kickapoos, Art. 3, 13 Stat. 623, 624; Treaty of July 4, 1866, with Delawares, Arts. 3 and 9, 14 Stat. 793, 794, 796. Treaty of February 23, 1867, with Senecas and others, Art. 13, 15 Stat. 513, 516, interpreted in *Wiggan* v. *Connolly*, 163 U. S. 56 (1896); Treaty of February 27, 1867, with Pottawatomies, Art. 6, 15 Stat. 531–533; Treaty of April 29, *et seq.*, 1868, with Sioux, Art. 6, 15 Stat. 635, 637. Act of March 3, 1873, 17 Stat. 631 (Miamies). Also see Appropriation Act to effectuate this provision, Act of June 22, 1874, 18 Stat. 146–175; and 2 Op. A. G. 462 (1831). It was hoped to eliminate reservations and to cause the disintegration of the tribe. Varney, The Indian Remnant in New England (1901), 13 Green Bag 399, 401–402; Thayer, A People Without Law (1891), 68 Atl. Month. 540, 546–547; Kyle, How Shall the Indians Be Educated (1894), 159 N. A. Rev. 434; Krieger, Principles of the Indian Law and the Act of June 18, 1934 (1935), 3 Geo. Wash. L. Rev. 279, 295; *United States* v. *Rickert*, 188 U. S. 432, 437 (1903); *Choteau* v. *Burnet*, 283 U. S. 691 (1931); *Oakes* v. *United States*, 172 Fed. 305 (C. C. A. 8, 1909).

[7] Treaty of September 27, 1830, with Choctaws, Arts. 14 and 16, 7 Stat. 333, 335–336.

[8] Art. 3, 12 Stat. 1191, 1192.

[9] Art. 13, 15 Stat. 513, 516 (Senecas and others); also see Arts. 17, 28, 34 for other provisions regarding citizenship.

[10] Also see Treaty of July 4, 1866, with Delawares, Arts. 3 and 9, 14 Stat. 793, 794, 796; Act of March 3, 1873, 17 Stat. 631 (Miamies). Unusual provisions are contained in the Treaty of February 27, 1867, with Pottawatomies, Arts. 4 and 6, 15 Stat. 531–533, which permits women who are heads of families or single women of adult age to become citizens in the same manner as males, and authorizes the Tribal Business Committee and the agent to determine the competency of an Indian to manage his own affairs. By the Treaty of June 24, 1862, Art. 4, 12 Stat. 1237, 1238, the Ottawa tribe, which was to be dissolved after 5 years, was given money to assist the members in establishing themselves in agricultural pursuits and thus gradually increase their preparation for assuming the responsibilities and duties of citizenship. Also see Treaty of July 31, 1855, with Ottowas and Chippewas, Art. 5, 11 Stat. 621.

[11] Act of March 3, 1839, 5 Stat. 349, 351 (Brothertown); Act of March 3, 1843, sec. 7, 5 Stat. 645, 647 (Stockbridge); Act of March 3, 1921, sec. 3, 41 Stat. 1249, 1250 (Osage). The right of the Cherokees to be naturalized was discussed in *Raymond* v. *Raymond*, 1 Ind. T. 334 (1896), reversed in 83 Fed. 721 (C. C. A. 8, 1897).

[12] Act of March 3, 1839, sec. 7, 5 Stat. 349, 351 (Brothertown); Act of March 3, 1843, sec. 7, 5 Stat. 645, 647 (Stockbridge).

[13] Act of March 3, 1865, sec. 4, 13 Stat. 541, 562, discussed in *Oakes* v. *United States*, 172 Fed. 305 (C. C. A. 8, 1909); Act of August 6, 1846, 9 Stat. 55 (Stockbridge).

[14] Sec. 10, 16 Stat. 335, 361–362. By the Act of March 3, 1873, sec. 3, 17 Stat. 631, 632, similar provision was made for the naturalization of adult members of any of the Miami Tribe of Kansas and their minor children.

and interests; that he had adopted the habits of civilized life and for the preceding 5 years supported himself and his family. If satisfied with the proof, the court would declare him a citizen and give him a certificate, which would enable the Secretary of the Interior to issue a patent in fee with powers of alienation of the land already held by the Indian in severalty and to pay to him his share of tribal property.[15] Thenceforth, the Indian ceased to be a member of the tribe and his land was subject to levy, taxation and sale the same as that of other citizens. Again, the statutory formula seems to rest on the assumed incompatability between tribal membership and United States citizenship.

The same idea underlay the Indian Territory Naturalization Act,[16] which provided:

> * * * That any member of any Indian tribe or nation residing in the Indian Territory may apply to the United States court therein to become a citizen of the United States, and such court shall have jurisdiction thereof and shall hear and determine such application as provided in the statutes of the United States * * * *Provided*, That the Indians who become citizens of the United States under the provisions of this act do not forfeit or lose any rights or privileges they enjoy or are entitled to as members of the tribe or nation to which they belong.

(3) **General statutes naturalizing allottees.**—Prior to the Citizenship Act, the General Allotment Act,[17] generally known as the Dawes Act, was the most important method of acquiring citizenship.[18] This law conferred citizenship upon two classes of Indians born within the limits of the United States:

> (1) An Indian to whom allotments were made in accordance with this act, or any law or treaty.
>
> (2) An Indian who had voluntarily taken up within said limits, residence separate and apart from any tribe of Indians therein and adopted the habits of civilized life.

President Theodore Roosevelt described this important law in his message to Congress of December 3, 1901, as "a mighty pulverizing engine to break up the tribal mass" whereby "some sixty thousand Indians have already become citizens of the United States."[19]

By an amendment adopted May 8, 1906,[20] known as the Burke Act, the Indian became a citizen after the patent in fee simple was granted instead of upon the completion of his allotment and the issuance of a trust patent.[21] It has been administratively held that an Indian to whom an allotment was made subsequent to the Burke Act is a citizen upon the issuance of a patent in fee for part of his allotment,[22] because the conveyance was also an adjudication that the Indian allottee is "competent and capable" to manage his own affairs.

The Supreme Court of the United States in the case of *United States* v. *Celestine*[23] suggested "that Congress in granting full rights of citizenship to Indians, believed that it had been too hasty." The purpose of the Burke Act was stated by the court in the case of *United States* v. *Pelican:*[24] "distinctly to postpone to the expiration of the trust period the subjection of allottees under that act to state laws."

(4) **General statutes naturalizing other classes of Indians.**—Indian women marrying citizens became citizens by the Act of August 9, 1888,[25] and Indian men who enlisted to fight in the World War could become citizens under the Act of November 6, 1919.[26]

B. NONCITIZEN INDIANS

Until the Citizenship Act of 1924 those Indians who had not acquired citizenship by marriage to white men, by military service, by receipt of allotments, or through special treaties or special statutes, occupied a peculiar status under Federal law. Not only were they noncitizens but they were barred from the ordinary processes of naturalization open to foreigners. Such remained the status of Indians living in the United States who were born in Canada, Mexico, or other foreign lands, since the 1924 Act referred only to "Indians born within the territorial limits of the United States."[27]

[15] Beginning with the Act of March 3, 1865, sec. 4, 13 Stat. 541, 562, the statutes granting citizenship to Indians abandoning their tribal relationships safeguarded their rights in tribal property. Act of February 8, 1887, sec. 6, 24 Stat. 388, 390, 25 U. S. C. 349; amended by Act of May 8, 1906, 34 Stat. 182; Act of August 9, 1888, sec. 2, 25 Stat. 392, 25 U. S. C. 182; also see *Oakes* v. *United States*, 172 Fed. 305, 308–309 (C. C. A. 8, 1909); *United States ex rel. Besaw* v. *Work*, 6 F. 2d 694, 697 (App. D. C. 1925).

[16] Act of May 2, 1890, sec. 43, 26 Stat. 81, 99–100. This section also grants citizenship to the Confederated Peoria Indians residing in the Quapaw Indian Agency, who accept land in severalty.

[17] Act of February 8, 1887, sec. 4, 24 Stat. 388, 389; amended, Act of February 28, 1891, 26 Stat. 794. For other allotment acts see Act of March 3, 1875, 18 Stat. 420; Act of March 3, 1921, 41 Stat. 1355 (Fort Belknap); see also Chapter 11. In the Act of June 4, 1924, 43 Stat. 376 (Cherokees of North Carolina), providing for the allotment of land, which was enacted after the Citizenship Act, there was a provision in accordance with the old formula that each allottee shall become a citizen of the United States and of the state where he resides, with all the privileges of citizenship (sec. 19, p. 380). The Act of January 25, 1929, c. 101, 45 Stat. 1094, stated that it was not the purpose of the former act to abridge or modify the Citizenship Act. Also see *Monson* v. *Simonson*, 231 U. S. 341 (1913); *United States* v. *Rickert*, 188 U. S. 432 (1903); 42 L. D. 489 (1913); 7 Yale L. J. 193 (1898). On policy of Osage Indian Allotment Act, Act of June 28, 1906, 34 Stat. 539, see *Levindale Lead Co.* v. *Coleman*, 241 U. S. 432 (1916) and Chapter 23, sec. 12A.

[18] Senator Orville H. Platt of Connecticut wrote: "Modern observation and thought have reached the conclusion that allotment of land in severalty, and citizenship, are the indispensable conditions of Indian progress." Problems in the Indian Territory (1895), 160 N. Am. Rev. 195, 200. See also Thayer, A People Without Law (1891), 68 Atl. Month. 540, 676, 680. Usually the children of tribal members who elected citizenship received a smaller allotment. The Treaty of July 4, 1866, with the Delaware Indians, 14 Stat. 793, 796, contained an unusual provision permitting a child reaching majority to elect whether he desired to become a citizen.

The Act of June 22, 1874, 18 Stat. 146, 175, appropriated money to enable the Secretary of the Interior to pay to the children of the Delaware Indians who had become citizens of the United States their share of the tribal funds.

[19] 35 Congressional Record, Pt. 1, 57th Cong., 1st sess. (1901), p. 90. *Cf.* Kyle, How Shall the Indians be Educated? (1894), 159 N. Am. Rev. 434, 437. According to Wise, Indian Law and Needed Reforms (1926), 12 A. B. A. Jour. 37, there were about 150,000 Indians holding tribal lands not yet allotted.

[20] 34 Stat. 182.

[21] "This change was due largely to a misunderstanding as to the real legal significance. At that time it was the belief that wardship and citizenship were incompatible." Flickinger, A Lawyer Looks at the American Indian, Past and Present (1939), 6 Indians at Work, No. 8, pp. 24, 26.

[22] Op. Sol. I. D., M.4018, July 29, 1921.

[23] 215 U. S. 278, 291 (1909).

[24] 232 U. S. 442, 450 (1914).

[25] Sec. 2, 25 Stat. 392, 25 U. S. C. 182.

[26] 41 Stat. 350. This measure was endorsed by the Commissioner of Indian Affairs. Only a few Indians acquired citizenship in this way. Annual Reports of Commissioner of Indian Affairs (1920), pp. 10–11; (1921), p. 33. *Cf.* special provision relating to honorably discharged alien veterans of foreign birth, Act of July 19, 1919, 41 Stat. 163, 222.

[27] See *Morrison* v. *California*, 291 U. S. 82, 95 (1934). This restriction was eliminated by sec. 303 of the Nationality Act of October 14, 1940 (Public No. 853, 76th Cong.), which declares:

> The right to become a naturalized citizen under the provisions of this Act shall extend only to white persons, persons of African nativity or descent, and descendants of races indigenous to the Western Hemisphere.

The naturalization laws applied only to free white persons and did not include Indians,[28] who were regarded as domestic subjects or nationals.[29] As members of domestic dependent nations, owing allegiance to their tribe, they were analogized to children of foreign diplomats, born in the United States.[30]

Thus noncitizen Indians were not able to secure passports, but were sometimes granted documents specifying that they were not citizens but requesting protection for them.[31]

Caleb Cushing, Attorney General of the United States, formulated the following theory of the status of Indians:[32]

> The fact, therefore, that Indians are born in the country does not make them citizens of the United States. The simple truth is plain, that the Indians are the *subjects* of the United States, and therefore are not, in mere right of home-birth, citizens of the United States.
>
> * * * * *
>
> But they cannot become citizens by naturalization under existing general acts of Congress. (ii Kent's Com., p. 72.)
>
> Those acts apply only to *foreigners*, subjects of another allegiance. The Indians are not foreigners, and they are in our allegiance, without being *citizens* of the United States. Moreover, those acts only apply to "white" men.
>
> * * * * *
>
> Indians, of course, can be made citizens of the United States only by some competent act of the General Government, either a treaty or an act of Congress. (Pp. 749–750.)

This theory was reiterated after the adoption of the Fourteenth Amendment, which first defined federal citizenship. At the time of its adoption, eminent lawyers differed on its effect on the Indians.[33] Hope that a liberal interpretation would make Indians citizens was shattered by an early case,[34] holding that the amendment was merely declaratory of the common-law rule of citizenship by birth and that Indians born in tribal allegiance were not born in the United States and subject to the jurisdiction thereof, because:

> To be a citizen of the United States by reason of his birth, a person must not only be born within its territorial limits, but he must also be born subject to its jurisdiction—that is, in its power and obedience. * * * But the Indian tribes within the limits of the United States have always been held to be distinct and independent political communities, retaining the right of self-government, though subject to the protecting power of the United States. (Pp. 165, 166.)

This view was sustained by two leading naturalization opinions of the Supreme Court of the United States, the holding of *Elk* v. *Wilkins*,[35] and the dicta of *United States* v. *Wong Kim Ark*,[36] which excepted from its doctrine of citizenship by birth "children of Indian tribes owing direct allegiance to their several tribes."

Other theories have been advanced as additional justification for this unique status of the Indians, which departed from the common-law doctrine of *ius soli*.[37] One writer[38] believes that the economic interests of the land grabbers and Indian traders caused their opposition to citizenship for the Indians. They feared the destruction of their business with the coming of Indian suffrage, which was expected to accompany citizenship. Other writers maintained that citizenship should be denied Indians because they were strangers to our laws, customs, and privileges,[39] because they would add to burdens imposed by naturalization of aliens,[40] and because they enjoyed special privileges, such as exemption from taxation.[41]

The Indian question, which had been overshadowed after the Civil War by discussion of the economic welfare, freedom, and citizenship of the Negro, became a live issue toward the close of the nineteenth century. Many writers realized the incongruity of disenfranchisement and noncitizenship of Indians in a country founded on the principle of the equality of man and agreed that "the ultimate objective point to which all efforts for progress should be directed is to fix upon the Indian the same personal, legal, and political status which is common to all other inhabitants."[42]

The Indians, however, frequently did not welcome federal citizenship;[43] they often chose to leave their homes in order to retain their tribal membership.[44] A report of the Bureau of Municipal Research submitted in 1915 to a Joint Commission of Congress which requested its preparation, stated that "the Indian (except in rare individual cases) does not desire citizenship."[45]

The delegates of the Five Civilized Tribes opposed the grant of federal citizenship to their people because they feared it would terminate their tribal government.[46] Indians were often un-

---

[28] An Indian was not regarded as "a white person" within the naturalization laws. *In re Camille*, 6 Fed. 256 (C. C. Ore. 1880); *In re Burton*, 1 Alaska 111 (1900); 13 Yale L. J. 250, 252 (1904). In 1870 these laws were extended to include aliens of African nativity and to persons of African descent. Act of July 14, 1870, sec. 7, 16 Stat. 254, 256.

[29] 7 Op. A. G. 746 (1856).

[30] Pound, Nationals Without a Nation (1922), 22 Col. L. Rev. 97, 99; *Elk* v. *Wilkins*, 112 U. S. 94, 102 (1884); *cf. United States* v. *Elm*, 25 Fed. Cas. No. 15048 (D. C. N. D. N. Y., 1877).

[31] Hunt, The American Passport (1898), pp. 146–148. Manuscript instructions of the Department of State provided:

> Even if he [an Indian] has not acquired citizenship, he is a ward of the Government and entitled to the consideration and assistance of our diplomatic and consular officers. (P. 147.)

[32] 7 Op. A. G. 746 (1856).

[33] To clarify its effect, the Senate Judiciary Committee filed a report pursuant to Senate Resolution of April 7, 1870, concluding that the Indians did not attain citizenship by the Fourteenth Amendment; Sen. Rept. No. 268, 41st Cong., 3d sess. (1870), pp. 1–11.

[34] *McKay* v. *Campbell*, 16 Fed. Cas. No. 8840 (D. C. Ore. 1871).

[35] 112 U. S. 94 (1884). The Court also held that citizenship was not acquired by abandonment of tribal membership. Also see *United States* v. *Osborn*, 2 Fed. 58 (D. C. Ore. 1880). On the effect of tribal membership upon citizenship see *Katzenmeyer* v. *United States*, 225 Fed. 523 (C. C. A. 7, 1915).

[36] 169 U. S. 649, 693 (1898).

[37] Krieger, Principles of the Indian Law and the Act of June 18, 1934 (1935), 3 Geo. Wash. L. Rev. 279, 282–283.

[38] Abel, The Slaveholding Indians (1915), vol. 1, p. 170.

[39] Russell, The Indian Before the Law (1909), 18 Yale L. J. 328; Canfield, Legal Position of the Indian (1881), 15 Am. L. Rev. 21, 27–28, 37; *cf.* Lambertson, Indian Citizenship (1886), 20 Am. L. Rev. 183, 189; Harsha, Law for the Indians (1882), 134 N. Am. Rev. 272, 277; Blackmar, Indian Education (1892), 2 Am. Acad. Pol. & Soc. Sci. 813, 833; *Labadie* v. *United States*, 6 Okla. 400, 51 Pac. 666 (1897).

[40] Krieger, Principles of the Indian Law and the Act of June 18, 1934 (1935), 3 Geo. Wash. L. Rev. 279, 286; Lambertson, Indian Citizenship (1886), 20 Am. L. Rev. 183, 187–189.

[41] Lambertson, Indian Citizenship, 20 Am. L. Rev. (1886), 183, 188. For a discussion of the discrimination against Indians because of exemption from taxation, see sec. 10; on tax exemption generally, see Chapter 13.

[42] Abbot, Indians and the Law (1888), 2 Harv. L. Rev. 167, 174. Also see Harsha, Law for the Indians (1882), 134 N. A. Rev. 272; Blackmar, Indian Education (1892), 2 Am. Acad. Pol. & Soc. Sci. 813, 834. U. S. Senator J. H. Kyle contended that the Indians have a good character for citizenship. How Shall the Indians be Educated? (1894), 159 N. A. Rev. 434, 441. *Contra* Canfield, Legal Position of the Indian (1881), 15 Am. L. Rev. 21, 36–37.

[43] Leupp, The Indian and His Problem (1910), p. 35. Sometimes Indians were made citizens willy-nilly, Willoughby, The Constitutional Law of the United States (1929), pp. 390–391.

[44] See Chapter 8, secs. 4E, 4G.

[45] Administration of the Indian Office (Bureau of Municipal Research Publication no. 65) (1915), p. 17.

[46] Memorial relating to the Indians, Choctaw delegates, Sen. Misc. Doc. No. 7, 45th Cong., 2d sess., December 10, 1877, vol. I; Memorial against bill to enable Indians to become citizens, Sen. Misc. Doc. No. 18, 45th Cong., 2d sess., January 14, 1877, vol. I. The Five Civilized Tribes were excluded from the General Allotment Act of February 8, 1887 secs. 6 and 8, 24 Stat. 388, 390, 391.

familiar with the significance of federal citizenship and sometimes recanted choosing it.[47]

C. EFFECT OF CITIZENSHIP

Many people who know that Indians are citizens are unaware of the legal consequences of citizenship.[48] The more common errors in this field may be disposed of briefly.

1. By virtue of the Fourteenth Amendment to the Federal Constitution, Indians, as citizens of the United States, automatically become citizens of the state of their residence.[49]

2. Except when a special statute or treaty has provided otherwise, citizenship does not impair the force of tribal law[50] or affect tribal existence.[51] Statutes or treaties naturalizing Indians often expressly permit those who become citizens to retain their tribal rights.[52] Citizenship and tribal membership are not incompatible.[53]

3. Citizenship, though it is today usually a prerequisite of suffrage, does not confer the right.[54] Before securing the franchise, a voter must comply with the requirements of the state law, which regularly include attainment of the age of majority and residence in the state for a specified period, and sometimes include payment of poll tax, literacy, or other special requirements.[55]

4. Citizenship is not incompatible with federal powers of guardianship.[56] The United States Supreme Court has said:[57]

> It is thoroughly established that Congress has plenary authority over the Indians and all their tribal relations, and full power to legislate concerning their tribal property. The guardianship arises from their condition of tutelage or dependency; and it rests with Congress to determine when the relationship shall cease; the mere grant of rights of citizenship not being sufficient to terminate it. (Pp. 391–392.)

Citizenship does not affect the rights of the United States Government over the Indian. It retains jurisdiction over a citizen Indian for offenses committed within the reservation.[58] Citizenship does not impair the government's right to sue on behalf of a citizen allottee to protect his restricted lands,[59] nor affect its power to prevent state taxation of his property while he is living on the reservation,[60] or to exercise control over tribal property,[61] or to exclude bill collectors from coming on the reservation on days when payments are made to the Indians,[62] or to exempt unrestricted property from levy, sale, or forfeiture.[63] Many rights, such as the right to sue or contract, are not derived from or dependent on citizenship.[64]

It has been held that the citizenship of the Pueblos and many of the Alaskan Indians did not terminate their subjection to federal jurisdiction.[65] The conferring of citizenship does not

---

[47] This is shown by Art. 13 of the Treaty of February 23, 1867, with the Senecas and others, 15 Stat. 513, 516, which provides that a member who changes his mind after becoming a citizen shall not be allowed to rejoin the tribe unless the agent shall signify that he is "through poverty or incapacity, unfit to continue in the exercise of the responsibilities of citizenship of the United States, and likely to become a public charge."

[48] Op. Sol. I. D., M.28869, February 13, 1937, p. 5. When the Citizenship Act was passed in 1924, many tax officials in New Mexico thought that all Indians were subject to taxation. Goodrich, The Legal Status of the California Indian (1926), 14 Calif. L. Rev. 83, 157, 180–181. On taxation of Indians, see Chapter 13.

[49] *Deere* v. *State of New York*, 22 F. 2d 851, 852 (D. C. N. D. N. Y. 1927). Also see *Porter* v. *Hall*, 34 Ariz. 308, 271 Pac. 411 (1928).

[50] *Yakima Joe* v. *To-is-lap*, 191 Fed. 516 (C. C. Ore. 1910). Also see Chapter 7.

[51] See *Cherokee Nation* v. *Hitchcock*, 187 U. S. 294, 308 (1902); *United States* v. *Celestine*, 215 U. S. 278, 288–290 (1909); *Hallowell* v. *United States*, 221 U. S. 317, 324 (1911); *Tiger* v. *Western Investment Co.*, 221 U. S. 286 (1911); *United States* v. *Sandoval*, 231 U. S. 28, 38 (1913); *United States* v. *Noble*, 237 U. S. 74 (1915); *Williams* v. *Johnson*, 239 U. S. 414 (1915); *United States* v. *Nice*, 241 U. S. 591 (1916); *Winton* v. *Amos*, 255 U. S. 373 (1921). Also see Knoepfler, Legal Status of American Indian and His Property (1922), 7 Ia. L. B. 232, 240–241; and Chapter 14, sec. 2.

[52] Act of May 2, 1890, sec. 43, 26 Stat. 81, 99, provides for the naturalization of the Indian tribes in the Indian Territory and states that Indians who become citizens retain their rights as tribal members.

[53] *United States* v. *Nice*, 241 U. S. 591 (1916); *Halbert* v. *United States*, 283 U. S. 753, 762–763 (1931), rev'g *United States* v. *Halbert*, 38 F. 2d 795 (C. C. A. 9, 1930), cert. granted 282 U. S. 818; *United States* v. *Boylan*, 265 Fed. 165, 171 (C. C. A. 2, 1920), aff'g 256 Fed. 468 (D. C. N. D. N. Y. 1919), app. dism. 257 U. S. 614 (1921); *Farrell* v. *United States*, 110 Fed. 942 (C. C. A. 8, 1901).

[54] See sec. 3, *infra*. Also see Act of June 19, 1930, 46 Stat. 787, 8 U. S. C. 3a (Cherokee Indians resident in North Carolina).

[55] See *United States* v. *Rickert*, 188 U. S. 432, 445 (1903); 8 Op. A. G. 300 (1857). In some states citizenship is the only qualification. Calif. Const. (1879), Art. II, sec. 1, "Every native citizen of the United States * * * shall be entitled to vote at all elections * * *."

[56] The contrary opinion of the United States Supreme Court in Matter of Heff, 197 U. S. 488 (1905) holding that Congress could not regulate the sale of liquor to Indians who were citizens was expressly overruled by *United States* v. *Nice*, 241 U. S. 591, 598 (1916), which held:

> * * * Citizenship is not incompatible with tribal existence or continued guardianship, and so may be conferred without completely emancipating the Indians or placing them beyond the reach of congressional regulations adopted for their protection.

Bledsoe, Indian Land Laws, 2d ed. (1913), though recognizing that citizenship does not remove the restrictions on allotments, pp. 34–36, does not share this view, pp. 3–33.

See Op. Sol. I. D., M.28869, February 13, 1937, p. 5; 20 L. D. 157, 159 (1895); 31 L. D. 439 (1902), and 55 I. D. 14, 29 (1934). In rejecting a claim by courts of the State of New York to jurisdiction over certain Indians for acts committed on an Indian reservation, the court in *United States* v. *Boylan*, 265 Fed. 165 (C. C. A. 2, 1920), aff'g. 256 Fed. 465 (D. C. N. D. N. Y. 1919), app. dism. 257 U. S. 614 (1921), said:

> * * * even a grant of citizenship does not terminate the tribal status or relieve the Indian from the guardianship of the government. (P. 171.)

Accord: *United States* v. *Abrams*, 194 Fed. 82 (C. C. A. 8, 1912), aff'g 181 Fed. 847 (C. C. E. D. Okla., 1910); *United States* v. *Noble*, 237 U. S. 74, 79 (1915); *Hallowell* v. *United States*, 221 U. S. 317 (1911). Also see *Williams* v. *Johnson*, 239 U. S. 414 (1915); *United States* v. *Sandoval*, 231 U. S. 28, 48 (1913), rev'g 198 Fed. 539 (D. C. N. M. 1912); *Farrell* v. *United States*, 110 Fed. 942 (C. C. A. 8, 1901); *Renfrow* v. *United States*, 3 Okla. 161, 41 Pac. 88 (1895). The last sentence of the Citizenship Act clearly shows the congressional intention to continue federal trusteeship despite the conferring of citizenship. Butte, The Legal Status of the American Indian (1912), p. 17, criticizes the dual relationship of citizenship and wardship.

[57] *Winton* v. *Amos*, 255 U. S. 373 (1921).

[58] Chapter 18. Also see *United States* v. *Celestine*, 215 U. S. 278 (1909).

[59] *Bowling* v. *United States*, 233 U. S. 528 (1914), aff'g 191 Fed. 19 (C. C. A. 8, 1911); *United States* v. *Sherburne Mercantile Co.*, 68 F. 2d 155 (C. C. A. 9, 1933). Also see Chapter 19, sec. 2A(1).

[60] See Chapter 13, sec. 3.

[61] *Cherokee Nation* v. *Hitchcock*, 187 U. S. 294, 308 (1902).

[62] *Rainbow* v. *Young*, 161 Fed. 835 (C. C. A. 8, 1908), rev'g. 154 Fed. 489.

[63] The Congressional intent must be clear. *Goudy* v. *Meath*, 203 U. S. 146 (1906).

[64] See secs. 6, 7. Exceptions to this rule are cases in the federal courts dependent upon diversity of citizenship.

[65] For discussion of the status of Pueblos of New Mexico, see Chapter 20; and of the Alaskan Indians, see Chapter 21.

"necessarily end the right or duty of the United States to pass laws in their interest as a dependent people."[66]

5. Citizenship is not inconsistent with restrictions on property and does not confer on incompetent persons, like minors, the right to control or dispose of their property.[67]

Although prior to the Citizenship Act[68] Indian citizenship was often associated with the possession of unrestricted property, there is no intrinsic relation between the two. It does not detract from the dignity or value of citizenship when a person possessed of an estate is deprived of the right of alienation.[69]

[66] *Hallowell* v. *United States*, 221 U. S. 317, 324 (1911). Even though the members of the Choctaw Nation were citizens of the United States and of the State of Mississippi, Congress by a series of acts from 1891 to 1908, cited in Houghton, The Legal Status of Indian Suffrage in the United States (1931), 19 Calif. L. Rev. 507, 515, fn. 39, rescued them from destitution, removed them to the Indian Territory, and equipped them with tools and food to last for 6 months.

[67] The Supreme Court in *Tiger* v. *Western Investment Co.*, 221 U. S. 286 (1911), said:

> The privileges and immunities of Federal citizenship have never been held to prevent governmental authority from placing such restraints upon the conduct or property of citizens as is necessary for the general good. Incompetent persons, though citizens, may not have the full right to control their persons and property. The privileges and immunities of citizenship were said, in the *Slaughter-House Cases*, (16 Wall. 36, 76), to comprehend:
>
> "Protection by the Government with the right to acquire and possess property of every kind, and to pursue and obtain happiness and safety, subject, nevertheless, to such restraints as the Government may prescribe for the general good of the whole." (Pp. 315–316.)

Also see *Brader* v. *James*, 246 U. S. 88 (1918); *United States* v. *Nice*, 241 U. S. 591 (1916); *United States* v. *Logan*, 105 Fed. 240 (C. C. Ore. 1900); *United States* v. *Sandoval*, 231 U. S. 28 (1913), rev'g 198 Fed. 539 (D. C. N. M. 1912); *Beck* v. *Flournoy Live-Stock and Real Estate Co.*, 65 Fed. 30 (C. C. A. 8, 1894), app. dism. 163 U. S. 686; Contra: *Territory of N. Mex.* v. *Delinquent Taxpayers*, 12 N. M. 139 (1904).

[68] Act of June 2, 1924, 43 Stat. 253, 8 U. S. C. 3.

[69] *Williams* v. *Steinmetz*, 16 Okla. 104, 82 Pac. 986 (1905); Meriam, Problem of Indian Administration (1928), p. 753.

SECTION 3. SUFFRAGE

In a democracy suffrage is the most basic civil right, since its exercise is the chief means whereby other rights may be safeguarded.[70] The enfranchisement of the Indians has been a slow and is still an incomplete process. In most states Indians meeting the ordinary suffrage requirements can and do vote. In some of the sparsely settled western states, where they form a large proportion of the population, their vote is of considerable importance in close primaries and elections.[71] While at first it was asserted that unscrupulous whites could control the vote of the ignorant,[72] many Indians are becoming increasingly aware of their political power and responsibility, and are directing considerable attention to matters directly affecting them, such as tribal claims and water rights.[73]

A. INDIAN DISENFRANCHISEMENT

The term "Indians not taxed" has been frequently used in statutes excluding Indians from voting. It appears in one of the two places in the original Constitution relating specifically to the Indians: viz, Article 1, section 2, which declares that Indians not taxed shall not be counted as "free persons" in determining the representations of any state in Congress or in computing direct taxes to be levied by the United States. This phrase is used in the Act of March 1, 1790, providing for the first census,[74] reappears in section 2 of the Fourteenth Amendment and the Civil Rights Act of April 9, 1866,[75] declaring who shall be federal citizens, and was used to exclude Indians in the apportionment of representatives to a territorial or state legislature[76] or constitutional convention, or from participation in a referendum to determine whether the inhabitants of a territory desired statehood.[77]

Various state and federal laws enacted from the beginning of the nineteenth century to the early part of the twentieth disenfranchised "Indians not taxed,"[78] or limited voters to white citizens.[79]

Though permitted to vote in their former country, Mexico, the California Indians were disenfranchised by the constitutional convention which established a government for the State of California.[80] In order to leave a loophole for compliance with the spirit of the Treaty of Guadalupe Hidalgo,[81] the new constitution[82] permitted the legislature, "by a two-thirds concurrent vote, to admit to the right of suffrage 'Indians, or the descendants of Indians, in such special cases as such a proportion of the legislative body may deem just or proper.'" As was expected, the first legislature restricted the vote to white citizens.[83]

Some state constitutions and statutes still reflect early legal theory that "Indians not taxed," being generally identified as persons born subject to the jurisdiction of the tribe of which they are members, were not citizens of the United States. The clearest cases of such racial discrimination are found in the constitutions of the States of Idaho,[84] New Mexico,[85] and Wash-

[70] See Thayer, A People Without Law (1891), 68 Atl. Month. 540, pp. 676, 682, 686.

[71] "* * * where they are a substantial element of the population, candidates for state office have found it worth while to hold rallies and barbecues, Democratic, Republican and Progressive, on the reservations." (Goodrich, The Legal Status of the California Indian (1926), 14 Calif. L. Rev. 83, 157, 179.)

[72] Leupp, The Indian and His Problem (1910), pp. 35, 64; also see pp. 358, 360.

[73] Meriam, Problem of Indian Administration (1928), pp. 756–757.

[74] 1 Stat. 101; also in subsequent census statutes. See Act of June 18, 1929, sec. 22, 46 Stat. 21, 26.

[75] Sec. 1, 14 Stat. 27.

[76] Act of June 19, 1878, 20 Stat. 178, 193; Act of March 3, 1887, sec. 22, 24 Stat. 635, 639; Act of March 3, 1891, 26 Stat. 908, 930: Act of July 16, 1894, 28 Stat. 107. For other terms of exclusion see Act of March 3, 1849, sec. 4, 9 Stat. 403, 404; Act of September 9, 1850, 9 Stat. 446; Act of June 8, 1880, sec. 5, 21 Stat. 154.

[77] Act of May 4, 1858, sec. 3, 11 Stat. 269, 271; Act of June 19, 1878, 20 Stat. 178, 193.

[78] See *United States* v. *Kagama*, 118 U. S. 375, 378 (1886); *Elk* v. *Wilkins*, 112 U. S. 94, 99 (1884); Act of June 16, 1906, sec. 25, 34 Stat. 267, 280. New Mexico still excludes Indians on this ground. This state was admitted to statehood under a special compact with the United States exempting Indian lands from taxation; and with a constitution excluding "Indians not taxed" from the electorate. New Mexico Constitution, Art. XII, sec. 1.

[79] Act of October 25, 1914, 3 Stat. 143; Act of March 2, 1819, sec. 4, 3 Stat. 489, 490; Act of April 20, 1836, c. 54, sec. 5, 5 Stat. 10, 12; Act of March 2, 1861, sec. 5, 12 Stat. 209, 211; Act of May 3, 1887, sec. 22, 24 Stat. 635, 639. By the Act of February 28, 1861, sec. 5, 12 Stat. 172, 173, whites and citizens recognized by Treaty with Mexico were eligible to vote and hold office.

[80] Goodrich, The Legal Status of the California Indian (1926), 14 Calif. L. Rev., 83–99.

[81] Signed February 12, 1848, ratification exchanged May 12, 1848, Treaty proclaimed July 4, 1948, 9 Stat. 922, discussed in Chapter 25, sec. 3. See *United States* v. *Ritchie*, 17 How. 525 (1854).

[82] Goodrich, *op. cit.*, p. 91.

[83] *Ibid.*

[84] Idaho Constitution, Art. 6, sec. 3. This restriction is applicable to "Indians not taxed," who have not severed their tribal relations and adopted the habits of civilization.

[85] Art. 7. *Cf.* Act of June 20, 1910, sec. 2, 36 Stat. 557, providing that the Constitution of New Mexico shall make no distinction in civil or political rights on account of race or color and shall not be repugnant to the Constitution of the United States and the Declaration of Independence. Also Provision Fifth providing that the State shall not restrict the right of suffrage on account of race, color, or previous condition of servitude.

ington,[86] which deny the right to vote to "Indians not taxed," while granting the ballot to whites not taxed.

The laws of a few other states, though not specifically discriminating against Indians, are construed and applied so as to result in discrimination. In Arizona, Indians are denied the right to vote on the ground that they are within the provisions[87] denying suffrage to "persons under guardianship."[88] The law of South Dakota excludes from voting Indians who maintain tribal relations, but has not been enforced for many years.

The Attorney General of Colorado rendered an opinion on November 14, 1936, that Indians had no right to vote under Colorado law because they were not citizens. This ruling is clearly erroneous.[89] The Utah Attorney General, on January 23, 1937, held that Indians residing on a reservation within the state were not residents and therefore not entitled to vote. This ruling conflicts with the opinion of the United States Supreme Court, holding that the land of an Indian reservation is part of the state within which the reservation is located.[90]

B. CONSTITUTIONAL PROTECTION OF INDIAN VOTING RIGHTS[91]

On March 30, 1870, the Fifteenth Amendment to the United States Constitution was adopted, providing:

> SEC. 1. The right of citizens of the United States to vote shall not be denied or abridged by the United States or by any State on account of race, color, or previous condition of servitude.
>
> SEC. 2. The Congress shall have the power to enforce this article by appropriate legislation.

With the passage of the Citizenship Act in 1924, considerations of disability because of allegiance to a tribe became irrelevant to the question of citizenship. The provisions of state constitutions and statutes based on these considerations which would operate to exclude Indian citizens from voting are probably void under the Fifteenth Amendment.[92]

The year following the passage of the Civil Rights Act of 1870,[93] the United States District Court for Oregon stated[94] that "an Indian * * * who is a citizen of the United States * * * cannot be excluded from this privilege [of voting] on the ground of being an Indian, as that would be to exclude him on account of race." (P. 166.) As was said by the United States Supreme Court in the case of *United States* v. *Reese*,[95]

> If citizens of one race having certain qualifications are permitted by law to vote, those of another having the same qualifications must be. Previous to this amendment, there was no constitutional guaranty against this discrimination: now there is. It follows that the amendment has invested the citizens of the United States with a new constitutional right which is within the protecting power of Congress. That right is exemption from discrimination in the exercise of the elective franchise on account of race, color, or previous condition of servitude. This, under the express provisions of the second section of the amendment, Congress may enforce by "appropriate legislation." (P. 218.)

This doctrine was applied in the case of *Neal* v. *Delaware*,[96] which invalidated a provision of the Delaware Constitution restricting suffrage to the white race. The court declared:

> Beyond question the adoption of the Fifteenth Amendment had the effect, in law, to remove from the State Constitution, or render inoperative, that provision which restricts the right of suffrage to the white race. (P. 389.)

These cases leave no doubt that, under the Fifteenth Amendment, Indians are protected against all legislation which discriminates against them in prescribing the qualifications of voters, and that it is immaterial whether the disenfranchisement is direct or indirect. This view does not conflict with the theory of *Elk* v. *Wilkins*, *supra*, which held simply that a noncitizen Indian might be disenfranchised by state legislation along with noncitizens of other races.

On January 26, 1938, the Solicitor of the Department of the Interior issued an opinion on the question of whether a state can constitutionally deny the franchise to Indians. The opinion concluded:

> * * * I am of the opinion that the Fifteenth Amendment clearly prohibits any denial of the right to vote to Indians under circumstances in which non-Indians would be permitted to vote. The laws of Idaho, New Mexico, and Washington which would exclude Indians not taxed from voting in effect exclude citizens of one race from voting on grounds which are not applied to citizens of other races. For this reason I believe such laws are unconstitutional under the Fifteenth Amendment. Similarly, the laws of Idaho and South Dakota which would exclude Indians who maintain tribal relations from voting are believed to be unconstitutional as such laws exclude citizens from voting on grounds which apply only to one race.[97] (P. 8.)

Two Attorneys General of the State of Washington have ruled that the Indian disenfranchisement clause in the Constitution of Washington is invalid.[98]

The Attorney General of New York in 1928 rendered an opinion to the effect that Indians resident upon reservations in that state are entitled to vote the same as any other qualified citizen.[99]

Congress has implemented the provisions of the Fifteenth Amendment in various general and special statutes.

The Reconstruction Acts, providing for the admission of the Confederate states to the Union, prohibited these states from depriving of the right to vote any class of citizens of the United

---

[86] Art. 6.

[87] Arizona Laws, 1933, Chapter 62.

[88] *Porter* v. *Hall*, 34 Ariz. 308, 271 Pac. 411 (1928); discussed by N. D. Houghton, The Legal Status of Indian Suffrage in the United States (1931), 19 Calif. L. Rev. 507, 509, 518. The decision was based on the ground that Indians living on the reservations are "persons under guardianship" and hence "wards of the national Government" within the meaning of the Constitution of the State of Arizona. This opinion appears to be based on an erroneous conception of the status of Indians, especially of the relationship of guardian and wards. See contra: *Swift* v. *Leach*, 45 N. D. 437, 178 N. W. 437 (1920), cited in the dissenting opinion in the *Porter* case. Also see sec. 9, *infra*.

[89] See discussion of citizenship, sec. 2, *supra*.

[90] *United States* v. *McBratney*, 104 U. S. 621 (1881).

[91] No attempt is made in this chapter to treat of the rights of Indians to vote in tribal elections. This subject has been covered in Chapter 7. It may be noted, however, that many of the Indian constitutions contain bills of rights, including guarantees of the right of suffrage. Thus, for example, the Constitution of the Blackfeet Tribe, approved December 13, 1935, provides: "Any member of the Blackfeet Tribe, twenty-one (21) years of age or over, shall be eligible to vote at any election when he or she presents himself or herself at a polling place within his or her voting district." (Art. VIII, sec. 1.)

[92] Op. Sol. I. D., M.29596, January 26, 1938; *Guinn* v. *United States*, 238 U. S. 347 (1915), holding unconstitutional the grandfather clause in the Constitution of Oklahoma; *Myers* v. *Anderson*, 238 U. S. 368 (1915), invalidating a similar clause in a Maryland statute; and see *Nixon* v. *Herndon*, 273 U. S. 536 (1927).

[93] Act of May 31, 1870, 16 Stat. 140.

[94] *McKay* v. *Campbell*, 16 Fed. Cas. No. 8840 (D. C. Ore. 1871).

[95] 92 U. S. 214 (1875).

[96] 103 U. S. 370 (1880).

[97] Op. Sol. I. D., M.29596, January 26, 1938.

[98] Op. A. G., W. V. Tanner, June 15, 1916, and Op. No. 4086 of G. W. Hamilton, April 1, 1936.

[99] Op. A. G. N. Y. (1928), p. 204. Informal opinions have also been rendered to the same effect by attorneys general of many other states. For example, the Attorney General of Florida in a letter dated March 13, 1923, to the Chairman of the County Commissioners, Everglades, Fla.

States who are entitled to vote under the Federal Constitution, dealing similarly with the right to hold office.[100] There are also many general civil rights laws which are applicable to the disenfranchisement of Indians because of their race. In 1906 the Enabling Act for the State of Oklahoma expressly permitted members of an Indian nation or tribe in the Indian Territory in Oklahoma to vote for delegates[101] and prohibited any law restricting the right of suffrage because of race or color.[102]

[100] Act of January 26, 1870, 16 Stat. 62, 63; Act of February 23, 1870, 16 Stat. 67; Act of March 30, 1870, 16 Stat. 80.

[101] Act of June 16, 1906, sec. 2, 34 Stat. 267, 268; also see Act of June 20, 1910, secs. 2 and 20, 36 Stat. 557, 559, 569 (N. M.).

[102] Act of June 16, 1906, secs. 2 and 3, 34 Stat. 267. *Cf.* sec. 25, p. 279, applying to New Mexico and permitting discrimination against "Indians not taxed."

SECTION 4. ELIGIBILITY FOR PUBLIC OFFICE AND EMPLOYMENT

A. PUBLIC OFFICE

The fact that one is an Indian is not, generally speaking, a disqualification for public office. Exclusionary statutes based on race are probably unconstitutional.[103] General Parker, a Seneca Indian, was qualified, according to an opinion of the Attorney General of the United States, to hold the office of the Commissioner of Indian Affairs.[104]

Many early statutes disqualified noncitizen Indians from holding public offices by limiting incumbents to citizens of the United States[105] or to whites.[106] After the Civil War, the acts admitting the Confederate states to the Union prohibited the exclusion of elected officials because of race, color, or previous condition of servitude.[107] These acts were implemented by the Act of April 20, 1871.[108] A number of Indians were elected as delegates to the Constitutional Convention of the Territory of Oklahoma.[109] Nevertheless, even now a few states still bar Indians from public office, by provisions which are probably unconstitutional. Idaho[110] prohibits from holding any civil office Indians not taxed who have not severed their tribal relations and adopted the habits of civilization. The law of South Dakota excludes Indians "while maintaining tribal relations."[111]

B. PREFERENCE IN INDIAN AND OTHER GOVERNMENTAL SERVICE.

(1) **Extent of employment.**—Congress has frequently manifested its intention to grant preferences to Indians in certain positions. Unfortunately, many such preferential statutes have become "dead letters," or been only partially fulfilled.[112] Officials have sometimes justified their failures in this respect by maintaining the impossibility of securing competent Indians, especially for the more important positions.[113] Some critics have ascribed this failure to the fact that many positions, like that of Indian agent, were regarded for decades as political plums,[114] and that the Indian Office comprised one of the largest fields for political plunder in the Federal Government.[115]

Some notable increases in Indian employment have been effected in recent years.[116] The number of Indians employed in the Washington office increased between 1934 and 1937 from 10 percent of the total staff to about 35 percent. By 1939 Indians occupied more than half of the regular positions of the Indian Service and more than 70 percent of the emergency positions.[117]

(2) **Civil service.**—The Indian Office was one of the first bureaus to be placed under civil service.[118] Indians entering the Office of Indian Affairs were required to qualify in regular civil service examinations, except that certain preferences were allowed in compliance with statutes providing that Indians shall be employed whenever practicable. The formulation of a competitive civil service for Indians under authority of the Indian Reorganization Act is now in progress.[119] Standards have been established and examinations conducted for nurses and organization field agents, and a number of appointments have been made from the registers established as a result of these examinations. Executive Order No. 8043 of January 31, 1939, permits the appointment of Indians of one-quarter or more Indian blood to any position in the Indian Service without examination.[120] By Executive Order No. 8383 of March 28, 1940, Indians in the Office

[103] See *Nixon v. Herndon*, 273 U. S. 536 (1927).

[104] 13 Op. A. G. 27 (1869). A later opinion held that an Indian, while a member of a tribe and subject to tribal jurisdiction and residing in the Indian Territory, was not competent to take the official oath as postmaster. The basis for this ruling was that the government could not enforce the required bond because the Indian would be immune to suit. 18 Op. A. G. 181 (1885).

[105] Act of September 9, 1850, sec. 6, 9 Stat. 446, 449; Act of May 30, 1854, sec. 5, 10 Stat. 277, 279; Act of August 18, 1856, sec. 21, 11 Stat. 52, 60, provided that noncitizens holding office in the Department of State shall not be paid.

[106] Act of August 14, 1848, sec. 5, 9 Stat. 323, 325; Act of March 3, 1849, sec. 5, 9 Stat. 403, 405; Act of March 2, 1853, sec. 5, 10 Stat. 172, 174; Act of December 22, 1869, sec. 6, 16 Stat. 59.

[107] Act of March 30, 1870, 16 Stat. 80, 81, admitting Texas to the Union.

[108] Act of April 20, 1871, sec. 2, 17 Stat. 5.

[109] Leupp, The Indian and His Problem (1910), pp. 341–342.

[110] Constitution of Idaho, Art. 6, sec. 3.

[111] Compiled Laws of S. D., sec. 92 (1929).

[112] See 3(b) *infra*.

[113] "* * * the policy of all administrations since Commissioner Morgan took office has been to give educated Indians every practicable chance to serve their people; but * * * the experiment of putting them into the places of highest responsibility has, except in rare instances, not worked so successfully, * * *." Leupp, The Indian and His Problem (1910), p. 110. Also see Schmeckebier, The Office of Indian Affairs. Its History, Activities, and Organization (1927), pp. 295–296, and 7 Indians at Work (September 1939), No. 1, p. 41.

[114] Leupp, The Indian and His Problem (1910), pp. 98–99.

[115] Administration of the Indian Office (Bureau of Municipal Research Publication No. 65) (1915), pp. 24–25.

[116] Annual Report of the Secretary of the Interior (1937), pp. 241–242. In 1910 there were about 200 Indians in the Office of Indian Affairs. Leupp, The Indian and His Problem (1910), p. 96.

The Annual Report of the Secretary of the Interior for 1938 states:

> On July 1, 1937, there were authorized in the Indian field service and Alaska 6,933 permanent year-round positions. On April 30, 1938, there were 3,916 Indians employed in the Indian Service, of whom 3,627 were in regular year-round positions. Approximately one-half of the regular employees of the Indian Service are Indians. Slightly more than 40 percent of the Indians employed are full-bloods. (P. XIV.)

Slightly more than 70 percent of the Indians employed were of one-half or more degrees Indian blood. (*Ibid.*, p. 257.) The personnel records do not classify as Indians those with a smaller amount of Indian blood than one-fourth.

[117] Between July 1, 1933, and May 1, 1937, the number of Indians in the Washington office increased from 11 to 83. 4 Indians At Work, No. 20 (June 1, 1937), p. 39. According to data submitted by the Indian Office on November 7, 1939, 109 of the 384 employees of the Washington office were Indians.

[118] Administration of the Indian Office. (Bureau of Municipal Research Publication No. 65) (1915), p. 24.

[119] Aberle, Some Aspects of the Personnel Problem of the Indian Service in the United States in Indians of the United States, Contributions by the delegation of the United States First Inter-American Conference on Indian Life, Patzcuaro, Mexico, published by Office of Indian Affairs (April 1940), pp. 61, 64. Also see subsection 3(b) *infra*.

[120] There have been numerous Executive orders affecting the employment of Indians, *e. g.*, Executive orders of August 14, 1928; July 2, 1930; April 14, 1934; July 26, 1936.

of Indian Affairs on February 1, 1939, who met certain requirements were given a classified civil-service status.

(3) **Treaties and statutes.**—With a few exceptions, throughout the history of the United States Indians have generally been granted preference in the actual hiring of employees for public positions in the Indian Service which require little or no skill or which, like the post of interpreter, can be filled only by them, or in the Army as scouts, because of their unusual qualifications,[121] or for laboring positions.[122] These positions, which were often created by appropriation acts, usually paid low wages,[123] and were sometimes supported by tribal funds.[124] Similarly today most Indians in the Government Service are employed in clerical, stenographic, or laboring work, though a few hold supervisory positions.[125]

(*a*) *Treaties.*—Treaties occasionally provided for preference in employment of Indians.[126] The Treaty of April 28, 1866,[127] between the United States and the Choctaw and Chickasaw Nations contains an interesting provision:

> And the United States agree that in the appointment of marshals and deputies, preference, qualifications being equal, shall be given to competent members of the said nations, the object being to create a laudable ambition to acquire the experience necessary for political offices of importance in the respective nations.

(*b*) *General statutes.*—The Act of June 30, 1834, the first important employment statute for Indians, gave them preference for positions as "interpreters or other persons employed for the benefit of the Indians," if "properly qualified for the execution of the duties."[128] Section 5 of the Act of March 3, 1875,[129] provided that "where Indians can perform the duties they shall be employed" in Indian agencies. Again in the Act of March 1, 1883,[130] Congress manifested its desire to increase the employment of Indians in the Indian Service, by providing: "* * * preference shall at all times, as far as practicable, be given to Indians in the employment of clerical, mechanical, and other help on reservations and about agencies."

A broader provision, which also includes positions outside the Indian Bureau, appears in the General Allotment Act.[131] Offered as an additional inducement to the abandonment of tribal relations, it provides:

> * * * And hereafter in the employment of Indian police, or any other employees in the public service among any of the Indian tribes or bands affected by this act, and where Indians can perform the duties required, those Indians who have availed themselves of the provisions of this act and become citizens of the United States shall be preferred.

Seven years later a law provided for preference for "herders, teamsters, and laborers, and where practicable in all other employments in connection with the agencies and the Indian service."[132]

Section 12 of the Wheeler-Howard Act,[133] the sixth major attempt in the space of a century, to give preference to Indians in the Indian Service, provides:

> The Secretary of the Interior is directed to establish standards of health, age, character, experience, knowledge, and ability for Indians who may be appointed, without regard to civil-service laws, to the various positions maintained, now or hereafter, by the Indian Office, in the administration of functions or services affecting any Indian tribe. Such qualified Indians shall hereafter have the preference to appointment to vacancies in any such positions.

This provision contemplates the establishment within the Interior Department of a special civil service for Indians alone. The failure of the Interior Department to complete such a system has been ascribed to lack of adequate appropriations.[134]

(4) **Statutes of limited application.**—

(*a*) *Construction work on reservation.*—Agreements with Indian tribes[135] or statutes appropriating money for the con-

---

[121] For a discussion of the policy of preferring Indians for appointment in the Indian Service, see Meriam and Associates, Problem of Indian Administration (1928), pp. 156–159.

[122] Act of April 27, 1904, 33 Stat. 352, 354 (Crows), "* * * nothing herein contained shall be construed to prevent the employment of such engineers or other skilled employees, or to prevent the employment of white labor where it is impracticable for the Crows to perform the same." Also see Act of June 7, 1924, c. 318, 43 Stat. 606 (Navajo); Act of March 1, 1926, 44 Stat. 135 (Quinaielts); Act of April 19, 1926, 44 Stat. 303 (Quinaielts); Act of July 3, 1926, 44 Stat. 888 (Chippewas); Act of May 12, 1928, c. 531, 45 Stat. 501 (Zuni); Act of May 27, 1930, c. 343, 46 Stat. 430 (Wind River) ("only Indian labor shall be employed except for engineering and supervision"); amended by Act of April 21, 1932, c. 123, 47 Stat. 88.

[123] Sec. 9 of the Act of June 30, 1834, 4 Stat. 735, provides that the pay of an agency interpreter shall be $300 annually (congressional statutes regarding the pay of interpreters are discussed in *United States v. Mitchell*, 109 U. S. 146 (1883)), while the Act of February 24, 1891, 26 Stat. 783, 784, provides for the employment of Indian scouts and guides without pay. In one of the treaties relating to the pensioning of Indians, the Treaty of September 27, 1830, with the Choctaws, Art. 21, 7 Stat. 333, 338, annual pensions of $25 were granted to a few surviving "Choctaw Warriors," not exceeding 20, "who marched and fought in the army with General Wayne." Provision was made for one of the few comparatively high-salaried Indians in the Treaty of August 7, 1790, unpublished treaty, Art. 3, Archives No. 17, which appoints McGillivray, Chief of the Creek Nation, as agent of the United States in said nation with the rank of brigadier general, and the annual salary of $1,200. Treaty of January 21, 1785, with the Wiandot, Delaware, Chippewa, and Ottawa Nations, 7 Stat. 16, Separate Article following Art. 10, which provides that two Delaware chiefs "who took up the hatchet" for the United States as lieutenant colonel and captain shall be restored to rank in the Delaware Nation as before the Revolutionary War. Also see Treaty of September 27, 1830, Art. 15, 7 Stat. 333, 335–336, providing that one chief of the Choctaw Nation when in military service shall receive the pay of a lieutenant colonel, and other chiefs the pay of majors and captains in the United States Army.

[124] Act of April 27, 1904, 33 Stat. 352, 354 (Crows); Act of March 3, 1905, Art. IV, 33 Stat. 1016, 1017 (Shoshones); Act of June 7, 1924, 43 Stat. 606 (Navajos); Act of March 1, 1926, c. 41, 44 Stat. 135 (Quinaielts); Act of April 19, 1926, c. 165, 44 Stat. 303 (Fort Peck and Blackfeet); Act of July 3, 1926, 44 Stat. 888 (Chippewas).

[125] Annual Report of the Secretary of the Interior (1937), p. 241.

[126] Article 11 of the Treaty of March 11, 1863, with the Chippewas, 12 Stat. 1249, 1251: "Whenever the services of laborers are required upon the reservation, preference shall be given to full or mixed bloods, if they shall be found competent to perform them." Also see Treaty of May 7, 1864, with the Chippewas, Art. 11, 13 Stat. 693: Article 13 of the Treaty of October 21, 1867, with the Kiowas and Comanches, 15 Stat. 581, 585, provides: "The Indian agent, in employing a farmer, blacksmith, miller, and other employees herein provided for, qualifications being equal, shall give the preference to Indians."

[127] Art. 8, cl. 12, 14 Stat. 769.

[128] Act of June 30, 1834, sec. 9, 4 Stat. 735, 737.

[129] 18 Stat. 402, 449.

[130] Sec. 6, 22 Stat. 432, 451.

[131] Act of February 8, 1887, sec. 5, 24 Stat. 388, 389–390. The Act of February 14, 1923, 42 Stat. 1246 (Piutes), extended the provisions of this act, as amended, to lands purchased for Indians.

[132] Act of August 15, 1894, sec. 10, 28 Stat. 286, 313, 25 U. S. C. 44. Also see Act of May 17, 1882, 22 Stat. 68, 88; Act of July 4, 1884, 23 Stat. 76, 97.

[133] June 18, 1934, sec. 12, 48 Stat. 984, 986, 25 U. S. C. 472.

[134] 7 Indians at Work, No. 1, pp. 41–42 (1939); vol. 7, No. 5 p. 2 (1940).

[135] Act of June 10, 1896, Art. 3, 29 Stat. 321, 355: "It is agreed that in the employment of all agency and school employees preference in all cases be given to Indians residing on the reservation, who are well qualified for such positions." Also see Act of April 27, 1904, Art. 2, 33 Stat. 352, 354 (Crows); Act of March 3, 1905, Art. 4, 33 Stat. 1016, 1017 (Shoshones).

struction of roads[136] or for other public[137] or private work[138] on the reservations often require the employment of members of the tribe[139] or Indian labor.[140]

(*b*) *Purchase of Indian products.*—The Act of April 30, 1908,[141] provides that Indian labor shall be employed as far as practicable and that purchases of the products of Indian industry may be made in the open market in the discretion of the Secretary of the Interior. By subsequent amendments,[142] the portion of this provision regarding purchases was made applicable only to those purchases and contracts for supplies and services, except personal services, for the Indian Field Service, which exceed in amount $100 each.[143]

The Act of May 11, 1880,[144] authorizes the Secretary to purchase for use in the Indian Service articles manufactured at Indian manual and training schools.

(*c*) *Military service.*—The skill and bravery of Indians were utilized in fighting foreign foes[145] and other Indians.[146] Article III of the Treaty of September 17, 1778,[147] provided that the Delawares "* * * engage to join the troops of the United States aforesaid, with such a number of their best and most expert warriors as they can spare * * *." The Act of March 5, 1792,[148] provided for the employment of Indians to protect the frontiers of the nation. Some of the tribes agreed to furnish such warriors as "the president of the United States, or any officer having his authority therefor, may require," in prosecuting the War of 1812 against Great Britain.[149] A decade before the Civil War the Army contained a company of Shawnee and Delaware mounted volunteers.[150] Three full regiments of Indians were enlisted in the Union Army.[151] With the coming of peace, the President was authorized to employ in the territories and Indian country a maximum of 1,000 Indian scouts, to be paid like cavalry soldiers.[152] The Act of August 1, 1894,[153] permitted the enlistment of noncitizen Indians in the Army in times of peace.[154] Over 17,000 Indians served in the World War.[155] There are Indian scouts in the regular army of the United States.[156]

(*d*) *Youth.*—The Act of June 7, 1897,[157] requires the Commissioner of Indian Affairs to "employ Indian girls as assistant

---

[136] Act of May 1, 1888, Art. III, 25 Stat. 113, 114; Act of June 7, 1924, 43 Stat. 606, 607 (Navajos); Act of March 1, 1926, 44 Stat. 135. The Act of May 26, 1928, 45 Stat. 750, authorizes an appropriation for reservation roads not eligible for Government aid under the Federal Highway Act for which no other appropriation is available. $1,000,000 was appropriated for this purpose by the Act of July 21, 1932, sec. 301 (a)(2)(D), 47 Stat. 709, 717. The Act of May 27, 1930, c. 343, 46 Stat. 430, amended April 21, 1932, 47 Stat. 88, exempts from the requirement of employment of Indian labor roads built by funds provided by the State of Wyoming.

[137] Act of April 27, 1904, Art. 2, 33 Stat. 352, 354 (Crows), irrigation; Act of March 3, 1905, Art. 4, 33 Stat. 1016, 1017 (Shoshones); Act of April 19, 1926, 44 Stat. 303 (Quinaielts), water supply.

[138] Act of April 27, 1904, 33 Stat. 352, 354 (Crows), ditches, dams, canals, and fences; Act of June 28, 1906, 34 Stat. 547; Act of March 28, 1908, sec. 2, 35 Stat. 51, amended by Act of January 27, 1925, 43 Stat. 793, timber work on Menominee Indian reservation.

[139] Statutes cited in fn. 138, *supra*. Agreement with Shoshone and Arapahoe tribes on Shoshone reservation, Act of March 3, 1905, Art. 4, 33 Stat. 1016, 1017; Agreement with Indians of Crow Reservation, April 27, 1904, 33 Stat. 352, 354, "* * * no contract shall be awarded; nor employment given to other than Crow Indians, or whites intermarried with them, except that any Indian employed in construction may hire white men to work for him * * *."

[140] The Act of June 27, 1902, 32 Stat. 400, 402 (Chippewas), provides that purchasers of timber shall be required "when practicable, to employ Indian labor in the cutting, handling, and manufacture of said timber." The proceeds of such sales are received by the Indian Bureau and used for the benefit of the Indian children in the schools. 17 Op. A. G. 531 (1883). The Act of May 26, 1928, 45 Stat. 750, authorizes the employment of Indian labor on certain Shoshone Indian reservation roads; supplemented by Act of July 21, 1932, sec. 301(a)(2)(D), 47 Stat. 709, 717. The Act of May 27, 1930, c. 343, 46 Stat. 430, amended Act of April 21, 1932, 47 Stat. 88 (Wind River), excepts engineers and supervisors from the requirement for Indian labor.

[141] 35 Stat. 70.

[142] Act of June 25, 1910, sec. 23, 36 Stat. 855, 861, 25 U. S. C. 47, 93; Act of May 18, 1916, 39 Stat. 123, 126. Also see Act of January 12, 1927, 44 Stat. 934, 936, which creates an Indian Service supply fund.

[143] Sometimes appropriation acts contain special provisions empowering the Secretary of the Interior, when practicable, to buy Indian goods. For example, c. 290, sec. 3, of the Act of August 15, 1894, 28 Stat. 286, 312, and the Act of March 2, 1895, 28 Stat. 876, 907, contain the following provisions: "* * * That purchase [of supplies] in open market shall, as far as practicable, be made from Indians, under the direction of the Secretary of the Interior. * * * That the Secretary of the Interior may, when practicable, arrange for the manufacture by Indians upon the reservation of shoes, clothing, leather, harness, and wagons."

[144] Sec. 1, 21 Stat. 114, 131.

[145] Treaty of September 27, 1830, with the Choctaws, Art. 21, 7 Stat. 333, 338.

[146] Treaty of September 24, 1857, with the Pawnees, Art. 11, 11 Stat. 729, 732, provides for compensation or replacement of property stolen from Pawnee scouts returning from an expedition with the American Army against the Cheyenne Indians.

[147] With the Delawares, 7 Stat. 13. The Treaty of December 2, 1794, with the Oneida, Tuscorora, and Stockbridge Indians, 7 Stat. 47, cites in its preamble the faithful assistance of a body of the Oneida, Tuscorora, and Stockbridge Indians who, because of their services during the Revolution, were driven from their homes, their houses and property destroyed. Arts. 1 and 5 of this treaty provided that $5,000 shall be distributed for individual losses and services in return for relinquishment of further claims. The Act of July 29, 1848, 9 Stat. 265, provided for the granting of a pension for widows of "Indian spies, who shall have served in the Continental line."

[148] 1 Stat. 241.

[149] Treaty of July 22, 1814, with the Wyandots and others, Art. 2, 7 Stat. 118. Also see Treaty of September 29, 1817, with the Wyandots and others, Art. 12, 7 Stat. 160, providing for payment for property destroyed during this war. Part of the Creeks assisted the British. See preamble to Treaty of August 9, 1814, with the Creeks, 7 Stat. 120. Other tribes did the same. For example see Treaty of September 8, 1815, with the Wyandots and others, 7 Stat. 131.

Cherokee warriors fought against Great Britain and the southern Indians. See Act of April 14, 1842, 5 Stat. 473. Shawnee warriors fought in the Florida War. See Joint Resolution March 3, 1845, 5 Stat. 800; and Treaty of October 18, 1820, with the Choctaws, Art. 11, 7 Stat. 210. The Navajos offered to fight the Apaches. See 16 Op. A. G. 451 (1880).

[150] Act of September 28, 1850, 9 Stat. 519.

[151] Bounties were provided for these regiments. Joint Resolution June 18, 1866, 14 Stat. 360. Also see Joint Resolution July 14, 1870, 16 Stat. 390; Abel, The Slaveholding Indians (1919), vol. 2, p. 76, stating that the Secretary of War was opposed to having Indians in the Army during the Civil War.

[152] Act of July 28, 1866, sec. 6, 14 Stat. 332, 333; Treaty of February 19, 1867, with the Dakotas and Sioux, Arts. 11–13, 15 Stat. 505, 507–508. Also see 16 Op. A. G. 451 (1880), and Act of August 12, 1876, 19 Stat. 131; Act of February 24, 1891, 26 Stat. 770, 774, and R. S. §1094, repealed by Act of March 3, 1933, 47 Stat. 1428.

[153] Sec. 2, 28 Stat. 215, 216, amended June 14, 1920, 41 Stat. 1077. Also see Act of April 22, 1898, sec. 5, 30 Stat. 364.

[154] Repealed by Act of June 14, 1920, 41 Stat. 1077.

[155] Flickinger, A Lawyer Looks at the American Indian, Past and Present, pt. 2 (1939), 6 Indians at Work, No. 9, pp. 26, 29.

[156] 10 U. S. C. 4, 786, R. S. § 1276, provides:

> Indians, enlisted or employed by order of the President as scouts, shall receive the pay and allowances of Cavalry soldiers.

10 U. S. C. 915 grants Indian scouts an allowance for horses. The Act of May 19, 1924, sec. 202(c), 43 Stat. 121, grants adjusted compensation, commonly called a bonus, to Indian scouts who were veterans of the World War.

[157] Indian Appropriation Act, fiscal year ending June 30, 1898, 30 Stat. 62–83. For similar provisions in previous appropriation acts see Act of June 10, 1896, 29 Stat. 321, 348, and Act of March 2, 1895, 28 Stat. 876, 906.

matrons and Indian boys as farmers and industrial teachers in all Indian schools when it is practicable to do so."

Sections 1 and 9 of the Act of June 28, 1937,[158] which establishes a permanent Civilian Conservation Corps, provide that camps may be established for a maximum of 10,000 Indian enrollees, who need not be unemployed or in need of employment, and who may be exempted from the requirement that part of the wages shall be paid to dependents.[159]

[158] 50 Stat. 319, 320. The original law, Act of March 31, 1933, c. 17, 48 Stat. 22, did not contain such a provision.

[159] Sec. 7, 50 Stat. 319. On regulations regarding operations of Indian Division of C. C. C., see 25 C. F. R. 18.1–18.29.

SECTION 5. ELIGIBILITY FOR STATE ASSISTANCE [160]

Some state administrators are unaware that Indians maintaining tribal relations or living on reservations are citizens,[161] or mistakenly assume that they are supported by the Federal Government,[162] and deny them relief. This discrimination in state aid has made more acute the economic distress of many Indians who are poor and live below any reasonable standard of health and decency.[163]

It has been administratively held that Indians are entitled to share in the aids and services provided by state laws, subsidized by federal grants-in-aid under the Social Security Act,[164] or direct or work-relief statutes.[165]

The Solicitor for the Department of the Interior in a memorandum dated April 22, 1936, holding that the Social Security Act was applicable to Indians, stated:

> * * * An Indian ward votes or is entitled to vote. *United States* v. *Dewey County, supra; Anderson* v. *Mathews*, 174 Cal. 537, 163 Pac. 902; *Swift* v. *Leach*, 45 N. D. 437, 178 N. W. 437. His children are entitled to attend public schools even though a Federal Indian school is available. *LaDuke* v. *Melin, supra; United States* v. *Dewey County, supra; Piper* v. *Big Pine School Dist.*, 193 Cal. 664, 226 Pac. 926. He may sue and be sued in State courts. *In re Celestine*, 114 Fed. 551 (D. Wash. 1902); *Swift* v. *Leach, supra, Brown* v. *Anderson*, 61 Okla. 136, 160 Pac. 724. His ordinary contracts and engagements are subject to State law, *Luigi Marre and Cattle Co.* v. *Roses*, 34 P. (2) 195 (Cal. 1934), and his personal conduct is subject to State law except upon reserved land. *State* v. *Morris*, 136 Wis. 552, 117 N. W. 1006. He must pay State taxes on all non-trust property which he may own and all fees and taxes for the enjoyment of State privileges, such as driving on State highways, and all taxes, such as sales taxes, which reach the entire population. Where the taxes paid by the Indians are insufficient to provide necessary support for State schools, hospitals, and other institutions caring for Indians, the Federal Government often pays for such services with trust or tribal funds or with gratuity appropriations. (See, e. g., act of April 16, 1934, 48 Stat. 596). 17 Decisions of the Comptroller of the Treasury 678. And Indian wards are constantly receiving care in State institutions either without charge or with payment from their unrestricted resources. Furthermore, the United States has not provided any old-age pension system for the Indians nor has it made any general provision for Indians for the types of services which it is assisting the States to render under the Security Act. (Pp. 5–6.)

[160] For a discussion of their right to federal assistance, see Chapter 12, sec. 5; on right to rations, clothing, etc., under treaties, see Chapter 15, sec. 23. For a discussion of rations, see Schmeckebier, The Office of Indian Affairs, Its History, Activities, and Organization (1927), pp. 66–70; for a discussion of support of Indians, see pp. 252–255.

Often treaties provided that the United States would give an Indian tribe provisions and clothing. See Chapter 3, sec. 3C(3). This was generally a partial consideration for the cession of land by the Indians and sometimes a recognition of a moral obligation as guardian. Sometimes Congress provided food and clothing in lieu of annuities. For an example of a statute providing subsistence to Indians, see Act of April 29, 1902, 32 Stat. 177 (Choctaws and Chickasaws). On regulations regarding the operations of the Indian Division of the Civilian Conservation Corps, see C. F. R. 18.1–18.29.

[161] Op. Sol. I. D., M. 28869, February 13, 1937, p. 5.

[162] See Chapter 12.

[163] Annual Report of Secretary of Interior (1938), p. 237. "The income of the typical Indian family is low and the earned income extremely low"; Meriam, Problem of Indian Administration (1928), p. 4; for a discussion of the general economic condition of the Indians, see pp. 3–8, and pp. 430–546; on health conditions, pp. 189–345; also see Schmeckebier, *op. cit.* pp. 227–236.

[164] Memo. Sol. I. D., April 22, 1936; Act of August 13, 1935, 49 Stat. 612, 620, amended August 10, 1939, Public No. 379, 76th Cong., 1st sess. See Chapter 12, sec 5.

[165] Act of May 12, 1933, 48 Stat. 55; Resolution of April 8, 1935, 49 Stat. 115; Letters of July 17, 1933, and November 1, 1934, of the Federal Relief Administration to State Emergency Relief Administration.

SECTION 6. RIGHT TO SUE

Even before attaining citizenship, Indians had the capacity to sue and be sued in state and federal courts.[166] Though some writers [167] have sought to deny the right of reservation Indians to sue,[168] this view is rejected by the weight of authority [169]

[166] Ray A. Brown, the Indian Problem & the Law (1930), 39 Yale L. J. 307, 315. In *Felix* v. *Patrick*, 145 U. S. 317, 332 (1892), the court said that there was no doubt that before he became a citizen the Indian was capable of suing in the state courts which were open to all persons irrespective of race or color, and that upon becoming a citizen he could also sue in the federal courts. Also see *Yick Wo* v. *Hopkins*, 118 U. S. 356, 367 (1886), and holding that aliens had access to the courts for the protection of their person and property and a redress of their wrongs. Accord: *Deere* v. *St. Lawrence River Power Co.*, 32 F. 2d 550 (C. C. A. 2, 1929); *Missouri Pacific Ry. Co.* v. *Cullers*, 81 Tex. 382, 17 S. W. 19 (1891), discussed in 13 L. R. A. 542 (1891); *Johnson* v. *Pacific Coast S. S. Co.*, 2 Alaska 224, 239 (1904); *Keokuk* v. *Ulam*, 4 Okla. 5, 14 (1895); Canfield, Legal Position of the Indian (1881), 15 Am. L. Rev. 21, 33. Also see Chapter 23, sec. 4.

Indians may sue out a writ of habeas corpus. *United States ex rel. Standing Bear* v. *Crook*, 25 Fed. Cas. No. 14891 (C. C. Nebr. 1879). Also see *United States ex rel. Kennedy* v. *Tyler*, 269 U. S. 13 (1925); and *Bird* v. *Terry*, 129 Fed. 472 (C. C. Wash. 1903), app. dism. 129 Fed. 592 (C. C. A. 9, 1904). A judgment may be obtained against an Indian for breach of contract even though unenforceable because his property is restricted. *Stacy* v. *La Belle*, 99 Wis. 520, 75 N. W. 60 (1898).

[167] Canfield contended that the common law did not prevail on the reservations and that since Indian tribes were distinct political entities, Indians should not be able to enforce in state courts rights acquired under Indian laws or customs. Legal Position of the Indian (1881), 15 Am. L. Rev. 21, 32, 33.

[168] Suits by and against tribes are elsewhere analyzed. See Chapter 14, sec. 6. *Cf. Johnson* v. *Long Island Railroad Company*, 162 N. Y 462, 56 N. E. 992 (1900). Plaintiff, a member of the Montauk Tribe, brought an action of ejectment on behalf of himself and any members of the tribe who would come in and contribute to the expenses. The court held (two judges dissenting) that Indian tribes are wards of the state and are only possessed of such rights to litigate in courts of justice as are conferred on them by statutes. Accord: *Onondago Nation* v. *Thacher*, 169 N. Y. 584, 62 N. E. 1098 (1901), aff'g 53 App. Div. 561, 65 N. Y. Supp. 1014 (1900). A New York statute giving Indians such power was not questioned. McKinney, New York Consol. Laws (1917), book 25, sec. 5; *George* v. *Pierce*, N. Y. Sup. Ct. 85 Misc. 105, 148 N. Y. Supp. 230 (1914).

[169] Pound, Nationals without a Nation (1922), 22 Col. L. Rev. 97, 101, 102.

on the ground that Indians are not extraterritorial but only subject to special rules of substantive law.[170] An Indian has the same right as anyone else to be represented by counsel of his own selection, who may not be subordinated to counsel appointed by the court.[171] As an additional protection, the United States District Attorney has the duty to represent him in all suits at law or in equity.[172]

As a practical matter, the Indians have frequently been at a decided disadvantage in safeguarding their legal rights.

The courts were often at such a distance that the Indians could not avail themselves of their right to sue.[173] Their ignorance of the language, customs, usages, rules of law, and forms of procedure of the white man, the disparities of race, the animosities caused by hostilities, frequently deprived them of a fair trial by jury.[174] They were sometimes barred by state statutes from serving on juries,[175] and deemed incompetent as witnesses.[176]

The Committee on Indian Affairs of the House of Representatives, in a report [177] on the Trade and Intercourse Act of 1834 said:

> Complaints have been made by Indians that they are not admitted to testify as witnesses; and it is understood that they are in some of the States excluded by law. Those laws, however, do not bind the courts or tribunals of the United States. The committee have made no provision on the subject, believing that none is necessary: that the rules of law are sufficient, if properly applied, to remove every ground of complaint. (P. 13.)

Even at the present time, many Indians, particularly the older people, do not know any language but their native Indian tongue, and lack familiarity with most of the customs and ideas of the white people.[178] Most of the Indians live far from the county seats and cities where courts meet and legal business is transacted.[179] Prejudice,[180] lack of education,[181] of money,[182] and of a sufficient number of lawyers of their race who have their confidence also hamper them in securing adequate legal advice and enforcing their rights. Prof. Ray A. Brown, an eminent authority on Indian Law, has written: "* * * The majority of these people are not able either in understanding or financial ability to take advantage of the courts of justice * * *."[183]

In order to minimize the foregoing disadvantages a number of statutes have been enacted, establishing a separate administrative procedure to safeguard the rights of the Indians. One of the most important laws of this nature is the Act of June 25, 1910,[184] which vests in the Secretary of the Interior conclusive power to ascertain the heirs of a deceased allottee.

During the era of the westward expansion of railroads, statutes authorizing the construction and operation of railways through the Indian Territory usually provided that in case of the failure of the railroad to make amicable settlements with the Indian occupants of the land a commission of three disinterested referees should be appointed as appraisers, the chairman by the President, one by the chief of the nation to which the occupant belongs, and the other by the railway.[185]

In the absence of statute, Indian litigants are subject to the same defenses as other people. Except with respect to restricted property,[186] they may lose their rights because of laches, and the running of the statute of limitations.[187] They are also subject to the restrictions against suing sovereigns without their consent.

---

[170] Rice, The Position of the American Indian in the Law of the United States (1934), 16 J. Comp. Leg. 78; 14 Col. L. Rev., pp. 587–590 (1914).

[171] *Roberts* v. *Anderson*, 66 F. 2d 874 (C. C. A. 10, 1933).

[172] Act of March 3, 1893, 27 Stat. 612, 631, 25 U. S. C. 175, 178. On the interpretation of this law, see Chapter 12, sec. 8.

[173] Abel, vol. 1, *op. cit.*, p. 23, fn. 14. Toward the close of the nineteenth century, many writers criticized the government for not giving the Indians courts for the redress of their wrongs, especially the arbitrary action of administrators. Thayer, A People Without Law (1891), 68 Atl. Month, 540, 542, 676, 683. Wise describes the disadvantages under which Indians labor in their legal struggles with the Federal Government, Indian Law and Needed Reforms (1926), 12 A. B. A. J. 37, 39–40.

[174] Abbot, Indians and the Law (1888), 2 Harv. L. Rev. 167, 175–176; Harsha, Law for the Indians (1882), 134 N. A. Rev. 272, 274–275; Kyle, How Shall the Indians be Educated (1894), 159 N. A. Rev. 434.

[175] See Const. Idaho, Art. 6, sec. 3; *Kie* v. *United States*, 27 Fed. 351, 357–358 (C. C. Ore. 1886); *People* v. *Howard*, 17 Calif. 64 (1860).

[176] For early texts discussing their incompetency as witnesses, see Rapalje, A Treatise on the Law of Witnesses (1887), p. 26; Appleton, Rules of Evidence (1860), pp. 271–272. *Pumphrey* v. *State*, 84 Nebr. 636, 122 N. W. 19 (1909). Sometimes their incompetency as witnesses was restricted to cases where whites were parties. *People* v. *Hall*, 4 Calif. 399 (1854), aff'd by *Speer* v. *See Yup Co.*, 13 Cal. 73 (1859), held that the term "Indian" as used in section 394 of the Civil Practice Act (Calif. Stats. 1850, p. 230, subsequently reenacted) excluded a Chinese from testifying as a witness. See Goodrich, The Legal Status of the California Indian (1926), 14 Calif. L. Rev. 83, pp. 156 and 174; *Carter* v. *United States*, 1 Ind. T. 342 (1896). Even when competent, prejudice against their testimony was not infrequent. See *Shelp* v. *United States*, 81 Fed. 694 (C. C. A. 9. 1897). The Confederate States signed treaties with many of the southern tribes giving the members the right to be competent as witnesses in state courts and if indicted to subpoena witnesses and employ counsel. Abel, vol. 1, The American Indian as Slaveholder & Secessionist (1915), pp. 172–173. The Act of March 1, 1889, sec. 15, 25 Stat. 783, limited jurors in criminal cases in the United States courts in the Indian Territory in which the defendant is a citizen to citizens and thus excluded most Indians.

[177] 23d Cong., 1st sess., Repts. of Committees, No. 474, May 20, 1834.

[178] Meriam, Problem of Indian Administration (1928), pp. 777, 783, 790.

[179] *Ibid.*, pp. 713–714.

[180] *Ibid.*, p. 776.

[181] *Ibid.*, pp. 346–429.

[182] *Ibid.*, p. 776.

[183] The Indian Problem and the Law, 39 Yale L. J. 307, 331 (1930).

[184] 36 Stat. 855, amended March 3, 1928, 45 Stat. 161, April 30, 1934, 48 Stat. 647, 25 U. S. C. 372, discussed in *Hallowell* v. *Commons*, 239 U. S. 506 (1916), aff'g 210 Fed. 793 (C. C. A. 8, 1914); Knoepfler, Legal Status of American Indian & His Property (1922), 7 Ia. L. B. 232, 247, 248; Meriam, Problem of Indian Administration (1928), pp. 787–795; Schmeckebier, The Office of Indian Affairs, Its History, Activities, and Organization (1927), pp. 166–175.

[185] For an example of such a provision, see Act of September 26, 1890, 26 Stat. 485, 486. The Act of May 21, 1934, 48 Stat. 787, repealed sec. 186 of title 25, U. S. C., derived from sec. 2 of the Act of June 14, 1862, 12 Stat. 427, which empowered the superintendent or agent to ascertain the damages caused by a tribal Indian trespassing upon the allotments of an Indian; to deduct from the annuities due to the trespassing Indian the amount ascertained and, with the approval of the Secretary, to pay it to the party injured.

[186] See Chapter 11; Chapter 19, sec. 5.

[187] *Felix* v. *Patrick*, 145 U. S. 317, 331 (1892), discussing laches, aff'g 36 Fed. 457, discussing the statute of limitations. Also see *Lemieux* v. *United States*, 15 F. 2d 518 (C. C. A. 8, 1926), cert. den. 273 U. S. 749; 14 Col. L. Rev. 587–589 (1914). Also see Act of May 31, 1902, sec. 1, 32 Stat. 284, 25 U. S. C. 347, which provides for the application of the state statute of limitations in certain suits involving lands patented in severalty under treaties. While a deed of an Indian who received patent prohibiting alienation of property without the approval of the Secretary of Interior is void and the statute of limitations does not run against him and his heirs so long as the condition of incompetency remains, when by treaty subsequent to the issuance of the deed all restrictions were removed and the Indian became a citizen, the statute of limitations began to run against the grantor and his heirs. *Schrimpscher* v. *Stockton*, 183 U. S. 290 (1902). Also see *Bluejacket* v. *Ewert*, 265 Fed. 823 (C. C. A. 8, 1920), aff'd in part and rev'd in part, 259 U. S. 129 (1922). Cf. Op. Sol. I. D., M.20858, January 14, 1927, p. 2, to the effect that in view of the guardianship relation existing between the Government and the Indians, and the fact that so long as they maintain tribal relations, they are perhaps not chargeable with laches, the Department [of Interior] has been slow to establish a definite rule limiting the reopening of heirship proceedings or invoking the maxims of *res adjudicata* and *stare decisis*.

The right to sue is not conferred upon an individual member by a statute granting to a tribe the right to sue to recover tribal property.[188] In the absence of congressional legislation bestowing upon individual Indians the right to litigate in the federal courts internal questions relating to tribal property, the courts will not assume jurisdiction.[189]

[188] *Blackfeather* v. *United States*, 190 U. S. 368 (1903), aff'g 37 C. Cls. 233 (1902); *Casteel* v. *McNeely*, 4 Ind. T. 1 (1901).

[189] *United States* v. *Seneca Nation of New York Indians*, 274 Fed. 946 (D. C. W. D. N. Y. 1921). Also see *Lane* v. *Pueblo of Santa Rosa*, 249 U. S. 110 (1919).

The judgment entered in a suit against an Indian may be enforced against any unrestricted property which the Indian judgment debtor may own free from federal control. The restricted property of the judgment debtor is exempt from levy and sale under such a judgment.[190]

The Secretary of the Interior has authority to make payment of a judgment obtained in a state court against a restricted member of the Osage tribe of Indians or his estate.[191]

[190] *Mullen* v. *Simmons*, 234 U. S. 192 (1914).

[191] Act of February 27, 1925, 43 Stat. 1008 (Osage).

SECTION 7. RIGHT TO CONTRACT

Indians may make contracts in the same way as any other people,[192] except where prohibited by statutes which primarily regulate contracts affecting trust property.[193]

The contractual capacity of Indians is discussed in the case of *Gho* v. *Julles:*[194]

> We are unable to see why an Indian alien, preserving his tribal relations, is not as capable of making a binding contract (other than such as we have defined to be void by Statute), as an Englishman, or Spaniard, or a Dane, who while still retaining his native allegiance makes contracts here. (P. 328.)

Similarly, a more recent opinion[195] holds:

> * * * The fact that one of the parties to the contract was a full-blood Indian did not incapacitate him or impair his right to enter into this contract. He had the same right as other persons to make contracts generally. The only restriction on this right peculiar to an Indian was in regard to contracts affecting his allotment. These he could not make without the consent and approval provided by law. * * * (P. 156.)

Some treaties contained contractual restrictions.[196]

The most important limitation on the alienability of land is found in the Allotment Act of February 8, 1887,[197] which prevents an Indian allottee from making a binding contract in respect to land which the United States holds for him as trustee.[198]

The Act of May 21, 1872,[199] imposing restrictions on the contractual rights of noncitizen Indians, which has lost most of its importance because of the passage of the Citizenship Act, voids any contract with a noncitizen Indian (or an Indian tribe) for services concerning his lands or claims against the United States, unless it is executed in accordance with prescribed formalities and approved by the Secretary of the Interior.

An important statute restricting the contractual power of Indians with respect to certain types of property is the Act of June 30, 1913,[200] which provides:

> No contract made with any Indian, where such contract relates to the tribal funds or property in the hands of the United States, shall be valid, nor shall any payment for services rendered in relation thereto be made unless the consent of the United States has previously been given.

A. POWER OF ATTORNEY

Though an Indian may grant a power of attorney to another, and such grants of power have been extensively used in the award of grazing permits in allotted lands,[201] such a power will not ordinarily be implied.[202] If there is any doubt about the method of exercising the power, it will be resolved in favor of the grantors of the power.[203]

The government examines closely the circumstances surrounding the issuance and exercise of a power of attorney in order

[192] An Indian may contract freely concerning unrestricted real and personal property, *Jones* v. *Meehan*, 175 U. S. 1 (1899); also see *United States* v. *Paine Lumber Co.*, 206 U. S. 467 (1907). Accord: *Ke-tuc-e-mun-guah* v. *McClure*, 122 Ind. 541, 23 N. E. 1080 (1890); *Stacy* v. *La Belle*, 99 Wis. 520, 75 N. W. 60 (1898). Recognition of this capacity was contained in the Act of May 2, 1890, sec. 29, 26 Stat. 81, 93, which gave to the United States Courts in the Indian Territory jurisdiction of all contracts between citizens of Indian nations and citizens of the United States, provided such contracts were made in good faith and in accordance with the laws of such tribe or nation. As to individual rights in restricted personalty, see Chapter 10.

[193] Op. Sol. I. D., M.28869, February 13, 1937, p. 8: "It should be pointed out that an Indian, although a tribal member and a ward of the Government, is capable of making contracts and that these contracts require supervision only insofar as they may deal with the disposition of property held in trust by the United States." *Cf. Owen* v. *Dudley*, 217 U. S. 488 (1910). Questions frequently arise as to whether property is restricted. For example, crops growing on Indian trust land are considered trust property. *United States* v. *First National Bank*, 282 Fed. 330 (D. C. E. D. Wash. 1922), repudiating the case of *Rider* v. *LaClair*, 77 Wash. 488, 138 Pac. 3 (1914), which held that Indians could mortgage crops growing on allotments without the Government's consent. Also see Act of May 31, 1870, sec. 16, 16 Stat 140, 144, guaranteeing the right to enforce contracts to all persons "within the jurisdiction of the United States." The Act of February 27 1925, sec. 6, 43 Stat. 1008, 1011, exemplifies a restriction of the right to contract. It requires the approval of the Secretary of the Interior for contracts of debts of Osage tribesmen not having a certificate of competency. And see Act of February 21, 1863, 12 Stat. 658 (Winnebago).

[194] 1 Wash. Terr. (new series) 325 (1871).

[195] *Postoak* v. *Lee*, 46 Okla. 477, 149 Pac. 155 (1915).

[196] Section 15 of the Treaty of March 3, 1863, 12 Stat. 819, 820 provided that the Sioux Indians shall be incapable of making any valid civil contract with anyone other than a native member of their tribe without consent of the President. The Cherokees obtained an interesting provision in Article X of the Treaty of July 19, 1866, 14 Stat. 799, 801, permitting their members and resident freedmen to sell their farm or manufacured products and to ship and drive them to market without restraint.

[197] Sec. 5, 24 Stat. 388, 389. Also see Act of June 25, 1910, 36 Stat. 55. See Chapter 11.

[198] See Chapter 11. A few treaties also restrict the alienability of land. The Treaty with the Nez Perce of June 9, 1863, Art. III, 14 Stat. 647, 649, provides that lands belonging to individual Indians shall be inalienable without the permission of the President and shall be subject to regulations of the Secretary of the Interior.

[199] 17 Stat. 136, 25 U. S. C. 81, amended by Act of June 26, 1936, 49 Stat. 1984. The Act of April 29, 1874, 18 Stat. 35, contains similar provisions for contracts, made prior to May 21, 1872. Also see prior statute restricting contracts—Act of March 3, 1871, 16 Stat. 544, 570. To the effect that a contract by which Indian residents and subjects of the Dominion of Canada propose to employ an attorney to prosecute claims against the United States is not subject to the approval of the Secretary of the Interior and the Commissioner of Indian Affairs, see Op. Sol. I. D., M.30146, February 8, 1939. On the application of this law to tribes, see Chapter 14, sec. 5.

[200] Sec. 18, 38 Stat. 77, 97, 25 U. S. C. 85.

[201] See 25 C. F. R. 71.10–71.19.

[202] *Richardville* v. *Thorp*, 28 Fed. 52, 53 (C. C. Kan. 1886).

[203] 18 Op. A. G. 447, 497 (1886); 5 Op. A. G. 36 (1848).

to safeguard the interests of the Indian.[204] Subterfuges whereby such powers are used to take away control of restricted lands are held invalid[205] because "the restraints upon alienation and incumbrance were intended by Congress to instill into the Indians habits of thrift and industry and a sense of independence, and to protect them in the meantime from improvident contracts." (P. 799.)

B. COOPERATIVES AND BUSINESS ORGANIZATIONS

In some types of work, Indians, like other people, cannot compete with large aggregations of capital which dominate an increasing number of types of business, unless many of them combine their resources and energies.[206] Indian cooperatives have been chartered by the Secretary of the Interior, by organized tribes, and by states.[207]

Many recent statutes encourage the formation of cooperatives, including the Wheeler-Howard Act,[208] the Act of May 1, 1936,[209] applying its main provisions to Alaska, the Oklahoma Welfare Act,[210] and the Alaskan Reindeer Act.[211] Other legislation permitting loans to cooperatives is discussed under another heading.[212]

Thus encouraged by the Federal Government, Indians have established many different kinds of cooperatives.[213] Several statutes and tribal ordinances are designed to encourage Indian cooperatives in a particular tribe.[214]

The Constitution of the Blackfeet Tribe contains provisions typical of many tribal constitutions. Article VII, section 3, gives preference in the leasing of tribal land to members and associations of members, such as oil producers' cooperatives.[215] Section 1h of Article VI authorizes the Tribal Business Council to regulate and license all business or professional activities upon the reservation, subject to the approval of the Secretary of the Interior.[216]

Indian business organizations have been aided by some important laws relating to both Indians and non-Indians, such as the Taylor Grazing Act,[217] which provides for the granting of privileges to stockowners, including groups, associations, or corporations, authorized to conduct business under the laws of the state in which a grazing district is located. An Indian or group of Indians is capable of applying for grazing privileges under this act without the intervention of agency officials.[218]

C. RIGHTS OF CREDITORS

In the absence of statutory authorization, a third person may not discharge the duty of the Government and then recover the expenses incurred in performing such governmental duty.[219] Governmental liability for the debts of Indians arises solely from acts of Congress or treaties with the tribes. Treaties often provided payments even for substantial debts.[220]

The treaty provisions were often worded in justification for the payments of claims. The Indians were "anxious" to pay the claims,[221] or the payments were made at the "request" of the Indians, and the money was acknowledged by them to be due or to be a just claim.[222] The good deed of the creditor or a friend of the tribe would be glowingly described.[223]

---

[204] *United States* v. *Sands*, 94 F. 2d 156 (C. C. A. 10, 1938). Individual Indian owners frequently empower superintendents to issue leases or permits for them. Also see Chapter 11, sec. 5.

[205] *Williams* v. *White*, 218 Fed. 797 (C. C. A. 8, 1914).

[206] Senator O'Mahoney, Chairman of the Temporary National Economic Committee, alluded to one of the many causes for the trend toward concentration of economic power:

> * * * it is a common experience that the large aggregations of capital are able to secure money at a very much lower rate and for longer terms and on better conditions than the small business corporation may, and that in itself is an inherent difficulty which tends to magnify the big and reduce the little. Hearings before the Temporary National Economic Committee, Pt. V, p. 1669 (1939).

These hearings report the growth of monopoly in general and in specific industries. Also see Berle and Means, The Modern Corporation and Private Property (1932), pp. 18–46.

[207] In Oklahoma the Secretary may issue charters of incorporation to Indian cooperatives; in other states they generally operate as unincorporated associations. J. E. Curry, Principles of Cooperation, 4 Indians at Work, No. 16 (April 1, 1937), p. 8. For regulations on cooperatives see 25 C. F. R. 21.1–25.26.

[208] Secs. 10 (25 U. S. C. 470) and 17 (25 U. S. C. 477), June 18, 1934, 48 Stat. 984. The regulations governing the administration of the revolving credit fund make special provision for loans by incorporated tribes to Indian cooperatives. For example, see 25 C. F. R. 22.1–23.27 relating to cooperatives in Oklahoma.

[209] 49 Stat. 1250.

[210] Act of June 26, 1936, sec. 4, 49 Stat. 1967, 25 U. S. C. 504.

[211] Act of September 1, 1937, sec. 10, 50 Stat. 900, authorizing transfer of reindeer to cooperative associations or other organizations.

[212] See Chapter 12, sec. 6A.

[213] Some of these enterprises were discussed by John Collier, Commissioner of Indian Affairs, in a radio address on December 4, 1939, entitled "America's Handling of its Indigenous Indian Minority," and in the Annual Report of the Secretary of the Interior (1939), pp. 30–31, and (1938), pp. 251–252.

> The most important development in the Indian livestock field, perhaps, has been the marked increase in Indian initiative and management. Indians, through cooperative livestock associations, are managing controlled grazing, round-ups, sales, and other business affecting their livestock enterprises. Cooperative livestock associations have increased from a comparatively small number in 1933 to 53 in 1935 and to 119 in 1936. (Annual Report of Secretary of Interior (1937), p. 213.)

Also see Indian Land Tenure, Economic Status, and Population Trends, Pt. X of the Supplementary Report of the Land Planning Committee to the National Resources Board (1935), pp. 24–25, 56.

[214] The Act of August 15, 1935, 49 Stat. 654, authorizes the loaning of tribal moneys as a capital fund to the Chippewa Indian Cooperative Marketing Association.

[215] Discussed in Memo. Sol. I. D., March 16, 1939.

[216] It has been held that this provision does not require a group of Indians forming an unincorporated or incorporated cooperative association to secure departmental approval of the articles of association and bylaws. Memo. Sol. I. D., March 14, 1938.

[217] Act of June 28, 1934, 48 Stat. 1269, amended Act of June 26, 1936, 49 Stat. 1967, 1976.

[218] Op. Sol. I. D., M.28869, February 13, 1937.

[219] *McCalib, Adm'r* v. *United States*, 83 C. Cls. 79 (1936).

[220] The Treaty of September 26, 1833, with the United Nation of Chippewa, Ottowa, and Potawatamie, Art. 3, 7 Stat. 431, 432, provided for the payment of $100,000 and the supplementary Treaty of September 27, 1833, Art. 7, 7 Stat. 442, provided for an additional sum of $25,000.

[221] Treaty of October 23, 1826, with the Miami Tribe, Art. 5, 7 Stat. 300, 301.

[222] To show satisfaction of claims acknowledged to be due, see Treaty of July 29, 1929, with the United Nation of Chippewa, Ottawa, and Potawatamie Indians, Art. 5, 7 Stat. 320; Treaty of August 1, 1829, with the Winnebaygo Indians, Art. 4, 7 Stat. 323, 324; Treaty of September 15, 1832, with the Winnebago Nation, Art. 8, 7 Stat. 370, 374; payment of debts acknowledged to be due, Treaty of October 26, 1832, with the Shawnoes and Delawares, Art. 3, 7 Stat. 397, 398; also see Treaty of October 16, 1826, with the Potawatamie Tribe, Art. 5, 7 Stat. 295, 296; and (at the request of Indians) Treaties of August 5, 1836, with the Potawattimie Tribe, 7 Stat. 505, and of September 20, 1836, with the Patawattimie Tribe, Art. 4, 7 Stat. 513.

[223] Treaty of February 18, 1833, with the Ottawa Indians, Art. 2, 7 Stat. 420, 421, 422, land was ceded to people who had resided with or been kind to the tribe; Treaty of September 28, 1836, with the Sac and Fox Tribe, Art. 4, 7 Stat. 517, 525, 526, compensation was provided in view of liberality of individuals extending large credit to the chiefs or braves; Treaty of October 15, 1836 (articles of a convention) with the Otoes, Missouries, and others, Art. 4, 7 Stat. 524, 525:

> * * * feeling sensible of the many acts of kindness and liberality manifested towards them, and their respective tribes by their good friends * * * during an intercourse of many years; aware of the heavy losses sustained by them at different times by their liberality in extending large credits to them and their people, which have never been paid, and which (owing to the impoverished situation of their country and their scanty means of living) never can be; are anxious to evince some evidence of gratitude for such benefits and favours, and compensate the said individuals in some measure for their losses. * * *

Often the United States would agree to pay creditors[224] of the Indians for some consideration or partial consideration, such as the cession of land,[225] reduction or omission of annuities,[226] or relinquishment of claims against the United States,[227] or described services and goods.[228]

The names of the creditors were often enumerated in an attached schedule[229] or separate schedule,[230] but sometimes they were listed in the body of the treaty.[231]

Other provisions included an acknowledgment of special services and a provision for their payment. One, for example, provided that money should be paid to a designated captain to repay him for expenditures in defending Chickasaw towns against the invasion of the Creeks.[232]

Sometimes claims already brought against the Indians were acknowledged as due and the United States agreed to make payments for them.[233] Occasional provisions include a prohibition against the payments of debts of individuals[234] or payments for depredations;[235] a requirement that the superintendent shall pay the debts;[236] a prohibition against the sale of land for prior debts.[237]

The limitation of the rights of creditors is in accordance with the well established policy of the Federal Government to protect Indians from their own improvidence.[238]

A number of restrictive statutes hamper creditors from executing on their judgments.[239] An important general provision of this type is contained in the Appropriation Act of June 21, 1906,[240] which amended the General Allotment Act[241] by adding the following:

> No lands acquired under the provisions of this Act shall, in any event, become liable to the satisfaction of any debt contracted prior to the issuing of the final patent in fee therefor.

The same principle is also applicable to restricted money.[242]

The United States cannot restrain the enforcement, in a state court, of claims against property of Indian allottees for which they had received patents in fee,[243] but it can restrain a state receiver from disposing of the proceeds of a lease of restricted lands,[244] and of a growing crop on allotted lands.[245]

In holding that a mortgage by an allottee of growing crops is void, the District Court said:[246]

> The crops growing upon an Indian allotment are a part of the land and are held in trust by the government the same as the allotment itself, at least until the crops are severed from the land. The use and occupancy of these lands by the Indians, together with the crops grown thereon, are a part of the means which the government has employed to carry out its policy of protection, and I am satisfied that a mortgage of any of these means by the Indian, without the consent of the government, is necessarily null and void. If the lien is valid, it carries with it all the incidents of a valid lien, including the right to appoint a receiver to take charge of and garner the crops, if necessary, and the right to send an officer upon the allotment armed with process to seize and sell the crops without the consent and even over the protest of the government and its agents. That this cannot be done does not, in my opinion, admit of question. (P. 332.)

Though an Indian may be a bankrupt, land allotted to him does not pass to a trustee in bankruptcy.[247] This decision is based on the fact that it is not the policy of the Bankruptcy Act to interfere with congressional statutes relating to the disposition and control of property which is set apart for the benefit of the bankrupt, and that a man presumably deals with an Indian with full knowledge of his disability, and does not give credit on his allotments,[248] or his other restricted property.

[224] For early opinions on method of determining amount of claims against Indians, see 5 Op. A. G. 284 (1851) and 572 (1852). Treaty of October 27, 1822, with the Potowatomies, Art. 4, 7 Stat. 399, 401.

[225] Treaty of August 30, 1831 (articles of agreement and convention), with Ottoway Indians, Arts. 2 and 6, 7 Stat. 359, 360–361; Treaty of October 27, 1832, with the Potowatomies, Art. 4, 7 Stat. 399, 401; Act of February 21, 1863, Art. 4, 12 Stat. 658, 659 (Winnebago).

[226] Treaty of May 13, 1833 (articles of agreement), with the Quapaw Indians, Art. 4, 7 Stat. 424, 425–426.

[227] Treaty of January 20, 1825 (articles of a convention), with the Choctaw Nation, Art. 5, 7 Stat. 234, 235; Treaty of October 16, 1826, with the Potawatamie Tribe, Art. 4, 7 Stat. 295, 296; Treaty of October 23, 1826, with the Miami Tribe, Art. 4, 7 Stat. 300, 301.

[228] Treaty of July 23, 1805, with the Chickasaw Nation, Art. 2, 7 Stat. 89, 90; Treaty of February 11, 1828, with the Eel River, or Thorntown party of Miami Indians, Art. 3, 7 Stat. 309, 310; Treaty of March 24, 1832, with the Creek Tribe, Art. 9, 7 Stat. 366, 367.

[229] Treaty of October 11, 1842, with the Sac and Fox Indians, Art. 2, 7 Stat. 596.

[230] Treaty of October 16, 1826, with the Potawatamie, Art. 5, 7 Stat. 295, 296, 297.

[231] Treaty of July 23, 1805, with the Chickasaw Nation, Art. 2, 7 Stat. 89, 90; Treaty of October 19, 1818, with the Chickasaws, Art. 3, 7 Stat. 192, 193; Treaty of February 11, 1828, with the Eel River, or Thorntown party of Miami Indians, Art. 3, 7 Stat. 309, 310.

[232] Treaty of October 19, 1818, with the Chickasaws, Art. 3, 7 Stat. 192, 193. Also see Treaty of July 23, 1805, with the Chickasaw Nation, Art. 2, 7 Stat. 89, 90.

[233] Treaty of July 29, 1829, with the United Nations of Chippewa, Ottowa, and Potawatamie, Art. 5, 7 Stat. 320, 321; Treaty of August 1, 1829, with the Winnebaygo, Art. 4, 7 Stat. 323, 324.

[234] Treaty of October 17, 1855, with the Blackfoot, Art. 15, 11 Stat. 657, 660.

[235] Treaty of November 1, 1837, with the Winnebago Nation, Art. 4, 7 Stat. 544, 545.

[236] Treaty of October 26, 1832, with the Shawnoes and Delawares, Art. 3, 7 Stat. 397, 398.

[237] Act of June 1, 1872, Art. 4, 17 Stat. 213, 214 (Miami).

[238] Knoepfler, Legal Status of American Indian & His Property (1922), 7 Ia. L. B. 232, 245. On creditor's rights against restricted money and estates of allottees, see Chapter 11, sec. 6, and 25 C. F. R. 81.23, 81.46–81.49, 221.1–221.39.

[239] Act of May 2, 1890, 26 Stat. 81, 94 (Indian Territory), discussed in *Crowell v. Young*, 4 Ind. T. 36 (1901), mod. 4 Ind. T. 148 (1902). Also see *In re Grayson*, 3 Ind. T. 497 (1901), concerning foreclosure of mortgage.

[240] 34 Stat. 325, 327.

[241] Act of February 8, 1887, 24 Stat. 388.

[242] See Chapter 5, sec. 5B and D.

[243] *United States v. Parkhurst-Davis Co.*, 176 U. S. 317 (1900).

[244] *United States v. Inaba*, 291 Fed. 416 (D. C. E. D. Wash. 1923). On the right of the United States to sue on behalf of Indians, see Chapter 19, sec. 2A(1).

[245] See *United States v. First Nat. Bank*, 282 Fed. 330 (D. C. E. D. Wash. 1922). On the rights of conveyees of allotted lands, see Chapter 11, sec. 4H.

[246] *Ibid.* For a decision holding invalid a mortgage executed by a tribal member of his interest in the tribal lands, see *United States v. Boylan*, 265 Fed. 165 (C. C. A. 2, 1920).

[247] *In re Russie*, 96 Fed. 609 (D. C. Ore. 1899). See Chapter 11, sec. 4A. State laws relating to assignments for the benefit of creditors were extended to the Indian debtor by the Act of May 2, 1890, 26 Stat. 81 (Indian Territory), discussed in *Robinson & Co. v. Belt*, 187 U. S. 41 (1902), aff'g 100 Fed. 718 (C. C. A. 8, 1900).

[248] *In re Russie*, 96 Fed. 609 (D. C. Ore. 1899).

SECTION 8. THE MEANINGS OF "INCOMPETENCY"

The word "incompetency" has varied applications in many branches of law. Thus a person may be incompetent to serve on a jury, or evidence may be inadmissible as incompetent. Perhaps the most common meaning of the term is lack of capacity to enter into legally binding contracts.[349]

In addition to its ordinary legal meaning, the term "incompetency," as used in Indian law, has several special or restricted meanings, relating to particular types of transactions, such as land alienation.

A. GENERAL LACK OF LEGAL CAPACITY[350]

Treaties and statutes contain numerous illustrations of the ordinary use of the term "incompetency," and various provisions to safeguard the interests of Indians who are deemed unfit to manage their own affairs. They empower guardians or other persons authorized by the Department of the Interior,[351] parents or guardians,[352] heads of families,[353] chiefs,[354] collectors of customs,[355] and agents,[356] and superintendents or other bonded officers of the Indian Service,[357] to select allotments,[358] or homestead entries,[359] receive payments due,[360] appraise property in condemnation proceedings, or perform other functions for minors or persons *non compos mentis*.[361]

Special provisions were often made for minor orphan children,[362] such as making the chiefs responsible for the school attendance of orphan children between 7 and 18 who had no guardians.[363]

Congress has conferred on parents certain rights with respect to the property of minor children.[364] The administrative practice of the Department of the Interior requires that a minor be represented in some cases, such as the relinquishment or inheritance of Indian trust lands.[365]

B. RESTRICTED MEANINGS

(1) Inability to alienate land.[366]—Perhaps the most frequent special use of the term "incompetency" is to describe the status of an Indian incapable of alienating some[367] or all of his real property. Such an Indian may be competent in the ordinary legal sense. An outstanding example is Charles Curtis, who, though he became Senator and Vice President of the United States, remained all his life an incompetent Indian, incapable of disposing of his trust property by deed or devise, without securing the approval of the Secretary of the Interior.

This striking example indicates that a determination of general competency is not always sufficient to cause the Secretary to issue a certificate of competency permitting the Indian to dispose of his restricted property. In determining whether to remove restrictions, the Secretary must decide, not only the "competency" of the Indian, but also whether such removal would be for the best interest of the Indian.[368]

---

[349] See *In re Blochowitz Guardianship*, 135 Neb. 163, 169, 280 N. W. 438, 441 (1938); *In re Mathews*, 174 Cal. 679, 164 Pac. 8 (1917).

[350] See *Stewart* v. *Keyes*, 295 U. S. 403 (1935). Pet. for rehearing den. 296 U. S. 661 (1935).

[351] Act of March 3, 1885, 23 Stat. 340, 341 (Umatilla Reservation).

[352] Treaty of April 28, 1866, with the Choctaws and Chickasaws, Art. 15, 14 Stat. 769, 775; Treaty of July 4, 1866, with the Delawares, Art. 8, 14 Stat. 793, 794; Act of February 13, 1891, Art. 2, 26 Stat. 749, 750, 751 (Sac and Fox).

[353] Act of April 11, 1882, 22 Stat. 42 (Crow); Act of August 7, 1882, sec. 5, 22 Stat. 341, 342 (Omahas).

[354] Act of March 2, 1889, sec. 2, 25 Stat. 1013, 1015 (Peorias and Miamies).

[355] Act of June 10, 1872, sec. 6, 17 Stat. 381, repealed by Act of March 3, 1933, 47 Stat. 1428.

[356] The agents often made selections for orphans, Act of March 2, 1889, sec. 9, 25 Stat. 888, 891 (Sioux); Act of February 23, 1889, Art. 4, 25 Stat. 687, 688 (Shoshones and others).

[357] Act of February 25, 1933, 47 Stat. 907, 25 U. S. C. 14.

[358] Treaty of April 28, 1866, with the Choctaws and Chickasaws, Art. 15, 14 Stat. 769, 775.

[359] Act of June 10, 1872, sec. 6, 17 Stat. 381.

[360] Act of June 10, 1872, sec. 6, 17 Stat. 381. Also see Appropriation Act of July 5, 1862, sec. 6, 12 Stat. 512, 529, R. S. § 2108, 25 U. S. C. 159, providing for payment to persons appointed by Indian councils to receive money due to incompetent or orphan Indians.

[361] Allotments to minors were sometimes not selected until their majority or marriage, Treaty of June 19, 1858, with the Sioux, Art. 1, 12 Stat. 1031; Treaty of June 19, 1858, with the Sioux, Art. 1, 12 Stat. 1037.

[362] Treaty of May 10, 1854, with the Shawnees, Art. 2, 10 Stat. 1053, providing that the selections for incompetents and minor orphans shall be made as near as practical to their friends by some disinterested person appointed by the council and approved by the United States agent. Also see Treaty of January 31, 1855, with the Wyandotts, 10 Stat. 1159; Treaty of August 2, 1855, with the Chippewas, Art. 1, 11 Stat. 633; Act of June 28, 1898, 30 Stat. 495, 513 (Indian Territory); Act of April 11, 1882, 22 Stat. 42 (Crow); Act of August 7, 1882, sec. 5, 22 Stat. 341, 342 (Omaha Tribe). The Act of March 2, 1889, sec. 2, 25 Stat. 1013, 1015 (Peorias and Miamies), empowers the father to make grazing lease not exceeding 3 years for minors; and chiefs, for orphans. No allotment to orphan until 21 or married, Act of February 13, 1891, Art. 8, 26 Stat. 749, 751 (Sac and Fox Nation and Iowa Tribe). Heads of family choose lands for minor children, but agent chooses lands for orphans and persons of unsound mind, Treaty of November 15, 1861, with the Pottawatomies, Art. 2, 12 Stat. 1191, 1192; Treaty of October 18, 1864, with the Chippewas, Art. 3, 14 Stat. 657, 658; Act of February 8, 1887, 24 Stat. 388.

[363] Treaty of September 24, 1857, with the Pawnees, Art. 3, 11 Stat. 729, 730.

[364] See Act of June 28, 1906, sec. 7, 34 Stat. 539, 545 (Osage), which confers on parents of minor members of the tribe the control and use of their lands, together with its proceeds, until the minors reach majority.

Allotments to minor children under sec. 4 of the General Allotment Act, as amended, are made when the parent has settled upon the public lands, is himself entitled to an allotment, and is a recognized member of an Indian tribe or entitled to such recognition according to the tribal laws and usages. 35 L. D. 549 (1907); 40 L. D. 148 (1911); 41 L. D. 626 (1913); 43 L. D. 149 (1914).

An administrative finding that an Indian had reached majority is not conclusive upon a determination of whether a deed of land made by him after the issuance of a patent was subject to a state law permitting disaffirmance of a contract made in infancy. *Dickson* v. *Luck Land Co.*, 242 U. S. 371 (1917).

The rights of minors are discussed in 13 L. D. 318 (1891), 30 L. D. 532, 536 (1901), 35 L. D. 145 (1906), 38 L. D. 422 (1910), and 43 L. D. 125 (1914).

The rights of heirs upon death of allottee before expiration of trust period and before issuance of fee simple patent without having made will, are discussed in 40 L. D. 120 (1911). Also see 38 L. D. 422 (1910); 38 L. D. 427 (1910).

For interpretation of sec. 4 of the General Allotment Act, authorizing the allotment of public lands on behalf of minor children where the parent settled and made his home on public domain, see 40 L. D. 148 (1911); 43 L. D. 125, 128 (1914). This section includes step children and all other children to whom the settler stands *in loco parentis*, 41 L. D. 626 (1913), 43 L. D. 149 (1914), 44 L. D. 520 (1916); who are recognized members of the tribe or entitled to be recognized, 35 L. D. 549 (1907); but orphan children under 18 are not entitled to benefits, 8 L. D. 647 (1889); nor children of parents who are disqualified from benefits, 44 L. D. 188 (1915). For interpretations of other allotment acts affecting minors, see: 15 L. D. 287 (1892); 24 L. D. 511 (1897); 40 L. D. 4, 9 (1911); 43 L. D. 125, 149, 504 (1914).

[365] This practice has been upheld by the courts. *Henkel* v. *United States*, 237 U. S. 43 (1915), aff'g 196 Fed. 345 (C. C. A. 9, 1912).

[366] On restrictions on alienation, see Chapter 11, sec. 4; on leasing, sec. 5 and *Smith* v. *McCullough*, 270 U. S. 456 (1926).

[367] The Act of April 18, 1912, sec. 9, 37 Stat. 86, defined "competent" as used therein to "mean a person to whom a certificate has been issued authorizing alienation of all the lands comprising his allotment, except his homestead."

[368] *Williams* v. *Johnson*, 239 U. S. 414, 418, 419, (1915). While the Secretary may permit the sale of trust lands, he may retain control

An Indian may be declared competent to alienate his land, and then, having become landless, may inherit property in a restricted estate and thus become incompetent again.[369]

An administrative holding analyzes the material difference between the removal of restrictions against alienation and the issuance of a certificate of competency:[370]

> * * * At times and under given circumstances restrictions against alienation as applied to lands allotted to the Indians, savor largely of covenants running with the land. Competency, of course, is a personal attribute or equation. These two, competency and the power to alienate certain lands are not synonymous or even coexistent factors in all cases. Frequently they go hand in hand but not necessarily always so. Congress itself, at times, has lifted restrictions against alienation, in masse, without special regard to the competency of the individual Indian land owners. With respect to the Osages, as previously shown, under the act of 1906, the issuance of a certificate of competency did not remove the restrictions against alienation of the homestead and under other legislation dealing with these people, the Secretary of the Interior is empowered to lift the restrictions against alienation on part or all of their allotted lands including the homesteads even in the hands of incompetent members of the tribe; act of March 3, 1909 (35 Stat. 778); act of May 25, 1918 (40 Stat. 561–579). This but again emphasizes the fact that removal of restrictions against alienation is not synonymous with competency, or the right to a certificate of that character. (Pp. 8–9.)

(*a*) *Statutes.*—The following provision of the Act of May 8, 1906,[371] illustrates this use of the term:

> * * * *Provided*, That the Secretary of the Interior may, in his discretion, and he is hereby authorized, whenever he shall be satisfied that any Indian allottee is competent and capable of managing his or her affairs at any time to cause to be issued to such allottee a patent in fee simple, and thereafter all restrictions as to sale, incumbrance, or taxation of said land shall be removed and said land shall not be liable to the satisfaction of any debt contracted prior to the issuing of such patent: * * *.

The Circuit of Appeals,[372] in construing this provision, said that the Indian "shall have at least sufficient ability, knowledge, experience, and judgment to enable him to conduct the negotiations for the sale of his land and to care for, manage, invest, and dispose of its proceeds with such a reasonable degree of prudence and wisdom as will be likely to prevent him from losing the benefit of his property or its proceeds."

The same court, in another case,[373] said:

> * * * The chief purpose and main object of the restriction upon alienation is not to prevent the incompetent Indian from selling his land for a price too low, but to prevent him from selling it at all, to the end that he shall be prevented from losing, giving away, or squandering its proceeds and thus be left dependent upon the government or upon charity for his support. * * * (P. 776.)

Another important act, illustrating a somewhat similar concept of incompetency is the Act of March 1, 1907,[374] which provides:

> That any noncompetent Indian to whom a patent containing restrictions against alienation has been issued for an allotment of land in severalty, under any law or treaty, or who may have an interest in any allotment by inheritance, may sell or convey all or any part of such allotment or such inherited interest on such terms and conditions and under such rules and regulations as the Secretary of the Interior may prescribe, and the proceeds derived therefrom shall be used for the benefit of the allottee or heir so disposing of his land or interest, under the supervision of the Commissioner of Indian Affairs; * * *

A federal district court[375] in construing this provision at first treated the term "noncompetent" as equivalent to "incompetent," and as implying the ordinary legal meaning of incompetency "legal incapacity, due to nonage, imbecility, or insanity." Upon reconsideration the court thought such restriction of its meaning was too narrow. It also discussed the provisions of section 1 of the Act of June 25, 1910,[376] which authorizes the Secretary of the Interior

> * * * in his discretion to issue a certificate of competency, upon application therefor, to any Indian, or, in case of his death, to his heirs, to whom a patent in fee containing restrictions on alienation has been or may hereafter be issued, and such certificate shall have the effect of removing the restrictions on alienation contained in such patent. (P. 497.)

The court concluded:

> * * * while as applied to Indians the terms "competency" and "noncompetency" or "incompetency" are used in their ordinary legal sense, there is a presumption, conclusive upon the courts, that until the restriction against alienation is removed in the manner provided by law, either through the lapse of time or the positive action of the Secretary of the Interior, the allottee continues to be an "incompetent" Indian, at least in so far as concerns the land to which the restriction relates. (Pp. 497–498.)

Under the 1910 act the determination of competency and the issuance of a patent in fee simple were both conditions precedent to the removal of restrictions on alienation and "the issuance of a patent in fee simple by the Secretary is not mandatory upon his being satisfied that a trust allottee is competent and capable of managing his own affairs."[377]

---

over the investment of the proceeds. *Sunderland* v. *United States*, 266 U. S. 226 (1924), aff'g 287 Fed. 468 (C. C. A. 8, 1923). Also see Chapter 5, sec. 11.

[369] Indian Land Tenure, Economic Status, and Population Trends, Pt. X, of the Supplementary Report of the Land Planning Committee to the National Resources Board (1935), p. 1.

[370] Op. Sol. I. D., M.19190, June 2, 1926.

[371] 34 Stat. 182, 183, 25 U. S. C. 349. For regulations regarding this statute see 25 C. F. R. 241.1–241.2.

[372] *United States* v. *Debell*, 227 Fed. 760, 770 (C. C. A. 8, 1915). This case held that the Secretary may not determine such competency by an arbitrary test, such as the Indian's awareness of the effect of his deeding restricted property, saying, "* * * a person might know he was making a deed to his property, and that after he made and delivered the deed he could not regain his property, and yet be utterly incapable of managing his affairs, the sale of his property, or the care or disposition of the proceeds. * * *." (P. 770.) Also see *Miller* v. *United States*, 57 F. 2d 987 (C. C. A. 10, 1932).

[373] *United States* v. *Debell*, 227 Fed. 775 (C. C. A. 8, 1915).

[374] 34 Stat. 1015, 1018, 25 U. S. C. 405.

[375] *United States* v. *Nez Perce County, Idaho*, 267 Fed. 495, 497 (D. C. D. Idaho 1917).

[376] 36 Stat. 855, 25 U. S. C. 372. For regulations regarding certificates of competency see 25 C. F. R. 241.3–241.7.

[377] *Ex parte Pero*, 99 F. 2d 28, 34 (C. C. A. 7, 1938), cert. den. 306 U. S. 643.

Statutory [378] and administrative [379] distinctions in the determination of competency to alienate freely often hinge on the quantum of the Indian blood of the allottee.[380]

(*b*) *Treaties.*—Many treaties contain special provisions providing for the separation of competent and incompetent Indians.[381] The Treaty of October 18, 1864,[382] between the United States and the Chippewas provides that the agent shall divide the Indians who have selected lands into two classes:

> Those who are intelligent, and have sufficient education, and are qualified by business habits to prudently manage their affairs, shall be set down as "competents," and those who are uneducated, or unqualified in other respects to prudently manage their affairs, or who are of idle, wandering, or dissolute habits, and all orphans, shall be set down as "those not so competent."

The United States agreed to issue fee patents to the competent Indians, but the incompetents could not alienate their land without the consent of the Secretary of the Interior.

(2) Inability to receive or spend funds.—Another special meaning of "incompetency" is inability to control funds, illustrated by the Act of March 2, 1907,[383] which authorizes the Secretary of the Interior to designate any individual Indian belonging to any tribe whom he deems capable of managing his affairs to be apportioned his pro rata shares of tribal funds.[384]

[378] For example the Act of February 27, 1925, 43 Stat. 1008 (Osage), distinguishes between a member of the Osage tribe of more than one-half blood and one with less. Also see Act of March 1, 1907, 34 Stat. 1015, 1034, which removed the restrictions upon alienation of allotments of Chippewas of mixed blood imposed by the General Allotment Act; Act of May 27, 1908, 35 Stat. 312 (Five Civilized Tribes), discussed in *United States* v. *Bartlett*, 235 U. S. 72 (1914), aff'g 203 Fed. 410 (C. C. A. 8, 1913), and *Whitchurch* v. *Crawford*, 92 F. 2d 249 (C. C. A. 10, 1937), aff'g sub nom. *Whitchurch* v. *Burge*, 17 F. Supp. 234 (D. C. Okla. 1936). Act of June 21, 1906, 34 Stat. 325, 353, interpreted in *United States* v. *First National Bank*, 234 U. S. 245 (1914), aff'g 208 Fed. 988 (C. C. A. 8, 1913). Act of June 25, 1910, sec. 1, 36 Stat. 855, 25 U. S. C. 372, interpreted in *United States* v. *Sherburne Mercantile Co.*, 68 F. 2d 155, 156 (C. C. A. 9, 1933).

The courts have justified these distinctions. The court in *United States* v. *Shock*, 187 Fed. 862 (C. C. E. D. Okla. 1911), said:

> * * * The varying degrees of blood most naturally become the lines of demarcation between the different classes, because experience shows that generally speaking the greater percentage of Indian blood a given allottee has, the less capable he is by natural qualification and experience to manage his property. * * * (P. 870.)

Also see *Tiger* v. *Western Investment Co.*, 221 U. S. 286, 306, 308 (1911); *United States* v. *Waller*, 243 U. S. 452, 462 (1917); *United States* v. *Ferguson*, 247 U. S. 175 (1918), aff'g 225 Fed. 974 (C. C. A. 8, 1915); 34 Op. A. G. 275, 281 (1924).

[379] Annual Report of Commissioner of Indian Affairs, p. 3 (1917):

> While ethnologically a preponderance of white blood has not heretofore been a criterion of competency, nor even now is it always a safe standard, it is almost an axiom that an Indian who has a larger proportion of white blood than Indian partakes more of the characteristics of the former than of the latter. In thought and action, so far as the business world is concerned, he approximates more closely to the white blood ancestry.

[380] The determination of competency is often a difficult administrative decision. Leupp, The Indian and His Problem (1910), pp. 67–78. Also see Schmeckebier, The Office of Indian Affairs, Its History, Activities, and Organization (1927), p. 29. During some periods the Indian Service was desirous of declaring Indians competent. Annual Report of the Commissioner of Indian Affairs (1918), pp. 22, 47, id. (1917), p. 11. Congress sometimes authorizes the Secretary of the Interior to appoint a commission to classify the competent and incompetent Indians of an Indian tribe (Crow Act of June 4, 1920, sec. 12, 41 Stat. 751). For further discussion see Chapter 5, sec. 13, and Chapter 12, sec. 2.

The Circuit Court of Appeals in *Cully* v. *Mitchell*, 37 F. 2d 493 (C. C. A. 10, 1930), wrote:

> If Congress were concerned alone with incompetency in fact, some intelligence tests would have been more appropriate, for Indians, like whites, differ in mental stature, and some full-bloods are actually more competent than other half-bloods. (P. 498.)

Also see *United States* v. *First National Bank of Detroit*, 234 U. S. 245 (1914).

[381] Treaty of May 24, 1834, with the Chickasaws, Art. 4, 7 Stat. 450; Treaty of January 31, 1855, with the Wyandotts, Art. 2, 10 Stat. 1159, interpreted in 11 Op. A. G. 197 (1865). Treaty of October 18, 1864, with the Chippewa, Art. 3, 14 Stat. 657, 658. Treaties providing for restrictions on alienation: Treaty of July 16, 1859, with the Swan Creek and Black River Chippewa and the Munsee or Christian Indians, 12 Stat. 1105; Treaty of October 5, 1859, with the Kansas Tribe, Art. 3, 12 Stat. 1111, 1112; Treaty of February 18, 1861, with the Arapahoes and Cheyenne Indians, Art. 3, 12 Stat. 1163, 1164.

[382] 14 Stat. 657, 658.

[383] 34 Stat. 1221.

[384] Another use of the term is to describe the legal incapacity of an Osage to expend his income. See Chapter 23, sec. 12B. *Ex parte Pero*, 99 F. 2d 28, 34 (C. C. A. 7, 1938) cert. den. 306 U. S. 643. Also see *Darks* v. *Ickes*, 69 F. 2d 231 (App. D. C. 1934), *Barnett* v. *United States*, 82 F. 2d 765 (C. C. A. 9, 1936), cert. den. 299 U. S. 546, rehearing den. 299 U. S. 620.

SECTION 9. THE MEANINGS OF "WARDSHIP"

The relationship of guardian and ward, at common law, is a relation under which, typically, the guardian (*a*) has custody of the ward's person and can decide where the ward is to reside, (*b*) is required to educate and maintain the ward, out of the ward's estate, (*c*) is authorized to manage the ward's property, for the benefit of the ward, (*d*) is precluded from profiting at the expense of the ward's estate, or acquiring any interest therein, (*e*) is responsible to the courts and to the ward, at such time as the ward may become *sui juris*, for an accounting with respect to the conduct of the guardianship.[385]

It is clear that this relationship does not exist between the United States and the Indians, although there are important similarities and suggestive parallels between the two relationships. The relationship of the United States to the Indian tribes and their members is analyzed in many other sections and chapters of this work, and it would be futile to treat under the heading of "wardship" the many aspects of that relation which are analyzed elsewhere under more precise topical headings. Rather we shall attempt in the present section to clarify and separate the various questions that have frequently been fused or confused under the term "wardship."

The term "ward" has been applied to Indians in many different senses and the failure to distinguish among these different senses is responsible for a considerable amount of confusion. Today a careful draftsman of statutes will not use the term "ward Indian" or, if he uses the term at all, will expressly define it for the purposes of the statute. The fact remains, however, that the term "ward Indian" has been used in several statutes.[386]

[385] 1 Schouler, Marriage, Divorce, Separation, and Domestic Relations (6th ed., 1921), pt. IV.

[386] See, for example, Act of June 15, 1938, sec. 1, 52 Stat. 696, 25 U. S. C. A. 241, amending R. S. sec. 2139; Act of May 27, 1908, 35 Stat. 312 (Five Civilized Tribes). The Act of February 25, 1933, 47 Stat. 907, 25 U. S. C. 14, refers to Indians "who are recognized wards of the Federal Government," and the Act of February 14, 1920, 41 Stat. 408, 410, 25 U. S. C. 282, refers to "Indian children who are wards of the Government."

a few treaties,[287] and many judicial opinions.[288] It may help us to avoid some of the fallacies that result from a shuffling of the different meanings of the term "wardship" to survey these various meanings. We shall find at least 10 distinct connotations of the term in various contexts.[289]

A. WARDS AS DOMESTIC DEPENDENT NATIONS

Like so many other concepts in Indian law, the idea of "wardship" appears to have been first utilized by Chief Justice Marshall.[290] In fairness to the great Chief Justice, however, it must be said that he used the term with more respect for its accepted legal significance than some of his successors have shown. He did not apply the term "ward" to individual Indians; he applied the term to Indian tribes. He did not say that Indian tribes were wards of the Government but only that the relation to the United States of the Indian tribes within its territorial limits *resembles* that of a ward to his guardian.[291] The Chief Justice hastened to explain this sentence by offering a bill of particulars (pp. 17–18):

> They look to our government for protection; rely upon its kindness and its power; appeal to it for relief to their wants; and address the president as their great father. They and their country are considered by foreign nations, as well as by ourselves, as being so completely under the sovereignty and dominion of the United States, that any attempt to acquire their lands, or to form a political connection with them, would be considered by all as an invasion of our territory and an act of hostility.

The court went on to say (p. 18):

> These considerations go far to support the opinion, that the framers of our constitution had not the Indian tribes in view, when they opened the courts of the Union to controversies between a state or the citizens thereof and foreign states.

The question in the case was whether the Supreme Court had jurisdiction to entertain a suit by the Cherokee Nation against the State of Georgia under that provision of the Constitution (Art. III, sec. 2) which provides for the extension of the federal judicial power "to controversies * * * between a State * * * and foreign States * * *." To that question the following answer was given:

> The Court has bestowed its best attention on this question, and, after mature deliberation, the majority is of opinion, that an Indian tribe or nation within the United States is not a foreign state, in the sense of the constitution; and cannot maintain an action in the courts of the United States. (P. 20.)

[287] Art. 10 of the Treaty of April 1, 1850, with the Wyandots, 9 Stat. 987, which provides that "persons adjudged to be incompetent to take care of their property * * * shall become the wards of the United States * * *."

[288] Often the courts have described specific tribes of Indians as wards. See *Oregon* v. *Hitchcock*, 202 U. S. 60, 70 (1906) (Klamath); *Ex parte Webb*, 225 U. S. 663, 684 (1912) (Five Civilized Tribes); *LaMotte* v. *United States*, 254 U. S. 570, 575 (1921) (Osage); *Jaybird Mining Co.* v. *Weir*, 271 U. S. 609, 612 (1926) (Quapaw); *United States* v. *Candelaria*, 271 U. S. 432, 443 (1926) (Pueblo); *British-American Co.* v. *Board*, 299 U. S. 159, 160 (1936) (Blackfeet).

[289] The number of ways in which these 10 meanings can be combined is two to the tenth power minus one, that is to say, 1,023. It would be obviously impossible to analyze all of these combinations within the confines of this work.

[290] Analogies to the common law concept of wardship may be found in the early Spanish and French recognition that the Indians were not able to deal with the whites on an equal footing and required special governmental protection. See *Choteau* v. *Molony*, 16 How. 203 (1853). Also see *United States* v. *Douglas*, 190 Fed. 482 (C. C. A. 8, 1911), for a theory of the origin of guardianship.

[291] *Cherokee Nation* v. *Georgia*, 5 Pet. 1, 17, 18, 20 (1831).

Thus in its original and most precise signification the term "ward" was applied (*a*) to tribes rather than to individuals, (*b*) as a suggestive analogy rather than as an exact description, and (*c*) to distinguish an Indian tribe from a foreign state.

It should be noted that the basis upon which the Supreme Court applied the concept of wardship was the acceptance of that status, in effect, by the Indian tribes themselves: "They look to our government for protection * * *." For many years after the decision in *Cherokee Nation* v. *Georgia*, the Indian tribes continued to emphasize, in their treaties with the United States, their dependence upon the protection of the Federal Government.[292]

B. WARDS AS TRIBES SUBJECT TO CONGRESSIONAL POWER

By a natural extension of the term, "wardship" came to be commonly used to connote the submission of Indian tribes to congressional legislation. The power of Congress to legislate in matters affecting the Indian tribes was expressly recognized by the tribes themselves in many early treaties.[293] Thus, quite apart from the specific power given by the Constitution to Congress to regulate commerce with the Indian tribes, there came to be recognized, as an outgrowth of the federal treaty-making power and the power of Congress to legislate for the effectuation of treaties, a broad and vaguely defined congressional power over Indian affairs.[294] By virtue of this power, congressional legislation that would have been unconstitutional if applied to non-Indians was held to be constitutional when limited in its application to Indians. In this sense, "wardship" was still a concept applicable primarily to the Indian tribe, rather than to the individual members thereof, since it was the tribe as such that entered into treaties. As with the original meaning of the term "wardship," the justification of the result reached, in this case the extension of congressional power, was found in a course of action to which the Indian tribes themselves had expressly consented.

The effective meaning of the term "wardship," in the sense of special subjection to congressional power, is to be found entirely in the realm of constitutional law. The extent of this constitutional power is a matter dealt with in other chapters. For the present it is enough to note that this power is utilized in two general ways: (1) as a justification for congressional legislation in matters ordinarily within the exclusive control of the states,[295] and (2) as a justification for federal legislation which would be considered "confiscatory" if applied to non-Indians.[296]

In upholding the power of Congress to confer jurisdiction upon the federal courts over certain crimes committed on Indian reservations within a state, the Supreme Court of the United States said:[297]

> * * * These Indian tribes *are* the wards of the nation. They are communities *dependent* on the United States. Dependent largely for their daily food. Dependent for their political rights. They owe no allegiance to the States, and receive from them no protection. Because of the local ill feeling, the people of the States where they are found are often their deadliest enemies. From their

[292] See Chapter 3, sec. 3B(1).

[293] See Chapter 3, sec. 3B(4) and Chapter 5, sec. 2.

[294] See Chapter 5, sec. 2.

[295] See Chapters 5 and 6.

[296] See Chapter 5, sec. 1.

[297] *United States* v. *Kagama*, 118 U. S. 375 (1886); also see *United States* v. *McBratney*, 104 U. S. 621 (1881). See Introduction, footnote 22.

very weakness and helplessness, so largely due to the course of dealing of the Federal Government with them, and the treaties in which it has been promised, there arises the duty of protection, and with it the power. This has always been recognized by the Executive and by Congress, and by this court, whenever the question has arisen. (Pp. 383-384.)

Though state courts have justified the regulation of Indian tribes by the doctrine of state wardship,[298] it is settled that federal guardianship does not terminate with the admission of a state into the Union.[299] Although the power ascribed to wardship is not unlimited and is subject to constitutional restrictions,[300] the practical significance of the wardship concept in these cases is to justify certain types of legislation that would otherwise be held unconstitutional. There is thus not only an important difference but indeed a striking contrast between the use of the wardship concept in relation to Indian tribes and the use of the concept in private law. In private law, a guardian is subject to rigid court control in the administration of the ward's affairs and property. In constitutional law the guardianship relation has generally been invoked as a reason for *relaxing* court control over the action of the "guardian."[301]

C. WARDS AS INDIVIDUALS SUBJECT TO CONGRESSIONAL POWER

When Congress legislates with reference to tribal rights and duties it necessarily affects, indirectly, the rights and duties of the individual members of the tribes. Thus the courts, in holding that Congress had extraordinary powers over Indian tribes as "wards," were indirectly holding that Congress had extensive powers in dealing with the members of such tribes in matters affecting their tribal relations. The courts soon made this logical implication explicit and came to apply the term "wards" to individual Indians, signifying the susceptibility of individual Indians to an extraordinary measure of congressional control in matters affecting their tribal relations.[302]

The use of the concept of wardship to justify a very broad exercise of power is also exemplified by judicial utterances to the effect that state control is superseded because of federal wardship.[303]

D. WARDS AS SUBJECTS OF FEDERAL COURT JURISDICTION

The term "wards of the United States" has been applied to Indians in still a fourth sense, as equivalent to the phrase "subject to the jurisdiction of the federal courts."[304] Certain federal laws are, in terms, applicable only to Indians. By such laws, and by treaties, Indians have been subjected to federal court jurisdiction in many realms where non-Indians are amenable only to courts of the states. It would be foolish to quarrel with this use of the term "wardship" to express a jurisdictional relationship, but it is important to recognize that "wardship" in this sense has no necessary connection with the other senses of the term that have been examined. A group of individuals, whether identified by race or in any other manner, may be subjected to a particular set of laws administered by federal courts, and in this sense they might be considered "wards of the Federal Government." This might be the case even though the extent of constitutional power vested in Congress over the group in question were no greater than the extent of the power which Congress could exercise, but has not exercised, over other groups. Thus the fact that certain individuals are "wards" in the jurisdictional sense does not mean that they must be "wards" in the constitutional sense. Conversely, individuals may be "wards" in the constitutional sense, and yet if Congress has not actually exercised its powers over that group but has allowed them to be dealt with by the states, the individuals concerned would not be "wards" in the sense of "subjects of federal jurisdiction."

E. WARDS AS SUBJECTS OF ADMINISTRATIVE POWER

Still another distinct sense of the term "wardship" involves the concept of administrative power. To say that the United States has certain extraordinary powers over Indians is to say that the President and the Senate, by treaty, and that Congress, by statute, may exercise certain extraordinary powers over the Indians, powers which could not constitutionally be exercised over non-Indians generally, and it is to say that courts and administrators may thereupon enforce such measures. It is however, another thing entirely to say that administrators, in the absence of such laws or treaty provisions, may in their wisdom govern Indians by issuing and enforcing administrative regulations. There is, therefore, an important distinction between the concept of an Indian tribe or an individual Indian as a "ward of the United States" and the concept of an Indian tribe or individual as a "ward of the Interior Department." To identify these concepts is to identify the United States with a particular branch of its government and to assume that the powers of the Interior Department over the Indians, in the absence of treaty or statutory authorization, are as broad as the powers of Congress. The error of this assumption is ob-

---

[298] For a case holding that the New York Indians are under the wardship of New York State, see *George* v. *Pierce*, 85 Misc. 105, 148 N. Y. Supp. 230 (1914). Also see *John* v. *Sabattis*, 69 Me. 478 (1879):

> The wandering and improvident habits of the remnants of Indian tribes within our borders led our legislature at an early period to make them, in a manner, the wards of the state, and especially to take the control and regulate the tenure of their lands. (P. 476.)

and *Moor* v. *Veazie*, 32 Me. 343 (1850), aff'd on other grounds, 55 U. S. 567 (1852):

> By the agreed statement it appears, that the Penobscot tribe of Indians "always have been, and now are under the jurisdiction and guardianship of this State." This tribe cannot, therefore, be one of those referred to in the constitution of the United States. (P. 368.)

Also see Minnesota Laws, 1925, chapter 291, p. 365; 13 Yale L. J. (1904) 250; Rice, The Position of the American Indian in the Law of the United States, 16 J. Comp. Leg. (1934), pp. 78-80, and memorandum filed by the Attorney General of the United States in *United States* v. *Hamilton*, 233 Fed. 685, 686-690 (D. C. W. D. N. Y. 1915).

[299] *United States* v. *Ramsey*, 271 U. S. 467 (1926); *Surplus Trading Co.* v. *Cook*, 281 U. S. 647, 651 (1930).

[300] *Choate* v. *Trapp*, 224 U. S. 665 (1912). Also see Chapter 5 sec. 1.

[301] Consider the significance of the word "although" in the following sentence, referring to the Five Civilized Tribes, taken from the opinion of the Supreme Court in *Ex parte Webb*, 225 U. S. 663 (1912): "Although those tribes had long been treated more liberally than other Indians, they remained none the less wards of the Government, and in all respects subject to its control." (P. 684.)

[302] In *Elk* v. *Wilkins*, 112 U. S. 94, 106 (1884), the Court said:

> * * * But the question whether any Indian tribes, or any members thereof, have become so far advanced in civilization, that they should be let out of a state of pupilage, * * * is a question to be decided by the nation whose wards they are * * *.

5 Op. A. G. 36, 40 (1848):

> * * * The government deals directly not only with the tribe, but with the individuals of the tribe. It exercises a parental or guardian authority over them as a dependent people, in a state of pupilage. * * *

See also *United States* v. *Pelican*, 232 U. S. 442 (1914); 19 Op. A. G. 161, 165 (1888).

[303] *United States* v. *Kagama*, 118 U. S. 375, 383 (1886); *Ward* v. *Love County*, 253 U. S. 17 (1920); but see *United States ex rel. Kennedy* v. *Tyler*, 269 U. S. 13 (1925). On the sharp difference of opinion among Indians on the question of termination of guardianship see Meriam, *op. cit.* pp. 100, 105.

[304] See *United States* v. *Thomas*, 151 U. S. 577, 585 (1894), and see Chapters 5, 6, 18 and 19.

vious and the implications of this error have elsewhere been analyzed.[305]

F. WARDS AS BENEFICIARIES OF A TRUST

The term "ward" has sometimes been loosely used as a synonym for "beneficiary of a trust" or "cestui que trust." Thus when land is held by the United States in trust for an Indian tribe or in trust for an individual or group of individuals, it is sometimes said that this creates a wardship relationship by virtue of which Indians are unable to alienate the land. The futility of this method of argument is shown by the fact that even where no trust relationship is found, and the land of an Indian tribe is vested in fee simple in the tribe itself, the land is nevertheless inalienable (except in certain special cases) by virtue of general federal legislation.[306] There is thus no practical justification for the use of the term "ward" as synonymous with "cestui que trust." Obviously property, real or personal, may be held in trust for a perfectly competent individual who is nobody's ward, and on the other hand perfect title to land or any other property may be vested in a lunatic or a minor whose every act is subject to a guardian's physical and legal control.

G. WARDS AS NONCITIZENS

Occasionally the term "ward Indian" has been used as synonymous with "noncitizen" Indian. This appears to be the case, for instance in the following sentence from the opinion of the Supreme Court (*per* Harlan, *J.*) in the case of *United States* v. *Rickert:*[307]

> * * * It is for the legislative branch of the Government to say when these Indians shall cease to be dependent and assume the responsibilities attaching to citizenship.

The frequent confusion regarding the supposed incompatibility of the terms "wardship" and "citizenship" has already been discussed in this chapter. It has been seen that the extent of congressional power over Indians is not diminished by the grant of citizenship. As was said by the United States Supreme Court in *United States* v. *Waller*.[308]

> * * * The tribal Indians are wards of the Government, and as such under its guardianship. It rests with Congress to determine the time and extent of emancipation. Conferring citizenship is not inconsistent with the continuation of such guardianship, for it has been held that even after the Indians have been made citizens *the relation of guardian and ward for some purposes* may continue. On the other hand, Congress may relieve the Indians from such guardianship and control, in whole or in part, and may, if it sees fit, clothe them with full rights and responsibilities concerning their property or give to them a partial emancipation if it thinks that course better for their protection. *United States* v. *Nice*, 241 U. S. 591, 598, and cases cited. (Pp. 459–460.) [Italics added.]

H. WARDSHIP AND RESTRAINTS ON ALIENATION

The term "ward" has sometimes been applied to an Indian allottee who holds land subject to restraints upon alienation. According to this usage, when the Indian has received a fee patent, or has been adjudged "competent" to manage his own affairs and his property has been released from the protection of the Federal Government, he ceases to be a "ward." The distinction between this use of the term "ward" and the constitutional sense of the term discussed above becomes apparent in the situation in which Congress reimposes a restriction on alienation which has already expired. The individual allottee ceased to be a "ward," in the sense that he was freed from restrictions upon alienation, but the courts say that Congress can reimpose those restrictions because the Indian is a "ward" of the Federal Government.[309] It is obvious that in this situation the term "wardship" is being used in two distinct senses.

I. WARDSHIP AND INEQUALITY OF BARGAINING POWER

Doubtful clauses in treaties or agreements between the United States and Indian tribes have often been resolved by the courts in a nontechnical way, as the Indians would have understood the language and in their favor. The Supreme Court of the United States stated, *per* Justice Matthews, in the case of *Choctaw Nation* v. *United States:*[310]

> The recognized relation between the parties to this controversy, therefore, is that between a superior and an inferior, whereby the latter is placed under the care and control of the former, and which, while it authorizes the adoption on the part of the United States of such policy as their own public interests may dictate, recognizes, on the other hand, such an interpretation of their acts and promises as justice and reason demand in all cases where power is exerted by the strong over those to whom they owe care and protection. (P. 28.)

The principle of construction in favor of the Indians is also applicable to congressional statutes.[311]

---

[305] See Chapter 5, sec. 8. *Cf.* comment of court in *Ex parte Bi-a-lille*, 100 Pac. 450 (Ariz. 1909):

> Indians are not wards of the executive officers, but wards of the United States, acting through executive officers, it is true, but expressing its fostering will by legislation. (P. 451.)

[306] See Chapter 15, sec. 18; Chapter 20, sec. 7.

[307] 188 U. S. 432, 445 (1903).

[308] 243 U. S. 452, 459–60 (1917). In *United States* v. *Nice*, 241 U. S. 591 (1916), the court said:

> Of course, when the Indians are prepared to exercise the privileges and bear the burdens of one *sui juris*, the tribal relation may be dissolved and the national guardianship brought to an end, but it rests with Congress to determine when and how this shall be done, and whether the emancipation shall at first be complete or only partial. Citizenship is not incompatible with tribal existence or continued guardianship, and so may be conferred without completely emancipating the Indians or placing them beyond the reach of congressional regulations adopted for their protection. (P. 598.)

Congress has the exclusive power to determine when guardianship shall terminate. *Tiger* v. *Western Investment Co.*, 221 U. S. 286 315 (1911). Accord: *Surplus Trading Co.* v. *Cook*, 281 U. S. 647, 651, (1930); *Dewey County, S. D.* v. *United States*, 26 F. 2d 434 (C. C. A. 8, 1928), aff'g sub nom. *United States* v. *Dewey County, S. D.*, 14 F. 2d 784 (D. C. S. Dak. 1926), cert. den. 278 U. S. 649 (1928); *Katzenmeyer* v *United States*, 225 Fed. 523 (C. C. A. 7, 1915); *Lone Wolf* v. *Hitchcock*, 187 U. S. 553 (1903). Also see Chapter 5.

[309] *Cf. Brader* v. *James*, 246 U. S. 88 (1918); *Tiger* v. *Western Investment Co.* 221 U. S. 286 (1911).

[310] 119 U. S. 1 (1886), rev'g 21 C. Cls. 59 (1886). Also see Chapter 3, sec. 2; *United States* v. *Seufert Bros. Co.*, 249 U. S. 194 (1919), aff'g sub nom. *United States ex rel. Williams* v. *Seufert Bros. Co.*, 233 Fed. 579 (D. C. Ore. 1916). "* * * there is no rule that the language of Congressional statutes giving rise to a controversy between the Indians and the states should likewise be construed in favor of the Indians." (Brown, The Taxation of Indian Property (1931), 15 Minn. L. Rev., pp. 182, 185, referring to *Goudy* v. *Meath*, 203 U. S. 146 (1906).) Justice Stone, while Attorney General, referred to the judicial "disinclination to invoke technical rules of law to the prejudice of Indian tribes or members thereof * * *." 34 Op. A. G. 302, 304 (1924).

[311] Legislation of Congress is to be construed in the interest of the Indian. *United States* v. *Celestine*, 215 U. S. 278, 290 (1909). *Red*

The Supreme Court has said:[312]

> But in the Government's dealings with the Indians the rule is exactly the contrary. The construction, instead of being strict, is liberal; doubtful expressions, instead of being resolved in favor of the United States, are to be resolved in favor of a weak and defenseless people, who are wards of the nation, and dependent wholly upon its protection and good faith. This rule of construction has been recognized, without exception, for more than a hundred years and has been applied in tax cases. (P. 675.)

The theory also helps to explain the rule of statutory construction, often recited but not always followed, that general acts of Congress do not apply to Indians, if their application would affect the Indians adversely,[313] unless congressional intent to include them is clear.[314]

It should be clear that the use of the terms "guardian" and "ward" in these cases has no necessary connection in the other senses in which the ward concept has been invoked.

J. WARDS AS SUBJECTS OF FEDERAL BOUNTY

The terms "wardship" and "guardianship" have been frequently used to convey the thought that Indians have a racial right to receive rations and other special favors of various sorts from the Federal Government. The error of this notion has been pointed out in other chapters,[315] and the fact that this notion does not logically follow from, or imply, any of the other senses of the terms discussed in the foregoing pages is too clear for argument.

Bird v. *United States*. 203 U. S. 76 (1906); 34 Op. A. G. 439, 444 (1925). *United States* v. *First National Bank*, 234 U. S. 245 (1914), aff'g 208 Fed. 988 (C. C. A. 8, 1913), excludes from this rule statutes having none of the features of an agreement. This decision is critized by R. C. Brown, The Taxation of Indian Property (1931), 15 Minn. L. Rev., pp. 182, 185, fn. 17. It is also a settled rule, the Supreme Court has said, "that as between the whites and the Indians the laws are to be construed most favorably to the latter." *Cherokee Intermarriage Cases*, 203 U. S. 76, 94 (1906).

[312] *Choate* v. *Trapp*, 224 U. S. 665 (1912); quoted with approval in *Blackbird* v. *Commissioner of Internal Revenue*, 38 F. 2d 978 (C. C. A. 10, 1930). Accord: *Gleason* v. *Wood*, 224 U. S. 679 (1912); *English* v. *Richardson, Treasurer of Tulsa County, Oklahoma*, 224 U. S. 680 (1912).

[313] *Ex parte Crow Dog*, 109 U. S. 556 (1883); 12 Op. A. G. 208 (1867). See *Lewellyn* v. *Colonial Trust Co.*, 275 U. S. 232 (1927). *Cf. McCandless* v. *United States ex rel. Diabo*, 25 F. 2d 71 (C. C. A. 3, 1928), aff'g sub nom. *United States ex rel. Diabo* v. *McCandless*, 18 F. 2d 282 (D. C. E. D. Pa. 1927); *United States* v. *Rickert*, 188 U. S. 432 (1903).

[314] *Cherokee Tobacco*, 11 Wall. 616 (1870), aff'g sub nom. *United States* v. *Tobacco Factory*, 28 Fed. Cas. No. 16,528 (D. C. W. D. Ark. 1870); *United States* v. *43 Gallons of Whiskey*, 93 U. S. 188 (1876); 21 Op. A. G. 466 (1897); *Elk* v. *Wilkins*, 112 U. S. 94, 100 (1884).

[315] See especially Chapter 12, sec. 1.

SECTION 10. CIVIL LIBERTIES

The term "civil liberties" has been used in many senses. In this chapter we shall use the term to cover those immunities from governmental interference which are enjoyed by individuals and which are not derived from the ownership of property. The category of "civil liberties" thus defined includes certain subjects which are elsewhere treated in this chapter, such as the rights of citizenship, the right to vote, the right to sue, the right to contract, and the right to hold public office. These rights, of course, are fundamental in the field of civil liberties. There are other rights, however, which are of great importance.

The civil liberties of the Indian are, generally speaking, those liberties which have been conferred constitutionally or otherwise upon all citizens of the United States.[316] The legal problems arising in the defense of Indian civil liberties, however, differ fundamentally from those problems which arise in the defense of the civil liberties of other groups. This is because infringements upon civil liberties are byproducts of Government action and the action of the federal and state governments with respect to Indians constitutes a special, and in many ways peculiar, body of law and administration. In this mass of special legislation and special administration we find a number of civil liberties problems that have not arisen elsewhere in American law.

The principle of government protection of the Indians runs through the course of federal legislation and administration. The line of distinction between protection and oppression is often difficult to draw. What may seem to administrative officials and even to Congress to be a wise measure to protect the Indian against supposed infirmities of his own character, may seem to the Indian concerned a piece of presumptuous and intolerable interference with precious individual rights. These differences in appraising a given measure of government regulation are natural where differences in standards of value exist. In the interaction between two groups with divergent histories, traditions, and ways of life, such differences of value standards are common. They must be continually reckoned with by one who seeks to understand divergent viewpoints in the field of Indian civil liberties.

A. DISCRIMINATION

(1) Discriminatory state laws.—One set of problems in the field of Indian civil liberties arises out of discriminatory state statutes and state constitutional provisions. Laws and constitutional provisions which deprive Indians of their privileges of voting,[317] serving on a jury,[318] or testifying in a lawsuit[319] have already been discussed.

Some states enacted a series of discriminatory and oppressive laws against the Indians. After discussing some of the flagrant laws of this type passed by the early legislature of California,[320] Mr. Goodrich concludes:

> * * * Enough has been said to indicate what the legal status of the Indian was in the California of the fifties and sixties, without touching upon the treatment meted to him outside the law. The legislation affecting him reflects the pioneer spirit, one of whose necessary virtues is ruthlessness toward any element, human or other, which may be thought to endanger the new community. The swift economic development of California was bought at

[316] *In re Sah Quah*, 31 Fed. 327 (D. C. Alaska, 1886), holding that despite custom, slaveholding was illegal after the passage of the Thirteenth Amendment. In *Strauder* v. *West Virginia*, 100 U. S. 303, 306 (1879), the Supreme Court of the United States said that the colored race was entitled to all "the civil rights that the superior race enjoy." The court held in *Yick Wo* v. *Hopkins*, 118 U. S. 356 (1886), that the guarantees of protection of the Fourteenth Amendment extend to all persons within the territorial jurisdiction of the United States, without regard to differences of race, color, or nationality, and that a statute, though impartial on its face, was unconstitutional if "applied" and administered with an evil eye and an unequal hand so as practically to make unjust and illegal discrimination between persons in similar circumstances (p. 374).

[317] See sec. 3, *supra*.

[318] See sec. 6, *supra*.

[319] See sec. 6, *supra*.

[320] Goodrich, The Legal Status of the California Indian (1926), 14 Calif. L. Rev., pp. 83, 91–94; also see pp. 157, 170–176.

> a certain cost of human values. It was the Indian who paid the price.[321] (P. 94.)

Although laws of this type are less frequently passed today than in the early state history, some have never been repealed.[322]

A more recent picture of discrimination is given in the case of *United States* v. *Wright*,[323] dealing with the Eastern Cherokees:

> * * * the state of North Carolina has afforded them few of the privileges of citizenship. It has not furnished them schools, and forbids their attendance upon schools maintained for the white and colored people of the state. It will not receive their unfortunate insane or their deaf, dumb, or blind in state institutions. It makes no provision for their instruction in the arts of agriculture or for the care of their sick or destitute. It supervises their roads; but until comparatively recent years these were maintained by their own labor. * * * Politically they have been subject to the laws of the state, but economically they have been wards of the federal government and cared for as such under the provisions of its laws. (Pp. 304–305.)

(2) **Discriminatory federal laws.**—During much of the history of the United States, the original occupants of the continent were imprisoned on reservations.[324] As late as May 8, 1890, Congress provided that the Spokane Falls and Northern Railway Co. should prohibit the riding by the Indians of the Colville Indian Reservation upon any of its trains unless they were provided with passes signed by the Indian agent.[325]

The statute admitting Utah to statehood[326] illustrates a comprehensive form of discrimination:

> The constitution shall be republican in form, and make no distinction in civil or political rights on account of race or color, except as to Indians not taxed, and not to be repugnant to the Constitution of the United States and the principles of the Declaration of Independence. * * *

Early laws, only recently repealed by the Act of May 21, 1934,[327] hampered freedom of speech, empowered the Commissioner of Indian Affairs to remove from an Indian reservation "detrimental" persons, and sanctioned various measures of military control within the boundaries of the reservations.

A summary of these repealed laws conveys an excellent insight into early congressional disregard of the civil liberties of Indians.

Sections 171, 172, and 173 of the United States Code were derived from the Trade and Intercourse Act.[328] They prohibited the sending or carrying of seditious messages to Indians and correspondence with foreign nations to excite Indians to war.[329] Like many other archaic espionage laws, they were broad, ambiguous, and liable to be applied to situations beyond the contemplation of the Congress,[330] as when the Federal Government arrested an individual who conferred with the Sandia Pueblo in order to join in opposing a Government engineering project in the Pueblo.[331]

Section 219[332] required foreigners[333] entering the Indian country to secure a passport from the Department of the Interior or officer of the United States commanding the nearest military post on the frontiers.

Section 220[334] empowered the superintendent of Indian affairs and the Indian agents and subagents to remove persons illegally in the Indian country and authorized the President to direct the military force to be employed in such removal.

Section 221[335] provided that a person returning after removal from the Indian country would be liable to a penalty of $1,000.

Section 222 authorized the Commissioner of Indian Affairs with the approval of the Secretary of the Interior to remove any person from a reservation whose presence in his judgment may be "detrimental to the peace and welfare of the Indians."[336]

In an opinion of the Solicitor of the Department of the Interior discussing this section, it was said:

> * * * The power of removal under this section has been held to cover not only collectors, but even an alderman of an incorporated town in a Territory. The alderman in that case was not a State official, since the reservation was not then included within a State, but the decision would be equally applicable if he were. *Ex parte Carter* (1903, 76 S. W. 102, 4 I. T. 539). The question of whether the presence of any person in Indian country is detrimental to the welfare of the Indians is one for the Commissioner of Indian Affairs and the Secretary of the Interior, and the courts will not review their decision. *United States* v. *Sturgeon* (1879, Fed. Cas. No. 16,413, D. C. Nev.). See *United States* v. *Mullin* (1895, 71 Fed. 682, 684, D. C. Neb.).[337]

The Attorney General held that the Commissioner and his agents have full discretion to remove from an Indian reservation any person not of the tribe entitled to remain thereon, and that they could not be interfered with by mandamus or injunction of any court.[338]

---

[321] Schmeckebier, in The Office of Indian Affairs: Its History, Activities, and Organization (1927), writes:

> * * * public opinion on the frontier justified practically any action taken by settlers against the Indians, regardless of law or equity. (P. 23.)

The Government was powerless to prevent constant violation of treaty stipulations by the whites; *ibid.*, p. 62. Also see *United States* v. *Kagama*, 118 U. S. 375 (1886), and 19 Op. A. G. 511 (1890). The present attitude towards the Indian is described as follows:

> In the generation that has passed * * * the white neighbors have ceased to be deadly enemies in the physical sense, but in too many places they are deadly enough as regards the Indian's property. It is not true that all communities near the Indian are indifferent to his welfare, but it is an unfortunate fact that the Indian is too often regarded as legitimate prey and that public opinion is indifferent to the wrongs perpetrated upon him. * * * (Schmeckebier *op. cit.* p. 11.)

Also see 9 Op. A. G. 110, 111 (1857).

[322] Considerable discrimination still exists against Indians in several states. Rice, The Position of the American Indian in the Law of the United States (1934), 16 J. Comp. Leg. 78, 79.

[323] 53 F. 2d 300 (C. C. A. 4, 1931).

[324] Kinney, A Continent Lost—A Civilization Won (1937), pp. 168–170, 209, 231, 311, 314.

[325] Sec. 8, 26 Stat. 102, 103. A series of treaties in 1865 restricted the freedom of the Indians to leave the reservation without the written consent of the agent or superintendent. Treaty of August 12, 1865, with the Snake, Art. 3, 14 Stat. 683; Treaty of October 14, 1865, with the Cheyenne and Arrapahoe, Art. 2, 14 Stat. 703, 704; Treaty of October 18, 1865, with the Camanche and Kiowa, Art. 2, 14 Stat. 717, 718.

[326] Act of July 16, 1894, sec. 3, 28 Stat. 107, 108. A similar provision is found in the act providing for the division of Dakota into two states and enabling the people of North Dakota, South Dakota, Montana, and Washington to form constitutions and state governments; Act of February 22, 1889, sec. 4, 25 Stat. 676.

[327] 48 Stat. 787, repealing secs. 171–173, 186, 219–226 of title 25 of U. S. C. Some of these provisions are interpreted in 18 Op. A. G. 855 (1887).

[328] Act of June 30, 1834, 4 Stat. 729, 731. See Chapter 4, secs. 3, 6.

[329] A similar law, Act of January 17, 1800, 2 Stat. 6, expired by its terms (sec. 5) on March 3, 1802.

[330] See *In re Lelah-Puc-Ka-Chee*, 98 Fed. 429, 435 (D. C. N. D. Iowa, 1899).

[331] American Indian Life, Bull. No. 16, American Indian Defense Association, Inc. (1930), pp. 35–36.

[332] Derived from sec. 6 of the Act of June 30, 1834, c. 161, 4 Stat. 729, 730, R. S. § 2134. See Chapter 4, sec. 6.

[333] For the interpretation of "foreigner" see 18 Op. A. G. 555 (1887).

[334] Derived from sec. 10 of the Act of June 30, 1834, c. 161, 4 Stat. 729, 730, R. S. § 2147. See Chapter 4, sec. 6.

[335] Derived from sec. 2 of the Act of August 18, 1856, c. 128, 11 Stat. 65, 80, R. S. § 2148.

[336] Derived from sec. 2 of the Act of June 12, 1858, c. 155, 11 Stat. 329, 332, R. S. § 2149. See Chapter 4, sec. 8.

[337] Op. Sol. I. D., M.27487, July 26, 1933. Also see *Rainbow* v. *Young*, 161 Fed. 835 (C. C. A. 8, 1908).

[338] 20 Op. A. G. 245 (1891).

Sections 223, 224, 225 empowered the President to employ military forces for the enforcement of various laws and in the arrest of absconding Indians.[338a]

Section 226 authorized the marshal in executing process in Indian country to employ a posse comitatus, not exceeding three persons in any of the states respectively, to assist in executing process by arresting and bringing in prisoners from the Indian country.[339]

(3) Oppressive federal administrative action.—Administrative oppression has often infringed on the civil liberties of Indians. The oppression depended upon two main factors: (*a*) The great concentration of power in administrative officials; (*b*) the practice of confining Indian tribes on reservations. Both of these conditions were described by the Court of Claims in the case of *Conners* v. *United States*,[340] involving Indians of the Cheyenne Reservation:

> These Indians, indeed, in 1878 occupied an anomalous position, unknown to the common or the civil law or to any system of municipal law. They were neither citizens nor aliens; they were neither free persons nor slaves; they were the wards of the nation, and yet, on a reservation under a military guard, were little else than prisoners of war while war did not exist. Dull Knife and his daughters could be invited guests at the table of officers and gentlemen, behaving with dignity and propriety, and yet could be confined for life on a reservation which was to them little better than a dungeon, on the mere order of an executive officer.

(*a*) *Concentration of administrative power.*[341]—All persons living in civilized society are subjected to the orders of many public officials and employees, including policemen, tax collectors, judges, and administrative boards, and numerous private agencies and individuals, such as employers, creditors, utility companies, and landlords. Up to a few years ago the 200,000 reservation Indians were subjected to perhaps the greatest concentration of administrative absolutism in our governmental structure. At that time the Indian Bureau, represented by the superintendent, combined, for these Indians, the functions of an employer, landlord, policeman, judge, physician, banker, teacher, relief administrator, and employment agency. According to the report of the Bureau of Municipal Research, "the Indian superintendent is a czar within the territorial jurisdiction prescribed for him. He is ex-officio both guardian and trustee. In both of these capacities he acts while deciding what is needed for the Indian and while disbursing funds."[342]

As early as 1834 the great power of Indian agents was commented upon by the House Committee of Indian Affairs in a report[343] which stated:

> The tribes are placed at too great a distance from the Government to enable them to make their complaints against the arbitrary acts of our agents heard; and it is believed they have had much cause of complaint. Hitherto they have suffered in silence. The agents, being subject to no immediate control, have acted under scarcely any other responsibility than that of accountability for moneys received. Although much is expected from the personal character of the agents, yet it is not deemed safe to depend entirely upon it. (P. 8.)

Since 1884, Indian Service officials and judges chosen and removable by the superintendent of the reservation could arrest, try, and imprison reservation Indians. This system has been subjected to continued criticism by Congressmen, Indians, and Indian welfare societies. Prior to the election of President Franklin D. Roosevelt, several earlier administrations initiated studies to reform this condition but few substantial changes resulted.[344]

On November 27, 1935, the Secretary of the Interior revoked the regulations of the office, in force since 1884,[345] which empowered the superintendent of an Indian reservation to act as judge, jury, prosecuting attorney, police officer, and jailer. A judicial system was established giving the defendants the right to formal charges, jury trial, power to summon witnesses, and the privilege of bail.

John Collier, Commissioner of Indian Affairs, has described the revised Law and Order Regulations in these terms:[346]

> * * * Indian Service Officials are prohibited from controlling, obstructing, or interfering with the functions of the Indian courts. The appointment and removal of Indian judges on those reservations where courts of Indian offenses are now maintained is made subject to confirmation by the Indians of the reservation. Indian defendants will hereafter have the benefit of formal charges, the power to summon witnesses, the privilege of bail, and the right to trial by jury. The offenses for which punishment may be imposed are specifically enumerated, the maximum of 6 months labor or $360 fine being imposed for such offenses as assault and battery, abduction, embezzlement, fraud, forgery, misbranding and bribery. * * *
>
> * * * * *
>
> The revision of law and order regulations is one step in the program of the present administration to eliminate obsolete regulations and bureaucratic procedures governing the conduct of Indians, and to endow the Indian tribes themselves with increased responsibility and freedom in local self-government. * * *
>
> These regulations are subject to modifications in the light of local conditions by each tribe organized under the Indian Reorganization Act.

Administrative control of Indian life, until recently, recognized no right of religious freedom.

Administrators who identified civilization with a particular sect infringed the religious liberty of the Indians and interfered, on the ground of immorality, with many of the dances and other cherished customs of some of the tribes.[347] On January 3, 1934,

---

[338a] Section 223 is derived from secs. 21 and 23 of the Act of June 30, 1834, c. 161, 4 Stat. 729, 732, 733, R. S. § 2141; section 224, from sec. 23 of the same act, R. S. § 2150; and section 225 from sec. 19 of the same act, R. S. § 2151. See Chapter 4, sec. 6.

[339] Derived from sec. 8 of the Act of June 14, 1858, c. 163, 11 Stat. 362, 363, R. S. § 2153. An obsolete provision, which is still unrepealed is sec. 187, 25 U. S. C., which permits the Superintendent of Indian Affairs to suspend a chief or headman of a band or tribe for trespassing on allotments. See Chapter 4, sec. 9.

[340] 33 C. Cls. 317, 323–324 (1898).

[341] See chapter 5, secs. 7–13.

[342] Administration of the Indian Office (Bureau of Municipal Research Publication No. 65) (1915), p. 21. "'All offences,' wrote an Indian agent to the commissioner in September, 1890, 'are punished *as I deem expedient*, and the Indians offer no resistance.'" Thayer, A People Without Law (1891), 68 Atl. Month. 540, 551.

[343] 23d Cong., 1st sess., Repts. of Committees, No. 474, May 20, 1834.

[344] Annual Report of Secretary of the Interior (1936), pp. 165–166.

[345] Slightly modified in 1904. F. S. Cohen, Indian Rights and the Federal Courts (1940), 24 Minn. L. Rev. 145, 153, 194.

[346] Annual Report of Secretary of the Interior (1936), p. 166. For a history of Courts of Indian Offences, see Leupp, The Indian and His Problem (1910), pp. 241–247.

[347] Office of Indian Affairs, Circular No. 1665, April 26, 1921, reads in part:

> The sun-dance, and all other similar dances and so-called religious ceremonies are considered "Indian Offences" under existing regulations, and corrective penalties are provided. I regard such restriction as applicable to any [religious] dance which involves * * * the reckless giving away of property * * * frequent or prolonged periods of celebration * * * in fact any disorderly or plainly excessive performance that promotes superstitious cruelty, licentiousness, idleness, danger to health, and shiftless indifference to family welfare.

In all such instances, the regulations should be enforced. The Supplement to this Circular, February 14, 1923, contained recommendations endorsed by the Commissioner of Indian Affairs, including the following:

> That the Indian dances be limited to one in each month in the daylight hours of one day in the midweek, and at one center in

the employees of the Indian Service were warned against interfering with the religious liberties guaranteed by the Federal Constitution.[348]

Recent statutes, notably the Wheeler-Howard Act, have laid down a policy which is designated to grant greater self-government to the Indians and thus eventually lessen or end the great administrative powers now exercised by the Federal Government over Indians.[349] The monopolistic control of Indians by the Indian Office has been displaced by increased activities in matters affecting the Indians by many federal, state, and county agencies.[350]

(*b*) *Confinement on reservations.*—The great administrative power of the Indian Bureau was sometimes abused or misdirected.[351] One of the objectives of Indian Service policy, for many years, was the segregation of Indians.[352] The location of these settlements was changed as the white man moved westward.

The attitude of the administrators towards the reservation Indians may be gleaned from annual reports and judicial opinions. In *Dobbs v. United States* [353] the Court of Claims characterized Indians on a reservation as "little better than prisoners of war." The same court in the case of *Tully* v. *United States*,[354] said:

> General Ord, in his report for September, 1869 (Messages and Documents War Department, 1, 1869 and 1870, p. 121), in substance says that on taking command of the department he became satisfied that the few settlers and scattered miners of Arizona were the sheep upon which these wolves habitually preyed, and that a temporizing policy would not answer, and so he "encouraged the troops to capture and root out the Apaches by every means and to hunt them as they would wild animals." "This," he says, "they have done with unrelenting vigor, and as a result" he says, "since my last report over 200 have been killed, generally by parties who have trailed them for days and weeks into the mountain recesses, over snows, among gorges and precipices, lying in wait for them by day and following them by night."
>
> In the table appended to this report, pages 127–129, it appears that 66 parties were sent out in search of Indians, traveling over 11,000 miles, and that as a result of these expeditions 207 Indians were killed, 75 wounded, and 65 men, women, and children taken prisoners, while 1 enlisted man was killed or captured and 3 wounded.

The Court of Claims in the case of *Conners* v. *United States et al.*,[355] described another illuminating incident. After telling of the surrender of Dull Knife's band, the last of the Northern Cheyennes to make peace, the court said:

> After a year of sickness, misery, and bitterness in the Indian Territory, and repeated prayers to be taken back to the country where their children could live, 320 of them, in September, 1878, broke away from the reservation. Dull Knife and Little Wolf were the leaders of this escaping party, which consisted of their bands.
>
> They were pursued and overtaken. A parley ensued in which Little Wolf, whom Captain Bourke characterizes as "one of the bravest in fights where all were brave," said, "We do not want to fight you, but we will not go back." The troops instantly fired upon the Cheyennes and a new Indian war began.
>
> That volley was one of the many mistakes, military and civil, which have been the fatality of our Indian administration, for the officer who ordered it thereby instituted an Indian war, and at the same instant turned hostile savages loose upon the unprotected homes of the frontier and their unwarned, unsuspecting inmates. (P. 321.)

After fierce fighting the Cheyenne surrendered and forty-nine men, fifty-one women and forty-eight children were carried as prisoners of war to Fort Robinson.

The court continued:

> * * * Dull Knife and his band were carried to Fort Robinson. There they persistently refused to return to the reservation and were kept in close custody. In January, 1879, orders from the Interior Department arrived at Fort Robinson peremptorily directing the commanding officer to remove them to the reservation. On the 3d of January, 1879, the Indians were told of this, and on the next day gave, through Wild Hog, their spokesman, their unequivocal answer, "We will die, but we will not go back."
>
> The commanding officer apparently shrunk from shooting them down; removing them meant nothing short of that, or of actually carrying each one forcibly to the detested place from which they had escaped. The military authorities therefore resorted to the means for subduing the Cheyennes by which a former generation of animal tamers subdued wild beasts. In the midst of the dreadful winter, with the thermometer 40° below zero, the Indians, including the women and children, were kept for five days and nights without food or fuel, and for three days without water. At the end of that time they broke out of the barracks in which they were confined and

---

> each district; the months of March and April, June, July, and August being excepted.
>
> That none take part in the dances or be present who are under 50 years of age.
>
> That a careful propaganda be undertaken to educate public opinion against the dance. * * *

The religious persecutions caused by these circulars, as well as the Taos persecution, during which the education for the tribal priesthood of the boys of the ancient Pueblo of Taos in New Mexico was forbidden by the Indian Bureau, are discussed in two pamphlets of the American Indian Defense Association, Inc.: The Indian and Religious Freedom (1924), and Even as You Do Unto the Least of These, so You Do Unto Me (1924).

> * * * children enrolled in Government schools were forced to join a Christian sect, to receive instruction in that sect, and to attend its church. On many reservations native ceremonies were flatly forbidden, regardless of their harmless nature. In some cases force was used to make the Indians of a reservation cut their hair short. (The New Day for the Indians, edited by Nash (1938), p. 12.
>
> Official policy in the United States toward the religions of the Indians, through the 70 years preceding 1929, definitely ruled out the concept of liberty of conscience. * * * (7 Indians at Work, No. 8 (April 1940), p. 46.)

[348] Office of Indian Affairs, Circular No. 2970, January 3, 1934.

[349] The new policy and possible dangers in its consummation are described in the Annual Report of the Secretary of the Interior (1936):

> * * * Many of these legislative acts, as provided for in tribal constitutions, require formal approval by the Secretary of the Interior; also, many new and unsolved questions of law and policy have arisen * * *. It will be increasingly important, as organization takes effect among the tribes, that the Indian Office shall devise a new practice in Indian administration. The temptation will be great, on occasion, to make decisions in Washington on matters which, when referred to the Office or the Department for decision, should be returned to the point of origin for local action. With the best intentions in the world, the Office can in effect fasten a blight upon local self-government before it is ever an established fact. (P. 164.)

[350] McCaskill, The Cessation of Monopolistic Control of Indians by the Indian Office, Indians of the United States, contributions by the delegation of the United States First Inter-American Conference on Indian Life, Patzcuaro, Mexico, Office of Indian Affairs (April 1940), p. 69.

[351] Harold L. Ickes wrote in 1929: "There has been no more shameful page in our whole history than our treatment of the American Indians." Federal Senate & Indian Affairs (1930), 24 Ill. L. Rev. 570, 577. The attitude of some public officials and employees is exemplified by the cruel treatment of Indian children at some of the Indian schools; Schmeckebier, *op. cit.*, pp. 71–76. Meriam, The Problem of Indian Administration (1928), pp. 332–333, 779; and such educational policies as the forcible removal of children from their families to distant boarding schools; *id.*, 373–579. See also Chapter 12, sec. 2; Harsha, Law for the Indians (1882), 134 N. A. Rev. 272, 275, and *In re Lelah-Puc-Ka-Chee*, 98 Fed. 429 (D. C. N. D. Iowa, 1899).

[352] See Chapter 2, sec. 2.

[353] 33 C. Cls. 308, 317 (1898).

[354] 32 C. Cls. 1, 13 (1896).

[355] 33 C. Cls. 317 (1898).

rushed forth into the night. The troops pursued, firing upon them as upon enemies in war; those who escaped the sword perished in the storm. Twelve days later the pursuing cavalry came upon the remnant of the band in a ravine 50 miles from Fort Robinson. "The troops encircled the Indians, leaving no possible avenue of escape." The Indians fired on them, killing a lieutenant and two privates. The troops advanced; "the Indians, then without ammunition, rushed in desperation toward the troops with their hunting knives in hand; but before they had advanced many paces a volley was discharged by the troops and all was over." "The bodies of 24 Indians were found in the ravine—17 bucks, 5 squaws, and 2 papooses." Nine prisoners were taken—1 wounded man, and 8 women, 5 of whom were wounded. The officer in command unconsciously wrote the epitaph of the slain in his dispatch announcing the result: "The Cheyennes fought with extraordinary courage and firmness, and refused all terms but death." The final result of the last Cheyenne war was, that of the 320 who broke away in September, 7 wounded Cheyennes were sent back to the reservation. (Pp. 322–323.)

Although there never was any statutory authority for confining Indians on reservations, administrators relied upon the magic solving word "wardship" to justify the assertion of such authority. Thus the statement on "Policy and Administration of Indian Affairs" which appears in the "Report on Indians Taxed and Not Taxed, at the Eleventh Census, 1890" declares:

> The Indian not being considered a citizen of the United States, but a ward of the nation, he can not even leave the reservation without permission.[355a]

It is now recognized that there is no legal authority for confining any Indian within a reservation.

B. REMEDIES

The courts have pointed to two ways in which an Indian may meet injustices directed at him as an Indian. One way is to give up the status that subjects him to oppression: If he is a member of an oppressed tribe, he may give up his citizenship in that tribe. The other way is to attack the oppressive measure itself.

The former alternative is based upon the individual right of expatriation. The latter is based upon the right of a racial minority to be immune from racial discrimination. This latter right our Indian population shares with every other minority group in the United States, and since all the minority groups that have reason to fear discriminatory legislation make up together a great majority of our population, the asserted right to be immune from racial discrimination lies at the heart of our democratic institutions.

(1) The right of expatriation.[356]—Oppression against a racial minority is more terrible than most other forms of oppression, because there is no escape from one's race. The victim of economic oppression may be buoyed up in the struggle by the hope that he can improve his economic status. The victim of religious oppression may embrace the religion of his oppressors. The victim of political oppression may change his political affiliation. But the victim of racial persecution cannot change his race. For these victims there is no sanctuary and no escape.

If special legislation governing Indians refers to a racial group,[357] there is no way in which the individual Indian can avoid the impact of such laws. If, on the other hand, as we have elsewhere suggested,[358] such laws refer primarily to persons having a certain social or political status, then, presumably, the oppressed Indian, by changing that status, can escape the force of such legislation.

This issue never has been squarely before the United States Supreme Court, but the viewpoint here put forward is confirmed by the only statement the Supreme Court has made upon the question, the dictum of the majority opinion in the *Dred Scott Case:*

> * * * if an individual should leave his nation or tribe, and take up his abode among the white population, he would be entitled to all the rights and privileges which would belong to an emigrant from any other foreign people.[359]

There is one federal case which squarely raised the question whether Indians can avoid oppression at the hands of the Federal Government by renouncing their allegiance to their tribe and abandoning the reservation assigned to their use.

The case of *United States ex rel. Standing Bear* v. *Crook*[360] arose out of an attempt of a band of Ponca Indians led by Chief Standing Bear to escape from a reservation in Indian Territory to which they had been removed by the Interior Department. After a few months on their new reservation they succeeded in escaping to Nebraska, where they took up a residence with friendly Omaha Indians. Brigadier General Crook, Commander of the Military Department of the Platte, was ordered to arrest Standing Bear and his followers and to return them to the Ponca Reservation in Indian Territory. Standing Bear managed to secure attorneys, who sued out a writ of habeas corpus against General Crook. The principal ground of the writ was the claim that Standing Bear and his followers had renounced their membership in the Ponca tribe. Since they were no longer members of the tribe, it was argued that neither the Interior Department nor the United States Army could force these Indians to live upon the Ponca Reservation.

The issue of fact was thus formulated by the court, *per* Dundy, *J.*:

> It is claimed upon the one side, and denied upon the other, that the relators had withdrawn and severed, for all time, their connection with the tribe to which they belonged; and upon this point alone was there any testimony produced by either party hereto.[361] (P. 696.)

On the issue of fact the court found as follows:

> Standing Bear, the principal witness, states that out of five hundred and eighty-one Indians who went from the reservation in Dakota to the Indian Territory, one hundred and fifty-eight died within a year or so, and a great proportion of the others were sick and disabled, caused,

[355a] H. R. Misc. Doc. No. 340, 52d Cong., 1st sess., pt. 15 (1894), p. 68.

[356] Expatriation is the voluntary act of changing one's allegiance from one country to another. In Indian law it connotes the giving up of membership in a tribe. On the general subject of expatriation see 3 Moore International Law Digest (1906), pp. 552–735; Hunt, The American Passport (1898), pp. 127–144; Moore, American Diplomacy (1918), c. VII.

[357] The thesis that our law governing Indians is "racial law" is defended by Heinrich Krieger, of the Notgemeinschaft der Deutschen Wissenschaft, in an article, Principles of the Indian Law and the Act of June 18, 1934 (1935), 3 Geo. Wash. L. Rev. 279 (announced as part of a dissertation on "American Racial Law").

[358] See Chapter 14, sec. 1.

[359] *Dred Scott* v. *Sandford*, 19 How. 393, 404 (1856). A tribal council cannot prevent a member from expatriating himself. Memo. Sol. I. D., March 19, 1938.

[360] 25 Fed. Cas. No. 14891 (C. C. Nebr. 1879). See Canfield, The Legal Position of the Indian (1881), 15 Am. L. Rev. 21, 33. *Cf. The New York Indians* v. *United States*, 40 C. Cls. 448, 459 (1905), and *United States* v. *Earl*, 17 Fed. 75 (C. C. Ore. 1883), holding that an Indian who absented himself from the reservation to obtain liquor, did not expatriate himself.

[361] *Ibid.*, p. 696. *United States ex rel. Standing Bear* v. *Crook*, *supra*.

> in a great measure, no doubt, from change of climate; and to save himself and the survivors of his wasted family, and the feeble remnants of his little band of followers, he determined to leave the Indian Territory and return to his old home, where, to use his own language, "he might live and die in peace, and be buried with his fathers." He also states that he informed the agent of their final purpose to leave, never to return, and that he and his followers had finally, fully, and forever severed his and their connection with the Ponca tribe of Indians, and had resolved to disband as a tribe, or band, of Indians, and to cut loose from the government, go to work, become self-sustaining, and adopt the habits and customs of a higher civilization. To accomplish what would seem to be a desirable and laudable purpose, all who were able so to do went to work to earn a living. The Omaha Indians, who speak the same language, and with whom many of the Poncas have long continued to intermarry, gave them employment and ground to cultivate, so as to make them self-sustaining. And it was when at the Omaha reservation, and when thus employed, that they were arrested by order of the government, for the purpose of being taken back to the Indian Territory. They claim to be unable to see the justice, or reason, or wisdom, or necessity, of removing them by force from their own native plains and blood relations to a far-off country, in which they can see little but new-made graves opening for their reception. The land from which they fled in fear has no attractions for them. The love of home and native land was strong enough in the minds of these people to induce them to brave every peril to return and live and die where they had been reared. The bones of the dead son of Standing Bear were not to repose in the land they hoped to be leaving forever, but were carefully preserved and protected, and formed a part of what was to them a melancholy procession homeward. * * * (Pp. 698, 699.)

In view of the foregoing facts the court reached the conclusion that the Indian relators

> * * * did all they could to separate themselves from their tribe and to sever their tribal relations, for the purpose of becoming self-sustaining and living without support from the government. This being so, it presents the question as to whether or not an Indian can withdraw from his tribe, sever his tribal relation therewith, and terminate his allegiance thereto, for the purpose of making an independent living and adopting our own civilization.
>
> If Indian tribes are to be regarded and treated as separate but dependent nations, there can be no serious difficulty about the question. If they are not to be regarded and treated as separate, dependent nations, then no allegiance is owing from an individual Indian to his tribe, and he could, therefore, withdraw therefrom at any time. The question of expatriation has engaged the attention of our government from the time of its very foundation. Many heated discussions have been carried on between our own and foreign governments on this great question, until diplomacy has triumphantly secured the right to every person found within our jurisdiction. This right has always been claimed and admitted by our government, and it is now no longer an open question. It can make but little difference, then, whether we accord to the Indian tribes a national character or not, as in either case I think the individual Indian possesses the clear and God-given right to withdraw from his tribe and forever live away from it, as though it had no further existence. If the right of expatriation was open to doubt in this country down to the year 1868, certainly since that time no sort of question as to the right can now exist. On the 27th of July of that year congress passed an act, now appearing as section 1999 of the Revised Statutes, which declares that: "Whereas, the right of expatriation is a natural and inherent right of all people, indispensable to the enjoyment of the rights of life, liberty, and the pursuit of happiness; and, whereas, in the recognition of this principle the government has freely received emigrants from all nations, and invested them with the rights of citizenship. * * * Therefore, any declaration, instruction, opinion, order, or decision of any officer of the United States which denies, restricts, impairs, or questions the right of expatriation, is declared inconsistent with the fundamental principles of the republic."
>
> This declaration must forever settle the question until it is reopened by other legislation upon the same subject. (P. 699.)

The federal court, in granting a writ of habeas corpus to Standing Bear against General Crook, established a precedent which many Indians since Standing Bear have followed, and which many administrators since General Crook have recognized. In the closing decades of the nineteenth century and down to very recent times, the trend of legislation and of administration with respect to Indian affairs was to decrease the area of tribal land and the authority of tribal councils, to multiply the restrictions upon the use that Indian tribes might make of their remaining property, and to break down tribal governments, tribal customs, and tribal social life. But always one door to freedom was left open: the individual Indian might accept an allotment of land, have the restrictions upon his land tenure removed, adopt "the habits of civilized life," abandon his tribal relations, attain citizenship, and thus achieve freedom from the oppression of Indian Bureau control. This was the way in which the Indian Bureau was to dissolve the Indian problem. The more intolerable the oppression of the Bureau upon the life of the tribe, the more successful was the Bureau in achieving its objective. The year's quota of spiritual refugees from the tribal life was, on each reservation, the criterion of the Indian superintendent's success.[362] It did not matter much that those who grasped at freedom through renunciation of tribal relations and federal property frequently reached their goal broken in spirit and swindled of their lands. To many Indians, as well as to many Indian administrators, this was an advance from serfdom to freedom, from barbarism to civilization.

The right of expatriation established by the Standing Bear case remains a significant human right, even where Indian tribes are actually moving in an organized way toward the ideal of freedom from Indian Bureau supervision. The right of expatriation is an answer not only to federal oppression but to tribal oppression as well. It would be remarkable if the development of Indian self-government failed to give rise to dissatisfied individuals and minority groups who considered their tribal status a misfortune. History shows that nations lose in strength when they seek to prevent such unwilling subjects from renouncing allegiance.

(2) Antidiscrimination statutes and treaties.—Against the somber background of discriminatory state and federal statutes, administrative oppression, and public discrimination, prejudice and unfair treatment, stand treaties, state and federal statutes and administrative rulings prohibiting discrimination against Indians or any races.[363]

Treaties ceding Louisiana, New Mexico, and Alaska to the United States contained guarantees of civil liberties to all the inhabitants of the ceded territory. Later, federal statutes provided for equality of treatment between Indians and whites. Many recent statutes prohibit discrimination against the Indians or against any races.

(a) Federal statutes affecting Indians only.—The Act of March 3, 1855,[364] granting bounty lands to soldiers, provided that Indians shall be granted lands on the same terms as white men. Recent statutes appropriating money or ceding land from a reservation for school purposes, often contain a condition that the

---

[362] See Chapter 2, sec. 2.

[363] On legislative attempts to eliminate racial and religious discrimination, see 39 Col. L. Rev. 986 (1939).

[364] Sec. 7, 10 Stat. 701, 702.

schools shall be available to Indian children on an equality with white children.[365]

(*b*) *Federal statutes affecting all races.*—Civil-rights laws protect Indians as well as other races against various forms of governmental and public discrimination.[366] Some recent laws expressly prohibit discrimination against any races. An excellent illustration is a clause in section 8 of the Act of June 28, 1937,[367] establishing the Civilian Conservation Corps, which provides: " * * * no person shall be excluded on account of race, color, or creed." A frequent provision is a condition in grants of land to the state that its institutions shall be open to all races.[368]

Other statutes which do not contain express guarantees of equality, have been administratively interpreted to prohibit discrimination against Indians. A recent administrative ruling of this kind by the Solicitor of the Department of Agriculture on February 17, 1937, declared unlawful the exclusion of Indians and Indian lands from soil conservation benefit payments.[369]

(*c*) *State statutes affecting all races.*—Over one-third of the states have enacted civil rights statutes prohibiting various kinds of racial discrimination.[370]

(*d*) *Treaties affecting all races.*—The civil liberties of the Indians of the Territories of Louisiana and New Mexico and the Alaskan natives were protected by treaty guarantees until they became citizens.

Article 3 of the Treaty of April 30, 1803,[371] whereby the United States purchased the Territory of Louisiana from the French Republic, provides:

> The inhabitants of the ceded territory shall be incorporated in the Union of the United States, and admitted as soon as possible, according to the principles of the Federal constitution, to the enjoyment of all the rights, advantages and imunities of citizens of the United States; and in the mean time they shall be maintained and protected in the free enjoyment of their liberty, property, and the religion which they profess.

A provision along the same lines is contained in the treaties whereby the Territories of New Mexico[372] and Alaska[373] were ceded to the United States.

(3) **Constitutional protection.**—The right of the Indian to be immune from racial discrimination by Government officials is protected by the Fifth, Fourteenth, and Fifteenth Amendments of the United States Constitution.[374]

Although the Fourteenth and Fifteenth Amendments were primarily passed to protect the Negroes, they have been successfully invoked to protect the civil liberties of other races.

While the reasons for discrimination against Indians include economic competition and ignorance, the exemption of some of the Indians from property taxation perhaps constitutes the most common avowed reason for this discrimination.[375] Obviously this argument is inapplicable to the many Indians who do not possess exempt property.[376]

It is also probably invalid as to other Indians. Until recently state and federal officials were exempt from the income tax of the federal and state governments respectively. The possession of tax-exempt securities has never been considered a justification for denying a wealthy citizen possessing such securities the right to vote.

Another justification for discrimination, the grant of special federal benefits to the Indians, sometimes springs from the erroneous impression that the Government supports most Indians. The majority of the Indian population supports itself and does not receive direct and continuous federal dole.[377] This argument is clearly invalid in so far as it is applied to discrimination against political rights, unless it be applied equally to non-Indian beneficiaries of federal subsidies such as shipowners, farmers, beneficiaries of tariffs, and relief recipients. On the other hand, it may be argued with some force that special Government assistance and facilities rendered tribal Indians may give legal validity to a state law or regulation discriminating against such Indians in the dispensing of similar state benefits and services.

Indians, like other races, are constitutionally protected against legislative or administrative discrimination because of color or race.[378] In a leading early case, *Strauder* v. *West Virginia*,[379] the Supreme Court of the United States, in discussing the Fourteenth Amendment, said:

> * * * The words of the amendment, it is true, are prohibitory, but they contain a necessary implication of a

---

[365] Act of August 21, 1916, 39 Stat. 524 (City of Flandreau, S. D.); Act of May 31, 1918, 40 Stat. 592 (Fort Hall Indian Reservation); Act of January 7, 1919, 40 Stat. 1053; Act of April 1, 1920, 41 Stat. 549 (Blackfeet); Act of June 4, 1920, 41 Stat. 751 (Crow); Act of March 3, 1921, 41 Stat. 1355 (Fort Belknap); Act of May 15, 1930, 46 Stat. 334 (Blackfeet); Act of February 14, 1931, 46 Stat. 1105 (Klamath); Act of February 14, 1931, 46 Stat. 1106 (Fort Peck); Act of June 7, 1935, c. 188, 49 Stat. 327; Act of June 7, 1935, 49 Stat. 330; Act of June 7, 1935, c. 198, 49 Stat. 331; Act of June 7, 1935, c. 199, 49 Stat. 331.

[366] Sec. 1 of the Act of April 20, 1871, 17 Stat. 13, provides for recovery in tort against any person depriving another person of civil rights guaranteed by the Constitution and laws. Other federal statutes protecting civil rights include Act of May 31, 1870, sec. 1, 16 Stat. 140, R. S. § 629, 2004; Act of March 4, 1909, secs. 19–20, 35 Stat. 1088, 1092.

[367] 50 Stat. 319, 320, extended until July 1, 1943, by Act of August 7, 1939, 53 Stat. 1253, 16 U. S. C. 584a. The original law creating a temporary Civilian Conservation Corps contains a similar provision, Act of March 31, 1933, c. 17, sec. 1, 48 Stat. 22, 23.

[368] Act of February 19, 1934, 48 Stat. 353; Act of May 21, 1934, 48 Stat. 786. And *cf.* Act of October 1, 1890, sec. 10, 26 Stat. 655 (Indian Territory), R. S. § 2434.

[369] See Chapter 15, sec. 10, fn. 511.

[370] Colorado: Statutes Annotated (1935), c. 35; Connecticut: Supplement to General Statutes (1935), c. 319, sec. 1676c; General Statutes (Revision of 1930), c. 323, sec. 6065–6066; Illinois: Revised Statutes (1939), c. 38, sec. 125–128; Indiana: Burns Annotated Statutes (1933) sec. 10–901, 10–902; Iowa: Code (1939), c. 602, sec. 13251–13252; Kansas: General Statutes (1935), c. 21, sec. 2424–2425; Louisiana: Dart's General Statutes (1939), title 13, sec. 1070–1073; Massachusetts: Acts and Resolves (1933), c. 117, (1934), c. 138; Michigan: Compiled Laws (1929), sec. 16809–16811; Minnesota: Mason's Minnesota Statutes (1927), c. 55, sec. 7321; Nebraska: Compiled Statutes (1929), c. 23, sec. 101–102; New Jersey: Revised Statutes (1937), title 10, c. 1, sec. 1–9; New York: Thompson's Laws of New York (1939), sec. 40, amended c. 810, Laws of 1939, and sec. 40a, 41 and 42; Ohio: Throckmorton's Ohio Code Annotated (Baldwin's) (1936), sec. 12940–12942; Pennsylvania: Laws of Pennsylvania (1935), Act No. 132; Rhode Island: General Laws (1938), c. 606, sec. 28; Washington: Remington's Revised Statutes (1932), title 14, c. 10, sec. 2686; Wisconsin: Statutes (1937), sec. 340.75.

[371] 8 Stat. 200, 202.

[372] Treaty of Guadalupe Hidalgo, signed February 2, 1848, 9 Stat. 922.

[373] Art. 3, 15 Stat. 539. See Chapter 21, sec. 3, for the text of this article.

[374] F. S. Cohen, Indian Rights and the Federal Courts (1940), 24 Minn. L. Rev. 145, 191.

[375] See Usher, Pan Americanism (1915), p. 296.

[376] It is estimated that approximately 100,000 Indians are totally landless and in many cases homeless. Indian Land Tenure, Economic Status, and Population Trends, Part X of the Supplementary Report of the Land Planning Committee to the National Resources Board (1935), p. 2.

[377] Indian Land Tenure, Economic Status, and Population Trends, Part X of the Supplementary Report of the Land Planning Committee to the National Resources Board (1935), pp. 2, 11.

[378] 45 Yale L. J. 1296 (1936).

[379] 100 U. S. 303 (1879). Also see *Nixon* v. *Herndon*, 273 U. S. 536 (1927); and see sec. 3, *supra*. The Court in *Buchanan* v. *Warley*, 245 U. S. 60 (1917), said that while a principal purpose of the Fourteenth Amendment "was to protect persons of color, the broad language used was deemed sufficient to protect all persons, white and black, against discriminatory legislation by the States. This is now the settled law." (P. 76.)

> positive immunity, or right, most valuable to the colored race,—the right to exemption from unfriendly legislation against them distinctively as colored,—exemption from legal discriminations, implying inferiority in civil society, lessening the security of their enjoyment of the rights which others enjoy, and discriminations which are steps towards reducing them to the condition of a subject race. (Pp. 307–308.) * * * Its aim was against discrimination because of race or color. * * * (P. 310.)

In this case the court held that discrimination by any state agency in selection for jury service because of race is a denial of equal protection of law. The court has subsequently reaffirmed this doctrine in many cases, usually involving a Negro, the most recent being *Norris* v. *Alabama*[380] and *Hale* v. *Kentucky*.[381]

While segregation *per se* is not held to be discriminatory,[382] the facilities offered must be substantially equal. This doctrine was reenunciated in the case of *Missouri ex rel. Gaines* v. *Canada*.[383] The petitioner Gaines, a Negro, was granted a writ of mandamus compelling the board of curators of the University of Missouri to admit him to the law school of the university. The qualifications of Gaines for admission, apart from race, were admitted. In holding that this discrimination constituted a denial of the Negro's constitutional right, Chief Justice Hughes, speaking for the majority of the court, said:

> * * * The basic consideration is * * * what opportunities Missouri itself furnishes to white students and denies to negroes solely upon the ground of color. The admissibility of laws separating the races in the enjoyment of privileges afforded by the State rests wholly upon the equality of the privileges which the laws give to the separated groups within the State. The question here is not of a duty of the State to supply legal training, or of the quality of the training which it does supply, but of its duty when it provides such training to furnish it to the residents of the State upon the basis of an equality of right. By the operation of the laws of Missouri a privilege has been created for white law students which is denied to negroes by reason of their race. The white resident is afforded legal education within the State; the negro resident having the same qualifications is refused it there and must go outside the State to obtain it. That is a denial of the equality of legal right to the enjoyment of the privilege which the State has set up, and the provision for the payment of tuition fees in another State does not remove the discrimination. (Pp. 349–350.)

As in the case of the Negro,[384] one of the principal battlegrounds regarding discrimination against the Indian is exclusion from public schools. The only case which has squarely considered the Indian's right to state education held that the Fourteenth Amendment requires a state to grant equal educational opportunities to persons of the Indian race.[385]

In 1924 admittance to a state public school was sought by Alice Piper, a full-blooded Indian, a citizen of the United States and of California, who had never lived in tribal relations with any tribe of Indians, nor owed or acknowledged allegiance or fealty of any kind to any tribe or "nation" of Indians, nor lived on an Indian reservation. A law of California declared that the governing body of the public school could exclude Indian children from attending, provided the United States Government maintained a school for Indians within the school district. Refused admission, she sought a writ of mandamus to compel the board to admit her. The Supreme Court of California granted the writ and held that the law violated the state and federal constitutions, saying:

> The privilege of receiving an education at the expense of the state is not one belonging to those upon whom it is conferred as citizens of the United States. The federal Constitution does not provide for any general system of education to be conducted and controlled by the national government. It is distinctly a state affair. * * * But the denial to children whose parents, as well as themselves, are citizens of the United States and of this state, admittance to the common schools solely because of color or racial differences without having made provision for their education equal in all respects to that afforded persons of any other race or color, is a violation of the provisions of the Fourteenth Amendment of the Constitution of the United States * * *.[386] (Pp. 928–929.)

The following dicta in the *Piper* case indicate that, as in the case of Negroes, state laws segregating Indian pupils from white pupils are constitutional so long as there is no disparity between the educational advantages offered to both races. The California Supreme Court said:

> The establishment by the state of separate schools for Indians, as provided by the statute, does not offend against either the federal or state Constitutions. Questions of racial differences have arisen in various forms in the several states of the Union and it is now finally settled that it is not in violation of the organic law of the state or nation, under the authority of a statute so providing, to require Indian children or others in whom racial differences exist, to attend separate schools, provided such schools are equal in every substantial respect with those furnished for children of the white race. "Equality, and not identity of privileges and rights, is what is guaranteed to the citizen."[387]

Since the *Piper* case dealt with an Indian who was not a member of any tribe, the scope of the decision is not entirely certain.

Indian children are entitled to state educational benefits financed by federal grants-in-aid with the proviso that there shall be no discrimination against Indian children.[388] A federal statute disposing of Indian lands upon which schools are to be established may provide that Indian children shall be allowed to attend the schools.[389]

---

[380] 294 U. S. 587 (1935).

[381] 303 U. S. 613 (1938). On discrimination in housing, see *Buchanan* v. *Warley*, 245 U. S. 60 (1917), and *Harmon* v. *Tyler*, 273 U. S. 668 (1927). On barring Negroes from party primaries, see *Nixon* v. *Herndon*, 273 U. S. 536 (1927). Also see *Yick Wo* v. *Hopkins*, 118 U. S. 356 (1886) and the *Slaughter-House Cases*, 16 Wall. 36 (1872). On discrimination against voting, see sec. 3, *supra*.

[382] *Plessy* v. *Ferguson*, 163 U. S. 537, 544 (1896); *McCabe* v. *Atchison, T. & S. F. Ry Co.*, 235 U. S. 151, 160 (1914); *Gong Lum* v. *Rice*, 275 U. S. 78, 85, 86 (1927). *Cf. Cumming* v. *Board of Education*, 175 U. S. 528, 544, 545 (1899).

[383] 305 U. S. 337 (1938).

[384] The Courts and the Negro Separate School (1935), 4 Journal of Negro Education, pp. 289 *et seq.*, especially pp. 351–441.

[385] *Piper* v. *Big Pine School Dist. of Inyo County*, 193 Cal. 664, 226 Pac. 926 (1924). For a subsequent law permitting the segregation of Indians, see Cal. School Laws, 1931, Div. III, c. 1, Art. 1, sec. 3.3–3.4, repealed by Act of June 15, 1935; Session Laws 1935, pp. 1562–1563. Also see Delaware Session Laws of 1935, Act of April 15, 1935, p. 700.

[386] *Piper* v. *Big Pine School Dist. of Inyo County*, 193 Cal. 664, 226 Pac. 926, 928–929 (1924). Also see *Crawford* v. *District School Board for School Dist. No. 7*, 68 Ore. 388, 137 Pac. 217, 219 (1913), wherein the court said:

> The facts stated in the amended writ show prima facie that the petitioner's children were entitled to be admitted as pupils of said school district No. 7, and to receive instructions therein in all respects as the white children. They and their parents are citizens of the United States and of the State of Oregon, and reside in said school district. They are not members of any Indian tribe, and they conform to the customs and habits of civilization. These children are half white, and their rights are the same as they would be if they were wholly white.

[387] *Piper* v. *Big Pine School Dist. of Inyo County*, 193 Cal. 664, 226 Pac. 926, 929 (1924). See also *McMillan* v. *School Committee*, 107 N. C. 609, 12 S. E. 330 (1890). For construction of legislative intent in this respect, see *Ammons* v. *School District No. 5*, 7 R. I. 596 (1864).

[388] Act of June 15, 1938, 52 Stat. 685, is typical in this regard.

[389] A typical provision is "*Provided*, That said school shall be conducted for both white and Indian children without discrimination." Act of June 15, 1938, 52 Stat. 685; also see Chapter 12, sec. 2.

Many important prohibitions, including the Bill of Rights[390] of the Federal Constitution, are limitations only on the power of the Federal Government. Other provisions limit the activities of state governments only,[391] or of the federal and state governments,[392] and hence are inapplicable to Indian tribes, which are not creatures of either the federal or state governments.[393]

The provisions of the Federal Constitution protecting personal liberty and property rights do not apply to tribal action.[394] In *Talton* v. *Mayes*,[395] the court held that the Fifth Amendment of the Federal Constitution, requiring indictment by a grand jury in most infamous crimes, does not apply to the acts of a tribal government.

[390] Amendments 1 to 10 inclusive.

[391] Articles 13 and 14.

[392] Amendment 19.

[393] *Talton* v. *Mayes*, 163 U.S. 376 (1896), and *Cf. Patterson* v. *Council of Seneca Nation*, 245 N. Y. 433, 157 N. E. 734 (1927); *Worcester* v. *Georgia*, 6 Pet. 515 (1832); *United States* v. *Kagama*, 118 U. S. 375 (1886); *Turner* v. *United States*, 248 U. S. 354 (1919), aff'g 51 C. Cls. 125 (1916); and *Roff* v. *Burney*, 168 U. S. 218, 222 (1897).

[394] Op. Sol. I. D., M.27810, October 23, 1934; Op. Sol. I. D., M.27810, December 13, 1934. See Chapter 7, sec. 2.

[395] 163 U. S. 376 (1896), discussed in Memo. Sol. I. D., August 8, 1938.

SECTION 11. THE STATUS OF FREEDMEN AND SLAVES

Although a minority race treated as inferiors, some of the members of the southern tribes, especially the plantation owners of mixed breed, possessed slaves.[396] Among some of the tribes, particularly the Choctaws, Chickasaws, and Seminoles, the slaves and freedmen[397] numbered from one-fourth to one-third of the population.[398]

The agents with the Cherokees, Choctaws, Chickasaws, and Creeks went over to the Confederacy.[399] After the Union troops withdrew despite treaty obligations to protect them,[400] their friendship was cultivated by Albert Pike acting for the Confederate State Department because of the strategic importance of the Indian country from a military and economic view.[401] The success of the southern troops in Arkansas aided his diplomacy.[402]

Although many of their members remained loyal to the Union and in consequence suffered great privation,[403] most of the southern tribes supported the Confederacy,[404] largely because of economic considerations.

Influenced by the Emancipation Proclamation, the Cherokee Nation, when severing its connection with the Confederacy, abolished slavery in February of 1863.[405] The exact date when the slaves of other Indians were emancipated is doubtful. Some contend that they were freed by the Emancipation Proclamation prior to the Thirteenth Amendment of the Constitution of the United States,[406] which prohibits slavery within the United States or any place subject to their jurisdiction. Others[407] more accurately point out that the Emancipation Proclamation referred only to the states and did not extend to the Indian Territory. Although it has been suggested that the reasoning in *Elk* v. *Wilkins*[408] and *Jackson* v. *United States*,[409] holding that the Fourteenth Amendment to the United States Constitution did not grant citizenship to the Indians might also be applied in interpreting the Thirteenth Amendment,[410] it is now established that the Thirteenth Amednment freed the slaves of the United States,[411] and its incorporated territories,[412] of African, Indian, or mixed descent.[413]

The year following the adoption of the Fourteenth Amendment and 4 months after the end of the Civil War a convention of the principal southern tribes was held at Fort Smith.[414] Treaties were effected with each of the tribes, which provided for peace and recognized the abolition of slavery.[415]

Treaties containing provisions freeing slaves were also consummated with several northwestern tribes,[416] both before and after the Civil War.

[396] The Act of July 30, 1852, c. 76, 10 Stat. 734, authorized repayment to legal representatives of a general of Georgia for purchasing captured slaves from Creek warriors while these warriors were serving the United States against the Seminole Indians in Florida.

[397] The freedmen were persons of African descent embracing free slaves and their descendants who had been admitted to the rights of citizens *Goat* v. *United States*, 224 U. S. 458 (1912). See Abel, The Slaveholding Indians, vol. 3, p. 260 *et seq.*

[398] Sen. Ex. Doc. No. 71, 41st Cong., 2d sess., vol. 2, p. 3, March 24 1870; *Goat* v. *United States*, 224 U. S. 458, 462 (1912). Reports of the Dawes Commission, p. 13 (1898). The earliest reference to slaves was found in the Treaty of September 17, 1778, with the Delawares, Art. 4, 7 Stat. 13, 14.

[399] Schmeckebier, The Office of Indian Affairs, *op. cit.*, p. 49. The *Chickasaw Freedmen* v. *Choctaw Nation and Chickasaw Nation*, 193 U. S. 115, 124 (1904). Part of the Osage, Quapaw, Seminole, and Shawnee tribes signed treaties of alliance with the Confederacy on October 2 and 4, 1861. The Cherokees signed such a treaty on October 7, 1861, and on October 28, 1861, adopted a declaration of independence Wardwell, Political History of Cherokee Nation (1938), pp. 132–133, 139. Also see Op. Sol. I. D., M.27759, January 22, 1935. For a list of treaties negotiated by the Confederacy with the Indians, see Abel, supra, vol. 1 (1915), pp. 157, 158. Their terms are discussed at pp 158–180. The Confederacy recognized slavery as a legal institution within the Indian country, p. 166.

[400] Abel, vol. 1, *supra*, pp. 14, 266.

[401] *Ibid.*, p. 14.

[402] Schmeckebier, *op. cit.*, p. 49.

[403] *Ibid.* The Cherokees, Creeks, and Seminoles were fairly evenly divided. Abel, vol. 1, *supra*, pp. 265, 266, vol. 3, *supra*, pp. 12, 304–306 Several appropriation acts authorized the President to expend part of the appropriations for the hostile tribes on the loyal members of such tribes, who were driven from their homes during the Civil War. Act of July 5, 1862, 12 Stat. 512, 528; Act of March 3, 1863, sec. 3, 12 Stat. 774, 793.

[404] See *The Chickasaw Freedmen*, *supra*, p. 116.

[405] Treaty of July 19, 1866, with the Cherokee Nation, Art. 9, 14 Stat. 799, 801. However, the large slave owners among the Cherokee Nation did not recognize this law until the fall of the Confederacy. Wardwell, *op. cit.*, pp. 173–174.

[406] Adopted September 3, 1865. *The Chickasaw Freedmen*, *supra*, p. 124. See Abel, vol. 3, *supra*, p. 269.

[407] Abel, vol. 3, *supra*, p. 269.

[408] 112 U. S. 94 (1884).

[409] 34 C. Cls. 441 (1899).

[410] See *Nunn* v. *Hazelrigg*, 216 Fed. 330, 333 (C. C. A. 8, 1914); Thompson, The Constitution & the Courts (1924), p. 556.

[411] *United States* v. *Choctaw Nation*, 38 C. Cls. 558, 566 (1903), aff'd sub nom. *Chickasaw Freedmen*, 193 U. S. 115 (1904). The day before the proclamation of the Thirteenth Amendment, the President approved the Joint Resolution of July 27, 1868, 15 Stat. 264, commissioning General Sherman to reclaim from peonage women and children of the Navajo Indians enslaved in the Indian Territory.

[412] *In re Sah Quah*, 31 Fed. 327 (D. C. Alaska, 1886) in which the court refused to recognize the tribal law of slavery because it contravenes the Federal Constitution.

[413] *Hodges* v. *United States*, 203 U. S. 1 (1906).

[414] Sen. Ex. Doc., No. 71, *supra*.

[415] Treaty of March 21, 1866, with the Seminoles, Art. 2, 14 Stat. 755, 756; Treaty of June 14, 1866, with the Creeks, Art. 2, 14 Stat. 785, 786; Treaty of July 19, 1866, with the Cherokee, Art. 9, 14 Stat. 799, 801.

[416] Treaty of January 22, 1855, with the Dwamish and others, Art. 11, 12 Stat. 927, 929; Treaty of January 26, 1855, with the S'Klallams, Art. 12, 12 Stat. 933, 935; Treaty of August 12, 1865, with the Snakes, Art. 1, 14 Stat. 683.

Even before the war there were many freedmen in the Indian Territory[417] and considerable intermarriage between Negroes and southern Indians.[418] Fearful that the emancipation of the slaves might cause prejudice against them, the United States Commissioners required the adoption of important provisions regarding the freedmen in many of the treaties, which included recognition as citizens, the granting of equal rights with Indians[419] and the right to share in tribal funds and property.[420]

The Court of Claims said:[421]

> * * * It is impossible to find in the history of the Seminoles a trace of hostility towards their slaves or freemen * * *. (P. 464.)
>
> * * * The wife of Osceola, one of their most noted, brave, and celebrated chiefs, was a descendant of a fugitive slave, and it was on account of her recapture as a fugitive that this intrepid half-breed chief waged a cruel and protracted warfare against the whites * * *. (P. 459.)

The court added:

> An examination of the treaties made immediately after the close of the Civil War with the tribes who had entered into treaties with the Confederacy, unmistakably discloses that the predominant purpose and intent of the Government as to preexisting slavery was to protect and care for the freedmen. (P. 466.)

The setting up of the freedmen as worthy of special consideration at a time when the Indians were suffering from economic dislocation[422] caused increased prejudice and among the Choctaws and Chickasaws, a reign of terror.[423]

Until the passage of the Citizenship Act, tribal Indians were unable to become citizens by the regular naturalization laws, but by the Thirteenth Amendment Negroes who were formerly slaves could become citizens in this way.[424]

Other types of statutes distinguished between Indians and freedmen. For example, the prohibition against the execution and sale of improvements on Indian lands contained in the Act of May 2, 1890,[425] is applicable only to improvements owned by Indians by blood and not Indians by adoption or marriage.[426]

---

[417] Abel, vol. 3, *supra*, p. 272.

[418] Abel, vol. 3, *supra*, p. 23, fn. 14. Even before the Civil War some Indians actively opposed slavery. Opposition to slavery was one of the main objectives of the Keetowah Society, secret organization of Cherokees, formed almost a century ago. Memo. Sol. I. D., July 29, 1937.

[419] Cherokee Treaty of July 19, 1866, 14 Stat. 799; Treaty of March 21, 1866, with the Seminole Nation, Art. 2, 14 Stat. 755, 756, interpreted by *Seminole Nation* v. *United States*, 78 C. Cls. 455 (1933).

[420] Treaty of March 21, 1866, with the Seminole Nation, Art. 15, 14 Stat. 755. See Chapter 3, sec. 4I. On the subsequent history of these provisions, see Chapter 23, sec. 4.

[421] *Seminole Nation* v. *United States*, 78 C. Cls. 455 (1933).

[422] Abel, vol. 3, *supra*, pp. 290–292, 295.

[423] *Ibid.* p. 273.

[424] *Cf. United States* v. *Wildcat*, 244 U. S. 111 (1917).

[425] Sec. 31, 26 Stat. 81, 95.

[426] *Hampton* v. *Mays*, 4 Ind. T. 503 (1902).

CHAPTER 9

INDIVIDUAL RIGHTS IN TRIBAL PROPERTY

TABLE OF CONTENTS

SECTION 1. THE NATURE OF INDIVIDUAL RIGHTS IN TRIBAL PROPERTY [1]

The nature of the individual Indian's interest in tribal property presents one of the most difficult problems in the law of Indian property. It is clearly established that where legal or equitable title to real or personal property is vested in the tribe it is not vested in the individual members thereof, and yet these individual members are not entirely without legal or equitable rights in such property. The right of the individual Indian is, in effect, a right of participation similar in some respects to the rights of a stockholder in the property of a corporation.

In analyzing this right of participation, we shall be concerned, in the present chapter, with six questions:

(1) How does the right of participation in tribal property resemble, or differ from, other forms of property right?

(2) How far is this right of participation limited by the character and extent of the tribal property?

(3) Who is entitled to participate in tribal property?

(4) Under what circumstances, if any, is the individual's right of participation transferable?

(5) What rights of *user* may the individual participant exercise while property remains in tribal status?

(6) What rights does the individual enjoy in the *distribution* of tribal property?

We must recognize that just as the nature of rights of participation in corporate property varies among corporations and among various classes of security holders within a single corporation, so the rights of individual Indians in tribal property exhibit a wide range of variation, and depend, in the last analysis, upon the governmental acts and contractual agreements of the Federal Government, the tribe, and the individual Indian himself.

Answers to our questions are to be found primarily in a series of statutes and treaties, nearly all of which deal with particular tribes. The judicial and administrative decisions in this field are, in nearly every case, dependent upon such particular acts and treaties.

Here, even more than in most fields of law, general principles, no matter how confidently announced by the highest authorities, must be pared down to the facts with which they deal before we are entitled to rely upon them.

With this cautionary introduction we turn to our first question: How does the right of participation in tribal property resemble, or differ from, other forms of property right?

The right of participation in tribal property must be distinguished, in the first place, from tenancy in common. This distinction is particularly important because a good deal of the discussion of tribal property in the decided cases invokes such terms as "ownership in common," which is occasionally used to mean "tenancy in common." The distinction between tribal ownership and tenancy in common may be clearly seen if we consider the fractional interest of an Indian in an allotment in heirship status where there are so many heirs that every member of the tribe has a fractional interest, and then consider the interest which the same Indian would have in the same land if the land belonged to the tribe. In the first case, the individual Indian is a tenant in common. He may, under certain circumstances, obtain a partition of the estate. His consent is, generally, necessary to authorize the leasing of the land. His interest in the land is transferable, devisable, and inheritable. In the second case, his interest is legally more indirect, although economically it may be more valuable. He cannot, generally, secure partition of the tribal estate. He can act only as a voter in the leasing of tribal land. His interest in the tribal property is personal and cannot be transferred or inherited, but his heirs, if they are members of the tribe, will participate in the tribal property in their own right.

Observing that the Cherokee lands were held in communal ownership, the Supreme Court, speaking in the case of *The Cherokee Trust Funds* [2] remarks:

> * * * that does not mean that each member had such an interest, as a tenant in common, that he could claim a *pro rata* proportion of the proceeds of sales made of any part of them. (P. 308.)

In the absence of legislation to the contrary, the individual Indian has no right as against the tribe to any specific part of the tribal property.[3] It is often said that the individual has only

[1] On the nature of tribal property see Chapter 15. On individual property see Chapters 10 and 11.

[2] 117 U. S. 288 (1886).

[3] *Delaware Indians* v. *Cherokee Nation*, 193 U. S. 127 (1904); *United States* v. *Chase*, 245 U. S. 89 (1917). See *McDougal* v. *McKay*, 237 U. S. 372 (1915); *Shulthis* v. *McDougal*, 170 Fed. 529 (C. C. A. 8, 1909), app. dism. 225 U. S. 561 (1912).

a "prospective right" [4] to future income from tribal property in which he has no present interest.[5] Other terms used to picture this right are "an inchoate interest," [6] and a "float." [7] These terms aptly characterize the intangible right of the Indian to share in tribal property. Until the property loses its tribal character and becomes individualized, his right can be no more than this, except insofar as federal law, tribal law, or tribal custom may give him a more definite right of occupancy in a particular tract. In the case of tribal funds, he has, ordinarily, no vested right in them until they have been paid over to him or have been set over to his credit, perhaps subject to certain restrictions.[8] In the case of lands, he has no vested right unless the land or some designated interest therein has been set aside for him either severally or as tenant in common.[9]

The statement has often been made that the tribe holds its property in trust for its members.[10] This statement may be compared with the assertion frequently made that corporate property is held in trust for the stockholders, though, strictly speaking, no technical trust relationship exists in either case.

In speaking of the title to the lands of the Creek Nation, the court in *Shulthis* v. *McDougal*,[11] declared:

> The tribal lands belonged to the tribe. The legal title stood in the tribe as a political society; but those lands were not held by the tribe as the public lands of the United States are held by the nation. They constituted the home or seat of the tribe. Every member, by virtue of his membership in the tribe, was entitled to dwell upon and share in the tribal property. It was granted to the tribe by the federal government not only as the home of the tribe, but as a home for each of the members.[12]

Indian lands were generally looked upon as a permanent home for the Indians. "Considered as such, * * * it was not unnatural or unequal that the vast body of lands not thus specifically and personally appropriated should be treated as the common property of the Nation * * *." [13]

That tribal property should be held in common for the benefit of the members of the Indian community as a whole was, according to the Supreme Court in the case of *Woodward* v. *de Graffenried*, the principle upon which conveyances of land to the Five Civilized Tribes were made.[14] Treaties often provided that the land conveyed to the tribe was to be held in common.[15]

Likewise certain statutes specify that tribal lands are to be held or occupied in common.[16]

Indian tribal laws and customs led governments dealing with Indian lands to adopt the theory that tribal property was held for the common benefit of all.[17] The constitution of the Cherokee Nation, both as originally adopted in 1839 and as amended in 1866, declared in section 2, article 1, that the lands of the Cherokee Nation were to remain the common property of the tribe.[18]

In the case of *United States* v. *Charles*,[19] the court, in referring to the lands occupied by the Tonawanda Band of Seneca Indians, stated, "The reservation lands are held in common by the tribe, although individual members of the tribe may be in possession of a particular tract, and such possession is recognized by the tribe." (P. 348.) Many tribal constitutions, adopted under the Wheeler-Howard Act,[20] provide that all lands hitherto unallotted shall be held in the future as tribal property.[21]

Although tribal property is vested in the tribe as an entity, rather than in the individual members thereof, each member of the tribe may have an interest in the property.

The nature of the individual member's right in tribal property is discussed in *Seufert Bros. Co.* v. *United States*.[22] The court quotes the words of an Indian witness who compared a river in which there was a common right to fish to a "great table where all the Indians came to partake." (P. 197.)

In the case of *Mason* v. *Sams*, the Treaty of 1855 between the United States and the Quinaielts [23] is discussed. By the terms of article two of the treaty, a tract of land was to be "reserved for the use and occupation of the tribes * * * and set apart for their exclusive use." The court construed the treaty to give the Indians an exclusive right of fishing in the waters on these lands; the right to fish being enjoyed by all members, even though the treaty was made with the tribe.[24]

---

[4] Op. Sol. I. D., M.8370, August 15, 1922.

[5] *Taylor* v. *Tayrien*, 51 F. 2d 884 (C. C. A. 10, 1931), cert. den. 284 U. S. 672 (1931). This case involved individual rights in Osage tribal minerals. For a discussion of special laws governing Osage tribe see Chapter 23, sec. 12.

[6] *Taylor* v. *Tayrien*, 51 F. 2d 884 (C. C. A. 10, 1931), cert. den. 284 U. S. 672 (1931).

[7] *McKee* v. *Henry*, 201 Fed. 74 (C. C. A. 8, 1912); *Woodbury* v. *United States*, 170 Fed. 302 (C. C. A. 8, 1909). The cases involved rights of an enrollee before allotments had been made. In an opinion involving back annuity payments, the Solicitor of the Department of the Interior wrote: "The members of a tribe have an inherent interest in the tribal lands and funds but until segregated by allotment or payment in severalty they remain the common property of the tribe." Op. Sol. I. D., D. 42071, December 29, 1921.

[8] Funds due Osage as share in royalties and proceeds from sale of land, not his until actually paid to him or placed to his credit—Op. Sol. I. D., M.8370, August 15, 1922. See Chapter 23, sec. 12B. So long as a judgment in favor of a tribe is not prorated among individual members, no present or former member has a vested right—Letter of Commissioner of Indian Affairs to Indian Agents, October 9, 1937.

[9] *Gritts* v. *Fisher*, 224 U. S. 640 (1912); *St. Marie* v. *United States*, 24 F. Supp. 237 (D. C. S. D. Cal. 1938), aff'd — F. 2d — (C. C. A. 10, 1940); 56 I. D. 102 (1937); *McKee* v. *Henry*, 201 Fed. 74 (C. C. A. 8, 1912).

[10] *L'gon* v. *Johnston*, 164 Fed. 670 (C. C. A. 8, 1908), app. dism. 223 U. S. 741; *Cherokee Nation* v. *Hitchcock*, 187 U. S. 294 (1902).

[11] 170 Fed. 529, 533 (C. C. A. 8, 1909), aff'd 225 U. S. 561 (1912).

[12] Also see *W. O. Whitney Lumber & Grain Co.* v. *Crabtree*, 166 Fed. 738 (C. C. A. 8, 1908). Title to Creek lands were in nation; occupants had no more than possessory rights.

[13] *Cherokee Nation* v. *Journeycake*, 155 U. S. 196, 215 (1894).

[14] 238 U S. 284 (1915). Accord: *Heckman* v. *United States*, 224 U. S. 413 (1912), modify'g and aff'g sub nom. *United States* v. *Allen*, 179 Fed. 13 (C. C. A. 8, 1910). See *Shulthis* v. *McDougal*, 170 Fed. 529 (C. C. A. 8, 1909), app. dism. 225 U. S. 561 (1912).

[15] See, for example: Treaty of December 29, 1832, with the United Nation of the Senecas and Shawnee Indians, 7 Stat. 411; Treaty of May 30, 1854, with the United Tribes of Kaskaskia and Peoria, Piankeshaw, and Wea Indians, 10 Stat. 1082; Treaty of June 22, 1855, with Choctaws and Chickasaws, 11 Stat. 611; Treaty of August 6, 1846, with Cherokee, 9 Stat. 871, discussed in *The Cherokee Trust Funds*, 117 U. S. 288 (1886), and *United States* v. *Cherokee Nation*, 202 U. S. 101 (1906).

[16] See, for example, Joint Resolution, June 19, 1902, 32 Stat. 744 (Walker River, Uintah, and White River Utes). Various allotment statutes reserve from allotment lands to be held "in common," specifying occasionally for the reservation of grazing or timber lands, lands containing springs, etc. See, for example: Act of March 3, 1885, 23 Stat. 340 (Umatilla Reservation); Act of March 2, 1889, 25 Stat. 1013 (United Peorias and Miamies); Act of June 3, 1926, 44 Stat. 690 (Northern Cheyenne Indian Reservation). See, also, Chapter 15.

[17] See *Mitchel* v. *United States*, 9 Pet. 711, 746 (1835).

[18] Cited and discussed in *Cherokee Intermarriage Cases*, 203 U. S. 76 (1906), and in *The Cherokee Trust Funds*, 117 U. S. 288 (1886).

[19] 23 F. Supp. 346, 348 (D. C. W. D. N. Y. 1938).

[20] Act of June 18, 1934, 48 Stat. 984, 25 U. S. C. 461, *et seq.*

[21] *E. g.*, Art. 8, sec. 2, of the Constitution and Bylaws for the Shoshone-Bannock Tribes of the Fort Hall Reservation, Idaho, approved Apr'l 30, 1936.

[22] 249 U. S. 194 (1919), aff'g sub nom. *United States ex rel. Williams* v. *Seufert Bros. Co.*, 233 Fed. 579 (D. C. Ore. 1916).

[23] 12 Stat. 971.

[24] 5 F. 2d 255 (D. C. W. D. Wash. 1925). Accord: *Halbert* v. *United States*, 283 U. S. 753 (1931), rev'g sub nom. *United States* v. *Halbert*, 38 F. 2d 795 (C. C. A. 9, 1930).

Where certain lands have been reserved for the use and occupation of a tribe, members of the tribe are entitled to use bodies of navigable water within the reservation.[25]

In all these cases, the individual enjoys a right of user derived from the legal or equitable property right of the tribe in which he is a member.[26]

[25] Op. Sol. I. D., M.24358, May 14, 1928. *Cf. United States* v. *Powers*, 305 U. S. 527 (1939), aff'g 94 F. 2d 783 (C. C. A. 9, 1938), and modify'g 16 F. Supp. 155 (D. C. Mont. 1936), holding that under the Treaty of May 7, 1868, with the Crow Indians, 15 Stat. 649, the waters within the reservation were reserved for the equal benefit of tribal members and when allotments of these lands were made, the right to use the waters passed to the allottees. See also *Skeem* v. *United States*, 273 Fed. 93 (C. C. A. 9, 1921), holding that the members of the Shoshone Tribe who occupied tribal lands under Art. 6 of the Fort Bridger Treaty, July 3, 1868, 15 Stat. 673, and who were awarded allotments of these lands under Art. 8 of the agreement ratified by Act of June 6, 1900, 31 Stat. 672, were entitled to the water rights.

[26] See sec. 5, *infra*.

SECTION 2. DEPENDENCY OF INDIVIDUAL RIGHTS UPON EXTENT OF TRIBAL PROPERTY

The individual Indian claiming a share in tribal assets is subject to the general rule that he can obtain no greater interest than that possessed by the tribe in whose assets he participates.[27] The use that an individual Indian may make of tribal lands is limited by the nature of the estate in the land held by the tribe. Thus in the case of *United States* v. *Chase*,[28] the court held that where the Omaha tribe held only a right of occupancy in certain lands, with the fee remaining in the United States, the tribe could not convey more than its right of occupancy to a member without the consent of the United States.

Viewed in this fashion, an allotment system or any act or treaty which extinguishes tribal title decreases to that extent the quantity of tribal property in which the individual may share.[29]

In the case of *The Cherokee Trust Funds*,[30] the court said,

> Their [Cherokee Nation] treaties of cession must, therefore, be held not only to convey the common property of the Nation, but to divest the interest therein of each of its members. (P. 308.)

The individual's rights in tribal property are affected by any set-offs or claims against the tribe, because the amount of his share that he would otherwise be entitled to is decreased.

[27] "The right of the individual member in tribal land is derived from and is no greater than the right of the tribe itself." If the tribe cannot make a lease without the approval of the Department of the Interior, neither can the individual. Memo. Sol. I. D., October 21, 1938.

[28] 245 U. S. 89 (1917), rev'g 222 Fed. 593 (C. C. A. 8, 1915).

[29] For examples of this fact situation see: *Moore* v. *Carter Oil Co.*, 43 F. 2d 322 (C. C. A. 10, 1930), cert. den. 282 U. S. 903; *United States* v. *Ft. Smith & W. R. Co.*, 195 Fed. 211 (C. C. A. 8, 1912); *Choate* v. *Trapp*, 224 U. S. 665 (1912); *The Kansas Indians*, 5 Wall. 737 (1866).

[30] 117 U. S. 288 (1886).

SECTION 3. ELIGIBILITY TO SHARE IN TRIBAL PROPERTY

Originally the only requisite to share in tribal property was membership.[31] Abandonment or loss of membership forfeited the right to share.[32] Acquisition of membership ordinarily carried with it the right to share in tribal property.[33] The question of what constitutes tribal membership is discussed elsewhere.[34]

Under the rule that membership was necessary to share in tribal property, the right to participate in the distribution could not pass to the member's heirs, nor could it be assigned by the member.[35] The children of a member could not inherit their parent's right to share. Their only right to share in the distribution of tribal property came from being members themselves. However, had their parent's right to participate in the distribution of tribal assets attached itself to certain property in which he had a vested right, his children might inherit this property.[36] But as soon as the member's right had vested, the property was no longer tribal property. It had become individualized; it was individual property and not tribal property that was being passed on by descent.[37]

Although originally the right to participate in tribal property was coextensive with tribal membership, this rule has been modified by various congressional enactments. On the one hand, the

[31] *Halbert* v. *United States*, 283 U. S. 753 (1931), rev'g sub nom. *United States* v. *Halbert*, 38 F. 2d 795 (C. C. A. 9, 1930); *Tiger* v. *Fewell*, 22 F. 2d 786 (C. C. A. 8, 1927); *La Roque* v. *United States*, 239 U. S. 62 (1915), aff'g 198 Fed. 645 (C. C. A. 8, 1912); *Sizemore* v. *Brady*, 235 U. S. 441 (1914); *Gritts* v. *Fisher*, 224 U. S. 640 (1912); *Oakes* v. *United States*, 172 Fed. 305 (C. C. A. 8, 1909); *Fleming* v. *McCurtain*, 215 U. S. 56 (1909); *Cherokee Nation* v. *Hitchcock*, 187 U. S. 294 (1902); Op. Sol. I. D., M.15954, January 8, 1927. For regulations governing pro-rata shares of tribal funds, see 25 C. F. R. 233.1–233.7; for regulations governing annuity and other per capita payments, see 25 C. F. R. 224.1–224.5.

[32] See Memo. Sol. I. D., March 19, 1938 (Cheyenne River Sioux). In the case of *The Cherokee Trust Funds*, 117 U. S. 288 (1886), in which the Court denied the right of those who had remained East and abandoned their membership, to share in proceeds arising from sale of lands of Cherokee Nation, the Court stated:

> If Indians * * * wish to enjoy the benefits of the common property of the Cherokee Nation, in whatever form it may exist, they must * * * be readmitted to citizenship * * *. They cannot live out of its Territory, evade the obligations and burdens of citizenship, and at the same time enjoy the benefits of the funds and common property of the Nation. (P. 311.)

[33] In the case of *Cherokee Nation* v. *Journeycake*, 155 U. S. 196 (1894), the Supreme Court discussed the rights of the Delaware Indians to share in the property rights of the Cherokee Nation, under the contract entered into between the Delawares and the Cherokees on April 8, 1867, in pursuance of a treaty entered into between the United States and the Cherokee Nation, July 19, 1866 (14 Stat. 799, 803). The court decided:

> Given therefore, the two propositions that the lands are the common property of the Cherokee Nation, and that the registered Delawares have become incorporated into the Cherokee Nation and are members and citizens thereof, it follows necessarily that they are equally with the native Cherokees the owners of and entitled to share in the profits and proceeds of these lands. (Pp. 210–211.)

See also *Cherokee Intermarriage Cases*, 203 U. S. 76 (1906), and *Delaware Indians* v. *Cherokee Nation*, 193 U. S. 127 (1904), for a discussion of the rights of the Delawares in Cherokee property.

In the case of the *Cherokee Nation* v. *Blackfeather*, 155 U. S. 218 (1894), the court applied the rule of the *Journeycake* case to the Shawnees who were admitted to the Cherokee Nation.

[34] See Chapters 1, 5, 7.

[35] *Gritts* v. *Fisher*, 224 U. S. 640, 642 (1912); *La Roque* v. *United States*, 239 U. S. 62 (1915).

[36] See Op. Sol. I. D., D42071, December 29, 1921.

[37] Op. Sol. I. D., M.15954, January 8, 1927; Op. Sol. I. D., M.13270, November 6, 1924; Op. Sol. I. D., M.27381, December 13, 1934.

right to share in tribal property has been denied to certain special classes of tribal members. On the other hand, the right to share in tribal property has been extended to various classes of nonmembers.

The most important class of members excluded from the right to share in tribal property comprised white men marrying Indian women who, under special tribal laws, were admitted to tribal membership or "citizenship," but were not, in many cases, given any rights at all in tribal property.

The problem created by the claims of those people is discussed in the *Cherokee Intermarriage Cases*.[38] The court traces the policy of the United States and the tribal government to keep tribal property from coming into the hands of whites who married Indians solely for the purpose of sharing in the tribal wealth.[39]

The policy of the United States toward the rights of non-Indians who claimed rights because of intermarriage is indicated by the Act of August 9, 1888,[40] which, excluding the Five Civilized Tribes from its scope, provided:

> * * * no white man, not otherwise a member of any tribe of Indians, who may hereafter marry, an Indian woman, member of any Indian tribe * * * shall by such marriage hereafter acquire any right in any tribal property, privilege, or interest whatever to which any member of such tribe is entitled.

An analogous problem arose when the slaves residing in the Indian Territory were granted freedom and citizenship by the Emancipation Proclamation and the Thirteenth Amendment to the United States Constitution. The rights of these "freedmen" in tribal property are elsewhere discussed.[41]

As already noted, the original rule was that existing membership was the requisite for sharing in tribal property. But the beginning of the allotment system, and the policy of encouraging the abandonment of tribal relations led to the modification of this rule.[42]

In order to persuade Indians to forsake tribal habits and adopt the white man's civilization, various acts[43] were passed and treaties[44] adopted, guaranteeing to those Indians who complied with this policy the same rights to share in tribal property, as if they had remained with the tribe.[45] Four of these acts, general in their terms, deserve special mention:

(1) The Act of March 3, 1875,[46] applying to Indians who had abandoned or who should thereafter abandon their tribal relations to settle under federal homestead laws,[47] declares:

> That any such Indian shall be entitled to his distributive share of * * * tribal funds, lands, and other property, the same as though he had maintained his tribal relations * * *.[48]

However, where specially provided, such as in the Act of February 6, 1871,[49] Indians who wished to leave the tribe and at the same time receive certain lands as their allotments, had to relinquish their rights to share in any further distribution of tribal assets. The Treaty of November 15, 1861,[50] with the Pottawatomie Nation, discussed in *Goodfellow* v. *Muckey*,[51] provided that those of the tribe who had adopted the customs of the whites and who were willing to abandon all claims to the common lands and funds would have lands allotted to them in severalty.

(2) Section 6[52] of the Act of February 8, 1887,[53] declares:

> * * * and every Indian born within the territorial limits of the United States who has voluntarily taken up, within said limits, his residence separate and apart from any tribe of Indians therein, and has adopted the habits of civilized life, is hereby declared to be a citizen of the United States, and is entitled to all the rights, privileges, and immunities of such citizens, whether said Indian has been or not, by birth or otherwise, a member of any tribe of Indians within the territorial limits of the United

---

[38] 203 U. S. 76 (1906).

[39] In 1874, the Cherokee National Council adopted a code which admitted white men to citizenship, and if one paid a sum of $500 (the approximate value of the share of each Indian) into the national treasury, he became entitled to a share in tribal property. But even this privilege was withdrawn in 1877, and so from that date, whites intermarrying into the Cherokee Nation were admitted to citizenship upon the condition that they should not thereby acquire an estate or interest in the communal property of the nation. In the case of *Whitmire* v. *Cherokee Nation*, 30 C. Cls. 138, 152 (1895), the court quotes a section of the Cherokee code and adds: "The idea therefore existed, both in the mind and in the laws of the Cherokee people, that citizenship did not necessarily extend to or invest in the citizen a personal or individual interest in what the constitution termed the 'common property,' 'the lands of the Cherokee Nation.'"

[40] C. 818, sec. 1, 25 Stat. 392, 25 U. S. C. 181.

[41] See Chapter 8, sec. 11.

[42] In 1909, Mr. Justice Van Devanter, then on the Circuit Court of Appeals, wrote:

> For many years the treaties and legislation relating to the Indians proceeded largely upon the theory that the welfare of both the Indians and the whites required that the former be kept in tribal communities separated from the latter, and while that policy prevailed, effect was given to the original rule respecting the right to share in tribal property; but Congress later adopted the policy of encouraging individual Indians to abandon their tribal relations and to adopt the customs, habits, and manners of civilized life, and, as an incident to this change in policy, statutes were enacted declaring that the right to share in tribal property should not be impaired or affected by such a severance of tribal relations, whether occurring theretofore or thereafter. (*Oakes* v. *United States*, 172 Fed. 305, 308 (C. C. A. 8, 1909).) See Chapter 11, sec. 1.

[43] *E. g.*, the Act of December 19, 1854, 10 Stat. 598, 599, promised that the property rights of the mixed bloods in the tribal property of the Chippewas would not be impaired if they remained on the lands ceded to the United States and separated from the tribe.

[44] *E. g.*, Treaty with Choctaws, September 27, 1830, 7 Stat. 333, discussed in *Winton* v. *Amos*, 255 U. S. 373, 388 (1921).

[45] *Oakes* v. *United States*, 172 Fed. 305 (C. C. A. 8, 1909); *United States ex rel. Besaw* v. *Work*, 6 F. 2d 694 (App. D. C. 1925); *Pape* v. *United States*, 19 F. 2d 219 (C. C. A. 9, 1927).

[46] 18 Stat. 402, 420.

[47] While this act is directed particularly at Indians acquiring homesteads on the public domain, it has been referred to as applying to any Indians abandoning their tribal relations. *Oakes* v. *United States*, 172 Fed. 305. It is believed, however, that this act can be restricted in the following manner. The well-recognized purpose of this act and of similar acts preserving interests in tribal property to Indians abandoning their tribal relations was to induce Indians to leave their tribal life on the reservations and to take up the habits and customs of civilized life in white communities. See *Oakes* v. *United States*, at 308; *United States* v. *Besaw*, 6 F. (2d) 694, 697 (Ct. App. D. C. 1925). In fact, the phrase "abandonment of tribal relations" has continuously been interpreted as meaning a physical abandonment of the tribe and the reservation and an undertaking to live as a white person. An example of such an interpretation of the phrase in the Act of 1875 is the Circular of Instructions issued by the General Land Office on March 25, 1875, requiring Indians desiring to take advantage of the benefits of the Act of 1875 to make affidavit that they have adopted the habits and pursuits of civilized life (2 C. L. O. 44). In all cases of which I have knowledge so far brought into court or before the Department for adjudication of the rights of Indians under the 1875 or 1887 acts, the Indians had physically abandoned their tribe and reservation and this was assumed to prove abandonment of tribal relations.

In view of this purpose of Congress to induce Indians to leave the reservations and the interpretation of the statutory language "abandonment of tribal relations" it may be said that the Act of 1875 would not apply to Indians who wish to relieve themselves of membership in a tribe but who, nevertheless, remain upon the reservation of the tribe and continue living as other members of the tribe and continue enjoying the Federal protection of reservation life. Memo. Sol. I. D., March 19, 1938.

[48] The Act of January 18, 1881, 21 Stat. 315, 316, gave to those Winnebago Indians of Wisconsin who abandoned their tribal relations and wished to use the money for purposes of settling a homestead on the public domain a pro rata share in the distribution of tribal funds.

[49] 16 Stat. 404 (Stockbridge and Munsee).

[50] 12 Stat. 1191.

[51] 10 Fed. Cas. No. 5537 (C. C. Kans. 1881).

[52] This section was amended by the Act of May 8, 1906, 34 Stat. 182, 25 U. S. C. 349.

[53] 24 Stat. 388, 390.

> States without in any manner impairing or otherwise affecting the right of any such Indian to tribal or other property.[54]

In the case of *Reynolds* v. *United States*,[55] a Sioux woman who had been born on the reservation and was a member of the tribe was taken from the reservation by her father. She moved away from the reservation, adopted the habits of white people and married a white man. Her rights to share in the tribal property were recognized, under the 1887 statute.

(3) By section 2 of the Act of August 9, 1888,[56] rights in tribal property were preserved to Indian women who thereafter married citizens of the United States and became citizens also.

(4) In furtherance of its policy to induce Indians to break away from the tribal mode of life, Congress included in the Appropriation Act of June 7, 1897,[57] the following provision granting rights in tribal property to the children of certain Indian women who had left the tribe:

> That all children born of a marriage heretofore solemnized between a white man and an Indian woman by blood and not by adoption, where said Indian woman is at this time, or was at the time of her death, recognized by the tribe shall have the same rights and privileges to the property of the tribe to which the mother belongs, or belonged at the time of her death, by blood, as any other member of the tribe * * *.[58]

Because this statute creates a new class of distributees in tribal property and, to that extent, decreases the property right of those distributees otherwise entitled to share, it has been strictly construed. It does not include the children of a marriage between two Indians;[59] it does not include the children of a marriage between an Indian man and a white woman;[60] it does not save any rights of children of an Indian woman who married a white man after June 7, 1897;[61] it does not save the rights of children whose Indian mother had married a white man before that date, but who was a member by adoption only, or if she had been a member by blood, who was not considered a member at that date or at her death if it had occurred prior to that time.[62] Nor does it create any rights in any lineal descendants other than children of the Indian woman.

The rights of children of a tribal member are discussed in *Halbert* v. *United States:*[63]

> The children of a marriage between an Indian woman and a white man usually take the status of the father; but if the wife retains her tribal membership and the children are born in the tribal environment and there reared by her, with the husband failing to discharge his duties to them, they take the status of the mother.
>
> Whether grandchildren of such a marriage have tribal membership or otherwise depends on the status of the father or mother as the case may be, and not on that of a grandparent.
>
> As to marriages occurring before June 7, 1897 (as the marriages here did), between a white man and an Indian woman, who was Indian by blood rather than by adoption—and who on June 7, 1897, or at the time of her death, was recognized by the tribe—the children have the same right to share in the division or distribution of the property of the tribe of the mother as any other member of the tribe, but this is in virtue of the Act of June 7, 1897.

In the distribution of tribal assets, the visible evidence of one's right to share is the appearance of his name on the appropriate "roll." If membership was the requisite, he had to be on the "membership roll." As a practical matter, acts and treaties providing for distribution of tribal property had to and did set a specific date as to when status must exist. Generally those who did not have a status entitling them to share on that date could not participate even though they might have had such a status before and after that date.[64]

[54] In view of this act, "the mere transfer of citizenship is not important, so far as the question of the rights in tribal property is concerned." *United States ex rel. Besaw* v. *Work*, 6 F. 2d 694, 698 (App. D. C. 1925).

[55] 205 Fed. 685 (D. C. S. D. 1913).

[56] C. 818, 25 Stat. 392. See also *Pape* v. *United States*, 19 F. 2d 219 (C. C. A. 9, 1927), holding that an Indian woman may receive a share in tribal property even if she marries a white man, becomes a citizen of the United States, has severed tribal relations and has adopted civilized life. *Work* v. *Gouin*, 18 F. 2d 820 (App. D. C. 1927), holding that a Chippewa woman, though married to a white man and separated from the tribe, was entitled to share in tribal fund.

[57] 30 Stat. 62, 90, 25 U. S. C. 184.

[58] *Cf. Stookey* v. *Wilbur*, 58 F. 2d 522 (App. D. C. 1932). (Act invoked by Secretary of the Interior; court declined to issue mandamus to compel Secretary to restore certain names to tribal rolls.)

[59] Memo. Sol. I. D., December 18, 1934.

[60] *Ibid.*

[61] *Pape* v. *United States*, 19 F. 2d 219 (C. C. A. 9, 1927).

[62] *Oakes* v. *United States*, 172 Fed. 305 (C. C. A. 8, 1909).

[63] 283 U. S. 753, 763–764 (1931), rev'g sub nom. *United States* v. *Halbert*, 38 F. 2d 795 (C. C. A. 9, 1930).

[64] For examples of such rolls, see the Act of March 1, 1901, 31 Stat. 861, 869–870 (Creek) and the Act of June 30, 1902, 32 Stat. 500, 501–502 (Creek). See Chapter 23, sec. 7. For a discussion of the power of Congress and the Secretary over enrollment, see Chapter 5, secs. 6 and 13.

SECTION 4. TRANSFERABILITY OF THE RIGHT TO SHARE

Ordinarily, a right to participate in tribal property cannot be alienated, either voluntarily or by operation of law.[65] To be entitled to share, the participant's children must have a status in their own right; they may be entitled to share as members, but not as heirs.[66]

However, interests in tribal property may be made transferable by congressional act[67] or tribal law and custom.[68] In such event, alienability may be limited to transfer only by operation of law.[69]

Under the Wheeler-Howard Act, shares in the assets of an Indian tribe or corporation may be disposed of to the Indian tribe or corporation from which the shares were derived or to its successor with the approval of the Secretary of the Interior, but alienation to others is prohibited. The Secretary of the Interior is authorized to permit exchanges of shares of equal value whenever such exchange is expedient and for the benefit of cooperative organizations.[70]

[65] *Sloan* v. *United States*, 118 Fed. 283 (C. C. Nebr. 1902), app. dism. 193 U. S. 614 (1904). *Woodbury* v. *United States*, 170 Fed. 302 (C. C. A. 8, 1909); *cf. Doe* v. *Wilson*, 23 How. 457 (1859); *Crews* v. *Burcham*, 1 Black 352 (1861).

[66] *Cf. Woodbury* v. *United States*, 170 Fed. 302 (C. C. A. 8, 1909).

[67] *E. g.*, Act of March 1, 1901, 31 Stat. 861, 864, and Act of June 30, 1902, c. 1323, 32 Stat. 500 (Creek allotments and funds). Act of June 28, 1906, c. 3572, 34 Stat. 539, and Act of April 18, 1912, 37 Stat. 86 (Osage allotments and funds). For a discussion of these statutes, see Chapter 23.

[68] See sec. 5.

[69] Act of June 28, 1906, c. 3572, 34 Stat. 539 (Osage), providing for descendibility did not make interest assignable. Op. Sol. I. D., M.8370, August 15, 1922. Act of April 18, 1912, 37 Stat. 86 (Osage), providing for descendibility did not make right assignable. *Taylor* v. *Tayrien*, 51 F. 2d 884 (C. C. A. 10, 1931), cert. den., 284 U. S. 672 (1931).

[70] Act of June 18, 1934, sec. 4, 48 Stat. 984, 985; 25 U. S. C. 464.

SECTION 5. RIGHTS OF USER IN TRIBAL PROPERTY

While property may be vested in a tribe, it is generally the individual members of the tribe who enjoy the use of such property. The question of what rights of user are enjoyed by individual Indians in tribal property may conveniently be considered under four headings:

(A) Occupancy of particular tracts.
(B) Improvements.
(C) Grazing and fishing rights.
(D) Rights in tribal timber.

A. OCCUPANCY OF PARTICULAR TRACTS

We have elsewhere noted [74] that it is a distinctive characteristic of tribal property that the right of possession is vested in the tribe as such, rather than in individual members.

Nevertheless, as a practical matter, some orderly distribution of occupancy among the members of the tribe is generally necessary in order that the land may be used. Hence, it comes about that individuals are given rights of occupancy in certain tracts of tribal land. The tribe may formally assign a right of occupancy to an individual, or if an individual is in possession by tribal law, usage and custom, a right of occupancy may come to be recognized without such formal assignment.[75]

The right of an Indian tribe to grant occupancy rights in designated tracts is specified in certain treaties.[76]

Many treaties recognize the value of individual occupancy rights on tribal land as well as the individual ownership of improvements, and provide for payments to such individuals for loss or destruction of such rights and improvements.[77]

The limitations on the rights of an individual occupant have been defined in several cases. In *Reservation Gas Co.* v. *Snyder*,[78] it was held that an Indian tribe might dispose of minerals on tribal lands which had been assigned to individual Indians for private occupancy, since the individual occupants had never been granted any specific mineral rights by the tribe.

In *Terrance* v. *Gray*,[79] it was held that no act of the occupant of assigned tribal land could terminate the control duly exercised by the chiefs of the tribe over the use and disposition of the land.

In *Application of Parker*,[80] it was held that the Tonawanda Nation of Seneca Indians had the right to dispose of minerals on the tribal allotments of its members and that the individual allottee had no valid claim for damages.

The nature of the rights conferred by an Indian tribe upon its members with respect to land occupancy depends upon the laws, customs, and agreements of the tribe. In the case of *United States* v. *Chase*,[81] the Supreme Court held that the making of assignments of land of the Omaha tribe to individual members did not preclude a later revocation of such assignments when the tribe decided that the reservation should be allotted, even though the original assignments were made pursuant to a specific treaty provision, were approved by the Commissioner of Indian Affairs, and guaranteed the possessory right of the assignee. The court *per* Van Devanter, *J.*, characterized these arrangements as:

> * * * leaving the United States and the tribe free to take such measures for the ultimate and permanent disposal of the lands, including the fee, as might become essential or appropriate in view of changing conditions, the welfare of the Indians and the public interests. (P. 100.)

Referring to the rights of an occupant of lands of the Cherokee Nation, the court in *The Cherokee Trust Funds*,[82] declared:

> He had a right to use parcels of the lands thus held by the Nation, subject to such rules as its governing authority might prescribe; but that right neither prevented nor qualified the legal power of that authority to cede the lands and the title of the Nation to the United States.

The right of the occupant has been likened to that of a licensee or tenant at will. But, in order to assure the occupant of land some security in his possession, tribal law and custom may recognize his right of possession to the extent that the right of occupancy may not be revoked at the mere caprice of tribal officials.

Typical of the laws of the Five Civilized Tribes with respect to occupancy rights was the Creek Act of 1880 by which the Creek Nation conferred on each citizen of the nation who was the head of a family and engaged in grazing livestock the right to enclose for that purpose one square mile of public domain without paying compensation. Provision was made for establishing, under certain conditions, more extensive pastures near the frontiers to protect the occupants against the influx of stock from adjacent territories.[83] Various laws of the Five Civilized Tribes provided for the sale or lease of these rights in tribal lands to other members of the tribe.[84] Under these laws, the rights of the grantor and the grantee or the lessor and lessee were protected in tribal and territorial courts. If the lessee refused to surrender possession after the expiration of his term, the lessor could maintain an action of ejectment in federal courts.[85] Adverse possession could run against an occupant. The occupant could maintain an action of forcible entry and detainer against

---

[74] Chapter 15, sec. 1.

[75] Memo. Sol. I. D., October 21, 1938. "If no definite land assignments are made, it is possible that individual members may assert occupancy rights in tribal land based upon long-continued usage." On the power of the tribe over individual rights of occupancy in tribal land, see Chapter 7.

[76] See, for example, Art. VI of the Treaty of September 24, 1857, with the Pawnee Indians, 11 Stat. 729, which provided in part:

> * * * if they think proper to do so, they may divide said lands among themselves, giving to each person, or each head of a family, a farm, subject to their tribal regulations, but in no instance to be sold or disposed of to persons outside, or not themselves of the Pawnee tribe.

And see Art. IV of the Treaty of March 6, 1865, with the Omaha Indians, 14 Stat. 661, construed in *United States* v. *Chase*, 245 U. S. 89 (1917).

On the development of individual allotments, see Chapter 11.

[77] See, for example: Treaty of January 24, 1826, with the Creek Nation of Indians, 7 Stat. 286; Treaty of August 8, 1831, with the Shawnees, Senecas, and Wyandots, 7 Stat. 355; Treaty of May 20, 1842, with the Seneca Nation of Indians, 7 Stat. 586; Treaty of June 5 and 17, 1846, with the various Bands of Pottawautomie, Chippewa, and Ottawa Indians, 9 Stat. 853; Treaty of August 6, 1846, with the Cherokee Nation, 9 Stat. 871; Treaty of October 18, 1846, with the Menomonee Tribe of Indians, 9 Stat. 952; Treaty of February 5, 1856, with the Stockbridge and Munsee Tribes of Indians, 11 Stat. 663; Treaty of June 9, 1855, with the Walla-Walla, Cayuse, and Umatilla Tribes and Bands of Indians, 12 Stat. 945; Treaty of June 9, 1855, with the Yakama, 12 Stat. 951.

[78] 150 N. Y. Supp. 216 (1914).

[79] 156 N. Y. Supp. 916 (1916).

[80] 237 N. Y. Supp. 134 (1929).

[81] 245 U. S. 89 (1917).

[82] 117 U. S. 288, 308 (1886).

[83] See *Turner* v. *United States*, 248 U. S. 354 (1919). Art. X of the Compiled Laws of the Cherokee Nation (1892) limited each citizen of the nation to 50 acres of land for grazing purposes, attached to his farm.

[84] *E. g.*, Compiled Laws of Cherokee Nation (1892), Art. XXIII, sec. 706.

[85] *Gooding* v. *Watkins*, 5 Ind. T. 578, 82 S. W. 913 (1904), rev'd on other grounds, 142 Fed. 112 (C. C. A. 8, 1905) (Chickasaw).

a trespasser.[86] *Shulthis* v. *McDougal*,[87] describes the nature of the interest held by an occupant of Creek lands, as follows:

> From the time they took up their residence west of the Mississippi, the Constitutions of the Five Nations provided that their land should remain "common property; but the improvements made thereon, and in the possession of the citizens of the nation, are the exclusive and indefeasible property of the citizens respectively who made, or may rightfully be in possession of them." The term "improvements," as here used, meant not only betterments, but occupancy. *Cherokee Nation* v. *Journeycake*, 155 U. S. 196, 210, * * *. These "improvements" passed from father to son, and were the subject of sale, with the single restriction that they should not be sold to the United States, individual states, or to individual citizens thereof.

As the foregoing cases indicate, the federal courts have given full weight to the arrangements made by the various tribes with respect to the individual occupancy rights of tribal members.

Congress has repeatedly given recognition to such occupancy rights, as, for example, by providing that compensation be made directly to occupants of tribal land for damage done or property taken in railroad building across such land.[88] There have been occasions, however, when Congress has felt compelled to modify these tribal arrangements by federal legislation. The Five Civilized Tribes are a case in point.

The following statement of conditions in the lands of the Five Civilized Tribes is found in the Report by the Senate Committee on the Five Civilized Tribes, May 1894:[89]

> A few enterprising citizens of the tribe, frequently not Indians by blood but by intermarriage, have in fact become the practical owners of the best and greatest part of these lands, while the title still remains in the tribe—theoretically for all, yet in fact the great body of the tribe derives no more benefit from their title than the neighbors in Kansas, Arkansas or Missouri * * *.[90]

These conditions were cited in justification of congressional acts providing for the redistribution of occupancy rights and ultimately for the allotment of lands of the Five Civilized Tribes.[91]

Under the Act of June 18, 1934,[92] the problem of individual rights in tribal land assumes a new importance by reason of the provision prohibiting future allotments in severalty.[93]

On unallotted reservations, tribal constitutions often provide for a single form of assignment, under which each head of a family is entitled to secure the occupancy of a tract of standard acreage under a tenure dependent upon use.[94]

On allotted reservations, the land problem is more complicated, and two types of assignment are common, "standard" assignments and "exchange"[95] assignments. Standard assignments are usually made to landless Indians or to Indians having a lesser amount of land than the standard acreage fixed by the tribe, and are generally made for the purpose of establishing homes. The tribal constitution and the assignment form generally provide that a standard assignment shall be canceled if the land is not beneficially utilized by the assignee for a specified period of time. Exchange assignments may be made to Indians who have an interest in severalty in some land in consideration of their surrendering such interest. Exchange assignments generally include more extensive rights of lease and transfer than are provided in connection with standard assignments, and in this respect approach more nearly to the character of allotments. The chief respects in which exchange assignments differ from allotments are: (1) land under such assignment cannot be alienated (apart from exchanges of land of equal value) during the life of the assignee except to the tribe, whereas allotted land may be transferred, upon the removal of restrictions or the issuance of a fee patent by the Secretary of the Interior, to any individual, Indian or non-Indian; (2) land under an exchange assignment is not inheritable in the strict sense of the term, as is allotted land, but is subject to reassignment to qualified members of the tribe designated by the original assignee, provided the land is neither subdivided into portions too minute for economic use nor reassigned to persons holding more than a designated maximum acreage of tribal land; (3) land under an exchange assignment is tribal land and is subject to all the protections which the law throws about tribal land.

The rights to improvements placed by individual Indians on the land are, under many constitutions, distinguished from the assigned right of user in the land itself, and are made transferable by devise, lease, or operation of law to certain members of the tribe upon approval by the tribe.[96]

It has been administratively held that a tribal grant of occupancy rights to its members does not necessarily involve the conveyance of any *interest* in tribal land, since the occupant may hold a position similar to that of a licensee.[97]

On the other hand, it has been held that an individual member of an Indian Pueblo has such an occupancy interest as will, under the Taylor Grazing Act,[98] justify a preference in the award of grazing rights on the public domain.[99]

At this stage in the development of the forms of assignment it is important to avoid over-generalizations on the nature of the legal rights thus created. Possibly a suggestive analogy to the member's occupancy right in tribal land is the right of a member of a membership corporation to reside in an allocated tract of the society's estate.

B. IMPROVEMENTS

With reference to improvements placed upon the land, an occupant may acquire a vested right, subject to the limitations of tribal rules and customs.[100] It has been said that the individual has a vested right in such improvements, even as against the tribe because they are his own property; they are not the

[86] *Hunt* v. *Hicks*, 3 Ind. T. 275, 54 S. W. 818 (1900) (Cherokee).

[87] 170 Fed. 529, 533–534 (C. C. A. 8, 1909), app. dism. 225 U. S. 561 (1912).

[88] See, for example, sec. 3 of the Act of March 2, 1899, 30 Stat. 990, 991, amended by the Act of February 28, 1902, 32 Stat. 50, 25 U. S. C. 314. And see acts cited in Chapter 15, fn. 14.

[89] Sen. Rept. No. 377, 53d Cong. 2d sess. (1894), cited in *Stephens* v. *Cherokee Nation*, 174 U. S. 445 (1899), and *Heckman* v. *United States*, 224 U. S. 413, 434 (1912).

[90] For a further statement of conditions, see *Woodward* v. *de Graffenried*, 238 U. S. 284 (1915).

[91] See Chapter 23.

[92] Secs. 1 to 19, 48 Stat. 984, 25 U. S. C. 461–479.

[93] Op. Sol. I. D., M. 27770, May 22, 1935.

[94] E. g., Constitution and Bylaws of Papago Tribe, Ariz., approved January 6, 1937, Art. 8, sec. 3. Constitution and Bylaws of Pyramid Lake Paiute Tribe, Nev., approved January 15, 1936, Art. 7, sec. 3.

[95] E. g., Constitution and Bylaws of Cheyenne River Sioux, S. D., approved December 27, 1935, Art. 8, sec. 4.

Constitution and Bylaws of Lower Sioux Community, Minn., approved June 11, 1936, Art. 9, secs. 1, 5.

[96] E. g., Constitution and Bylaws of Fort Belknap Community, Mont., approved December 13, 1935, Art. V, secs. 5, 7, 8.

[97] Memo. Sol. I. D., October 21, 1938 (Palm Springs); Memo. Sol. I. D. April 14, 1939 (Pueblo of Santa Clara).

[98] Act of June 28, 1934, 48 Stat. 1269, as amended June 26, 1936, 49 Stat. 1976, and July 14, 1939 (Pub., No. 173—76th Cong., 1st sess.).

[99] Eligibility of Indians and Indian Pueblos for Grazing Privileges under the Taylor Grazing Act, 56 I. D. 79 (1937); see, also, Rights of Pueblos and Members of Pueblo Tribes under the Taylor Grazing Act, 56 I. D. 808 (1938).

[100] See Chapter 7, sec. 8.

property of the tribe and his right to them is not derived as an interest in tribal property.[101]

However, the occupant's right of use and disposition of the improvements is qualified by the fact that he does not own the land and that the tribe, in granting him the right of occupancy, may impose as conditions certain terms affecting improvements. In effect, tribal laws and customs represent conditions upon the grant of individual occupancy rights, to which the individual is deemed to consent upon receiving such rights.[102]

The laws of many tribes contain provisions regarding the placing of improvements upon tribal land by an occupant.[103] For example, the laws of the Cherokee Nation compelled the occupant to place at least $50 worth of improvements upon the land he occupied within 6 months of locating thereon or else the land reverted to the nation.[104] Various tribal constitutions permit the holder of an assignment of land from the tribe to make improvements on the land and allow him to dispose of them by will or by other methods, under such rules and regulations as the tribal council may direct. It is also generally provided that permanent improvements may not be removed from the land without the consent of the tribal council.[105]

The claim of the individual Indian to the improvements he has placed upon tribal land has been frequently recognized by Congress. Allotment acts generally provided that the Indian who held certain lands as an occupant and had made improvements thereon had prior right of selecting these lands as his allotment.[106] The practical value of this was that he could, if he wished, retain a favorable location and save himself the expense of moving and making improvements elsewhere.[107]

Various statutes recognize the right of the individual who has occupied or placed improvements upon tribal land to the value of these improvements when they have been taken from him or destroyed.[108]

C. GRAZING AND FISHING RIGHTS[109]

Even in the absence of particular assignments of individual tracts, arrangements limiting the use of tribal lands are frequently imposed, either by tribal or by federal authorities, for the purpose of defining and protecting the rights of all the members of the tribe, including those yet unborn.[110] This control has been exercised most notably to prevent exploitation of tribal grazing lands by a small number of stock owners and to protect the economic life of the tribe against the damages resulting from serious overstocking of the range and soil erosion.[111]

In the case of *United States* v. *Barquin*,[112] the court considered regulations promulgated by the Commissioner of Indian Affairs governing grazing on the Shoshone Indian tribal lands. The regulations provided generally for the free grazing by each family of a limited number of stock, which were to be branded. Indians were allowed to graze cattle in excess of this number by securing a permit and paying a small fee. The court held that an Indian who grazed cattle in violation of these regulations was guilty of trespass and enjoined him from so using the tribal lands.[113]

In the case of *United States* v. *Bega*,[114] and related cases, the court had before it the power of the Department of the Interior to make grazing regulations on Navajo tribal lands.[115] Consent

---

[101] Memo. Sol. I. D., October 21, 1938 (Palm Springs). The tribe does not own the improvements placed on tribal land by or under direction of individual members of the tribe. Where the occupant leases, with approval of the tribe and the Department of the Interior, the land and improvements, "there should be a definite provision as to the division of rentals between the individual as the owner of improvements, and the tribe as the owner of the land." *Cf.* Memo. Sol. I. D., October 20, 1937 (Ft. Belknap).

[102] See Chapter 7. sec. 8.

[103] See Chapter 15, secs. 9 and 18B.

[104] Compiled 1892, Art. III.

[105] *E. g.*, Constitution and Bylaws of the Oglala Sioux of Pine Ridge Reservation, approved January 15, 1936, Art. 10, sec. 9; Constitution and Bylaws of the Colorado Pine Indians, approved August 13, 1937, Art. 8, sec. 9; Art. 1, sec. 2 of the Cherokee Constitution (1892) provided that improvements might be made by the individual occupant and recognized his vested rights therein. The improvements were inheritable and subject to sale, the only restriction being that they were not to be sold to the United States, to any of the states, or to any citizen of the state. The purpose of this restriction was to keep tribal members in possession. See *Cherokee Trust Funds*, 117 U. S. 288, 305 (1886); *Shulthis* v. *McDougal*, 170 Fed. 529, 534 (C. C. A. 8, 1909), app. dism. 225 U. S. 561 (1912).

Improvements and inclosures on lands held in occupancy made in furtherance of agriculture and grazing purposes by members of the Five Civilized Tribes were permitted to pass by quitclaim deed or bill of sale from one member to another. See *United States* v. *Rea-Read Mill & Elevator Co.*, 171 Fed. 501, 504 (C. C. E. D. Okla. 1909).

[106] "That all allotments * * * shall be selected * * * in such manner as to embrace the improvements of the Indians making the selection," is the provision found in sec. 2. of the General Allotment Act of February 8, 1887, 24 Stat. 388, 25 U. S. C., secs. 331, 332, 333, 334, 348, 349, 381, 339, 341, 342, and sec. 9 of the Act of March 2, 1889, 25 Stat. 888 (Sioux).

Art. 3 of the Agreement of June 6, 1900, 31 Stat. 672, between the Shoshones and the United States provided that the Indians who had taken possession of lands under a prior agreement (Act of February 23, 1889, 25 Stat. 687) and were occupying them as tribal lands and had made improvements thereon had a preference in selecting such lands as contained the improvements for their allotments. See *Skeem* v. *United States*, 273 Fed. 93 (C. C. A. 9, 1921), and see Art. 3 of the Agreement with the Crow Indians, ratified April 27, 1904, c. 1924, 33 Stat. 352.

[107] This explains why, in the selection of allotments, contention arose as to who had been entitled to occupancy rights.

[108] Act of February 13, 1871, 16 Stat. 410 (Menomonee); Act of May 8, 1872, 17 Stat. 85 (Kansas); Act of February 19, 1875, 18 Stat. 330 (Seneca); Act of May 15, 1882, 22 Stat. 63 (Miami); Act of February 20, 1895, 28 Stat. 677 (Ute); Act of March 2, 1907, 34 Stat. 1220 (Cherokee); Act of June 3, 1924, 43 Stat. 357 (Red Lake); Act of January 20, 1925, 43 Stat. 795 (Indians in New Mexico or California).

[109] This section deals only with rights in tribal property. On rights pertaining to adjacent public lands, under the Taylor Grazing Act, see fns. 98 and 99, *supra*.

[110] Tribal constitutions sometimes provide that in issuing grazing permits or leasing tribal lands preferences shall be given to Indian cooperative associations and to individual members of the tribe. See, *e. g.*, Constitution of the Cheyenne River Sioux Tribe, South Dakota, Art. VIII, sec. 3.

[111] The purposes of the general grazing regulations issued by the Secretary of the Interior is set forth as follows:

> (a) The preservation * * * of the forest, the forage, the land, and the water resources. * * * and the building up of these resources where they have deteriorated. (b) The utilization of these resources for the purpose of giving the Indians an opportunity to earn a living through the grazing of their own livestock. (c) The granting of grazing privileges on surplus range lands * * * in a manner which will yield the highest return consistent with undiminished future use. (d) The protection of the interests of the Indians from the encroachment of unduly aggressive and anti-social individuals. 25 C. F. R. 71.3.

[112] (D. C. Wyo. 1928, unreported) D. J. File No. 90-2-8-24.

[113] In the case of *United States* v. *Jensen*, unreported (D. C. E. D. Wash. 1926), a member of the Yakima tribe was adjudged guilty of trespassing on tribal lands when he grazed sheep upon the tribal reservation without securing a permit from the Secretary of the Interior, in accordance with regulations promulgated by the Secretary. See also *United States* v. *Olney*, unreported (D. C. E. D. Wash. 1919), holding that the Secretary of the Interior has the authority to require an Indian user of tribal grazing lands to first secure a permit and to require him to pay a fee for cattle grazed in excess of the number prescribed as "free" under Department of the Interior regulations.

[114] (D. C. Ariz. 1939, unreported) D. J. File No. 90-2-8-24-3.

[115] As promulgated, June 2, 1937, these regulations provided, in part:

> 1. The Commissioner of Indian Affairs shall establish land-management districts within the Navajo and Hopi Indian Reservations, based upon the social and economic requirements of the Indians and the necessity of rehabilitating the grazing lands.
>
> 2. The Commissioner of Indian Affairs shall promulgate for each land management district the carrying capacity for livestock.
>
> 3. The Superintendent shall keep accurate records of ownership of all livestock.
>
> 4. The Superintendent shall reduce the livestock in each district to the carrying capacity of the range.
>
> 5. The Superintendent is authorized to assess and collect trespass fees and, with the consent of the tribal council of the Navajo Indians, he may also assess and collect grazing fees upon all stock owned in excess of the base preference number and upon all nonproductive stock owned below the base preference number. * * *

Regulations governing grazing in the Navajo and Hopi Reservations are codified in 25 C. F. R. 72.1-72.13.

of the Navajo tribe to the federal grazing regulations had been duly obtained. The court held that under these regulations the Secretary of the Interior could require the removal of horses from the reservation in excess of the number permitted, and in its decree the court compelled the individual stock owners to remove their excess stock. In addition, the court disposed of questions that might cause future litigation by including a declaratory judgment to the following effect:

> * * * the Secretary of the Interior of the United States is vested with the power, right, and authority to promulgate rules and regulations for the protection of the tribal lands of the Navajo Reservation within the State of Arizona, and to the effect and extent necessary to prevent waste caused by overgrazing and to prevent unfair or unreasonable monopolization of tribal range by individuals, and to provide by rules and regulations a maximum carrying capacity of such districts as may be fixed and determined by said rules and regulations.

A similar problem has arisen in connection with the regulation of individual fishing rights in tribal waters. In the case of *Mason* v. *Sams*,[116] the court considered the power of the Secretary of the Interior to promulgate regulations with respect to the use by tribal Indians of waters in the Quinaielt Reservation which had been reserved for the exclusive use of the Indians by the Treaty of July 1, 1855, and January 25, 1856, with the Qui-nai-elts and Quil-leh-utes.[117] The scheme of regulations in question has been promulgated by the Department of the Interior, without tribal consent. Under these regulations certain members of the tribe were granted exclusive fishing rights at favored locations upon payment of prescribed fees, and other members were excluded therefrom. The court held that these regulations were invalid. The decision in *Mason* v. *Sams* is distinguishable from the grazing cases discussed above in two respects: first, certain individual members of the tribe were entirely excluded from the right to fish in tribal waters, in *Mason* v. *Sams*, while in the grazing cases no member of the tribe was entirely deprived of grazing rights on tribal land; secondly, tribal authority for the regulations in question was lacking in *Mason* v. *Sams* and present in the *Bega* case. (Whether it was present in the other grazing cases is not clear.)

D. RIGHTS IN TRIBAL TIMBER

Where a tribe possesses property rights in timber, the question arises: What right has a member of the tribe to cut and to use or sell tribal timber?

By the general Act of February 16, 1889,[118] for example, the President of the United States was authorized to permit, at his discretion and under such regulations as he might prescribe, Indians living on reservations or allotments, the fee to which was in the United States, to cut, remove, sell or otherwise dispose of dead timber, standing or fallen, on such lands. Pursuant to this statute, permission was given to Indians of the Chippewa reservation in Minnesota to cut tribal timber, subject to certain regulations. As discussed in the case of *Pine River Logging Co.* v. *United States*,[119] the regulations permitted "deserving Indians, who had no other means of support, to cut for a single season a limited quantity of dead and down timber * * *, and to use the proceeds for their support in exact proportion to the scale of logs banked by each, provided that ten per cent of the gross proceeds should go to the stumpage or poor fund of the tribe * * *."[120] The facts in the *Pine River Logging Co.* case disclosed that the Commissioner of Indian Affairs had approved contracts between several Indians and a logging company for the cutting of a certain amount of dead timber. In its decision the court held that both the Indians and the logging company were trespassers and were liable to the United States for the value of the timber cut in excess of the amount stated in the contract.[121]

Other acts relating to specific tribes provided that the timber on tribal lands was to be cut and sold under federal supervision and the proceeds thereof were either to be spent for the benefit of the tribe or distributed per capita.[122]

The general Act of June 25, 1910,[123] contains authority for the sale of mature living and dead and down timber from the unallotted lands of any reservation, except the Osages, the Five Civilized Tribes, and the reservations of Minnesota and Wisconsin.

Pursuant to the foregoing acts, the Department of the Interior has issued general forest regulations.[124] Insofar as these acts and regulations deal with the rights of the tribe in tribal timber they are elsewhere considered.[125] The right of the individual Indian to cut tribal timber is covered by section 20 of the current regulations which appears as section 61.27 of Title 25 of the Code of Federal Regulations.

Section 61.27 establishes a permit system whereby permits approved by duly authorized representatives of the tribe are required for the cutting of timber by individual Indians on tribal lands. As stated in the regulation, the system was devised to meet the needs of "Indians and other persons for limited quantities of timber for domestic, agricultural, and grazing purposes." Individual Indians who need timber for personal use may receive permits without the payment of stumpage charge, but the trees so cut are to be designated by a forest officer or other agency employee. The maximum value of the stumpage which may be thus cut by one person in any one year is not to exceed $100. Should the individual require more timber for his needs, he may purchase the surplus tribal timber or timber otherwise authorized for sale (61.13). The Indian is given the preference of buying stumpage not exceeding $5,000 in value in open market without having to bid therefor, provided the tribe consents to the sale (61.17).

---

[116] 5 F. 2d 255 (D. C. W. D. Wash. 1925).

[117] 12 Stat. 971.

[118] C. 172, 25 Stat. 673, 25 U. S. C. 196. On the right of Indians, under departmental regulations, to cut and sell tribal timber, see Act of March 31, 1882, 22 Stat. 36, entitled:

> An act to confirm certain instructions given by the Department of the Interior to the Indian agent at Green Bay Agency, in the State of Wisconsin, and to legalize the acts done and permitted by said Indian agent pursuant thereto.

[119] 186 U. S. 279, 285–286 (1902).

[120] *Ibid.*

[121] For a later act relating to rights of individual Chippewas in tribal timber, see the Act of June 27, 1902, 32 Stat. 400.

[122] *E. g.*, Act of June 12, 1890, c. 418, 26 Stat. 146 (Menomonee), discussed in *United States ex rel. Besaw* v. *Work*, 6 F. 2d 694 (App. D. C. 1925), and supplemented by the Act of June 28, 1906, c. 3578, 34 Stat. 547; Act of December 21, 1904, c. 22, 33 Stat. 595 (Yakima); Act of April 23, 1904, 33 Stat. 302 (Flathead). *Cf.* sec. 4 of the Act of March 3, 1921, 41 Stat. 1355 (Fort Belknap), which affirms the right of the individual Indian to cut timber on tribal land. The foregoing statute also provides that the head of a family may take coal from unleased tribal lands for domestic use (sec. 6).

[123] 36 Stat. 855, 857, sec. 7, 25 U. S. C. 407. The disposition of timber belonging to the Five Civilized Tribes is governed by the Act of June 28, 1898, 30 Stat. 495; Act of January 21, 1903, 32 Stat. 774; Act of April 26, 1906, 34 Stat. 137; Act of August 24, 1912, 37 Stat. 497. Timber on reservation lands in Minnesota and Wisconsin may be sold in accordance with the provisions of the Acts of February 16, 1889, 25 Stat. 673, 25 U. S. C. 196, the Act of March 28, 1908, 35 Stat. 51 (Menominee), and the Act of May 18, 1916, 39 Stat. 123, 137 (Red Lake).

[124] 25 C. F. R. 61.1–61.29. Office of Indian Affairs, Department of the Interior, General Forest Regulations, approved April 23, 1936. It is provided that the regulations may be superseded by special instructions to particular reservations or by provisions of tribal constitutions, bylaws, or charters, or any authorized tribal action of the tribes thereunder. 25 C. F. R. 61.6.

[125] See Chapter 15, secs. 15, 19.

SECTION 6. INDIVIDUAL RIGHTS UPON DISTRIBUTION OF TRIBAL PROPERTY

The extent of individual participation in the distribution of tribal property is governed, in the first instance by the federal statute or treaty authorizing the distribution, or, where the federal law is silent, by the law or custom of the tribe.

Apportionment and distribution of tribal funds may be affected by acts passed by Congress in the exercise of its plenary power over tribal property.[126] The manner in which the plenary power over tribal property could be exercised to affect the individual's rights is discussed elsewhere.[127]

A. MODES OF DISTRIBUTION

Where Congress has prescribed the method of distributing tribal property, equal division per capita has been the general rule.[128] This method of apportionment is consistent with the nature of the individual's interest in tribal property and is found in numerous treaties and acts providing for the distribution of tribal property.[129] "Every member of the tribe has an interest in preventing one member from getting more than his share * * *."[130]

However, the act, treaty, or custom providing for distribution may restrict the class of those entitled to participate in a given distribution or deviate from the equality rule by differentiating among various classes of participants. Certain classes of members may receive more tribal property at given times than others.[131]

Even in the same class there have been inequalities in the distribution of tribal assets. For example, many allotments were made on the basis of acreage rather than value, although equality of acreage might co-exist with wide inequality of values.

Ordinarily, in the distribution of money, the wants of all individuals are, for all practical purposes, infinite and equal, and equal per capita distribution is a well-nigh universal rule.[132]

Where, however, the Federal Government has provided for a distribution of land or overcoats or teams of oxen, differentiations have frequently been made between adults and infants or between heads of families and dependents or between men and women.[133] Likewise, where divisions exist within a tribe, based upon separations in migration, degree of blood, or other historical factors, these factors have frequently been taken into account in treaties and statutes.[134]

Occasionally Congress, instead of specifying a total amount to be distributed within a given class, has allocated out of the tribal estate a fixed amount of money or property to each member of a tribe,[135] or to each member who meets certain qualifications.[136]

---

[126] See Chapter 5, sec. 5B.

[127] See Chapter 5, sec. 5.

[128] On the application of this rule to the allotment of tribal land, see Chapter 11. The application of this rule in the distribution of annuities is discussed in Chapters 10 and 15.

[129] *E. g.*, Act of April 30, 1888, c. 206, 25 Stat. 94 (Sioux Nation); Act of April 27, 1904, c. 1620, 33 Stat. 319 (Devils Lake Reservation Indians); Act of June 28, 1906, c. 3578, 34 Stat. 547 (Menominee); Act of March 2, 1907, c. 2536, 34 Stat. 1230 (Rosebud Sioux).

[130] *Tiger* v. *Twin State Oil Co.*, 48 F. 2d 509, 511 (C. C. A. 10, 1931), aff'g sub nom. *Kemohah* v. *Shaffer Oil and Refining Co.*, 38 F. 2d 665 (D. C. N. D. Okla. 1930).

[131] In passing upon the distributing of a tribal fund created for the purpose of paying to certain Stockbridge-Munsee Indians their share in tribal property, said Indians having been erroneously omitted from the distribution of an earlier fund, the Solicitor of the Department of the Interior declared:

> The fund created was for one purpose only. Consequently there is no merit to the contention that if the fund be tribal or communal then it must be subject to disbursement for tribal expenditures generally, and that it is necessarily individual and not tribal because all members do not participate in its distribution. The very purpose of the appropriation refutes the contention. Op. Sol. I. D., D. 42071, December 29, 1921.

Cf. Treaty of March 28, 1836, with the Ottawas and Chippewas, 7 Sat. 491, providing for payments of different amounts to different classes of half-breeds.

[132] Per capita payment was made the general rule, except where the interest of the Indians or some treaty stipulation otherwise required, by sec. 3 of the Act of March 3, 1853, 10 Stat. 226, 239. This provision superseded a provision to the same general effect in sec. 3 of the Act of August 30. 1852, 10 Stat. 41, 56, which made permanent the clause which had been included as a limitation upon the appropriations made by earlier appropriation acts. See section 3 of Act of July 21, 1852, 10 Stat. 15, 23. Recent statutes providing for per capita distribution of various funds are cited in fn. 135 and 144 *infra*.

[133] Thus, for example, the original General Allotment Act of February 8, 1887, sec. 1, 24 Stat. 388, 25 U. S. C. 331, authorized the allotment of land in these terms:

> To each head of a family, one-quarter of a section;
> To each single person over eighteen years of age, one-eighth of a section;
> To each orphan child under eighteen years of age, one-eighth of a section; and
> To each other single person under eighteen years now living, or who may be born prior to the date of the order of the President directing an allotment of the lands embraced in any reservation, one-sixteenth of a section.

[134] An example of a treaty provision modifying the general rule of equality is Art. 10 of the Treaty of October 1, 1859, with the Sacs and Foxes of the Mississippi, 15 Stat. 467, 470. Under this treaty half-bloods and intermarried Indians might receive certain tribal lands assigned to them in severalty, but then they would have no share in other tribal property, even though they remained members of the tribe.

See, for example, secs. 4 and 5, Act of July 29, 1848, 9 Stat. 252, 264–265 (N. C. Cherokees); Act of January 18, 1881, 21 Stat. 315 (Winnebago Indians); Act of October 19, 1888, 25 Stat. 608 (Cherokee freedmen); Act of October 1, 1890, 26 Stat. 636 (Shawnee and Delaware Indians and Cherokee freedmen); Act of March 3, 1893, 27 Stat. 744 (Stockbridge and Munsee tribe); Act of April 28, 1904, 33 Stat. 519 (Wyandotte Indians); Act of March 1, 1907, 34 Stat. 1055 (Sac and Fox Indians); Act of August 11, 1916, 39 Stat. 509 (Rosebud Sioux Reservation); Act of March 4, 1917, 39 Stat. 1195 (Santee Sioux); Act of April 14, 1924, 43 Stat. 95 (Chippewas of Minnesota); Act of May 3, 1928, 45 Stat. 484 (Sioux Tribe); Act of March 4, 1929, 45 Stat. 1550 (Loyal Shawnee Indians); Act of March 3, 1931, 46 Stat. 1495 (Blackfeet Tribe).

The following Appropriation Acts include special provisions for per capita payments to specified individuals or classes of individuals within a given tribe; Act of March 3, 1855, sec. 3, 10 Stat. 686 (North Carolina Cherokees); Act of July 31, 1854, sec 8(7), 10 Stat. 315, 333 (Cherokees); Act of August 18, 1856, sec. 14, 11 Stat. 81, 92 (Cherokees east of the Mississippi); Act of June 14, 1858, 11 Stat. 362 (Cherokees); Act of March 3, 1875, 18 Stat. 402, 412 (Kickapoo); Act of July 4, 1884, 23 Stat. 76, 81 (Kickapoo); Act of June 29, 1888, 25 Stat. 217, 222–223 (Kickapoo); Act of March 3, 1891, 26 Stat. 989, 1010 (Creek Nation of Indians); Act of June 10, 1896, 29 Stat. 321, 334 (Flandreau Band of Sioux and Santee Sioux in Nebraska) and pp. 358–359, Art. II (Apache, Mohave, and Yuma); Act of July 1, 1898, 30 Stat. 571, 578 (Kickapoo); Act of March 1, 1899, 30 Stat. 924, 931 (Kickapoo); Act of March 3, 1905, 33 Stat. 1048, 1052 (Kickapoo) and pp. 1078–1079, Art. II (Port Madison Indian Reservation) Act of March 4, 1929, 45 Stat. 1562, 1587 (Saint Croix Chippewas of Minnesota); Act of May 14, 1930, 46 Stat. 279, 285 (Sioux).

Special rights of participation in tribal property granted to mixed bloods of various tribes gave rise to "half-breed scrip." Act of July 17, 1854, 10 Stat. 304 (Sioux Nation). See also Appropriation Act of March 3, 1885, 23 Stat. 362, 368 (Kaw or Kansas Tribe).

[135] Act of August 22, 1911, 37 Stat. 44 (Choctaw, Chickasaw, Cherokee, and Seminole Indians); Act of November 19, 1921, 42 Stat. 221 (Chippewas of Minnesota); Act of January 25, 1924, 43 Stat. 1 (Chippewas of Minnesota); Act of January 30, 1925, 43 Stat. 798 (Chippewas of Minnesota); Act of February 19, 1926, 44 Stat. 7 (Chippewas of Minnesota); Act of March 15, 1928, 45 Stat. 314 (Chippewas of Minnesota); Act of April 28, 1928, 45 Stat. 467 (Shoshones and Arapahoes of Wyoming); Act of May 11, 1928, 45 Stat. 497 (Rosebud Sioux Indians); Act of May 26, 1928, 45 Stat. 747 (Pine Ridge Sioux Indians); Act of December 23, 1929, 46 Stat. 54 (Chippewas of Minnesota); Act of March 24, 1930, 46 Stat. 88 (Shoshone and Arapahoe); Act of April 15, 1930, 46 Stat. 169 (Pine Ridge, South Dakota); Act of February 3, 1931, 46 Stat. 1060 (Shoshone and Arapahoe); Act of February 14, 1931, 46 Stat. 1102 (Menominees of Wisconsin); Act of February 14, 1931, 46 Stat. 1107 (Chippewas of Minnesota); Act of February 12, 1932, 47 Stat. 49

To equalize allotments, various acts provide for the payment [137] or the withholding of payment [138] of tribal funds to individuals.

B. TIME OF DISTRIBUTION

Ordinarily, acts providing for the distribution of tribal assets provide for the immediate payment of the entire share to those entitled to it. Individual rights vest immediately upon segregation, and the tribal character of the property is extinguished.[139]

In some special acts providing for distribution of tribal property, Congress has seen fit to withhold payment of some or all of the Indian's share until some future time.[140]

C. THE LIMITS OF LEGISLATIVE DISTRIBUTION

Oftentimes, the act or treaty providing for the distribution of tribal lands or tribal funds does not state specifically the proportion each member is to receive, but leaves the distribution to the decision of the tribe.[141] Tribal charters generally limit the amount and mode in which tribal property may be distributed,[142] and in some cases prohibit any per capita distribution of tribal funds.[143]

So long as the Federal Government sought to achieve the breaking up of tribal estates, legislative distribution of tribal funds was the order of the day.[144]

(Chippewas of Minnesota); Act of June 14, 1932, 47 Stat. 306 (Red Lake of Minnesota); Act of June 14, 1932, 47 Stat. 307 (Menominees of Wisconsin); Act of January 20, 1933, 47 Stat. 773 (Chippewas of Minnesota); Act of June 3, 1933, 48 Stat. 112 (Menominee); Act of June 15, 1933, 48 Stat. 146 (Seminole); Act of June 16, 1933, 48 Stat. 254 (Red Lake); Act of May 7, 1934, 48 Stat. 668 (Chippewas of Minnesota); Act of July 2, 1935, 49 Stat. 444 (Red Lake); Act of June 20, 1936, 49 Stat. 1568 (Blackfeet).

[136] The Act of April 30, 1888, 25 Stat. 94 (later amended by the Act of June 21, 1906, 34 Stat. 325, 326), established the right to "Sioux benefits" in the following terms:

> * * * That each head of family or single person over the age of eighteen years, who shall have or may hereafter take his or her allotment of land in severalty, shall be provided with two milch cows, one pair of oxen, with yoke and chain, one plow, one wagon, one harrow, one hoe, one axe, and one pitchfork, all suitable to the work they may have to do, and also twenty dollars in cash. (P. 101.)

And see Act of March 3, 1909, 35 Stat. 751 (Quapaw, Modoc, Klamaths); Act of June 1, 1938, 52 Stat. 605 (Klamath).

[137] See the Act of April 26, 1906, c. 1876, 34 Stat. 137 (Five Civilized Tribes).

[138] See the Act of March 1, 1901, 31 Stat. 861, 862–863 (Creek).

[139] Parallel problems arise in the law of corporations, future interests, and trusts. See *Cogswell* v. *Second Nat. Bank*, 78 Conn. 75, 60 Atl. 1059 (1905), aff'd sub nom. *Jerome* v. *Cogswell*, 204 U. S. 1 (1907), holding that the declaration of a dividend, payable at some future date, creates a debt in favor of the stockholder against the corporation. When a fund out of which the dividend is to be paid is segregated, a trust for the benefit of the stockholders is imposed upon the segregated fund. See *New York Trust Co.* v. *Edwards*, 274 Fed. 952 (D. C. S. D. N. Y. 1921); *Staats* v. *Biograph Co.*, 236 Fed. 454 (C. C. A. 2, 1916). See also *Hayward* v. *Blake*, 247 Mass. 430, 142 N. E. 52 (1924), to the effect that income accruing to a life tenant during his lifetime, but not yet payable at the date of his death, is payable to his estate.

[140] The Act of January 14, 1889, 25 Stat. 642, provided for the sale of certain tribal lands of the Chippewa Indians of Minnesota. Sec. 7 provided in part:

> That all money accruing from the disposal of said lands * * * shall * * * be placed in the Treasury of the United States to the credit of all the Chippewa Indians in the State of Minnesota as a permanent fund, which shall draw interest at the rate of five per centum per annum, payable annually for the period of fifty years * * * and which interest and permanent fund shall be expended for the benefit of said Indians in manner following: One-half of said interest shall, during the said period of fifty years, except in the cases hereinafter otherwise provided, be annually paid in cash in equal shares to the heads of families and guardians of orphan minors for their use; and one-fourth of said interest shall, during the same period and with the like exception, be annually paid in cash in equal shares per capita to all other classes of said Indians; and the remaining one-fourth of said interest shall, during the said period of fifty years * * * be devoted exclusively to the establishment and maintenance of a system of free schools among said Indians * * *; and at the expiration of the said fifty years, the said permanent fund shall be divided and paid to all of said Chippewa Indians and their issue then living, in cash, in equal shares: * * * The United States shall, for the benefit of said Indians, advance to them as such interest as aforesaid the sum of ninety thousand dollars annually * * * until such time as said permanent fund * * * shall equal or exceed the sum of three million dollars, less any actual interest that may in the meantime accrue from accumulations of said permanent fund * * *.

Under this act, three-fourths of the interest is to be paid annually to the eligible Indians in equal shares per capita. Any advances made can come only from the interest, and the Secretary of the Interior cannot segregate and advance to any individual Chippewa his pro rata share of the permanent fund. If he were allowed to do this, there is a possibility that the permanent fund set apart for the benefit of all Chippewas might be seriously depleted or exhausted (Op. Sol. I. D., M.11879, May 31, 1924). The policy behind keeping the fund intact for the period of 50 years was to prevent the Indians from squandering their wealth; it was supposed that, during the 50-year period, they would have become sufficiently educated to realize the value of their property.

However, by virtue of the Act of May 18, 1916, c. 125, 39 Stat. 123, 135, the Secretary of the Interior was authorized in his discretion to advance to any individual entitled to participate in the permanent fund of the Chippewas

> * * * one-fourth of the amount which would now be coming to said Indian under a pro rata distribution of said permanent fund: *Provided further*, That any money received hereunder by any member of said tribe or used for his or her benefit shall be deducted from the share of said member in the permanent fund of the said Chippewa Indians in Minnesota to which he or she would be entitled * * *.

(Discussed Op. Sol. I. D., M.15954, January 8, 1927.)

The question of the proportionate distribution of the interest accruing upon the Chippewa fund was discussed in an opinion of the Solicitor of the Interior Department (Op. Sol. I. D., M.15954, January 8, 1927).

[141] The Act of March 3, 1839, 5 Stat. 349, 350, providing for the division and distribution of lands belonging to the Brothertown Indians by a board of commissioners, stated that it was the duty of the board "to make a just and fair partition and division of said lands among the members of said tribe, or among such of them as, by the laws and customs and regulations of said tribe, are entitled to the same, and in such proportions and in such manner as shall be consistent with equity and justice, and in accordance with the existing laws, customs, usages, or agreements of said tribe." Numerous other acts which leave the distribution of tribal property to the tribe itself are discussed in Chapter 15, secs. 23 and 24.

[142] For example, the corporate charter of the Winnebago Tribe of Nebraska, ratified August 15, 1936, provides:

> The Tribe may issue to each of its members a nontransferable certificate of membership evidencing the equal share of each member in the assets of the Tribe and may distribute per capita, among the recognized members of the Tribe, all profits of corporate enterprises or income over and above sums necessary to defray corporate obligations and over and above all sums which may be devoted to the establishment of a reserve fund, the construction of public works, the costs of public enterprises, the expenses of tribal government, the needs of charity, or other corporate purpose. No such distribution of profits or income in any one year amounting to a distribution of more than one-half of the accrued surplus, shall be made without the approval of the Secretary of the Interior. No distribution of the financial assets of the Tribe shall be made except as provided herein or as authorized by Congress.

[143] For example, the corporate charter of the Gila River Pima-Maricopa Indian Community (ratified February 28, 1938) provides, in sec. 8: "No per capita distribution of any assets of the community shall be made."

[144] Act of June 10, 1872, 17 Stat. 388 (Ottawa); Act of March 3, 1873, 17 Stat. 623 (Ottawa); Act of May 15, 1888, 25 Stat. 150 (Omaha); Act of August 19, 1890, 26 Stat. 329 (Omaha tribe); Act of February 13, 1891, 26 Stat. 749 (Sac and Fox and Iowa); Act of August 11, 1894, 28 Stat. 276 (Omaha); Act of February 20, 1895, 28 Stat. 677 (Ute); Act of February 28, 1899, 30 Stat. 909 (Pottawatomie and Kickapoo); Act of June 6, 1900, 31 Stat. 672 (Fort Hall); Act of February 28, 1901, 31 Stat. 819 (Seneca); Act of February 20, 1904, 33 Stat. 46 (Red Lake); Act of April 23, 1904, 33 Stat. 254 (Sioux); Act of April 23, 1904, 33 Stat. 302 (Flathead); Act of April 27, 1904, 33 Stat. 319 (Devils Lake); Act of April 27, 1904, 33 Stat. 352 (Crow); Act of April 28, 1904, 33 Stat. 567 (Grande Ronde); Act of December 21, 1904, 33 Stat. 595 (Yakima); Act of March 3, 1905, 33 Stat. 1016 (Shoshone or Wind River); Act of March 20, 1906, 34 Stat. 80 (Kiowa, Comanche, and Apache); Act of March 22, 1906, 34 Stat. 80 (Colville); Act of June 14, 1906, 34 Stat. 262 (Indians in Richardson County, Nebraska); Act of May 30, 1908, 35 Stat. 558 (Fort Peck); Act of February 18, 1909, 35 Stat. 628 (Omaha and Winebago); Act of March 3, 1909, 35 Stat. 75) (Quapaw); Act of May 13, 1910, 36 Stat. 368 (Richardson County, Nebraska); Act of May 11, 1912, 37 Stat. 111 (Omaha); Act of July 1, 1912, 37 Stat. 187 (Winnebago); Act of February 14, 1913, 37 Stat.

In recent years, however, the Federal Government, recognizing that per capita payments would lead to the dissipation of the tribal estate and the creation of new demands upon the Federal Treasury on the part of individual Indians, has sought to discourage the per capita distribution of tribal funds,[145] except where such funds represent continuing income,[146] or where prior legislative commitments preclude application of the current policy of conserving the tribal estate.

The federal policy of discouraging per capita distribution of tribal funds, coupled with a tendency to cut down federal use of tribal funds for Indian Service administration, has made the activity of the tribe itself in distributing tribal property or rights of user therein a matter of increasing importance.[147]

675 (Standing Rock); Act of August 26, 1922, 42 Stat. 832 (Riverside County, California); Act of May 19, 1924, 43 Stat. 132 (Lac du Flambeau Band of Chippewas); Act of January 7, 1925, 43 Stat. 726 (Omaha); Act of February 9, 1925, 43 Stat. 820 (Omaha); Act of March 3, 1927, 44 Stat. 1369 (Kiowa, Comanche, and Apache); Act of March 3, 1927, 44 Stat. 1389 (Cheyenne River); Act of March 3, 1927, 44 Stat. 1397 (Fort Hall); Act of April 29, 1930, 46 Stat. 260 (Iowa); Act of March 2, 1931, 46 Stat. 1481 (Fort Berthold); Act of March 4, 1931, 46 Stat. 1526 (Puyallup); Act of March 3, 1933, 47 Stat. 1488 (Utes); Act of June 20, 1936, 49 Stat. 1543 (Crow); Joint Resolution of June 20, 1936, 49 Stat. 1569 (Fort Belknap). For a fuller discussion of problems involved in pro rata division of tribal property, and general statutes on the subject, see Chapter 15, secs. 22–24, and Chapter 10, secs. 4–5.

[145] Prohibitions against or limitations upon per capita payments are found in the following general statutes: Act of March 3, 1927, 44 Stat. 1347 (tribal oil and gas rentals); Act of June 18, 1934, 48 Stat. 984 (making distribution of tribal assets subject to tribal consent). Prohibitions against per capita payments are likewise found in the following special statutes: Act of May 18, 1928, 45 Stat. 602 (Indians of California); Act of December 17, 1928, 45 Stat. 1027 (Winnebago); Act of February 20, 1929, 45 Stat. 1249 (Nez Perce); Act of February 23, 1929, 45 Stat. 1256 (Coos Bay, Lower Umpqua and Siuslaw); Act of February 23, 1929, 45 Stat. 1258 (Kansas); Act of April 21, 1932, 47 Stat. 87 (Wichita and affiliated bands); Act of June 19, 1935, 49 Stat. 388 (Tlingit and Haida); Act of August 30, 1935, 49 Stat. 1049 (Chippewa). A precursor of this prohibition against per capita distribution is found in the Act of March 3, 1863, 12 Stat. 819 (Sioux).

[146] Act of June 15, 1934, 48 Stat. 964 (Menominee); Act of August 25, 1937, 50 Stat. 811 (Palm Springs).

[147] See Chapter 7, sec. 8.

CHAPTER 10

THE RIGHTS OF THE INDIAN IN HIS PERSONALTY

TABLE OF CONTENTS

SECTION 1. NATURE AND FORMS OF INDIVIDUAL PERSONAL PROPERTY

The forms of personalty held by Indians (*e. g.* funds, personal belongings, notes, mortgages, growing crops, livestock, and choses in action) may be as diverse as those held by non-Indians. So, too, the forms of legal and equitable interests in personal property which may be vested in individual Indians are probably as diverse as among non-Indians. It is not our purpose to analyze those rights in personalty which Indians enjoy in common with other citizens. Yet in so far as the Indian is subject to the special guardianship[1] of the Federal Government, problems peculiar to him arise concerning his acquisition, use, and disposition of his goods and chattels.

Under the United States Constitution, the rights of the Indian in his private property, whatever they may be, are "secured and enforced to the same extent and in the same way as other residents or citizens of the United States."[2] Nonetheless, Congress may, acting within the scope of its constitutional power, control and manage his affairs and property.[3] The rights of the Indian in his personalty are primarily dependent upon the answer to the question: Has Congress, in the particular instance, undertaken to manage the property, and if so, to what extent have powers of management been conferred upon administrative officials?

Where Congress has not imposed restrictions upon the Indian's personal property he may exercise the same power to use, destroy, or alienate his personal property which any other citizen possesses. There is nothing about the status of the individual Indian as such that incapacitates him from exercising the ordinary rights enjoyed by other owners of personal property.[4] Whatever peculiar limitations are to be found in this field are limitations attached to the property rather than limitations affecting the person.

[1] "Guardian-ward" concepts are discussed in Chapter 8, sec. 9.

[2] See *Choate* v. *Trapp*, 224 U. S. 665, 677 (1912).

[3] For the extent of congressional power over Indian affairs and Indian property, see Chapter 5.

[4] See Chapter 8.

If legal problems in the field of Indian-owned personal property are viewed from this standpoint, the statutory or treaty origin of any property is of final importance in determining what limitations are attached to its use or disposition. If the treaty or statute provides that funds or teakettles are to be turned over to an Indian without restriction, that ordinarily ends the matter. The funds or the teakettles become the absolute property of the recipient, who may thereafter utilize, destroy, conserve, or give away his property without the consent of any official. On the other hand, if Congress provides that certain property shall be distributed to Indians "under such rules and regulations as the Secretary of the Interior may prescribe," it becomes necessary to examine what those rules and regulations provide in order to determine how far rights ordinarily associated with ownership can be exercised by the Indian and how far they rest with the reservation superintendent or some other government official.

Generally, but not universally, restricted personal property represents a carry-over of restrictions imposed upon land ownership. Since Indian lands have generally been subjected to restrictions on lease or sale,[5] the treaties and statutes authorizing such lease or sale might, and often did, provide that the cash returns derived from such disposition of lands should be held by the United States in trust for the Indians concerned or should be turned over to the Indians subject to specific restrictions upon use or disposition. The legal justification for such provisions was that the Federal Government, having power to forbid or permit land alienation might condition its permission by extending restrictions to the proceeds derived from restricted lands. The factual justification was, generally, that the Indians might squander the proceeds of their lands and thus render themselves a burden to the Government or a danger to their neighbors unless restrained from doing so by governmental restrictions.

[5] See Chapter 11, secs. 4 and 5.

The policy problems which are raised in this field involve a balancing of two objectives: on the one hand to safeguard the economic future of the Indian and the purse strings of the Federal Government by preventing the dissipation of the Indian's capital assets; on the other hand to minimize the cost of paternal supervision that such safeguarding entails and to give the individual Indian the right to exercise his own judgment, and to make mistakes in the process, without which practical education in economics is impossible. At different times and in diverging circumstances, the balance between these conflicting objectives has naturally varied. No simple formula will explain why certain property has been restricted and other property turned over to Indian owners without strings. All that can be attempted in this chapter in that regard is to indicate the principal types of legislation in the field.

SECTION 2. SOURCES OF INDIVIDUAL PERSONAL PROPERTY

The same Indian may possess at one time restricted and unrestricted funds. With unrestricted funds, as, for example, wages earned by the Indian in private employment, he may do just as he wishes, as any other person might.[6] Funds may come from sources not subject to control by the Federal Government; yet Congress may restrict the Indian's use of such funds as long as it retains its guardianship over the Indian.[7] On the other hand, funds, presently unrestricted, may have had their source in other restricted property.

The chief sources of funds which have given rise to special problems of Indian law are:[8]

1. Proceeds, including income, from restricted allotted lands.
2. Tribal funds individualized by per capita distributions to the Indians.
3. Payments from the Federal Government.
4. Payments of damages for loss of property.
5. Proceeds from the sale of restricted crops and livestock.

[6] See *Choteau* v. *Burnet*, 283 U. S. 691 (1931), aff'g sub nom. *Choteau* v. *Commissioner of Internal Revenue*, 38 F. 2d 976 (C. C. A. 10, 1930).

[7] See *Hickey* v. *United States*, 64 F. 2d 628 (C. C. A. 10, 1933); *United States* v. *Waller*, 243 U. S. 452 (1917); *Brader* v. *James*, 246 U. S. 88 (1918); and see Chapter 5, secs. 5C, D.

[8] Op. Sol. I. D., M.25258, June 26, 1929.

SECTION 3. SOURCES OF INDIVIDUAL PERSONAL PROPERTY—PROCEEDS FROM ALLOTTED LANDS

Comparatively few of the allotment acts have any specific direction governing the distribution of the proceeds from the disposition of the individual's land, either by sale or lease.[9] The General Allotment Act of 1887[10] did not permit any disposition, except by descent, of allotted lands for certain periods of time, during which the lands were to be held in trust by the United States. But realizing that the heirs might not want the inherited lands, since they might have allotted lands of their own, and desiring to encourage the sale of such lands,[11] Congress, in the Appropriation Act of May 27, 1902,[12] provided that trust lands inherited from Indians might be conveyed in fee by them subject to the approval of the Secretary of the Interior.[13]

The rights of the heirs to the proceeds derived from conveyance are discussed in the cases of *National Bank of Commerce* v. *Anderson*[14] and *United States* v. *Thurston County, Nebraska*,[15] which sustain the regulations of the Secretary of the Interior controlling the proceeds under the Act of 1902. The court in the *National Bank of Commerce* case holds that the Act of 1902 does not indicate an intent by Congress to vacate the trust of the lands held in trust. When the lands are sold with the consent of the Secretary, the trust attaches to the proceeds, which are payable to the heirs under the rules prescribed by the Interior Department. In approving sales by heirs, the Secretary of the Interior had prescribed that all proceeds of such sales be deposited in United States depositories to the individual credit of each heir as his interest in the estate indicated and subject to checks of $10 per month with the approval of the agent in charge and in larger amounts only when authorized by the Commissioner of Indian Affairs.[16]

In *United States Fidelity and Guaranty Co.* v. *Hansen*,[17] the court holds that the purchase price derived from the sale of the land by the heir is a trust fund; that under the provision of the act requiring the Secretary of the Interior to approve a conveyance, he has the authority to exercise the government's option of continuing control or relinquishing it.

In 1907, Congress took the further step and permitted the sale or lease of allotted lands by either the allottee or his heirs during the trust period,

> * * * on such terms and conditions and under such rules and regulations as the Secretary of the Interior may prescribe, and the proceeds derived therefrom shall be used for the benefit of the allottee or heir so disposing of his land or interest, under the supervision of the Commissioner of Indian Affairs; * * *.[18]

In the same Act of March 1, 1907,[19] Congress amended the Act of 1902, and relinquished some control over the proceeds derived from the sale of allotments in the White Earth Reservation in Minnesota. The amendment provides for the removal of re-

[9] See Chapter 11.

[10] Sec. 5, Act of February 8, 1887, 24 Stat. 388, 389.

[11] The Act of 1902 permits alienation by the heirs, subject to the approval of the Secretary of the Interior, on the assumption that they would be "more competent in many cases to manage their own affairs than would the original allottee have been; and that the Secretary of the Interior should be the judge as to whether that condition has come about." *United States* v. *Park Land Co.*, 188 Fed. 383, 387 (C. C. Minn. 1911).

> The purpose of the statute evidently is that lands inherited from deceased allottees by heirs who had and were living upon allotments of their own, might be sold and converted into money, rather than remain untilled and unoccupied.

National Bank of Commerce v. *Anderson*, 147 Fed. 87, 89 (C. C. A. 9, 1906).

[12] Sec. 7, 32 Stat. 245, 275, 25 U. S. C. 379.

[13] The approval of the Secretary of the Interior was necessary to the validity of a conveyance by an adult heir of an Indian allottee. *United States* v. *Leslie*, 167 Fed. 670 (C. C. S. D. 1909).

[14] 147 Fed. 87 (C. C. A. 9, 1906).

[15] 143 Fed. 287 (C. C. A. 8, 1906), rev'g 140 Fed. 456 (C. C. Nebr. 1905).

[16] Rules promulgated September 16, 1904, sustained in *United States* v. *Thurston County*, *supra*, fn. 15. See Chapter 13, sec. 4.

[17] 36 Okla. 459, 129 Pac. 60 (1912).

[18] Appropriation Act of March 1, 1907, 34 Stat. 1015, 1018, 25 U. S. C. 405. See Chapter 11.

[19] 34 Stat. 1015, 1034.

strictions on allotments held by adult mixed bloods. In *United States* v. *Park Land Co.*,[20] the court construes this amendment to remove from federal control the sale of lands in the White Earth Reservation and the proceeds derived therefrom by the adult mixed-blood Indian, no matter how it has come to him. As for an adult full blood, the act provides that the Secretary of the Interior may remove the restrictions upon the sale of his allotment if satisfied that that Indian is competent to handle his own affairs. Till then, Congress retains control over the land and the proceeds therefrom.

Section 1 of the Act of May 29, 1908,[21] which expressly excludes from its scope lands in Oklahoma, Minnesota, and South Dakota, permits the sale of allotments on petition of the allottee, his heir, or duly authorized representative,

> *Provided*, That the proceeds derived from all sales hereunder shall be used, during the trust period, for the benefit of the allottee, or heir, so disposing of his interest, under the supervision of the Commissioner of Indian Affairs: * * *

Sections 1[22] and 4[23] of the Act of June 25, 1910,[24] provide generally for the control of the proceeds from the sale or lease of the Indian's restricted lands. Section 8 of the act allows the sale of timber on trust allotments with the consent of the Secretary of the Interior and the distribution of the proceeds to the allottee or disposal for his benefit under rules and regulations prescribed by the Secretary of the Interior.[25]

The imposition of a trust over Indian funds may be effectuated by treaty as well as by statute. In the treaty concluded September 30, 1854,[26] between the United States and certain Chippewa Indians, a system of allotting tribal lands was established. Article 3 of the treaty provided that the President was to assign the allotments and that he might issue patents "with such restrictions of the power of alienation as he might see fit to impose." In the exercise of this power, he may include in the patent a restriction against alienation without his consent. In the case of *Starr* v. *Campbell*,[27] it is held that this restriction extends to the timber on the land and therefore the President could regulate the distribution of the proceeds from the sale of the timber.[28]

On the other hand, Congress may permit the leasing of allotted lands, subject to the approval of the Secretary of the Interior, but specifically providing that the allottees "* * * shall have full control of the same, including the proceeds thereof * * *."[29]

A perusal of the acts cited indicates a general intent of Congress to retain, for a time, governmental control of the proceeds from the disposition of restricted allotted lands and to leave to the discretion of administrative officials the time and manner in which such funds are to be distributed or expended, subject to the qualification that the funds be used for the benefit of the Indian.

---

[20] 188 Fed. 383 (C. C. Minn. 1911). In *United States* v. *First National Bank*, 234 U. S. 245 (1914), aff'g 208 Fed. 988 (C. C. A. 8, 1913), a case involving an attempt by the United States to set aside a conveyance of land by an Indian having less than one-eighth white blood, the Supreme Court held that any identifiable amount of white blood brought an Indian within the scope of the provision of the Act of March 1, 1907, removing restrictions upon the allotments of mixed-blood Indians.

[21] 35 Stat. 444, 25 U. S. C. 404.

[22] * * * All sales of lands allotted to Indians * * * shall be made under such rules and regulations * * * as the Secretary of the Interior may prescribe * * * *Provided*, That the proceeds of the sale of inherited lands shall be paid to such heir or heirs as may be competent and held in trust subject to use and expenditure during the trust period for such heir or heirs as may be incompetent, as their respective interests shall appear * * *.

The section permits the deposit of Indian funds held by federal disbursing agents in banks. This provision is not affected by the Act of March 3, 1928, 45 Stat. 161, amending sec. 1. See 25 U. S. C. 372.

[23] Sec. 4 provides for the leasing of allotted lands for a period not to exceed 5 years, subject to and in conformity with such rules and regulations as the Secretary of the Interior may prescribe, and the proceeds of any such lease shall be paid to the allottee or his heirs, or expended for his or their benefit, in the discretion of the Secretary of the Interior. See 25 U. S. C. 403.

[24] 36 Stat. 855. This act applies to proceeds derived from the sale of lands held in trust as well as lands in which the power of alienation is restricted. *United States* v. *Bowling*, 256 U. S. 484 (1921), rev'g 261 Fed. 657 (D. C. E. D. N. Y. 1919).

[25] The Act of March 4, 1907, 34 Stat. 1413, provides also for the sale of merchantable timber on allotments on the Jicarilla Reservation and declares that the proceeds therefrom are to be expended under the direction of the Secretary of the Interior for purposes beneficial to the Indian.

In the Appropriation Act of May 18, 1916, 39 Stat. 123. Congress provided for the disposal of flowage rights on the allotments of Indians of the Lac Court Oreilles Tribe. The provision states that,

> any allottee or the heirs of any deceased allottee, as a condition to giving his or their consent to the leasing or granting of flowage rights on their respective allotments, may determine, subject to the approval of the Secretary of the Interior, what consideration or rental shall be received for such flowage rights, and in what manner and for what purposes such consideration or rental shall be paid or expended; and the consideration or rental shall be paid or expended under such rules and regulations as the Secretary of the Interior may prescribe. (P. 158.)

Under the agreement concluded between the Columbia and Colville Indians and the United States on July 7, 1883, ratified by the Appropriation Act of July 4, 1884, 23 Stat. 76, 79–80, allotments of tribal lands are made, but no provision is made for the sale of allotments; hence no problem of rights in funds therefrom could arise. However, by the Act of March 4, 1911, 36 Stat. 1358, Congress authorizes the Secretary of the Interior to sell some of the land held in trust for certain named Indians and to conserve the funds for the benefit of the allottee or to invest or expend them for the individual's benefit in such manner as he might determine. The Act of May 20, 1924, c. 160, 43 Stat. 133, permits the disposition of patented lands by the Columbia or Colville allottee, or if he were deceased; the heirs might convey the land in accordance with the provisions of the Act of June 25, 1910, 36 Stat. 855.

[26] 10 Stat. 1109.

[27] 208 U. S. 527 (1908).

[28] See Chapter 11, sec. 4B. Under the regulations approved by the President December 8, 1893, proceeds from the sale of timber from allotted lands, after the deduction of expenses, were to be deposited in some national bank, subject to the check of the allottee, countersigned by the Indian agent. In December 1902 the regulations were amended so that if the allottee were deemed incompetent to manage his own affairs, the agent had the authority, subject to the approval of the Commissioner of Indian Affairs, to fix the amounts the Indian could withdraw. For regulations regarding timber, see 25 C. F. R. 61.1–61.29.

[29] Osage Allotment Act of June 28, 1906, sec. 7, 34 Stat. 539, 545. For a discussion of this statute, see Chapter 23, sec. 12A.

SECTION 4. SOURCES OF INDIVIDUAL PERSONAL PROPERTY—INDIVIDUALIZATION OF TRIBAL FUNDS

A second important source of individual funds is the individualization of tribal funds.[30] Since tribal funds generally represent the income from disposition of tribal lands, the Federal Government has commonly extended the restrictions on the land to the proceeds therefrom. By a further extension, Congress has frequently imposed, as conditions to the right of the individual to participate in tribal funds, certain restrictions affecting his use of the funds after they have become individualized.[31]

---

[30] The nature of tribal funds is discussed in Chapter 15; the right of the individual to share in tribal funds is discussed in Chapter 9. On administrative power over tribal funds, see Chapter 5, sec. 10, and over individual funds, see *ibid.*, sec. 12. On regulations regarding moneys, tribal and individual, see 25 C. F. R. 221.1–233.7.

[31] See Chapter 9.

By the Act of March 2, 1907,[32] Congress provided generally for the distribution of tribal funds among individuals. Those Indians whom the Secretary of the Interior believed capable of managing their affairs could have placed to their credit upon the books of the United States Treasury their pro rata share of the tribal funds held in trust by the United States, and they could draw upon this credit without any further governmental control.[33] Section 2 of the act provided that the Secretary of the Interior might pay to disabled Indians their shares in tribal property, under such rules and conditions as he might prescribe. As later amended[34] this section authorizes the Secretary of the Interior upon application by an Indian "mentally or physically incapable of managing his or her own affairs," to withdraw the pro rata share of such Indian in the tribal funds, and to expend such sums on behalf of the Indian.

Section 28 of the Appropriation Act of May 25, 1918,[35] which specifically excluded from its scope the funds of the Five Civilized Tribes and the Osages, in Oklahoma, authorized the Secretary of the Interior to withdraw tribal funds from the Treasury of the United States and to credit recognized members of the tribe with equal shares. However, this authority was revoked by section 2 of the Act of June 24, 1938.[36] Nevertheless, the Indian may still apply for funds as his pro rata share in tribal assets, under the Act of 1907.[37] The granting of such applications is contrary to the general administrative policy of conserving tribal funds, but in special circumstances such pro rata distributions are still made. It has been held by the Interior Department that, under section 16 of the Act of June 18, 1934,[38] such applications must receive the approval of the tribal council, if the tribe in question is organized under that act.[39]

The individual may be awarded, by special statute, a specified sum from the tribal funds on deposit in the United States Treasury. A typical act is the Act of February 12, 1932,[40] providing for payment of $25 to each enrolled Chippewa of Minnesota from tribal funds, under such regulations as the Secretary of the Interior may prescribe.

In the individualization of tribal funds, Congress has at various times laid down directions under which the Secretary of the Interior should expend the funds.

In the Act of March 3, 1933,[41] Congress provided for the distribution of tribal funds of the Ute Indians. The shares of all were to be deposited as individual Indian moneys[42] and subject to disbursement for the individual's benefit in the following ways: for improving lands, erecting homes, purchase of equipment, livestock, household goods and in other ways as will enable them to become self-supporting. The shares of the aged, infirm, and other incapacitated members were to be used for their support and maintenance. As for minors, their shares might be invested or spent in the same fashion as prescribed for adults, but when their funds were to be invested or expended, the consent of the parents and the approval of the Secretary of the Interior was necessary.[43]

Acts providing for the payment of judgments in favor of a tribe may limit the rights of the Indian in individualized tribal funds by the qualification that "the per-capita share due each member * * * be credited to the individual Indian money account of such member for expenditure in accordance with the individual Indian money regulations."[44] Various resolutions authorizing the distribution of judgments rendered in favor of Indian tribes provide for per capita payments to each enrolled member, such distribution to be made under such rules and regulations as the Secretary of the Interior may prescribe.[45]

By virtue of these acts, Congress has given to the Secretary of the Interior authority over individual funds derived from the tribal property held in trust comparable to the authority over funds derived from the individual's restricted property.[46]

[32] 34 Stat. 1221, 25 U. S. C. 119.
[33] Op. Sol. I. D. M.25258, June 26, 1929.
[34] Amended by Act of May 18, 1916, 39 Stat. 123, 128, 25 U. S. C. 121.
[35] 40 Stat. 561, 591–592.
[36] 52 Stat. 1037.
[37] 34 Stat. 1221.
[38] Memo. Sol. I. D., September 21, 1939.
[39] 48 Stat. 984, 987, 25 U. S. C. 476.
[40] 47 Stat. 49. Acts of similar nature are cited in Chapter 9, sec. 6.
[41] 47 Stat. 1488.

[42] "Individual Indian moneys are funds, regardless of derivation, belonging to individual Indians which come into the custody of a disbursing agent." 25 C. F. R. 221.1. See sec. 8, *infra*, for a discussion of these regulations.

[43] *Cf.*, Act of June 1, 1938, 52 Stat. 605, as amended by sec. 2(b), Act of August 7, 1939, Pub. No. 325, 76th Cong., 1st sess. (Klamath).

[44] Joint Resolution, June 20, 1936, 49 Stat. 1569, authorizing distribution of judgment in favor of Gros Ventre Indians among enrolled members.

[45] The Joint Resolution of June 20, 1936, 49 Stat. 1568, provides for a per capita payment of $85, and places the remainder of the fund awarded to the Blackfeet Tribe at the disposal of the tribal council and the Secretary of the Interior.

Under the Joint Resolution of April 29, 1930, 46 Stat. 260, the Secretary of the Interior is authorized to pay a judgment in favor of the Iowa Tribe to members of the tribe in pro-rata shares. The competent members receive their entire shares in cash; the shares of the others, including minors, are deposited to the individual credit of each and subject to existing laws governing Indian moneys.

The right of the Chippewa allottee on the Lac du Flambeau Reservation to the proceeds derived from the sale of tribal timber is controlled by the Act of May 19, 1924, 43 Stat. 132. After providing for the sale under rules and regulations prescribed by the Secretary of the Interior, the act states that the net proceeds are to be distributed per capita. Those whom the Secretary shall deem competent to handle their own affairs shall receive their shares. As for the others, their shares are deposited to their individual credit and paid to them or used for their benefit under the Secretary's supervision.

[46] See Chapter 5, secs. 11 and 12.

SECTION 5. SOURCES OF INDIVIDUAL PERSONAL PROPERTY—PAYMENTS FROM THE FEDERAL GOVERNMENT

A third source of individual personalty comprises the various forms of direct payment to individual Indians from the Federal Government. In this connection a distinction must be drawn between obligations assumed by the Federal Government towards the various tribes, by reason of the sale of tribal lands or otherwise, and obligations running directly to the members of the tribes. Problems arising out of the former situation are dealt with elsewhere.[47] For the present we are concerned only with the situations in which the Federal Government has undertaken to make payments, in money or goods, to individual Indians.

Gifts were sometimes made for the purpose of civilizing the Indians by giving them agricultural aids and clothes.[48] Gifts

[47] See Chapters 9 and 15.

[48] The Act of March 30, 1802, sec. 13, 2 Stat. 139, 143, provides in part:

> That in order to promote civilization among the friendly Indian tribes, and to secure the continuance of their friendship, it shall be lawful for the President of the United States, to cause them to be furnished with useful domestic animals, and implements of husbandry, and with goods or money, as he shall judge proper * * *.

In the Appropriation Act of March 3, 1875, 18 Stat. 420, are numerous appropriations for agricultural pursuits. Miamies of Kansas are given

were also justified simply on the ground that the Indian needed the bounty for subsistence.[49]

A. ANNUITIES [50]

Periodic payments of either money or goods are called "annuities." According to the terms of the instrument, an annuity may be a specific amount for a specified number of years,[51] or it may be a specified amount for life [52] or while the Indians are at peace.[53]

Frequently the individual recipients of annuities were the chiefs or others of the tribe who were influential in keeping the peace and in treaty making.[54] Treaties often provided that a sum of money or other gifts would be paid when a particular treaty went into effect.[55] At times the United States would promise to pay the salary of the chief annually [56] but the policy behind this was probably no different than that fostering the payment of annuities.

In order to induce Indians to settle upon homesteads [57] or accept allotments,[58] Congress generally provided that those Indians who accepted the benefits of homestead and allotment acts would not lose any rights in annuities and other personalty and that those Indians who did receive allotments would be assured of receiving compensation for damages occasioned by trespass of Indians who had not received allotments by payments from annuities due the trespassers.[59]

B. METHOD OF PAYMENT

While ordinarily the obligations of the United States under treaties and agreements with the Indian tribes were considered obligations owing to the tribes, even where the Federal Government assumed the task of paying over the promised sums per capita to the members of the tribe,[60] there have been cases in which the obligation of the United States ran directly to individual Indians.

In the treaty with the Shawnees on May 10, 1854,[61] the United States was to pay certain sums to these Indians. Section 8 of the treaty provides that competent Shawnees should receive their portions in seven annual payments and in money. As for those incompetent to manage their own affairs, the President was to dispose of their portion in a manner he believed to be for the best interests of them and of their families after consulting the Shawnee Council. The funds due the minor orphan children were to be appropriated by the President in a manner considered to be for their best interest.

The payments due the orphan children became a matter of litigation which reached the Supreme Court of the United States in 1894 in the case of *United States* v. *Blackfeather*.[62] The Court discusses the treaty of 1854 and finds that under it the President had determined that the orphans' funds should be paid to them in severalty. He committed some of the money to a United States Indian superintendent for distribution but said officer embezzled it. Another portion was paid to guardians of the orphans who were created by the Shawnee Council, but because of laches or dishonesty, this portion never reached the orphans. The Shawnee Tribe brought this action to collect this money from the Government. In its decision, the court holds that the tribe has no authority to sue for these moneys under a jurisdictional act authorizing suit for moneys claimed in tribal capacity. The Court also holds that the Government is not liable to the tribe for the portion paid to the guardians appointed by the tribal council, but intimates that the Government may have a moral obligation to reimburse the money embezzled by the Indian superintendent.[63]

Because of difficulties of the type that arose under the Shawnee treaty and described above, Congress in 1862 passed an act prohibiting the payment of money to any person appointed by any Indian council on behalf of incompetent or orphan Indians, and providing that said moneys shall remain in the United States Treasury at 6 percent interest until ordered to be paid by the Secretary of the Interior.[64]

---

money for grain and seed for farming purposes (p. 432); money in aid of agricultural pursuits, to be given to Poncas (p. 436); River-Crows (p. 437). Appropriations for clothes are made to Bannocks (p. 440); to Shoshones (p. 440); Six Nations of New York (p. 441); Cheyennes and Arapahoes (p. 424); Crows (p. 429).

The Acts of April 30, 1888, sec. 17, 25 Stat. 94, 101, and of March 2, 1889, sec. 17, 25 Stat. 888, 895, dividing the Sioux lands, provide for the distribution of cattle and farming implements among the Sioux allottees.

[49] The Appropriation Act of March 3, 1875, 18 Stat. 420, makes an appropriation for subsistence to those Apaches of Arizona and New Mexico "who go and remain upon said reservations and refrain from hostilities, * * *" (p. 423); appropriation for the aged, sick, infirm and orphans among the Assiniboines (p. 424); the Blackfeet, Bloods, and Piegans (p. 424).

The Appropriation Act of June 25, 1864, 13 Stat. 161, provides for the subsistence of Indians who remain loyal to the United States, including members of the Five Civilized Tribes and affiliated tribes (pp. 180–181). The Appropriation Act of March 3, 1865, 13 Stat. 541, provides for the subsistence of a number of Chippewas of the Mississippi.

In the Treaty of August 9, 1814, with the Creek Nation, 7 Stat. 120, the United States agreed to furnish members of the Creek Nation with the necessaries of life until they were able to take care of themselves to some extent.

[50] For regulations regarding annuity and other per capita payments, see 25 C. F. R. 224.1–224.5.

[51] By the Treaty of October 7, 1863, Art. 10, 13 Stat. 673, 675, with the Tabeguache Band of Utah Indians, each family receives a number of sheep and cattle annually for 5 years.

[52] Treaty of January 20, 1825, with Choctaw Nation, 7 Stat. 234; Treaty of September 26, 1833, with Chippewa, Ottowa, and Potawatamie Indians, 7 Stat. 431; Treaty of September 24, 1829, with Delaware Indians, 7 Stat. 327; Treaty of January 7, 1806, 7 Stat. 101, 102 (Cherokee chief receives $100 per year for life); Treaty of September 20, 1828, 7 Stat. 317, 318 (Potowatamie chief receives $100 per year in goods for life).

[53] Appropriation Act of March 3, 1875, 18 Stat. 420, 423 (supplies to those who refrain from fighting). Act ratifying agreement with Utes, April 29, 1874, 18 Stat. 36, 38.

[54] Art. V of the Treaty with the Chippewas, October 2, 1863, 13 Stat. 667, provides that the Chippewa chiefs may receive a house and annuity, to encourage peace and to encourage others to become orderly.

Treaty with the Chickasaw, October 19, 1818, 7 Stat. 192, 194. Because of their friendliness to the United States, the chiefs receive $150 in cash or in goods.

[55] Appropriation Act of July 2, 1836, 5 Stat. 73, 75.

[56] The Act of April 29, 1874, 18 Stat. 36, provides for the payment of salary to the head chief of the Ute Nation by the United States at the rate of $1,000 per year for the term of 10 years, or as long as he remains head chief and at peace with the United States.

The Act of December 15, 1874, 18 Stat. 291, provides for a salary of $500 per year by the United States for a term of 5 years. Accord: Treaty of June 11, 1855, 12 Stat. 957 (salary of Nez Perce chief to be paid); Treaty of June 25, 1855, 12 Stat. 963 (salary of chief of Oregon bands to be paid); Treaty of June 9, 1855, 12 Stat. 951 (salary to be paid to Yakama chief).

[57] Appropriation Act of March 3, 1865, 13 Stat. 541, 562, sec. 4, relating to Stockbridge and Munsee Indians; Appropriation Act of March 3, 1875, 18 Stat. 402, 420, sec. 15 (general act).

[58] Act of March 3, 1843, 5 Stat. 645 (Stockbridge).

[59] Act of June 14, 1862, 12 Stat. 427 (general act).

[60] See Chapter 15, secs. 22–23.

[61] 10 Stat. 1053.

[62] 155 U. S. 180 (1894).

[63] In the Appropriation Act of July 7, 1884, 23 Stat. 236, 247, an appropriation was made for that purpose.

[64] Sec. 6, Act of July 5, 1862, 12 Stat. 512, 529–530, which is embodied in R. S. § 2108 and 25 U. S. C. 159.

SECTION 6. SOURCES OF INDIVIDUAL PERSONAL PROPERTY—PAYMENTS OF DAMAGES

The Indian may receive funds because of being dispossessed from all or some of his lands. Acts or treaties which convey or reserve to the Indian tribe or to its members certain rights in land usually provide that the United States guarantees to them security and protection in the exercise of such rights.[65] The right of the individual to receive compensation for damages to his lands and property used in connection with it is derived in part from such provisions.

The loss of his land may be occasioned by the Government's taking.[66] A more frequent disposition of the Indian's land occurs when Congress grants rights-of-way across the land for railroad and similar purposes. Some treaties, such as the 1854 treaty with the Shawnees,[67] provide specifically for payment to Indians for any roads made through their lands. The acts granting such rights-of-way provide for payment of compensation for the taking of the land and for any damages done to his other property, such as chattels.[68] Although the property taken may have been restricted, nevertheless, it is a general policy of the acts to free from Government control the expenditure of the funds by making provision only for the supervision of payment to the Indians. The Act of May 6, 1910,[69] is a typical illustration. It provides that the railroad company shall pay to the Secretary of the Interior the amount of the damages and compensation. The act continues: "that the damages and compensation paid to the Secretary of the Interior by the railway company taking any such land shall be paid by said Secretary to the allottee sustaining such damages."

Similarly, many acts or treaties providing for the removal of the Indian from the land of which he has possession stipulate that he is to receive money or other goods as payment for any improvements he made on the land or chattels he must leave behind.[70]

Related to moneys and other personal property given to Indians for property left behind are the gifts made to the individual Indians to aid them in their emigration from the lands ceded.[71]

[65] Treaty with Miamies, November 6, 1838, 7 Stat. 569, 571. See Chapter 15, sec. 10.

[66] The Act of April 28, 1924, c. 134, 43 Stat. 111, appropriates a sum of $85,000 for the benefit of dispossessed Nisqually Indians. Sec. 2 provides that the sum "shall be expended, in the discretion of the Secretary of the Interior, for the benefit of the said dispossessed families or individual Indians, under such rules and regulations as he may prescribe."

[67] May 10, 1854, sec. 13, 10 Stat. 1053, 1058.

[68] See Chapter 15, secs. 1, 17.

[69] 36 Stat. 349.

[70] Treaty with Cherokees, July 8, 1817, 7 Stat. 156, 158, provides that the Cherokee emigrants are to be paid for loss of improvements by receiving rifles and other personal property; Treaty with Wyandots, etc., September 29, 1817, 7 Stat. 160, 166; Treaty with Chickasaws, October 19, 1818, 7 Stat. 192, 194; Treaty with Choctaws, October 18, 1820, 7 Stat. 210, 212–213; Treaty with Quapaws, November 15, 1824, 7 Stat. 232; Article 11, Treaty with Creeks, January 24, 1826, 7 Stat. 286, 288; Treaty with Cherokees, May 6, 1828, 7 Stat. 311, 313–314; Treaty with Senecas, February 28, 1831, 7 Stat. 348, 349; Treaty with Wyandots, etc., July 20, 1831, 7 Stat. 351, 352; Treaty with Ottaways, August 30, 1831, 7 Stat. 359, 360; Article 9, Treaty with Cherokees, December 29, 1835, 7 Stat. 478, 482; Treaty with New York Indians, January 15, 1838, 7 Stat. 550; Treaty with Menominees, October 18, 1848, 9 Stat. 952, 953; Treaty with Stockbridges and Munsees, February 5, 1856, 11 Stat. 663, 667; Treaty with Senecas, November 5, 1857, 11 Stat. 735, 737; Act of April 30, 1888, 25 Stat. 94, 103 (Sioux); Act of March 2, 1889, 25 Stat. 888, 897–898 (Sioux); Act of February 20, 1895, 28 Stat. 677 (Ute).

[71] Appropriation Act of July 29, 1848, sec. 4 (R. S. § 3689) and 5, 9 Stat. 252, 264–265 (Each Cherokee to receive a sum of money when he moves west); Joint Resolution, March 3, 1845, 6 Stat. 942 (Those Miamies moving west of the Mississippi receive tribal annuities); Treaty with Choctaws, September 27, 1830, Art. 20, 7 Stat. 333, 338 (Each emigrating Choctaw warrior receives rifle, etc.); Treaty with Cherokees, December 29, 1835, Art. 8, 7 Stat. 478, 482 (Money for moving expenses paid).

SECTION 7. FEDERAL PROTECTION OF INDIVIDUAL PERSONAL PROPERTY

Though the Indian enjoys the legal capacity to enforce his property rights in court, nevertheless his ability to do so has often been handicapped by unfamiliarity with legal processes and rules of law.[72] To aid the Indian in the protection of his rights and to supplement these rights, the Government has at various times sought to give additional protection to the individual Indian. The exent to which the United States may bring suit or intervene in litigation affecting Indian property[73] and the statutory responsibility of the United States attorneys in Indian litigation are discussed elsewhere.[74]

In various treaties and acts of Congress may be found provisions informing the Indian of his rights respecting depredations committed by whites and by other Indians, or provisions creating rights of damages therefrom.

Treaties may contain declaratory provisions stating the Indian's rights of property. Article 10 of the Treaty of November 6, 1838, with the Miamies[75] provides in part: "the United States shall protect the said tribe and the people thereof, in their rights and possessions, against injuries, encroachments, and oppressions of any person or persons, tribe or tribes whatsoever."

In the Treaty of Dancing Rabbit Creek[76] with the Choctaws, Article 12 protected the Indian's personalty. It provided in part:

> Private property to be always respected and on no occasion taken for public purposes without just compensation being made therefor to the rightful owner. * * * And if a white man unlawfully take or steal any thing from an Indian, the property shall be restored and the offender punished.

Similar provisions protecting the Indians' rights to their personalty are found in acts of Congress. As early as 1796 Congress indicated a policy to protect Indian property by the passage of the Indian Trade and Intercourse Act of May 19, 1796.[77] It provided that any white person who takes Indian property shall upon conviction of crime be sentenced (in addition to the usual sentence) to pay to the Indian to whom the property taken belongs, a sum twice the just value of such property. Furthermore, the United States Treasury is directed to pay the Indian the just value of stolen or destroyed property if compensation cannot be secured from the white criminal. This protection was continued by subsequent acts.[78]

[72] See Chapter 8, sec. 6.

[73] See Chapter 19, sec. 2A(1) and (3).

[74] See Chapter 12, sec. 8.

[75] 7 Stat. 569, 571.

[76] Entered into September 27, 1830, 7 Stat. 333, 335, proclaimed February 24, 1831.

[77] Sec. 4, 1 Stat. 469, 470.

[78] Act of March 3, 1799, sec. 4, 1 Stat. 743, 744–745; Act of January 17, 1800, sec. 4, 2 Stat. 6; Act of March 30, 1802, sec. 4, 2 Stat. 139, 141; Act of June 30, 1834, sec. 16, 4 Stat. 729, 731, R. S. § 2154, § 2155, 25 U. S. C. 227, 228.

Other treaties provide for reimbursement to the Indian for damages to his personalty. For example, Article 4 of the Treaty of 1832 with the Potawatamies[79] contains a schedule listing the names of various Indians whom the United States agrees to reimburse for horses stolen from them during a war between the United States and the Sacs and Foxes.[80]

[79] Concluded October 20, 1832, proclaimed January 21, 1833, 7 Stat. 378, 379.

[80] For examples of other treaties containing provision of payment by the United States for damages sustained, see Treaty with Shawnees, May 10, 1854, Art. 11, 10 Stat. 1053, 1057; Treaty with Shawnees, etc., February 23, 1867, Art. 12, 15 Stat. 513, 516; Treaty with Kickapoos, June 28, 1862, Art. 9, 13 Stat. 623; Treaty with Tabeguache Band of Utah Indians, October 7, 1863, Art. 6, 13 Stat. 673; Treaty with Pawnee Marhar Tribe, June 22, 1818, Art. 6, 7 Stat. 175, 178; Treaty with Chippewas of the Mississippi, May 7, 1864, Art. 3, 13 Stat. 693.

In accordance with treaties and acts of this type, Congress has at various times caused to be paid to Indians sums for property taken from them.[81]

[81] Act of March 15, 1832, 6 Stat. 480 (Cherokee paid for slaves taken by white man); Act of July 13, 1832, 4 Stat. 576 (Cherokee Indians paid for livestock taken by United States citizens); Act of June 30, 1834, 6 Stat. 592 (Creek to be paid for horse stolen by white men); Appropriation Act of September 30, 1850, 9 Stat. 544, 588 (Seminole reimbursed for money stolen by United States soldier); Appropriation Act of March 3, 1863, 12 Stat. 774, 791 (Omaha chief paid for horses killed by white settlers); Appropriation Act of March 3, 1865, 13 Stat. 541, 560 (Chippewa chief paid for loss of house and furniture); Act of January 19, 1891, 26 Stat. 720 (Indians of Standing Rock and Cheyenne River agencies to be paid for ponies taken by United States); Appropriation Acts of December 22, 1927, 45 Stat. 2, 16, and of March 4, 1929, 45 Stat. 1550.

SECTION 8. EXPENDITURE AND INVESTMENT OF INDIVIDUAL INDIAN MONEYS

As may be noted in the statutes cited in this chapter, the rules and regulations prescribed by the Secretary of the Interior with reference to the disposition of individual Indian moneys are subject to the congressional requirement that the funds shall be used for the use and benefit of the Indian. The Secretary may not make gifts or donations on behalf of the Indian; nor create private trusts to which he might transfer the supervision and control that was intrusted to him.[82] Nevertheless, the meaning of the term "for the use and benefit of the Indian" is relative, and in absence of a showing of fraud or a lack of understanding as to what might be within the purview of this phrase, the court will not set aside the act and judgment of the Secretary of the Interior.[83]

It has been held by the Solicitor for the Interior Department that the money is not spent for the use and benefit of the Indian when the Secretary of the Interior deducts from the royalties accruing to respective allottees from mining leases money to pay for the upkeep of the local Indian agency. For by his so doing the allottees who have royalties accruing pay for an object of general welfare, while other Indians who benefit from the maintenance of an agency but who have no such royalties accruing to them pay nothing.[84]

Large amounts of individual moneys are under the control of the Secretary of the Interior.[85]

The regulations provide that withdrawal of money from the Indian's account shall be made by check, upon the application of the disbursing agent, approved by the Commissioner of Indian Affairs.[86] Minors and adults may receive monthly allowances not to exceed $50 per month; specific authority from the Secretary of the Interior must be obtained for payment of larger amounts.[87] Another regulation provides that the disbursing agents, in their discretion, may turn over to any Indian who has received a patent in fee of his allotted land any individual funds then on deposit to his credit or which in the future accrue to his credit.[88]

[82] See Chapter 5, secs. 5D and 12.

[83] *United States* v. *McGugin*, 28 F. 2d 76 (D. C. Kans. 1928), and *United States* v. *Mott*, 37 F. 2d 860 (C. C. A. 10, 1930), cert. granted 281 U. S. 714 (1930), aff'd sub nom. *Mott* v. *United States*, 283 U. S. 747 (1931), indicate how different courts can disagree as to whether an act of the Secretary of the Interior was in fact for the use and benefit of the Indian.

[84] Op. Sol. I. D., M.23117, October 6, 1927.

[85] The statement of the Indian Office shows that as of June 30, 1939, it had in its control the sum of $53,200,000 belonging to individual Indians.

[86] 25 C. F. R. 221.2.

[87] *Ibid.*, 221.4.

[88] *Ibid.*, 221.6.

Among the regulations are found several which provide that certain payments of money may be made to the Indian for his unrestricted use.[89] The purpose of this is stated to be the encouragement of personal responsibility, self-reliance, and business experience which will enable the Indian to become an independent and progressive member of the community.[90]

The regulations authorize the expenditure of money for educational and agricultural purposes.[91] Further regulations provide that disbursing agents may pay necessary medical and funeral expenses, within specified maximum limits.[92] Administrative practice permits the superintendent to apply restricted funds of an Indian toward the support of an illegitimate child of such Indian.[93]

"Debts of Indians will not be paid from funds under the control of the United States * * * unless previously authorized by the Superintendent, except in emergency cases necessitating medical treatment or in the payment of last illness or funeral expenses * * * and any other exceptional cases where specific authority is granted by the Indian Office."[94]

The regulations provide that when personal property, such as wagons, horses, farm implements, etc., is purchased for an Indian, singly or in the aggregate value of $50 or more, the superintendent shall take a bill of sale therefor in his name as vendee, expressly in trust for the Indian.[95]

In the case of *United States* v. *O'Gorman*,[96] under a regulation such as the above, the superintendent of the Winnebago Agency bought several horses with the trust money held by him for an incompetent Indian. The bill of sale, which was promptly recorded, recited that the horses were bought with trust funds and that the sale was made to the superintendent. The Indian was permitted to have the use of the team of horses and hired the defendant to care for it. When he failed to receive payment for his services, the defendant asserted a claim of lien against the team. The court held that as trustee, the United States could maintain an action of replevin to recover the team from the possession of the defendant.[97]

[89] *Ibid.*, 221.5, 221.6, 221.18.

[90] *Ibid.*, 221.5.

[91] *Ibid.*, 221.10–221.14.

[92] *Ibid.*, 221.8, 221.17.

[93] Memo. Sol. I. D., September 8, 1938.

[94] 25 C. F. R. 221.20.

[95] *Ibid.*, 221.27.

[96] 287 Fed. 135 (C. C. A. 8, 1923).

[97] In accord, *Cochran* v. *United States*, 276 Fed. 701 (C. C. A. 8, 1921). For a fuller discussion of the rights of the United States with respect to trust property, see Chapter 5. On the protection from State taxation of property, purchased with restricted funds, see *United States* v. *Hughes*, 6 F. Supp. 972 (D. C. N. D. Okla. 1934); and see Chapter 13.

683058—45——15

SECTION 9. DEPOSITS OF INDIVIDUAL INDIAN MONEYS

Ordinarily, restricted Indian funds are held in the custody of a Government official. Several statutes, however, authorize the deposit of such funds under prescribed conditions.

Section 1 of the Act of June 25, 1910,[98] provided that any "Indian agent, superintendent or other disbursing agent of the Indian Service" might "deposit Indian moneys, individual or tribal, coming into his hands as custodian, in such bank or banks as he may select," subject to certain bond requirements.

The Appropriation Act of May 25, 1918,[99] provided for the segregation of tribal funds to the credit of the individual member. The funds so segregated were to be deposited to the individual's credit in any bank selected by the Secretary of the Interior, in the state or states in which the tribe is located. The act contained general legislation in the form of a proviso:

> That no * * * individual Indian money shall be deposited in any bank until the bank shall have agreed to pay interest thereon at a reasonable rate and shall have furnished an acceptable bond or collateral security therefor, and United States bonds may be furnished as collateral security for * * * individual funds so deposited, in lieu of surety bonds: *Provided further*, That the Secretary of the Interior * * * may invest the trust funds of any * * * individual Indian in United States Government bonds: * * *

The Act of June 24, 1938,[100] superseding section 2 of the Act of June 25, 1910, and section 28 of the Appropriation Act of May 25, 1918,[101] provides that the Secretary of the Interior may deposit individual trust moneys in banks selected by him, under such rules and regulations as he may prescribe, provided that the bank agrees to pay a reasonable rate of interest thereon and to furnish security of a specified type. The Secretary of the Interior may waive interest on demand deposits. The act also permits the Secretary, if he deems it for the best interest of the Indian, to invest the Indian moneys in any federal public-debt obligations and in any other obligations which are unconditionally guaranteed both as to interest and principal by the United States.[102]

In practice, the deposit of individual Indian moneys is made in the name of the United States; the disbursing agent keeps account of the amounts due the various individuals; the bank in which the funds are deposited has no account with the various individuals on whose behalf the funds were deposited.

Though these funds are deposited by the United States in its representative capacity, yet in case the bank fails, such deposits, being debts due to the United States, are entitled to priority under R. S. Sec. 3466. In the case of *Bramwell* v. *United States Fidelity & Guaranty Co.*,[103] the court under R. S. Sec. 3466, giving the United States priority in payment of claims against an insolvent estate, granted priority to deposits of Indian moneys, individual and tribal, made by the superintendent of the Klamath Reservation.

In enforcing the terms laid down by Congress for the deposit of Indian funds, the Department of the Interior issued regulations governing deposits. Under regulations approved March 5, 1938,[104] a bank seeking to qualify as a depository must file an application showing its financial condition, the amounts of money it will accept, the rate of interest that will be paid and the type of security that will be furnished. The regulations provide for deposits in the name of the disbursing agent and interest is payable semiannually. Monthly statements of receipts and checks on the Indian money account and other statements of information shall be furnished when required. Definite provisions as to the type of security, such as bonds of corporations, individuals, or of the United States are made.

[98] Sec. 1, 36 Stat. 855, 856, amended in other respects by Act of February 14, 1913, 37 Stat. 678, 25 U. S. C 373. This provision was unchanged by the Act of March 3, 1928, 45 Stat. 161, and the Act of April 30, 1934, 48 Stat 647, 25 U. S. C. 372, amending the Act of 1910 but was superseded by the Act of June 24, 1938, discussed below.

[99] 40 Stat. 561, 591, 25 U. S. C. 162.

[100] 52 Stat. 1037, 25 U. S. C. 162a.

[101] Sec. 28, 40 Stat. 561, 591, 25 U. S. C. 162.

[102] The authority to waive interest on demand deposits included in the 1938 act, was occasioned by the passage of the Banking Act of August 23, 1935, 49 Stat. 684, 714, 715. The Act of May 25, 1918, had limited the class of eligible depositories of Indian funds to those paying reasonable interest. But under the 1935 act, as interpreted by the Solicitor of the Department of the Interior (Op. Sol. I. D., M.28231, March 12, 1936), banks which are members of the Federal Reserve System or of the Federal Deposit Insurance Corporation are prohibited from paying any interest on demand deposits and all statutory requirements inconsistent with this prohibition are repealed. Following a parallel opinion of the Attorney General in the case of postal savings funds, the Solicitor of the Interior Department held that deposits might be made without interest in banks prohibited, under the 1935 Banking Act, from paying interest.

[103] 269 U. S. 483 (1926), aff'g 299 Fed. 705 (C. C. A. 9, 1924), aff'g 295 Fed. 331. See also *United States* v. *Barnett*, 7 F. Supp. 573 (D. C. N. D. Okla. 1934). Cf. *United States* v. *Johnson*, 11 F. Supp. 897 (D. C. N. D. Okla. 1935), aff'd 87 F. 2d 155 (C. C. A. 10, 1936) (holding United States not entitled to priority in debt of bank to guardian to whom funds had been unlawfully paid). On rights of creditors of Indians, see Chapter 8, sec. 7C.

[104] Regulations of March 2, 1938, Department of the Interior, Office of Indian Affairs; 25 C. F. R. 230.1–230.18.

SECTION 10. BEQUEST, DESCENT, AND DISTRIBUTION OF PERSONAL PROPERTY

A. IN THE ABSENCE OF FEDERAL LEGISLATION

In the absence of federal legislation, the bequest, descent, and distribution of the Indian's personalty is subject to tribal rule and custom.[105]

Because the inheritance of allotted lands is governed on substantive questions by state law,[106] the Indians of allotted reservations have, in some cases, adopted the state law as their own with respect to the descent of personalty, thus achieving the advantage of having a single body of law determine the descent of real and personal property.[107] A typical body of rules governing descent and distribution of unrestricted personalty is that set forth in the Code of Ordinances of the Gila River Pima-Maricopa

[105] See Chapter 7, sec. 6. *Cf. Trujillo* v. *Prince*, 42 N. M. 337, 78 P. 2d 145 (1938), holding that the state court has power to appoint an administrator for a deceased tribal Indian to enforce a right of action created by a state wrongful death statute.

[106] See Chapter 11, sec. 6.

[107] Swinomish Law and Order Code, chap. 3, sec. 5 (adopted March 15, 1938, approved March 24, 1938); Pine Ridge Tribal Court and Code of Offenses, chap. 4, sec. 1 (adopted February 20, 1937, approved March 2, 1937); Cheyenne River Code, chap. 3, sec. 2 (adopted October 6, 1938, approved October 8, 1938). The Blackfeet Code of Law and Order (May 6, 1937) provides that the tribal court shall apply its own law if proved; otherwise, the state law is to be used. Similar provisions are to be found in the Flathead Code (adopted December 22, 1936, approved December 24, 1936), and the Makah Tribal Court and Code of Offenses (adopted February 15, 1938, approved February 28, 1938). And *cf. Gray* v. *Coffman*, 10 Fed. Cas. No. 5, 714 (C. C. Kans. 1874), where the court points out that the Wyandot probate laws have been copied from the laws of Ohio with certain modifications, such as a provision that only living children should inherit.

Indian Community, adopted June 3, 1936, approved August 24, 1936. The governing ordinance [108] provides that after the payment of the debts and funeral expenses, the remainder passes to the surviving spouse. If no spouse survives, then the property descends to the children or grandchildren of the deceased. If none of these exist, then the property goes to the parents or parent of the deceased. And if no parents survive, the nearest relatives take. The code provides that if there is more than one heir, the heirs are to meet and decide among themselves what share each shall take and file their decision with the tribal court. If these heirs cannot agree, upon petition by any one of them, the tribal court will pass upon the distribution.

B. UNDER FEDERAL ACTS [109]

By virtue of its power over Indian property,[110] Congress may provide for a system of bequest, descent, and distribution of an Indian's personalty.

1. *Descent.*—Congress has never enacted general legislation [111] governing the descent of an Indian's personal property, and this is a matter, therefore, that remains generally subject to tribal jurisdiction.[112] Congress has provided, however, that upon the death, intestate, of "any Indian to whom an allotment of land has been made * * * before the expiration of the trust period and before the issuance of a fee simple patent," the Secretary of the Interior shall determine the heirs of the allottee and his decision shall be final.[113] Although this statute is directed primarily to the problem of the inheritance of allotments, and is discussed in more detail in connection with that subject,[114] the Interior Department has construed the power to determine heirs in the cases specified, as a power to determine *heirs for all purposes.*[115] Thus, in determining the heirs of an allottee, the Secretary of the Interior actually rules on the descent of personal property in the decedent's estate. This practice probably has the force of law, with respect to the estates of allottees, and it may be argued that an established course of administrative construction has extended the power of the Department to persons who are not within the language of the statute because they are not Indians "to whom an allotment of land has been made."

The regulations of the Interior Department refer to "an Indian of any allotted reservation," [116] which obviously defines a broader class than the class defined by the statute, since there are many Indians on allotted reservations who were born too late to receive allotments. The regulations of the Interior Department do not provide for departmental distribution of estates on unallotted reservations, although this practice is occasionally resorted to with the consent of all parties in interest where tribal judicial agencies are unavailable.

Under the Law and Order Regulations of the Indian Service, the Court of Indian Offenses determines heirship with respect to "property other than an allotment or other trust property subject to the jurisdiction of the United States." [117]

Tribal courts of organized tribes sometimes exercise like jurisdiction over all personal property.[118]

In some cases, tribal councils have requested the Interior Department to handle estates involving personal property, and the Department has done so.

The question of what law applies to an estate of personal property should be distinguished from the question of what agency shall administer the estate. The Secretary of the Interior may apply tribal custom and the tribal councils may apply state law. As a matter of practice, the examiners of inheritance, acting for the Interior Department and applying state law to the determination of the inheritance of real property, commonly apply the same rules to the inheritance of personal property. Where, however, the record shows a discrepancy between tribal custom and state law, a determination by an inheritance examiner of the descent of the personal estate of an unallotted Indian in accordance with state law and in violation of tribal custom has been held illegal. In *Estate of Yellow Hair, Unallotted Navajo,*[119] the Solicitor for the Interior Department disapproved such a determination, declaring:

> I believe that this conclusion is unjustified either as a matter of strict law or as a matter of policy. On the legal question I call your attention to the following paragraphs in the opinion of this Department, approved October 25, 1934, on "Powers of Indian Tribes" (M-27781). [See 55 I. D. 14]:
>
> > * * * With respect to all property other than allotments of land made under the General Allotment Act, the inheritance laws and customs of the Indian tribe are still of supreme authority.
>
> On the policy question involved I can see no necessity for departmental regulation of inheritance of personal property of Navajo Indians. The recently promulgated departmental regulations relating to the determination of heirs and the approval of wills specifically restrict departmental supervision over the inheritance of personal property to reservations which have been allotted. (Sections 13 and 22.) Likewise, the recently approved law and order regulations provide that Indian judges shall apply tribal custom in the distribution of personal property.
>
> I therefore recommend that instead of returning this case for the purpose of redistributing in accordance with Arizona law the personal property which has been distributed in accordance with tribal custom, it should be returned so that the entire estate may be distributed in accordance with tribal custom. The Examiner of Inheritance should take testimony as to such customs of inheritance, in their application to the facts of this case, and submit a revised order determining heirs for departmental approval.

2. *Bequest.*—The power to bequeath personalty is specifically granted by Act of February 14, 1913,[120] amending the Act of June 25, 1910.[121] It provides that any person of the age of 21 years or over may dispose of his interest in any restricted allotment, trust moneys, or other property held in trust by the United States before expiration of the restrictive period, by will in accordance with regulations prescribed by the Secretary of the Interior. To be valid, the will must be approved by the Secretary of the Interior. The act provides further:

> That the Secretary of the Interior may approve or disapprove the will either before or after the death of the testator, and in case where a will has been approved and it is subsequently discovered that there has been fraud in

[108] Chapter 4, sec. 7.

[109] This discussion excludes the Five Civilized Tribes and Osages. For a discussion of descent and related problems affecting them, see Chapter 23, secs. 9, 12D.

[110] See Chapter 5, sec. 5.

[111] The Act of January 19, 1891, 26 Stat. 720, provides for the payment to individual Indians of the Standing Rock and Cheyenne River agencies for ponies they were deprived of and states that "if any Indian entitled to such compensation shall have deceased the sum to which such Indian would be entitled shall be paid to his heirs at law, according to the laws of the State of Dakota * * *."

[112] See Chapter 7, sec. 6.

[113] Act of June 25, 1910, sec. 1, 36 Stat. 855, 25 U. S. C. 372.

[114] See Chapter 11, sec. 6.

[115] 25 C. F. R. 81.13, 81.23. Regulations governing Determination of Heirs and Approval of Wills of Indians, approved May 31, 1935, secs. 13, 22, 55 I. D. 263, 266, 268. This rule does not bind organized tribes.

[116] See fn. 115, *supra.*

[117] 25 C. F. R. 161.81; 55 I. D. 401, 407 (1935).

[118] See Chapter 7, sec. 6.

[119] 55 I. D. 426, 427–429 (1935). Also see Chapter 7, sec. 6.

[120] Sec. 2, 37 Stat. 678, 679, 25 U. S. C. 373.

[121] 36 Stat. 855.

> connection with the execution or procurement of the will the Secretary of the Interior is hereby authorized * * * to cancel the approval of the will, and the property of the testator shall thereupon descend or be distributed in accordance with the laws of the State wherein the property is located:[122] * * *.

In the case of *Blanset* v. *Cardin*,[123] the Supreme Court held that a will by a Quapaw allottee disposing of her moneys derived from her restricted lands and which were held in trust by the United States is governed by the 1913 act. The Court held inapplicable a statute of the State of Oklahoma regulating the portion of an estate that may be transferred by will, stating that the will is valid if approved by the Secretary of the Interior and executed in accordance with his regulations.

[122] The act provides also that the death of testator and the approval of the will does not terminate the trust, and that the Secretary of the Interior may in his discretion regulate the distribution and expenditure of the money belonging to the legatee.

[123] 256 U. S. 319 (1921), aff'g 261 Fed. 309 (C. C. A. 8, 1919). This case is also discussed in Chapter 5, sec. 11C(2), Chapter 6, sec. 2A and Chapter 11, sec. 6B. See also *Blundell* v. *Wallace*, 267 U. S. 373 (1925).

The right of the Indian to bequeath his shares in a tribal corporation organized under the Wheeler-Howard Act[124] is limited to the extent that he can give them only to his heirs, to tribal members, or to the tribal corporation.[125]

Since the statute governing the bequest of restricted personalty does not apply to unrestricted personalty, the tribal law on testamentary disposition of unrestricted personalty is supreme.[126] Even though the bequest of restricted personalty be subject to the rules and regulations of the Secretary of the Interior, nevertheless such rules and regulations[127] implicitly authorize approval of wills made in accord with tribal customs or tribal laws regarding testamentary disposition where there has been no compliance with state law.[128]

[124] Act of June 18, 1934, sec. 4, 48 Stat. 984, 985, 25 U. S. C. 464.

[125] 55 I. D. 263, 279 (1935).

[126] *Estate of Yellow Hair, Unallotted Navajo*, 55 I. D. 426 (1935).

[127] The rules and regulations prescribed by the Department of the Interior for the execution of wills, as approved May 31, 1935, may be found in 55 I. D. 263, 275–280.

[128] 55 I. D. 14, 42 (1934). See also *Estate of Yellow Hair, Unallotted Navajo*, 55 I. D. 426 (1935).

SECTION 11. INDIVIDUAL RIGHTS IN PERSONALTY—CROPS

Early in its dealings with the Indians, the government sought, by granting them agricultural aids, to encourage them in peaceful pursuits, that would provide a means of subsistence.[129]

As has been observed elsewhere in this chapter, when the Indian was compelled to vacate his land, provision was made for his reimbursement for the property he could not take with him, including crops.[130] Where possible, the Indian may have been permitted to remain on the land until he harvested his growing crops.[131]

Problems arising today concern chiefly the Indian's rights to dispose of all or some of his interest in his crops grown on restricted lands.

The law is not settled as to whether an Indian may without departmental approval, sell or mortgage[132] crops grown on restricted lands, but severed therefrom. A memorandum of the Solicitor of the Department of the Interior[133] presents the arguments on either side. On the one hand, it may be contended that even though severed from the restricted land, the crops are trust property while situated on the land. For as long as they remain there, the mortgagee cannot enter upon the land without the Government's consent. The contrary argument is that the sale or mortgage of severed crops does not come within the restrictions of the Indian's privilege to contract[134] nor does it affect the realty since severed crops are not part of the land; that there are no restrictions on the Indian's disposing of his crop as best he can.

To secure a loan from a tribal corporation under the Wheeler-Howard Act,[135] an Indian may mortgage his crops to the corporation,[136] since he might convey the land itself to the corporation.[137]

[129] *United States* v. *Gray*, 201 Fed. 291, 293 (C. C. A. 8, 1912).

[130] See sec. 6, *supra*.

[131] Treaty with Cherokees, February 27, 1819, 7 Stat. 195, 197.

[132] As for the sale or mortgage of the crops before severance, the case of *United States* v. *First Nat. Bank*, 282 Fed. 330 (D. C. E. D. Wash. 1922), holds that the United States may enjoin the foreclosure sale of mortgaged crops, the mortgage having been made on growing crops and crops to be grown during that year. Memo. Sol. I. D., March 25, 1936.

[133] Dated January 5, 1938.

[134] For restrictions on the power to contract, see Chapter 8, sec. 7.

[135] 48 Stat. 984, 25 U. S. C. 461, *et seq.*

[136] Memo. Asst. Sec'y I. D., August 17, 1938. This memorandum discusses an opinion of the Attorney General of North Dakota, which holds that the 1932 Crop Mortgage Act of North Dakota, which declares void mortgages on growing and unharvested crops does not apply to such mortgages given by Indians to Indian corporations. The opinion holds that the proviso in the amendment of 1933 excepting from the scope of the 1932 act "any mortgage or lien in favor of the United States * * * or any department or agency of either thereof" excepts such tribal corporation as a federal instrumentality.

[137] Memo. Sol. I. D., March 25, 1936.

SECTION 12. INDIVIDUAL RIGHTS IN PERSONALTY—LIVESTOCK

To induce Indians to adopt agricultural pursuits, treaties with Indians frequently contained a promise by the United States that it would furnish livestock to them.[138] When these promises were fulfilled, the livestock remained the property of the United States, the Indian having the right to possession and use.[139] Livestock was also purchased by the United States for the Indian, with his own money.[140]

[138] *E. g.*, Treaty with the Sioux, April 29, 1868, Art. 10, 15 Stat. 635, 639.

[139] See *United States* v. *Anderson*, 228 U. S. 52 (1913), rev'g 189 Fed. 262 (D. C. Ore. 1911).

[140] *United States* v. *Anderson*, 228 U. S. 52 (1913), rev'g 189 Fed. 262 (D. C. Ore. 1911).

In the Appropriation Act of July 4, 1884,[141] Congress prohibited the sale of any cattle or their increase, in possession or control of an Indian, which were purchased by the Government, to any person not belonging to the tribe to which said Indian belonged or to any citizen of the United States, except with the written consent of the agent of the tribe to which said Indian belonged. In the case of *United States* v. *Anderson*,[142] the Court held that this act applied to cattle purchased by the Government even with the Indian's funds. It has also been held that the Act of 1884 is not limited in application to cattle in possession of Indians

[141] 23 Stat. 76, 94. 25 U. S. C. 195.

[142] 228 U. S. 52 (1913), rev'g 189 Fed. 262 (D. C. Ore. 1911).

at the time of its enactment.[143] Since a sale cannot be made without the written consent of the agent, a mortgage on the cattle without such consent has been held void.[144]

However, a sale or other disposition of the livestock to nonmembers of the tribe, even with the consent of the agent, may be made illegal, as where the statute making the appropriation specifically states that no sales to such outsiders shall be made.[145]

The Appropriation Act of June 30, 1919,[146] also restricted the disposition of livestock purchased or issued by the United States and any increase. It provided that such animals could not be sold, mortgaged, or otherwise disposed of, except with the written consent of the federal officer in charge of the tribe; any transaction in violation of the statute would be void. It was further provided that all such stock was to be branded with the initials I. D. (referring to Interior Department) or with the reservation brand and could not be removed from the Indian country without the consent of the federal officer or by order of the Secretary of War in connection with troop movements.

An additional act affecting an Indian's interest in his livestock is the Appropriation Act of March 3, 1865,[147] which permits an Indian agent to sell livestock belonging to Indians which is not needed for subsistence. The sale is to be under rules and regulations prescribed by the Secretary of the Interior and the proceeds used for the benefit of the Indian.

In accordance with the federal policy of encouraging Indians in peaceful agricultural pursuits and of providing them with a means of livelihood and subsistence, the Secretary of the Interior has provided for certain preferential rights to Indians in the acquisition of grazing permits on Indian lands for his livestock.[148]

On reservations where sufficient tribal land is available, free grazing privileges may be granted to Indians by the tribal authorities, as an encouragement for the breeding and raising of livestock.[149]

The Indian is protected in his care of livestock by regulations seeking to prevent the spread of contagious diseases among stock on Indian lands.[150]

---

[143] *Rider* v. *La Clair*, 77 Wash. 488, 138 Pac. 3 (1914).

[144] *Ibid.*

[145] Appropriation Act of March 2, 1889, sec. 17, 25 Stat. 888, 894 making provision for distribution of livestock among Sioux. Effect of this act upon Act of 1884 is discussed in *Fisher* v. *United States*, 226 Fed. 156 (C. C. A. 8, 1915).

[146] Sec. 1, 41 Stat. 3, 9, 25 U. S. C. 163.

[147] Sec. 9, 13 Stat. 541, 563, R. S. § 2127, 25 U. S. C. 192. See Chapter 4, sec. 9.

[148] 25 C. F. R. 71.11, 71.13, 72.8.

[149] *Ibid.*, 71.9.

[150] *Ibid.*, 71.22, 72.10.

CHAPTER 11

INDIVIDUAL RIGHTS IN REAL PROPERTY

TABLE OF CONTENTS

The process of allotment shifted the rights of individual Indians in real property from the rights of participation in tribal property, already discussed,[1] to rights of ownership in individual tracts.

[1] See Chapter 9. Also see Chapter 2, secs. 2B, 2C, 2D.

SECTION 1. BACKGROUND OF THE ALLOTMENT SYSTEM

The background, the inception, and the operation of this system are set forth with a wealth of detail in J. P. Kinney's study, *A Continent Lost—A Civilization Won* (1937) and, more briefly, in a "History of the Allotment Policy" by D. S. Otis, which, presented in hearings[2] leading to the enactment of the Act of June 18, 1934,[3] provided the chief factual basis for the termination of the allotment system by that act.

A. EARLY DEVELOPMENT OF THE ALLOTMENT SYSTEM

The origins of the allotment system, as of every other important legal institution in the field of Indian affairs, are to be found in Indian treaties. As early as 1798 tribal lands were allotted to individuals or families.[4] Allotment was then, as it has been generally ever since, an incident in the transfer of Indian lands to white ownership. Chiefs and councils might cede vast areas over which a tribe claimed ownership, but when it came to ceding a plot of land which some member of the tribe had improved and on which he lived, a different situation was presented. In this situation many treaties provided that there should be "reserved" from the cession tracts of land for the use, or occupancy, or ownership, of designated individuals or families.[5] These early allotments were commonly known as reservations. Various forms of tenure were imposed upon these reservations. In some cases lands were held in trust for the individual.[6] In other cases the Indian acquired title either

[2] Hearings, Committee on Ind. Aff., 73d Cong., 2d sess., on H. R. 7902, 1934, pt. 9, pp. 428 *et. seq.*

[3] 48 Stat. 984, 25 U. S. C. 461 *et seq.*

[4] Treaty of June 1, 1798, with the Oneida Nation, unpublished treaty, Archives No. 28.

[5] Treaty of September 20, 1816, with the Chickasaw Nation, 7 Stat. 150; Treaty of July 8, 1817, with the Cherokee Nation, 7 Stat. 156; Treaty of September 29, 1817, with the Wyandot, Seneca, and other tribes, 7 Stat. 160; Treaty of October 2, 1818, with the Potawatamie Nation, 7 Stat. 185; Treaty of October 2, 1818, with the Wea Tribe, 7 Stat. 186; Treaty of October 3, 1818, with the Delaware Nation, 7 Stat. 188; Treaty of October 6, 1818, with the Miame Nation, 7 Stat. 189; Treaty of February 27, 1819, with the Cherokee Nation, 7 Stat. 195; Treaty of August 29, 1821, with the Ottawa, Chippewa, and Pottawatamie Nations, 7 Stat. 218; Treaty of June 2, 1825, with the Great and Little Osage Tribes, 7 Stat. 240 (reservations for "half-breeds"); Treaty of June 3, 1825, with the Kansas Nation, 7 Stat. 244 (reservations for "half-breeds"); Treaty of October 16, 1826, with the Potawatamie Tribe, 7 Stat. 295; Treaty of October 23, 1826, with the Miami Tribe, 7 Stat. 300; Treaty of July 29, 1829, with the United Nations of Chippewa, Ottawa, and Potawatamie Indians, 7 Stat. 320; Treaty of August 1, 1829, with the Winnebaygo Nation, 7 Stat. 323; Treaty of September 27, 1830, with the Choctaw Nation, 7 Stat. 333; Treaty of August 30, 1831, with the Ottoway Indians, 7 Stat. 359; Treaty of March 24, 1832, with the Creek Tribe, 7 Stat. 366; Treaty of September 15, 1832, with the Winnebago Nation, 7 Stat. 370; Treaty of October 20, 1832, with the Potawatamie Tribe, 7 Stat. 378; Treaty of October 20, 1832, with the Chickasaw Nation, 7 Stat. 381; Treaty of October 27, 1832, with the Potowatomies, 7 Stat. 399; Treaty of October 27, 1832, with the Kaskaskia Tribe, 7 Stat. 403; Treaty of February 18, 1833, with the Ottawas, 7 Stat. 420; Treaty of September 26, 1833, with the United Nation of Chippewa, Ottawa, and Potawatamie Indians, 7 Stat. 431; Treaty of May 24, 1834, with the Chickasaw Nation, 7 Stat. 450; Treaty of October 23, 1834, with the Miami Tribe, 7 Stat. 458; Treaty of December 29, 1835, with the Cherokee Tribe, 7 Stat. 478; Treaty of April 23, 1836, with the Wyandot Tribe, 7 Stat. 502; Treaty of November 6, 1838, with the Miami Tribe, 7 Stat. 569.

[6] Treaty of June 1, 1798, with the Oneida Nation, unpublished treaty, Archives No. 28; Treaty of September 20, 1816, with the Chickasaw Nation, 7 Stat. 150.

under a restriction against alienation without the consent of the President,[7] or in fee simple.[8]

Somewhat later allotment came to be used as an instrument for terminating tribal existence. Allottees surrendered their interest in the tribal estate and became citizens.[9]

During the 1850's, this break-up of tribal lands and tribal existence through allotment assumed a standard pattern.[10]

During the last years of the treaty-making period, and for two decades thereafter, the treaty provisions on allotment served as models for legislation.

The legislative development leading up to the General Allotment Act, and the purposes and background of that act are analyzed in Otis' study from which the following excerpts are taken:

> In the 1870's the Government's policy of general allotment of Indian lands in severalty gradually took form. * * * By 1885 the Government had, under various treaties and laws issued over 11,000 patents to individual Indians and 1,290 certificates of allotment.[4] The fact that 8,595 of these patents and 1,195 of these certificates were issued under laws passed and treaties ratified during the period 1850–69 suggests that the forces which produced the General Allotment Act of 1887 were coming to life in the mid-century. In 1862 Congress saw fit to pass a law for the special protection of the Indian allottee in the enjoyment and use of his land.[5] And in 1875 Congress gave further momentum to the whole lands-in-severalty movement by extending to the Indian homesteading privileges. (18 Stat. L. 420.)
>
> [4] Commissioner of Indian Affairs (1885), 320, 321.
> [5] H. Rep. No. 1576, May 28, 1880, 46th Cong., 2d sess., 7.
>
> In the meantime, the Indian Administration was gravitating steadily to the position of supporting allotment as a general principle. * * *
>
> * * * In 1877 Secretary Schurz recommended allotment to heads of families on all reservations, "the enjoyment and pride of the individual ownership of property being one of the most effective civilizing agencies."[15] From that date onward the Service as a whole worked for the speeding up of allotment under previous acts and treaties and the passage of a general law. * * *
>
> [15] Report of the Secretary of the Interior, 1877, xi.
>
> LEGISLATION
>
> In the late seventies there was a growing public opinion in support of the allotment movement. The Commissioner in 1878 declared,
>
>> "It [allotment] is a measure correspondent with the progressive age in which we live, and is endorsed by all true friends of the Indian, as is evidenced by the numerous petitions to this effect presented to Congress from citizens of the various States."[20]
>
> [20] Commissioner of Indian Affairs (1880), xvii.
>
> Early the following year a joint committee of Congress, appointed to consider the matter of transferring the Indian Bureau to the War Department, reported a decision adverse to the change and proceeded to make recommendations of measures to civilize the Indians. One of their proposals was a general allotment law providing for a title in fee with a 25-year restriction upon alienation.[21] That same day, January 31, 1879, Chairman Scales of the House Committee on Indian Affairs reported a general allotment bill.[22] In the next Congress various bills were introduced to the same effect.[23] The House committee on May 28, 1880, reported favorably an allotment bill and accompanied it with statements of the majority and minority views.[24] In the Senate the measure which was to be known for the next few years as the "Coke bill" was introduced.[25]
>
> [21] H. Rep. No. 93, Jan. 31, 1879, 45th Cong., 3d sess., 3–20.
> [22] Congressional Record, Jan. 31, 1879, 864. (See also H. Rep., Mar. 3, 1879, 45th Cong., 3d sess.).
> [23] Congressional Record, Jan. 12, 1880, 274; Mar. 8, 1880, 1394; May 19, 1880, 3507.
> [24] H. Rep. No. 1576, May 28, 1880, 46th Cong., 2d sess.
> [25] Congressional Record, May 19, 1880, 3507.

B. THE GENERAL ALLOTMENT ACT

The circumstances surrounding the enactment of the General Allotment Act are thus summarized in Dr. Otis' study:

> Senator Dawes in 1885 credited Carl Schurz with having originated the bill.[26] Its provisions were substantially the same as those of the ultimate Dawes Act, except that the Indian was not thereby declared a citizen.[27] The Coke bill passed the Senate in 1884 and in 1885 and in this latter year was favorably reported in the House.[28] In the meantime certain tribes by special laws were given the privilege of allotments in severalty—the Crows on April 11, 1882 (22 Stat. L. 42), the Omahas on August 7, 1882 (22 Stat. L. 341), and the Umatillas on March 3, 1885 (23 Stat. L. 340). These acts applied to specific reservations the principles of the Coke bill.
>
> [26] Proceedings of the Third Annual Meeting of the Lake Mohonk Conference of Friends of the Indian (1885) in Miscellaneous Document, XIII, 1013'.
> [27] Congressional Record, Jan. 20, 1881, 778, 779. For debate on the question of amending the bill to extend citizenship to the Indian, see Congressional Record, Jan. 24, 18 1, 875–982.
> [28] Reports of the Commissioner of Indian Affairs (1884), xiii; Reports of the Commissioner of Indian Affairs (1885), xv; H. Rept. No. 2247, Jan. 9, 1885, 48th Cong., 2d sess.
>
> The allotment movement seemed rapidly to be gaining strength in 1886. President Cleveland in his annual messages in 1885 and 1886 advocated the policy.[29] In 1886 General Sheridan, reporting as lieutenant general of the Army to the Secretary of War, likewise urged an allotment scheme.[30] Finally, Congress acted early in the following year and the President signed the Dawes Act on February 8, 1887 (24 Stat. L. 388).[31] The chief provisions of the act were:
>
>> (1) a grant of 160 acres to each family head, of 80 acres to each single person over 18 years of age
>
> [29] George F. Parker (ed.), The Writings and Speeches of Grover Cleveland (New York, 1892), 410–415.
> [30] In Miscellaneous Documents Relating to Indian Affairs (collected in Indian Office Library), XV, 11660–11663.
> [31] The writer regrets that time has not permitted a careful study of the Government documents, especially of the Congressional Record, relating to the Dawes bill. Such a study might by implication throw some light on the forces at work to secure its passage. There is a well-founded suspicion that all the motives of the legislators were not concerned merely with the Indian's welfare. The study would at least show the drift of opinion. In 1887 President Quinton told the Women's National Indian Association that passage of the Dawes bill 8 years previously would have been "an absolute impossibility." She said that the women's petition with 100 000 signatures, which was presented to Congress in 1882, met with "dense ignorance," "prejudice," and the influence of the "Indian Ring." Miscellaneous Documents Relating to Indian Affairs (collected in Indian Office Library), XV, 11968, 11969. In its last stages the bill met with no opposition at all. Debate dealt only with details.

[7] Treaty of October 2, 1818, with the Potawatamie Nation, 7 Stat. 185; Treaty of October 2, 1818, with the Wea Tribe, 7 Stat. 186; Treaty of October 3, 1818, with the Delaware Nation, 7 Stat. 188; Treaty of October 16, 1826, with the Potawatamie Tribe, 7 Stat. 295; Treaty of October 23, 1826, with the Miami Tribe, 7 Stat. 300; Treaty of July 29, 1829, with the United Nations of Chippewa, Ottawa, and Potawatamie Indians, 7 Stat. 320; Treaty of August 1, 1829, with the Winnebaygo Nation, 7 Stat. 323.

[8] Treaty of September 29, 1817, with the Wyandot, Seneca, and other tribes, 7 Stat. 160; Treaty of October 6, 1818, with the Miame Nation, 7 Stat. 189; Treaty of August 29, 1821, with the Ottawa, Chippewa, and Pottawatamie Nations, 7 Stat. 218; Treaty of June 2, 1825, with the Great and Little Osage Tribes, 7 Stat. 240 (reservations for "half-breeds"); Treaty of June 3, 1825, with the Kansas Nation, 7 Stat. 244 (reservations for "half-breeds"); Treaty of September 15, 1832, with the Winnebago Nation, 7 Stat. 370.

[9] Treaty of November 24, 1848, with the Stockbridge Tribe, 9 Stat. 955 (division of tribe into "citizen" party and "Indian" party); Treaty of April 1, 1850, with the Wyandot, 9 Stat. 987. *Cf.*, Treaty of August 5, 1826 with the Chippewa Tribe, 7 Stat. 290, providing for allotments to half-breeds; Treaty of September 27, 1830, with the Choctaw Nation, 7 Stat. 333; Treaty of December 29, 1835, with the Cherokee Tribe, 7 Stat. 478; Treaty of July 8, 1817, with the Cherokee Nation, 7 Stat. 156.

[10] See Chapter 3, sec. 4G.

and to each orphan under 18, and of 40 acres to each other single person under eighteen; [38]

[38] Certain tribes were exempted from the provisions of the act, viz, the Five Civilized Tribes, the Osages, Miamies and Peorias, Sacs and Foxes, in Indian Territory, the Senecas in New York State, and the inhabitants of the strip south of the Sioux in Nebraska (sec. 8).

(2) a patent in fee to be issued to every allottee but to be held in trust by the Government for 25 years, during which time the land could not be alienated or encumbered;

(3) a period of 4 years to be allowed the Indians in which they should make their selections after allotment should be applied to any tribe—failure of the Indians to do so should result in selection for them at the order of the Secretary of the Interior;

(4) citizenship to be conferred upon allottees and upon any other Indians who had abandoned their tribes and adopted "the habits of civilized life." * * *

AIMS AND MOTIVES OF THE ALLOTMENT MOVEMENT

That the leading proponents of allotment were inspired by the highest motives seems conclusively true. A Member of Congress, speaking on the Dawes bill in 1886 said, "It has * * * the endorsement of the Indian rights associations throughout the country, and of the best sentiment of the land." [39] * * *

[39] Congressional Record, Dec. 15, 1886, 196.

* * * * *

The supreme aim of the friends of the Indian was to substitute white civilization for his tribal culture, and they shrewdly sensed that the difference in the concepts of property was fundamental in the contrast between the two ways of life. That the white man's way was good and the Indian's way was bad, all agreed. So, on the one hand, allotment was counted on to break up tribal life. This blessing was dwelt upon at length. The agent for the Yankton Sioux wrote in 1877: [40]

> "As long as Indians live in villages they will retain many of their old and injurious habits. Frequent feasts, community in food, heathen ceremonies, and dances, constant visiting—these will continue as long as the people live together in close neighborhoods and villages * * * I trust that before another year is ended they will generally be located upon individual lands of farms. From that date will begin their real and permanent progress."

[40] Reports of the Commissioner of Indian Affairs (1877), 75, 76. (See also Reports of the Commissioner of Indian Affairs (1879), 25 (1885), 21 (1886), ix, x.)

On the other hand, the allotment system was to enable the Indian to acquire the benefits of civilization. The Indian agents of the period made no effort to conceal their disgust for tribal economy. * * *

But voices of doubt were here and there raised about allotment as a wholesale civilizing program. "Barbarism" was not without its defenders. Especially were the Five Civilized Tribes held up as an example of felicity under a communal system in contrast to the deplorable condition of certain Indians upon whom allotment had been tried. [41] A minority report of the House Committee on Indian Affairs in 1880 went so far as to state that Indians had made progress only under communism. [42] At this point it is worth remarking that friends and enemies of allotment alike showed no clear understanding of Indian agricultural economy. Both were prone to use the word "communism" in a loose sense, in describing Indian enterprise. It was in the main an inaccurate term. Gen. O. O. Howard told the Lake Mohonk Conference in 1889 about a band of Spokane Indians who worked their lands in common in the latter part of the 1870's, [43] but certainly in the vast majority of cases Indian economic pursuits were carried on directly with individual rewards in view. This was primarily true even of such essentially group activities as the Omahas' annual buffalo hunt. [44] Agriculture was certainly but rarely a communal undertaking. The Pueblos, who had probably the oldest and most established agricultural economy, were individualistic in farming and pooled their efforts only in the care of the irrigation system. [45] What the allotment debaters meant by communism was that the title to land invariably vested in the tribe and the actual holding of the land was dependent on its use and occupancy. They also meant vaguely the cooperativeness and clannishness—the strong communal sense—of barbaric life, which allotment was calculated to disrupt.

[41] Memorial to Congress from Cherokee Nation in Congressional Record, January 20, 1881, 781.
[42] H. Rept. No. 1576, May 28, 1880, 46th Cong., 2d sess., 10.
[43] Twenty-first Reports of the Board of Indian Commissioners (1889), 111.
[44] Alice C. Fletcher and Francis La Flesche, the Omaha Tribe, in Twenty-seventh Annual Report of the Bureau of American Ethnology to the Secretary of the Smithsonian Institution, 1905–6 (Washington, 1911), 273–275.
[45] Reports of the Commissioner of Indian Affairs (1864), 332.

In any event, the doubters were skeptical as to whether this allotment method of civilizing would work. They placed much emphasis upon the fact that Indian life was bound up with the communal holding of land. In 1881 Senator Teller quoted a chief's explanation why the Nez Perces went on the warpath:

> "They asked us to divide the land, to divide our mother upon whose bosom we had been born, upon whose lap we had been reared." [46]

[46] Congressional Record, January 20, 1881, 781, 782. (See also H. Rept. No. 1576, May 28, 1880, 46th Cong., 2d sess., 7–10.)

* * * The minority of the House Committee on Indian Affairs doubted whether private property would transform the Indian. The minority report said: [47]

> "However much we may differ with the humanitarians who are riding this hobby, we are certain that they will agree with us in the proposition that it does not make a farmer out of an Indian to give him a quarter-section of land. There are hundreds of thousands of white men, rich with the experiences of centuries of Anglo-Saxon civilization, who cannot be transformed into cultivators of the land by any such gift."

[47] H. Rept. No. 1576, May 28, 1880, 46th Cong., 2d sess., 8.

The believers in allotment had another philanthropic aim, which was to protect the Indian in his present land holding. They were confident that if every Indian had his own strip of land, guaranteed by a patent from the Government, he would enjoy a security which no tribal possession could afford him. If the Indians possession was further safeguarded by a restriction upon his right to sell it they believed that the system would be foolproof. * * *

* * * * *

It must also be noted that while the advocates of allotment were primarily and sincerely concerned with the advancement of the Indian they at the same time regarded the scheme as promoting the best interest of the whites as well. For one thing, it was fondly but erroneously hoped that setting the Indian on his own feet would relieve the Government of a great expense. In 1879 the Indian Commissioner, in recommending an allotment bill to Secretary Schurz, wrote, "The evidently growing feeling in the country against the continued appropriations for the care and comfort of the Indians indicates the necessity for a radical change of policy in affairs connected with their lands." [48] Speaking in favor of the Dawes bill, a member of Congress said in 1886, "What shall be his future status? Shall he remain a pauper savage, blocking the pathway of civilization, an increasing burden upon the people? Or shall he be converted into a civilized taxpayer, contributing toward the support of the Government and adding to the material prosperity of the country? * * * We desire, I say, that the latter shall be his destiny." [49]

[48] Commissioner to Secretary Schurz in H. Rept. No. 165, March 8, 1879, 45th Cong., 3d sess., 3. (See also Reports of the Commissioner of Indian Affairs (1881), xxiii.)
[49] Congressional Record, December 15, 1886, 190.

The chief advantages that the new system was to bring to the country as a whole were to be found in the opening up of surplus lands on the reservations and in the attendant march of progress and civilization westward. In his report of 1880, Secretary Schurz wrote: [50]

"[Allotment] will eventually open to settlement by white men the large tracts of land now belonging to the reservations, but not used by the Indians. It will thus put the relations between the Indians and their white neighbors in the western country upon a new basis, by gradually doing away with the system of large reservations, which has so frequently provoked those encroachments which in the past have led to so much cruel injustice and so many disastrous collisions."

[63] Report of the Secretary of the Interior, 1880, 12.

* * * * *

It must be reported that the using of these lands which the Indians did not "need" for the advancement of civilization was a logical part of a whole and sincerely idealistic philosophy. The civilizing policy was in the long run to benefit Indian and white man alike. But doubters of the allotment system could see nothing in the policy but dire consequences for the Indian. Senator Teller in 1881 called the Coke bill "a bill to despoil the Indians of their lands and to make them vagabonds on the face of the earth."[64]

[64] Congressional Record, January 26, 1881, 934.

At another time he said,[65]

"If I stand alone in the Senate, I want to put upon the record my prophecy in this matter, that when 30 or 40 years shall have passed and these Indians shall have parted with their title, they will curse the hand that was raised professedly in their defense to secure this kind of legislation and if the people who are clamoring for it understood Indian character, and Indian laws, and Indian morals, and Indian religion, they would not be here clamoring for this at all."

[65] Ibid., January 20, 1881, 783.

* * * Senator Teller had charged that allotment was in the interests of the land-grabbing speculators,[67] but the minority report of the House Indian Affairs Committee in 1880 had gone even further in its accusations. It said:[68]

"The real aim of this bill is to get at the Indian lands and open them up to settlement. The provisions for the apparent benefit of the Indian are but the pretext to get at his lands and occupy them * * *. If this were done in the name of greed, it would be bad enough; but to do it in the name of humanity, and under the cloak of an ardent desire to promote the Indian's welfare by making him like ourselves, whether he will or not, is infinitely worse."

[67] Congressional Record, January 20, 1881. 783.
[68] H. Rept. No. 1576, May 28, 1880, 46th Cong., 2d sess., 10.

* * * * *

It is probably true that the most powerful force motivating the allotment policy was the pressure of the land-hungry western settlers. A very able prize thesis written at Harvard by Samuel Taylor puts forth this theory. The author copiously and convincingly cites evidence to show the cupidity of the westerners for the Indian's lands and their unrestrained zeal in acquiring them.[70] * * *

[70] Samuel Taylor, The Origins of the Dawes Act of 1887 (unpublished manuscript, Philip Washburn Prize Thesis, Harvard, 1927), 25–42.

* * * * *

A special enterprise which undoubtedly affected the establishing and working out of the allotment program was the railroads. It must again be remembered that the 1880's were a time of feverish railroad building. * * *

* * * * *

* * * It is interesting that the same session of the same Congress that passed the Dawes Act went in for grants of railroad rights-of-way through Indian lands on a new and enlarged scale. Of 9 Indian bills that became law, 6 were railroad grants.[80] Of the remaining 3, 1 was the Dawes Act, 1 was the appropriation act, and the third was an amendment to the land-sales law. In September 1887 the Indian Commissioner remarked in his report, "The past year has been one of unusual activity in the projection and building of numerous additional railroads through Indian lands."

[80] Reports of the Commissioner of Indian Affairs (1887), 272–285.

* * * * *

It is significant that one of the foremost of these empire builders was discovering that under the old reservation system the way of the railroaders was hard. The biographer of James J. Hill tells of the difficulties which the builder of the St. Paul, Minneapolis & Manitoba Railroad experienced in securing a right-of-way across the Fort Berthold and Blackfeet Reservations in 1886 and 1887.[86] Eventually the railroad got its grant (24 Stat. L. 402), but the way was paved for acquiring more easily a second grant, extending the right-of-way westward, by the Blackfeet agreement of 1888.[87] This agreement (25 Stat. L. 113) cut the reservation up into several smaller ones (art. I), allowed the sale of the surplus land, provided for allotment in severalty (art. VI), and stipulated that rights-of-way might be granted through any of the separate reservations "whenever in the opinion of the President the public interests require the construction of railroads, or other highways, or telegraph lines * * *" (art. VIII). Again, the writer of this paper has no evidence to show that the railroad was active in promoting this agreement. But a later comment of James J. Hill indicates that he had been well aware of the disadvantages of the old reservations for railroading. He said:[88]

"When we built into northern Montana, and I want to tell you that it took faith to do it, from the eastern boundary of the State to Fort Benton was unceded Indian land; no white man had a right to put two logs one on top of the other. If he undertook to remain too long in passing through the country, he was told to move on. Even when cattle crossed the Missouri River during the first years to come to our trains, the Indians asked $50 a head for walking across the land a distance of 3 miles, and they wanted an additional amount per head, I don't remember what it was, for the water they drank in crossing the Missouri."

[86] Jos. G. Pyle, Life of James J. Hill (2 vols., Garden City, N. Y., 1917), I, 384.
[87] Jos. G. Pyle, Life of James J. Hill (2 vols., Garden City, N. Y., 1917), I, 386
[88] Jos. G. Pyle, Life of James J. Hill (2 vols., Garden City, N. Y., 1917), I, 385, 386.

* * * * *

INDIAN ATTITUDES AND CAPACITIES

* * * In 1881 the Commissioner, in a letter to Senator Hill, listed the particular tribes that had petitioned for allotment and concluded by saying, "* * * It may truthfully be said that there are at this time but few tribes of Indians, outside of the Five Civilized Tribes in the Indian Territory, who are not ready for this movement."[36] As early as 1876 agents were reporting Indian sentiment in favor of allotment and presenting Indian petitions and this activity increased up to 1887.[37] * * *

[36] Congressional Record, Jan. 20, 1881.
[37] See agents' reports, Reports of the Commissioner of Indian Affairs (1876), passim; ibid., (1878), 142 (1880), 25, 50, 87, 171, (1881), 22, 25, 132, 177; especially agents' reports, ibid. (1882) and (1883).

* * * * *

From the repeated statements of those Indians who favored allotment it is clear that what was first and foremost in their minds was a hope that patents in fee would protect them against white inroads upon their lands and against the danger of removal by the Government. A comment as early as 1876 from the Siletz agent in Oregon as to his charges' desire for allotment is typical. He said: "Nothing gives them so much uneasiness as the constant efforts of some white men to have them removed to some other country."[41] There seems to have been little understanding of or desire for a new agricultural economy on the part of the Indians. This was quite as true of the Omahas who at the time were regarded by white proponents of allotment as especially enlightened.

[41] Ibid. [Reports of the Commissioner of Indian Affairs] (1876), 124; see also Miscellaneous Documents relating to Indian Affairs (collected in Indian Office library), IX, 7553–7558, Reports of the Commissioner of Indian Affairs (1880), 25.

One of the 55 members of the tribe who asked for allotment expressed his sense of the changing order but concluded his statement (as nearly all the fifty-five did) with the usual argument. He said:

> "The road our fathers walked is gone; the game is gone; the white people are all about us. There is no use in any Indian thinking of the old ways; he must now go to work as the white man does. We want titles to our lands, that the land may be secure to our children." [42]

[42] Fletcher and La Flesche, 636, 637; see also Reports of the Commissioner of Indian Affairs (1882), 112.

There were many expressions of Indian opposition to allotment in the early 1880's. The minority report of the House Committee on Indian Affairs in 1880 noted that since the act of 1862 provided for special protection of allottees in their holdings it was "passing strange" that so few had availed themselves of their privileges.[43] The Senecas and the Creeks made bold to memorialize Congress against disrupting with allotment their systems of common holding.[44] Realizing that they were opposing the trend of official policy the Creeks remarked:

> "In opposing the change of Indian land titles from the tenure in common to the tenure in severalty your memorialists are aware that they differ from nearly every one of note holding office under the Government in connection with Indian affairs, and with the great body of philanthropists whose desire to promote the welfare of the Indian cannot be questioned." * * *[45]

[43] H. Rept. No. 1576, May 28, 1880, 46th Cong., 2d sess., 7.
[44] H Ex. Doc., No. 83, Mar. 1, 1882, 47th Cong., 1st sess.
[45] Ibid., 26.

Certain tribes had specific objections to allotment. A memorial from the Creeks, Choctaws, and Cherokees in 1881 read:

> "The change to an individual title would throw the whole of our domain in a few years into the hands of a few persons." [46]

[46] Congressional Record, Jan. 20, 1881, 781.

* * * * *

* * * There is a final fact which must be taken into consideration in interpreting reports of Indian sentiments and of the results of allotment experiments, namely, that allotment had become an official policy. As Senator Teller maintained with probable accuracy there would be a tendency on the part of agents and subordinate officials to be influenced in their estimates consciously or unconsciously by the knowledge that allotment was the program to be furthered.[52]

[52] Congressional Record, Jan. 20, 1881, 783.

What can be said from this survey is that there was no apparent widespread demand from the Indians for allotment.

C. CONSEQUENCES OF THE ALLOTMENT SYSTEM

The General Allotment Act proved to be the cornerstone of a system which involved a considerable amount of legislation that supplemented and amended the terms of that act. The working out of the allotment system in its early years is sketched in Part II of Dr. Otis' study, from which the following quotations are taken:

> There was no doubt in the minds of the proponents of the allotment system that they were on the road to the complete solution of the Indian problem. * * * Senator Dawes went so far as to say that the general allotment law had obviated the need for tinkering with the organization of the [Indian] service. He said:[3]
>
> > "It seems to me that this is a self-acting machine that we have set going, and if we only run it on the track it will work itself all out, and all these difficulties that have troubled my friend will pass away like snow in the spring time, and we will never know when they go; we will only know they are gone."
>
> [3] Nineteenth Report of the Board of Indian Commissioners (1887), 54.
>
> Indeed this "self-acting machine" would finally render obsolete all Government machinery whatever. Senator Dawes went on to express a prediction of which an echo has been heard in discussions of the present proposed policy:[4]
>
> > "Suppose these Indians become citizens of the United States with this 160 acres of land to their sole use, what becomes of the Indian reservations, what becomes of the Indian Bureau, what becomes of all this machinery, what becomes of the six commissioners appointed for life? Their occupation is gone; they have all vanished; the work for which they have been created * * * is all gone, while you are making them citizens * * * That is why I don't trouble myself at all about how to change it [the machinery of administration]."
>
> Dr. Lyman Abbot said:
>
> > "The Indian is no longer to be cared for by the executive department of the Government; he is coming under the general protection under which we all live, namely, the protection of the courts."[5]
>
> [4] Ibid. (1887), 55.
> [5] Ibid. (1887), 53.
>
> * * * * *
>
> THE APPLICATION OF ALLOTMENT
>
> The application of allotment to the reservations was above all characterized by extreme haste.
>
> In September 1887—7 months after the passage of the Dawes Act—the author of the measure told the Lake Mohonk Conference how President Cleveland had remarked when signing the bill that he intended to apply it to one reservation at first, and then gradually to others. Senator Dawes went on to say:[89]
>
> > "But you see he has been led to apply it to half a dozen. The bill provides for capitalizing the remainder of the land for the benefit of the Indian, but the greed of the landgrabber is such as to press the application of this bill to the utmost * * * There is no danger but this will come most rapidly, too rapidly, I think; the greed and hunger and thirst of the white man for the Indian's land is almost equal to his 'hunger and thirst for righteousness.'"
>
> [89] Nineteenth Report of the Board of Indian Commissioners (1887), 88.
>
> * * * * *
>
> In 1890 the Commissioner reported,
>
> > "In numerous instances, where clearly desirable, Congress has by special legislation authorized negotiations with the Indians for portions of their reservations without waiting for the slower process of the general allotment law."[93]
>
> [93] Ibid. [Report of the Commissioner of Indian Affairs] (1890), xxxviii.
>
> In 1888 Congress had ratified five agreements with different Indian tribes providing for allotment and for the sale of surplus lands.[94] The following year Congress passed eight such laws.[95] A member of the Board of Indian Commissioners in 1891 estimated that the 104,314,349 acres of Indian reservations in 1889 had been reduced by 12,000,000 acres in 1890 and by 8,000,000 acres in the first 9 months of 1891.[96] * * *
>
> [94] Ibid. (1888), 294, 302, 320, 322, 335–336, 340–344.
> [95] Ibid. (1889), 421, 432, 438, 440, 447, 449, 460, 463, 464.
> [96] Twenty-third Report of the Board of Indian Commissioners (1891), 51.
>
> * * * * *
>
> In the meantime, the work of applying allotment was pushed rapidly forward. * * * In 1888 the Commissioner had reported that 3,349 allotments had been approved since the passage of the Dawes Act.[7] There were 1 958 allotments approved in 1890, 2,830 in 1891, 8,704 in 1892; and in this last year Commissioner Morgan reported that since February 1887 the Indian Office had given its approval to 21,274 allotments.[8] In this same year, 1892, he told the Mohonk Conference that the allotments which were about to be made would bring the grand total of all the allotments which the Government had made to over

80,000. He concluded it was time to slow down.[4] His successors seem to have acted upon his advice until the opening of the new century, as the following figures show:[5]

Allotments approved 1893–1900

Years:	Number	Year:	Number
1893	4,561	1897	8,229
1894	3,061	1898	2,015
1895	4,851	1899	1,011
1896	4,414	1900	8,752

[3] Table in Report of the Commissioner of Indian Affairs (1916), 94.

[3] Ibid. (1892), 184.

[4] Twenty-fourth Report of the Board of Indian Commissioners (1892), 37.

[5] Report of the Commissioner of Indian Affairs (1893), 23 (1894), 20 (1895), 19 (1896), 25 (1897), 21 (1898), 40 (1899), 43 (1900), 53, 54.

In the years prior to 1887 the Government had approved 7,463 allotments with a total acreage of 584,423; from 1887 through 1900 it approved a total of 53,168 with an acreage of nearly 5,000,000.[6] * * *

[6] Ibid. (1916), 93, 94.

* * * * *

* * * So satisfactory was the speed of allotment to Board of Indian Commissioners that in 1891 it was contemplating a very early disappearance of Government supervision over the Indian. The Board's report stated in that year:[9]

> "* * * When patents have been issued and homesteads secured, when Indians are declared and acknowledged citizens, and are actually self-supporting, the supervision of the Government and the arbitrary rule of the agent may be safely withdrawn. * * *"

This faith that the allotment system would mean an early decline of Government supervision and placing the Indian on his own responsibility continued to be expressed by the friends of the Indian through the 1890's. But the hope was not realized. In 1900 there were in existence 61 agencies—3 more than in 1890.[10] But while the maintenance of the agency system was in large measure dependent upon the needs of the service, it was apparently even more dependent on the needs of the agents. The Indian Rights Association reported in 1900 that Commissioner Jones had recommended to Congress the discontinuing of 15 agencies but that the agents had been able to bring such pressure through their friends at the Capitol that Congress had agreed to the eliminating of only one.[11]

[9] Twenty-second Report of the Board of Indian Commissioners (1890), 9.

[10] Report of the Commissioner of Indian Affairs (1890), 512–514; Ibid. (1900), 743–745.

[11] Eighteenth Annual Report Indian Rights Association (1900), 57. This report lists the agencies as 56 in 1900 but Report of the Commissioner of Indian Affairs (1900) lists 61. See pp. 743–745.

* * * * *

There is no doubt that the idea of allotment was making headway with the Indians, but there is considerable doubt that its progress was the result of a spontaneous and wide-spread interest of the Indians in becoming hard-working American farmers. * * * In that same year [1888] the Yankton agent wrote about a determined opposition to allotment which was led by the old chiefs and which was successfully overcome by two companies of soldiers from Fort Randall.

The agent concluded by remarking that when the survey was finished there was not one Indian on the reservation who did not want his allotment.[18] * * *

[18] Ibid. [Report of the Commissioner of Indian Affairs] (1888). 70, 208.

* * * * *

There is considerable testimony to the fact that the Indians knew pretty well what the white man's system had meant for their race. One of the members of the Board of Indian Commissioners reported in 1890:[20]

> "The Osages as a tribe are almost unanimously opposed to taking their land in severalty. Eighteen years ago they purchased this reservation of the Cherokees for a home, and as such they want it to be. They argue that the time for such action has not yet come; that they are not prepared in any way to have white settlers for neighbors, and especially that variety of white men with whom it has been their misfortune to come in contact. About 250,000 acres of an area of over 1,500,000 is tillable land, the other is only suitable for grazing, and this they contend is no more than is needed for themselves and children."

[20] Ibid. [Twenty-first Report of the Board of Indian Commissioners] (1890), 27. The Osage population was about 1,500 in 1890, which would allow for an average of about 166 acres of arable land per capita.

This refrain is repeated in the reports of various agents. * * *

* * * In that year [1887] the International Council of Indian Territory, to which 19 tribes sent 57 representatives, voted unanimously against allotment and the granting of railroad rights-of-way through their lands. The council's resolution on the allotment question, which was sent to the President of the United States, cited these tribes' "sad experience" with allotment and assailed the policy as one which would "engulf all of the nations and tribes of the territory in one common catastrophe, to the enrichment of land monopolists."[23]

[23] Report of the Commissioner of Indian Affairs (1887), 116, 117.

* * * there is a compelling ring to the appeal of the International Council of 1887:[24]

> "Like other people, the Indian needs at least the germ of political identity, some governmental organization of his own, however crude, to which his pride and manhood may cling and claim allegiance, in order to make true progress in the affairs of life. This peculiarity in the Indian character is elsewhere called patriotism, the wise and patient fashioning and guidance of which alone will successfully solve the question of civilization. Preclude him from this and he has little else to live for. The law to which objection is urged does this by enabling any member of a tribe to become a member of some other body politic by electing and taking to himself a quantity of land which at the present time is the common property of all."

[24] Ibid. [Report of the Commissioner of Indian Affairs] (1887), 117.

The following year the agent to the Five Tribes observed that the half-breeds were becoming favorably inclined toward allotment but, he said,

> "The full-bloods are against it, as a rule, as they fear it will destroy their present government, to which they appear attached.[25]"

[25] Ibid. (1888), 135.

This same cleavage which characterized Indian opinion before the passage of the Dawes Act is apparent all through the nineties.[26] This cleavage expresses the fundamental fact that the allotment controversy was a struggle between two cultures. With the irresistible penetration of the white civilization, the conflict within the tribes crystallized into two factions, the half-breeds and the full-bloods, the young and the old, the "progressives" and the "conservatives", the sheep and the goats.

[26] See miscellaneous documents relating to Indian Affairs (collected in Indian Office library), xvii, 14066; Report of the Commissioner of Indian Affairs (1888), 93 (1889), 182, 230 (1890), 31 (1892), 294, 457 (1895), 255 (1900), 233, 381.

* * * * *

ADMINISTRATION AND CHANGES IN POLICY: LEASING

* * * * *

Those who were dissatisfied with the results achieved by the Dawes Act saw various causes of failure. For one thing, the whole emphasis of the allotment policy was laid upon farming, and critics from time to time pointed out that large sections of the Indians' lands were not suitable for agriculture. * * *

For another thing, the Government was continuing a policy which was a cause, as well as an index, of allotment's failure. A speaker at the 1890 Mohonk Conference described at length the evil consequences of the rationing system. He showed how it had pauperized the Indians and now deterred them from farming, since they feared if they raised crops the Government would cut down their allowances.[54]

[54] Ibid. [Twenty-second Report of the Board of Indian Commissioners] (1890), 142.

* * * * *

Many friends of the Indian who believed that the allotment system was not accomplishing all that it should were inclined to hold the Government responsible because of its failure to give adequate aid to the allottees. * * * It was not true that the Government made no efforts whatever to equip the Indians for farming. But it made very slight efforts. The appropriation act passed in 1888 provided for the allocation of $30,000 to the purchase of seed, farming implements, and other things "necessary for the commencement of farming" (25 Stat. L. 234). In 1888 alone 3,568 allotments had been made.[57] The appropriation, therefore, granted less than $10 to every new allottee setting out on his farming career. There is, furthermore, no way of knowing how much of this money was expended for this purpose. * * *

[57] Report of the Commissioner of Indian Affairs (1888), 444.

The following year the same amount was provided (25 Stat. L. 998) but in 1890 no such appropriation was made. In 1891 Congress raised $15,000 for the purpose (26 Stat. L. 1007) and this sum was continued through the next 2 years (27 Stat. L. 137, 630). After 1893 the appropriation acts up to 1900 included no such items. * * * The Omaha treaties of 1854 (10 Stat. L. 1043) and of 1868 (14 Stat. L. 667), which provided for a form of allotment, required the Government to furnish the Indians with implements, stock, and milling services. Yet these promises were never carried out.[68] One of the Indians who signed the petition for the Omaha allotment bill in 1881 said:

> "Three times I have cut wood to build a house. Each time the agent told me the Government wished to build me a house. Every time my wood has lain and rotted, and now I feel ashamed when I hear an agent telling me such things."[69]

[68] Fletcher and La Flesche, 623, 624.
[69] Ibid., 637.

* * * * *

Defects in the system which * * * occupied the attention of the friends of the Indian were those resulting from the fact that allotted lands must be free from State taxation. The Dawes Act, providing for the 25-year Federal trust period during which time the land might not be encumbered (24 Stat. L. 389), meant, it was clear, that no State could tax the allottee's holdings. As a result, the friends of the Indian were noting in 1889, States were refusing to assume any responsibilities for Indian communities and were withholding such services as the upkeep of schools and roads. It was also apparent that this situation was a source of great hostility to Indians on the part of white neighbors.[73] * * *

[73] Twenty-first Report of the Board of Indian Commissioners, (1889). 107–109.

* * * the most enthusiastic supporters of the allotment policy felt that its first results showed that it needed important revision, itself. In his report for 1889 the Commissioner observed that Indians were asking for equal allotments to all individuals, and he recommended that the law should be so amended. He noted that there was a special need to protect the married women whom the Dawes Act had excluded from allotment benefits. * * *[74] The Board of Indian Commissioners that same year urged upon Congress the equalization of allotments.[75]

[74] Report of the Commissioner of Indian Affairs (1889), 17.
[75] Ibid. [Twenty-first Report of the Board of Indian Commissioners] (1889), 9.

This proposed change was, significantly, bound up with another and still more important change which most friends of the Indian came to demand. * * * The Mohonk Conference that year heard some talk about the leasing of Indian lands and the freeing of the Indian from bondage. Justice Strong, previously associate justice of the United States Supreme Court, said:

> "But on one subject I am perfectly convinced; namely, that the Government has not the shadow of a right to interfere with an Indian's having an allotment, either with the use of his property or with the manner in which he shall educate his children * * *"[80]

[80] Idem. [Ibid. (1889), 105–109].

But especially the point was emphasized that leasing part of his land would bring the Indian the wherewithal to cultivate the rest.[81] Other arguments from time to time were brought forward by Indian sympathizers to show how leasing would help him.

[81] Ibid. (1889), 110, 112.

* * * * *

The decision to allow the Indian to lease his land was fraught with grave consequences for the whole allotment system. Probably it was the most important decision as to Indian policy that was made after the passage of the Dawes Act. Yet, interestingly enough, the significance of the leasing question seemed to be dwarfed in the eyes of contemporaries by the pressing matter of equal allotments. It is true that after the Attorney General ruled in 1885 that tribal grazing leases were illegal, the Commissioner of Indian Affairs recommended annually until 1889 a law permitting such leases.[88] But he made no proposal of leasing allotments.

[88] Report of the Commissioner of Indian Affairs (1888), xxxix.

And no doubt his advocating of grazing leases was looked at with suspicion by the friends of the Indian, as were most of his official acts.[89] The question of leasing allotments had been raised at the 1889 Mohonk Conference,[90] but the Indian Office took no stand on the question in that year. As has been said, Commissioner Morgan was interested in the question of granting equal allotments to Indians of all ages and both sexes.[91] In January 1890 he wrote a letter to the Secretary of the Interior enclosing a bill providing for the granting of 160 acres to every Indian—man, woman, and child. The following month the President transmitted the bill, together with Commissioner Morgan's letter to the Senate Committee on Indian Affairs.[92] The Commissioner mentioned several tribes which had opposed allotment because they disliked the system of unequal grants to the different classifications and he thought that if 160 acres were given each Indian "there would be less hesitation on the part of many of the tribes to the taking of land in severalty."[93] He also stressed the predicament of cast-off Indian wives under the existing system and the importance of dealing more liberally with the young Indians who were the future hope of the race.[94]

[89] The criticism directed at the Commissioner especially by the Indian Rights Association was claimed by that organization to be the cause of the Commissioner's dismissal and of the appointment of J. H. Oberly in his place. Seventh Annual Report Executive Commissioner Indian Rights Association (1889), 9, 10.
[90] See above p. 101.
[91] Ibid., p. 100.
[92] S. Ex. Doc. No. 64, February 17, 1890, 51st Cong., 1st sess., 1–4.
[93] Ibid., 2.
[94] Ibid., 3.

Accordingly, on March 10, 1890, Senator Dawes introduced in the Senate a bill to "amend and further extend the benefits" of the Dawes Act.[95] Section 1 of the bill provided for the granting of 160 acres to every Indian. The previous agitation of this question by the official and unofficial friends of the Indian furnished an adequate introduction to this legislative proposal. But section 2 of the bill seems to have come almost unheralded from Senator Dawes, the man who a few months later publicly expressed his misgivings about the leasing policy.[96] Section 2 of the Senator's bill read:[97]

> "That whenever it shall be made to appear to the Secretary of the Interior that, by reason of age or other disability, any allottee under the provisions of said act or any other act or treaty cannot personally and with benefit to himself occupy or improve his allotment, or any part thereof, the same may be leased upon such terms, regulations, and conditions as shall be prescribed by said Secretary, for a term not exceeding 3 years for farming or grazing, or 10 years for mining purposes."

[65] Congressional Record, March 10, 1890, 2068.
[66] See above, p. 102.
[67] Copy of bill in Senate Document Room files.

* * * a conference committee reached a compromise which was accepted by both Senate and House on February 23, 1891.[4] Eighty acres were to go to each Indian, but an Indian could rent his land only when unable to work it "by reason of age or other disability." The Indian must apply for a lease to the Secretary of the Interior directly and not to the agent, and farming and grazing leases of allotted lands could be for no longer than 3 years.[5] In other words, there was to be something in the way of restraint exercised upon Indian leasing. The President signed the bill on February 28, 1891 (26 Stat. L. 794).

* * * * *

The Indian administration set out at a very cautious gait to apply the leasing provision to allotments. The

[4] Ibid. [Congressional Record], Feb. 23, 1891, 3118, 3152.
[5] Sec. 3, 26 Stat. L. 794.

Commissioner in his report for 1892 said:

> "Agents are expressly directed that it is not intended to authorize the making of any lease by an allottee who possesses the necessary physical and mental qualifications to enable him to cultivate his allotment, either personally or by hired help." [17]

[17] Ibid. [Report of the Commissioner of Indian Affairs] (1892), 71.

He said that but two allotment leases had thus far been approved by him.[18] The next year the Commissioner promulgated a set of rules for the making of leases. The rules were primarily concerned with defining the terms in the phrase, "by reason of age or other disability." "Age" applied to all Indians under 18 and all those disabled by senility. "Other disability" applied to all unmarried Indian women, married women whose husband or sons were unable to work the land, widows without able-bodied sons, all Indians with chronic sickness or incurable physical defect, and those with "native defect of mind or permanent incurable mental disease." [19] The Commissioner reported that four allotment leases had been allowed that year.[20] * * *

[18] Ibid. (1892), 72.
[19] Ibid. (1893), 477, 476.
[20] Ibid. (1893), 27.

The Senator [Dawes] had secured an amendment to the House bill taking away from the agents the power of recommending leases and requiring the Indians to apply directly to the Secretary of the Interior.[21] But in 1893 the Commissioner wrote:

> "The matter of leasing allotted lands has been placed largely in the hands of Indian agents in charge of the agencies where allotments in severalty have been made."

[21] Congressional Record, Feb. 23, 1891, 3118.

He went on to say that all leases must be approved by the Secretary after recommendation by the agent.[22] How much this administrative ruling was in itself responsible for the subsequent speeding up of leasing cannot be said for at that point a most important change was made in the law. * * *

[22] Report of the Commissioner of Indian Affairs (1893), 27.

* * * * *

* * * the general Indian appropriation act which became law August 15, 1894, contained a provision which changed the critical phrase in the act of 1891 to read "by reason of age, disability or inability", extended the term of agricultural and grazing leases to 5 years and permitted 10-year leases for business as well as mining purposes (28 Stat. L. 305). Nevertheless, the Commissioner said in his report that year:

> "It has been repeatedly stated that it was not the intent of the law nor the policy of the office to allow indiscriminate leasing of allotted lands * * * If an allottee has physical or mental ability to cultivate an allotment by personal labor or by hired help, the leasing of such allotment should not be permitted." [24]

[24] Ibid. [Report of the Commissioner of Indian Affairs] (1894), 32, 33.

But a new rule which the Commissioner added to those defining "age" and "disability" read:

> "The term 'inability' as used in said amended act, cannot be specifically defined as the other terms have been. Any allottee not embraced in any of the foregoing classes who for any reason other than those stated is unable to cultivate his lands or a portion of them, and desires to lease same may make application therefor to the proper Indian agent." [25]

* * * * *

* * * the Indian Appropriation Act of 1897 changed the leasing system back to its original form. Indeed in one respect the provisions were even more restrictive than were those of the 1891 law. The maximum term for mining and business leases was fixed at 5 years. The term for farming and grazing leases was changed back to 3 years, and the word "inability" was dropped so that "age or other disability" became the only legal grounds for permitting leases (30 Stat. L. 85). The Commissioner's report for 1897 commented on the fact that the leasing periods had been changed by the Indian appropriation act but, interestingly enough, he made no mention of the dropping of the word "inability." [26] * * * The Commissioner approved 1.185 allotment leases in 1899 and 2,590 in 1900.[27] In this latter year, the system was again changed by the Indian appropriation act. "Inability" was restored as a reason for permitting allotment leases, and the maximum period of leasing for farming purposes was extended once more to 5 years (31 Stat. L. 229). * * * Apparently the change in policy had not been the doing of the Commissioner. He wrote in his report for 1900:[28]

> "The better to assist them the allottees should be divided into small communities, each to be put in charge of persons who by precept and example would teach them how to work and how to live.
>
> "This is the theory. The practice is very different. The Indian is allotted and then allowed to turn over his land to the whites and go on his aimless way. This pernicious practice is the direct growth of vicious legislation. The first law on the subject was passed in 1891. * * *
>
> "It is conceded that where an Indian allottee is incapacitated by physical disability or decrepitude of age from occupying and working his allotment, it is proper to permit him to lease it, and it was to meet such cases as this that the law referred to was made * * * But "inability" has opened the door for leasing in general, until on some of the reservations leasing is the rule and not the exception, while on others the practice is growing.
>
> "To the thoughtful mind it is apparent that the effect of the general leasing of allotments is bad. Like the gratuitous issue of rations and the periodical distribution of money it fosters indolence with its train of attendant vices. By taking away the incentive to labor it defeats the very object for which the allotment system was devised, which was, by giving the

Indian something tangible that he could call his own, to incite him to personal effort in his own behalf."

[35] Ibid. (1894), 421.
[36] Report of the Commissioner of Indian Affairs (1897), 40–43.
[37] Ibid. [Report of the Commissioner of Indian Affairs] (1899), 60 (1900), 76–78.
[38] Report of the Commissioner of Indian Affairs (1900), 13.

Thus it seems that the leasing policy had been pushed much further than the friends of the Indian desired. As to who had been pushing it there one can only guess. It is apparent that white settlers and promoters had found leasing a new and effective technique for exploiting Indian lands. So had Indian agents—according to the Indian Rights Association. The association's report for 1900 described the evil consequences of the leasing system under the new law and set forth grave charges.[40]

[40] Eighteenth Annual Report of the Executive Committee Indian Rights Association (1900), 58.

* * * * *

RESULTS OF ALLOTMENT TO 1900

Analysis of the achievements of the allotment system requires first some appraisal of the leasing practice which vitally affected allotment results. There were defenders of the leasing system all through the 1890's. It had certain immediate consequences which recommended it to friends of the Indian who were sincere if lacking in vision. There was the simple fact of allotted lands lying idle which the Indians either could not or would not cultivate. Such waste seemed wicked to a generation that was coming increasingly to set store by efficiency. How much better it was for the lands to be used and the Indians to be deriving an income from them. In 1890, before the passage of the leasing act, a member of the Board of Indian Commissioners regretted that the Government had ousted white share workers from the Kiowa, Comanche, and Apache Reservations. He said:

"Farms that could only be worked in this way, owing to peculiar circumstances, are now lying tenantless and abandoned." [41]

[41] Twenty-second Report of the Board of Indian Commissioners (1890), 31.

In 1895 various agents expressed their approval of the way leasing was working since it was bringing in to the Indians a sizeable revenue.[42] * * *

[42] Report of the Commissioner of Indian Affairs (1895), 260, 262, 335.

But for the most part, the agents who expressed their approval of allotment leasing saw it as productive of practical results. It took care of minors, women, and the old folks,[43] and it was economically profitable. One agent said the Indians got more out of the leased lands than if they worked them themselves.[44] * * * Leasing was undoubtedly a spur to the taking of allotments. But it seems hardly to have been a spur to the Indian becoming a farmer. * * *

[43] Thirtieth Report of the Board of Indian Commissioners (1898), 14.
[44] Ibid. (1898) 18; see also p. 15, and Report of the Commissioner of Indian Affairs (1900), 361.

* * * * *

Perhaps the most flagrant example of the corrosive influence of leasing was that of the Omahas and Winnebagoes, in Nebraska. The Omahas were the great hope of the allotment enthusiasts. But in 1893 the agent wrote that leasing had gone far among the Omahas and Winnebagoes and that the former were renting their lands without the consent of the agent or Government.[57] In 1894 * * * Professor Painter told the Mohonk conference of his bitter disappointment in the Omahas especially, about whom he had been satisfied and enthusiastic as they had started out under the allotment system. He had recently visited the two reservations and found most of the land in white hands. Real-estate syndicates had leased lands even before the allotment was completed. One company had rented 47,000 acres from the Winnebagoes at from 8 to 10 cents an acre and sublet to white farmers for $1 to $2 an acre. The Winnebagoes got enough income from these lands to stay drunk part of the time. But the Omahas got much more.[60]

[57] Ibid. [Report of the Commissioner of Indian Affairs] (1893), 193–195; see also (1892), 186.
[60] Twenty-sixth Report of the Board of Indian Commissioners (1894), 120.

The illegal leasing of allotments had apparently gone to great lengths on these two reservations.[61] In 1894 the agent thought that the Indians were anxious to recover their lands and till some portion of them.[62] The following year this fighting agent set out in a vain effort to bring to heel a powerful land company. The Government ultimately furnished him with 50 extra police and 70 rifles as the local authorities rallied to the support of the land company and were reported to be arming a hundred deputies. Confronted by an injunction in the State courts restraining him from evicting the company's tenants, the agent at last gave in.[63] In 1894 the agent had written,

"The settlers would almost unanimously prefer to lease under the rules and regulations of the Department; but are held, pecuniarily, by the lawless corporations and individuals who have subleased to them." [64]

[61] Report of the Commissioner of Indian Affairs (1895), 37, 38.
[62] Ibid. (1894), 187, 188.
[63] Report of the Commissioner of Indian Affairs (1895), 37–41.
[64] Ibid. (1894), 188.

In 1895 the Commissioner explained the effective technique of this particular land company which had been able to flout the Federal authority. His explanation suggests very clearly why this outlaw corporation received the community's support. In many instances the company accepted notes from their subtenants in place of money rent. These notes in turn came into the hands of local bankers. As a result all of the powerful interests in the community were galvanized in opposition to the Government in its attempt to force evictions or collect legal rents.[65]

[65] Ibid. (1895), 41.

Whatever progress the Omahas, especially, might have made under the original allotment system it is clear that the leasing policy doomed their efforts to failure and themselves to demoralization. * * *

The passionate denunciation of leasing by the Omaha and Winnebago agent in 1898 perhaps says the last word on the matter. He wrote that out of 140,000 acres allotted on the two reservations, 112,000 acres had been leased. He then wrote:[67]

"Leasing of allotted agricultural lands should never be permitted. The Indians should be compelled to live upon their allotments and support themselves by cultivating the land. They can do it, but will not unless compelled to. Not 1 acre of allotted agricultural land should be leased to a white man, and it would be far better to burn the grass on the allotted lands than to lease them for pastures to the white man. * * *"

[67] Thirtieth [R]eport of the Board of Indian Commissioners (1898), 25.

* * * * *

* * * the allotment policy began and continued as an act of faith. So it was possible for an agent to report that allotment was working well on his reservation and at the same time submit figures which showed that the greater portion of the Indian lands were leased to white men. Indeed, the testimony which comes even from the friends of the Indian as to the dire results of the leasing policy toward the end of the century makes it seem improbable that the allotment system in the main was working well.

The writer's scepticism as to the real success of the allotment system in the period of the 1890's is based not alone on inference and deduction. The following table contains figures that are pertinent to the question whether or not allotment was producing results:

Land and crop statistics

[Unless otherwise indicated the figures are taken from the current volume of the Annual Reports of the Commissioner of Indian Affairs. The figures in parentheses are page references]

Date	Total number of allotments to date	Total number of leases to date	Number of families living on and cultivating allotments	Number of acres cultivated by Indians	Indian agricultural production (in bushels)				Page
					Wheat	Oats and barley	Corn	Vegetables	
1890	15,166	.....	5,554	288,613	881,419	545,032	1,139,297	482,500	(480)
1891	17,996	.....	5,883	......	1,318,218	793,001	1,830,704	541,974	(106)
1892	26,700	2	7,302	......	1,825,715	875,631	1,515,464	558,162	(816)
1893	31,261	6	7,579	......	[1]1,722,656	883,170	1,373,230	462,871	(723)
1894	34,322	301	8,359	......	887,809	653,631	911,655	398,133	(593)
1895	39,173	631	8,366	369,974	[2]1,016,751	[2]875,349	[2]2,226,944	476,272	(594)
1896	43,587	1,564	10,045	......	753,577	731,806	2,100,316	542,538	(551)
1897	46,816	2,851	10,659	......	788,192	805,466	1,123,200	703,770	(510)
1898	48,831	3,799	11,789	......	664,930	599,665	1,339,444	494,509	(630)
1899	49,842	4,984	10,704	......	982,120	850,387	1,386,977	445,935	(597)
1900	58,594	7,574	10,835	343,351	935,731	722,925	1,655,504	396,067	(677)

[1] Over 850,000 bushels of wheat raised by white lessees on Umatilla Reservation.

[2] Unspecified amount of wheat, oats, barley, and corn raised by white lessees on Indian lands.

NOTE.—Allotment and leasing totals, 1891–1900 taken from figures given above pp. 81, 111–113.

The figures given above, while by no means conclusive, indicate that the allotment system was not producing the results which the originators of the policy hoped for. In comparing the number of allotments with the number of families living and working on them, one must bear in mind that several allotments might be made to one family. The act of 1891 which granted 80 acres to every Indian made it possible for one family to possess an even greater number of allotments than before. It is unfortunate that there is no way of knowing the number of specific families allotted and the average number of allotments to each. But the above figures show that the number of families cultivating their allotments was by no means keeping pace with the allotment figures. The number of allotments per family grew from 2.7 in 1890 to 5.4 in 1900. Since it may be supposed that when Indians accepted allotments the family took as many as they could get, and since the only change in the law after 1890 which affected the question of eligibility for allotment was the extension of the privilege to married women, this increasing ratio of allotments to families cultivating them suggests a decline of Indian husbandry. Or at least it suggests a failure to reach the goal envisaged by the friends of the Indian. Even more disquieting are the statistics of Indian agriculture. The above figures show an increase in acreage of Indian farming from 1890 to 1895 which was far from proportionate to the number of allotments made in those years. Then from 1895 to 1900, although more than 19,000 allotments were made, the area of the land tilled by Indians actually decreased by over 26,000 acres. Nor if one takes the figures of crop production for what they are worth, can one observe the progress in Indian agriculture during these 10 years which the friends of allotment expected. * * *

* * * * *

* * * If the allotment system were to have succeeded the Indian would, culturally, have had to be made over. The significance of this fact was never fully grasped by the philanthropists and the Government. * * * So the Indian hopefully if not enthusiastically, went, unprepared, out upon his allotment, as an unarmed man would go unwittingly into a forest of wild beasts.

For if white land seekers and business promoters did not create the allotment system, they at least turned it to their own good use. * * *

* * * * *

Besides the lands that were thrown open to settlement, white men were interested in tribal lands that remained. This was especially true of the cattlemen. * * *

When it came to the actual designation of allotments, white influence was also busy. General Whittlesey, of the Board of Indian Commissioners, said to the Mohonk Conference in 1891, "Another hindrance [to the allotting of lands] is the influence brought to bear by surrounding white settlers, who are waiting to get possession of the lands that may be reserved after allotments are completed. If there are valuable tracts of land, they try to prevent those lands from being allotted, and to prevent Indians from selecting them, by bribery and by other means."[97] * * *

[97] Ibid. [Report of the Board of Indian Commissioners] (1891), 96.

* * * * *

* * * In 1890, General Whittlesey reported that there was a growing demand for the Government to distribute among the Indians on a per capita basis tribal funds that had been so heavily swelled by sales of surplus lands. He said, "That is their own desire, and the desire of many of those who surround them, who know how soon such money disappears."[1] The Umatilla agent who found agriculture languishing on his reservation in 1894—especially among the full bloods—wrote:

> "The few mixed bloods who farm their allotments do so with stock, machinery, and provisions furnished by merchants or bankers, who take a mortgage on the crop, afterwards taking all the crop."[2]

[1] Ibid. [Report of the Board of Indian Commissioners] (1890), 129.

[2] Report of the Commissioner of Indian Affairs (1894), 269.

And there was a long story of flagrant corruption and exploitation in the activities of lumbering companies who manipulated the allotment system to their great profit, on up into the twentieth century.[3]

[3] See W. K. Moorehead, The American Indian in the United States (Andover, Mass., 1914), 59, 62, 71 ff.

By the middle of the 1890's the friends of the Indian began to express dismay at the course their humanitarian policy had taken in the hands of persons who were not always humanitarians. * * *

* * * * *

In 1895 the Commissioner showed himself well aware of the forces that were crippling Indian development. He made a shrewd comment on his times and a significant forecast. He said:

> "The whites in some sections of the country seem to have very little respect for the rights of Indians who have segregated themselves from their tribes and sought to avail themselves of the benefits of the Indian homestead and allotment laws enacted expressly for them by Congress, and I apprehend that the opposition to them will increase as the public domain grows less and less."[7]

[7] Report of the Commissioner of Indian Affairs (1895), 22.

* * * One student of the allotment movement believes that the act of 1891 was the most important step toward ruin. This law by granting the Indian the right to lease and at the same time allotting to each member of the family—to babies and octogenarians—an equal amount of land developed in the Indian idleness and avarice. Children ceased to be a responsibility and became indirectly a source of revenue through their leased allotments. As a result the family was disrupted as a producing unit and the Indian's interest became pecuniary instead of industrial.[8] The present writer agrees with this analysis, but he is inclined to think that basically the leasing policy in almost any form would have meant ultimate defeat for the allotment system.

[8] Flora Warren Seymour, Story of the Red Man (New York, 1929), 376; letter from Mrs. Seymour to the writer.

D. APPRAISAL OF THE ALLOTMENT SYSTEM

A critical appraisal of the consequences of the allotment system is found in a memorandum submitted to the Senate and House Committees on Indian Affairs by Commissioner Collier on February 19, 1934.[11] This memorandum provided at least part of the basis for those provisions of the Act of June 18, 1934,[12] which put an end to the process of allotment:

> The Indians are continuing to lose ground; yet Government costs must increase, while the Indians must still continue to lose ground, unless existing law be changed.
>
> Two thirds of the Indians in two thirds of the Indian country for many years have been drifting toward complete impoverishment.
>
> While being stripped of their property, these same Indians cumulatively have been disorganized as groups and pushed to a lower social level as individuals.
>
> During this time, when Indian wealth has been shrinking and Indian life has been diminishing, the costs of Indian administration in the identical areas have been increasing. The complications of bureaucratic management have grown steadily greater.
>
> Ruin for the Indians, and still larger costs to the Government, are insur[ed] by the existing system.
>
> Neither the Indians themselves, nor the Indian Service, can reverse the downhill process, or even materially delay it, unless certain fundamental impracticabilities of law can be changed.
>
> The disastrous condition, peculiar to the Indian situation in the United States, and sharply in contrast with the Indian situations both of Canada and of Mexico, is directly and inevitably the result of existing law—principally, but not exclusively, the allotment law and its amendments and its administrative complications.
>
> The approximately one third of the Indians who as yet are outside the allotment system are not losing their property; and generally they are increasing in industry and are rising, not falling, in the social scale. The costs of Indian administration are markedly lower in these unallotted areas.
>
> * * * * *
>
> The backbone of Indian law since 1887 has been the allotment act and its amendments and administrative regulations.
>
> The law originally possessed, and still possesses, virtues which can be preserved and made effective. The bill does preserve them. But these virtues, potential rather than realized, have been slight indeed when contrasted with the destructive effects of the law and the system.
>
> HOW ALLOTMENT HAS WORKED AND NOW WORKS
>
> Land allotment, under the general and special allotment acts, has been mandatory. To each Indian—man, woman, and child—living and enrolled at a specified date, a separate parcel of land has been attached. The residual lands, fictitiously called "surplus," have been mandatorily bought from the tribes by the government and thereafter have been disposed of to whites.
>
> The individualized parcels of land have been held under Government trust over longer or shorter periods. Sometimes, where the land was agricultural, the Indian family has lived upon and has used one or more of the allotments attached to its several members. Where the land was of grazing character, or was timberland, allotment precluded the integrated use of the land by individuals or families, even at the start.
>
> Upon the allottees' death, it has been necessary to partition the land equally among heirs, or to sell it, and in the interim it has been leased.
>
> Most likewise of the land of living allottees has been leased to whites.
>
> STATISTICS OF LOSS OF LAND THROUGH ALLOTMENT
>
> Through sales by the Government of the fictitiously designated "surplus" lands; through sales by allottees after the trust period had ended or had been terminated by administrative act; and through sales by the Government of heirship land, virtually mandatory under the allotment act: Through these three methods, the total of Indian landholdings has been cut from 138,000,000 acres in 1887 to 48,000,000 acres in 1934.
>
> These gross statistics, however, are misleading, for, of the remaining 48,000,000 acres, more than 20,000 acres are contained within areas which for special reasons have been exempted from the allotment law; whereas the land loss is chargeable exclusively against the allotment system.
>
> Furthermore, that part of the allotted lands which has been lost is the most valuable part. Of the residual lands, taking all Indian-owned lands into account, nearly one half, or nearly 20,000,000 acres, are desert or semidesert lands.
>
> Allotment, commenced at different dates and applied under varying conditions, has divested the Indians of their property at unequal speeds. For about 100,000 Indians the divestment has been absolute. They are totally landless as a result of allotment. On some of the reservations the divestment is as yet only partial and in part is only provisional. Many of the heirship lands, awaiting sale to whites under existing law, have not yet been sold, and the Indian title is not yet extinguished. Under the allotment system it inevitably will be extinguished.
>
> The above statement relates solely to land losses. The facts can be summarized thus:
>
> Through the allotment system, more than 80 percent of the land value belonging to all the Indians in 1887 has been taken away from them; more than 85 percent of the land value of all the allotted Indians has been taken away.
>
> And the allotment system, working down through the partitionment or sale of the land of deceased allottees, mathematically insures and practically requires that the remaining Indian allotted lands shall pass to whites. The allotment act contemplates total landlessness for the Indians of the third generation of each allotted tribe.
>
> THE REMAINING LANDS RENDERED UNUSABLE
>
> A yet more disheartening picture will immediately follow the above statement. For equally important with the outright loss of land is the effect of the allotment system in making such lands as remain in Indian ownership unusable.
>
> There have been presented to the House Indian Committee numerous land maps, showing the condition of Indian-owned lands on allotted reservations. The Indian-owned lands are parcels belonging (*a*) to allottees and (*b*) to the heirs of deceased allottees. Both of these classes of Indian-owned land are checkerboarded with white-owned land already lost to the Indians, and on many reservations the Indian-owned parcels are mere islands within a sea of white-owned property.
>
> Farming, at least at the subsistence level, and commercial farming within irrigated areas, is still possible on those parcels belonging to living allottees. But grazing, upon the grazing land of living allottees, and businesslike or conservative forest operation, upon the allotted forest land of living allottees, are largely, often absolutely, impossible.
>
> On the checkerboarded land maps, the heirship lands each year become a greater proportion of the total of the remaining Indian land. These heirship lands belong to numerous heirs, even up to the number of hundreds.
>
> And one heir possessed equities in numerous allotments, up to the number of hundreds.
>
> The above conditions force some of the Indian allotted land out of any profitable use whatsoever, and they force nearly all of it into the condition of land rented to whites, and rented under conditions disadvantageous to the Indians. The denial of financial credit to Indians is, of course, an added influence.
>
> The Indians are practically compelled to become absentee landlords with petty and fast-dwindling estates, living upon the always diminishing pittances of lease money.
>
> And here there becomes apparent the administrative impossibility created by the allotment system.
>
> ALLOTMENT COSTS THE GOVERNMENT MILLIONS IN BARREN EXPENDITURES THAT CANNOT SAVE THE INDIAN LANDS OR CAPITAL, WHILE EMBITTERING AND RUINING THE INDIANS
>
> The Indian Service is compelled to be a real-estate agent in behalf of the living allottees; and in behalf of the more numerous heirs of deceased allottees. As such

[11] See Hearings, Committee on Ind. Aff., 73d Cong., 2d sess., on H. R. 7902, pp. 15–18.

[12] 48 Stat. 984, 25 U. S. C. 461, *et seq.*

real-estate agent, selling and renting the hundreds of thousands of parcels of land and fragmented equities of parcels, and disbursing the rentals (sometimes to more than a hundred heirs of one parcel, and again to an individual heir with an equity in a hundred parcels), the Indian Service is forced to expend millions of dollars a year. The expenditure does not and cannot save the land, or conserve the capital accruing from land sales or from rentals.

The operation gets nowhere at all; under the existing system of law it cannot get anywhere; it creates between the Indians and the Government a relationship barren, embittered, full of contempt and despair; it keeps the Indians' own minds focused upon petty and dwindling equities which inexorably vanish to nothing at all.

For the Indians the situation is necessarily one of frustration, of impotent discontent. They are forced into the status of a landlord class, yet it is impossible for them to control their own estates; and the estates are insufficient to yield a decent living, and the yield diminishes year by year and finally stops altogether.

It is difficult to imagine any other system which with equal effectiveness would pauperize the Indian while impoverishing him, and sicken and kill his soul while pauperizing him, and cast him in so ruined a condition into the final status of a nonward dependent upon the States and counties.

The Indian Bureau's costs must rise, as the allotted lands pass to the heirship class. The multiplication of individual paternalistic actions by the Indian Service must grow as the complications of heirship grow wtih each year. Such has been the record, and such it will be, unless the Government, in impatience or despair, shall summarily retreat from a hopeless situation, abandoning the victims of its allotment system. The alternative will be to apply a constructi[ve] remedy as proposed by the present bill.

The bill breaks this hopeless impasse.

For a number of years, it has been clearly recognized within the Indian Service that conditions must continue to grow worse, regardless of attempted administrative reforms, unless the allotment situation in its totality be modified.

And for a number of years the directions of practicable modification have become increasingly clear, both within the Indian Service and among observers outside it. The indicated solution has been stated with clarity, and more than once, in debates on the Senate floor and in reports by the Indian Investigation Committee of the Senate. The preceding administration recognized the impasse which had been reached under the allotment system, but did not put forward legislation to break the impasse.

The present bill, in those aspects which are most truly emergency items, is a bill to correct the allotment system, saving the remaining lands, enabling the Indians to get their lands into usable shape, and providing the machinery and authority for restoring, to those Indians already rendered landless, usable lands, if they will demonstrate their wish to possess and use the restored lands.

E. TERMINATION OF THE ALLOTMENT SYSTEM

The allotment system involved four critical steps:

1. The allotting of tribal lands.
2. The termination of trust periods or periods of restricted alienability, after a fixed term of years.
3. The termination of such restrictions prior to the expiration of the statutory period by administrative action.
4. The alienation of allotted lands prior to the termination of such periods.

The Act of June 18, 1934, stopped the continuance of the allotment system at points 1 and 2 [13] and placed severe limitations on the operation of the system at points 3 and 4.[14]

The operation of the Act of June 18, 1934, upon the statutory fabric of the allotment system at each of these points is analyzed in the following pages.

[13] See Act of June 18, 1934, secs. 1 and 2, 48 Stat. 984, 25 U. S. C. 461–462.

[14] See Act of June 18, 1934, secs. 4 and 5, 48 Stat. 984, 985, 25 U. S. C. 464–465.

SECTION 2. RIGHT TO RECEIVE ALLOTMENT

Section 1 of the Act of June 18, 1934 [15] provides:

> That hereafter no land of any Indian reservation, created or set apart by treaty or agreement with the Indians, Act of Congress, Executive order, purchase, or otherwise, shall be allotted in severalty to any Indian.

Its obvious purpose is to preserve in communal ownership all tribal lands of Indian reservations. It accomplishes that purpose by the declaration that no such lands shall be allotted. To that extent, the act is incompatible with and, therefore, supplants all prior laws, both general and special, purporting to authorize allotments in severalty in any form on any reservation to which the act applies, and this notwithstanding the fact that the act contains no general repeal provision.[16]

The act extends to and binds all Indians under the jurisdiction of the Federal Government save those tribes expressly excluded by section 13 and those reservations which, in the exercise of the privilege conferred by section 18, vote against its application.

Since allotments have been discontinued under the mandate of this statute, and under a policy preceding this enactment which applies even to tribes not under the act, a detailed study of the allotment statutes will not be attempted. However, inasmuch as allotments may be made on reservations which have rejected the Wheeler-Howard Act until the surplus lands have been completely disposed of or until prohibited by Congress,[17] and individual rights of Indians in real property have vested under the allotment statutes, it may be useful to offer a short summary of the provisions and legal effect of such statutes.

Section 1 of the General Allotment Act of February 8, 1887,[18] later amended by general acts of February 28, 1891,[19] and of June 25, 1910,[20] and now embodied in section 331 of title 25 of the United States Code authorized the President of the United States to allot land [21] in severalty to Indians living on reserva-

[15] 48 Stat. 984, 25 U. S. C. 461.

[16] Where a reservation has by vote come under the act, land may not thereafter be allotted under a prior statute. Op. Sol. I. D., M.27770, May 22, 1935. But where an Indian acquired rights by a proper selection which was approved prior to the passage of the act, it has been ruled that the Secretary may issue a patent, and where lands had been selected but not approved before the passage of the act, they could be approved and patented to the allottee, the approval not requiring the exercise of discretion. Op. Sol. I. D. M.28086, July 17, 1935, 55 I. D. 295.

[17] Op. Sol., I. D., M.30256, May 31, 1939. The Act of June 15, 1935, 49 Stat. 378, provided that all laws affecting any Indian reservation which voted to exclude itself from the application of the Indian Reorganization Act shall be deemed to have been continuously effective as to such reservation notwithstanding the passage of that act. *Ibid.* On the power of the Secretary over individual lands, see Chapter 5, sec. 11.

[18] 24 Stat. 388.

[19] C. 383, sec. 1, 26 Stat. 794.

[20] C. 431, sec. 17, 36 Stat. 855, 859, 25 U. S. C. 331.

[21] Section 335 of title 25 of the Code, derived from the Act of February 14, 1923, c. 76, 42 Stat. 1246, makes the provisions of secs. 331–334, inclusive, and 336 and 341 heretofore discussed (and secs. 348–350, inclusive, and 381 to be discussed subsequently) applicable to "all lands heretofore purchased or which may be purchased by authority of Congress for the use or benefit of any individual Indian or band or tribe of Indians."

tions, whenever, in his opinion, the reservation or any part thereof might be advantageously utilized for agricultural or grazing purposes. Provision is made for allotments "not to exceed eighty acres of agricultural or one hundred and sixty acres of grazing land." [22]

The allotment policy was by no means uniform, certain tribes, for example, being excepted from provisions of the General Allotment Act of 1887.[23]

In addition to the general statute of 1887, Congress passed special acts authorizing the allotment of lands of specific tribes.[24] For those Indians not residing on reservations and who could otherwise not receive an allotment, Congress provided in section 4 of the General Allotment Act (incorporated in title 25 of the Code as sec. 334) for their receiving allotments upon any surveyed or unsurveyed lands of the United States not otherwise appropriated.

Where under this section an allotment was erroneously made and a person thereafter applied for homestead entry upon such an allotment, the Secretary of the Interior was held to have authority to protect the Indian in his allotment even though erroneously made and to deny the application for homestead entry, since to have allowed the entry would have been to visit a considerable injustice upon the allottee.[25]

Section 336 [26] of title 25 of the United States Code provides that where any Indian entitled to an allotment should settle upon lands of the United States not otherwise appropriated he should be entitled to have the same allotted to him in the manner provided for allotments to Indians residing upon reservations, and such allotments were not to exceed 40 acres of irrigable land or 80 acres of nonirrigable agricultural land, or 160 acres of nonirrigable grazing land.

Under section 337 of title 25 of the United States Code,[27] the Secretary of the Interior is permitted in his discretion to make allotments within the national forests to Indians who were living on lands included in a national forest or who had made improvements thereon and were not entitled to an allotment on any existing reservation or whose tribal reservation was not sufficient to give each member an allotment.

As pointed out in Chapter 8, the allotment of lands in severalty did not in any way affect the guardian-ward relationship existing between the national government and the Indian [28] nor did it affect the authority of the Commissioner of Indian Affairs to remove collectors from the reservation.[29] It has also been held that an allotment system does not deprive the tribe of the right to regulate the domestic affairs of its members.[30]

A. ELIGIBILITY

Insofar as eligibility to receive an allotment depends upon tribal membership the cases and statutes on the subject have been elsewhere discussed.[31]

In litigation dealing with the eligibility of Indians entitled to allotments, it has been held that the fact that a member of a tribe is born after the passage of the General Allotment Act does not disqualify him.[32] It has also been held that an Indian woman, though married to a white man, is head of her family and that her children who maintained their tribal relations were entitled to allotments as members of the tribe.[33] In the case of *La Clair* v. *United States* [34] the court held that adopted members of the Yakima tribe, who were formerly Puyallup Indians and whose parents had received allotments on the Puyallup Reservation as heads of families, were nevertheless entitled to allotments in the Yakima Reservation.[35] On the other hand, it

[22] The Act of 1887 provided for allotments of varying amount to various classes of Indians. For example, a head of a family was to receive a quarter of a section, while only one-eighth of a section was to be allotted to a single person over 18 years of age or an orphan under 18. To "each other single person under eighteen years now living, or who may be born prior to the date of the order of the President," sec. 1 specifies the allotment of one-sixteenth of a section.

[23] Thus sec. 339 of title 25 of U. S. C. which is derived from sec. 8 of the General Allotment Act expressly provided that:

> * * * sections 331 to 334, inclusive, 336, 341, 348 to 350, inclusive, and 381 [of this title] shall not extend to the territory occupied by the Cherokees, Creeks, Choctaws, Chickasaws, Seminoles, and Osage, Miamies and Peorias, and Sacs and Foxes, in Oklahoma nor to any of the reservations of the Seneca Nation of New York Indians in the State of New York, nor to that strip of territory in the State of Nebraska adjoining the Sioux Nation on the south added by Executive order.

By a proviso annexed to the Act of February 28, 1891, 26 Stat. 796 it was provided that no allotment of lands shall be made or annuities of money paid to any of the Sacs and Foxes of Missouri who are not enrolled as members of said tribe on January 1, 1890.

On the other hand the provisions of secs. 331 to 334, 336, 341, 348, 350, and 381 of title 25 of U. S. C. (Supp.) have by sec. 340, which is derived from the Act of March 2, 1889, 25 Stat. 1013, been extended to

> * * * the Confederated Wea, Peoria, Kaskaskia, and Piankeshaw tribes of Indians, and the Western Miami tribe of Indians, located in the northeastern part of the former Indian Territory and to their reservation, in the same manner and to the same extent as if said tribes had not been excepted from the provisions of said sections, except and as otherwise hereinafter provided.

[24] See Act of February 25, 1920, c. 87, 41 Stat. 452 for the Flathead Indians and the Act of March 3, 1921, c. 135, 41 Stat. 1355 for the Gros Ventre and Assiniboine Tribes in the Fort Belknap Reservation.

> Broadly speaking, the act of 1889, known as the Nelson act, provided for the cession by "all the different bands or tribes of Chippewa Indians in the State of Minnesota" of all their title and interest in and to their reservations in said State not needed for allotments; for allotments of land in severalty in conformity with the act of February 8, 1887 (24 Stat. 388), and for the sale of the remaining lands. * * *
>
> The act of April 28, 1904 (33 Stat. 539), known as the Steenerson act, providing for allotments to Indians on the White Earth reservation in Minnesota, authorized allotment "to each Chippewa Indian now legally residing upon" that reservation under treaty or laws of the United States in accordance with the express promise made by the Commissioners appointed under the act of January 14, 1889. (Op. Sol. I. D., M. 15954, January 8, 1927.)
>
> * * * We frequently find acts of Congress directing allotments on particular Indian reservations to be made in accordance with the general allotment laws of the United States. When so made, for all practical purposes, such allotments are to be regarded as coming within the scope of the general allotment act. The chief difference lies in the area received by the allottees. Under the general allotment act, ordinarily, each Indian receives 80 acres of agricultural or 160 acres of grazing land, while under the special acts relating to particular reservations they frequently receive considerably more. See the act of May 30, 1908 (35 Stat. 558), relating to the Fort Peck Reservation and the act of March 1, 1907 (34 Stat. 1035) as amended June 30, 1919 (41 Stat. 16), relating to the Blackfoot reservation, both of which are also in the State of Montana. Both of these acts authorize allotments under the general allotment laws of the United States and on each reservation the allottees received in excess of 320 acres. Patents for such allotments however were issued in accordance with the general allotment act of February 8, 1887, as amended. (Op. Sol. I. D., M.12498, June 6, 1924.)

[25] *Baldwin* v. *Keith*, 13 Okla. 624, 75 Pac. 1124 (1904). For a discussion of the Secretary's power over Indian lands, see Chapter 5, sec. 11.

[26] This section was derived from sec. 4 of the Act of February 28, 1891, 26 Stat. 794, 795, as amended by sec. 17 of the Act of June 25, 1910, 36 Stat. 855, 860.

[27] Act of June 25, 1910, sec. 31, 36 Stat. 855, 863.

[28] See sec. 2C, and *Hollister* v. *United States*, 145 Fed. 773 (C. C. A. 8, 1906).

[29] *Rainbow* v. *Young*, 161 Fed. 835 (C. C. A. 8, 1908).

[30] *Yakima Joe* v. *To-is-lap*, 191 Fed. 516 (C. C. Ore. 1910). And see Chapter 7, sec. 5.

[31] See Chapter 1, sec. 2; Chapter 5, sec. 13; Chapter 7, sec. 4.

[32] *United States* v. *Fairbanks*, 171 Fed. 837, 839 (C. C. A. 8, 1909) aff'd sub nom. *Fairbanks* v. *United States*, 223 U. S. 215, 224 (1912).

[33] *Bonifer* v. *Smith*, 166 Fed. 846 (C. C. A. 9, 1909). And *cf. Ladiga* v. *Roland*, 2 How. 581 (1844), holding that widow living with grandchildren was head of family, entitled to allotment under Creek Treaty of March 24, 1932, 7 Stat. 366, and obtained title thereto by application, although President attempted to award title to another.

[34] 184 Fed. 128 (C. C. E. D. Wash. 1910).

[35] In *Mitchell* v. *United States*, 22 F. 2d 771 (C. C. A. 9, 1927), it was held that under a regulation requiring that adoptions be approved by the Secretary of the Interior and the Indian Commissioner, an adoption without such approval did not entitle the Indian to an allotment.

has been held that a tribal Indian living apart from the tribe and off the reservation is not entitled to an allotment on the reservation.[36] This does not mean, of course, that the Indian had to be on the reservation the instant the Allotment Act was passed.[37]

An Indian may not have allotments from two different tribes;[38] nor claim an allotment under his English name and thereafter claim one under an Indian name.[39]

Although the allotment rolls have been deemed conclusive and final evidence of the right of any Indians of a reservation to an allotment[40] it has been held that they may be changed by the Secretary to correct mistakes.[41]

B. SELECTION OF ALLOTMENT

Section 332[42] of title 25 of the United States Code deals with the selection of allotments and provides that the Indians are to do the selecting, the heads of families selecting for their minor children, and the Indian agent is to make the selection for each orphan. The selections are to be made in such manner as to include the improvements of the Indian making the selection. The Supreme Court has upheld the validity of this clause giving a preferential right to certain lands to Indians who had occupied them and had made improvements thereon, prior to the passage of the Allotment Act affecting the lands of his tribe.[43]

Congress also provided that, if an Indian failed to make his selection within four years after the President authorized an allotment on a particular reservation, the Secretary of the Interior could direct the agent of such tribe or a special agent, if there were no agent, to make the selection. The Supreme Court has sustained the power of the Dawes Commission to place members of the Creek Nation on the allotment roll, upon their refusal to select allotments.[44]

The term "select," used with reference to selection of allotments by Indians, as defined by the Cherokee Allotment Agreement[45] and the Choctaw-Chickasaw Supplemental Agreement,[46] means a formal application for a particular tract or tracts of land in the land office established by the commission for the particular tribe or nation.[47]

It has been held that section 332 contemplates a selection by a living Indian only. Thus the death of a Chippewa Indian before making a selection of an allotment under the Nelson Act terminated his right to an allotment.[48] Where a right to the allotment becomes equitably vested in the allottee,[49] the act of the allotting commissioners in thereafter wrongfully allotting the land to another does not operate to cut off the heirs of the person originally entitled to the allotment.[50]

C. APPROVAL OF ALLOTMENT

Section 333[51] provides that after the filing of the selection the allotments shall be made by special allotting agents or by the agents or superintendents in charge of the reservations on which the allotments are directed to be made.[52]

After an allotment has been approved, the allottee is entitled to have the land patented to him,[53] even after the passage of the Wheeler-Howard Act which provided that "* * * no land * * * shall be allotted * * * to any Indian."[54]

D. CANCELLATION

As might be expected, the wholesale allotment of lands in severalty which characterized Indian administration for many years resulted in numerous instances in injustice to the allottee.[55] This injustice took the form very often of the allotment of a parcel of land which was unsuitable for any purpose to which the allottee could reasonably be expected to put it. To remedy in part this situation, Congress in 1909[56] provided for the can-

---

[36] *Lemieux* v. *United States*, 15 F. 2d 518 (C. C. A. 8, 1926), cert. den. 273 U. S. 749. But *cf. Vezina* v. *United States*, 245 Fed. 411 (C. C. A. 8, 1917), under Act of June 7, 1897, c. 3, 30 Stat. 62, 90, 25 U. S. C. 184.

[37] *Hy-yu-tse-mil-kin* v. *Smith*, 194 U. S. 401 (1904). And see *Fairbanks* v. *United States*, 223 U. S. 215, 225 (1912).

[38] *Josephine Valley et al.*, 19 L. D. 329 (1894).

[39] *Tiger* v. *Twin State Oil Co.*, 48 F. 2d 509 (C. C. A. 10, 1931).

[40] See Act of March 3, 1921, 41 Stat. 1355 (Fort Belknap Reservation); Op. Sol. I. D., M.7599, June 9, 1922. See also Chapter 5, sec. 13.

[41] Op. Sol. I. D., M.7599, June 9, 1922. See also Chapter 5, sec. 13.

[42] This section was derived from sec. 2 of the General Allotment Act. On selection of allotment for minors and incompetents, see Chapter 8, sec. 8A.

[43] *E. g.*, *Harnage* v. *Martin*, 242 U. S. 386 (1917). See also *Smith* v. *Bonifer*, 154 Fed. 883 (C. C. Ore. 1907), aff'd sub nom. *Bonifer* v. *Smith*, 166 Fed. 846 (C. C. A. 9, 1909).

[44] *United States* v. *Wildcat*, 244 U. S. 111 (1917). See Chapter 5, secs. 6 and 13.

[45] Act of March 1, 1901, 31 Stat. 861.

[46] Act of June 30, 1902, 32 Stat. 500.

[47] See *Millet* v. *Bilby*, 110 Okla. 241, 237 Pac. 859 (1925).

[48] *La Roque* v. *United States*, 239 U. S. 62 (1915). See also Chapter 9, sec. 3; *Taylor* v. *United States*, 230 Fed. 580 (C. C. A. 8, 1916).

[49] See Op. Sol. I. D., M.28086, July 17, 1935, 55 I. D. 295. Where Indians had made selections prior to the passage of the Wheeler-Howard Act and approval was not of a discretionary nature but was lacking because of clerical error, it was held that the Indians were entitled to the approval and patenting of their selections, even after the passage of the said act which provided that "* * * no land * * * shall be allotted * * * to any Indian." Act of June 18, 1934, 48 Stat. 984. But *cf. Lemieux* v. *United States*, 15 F. 2d 518 (C. C. A. 8, 1926), cert. den, 273 U. S. 749, where the approval was of a discretionary nature; *United States ex rel. West* v. *Hitchcock*, 205 U. S. 80 (1907); *St. Marie* v. *United States*, 24 F. Supp. 237 (D. C. S. D. Cal. 1938).

[50] *Bonifer* v. *Smith*, 166 Fed. 846 (C. C. A. 9, 1909); *Smith* v. *Bonifer*, 132 Fed. 889 (C. C. Ore. 1904).

[51] 25 U. S. C. 333, derived from Act of February 8, 1887, 24 Stat. 388 and Act of June 25, 1910, 36 Stat. 855, 858.

[52] Sec. 3 of Act of February 8, 1887, 24 Stat. 388, provided only for agents and special agents fulfilling this duty, but sec. 9 of the Act of June 25, 1910, 36 Stat. 855, 858, provided for the inclusion of superintendents as performers of this function.

25 U. S. C. 338, derived from the Appropriation Act of April 4, 1910, sec. 1, 36 Stat. 269, 270, required the Secretary of the Interior to transmit annual reports to Congress of the cost of survey and allotment work on Indian reservations generally. This section was repealed by the Act of May 29, 1928, sec. 64, 45 Stat. 986.

[53] The allottee may bring mandamus to obtain the patent. See *Vachon* v. *Nichols-Chisholm Lumber Co.*, 126 Minn. 303, 148 N. W. 288, 290 (1914). But when an allotment has not been approved, approval and issuance of patent cannot be compelled by mandamus. *United States ex rel. West* v. *Hitchcock*, 205 U. S. 80 (1907); *St. Marie* v. *United States*, 24 F. Supp. 237, (D. C. S. D. Calif. 1938). On when mandamus will issue, see Chapter 5, sec. 13B.

[54] Op. Sol. I. D. M.28086, July 17, 1935, 55 I. D. 295.

[55] Section 343 of title 25 of the U. S. Code provides:

> In all cases where it shall appear that a double allotment of land has been wrongfully or erroneously made by the Secretary of the Interior to any Indian by an assumed name or otherwise, or where a mistake has been made in the description of the land inserted in any patent, said Secretary is authorized and directed, during the time that the United States may hold the title to the land in trust for any such Indian, and for which a conditional patent may have been issued, to rectify and correct such mistakes and cancel any patent which may have been thus erroneously and wrongfully issued whenever in his opinion the same ought to be canceled for error in the issue thereof, * * *

[56] Act of March 3, 1909, 35 Stat. 781, 784.

From time to time Congress has enacted sundry statutes permitting Indians to surrender the lands allotted to them and select other lands in lieu thereof. See Acts of October 19, 1888, 25 Stat. 611, 612, 25 U. S. C. 350; January 26, 1895, 28 Stat. 641, 25 U. S. C. 343; April 23, 1904, 33 Stat. 297, 25 U. S. C. 343; March 3, 1909, 35 Stat. 781, 784, 25 U. S. C. 344. Sec. 2 of the Act of 1888, *supra*, which has been incorporated in sec. 350 of 25 U. S. C., reads:

> The Secretary of the Interior is hereby authorized, in his discretion, and whenever for good and sufficient reason he shall consider it to be for the best interest of the Indians, in making allotments under the statute aforesaid, to permit any Indian to whom a patent has been issued for land on the reservation to which such Indian belongs, under treaty or existing law, to surrender such patent with formal relinquishment by such Indian to the United States of all his or her right, title, and interest

cellation of an allotment of unsuitable land and the exchange therefor of other land. This act has been incorporated in section 344 of title 25 of the United States Code.[57] Its provisions are:

> If any Indian of a tribe whose surplus lands have been ceded or opened to disposal has received an allotment embracing lands unsuitable for allotment purposes, such allotment may be canceled and other unappropriated, unoccupied, and unreserved land of equal area, within the ceded portions of the reservation upon which such Indian belongs, allotted to him upon the same terms and with the same restrictions as the original allotment, and lands described in any such canceled allotment shall be disposed of as other ceded lands of such reservation. This provision shall not apply to the lands formerly comprising Indian Territory. The Secretary of the Interior is authorized to prescribe rules and regulations to carry this law into effect.

In 1927 Congress also provided for the cancellation of fee patents issued without the consent of the Indian:[58]

> * * * the Secretary of the Interior is hereby authorized, in his discretion, to cancel any patent in fee simple issued to an Indian allottee or to his heirs before the end of the period of trust described in the original or trust patent issued to such allottee, or before the expiration of any extension of such period of trust by the President, where such patent in fee simple was issued without the consent or an application therefor by the allottee or by his heirs: *Provided*, That the patentee has not mortgaged or sold any part of the land described in such patent: *Provided also*, That upon cancellation of such patent in fee simple the land shall have the same status as though such fee patent had never been issued.

E. SURRENDER

Section 408, title 25, of the United States Code[59] provides:

> In any case where an Indian has an allotment of land, or any right, title, or interest in such an allotment, the Secretary of the Interior, in his discretion, may permit such Indian to surrender such allotment, or any right, title, or interest therein, by such formal relinquishment as may be prescribed by the Secretary of the Interior, for the benefit of any of his or her children to whom no allotment of land shall have been made; and thereupon the Secretary of the Interior shall cause the estate so relinquished to be allotted to such child or children subject to all conditions which attached to it before such relinquishment.

---

in the land conveyed thereby, properly indorsed thereon, and to cancel such surrendered patent: *Provided*, That the Indian so surrendering the same shall make a selection, in lieu thereof, of other land and receive patent therefor, under the provisions of the act of February eighth, eighteen hundred and eighty-seven.

[57] On the question of the necessity for notice and an opportunity to be heard, see *Fairbanks* v. *United States*, 223 U. S. 215 (1912).

[58] Act of February 26, 1927, c. 215, 44 Stat. 1247, 25 U. S. C. 352a. Partial cancellation was also provided for. Act of February 26, 1927, c. 215, sec. 2, 44 Stat. 1247, as amended February 21, 1931, c. 271, 46 Stat. 1205, 25 U. S. C. 352b. For an analysis of the power of the Secretary to cancel a fee patent issued without request from the Indian concerned, see Op. Sol. I. D., M.28297, August 1, 1939. See Chapter 2, sec. 2E; Chapter 13, sec. 3B.

[59] Act of June 25, 1910, sec. 3, 36 Stat. 855, 856. For regulations regarding reallotment of lands to unallotted Indian children, see 25 C. F. R. 52.1–52.2.

SECTION 3. POSSESSORY RIGHTS IN ALLOTTED LANDS

An allottee ordinarily acquires by virtue of his allotment full possessory right with respect to the improvements and the timber upon his allotment as well as the minerals beneath it. Occasionally, by the term of special allotment acts, the minerals are reserved to the tribe in which event the allottee acquires at best a right to share in the income flowing therefrom.[60] His right of ownership in timber is limited only by the statutory restriction on alienation.[61] These restrictions upon alienation are elsewhere discussed.[62] When the allottee acquires his patent in fee, however, his right of use and enjoyment becomes an absolute right of ownership.

The allottee's right to water is recognized by the General Allotment Act,[63] section 7 of which provides:

> That in cases where the use of water for irrigation is necessary to render the lands within any Indian reservation available for agricultural purposes, the Secretary of the Interior be, and he is hereby, authorized to prescribe such rules and regulations as he may deem necessary to secure a just and equal distribution thereof among the Indians residing upon any such reservations; and no other appropriation or grant of water by any riparian proprietor shall be authorized or permitted to the damage of any other riparian proprietor.

The Supreme Court in *United States* v. *Powers*[64] declared that under the doctrine of the *Winters* case[65] waters are reserved for the equal benefit of tribal members and that the Secretary of the Interior is without power affirmatively to authorize unjust and unequal distribution of water. It further declared that when allotments of land were duly made for exclusive use and thereafter conveyed in fee, the right to use some portion of tribal waters essential to cultivation passed to the owner of the allotted land, including both the allottees and those who took from them by conveyance or by purchase of land of deceased allottees at Government sales.

The *Powers* case compels the view that the right to use water is a right appurtenant to the land within the reservation, and that unless excluded it passes to each grantee in subsequent conveyances of allotted land.[66]

In accordance with the doctrine that the United States has exclusive jurisdiction over reservation lands unless it has specified that state statutes shall be controlling, it has been held[67] that an allottee cannot under the state laws relating to the appropriation of water acquire any right whatsoever in waters reserved to the tribe.

---

[60] See Chapter 15, sec. 14, fn. 286.

[61] See sec. 4 of this chapter.

[62] *Ibid.*

[63] Act of February 8, 1887, 24 Stat. 388, 25 U. S. C. 381. Also see Chapter 12, sec. 7.

[64] 305 U. S. 527, 532–533 (1939).

[65] *Winters* v. *United States*, 207 U. S. 564 (1908). For a further discussion of this case in connection with tribal water rights, see Chapter 15, sec. 16.

[66] In *Anderson* v. *Spear-Morgan Livestock Co.*, 79 P. 2d 667 (1938), the court had occasion to restate the doctrine of the *Powers* case. It said:

> * * * The purpose of this statute is to provide for the distribution of the right to use the water to the individual Indians. *United States* v. *Powers*, * * *. The right to use the water prior to a distribution of it by the Secretary of the Interior may be said to be inchoate in the sense that the precise amount or extent of the right assigned to an individual allottee would be undetermined, but the right is vested in so far as the existence of the right to use the water in the allottee is concerned. This right is appurtenant to the land upon which it is to be used by the allottee. When the allottee became seized of fee simple title, after the removal of the restrictions of the trust patent, then a conveyance of the land, in the absence of a contrary intention, would operate to convey the right to use the water as an appurtenance. *United States* v. *Powers*, *supra*. (P. 669)

[67] *United States* v. *McIntire*, 101 F. 2d 650 (C. C. A. 9, 1939), rev'g 22 F. Supp. 316 (D. C. D. Mont. 1937).

Likewise, where statutory attempts have been made to relegate water rights of Indians on certain reservations to the jurisdiction of particular states by requiring that state statutes be complied with in securing water rights for the irrigation of Indian land,[68] it has been held[69] that since the statute contained no specific grant of the reserved waters to the state it could not be construed as the intent of Congress to take from the Indians a vested right and provide in lieu thereof only a means for acquiring an inferior and secondary right.

The water right guaranteed an allottee of Indian land has sometimes been defined in treaty or agreement.[70] In *United States v. Hibner*,[71] involving such an agreement, it was held that a purchaser from the allottee acquires a water right for the actual acreage under irrigation at the time title passes from the Indians, and for such additional acreage as can be placed under irrigation within a reasonable time.

On the other hand, a purchaser from an allottee is without right to appropriate to his private use water from a creek, most of which comes primarily from a Government irrigation system constructed after he acquired title to the land, which uses the creek bed for a distance as a canal to reach customers below.[72]

[68] Act of June 21, 1906, 34 Stat. 325, 375 (Uintah Project in Utah); Act of March 3, 1905, 33 Stat. 1016 (Shoshone Project in Wyoming).

[69] *United States* v. *Parkins*, 18 F. 2d 642 (D. C. Wyo. 1926).

[70] Act of June 6, 1900, with the Fort Hall Indians, 31 Stat. 672. For a statute guaranteeing a similar right, see Act of May 18, 1916, 39 Stat. 123, 130.

[71] 27 F. 2d 909 (D. C. E. D. Idaho 1928).

[72] *United States* v. *Parkins*, 18 F. 2d 642 (D. C. Wyo. 1926). For a holding that one who purchases land in what was formerly an Indian reservation from the United States may not appropriate water for the irrigation of his land from an irrigation ditch, which the United States had constructed for the benefit of Indian allottees, see *United States* v. *Morrison*, 203 Fed. 364 (C. C. Colo. 1901).

SECTION 4. ALIENATION OF ALLOTTED LANDS

Since tribal lands are generally nonalienable without the consent of the Federal Government it was natural that Congress should continue federal control of land alienation when tribal land passed into the hands of individual Indians. The same considerations that lay behind the former restrictions—the desire to protect the Indian against sharp practices leading to Indian landlessness, the desire to safeguard the certainty of titles, and the urge to continue an important basis of governmental activity—operated in the case of allotted lands. The first of these motives is usually stressed in the opinions. Typical of the cases is the discussion by the Court of Appeals in *Beck* v. *Flournoy Live-Stock & Real-Estate Co.*[73]:

> * * * These limitations upon the power of the Indians to sell or make contracts respecting land that might be set apart to them for their individual use and benefit were imposed to protect them from the greed and superior intelligence of the white man. Congress well knew that if these wards of the nation were placed in possession of real estate, and were given capacity to sell or lease the same, or to make contracts with white men with reference thereto, they would soon be deprived of their several holdings; and that, instead of adopting the customs and habits of civilized life and becoming self-supporting, they would speedily waste their substance and very likely become paupers. The motive that actuated the lawmaker in depriving the Indians of the power of alienation is so obvious, and the language of the statute in that behalf is so plain, as to leave no room for doubt that congress intended to put it beyond the power of white men to secure any interest whatsoever in lands situated within Indian reservations that might be allotted to Indians. This conclusion is fortified by an amendment to the act of February 8, 1887, which was adopted on February 28, 1891 (26 Stat. 794, c. 383), whereby power was conferred upon the secretary of the interior to prescribe regulations and conditions for the leasing of lands allotted to Indians under the previous act of February 8, 1887, whenever, by reason of "age or other disability," the allottee was not able to occupy or improve the land assigned to him with benefit to himself. It is manifest that the amendment in question, authorizing allotted land to be leased in certain cases, under the direction of the secretary of the interior, was unnecessary if power to execute leases of allotted lands had already been conferred by previous enactments or treaty stipulations. The last-mentioned act, therefore, is a legislative declaration that congress did not intend by any previous statute to authorize the leasing of any lands that might be assigned to Indians to be held by them in severalty. (P. 34–35.)

[73] 65 Fed. 30 (C. C. A. 8, 1894), app. dism. 163 U. S. 686.

The opinion in *Lykins* v. *McGrath*[74] throws added light upon this basic policy:

> * * * What was the purpose of imposing a restriction upon the Indian's power of conveyance? Title passed to him by the patent, and but for the restriction he would have had the full power of alienation the same as any holder of a fee simple title. The restriction was placed upon his alienation in order that he should not be wronged in any sale he might desire to make; that the consideration should be ample; that he should in fact receive it, and that the conveyance should be subject to no unreasonable conditions or qualifications. It was not to prevent a sale and conveyance, but only to guard against imposition therein. When the Secretary approved the conveyance it was a determination that the purposes for which the restriction was imposed had been fully satisfied; that the consideration was ample; that the Indian grantor had received it, and that there were no unreasonable stipulations attending the transaction. All this being accomplished, justice requires that the conveyance should be upheld, and to that end the doctrine of relation attaches the approval to the conveyance and makes it operative as of the date of the latter.

The broad power of Congress to effectuate this policy and the extent to which the enforcement and relaxation of restraints upon alienation have been entrusted to the Secretary of the Interior have been discussed in Chapter 5.[75]

A. LAND[76]

The policy of restricting alienation finds expression in provisions of allotment acts forbidding alienation of lands during a fixed period of years without the consent of some administrative officer, generally the Secretary of the Interior. The provision contained in section 5 of the General Allotment Act[77] declares:

> * * * And if any conveyance shall be made of the lands set apart and allotted as herein provided, or any contract made touching the same, before the expiration of the time above mentioned, such conveyance or contract shall be absolutely null and void: * * *.

[74] 184 U. S. 169, 171–172 (1902).

[75] See secs. 5C and 11.

[76] For regulations relating to sale of allotted lands, exclusive of Five Civilized Tribes lands, see 25 C. F. R. 241.9–241.38.

[77] 24 Stat. 388, 389, 25 U. S. C. 348, amended in other particulars by Act of March 3, 1901, 31 Stat. 1058, 1085. Subsequent statutes authorizing alienation of lands with departmental approval are noted in Chapter 5, sec. 11B.

We have elsewhere noted the various forms in which restrictions on alienation are embodied, notably the "trust patent" and the "restricted fee."[78]

Prohibitions against alienation have been broadly interpreted in the light of the policy of Congress to prevent whites from taking advantage of the Indians.[79] This is shown by the interpretation of the term "conveyance" by the Supreme Court of Oklahoma in the case of *Potter* v. *Vernon:*[80]

> Under the general rule that all instruments affecting real estate are included under the word "conveyance" are included the following: A mortgage of an equitable interest (*Sullivan* v. *Corn Exchange Bank*, 154 App. Div. 292, 139 N. Y. S. 97); a leasehold (Lembeck, etc., *Eagle Brewing Co.* v. *Kelly*, 63 N. J. Eq. 401, 406, 51 A. 794); of personal property (*Patterson* v. *Jones*, 89 Ala. 388, 390, 8 So. 77); an agreement to execute a mortgage (*In re Wight's Mortg. Trust*, L. R. 16 Eq. 41, 46); an assignment for the benefit of creditors (*Prouty* v. *Clark*, 73 Iowa, 55, 56, 34 N. W. 614); an assignment of a chose in action (*Wilson* v. *Beadle*, 2 Head [Tenn.] 510); the satisfaction of a mortgage (*Foss* v. *Dullam*, 111 Minn. 220, 126 N. W. 820); an instrument in the nature of a trust deed, even without a seal, acknowledgement, or witness (*White* v. *Fitzgerald*, 19 Wis. 480); a release, as an instrument by which the title to real estate might be affected in law or equity (*Palmer* v. *Bates*, 22 Minn. 532); a release of a mortgage (*Baker* v. *Thomas*, 61 Hun, 17, 15 N. Y. S. 359); or part of land covered by a mortgage (*Merchant* v. *Woods*, 27 Minn. 396, 7 N. W. 826).
>
> It is true that under our statute a mortgage of real estate is to be regarded as a lien only, but the lands in question are Indian lands, with reference to which the federal government has dealt in a peculiar manner, due to peculiar conditions. Under our Oklahoma laws our citizens have the right to transfer without let or hindrance, all or part of their real property, but, with respect to its awards, the Indians, the government has always dealt exclusively with the transfer of their lands, not only placing restrictions upon the lands themselves, but upon those who owned them. In this case the legality of the transfer is to be determined by interpretation of the act of Congress, and the meaning of this act is ascertained by discovering, not what was in the minds of the lawmakers of Oklahoma in passing the several statutes with reference to conveyances and transfers, but what was in the mind of Congress when it passed the Act of May 27, 1908, and its use of the word "conveyances" in said act. We must assume that in an act of such sweeping proportions it was intended by Congress to deal finally and comprehensively with the subject in hand. Section 5 of the act uses very general terms:
>
> "That any attempted alienation or incumbrance by deed, mortgage, contract to sell, power of attorney, or other instrument or method of incumbering real estate, made before or after the approval of this act, which affects the title of the land allotted to allottees of the Five Civilized Tribes * * * shall be absolutely null and void." 35 Stat. 313.
>
> Section 9 seems to be just as comprehensive in the following words:
>
> "That the death of any allottee of the Five Civilized Tribes shall operate to remove all restrictions upon the alienation of said allottee's land: *Provided*, That no conveyance of any interest of any full-blood Indian heir in such land shall be valid unless approved by the court having jurisdiction of the settlement of the estate of said deceased allottee. * * *" 35 Stat. 315.
>
> It appears to us that the words "provided that no conveyance of any interest of any full-blood Indian heir in such land" could hardly be more comprehensive. We think that the words "conveyance of any interest" is just as comprehensive and perhaps more so than the word "alienation," and yet a valid mortgage is often the first step in a final alienation of land and even a foreclosure has reference back to the date of the mortgage and must follow the terms thereof.
>
> To give too limited or restricted a meaning to the word "conveyance" and yet a comprehensive meaning to the word "alienation" in the act, the result would be illogical, for it would require, for the making of a deed by the full-blood Indian heir, an approval of the county court, but for the execution of a mortgage upon his land, which might easily be effective to transfer his title, no such approval was necessary. This could not have been in the mind of Congress. It is not to be supposed that Congress inadvertently or through oversight failed to take into consideration that the Indian might wish to mortgage his land, for the mortgaging of real estate is almost as old as our assurances of title, so that, in our judgment, they either entirely overlooked this contingency, or they meant the words "conveyance of any interest" should include every written instrument which might affect the title. It has been, and properly so we think, the design of the government as rapidly as they could with safety to permit the Indians to deal with and have charge of their property, not only for the benefit of the community, but for the distinct benefit of the Indians, by casting responsibility upon them, and we interpret and understand this act of Congress as evidencing that disposition of the government. (P. 614.)

The courts have also considered the remedial nature of this legislation in construing the extent of its coverage. In holding that homesteads were within the purview of the General Allotment Act, Chief Justice Taft said:[81]

> We find that the Indian Homestead Act of July 4, 1884, and the General Allotment Act of February 8, 1887, with its various amendments, constitute part of a single system evidencing a continuous purpose on the part of the Congress. The statutes are *in pari materia*, and must be so construed. It cannot be supposed that Congress, in any part of this legislation, all of which is directed toward the benefit and protection of the Indians, as such, intended to exclude from the beneficent policy which each Act evidences, an Indian claiming under the homestead act, even though the statute uses the term "allottee." If there were any doubt on the question, the silence of Congress in the face of the long-continued practice of the Department of the Interior in construing statutes which refer only to Indian "allottees," or Indian "allotments," as applicable also to Indians claiming under the homestead laws, must be considered as "equivalent to consent to continue the practice until the power was revoked by some subsequent action by Congress." *United States* v. *Midwest Oil Co.*, 236 U. S. 459, 481. (Pp. 196–197.)

B. TIMBER

Section 406 of title 25 of the United States Code provides:[82]

> The timber on any Indian allotment held under a trust or other patent containing restrictions on alienations may be sold by the allottee, with the consent of the Secretary of the Interior, and the proceeds thereof shall be paid to

[78] See Chapter 5, sec. 11B. The inability of incompetent Indians to alienate land has been discussed in Chapter 8, sec. 8B(1).

[79] The effect of bankruptcy of an allottee is discussed in Chapter 8, sec. 7C.

A deed is not executed until delivered; hence, until the Secretary has removed the restrictions upon alienation of allotted lands effective upon the executing of a deed by an allottee, a deed signed by the allottee and given to an Indian superintendent for transmission to a purchaser does not pass title and is subject to cancellation by the Secretary since the execution of a deed had not been completed by delivery. *United States* v. *Lane*, 258 Fed. 520 (App. D. C. 1919).

An order of the Secretary of the Interior approving an Indian agent's recommendation that restrictions on alienation be removed from an allotment to be effective thirty days from date would become effective on the thirtieth day after its date and the allottee is enabled to make a valid conveyance on that date. *Lanham* v. *McKeel*, 244 U. S. 582 (1917).

Also see *Taylor* v. *Brown*, 147 U. S. 640 (1893); *Nixon* v. *Woodcock*, 64 Okla. 86, 166 Pac. 133 (1917).

[80] 129 Okla. 251, 264 Pac. 611 (1928).

[81] *United States* v. *Jackson*, 280 U. S. 183 (1930); also see *Wiggan* v. *Conolly*, 163 U. S. 56 (1896).

[82] Derived from Act of June 25, 1910, sec. 8, 36 Stat. 855, 857. For regulations regarding timber, see 25 C. F. R. 61.1–61.29.

the allottee or disposed of for his benefit under regulations to be prescribed by the Secretary of the Interior.

The rights of an allottee to sell timber on his allotment without administrative approval had been determined by the Supreme Court a few years before the enactment of this provision. The Court in the first case held that the restrictions on alienation did not preclude a sale by the allottee of timber of land which was capable of cultivation after the cutting of the timber. The Court said:[83]

> * * * it hardly needs to be said that the allotments were intended to be of some use and benefit to the Indians. And, it will be observed, that on that use there is no restraint whatever. A restraint, however, is deduced from the provision against alienation, the supervision to which, it is asserted, the Indians are subject and the character of their title. It is contended that the right of the Indians is that of occupation only, and that the measure of power over the timber on their allotments is expressed in *United States* v. *Cook*, 19 Wall. 592. We do not regard that case as controlling. The ultimate conclusion of the court was determined by the limited right which the Indians had in the lands from which the timber there in controversy was cut.
>
> Certain parties of the Oneida Indians ceded to the United States all the lands set apart to them, except a tract containing one hundred acres for each individual, or in all about 65,000 acres, which they reserved to themselves, *to be held as other Indian lands are held.* Some of the lands were held in severalty by individuals of the tribe with the consent of the tribe, but the timber sued for was cut by a small number of the tribe from a part of the reservation not occupied in severalty. It was held, citing *Johnson* v. *McIntosh*, 8 Wheat. 574, that the right of the Indians in the land from which the logs were taken was that of occupancy only. Necessarily the timber when cut "became the property of the United States absolutely, discharged of any rights of the Indians therein." It was hence concluded "the cutting was waste, and, in accordance with well-settled principles, the owner of the fee may seize the timber cut, arrest it by replevin, or proceed in trover for its conversion." If such were the title in the case at bar, such would be the conclusions. But such is not the title. We need not, however, exactly define it. It is certainly more than a right of mere occupation. The restraint upon alienation must not be exaggerated. It does not of itself debase the right below a fee simple. *Schly* v. *Clark*, 118 U. S. 250. The title is held by the United States, it is true, but it is held "in trust for individuals and their heirs to whom the same were allotted." The considerations, therefore, which determined the decision in *United States* v. *Cook* do not exist. The land is not the land of the United States, and the timber when cut did not become the property of the United States. And we cannot extend the restraint upon the alienation of the land to a restraint upon the sale of the timber consistently with a proper and beneficial use of the land by the Indians, a use which can in no way affect any interest of the United States. It was recognized in *United States* v *Clark* that "in theory, at least," that land might be "better and more valuable with the timber off than with it on." Indeed, it may be said that arable land is of no use until the timber is off, and it was of arable land that the treaty contemplated the allotments would be made. We encounter difficulties and baffling inquiries when we concede a cutting for clearing the land for cultivation, and deny it for other purpose. At what time shall we date the preparation for cultivation and make the right to sell the timber depend? Must the axe immediately precede the plow and do no more than keep out of its way? And if that close relation be not always maintained, may the purpose of an allottee be questioned and referred to some advantage other than the cultivation of the land, and his title or that of his vendee to the timber be denied? Nor does the argument which makes the occupation of the land a test of the title to the timber seem to us more adequate to justify the qualification of the Indians' rights. It is based upon the necessity of superintending the weakness of the Indians and protecting them from imposition. The argument proves too much. If the provision against alienation of the land be extended to timber cut for purposes other than the cultivation of the land it would extend to timber cut for the purpose of cultivation. What is there in the latter purpose to protect from imposition that there is not in the other? Shall we say such evil was contemplated and considered as counterbalanced by benefit? And what was the benefit? The allotments, as we have said, were to be of arable lands useless, may be, certainly improved by being clear of their timber, and yet, it is insisted, that this improvement may not be made, though it have the additional inducement of providing means for the support of the Indians and their families. We are unable to assent to this view. (Pp. 472–474.)

The Supreme Court held in *Starr* v. *Campbell*[84] that where the allotment is all timber and nonarable land the restriction upon alienation extended to timber. The Court said:

> The restriction upon alienation, however, it is contended, does not extend to the timber, and *United States* v. *Paine Lumber Co.*, 206 U. S. 467, is adduced as conclusive of this. We do not think so. There, as said by the Solicitor General, the land granted was arable, and could be of no use until the timber was cut; here the land granted is all timber land. And that the distinction is important to observe is illustrated by the allegations of the complaint. It is alleged that the value of the land, exclusive of the timber, is no more than $1,000; fifteen thousand dollars' worth of lumber has been cut from the land. The restraint upon alienation would be reduced to small consequence if it be confined to one-sixteenth of the value of the land and fifteen-sixteenths left to the unrestrained or unqualified disposition of the Indian. Such is not the legal effect of the patent. (P. 534.)

C. EXCHANGE OF ALLOTTED LANDS

The Act of October 19, 1888,[85] authorized the Secretary of the Interior in his discretion and when deemed for the best interest of the Indians to permit any Indian to whom a patent was issued for land on a reservation to surrender such patent and authorizes the Secretary to cancel such patent provided that the Indian shall make a lieu selection of other land and receive a patent for it under the General Allotment Act. This provision was interpreted by the Circuit Court of Appeals in *United States* v. *Getzelman*, as follows:[86]

> The plain language of the statute indicates that it is intended to effect a change in allotments; that is, to acquire other and different land when that is deemed for the best interest of the Indians. And that conclusion finds support in the history of the act. It originated in the

[83] *United States* v. *Paine Lumber Co.*, 206 U. S. 467 (1907).

[84] 208 U. S. 527 (1908).

However, an Indian allottee under the General Allotment Act may remove and sell dead timber, standing or fallen, from his allotment. The Attorney General said in 19 Op. A. G. 559 (1890):

> The effect of the allotment and declaration of trust are to place the allottee in possession of the land allotted and give him a qualified ownership therein, and the extent to which the allottee is thus restricted as a proprietor remains now to be considered, insofar as necessary to answer the questions submitted.
>
> (1) And first as to timber: In an opinion of Attorney-General Garland dated January 26, 1880, it was held to be waste for an allottee to cut timber standing on his allotment for the direct purpose of selling it, by which I understand him to mean timber that is live and growing. The question before me, however, namely, whether the allottee has the right to sell and remove from his allotment *dead* timber, standing or fallen, is essentially different from that passed upon by my predecessor, and as I have reached the conclusion that appropriating and selling dead timber of any kind is not waste at common law or by the law of Wisconsin, within the limits of which State the timber in question is situated, it is not necessary to reexamine the question whether an allottee is impeachable for waste. (P. 562.)

In this opinion the Attorney General also held that an Indian cannot contract for or permit the erection of mills on his allotment for the manufacture of lumber or other purposes.

On construction of the word "land" in statutes restricting alienation, see *Holmes* v. *United States*, 53 F. 2d 960 (C. C. A. 10, 1931).

[85] Sec. 2, 25 Stat. 611, 25 U. S. C. 350.

[86] 89 F. 2d 531 (C. C. A. 10, 1937), cert. den. 302 U. S. 708.

Department of the Interior. The Secretary wrote the President pro tempore of the Senate on June 7, 1888, transmitting a proposed draft of a resolution. The letter recited that four members of the Sisseton and Wahpeton Indians on the Lake Traverse Reservation, in South Dakota, who had obtained allotments under the General Allotment Act, desired to make changes because it had been discovered that in three of these cases the lands allotted were not the lands on which the allottees lived and had made improvements, and in the fourth case the land allotted was not desirable farm land; that steps had been taken to effect relinquishment and new allotments; and that on further investigation it was found that no statutory authority existed for action of that kind. It was further stated that similar cases would likely arise on other reservations; and that for such reason the proposed resolution had been prepared and was transmitted with recommendation that it be passed. The proposed legislation was amended in form from a resolution to an act, and enacted into law. It thus clearly appears that the contemplated object, purpose, and function of the act is to enable an Indian allottee to whom a patent has been issued to make relinquishment and secure other and different land in lieu thereof. It was never intended as a means through which an agreement of the kind outlined in the bill before us could be achieved. The relinquishment of the patent was not for the purpose of enabling John to acquire other and different land more suited and better adapted to his uses and purposes. It was not intended to enable Mary to relinquish the remaining 80 acres of her original allotment and acquire a new allotment for other and different land in lieu of it. The purpose was to enable John to convey 80 acres of his remaining land, to acquire a new patent for the other 80 acres which he already owned, and to receive the $625 from Chapman to be used in making improvements on his remaining 80-acre tract; and further to enable Mary to part with the last 80 acres of her original allotment by conveying it to Chapman and at the same time to acquire 80 acres of the land originally allotted to John. A transaction of that kind falls well outside the intended scope, purpose, and function of the act permitting relinquishment and lieu allotments. In the absence of express authority granted by statute, the Secretary has no power to cancel a patent which has been regularly issued and delivered. See *Ballinger* v. *United States ex rel.* Frost, 216 U. S. 240, 30 S. Ct. 338, 54 L. Ed. 464; *United States* v. *Dowden* (C. C. A.) 220 F. 277. Measured by the doctrine announced in these cases, it is manifest that the Secretary was without power to cancel the patent for the purpose of accomplishing the unauthorized end. (P. 535.)

The restriction on alienation of allotted lands was held not to prohibit an allottee Indian from selling his improvements to the United States and selecting other lands so that the United States could use the lands for irrigation purposes. The Supreme Court in *Henkel* v. *United States*[37] explained:

> The Circuit Court of Appeals in its decision laid emphasis upon the case of *Williams* v. *First National Bank*. 216 U. S. 582, in which this court recognized the right of one Indian to surrender and relinquish to another Indian a preference right to an allotment of a tract of land In that case it was held that one Indian might sell his improvements and holdings to another Indian for allotment, and lay his own on other land which he might find vacant, or which he might, in turn, purchase from another Indian, and the Circuit Court of Appeals held that. this being so, as a matter of course, and for stronger reasons, an Indian might relinquish his rights to the United States, and that restrictions had been placed upon the power of the Indians to alienate their lands or convey their rights of possession only for their protection, and not for the purpose of restricting their right to deal with the United States or to relinquish their rights to the Government, citing *Lykins* v. *McGrath*, 184 U. S. 169, and *Jones* v. *Meehan*, 175 U. S. 1. Without questioning the correctness of this reasoning, we think the purpose of the United States to acquire any property necessary for the reclamation project embraced such transactions as the Secretary had in this case with the Indians, and the action which he took under the authority conferred by that act wholly justified all that was done in the premises.

The effect of the Wheeler-Howard Act on the exchange of allotted lands has been the subject of many administrative rulings.

On March 22, 1935,[38] the Solicitor of the Department of the Interior discussed as follows these features of the act:

> Section 1 of the act of June 18, 1934 (48 Stat. 984), declares that no land of any Indian reservation created or set apart by treaty or agreement with the Indians, act of Congress, Executive Order, purchase or otherwise, shall be allotted in severalty to any Indian. It may be argued with some force that an exchange of a tract of tribal land for an individual allotment of equal value does not come within the class of transactions which this section of the act was designed to prevent. In such case, the tribal land is not depleted. There is no new allotment as such—merely a change of an existing allotment. However this may be, the authority to make an exchange of this sort appears to be conferred by section 4 of the act which, so far as material, reads:
>
> > "Except as herein provided, no * * * exchange * * * of restricted Indian lands or of shares in the assets of any Indian tribe or corporation organized hereunder, shall be made or approved: * * * *Provided* * * * That the Secretary of the Interior may authorize voluntary exchanges of lands of equal value and the voluntary exchange of shares of equal value whenever such exchange, in his judgment, is expedient and beneficial for or compatible with the proper consolidation of Indian lands and for the benefit of cooperative organizations."
>
> The exchanges authorized to be made under the foregoing section do not appear to be confined to lands in individual ownership. The main clause refers to "restricted Indian lands" and the proviso refers to "voluntary exchanges of lands of equal value." The terms so used are broad and when given their natural meaning they embrace both tribal and individually owned lands. As I view the section, therefore, it operates to prevent the exchange of a tract of unallotted land for a tract in individual ownership unless the lands are of equal value, the exchange is voluntary and is not inconsistent with the proper consolidation of Indian lands. * * *

In a subsequent memorandum, dated February 3, 1937,[39] the Solicitor further stated:

> Section 4, as I read it, authorizes exchanges of lands of equal value. The parties to the exchange may be two individual Indians, an Indian and a white man, an Indian and an Indian tribe, or a white man and an Indian tribe. The requirement of equality of value is substantially complied with if the difference is so small that both parties are ready to disregard it. It is arguable that an exchange transaction involving a small cash payment to boot falls within the scope of section 4. I would suggest that 5 percent of the value of the land might be regarded as a safe margin within which the maxim, *de minimis non curat lex*, may operate. Where tracts of land are substantially unequal in value, an exchange transaction under section 4 is not authorized. However, where two parties wish to exchange tracts of land and are willing to put improvements on the less valuable tract to make it equal in value to the other tract, no objection can be raised to an exchange. The validity of this proposition is not affected by the question of which party makes the improvements, or whether the improved land goes to an Indian or a white man. In this situation no Indian loses any land, in point of value. The transaction is therefore consistent with the whole purpose of the Reorganization Act. In these cases the report from the field should show that the lands are of equal value and that the exchange is at least compatible with the proper consolidation of Indian lands.

[37] 237 U. S. 43, 51 (1915).

[38] Memo. Sol. I. D., March 22, 1935.

[39] Memo. Sol. I. D., February 3, 1937.

Section 5 of the act, in my opinion, so far as it authorizes land exchanges has an entirely different purpose from section 4. Under section 5 the two tracts of land may be either equal or unequal in value, but if they are unequal in value it must be the Indians rather than the whites involved in the transaction who emerge from the transaction with an increased land value. Thus, an Indian may not convey $2,000 worth of land to a white man where the white man transfers to the Secretary for the Indian's use a tract of land worth only $500 and a cash payment to boot of $1,500. On the other hand, an Indian may transfer the lesser tract to a white man and make an additional payment of $1,500 in exchange for a transfer of the more valuable tract to the Secretary for the benefit of the Indian. The difference between the two cases is not technical or abstruse. In the one case the Indian is selling land; in the other case land is being bought for the Indian's benefit. The former is forbidden and the latter is authorized by the terms of the act. This distinction, based on the major purpose of the act, should eliminate some of the confusion that appears in certain memoranda on this subject in the attached file.

Where exchanges under section 5 affect only Indians it seems to me that the same principles should be applied. Ordinary commercial transactions in land between Indians are not within the purpose of section 5. It seems to me that a transaction under which an Indian surrenders land does not come within the true purpose of section 5 unless some special circumstances such as are mentioned in the land circular referred to above* are shown. I would suggest, therefore, that any recommendation for approval of a sale or surrender of Indian land under section 5 should be based upon a finding supported by facts that the result of the transaction will be to bring more land into effective Indian use.

* Indian Office Land Circular No. 3162, June 30, 1936.

Familiar cases in which such exchanges may advantageously be made are cases involving the exchange of inherited interests, and cases involving the transfer of a more valuable tract of land by a nonresident Indian in exchange for a less valuable tract and a money payment by a resident Indian able to use the newly acquired land.

Without attempting to analyze every possible transaction, I believe that such cases as the attached will be dealt with more expeditiously in the future if it is borne in mind that section 5 contemplates a land acquisition program looking to general improvement in the land status of the Indians and that section 4 contemplates private transactions which do not interfere with that program.

D. MORTGAGES

Mortgages of restricted lands are also prohibited. The court in *United States* v. *First Nat. Bank of Yakima, Wash.* said:[60]

> The crops growing upon an Indian allotment are a part of the land and are held in trust by the government the same as the allotment itself, at least until the crops are severed from the land. The use and occupancy of these lands by the Indians, together with the crops grown thereon, are a part of the means which the government has employed to carry out its policy of protection, and I am satisfied that a mortgage of any of these means by the Indian, without the consent of the government, is necessarily null and void. If the lien is valid, it carries with it all the incidents of a valid lien, including the right to appoint a receiver to take charge of and garner the crops, if necessary, and the right to send an officer upon the allotment armed with process to seize and sell the crops without the consent and even over the protest of the government and its agents. That this cannot be done does not, in my opinion, admit of question. (P. 332.)

E. JUDGMENTS

The Supreme Court in *Mullen* v. *Simmons*,[61] in holding that restricted lands could not be encumbered by judgments entered against an allottee, whether based on tort or contract, said:

> The section referred to is as follows: "Lands allotted to members and freedmen shall not be affected or encumbered by any deed, debt or obligation of any character contracted prior to the time at which said land may be alienated under this Act, nor shall said lands be sold except as herein provided." c. 1362, 32 Stat. 641, 642.
>
> The Supreme Court of Oklahoma in deciding that this provision did not apply distinguished between the obligations resulting from an Indian's wrongful conduct and the obligations resulting from his contracts, saying, p. 187, "A judgment in damages for tort is not a 'debt contracted'" within the contemplation of § 15. In other words, the court was of the view that the tort retained its identity, though merged in the judgment. However, we need not enter into the controversy of the cases and the books as to whether a judgment is a contract. Passing such considerations, and regarding the policy of § 15 and its language, we are unable to concur with the Supreme Court of Oklahoma.
>
> This court said, in *Starr* v. *Long Jim*, 227 U. S. 613, 625, that the title to lands allotted to Indians was "retained by the United States for reasons of public policy, and in order to protect the Indians against their own improvidence." It was held, applying the principle, that a warranty deed made by Long Jim at a time when he did not have the power of alienation "was in the very teeth of the policy of the law, and could not operate as a conveyance, either by its primary force or by way of estoppel" after he had received a patent for the land.
>
> The principle was applied again in *Franklin* v. *Lynch*, 233 U. S. 269, and its strict character enforced against the deed of a white woman who acquired title in an Indian right. It is true, in these cases the act of the Indian was voluntary or contractual, and, it is contended, a different effect can be ascribed to the wrongs done by an Indian and that in reparation or retribution of them the state law may subject his inalienable lands—inalienable by the National law—to alienation. The consequence of the contention repels its acceptance. Torts are of variable degree. In the present case that counted on reached, perhaps, the degree of a crime, but a tort may be a breach of a mere legal duty, a consequence of negligent conduct. The policy of the law is, as we have said, to protect the Indians against their improvidence, and improvidence may affect all of their acts, those of commission and omission, contracts and torts. And we think § 15 of the act of July 1, 1902, was purposely made broadly protective, broadly preclusive of alienation by any conduct of the Indian, and not only its policy but its language distinguishes it from the statute passed on in *Brun* v. *Mann*, 151 Fed. Rep. 145. Its language is that "lands allotted * * * shall not be *affected* or encumbered by any deed, debt or *obligation* of any *character contracted* prior to the time at which" the lands may be alienated, "nor shall said lands be sold except" as in the act provided. The prohibition then is that the lands shall not be "affected * * * by any obligation of any character," and, as we have seen, an obligation may arise from a tort as well as from a contract, from a breach of duty or the violation of a right. *Exchange Bank* v. *Ford*, 7 Colorado, 314, 316. If this were not so, a prearranged tort and a judgment confessed would become an easy means of circumventing the policy of the law.

F. CONDEMNATION

Section 357 of title 25 of the United States Code, derived from the Act of March 3, 1901,[62] provides:

> Lands allotted in severalty to Indians may be condemned for any public purpose under the laws of the State or

[60] 282 Fed. 330 (D. C. E. D. Wash., 1922). But see *Miller* v. *McClain*, 249 U. S. 308, 311 (1919).

[61] 234 U. S. 192, 197–199 (1914).

[62] 31 Stat. 1058, 1084. The preceding provision of this section relating to grants of rights-of-way for telephone and telegraph lines through Indian reservations are set forth under sec. 319 of title 25. Permission to state or local authorities for the opening of public highways through Indian reservations or lands allotted to Indians in severalty was authorized by sec. 4 of this act, 25 U. S. C. 311.

The United States is an indispensable party defendant in a condemnation proceeding brought by a state to acquire a right-of-way over lands which the United States owns and holds in trust for Indian allottees. *Minnesota* v. *United States*, 305 U. S. 382 (1939). For regulations regarding condemnation of allotted lands, see 25 C. F. R. 256.71–256.74.

> Territory where located in the same manner as land owned in fee may be condemned, and the money awarded as damages shall be paid to the allottee.

Subsequent legislation concerning rights-of-way through Indian reservations is found in the Act of February 28, 1902[93] and of May 27, 1908.[94] The first-mentioned act authorized any railroad company to condemn a right-of-way through Indian lands, the second provided that no restriction upon alienation should be construed to prevent the exercise of the right of eminent domain in condemning rights-of-way for public purposes over allotted lands.

G. REMOVAL[95] OF RESTRICTIONS[96]

Restrictions on alienation of lands imposed by the allotment acts run with the land and are not personal to the allottee. Hence the removal of such restrictions as to an allotment by the Secretary in accordance with a statute does not operate to remove restrictions as to other tracts in which the Indian may be interested. In reaching this holding the Circuit Court of Appeals in *Johnson* v. *United States* said:[97]

> Appellants rely also on that part of the act of February 8, 1887, as the sixth section thereof is amended by the act of May 8, 1906 (34 Stat. 183 [Comp. St. § 4203]), reading:
>
> > "Provided, that the Secretary of the Interior may, in his discretion, and he is hereby authorized, whenever he shall be satisfied that any Indian allottee is competent and capable of managing his or her affairs at any time to cause to be issued to such allottee a patent in fee simple, and thereafter all restrictions as to sale, incumbrance, or taxation of said land shall be removed * * *"
>
> and also on subsequent acts (35 Stat. 444; 36 Stat. 855; 37 Stat. 678) which extend the power of the Secretary to determine the heirs of deceased allottees, and provide that, if he is satisfied of their ability to manage their own affairs, he may cause patents in fee simple to be issued to them for their inherited interest. The contention, as we understand it, is that, if the Secretary, acting under these statutes, removes the restriction as to any allotment or an inherited interest therein, such action on his part operates to remove restrictions on other tracts in which the Indian may be interested. But the effect of this contention is to make the restriction against alienation personal to the Indian, whereas the uniform ruling is that it attaches to and runs with the land. In *U. S.* v. *Noble*, 237 U. S. 74, it is said, at page 80, 35 Sup. Ct. 532, 59 L. Ed. 844, that the restriction binds the land for the time stated. See, also, *Bowling* v. *U. S.*, 233 U. S. 528, 34 Sup. Ct. 659, 58 L. Ed. 1080; Id., 191 Fed. 19, 111 C. C. A. 561; *Goodrum* v. *Buffalo*, 162 Fed. 817, 89 C. C. A. 525. Furthermore, the facts as we obtain them from the record do not show a removal of restrictions, as claimed, in behalf of any Indian other than those that have been heretofore named and whose conveyances we held to be valid under the act of June 21, 1906, as above stated. (Pp. 956–957.)

H. RIGHTS OF CONVEYEES OF ALLOTTED LANDS

Contracts involving allotted lands which are not yet freed from restrictions have been held void.[98] Justice Holmes in the case of *Sage* v. *Hampe*[99] explained:

> * * * The purpose of the law still is to protect the Indian interest and a contract that tends to bring to bear improper influence upon the Secretary of the Interior and to induce attempts to mislead him as to what the welfare of the Indian requires are as contrary to the policy of the law as others that have been condemned by the courts. *Kelly* v. *Harper*, 7 Ind. Terr. 541. See *Larson* v. *First National Bank*, 62 Nebraska, 303, 308.

Courts and administrators have consistently refused to order the restoration of consideration received by an Indian for a conveyance which violates such laws, despite the good faith of the party dealing with the Indian[100] and the bad faith of the Indian who intended to deceive the purchaser.[101]

In the case of *Bartlett* v. *Okla. Oil Co.*,[102] the District Court stated:

> * * * The disabilities under which these wards of the government are placed as to the alienation of restricted lands is very similar to those attaching to minors with reference to their contracts, and in the latter case it is established that the acts and declarations of a minor during infancy cannot estop him from asserting the invalidity of his debts after he has attained his majority. *Sims* v. *Everhardt*, 102 U. S. 300, 26 L. Ed. 87. (P. 391.)

The Supreme Court in the case of *Heckman* v. *United States*,[103] *per* Hughes, J., said:

> It is said that the allottees have received the consideration and should be made parties in order that equitable

---

[93] 32 Stat. 43.

[94] 35 Stat. 312 (Five Civilized Tribes).

[95] The Supreme Court in the case of *United States* v. *Bartlett*, 235 U. S. 72, 80 (1914), discussed a meaning of the word "removed":

> The real controversy is over the meaning of the word "removed." It is not questioned that it embraces the action of Congress and of the Secretary of the Interior in abrogating or cancelling restrictions in advance of the time fixed for their expiration, but it is insisted that it does not embrace their termination by the lapse of time. In short, the contention is that the word is used in a sense which comprehends only an affirmative act, such as a rescission or revocation while the statutory period was still running. Although having support in some definitions of the word, the contention is, in our opinion, untenable, for other parts of the same act, as also other acts dealing with the same subject, show that the word is employed in this legislation in a broad sense plainly including a termination of the restrictions through the expiration of the prescribed period. This is illustrated in §§ 4 and 5 of the act of 1908 and § 19 of the act of April 26, 1906, c. 1876, 34 Stat. 137, 144, and is recognized in *Choate* v. *Trapp*, 224 U. S. 665, 673, where, in dealing with some of these allotments, it was said that "restrictions on alienation were removed by lapse of time."

[96] On the power of the Secretary of the Interior to remove and reimpose restrictions, see Chapter 5, sec. 11. For regulations regarding issuance of patents in fee, see 25 C. F. R. 241.1–241.2.

[97] 283 Fed. 954 (C. C. A. 8, 1922). Accord: *United States* v. *Estill*, 62 F. 2d 620 (C. C. A. 10, 1932).

[98] Allotted lands are declared not liable for debts contracted prior to the issuance of the final patent in fee therefor. 25 U. S. C. 354, derived from Act of June 21, 1906, 34 Stat. 325, 327. And see Act of February 8, 1887, sec. 5, 24 Stat. 388, 389, as amended, 25 U. S. C. 348.

[99] 235 U. S. 99, 105 (1914).

[100] *United States* v. *Walters*, 17 F. 2d 116 (D. C. Minn. 1926), holding that a purchaser of land from an Indian allottee during the trust period is not entitled to return of the purchase money as a condition to the cancellation of the deed at suit of the United States. In *United States v. Brown*, 8 F. 2d 564 (C. C. A. 8, 1925), cert. den. 270 U. S. 644 (1926), the court said that "Whether the disposition of this land was made in good faith or upon commendable considerations cannot be made to affect this decision, which involves a public policy of far-reaching consequences." (P. 568.) Also see *Sage* v. *Hampe*, 235 U. S. 99, 105 (1914), and *Smith* v. *McCullough*, 270 U. S. 456 (1926), rev'g 285 Fed. 698 (C. C. A. 8, 1922), invalidating leases negotiated for a forbidden term.

The Circuit Court of Appeals in *United States* v. *Raiche*, 31 F. 2d 624 (D. C. W. D. Wis. 1928) said:

> The bona fides of the transaction was held to be beside the point in *United States* v. *Brown*, 8 F. (2d) 564 (C. C. A. 8), in which it is said: "The bona fides of these conveyances is unimportant. Whether the disposition of this land was made in good faith or upon commendable considerations cannot be made to affect this decision, which involves a public policy of far-reaching consequences."
>
> Indeed, it seems this must be the correct rule, else the effectiveness of such restrictions would be readily frittered away. * * * (P. 627.)

[101] *United States* v. *Walters*, 17 F. 2d 116 (D. C. Minn. 1926).

[102] 218 Fed. 380 (D. C. E. D. Okla. 1914), aff'd sub nom. *Okla. Oil Co.* v. *Bartlett*, 236 Fed. 488 (C. C. A. 8, 1916).

[103] 224 U. S. 413 (1912), mod'g. and aff'g. in part *United States* v. *Allen*, 179 Fed. 13 (C. C. A. 8, 1910).

restoration may be enforced. Where, however, conveyance has been made in violation of the restrictions, it is plain that the return of the consideration cannot be regarded as an essential prerequisite to a decree of cancelation. Otherwise, if the Indian grantor had squandered the money, he would lose the land which Congress intended he should hold, and the very incompetence and thriftlessness which were the occasion of the measures for his protection would render them of no avail. The effectiveness of the acts of Congress is not thus to be destroyed. The restrictions were set forth in public laws, and were matters of general knowledge. Those who dealt with the Indians contrary to these provisions are not entitled to insist that they should keep the land if the purchase price is not repaid and thus frustrate the policy of the statute. *United States* v. *Trinidad Coal Co.*, 137 U. S. 160, 170, 171. (Pp. 446, 447.)

SECTION 5. LEASING OF ALLOTTED LANDS

We have elsewhere noted that by virtue of a general statutory prohibition against leasing of tribal lands dating from the Act of May 19, 1796,[104] valid leases of tribal lands can be made only pursuant to specific statutes expressly authorizing such leases. Such is not the case with allotted lands. There is no general statutory prohibition against leasing of allotted lands. Limitations, if they exist, are to be found in the treaty or statute prescribing the tenure under which the allotment is to be held.

No attempt will be made in these pages to analyze the various leasing provisions of statutes applicable to particular tribes.[105]

The prohibition against leases contained in the General Allotment Act is found in section 5[106] of that act, which is embodied in the United States Code as section 348 of title 25, providing:

> * * * And if any conveyance shall be made of the land set apart and allotted as herein provided, or any contract made touching the same, before the expiration of the time above mentioned, such conveyance or contract shall be absolutely null and void. * * *

This general provision has been modified by a series of statutes authorizing leases, subject to Interior Department control, in a variety of cases. Note has already been taken of the historical process, which began in 1891, of amending this provision contained in the General Allotment Act so as to permit leasing in a growing class of cases. These amendments authorizing the leasing of allotted lands vary in four major respects: (1) The purpose of the lease; (2) the term of the lease; (3) who is to make the lease; and (4) who is to approve the lease.

A brief comment on each of these points is in order.

(1) Leasing of restricted Indian allotments, without regard to the purpose of the lease, is authorized by section 4 of the Act of June 25, 1910,[107] which authorizes the Secretary of the Interior to consent to the alienation of allotments "by deed, will, lease, or any other form of conveyance" in cases where, by the terms of special allotment laws or treaties, land is inalienable without the consent of the President.

Other statutes in the field limit the leases which they authorize to those made for specific purposes such as "farming and grazing purposes";[108] "irrigation farming";[109] "farming purposes only";[110] and "mining purposes".[111]

(2) The statutes permitting the Secretary to lease certain heirship lands,[112] to approve leases on lands the alienation of which originally required Presidential consent[113] and authorizing mining leases on allotted lands[114] contain no limitations as to the term of years for which the lease may be made. Other statutes limit the term to 5[115] or 10 years.[116]

---

[104] Sec. 12, 1 Stat. 469, 472. See Chapter 15, sec. 19.

[105] Acts applying to particular tribes include the following:

Allotted lands on the Fort Belknap Reservation, susceptible of irrigation, may be leased for not to exceed ten years for sugar beets "and other crops in rotation" (Act of March 1, 1907, 34 Stat. 1015, 1034).

Allotted lands in the Shoshone Reservation may be leased for maximum terms of twenty years (Act of April 30, 1908, 35 Stat. 70, 97).

Yakima Reservation allottees may lease unimproved allotted lands for agricultural purposes for a period of not more than ten years (Act of March 1, 1899, 30 Stat. 924, 941, and Act of May 31, 1900, 31 Stat. 221, 246).

The Secretary of the Interior may lease, for a maximum of ten years, the irrigable allotments of any Indian allottees of the former Uintah and Uncompahgre Reservation in Utah when the allottee is unable to cultivate the same or any portion (Act of April 30, 1908, 35 Stat. 70, 95).

Competent Crow allottees may lease their own and their minor children's allotments for five years. Adult incompetent Crows may lease their own and their children's allotments with the approval of the agency superintendent for terms up to five years. Lands of Crow minor orphans may be leased by their superintendent for the same term (Act of May 26, 1926, 44 Stat. 658).

Most of the foregoing acts place the leasing of Indian allotted lands under the superintendent of the reservations. Competent adult Crow Indians may execute farming and grazing leases without restraint of the Indian Service (Act of May 26, 1929, 44 Stat. 658).

Allottees under the Quapaw Agency may lease lands for not to exceed three years for farming or grazing purposes or ten years for mining or business purposes (Act of June 7, 1897, 30 Stat. 62, 72).

On Five Tribes leasing statutes, see Chapter 23, sec. 10. On Osage leasing statutes see *ibid.*, sec. 12D.

[106] Act of February 8, 1887, 24 Stat. 388, 389, amended Act of March 3, 1901, sec. 9, 31 Stat. 1058, 1084.

It has been held that an assignment by an Indian of royalties from a mining lease of restricted lands is void as constituting an assignment of part of his inalienable reversion. *United States* v. *Moore*, 284 Fed. 86 (C. C. A. 8, 1922).

[107] 36 Stat. 855, 856, 25 U. S. C. 403.

Sec. 5 of this act (36 Stat. 855, 857) makes it unlawful and punishable by fine and imprisonment "for any person to induce any Indian to execute any contract, deed, mortgage, or other instrument purporting to convey any land or any interest therein held by the United States in trust for such Indian, or to offer any such contract, deed, mortgage, or other instrument for record in the office of any recorder of deeds."

On administrative power of the Secretary over leasing, see Chapter 5, sec. 11E. When approval is secured, the lease is effective as of the date of execution. *Hallam* v. *Commerce Mining and Royalty Co.*, 49 F. 2d 103 (C. C. A. 10, 1931), aff'g 32 F. 2d 371 (D. C. N. D. Okla. 1929), cert. den. 284 U. S. 643 (1931). Also see *Hampton* v. *Ewert*, 22 F. 2d 81 (C. C. A. 8, 1927), cert. den. 276 U. S. 623 (1928).

[108] Act of March 3, 1921, sec. 1, 41 Stat. 1225, 1232, 25 U. S. C. 393. On general grazing regulations, see 25 C. F. R. 71.1–71.26. On regulations for leasing of certain restricted allotted Indian lands for mining, see 25 C. F. R. 189.1–189.32.

[109] Act of May 18, 1916, sec. 1, 39 Stat. 123, 128, 25 U. S. C. 394.

[110] Act of May 31, 1900, sec. 1, 31 Stat. 221, 229, 25 U. S. C. 395.

[111] Act of March 3, 1909, 35 Stat. 781, 783, 25 U. S. C. 396, amended by Act of May 11, 1938, 52 Stat. 347, 25 U. S. C. 396A–396F.

Leases of Indian mineral lands frequently concern only certain specified minerals. For example, when only oil is named in the lease, it is a wrongful conversion to sell the gas issued from the well, except that such an oil lessee may use gas necessary to facilitate production upon the leased land, such as to run compressors and to repressure his well. *Utilities Production Corp.* v. *Carter Oil Co.*, 2 F. Supp. 81 (D. C. N. D. Okla. 1933).

[112] Act of July 8, 1940 (Pub. No. 732, 76th Cong.).

[113] Act of September 21, 1922, sec. 6, 42 Stat. 994, 995, 25 U. S. C. 392.

[114] Act of March 3, 1909, 35 Stat. 781, 783, 25 U. S. C. 396.

[115] Act of June 25, 1910, sec. 4, 36 Stat. 855, 856, 25 U. S. C. 403.

[116] Act of May 18, 1916, sec. 1, 39 Stat. 123, 128, 25 U. S. C. 394.

The policy behind this limitation of term has been considered in interpreting other statutes relating to leases of Indian lands. Thus the Circuit Court in *United States* v. *Haddock*, 21 F. 2d 165 (C. C. A. 8, 1927) said:

> Whenever Congress has authorized Indian allottees to lease their lands without the approval of the Secretary of the Interior

(3) Most of the statutes provide specifically that the lease shall be made by the allottee or by the heirs to whom the allotment has descended.[117] Other statutes leave this to inference.[118] A statute authorizing leasing of lands in heirship status allows the local superintendent to execute leases under specified conditions.[119]

It has been administratively ruled that the statutory requirement of execution by the allottee cannot be waived so as to authorize the execution of leases by the superintendent of the reservation.[120]

(4) Several of the statutes specifically require the "approval" or "consent or approval" of the Secretary to a lease of allotted lands.[121]

Other statutes require approval "of the superintendent or other officer in charge of the reservation where the land is located."[122] Still other statutes leave it to the regulations of the Secretary to determine whether approval shall be by the Secretary, by the Commissioner, or by a local reservation official.[123]

A lease made without the approval required by the statute or by regulations issued pursuant to such statute is generally considered to be void.[124] There are, however, a number of unsettled

---

> it has limited the period for which the leases can be made, and in order to protect the Indian allottees it has been held that Congress intended thereby to authorize the allottees to make leases in possession, and not in future or reversion, and such is the doctrine of the Noble Case. But as to leases where the approval of the Secretary of the Interior is necessary to give validity thereto the reason for the rule fails. The allottee is protected by the requirement of departmental approval. The lease here was made and approved as provided by law. * * * (P. 167.)

Also see *Bunch* v. *Cole*, 263 U. S. 250 (1923), and *United States* v. *Noble*, 237 U. S. 74 (1915), rev'g 197 Fed. 292 (C. C. A. 8, 1912).

The broad outlines of administrative policy concerning the leasing of allotted lands are shown by many of the regulations. For instance, sec. 171.1 of 25 C. F. R. provides "* * * leases should be made for the shortest term for which advantageous contracts can be secured with responsible parties."

[117] Act of March 3, 1921, sec. 1, 41 Stat. 1225, 1232, 25 U. S. C. 393 (farming and grazing leases); Act of March 3, 1909, 35 Stat. 781, 783, 25 U. S. C. 396 (mining leases).

[118] Act of May 18, 1916, sec. 1, 39 Stat. 123, 128, 25 U. S. C. 394 (leases of irrigable allotments); Act of May 31, 1900, sec. 1, 31 Stat. 221, 229, 25 U. S. C. 395 (leases where allottee is incapacitated).

[119] The Act of July 8, 1940, Public, No. 732; 76th Cong., 3d sess., provides:

> That restricted allotments of deceased Indians may be leased, except for oil and gas mining purposes, by the superintendents of the reservation within which the lands are located (1) when the heirs or devisees of such decedents have not been determined and (2) when the heirs or devisees of the decedents have been determined, and such lands are not in use by any of the heirs and the heirs have not been able during a three-months' period to agree upon a lease by reason of the number of the heirs, their absence from the reservation, or for other cause, under such rules and regulations as the Secretary of the Interior may prescribe. The proceeds derived from such leases shall be credited to the estates or other accounts of the individuals entitled thereto in accordance with their respective interests.

[120] "This office has had occasion frequently to point out that the general rule for the leasing of Indian allotments is that the signatures of the Indian owner or owners must be obtained before approval can be given to a lease. In a memorandum dated October 28, 1937, the Solicitor, in dealing with a similar factual situation, held that section 7 of the Leasing Regulations as revised by departmental circular of December 18, 1936, while authorizing a substantial majority of the heirs of allotted land in heirship status to execute a lease thereof does not authorize an heir or heirs representing only a half interest in the land to do likewise. It was pointed out that the Department was without legal power to approve a lease, where the owner, or the owners of a majority interest, were unable to agree to the lease, except in such special cases as infancy, mental disability, or pending heirship determinations. These exceptions are not to be broadened into unlimited administrative discretion. The special circumstances where the Department may act without the consent of the Indian owner, or a majority interest, are those cases where there is no owner, or owners, legally capable of executing a valid lease of the land. They are not every case where Department officials may feel that some of the Indians are acting unwisely or capriciously, or to the detriment of the other Indians interested in the land.

In the present case, one heir, Jennie Kills First, has signed the lease. The other heir, Benjamin Kills First, refuses, however, to sign it. There is no legal authority, therefore, to take the action proposed in the letter. Neither heir holds such a substantial majority interest in the land as to enable him or her to bind the other. The Indian owners are known and are capable of executing a valid lease. Their motives in signing, or not signing, are not relevant at this point." (Memo. Sol. I. D. June 15, 1938.)

Sec. 7 of the leasing regulations above referred to, embodied in 25 C. F. R. 171.8, declares:

> When the heirs owning a substantial majority in interest are desirous of leasing their inherited trust or restricted lands, the Superintendent is authorized to approve such a lease provided the heirs holding a minority interest in the estate have been notified of the proposed lease and have not objected to such a lease. In case the heirs holding such minority interest have objected to the approval of a lease on such inherited lands, the Superintendent, if in his judgment owners of the majority interest are best served, may approve the lease, and in such case, the share of the rentals that would accrue thereunder to the owners of the minority interest shall be held in escrow by the Superintendent to be paid to such heirs upon their request or when and if they sign the lease. Such minority owners may, however, be permitted through partition or other arrangement with their coheirs to make use of such part of the land as may be equivalent to their undivided interests in the whole, in which event the rentals otherwise due them and held in escrow shall be refunded to the lessee. Approved leases executed by the heirs holding a majority interest shall be regarded as covering the entire acreage included in the lease and no refund of any portion of the rentals paid thereunder shall be made to the lessee save when by partition or other arrangement, heirs not parties to the lease have been permitted to use a portion of the land included in the lease. * * * (P. 268.)

For a discussion of the lack of power of the Secretary, or the superintendent on his behalf, to change the terms of a lease, see *Holmes* v. *United States*, 33 F. 2d 688 (C. C. A. 8, 1929), and *United States* v. *Sandstrom*, 22 F. Supp. 190 (D. C. N. D. Okla. 1938).

[121] Act of September 21, 1922, sec. 6, 42 Stat. 994, 995, 25 U. S. C. 392. And see sec. 1C, *supra*. Also see Chapter 5, sec. 1E. For a discussion of early statutes giving the Secretary power to approve leases, see *Miller* v. *McClain*, 249 U. S. 308 (1919).

[122] Act of March 3, 1921, sec. 1, 41 Stat. 1225, 1232, 25 U. S. C. 393.

[123] Act of May 18, 1916, sec. 1, 39 Stat. 123, 128, 25 U. S. C. 394 (leasing of irrigable land); Act of May 31, 1900, sec. 1, 31 Stat. 221, 229, 25 U. S. C. 395 (leasing where allottee is incapacitated); Act of March 3, 1909, 35 Stat. 781, 783, 25 U. S. C. 396 (mining leases); Act of June 25, 1910, sec. 4, 36 Stat. 855, 856, 25 U. S. C. 403 (leasing of trust allotments generally).

By the Act of May 11, 1938, 52 Stat. 347, 25 U. S. C. 396e, the Secretary of the Interior may delegate his power of approval of mining leases to superintendents or other Indian Service officials. Previously it was held that the superintendent had no power of approval of leases. See *Central National Bank of Tulsa, Oklahoma*, v. *United States*, 283 Fed. 368 (C. C. A. 8, 1922). By statute, however, the superintendent for the Five Civilized Tribes could previously act for the Secretary in approving leases. See Act of May 27, 1908, sec. 2, 35 Stat. 312, interpreted in *Holmes* v. *United States*, 33 F. 2d 688 (C. C. A. 8, 1929). The superintendent for the Osage Tribe also possessed such power pursuant to the Act of June 28, 1906, sec. 7, 34 Stat. 539, 545, interpreted in *United States* v. *Sandstrom*, 22 F. Supp. 190 (D. C. N. D. Okla. 1938).

The regulation which is specifically concerned with business leases provides:

> Whenever it is deemed advisable to lease allotted Indian land for business purposes, the Superintendent should report the facts, object, terms, and conditions of the proposed lease to the Commissioner of Indian Affairs, who, if he deems it proper, may grant authority therefor, and no lease of this nature should be made without such prior approval. (25 C. F. R. 171.10.)

[124] "* * * It thus appears that the leases under which the defendants claim the right to the possession of the lands allotted in severalty are wholly void, having been taken in direct violation of the provisions of the acts of congress under which the allotments in severalty were made; that the occupancy of the lands and the cultivation thereof by the defendants is wholly inconsistent with the purpose for which the lands were originally set apart as a reservation for the Indians, and with the object of the government in providing for allotments in severalty; that such occupancy is held contrary to the rules and regulations of the department of the interior, and is held, not for the benefit, protection, and advancement of the Indians, but for the benefit of the original lessees and their subtenants; that such occupancy of said lands by the defendants results in antagonizing the authority and control of the government over the Indians, and is clearly detrimental to their best interests, and materially interferes with the rules and regulations of the department charged with the duty of carrying out the treaty stipulations under which the land forming the reservations was set apart for the benefit and occupancy of the Indians. Having

questions as to the legal position of the parties under such an illegal lease.[135]

Apart from the four matters above considered, as to which different leasing statutes vary, it remains to be said that all the statutes subject the leasing of allotments to regulations prescribed by the Secretary of the Interior. Such regulations require the payment of filing fees[136] and the execution of a bond by the lessee.[137] Rents, and, in the case of mineral leases, royalties are ordinarily payable to the superintendent on behalf of the allottee.[138]

Employees of the Office of Indian Affairs may not purchase any lease or have any interest therein, or have any interest in any corporation holding leases on Indian land.[129]

In matters not covered by the statutes or by the regulations authorized thereunder the courts have applied familiar rules of law governing leases. Thus it has been held that a tenant is estopped from denying his landlord's title[130] and that this estoppel continues until the tenant yields title.[131] But the landlord's title means the title which the landlord purported to have at the creation of the tenancy, and termination of such title afterwards may be shown.[132]

assumed the duty of securing the use and occupancy of these lands to the Indians, and being charged with the duty of enforcing the provisions of the acts of congress forbidding all alienations of the lands until the expiration of the period of 25 years after the allotment thereof, the government of the United States, through the executive branch thereof, has the right to invoke the aid of the courts, by mandatory injunction and other proper process, to compel parties wrongfully in possession of the lands held in trust by the United States for the Indians to yield the possession thereof, and to restrain such parties from endeavoring to obtain or retain the possession of these lands in violation of law. * * *" (*United States* v. *Flournoy Live-Stock & Real-Estate Co.*, 69 Fed. 886, 894 (C. C. Neb. 1895).)

[135] See with respect to the parallel situation under unauthorized leases of tribal land, Chapter 15, sec. 19.

[136] See 25 C. F. R. 183.7; also see 189.31 (mining leases). For statutory authority for such fees, see Act of February 14, 1920, 41 Stat. 408, 415, as amended by Act of March 1, 1933, 47 Stat. 1417, 25 U. S. C. 413.

[137] See, *e. g.*, 25 C. F. R. 183.15.

Many statutory requirements are designed to insure the proper payment of rents and royalties.

The Act of May 11, 1938, 52 Stat. 347, 348, 25 U. S. C. 396c, requires lessees of restricted lands for mineral purposes, including oil and gas, to furnish surety bonds for the faithful performance of the terms of the leases.

Lease forms are often prepared by the Department of the Interior. See *Montana Eastern Ltd.* v. *United States*, 95 F. 2d 897 (C. C. A. 9, 1938). For a discussion of the power of the United States with respect to violations of leases on restricted lands, see Chapter 19, sec. 2A(1).

[138] 25 C. F. R. 186.12, 189.14. Circumstances under which allottees are permitted to make their own leases are defined in current regulations in these terms:

> Any adult allottees deemed by the Superintendent to have the requisite knowledge, experience, and business capacity may be permitted to negotiate their own leases and collect the rentals therefor. All such leases, however, must be approved by the Superintendent. This privilege should be granted in writing, and with some liberality, and be subject to revocation at any time the allotte proves himself unworthy of it by wasteful expenditure of the money. Indians of this class may also be permitted to negotiate leases on the land of their minor children, but not to collect the rentals, which shall be paid to the Superintendent for deposit to the minors' credit as individual Indian money. Such leases must be approved by the Superintendent. (25 C. F. R. 171.4.)

[129] Act of June 30, 1834, 4 Stat. 735, 738; 25 U. S. C. 68. See Chapter 2, sec. 3B, fn. 335.

[130] *Eagle-Picher Lead Co.* v. *Fullerton*, 28 F. 2d 472 (C. C. A. 8, 1928).

[131] *Sittel* v. *Wright*, 122 Fed. 434 (C. C. A. 8, 1903).

[132] *Eagle-Picher Lead Co.* v. *Fullerton*, *supra*.

SECTION 6. DESCENT AND DISTRIBUTION OF ALLOTTED LANDS[133]

No feature of the allotment system has provoked more criticism than the "heirship problem" and it is against the background of this problem that existing law must be reviewed.

> It is doubtful if the serious nature of this problem was appreciated at the time the allotment acts were passed. Because of this feature of the allotment system the land of the Indians is rapidly passing into the hands of the whites, and a generation of landless, almost penniless, unadjusted Indians is coming on. What happens is this: The Indian to whom the land was allotted dies leaving several heirs. Actual division of the land among them is impracticable. The estate is either leased or sold to whites and the proceeds are divided among the heirs and are used for living expenses. So long as one member of the family of heirs has land the family is not landless or homeless, but as time goes on the last of the original allottees will die and the public will have the landless, unadjusted Indians on its hands.[134]

The problem of the landless younger generations on those reservations which were earliest allotted was the chief problem leading to the termination of the allotment system.[135] In place of alienable titles, the tendency today is to grant, out of tribal lands, "assignments" of land which are to be used by the "assignee" and which revert to the tribe for reassignment when no longer so used. This development has occurred on reservations which still retain sufficient areas of unallotted land. As for the other areas, any development along these lines depends upon (*a*) federal acquisition of land for the tribe, under section 5 of the Wheeler-Howard Act[136] or restoration of ceded lands, under section 3;[137] or (*b*) the acquisition of land by a tribe, through exchange of allotments for assignments, or through land purchase or through other legal means.[138]

Meanwhile, on the allotted reservations, the complexities of the "heirship" problem increase in geometric progression.

> The problem of land is still the greatest unsolved problem of Indian administration. The condition of allotted lands in heirship status grows more complicated each year. Commissioner Collier supplied the House Appropriations Committee a year ago with examples showing probate and administrative expenditures upon heirship lands totaling costs seventy times the value of the land; and under existing law these costs are destined to increase indefinitely. Responsibility lies with Congress and the administration to work out a practical solution to this problem, either in terms of corporate ownership of lands, or through some modification of the existing inheritance system. (P. 34.)[139]

The chief reasons for this complexity appear to be: (1) The Indian allottee does not ordinarily have ready cash or credit facilities for the settlement of estates where physical partition is not practicable.[140]

(2) The Indian allottee frequently does not consider land in a commercial aspect, and in many cases he could not get as much cash income from the land as a non-Indian, and therefore cannot outbid non-Indian purchasers of heirship lands.[141]

[133] Questions of administrative power in this field are dealt with in Chapter 5, sec. 11C. Questions of jurisdiction are considered in Chapter 19, sec. 5.

[134] Meriam, The Problem of Indian Administration (1928), p. 40.

[135] See sec. 1D, *supra*.

[136] See Chapter 15, sec. 8.

[137] See Chapter 15, sec. 7.

[138] See Chapter 15, sec. 8.

[139] Abeita *et al.*, The New Day for the Indians (1938).

[140] See quotation from Meriam, *supra*.

[141] See sec. 1C, *supra*.

(3) It may be that Indian family relations are more complicated than the family relations of non-Indians in rural areas, although there do not appear to be any authoritative figures on this point

(4) The Indian population, on most allotted reservations, is without channels by which members of families too large for the family homestead and too poor to increase it move off to other rural or urban areas The application to the allotted Indians of state inheritance laws adapted to a more fluid population and economy has therefore had striking and largely unforeseen results

(5) Under existing law the cost of administration is borne by the Federal Government rather than by the individual Indians concerned in the estate There is thus no economic incentive on the part of the Indians concerned to simplify the status of heirship lands

A INTESTACY

In the absence of statute, heirs to an allotment are determined in accordance with tribal custom [142]

The General Allotment Act, like several special allotment acts, modifies this rule and substitutes state law as a standard for the determination of heirs The most important consequence of this shift has been the multiplication of the number of heirs and the subdivision of interests in "dead allotments"

This result is achieved by section 5 of the General Allotment Act,[143] which prescribes that the patent issued to each allottee under the General Allotment Act shall

> * * * declare that the United States does and will hold the land thus allotted, for the period of twenty-five years, in trust for the sole use and benefit of the Indian to whom such allotment shall have been made, or, in case of his decease, of his heirs according to the laws of the State or Territory where such land is located * * *.

Where an Indian to whom an allotment of land has been made dies before the expiration of the trust period and before the issuance of a fee simple patent without having made a will disposing of said allotment the Secretary of the Interior may, under rules prescribed by him and upon notice and hearing, determine the heirs; his decision is final and conclusive [144] The statute [145] granting him this right further provides

(1) If the Secretary finds the heirs competent to manage their own affairs he may issue a patent in fee to them for the allotment.

(2) If he finds partition to be to the advantage of the heirs, he may, on petition of the competent heirs, issue patents in fee to them for their shares.

(3) If he finds one or more of them incompetent, he may cause the land to be sold, under certain rules of sale

(4) The shares of the proceeds of the sale due the competent Indians are to be paid to them

(5) The shares due the incompetent ones are to be held in trust for their use during the trust period

(6) The purchaser of the land receives a patent in fee

The foregoing provision, though phrased to apply to trust allotments, has been held by the Supreme Court to be applicable to restricted allotments in fee as well [146]

The power of Congress to enact this statute and the power of the Secretary thereunder have been elsewhere treated.[147]

The Act of June 18, 1934, has not affected the mode of intestate descent of allotted lands

Certain of the regulations pertaining to the determination of heirs define the manner in which the Secretary determines heirs [148] Eight examiners of inheritance are appointed, one for each probate district in the Indian country.[149] It is made the duty of the superintendent in charge of any allotted reservation, as soon as he is informed of the death of an allottee or an Indian possessed of trust property within the jurisdiction, to cause to be prepared an inventory showing in detail the estate of the decedent and also a certificate of appraisement thereof and statement as to reimbursable claims [150]

Notice of hearing is provided for by the requirement that the examiner of inheritance shall post, for 20 days in five or more conspicuous places on the reservation or in the vicinity of the place of hearing, notices of the time and place at which he will take testimony to determine the legal heirs of the deceased Indian, calling upon all persons interested to attend the hearing [151] Copies of the notice are usually served personally on all persons who the superintendent believes are probable heirs or creditors of the deceased [152] A further requirement is made of the examiner that he inspect carefully the allotment, census, and annuity rolls, and any other records on file at the agency, and obtain all other information which may enable him to make a prima facie list of the heirs of such deceased Indian [153]

Minors in interest must be represented at the hearings by a natural guardian or by a guardian ad litem appointed by the examiner.[154]

Parties interested in any probate case before an examiner of inheritance may appear by attorney [155] Attorneys appearing before the examiner of inheritance, the Indian Office, or the Department of the Interior, must have a power of attorney from their respective clients and must be licensed attorneys, *admitted* to practice [156] Written arguments or briefs may be presented [157]

All claimants are required to be summoned to appear and testify at the hearings There must be present at least two disinterested witnesses, who are acquainted with and have direct knowledge of the family history of the decedent [158] In case the decedent is a minor, unmarried and without issue, and the heirs are members of the immediate families of the decedent, the ex-

[142] See Chapter 7, sec 6, Chapter 10, sec 10

[143] Act of February 8, 1887, 24 Stat 388, 389, amended Act March 3, 1901, sec 9, 31 Stat 1058, 1085, 25 U S. C 348.

[144] In *Chase* v *United States*, 272 Fed 684 (C C A 8, 1921), the court held that the determination by the Secretary of the Interior that a certain person was the heir of a deceased Omaha allottee who as such had a life estate in the allotment under the Nebraska laws was conclusive The same principle was followed in *Lane* v *United States ex rel Mickadiet*, 241 U. S 201 (1916), wherein it was further held that even after determining the heirs the Secretary may reopen his decision at any time during the trust period.

[145] Act of June 25, 1910, sec. 1, 36 Stat 855; Act of March 3, 1928, 45 Stat. 161; Act of April 30, 1934, 48 Stat 647; 25 U. S C 372.

[146] *United States v. Bowling*, 256 U S 484 (1921)

[147] See Chapter 5, secs 5C, 11C.

[148] The procedure in Indian probate cases is discussed in Monograph No 20, Attorney General's Committee on Administrative Procedure (1940)

[149] 25 C F R. 81 1, 81.2, 81 3

[150] 25 C F. R 81 5 The superintendent also notifies the examiner for the district and the Probate Division of the Office of Indian Affairs of the demise of an Indian with restricted property. When an Indian of any allotted reservation dies leaving only personal property or cash of a value less than $250, the superintendent of the reservation where the property is found is authorized to assemble the apparent heirs and hold an informal hearing, with a view to the proper distribution thereof. In the disposition of such funds, the superintendent is authorized to pay funeral charges and expenses of last illness and any just claims for necessaries furnished decedent 25 C. F R. 81.28 (1940).

[151] 25 C F R 81 6 Also see 81 10–81 11

[152] The rules also permit service by mail 25 C F R 81 5

[153] 25 C F R 81 7

[154] 25 C F R. 81 12

[155] 25 C. F R. 81 15 Attorneys appear very rarely.

[156] 25 C. F. R. 81.17.

[157] 25 C F. R. 81 18.

[158] 25 C. F. R. 81.19–81.21.

aminer may, in his discretion, dispense with the presence of disinterested witnesses, provided the testimony of the interested witnesses is corroborated by the records of the Department [159]

When, subsequent to the determination of heirs by the Department, property is found which is not included in the examiner's report, this fact must be brought to the attention of the Commissioner, together with an appraisal thereof The superintendent will then be instructed to include this property in the original findings with instructions as to any additional fee to be charged However, where newly discovered property takes a different line of descent from that shown by the original findings, a redetermination relative thereto must be ordered and had [160]

The Solicitor for the Department of the Interior, discussing the authority of the Secretary of the Interior relative to claims against estates of deceased Indians, declared [161]

> The Secretary of the Interior is authorized to probate Indian estates under the Acts of June 25, 1910 (36 Stat 855), and February 14, 1913 (37 Stat 678) No specific authority is indicated in these acts relative to the allowance or disallowance of claims against the estate As an incident to the power granted, however, ever since the passage of the acts mentioned, the Secretary of the Interior has passed on claims based on indebtedness incurred by the decedent during his lifetime, and on expense of last illness and funeral charges While the allotted lands of the Indian are not subject to the liens of indebtedness incurred while the title is held in trust for the Indian (Section 354, Title 25, U S Code), the right of the Secretary administratively to allow and settle indebtedness against the Indian decedent has never been seriously questioned
>
> The priority accorded claims of the United States by virtue of 31 U S C 191, does not apply to the estates of deceased Indians No administrator or executor is appointed in these Indian estates, and claims against them are not such liens as may be enforced through the sale of the restricted lands involved Allowed claims are paid from the accruals to the land or from such cash as may be available at the time of death of the decedent
>
> Priority is however given to claims of the United States against estates of deceased Indians, administratively There are some qualifications which are covered by Departmental Regulations
>
> * * * *
>
> Except when the expenditures above mentioned [medical and funeral] affect the order of priority this Department allows claims administratively as follows
>
> 1 The probate fee (25 U S C 377, 25 C F R 81 40)
> 2 Funeral bills and expense of last illness in reasonable amount (25 C F R 221 9 and 81 46)
> 3 Claims of the United States
> 4 General creditors (25 C F R 81 44, 81 46)

Any aggrieved person claiming an interest in the trust or restricted property of an Indian, who has received notice of the hearing to determine heirs or consideration of a will, or who was present at the hearing, may file a motion for rehearing within 60 days from the date of notice on him of the determination of heirs or action on a will, or within such shorter period of time as the Secretary of the Interior may determine to be appropriate in any particular case A motion so filed operates as a supersedeas until otherwise directed by the Secretary of the Interior

Any such motion must state concisely and specifically the grounds upon which the motion for rehearing is based and be accompanied by brief and argument in support thereof

If proper grounds are not shown, the rehearing will be denied If upon examination grounds sufficient for rehearing are shown, a rehearing will be granted and the moving party will be notified that he will be allowed 15 days from the receipt of notice within which to serve a copy of this motion, together with all argument in support thereof, on the opposite party or parties, who will be allowed 30 days thereafter in which to file and serve answer, brief, and argument Thereafter, the case will be again considered and appropriate action taken, which may consist either in adhering to the former decision or modifying or vacating same, or the making of any further or other order deemed warranted [162]

No case will be reopened at the petition of any person who received notice of the hearing or who was present at such hearing, and received notice of the final decision, except as provided in § 81 34 Any other aggrieved person, claiming an interest in the estate, may apply for reopening of the case by petition, in writing, addressed to the Secretary of the Interior, to be submitted through the Commissioner of Indian Affairs All such petitions must set forth fully the alleged grounds for reopening, and when such petitions are based on alleged errors of fact are to be accompanied by affidavits or other supporting evidence On receipt of such petition, the Commissioner of Indian Affairs, if he deems it essential, will give the previously determined heirs an opportunity to present such showing in the matter as they may care to offer Thereafter, the petition together with the record in the case will be submitted to the Secretary of the Interior with such recommendation in the premises as the Commissioner of Indian Affairs may deem appropriate Aside from filing the papers specifically referred to, no further proceedings by the respective parties are required prior to a determination by the Secretary of the question whether a reopening will be granted or not

Petitions for reopening will not be considered when 10 years or longer have elapsed since the heirs were previously determined nor in those cases in which the estate of the decedent or any considerable part thereof has been disposed of under the previous finding of heirs Claims for expenses, attorneys' fees, etc, in connection with petitions for reopening will not be considered or recognized prior to a determination of the question whether or not a reopening is to be had, and neither the estate of the decendent nor the determined heirs thereto will be subject to any expense incurred prior to allowance by the Secretary of a reopening of the case [163]

B TESTAMENTARY DISPOSITION

Statutory provision has been made for the disposal by will of allotments held under trust [164] This provision, as it appears in

[159] 25 C F R 81 20 According to the Court of Appeals of the District of Columbia in *Nimrod v Jandron*, 24 F 2d 613 (App D C 1928)

> The duty of the examiner is clearly defined under the regulations which require a complete investigation of the mental capacity of the testator at the time of the making of the will, and of the influences to which she may have been subjected at the time, as well as the ascertainment of the legal heirs to her estate He was required likewise to give a full and complete hearing to all parties interested, * * * (P 616)

The report of the examiner of inheritance, which contains a proposed order for the determination of heirs, is reviewed by the Probate Division of the Office of Indian Affairs and the Office of the Solicitor, and is then submitted to the Secretary of the Interior for approval While the Probate Division is nominally a branch of the Office of Indian Affairs, it is also subject to the supervision of the Solicitor by virtue of a departmental order which placed all attorneys under the administrative jurisdiction of the Solicitor Personnel Order No 8890 of June 30, 1931, supplementing Order No 689, issued June 9, 1933

[160] 25 C F R 81 22

[161] Letter Sol I D to Sol of Dept of Agr, June 20, 1940

[162] 25 C F R 81 34

[163] 25 C F R 81 35.

[164] Acts of June 25, 1910, 36 Stat 855, 856, and February 14, 1913, 37 Stat 678, 25 U. S. C 373

the United States Code,[165] permits the disposal by will of interests in allotments (as well as other property) held under trust by anyone having such an interest who is at least 21 years old. The will is to be executed in accordance with regulations prescribed by the Secretary of the Interior and each will must be approved by him. If after an Indian's decease the will is disapproved, the allotment descends according to the law of the state wherein it is located.[166]

Approval of a will and death of the testator do not automatically terminate the trust. The Secretary may cause the lands to be sold and the proceeds to be held for the legatees or devisees and used for their benefit.

In the case of *Blanset* v. *Cardin*,[167] the Supreme Court was of the opinion that this provision was exclusive and that state statutes regarding devises of property have no effect upon allotments held in trust. Thus it held that the death of an allottee who had made a will did not terminate the restrictions[168] and subject the land to the Oklahoma law of wills, under which a wife could not devise more than two-thirds of her property away from her husband.

The power of the Secretary in connection with the approval or disapproval of wills is broad enough to enable him to determine whether he has mistakenly approved a will and whether the hearing before the examiner has been conducted in accordance with statute and regulations even after more than a year has elapsed since the death of the allottee.[169]

The authority of the Secretary of the Interior is limited to approval or disapproval of an Indian will, and he is without authority to change the provisions of the will by making a different provision than that provided by the testator.[170]

But after the will has been approved, the parties interested in the estate may agree upon a different disposition of property, subject, of course, to the approval of the Secretary of the Interior.

Certain of the federal regulations pertaining to the approval of wills illuminate the meaning of the statutory provisions above quoted. It is provided[171] that the will of any Indian who may make such an instrument shall be filed with the superintendent and that the officials of the Indian Office shall aid and assist the Indian as far as possible in the drawing of the instrument so that it will clearly and unequivocally express his wishes and intentions. Statements preferably under oath by the person drawing the will and the witnesses thereto that the testator was mentally competent and that there was no evidence of fraud, duress, or undue influence in connection therewith should be attached to the instrument. Where such evidence exists, a detailed statement should accompany the will setting forth the nature and extent thereof.

Other important regulations as they appear in title 25 of the Code of Federal Regulations are noted in the following summary:

> Section 81.53 requires the examiner, Superintendent, or other officer to make a specific recommendation as to whether the will of a deceased Indian should be approved by the Secretary, based upon a full inquiry into his mental competency; "the circumstances attending the execution of the will; the influences which induced its execution." In the event that the distribution is contrary to the laws of the State in which the testator resides, the examiner is required to seek the best available evidence as to the reasons for such action, including the affidavit of the testator, if living. He must also investigate the competency of all devisees and legatees to manage their affairs and note if any beneficiary is a person not of Indian blood.
>
> Section 81.54 provides that "No will executed in conformity with the Act of February 14, 1913 (37 Stat. 678; 25 U. S. C. 373), shall be valid or have any force or effect so far as it relates to property under the control of the United States, unless and until it shall have been approved by the Secretary of the Interior, who may approve or disapprove the will after a due and proper hearing to determine the heirs to the estate of the testator or testatrix shall have been held, required notice of such hearing first having been given to all persons interested, including the presumptive legal heirs, so far as they may be ascertained, and at which hearing the circumstances attendant upon the execution of said will shall have been fully shown by proper and credible testimony, and after the legal heir or heirs have had ample opportunity to object to the will and its approval. * * *"
>
> Section 81.55 provides that no action on wills will be taken until after the death of the testator, except that during the life of the testator the Office of Indian Affairs shall pass on the form of the will.
>
> Section 81.56 provides that in the absence of a contest, the examiner may secure affidavits of attesting witnesses to the will, in lieu of their personal appearance at the hearing.

Under section 4 of the Act of June 18, 1934,[172] an Indian's real property and shares in a tribal corporation may be devised only to his heirs, to members of the tribe having jurisdiction over the property, or to the tribe itself. In a recent opinion, the Solicitor of the Department of the Interior was called upon to construe this section. His opinion throws considerable light upon the limitation placed by that act upon a testator:[173]

> My opinion has been requested upon the proper construction of section 4 of the Wheeler-Howard Act (48

[165] "Any persons of the age of twenty-one years having any right, title, or interest in any allotment held under trust or other patent containing restrictions on alienation or individual Indian moneys or other property held in trust by the United States shall have the right prior to the expiration of the trust or restrictive period, and before the issuance of a fee simple patent or the removal of restrictions, to dispose of such property by will, in accordance with regulations to be prescribed by the Secretary of the Interior: *Provided, however,* That no will so executed shall be valid or have any force or effect unless and until it shall have been approved by the Secretary of the Interior: *Provided further,* That the Secretary of the Interior may approve or disapprove the will either before or after the death of the testator, and in case where a will has been approved and it is subsequently discovered that there has been fraud in connection with the execution or procurement of the will the Secretary of the Interior is authorized within one year after the death of the testator to cancel the approval of the will, and the property of the testator shall thereupon descend or be distributed in accordance with the laws of the State wherein the property is located: *Provided further,* That the approval of the will and the death of the testator shall not operate to terminate the trust or restrictive period, but the Secretary of the Interior may, in his discretion, cause the lands to be sold and the money derived therefrom, or so much thereof as may be necessary, used for the benefit of the heir or heirs entitled thereto, remove the restrictions, or cause patent in fee to be issued to the devisee or devisees, and pay the moneys to the legatee or legatees either in whole or in part from time to time as he may deem advisable, or use it for their benefit: *Provided also,* That this and the preceding section shall not apply to the Five Civilized Tribes or the Osage Indians." (25 U. S. C. 373.)

[166] See subsection A, *supra.* Also see Chapter 7, sec. 6.

[167] 256 U. S. 319 (1921).

[168] Where, on the other hand, an Indian died testate prior to the enactment of June 25, 1910, 36 Stat. 855, his will made under an authorizing statute which was silent as to its effect upon the removal by will of restrictions made upon approval by the President serves to remove such restrictions. Op. Sol. I. D., M.27700, August 3, 1934. See *La Motte* v. *United States*, 254 U. S. 570 (1921).

[169] *Nimrod* v. *Jandron*, 24 F. 2d 613 (App. D. C. 1928).

[170] In the case of *In Re Wah-shah-she-Me-tsa-he's Estate,* 111 Okla. 177, 239 Pac. 177 (1925), the Supreme Court of Oklahoma, speaking with reference to the probating of a will of an Osage Indian which had been approved by the Secretary of the Interior as provided by law, said:

> If the will is void for any reason the husband would take under the provisions of section 11301, C. S. 1921, but so long as the will stands the disposition of the property made by its terms must also stand, as the court cannot make a new will nor direct a different division of the property from that made by the testatrix with the approval of the Secretary of the Interior. (P. 179.)

[171] 25 C. F. R. 81.50.

[172] 48 Stat. 984, 985, 25 U. S. C. 464. See 25 C. F. R. 81.58.

[173] Op. Sol. I. D., M.27776, August 17, 1934; 54 I. D. 584.

Stat. 984, 985) in so far as this section limits the class of persons to whom an Indian may devise restricted lands. The relevant language of this section declares:

> Except as herein provided, no sale, devise, gift, exchange, or other transfer of restricted Indian lands or of shares in the assets of any Indian tribe, or corporation organized hereunder, shall be made or approved: *Provided, however,* That such lands or interests may, with the approval of the Secretary of the Interior, be sold, devised, or otherwise transferred to the Indian tribe in which the lands or shares are located or from which the shares were derived or to a successor corporation; and in all instances such lands or interests shall descend or be devised, in accordance with the then existing laws of the State, or Federal laws where applicable, in which said lands are located or in which the subject matter of the corporation is located, to any member of such tribe or of such corporation or any heirs of such member: * * *

The question of what persons other than members of the testator's tribe may lawfully be designated as devisees of his restricted property, where such property is subject to the terms of the Wheeler-Howard Act, is raised by the ambiguity of the last two words in the passage above quoted, namely, "such member." If "such member" refers to the testator himself, then the class of nonmembers entitled to receive restricted Indian property will be limited to those who through marriage, descent or adoption have acquired a relationship to the testator sufficient to constitute them heirs at law.

If the words "such member" be construed to mean *any member to whom the property in question might be devised,* then, apparently, nonmember heirs of other Indians than the testator might be made devisees of the testator's restricted property.

In the third place, the phrase "such member" might be construed to refer *to a member who is a devisee under the will in question.*

* * * * *

The circumstances under which the phrase "or any heirs of such member" was inserted in the Wheeler-Howard Bill indicate the proper meaning to be attached to that phrase. Early drafts of the legislation (e. g. H. R. 7902, Title III, Sec. 5, April House Committee Print; S. 2755, Sec. 4, May Senate Committee Print), both in the House and in the Senate, limited the privilege of inheriting restricted property to the members of the testator's tribe, in accordance with the fundamental purpose of the legislation to conserve Indian lands in Indian ownership and to prevent the further checker-boarding of Indian lands through the acquisition of parcels of such lands by persons not subject to the authority of the Indian tribe or reservation. To this limitation the objection was urged that in some cases the heirs of a deceased Indian would not be members of the tribe or corporation to which the deceased had adhered, and that it would be unfair to deny such natural heirs the right to participate in a devise of property. The House Committee on Indian Affairs, therefore, added to the clause first considered the phrase "or any heirs of such member." (H. R. 7902, Sec. 4, as reported to the House.) Independently, the Senate Committee on Indian Affairs added to the draft under its consideration a parallel phrase more restricted in scope, "or the Indian heirs of such member." (S. 2755, Sec. 4, Committee Print No. 2; S. 3645, Sec. 4, as reported to the Senate.) It seems clear that the purpose of these legislative after-thoughts was not to alter fundamentally the intent and scope of the original restriction but rather to provide for the exigencies of a special case that had not been distinctly considered, namely, the case of an Indian testor desiring to divide his estate by will among those who would, in the absence of a will, have been entitled to share in the estate, namely, his own heirs.

That the Chairman of the House Committee on Indian Affairs so construed the phrase here in question is indicated by his explanatory statement to the House of Representatives:

> Section 4 stops a dangerous leak through which the restricted allotted lands still in Indian ownership pass therefrom. Upon the death of an allottee the number of heirs frequently makes partition of the land impractical, and it must be sold at partition sale, when it generally passes into the hands of whites. This section endeavors to restrict such sales to Indian buyers or to Indian tribes or organizations. It however permits the devise of restricted lands to the heirs, whether Indian or not. (Cong. Rec. June 15, 1934, p. 12051.)

It requires no strained construction of language to interpret the phrase "or any heirs of such member" in accordance with this intent and purpose. The phraseology of section 4 suffers from the looseness of syntax incident to the agglutinative process of amendment. Grammatical rules, such as that requiring a definite antecedent for the word "such", are not always religiously observed in the closing days of a Congressional session. In the phrase "heirs of such member" the reference of the word "such" is supplied not by any clear grammatical antecedent but by the fact that the "member" chiefly considered throughout the section, though never expressly named, is the testator. This is not the only instance in the statute where the word "such" cannot be construed by simple application of the rules of grammar. (See the initial words of Sec. 17.)

To conclude, legal usage requires that the phrase "heirs of such member" must refer to the heirs of one who is deceased. *Memo est haeres viventis.* The only deceased person considered in the section is the testator. Evidence of the intent of Congress indicates that it is the testator's heirs that are being considered. I am of the opinion that the phrase "heirs of such member" should properly be construed to mean "heirs of the testator."

C. PARTITION AND SALE OF INHERITED ALLOTMENTS

In 1935, the National Resources Board published a study entitled "Indian Land Tenure, Economic Status, and Population Trends." Its authors had studied, among others, the problems resulting from the partition and sale of inherited allotments. Their comments on this subject are particularly enlightening:

> In 1902 pressure for legislation which would authorize the sale of heirship allotments could no longer be resisted. The passage of the act of May 27, 1902 (32 Stat. 245, 275)[174] opened the sluiceway for a wholesale dissipation of the Indian landed estate.[38] A few years later (1906) it was complemented by another law which permitted the Secretary of the Interior to sell original allotments, as well.
>
> [38] The act of 1902 was later modified to provide a more orderly method of determining heirs, principally by the act of May 8, 1906 (34 Stat. 182), and the act of June 25, 1910 (36 Stat. 855, 859).

---

[174] Although such sale was provided for as early as 1902, no statutory provision for the determination of heirs by the Secretary of the Interior was made until 1910 (Act of June 25, 1910, 36 Stat. 855). As a result, purchasers of allotted Indian lands from heirs of the allottee prior to 1910 found difficulty in obtaining loans upon such property because of the contention of the loan companies that there had not been formal determination of the heirs of the deceased allottees by a court or official clothed with authority to make such determination and that in the absence of such proceedings the title was defective. A letter from the Secretary of the Interior to the Chairman of the Federal Home Loan Bank Board, presents a rather exhaustive review of authority on the validity of sale under the foregoing statutory provisions:

> It has come to the attention of this Department that owners of lands whose titles are founded upon deeds executed by the heirs of deceased Indian allottees and approved by the Secretary of the Interior prior to the enactment of the act of June 25, 1910 (36 Stat. 855), conferring jurisdiction upon the Secretary of the Interior to determine the heirs of such deceased Indians, are experiencing difficulty in obtaining loans from the Federal land banks and other governmental lending agencies.
>
> The principal trouble appears to be that the abstracts of title furnished by the applicants for loans fail to show that there has been a formal determination of the heirs of the deceased Indian allottees by a court or official clothed with authority to make such determination, and in the absence of such proceedings, the position has been taken that the title is defective. We believe that the position so taken is based upon a misconception of the legal effect of the deeds from these Indian heirs.
>
> The deeds under consideration were executed and approved in accordance with regulations prescribed by the Secretary of

Upon the death of an allottee there were four possible methods of disposing of the estate:

(1) The Secretary of the Interior could issue fee patents to the heirs as a group or otherwise remove the restrictions.

(2) The estate could be physically partitioned among the heirs and either trust or fee patents issued to them individually.[175]

(3) The estate could be retained by the superintendent and leased for the benefit of the heirs.

(4) The estate could be sold under Government supervision and the proceeds distributed among the heirs.

Partition of estates is a common procedure when the number of heirs is small; but small families are not the rule among Indians, and the very tardy process of probute in the Office of Indian Affairs causes long periods of time, often running into years, to elapse before the heirs are determined. In the meantime, new heirs may have been born, and the heirs of the original allottee may have died.

The leasing of heirship allotments is a more frequent procedure, with consequences to be noted later. But it is more important to note here that under the act of 1902 a single "competent" heir could demand the sale of the whole allotment. Even though an administration may frown upon the sale of the heirship lands, it is actually powerless to prevent it. It perpetually faces the dilemma of either permitting the land to be sold, or exerting its influence to retain the land in the ownership of the heirs and to lease it. So long as the allotment is held intact, it is subject to progressive subdivision by the death of heirs and the resulting fragmentation of the equities.

If the estate is put up for sale, Indians rarely have the cash to buy it and the allotment almost invariably passes to white ownership. A strong pressure to sell comes from the Indian heirs themselves because of their lack of experience with the white man's property system. Contrary to the hopeful idealism of the proponents of the allotment system, the Indians have not acquired the white man's respect for "land in severalty." Unrestricted, individual ownership, as contrasted with their own communal ownership, tempts Indians to look on land as an asset to be disposed of for cash to meet everyday wants rather than to work it for an income.[29]

[29] Dr. John R. Swanton of the Bureau of American Ethnology recently wrote: "Our own attempts to substitute land for a living fails to attain its object because there is no insistence that land shall be used to furnish a living with the addition of labor instead of being sold outright."

The result of this legislation was exactly what would be expected—a rapid dissipation of capital assets. From 1903, when the first sales were made, to 1934, sales of heirship land totaled 1,426,061 acres, most of which was spent as income. Desperately in need of the steady income which the application of labor to these lands would have provided, Indians were nevertheless permitted to divest themselves of the one asset which they needed most to insure their own survival. (Pp. 15–17.)

* * * * * *

With the stoppage of further allotment virtually assured under the Wheeler-Howard Act,[30] all the land now in the possession of original allottees will pass into the heirship stage in the next generation. Sales of land to other than Indian tribes or corporations were also prohibited.[31] It is, therefore, a definite certainty that the area of heirship lands will steadily increase in the immediate future; and inasmuch as the Wheeler-Howard Act left untouched the present system of heirship, except to restrict inheritance to members of a tribe or their descendants (thus preventing acquisition by whites), the problem of what to do with these lands becomes of paramount importance. At present the heirship lands are 12

---

the Interior under authority of section 7 of the act of May 27, 1902 (32 Stat. 245–275) and the act of March 1, 1907 (34 Stat. 1015–1018). The pertinent provisions of these acts read:

Sec 7, Act of 1902

"That the adult heirs of any deceased Indian to whom a trust or other patent containing restrictions upon alienation has been or shall be issued for lands allotted to him may sell and convey the lands inherited from such decedent, but in case of minor heirs their interests shall be sold only by a guardian duly appointed by the proper court upon the order of such court, made upon petition filed by the guardian, but all such conveyances shall be subect to the approval of the Secretary of the Interior, and *when so approved shall convey a full title to the purchaser the same as if a final patent without restriction upon the alienation had been issued to the allottee.* * * *" [Italics supplied.]

Act of 1907

"That any noncompetent Indian to whom a patent containing restrictions against alienation has been issued for an allotment of land in severalty, under any law or treaty or who may have an interest in any allotment by inheritance, *may sell or convey all or any part of such allotment or such inherited interest on such terms and conditions and under such rules and regulations as the Secretary of the Interior may prescribe*, and the proceeds derived therefrom shall be used for the benefit of the allottee or heir so disposing of his land or interest, under the supervision of the Commissioner of Indian Affairs; *and any conveyance made hereunder and approved by the Secretary of the Interior shall convey full title to the land or interest so sold, the same as if fee simple patent had been issued to the allottee.*" [Italics supplied.]

In considering the foregoing statutory provisions, it is well to point out that the courts were without jurisdiction to determine the heirs of deceased Indian allottees (*McKay* v. *Kalyton*, 204 U. S. 458), and that, other than the Secretary of the Interior, there existed no tribunal with jurisdiction to make such determination. Before any conveyance could be made of the lands of deceased allottees, it was, of course, essential that the heirs be first determined, and the acts of 1902 and 1907, reasonably construed, appear to confer upon the Secretary of the Interior, by necessary implication, the authority to determine the facts of heirship. Neither act makes provision for formal notice and hearing for the determination of heirs, but regulations were approved and promulgated by the Secretary of the Interior providing that when a deed or other instrument conveying inherited lands was submitted to him for approval, it should be accompanied by the following data concerning the heirs of the deceased allottee:

"By a certificate signed by two members of a business committee, if there be such, or by at least two recognized chiefs, or by two or more reliable members of the tribe, setting forth that the allottee to whom he land was originally allotted is dead, giving as nearly as possible the date of death. Such certificate shall also show the names and ages of the heirs, adults and minors, of such deceased allottee, but the Department reserves the right to require, if in its judgment it shall be considered necessary, such further and additional evidence relative to heirship as may be deemed proper. If the persons who certify to the death of the allottee are, from their own knowledge, unable to certify as to who are the heirs (with their names and ages) of such deceased allottee, an additional certificate made by persons of one of the three classes herein specified, showing who are the heirs and giving their names and ages (adults and minors), must be furnished."

It has been the uniform practice and policy of this Department to regard the approval by the Secretary of the Interior of a deed based upon proof of heirship furnished in accordance with the above regulations as having the effect of finally determining the heirs and conveying the full title, particularly in view of the legislative declaration in the acts of 1902 and 1907 that such an approved deed shall convey full title to the purchaser the same as if a final fee simple patent had been issued to the allottee or purchaser. While the authorities are not in entire harmony, the better view supports the departmental position.

The remainder of the letter above quoted analyzes the cases supporting (*Brown* v. *Boston Steele, et al.*, 23 Kans. 672 (1880); *Egan* v. *McDonald*, 153 N. W. 915 (1915): *Hellen* v. *Morgan*, 283 Fed. 433 (D. C. E. D. Wash. 1922); *Davidson* v. *Roberson*, 92 Okla. 161, 218 Pac. 878 (1923)) and opposing the foregoing conclusion. (Even cases which deny binding force to secretarial determination of heirs under the circumstances considered indicate that secretarial approval conveys a prima facie title good until someone else shows a better title. See *Highrock* v. *Gavin*, 179 N. W. 12 (1920); *Tripp* v. *Stieler*, 161 N. W. 337 (1917); *Horn* v. *Ne-Gon-Ah-E-Quainoe*, 192 N. W. 363 (1923).)

[175] The Act of May 18, 1916, 39 Stat. 123, 127, 25 U. S. C. 378 provides:

* * * if the Secretary of the Interior shall find that any inherited trust allotment or allotments are capable of partition to the advantage of the heirs, he may cause such lands to be partitioned among them, regardless of their competency, patents in fee to be issued to the competent heirs for their shares and trust patents to be issued to the incompetent heirs for the lands respectively or jointly set apart to them, the trust period to terminate in accordance with the terms of the original patent or order of extension of the trust period set out in said patent.

For regulations regarding applications for partitions of inherited allotments, see 25 C. F. R. 241.8; regarding sale of heirship lands, see 25 C. F. R. 241.9–241.12.

percent of all Indian lands and 35 percent of the allotted lands.

[36] Sec. 1 prohibits further allotment, but by sec. 18 the whole act may be rejected by a negative vote of a majority of eligible voters of a band or tribe.
[37] Sec. 4.

These heirship tracts are potentially one of the most important of the Indian resources. (P. 15.)

The present Federal policy and objectives relating to Indian land have recently been stated in a Handbook of Indian Land Policy and Manual of Procedures prepared by the Office of Indian Affairs.[176]

By exchange of allotments for assignments the problem of the sale and partition of inherited lands is finding a solution and the federal Indian land policy is being carried forward. Section 5 of the Act of June 18, 1934,[177] has provided for the acquisition of land by the Secretary of the Interior for an Indian tribe, through purchase, gift, exchange, or assignment, or through relinquishment of land by individual Indians. It has been held that the purpose of "providing land for Indians" is served by an exchange transaction whereby an individual Indian transfers allotted land to the tribe in exchange for an assignment of occupancy rights in the same or in another tract, since the tribe through this transaction acquires a definite interest in the land over and above the transferor's retained occupancy right.[178] By means of this exchange provision the tribe may acquire Indian allotments or heirship lands and may designate various parcels of tribal land which are not needed for any tribal enterprise as available for exchange. Where a tribe has funds in its tribal treasury or in the United States Treasury, it may decide to use a portion of such funds to buy up lands from Indians who have holdings in the area under consideration. Where the land is in heirship status, if the tribe and all the heirs are unable to agree among themselves on the terms of purchase, the Secretary of the Interior may prescribe the method of sale and valuation.

There is no reason why a tribe may not purchase allotted lands in heirship status where such lands are offered for sale by the Secretary of the Interior. The mechanics of such a transaction are set forth in a memorandum of the Solicitor of the Department of the Interior [179] in the following words:

> It will be noted that section 372 of United States Code, title 25, requires that upon completion of the payment of the purchase price a patent in fee shall issue to the purchaser. Does this requirement make impossible sales to individual Indians, to Indian tribes, or to the Secretary of the Interior in trust for such tribes or individuals?
>
> So far as direct sales to Indian tribes are concerned, there is nothing to prevent the issuance of a patent in fee to an Indian tribe. The issuance of patents to an Indian tribe is provided for by the following statutes: Act of January 12, 1891 (26 Stat. 762), providing for patents to Mission Bands; treaty with Cherokees, December 29, 1835 (7 Stat. 478) granting land to Cherokee Nation.
>
> After issuance of such patent, however, an organized tribe might, under section 5 of the act of June 18, 1934, surrender legal title to the land, if it so chose, to the United States, retaining equitable ownership of the land. A tribe not within the provisions of that act could not surrender such legal title.
>
> * * * * *
>
> The necessity for issuance of a fee patent which arises when heirship land is sold by the Secretary of the Interior, does not arise where the conveyance of land is made by all the interested heirs. Such conveyance, made on a restricted deed form, conveys only the same interest as is held by the heirs.
>
> The question of issuing fee patents to Indian purchasers of land does not arise on reservations subject to the act of June 18, 1934, since on such reservations direct sales to individual Indians are prohibited. A related question, however, arises with respect to sales of land to the United States in trust for a tribe or individual Indian under the provisions of section 5 of the said act, which authorizes the Secretary of the Interior,
>
> > "to acquire through purchase, relinquishment, gift, exchange, or assignment, any interest in lands, water rights, or surface rights to lands, within or without existing reservations, including trust or otherwise restricted allotments, whether the allottee be living or deceased, for the purpose of providing land for Indians."
>
> The statute in question specifically provides, with respect to the tenure of lands so acquired:
>
> > "Title to any lands or rights acquired pursuant to this act shall be taken in the name of the United States in trust for the Indian tribe or individual Indian for which the land is acquired, and such lands or rights shall be exempt from State and local taxation."

[176] The primary object of Indian land policy is to save and to provide for the Indian people adequate land, in such a tenure and in accordance with such proper usage that they may subsist on it permanently by their own labor.

Indian land policy shall have for its purpose the organization and consolidation of Indian lands into proper units, considering the use to be made of the land, the type of labor and capital investment to be applied thereon, and the technical capacities and habits of co-operation of the Indians concerned.

Indian land policy definitely looks toward the substitution of Indian use for non-Indian use of Indian lands.

Implicit in all of the above is the responsibility of affording the Indians the necessary credit and technical training to make possible the best economic use of their lands.

Indian land tenure policy shall be searchingly adapted to various solutions not only as to whole tribes, but also as to natural communities within any particular tribe, and where the facts so indicate, to individual cases.

Indian land policy should take into account and should seek to contribute to the solution of the land policy problems of the Government as a whole.

In the protection and enlargement of an adequate land base, due consideration must be given to the preservation of those Indian cultural, social, and economic values and institutions which have in the past sustained, and are now sustaining, their economic and spiritual integrity and which may hold important possibilities for the future.

Indian land policy shall seek the most rapid possible reduction of uneconomic and nonproductive administrative expenditures, particularly in connection with the management of heirship lands.

In view of the limited amount of funds available for the enlargement of the Indian land base, preference in the application of these funds shall be given to those reservations showing a readiness to co-operate in order to secure the advantages, and to those showing a critical shortage of resources; and within these reservations, preference shall be given to those communities definitely Indian in character.

In the process of simplifying the ownership pattern on Indian reservations, tribal funds, IRA land-acquisition appropriations, or other applicable funds may be used (in default of other and preferable methods) for the consolidation of Indian-owned lands whenever such use supplies an essential element in improving the economy of the tribe, and reducing costs of administration.

The acquisition of land for Indians shall be for Indian use and upon adequate evidence that it will be used by Indians. In all cases where it is practicable, the acquisition should be carried out in response to the request of the Indians and upon evidence furnished by them of their determination to use the land.

Funds accruing to tribes from the past or present disposal of capital assets shall be used to the largest feasible extent for the creation of new productive resources. (Handbook, *supra*, Pt. III (1938), pp. 1-3.)

[177] 48 Stat. 984, 25 U. S. C. 465.

[178] Memo Sol. I. D., April 4, 1935.

[179] Memo Sol. I. D., August 14, 1937.

In the light of these provisions it may be asked whether the requirement of section 372 that a fee patent issued to the purchaser of heirship lands remains in force, on reservations subject to the act of June 18, 1934. If it is in force then either the Secretary of the Interior must issue a fee patent to the United States, or, if this is impossible, he must refrain from acquiring heirship land under the provisions of section 372. If the latter view is taken one of the principal objects of section 5 of the act of June 18, 1934, would be defeated. If the former view is taken a legal absurdity is presented. In the face of this dilemma it appears to be a reasonable view that the requirement of section 372 that a patent in fee be issued to the purchaser, is inapplicable where the United States is itself the purchaser, and that in this case section 5 of the act of June 18, 1934, supersedes and amends the relevant provisions of section 372. This view is in accord with the familiar rule that a limiting statute does not run against the sovereign.

It is my opinion, therefore, that the Secretary of the Interior, on reservations subject to the act of June 18, 1934, may acquire heirship land on behalf of individual Indians or Indian tribes, on the same terms as a private individual might acquire such lands under section 372, and that title to such lands is to be held by the United States in trust for the Indian or Indian tribe for which the land is purchased.

In accordance with the foregoing analysis you are advised that existing departmental regulations and orders affecting the sale of heirship lands may be amended to provide for the following transactions, under existing law:

1. On all reservations heirship lands may be sold by the Secretary of the Interior to an Indian tribe. Such sale may be made with or without the consent of the interested heirs. It is necessary that reasonable compensation be paid by the tribe for the land thus sold. Such reasonable compensation may be based upon the actual income-producing prospects and record of the land, due consideration being given to the expenses of leasing created by [the] heirship status insofar as these expenses would, be deducted from the sums paid to the lessors. Except for the requirement that 10 percent of the purchase price be paid in advance, the terms of payment are within the discretion of the Secretary of the Interior.

2. On reservations within the act of June 18, 1934, sales of heirship land may be made to the United States in trust for the tribe or for individual Indians. With respect to the terms and manner of sale and the basis of valuation the comments noted in the preceding paragraph appear equally applicable.

3. On reservations not within the act of June 18, 1934, heirship lands may be sold directly to individual Indians or to an Indian cooperative or tribe. It is within the discretion of the Secretary of the Interior to make such sales with or without the consent of the heirs, without calling for bids or after bids have been called for. Patents in fee must issue to the purchaser upon final completion of payments for the land, unless all the heirs join in making a conveyance of the trust title. If bids are called for it would be proper to limit the bidders either to Indians or to Indians of a particular tribe or to Indians interested in the particular estate or to any other reasonably defined class of Indians, provided that in any case a fair price, in the light of all circumstances, is obtained for the land that is sold. With respect to the terms and manner of sale, and the basis of valuation the comments noted in the first paragraph of this summary appear equally applicable.

CHAPTER 12

FEDERAL SERVICES FOR INDIANS

TABLE OF CONTENTS

SECTION 1. INTRODUCTION

Federal services which the United States provides for Indians are frequently viewed as a matter of charity. The erroneous notion is widely prevalent that in their relationship with the Federal Government the Indians have been the regular recipients of unearned bounties. In reality, federal services were, in earlier years, largely a matter of self-protection for the white man or partial compensation to the Indian for land cessions or other benefits received by the United States. In recent years such services have been continued, partly as a result of the failure of the states to render certain essential public services to the Indians, because of their special relation to the Federal Government.

In the treaty period[1] of our Indian relations, in order to induce the Indian to cease active resistance to further encroachment upon his domain, it was thought wise to educate him in the white man's culture. The Indian's white neighbors would instruct him to seek paths of peace rather than the ways of war, to replace the tomahawk with a religion of love for his fellow man. To obviate responsibility for his support, or the alternative of slow starvation, they would instruct him in the ways of the farm, in the arts of the fireside, and in means of earning a livelihood on his greatly reduced land.[2] This offered a practical alternative to a policy of warfare which, it has been estimated, cost the Federal Government in the neighborhood of one million dollars for each dead Indian.

Reservations were located in the vicinities of army posts. In the panic of an epidemic of smallpox, as a matter of protection to prevent the spread of this disease through the entire population, a statute[3] was enacted which provided for vaccination of Indians by army surgeons.[4] This statute is illustrative of the way in which the Indian health service and other federal services originated.

In making treaties with the Indian tribes, the United States generally offered a more or less substantial *quid pro quo* for land ceded by the Indian tribes in such treaties and for other promises contained in such treaties that were advantageous to the United States.[5] This *quid pro quo* might be, and generally was, defined in terms of money, although in some cases the United States undertook to furnish specified supplies or services for a designated period of years. The Indians had little use for money. The practice therefore arose of placing the money in trust in the United States Treasury and expending either the principal or the interest of such funds, in accordance with the wishes of the Indians, for food, clothing, livestock, farm implements, and the pay of blacksmiths, teachers, physicians, and other skilled employees. To this day tribal funds are expended for these purposes.[6]

When treaty and tribal funds of a given tribe came to an end, the Federal Government might have discharged the teachers, physicians, blacksmiths, and other employees maintained by it pursuant to treaty obligation; but many factors, some of them humanitarian, combined to prevent the abandonment of these services. Instead, an increasing amount of what were called "gratuity appropriations," as distinct from treaty appropriations and tribal fund appropriations, was devoted to the maintenance of these various federal services in the Indian country. According to contemporary critics, and according to subsequent official investigations, these funds were in many

[1] See Chapter 3.

[2] 8 Am. State Papers (Indian Affairs, class II, vol. 2) 1815–27, pp. 150–151.

[3] Act of May 5, 1832, 4 Stat. 514.

[4] Appropriations for this service have since been regularly enacted. See Chapter 4, sec. 17.

[5] See Chapter 3, sec. 3C(3).

[6] See Chapter 15, sec. 23.

cases extravagantly and wastefully disbursed. Irrigation projects, for example, frequently were launched without the benefit of expert technical advice and were consequently improperly constructed and ill-advised.[7]

With the increase of gratuity appropriations, the picture of the Indian as a charity ward came to loom large in the public eye. In 1875 Congress provided that Indians receiving supplies from the Federal Government might be required to perform useful labor as a condition precedent,[8] quite ignoring the fact that many Indians were no more "charity wards" than were holders of federal bonds or other legal obligations of the Federal Government.

In an effort to remove federal services to Indians from a gratuity basis, Congress has frequently provided that various expenditures made for the benefit, or supposed benefit, of Indians should be "reimbursable," that is to say, repaid to the United States Treasury out of the future income of the tribes concerned. Even where Congress has not so provided, the rule has been developed in many jurisdictional acts and court cases that appropriations which were supposed to be gratuities when made are to be reimbursed out of judgments rendered in favor of an Indian tribe.[9]

More recently the effort to remove federal Indian services from a charitable basis has taken the form of legislation authorizing the Secretary of the Interior to assess fees for various acts and services benefiting Indians.[10]

[7] See Hearings, Sen. Subcom. of Comm. on Ind. Aff., 71st Cong., 2d sess., Survey of Conditions of the Indians in the United States, pt. 6, Engle Report, January 21, 1930, p. 2285.

[8] Act of March 3, 1875, 18 Stat. 420, 449, 25 U. S. C. 137.

[9] *Osage Tribe of Indians* v. *United States*, 66 C. Cls. 64 (1928), app. dism. 279 U. S. 811, 68 C. Cls. 788; *Choctaw Nation* v. *United States*, 81 C. Cls. 1 (1935), cert. den. 296 U. S. 643; Act of June 7, 1924, 43 Stat. 537 (Choctaw and Chickasaw); *Fort Berthold Indians* v. *United States*, 71 C. Cls. 308 (1930); Act of February 11, 1920, 41 Stat. 404.

[10] Section 1 of the Act of May 9, 1938, 52 Stat. 291, 312, 318, as amended by the Act of May 10, 1939, 53 Stat. 708, 25 U. S. C. 561, provides:

> In the discretion of the Secretary of the Interior, and under such rules and regulations as may be prescribed by him, fees may be collected from individual Indians for services performed for them, and any fees so collected shall be covered into the Treasury of the United States.

Cf. Act of January 24, 1923, 42 Stat. 1174, 1185, 25 U. S. C. 377 relating to probate fees, and Act of February 14, 1920, 41 Stat. 408, 415, amended March 1, 1933, 47 Stat. 1417, 25 U. S. C. 413, relating to various management fees for Indian forestry work.

In recent years, and particularly since 1924, when citizenship was granted to all Indians not already citizens,[11] the states have assumed a larger role in supplying the Indians with essential public services. In 1929[12] the Secretary of the Interior was authorized to permit state agents to make inspections of health and educational conditions on the reservations and to enforce sanitation and quarantine regulations or to enforce compulsory school attendance of Indian pupils, as provided by the law of the state, and since 1934[13] the Secretary has been authorized to enter into contracts with state or other bodies for education, medical attention, agricultural assistance, and social welfare, including relief of distress, of Indians, and to authorize the state to utilize existing federal school buildings, hospitals, and other facilities.

Some states have taken kindly to their added responsibility; others have continued to discriminate against the Indian, as, for instance, those states which deny the Indian services available under the Social Security Act.[14]

The year 1934 marked a momentous change in Indian policy. The then prevalent economic conditions brought on by the depression emphasized the desperate plight of the Indian. The Wheeler-Howard Act[15] was passed. A program was launched, with the assistance of federal and tribal funds, to organize and incorporate Indian tribes, to launch tribal enterprises, to enable tribes and tribal members to become self-sufficient by their own efforts in lines of endeavor congenial to native tastes and talents, and to make possible the transfer to the organized tribes of responsibility for services hitherto performed by the Federal Government.

This program is still too close to its inception to warrant estimation of its success. It may be said, however, that the prevailing tendency today is to turn over to the organized tribes, or to the states, where such tribes and states are willing to accept such burdens, an increasing measure of responsibility for the performance of services which have historically been rendered to the Indians by the Federal Government.[16]

[11] See Chapter 8, sec. 2.

[12] Act of February 15, 1929, 45 Stat. 1185, 25 U. S. C. 231. See Chapter 6, sec. 2.

[13] Act of April 16, 1934, 48 Stat. 596, amended June 4, 1936, 49 Stat. 1458, 25 U. S. C. 452, 454.

[14] Act of August 14, 1935, 49 Stat. 620. See sec. 5, *infra*, and see Chapter 8, sec. 5.

[15] Act of June 18, 1934, 48 Stat. 984, 25 U. S. C. 461 *et seq.* See Chapter 4, sec. 16.

[16] See Chapter 2, sec. 3C.

SECTION 2. EDUCATION

A. DEVELOPMENT OF FEDERAL POLICY

"Father," requested Cornplanter, speaking for the Senecas in 1792, "you give us leave to speak our minds concerning the tilling of the ground. We ask you to teach us to plough and to grind corn; * * * that you will send smiths among us, and, above all, that you will teach our children to read and write, and our women to spin and to weave."[17] With equal warmth George Washington replied, through the Secretary of War, that the Senecas might be sure of his willingness and desire to impart to them "the blessings of husbandry, and the arts" and that a number of their children would be received to be educated either at the time of the treaty, or at such a time and place as they might agree upon.[18]

In such a fashion did the President of the United States and a chief of an Indian tribe first discuss the possibility of governmental assistance in bringing to the red man the advan-

[17] 7 American State Papers (Indian Affairs, class II, vol. 1) (1789–1815) p. 144.

That such was not always the attitude of all Indians is clear in an excerpt from Benjamin Franklin's "Remarks Concerning the Savages of North America." In 1744, after the Treaty of Lancaster in Pennsylvania between the government of Virginia and the Six Nations, the Virginia Commissioners offered to the chiefs to educate six of their sons at a college in Williamsburg, Va. They received this reply:

> Several of our young people were formerly brought up at the colleges of the Northern Provinces; they were instructed in all your sciences; but when they came back to us, they were bad runners; ignorant of every means of living in the woods; unable to bear either cold or hunger; knew neither how to build a cabin, take a deer, or kill an enemy; spoke our language imperfectly; were therefore neither fit for hunters, warriors, or counsellors; they were totally good for nothing. We are however not the less obliged by your kind offer, though we decline accepting it: And to show our greatful sense of it, if the Gentlemen of Virginia will send us a dozen of their sons, we will take great care of their education, instruct them in all we know, and make *men* of them. (Benjamin Franklin, Two Tracts etc. (2d ed., 1794), pp. 28–29.)

[18] *Ibid.*, p. 166.

tages of a European civilization.[19] Although this particular arrangement was destined not to materialize, the interest it aroused quickened, and on December 2, 1794, educational provisions were included in a treaty negotiated with the Oneida, Tuscarora, and Stockbridge Indians.[20] This was followed in 1803 by a treaty with the Kaskaskia Indians which provided an annual contribution for 7 years for a Roman Catholic priest who, among other things, was to instruct in literature.[21] Thus began the practice, which persisted up to the end of treaty-making in 1871, of including educational provisions in treaties.[22] The provisions covered technical education in agriculture and the mechanical arts,[23] support of reservation schools,[24] boarding schools,[25] or schools and teachers generally,[26] and contributions for educational purposes.[27]

On March 30, 1802, Congress made provision for the expenditure of a sum of money not to exceed $15,000 per annum to promote civilization among the aborigines.[28] For another decade this action stood as the sole indication that Congress had recognized responsibility for Indian education; then, in his first message to Congress, President Monroe called for additional efforts to preserve, improve, and civilize the original inhabitants.[29] This recommendation was acted upon 2 years later when Congress enacted a provision which still stands as the organic legal basis for most of the educational work of the Indian Service. As embodied in the United States Code, the law declares:[30]

> * * * The President may, in every case where he shall judge improvement in the habits and conditions of such

---

[19] For additional examples see Bureau of Education, Special Report on Indian Education and Civilization (1888), Sen. Ex. Doc. No. 95, 48th Cong., 2d sess. pp. 161–197. The annual reports of the Commissioners of Indian Affairs throw considerable light on the development of the federal educational policies regarding the Indians. See Chapter 2, sec. 2.

[20] 7 Stat. 47, 48. These provisions allowed for the employment of one or two persons for 3 years to instruct in the arts of the miller and sawyer.

[21] Treaty of August 13, 1803, 7 Stat. 78, 79.

[22] The educational provisions of the various treaties are analyzed and summarized in the following government documents: Industrial Training Schools for Indian Youths, H. Rept. No. 29, 46th Cong., 1st sess. (1879); Industrial Training Schools for Indians, H. Rept. No. 752, 46th Cong., 2d sess. (1880); Treaty Items, Indian Appropriation Bill, H. Doc. No. 1030, 63d Cong., 2d sess. (1914).

[23] Treaty of August 18, 1804, with Delaware Tribe, 7 Stat. 81; Treaty of August 29, 1821, with Ottawa, Chippewa, and Pottawatamie, 7 Stat. 218; Treaty of February 12, 1825, with Creek Nation, 7 Stat. 237; Treaty of February 8, 1831, with the Menomonee Indians, 7 Stat. 342; Treaty of September 21, 1833, with the Otoes and Missourias, 7 Stat. 429; Treaty of March 28, 1836, with the Ottawa and Chippewa, 7 Stat. 491; Treaty of September 17, 1836, with the Sacks and Foxes, etc., 7 Stat. 511; Treaty of October 15, 1836, with the Otoes, etc., 7 Stat. 524; Treaty of January 4, 1845, with the Creeks and Seminoles, 9 Stat. 821, 822; Treaty of October 13, 1846, with the Winnebago Indians, 9 Stat. 878; Treaty of August 2, 1847, with the Chippewas, 9 Stat. 904; Treaty of October 18, 1848, with the Menomonee Tribe, 9 Stat. 952; Treaty of July 23, 1851, with the Sioux, 10 Stat. 949; Treaty of August 5, 1851, with the Sioux Indians, 10 Stat. 954; Treaty of May 12, 1854, with the Menomonee, 10 Stat. 1064; Treaty of December 26, 1854, with the Nisqually, etc., Indians, 10 Stat. 1132; Treaty of October 17, 1855, with the Blackfoot Indians, 11 Stat. 657; Treaty of September 24, 1857, with the Pawnees, 11 Stat. 729; Treaty of January 22, 1855, with the Dwamish, etc., 12 Stat. 927; Treaty of January 26, 1855, with the S'Klallams, 12 Stat. 933; Treaty of January 31, 1855, with the Makah Tribe, 12 Stat. 939; Treaty of July 1, 1855, with the Qui-nai-elt, etc., Indians, 12 Stat. 971; Treaty of July 16, 1855, with the Flathead, etc., Indians, 12 Stat. 975; Treaty of December 21, 1855, with the Molels, 12 Stat. 981; Treaty of October 18, 1864, with the Chippewa Indians, 14 Stat. 657; Treaty of June 14, 1866, with the Creek Nation, 14 Stat. 785; Treaty of February 18, 1867, with the Sac and Fox Indians, 15 Stat. 495; Treaty of February 19, 1867, with the Sissiton, etc., Sioux, 15 Stat. 505.

[24] Treaty of May 6, 1828, with the Cherokee Nation, 7 Stat. 311; Treaty of New Echota, December 29, 1835, with the Cherokee, 7 Stat. 478 (provides for common schools and "* * * a literary institution of a higher order * * *"); Treaty of June 5, and 17, 1846, with the Pottowautomie Nation, 9 Stat. 853; Treaty of September 30, 1854, with the Chippewa Indians, 10 Stat. 1109; Treaty of November 18, 1854, with the Chastas, etc., Indians, 10 Stat. 1122; Treaty of April 19, 1858, with the Yancton Sioux, 11 Stat. 743; Treaty of June 9, 1855, with the Walla-Wallas, etc., Tribes, 12 Stat. 945; Treaty of June 11, 1855, with the Nez Perces, 12 Stat. 957; Treaty of March 12, 1858, with the Poncas, 12 Stat. 997; Treaty of October 14, 1865, with the Lower Brule Sioux, 14 Stat. 699; Treaty of February 23, 1867, with the Senecas, etc., 15 Stat. 513; Treaty of October 21, 1867, with the Kiowa and Comanche Indians, 15 Stat. 581; Treaty of October 21, 1867, with the Kiowa, Comanche, and Apache Indians, 15 Stat. 589; Treaty of October 28, 1867, with the Cheyenne and Arapahoe Indians, 15 Stat. 593; Treaty of March 2, 1868, with the Ute Indians, 15 Stat. 619; Treaty of April 29 *et seq.*, 1868, with the Sioux Nation, 15 Stat. 635; Treaty of May 7, 1868, with the Crow Indians, 15 Stat. 649; Treaty of May 10, 1868, with the Northern Cheyenne and Northern Arapahoe Indians, 15 Stat. 655; Treaty of June 1, 1868, with the Navajo Tribe, 15 Stat. 667; Treaty of July 3, 1868, with the Eastern Band Shoshones and Bannock Tribe of Indians, 15 Stat. 673.

An unusual educational provision appears in the Treaty of May 6, 1828, with the Cherokee Nation, *supra*. Art. 5 reads in part:

> * * * It is further agreed by the United States, to pay two thousand dollars, annually, to the Cherokees, for ten years, to be expended under the direction of the President of the United States in the education of their children, in their own country, in letters and the mechanick arts; also, one thousand dollars towards the purchase of a Printing Press and Types to aid the Cherokees in the progress of education, and to benefit and enlighten them as a people, in their own, and our language. (P. 313.)

[25] Treaty of November 15, 1827, with the Creek Nation, 7 Stat. 307; Treaty of September 15, 1832, with the Winnebago Nation, 7 Stat. 370; Treaty of May 24, 1834, with the Chickasaw Indians, 7 Stat. 450; Treaty of June 9, 1863, with the Nez Perce Tribe, 14 Stat. 647; Treaty of March 19, 1867, with the Chippewa of Mississippi, 16 Stat. 719.

[26] Treaty of October 18, 1820, with the Choctaw Nation, 7 Stat. 210; Treaty of June 3, 1825, with the Kansas Nation, 7 Stat. 244; Treaty of August 5, 1826, with the Chippewa Tribe, 7 Stat. 290; Treaty of October 21, 1837, with the Sac and Fox Indians, 7 Stat. 543; Treaty of March 17, 1842, with the Wyandott Nation, 11 Stat. 581; Treaty of May 15, 1846, with the Comanche, etc., Indians, 9 Stat. 844; Treaty of June 5, 1854, with the Miami Indians, 10 Stat. 1093; Treaty of November 15, 1854, with the Rogue Rivers, 10 Stat. 1119; Treaty of November 29, 1854, with the Umpqua, etc., Indians, 10 Stat. 1125; Treaty of July 31, 1855, with the Ottowas and Chippewas, 11 Stat. 621; Treaty of February 5, 1856, with the Stockbridge and Munsee Tribes, 11 Stat. 663; Treaty of June 9, 1855, with the Yakama Indians, 12 Stat. 951; Treaty of June 25, 1855, with the Oregon Indians, 12 Stat. 963; Treaty of June 19, 1858, with Sioux Bands, 12 Stat. 1031; Treaty of July 16, 1859, with the Chippewa Bands, 12 Stat. 1105; Treaty of February 18, 1861, with the Arapahoes and Cheyenne Indians, 12 Stat. 1163; Treaty of March 6, 1861, with the Sacs, Foxes and Iowas, 12 Stat. 1171; Treaty of June 24, 1862, with the Ottawa Indians, 12 Stat. 1237; Treaty of May 7, 1864, with the Chippewas, 13 Stat. 693; Treaty of August 12, 1865, with the Snake Indians, 14 Stat. 683; Treaty of March 21, 1866, with the Seminole Indians, 14 Stat. 755; Treaty of April 28, 1866, with the Choctaw and Chickasaw Nation, 14 Stat. 769; Treaty of August 13, 1868, with the Nez Perce Tribe, 15 Stat. 693.

[27] Treaty of October 16, 1826, with the Potawatamie Tribe, 7 Stat. 295; Treaty of September 20, 1828, with the Potowatamie Indians, 7 Stat. 317; Treaty of July 15, 1830, with the Sacs and Foxes, etc., 7 Stat. 328; Treaty of September 27, 1830, with the Choctaw Nation, 7 Stat. 333; Treaty of March 24, 1832, with the Creek Tribe, 7 Stat. 366; Treaty of February 14, 1833, with the Creek Nation, 7 Stat. 417; Treaty of January 14, 1846, with the Kansas Indians, 9 Stat. 842; Treaty of April 1, 1850, with the Wyandot Tribe, 9 Stat. 987; Treaty of March 15, 1854, with the Ottoe and Missouria Indians, 10 Stat. 1038; Treaty of May 6, 1854, with the Delaware Tribe, 10 Stat. 1048; Treaty of May 10, 1854, with the Shawnees, 10 Stat. 1053; Treaty of May 17, 1854, with the Ioway Tribe, 10 Stat. 1069; Treaty of May 30, 1854, with the Kaskaskia, etc., Indians, 10 Stat. 1082; Treaty of January 22, 1855, with the Willamette Bands, 10 Stat. 1143; Treaty of February 22, 1855; with the Chippewa Indians of Mississippi, 10 Stat. 1165; Treaty of June 22, 1855, with the Choctaw and Chickasaw Indians, 11 Stat. 611; Treaty of August 2, 1855, with the Chippewa Indians of Saginaw, 11 Stat. 633; Treaty of August 7, 1856, with the Creeks and Seminoles, 11 Stat. 699; Treaty of June 28, 1862, with the Kickapoo Tribe, 13 Stat. 623; Treaty of October 2, 1863, with the Chippewa Indians (Red Lake and Pembina Bands), 13 Stat. 667; Treaty of September 29, 1865, with the Osage Indians, 14 Stat. 687.

[28] Act of March 30, 1802, 2 Stat. 139, 143.

[29] XXXI Annals of Congress, 15th Cong., 1st sess. (1817–18), p. 12.

[30] Act of March 3, 1819, 3 Stat. 516, R. S. § 2071, 25 U. S. C. 271.

> Indians practicable, and that the means of instruction can be introduced with their own consent, employ capable persons of good moral character to instruct them in the mode of agriculture suited to their situation; and for teaching their children in reading, writing, and arithmetic, and performing such other duties as may be enjoined according to such instructions and rules as the President may give and prescribe for the regulation of their conduct, in the discharge of their duties. A report of the proceedings adopted in the execution of this provision shall be annually laid before Congress.

This statute carried with it a permanent annual appropriation of $10,000 "for the purpose of providing against the further decline and final extinction of the Indian tribes, adjoining the frontier settlements of the United States, and for introducing among them the habits and arts of civilization." [31]

The expenditure of this fund occasioned no little difficulty. The President, anxious to apply it in the most effective manner possible, addressed a circular letter to those societies and individuals—usually missionary organizations—that had been prominent in the effort to civilize the Indians, offering the cooperation of the Government in their various enterprises.[32] Soon the $10,000 was apportioned among them, and later, as treaty funds became available for this purpose, these, too, generally were disbursed to such establishments.[33]

A significant development in the history of Indian education was the establishment by a number of Indian tribes of their own schools. As early as 1805, the Choctaw chieftains maintained a school with annuity funds.[34] In 1841 and 1842, before a number of states had provided for public schools, the Cherokee and Choctaw nations had put into operation a common-school system.[35]

In 1855, the Commissioner of Indian Affairs, George W. Manypenny, noted that total expenditures for education among the Indian tribes during the 10-year period ending January 1, 1855, exceeded $2,150,000. Apparently only a small portion of this sum was contributed directly by the Government, for the Commissioner's report shows that while $102,107.14 had been furnished by the United States, $824,160.61 had been added from Indian treaty funds, over $400,000 had been paid out by Indian nations themselves, and $830,000 had come from private benevolence.[36]

After the Civil War a more liberal policy for participation of the Government in the education of the Indians was pursued. In 1870, $100,000 was set aside for this purpose,[37] and in succeeding years the sums allocated were sufficiently liberal to permit a definite expansion of activities.

By 1878, several nonreservation boarding schools had been opened. Indian youths from all parts of the country attended the United States Indian Training and Industrial School at Carlisle, Pennsylvania. Other schools were located at Chemawa, Oregon; Lawrence, Kansas (Haskell Institute); Genoa, Nebraska; and Chilocco, Indian Territory.[38]

By the Act of July 31, 1882,[39] it was provided that abandoned military posts might be turned over to the Interior Department for the purpose of conducting therein Indian schools.

Government participation increased when, in 1890, the Indian Service

> * * * began to use public schools for the instruction of Indian children. Individual Indians had attended public schools before, but under the policy adopted in 1890 the Office of Indian Affairs reimbursed public schools for the actual increase in cost incurred by instructing the Indian children. The practice was in accordance with the ultimate plan of the Office of turning over the Indian day schools to the States as soon as white settlers and taxpayers were present in sufficient numbers to justify the establishment of local systems of schools. However, the use of public schools for educating Indian children did not become a common practice until after 1900, when it developed rapidly.[40]

The recent course of federal activity with respect to Indian education is charted in the following excerpt from a recent study prepared under the auspices of the President's Advisory Committee on Education:

> The period since 1900 is marked by a number of changes. In 1906 the schools—several hundred day schools and a number of boarding schools—of the Five Civilized Tribes in Oklahoma, previously operated by the tribal governments, were placed in charge of the Office of Indian Affairs. At first they were operated under contract but later by the Office of Indian Affairs. * * * A uniform course of study for the Indian schools—now hardly to be regarded as a progressive step—was provided in 1916. In order to increase the efficiency of the teachers, provision was made in 1912 for educational leave not to exceed 15 days a year to attend teachers' institutes or training schools, and in 1922 this leave was increased to 30 days. A provision in 1928 permitted 60 days of educational leave in any 2-year period.
>
> * * * * *
>
> Some of the changes which occurred are reflected in the data on enrollment of Indians in schools. * * * From 1900 to 1926 the enrollment increased from 26,451 to 69,892 or 164 percent. * * *[41]

Since then, a number of other changes have taken place, largely in response to criticism voiced by the Report of the Institute for Government Research, in 1928[42] and the Report of the National Advisory Committee on Education in 1931.[43] These changes are summarized in additional passages from the 1939 Advisory Committee study:

> * * * A material change has occurred in the point of view of the education of Indians, and a program is being developed which seeks to relate instruction to the needs and interests of children as well as to develop initiative and independence. Much of the deadening routinization has been eliminated. Increased emphasis has been placed on community day schools, there has been a notable decrease in the enrollments of Government boarding schools, and the programs of the boarding schools have been improved to serve primarily the need for secondary education. Vocational education adapted to the needs of Indian children has received some attention. Provision has been made for the higher and technical education of Indian youth. Child labor in the schools has been reduced, although there is still too much of it in the elementary boarding schools. Improvement has been made in the educational personnel through higher requirements and increases in salaries. Congress has also made larger

[31] Act of March 3, 1819, 3 Stat. 516. The repeal of this permanent appropriation was contemplated several times and finally accomplished in the Act of February 14, 1873, c. 138, 17 Stat. 437, 461. This appropriation became known as the "civilization fund." Blauch, Educational Service for Indians, Staff Study No. 18, prepared for the Advisory Committee on Education (1939), p. 32.

[32] 8 Am. State Papers (Indian Affairs, class II, vol. 2) 1815–27, pp. 200, 201.

[33] Blauch, *op. cit.*, p. 33.

[34] Treaty of October 18, 1820, with the Choctaw Nation, Arts. 7 and 8, 7 Stat. 210.

[35] Blauch, *op. cit.*, p. 33.

[36] Report of the Secretary of the Interior, Sen. Ex. Doc. No. 1, pt. 1, 34th Cong., 1st sess. (1855), p. 561.

[37] Act of July 15, 1870, 16 Stat. 335, 359.

[38] Blauch, *op. cit.*, p. 34.

[39] 22 Stat. 181.

[40] Blauch, *op. cit.*, pp. 34, 35.

[41] Blauch, *op. cit.*, pp. 37, 38.

[42] Meriam, The Problem of Indian Administration (1928), c. IX.

[43] Federal Relations to Education (1931). The National Advisory Committee on Education was organized in 1929 by the Secretary of the Interior acting for the President.

appropriations to provide for larger expenditures per child in the schools. Educational management has been somewhat decentralized, more control being given to the regional and local superintendents.[44]

Another innovation is the Act of April 16, 1934,[45] commonly known as the Johnson-O'Malley Act providing for federal-state cooperation. Under the terms of this legislation, moneys appropriated by Congress for Indian education may be turned over to "any State or Territory, or political subdivision thereof" or to "any State university, college, or school" or "any appropriate State or private corporation, agency, or institution" under a contract by which the recipient of federal funds undertakes to provide educational facilities in accord with standards established by the Secretary of the Interior to a specified number of Indian students. So far contracts in accordance with this act have been made with Arizona, California, Minnesota, and Washington.

In line with the foregoing tendency towards decentralization of federal educational activities it should be noted that in a long series of special statutes Congress has appropriated money directly to various counties and school districts for the maintenance of public schools attended by Indians.[46] Generally such statutes contain some such provision as the following:

> * * * That there is hereby authorized to be appropriated, out of any moneys * * * for the purpose of cooperating with school district * * * in the improvement and extension of public-school buildings: *Provided*, That the schools * * * shall be available to both Indian and white children without discrimination, except that tuition may be paid for Indian children attending in the discretion of the Secretary of the Interior * * *.[47]

From these varying treaty stipulations, statutory provisions and governmental policies have emerged a number of problems concerning education of the Indian. Are all Indians eligible to attend federal schools; state schools? Can Indians be compelled to attend schools? What are the limitations upon the use of funds for Indian education? At various times these and other questions have been dealt with judicially and the substance and application of these decisions must be examined.

B. ELIGIBILITY FOR SCHOOL ATTENDANCE

The most important restriction imposed on the Indian's right to attend federal schools is found in the provision that

> * * * No appropriation, except appropriations made pursuant to treaties, shall be used to educate children of less than one-fourth Indian blood whose parents are citizens of the United States and of the State wherein they live and where there are adequate free school facilities provided.

This restriction, contained in the Appropriation Act of May 25, 1918[48] has been embodied in title 25 of the United States Code as section 297.

At a time when allotment was considered a step towards the termination of governmental obligations, Congress thought it proper to enact a specific statute which declares that the fact of allotment shall not be construed as a reason for excluding the children of allottees from the benefit of federal appropriations for education.[49]

The eligibility of Indians to attend state schools is primarily a matter of state law, and therefore need not be considered at this point. The existence of various federal statutes designed to induce the states to offer educational facilities to Indians has already been noted,[50] and the constitutional issues involved in state discrimination are elsewhere analyzed.[51]

Under certain conditions non-Indian children have the right to attend Indian schools.[52]

C. COMPULSORY EDUCATION

The Secretary of the Interior is authorized at the present time to make and enforce regulations necessary to secure regular attendance of Indian children at Indian or public schools.[53]

Several treaties contained provisions for compulsory school attendance for children between specified ages and for a specified part of the year.[54] Failure to comply with those provisions might involve penalties.[55] However, compulsory education was not a common feature of treaties up to the cessation of treaty-making in 1871.

At least as early as 1877, common schools and compulsory education were urged by the Commissioner of Indian affairs as a general policy.[56]

In 1891,[57] Congress provided for regulations to enforce, by proper means, the regular attendance of Indian children of suitable age and health at schools established for their benefit. In 1893 much stronger methods were adopted. In the discretion of the Secretary of the Interior, parents were given the alternative of sending their children to school or losing their portion of the annual rations or subsistence.[58]

A year later, Congress made it clear that compulsory attendance was not to apply to nonreservation schools, enacting legislation[59] which forbade the removal of Indian children to reservations outside the state or territory in which they resided without the consent of parents or next of kin, and further declared:

> * * * And it shall be unlawful for any Indian agent or other employe of the Government to induce, or seek to induce, by withholding rations or by other improper

---

[44] Blauch, *op. cit.*, p. 44.

[45] Act of April 16, 1934, c. 147, 48 Stat. 596, amended by Act of June 4, 1936, 49 Stat. 1458, 25 U. S. C. 452–456.

[46] Act of June 7, 1935, c. 188, 49 Stat. 827; Act of June 7, 1935, c. 189, 49 Stat. 827; Act of June 7, 1935, c. 190, 49 Stat. 828; Act of June 7, 1935, c. 191, 49 Stat. 828; Act of June 7, 1935, c. 192, 49 Stat. 828; Act of June 7, 1935, c. 193, 49 Stat. 829; Act of June 7, 1935, c. 195, 49 Stat. 829; Act of June 7, 1935, c. 196, 49 Stat. 830; Act of June 7, 1935, c. 197, 49 Stat. 330; Act of June 7, 1935, c. 198, 49 Stat. 331; Act of June 7, 1935, c. 199, 49 Stat. 331; Act of June 7, 1935, c. 204, 49 Stat. 333; Act of June 7, 1935, c. 205, 49 Stat. 333; Act of June 11, 1935, c. 215, 49 Stat. 836; Act of June 11, 1935, c. 216, 49 Stat. 836; Act of August 30, 1935, c. 827, 49 Stat. 1013; Act of August 30, 1935, c. 828, 49 Stat. 1014.

[47] Act of June 7, 1935, c. 190, 49 Stat. 328, *supra*.

[48] C. 86, 40 Stat. 561, 564; Act of May 24, 1922, c. 199, 42 Stat. 552, 576; Act of May 18, 1916, c. 125, 39 Stat. 123, 125.

The Appropriation Act of May 18, 1916, declared that "the facilities of the Indian schools are needed for pupils of more than one-fourth Indian blood." (*Davis v. Sitka School Board*, 3 Alaska 481, 491 (1908).) See also Chapter 21, sec. 7.

[49] Act of August 15, 1894, 28 Stat. 286, 311.

[50] See fn. 45, *supra*.

[51] See Chapter 8, sec. 10.

[52] Act of March 1, 1907, 34 Stat. 1015, 1018, 25 U. S. C. 288; Act of March 3, 1909, 35 Stat. 781, 783, 25 U. S. C. 289.

[53] Act of February 14, 1920, 41 Stat. 408, 410, 25 U. S. C. 282. For regulations regarding education of Indians, see 25 C. F. R. 41.1–47.7.

[54] *E. g.*, Treaty of April 19, 1858, with the Yancton Tribe, Art. 4, sec. 4, 11 Stat. 743; Treaty of March 12, 1858, with the Ponca Tribe, Art. 2, sec. 4, 12 Stat. 997; Treaty of April 29, 1868, *et seq.*, with the Sioux Tribes, 15 Stat. 635, Art. 7.

[55] Treaties of April 19, 1858, 11 Stat. 743, and March 12, 1858, 12 Stat. 997, carried the definite penalty for failure to comply of withholding annuities by the Secretary of the Interior. The Treaty of April 29, 1868, *et seq.*, 15 Stat. 635, contained a pledge to comply. See fn. 72, *infra*.

[56] Report of the Commissioner of Indian Affairs, 1877, p. 1.

[57] Act of March 3, 1891, 26 Stat. 989, 1014, 25 U. S. C. 284. The Commissioner of Indian Affairs was authorized to make regulations to secure attendance by the Act of July 13, 1892, 27 Stat. 120, 143, 25 U. S. C. 284.

[58] Act of March 3, 1893, 27 Stat. 612, 628, 635, 25 U. S. C. 283.

[59] Act of August 15, 1894, c. 290, sec. 11, 28 Stat. 286, 313.

> means, the parents or next of kin of any Indian to consent to the removal of any Indian child beyond the limits of any reservation.

This provision was reenacted a year later,[60] and has been incorporated in title 25 of the United States Code as section 286.

Under this statute it has been suggested that a writ of habeas corpus will be issued to compel the release of an Indian child placed in a nonreservation school without parental consent.[61]

The Indian Service sought to evade the force of this statute by having a local Indian agent apply in the courts of the state to be appointed the guardian of the persons of the Indian children. His application was granted and he was directed to place the children at the industrial school, which was done. Later this proceeding was declared invalid by the federal court, which declared that if a county court could appoint a guardian of Indian children and could direct the placing of these children in any of the schools of the state, then the tribal condition of the Indians could be speedily broken up, not in pursuance of the acts of the National Government, but through the enforcement of the laws of the state acting upon the persons and property of the Indians.[62]

Consent of parents, guardians, or next of kin is not required to place Indian youths in an "Indian Reform School."[63]

No Indian pupil under the age of 14 may be transported at Government expense beyond the limits of the state or territory where its parents reside or of the adjoining state or territory.[64]

In 1913 an act was passed which authorized retention of annuities due Osage minors from parents who refused to send their children to some established school.[65]

After Indians became citizens and responsibility for the Indian devolved to some extent at least upon the states, state agents and employees, under regulations of the Secretary of the Interior, were authorised to enter reservations as truant officers to enforce laws of states requiring regular school attendance.[66]

D. USE OF FUNDS FOR INDIAN EDUCATION

From time to time Congress has placed certain restrictions on its appropriations for the support of Indian schools.

In 1897, Congress declared it to be the policy of the government thereafter to make no appropriation whatever for education in any sectarian school.[67] In 1905,[68] contracts were made with mission schools, the money being taken from treaty and trust funds (tribal funds) on request of Indians. This use of tribal funds was challenged as being contrary to the policy stated in the appropriation act for 1897. The Supreme Court held, in 1908,[69] that both treaty and trust funds to which the Indians could lay claim as a matter of right, were not within the scope of the statute and could be used for sectarian schools.

In 1917, a statute was enacted which provided that "no appropriation whatever out of the Treasury of the United States" should be used "for education of Indian children in any sectarian school."[70] The effect of the newly added phrase "out of the Treasury of the United States" is not clear. At the present time money is appropriated for the institutional care[71] of Indian children in sectarian schools rather than for their instruction.

Controversies in the Court of Claims involve educational provisions of treaties and the use of tribal funds for educational purposes.[72]

Legislation[73] limiting the annual per capita cost in Indian schools has been repealed.[74]

All expenditures of money appropriated for school purposes among Indians are under the direction of the Commissioner of Indian Affairs, subject to the supervision of the Secretary of the Interior.[75]

Tribal and gratuity funds are made available for advances to worthy Indian youth to enable them to take educational courses, including special courses in nursing, home economics, forestry, and other industrial subjects in colleges, universities, or other institutions, the advances to be reimbursed in not to exceed 8 years.[76]

The status of Indian Service educational personnel involves problems of Indian Office structure and policy, which are separately treated.[77]

---

[60] Act of March 2, 1895, 28 Stat. 876, 906. See also Act of June 10, 1896, 29 Stat. 321, 348, 25 U. S. C. 287.

[61] See *In re Lelah-puc-ka-chee*, 98 Fed. 429 (D. C. N. D. Iowa, 1899).

[62] *Peters* v. *Malin*, 111 Fed. 244 (C. C. N. D. Iowa 1901). *Cf. State* v. *Wolf*, 145 N. C. 440, 59 S. E. 40 (1907) (state law compelling school attendance applied to Indian children and federal Indian school). In an Alaskan case, *In re Can-ah-couqua*, 29 Fed. 687 (D. C. Alaska, 1887), the question of continued attendance at school was at issue. It is interesting to note that the decision was put on a quasi-contract basis, the Alaska district court holding the mother of the child could not reclaim him from the custody of a Presbyterian mission school because she had agreed to allow him to attend for 5 years, and unless a clear breach or abuse of the child or a failure to educate and provide for and properly superintend its moral training was shown, it would be presumed that the best interests of the child would be served by continuance at school. Contrast with this the accepted view that when a white parent agrees to transfer custody of the child to another not *in loco parentis*, he may ordinarily repudiate that agreement and the courts will return custody to him unless a reciprocal affection has grown up between the custodian and child. The primary concern in these situations is still the best interest of the child, but the courts ordinarily hold that when the parents are alive and competent, it is to the best interest of the child to return him to the parents. *Sandro* v. *Villapiano*, 81 F. 2d 255 (App. D. C. 1936).

[63] Act of June 21, 1906, 34 Stat. 325, 328, 25 U. S. C. 302.

[64] Act of March 3, 1909, 35 Stat. 781, 783; 25 U. S. C. 290.

[65] Act of June 30, 1913, 38 Stat. 77, 96, 25 U. S. C. 285. *Cf.* fns. 54–55, *supra*.

It is no longer the practice to withhold annuities to compel attendance.

[66] Act of February 15, 1929, 45 Stat. 1185, 25 U. S. C. 231.

[67] Act of June 7, 1897, 30 Stat. 62, 79, 25 U. S. C. 278. And see Act of June 10, 1896, 29 Stat. 321, 345.

[68] Act of March 3, 1905, 33 Stat. 1048, 1055.

[69] *Quick Bear* v. *Leupp*, 210 U. S. 50, 80 (1908).

[70] Act of March 2, 1917, 39 Stat. 969, 988, 25 U. S. C. 278.

[71] The Act of June 21, 1906, 34 Stat. 325, 326, 25 U. S. C. 279, provided for receipt of rations by mission schools for children enrolled in such schools who were entitled to rations under treaty stipulations.

[72] See fns. 22–27, fns. 54 and 55, *supra*.

The educational provisions of the Treaty of April 29, *et seq.*, 1868, with the Sioux Tribe of Indians, 15 Stat. 635, formed the basis of a petition filed May 7, 1928, in the Court of Claims, under authority of the Act of June 3, 1920, 41 Stat. 738 (Sioux). The petitioner alleged that treaty provisions for a teacher and schoolhouse for every 30 children were unfulfilled and asked compensatory damages. The court in dismissing the petition held that the treaty imposed an obligation upon the Indian parents to compel attendance which had not been discharged and that, moreover, there existed no logical basis for computing damages. *Sioux Tribe of Indians* v. *United States*, 84 C. Cls. 16 (1936), cert. den. 302 U. S. 740. Other Court of Claims cases concern the possibility of a counterclaim by the United States for gratuitous expenditures for education against Indian tribal claims. The language of pertinent jurisdictional acts on this point varies. *Osage Tribe of Indians* v. *United States*, 66 C. Cls. 64 (1928), app. dism. 279 U. S. 811, 68 C. Cls. 788; *Fort Berthold Indians* v. *United States*, 71 C. Cls. 308 (1930); *Blackfeet et al. Nations* v. *United States*, 81 C. Cls. 101 (1935). *Cf. Chickasaw Nation* v. *United States*, 87 C. Cls. 91 (1938), cert. den. 307 U. S. 646.

[73] Act of April 30, 1908, 35 Stat. 70, 72; Act of June 30, 1919, 41 Stat. 3, 6; Act of February 21, 1925, 43 Stat. 958; 25 U. S. C. 296.

[74] Act of March 2, 1929, 45 Stat. 1534.

[75] Act of April 30, 1908, 35 Stat. 70, 72, 25 U. S. C. 295.

[76] See sec. 6, *infra*.

[77] See Chapter 2.

SECTION 3. HEALTH SERVICES [78]

When the Federal Government assumed the education of Indians, some degree of responsibility for their health was incidentally involved, and the first expenditures for Indian health were made from funds appropriated for education and civilization.[79] Early expenditures for health and medical care were made from tribal funds under treaties and from general appropriations for education or incidentals.[80] These appropriations were allotted among various religious and philanthropic societies already active in educational and missionary work among the various Indian tribes.[81]

While the superintendency of Indian Affairs was under the War Department,[82] the Indians were for the most part in the vicinities of military posts. It was a natural and convenient thing that dispensation of medical care and sanitary regulation be assumed by members of the army medical staff located on the nearby posts.

In 1832, Congress [83] authorized the Secretary of War to provide vaccination against smallpox for the Indians and made an appropriation for that purpose.

In 1849,[84] when the Department of the Interior was established, medical care of the Indian under the Bureau of Indian Affairs passed from military to civil control. Under this department, agency physicians on the reservation at first gave little attention to the Indians and acted more in the capacity of doctors for the government employees, or in connection with Indian schools.[85] Treaties [86] entered into included provisions for physicians and hospitals. In 1878, measures were taken towards furnishing organized medical facilities and an educational and medical division which continued until 1877.[87] By 1874,[88] about one-half of the Indian agencies were each supplied with a physician. After 1878 [89] physicians on Indian reservations were required to be graduates of medical colleges. Between 1880 and 1890,[90] several hospitals were established. In 1909,[91] prevalence of trachoma among the Indians had become so devastating that funds were appropriated for investigation, treatment, and prevention of this disease, and in 1912 [92] money was allotted to the Public Health and Marine Service for a survey of trachoma and tuberculosis.

After 1911,[93] appropriations under the heading "relief of distress and prevention of contagious diseases" were greatly increased and were spent on correspondingly increased medical care and hospital facilities.[94] Since 1921,[95] when the Bureau of Indian Affairs was authorized to expend funds for the conservation of health, funds have been appropriated specifically for that purpose. In 1924, a special division of health was established in the Office of Indian Affairs.

Fees may be charged for medical, dental, and hospital services under such rules and regulations as the Secretary of the Interior may prescribe.[96] Other regulations [97] in force relative to health activities of the Indian Service, briefly summarized, state that health personnel is subject to civil service regulations; physicians may not engage in outside practice; they are responsible for health conditions on the reservation, prevention of diseases and are required to treat and medically instruct Indians at established offices, clinics, or in their homes; they are required to make reports of all contagious diseases, inoculations, immunizations, vital statistics; cooperate with state officials and otherwise enforce necessary quarantine regulations and sanitary inspections; immunize and inoculate against contagious diseases.[98] All admissions and discharges to and from hospitals are upon order of physician. Adults leaving the hospital against the advice of physician in charge must give a written release of all liability to the Indian Service. Parents or guardians must give written permission for hospitalization of a minor or incompetent person and consent for surgical operations must be obtained from

---

[78] For regulations concerning hospital and medical care of Indians, see 25 C. F. R. 84.1–85.15.

[79] See sec. 2, *supra*.

[80] Sen. Ex. Doc. 48th Cong., 2d sess., vol. 2, pt. 2, Special Report of 1888 on Indian Education and Civilization, p. 168.

[81] American Board of Foreign Missions, Moravians, Baptist Board of Foreign Missions, Society of Friends. The reports of religious and educational societies even in prerevolutionary days refer to health and medical care for students. Mass. Hist. Coll., 1st series, vol. I (1792 ed.) p. 173. Regarding two Indian students at Cambridge, Mass. in 1654: "The other called Caleb, not long after took his degree * * * died of a consumption at Charlestown, where he was placed * * * under the care of a physician * * * where he wanted not for the best means the country could afford, both of food and physick * * *." Accounts of the Superintendent of Indian Affairs of 1820–21 include items for medical service and supplies. 8 Am. State Papers (class II, Indian Affairs, vol. 2) 1815–27, p. 299.

[82] Act of May 25, 1824, 4 Stat. 35.

[83] Act of May 5, 1832, 4 Stat. 514. "For vaccine matter and vaccination of Indians" was a regular item in appropriation bills.

[84] Act of March 3, 1849, 9 Stat. 395.

[85] Speech of Dr. James Townsend before Western Branch, American Public Health Ass'n., July 24, 1939, "Government and Indian Health."

[86] Treaty of January 22, 1855, with the Dwamish, etc., Indians, 12 Stat. 927, 929; Treaty of January 26, 1855, with the S'Klallam Indians, 12 Stat, 933, 935; Treaty of January 31, 1855, with the Makahs, 12 Stat. 939, 941; Treaty of June 9, 1855, with the Walla-Wallas, Cayuses, and Umatilla Bands, 12 Stat. 945, 947; Treaty of June 9, 1855, with the Yakama Nation, 12 Stat. 951, 953; Treaty of June 11, 1855, with the Nez Perce Indians, 12 Stat. 957, 959; Treaty of June 25, 1855, with the Indians in Middle Oregon, 12 Stat. 963, 965; Treaty of July 1, 1855, and January 25, 1856, with the Qui-nai-elts and Quil-leh-ute, 12 Stat. 971, 973; Treaty of July 16, 1855, with the Flatheads, etc., 12 Stat. 975, 977; Treaty of October 21, 1867, with the Kiowa and Comanche Tribes, 15 Stat. 581, 584; Treaty of October 28, 1867, with the Cheyenne and Arapahoe Tribes, 15 Stat. 593, 597; Treaty of April 29, 1868, *et. seq.*, with the Sioux, 15 Stat.. 635, 638; Treaty of May 7, 1868, with the Crow Tribe, 15 Stat. 649, 652; Treaty of May 10, 1868, with the Northern Cheyenne and Arapahoe Tribes, 15 Stat. 655, 658; Treaty of July 3, 1868, with the Eastern Band of Shoshones and Bannock Tribe, 15 State. 673, 676.

[87] Sen. Ex. Doc., 48th Cong., 2d sess., vol. 2, pt. 2, Special Report of 1888 on Indian Education and Civilization, p. 168. Annual Report of the Commissioner of Indian Affairs, 1885, p. LXXVI.

[88] Speech of Dr. Townsend, *op. cit.*,

[89] *Ibid.*

[90] Annual Reports of the Commissioner of Indian Affairs, 1887, pp. 227, 264; 1888, p. XXXV.

[91] Act of February 20, 1909, 35 Stat. 642.

[92] Act of August 24, 1912, 37 Stat. 518, 519.

[93] Act of March 3, 1911, 36 Stat. 1058.

[94] Specific appropriations for health work among Indians: 1911, $40,000; 1912, $60,000; 1913, $90,000; 1914, $200,000; 1915, $300,000; 1916, $300,000; 1917, $350,000; 1918, $350,000; 1919, $350,000; 1920, $375,000; 1921, $350,000; 1922, $375,000; 1923, $370,000; 1924, $370,000; 1925, $596,270; 1926, $700,000; 1927, $756,000; 1928, $948,000; 1929, $1,514,000; 1930, $2,658,000; 1931, $3,074,110; 1932, $4,050,000; 1933, $3,213,000; 1934, $2,996,200; 1935, $2,981,040; 1936, $3,534,620; 1937, $4,062,360; 1938, $4,595,690; 1939, $5,024,000; 1940, $5,088,170. See appropriation acts listed in Chapter 4.

[95] Act of November 2, 1921, 42 Stat. 208, 25 U. S. C. 13.

[96] Act of May 9, 1938, 52 Stat. 291, 312, 25 U. S. C. 562.

[97] 25 C. F. R. 84.1–85.15. Regulations apply to tribes organized pursuant to the Reorganization Act of June 18, 1934, 48 Stat. 984, amended, Act of June 15, 1935, 49 Stat. 378, and the Oklahoma Welfare Act of June 26, 1936, 49 Stat. 1967, 25 U. S. C. 500, 501, except where inconsistent with tribal constitutions or bylaws. In case of conflict, tribal law provisions supersede regulations.

[98] Act of August 1, 1914, 38 Stat. 582, 584, 25 U. S. C. 198.

the patient, if an adult; if a minor or incompetent, from parents or guardians.[99]

Under regulations[100] relating to hospitals, indigent Indians recognized as tribal members are admitted without cost. In tribal hospitals supported by tribal funds, all tribal members are entitled to free hospitalization. Priority of admission is based on necessity for hospitalization and degree of Indian blood. White wives of Indians, Indian children from Government schools, Indian widows of whites or of nonrestricted Indians, if residing on reservations, are eligible for admission. Indian wives and children of white men are not admitted unless residents on reservations and participants in tribal affairs.

Indians as citizens of the states in which they reside frequently claim and sometimes obtain the public health protection of the various states. To facilitate cooperation between the state and Federal Government, the Secretary of the Interior in 1929[101] was authorized to permit agents and employees of any state to enter on tribal land, reservation, or allotment therein for the purpose of making inspections of health and enforcing sanitation and quarantine regulations

In 1934, the Johnson-O'Malley Act[102] became law and provided that the Secretary of the Interior might enter into contracts with states or territories for medical attention to Indians.

In 1935, under the Social Security Act, increased health benefits were made available to the Indians.[103]

In 1936,[104] the President, by Executive order, provided that officials and employees of the Indian Service serving in a medical or sanitary capacity could hold state, county, or municipal positions of similar character without additional compensation, with the consent of the Secretary of the Interior.

In the enforcement of public health regulations the Secretary of the Interior has been authorized to impose quarantine and when necessary to confine persons afflicted with infectious diseases.[105]

99 25 C. F. R. 84, 85.

100 *Ibid.*

101 Act of February 15, 1929, 45 Stat. 1185, 25 U. S. C. 231.

102 Act of April 16, 1934, 48 Stat. 596, amended June 4, 1936, 49 Stat. 1458, 25 U. S. C. 452–454.

103 See sec. 5 of this Chapter.

104 Executive Order 7369, May 13, 1936.

105 Act of August 1, 1914, 38 Stat. 582, 584.

Care of insane Indians has for many years been considered within the powers of the Secretary.[106] Payment for their care is made to various hospitals for the insane including St. Elizabeths Hospital in the District of Columbia, which is a federal institution.[107]

Commitment of an Indian to a hospital for the insane requires a sanity hearing to insure due process.[108] The laws of the states where reservations are located are conformed to in the commitment of insane Indians to state mental hospitals or state institutions for the insane. An insane Indian residing on an Indian reservation under the jurisdiction of the United States may be committed to St. Elizabeths Hospital by order of the Secretary of the Interior. A certificate of insanity made by two reputable physicians who have conducted an examination of the Indian is required before issuance of an order of the Secretary. Notice of the time and place of such examination must be personally served upon the alleged insane Indian, the spouse, parent, or other next of kin known to be residing on the reservation. The Indian alleged to be insane has the right to present witnesses and to submit evidence of his sanity.[109]

In any case in which an Indian is alleged to be insane or of unsound mind, and such Indian has displayed homicidal tendencies or has otherwise demonstrated that if permitted to remain at large or to go unrestrained, the rights of persons and of property will be jeopardized or the preservation of the public peace imperiled and the commission of crime rendered probable, the superintendent has authority to take such Indian into custody and to detain him temporarily in some suitable place pending proper legal adjudication of his insanity.

106 25 U. S. C. 13, derived from Act of November 2, 1921, 42 Stat. 208, grants the Bureau of Indian Affairs power to expend money for relief of distress and conservation of health.

107 Act of April 28, 1904, 33 Stat. 589, directs that insane Indians in Indian Territory be cared for at the asylum for insane Indians at Canton, S. Dak. The Appropriation Act of May 10, 1939, 53 Stat. 685, 736, provides for the admission to St. Elizabeths Hospital of "insane Indian beneficaries of the Bureau of Indian Affairs."

108 *Cf. Barry* v. *Hall*, 98 F. 2d 222 (App. D. C., 1938). This case requires all persons admitted to St. Elizabeths Hospital to have been determined insane upon hearing with an opportunity for defense. Memo. Sol. I. D., July 27, 1939.

109 25 C. F. R. 84.

SECTION 4. RATIONS, RELIEF, AND REHABILITATION

The common belief that Indians, as such, receive rations from the Federal Government is not in accord with the facts.[110]

As noted in the introduction to this chapter, frequently in sales of Indian land[111] supplies were used instead of cash as the *quid pro quo* offered to compensate the Indian for value received by the United States. Later, as the Indians advanced sufficiently in the knowledge of white man's civilization to purchase their own supplies and clothing, the value of promised supplies was frequently commuted and paid in money per capita to the members of various tribes.[112]

As a matter of hospitality, a law[113] authorizing food for Indians visiting at army posts has remained on the statute book for over a hundred years. Relief, frequently dispensed in the form of food, has been authorized in general appropriations[114] for indigent Indians. The charitable nature of these limited appropriations, however, has been mistakenly attributed generally to all provisions relating to rations. The failure to recognize that issuance of rations may be a form of payment of obligations to Indians resulted in the provision in the Act of March 3, 1875,[115] that able-bodied male Indians give service and labor in return for supplies distributed to them.

At the present time, when relief is given in the form of food and supplies, labor is required of recipients of relief rations wherever possible. Such rations may not be sold or exchanged. They can be shared only with dependents of the recipients.[116]

Under recent appropriation acts[117] tribal funds have been made available for relief purposes.

110 25 C. F. R. 251.1. Also see 251.2–251.8.

111 For example, see treaties of February 19, 1867, with the Sisseton and Warpeton, 15 Stat. 505; October 21, 1867, with the Kiowa and Comanche, 15 Stat. 581; May 7, 1868, with the Crow, 15 Stat. 649.

112 Act of July 1, 1898, 30 Stat. 571, 596, 25 U. S. C. 186.

113 Act of May 13, 1800, 2 Stat. 85; R. S. § 2110, 25 U. S. C. 141.

114 See appropriation acts, Chapter 4.

115 18 Stat. 420, 449, 25 U. S. C. 137.

116 25 C. F. R. 251.2, 251.3.

117 Act of May 9, 1938, 52 Stat. 291, 314. Tribal funds are appropriated for relief of Indians, "in need of assistance, including cash grants; the purchase of subsistence supplies * * * and household goods; * * * transportation, and all other necessary expenses, $100,000, payable from funds on deposit to the credit of the particular tribe concerned."

Allotments are made to the superintendents of the various agencies for the relief of indigent Indians under their supervision. These allotments are spent chiefly for supplies, food, and clothing;[118] a limited amount being spent also for work relief and for subsistence grants when unusual circumstances warrant such procedure. Rarely is relief given in the form of cash.

A chief object of recent rehabilitation work has been to provide landless Indians with land, houses, outbuildings, fencing, water supply, etc., so that with equipment and livestock provided from other sources they may be enabled to work the land in a self-supporting manner.[119] Aid to individual Indians in this field has generally taken the form of loans rather than grants, and is therefore considered under section 6 of this Chapter.

[118] Relief situations are often of an emergency nature and purchases for relief dispensation are permitted without usual advertisement required by R. S. § 3709. Compliance is apparently required with the provisions of the Act of May 27, 1930, 46 Stat. 391, requiring purchases of shoes or other articles available from prison manufacture to be made through the Federal Prison Industries, Inc.—Hearings, H. Subcomm. of Comm. on Appropriations, Interior Dept., 76th Cong., 3d sess., pt. II, p. 502.

[119] *Ibid.* The National Resources Board, as the result of a survey of Indian homes in 1935, has reported that some 70 percent of Indian dwellings are probably below a reasonable living standard.

SECTION 5. SOCIAL SECURITY BENEFITS

In 1936[120] the Solicitor of the Interior Department rendered an opinion which held that the Social Security Act[121] was applicable to the Indians. The act contemplates three types of direct aid by states in cooperation with the Government to their needy citizens, that is, aid to needy aged individuals, to needy dependent children, and to needy individuals who are blind.

In connection with these three types of direct aid, it was determined that as a state plan must be "in effect in all political subdivisions of the State," and as Indian reservations are included within states, counties, and other political subdivisions, Indians are entitled to aid under state plans.

Other provisions of the Social Security Act provide federal assistance in the care of crippled children, maternal health service and public health service, special attention being given to rural areas and areas suffering from severe economic distress. One of the bases for allotment of federal funds was population of states. Statistics relating to population included Indians. Their inclusion in the compilation would seem to prohibit any implication that Indians were to be deprived of the benefits of the act. To quote the Solicitor,

> In computing these statistics no omission is made of the Indians and official registration and census rolls have been used which, of course, include the Indian population. It would be manifestly contrary to the intention of the act that funds allotted to cover a certain number of people should be used only for a chosen group to the exclusion of others included in the count.

Furthermore it was held that, as citizens, Indians were entitled to social security benefits, all Indians who were not already citizens having become so by the Act of June 2, 1924.[122]

In view of these considerations, the Solicitor held that no distinction is justified between the Indian and other state citizens, and that the law requires that social security benefits be distributed without discrimination against the Indians.

According to Dr. James Townsend,[123] Director of Health, Office of Indian Affairs, most states are actively assisting in the application of the Social Security Act to Indians, others are assisting to a lesser degree, and still others resist expenditure of state and local funds for Indians, even to the point of failure to accept Indian applications.

[120] Memo. Sol. I. D., April 22, 1936.

[121] Act of August 14, 1935, 49 Stat. 620.

[122] 43 Stat. 253. See Chapter 8, sec. 2.

[123] Speech by Dr. Townsend, *op. cit.*

SECTION 6. FEDERAL LOANS

Loans advanced by the Federal Government to the Indians are financed from gratuity appropriations,[124] appropriations from tribal funds,[125] and revolving credit funds established under the Indian Reorganization Act[126] and the Oklahoma Welfare Act.[127] The Klamath Indians may borrow from a revolving credit fund specifically set up for that tribe.[128]

In addition, loans and grants have been made available to the tribe and their members under emergency relief appropriation acts beginning in 1935 for financing rehabilitation of families in stricken agricultural areas.[129] It is also possible for Indian tribes to borrow from other federal agencies funds appropriated for such purposes in promotion of the general welfare of the nation as low-rent housing development, when the tribes meet the eligibility requirements of the controlling federal legislation.[130]

A. LOANS UNDER SPECIAL INDIAN LEGISLATION

Since 1912, Congress has appropriated[131] gratuity funds for reimbursable loans direct from the Government to individual Indians. Prior to 1938 loans were made in the form of property, but since that year Indians have received cash loans. These loans were designed to establish Indians in self-supporting individual enterprises including farming, stock raising, and other industries. Loans have been granted also to assist old and indigent Indians who have land they cannot use.

A limited number of qualified Indians are able to obtain loans from gratuity and tribal funds for educational purposes, for payment of tuition, and other expenses in recognized vocational and trade schools.[132]

Recipients of loans from gratuity funds are for the most part members of tribes not organized under the Indian Reorganization Act,[133] who therefore are not eligible to borrow funds under that act. With the exception of members of the Osage Tribe, loans from gratuity funds are not made to residents of the State of Oklahoma.

Congress has also made available for loans to the members of certain tribes a part of their tribal funds. These are handled as tribal revolving credit funds under which loans are made to

[124] 25 U. S. C. 13; annual appropriation acts.

[125] 25 U. S. C. 123; annual appropriation acts.

[126] Act of June 18, 1934, sec. 10, 48 Stat. 984, 986, 25 U. S. C. 470.

[127] Act of June 26, 1936, sec. 6, 49 Stat. 1967, 1968, 25 U. S. C. 506.

[128] Act of August 28, 1937, 50 Stat. 872.

[129] See subsection B, *infra*.

[130] See subsection B, *infra*.

[131] 25 U. S. C. 13, 123. And see annual appropriation acts. Chapter 4.

[132] Hearings, H. Subcomm. of Comm. on Appropriations, Interior Dept., 76th Cong. 3d sess., pt. II, p. 175.

[133] Act of June 18, 1934, 48 Stat. 984, 986, 25 U. S. C. 470. Under sec. 11 of the Indian Reorganization Act similar provisions are made for loans for educational purposes.

individual Indians whose repayments are returned to the fund and are available for further loans.[134]

Under the Act of May 10, 1939,[135] Congress authorized transfer of tribal revolving funds to the revolving credit funds of organized tribes to supplement credit funds and to be administered under the rules and regulations applicable thereto. In the case of organized tribes, tribal consent is necessary to authorise use of tribal funds for loans or other purposes.[136]

Federal credit to the Indians was greatly extended by the establishment of revolving credit funds under the Acts of June 18, 1934,[137] and June 26, 1936.[138] These statutes authorized the establishment of a revolving fund totaling $12,000,000, from which the Secretary of the Interior may make loans to incorporated tribes, and in the State of Oklahoma to cooperatives,[139] credit associations,[140] and individuals[141] for economic development. Loans as repaid are credited to the revolving fund and reports are made annually to Congress of transactions under this authorization.

Regulations governing loans from revolving credit funds to a tribal corporation, cooperative, credit association, or an individual provide that the tribal application must be accompanied by an economic program.[142] Security or other guarantee of repayment, terms of payment, and plans for managing credit operations must be included in the application. Upon approval of the application a commitment order covering the terms and conditions for making advances of funds is prepared. Any changes to be made in the application or any additional conditions are incorporated in the commitment order, which is then returned to the applicant for acceptance. Advances are made contingent upon accomplishment of certain features of the program. Failure to carry out these provisions is ground for refusing further advances. The tribe, if the loan contract so provides, may relend funds to individuals, partnerships, and to cooperatives, and may use funds for the development and operation of corporate (tribal) enterprises. Credit associations may lend only to individuals.[143]

Definite plans for the use of funds likewise are required of any individual or association of individuals borrowing from the tribe or credit association. These loans may not extend for a greater period than the duration of the agreement of the tribe or credit association with the government. This period varies, ranging from short-term crop loans and intermediate-term loans for livestock products, to long-term loans for permanent improvements. Loans for permanent improvements are made only in exceptional circumstances, preference being given to income-producing enterprises. As a matter of policy loans are not made for land purchases under the revolving fund except in very unusual cases and then in small amounts.[144]

Final approval of all loans made by corporations, or credit associations, is vested in representatives of the Indian Service at the present time.

[134] See for example 25 C. F. R. 28.1–28.56, governing administration of Klamath Tribal Loan Fund, created by Act of August 28, 1937, 50 Stat. 872, 25 U. S. C. 530–535.

[135] Public Act No. 68, 76th Cong., 1st sess.

[136] Act of June 18, 1934, sec. 16, 48 Stat. 984, 987, 25 U. S. C. 476, giving such tribe power to veto unauthorized use of tribal assets. And see Memo. Sol. I. D. October 18, 1932.

[137] Sec. 10, 48 Stat. 984, 986, 25 U. S. C. 470. For regulations governing loans to Indian chartered corporations, see 25 C. F. R. 21.1–21.49.

[138] 49 Stat. 1967.

[139] For regulations governing loans to Indian cooperatives in Oklahoma, see 25 C. F. R. 23.1–23.27.

[140] See *ibid.*, 24.1–24.15. For regulations governing loans by Indian credit associations in Oklahoma, see 25 C. F. R. 25.1–25.26.

[141] For regulations governing loans by the United States to individual Indians in Oklahoma, see *ibid.*, 26.1–26.26.

[142] 25 C. F. R., subchapter E.

[143] *Ibid.*

[144] *Ibid.*, part 27.

Legislation authorizing revolving credit fund loans to incorporated tribes has been construed in the light of the avowed purpose of increasing tribal control over tribal resources.

In discussing this legislation the Solicitor of the Interior Department[145] pointed out:

> Money from the revolving credit fund may not be loaned to individual Indians directly. In relation to this fund the Secretary of the Interior can deal only with the tribal corporations representing the interests of all the Indians who are members of the tribes. In this respect the loans contemplated * * * are in distinct contrast to those heretofore authorized by Congress. Under reimbursable appropriations loans have been made to the Indians for designated purposes, * * * are carried on by the Government with individual Indians. * * * The tribal bodies, where such exist, have no responsibility in the administration of such funds.

Under section 10 of the Wheeler-Howard Act,[146] governing the revolving credit fund the Government can deal only with the tribal authorities, and these are charged with the responsibility for making such loans to their members, or for using the funds in such ways as will enable them to create a basis for expanding self-sufficiency. In accordance with the purpose expressed in sections 16 and 17 of the act, by which a large and increasing responsibility for taking care of their own welfare is placed upon the various tribes, organized for local self-government and economic activity, section 10 contemplates that funds loaned to the tribes will be, in large measure, subject to their disposition, consistent with the terms of said provision.

This section was construed by the Solicitor:

> Under section 10 the Secretary of the Interior may determine the conditions upon which he will make loans to Indian corporations. He may prescribe such rules and regulations as are reasonably appropriate to this purpose. He may require reasonable guarantees by the borrowing corporation that the money loaned to it will be used for specified purposes and handled in specified ways. If the Secretary is to exercise any control over money already loaned to the corporation it must be a control which is authorized by mutual agreement, and is designed to enforce the terms of such agreement. The strictly regulatory power of the Secretary, conferred by section 10, ceases when the loan to the tribe is completed. Thereafter the powers of the Department are limited to enforcement of the terms of the tribal loan agreement. The Indian corporation, upon which responsibility is placed for the repayment of the loan, may properly expect, under the terms of section 10, that moneys will not be disbursed to individual members of the tribe in the discretion of the Interior Department, on behalf of the corporation, but that the money will actually be loaned to the corporation to be used or disbursed by the duly elected officers of the corporation in accordance with the terms of a loan agreement and in accordance with the mandates given these officers in tribal constitutions, bylaws and charters.[147]

In view of these purposes, the Solicitor of the Interior Department held, any arrangement placing upon Indian Service officials primary responsibility for the administration of loans from the tribe to the individual would be " a serious invasion of tribal responsibility and initiative" and would "nullify in large measure the promises contained in other sections of the Act." Equally inconsistent with the purposes of the act and with the terms of constitutions and charters adopted thereunder, the Solicitor held, would be any arrangement whereby the tribal authorities administering such loans were subjected to the control of Indian Service officials. Any such arrangement would constitute an assumption of "political control of matters internal to the tribe."

[145] Memo. Sol. I. D., December 5, 1935.

[146] Act of June 18, 1934, 48 Stat. 984, 986, 25 U. S. C. 470.

[147] Memo. Sol. I. D., December 5, 1935.

Safeguards against improper disposition of funds by the borrowing tribe must be set forth in the loan agreements between the tribe and the Secretary of the Interior.[148]

The Oklahoma Welfare Act[149] made funds appropriated for loans under the Indian Reorganization Act available for loans to Oklahoma tribes, individual Indians, and cooperatives for land management, credit, administration, consumers' protection, production, and marketing purposes. The act also authorized additional appropriations of an additional $2,000,000 for loans.

The benefit of the revolving credit fund was extended to Alaska by the Act of May 1, 1936.[150]

B. LOANS UNDER GENERAL LEGISLATION

Under various acts making appropriations for rural rehabilitation, and relief,[151] Indians, like other citizens, have received loans and grants. At the same time certain Indian tribes have undertaken to handle their own rehabilitation and relief problems, with federal aid. Thus funds for rehabilitation were granted to various tribes under agreements[152] executed by the Commissioner of Indian Affairs for, and on behalf of, the United States. Agreements on behalf of organized tribes are signed by tribal officers. Unorganized tribes are represented by trustees. Submission of programs approved by such officers or trustees is required as a condition precedent to the execution of a trust agreement. The funds may be set up by the tribe as a revolving fund and money may be advanced by the tribe to individual Indians, all contracts with individuals being executed by the tribes.

In some cases the tribe, instead of loaning money, uses rehabilitation funds to improve tribal land, and then assigns the use of the land to members. Improvements on tribal land remain the property of the tribe, individual Indians paying fees for the use of the improvements. These payments are, in most cases, to be collected until the original value, or partial value at least, of the improvement has been collected. Payments are placed in a tribal revolving fund.

Property improved under rehabilitation loans is ordinarily held under revocable assignments, subject to revocation upon failure to pay. The assignee may ordinarily designate a successor subject to joint approval of the tribal officers or trustees and superintendent.

Another phase of rehabilitation involves self-help projects. Money is advanced to the tribes for community buildings, in which Indians are engaged in sewing, canning, weaving, and handicrafts. Machine sheds, storehouses, shearing sheds, smithies, shops, grist mills, tanneries have been constructed. Water development and irrigation projects have been financed. Frequently materials are supplied at tribal expense and the workers are paid wages, the products being property of the tribe. By these activities not only have numerous Indian workers received wages but thousands of Indian families have been more adequately fed and clothed.[153]

The tribal programs of rehabilitation were first financed out of appropriations under the Joint Resolution of April 8, 1935,[154] allocated to the Office of Indian Affairs by a Presidential letter of January 11, 1936.[155] This work was continued under the Emergency Relief Acts of 1937[156] and 1938.[157] The Emergency Relief Appropriation Act of 1939[158] made a special appropriation direct to the Office of Indian Affairs.

Those Indians whose needs are not met by the tribal rehabilitation program are entitled to treatment on a parity with other citizens when they apply to the Farm Security Administration for individual rehabilitation loans.[159]

Under the same principle that prompted the holding that individual Indians are eligible to receive assistance under the Social Security Act and from the Farm Security Administration for rehabilitation loans,[160] Indian tribes are eligible to apply for loans under such legislation for the general welfare as that

---

[148] *Ibid.* In this memorandum the Solicitor declared:

> * * * If the loan agreement is to be regarded as a contract, observance of which by the corporation is a prerequisite to the obtaining and the continued use of funds from the revolving fund, then such contract should be equally binding on the Government. The Secretary of the Interior has no authority, under the power to make rules and regulations contained in section 10 of the Act, to require that the Indians shall observe such agreements on pain of drastic penalties, while the Government is free to change its policies in such ways as it deems best, and to force new terms upon the Indians which were not included in the original agreements. Such an illusory agreement is clearly not justified as a matter of law.
>
> I believe that the rules and regulations should state clearly the minimum terms and conditions which must be inserted in every agreement for a loan from the revolving fund, and further that this agreement should be binding, not only upon the Indians, but also upon the Government. If the Secretary of the Interior and the Indians of a particular tribe agree upon a credit program and upon plans for the economic development of such tribe, and of its members, I do not believe that a subsequent Secretary should have the power at a later date to change the terms of that agreement.

[149] Act of June 26, 1936, 49 Stat. 1967, 25 U. S. C. *et seq.* For regulations governing loans by United States to individual Indians in Oklahoma, see 25 C. F. R. 26.1–26.26.

[150] 49 Stat. 1250, 48 U. S. C. See Chapter 21, sec. 9.

[151] Joint Resolution of April 8, 1935, 49 Stat. 115; Joint Resolution of June 29, 1937, 50 Stat. 352; Joint Resolution of June 21, 1938, 52 Stat. 809.

[152] Under these agreements, the United States grants to the tribe all of the allocation of emergency funds required to cover the cost of the approved projects, excepting such part of the cost as represents necessary administrative and supervisory expenses. The grant is made subject to the condition that it will be used for approved objects.

[153] Hearings H. Subcomm. of Comm. on Appropriations, Interior Dept., 76th Cong., 3d sess., pt. II, p. 461.

[154] 49 Stat. 115. This act appropriated for rural rehabilitation and relief of stricken agricultural areas.

[155] Presidential letter No. 1323, January 11, 1936.

[156] Joint Resolution of June 29, 1937, 50 Stat. 352, 353. This act appropriated for expenditure by the Resettlement Administration for rehabilitation of needy persons as the President may direct.

[157] Joint Resolution of June 21, 1938, 52 Stat. 809. Under this act only Indians are eligible to positions on Indian work relief projects until these needs have been met. Memo. Sol. I. D., December 18, 1938.

[158] Public Res. No. 24, 76th Cong., 1st sess., 252.

> SEC. 5. (a) In order to continue to provide relief and rural rehabilitation for needy Indians in the United States, there is hereby appropriated to the Bureau of Indian Affairs, Department of the Interior, out of any money in the Treasury not otherwise appropriated for the fiscal year ending June 30, 1940, $1,350,000.
>
> (b) The funds provided in this section shall be available for (1) administration, not to exceed $67,500; (2) loans; (3) relief; (4) the prosecution of projects approved by the President for the Farm Security Administration for the benefit of Indians under the provisions of the Emergency Relief Appropriation Act of 1938; and (5) subject to the approval of the President, for projects involving rural rehabilitation of needy Indians.

[159] The argument that Indians should be excluded from benefits available to other needy persons under the appropriations to the Farm Security Administration, because of the special appropriation to the Office of Indian Affairs, was considered and rejected by the Solicitor for the Department of Agriculture, in view of the ruling of the Solicitor for the Interior Department that the appropriation to the Office of Indian Affairs

> * * * should be narrowly construed in such a manner as to limit expenditures by the Indian Service to those purposes for which expenditures were made during the fiscal year 1939 out of the fund transferred in that year to the Indian Service by the Farm Security Administration. These purposes are, in substance: (1) grants to Indian tribes for the benefit of Indians through a program of tribal or community projects for the construction of buildings and other tribal and community enterprises; and (2) administrative expenses, loans, and relief payments incidental to the foregoing primary purpose or otherwise affecting Indians who are ineligible to receive benefits under section 3 of the act. (Memo. Sol. I. D., December 14, 1939.)

The Solicitor for the Department of Agriculture thereupon ruled:

> * * * there is no occasion for applying the rule that an appropriation for a specific purpose cannot be augmented by the use of funds appropriated in more general terms. * * * funds appropriated to that [Farm Security] Administration under the current [Emergency] Relief Act [of 1939] may be used for loans and grants to Indians, except those Indians who are receiving aid directly from the Indian Office under Section 5 of the Act. (Letter Sol. Dept. of Agriculture, December 22, 1939.)

[160] See secs. 5 and 6, *supra*.

providing for low-rent housing development, when they are otherwise qualified under the terms of the legislation. The United States Housing Act of 1937[161] authorizes loans to "public housing agencies," which are defined to include a "governmental entity or public body * * * which is authorized to engage in the development or administration of low-rent housing or slum clearance."[162] In an opinion of the Solicitor,[163] the Interior Department has held that Indian tribes are governmental entities capable of undertaking housing enterprises and that, where a tribe is incorporated under the Act of June 18, 1934,[164] it may be said to be authorized to engage in the low-rent housing and slum clearance projects contemplated by the United States Housing Act of 1937 and it is, therefore, eligible to apply for a loan under that act.

[161] Act of September 1, 1937, 50 Stat. 888, 42 U. S. C. chap. 8.
[162] Sec. 2 (11), Act of September 1, 1937, 50 Stat. 888.
[163] Op. Sol. I. D., M. 30807, August 6, 1940.
[164] 48 Stat. 984.

SECTION 7. RECLAMATION AND IRRIGATION

Evidence of ancient irrigation works abounds in the more arid regions of the western part of the United States, indicating that irrigation was practiced by the Indian in prehistoric times. Without irrigation, much of this land is unproductive and unsuited to human life. When Indian reservations were established in this country, the Federal Government, in order to make it possible for the Indian to become self-supporting, embarked on a program of irrigation development.[165]

At the present time, the Irrigation Division of the Bureau of Indian Affairs is responsible for the administration of over 100 individual irrigation projects embracing approximately 1,250,000 acres, of which some 800,000 acres are under constructed works. The total investment in these projects exceeds $51,000,000. The area under constructed works is being increased each year. The annual operation and maintenance expenditures average about $1,500,000, and the construction expenditures vary from $3,000,000 to $7,000,000 annually.[166]

The field administration is handled from four offices: The assistant director's office in Los Angeles; the supervising engineer's offices in San Francisco and Billings, and a district office in Oklahoma City. There is also maintained a chief counsel's office in Los Angeles and a district counsel's office in Billings. On each of the projects a local operating force is maintained.[167]

Until 1902[168] irrigation construction, maintenance, and operation were carried on under the direction of the reservation superintendents, with occasional assistance from local engineers temporarily employed.

In 1906,[169] a chief engineer was appointed and gradually since that time a technical staff and organization has been developed to supervise and carry on Indian irrigation.

In 1907,[170] a plan contemplating close cooperation between the Bureau of Reclamation and the Indian Service was formulated. Some of the Indian projects were transferred to the Bureau of Reclamation. Under this agreement construction was carried on by the Reclamation Service on the Flathead, Fort Peck, and Blackfeet projects in Montana and on the Pima and Yuma reservations in Arizona. In 1924,[171] these projects were returned to the Indian Service. In the past few years the Bureau of Reclamation and the Office of Indian Affairs frequently have cooperated on engineering features of various irrigation projects.

The irrigable land on Indian reservations in the Northwest, in almost every instance, is allotted. In the Southwest a few allotments of irrigable land have been made, but on most of the reservations in that area the Indians occupy and use certain small tracts so long as the individual makes beneficial use of the land and irrigation facilities, the ownership remaining in a tribal status. This condition applies to practically all the projects in the Navajo and Hopi country and also to the Pueblo projects.

In the North and Northwest the allotments range from 20 acres to 80 acres, the average being about 40 acres of irrigable land per individual. The southern projects are subdivided into small tracts, the majority being about 10 acres. In areas where fruit or garden is the prevailing crop, individual tracts are frequently as small as 2 acres.[172]

In addition to construction, operation, and maintenance of systems of canals and ditches, the Indian irrigation service has supervised the construction and operation and maintenance of numerous drainage systems, pumping plants, storage and flood control dams, and miscellaneous irrigation developments in connection with subsistence gardens or homesteads. Hydroelectric and Diesel engine power generating plants[173] have been constructed in some instances with transmission lines supplying power to neighboring communities, factories, farms, and mining operations.

The government's first venture in irrigation construction in 1867[174] was provided for by an appropriation of $50,000 for the "expense of collecting and locating the Colorado River Indians in Arizona * * * including the expense of constructing a canal for irrigating said reservation." The work was finally completed, under supplementary appropriations,[175] only to be abandoned, however, after several unsuccessful attempts at operation and maintenance. In 1884,[176] a general appropriation of $50,000 for irrigation was to be spent for irrigation in the discretion of the Secretary of the Interior. A similar appropriation followed in 1892,[177] and beginning with 1893,[178] Congress annually made general appropriations[179] under the description "Irrigation, Indian Reservations" for use on such reservations or for such purposes as were not provided for by specific appropriation. By the Act of April 4, 1910,[180] no new irrigation project on any Indian reservation or land could be undertaken without

[165] The extent to which water rights have been reserved is considered in Chapter 15.
[166] Annual statement of "Costs, Cancellations, and Miscellaneous Irrigation Data of Indian Irrigation Projects, Fiscal year 1939," Interior Department.
[167] *Ibid.*
[168] By the Act of June 17, 1902, 32 Stat. 388, the Secretary was authorized to contract for construction of projects.
[169] Act of June 21, 1906, 34 Stat. 386.
[170] Hearings, Sen. Subcomm. of Comm. on Ind. Aff., Survey of Conditions of the Indians in the United States, 71st Cong., 2d sess., pt. 6, Engle report. January 21, 1930, p. 2259.
[171] Act of June 5, 1924, 43 Stat. 390, 402.
[172] Data to support Request for Public Works Funds, The Indian Service, August 31, 1933.
[173] San Carlos Project. See subsec. I, *infra*.
[174] Act of March 2, 1867, 14 Stat. 492, 514.
[175] Act of July 27, 1868, 15 Stat. 198, 222; Act of May 29, 1872, 17 Stat. 165, 188.
[176] Act of July 4, 1884, 23 Stat. 76, 94.
[177] Act of July 13, 1892, 27 Stat. 120, 137.
[178] Act of March 3, 1893, 27 Stat. 612, 631.
[179] Appropriation acts: Act of March 2, 1867, 14 Stat. 492, 514; Act of July 27, 1868, 15 Stat. 198, 222; Act of May 29, 1872, 17 Stat. 165, 188; Act of July 4, 1884, 23 Stat. 76, 94; Act of March 3, 1891, 26 Stat. 989, 1011.
[180] 36 Stat. 269, 270, 272, 25 U. S. C. 388.

express authorization by Congress upon presentation of an estimate of the cost of the work to be constructed.

Basic authorization for expenditures for irrigation purposes was conferred by the Act of November 2, 1921.[181] After 1933, emergency funds were allocated for irrigation purposes.

For projects involving a large expenditure from the United States Treasury or from tribal funds and benefiting, in many instances, both white and Indian water users, it has been customary for Congress to pass special acts of authorization.[182] For the most part reimbursement was provided for by these special acts.

Until 1914,[183] costs of irrigation work on Indian reservations under general appropriations since 1884 were borne by the United States. Appropriations for this purpose were considered gratuities. Also, until that year, projects reimbursable from tribal funds were operated on the theory that irrigation conferred collective tribal benefit. In effect, all members of the tribe were required to pay an equal part of the cost regardless of whether or not their lands were irrigated.

By the Act of August 1, 1914,[184] Congress changed its legislative policy as to reimbursable appropriations for specific projects, and thereafter required reimbursement of construction charges on the basis of individual benefits received. It provided also for reimbursement, under the direction of the Secretary of the Interior, of general appropriations, hitherto considered as gratuities and gifts. Maintenance and operation charges were to be fixed upon the same basis.

Enforcement of this act proved difficult. One reason given was that computation of construction charges was impossible in the uncompleted state of numerous projects.[185] Furthermore, reimbursement in the discretion of the Secretary of the Interior by the Act of August 1, 1914, was made dependent upon ability of the Indians to pay assessments. In 1920,[186] when Congress made it mandatory that the Secretary of the Interior begin to enforce at least partial reimbursement, the retroactive provision of the reimbursement act was strenuously opposed. Some of the projects included ceded tribal lands which had been appraised and open to entry, the entryman paying the appraised price which apparently included water rights. Numerous individual allotments had been sold under Indian agency advertisements with the understanding that water rights were included in the conveyance. An opinion by the Attorney General[187] held that reimbursement could not be enforced where vested rights had been acquired. Regulations[188] were issued requiring that in all future contracts for the purchase of Indian allotments, the purchaser assume accrued irrigation charges and undertake to pay future charges until the total assessable costs had been paid. Likewise many Indians had received fee patents containing affirmations that their lands were free of all encumbrances and these lands later had been sold under warranty deed. The Solicitor of the Department of the Interior[189] held that where no specific lien was created by act of Congress for repayment of irrigation charges, the obligation was personal against the individual Indian and the land was not subject to construction charges accrued prior to the issuance of the fee patent.

Unpaid charges were made liens on the land under the Blackfeet, Fort Peck, Flathead, Crow, Wahpeto, Fort Hall, Fort Belknap, and Gila River (or San Carlos) projects by specific acts.[190] To facilitate collection of reimbursement charges generally by the Act of March 7, 1928,[191] all unpaid apportioned construction and maintenance costs were made a lien on land in all irrigation projects.

Practically all assessments that were collected under the 1914[192] and 1920[193] acts were paid by white landowners on Indian projects. In 1932 a statute known as the Leavitt Act[194]

---

[181] 42 Stat. 208, 25 U. S. C. 13.

[182] See statutes relating to the more important projects in subsections A through L of this section. The major projects in the Indian Service such as the San Carlos, Ariz., the Wapato and Yakima in Washington, the Flathead, Fort Belknap, and Crow in Montana, and the Wind River in Wyoming, were constructed under specific acts of Congress.

[183] Act of August 1, 1914, 38 Stat. 582, 583, 25 U. S. C. 385. This act provided:

> * * * That all moneys expended heretofore or hereafter under this provision shall be reimbursable where the Indians have adequate funds to repay the Government, such reimbursements to be made under such rules and regulations as the Secretary of the Interior may prescribe: *Provided further*, That the Secretary of the Interior is hereby authorized and directed to apportion the cost of any irrigation project constructed for Indians and made reimbursable out of tribal funds of said Indians in accordance with the benefits received by each individual Indian so far as practicable from said irrigation project, said cost to be apportioned against such individual Indian under such rules, regulations, and conditions as the Secretary of the Interior may prescribe. * * *

Prior to the year 1914 there were two classes of funds utilized: (1) Funds specified as reimbursable in the legislative act making appropriation and in most cases reimbursable from tribal funds. (2) Funds concerning which nothing was stipulated as to reimbursement. The Crow, Blackfeet, Flathead, Fort Peck, Fort Belknap, Fort Hall, and Yakima projects were in this class. Hearings, Sen. Subcomm. of Comm. on Ind. Aff., Survey of Conditions of the Indians in the United States, 71st Cong., 2nd sess., pt. 6, Engle report, January 21, 1930, p. 2285.

[184] 38 Stat. 582, 583.

[185] See fn. 183, *supra*.

[186] Act of February 14, 1920, 41 Stat. 408, 409, 25 U.S.C. 386. This act provided:

> The Secretary of the Interior is hereby authorised and directed to require the owners of irrigable land under any irrigation system heretofore or hereafter constructed for the benefit of Indians and to which water for irrigation purposes can be delivered to begin partial reimbursement of the construction charges, where reimbursement is required by law, at such times and in such amounts as he may deem best; all payments hereunder to be credited on a per acre basis in favor of the land in behalf of which such payments shall have been made and to be deducted from the total per acre charge assessable against said land. * * *

Op. Sol. I. D., M.6376, November 15, 1921, held no interest charge could be assessed for overdue charges under the Act of February 14, 1920, 41 Stat. 408, 409.

[187] 33 Op. A. G. 25 (1921).

[188] Office of Indian Affairs, Circular No. 1677, May 12, 1921.

[189] 52 L. D. 709 (1929).

[190] Acts creating liens against lands for repayment of irrigation charges are: Act of March 3, 1911, 36 Stat. 1058, 1063, Yuma Reservation; Act of March 3, 1911, 36 Stat. 1058, 1063, Colorado River Reservation; Act of August 24, 1912, 37 Stat. 518, 522, Gila River Reservation; Act of May 18, 1916, 39 Stat. 123, 140, Flathead Reservation; Act of May 18, 1916, 39 Stat. 123, 140, etc., Blackfeet Reservation, discussed in 46 L. D. 600 (1917); Act of May 18, 1916, 39 Stat. 123, 154, Yakima Reservation; Act of May 18, 1916, 39 Stat. 123, 156, West Okanogan Irrigation District, Colville Reservation; Act of June 4, 1920, 41 Stat. 751, Crow Reservation; Act of March 3, 1921, 41 Stat. 1355, Fort Belknap Reservation; Act of May 24, 1922, 42 Stat. 552, 568, Fort Hall Reservation; Act of June 7, 1924, 43 Stat. 475, Gila River Reservation, San Carlos Project.

[191] 45 Stat. 200, 210.

[192] Act of August 1, 1914, 38 Stat. 582, 583.

[193] Act of February 14, 1920, 41 Stat. 408.

[194] Act of July 1, 1932, 47 Stat. 564. The House Committee on Indian Affairs in recommending the passage of this law said:

> * * * The progress of many Indians is retarded by old debts held against them by the Government and incurred under circumstances which dictate adjustment as a matter of simple justice. There is at the present time no authority to make any such adjustments. As a consequence, while the Indian Bureau has been liberal in making collections, these accumulated debts, many of long years standing, exist against lands, against restricted funds of individual Indians, and against some tribal funds. This decreases the value of lands and interferes with the credit necessary to make Indians self-supporting through farming, livestock raising, etc.
>
> "It is not the purpose of this measure to wipe out any just or proper debts. The record of the Indians in making repayment of revolving funds and proper obligations is worthy of emulation by our citizens generally. It is intended to enable the Secretary of the Interior to do justice in connection with ill-founded or unjust obligations. (House Report No. 951, 72d Cong., 1st sess. p. 1.)

For an analysis of the legislative history of this act leading to the conclusion that it applies to Indian lands subsequently acquired, see Op. Sol. I. D., M.30133, April 13, 1939.

Cf. Letter of Secretary of the Interior to Comptroller General, September 28, 1932, with regard to availability after passage of the

was enacted. Under this act, the Secretary of the Interior was given authority to adjust and eliminate reimbursable charges due from Indians or tribes of Indians, taking into consideration the equities existing at the time of the expenditure. It was specifically provided with respect to irrigation that all uncollected construction assessments theretofore levied were cancelled and that no more assessments of construction charges should be made as long as lands remain in Indian ownership. This act in effect recognized the need for and provided a subsidy in favor of the Indians to the extent of construction costs.

A. OPERATION AND MAINTENANCE CHARGES

Although the Leavitt Act [195] relieved the Indian of liability for future construction charges, he remained liable for the current assessments for operation and maintenance charges. However, as the Act of August 1, 1914, made reimbursement of all charges dependent upon ability of the Indian to pay,[196] when an agency superintendent certifies as to the indigent circumstances of an Indian, payments of current operation and maintenance charges are also deferred and remain charges against the land. In such cases a reimbursable appropriation is secured to defray the Indian's share of such costs.

Land of non-Indian owners on Indian projects continued liable for irrigation construction charges. Several moratorium acts [197] have been enacted for their relief. In 1936 [198] Congress authorized an investigation and adjustment of irrigation charges on non-Indian lands. A survey is now in process. Under this act, costs which are found improper upon investigation under direction of the Secretary of the Interior may be adjusted, subject to report of the proposed adjustments to Congress for approval. Further, the Secretary is authorized to declare land nonirrigable for a period not exceeding 5 years, which could not be properly irrigated with existing facilities and no charges may be assessed during that period. He may, also, cancel all charges, construction and operation and maintenance, which remained unpaid at the time Indian title was extinguished which were not a lien against the land.

Regulations relative to time of payment, delivery, penalties for nonpayment, both as to fine and stoppage of water upon failure to pay, apportionment of water and other distinctions as to various classes of water users, Indians, Indian lessees, and non-Indians, and the effect of contracts with state or local water-users' projects are in force.[199]

The various irrigation projects were instituted and are operated under dissimilar conditions and different statutory authority, and consequently regulations are not uniform.

General statutory provisions dealing with irrigation are noted below.[200]

The more important pertinent legislation of the several more important irrigation projects are enumerated subsequently.

B. BLACKFEET PROJECT [201]

Under an agreement of June 10, 1896,[202] upon cession of Indian land, the United States was committed to irrigate the farms of the Blackfeet Tribe of Indians. Their reservation consisting of 1,492,042 acres inhabited by approximately 4,500 Indians is located in the northwestern part of Montana. In connection with the livestock industry, the basis upon which the Blackfeet Indians expect to attain a sustaining economy, irrigation is necessary to raise winter feed for cattle. Operation costs were apportioned to the land irrigated,[203] and Indian landowners, when self-supporting, were to repay construction charges over and above the amount paid from tribal funds.

C. COLORADO RIVER PROJECT [204]

The Colorado River project irrigates 6,500 acres on the Colorado River Reservation in Arizona. In 1916, a policy of leasing was

---

Leavitt Act of funds appropriated for irrigation projects without consent of Indian owners to pay construction costs.

After an assessment has accrued, the Secretary of the Interior is without authority to extend time of payment in the absence of specific enactment of Congress, except as modified by the Leavitt Act. Op. Sol. I. D., M.26084, July 8, 1930; 50 L. D. 228.

[195] Act of July 1, 1932, 47 Stat. 564.

[196] See quotation of act, fn. 186, *supra*.

[197] Act of February 14, 1931, 46 Stat. 1115, 1127; Act of June 1. 1932, 47 Stat. 564; Act of January 26, 1933, 47 Stat. 776; Act of March 3, 1933, 47 Stat. 1427; Act of May 9, 1935, 49 Stat. 176, 187; Act of June 13, 1935, 49 Stat. 337; Act of April 14, 1936, 49 Stat. 1206; Act of May 31, 1939, Pub. No. 97, 76th Cong., 1st sess.; Pub. Res. No. 40 of August 5, 1939, 76th Cong., 1st sess. These moratorium acts deferred only construction charges and not assessment for operation and maintenance. For regulations, see 25 C. F. R. 130.1–130.100 and 151.1–151.4 and 154.1

[198] Act of June 22, 1936, 49 Stat. 1803.

[199] 25 C. F. R., subchaps. L. M. N. O.

[200] Act of February 8, 1887, 24 Stat. 388, 390 (Secretary of the Interior authorized to provide for equal distribution of water supply among the Indians on any reservation); Act of March 3, 1891, 26 Stat. 1095, 1101 (rights-of-way to public land and reservations were granted the canal and ditch companies under certain rules and regulations); Act of February 26, 1897, 29 Stat. 599 (opened reservoir sites on reservations); Act of May 11, 1898, 30 Stat. 404 (authorized rights-of-way for ditches, canals, reservoirs, and other purposes subsidiary to irrigation); Act of February 15, 1901, 31 Stat. 790 (required the approval of the Secretary of the Interior and the chief officer of the department in charge of the reservation for right-of-way for ditches, canals, and reservoirs through reservations. No easements were conferred by grants of the right-of-way); Act of June 21, 1906, 34 Stat. 325, 327 (provided for the sale of any allotted land within a reclamation project with the approval of the Secretary of the Interior, compensation to be used first to pay construction charges); Act of April 4, 1910, 36 Stat. 269, 270 (provided for express authorization of Congress of any irrigation project and then only after estimation of probable cost of undertaking); Act of June 25, 1910. 36 Stat. 855. 858 (provided for the reservation of power sites on Indian irrigation projects); Act of August 1, 1914, 38 Stat. 582, 583 (made irrigation expenditures reimbursable and apportionate costs to benefits received); Act of February 14, 1920, 41 Stat. 408 (made mandatory that the Secretary of the Interior begin collection of at least partial reimbursement of construction costs); for regulations issued in pursuance of this act, see 25 U. S. C. 141.1–141.7; Act of March 7, 1928, 45 Stat. 200, 210 (provided that all unpaid charges reimbursable by law become a first lien against the land): Act of July 1, 1932, 47 Stat. 564 (provided that no construction assessments be levied against Indian lands until Indian title thereto had been extinguished); Act of June 22, 1936, 49 Stat. 1803 (provided for the investigation and adjustment of irrigation charges subject to the approval of Congress); moratorium acts, see fn. 197.

[201] Principal statutory provisions, other than appropriation acts, or acts generally applicable to all projects, which relate specifically to the Blackfeet project are: Act of March 1, 1907, 34 Stat. 1015, 1035 (authorized construction); Act of May 18, 1916, 39 Stat. 123, 140 (irrigation charges were made a lien on the lands); Act of June 30, 1919, 41 Stat. 3, 16 (replaced provisions of the Act of March 1, 1907, 34 Stat. 1015, 1035, relating to the disposal of allotted land and provided for further allotment to tribal members; Act of April 1, 1920, 41 Stat. 549 (authorized the Secretary of the Interior to acquire land for reservoir purposes); Act of February 26, 1923, 42 Stat. 1289 (authorized the Secretary of the Interior to enter into an agreement with Toole County irrigation district to settle water rights of the Blackfeet Indians); Act of February 18, 1931, 46 Stat. 1093 (authorized the Secretary of the Interior to adjust payment of charges on Blackfeet Indian irrigation projects); Act of August 28, 1937, 50 Stat. 864, 865 (provided that the Secretary of the Interior release to the Blackfeet Tribe the interest in certain lands acquired by the United States under reclamation laws, land to be held in trust for the Indians by the Secretary of the Interior). For discussion of Act of May 1, 1888, 25 Stat. 113, as affecting water rights of Blackfeet Indians, see Op. Sol. I. D., M.15849, May 12, 1925. For regulations, see 25 C. F. R. 91.1–91.22.

[202] 29 Stat. 321, 354.

[203] Act of March 1, 1907, 34 Stat. 1015, 1035.

[204] Principal statutory provisions, other than those relating to appropriations or those generally applicable to all projects, which relate specifically to the Colorado River project are: Act of March 2, 1867, 14 Stat. 492, 514 (appropriated for construction of canal); Act of July

instituted whereby lessees in consideration of clearing and improving the land received the use of it for from 3 to 7 years, operations and maintenance charges being paid by lessee. Since 1925 the lessee has paid construction charges. Crop returns from this project have in the past been as high as $500,000 and it is expected that the land of this reservation properly drained will produce profitably. A diversion dam is under construction in the Colorado River near Parker, which will divert water for 100,000 acres of Indian-owned land.

D. CROW IRRIGATION PROJECT [305]

Construction of the present irrigation system on the Crow Indian Reservation [306] in southeastern Montana was begun in 1885.

Under the agreement with the Crow Tribe [307] the United States agreed to construct an irrigation project, and facilities were extended more or less continuously until 1925. Many private systems are operated from the streams supplying the Indian project. To provide a sufficient water supply for the area now under cultivation a storage dam is being constructed.

All money expended for irrigation, both construction and operation and maintenance, were from tribal funds until 1924. Beginning with 1918,[308] these funds were made reimbursable.

E. FLATHEAD IRRIGATION PROJECT [309]

The Flathead project [310] on the Flathead Reservation in western Montana irrigates approximately 105,000 acres. Less than one-fourth of the land is owned by Indians. Repayment contracts providing for payment of construction and operation and maintenance costs have been executed by non-Indian owners. A power system is operated in connection with the irrigation project.

Tribal money was expended for a part of the construction. By the Act of May 18, 1916,[311] these funds were refunded and placed to the credit of the tribe.

F. FORT BELKNAP PROJECT [312]

The Fort Belknap project, on the reservation of that name, in north central Montana, has been in operation about 40 years. The irrigated land is all Indian owned. Tribal money has been used extensively in the construction of this project. All construction appropriations were made reimbursable but water users on this project have not had sufficient income to pay charges.

G. FORT HALL PROJECT [313]

The Fort Hall project on the Fort Hall Reservation in the southeastern part of Idaho contains a total irrigable area of 90,000 acres of which 60,000 acres are under constructed works. Additional storage on Snake River will be necessary to provide a water supply for the remaining 30,000 acres of irrigable land. Irrigation on this reservation is vital as the key to the agricultural enterprises by which the Indians expect to become self-sustaining. In the agreement of the United States with this tribe [314] it was provided "that water rights are to be without cost to the Indians so long as title remained in said Indians or tribe." The white-owned lands pay both construction and operation and maintenance charges. A nonreimbursable appropriation has been made each year to cover the Indian share of the costs.

H. FORT PECK RESERVATION [315]

By the Act of May 30, 1908, under the direction of the Reclamation Service, irrigation projects were built on Fort Peck

---

27, 1868, 15 Stat. 198, 222 (provided further for irrigation canals); Act of April 21, 1904, 33 Stat. 189, 224 (authorized irrigation under Reclamation Act); Act of April 4, 1910, 36 Stat. 269, 273 (authorized further construction funds to be reimbursed from the sale of lands); Act of March 3, 1911, 36 Stat. 1058, 1063 (made construction charges a lien on the land, not to be enforced as long as original allottee occupied land as a homestead).

[305] Principal statutory provisions, other than those relating to appropriations or those generally applicable to all projects, which relate specifically to the Crow Reservation are: Act of April 27, 1904, 33 Stat. 352, 367 (agreement by which proceeds from ceded lands were to be used in irrigation); Act of March 3, 1909, 35 Stat. 781, 797 (extended provisions for entry upon ceded lands); Act of May 25, 1918, 40 Stat. 561, 574 (made reimbursable appropriation from tribal funds); Act of June 4, 1920, 41 Stat. 751 (made irrigation charges a lien on the land. Since that year funds have been appropriated from the United States Treasury; Act of May 26, 1926, 44 Stat. 658 (amends the Act of June 4, 1920, 41 Stat. 751, by providing previous expenditure of tribal funds not approved by the tribal council be reimbursed to the tribe). For regulations see 25 C. F. R. 94.1–94.22.

[306] See *United States* v. *Powers*, 305 U. S. 581 (1938); *Anderson* v. *Spear Morgan Livestock Co.*, 79 P. 2d 667 (1938).

[307] Act of March 3, 1909, 35 Stat. 781, 797.

[308] Act of May 25, 1918, 40 Stat. 561, 574.

[309] Principal statutory provisions, other than those relating to appropriations or those generally applicable to all projects, which relate specifically to the Flathead project are: Act of April 23, 1904, 33 Stat. 302, 305 (authorized survey for irrigation purposes); Act of June 21, 1906, 34 Stat. 325, 354, and Act of April 30, 1908, 35 Stat. 70, 83 (amended and extended Act of April 23, 1904, 33 Stat. 302, 305); Act of May 29, 1908, 35 Stat. 444, 448 (provided that entrymen on the portion of reservation pay proportionate cost of irrigation construction. Allotted Indian lands were relieved of construction costs); Act of April 4, 1910, 36 Stat. 269, 277 (authorized construction); Act of August 24, 1912, 37 Stat. 518, 526 (related to the disposal of allotted land); Act of July 17, 1914, 38 Stat. 510 (provided for reimbursement of funds spent for irrigation); Act of May 18, 1916, 39 Stat. 123, 139 (provided for operation and maintenance charges and amended the Act of May 29, 1908, 35 Stat. 444, 448, so that purchasers of allotted Indian Lands were liable for construction charges; refunded money spent from tribal funds for irrigation); Act of June 5, 1924, 43 Stat. 390, 402 (transferred the Flathead reservation from the Bureau of Reclamation to the Indian Service). For regulations see 25 C. F. R. 97.1–100.10. For regulations relating to electric power system see *ibid.*, 131.1–131.52.

[310] *Moody* v. *Johnston*, 66 F. 2d 999 (C. C. A. 9, 1933) and *United States* v. *McIntire*, 101 F. 2d 650 (C. C. A. 10, 1939) relate to water rights of this tribe.

[311] 39 Stat. 123, 141.

[312] Principal statutory provisions, other than those relating to appropriations or those generally applicable to all projects, which relate specifically to the Fort Belknap project are: Act of June 10, 1896, 29 Stat. 321, 351 (agreement of the United States to irrigate lands on Fort Belknap Reservation); Act of April 4, 1910, 36 Stat. 269, 277 (provided that costs of irrigation be reimbursed from tribal funds); Act of March 3, 1911, 36 Stat. 1058, 1066, provided charges become a first lien when land ceases to be used as a homestead); Act of March 3, 1921, 41 Stat. 1355, 1357 (provided all charges become a lien on the land). For regulations see 25 C. F. R. 103.1–103.22.

[313] Principal statutory provisions, other than those relating to appropriations or those generally applicable to all projects, which relate specifically to the Fort Hall project are: Act of March 1, 1907, 34 Stat. 1015, 1024 (instituted construction); Act of April 4, 1910, 36 Stat. 269, 274 (provided for the payment of construction charges on lands in private ownership); Act of March 3, 1911, 36 Stat. 1058, 1063 (provided for the completion of the project and that charges should be a lien on land not used as Indian homestead); Act of May 24, 1922, 42 Stat. 552, 568 (provided that the cost of rehabilitation to be paid by both Indian and non-Indian owners, making proportionate reimbursable expenditures a lien on Indian lands); Act of March 3, 1927, 44 Stat. 1398 (required contracts for the repayment of further charges by white owners and created a lien on Indian lands. This applied to the Gibson unit only). For regulations see 25 C. F. R. 106.1–106.25.

[314] Op. Sol. I. D., M.5386, June 19, 1923 (authority of the Secretary of the Interior to appropriate land in Fort Hall Reservation as a reservoir site without consent of the Indians).

[315] Principal statutory provisions, other than those relating to appropriations or those generally applicable to all projects which relate specifically to the Fort Peck Reservation are: Act of May 30, 1908, 35 Stat. 558 (authorized construction); Act of May 18, 1916, 39 Stat. 123, 140 (provided that a lien was to be recited in patents for unpaid charges; that tribal funds hitherto used for construction be returned to the tribal account); Act of June 5, 1924, 43 Stat. 390, 402 (transferred jurisdiction from the Bureau of Reclamation to the Indian Service).

Reservation, Mont., into which both white and Indian interests entered. The proceeds of the sale of surplus land were used for original construction.

I. SAN CARLOS PROJECT [316]

The San Carlos irrigation project,[317] was designed to irrigate 100,000 acres of which 50,000 are owned by whites and 50,000 acres on the Gila River Indian Reservation owned in part by individual Indians and in part by the Gila River Pima-Maricopa Indian Community.[318] The project has a hydroelectric plant at Coolidge Dam and a Diesel electric plant located near the town of Coolidge, with high voltage and low voltage lines to carry power to project irrigation wells, nearby towns, mining camps, and rural farm consumers.

J. UINTAH [319]

On the Uintah Reservation in Utah an irrigation project was constructed over a period of years, from 1906 to 1912. A systematic program of replacement is now in process.

This project is designed to irrigate 77,194 acres of project land and to carry water to approximately 28,000 acres of private lands through carrying capacity granted to companies and individuals who pay a proportionate share in the operation and maintenance of the project.

[316] Principal statutory provisions, other than appropriations or those generally applicable to all projects, which relate specifically to the San Carlos project are: Act of March 3, 1905, 33 Stat. 1048, 1081 (authorized construction and provided that costs of the project for the Pima Indians be repaid within 30 years after the Indians have become supporting); Act of August 24, 1912, 37 Stat. 518, 522 (provided that the cost of the irrigation work be reimbursable and created a lien upon Indian lands); Act of May 18, 1916, 39 Stat. 123, 129 (provided for the construction of a dam to irrigate white- and Indian-owned lands. Costs of this construction made reimbursable with respect to Indian lands under the Act of August 24, 1912. Costs of non-Indian-owned land were to be paid in accordance with the Act of August 13, 1914, 38 Stat. 686); Act of June 7, 1924, 43 Stat. 475, 476 (enabling act for the San Carlos project provided for contracts for irrigation of the Gila River Reservation and of white-owned land).

[317] Preference of Indians to waters stored by Coolidge Dam. Memo. Sol. I. D., February 19, 1933.

[318] Memo. Sol. I. D., August 25, 1936 (collection of charges).

[319] Principal statutory provisions, other than those relating to appropriations or those generally applicable to all projects, which relate specifically to the Uintah irrigation projects are: Act of June 21, 1906, 34 Stat. 325, 375 (authorized the project and provided that the cost should be repaid within 30 years after becoming self-supporting); Act of April 30, 1908, 35 Stat. 70, 95 (provided for the leasing of allotted irrigated lands with the consent of the allottee with the approval of the Secretary of the Interior); Act of May 24, 1922, 42 Stat. 552, 578 (provided for extension and rehabilitation of this project, repaid from the principal funds held in trust for the Confederated Band of Ute Indians). For regulations see 25 C. F. R. 121.1–121.23.

K. WIND RIVER [320]

The Wind River irrigation project includes the diminished and ceded portions of the Wind River Reservation, Wyoming. The project consists of five systems embracing irrigable areas of approximately 65,000 acres. The funds furnished for this project were made reimbursable. Assessments of operation and maintenance costs are made against all land to which water can be delivered except tribal lands not farmed. Regulations covering the first sale of the irrigated land provided for paid-up water rights. These lands are not charged with construction costs.[321]

L. YAKIMA [322]

The Yakima Reservation irrigation projects in the State of Washington include the Wapato, Toppenish-Simcoe, Satus, and Ahtanum units containing a total irrigable area of 170,000 acres, of which 120,000 acres are in Indian ownership and 50,000 acres in private ownership. Of this area some 128,000 acres are supplied with irrigation facilities.

[320] Principal statutory provisions, other than appropriations or acts generally applicable to all irrigation projects, which relate specifically to the Wind River project are: Act of March 3, 1905, 33 Stat. 1016 (provided for the construction of the project from proceeds of sale of ceded lands); Act of April 30, 1908, 35 Stat. 70, 97 (appropriations with provision for reimbursement of funds appropriated by this act); Act of May 25, 1918, 40 Stat. 561, 590 (provided that private lands under this project pay their pro rata share of the cost of construction). For regulations see 25 C. F. R. 127.1–127.22.

[321] Op. Sol. I. D., M.14051, July 8, 1925.

[322] Principal statutory provisions, other than those relating to appropriations or those generally applicable to all projects, which relate specifically to the Yakima project are: Acts of December 21, 1904, 33 Stat. 595 (provided for the construction of irrigation works on the Yakima Indian Reservation, such benefit to compensate the Indians for any valid right hitherto acquired by settlers. This act provided that the proceeds of the sale of land be used in the construction of the project); Act of June 21, 1906, 34 Stat. 325 (appropriated reimbursable funds); Act of April 4, 1910, 36 Stat. 269, 286 (provided for the construction of a drainage system for the Wapato project); Act of June 30, 1913, 38 Stat. 77, 100 (provided for the appointment of a joint congressional committee to report on the feasibility of constructing irrigation systems on this reservation); Act of August 1, 1914, 38 Stat. 582, 604 (provided that the Indians who had been unjustly deprived of the Yakima River be entitled to 147 cubic feet per second in perpetuity); Act of August 1, 1914, 38 Stat. 582, 604 (construed in Op. Sol. I. D., M.3403, April 14, 1921, holding that no penalty could be charged on delinquency. This applied to the Wapato and Satus unit only); Act of May 18, 1916, 39 Stat. 123, 153, 154 (provided costs in extension of project be reimbursed in 20 annual installments and created a first lien on Indian lands in the Wapato and Satus unit; authorized the Secretary of the Interior to fix operation and maintenance charges, construed in Ind. Off. Memo., June 12, 1933); Act of June 30, 1919, 41 Stat. 3, 28 (made uncollected charges liens on land under the Toppenish-Simcoe units); Act of February 14, 1920, 41 Stat. 408, 431 (provided that landowners under the Wapato and Satus units repay construction costs of land at $5 per acre per year); Act of May 25, 1922, 42 Stat. 595 (reduced annual construction payment from $5 to $2.50 per acre on the Wapato and Satus units). For regulations regarding the Wapato irrigation project, Washington, see 25 C. F. R. 124.1–124.19.

SECTION 8. FEDERAL LEGAL SERVICES

The United States without specific statutory authority represents the Indian generally in legal matters in which the United States has an interest. Federal legal services, therefore, are available to the Indian in cases involving the protection of property allotted or furnished to the Indian by the Government in which an interest of the United States may be found, either in the fact that it holds such property in trust for the Indians or in the fact that the property may be held by the Indians subject to restrictions against alienation.[323]

The Federal Government, as a routine service to the Indian, brings actions to enforce terms of leases or other contracts arising in connection with restricted property. It institutes or defends litigation relating to oil royalties or other mineral rights and represents the Indians in suits involving federal and state taxes.[324]

The Department of Justice has, for the most part, followed the policy of representing Indians in matters relating to their allotments or reservations or to property of Indians over which

[323] See Chapter 19, sec. 2A(1).

[324] Justice Department File No. 90–2–012–1, Memo. of July 29, 1932.

Congress has provided that the United States maintain control and supervision.[225]

Legal representation is also given the Indian in other cases involving interests of the United States, as expressed in treaty provisions or acts of Congress. These cases for the most part relate to hunting and fishing privileges, water rights, suits for trespass, or other rights arising out of reservation property.[226]

A specific statutory duty to represent the Indian in all suits at law and in equity is found in section 175, title 25, of the United States Code. This section provides:

> In all States and Territories where there are reservations or allotted Indians the United States district attorney shall represent them in all suits at law and in equity.

The language of this provision is very broad, and this probably has been a factor in the failure of the Department of Justice to adopt a consistent policy as to when it will authorize or require the United States district attorneys to appear on behalf of the Indian.

The original enactment, as found in the Act of March 3, 1893,[227] is part of a paragraph which reads:

> To enable the Secretary of the Interior, in his discretion, to pay the legal costs incurred by Indians in contests initiated by or against them, to any entry, filing, or other claims, under the laws of Congress relating to public lands, for any sufficient cause affecting the legality or validity of the entry, filing or claim, five thousand dollars: *Provided*, That the fees to be paid by and on behalf of the Indian party in any case shall be one-half of the fees provided by law in such cases, and said fees shall be paid by the Commissioner of Indian Affairs, with the approval of the Secretary of the Interior, on an account stated by the proper land officers through the Commissioner of the General Land Office. In all states and Territories where there are reservations or allotted Indians the United States District Attorney shall represent them in all suits at law and in equity.

It may be argued that the last sentence of the paragraph should be construed as relating only to the first sentence, and the circumstance that the last sentence was introduced on the floor of the House in the course of a discussion of the first sentence may be thought to give support to this construction.[228] Such a construction, however, would subordinate the plain language of the statute to the form of paragraphing, and would ignore the long established custom of including items of permanent general legislation on Indian affairs in scattered paragraphs of appropriation acts. This narrow construction has never been adopted by the Attorney General, and it was rejected by the codifiers of the United States Code, who accepted the proviso in the first sentence, and the last sentence of the paragraph, as distinct statements of general and permanent legislation.

While rejecting the construction which would limit the duty of legal representation to public land contests, the Department of Justice has occasionally taken the view that the statute in question contains an implied proviso, and that the phrase "all suits at law and in equity" really means "all suits at law and in equity in which the United States has an interest."[229] The Department of Justice has not been consistent, however, in the use of this construction, and has on occasion given a less narrow interpretation to the words of Congress.[230] Carried out consistently, this narrow construction would nullify the statute, since, as we have noted, the United States has represented Indians in such cases without special statutory authorization.

In criminal prosecutions[231] for alleged violations of state laws committed outside the reservation, where the jurisdiction of the state is plenary and unquestionable, the United States has not represented the Indians in any such criminal prosecutions brought by state authorities, unless the Indian claims immunity from such state laws by reason of the status of the *locus in quo*, or because of some treaty stipulation or provision of a federal law affecting the act, the commission of which is regarded as a crime by the state law. Within this latter class of cases may be included, for instance, the defense of Indians who are prosecuted for alleged violations of the state fish and game laws,[232] the Indian claiming a right to fish or hunt in the particular place where the offense is alleged to have been committed, or prosecuted for the driving of a truck without a state license.

Special provision has been made by Congress to provide legal services for the Five Civilized Tribes,[233] the Osages,[234] and the Pueblo Indians.[235?]

---

[225] Justice Department File No. 90-2-012-1, Memo. of July 29, 1932.

[226] Where the State of Idaho prosecuted several Indians of the Coeur d'Alene Agency in that state for the killing of deer out of season in alleged violation of the state game laws, the Department of Justice took the position that, since the United States had the duty to protect the Indians in their treaty rights of fishing, it could maintain an action to restrain the state authorities from interfering with the exercise of such treaty rights by the Indians, and the United States Attorney appeared for the purpose of protecting and defending the Indians. (Justice Department File No. 90-2-0-71.)

[227] 27 Stat. 612, 631. Compare the statute of September 6, 1563, embodied in the Laws of the Indies, requiring the King's Solicitors to "be protectors of the Indians * * * and plead for them in all civil and criminal suits, whether official or between parties, with Spaniards demanding or defending." 2 White's Recopilacion (1839) 95.

[228] Cong. Rec., 52d Cong., 2d sess., February 24, 1893, p. 2182. This narrow view of the law is criticized in a memorandum of Assistant Attorney General Van Devanter, dated November 23, 1897, 25 L. D. 426.

[229] In the *Constitution Indemnity Company* case in California, no legal representation was furnished in a suit for negligence resulting in personal injuries or death of Indians, even though such Indians were still wards of the government (Justice Department File No. 90-2-0-63). And again representation was denied in suit to recover damages for the death of restricted Fort Peck Agency Indians from the Great Northern Railway (Justice Department File No. 90-2-0-135).

[230] On December 26, 1929, the Attorney General advised a United States Attorney to represent a Hopi Indian, Tom Pavatea, sued for accidental shooting of a white man off the reservation. See Ind. Off. Memo., May 20, 1930. In the case of the claim of the Indians of the Warm Springs Reservation against the Montana Horse Products Company, the United States Attorney brought suit in the name and behalf of the Indian to compel the said company to pay to individual Indians the stipulated consideration for catching a number of wild horses roaming on the reservation (Justice Department File No. 90-2-19-6).

[231] In the Jimerson murder case in New York the position was taken that section 175 has no relation to criminal prosecutions and had never been so construed (Justice Department File No. 90-2-7-42).

[232] See fn. 227, *supra*.

[233] See Chapter 23, sec. 9.

[234] See Chapter 23, sec. 12.

[235] See Chapter 20, sec. 3A.

CHAPTER 13

TAXATION

TABLE OF CONTENTS

The use of the phrase "Indians not taxed" in the provisions of the Federal Constitution relating to representation in Congress[1] has given color to the popular belief that tribal Indians are exempt from taxes. Whatever the situation may have been when this phrase was first used, it is a fact today that Indians pay a great variety of taxes, federal, state, and tribal. It is, however, a fact that peculiarities of property ownership and special jurisdictional factors affecting Indian reservations result in certain tax exemptions not generally applicable to non-Indians. These exemptions involve a series of difficult legal and political problems.[2]

Limitations upon the power to tax, which has been called an attribute of sovereignty,[3] give rise to certain immunities. Such limitation may be expressed in federal, state, and tribal constitutions[4] or laws[5] or they may be imposed by contract.[6]

[1] Art. I, sec. 2; amendment XIV, sec. 2. For an analysis of the legislative and administrative history of this phrase, leading to the conclusion that there is no longer any class of "Indians not taxed," see Op. Sol. I. D., M.31039, November 7, 1940. And see 87 Cong. Rec. 79 (January 8, 1941) for Census report following this opinion.

[2] See Sen. Rept. 168, 75th Cong., 3d sess. (May 6, 1938); Sen. Rept. 1365, 72d Cong., 2d sess.; Hearings, Sen. Comm. on Ind. Aff., on S. Res. 282, 72d Cong., 1st sess. The proposal has been made for many years that the Federal Government pay to counties and states in which tax-exempt Indian lands are located sums in lieu of taxes to pay for educational and other services. See Twenty-first Report of the Board of Indian Commissioners (1889). This principle has been occasionally embodied in special legislation. Act of July 1, 1892, sec. 2, 27 Stat. 62, 63 (Colville). And see Chapter 12, sec. 2A.

[3] See *McCulloch* v. *Maryland*, 4 Wheat. 316, 428–429 (1819); 1 Cooley, Taxation (4th ed. 1924) c. 1, sec. 1, p. 61.

[4] See secs. 1C and 8, *infra*.

[5] Act of June 18, 1934, sec. 5, 48 Stat. 984, 985, 25 U. S. C. 465; Act of June 20, 1936, 49 Stat. 1542.

[6] 1 Cooley, Taxation (4th ed. 1924) c. 2, sec. 58, p. 151.

SECTION 1. SOURCES OF LIMITATIONS ON TAXING POWER OF THE STATES

To the extent that Indians and Indian property within an Indian reservation are not subject to state laws, they are not subject to state tax laws.[7]

We have seen, elsewhere, that state laws, are not applicable to tribal Indians on an Indian reservation except where Congress has expressly provided that state laws shall apply.[8] It follows that Indians and Indian property on an Indian reservation are not subject to state taxation except by virtue of express authority conferred upon the state by act of Congress. Conversely Indian property outside of an Indian reservation is subject to state taxation unless congressional authority for a claim of tax exemption can be found.[9] This jurisdictional immunity from state taxation is sometimes buttressed by:

(*a*) The judicial doctrine that states may not tax a federal instrumentality, operating upon the assumption that various incidents of Indian property are federal instrumentalities;

(*b*) Express prohibition in enabling acts and other federal statutes against taxation of Indians and Indian property;

(*c*) Explicit waiver in state constitutions of the right to tax Indians or Indian property;

(*d*) Express prohibition in state statutes against taxation of Indians or Indian property.

It is not clear whether any of these added reasons need be advanced to justify the immunity of Indian property on an Indian reservation from state property taxes. Since, however, they often figure largely in the reasoning used by the courts in attaining a particular result, they will hereinafter be discussed in some detail.

A. "INSTRUMENTALITY" DOCTRINE

Perhaps the most frequent reason stressed by the courts for the exemption of Indian property from state taxation is the federal instrumentality doctrine. The doctrine in its application to Indians and Indian property is founded upon the premise that the power and duty of governing and protecting tribal Indians is

[7] See *Surplus Trading Co.* v. *Cook*, 281 U. S. 647, 651 (1930).

[8] See Chapter 6.

[9] Act of June 18, 1934, sec. 5, 48 Stat. 984, 985, 25 U. S. C. 465; Act of June 20, 1936, 49 Stat. 1542.

primarily a federal function,[10] and that a state cannot impose a tax which will substantially impede or burden the functioning of the Federal Government.[11]

The doctrine is limited in its application to the property or functions of those Indians who are in some degree under federal control or supervision. Thus it has afforded immunity to the property and functions of tribal Indians whether allotted or unallotted.[12]

Something of the nature of the doctrine as well as its scope may be found in the illuminating opinion of the Circuit Court of Appeals in the case of *United States* v. *Thurston County* [13] where the proceeds of the sale of restricted Indian lands were held exempt from state taxation:

> * * * The experience of more than a century has demonstrated the fact that the unrestrained greed, rapacity, cunning, and perfidy of members of the superior race in their dealings with the Indians unavoidably drive them to poverty, despair, and war. To protect them from want and despair, and the superior race from the inevitable attacks which these evils produce, to lead them to abandon their nomadic habits and to learn the arts of civilized life, the government of the United States has long exercised the power granted to it by the Constitution (article 1, § 8, subd. 3) to reserve and hold in trust for them large tracts of land and large sums of money derived from the release of their rights of occupancy of the lands of the continent, to manage and control their property, to furnish them with agricultural implements, houses, barns, and other permanent improvements upon their lands, domestic animals, means of subsistence, and small amounts of money, and to provide them with physicians, farmers, schools and teachers. The Indian reservations, the funds derived from the release of the Indian right of occupancy, the lands alloted to individual Indians, but still held in trust by the nation for their benefit, the improvements upon these lands, the agricultural implements, the domestic animals and other property of like character furnished to them by the nation to enable and induce them to cultivate the soil and to establish and maintain permanent homes and families, are the means by which the nation pursues its wise policy of protection and instruction and exercises its lawful powers of government.
> * * * Every instrumentality lawfully employed by the United States to execute its constitutional laws and to exercise its lawful governmental authority is necessarily exempt from state taxation and interference. *McCullough* v. *Maryland*, 6 Wheat. 316, 4 L. Ed. 479; *Van Brocklin* v. *State of Tennessee*, 117 U. S. 151, 155, 6 Sup. Ct. 670, 29 L. Ed. 845; *Wisconsin Central Railroad Co.* v. *Price County*, 133 U. S. 496, 504, 10 Sup. Ct. 341, 33 L. Ed. 687. It is for this reason that the Supreme Court decided that lands held by Indian allottees under Act Feb. 8, 1887, 24 Stat. 389, c. 119, § 5, within 25 years after their allotment, houses and other permanent improvements thereon, and the cattle, horses, and other property of like character which had been issued to the allottees by the United States and which they were using upon their allotments, were exempt from state taxation, and declared that "no authority exists for the state to tax lands which are held in trust by the United States for the purpose of carrying out its policy in reference to these Indians." *U. S.* v. *Rickert*, 188 U. S. 432, 441, 23 Sup. Ct. 478, 482, 47 L. Ed. 532.
>
> * * * * *
>
> * * * The proceeds of the sales of these lands have been lawfully substituted for the lands themselves by the trustee. The substitutes partake of the nature of the originals, and stand charged with the same trust. The lands and their proceeds, so long as they are held or controlled by the United States and the term of the trust has not expired, are alike instrumentalities employed by it in the lawful exercise of its powers of government to protect, support, and instruct the Indians, for whose benefit the complainant holds them, and they are not subject to taxation by any state or county. (Pp. 289–290, 292.)

B. FEDERAL STATUTES

Congressional power to exempt land from state taxation [14] is limited only by the requirement that the property or function in question be reasonably considered incident to a federal function. So large is the discretion permitted the legislature by the courts [15] in this connection that no case has been found in which the court refused to sustain Congress' power to exempt.

When a tax immunity is offered to individual Indians by federal statute or treaty, by way of inducement to a voluntary transaction, the courts have held that the immunity becomes contractual in the sense that the individual Indians acquire a vested right to the exemption which is protected against Congress itself by the Fifth Amendment.[16]

Other federal statutes limiting the power of the states to tax are the enabling and organic acts authorizing the formation of state and territorial governments,[17] expressly exempting Indians and Indian property from the application of state laws.

[10] See Chapter 5.

[11] *United States* v. *Rickert*, 188 U. S. 432 (1903); *United States* v. *Pearson*, 231 Fed. 270 (D. C. S. D. 1916); *Dewey County, S. D.* v. *United States*, 26 F. 2d 434 (C. C. A. 8, 1928), cert. den. 278 U. S. 649 (1928); *United States* v. *Thurston County*, 143 Fed. 287 (C. C. A. 8, 1906); *United States* v. *Wright*, 53 F. 2d 300 (C. C. A. 4. 1931), cert. den. 285 U. S. 539; *Morrow* v. *United States*, 243 Fed. 854 (C. C. A. 8, 1917).

[12] *New York Indians*, 5 Wall. 761 (1866).

[13] 143 Fed. 287 (C. C. A. 8, 1906).

[14] Act of June 18, 1934, sec. 5, 48 Stat. 984, 25 U. S. C. 465, provides:

> The Secretary of the Interior is hereby authorized, in his discretion, to acquire * * * any interest in lands, * * * within or without existing reservations, * * * for the purpose of providing land for Indians.
> Title to any lands * * * shall be taken in the name of the United States * * * and such lands or rights shall be exempt from State and local taxation.

See also Act of June 20, 1936, 49 Stat. 1542, upheld in *United States* v. *Board of Comm'rs*, 26 F. Supp. 270 (D. C. N. D. Okla. 1939).

[15] *Cf. United States* v. *Board of County Commissioners of Osage County, Okla.*, 193 Fed. 485 (C. C. W. D. Okla. 1911), aff'd 216 Fed. 883 (C. C. A. 8, 1914), app. dism. 244 U. S. 663 (1917).

[16] The leading case is *Choate* v. *Trapp*, 224 U. S. 665 (1912), holding that the Act of May 27, 1908, 35 Stat. 312, was invalid insofar as it attempted to remove the tax exemption accruing to Choctaw and Chickasaw allottees under the Atoka Agreement and Curtis Act of June 28, 1898, 30 Stat. 495. The rationale of this decision has been followed in many cases. See for example, *Carpenter* v. *Shaw*, 280 U. S. 363 (1930); *Ward* v. *Love County*, 253 U. S. 17 (1920); *Board of Com'rs* v. *United States*, 110 F. 2d 929 (C. C. A. 10, 1938), cert. granted 306 U. S. 629, mod. 60 Sup. Ct. 285; *Board of Com'rs of Caddo County, Okla.* v. *United States*, 87 F. 2d 55 (C. C. A. 10, 1936); *Glacier County, Mont.* v. *United States*, 99 F. 2d 733 (C. C. A. 9, 1938); *Morrow* v. *United States*, 243 Fed. 854 (C. C. A. 8, 1917).

The doctrine is not without limitations. The immunity can only vest in an Indian and does not accrue to a purchaser from him. *Fink* v. *County Commissioners*, 248 U. S. 399 (1919). This conclusion is sometimes based upon the ground that tax immunity has been contractually relinquished by the Indian in consideration for a removal of restrictions. *Sweet* v. *Shock*, 245 U. S. 192 (1917). This immunity, finally, extends only for the time prescribed in the defining statute. *United States* v. *Spaeth*, 24 F. Supp. 465 (D. C. Minn. 1938).

[17] *United States* v. *Pearson*, 231 Fed. 270 (D. C. S. D. 1916) (Enabling Act for North Dakota, South Dakota, Montana, and Wyoming, Act of February 22, 1889, 25 Stat. 676, 677); *Wau-Pe-Man-Qua* v. *Aldrich*, 28 Fed. 489 (C. C. Ind. 1886) (Northwest Ordinance, July 13, 1787, U. S. C. (1934 ed.) p. xxiii); *United States* v. *Yakima County*, 274 Fed. 115 (D. C. E. D. Wash. 1921) (Enabling Act for Washington, Act of February 22, 1889, 25 Stat. 677); see *United States* v. *Ferry County, Wash.*, 24 F. Supp. 399 (D. C. E. D. Wash. 1938) (Enabling Act for Washington, Act of February 22, 1889, 25 Stat. 676, 677), *Fink* v. *County Com'rs*, 248 U. S. 399, 401 (1919); *United States* v. *Board of Com'rs of McIntosh County*, 271 Fed. 747 (D. C. E. D. Okla. 1921), aff'd 284 Fed. 103 (C. C. A. 8, 1922), app. dism. 263 U. S. 689 (1924), 263 U. S. 691 (1924); *United States* v. *Board of Com'rs*, 26 F. Supp. 270, 275 (D. C. N. D. Okla. 1939) (Enabling Act for Oklahoma, Act of June 16, 1906, 34 Stat. 267); *Truscott* v. *Hurlbut Land & Cattle Co.*, 73 Fed. 60 (C. C. A. 9, 1896) (Enabling Act for Montana, Act of February 22, 1889, 25 Stat. 676, 677), app. dism. sub nom. *Hurlbut Land & Cattle Co.* v. *Truscott*, 165 U. S. 719 (1897).

Thus Indian immunity from taxation has been predicated[18] upon clauses providing that nothing in the enabling act shall impair the rights of persons or property pertaining to the Indians, or that Indian lands shall remain subject to the absolute jurisdiction of Congress.[19]

C. STATE CONSTITUTIONS

Most of these enabling act provisions have been written into state constitutions, thus adding additional reason for limitation upon the power of the state.[20]

[18] *The Kansas Indians*, 5 Wall. 737, 756 (1866); *United States* v. *Yakima County*, 274 Fed. 115 (D. C. E. D. Wash. 1921); *United States* v. *Pearson*, 231 Fed. 270 (D. C. S. D. 1916); see *United States* v. *Stahl*, 27 Fed. Case No. 16373 (C. C. Kans. 1868); see *United States* v. *Board of Com'rs of McIntosh County*, 271 Fed. 747, (D. C. E. D. Okla., 1921), aff'd 284 Fed. 103 (C. C. A. 8, 1922), app. dism., 263 U. S. 689 (1924), 263 U. S. 691 (1924).

[19] See for example, Arizona: Act of June 20, 1910, 36 Stat. 557; Colorado: Act of February 28, 1861, 12 Stat. 172; Dakota Territory: Act of March 2, 1861, 12 Stat. 239; Idaho Territory: Act of March 3, 1863, 12 Stat. 808, 809; Kansas; Act of January 29, 1861, 12 Stat. 126, 127; Montana Territory: Act of May 26, 1864, 13 Stat. 85, 86; New Mexico: Act of June 20, 1910, 36 Stat. 557; Oklahoma: Act of May 2, 1890, 26 Stat. 81, 82; Act of June 16, 1906, 34 Stat. 267, 270; Utah: Act of July 16, 1894, 28 Stat. 107; Wyoming Territory: Act of July 25, 1868, 15 Stat. 178.

D. STATE STATUTES

A state may also limit its own power to tax the property of an Indian tribe by entering into an agreement with the tribe guaranteeing exemption of its lands from taxation, which guarantee is protected against violation by the obligation of contracts clause of the Federal Constitution.[21] This source of immunity, however, is of little importance today because states seldom make agreements with Indian tribes.

The agreement may sometimes take the form of a statutory enactment.[22]

[20] Oklahoma Const., Art. 1, sec. 3; South Dakota Const. Art. XXII, sec. 2. See *United States* v. *Rickert*, 188 U. S. 432 (1903); *United States* v. *Yakima County*, 274 Fed. 115 (D. C. E. D. Wash. 1921).

[21] United States Const., Art. 1, sec. 10, cl. 1. *New Jersey* v. *Wilson*, 7 Cranch 164 (1812). *Cf.* fn. 35, *infra*.

[22] *New Jersey* v. *Wilson*, 7 Cranch 164 (1812); and see *Wau-Pe-Man-Qua* v. *Aldrich*, 28 Fed. 489 (C. C. Ind. 1886).

SECTION 2. STATE TAXATION OF TRIBAL LANDS

Lands which are occupied by a tribe or tribes of Indians have always been regarded as not within the jurisdiction of the state for purposes of state property taxation. The principal reason for this immunity has been the fact that the tribes have been regarded as distinct political communities exercising many of the attributes of a sovereign body.[23] A landmark in this field is the case of *The Kansas Indians*.[24] In holding that the tribal lands (as well as lands held by individual members thereof) were not subject to state tax laws, the court said:

> * * * If the tribal organization of the Shawnees is preserved intact, and recognized by the political department of the government as existing, then they are a "people distinct from other," capable of making treaties, separated from the jurisdiction of Kansas, and to be governed exclusively by the government of the Union. If under the control of Congress, from necessity there can be no divided authority. If they have outlived many things, they have not outlived the protection afforded by the Constitution, treaties, and laws of Congress. It may be, that they cannot exist much longer as a distinct people in the presence of the civilization of Kansas, "but until they are clothed with the rights and bound to all the duties of citizens," they enjoy the privilege of total immunity from State taxation. There can be no question of State sovereignty in the case, as Kansas accepted her admission into the family of States on condition that the Indian rights should remain unimpaired and the general government at liberty to make any regulation respecting them, their lands, property, or other rights, which it would have been competent to make if Kansas had not been admitted into the Union.* * * While the general government has a superintending care over their interests, and continues to treat with them as a nation, the State of Kansas is estopped from denying their title to it. She accepted this status when she accepted the act admitting her into the Union. Conferring rights and privileges on these Indians cannot affect their situation, which can only be changed by treaty stipulation, or a voluntary abandonment of their tribal organization. As long as the United States recognizes their national character they are under the protection of treaties and the laws of Congress, and their property is withdrawn from the operation of State laws. (Pp. 755–757.)

When the State of New York attempted to levy taxes upon the lands occupied by various tribes of Indians, contending that though the lands might be sold for nonpayment of the taxes the right of occupancy of the tribe would continue unchallenged, its attempt was frustrated by the Supreme Court[25] in the following words:

> It will be seen on looking into the general laws of the State imposing taxes for town and county charges, as well as into the special acts of 1840 and 1841, that the taxes are imposed upon the lands in these reservations, and it is the lands which are sold in default of payment. They are dealt with by the town and county authorities in the same way in making this assessment, and in levying the same, as other real property in these subdivisions of the State. We must say, regarding these reservations as wholly exempt from State taxation, and which, as we understand the opinion of the learned judge below, is not denied, the exercise of this authority over them is an unwarrantable interference, inconsistent with the original title of the Indians, and offensive to their tribal relations.
>
> The tax titles purporting to convey these lands to the purchaser, even with the qualification suggested that the right of occupation is not to be affected, may well embarrass the occupants and be used by unworthy persons to the disturbance of the tribe. All agree that the Indian right of occupancy creates an indefeasible title to the reservations that may extend from generation to generation, and will cease only by the dissolution of the tribe, or their consent to sell to the party possessed of the right of pre emption. He is the only party that is authorized to deal with the tribe in respect to their property, and this with the consent of the government. Any other party is an intruder, and may be proceeded against under the twelfth section of the act of 30th June, 1834.* (P. 771.)

*4 Stat. at Large, 730.

On the other hand, though a state may not tax the lands which the tribe occupies, it was early held that the state might tax cattle of non-Indians grazing upon tribal land under a lease from the Indians.[26] "But it is obvious," said the court, "that a tax put upon the cattle of the lessees is too remote and indirect to be deemed a tax upon the lands or privileges of the Indians."

[23] See Chapter 14.

[24] 5 Wall. 737 (1866). Where, however, the tribe has ceased to exist as such within the state, lands owned by Indians formerly members of the tribe are subject to state taxation unless forbidden by some other federal law. *Pennock* v. *Commissioners*, 103 U. S. 44 (1880).

[25] *The New York Indians*, 5 Wall. 761 (1866).

[26] *Thomas* v. *Gay*, 169 U. S. 264 (1898).

Until recently, the federal instrumentality doctrine was employed to exempt from state taxation the income of non-Indian lessees of tribal or restricted Indian lands. However, in sustaining a federal tax on the income accruing to a lessee under a lease of state lands the Supreme Court in *Helvering* v. *Producers Corp.*[27] expressly overruled the leading case of *Gillespie* v. *Oklahoma*,[28] which held that a state tax on income derived by a lessee from leases of Creek or Osage restricted lands was invalid because it hampered the United States in making the best terms possible for its Indian wards.[29]

The *Gillespie* case seems to have rested on the premise that a lessee of lands from which a Government derives income for its governmental functions becomes thereby an instrumentality of that Government.

The Supreme Court, in 1938, was more concerned with the immunity from state and federal taxation which its decision 6 years earlier in the *Gillespie* case had granted to large private incomes than with any question of interference with federal power in Indian affairs.

As said by the court, in the *Helvering* case:

> * * * immunity from non-discriminatory taxation sought by a private person for his property or gains because he is engaged in operations under a government contract or lease cannot be supported by merely theoretical conceptions of interference with the functions of government. Regard must be had to substance and direct effects. And where it merely appears that one operating under a government contract or lease is subjected to a tax with respect to his profits on the same basis as others who are engaged in similar businesses, there is no sufficient ground for holding that the effect upon the Government is other than indirect and remote * * * (Pp. 386–387.)

And even if the lessee were in fact an agency of the Government, "no constitutional implications prohibit a State tax upon the property of an agent of the Government merely because it is the property of such an agent."[30]

It is to be noted, however, that in the cases overruled the taxes were levied on private individuals or corporations organized for profit and which were only incidentally performing a federal function. A distinction may be drawn between these cases, and cases involving a corporation organized solely to carry out governmental objectives, such as the tribal corporations organized under the Indian Reorganization Act of June 18, 1934,[31] and it is probable that an attempt by a state to impose income or other types of taxes on such business organizations would still be held a direct burden on a federal instrumentality.[32]

There seems little doubt in view of the foregoing that the validity, if not the scope, of the instrumentality doctrine, in so far as it relates to Indians, their property and their affairs, remains unchanged. For just as the right to tax the lessee of state lands does not include the right to tax the state itself, so the right to tax the lessee of Indian lands does not imply a right to tax the Indians or their property.

When the lands pass from the tribe to non-Indians they become, ordinarily, subject to state taxation. Thus a railroad purchasing a right-of-way through a reservation must pay taxes on that right-of-way as though the lands were entirely withdrawn from the reservation,[33] and the fact that property owned by a railroad is subject to a right of reverter in an Indian tribe does not preclude the state from taxing such property while owned by the railroad.[34]

On the other hand a state may contract with a tribe that designated lands be tax exempt. In such a case it has been held that the exemption runs with the lands even into the hands of a non-Indian purchaser.[35] Nevertheless, as pointed out by the Court, the state could, as a condition to permitting the sale of the lands, require that the right to exemption be waived, in which event the lands in the hands of the purchaser would be subject to state property taxes.

In the exercise of its plenary power over the Indian tribes, Congress may expressly subject a privilege or a property right of the tribe to state taxation. Thus the Act of May 29, 1924,[36] provided that—

> * * * the production of oil and gas and other minerals on [unallotted Indian reservation land, other than land of the Five Civilized Tribes and the Osage reservation,] may be taxed by the State in which said lands are located * * * the same as production on unrestricted lands, * * *. *Provided, however*, That such tax shall not become a lien or charge of any kind or character against the land or the property of the Indian owner.

[27] 303 U. S. 376 (1938).

[28] 257 U. S. 501 (1922). But see dissenting opinion in *Helvering* v. *Producers Corp.*, 303 U. S. 376, 387 (1938).

[29] In its original form the tax immunity of governmental lessees seemed a relatively innocuous doctrine designed to protect the income of the Indian wards of the nation. See Note, 51 Harv. L. Rev. 707, 712, fn. 36 (1938). But from exemption of the gross income of the lessee of Indian lands, the cases progressed through exemption of net receipts to serious impairment of the taxing powers of Oklahoma. *Choctaw, Okla. & G. R. R.* v. *Harrison*, 235 U. S. 292 (1914) (gross income tax; rent paid directly to Federal Government); *Indian Territory Illuminating Oil Co.* v. *Oklahoma*, 240 U. S. 522 (1916) (leaseholds of Indian land exempt from general property tax); *Howard* v. *Gipsy Oil Co.*, 247 U. S. 503 (1918) (gross production tax in lieu of property taxes); *Gillespie* v. *Oklahoma*, 257 U. S. 501 (1922) (net income tax; interstate commerce analogy rejected); *Jaybird Mining Co.* v. *Weir*, 271 U. S. 609 (1926) (non-discriminatory property tax on ore at mine before sale). But *cf. Indian Territory Illuminating Oil Co.* v. *Board*, 288 U. S. 325 (1933) (oil taxable before sale, where royalty already paid to Indians).

[30] *Railroad Co.* v. *Peniston*, 18 Wall. 5, 33 (1873). *Cf. Clallum County* v. *United States*, 263 U. S. 341 (1923). See also discussion of federal income tax, *infra*, sec. 7B.

[31] 48 Stat. 984.

[32] See *Clallum County* v. *United States*, 263 U. S. 341 (1923).

[33] *Utah and Northern Railway* v. *Fisher*, 116 U. S. 28 (1885); *Maricopa and Phoenix Railroad* v. *Arizona*, 156 U. S. 347 (1895).

[34] *Choctaw, O. & G. R. R.* v. *Mackey*, 256 U. S. 531 (1921).

[35] *New Jersey* v. *Wilson*, 7 Cranch 164 (1812), *Cf. Fink* v. *County Commissioners*, 248 U. S. 399 (1919); *Sweet* v. *Schock*, 245 U. S. 192 (1917).

[36] 43 Stat. 244.

SECTION 3. STATE TAXATION OF INDIVIDUAL INDIAN LANDS

A. TREATY ALLOTMENTS

The earliest individual Indian land holdings with which the cases are concerned are those resulting from treaty. The early case of *The Kansas Indians* involved, among others, the question of whether tribal lands conveyed, pursuant to treaty, to tribal members in severalty were exempt from state taxation. As we have seen[37] the Court was of the opinion that since "There is no evidence * * * to show that the Indians with separate estates have not the same rights in the tribe as those whose estates are held in common," and since "as long as the United States recognizes their [the tribes'] national character they are under the protection of treaties and the laws of Congress, and their property is withdrawn from the operation of State laws," the individual Indian holdings, as those of the tribe, are exempt from state taxation.

Similarly, lands allotted pursuant to treaty to a chief of the

[37] 5 Wall. 737, 756, 757 (1866). See Fn. 24 *supra*.

Miamies and restricted as to alienation remain tax exempt even in the hands of the heirs of the allottee, provided that tribal relations are maintained.[38]

With the growth of the practice of allotting tribal lands in severalty the question of their exemption from state taxation became of increasing importance. We find the courts holding uniformly that restricted lands within an Indian reservation remain exempt from taxation. The extent, however, of their immunity from taxation is dependent in each case upon the statute under which the allotment is made. Conversely, land held by individual Indians outside an Indian reservation is exempt only to the extent that it is declared exempt by statute or state constitution or is recognized by the court as a federal instrumentality.[39]

B. THE GENERAL ALLOTMENT ACT

The division of tribal lands in severalty to individual Indians was largely accomplished by the General Allotment Act of 1887.[40] This act did not apply to all the Indians, several tribes, including the Five Civilized Tribes inhabiting the Indian Territory, which has since become a part of Oklahoma, being omitted.[41] However, it covered all Indian tribes except those explicitly named, and provided for the allotment to individual Indians of tracts of land for their own use. Under it the President was authorized to allot to individual Indians plots of land, and the Secretary of the Interior to issue patents

> * * * in the name of the allottees, which patents shall be of the legal effect, and declare that the United States does and will hold the land thus allotted, for the period of twenty-five years, in trust for the sole use and benefit of the Indian to whom such allotment shall have been made, * * * and that at the expiration of said period the United States will convey the same by patent to said Indian, or his heirs as aforesaid, in fee, discharged of said trust and free of all charge or incumbrance whatsoever.[42] * * * (P. 389.)

Buttressing their holding with the argument that the "trust" is the means whereby the Federal Government exercises control over the Indian ward in order to fulfill the duty of care and protection which it owes him, the courts have uniformly declared the subject of that trust a federal instrumentality and hence not subject to state taxation. As said by the Supreme Court[43] in quoting a statement of the Attorney General:

> It was therefore well said by the Attorney General of the United States, in an opinion delivered in 1888, "that the allotment lands provided for in the Act of 1887 are exempt from state or territorial taxation upon the ground above stated, * * * namely, that the lands covered by the act are held by the United States for the period of twenty-five years in trust for the Indians, such trust being an agency for the exercise of a Federal power, and therefore outside the province of state or territorial authority. 19 Op. Atty. Gen. 161, 169. (P. 439.)

The courts have also argued that the lands allotted under this act are not subject to state taxation, on the theory that if the lands were taxable, they could be incumbered, and any incumbrance would prevent the United States from fulfilling its trust obligation.[44]

Similarly, lands allotted under authority of acts incorporating the General Allotment Act by reference are not taxable.[45] In *Morrow* v. *United States*[46] the court said that the exemption arose from the legal trusteeship obligating the United States to convey free of encumbrance, rather than from any concept of "governmental wardship over a dependent and inferior people." (P. 859.)

The futility of exempting the lands and not the improvements thereon was recognized in *United States* v. *Rickert*[47] wherein the court said:

> Looking at the object to be accomplished by allotting Indian lands in severalty, it is evident that Congress expected that the lands so allotted would be improved and cultivated by the allottee. But that object would be defeated if the improvements could be assessed and sold for taxes. The improvements to which the question refers were of a permanent kind. While the title to the land remained in the United States, the permanent improvements could no more be sold for local taxes than could the land to which they belonged. Every reason that can be urged to show that the land was not subject to local taxation applies to the assessment and taxation of the permanent improvements.
>
> * * * * *
>
> * * * The fact remains that the improvements here in question are essentially a part of the lands, and their use by the Indians is necessary to effectuate the policy of the United States. (P. 442.)

It is clear, of course, that an allotment made under the General Allotment Act[48] remained exempt from taxation so long as the land was held in trust by the United States.[49] The allottee was thus assured that his lands would be tax exempt for at least 25 years and perhaps longer. However, in 1906[50] Congress empowered the Secretary of the Interior, before the expiration of the 25-year trust period, to issue a patent in fee "whenever he shall be satisfied that any Indian allottee is competent and capable of managing his or her affairs * * *." The duration of the exemption came thus to be determined according to the federal Indian policy in vogue at any particular time.[51] Yet, the importance to the Indian of his tax immunity can hardly be underestimated. The consequences of the vesting of a fee patent have been expressed in Meriam, The Problem of Indian Administration as follows:

> * * * The statistics of Indian property previously given in this chapter demonstrate the fact, so obvious to persons who visit the Indian country, that the value of the Indian lands is relatively high as compared with the

[38] *Wau-Pe-Man-Qua* v. *Aldrich*, 28 Fed. 489 (C. C. Ind. 1886). *Cf.* *Lowry* v. *Weaver*, 15 Fed. Cas. No. 8584 (C. C. Ind. 1846).

[39] *Pennock* v. *Commissioners*, 103 U. S. 44 (1880).

[40] Act of February 8, 1887, 24 Stat. 388. See Chapter 4, sec. 11, and Chapter 11.

[41] The act, by its terms, did not apply to territory occupied by the Cherokees, Creeks, Choctaws, Chickasaws, Seminoles, Osages, Miamies, Peorias, Sacs, and Foxes, in the Indian Territory, nor to any reservations occupied by the Seneca Nation in New York, nor to a certain strip of land in Nebraska, adjoining the Sioux Nation on the south. For a discussion of state taxation of the lands of the Five Civilized Tribes and the Osages see Chapter 23.

[42] The trust period was extended from time to time by various Executive orders, and indefinitely by the Act of June 18, 1934, 48 Stat. 984.

[43] *United States* v. *Rickert*, 188 U. S. 432 (1903).

[44] *Morrow* v. *United States*, 243 Fed. 854 (C. C. A. 8, 1917); *Board of Com'rs.* v. *United States*, 100 F. 2d 929 (C. C. A. 10, 1938), mod. 60 Sup. Ct. 285 (1939); *Glacier County, Mont.* v. *United States*, 99 F. 2d 733 (C. C. A. 9, 1938); *United States* v. *Benewah County, Idaho*, 290 Fed. 628 (C. C. A. 9, 1923); *United States* v. *Chehalis County*, 217 Fed. 281 (D. C. W. D. Wash. 1914); *United States* v. *Ferry County, Washington*, 24 F. Supp. 399 (D. C. E. D. Wash., 1938); see *United States* v. *Nez Perce County, Idaho*, 95 F. 2d 232 (C. C. A. 9, 1938), rehearing den. 95 F. 2d 238 (C. C. A. 9, 1938).

[45] *E. g.*, Nelson Act of January 14, 1889, 25 Stat. 642, 643, sec. 3, applied to Minnesota Chippewas in *Morrow* v. *United States*, 243 Fed. 854 (C. C. A. 8, 1917); *cf.*, *United States* v. *Spaeth*, 24 F. Supp. 465 (D. C. Minn. 1938); Act of June 6, 1900, 31 Stat. 672, 678, sec. 5 (Comanches, Kiowas, and Apaches) discussed in *United States* v. *Board of Com'rs (Comanche County)*, 6 F. Supp. 401 (D. C. W. D. Okla. 1934); Act of March 3, 1893, 27 Stat. 557, applying to the Kickapoos in Indian Territory. *Cf. United States* v. *Matthewson*, 32 F. 2d 745 (C. C. A. 8, 1929).

[46] 243 Fed. 854 (C. C. A. 8, 1917).

[47] 188 U. S. 432 (1903).

[48] Act of February 8, 1887, 24 Stat. 388.

[49] *United States* v. *Rickert*, 188 U. S. 432 (1903).

[50] Act of May 8, 1906, 34 Stat. 182.

[51] For a discussion of such policy and its effects, see Chapters 2 and 11.

> Indians' income from the use of that land. The general property tax, although based on the value of land, must be paid from income unless it is to result in the forfeiture of the land itself. Bad as is the general property tax from many points of view, it is peculiarly bad when applied to Indians suddenly removed from the status of a tax exempt incompetent and subjected to the full weight of state and local taxation. So far as the Indians are concerned, the tax violates the accepted canon of taxation that a tax shall be related to the capacity to pay. The levying of these taxes has without doubt been an important factor in causing the loss of Indian lands by so large a proportion of those Indians who have been declared competent.
>
> The policies involved in making individual allotments and issuing fee patents brought into the economic problems of the Indian Service the difficult subject of taxation. Under the allotment act the incompetent Indian holding a trust patent is generally exempt from taxation. On the day he is declared competent and is given his fee patent, he straightway becomes subject to the full burden of state and local taxation. The more common form of taxation is the general property tax, the basis of which is the value of the property owned and the burden of which falls heavily on land, because it cannot slip out from under in the way other forms of property frequently do.
>
> Many wise, conservative Indians, with a keen power to observe the experience of others, have no desire to progress to the point where they will be declared competent and be obliged to pay taxes. They know that the taxes will consume a large proportion of their total income and that taxes are inescapable. To them to achieve the status of competency means in all probability the ultimate loss of their lands. From their point of view the reward for success is the imposition of an annual fine. (P. 477.)

A policy of "great liberalism" inaugurated in 1917 led to wholesale patenting in fee whether the allottee desired the patent or not. Fairly typical is the following description by the Court of Appeals for the Tenth Circuit:[52]

> * * * Briefly, the record discloses that in the year 1918 patents covering the lands involved were issued to the United States in trust for twenty-seven Indians to whom the lands had been allotted in severalty. Within two years thereafter, fee patents were issued to these Indians. It is stipulated that the fee title was granted to the Indians without any application on their part and without their consent. Apparently there was some opposition among the Indians to the policy of the Department and some had said that they would not receipt for the fee patents. There is a letter in the record written under date of April 24, 1918 from the office of the Commissioner of Indian Affairs to the special superintendent in charge at the reservation, instructing the latter to inform the Indians that the Secretary of the Interior "has the right to issue these patents, and if they refuse to accept them, you are directed to have the patents recorded and after recording same, to send them to the patentees by registered mail and retain the receipt cards for the files in your office." (P. 734.)

The year 1921 saw a reversal of policy in the issuing of patents and recent years have witnessed the cancellation of such patents[53] and a variety of suits by the Federal Government seeking to recover taxes paid the state by the allottee, to enjoin further taxation and to strike allotments from the tax rolls.[54] In all these cases the Government was successful on a rationale perhaps best expressed in *United States* v. *Nez Perce County, Idaho*,[55] as follows:

> * * * The Allotment Act, as well as the trust patent, by plain implication granted the Indian immunity from taxation during the trust period or any extension of it, and he had the right finally to receive his lands "free of all charge or incumbrance whatsoever." The authorities are uniform to the effect that this right of exemption is a vested right, as much a part of the grant as the land itself, and the Indian may not be deprived of it by the unwanted issuance to him of a fee patent prior to the end of the trust period. *Choate* v. *Trapp*, 224 U. S. 665, 32 S. Ct. 565, 56 L. Ed. 941; *Ward* v. *Love County*, 253 U. S. 17, 40 S. Ct. 419, 64 L. Ed. 751; *United States* v. *Benewah County*, 9 Cir., 290 F. 628; *Morrow* v. *United States*, 8 Cir., 243 F. 854; *Board of Com'rs of Caddo County* v. *United States*, 10 Cir., 87 F. 2d 55; *United States* v. *Dewey County*, D. C., 14 F. 2d 784; *United States* v. *Comanche County*, D. C., 6 F. Supp. 401; *United States* v. *Chehalis County*, D. C., 217 F. 281. Treaties with the Indians and acts of Congress relative to their rights in property reserved to them have always been liberally construed by the courts. The dependent condition of these wards of the Government makes it imperative that doubtful provisions in treaties and statutes be resolved in their favor. This court in *United States* v. *Benewah County*, *supra*, as early as 1923 declared that the Act of May 8, 1906, should be held to mean that the action of the Secretary of the Interior authorized by it can be had only on the application of the allottee or with his consent. The Act of February 26, 1927, was little more than a statutory recognition of the principle there announced. The fee patent in the present instance was issued during the trust period, or at least during an extension of that period. It follows from what has been said that, if it was issued to Carter without his application or consent, his land remained immune from taxation during the whole of the time from 1921 to 1932, and the lien of the county should be held void. (Pp. 235–236.)

Therefore, it would appear that the allottee under the General Allotment Act obtains a vested right to tax exemption which cannot be taken from him without his consent.[56] Should he, on the other hand, apply for the issuance of a fee patent and be accorded one pursuant to law, there seems no reason to believe that his lands would not thereby become subject to state taxation.[57]

C. HOMESTEAD ALLOTMENTS

Lands acquired by individual Indians under the general homestead laws are exempt from taxation for specified periods following the date of issuance of the patent. Section 15 of the Homestead Act of March 3, 1875,[58] extended to Indians born in the United States who were heads of families or over 21 years of age and who have abandoned or shall abandon tribal relations, the benefits of the General Homestead Act of 1862.[59] The 1875 Act defined a tax exemption for a 5-year period by providing that the title to the lands acquired under it

> * * * shall not be subject to alienation or incumbrance, either by voluntary conveyance or the judgment,

[52] *Glacier County, Mont.* v. *United States*, 99 F. 2d 733 (C. C. A. 9, 1938).

[53] Authority for such cancellation is accorded by the Act of February 26, 1927, 44 Stat. 1247, which provides:

> * * * That the Secretary of the Interior is hereby authorized, in his discretion, to cancel any patent in fee simple issued to an Indian allottee or to his heirs before the end of the period of trust described in the original or trust patent issued to such allottee, or before the expiration of any extension of such period of trust by the President, where such patent in fee simple was issued without the consent or an application therefor by the allottee or by his heirs: *Provided*, That the patentee has not mortgaged or sold any part of the land described in such patent: *Provided also*, That upon cancellation of such patent in fee simple the land shall have the same status as though such fee patent had never been issued.

See also Act of February 21, 1931, 46 Stat. 1205.

[54] *United States* v. *Benewah County*, 290 Fed. 628 (C. C. A. 9, 1923); *United States* v. *Board of Com'rs*, 6 F. Supp. 401 (D. C. W. D. Okla. 1934); *United States* v. *Ferry County, Washington*, 24 F. Supp. 399 (D. C. E. D. Wash. 1938).

[55] 95 F. 2d 232 (C. C. A. 9, 1938).

[56] *United States* v. *Ferry County, Washington*, 24 F. Supp. 399 (D. C. E. D. Wash., 1938). For an account of legislation designed to deal with this situation, see Chapter 5, sec. 11B.

[57] *Ibid.* Accord: 50 L. D. 691 (1924).

[58] 18 Stat. 402, 420.

[59] Act of May 20, 1862, 12 Stat. 392, allowing citizens over 21 or heads of families to enter a quarter section of public lands. This act was thought not to include Indians because they were not considered citizens. *United States* v. *Joyce*, 240 Fed. 610 (C. C. A. 8, 1917).

> decree, or order of any court, and shall be and remain inalienable for a period of five years from the date of the patent issued therefor.[34] * * *

This act was supplemented by the Act of July 4, 1884,[35] which applied the homestead laws to Indians generally who had located on public lands rather than to a specified class,[36] and contained a 25-year[37] trust period provision almost identical to that contained in the General Allotment Act.[38] The same principles applied to the General Allotment Act allotments would seem, therefore, applicable to lands acquired under the 1884 Act.[39]

D. LAND PURCHASED WITH RESTRICTED FUNDS

In 1928 the Meriam report on "The Problem of Indian Administration" was published. Its authors had had occasion to study the then perplexing problem of the taxability of lands purchased with restricted funds and their comments concerning it are particularly enlightening:

> * * * A perplexing problem confronting the Indian Office today is the taxation by the states of the lands purchased for the Indians with their restricted funds which are under the supervision of the Office. The volume of such purchases is large because the allotments originally made to the Indians are often not suitable for homes. These original allotments must be sold and new property purchased if the Indians are to be started on the road to better social and economic conditions. In order to preserve these new lands for the use and benefit of the Indian owner, it has been the uniform rule to impose upon them the restrictions which existed upon the funds with which they were obtained. Some states are claiming and exercising the power to tax such lands. Since the Indian owner, on account of his lack of ready funds or his insufficient sense of public responsibility, either cannot or will not pay taxes, the result is that the lands purchased for his permanent home are speedily slipping from him and he himself is becoming a homeless public charge. This unfortunate situation is rendered more acute because the terms of the deeds prohibit alienation by voluntary act, and thus the Indian owner is not able either to mortgage or sell his lands to secure for himself the interest that he may have in the land over and above the delinquent taxes.
>
> The United States Supreme Court[40] held at an early date that the allotted lands of the Indians, the title to which was held in trust by the United States, were not taxable by the states. The policy of allotting land to the Indians and holding the title to it in abeyance until such time as they could be trusted with its full and free control had been adopted by the national government as a means for more fully civilizing the Indians and bringing them to the position where they could assume the full responsibility of citizenship. The lands were therefore the instrumentalities of the United States, and as such, by virtue of longstanding principles of constitutional law, not taxable by the several states. To this unquestioned decision may be added the ruling that, in the event of the sale of the allotted lands by governmental consent, the proceeds, being simply the medium for which the lands were exchanged, were likewise held in trust by the government and not taxable.[41] The Supreme Court has also sustained the power of the Secretary of the Interior, in whom is vested the discretion to permit the conveyance of Indian lands, to allow such conveyance on the sole condition that the proceeds be invested in lands subject to his control in the matter of sale.[42]

[34] See *United States* v. *Hemmer*, 241 U. S. 379 (1916).

[35] 23 Stat. 76, 96.

The 1875 Act was also supplemented by the Act of January 18, 1881, 21 Stat. 315, making funds available to the Winnebagoes of Wisconsin so they could avail themselves of the benefits of it. That act expressly provided that titles acquired by the Winnebagoes should be nontaxable for 20 years from date of issuance of the patent.

[36] For discussions comparing the two acts, see *United States* v. *Hemmer*, 241 U. S. 379, 384–385 (1916); *United States* v. *Corporation of the President Etc.*, 101 F. 2d 156 (C. C. A. 10, 1939).

[37] This trust period was extended to 1945 by Executive orders issued under authority of Act of June 21, 1906, 34 Stat. 325, 326, and indefinitely under the Act of June 18, 1934, 48 Stat. 984.

[38] See sec. 3B, *supra*.

[39] See discussion of General Allotment Act, *supra*, sec. 3B. Also see *United States* v. *Jackson*, 280 U. S. 183 (1930).

[40] *United States* v. *Rickert*, 188 U. S. 432, (1903).

[41] *National Bank of Commerce* v. *Anderson*, 147 Fed. 87 (C. C. A. 9th Cir. 1906); *United States* v. *Thurston County*, 143 Fed. 287 (C. C. A. 8th Cir. 1906).

[42] *United States* v. *Sunderland*, 266 U. S. 226 (1924). See also *United States* v. *Brown*, 8 Fed. 2nd 564 (C. C. A. 8th Cir. 1925), holding that the Secretary of the Interior may purchase lands for the Indians with money arising from the lease of restricted lands, and restrict the title of the lands purchased.

In spite of the intimation from these cases and from the express decisions of two district courts of the Northwest[43] more favorable to the Indians, the exemption from state taxes of restricted lands purchased for them by the government with their restricted funds is in a precarious situation. In a case which was taken to the United States Supreme Court[44] it was held that lands purchased with trust funds for an Osage Indian, and made inalienable without the consent of the Secretary of the Interior, were yet taxable. This decision, however, did not involve necessarily the declaration of a general principle, since the ruling was occasioned by the fact that the special act[45] under which these particular funds were released to the allottee gave to the Secretary no authority to control said funds after such release. In this case, moreover, it was not shown that the money released from the trust was invested directly in the property purchased. The thought of the court is perhaps shown in its closing remark, "Congress did not confer upon the Secretary of the Interior authority * * * to give to property purchased with released funds immunity from state taxation." By a series of recent decisions[46] the Circuit Court of Appeals for the Eighth Circuit, although omitting some dicta favorable to the Indian position, has uniformly sustained state taxation of lands purchased for the Indians with their restricted funds and made subject to alienation only with the consent of the Secretary of the Interior, and has declared itself committed to the proposition that such lands are taxable.[46a] One of these cases was affirmed by the United States Supreme Court[47] in a *per curiam* decision on the somewhat doubtful authority of the McCurdy case *supra*.[48]

[43] *United States* v. *Nez Perce County*, 267 Fed. 495 (D. C. Idaho, 1917); *United States* v. *Yakima County*, 274 Fed. 115 (D. C. E. D. Wash. 1921).

[44] *United States* v. *McCurdy*, 246 U. S. 263 (1918).

[45] Section 5 of the act of April 18, 1912.

[46] *United States* v. *Gray*, 284 Fed. 103 (1922); *United States* v. *Ransom*, 284 Fed. 108 (1922); *United States* v. *Brown*, 8 Fed. 2nd 584 (1925), dictum; *United States* v. *Mummert*, 15 Fed. 2nd 926 (1926).

[47] *United States* v. *Ransom*, 263 U. S. 691 (1924).

[48] *United States* v. *McCurdy*, 246 U. S. 263 (1918).

The declaration by the Circuit Court of Appeals[49] that the national government has no authority to withdraw from state taxation lands formerly subject thereto is certainly not tenable. Congress has the power to relieve from the burden of state taxes a governmental instrumentality, whether a post office or a home for the government's Indian wards, and it matters not that the prior status of the property may have been such that the state could freely tax it.

[49] *United States* v. *Brown*, 8 F. 2d 584 (1925), dictum.

[46a] On the other hand, some courts have held that where land is purchased for an Indian with restricted funds from another Indian who held it tax exempt, it is tax exempt in the hands of the new purchaser, the reason given being that the lands and funds involved were at all times used by the United States in the discharge of its obligation to its Indian wards. *McGeehan* v. *Ashland County*, 192 Wis. 177, 212 N. W. 283 (1927); *United States* v. *G. Meriwether* (D. C. E. D. Okla. June 14, 1934), Justice file No. 90–2–11–431; *Marble* v. *King* (D. C. N. D. Okla. August 27, 1934) Justice File No. 90–2–5–36; *United States* v. *Stone* (D. C. W. D. Okla. September 29, 1934), Justice File No. 90–2–11–322.

If, as has been inferred, there be doubt as to the intention of Congress to give immunity from state taxation, it is recommended that legislation be secured expressly conferring the exemption. The states will not suffer from such a practice, for in return for the lost taxes on the purchased lands will be the subjection to the state taxing power of the relinquished lands, or of the funds used in making the new purchase.

Pending litigation should, of course, be pressed to a final conclusion with all possible speed in order that the existing uncertainty be ended. Should it transpire that these Indian lands are taxable, then the national government must fairly consider the nature of the duty to the ward of the guardian who has employed the ward's tax-exempt funds to purchase property on the express or implied misrepresentation that the newly-acquired property is likewise exempt. Several Indians have complained to the survey staff that they are being taxed despite the formal assurance of Indian Service employees that the land purchased for them would be exempt from taxation.[67] (Pp. 795–798.)

In the case of *Shaw* v. *Gibson-Zahniser Oil Corp.*,[68] lands outside a reservation purchased with restricted Indian funds and subject to a restraint against alienation were held subject to state property taxation. The court, however, recognized the fact that:

> There are some instrumentalities which, though Congress may protect them from state taxation, will nevertheless be subject to that taxation unless Congress speaks. (P. 581.)

Thereafter by the Act of June 20, 1936,[69] Congress expressly exempted such lands from state taxation. In order that its purpose and meaning may be more fully understood, both section 1 and section 2 of the 1936 Act are quoted in full:

> That there is hereby authorized to be appropriated, out of any money in the Treasury of the United States not otherwise appropriated, the sum of $25,000, to be expended under such rules and regulations as the Secretary of the Interior may prescribe, for payment of taxes, including penalties and interest, assessed against individually owned Indian land the title to which is held subject to restrictions against alienation or encumbrance except with the consent or approval of the Secretary of the Interior, heretofore purchased out of trust or restricted funds of an Indian, where the Secretary finds that such land was purchased with the understanding and belief on the part of said Indian that after purchase it would be nontaxable, and for redemption or reacquisition of any such land heretofore or hereafter sold for nonpayment of taxes.
>
> SEC. 2. All lands the title to which is now held by an Indian subject to restrictions against alienation or encumbrance except with the consent or approval of the Secretary of the Interior, heretofore purchased out of trust or restricted funds of said Indian, are hereby declared to be instrumentalities of the Federal Government and shall be nontaxable until otherwise directed by Congress.

The 1937 amendment[70] to section 2 of the above act reads as follows:

> All homesteads, heretofore purchased out of the trust or restricted funds of individual Indians, are hereby declared to be instrumentalities of the Federal Government and shall be nontaxable until otherwise directed by Congress: *Provided*, That the title to such homesteads shall be held subject to restrictions against alienation or encumbrance except with the approval of the Secretary of the Interior: *And provided further*, That the Indian owner or owners shall select, with the approval of the Secretary of the Interior, either the agricultural and grazing lands, not exceeding a total of one hundred and sixty acres, or the village, town, or city property, not exceeding in cost $5,000, to be designated as a homestead.

The 1936 Act was passed to establish the tax-exemption of the lands purchased with restricted funds under the guidance and direction of the Interior Department as tax-exempt lands. After the passage of the act it was found that section 2 had application to such a large quantity of lands that a bill was introduced in Congress for its repeal. This bill was, however, amended on the recommendation of the Senate Committee on Indian Affairs to provide for restricting the tax exemption to homesteads purchased with trust or restricted funds rather than for repealing the tax exemption entirely, and the bill was passed in this amended form. The report of the Senate Committee in which this recommendation was made contains the following pertinent statement of the purpose of the 1936 Act and the 1937 amendment:

> The said act of June 20, 1936 (49 Stat. L. 1542) was designed to bring relief and reimbursement to Indians who by failure to pay taxes have lost or now are in danger of losing lands purchased for them under supervision, advice, and guidance of the Federal Government, which losses were not the fault of the Indians, but were purchased with the understanding and belief on their part and induced by representations of the Government that the lands be nontaxable after purchase. It was intended that such lands would be redeemed out of the fund of $25,000 authorized to be appropriated under the provisions of said act of June 20, 1936 (49 Stat. L. 1542).
>
> Since the passage of said act of June 20, 1936 (49 Stat. L. 1542), it was found the provisions of section 2 thereof would apply to lands and other property purchased by restricted Indian funds, which would exempt from taxation vast quantities of property, such as business buildings, farm lands which are not homesteads, etc.
>
> The Commissioner of Indian Affairs appeared before the committee and suggested the amendment herein proposed, which proposed amendment was adopted and herein recommended by your committee. (Senate Report No. 332, 75th Cong., 1st sess.)

In *United States* v. *Board of Com'rs.*,[71] the court, in construing these statutes, held that Congress had the power to define federal instrumentalities, and that the 1936 Act clearly applied to prevent taxation for 1936[72] of real estate used for both residence and business purposes which was purchased with restricted funds of Osage Indians. The court said that the act applied to Indians in general, and was not made inapplicable to the Osages by reason of prior acts referring specifically to Osage homesteads.

In an unreported case, the same court applied these statutes to prevent taxation of homesteads purchased with trust funds held on deposit by the United States for Pawnee Indians in lieu of allotment.[73]

The further extent of the operation of these statutes is not known at the present time, but they express the clear intent of Congress to continue homesteads of Indians tax exempt, whether the homestead was purchased for the Indian or allotted to him.[74]

---

[67] The legislation referred to was finally enacted in 1936. Act of June 20, 1936, 49 Stat. 1542. *Cf.*, Act of June 30, 1932, 47 Stat. 474.

[68] 276 U. S. 575 (1928).

[69] 49 Stat. 1542. Upheld in *United States* v. *Board of Comm'rs*, 26 F. Supp. 270 (D. C. N. D. Okla. 1939).

[70] Act of May 19, 1937, 50 Stat. 188.

[71] 26 F. Supp. 270 (D. C. N. D. Okla. 1939) (Osage County). The court followed the view expressed in 56 I. D. 48 (1937) as to the applicability of the 1936 act to the Osages.

[72] The court held that the act was in force at the date of levy which was the critical date.

[73] *United States* v. *Board of County Com'rs. of Pawnee County, Okla.* (D. C. N. D. Okla., January 19, 1939), Justice File No. 90-2-11-610.

[74] For a discussion of questions of tax exemption not yet passed upon by the courts, see Op. Sol. I. D., M.29867 (1939). And *cf.* letter of Attorney General dated October 6, 1939, declining to pass upon cases therein discussed.

SECTION 4. STATE TAXATION OF PERSONAL PROPERTY

Wherever personal property is acquired by or for tribal Indians for use on Indian reservation lands in connection with or in furtherance of the policy adopted by the Government in encouraging the Indians to cultivate the soil and to establish permament homes and families, or otherwise aid in their economic rehabilitation, such property may not be taxed by the state.[75] The immunity exists whether the property be purchased with moneys held in trust by the United States for the Indians or with moneys accruing to the Indians from other federal sources. The reason behind this doctrine of immunity is that the state has no power, by taxation or otherwise, to retard, impede, burden, or control the operations or instrumentalities employed by the Federal Government in carrying into execution the powers lawfully vested in it.

In *United States* v. *Thurston County*[76] the Circuit Court of Appeals for the Eighth Circuit ruled that the proceeds of the sales of allotted lands held in trust by the United States were exempt from state taxation for the reason that the proceeds like the lands from which they were derived constituted an instrumentality lawfully employed by the Government in the exercise of its powers to protect, support and instruct the Indians. The court said, among other things:

> The allotted lands were held in trust by the United States for the benefit of those to whom they were assigned, and their heirs, under the acts of August 7, 1882, and February 8, 1887. The proceeds of the sales of these lands have been lawfully substituted for the lands themselves by the trustee. The substitutes partake of the nature of the originals, and stand charged with the same trust. The lands and their proceeds, so long as they are held or controlled by the United States and the term of the trust has not expired, are alike instrumentalities employed by it in the lawful exercise of its powers of government to protect, support, and instruct the Indians, for whose benefit the complainant holds them, and they are not subject to taxation by any state or county. (P. 292.)

The doctrine of the foregoing case was approved in *United States* v. *Pearson*,[77] a case involving issue property, that is, property issued to the Indians by the Federal Government. Immunity from state taxation was there extended to personal property which could be traced and identified as issue property, the increase of issue property, property purchased with the proceeds of the sale of issue property, property purchased with the proceeds of the sale of the increase of issue property, property for which similar issue property has been exchanged for similar use, the increase of property received in such exchange, the increase of issue property exchanged for similar property for similar use, and property purchased with money given to the Indians by the United States.

To the same general effect is *United States* v. *Dewey County*[78] and *United States* v. *Rickert*.[79] In the case last cited the court held that personal property consisting of horses, cattle, and other property issued by the United States to the Indians and used by them on their allotments was not subject to assessment and taxation by the state.

For the same reason that property purchased by Indians with restricted funds and property issued to the Indians by the Government are Government instrumentalities, property purchased by the Indians pursuant to a specific plan for economic rehabilitation approved by the Government and carried out under Government supervision should likewise be recognized as a Government instrumentality. As said by the Solicitor of the Interior Department:[80]

> The purchase of property by the Indians themselves in accordance with an economic plan worked out with the Government is supplanting, as a method of assuring the possession by Indians of productive property, the old method of the Government's issuing such property to the Indians. From a legal viewpoint the purpose and concern of the Government are identical whether the plow or the cattle are bought by the Indian with Individual Indian Moneys, the expenditure of which has been approved by the Superintendent, or bought by the Indians with revolving loan funds or judgment fund money, pursuant to a plan of rehabilitation approved by the Superintendent, or bought by the Superintendent with gratuity funds and issued to the Indians. The reasoning of the courts applies equally to these procedures, except that in the cases above cited the Government had an ownership interest as the title to the property was found to be in the United States. The form of title, while indicative of the interest of the Government, is not, in my opinion, the determining factor. The important factor is the acquisition and use of the property in execution of a government plan for the Indians.

There are apparently no cases determining the right of the state to tax personal property of an Indian on a reservation which is not used pursuant to some federal plan. Apparently no state has attempted to collect such a tax. The doctrine that Indians on a reservation are not subject to state law in the absence of congressional authority[81] would indicate that any such tax would be invalid.

On the other hand, personalty issued to an Indian by the Federal Government and used by him outside the reservation is taxable by the state.[82]

Personalty owned by non-Indians but held on an Indian reservation is subject to state taxation.[83] This is true even though the personalty belongs to a Catholic mission situated on an Indian reservation and devoting both the personalty and the proceeds therefrom to the welfare of the Indians. In so deciding the Supreme Court declared:[84]

> Taking the complaint as it is, it shows on its face that the Indians have neither any legal nor equitable title to the property, neither have they any legal or equitable right to its beneficial use, and it also appears from the complaint that the property is owned unconditionally and absolutely by the plaintiff. The plaintiff, as the owner of these cattle, may, at any time, abandon its present manner of using them and may devote them, or any income arising from their ownership, to any other purpose it may choose, and the Indians would have no legal right of complaint. The plaintiff might refuse to spend another dollar upon the Indians upon these reservations, and refuse to further maintain or aid them in any way whatever, and no right of the Indians would be thereby violated, nor could they call upon the courts to enforce the application of the plaintiff's property, or the income thereof, to the same purposes the plaintiff had theretofore applied them. There is noth-

[75] This immunity extends to the personalty of a half-blood Indian adopted into a tribe, *United States* v. *Heyfron*, 138 Fed. 964 (C. C. Mont. 1905), and in fact to the personalty of any recognized member of an Indian tribe. *United States* v. *Higgins*, 103 Fed. 348 (C. C. Mont. 1900). But *cf. United States* v. *Higgins*, 110 Fed. 609 (C. C. Mont. 1901).

[76] 143 Fed. 287 (C. C. A. 8, 1906).

[77] 231 Fed. 270 (D. C. S. Dak. 1916).

[78] 14 F. 2d 784 (D. C. S. Dak. 1926), aff'd. sub nom. *Dewey County* v. *United States*, 26 F. 2d 434 (C. C. A. 8, 1928), cert. den. 278 U. S. 649.

[79] 188 U. S. 432 (1903). And see *McKnight* v. *United States*, 130 Fed. 659 (C. C. A. 9, 1904).

[80] Op. Sol. I. D., M.30449, May 8, 1940.

[81] See Chapter 6.

[82] *United States* v. *Porter*, 22 F. 2d 365 (C. C. A. 9, 1927).

[83] *Thomas* v. *Gay*, 169 U. S. 264 (1898); *Wagoner* v. *Evans*, 170 U. S. 588 (1898); *Catholic Missions* v. *Missoula County*, 200 U. S. 118 (1906); *Truscott* v. *Hurlbut Land & Cattle Co.*, 73 Fed. 60 (C. C. A. 9, 1896), app. dism. sub nom. *Hurlbut Land & Cattle Co.* v. *Truscott*, 165 U. S. 719 (1897).

[84] *Catholic Missions* v. *Missoula County*, 200 U. S. 118 (1906).

ing in *Mormon Church* v. *United States*, 136 U. S. 1, which in the remotest degree applies to this case. This court has heretofore determined that the Indians' interest in this kind of property, situated on their reservations, was not sufficient to exempt such property, when owned by private individuals, from taxation. *Thomas* v. *Gay*, 169 U. S. 264: *Wagoner* v. *Evans*, 170 U. S. 588. In the first of above-cited cases the right to graze over the reservation was leased by the Indians to the owners of the cattle, and it was alleged that if the cattle were taxed the value of the lands would be reduced, because the owners of the cattle would not pay as much for the right to graze as they would if their cattle were not subjected to taxation, and that therefore the tax was, in effect and substance, upon the land. This court held that the tax put upon the cattle of the lessees was too remote and indirect to be deemed a tax upon the lands or privileges of the Indians, citing *Erie Railroad* v. *Pennsylvania*, 158 U. S. 431, and other cases, as authority for the decision. This is reaffirmed in the second case above cited. In this case the Indians have not even given a lease, and the owners are not obliged to pay anything for the privilege of grazing, and may, as we have said, devote the property, or the income thereof, to purposes wholly foreign to the Indians themselves. However meritorious the conduct of the owners of the cattle may be, in devoting the income or any portion of the principal of their property to the charitable work of improving and educating the Indians (and we cordially admit the merit of such conduct), we cannot see that there is, on that account, the least claim for exemption from taxation because of any Federal provision, constitutional or otherwise. (Pp. 128–129.)

SECTION 5. STATE SALES TAXES

The question of the extent to which Indians and persons trading with Indians are subject to state sales taxes has been treated in a recent opinion of the Solicitor of the Interior Department.[58] Though the questions treated arose under Arizona statutes, the problem they present is a general one and the Arizona statutes involved are not dissimilar in substance from the sales tax laws of other states. For this reason the following copious quotations from the opinion serve to illuminate the entire subject:

> There are two Arizona statutes particularly involved, each of which is illustrative of a type of sales tax law. The Excise Revenue Act of 1935, Chapter 77, Laws Regular Session 1935, as amended by Chapter 2, Laws of First Special Session 1937, places an annual privilege tax on the business of selling at retail measured by the gross proceeds or the gross income from the business. Provision is made by the law for the use of tokens by purchasers to reimburse the dealers for the tax applicable to any sale. The other statute in question, Chapter 78, Laws Regular Session 1935, as amended in 1936, 1937, and 1939, places a tax on certain designated luxuries to be paid by stamps to be affixed to the articles by the dealers. Both statutes contain, as a method of enforcement, the requirement that all dealers shall take out State licenses. Both statutes provide for an exemption from the tax of businesses and transactions not subject to tax under the United States Constitution, and provide for refund to the dealer of the tax paid by him when proof is made that the transactions and articles taxed were not subject to tax under the law. In both statutes the tax is, on its face, a tax to be paid by dealers, whether wholesalers or retailers, and to be enforced against them, although both acts contemplate that the amount of the tax shall be added to the price paid by the consumer.
>
> 1. *Application of State taxes to persons trading with Indians.*
>
> The question of the application of these taxes to persons trading with Indians is subject to different answers depending upon the location of the trade and upon whether the traders or the persons dealt with are Indians. The regulation of trade with Indian tribes is one of the powers expressly delegated to Congress by section 8 of Article I of the United States Constitution. Congress has exercised this power in statutes restricting trade with the Indians and giving exclusive authority to the Commissioner of Indian Affairs to regulate such trade and the prices at which goods shall be sold to the Indians. (Sections 261 through 266, Title 25 of the United States Code.) These statutes, by their terms or by judicial construction, are limited in their application to Indian reservations. *United States* v. *Taylor*, 44 F. (2d) 537 (C. C. A. 9th, 1930), cert. den. 283 U. S. 820; *Rider* v. *La Clair*, 77 Wash. 488, 138 Pac. 3; *United States* v. *Certain Property*, 25 Pac. 517 (Ariz. 1871). Congress has not exercised its power to regulate trade with the Indians in so far as trade off the reservation is concerned except in the case of traffic in liquor.
>
> (a) Where Congress has exercised its authority it is axiomatic that the field is closed to State action. *Sperry Oil and Gas Co.* v. *Chisholm*, 264 U. S. 488. Therefore, persons selling to or buying from Indians on Indian reservations are not subject to State laws which regulate or tax such transactions. However, it should be emphasized that it is trade with the Indians which is removed from State interference and not the trader himself, if the trader is a white person and is dealing with other white persons, even though such transactions occur on a reservation.
>
> The Supreme Court has repeatedly permitted the taxation by the State of the property of white persons located on Indian reservations on the theory that such taxation did not interfere with the exercise of Federal authority within the reservation. *Thomas* v. *Gay*, 169 U. S. 264; *Wagoner* v. *Evans*, 170 U. S. 588; *Catholic Missions* v. *Missoula County*, 200 U. S. 118. This principle has been carried by the State courts to the extent of permitting State taxation of the property of Indian traders, including their stock in trade. *Moore* v. *Beason*, 7 Wyo. 292, 51 Pac. 875; *Cosier* v. *McMillan*, 22 Mont. 484, 56 Pac. 965; *Noble* v. *Amoretti*, 71 Pac. 879 (Wyo. 1903). In the review of the relationship between the Federal Government and the State government on an Indian reservation, in *Surplus Trading Co.* v. *Cook*, 281 U. S. 647, the Supreme Court stated that the jurisdiction of the State over the reservation is full and complete save as to the Indians and their property.
>
> In view of this jurisdiction of the State I held in my memorandum to the Commissioner of Indian Affairs of February 4, 1938, that white traders in their dealings with non-Indians must comply with the State laws, including those imposing sales taxes. I believe this ruling was correct. Traders on Indian reservations who are non-Indians are, in my opinion, required to take out licenses under the Arizona laws in question to carry on trade with non-Indians on the reservation, and must account to the State authorities for sales taxes on so much of their business as is done with non-Indians.[59] They are not required to account to the State authorities for their transactions with Indians on the reservations, but are, if they do deal with the Indians, required to conform with the licensing provisions in the Federal statutes regulating trade with Indians. Traders who are themselves Indians are not subject to the State laws whether they deal with Indians or non-Indians.
>
> (b) Where traders are not located on Indian reservations they are, in my opinion, responsible for the State taxes and subject to license whether or not they are Indians and whether or not they deal with Indians. Since

[58] Op. Sol. I. D., M.30449, May 8, 1940.

[59] The position of the Solicitor in this connection has been substantiated by the recent case of *Neah Bay Fish Co.* v. *Krummel*, 101 P. 2d 600 (Wash. 1940). The court there held that the State of Washington may levy a sales tax upon a company conducting business solely within the Indian reservation under a license from the Commissioner of Indian Affairs and the tribe, for sales made to persons other than Indians.

Congress has not attempted to regulate such trade and since such trade has been carried on subject to State laws for a long number of years, there is no ground for exemption of such trade in the absence of congressional authority, except in the special types of Indian purchases discussed in part 2 (b) of this opinion.

2. *Application of State taxes to sales to Indians.*

This subject falls into two parts—sales to Indians on the reservation and sales to Indians off the reservation.

(a) The preceding part of this opinion demonstrates that sales to Indians on the reservation are not subject to State taxation and Indian purchasers are not required to pay the additional cost which is added to the price of the article to cover the tax. Such additions to the price of articles by State action are clearly interferences with the authority of the Commissioner of Indian Affairs to regulate the prices at which goods shall be sold to the Indians.

(b) The preceding part of this opinion likewise demonstrates that when Indians purchase goods off the reservation they are not exempt from sales taxes on the ground of State interference with Federal regulation of Indian trade. However, certain purchases by Indians may be exempt on the ground that these purchases are instrumentalities of the Federal Government used to improve the economic conditions of its wards. Where this is the case, the purchase may be considered not subject to State taxation under the principle that the State, through the use of its taxing power, cannot hinder or interfere with an instrumentality of the Federal Government.

After noting the fact that personal property purchased by Indians with restricted funds and property issued to the Indians by the Government are Government instrumentalities, and that property purchased by the Indians pursuant to a specific plan for economic rehabilitation approved by the Government and carried out under Government supervision should likewise be recognized as a Government instrumentality, the opinion continues with a review of the authorities on the question of whether a state tax upon the acquisition of such property places an unconstitutional burden upon a federal instrumentality and concludes:

> The Supreme Court has held that the application of a State tax on the selling of gasoline to sales of gasoline to the United States is unconstitutional as placing a direct burden on the Federal Government. *Panhandle Oil Co.* v. *Mississippi*, 277 U. S. 218; *Graves* v. *Texas Co.*, 298 U. S. 393. However, in *James* v. *Dravo Contracting Co.*, 302 U. S. 313, the Supreme Court said that the *Panhandle* and *Graves* cases had been distinguished and should be limited to their particular facts. In the *James* case a State tax on the gross proceeds of a contractor on Government work was held constitutional as having only an indirect effect on the Federal Government. That case is representative of the recent Supreme Court cases tending to restrict the tax immunity of agencies of Government where the burden on the Government was not clear and direct. *Helvering* v. *Mountain Producers Corp.*, 303 U. S. 376; *Helvering* v. *Gerhardt*, 304 U. S. 405.
>
> * * * * *
>
> Although the law on the question is in a state of flux, the proper holding at the present time is, in my opinion, that where purchases are made either by the Indians themselves or by Government agents in carrying out a specific economic program for the Indians approved and supervised by the Federal Government, or where such purchases are made with restricted funds, the purchases are not subject to the State sales taxes even though they are made off the reservation.
>
> SUMMARY
>
> 1. Persons trading with the Indians on Indian reservations are not subject to the Arizona sales tax laws. However, where such traders are non-Indians, they are subject to the sales tax laws on so much of their business as is carried on with other non-Indians. Traders off an Indian reservation are subject to the State sales tax laws whether or not they are Indians or dealing with Indians.
>
> 2. Purchases made by Indians on Indian reservations are not subject to the Arizona sales taxes nor are purchases made by Indians or Government agents off the reservation where they are made with restricted funds or in carrying out a specific program for the economic rehabilitation of the Indians approved and supervised by the Federal Government.

In another recent opinion of the Solicitor of the Interior Department[97] the application of certain state taxes to sales of tobacco and gasoline to the Menominee Indian Mills was considered. The state taxes in question were: (1) the State excise tax on the sales of gasoline, levied under chapter 78 of the Wisconsin Statutes of 1937; and (2) the State occupational tax on the sale of tobacco products, levied under chapters 443 and 518 of the Laws of Wisconsin, 1939.

After a searching analysis of the problems presented, the Solicitor made a twofold finding, to wit:

1. State gasoline sales taxes (*a*) do not apply to sales of gasoline to the Menominee Indian Mills for use in the operation of the mills, but (*b*) do apply to sales of gasoline to the mills for resale through the commissary of the mills to employees and the general public. This latter ruling was occasioned by the fact that title IV of the Internal Revenue Act of 1932 and the regulations issued thereunder exempted from the operation of the tax only gasoline sold "for the exclusive use of the United States."

2. The state tax on the selling of tobacco products does not apply to the selling of such products by the commissary of the Menominee Indian Mills to employees and the general public.

[97] Op. Sol. I. D., M.30544, May 31, 1940.

SECTION 6. STATE INHERITANCE TAXES

There appears to be meager authority on the question of the liability of an Indian's estate to the payment of state inheritance taxes. The only case to reach the Supreme Court involved allotted lands of a restricted full-blood Quapaw Indian which had been declared inalienable for a period of 25 years by the Act of March 2, 1895.[98] By the Act of June 25, 1910,[99] the Secretary of the Interior was directed to determine the heirs of deceased allottees according to state statutes of descent. According to the state statute the land herein involved descended to two full-blood Quapaws. The state auditor of Oklahoma attempted to subject the lands to the state inheritance tax. Upon appeal the Supreme Court declared:[100]

> Apparently appellant supposed that the lands passed to the heirs by virtue of the laws of the State and were subject to the inheritance taxes which she laid. He accordingly demanded the payment of appellees and threatened enforcement by summary process and sale of the lands. The court below held that the State had no right to demand the taxes and restrained appellant from attempting to collect them.
>
> The duty of the Secretary of the Interior to determine the heirs according to the State law of descent is not questioned. Congress provided that the lands should de-

[98] 28 Stat. 876.

[99] 36 Stat. 855.

[100] *Childers* v. *Beaver*, 270 U. S. 555 (1926).

scend and directed how the heirs should be ascertained. It adopted the provisions of the Oklahoma statute as an expression of its own will—the laws of Missouri or Kansas, or any other State, might have been accepted. The lands really passed under a law of the United States, and not by Oklahoma's permission.

It must be accepted as established that during the trust or restricted period Congress has power to control lands within a State which have been duly allotted to Indians by the United States and thereafter conveyed through trust or restrictive patents. This is essential to the proper discharge of their duty to a dependent people; and the means or instrumentalities utilized therein cannot be subjected to taxation by the State without assent of the federal government. (P. 559.)

SECTION 7. FEDERAL TAXATION

A. SOURCES OF LIMITATIONS

While the tax which was declared invalid in *Choate* v. *Trapp*[91] was payable to the State of Oklahoma, the question to which the Supreme Court addressed its primary attention in that case was the validity of the congressional enactment which purportedly subjected the land to state taxation. In holding that Congress had no power to subject the land to taxation after agreeing, in exchange for a valuable consideration, that the land should be tax-exempt, the Supreme Court enunciated and went far to support a rule which would lay limits upon federal taxation as well as upon state taxation. Thus if, in circumstances similar to those exemplified in *Choate* v. *Trapp*, the Federal Government, pursuant to an agreement with an Indian tribe, issues a trust patent promising clear title to the patentee after a fixed period, it seems probable that any attempt, for example, to impose a federal inheritance tax upon such land would be held violative of the Fifth Amendment.

Nevertheless, in the only Supreme Court case in which the constitutionality of a federal tax violating an agreement with an Indian tribe was considered, the case of *The Cherokee Tobacco*,[92] the Supreme Court held that the violation of a treaty provision by an act of Congress presented a purely political question which the courts were powerless to remedy. This doctrine would, of course, preclude the relief which the Supreme Court gave in *Choate* v. *Trapp*.

It seems clear, then, that the holding in *Choate* v. *Trapp* is inconsistent with the doctrine of *The Cherokee Tobacco*, and that the holding in that case is incompatible with the doctrine of *Choate* v. *Trapp*. The opinion in the later case does not attempt to distinguish the earlier case—does not even mention the earlier case. It is easy to make verbal distinctions, to say that *The Cherokee Case* involved a question of the plenary power of Congress over tribal affairs and that *Choate* v. *Trapp* involved individual property rights. But one might as easily say that plenary power of Congress over tribal affairs was involved in *Choate* v. *Trapp*, since all the legislation in that case dealt with tribes, and that the individual rights of the Indian Elias Boudinot in *The Cherokee Tobacco*, which in fact Congress felt called upon to recognize and compensate 4 years after the Supreme Court decision,[93] were even more individual than the rights of the 8,000 plaintiff members of the Choctaw and Chickasaw tribes in *Choate* v. *Trapp*. To say that property rights existed in one case and not in the other is to describe the result rather than to explain it or to aid in predicting future decisions.[94]

Whether the *Choate* case overruled the case of *The Cherokee Tobacco*, *sub silentio*, or whether the doctrine of the earlier case is to prevail outside the narrow fact situation presented in the *Choate* case, the future will determine. Some support is given to the former hypothesis by the consideration that the decision of the Supreme Court in *Choate* v. *Trapp* was unanimous, while that in *The Cherokee Tobacco* was a four-to-two decision with three members of the court not hearing argument.[95]

In recent years Congress has occasionally made certain that no claim to permanent tax exemption would arise, by specifying that designated Indian property should be "nontaxable until otherwise directed by Congress."[96]

[91] 224 U. S. 665 (1912).

[92] 11 Wall. 616 (1870).

[93] Act of May 14, 1874; c. 173, 18 Stat. 549.

[94] *Cf.* F. S. Cohen, Transcendental Nonsense and the Functional Approach (1935) 35 Col. L. Rev. 809, 813–820.

B. FEDERAL INCOME TAXES

In considering federal taxation of Indian income, one finds the courts concerned not, as in the case of the state, with the question of whether the state may tax, but with the question of whether the Federal Government has intended to tax. Whether it has done so in a particular case depends on the construction accorded the taxing statute by the courts. The rule of construction most recently announced[97] is that the federal income tax law, applying as it does to the income of "every individual" and to income derived "from any source whatever," includes within its application Indians and their income unless they are by agreement or statute exempted.

It is clear that the exemption accorded tribal and restricted Indian lands extends to the income derived directly therefrom.[98] Accordingly, rents, royalties, and other income of Quapaw,[99] Otoe,[100] Otoe and Missouri,[101] and Ponca[102] Indians have been held tax-exempt. Likewise, the income derived by individual Indians as their share in the oil or mineral deposits in tribal lands has been held tax-exempt.[103]

[95] "The case of the Cherokee Tobacco Tax, 11 Wall. 616, cannot be treated as authority against the conclusion we have reached. The decision only disposed of that case, as three of the judges of the court did not sit in it and two dissented from the judgment pronounced by the other four." *United States* v. *Forty-Three Gallons of Whiskey*, 108 U. S. 491, 497–498 (1883).

[96] Act of June 20, 1936, sec. 2, 49 Stat. 1542, amended May 19, 1937, 50 Stat. 188, 25 U. S. C. 412a. No such limitation is found in various other statutes, *e. g.*, Act of June 18, 1934, sec. 5, 48 Stat. 984, 985. 25 U. S. C. 465.

[97] *Superintendent* v. *Commissioner of Internal Revenue*, 295 U. S. 418 (1935).

[98] *United States* v. *Homeratha*, 40 F. 2d 305 (D. C. W. D. Okla. 1930). app. dism. 49 F. 2d 1086; *Blackbird* v. *Commissioner of Internal Revenue*, 38 F. 2d 976 (C. C. A. 10, 1930); *Pitman* v. *Commissioner*, 64 F. 2d 740 (C. C. A. 10, 1933).

[99] T. D. 3754, c. B. IV–2, p. 37; G. C. M. 2056, c. B. VI–a, p. 65.

The following abbreviations, referring to Treasury Department rulings, are used in this and succeeding footnotes:

G. C. M.—General Counsel Memo.
C. B.—Cumulative Bulletin, Treasury Department.
B. T. A.—Board of Tax Appeals.
A. F. T. R.—American Federal Tax Reports.
S. M.—Solicitor's Memo.
T. D.—Treasury Decisions.

[100] G. C. M. 2715, C. B. VII–1, p. 56, revoked, however, in G. C. M. 6020, C. B. VIII–1, p. 63.

[101] *United States* v. *Homeratha*, 40 F. 2d 305 (D. C. W. D. Okla. 1930).

[102] S. M. 5682, C. B. V–1, p. 198.

[103] *Blackbird* v. *Commissioner of Internal Revenue*, 38 F. 2d 976 (C. C. A. 10, 1930).

633058—45——19

Conversely, income which is derived from unrestricted lands has been held taxable,[104] and the Circuit Court of Appeals has held that upon the death of a restricted Creek allottee, his surplus allotment having been freed of restrictions by the Act of May 27, 1908,[105] the income therefrom was taxable in the hands of a noncompetent heir although income from the homestead which remained restricted was nontaxable.[106] It has been held, too, by the United States Supreme Court[107] that where an Indian holds a certificate of competency the income paid to him as royalties from oil and gas leases is taxable. And the income of a Hopi Indian derived from his commercial business in trading with other Indians and from the sale of cattle given him by the Government is taxable.[108]

Though income derived directly from restricted allotted lands is exempt from federal income taxation, so-called reinvestment income is subject to such taxation.[109] The case of *Superintendent, Five Civilized Tribes* v. *Commissioner*,[110] involved the taxability of the income of a noncompetent Indian derived from the reinvestment of income from restricted allotted lands. The court there said that the taxation of the income from trust property of its Indian wards by the Federal Government, under federal revenue acts general in scope, is not so inconsistent with the relationship between the Government and its Indian wards that exemption is a necessary implication, and held that reinvestment income is clearly taxable under the federal revenue laws.[111]

It has been held that the income of a non-Indian lessee derived from a lease of restricted Indian lands is subject to the federal income tax.[112]

The courts in considering an Indian claim for refund of taxes erroneously paid, have looked upon an unrestricted Indian claimant as upon any other taxpayer. Thus an unrestricted Indian member of the Choctaw Tribe of Indians is not entitled to a refund of taxes erroneously paid upon income from tax-exempt lands where no claim for refund was filed until after the running of the statute of limitations.[113] But there is no limitation on refunds to restricted Indians if (1) a tax was assessed against their nontaxable income, and (2) such tax was paid by an Indian superintendent, or other such officer of the United States, out of funds in his possession belonging eventually to his ward.[114]

Provision has been made by public resolution [115] for the allowance of claims for refund of taxes erroneously or illegally collected from a duly enrolled member of an Indian tribe who received in pursuance of a tribal treaty or agreement with the United States an allotment of land which by the terms of said treaty or agreement was exempted from taxation, notwithstanding his failure to file a claim for refund within the time prescribed by law. A recent statute,[116] similar in nature to the foregoing resolution, has expressly stated that it is not the policy of the Government to invoke or plead the statute of limitations in order to escape its obligation to its Indian wards.

C. OTHER FEDERAL TAXES

By section 617 of title 4 of the Revenue Act of 1932,[117] an excise tax was levied on sales of gasoline. In considering the application of this tax to sales of gasoline to the Menominee Indian Mills, the Solicitor of the Interior Department in a recent opinion [118] made the following finding, to wit:

1. Federal gasoline sales taxes (*a*) do not apply to sales of gasoline to the Menominee Indian Mills for use in the operation of the mills, but (*b*) do apply to sales of gasoline to the mills for resale through the commissary of the mills to employees and the general public. This latter ruling was occasioned by the fact that title 4 of the Internal Revenue Act of 1932 and the regulations issued thereunder exempted from the operation of the tax only gasoline sold "for the exclusive use of the United States."

From an early date Congress has expressly provided that no duty shall be levied or collected from Indians on the importation of peltries brought by them into the territories of the United States [119] and the desire to encourage native Indian handicraft has been clearly evidenced by the express exemption from the operation of the Revenue Act of 1932 [120] of "any article of native Indian handicraft manufactured or produced by Indians on Indian reservations, or in Indian schools, or by Indians under the jurisdiction of the United States Government in Alaska."

[104] Esther Rentie, 21 B. T. A. 1230, involving a full-blood Creek Indian; G. C. M. 2008, C. B. VII–1, p. 209, involving a half-blood, incompetent Creek Indian; G. C. M. 8066, C. B. IX–2, p. 316.

[105] 35 Stat. 312. *Cf. Bagby* v. *United States*, 60 Fed. 80 (C. C. A. 10, 1932).

[106] *Pitman* v. *Commissioner*, 64 F. 2d 740 (C. C. A. 10, 1933). *Cf. Commr.* v. *Owens*, 78 F. 2d 768 (C. C. A. 10, 1935).

[107] *Choteau* v. *Burnet*, 283 U. S. 691 (1931).

[108] S. M. 4527, C. B. IV–2, p. 29.

[109] *Katie Snell et al.* v. *Commissioner*, 10 B. T. A. 1081, and G. C. M. 9621, C. B. December 1931, chap. 111.

[110] 295 U. S. 418 (1935), affg. 75 F. 2d 183 (C. C. A. 10, 1935).

[111] For a discussion and construction of this case see the rulings of the Board of Tax Appeals, as contained in Prentis Hall, Federal Tax Service, pars. 8335, 8336.

[112] *Heiner* v. *Colonial Trust Co.*, 275 U. S. 232 (1927). To the same effect, S. R. 8498, C. B. June 1926, p. 183; *Cortez Oil Co.* v. *United States*, 64 C. Cls. 390 (1928), T. D. 4146, C. B. June 1928, p. 282; 6 A. F. T. R. 7130 (cert. den. May 28, 1928); *The Terrell Co.*, 9 B. T. A. 1131 (involving a lessee of Indian lands expressly exempted from taxation); *Western American Oil Co.*, 10 B. T. A. 17; *Ernest L. Henton*, 10 B. T. A. 21; *Thomas Coal Co.*, 10 B. T. A. 639; *McAlester-Edwards Coal Co.*, 10 B. T. A. 1368; *Philadelphia Quartz Co.*, 13 B. T. A. 1146 (nonacquiescence, C. B. December 1929, p. 69).

[113] G. C. M. 762, C. B. June 1927, p. 123. To the same effect: *United States* v. *Richards*, 27 F. 2d. 284 (C. C. A. 8, 1928), cert. den. 278 U. S. 530; *Lundman* v. *Alexander*, 26 F. Supp. 752 (D. C. Okla. 1939), sec. 5,207 of P. H. Fed. Tax Service for 1939, app. dism., 105 F. 2d 1018 (C. C. A. 10), sec. 5.627 of P. H. Fed. Tax Service for 1939.

[114] S. M. 5632, C. B. June 1926, p. 193.

[115] Public Resolution No. 74, 71st Cong. (S. J. Res. 163), approved May 19, 1930.

[116] Act of February 14, 1933, 47 Stat. 807.

[117] 26 U. S. C. 1481, *et seq.*; chap. 29 of the Internal Revenue Code, approved February 10, 1939, 53 Stat. 409.

[118] Op. Sol. I. D., M.30544, May 31, 1940. See sec. 5, *supra*.

[119] Act of March 2, 1799, 4 Stat. 627; Act of October 1, 1890, 26 Stat. 567; Act of August 27, 1894, 28 Stat. 509.

[120] Act of June 6, 1932, sec. 624, 47 Stat. 169.

SECTION 8. TRIBAL TAXATION

As distinct political communities, the Indian tribes possess some of the attributes of sovereignty, among which is the power to legislate regarding their internal relations.[121] This power, with certain exceptions, includes the power to levy local taxes on all property within tribal limits, belonging to members of the tribe.[122] Though the scope of the power as applied to nonmembers is not clear, it extends at least to property of nonmembers used in connection with Indian property as well as to privileges enjoyed by nonmembers in trading with the Indians.[123] The power to tax nonmembers is derived in the cases from the authority, founded on original sovereignty and guaranteed in some instances by treaties, to remove property of nonmembers from

[121] See Chapter 7.

[122] 55 I. D. 14, 46 (1934).

[123] See *Morris* v. *Hitchcock*, 21 App. D. C. 565, 593 (1903), aff'd 194 U. S. 384 (1904).

the territorial limits of the tribe. Since the tribal government has the power to exclude, it can extract a fee from nonmembers as a condition precedent to granting permission to remain or to operate within the tribal domain.[124] Since, however, the exclusive power to regulate trade with the Indians is vested in the Commissioner of Indian Affairs,[125] it would seem that, in the absence of specific federal authorization, the tribe has no power to tax licensed traders.[126]

Limitations on the taxing power of the state governments arising from the federal instrumentality doctrine logically also apply to the tribal governments.[127]

It would seem that the tribal taxing power is not subject to limitations imposed upon state or federal legislation by the Federal Constitution.[128] In the only Supreme Court case on the point the court remarked in approving such a tax that the act of the tribal legislature was not arbitrary and did not violate the Federal Constitution.[129]

Under section 16 of the Act of June 18, 1934,[130] tribal constitutions containing provisions authorizing taxation of members and nonmembers have been adopted by many tribes and approved by the Secretary of the Interior. Since there is no express grant of taxing power in the act, such power must be traced to tribal sovereignty, the power to exclude, or some federal statute or treaty. Several types of limitations are imposed on the tribal taxing power by the constitutions.

Some of the constitutions provide that taxes may be levied upon members of the tribe without review by the Secretary of the Interior, but that taxes upon nonmembers shall be subject to such review,[131] and another group provides for general review of all taxing ordinances by the Secretary.[132] Still another group provides that an assessment upon members of the tribe shall not be effective unless the eligible voters of the tribe approve.[133]

Under some of the constitutions only a per capita tax on eligible voters can be levied.[134] One constitution providing for assessments to obtain funds for carrying out any project for the benefit of the community as a whole allows any district not directly benefited by the project to exempt itself from the assessment by a majority vote.[135]

---

[124] *Morris* v. *Hitchcock*, 194 U. S. 384 (1904) (Chickasaw); *Buster* v. *Wright*, 135 Fed. 947 (C. C. A. 8, 1905) (Creek), app. dism. 203 U. S. 599; *Maxey* v. *Wright*, 3 Ind. T. 243, 54 S. W. 807 (1900), aff'd 105 Fed. 1003 (C. C. A. 8. 1900); 23 Op. A. G. 214 (1900) (Five Civilized Tribes); 18 Op. A. G. 34 (1884); 17 Op. A. G. 134 (1881) (Choctaw and Chickasaw); *cf. Crabtree* v. *Madden*, 54 Fed. 426 (C. C. A. 8, 1893). This rationale is more like the exercise of a police power than tax power.

[125] 25 U. S. C. 261, derived from Act of August 15, 1876, sec. 5, 19 Stat. 176, 200; and 25 U. S. C. 262, derived from Acts of March 3, 1901, sec 1, 31 Stat. 1058, 1066; March 3, 1903, sec. 10, 32 Stat. 982, 1000.

[126] 1 Op. A. G. 645 (1824) (Cherokee); 55 I. D. 14, 48 (1934).

[127] For example, it has been administratively determined that the tribe may not tax employees of the Federal Government. See Memo. Sol. I. D., February 17, 1939.

[128] See Chapter 7, sec. 2. Cf. *Talton* v. *Mayes*, 163 U. S. 376 (1896); *Worcester* v. *Georgia*, 6 Pet. 515, 559 (1832); Memo. Sol. I. D., February 17, 1939.

[129] See *Morris* v. *Hitchcock*, 194 U. S. 384, 393 (1904).

[130] 48 Stat. 984, 987, 25 U. S. C. 476.

[131] Constitution, Hannahville Indian Community, Art. V, sec. 1 (3); Constitution, Keweenaw Bay Indian Community, Art. VI, sec. 1 (i).

[132] Constitution, Oneida Tribe of Indians of Wisconsin, Art. IV, sec. 1 (f); Constitution, Kalispel Indian Community, Wash., Art. IV, sec. 1 (f); Constitution, Fort McDermitt Paiute and Shoshone Tribe, Art. VI, sec. 1 (f); Constitution, Flandreau Santee Sioux Tribe, Art. IV, sec. 1 (f).

[133] Constitution, Omaha Tribe of Nebraska, Art. IV, sec. 1 (h); Constitution, Lac du Flambeau Band of Lake Superior Chippewa Indians of Wisconsin, Art. VI, sec. 1 (i); Constitution, Lower Sioux Indian Community in Minnesota, Art. V, sec. 1 (h); Constitution, Hydaburg Cooperative Association, Alaska, Art. 4, sec. 1 (d).

[134] Constitution, Colorado River Indian Tribe, Art. VI, sec. 1 (g); Constitution, Cheyenne River Sioux Tribe, Art. IV, sec. 1 (i); Constitution, Three Affiliated Tribes, Fort Berthold Reservation, Art. VI, sec. 5 (b).

[135] Constitution, Fort Belknap Indian Community, Art. V, sec. 1 (g).

CHAPTER 14

THE LEGAL STATUS OF INDIAN TRIBES

TABLE OF CONTENTS

SECTION 1. TRIBAL EXISTENCE

The term "tribe" is commonly used in two senses, an ethnological sense and a political sense. It is important to distinguish between these two meanings of the term.[1] Groups that consist of several ethnological tribes, sometimes speaking different languages, have been recognized as single tribes for administrative and political purposes. Examples are the Fort Belknap Indian Community[2] (Gros Ventre and Assiniboine), the Cheyenne and Arapahoe Indians of Oklahoma,[3] the Cherokee Nation (in which Delawares, Shawnees, and others were amalgamated), and the Confederated Salish and Kootenai Tribes of the Flathead Reservation. Despite the use of the plural "Tribes" in this last case, and other similar cases, the group has been treated, politically, as a single tribe. Likewise what is a single tribe, from the ethnological standpoint, may sometimes be divided into a number of independent tribes in the political sense. Examples of this situation are offered by the Sioux, the Chippewa, and the Shoshone.

The question of tribal existence, in the legal or political sense, has generally arisen in determining whether some legislative, administrative, or judicial power with respect to Indian "tribes" extended to a particular group of Indians.

The most basic of these issues has been the constitutional issue arising from the grant of power to Congress to regulate "commerce with * * * the Indian Tribes."[4] The Supreme Court has, in a number of cases, taken the position that the applicability or constitutionality of congressional legislation affecting individual Indians, and the inapplicability or unconstitutionality of state legislation affecting such individuals, depended upon whether or not the individuals concerned were living in tribal relations.

While thus making the validity of congressional and administrative actions depend upon the existence of tribes, the courts have said that it is up to Congress and the executive to determine whether a tribe exists. Thus the "political arm of the Government" would seem to be in a position to determine the extent of its power. In this respect the question of tribal existence and congressional power has been classed as a "political question" along with the recognition of foreign governments and other issues of international relations.[5]

Thus in the case of *United States* v. *Holliday*,[6] the Supreme Court held that federal liquor laws were applicable to a sale of liquor to a Michigan Chippewa Indian, despite a treaty provision looking to the dissolution of the tribe, for the reason that the Interior Department regarded the tribe as still existing. The Court declared:

> In reference to all matters of this kind, it is the rule of this court to follow the action of the executive and other political departments of the government, whose more special duty it is to determine such affairs. If by them those Indians are recognized as a tribe, this court must do the same. (P. 419.)

Again, in the case of *The Kansas Indians*,[7] the Supreme Court dealt with the converse situation, involving an attempt to apply state tax laws to Shawnee, Wea, and Miami Indians of Kansas, and held such laws to be unconstitutional on the ground that the tribal relations of these Indians were still recognized by the Interior Department. In this case the Court declared:

> If the tribal organization of the Shawnees is preserved intact, and recognized by the political department of the government as existing, then they are a "people distinct from others," capable of making treaties, separated from the jurisdiction of Kansas, and to be governed exclusively by the government of the Union. * * * Conferring rights and privileges on these Indians cannot affect their situation, which can only be changed by treaty stipulation, or a voluntary abandonment of their tribal organization. As long as the United States recognizes their national character they are under the protection of treaties and the laws of Congress, and their property is withdrawn from the operation of State laws. (Pp. 755–757.)

[1] *Cf. Cherokee Nation* v. *United States*, 80 C. Cls. 1 (1932), holding that Cherokees by blood, calling themselves "the Cherokee Tribe of Indians," excluding the various tribes and groups incorporated into or adopted by the Cherokee Nation, had no standing to bring a suit in the Court of Claims under the special Cherokee jurisdictional Act of March 19, 1924, 43 Stat. 27. For examples of tribal consolidation effected by intertribal agreement authorized by a general treaty provision, see: *Cherokee Nation* v. *Blackfeather*, 155 U. S. 218 (1894) (Shawnee and Cherokee), and *Cherokee Nation* v. *Journeycake*, 155 U. S. 196 (1894) (Cherokees and Delawares). To the effect that the dissolution of a union between two tribes requires consent of the United States where such consent was a condition of the original act of union, see Choctaw and Chickasaw Union, 7 Op. A. G. 142 (1855). On the situation in Alaska, see Chapter 21.

For an anthropological definition of "tribe," see Handbook of American Indians (Bureau of American Ethnology, Bulletin No. 30, 1910), pt. 2, p. 814.

[2] See Memo. Sol. I. D., March 20, 1936.

[3] See Treaty of October 28, 1867, with these Indians, 15 Stat. 593, particularly Arts. XII and XIV.

[4] U. S. Const., Art. I, sec. 8.

[5] See *United States* v. *Rickert*, 188 U. S. 432 (1903); *United States* v. *Boyd*, 83 Fed. 547 (C. C. A. 4, 1897).

[6] 3 Wall. 407 (1865).

[7] 5 Wall. 737 (1866).

In the case of *Chippewa Indians* v. *United States*,[9] the power of Congress over Chippewa funds was challenged on the theory that the tribe had been dissolved and the funds individualized, and that Congress had therefore no right to expend the funds for various tribal purposes. In rejecting this argument, the Supreme Court put its criterion of tribal existence in these terms:

> It is true that, prior to the adoption of the Act of 1889, the tribe had been broken up into numerous bands, some of which held Indian title to tracts in the State of Minnesota. The Act refers to these collectively as "The Chippewas in the State of Minnesota." Whether or not the tribal relation had been dissolved prior to its adoption, the Act contemplates future dealings with the Indians upon a tribal basis. It exhibits a purpose gradually to emancipate the Indians and to bring about a status comparable to that of citizens of the United States. But it is plain that, in the interim, Congress did not intend to surrender its guardianship over the Indians or treat them otherwise than as tribal Indians.
>
> This is evidenced by a series of acts, the first of which was adopted nineteen months after the Act of 1889, which are inconsistent with the view that the Congress considered the Indians as emancipated or intended to enter into a binding contract with them as individuals. [Citing findings.] Many of these statutes refer to the Chippewas of Minnesota as a tribe. [Citing statutes.] Moreover, an examination of the Act of 1889 discloses that it is not cast in the form of an agreement; and we may not assume that Congress abandoned its guardianship of the tribe or the bands and entered into a formal trust agreement with the Indians, in the absence of a clear expression of that intent. (Pp. 4–5.)

Issues similar to the above have been raised in many other cases, and determined in accordance with the foregoing principles.[9]

The limits of legislative power in this field were suggested in the opinion written by Mr. Justice Van Devanter, for a unanimous court, in *United States* v. *Sandoval*:[10]

> Of course, it is not meant by this that Congress may bring a community or body of people within the range of this power by arbitrarily calling them an Indian tribe, but only that in respect of distinctly Indian communities the questions whether, to what extent, and for what time they shall be recognized and dealt with as dependent tribes requiring the guardianship and protection of the United States are to be determined by Congress, and not by the courts. (P. 46.)

Aside from those cases which have dealt with the term "Indian tribes" as used in the Constitution, there have been a few statutes which have used the term and about which legal questions of tribal existence have been raised.

One such statute is that regulating the purchase or leasing of land "from any Indian nation or tribe of Indians."[11] Under this statute a state court decree partitioning Oneida Indian lands in New York, based upon the theory that the Oneidas in New York had ceased to exist as a tribe, was set aside. The federal court held that the Oneidas of New York still existed as a tribe, in the eyes of the Federal Government, and that it was for Congress, and not the state courts, to say when this tribal existence was at an end.[12]

A similar holding with respect to the Pueblos of New Mexico is elsewhere discussed.[13]

Questions of tribal existence were extensively litigated under the Indian Depredation Act of 1891,[14] which gave to the Court of Claims jurisdiction over "all claims for property of citizens of the United States taken or destroyed by Indians belonging to any band, tribe, or nation, in amity with the United States, without just cause or provocation on the part of the owner or agent in charge, and not returned or paid for." Under the statute it became necessary, in each case, to determine whether the band or tribe to which the offender belonged was in amity with the United States.[15]

The question of tribal existence presented little difficulty under the 1891 Act where the group in question had entered into treaty relations with the United States, or where a separate

[8] 307 U. S. 1 (1939).

[9] *United States* v. *Kagama*, 118 U. S. 375 (1886) (upholding constitutionality of federal statute on murder of one Indian by another, as applied to Hoopa Valley Indians); *Lone Wolf* v. *Hitchcock*, 187 U. S. 553 (1903) (upholding constitutionality of federal allotment statute for Kiowa, Comanche, and Apache tribes); *Tiger* v. *Western Investment Co.*, 221 U. S. 286, 316 (1911) (upholding constitutionality of congressional restriction upon alienation of lands of "a member of the existing Creek Nation"); *United States* v. *Wright*, 53 F. 2d 300 (C. C. A. 4, 1931), revg. sub nom. *United States* v. *Swain County*, 46 F. 2d 99 (D. C. W. D. N. C. 1930), cert. den. 285 U. S. 539 (upholding constitutionality of congressional act exempting Eastern Cherokee lands from state taxation, declaring, at p. 304, "they live under a primitive tribal organization"); *United States* v. *7,405.3 Acres of Land*, 97 F. 2d 417 (C. C. A. 4, 1938) (Eastern Cherokee lands held "tribal" land exempt from condemnation by state); *Perrin* v. *United States*, 232 U. S. 478, 487 (1914) (upholding constitutionality of liquor legislation covering lands ceded by Yankton Sioux Tribe, where "the tribal relation has not been dissolved"). And see Chapter 5, sec. 8.

[10] 231 U. S. 28 (1913), revg. 198 Fed. 539 (D. C. N. M., 1912).

[11] Act of June 30, 1834, sec. 12, 4 Stat. 729, 730, R. S. § 2116, 25 U. S. C. 177.

[12] *United States* v. *Boylan*, 265 Fed. 165 (C. C. A. 2, 1920), app. dism. 257 U. S. 614 (1921). Accord: *United States* v. *Charles*, 23 F. Supp. 346 (D. C. W. D. N. Y., 1938) (Tonawanda Band).

[13] See Chapter 20, sec. 4.

[14] Act of March 3, 1891, 26 Stat. 851, 852. *Cf.* the Act of March 3, 1885, 23 Stat. 362, 376, which dealt with depredation claims where treaties made provision for redress. An illuminating account of Indian depredation legislation will be found in the opinion of the Court of Claims in *Leighton* v. *United States and Ogalalla Band*, 29 C. Cls. 288 (1894), affd. 161 U. S. 291 (1895). See also *United States* v. *Martinez*, 195 U. S. 469 (1904); *Corralitos Co.* v. *United States*, 178 U. S. 280 (1900), affg. sub nom. *Corralitos Stock Co.* v. *United States*, 33 C. Cls. 342 (1898). The subjection of tribal funds to damage claims by private citizens was an outgrowth of the collective responsibility imposed by early statutes and treaties upon the tribes for the torts of their members. See sec. 14 of Indian Intercourse Act of May 19, 1796, 1 Stat. 469, 472; reenacted sec. 14 of Indian Intercourse Act of March 3, 1799, 1 Stat. 743, 747, made permanent in sec. 14 of Indian Intercourse Act of March 30, 1802, 2 Stat. 139, 143; reenacted as sec. 17 of Indian Intercourse Act of June 30, 1834, 4 Stat. 729, 25 U. S. C. 229. See also secs. 3 and 6, *infra*.

[15] The following cases involved decisions on tribal existence reached under this statute: *Marks* v. *United States*, 28 C. Cls. 147 (1893), affd. 161 U. S. 297 (1896) (Piute and Bannock Tribes); *Valk* v. *United States and Rogue River Indians*, 29 C. Cls. 62 (1894), affd. 168 U. S. 703 (1897); *Woolverton, Admr.* v. *United States and Nez Perce Indians*, 29 C. Cls. 107 (1894); *Jaeger* v. *United States and Yuma Indians*, 29 C. Cls. 172 (1894); *Leighton* v. *United States and Ogalalla Band*, 29 C. Cls. 288 (1894), affd. 161 U. S. 291 (1895); *Love, Admr.* v. *United States, Rogue River Indians, et al.*, 29 C. Cls. 332 (1894); *Barrow, Porter & Co.* v. *United States, Mojave, Coosnejo, and Navajo Indians*, 30 C. Cls. 54 (1895); *Graham* v. *United States and Sioux Tribe of Indians*, 30 C. Cls. 318 (1895); *Gamel* v. *United States, and Apache Indians*, 31 C. Cls. 321 (1896); *Carter* v. *United States*, 31 C. Cls. 441 (1896); *Tully* v. *United States*, 32 C. Cls. 1 (1896) (Apache); *Salois* v. *United States and Sioux Indians*, 32 C. Cls. 68 (1896); *Duran, Admr.* v. *United States and Navajo Indians*, 32 C. Cls. 273 (1897); *Brown* v. *United States and Brulé Sioux*, 32 C. Cls. 432 (1897); *Herring* v. *United States and Ute Indians*, 32 C. Cls. 536 (1897); *Litchfield* v. *United States and Sioux and Cheyenne Indians*, 32 C. Cls. 585 (1897); *Grow* v. *United States and Nisqually Indians*, 32 C. Cls. 599 (1897); *McKee* v. *United States and Comanche Indians*, 33 C. Cls. 99 (1897); *Painter* v. *United States, Humboldt, Eel River, Yaga Creek, Redwood, Mad River, and Klamath Indians*, 33 C. Cls. 114 (1897); *Dobbs* v. *United States and Apache Indians*, 33 C. Cls. 308 (1898); *Conners* v. *United States and Cheyenne Indians*, 33 C. Cls. 317 (1898), affd. 180 U. S. 271 (1901); *Labadie* v. *United States and Cheyenne Indians*, 33 C. Cls. 476 (1898); *Scott* v. *United States and Apache Indians*, 33 C. Cls. 486 (1898); *Luke* v. *United States and Hualapai Indians*, 35 C. Cls. 15 (1899); *Allred* v. *United States and Ute Indians*, 36 C. Cls. 280 (1901); *Lowe* v. *United States and Kickapoo Indians*, 37 C. Cls. 413 (1902); *Thompson* v. *United States and Klamath Indians*, 44 C. Cls. 359 (1909).

reservation had been set aside for the group.[16] A more difficult question, however, was presented in cases where a portion of a tribe went on the warpath. In this situation the rule was established that if the hostile party constituted *a distinct band* the original tribe was not responsible for its depredations.[17] In the case of *Montoya* v. *United States*,[18] the Supreme Court upheld the rule laid down by the Court of Claims, and sought to establish working definitions of the terms "tribe" and "band," in these words:

> We are more concerned in this case with the meaning of the words "tribe" and "band." By a "tribe" we understand a body of Indians of the same or a similar race, united in a community under one leadership or government, and inhabiting a particular though sometimes ill-defined territory; by a "band," a company of Indians not necessarily, though often of the same race or tribe, but united under the same leadership in a common design. While a "band" does not imply the separate racial origin characteristic of a tribe, of which it is usually an offshoot, it does imply a leadership and a concert of action. How large the company must be to constitute a "band" within the meaning of the act it is unnecessary to decide. It may be doubtful whether it requires more than independence of action, continuity of existence, a common leadership and concert of action. (P. 266.)

In the parallel case of *Conners* v. *United States*,[19] the Supreme Court declared:

> To constitute a "band" we do not think it necessary that the Indians composing it be a separate political entity, recognized as such, inhabiting a particular territory, and with whom treaties had been or might be made. These peculiarities would rather give them the character of tribes. The word "band" implies an inferior and less permanent organization, though it must be of sufficient strength to be capable of initiating hostile proceedings. (P. 275.)

In the case of *Dobbs* v. *United States*,[20] the Court of Claims declared:

> It has been urged in this and other cases that when a number of Indian tribes have been removed to a reservation the tribal entity of each ceases; that they become in legal effect one tribe, and that the question of amity is to be directed to all of the Indians thus brought together.
>
> * * * * *
>
> In dealing with the question of the amity of such a tribe as a band of the Apaches, the court has been more and more compelled to fall back upon the purpose of the earlier statutes which created a liability and gave to these claimants their right of action. That purpose, as has been said before, was to keep the peace—to prevent Indian warfare upon the frontier. The Government said both to the white man and to the Indian, "This depredation or this outrage is wrong, is indefensible, and you shall be indemnified for your losses so far as property is involved, provided always that you refrain from war." If the frontiersmen and the Indians did not comply with this simple condition, if the purpose of offering the indemnity was not effective, the claimants have no right to seek it under the act of 1891.
>
> The practical question, then, is, Who were the Indians whose amity was to be maintained? Who were the Indians so affiliated with the depredators in fact that the depredators might reasonably be regarded as a part of them and they be regarded as a body whose amity it was desirable to maintain?
>
> In dealing with this question the court has held, first, that a nation, tribe, or band will be regarded as an Indian entity where the relations of the Indians in their organized or tribal capacity has been fixed and recognized by treaty; second, that where there is no treaty by which the Government has recognized a body of Indians, the court will recognize a subdivision of tribes or bands which has been recognized by those officers of the Government whose duty it was to deal with and report the condition of the Indians to the executive branch of the Government; third, that where there has been no such recognition by the Government, the court will accept the subdivision into tribes or bands made by the Indians themselves. (*Tully* v. *The Apache Indians*, 32 C. Cls. R., 1.)
>
> But in the application of this rule the court has had to go further and recognize bands which simply in fact existed, irrespective of recognition, either by the Department of the Interior or the Indian tribes from which the members of the band came. Victoria's band of Apaches was merely a combination of individuals from different bands associated together for the purpose of waging war against the United States. The band did not exist until its warfare began. It had no geographical home or habitat. A ferocious sense of injustice induced the Indians to prefer death to submission, and they fought the troops of the United States until the band and its members were extinct. (*Montoya* v. *The Mescalero Apaches*, 32 Id., 349.) * * *
>
> The Chiricahuas were an isolated mountain band; they had their own habitat in remote valleys distinct from the valleys or mountains of the other bands; they fought their own battles; they pursued their own policy; they were hunted down and captured as Chiricahuas and were brought in and placed upon a reservation as a distinct and well-known military enemy. On the reservation they remained distinct, neither in fact nor in a legal sense merging with the other tribes. In their outbreak and escape from the San Carlos Reservation, in 1881, they still retained their tribal distinctiveness. For the court to hold that they had become an integral part of all the Indians upon the reservation and that all of the Indians upon the reservation, little better than prisoners of war, had become a new, distinctive Indian nation or tribal organization would be to introduce a new and artificial element into this branch of litigation founded not on the facts of the case but on a speculative theory. (Pp. 313–317.)

The question of what groups constitute tribes or bands has been extensively considered in recent years by the administrative authorities of the Federal Government in connection with tribal organization effected pursuant to section 16 of the Act of June 18, 1934.[21] A showing that the group seeking to organize is entitled to be considered as a tribe, within the meaning of the act,[22] is deemed a prerequisite to the holding of a referendum on

[16] *Thompson* v. *United States and Klamath Indians*, 44 C. Cls. 359 (1909).

[17] *Herring* v. *United States and Ute Indians*, 32 C. Cls. 536 (1897); *Allred* v. *United States and Ute Indians*, 36 C. Cls. 280 (1901); *Montoya* v. *United States and Mescalero Apaches*, 32 C. Cls. 349 (1897), aff'd 180 U. S. 261 (1901); *Dobbs* v. *United States and Apache Indians*, 33 C. Cls. 308 (1898); *Conners* v. *United States and Cheyenne Indians*, 33 C. Cls. 317 (1898), aff'd 180 U. S. 271 (1901). In the case of *Herring* v. *United States and Ute Indians*, the Court of Claims held that while the Ute Tribe was in amity with the United States, the members of Black Hawk's band had dissociated themselves from the tribe in order to engage in hostile acts, so that neither the tribe nor the band was liable for depredations which had been committed, the tribe being immune because not involved, the band immune because engaged in war. The Court declared:

> A band, being the lowest and smallest subdivision, confederates more readily than any other form of corporate existence, so to speak, and may be composed of Indians of different tribes or nations, and becomes a de facto band by the extent of its membership, its continuity of existence, and its persistent cohesion, subject to the control and power of a leader having the recognized authority of a commander and chief.
>
> The different divisions of the Indians have not usually originated from the conventional mode which organizes white persons into political communities, but have originated as a condition in fact, and when so existing they are recognized by the laws and treaties as a separate entity, and held responsible as such. (P. 538.)

[18] 180 U. S. 261 (1901), aff'g 32 C. Cls. 349 (1897).

[19] *Conners* v. *United States*, 180 U. S. 271 (1901), aff'g 33 C. Cls. 317 (1898).

[20] 33 C. Cls. 308 (1898).

[21] 48 Stat. 984, 986, 25 U. S. C. 476.

[22] Sec. 16 of the act covers "any Indian tribe, or tribes, residing on the same reservation." Sec. 19 defines "tribe" as follows: "The term 'tribe' wherever used in this Act shall be construed to refer to any Indian tribe, organized band, pueblo, or the Indians residing on one reservation." Critical cases arise particularly where the last phrase is inapplicable. Where this phrase is applicable, and the Indians of a given reservation

a proposed tribal constitution, and the basis for such a holding is regularly set forth in the letter from the Commissioner of Indian Affairs to the Secretary of the Interior recommending the submission of a tribal constitution to a referendum vote. In cases of special difficulty, a ruling has generally been obtained from the Solicitor for the Interior Department as to the tribal status of the group seeking to organize. The considerations which, singly or jointly, have been particularly relied upon in reaching the conclusion that a group constitutes a "tribe" or "band" have been:

(1) That the group has had treaty relations with the United States.

(2) That the group has been denominated a tribe by act of Congress or Executive order.

(3) That the group has been treated as having collective rights in tribal lands or funds, even though not expressly designated a tribe.

(4) That the group has been treated as a tribe or band by other Indian tribes.[33]

(5) That the group has exercised political authority over its members, through a tribal council or other governmental forms.[34]

Other factors considered, though not conclusive, are the existence of special appropriation items for the group[35] and the social solidarity of the group.

Ethnological and historical considerations, although not conclusive, are entitled to great weight in determining the question of tribal existence. A situation of peculiar difficulty and complexity arose in connection with the application of two tribal towns of the Creek Nation to organize under the Oklahoma Indian Welfare Act. In upholding the tribal status of the applicants, the Solicitor for the Interior Department declared:

> For the information of the Solicitor's Office an anthropological report, compiled by Mr. Morris Opler, was submitted which deals with the history and present character of these towns. This report provides data and opinions of authorities on the Creeks showing that the Creeks were originally a confederacy composed of a number of tribes, each referred to as a "Talwa." This word was generally translated into the English word "town" but rather covers the conception contained in the word "tribe." Each Talwa was self-governing. It was composed of people living in a single locality, but membership was dependent on birth rather than residence since a Creek Indian belonged to the Talwa of his mother. These towns were originally recognized by the Federal Government as the governing units in the Creek confederacy. The treaties of 1790 and 1796 with the Creeks were signed by the representatives of the various towns.[36] However, because of the pressure of the white people for land and the fact that the towns declared war and peace independently of each other, the Federal authorities found it advisable to insist upon centralization of the Creeks to avoid dealing with each Talwa. The Indians opposed this centralization and it was not until after the Civil War, in which the towns took opposing positions, that the Federal Government achieved the formation of a single government among the Creek Indians. And even then the union was opposed by the full-blood element. In spite of the centralization, however, the towns were still used for the official purposes of census and annuity payments and as a basis for representation in the central body. The census was kept on the basis of these towns until the making of the allotment rolls by the Dawes Commission. It was thought that the allotting of the Creek Indians would destroy their town organization but this did not in fact occur as the members of the town took allotments in the same locality and continued their social and political organization. The report states that at the present time the same offices described by members of De Soto's expedition are still maintained. Many of the old traditions and distinctions between the towns are likewise maintained, including the matrilineal membership.
>
> There is other evidence besides the report of this anthropologist now available which indicates the tribal character of these towns. The federated government formed in the latter part of the nineteenth century was a modified replica of the United States government, with representatives elected from the self-governing towns to the two Houses of legislature, the House of Kings and the House of Warriors. These titles represented the Creek designation of the chiefs and headmen of the towns. The present Principal Chief of the Creek Nation has informed the office that these elections still continue, though the National Council has few functions, and that the towns still have their kings and warriors. The petition for an election connected with one of the constitutions and the provisions of the constitutions themselves show the existence of a fairly elaborate local organization with a chief, governing committee and various special offices. Some towns have a square dedicated by their members used for meetings, ceremonies and social functions and there is at least one case of communal ground, also given by the members, worked by them to the benefit of indigent persons in the town. The principal Chief reports various ways in which the towns are active in providing assistance and relief to the members of the town.
>
> * * * * *
>
> That the Indians themselves recognized the existence of the Creek tribal towns is clear from an examination of the constitution and laws of the Muskogee Nation.
>
> * * * * *
>
> Under the foregoing legal authorities it appears to me that the Creek towns can lay a substantial claim to the right to be considered as recognized bands within the meaning of section 3 of the Oklahoma Indian Welfare Act of June 26, 1936.[37]

It is not enough, however, to show that any of the foregoing elements existed at some time in remote past. As was said by the Solicitor in passing upon the status of the Miami and Peoria Indians under the Oklahoma Indian Warfare Act:[38]

> It is not enough that the ethnographic history of the two groups shows them in the past to have been distinct and well-recognized tribes or bands. A particular tribe or band may well pass out of existence as such in the course of time. The word "recognized" as used in the Oklahoma Indian Welfare Act involves more than past

---

organize and adopt a constitution under sec. 16, it has been administratively held that they thereby become a tribe, but do not thereby acquire nonstatutory powers of government which they have never exercised. See Chapter 7, fn. 67.

[33] The case of *Tully* v. *United States*, 32 C. Cls. 1 (1896), indicates that where the Indians themselves have treated a group as a band separate from or subordinate to a given tribe, the courts will accept the subdivisions so recognized.

> The policy of the United States in dealing with the Indians has been, as we understand, to accept the subdivisions of the Indians into such tribes or bands as the Indians themselves adopted, and to treat with them accordingly.
>
> So that if such subdivisions, whether into tribes or bands, have not been recognized by treaty, but have been by the officers of the Government whose duty it was to report in respect thereto, then the court will accept that as sufficient recognition of the tribe or band upon which to predicate a judgment.
>
> Or if there be no such recognition by the Government, then the court will accept the subdivisions into such tribes or bands as made by the Indians themselves, whether such tribes and bands be named by reason of their geographical location or otherwise. (Pp. 7 and 8.)

[34] See, for an example of the consideration given to the foregoing elements of tribal existence, Memo. Sol. I. D., February 8, 1937 (Mole Lake and St. Croix Chippewa).

[35] This appears to be given considerable weight by the Court of Claims in *McKee* v. *United States and Comanche Indians*, 33 C. Cls. 99, 104 (1897).

[36] Treaty of August 7, 1790, with the Creek Nation, 7 Stat. 35; Treaty of June 29, 1796, with the Creek Nation, 7 Stat. 56.

[37] Memo. Sol. I. D., July 15, 1937. The Constitution of the Thlopthlocco Tribal Town was ratified on December 27, 1938, that of the Alabama-Quassarte Tribal Town on January 10, 1939. Both constitutions recognise that membership in the town is not inconsistent with membership in the Creek Nation.

[38] Act of June 26, 1936, 49 Stat. 1967, 25 U. S. C. 501 *et seq.*

existence as a tribe and its historical recognition as such. There must be a currently existing group distinct and functioning as a group in certain respects and recognition of such activity must have been shown by specific actions of the Indian Office, the Department, or by Congress.[28]

The distinction between a band or tribe and a voluntary association or society is at times difficult to draw with precision. The Acting Solicitor for the Interior Department, ruling that a particular group could not be considered a tribe or band for purposes of organization under the Oklahoma Indian Welfare Act,[29] declared:

> The primary distinction between a band and a society is that a band is a political body. In other words, a band has functions and powers of government. It is generally the historic unit of government in those tribes where bands exist. Because of Federal intervention aimed to destroy tribal organization many recognized bands have lost most if not all of their governmental functions. But their identity as a political organization must remain if the group of Indians can be considered a band or tribe.
>
> This character of a band as an existing or historical unit of Indian government seems to be recognized in sections 16 and 19 of the Indian Reorganization Act which refer to "powers vested in any tribe or tribal council by existing law," and define tribe to include an "organized band." In the administration of the act, organizations of tribes or bands have included such limited powers of government as remain and are considered appropriate. It is this feature which distinguishes organization under section 3 of the Oklahoma Act from organization of voluntary associations under section 4.[31]

The question of tribal existence has generally been treated by the courts as a simple yes-or-no question. It remains true, however, that an Indian tribe may "exist" for certain purposes, and not for others. Where several Indian groups are considered a single tribe generally for political and administrative purposes, Congress may nevertheless assign tribal status to a component group for specified purposes. This has frequently occurred in connection with claims. Tribe A and Tribe B have amalgamated to form Tribe C and share a common reservation and common funds. But at some time prior to amalgamation, Tribe A had suffered some injury for which a later generation offers redress in the form of a jurisdictional act. In such cases, Congress occasionally recognizes as a tribe, entitled to bring suit in the Court of Claims, what is for most purposes only a part of a tribe.[32]

[28] Memo. Sol. I. D., December 13, 1938.

[29] Act of June 26, 1936, 49 Stat. 1967, 25 U. S. C. 501, *et seq.*

[31] Memo. Acting Sol. I. D., July 29, 1937.

[32] Examples of this situation are involved in the Act of February 25, 1889, 25 Stat. 694 (authorizing suit by "Old Settlers"), construed in *United States* v. *Old Settlers*, 148 U. S. 427 (1893); Act of October 1, 1890, 26 Stat. 636 (Shawnee and Delaware Indians, incorporated in the Cherokee Nation, allowed to bring tribal suits against the Cherokee Nation and the United States); Act of June 28, 1898, sec. 25, 30 Stat. 495 (authorizing suit by Delaware Indians), construed in *Delaware Indians* v. *Cherokee Nation*, 193 U. S. 127 (1904); Joint Resolution of June 9, 1930, 46 Stat. 531 (authorizing suit by Assiniboine Indians).

SECTION 2. TERMINATION OF TRIBAL EXISTENCE

Given adequate evidence of the existence of a tribe during some period in the remote or recent past, the question may always be raised: Has the existence of this tribe been terminated in some way?

Generally speaking, the termination of tribal existence is shown positively by act of Congress, treaty provision, or tribal action[33] or negatively by the cessation of collective action and collective recognition. The forms of such collective action and collective recognition which are considered criteria of tribal existence have already been discussed.

The view was once widely entertained that tribal membership was legally incompatible with United States citizenship. Thus a number of early treaties and statutes provided that a given tribe should be dissolved when its members became citizens.[34] Dissolution of the tribe required division of property, and this meant allotment of tribal lands and per capita division of tribal funds.[35]

The Supreme Court in *Matter of Heff*,[36] took the view that citizenship and allotment involved a termination of tribal relations, and that such termination of tribal relations removed citizen allottees from the scope of the Indian liquor laws.

The defendant in the case was a Kickapoo Indian, and the Treaty of June 28, 1862, with that tribe[37] had provided that upon allotment these Indians "shall cease to be members of said tribe, and shall become citizens of the United States." This provision provides a possible justification for the actual decision in *Matter of Heff*, but the opinion in the case put the decision upon the broader ground that under section 6 of the General Allotment Act,[38] which provides that allottees shall be citizens of the United States "entitled to all the rights, privileges, and immunities of such citizens," every allottee became emancipated from federal control.

This doctrine was rejected in the case of *United States* v. *Nice*,[39] which held that allotment did not terminate tribal existence so as to take allottees outside the scope of Indian liquor laws adopted pursuant to congressional power to regulate commerce with Indian tribes. The Supreme Court declared:

> We recognize that a different construction was placed upon section 6 of the act of 1887 in *Matter of Heff*, 197 U. S. 488, but after reexamining the question in the light of other provisions in the act and of many later enactments clearly reflecting what was intended by Congress, we are constrained to hold that the decision in that case is not well grounded, and it is accordingly overruled. (P. 601.)

The view taken in the *Nice* case has prevailed ever since.[40]

While it is thus clear that neither allotment nor citizenship,[41] *per se*, nor both together, imply a termination of tribal existence, in the absence of express provision of treaty or statute asserting such a connection, presumably these are factors to be considered

[33] See *United States* v. *Anderson*, 225 Fed. 825 (D. C. E. D. Wis. 1915) (dissolution of Stockbridge Munsee Tribe by tribal agreement ratified by Congress).

[34] See Chapter 8, sec. 2A. And see Act of March 3, 1873, 17 Stat. 631 (Miami).

[35] See Chapter 15, sec. 23.

[36] 197 U. S. 488 (1905).

[37] 13 Stat. 623, 624.

[38] February 8, 1887, 24 Stat. 388, 390, 25 U. S. C. 349. See Chapter 8, sec. 2A(3).

[39] 241 U. S. 591 (1916).

[40] *United States* v. *Boylan*, 265 Fed. 165 (C. C. A. 2, 1920) aff'g. 256 Fed. 468 (D. C. N. D. Y. N. 1919), app. dism. 257 U. S. 614 (1921). Accord: *Farrell* v. *United States*, 110 Fed. 942 (C. C. A. 8, 1901).

[41] Of the argument that the Fourteenth Amendment conferred citizenship upon Indians and thereby dissolved tribal relations, the Senate Committee on Judiciary said, in 1870:

> To maintain that the United States intended, by a change of its fundamental law, which was not ratified by these tribes, * * * to annul treaties then existing * * * would be to charge upon the United States repudiation of national obligations, repudiation doubly infamous from the fact that the parties whose claims were thus annulled are too weak to enforce their just rights, and were enjoying the voluntarily assumed guardianship and protection of this Government. (Sen. Rept. No. 268, 41st Cong., 3d sess., December 14, 1870, p. 11.)

See Chapter 8, sec. 2(C), fn. 51.

in determining whether a given group has ceased to maintain tribal relations. Other factors considered by courts and administrative authorities in determining whether the tribal relations of a given group have come to an end are: the physical separation of a group from the main body of the tribe, and the cessation of participation in tribal resources and tribal government.

In the case of *The Cherokee Trust Funds*,[42] it was held that those Cherokees who remained in North Carolina when the main body of the Cherokees were removed to Indian Territory thereby lost their tribal status. The Supreme Court declared:

> * * * Whatever union they have had among themselves has been merely a social or business one. It was formed in 1868, at the suggestion of an officer of the Indian office, for the purpose of enabling them to transact business with the Government with greater convenience. Although its articles are drawn in the form of a constitution for a separate civil government, they have never been recognized as a separate Nation by the United States; no treaty has been made with them; they can pass no laws; they are citizens of that State and bound by its laws. * * * (P. 309.)

As the Court of Claims pointed out, in this case, the nonmigrating Cherokees "had expatriated themselves from the Cherokee Nation. * * * The only privilege ever accorded to them by the nation was that they might become citizens and subjects upon removal within its territorial boundaries * * *".[43]

It has been administratively determined that those Choctaws remaining in Mississippi when the Choctaw Tribe removed to Indian Territory lost their tribal status and could not be recognized as a separate tribe,[44] and, similarly, that the Indians of the Georgetown or Shoalwater Reservation in Washington, all of whom, apparently, took allotments at other reservations or otherwise abandoned the reservation in question, could no longer be recognized as a separate tribe entitled to the use of receipts from timber sales on the Georgetown Reservation.[45]

Many of the attempts made by Congress to terminate the existence of particular tribes have proved abortive. Tribes which have been dissolved not once but several times have been recognized, in later congressional legislation, as still existing.

An example in point is the group of Winnebago Indians who, separating from their brothers in Nebraska, took up homestead allotments in Wisconsin, under the Act of March 3, 1875,[46] which provided for the issuance of homestead allotments to Indians upon proof of the abandonment of tribal relations. The intent of these Indians "to abandon their tribal relations and adopt the habits and customs of civilized people" was given special legislative confirmation in the Act of January 18, 1881.[47] Nevertheless, in many subsequent statutes Congress recognized the continued existence of the Winnebago Indians of Wisconsin as a separate band.[48] In 1937 the right of this group to organize as a separate band was affirmed by the Interior Department.[49]

The efforts of Congress to terminate the existence of the Five Civilized Tribes are elsewhere discussed.[50]

The efforts to terminate the existence of the Wyandotte Tribe apparently began in 1850, in a treaty by which that tribe, having "manifest an anxious desire to extinguish their *tribal* or *national* character and become citizens of the United States," agreed "that their existence, as a nation or tribe, shall terminate and become extinct upon the ratification of this treaty * * *."[51] The treaty was ratified on September 24, 1850. Apparently the extinguisher clause did not work, for another treaty containing similar provisions for the extinguishment of tribal existence was entered into by the supposedly nonexistent tribe some 5 years later.[52] In 1935, Congress again provided for the final distribution of the funds belonging to the Wyandotte Tribe.[53] Even this, apparently, did not interfere with the continued functioning of the tribe, and on July 24, 1937, the chief of the tribe certified that the members of the tribe, by a unanimous vote, had adopted a tribal constitution under the Oklahoma Indian Welfare Act[54] perpetuating the traditional tribal organization.

Various other attempts to terminate tribal relations by treaty or act of Congress have proved abortive.[56] These legislative experiences suggest that the dissolution of tribal existence is easier to decree than to effect, and indicate the value of a certain skepticism in considering current legislative proposals looking to the dissolution of all or some Indian tribes. They also point to the reasons for the judicial rule that an exercise of the federal power to dissolve a tribe must be demonstrated by statutory or treaty provisions which are positive and unambiguous.[57]

---

[42] *Eastern Band of Cherokee Indians* v. *United States and Cherokee Nation*, 117 U. S. 288 (1886), aff'g 20 C. Cls. 449 (1885).

[43] 20 C. Cls. 449, 473. Accord: *United States* v. *Elm*. 25 Fed. Cas. No. 15048 (D. C. N. D. N. Y., 1877) (Oneida).

[44] Memo. Sol. I. D., August 31, 1936. *Cf.* note on the status of Pojoaque Pueblo, Chapter 20, sec. 1.

[45] Op. Sol. I. D., M.24173, September 23, 1932, 54 I. D. 71.

[46] Sec. 15, 18 Stat. 402, 420.

[47] 21 Stat. 315.

[48] Act of March 3, 1909, 35 Stat. 781, 798; Act of January 20, 1910, 36 Stat. 873; Act of July 1, 1912, 37 Stat. 187; Act of December 17, 1928, 45 Stat. 1027.

[49] Memo. Sol. I. D., March 6, 1937.

[50] See Chapter 23, sec. 6.

[51] Treaty of April 1, 1850, with the Wyandot, 9 Stat. 987, 989.

[52] Treaty of January 31, 1855, 10 Stat. 1159, construed in *Schrimpscher* v. *Stockton*, 183 U. S. 290 (1902). *Cf.* Art. XIII of the Treaty of February 23, 1867, with the Senecas and others, including certain Wyandottes, 15 Stat. 513, 516, providing for Wyandottes, "many of whom have been in a disorganized and unfortunate condition since their treaty of one thousand eight hundred and fifty-five." And see *Gray* v. *Coffman*, 10 Fed. Cas. No. 5714 (C. C. Kans. 1874); *Conley* v. *Ballinger*, 216 U. S. 84 (1910).

[53] Act of August 27, 1935, 49 Stat. 894.

[54] Act of June 16, 1936, 49 Stat. 1967.

[56] *Wiggan* v. *Conolly*, 163 U. S. 56 (1896), construing the Treaty of June 24, 1862, with the Ottawa Indians of the United Bands of Blanchard's Fork, etc., 12 Stat. 1237, providing for the termination of tribal relations on July 16, 1867, and also the Treaty of February 23, 1867, with the Ottawa and other tribes, 15 Stat. 513, repealing this provision. And see Act of August 6, 1846, 9 Stat. 55.

[57] *Jones* v. *Meehan*, 175 U. S. 1 (1899); *Morrow* v. *Blevins*, 23 Tenn. 223 (1843).

SECTION 3. POLITICAL STATUS

The political status of Indian tribes may be considered with respect to the relations subsisting between the tribe and (*a*) its members, (*b*) other governments, and (*c*) private persons not members of the tribe.

(*a*) So far as concerns the political relation between a tribe and its members, this is a subject which has already been considered in treating of the nature and scope of tribal self-government.[58]

(*b*) The relation of an Indian tribe to other governments presents a series of difficult problems of international law. These problems involve: (1) The treaty-making capacity of an Indian tribe; (2) the capacity of a tribe to wage war; (3) its capacity to sue as a "foreign nation"; (4) its relationship to a foreign country; (5) the recognition which it may demand of the several states; (6) its relation to the federal power of eminent domain; (7) its relation to the state power of eminent domain; and (8) its status as a federal instrumentality.

---

[58] See Chapter 7.

(1) The Indian tribes were recognized as powers capable of making treaties before the United States was.[59] The validity of the many treaties made and ratified between the United States and nearly all the tribes within its boundaries, is clearly established, as a matter of law.[60] Treaty making, however, depends upon the will of two parties, and either the United States or an Indian tribe may refuse, and frequently has refused, to make treaties which the other party desired. Thus, since Congress expressed its opposition to the continued making of treaties with the Indian tribes, in a rider which the House of Representatives attached to the Indian Department Appropriation Act of March 3, 1871,[61] the President and the Senate have refused to make such treaties. Whether Congress, which is not the treaty-making department of the Government, has the power thus to lay down a binding limitation upon the treaty-making power, viz, the President and the Senate, and whether a treaty made next year with an Indian tribe and constitutionally ratified would be valid or invalid, are probably academic questions. They are also primarily verbal questions. When Congress condemned the use of treaties, it did not prevent the practice of dealing with Indian tribes by means of "conventions," "agreements," "charters," and "constitutions." From the standpoint of the Indian tribes, it made little difference what manner of ratification and procedure was incumbent upon the representative of the United States who treated with them.[62]

(2) A second fundamental attribute of sovereignty, in international law, is the power to make war. This power has been recognized in Indian tribes down to recent times,[63] and there are still on the statute books laws which contemplate the possibility of hostilities by an Indian tribe.[64] The capacity of an Indian tribe to make war involves certain definite consequences for domestic law. Acts which would constitute murder or manslaughter in the absence of a state of war, whether committed by Indians[65] or by the military forces[66] of the United States, may be justified as acts of war where a state of war exists. Hostile Indians surrendering to armed forces are subject to the disabilities and entitled to the rights of prisoners of war.[67] While the existence of a state of war at some time in the past continues to be a current question in Indian litigation, particularly claims litigation, it may be doubted whether the courts would recognize the legal capacity of an Indian tribe to engage in war today.

(3) A third issue in the relations between an Indian tribe and other governments relates to the possibility of suit by an Indian tribe against a state or its citizens in the federal courts.

It was settled in the historic case of *Cherokee Nation* v. *Georgia*[68] that the Cherokee Nation was not a foreign state entitled to bring suit in the federal courts against the State of Georgia to restrain the enforcement of unconstitutional laws.[69] The Supreme Court, *per* Marshall, *C. J.*, laid down the classic outlines of the doctrine which has since prevailed:

> * * * Is the Cherokee nation a foreign state, in the sense in which that term is used in the constitution? The counsel for the plaintiffs have maintained the affirmative of this proposition with great earnestness and ability. So much of the argument as was intended to prove the character of the Cherokees as a state, as a distinct political society, separated from others, capable of managing its own affairs and governing itself, has, in the opinion of a majority of the judges, been completely successful. * * *
>
> A question of much more difficulty remains. Do the Cherokees constitute a *foreign* statein the sense of the construction? The counsel have shown conclusively, that they are not a state of the Union, and have insisted that, individually, they are aliens, not owing allegiance to the United States. An aggregate of aliens composing a state must, they say, be a foreign state each individual being foreign, the whole must be foreign.
>
> This argument is imposing, but we must examine it more closely, before we yield to it. The condition of the Indians in relation to the United States is, perhaps, unlike that of any other two people in existence. In general, nations not owing a common allegiance, are foreign to each other. The term *foreign* nation is, with strict propriety, applicable by either to the other. But the relation of the Indians to the United States is marked by peculiar and cardinal distinctions which exist nowhere else. The Indian territory is admitted to compose a part of the United States. In all our maps, geographical treatises, histories, and laws, it is so considered. In all our intercourse with foreign nations, in our commercial regulations, in any attempt at intercourse between Indians and foreign nations, they are considered as within the jurisdictional limits of the United States, subject to many of those restraints which are imposed upon our own citizens. They acknowledge themselves, in their treaties, to be under the protection of the United States; they admit, that the United States shall have the sole and exclusive right of regulating the trade with them, and managing all their affairs as they think proper; and the Cherokees in particular were allowed by the treaty of Hopewell, which preceded the constitution, "to send a deputy of their choice, whenever they think fit, to congress." Treaties were made with some tribes, by the state of New York, under a then unsettled construction of the confederation, by which they ceded all their lands to that state, taking back a limited grant to themselves, in which they admit their dependence. Though the Indians are acknowledged to have an unquestionable, and heretofore unquestioned, right to the lands they occupy, until that right shall be extinguished by a voluntary cession to our government; yet it may well be doubted, whether those tribes which reside within the acknowledged boundaries of the United States can, with strict accuracy, be denominated foreign nations. They may, more correctly, perhaps, be denominated domestic dependent nations. They occupy a territory to which we assert a title independent of their will, which must take effect in point of possession, when their right of possession ceases. Meanwhile, they are in a state of pupilage; their relation to the United States resembles that of a ward to his guardian. They look to our government for protection; rely upon its kindness and its power; appeal to it for relief to their wants; and address the president as their great father. They and their country are considered by foreign nations, as well

[59] See *Preston* v. *Browder*, 1 Wheat. 115 (1816); *Patterson* v. *Jenks*, 2 Pet. 216 (1829); *Worcester* v. *Georgia*, 6 Pet. 515 (1832); *Lattimer* v. *Poteet*, 14 Pet. 4 (1840); *Porterfield* v. *Clark*, 2 How. 76 (1844); *Seneca Nation* v. *Christy*, 162 U. S. 283 (1896); *Mitchel* v. *United States*, 9 Pet. 711 (1835). Also see Chapter 3, sec. 4A.

[60] See Chapter 3.

[61] 16 Stat. 544, 566.

[62] See Chapter 3, sec. 6.

[63] *Montoya* v. *United States*, 180 U. S. 261 (1901); *Scott* v. *United States and Apache Indians*, 33 C. Cls. 486 (1898); *Dobbs* v. *United States and Apache Indians*, 33 C. Cls. 308 (1898). Warfare among the Indian tribes themselves was long a matter of concern to the Federal Government. See, for example, the Act of July 14, 1832, 4 Stat. 595.

[64] Act of July 5, 1862, 12 Stat. 512, 528, R. S. § 2080, 25 U. S. C. 72 (authorizing abrogation of treaties with tribe engaged in hostilities); Act of March 2, 1867, 14 Stat. 492, 515, R. S. § 2100, 25 U. S. C. 127 (authorizing withholding of annuities from hostile Indians); Act of February 14, 1873, 17 Stat. 437, 457, 459, R. S. §§ 467, 2136, 25 U. S. C. 266 (regulating sale of arms to hostile Indians); Act of March 3, 1875, 18 Stat. 420, 449, 25 U. S. C. 128 (forbidding payments to Indian bands at war).

[65] "The fact that they were treated as prisoners of war also refutes the idea that they were murderers, brigands or other common criminals." *Conners* v. *United States*, 180 U. S. 271, 275 (1901). And *cf. United States* v. *Cha-to-kah-na-pe-sha*, 25 Fed. Cas. No. 14789a (Superior Court, Ark. 1824) (holding Osage Indians guilty of murder, tribe being in amity). *Cf.* also *Ke-tuo-e-mun-guah* v. *McClure*, 122 Ind. 541, 23 N. E. 1080 (1890).

[66] See *Conners* v. *United States and Cheyenne Indians*, 33 C. Cls. 317, 325 (1898), aff'd. 180 U. S. 271 (1901) (killing of "escaping prisoners of war" legally justified).

[67] *Ibid.* And see *Montoya* v. *United States and Mescalero Apaches*, 180 U. S. 261 (1901), aff'g. 32 C. Cls. 349 (1897).

[68] 5 Pet. 1 (1831).

[69] *Cf. Worcester* v. *Georgia*, 6 Pet. 515 (1832), discussed in Chapter 7.

> as by ourselves, as being so completely under the sovereignty and dominion of the United States that any attempt to acquire their lands, or to form a political connection with them, would be considered by all as an invasion of our territory and an act of hostility. These considerations go far to support the opinion, that the framers of our constitution had not the Indian tribes in view, when they opened the courts of the Union to controversies between a state or the citizens thereof and foreign states.
>
> * * * we should feel much difficulty in considering them as designated by the term foreign state, were there no other part of the constitution which might shed light on the meaning of these words. But we think that in construing them, considerable aid is furnished by that clause in the eighth section of the third article, which empowers congress to "regulate commerce with foreign nations, and among the several states, and with the Indian tribes." In this clause, they are as clearly contradistinguished, by a name appropriate to themselves, from foreign nations, as from the several states composing the Union. * * *
>
> * * * * *
>
> The court has bestowed its best attention on this question, and, after mature deliberation, the majority is of opinion, that an Indian tribe or nation within the United States is not a foreign state, in the sense of the constitution, and cannot maintain an action in the courts of the United States. (Pp. 16–18, 20.)

(4) It has been held that the relation of dependence existing between an Indian tribe and the Federal Government is not terminated by the flight of the tribe to foreign soil or by its sojourn on such soil for 9 years. Thus the return of a refugee tribe has been demanded of the foreign country in which it was sojourning.[70]

(5) The Indian tribes have been treated, for certain purposes as similar to states, territories, or dependencies of the United States.[71] Thus, in the case of *Mackey* v. *Coxe*,[72] the Supreme Court held that an administrator appointed by a probate court of the Cherokee Nation occupied the same position as an administrator appointed by any state or territory of the United States. The court declared:

> * * * In some respects they bear the same relation to the federal government as a territory did in its second grade of government, under the ordinance of 1787. Such territory passed its own laws, subject to the approval of congress, and its inhabitants were subject to the constitution and acts of congress. The principal difference consists in the fact that the Cherokees enact their own laws, under the restriction stated, appoint their own officers, and pay their own expenses. This, however, is no reason why the laws and proceedings of the Cherokee territory, so far as relates to rights claimed under them, should not be placed upon the same footing as other territories in the Union. It is not a foreign, but a domestic territory,—a territory which originated under our constitution and laws.
>
> By the 11th section of the act of 24th of June, 1812, it is provided "that it shall be lawful for any person or persons to whom letters testamentary or of administration hath been or may hereafter be granted, by the proper authority in any of the United States or the territories thereof, to maintain any suit or action, and to prosecute and recover any claim in the District of Columbia, in the same manner as if the letters testamentary or administration had been granted in the District." * * *
>
> The Cherokee country, we think, may be considered a territory of the United States, within the act of 1812. In no respect can it be considered a foreign State or territory, as it is within our jurisdiction and subject to our laws. (Pp. 103–104.)

Again, in the case of *Standley* v. *Roberts*[73] the question arose whether a federal court might, by injunction, restrain the enforcement of a judgment rendered by the circuit court of the Choctaw Nation and affirmed by the supreme court of that nation, affecting title to land and rights to rentals within the Choctaw Nation. This issue was resolved in favor of the Choctaw Nation by the Circuit Court of Appeals, and the decision was sustained by the Supreme Court. In the opinion of the former court, rendered by Judge Sanborn, it was said:

> * * * the judgments of the courts of these nations, in cases within their jurisdiction, stand on the same footing with those of the courts of the territories of the Union and are entitled to the same faith and credit. (P. 845.)

A similar decision was reached in the case of *Raymond* v. *Raymond*, where the validity of a tribal divorce decree[74] was upheld.

The Interior Department has taken the view that tribal elections are within those provisions of the Hatch Act[75] applicable to "any election."[76]

(6) Again, it is held that an Indian tribe is not exempt from the power of federal eminent domain.[77]

(7) The rule has likewise been established that an Indian tribe is exempt from the eminent domain power of the several states, in the absence of federal legislation subjecting the tribe to such power.[78]

(8) In its relations with state and municipal governments, an Indian tribe is treated for certain purposes as an instrumentality of the Federal Government.[79] Following a ruling of the Attorney General of North Dakota to the effect that a state crop mortgage law did not apply to mortgages made to an Indian tribe, for the reason that such tribe was deemed an "agency" of the United States within the meaning of the statutory exemption, the Interior Department authorized the acceptance of such mortgages as security for revolving fund loans. The Assistant Secretary declared:

> * * * This Department has previously held in various connections that an Indian tribe, particularly where incorporated, is a Federal agency. In the Solicitor's Opinion M. 27810, of December 13, 1934, the following statement is made:
>
> "The Indian tribes have long been recognized as vested with governmental powers, subject to limitations imposed by Federal statutes. The powers of an Indian tribe cannot be restricted or controlled by the governments of the several States. The tribe is, therefore, so far as its original absolute sovereignty has been limited, an instrumentality and agency of the Federal Government. (See the recent opinion of this Department, 'Powers of Indian Tribes,' approved October 25, 1934—M.27781.)
>
> "Various statutes authorize the delegation of new powers of government to the Indian tribes. (See opinion cited above.) The most recent of such

---

[70] *Lowe* v. *United States and Kickapoo Indians*, 37 C. Cls. 413 (1902). Compare, however, *McCandless* v. *United States ex rel. Diabo*, 25 F. 2d 71 (C. C. A. 3, 1928) (Iroquois in Canada).

[71] See, for example, the Joint Resolution of June 15, 1860, 12 Stat. 116, providing that certain tribes should receive all congressional documents supplied to states and territories.

[72] 18 How. 100 (1855).

[73] 59 Fed. 836 (C. C. A. 8, 1894), app. dism. 17 Sup. Ct. 999 (1896).

[74] "The Cherokee Nation * * * may maintain its own judicial tribunals, and their judgments and decrees upon the rights of the persons and property of members of the Cherokee Nation as against each other are entitled to all the faith and credit accorded to the judgments and decrees of territorial courts." (*Per* Sanborn, *J.*) *Raymond* v. *Raymond*, 83 Fed. 721, 722 (C. C. A. 8, 1897). But *cf. Ex parte Morgan*, 20 Fed. 298 (D. C. W. D. Ark., 1883) (holding Cherokee Nation not a "state" for purposes of extradition).

[75] Act of August 2, 1939, 76th Cong., Pub. No. 252.

[76] Memo. Sol. I. D., April 6, 1940.

[77] *Cherokee Nation* v. *Kansas Railway Co.*, 135 U. S. 641 (1890), rev'g 33 Fed. 900 (D. C. W. D. Ark. 1888). And see Chapter 15, sec. 18D; and Federal Eminent Domain (Dept. Justice 1940).

[78] See Chapter 15, sec. 11.

[79] The "instrumentality" and "wardship" concepts are sometimes used interchangeably. See *United States* v. *4,450.72 Acres of Land*, 27 F. Supp. 167 (D. C. Minn. 1939) ("wardship" offered as basis of federal legislative power to condemn land for Indian use.) And see Chapter 8, sec. 9.

> statutes is the Wheeler-Howard Act, which sets up as one of its primary objectives, the purpose 'to grant certain rights of home rule to Indians.' This Act contemplates the devolution to the duly organized Indian tribes of many powers over property and personal conduct which are now exercised by officials of the Interior Department. The granting of a Federal corporate charter to an Indian tribe confirms the character of such a tribe as a Federal instrumentality and agency."

Again it has been ruled that Indian tribes handling rehabilitation funds are exempt from federal unemployment insurance and social security laws by reason of the exception in the application of those laws in favor of "an instrumentality of the United States." [80]

On the other hand, an Indian tribe has been held not a federal instrumentality within the meaning of various statutory and constitutional restrictions upon federal instrumentalities.[81]

The question of how far an Indian tribe is a federal instrumentality for tax purposes is elsewhere considered.[82]

(c) The relations between an Indian tribe and private persons not members of the tribe apart from questions of contract, which are elsewhere considered, raise the question of tribal liability for the acts of tribal members. This question involves the balancing of two opposing principles. On the one hand, an Indian tribe, as a municipality, falls within the ordinary rule that a municipality is not liable for damage inflicted by its citizens upon third parties. On the other hand, an Indian tribe is, in some measure, responsible, under principles of international law, for the conduct of its citizens towards the citizens of another friendly power.

An illuminating analysis of the problem which this conflict of principles creates is found in the opinion of the Court of Claims in the case of *Brown* v. *United States.*[83] The responsibility of an Indian tribe from the international law standpoint is, from the domestic law standpoint, no more than a proper consideration explaining certain treaty provisions and statutes. Where no treaties or statutes impose liability upon a tribe for acts of individual members, the courts will not do so.

In *Turner* v. *United States,*[84] the leading case on this point,

---

[80] This office has frequently taken the position that an Indian tribe is an instrumentality of the United States, particularly insofar as its powers have been limited or expanded by the Federal Government * * *. However, even if the tribe could not otherwise be considered as an instrumentality of the United States, the trust agreement entered into between the Government and the tribe would give it that character, since the tribe becomes the means whereby the Government carries on the Rehabilitation activities provided for by Congress and administers to the needs of the tribes and their members. (Op. Sol. I. D., M. 29156. June 30, 1937.)

[81] To the effect that an Indian tribe is not an agency of the Federal Government in such a sense as to subject tribal officers to penalties for embezzlement by federal officers, see Memo. Sol. I. D., March 9, 1935 (Klamath).

To the effect that constitutional restrictions upon federal power do not limit tribal powers, see *Talton v. Mayes,* 163 U. S. 376 (1896), and see Chapter 7, sec. 1.

On the distinction between tribal employees and federal employees, see Op. Sol. I. D., December 9, 1932 (teachers in Choctaw-Chickasaw schools, after Curtis Act of June 28, 1898, 30 Stat. 495, held not federal employees although under federal supervision). And see Memo. Sol. I. D., Oct. 20, 1936 (Menominee); 27 Op. A. G. 139 (holding Menominee Mills employees not subject to federal employee 8-hour legislation); Op. Comp. Gen. A–51847, Nov. 16, 1933 (same employees held not subject to Economy Act reducing federal salaries).

[82] See Chapter 13, sec. 1A and 2.

[83] It is an established principle of international law that a nation is responsible for wrongs done by its citizens to the citizens of a friendly power. Ordinarily this responsibility is discharged by a government rendering to a resident alien the same protection which it affords to its own citizens and bringing the perpetrators to trial and punishment. This responsibility of a nation for the acts of its individual members is so well established and regulated by international law that it falls little short of being a natural right.

In like manner, though in a varying degree, the Government of the United States has always held an Indian tribe in amity to a like responsibility. The maintenance of peace on the one hand and the protection of its citizens on the other may be said to have been the two fundamental principles of the Government's Indian policy. The Indian tribes did not rise to the rank of independent nations, and the relations between them and the United States were peculiar. Consequently the assertion of the right to demand satisfaction for outrages committed upon property was generally made by statutes and not by treaties. These statutory declarations began in 1796 (1 Stat. L., 469) and continued until 1874 (Revised Stat., Sec. 2156). Between these there came the very important and elaborate statute of *30th June, 1834* (4 Stat. L. 731, Sec. 17), which codified our Indian policy, and which, with some modifications in 1859 (11 Stat. L. 401) and 1872 (17 Stat. L. 190), was reenacted in the Revised Statutes, and thus continued until the present day, or at least until the Indian Depredation Act of 1891. These statutes may not be binding upon the Indians in one sense, when the Indians are considered as treaty-making powers; but they are nevertheless declarations of the intention of the United States to hold the Indian tribes to a national or quasi international responsibility, and they indicate and define the extent or limits of this national or tribal liability as the United States understand it to exist. In the courts of the United States that effect must be given to the statutes. They must be regarded as an authoritative declaration of the quasi international law applicable to dependent Indian nations; that is to say, they must be regarded as correctly defining and laying down the limitations of tribal responsibility.

From 1796 until 1867 this declaration of the United States, that "satisfaction" must be made by a tribe for the unlawful depredations of its members, was thus proclaimed generally through their statutes. In 1867 the Government first introduced into an Indian treaty a provision looking toward the surrender of the wrongdoers as the tribal "satisfaction" which might be made for wrongs inflicted by its members in the stead of money indemnification. The act of 1834 had said and in 1867 continued to say:

> "*And be it further enacted*, That if any Indian or Indians belonging to any tribe in amity with the United States shall, within the Indian country, take or destroy the property of any person lawfully within such country, or shall pass from the Indian country into any State or Territory inhabited by citizens of the United States, and there take, steal, or destroy any horse, horses, or other property belonging to any citizen or inhabitant of the United States, such citizen or inhabitant, his representative, attorney, or agent, may make application to the proper superintendent, agent, or subagent, who, upon being furnished with the necessary documents and proofs, shall, under the direction of the President, make application to the nation or tribe to which said Indian or Indians shall belong for satisfaction; and if such nation or tribe shall neglect or refuse to make satisfaction in a reasonable time, not exceeding twelve months, it shall be the duty of such superintendent, agent, or subagent to make return of his doings to the Commissioner of Indian Affairs that such further steps may be taken as shall be proper, in the opinion of the President, to obtain satisfaction for the injury; and, in the meantime, in respect to the property so taken, stolen, or destroyed, the United States guarantee to the party so injured an eventual indemnification." (Sec. 17.)

The treaty 21st October, 1867, with the Kiowas and Comanches (15 Stat. L. 581) then introduced into our Indian policy a new element, thus declared:

> "If bad men among the Indians shall commit a wrong or depredation upon the person or property of anyone, white, black, or Indians, subject to the authority of the United States and at peace therewith, the tribes herein named solemnly agree that they will, on proof made to their agent and notice by him, deliver up the wrongdoer to the United States, to be tried and punished according to its laws, and in case they wilfully refuse so to do, the person injured shall be reimbursed for his loss from the annuities or other moneys due or to become due to them under this or other treaties made with the United States. And the President, on advising with the Commissioner of Indian Affairs, shall prescribe such rules and regulations for ascertaining damages under the provisions of this article as, in his judgment, may be proper; but no such damages shall be adjusted and paid until thoroughly examined and passed upon by the Commissioner of Indian Affairs and the Secretary of the Interior; and no one sustaining loss, while violating or because of his violating, the provisions of this treaty or the laws of the United States, shall be reimbursed therefor." (Art. 1.)

* * * * *

The making of the treaties was apparently the institution of a new Indian policy—a policy which would induce the tribes to give up their offenders instead of paying for their offenses by a communal tax upon their annuities—a policy which would tend to weed out the worst criminals among the Indians and stamp in their estimation depredations as crimes. But the policy instituted by the treaties never was instituted in fact. The provision of the first article remained a dead letter. The President never "prescribed rules and regulations for ascertaining damages;" the United States never notified an Indian tribe to deliver up a wrongdoer; no tribe ever willfully refused so to do, or was offered an opportunity to refuse; no person, by virtue of any one of these nine treaties ever became entitled to "be reimbursed for his loss from the annuities or other moneys due or to become due" to any one of these treaty-making tribes.

(*Brown* v. *United States*, 32 C. Cls. 432, 433–436 (1897).)

[84] 248 U. S. 354 (1919), aff'g. 51 C. Cls. 125 (1916).

the plaintiffs were white men, who, by procedures of questionable legality, had secured a lease to approximately 400 square miles of Creek tribal land. When they proceeded to fence the land, the tribal treasurer and many other Indians of the vicinity rose in protest and destroyed 60 miles of fence, which was as much as the plaintiffs had built. Congress thereafter enacted a statute authorizing the Court of Claims to hear the plaintiffs' claim against the Creek Nation. The Court of Claims finally dismissed the plaintiffs' suit, declaring:

> Plaintiff's petition avers that the damage was inflicted by "a mob of Indians of the Creek or Muskogee Nation or Tribe"; and if that be true the Creek Nation is not to be held responsible for the mob's action. It can be said of the Creek Nation, as was said of the Cherokee Nation that it has "many of the rights and privileges of an independent people. They have their own constitution and laws and power to administer their internal affairs. They are recognized as a distinct political community, and treaties have been made with them in that capacity." *Delaware Indians* v. *Cherokee Nation*, 193 U. S. 127, 144 They are not sovereign to the extent that the federal or state governments are sovereign, but this suit is predicated upon the assumption that their laws are valid enactments, and it recognizes the separate existence of the Creek Nation. When, therefore, the effort is made to hold them responsible as a nation for the illegal action of a mob we must apply the rule of law applicable to established governments under similar conditions. It is a familiar rule that in the absence of a statute declaring a liability therefor neither the sovereign nor the governmental subdivisions, such as counties or municipalities, are responsible to the party injured in his person or estate by mob violence.[85] (Pp. 152–153.)

The decision of the Court of Claims, affirmed by the Supreme Court, clearly establishes that an Indian tribe is not a mere collection of individuals, and that the action of a mob, even though it should include all the members of a municipality, is not the action of the municipality.

[85] Citing: *Louisiana* v. *Mayor*, 109 U. S. 285, 291 (1883); *Hart* v. *Bridgeport*, 11 Fed. Cas. No. 1649 (C. C. Conn. 1876); *Gianfortone* v. *New Orleans*, 61 Fed. 64 (C. C. E. D. La. 1894); *City* v. *Abbagnato*, 62 Fed. 240 (C. C. A. 5, 1894); *Murdock Grate Co.* v. *Commonwealth*, 152 Mass. 28, 31, 24 N. E. 854 (1890).

Under the Act of March 3, 1885,[86] the Secretary of the Interior was authorized to pass on claims for depredations where the tribe concerned had, by treaty, assumed collective responsibility for the acts of its members. This statute was narrowly construed. The Court of Claims held that in order to bring a case within the terms of the statute it had to be shown that the tribe had expressly undertaken to make compensation for injuries committed by individual members.

> While Congress has the undoubted right to provide that an obligation to pay may arise from an act of Congress, the policy of the Government has confined the responsibility of the Indian and the consequent power of the Secretary to the obligation arising from treaties in which there is an express undertaking on the part of the Indians to pay for depredations.[87] (P. 22.)

As was said by the Court of Claims, with respect to a depredation suit brought against an Indian tribe under the statute:

> * * * the Indian defendants were not liable, for they were a tribe, a quasi body politic, and the trespassers were individuals. There was no natural right * * * except that of pursuing and proceeding against the depredators individually. They were the only wrongdoers known to the common law—to any law. As against both of the defendants in this suit, the Government and the Cheyenne tribe, the only semblance of liability that existed, or exists, is that which has been expressly declared and created by treaties and statutes.[88] (P. 479.)

We have already noted that a later act imposed upon Indian tribes a liability for depredations which was statutory and not based upon treaty provisions. While the power of Congress thus to impose a corporate liability for individual wrongs is unquestioned, it remains true that clear and unambiguous language must be used to show such an intention.[89]

[86] 23 Stat. 362, 376.

[87] *Crow* v. *United States and Arapahoe and Kiowa Indians*, 32 C. Cls. 16 (1896). Accord: *Mares, Adm'r.* v. *United States and Jicarilla Apache Indians*, 29 C. Cls. 197 (1894).

[88] *Labadie, Adm'r.* v. *United States and Cheyenne Indians*, 33 C. Cls. 476 (1898).

[89] See fn. 85, *supra*.

SECTION 4. CORPORATE CAPACITY

Whether an Indian tribe, in the absence of some act of incorporation, is to be regarded as a corporate body is an interesting question. The answer to it must depend, in part, upon one's definition of the term "corporation." In the narrow sense in which the term is frequently used, a corporation is something chartered by a government, and in this sense only those Indian tribes which have been chartered by some government, *e. g.*, the Pueblos of New Mexico incorporated by territorial legislation,[90] and the tribes incorporated under section 17 of the Act of June 18, 1934,[91] are to be considered corporations.

The term "corporation," however, is frequently used in a broader sense,[92] as when it is stated, for instance, that the City of London, or the United States, is a body corporate, even though a charter of incorporation cannot be discovered. The term "corporation," in this sense, might be defined as designating a group of individuals to which the law ascribes legal personality, *i. e.*, the complex of rights, privileges, powers, and immunities enjoyed by natural persons generally. This definition is not precise, because the rights, privileges, powers, and immunities of different classes of natural persons vary, and various organized groups may enjoy the status of individuals in some respects and not in others. The definition does, however, establish a direction and a method of analysis, and enables us to say that for certain purposes a group has corporate status.

In this sense, we may say that Indian tribes have been assigned corporate status for many different purposes.[93] Among these purposes are the right to sue, the capacity of being sued, the capacity to hold and exercise property rights not vested in any of the members of the tribe, the power to execute contracts that bind the tribe even when in the course of time its entire membership has changed, and the separation of tribal liability from the liability of tribal members.

Various general statutes on Indian depredations, for instance, have authorized suits by injured citizens of the United States against Indian tribes whose members had committed such depre-

[90] Laws of New Mexico, 1851–52, pp. 176, 418; see Chapter 20, sec. 2.

[91] 48 Stat. 984, 988, 25 U. S. C. 477.

[92] See Stevens on Corporations (1936), c. 1.

[93] In *Farmers' Loan and Trust Co.* v. *Pierson*, 130 Misc. 110, 119, 222 N. Y. S. 532 (1927), Justice Bijur of the New York Supreme Court wrote that "a corporation is more nearly a method than a thing, and that the law in dealing with a corporation has no need of defining it as a person or an entity, or even as an embodiment of functions, rights and duties, but may treat it as a name for a useful and usual collection of jural relations, each one of which must in every instance be ascertained, analyzed and assigned to its appropriate place according to the circumstances of the particular case, having due regard to the purposes to be achieved."

dations.[94] None of these statutes imposes individual liability upon the members of the tribe; the liability imposed is purely tribal. It is, in the sense above defined, corporate, and has been so described by the Court of Claims.[95] The extent to which Indian tribes have been subjected to suit under these and similar statutes is elsewhere noted.[96]

The distinction between property rights of a tribe and rights of individual members is elsewhere analyzed in some detail,[97] and for the present it is pertinent only to cite examples of this corporate attribute of the Indian tribes.

In the case of *Fleming* v. *McCurtain*[98] the Supreme Court, *per* Holmes, *J.*, referred to "the corporate existence of the nation as such," in construing a treaty provision granting a tract to the Choctaw Nation "in fee simple to them and their descendants to inure to them while they shall exist as a nation and live on it," and emphasized the distinction between the nation and its members, in reaching the conclusion that title to the tract rested with the former and that no trust was imposed in favor of the latter. The same distinction is confirmed in the case of *Gritts* v. *Fisher*,[99] holding that the particular members alive when the distribution of tribal property was ordered did not obtain any vested right which would preclude the legislature of the tribe and Congress from later decreeing that a new list of tribal members should participate in the property.[100]

Another example of the distinction between tribal and individual property rights is found in claims cases which seek to distinguish between the claims of the tribe and the claims of individual members,[101] holding that damages to members, through denial of education promised in treaty, are not damages to a tribe, except in a sense too remote to serve as a basis of recovery.

Further examples of the distinction between corporate liability and individual liability are found in the cases of *Parks* v. *Ross*[102] and *Turner* v. *United States*,[103] the former case holding that an officer of a tribe was not personally responsible for the debts of the tribe; the latter case holding that the tribe itself was not liable at common law for torts committed by its members.[104]

The distinction between tribe and members is emphasized in *United States* v. *Cherokee Nation*,[105] in holding that where Congress allows a tribe to bring suit not on its own behalf but on behalf of a designated class of individuals, some of them nonmembers, and excluding from the class certain members, the beneficial interest in a judgment rests in the class and not in the tribe.

The practical significance of the corporate concept lies in the form of analogical argument that proceeds from the fact that a tribe is treated as a corporation for some purposes to the conclusion that it may be so treated for other purposes.[106]

Recognizing that the corporate existence and corporate powers of Indian tribes are at least subject to considerable uncertainties, Congress may enact special or general legislation providing for the issuance of charters of incorporation upon application by the Indian tribes. The constitutional power of Congress to incorporate an Indian tribe is clear.[107] The only general legislation on this subject is found in section 17 of the Act of June 18, 1934,[108] which provides for the establishment of tribal corporate status in the following language:

> The Secretary of the Interior may, upon petition by at least one-third of the adult Indians, issue a charter of incorporation to such tribe: *Provided*, That such charter shall not become operative until ratified at a special election by a majority vote of the adult Indians living on the reservation. Such charter may convey to the incorporated tribe the power to purchase, take by gift, or bequest, or otherwise, own, hold, manage, operate, and dispose of property of every description, real and personal, including the power to purchase restricted Indian lands and to issue in exchange therefor interests in corporate property, and such further powers as may be incidental to the conduct of corporate business, not inconsistent with law, but no authority shall be granted to sell, mortgage, or lease for a period exceeding ten years any of the land included in the limits of the reservation. Any charter so issued shall not be revoked or surrendered except by Act of Congress.

Various special acts establish procedures for acquiring corporate status applicable to designated tribes or areas.

Section 1 of the Act of May 1, 1936,[109] extending the foregoing section to Alaska, contains the following proviso:

> * * * That groups of Indians in Alaska not heretofore recognized as bands or tribes, but having a common bond of occupation, or association, or residence within a well-defined neighborhood, community, or rural district, may organize to adopt constitutions and bylaws and to receive charters of incorporation and Federal loans under sections 16, 17, and 10 of the Act of June 18, 1934 (48 Stat. 984).

Section 3 of the Oklahoma Indian Welfare Act of June 26, 1936,[110] provides:

> Any recognized tribe or band of Indians residing in Oklahoma shall have the right to organize for its common welfare and to adopt a constitution and bylaws, under such rules and regulations as the Secretary of the Interior may prescribe. The Secretary of the Interior may issue to any such organized group a charter of incorporation, which shall become operative when ratified by a majority vote of the adult members of the organization voting: *Provided, however*, That such election shall be void unless the total vote cast be at least 30 per centum of those entitled to vote. Such charter may convey to the incorporated group, in addition to any powers which may properly be vested in a body corporate under the laws of the State of Oklahoma, the right to participate in the revolving credit fund and to enjoy any other rights or privileges secured to an organized Indian tribe under the Act of June 18, 1934 (48 Stat. 984): *Provided*, That the corporate funds of any such chartered group may be deposited in any national bank within the State of Oklahoma or otherwise invested, utilized, or disbursed in accordance with the terms of the corporate charter.

Where the corporate status of an Indian tribe is established, it will ordinarily be held to be within the scope of federal legislation extending certain benefits to corporations. Thus it has been administratively determined[111] that the Pueblos of

[94] Act of March 3, 1885, 23 Stat. 362, 376; Act of March 3, 1891, 26 Stat. 851. See secs. 1, 3, *supra*.

[95] *Graham* v. *United States and Sioux Tribe*, 30 C. Cls. 318, 331–338 (1895).

[96] See sec. 5, *infra*.

[97] See Chapters 9 and 15.

[98] 215 U. S. 56, 61 (1909).

[99] 224 U. S. 640 (1912).

[100] And see analysis of status of Seminole lands in terms of "corporate capacity," in 26 Op. A. G. 340 (1907).

[101] See, for example, *Sioux Tribe of Indians* v. *United States*, 84 C. Cls. 16 (1936), cert. den. 302 U. S. 740.

[102] 11 How. 362 (1850).

[103] 248 U. S. 354 (1919), aff'g. 51 C. Cls. 125 (1916). See sec. 3, *supra*.

[104] Characteristic of holdings on tribal "entity" is the decision in *Crow Nation* v. *United States*, 81 C. Cls. 238 (1935), to the effect that a treaty or agreement with an Indian nation or tribe is binding upon all the bands and divisions thereof.

[105] 202 U. S. 101 (1906).

[106] See, for example, the opinion of the Supreme Court in *Lane* v. *Pueblo of Santa Rosa*, 249 U. S. 110 (1919), discussed in Chapter 20, sec. 9. And *cf.* G. F. Canfield, Legal Position of the Indian (1881), 15 Am. L. Rev. 21, 33.

[107] See Memo. Acting Sol. I. D., May 15, 1934, citing *McCulloch* v. *Maryland*, 4 Wheat. 316 (1819); *Lurton* v. *North River Bridge Co.*, 153 U. S. 525 (1894); *Pacific Railroad Removal Cases*, 115 U. S. 2 (1885).

[108] 48 Stat. 984, 988; 25 U. S. C. 477.

[109] 49 Stat. 1250, 48 U. S. C. 362.

[110] 49 Stat. 1967, 25 U. S. C. 503.

[111] Op. Sol. I. D., M.28869, February 13, 1937, 56 I. D. 79.

New Mexico are entitled to receive grazing privileges under the Taylor Grazing Act, under the clause in section 3 of that act [111a] conferring such rights upon "corporations authorized to conduct business under the laws of the State." The principle involved would appear to be equally applicable to any Indian tribe which has a recognized corporate status, either under the Act of June 18, 1934, or otherwise.[112]

Where a tribe is incorporated under the Act of June 18, 1934,[113] or similar legislation, the question may be raised, "How far does the incorporated tribe remain possessed of the rights and subject to the obligations vested in it prior to the issuance of its corporate charter?"

That an incorporated Indian tribe is not responsible for debts contracted by individual members, jointly or severally, prior to incorporation was the holding of the Massachusetts Supreme Judicial Court in *Mayhew* v. *Gay Head*,[114] where the court declared, *per* Bigelow, *C. J.*:

> The claim which the plaintiff seeks to enforce is for a debt alleged to have been incurred by various persons belonging to the Gay Head tribe of Indians, now included within the district of Gay Head, for goods sold and delivered prior to the incorporation of said district by *St.* 1862, *c.* 184. The obvious and decisive objection to the enforcement of this claim is, that it is not due and owing from the "body politic and corporate" which that act creates. No contract, either express or implied, exists by force of which the corporate body can be held liable. There is no rule or principle of the common law by virtue of which the creation of a municipal corporation can be held to convert the debts previously due, either jointly or severally, from the persons who become members of the new municipality, into corporate liabilities. In the absence of any express legislative enactment, the corporation cannot be said to be the successors of or in privity with its members, so as to be responsible for their previously existing liabilities. There is no legal identity between a corporation and the individuals who compose it. The corporate body is a distinct legal entity, and can be held liable only by showing some breach of corporate duty or contract. * * * (Pp. 134–135.)

While the distinction here specified between obligations of members and corporate obligations would probably be followed today, it does not follow that an obligation of the tribe as such would be dissolved by incorporation. In fact, the incorporation provisions of the Act of June 18, 1934, have been consistently interpreted by the administrative authorities of the Federal Government and by the tribes themselves as modifying only the structure of the tribe and not relieving it of any tribal obligations or depriving it of any tribal property. A customary provision of a tribal charter declares:[115]

> 7. No property rights of the Northern Cheyenne Tribe, as heretofore constituted, shall be in any way impaired by anything contained in this charter, and the tribal ownership of unallotted lands, whether or not assigned to the use of any particular individuals, is hereby expressly recognized. The individually owned property of members of the Tribe shall not be subject to any corporate debts or liabilities, without such owners' consent. Any existing lawful debts of the Tribe shall continue in force, except as such debts may be satisfied or cancelled pursuant to law.

[111a] Act of June 28, 1934, 48 Stat. 1269, 1270, 43 U. S. S. 315b.

[112] Sec. 17, 48 Stat. 984, 988, 25 U. S. C. 477.

[113] 48 Stat. 984, 25 U. S. C. 461, *et seq.*

[114] 95 Mass. 129 (1866). The statute of incorporation was Mass. St. 1862, c. 184.

[115] Corporate Charter of the Northern Cheyenne Tribe of the Tongue River Reservation, ratified November 7, 1936.

SECTION 5. CONTRACTUAL CAPACITY

That an Indian tribe has legal capacity to enter into binding contracts is clearly established.[116] Except where federal or tribal law otherwise provides, such contracts are subject to the same rules of contract law that are applied to contracts of non-Indians.

Thus it is held that contractual relations between a tribe and the United States may confer vested rights upon tribal members, which rights are not subject to invasion by Congress or the states.[117] Likewise, it has been held that a convention or treaty between the Colony of New Jersey and the Delaware Tribe is a contract, constitutionally protected against impairment by the legislature of the State of New Jersey.[118]

In accordance with the usual rule, a tribe is not bound by a contract which is not made by a proper representative or agent of the tribe,[119] although a tribe, like any other party, may be estopped from denying the authority of its agent by accepting the benefit of services for which he has contracted.[120] Again following the usual rule of contract law, the Supreme Court has held that a tribal representative is not personally liable on a contract signed in the name of the principal, or reasonably to be construed as executed on behalf of such principal. This rule was laid down in *Parks* v. *Ross*,[121] a case arising out of the forced migration of Cherokee Indians, in 1838 and 1839, from Georgia to what is now Oklahoma. John Ross, the Principal Chief of the Cherokee Nation, was authorized to contract for the hire of wagons to transport the Cherokee Indians and as much of their belongings as they had managed to save from the whites who had overrun their lands. One of the wagon owners who entered into such a contract later brought suit against John Ross to recover extra compensation to which he deemed himself entitled. The Supreme Court held that there was no basis for a claim against Principal Chief Ross, since he had entered into the contract on behalf of the tribe. The Court declared, *per* Grier, *J.*:

> Now, it is an established rule of law, that an agent who contracts in the name of his principal is not liable to a suit on such contract; much less a public officer, acting for his government. As regards him the rule is, that he is not responsible on any contract he may make in that capacity; and wherever his contract or engagement is connected with a subject fairly within the scope of his authority, it shall be intended to have been made officially, and in his public character, unless the contrary appears by satisfactory evidence of an absolute and unqualified engagement to be personally liable.
>
> The Cherokees are in many respects a foreign and independent nation. They are governed by their own laws and officers, chosen by themselves. And though in a state of pupilage, and under the guardianship of the United States, this government has delegated no power to the courts of this District to arrest the public representatives or agents of Indian nations, who may be casually within their local jurisdiction, and compel them to pay the debts

[116] The argument noted in *United States* v. *Boyd*, 83 Fed. 547 (C. C. A. 4, 1897). "That as said Indians are the wards of the nation, all contracts made by them are void, unless they are approved by the proper officials of the government", is not supported by any statutes or judicial holdings. As to contracts involving tribal property, see Chapter 15, sec. 24.

[117] *Choate* v. *Trapp*, 224 U. S. 665 (1912); *Board of Commissioners of Tulsa County* v. *United States*, 94 F. 2d, 450 (C. C. A. 10, 1938), affg. 19 F. Supp. 635 (D. C. N. D. Okla. 1937).

[118] *New Jersey* v. *Wilson*, 7 Cranch 164 (1812).

[119] *Pueblo of Santa Rosa* v. *Fall*, 273 U. S. 315 (1927), revg. 12 F. 2d 332 (App. D. C. 1926), discussed in Chapter 20, sec. 5.

[120] *Rollins and Presbrey* v. *United States*, 23 C. Cls. 106 (1888).

[121] 11 How. 362 (1850).

> of their nation, either to an individual of their own nation or a citizen of the United States. (P. 374.)

The usual rules of contract law relating to the interpretation of contracts, the validity of releases, the statute of frauds, and various other matters have been affirmed in a considerable number of cases involving Indian tribes.[122] Congress, however, may and frequently does, modify the usual rules of contract law with respect to particular tribal agreements. Thus, for example, oral agreements may be given legal effect, by congressional legislation, in a case where such agreements would otherwise be deemed invalid. In the case of *Iowa Tribe of Indians* v. *United States*[123] the Court of Claims noted that while ordinarily the terms of a transfer of land must be spelled out within the four corners of a written instrument, where Congress, in view of the disparity of intelligence and bargaining power involved in an agreement between an Indian tribe and the Federal Government, had expressly authorized the court to pass upon "stipulations or agreements, whether written or oral," [124] the Court was bound to give legal weight to oral assurances and explanations given to the Indians upon the execution of an agreement for land cession.

Where Congress has fixed the consideration for a tribal agreement releasing claims, the courts will not assume to reconsider the adequacy of the amount so fixed.[125] The courts have likewise refused to review the propriety of congressional legislation which in effect nullifies an assignment of proceeds of a judgment made by an Indian tribe to an attorney.[126]

Certain special applications of general rules of contract law may be noted in the Indian cases. The usual rule that where disparity of bargaining power is found the contract will be interpreted in favor of the weaker party has particular application to agreements made between an Indian tribe and the United States.[127] This rule, however, has no application to contracts or agreements made between two Indian tribes.[128] The question of the effective date of an agreement between the United States and an Indian tribe arose in the case of *Beam* v. *United States and Sioux Indians*.[129] It was held that such agreements become effective only upon ratification by Congress, and that such ratification does not relate back to the date of the agreement so as to legalize acts which amounted to trespass if the agreement (for land cession) was not in effect.

There are few, if any, cases which give careful consideration to the question of what law is applicable to a contract made between an Indian tribe and third parties. In most cases the ordinary rules of the common law with respect to the execution and interpretation of contracts have been applied, by common consent of the parties. That tribal law is applicable to a contract by which one tribe was incorporated into another was the holding in the case of *Delaware Indians* v. *Cherokee Nation*,[130] in which the court declared:

> The common law did not prevail in the Cherokee country * * *. The agreement must be construed with reference to the constitution and laws of the Cherokee Nation. (P. 253.)

It is by no means clear, however, that this rule would apply to an agreement between a tribe and the United States.

The question of whether the state law of contract applies to a contract made by the United States, on behalf of an Indian tribe, with a third party was expressly left open in the case of *Kirby* v. *United States*,[131] in which the Supreme Court said:

> Whether the state statute [on penalties and liquidated damages] could affect a contract made by the United States on behalf of Indian wards need not be considered. (P. 427.)

General doctrines of conflict of laws would justify the application of the law of the forum where the tribal law that is applicable is not shown. As was said by Caldwell, *J.*, in *Davison* v. *Gibson*:[132]

> It is very well settled that it will not be presumed that the English common law is in force in any state not settled by English colonists, (*Whitford* v. *Railroad Co.*, 23 N. Y. 465; *Savage* v. *O'Neil*, 44 N. Y. 298; *Flato* v. *Mulhall*, 72 Mo. 522; *Marsters* v. *Lash*, 61 Cal. 622), and it has been expressly decided that it will not be presumed to be in force in the Creek nation (*Du Val* v. *Marshall*, 30 Ark. 230), or in the Indian Territory, (*Pycatt* v. *Powell*, 2 C. C. A. 367, 51 Fed. Rep. 551). * * *
>
> If, therefore, the court had no means of ascertaining what the law or custom of the Creek nation was on this question it should have applied the law of the forum.

The interpretation of attorneys' contracts in connection with claims against the United States has been a source of considerable litigation.[133] No principles peculiar to Indian law appear to be involved in these cases.

The foregoing discussion of the validity and interpretation of contracts made by an Indian tribe assumes that the contract in question is not one forbidden by federal law. It must be recognized, however, that the Federal Government has seriously curtailed the contractual powers of an Indian tribe. Those restrictions which relate particularly to the disposition of real property will be considered in a subsequent chapter dealing with tribal property. A broader restriction upon the scope of tribal contracts was imposed by the Act of March 3, 1871,[134] as amended by the Act of May 21, 1872.[135] These provisions were embodied in the Revised Statutes as sections 2103 to 2106, and are now embodied in title 25 of the United States Code as sections 81 to 84. Section 81 contains this important provision:

> No agreement shall be made by any person with any tribe of Indians, or individual Indians not citizens of the United States, for the payment or delivery of any money or other thing of value, in present or in prospective, or for the granting or procuring any privilege to him, or any other person in consideration of services for said Indians relative to their lands, or to any claims growing out of, or in reference to, annuities, installments, or other moneys, claims, demands, or thing, under laws or treaties with the United States, or official acts of any officers thereof, or in any way connected with or due from the United States, unless such contract or agreement be executed and approved as follows:

The section then lists six distinct requirements as to form and manner of execution, the most important of which is the re-

[122] *Klamath and Moadoc Tribes* v. *United States*, 296 U. S. 244 (1935), aff'g 81 C. Cls. 79 (1935); *Kirby* v. *United States*, 260 U. S. 423 (1922), aff'g 273 Fed. 391 (C. C. A. 9, 1921); *Sioux Tribe of Indians* v. *United States*, 84 C. Cls. 16 (1936), cert. den. 302 U. S. 740; *Green* v. *Menominee Tribe of Indians*, 46 C. Cls. 68 (1911), aff'd 233 U. S. 558 (1914); *Peel* v. *Choctaw Nation and United States*, 45 C. Cls. 154 (1910).

[123] 68 C. Cls. 585 (1929).

[124] Act of April 28, 1920, 41 Stat. 585, amended Joint Resolution of January 11, 1929, 45 Stat, 1073 (Iowa).

[125] *Klamath Indians* v. *United States*, 296 U. S. 244 (1935).

[126] *Kendall* v. *United States*, 1 C. Cls. 261 (1865), aff'd 7 Wall. 113 (1868).

[127] *Iowa Tribe of Indians* v. *United States*, 68 C. Cls. 585 (1929).

[128] See *Delaware Indians* v. *Cherokee Nation*, 38 C. Cls. 234, 249–250 (1903), aff'd 193 U. S. 127 (1904); *Choctaw Nation* v. *United States and Chickasaw Nation*, 83 C. Cls. 140 (1936), cert. den. 287 U. S. 643.

[129] 43 C. Cls. 61 (1907).

[130] 38 C. Cls. 234 (1903).

[131] 260 U. S. 423 (1922), aff'g 273 Fed. 391 (C. C. A. 9, 1921).

[132] 56 Fed. 443 (C. C. A. 8, 1893).

[133] *Garland's Heirs* v. *Choctaw Nation*, 256 U. S. 439 (1921), s. c. 272 U. S. 728 (1927); *Eastern Cherokees* v. *United States*, 225 U. S. 572 (1912); *Owen* v. *Dudley*, 217 U. S. 488 (1910); *Gilfillan* v. *McKee*, 159 U. S. 303 (1895); *In re Sanborn*, 148 U. S. 222 (1893); And see: Contract with the Osage Nation of Indians, 17 Op. A. G. 445 (1882); *cf. Gordon* v. *Gwydir*, 34 App. D. C. 508 (1910); *United States* v. *Crawford*, 47 Fed. 561 (C. C. W. D. Ark. 1891); *Eastern Cherokees* v. *United States*, 225 U. S. 572 (1912).

[134] 16 Stat. 544, 570.

[135] 17 Stat. 186.

quirement that such an agreement must "be executed before a judge of a court of record, and bear the approval of the Secretary of the Interior and the Commissioner of Indian Affairs indorsed upon it."

The section further provides that, "all contracts or agreements made in violation of this section shall be null and void * * *" and establishes a special procedure for suit to recover moneys improperly paid out by or on behalf of an Indian tribe under a prohibited contract.

Section 82 provides for departmental supervision of payments made "to any agent or attorney" under such contract or agreement. Section 83 provides for the prosecution of persons receiving money contrary to the provisions of sections 81 and 82, and provides that any district attorney who fails to prosecute such a case upon application shall be removed from office and that any person in the employ of the United States who shall assist in the making of such a contract shall be "dismissed from the service of the United States, and be forever disqualified from holding any office of profit or trust under the same."

Section 84 provides that no assignment of any contract embraced by section 81 shall be valid unless approved by the Commissioner of Indian Affairs and the Secretary of the Interior.

A specific modification of the foregoing statutory provisions was made by the Act of June 26, 1936,[136] which applied only to contracts made and approved prior to that date and declared that as to such contracts the requirement of the original statute that the contract "have a fixed limited time to run, which shall be distinctly stated" and that the contract shall fix "the amount or rate per centum of the fee" should be considered satisfied by attorneys' contracts "for the prosecution of claims against the United States, which provide that such contracts or agreements shall run for a period of years therein specified, and as long thereafter as may be required to complete the business therein provided for, or words of like import, or which provide that compensation for services rendered shall be on a quantum-meruit basis not to exceed a specified percentage * * *."

In the case of *McMurray* v. *Choctaw Nation*,[137] the Court of Claims declared:

> Section 2103, Revised Statutes, is a most stringent and protective enactment. The section points out in precise terms the method of contracting with Indian tribes * * *. If this method is not followed, any proceeding contrary thereto is absolutely void. Any money paid upon contracts not executed according to its terms and approved by the Secretary of the Interior and Commissioner of Indian Affairs may be recovered back by the Indians. (P. 495.)

The scope of the prohibitions imposed by the statutes in question was given careful consideration in two important Supreme Court cases. In the case of *Green* v. *Menominee Tribe*[138] it was held that this statute rendered invalid a contract between an Indian tribe and a licensed trader whereby the tribe undertook to compensate the trader for his services in making lumber equipment available to individual members of the tribe. The fact that a representative of the Interior Department participated in the making of the contract and was to participate in its performance was held not to remove the agreement from the prohibitions of the statute.

In *Pueblo of Santa Rosa* v. *Fall*[139] the prohibitory statute was held applicable to an alleged contract by which an attorney sought to prosecute certain claims on behalf of an alleged Indian pueblo of Arizona.

[136] 49 Stat. 1984, 25 U. S. C. 81a.

[137] 62 C. Cls. 458 (1926), cert. den. 275 U. S. 524 (1927).

[138] 233 U. S. 558 (1914), aff'g 47 C. Cls. 281 (1912).

[139] 273 U. S. 315 (1927), rev'g. 12 F. 2d 332 (App. D. C. 1926).

While the foregoing cases leave some doubt as to the exact scope of the statute, it is at least clear that the statute applies only to contracts with Indians "relative to their lands, or to any claims" and does not apply to matters not comprised within these two categories.

Some light is thrown upon the intended scope of the statute by the extensive report of the House Committee on Indian Affairs on the frauds which the statute was designed to circumvent, and the expected consequences of the legislation. In general the legislation was directed against the "godless robbery of those defenseless people" by attorneys and claim-agents.[140]

The statutory restrictions upon tribal contracts have been modified by sections 16 and 17 of the Act of June 18, 1934.[141] By the former section each tribe adopting a constitution under this act became entitled to employ legal counsel, the choice of counsel and the fixing of fees to be subject to the approval of the Secretary of the Interior. The effect of this provision was thus stated in a memorandum of the Solicitor for the Interior Department:[142]

> The Minnesota Chippewa Tribe has organized and adopted a constitution and bylaws pursuant to section 16 of the Indian Reorganization Act of June 18, 1934 (49 Stat. 984). That section declares, among other things, that such an organized tribe shall have the power "to employ legal counsel, the choice of counsel and fixing of fees to be subject to the approval of the Secretary of the Interior." Your proposed letter raises the question of whether the provision in section 16 just quoted supersedes, as to contracts to which section 81, Title 25, U. S. C., otherwise would be applicable, the specific requirements set forth in said section 81. Section 81 is confined to a certain class of contracts; that is, contracts for services relating to Indian lands, or to any claims growing out of or in reference to annuities, installments or other moneys, claims, demands or thing under the laws or treaties with the United States, or official acts of any official thereof, or in any way connected with or due from the United States. Contracts not calling for the performance of legal services connected with any of the matters or things mentioned in section 81 obviously are controlled by section 16 of the Reorganization Act and may be entered into without regard to the requirements of section 81.
>
> The Minnesota Chippewa contract provides for the performance of legal services in relation to claims of the tribes against the United States Government. This is the sort of contract to which section 81 applies and the requirements of that section should be observed unless they are superseded by section 16 of the Reorganization Act. To the extent of any conflict or inconsistency, it is clear that section 16 is controlling and supersedes the prior law. Requirements of the prior law not directly inconsistent or conflicting may also be superseded as to the particular kind of contract to which section 16 applies if such was the intent of Congress. A consideration of the general background and purpose of the Indian Reorganization Act leaves no doubt that the purpose of the statutory provision in question was to increase the scope of responsibility and discretion afforded the tribe in its dealings with attorneys. Earlier drafts of legislation contained provisions limiting the fees that might be charged. After considerable discussion before the Senate Committee (Hearings before the Committee on Indian Affairs, United States Senate, 73rd Congress, 2d session, S. 2755 and S. 3645, part 2, pages 244–247), it was decided that the Secretary of the Interior should have the added power to approve or veto the choice of counsel. This discussion would have been futile and the statutory provision would have been meaningless if the intention had

[140] Investigation of Indian Frauds, H. Rept. No. 98, 42nd Cong., 3d sess., March 3, 1873, especially pp. 4–7.

[141] 48 Stat. 984, 987–988, 25 U. S. C. 476, 477.

[142] Memo. Sol. I. D., January 23, 1937. Also see 25 C. F. R. 14.1–14.17, relative to the recognition of attorneys and agents to represent claimants of organized and unorganized tribes or individual claimants before the Indian Bureau and the Department of the Interior and 15.1–15.25, relative to attorney contracts with Indian tribes.

been to make those contracts subject to the provisions of section 81, Title 25 of the Code.

I am inclined to the view that insofar as contracts for the employment of legal counsel are concerned, Congress intended to empower the organized tribe to make such contracts, subject only to the limitations imposed by section 16 of the Reorganization Act. The matter is by no means free from difficulty, however, and it may be that the courts when called upon to consider the question, will hold that the two statutes should be treated as one and that the requirements of both in the absence of conflict or inconsistency must be observed. In this situation it is appreciated that attorneys may desire for their own protection to have the contract executed in conformity with the requirements of both statutes. Such appears to be the position of the attorneys seeking employment by the Minnesota Chippewa Tribe. Such a position is not unreasonable and I recommend that no objection be raised to approval of this or any other contract so executed.

Constitutions of Indian tribes adopted pursuant to the Act of June 18, 1934, generally contain some such provision as the following, in line with the statutory requirement on the point:[143]

ARTICLE V. POWERS OF THE COMMUNITY COUNCIL

SECTION 1. *Enumerated powers.*—The council of the Fort Belknap Community shall have the following powers, the exercise of which shall be subject to popular referendum as provided hereafter:

* * * * *

(b) To employ legal counsel for the protection and advancement of the rights of the community and its members, the choice of counsel and fixing of fees to be subject to the approval of the Secretary of the Interior.

Apart from contracts involving a disposition of tribal property, the contracts made by chartered tribes are subject to the limitations imposed by the corporate charter. Typical of such limiting provisions are the following, taken from the charter of the Covelo Indian Community of the Round Valley Indian Reservation, California:[144]

5. The Covelo Indian Community, subject to any restrictions contained in the Constitution and laws of the United States, or in the Constitution and By-laws of the Covelo Indian Community, shall have the following corporate powers * * *:

* * * * *

(d) To borrow money from the Indian Credit Fund in accordance with the terms of section 10 of the Act of June 18, 1934 (48 Stat. 984), or from any other governmental agency, or from any member or association of members of the Covelo Indian Community, and to use such funds directly for productive Community enterprises, or to loan money thus borrowed to individual members or associations of members of the Community: *Provided*, That the amount of indebtedness to which the Covelo Indian Community may subject itself, aside from loans from the Indian Credit Fund, shall not exceed $10,000 except with the express approval of the Secretary of the Interior.

(e) To engage in any business that will further the economic well-being of the members of the Covelo Indian Community or to undertake any activity of any nature whatever, not inconsistent with law or with any provisions of this Charter.

(f) To make and perform contracts and agreements of every description, not inconsistent with law or with any provisions of this Charter, with any person partnership, association, or corporation, with any municipality or any county, or with the United States or the State of California, including agreements with the State of California for the rendition of public services: *Provided*, That any contract involving payment of money by the corporation in excess of $2,000 in any one fiscal year other than a contract for the use of the revolving loan fund established under section 10 of the Act of June 18, 1934 (48 Stat. 984), shall be subject to the approval of the Secretary of the Interior or his duly authorized representative.

(g) To pledge or assign chattels or future Community income due or to become due to the Community under any notes, leases, or other contracts whether or not such notes, leases, or contracts are in existence at the time, or from any source: *Provided*, That such agreements of pledge or assignment except to the Federal Government shall not extend more than ten years from the date of execution and shall not cover more than one-half of the net Community income in any one year: *And provided further*, That any such agreement shall be subject to the approval of the Secretary of the Interior or his duly authorized representative.

(h) To deposit corporate funds, from whatever source derived, in any national or state bank to the extent that such funds are insured by the Federal Deposit Insurance Corporation, or secured by a surety bond, or other security, approved by the Secretary of the Interior; or to deposit such funds in the Postal Savings Bank or with a bonded disbursing officer of the United States to the credit of the Covelo Indian Community.

The supervisory provisions of sections 5 (d), 5 (e), 5 (f), 5 (g), and 5 (h), above set forth, are subject to termination under section 6 of the corporate charter, which reads:

6. Upon the request of the Covelo Indian Community Council for the termination of any supervisory powers reserved to the Secretary of the Interior under Sections 5 (b) 3, 5 (c), 5 (d), 5 (f), 5 (g), 5 (h), and section 8 of this Charter, the Secretary of the Interior, if he shall approve such request, shall thereupon submit the question of such termination to the Covelo Indian Community for a referendum vote. The termination shall be effective upon ratification by a majority vote at an election in which at least 30 per cent of the adult members of the Covelo Indian Community residing on the reservation shall vote. If at any time after ten years from the effective date of this Charter, such request shall be made and the Secretary shall disapprove such request or fail to approve or disapprove it within 90 days after its receipt, the question of the termination of any such supervisory power may then be submitted by the Secretary of the Interior or by the Community Council to popular referendum of the adult members of the Covelo Indian Community actually living within the reservation and if the termination is approved by two-thirds of the eligible voters, it shall be effective.

By section 17 of the act quoted, each tribe receiving a charter of incorporation might be empowered thereby

to purchase, take by gift, or bequest, or otherwise, own, hold, manage, operate, and dispose of property of every description, real and personal, * * * and such further powers as may be incidental to the conduct of corporate business, not inconsistent with law, but no authority shall be granted to sell, mortgage, or lease for a period exceeding ten years any of the land included in the limits of the reservation.

This provision has been construed as granting to the incorporated Indian tribes very extensive powers to contract with respect to all matters of tribal concern, including tribal property. The extent to which this section legalized agreements with respect to tribal property which were formerly prohibited is a matter which must be reserved for further discussion in connection with our analysis of tribal property rights.[145]

[143] Constitution of the Fort Belknap Indian Community, approved December 13, 1935.

[144] Ratified November 6, 1937. Under the terms of this charter, the incorporated tribe handled all sales of Indian arts and crafts work at the San Francisco Fair in 1939.

[145] See Chapter 15, sec. 22.

SECTION 6. CAPACITY TO SUE

That Indian tribes may, under certain circumstances, sue and be sued is clear from the large number of such suits which are analyzed in this chapter and other chapters of this work. Since, however, nearly all such suits have been expressly authorized by general or special statutes, the question of whether an Indian tribe may sue or be sued in the absence of such express statutory authorization is more difficult to answer.

A. STATUTES AUTHORIZING SUITS BY TRIBES

Statutes authorizing suits by Indian tribes include: (*a*) jurisdictional acts authorizing suits against the United States, and sometimes against other tribes, in the Court of Claims, (*b*) statutes authorizing suits against third parties to determine questions of ownership, and (*c*) statutes authorizing suits against third parties to determine the measure of compensation due from third parties for property taken.

(*a*) Within the scope of this chapter it is not possible to include more than a simple reference to statutes conferring jurisdiction upon the Court of Claims to hear tribal claims,[146] cases in which these claims are adjudicated,[147] and statutes compromising claims.[148]

The language of special jurisdictional acts varies so fundamentally from act to act that it is impossible to list any common principles applicable to all Indian claims cases and not applicable to other cases. There are certain maxims which frequently recur, in these cases, such as the maxim that acts authorizing suit on claims against the Government are to be narrowly construed,[149] that such acts will ordinarily be construed as granting a forum rather than determining liability, and that such acts will not be construed, in the absence of clear language to the contrary, as empowering a court to consider the justice or injustice of a law, treaty, or agreement.[150] It may be doubted however, whether these maxims show more than verbal uniformities, and they are certainly of little help in predicting the outcome of cases. Indian claims cases, like other Indian cases, involve questions with respect to tribal property rights, tribal powers, the powers of the Federal Government, and similar questions of substantive law, elsewhere considered,[151] and which have a greater bearing upon the actual decisions in claims cases than any rules which might be derived from considerations limited purely to these cases.

(*b*) Various statutes provide for suits by Indian tribes against third parties to determine land ownership. Perhaps the most important of these statutes is the Pueblo Lands Act,[152] which is discussed elsewhere.[153]

(*c*) Tribal capacity to sue is implied in the various right-of-way statutes which permit appeals from administrative decisions on the amount of damages due for tribal property taken or damaged.[154]

(*d*) As we have already noted, capacity to sue is *not* conferred by Article III, section 2, of the Federal Constitution, providing for federal jurisdiction over controversies "between a state * * * and foreign states." The learned opinion of Chief Justice Marshall established the proposition, which has not since been questioned by any federal court, that an Indian tribe is not a foreign state within the meaning of this provision.[155]

B. STATUTES AUTHORIZING SUITS AGAINST TRIBES

Just as there are various statutes allowing suits by Indian tribes, so there are a number of statutes which authorize suits against Indian tribes.

We have already noted and need not here reconsider, the various depredation statutes which authorized suits against Indian tribes and allowed, in effect, the execution of judgment upon the tribal funds of the tribe in the United States Treasury, subject to the approval of the Secretary of the Interior.[156]

Congress has from time to time authorized various other suits against Indian tribes by private citizens. Thus, for example, the Act of May 29, 1908,[157] confers jurisdiction upon the Court of Claims to adjudicate a suit by designated traders against the Menominee tribe and members thereof, and requires that the Secretary of the Interior

> shall thereupon, in case judgments be against the said Menominee tribe of Indians as a tribe, direct the payment of said judgments out of any funds in the Treasury of the United States to the credit of said tribe, and who, in case judgments be against individual members of said Menominee tribe of Indians, shall, through the disbursing officers in charge of said Green Bay Agency, pay, from any annuity due or which may become due said Indian as an individual or as the head of a family from the United States or from the share of such Indian as an individual or as the head of a family in any distribution of tribal funds deposited in the Treasury of the United States, the amounts of such judgments to the claimants in whose favor such judgments have been rendered * * *.[158]

C. JURISTIC CAPACITY IN THE ABSENCE OF SPECIFIC STATUTES

There remains the question of whether suit may be brought by or against an Indian tribe where Congress is silent.

The latter portion of this question is easier to answer than the former. We have noted that an Indian tribe is a municipality.[159] As such it would appear to be exempt from suit unless it has consented thereto or been subjected thereto by a superior power.

The general attitude of Congress and the courts towards suits against Indian tribes is clarified in an opinion of Caldwell, J., in *Thebo* v. *Choctaw Tribe of Indians*,[160] where it was held that a suit against an Indian tribe could not be maintained in the absence of clear congressional authorization.

The court declared:

> It may be conceded that it would be competent for congress to authorize suit to be brought against the Choctaw Nation upon any and all the causes of action

[146] See Chapter 19, sec. 3.

[147] See Chapter 19, sec. 3.

[148] Joint Resolution of June 19, 1902, 32 Stat. 744, 745 (Utes); Act of February 9, 1925, 43 Stat. 820 (Omahas). See Loyal Creek Claims—Attorneys' Fees, 24 Op. A. G. 623 (1903).

[149] *Choctaw and Chickasaw Nations* v. *United States*, 75 C. Cls. 494 (1932).

[150] *Otoe and Missouria Indians* v. *United States*, 52 C. Cls. 424 (1917).

[151] See, particularly, Chapters 5 and 15.

[152] Act of June 7, 1924, 43 Stat. 636, 637, 638, construed in *Pueblo de Taos* v. *Gusdorf*, 50 F. 2d 721 (C. C. A. 10, 1931); *Pueblo of Picuris* v. *Abeyta*, 50 F. 2d 12 (C. C. A. 10, 1931).

[153] See Chapter 20, sec. 4.

[154] *Cf. Cherokee Nation* v. *Southern Kansas Ry. Co.*, 135 U. S. 641 (1890).

[155] *Cherokee Nation* v. *Georgia*, 5 Pet. 1 (1831). See sec. 3, *supra*.

[156] See secs. 1 and 3, *supra*. Suits for depredations were "forever barred" unless brought within 3 years of the enactment of the Indian Depredation Act of March 3, 1891. *United States and Kiowa Indians* v. *Martinez*, 195 U. S. 469 (1904).

[157] 35 Stat. 444.

[158] Sec. 2. The same act authorizes suits in the Court of Claims against the Choctaw Nation (sec. 5, 35 Stat. 445), against the Creek Nation (sec. 26, 35 Stat. 457), and against the Mississippi Choctaws (sec. 27, 35 Stat. 457).

[159] See sec. 3, *supra*.

[160] 66 Fed. 372 (C. C. A. 8, 1895).

in any court it might designate. Acts of congress have been passed, specially conferring on the courts therein named jurisdiction over all controversies arising between the railroad companies authorized to construct their roads through the Indian Territory and the Choctaw Nation and the other nations and tribes of Indians owning lands in the territory through which the railroads might be constructed. Other acts have been passed authorizing suits to be brought by or against these Indian Nations in the Indian Territory to settle controversies between them and the United States and between themselves.

Among such acts are the following: "An act for the ascertainment of amount due the Choctaw Nation." 21 Stat. 504. Act of July 4, 1884 (23 Stat. 73), granting the right of way through the Indian Territory to the Southern Kansas Railway Company. An act granting right of way through Indian Territory to Kansas & Arkansas Valley Railway Company, 24 Stat. 73. An act granting the right of way to the Denison & Wichita Valley Railway Company through the Indian Territory. Id. 117. An act granting the right of way through the Indian Territory to the Kansas City, Ft. Scott & Gulf Railway Company. Id. 124. An act granting the right of way through Indian Territory to Ft. Worth & Denver City Railway Company. Id. 419. An act granting the right of way through Indian Territory to the Chicago, Kansas & Nebraska Railway Company. Id. 446. An act granting right of way through the Indian Territory to the Choctaw Coal & Railway Company. 25 Stat. 35. An act granting right of way to the Ft. Smith & El Paso Railway Company through the Indian Territory. Id 162. An act granting the right of way to Kansas City & Pacific Railway Company through the Indian Territory. Id. 140. An act granting the right of way to Paris. Choctaw & Little Rock Railway Company through the Indian Territory. Id. 205. An act granting right of way to Ft. Smith, Paris & Dardanelle Railway Company through Indian Territory. Id. 745. An act to authorize the Kansas & Arkansas Valley Railway Company to construct an additional railroad through the Indian Territory. 26 Stat. 783.

The constitutional competency of congress to pass such acts has never been questioned, but no court has ever presumed to take jurisdiction of a cause against any of the five civilized Nations in the Indian Territory in the absence of an act of congress expressly conferring the jurisdiction in the particular case. (Pp. 373–374.)

* * * * *

* * * Being a domestic and dependent state, the United States may authorize suit to be brought against it. But, for obvious reasons, this power has been sparingly exercised. It has been the settled policy of the United States not to authorize such suits except in a few cases, where the subject-matter of the controversy was particularly specified, and was of such a nature that the public interests, as well as the interests of the Nation, seemed to require the exercise of the jurisdiction. It has been the policy of the United States to place and maintain the Choctaw Nation and the other civilized Indian Nations in the Indian Territory, so far as relates to suits against them, on the plane of independent states. A state, without its consent, cannot be sued by an individual. "It is a well-established principle of jurisprudence in all civilized nations that the sovereign cannot be sued in its own courts or any other without its consent and permission; but it may, if it thinks proper, waive this privilege, and permit itself to be made a defendant in a suit by individuals or by another state." *Beers* v. *Arkansas*, 20 How. 527. The United States has waived its privilege in this regard, and allowed suits to be brought against it in a few specified cases. Some of the states of the Union have at times claimed no immunity from suits, but experience soon demonstrated this to be an unwise and extremely injurious policy, and most, if not all, of the states after a brief experience, abandoned it, and refused to submit themselves to the coercive process of judicial tribunals. When the Supreme Court of the United States in *Chisholm* v. *Georgia*, 2 Dall. 419, decided that under the constitution that court had original jurisdiction of a suit by a citizen of one state against another state, the eleventh amendment to the constitution was straightway adopted, taking away this jurisdiction. Since the adoption of this amendment, the contract of a state "is substantially without sanction, except that which arises out of the honor and good faith of the state itself; and these are not subject to coercion." *In re Ayers*, 123 U. S. 443, 505, 8 Sup. Ct. 164. One claiming to be creditor of a state is remitted to the justice of its legislature. It has been the settled policy of congress not to sanction suits generally against these Indian Nations, or subject them to suits upon contracts or other causes of action at the instance of private parties. In respect to their liability to be sued by individuals, except in the few cases we have mentioned, they have been placed by the United States, substantially, on the plane occupied by the states under the eleventh amendment to the constitution. The civilized Nations in the Indian Territory are probably better guarded against oppression from this source than the states themselves, for the states may consent to be sued, but the United States has never given its permission that these Indian Nations might be sued generally, even with their consent. As rich as the Choctaw Nation is said to be in lands and money, it would soon be impoverished if it was subject to the jurisdiction of the courts, and required to respond to all the demands which private parties chose to prefer against it. The intention of congress to confer such a jurisdiction upon any court would have to be expressed in plain and unambiguous terms. (Pp. 375–376.)

There is at least language supporting the rule that a tribe cannot be sued without its consent, in the Supreme Court opinion in *Turner* v. *United States*.[161] And in the case of *United States* v. *U. S. Fidelity & Guar. Co.*,[162] the Circuit Court of Appeals for the Tenth Circuit declared, citing the two cases above noted:

> * * * the Indian tribes, like the United States, are sovereigns immune from civil suit except when expressly authorized. (P. 810.)

In line with the policy set forth in the *Thebo* case, it has been held that where the tribe itself is not subject to suit, tribal officers cannot be sued on the basis of tribal obligations.[163]

Although a tribe, as a municipality, is not subject to suit without its consent, it may be argued that a tribe has legal capacity to consent to such a suit. The power to consent to such suit must be regarded as cognate with the power to bring suit.

Some support for the view that an Indian tribe is capable of appearing in litigation as a plaintiff or voluntary defendant is found in the statement of the Supreme Court in *United States* v. *Candelaria*:[164]

> It was settled in *Lane* v. *Pueblo of Santa Rosa*, 249 U. S. 110, that under territorial laws enacted with congressional sanction each pueblo in New Mexico—meaning the Indians comprising the community—became a juristic person and enabled to sue and defend in respect of its lands. (Pp. 442–443.)

This statement, standing by itself, could be given a limited scope on the ground that the Pueblos are statutory corporations. The fact remains, however, that the Supreme Court has entertained suits in which Indian tribes were parties litigant, without any question of legal capacity being raised. An outstanding case in point is the case of *Cherokee Nation* v. *Hitchcock*.[165] This was a suit brought by an Indian tribe against the Secretary of the Interior. Although judgment was rendered for the defendant, no question was raised, apparently, as to the capacity of the principal plaintiff (individual members were joined as parties plaintiff) to bring the suit.

The decision of the Supreme Court in the *Coronado* case,[166] holding labor unions suable in view of the legislative recognition

---

[161] 248 U. S. 354 (1919).

[162] 106 F. 2d 804 (C. C. A. 10, 1939).

[163] *Adams* v. *Murphy*, 165 Fed. 304 (C. C. A. 8, 1908) (suit by attorney on tribal attorney's contract).

[164] 271 U. S. 432 (1926).

[165] 187 U. S. 294 (1902).

[166] *United Mine Workers of America* v. *Coronado Coal Co.*, 259 U. S. 344 (1922). And *cf.* F. S. Cohen, Transcendental Nonsense and the Functional Approach, 35 Col. L. Rev. 809, 813 (1935).

given them as subjects of rights and duties, and the extent to which such rights and duties have been recognized in Indian tribes,[167] suggests that the courts may hold that even a tribe not expressly chartered as a corporation may bring and defend suits.[168] There are, however, some dicta *contra*,[169] and in the absence of any clear holding, judgment must be reserved.

What can be said is that even if a tribe lacks legal capacity to appear in courts of proper jurisdiction against third parties, the objects of such a suit can frequently be attained by a representative suit brought by individual members of the tribe.[170]

[167] See sec. 4, *supra*.

[168] The right to sue the United States of course presents an independent question.

> The reason the Indians could not bring the suits suggested lies in the general immunity of the State and the United States from suit in the absence of consent. (*United States* v. *Minnesota*, 270 U. S. 181, 195 (1926).)

[169] In *Jaeger* v. *United States and Yuma Indians*, 27 C. Cls. 278 (1892), for instance, the Court of Claims, holding that the Indian Depredations Act of March 3, 1891, 26 Stat. 851, in allowing suits to be brought against tribes and execution to be made against tribal funds, did not require notice to the tribal defendants, declared (*a*) that

> The civil rights incident to States and individuals as recognized by what may be called the "law of the land" have not been accorded either to Indian nations, tribes, or Indians. Whenever they have asserted a legal capacity in the maintenance of their rights, it has been in pursuance of some statute of the United States specially conferring upon them the civil rights of suitors. (P. 285.)

and (*b*) that the statute expressly required the service of notice upon the Attorney General, who was competent to protect the interests of the Indian tribe.

The first of these arguments is clearly unsound as regards individual Indians (see Chapter 8, sec. 6), and its soundness as applied to a tribal plaintiff or a tribe defending a suit to which it has consented may be seriously questioned.

[170] *Lone Wolf* v. *Hitchcock*, 187 U. S. 553 (1903); *Choate* v. *Trapp*, 224 U. S. 665 (1912); *Western Cherokees* v. *United States*, 27 C. Cls. 1 (1891). *Cf. Fleming* v. *McCurtain*, 215 U. S. 56 (1909) (suit in equity by and on behalf of some 13,000 persons, "all persons of Choctaw or Chickasaw Indian blood and descent and members of a designated class of persons for whose exclusive use and benefit a special grant was made").

SECTION 7. TRIBAL HUNTING AND FISHING RIGHTS

Rights of hunting and fishing guaranteed to Indian tribes by treaty[171] or statute[172] are in some respects treated as property rights, and are so dealt with in a following chapter.[173] These rights, however, differ in several respects from ordinary property rights, and therefore deserve brief mention in a discussion of the general legal status of Indian tribes.

Indian hunting and fishing rights are, in general, of two sorts, those pertaining to Indian reservation lands and those pertaining to nonreservation (generally ceded) lands.

The extent of Indian rights with respect to reservation lands is noted in an opinion of the Acting Solicitor[174] for the Interior Department, upholding the exclusive right of the Red Lake Chippewa Tribe to fish in the waters of Red Lake, and declaring:

> An examination of the various treaties between the United States and the Chippewa Indians discloses that while the right in the Indians to hunt and fish on ceded lands was reserved in some of the earlier treaties (see Article 5, Treaty of July 20, 1837, 7 Stat. 536; Article 2, Treaty of October 4, 1842, 7 Stat. 591; and Article 11, Treaty of September 30, 1854, 10 Stat. 1109), no reservation of the right to hunt and fish was made with respect to the unceded lands of the Red Lake Reservation. But such a reservation was not necessary to preserve the right on the lands reserved or retained in Indian ownership. The right to hunt and fish was part of the larger rights possessed by the Indians in the lands used and occupied by them. Such right, which was "not much less necessary to the existence of the Indians than the atmosphere they breathed" remained in them unless granted away. *United States* v. *Winans*, 198 U. S. 371. Speaking of a

[171] Treaty of January 9, 1789, with the Wyandots and others, 7 Stat. 28; Treaty of August 3, 1795, with the Wyandots and others, 7 Stat. 49; Treaty of October 2, 1798, with the Cherokees, 7 Stat. 62; Treaty of August 13, 1803, with the Kaskaskias, 7 Stat. 78; Treaty of November 3, 1804, with the Sacs and Foxes, 7 Stat. 84; Treaty of July 4, 1805, with the Wyandots and others, 7 Stat. 87; Treaty of December 30, 1805, with the Piankishaws, 7 Stat. 100; Treaty of January 7, 1806, with the Cherokees, 7 Stat. 101; Treaty of November 17, 1807, with the Ottoways and others, 7 Stat. 105; Treaty of November 10, 1808, with the Osage Nations, 7 Stat. 107; Treaty of November 25, 1808, with the Chippewas and others, 7 Stat. 112; Treaty of September 30, 1809, with the Delawares and others, 7 Stat. 113; Treaty of December 9, 1809, with the Kickapoos, 7 Stat. 117; Treaty of August 24, 1816, with the Ottawas, Chipawas, and Pottowotomees, 7 Stat. 146; Treaty of September 29, 1817, with the Wyandots and others, 7 Stat. 160; Treaty of August 24, 1818, with the Quapaws, 7 Stat. 176; Treaty of September 24, 1819, with the Chippewas, 7 Stat. 203; Treaty of June 16, 1820, with the Chippeways, 7 Stat. 206; Treaty of August 29, 1821, with the Ottawas, Chippewas, and Pottawatomies, 7 Stat. 218; Treaty of August 4, 1824, with the Sock and Fox tribes, 7 Stat. 229; Treaty of November 15, 1824, with the Quapaws, 7 Stat. 232; Treaty of August 19, 1825, with Sioux, Chippewas, and others, 7 Stat. 272; Treaty of August 5, 1826, with the Chippewas, 7 Stat. 290; Treaty of October 16, 1826, with the Potawatamies, 7 Stat. 295; Treaty of October 23, 1826, with the Miamies, 7 Stat. 300; Treaty of July 29, 1829, with the Chippewas and others, 7 Stat. 320; Treaty of February 8, 1831, with the Menomonees, 7 Stat. 342; Treaty of September 15, 1832, with the Winnebagoes, 7 Stat. 370; Treaty of September 21, 1832, with the Sacs and Foxes, 7 Stat. 374; Treaty of October 20, 1832, with the Potawatamies, 7 Stat. 378; Treaty of September 26, 1833, with the Chippewa, Ottowa, and Potawatamie Nation, 7 Stat. 431; Treaty of October 9, 1833, with the Pawnees, 7 Stat. 448; Treaty of August 24, 1835, with the Comanches and Witchetaws, 7 Stat. 474; Treaty of March 28, 1836, with the Ottawas and Chippewas, 7 Stat. 491; Treaty of September 28, 1836, with the Sacs and Foxes, 7 Stat. 517; Treaty of July 29, 1837, with the Chippewas, 7 Stat. 536; Treaty of November 1, 1837, with the Winnebagos, 7 Stat. 544; Treaty of October 4, 1842, with the Chippewas, 7 Stat. 591; Treaty of September 15, 1797, with the Senekas, 7 Stat. 601; Treaty of October 13, 1846, with the Winnebagos, 9 Stat. 878; Treaty of September 30, 1854, with the Chippewas, 10 Stat. 1109; Treaty of July 31, 1855, with Ottowas and Chippewas, 11 Stat. 621; Treaty of August 2, 1855, with the Chippewas, 11 Stat. 631; Treaty of June 11, 1855, with Nez Perces, 12 Stat. 957; Treaty of October 7, 1863, with the Tabeguaches, 13 Stat. 673; Treaty of October 21, 1867, with the Kiowas and Comanches, 15 Stat. 581; Treaty of October 28, 1867, with the Cheyennes and Arapahoes, 15 Stat. 593; Treaty of April 29, *et seq.*, 1868, with Sioux, 15 Stat. 635; Treaty of May 7, 1868, with the Crows, 15 Stat. 649; Treaty of June 1, 1868, with the Navajos, 15 Stat. 667; Treaty of July 3, 1868, with Shoshones and Bannock tribes, 15 Stat. 673; Treaty of October 14, 1864, with the Yahooskins, 16 Stat. 707. The Treaty of February 7, 1911, between the United States and the United Kingdom, 37 Stat. 1538, and the Treaty of July 7, 1911, between the United States and Great Britain, Japan, and Russia, 37 Stat. 1542, restricting pelagic sealing in certain waters, specifically exempt from such restrictions the natives dwelling on the coasts of those waters.

[172] Act of April 29, 1874, 18 Stat. 36 (Ute); Act of May 9, 1924, 43 Stat. 117 (granting to Fort Hall Indians reservation of an easement, in lands sold to United States, to use said lands for grazing, hunting, fishing, and gathering of wood "the same way as obtained prior to this enactment, insofar as such uses shall not interfere with the use of said lands for reservoir purposes"). The Act of June 30, 1864, 13 Stat. 324, authorized the President of the United States to negotiate with the Confederated Indian Tribes of Middle Oregon

> * * * for the relinquishment of certain rights guaranteed to them by the first article of the treaty made with them April eighteenth, eighteen hundred and fifty-nine, by which they are permitted to fish, hunt, gather roots and berries, and pasture stock, in common with citizens of the United States, upon the lands and territories of the United States outside their reservations * * *.

and appropriated the sum of five thousand dollars to defray the expenses of the treaty and pay the Indians for their relinquishment of such rights.

[173] See Chapter 15, especially sec. 21.

[174] Op. Acting Sol. I. D., M.28107, June 30, 1936.

similar situation, the Supreme Court of Wisconsin in *State* v. *Johnson*, 249 N. W. 285, 288, said:

> "While the treaty entered into did not specifically reserve to the Indians such hunting and fishing rights as they had theretofore enjoyed, we think it reasonably appears that there was no necessity for specifically mentioning such hunting and fishing rights with respect to the lands reserved to them. At the time the treaty of 1854 was entered into there was not a 'shadow of impediment upon the hunting rights of the Indians' on the lands retained by them. 'The treaty was not a grant of rights to the Indians, but a grant of rights from them—a reservation of those not granted.' *United States* v. *Winans*, 198 U. S. 371, 25 S. Ct. 662, 664, 49 L. Ed. 1089. We entertain no doubt that the rights of the Indians to hunt and fish upon their own lands continued."

The court further recognized that as to unpatented lands inside the reservation, the fish and game laws of the State of Wisconsin were without force and effect.

By tradition and habit the Indians as a race are hunters and fishermen, depending largely upon these pursuits for their livelihood. Their ancient and immemorial right to follow these pursuits on the lands and in the waters of their reservations is universally recognized. The Indians of the Red Lake Reservation appear to have asserted and exercised an exclusive right of fishing in the waters of Upper and Lower Red Lakes from the beginning subject only to Federal control and regulation. The right of the Indians so to do has not heretofore been disputed by the State of Minnesota but has been recognized and acquiesced in. * * * Circumstances somewhat similar to these, coupled with the rule of liberal construction uniformly invoked in determining the rights of Indians, were cited by the Supreme Court of the United States in support of its conclusion that the Metlakahtla Indians had an exclusive right to fish in the waters adjacent to Annette Islands in Alaska notwithstanding the fact that the Act of Congress setting aside the Islands as a reservation for the Indians made no mention of the surrounding waters or the fishing rights of the Indians therein. *Alaska Pacific Fisheries* v. *United States*, 248 U. S. 86. * * *

In *United States* v. *Sturgeon* (27 Federal Cases, Case No. 16413), the court gave consideration to the rights of the Indians of the Pyramid Lake Indian Reservation in Nevada to fish in the waters of a lake inside the boundaries of their reservation and held:

> "The president has set apart the reservation for the use of the Pah Utes and other Indians residing thereon. He has done this by authority of law. We know that the lake was included in the reservation, that it might be a fishing ground for the Indians. The lines of the reservation have been drawn around it for the purpose of excluding white people from fishing there except by proper authority. It is plain that nothing of value to the Indians will be left of their reservation if all the whites who choose may resort there to fish. In my judgment, those who thus encroach on the reservation and fishing ground violate the order setting it apart for the use of the Indians, and consequently do so contrary to law."

In an opinion dated May 14, 1928 (M.24358), the Solicitor for this Department ruled that the State of Washington was without right to regulate or control the use of boats on navigable bodies of water within the Quinaielt Reservation in that State. The Solicitor said, and his remarks apply with equal force here:

> "Manifestly, unless the Indians of the Quinaielt Reservation are protected in the exclusive use and occupancy of their reservation including the waters therein, navigable or nonnavigable, then their rights may become subject to serious interference, if not jeopardy, by outsiders. If we admit the right of the State to invade the reservation for the purpose of regulating or controlling the use of boats on the Queets or any other body of navigable water therein. It would be tantamount to recognizing the right of the State to regulate other activities there, including fishing. This we cannot afford to do."

Minnesota was admitted into the Union in 1858. The Indian title, as subsequently recognized by treaty and Act of Congress, then extended to all of the lands surrounding Upper and Lower Red Lakes. The Indian title was that of occupancy only, the ultimate fee being in the United States, but the right of occupancy extended to and included the right to fish in the waters of the Lakes. *United States* v. *Winans*, *supra*. These rights insofar as the diminished reservation is concerned have never been surrendered or relinquished by the Indians nor have they been taken away by any Act of Congress of which I am aware. In these circumstances, it is not unreasonable to hold that the State upon its admission into the Union took title to the submerged lands subject to the occupancy rights of the Indians in virtue of which the Indians possess an exclusive right of fishing in the waters of the Lakes. *Beecher* v. *Wetherby*, *supra*; *United States* v. *Thomas*, *supra*. If this be the correct view, and I think it is, the exercise by the Indians of the right of fishing is subject to Federal and not State regulation and control. *United States* v. *Kagama*, 118 U. S. 375; *In re Blackbird*, 109 Fed. 139; *Peters v. Malin*, 111 Fed. 244; *In re Lincoln*, 129 Fed. 246; *United States* v. *Hamilton*, 233 Fed. 685; *State* v. *Campbell*, 53 Minn. 354, 55 N. W. 553.

In expressing the foregoing view, I am mindful of the statement of the Supreme Court in *United States* v. *Holt Bank*, *supra*, that while the Indians of the Red Lake Reservation were to have access to the navigable waters therein and were to be entitled to use them in accustomed ways, "these were common rights vouchsafed to all, whether Indian or white." But when this statement is read, as it should be, in the light of the decisions cited in its support, it becomes apparent that the court had in mind rights of navigation of a public nature and not private rights of ownership such as the Indian right of fishing. The latter right was not involved and was neither considered nor discussed.

Accordingly, since the Indians' exclusive rights to fish in the waters of Lower Red Lake and that part of Upper Red Lake inside the Indian reservation is supported by all of the decided cases touching on the subject, it is my opinion that continued administrative recognition of such rights as exclusive in the Indians is fully justified.

Such rights of hunting and fishing as the Indian tribes may enjoy are subject, in the first instance, to federal regulation. Thus it has been held that Congress may restrict tribal rights by conferring on a state powers inconsistent with such rights, through an enabling act.[175]

Likewise, the United States may limit Indian hunting and fishing rights by international treaty.[176] The extent and constitutional limits of such regulatory powers of State and Federal Governments are questions more fully considered in other chapters of this volume.[177] Within the limits suggested tribal rights of hunting and fishing have received judicial recognition and protection against state and private interference[178] and even against interference by federal administrative officials.[179]

---

[175] *Ward* v. *Race Horse*, 163 U. S. 504 (1896). But *cf. Seufert Bros. Co.* v. *United States*, 249 U. S. 194 (1919).

[176] See Op. Sol. I. D., M.27690, June 15, 1934, 54 I. D. 517 (holding Migratory Bird Treaty Act of July 3, 1918, 40 Stat. 755, applicable to Swinomish Indian Reservation).

[177] See Chapters 5, 6.

[178] *Seufert Bros. Co.* v. *United States*, 249 U. S. 194 (1919); *United States* v. *Winans*, 198 U. S. 371. *In re Blackbird*, 109 Fed. 139 (D. C. W. D. Wis. 1901). And see *Halbert* v. *United States*, 283 U. S. 753, 756 (1931); *Hy-Yu-Tse-Mil-Kin* v. *Smith*, 194 U. S. 401, 410 (1904); *Spalding* v. *Chandler*, 160 U. S. 394 (1896); *Taylor* v. *United States*, 44 F. 2d 531, 532-536 (C. C. A. 9. 1930), cert. den. 283 U. S. 820.

[179] *Mason* v. *Sams*, 5 F. 2d 255 (D. C. W. D. Wash. 1925), discussed in Chapter 9, sec. 5C.

Chapter 15

TRIBAL PROPERTY

TABLE OF CONTENTS

SECTION 1. DEFINITION OF TRIBAL PROPERTY

Tribal property may be formally defined as property in which an Indian tribe has a legally enforceable interest. The exact nature of this interest it will be the purpose of this chapter to delineate. It will, however, clarify the scope and purpose of the chapter to note certain implications of the formal definition of tribal property here presented.

If tribal property is property in which a tribe has a legally enforceable interest, it must be distinguished, on the one hand, from property of individual Indians, and, on the other hand, from public property of the United States. Actually, we find that tribal property partakes of some of the incidents of both individual private property and public property of the United States. The distinctions on both sides, however, are as significant as the similarities. It may be noted that historically, conceptions of tribal property have oscillated between the two limits of individual private property and public property. When, for instance, Pueblo property was treated like any other private corporate property in the Territory of New Mexico,[1] no special problems of Indian law were presented. Likewise, where lands, although set aside for Indian purposes, have not been the subject of any legally enforceable Indian rights, as is the case perhaps with public lands set aside for the establishment of an Indian hospital or school not restricted to any particular tribe, the lands remain public property of the United States and no question of tribal property is presented.[2]

[1] See Chapter 20, sec. 8.

[2] See Chapter 1, sec. 3, fn 76. Even in the Indian school situation, tribal property rights *may* be created. In Alaska, for instance, reservations for native education have come to be treated, for most purposes, as Indian reservations. See Chapter 21, sec. 7. Similarly, we may note that the Joint Resolution of January 30, 1897, 29 Stat. 698, authorizing the use of the Fort Bidwell, abandoned military reservation, "for the purposes of an Indian training school," has been construed as establishing an Indian reservation. The Act of January 27, 1913, 37 Stat. 652, refers to "Indians having rights on said reservation."

The distinction between the *fact* of use and enjoyment and the *right* of possession is essential in the understanding of Indian tribal property. The area of land reserved in the Washington Zoo for the exclusive use and occupancy of a herd of buffalo does not, by the fact of such reservation, cease to be the public property of the United States. The buffalo have no legally enforceable interest, no possessory right, in the land. It is true that they are allowed to occupy an area from which other animals and, except for certain Government employees, human beings, may be lawfully excluded. The buffalo, however, cannot bring an action of ejectment and no other party can bring such an action on behalf of the buffalo.

From time to time, distinguished advocates have upheld what may be called the "menagerie theory" of tribal property, under which no rights whatsoever are vested in the Indian tribe.[3] In every case, however, in which this theory has been presented to the Supreme Court of the United States, it has been rejected.[4]

A. TRIBAL OWNERSHIP AND TENANCY IN COMMON

The distinction between tribal property and property owned in common by a group of Indians appears most clearly in connection with the claims repeatedly put forward by descendants of tribal members who are not themselves tribal members and who, under a theory of tenancy in common, would be entitled to share in the common property but, if the property is indeed tribal, have no valid claim thereon. The Supreme Court has made it clear in such cases as *Fleming* v. *McCurtain*,[5] and *Chippewa Indians of Minnesota* v. *United States*,[6] that where the Federal Government has dealt with Indians as a tribe no tenancy in common is created, and no descendible or alienable right accrues to the individual members of the tribe in being at the time the property vests. The fact that the plural form is used in describing the grantee does not show an intent to create a tenancy in common[7] nor does a limitation to a tribe "and their descendants" establish any basis for declaring a trust for descendants of individual members.[8]

A second distinction between tribal ownership and tenancy in common relates to the method of transfer. As the Attorney General declared, in the early case of the Christian Indians,[9]

> The gravest of your questions remains to be answered. Can these Christian Indians sell the lands thus acquired? The right of alienation is incident to an absolute title. If the patent is not to a nation, tribe, or band, called by the name of the Christian Indians, but to the individual persons included within that designation, then all those persons are patentees, and all hold as tenants in common. No conveyance can be made but by the lawful deed of all. If any one refuses or is unable to consent, he cannot be deprived of his interest by an act of the others. Some of these persons being children, and some, perhaps, being under other legal disabilities, it will be impossible for any purchaser to get a good title if they are tenants in common.
>
> But I think the patent will vest the title in the tribe. You have mentioned no fact to make me believe that their national or tribal character was ever lost or merged into that of the Delawares. They are treated as a separate people, wholly distinct and different from the Delawares. The land, therefore, belongs to the nation or band, and can be disposed of only by treaty. * * * (Pp. 26–27.)

A third distinction lies in the fact that debts of individuals may be set off against claims of tenants in common but not against claims of tribes. Thus in the case of *Shoshone Tribe of Indians* v. *United States*,[10] the Government sought to offset, against allowed tribal claims, debts due from individual allottees to the United States for irrigation construction costs. This contention was rejected on the ground that debts of individual allottees were not debts of the Indian tribe.

The essential differences between tribal ownership and tenancy in common are thus analyzed by the Court of Claims in the case of *Journeycake* v. *Cherokee Nation and the United States*,[11] in an opinion quoted and affirmed by the Supreme Court:

> The distinctive characteristic of communal property is that every member of the community is an owner of it as such. He does not take as heir, or purchaser, or grantee; if he dies his right of property does not descend; if he removes from the community it expires; if he wishes to dispose of it he has nothing which he can convey; and yet he has a right of property in the land as perfect as that of any other person; and his children after him will enjoy all that he enjoyed, not as heirs but as communal owners. * * * (P. 302.)

Perhaps all of these differences can be summed up in the conception of tribal property as *corporate* property.[12]

B. TRIBAL OWNERSHIP AND INDIVIDUAL OCCUPANCY

Congress has consistently distinguished between the tribal interest in land and the complementary interest of the individual Indian in improvements thereon.[13] Thus, a long series of congressional acts granting rights-of-way across Indian reservations to various railroad companies contain the specification that damages shall be payable not only to the tribe but to individuals, wherever lands are "held by individual occupants according to the laws, customs, and usages" of the tribe in question.[14] Other right-of-way statutes provide in slightly different

[3] Thus, Attorney General Cushing, in his opinion in the *Portage City Case*, 8 Op. A. G. 255 (1856), declared that the making of treaties with Indians and the references in such treaties to "their lands" were errors on the part of the United States.

Today a basic issue of policy in the administration of tribal property "is whether the tribe that 'owns' land will be allowed to exercise the powers of a landowner, to receive rentals and fees, to regulate land-use and to withdraw land-use privileges from those who flout the tribal regulations; or whether the Federal Government will administer 'tribal' lands for the benefit of the Indians as it administers National Monuments, for instance, for the benefit of posterity, with the Indians having perhaps as much actual voice in the former case as posterity has in the latter." F. S. Cohen, How Long Will Indian Constitutions Last? (1939), 6 Indians at Work, No. 10, pp. 40, 41.

[4] See secs. 10–20, *infra*.

[5] 215 U. S. 56 (1909). Accord: *Ligon* v. *Johnston*, 164 Fed. 670 (C. C. A. 8, 1908), app. dism., 223 U. S. 741. *Cf. United States* v. *Charles*, 23 F. Supp. 346 (D. C. W. D., N. Y. 1938).

[6] 307 U. S. 1 (1939).

[7] See *Fleming* v. *McCurtain*, 215 U. S. 56, 59 (1909).

[8] *Ibid.*, p. 60.

[9] 9 Op. A. G. 24, 26, 27 (1857).

[10] 82 C. Cls. 23 (1935), reversed on other grounds in 299 U. S. 476 (1937). It should be noted that the tribe sued *inter alia*, for the value of timber and hay unlawfully cut from tribal property and sold by members of the tribe. This contention was rejected by the court on the ground that the tribe was not damaged where the entire membership was permitted to utilize or sell tribal property.

[11] 28 C. Cls. 281 (1893), aff'd. sub nom. *Cherokee Nation* v. *Journeycake*, 155 U. S. 196 (1894).

[12] On the concept of Indian tribes as membership corporations, see Chapter 14, sec. 4.

[13] See Chapter 9, sec. 5B.

[14] Act of August 2, 1882, 22 Stat. 181; Act of July 4, 1884, 23 Stat. 69; Act of July 4, 1884, 23 Stat. 73; Act of June 1, 1886, 24 Stat. 73; Act of July 1, 1886, 24 Stat. 117; Act of July 6, 1886, 24 Stat. 124; Act of February 24, 1887, 24 Stat. 419; Act of March 2, 1887, 24 Stat. 446; Act of February 18, 1888, 25 Stat. 35; Act of May 14, 1888, 25 Stat. 140; Act of May 30, 1888, 25 Stat. 162; Act of January 16, 1889, 25 Stat. 647; Act of May 8, 1890, 26 Stat. 102; Act of June 21, 1890, 26 Stat. 170; Act of June 30, 1890, 26 Stat. 184; Act of September 26, 1890, 26 Stat. 485; Act of October 1, 1890, 26 Stat. 632; Act of February 24, 1891, 26 Stat. 783; Act of March 3, 1891, 26 Stat. 844; Act of July 6, 1892, 27 Stat. 83; Act of July 30, 1892, 27 Stat. 336; Act of February 20, 1893, 27 Stat. 465; Act of March 2, 1896, sec. 3, 29 Stat. 40; Act of March 18, 1896, sec. 2, 29 Stat. 69; Act of March 30, 1896, sec. 2, 29 Stat. 80, 81; Act of April 6, 1896, 29 Stat. 87; Act of January 29, 1897, 29 Stat. 502; Act of February 14, 1898, 30 Stat. 241; Act of March 30, 1898, 30 Stat. 347.

terms for damages to individual occupants injured by the granting of such rights-of-way.[15] Under such statutes, it has been said,

> Where one has a base fee, it has been held that he should receive the full value of the land, as the interest of the grantor is too remote to be treated as property. The fee of the territory of the Cherokee Nation is in the Nation, but the occupants of the land have so complete a right of enjoyment that, when a right of way is condemned, they are entitled to the compensation.[16]

Where Congress has provided for the sale of tribal lands, special provision has frequently been made for the payment of damages to individual occupants.[17]

While the Indian occupant of tribal land has such an interest as will entitle him to compensation when a right-of-way is granted across the land he occupies, it has been held administratively that such payments made to individual Indian occupants cannot satisfy the tribal right to compensation.[18]

C. TRIBAL LANDS AND PUBLIC LANDS OF THE UNITED STATES

Although Indian tribal lands have been distinguished from public lands in various ways, there are certain situations in which tribal lands have been treated as public lands. For example it has been held that tribal lands, even though held by the tribe in fee, may be considered public lands of the United States for the purpose of erecting federal buildings thereon, at least where Congress has directed such action, or where the tribe itself has consented to the action.[19]

Again, it has been held that Indian lands are "public lands" within the meaning of a statute granting a right-of-way to a railroad company across "public lands," where the United States specifically undertakes to extinguish Indian title on the lands affected and where the statute is interpreted to cover Indian lands by the "Executive Department charged with the administration of the act." [20]

Likewise, it has been held that land acquired by the United States in trust for an Indian tribe is immune from state zoning regulations which, in terms, do not apply to lands "belonging to and occupied by the United States." [21]

As already noted, the fact that Indian lands may be classified as "public lands" for certain purposes, does not negate their character as tribal property. Thus, surplus Indian lands although denominated "public lands of the United States" for purposes of disposition, are subject to restoration as tribal lands under section 3 of the Act of June 18, 1934.[22]

And where "public lands" are granted to a state or railroad, Indian lands will not be deemed to be covered by the grant in the absence of clear evidence of a congressional intent to include such lands.[23]

Similarly, it has been held that Indian tribal lands are not covered by statutes opening "public lands" to settlement,[24] nor are they comprised within the mineral laws affecting the public domain.[25]

D. THE COMPOSITION OF THE TRIBE AS PROPRIETOR

To mark out the tribe in which any form of tribal property is vested is ordinarily a simple enough matter. There are, however, a number of cases in which, because of tribal amalgamation or dissolution, modification of membership rules, or inconsistencies and ambiguities in treaty or statutory designations, serious questions arise as to the composition of the tribe in which particular rights of property are vested. Insofar as these questions involve the issue of the tribal status, they have already received our consideration in Chapter 14. For present purposes it is enough to designate briefly the chief complications that have arisen in designating the tribe in which given property rights are vested.

One of these complications arises out of the practice in numerous early statutes and treaties, of dividing a tribal estate between those Indians desiring to maintain tribal relationships and communal property and those desiring to separate themselves from the tribe and hold their shares of tribal property in individual ownership. Typical of this arrangement is the Act of February 6, 1871.[26] Under this statute the tribal estate was divided be-

[15] Act of May 30, 1888, 25 Stat. 160; Act of June 4, 1888, 25 Stat. 167; Act of June 26, 1888, 25 Stat. 205; Act of July 26, 1888, 25 Stat. 347; Act of July 26, 1888, 25 Stat. 349; Act of October 17, 1888, 25 Stat. 558; Act of February 23, 1889, 25 Stat. 684 (Dakota); Act of February 26, 1889, 25 Stat. 745 (Kansas); Act of May 8, 1890, 26 Stat. 104; Act of October 1, 1890, 26 Stat. 663; Act of December 21, 1893, 28 Stat. 22; Act of August 4, 1894, 28 Stat. 229; Act of February 28, 1899, sec. 3, 30 Stat. 906; Act of March 2, 1899, sec. 3, 30 Stat. 990.

[16] Randolph, Eminent Domain (1894), sec. 301, citing *Payne* v. *Kansas & A. Val. R. Co.*, 46 Fed. 546 (C. C. W. D. Ark., 1891).

[17] Act of May 28, 1830, 4 Stat. 411 (providing that where tribal lands were exchanged for lands west of the Mississippi, by tribal consent, the individual members of the tribe shall be paid the value of improvements upon the land they occupy); Act of February 6, 1871, sec. 1, 16 Stat. 404 (ownership of improvements on land offered for sale to be "certified by the sachem and councillors of said [Stockbridge and Munsee] tribe"); Act of March 3, 1885, 23 Stat. 351 (Sac and Fox); Act of February 20, 1895, 28 Stat. 677 (Southern Ute); Act of June 28, 1898, 30 Stat. 495 (Indian Territory).

[18] Memo. Sol. I. D., August 11, 1937.

[19] In a decision dated June 25, 1900, 6 Comp. Dec. 957, the Comptroller of the Treasury considered the question of the construction of a school on the Pipestone Indian reservation owned by the Yankton Sioux Tribe in fee simple. The Comptroller held that neither sec. 355 of the Revised Statutes, 33 U. S. C. 733, nor the general policy exemplified by that section against the expenditure of public funds on private property had any application, stating:

> * * * The same acts which make the appropriations for new buildings make large appropriations for the support of the school on the reservation, and as the funds provided for the support of the school is a gift it may, with some show of reason, be contended that it was the intention of Congress that the provisions for new buildings should be considered as a gift, and that the money should be expended on the land known to belong to the Indians in fee. (P. 960.)

A subsequent decision dated February 23, 1918, 24 Comp. Dec. 477, subscribes to the same doctrine. There the Comptroller ruled that public moneys could not be expended in erecting school buildings on Indian reservation lands the title to which was in the State. But he said:

> If the legal title to the land upon which it is contemplated to erect the buildings were in the Seminole Indians, then it might not be improper to use Government appropriations for the construction of the required buildings. * * * (P. 479.)

[20] *Kindred* v. *Union Pacific R. R. Co.*, 225 U. S. 582, 596 (1912), aff'g. 168 Fed. 648 (C. C. A. 8, 1909). The doctrine of this case is stretched to cover a case where no administrative construction supported the decision and where the land had been promised to a given tribe of Indians "as their land and home forever" (Treaty of June 5 and 17, 1846, with the Pottowautomie, 9 Stat. 853, 854), in the case of *Nadeau* v. *Union Pac. R. Co.* 253 U. S. 422 (1920) (construing the Act of July 1, 1862, 12 Stat. 489, as amended by the Act of July 3, 1866, 14 Stat. 79). *Cf.*, however, *Leavenworth, etc., R. R. Co.*, v. *United States*, 92 U. S. 733, 743 (1875), holding that a congressional grant of Indian lands is not to be presumed "in the absence of words of unmistakable import." Accord: *Missouri, Kans. & Tex. Ry. Co.* v. *United States*, 235 U. S. 37 (1914). *Cf.* also *Beecher* v. *Wetherby*, 95 U. S. 517 (1877) (holding that a grant of "public lands" may convey the fee to an Indian reservation subject to the Indians' right of occupancy, if such congressional intention is shown). And see fns. 215, 217, *infra*.

[21] Memo. Sol. I. D., October 5, 1936.

[22] 48 Stat. 984, 25 U. S. C. 463; Op. Sol. I. D., M.29798, June 15, 1938.

[23] *Minnesota* v. *Hitchcock*, 185 U. S. 373 (1902). And see *Leavenworth, etc. R. R. Co.* v. *United States*, 92 U. S. 733, 741 (1875). See *Missouri, Kansas & Texas Ry. Co.* v. *Roberts*, 152 U. S. 114, 119 (1894); *Dubuque, etc., Railroad* v. *D. M. V. Railroad*, 109 U. S. 329, 334 (1883); but *cf.* *Shepard* v. *Northwestern Life Ins. Co.*, 40 Fed. 341, 348 (C. C. E. D. Mich., 1889). And *cf.* fn. 20, *supra*.

[24] *United States* v. *McIntire*, 101 F. 2d 650 (C. C. A. 9. 1939), rev'g. *McIntire* v. *United States*, 22 F. Supp. 316 (D. C. Mont. 1937).

[25] See secs. 7 and 14, *infra*.

[26] 16 Stat. 404 (Stockbridge and Munsee).

tween a "citizen party" and an "Indian party," the former to receive per capita shares of the tribal funds, and the latter to enjoy exclusive rights in the remaining tribal fund. Members of the "citizen party" were deemed to have made "full surrender and relinquishment" of all claims "to be thereafter known and considered as members of said tribe, or in any manner interested in any provision heretofore or hereafter to be made by any treaty or law of the United States for the benefit of said tribes * * *." (Sec. 6.)[27]

A similar procedure was employed in certain cases where tribes were induced to migrate westward and those individuals remaining behind severed tribal connections and thus lost any rights in the tribal property of the migrant tribe.[28]

The problem of proportionate common ownership by two tribes is raised by the Act of March 2, 1889.[29]

A related problem is raised by the existence of separate treaty rights enjoyed by the Gros Ventre and the Assiniboine tribes of the Fort Belknap Reservation, which tribes, as a result of occupying a single reservation,[30] holding land in common, and acting through a single tribal council, have come to be amalgamated as a single tribe.[31]

The pooling of lands held by different Chippewa bands under the Act of January 14, 1889,[32] has raised a number of complex questions which can hardly be noted within the confines of this discussion.[33] While it is impossible to lay down a simple rule to determine when title to reservation lands is located in a tribe and when it is located in a component band, the opinion of the Supreme Court in *Chippewa Indians* v. *United States*[34] indicates the factors that will be considered in such a determination. Among such factors particular importance attaches to the attitudes of other bands towards the claim of the band in occupancy, the nature of the treaties made, whether with individual bands or with the entire tribe or nation, and the administrative practice of the Interior Department with respect to the use of lands and the disposition of proceeds therefrom.

The clarification of ambiguities in the designation of the Indian group for which a reservation has been set aside is exemplified in the case of the Colorado River Reservation. This reservation was originally set aside "for the Indians of the said river and its tributaries."[35] It was held by the Solicitor of the Interior Department that the Indians located on the reservation over a long period of years and recognized as a single tribe came to enjoy rights in the reservation which administrative officers could not thereafter diminish by locating, on the reservation, Indians of other tribes residing within the Colorado River watershed.[36]

[27] Accord: Act of February 20, 1895, 28 Stat. 677 (Ute).

[28] 17 Op. A. G. 410 (1882) (Miami tribe). See Chapter 3, secs. 3 and 4.

[29] 25 Stat. 1013.

[30] Act of May 1, 1888, 25 Stat. 113, 124.

[31] Memo. Sol. I. D., March 20, 1936.

[32] 25 Stat. 642.

[33] For an account of these arrangements, see *United States* v. *Mille Lac Band of Chippewa Indians*, 229 U. S. 498 (1913); *Chippewa Indians of Minnesota* v. *United States*, 301 U. S. 358 (1937), aff'g 80 C. Cls. 410 (1935); *United States* v. *Minnesota*, 270 U. S. 181 (1926); Op. Sol. I. D., M.29616, February 19, 1938.

[34] *Supra*, fn. 33. And see *Chippewa Indians of Minnesota* v. *United States*, 307 U. S. 1 (1939).

[35] Act of March 3, 1865, 13 Stat. 541, 559.

[36] Memo. Sol. I. D., September 15, 1936; Memo. Sol. I. D. October 29, 1936. Accord: *United States* v. *Choctaw Nation*, 179 U. S. 494, 548 (1900).

SECTION 2. FORMS OF TRIBAL PROPERTY

In the whole range of ownership forms known to our legal system, from simple ownership of money or chattels and fee simple title in real estate, through the many varieties of restricted and conditioned titles, trust titles and future interests, to the shadowy rights of permittees and contingent remaindermen, there is probably no form of property right that has not been lodged in an Indian tribe. The term *tribal property*, therefore, does not designate a single and definite legal institution, but rather a broad range within which important variations exist. These variations occur in every aspect of property law—in the duration of the possessory right, whether perpetual or limited, in the extent of that right, with respect, *e. g.*, to timber, minerals, water, and improvements on tribal land, in the measure of supervision which the Federal Government reserves over the tribal property, and in the types of use and disposition which may be made of the property by the tribal "owner." In view of these diversities, generalizations about "tribal property" should be scrutinized as critically as assertions about "property" in general.

A brief and incomplete list of the various tenures by which tribal property is held may serve to indicate the need for caution in dealing with generalizations about "Indian title" and "tribal ownership": (1) fee simple ownership of land;[37] (2) equitable ownership of land;[38] (3) leasehold interest in land;[39] (4) rights of reverter established by statutes granting to various railroads rights-of-way across Indian reservations with a provision that the land shall revert to the tribe in the event that the grantee ceases to use it for the designated purpose,[40] and similar rights of reverter established by various other types of legislation;[41] (5) easements;[42] (6) ownership of minerals underlying allotted

[37] See sec. 6 of this Chapter.

[38] See sec. 6 of this Chapter.

[39] See, for example, the Act of February 28, 1809, 2 Stat. 527, conferring a 50-year leasehold upon the Alibama and the Wyandott tribes, subject to termination upon abandonment.

[40] Act of July 4, 1884, 23 Stat. 69; Act of July 4, 1884, 23 Stat. 73; Act of June 1, 1886, 24 Stat. 73; Act of July 1, 1886, 24 Stat. 117; Act of July 6, 1886, 24 Stat. 124; Act of February 24, 1887, 24 Stat. 419; Act of March 2, 1887, 24 Stat. 446; Act of February 18, 1888, 25 Stat. 35; Act of May 14, 1888, 25 Stat. 140; Act of May 30, 1888, 25 Stat. 162; Act of June 26, 1888, 25 Stat. 205; Act of September 1, 1888, 25 Stat. 452; Act of January 16, 1889, 25 Stat. 647; Act of February 26, 1889, 25 Stat. 745; Act of May 8, 1890, 26 Stat. 102; Act of June 21, 1890, 26 Stat. 170; Act of June 30, 1890, 26 Stat. 184; Act of September 26, 1890, 26 Stat. 485; Act of October 1, 1890, 26 Stat. 632; Act of February 24, 1891, 26 Stat. 783; Act of March 3, 1891, 26 Stat. 844; Act of July 6, 1892, 27 Stat. 83; Act of July 30, 1892, 27 Stat. 336; Act of February 20, 1893, 27 Stat. 465; Act of December 21, 1893, 28 Stat. 22; Act of August 4, 1894, 28 Stat. 229; Act of March 2, 1896, 29 Stat. 40; Act of March 18, 1896, 29 Stat. 69; Act of March 30, 1896, 29 Stat. 80; Act of April 6, 1896, 29 Stat. 87; Act of January 29, 1897, 29 Stat. 502; Act of February 14, 1898, 30 Stat. 241; Act of March 30, 1898, 30 Stat. 347; Act of February 28, 1899, 30 Stat. 906.

[41] See, for example, *United States* v. *Board of Nat. Missions of Presbyterian Church*, 37 F. 2d 272 (C. C. A. 10, 1929). Compare sec. 2, paragraph 12, of the Act of June 28, 1906, 34 Stat. 539, providing for the conveyance of Osage lands to a cemetery association with a right of reverter to "the use and benefit of the individual members of the Osage tribe, according to the roll herein provided, or to their heirs."

[42] See, for example, the Act of May 9, 1924, 43 Stat. 117, providing that lands withdrawn from the Fort Hall Indian reservation for reservoir purposes shall be subject to a "reservation of an easement to the Fort Hall Indians to use the said lands for grazing, hunting, fishing, and gathering of wood, and so forth, the same way as obtained prior to this enactment, insofar as such uses shall not interfere with the use of said lands for reservoir purposes." Compare the Act of February 26, 1919, 40 Stat. 1175, conferring upon the Havasupai tribe rights of "use and occupancy" in lands within the Grand Canyon National Park.

lands;[43] (7) water rights;[44] (8) rights of interment;[45] (9) tribal trust funds;[46] (10) accounts payable to tribe.[47]

Various other types of property rights[48] vested in Indian tribes might be noted, but the foregoing list should serve to convey a fair idea of the complexity of the subject matter and the danger of overgeneralization.

[43] Act of June 4, 1920, sec. 6, 41 Stat. 751, 753 (Crow); Act of June 28, 1898, sec. 11, 30 Stat. 495, 497 (Indian Territory); Act of June 28, 1906, 34 Stat. 539 (Osage); Act of March 3, 1921, sec. 4, 41 Stat. 1355 (Fort Belknap). See sec. 14, *infra*.

[44] See, for example, Act of June 6, 1900, 31 Stat. 672 (Fort Hall; reserving water rights by agreement where surplus lands were sold on Fort Hall Reservation); Act of March 3, 1905, 33 Stat. 1016 (authorizing the use of tribal funds to purchase water rights for Indian lands on the Wind River Reservation in accordance with the statutes of Wyoming). And see sec. 16 of this Chapter.

[45] Act of March 1, 1883, 22 Stat. 432 (rights of interment reserved for Indians of Alleghany Indian Reservation when lands are transferred to cemetery association); Act of January 27, 1913, 37 Stat. 652 (Fort Bidwell Indian School Reservation).

[46] Act of June 8, 1858, sec. 2, 11 Stat. 312; Act of March 3, 1863, secs. 4, 5, 12 Stat. 819; Act of April 29, 1874, sec. 2, 18 Stat. 36, 41; Act of March 3, 1881, sec. 4, 21 Stat. 380; Act of March 3, 1885, 23 Stat. 351 (Sac and Fox, and Iowa); Act of September 1, 1888, sec. 6, 25 Stat. 452; Act of February 20, 1893, 27 Stat. 469 (White Mountain Apache); Act of March 2, 1901, 31 Stat. 952; Act of April 23, 1904, 33 Stat. 302 (Flathead); Act of December 21, 1904, 33 Stat. 595 (Yakima); Act of June 5, 1906, 34 Stat. 213; Act of February 10, 1912, 37 Stat. 64 (Blackfeet); Act of February 14, 1913, 37 Stat. 675 (Standing Rock); Act of March 3, 1925, 43 Stat. 1101. See sec. 22, *infra*.

[47] See, for example, Act of March 3, 1921, sec. 5, 41 Stat. 1355.

[48] See, for example, Act of August 6, 1846, 9 Stat. 55 (claims); Joint Resolution of January 18, 1893, 27 Stat. 753; Act of February 13, 1913, 37 Stat. 668 (right of ferriage); Act of February 9, 1925, 43 Stat. 820 (claims).

SECTION 3. SOURCES OF TRIBAL RIGHTS IN REAL PROPERTY

The definition of tribal property rights in every decided case and in every actual situation involves some document or course of action which defines those rights. An analysis of the different ways in which tribal rights over property come into being is therefore prerequisite to a proper definition of those rights.

Interests in real property have been acquired by Indian tribes in at least six ways:

1. By aboriginal possession.
2. By treaty.
3. By act of Congress.
4. By Executive action.
5. By purchase.
6. By action of a colony, state, or foreign nation.

In sections 4 to 9 of this chapter, these six sources of tribal right will be analyzed.

A word of caution, however, must be offered against the assumption that the foregoing six methods are clearly distinguished from each other. In fact, there is an interconnection of all methods: aboriginal possession may be confirmed by treaty or statute; a treaty may carry out objectives laid down in a statute, and vice versa; either may be implemented by Executive order or purchase. Action of the United States along any of these lines may parallel or confirm acts of prior sovereignties. But with all these qualifications, the six-fold division above proposed does offer a convenient method of arranging in workable compass the material pertaining to the creation of tribal property rights in land.

By way of corrective to any illusion of certainty that this division of material may stimulate, it is well to quote the words of the Supreme Court in *Minnesota* v. *Hitchcock*.[49]

> * * * Now, in order to create a reservation it is not necessary that there should be a formal cession or a formal act setting apart a particular tract. It is enough that from what has been done there results a certain defined tract appropriated to certain purposes. * * *

[49] 185 U. S. 373, 389–390 (1902).

SECTION 4. ABORIGINAL POSSESSION

The derivation of Indian property rights from aboriginal possession[50] is not only the first source of tribal property rights in a historical sense, but is of first importance in that this source of property has greatly influenced tribal tenures established in other ways. Except in the light of this influence, it is difficult to understand why peculiar incidents should attach to property which has been purchased outright by an Indian tribe from a private person, or has been patented to the tribe by the United States in the same way that other public lands are patented to private individuals. That there are peculiar incidents attached even to fee-simple tenure by an Indian tribe is an undoubted fact, and the explanation of this fact is probably to be found in the contagion that has emanated from the concept of aboriginal possession.

The problem of recognizing or denying possessory rights claimed by the aborigines in the soil of America engaged the attention of jurists and publicists from the discovery of America. A clear expression of the classical view, which influenced Chief Justice Marshall and other founders of American legal doctrine in this field, was given by Vattel.[51] The conflicting claims of European powers to unpopulated areas in the new world were to be resolved, according to Vattel, in accordance with the precept of natural law (or, as we should say today, the precept of international morality) that no nations can

> * * * exclusively appropriate to themselves more land than they have occasion for, or more than they are able to settle and cultivate. * * * We do not, therefore, deviate from the views of nature in confining the Indians within narrower limits. However, we cannot help praising the moderation of the English puritans who first settled in New England; who, notwithstanding their being furnished with a charter from their sovereign, purchased of the Indians the land of which they intended to take possession. This laudable example was followed by William Penn, and the colony of quakers that he conducted to Pennsylvania.

The basic issues in the field of aboriginal possessory right were first presented to the United States Supreme Court in the case of *Johnson* v. *McIntosh*.[52] Of the opinion of Chief Justice Marshall in that case, a leading writer on American consti-

[50] The significance of this concept is summarized in these words from the opinion in *Deere* v. *State of New York*, 22 F. 2d 851, 854 (D. C. N. D. N. Y., 1927):

> * * * The source of title here is not letters patent or other form of grant by the federal government. Here the Indians claim immemorial rights, arising prior to white occupation, and recognized and protected by treaties between Great Britain and the United States and between the United States and the Indians. By the treaty of 1784 between the United States and the Six Nations of Indians, and the treaty of 1796 between the United States, the state of New York and the Seven Nations of Canada, the right of occupation of the lands in question by the St. Regis Indians, was not granted, but recognized and confirmed.

[51] Vattel's *Law of Nations* (1758), Book I, c. XVIII. The passage quoted is from the edition of Chitty published in 1839.

[52] 8 Wheat. 543 (1823).

tutional law remarks: "the principles there laid down have ever since been accepted as correct." [83] In this case the plaintiffs claimed land under a grant by the chiefs of the Illinois and Piankeshaw Nations, and in the words of the opinion, "the question is, whether this title can be recognized in the courts of the United States?" In reaching the conclusion that the Indian tribes did not enjoy and could not convey complete title to the soil, the Court analyzed in some detail the extent and origin of the Indians' possessory right. From this opinion the following pertinent excerpts are taken:

> On the discovery of this immense continent, the great nations of Europe were eager to appropriate to themselves so much of it as they could respectively acquire. Its vast extent offered an ample field to the ambition and enterprise of all; and the character and religion of its inhabitants afforded an apology for considering them as a people over whom the superior genius of Europe might claim an ascendency. The potentates of the old world found no difficulty in convincing themselves that they made ample compensation to the inhabitants of the new, by bestowing on them civilization and Christianity, in exchange for unlimited independence. But, as they were all in pursuit of nearly the same object, it was necessary, in order to avoid conflicting settlements, and consequent war with each other, to establish a principle, which all should acknowledge as the law by which the right of acquisition, which they all asserted, should be regulated as between themselves. This principle was, that discovery gave title to the government by whose subjects, or by whose authority, it was made, against all other European governments, which title might be consummated by possession.
>
> The exclusion of all other Europeans, necessarily gave to the nation making the discovery the sole right of acquiring the soil from the natives, and establishing settlements upon it. It was a right with which no Europeans could interfere. It was a right which all asserted for themselves, and to the assertion of which, by others, all assented.
>
> Those relations which were to exist between the discoverer and the natives, were to be regulated by themselves. The rights thus acquired being exclusive, no other power could interpose between them.
>
> In the establishment of these relations, the rights of the original inhabitants were, in no instance, entirely disregarded; but were necessarily, to a considerable extent, impaired. They were admitted to be the rightful occupants of the soil, with a legal as well as just claim to retain possession of it, and to use it according to their own discretion; but their rights to complete sovereignty, as independent nations, were necessarily diminished, and their power to dispose of the soil at their own will, to whomsoever they pleased, was denied by the original fundamental principle, that discovery gave exclusive title to those who made it.
>
> While the different nations of Europe respected the right of the natives, as occupants, they asserted the ultimate dominion to be in themselves; and claimed and exercised, as a consequence of this ultimate dominion, a power to grant the soil, while yet in possession of the natives. These grants have been understood by all, to convey a title to the grantees, subject only to the Indian right of occupancy.
>
> The history of America, from its discovery to the present day, proves, we think, the universal recognition of these principles. (Pp. 572–574.)
>
> * * * * *
>
> The United States, then, have unequivocally acceded to that great and broad rule by which its civilized inhabitants now hold this country. They hold, and assert in themselves, the title by which it was acquired. They maintain, as all others have maintained, that discovery gave an exclusive right to extinguish the Indian title of occupancy, either by purchase or by conquest; and gave also a right to such a degree of sovereignty as the circumstances of the people would allow them to exercise.
>
> The power now possessed by the government of the United States to grant lands, resided, while we were colonies, in the crown, or its grantees. The validity of the titles given by either has never been questioned in our courts. It has been exercised uniformly over territory in possession of the Indians. The existence of this power must negative the existence of any right which may conflict with and control it. An absolute title to lands cannot exist, at the same time, in different persons, or in different governments. An absolute, must be an exclusive title, or at least a title which excludes all others not compatible with it. All our institutions recognize the absolute title of the crown, subject only to the Indian right of occupancy, and recognize the absolute title of the crown to extinguish that right. This is incompatible with an absolute and complete title in the Indians.
>
> We will not enter into the controversy, whether agriculturists, merchants, and manufacturers, have a right, on abstract principles, to expel hunters from the territory they possess, or to contract their limits. Conquest gives a title which the courts of the conqueror cannot deny, whatever the private and speculative opinions of individuals may be, respecting the original justice of the claim which has been successfully asserted. The British government, which was then our government, and whose rights have passed to the United States, asserted a title to all the lands occupied by Indians, within the chartered limits of the British colonies. It asserted also a limited sovereignty over them, and the exclusive right of extinguishing the title which occupancy gave to them. These claims have been maintained and established as far west as the River Mississippi, by the sword. The title to a vast portion of the lands we now hold, originates in them. It is not for the courts of this country to question the validity of this title, or to sustain one which is incompatible with it. (Pp. 587–589.)
>
> * * * * *
>
> However extravagant the pretension of converting the discovery of an inhabited country into conquest may appear; if the principle has been asserted in the first instance, and afterwards sustained; if a country has been acquired and held under it; if the property of the great mass of the community originates in it, it becomes the law of the land, and cannot be questioned. So, too, with respect to the concomitant principle, that the Indian inhabitants are to be considered merely as occupants, to be protected, indeed, while in peace, in the possession of their lands, but to be deemed incapable of transferring the absolute title to others. However this restriction may be opposed to natural right, and to the usages of civilized nations, yet, if it be indispensable to that system under which the country has been settled, and be adapted to the actual condition of the two people, it may, perhaps, be supported by reason, and certainly cannot be rejected by courts of justice. (Pp. 591–592.)

The limitations upon Indian rights emphasized by Chief Justice Marshall in his opinion in the *McIntosh* case were supplemented a few years later by a second notable opinion of the Chief Justice emphasizing the positive content of the Indian possessory right. In the case of *Worcester v. Georgia*,[84] which dealt with the constitutionality of action by the State of Georgia leading to the imprisonment of individuals admitted to residence in the Cherokee Reservation by the authorities of that nation and by the United States, the Supreme Court took occasion again to analyze in detail the extent of the Indian right in the soil of the Cherokee Nation. "It is difficult" the Chief Justice ironically noted

> * * * to comprehend the proposition, that the inhabitants of either quarter of the globe could have rightful original claims of dominion over the inhabitants of the other, or over the lands they occupied; or that the discovery of either by the other should give the discoverer rights in the country discovered, which annuled the preexisting rights of its ancient possessors.
>
> * * * * *

[83] C. K. Burdick, The Law of the American Constitution, Its Origin and Development (1922) sec. 107.

[84] 6 Pet. 515 (1832).

> But power, war, conquest, give rights which, after possession, are conceded by the world, and which can never be controverted by those on whom they descend. (P. 543.)

"The great maritime powers of Europe," the Chief Justice observed, agreed upon the mutually advantageous rule, formulated in the *McIntosh* case "'that discovery gave title to the government by whose subjects or by whose authority it was made, against all other European governments, which title might be consummated by possession.' 8 Wheat. 573." (Pp. 543–4.)

Such a rule, however, bound the European governments, but not the Indian tribes.

> This principle, acknowledged by all Europeans, because it was the interest of all to acknowledge it, gave to the nation making the discovery, as its inevitable consequence, the sole right of acquiring the soil and of making settlements on it. It was an exclusive principle which shut out the right of competition among those who had agreed to it; not one which could annul the previous rights of those who had not agreed to it. It regulated the right given by discovery among the European discoverers; but could not affect the rights of those already in possession, either as aboriginal occupants, or as occupants by virtue of a discovery made before the memory of man. It gave the exclusive right to purchase, but did not found that right on a denial of the right of the possessor to sell.
>
> The relation between the Europeans and the natives was determined in each case by the particular government which asserted and could maintain this preemptive privilege in the particular place. The United States succeeded to all the claims of Great Britain, both territorial and political; but no attempt, so far as is known, has been made to enlarge them. So far as they existed merely in theory, or were in their nature only exclusive of the claims of other European nations, they still retain their original character, and remain dormant. So far as they have been practically exerted, they exist in fact, are understood by both parties, are asserted by the one, and admitted by the other.
>
> Soon after Great Britain determined on planting colonies in America, the king granted charters to companies of his subjects, who associated for the purpose of carrying the views of the crown into effect, and of enriching themselves. The first of these charters was made before possession was taken of any part of the country. They purport, generally, to convey the soil, from the Atlantic to the South Sea. This soil was occupied by numerous and warlike nations, equally willing and able to defend their possessions. The extravagant and absurd idea, that the feeble settlements made on the sea-coast, or the companies under whom they were made, acquired legitimate power by them to govern the people, or occupy the lands from sea to sea, did not enter the mind of any man. They were well understood to convey the title which, according to the common law of European sovereigns respecting America, they might rightfully convey, and no more. This was the exclusive right of purchasing such lands as the natives were willing to sell. The crown could not be understood to grant what the crown did not affect to claim; nor was it so understood. (Pp. 544–545.)

Viewing the problem in these terms, the Supreme Court had no difficulty in reaching the conclusion that a possessory right in the area concerned was vested in the Cherokee Nation and that the State of Georgia had no authority to enter upon the Cherokee lands without the consent of the Cherokee Nation.

These views were reaffirmed by the Supreme Court, *per* Clifford, *J.*, in the subsequent case of *Holden* v. *Joy*.[55]

> Enough has already been remarked to show that the lands conveyed to the United States by the treaty were held by the Cherokees under their original title, acquired by immemorial possession, commencing ages before the New World was known to civilized man. Unmistakably their title was absolute, subject only to the pre-emption right of purchase acquired by the United States as the successors of Great Britain, and the right also on their part as such successors of the discoverer to prohibit the sale of the land to any other governments or their subjects, and to exclude all other governments from any interference in their affairs.*
>
> **Mitchel et al.* v. *United States*, 9 Peters, 748.

A similar view of the aboriginal Indian title was taken by the Attorney General in answering the question whether a certain Mr. Ogden, owner of the reversionary fee in Seneca Indian lands, might lawfully enter these lands for the purpose of making a survey. In answering this question in the negative, Attorney General Wirt declared:

> The answer to this question depends on the character of the title which the Indians retain in these lands. The practical admission of the European conquerors of this country renders it unnecessary for us to speculate on the extent of that right which they might have asserted from conquest, and from the migratory habits and hunter state of its aboriginal occupants. (See the authorities cited in Fletcher and Peck, 6 Cranch, 121.) The conquerors have never claimed more than the exclusive right of purchase from the Indians, and the right of succession to a tribe which shall have removed voluntarily, or become extinguished by death. So long as a tribe exists and remains in possession of its lands, its title and possession are sovereign and exclusive; and there exists no authority to enter upon their lands, for any purpose whatever, without their consent. * * * Although the Indian title continues only during their possession, yet that possession has been always held sacred, and can never be disturbed but by their consent. They do not hold under the States, nor under the United States; their title is original, sovereign, and exclusive. We treat with them as separate sovereignties; and while an Indian nation continues to exist within its acknowledged limits, we have no more right to enter upon their territory, without their consent, than we have to enter upon the territory of a foreign prince.
>
> It is said that the act of ownership proposed to be exercised by the grantees under the State of Massachusetts will not injure the Indians, nor disturb them in the usual enjoyment of these lands; but of this the Indians, whose title, while it continues, is sovereign and exclusive, are the proper and the only judges. * * *
>
> I am of opinion that it is inconsistent, both with the character of the Indian title and the stipulations of their treaty, to enter upon these lands, for the purpose of making the proposed surveys, without the consent of the Indians, *freely rendered, and on a full understanding of the case*.[56] (Pp. 466–467.)

Cases and opinions subsequent to the *McIntosh* case oscillate between a stress on the content of the Indian possessory right and stress on the limitations of that right. These opinions and cases might perhaps be classified according to whether they refer to the Indian right of occupancy as a "mere" right of occupancy or as a "sacred" right of occupancy. All the cases, however, agree in saying that the aboriginal Indian title involves an exclusive right of occupancy and does not involve an ultimate fee. The cases dealing with Indian lands in the territory of the original colonies locate the ultimate fee in the state wherein the lands are situated.[57] Outside of the territory of the original

[55] 84 U. S. 211, 244 (1872). Accord: 1 Op. A. G. 465 (1821).

[56] The Seneca Lands, 1 Op. A. G. 465 (1821).

[57] *Clark* v. *Smith*, 13 Pet. 195 (1839); *Lattimer* v. *Poteet*, 14 Pet. 4 (1840); *Seneca Nation* v. *Christy*, 162 U. S. 283 (1896); The Cherokees and their Lands, 2 Op. A. G. 321 (1830) (holding that Cherokee lands became the property of Georgia upon the migration of the occupants); Tennessee Land Titles, 30 Op. A. G. 284 (1914) (holding that such lands within the boundaries of the State of Tennessee became the property of that state upon the migration of the Cherokees); *Spalding* v. *Chandler*, 160 U. S. 394 (1896), and see *Fletcher* v. *Peck*, 6 Cranch 87 (1810); *Johnson* v. *McIntosh*, 8 Wheat. 543, 590 (1823); *Cherokee Nation* v. *Georgia*, 5 Pet. 1, 38 (1831); *United States* v. *Joseph*, 94 U. S. 614, 618 (1876), aff'g. 1 N. M. 593 (1894); 5 L. D. Memo. 286 (New York Indians).

colonies, the ultimate fee is located in the United States and may be granted to individuals subject to the Indian right of occupancy.[58]

The question of what evidenciary facts must be shown to establish the aboriginal possession described in the foregoing opinions would carry us beyond the limits of this volume, but certain elementary principles are readily established. It has been held that title by aboriginal possession is not established by proof that an area was used for hunting purposes where other tribes also hunted on the lands in question.[59]

Where exclusive occupancy over a considerable period is shown, rights of possession are not lost by forced abandonment.[60] In the words of the Court of Claims,

> The Supreme Court has repeatedly held that the Indians' claim of right of occupancy of lands is dependent upon actual and not constructive possession. *Mitchel* v. *United States*, 9 Pet. 711; *Williams* v. *Chicago*, 242 U. S. 434; *Choctaw Nation* v. *United States*, 34 C. Cls. 17. Beyond doubt, abandonment of claimed Indian territory by the Indians will extinguish Indian title. In this case the Government interposes the defense of abandonment, asserting that the facts sustain the contention. It is of course conceded that the issue of abandonment is one of intention to relinquish, surrender, and unreservedly give up all claims to title to the lands described in the treaty, and the source from which to arrive at such an intention is the facts and circumstances of the transaction involved. Forcible ejection from the premises, or nonuser under certain circumstances, as well as lapse of time, are not standing alone sufficient to warrant an abandonment. *Welsh* v. *Taylor*, 18 L. R. A. 535; *Gassert* v. *Noyes*, 44 Pacific 959; *Mitchell* v. *Corder*, 21 W. Va. 277. (P. 334.)

[58] *Missouri* v. *Iowa*, 7 How. 660 (1849); *Portage City Case*, 8 Op. A. G. 255 (1856). *Cf.* Act of June 7, 1836, 5 Stat. 34 (granting state jurisdiction over given territory, to take effect when Indian title to the country was extinguished).

[59] *Assiniboine Indian Tribe* v. *United States*, 77 C. Cls. 347 (1933), app. dism. 292 U. S. 606.

[60] *Fort Berthold Indians* v. *United States*, 71 C. Cls. 308 (1930).

SECTION 5. TREATY RESERVATIONS

The various ways in which treaty reservations have been established and the different forms of language used in defining the tenure by which such reservations are held, together with the judicial and administrative interpretations placed upon these phrases, have been noted in some detail in Chapter 3, and need not be restated here. It is enough for our present purposes merely to list (*a*) the principal ways in which treaty reservations have been established; (*b*) the principal forms of language used in defining tribal tenure; and (*c*) the more important rules of interpretation placed upon such phraseology.

A. METHODS OF ESTABLISHING TREATY RESERVATIONS

In general, three methods of establishing tribal ownership of lands by treaty were in common use: (1) the recognition of aboriginal title; (2) the exchange of lands; and (3) the purchase of lands.

(1) Usually the first treaty made by the United States with a given tribe recognizes the aboriginal possession of the tribe and defines its geographical extent. When this geographical extent has been defined by treaty with another sovereign, the treaty with the United States may simply confirm such prior definition. Thus, the first published Indian treaty, that of September 17, 1778, with the Delaware Nation,[61] provides:

> Whereas the enemies of the United States have endeavoured, by every artifice in their power, to possess the Indians in general with an opinion, that it is the design of the States aforesaid, to extirpate the Indians and take possession of their country: to obviate such false suggestion, the United States do engage to guarantee to the aforesaid nation of Delawares, and their heirs, all their territorial rights in the fullest and most ample manner, as it hath been bounded by former treaties,[62] as long as they the said Delaware nation shall abide by, and hold fast the chain of friendship now entered into.

A typical treaty fixed a "boundary line between the United States and the Wiandot and Delaware nations."[63]

In many treaties the recognition of aboriginal title was coupled with a cession of portions of the aboriginal domain.[64] Thus, Article 6 of the Treaty of January 31, 1786, with the Shawanoe Nation[65] provides:

> The United States do allot to the Shawanoe nation, lands within their territory to live and hunt upon, beginning at * * *, beyond which lines none of the citizens of the United States shall settle, nor disturb the Shawanoes in their settlement and possessions; and the Shawanoes do relinquish to the United States, all title, or pretence of title, they ever had to the lands east, west, and south, of the east, west and south lines before described.

In some of these treaties the tribe was given a right at a future date to select from the ceded portions additional land for reservation purposes.[66]

(2) A second method of establishing tribal land ownership by treaty was through the exchange of lands held in aboriginal possession for other lands which the United States presumed to grant to the tribe.[67] A typical treaty of this type is that of

[61] Art 6, 7 Stat. 13.

[62] The "former treaties" referred to in this article were treaties with the British Crown and with the Colonies. A similar reference is made in the Treaty of December 17, 1801, with the Chactaw Nation, Art. 3, 7 Stat. 66. ("The two contracting parties covenant and agree that the old line of demarkation heretofore established by and between the officers of his Britannic Majesty and the Chactaw nation * * * shall be retraced and plainly marked, * * * and that the said line shall be the boundary between the settlements of the Mississippi Territory and the Chactaw nation.")

[63] Art 3 of Treaty of January 21, 1785, with the Wiandot, Delaware Chippawa, and Ottawa Nations, 7 Stat. 16. Art. 3 of Treaty of January 3, 1786, with the Choctaw Nation, 7 Stat. 21. ("The boundary of the lands hereby allotted to the Choctaw nation to live and hunt on * * *, is and shall be the following * * *"); Art. 4 of Treaty of August 7, 1790, with the Creek Nation, 7 Stat. 35. ("The boundary between the citizens of the United States and the Creek Nation is, and shall be, * * *.")

[64] Treaty of August 3, 1795, with the Wyandots, Delawares, Shawanoes, Ottawas, Chipewas, Putawatimes, Miamis, Eel River, Weea's, Kickapoos, Piankashaws, and Kaskaskias, 7 Stat. 49; Treaty of May 31, 1796, with the Seven Nations of Canada, 7 Stat. 55; *cf.* Treaty of July 2, 1791, with the Cherokee Nation, 7 Stat. 39, 40; ("The United States solemnly guarantee to the Cherokee nation all their lands not hereby ceded."); Treaty of October 17, 1802, with the Choctaw Nation, 7 Stat. 73; Treaty of December 30, 1805, with the Piankishaw Tribe, 7 Stat. 100; Treaty of November 17, 1807, with the Ottoway, Chippeway, Wyandotte and Pottawatamie Nations, 7 Stat. 105; Treaty of August 24, 1818, with the Quapaw Tribe, 7 Stat. 176; Treaty of September 24, 1819, with the Chippewa Nation, 7 Stat. 203; Treaty of September 18, 1823, with the Florida Tribes, 7 Stat. 224; Treaty of June 2, 1825, with the Great and Little Osage Tribes, 7 Stat. 240; Treaty of June 3, 1825, with the Kansas Nation, 7 Stat. 244; Treaty of October 23, 1826, with the Miami Tribe, 7 Stat. 300.

[65] 7 Stat. 26, 27.

[66] Treaty of August 13, 1803, with the Kaskaskia Nation, 7 Stat. 78.

[67] Treaty of September 29, 1817, with the Wyandot, Seneca, Delaware, Shawanese, Potawatomees, Ottawas, and Chippeway Tribes, 7 Stat. 160;

October 3, 1818, with the Delaware Nation.[68] The first two articles of this treaty provided:

> ART. 1. The Delaware nation of Indians cede to the United States all their claim to land in the state of Indiana.
>
> ART. 2. In consideration of the aforesaid cession, the United States agree to provide for the Delawares a country to reside in, upon the west side of the Mississippi, and to guaranty to them the peaceable possession of the same.

This type of exchange is characteristic of the "removal" treaties whereby many of the eastern and central tribes were induced to move westward.[69]

Another type of treaty wherein an aboriginal domain is ceded to the United States in exchange for other lands arises where a particular tribe combines with another and cedes to the United States its land in exchange for the privilege of participating in the reservation privileges accorded the other tribe.[70] Yet another variation combines the two foregoing basic methods. A typical treaty of this type is that of July 8, 1817, with the Cherokee Nation,[71] wherein it was provided that a portion of the aboriginal lands be ceded in exchange for lands west of the Mississippi but that a portion be retained for those Indians not desirous of migrating west.[72]

(3) A third type of treaty provision for the establishing of reservations, frequently connected with the above two methods, directed the purchase of lands on behalf of the tribe. Generally tribal funds were utilized for such purchase and the purchase was made either from the United States or from another tribe. A typical provision of this type is the following, taken from the Treaty of March 21, 1866, with the Seminoles:

> * * * The United States having obtained by grant of the Creek nation the westerly half of their lands, hereby grant to the Seminole nation the portion thereof hereafter described, * * *. In consideration of said cession of two hundred thousand acres of land described above, the Seminole nation agrees to pay therefor the price of fifty cents per acre, amounting to the sum of one hundred thousand dollars, which amount shall be deducted from the sum paid by the United States for Seminole lands under the stipulations above written.[73]

B. TREATY DEFINITIONS OF TRIBAL PROPERTY RIGHTS

The language used to define the character of the estate guaranteed to an Indian tribe varies so considerably that any detailed classification is likely to be nearly useless. It is possible, however, to distinguish five general types of language commonly utilized.

(1) In a number of treaties the United States undertakes to grant to the tribe concerned a patent in fee simple.[74] In some cases reference is made to the tribe "and their descendants."[75] In a few cases the terms "patent" and "fee simple" are coupled with language indicating that if the tribe ceases to exist as an entity the land will revert or escheat to the United States.[76] In some cases express provision is made restricting alienation.[77] Occasionally the language of the ordinary patent or deed in fee simple is embellished with guarantees stressing the permanent character of the tenure, as in the following language, taken from the Treaty of May 6, 1828, with the Cherokee Nation:[78]

> * * * *a permanent* home, and which shall, under the most solemn guarantee of the United States, be, and remain, theirs forever—a home that shall never, in all future time, be embarrassed by having extended around it the lines, or placed over it the jurisdiction of a Territory or State, nor be pressed upon by the extension, in any way, of any of the limits of any existing Territory or State; * * *.

(2) Other treaties guaranteed ownership or possession, or permanent possession, without using the technical language of the typical patent or grant in fee simple.[79] Thus, for instance,

---

Treaty of July 30, 1819, and July 19, 1820, with the Kickapoo Tribe, 7 Stat. 200, 208; Treaty of November 7, 1825, with the Shawanee Nation, 7 Stat. 284; Treaty of September 27, 1830, with the Choctaw Nation 7 Stat. 333; Treaty of February 28, 1831, with the Seneca Tribe, 7 Stat. 348; Treaty of July 20, 1831, with the Mixed Band of Seneca and Shawnee Indians, 7 Stat. 351; Treaty of August 8, 1831, with the Shawnee Tribe, 7 Stat. 355; Treaty of August 30, 1831, with the Ottoway Indians, 7 Stat. 359; Treaty of September 15, 1832, with the Winnebago Nation, 7 Stat. 370; Treaty of October 24, 1832, with the Kickapoo Tribe, 7 Stat. 391; Treaty of November 6, 1838, with the Miami Tribe, 7 Stat. 569; Treaty of October 11, 1842, with the Confederated Tribes of Sac and Fox, 7 Stat. 596; Treaty of March 17, 1842, with the Wyandott Nation, 11 Stat. 581.

[68] 7 Stat. 188.

[69] See Chapter 3, sec. 4E.

[70] Treaty of September 25, 1818, with the Peoria, Kaskaskia, Mitchigamia, Cahokia and Tamarois Tribes of the Illinois Nation, 7 Stat. 181; Treaty of November 15, 1824, with the Quapaw Nation, 7 Stat. 232.

[71] 7 Stat. 156.

[72] Treaty of January 24, 1826, with the Creek Nation, 7 Stat. 286. See also Treaty of October 18, 1820, with the Choctaw Nation, 7 Stat. 210 ("Whereas it is an important object with the President of the United States, to promote the civilization of the Choctaw Indians, by the establishment of schools amongst them; and to perpetuate them as a nation, by exchanging, for a small part of their land here, a country beyond the Mississippi River, where all, who live by hunting and will not work, may be collected and settled together. * * *").

[73] Art. 3, 14 Stat. 755. See also Treaty of December 29, 1835, with the Cherokee Tribe, 7 Stat. 478, 480 ("* * * the United States in consideration of the sum of five hundred thousand dollars therefore hereby covenant and agree to convey to the said Indians * * * the following additional tract of land").

[74] Treaty of March 17, 1842, with the Wyandott Nation, 11 Stat. 581 ("both of these cessions to be made in fee simple to the Wyandotts, and to their heirs forever"). And see Chapter 3, sec. 4

[75] Treaty of December 29, 1835, with the Cherokee Tribe, 7 Stat. 478 ("the United States * * * hereby covenant and agree to convey to the said Indians, and their descendants by patent, in fee simple * * *").

[76] Treaty of September 20, 1816, with the Chickasaw Nation, 7 Stat. 150; Treaty of September 27, 1830, with the Choctaw Nation, 7 Stat. 333 ("in fee simple to them and their descendants, to inure to them while they shall exist as a nation and live on it"); Treaty of February 28, 1831, with the Seneca Tribe, 7 Stat. 348; Treaty of July 20, 1831, with the Mixed Band of Seneca and Shawnee Indians, 7 Stat. 351; Treaty of August 8, 1831, with the Shawnee Tribe, 7 Stat. 355; Treaty of August 30, 1831, with the Ottoway Indians, 7 Stat. 359; Treaty of February 14, 1833, with the Creek Nation, Art. 3, 7 Stat. 417 ("The United States will grant a patent, in fee simple, to the Creek nation of Indians * * *, and the right thus guarranteed by the United States shall be continued to said tribe of Indians, so long as they shall exist as a nation, and continue to occupy the country hereby assigned them").

[77] Treaty of December 29, 1832, with the United Nation of Senecas and Shawnee Indians, 7 Stat. 411, 412 ("The said patents shall be granted in fee simple; but the lands shall not be sold or ceded without the consent of the United States"); *cf.* Treaty of July 30, 1819, and July 19, 1820, with the Kickapoo Tribe, 7 Stat. 200, 208 ("to them, and their heirs for ever * * *. *Provided, nevertheless,* That the said tribe shall never sell the said land without the consent of the President of the United States").

[78] 7 Stat. 311.

[79] Treaty of September 24, 1829, with the Delaware Indians, 7 Stat. 327 ("And the United States hereby pledges the faith of the government to guarantee to the said Delaware Nation forever, the quiet and peaceable possession and undisturbed enjoyment of the same, against the claims and assaults of all and every other people whatever."); Treaty of October 11, 1842, with the Confederated Tribes of Sac and Fox, 7 Stat. 596 ("to the Sacs and Foxes for a permanent and perpetual residence for them and their descendants * * *"); Treaty of August 3, 1795, with the Wyandots, Delawares, Shawanoes, Ottawas, Chipewas, Putawatimes, Miamis, Eel-river, Weea's, Kickapoos, Piankashaws, and Kaskaskias, 7 Stat. 49, 52 ("The Indian tribes who have a right to those lands, are quietly to enjoy them, hunting, planting, and dwelling thereon so long as they please * * *"); Treaty of October 24, 1832, with the Kickapoo Tribe, 7 Stat. 391 ("and secured by the United States, to the said Kickapoo tribe, as their permanent residence").

Article 4 of the Treaty of August 18, 1804, with the Delaware Nation [80] recognized the Delawares "as the rightful owners of all the country which is bounded * * *."[81]

(3) Various other treaties used language which if literally construed restricts the Indian possession to a particular form of land utilization, but which may be construed as an outright grant in nontechnical language. Phraseology of this sort was analyzed by Marshall, *C. J.*, in *Worcester* v. *Georgia*,[82] where he noted that the use of the term "hunting grounds" in describing the country guaranteed to the Cherokees did not mean that the land could not be used for the establishment of villages or the planting of cornfields.

(4) Particularly in the later treaties, phrases such as "use and occupancy" are increasingly utilized.[83]

(5) Finally, a number of treaties dodge the problem of defining the Indian estate by providing that specified lands shall be held "as Indian lands are held,"[84] or as an Indian reservation,[85] thus ignoring the fact that considerable differences may exist with respect to the tenures by which various tribes hold their land.

C. PRINCIPLES OF TREATY INTERPRETATION

Apart from general principles of treaty interpretation discussed in Chapter 3, certain holdings with respect to the interpretation of treaty provisions establishing tribal land ownership deserve special note at this point.

(1) By way of caution against the notion that all Indian treaty reservations are held under a single form of ownership, one may note the comment of the Court of Claims in the case of *Crow Nation* v. *United States:*[86]

> * * * the title derived by an Indian tribe, through the setting apart of a reservation, depends entirely upon the terms of the treaty which is entered into between the parties, and that, where there is simply a reservation set apart for the Indian Nation, no fee simple or base fee is granted to the tribe, but only a right of occupancy.

(2) The question whether a treaty incorporates a grant *in praesenti*, or an executory promise, was considered in the case of the *New York Indians* v. *United States.*[87] Although the treaty used the words "agreed to set apart," the court held that the context and circumstances showed that the treaty was understood to effectuate a grant *in praesenti.*[88]

(3) It has been held that the mere use of the term "grant" in Indian treaties does not indicate an intent to establish fee simple tenure.[89]

(4) Likewise, it has been held that the language of a "grant" does not necessarily evidence a desire to grant new property rights but may constitute simply a method of defining and reserving aboriginal rights.[90]

(5) Where the United States has made a treaty promise that certain land "shall be confirmed by patent to the said Christian Indians, subject to such restrictions as Congress may provide,"[91] and Congress has not provided any restrictions, the tribe is entitled to receive an ordinary patent granting title in fee simple, rather than "the usual Indian title."[92]

Other questions of the interpretation of treaty clauses are considered in later portions of this chapter, particularly in sections 12 to 16, and in Chapter 3, section 2.

It is doubtful whether any broad principles of interpretation that would be at all useful can be derived from the cases in this field, but in subsequent sections of this chapter we shall be concerned to analyze specific questions concerning the nature of the estate granted by the various phrases classified in the foregoing sections.

---

[80] 7 Stat. 81.

[81] See Treaty of January 7, 1806, with the Cherokee Nation, 7 Stat. 101, 103 ("and will secure to the Cherokees the title to the said reservations").

[82] 6 Pet. 515, 553 (1832).

[83] Treaty of May 31, 1796, with the Seven Nations of Canada, 7 Stat. 55 ("to be applied to the use of the Indians of * * * St. Regis"); *cf.* Treaty of January 9, 1789, with the Wiandot, Delaware, Ottawa, Chippewa, Pattawattima, and Sac Nations, 7 Stat. 28, 29 ("to live and hunt upon, and otherwise to occupy as they shall see fit").

[84] Treaty of May 12, 1854, with the Menomonees, 10 Stat. 1064. *Cf.* Art. 2, Treaty of September 26, 1833, with the United Nation of Chippewas, Potawatamies and Ottowas, 7 Stat. 431.

[85] Treaty of October 2, 1818, with the Wea Tribe, 7 Stat. 186 ("to be holden by the said tribe as Indian reservations are usually held"). *Cf.* Treaty of September 17, 1818, with the Wyandot, Seneca, Shawnese, and Ottawa Tribes, 7 Stat. 178 ("and held by them in the same manner as Indian reservations have been heretofore held. But [it] is further agreed, that the tracts thus reserved shall be reserved for the use of the Indians named * * * and held by them and their heirs forever, unless ceded to the United States."); Treaty of September 20, 1817, with the Wyandot, Seneca, Delaware, Shawanese, Potawatomees, Ottawas and Chippeway Tribes, 7 Stat. 160 ("grant, by patent, to the chiefs * * * for the use of the said tribe, * * * which tracts, thus granted, shall be held by the said tribe, upon the usual conditions of Indian reservations, as though no patent were issued.")

[86] 81 C. Cls. 238, 275 (1935).

[87] 170 U. S. 1 (1898); followed in *United States* v. *New York Indians*, 173 U. S. 464 (1899).

[88] Treaty of January 15, 1838, with New York Indians, 7 Stat. 550. See also *Godfrey* v. *Beardsley*, 10 Fed. Cas. No. 5497 (C. C. Ind. 1841), holding that a treaty can operate as a grant of title to lands. Accord: *Jones* v. *Meehan*, 175 U. S. 1 (1899).

[89] Title of the Brothertowns under the Menominie Treaty, 3 Op. A. G. 322 (1838) ("the Indian tribes, under the policy of this government, in their natural capacity, cannot hold the absolute title to lands occupied by them, except when specially provided for by treaty; * * *"); *Goodfellow* v. *Muckey*, 10 Fed. Cas. No. 5537 (C. C. Kans. 1881), holding that unless there is a clear and explicit provision in the treaty showing that the Government intended to make the grant in fee simple the court will presume that the treaty granted but a right of occupancy to the Indians.

[90] See *United States* v. *Romaine*, 255 Fed. 253, 260 (C. C. A. 9, 1919) (interpreting Treaty of January 22, 1855, with various tribes of Oregon Territory, 12 Stat. 927); *Gaines* v. *Nicholson*, 9 How. 356, 364 (1850); *United States* v. *Winans*, 198 U. S. 371 (1905), rev'g. 73 Fed. 72 (C. C. Wash. 1896).

[91] Treaty of May 6, 1854, with the Delaware Indians, 10 Stat. 1048.

[92] 9 Op. A. G. 24 (1857).

SECTION 6. STATUTORY RESERVATIONS

Sporadically during the treaty-making period and regularly since its expiration, tribal property rights in land have been established by specific acts of Congress. These acts vary from specific grants of fee simple rights to broad designations that a given area shall be used for the benefit of Indians, or that Indian occupancy of designated areas shall be respected by third parties. Legislation establishing Indian reservations follows various patterns.

(1) Perhaps the most common type of such legislation today is that which *reserves* a portion of the public domain from entry or sale and dedicates the reserved area to Indian use. The designated area is "set aside" or "reserved" for a given tribe, band, or group of Indians.[93] Frequently the statute uses the

---

[93] *E. g.*, Act of March 3, 1863, 12 Stat. 819 ("assign to and set apart for the Sisseton, Wahpaton, Medawakanton, and Wahpakoota bands of Sioux Indians"); Act of May 21, 1926, 44 Stat. 614 (Makah and Quileute Indians); Act of March 3, 1928, 45 Stat. 162 (Indians of Indian Ranch, Inyo County, California).

phrase "reserved for the sole use and occupancy" [94] or some similar phrase.[95] Other statutes of this type provide that designated lands shall be "reserved as additions to" named reservations,[96] or, that the boundaries of a designated reservation are "extended to include" specified lands.[97] Occasionally the public lands so set aside are lands which have previously been used for another purpose and the prior purpose may be mentioned in the statute.[98] In some of these statutes the designation of the Indian beneficiaries of the reservation to be established is delegated to administrative discretion. These statutes, typically, provide that given lands shall be reserved for the use and occupancy of certain named bands or tribes "and such other Indians as the Secretary of the Interior may see fit to settle thereon." [99]

(2) Another and a distinct type of statute authorizes the purchase either by voluntary sale or by condemnation [100] of private lands for Indian use, and allocates therefor funds in the United States Treasury not otherwise appropriated,[101] or, in the alternative, tribal funds of the tribe benefited.[102] Some of these statutes authorize the purchase of land for Indians without using the word "reservation." [103] Since the decision of the Supreme Court in *United States* v. *McGowan*,[104] it has been clear that there is no magic in the word "reservation" and that land purchased for Indian use and occupancy is a "reservation," at least within the meaning of the Indian liquor laws, whether or not the statute uses the term. Although the issue presented in the *McGowan* case was one of criminal jurisdiction rather than of property right, the views therein expressed appear to be as pertinent to the demarcation of tribal property as to the delimitation of federal jurisdiction. The Court declared, *per* Black, J., "It is immaterial whether Congress designates a settlement as a 'reservation' or 'colony' " (pp. 538, 539). The Court, quoting from its earlier opinion in *United States* v. *Pelican*,[105] indicated that the important issue was whether the land had "been validly set apart for the use of the Indians as such, under the superintendence of the Government" (p. 539). The determination of this question requires an ascertainment of the purpose underlying the particular legislation, to which end consideration may be given to committee hearings and reports (p. 537).

(3) In addition to the two major methods of establishing Indian reservations by statute, *public land withdrawal* and *purchase of private land*, a third method, the surrender of private lands in exchange for public lands, is followed in a number of statutes. A typical statute is that of June 14, 1934,[106] commonly known as the Arizona Navajo Boundary Act, which authorizes the Secretary of the Interior in his discretion to accept relinquishments and reconveyances to the United States of such privately owned lands as in his opinion are desirable for, and should be reserved for the use and benefit of, a particular tribe of Indians, "so that the lands retained for Indian purposes may be consolidated and held in a solid area as far as may be possible." [107] Upon conveyance to the United States of a good and sufficient title to such privately owned land, the owners thereof, or their asigns, are authorized under regulations of the Secretary of the Interior, to select lands approximately equal in value to the lands thus conveyed. Similar in effect are statutes authorizing the grant of public lands to a state in exchange for the relinquishment of state lands for Indian use.[108]

---

[94] Act of March 3. 1928. 45 Stat. 162 (Koosharem Band of Indians in Utah); Act of May 23. 1928. 45 Stat. 717 (Indians of the Acoma Pueblo); Act of February 11, 1929, 45 Stat. 1161 (Kanosh Band of Indians in Utah); Act of June 20, 1935, 49 Stat. 393 (Kanosh Band of Indians of Utah).

[95] Act of March 3. 1807. 2 Stat. 448 ("reserved for the use of the said [Delaware] tribe and their descendants, so long as they continue to reside thereon, and cultivate the same"). Act of April 12. 1924. 43 Stat. 92 (Zia Pueblo); Act of March 3, 1925, 43 Stat. 1114 ("Navajo Indians residing in that immediate vicinity"); Act of May 10. 1926. 44 Stat. 496 (Mesa Grande Reservation); Act of June 1. 1926, 44 Stat. 679 (Morongo Indian Reservation); Act of March 3, 1928. 45 Stat. 160 (Indians of the Walker River Reservation); Act of February 11. 1929. 45 Stat. 1161 (San Ildefonso Pueblo); Act of January 17. 1936. 49 Stat. 1094 (Indians of the former Fort McDermitt Military Reservation, Nev.).

[96] Act of February 21. 1931. 46 Stat. 1201 (Temecula or Pechanga Indian Reservation); Act of February 12. 1932. 47 Stat. 50 (Skull Valley Indian Reservation); Act of May 14. 1935. 49 Stat. 217 (Rocky Boy Indian Reservation); Act of June 22. 1936, 49 Stat. 1806 (Walker River Indian Reservation). and *cf.* Act of April 22. 1937. 50 Stat. 72 ("set aside as an addition to the Barona Ranch, a tract of land purchased for the Capitan Grande Band of Mission Indians under authority contained in the Act of May 4. 1932. 47 Stat. L. 146").

[97] Act of May 28, 1937, 50 Stat. 241 (Koosharem Indian Reservation in Utah).

[98] Act of June 7. 1935. 49 Stat. 332 (Veterans' Administration lands to be held by the United States in trust for the Yavapai Indians); Act of June 20. 1935. 49 Stat. 393 (National Forest lands "eliminated from the Cibola National Forest and withdrawn as an addition to the Zuni Indian Reservation").

[99] Act of April 15. 1874. 18 Stat. 28 ("use and occupation of the Gros Ventre, Piegan, Blood, Blackfoot, River Crow, and such other Indians as the President may, from time to time, see fit to locate thereon"); Act of September 7. 1916. 39 Stat. 739 ("set apart as a reservation for Rocky Boy's Band of Chippewa and such other homeless Indians in the State of Montana as the Secretary of the Interior may see fit to locate thereon"); Act of May 31. 1924, 43 Stat. 246 ("certain bands of Paiute Indians, and such other Indians of this tribe as the Secretary of the Interior may see fit to settle thereon"); Act of March 3 1928. 45 Stat. 160 (Paiute and Shoshone); Act of April 13. 1938. 52 Stat. 216 (Goshute). *Cf.* Act of April 8. 1864, sec. 2, 13 Stat. 39 ("tracts of land * * * to be retained by the United States for the purposes of Indian reservations, which shall be of suitable extent for the accommodation of the Indians of said state [California]"); Act of May 5. 1864, sec. 2, 13 Stat. 63 ("set apart for the permanent settlement and exclusive occupation of such of the different tribes of Indians of said territory [Utah] as may be induced to inhabit the same").

On the interpretation of this language, see sec. 1D, *supra*, and sec. 7, *infra*.

[100] Act of June 23. 1926. 44 Stat. 763: applied in *United States* v. *4,450.72 Acres of Land*, 27 F. Supp. 167 (D. C. Minn. 1939).

[101] Act of June 7. 1924. 43 Stat. 596 ("to purchase a tract of land, with sufficient water right attached, for the use and occupancy of the Temoak Band of homeless Indians, located at Ruby Valley, Nevada: *Provided*, That the title to said land is to be held in the United States for the benefit of said Indians"); Act of April 14. 1926. 44 Stat. 252 (Cahuilla); Act of June 8. 1926. 44 Stat. 690 (Santa Ysabel Indian Reservation); Act of January 31. 1931. 46 Stat. 1046 ("purchase of a village site for the Indians now living near Elko. Nevada"); Act of April 17, 1937, 50 Stat. 69 (Santa Rosa Band of Mission Indians).

[102] Act of February 12. 1927. 44 Stat. 1089 (Jicarilla Reservation); Act of May 29. 1928. 45 Stat. 962 (Fort Apache Reservation); Act of April 18, 1930, 46 Stat. 218 (Wind River Reservation); Act of March 4, 1931, 46 Stat. 1517 (Fort Apache Indian Reservation) ("title thereto to be taken in the name of the United States in trust for said [Fort Apache] Indians"); Act of March 4, 1931, 46 Stat. 1522 (Cahuilla Reservation).

[103] Act of July 1, 1922. 37 Stat. 187 (Wisconsin Winnebagoes); Act of September 21. 1922. 42 Stat. 991 (Apache Indians of Oklahoma); Act of March 2. 1925, 43 Stat. 1096 ("for the use and occupancy of a small band of the Piute Indians now residing thereon: *Provided*, That the title to said lots is to be held in the United States for the benefit of said Indians"); Act of May 10. 1926. 44 Stat. 496 ("added to and become a part of the site for the Reno Indian colony"); Act of June 27, 1930. 46 Stat. 820 (lands occupied by "Indian colony" to be purchased. "the title to be held in the name of the United States Government, for the use of the Indians").

[104] 302 U. S. 535 (1938), rev'g 89 F. 2d 201 (C. C. A. 9, 1937), aff'g sub nom. *United States* v. *One Chevrolet Sedan*, 16 F. Supp. 453 (D. C. Nev. 1936).

[105] 232 U. S 442, 449 (1914).

[106] 48 Stat. 960.

[107] Act of March 3, 1925, 43 Stat. 1115. See also: Act of May 23, 1930, 46 Stat. 378, as amended by Act of February 21. 1931, 46 Stat. 1204 (Western Navajo Indian Reservation); Act of March 1, 1933, 47 Stat. 1418 (Navajo Reservation in Utah); Act of May 23, 1934, 48 Stat. 795 (Fort Mojave).

[108] Act of February 11, 1903, 32 Stat. 822 (disputed lands confirmed to Torros Band of Mission Indians and new public domain lands transferred to state); Act of March 1, 1921, 41 Stat. 1103; Act of June 14,

Various combinations[109] as well as minor variations[110] of the foregoing three basic methods have been used in other statutes.

(4) Distinct mention should be made of "reservation removal" statutes which authorize the sale of reservation lands and the reinvestment of the proceeds of such sale in the acquisition of new lands for the benefit of the tribe concerned.[111] Generally such statutes provide for the consent of the Indians.[112]

(5) A fifth type of statute establishing tribal property in reservation lands involves the restoration to a tribe of lands previously removed from tribal ownership.[113]

(6) A sixth source of tribal title is congressional legislation approving voluntary transfers of lands by another tribe,[114] state,[115] or individual.[116]

(7) Finally, it should be noted that tribal ownership is frequently confirmed, if not created, in allotment and cession acts, with respect to lands withheld from allotment or cession.[117] Similar are statutes which divide up a single reservation among various component tribes or bands,[118] such division being based upon the consent of the Indians concerned.

A. LEGISLATIVE DEFINITIONS OF TRIBAL PROPERTY RIGHTS

The foregoing statutes, except as otherwise noted, generally provide for the establishment of tribal lands, or reservations, without defining the precise character of the tribal interest therein. Certain statutes, however, seek to define precisely the extent of such tribal interest.

A number of these statutes, for instance, specify that a fee-simple title shall be vested in the Indian tribe.[119] Of particular importance in this category are the statutes authorizing the patenting of land to the Pueblos of New Mexico and to the Mission Bands of California Indians. The former of these statutes[120] is analyzed in Chapter 20, section 6, of this volume. The latter statute[121] directed the Secretary of the Interior to appoint three commissioners (sec. 1) for the purpose of selecting

> * * * a reservation for each band or village of the Mission Indians residing within said State, which reservation shall include, as far as practicable, the lands and villages which have been in the actual occupation and possession of said Indians, and which shall be sufficient in extent to meet their just requirements, which selection shall be valid when approved by the President and Secretary of the Interior. (Sec. 2.)

The Secretary of the Interior was directed to issue a patent for each of the reservations,

> * * * which patents shall be of the legal effect, and declare that the United States does and will hold the land thus patented, subject to the provisions of section four of this act, for the period of twenty-five years, in trust, for the sole use and benefit of the band or village to which it it issued, and that at the expiration of said period the United States will convey the same or the remaining portion not previously patented in severalty by patent to said band or village, discharged of said trust, and free of all charge or incumbrance whatsoever * * *. (Sec. 3.)

The Secretary of the Interior was further authorized to cause allotments to be made out of such reservation land to any Indian residing upon such patented land who shall be so advanced in civilization as to be capable of owning and managing land in severalty (sec. 4). Individual patents were to "override" the group patent (sec. 5). The Attorney General was directed to

---

1935. 49 Stat. 339 ("Upon conveyance to the United States by the State of Florida of a sufficient title to the lands to be acquired for the use of Seminole Indians, the Secretary of the Interior is authorized to issue a patent * * * to the State of Florida * * *").

[109] Act of June 23, 1926, 44 Stat. 763 (Chippewa); Act of February 21, 1931, sec. 1, 46 Stat. 1202 (public lands "reserved for the use and occupancy of the Papago Indians as an addition to the Papago Indian Reservation, Arizona, whenever all privately owned lands except mining claims within said addition have been purchased and acquired as hereinafter authorized"); Act of April 13, 1938, 52 Stat. 216 (Goshute). The first named statute provides for the use of condemnation powers to complete consolidation of a given reservation, and authorizes the use of tribal funds to pay for lands acquired.

[110] Act of May 29, 1935, 49 Stat. 312 (Minnesota National Park Reserve lands transferred to Chippewa tribe upon repayment of sums originally paid tribe for such lands); Act of August 28, 1937, 50 Stat. 864 (interests in Blackfeet lands acquired for federal reclamation purposes resold to tribe). *Cf.* Act of February 26, 1925, 43 Stat. 1003 (Kiowa, Comanche, and Apache).

[111] Act of June 5, 1872, 17 Stat. 228, 229 ("set apart for and confirmed as their [Osage] reservation"); Act of April 10, 1876, 19 Stat. 28 ("purchase of a suitable reservation in the Indian territory for the Pawnee tribe of Indians"); Act of February 28, 1919, 40 Stat. 1206 ("purchase of additional lands for the Capitan Grande Band of Indians * * * to properly establish these Indians permanently on the lands purchased for them").

[112] Act of March 3, 1885, sec. 5, 23 Stat. 351, 352 (Sac and Fox and Iowa); Act of March 3, 1881, sec. 5, 21 Stat. 380, 381 ("That the Secretary of the Interior may, with the consent of the [Otoe and Missouria] Indians, expressed in open council, secure other reservation lands upon which to locate said Indians * * * and expend such sum * * * to be drawn from the fund arising from the sale of their reservation lands").

[113] Act of May 24, 1924, 43 Stat. 138 (trust patents canceled and lands restored to the status of tribal property). Accord: Act of May 24, 1924, 43 Stat. 138 (Winnebago); Act of February 13, 1929, 45 Stat. 1167 (agency lands revested in Yankton Sioux Tribe); Act of March 3, 1927, 44 Stat. 1401 (Fort Peck; payments for agency land refunded to Federal Government); see also the Indian Reorganization Act, June 18, 1934, 48 Stat. 984, which in sec. 3 provides that, "The Secretary of the Interior, if he shall find it to be in the public interest, is hereby authorized to restore to tribal ownership the remaining surplus lands of any Indian reservation heretofore opened, or authorized to be opened, to sale, or any other form of disposal by Presidential proclamation, or by any of the public-land laws of the United States: * * *." For a more detailed discussion see section 7 of this chapter.

[114] Joint Resolution of July 25, 1848, 9 Stat. 337 (cession by Delaware Tribe to Wyandottes); Act of February 23, 1889, 25 Stat. 687 (agreement for the settlement of Lemhi Indians upon Fort Hall Reservation).

[115] Act of February 15, 1929, 45 Stat. 1186 (Alabama and Coushatta Indians of Texas).

[116] Act of August 14, 1876, 19 Stat. 139 (lands to be accepted by the Commissioner of Indian Affairs "and conveyed to the Eastern Band of Cherokee Indians in fee-simple").

[117] "* * * set apart * * * for school, church, and cemetery purposes * * * shall be held as common property of the respective tribes." Act of March 2, 1889, sec. 1, 25 Stat. 1013 (United Peorias and Miamies); Act of June 28, 1898, sec. 11, 30 Stat. 495, 497 (Indian Territory); Act of June 6, 1900, sec. 6, 31 Stat. 672, 677 (set aside for the use in common by said Indian tribes [Kiowa, Comanche, and Apache] 400,000 acres of grazing land); Joint Resolution of June 19, 1902, 32 Stat. 744 (Walker River, Uintah); Act of December 21, 1904, 33 Stat. 595 (Yakima); Act of June 4, 1920, 41 Stat. 751 (Crow); Act of May 19, 1924, 43 Stat. 132 (Lac du Flambeau Band of Chippewas); Act of February 13, 1929, 45 Stat. 1167 (Yankton Sioux).

[118] Act of April 30, 1888, 25 Stat. 94 (Sioux); Act of May 1, 1888; 25 Stat. 113 (Fort Peck, Fort Belknap, Blackfeet).

[119] Act of August 14, 1876, 19 Stat. 139 (Eastern Cherokees); Act of March 3, 1885, secs. 7 and 8, 23 Stat. 351, 352 (Sac and Fox and Iowa); Act of May 17, 1926, 44 Stat. 561 ("Title to * * * is hereby confirmed to the Sac and Fox Nation or Tribe of Indians unconditionally"); Act of June 6, 1932, 47 Stat. 169 (Secretary of the Interior authorized to "convey by deed" abandoned Indian school lands "to the L'Anse Band of Lake Superior Indians for community meetings and other like purposes * * * *Provided,* That said conveyance shall be made to three members of the band duly elected by said Indians as trustees for the band and their successors in office"); Act of February 13, 1929, 45 Stat. 1167 ("all claim, right, title, and interest in and to" agency lands revested in Yankton Sioux Tribe). *Cf.* Act of June 3, 1926, 44 Stat. 690 (declaring executive order reservation lands set apart for "permanent use and occupancy" to be "the property of said Indians, subject to such control and management of said property as the Congress of the United States may direct.")

[120] Act of December 22, 1858, 11 Stat. 374 ("a patent to issue therefor as in ordinary cases to private individuals"); extended to Zuni Pueblo by Act of March 3, 1931, 46 Stat. 1509.

[121] Act of January 12, 1891, 26 Stat. 712.

defend the rights of Indian groups "secured to them in the original grants from the Mexican Government" (sec. 6).

The provisions of this legislation have been modified in certain respects by later enactments[132] and have been incorporated by reference in a number of subsequent acts dealing with the Mission Indians of California.[133]

While the foregoing statutes may be construed to grant an estate greater than the ordinary tribal title, there are other statutes which rigidly confine the interest of the Indians in a given tract by specifying the particular purpose for which the tract is to be used.[134] Other statutes specify that the land is established for Indian use under the supervision of the Secretary of the Interior or under rules and regulations to be prescribed by him,[135] or that the land shall not be subject to allotment.[136]

[132] The Act of March 2, 1917, 39 Stat. 969, 976, provided that the President might extend the 25-year trust period. Such power to extend must be exercised before the expiration of the period or it lapses. Op. Sol. I. D., M. 27939, April 9, 1935. After expiration, the period may be extended by Congress. Act of February 11, 1936, 49 Stat. 1106 (Pala Band of Mission Indians). Other acts extending these trust periods include Act of February 8, 1927, 44 Stat. 1061.

[133] Act of February 21, 1931, 46 Stat. 1201 (Temecula or Pechanga Mission); Act of March 4, 1931, 46 Stat. 1522 (Cahuilla Mission).

[134] Act of February 20, 1895, 28 Stat. 677 (Southern Ute) ("That for the sole and exclusive use and occupancy of such of said Indians as may not elect or be deemed qualified to take allotments of land in severalty, as provided in the preceding section, there shall be, and is hereby, set apart and reserved all that portion of their present reservation lying * * * subject, however, to the right of the Government to erect and maintain agency buildings thereon and to grant rights of way through the same for railroads, irrigation ditches, highways, and other necessary purposes; and the Government shall maintain an agency at some suitable place on said lands so reserved"). *Cf.* Act of June 30, 1864 sec. 2, 13 Stat. 323 (Navajoe and Apache). Joint Resolution of January 30, 1897, 29 Stat. 698 (Fort Bidwell; lands to be used by the Secretary of the Interior "for the purposes of an Indian training school"); Act of May 14, 1898, sec. 10, 30 Stat. 409, 413; Act of May 27, 1910, 36 Stat. 440 (Pine Ridge); Act of May 30, 1910, 36 Stat. 448 (Rosebud) (Secretary of the Interior authorized to reserve "such lands as he may deem necessary for agency, school and religious purposes, to remain reserved as long as needed and as long as agency, school, or religious institutions are maintained thereon for the benefit of said Indians"); Act of May 31, 1924, 43 Stat. 246 ("reserved for and as a school site" for the Ute Indians); Act of June 23, 1926, 44 Stat. 763; Act of June 24, 1926, 44 Stat. 768 (for the use of the Yakima Indians and confederated tribes as a burial ground); Act of June 28, 1926, 44 Stat. 775 ("agency reserve of the Papago Indian Reservation"); Act of March 3, 1927, 44 Stat. 1389 (addition to United States Indian school farm); Act of May 21, 1928, 45 Stat. 684 (public lands "permanently reserved for said village site for said [Chippewa] Indians"); Act of March 28, 1932, 47 Stat. 74 (for cemetery purposes).

[135] Act of March 3, 1891, sec. 15, 26 Stat. 1095 (Metlakatla Indians); Act of June 23, 1926, 44 Stat. 763 (Chippewa Indians of Minnesota).

[136] Act of March 3, 1891, sec. 15, 26 Stat. 1095 (Metlakatla Indians); Act of February 13, 1929, 45 Stat. 1167 (Yankton Sioux).

SECTION 7. EXECUTIVE ORDER RESERVATIONS

Although the practice of establishing Indian reservations by Executive order goes back at least to May 18, 1855,[137] the practice rested on an uncertain legislative foundation prior to the General Allotment Act.[138] In fact, so uncertain was the legislative foundation for the exercising of the power by the Executive that the Attorney General in upholding its legality in an opinion rendered in 1882, did so chiefly on the basis that the practice had been followed for many years and Congress had never objected.[139]

Questions as to the validity of already established Executive order reservations were settled[140] by the language of the General Allotment Act which referred to "any reservation created for their use, either by treaty stipulation or by virtue of an Act of Congress or Executive order setting apart the same for their use * * *" (sec. 1). The view that Executive order reservations have exactly the same validity and status as any other type of reservation is expressed in a carefully documented opinion of Attorney General Stone, rendered with respect to the validity of attempts by Secretary of the Interior Fall to dispose of minerals within Executive order Indian reservations under the laws governing minerals within the public domain. In holding the proposed practice to be illegal, the Attorney General declared:

> That the President had authority at the date of the orders to withdraw public lands and set them apart for the benefit of the Indians, or for other public purposes, is now settled beyond the possibility of controversy. *United States* v. *Midwest Oil Co.*, 236 U. S. 459; *Mason* v. *United States*, 260 U. S. 545. And aside from this, the General Indian Allotment Act of February 8, 1887 (24 Stat. 388, Sec. 1), clearly recognizes and by necessary implication confirms Indian reservations "heretofore" or "hereafter" established by executive orders.
>
> Whether the President might legally abolish, in whole or in part, Indian reservations once created by him, has been seriously questioned (12 L. D. 205; 13 L. D. 628) and not without strong reason; for the Indian rights attach when the lands are thus set aside; and moreover, the lands then at once become subject to allotment under the General Allotment Act. Nevertheless, the President has in fact, and in a number of instances, changed the boundaries of executive order Indian reservations by excluding lands therefrom, and the question of his authority to do so has not apparently come before the courts.
>
> When, by an executive order, public lands are set aside, either as a new Indian reservation or an addition to an old one without further language indicating that the action is a mere temporary expedient, such lands are thereafter properly known and designated as an "Indian reservation;" and so long, at least, as the order continues in force, the Indians have the right of occupancy and use and the United States has the title in fee. *Spalding* v. *Chandler*, 160 U. S. 394; *In re Wilson*, 140 U. S. 575.
>
> But a right of "occupancy" or "occupancy and use" in the Indians with the fee title in the sovereign (the Crown, the original States, the United States) is the same condition of title which has prevailed in this country from the beginning, except in a few instances like those of the Cherokees and Choctaws, who received patents for their new tribal lands on removing to the West. And the Indian right of occupancy is as sacred as the fee title of the sovereign.
>
> The courts have applied this legal theory indiscriminately to lands subject to the original Indian occupancy, to reservations resulting from the cession by Indians of part of their original lands and the retention of the remainder, to reservations established in the West in exchange for lands in the East, and to reservations created by treaty, Act of Congress, or executive order, out of "public lands." The rights of the Indians were always those of occupancy and use and the fee was in the United States. *Johnson* v. *McIntosh*, 8 Wheat. 543; *Mitchell* v. *United States*, 9 Pet. 711, 745; *United States* v. *Cook*, 19 Wall. 591; *Leavenworth, etc. R. R. Co.* v. *United States*, 92 U. S. 733, 742; *Seneca Nation* v. *Christy*, 162 U. S. 283, 288–9; *Beecher* v. *Wetherby*, 95 U. S. 517, 525; *Minnesota* v. *Hitchcock*, 185 U. S. 373, 388 et seq.; *Lone Wolf* v. *Hitchcock*, 187 U. S. 553; *Jones* v. *Meehan*, 175 U. S. 1;

[137] 34 Op. A. G. 181, 186–189 (1924).

[138] Act of February 8, 1887, 24 Stat. 388.

[139] Indian Reservations, 17 Op. A. G. 258 (1882); in 1887 the Attorney General ruled that an act of Congress would be necessary in order to establish a reservation in Alaska for Indians emigrating from Canada since the President's "power to declare permanent reservation for Indians to the exclusion of others on the public domain does not extend to Indians not born or resident in the United States." 18 Op. A. G. 557, 559 (1887).

[140] See 29 Op. A. G. 239, 241 (1911); and see *In re Wilson*, 140 U. S. 575, 577 (1891).

Spalding v. *Chandler*, 160 U. S. 394; *M'Fadden* v. *Mountain View Min. & Mill. Co.*, 97 Fed. 670, 673; *Gibson* v. *Anderson*, 131 Fed. 39.

In *Spalding* v. *Chandler*, *supra*, which involved an executive order Indian reservation, the Supreme Court said (pp. 402, 403):

> "It has been settled by repeated adjudications of this court that the fee of the land in this country in the original occupation of the Indian tribes was from the time of the formation of this government vested in the United States. The Indian title as against the United States was merely a title and right to the perpetual occupancy of the land with the privilege of using it in such mode as they saw fit until such right of occupation had been surrendered to the government. When Indian reservations were created, either by treaty or executive order, the Indians held the land by the same character of title, to wit, the right to possess and occupy the lands for the uses and purposes designated."

In *M'Fadden* v. *Mountain View Min. & Mill. Co.*, *supra*, the Circuit Court of Appeals for the Ninth Circuit said (p. 673):

> "On the 9th day of April, 1872, an executive order was issued by President Grant, by which was set apart as a reservation for certain specified Indians, and for such other Indians as the department of the interior should see fit to locate thereon, a certain scope of country 'bounded on the east and south by the Columbia river, on the west by the Okanagon river, and on the north by the British possessions,' thereafter known as the 'Colville Indian Reservation.' There can be no doubt of the power of the president to reserve those lands of the United States for the use of the Indians. The effect of that executive order was the same as would have been a treaty with the Indians for the same purpose, and was to exclude all intrusion upon the territory thus reserved by any and every person, other than the Indians for whose benefit the reservation was made, for mining as well as other purposes."

The latter decision was reversed by the Supreme Court and on an entirely different ground (180 U. S. 533). The views expressed in the *M'Fadden* case were reaffirmed by the same court in *Gibson* v. *Anderson*, *supra*, involving a reservation created by executive order for the Spokane Indians.

The General Indian Allotment Act of February 8, 1887 (24 Stat. 388, Sec. 1), is based upon the same legal theory as the decisions of the courts; for it is expressly made applicable to "any reservation created for their use, either by treaty stipulation or by virtue of an Act of Congress or *executive order setting apart the same for their use,*" * * *.[131]

A few years after the foregoing opinion was rendered, the question raised by Attorney General Stone as to the propriety of modifying Executive order reservations by new Executive orders received its legislative answer in section 4 of the Act of March 3, 1927,[132] which declared:

> That hereafter changes in the boundaries of reservations created by Executive order, proclamation, or otherwise for the use and occupation of Indians shall not be made except by Act of Congress: *Provided*, That this shall not apply to temporary withdrawals by the Secretary of the Interior.

Some years earlier, a general prohibition against the creation of new Executive order reservations or new additions to existing reservations had been enacted, in these terms:

> That hereafter no public lands of the United States shall be withdrawn by Executive Order, proclamation, or otherwise, for or as an Indian reservation except by act of Congress.[133]

[131] 34 Op. A. G. 181, 186–189 (1924).

[132] 44 Stat. 1347.

[133] Act of June 30, 1919, sec. 27, 41 Stat. 3, 34; *Cf.* Chapter 20, fn. 90.

The foregoing statute, which terminates the practice of establishing Indian reservations by Executive order, remains in force to this day, except with respect to the Territory of Alaska, where it has been substantially repealed by section 2 of the Act of May 1, 1936.[134] It may be argued that the procedure of establishing reservations by Executive order is revived, *pro tanto*, by section 3 of the Act of June 18, 1934,[135] which authorizes the Secretary of the Interior to add to existing reservations by restoring to Indian ownership "the remaining surplus lands of any Indian reservation heretofore opened, or authorized to be opened, to sale, or any other form of disposal by Presidential proclamation, or by any of the public-land laws of the United States." Under this provision, it has been administratively held that the restoration of land must be for the benefit of the entire tribe that would, according to the terms of the cession, be entitled to receipts from the sale thereof, rather than to a fraction of the tribe to which the land formerly belonged.[136]

Executive orders setting apart public lands for Indian reservations or Indian use are by no means uniform. Perhaps the most common type of order is that which presumes to set apart a designated area for the use,[137] or use and occupancy,[138] or as a reservation [139] for a particular tribe or tribes of Indians. Frequently the order uses the term "permanent use and occupancy."[140] Other orders of this type provide that designated

[134] 49 Stat. 1250. See Chapter 21, sec. 8.

[135] 48 Stat. 984. 25 U. S. C. 463.

[136] Op. Sol. I. D., M.29616, February 19, 1938 (Chippewa); Op. Sol. I. D., M.29791, August 1, 1938 (Red Lake Chippewa). Where there is a preexisting lien against land restored to tribal ownership, it has been administratively decided that such lien remains unaffected by the restoration and may be enforced by judicial process.

[137] Executive order, March 12, 1873 (Moapa River); Executive order, November 4, 1873 (Leech Lake); Executive order, November 4, 1873 (Quinaielt); Executive order, February 25, 1874 (Skokomish); Executive order, May 26, 1874 (Leech Lake); Executive order May 26, 1874 Winnebagoshish); Executive order, November 11, 1907 (Jicarilla Apache); Executive order, June 2, 1911 (Hualapai); Executive order, May 29, 1912 (Hualapai); Executive order, March 11, 1912 (Smith River); Executive order, April 24, 1912 (Chuckekansies Band); Executive order, February 10, 1913 (Navajo); Executive order, May 6, 1913 (Navajo); *cf.* Executive order, February 12, 1875 (Lembi) ("for the exclusive use"); see Executive order, December 19, 1906 (Jemez Pueblo) ("for the use and benefit of"), amended by Executive order, September 1, 1911 (Jemez Pueblo); Executive order, March 23, 1914 (Goshute); Executive order, November 10, 1914 (Cold Springs); Executive order, October 4, 1915 (Jemez Pueblo); Executive order, June 18, 1917 (Winnemucca); Executive order, February 8, 1918 (Winnemucca).

[138] Executive order, November 22, 1873 (Lummi); Executive order, March 16, 1877 (Zuni Pueblo), amended by Executive order, May 1, 1883 (Zuni Pueblo); Executive order, June 8, 1880 (Suppai); Executive order, November 23, 1880 (Suppai); Executive order, January 18, 1881 (Spokane); Executive order, March 31, 1882 (Suppai); Executive order, December 16, 1882 (Moqui); Executive order, January 4, 1883 (Hualapai); Executive order, November 26, 1884 (Northern Cheyenne); Executive order, February 11, 1887 (Jicarilla Apache); Executive order, March 14, 1887 (Mission); Executive order, June 13, 1902 (San Felipe Pueblo); Executive order, September 4, 1902 (Nambe Pueblo); Executive order, July 29, 1905 (Santa Clara Pueblo); *cf.* Executive order, May 6, 1913 (Colony or Nevada) ("for the Nevada or Colony Tribe"); Executive order, September 27, 1917 (Cocopah).

[139] Executive order, November 8, 1873 (Coeur D'Alene); Executive order, July 3, 1875 (Moapa River); Executive order, May 10, 1877 (Carlin Farms); Executive order, April 16, 1877 (Duck Valley); Executive order, February 7, 1879 (Southern Ute); Executive order, March 18, 1879 (White Earth); Executive order, June 27, 1879 (Drifting Goose); Executive order, September 21, 1880 (Jicarilla Apache); Executive order, December 20, 1881 (Vermillion Lake); Executive order, January 5, 1882 (Uncompahgre); Executive order, September 11, 1893 (Hoh); Executive order, May 6, 1889 (Mission); Executive order, April 12, 1893 (Osette); Executive order, June 28, 1911 (Seminole); Executive order, March 23, 1914 (Kalispel); Executive order, January 14, 1916 (Papago).

[140] Executive order, December 27, 1875 (Mission); Executive order, May 15, 1876 (Mission); Executive order, April 19, 1879 (Columbia or Moses); Executive order, March 6, 1880 (Columbia or Moses); Executive order, March 2, 1881 (Mission); Executive order, June 19, 1883 (Mis-

lands shall be "set apart as additions to" named reservations,[141] or, that the boundaries of a designated reservation are "extended to include"[142] specified lands. Occasionally an order merely recites the boundary of the reservation it presumes to establish.[143] Another type of order restores theretofore reserved lands to the public domain and withdraws in lieu thereof certain designated land to be set apart for an Indian reservation,[144] or as an addition to an established reservation.[145] Various combinations of the foregoing types may be found in other orders.[146]

In some of the orders the designation of additional Indian beneficiaries of the reservation to be established is delegated to administrative discretion. These orders, typically, provide that given lands shall be set apart for the use and occupancy of certain named bands or tribes and "such Indians as the Secretary of the Interior may see fit to locate thereon."[147] Under another type of order the land is withdrawn and set apart for an indefinite period, the duration of which is conditioned upon the happening of a named event. For example, the Executive order of November 14, 1901, provides that designated land be "withdrawn from sale and settlement until such time as the [Navajo] Indians residing thereon shall have been settled permanently under the provisions of the homestead laws or the general allotment act * * *".[148] Yet another type of order, merely provides that designated land be set apart for Indian purposes.[149] In some cases a particular purpose is designated.[150]

---

sion); Executive order, June 30, 1883 (Deer Creek); Executive order, August 15, 1883 (Iowa); Executive order, August 15, 1883 (Kickapoo); Executive order, January 29, 1887 (Mission); Executive order, February 19, 1889 (Quillehute); Executive order, March 19, 1900 (Northern Cheyenne); Executive order, August 2, 1915 (Paiute).

[141] Executive order, October 26, 1872 (Makah); Executive order, October 29, 1873 (Winnebagoshish); Executive order, November 22, 1873 (Colorado River); Executive order, April 9, 1874 (Muckleshoot); Executive order, November 16, 1874 (Colorado River); Executive order, January 11, 1875 (Standing Rock); Executive order, January 11, 1875 (Cheyenne River); Executive order, January 11, 1875 (Crow Creek); Executive order, January 11, 1875 (Lower Brule); Executive order, January 11, 1875 (Rosebud); Executive order, March 16, 1875 (Standing Rock); Executive order, April 13, 1875 (Blackfeet); Executive order, October 20, 1875 (Crow); Executive order, April 13, 1875 (Fort Belknap); Executive order, April 13, 1875 (Fort Peck); Executive order, May 15, 1875 (Malheur); Executive order, May 20, 1875 (Crow Creek); Executive order, May 20, 1875 (Rosebud); Executive order, November 22, 1875 (Confederated Ute); Executive order, May 15, 1876 (Colorado River); Executive order, August 31, 1876 (Pima and Maricopa); Executive order, November 28, 1876 (Standing Rock); Executive order, October 29, 1878 (Navajo); Executive order, January 10, 1879 (Pima and Maricopa); Executive order, January 6, 1880 (Navajo); Executive order, January 24, 1882 (Great Sioux); Executive order, January 24, 1882 (Pine Ridge); Executive order, May 5, 1882 (Pima and Maricopa); Executive order, November 15, 1883 (Pima and Maricopa); Executive order, May 4, 1886 (Duck Valley); Executive order, November 21, 1892 (Red Lake); Executive order, July 31, 1903 (Moapa River); Executive order, March 10, 1905 (Navajo); Executive order, November 9, 1907 (Navajo); Executive order, July 1, 1910 (Duck Valley); Executive order, October 20, 1910 (Salt River); Executive order, December 1, 1910 (Fort Mojave); Executive order, July 31, 1911 (Pima and Maricopa); Executive order, October 28, 1912 (Moapa River); Executive order, November 26, 1912 (Moapa River); Executive order, June 2, 1913 (Gila River); Executive order, April 13, 1914 (Los Coyotes); Executive order, November 12, 1915 (Ute); Executive order, April 29, 1916 (Camp or Fort Independence); cf. Executive order, September 4, 1902 (Nambe Pueblo) (*"Provided further*, That if at any time the lands covered by any valid claims shall be relinquished to the United States, or the claim lapse, or the entry be canceled * * *, such lands shall be added to * * * the reservation hereby set apart * * *"). Accord: Executive order, June 13, 1902 (San Felipe Pueblo); Executive order, July 29, 1905 (Santa Clara Pueblo).

[142] Executive order, October 16, 1891 (Hoopa); *cf.* Executive order, July 26, 1876 (Round Valley) ("as an extension thereof"); Executive order, August 17, 1876 (Confederated Ute) ("set aside as a part of"). Accord: Executive order, August 8, 1917 (Fort Bidwell).

[143] Executive order, September 9, 1873 (Swinomish Reservation-Perrys Island); Executive order, December 23, 1873 (Tulalip or Snohomish).

[144] Executive order, November 9, 1855 (Siletz); Executive order, February 21, 1856 (Red Cliff); Executive order, January 20, 1857 (Muckleshoot); Executive order, January 20, 1857 (Nisqually); Executive order, January 20, 1857 (Puyallup); Executive order, June 30, 1857 (Grande Ronde); Executive order, October 3, 1861 (Uintah Valley); Executive order, January 15, 1864 (Bosque Redondo); Executive order, July 8, 1864 (Chehalis); Executive order, October 21, 1864 (Port Madison); Executive order, March 20, 1867 (Santee); Executive order, August 10, 1869 (Cheyenne and Arapaho); Executive order, April 12, 1870 (Fort Berthold); Executive order, March 14, 1871 (Malheur); Executive order, April 9, 1872 (Colville); Executive order, July 2, 1872 (Colville); Executive order, September 12, 1872 (Malheur); Executive order, January 2, 1873 (Makah); Executive order, May 29, 1873 (Fort Stanton or Mescalero Apache); Executive order, September 6, 1873 (Puyallup); Executive order, October 3, 1873 (Tule River); Executive order, October 21, 1873 (Makah); Executive order, February 2, 1874 (Fort Stanton or Mescalero Apache); Executive order, February 12, 1874 (Moapa River); Executive order, March 19, 1874 (Walker River); Executive order, March 23, 1874 (Pyramid Lake or Truckee); Executive order, October 20, 1875 (Fort Stanton or Mescalero Apache); Executive order, December 21, 1875 (Hot Springs); Executive order, June 14, 1879 (Pima and Maricopa); Executive order, July 13, 1880 (Fort Berthold); Executive order, May 19, 1882 (Fort Stanton or Mescalero Apache); Executive order, January 9, 1884 (Yuma); Executive order, June 3, 1884 (Turtle Mountain); Executive order, October 1, 1886 (Chehalis); Executive order, December 4, 1888 (Umatilla); Executive order, July 12, 1895 (Cheyenne and Arapaho); Executive order, February 17, 1912 (Navajo); Executive order, December 5, 1912 (Papago); Executive order, February 1, 1917 (Papago).

[145] Executive order, February 2, 1911 (Fort Mohave); Executive order, May 15, 1905 (Navajo).

[146] *E. g.*, Executive order, December 14, 1872 (Chiricahua and White Mountain) ("It is hereby ordered that the following tract of country be * * * set apart * * * for certain Apache Indians * * * to be known as the 'Chiricahua Indian Reservation' * * *. It is also hereby ordered that the reservation heretofore set apart for certain Apache Indians * * * known as the 'Camp Grant Indian Reservation,' be * * * restored to the public domain. It is also ordered that the following tract of country be * * * added to the White Mountain Indian Reservation * * *").

[147] Executive order, April 9, 1874 (Hot Springs); Executive order, July 1, 1874 (Papago); Executive order, December 12, 1882 (Gila Bend); Executive order, December 21, 1882 (Turtle Mountain); Executive order, July 6, 1883 (Yuma); Executive order, August 15, 1883 (Iowa); Executive order, January 9, 1884 (Yuma); Executive order, September 15, 1903 (Camp McDowell); Executive order, December 1, 1910 (Fort Mojave); Executive order, February 2, 1911 (Fort Mojave); Executive order, March 22, 1911 (Salt River); Executive order, September 28, 1911 (Salt River); Executive order, May 8, 1911 (Pima and Maricopa); Executive order, May 28, 1912 (Papago); Executive order, January 14, 1913 (Paiute and Shoshone); Executive order, March 4, 1915 (Fond Du Lac); Executive order, August 2, 1915 (Paiute); Executive order, April 21, 1916 (Shebit or Shivwits); Executive order, January 15, 1917 (Navajo); Executive order, March 21, 1917 (Laguna Pueblo); Executive order, July 17, 1917 (Kaibab); Executive order, February 15, 1918 (Skull Valley); Executive order, March 23, 1918 (Western Shoshone).

[148] Similar in effect is the Executive order of May 7, 1917 (Navajo) which provides that designated land be "set aside temporarily until allotments in severalty can be made to the Navajo Indians living thereon, or until some other provision can be made for their welfare." Accord: Executive order, January 19, 1918 (Navajo). See also Executive order, May 9, 1912 (Paiute) ("until their suitableness for allotment purposes * * * may be fully investigated"); Executive order, December 13, 1910 (Coeur d'Alene) ("as an addition to the Indian school and agency site * * * until such time as it shall be no longer needed and used for this purpose").

[149] Executive order, September 22, 1866 (Shoalwater); Executive order, June 23, 1876 (Hoopa); Executive order, August 25, 1877 (Mission); Executive order, September 29, 1877 (Mission); Executive order, March 9, 1881 (Mission); Executive order, June 27, 1882 (Mission); Executive order, November 19, 1892 (Navajo); Executive order, May 24, 1911 (Navajo). *Cf.* Executive order, August 14, 1914 (Chuckekanzie) ("for Indian use"); Presidential proclamation, August 31, 1915 (Cleveland National Forest—Mission Indians).

[150] Executive order, July 12, 1884 (Chilocco School Reservation) ("for the settlement of such friendly Indians * * * as have been or who may hereafter be educated at the Chilocco Indian Industrial School"); Executive order, October 3, 1884 (Pueblo Industrial School Reservation); Executive order, July 9, 1895 (Cheyenne and Arapaho); Executive order, December 22, 1898 (Hualapai) ("for Indian school purposes"). Accord: Executive order, May 14, 1900 (Hualapai); Executive order, November 26, 1902 (Greenville Indian School); Executive order February 5, 1906 (Uintah) ("be * * * temporarily set apart to the Protestant

It will be noted that the foregoing types of order are all similar in certain respects. In each it is decreed that certain designated land be set apart in a designated manner for a named purpose. In contradistinction to these is the type of Executive order which, though it effects the same purpose, namely, the setting apart of designated land for a particular purpose, may more accurately be termed Executive approval than Executive order. The typical situation wherein this Executive approval is found arises where agents of the War or Interior Departments of their own discretion set aside designated lands and notify the Executive department of such action. In confirmance thereof the Executive may indicate his approval either by affixing his signature to the official notification or by issuing an order confirming same.[151] Needless to say this type of Executive order is of equal validity with the orders hereinbefore mentioned.[152]

Comparatively few questions have arisen as to the interpretation of Executive orders establishing Indian reservations. One such question was raised before the Court of Claims in the case of *Crow Nation* v. *United States.*[153] According to that court, the phrase in controversy reserving an area for the Crow tribe "and such other Indians as the President may, from time to time, locate thereon"[154] gave to the Crow tribe

> * * * only the right to reside upon the reservation, so set apart by Executive order, and did not confer upon them any definite title or particular interest in the land. It was in the nature of a tenancy by sufferance or residential title. * * * The Executive order reserves to the President the right to put other Indians on the reservation and this could not be done if a statutory title, as tenants in common, was given to these five tribes alone. (Pp. 278, 279.)

Where an Executive order establishes an Indian reservation in an area previously reserved for reservoir purposes, it has been held that the later Executive order supersedes the earlier order.[155]

It has been held that a reservation in the nature of an Executive order reservation may be established without a formal Executive order if a course of administrative action is shown which had for its purpose the inducing of an Indian tribe to settle in a given area and if the area has thereafter been referred to and dealt with as an Indian reservation by the Executive branch of the Government.[156]

Likewise it has been held that an Executive reservation may be created by administrative action prior to the formal issuance of an Executive order, the effect of such order being simply to give "formal sanction to what had been done before."[157]

Occasionally a treaty leaves a good deal of discretion to administrative authorities in establishing a reservation, and the courts must look to administrative correspondence, maps, and other records to determine the date, extent, and character of the reservation. Here we are on the borderline between treaty and Executive order reservations.[158] In fact, the connection between treaty and Executive order is characteristic of many, if not most, of the early Executive orders and provides a legal basis of unquestioned validity for such Executive orders.[159]

Episcopal Church for missionary and cemetery purposes for the benefit of the Ute Indians so long as used therefor."); Executive order, July 6, 1912 (Rosebud). *Cf.* Executive order, June 16, 1911 (Papago) ("for school, agency, and other necessary uses"); Executive order, January 17, 1912 (Skull Valley Band); Executive order, May 29, 1912 (Deep Creek Band); Executive order, July 22, 1915 (Paiute) ("for use * * * as a cemetery and camping ground"); Executive order, March 15, 1918 (Walker River) ("as a grazing reservation").

[151] Executive order, May 14, 1855 (Isabella); Executive order, August 9, 1855 (Ottawa and Chippewa); Executive order, September 25, 1855 (Ontonagon); Executive order, May 22, 1856 (Mendocino); Executive order, December 21, 1858 (Fond Du Lac); Executive order, April 16, 1864 (Little Traverse); Executive order, February 27, 1866 (Niobrara or Santee Sioux); Executive order, July 20, 1866 (Niobrara or Santee Sioux); Executive order, June 14, 1867 (Fort Hall); Executive order, June 14, 1867 (Coeur D'Alene); Executive order, November 16, 1867 (Niobrara or Santee Sioux); Executive order, January 16, 1868 (Cheyenne and Arapaho Halfbreed); Executive order, July 30, 1869 (Fort Hall); Executive order, January 31, 1870 (Mission); Executive order, March 30, 1870 (Round Valley); Executive order, November 9, 1871 (Fort Apache); Executive order, November 9, 1871 (White Mountain); Executive order, January 9, 1873 (Tule River); Executive order, July 5, 1873 (Blackfeet); Executive order, July 5, 1873 (Fort Belknap); Executive order, July 5, 1873 (Fort Peck); Executive order, March 19, 1874 (Walker River); Executive order, September 19, 1880 (Fort Mojave); Executive order, November 16, 1885 (Klamath River).

[152] *Cf. United States* v. *Walker River Irr. Dist.*, 104 F. 2d 334 (C. C. A. 9, 1939).

[153] 81 C. Cls. 238 (1935).

[154] *Cf.* fn. 36, *supra.*

[155] Op. Sol. I. D., M.28589, August 24, 1936.

[156] Old Winnebago and Crow Creek Reservation, 18 Op. A. G. 141 (1885).

[157] *Northern Pacific Ry. Co.* v. *Wismer*, 246 U. S. 283 (1918), aff'g 230 Fed. 591 (C. C. A. 9, 1916).

[158] *Spalding* v. *Chandler*, 160 U. S. 394 (1896).

[159] In the present instance, the orders of May 29, 1873, February 2, 1874, and October 20, 1875, not only confirmed Indian rights of use and occupancy (34 Op. Atty. Gen. 181, 187), but were issued in pursuance of obligations toward the Apache Indians undertaken by the United States in the Treaty of July 1, 1852, 10 Stat. 979, in which the Government agreed "at its earliest convenience" to "designate, settle, and adjust their territorial boundaries." Memo. Sol. I. D., June 28, 1940 (Mescalero Apache).

SECTION 8. TRIBAL LAND PURCHASE

That a tribe may acquire land in its own name is a consequence of its general contractual capacity, discussed in Chapter 14 of this volume. In the exercise of this capacity various tribes have, from time to time, purchased lands (using the term "purchase" in its technical sense to include acquisition through gift and devise as well as bargain and sale), and the validity of such purchases has been recognized legislatively[160] and judicially.[161]

A notable instance of land acquisition is found in the history of the Eastern Band of Cherokee Indians of North Carolina. The individual members of the band had the foresight to provide that land purchased with individual funds should be held under a single title, first by a private trustee, then by the incorporated band, and finally (by cession from the band)[162] by the United States in trust for the band. Always resisting allotment, the band has maintained its lands intact, in sharp contrast to the fate of its fellow tribesmen in Oklahoma.[163]

From time to time, the Secretary of the Interior has been authorized to purchase lands for Indian tribes. Such legislation, where specific, has been dealt with under the heading "Statutory Reservations." Where the legislation creates a general authority, the process of establishing reservations by purchase resembles the process whereby the tribe itself undertakes to acquire lands.

The acquisition of land by the Secretary of the Interior for

[160] Pueblo Lands Act of June 7, 1924, 43 Stat. 636; Act of March 3, 1875, 18 Stat. 420, 447 (Eastern Cherokees); Act of August 4, 1892, 27 Stat. 348 (Eastern Cherokees); Act of March 3, 1925, 43 Stat. 1141, 1148–1149 (Choctaw).

[161] *Garcia* v. *United States*, 43 F. 2d 873 (C. C. A. 10, 1930); *Pueblo De-Taos* v. *Archuleta*, 64 F. 2d 807 (C. C. A. 10, 1933); *United States* v. *7,405.3 Acres of Land*, 97 F. 2d 417 (C. C. A. 4, 1938).

[162] See Act of June 4, 1924, 43 Stat. 376.

[163] See *United States* v. *7,405.3 Acres*, 97 F. 2d 417.

an Indian tribe, through purchase, gift, exchange or assignment or through relinquishment of land by individual Indians, is authorized by section 5 of the Act of June 18, 1934.[164] It has been held that the purpose of "providing land for Indians" is served by an exchange transaction whereby an individual Indian transfers allotted land to the tribe in exchange for an assignment of occupancy rights in the same or in another tract, since the tribe through this transaction acquires a definite interest in the land over and above the transferror's retained occupancy right.[165] Where a tribe exchanges land with a non-Indian, under this section, the value of the land acquired must be equal to, or greater than, the value of the land ceded, since the purpose of section 5 is to increase the tribal estate rather than to open the way to its alienation.[166]

Relinquishments of individual timber and mineral rights to the tribe have been made in consideration of other similar relinquishments by other members of the tribe.[167] The result of such a transaction is that each member of the tribe has an undivided interest in the entire mineral and timber wealth of the reservation, instead of a particular interest in the possible timber and mineral wealth of his own allotment.

It has been held that a tribe may purchase allotted lands in heirship status where such lands are offered for sale by the Secretary of the Interior.[168] The mechanics of such a transaction are elsewhere discussed.[169]

The acquisition of land by one tribe from another was at one time a common method of acquiring tribal property. The distinction between such a transfer and a transaction whereby one tribe is dissolved and its members incorporated in another tribe, is carefully analyzed by the Supreme Court in the case of *Cherokee Nation* v. *Journeycake*.[170]

For some time it was doubted whether land conveyed to an Indian tribe by private parties was within the protection of the Federal Government. These doubts were largely dissipated by the case of *United States* v. *7,405.3 Acres of Land*,[171] in which it was held that lands of the Eastern Cherokees of North Carolina were not subject to a claim of adverse possession. In an opinion which illuminates the subject, the court declared, *per* Parker, *J.*:

> As we were at pains to point out in the *Wright Case*, it makes no difference that title to the land in controversy was originally obtained by grant from the state of North Carolina, or that the Indians are citizens of that state and subject to its laws. The determinative fact is that the federal government has assumed towards them the same sort of guardianship that it exercises over other tribes of Indians, from which it results that their property becomes an instrumentality of that government for the accomplishment of a proper governmental purpose and may not be taken from them by contract, adverse possession, or otherwise, without its consent. *United States* v. *Candelaria*, 271 U. S. 432, 440, 46 S. Ct. 561, 562, 70 L. Ed. 1023; *United States* v. *Minnesota*, 270 U. S. 181, 196, 46 S. Ct. 298, 301, 70 L. Ed. 539; *United States* v. *Sandoval*, 231 U. S. 28, 34 S. Ct. 1, 58 L. Ed. 107; *Heckman* v. *United States*, 224 U. S. 413, 438, 32 S. Ct. 424, 56 L. Ed. 820. Indeed, a statute of the United States expressly forbids the acquisition of lands of any Indian tribe by purchase, grant, lease or other conveyance, except by treaty or convention and subjects to penalty anyone not being employed under the authority of the United States who attempts to negotiate such treaty. R. S. § 2116, 25 U. S. C. A. § 177. This statute protects Indians such as these as well as the nomadic tribes. *United States* v. *Candelaria*, *supra*. And the protection is not affected by reason of the fact that the band has been incorporated under a state charter and attempts to take action thereunder. *United States* v. *Boyd*, *supra*, 4 Cir., 83 F. 547, 553. Certainly if the land was not alienable by the Indians, title could not be obtained as against them by adverse possession. *Schrimpscher* v. *Stockton*, 183 U. S. 290, 295, 22 S. Ct. 107, 46 L. Ed. 203; *Garcia* v. *United States*, 10 Cir., 43 F. 2d 873. (Pp. 422–423.)
>
> * * * * *
>
> If adverse possession will not give title under state statutes of limitation against restricted allotments of individual Indians, a fortiori such possession cannot give title to lands held in trust for the common benefit of the tribe over which the United States exercises guardianship. It is beyond the power of the state, either through statutes of limitation or adverse possession, to affect the interest of the United States; and the United States manifestly has an interest in preserving the property of these wards of the government for their use and benefit. As said in the *Heckman Case*, *supra* (32 S. Ct. page 432), "If these Indians may be divested of their lands, they will be thrown back upon the Nation a pauperized, discontented * * * people." The lands held for them are thus an instrumentality in the discharge of the duty which the government has assumed toward them. Title to it can no more be acquired by adverse possession under state statute, than to land held for other governmental purposes. (P. 423.)

A further step in assimilating the status of lands purchased for Indians to the status of treaty, Executive order, and statutory reservations was taken in the Act of February 14, 1923,[172] which extended the provisions of the General Allotment Act[173] as amended, which in terms covered only reservations created "either by treaty stipulation or by virtue of an act of Congress or executive order setting apart the same for their use," to "all lands heretofore purchased or which may hereafter be purchased by authority of Congress for the use or benefit of any individual Indian or band or tribe of Indians."

[164] 48 Stat. 984. 25 U. S. C. 465.

[165] Memo. Sol. I. D., April 4, 1935.

[166] Memo. Sol. I. D., February 3, 1937.

[167] Memo. Sol. I. D., October 7, 1937 (Jicarilla Apache).

[168] Memo. Sol. I. D., August 14, 1937.

[169] See Chapter 11, sec. 6C. On the disposition of reimbursable debts chargeable to the estate, see Memo. Sol. I. D., January 2, 1940.

[170] 155 U. S. 196 (1894), aff'g. *Journeycake* v. *Cherokee Nation*, 28 C. Cls. 281 (1893). Accord: *Cherokee Nation* v. *Blackfeather*, 155 U. S. 218 (1894).

[171] 97 F. 2d 417 (C. C. A. 4, 1938).

[172] 42 Stat. 1246.

[173] Act of February 8, 1887, 24 Stat. 388.

SECTION 9. TRIBAL TITLE DERIVED FROM OTHER SOVEREIGNTIES

The analysis of tribal rights in land is complicated by the fact that all of the territory of the United States (with the possible exception of Oregon territory) was at one time subject to some other sovereignty, and it has been the consistent policy of the United States to respect rights in real property recognized under such prior sovereignty. This policy, based upon international law,[174] has been affirmed in our various treaties with Spain, France, Great Britain, Mexico, and Russia. It would take us far beyond the limits of this volume to analyze in any detail the principles of Spanish, French, British, Mexican, and Russian law governing aboriginal titles. It is necessary, however, to refer to the statutes and judicial decisions of this country which interpret the applicable principles of foreign law and mark out the authority which the courts of this Nation will accord to such principles.

In some measure the Spanish and Mexican law relating to the Pueblos of New Mexico and the Russian law relating to the

[174] See *Barker* v. *Harvey*, 181 U. S. 481 (1901) (discussing Treaty of Guadalupe Hidalgo).

natives of Alaska are dealt with in separate chapters[175] and need not be discussed at this point. The relevance of Spanish and Mexican law is not, however, limited to the problems of the Pueblos of New Mexico. The cession of Florida and the land claims of nomadic Indians in the later Mexican cessions often involve difficult questions of Spanish law.

The California Private Land Claims Act of March 3, 1851,[176] provided a means for determining land titles established under Mexican law, including rights of permanent occupancy vested in Indian tribes. It has been held that claims not presented to the Commission established under this act have been waived, even though such claims emanate from Indian tribes not practically in a position to present them at the time when the commission was functioning.[177]

The effect of Spanish and British law upon Indian rights within the Florida cession was analyzed by the Supreme Court in the case of *Mitchel* v. *United States*,[178] from which the following excerpts are taken:

> We now come to consider the nature and extent of the Indian title to these lands.
>
> As Florida was for 20 years under the dominion of Great Britain, the laws of that country were in force as the rule by which lands were held and sold; it will be necessary to examine what they were as applicable to the British provinces before the acquisition of the Floridas by the treaty of peace in 1763. One uniform rule seems to have prevailed from their first settlement, as appears by their laws; that friendly Indians were protected in the possession of the lands they occupied, and were considered as owning them by a perpetual right of possession in the tribe or nation inhabiting them, as their common property, from generation to generation, not as the right of the individuals located on particular spots.
>
> Subject to this right of possession, the ultimate fee was in the crown and its grantees, which could be granted by the crown or colonial legislatures while the lands remained in possession of the Indians, though possession could not be taken without their consent.
>
> Individuals could not purchase Indian lands without permission or license from the crown, colonial governors, or according to the rules prescribed by colonial laws; but such purchases were valid with such license, or in conformity with the local laws; and by this union of the perpetual right of occupancy with the ultimate fee, which passed from the crown by the license, the title of the purchaser became complete.
>
> Indian possession or occupation was considered with reference to their habits and modes of life; their hunting-grounds were as much in their actual possession as the cleared fields of the whites; and their rights to its [ex]clusive enjoyment in their own way and for their own purposes were as much respected, until they abandoned them, made a cession to the government, or an authorized sale to individuals. In either case their right became extinct, the lands could be granted disencumbered of the right of occupancy, or enjoyed in full dominion by the purchasers from the Indians. Such was the tenure of Indian lands by the laws of Massachusetts Indian Laws, 9, 10, 15, 16, 17, 18, 19, 21; in Connecticut, 40, 41, 42; Rhode Island, 52, 55; New Hampshire, 60; New York, 62, 64, 71, 85, 102; New Jersey, 133; Pennsylvania, 138; Maryland, 141, 143, 144, 145; Virginia, 147, 148, 150, 153, 154; North Carolina, 163, 4, 58; South Carolina, 178, 179; Georgia, 186, 187; by Congress, Appendix, 16; by their respective laws, and the decisions of courts in their construction. See cases collected in 2 Johnson's Dig. 15, tit. Indians; and Wharton's Dig. tit. Land, &c. 488. Such, too, was the view taken by this court of Indian rights in the case of *Johnson* v. *M'Intosh*, 8 Wheat. 571, 604, which has received universal assent.
>
> The merits of this case do not make it necessary to inquire whether the Indians within the United States had any other rights of soil or jurisdiction; it is enough to consider it as a settled principle, that their right of occupancy is considered as sacred as the fee-simple of the whites. 5 Pet. 48. The principles which had been established in the colonies were adopted by the king in the proclamation of October, 1763, and applied to the provinces acquired by the treaty of peace and the crown lands in the royal provinces, now composing the United States, as the law which should govern the enjoyment and transmission of Indian and vacant lands. After providing for the government of the acquired provinces, 1 Laws U. S. 443, 444, it authorizes the governors of Quebec, East and West Florida, to make grants of such lands as the king had power to dispose of, upon such terms as have been usual in other colonies, and such other conditions as the crown might deem necessary and expedient, without any other restriction. It also authorized warrants to be issued by the governors for military and naval services rendered in the then late war. It reserved to the Indians the possession of their lands and hunting-grounds; and prohibited the granting any warrant of survey, or patent for any lands west of the heads of the Atlantic waters, or which, not having been ceded or purchased by the crown, were reserved to the Indians; and prohibited all purchases from them without its special license. The warrants issued pursuant to this proclamation for lands then within the Indian boundary, before the treaty of Fort Stanwick's in 1768, have been held to pass the title to the lands surveyed on them, in opposition to a Pennsylvania patent afterwards issued. *Sims* v. *Irvine*, 3 Dallas, 427–456. And all titles held under the charter of license of the crown to purchase from the Indians have been held good, and such power has never been denied; the right of the crown to grant being complete, this proclamation had the effect of a law in relation to such purchases; so it has been considered by this court. 8 Wheat. 595–604. (Pp. 745–747.)[179]

A classic historical account of the extent to which Indian rights were recognized under British and colonial rule is given by Chief Justice Marshall in his epic opinion in *Worcester* v. *Georgia*.[180] After analyzing the claims of the European nations on the subject of aboriginal right,[181] the Chief Justice offered these comments on the colonial charters issued by the European powers and the recognition of Indian rights implicit in the language of these charters:

> The power of making war is conferred by these charters on the colonies, but defensive war alone seems to have been contemplated. In the first charter to the first and second colonies, they are empowered, "for their several defences, to encounter, expulse, repel, and resist all persons who shall, without license," attempt to inhabit "within the said precincts and limits of the said several colonies, or that shall enterprise or attempt at any time hereafter the least detriment or annoyance of the said several colonies or plantations."

After analyzing various colonial charters, the court concluded:

> These motives for planting the new colony are incompatible with the lofty ideas of granting the soil, and all its inhabitants from sea to sea. They demonstrate the truth that these grants asserted a title against Europeans only, and were considered as blank paper so far as the rights of the natives were concerned. The power of war is given only for defence, not for conquest.
>
> The charters contain passages showing one of their objects to be the civilization of the Indians, and their conversion to Christianity—objects to be accomplished by conciliatory conduct and good example; not by extermination.
>
> The actual state of things, and the practice of European nations, on so much of the American continent as lies

[175] Chapter 20 (Pueblos of New Mexico); Chapter 21 (Alaskan Natives).

[176] 9 Stat. 631.

[177] *Barker* v. *Harvey*, 181 U. S. 481 (1901); *United States* v. *Title Ins. Co.*, 265 U. S. 472 (1924), aff'g 288 Fed. 821 (C. C. A. 9, 1923).

[178] 9 Pet. (11 Curtis) 711 (1835).

[179] Apparently the Supreme Court was of the opinion that the principles applicable to Indian possessions in Florida under Spanish rule were not identical with those applicable in the Territory of New Mexico. The court declared that, to Spain, "the friendship of the Indians was a most important consideration. It would have been lost by adopting towards them a less liberal, just, or kind policy than had been pursued by Great Britain, or acting according to the laws of the Indies in force in Mexico and Peru." (P. 751.)

[180] 6 Pet. (10 Curtis) 515 (1832).

[181] See sec. 4 of this chapter.

between the Mississippi and the Atlantic, explain their claims and the charters they granted. Their pretensions unavoidably interfered with each other; though the discovery of one was admitted by all to exclude the claim of any other, the extent of that discovery was the subject of unceasing contest. Bloody conflicts arose between them, which gave importance and security to the neighboring nations. Fierce and warlike in their character, they might be formidable enemies, or effective friends. Instead of rousing their resentments, by asserting claims to their lands, or to dominion over their persons, their alliance was sought by flattering professions, and purchased by rich presents. The English, the French, and the Spaniards were equally competitors for their friendship and their aid. Not well acquainted with the exact meaning of words, nor supposing it to be material whether they were called the subjects, or the children of their father in Europe; lavish in professions of duty and affection, in return for the rich presents they received; so long as their actual independence was untouched, and their right to self-government acknowledged, they were willing to profess dependence on the power which furnished supplies of which they were in absolute need, and restrained dangerous intruders from entering their country; and this was probably the sense in which the term was understood by them.

Certain it is that our history furnishes no example, from the first settlement of our country, of any attempt, on the part of the crown, to interfere with the internal affairs of the Indians, further than to keep out the agents of foreign powers, who, as traders or otherwise, might seduce them into foreign alliances. The king purchased their lands when they were willing to sell, at a price they were willing to take; but never coerced a surrender of them. He also purchased their alliance and dependence by subsidies; but never intruded into the interior of their affairs, or interfered with their self-government, so far as respected themselves only.

The general views of Great Britain, with regard to the Indians, were detailed by Mr. Stuart, superintendent of Indian affairs, in a speech delivered at Mobile, in presence of several persons of distinction, soon after the peace of 1763. Towards the conclusion, he says: "Lastly, I inform you that it is the king's order to all his governors and subjects, to treat Indians with justice and humanity, and to forbear all encroachments on the territories allotted to them; accordingly, all individuals are prohibited from purchasing any of your lands; but, as you know that, as your white brethren cannot feed you when you visit them unless you give them ground to plant, it is expected that you will cede lands to the king for that purpose. But whenever you shall be pleased to surrender any of your territories to his Majesty, it must be done, for the future, at a public meeting of your nation, when the governors of the provinces, or the superintendent shall be present, and obtain the consent of all your people. The boundaries of your hunting grounds will be accurately fixed, and no settlement permitted to be made upon them. As you may be assured that all treaties with your people will be faithfully kept, so it is expected that you, also, will be careful strictly to observe them."

The proclamation issued by the king of Great Britain, in 1763, soon after the ratification of the articles of peace, forbids the governors of any of the colonies to grant warrants of survey, or pass patents upon any lands whatever, which, not having been ceded to or purchased by us, (the king), as aforesaid, are reserved to the said Indians, or any of them.

The proclamation proceeds: "and we do further declare it to be our royal will and pleasure, for the present, as aforesaid, to reserve, under our sovereignty, protection, and dominion, for the use of the said Indians, all the lands and territories lying to the westward of the sources of the rivers which fall into the sea, from the west and northwest as aforesaid; and we do hereby strictly forbid, on pain of our displeasure, all our loving subjects from making any purchases or settlements whatever, or taking possession of any of the lands above reserved, without our special leave and license for that purpose first obtained.

"And we do further strictly enjoin and require all persons whatever, who have, either wilfully or inadvertently, seated themselves upon any lands within the countries above described, or upon any other lands which, not having been ceded to or purchased by us, are still reserved to the said Indians, as aforesaid, forthwith to remove themselves from such settlements."

A proclamation, issued by Governor Gage, in 1772, contains the following passage: "Whereas many persons, contrary to the positive orders of the king, upon this subject, have undertaken to make settlements beyond the boundaries fixed by the treaties made with the Indian nations, which boundaries ought to serve as a barrier between the whites and the said nations; particularly on the Ouabache." The proclamation orders such persons to quit those countries without delay.

Such was the policy of Great Britain towards the Indian nations inhabiting the territory from which she excluded all other Europeans; such her claims, and such her practical exposition of the charters she had granted; she considered them as nations capable of maintaining the relations of peace and war; of governing themselves, under her protection; and she made treaties with them, the obligation of which she acknowledged. (Pp. 545–549.)

The question of how far Spain and Mexico recognized rights of possession in nomadic tribes is a question upon which conflicting views have been expressed. In *Hoyt* v. *United States and Utah Indians*,[182] the Court of Claims took the position that Spain and Mexico had never recognized any right of exclusive possession in any of the nomadic tribes, and that only areas affirmatively designated as Indian reservations could be considered Indian country within the meaning of the Indian Intercourse Act of 1834. The actual decision in the case, however, was simply that a plaintiff was not precluded from maintaining a suit for depredations committed by Ute Indians by the mere fact that he was on territory which later became recognized as an Indian reservation. On the other hand, the Supreme Court, in the case of *Chouteau* v. *Molony*[183] held that under the Spanish law applicable to what is now the State of Iowa when that territory was under Spanish dominion, the Fox tribe of Indians had rights of ownership in the land they occupied which were of such dignity that a purported grant of such land by the Spanish Governor would be

> * * * an unaccountable and capricious exercise of official power, contrary to the uniform usage of his predecessors in respect to the sales of Indian lands, and that it could give no property to the grantee. It is not meant, by what has just been said, that the Spanish governors could not relinquish the interest or title of the Crown in Indian lands and for more than a mile square; but when that was done, the grants were made subject to the rights of Indian occupancy. They did not take effect until that occupancy had ceased, and whilst it continued it was not in the power of the Spanish governor to authorize any one to interfere with it. (P. 239.)

Apparently the Foxes were as nomadic in their habits as most of the other Plains tribes, so that the correct historical view would seem to be that if Spanish law ever denied title by aboriginal occupancy to certain Indian tribes it was because these tribes did not in fact maintain exclusive occupancy of any territory at all but merely wandered over lands which were traversed by other tribes as well. In this situation even our own law recognizes that no possessory rights are created.[184] There would seem, therefore, to be no valid reason to suppose that the Spanish law was more rigorous than the law of Great Britain or the United States with respect to the recognition of Indian possessory rights derived from aboriginal occupancy.[185]

---

[182] 38 C. Cls. 455 (1903).

[183] 16 How. 203 (1853).

[184] *Assiniboine Indian Tribe* v. *United States*, 77 C. Cl. 347 (1933), app. dism. 292 U. S. 606.

[185] For a classical statement of Spanish legal theory on the subject of Indian title, see Victoria, De Indis et De Jure Belli Relectiones (trans. by John Pawley Bate, 1917), originally published in 1557. And see: Hall, Laws of Mexico (1885), secs. 36, 38, 40, 45, 49, 85, 195; 2 White's Recopilacion (1839), 34, 51–52, 54–55, 59, 95–98. See also Chapter 3, sec. 4A, *supra*.

SECTION 10. PROTECTION OF TRIBAL POSSESSION

Tribal possessory right may be defined as a power to command the aid of the law against trespassers, coupled with a privilege to use reasonable force in excluding such trespassers. An assertion of possessory right, whether contained in statute, treaty, Executive order, or judicial decision, is meaningless if both these elements are lacking, and imperfect if one is lacking.

The right to protection of tribal possession through an action of ejectment or other similar possessory action was affirmed at an early period. Thus, the Supreme Court in the case of *Marsh* v. *Brooks*[186] declared:

> * * * This Indian title consisted of the usufruct and right of occupancy and enjoyment; * * *
> That an action of ejectment could be maintained on an Indian right to occupancy and use, is not open to question. This is the result of the decision in *Johnson* v. *McIntosh*, 8 Wheat. 574, and was the question directly decided, in the case of *Cornet* v. *Winton*, 2 Yerger's Ten. Rep. 143, on the effect of reserves to individual Indians of a mile square each, secured to heads of families by the Cherokee treaties of 1817[1] and 1819.[2] * * * (Pp. 232–233.)
>
> [1] 7 Stats. at Large, 156.
> [2] Ibid, 195

This measure of common law protection was amplified from time to time by treaty and statute provisions designed to prevent or punish various types of trespass upon Indian land. These provisions were generally limited either to a particular tribe or reservation or to a particular type of trespass, *e. g.*, trespass for purposes of trading, driving livestock, stealing horses, and settlement. At no time has there been comprehensive legislation on the general problem of the protection of tribal property against trespass.[186a] The law on the subject is therefore a historical patchwork which can hardly be understood without reference to historical considerations.

A. LEGISLATION ON TRESPASS

The early legislation, whether emanating from the United States,[186b] from the colonies,[186c] or from the European powers,[187] purported not to create new possessory rights, but to recognize existing rights inherent in the Indian nations. This recognition took the form of (*a*) disclaiming the right or intention to interfere with the action of the Indian tribes, in their own territories, in excluding or removing intruders, or (*b*) establishing forms of civil or criminal proceedings in non-Indian courts against such intruders. Thus, we find in many of the early treaties, provisions recognizing the right of the Indian tribes to proceed against trespassers in accordance with their own laws and customs,[188] which, of course, antedated the discovery of America by Europeans and applied, originally, only to intruders from other Indian tribes.

The historic source of tribal possessory right is a matter of more than antiquarian interest, since even today the limitations upon the right depend in part upon its source. Perhaps the clearest authoritative analysis of the basis and origin of tribal possessory right is that given in the case of *Buster* v. *Wright*.[189]

> The authority of the Creek Nation to prescribe the terms upon which noncitizens may transact business within its borders did not have its origin in act of Congress, treaty, or agreement of the United States. It was one of the inherent and essential attributes of its original sovereignty. It was a natural right of that people, indispensable to its autonomy as a distinct tribe or nation, and it must remain an attribute of its government until by the agreement of the nation itself or by the superior power of the republic it is taken from it. Neither the authority nor the power of the United States to license its citizens to trade in the Creek Nation, with or without the consent of that tribe, is in issue in this case, because the complainants have no such licenses. The plenary power and lawful authority of the government of the United States by license, by treaty, or by act of Congress to take from the Creek Nation every vestige of its original or acquired governmental authority and power may be admitted, and for the purposes of this decision are here conceded. The fact remains nevertheless that every original attribute of the government of the Creek Nation still exists intact which has not been destroyed or limited by act of Congress or by the contracts of the Creek tribe itself. (P. 950.)

The proposition that a tribe needs no grant of authority from the Federal Government in order to exercise its inherent power of excluding trespassers has been repeatedly affirmed by the Attorney General.[190] It is against the background of this recognition of tribal power that the course of federal legislation must be viewed. Thus viewed, legislative prohibitions against trespass on Indian land are seen as implementing the assumed international obligations of the United States.[191]

The early Indian Intercourse Acts, culminating in the Act of June 30, 1834,[192] dealt with five distinct types of trespassers: (1) trespassers seeking to trade with Indians; (2) trespassers

---

[186] 8 How. 223 (1850). A suit in trespass, brought by the individual occupant of tribal land against a non-Indian, was successfully maintained in *Fellows* v. *Blacksmith*, 19 How. 366 (1856).

In a case where a conveyee under a congressional grant brought a successful suit in ejectment in a state court against the local Indian superintendent, the Attorney General held that the writ of execution founded on that judgment did not give the conveyee legal possession of the land and that the plaintiff was an intruder who could be removed by federal authorities under R. S. §2118, and said:

> * * * the tribe hold the reservation, not under the treaty, but under their original title, which is confirmed by the Government in agreeing to the reservation. (See *Gaines* v. *Nicholson*, 9 How. 365.)
> Thus it would seem that the title imparted by the acts of 1848 and 1853 was at that period, and has ever since continued to be, subject to the Indian right of occupancy in said tribe, the enjoyment of which right, moreover, is assured thereto by the Government by solemn treaty stipulations. * * * (P. 573.)

Nez Perce Reservation—Claim of W. G. Langford, 14 Op. A. G. 568 (1875), decision reaffirmed in 17 Op. A. G. 306 (1882), and 20 Op. A. G. 42 (1891), the latter case holding that Langford held "nothing but a naked title" (p. 47, *per* Taft, Sol. G.), which could not be invoked to prevent allotment. "What is the Indian right of occupancy? It is the right to enjoy the land forever with the right of alienation limited to one alienee, the United States, or to such persons as the United States, in its capacity of guardian over the Indians, may permit." (P. 48.)

[186a] The nearest approach to such general legislation was legislation authorizing Indian Service officials, with the aid of the military, "to remove from the Indian country all persons found therein contrary to law." See Act of June 30, 1834, sec. 10, 4 Stat. 729, 730, R. S. § 2147, 25 U. S. C. 220, repealed by Act of May 21, 1934, 48 Stat. 787. And see *United States ex rel. Gordon* v. *Crook*, 179 Fed. 391, 398–399 (D. C. Neb. 1875).

[186b] Reference to legislation of the United States on this subject under the Articles of Confederation is found in 18 Op. A. G. 235, 236–237 (1885).

[186c] *Preston* v. *Browder*, 1 Wheat. 115, 121 (1816).

[187] See *United States* v. *Ritchie*, 17 How. 525 (1854) (dealing with the Act of March 3, 1851, 9 Stat. 631).

[188] Treaty of January 21, 1785 with the Wiandot, Delaware, Chippewa, and Ottawa Nations, Art. V, 7 Stat. 16, 17. *Accord:* Art. VII of Treaty of January 31, 1786, with the Shawanoe Nation, 7 Stat. 26, and see Chapter 3, sec. 3D (1).

[189] 135 Fed. 947 (C. C. A. 8, 1905), app. dism. 203 U. S. 599 (1906).

[190] * * * So long as a tribe exists and remains in possession of its lands, its title and possession are sovereign and exclusive; and there exists no authority to enter upon their lands, for any purpose whatever, without their consent. * * * 1 Op. A. G. 465, 466 (1821).

See to the same effect, 17 Op. A. G. 134 (1881); 18 Op. A. G. 34 (1884.)

[191] See, for example, Art. 7 of Treaty of August 7, 1790, with Creek Nation, 7 Stat. 35, 37; Art. 2 of Treaty of October 3, 1818, with Delawares, 7 Stat. 188.

[192] Act of July 22, 1790, 1 Stat. 137; Act of March 1, 1793, 1 Stat. 329; Act of May 19, 1796, 1 Stat. 469; Act of March 3, 1799, 1 Stat. 743; Act of March 30, 1802, 2 Stat. 139; Act of June 30, 1834, 4 Stat. 729.

committing injuries against Indians; (3) trespassers settling on Indian lands; (4) trespassers driving livestock upon Indian lands; and (5) trespassers hunting or trapping game on Indian lands.

Section 3 of the first Indian Intercourse Act,[193] approved by President Washington on July 22, 1790, provided for the punishment of any person found in the Indian country "with such merchandise in his possession as are usually vended to the Indians. without a license first had and obtained," and this provision, with minor modifications,[194] remains the law to this day. Section 5 of the same act[195] contained a further provision making it an offense for any inhabitant of the United States to "go into any town, settlement, or territory belonging to any nation or tribe of Indians, and * * * there commit any crime upon, or trespass against, the person or property of any peaceable and friendly Indian or Indians, which, if committed within the jurisdiction of any state, or within the jurisdiction of either of said districts, against a citizen or white inhabitant thereof, would be punishable by the laws of such state or district." This provision was likewise incorporated with minor modifications in subsequent statutes.[196]

The first Indian Intercourse Act was temporary, to continue "in force for the term of two years, and from thence to the end of the next session of Congress, and no longer."[197]

The second Intercourse Act, that of March 1, 1793,[198] introduced a new provision of importance. Section 5 of that act provided:

> *And be it further enacted*, That if any such citizen or inhabitant shall make a settlement on lands belonging to any Indian tribe, or shall survey such lands, or designate their boundaries, by marking trees, or otherwise, for the purpose of settlement, he shall forfeit a sum not exceeding one thousand dollars, nor less than one hundred dollars, and suffer imprisonment not exceeding twelve months, in the discretion of the court, before whom the trial shall be: And it shall, moreover, be lawful for the President of the United States, to take such measures, as he may judge necessary, to remove from lands belonging to any Indian tribe, any citizens or inhabitants of the United States, who have made, or shall hereafter make, or attempt to make a settlement thereon. (P. 330.)

The reference to "lands belonging to any Indian tribe" was amplified in later legislation to refer to "lands belonging, or secured, or granted by treaty with the United States, to any Indian tribe".[199] Various other minor modifications are found in the language of this provision, but in essence it sets forth the present-day law on the subject.

The second Indian Intercourse Act, like the first, was a temporary act, to continue "in force, for the term of two years, and from thence to the end of the then next session of Congress, and no longer."[200]

The Third Indian Intercourse Act, that of May 19, 1796,[201] dealt for the first time with two new kinds of trespasser, the hunter and the ranger. Section 2 of that act provided:

> *And be it further enacted*, That if any citizen of, or other person resident in the United States, or either of the territorial districts of the United States, shall cross over, or go within the said boundary line, to hunt, or in any wise destroy the game; or shall drive, or otherwise convey any stock of horses or cattle to range, on any lands allotted or secured by treaty with the United States, to any Indian tribes, he shall forfeit a sum not exceeding one hundred dollars, or be imprisoned not exceeding six months.

These provisions, reaffirmed and made permanent in the second section of the fifth Indian Intercourse Act,[202] were subsequently separated and elaborated in the Act of June 30, 1834,[203] which was a comprehensive statute on Indian relations:

> SEC. 8. *And be it further enacted*, That if any person, other than an Indian, shall, within the limits of any tribe with whom the United States shall have existing treaties, hunt, or trap, or take and destroy, any peltries or game, except for subsistence in the Indian country, such person shall forfeit the sum of five hundred dollars, and forfeit all the traps, guns, and ammunition in his possession, used or procured to be used for that purpose, and peltries so taken. (P. 730.)
>
> SEC. 9. *And be it further enacted*, That if any person shall drive, or otherwise convey any stock of horses, mules, or cattle, to range and feed on any land belonging to any Indian or Indian tribe, without the consent of such tribe, such person shall forfeit the sum of one dollar for each animal of such stock. (P. 730.)

The last of these provisions, which is still in force,[204] has been interpreted to cover only the case where cattle are "driven" to the reservation, or to the vicinity of the reservation.[205] It has been held that sheep are "cattle" within the meaning of this section.[206]

Following the 1834 act, Congress provided for the protection of Indian lands against trespass in various other statutes. Thus, the Act of July 20, 1867,[207] entitled "An Act to establish Peace with certain Hostile Indian Tribes" provided that "all the Indian tribes now occupying territory east of the Rocky mountains, not now peacefully residing on permanent reservations under treaty stipulations" should be offered reservations. The In-

[193] Act of July 22, 1790, 1 Stat. 137.

[194] Act of March 1, 1793, 1 Stat. 329 ("without lawful license"); Acts of May 19, 1796, 1 Stat. 469; March 3, 1799, 1 Stat. 743; March 30, 1802, 2 Stat. 139; ("That no such citizen, or other person, shall be permitted to reside at any of the towns, or hunting camps of any of the Indian tribes as a trader without a license"); Act of June 30, 1834, 4 Stat. 729 ("That any person other than an Indian who shall attempt to reside in the Indian country as a trader, or to introduce goods, or to trade therein without such license, shall forfeit * * *"); Act of July 31, 1882, 22 Stat. 179; R. S. § 2133; 25 U. S. C. 264 ("Any person other than an Indian of the full blood who shall attempt to reside in the Indian country, or on any Indian reservation, as a trader, or to introduce goods, or to trade therein, without such license, shall forfeit * * * *Provided*, That this section shall not apply to any person residing among or trading with * * * the five civilized tribes, residing in said Indian country, and belonging to the Union Agency therein").

[195] Act of July 22, 1790, 1 Stat. 137, 138. See Chapter 1, sec. 2.

[196] Act of March 1, 1793, 1 Stat. 329 ("and shall there commit murder, robbery, larceny, trespass or other crime, against the person or property of any friendly Indian or Indians"); Act of May 19, 1796, 1 Stat. 469, and Acts of March 3, 1799, 1 Stat. 743; March 30, 1802, 2 Stat. 139 ("and shall there commit murder, robbery, larceny, trespass or other crime, against the person or property of any friendly Indian or Indians, which would be punishable, if committed within the jurisdiction of any state, against a citizen of the United States: or, unauthorized by law, and with a hostile intention, shall be found on any Indian land"); Act of June 30, 1834, 4 Stat. 729 ("That where, in the commission, by a white person, of any crime, offense, or misdemeanor, within the Indian country, the property of any friendly Indian is taken, injured or destroyed, and a conviction is had for such crime, offense, or misdemeanor, the person so convicted shall be sentenced to pay to such friendly Indian to whom the property may belong, or whose person may be injured, a sum equal to twice the just value of the property so taken, injured, or destroyed."): *cf.* R. S. § 2143, 25 U. S. C. 212 (imposing penalty for offense of arson in Indian country); R. S. § 2142, 25 U. S. C. 213 (imposing penalty for crime of assault in Indian country).

[197] Sec. 7.

[198] 1 Stat. 329. See Chapter 4, sec. 2.

[199] Act of March 3, 1799, sec. 5, 1 Stat. 743, 745.

[200] Act of March 1, 1793, sec. 15, 1 Stat. 329, 332.

[201] 1 Stat. 469. See Chapter 4, sec. 2.

[202] Act of March 30, 1802, 2 Stat. 139, 141. See Chapter 4, sec. 3.

[203] 4 Stat. 729. See Chapter 4, sec. 6.

[204] R. S. § 2117, 25 U. S. C. 179.

[205] Trespass on Indian Lands, 16 Op. A. G. 568 (1880).

[206] *Ash Sheep Co.* v. *United States*, 252 U. S. 159 (1920), a'ffg 250 Fed. 591 (C. C. A. 9, 1918), and 254 Fed. 59 (C. C. A. 9, 1918); Driving Stock on Indian Lands, 18 Op. A. G. 91 (1884); *United States* v. *Matlock*, 26 Fed Cas. No. 15744 (D. C. Ore. 1872), holding that the word cattle includes both sheep and all other animals used by man for labor or food.

[207] 15 Stat. 17.

dians' possessory right in such reservations was secured by the following statutory language:

> * * * Said district or districts, when so selected, and the selection approved by Congress, shall be and remain permanent homes for said Indians to be located thereon, and no person[s] not members of said tribes shall ever be permitted to enter thereon without the permission of the tribes interested, except officers and employees of the United States. (Sec. 2.)

B. CONGRESSIONAL RESPECT FOR TRIBAL POSSESSION

In addition to the foregoing statutes prohibiting various forms of trespass upon Indian lands, there is a considerable body of legislation which extends recognition to tribal possession by exempting tribal lands from provisions designed to open up the public domain to settlement.[208] Thus, for example, the Act of March 3, 1853,[209] relating to public lands in California, protects from settlement "any tract of land in the occupation or possession of any Indian tribe."[210]

The Act of May 17, 1884,[211] relating to Alaska contains a special proviso:

> *Provided*, That the Indians or other persons in said district shall not be disturbed in the possession of any lands actually in their use or occupation or now claimed by them but the terms under which such persons may acquire title to such lands is reserved for future legislation by Congress: * * * (P. 26.)

Protection of Indian possession is likewise the purpose of a provision in the Act of March 3, 1891,[212] establishing a court of private land claims to determine land claims in former Mexican territory within New Mexico, Arizona, Utah, Nevada, Colorado, and Wyoming:

> No claim shall be allowed that shall interfere with or overthrow any just and unextinguished Indian title or right to any land or place.

In the same spirit, grants of rights-of-way were frequently conditioned upon a special undertaking by the grantee that it

> * * * will neither aid, advise, nor assist in any effort looking towards the changing or extinguishing the present tenure of the Indians in their remaining lands, and will not attempt to secure from the Indian tribes any further grant of land or its occupancy than is hereinbefore provided: *Provided*, That any violation of the condition mentioned in this section shall operate as a forfeiture of all the rights and privileges of said railway company under this act.[213]

In 1888 the Attorney General was able to say:[214]

> * * * it was and is a well-known usage of the Government not to sell lands until the Indian title of occupancy should be extinguished * * *.

Even where Congress has not specifically provided for the protection of Indian possessory rights, the courts have read an implicit qualification into general legislation relating to the public domain, in order to protect such possession. Thus, in the case of *Spalding* v. *Chandler*, the Supreme Court declared:[215]

> * * * The general grant of authority conferred upon the President by the act of March 1, 1847, c. 32, 9 Stat. 146, to set apart such portion of lands within the land district then created as were necessary for public uses, cannot be considered as empowering him to interfere with reservations existing by force of a treaty. (P. 405.)

Likewise, school land grants have never been made in disregard of tribal possessory rights.[216] In the absence of an expressed intent of Congress to the contrary, railroad land grants have not affected tribal possessory rights.[217] Even where Congress expressly stipulated to extinguish Indian title, railroad land grants conveyed only the naked fee, subject to tribal occupancy and possessory rights.[218] Only where it was necessary to give emigrants possessory rights to parts of the public domain, has Congress ever granted tribal lands in disregard of tribal possessory rights.[219]

C. WHO MAY PROTECT TRIBAL POSSESSION

The protection of tribal possessory rights has been recognized as a proper function of the Army,[220] of the Interior Department,[221] and of the Department of Justice.[222] At the same time, the interest of the tribes themselves in self-protection has been recognized repeatedly in statutes.[223]

Although primary concern for the protection of Indian lands against trespass rests with the Indian tribe and the Federal Government, it has been held that the individual states have a legitimate interest in protecting Indian possession against trespass. Thus, it was early held by the Supreme Court that state laws protecting Indian lands against trespass were valid, and state decisions thereon entitled to great weight.[224] Where a state patent to land included land reserved for Indians under state law, it was held that such patent was void as to the erroneously

[208] Act of March 2, 1907, 34 Stat. 1229 (permission to landowners or entrymen to complete tracts at expense of reservation limited so as to exclude "lands in the use or occupation of any Indian having tribal rights on the Coeur d'Alene Reservation").

[209] 10 Stat. 244.

[210] Accord: Act of March 25, 1864, 13 Stat. 37.

[211] 23 Stat. 24. See chapter 21, sec. 8C.

[212] 26 Stat. 854.

[213] Act of September 1, 1888, 25 Stat. 452, 457 (Shoshone and Bannock); Act of March 3, 1887, 24 Stat. 545; Act of October 1, 1890, 26 Stat. 663.

[214] 19 Op. A. G. 117 (1888).

[215] 160 U. S. 394, 405 (1896). Accord: *United States* v. *McIntire*, 101 F. 2d 650 (C. C. A. 9. 1939), rev'g *McIntire* v. *United States*, 22 F. Supp. 316 (D. C. Mont. 1937); *United States* v. *Minnesota*, 270 U. S. 181 (1926). But *cf. United States* v. *Portneuf-Marsh Valley Irr. Co.*, 213 Fed. 601 (C. C. A. 9, 1914, aff'g 205 Fed. 416 (D. C. Idaho 1913). And see *Hot Springs Cases*, 92 U. S. 698, 703–704 (1875) (Indian possession protected against settlers by deny'ng them preemption claims).

[216] *Beecher* v. *Wetherby*, 95 U. S. 517, 526 (1877); *Wisconsin* v. *Hitchcock*, 201 U. S. 202 (1906).

[217] *Leavenworth, etc. R. R. Co.* v. *United States*, 92 U. S. 733 (1875); *Northern Pac. Ry. Co.* v. *United States*, 227 U. S. 355 (1913).

[218] *Buttz* v. *Northern Pac. Railroad*, 119 U. S. 55 (1886).

[219] Oregon Donation Act of September 27, 1850, c. 76 secs. 4, 5, 9 Stat. 496, 497, 498; New Mexico Donation Act of July 22, 1854, c. 103, sec. 2, 10 Stat. 308; Homestead Act of May 20, 1862, c. 75, 12 Stat. 392.

[220] See *United States ex rel. Gordon* v. *Crook*, 179 Fed. 391 (D. C. Nebr. 1875).

[221] *United States* v. *Mullin*, 71 Fed. 682 (D. C. Nebr., 1895).

[222] See, for instance, Joint Resolution of March 3, 1879, 20 Stat. 488, superseded by Act of March 1, 1889, 25 Stat. 768 (instructing Attorney General to bring suit to quiet tribal title); sec. 3, Pueblo Lands Act of June 7, 1924, 43 Stat. 636 (discussed in Chapter 20, sec. 4). And see Chapter 19, sec. 2A(1).

[223] Thus, for instance, sec. 2 of the Act of June 28, 1898, 30 Stat. 495 requires the courts in the Indian Territory to make tribes parties to suits affecting their possessory rights "by service upon a chief or governor of the tribe" whenever it appears "that the property of any tribe is in any way affected by the issues being heard." Sec. 4 of the Pueblo Lands Act of June 7, 1924, 43 Stat. 636, expressly protects the right of the individual Pueblos to bring suit in vindication of their land claims. The right to protect tribal property against trespass, inures only to the tribe whose land it is and not to Indians of another tribe who happen to be on the land. *Merchant* v. *United States*, 35 C. Cls. 403 (1900).

[224] *Danforth's Lessee* v. *Thomas*, 1 Wheat. 155 (1816); *Preston* v. *Browder*, 1 Wheat, 115 (1816). See also *Danforth* v. *Weur*, 9 Wheat, 673, 677 (1824).

included Indian lands.[225] The constitutionality of state legislation designed to protect Indian lands from trespass was upheld by the Supreme Court in *State of New York* v. *Dibble*.[226]

In that case the court declared, *per* Grier, *J.*:

> The statute in question is a police regulation for the protection of the Indians from intrusion of the white people, and to preserve the peace. * * * The power of a State to make such regulations to preserve the peace of the community is absolute, and has never been surrendered. (P. 370.)

D. EFFECT OF TITLE UPON POSSESSORY RIGHT

The protection which the Federal Government gives to tribal possession is not limited to the cases where title to tribal land is held in the name of the United States, but extends equally to lands where ultimate title is vested in the state. An illuminating analysis of this problem is found in a memorandum to the Assistant Attorney General dated April 29, 1935, regarding the Onondaga Reservation.[227] Copious authority is cited to show that even where the United States does not own the ultimate fee in the land of an Indian reservation, its relation of guardianship to the Indian tribe carries the power and duty of protecting the Indian possessory right against condemnation proceedings or other infringements by the state:

> As guardian of the Indians there is imposed upon the Government a duty to protect these Indians in their property; it follows that this duty extends to protecting them against the unlawful acts of the State of New York. (P. 222.)[228]

Likewise, it has been held that protection of tribal property by the Federal Government is not forsworn where a tribe incorporates under state law and thus achieves corporate capacity.[229]

E. AGAINST WHOM PROTECTION EXTENDS

Tribal possessory right in tribal land requires protection not only against private parties but against administrative officers acting without legal authority and against persons purporting to act with the permission of such officers. Thus where Indians were induced by administrative authorities to settle on a given area and the area was designated as the "Old Winnebagoe and Crow Creek Reservation" on Indian office maps, it was held that such lands were a "reservation" within the meaning of a subsequent treaty which set "reservation" lands apart "for the absolute and undisturbed use and occupation of the Indians herein named, and for such other friendly tribes or individual Indians as from time to time they may be willing, with the consent of the United States, to admit amongst them; * * *."[230] It was further held that a later Executive order of February 27, 1885, opening these lands to entry was invalid and inoperative.[231]

It was likewise ruled by the Attorney General that an application for permission to construct a ditch across an Executive order reservation, without the consent of the Indians, could not be legally granted by Interior Department officials, even though the ditch was supposed to be beneficial to the Indians. The Attorney General declared:

> But the petitioners allege the reservation is not a legal one, and in consequence thereof the Indians for whom the reservation was made are only tenants at will of the Government. But the rights of tenants at will, so long as the landlord does not elect to determine the tenancy, are as sacred as those of a tenant in fee.[232]

It has also been held [233] that the Federal Government is under an obligation to protect tribal lands even against fellow tribesmen.

The respect for tribal possessory rights shown by Congress and the courts has not always been shared by administrative authorities. In recent years, however, the Department of the Interior has strictly adhered to the view that a tribe may exclude from tribal property any nonmembers not specially authorized by law to enter thereon, that, having the right so to exclude outsiders, the tribe may condition the entry of such persons by requiring payments of fees, and that federal authorities, in the absence of specific legislative authorization, may not invite outsiders to enter upon tribal lands without tribal consent.

Indian possessory rights are enforceable against state authorities as well as against federal authorities.[234] Thus, where a treaty between the United States and the Seneca Nation provided:

> The United States acknowledge all the land within the aforementioned boundaries (which include the reservations in question) to be the property of the Seneca nation, and the United States will never claim the same nor disturb the Seneca nation, * * * in the free use and enjoyment thereof; but it shall remain theirs until they choose to sell the same * * *. (Pp. 766–767.)

the Supreme Court held that state taxation of tribal lands was inconsistent with the treaty and invalid.[235] The court declared:

> The tax titles purporting to convey these lands to the purchaser, even with the qualification suggested that the right of occupation is not to be affected, may well embarrass the occupants and be used by unworthy persons to the disturbance of the tribe. All agree that the Indian right of occupancy creates an indefeasible title to the reservations that may extend from generation to generation, and will cease only by the dissolution of the tribe, or their consent to sell to the party possessed of the right of pre-emption. He is the only party that is authorized to deal with the tribe in respect to their property, and this with the consent of the government. Any other party is an intruder, and may be proceeded against under the twelfth section of the act of 30th June, 1834.* (P. 771.)
>
> *4 Stat. at Large, 730. (P. 771.)

The question of how far Indian possessory rights are protected against Congress raises a problem of constitutional law considered earlier in Chapter 5.

With the establishment of the right of Indian tribes to the protection of federal and state governments (as well as self-protection) against trespass, whether by private parties or by state or federal officers, it becomes pertinent to consider the exact extent of the possessory right to which this protection attaches.

[225] *Danforth* v. *Wear*, *supra*; *Patterson* v. *Jenks*, 2 Pet. 216 (1829).

[226] 62 U. S. 366 (1858).

[227] 5 L. D. Memo. 179, April 29, 1935.

[228] *Ibid.*

[229] *United States* v. *7,405.3 Acres of Land*, 97 F. 2d 417 (C. C. A. 4, 1938.) And see 12 L. D. Memo. 206, January 14, 1938.

[230] Treaty of April 29 *et seq*, 1868, 15 Stat. 635.

[231] Old Winnebago and Crow Creek Reservation, 18 Op. A. G. 141 (1886).

[232] Lemhi Indian Reservation, 18 Op. A. G. 563 (1887).

[233] *St. Marie* v. *United States*, 24 F. Supp. 237 (D. C. S. D. Cal. 1938). See also Chapter 9, sec. 5C.

[234] *Danforth* v. *Wear*, 9 Wheat. 673 (1824).

[235] *The New York Indians*, 5 Wall. 761 (1866). See Chapter 18, secs. 1–3.

SECTION 11. EXTENT OF TRIBAL POSSESSORY RIGHTS

The extent of possessory right vested in an Indian tribe may differ in important respects from that of ordinary private possessory rights. Some of these differences run to the advantage of the Indian tribe; others, to its disadvantage.

Because an Indian tribe is a ward of the Government, it has been held that adverse possession under the statute of limitations does not run against an Indian tribe, even where title to the land is vested in the tribe and the tribe is incorporated under state law.[236] This rule was slightly modified by Congress, with respect to the Pueblos of New Mexico, in view of the fact that for many years these Pueblos had enjoyed the right to sue and be sued under territorial law.[237] The compromise adopted in the Pueblo Lands Act of June 7, 1924,[238] was to the effect that adverse possession might be established by proof of (*a*) "open, notorious, actual, exclusive, continuous, adverse possession of the premises claimed, under color of title from the 6th day of January, 1902, to the date of the passage of this Act" together with proof of tax payments, or (*b*) such possession "with claim of ownership, but without color of title from the 16th day of March, 1889."

While tribal lands are, like other lands, subject to the federal power of eminent domain,[239] they are not subject to the state power of eminent domain except where Congress has specifically so provided.[240] The constitutionality of congressional acts conferring upon state or private agencies the power to condemn tribal land is established beyond question.[241]

Tribal possessory rights may, as we have already noted, be expressly qualified by the statute, treaty, or Executive order establishing the right, and in this way made subject, for instance, to entry under public land mineral laws.[242]

Except for special limitations and special advantages of the type above noted, tribal possessory rights are equivalent in extent to the possessory rights of private persons.[243]

[236] *United States* v. *7,405.3 Acres of Land*, 97 F. 2d 417 (C. C. A. 4, 1938); *United States* v. *Wright*, 53 F. 2d 300 (C. C. A. 4, 1931); Memo. *re* Eastern Band of Cherokee Indians of North Carolina, 7 L. D. Memo. 517, 531, 534, August 4, 1936. Memo. *re* 97 F. 2d 417, 12 L. D. Memo. 206, 210, January 14, 1938. Accord: *United States* v. *Candelaria*, 271 U. S. 432, 440 (1926); *United States* v. *Minnesota*, 270 U. S. 181, 196 (1926); *United States* v. *Sandoval*, 231 U. S. 28 (1913); *Heckman* v. *United States*, 224 U. S. 413, 438 (1912).

[237] See Chapter 20, sec. 4.

[238] 43 Stat. 636.

[239] *Cherokee Nation* v. *Southern Kansas Ry. Co.*, 135 U. S. 641 (1890), reversing 33 Fed. 900 (D. C. W. D. Ark. 1888) (interpreting Act of July 4, 1884, 23 Stat. 73).

[240] *United States* v. *Minnesota*, 95 F. 2d 468 (C. C. A. 8, 1938), aff'd. sub nom. *Minnesota* v. *United States*, 305 U. S. 382 (1939); *United States* v. *Colvard*, 89 F. 2d 312 (C. C. A. 4, 1937); Op. Sol. I. D., M.29961, October 4, 1938 (Eastern Cherokees); see Act of February 28, 1919, 40 Stat. 1206, authorizing condemnation of lands of Capitan Grande Reservation by the City of San Diego, subject to the approval of the terms of the judgment by the Secretary of the Interior. Accord: Act of June 28, 1898, sec. 11, 30 Stat. 495, 498 (authorizing towns and cities in Indian Territory to condemn tribal lands).

[241] The extent and basis of this power is analyzed in Federal Eminent Domain (1939), Secs. 9 and 15N. See also Randolph, Eminent Domain (1894) sec. 30 and cases cited.

[242] Op. Sol. I. D., M.28183, October 16, 1935, holding that prospectors taking by claim on Papago Indian lands under public land mineral laws, must pay tribe for surface use if claim was taken up after passage of Act of June 18, 1934, 48 Stat. 984, but not if claim was taken up prior to such act.

[243] See Act of July 14, 1862, 12 Stat. 566, granting to white settlers the value of improvements on lands occupied by them which are reserved for Indian use, showing Congress' assumption that the establishment of the Indian reservation wiped out the claims of the prior settlers. Accord: Act of June 3, 1874, 18 Stat. 555 (Makah); Act of March 3, 1885, 23 Stat. 677 (Duck Valley). See also Act of August 4, 1886, 24 Stat. 876 (refund to entryman of payments made to land office where entry on Indian reservation was subsequently cancelled). *Cf.* Joint Resolution, of February 8, 1887, 14 Stat. 640 (Sioux); Act of February 11, 1920, 41 Stat. 1459 (Siletz); Act of March 3, 1925, 43 Stat. 1586 (L'Anse and Vieux Desert).

SECTION 12. THE TERRITORIAL EXTENT OF INDIAN RESERVATIONS

In determining the extent of Indian tribal lands, first importance naturally attaches to the treaty, statute, or other document upon which tribal ownership is predicated or by which it is defined. The fixing of boundaries of Indian reservations was a major part of early governmental policy in Indian affairs, as a means of securing peace between Indians and whites and among the Indian tribes themselves.[244] Both by treaty[245] and by statute[246] the United States has endeavored to settle conflicting claims and to resolve ambiguities in the definition of reservation boundaries.[247]

Where the delimitation of tribal lands has proved to be of special difficulty, Congress has occasionally referred the determination of such boundaries to the Court of Claims,[248] or the Secretary of the Interior,[249] or has established a special tribunal to determine such questions.[250]

In interpreting treaties and statutes defining Indian boundaries, the Supreme Court has said:

> * * * our effort must be to ascertain and execute the intention of the treaty makers, and as an element in the effort we have declared that concession must be made to the understanding of the Indians in redress of the differences in the power and intelligence of the contracting parties. *United States* v. *Winans*, 198 U. S. 371. The present case invokes in special degree the principle.[251]

Apart from the foregoing principle, the same rules apply to the resolution of ambiguities in reservation boundaries as are applied to similar ambiguities in other deeds or patents.[252]

It is presumed that the bed of a navigable stream is not conveyed to an Indian tribe but is reserved by the United States for the future state to be established.[253] However, an intent to confer ownership rights upon the Indian tribe in such stream bed may be shown by the context of the boundary description,[254] and such intent appears definitely where territory on both sides of the river is reserved to the Indian tribe. As was said in *Donnelly* v. *United States*:[255] "It would be absurd to treat the order as intended to include the uplands to the width of one mile to each side of the river, and at the same time to exclude the river" (at p. 259).[256] Tide lands and beds of navigable streams which have been made a part of an Indian reservation

[244] See Chapter 3, sec. 3A(2). The fixing of intertribal boundaries was the chief purpose of certain treaties, *e. g.*, Treaty of August 19, 1825, with Chippewas *et al.*, 7 Stat. 272; see 5 Op. A. G. 31 (1848).

[245] See Chapter 3, sec. 3A(2).

[246] Act of March 3, 1875, 18 Stat. 476 (boundary between State of Arkansas and Indian country); Act of June 6, 1894, 28 Stat. 86 (Warm Springs Reservation); Act of June 6, 1900, 31 Stat. 672 (conflicting tribal claims of Choctaw-Chickasaw and Comanche, Kiowa, and Apache).

[247] To the effect that the parties to a treaty are authorised to determine its meaning, and to define boundaries which the terms of the treaty leave unclear, see *Lattimer* v. *Poteet*, 14 Pet. 4 (1840).

[248] Act of January 9, 1925, 43 Stat. 730 (title to Red Pipestone Quarries); *cf.* Act of June 28, 1898, sec. 29, 30 Stat. 495, 513.

[249] Act of June 7, 1872, 17 Stat. 281 (Sisseton and Wahpeton).

[250] Act of March 3, 1851, sec. 16, 9 Stat. 631, 634 (California private land claims); Pueblo Lands Act of June 7, 1924, 43 Stat. 636, discussed in Chapter 20, sec. 4.

[251] *Northern Pacific Ry. Co.* v. *United States*, 227 U. S. 355, at p. 362 (1913), aff'g 191 Fed. 947 (C. C. A. 9, 1911).

[252] *Meigs* v. *M'Clung's Lessee*, 9 Cranch 11 (1815) (holding that unilateral action of United States agents cannot give meaning to treaty, which is a bilateral contract). See also 29 Op. A. G. 455 (1912) (Chippewa).

[253] *United States* v. *Holt State Bank*, 270 U. S. 49, 55 (1926), aff'g 294 Fed. 161 (C. C. A. 8, 1923).

[254] *United States* v. *Hutchings*, 252 Fed. 841 (D. C. W. D. Okla. 1918), aff'd sub nom. *Commissioners* v. *United States*, 270 Fed. 110 (C. C. A. 8, 1920), app. dism. 260 U. S. 753 (land to middle of nonnavigable river included in Osage Reservation). Accord: *Brewer-Elliott Oil & Gas Co.* v. *United States*, 260 U. S. 77 (1922), aff'g 270 Fed. 100 (C. C. A. 8, 1920), and 249 Fed. 609 (D. C. W. D. Okla. 1918).

[255] 228 U. S. 243 (1913).

[256] Followed in 55 I. D. 475 (1936) (Fort Berthold Reservation), Memo. Sol. I. D., July 5, 1939 (Owhi Lake in Colville Reservation).

by treaty or otherwise [257] do not pass to a state subsequently created, as do public lands similarly situated.[258] Where the high-water mark is referred to in designating the boundaries of an Indian reservation, there is no implied reservation of tide lands.[259]

The principles of international law applicable to boundary disputes have been invoked in reaching the determination that an island once part of an Indian reservation remains so although it becomes attached to the opposite bank of the river through a sudden change in the stream bed.[260]

In other cases local state law has been invoked to settle ambiguities,[261] and it has been held that where, under Minnesota law, the title of the riparian owner stops at the water's edge, the ownership by an Indian tribe of the entire shore line of a lake will not disturb state ownership of the lake bed.[262]

Errors in surveying boundaries fixed by treaties or statutes have occasionally given rise to tribal claims.[263]

[257] *United States* v. *Boynton*, 53 F. 2d 297 (C. C. A. 9, 1931) rev'g 49 F. 2d 810 (D. C. W. D. Wash. 1931) (land between high and low tide reserved for tribe, not allottees); *United States* v. *Romaine*, 255 Fed. 253 (C. C. A. 9, 1919). But *cf. United States* v. *Snohomish River Boom Co.*, 246 Fed. 112 (C. C. A. 9, 1917).

[258] *United States* v. *Stotts*. 49 F. 2d 619 (D. C. W. D. Wash. 1930); *Taylor* v. *United States*, 44 F. 2d 531 (C. C. A. 9, 1930); Op. Sol. I. D., M. 28120, March 31, 1936.

[259] *United States* v. *Holt State Bank*, 270 U. S. 49, 55 (1926), aff'g 294 Fed. 161 (C. C. A. 8, 1923); *Taylor* v. *United States*, 44 F. 2d 531 (C. C. A. 9, 1930), cert. den. 283 U. S. 820; *United States* v. *Ashton*, 170 Fed. 509 (C. C. W. D. Wash. 1909), app. dism. sub nom. *Bird* v. *Ashton*, 220 U. S. 604 (1911), without opinion.

[260] Sheyenne Island, Missouri River, 18 Op. A. G. 230 (1885).

[261] *United States* v. *Ladley*, 4 F. Supp. 580 (D. C. N. D. Idaho, 1933).

[262] Memo Sol. I. D., December 19, 1936.

[263] See, for example, *Creek Nation* v. *United States*, 302 U. S. 620 (1938), rev'g 84 C. Cls. 12. Other aspects of the case are considered in 295 U. S. 103 (1935), rev'g 77 C. Cls. 159, and in 87 C. Cls. 280 (1938).

SECTION 13. THE TEMPORAL EXTENT OF INDIAN TITLES

The question of when Indian possessory rights in a given tract of land come to an end, or, in technical terms, the question of the quantum of the tribal estate in land, has generally been raised in connection with such title as depends upon actual occupancy. The assumption that all possession of lands by Indian tribes is of an identical type has elsewhere been discussed and criticized and need not be reexamined at this point.[264]

Within the diversity of tenures by which tribal lands are held, there undoubtedly exists a type of ownership that ceases when the tribe becomes extinct or abandons the land. Although this circumstance is commonly cited as indicating a peculiar tenure by which Indian lands are held, an examination of the prevailing doctrines of real property law at the time when the theory of "Indian title" was first advanced, shows that there is nothing novel or peculiar about the legal justification or the practical significance of the doctrine. Under the feudal theory of English law, where the owner of land died without heirs or committed a felony, the land escheated to the Crown, or to the mesne lord. This right of escheat was not, strictly speaking, a form of inheritance but was a sovereign right superior to the property right of any landlord.[265] The right of escheat became less valuable, with respect to individual landowners, when the statutory right of testamentary disposition was extended to real property. An Indian tribe, however, could not, under British or American law, alienate its land without the consent of the Crown or the Federal Government. Therefore, the possibility that land would be left vacant when a tribe disintegrated or abandoned the land was a real possibility and the rule of escheat served the same purpose that it served under early feudal conditions in England. Land held by a tribe in fee simple would be subject to escheat and it is unnecessary to assume any peculiarity of "Indian title" to explain this result.

Although technically the right of escheat was something entirely distinct from a possibility of reverter, there is ample precedent for confusing the two institutions.[266] Thus, although one might say with perfect accuracy that land held by an Indian tribe in fee simple would escheat to the United States when the tribe became extinct or abandoned the property, it became fashionable to refer to this incident as a possibility of reverter, rather than escheat. This use of language was not restricted to Indian tribes, but was applied, in the early nineteenth century, to all corporations under the doctrine that a corporation had "only a determinable fee for the purposes of enjoyment. On the dissolution of the corporation, the reverter is to the original grantor or his heirs." [267] It was generally agreed that "corporations have a fee simple for the purpose of alienation," [268] but this portion of the doctrine was, of course, inapplicable to Indian tribes.

If these observations are well taken, we should conclude that it makes little practical difference whether we describe an Indian estate as a fee simple absolute subject to the ordinary sovereign right of escheat, or call the Indians' estate a determinable fee with a possibility of reverter in the sovereign, or refer to "Indian title of use and occupancy."

The only point at which these various theories may perhaps diverge lies in the test to be applied to determine when land has been "abandoned."

In *Holden* v. *Joy* [269] the Indian estate in question was to be, according to the governing treaty, a fee simple, but the patent issued by the President included the condition "that the lands hereby granted shall revert to the United States, if the said Cherokees become extinct, or *abandon* the same." [270] The Supreme Court rejected the argument that such abandonment took place by reason of (*a*) Cherokee participation in the Civil War on the part of the Confederacy, or (*b*) an agreement whereby the Cherokees allowed Congress to sell the land for their benefit. The Court held that the Cherokee title continued until, by the agreement in question, title became vested in the United States. The Court further declared:

> Beyond doubt the Cherokees were the owners and occupants of the territory where they resided before the first approach of civilized man to the western continent, deriving their title, as they claimed, from the Great Spirit, to whom the whole earth belongs, and they were unquestionably the sole and exclusive masters of the territory, and claimed the right to govern themselves by their own laws, usages, and customs. * * *
>
> * * * * *
>
> Enough has already been remarked to show that the lands conveyed to the United States by the treaty were held by the Cherokees under their original title, acquired by immemorial possession, commencing ages before the New World was known to civilized man. Unmistak-

[264] See secs. 5, 6, 10, and 18 of this chapter.

[265] See "Escheat," 5 Encyc. Soc. Sci. 591 (T. F. T. Plucknett).

[266] *Op. cit.* note 131.

[267] 2 Kent Commentaries 282. And see 4 Thompson on Corporations, 3d ed., 1927, sec. 2455.

[268] *Ibid.*

[269] 17 Wall. 211 (1872).

[270] Quotation from patent. *Ibid.*

> ably their title was absolute, subject only to the preemption right of purchase acquired by the United States as the successors of Great Britain, and the right also on their part as such successors of the discoverer to prohibit the sale of the land to any other governments or their subjects, and to exclude all other governments from any interference in their affairs. (Pp. 243–244.)

Again, the Supreme Court held in *New York Indians* v. *United States*,[371] that delay in the settlement of new lands did not constitute abandonment.[372] On the other hand, the Supreme Court, holding that the Pottawatomies do not own a large part of the city of Chicago, indicated as one basis for its decision the fact that the Pottawatomies had, after conveying at least all the lands above the lake level, abandoned the district for more than half a century.[373] It appears to be settled law that actual removal of an entire tribe from one reservation to another, where such removal is voluntary, constitutes abandonment.[374]

Although various dicta may be found asserting that the title of Indian tribes is less, in point of temporal extent, than a fee simple, reliance upon such dicta has proven extremely hazardous.[375] A realistic analysis of the cases suggests that the only clear distinction between "Indian title" and "fee simple title" lies in the fact that Indian lands are subject to statutory restrictions upon alienation.[376]

[371] 170 U. S. 1 (1898), app. dism. 173 U. S. 464.

[372] *Cf. The New York Indians*, 5 Wall. 761 (1866) (holding that interest in original land continues until date fixed for removal).

[373] *Williams* v. *City of Chicago*, 242 U. S. 434 (1917).

[374] *Butts* v. *Northern Pacific Railroad*, 119 U. S. 55 (1886); *Shore* v. *Shell Pet. Corp.*, 60 F. 2d 1 (C. C. A. 10, 1932), aff'g. 55 F. 2d 696, cert. den. 287 U. S. 656. And see cases cited in sec. 4, *supra*.

[375] See, for instance, the discussion of "waste" in *United States* v. *Cook*, 19 Wall. 591, 593 (1873), and erroneous decisions, based on this discussion, which are noted in sec. 15, *infra*.

[376] See sec. 18, *infra*.

SECTION 14. SUBSURFACE RIGHTS

Whether the possessory right of an Indian tribe includes minerals depends, as does every other question relating to the extent of Indian possessory rights, upon the treaty, statute, Executive order or other document or course of action upon which the right is based. Where a treaty, statute, or Executive order specifically provides that minerals on Indian land shall be reserved to the United States[377] or where a statute specifies that title to land purchased for an Indian tribe shall not extend to mineral rights,[378] no question is likely to arise. So, too, a treaty or statute may provide that the Indian tribe shall have specified rights of mining or quarrying in land belonging to the United States.[379]

Questions as to the Indian right to minerals have generally arisen where nothing specific appears in the treaty, statute, or other document upon which the Indian claim is based, or where the Indian claim is based simply on aboriginal occupancy. Confirmation of the view that aboriginal occupancy may include subsurface rights as well as surface rights is found in the case of *Chouteau* v. *Molony*.[380] A treaty provision by which designated lands were "set apart for the absolute and undisturbed use and occupation of the Shoshone Indians" was held to convey to the Indians full mineral, as well as timber, rights, in the case of *United States* v. *Shoshone Tribe*.[381]

Further analysis of the extent of Indian mineral rights is found in the opinion [382] of Attorney General (afterwards Justice) Stone rendered on May 27, 1924, with reference to the proposal of Secretary of the Interior Fall to open Executive order reservation lands to mineral entry under the laws governing minerals within the public domain. After analyzing the terms of the general mining laws, the Attorney General declared:

> The general mining laws never applied to Indian reservations, whether created by treaty, Act of Congress, or executive order. *Noonan* v. *Caledonia Min. Co.*, 121 U. S. 393; *Kendall* v. *San Juan Silver Mining Co.*, 144 U. S. 658; *M'Fadden* v. *Mountain View M. & M. Co.*, 97 Fed. 670; *Gibson* v. *Anderson*, 131 Fed. 39.

In support of this conclusion, based upon the language of the general mining laws, the Attorney General presented an analysis of Indian mineral rights which may well be set forth in full, without comment, as a complete exposition of the subject.

> If the extent of the Indian rights depended merely on definitions, or on deductions to be drawn from descriptive terms, there might be some question whether the right of "occupancy and use" included any right to the hidden or latent resources of the land, such as minerals or potential water power, of which the Indians in their original state had no knowledge. As a practical matter, however, that question has been resolved in favor of the Indians by a uniform series of legislative and treaty provisions beginning many years ago and extending to the present time. Thus the treaty provisions for the allotment of reservation lands all contemplate the final passing of a perfect fee title to the individuals of the tribe. And that meant, of course, that minerals and all other hidden or latent resources would go with the fee. The same is true of the General Allotment Act of 1887, which applies expressly to executive order reservations as well as to others. Then, beginning years ago, many special acts were passed (with or without previous agreements with the Indians concerned) whereby surplus lands remaining to the tribe after completion of the allotments were to be sold for their benefit. In all these instances Congress has recognized the right of the Indians to receive the full sales value of the land, including the value of the timber, the minerals, and all other elements of value, less only the expenses of the Government in surveying and selling the land. Legislation and treaties of this character were dealt with in *Frost* v. *Wenie*, 157 U. S. 46, 50; *Minnesota* v. *Hitchcock*, 185 U. S. 373; *Lone Wolf* v. *Hitchcock*, 187 U. S. 553; *United States* v. *Blendaur*, 128 Fed. 910, 913; *Ash Sheep Co.* v. *United States*, 252 U. S. 159.
>
> Similar provisions have been made in many other cases for the sale of surplus tribal lands, all the proceeds of all elements of value to go to the tribe. In a recent Act for further allotment of Crow Indian lands (41 Stat. 751), the minerals are reserved to the tribe instead of passing to the allottees (Sec. 6); and moreover, unallotted lands chiefly valuable for the development of water power are

[377] See, for example, Art. III of Treaty of August 5, 1826, with the Chippewa Indians, 7 Stat. 290; Act of February 21, 1931, 46 Stat. 1202 (Papago Indians), construed in Op. Sol. I. D., M.27656, March 7, 1934, and Op. Sol. I. D., M.27656, May 7, 1934.

[378] Act of February 15, 1929, 45 Stat. 1186 (Alabama and Coushatta); Act of June 22, 1936, 49 Stat. 1806 (Walker River); Act of June 26, 1936, sec. 1, 49 Stat. 1967, 1968, 25 U. S. C. 507 (Oklahoma).

[379] *Yankton Sioux Tribe* v. *United States*, 61 C. Cls. 40 (1925). In this case it was held that a treaty reservation of the right to quarry pipestone in a given area did not confer upon the tribe concerned a right of occupancy. The suit was brought under sec. 22 of the Act of April 4, 1910 36 Stat. 269, 284, on the basis of the Treaty of April 19, 1858, 11 Stat. 743. The decision was reversed on other grounds in 272 U. S. 351 (1926).

[380] 16 How. 203 (1853). *Cf.* Joint Resolution of April 16, 1800, 2 Stat. 87, authorizing the President to determine whether Indian title to copper lands adjacent to Lake Superior was "yet subsisting, and if so, the terms on which the same can be extinguished." But *cf.* discussion of separation of surface and mineral rights under Spanish law, in Op. Sol. I. D., M.27656, March 7, 1934.

[381] 304 U. S. 111 (1938), aff'g *Shoshone Tribe* v. *United States*, 85 C. Cls. 331 (1937); the argument *contra* will be found in a memorandum of the Assistant Attorney General dated December 8, 1937 (11 L. D. Memo. 468).

[382] 34 Op. A. G. 181 (1924). This opinion follows that of Solicitor Edwards of the Department of the Interior (A.2592), dated February 12, 1924.

reserved from allotment "for the benefit of the Crow Tribe of Indians" (Sec. 10). The Federal Water Power Act of June 10, 1920 (41 Stat. 1063), applies to tribal lands in Indian reservations of all kinds, but it provides (Sec. 17) that "all proceeds from any Indian reservation shall be placed to the credit of the Indians," etc.

Again, by a provision in the Indian Appropriation Act of June 30, 1919, the Secretary of the Interior was authorized to lease, for the purpose "of mining for deposits of gold, silver, copper, and other valuable metalliferous minerals," any part of the unallotted lands within "any Indian reservation" within the States of Arizona, California, Idaho, Montana, Nevada, New Mexico, Oregon, Washington, or Wyoming" heretofore withdrawn from entry under the mining laws. These States contain numerous executive order reservations, and yet the Act declares that all the royalties accruing from such leases shall be paid to the United States "for the benefit of the Indians." (41 Stat. 3, 31–33.)

The opening to entry by Congress of a part of the Colville Reservation established in Washington by executive order has been cited as an exception to this line of precedents. (Act July 1, 1892, 27 Stat. 62.) But the exception is more apparent than real; for Congress, though it expressly declined to recognize affirmatively any right in the Indians "to any part" of that reservation (Sec. 8), yet, in fact, preserved the right of allotment, required the entrymen to pay for the lands, and set aside the proceeds for the benefit of the Indians for an indefinite period. Later, the proceeds of timber sales from the former reservation lands were secured to the Indians, but the mineral lands were subjected to the mineral laws without any express direction for the disposal of the proceeds, if any. (Act July 1, 1898, 30 Stat. 571, 593.) The Committee reports show that the reservation was considered as improvidently made, excessive in area, and that the action taken was really for the best interests of the Indians. (Senate Report No. 664, 52d Cong., 1st sess., vol. 3; House Report No. 1035, 52d Cong., 1st sess., vol. 4.)

In respect to legislation and treaties of this character two views are possible. First, that the right of occupancy and use extends merely to the surface and the United States, in providing that the Indians shall ultimately receive the value of the hidden and latent resources, merely gives them its own property as an act of grace. Second, that the Indian possession extended to all elements of value in or connected with their lands, and the Government, in securing those values to the Indians recognizes and confirms their pre-existing right. If it were necessary here to decide as between these opposing views, I should incline strongly to the latter; mainly because the Indian possession has always been recognized as complete and exclusive until terminated by conquest or treaty, or by the exercise of that plenary power of guardianship to dispose of tribal property of the Nation's wards without their consent. *Lone Wolf* v. *Hitchcock*, 187 U. S. 553. Moreover, support for this view is found in many expressions of the courts.* * *

* * * * * * *

The important matter here, however, is that neither the courts nor Congress have made any distinction as to the character or extent of the Indian rights, as between executive order reservations and reservations established by treaty or Act of Congress. So that if the General Leasing Act applies to one class, there seems to be no ground for holding that it does not apply to the others. (Pp. 189–192.)

Various special acts relating to the disposition of minerals on Indian reservations proceed on the assumption that, in the absence of a clear expression to the contrary, tribal possession extends "to the center of the earth." [283] Generally such statutes provide that the proceeds of such disposition shall inure to the benefit of the tribe concerned.[284]

Recognition of Indian mineral rights is also found in special statutes authorizing Indian tribes to execute mineral leases.[285] Further recognition of tribal mineral leases is found in the statutes referred to in Attorney General Stone's opinion, which, in allotting lands, reserved to the tribe the underlying mineral rights.[286]

Further recognition of Indian mineral rights is found in various jurisdictional acts.[287]

As noted in Attorney General Stone's opinion, the authorities are uniform in holding that minerals underlying Indian lands which have not been expressly reserved to the United States are not subject to disposition under the general mining laws.[288]

Under the foregoing authorities it must be held that Indian title to minerals is valid as against federal administrative authorities, as well as against private parties.[289]

[283] Act of July 1, 1902, 32 Stat. 641 (Choctaw-Chickasaw), construed in 35 Op. A. G. 259 (1927); Act of January 21, 1903, 32 Stat. 774 (timber and stone in Indian Territory). *Cf.* Act of February 20, 1896, 29 Stat. 9 (opening designated area of Colville Reservation to entry under general mineral land laws) construed in *United States* v. *Four Bottles Sour-Mash Whiskey*, 90 Fed. 720 (D. C. Wash. 1898). *Cf.* also Act of August 14, 1848, 9 Stat. 741 (Ottawa, Pottawatomie, Chippewa, etc.).

[284] Act of May 30, 1908, 35 Stat. 558 (Fort Peck Indian Reservation); Act of June 1, 1910, 36 Stat. 455 (Fort Berthold Indian Reservation); Act of January 11, 1915, 38 Stat. 792 (Rosebud Indian Reservation); Act of February 27, 1917, 39 Stat. 944 (an act to authorize agricultural entries on surplus coal lands in Indian reservations).

[285] Act of August 7, 1882, 22 Stat. 349 (Cherokee salt mines). And see sec. 19, *infra*.

[286] Act of March 3, 1927, 44 Stat. 1401 (Fort Peck); Act of June 28, 1906, 34 Stat. 539 (Osage), construed in 33 Op. A. G. 60 (1921), recognized in the Act of March 3, 1909, 35 Stat. 778, period of tribal ownership extended by Act of March 3, 1921, 41 Stat. 1249 and Act of March 2, 1929, 45 Stat. 1478; constitutionality of extension upheld in *Adams* v. *Osage Tribe of Indians*, 59 F. 2d 653 (C. C. A. 10, 1932), aff'g. 50 F. 2d 918 (D. C. N. D. Okla. 1931), cert. den. 287 U. S. 652; Act of July 1, 1898, 30 Stat. 567 (reserving to Seminole tribe half interest in minerals underlying allotted lands).

[287] Act of February 20, 1929, 45 Stat. 1249 (Nez Perce jurisdictional act recognizing propriety of tribal claim for gold mined by trespassers).

[288] *French* v. *Lancaster*, 2 Dak. 346 (1880) and cases cited in text quotation. See Martin, Mining Law and Land-Office Procedure (1908), sec. 46, and authorities cited in support of the conclusion, "Lands embraced in an Indian reservation are not subject to mining laws, or to mineral exploration and entry." Accord: Morrison's Mining Rights (16th ed., 1936), pp. 426–427; Costigan, American Mining Law (1908), sec. 23, and see early Land Office rulings cited in Copp, United States Mineral Lands (1881), 142, 253.

[289] *Cf.* Memo. Sol. I. D., July 1, 1936 (holding Government officials are not authorized to mine coal on the Navajo Reservation without the consent of the Indians).

SECTION 15. TRIBAL TIMBER [290]

With respect to every concrete question of tribal ownership of timber, as with all other questions relating to the extent of tribal possessory right, our starting point must be the language of the treaty, statute, or other document which establishes that right. Where by treaty the United States expressly reserves the right to use timber on tribal land,[291] or where the treaty specifically confirms the interest of the Indian tribe in timber,[292] no question is likely to arise as to the extent of the tribal possessory right.[293] Serious questions have arisen, however, where

[290] For general forest regulations, see 25 C. F. R. 61.1–61.29.

[291] Art. 9 of Treaty of April 19, 1858, with Yankton Tribe of Sioux, 11 Stat. 743.

[292] Art. 10 of Treaty of January 15, 1838, with New York Indians, 7 Stat. 550; Art. 2 of Treaty of August 13, 1868, with Nez Perce Tribe, 15 Stat. 693.

[293] Nor is this question likely to arise where a statute specifies that title to land purchased for Indians may be taken subject to existing contracts for sale of timber. Act of February 15, 1929, 45 Stat. 1186 (Alabama and Coushatta).

the treaty or statute establishing the reservation has referred to "Indian use and occupancy" or used some similar phrase. These questions were seriously complicated by the interpretations placed on language of the Supreme Court in the cases of *United States* v. *Cook*[294] and *Pine River Logging Co.* v. *United States*.[295]

In the former of these cases, timber standing on tribal land was cut by individual Indians, without the authority of the Interior Department.[296] The United States brought an action of replevin against the vendee, and the Supreme Court held that the United States was entitled to recover possession of the timber. The Court based its decision upon the argument that since the timber while standing is a part of the realty, standing timber cannot be sold by the Indians, and only timber rightfully severed from the soil can be legally sold.[297] Whether timber was rightfully severed depended upon whether its cutting resulted in improvement of the land or on the contrary, amounted to waste. Since the facts of the case established the latter situation, the Court held that the possession of the vendee was illegal. The Court did *not* decide whether, in recovering the timber or its value, the United States was to hold such timber or funds in trust for the Indian tribe concerned, or whether such recovery was to accrue to the general funds of the United States Treasury.

In the course of its opinion, the Supreme Court, *per* Waite, *C. J.*, declared:

> These are familiar principles in this country and well settled, as applicable to tenants for life and remainder-men. But a tenant for life has all the rights of occupancy in the lands of a remainder-man. The Indians have the same rights in the lands of their reservations. What a tenant for life may do upon the lands of a remainder-man the Indians may do upon their reservations, but no more. (P. 594.)

The view thus expressed was confirmed by the Supreme Court in the *Pine River Logging Co.* case,[298] where an action in the nature of trover, brought by the United States against the vendees of unlawfully cut timber, was upheld by the Court. In the course of its opinion, the Court, *per* Brown, *J.*, declared:

> The argument overlooks the fact that the Indians had no right to the timber upon this land other than to provide themselves with the necessary wood for their individual use, or to improve their land, *United States* v. *Cook*, 19 Wall. 591, except so far as Congress chose to extend such right; that they had no right even to contract for the cutting of dead and down timber, unless such contracts were approved by the Commissioner of Indian Affairs; that the Indians in fact were not treated as *sui juris*. but every movement made by them, either in the execution or the performance of the contract, was subject to government supervision for the express purpose of securing the latter against the abuse of the right given by the statute. (P. 290.)

In the *Pine River Logging Co.* case (and probably in the *Cook* case) the Department of the Interior and the Department of Justice apparently construed the decision as implying that the tribe concerned had no property interest in the timber or in the funds recovered. In an opinion rendered in 1888, the Attorney General answered in the negative the following question presented by the Secretary of the Interior:[299]

> (1) Whether the Indians occupying reservations, the title to which is in the United States, have the right, in view of the opinion of the Supreme Court of the United States in the case of the *United States* v. *George Cook* (19 Wall. 591), to cut and sell for their use and benefit the dead and down timber which is found to a greater or less extent on many of the reservations and which will go to waste if not used? (Pp. 194–195.)

Two years later the Attorney General ruled that where timber on land of the Fond du Lac tribe was cut by trespassers, with the connivance of Indian Service officials, the timber should be sold by the Commissioner of the General Land Office, the proceeds to "belong to the Government absolutely."[300]

This view was supported by the argument that, under the *Cook* case, the Indians have "the mere right to use and enjoy the land as occupants" and that, therefore, "the Indians have no interest in this timber." The Board of Indian Commissioners had protested immediately after the decision in the *Cook* case, against an interpretation of that case which would "prevent the Indians from cutting and marketing their timber," alleging that such a construction, particularly when applied to dead and down timber, "would prove not only a loss to the Indians, but an absolute damage to the United States."[301] In 1889 Congress enacted a statute authorizing the sale of dead timber on Indian reservations by the Indians of the reservation, under Presidential regulations,[302] thus recognizing an Indian possessory right but leaving its extent still uncertain.

In a later opinion of the Attorney General, it was held that the Indian occupants of an Executive order reservation were entitled to the proceeds of timber sales.[303]

In the case of the *Shoshone Indians* v. *United States*,[304] the Court of Claims pointed out that the interpretation of the *Cook* case as denying the validity of the Indian interest in timber was unnecessary and unjustifiable. In the *Cook* case, it was pointed out, "The court decided that the members of the Oneida Tribe had no right to cut the timber on the land solely for the purpose of sale; that to do so was waste as in the case of the cutting of timber by a trespasser; and that the United States as the owner of the fee became the owner of the logs." The court further declared:

> In that case two points were decided: first, it was decided by analogy to the law relating to the respective rights of life-tenant and remainder-man, that the Indians have no right to cut the timber on an Indian reservation for the purpose of sale only; that to do so is waste, and that the

---

[294] 19 Wall. 591 (1873).

[295] 186 U. S. 279 (1902).

[296] Apparently the Interior Department took the position at this time that tribal timber might be sold by the Indian agent for the benefit of the tribe and that the tribe itself might give a valid permit for the cutting and marketing of timber. Sen. Ex. Doc. No. 72, 40th Cong., 2d sess., vol. 2, July 6, 1868.

[297] As was said in the case of *Starr* v. *Campbell*, 208 U. S. 527 (1908), involving timber on allotted lands.

> It is alleged that the value of the land, exclusive of the timber, is no more than $1,000; fifteen thousand dollars' worth of lumber has been cut from the land. The restraint upon alienation would be reduced to small consequence if it be confined to one-sixteenth of the value of the land and fifteen-sixteenths left to the unrestrained or unqualified disposition of the Indian. Such is not the legal effect of the patent. (P. 534.)

Accord: *United States* v. *Boyd*, 83 Fed. 547 (C. C. A. 4, 1897).

[298] *Op. cit.*, fn. 295.

[299] Timber on Indian Reservations, 19 Op. A. G. 194 (1888).

[300] Timber Unlawfully Cut on Indian Lands, 19 Op. A. G. 710 (1890).

[301] Letter from the Secretary of the Interior, House Ex. Doc. No. 61, 43d Cong., 2d sess., vol. 12, December 17, 1874. And *cf.* remarks of court in *United States* v. *Foster*, 25 Fed. Cas. No. 15141 (C. C. E. D., Wis. 1870):

> * * * while, perhaps, there may be some question whether the Indians would have the right to commit waste, properly so called, upon the land, or to use the timber for the purpose of speculation, still there can be no doubt they would have the right to clear the land for cultivation; and, if so, it would seem, to sell the wood thus obtained from the land; and to say that they could have the right to cut and use the wood and timber for these purposes, and that they could not sell it to enable them to obtain necessary articles, such as nails and other materials for the construction of their buildings and fences, would seem to be making a very refined distinction and one not warranted under the circumstances of the case.

[302] Act of February 16, 1889, 25 Stat. 673, 25 U. S. C. 196.

[303] Sales of Timber from Unallotted Lands of Indian Reservation, 29 Op. A. G. 239 (1911) (White Mountain Apache).

[304] 85 C. Cls. 331 (1937), aff'd 304 U. S. 111 (1938).

title to timber so cut vests in the United States as the owner of the fee or "ultimate domain"; second, that the Indians have an exclusive right of use and occupancy of *unlimited duration*, and the right to cut the standing timber *during the whole period of such occupancy* not only for use upon the premises but "for the purpose of improving the land or the better adapting it to convenient occupation"; also the right to sell all timber cut for the latter purpose. It is clear therefore that this decision did not hold that the government had the right to cut or dispose of the timber on Indian Reservations, or to sell Indian lands for its own use and benefit without accounting therefor to the Indian tribe. When a reservation is definitely set apart for an Indian tribe by treaty or statute, the Government has only the right and power to control and manage the property and affairs of the Indians in good faith for their betterment, but, as stated by the court in *Shoshone Tribe of Indians* v. *United States*, 299 U. S. 476:

> Power to control and manage the property and affairs of Indians in good faith for their betterment and welfare may be exerted in many ways and at times even in derogation of the provisions of a treaty. *Lone Wolf* v. *Hitchcock*, 187 U. S. 553, 564, 565, 566. The power does not extend so far as to enable the Government "to give the tribal lands to others, or to appropriate them to its own purposes, without rendering, or assuming an obligation to render, just compensation * * *; for that 'would not be an exercise of guardianship, but an act of confiscation.'" *United States* v. *Creek Nation*, *supra*, p. 110, 113; * * *.
>
> Government counsel argue here that *United States* v. *Cook*, *supra*, decided that the *interest* of the Indians in the reservation lands and timber thereon is that of a life-tenant and no more. In that case the court did say that "What a tenant for life may do upon the lands of a remainder-man the Indians may do upon their reservations, but no more." But in thus comparing the position of the Indian with that of a life-tenant for the purpose of stating what the Indians may or may not do on their reservations, we think the court did not intend definitely to hold that the *interest* of the Indians in the lands of their reservations is only that of a tenant for life. Such a holding would have been in conflict with the statement of the court after reviewing prior cases concerning the nature of Indian title, that the Indians have the right of use and occupancy of unlimited duration. We think also that the contention of counsel for defendant is inconsistent with the holding of the Supreme Court in the case at bar—that the power of the government to control and manage the property and affairs of the Indians in good faith for their betterment and welfare does not extend so far as to enable the government to give the land to others or to appropriate them to its own purposes. (Pp. 364–365.)

The decision of the Court of Claims, that the value of Shoshone lands taken by the Government must include the value of the timber thereon, was upheld by the Supreme Court on appeal,[305] and confirmed in the later case of *United States* v. *Klamath Indians*.[306] Following this decision, Congress by special statute directed the Secretary of the Treasury to credit to the tribal funds of the Chippewa Indians the amount of the judgment in the *Pine River Logging Co.* case, which had been erroneously deposited in the Treasury of the United States as public money, together with interest thereon.[307]

It must, therefore, be taken as settled law at the present time, that in the absence of specific language to the contrary the establishment of an Indian reservation for the use and occupancy of the Indians conveys to the Indians an interest in the timber of the reservation as complete as is the tribal interest in the land itself, that the cutting and alienation of such timber is subject to congressional legislation, and that the wrongful acts of individual Indians, vendees of timber, or agents of the United States Government cannot deprive an Indian tribe of its interest in tribal timber, or of its right to receive the proceeds of timber cut and alienated without the consent of the tribe.

These views are supported by the course of congressional legislation relating to timber growing on tribal land. Congress has repeatedly enacted special legislation authorizing disposition of timber on various designated reservations, providing always that the proceeds of such disposition should accrue to the benefit of the tribe concerned.[308]

Apart from these special statutes, Congress has enacted various laws of general application relating to the disposition of tribal timber, and providing that proceeds therefrom shall accrue to the benefit of the tribe concerned. Thus, section 7 of the Act of June 25, 1910,[309] reads:

> That the mature living and dead and down timber on unallotted lands of any Indian reservation may be sold under regulations to be prescribed by the Secretary of the Interior, and the proceeds from such sales shall be used for the benefit of the Indians of the reservation in such manner as he may direct: *Provided*, That this section shall not apply to the States of Minnesota and Wisconsin. (P. 857.)

Again Congress, by the Act of July 3, 1926,[310] provided that the net proceeds derived from the sale of timber on Indian lands should be credited to the funds of the tribe.

Similarly, various treaties have recognized the Indian right in timber on tribal land by providing for payments to the Indian tribe where such timber was destroyed without tribal consent.[311] Many other treaties provide for the establishment of Indian sawmills, and this has been construed as evidencing an understanding that the Indians would own the timber on the reservation.[312]

Further recognition of the possessory interest of an Indian tribe in the timber growing upon its land is found in statutory provisions reserving timber on allotted land for the benefit of the tribe,[313] or reserving tribal timberlands from sale, where other lands are offered for sale.[314]

The action of Congress in exercising a large measure of supervision, through the Department of the Interior, over the disposition of Indian timber is no more a denial of the Indian

[305] 304 U. S. 111 (1938). Commenting on the Cook case, the Supreme Court declared, *per* Butler, *J.* (Reed, *J.*, dissenting):

> *United States* v. *Cook*, *supra*, gives no support to the contention that in ascertaining just compensation for the Indian right taken, the value of mineral and timber resources in the reservation should be excluded. That case did not involve adjudication of the scope of Indian title to land, minerals or standing timber but only the right of the United States to replevin logs cut and sold by a few unauthorized members of the tribe. We held that, as against the purchaser from the wrongdoers, the United States was entitled to possession. It was not there decided that the tribe's right of occupancy in perpetuity did not include ownership of the land or mineral deposits or standing timber upon the reservation, or that the tribe's right was the mere equivalent of, or like, the title of a life tenant. (P. 118.)

The argument contra is presented in a Memorandum of the Asst. Attorney General, dated December 8, 1937, 11 L. D. Memo. 468.

[306] 304 U. S. 119 (1938). In this case, the Court ruled:

> The clause declaring that the district retained should, until otherwise directed by the President, be set apart as a residence for the Indians and "held and regarded as an Indian reservation" clearly did not detract from the tribes' right of occupancy. The worth attributable to the timber was a part of the value of the land upon which it was standing. (P. 123.)

[307] Act of June 15, 1938, 52 Stat. 688.

[308] Act of April 25, 1876, 19 Stat. 37 (Menomonee); Act of July 5, 1876, 19 Stat. 74 (Kansas Indians); Act of June 17, 1892, 27 Stat. 52 (Klamath River Indian Reservation); Act of April 23, 1904, sec. 11, 33 Stat. 302, 304 (Flathead Indian Reservation); Act of June 5, 1906, 34 Stat. 213 (Kiowa, Comanche, and Apache); Act of March 28, 1908, 35 Stat. 51 (Menominee); Act of May 29, 1908, 35 Stat. 458 (Spokane).

[309] 36 Stat. 855. Sec. 27 of this act provides for the sale of pine timber on ceded Chippewa Indian Reservation in Minnesota. See also 25 U. S. C. A. 196.

[310] 44 Stat. 890.

[311] Art. 8 of Treaty of March 6, 1865, with Omaha Tribe, 14 Stat. 667; Art. 14 of Treaty of July 4, 1866, with the Delaware Tribe, 14 Stat. 793.

[312] *United States* v. *Sinnott*, 26 Fed. 84 (C. C. Ore. 1886) (Grand Ronde).

[313] Act of February 25, 1920, 41 Stat. 452.

[314] Act of May 27, 1910, 36 Stat. 440 (Pine Ridge Indian Reservation); Act of May 30, 1910, 36 Stat. 448 (Rosebud Indian Reservation).

interest in such timber than is the equally large measure of control over alienation of Indian lands a denial of the Indian interest in such lands. On the contrary, the underlying purpose of such regulation, for many years, has been the protection of the interests of the tribe as a whole against overaggressive individuals and generations heedless of posterity.[315] It is believed that the first federal law establishing the principle of sustained yield timber production was the Act of March 28, 1908,[316] relating to timber-cutting on the Menominee Reservation.

Federal control over the disposition of tribal timber applies even where the tribe concerned holds the land in fee simple,[317] which is a clear indication that limitations upon the disposition of Indian tribal timber are in no way inconsistent with a recognition that the full beneficial interest therein is vested in the Indian tribe.

The tribal possessory right in timber may be protected both by civil and by criminal proceedings. Actions in the nature of replevin [318] or trover [319] and injunction [320] suits have been brought by the United States, as already noted, where timber has been disposed of unlawfully. In addition, criminal sanctions have been applied.

Section 5388 of the Revised Statutes, making it an offense to cut timber on lands of the United States reserved for military or other purposes, was apparently the only statute on the books that might be construed to make unlawful cutting of Indian tribal timber [321] a criminal offense, until June 4, 1888, when an amendment to this section was adopted which added to the section the words "or upon any Indian reservation, or lands belonging to or occupied by any tribe of Indians under authority of the United States." [322] In 1909, this statute was incorporated, with slight verbal changes, in the Penal Code,[323] as section 50. The provision in question, as subsequently amended, reads: [324]

> SEC. 50. Whoever shall unlawfully cut, or aid in unlawfully cutting, or shall wantonly injure or destroy, or procure to be wantonly injured or destroyed, any tree, growing, standing, or being upon any land of the United States which, in pursuance of law, has been reserved or purchased by the United States for any public use, or upon any Indian reservation, or lands belonging to or occupied by any tribe of Indians under the authority of the United States, or any Indian allotment while the title to the same shall be held in trust by the Government, or while the same shall remain inalienable by the allottee without the consent of the United States, shall be fined not more than five hundred dollars, or imprisoned not more than one year, or both.[325]

The validity of federal penal legislation in this field appears to be beyond question,[326] and its applicability to individual members of the tribe that owns the timber has been maintained even in an extreme case where the court was forced to say:

> It is plain that by cutting trees on the reservation Konkapot brought himself within the letter of the section as amended. He did not, however, cut the trees for sale or profit. To occupy and cultivate the tract allotted to him in severalty he needed a house and barn, and the trees were cut for the sole purpose of erecting such buildings upon his premises. It seems harsh to visit upon him the penalty of the statute for this act; but the court must administer the law as it finds it.[327]

[315] The Department of the Interior in General Forest Regulations dated April 23, 1936, 25 C. F. R. 61, states as among its objects the following:

> The preservation of Indian forest lands in a perpetually productive state by providing effective protection, preventing clear cutting of large contiguous areas, and making adequate provision for new forest growth when the mature timber is removed.

Regulation 9 provides for sale of timber only where the volume produced by the forest annually is in excess of that which is practicable of development by the Indians, or where the stand is rapidly deteriorating for various reasons, and then only after the timber to be sold has been inspected and the contract of sale approved.

[316] 35 Stat. 51. The question of whether the Department of the Interior has complied with this statute has been referred by Congress to the Court of Claims for determination. Act of September 3, 1935, 49 Stat. 1085, amended by Act of April 8, 1938, 52 Stat. 208. *Cf. United States ex rel. Besaw* v. *Work*, 6 F. 2d 694 (App. D. C. 1925).

[317] *United States* v. *Boyd*, 83 Fed. 547 (C. C. A. 4, 1897).

[318] *United States* v. *Cook*, *supra*, fn. 294.

[319] *Pine River Logging Co.* v. *United States*, *supra*, fn. 295.

[320] *United States* v. *Boyd*, *supra*, fn. 317.

[321] See *United States* v. *Konkapot*, 43 Fed. 64, 65 (C. C. Wis. 1890).

[322] 25 Stat. 166.

[323] Act of March 4, 1909, 35 Stat. 1088. The Act of June 4, 1888, is included in the repealing clause, sec. 341.

[324] Act of June 25, 1910, sec. 6, 36 Stat. 855, 857.

[325] This section is made inapplicable to the Osage Indians and the Five Civilized Tribes by sec. 33 of the same act. Separate similar legislation relating to the Five Civilized Tribes is found in the Act of June 6, 1900, 31 Stat. 660, as amended by the Act of January 21, 1903, 32 Stat. 774. See Op. Sol. I. D., M 22121, April 12, 1927.

[326] *United States* v. *Kempf*, 171 Fed. 1021 (D. C. E. D. Wis. 1909).

[327] *United States* v. *Konkapot*, 43 Fed. 64, 66 (C. C. Wis. 1890); *Labadie* v. *United States*, 6 Okla. 400 (1897). In the former case, the court held erroneous the conviction of a second Indian defendant who had removed and used tribal timber unlawfully cut by the first defendant.

SECTION 16. TRIBAL WATER RIGHTS

Whether water rights inure to a tribe and to what extent is largely a matter of judicial interpretation. The early treaties with the Indians seldom mentioned and never defined water rights. And yet, since the Indian economy was built at that time in part on fishing and later on agriculture, it was essential that a tribe be assured some right to the water within or bordering the reservation.

That the Federal Government had the power to reserve the waters flowing through the territories and except them from appropriation under the state laws had early been decided.[328] Thus, when the question of tribal water right first arose the Supreme Court in the case of *Winters* v. *United States* [329] held that where land in territorial status was reserved by treaty to an Indian tribe, there was impliedly reserved for the Indians, and withheld from subsequent appropriation by others, water of the streams of the reservations necessary for the irrigation of their lands.

> The reservation was a part of a very much larger tract which the Indians had the right to occupy and use and which was adequate for the habits and wants of a

[328] *United States* v. *Rio Grande Irrigation Co.*, 174 U. S. 690 (1899); *United States* v. *Winans*, 198 U. S. 371 (1905), rev'g. 73 Fed. 72 (C. C. Wash. 1896).

[329] 207 U. S. 564 (C. C. A. 9, 1908). Followed in *United States* v. *Powers*, 305 U. S. 527 (1939), aff'g. 94 F. 2d 783 (C. C. A. 9, 1938), mod'g. 16 F. Supp. 155 (D. C. Mont. 1936); *United States* v. *McIntire*, 101 F. 2d. 650 (C. C. A. 9. 1939), rev'g. *McIntire* v. *United States*, 22 F. Supp. 316 (D. C. Mont. 1937); *United States* v. *Parkins*, 18 F. 2d 643 (D. C. Wyo. 1926); *United States* v. *Hibner*, 27 F. 2d 909, 911 (D. C. Idaho 1928); *United States* v. *Cedarview Irrigation Co.* and *United States* v. *Dry Gulch Irrigation Co.* (Equity Nos. 4427 and 4418, D. C. Utah, 1923—unreported); *United States* v. *Orr Water Ditch Co.* (Equity Docket A-3, D. C., Nev. 1926—unreported); *United States* v. *Morrison Consol. Ditch Co.* (Equity No. 7736, D. C. Colo. 1931—unreported); *Anderson* v. *Spear-Morgan Livestock Co.*, 79 P. 2d 667 (Mont. 1938); *Conrad Inv. Co.* v. *United States*, 161 Fed. 829 (C. C. A. 9, 1908), aff'g 156 Fed. 123 (C. C. Mont. 1907); and compare *Skeem* v. *United States*, 273 Fed. 93 (C. C. A. 9, 1921); *Mason* v. *Sams*, 5 F. 2d 255 (D. C. W. D. Wash. 1925); but *cf. United States* v. *Wightman*, 230 Fed. 277 (D. C. Ariz. 1916); *Byers* v. *Wa-Wa-Ne*, 86 Ore. 617, 169 Pac. 121 (1917).

> nomadic and uncivilized people. It was the policy of the Government, it was the desire of the Indians, to change those habits and to become a pastoral and civilized people.[330] If they should become such the original tract was too extensive, but a smaller tract would be inadequate without a change of conditions. The lands were arid and, without irrigation, were practically valueless. And yet, it is contended, the means of irrigation were deliberately given up by the Indians and deliberately accepted by the Government. (P. 576.)

This contention, the Court said, could not be accepted, especially in view of the rule that agreements with Indians are to be construed in favor of the Indians. The Court rejected also the further contention that the United States had repealed the reservation of water for the Indians by the admission into the Union of Montana, the state in which the reservation was situated. It would be extreme to believe, the Court said, that Congress—

> * * * took from them the means of continuing their old habits, yet did not leave them the power to change to new ones. (P. 577.)

The Winters decision effects a prohibition against the diversion of water from a stream above and outside the reservation insofar as such diversion deprives the tribe of water necessary for the irrigation of tribal lands. In other words, these reserved rights are the property of the Indians to be protected by the Federal Government and no appropriation of water either under state or federal laws which reduces the amount of water in a stream within an Indian reservation below the amount necessary for irrigation of Indian lands is valid.

The Winters decision was thus followed in *Conrad Inv. Co.* v. *United States:*[331]

> * * * This court affirmed the decree [in the Winters case], holding that the United States, by treaties with the Indians on the reservation, had impliedly reserved the waters of Milk river for the benefit of the Indians on the reservation to the extent reasonably necessary to enable them to irrigate their lands, and that grantees and settlers on public lands outside of their reservation could not acquire, under the desert land laws of the United States or the laws of the state of Montana relating to the appropriation of the waters of the streams of that state, the right to divert the waters of Milk river to the prejudice of the rights of the Indians residing upon that reservation. * * * The law of that case is applicable to the present case, and determines the paramount right of the Indians of the Blackfeet Indian reservation to the use of the waters of Birch creek to the extent reasonably necessary for the purposes of irrigation and stock raising, and domestic and other useful purposes. The government has undertaken, by agreement with the Indians on these reservations, to promote their improvement, comfort, and welfare, by aiding them to become self-supporting as a peaceable and agricultural people. The lands within these reservations are dry and arid, and require the diversion of waters from the streams to make them productive and suitable for agricultural, stock-raising, and domestic purposes.

The doctrine enunciated in the Winters case as applied to reservations created by treaty was later recognized by the courts as applicable to reservations created by Executive order. In *United States* v. *Walker River Irrigation District*[332] the Circuit Court of Appeals had this to say:

> * * * The trial court thought *Winters* v. *United States* distinguishable, as being based on an agreement or treaty with the Indians. Here there was no treaty. It said that at the time the Walker River reservation was set apart, the Pahutes were at war with the whites, hence no agreement between them and the Government was possible.
>
> (a) In the Winters case, as in this, the basic question for determination was one of intent—whether the waters of the stream were intended to be reserved for the use of the Indians, or whether the lands only were reserved. We see no reason to believe that the intention to reserve need be evidenced by treaty or agreement. A statute or an executive order setting apart the reservation may be equally indicative of the intent. While in the Winters case the court emphasized the treaty, there was in fact no express reservation of water to be found in that document. The intention had to be arrived at by taking account of the circumstances, the situation and needs of the Indians and the purpose for which the lands had been reserved. (P. 336.)

The views expressed in the foregoing cases are supported by the course of congressional legislation relating to tribal rights in water. Congress has repeatedly enacted special legislation authorizing the construction of irrigation projects on various designated reservations, providing always that the Indians shall be supplied with water from the project.[333]

Again, in opening reservation land to mineral entry Congress has expressly excepted "lands containing springs, water holes, or other bodies of water needed or used by the Indians for watering livestock, irrigation, or water-power purposes."[334] By the Act of March 7, 1928,[335] Congress provided for the purchase of land with sufficient water right for the use and occupancy of the Tamoak Band of Homeless Indians. When the Yakima Reservation was receiving less water than the amount to which it was entitled under the doctrine of the Winters case, Congress appropriated a sum of money for the purchase of an additional water right for the Indians.[336] To protect the water rights of the Indians of the Taos Pueblo, Congress has authorized the President to withdraw from entry lands within the watershed and to protect said lands from any act or condition which would impair the purity or the volume of the water flowing therefrom.[337] Water from streams on the ceded portion of the Fort Hall Reservation necesary for irrigation of land under cultivation has been reserved to the Indians using same so long as the Indians "remain where they now live."[338]

Similarly, various statutes have provided for payment of compensation to be credited to tribal funds in the event Indian water rights are sold, appropriated, or otherwise damaged.[339]

Apart from the foregoing statutes Congress has enacted various laws of general application relating to the water rights of Indian allotees.[340]

---

[330] See sec. 23, *infra;* and see Chapters 2, 3, and 4.

[331] 161 Fed. 829, 831–832 (C. C. A. 9, 1908), aff'g 156 Fed. 123 (C. C. Mont. 1907).

[332] 104 F. 2d 334 (C. C. A. 9, 1939).

[333] Act of January 1, 1889, 25 Stat. 639 (Papago Reservation), Act of January 12, 1893, 27 Stat. 417 (Umatilla Reservation); Act of February 10, 1891, 26 Stat. 745 (Umatilla Reservation); Act of February 15, 1893, 27 Stat. 456 (Yuma Reservation); Act of January 20, 1893, 27 Stat. 420 (Yuma Reservation); Act of March 6, 1906, 34 Stat. 53 (Yakima Reservation); *cf.* Act of March 13, 1928, 45 Stat. 312 (*"Provided further,* That all present water rights now appurtenant to the * * * irrigated Pueblo lands owned individually or as pueblos * * *, and all water for the domestic purposes of the Indians and for their stock shall be prior and paramount to any rights of the district or of any property holder therein."); Act of March 1, 1899, 30 Stat. 924, 941 (Uintah Reservation).

[334] Act of December 16, 1926, 44 Stat. 922; *cf.* Act of August 26, 1922, 42 Stat. 832 (Agua Caliente Band).

[335] 45 Stat. 200, 207.

[336] Act of August 1, 1914, 38 Stat. 582, 604.

[337] Act of March 27, 1928, 45 Stat. 372.

[338] Act of June 6, 1900, 31 Stat. 672.

[339] Act of August 26, 1935, 49 Stat. 803; Act of March 3, 1927, 44 Stat. 1370 (Choctaw and Chickasaw Indians); Act of March 22, 1906, 34 Stat. 80 (Colville Reservation); Act of January 12, 1893, 27 Stat. 417 (Umatilla Reservation).

[340] Act of February 8, 1887, sec. 7, 24 Stat. 388, 390–391; Act of May 29, 1908, 35 Stat. 444; *cf.* Act of March 2, 1889, 25 Stat. 888 (pertaining to both allotted and tribal lands).

A. TRIBAL RIGHT *versus* STATE RIGHT IN NAVIGABLE WATERS

The ownership by the United States of lands in territorial status extends to the lands underlying all bodies of water therein.[341] Where unreserved, the title to land underlying navigable waters is held to pass to a state upon admission into the Union, while title to the land underlying non-navigable waters remains in the United States.[342]

If navigable waters have not been reserved the tribe has but a right of use in common with citizens of the state.[343] It becomes pertinent therefore to examine the criteria for determining whether such waters have been reserved to a tribe. Here again questions of intent and of circumstances surrounding the creation of the reservation are of paramount importance. Thus, in holding that the lands underlying the navigable waters within the Red Lake Indian Reservation passed to the State of Minnesota upon its admission into the Union, the Supreme Court said:[344]

> We come then to the question whether the lands under the lake were disposed of by the United States before Minnesota became a State. An affirmative disposal is not asserted, but only that the lake, and therefore the lands under it, was within the limits of the Red Lake Reservation when the State was admitted. The existence of the reservation is conceded, but that it operated as a disposal of lands underlying navigable waters within its limits is disputed. We are of opinion that the reservation was not intended to effect such a disposal and that there was none. If the reservation operated as a disposal of the lands under a part of the navigable waters within its limits it equally worked a disposal of the lands under all. Besides Mud Lake, the reservation limits included Red Lake, having an area of 400 square miles, the greater part of the Lake of the Woods, having approximately the same area, and several navigable streams. The reservation came into being through a succession of treaties with the Chippewas whereby they ceded to the United States their aboriginal right of occupancy to the surrounding lands. The last treaties preceding the admission of the State were concluded September 30, 1854, 10 Stat. 1109, and February 22, 1855, 10 Stat. 1165. There was no formal setting apart of what was not ceded, nor an affirmative declaration of the rights of the Indians therein, nor any attempted exclusion of others from the use of navigable waters. The effect of what was done was to reserve in a general way for the continued occupation of the Indians what remained of their aboriginal territory; and thus it came to be known and recognized as a reservation. *Minnesota* v. *Hitchcock*, 185 U. S. 373, 389. There was nothing in this which even approaches a grant of rights in lands underlying navigable waters; nor anything evincing a purpose to depart from the established policy, before stated, of treating such lands as held for the benefit of the future State. Without doubt the Indians were to have access to the navigable waters and to be entitled to use them in accustomed ways; but these were common rights vouchsafed to all, whether white or Indian, by the early legislation reviewed in *Railroad Co.* v. *Schurmeir*, 7 Wall. 272, 287–289, and *Economy Light & Power Co.* v. *United States*, *supra*, pp. 118–120, and emphasized in the Enabling Act under which Minnesota was admitted as a State, c. 60, 11 Stat. 166, which declared that the rivers and waters bounding the State 'and the navigable waters leading into the same shall be common highways, and forever free, as well to the inhabitants of said State as to all other citizens of the United States'. (Pp. 57–59.)

A similar result was reached in *Taylor* v. *United States*[345] on the theory that since the Executive order creating the Quileute Indian Reservation made no express reference to the Quileute River as the northern boundary, no reservation of its waters was intended, nor any exception to the general policy of the Government to hold such property in trust for the future states.

Where a reservation is created after admission of a state into the Union, there is some question as to whether the unappropriated navigable waters within the reservation are reserved to the tribe. An affirmative answer would seem to deprive the state of an acquired right unless it can be said that the creation of the reservation serves as a notice of the appropriation of unappropriated navigable waters within its border for the use of the Indians.

Where California by statute classified a river as nonnavigable, it has been held that by the subsequent creation of a reservation the waters therein were reserved for the benefit of the Indians.[346]

B. EXTENT OF RESERVED WATER RIGHT

It will be remembered that the Court in the *Winters* case decreed only that there was an implied reservation to a tribe of an amount of water reasonably necessary for irrigation and domestic purposes. There was left open the further question of whether the water right impliedly reserved for use for irrigation includes a flow of water sufficient merely to supply the needs of the Indians at the time of the creation of the reservation, or whether it includes a flow sufficient in quantity to irrigate all the irrigable lands of the reservation.

The policy which underlies the doctrine of implied reservation of water has been given effect by holdings that when an Indian reservation is set apart, the water right impliedly reserved is large enough to irrigate the entire irrigable acreage of the reservation.[347] In *Conrad Inv. Co.* v. *United States*,[348] the court granted a right to a designated amount of water with leave to the Government to apply for modification of the decree at any time it might determine that its needs would be in excess of that amount. The District Court decision[349] shows clearly that the water right reserved was based on total irrigable acreage (p. 130) and increased need was anticipated only because of probable change in use of the land resulting from the Indians' progress in agriculture (p. 129). Likewise, in *Skeem* v. *United States*,[350] where water was expressly reserved by treaty for irrigation "on land actually cultivated and in use," the court held that the water right reserved was not limited in quantity to the amount of water necessary to the irrigation of such portion of the Indian lands as were at the time of the treaty actually irrigated. The court said (p. 95):

> The purpose of the government was to induce the Indians to relinquish their nomadic habits and to till the soil, and the treaties should be construed in the light of that purpose and such meaning should be given them as will enable the Indians to cultivate eventually the whole of their lands so reserved to their use.

---

[341] *Shively* v. *Bowlby*, 152 U. S. 1 (1894); *Alaska Pacific Fisheries* v. *United States*, 248 U. S. 78 (1918), aff'g 240 Fed. 274 (C. C. A. 9, 1917).

[342] *Donnelly* v. *United States*, 228 U. S. 243 (1913).

[343] *United States* v. *Holt State Bank*, 270 U. S. 49 (1926), aff'g 294 Fed. 161 (C. C. A. 8, 1923); *The James G. Swan*, 50 Fed. 108 (D. C. Wash. 1892); *Taylor* v. *United States* 44 F. 2d 53 (C. C. A. 9, 1930).

[344] *United States* v. *Holt State Bank*, 270 U. S. 49 (1926), aff'g 294 Fed. 161 (C. C. A. 8, 1923). It has been administratively held that even in the light of *United States* v. *Holt State Bank* the reservation of lands for the "use and occupancy" of the Chippewas had the effect of reserving to them the exclusive right of fishing in the waters of the Upper and Lower Red Lakes, a right which the state could neither deprive them of nor regulate. Op. Sol. I. D., M.28107, June 30, 1936. And compare *The James G. Swan*, 50 Fed. 108 (D. C. Wash. 1892).

[345] 44 F. 2d 53 (C. C. A. 9, 1930).

[346] *Donnelly* v. *United States*, 228 U. S. 243 (1913).

[347] *Conrad Inv. Co.* v. *United States*, 161 Fed. 829 (C. C. A. 9, 1908). aff'g. 156 Fed. 123 (C. C. Mont. 1907); *Skeem* v. *United States*, 273 Fed. 93 (C. C. A. 9, 1921); Op. Sol. I. D., M.15849, May 12, 1925.

[348] *Ibid.*

[349] *United States* v. *Conrad Inv. Co.*, 156 Fed. 123, 130–131 (C. C. Mont. 1907), aff'd. by 161 Fed. 829 (C. C. A. 9, 1908).

[350] *Op. cit.* fn. 347.

The decision of the Circuit Court of Appeals in the case of *United States* v. *Walker River Irrigation District*[351] would seem to constrict the foregoing decisions. The court there held, in accordance with the Winters decision, that by the establishment of the Walker River Reservation in 1859 there was impliedly reserved water to the extent reasonably necessary to supply the needs of the Indians. However, in determining the *quantity* of water "to which the United States is entitled" the court held:

> The area of irrigable land included in the reservation is not necessarily the criterion for measuring the amount of water reserved, whether the standard be applied as of 1859 or as of the present. The extent to which the use of the stream might be necessary could only be demonstrated by experience. (P. 340.)

The court found from the record that about 1,900 acres were under cultivation as early as 1886; that this area had not been substantially increased up to the time of trial; and that the number of Indians on the reservation was not increasing. Adverting to the master's finding that a demand for the cultivation of more than 2,100 acres, or a water right of 26.25 cubic feet per second, had not been shown, the court concluded:

> We are constrained to accept this estimate as a fair measure of the needs of the Government as demonstrated by seventy years' experience. (P. 340.)

While lands were reserved in tribal status questions of water right were confined largely to whether particular waters had been reserved to the tribe. With the growth of the practice of allotting tribal lands to individual Indians there arose the question of whether the allottee, or a party holding under the allottee, was entitled to divert a part of the water reserved under the doctrine of the *Winters* case to the tribe. The problems to which this question gives rise are elsewhere discussed.[352]

[351] 104 F. 2d 334 (C. C. A. 9, 1939).

[352] See Chapter 11, sec. 3.

SECTION 17. TRIBAL RIGHTS IN IMPROVEMENTS

The extent of tribal possessory rights in improvements on tribal land raises two issues: (*a*) the demarcation of rights between the tribe and the individual member of the tribe who has made the improvements or who resides on the improved land, and (*b*) the demarcation of interests between the tribe and third parties.

Of these issues, the first is an issue internal to the affairs of the tribe and therefore dealt with in accordance with tribal law and customs, [353] except as statute or treaty otherwise provides. The matter has been specially dealt with in several types of statutes and treaties. Perhaps the most common case in which the ownership of improvements must be determined arises in connection with the sale or cession of improved tribal lands. The earlier treaties generally provided that compensation for improvements was to be paid directly to the tribe,[354] thus leaving to the determination of the tribe itself the question of whether any individual Indian should receive special compensation by reason of such improvements. A few treaties and statutes provide for payment by the United States to the member of the tribe who has made the improvements,[355] and others leave uncertain the manner in which compensation for improvements is to be made.[356] The early practice of making compensation directly to the tribe permitted adjustments between the tribe and the individual concerned, but under modern legislation restricting the use of tribal funds such adjustments became impracticable. Thus when the Act of June 18, 1934,[357] was adopted, containing a provision opening up the lands of the Papago Reservation, improved and unimproved, to appropriation by mineral prospectors, the requirement that damages should be paid "to the Papago Tribe for loss of any improvements on any land located for mining in such a sum as may be determined by the Secretary of the Interior but not to exceed the cost of said improvements," failed to do justice to the individual Indians deprived of their homes, gardens, and corrals. Accordingly, following the referendum vote of the Papago Indians favoring the application of the Act of June 18, 1934, to the Papago Reservation,[358] amendatory legislation was enacted providing that the individual Indians concerned should receive payment for improvements of which they might be deprived.[359]

For many years it was the policy of the Government to encourage the improvement of tribal lands occupied by individual members of a tribe.[360] The Federal Government, having encouraged such improvements, frequently provided, in disposing of improved tribal lands, that the individual Indian who had made, or come to enjoy, the improvements should, if possible, receive the lands improved.[361] Likewise an attempt was sometimes made to safeguard Indian improvements in marking or revising reservation boundaries,[362] and where lands were ceded provision was sometimes made for making improvements on retained or new

[353] *Rush* v. *Thompson*, 2 Ind. T. 557, 53 S. W. 333 (1899); and see Chapter 7, sec. 8, and Chapter 9, sec. 5. In the absence of proved custom to the contrary, and where laws and treaties are silent, the Interior Department has taken the position that:

> The tribe does not own the improvements placed upon tribal land by or under the direction of individual members of the tribe. (Memo. Sol. I. D., October 21, 1938 (Palm Springs).)

[354] Art. III of Treaty of September 20, 1816, 7 Stat. 150 (Chickasaw Nation); Art. V of Treaty of July 20, 1831, 7 Stat. 351 (Senecas and Shawnees); Treaty of February 8, 1831, 7 Stat. 342 (Menomonee); Art. V of Treaty of February 28, 1831, 7 Stat. 348 (Senecas); Art. V of Treaty of August 8, 1831, 7 Stat. 355 (Shawnees); Art. V of Treaty of August 30, 1831, 7 Stat. 359 (Ottaways); Art. III of Treaty of January 19, 1832, 7 Stat. 364 (Wyandots); Art. IX of Treaty of December 29, 1835, 7 Stat. 478 (Cherokees); Art. I of Treaty of November 23, 1838, 7 Stat. 574 (Creeks); Art III of Treaty of May 20, 1842, 7 Stat. 586 (Senecas); Art. VI of Treaty of October 27, 1832, 7 Stat. 403 (Kaskaskias and Peorias); Art. VIII of Treaty of January 4, 1845, 9 Stat. 821 (Creeks and Seminoles); Art. V of Treaty of June 5 and 17, 1846, 9 Stat. 853 (Pottowautomie, Chippewas, and Ottawas); Art. IV of Treaty of June 5, 1854, 10 Stat. 1093 (Miamies); Art. V of Treaty of March 17, 1842, 11 Stat. 581 (Wyandotts); Art. IV of Treaty of February 5, 1856, 11 Stat. 663 (Munsees); Act of July 21, 1852, 10 Stat. 15 (Pottawatomies); Act of July 31, 1854, 10 Stat. 315 (Kickapoos); Art. III of Treaty of March 11, 1863, 12 Stat. 1249 (Chippewas); Act of April 10, 1876, 19 Stat. 28 (Pawnee).

[355] Art. XI of Treaty of January 24, 1826, 7 Stat. 286, 288 (Creek Nation); Art. XIV of Treaty of January 15, 1838, 7 Stat. 550 (New York Indians); Art. III of Treaty of September 3, 1839, 11 Stat. 577 (Munsees); Art. VII of Treaty of November 5, 1857, 12 Stat. 991 (Tonawanda Band of Senecas); Act of May 8, 1872, 17 Stat. 85 (Kansas Tribe).

[356] Art. VI of Treaty of December 26, 1854, 10 Stat. 1132 (Nisqually); Art. VII of Treaty of January 26, 1855, 12 Stat. 933 (S'Klallams); Art. VI of Treaty of January 31, 1855, 12 Stat. 939 (Makah); Art. V of Treaty of June 19, 1858, 12 Stat. 1037 (Sisseton and Wahpeton Bands of Sioux); Art. V of Treaty of November 15, 1861, 12 Stat. 1191 (Pottawatomie); Art. VI of Treaty of June 28, 1862, 13 Stat. 623 (Kickapoo). And *cf.* Art IV of Treaty of October 18, 1848 with Menomonee Tribe, 9 Stat. 952; Act of April 26, 1906, 34 Stat. 137 (Choctaw, Chickasaw, and Seminole).

[357] 48 Stat. 984.

[358] See 38 Op. A. G. 121 (1934).

[359] Act of August 28, 1937, 50 Stat. 862.

[360] Art. IX of Treaty of May 17, 1854, 10 Stat. 1069 (Ioways); Art. IX of Treaty of August 7, 1856, 11 Stat. 699 (Seminoles and Creeks); Act of May 15, 1888, 25 Stat. 150 (Omaha Tribe).

[361] Act of March 24, 1832, 7 Stat. 366 (Creeks); Treaty of February 18, 1833, 7 Stat. 420 (Ottawa); sec. 6 of Act of June 6, 1900, 31 Stat. 672 (Fort Hall Indian Reservation); sec. 4 of the Act of March 1, 1901, 31 Stat. 848 (Cherokees).

[362] Art. II of Treaty of February 3, 1838, 7 Stat. 566 (Oneidas).

lands to take the place of those lost,[363] or for having that portion of the tribe remaining on its original lands compensate emigrants for their improvements on such lands.[364]

The issue of possessory right in improvements that may arise between the tribe and third parties is an issue which depends not on the internal law and customs of the tribe but rather on the law governing the transaction under which the property in question has come to be recognized as tribal property. Certain statutes providing for the acquisition of land for the benefit of Indians specifically determine that the improvements thereon shall likewise be acquired for the benefit of the Indians.[365] Under such statutes there is no question but that the Indians have the same right in the improvements that they have in the land itself.

Where the statute is silent, a more difficult question is presented. Thus where, under the Act of February 13, 1929,[366] improved lands used for agency, school, and other purposes were reinvested in the Yankton Sioux Tribe, the question was presented whether the buildings on such land thereby became the property of the Indian tribe. The Solicitor of the Interior Department, answering this question in the affirmative declared:[367]

> The use of the term "reinvested" implies that the purpose of Congress was to restore to the Indians the title which they held prior to the cession of 1892, that is, the Indian title of occupancy and use, the United States still retaining the title in fee. But the Indian title of use and occupancy is as sacred as the fee title of the sovereign, *United States* v. *Cook* (19 Wall. 591), and the Indians have the full beneficial ownership with all the rights incident thereto. See 34 Op. Atty. Gen. 171. Whether the ownership of the Indians extends to the buildings upon the lands is essentially a question of what was intended and where that intention is not otherwise shown, it has been held that the Government will be deemed to have assented that its conveyance be construed according to the law of the State in which the land lies. See in this connection *Oklahoma* v. *Texas* (258 U. S. 574, 595). The act of 1929 contains nothing to indicate any intention upon the part of the Government to retain ownership of the buildings. They are neither excepted nor reserved. In the absence of such an exception or reservation, the rule is universal that the buildings are part of and pass with the land. *Isham* v. *Morgan* (9 Conn. 374; 23 Am. Dec. 361); *Oesting* v. *New Bedford* (210 Mass. 396; 96 N. E. 1095); *Blake McFall Co.* v. *Wilson* (98 Ore. 626; 193 Pac. 902); *Holmes* v. *Neill* (222 Pac. 670); *Schiltz* v. *Ferguson* (231 N. W. 358). Under this rule, the grant to the Indians carried with it the buildings upon the lands.
>
> Nothing in the legislative history of the enactment is to the contrary. In reports to the Senate and House Committees on Indian Affairs recommending that the bill which became the act of 1929 be not enacted, the Secretary of the Interior called specific attention to the fact that "there are forty buildings on the land used in connection with school and administrative activities." See House Report No. 1852 and Senate Report No. 1130 on S-2792, 70th Congress, 1st sess. The debates before the House and Senate also show that Congress was advised of the existence of the buildings upon the premises. See Congressional Record, Volume 69, Part 8, 70th Congress, 1st Session, page 8837, and Volume 70, Part 3, 70th Congress, 2nd Session, page 2489–2490.
>
> * * * * *
>
> Aside from the fact that the failure of Congress, with knowledge of the existence of the buildings, to reserve them, reasonably warrants the assumption that no such reservation was intended, the statements of Congressman Leavitt and Senator McMaster strongly indicate that it was the undertsanding of Congress that enactment of the measure would confer upon the Indians ownership of the buildings along with the lands, such ownership, under the terms of the statute, to take effect when the property was no longer required for agency, school, and other purposes.
>
> It is understood from the information submitted by the Assistant Commissioner of Indian Affairs that the use of the reserved lands for the purposes for which they were reserved has been permanently discontinued and that the lands are no longer needed for any of such purposes. Upon that understanding, I hold, for reasons stated above, that the lands and buildings located thereon are now tribal property belonging to the Yankton Sioux Tribe of Indians.

The approach taken in the foregoing opinion suggests that in passing upon any specific tribal claim of possessory right in improvements on tribal land, first resort must be had to the governing statute or treaty. Silence or ambiguity may be resolved (*a*) by reference to legislative history, or (*b*) by reference to the state or the common law rule. In general, it may be said that Congress has frequently subordinated the traditional common law rule that improvements run with the land to the equitable principle that one who has built improvements, in good faith, on another's land should not be entirely deprived of the fruit of his labor. Attempts to do justice to the claims of those who have improved tribal lands include provisions allowing non-Indians who have improved tribal lands to sell their improvements at their appraised value,[367a] or allowing Indians of another tribe to purchase the lands on which their improvements stand.[368] As a matter of history, the improvements on land conveyed to Indians were frequently more important inducements of reciprocal cessions than the land itself.[369]

[363] Art. VII of Treaty of November 6, 1838, 7 Stat. 569 (Miamies); Art. I of Treaty of January 22, 1855, 10 Stat. 1143 (Oregon Bands); and *cf.* Art. III of Treaty of February 27, 1855, 10 Stat. 1172 (Cherokees); Art. II of Treaty of June 9, 1863, 14 Stat. 647 (Nez Perce); Treaty of May 6, 1828, 7 Stat. 311 (Cherokees).

[364] Art. 6 of Treaty of May 20, 1842, with Seneca Nation, 7 Stat. 586.

[365] Act of July 1, 1892, 27 Stat. 61 (Mission Indians). The Act of March 2, 1889, 25 Stat. 1013 (United Peorias and Miamies) provides that certain lands, together with all improvements thereon, shall be held as tribal property. *Cf. Donohoo* v. *Howard*, 4 Ind. T. 433 (1902) (Cherokee legislation relating to "intruder improvements").

[366] 45 Stat. 1167.

[367] Op. Sol. I. D., M.27671, March 1, 1934.

[367a] Act of March 2, 1907, 34 Stat. 1220 (intermarried whites on Cherokee lands).

[368] Art. 13 of Treaty of May 6, 1854, with Delaware Tribe, 10 Stat. 1048 (for benefit of Christian Indians). *Cf.* Memo. Sol. I. D., October 20, 1937, and cases cited (log house on Fort Belknap tribal land).

[369] *Cf.* Art. I of Treaty of January 22, 1855, 10 Stat. 1143.

SECTION 18. TRIBAL CONVEYANCES

A. RESTRAINTS ON ALIENATION

It is frequently assumed that the inability of an Indian tribe to alienate tribal land is a consequence of the peculiar tenure by which such lands are held.[370] This tenure is commonly designated as "occupancy," "mere occupancy," "possession," or "Indian title," and these phrases are sometimes deemed a sufficient explanation for the conclusion that Indian lands are inalienable. Careful examination of the cases and of the historical practice of the United States shows that this view is inaccurate. This inaccuracy appears most clearly in five situations:

(1) If the inalienability of tribal land is caused simply by the peculiarity that tribal land is not held in fee simple, then an Indian tribe which does hold land in fee simple should be able

[370] See *United States* v. *Cook*, 19 Wall. 591, 592–593 (1873); *Howard* v. *Moot*, 64 N. Y. 262, 271 (1876); Kerr, Real Property (1895), sec. 221.

to alienate it. But the decisions are uniform that a tribe holding land in fee simple is subject to exactly the same restraints upon alienation as any other tribe.[371]

(2) If "Indian title" is something less than a fee simple,[372] then an Indian conveyance of tribal land to private parties should convey something less than a fee simple. But the cases uniformly hold that a conveyee of tribal property under a valid conveyance acquires a complete title.[373]

(3) If title by aboriginal occupancy is simply equivalent to a tenancy at will, the land cannot be sold to the sovereign. Yet the practice of the United States[374] and of the British Crown, before 1776, of purchasing land from Indians, and the validity of conveyances thus effectuated, has never been questioned. As Marshall, *C. J.*, observed, when sovereigns claimed "the exclusive right to purchase" they "did not found that right on a denial of the right of the possessor to sell."[375]

> The king purchased their lands, when they were willing to sell, at a price they were willing to take, but never coerced a surrender of them.[376]
> * * * the Indian nations possessed a full right to the lands they occupied, until that right should be extinguished by the United States, with their consent.[377]

(4) If "Indian title" is something substantially less than a fee simple, then in cases of involuntary alienation damages should be based upon something less than the value of the land itself. Yet the courts hold that in such cases the value of the land is the measure of damages.[378]

(5) If "Indian title" is something less than a fee simple subject to restraints on alienation, then when the sovereign grants a right of preemption to a third party, there should be a fee left in the sovereign. But the cases hold that this is not the case and that all interest in the land outside of the right of preemption rests with the Indian tribe.[379]

These defects in the theory of "Indian title" do not show that all tribes hold property in fee simple or that any tribe can alienate any property at will, but they should serve to direct our consideration of well-established restraints on alienation[380] towards the field of commercial legislation rather than the morass of medieval doctrine that surrounds the feudal fiction of "title in the sovereign."[381]

B. HISTORICAL VIEW OF RESTRAINTS

The historical fact is that the alienation of Indian lands, far from being a legal impossibility because of peculiarities of Indian title, was probably the chief objective attained by the Indian land law of Britain, Spain, France, the Colonies, and the United States, for some four centuries. None of these sovereigns forbade such alienation but each sought to regulate it and, generally, to profit from it. Thus, the Supreme Court declared in the case of *Mitchel* v. *United States:*[382]

> The Indian right to the lands as property, was not merely of possession; that of alienation was concomitant; both were equally secured, protected and guaranteed by Great Britain and Spain, subject only to ratification and confirmation by the license, charter or deed from the governor representing the king. Such purchases enabled the Indians to pay their debts, compensate for their depredations on the traders resident among them, to provide for their wants; while they were available to the purchasers as payment of the considerations which at their expense had been received by the Indians. It would have been a violation of the faith of the government to both, to encourage traders to settle in the province, to put themselves and property in the power of the Indians, to suffer the latter to contract debts, and when willing

---

[371] *United States* v. *Candelaria*, 271 U. S. 432 (1926); Christian Indians, 9 Op. A. G. 24 (1857); *Goodell* v. *Jackson*, 20 Johns. 693 (1823).

[372] *Cf. United States* v. *Paine Lumber Co.*, 206 U. S. 467, 473 (1907), aff'g 154 Fed. 263 (C. C. E. D. Wis. 1904):

> The restraint upon alienation must not be exaggerated. It does not of itself debase the right below a fee simple. [Said of allotted land]

Apparently the theory that Indian title is something less than a fee was invented to justify the holding that when the sovereign granted an individual land owned by Indians and the Indians afterwards abandoned the land the grantee was entitled to the land in fee simple. See, for example, *United States* v. *Fernandez*, 10 Pet. 303 (1836). But this result, which seems eminently sensible, can be justified on the ground that the grantee received a contingent future interest which ripened into a fee simple on the happening of the contingency contemplated. Even under the classical theory of land tenures, a grant of a possibility of reverter by the sovereign is not inconsistent with the retention of a fee simple in the Indian tribe. It must be remembered that a fee simple, according to classical theory, may be either "absolute" or "qualified," or "conditional," and the possibility of death without issue was a standard condition for the termination of an estate. In fact, the general right of escheat was vested in the sovereign, so it was only natural that if a tribal owner became extinct the land would pass to the sovereign and there was nothing to prevent the sovereign from speculating on that contingency and making grants limited to take effect upon its happening.

[373] *United States* v. *Brooks*, 51 U. S. 442 (1850); *Godfrey* v. *Beardsley*, 10 Fed. Cas. No. 5497 (C. C. Ind. 1841). And note sec. 28 of the Act of June 4, 1924, 43 Stat. 376, which declares:

> That the authority of the Eastern Band of Cherokee Indians of North Carolina to execute conveyances of lands owned by said band, or any interest therein, is recognized, and any such conveyance heretofore made, whether to the United States or to others, shall not be questioned in any case where the title conveyed or the instrument of conveyance has been or shall be accepted or approved by the Secretary of the Interior. (P. 381.)

[374] See Chapter 3; and *cf. Omaha Tribe of Indians* v. *United States*, 53 C. Cls. 549 (1918), holding that where the United States undertook by treaty to compensate the tribe for ceded land it was estopped from thereafter denying the title of the Omaha Tribe:

> * * * the defendants can not now be heard to say that the Indians did not own the land when the treaty was made and had no right to make a cession of it. (P. 560.)

But *cf. Shore* v. *Shell Petroleum Corp.*, 60 F. 2d 1 (C. C. A. 10, 1932), cert. den. 287 U. S. 656.

[375] *Worcester* v. *Georgia*, 6 Pet. 515, 543 (1832).

[376] *Ibid.*, 546.

[377] *Ibid.*, 559.

[378] "For all practical purposes, they [the tribe] owned the land," *United States* v. *Shoshone Tribe*, *infra*, at p. 116. Grants of land subject to the Indian title by the United States, which had only the naked fee, would transfer no beneficial interest. *Leavenworth, L. & G. R. Co.* v. *United States*, 92 U. S. 733, 742–743 (1875); *Beecher* v. *Wetherby*, 95 U. S. 517, 525 (1877). The right of perpetual and exclusive occupancy of the land is not less valuable than full title in fee. See *Holden* v. *Joy*, 17 Wall. 211, 244 (1872); *Western Union Tel. Co.* v. *Pennsylvania R. Co.*, 195 U. S. 540, 557 (1904); *United States* v. *Shoshone Tribe*, 304 U. S. 111, 117 (1938), aff'g *Shoshone Tribe* v. *United States*, 85 C. Cls. 331 (1937.) See secs. 11–15 of this chapter and cases cited. See also Op. Sol. I. D., M.28589, August 24, 1936 (damages for flooding tribal land).

[379] *Blacksmith* v. *Fellows*, 7 N. Y. 401 (1852):

> The lands were then in the independent occupancy of a nation of Indians, and were owned by them, and all that Massachusetts acquired by the cession to her, was the exclusive right of buying from the Indians, when they should be disposed to sell. (P. 411.)

Cf. United States v. *Oregon Central Military Road Co.*, 103 Fed. 549 (C. C. Ore. 1900), holding that a floating grant to road company did not extend to Indian reservation, and declaring:

> The intention to bestow the fee subject to the burden of the Indian occupation must necessarily refer to the temporary character of that occupation. Here the treaty provides for allotment of the reserved lands, and guaranties to the allottees the perpetual possession and use of the tracts so granted, reserving to the United States the right of sale for the benefit of the Indians whenever their prosperity will be advanced thereby. This leaves nothing to be taken cum onere, and where there is nothing there is no fee. (P. 558.)

This case was reversed on other grounds in 192 U. S. 355 (1904), sub nom. *United States* v. *Calif. and Ore. Ld. Co.* *Cf.* also 8 Op. A. G. 458 (1839) (holding that land may be held by tribe according to "same manner as Indian reservations, have been heretofore held," and yet be subject to trust for named Indians "and their heirs forever").

[380] For recognition of these restraints see 3 Kent's Comm. 377; 3 Washburn, Real Property (6th ed. 1902) sec. 2009; Rice, Modern Law of Real Property (1897) sec. 32; 1 Dembitz, Land Titles (1895) sec. 65.

[381] The character of the "Indian title" theory as a fiction of feudalism was recognized a hundred years ago by Kent, *op. cit.* p. 378.

[382] 9 Pet. 711, 758–759 (1835).

> to pay them by the only means in their power, a cession of their lands, withhold an assent to the purchase, which, by their laws or municipal regulations, was necessary to vest a title. (Pp. 758–759.)

Again, in the case of *United States* v. *Pico*,[383] the Supreme Court declared, in upholding the validity of a grant made by an Indian pueblo:

> The transfer of land to the Picos was made in conformity with the existing regulations established for the protection of the Indians, under the supervision and with the approval of the local authorities, and appears to have been satisfactory to all parties. (P. 540.)

Again, in the case of *Chouteau* v. *Molony*,[384] where it was held that an instrument executed by the Fox Tribe amounted to a permit to mine rather than a conveyance in fee, the Supreme Court declared:

> It is a fact in the case, that the Indian title to the country had not been extinguished by Spain, and that Spain had not the right of occupancy. The Indians had the right to continue it as long as they pleased, or to sell out parts of it—the sale being made conformably to the laws of Spain, and being afterwards confirmed by the king or his representative, the Governor of Louisiana. Without such conformity and confirmation no one could, lawfully, take possession of lands under an Indian sale. We know it was frequently done, but always with the expectation that the sale would be confirmed, and that until it was, the purchaser would have the benefit of the forbearance of the government. We are now speaking of Indian lands, such as these were, and not of those portions of land which were assigned to the Christian Indians for villages and residences, where the Indian occupancy had been abandoned by them, or where it had been yielded to the king by treaty. Such sales did not need ratification by the governor, if they were passed before the proper Spanish officer, and put upon record. (Pp. 236–237.)

Similarly did the various colonies, at least since 1633, make provision for the confirmation of Indian conveyances by proper governmental authorities.[385]

Indian grants in Massachusetts Colony, for example, required the approval of the General Court.[386] In New York, under the Constitution of 1777, Indian tribal conveyances required the assent of the legislature, or, after the Act of March 7, 1809, of the State Surveyor-General.[387]

The legislation of the United States on the sale of Indian lands has followed the course thus fixed by European and colonial sovereignties, and under this legislation the existence of a transferable estate in land has not been denied but the method of transfer has been rigidly circumscribed. This regulation of land sales by Indians to non-Indians has been an essential part of the general power of supervision over "Indian intercourse," claimed by each of the European sovereigns exercising dominion in North America. This power the United States likewise claimed, in its Constitution, and to this claim many Indian tribes were induced to give explicit assent.[388] The most substantial subject of such intercourse was land, since this was the most valuable possession of the Indian tribes. The United States asserted the power, as did other sovereign nations, of regulating the sale of land by Indians. As an essential part of such regulation the United States claimed the right, either for itself or for the state in which the land was situated, of purchasing land from the Indian tribes and of excluding other would-be purchasers from the market, and various treaties assented to this claim.[389] This policy was parallel to a policy which excluded from the Indian country unlicensed private traders in commodities other than land.

C. FEDERAL LEGISLATION

Section 4 of the first Indian Intercourse Act[390] covered the sale of lands, together with other types of trade, and declared:

> That no sale of lands made by any Indians, or any nation or tribe of Indians within the United States, shall be valid to any person or persons, or to any state, whether having the right of pre-emption to such lands or not, unless the same shall be made and duly executed at some public treaty, held under the authority of the United States.

This provision was amplified in the Second Indian Intercourse Act, approved March 1, 1793,[391] section 8 of which provided:

> That no purchase or grant of lands, or of any title or claim thereto, from any Indians or nation or tribe of Indians, within the bounds of the United States, shall be of any validity in law or equity, unless the same be made by a treaty or convention entered into pursuant to the constitution; and it shall be a misdemeanor, in any person not employed under the authority of the United States, in negotiating such treaty or convention, punishable by fine not exceeding one thousand dollars, and imprisonment not exceeding twelve months, directly or indirectly to treat with any such Indians, nation or tribe of Indians, for the title or purchase of any lands by them held, or claimed: *Provided, nevertheless*, That it shall be lawful for the agent or agents of any state, who may be present at any treaty, held with Indians under the authority of the United States, in the presence, and with the approbation of the commissioner or commissioners of the United States, appointed to hold the same, to propose to, and adjust with the Indians, the compensation to be made for their claims to the lands within such state, which shall be extinguished by the treaty.

This provision was reenacted from time to time with various minor modifications.[392] It should be noted that this provision was

[383] 5 Wall. 536 (1866). Accord: *Pueblo de San Juan* v. *United States*, 47 F. 2d 446 (C. C. A. 10, 1931), cert. den. 284 U. S. 626.

[384] 16 How. 203 (1853). See comment in Blanchard and Weeks, Law of Mines, Minerals, and Mining Water Rights (1877) pp. 93–94.

[385] See 3 Kent, Comm. 391 *et seq.* for an analysis of the colonial legislation.

[386] *Lynn* v. *Nahant*, 113 Mass. 433 (1873) (citing colonial authorities; Indian deed dated September 4, 1686). And see *Danzell* v. *Webquish*, 108 Mass. 133 (1871).

[387] See *Goodell* v. *Jackson*, 20 Johns. 693, 722, 733 (1823).

[388] Art. IV of Treaty of December 30, 1849, 9 Stat. 984 (Utahs); Art. VII of Treaty of June 22, 1852, 10 Stat. 974 (Chickasaws); Art. VII of Treaty of February 22, 1855, 10 Stat. 1165 (Mississippi Bands of Chippewas); Art. VIII of Treaty of February 27, 1855, 10 Stat. 1172 (Winnebagoes); Art. XV of Treaty of August 7, 1856, 11 Stat. 699 (Seminoles); Art. XIII of Treaty of April 19, 1858, 11 Stat. 743 (Yankton Tribe of Sioux); Art. X of the Treaty of June 11, 1855, 12 Stat. 957 (Nez Perces); Art. IX of Treaty of March 12, 1858, 12 Stat. 997 (Poncas); Art. IV of Treaty of June 19, 1858, 12 Stat. 1031 (Mendawakanton and Wahpakoota Bands of Sioux); Art. IV of Treaty of June 19, 1858, 12 Stat. 1037 (Sisseeton and Wahpaton Bands of Sioux); Art. I of Treaty of April 15, 1859, 12 Stat. 1101 (Winnebagoes); Art. I of Treaty of July 16, 1859, 12 Stat. 1105 (Swan Creek and Black River Chippewas and Munsees or Christians); Art. II of Treaty of February 18, 1861, 12 Stat. 1163 (Arapahoes and Cheyenne Indians); Art. VIII of Treaty of June 9, 1863, 14 Stat. 647 (Nez Perces); Art. IV of Treaty of March 6, 1865, 14 Stat. 667 (Omahas); Art. XI of Treaty of July 19, 1866, 14 Stat. 799 (Cherokees); Art. II of Treaty of October 1, 1859, 15 Stat. 467 (Sacs and Foxes of Mississippi). And see Chapter 8, sec. 8C(1).

[389] See, for example, Art. III of the Treaty of January 9, 1789, with the Wiandot, Delaware, Ottawa, Chippewa, Pattawattima, and Sac Nations, 7 Stat. 28, 29; Art. V of the Treaty of August 3, 1795, with the Wyandots, Delawares, Chipewas, and other tribes, 7 Stat. 49, 52; Art. VI of the Treaty of September 24, 1857, with the Pawnee Tribe, 11 Stat. 729; Art. V of the Treaty of March 12, 1858, with the Ponca Tribe, 12 Stat. 997. And see Chapter 8, sec. 3B(2). That similar provisions were included in colonial legislation is manifest in the reference of Marshall, *C. J.*, in *State of New Jersey* v. *Wilson*, 7 Cranch 164 (1812), to the New Jersey Act of August 12, 1758, restraining the Delaware Indians from alienating lands reserved to them by agreement.

[390] Act of July 22, 1790, 1 Stat. 137. See sec. 10, this Chapter, and see Chapter 16.

[391] 1 Stat. 329.

[392] Act of March 1, 1793, sec. 8, 1 Stat. 329, 330; Act of May 19, 1796, sec. 12, 1 Stat. 469, 472; Act of March 3, 1799, sec. 12, 1 Stat. 743, 746; Act of March 30, 1802, sec. 12, 2 Stat. 139, 143; Act of June

not intended to prevent the alienation of Indian lands and in fact many Indian treaties thereafter concluded provided for the alienation of Indian lands to parties other than the United States,[393] notably to religious bodies,[394] railroads,[395] or other Indian tribes.[396] In some instances a particular grant is validated.[397] In other cases authority is given to some administrative officer, generally the Secretary of the Interior, to sell at public sale,[398] and in a few cases the tribe itself is given authority to sell land to a named grantee [399] or to any purchaser.[400] A number of treaties provide for tribal grants of land by the tribe to individual members.[401] In effect this statutory requirement that all tribal grants be made by treaty simply applied to the American constitutional scene the principle that had been developed under British rule, that the consent of the Crown was necessary to validate a tribal conveyance.[402] This principle is not dependent upon the character of the Indian title and applied as much to land held in fee simple by an incorporated tribe as to land held under any lesser tenure.[403]

So firmly has this principle been established that the Supreme Court suggested, in the *Candelaria* case, that quite apart from any particular statute, the United States sustained a relation of guardianship towards an Indian pueblo such that even land held in fee simple could not be granted or lost by court action unless the United States was represented by an attorney.[404] It is difficult to understand how the appearance of a United States attorney would validate a conveyance of tribal land which is invalid by statute,[405] and the scope of this doctrine remains uncertain.

General limitations on the conveyance by an Indian tribe of interests in real property have been supplemented, from time to time, by special statutes prohibiting such conveyances with respect to particular tribes.[406]

On the other hand, general limitations upon the manner of disposing of tribal property have been qualified by numerous special acts of Congress. Since 1871, transfers of tribal land have generally been made pursuant to statutes relating to particular reservations or areas and authorizing sales by the Secretary of the Interior. Some of these statutes require tribal consent to such sale.[407] Other statutes validate conveyances by one tribe to another tribe,[408] or by a tribe to non-Indians,[409] or

---

30, 1834, sec. 12, 4 Stat. 729, 730; R. S. § 2116; 25 U. S. C. 177. Of the scope of this statute, an opinion of the Attorney General declares:

> I cannot think that it applies merely to those Indian tribes who hold their land by the original Indian title. The words are broad enough to include a tribe holding lands by patent from the United States, and the purpose of the statute manifestly requires it to receive that construction. (Christian Indians, 9 Op. A. G. 24, 27 (1857).)

Accord: *United States* v. *Candelaria* and *Goodell* v. *Jackson*, discussed above. Contra: *Clark* v. *Williams*, 36 Mass. 499, 501 (1837) (holding that similar colonial statute applies to aboriginal occupancy but not to land held by individual Indian in fee simple, and such tenure is presumed where land is in settled community).

[393] Various treaty provisions by which the New York Indians conveyed lands are analyzed in 1 L. D. Memo. 35 (1929); 5 L. D. Memo. 236 (May 18, 1935). Other treaty provisions empower prospectors to take minerals from an Indian reservation, *e. g.*, Art. IV of Treaty of October 12, 1863, with the Shoshone-Goship Bands, 13 Stat. 681, 682. An example of a tribal land grant disapproved by treaty will be found in Art. VI of the Treaty of March 29, 1836, with the Pottawatamies, 7 Stat. 498. A contract for the transfer of land is modified in a supplemental article concluded April 27, 1868, 16 Stat. 727, to the Treaty of July 19, 1866, 14 Stat. 799, with the Cherokee Nation.

[394] Art. II of Treaty of January 31, 1855, with the Wyandotts, 10 Stat. 1159.

[395] Art. II of Treaty of July 19, 1866, 14 Stat. 799, with Cherokee Nation, construed in *Bell* v. *Atlantic & P. R. Co.*, 63 Fed. 417 (C. C. A. 8, 1894). Art. V of Treaty of June 28, 1862, with the Kickapoos, 13 Stat. 623; Art V of Treaty of March 21, 1866, with the Seminoles, 14 Stat. 755; Art. V of Treaty of June 14, 1866, with the Creeks, 14 Stat. 785; Art. I of Treaty of July 4, 1866, with the Delawares, 14 Stat. 793; Treaty of June 22, 1855, with Choctaw-Chickasaws, 11 Stat. 611 (conferring power on President to prescribe manner of fixing compensation, construed in 17 Op. A. G. 265 (1882)); Treaty of April 28, 1866, with Choctaws and Chickasaws, 14 Stat. 769. And *cf.* "agreements" ratified by Act of July 10, 1882, 22 Stat. 157 (Crow) and Act of September 1, 1888, 25 Stat. 452.

[396] See sec. 8, this chapter.

[397] Treaty of June 30, 1802, with the Senecas, 7 Stat. 72; Art. XIV of Treaty of January 15, 1838, with New York Indians, 7 Stat. 550.

[398] Art. II of Treaty of January 31, 1855, with Wyandotts, 10 Stat. 1159; Art. IX of Treaty of June 24, 1862, with the Ottawas, 12 Stat. 1237.

[399] Art. X of Treaty of January 15, 1838, with the New York Indians, 7 Stat. 550.

[400] Art. XVIII of Treaty of July 19, 1866, with the Cherokees, 14 Stat. 799; Art. I of Act of February 13, 1891, 26 Stat. 749 (Sac and Fox Nation).

[401] Sec. 5 of Act of July 1, 1902, 32 Stat. 636 (confirming agreement submitted by Kansas Indians).

[402] See *Jackson* v. *Porter*, 13 Fed. Cas. No. 7143 (C. C. N. D. N. Y., 1825), p. 241.

[403] See fn. 370 *supra*. A similar provision in the Constitution of New York of 1777 (Art. 37) ("that no purchases or contracts for the sale of lands, made with, or of the said *Indians*, shall be binding on them, or deemed valid, unless made under the authority, and with the consent of the legislature") was construed in *Goodell* v. *Jackson* (20 Johns. 693, 1823). The court, holding that such limitations applied to an Indian holding land under a patent, declared:

> This is the provision; and the constitution states one important fact as the basis, and the sole governing motive for the whole of it, and that is, that *frauds* were too often practised towards the *Indians* in contracts made for their lands. It was this, and this only, that endangered our peace and amity with them. There was no suggestion of fraud or imposition committed by them upon the whites. That, indeed, would have been an idle suggestion, and about as reasonable as the complaint of the wolf in the fable, that the lamb, standing far below him, was disturbing him in the enjoyment of the running stream. * * *
> Thus, in the resolution of congress of *January*, 1776, regulating trade with the *Indians*, it was declared, that no person should be permitted to trade with them without license, and that the traders should take no unjust advantage of *their distress and intemperance*. In a speech, on behalf of congress, to the six nations, in *April* 1776, it was said to them, that congress were determined to cultivate peace and friendship with them, and prevent the white people from *wronging them in any manner, or taking their lands*. That congress wished to afford protection to all their brothers the *Indians*, who lived with them on this great island, and that the white people should not be suffered, by *force or fraud, to deprive them of any of their lands*. And in *November*, 1779, when congress were discussing the conditions of peace to be allowed to the six nations, they resolved, that one condition should be, that no land should be sold or ceded *by any of the said Indians*, either *as individuals*, or as a nation, unless by consent of congress. (Pp. 722–723.)
>
> * * * * *
>
> It was immaterial whether the *Indians* held their lands by immemorial possession, or by gift or grant from the whites, provided they had an acknowledged title. In either case, the lands were of equal value to them, and required the same protection, and exposed them to the like frauds. (Pp. 729.)
>
> * * * * *
>
> My conclusion upon the whole case is, 1. That the patent of *John Sagoharase* and his heirs, was a patent to him and his *Indian* heirs, whatever their civil condition and character might be, whether aliens or natives.
>
> * * * * *
>
> 4. That by the constitution and statute law of this state, no white person can purchase any right or title to land from any one or more *Indians*, either individually or collectively, without the authority and consent of the legislature, and none such existed, when the land in question was purchased by *Peter Smith*, in 1797. (P. 734.)

[404] 271 U. S. 432 (1926). See Chapter 20, sec. 7.

[405] "* * the Department of Justice has no greater authority than has the Interior Department to legalize such use or to divest the Indians of their land, no authority to do so, and no authority to bring the action having been conferred by Congress, and there being no theory in law upon which compensation may be awarded by the court." *United States* v. *Portneuf-Marsh Valley Irr. Co.*, 213 Fed. 601, 605 (C. C. A. 9, 1914), aff'g 205 Fed. 416 (D. C. Idaho 1913).

[406] Act of February 28, 1809, 2 Stat. 527 (Alibama and Wyandott).

[407] Sec. 4 of Act of May 8, 1872, 17 Stat. 85 (Kansas); Act of June 10, 1872, 17 Stat. 388 (Ottawas); Act of June 10, 1872, 17 Stat. 391 (Omahas); Act of March 3, 1873, 17 Stat. 631 (Miamis); Act of August 27, 1894, 28 Stat. 507 (recital shows tribal consent to exchange of lands for missionary use); Act of May 28, 1928, 45 Stat. 774 (Fort Peck Indian Reservation).

[408] Joint Resolution of July 25, 1848, 9 Stat. 337 (Wyandotts and Delawares); Act of June 8, 1858, 11 Stat. 312 (grant by Delaware Indians to Christian Indians); Act of June 22, 1874, 18 Stat. 146, 170 (Omaha and Winnebago); Act of March 3, 1875, 18 Stat. 420, 451 (Senecas and Kaskaskias); Act of March 3, 1883, 22 Stat. 603 (Cherokees, Pawnees,

by a tribe to its members,[410] which amounts, of course, to allotment. Other statutes authorizing sales by the Secretary of the Interior are silent on the issue of tribal consent. Statutes of this character are generally limited to surplus lands left after the completion of allotment.[411] Between 1912 and 1932 a number of statutes were enacted authorizing the Secretary of the Interior to sell or otherwise dispose of specific areas of tribal land to municipalities, religious bodies, and public utilities, without reference to the wishes of the tribe.[412] Questions raised by these statutes are dealt with separately, insofar as they present a question of the extent of federal power over Indian lands.[413]

Statutes authorizing the sale of tribal lands were superseded,[414] with respect to Indian tribes subject to the Act of June 18, 1934,[415] by section 4 of that act, which provides:

> Except as herein provided, no sale, devise, gift, exchange, or other transfer of restricted Indian lands or of shares in the assets of any Indian tribe or corporation organized hereunder, shall be made or approved: *Provided, however*, That such lands or interests may, with the approval of the Secretary of the Interior, be sold, devised, or otherwise transferred to the Indian tribe in which the lands or shares are located or from which the shares were derived or to a successor corporation; and in all instances such lands or interests shall descend or be devised, in accordance with the then existing laws of the State, or Federal laws where applicable, in which said lands are located or in which the subject matter of the corporation is located, to any member of such tribe or of such corporation or any heirs of such member: *Provided further*, That the Secretary of the Interior may authorize voluntary exchanges of lands of equal value and the voluntary exchange of shares of equal value whenever such exchange, in his judgment, is expedient and beneficial for or compatible with the proper consolidation of Indian lands and for the benefit of cooperative organizations.

The prohibitions of that section have been supplemented by prohibitions against alienation contained in tribal constitutions adopted pursuant to section 16 of the act and tribal charters adopted pursuant to section 17.

On the other hand, the proviso in section 4 allowing exchanges of land of equal value, and section 5 of the act allowing acquisition of lands by exchange, make it possible for tribes subject to the act to execute valid conveyances of tribal land by deed, approved by the Secretary of the Interior, provided the consideration is land of equal or greater value.[416]

D. INVOLUNTARY ALIENATION

Generally speaking, restraints on alienation of Indian land apply to involuntary alienation as well as to voluntary alienation. Thus, treaty guarantees of tribal possession are held to protect tribal land against sale by state authorities for nonpayment of taxes and therefore, inferentially, to protect such lands against taxation.[417] Restraints on alienation of tribal lands which prevent a tribe from making a valid conveyance of its property equally prevent individual members of the tribe from conveying such property.[418] Restraints on alienation of tribal lands likewise operate to prevent partition of such lands by state court at the suit of a tribal member.[419]

E. INVALID CONVEYANCES

Despite all statutes, Indian tribes have, from time to time, executed grants of tribal land. Although such grants are clearly invalid to convey a legal or equitable estate, it would be rash to say that all such grants are meaningless acts that cannot affect any rights. There are at least two federal cases which suggest that rights may accrue under tribal law, though not under federal or state law.

In *Johnson* v. *McIntosh*, [420] Marshal, *C. J.*, intimated that an Indian tribe might make a grant under its own laws even though such a grant would not be enforceable in the courts of the United States:

> If an individual might extinguish the Indian title, for his own benefit, or, in other words, might purchase it, still he could acquire only that title. Admitting their [the Indians'] power to change their laws or usages, so far as to allow an individual to separate a portion of their lands from the common stock, and hold it in severalty, still it is a part of their territory, and is held under them, by a title dependent on their laws. The grant derives its efficacy from their will; and, if they choose to resume it, and make a different disposition of the land, the courts of the United States cannot interpose for the protection of the title. (P. 593.)

A similar view is taken in the case of *Jackson* v. *Porter*,[421] where it was held that a grant made by an Indian tribe might be revoked by the tribe and that the grantee would have no redress in the courts of the United States.

> A purchaser, from the natives, at all events, could acquire only the Indian title, and must hold under them and according to their laws. The grant must derive its efficacy from their will, and if they choose to resume it and make a different disposition of it, courts cannot protect the right before granted. The purchaser incorporates himself with the Indians, and the purchase is to be considered in the same light as if the grant had been made to an Indian; and might be resumed by the tribe, and granted over again at their pleasure.

Poncas, Nez Perces, Otoes and Missourias and Osages); on the distinction between a sale by one tribe to another, and an amalgamation of tribes, note *Delaware Indians* v. *Cherokee Nation*, 38 C. Cls. 234 (1903); aff'd 193 U. S. 127 (1904).

[409] Act of March 3, 1871, 16 Stat. 588 (conveyance to railway company by Oneida tribe, Wisconsin).

[410] Act of April 20, 1878, 20 Stat. 513 (Brothertown Indians and Menomonees). And see Chapter 11.

[411] Act of February 26, 1896, 29 Stat. 17 (Chippewa); Act of February 19, 1912, 37 Stat. 67 (Choctaw and Chickasaw); Act of August 24, 1912, 37 Stat. 497 (Five Civilized Tribes); Act of February 14, 1913, 37 Stat. 675 (Standing Rock Reservation); Joint Resolution of December 8, 1913, 38 Stat. 767 (Choctaw-Chickasaw); Joint Resolution of January 11, 1917, 39 Stat. 866 (Choctaw-Chickasaw); Act of January 25, 1917 39 Stat. 870 (Choctaw-Chickasaw); Act of February 27, 1917, 39 Stat 944; Act of April 12, 1924, 43 Stat. 93; Act of May 26, 1930, 46 Stat 385 (Chickasaw-Choctaw); on the sale of coal deposits in the segregated mineral lands of the Choctaw and Chickasaw tribes, see Memo. Sol. I. D. December 11, 1918; Op. Sol. I. D., M.7316, April 5, 1922; Op. Sol. I. D., M.7316, May 28, 1924; Op. Sol. I. D., M.24735, November 19, 1928.

[412] Act of July 1, 1912, 37 Stat. 186 (Umatilla Reservation); Act of July 10, 1912, 37 Stat. 192 (Flathead Reservation); Act of September 8, 1916, 39 Stat. 846 (Chippewa); Act of January 7, 1919, 40 Stat. 1053 (Flathead Reservation); Act of February 28, 1919, 40 Stat. 1206 (Capitan Grande Reservation); Act of April 15, 1920, 41 Stat. 553 (Nez Perce); Act of February 21, 1921, 41 Stat. 1105 (Choctaw and Chickasaw); Act of March 3, 1921, 41 Stat. 1355 (Fort Belknap); Act of May 4, 1932, 47 Stat. 146 (Capitan Grande Reservation). And see Chapter 5, sec. 9C.

[413] See Chapter 5.

[414] Memo. Sol. I. D., August 22, 1936 (Pyramid Lake). Sec. 4 does not, however, prevent foreclosure of a lien on land existing when land is restored to tribal ownership under sec. 3. Op. Sol. I. D., M.29791, August 1, 1938.

[415] 48 Stat. 984, 25 U. S. C. 451 *et seq.*

[416] Memo. Sol. I. D., February 3, 1937. The problem of what officials of a tribe may execute a deed is dealt with in *Pueblo of Santa Rosa* v. *Fall*, 273 U. S. 315 (1927), rev'g. 12 F. 2d 332 (App. D. C. 1926); 55 I. D. 14 (1934); Memo. Sol. I. D., March 11, 1935.

[417] See Chapter 13, sec. 2.

[418] *United States* v. *Boylan*, 265 Fed. 165 (C. C. A. 2, 1920), aff'g. 256 Fed. 468 (D. C. N. D. N. Y. 1919), app. dism. 257 U. S. 614 (1921); *Franklin* v. *Lynch*, 233 U. S. 269 (1914) (holding adopted white member of tribe subject to restraint on alienation). And see authorities cited in Chapter 9, sec. 2.

[419] *United States* v. *Charles*, 23 F. Supp. 346 (D. C. W. D. N. Y. 1938).

[420] 8 Wheat. 543 (1823).

[421] 13 Fed. Cas. No. 7143 (C. C. N. D. N. Y. 1825). And see 1 Dembitz. Land Titles (1895), p. 494.

If this be the view which we are to take of the Indian right of occupancy, the claim of John Stedman considered in the most favourable manner, could never have been any thing more than a mere right of possession, subject to be reclaimed, and extinguished at the will of the Indians, and which has been done, as will be seen hereafter. But it may very well be questioned, whether this claim is entitled even to so favourable a consideration. (P. 240.)

* * * * *

It has already been shown, that admitting a purchaser from the Indians acquires their right of occupancy, the Indians may whenever they choose, resume it, and make a different disposition of the land, which in the present case has been done by the 3d article of a treaty between his Britannic majesty and the Seneca Nation of Indians, dated the 3d of April, 1764. * * * There can therefore be no doubt, but that the Indian right to the land in question was ceded to the king by the treaty of 1764; and all Stedman's right of occupancy must then have ceased, and been extinguished; and he stood upon his mere naked possession, without title, and without the right of possession. (P. 242.)

In 1882 the Attorney General in an opinion on the claim of William G. Langford, declared:[432]

The occupancy of the land by the American Board of Commissioners for Foreign Missions from 1836 to 1847 was by the consent and allotment of the tribe; the occupancy by the United States since 1862 has been by a similar consent, manifested by the treaties of 1855 (12 Stat., 957), and 1863 (14 Stat., 467). Chief Justice Marshall, in *Johnson* v. *McIntosh* (8 Wheaton, 543), speaking of a deed poll executed by the Illinois Indians, said (p. 593): (Quoting the passage above set forth.)

It is not suggested in the present case that any grant was made by the Nez Perces to the board, and it is fair to assume that the inducement for the allotment was the appreciation by the tribe of the benefits which the agents of the board had come there to confer on them. If the presence of the board became distasteful to them, I know of no law to prevent the annulment of the allotment and the resumption of the land. (P. 307.)

The possibility suggested in these cases, that a tribe may give effect under its own laws and customs to grants that would be held invalid in state or federal courts, assumes that this is a subject not within the scope of the federal statutes and one on which the local law of the tribe is therefore conclusive. Authority for this view is available but not conclusive.[433]

Speaking of a colonial statute similar to 25 U. S. C. 177,[434] Chief Justice Shaw of Massachusetts, holding the statute inapplicable where the land was within a settled community, declared:[435]

In the first place, we think it manifest, that this law was made for the personal relief and protection of the Indians, and is to be so limited in its operation. It is to be used as a shield, not as a sword.

[432] 17 Op. A. G. 306 (1882). See sec. 6, fn. 101, this chapter.

[433] The law of real property is to be found in the law of the situs. The law of real property in the Cherokee country therefore is to be found in the constitution and laws of the Cherokee Nation.

Delaware Indians v. *Cherokee Nation*, 38 C. Cls. 234, 251 (1903).

* * * that neither the establishment of town sites nor the purchase nor the occupancy by noncitizens of lots therein withdraws those lots or the town sites or their occupants from the jurisdiction of the government of the Creek Nation * * * (P. 953.)

[434] See fn. 403, *supra*.

Buster v. *Wright*, 135 Fed. 947 (C. C. A. 8, 1905), app. dism. 203 U. S. 599 (holding that deeded land is subject to tribal jurisdiction where tribe holds determinable fee).

[435] *Clark* v. *Williams*, 36 Mass. 499, 501 (1837).

SECTION 19. TRIBAL LEASES'

The question whether leases of tribal lands executed by tribes are valid in the absence of statutory prohibition or invalid in the absence of positive statutory authorization can be answered only on the basis of an analysis of the entire course of federal legislation and litigation on the subject.

The first explicit statutory limitation upon the power of a tribe to lease tribal land is found in section 12 of the Act of May 19, 1796,[436] reading as follows:

And be it further enacted, That no purchase, grant, lease, or other conveyance of lands, or of any title or claim thereto, from any Indian, or nation or tribe of Indians, within the bounds of the United States, shall be of any validity, in law or equity, unless the same be made by treaty, or convention, entered into pursuant to the constitution: * * *.

[436] 1 Stat. 469, 472. The background of the 1796 act is indicated by the two following quotations. The first is from a resolution proposed by the Indian Affairs Committeee of the House of Representatives, in 1795 with reference to the rights of states and individuals to extinguish the right of possession and occupancy held by the Indians:

That, it appears to your committee, that the Legislature of the State of Georgia, by an act of the 7th day of January last, have contracted and provided for an absolute conveyance of certain portions of lands held by the Creek and other Indian tribes, within the limits claimed by that State, under the sanction of treaties made with the United States, amounting to three-fourths of the lands so held by said Indians.

That your committee cannot but foresee great danger to the peace of the United States, in vesting interests in individuals, the enjoyment of which is to depend on the extinguishment of the Indian titles, from the constant excitement which they produce, to embroil the Government with the neighboring Indians, in hope of their extinction or banishment.

That rights, so dangerous to the general happiness, should reside only in the bodies constituted for the guardianship of the general good of society, as being alone capable of comparing the various interests, alone disposed to promote a happy result to the community.

That your committee are of opinion, that it is highly incumbent on the United States to secure to the neighboring Indians, the rights acquired by treaty, not only for obtaining their confidence in our Government, but, for preserving an inviolate respect in the citizens of the United States, to its constitutional acts.

Your committee, therefore, submit the following resolutions:

Resolved, That it be recommended to the President of the United States, to use all constitutional and legal means, to prevent the infraction of the treaties made with the Indian tribes by the citizens of the United States, with an assurance, that Congress will cooperate in such other acts, as will be proper for the same end.

Resolved, That it be further recommended to the President of the United States, not to permit treaties for the extinguishment of the Indian title to any lands, to be holden at the instance of individuals or of States, where it shall appear that the property of such lands, when the Indian title shall be extinguished, will be in particular persons: And that, wherever treaties are held for the benefit of the United States, individuals claiming rights of pre-emption, shall be prevented from treating with Indians, concerning the same; and that, generally, such private claims be postponed to those of the several States, whenever the same may be consistent with the welfare and defence of the United States.

Resolved, That the President of the United States be authorised, whenever claims under prior contracts may cease to exist, to obtain a cession of the State of Georgia, of their claim to the whole or any part of the land within the present Indian boundaries, and that __________ dollars ought to be appropriated to enable him to effect the same.

President Washington in the same year and shortly thereafter addressed a communication to the United States Senate with reference to certain treaties requested by the State of Georgia:

Gentlemen of the Senate:

Just at the close of the last session of Congress, I received from one of the Senators and one of the Representatives of the State of Georgia, an application for a treaty to be held with the tribes or nations of Indians claiming the right of soil to certain lands lying beyond the present temporary boundary line of that State, and which were described in an act of the Legislature of Georgia, passed on the 28th of December last, which has already been laid before the Senate. This application, and the subsequent correspondence with the Governor of Georgia, are herewith transmitted. The subject being very important, I thought proper to postpone a decision upon that application. The views I have

This provision amplifies earlier provisions relating to the alienation of Indian lands.[427]

The foregoing provision was reenacted as section 12 of the Act of March 3, 1799,[428] and as section 12 of the Act of March 30, 1802.[429] The Act of March 30, 1802, was the first piece of permanent legislation on the subject, the earlier statutes, having been limited in duration to a term of years.

The Act of June 30, 1834,[430] which, as elsewhere noted,[431] represented, in a measure, a codification of general Indian legislation, copied the language of the earlier acts, except that it omitted from its scope any reference to leases by individual Indians.[432] This omission apparently took account of the beginnings of the allotment system, and the encouragement, under that system, of leases by individual Indians to whom "reservations," later called "allotments," had been made.

The provision denying legal validity to tribal leases not made by treaty, contained in the Act of June 30, 1834, was embodied in Section 2116 of the Revised Statutes and in the United States Code in section 177 of title 25. This enactment is law today, except for (*a*) incorporated tribes which have been given general power to lease tribal lands, pursuant to the Act of June 18, 1934,[433] (*b*) other tribes authorized by special law or treaty to execute leases of tribal land, and (*c*) various types of lease generally authorized by act of Congress.[434]

This statutory limitation of the power to lease tribal lands, according to an opinion of the Attorney General, is not dependent upon the nature of the tribal possessory right in the land,[435] nor can the Interior Department by its approval, bestow validity upon a lease of tribal land declared invalid by the statute.[436]

The drastic character of the statute cited raises questions upon which history may throw some light. Today we are likely to think of a lease, particularly a lease of agricultural lands, as a short-term transaction. This is in part the result of widespread state legislation outlawing long-term agricultural leases. In 1796, however, leases having the practical effect of outright grants were common,[437] and even as late as 1855 an agreement was made by treaty between the Choctaw and Chickasaw tribes and the United States whereby these tribes agreed to "lease to the United States * * * for the permanent settlement of the Wichita and such other tribes or bands of Indians as the Government may desire to locate therein." [438]

Under these circumstances a statute denying validity to Indian grants not made pursuant to treaty would be ineffective unless leasing were brought within its scope. We have already noted the insistence of the Federal Government that all grants of Indian land should be made by treaty, this being considered necessary to prevent frauds on non-Indian vendees as well as on Indian vendors. So long as it was possible to grant or lease tribal land by treaty,[439] the statute which declared this to be

---

since taken of the matter, with the information received, of a more pacific disposition on the part of the Creeks, have induced me, now, to accede to the request, but with this explicit declaration: That neither my assent, nor the treaty which may be made, shall be considered as affecting any question which may arise, upon the supplementary act, passed by the Legislature of the State of Georgia, on the 7th of January last, upon which inquiries have been instituted, in pursuance of a resolution of the Senate and House of Representatives; and that any cession or relinquishment of the Indian claims, shall be made in the general terms of the treaty of New York, which are contemplated as the form proper to be generally used on such occasions; and on the condition that one half of the expense of the supplies of provisions for the Indians assembled at the treaty be borne by the State of Georgia.

Having concluded to hold the treaty requested by that State, I was willing to embrace the opportunity it would present, of inquiring into the causes of the dissatisfaction of the Creeks, which has been manifested since the treaty of New York, by their numerous and distressing depredations on our Southwestern frontiers. Their depredations on the Cumberland have been so frequent, and so peculiarly destructive, as to lead me to think they must originate in some claim to the lands upon that river. But, whatever may have been the cause, it is important to trace it to its source: for, independent of the destruction of lives and property, it occasions a very serious annual expense to the United States. The commissioners for holding the proposed treaty will, therefore, be instructed to inquire into the causes of the hostilities to which I have referred, and to enter into such reasonable stipulations as will remove them, and give permanent peace to those parts of the United States.

I now nominate Benjamin Hawkins, of North Carolina, George Clymer, of Pennsylvania, and Andrew Pickens, of South Carolina, to be commissioners to hold a treaty with the Creek nation of Indians, for the purposes hereinbefore expressed.

(American State Papers, vol. 7 (Indian Affairs, class 2, vol. 1), pp. 558, 560.)

And see American State Papers, vol. 7 (Indian Affairs, class 2, vol. 1), pp. 165, 585, 626, 655, 663, 665; vol. 2, p. 323. The Memorandum of the Justice Department, dated May 13, 1935 (5 L. D. Memo. 248), from which the foregoing citations are taken, comments:

> The procedure as above outlined was followed consistently by the Federal Government until Congress assumed full control over the Indians in 1871. (P. 253.)
>
> It should be noted that all treaties made pursuant to Section 12 of the Act of March 30, 1802, show on their face the attendance of a United States Commissioner appointed under the authority of the United States to hold such treaty (See Appendix pp. 39–44). This particular form was approved by President Washington. (See his letter to the Senate at pp. 16–17 hereof). (P. 258.)

[427] See sec. 4, Act of July 22, 1790, 1 Stat. 137, 138, reenacted as sec. 8 of the Act of March 1, 1793, 1 Stat. 329, 330. A similar provision under the Articles of Confederation is noted in 18 Op. A. G. 235 at p. 236, (1885).

[428] 1 Stat. 743, 746.

[429] 2 Stat. 139, 143.

[430] 4 Stat. 729.

[431] See Chapter 4, sec. 6.

[432] Sec. 12:

> That no purchase, grant, lease, or other conveyance of lands, or of any title or claim thereto, from any Indian nation or tribe of Indians, shall be of any validity in law or equity, unless the same be made by treaty or convention entered into pursuant to the constitution. * * *

[433] Sec. 17, 48 Stat. 984, 986, 25 U. S. C. 477.

[434] See pp. 327–382 *infra*.

[435] This statutory provision is very general and comprehensive. Its operation does not depend upon the nature or extent of the title to the land which the tribe or nation may hold. Whether such title be a fee simple, or a right of occupancy merely, is not material; in either case the statute applies. It is not therefore deemed necessary or important, in connection with the subject under consideration, to inquire into the particular right or title to the above-mentioned reservations held by the Indian tribes or nations respectively which claim them. Whatever the right or title may be, each of these tribes or nations is precluded, by the force and effect of the statute, from either alienating or leasing any part of its reservation, or imparting any interest or claim in or to the same, without the consent of the Government of the United States. A lease of the land for grazing purposes is as clearly within the statute as a lease for any other or for general purposes, and the duration of the term is immaterial. One who enters with cattle or other livestock upon an Indian reservation under a lease of that description, made in violation of the statute, is an intruder, and may be removed therefrom as such, notwithstanding his entry is with consent of the tribe. Such consent may exempt him from the penalty imposed by section 2117, Revised Statutes, for taking his stock there, but it cannot validate the lease or confer upon him any legal right whatsoever to remain upon the land; and to this extent and no further was the decision of Judge Brewer in *United States v. Hunter*, 21 Fed. Rep., 615.

But the present inquiry in substance is, (1) whether the Department of the Interior can authorize these Indians to make leases of their lands for grazing purposes, or whether the approval of such leases by the President or the Secretary of the Interior would make them lawful and valid; (2) whether the President or the Department of the Interior has authority to lease for such purposes any part of an Indian Reservation.

I submit that the power of the Department to authorize such leases to be made, or that of the President or Secretary to approve or to make the same, if it exists at all, must rest upon some *law*, and therefore be derived from either a treaty or a statutory provision. * * *

In my opinion, therefore, each of the questions proposed in your letter should be answered in the negative, and I so answer them. (18 Op. A. G. 235, 237–238 (1885).

[436] *Ibid.*

[437] See *Goodell* v. *Jackson*, 20 Johns, 693, 728 (N. Y. 1823).

[438] Art. IX of the Treaty of June 22, 1855, 11 Stat. 611, 613, carried into effect in Acts of June 19, 1860, 12 Stat. 44, 56 and March 2, 1861, 12 Stat. 221, 236. For an analysis of this lease see *United States* v. *Choctaw etc., Nations*, 179 U. S. 494, 510 (1900); *Chickasaw Nation* v. *United States*, 75 C. Cls. 426 (1932), cert. den. 287 U. S. 643.

[439] Leasing provisions are to be found in some of the earlier treaties: Art. IV of the Treaty of October 19, 1818, with the Chickasaws, 7 Stat. 192, provided for a lease of tribal salt springs by trustees for the benefit of the tribe, with a limit of $1 per bushel upon the selling price of the salt mined by the lessee. Such lease needed no approval by federal authorities. The Treaty of February 27, 1819, with the Cherokees, 7 Stat. 195, provided for a lease or license of a roadway, adjacent land and a ferry site.

the exclusive method of making grants or leases apparently worked no hardship.

A new situation, however, was created with the passage of the Act of March 3, 1871,[440] prohibiting the execution of treaties with Indian tribes. The passage of this act blocked the only valid method of leasing land which existing legislation permitted.

There is some evidence, in the statutes and decided cases, that invalid leases were made by various tribes before and after 1871 and that these leases, although denied legal validity, served the purposes of lessors and lessees.[441]

The first statutory breach in the general ban against tribal leasing appeared in a special act relating to the Seneca Indians, ratifying past invalid leases and authorizing new leases to be made by the authorities of the Seneca Nation in accordance witn the laws and customs of that nation.[442]

Since February 19, 1875, the date of the Seneca leasing act, various other special acts have provided for leases of tribal land of the Fort Peck,[443] Blackfeet,[444] Fort Belknap,[445] Kaw,[446] Crow,[447] Shoshone,[448] Spokane,[449] and Osage[450] reservations, the Five Civilized Tribes,[451] and Pueblos.[452]

The first general statutory authorization of tribal leasing is found in section 3 of the Act of February 28, 1891,[453] which in its present code[454] form reads as follows:

> * * * Where lands are occupied by Indians who have bought and paid for the same, and which lands are not needed for farming or agricultural purposes, and are not desired for individual allotments, the same may be leased by authority of the council speaking for such Indians, for a period not to exceed five years for grazing, or ten years for mining purposes in such quantities and upon such terms and conditions as the agent in charge of such reservation may recommend, subject to the approval of the Secretary of the Interior.

The Act of August 15, 1894 extended the foregoing authority as follows:[455]

> * * * the surplus lands of any tribe may be leased for farming purposes by the council of such tribe under the same rules and regulations and for the same term of years as is now allowed in the case of leases for grazing purposes.

The foregoing two statutes are, at the present time, the sole statutes of general application[456] under which tribal lands may be leased for grazing or farming purposes, except insofar as such lands are capable of irrigation, in which event the Act of July 3, 1926,[457] applies. This act extends the permissible leasing period for irrigable lands to 10 years, declaring:[458]

> The unallotted irrigable lands on any Indian reservation may be leased for farming purposes for not to exceed ten years with the consent of the tribal council, business committee, or other authorized body representative of the Indians, under such rules and regulations as the Secretary of the Interior may prescribe.

Insofar as the Act of 1891 authorized mining leases on lands "occupied by Indians who have bought and paid for the same," it has been extended and amplified by four later statutes.[459]

(1) Section 26 of the Act of June 30, 1919,[460] later amended by the Act of March 3, 1921,[461] and the Act of December 16, 192C,[462] authorized the Secretary of the Interior to lease tribal lands within the States of Arizona, California, Idaho, Montana, Nevada, New Mexico, Oregon, Washington, and Wyoming, for the purpose of mining for deposits of gold, silver, copper, and other valuable metalliferous minerals. The 1919 act, as was characteristic of acts relating to tribal property enacted at that time, made no provision for Indian consent to such leases. Leases made under this statute might be "for a period of twenty years with the preferential right in the lessee to renew the same for successive periods of ten years upon such reasonable terms and conditions as may be prescribed by the Secretary of the Interior,

---

[440] 16 Stat. 544, 566, R. S. § 2079, 25 U. S. C. 71.

[441] The existence of such invalid leases is discussed in the Rept. H. Comm. Ind. Aff., No. 478, 48d Cong., 1st sess., dated April 20, 1874, relating to the Seneca Indians of New York. In accordance with this report there was subsequently enacted the Act of February 19, 1875, 18 Stat. 330 ratifying earlier invalid leases. See also *Quigley* v. *Stephens,* 3 Ind. T. 265 (1900), aff'd 126 Fed. 148 (C. C. A. 8, 1903), in which leasing practices within the Indian Territory are discussed. In the case of *United States* v. *Rogers,* 23 Fed. 658 (D. C. W. D. Ark. 1885), in reaching the holding that certain lands were "occupied" by the Cherokee Nation, for purposes of criminal jurisdiction, the court described such "occupancy" in these terms:

> The evidence in this case shows that the Cherokee Nation has constantly, and all the time since it obtained the outlet, claimed it, and exercised acts of ownership and control over it. The nation has collected at different times a grazier's tax from white men who were grazing their stock on it. Individual Indians have gone on it and fenced up large tracts of land on the outlet. Different individual Indians have gone out and lived on it, and now live on it. That since the passage of this law of January 6, 1883, the Cherokee Nation has leased to citizens of the United States for grazing purposes 6,000,000 acres of this outlet. That under the provisions of the sixteenth article of the treaty of 1866 with the United States, it has sold tracts of land on this outlet for reservations to the Pawnees, Poncas, Nez Perces, Otoes, and Missouras. The very country where this alleged offense was committed, was, at the time of its commission, leased to the cattlemen as a part of the 6,000,000-acre lease. That the Cherokee Nation never has abandoned any part of the outlet except what it has sold. It claims the title and possession of the outlet and of that part of it where this alleged offense is shown to have been committed. The United States, the grantor, has admitted its title to it. (P. 665.)

[442] See preceding fn. 441. The Act of February 19, 1875, was amplified by the Act of September 30, 1890, 26 Stat. 558, and extended to cover additional particular cases by the Act of February 27, 1901, 31 Stat. 816; the Act of May 29, 1908, sec. 4, 35 Stat. 444, 445, and the Act of February 21, 1911, 36 Stat. 927. See also the Act of February 28, 1901, 31 Stat. 819, requiring payment of rentals to the United States agent for transmittal to tribal officers, in part, and in part to the heads of families of the Seneca Nation.

[443] Act of September 20, 1922, 42 Stat. 857; 25 U. S. C. 400 (mining leases on Fort Peck and Blackfeet Reservations).

[444] *Ibid.*

[445] Act of March 3, 1921, 41 Stat. 1355 (tribal leases of minerals and water power on Fort Belknap Reservation).

[446] Act of April 28, 1924, 43 Stat. 111; 25 U. S. C. 401 (mining leases on Kaw Reservation).

Act of February 28, 1891, 26 Stat. 794 (tribal permits, approved by tribal council).

[447] Act of June 4, 1920, 41 Stat. 751 (mining leases on Crow Reservation, approved by tribal council).

[448] Act of August 21, 1916, 39 Stat. 519 (20-year oil and gas leases on Shoshone Reservation, Wyo.).

[449] Act of May 18, 1916, 39 Stat. 155 (25-year mining leases on Spokane Reservation).

[450] Act of June 28, 1906, 34 Stat. 539 (tribal leases of oil, gas, and minerals on Osage Reservation). Act of March 3, 1921, 41 Stat. 1249; Act of March 2, 1929, 45 Stat. 1478. See Chapter 23.

[451] Act of August 7, 1882, 22 Stat. 349 (tribal leases of salt deposits in Cherokee Nation). Act of October 1, 1890, 26 Stat. 640 (giving the assent of the United States to coal leases on lands of the Choctaw Nation). The Act of June 28, 1898, 30 Stat. 495 terminates the making of tribal leases in the Indian Territory (sec. 23), grants power to the Secretary of the Interior to lease tribal minerals (sec. 13), provides for the deposit of rentals in the United States Treasury for the benefit of the tribe (sec. 16), and protects lessees under prior leases executed by individual occupants of tribal land (sec. 23). For other acts, see Chapter 23.

[452] Sec. 17 of the Pueblo Lands Act of June 7, 1924, 43 Stat. 636, provides that no lease made by any pueblo "shall be of any validity in law or in equity unless the same be first approved by the Secretary of the Interior."

[453] 26 Stat. 795.

[454] 25 U. S. C. 397.

[455] Act of August 15, 1894, sec. 1, 28 Stat. 305, 25 U. S. C., 402.

[456] For special statutes, see footnotes 442–452, *supra.*

[457] 44 Stat. 894, U. S. C. A. 402a.

[458] The leasing powers of incorporated tribes are discussed *infra.* For general grazing regulations see 25 C. F. R. 71.1–71.26. For regulations regarding grazing on the Navajo and Hopi Reservations, see 25 C. F. R. 72.1–72.13.

[459] For regulations relating to leasing of tribal lands for mining, see 25 C. F. R. 186.1–186.30.

[460] 41 Stat. 3, 31.

[461] Sec. 1, 41 Stat. 1225, 1231.

[462] 44 Stat. 922, 25 U. S. C. 399.

unless otherwise provided by law at the time of the expiration of such periods."

The 1919 act in effect extended to Indian reservations in the named states the procedure of exploration and discovery then in force on the public domain.

(2) A second extension of the law authorizing mineral leases on tribal land was brought about by the Act of May 29, 1924,[463] which provided that unallotted land on Indian reservations, other than lands of the Five Civilized Tribes and the Osage Reservation, subject to lease for mining purposes under the 1891 act, might be "leased at public auction by the Secretary of the Interior, with the consent of the council speaking for such Indians, for oil and gas mining purposes for a period of not to exceed ten years, and as much longer as oil or gas shall be found in paying quantities * * *"

(3) Secretarial authority to make mineral leases on tribal land was extended by the Act of April 17, 1926,[464] to cover lands "on any Indian reservation reserved for Indian agency or school purposes, in accordance with existing law applicable to other lands in such reservation." A royalty of at least one-eighth was to be reserved in all such leases, and the proceeds were to be deposited to the credit of the Indian tribe.

(4) The next statute on the subject of mineral leases was the Act of March 3, 1927,[465] which related to Executive order reservations, not covered by the 1891 act, and made special provision for oil and gas leases, in the following terms:[466]

> Unallotted lands within the limits of any reservation or withdrawal created by Executive order for Indian purposes or for the use or occupancy of any Indians or tribe may be leased for oil and gas mining purposes in accordance with the provisions contained in section 398 of this title.[467]

The foregoing statutes left the law governing mineral leases on tribal land in a patch-work state. This condition was remedied on May 11, 1938, by the enactment of comprehensive legislation governing the leasing of tribal lands for mining purposes. This legislation was advocated by the Secretary of the Interior in a letter to the Speaker of the House of Representatives dated June 17, 1937. As this letter was presented by the House Committee on Indian Affairs recommending the proposed legislation as the basis of its recommendation, it throws considerable light on the problems intended to be met by the above act.[468]

Section 1 of the Act of May 11, 1938,[469] lays down a comprehensive law covering mineral leases on unallotted land, in the following terms:

> Hereafter unallotted lands within any Indian reservation or lands owned by any tribe, group, or band of In-

---

[463] 43 Stat. 244. 25 U. S. C. 398.

[464] 44 Stat. 300. 25 U. S. C. 400a.

[465] 44 Stat. 1347. 25 U. S. C. 398a.

[466] 25 U. S. C. 398a.

[467] Other sections of this act relate to disposition of rentals (sec. 2, 25 U. S. C. 398b), taxes (sec. 3, 25 U. S. C. 398c), changes in reservation boundaries (sec. 4, 25 U. S. C. 398d), and prospecting permits (sec. 5, 25 U. S. C. 398e).

[468]

DEPARTMENT OF THE INTERIOR,
Washington, June 17, 1937.

THE SPEAKER OF THE HOUSE OF REPRESENTATIVES.

MY DEAR MR. SPEAKER: I transmit herewith a proposed bill to govern the leasing of Indian lands for mining purposes.

Under section 26 of the Act of June 30, 1919 (41 Stat. 31), as amended, leases for minerals other than oil and gas may be made on any reservation in the States of Arizona, California, Idaho, Montana, Nevada, New Mexico, Oregon, Washington, or Wyoming. Under the provisions of section 3 of the Act of February 28, 1891 (26 Stat. 785), as amended May 29, 1924 (43 Stat. 244), leases for oil, gas and other minerals may be made with the consent of the tribal council on treaty reservations in all States. Section 16 of the Indian Reorganization Act, approved June 18, 1934 (48 Stat. 984), provides that organized Indian tribes shall have the power to prevent the leasing of tribal lands. Under section 17 of that act Indian tribes to which charters of incorporation issue are empowered to lease their lands for periods of not more than ten years. There is at present no law under which Executive order lands may be leased for mining, outside of the States mentioned in the act of June 30, 1919, except for oil and gas mining purposes, unless the tribes are hereafter qualified under sections 16 and 17 of the Indian Reorganization Act. One of the purposes of the legislation now proposed, therefore, is to obtain uniformity so far as practicable of the law relating to the leasing of tribal lands for mining purposes.

The Act of June 30, 1919 requires the formal opening of lands for prospecting, location, and lease, by the Secretary of the Interior, before an application for a lease for minerals other than oil and gas can be considered. It also requires that a person desiring to lease shall locate the mining claims as under the United States mining laws, file formal location notice; and under the regulations he must have the lands surveyed if they have not already been surveyed, all in accordance with the mining laws applicable to the public domain. This frequently results in long delay and is often quite an expense to an applicant for a lease. Frequently we have requests for leases for the purpose of removing sand and gravel for road grading purposes, or for the quarrying of stone, either for building or grading purposes in connection with which there would be little or no undersurface workings. In such cases, applicants for leases are required to go through all the formality and expense necessary to acquiring actual mining leases. Sometimes the time and expense of making the locations and of having the land surveyed are more than they care to undertake although the material desired may be very conveniently located and could be profitably utilized; and consequently the opportunity to lease the land is lost and the revenue, while perhaps not a great deal in a particular instance would amount to considerable in such cases through the entire Indian Service.

Section 26 of the Act of June 30, 1919, *supra*, as amended by the Acts of March 3, 1921 (41 Stat. 1231) and December 16, 1926 (44 Stat. 922–923), places unallotted Indian lands within the States mentioned therein upon the same basis for prospecting and leasing for metalliferous minerals as lands of the public domain, after such Indian reservation lands have been declared opened by the Secretary of the Interior. It has been held that the Secretary of the Interior has no discretion under the said section in the matter of granting a lease to an applicant who has properly located his claim and complied with the laws and regulations of the Department thereunder; and in several instances it has been necessary to grant the lease notwithstanding the fact that the Indians of the reservation were opposed to leasing the lands. In other words, under that law, neither this Department nor the Indian Tribal Council is in a position to prevent the acquisition of a lease after the lands have been declared open to prospecting and lease, and the Indians at no time have any voice in the granting of such leases.

It is not believed that the present law is adequate to give the Indians the greatest return from their property. As stated, present law provides for locating and taking mineral leases in the same manner as mining locations are made on the public lands of the United States; but there are disadvantages in following this procedure on Indian lands that are not present in applying for a claim on the public domain. For instance, on the public domain the discoverer of a mineral deposit gets extralateral rights and can follow the ore beyond the side lines indefinitely, while on the Indian lands under the Act of June 30, 1919, he is limited to the confines of the survey markers not to exceed 600 feet by 1,500 feet in any one claim. The draft of the bill herewith would permit the obtaining of sufficient acreage to remove the necessity for extralateral rights with all its attending controversies.

The most urgent change is in the interest of leasing deposits of building stone, sand, gravel and metalliferous minerals. For instance, the well-known iron deposit on the Fort Apache Indian Reservation, outcropping along the canyon wall for a distance of about 2 miles and 20 feet thick, with an estimated ore reserve of over 15 million tons, now must be "discovered" and located and monumented and then an application made for a lease. Under the present law only the outcrop along the canyon wall can be taken up under the lease as there are no outcrops of iron ore back from the face of the cliff. This deposit, it is believed, could be leased to better advantage at public auction and in definite areas rather than to anyone who erects a few monuments along the outcrop and applies for a preference right to a lease, through tying up the land with a long strip 600 feet wide. This deposit of iron ore is about 20 miles from a railroad, and anyone interested and considering building a railroad and developing the property would want a reserve greater than 600 feet back from the edge of the cliff. This deposit should appropriately be laid out in blocks extending at least 1 mile back from the outcrop.

Coal deposits on the several reservations are not adaptable to the discovery and location feature of the present act which has very limited application. The presence of coal is usually known by geological association, and leases may be made with reasonable assurance before any coal is actually exposed on the land. Deposits of marl along the west side of Pyramid Lake, Nevada, can be seen for a distance of many miles yet they must be "discovered" and "located" in accordance with the provisions of law relating to placer mining claims and leased to the person who erects monuments thereon. Deposits of sand, gravel and building stone are now similarly leased, even though the deposits are well known and could be leased with greater advantage to the Indians in definite areas.

The attached draft of bill, it is believed, would be a more satisfactory law for the leasing of Indian lands for general mining purposes. It will bring all mineral leasing matters in harmony with the Indian Reorganization Act, and I recommend that it be enacted.

The Acting Director of the Bureau of the Budget has advised that there is no objection to the presentation of this report to the Congress.

Sincerely yours,

CHARLES WEST,
Acting Secretary of the Interior.

[469] 52 Stat. 347, 25 U. S. C. 396a.

> dians under Federal jurisdiction, except those hereinafter specifically excepted from the provisions of this Act, may, with the approval of the Secretary of the Interior, be leased for mining purposes, by authority of the tribal council or other authorized spokesmen for such Indians, for terms not to exceed ten years and as long thereafter as minerals are produced in paying quantities.

Section 2 of the act (25 U. S. C. 396b) provides for public auction of oil and gas leases and safeguards the right of tribes organized and incorporated under sections 16 and 17 of the Act of June 18, 1934,[470] "to lease lands for mining purposes as therein provided and in accordance with the provisions of any constitution and charter adopted by any Indian tribe pursuant to the Act of June 18, 1934." Section 3 of the act (25 U. S. C. 396c) specifies the type of bond to be furnished by lessees. Section 4 of the act (25 U. S. C. 396d) authorizes the Secretary of the Interior to promulgate regulations for the enforcement of the act. Section 5 (25 U. S. C. 396e) authorizes the Secretary of the Interior to delegate to subordinate officials power to approve leases. Section 6 of the act (25 U. S. C. 396f) provides that the act shall not apply to the "Papago Indian Reservation in Arizona, the Crow Reservation in Montana, the ceded lands of the Shoshone Reservation in Wyoming, the Osage Reservation in Oklahoma, nor to the coal and asphalt lands of the Choctaw and Chickasaw Tribes in Oklahoma."[471]

The 1891, 1894, and 1938 acts cover mining leases on all reservations and also grazing[472] and farming leases on lands "bought and paid for" by Indians. There is no comprehensive legislation authorizing agricultural and grazing leases on lands which the Indians never "bought and paid for," *e. g.*, lands held by aboriginal occupancy recognized by treaty. There is no general statute authorizing timber leases, but timber sales, which serve the purpose of leases, are made pursuant to section 7 of the Act of June 25, 1910.[473] Neither is there any general legislation authorizing leases for purposes other than farming, grazing, and mining.[474] This does not mean, of course, that tribal lands have not been utilized by third parties, under permits or under invalid tribal leases, for many other purposes, such as trading posts, power sites, summer cottages, and ordinary commercial development. The character of such use will be further considered in connection with the problem of invalid leases and the problem of tribal licenses or permits. For the present it is enough to point to the large gaps in the existing law governing tribal leases, gaps which, it may be hoped, Congress will soon cover.

For those Indian tribes within the scope of the Act of June 18, 1934, these gaps are largely covered by section 17 of that act, which provides that the Secretary of the Interior may issue a charter of incorporation to any tribe applying therefor, which charter may convey comprehensive power to manage and dispose of tribal property subject to the proviso that tribal land within the limits of the reservation may not be leased for periods exceeding 10 years. Such charter provisions may or may not provide for departmental approval of tribal leases. Most charters provide for a trial period during which all tribal leases are subject to departmental approval, to be followed by free tribal leasing within the limits prescribed by the act and the particular charter.[475]

---

[470] 48 Stat. 984, 986.

[471] Special statutes govern the exempted reservations. See fns. 463, 464, 466, *supra*. On Osage and Choctaw-Chickasaw lands, see Chapter 23. The Papago Reservation in Arizona was created by Executive order on February 1, 1917. The order provided that the mineral lands within the reservation should be open for exploration, location, and patent under the general mining laws of the United States. The subsequent acts of Congress enlarging and extending the boundaries of the Papago Reservation have provided that the lands added thereto should be subject to the proviso of the Executive order concerning mineral entries. Act of February 21, 1931, 46 Stat. 1202; Act of July 28, 1937, 50 Stat. 536; see also Op. Sol. I. D., M.28183, October 16, 1935. Since mineral lands of the Papago Reservation are subject to disposition as part of the public domain, the tribe cannot lease them.

[472] For grazing regulations see 25 C. F. R. 71.1–72.13. For leasing of Indian lands for farming, grazing and business purposes, see 25 C. F. R. 171.1–171.36.

[473] "The mature living and dead and down timber on unallotted lands of any Indian reservation may be sold under regulations to be prescribed by the Secretary of the Interior, and the proceeds from such sales shall be used for the benefit of the Indians of the reservation in such manner as he may direct: *Provided*, That this section shall not apply to the States of Minnesota and Wisconsin." (25 U. S. C. 407, 36 Stat. 857.) *Cf.* Act of February 16, 1889, 25 Stat. 673, 25 U. S. C. 196, discussed in sec. 15, *supra*; and see Act of March 4, 1913, 37 Stat. 1015, 16 U. S. C. 615 (authorizing sale of burnt timber on "public domain" and specifying that the proceeds from the sale of burnt timber on lands appropriated to an Indian tribe shall be transferred to the fund of such tribe. On the power of the Secretary to modify timber contracts, see Chapter 5.

[474] But see 25 C. F. R. 171.1, 171.12.

[475] The Corporate Charter of the Minnesota Chippewa Tribe, issued by the Secretary of the Interior on September 17, 1937, and ratified by vote of the tribe (1,480 for and 610 against) on November 13, 1937, contains the following provisions on the leasing of tribal lands and the termination of departmental supervisory powers over such leases:

> 5. The Tribe, subject to any restrictions contained in the Constitution and laws of the United States, or in the Constitution and By-Laws of the said tribe, shall have the following corporate powers, in addition to all powers already conferred or guaranteed by the Tribal Constitution and By-Laws:
>
> * * * (b) To purchase, take by gift, bequest, or otherwise, own, hold, manage, operate, and dispose of property of every description, real and personal, subject to the following limitations:
>
> * * * (3) No leases, permits (which terms shall not include land assignments to members of the Tribe) or timber sale contracts covering any land or interests in land now or hereafter held by the Tribe within the boundaries of any reservation of the Minnesota Chippewa Tribe shall be made by the Tribe for a longer term than ten years, and all such leases and permits, except to members of the Tribe, and all such contracts must be approved by the Secretary of the Interior or by his duly authorized representative; * * *
>
> 6. Upon the request of the Tribal Executive Committee for the termination of any supervisory power reserved to the Secretary of the Interior under sections 5 (b) 3, 5 (c), 5 (d), 5 (f), 5 (g), 5 (h), and section 8 of this Charter, the Secretary of the Interior, if he shall approve such request, shall thereupon submit the question of such termination to the tribe for referendum. The termination shall be effective upon ratification by a majority vote at an election in which at least thirty per cent of the adult members of the Tribe residing on the reservations of the Minnesota Chippewa Tribe shall vote. If at any time after ten years from the effective date of this Charter, such request shall be made and the Secretary shall disapprove it or fail to approve or disapprove it within ninety days after its receipt, the question of the termination of any such power may then be submitted by the Secretary of the Interior or by the Tribal Executive Committee to popular referendum of the adult members of the Tribe actually living within the reservations of the Minnesota Chippewa Tribe and if the termination is approved by two-thirds of the eligible voters, shall be effective.

A similar provision, without the 10-year minimum for continued supervision, is found in the Corporate Charter of the Fort Belknap Indian Community, issued by the Secretary of the Interior on July 29, 1937, and ratified by the Indian community on August 25, 1937.

An alternative form of charter, under which supervision terminates automatically, after a specified period, has been issued to a number of Oklahoma tribes, under the Act of June 26, 1936 (49 Stat. 1967; U. S. Code, title 25, sec. 503). A typical charter, that of the Kickapoo Tribe, issued by the Secretary of the Interior on December 11, 1937, and ratified by vote of the tribe on January 18, 1938, contains the following provisions:

> 3. The Kickapoo Tribe of Oklahoma, subject to any restrictions contained in the Constitution and laws of the United States or in the Constitution and By-Laws of the Tribe, and subject to the limitations of Sections 4 and 5 of this Charter, shall have the following corporate powers as provided by Section 3 of the Oklahoma Indian Welfare Act of June 26, 1936.
>
> * * * * *
>
> (q) To purchase, take by gift, bequest or otherwise, own hold, manage, operate, and dispose of property of every description, real or personal.
>
> * * * * *
>
> 4. The foregoing corporate powers shall be subject to the following limitations:
>
> * * * * *
>
> (b) No tribal land or interest in land shall be leased for a longer period than ten years, except that oil, gas, or mineral leases may be made for longer periods when authorized by law.
>
> * * * * *

Tribal constitutions adopted pursuant to section 16 of the act must be distinguished from charters issued pursuant to section 17. The former determine, primarily, the manner in which the tribe shall exercise powers based upon existing law, and leasing provisions in tribal constitutions are therefore to be read in the light of existing law; tribal charters, on the other hand, involve new grants of power, and leasing provisions are therefore not limited by prior law.[476]

Where a tribe has the power to execute a corporate lease, there are administrative determinations to the effect that ministerial details in the execution of such power may be delegated by the corporate authorities to a federal employee but that general responsibility for the execution of such leases and for fixing the terms thereof cannot be transferred to such an employee.[477]

Under the foregoing statutes it will be seen that the character of tribal ownership is, generally speaking, irrelevant to the question of whether the tribe may lease tribal lands. An exception to this general rule must be made respecting the Act of February 28, 1891,[478] which is limited to lands "bought and paid for" by the Indians,[479] and note should be taken of the early view, now superseded,[480] that Pueblo leases are not subject to departmental control.[481]

Within the limits fixed by acts of Congress and regulations issued pursuant thereto, the tribe may specify the terms upon which it will lease land. Thus where improvements for Indian rehabilitation are placed upon tribal land under the Emergency Appropriation Act of April 8, 1935,[482] the tribe may rent such improved lands to needy members and provide that rentals shall be impressed with a trust for a particular purpose.[483]

Congressional power over the leasing of tribal lands includes the power of controlling the receipts therefrom. It has been held that the tribal interest in rentals is subject to the same measure of plenary congressional control as is the tribal interest in land itself, so that a statute conveying the tribal interest in minerals to allottees raises no serious question of constitutionality and no reasonable basis for a suit by the tribe against the mineral lessees.[484] Conversely, where minerals are reserved to a tribe for a given period, with provision that they shall belong to the allottee thereafter, an extension of this period of tribal interest is not unconstitutional and tribal leases thereafter executed have been sustained as valid.[485]

Whatever its power over outstanding tribal leases may be, Congress has in certain cases provided that such outstanding leases shall continue in force despite the allotment of the land leased.[486] The present practice appears to be to include in tribal leases a provision permitting their termination in the event of the allotment of the land leased.

The execution of tribal leases which are not authorized by any existing federal law raises a series of difficult problems as to the legal rights of lessors, lessees, and third parties. The statute which denies legal validity to a lease not made "by treaty or convention entered into pursuant to the constitution" does not prohibit the execution of such a lease, and although the statute imposes a penalty upon private persons who, without legal authority, attempt to negotiate such treaties or conventions or otherwise "treat with any such nation or tribe of Indians for the title or purchase of any lands by them held or claimed," it has been held that this language does not make it an offense to execute, accept or negotiate for an unauthorized lease. This issue was squarely raised in the case of *United States v. Hunter*,[487] which was an action to recover the statutory penalty of $1,000 for an alleged violation, by a lessee of the Cherokee Nation, of Revised Statutes, section 2116. The court offered the following interpretation of the prohibitory language of this section:

> Obviously, it contemplates the casting of a penalty upon one who assumes to act for the United States, and, usurping an authority which he does not possess, attempts to negotiate a national compact or treaty with an Indian nation. But there is another clause in the sentence which renders the question of more doubt; that denounces the penalty on every person who attempts to treat with any such nation or tribe of Indians for the title or purchase of any lands by them held or claimed. This seems to refer to an attempt, by private contract and personal arrangement, to obtain the lands of an Indian nation. But what kind of a private contract is denounced? The description is not as broad as in the first sentence, for there it speaks of purchase, grant, lease, or other conveyance of lands, or of any title or claim thereto, while here it is for "*the title or purchase* of any lands." Does this include a mere lease for grazing purposes? I think not. A leasehold interest may be considered, for some purposes, a title, and sometimes the word "title" is used in a general sense so as to include any title or interest, and thus a mere leasehold interest; but here it is *the title*, and this, in common acceptance, means the full and absolute title; for when we speak of a man as having title to certain lands, the ordinary understanding is that he is the owner of the fee and not that he is a mere lessee; and, this being a penal statute, no extended, no strained construction should be put upon the words used in order to include acts not within their plain and ordinary significance. That this is the true construction is sustained by the section immediately following, which reads:
>
> > "Every person who drives or otherwise conveys any stock, or horses, mules, or cattle, to range and feed on any lands belonging to any Indian tribe, without the consent of such tribe, is liable to a penalty of one dollar for each animal of such stock."
>
> This imposes a penalty on any one who, *without* the *consent* of an Indian tribe drives his stock to range and feed on the lands of such tribe. This implies that an

---

> 5. Until ten years from the date of ratification of this Charter, or such other date as may be fixed pursuant to Section 6, the following corporate acts or transactions shall be valid only after approval by the Secretary of the Interior or his duly authorized representative:
>
> * * * * *
>
> (d) Any lease, grazing permit, or other contract affecting tribal land, tribal minerals, or other tribal interests in land.
>
> * * * * *
>
> 6. At any time within ten years after the ratification of this Charter, any power of review established by Section 5 may be terminated by the Secretary of the Interior with the consent of the Kickapoo Council. At or before the expiration of this ten-year period, the Secretary may propose a further extension of this period. Such proposed extension shall be effective unless disapproved by a three-fourths vote of the Kickapoo Council.

[476] Memo. Sol. I. D., January 12, 1937, and Memo. Sol. I. D., December 11, 1937 (holding that a statutory requirement of Secretarial approval for tribal leases applies to tribe organized under sec. 16, but not to tribe incorporated under sec. 17).

[477] Memo. Sol. I. D., September 11, 1937; Memo. Sol. I. D., December 22, 1938.

[478] 26 Stat. 795.

[479] It has been held by Assistant Attorney General, later Justice, Van Devanter that in order to bring land within the statutory category of "lands bought and paid for by the Indians," cash payment was not necessary, and that an exchange of other lands for other valuable consideration sufficed. Uintah Lands, 25 L. D. 408 (1897). Accord: *Strawberry Valley Cattle Co. v. Chipman*, 45 Pac. 348 (1896).

[480] *United States v. Candelaria*, 271 U. S. 432 (1926). And see Chapter 20.

[481] 19 L. D. 326 (1894).

[482] 49 Stat. 115. See Presidential Letter No. 1323-1, dated January 11, 1936, allocating emergency funds for "the rehabilitation of Indians in stricken rural agricultural areas."

[483] Op. Sol. I. D., M.28316, March 18, 1936.

[484] Attorney's Contract to Represent The Seminole Nation, 35 Op. A. G. 421 (1928).

[485] *Adams v. Osage Tribe of Indians*, 59 F. 2d 653 (C. C. A. 10, 1932) aff'g 50 F. 2d 918 (D. C. N. D. Okla. 1931), cert. den. 287 U. S. 652. Some later statutes seek to eliminate doubts on this point by expressly reserving to Congress the right to extend the period of tribal mineral ownership. Act of March 3, 1921, 41 Stat. 1355 (Fort Belknap).

[486] Act of June 4, 1920, 41 Stat. 751 (Crow); Act of March 3, 1921, 41 Stat. 1355 (Fort Belknap).

[487] 21 Fed. 615 (C. C. E. D. Mo. 1884).

Indian tribe may consent to the use of their lands for grazing purposes, or, at least, that if it does consent no penalty attaches; and, if the tribe may so consent, it may express such consent in writing, and for at least any brief and reasonable time. It was said by counsel for the government that if a lease for five years can be sustained, so may one for 999 years, and thus the Indian tribe be actually dispossessed of its lands. But, as was stated in the opening of the opinion, the question here is not as to the validity of a lease, long or short, but as to whether this penal statute reaches to the mere inducing or negotiating of the lease. For the reasons I have thus given, it seems to me that it cannot be so interpreted; and whatever may be the fact as to the validity of such a lease, and entering into no discussion as to how far it is binding on the Indian nation, or whether it could be set aside at the option of the nation or by the action of the national government, I am of the opinion that the acts charged upon the defendant are not within the scope of this penal statute. (Pp. 617–618.)

Under this analysis it would appear that the execution by tribal authorities of a lease covering tribal land may lead to the same consequences as the execution of a lease by an infant, a lunatic or a person under guardianship. The lease cannot be enforced, but the execution of the lease is not an offense, and valid rights may accrue under the lease.

Thus, it was held, in *Lemmon* v. *United States*,[488] that the United States could not recover rentals under an approved lease if rent had already been paid under an invalid lease. The court declared, *per* Circuit Judge (later Justice) Sanborn:

> * * * it is conceded on all hands that Robert H. Ashley, the United States Indian agent, had authority to collect the rents for these premises, and if, by his direction, the lessees under the invalid leases paid the rent to a representative of the Winnebago tribe of Indians, who accepted and distributed it, with Ashley's knowledge and consent, among those Indians, the government would undoubtedly be estopped from again collecting rent for the same premises of one who never had occupied them, and to whom it never delivered possession under its lease. The Winnebago tribe of Indians and its members were the cestuis que trustent of the government. They were the parties entitled to these rents. If by the direction of the trustee the rents were collected by a representative of the cestuis que trustent, and distributed with the consent of the trustee among the cestuis que trustent, it is difficult to perceive how the trustee can again collect the rents. All this rejected evidence was competent, pregnant, and persuasive upon the issue whether the Flournoy Company and Nick Fritz, who occupied during the term of the Lemmon lease, held under her or under their old leases from the Winnebago tribe of Indians, and it should have been received. (P. 653.)

A lease, although invalid, may be sufficient to bar a trespass action against the lessee under Revised Statutes, section 2117, above discussed.[489] Likewise a lessee under a void lease may justify his possession to the point of enjoining a trespasser.[490] Likewise, it has been held by a state court that the lessee under an invalid tribal lease may execute a binding agreement, amounting to a sublease, with a third party and may recover on a note given by such third party as consideration, in accordance with the principle that a lessee may not question the title of his lessor.[491] It has also been held in at least one state case[492] that the holder of an invalid tribal lease may recover upon a contract for the pasturage of cattle upon the land so leased. On the other hand, there are some state cases holding that an Indian tribe cannot recover rental under a void lease (although it is intimated that a *quantum meruit* recovery may be had),[493] and that a lessee under such a lease who is not in actual possession of the land leased, cannot secure possession of crops grown thereon.[494]

The foregoing decisions leave many gaps in a definition of the rights of lessors, lessees, and third parties under an invalid lease. These questions, however, are not peculiar to Indian law, and courts will probably answer them, as they arise, by reference to analogies in the general field of landlord and tenant relations. Such analogies, however, must be used cautiously, in view of the fundamental principle that, in matters affecting tribal affairs, where Congress is silent the law of the tribe rather than the law of the state must prevail.[495] In accordance with this principle, it has been held that the effect of a lease of tribal land must be determined in accordance with the statutes and judicial decisions of the tribe. Thus, in *Oolagah Coal Co.* v. *McCaleb*,[496] where the plaintiff company, operating under an instrument which, though called a "mineral license," apparently amounted to a "lease," sought an injunction against a trespasser, the court declared, *per* Thayer, *J.*:

> The bill averred * * * that the Cherokee Nation had theretofore lawfully issued five mineral licenses, pursuant to the laws of the Nation, to certain licensees therein named, which licenses conferred on said licensees the exclusive right to mine and sell coal on the various tracts of land described in said licenses. * * * that all of the licenses aforesaid were assigned by, and that the assignment thereof were obtained from, the licensees, by the plaintiff company, in accordance with the laws of the Nation. * * * From any point of view, we think that the bill stated a case entitling the plaintiff to some measure of equitable relief. It showed * * * that the plaintiff company had an exclusive right to mine coal on the lands in question * * *. (Pp. 87–89.)

Furthermore, it has been held that the judgment of a tribal court on the validity of a lease involving a member of the tribe, the tribe itself, and a nonmember is *res judicata* and will not be reexamined in a court of the United States.[497]

In the case of *Barbee* v. *Shannon*[498] the court declared:

> Much of the testimony in the record goes to show that the lease from the Creek Nation under which appellants claim is illegal because not made in compliance with the Creek laws upon the subject, and because the grant was in excess of the authority of the principal chief. The judgment of the Creek court precludes our consideration of these questions. We cannot review errors of law or practice in such courts, when their judgments are presented to us, unless such errors are jurisdictional. (P. 210.)

Moreover, it has been held that agents of the United States are without authority to remove as trespassers persons holding under an allegedly invalid lease. Thus, in the case of *Quigley* v. *Stephens*,[499] an Indian agent sought to determine a controversy

[488] 106 Fed. 650 (C. C. A. 8, 1901).

[489] 18 Op. A. G. 235 (1885).

[490] *Oolagah Coal Co.* v. *McCaleb*, 68 Fed. 86 (C. C. A. 8, 1895). While the opinion in this case refers to a "mineral license" rather than a "lease," it refers to the "estate" created by the transaction, which indicates that the instrument was a lease rather than a license.

[491] *Cherokee Strip Livestock Assn.* v. *Cass L. & C. Co.*, 138 Mo. 394, 40 S. W. 107 (1897).

[492] *Kansas & N. M. Land & Cattle Co.* v. *Thompson*, 57 Kans. 792, 797, 48 Pac. 34 (1897):

> Conceding that Thompson had at no time a right, as against the Indians or the government of the United States, to continue in the occupancy of the land, if he was there with the consent of the Indians, and in fact rendered the service to the defendant of caring for and feeding its cattle, he was entitled to compensation therefor.

[493] *Mayes* v. *Cherokee Strip Livestock Association*, 58 Kans. 712, 51 Pac. 215 (1897); and *cf. Light* v. *Conover*, 10 Okla. 732, 63 Pac. 966 (1901) (holding that an individual Indian attempting to lease tribal land cannot recover agreed rentals under the invalid lease); *Langford* v. *Monteith*, 1 Idaho 612 (1876), aff'd. 102 U. S. 145 (1880) (holding that white man attempting to lease tribal land cannot recover rentals); *Uhlig* v. *Garrison*, 2 Dak. 71, 2 N. W. 253 (1878) (holding that white man attempting to lease tribal land cannot recover in ejectment).

[494] *Ooey* v. *Low*, 36 Wash. 10, 77 Pac. 1077 (1904).

[495] See Chapter 7.

[496] 68 Fed. 86 (C. C. A. 8, 1895).

[497] *Barbee* v. *Shannon*, 1 Ind. T. 199, 40 S. W. 584 (1897).

[498] *Ibid.*

[499] 3 Ind. T. 265 (1900), aff'd. 126 Fed. 148 (C. C. A. 8, 1903).

as to the validity of a lease of tribal land executed by the owner of improvements thereon, and, reaching the conclusion that the lease was invalid, ordered the removal of the lessee. In a suit in ejectment which the alleged lessee then brought in the United States Court for the Northern District of the Indian Territory, it was held that the action of the agent was without legal authority or justification. The court declared:

> But whether the deed was void or valid, the rights of the parties to it, its construction, the disposition of the properties acquired under it, and the law and the equities of the case, cannot be passed upon or enforced by an Indian agent. The courts alone possess these powers. The Indian agent complains in his decree "that, if this rule were to prevail, noncitizens could take possession of the country, and practically control the tribes by connivance with their citizens." Whether this be issue or not, the fact is—and it is one of common knowledge—that nine-tenths of the farms of the Indian Territory have been opened up and made valuable by contracts substantially like this, and the Indian owners have been the direct beneficiaries. The courts here, without passing upon the validity of such contracts, have universally held that, until the improvements provided for in the contract were paid for, the Indian lessor was estopped to set up the invalidity of the lease; and recently, in harmony with these decisions, by act of Congress (the Curtis bill—Ind. T. Ann. St. 1899, §§ 57q–57z91) it is provided that the lessee shall not be ejected until he shall have been paid for his improvements. We hold that the Indian agent had no jurisdiction to try this case, and, therefore, when, at the instance of the appellee, he, using his police for that purpose, forcibly ejected the appellant from the premises, and put the appellee in possession, all the parties to the transaction—the appellees as well as the Indian police, who is made a party to this suit—were guilty of an act of forcible entry, and that, therefore, the court below erred in instructing the jury to find their verdict for the appellees. The judgment of the court below is reversed, and the cause remanded. (P. 274.)

Whether the foregoing decisions represent sound law may be open to discussion. They raise fundamentally a question that goes beyond the scope of Indian law and revolves about the principle that a lessee may not question the title of his lessor.[500] We may, however, in the following section on "Tribal Licenses," obtain some further light on the situation created by legally unauthorized tribal leases.

Whatever else these cases may show, they do indicate that a lease made by a tribe to a member of the tribe, being justiciable only in the courts of the tribe, may be valid under those laws although null and void under federal or state law. Such a view seems to have been implicitly accepted with respect to leases to tribal members in a number of decisions[501] and in a rather extensive administrative practice.

[500] See 1 Tiffany, Landlord and Tenant (1910), §§ 21, 182.

[501] *United States* v. *Rogers*, 23 Fed. 658 (D. C. W. D. Ark. 1885); *United States* v. *Foster*, 25 Fed. Cas. No. 15141 (C. C. E. D. Wis. 1870); and see case cited *supra*, fn. 497.

SECTION 20. TRIBAL LICENSES

That an Indian tribe may grant permission to third parties to enter upon tribal land, and may impose such conditions as it deems desirable upon such permission, is a proposition that has been repeatedly affirmed by the Attorney General. Perhaps the most persuasive of the opinions on this issue is that rendered by Acting Attorney General Phillips in 1884.[502] Three years earlier, the validity of the permit laws of the Choctaws and Chickasaws had been upheld in a formal opinion of the Attorney General, and the Interior Department had been advised that its activities in removing intruders should follow the definition of "intruders" provided by tribal law.[503] In 1884, a reconsideration of the question was asked "in consequence of earnest protest against that opinion from among the people of the two nations concerned—the more because such protest is in accordance with the judgments of some members of Congress and other prominent gentlemen from the States adjoining." The Attorney General declared:

> In the absence of a treaty or statute, it seems that the power of the nation thus to regulate its own rights of *occupancy*, and to say who shall participate therein and upon what conditions, cannot be doubted. The clear result of all the cases, as restated in 95 United States Reports, at page 526, is, "the right of the Indians to their occupancy is as sacred as that of the United States to the fee."
>
> I add, that so far as the United States recognize political organizations amongst Indians the right of occupancy is a right *in the tribe or nation*. It is of course competent for the United States to disregard such organizations and treat Indians individually, but their policy has generally been otherwise.* In such cases presumptively they remit all question of individual right to the definition of the nation, as being purely *domestic* in character. The practical importance here of this proposition is that in the absence of express contradictory provisions by treaty, or by statutes of the United States, the nation (and not a citizen) is to declare who shall come within the boundaries of its occupancy, and under what regulations and conditions. (P. 36.)

Finding no statute or treaty provision compelling variance from this rule, the Attorney General upheld the validity of the tribal laws in question. In answer to a second question put by the Interior Department "whether, supposing these laws to be valid, the United States, through the proper Department, have power to revise them so as to secure reasonableness in the amount of the fees which they require from persons who apply for permits," the Attorney General held:

> In conclusion I have to say, that my attention has not been called to any statute by which Congress has delegated to a Department or officer of the United States its power to control such taxation. I therefore conclude that no Department or officer has such power. (P. 39.)

While a tribe may thus issue and condition a permit covering entry upon tribal land, it cannot (any more than could a state) grant an exclusive permit which would interfere with interstate commerce and thus trespass upon a field constitutionally reserved to Congress. Thus in the case of *Muskogee National Telegraph Company* v. *Hall*,[504] the court held that a purported exclusive tribal license to a telephone company could not bar Congress from issuing a similar license to another company. The validity of the tribal license was not questioned, but the claim to exclusiveness "was invalid from the time the grant was made, being an attempt on the part of the nation to exercise a power vitally affecting interstate commerce, which did not belong to it." (P. 385, *per* Thayer, *J.*)

Under the foregoing analysis the power of a tribe "to declare who shall come within the boundaries of its occupancy and under what regulations and conditions" exists in the absence of treaty or statute as an inherent power of the tribe. We have already noted that such power is not limited by statutes restricting the power to lease.[505] The power to issue permits, while neither

[502] Choctaw and Chickasaw Permit Laws, 18 Op. A. G. 34 (1884).

[503] Intruders on Lands of the Chocktaws and Chickasaws; 17 Op. A. G. 234 (1881).

[504] 118 Fed. 382 (C. C. A. 8, 1902), rev'g 4 Ind. T. 18 (1901).

[505] See sec. 19, *supra*.

created nor limited by statute, has been occasionally recognized and confirmed by statute.[506]

There are administrative decisions upholding the validity of tribal permits approved by a superintendent, instead of by the Secretary of the Interior, who is required to approve tribal leases,[507] and upholding the validity of a tribal permit issued to a state conservation department for the establishment of a ranger station.[508] Tribal charters of incorporation issued by the Secretary of the Interior pursuant to section 17 of the Act of June 18, 1934,[509] sometimes distinguish between leases and permits, requiring departmental approval of leases but not requiring such approval of permits.[510]

For purposes of administering the payment of soil conservation benefits, the Department of Agriculture has ruled that in the case of grazing leases the lessee may receive conservation benefit payments but that in the case of permits neither the tribe nor the permittee may receive such benefits.[511]

The distinction between a lease and a permit or license received administrative consideration in connection with the validity of assignments made by a Pueblo to members of the Pueblo. The basic legal issues raised thereby must apply equally to transactions between the tribe and third parties:[512]

> This distinction has been considered by the courts in a great variety of cases, which seek to distinguish an interest in land from a mere license. A recent decision in the Circuit Court of Appeals for the Eighth Circuit holds:
>
> > "A mere permission to use land, dominion over it remaining in the owner and no interest or exclusive possession of it being given, is but a license. (Citing authorities)" *Tips* v. *United States*, 70 F. (2d) 525, 526.)
>
> The essential characteristic of a license to use real property, as distinguished from an interest in real property, is that in the former case the licensee has no vested right as against the licensor or third parties. He has only a privilege, which the licensor may terminate.
>
> As Justice Holmes pointed out, in *Marrone* v. *Washington Jockey Club*, 227 U. S. 633, "A contract binds the person of the maker but does not create an interest in the property that it may concern, unless it also operates as a conveyance. * * * But if it did not create such an interest, that is to say, a right *in rem* valid against the landowner and third persons, the holder had no right to enforce specific performance by self-help. His only right was to sue upon the contract for the breach." (At page 636.)
>
> Put in its simplest terms, the rule is that a landowner does not transfer an *interest* in his land by allowing another to *use* the land. Thus, for instance, a member of the landowner's family, inasmuch as he is "a bare licensee of the owner, who has no legal interest in the land," cannot derive from his legal privilege to *use* the land a right against the landowner or against third parties. *Elliott* v. *Town of Mason*, 81 Atl. 701 (N. H. 1911). See also *Keystone Lumber Co.* v. *Kolman*, 69 N. W. 165 (Wis. 1896). (Pp. 17–18.)

While it is easy to formulate a theoretical distinction between a lease and a license, there is actually a large "twilight zone" in which reasonable differences of interpretation may arise. Within this zone the courts have professed to look into the intention of the parties to determine whether the transaction was intended to create a right against the landowner and against third parties, in which case it must be considered a lease, or was intended merely to confer a privilege, in which case a mere license relationship is established:

> Even the language of leasing will not suffice to create a lease relationship if the transaction leaves complete power over the land in the hands of the landowner. Thus, in the case of *Tips* v. *United States*, 70 F. (2d) 525, the court found that an instrument which used the term "landlord," "tenant," "lease," etc., was nevertheless a mere license, because the so-called lessor, the War Department, had no power to lease the property or to grant more than a revocable permit to use the property. (P. 19.)[513]

Where the parties intend to create a bare license to use and enjoy tribal property, there is no statute under which the licensee may be barred from the use of such property nor can administrative authorities prevent the tribe concerned from peaceably tolerating such use. Whether, however, such permittee would be entitled to any protection against the tribe in the event of a breach of the conditions of the permit by the tribe is a question on which, unfortunately, no decisions are available.[514]

The terms and conditions of tribal permits have generally been agreed upon by the parties immediately concerned and the practical absence of litigation in this field leaves us without an authoritative basis for answering many questions which might be put. It has been administratively determined that a tribe may grant to an Indian service official a power of attorney to execute grazing permits covering tribal land, but that the Interior Department has no right to coerce the grant of such powers of attorney.[515]

The terms and conditions of tribal permits are prescribed in various of the constitutions and charters issued pursuant to sections 16 and 17 of the Act of June 18, 1934.[516] It has been administratively determined that a grant of a nonexclusive right-of-way across tribal land is not such a transfer of restricted Indian land as is absolutely prohibited by section 4 of the act cited, but that such a grant is a conveyance of an *interest* in land and therefore, even though the Secretary of the Interior is authorized by statute to grant rights-of-way across tribal land for specified purposes, such a grant by the Secretary is invalid, in the case of a tribe organized under section 16 of the act, unless the tribe consents thereto.[517]

---

[506] See, for instance, Act of January 5, 1927, 44 Stat. 932, safeguarding as an exclusive right of the Seneca Indians on their reservations in New York the right "to issue permits and licenses, for the taking of game and fish."

[507] Memo. Sol. I. D., December 11, 1937.

[508] Memo. Sol. I. D., December 22, 1938.

[509] 48 Stat. 984, 986.

[510] Memo. Sol. I. D., November 11, 1937. Charter of Lac du Flambeau Tribe, sec. 5(b) and 5(b3), and *cf.* Memo. Sol. I. D., May 25, 1937 (preference to tribal members in issuance of grazing permits).

[511] The permit (Form 5–512) prescribed by the Secretary of the Interior by which grazing privileges upon tribal lands may be granted expressly states that "this instrument is not a lease and is not to be taken or construed as granting any leasehold interest in or to the land described herein, but that it is a mere permit, terminable and revocable in the discretion of the approving officer." The permittee, therefore, in our opinion, has no such legal estate or interest in the land so as to give him control thereof. Furthermore, the operator having only a personal privilege to graze livestock on the land is neither an owner, cash tenant, share tenant, nor a person who acts in similar capacity; he is not within the definition of "ranch operator."

Whether the fee is or is not held by the United States Government in trust for the Indians, the land after it has been leased is outside the control of the Government or the Department of the Interior, except to prevent waste or other injury to the freehold, including the right to limit the numbers of livestock grazed on such lands by the lessee to the grazing capacity thereof, the lease conveying an estate or interest in the land for the period of the lease. The lessee, renting for cash, is a ranch operator by definition, and he has such estate or interest in the land upon which he operates as to give him control thereof. Memo. Sol. Dept. Agriculture, February 17, 1937.

[512] Op. Sol. I. D., M.29566, August 9, 1939.

[513] *Ibid.*

[514] The nearest case in point seems to be *Sharrock* v. *Kreiger*, 6 Ind. T. 466 (1906), but this situation was governed by sec. 3 of the Curtis Act of June 28, 1898, 30 Stat. 495, applicable only to the Five Tribes, which granted permittees the privilege of remaining on tribal land rent-free long enough to cover the value of their improvements.

[515] Memo. Sol. I. D., November 11, 1935.

[516] 48 Stat. 984, 986–987, 25 U. S. C. 476, 477.

[517] Memo. Sol. I. D., September 2, 1936.

SECTION 21. STATUS OF SURPLUS AND CEDED LANDS

In the preceding three sections dealing with the execution of conveyances, leases, and licenses covering Indian tribal lands, we have been primarily concerned with the validity of such instruments and with the power of the tribal owner to dispose of private property. When we turn to the subject of Indian land cessions to the United States, the question of validity is no longer a troublesome one, for, as we have noted, most of the historical peculiarities of Indian land law were designed to encourage the cession of tribal lands to the United States, and the courts have been reluctant to put obstacles in the way of this process.[518] Even where prior treaties guaranteed that no land cessions would ever be made or that such cessions would be made only with the consent of three-fourths of the Indians concerned, the Supreme Court has held that a subsequent statute providing for the cession of Indian land by a majority is entirely constitutional.[519] The problem in this field is, therefore, primarily one of the construction of treaties, agreements, and statutes, rather than their validity.

In dealing with the status of ceded lands, the basic question that constantly recurs is whether a cession of lands by an Indian tribe has finally and completely ended the interest of the tribe therein, or whether the tribe retains some equitable interest in the land conveyed.[520] Prior to 1880, most of the treaties, agreements, and statutes by which Indian tribes ceded land to the United States provided for an outright and final conveyance, in return for which the Indians received cash payments, annuities, substitute lands, or other things of value.[521]

For about four decades after the adoption of the General Allotment Act an alternative pattern prevails. "Surplus" reservation lands, not needed for allotment, are turned over to the Government for the purpose of sale. The Indians are credited with the proceeds only as the land is sold, and the United States is not itself bound to purchase any part of the lands so opened for disposal. Undisposed of lands of this class remain tribal property until disposed of as provided by law.[522]

In between these two recognized patterns of "cession and removal" and "relinquishment in trust," various hybrid forms appear.[523]

The "cession and removal" formula is found in the Treaty of March 16, 1854,[524] with the Omaha Indians, construed in *United States* v. *Omaha Tribe of Indians*.[525] In this treaty the language of present conveyance is used and the Indians undertake to remove from the land ceded within 1 year from the ratification of the treaty. The fact that payment was to be made over a long period of years, in the opinion of the Supreme Court, did not delay the passage of title to the United States.[526]

A clear case of the "relinquishment in trust" agreement appears in the Act of April 27, 1904,[527] ratifying an agreement with the Crow Indians. This agreement provided that the Indians "ceded, granted, and relinquished" to the United States all of their "right, title, and interest" in the lands described. The United States agreed to sell the land on prescribed terms and to pay the proceeds to the Indians, making semiannual reports as to the status and disposition of the sums realized. The agreement specifically declared "the intention of this Act that the United States shall act as trustee for said Indians to dispose of said lands and to expend and pay over the proceeds received from the sale thereof only as received, as herein provided." [528] Construing these provisions in the case of *Ash Sheep Co.* v. *United States*,[529] the Supreme Court declared:

> It is obvious that the relation thus established by the act between the Government and the tribe of Indians was essentially that of trustee and beneficiary and that the agreement contained many features appropriate to a trust agreement to sell lands and devote the proceeds to the interests of the *cestui que trust*. *Minnesota* v. *Hitchcock*, 185 U. S. 373, 394, 398.
>
> * * * * *
>
> Taking all of the provisions of the agreement together we cannot doubt that while the Indians by the agreement released their possessory right to the Government, the owner of the fee, so that, as their trustee, it could make perfect title to purchasers, nevertheless, until sales should be made any benefits which might be derived from the use of the lands would belong to the beneficiaries and not to the trustee, and that they did not become "Public lands" in the sense of being subject to sale, or other disposition, under the general land laws. *Union Pacific R. R. Co.* v. *Harris*, 215 U. S. 386, 388. They were subject to sale by the Government, to be sure, but in the manner and for the purposes provided for in the special agreement with the Indians, which was embodied in the Act of April 27, 1904, 33 Stat. 352, and as to this point the case is ruled by the *Hitchcock* and *Chippewa Cases, supra*. Thus, we conclude, that the lands described in the bill were "Indian lands" when the company pastured its sheep upon them, in violation of § 2117 of Revised Statutes, and the decree in No. 212 must be affirmed. (Pp. 165,166.)

Similar circumstances were present in the Act of January 14, 1889,[530] authorizing an agreement for the cession and sale of Chippewa lands. In construing this agreement the Supreme Court suggested:[531]

> * * * that the United States has no substantial interest in the lands; that it holds the legal title under a contract with the Indians and in trust for their benefit. (P. 387.)

[518] These claims have been maintained and established as far west as the river Mississippi, by the sword. The title to a vast portion of the lands we now hold, originates in them. It is not for the courts of this country to question the validity of this title, or to sustain one which is incompatible with it. *Johnson* v. *McIntosh*, 8 Wheat. 543, 588–589 (1823).

[519] *Lone Wolf* v. *Hitchcock*, 187 U. S. 553 (1903); *Cherokee Nation* v. *Hitchcock*, 187 U. S. 294 (1902).

[520] Whether or not the Government became trustee for the Indians or acquired an unrestricted title by the cession of their lands, depends in each case upon the terms of the agreement or treaty by which the cession was made. *Minnesota* v. *Hitchcock*, 185 U. S. 373, 394, 398 (1902); *United States* v. *Mille Lac Band of Chippewa Indians*, 229 U. S. 498, 509 (1913). *Ash Sheep Co.* v. *United States*, 252 U. S. 159, 164 (1920), aff'g 250 Fed. 591 (C. C. A. 9, 1918), and 254 Fed. 59 (C. A. A. 9, 1918). *Cf. United States* v. *Choctaw Nation*, 179 U. S. 494 (1900); Op. Sol. I. D., M. 29798, June 15, 1938 (Ute) (56 I. D. 330). Op. Sol. I. D., M.28198, January 8, 1936 (Yuma).

[521] See, for example, *Beaulieu* v. *Garfield*, 32 App. D. C. 398 (1909). See also fn. 64 of this chapter.

[522] *Ash Sheep Co.* v. *United States*, 252 U. S. 159 (1920), aff'g 250 Fed. 591 (C. C. A. 9, 1918); and 254 Fed. 59 (C. C. A. 9, 1918).

[523] See secs. 5–6, *supra*.

[524] 10 Stat. 1043.

[525] 253 U. S. 275 (1920).

[526] Accord: Op. Sol. I. D., M.28198, January 8, 1936. In this case the effect of Art. I of an agreement with the Yuma Indians, ratified by the Act of August 15, 1894, 28 Stat. 286, 332, was in issue. The Solicitor of the Interior Department ruled that although nonirrigable lands had been continuously administered as a part of the Indian reservation and leased for grazing and mining purposes for the benefit of the Yuma Indians, this administrative recognition of Indian ownership could not prevail in the face of clear language in the agreement indicating "in clear and precise terms a present relinquishment or cession of all of the interest of the Indians in the reservation lands." The unreported cases of *United States* v. *Sid Johnson and Mrs. Sid Johnson*, and *United States* v. *M. C. Walker and Mrs. M. C. Walker*, decided August 2, 1935, in the District Court of the United States for the Southern District of California, are cited in support of this ruling.

[527] 33 Stat. 352.

[528] 33 Stat. 352, 361.

[529] 252 U. S. 159 (1920), aff'g 250 Fed. 591 (C. C. A. 9, 1918), and 254 Fed. 59 (C. C. A. 9, 1918).

[530] 25 Stat. 642.

[531] *Minnesota* v. *Hitchcock*, 185 U. S. 373 (1902).

This was not a case, the Court pointed out, where "the interest of the tribe in the land from which it has been removed ceases and the full obligation of the Government to the Indians is satisfied when the pecuniary or real estate consideration for the cession is secured to them." (P. 401.) Under the circumstances the Indians had a right to expect that the entire tract would be used as declared in the act or agreement.[532]

Various other cases give effect to the equitable interest thus found to exist in the Indian tribe with respect to the land ceded.[533]

Several difficult border-line cases were presented when Congress, by section 3 of the Act of June 18, 1934,[534] authorized the Secretary of the Interior "to restore to tribal ownership the remaining surplus lands of any Indian reservation heretofore opened, or authorized to be opened, to sale, or any other form of disposal by Presidential proclamation, or by any of the public-land laws of the United States." The question arose whether this language was broad enough to cover land ceded by the Colorado Ute Indians under the Act of June 15, 1880.[535] The Solicitor of the Interior Department, holding that such lands came within the permissive scope of the statute,[536] declared:

> The 1880 cession agreement with the Colorado Ute Indians is one of the early examples of conditional surplus land cessions; in fact the provisions of the 1880 act set forth a plan of allotment and disposal of surplus lands which became stereotyped in later allotment acts. A commission was appointed to make a census of the Indians, to select lands to be allotted, to survey sufficient of these lands for allotment, and to cause allotments to be made. The provisions of section 3 of this act, quoted above, are significant, in that they provide for the disposal only of those lands within the reservation "not so allotted." The legislative history of this 1880 act makes clear that the chief purpose of the act was the immediate allotment within the Colorado Ute Reservation of the individual Indians of various Ute bands and the opening to disposal of the remaining surplus lands. The opening up of the surplus lands was described as essential in view of the thousands of settlers and prospectors on the borders of the reservation who could not successfully be kept from entering the reservation by military or other means. The plan of allotment of the Indians was favored and bitterly opposed as the entering wedge in the allotment of the tribes generally throughout the United States. In fact, a general allotment act was pending in that session of Congress. (See House debates on the 1880 agreement, Congressional Record, 46th Congress, 2d session, June 7, 1880, pages 4251–4263.)
>
> From the foregoing it definitely appears that the fact that this cession occurred several years before other allotment-cessions does not mean that this cession falls within the earlier type of outright cession and removal. This cession was rather a forerunner and a model of later allotment acts and differs in no important respect from these acts. The fact that two of the three main groups of Indians were subsequently not allotted within the borders of the Colorado Ute Reservation does not alter my conclusion. The 1880 act did not provide for establishing new reservations but for supplying the Indians with allotments, and where allotments occurred outside the reservation, the Indians were to be charged a price of $1.25 an acre to be paid from the proceeds of the land sold from the Colorado Ute Reservation. The allotments off the reservation were therefore in the nature of lieu allotments and, in the case of the Uncompahgre Utes, were made only because of the fact that insufficient agricultural lands were found within the Colorado Ute Reservation. (See Report of the Commissioner of Indian Affairs, 1881, at 19, 325, *et seq.*)

The fact that the Act of 1880 and the subsequent Act of 1882 provided that the lands ceded "shall be held and deemed to be public lands of the United States" was held not to affect the conclusion that the lands in question were lands in which the Indian tribe retained an interest:

> Surplus lands ceded to be disposed of for the Indians are in fact qualified public lands and also qualified Indian lands. They are public lands in that the United States has the legal title and has secured from the Indians a release of their right of occupancy and has arranged to dispose of them, but they are not public lands in the full sense of the term as they are to be disposed of only in limited ways and upon certain conditions. *Minnesota* v. *Hitchcock, supra.* It should be noted that both the 1880 and the 1882 acts concerning the Ute land qualified the reference to the land as public land and subject to disposal under the public land laws by stated conditions and restrictions. (Pp. 338–339.)

Where ceded lands are held by the United States to be disposed of for the benefit of an Indian tribe, all proceeds from the land belong, in equity, to the Indian tribe.[537] No part of such proceeds accrue to the state in which the lands are located, although such state is entitled to proceeds from the sale of ordinary "public lands".[538] Where such lands are subjected by statute to a flowage easement, Congress has provided for payment of damages to the tribe.[539]

Where surplus lands are disposed of as a result of fraud, the Secretary of the Interior, under proper statutory authorization, may sue on behalf of the tribe to recover the lands lost or the value thereof.[540]

The equitable right to the value of lands erroneously disposed of is vested in the Indian tribe.[541]

Where unsold ceded lands are held to be, in equity, the property of the tribe, it has been administratively determined that such lands are within the scope of the leasing provisions of approved tribal constitutions.[542]

The equity in ceded lands is vested in the tribe entitled to the proceeds therefrom, rather than the tribe or band making the original cession, and ceded lands restored to tribal ownership pursuant to section 3 of the Act of June 18, 1934[543] become the property of the tribe entitled to the proceeds therefrom.[544]

The manner in which ceded lands are to be disposed of is for Congress to determine, so long as the promised benefits accrue to

---

[532] *Ibid.*, pp. 401, 402.

[533] *United States* v. *Brindle*, 110 U. S. 688 (1884) (holding ceded lands remain property of Indians, in equity, until sold and are therefore not "public lands" within the official duties of an agent designated to sell "public lands"); *United States* v. *Blackfeather*, 155 U. S. 180 (1894); *United States v. Creek Nation*, 295 U. S. 103 (1935), rev'g. 77 C. Cls. 159 (1933); rehearing den. 295 U. S. 769 (1935); *cf. United States* v. *Mille Lac Band of Chippewas*, 229 U. S. 498 (1913) (certain lands ceded for present consideration, others for future disposition under trust).

[534] 48 Stat. 984. On the scope of sec. 3 of this act, see Memo. Sol. I. D., August 27, 1938 (Southern Ute; interpreting Act of June 15, 1880, 21 Stat. 199; Act of February 20, 1895, 28 Stat. 677), and see 54 I. D. 599 (1934).

[535] 21 Stat. 199.

[536] Op. Sol. I. D., M.29798, June 15, 1938 (56 I. D. 330). The restoration made pursuant to this opinion was superseded by the Act of June 28, 1938, 52 Stat. 1209.

[537] Op. Sol. I. D., M26075, August 5, 1930 (53 I. D. 154) (Flathead); Peter Fredericksen, 48 L. D. 440 (1922). *Cf.* Minnesota National Forest, 31 Op. A. G. 95 (1917) (ceded lands classified as National Forest under jurisdiction of Secretary of Agriculture); *Chippewa Indians of Minnesota* v. *United States*, 305 U. S. 479 (1939).

[538] Sales of Indian Lands in Kansas, 19 Op. A. G. 117 (1888).

[539] Act of April 13, 1938, 52 Stat. 215.

[540] *United States* v. *Rea-Read Mill & Elevator Co.*, 171 Fed. 501 (C. C. E. D. Okla., 1909).

[541] *United States* v. *Creek Nation*, 295 U. S. 103 (1935), rev'g. 77 C. Cls. 159 (1933); rehearing den. 295 U. S. 769 (1935).

[542] Memo. Acting Sol. I. D., May 25, 1937.

[543] 48 Op. Stat. 984, 25 U. S. C. 463.

[544] Op. Sol. I. D., M29616, February 19, 1938; Memo. Sol. Off. I. D., January 22, 1936. To the effect that proceeds of ceded lands are due to the tribe making the last cession, in the absence of clear contrary provisions in the governing statute, treaty, or agreement, see *United States* v. *Choctaw Nation*, 179 U. S. 494 (1900).

the tribe.[545] Whether ceded lands are subject to preemption laws applicable to the public domain generally[546] or exempt from such laws[547] depends upon the terms of the cession as well as the applicable public land laws.

Where Indians "cede and convey" certain lands to the United States "in compliance with the desire of the United States to locate other Indians and freedmen thereon"[548] it has been held that such lands become the property of the United States but are not subject to preemption rights as a part of the public domain and are "Indian country" within the meaning of criminal trespass laws.[549]

Where the Indians making the cession are given a certain period within which they may select a portion of the ceded land for their own use, it has been said that "until this privilege was exhausted, the land, in any proper sense, belonged to them," and accordingly it has been held that during such period the lands are not subject to "preemption" as public domain lands.[550]

It has been administratively determined that ceded lands in which an Indian tribe retains an equity may be temporarily withdrawn from entry as "public lands" under the Act of June 25, 1910.[551]

Cession agreements in acts of Congress are generally construed as contracts,[552] and where provision is made for subsequent tribal consent, the agreement becomes effective as of the time when such consent is given, although formal proclamation of such consent may be delayed.[553]

[545] Statutes governing appraisement of ceded lands for purposes of sale are construed in: Reappraisal of Land within Indian Reservation, 36 Op. A. G. 506 (1931); Stone Denham, 46 L. D. 375 (1918); Op. Sol. I. D., M.28028, May 24, 1935. Example of statute extending public land laws to ceded Indian lands is Act of March 19, 1906, 34 Stat. 78.

[546] *Stroud* v. *Missouri Ft. S. & G. R. Co.*, 23 Fed. Cas. No. 13547 (C. C. Kan., 1877); *Armsworthy* v. *Missouri River Ft. S. & G. R. Co.*, 1 Fed. Cas. No. 550 (C. C. Kan., 1879).

[547] Ceded Indian lands were held to be exempt from the preemption act of September 4, 1841, 5 Stat. 453; *Spalding* v. *Chandler*, 160 U. S. 394 (1896). Such lands were likewise held to be exempt from the preemption provisions of the Act of April 12, 1815, 3 Stat. 121; *Hot Springs Cases*, 92 U. S. 698 (1875).

[548] Treaty of March 21, 1866, with the Seminoles, 14 Stat. 755.

[549] *United States* v. *Payne*, 8 Fed. 883 (D. C. W. D. Ark., 1881).

[550] *Walker* v. *Henshaw*, 16 Wall. 436, 443 (1872).

[551] 36 Stat. 847. Memo. Sol. I. D., September 17, 1934.

[552] *Cf. New York Indians* v. *United States*, 170 U. S. 1 (1898) (time of exchange and removal). *Cf.* also, *Oklahoma* v. *Texas*, 258 U. S. 574 (1922) (conveyance of tribal land by United States construed in accordance with laws of state in which land is situated).

[553] Great Sioux Reservation, 19 Op. A. G. 467 (1890). See Chapter 14, sec. 5.

The question of civil and criminal jurisdiction over ceded lands involves, in addition to the question of property rights discussed in the *Ash Sheep* case, other questions which are separately treated in Chapters 18 and 19.

That reserved rights to hunt and fish on lands sold by an Indian tribe are property rights, rather than rights of sovereignty, and are therefore to be exercised under the police power of the state, was decided in the case of *Kennedy* v. *Becker*.[554] In that case the United States, on behalf of the plaintiff Indians, sought to maintain that lands sold by the Senecas with reservation of hunting and fishing rights "became thereby subject to a joint property ownership and the dual sovereignty of the two peoples, white and red, to fit the case intended, however infrequent such situation was to be."[555] The opinion of the Court, prepared by Hughes, *J.*, and read by White, *C. J.*, declared:

> We are unable to take this view. It is said that the State would regulate the whites and that the Indian tribe would regulate its members, but if neither could exercise authority with respect to the other at the *locus in quo*, either would be free to destroy the subject of the power. Such a duality of sovereignty instead of maintaining in each the essential power of preservation would in fact deny it to both.
> * * * We do not think that it is a proper construction of the reservation in the conveyance to regard it as an attempt either to reserve sovereign prerogative or so to divide the inherent power of preservation as to make its competent exercise impossible. Rather are we of the opinion that the clause is fully satisfied by considering it a reservation of a privilege of fishing and hunting upon the granted lands in common with the grantees, and others to whom the privilege might be extended, but subject nevertheless to that necessary power of appropriate regulation, as to all those privileged, which inhered in the sovereignty of the State over the lands where the privilege was exercised. This was clearly recognized in *United States* v. *Winans*, 198 U. S. 371, 384, where the court in sustaining the fishing rights of the Indians on the Columbia River, under the provisions of the treaty between the United States and the Yakima Indians, ratified in 1859, said (referring to the authority of the State of Washington): "Nor does it" (that is, the right of 'taking fish at all usual and accustomed places') "restrain the State unreasonably, if at all, in the regulation of the right. It only fixes in the land such easements as enable the right to be exercised." (Pp. 563, 564.)

[554] 241 U. S. 556 (1916). For a further discussion of tribal hunting and fishing rights, see Chapter 14, sec. 7; and see Chapter 8, sec. 2.

[555] *Ibid.* p. 563.

SECTION 22. TRIBAL RIGHTS IN PERSONAL PROPERTY[556]

The first white explorers, traders, settlers, and lawyers found the Indians possessing not only lands but various valuable chattels, such as furs, provisions, tobacco, wampum, and, in some parts of the country, slaves. Apparently no attempt was ever made to claim ownership of these chattels in the name of the sovereign, as was done, from time to time, with Indian lands. Possibly this may be ascribed to the fact that the Indians themselves had more definite notions of ownership with respect to chattels than they had with respect to land, or perhaps we may find a more adequate explanation in the historic fact that the feudal system was always pretty closely tied to land and never developed a theory of "seizin" and "fees" with respect to personal property. Whatever the reason, the result is that we are at least spared the confusions that the theory of seizin and fees has introduced into Indian land law. If an Indian tribe or clan owns a saint's picture[557] or a herd of cattle, no matter how many limitations the law may put upon the disposition of the property, nobody will explain the limitation in terms of a "fee in the sovereign."

Apart from this difference, the ownership of personal property by an Indian tribe raises problems essentially similar to those raised by tribal ownership of realty.

The same diversity noted in the types of interest in real property held by an Indian tribe is found with respect to personalty in tribal ownership.

The essential distinctions between tribal property and public

[556] For regulations regarding tribal moneys, see 25 C. F. R., subchapter S.

[557] *Pueblo of Laguna* v. *Pueblo of Acoma*, 1 N. M. 220 (1857).

property, which we have noted in the field of realty, are paralleled in the field of personalty.

The distinction between property vested in the tribe as an entity and property held by tribal members in common is likewise repeated in the field of personalty.

The question of who composes the tribe in which personal property is vested does not differ in principle from the parallel question which we have considered in the field of real property.

The problems raised by the concept of "equitable ownership" in tribal realty are repeated with respect to equitable ownership of tribal funds and other personal property.

Possibly a peculiar problem is raised in the field of tribal personalty by the question of when interest is payable on tribal funds helds by the United States, although this problem shows a basic similarity to the problem of the right to the proceeds of land held by the United States in trust for an Indian tribe.

Another problem that may appear peculiar to the field of tribal personalty, but is in fact basically analogous to problems in the field of tribal realty, is that of creditors' claims against tribal funds.

Because of these numerous parallels, it should be possible to deal with the foregoing questions rather briefly, relying upon analyses already made with respect to real property.

A. FORMS OF PERSONAL PROPERTY

The personal property of Indian tribes probably comprises all the forms of personal property known to non-Indians, including bonds, notes, mortgages, moneys, credits, shares of stock, choses in action,[558] and herds.[559]

A tribe may have an equitable interest in personal property held by the United States or by some other party, and, conversely, an Indian tribe may have in its possession funds which it holds as trustee.

Thus a tribe may hold funds as a trustee to carry out projects for the rehabilitation of needy Indians.[560]

Of all forms of property held by an Indian tribe, it is probable that a principal focus of discussion and controversy has been the category of choses in action and, in particular, claims against the United States and against other tribes.[561]

B. TRIBAL PROPERTY AND FEDERAL PROPERTY

As with realty, the distinction between personal property of an Indian tribe and public property of the United States has been recognized in a wide variety of cases.

The distinction between tribal funds and public moneys of the United States was the basis of the decision in *Quick Bear* v. *Leupp*.[562] In that case the Supreme Court held that payments to the Bureau of Catholic Indian Missions for the care, education, and maintenance of Indian pupils was not in violation of statutory provisions which declared it "to be the settled policy of the Government to hereafter make no appropriation whatever for education in any sectarian school."[563] The Supreme Court said:

> These appropriations rested on different grounds from the gratuitous appropriations of public moneys under the heading "Support of Schools." The two subjects were separately treated in each act, and, naturally, as they are essentially different in character. One is the gratuitous appropriation of public moneys for the purpose of Indian education, but the "Treaty Fund" is not public money in this sense. It is the Indians' money, or at least is dealt with by the Government as if it belonged to them, as morally it does. It differs from the "Trust Fund" in this: The "Trust Fund" has been set aside for the Indians and the income expended for their benefit, which expenditure required no annual appropriation. The whole amount due the Indians for certain land cessions was appropriated in one lump sum by the act of 1889, 25 Stat. 888, chap. 405. This "Trust Fund" is held for the Indians and not distributed *per capita*, being held as property in common. The money is distributed in accordance with the discretion of the Secretary of the Interior, but really belongs to the Indians. The President declared it to be the moral right of the Indians to have this "Trust Fund" applied to the education of the Indians in the schools of their choice, and the same view was entertained by the Supreme Court of the District of Columbia and the Court of Appeals of the District. But the "Treaty Fund" has exactly the same characteristics. They are moneys belonging really to the Indians. They are the price of land ceded by the Indians to the Government. The only difference is that in the "Treaty Fund" the debt to the Indians created and secured by the treaty is paid by annual appropriations. They are not gratuitous appropriations of public moneys, but the payment, as we repeat, of a treaty debt in installments. We perceive no justification for applying the proviso or declaration of policy to the payment of treaty obligations, the two things being distinct and different in nature and having no relation to each other, except that both are technically appropriations. (Pp. 80–81.)

Since the decision in *Quick Bear* v. *Leupp*, the Bureau of Indian Affairs has continued to make payments to sectarian schools out of Indian "trust" or "treaty" funds, at the request of the adult Indians concerned. Justifications for such expenditures have been regularly presented to Congress in hearings on Indian appropriations and regularly approved.[564]

In the case of *United States* v. *Sinnott*,[565] where the United States sought to recover upon an Indian agent's bond by reason of the agent's failure to deposit certain timber sale proceeds in the United States Treasury, the court found for the defendant, on this issue, declaring:

> The mill at which this lumber was sawed was erected by the United States for the Indians of this reservation in pursuance of the treaty with the Umpquas, of November 29, 1854 (10 St. 1125,) and that with the Mollallas, of December 21, 1885, (12 St. 981,) and in fact belongs to them; and therefore, in my judgment, such lumber was not the "property" of the United States, within the purview of section 3618 of the Revised Statutes, which requires the proceeds of any sale thereof to be conveyed into the treasury; nor was the money received therefor, received "for the use of the United States," within the purview of section 3617 of the Revised Statutes. (Pp. 85–86.)

[558] See, for example, Act of June 10, 1872, 17 Stat. 388 (sale of Ottawa tribal assets).

On debts to a tribe created by the appropriation of tribal funds for payment of irrigation construction charges on allotted lands, see Act of June 4, 1920, sec. 8, 41 Stat. 751, 753. See also Act of March 3, 1921, sec. 5, 41 Stat. 1355, and see Chapter 12, sec. 7. To the effect that a tribe may transfer or assign debts owing from the United States on the same basis as a private person, see Assignability of Indebtedness—Cherokee Nation, 20 Op. A. G. 749 (1894).

[559] See, for example, Act of April 27, 1904, 33 Stat. 352, 353 (Crow).

[560] See Letter of Acting Secretary I. D. to United States Employees' Compensation Commission, July 9, 1937, analyzing loans and grants to Indian tribes made pursuant to the Emergency Relief Appropriation Act of April 8, 1935.

> These agreements are known as trust agreements and contain the following significant provisions: The United States grants to the tribe all of the allocation of emergency funds required to cover the cost of the approved projects excepting such part of the cost as represents necessary administrative and supervisory expenses. The grant is made subject to the condition that it will be used for only the approved projects and that the projects will be carried on under the regulations and supervision of the Indian Office.

And see Sec. 24 of this chapter.

[561] See Chapter 14, sec. 6.

[562] 210 U. S. 50 (1908).

[563] Act of June 10, 1896, 29 Stat. 321, 345; Act of June 7, 1897, 30 Stat. 63, 79; similar provisions are found in more recent appropriation acts, e. g., Act of March 2, 1917, 39 Stat. 969, 988.

[564] Op. Sol. I. D., M.27514, August 1, 1933. See Chapter 12, sec. 2.

[565] 26 Fed. 84 (C. C. Ore. 1886).

In a somewhat similar case, the United States Supreme Court declared: [566]

> The moneys paid for the Indian lands were trust moneys, not public moneys. They were at all times in equity the moneys of the Indians, subject only to the expenses incurred by the United States for surveying, managing, and selling the lands. (P. 693.)

C. TRIBAL OWNERSHIP AND COMMON OWNERSHIP

Tribal funds, like tribal lands, are the property of the tribe as an entity rather than common property of the individual members.[567]

This general rule, however, does not settle the question of when a particular treaty or statute is to be construed as establishing tribal property rights in a given fund, for instance, and when individual rights are established. The problem is apt to become acute when the treaty or statute in question refers to "Indians" in the plural instead of to a tribe in the singular.

In the case of *Chippewa Indians of Minnesota* v. *United States*,[568] a possible ambiguity in the original statute [569] requiring payments to "the Chippewa Indians in the State of Minnesota" was resolved by the Supreme Court in view of a sustained course of administrative dealings treating the funds in question as the property of the tribe rather than of individuals.

Ordinarily a treaty promise to make annuity payments to a tribe *per capita* does not establish vested rights in individual members of the tribe, and no such vested right is established by the general statute requiring that payment of annuities be made directly to the Indians rather than to agents or attorneys.[570] Therefore individual members who separate from the tribe forfeit a legal claim to annuities.[571] As was said in the case of *The Sac and Fox Indians*,[572] *per* Holmes, *J.:*

> The Government did not deal with individuals but with tribes. *Blackfeather* v. *United States*, 190 U. S. 368, 377. See *Fleming* v. *McCurtain*, 215 U. S. 56. The promises in the treaties under which the annuities were due were promises to the tribes. Treaties of November 3, 1804, 7 Stat. 84; October 21, 1837, 7 Stat. 540; October 11, 1842, 7 Stat. 596. See treaty of October 1, 1859, 15 Stat. 467. (P. 484.)
>
> * * * * *
>
> The treaty contracts on which the plaintiff's claims are founded gave rights only to the tribe, not to the members. It was an accepted and reasonable rule, especially in the days when Indians' wars still were possible and troublesome, that payments to the tribe should be made only at their reservation and to persons present there. The acts of 1852 and 1867 did not shift the treaty rights from the tribe to the members, create new rights or enlarge old ones. The payments up to 1884 had the sanction of statute. The act of 1884 no more created individual rights than did the acts of 1852 and 1867. It confined its benefits to "original Sacs and Foxes now in Iowa," and made the Secretary of the Interior the judge. (Pp. 489-490.)

D. TRIBAL INTEREST IN TRUST PROPERTY

Numerous statutes refer to funds held by the United States for an Indian tribe as "trust funds" and to the Secretary of the Treasury or the Secretary of the Interior as "custodian." [573]

The strict language of "trust" is not, however, necessary to establish a trust relationship between the United States and the tribe where tribal personal property is held by the United States.

Incidents of the trust or depositary relationship are found in statutes providing for payments out of the Treasury to replace bonds held by the Secretary of the Interior for an Indian tribe and stolen while in his custody,[574] or to compensate for the defaults of states on state bonds.[575]

E. THE COMPOSITION OF THE TRIBE

As has been already noted, the question of what individuals are entitled to share in tribal personal property does not differ essentially from the parallel question considered with respect to realty.[576] The chief difficulties with respect to the proper distribution of tribal funds have arisen in connection with the amalgamation of distinct tribes,[577] the splitting of single tribes,[578] and the loss of membership by or adoption of particular individuals.

Where several tribes or bands are interested in a single fund, Congress has sometimes provided for distribution in accordance with respective numbers.[579]

The interest of the various groups of Cherokees in national funds has been a source of legislation [580] and litigation [581] for many years.

Special statutes occasionally provide for the payment of shares of tribal funds to persons newly added to tribal rolls.[582]

F. INTEREST ON TRIBAL FUNDS

When tribal funds are held by the United States for the benefit of the tribe, the question frequently arises whether interest on such funds is due to the tribe and, if such be the case, what the appropriate rate of interest may be. Ordinarily this question must be answered by reference to the terms of the treaty, act

---

[566] *United States* v. *Brindle*, 110 U. S. 688 (1884).

[567] *Dukes* v. *Goodall*, 5 Ind. T. 145 (1904) (holding individual Choctaw has no such interest in tribal property as will justify representative suit to prevent improper additions to tribal rolls); Seminole Indians—Modification of Agreement With, 26 Op. A. G. 340 (1907); see *Parks* v. *Ross*, 11 How. 362, 374 (1850). And *cf. Muskrat* v. *United States*, 219 U. S. 346 (1911), rev'g 44 C. Cls. 137 (1909) (holding unconstitutional provision in the Appropriation Act of March 1, 1907, 34 Stat. 1015, 1028, conferring jurisdiction upon the Court of Claims and the Supreme Court to determine the constitutionality of the Act of April 26, 1906, 34 Stat. 137, as amended by Act of June 21, 1906, 34 Stat. 325, adding new members to Cherokee rolls).

[568] 307 U. S. 1 (1939).

[569] Act of January 14, 1889, 25 Stat. 642.

[570] Act of August 30, 1852, sec. 3, 10 Stat. 41, 56.

[571] *Sac and Fox Indians of the Mississippi in Iowa* v. *Sac and Fox Indians of the Mississippi in Oklahoma*, 220 U. S. 481 (1911), aff'g. 43 C. Cls. 287 (1910).

[572] *Ibid.*

[573] Act of June 10, 1876, 19 Stat. 58; Act of June 16, 1880, sec. 2, 21 Stat. 291, 292 (Great and Little Osage).

[574] Act of July 12, 1862, sec. 1, 12 Stat. 539, 540 (Kaskaskias, Peorias, Piankeshaws, and Weas).

[575] Thus the Act of March 3, 1845, 5 Stat. 766, 777, includes an appropriation "To make good the interest on investments in State stocks and bonds, for various Indian tribes, not yet paid by the States, to be reimbursed out of the interest when collected * * *." Act of August 31, 1842, 5 Stat. 576 (Wyandott).

[576] Sec. 1, *supra*.

[577] See *e. g.*, Act of January 19, 1891, 26 Stat. 720 (division of Sioux Nation).

[578] See *e. g.*, Treaty of July 19, 1866, with Cherokee Nation, 14 Stat. 799 (incorporation of friendly tribes).

[579] Treaty of July 27, 1853, with Comanche, Kiowa, and Apache Indians, Art. 6, 10 Stat. 1013, 1014; Act of January 18, 1881, sec. 3, 21 Stat. 315, 316 (Winnebago); *cf.* Treaty of August 25, 1828, Art. 2, 7 Stat. 315, 316 (Winnebago, Potawatomie, Chippewa, and Ottawa Indians); *cf.* also Act of March 2, 1889, sec. 2, 25 Stat. 1013, 1015 (United Peorias and Miamies).

[580] See Act of August 7, 1882, 22 Stat. 302, 328; Act of March 3, 1883, 22 Stat. 582, 585-586; Act of August 23, 1894, 28 Stat. 424, 441, 451.

[581] *Cherokee Nation* v. *Blackfeather*, 155 U. S. 218 (1894); *Cherokee Nation* v. *Journeycake*, 155 U. S. 196 (1894), aff'g. *Journeycake* v. *Cherokee Nation*, 28 C. Cls. 281 (1893).

[582] Act of June 2, 1924, 43 Stat. 253 (Cheyenne and Arapaho).

of Congress, or agreement by which the fund in question was established.[583]

Under some treaties what amounted to interest payments were designated "annuities."[584]

The Act of April 1, 1880,[585] authorized the Secretary of the Interior to deposit such funds in the United States Treasury, in lieu of investment, with a provision that interest should be payable "semiannually * * * at the rate per annum stipulated by treaties or prescribed by law." The Act of February 12, 1929,[586] as amended by the Act of June 13, 1930,[587] provides for the payment of simple interest at the rate of 4 per centum per annum on tribal funds, "upon which interest is not otherwise authorized by law."[588]

When tribal funds held by the United States were segregated for pro rata distribution and deposited in banks, section 28 of the Act of May 25, 1918,[589] required as a condition of the deposit that the bank agree to pay interest on such funds "at a reasonable rate." Subsequently, section 324 (c) of the Banking Act of 1935[590] prohibited payment of interest by member banks of the Federal Reserve System on demand deposits, and repealed "so much of existing law as requires the payment of interest with respect to any funds deposited by the United States * * * as is inconsistent with the provision of this section as amended." It was administratively determined that this statute superseded the requirement of interest payment on funds on demand deposit in such banks, and that such funds might lawfully be deposited in banks not paying interest thereon.[591] This holding was limited to banks which are members of the Federal Reserve System,[592] and had no application to tribal funds not segregated for pro rata distribution, as to which a fixed interest is due to the tribe.

The Act of June 24, 1938,[593] authorized the Secretary of the Interior to withdraw from the United States Treasury and to deposit in banks tribal funds "on which the United States is not obliged by law to pay interest at higher rates than can be procured from the banks."

Although the right of an Indian tribe to interest in connection with recovery against the United States is beyond the scope of this chapter, we may note the general rule laid down by Taft, *C. J.*, in *Cherokee Nation* v. *United States*,[594] based upon section 177 of the Judicial Code:

> * * * we should begin with the premise, well established by the authorities, that a recovery of interest against the United States is not authorized under a special Act referring to the Court of Claims a suit founded upon a contract with the United States unless the contract or the act expressly authorizes such interest.[595]

G. CREDITORS' CLAIMS

The question of whether funds due to or held in trust for the tribe by the United States should be subjected to the claims of creditors has been expressly covered in a number of special statutes relating to the disposition of such funds.[596] In a few cases general payment by the Secretary of the Interior to all of the creditors of a given tribe is authorized, but generally the statute authorizes payment of a designated claim, based either upon tribal agreement,[597] or upon depredations.[598] General legislation on depredation claims authorized the Court of Claims to adjudicate such claims in suits against the United States, with permission to interested Indians to appear as parties defendant.[599] Judgments rendered against Indian tribes were to be satisfied out of annuities, other funds, or any appropriations for the benefit of the tribe, and, if all these sources failed, from the Treasury of the United States, such payments to be reimbursable out of future tribal annuities, funds, or appropriations. Thereafter the regular appropriation acts authorized the Secretary of the Interior to make payments to successful claimants under the Act of March 3, 1891, by deducting such sums from tribal funds, having due regard for the educational and other necessary requirements of the tribe or tribes affected.[600]

The general rule is that tribal funds held by the United States will not be subjected to claims of third parties unless payment of such claims is clearly authorized by statute or treaty,[601] or by lawful action of the tribe itself.[602]

[583] See Crow Indians of Montana, Modification of Agreement, 20 Op. A. G. 517 (1893).

[584] *United States* v. *Blackfeather*, 155 U. S. 180 (1894), revg. *Blackfeather* v. *United States*, 28 C. Cls. 447 (1893); but *cf. Sioux Indians* v. *United States*, 277 U. S. 424 (1928), affg. 58 C. Cls. 302 (1923).

[585] 21 Stat. 70, 25 U. S. C. 161.

[586] 45 Stat. 1164.

[587] 46 Stat. 584.

[588] Sec. 2 of this act fixes the same interest rate for "Indian Money, Proceeds of Labor" accounts over $500 (25 U. S. C. 161b). Secs. 3 and 4 relate to accounting and to deposit of accrued interest. (25 U. S. C. 161c, 161d).

[589] 40 Stat. 591.

[590] 49 Stat. 684, 714–715.

[591] Op. Sol. I. D., M.28231, March 12, 1936.

[592] Op. Sol. I. D., M.28519, May 27, 1936.

[593] 52 Stat. 1037.

[594] 270 U. S. 476, 487 (1926).

[595] For an example of such expression see *United States* v. *Blackfeather*, 155 U. S. 180 (1894), revg. *Blackfeather* v. *United States*, 28 C. Cls. 447 (1893), (holding that where interest is due on the proceeds of land ceded by the tribe, to be sold by the Federal Government in public sale, and such lands are actually sold at private sale at lower price than that designated, and subsequently, under a special jurisdictional act, it is adjudicated that the tribe is entitled to the difference, the tribe is also entitled to interest thereon; the case being brought within the exception to the rule above cited, by a treaty provision for the payment of "five per centum on the amount of said balance, as an annuity.") (P. 188.)

[596] Act of June 22, 1854, 10 Stat. 781 (Sac and Fox); Act of June 16, 1880, 21 Stat. 259, 277 (Cheyenne). Act of May 16, 1874, sec. 1, 18 Stat. 47 (Sioux).

[597] Act of August 5, 1882, 22 Stat. 728 (Kansas); Act of April 4, 1888, 25 Stat. 79 (Pottawatomie); Act of May 27, 1902, 32 Stat. 207 (Menominee).

[598] Act of March 3, 1883, 22 Stat. 804, 805 (Cheyenne and Arapaho); Act of March 3, 1885, 23 Stat. 478, 498 (Cheyenne and Arapaho).

[599] Act of March 3, 1891, 26 Stat. 851. For a discussion of the responsibility of tribes for depredations, see Chapter 14, secs. 1, 6.

[600] Act of August 23, 1894, 28 Stat. 424, 476; Act of June 8, 1896, 29 Stat. 267, 306; Act of February 9, 1900, 31 Stat. 7, 26; Act of February 14, 1902, 32 Stat. 5, 27.

[601] Claim of Board of Foreign Missions under Treaty with the Cherokees, 5 Op. A. G. 268 (1850); The Cherokee Fund Not Liable for Damages, etc., 3 Op. A. G. 431 (1839); Transfer of Stocks from the Chickasaw to the Choctaw Fund, 3 Op. A. G. 591 (1840).

[602] To the effect that a tribe may assume collective responsibility for debts incurred by individual members, and that the President, at the request of the tribe, may turn annuity funds over to the creditor, see: Contracts of the Potawatomie Indians, 6 Op. A. G. 49 (1853); Contracts of Indians, 6 Op. A. G. 462 (1854).

SECTION 23. TRIBAL RIGHT TO RECEIVE FUNDS

The right of an Indian tribe to receive funds or other personal property from the United States or from third parties depends, of course, upon the language of the treaty, statute, or agreement, in which such promise of payment appears.[603] In this section we shall attempt to determine the principal sources of tribal rights to income, and to analyze the manner in which such payments are handled.

[603] The right of an Indian tribe to recover funds, apart from agreement, by reason of torts committed against it, is treated elsewhere, in Chapter 14. The right to compensation under eminent domain proceedings is adverted to in sec. 11, *supra*. Powers with respect to taxes and fees are treated in Chapter 7.

A. SOURCES OF TRIBAL INCOME

The principal source of tribal income, at least since the Revolution, has been the sale of tribal resources—chiefly land, timber, minerals, and water power. Since sale of such resources was, for more than a century, largely restricted to the United States, most of the tribal income received prior to 1891, when the first general leasing law was enacted,[604] was paid to the tribe by the United States. Failure to appreciate the basis of such payments helped to create the popular misimpression that all payments made by the United States to Indians were matters of charity. An illustration of this sentiment is found in section 3 of the Act of June 22, 1874,[605] which provides that able-bodied male Indians receiving supplies pursuant to appropriation acts should perform useful labor "for the benefit of themselves or of the tribe, at a reasonable rate, to be fixed by the agent in charge, and to an amount equal in value to the supplies to be delivered."

The popular outcry that would have followed the application of a similar rule to white holders of Government bonds or pensions may well be imagined.

It is important to recognize that funds due to Indian tribes under treaties and agreements were viewed by the Indians either as commercial debts for value received or as indemnities due from a foe in war. The fact that such payments were otherwise viewed by the public and by many administrators helps to explain some of the bitter controversies which formerly were decided on the field of battle and are now decided in the Court of Claims.

In numerous treaties, agreements, and statutes, the United States has agreed to pay money to an Indian tribe, in consideration of land cessions or other disposition of Indian property.[606] Where the tribal organization permitted, provision was frequently made that payment should go directly to the treasurer of the tribe; in other cases payments were to be made to chiefs, or to heads of families, or per capita to all adults; in some cases payment was to be made in goods or services.[607]

[604] See sec. 19, *supra*.

[605] 18 Stat. 146. 176; reenacted as permanent legislation in sec. 3 of the Act of March 3, 1875, 18 Stat. 420, 449, 25 U. S. C. 137. See Chapter 4, sec. 10, Chapter 12, sec. 4.

[606] Art. 4 of Treaty of November 7, 1825, with Shawnee tribe, 7 Stat. 284, 285; Art. 4 of Treaty of October 27, 1832, with Potowatomies, 7 Stat. 399, 401; Art. 3 of Treaty of September 10, 1853, with Rogue River tribe, 10 Stat. 1018, 1019; Art. 3 of Treaty of May 12, 1854, with Menomonee tribe, 10 Stat. 1064, 1065; Art. 6 of Treaty of May 30, 1854, with Kaskaskia and Peoria and Piankeshaw and Wea tribes, 10 Stat. 1082, 1083; Art. 3 of Treaty of June 5, 1854, with Miami tribe, 10 Stat. 1093, 1094; Art. 4 of Treaty of September 30, 1854, with Chippewa Indians of Lake Superior and the Mississippi, 10 Stat. 1109, 1110; Arts. 3 and 4 of Treaty of September 3, 1839, with Stockbridge and Munsee tribes, 11 Stat. 577, 578; Art. 7 of Treaty of August 7, 1856, with Creek and Seminole tribes, 11 Stat. 699, 702; Art. 3 of Treaty of March 10, 1865, with Ponca tribe, 14 Stat. 675, 676; Art. 46 of Treaty of April 28, 1866, with Choctaws and Chickasaws, 14 Stat. 769, 780; Art. 11 of Treaty of October 1, 1859, with Sacs and Foxes of the Mississippi, 15 Stat. 467, 470; Treaty of February 23, 1867, with Senecas, mixed Senecas and Shawnees, Quapaws, Confederated Peorias, Kaskaskias, Weas, and Piankeshaws, Miamies, Ottawas of Blanchard's Fork and Roche de Boeuf, and certain Wyandottes, 15 Stat. 513; Act of April 15, 1874, 18 Stat. 29 (Seminoles); Act of February 19, 1875, 18 Stat. 330, 331 (Seneca Nation); Act of March 3, 1875, 18 Stat. 402, 413 (Choctaws); Act of February 28, 1877, 19 Stat. 265 (Cherokees); Act of June 16, 1880, 21 Stat. 238, 248 (Cherokee Nation); Act of July 7, 1884, 23 Stat. 194, 212 (Creek Nation); Act of March 1, 1889, 25 Stat. 757, 758 (Muscogee or Creek Nation); Act of August 19, 1890, 26 Stat. 329 (Omaha tribe); Act of February 13, 1891, 26 Stat. 749, 752 (Sac and Fox and Iowa); Joint Resolution of March 31, 1894, 28 Stat. 579, 580 (Cherokee Nation); Act of February 7, 1903, 32 Stat. 803 (Colville Indian Reservation); Act of August 26, 1922, 42 Stat. 832 (Agua Caliente Band).

[607] On the scope of obligations thereby assumed by the United States, see *United States* v. *Omaha Tribe of Indians*, 253 U. S. 275, 281 (1920); and *cf. United States* v. *Seminole Nation*, 299 U. S. 417 (1937).

Many of the early treaties provided for payments to be made in goods.[608]

Ordinarily payments promised in a treaty and paid in annual installments called annuities[609] were due to the tribe, and like obligations of one nation to another, were deemed satisfied when the tribal authorities had received the funds in question.[610] For the United States to have presumed to satisfy its obligation by direct payment to the individual members of the tribe would have been a departure from the canons of international law to which the Federal Government was trying to assimilate its relationship with the Indian tribes. Furthermore, payments to tribal authorities saved the Federal Government from the necessity of making difficult adjudications that might lead to dissatisfaction. On the other hand, payments to tribal authorities sometimes led to worse dissatisfactions on the part of individual members of the tribes who considered themselves discriminated against, and so the practice grew up of reserving to the United States, by treaty provision, the right to distribute to the members of the tribe the moneys or goods owing to the tribe.[611] Occasionally the treaty provided that this distribution was to be made on the basis of an agreement between the tribal authorities and the agents of the Federal Government.[612]

[608] See Chapter 3, sec. 3C(3).

[609] Although it has long been the custom to make new appropriations each year, Congress has made appropriations to Indian tribes payable over extended periods. Act of April 21, 1806, 2 Stat. 407; Act of March 3, 1819, 3 Stat. 517 ("annually, for ever"); Act of January 9, 1837, 5 Stat. 135; Act of March 3, 1811, 2 Stat. 660 ("five hundred dollars * * * to be paid annually to the said nations; which annuities shall be permanent").

[610] This was so self-evident that most of the early treaties did not mention the fact. A few treaties, however, did make explicit the understanding that distribution of payments made to the tribe was to be in the hands of the tribal authorities: Treaty of September 3, 1836, with the Menomonie Nation of Indians, 7 Stat. 506; Treaty of February 22, 1855, with the Mississippi bands of Chippewa Indians, 10 Stat. 1165. Other treaties emphasized this understanding, without making it explicit, by providing that the United States reserve the right to apportion annuities among the different bands or tribes with which a single treaty was made, but reserving no similar right to apportion funds within a band or tribe: Treaty of July 27, 1853, with the Comanche, Kiowa, and Apache tribes or nations of Indians, 10 Stat. 1013: Treaty of September 30, 1854, with the Chippewa Indians of Lake Superior and the Mississippi, 10 Stat. 1109.

[611] At first these treaties provided simply that the United States might "divide the said annuity amongst the individuals of the said tribe," Treaty of December 30, 1805, with the Piankeshaw, 7 Stat. 100. In the Treaty of January 8, 1821, with the Choctaw, 7 Stat. 210, per capita distribution is promised in order to remove "any discontent which may have arisen in the Choctaw Nation, in consequence of six thousand dollars of their annuity having been appropriated annually, for sixteen years, by some of the chiefs, for the support of their schools." Other treaties promising equal distribution are: Treaty of October 4, 1842, with the Chippewa Indians of the Mississippi and Lake Superior, 7 Stat. 591; Treaty of January 4, 1845, with the Creek and Seminole Tribes of Indians, 9 Stat. 821; Treaty of March 17, 1842, with the Wyandott Nation of Indians, 11 Stat. 581. Later treaties generally reserved a more comprehensive right in the President of the United States to determine how moneys due to the Indian tribe should be paid to the members of the tribe or expended for their use and benefit: Treaty of March 16, 1854, with the Omaha tribe of Indians, 10 Stat. 1043; Treaty of May 6, 1854, with the Delaware tribe of Indians, 10 Stat. 1048; Treaty of June 5, 1854, with the Miami tribe of Indians, 10 Stat. 1093; Treaty of October 17, 1855, with the Blackfoot and other tribes of Indians, 11 Stat. 657; Treaty of January 22, 1855, with the Dwamish and other tribes of Indians in Territory of Washington, 12 Stat. 927; Treaty of January 26, 1855, with the S'Klallams, 12 Stat. 933; Treaty of January 31, 1855, with the Makah tribe of Indians, 12 Stat. 939; Treaty of June 25, 1855, with the Confederated tribes of Indians in Middle Oregon, 12 Stat. 963; Treaty of July 1, 1855, with Qui-nai-elt and Quil-leh-ute Indians, 12 Stat. 971; Treaty of February 18, 1861, with the Confederated tribes of Arapahoe and Cheyenne Indians, 12 Stat. 1163; Treaty of March 6, 1865, with the Omaha Tribe of Indians, 14 Stat. 667; Treaty of September 29, 1865, with the Great and Little Osage Indians, 14 Stat. 687; Treaty of March 2, 1868, with the Ute Indians, 15 Stat. 619.

[612] See, for example: Treaty of September 29, 1837, with the Sioux Nation of Indians, 7 Stat. 538; Treaty of October 18, 1848, with the

Generally such per capita payments comprised only a portion of the funds due to the tribe, the remainder of such funds being invested or expended in other ways.[613] Occasionally an Indian treaty provided for complete per capita distribution of tribal funds.[614] Since 1871, and particularly during the years following the General Allotment Act, when per capita distribution of property was looked upon as an effective means of destroying tribal organization, numerous statutes provided for per capita payment of tribal funds.[615]

In recent decades compensation to Indian tribes for land or other property has generally taken the form of statutory provisions requiring that certain sums be placed "to the credit of" a given tribe.[616] Frequently specific provision is made covering the interest to be paid upon the fund and covering also the purposes for which and the manner in which the fund may be expended. Where a tribe has several different funds to its credit the statute, if clearly drafted, specifies the particular fund to which the sum in question is to be added.

Some statutes merely provide that funds shall be deposited in the United States Treasury and be subject to appropriations by the Congress for a designated group or tribe of Indians.[617]

Since 1847 the President has been empowered, in his discretion, to pay over moneys due to Indian tribes to the members thereof, per capita, instead of to the officers or agents of the tribe.[618] Questions of interpretation, however, continued to arise even after the 1847 statute.

Where the manner of payment is in issue it has been said that a requirement of execution of a receipt or release by the tribe indicates that payment to tribal officers rather than heads of families is intended.[619]

Again, it has been said:

> Ordinarily a debt due to a nation, by a treaty, ought to be paid to the constituted authorities of the nation; but where the treaty and the law appropriating the money both direct the payment to all the individuals of the nation *per capita*, the treaty and the statute must prevail.[620]

The statutes dealing with payments due from the United States to Indian tribes represented, until the end of the nineteenth century, the chief source of tribal income, supplemented only sporadically by special statutes or treaties authorizing the leasing or sale of tribal lands to other Indian tribes[621] or to non-Indians.

A further source of income of considerable importance during recent decades is constituted by judgment awards in suits against the United States.

In recent years, various jurisdictional acts have provided that no part of the judgment that may be awarded pursuant to the act shall be paid out in per capita payments to the Indians concerned.[622]

This proviso represents a well-established tendency to devote recoveries from judgments in claim cases to the rebuilding of the entire tribal estate rather than to temporary payments which are easily dissipated.

An important source of income due to Indian tribes from non-governmental sources developed with the building of railroads across Indian reservations.[623]

Most of the statutes which grant rights-of-way to railroads or other transportation or communication companies provide for payment of compensation to the Indian tribe. A majority of the statutes relating to railroads contain the phrase "that the

---

Menomonee Tribe of Indians, 9 Stat. 952; Treaty of May 10, 1854, with the Shawnees, 10 Stat. 1053; Treaty of June 19, 1858, with the Mendawakanton and Wahpakoota bands of the Sioux tribe of Indians, 12 Stat. 1031; Treaty of June 19, 1858, with the Sisseeton and Wahpaton bands of Sioux tribe of Indians, 12 Stat. 1037.

[613] Treaty of January 14, 1837, with Saganaw Chippewas, 7 Stat. 528; Treaty of October 21, 1837, with Sacs and Foxes, 7 Stat. 540; Treaty of October 19, 1838, with Ioways, 7 Stat. 568; Treaty of August 5, 1851, with Bands of Dakotas, 10 Stat. 954; Treaty of March 15, 1854, with Ottoes and Missourias, 10 Stat. 1038; Treaty of May 10, 1854, with Bands of Shawnees, 10 Stat. 1053; Treaty of April 19, 1858, with Yancton Sioux, 11 Stat. 743.

[614] Treaty of January 31, 1855, with Wyandott Tribe, 10 Stat. 1159.

[615] Act of March 3, 1881, sec. 5, 21 Stat. 414, 433–434; Act of May 15, 1888, sec. 1, 25 Stat. 150 (Omahas); Act of July 4, 1888, 25 Stat. 240 (Winnebago Reservation); Act of October 19, 1888, 25 Stat. 608 (Cherokee); Act of June 6, 1900, sec. 1, 31 Stat. 672, 673 (Fort Hall Reservation); Act of March 1, 1901, 31 Stat. 848, 859 (Cherokee); Act of March 1, 1901, 31 Stat. 861, 870 (Creek); Act of June 30, 1902, 32 Stat. 500, 503 (Creek); Act of March 3, 1909, 35 Stat. 751 (Quapaw); Act of June 25, 1910, sec. 21, 36 Stat. 855, 861 (Sisseton and Wahpeton); Joint Resolution of August 22, 1911, 37 Stat. 44; Act of April 18, 1912, 37 Stat. 86 (Osage Tribe); Act of May 11, 1912, sec. 3, 37 Stat. 111 (Omaha Tribe); Act of June 4, 1920, sec. 11, 41 Stat. 751, 755 (Crow); Act of March 3, 1921, 41 Stat. 1249 (Osage); Act of June 4, 1924, 43 Stat. 376 (Eastern Band of Cherokees).

[616] Act of December 15, 1874, 18 Stat. 291, 292 (Eastern band of Shoshones); Act of April 10, 1876, sec. 3, 19 Stat. 28, 29 (Pawnee tribe); Act of April 25, 1876, sec. 2, 19 Stat. 37 (Menomonee Indians); Act of August 15, 1876, sec. 4, 19 Stat. 208 (Otoe and Missouria and Sac and Fox of the Missouri tribes); Act of June 28, 1879, 21 Stat. 40, 41 (Osage Indians); Act of March 3, 1881, sec. 4, 21 Stat. 380, 381 (Otoe and Missouria Tribes); Act of March 3, 1885, sec. 3, 23 Stat. 340, 343 (Cayuse, Walla-Walla, and Umatilla Indians); Act of March 3, 1885, sec. 4, 23 Stat. 351, 352 (Sac and Fox and Iowa Indians); Act of September 1, 1888, sec. 6, 25 Stat. 452, 455 (Shoshone and Bannack tribes); Act of January 14, 1889, sec. 7, 25 Stat. 642, 645 (Chippewas); Act of June 12, 1890, sec. 3, 26 Stat. 146, 147 (Menomonees); Act of October 1, 1890, sec. 4, 26 Stat. 658, 659 (Round Valley Indian Reservation); Act of March 3, 1901, 31 Stat. 1455 (Chippewa Indians); Act of June 13, 1902, 32 Stat. 384 (Ute Indian Reservation); Act of August 17, 1911, 37 Stat. 21 (Rosebud Indian Reservation); Act of July 1, 1912, 37 Stat. 186 (Umatilla Indian Reservation); Act of July 10, 1912, 37 Stat. 192 (Flathead Indians); Act of February 14, 1913, sec. 6, 37 Stat. 675, 677 (Standing Rock Indian Reservation); Act of August 22, 1914, sec. 1, 38 Stat. 704 (Quinaielt Reservation); Act of March 2, 1917, sec. 2, 39 Stat. 994, 995 (Fort Peck Indians); Act of March 3, 1919, 40 Stat. 1320, 1321 (Rosebud Indians); Act of December 11, 1919, sec. 2, 41 Stat. 365, 366 (Fort Peck Indians); Act of May 31, 1924, sec. 1, 43 Stat. 247 (Quinaielt Reservation); Act of February 28, 1925, 43 Stat. 1052 (Chippewa Indians); Act of August 25, 1937, sec. 3, 50 Stat. 811 (Agua Caliente or Palm Springs Band).

[617] Act of June 7, 1924, sec. 1, 43 Stat. 596 (Pyramid Lake Indian Reservation).

[618] Act of March 3, 1847, sec. 3, 9 Stat. 203, amending Act of June 30, 1834, sec. 11, 4 Stat. 735, 737. The 1847 provision was subsequently embodied, with other material, in R. S. § 2086 and 25 U. S. C. 111.

[619] "The direction that the money shall be paid to the Creek nation is not decisive, because payment to the heads of families is a mode of making payment to the nation. But the condition that a release of all claim for the whole sum shall first be executed by the Creek nation, is not equivocal, because such a release could not be executed by the heads of families or by individuals. And when the act directs that the payment shall be made to the Creek nation, and that the release shall be executed by the Creek nation, the inference would seem to be very strong against a distribution *per capita*. But when the act goes one step further, and requires that the persons to whom the money shall be paid shall make satisfactory proof that they have full power and authority to receive and receipt for the same, the inference becomes irresistible against a distribution and payment to heads of families, which would be entirely irreconcilable with this provision." (Pp. 48–49.) Payment of Certain Moneys to the Creeks, 5 Op. A. G. 46, 48–49 (1848). The later portion of this opinion, apparently inconsistent with the above quotation, was revised in 5 Op. A. G. 98 (1849). *Cf.* Payment of Certain Moneys to the Cherokees, 5 Op. A. G. 320 (1851).

[620] Payment of Certain Moneys to the Cherokees, 5 Op. A. G. 320 (1851). Accord: Miami Indians, 6 Op. A. G. 440 (1854) (treaty provision, ambiguous, superseded by statute).

[621] Various early statutes provided for payment by one Indian tribe to another in connection with intertribal land transference. See, for example, Act of June 5, 1872, 17 Stat. 228 (payment by Kansas Tribe to Osage Tribe).

[622] See, for example, Act of March 3, 1931, 46 Stat. 1487 (Pillager Bands of Chippewa Indians). And see Chapter 9, sec. 6, fn. 145.

[623] See secs. 18–20, *supra*.

said railway company shall pay to the Secretary of the Interior, for the benefit of the particular nations or tribes through whose lands said line may be located," a specified sum,[624] which is frequently fixed at $50 per mile of road. In a few instances similar language referring to a definite tribe is used instead of the more general language above noted.[625] A few statutes provide that the railway company shall pay the required sum "to the Secretary of the Interior, for the benefit of the particular nations or tribes or individuals through whose lands said line may be located." [626] A few such statutes provide simply for payment directly to the tribe concerned.[627] Other statutes provide for payment without specifying the manner of such payment.[628]

In 1899 the matter of railroad rights-of-way, hitherto dealt with in piecemeal legislation, was covered by a general statute [629] which provided:

> SEC. 5. That where a railroad is constructed under the provisions of this Act through the Indian Territory there shall be paid by the railroad company to the Secretary of the Interior, for the benefit of the particular nation or tribe through whose lands the road may be located, such an annual charge as may be prescribed by the Secretary of the Interior, not less than fifteen dollars for each mile of road, the same to be paid so long as said land shall be owned and occupied by such nation or tribe, which payment shall be in addition to the compensation otherwise required herein.

The various general statutes authorizing the leasing of Indian lands, and other forms of disposition of Indian tribal property which have been analyzed in earlier sections of this chapter, generally provide that the proceeds from such transactions shall be deposited to the credit of the tribe concerned.

The following table shows the various general statutes directing that specified forms of tribal income be deposited to the credit of the tribe.[630]

U.S.C. sec. No.	Source of income	Date of act	Statute citation	Provision
25:314	Rights-of-way	Mar. 3, 1899, sec. 3, amended Feb. 28, 1902.	30 Stat. 991	"Payment to the Secretary of the Interior for the benefit of the tribe or nation."
25:319	Rights-of-way for telephone, etc.	Mar. 3, 1901, sec. 3.	31 Stat. 1083	"Pay to the Secretary of the Interior, for the use and benefit of the Indians, such annual tax as he may designate."
25:321	Right-of-way for pipe lines.	Mar. 11, 1904, amended Mar. 2, 1917, sec. 1.	33 Stat. 65, 39 Stat. 973.	"Pay to the Secretary of the Interior, for the use and benefit of the Indians, such annual tax as he may designate."
25:320	Acquisition of lands by railways for materials and reservoirs.	Mar. 3, 1909	35 Stat. 781	"Deposited in the Treasury of the United States to the credit of the tribe or tribes."
25:407	Sale of timber	June 25, 1910, sec. 7.	36 Stat. 857	"Shall be used for the benefit of the Indians of the reservation in such manner as he [Secretary of the Interior] may direct."
25:190	Sale of agency tracts, etc.	Apr. 12, 1924	43 Stat. 93	"Deposited in the Treasury of the United States to the credit of the Indians owning the same."
25:400a	Mining lease of agency reserves.	Apr. 17, 1926	44 Stat. 300	"Deposited in the Treasury of the United States to the credit of the Indians for whose benefit the lands are reserved subject to appropriation by Congress for educational work among the Indians or in paying expenses of administration of agencies."
16:615	Sale of burnt timber on "Public Domain."	Mar. 4, 1913, amended July 3, 1926.	37 Stat. 1015, amended 44 Stat. 891.	"Transferred to the fund of such tribe or otherwise credited or distributed as by law provided."
30:86	Agricultural entries on surplus coal lands.	Feb. 27, 1917, sec. 4.	39 Stat. 944, 945.	"Shall be paid into the Treasury of the United States to the credit o the same fund under the same conditions and limitations as are or may be prescribed by law for the dispositio of the proceeds arising from the disposal of other surplus lands in such Indian reservation."
16:810	Water power license rentals.	June 10, 1920, sec. 17.	41 Stat. 1063, 1072.	"Shall be placed to the credit of the Indians of such re ervation."

In addition to the foregoing specific provisions, there are other currently effective statutes relating to the leasing of Indian lands which do not specify the manner in which the receipts are to be handled.[631]

The Act of March 3, 1883, as amended,[632] provides:

> All miscellaneous revenues derived from Indian reservations, agencies, and schools, except those of the Five Civilized Tribes, and not the result of the labor of any member of such tribe, which are not required by existing law to be otherwise disposed of, shall be covered into the Treasury of the United States under the caption "Indian moneys, proceeds of labor", and are hereby made available for expenditure, in the discretion of the Secretary of the Interior, for the benefit of the Indian tribes, agencies, and schools on whose behalf they are collected, subject, how-

[624] Act of July 4, 1884, 23 Stat. 69, 71; Act of July 4, 1884, 23 Stat. 73, 74; Act of February 18, 1888, 25 Stat. 35, 37; Act of May 14, 1888, 25 Stat. 140, 142; Act of May 30, 1888, 25 Stat. 162, 163; Act of June 26, 1888, 25 Stat. 205, 207; Act of June 21, 1890, 26 Stat. 170, 171; Act of June 30, 1890, 26 Stat. 184, 185–186; Act of September 26, 1890, 26 Stat. 485, 487; Act of February 24, 1891, 26 Stat. 783, 785; Act of March 3, 1891, 26 Stat. 844, 846; Act of February 27, 1893, 27 Stat. 487, 489; Act of February 27, 1893, 27 Stat. 492, 493; Act of March 1, 1893, 27 Stat. 524, 525–526; Act of December 21, 1893, 28 Stat. 22, 24; Act of August 4, 1894, 28 Stat. 229, 231; Act of April 6, 1896, 29 Stat. 87, 89; Act of January 29, 1897, 29 Stat. 502, 504; Act of March 23, 1898, 30 Stat. 341, 342. The provision in question is found in sec. 5 of each of the foregoing statutes.

[625] Act of January 16, 1889, sec. 5, 25 Stat. 647, 649 (White Earth band of Chippewas); Act of February 23, 1889, sec. 5, 25 Stat. 684, 685 (Yankton Indian Reservation); Act of March 2, 1896, sec. 5, 29 Stat. 40, 41 (Choctaw).

[626] Act of March 18, 1896, sec. 5, 29 Stat. 69, 71; Act of March 30, 1896, sec. 5, 29 Stat. 80, 82; Act of February 28, 1899, sec. 4, 30 Stat. 912, 913.

[627] Act of April 25, 1896, 29 Stat. 109 ("deposit with the treasury of the tribe to which the lands belong").

[628] Act of April 24, 1888, sec. 4, 25 Stat. 90, 91; Act of July 26, 1888, sec. 3, 25 Stat. 350, 351 (Puyallup); Act of March 2, 1889, sec. 2, 25 Stat. 1010 (Leech Lake and White Earth Indian Reservations); Act of February 20, 1893, 27 Stat. 468 (Puyallup); Act of July 18, 1894, sec. 2, 28 Stat. 112 (White Earth, Leech Lake, Chippewa, and Fond du Lac Reservations); Act of August 23, 1894, sec. 2, 28 Stat. 489 (Leech Lake, Chippewa, and Winnebagoshish Reservations); Act of March 28, 1896, 29 Stat. 77.

[629] Act of March 2, 1899, 30 Stat. 990, 992.

[630] Special acts applying to particular tribes make similar provisions for depositing proceeds of leases, etc., in the United States Treasury to the credit of the designated tribe. Act of April 15, 1912, 37 Stat. 85 (homesteaders' payments on Coeur d'Alene Reservation); Act of August 9, 1916, 39 Stat. 445 (sale of Kiowa town-site reserve); Act of May 23, 1908, 35 Stat. 268 (sale of Chippewa timber); Act of May 29, 1908, 35 Stat. 458 (sale of Spokane surplus lands). *Cf.* Act of February 18, 1909, 35 Stat. 636 (Kiowa, Comanche, and Apache); Act of June 17, 1910, 36 Stat. 533 (Cheyenne-Arapahoe).

[631] Act of February 28, 1891, sec. 3, 26 Stat. 795, 25 U. S. C. 397 (grazing leases); Act of August 15, 1894, sec 1, 28 Stat. 305, 25 U. S. C. 402 (farming leases); Act of July 3, 1926, 44 Stat. 894, 25 U. S. C. 402a (lease of irrigable land); Act of May 11, 1938, 52 Stat. 347, 25 U. S. C. 396a (mining leases).

[632] Sec. 1, 22 Stat. 590, as amended by Act of March 2, 1887, 24 Stat. 463; Act of May 17, 1926, sec. 1, 44 Stat. 560; Act of May 29, 1928, sec. 1, 45 Stat. 986, 991, 25 U. S. C. A. 155 (Supp.).

ever, to the limitations as to tribal funds imposed by section 27 of the Act of May 18, 1916 (Thirty-ninth Statutes at Large, page 159).[633]

That this act does not limit the power of an Indian tribe to receive payments based on use of tribal land was the view taken by the Department of the Interior in holding that tribes organized under section 16 of the Act of June 18, 1934, but not incorporated under section 17, might deposit such receipts in their own treasury. This conclusion was concurred in by the Comptroller General. The position of the Interior Department and of the Comptroller General is set forth in an Opinion of the Comptroller General dated June 30, 1937,[634] from which the following excerpts are taken:

> "* * * the act of May 27, 1926 (44 Stat. 560), amending the act of March 3, 1883 (22 Stat. 590), governs the use of revenues received by officials or employees of the Interior Department, and has no application to such payments as may lawfully be made to tribal officers under the provisions of the act of June 18, 1934, and constitutions adopted thereunder and approved by the Secretary of the Interior. The legislative history of the act of 1883 and the act of 1926 shows that these statutes were designed to control and regularize departmental receipts and accounts. They were not intended to regulate or to prohibit payments made directly to tribal officers.[635] * * *
>
> "The question of whether an organized tribe may enter into negotiations and agreements respecting the use of tribal land and requiring payment to a regularly bounded tribal officer, by virtue of such agreements, is primarily an administrative question to be determined by the Secretary of the Interior in consideration of such factors as the experience of the Indian tribe in handling funds, the amount of the funds involved, the extent of the activity undertaken by tribal officers or other members of the tribe in developing sources of tribal revenue, and similar factors.
>
> "Under Article IX, section 3 of the Constitution of the Gila River Pima-Maricopa Indian Community, those community lands which are not assigned to particular individuals for their private benefit or to groups of individuals operating as districts may be used by the community or may be leased by the council to members of the community, rentals to accrue to the community treasury to be used for the support of the helpless or other public purposes. This provision supersedes prior administrative regulations requiring all leases to be approved by the superintendent of the agency and further requiring that all payments made on the leases should be deposited in the United States Treasury. Under the present constitutional provisions the receipts in question are not revenues or receipts of the United States, the agreements from which they arise are not agreements approved by the superintendent and consequently such receipts are not affected by the act of May 17, 1926, or regulations issued thereunder, with respect to the accounting and deposit of tribal trust funds."
>
> * * * * *
>
> CASE NO. 3
>
> "Article VIII, section 3 of the Constitution of the Cheyenne River Sioux Tribe, above referred to, provides 'Tribal lands may be leased by the tribal council, with the approval of the Secretary of the Interior, for such periods of time as are permitted by law.' Nothing is said in this section or in any other section of the constitution as to whether rentals paid under such leases shall be paid to the disbursing agent of the reservation for deposit in the United States Treasury or to the bonded treasurer of the tribe for deposit in the tribal treasury. Presumably this is left, like the other terms of the lease, to the discretion of the Tribal Council and the Secretary of the Interior."
>
> * * * * *
>
> * * * The additional powers granted in the new act do not expressly mention the control by the tribe of their own finances, and there is, therefore, some doubt whether such authorization was intended. However, having in view the broad purposes of the act, as shown by its legislative history, to extend to Indians the fundamental rights of political liberty and local self-government, and there having been shown the fact that some of the power so granted by the new act would require the use of tribal funds for their accomplishment—being necessary incidents of such powers—and the further fact that the act of June 25, 1936, 49 Stat. 1928, provides that section 20 of the Permanent Appropriation Repeal Act, 48 Stat. 1233, shall not apply to funds held in trust for individual Indians, associations of individual Indians, or for Indian corporations chartered under the act of June 18, 1934, this office would not be required to object to the procedures suggested in your memorandum for the handling of tribal funds of Indian tribes organized pursuant to the said act of June 18, 1934.

Whether the conclusion in which the Secretary of the Interior and the Comptroller General agreed, in the case of an organized tribe, applies equally to an unorganized tribe remains uncertain. Implicit in this problem is the question of whether legislation such as the 1883 act has any application to funds in the possession of an Indian tribe. To this question we shall return in the final section of this chapter.

B. MANNER OF MAKING PAYMENTS TO TRIBE

Although a good deal of the foregoing discussion has dealt inevitably with the manner as well as the source of payments made to an Indian tribe, it remains to note the various general statutes which have regulated the manner of making such payments. Generally such statutes have been limited to details of payment not covered by the treaty or act under which the payment is due. But in certain cases grave questions have arisen as to the compatibility between the statutes creating the debt and the statutes determining the manner of its discharge.

For the most part, these statutes are designed to guard against fraud and unfairness in the distribution of funds and supplies. The Act of June 30, 1834,[636] contained two general provisions covering the payment of Indian annuities:

> SEC. 11. *And be it further enacted*, That the payment of all annuities or other sums stipulated by treaty to be made to any Indian tribe, shall be made to the chiefs of such tribe, or to such person as said tribe shall appoint; or if any tribe shall appropriate their annuities to the purpose of education, or to any other specific use, then to such person or persons as such tribe shall designate.
>
> SEC. 12. *And be it furtther enacted*, That it shall be lawful for the President of the United States, at the request of any Indian tribe to which any annuity shall be payable in money, to cause the same to be paid in goods, purchased as provided in the next section of this act. (P. 737.)

As subsequently amended,[637] these provisions are embodied in the United States Code in the following form:

> § 111. Payment of annuities and distribution of goods. The payment of all moneys and the distribution of all goods stipulated to be furnished to any Indians, or tribe of Indians, shall be made in one of the following ways, as the President or the Secretary of the Interior may direct:
>
> First. To the chiefs of a tribe, for the tribe.
>
> Second. In cases where the imperious interest of the tribe or the individuals intended to be benefited, or any treaty stipulation, requires the intervention of an agency, then to such person as the tribe shall appoint to receive such moneys or goods; or if several persons be appointed, then upon the joint order or receipt of such persons.

[633] In its code form, the reference is to "secs. 123 and 142 of this title."

[634] A–86599.

[635] Material in quotations is quoted by the Comptroller General from the Interior Department letter of submission.

[636] 4 Stat. 735.

[637] Act of March 3, 1847, sec. 3, 9 Stat. 203; Act of August 30, 1852, sec. 3, 10 Stat. 41, 56; Act of July 15, 1870, secs. 2 and 3, 16 Stat. 335, 360, 25 U. S. C. 111.

Third. To the heads of the families and to the individuals entitled to participate in the moneys or goods.

Fourth. By consent of the tribe, such moneys or goods may be applied directly, under such regulations, not inconsistent with treaty stipulations, as may be prescribed by the Secretary of the Interior, to such purposes as will best promote the happiness and prosperity of the members of the tribe, and will encourage able-bodied Indians in the habits of industry and peace.

Various other early statutes still in force require civil and military officers to certify to the actual delivery of goods owing to Indians,[638] authorize the President to require that payments and deliveries be made by the various superintendents,[639] permit payment of annuities in coin,[640] or goods (at the request of the tribe)[641] authorize Indians 18 years of age or over to receive annuities,[642] require the Secretary of the Interior to designate disbursing officers handling per capita payments,[643] extend these safeguards to the payment of judgment moneys,[644] require the presence of the "original package" when goods are distributed,[645] and require reports as to the status of tribal fiscal affairs generally,[646] reimbursable accounts,[647] and attendance records for the occasions when goods are distributed.[648]

The foregoing statutes are designed primarily to protect the Indians against lax or dishonest officialdom. A separate body of legislation is directed against immorality on the part of the Indians.

Section 3 of the Act of March 3, 1847,[649] as it appears today in title 25 of the United States Code, provides:

> § 130. Withholding of moneys or goods on account of intoxicating liquors. No annuities, or moneys, or goods, shall be paid or distributed to Indians while they are under the influence of any description of intoxicating liquor, nor while there are good and sufficient reasons leading the officers or agents, whose duty it may be to make such payments or distribution, to believe that there is any species of intoxicating liquor within convenient reach of the Indians, nor until the chiefs and headmen of the tribe shall have pledged themselves to use all their influence and to make all proper exertions to prevent the introduction and sale of such liquor in their country.

The Act of March 2, 1867,[650] still in force, forbids the payment of treaty funds to an Indian tribe which, since the last distribution of funds, "has engaged in hostilities against the United States, or against its citizens * * *." The Act of April 10, 1869, also still in effect, forbids delivery of goods pursuant to treaty to chiefs who have violated a treaty.[651]

We have already noted that the Act of June 22, 1874,[652] required the beneficiaries of obligations from the United States to perform useful labor in order to secure the sums or supplies owing them. At various times provisions were made that tribes at war with the United States should not receive annuities or appropriations. Thus, section 2 of the Appropriation Act of March 3, 1875,[653] provided:

> That none of the appropriations herein made, or of any appropriations made for the Indian service, shall be paid to any band of Indians or any portion of any band while at war with the United States or with the white citizens of any of the States or Territories. (P. 449.)

Section 1 of the same act, now embodied in the United States Code as section 129 of title 25, provides:

> The Secretary of the Interior is authorized to withhold, from any tribe of Indians who may hold any captives other than Indians, any moneys due them from the United States until said captives shall be surrendered to the lawful authorities of the United States.

A third type of statute governing federal payments and distributions is concerned with the issue of tribal payments versus individual payments. During the allotment period a persistent effort was made to individualize annuities and funds, for approximately the same reasons that created the desire to individualize land.

The Appropriation Act of March 3, 1877,[654] contained a direction to each agent having supplies to distribute—

> * * * to make out rolls of the Indians entitled to supplies at the agency, with the names of the Indians and of the heads of families or lodges, with the number in each family or lodge, and to give out supplies to the heads of families, and not the heads of tribes or bands, and not to give out supplies for a greater length of time than one week in advance: *Provided, however*, That the Commissioner of Indian Affairs may, in his discretion, issue supplies for a greater period than one week to such Indians as are peaceably located upon their reservation and engaged in agriculture.

The purpose of this provision was apparently to break down the tribal control that chiefs might exercise through the distribution of food and clothing and to transfer the prestige attached to such offices to the Indian agents.

The Act of March 2, 1907,[655] authorizes the Secretary of the Interior to apportion "tribal or trust funds on deposit in the Treasury of the United States" among the members of the tribe concerned.[656]

General segregation and distribution of tribal funds to members appearing on "final rolls" made by the Secretary of the Interior was authorized by section 28 of the Act of May 25, 1918,[657] and section 1 of the Act of June 30, 1919.[658] The repeal of the distribution features of the latter statute by the Act of June 24, 1938,[659] parallels the termination of the allotment policy.

---

[638] Act of June 30, 1934. 4 Stat. 735. 737, R. S. § 2088, 25 U. S. C. 112.

[639] Act of March 3, 1857, sec. 1, 11 Stat. 169, R. S. § 2089, 25 U. S. C. 113.

[640] Act of March 3, 1865, sec. 3, 13 Stat. 541, 561, R. S. § 2081, 25 U. S. C. 114.

[641] Act of June 30, 1834, sec. 12, 4 Stat. 735, 737, R. S. § 2082, 25 U. S. C. 115.

[642] Act of March 1, 1899, sec. 8, 30 Stat. 924, 947; 25 U. S. C. 116.

[643] Act of June 10, 1896, sec. 1, 29 Stat. 321, 336, 25 U. S. C. 117.

[644] Act of March 3, 1911, sec. 28, 36 Stat. 1058, 1077, 25 U. S. C. 118.

[645] Act of April 10, 1869, 16 Stat. 13, 39, R. S. § 2090, 25 U. S. C. 132.

[646] Act of March 3, 1911, sec. 27, 36 Stat. 1058, 1077, 25 U. S. C. 143.

[647] Act of April 4, 1910, sec. 1, 36 Stat. 269, 270, amended June 10, 1921, sec. 304, 42 Stat. 20, 24; 25 U. S. C. 145.

[648] Act of February 14, 1873, 17 Stat. 437, 463, R. S. § 2109, 25 U. S. C. 146.

[649] 9 Stat. 203, R. S. § 2087, 25 U. S. C. 130.

[650] 14 Stat. 492, 515, R. S. § 2100, 25 U. S. C. 127.

[651] 16 Stat. 13, 39, R. S. § 2101, 25 U. S. C. 138.

[652] 18 Stat. 146; made permanent by Act of March 3, 1875, sec. 3, 18 Stat. 449; 25 U. S. C. 137.

[653] 18 Stat. 420.

[654] Sec. 2, 19 Stat. 271, 293.

[655] 34 Stat. 1221, 25 U. S. C. 119. See Chapter 4, sec. 13; Chapter 10, sec. 4.

[656] Sec. 2 of this act provides for payments to helpless Indians. 35 Stat. 1221, amended by Act of May 18, 1916, 39 Stat. 128; 25 U. S. C. 121.

[657] 40 Stat. 561, 591, 25 U. S. C. 162 (segregation of funds). To the effect that the preparation of a "final roll" under congressional direction cannot, in the nature of the case, prevent a later Congress from authorizing a new roll, see Op. Sol. I. D., M.27759, January 22, 1935 (Creek). And see Chapter 4, sec. 14; Chapter 10, sec. 4.

[658] 41 Stat. 3, 9, 25 U. S. C. 163 (enrollment).

[659] 52 Stat. 1037, 25 U. S. C. 162, 162a. See Chapter 4, sec. 16; Chapter 10, sec. 4.

Other miscellaneous statutes relating to the handling of funds due from the United States to Indian tribes relate primarily to matters of accounting procedure and the enforcement of appropriation limitations.[660]

[660] R. S. § 2097, 25 U. S. C. 122 (Limitation on application of tribal funds); Act of May 18, 1916, sec. 27, 39 Stat. 123, 158, 25 U. S. C. A. 123 (Expenditure from tribal funds without specific appropriations); Act of April 13, 1926, 44 Stat. 242, 25 U. S. C. A. 123a (Supp.) (Tribal funds; use to purchase insurance for protection of tribal property); Act of May 9, 1938, sec. 1, 52 Stat. 291, 315, 25 U. S. C. A. 123b (Supp.) (Tribal funds for traveling and other expenses); Act of May 24, 1922, 42 Stat. 552, 575, 25 U. S. C. 124 (Expenditures from tribal funds of Five Civilized Tribes without specific appropriations); Act of June 30, 1919, sec. 17, 41 Stat. 3, 20, 25 U. S. C. 125 (Expenditure of moneys of tribes of Quapaw Agency); R. S. § 2092, 25 U. S. C. 131 (Advances to disbursing officers); Act of March 1, 1907, 34 Stat. 1015, 1016, 25 U. S. C. 134 (Appropriations for supplies available immediately); Act of March 3, 1875, 18 Stat. 420, 450, 25 U. S. C. 135 (Supplies distributed so as to prevent deficiencies); Act of July 1, 1898, sec. 7, 30 Stat. 571, 596, 25 U. S. C. 136 (Commutation of rations and other supplies); Act of March 1, 1907, 34 Stat. 1015, 1016, 25 U. S. C. 139 (Appropriations for subsistence); Act of March 1, 1907, 34 Stat. 1015, 1016, 25 U. S. C. 140 (Diversion of appropriations for employees and supplies); Act of January 12, 1927, sec. 1, 44 Stat. 934, 989, 25 U. S. C. 148 (Supp.) (Appropriations for supplies; transfer to Indian Service supply fund; expenditure).

SECTION 24. TRIBAL RIGHT TO EXPEND FUNDS

Since the United States and the Indian tribe have each an interest in tribal funds held in the Treasury of the United States, the normal method of disposing of such funds has been by common consent of the tribe and the Federal Government. So far as treaty funds are concerned, treaty provisions, many of which are still in force, embodied a common agreement concerning the disposition of tribal money. Following the treaty period, agreements with Indian tribes, ratified by act of Congress, served a similar purpose. In recent years various new formulae have made their appearance embodying, in one way or another, the agreement of the tribe and the United States concerning expenditure of tribal funds.

Judgment moneys awarded to the Blackfeet Indians by the Court of Claims have been made "available for disposition by the tribal council of said Indians, with the approval of the Secretary of the Interior, in accordance with the constitution and bylaws of the Blackfeet Tribe * * *."[661] Other statutes provided for the expenditure of tribal funds for objects designated or approved by the tribal council concerned.[662] Perhaps the earliest of such provisions is found in section 3 of the Appropriation Act of February 17, 1879,[663] providing for the diversion of various appropriations to alternative uses "within the discretion of the President, and with the consent of said tribes, expressed in the usual manner." This provision was repeated in subsequent appropriation acts[664] and made permanent by the Act of March 1, 1907.[665]

There is an implied agreement between federal and tribal authorities in acts authorizing the Secretary of the Interior to appropriate money for the expenses of tribal councils,[666] tribal delegates,[667] and tribal attorneys.[668]

There are, of course, a great number of statutes authorizing the expenditure of tribal funds without express reference to the wishes of the tribe,[669] and the problem of federal power to expend tribal funds without Indian consent is dealt with elsewhere.[670] It may be noted, however, that the omission of express reference to tribal consent in appropriation provisions referring to tribal funds does not necessarily imply the absence of such consent. In fact, many provisions for the appropriation of tribal funds are sought at the request of the tribe concerned, although no reference to this fact appears on the face of the statute.

The present state of the law with respect to the power of an Indian tribe to expend funds or dispose of other personal property held by the United States in trust for the tribe is that any such expenditure must be authorized by act of Congress.[671] The situation is analogous to that of a private trust, where the trustee must consent to expenditures by the beneficiary out of the trust fund. In the case of the trust funds of an Indian tribe, the power to determine the propriety of expenditures is vested in Congress and only in a very few cases has Congress delegated its power of decision to administrative authorities.[672]

The history of Indian appropriation legislation shows a continuous struggle between two principles: on the one hand, it is

[661] Joint Resolution of June 20, 1936, 49 Stat. 1568. Accord: Act of March 2, 1889, 25 Stat. 1012 (Yankton).

[662] Act of June 20, 1936, 49 Stat. 1548 (Crow); Act of March 1, 1929, 45 Stat. 1439 (Klamath); Act of May 31, 1933, sec. 1, 48 Stat. 108 (Pueblos).

[663] 20 Stat. 295, 315.

[664] See, for example, Act of May 11, 1880, sec. 5, 21 Stat. 114, 133.

[665] 34 Stat. 1015, 1016, 25 U. S. C. 140.

[666] Act of March 2, 1929, 45 Stat. 1496 (Crow); Act of June 1, 1938, 52 Stat. 605 (Klamath).

[667] Act of March 3, 1881, 21 Stat. 435, 453 (Miami, Peoria, Wea, Kaskaskia, and Piankeshaw); Joint Resolution of June 7, 1924, 43 Stat. 667 (Fort Peck); Joint Resolution of May 10, 1926, 44 Stat. 498 (Fort Peck); Act of June 14, 1926, 44 Stat. 741 (Klamath).

[668] Act of April 11, 1928, 45 Stat. 423 (Chippewa of Minnesota); Act of June 26, 1934, 48 Stat. 1216 (Nez Perce).

[669] See, for example, Act of March 3, 1873, 17 Stat. 627 (Nez Perce); Act of June 27, 1902, 32 Stat. 400 (Chippewa of Minnesota); Act of June 28, 1906, 34 Stat. 547 (Menominee); Act of May 26, 1920, 41 Stat. 625 (Five Civilized Tribes).

Expenditure from tribal funds for a wide diversity of purposes considered beneficial to the tribe are authorized in a vast number of statutes. See, for example, Act of January 12, 1877, 19 Stat. 221 (Osage).

The cost of various improvements upon tribal lands has been met out of tribal funds, sometimes with a provision that the cost of the improvement shall be repaid to the tribe by the individual Indian benefited. Act of February 21, 1921, sec. 2, 41 Stat. 1105, 1106 (Red Lake Indian Reservation).

Federal appropriations for improvements upon tribal lands have frequently been made reimbursable obligations against future tribal funds or against such funds as might arise from disposal of the lands improved. Act of July 8, 1916, 39 Stat. 353 (Quinialt Indian Reservation); Act of March 3, 1921, sec. 6, 41 Stat. 1355, 1357 (Fort Belknap); Act of February 14, 1923, 42 Stat. 1246 (Paiute); Act of February 9, 1925, 43 Stat. 819 (Chippewa).

Various other statutes authorize payments from tribal funds to individual members of the tribe who have particular claims upon tribal bounty. Act of April 29, 1902, 32 Stat. 177 (Choctaw-Chickasaw); Act of June 3, 1924, 43 Stat. 357 (Red Lake Indians); cf. Joint Resolution of February 11, 1890, 26 Stat. 669.

Certain tribal funds have been made available for loans to individual members of the tribe. Act of March 4, 1925, 43 Stat. 1301 (Crow); Act of May 15, 1935, 49 Stat. 244 (Crow).

Between 1916 and 1925 a number of statutes were enacted appropriating tribal funds, or federal funds, to be reimbursed out of future tribal funds, for roads, bridges, public schools, and other public improvements. Act of June 26, 1916, 30 Stat. 237 (Ponca); Act of August 21, 1916, 39 Stat. 521 (Spokane); Act of February 20, 1917, 39 Stat. 926 (Navajo); Act of June 7, 1924, 43 Stat. 607 (Navajo); Act of February 26, 1925, 43 Stat. 994 (Navajo).

[670] See Chapter 5, secs. 5B, 10.

[671] Funds other than trust funds may be expended without such authorization. See Chapter 5, sec. 10.

[672] *Cf.* 25 U. S. C. 139, 140.

insisted that Congress, in which is vested constitutional power over appropriations, must retain full control of the subject; on the other hand, it is argued that continuity, prudent foresight in the expenditure of funds, and true economy require the setting aside of tribal funds for definite purposes in a manner that will avoid the red tape and delays of reappropriation.[673]

Actual practice has always been a compromise between these two principles. In section 27 of the Act of May 18, 1916,[674] Congress provided:

> § 123. *Expenditure from tribal funds without specific appropriations.*—No money shall be expended from Indian tribal funds without specific appropriation by Congress except as follows: Equalization of allotments, education of Indian children in accordance with existing law, per capita and other payments, all of which are hereby continued in full force and effect: *Provided further*, That this shall not change existing law with reference to the Five Civilized Tribes.

To this list of purposes for which expenditures may be made from tribal funds by administrative authorities without specific congressional appropriation, a specific addition was made by the Act of April 13, 1926,[675] which declares:

> § 123a. *Tribal funds; use to purchase insurance for protection of tribal property.*—The funds of any tribe of Indians under the control of the United States may be used for payments of insurance premiums for protection of the property of the tribe against fire, theft, tornado, hail, earthquake, and other elements and forces of nature.

Interior Department appropriation acts usually contain, in addition to specific appropriations out of designated tribal funds for specific purposes, general appropriations of the following form:[676]

> Expenses of tribal councils or committees thereof (tribal funds): For traveling and other expenses of members of tribal councils, business committees, or other tribal organizations, when engaged on business of the tribes, including supplies and equipment, not to exceed $5 per diem in lieu of subsistence, and not to exceed five cents per mile for use of personally owned automobiles, and including not more than $25,000 for visits to Washington, District of Columbia, when duly authorized or approved in advance by the Commissioner of Indian Affairs, $50,000, payable from funds on deposit to the credit of the particular tribe interested.

Furthermore, as we have already noted, "miscellaneous revenues * * * not the result of the labor of any member of such tribe" are deposited in a fund peculiarly misnamed "Indian moneys, proceeds of labor," and are thereafter available for expenditure "in the discretion of the Secretary of the Interior, for the benefit of the Indian tribes, agencies, and schools on whose behalf they are collected * * *" subject to the limitations as to tribal funds imposed by section 27 of the Act of May 18, 1916.[677]

In view of the present state of the law, an Indian tribe seeking a particular disposition of "tribal funds" or "trust funds" in the Treasury of the United States, must request a specific congressional appropriation unless "Indian Moneys, Proceeds of Labor" are available *or* the purpose is one of the four purposes for which Congress has given the Secretary of the Interior permanent spending authority, *or* the purpose is one as to which the current Interior Department appropriation act vests temporary spending authority in that Department. Under any of these three exceptions administrative authority rather than congressional appropriation must be obtained.

These limitations upon the power of an Indian tribe to dispose of funds or other personal property in which it has an equitable interest do not extend to funds or personal property over which the tribe has full legal ownership, even though such funds or property are voluntarily deposited for safekeeping with a local superintendent and therefore technically under the Permanent Appropriation Repeal Act of June 26, 1934,[678] within the Treasury of the United States. The Act of June 25, 1936,[679] specifically provides:

> That section 20 of the Permanent Appropriation Repeal Act, approved June 26, 1934 (48 Stat. 1233), shall not be applicable to funds held in trust for individual Indians, associations of individual Indians, or for Indian corporations chartered under the Act of June 18, 1934 (48 Stat. 984).

Since funds so deposited by an incorporated tribe are not subject to congressional appropriation, it must be held *a fortiori* that funds not so deposited but retained by the tribe are not subject to congressional appropriations. All charters issued to incorporated tribes recognize that funds held in the treasury of an incorporated tribe are subject to disposition, in accordance with the limitations of the charter, by the corporation, and are not in any way subject to congressional appropriation. This conclusion may be based upon the narrow ground that section 17 of the Act of June 18, 1934, expressly authorizes a chartered tribe to "dispose of property * * * real and personal," but it seems more satisfactory to place the conclusion upon the broader ground that the various statutes relating to appropriations of "tribal funds" and "trust funds" use these words in a technical sense, as terms of art, to refer to a well-understood category of funds which are held in the Treasury of the United States to the credit of the tribe pursuant to some law or treaty, and that, therefore, these limitations are utterly inapplicable to funds in the actual possession of the tribe itself.

This view is in accord with the historic fact that Congress has never presumed to interfere with the expenditure of funds held in tribal treasuries, even when the collection of such funds by tribal authorities is regulated by specific legislation requiring reports to Congress by a tribal treasurer.[680]

The difference between the power of an Indian tribe to dispose of personal property and its power over real property may be summed up in a sentence: A tribe may not validly alienate realty except with the consent of the Federal Government, given by Congress or by an official duly authorized by Congress to consent to particular forms of alienation; on the other hand, a tribe has complete power of disposition over tribal personal property, except in so far as such property has been removed from its control and placed in the possession of the Federal Government pursuant to some law or treaty.

Among the limitations voluntarily assumed by Indian tribes

---

[673] In other fields of Government, the public purpose corporation has been created to facilitate businesslike handling of appropriations, and this same objective was a major factor in the scheme of tribal incorporation established by the Act of June 18, 1934, 48 Stat. 984, 25 U. S. C. 461 *et seq.*

[674] 39 Stat. 123, 159, 25 U. S. C. A. 123 (Supp.) (incomplete in original edition). On the basis of this statute the Comptroller General has held that contracts with attorneys for payment of fees out of tribal funds should not be approved by the Secretary of the Interior in the absence of express statutory authorization. Comptroller's Decisions A. 24931, November 8, 1928; A. 27759, July 1, 1929; A. 29173, May 8, 1930; A. 34858, January 26, 1931; A. 45091, October 20, 1932; A. 81210, December 2, 1936; A. 44289, October 11, 1932. The Interior Department takes the position, in view of the Comptroller General's Opinion of June 30, 1937, discussed *supra*, that these decisions do not apply to funds in the treasury of an organized tribe. Memo. Sol. I. D., January 18, 1938.

[675] 44 Stat. 242, 25 U. S. C. A. 123a.

[676] Act of May 9, 1938, 52 Stat. 291, 315.

[677] 39 Stat. 123, 158, 25 U. S. C. A. 155 (Supp.). And see sec. 23, *supra*. See also Memo. Sol. I. D. January 24, 1936.

[678] 48 Stat. 1224.

[679] 49 Stat. 1928.

[680] See, for example, Act of February 28, 1901, 31 Stat. 819 (Seneca lease rentals).

with respect to the disposition of tribal moneys and other personalty, we may briefly note:

(1) Limitations contained in tribal constitutions.[681]

(2) Limitations contained in tribal charters.[682]

(3) Limitations contained in tribal loan agreements.[683]

(4) Limitations contained in tribal trust agreements.[684]

The grant of funds to Indian tribes for particular uses, under the Emergency Appropriation Act of April 8, 1935,[685] raised additional questions as to the powers of an Indian tribe in handling funds. In response to the question put by the Commissioner of Indian Affairs whether an Indian tribe might "use the proceeds of rentals of land improved through rehabilitation grants to finance additional construction projects or to meet general tribal expenses or to make per capita payments," the Solicitor of the Interior Department ruled:[686]

> 4. When money has been granted to an Indian tribe to be used for a particular purpose, e. g., the development of springs on tribal land or the construction of houses, the Presidential letter above set forth imposes no duty on the tribe when once the money has been properly expended. The fact that such expenditures may increase tribal income from the issuance of leases or permits on tribal land, or tribal income from other enterprises, does not subject a part of that income, or all of it, to any lien on the part of the Federal Government. Such income may, therefore, be received and disbursed by the Indian tribe in any manner not prohibited by Federal law or by the constitution, bylaws, or charter of the tribe, unless the tribe has specifically agreed to use such rentals or income for a specific purpose. It is, of course, within the power of a tribe to agree, through its representative council or other officers, that certain income available to the tribe shall be used only for designated purposes not inconsistent with law.

Following this determination, the Indian Office entered into trust agreements with various Indian tribes under which the Indian tribe became trustee of the funds granted and the proceeds thereof for the benefit of needy Indians entitled to the benefits of the act in question.[687]

---

[681] See, for example, the following provisions of the constitution and bylaws of the Hualapai tribe, approved December 17, 1938:

> Art. VI, Section 1. The Hualapai Tribal Council shall have the following powers:
>
> * * * * *
>
> (e) To deposit all Tribal Council Funds to the credit of the Hualapai Tribe in an Individual Indian Moneys Account, Hualapai Tribe of the Truxton Canon Agency, such funds to be expended only upon the recommendation of the Tribal Council in accordance with a budget having prior approval of the Secretary of the Interior.
>
> * * * * *
>
> BYLAWS OF THE HUALAPAI TRIBE OF THE HUALAPAI RESERVATION, ARIZONA
>
> ARTICLE 1—Duties of Officers.
>
> * * * * *
>
> SEC. 4. *Treasurer.*—The Treasurer shall accept, receive, receipt for, preserve, and safeguard all funds in the custody of the Tribal Council. He shall deposit all funds in such depository as the Council shall direct and shall make and preserve a faithful record of such funds and shall report on all receipts and expenditures and the amount and nature of all funds in his possession and custody, at such times at requested by the Tribal Council. He shall not pay out or disburse any funds in his possession or custody, except in accordance with a resolution duly passed by the Council. The books and records of the Treasurer shall be audited at least once each year by a competent auditor employed by the Council and at such other times as the Council or the Commissioner of Indian Affairs may direct. The Treasurer shall be required to give a bond satisfactory to the Tribal Council and to the Commissioner of Indian Affairs. Until the Treasurer is bonded, the Tribal Council may make such provision for the custody and disbursement of funds as shall guarantee their safety and proper disbursement and use.

[682] See, for example, the following provisions from sec. 5 of the corporate charter of the Confederated Salish and Kootenai tribes of the Flathead Reservation, ratified April 25, 1936:

> 5. The tribe, subject to any restrictions contained in the Constitution and laws of the United States, or in the constitution and bylaws of the said tribe, shall have the following corporate powers, in addition to all powers already conferred or guaranteed by the tribal constitution and bylaws:
>
> * * * * *
>
> (b) To purchase, take by gift, bequest, or otherwise, own, hold, manage, operate, and dispose of property of every description, real and personal, subject to the following limitations:
>
> * * * * *
>
> 5. No distribution of corporate property to members shall be made except out of net income.
>
> * * * * *
>
> (d) To borrow money from the Indian credit fund in accordance with the terms of section 10 of the act of June 18, 1934 (48 Stat. 984), or from any other governmental agency, or from any member or association of members of the tribe, and to use such funds directly for productive tribal enterprises, or to loan money thus borrowed to individual members or associations of members of the tribe: *Provided*, That the amount of indebtedness to which the tribe may subject itself shall not exceed $100,000, except with the express approval of the Secretary of the Interior.
>
> * * * * *
>
> (f) To make and perform contracts and agreements of every description, not inconsistent with law or with any provisions of this charter, with any person, association, or corporation, with any municipality or any county, or with the United States or the State of Montana, including agreements with the State of Montana for the rendition of public services and including contracts with the United States or the State of Montana or any agency of either for the development of water-power sites within the reservation: *Provided*, That all contracts involving payment of money by the corporation in excess of $5,000 in any one fiscal year, or involving the development of water-power sites within the reservation, shall be subject to the approval of the Secretary of the Interior or his duly authorized representative.
>
> (g) To pledge or assign chattels or future tribal income due or to become due to the tribe under any notes, leases, or other contracts, whether or not such notes, leases, or contracts are in existence at the time: *Provided*, That such agreements of pledge or assignment shall not exend more than 10 years from the date of execution and shall not cover more than one-half the net tribal income in any 1 year: *And provided further*, That any such agreement shall be subject to the approval of the Secretary of the Interior or his duly authorized representative.
>
> (h) To deposit corporate funds, from whatever source derived, in any National or State bank to the extent that such funds are insured by the Federal Deposit Insurance Corporation, or secured by a surety bond, or other security, approved by the Secretary of the Interior; or to deposit such funds in the postal-savings bank or with a bonded disbursing officer of the United States to the credit of the tribe.

[683] See Chapter 12, sec. 6.

[684] See Chapter 12, sec. 6.

[685] 49 Stat. 115.

[686] Op. Sol. I. D., M.28316, March 18, 1936.

[687] See Chapter 12, sec. 6.

CHAPTER 16

INDIAN TRADE

TABLE OF CONTENTS

SECTION 1. HISTORY OF LEGISLATION

Trade was one of the inevitable activities that arose from contact between Indians and whites, two distinct races, engaged in unlike activities and possessed of different types of goods.

To supervise trade with the Indian tribes, and to discourage individual avarice under conditions which presented unlimited opportunities for corruption and extortion, colonial governments continuously from early pioneer days licensed traders dealing with the Indian tribes [1] and the Congress of the United States since its first session has frequently legislated [2] with respect to Indian trade by virtue of its constitutional authority to regulate commerce with the Indian tribes.[3]

Provisions with respect to Indian trade were included in many treaties [4] between the Indian tribes and the United States.

By the Act of July 22, 1790,[5] the right to license traders was vested in the President or officers approved by him. All unauthorized persons [6] trading with the Indians were liable to forfeiture of their goods. By this act, Congress adopted the plan of leaving trading wholly to private enterprise and for a few years adhered exclusively to this policy. In 1796, however, the President was authorized to establish governmentally owned and operated trading posts along the far-flung western and southern frontiers or in Indian country within the limits of the United States.[7]

Trade for profit was not contemplated under this act and goods were sold to the Indians at cost. The trader in charge was an agent of the United States, paid by the Government and under oath to refrain directly or indirectly from personal business or commercial relations with any Indian or Indian tribe.

In 1822,[8] however, trading posts were closed. Accounts were rendered, and the system of governmental ownership and operation permanently abandoned. Indian trade again became for the most part private business under governmental supervision and license.

Until 1802 laws with reference to both private trading and Government trading posts were, by their terms, temporary. A permanent act to regulate private trade was enacted on March 30, 1802.[9]

[1] The irregularities and improper conduct of the traders received the attention of the General Court of the colony of Massachusetts in 1629. (Records of Mass., p. 48.) A proclamation of George III set forth the claim of the Crown to regulate trade and licensed traders (American Archives, 4th Series, 1774–1775, vol. I, Col. 174). On congressional power over trade, see Chapter 5, sec. 3.

[2] Act of July 22, 1790, 1 Stat. 137; Act of March 1, 1793, 1 Stat. 329; Act of April 18, 1796, 1 Stat. 452; Act of May 19, 1796, 1 Stat. 469; Act of March 3, 1799, 1 Stat. 743; Act of March 30, 1802, 2 Stat. 139; Act of April 21, 1806, 2 Stat. 402; Act of March 2, 1811, 2 Stat. 652; Act of June 30, 1834, 4 Stat. 729, R. S. §§ 2127–2138; Act of August 15 1876, 19 Stat. 176, 200, 25 U. S. C. 261; Act of July 31, 1882, 22 Stat. 179, R. S. § 2133, 25 U. S. C. 264; Act of March 3, 1901, 31 Stat. 1058, 1066, 25 U. S. C. 262; Act of March 3, 1903, 32 Stat. 982, 1009, 25 U. S. C. 262; Act of May 29, 1908, 35 Stat. 444.

[3] *United States* v. *Bridleman*, 7 Fed. 894 (D. C. Ore. 1881); *Green* v. *Menominee Tribe of Indians in Wisconsin*, 233 U. S. 558 (1914); *Worcester* v. *Georgia*, 6 Pet. 515 (1832); *Buster* v. *Wright*, 135 Fed. 947 (C. C. A. 8, 1905); *United States* v. *Cisna*, 25 Fed. Cas. No. 14795 (C. C. Ohio 1835); *United States* v. *Douglas*, 190 Fed. 482 (C. C. A. 8, 1911). See Chapter 5, sec. 3.

[4] See Chapter 3, sec. 3B(2).

[5] 1 Stat. 137. By the provisions of this statute, any proper person could obtain a license for 2 years to trade with the Indians upon giving bond for faithful observance of governmental regulations. The Act of March 1, 1793, 1 Stat. 329, was a statute similar in its provisions with an additional prohibition against purchase of horses in Indian country without a special license.

The Act of May 19, 1796, 1 Stat. 469, defined, according to existing treaties, "Indian country" where trading licenses were required. For subsequent definitions see Chapter 1, sec. 3.

[6] A provision relative to requiring licenses to trade with Indians was considered as interfering with a treaty of amity, commerce, and navigation between Great Britain and the United States, dated November 19, 1794, 8 Stat. 116. A Presidential proclamation of February 29, 1796, declared that trade regulations were not applicable to British subjects.

[7] Act of April 18, 1796, 1 Stat. 452. This act was a temporary measure succeeded by similar statutes enacted April 21, 1806, 2 Stat. 402; March 2, 1811, 2 Stat. 652; March 3, 1815, 3 Stat. 239; March 3, 1817, 3 Stat. 363; April 16, 1818, 3 Stat. 428; March 3, 1819, 3 Stat. 514; March 4, 1820, 3 Stat. 544; March 3, 1821, 3 Stat. 641. The Act of April 18, 1796, 1 Stat. 452, after two or three rejections, was enacted upon the insistence of President Washington. He recognized trade as a force for the maintenance of peaceful Indian relations. The congressional debates on this statute reveal a blending of benevolent desire to protect the Indians from the cupidity and vicious avarice of more commercially experienced whites and Yankee shrewdness, anxious to prevent British and Canadian interests from reaping increasing profits from lucrative Indian trade. Furthermore, the vast outlay of capital required to establish even a portion of the needed posts, presented too large a venture for private capital. See Annals of Congress, 4th Cong., 1st sess., 1796–97, pp. 229, 230.

[8] Act of May 6, 1822, 3 Stat. 682.

> * * * in relation to the general (trading) establishment * * * it has been a losing institution, owing, it is presumable, to adventitious circumstances, originating in our late belligerent state (War of 1812), and not growing out of any defect in the organization or government of the trade. From the first operation of this traffic up to December, 1809, it sustained a loss * * *. Since that period the trade has been more successful, it having yielded a profit * * * after covering a loss * * * which accrued in consequence of the capture of several trading posts by the enemy during the late war. (Annals of Congress, 15th Cong., 1st sess., 1817–18 pt. I, p. 801.)

[9] 2 Stat. 139. Construed in *United States* v. *Douglas*, 190 Fed. 482 (C. C. A. 8, 1911); *United States* v. *Cisna*, 25 Fed. Cas. No. 14795 (C. C. Ohio 1835); *Worcester* v. *Georgia*, 6 Pet. 515 (1832); *United States* v. *Leathers*, 26 Fed. Cas. No. 15581 (D. C. Nev. 1879); *Bates* v. *Clark*, 95 U. S. 204, 206 (1877).

This statute [10] made it unlawful for any citizen or other person to reside in Indian towns or hunting camps as a trader or to carry on commercial intercourse with Indians without a license. Suitable trading sites, it was later provided, were to be designated by Indian agents.[11]

On June 30, 1834, Congress passed an act revising and repealing the former legislation on the subject and particularly defining the term "Indian country" for the purposes of that act.[12]

Congress has not seen fit to regulate Indian traders outside of "Indian country." [13] By the Act of August 15, 1876,[14] the Commissioner of Indian Affairs was vested with sole authority to license traders to the Indian tribes and to make requisite rules and regulations. By the Act of July 31, 1882,[15] requirements for a license to trade were extended to include all but "an Indian of the full-blood." The Act of March 3, 1901,[16] as amended by the Act of March 3, 1903,[17] provides that a person desiring to trade with Indians on any Indian reservation must satisfy the Commissioner of Indian Affairs that he is "a proper person to engage in such trade." In addition, from time to time, Congress enacted appropriation or regulatory acts in connection with Indian trade.[18]

[10] This act was supplemented by the Act of April 29, 1816, 3 Stat. 332, so as to restrict issuance of trading licenses to citizens of the United States and to prohibit the transportation of foreign goods for purposes of Indian trade; the Act of May 6, 1822, 3 Stat. 682, amended administrative provisions of this act.

[11] Act of May 25, 1824, 4 Stat. 35.

[12] Act of June 30, 1834, 4 Stat. 729. On definitions of Indian country, see Chapter 1, sec. 3.

[13] Trade carried on from barges in streams adjacent to a reservation was held not to be trading in Indian country, *United States* v. *Taylor*, 33 F. 2d 608 (D. C. W. D. Wash. 1929), rev'd on other grounds, 44 F. 2d 531 (1930), cert. den. 283 U. S. 820 (1931).

In a state case privately owned land within the limits of a reservation to which Indian title had been extinguished was not considered as Indian country, so that traders located thereon were not required to be licensed before trading with Indian tribes, *Rider* v. *LaClair*, 138 Pac. 3 (1914).

United States v. *Certain Property*, 25 Pac. 517, 518–519 (1871), also held that no license is required to trade with Indians outside of Indian country. The opinion in this case stated that no other class of ordinary federal legislation is so full of pains, penalties, and forfeitures as that which regulates trade with the Indians. Indian country is the place, and no other, to which all pains and penalties are applied.

[14] 19 Stat. 176, 200, 25 U. S. C. 261.

[15] 22 Stat. 179, R. S. § 2133, 25 U. S. C. 264.

[16] 31 Stat. 1058, 1066 (Osage Reservation), 25 U. S. C. 262.

[17] 32 Stat. 982, 1009, 25 U. S. C. 262. This act amended the proviso in the 1901 act so as to make it applicable to all reservations.

[18] Acts appropriating funds for detecting and punishing violators of the Intercourse Acts of Congress; Act of March 3, 1893, 27 Stat. 572; Act of March 2, 1895, 28 Stat. 910; Act of June 4, 1897, 30 Stat. 11; Act of July 1, 1898, 30 Stat. 597; Act of March 3, 1899, 30 Stat. 1074; Act of June 6, 1900, 31 Stat. 280; Act of March 3, 1901, 31 Stat. 1133. The Treaty of May 7, 1864, with the Chippewas of the Mississippi and the Pillager and Lake Winnebageshish bands of Chippewa Indians in Minnesota, 13 Stat. 693, 695, Art. IX, provided that "no * * * trader * * * shall be * * * licensed, * * * who shall not have a family residing with them * * * whose moral habits * * * shall be reported upon annually by a board of visitors; * * *." A similar provision is found in the Act of February 28, 1877, 19 Stat. 254, 256, Art. 7 (Sioux Nation and Northern Arapahoe and Cheyenne Indians).

SECTION 2. PRESENT LAW

At the present time the Commissioner of Indian Affairs continues to exercise sole power and authority in the appointment of traders to the Indian tribes.[19] Under existing regulations,[20] any person who proves to the satisfaction of the Commissioner that he is a proper person may secure a trader's license.[21] Ordinarily the Commissioner will not issue a license without the approval of the tribal council. Bond with approved sureties [22] must accompany the application.[23] Any person other than an Indian of full blood [24] who attempts to reside in the Indian country [25] or on any Indian reservation as a trader without a license, or to introduce goods or trade therein, forfeits all merchandise offered for sale to the Indians or found in his possession and is liable to a penalty of $500. Licenses are granted for 1 year,[26] and, if at the end of that time the Commissioner is satisfied that all rules and regulations have been observed, a new license may be issued.[27] Introduction of liquor into the Indian country is statutory ground for the revocation of a trader's license.[28]

In order to prevent the acquisition of a share of the trade without approval of the Indian Service, Congress established the present rule that no appointed Indian trader could sell, share, or convey, in whole or in part, his right to trade with the Indians.[29] A sale of a license, being void, has been held not to

[19] Act of August 15, 1876, 19 Stat. 176, 200; Act of March 3, 1901, 31 Stat. 1058, 1066; Act of March 3, 1903, 32 Stat. 982, 1009; 25 U. S. C. 261–262.

[20] Regulations Governing Licensed Indian Traders, 25 C. F. R., pt. 276; Regulations Governing Traders on Navajo, Zuni, and Hopi Reservations, *ibid.*, pt. 277.

[21] See Act of August 15, 1876, sec. 5, 19 Stat. 176, 200; Act of March 3, 1901, 31 Stat. 1058, 1066; Act of March 3, 1903, sec. 10, 32 Stat. 982, 1009; 25 U. S. C. 261, 262. The view was expressed in 2 Op. A. G. 402 (1830), that no citizen of the United States can obtain exemption from laws of United States by entering Indian Territory and becoming an Indian by adoption and thereby claim the privilege of trading without a license. In 16 Op. A. G. 403 (1879), it was stated that a trader at a military post in Indian country must be licensed and licenses cannot be issued by military authorities.

[22] The Act of July 26, 1866, sec. 4, 14 Stat. 255, 280, which required traders to give a bond to the United States in the sum of not less than $5,000 nor more than $10,000 was incorporated in sec. 2128, Revised Statutes, but omitted from the United States Code of 1926. Sec. 2128 was repealed by the Act of March 3, 1933, 47 Stat. 1428. The regulations require a bond in the sum of $10,000 with at least two approved sureties or a bond of a qualified surety company, 25 C. F. R. 276.10.

[23] 25 U. S. C. 264. The words "of the full blood" and the words "on any Indian reservation" were added to the Revised Statutes by the Act of July 31, 1882, 22 Stat. 179.

Sections 261 and 262 of title 25, United States Code, giving the Commissioner of Indian Affairs authority to regulate trade with Indians, and requiring any person desiring to trade with the Indians on any Indian reservation to do so under the regulations of the Commissioner, are general in scope and would include the Indians themselves. However, section 264 of title 25 excludes from the enforcement provisions Indians of the full blood. Section 264 is the only statute which provides a method of enforcement of the laws governing trade with the Indians. Since the laws and regulations are unenforceable against Indians of the full blood, such Indians cannot be said to be required to operate under the regulations. Congress has evidently left to the tribe the regulation of traders who are Indians, restricting the term "Indian" for this purpose to persons with full Indian blood. The tribe itself could require the full-blood Indian traders to abide by the Federal laws and regulations. (Memo. Sol. I. D., April 29, 1940.)

[24] See fn. 13, *supra*.

[25] R. S. §§ 2127–2138. The Act of July 31, 1882, 22 Stat. 179, amended R. S. § 2133, 25 U. S. C. 264, by excluding the Five Civilized Tribes from its application. It also made nonapplicable to these tribes its provision that unlicensed white clerks could not be hired by Indian traders. The forfeiture provision has been regarded by the Department of Justice as not permitting seizure for forfeiture of an automobile used by an unlicensed trader to transport merchandise. D. J. File No. 90–2–7–858, Memorandum by O. J. R., July 13, 1939.

[26] Under the special regulations for the Navajo, Hopi, and Zuni Reservations, a 3-year term is allowed. See fn. 20.

[27] 25 C. F. R. 276.11–277.11.

[28] 25 U. S. C. 246, derived from Act of March 15, 1864, 13 Stat. 29, R. S. § 2140.

[29] *United States* v. *26 Buffalo Robes*, 1 Mont. 489 (1872).

constitute consideration for a note.[30] A contract by a holder of a trading license to pay a third person a portion of the proceeds of the trade, in consideration of the third person actually running the business, was considered by the courts as spurious, a subterfuge, violating the spirit and intent of the trading statutes.[31] The court, however, approved an arrangement whereby a licensed trader formed a partnership and the nonlicensed member of the partnership secured a permit to live on the reservation, to sell to the Indians and to share in the profits.[32]

While the general policy is to encourage resident ownership of Indian trading posts, in some instances the lack of local capital necessitates absentee ownership. At the present time, as a matter of actual practice, a license may be held by a resident manager instead of by a nonresident owner.[33]

To insure integrity of conduct on the part of persons employed in the Indian Service and to protect the Indians, no license is issued to any person employed in Indian affairs by the United States.[34]

A license to trade is not required in Alaska. The Act of June 30, 1834,[35] was not extended, *ex proprio vigore*, to that Territory upon its cession to the United States.[36]

The court, in *United States* v. *Seveloff*,[37] in 1872, decided that this new possession was not Indian country, as defined and limited by the Trade and Intercourse Act. After this decision, on March 3, 1873,[38] Congress extended to Alaska the provisions of sections 21 and 22 of this statute, relating principally to the interdiction of liquor traffic. The presumption seems clear that by singling out, mentioning, and extending two sections only, the intention of Congress was to withhold or exclude from the Territory all other sections of the act. Apparently Alaska was intended to be considered "Indian country," in connection with Indian trade, only to the extent of that specifically prohibited traffic.

By the regulations of the Department of the Interior, products sold to the Indians are required to be good and merchantable, and the prices must be fair and reasonable.[39] The President, whenever in his opinion public interest requires, is authorized to prohibit the introduction of goods, or any particular article, into the country of any tribe.

For many years the sale to the Indians of means of warfare has been restricted and regulated.[40] At the present time the Secretary of the Interior may adopt such rules as may be necessary to prohibit the sale of arms and ammunition in any district occupied by uncivilized or hostile Indians.[41] Arms and ammunition may not be sold to the Indians by traders except upon permission of a superintendent of an Indian agency who has clearly established that the weapons are for a lawful purpose.[42]

Congress has provided that no person other than an Indian may, within Indian country, purchase or receive of an Indian in the way of barter, trade, or pledge a gun, trap, or other article commonly used in hunting, any instrument of husbandry or cooking utensil of the kind commonly obtained by Indians in their intercourse with whites, or any article of clothing, except skins or furs.[43]

It is against the rules laid down by the Commissioner of Indian Affairs to sell tobacco, cigars, and cigarettes to minor Indians under 18 years of age.[44] Likewise, liquor traffic is suppressed.[45]

Sale of specified harmful drugs is illegal.[46] Gambling is prohibited in trading posts.[47] Trading on Sunday presents sufficient cause for revocation of a license.[48]

At the present time credit is given at the trader's risk.[49] Traders may not accept pawns or pledges of personal property by Indians to obtain credit or loans, and Indians may not be paid in store orders, in tokens, or in any other way than in money.[50]

To protect the Indians, traders are forbidden to buy, trade for, or have in their possession any annuity or other goods which have been purchased or furnished by the Government for the use or welfare of the Indians.[51] The business of a trader must be conducted on premises specified in the license.[52] Tribal or individual lands used by traders must be leased in the usual manner.[53]

No trader will be allowed to sublet or rent buildings which he occupies without the approval of the Commissioner of Indian Affairs[54] and, where the tribe is organized, without the consent of the tribal council.

The personal property, including the stock in trade of a licensed trader, is ordinarily subject to state taxation, although the privilege of doing business with Indians would appear to be exempt from state taxation.[55] As an Indian trader is not an officer of the Government, and as his goods are his own private property, which he may sell indiscriminately to Indians or non-Indians, a state tax on the personal property of a licensed trader is not a tax on an agency of the Federal Government, or an interference with the regulation of commerce with the Indian tribes.[56]

---

[30] *Hobbie* v. *Zaepffel*, 17 Neb. 536, 23 N. W. 514 (1885).

[31] *Gould* v. *Kendall*, 15 Neb. 549, 19 N. W. 483 (1884).

[32] *Dunn* v. *Carter*, 30 Kan. 294, 1 Pac. 66 (1883).

[33] Some traders' stores have licensed resident managers who are not the owners.

[34] 25 C. F. R. 276.5–277.4.

[35] 4 Stat. 729.

[36] *Waters* v. *Campbell*, 29 Fed. Cas. No. 17264 (C. C. Ore. 1876); *Kie* v. *United States*, 27 Fed. 351 (C. C. Ore. 1886); *In re Sah Quah*, 31 Fed. 327 (D. C. Alaska 1886); 16 Op. A. G. 141 (1878).

[37] 27 Fed. Cas. No. 16252 (D. C. Ore. 1872).

[38] 17 Stat. 530.

[39] 25 C. F. R. 276.22.

[40] Act of August 5, 1876, 19 Stat. 216, R. S. § 2136, 25 U. S. C. 266.

[41] 25 U. S. C. 266; R. S. §§ 467, 2136.

[42] 25 C. F. R. 276.8.

[43] 25 U. S. C. 265, R. S. § 2135. For other restrictions on trade see Chapter 5, sec. 3.

[44] 25 C. F. R. 276.17.

[45] See Chapter 17, Indian Liquor Laws.

[46] 25 C. F. R. 276.19.

[47] *Ibid.*, 276.21.

[48] *Ibid.*, 276.20.

[49] In *Tinker* v. *Midland Valley Co.*, 231 U. S. 681 (1914), it was held that a provision in the Indian Appropriation Act of June 21, 1906, 34 Stat. 325, 366, made it unlawful for traders on the Osage Indian Reservation to give credit to any individual Indian head of a family for any amount exceeding 75 per centum of his next quarterly allowance. Treaties with various tribes bear ample evidence of the grasp traders acquired by issuance of credit to their customers. A large portion of the money from the sale of ceded land passed directly to the trader for debts, and these debts in several instances necessitated cessions of land. See Chapter 8, sec. 7C.

[50] 25 C. F. R. 276.24.

[51] *Ibid.*, 276.16.

[52] *Ibid.*, 276.14.

[53] See Chapter 5, secs. 9B and 11E; Chapter 11, sec. 5; and Chapter 15, sec. 19.

[54] 25 C. F. R. 276.15.

[55] See Chapter 13, secs. 4 and 5.

[56] *Thomas* v. *Gay*, 169 U. S. 264 (1898). This case involved a tax on cattle owned by a lessee of Indian land. The court stated: "* * * it is not perceived that local taxation, by a State or Territory, of property of others than Indians would be an interference with Congressional power." Accord: *Wagoner* v. *Evans*, 170 U. S. 588 (1898); *Catholic Missions* v. *Missoula County*, 200 U. S. 118 (1906); *Surplus Trading Co.* v. *Cook*, 281 U. S. 647 (1930). In the *Surplus Trading Co.* case the opinion states: "Such reservations are part of the State within which they lie and her laws, civil and criminal, have the same force therein as elsewhere within her limits, save that they can have only restricted appli-

In view of the fact that Congress has conferred upon the Commissioner of Indian Affairs exclusive jurisdiction with respect to Indian traders[57] and since tribal constitutions generally provide that ordinances dealing with traders shall be subject to departmental review, tribal tax levy may not be made upon licensed traders unless such tax is authorized by the Commissioner of Indian Affairs.[58]

cation to the Indian wards. Private property within such a reservation, if not belonging to such Indians, is subject to taxation under the laws of the State" (at 651). Some state cases in accord are: *Moore* v. *Beason*, 51 Pac. 875 (1898); *Cosier* v. *McMillan*, 56 Pac. 965 (1899); *Noble* v. *Amoretti*, 71 Pac. 879 (1903). Contra. *Foster* v. *Board*, 7 Minn. 140 (1862).

[57] 25 U. S. C. 261-262, derived from Act of August 15, 1876, 19 Stat. 200, and the Act of March 3, 1903 (Osage Reservation), 31 Stat. 1058, 1066, as amended by Act of March 3, 1903, 32 Stat. 982, 1009.

[58] 55 I. D. 14, 46 (1934); 1 Op. A. G. 645 (1824). As the Treaty of November 28, 1785, with the Cherokees, 7 Stat. 18, and the Treaty of July 2, 1791, with the Cherokee Nation, 7 Stat. 39, provided that the United States have the sole and exclusive right of regulating trade with the Indians, the Attorney General herein expressed the opinion that the Cherokees had no right to impose a tribal tax on traders. 17 Op. A. G. 134 (1881) and 18 Op. A. G. 34 (1884) upheld the validity of permit laws of Choctaws and Chickasaws imposing a fee upon licensed traders under the provision of the treaties of June 22, 1855, 11 Stat. 611 and April 28, 1866, 14 Stat. 769 between the Choctaw and Chickasaw and the United States. Also see Chapter 23, sec. 3.

Cf. Crabtree v. *Madden*, 54 Fed. 426 (C. C. A. 8, 1893). The opinion in this case held a tax imposed by the Creek tribe upon licensed traders could not be enforced by the United States courts but recognized the power of the Department of the Interior to remove from Indian Territory any licensed trader who failed to pay taxes as lawfully levied by Indian tribes. *Morris* v. *Hitchcock*, 194 U. S. 384 (1904). On tribal power to tax, see Chapter 7, sec. 7.

CHAPTER 17

INDIAN LIQUOR LAWS

TABLE OF CONTENTS

SECTION 1. HISTORICAL BACKGROUND

Restrictions on traffic in liquor among the Indians began in early colonial times, in a few of the colonies.[1] The Indians themselves at various times sought to curb their consumption of strong drink,[2] and it is worthy of note that the first federal control measure[3] was enacted, at least in part, in response to the verbal plea of an Indian chief to President Thomas Jefferson on January 4, 1802.[4]

On January 28, 1802, President Jefferson called upon Congress to take some step to control the liquor traffic with the Indians in the following language:

> These people [the Indians] are becoming very sensible of the baneful effects produced on their morals, their health, and existence, by the abuse of ardent spirits: and some of them earnestly desire a prohibition of that article from being carried among them. The Legislature will consider whether the effectuating that desire would not be in the spirit of benevolence and liberality, which they have hitherto practised toward these, our neighbors, and which has had so happy an effect towards conciliating their friendship. It has been found, too, in experience, that the same abuse gives frequent rise to incidents tending much to commit our peace with the Indians.[5]

Congress forthwith adopted legislation which authorized the President of the United States "to take such measures, from time to time, as to him may appear expedient to prevent or restrain the vending or distributing of spirituous liquors among all or any of the said Indian tribes, anything herein contained to the contrary thereof notwithstanding."[6]

With control over treaty-making, the licensing of traders, and the management of Government trading houses, the Executive had ample power to control the situation without a general Indian prohibition law, and 30 years passed before such a law was enacted.[7]

The considerations of benefit to the Indians and protection to the whites thus suggested in Jefferson's message have since continued to influence the deliberations of Congress in its efforts to suppress the traffic in liquor with the Indians.[8]

[1] Mass. Colonial Laws, 1660–72 (Whitmore 1889), p. 161; The Charters of the Province of Pennsylvania and City of Philadelphia (Franklin 1742), c. 106, p. 41; Acts of the General Assembly of the Province of New Jersey, 1753–61 (Nevill 1761), sec. 2, p. 125.

[2] See F. W. Hodge, Handbook of American Indians, H. Doc. No. 926, pt. 2, 59th Cong., 1st sess. (1905–6), p. 799; American State Papers, vol. 7 (Indian Affairs, class II, vol. I) (1789–1815), p. 655.

[3] Act of March 30, 1802, sec. 21, 2 Stat. 139.

[4] In the course of his talk to the President, the Indian chief, Little Turtle, among other things, said:

> * * * But, father, nothing can be done to advantage unless the great council of the Sixteen Fires, now assembled, will prohibit any person from selling any spirituous liquors among their red brothers.
>
> * * * * * *
>
> Father: Your children are not wanting in industry; but it is the introduction of this fatal poison which keeps them poor. Your children have not that command over themselves, which you have, therefore, before anything can be done to advantage, this evil must be remedied.
>
> Father: When our white brothers came to this land, our forefathers were numerous and happy; but, since their intercourse with the white people, and owing to the introduction of this fatal poison, we have become less numerous and happy. (American State Papers, vol. 7 (Indian Affairs, class II, vol. I) (1789–1815) p. 655.)

[5] American State Papers, vol. 7 (Indian Affairs, class II, vol. I) (1789–1815) p. 653.

[6] Act of March 30, 1802, sec. 21, 2 Stat. 139, 146. An excellent account of the development of Indian liquor laws from 1802 to 1911 will be found in Ann. Cas. 1912 B, 1090, 1091.

[7] See fn. 35, *infra*.

[8] 23 Cong. Rec., pt. 3, p. 2187 (1892); 29 Cong. Rec., pt. 2, pp. 893–899 (1897). The view that liquor control aids in maintaining the peace is supported in the Annual Report of Louis C. Mueller, Chief Special Officer of the Office of Indian Affairs, March 28, 1939. The contention that practically every Indian war since the discovery of America has been caused, directly or indirectly, by the liquor traffic is put forward by William E. Johnson, The Federal Government and the Liquor Traffic (1911) pp. 183–238.

SECTION 2. SOURCES AND SCOPE OF FEDERAL POWER RE LIQUOR TRAFFIC

The power of the Federal Government over traffic in intoxicating liquors with the Indians may be said to be derived from several sources.[9] Among these may be mentioned, first, the clauses in the Constitution investing Congress with authority to regulate commerce with the Indian tribes,[10] and to dispose of and make all needful rules and regulations respecting the ter-

[9] In *United States Express Co.* v. *Friedman*, 191 Fed. 673 (C. C. A. 8, 1911), rev'g 180 Fed. 1006 (D. C. W. D. Ark. 1910), the power is said to be derived from five sources, as follows:

> First, the treaty-making power. Second, the power to regulate interstate commerce. Third, the power to regulate commerce with the Indian tribes. Fourth, the ownership, as sovereign, of lands to which the Indian title has not been extinguished. Fifth, the plenary authority arising out of its guardianship of the Indians as an alien but dependent people. (At p. 674.)

See also *Worcester* v. *Georgia*, 6 Pet. 515 (1832), where Chief Justice Marshall intimates that the authority of the Federal Government to control "all intercourse" with the Indians is traceable to the clauses in the Constitution relative to war and peace, of making treaties and of regulating commerce with foreign nations and among the several states and with the Indian tribes. For a further discussion of the sources and limits of federal power, see Chapter 5, sec. 1.

[10] U. S. Const., Art. I, sec. 8, cl. 3.

ritory and other property of the United States;[11] second, the clause in the Constitution relative to the making of treaties;[12] and third, the recognized relation of tribal Indians to the United States.[13] The first, of course, relates to the powers of Congress; the second to those of the treaty-making department, and the third, the broadest and most important of all, refers to the powers of both.

The treaty-making power has been exercised, in conjunction with the congressional power to carry out the terms of treaties by legislative enactments, to impose prohibitions against the liquor traffic by direct treaties with the Indians, as was done, for example, in the Treaty of October 2, 1863,[14] with the Chippewas, and by the Convention with Russia of April 5–17, 1824.[15] Treaties and legislative enactments of the United States are of equal dignity, so that the restrictions against intoxicants in the former have the force of law.[16] Similar in effect to treaties with the Indian tribes are "agreements," which were resorted to after the policy of dealing with the Indians by treaty was abandoned.[17] These agreements, however, received their legal force from acts of Congress ratifying and adopting them. They are exemplified by the agreements with the Nez Perce Indians and the Yankton Sioux.[18]

The power to regulate commerce with the Indian tribes is really the constitutional backbone of federal legislation against traffic in liquor with the Indians. The courts have upheld this power with respect to tribal Indians, and the Indian country.[19] The power over commerce with the Indians is distinct from that over interstate commerce in that traffic with the Indian tribes and may be regulated regardless of state lines. Thus, the Indian commerce power covers traffic which may be wholly within one state.[20]

It is to be noted that regulation under this power is not limited to transactions in which a tribe acts as an entity but extends to transactions with individual members of each tribe.[21] The Supreme Court has stated this principle in the following terms:

> Commerce with foreign nations, without doubt, means commerce between citizens of the United States and citizens or subjects of foreign governments, as individuals. And so commerce with the Indian tribes, means commerce with the individuals composing those tribes.[22]

In connection with the power to regulate commerce with the Indian tribes there exists also the authority granted by the Constitution to do all things necessary and proper by way of carrying out its provisions.[23] Pursuant to this power and the power over the territory and other property belonging to the United States,[24] the Federal Government has imposed liquor restrictions on lands ceded to it by the Indians when these lands adjoined Indian country.[25] The purpose of this measure was to prevent sale of liquor on the boundaries of the land retained by the Indians. Except for these extensions of the Indian liquor laws to "buffer" areas the states would have had the exclusive police power thereon. Such extensions have been repeatedly upheld by the United States Supreme Court.[26] The power lasts only so long as Indians are present on the retained reservation lands and remain wards of the Government.[27] In 1934, Congress withdrew liquor restrictions from the "buffer" lands.[28]

Congress may also enact such measures to aid in the enforcement of the prohibition statutes, as are "directed at the means and methods used in the accomplishing of the violation of the

---

[11] U. S. Const., Art. IV, sec. 3, cl. 2.

[12] U. S. Const., Art. II, sec. 2, cl. 2.

[13] See *United States* v. *Kagama*, 118 U. S. 375, 383–384 (1886). See also *United States* v. *Nice*, 241 U. S. 591 (1916); *United States* v. *Sandoval*, 231 U. S. 28 (1913), rev'g 198 Fed. 539 (D. C. N. M. 1912); *United States* v. *McGowan*, 302 U. S. 535 (1938), rev'g 89 F. 2d 201 (C. C. A. 9, 1937), aff'g *United States* v. *One Chevrolet Sedan*, 16 F. Supp. 453 (D. C. Nev. 1936).

[14] Ratified with amendments March 1, 1864; amendments assented to April 12, 1864; proclaimed May 5, 1864, 13 Stat. 667. Other treaty provisions containing prohibitions against the sale or introduction of liquor are: Treaty of April 5, 1824, with Russia, 8 Stat. 302, Art. 5; Treaty of May 15, 1846, with the Comanche, I-on-i, Ana-da-ca, Cadoe, Lepan, Long-wha, Keechy, Tah-qah, Carro, Wichita, and Wacoe Tribes of Indians, 9 Stat. 844, Art. XII; Treaty of July 23, 1851, with the See-see-toan and Way-pay-toan bands of Dakota or Sioux Indians, 10 Stat. 949, Art. 5; Treaty of August 5, 1851, with Med-ay-wa-kan-toan and Wah-pay-koo-tay bands of Dakota or Sioux Indians, 10 Stat. 954, Art. VI; Treaty of May 30, 1854, with the united tribes of Kaskaskia and Peoria, Piankeshaw and Wea Indians, 10 Stat. 1082, Art. 10; Treaty of October 17, 1855, with Blackfoot and other tribes of Indians, 11 Stat. 657, Art. 13; Treaty of February 11, 1856, with the Menomonee tribe of Indians, 11 Stat. 679, Art. 3; Treaty of April 19, 1858, with the Yancton Tribe of Sioux or Dacotah Indians, 11 Stat. 743, Art. XII; Treaty of October 14, 1864, with the Klamath tribe of Indians, Moadoc tribe of Indians and the Yahooskin band of Snake Indians, 16 Stat. 707, Art. IX.

[15] Ratified with amendments March 1, 1864; amendments assented to April 12, 1864; proclaimed May 5, 1864, 13 Stat. 667.

[16] U. S. Const., Art. VI, cl. 2; Willoughby, The Constitutional Law of the United States (2d ed. 1929), sec. 303, p. 548. See Chapter 3, sec. 1.

[17] Act of March 3, 1871, 16 Stat. 544, 566. See Chapter 3, sec. 6.

[18] See Act of August 15, 1894, 28 Stat. 286. The selling or giving away of intoxicants upon ceded territory is forever prohibited by Art. XVII of the Yankton agreement (p. 318). Introduction of intoxicants is prohibited for 25 years by Art. IX of the Nez Perce agreement (p. 330).

[19] *United States* v. *Forty-three Gals. Whiskey*, 108 U. S. 491 (1883); s. c. 93 U. S. 188 (1876); *Ex parte Webb*, 225 U. S. 663 (1912); *United States* v. *Wright*, 229 U. S. 226 (1913); *United States* v. *Sandoval*, 231 U. S. 28 (1913); *Perrin* v. *United States*, 232 U. S. 478 (1914); *United States* v. *Shaw-Mux*, 27 Fed. Cas. No. 16268 (D. C. Ore. 1873); *Farrell* v. *United States*, 110 Fed. 942 (C. C. A. 8, 1901); *United States* v. *Wirt*, 28 Fed. Cas. No. 16745 (D. C. Ore. 1874). In *Matter of Heff*, 197 U. S. 488 (1905), the Court held that a citizen allottee was not subject to federal Indian liquor laws. This holding governed the courts from 1905 to 1911, was ignored in *Hallowell* v. *United States*, 221 U. S. 317 (1911), and expressly overruled by *United States* v. *Nice*, 241 U. S. 591 (1916).

[20] F. H. Cooke, The Commerce Clause of the Federal Constitution (1908), pp. 62–64; 1 Willoughby, The Constitutional Law of the United States (2d ed. 1929), sec. 226, pp. 397–398; *Dick* v. *United States*, 208 U. S. 340 (1908); *United States* v. *Forty-three Gallons of Whiskey*, 93 U. S. 188 (1876), rev'g. 25 Fed. Cas. No. 15136 (D. C. Minn. 1874).

[21] *Browning* v. *United States*, 6 F. 2d 801 (C. C. A. 8, 1925), cert. den. 269 U. S. 568 (1925); *United States* v. *Shaw-Mux*, 27 Fed. Cas. No. 16268 (D. C. Ore. 1873); *United States* v. *Nice*, 241 U. S. 591 (1916); *United States* v. *Holliday*, 3 Wall. 407 (1865); *United States* v. *Flynn*, 25 Fed. Cas. No. 15124 (C. C. Minn. 1870).

[22] *United States* v. *Holliday*, *supra*, p. 417. Also see Chapter 5, sec. 3.

[23] U. S. Const., Art. I, sec. 8, cl. 18.

[24] U. S. Const., Art. IV, sec. 3, cl. 2.

[25] Act of December 19, 1854, 10 Stat. 598 (Chippewa); Act of March 1, 1895, 28 Stat. 693 (Indian Territory); Act of March 20, 1906, 34 Stat. 80 (Kiowa, Comanche, and Apache); Act of June 16, 1906, 34 Stat. 267 (Oklahoma, Indian Territory, New Mexico, and Arizona); Act of May 6, 1910, 36 Stat. 348 (Yakima); Act of June 20, 1910, 36 Stat. 557 (New Mexico and Arizona); Act of May 11, 1912, 37 Stat. 111 (Omaha); Act of July 22, 1912, 37 Stat. 197 (Colville); Act of February 14, 1913, 37 Stat. 675 (Standing Rock); Act of May 31, 1918, 40 Stat. 592 (Fort Hall); Act of June 4, 1920, 41 Stat. 751 (Crow).

[26] *Perrin* v. *United States*, 232 U. S. 478 (1914); *Dick* v. *United States*, 208 U. S. 340 (1908); *United States* v. *Forty-three Gallons of Whiskey*, 108 U. S. 491 (1883).

[27] *Perrin* v. *United States*, *supra*.

[28] Act of June 27, 1934, 48 Stat. 1245, 25 U. S. C. 254.

statute."[29] Statutes providing for search and seizure, and libel and forfeiture have been uniformly upheld.[30] As possession of intoxicants in Indian country leads to infractions of the Indian liquor laws, Congress may forbid possession.[31]

[29] *Commercial Investment Trust* v. *United States*, 261 Fed. 330, 333 (C. C. A. 8, 1919).

[30] Act of March 2, 1917, 39 Stat. 969, 970, was upheld in *Commercial Investment Trust* v. *United States*, *supra*; and *United States* v. *One Buick Roadster Automobile*, 244 Fed. 961 (D. C. E. D. Okla. 1917).

[31] Acts of May 25, 1918, 40 Stat. 561, 563, and June 30, 1919, 41 Stat. 3, 4, held valid in the following cases: *Kennedy* v. *United States*, 265 U. S. 344 (1924), question certified from *Kennedy* v. *United States*, 2 F. 2d 597 (C. C. A. 8, 1924); *Reynolds* v. *United States*, 48 F. 2d 762 (C. C. A. 10, 1931); *Morris* v. *United States*, 19 F. 2d 131 (C. C. A. 8, 1927); *Sharpe* v. *United States*, 16 F. 2d 876 (C. C. A. 8, 1926) aff'g *Ex parte Sharpe*, 13 F. 2d 651 (D. C. N. D. Okla. 1926); *Lucas* v. *United States*, 15 F. 2d 32 (C. C. A. 8, 1926); *Buchanan* v. *United States*, 15 F. 2d 496 (C. C. A. 8, 1926); *Renfro* v. *United States*, 15 F. 2d 991 (C. C. A. 8, 1926).

SECTION 3. EXISTING PROHIBITIONS AND ENFORCEMENT MEASURES

Pursuant to the foregoing federal powers, Congress has evolved a system of prohibitions and enforcement measures against traffic in liquor with the Indians, and in the Indian country.[32]

The most important of these measures is the Act of July 23, 1892,[33] as amended in 1938 to read as follows:[34]

> Any person who shall sell, give away, dispose of, exchange, or barter any malt, spirituous, vinous liquor, including beer, ale, and wine, or any ardent or other intoxicating liquor of any kind whatsoever, or any essence, extract, bitters, preparation, compound, composition, or any article whatsoever, under any name, label, or brand, which produces intoxication to any Indian to whom an allotment of land has been made while the title to the same shall be held in trust by the Government, or to any Indian who is a ward of the Government under charge of any Indian superintendent or agent, or to any Indian, including mixed bloods, over whom the Government, through its departments, exercises guardianship, and any person who shall introduce or attempt to introduce any malt, spirituous, or vinous liquor, including beer, ale, and wine, or any ardent or intoxicating liquor of any kind whatsoever into the Indian country, which term shall include any Indian allotment while the title to the same shall be held in trust by the Government, or while the same shall remain inalienable by the allottee without the consent of the United States, shall be punished for the first offense by imprisonment for not more than one year, and by a fine of not more than $500, and for the second offense and each offense thereafter by imprisonment for not more than five years, and by a fine of not more than $2,000: *Provided, however*, That the person convicted shall be committed until fine and costs are paid: *And provided further*, That first offenses under this section may be prosecuted by information, but no person convicted of a first offense under this section shall be sentenced to imprisonment in a penitentiary or required to perform hard labor. It shall be a sufficient defense to any charge of introducing or attempting to introduce ardent spirits, ale, beer, wine, or intoxicating liquors into the Indian country that the acts charged were done under authority, in writing, from the War Department or any officer duly authorized thereunto by the War Department. All complaints for the arrest of any person or persons made for violation of any of the provisions of this section shall be made in the county where the offense shall have been committed, or if committed upon or within any reservation not included in any county, then in any county adjoining such reservation; but in all cases such arrests shall be made before any United States court commissioner residing in such adjoining county, or before any magistrate or judicial officer authorized by the laws of the State in which such reservation is located to issue warrants for the arrest and examination of offenders by section 1014 of the Revised Statutes [18 U. S. C. 591] as amended. And all persons so arrested shall, unless discharged upon examination, be held to answer and stand trial before the court of the United States having jurisdiction of the offense.[35]

This statute defines two distinct prohibitions. The first is directed against any disposition of intoxicants to any Indian who has an allotment, title to which is restricted or held in trust by the Federal Government, or to any Indian who is a ward or under the guardianship of the United States.[36] The Indians included may be located in Indian country or outside of it.[37] Indians as well as whites and others may commit this crime,[38] but apparently an Indian purchasing or otherwise receiving illicit liquor is not offending against this law.[39]

The person disposing of liquor to an Indian allottee or ward is not excused because he did not know the recipient was an

[32] For a definition of "Indian country" see Chapter 1, sec. 3. For the purpose of the liquor laws it means all lands and reservations, Indian title to which has not been extinguished. The leading liquor cases applying this definition are *United States* v. *Le Bris*, 121 U. S. 278 (1887); *Bates* v. *Clark*, 95 U. S. 204 (1877). See also the Act of June 27, 1934, c. 846, 48 Stat. 1245, 25 U. S. C. 254.

[33] 27 Stat. 260.

[34] Act of June 15, 1938, 52 Stat. 696, 25 U. S. C. 241. This act expressly repealed similar provisions in the Act of January 30, 1897, 29 Stat. 506.

[35] Act of June 15, 1938, 52 Stat. 696, 25 U. S. C. 241. The first general statutory prohibition against liquor in Indian country was approved July 9, 1832, c. 174, 4 Stat. 564. Two years later Congress first included in sec. 20 of the Act to Regulate Trade and Intercourse with the Indian Tribes of June 30, 1834, 4 Stat. 729, the substance from which the above act was derived. By amendment of February 13, 1862, c. 24, 12 Stat. 338, Indians affected by the law were defined as those under charge of a superintendent or agent, and penalties for selling and introducing were made the same.

The Act of March 15, 1864, c. 33, 13 Stat. 29, added the words "or circuit court" giving that court jurisdiction concurrently with the district courts.

As the substance of this law was enacted in the R. S. § 2139, Indians "in the Indian country" were excepted from its penalties. This exception was repealed by the Act of February 27, 1877, 19 Stat. 240, 244, which was an act to correct errors in the Revised Statutes.

The words "ale, beer, wine, or intoxicating liquors of any kind" were added by the Act of July 23, 1892, 27 Stat. 260. This broadening was made necessary by decisions holding beer not to be within the earlier definition. See *Sarlis* v. *United States*, 152 U. S. 570 (1894); *In re McDonough*, 49 Fed. 360 (D. C. Mont. 1892).

Again, in the Act of January 30, 1897, 29 Stat. 506, the enumeration of liquors was extended to read as in the 1938 amendment above.

The acts of 1892 and 1897 were read together. See *Edwards* v. *United States*, 5 F. 2d 17 (C. C. A. 8, 1925); *Morgan* v. *Ward*, 224 Fed. 698 (C. C. A. 8, 1915), cert. den. 239 U. S. 648 (1915).

The sections of the 1938 amendment which are new are the penalty provisions and the provisions allowing prosecution by information for the first offense.

[36] Wardship of the Indians and termination of wardship is discussed in sec. 9 of Chapter 8. It may be noted here, however, that the granting of citizenship did not take citizen Indians out of the working of the liquor laws. *United States* v. *Nice*, 241 U. S. 591 (1916) [overruling *Matter of Heff*, 197 U. S. 488 (1905)]; *Katzenmeyer* v. *United States*, 225 Fed. 523 (C. C. A. 7, 1915); *Mosier* v. *United States*, 198 Fed. 54 (C. C. A. 8, 1912), cert. den. 229 U. S. 619 (1913). The privilege of buying liquor is not one of the privileges of citizenship. *Mulligan* v. *United States*, 120 Fed. 98 (C. C. A. 8, 1903); *Farrell* v. *United States*, 110 Fed. 942 (C. C. A. 8, 1901).

[37] *United States* v. *Belt*, 128 Fed. 68 (D. C. M. D. Pa. 1904).

[38] *United States* v. *Miller*, 105 Fed. 944 (D. C. Nev. 1901); *United States* v. *Shaw-Mux*, 27 Fed. Cas. No. 16268 (D. C. Ore. 1873).

[39] *Lott* v. *United States*, 205 Fed. 28 (C. C. A. 9, 1913) (under Alaska liquor law). But see Acts of May 25, 1918, 40 Stat. 561, 563, and June 30, 1919, 41 Stat. 34, prohibiting possession.

Indian or a "ward of the Government," or because he mistook him for a Mexican or white.[40]

The second prohibition defined in the statute is directed against the introduction or attempt to introduce any intoxicants into Indian country.[41] To offend against the ban on introducing liquor it is enough that one is the means of carrying the liquor within the limits of Indian country knowing of its presence and transportation.[42] The person so introducing alcohol need not have any interest in it.[43] Nor need he have any intent to introduce, that is, he need not know that he has entered Indian country.[44] But an intent is necessary to constitute the crime of *attempting* to introduce liquor into Indian country.[45] In both the introduction and the attempt to introduce, the destination, intentionally or unwittingly, must be the Indian country. The mere transportation through Indian country is not within this act when the destination is beyond.[46]

As the courts repeatedly held that possession of liquor in Indian country was not alone sufficient to show introduction,[47] Congress in 1916 enacted the following law to bolster this weak spot:

> * * * possession by a person of intoxicating liquors in the country where the introduction is prohibited by treaty or Federal statute shall be prima facie evidence of unlawful introduction.[48]

In 1918, as an additional aid to enforcement, Congress provided that *possession* in Indian country shall be an independent offense.[49] The statute reads:

> * * * possession by a person of intoxicating liquors in the Indian country where the introduction is or was prohibited by treaty or Federal statute shall be an offense and punished in accordance with the provisions of the Acts of July twenty-third, eighteen hundred and ninety-two (Twenty-seventh Statutes at Large, page two hundred and sixty), and January thirtieth, eighteen hundred and ninety-seven (Twenty-ninth Statutes at Large, page five hundred and six.[50]

The elements of this offense are possession, which means physical control and power to dispose of liquor, knowledge of possession,[51] and location of the liquor within the limits of Indian country.[52] Apparently, knowledge of possession in another is not enough, nor is drinking from the bottle of another enough.[53] But where the accused is found with a full liquor bottle which he breaks, it has been held that these facts are evidence of possession, knowledge, and control.[54] The wording of this statute, though not as detailed in defining prohibited liquors as the Act of June 15, 1938,[55] is apparently as broad, since it covers any intoxicant.[56]

The early Trade and Intercourse Act of 1834 contained a measure to facilitate enforcement of the liquor prohibitions, which is still in force. It provided:

> That if any person whatever shall, within the limits of the Indian country, set up or continue any distillery for manufacturing ardent spirits [beer and other intoxicating liquors named, in the Act of January thirtieth, eighteen hundred and ninety-seven (Twenty-ninth Statutes at Large, page five hundred and six)],[57] he shall forfeit and pay a penalty of one thousand dollars; and it shall be the duty of the superintendent of Indian affairs, Indian agent, or sub-agent, within the limits of whose agency the same shall be set up or continued, forthwith to destroy and break up the same * * *.[58]

Other enforcing acts, including provisions for search, seizure, and forfeiture of goods and vehicles, have been enacted from time to time as conditions required. This legislation also had its inception in the Trade and Intercourse Acts of May 6, 1822,[59] and of June 30, 1834,[60] and their modified provisions are as follows:

> SEC. 2140. If any superintendent of Indian affairs, Indian agent, or sub-agent, or commanding officer of a military post, has reason to suspect or is informed that any white person or Indian is about to introduce or has introduced any spirituous liquor or wine [beer and other intoxicating liquors named in the Act of January thirtieth, eighteen hundred and ninety-seven (Twenty-ninth Statutes at large, page five hundred and six)],[61] into the Indian country in violation of law, such superintendent, agent, sub-agent, or commanding officer, may cause the boats, stores, packages, wagons, sleds, and places of deposit of such person to be searched; and if any such liquor is found therein, the same, together with the boats, teams, wagons, and sleds used in conveying the same, and also the goods, packages, and peltries of such person, shall be seized and delivered to the proper officer, and shall be proceeded against, by libel in the proper court, and forfeited, one-half to the informer and the other half to the use of the United States; and if such person be a trader, his license shall be revoked and his bond put in suit. It shall moreover be the duty of any person in the service of the United States, or of any Indian, to take and destroy any ardent spirits or wine found in the Indian country, except such as may be introduced therein by the War Department. In all cases arising under this and the preceding section [27 Stat. 260 and 29 Stat. 506, as amended by 52 Stat. 696], Indians shall be competent witnesses.[62]

Under this statute federal enforcement officers have the right to search and seize the boats, stores, packages, wagons, etc., without warrant. But federal officers may not make unreasonable searches as they are subject to the Fourth Amendment to the United States Constitution. And the Act of August 27,

---

[40] *Scheff* v. *United States*, 38 F. 2d 263 (C. C. A. 8, 1929); *Feeley* v. *United States*, 236 Fed. 903 (C. C. A. 8, 1916); *Lott* v. *United States*, *supra*; *United States* v. *Stofello*, 8 Ariz. 461, 76 Pac. 611 (1904). Officers of the Indian Service, however, are instructed to resolve doubts in favor of the vendor in cases involving Indians resembling other nationalities.

[41] An Indian may be convicted of introducing liquor into Indian Territory, *Clairmont* v. *United States*, 225 U. S. 551 (1912). See also fn. 30, *supra*.

[42] *Archard* v. *United States*, 212 Fed. 146 (C. C. A. 8, 1914).

[43] *Ibid.*

[44] *United States* v. *Leathers*, 26 Fed. Cas. No. 15581 (D. C. Nev. 1879).

[45] *United States* v. *Stephens*, 12 Fed. 52 (D. C. Ore. 1882).

[46] *Butterfield* v. *United States*, 241 Fed. 556 (C. C. A. 8, 1917); *Townsend* v. *United States*, 265 Fed. 519 (C. C. A. 8, 1920); *United States* v. *Tadish*, 211 Fed. 490 (D. C. Ariz. 1913).

[47] *Collier* v. *United States*, 221 Fed. 64 (C. C. A. 8, 1915); *Chambliss* v. *United States*, 218 Fed. 154 (C. C. A. 8, 1914); *Parks* v. *United States*, 225 Fed. 369 (C. C. A. 8, 1915); *Cecil* v. *United States*, 225 Fed. 368 (C. C. A. 8. 1915); *Goff* v. *United States*, 257 Fed. 294 (C. C. A. 8, 1919).

[48] Act of May 18, 1916, 39 Stat. 123, 124, 25 U. S. C. 245.

[49] *Brown* v. *United States*, 265 Fed. 623 (C. C. A. 8, 1920), holds this act constitutional.

[50] Act of May 25, 1918, 40 Stat. 561, 563; and the Act of June 30, 1919, 41 Stat. 3, 4, 25 U. S. C. 244.

[51] *Buchanan* v. *United States*, 15 F. 2d 496 (C. C. A. 8, 1926); *Colbaugh* v. *United States*, 15 F. 2d 929 (C. C. A. 8, 1926).

[52] *Aldridge* v. *United States*, 67 F. 2d 956 (C. C. A. 10, 1933).

[53] *Colbaugh* v. *United States*, *supra*.

[54] *Morrison* v. *United States*, 6 F. 2d 809 (C. C. A. 8, 1925).

[55] 52 Stat. 696, 25 U. S. C. 241.

[56] *Sharp* v. *United States*, 16 F. 2d 876 (C. C. A. 8, 1926), aff'g. *Ex parte Sharp*, 13 F. 2d 651 (D. C. N. D. Okla. 1926).

[57] The bracketed clause was added to this act by the Act of May 18. 1916, 39 Stat. 123, 124, 25 U. S. C. 252.

[58] Act of June 30, 1834, 4 Stat. 729, 732, 733, 25 U. S. C. 251.

[59] 3 Stat. 682.

[60] 4 Stat. 729.

[61] The bracketed clause was made to apply to this act by the Act of May 18, 1916, 39 Stat. 123, 124, 25 U. S. C. 252.

[62] Enacted as it now appears in the R. S. § 2140, which is derived from the Act of March 15, 1864, 13 Stat. 29. This act changed the provisions of the Act of June 30, 1834, by omitting necessity for search under regulations provided by the President, and by making it a duty to destroy illicit liquor found in Indian country.

1935,[63] imposes criminal liability for unreasonable search of dwellings without a warrant. In case of such unreasonable search the officer, civil or military, also becomes civilly liable.[64] The early decision of the United States Supreme Court in *American Fur Co.* v. *United States*,[65] determined that this act gave authority to search and seize only in Indian country.[66] As to what might be seized and subject to libel action there was some doubt. The courts decided that the goods forfeited should be only those which were the property of the offender, and forfeited only to the extent of his interest.[67] When the automobile became perfected and widely used, it began to play an important role in the illicit liquor trade. The Government sought to subject it to libel proceedings under the foregoing statute. The courts determined that automobiles were not known to the legislators who passed the law in 1834, and that automobiles did not fit into the enumeration of wagons, boats, and sleds.[68] Congress quickly remedied this defect by the Act of March 2, 1917, which provided:

> That automobiles or any other vehicles or conveyances used in introducing, or attempting to introduce, intoxicants into the Indian country, or where the introduction is prohibited by treaty or Federal statute, whether used by the owner thereof or other person, shall be subject to the seizure, libel, and forfeiture provided in section twenty-two hundred and forty of the Revised Statutes of the United States.[69]

This act is broader than the search and seizure provisions in the Act of 1834 in these respects: (1) Search and seizure may be made *outside* Indian country when the vehicle taken is used in the attempt to introduce liquor into Indian country,[70] (2) automobiles and any other vehicles are included, (3) "the thing involved [automobile or other vehicle], and not its owner is the offender * * *."[71] The vehicle is forfeited without regard to ownership.[72] Finally, it should be noted that these enforcement measures apply solely to Indian liquor laws and cannot be used as a basis for search, seizure, and libel of goods, vehicles, etc., used in any other illicit traffic.[73]

The passage of the Eighteenth Amendment, the National Prohibition Act, and repeal of both had no effect to supplant or repeal any of the special Indian liquor laws.[74]

[63] 49 Stat. 872, 877, sec. 201.

[64] *Bates* v. *Clark*, 95 U. S. 204 (1877), holding a military officer liable though acting under superior's orders.

[65] 2 Peters 358 (1829).

[66] See also *Evans* v. *Victor*, 204 Fed. 361 (C. C. A. 8, 1913), rev'g 199 Fed. 504 (D. C. E. D. Okla., 1912); *United States* v. *Twelve Bottles of Whiskey*, 201 Fed. 191 (D. C. Mont., 1912); *Forty-three Cases Cognac Brandy*, 14 Fed. 539 (C. C. Minn., 1882), aff'g *Forty-three Gallons of Cognac Brandy*, 11 Fed. 47 (C. C. Minn. 1882); *United States* v. *Four Bottles Sour-Mash Whiskey*, 90 Fed. 720 (D. C. Wash., 1898).

[67] *Shawnee Nat. Bank* v. *United States*, 249 Fed. 583 (C. C. A. 8, 1918); *United States* v. *One Automobile*, 237 Fed. 891 (D. C. Mont., 1916); *United States* v. *Two Gallons of Whiskey*, 213 Fed. 986 (D. C. Mont., 1914).

[68] *United States* v. *One Automobile, supra*; *Shawnee Nat. Bank* v. *United States, supra*.

[69] 39 Stat. 969, 970.

[70] *One Buick Automobile* v. *United States*, 275 Fed. 809 (C. A. A. 8, 1921); *United States* v. *One Ford Five-Passenger Automobile*, 259 Fed. 645 (D. C. E. D. Okla. 1919).

[71] *United States* v. *One Buick Roadster Automobile*, 244 Fed. 961 (D. C. E. D. Okla. 1917); see also: *Hawley* v. *United States*, 15 F. 2d 621 (C. C. A. 8, 1926).

[72] *United States* v. *One Chevrolet Coupe Automobile*, 58 F. 2d 235 (C. C. A. 9, 1932). As to constitutionality of this legislation, see sec. 1, *supra*, and *Commercial Investment Trust* v. *United States*, 261 Fed. 330 (C. C. A. 8, 1919).

[73] *United States* v. *One Cadillac Eight Automobile*, 255 Fed. 173 (D. C. M. D. Tenn., 1918).

[74] *Elam* v. *United States*, 7 F. 2d 887 (C. C. A. 8, 1925); *Hawley* v. *United States*, 15 F. 2d 621 (C. C. A. 8, 1926); *Kennedy* v. *United States*, 265 U. S. 344 (1924), questions certified from *Kennedy* v. *United States*, 2 F. 2d 597 (C. C. A. 8, 1924); *McClintic* v. *United States*, 283 Fed. 781 (C. C. A. 8, 1922); *Morrison* v. *United States*, 6 F. 2d 809, 811 (C. C. A. 8, 1925); *Browning* v. *United States*, 6 F. 2d 801 (C. C. A. 8, 1925), cert. den. 269 U. S. 568 (1925).

SECTION 4. LOCALITY WHERE THESE MEASURES APPLY

The statutes examined above comprise the existing prohibitions and enforcement measures concerning the Indian liquor traffic. But the picture is not complete without an understanding of the locality where these measures apply. Recent statutes have made this fairly clear with regard to lands within the United States proper. First, the Act of June 27, 1934, provides:

> That hereafter the special Indian liquor laws shall not apply to former Indian lands now outside of any existing Indian reservation in any case where the land is no longer held by Indians under trust patents or under any other form of deed or patent which contains restrictions against alienation without the consent of some official of the United States Government: *Provided, however*, That nothing in this Act shall be construed to discontinue or repeal the provisions of the Indian liquor laws which prohibit the sale, gift, barter, exchange, or other disposition of beer, wine, and other liquors to Indians of the classes set forth in the Act of January 30, 1897 (29 Stat. L. 506), and section 241, title 25, of the United States Code.[75]

The purpose of this act is to repeal old treaty and statutory provisions whereby lands ceded to the United States, but adjoining Indian lands retained, were subjected to the Indian liquor laws.[76]

Second, ordinarily fee patented, unrestricted lands are not subject to the liquor laws. Congress has sometimes continued the Indian liquor laws in such lands.[77]

Third, the Act of March 2, 1917, brought Osage County, Oklahoma, within the Indian liquor laws.[78]

Fourth, by the Act of March 5, 1934[79] that part of Oklahoma, formerly known as "Indian Territory," in which all liquor traffic was forbidden by the Act of March 1, 1895,[80] was released from the restrictions of the Indian liquor laws except as to lands on which Indian schools are or may be located. Reservation lands, allotted lands under restrictions or covered by trust patents outside of Indian reservations, and Osage County, in Oklahoma, remain as Indian country in the enforcement of liquor laws.

An interesting question arises with regard to reservation lands newly purchased and set aside for the Indians. Are those lands subject to the Indian liquor laws? This question has been decisively settled in the affirmative in the recent opinion of the United States Supreme Court in *United States* v. *McGowan*.[81]

[75] 48 Stat. 1245, c. 846. Accord: Act of June 11, 1934, 48 Stat. 927 (Minnesota Chippewa). But *cf.* Act of August 31, 1937, 50 Stat. 884 (Crow).

[76] 73d Cong., 2d sess., Sen. Rept. No. 1423 (1934). And see Memo. Sol. I. D., September 28, 1939, holding that the 1934 act exempts from laws prohibiting introduction of liquor into Indian country certain surplus lands of the Colville Reservation sold to non-Indians.

[77] See for example Act of June 4, 1920, sec. 9, 41 Stat. 751, 754 (Crow Reservation).

[78] 39 Stat. 969, 983; amended to except the manufacture and sale of industrial and beverage alcohol for lawful purposes, Act of June 13, 1932, c. 245, 47 Stat. 302.

[79] 48 Stat. 396, c. 43.

[80] 28 Stat. 693, 697, sec. 8.

[81] 302 U. S. 535 (1938), rev'g 89 F. 2d 201 (C. C. A. 9, 1937), aff'g *United States* v. *One Chevrolet Sedan*, 16 F. Supp. 453 (D. C. Nev. 1936). See Chapter 1, sec. 8.

Only two statutory exceptions exist to the prohibitions against liquor in Indian country. The first relates to the use of sacramental wine, as follows:

> * * * it shall not be unlawful to introduce and use wines solely for sacramental purposes, under church authority, at any place within the Indian country or any Indian reservation, including the Pueblo Reservations in New Mexico: * * *[82]

The second exception permits liquor for lawful purposes in Osage County, Oklahoma.[83]

Perhaps still another exception may be found in the provisions of the Act of June 16, 1933,[84] making "3.2 beer" a matter of local option in Oklahoma.

Alaska is not covered by the Indian liquor laws.[85] Congress has always legislated specially for that territory with regard to liquor and has granted the power to control the liquor traffic to the territorial Legislature by the Act of April 13, 1934.[86]

[82] Act of August 24, 1912, 37 Stat. 518, 519, 25 U. S. C. 253.

[83] Act of June 13, 1932, c. 245, 47 Stat. 302, amending the Act of March 2, 1917, 39 Stat. 969, 983, 25 U. S. C. 242.

[84] 48 Stat. 311, c. 105.

[85] The legal status of Alaskan natives is discussed in Chapter 21, sec. 6. The Act of July 27, 1868, 15 Stat. 234, 241, R. S. § 1955, gave the President power to regulate importation and sale of distilled spirits in Alaska. Four years later the case of *United States* v. *Seveloff*, 27 Fed. Cas. No. 16252 (D. C. Ore., 1872) decided that Alaska was not Indian country and that the special Indian liquor laws did not extend to the new territory. In the following year, Congress extended the Indian liquor laws to Alaska by the Act of March 3, 1873, 17 Stat. 510, 530. Again by the Act of May 17, 1884, 23 Stat. 24, Congress prohibited importation, manufacture, and sale of intoxicants to all of Alaska and its inhabitants. This measure was amended by the Act of March 3, 1899, sec. 142, 30 Stat. 1253, 1274, to limit the prohibition to selling to Indians.

As amended by the Act of February 6, 1909, 35 Stat. 600, 603, the Act of 1899 remains in force. In answer to the question of the Secretary of the Interior as to whether the Indian liquor laws apply to Alaska, the Acting Solicitor of the Department of the Interior in 1937 gave his opinion that they do not. His opinion reached the following conclusion:

> It is evident, therefore, that Congress did not regard those provisions [i. e., the Indian liquor laws] as having application to the natives of Alaska; otherwise, the enactment of section 142 above [30 Stat. 1274] would not have been necessary. That the territorial legislature entertained a like view is shown by the fact that it has also seen fit to deal specially with the subject of liquor control among the Alaska natives (see section 4963, Compiled Laws of Alaska, 1933). In any event, the enactment by Congress of a special liquor law for the natives of Alaska makes the general enactment found in Section 241 [25 U. S. C.] locally inapplicable. * * *

Op. Sol., I. D., M.29147, May 6, 1937, pp. 18, 19.

[86] 48 Stat. 583, 584 (Alaska).

SECTION 5. ENFORCEMENT AGENCIES, JURISDICTION, AND PROCEDURE

The work of the Office of Indian Affairs in the field of prohibition enforcement was thus described by the Supreme Court, *per* Hughes, *J.*, in the case of *United States* v. *Birdsall*:[87]

> * * * From an early day, Congress has prohibited the liquor traffic among the Indians, and it has been one of the important duties of the Indian Office to aid in the enforcement of this legislation. See act of June 30, 1834, c. 161, sec. 20, 4 Stat. 729, 732; Rev. Stat., secs. 2139, 2140. 2141; act of July 23, 1892, c. 234, 27 Stat. 260; act of January 30, 1897, c. 109, 29 Stat. 506. It has furnished such aid by the detection of violations, by the collection of evidence, and by appropriate steps to secure the conviction and punishment of offenders. The regulations of the office, adopted under statutory authority (Rev. Stat., secs. 465, 2058), have been explicit as to the duties of Indian agents in this respect. In recent years, Congress has made special appropriations "to enable the Commissioner of Indian Affairs, under the direction of the Secretary of the Interior, to take action to suppress the traffic of intoxicating liquors among Indians" (34 Stat. 328, 1017; 35 Stat. 72, 782; 36 Stat. 271, 1059; 37 Stat. 519), and an organization of special officers and deputies, serving in various states, has been created in the department. Through these efforts numerous convictions have been obtained. The results have been reported to Congress annually by the Commissioner[1] and the appropriations for the continuance of the service have been increased.[2]
>
> [1] H. Doc. Vol. 27, 60th Cong., 1st sess., pp. 26–31; H. Doc. Vol. 43, 60th Cong., 2d sess., pp. 34–40; H. Doc. Vol. 44, 61st Cong., 2d sess., pp. 12–15; H. Doc. Vol. 32, 61st Cong., 3d sess., pp. 12–13; H. Doc. Vol. 41, 62d Cong., 2d sess., pp. 82–83.
>
> [2] The nature and extent of this authorized service of the department are shown by the following extract from the Commissioner's report for the fiscal year ending June 30, 1912: "Until 1906 * * * enforcement of these statutes and subsequent enactments" (as to the liquor traffic) "was left to Indian agents and superintendents and their Indian police, assisted so far as might be by local peace officers and by representatives of the Department of Justice. In 1906 criminal dockets in Indian Territory became so crowded and the possibility of early trial so remote that disregard of the statutes forbidding introduction of intoxicants asumed large importance. To meet the emergency Congress, in the act of June 21, 1906, appropriated $25,000 to be used to suppress the traffic in intoxicating liquors among Indians, and in August 1906, a special officer was commissioned and sent to Oklahoma, that he and his subordinates might, through detective operations, supplement the efforts of superintendents in charge of reservations. In the fiscal year 1909, when the appropriation had grown to $40,000, this service began to operate throughout all States where Indians needed protection. In 1911 the service had grown until it had an appropriation of $70,000 and an organization including 1 chief special officer, 1 assistant chief, 2 constables, 12 special officers, and 143 local deputies stationed in 21 States. The increasing success of the service appears in the fact that in 1909, 561 cases which the service secured came to issue in court, resulting in 548 convictions, whereas in 1911, 1,202 cases came to issue, 1,168 defendants were convicted, and but 34 defendants were acquitted by juries. In 1911 fines imposed amounted to $80,463, or more than the appropriation for the service." H. Doc. No. 933, 62d Cong., 3d sess., pp. 11, 12.

In the Act of March 1, 1907,[88] Congress empowered special officers to search and seize,[89] and in 1912 gave them the powers of the United States marshals and deputy marshals.[90]

Criminal or libel proceedings are cognizable in the Federal District Court in the district where the offense was committed.[91] The manner of complaint and arrest are governed by the Act of June 15, 1938, set out in full in section 3 of this chapter.

[87] 233 U. S. 223 (1914) (holding that prohibition enforcement was such an official responsibility as would provide basis for bribery indictment).

[88] 34 Stat. 1015, 1017.

[89] *Ibid.*

[90] Act of August 24, 1912, 37 Stat. 518, 519.

[91] Judicial Code, sec. 24, 28 U. S. C. 41.

Chapter 18

CRIMINAL JURISDICTION

TABLE OF CONTENTS

SECTION 1. INTRODUCTION

Criminal jurisdiction[1] in Indian law involves an allocation of authority among federal, tribal, and state courts. This allocation of authority depends in general upon three factors: subject matter, locus, and person.

Jurisdiction of the federal courts must be based, in every instance, upon some applicable statute, since there is no federal common law of crimes. From the standpoint of areas of application, the federal criminal statutes relating to Indian affairs are of three types:

(*a*) Those that apply regardless of the locus of the offense, such as the crime of selling liquor to an Indian;[2]

(*b*) Those that apply within areas under the exclusive jurisdiction of the Federal Government, such as the offense of receiving stolen goods;[3] and

(*c*) Offenses punishable only when committed within the "Indian country" or within "an Indian reservation," such as, for example, the offense of possessing intoxicating liquors in the Indian country.[4]

The jurisdiction of tribal courts depends also upon the factors of subject matter, locus, and person, and the same may be said of state court jurisdiction. Since this study is primarily devoted to federal Indian law, only incidental attention will be paid to tribal and state penal laws relating to Indian affairs. Limitations upon the application of such laws contained in federal statutes will, however, be examined.

[1] On civil jurisdiction see Chapter 19.

[2] See Chapter 17, sec. 3.

[3] R. S. § 5357, Act of March 4, 1909, sec. 288, 35 Stat. 1088, 1145, 17 U. S. C. 467.

[4] See 25 U. S. C. 244, and see Chapter 17, sec. 3.

SECTION 2. CRIMES IN INDIAN COUNTRY

Since there is a considerable body of federal legislation penalizing various acts committed on Indian reservations or within Indian country, the question may be raised in any case involving such legislation whether the offense charged was in fact committed within an Indian reservation or in the Indian country. The definition of these terms has been considered elsewhere.[5] For present purposes it is enough to summarize general conclusions which are elsewhere noted:

(1) Tribal land is considered Indian country for purposes of federal criminal jurisdiction.[6]

(2) An allotment held under patent in fee and subject to restraint against alienation is likewise considered Indian country for purposes of federal criminal jurisdiction.[7]

(3) An allotment held under trust patent, with title in the Government, is likewise considered Indian country during the trust period.[8]

(4) Rights-of-way across an Indian reservation are considered "Indian country" for some or all purposes of federal criminal jurisdiction.[9]

[5] See Chapter 1, sec. 3; Chapter 5; Chapter 6.

[6] See Chapter 1, sec. 3.

[7] *United States* v. *Ramsey*, 271 U. S. 467 (1926).

[8] *United States* v. *Sutton*, 215 U. S. 291 (1909), revg. 165 Fed. 253 (D. C. E. D. Wash., 1908); *Hallowell* v. *United States*, 221 U. S. 317 (1911); *United States* v. *Pelican*, 232 U. S. 442 (1914); *Ex parte Pero*, 99 F. 2d 28 (C. C. A. 7, 1938); *Ex parte Van Moore*, 221 Fed. 954 (D. C. S. D., 1915).

[9] The Act of June 28, 1932, 47 Stat. 336, amended sec. 548 of title 18 of the United States Code, which originally applied "within the limits of any Indian reservation" so as to apply "on and within any Indian reservation under the jurisdiction of the United States Government, including rights of way running through the reservation."

Interpreting this phrase, the Solicitor of the Interior Department declared:

> * * * it is my opinion that the amendment should be given its apparent and normal meaning; namely, that the specific reference to rights-of-way was intended to provide for Federal jurisdiction over all rights-of-way running through any Indian reservation. This is advanced as the proper position for this Department to take in view of the following considerations.
>
> 1. The probable judicial construction of the amendment would be that the amendment was intended to include within Federal jurisdiction all rights-of-way because of the previous division of jurisdiction over rights-of-way in Indian reservations. Prior to the passage of the amendment the courts had concluded that rights-of-way to which the Indian title had not been extinguished remained part of the reservation and within Federal jurisdiction, whereas other rights-of-way to which such title had been extinguished were subject to State jurisdiction. A court would presume that in view of this state of the law any amendment referring to rights-of-way generally would be intended to provide a uniform rule. If only a statement of existing law had been intended, the reference in the amendment would rather have been to rights-of-way to which the Indian title had not been extinguished, or no mention of the subject would have been made at all.
>
> Moreover, it would be presumed by a court that this Depart-

(5) It is questionable whether land held by an Indian under a fee patent without restriction is Indian country for purposes of federal criminal jurisdiction; the weight of authority is that the land is not "Indian country" within the meaning of federal penal statutes.[10]

The territorial limits of the jurisdiction of tribal courts and courts of Indian offenses[11] have not been considered in detail in any reported case. The following discussion is taken from an administrative ruling by the Solicitor for the Interior Department dealing with the question:[12]

> May an Indian court exercise jurisdiction over acts committed by Indians on unrestricted lands within an Indian reservation, where the Indians concerned are properly before the court?
>
> * * * * *
>
> Questions of court "jurisdiction" frequently turn out upon analysis to be a confused mixture of questions dealing with international law, constitutional law, statutory construction and common law principles. It is important, therefore, that we define the question that concerns us as clearly and realistically as possible. In asking whether an Indian court has "jurisdiction" over acts committed in certain areas we are concerned to ascertain whether such a court commits a wrongful act, that is to say, an act which is punishable, actionable, or enjoinable in a State or Federal court, if it orders the trial and punishment of an Indian who is before the court, on the basis of an act which that Indian has performed in the area designated.
>
> A question of jurisdiction arises when an Indian who is before an Indian court claims that the judges of such court are acting without proper authority and that such action, therefore, constitutes assault, false imprisonment, trespass, or some similar offense under State or Federal law. It is, therefore, necessary in passing upon such a jurisdictional question to inquire into the basis of authority upon which an Indian court acts. This is a subject which has been dealt with elsewhere at some length.[13]
>
> * * * * *
>
> Whether the Indian Court is an administrative Court of Indian Offenses or a tribal court, it appears that each has sufficient authority to include in its jurisdiction the trial and punishment of offenses by Indians which were committed on unrestricted land.
>
> If, on the one hand, Courts of Indian Offenses be considered, as suggested in the *Clapox* case, to be not regular judicial bodies but "mere educational and disciplinary instrumentalities," the propriety of educational and disciplinary action which such "courts" undertake will depend upon the relationship between the court and the person disciplined. On this view the location of the offense to which the discipline is directed becomes unimportant. An Indian Service hospital treats a diseased Indian regardless of where the disease was acquired. An Indian Service teacher may control the conduct of his pupils and administer discipline on a railroad car traveling through Texas, as well as on restricted Indian land. (See *Peck* v. *A. T. & S. F. Ry. Co.*, 91 S. W. 323.) An Indian will be regarded as married or divorced, a member of a given tribe, an eligible candidate for a certain position or office, regardless of where the acts leading to such a personal status may have taken place. So, if action of a Court of Indian Offenses is regarded as "educational and disciplinary" rather than strictly judicial, such action is not restricted in its horizon to a given territory. The Indian who assaults his fellow-tribesman on fee patented land within the reservation is subject to disciplinary action by the Court of Indian Offenses in the same measure as if the offense had been committed on restricted Indian land. Perhaps the closest analogy for this "educational and disciplinary" theory of the functions of a Court of Indian Offenses is to be found in the common law of domestic relations. The common law still confers a disciplinary power upon parents with respect to their children. To a certain extent guardians generally may exercise such power over their wards. In none of these cases is the exercise of such authority limited by any consideration of the locality of the misconduct. (See *Townsend* v. *Kendall*, 4 Minn. 412, 77 Amer. Dec. 534.)
>
> In *United States* v. *Earl*, 17 Fed. 75, it was held that an Indian ward off the reservation nevertheless was in the charge of an Indian agent within the meaning of a statute forbidding the sale of liquor to such Indians. In *Peters* v. *Malin*, 111 Fed. 244, the court stated that wherever Indians are maintaining their tribal relations, the control and management of their affairs is in the Federal Government irrespective of the title to the land upon which they might, for the time being, be located. In that case the State law of guardianship was held not to apply to tribal Indians either at an industrial school off the reservation or on a reservation the title to which was in the Governor of Iowa. Moreover, the State criminal law was held not to apply to the removal of a child from a reservation and his detention from a Government school, indicating that these acts outside the reservation were of concern only to the Federal Government because of the personal relationship between the Government and its wards. "The relation of dependency existing between tribal Indians and the national government does not grow out of the ownership of the land either by the Indians or the government." (Page 250.)
>
> This principle has been followed in administrative practice since the beginning. The Superintendents and the Courts of Indian Offenses have not in the past refrained from using corrective measures for violations of the regulations because the violations occurred on nontrust land. It may be doubted whether the Indian courts have ever made a practice of inquiring into the title of the land where the violation occurred. Nor have the departmental regulations required such inquiry and restraint. The 1904 law and order regulations of the Indian Office (sections 584–591, Regulations of the Indian Office, 1904) gave the Courts of Indian Offenses original jurisdiction over Indian offenses, including participating in the Sun Dance, contracting a plural marriage, preventing the attendance of children at school, and other misdemeanors committed by Indians "belonging to the reservation," without any limitation as to where the offense might be committed. It was not intended that Indians could dance the Sun Dance and practice polygamy with impunity simply because they did so on nontrust land. Such a distinction would have defeated the educational purpose of the regulations. On the contrary, the 1904 regulations went so far as to

ment and Congress would have been concerned to do away with the unsatisfactory situation resulting from the uncertain status of jurisdiction over rights-of-way on Indian reservations. This would be in conformity with the basic principle of statutory construction that legislation is intended to correct existing evils. The evil to be remedied in this instance was the uncertainty and confusion resulting from the fact that on each reservation there were a number of rights-of-way, whose ownership status depended on different statutes and regulations and the title to which could be definitely ascertained only through judicial statement, and that, although the title thereto had been determined, there was still the administrative difficulty arising from differences in jurisdiction over small strips of territory. This administrative difficulty was referred to by the Supreme Court in the case of *United States* v. *Soldana*, 246 U. S. 530, in which Justice Brandeis said that to except the highway strip from the reservation would cut the reservation in two and make it more difficult, if not impossible, to protect the Indians as the criminal statute intended.

2. If the amendment is given its obvious construction, that of covering all rights-of-way under Federal jurisdiction, the construction would be consistent with the policies of the Department based upon its own research and that of responsible organizations. The survey of law and order within Indian reservations in the Northwest made by the Institute for Government Research and submitted to the Senate Committee on Indian Affairs in 1932 (Hearings Before a Subcommittee of the Committee on Indian Affairs, United States Senate, 72d Congress, 1st session, Part 26, page 14137), recommended that legislation be drafted defining the term Indian reservation for purposes of Federal jurisdiction as including all rights-of-way regardless of their ownership. The Law and Order Regulations of the Department, approved November 27, 1935, and based upon a survey made by this Department of jurisdictional problems, defined Indian reservations for the purposes of tribal jurisdiction as including roads and other parts of the reservation not necessarily in Indian ownership. This type of provision has likewise been included in many tribal law and order codes. (Memo. Sol. I. D., July 3, 1940.)

[10] *Cf. Eugene Sol Louie* v. *United States*, 274 Fed. 47 (C. C. A. 9, 1921); *State* v. *Monroe*, 83 Mont. 556, 274 Pac. 840 (1929).

[11] See for regulations on Law and Order on Indian Reservations, 25 C. F. R. 161.1–161.306.

[12] Memo. Sol. I. D., April 27, 1939.

[13] See Chapter 7, sec. 9.

authorize police surveillance of the Indians leaving the reservation and to contemplate their arrest and punishment for infraction of the rules outside the reservation (sections 585-589).

However, whatever may be the disciplinary authority of the Secretary of the Interior over the conduct of Indian wards outside an Indian reservation, the Indian reservation itself has been considered an area peculiarly set apart as a domain within which the Federal Government exercises guardianship over the Indians. This guardianship is extended to all the Indians within the reservation, regardless of their residence or temporary location on unrestricted land. In the early days after the allotment act there was a tendency to withdraw protection from citizen and fee-patented Indians. This tendency was later reversed and Federal guardianship over tribal members has been recognized in spite of citizenship, possession of fee patents or residence on unrestricted land. A recent and far-reaching recognition of administrative supervision over all Indians within the boundaries of the reservation is found in the case of *United States* v. *Dewey County*, 14 F. (2d) 784 (D. C., S. D., 1926); Aff'd *Dewey County* v. *United States*, 26 F. (2d) 435 (C. C. A. 8th, 1928). The following quotations which uphold the authority of the Department to make rules and regulations governing all the Indians on the reservation, particularly fee-patent Indians residing on fee-patented lands, are set forth because of their peculiar applicability to the questions involved:

> "In the light of the plain determination of the question of the right, the power, and the duty of Congress to terminate this relation of guardian and ward, the [fee patent] Indians named in the complaint must be held to be wards of the government, unless there is legislation of Congress plainly indicating the intent and purpose to terminate the relation. Defendant urges consideration of the Act of June 25, 1910 (36 Stat. 855) * * *.
>
> "This, in my judgment, is far short of a congressional declaration that the relationship of guardian and ward shall, by the issuance of the [fee] patent, cease. It is simply a step recognizing some progress by the Indian as being competent to handle the particular piece of land, and the act grants to him only the power to manage and dispose of the particular land. There is neither language plainly expressing, nor from which it may be reasonably inferred, that there is any intent or purpose that they should be taken out of the tribe of Indians, that their tribal relations should cease, and they should have no further interest in the tribal lands or in the moneys to be paid for such lands; *that they should, from that time forward, not be subject to the agent provided for the band of Indians to which they belong, nor to the rules and regulations promulgated by the Indian Department as to the government of the reservation and all of the Indians thereon*, the education of their children, and the policy that the agent is required to work out with and for the members of the tribes. * * *
>
> "In the absence of further declaration on the part of Congress that the guardianship of the government shall terminate as to these Indians, it seems clear that it must be so held as to those Indians to whom [fee] patents have been issued, who are found by this record to be members of the Cheyenne band of Sioux Indians; that they all had their allotments; that they all resided on their [fee patent] allotments or near them *within the original limits of the Cheyenne River reservation, and some of them within the diminished portions thereof;* that all of said Indians, at all times mentioned in the complaint, appeared on the rolls at the Cheyenne River agency; that they are entitled to participate and partake of tribal funds and of the rents and profits of all tribal lands, together with the fact that the government maintains an agency and *agent in charge of said tribe of Indians, including these particular Indians named in the complaint*, are still wards of the government; that the government is still the guardian of all of these Indians, with control of their property, except in so far as that control of their property is released by the legislation above referred to, and the Indians are thereby granted the power to manage and control the particular piece of land involved in the fee-simple patent." [Italics supplied.]

The foregoing authorities make it clear that if Indian courts are viewed as administrative agencies of the Interior Department, their authority is not limited to offenses committed on restricted land.

If, on the other hand, the Indian courts are viewed as tribal courts, deriving their power from the unextinguished fragments of tribal sovereignty, it must be recognized that this sovereignty is primarily a personal rather than a territorial sovereignty. The tribal court has no jurisdiction over non-Indians unless they consent to such jurisdiction. Its jurisdiction is solely a jurisdiction over persons. We must therefore beware of reading into the measure of this jurisdiction the common law principle of the territoriality of criminal law. As was said in the case of *Ex parte Tiger*, 47 S. W. 304, 2 Ind. T. 41,

> "If the Creek Nation derived its system of jurisprudence through the common law, there would be much plausibility in this reasoning. But they are strangers to the common law. They derive their jurisprudence from an entirely different source, and they are as unfamiliar with common-law terms and definitions as they are with Sanskrit or Hebrew."

We must recognize that the general common law doctrine of the territoriality of criminal law has validity in practice only insofar as it is embodied in our criminal statutes. It is not a principle of logic or eternal reason. There are numerous well-recognized exceptions to this doctrine.

There are, in the first place, certain offenses for which citizens of the United States are punishable in United States courts, no matter where the offenses are committed (e. g., 18 U. S. C., Secs. 1, 5). The power of the Federal Government to govern the conduct of our citizens abroad by subjecting them, when they return to this jurisdiction, to trial and punishment for offenses committed abroad, has never been successfully challenged. (See The Appollon, 9 Wheat. 362, at 370.) If this power has been exercised, in fact, only in exceptional cases, that is because *as a matter of policy* it is generally believed that the power to punish for extra-territorial offenses should be invoked only under special circumstances.

A second departure from the general rule of territoriality is presented by the jurisdiction vested in Congress over Indian affairs. It is well settled that this Congressional jurisdiction does not apply simply to the "Indian country" but applies to offenses no matter where committed:

> "The question is not one of power in the national government, for, as has been shown, congress may provide for the punishment of this crime wherever committed in the United States. Its jurisdiction is coextensive with the subject-matter—the intercourse between the white man and the tribal Indian—and is not limited to place or other circumstances." (*United States* v. *Barnhart*, 22 Fed. 288.)

Again, it is a matter of policy, and not of law, to say how far Congress should extend its laws over Indians "off the reservation." The Indian liquor laws are the outstanding instance of a jurisdiction not limited to offenses committed within the reservation. (25 U. S. C. Sec. 241.)

A third recognized departure from the territorial principle is found in the application of Federal laws to our citizens in certain Eastern countries. Americans committing offenses in uncivilized countries, for instance, are triable before United States consuls (22 U. S. Code, Sec. 180), and Americans committing offenses in China are triable in the United States Court for China (*Biddle* v. *United States*, 156 Fed. 759) over which the Circuit Court of Appeals for the Ninth Circuit exercises appellate jurisdiction (22 U. S. Code, Secs. 191-202).

A fourth important limitation upon the doctrine of territoriality is the rule that in civil cases a court which has jurisdiction over the parties may consider all the elements of the case regardless of geographical considerations.

If, then, an Indian court is to be considered a judicial organ of Indian tribal sovereignty, he must recognize that this sovereignty is not a strictly territorial sovereignty, but primarily a personal sovereignty. We may therefore approach the problem of defining the scope of this sovereignty without begging the question by assuming in advance that the sovereignty is limited to any particular kind of land. The recognized exceptions to the usual rule of territoriality are closer to the situation here presented than the rule itself.

In defining the powers of an Indian tribe we look to Federal laws and treaties not for the basis of sovereignty but for the limitations on tribal powers.[14]

* * * * *

In the absence of Federal law to the contrary, it is for the tribe to decide as a matter of its own public policy whether members of the tribe who may properly appear before the judicial agency of the tribe, shall be triable and punishable for acts committed on unrestricted land. The answer given to this question in the Law and Order Regulations approved by the Secretary of the Interior November 27, 1935, and approved by numerous tribal councils before and after that date, is unmistakable. Section 1 of Chapter 1 reads:

> "A Court of Indian Offenses shall have jurisdiction over all offenses enumerated in Chapter 5, when committed by an Indian, within the reservation or reservations for which the Court is established.
>
> "With respect to any of the offenses enumerated in Chapter 5 over which Federal or State courts may have lawful jurisdiction, the jurisdiction of the Court of Indian Offenses shall be concurrent and not exclusive. It shall be the duty of the said Court of Indian Offenses to order delivery to the proper authorities of the State or Federal Government or of any other tribe or reservation, for prosecution, any offender, there to be dealt with according to law or regulations authorized by law, where such authorities consent to exercise jurisdiction lawfully vested in them over the said offender.
>
> "For the purpose of the enforcement of these regulations, an Indian shall be deemed to be any person of Indian descent who is a member of any recognized Indian tribe now under Federal jurisdiction, and a 'reservation' shall be taken to include all territory within reservation boundaries, including fee patented lands, roads, waters, bridges, and lands used for agency purposes."

The question remains, then, whether this statement of authority is in conflict with any Federal law.

That the original sovereignty of an Indian tribe extended to the punishment of a member by the proper tribal officers for depredations or other forms of misconduct committed outside the territory of the tribe cannot be challenged. Certainly we cannot read into the laws and customs of the Indian tribes a principle of territoriality of jurisdiction with which they were totally unfamiliar, and which no country has adopted as an absolute rule. That Indian tribes friendly to the United States acted to punish their members for depredations committed against whites outside of the Indian country is a matter of historical record. Will any one claim that such punishment was unconstitutional? The fact is that the United States, over a long period, encouraged the Indian tribes to help in controlling the conduct of their members outside of the Indian country, and in order to encourage such control made the tribe responsible for such individual offenses.

The analysis of Federal laws applicable to the situation under consideration indicates that the right of Indian tribal authorities to punish errant members of the tribe for offenses, no matter where committeed, has not only never been denied but has been positively recognized. The act of June 30, 1834 (4 Stat. 731), which is still in many respects the basis of Indian administration, placed upon the Indian "nation or tribe" the responsibility of securing redress for depredations committed by individual members of the nation or tribe outside of, as well as within, the Indian country.[15]

* * * * *

This provision placing responsibility upon the tribal authorities for the wrongs of individual Indians committed outside of the reservation clearly contemplates that the tribal authorities will deal in proper fashion with such individual Indians. While the occasion that gave rise to this legislation may have disappeared, the judicial basis of tribal action which the legislation assumed has never been challenged.

Provisions similar to that above quoted are found in many treaties with Indian tribes. (See for instance Treaty with the Kiowas, etc., May 26, 1837 (7 Stat. 533). Secs. 3, 5; Treaty with the Comanches, etc., July 27, 1853 (10 Stat. 1013), Art. 5; Treaty with the Rogue River Indians, September 10, 1853 (10 Stat. 1018), Art. 6; Treaty with the Blackfeet, October 17, 1855 (11 Stat. 657), Art. 11.)

Federal laws affecting the personal status of Indians have no direct bearing upon our present problem. The General Allotment Law of February 8, 1887 (24 Stat. 390), as amended by the act of May 8, 1906 (34 Stat. 182), provides:

> "At the expiration of the trust period and when the lands have been conveyed to the Indians by patent in fee, as provided in section 348, then each and every allottee shall have the benefit of and be subject to the laws, both civil and criminal, of the State or Territory in which they may reside * * *." (25 U. S. C. Sec. 349.)

Because of this provision fee patent allottees have been held to be subject to the laws of the State wherever they may be within the reservation. *Eugene Sol Louie* v. *United States*, 274 Fed. 47 (C. C. A. 9th, 1921); *State* v. *Monroe*, 83 Mont. 556, 274 Pac. 840 (1929). However, this fact does not mean that so long as the fee patent Indians live within the outer boundaries of the reservation and maintain tribal relations they are not also subject to the rules and regulations of the Department and to the tribal ordinances governing tribal members. That they are so subject is stated in the recent case of *United States* v. *Dewey County*, from which extensive quotation to this effect is given above.

Moreover, the allotment act certainly did not make a fee patented allotment a place of sanctuary on which even an unallotted member of the tribe may commit offenses without the risk of future punishment by his tribe. Fee patented lands are undoubtedly subject to State jurisdiction, but in the words of the Supreme Court, there is "no denial of the personal jurisdiction of the United States" (*United States* v. *Celestine*, 215 U. S. 278, 291), and neither is there any denial of the personal jurisdiction of the tribe. It is for the Federal Government itself to decide whether it shall retain jurisdiction over certain offenses by Indians, e. g., liquor offenses on fee patented land, and relinquish to the State jurisdiction over certain other offenses. Likewise, it is for the Indian tribe itself, subject only to limitation by Congress, to decide whether it shall retain jurisdiction over certain offenses committed by members of the tribe on such land.

The fact that Federal courts have refrained from taking jurisdiction of Indian offenses on fee patented lands does not negative the jurisdiction of the Indian courts. Since the fallacy of identifying the jurisdiction of the one with the other is a ready one, an analysis of the fundamental distinctions between them is desirable.

The Federal District Courts have been authorized by Congress to exercise jurisdiction over specific crimes committed by Indians or white people against Indians in the "Indian country" and in "Indian reservations." The Federal courts have no jurisdiction other than that granted by Federal statute. On the other hand, the Indian tribes retain all their original jurisdiction over their members except as may be limited by Federal statutes. Likewise, the authority of the Department to exercise administrative supervision over Indians is not based

[14] See Chapter 7, sec. 2.

[15] See R. S. § 2156, 25 U. S. C. 229.

upon a statutory specification of crimes and criminal jurisdiction but, as previously indicated, upon a statutory duty of guardianship and Congressional authorization to maintain order on Indian reservations. See *United States* v. *Quiver*, 241 U. S. 602, at 605.

The Federal court exercises an absolute and exclusive jurisdiction over Indians when their crimes fall within the circumstances covered by the statutes. There is no statutory authority for concurrent jurisdiction of State and Federal courts when an Indian or Indian land becomes subject to State jurisdiction.[16] If the Federal courts have jurisdiction, the State courts do not, and vice versa. However, there is no prohibition on a determination by the Interior Department to exercise corrective measures over Indians within the reservation when the State has jurisdiction but refuses to handle the case or upon a similar determination by the tribe that members uncorrected by State action shall be subject to correction by the tribal court.

Furthermore, the Federal courts are exercising judicial power as courts established by Congress pursuant to the United States Constitution, whereas the Department through the Court of Indian Offenses is not exercising judicial power but administrative guardianship powers and the tribe is exercising tribal powers over the persons of its members. The establishment of an Indian court and the extent of its jurisdiction is, therefore, in both cases an administrative policy question. No court is established where there is little restricted land. Courts are established, however, where there is much restricted land within a reservation. The Federal courts are obligated to take jurisdiction of crimes coming within the Federal statutes upon restricted lands regardless of administrative need. It would not be argued that there is any obligation on the part of the Department to provide corrective measures on such restricted lands if it is not advisable or necessary. In other words, it has often been recognized that the jurisdiction of the Federal courts and of the Indian courts does not coincide, since they derive their authority from different powers and function for different purposes.

I have reviewed the Federal laws which might be viewed as restricting or limiting the power of an Indian court to try and to punish an Indian for an offense committed on unrestricted land within a reservation. I find no Federal law imposing any such limitation.

Is there any provision of the Federal Constitution that precludes such exercise of jurisdiction? Would such an exercise of authority, in an area where the State may exercise a concurrent jurisdiction, constitute "double jeopardy" and violate the Fifth Amendment to the Federal Constitution?

Even if it could be maintained, in the face of the decision in *Talton* v. *Mayes*, 163 U. S. 376, that constitutional limitations under the "due process" clause are applicable to an Indian court, there is no force in the argument that the exercise of jurisdiction by such a court in these cases would subject the offender to "double jeopardy." The fact that an offense committed outside of restricted Indian lands may be subject to punishment in State courts does not make it unconstitutional for the court of another sovereignty to punish the same person for the same act. The decided cases clearly establish the principle that an individual who in a single act offends against the laws of several jurisdictions may be constitutionally punished by the agencies of each jurisdiction.[17]

* * * * *

In view of these decisions of the United States Supreme Court it is clear that the fact that an act is punishable in State courts is no bar to punishment in an Indian court. There remains, of course, a question of public policy to be considered in asserting jurisdiction over acts which are subject to another jurisdiction. This question is met by a specific provision in the Law and Order Regulations above set forth, under which cases in which Indian tribal jurisdiction is concurrent with State jurisdiction are to be turned over to State authorities, *if such authorities are willing to exercise jurisdiction.* This is undoubtedly a reasonable provision in view of the fact that the State may be, in many cases, unwilling to exercise even an admitted jurisdiction over Indians with respect to acts committed on unrestricted Indian lands within a reservation.

It should further be noted that the Law and Order Regulations do not purport to cover offenses committed outside of Indian reservations. There is therefore no immediate occasion to consider the legal and administrative problems that would be raised by any such exercise of jurisdiction. It is enough for our present purposes to note that the exercise of jurisdiction by an Indian court, under the departmental law and order or tribal codes, does not diminish the jurisdiction of State courts, does not subject the offender to "double jeopardy," and is not prohibited by any known Federal statute.

There remains the final question whether the action of an Indian court in trying and punishing an Indian for an offense committed within the jurisdiction of the State courts may violate any State law. While it is impossible to decide an issue of this sort in the abstract with entire certainty, it is enough to say that I know of no State legislation which would interfere with such exercise of jurisdiction by an Indian court, and since the matter is one that concerns the relations between an Indian and his tribe it would appear to be a matter on which State legislation would be ineffective. *Worcester* v. *State of Georgia*, 6 Pet. 514; *United States* v. *Quiver*, 241 U. S. 602; *United States* v. *Hamilton*, 233 Fed. 685; *In re Blackbird*, 109 Fed. 139; *In re Lincoln*, 129 Fed. 247; and see Opinion M. 28568, approved December 11, 1936, on the right of State game wardens to make searches on an Indian reservation.

In view of the foregoing authorities, I am of the opinion that an Indian court which orders the trial and punishment of an Indian before the court, on the basis of acts committed on unrestricted lands within an Indian reservation, does not offend against any State or Federal law.[18]

In certain offenses the nature of the offense and the character of the *locus in quo* establish federal jurisdiction without reference to the question whether the accused or the injured party is an Indian.[19] In other offenses, jurisdiction depends among other things upon the persons involved. In the following sections (3–6) we shall deal with jurisdiction over offenses in Indian country as affected by the character of the parties.

[16] This statement must now be qualified because of the passage of the Act of June 8, 1940, Public No. 565—76th Cong., which conferred jurisdiction on the State of Kansas over offenses committed by or against Indians on Indian reservations in the state.

[17] See *Moore* v. *Illinois*, 14 How. 13, 19 (1852); *United States* v. *Lanza*, 260 U. S. 377, 379–380, 382 (1922).

[18] Further discussion in the memorandum cited reaches the conclusion that Indian police may make arrests of Indians on unrestricted lands within a reservation.

[19] "In this offense (introducing liquor into Indian country) neither race or color are significant." *United States* v. *Sutton*, 215 U. S. 291, 295 (1909). Accord: *Perrin* v. *United States*, 232 U. S. 478 (1914).

SECTION 3. CRIMES IN INDIAN COUNTRY BY INDIAN AGAINST INDIAN

Offenses committed by Indians against Indians within the Indian country are ordinarily subject to the jurisdiction of tribal courts. This is a consequence of the doctrine of tribal self-government.[20] In determining whether an offense by an Indian against an Indian falls within the jurisdiction of tribal courts, we look to federal laws and treaties only for the limitations on tribal authority. The most important of such limitations is found in the Act of March 3, 1885.[21] This act brought

[20] See Chapter 7, sec. 9.

[21] 23 Stat. 362, 385, 18 U. S. C. 548. Later amendments of this act and problems raised in its application are discussed in Chapter 7, secs. 2 and 9.

under federal jurisdiction certain offenses committed by Indians against Indians, notably murder, manslaughter, rape, assault with intent to kill, arson, burglary, and larceny. In later years robbery, incest, and assault with a dangerous weapon were added to this list.[22] A few other federal statutes relating, mostly to non-Indians as well as Indians are applicable to offenses by Indians against Indians committed on an Indian reservation.[23]

It has been held that where jurisdiction over murder or manslaughter is thus conferred upon the federal courts such jurisdiction is exclusive and the tribal courts may not act to punish a member of the tribe who has killed another member.[24] Authority on this point, however, is not conclusive, and it would be a rash inference that a tribe is precluded from dealing with such matters as petty larceny between members of a tribe.

While, as noted, the jurisdiction of the tribe over offenses between Indians does not depend upon federal statutory authority, it may be noted that the policy of the Federal Government to respect such tribal jurisdiction is embodied in a series of statutes stretching back to the Act of March 3, 1817,[25] which, after establishing federal jurisdiction over Indian offenses, declared:

> *Provided*, That nothing in this act shall be so construed as to affect any treaty now in force between the United States and any Indian nation, or to extend to any offence committed by one Indian against another, within any Indian boundary.

Early treaties guaranteeing tribal jurisdiction over matters affecting only Indians have been elsewhere discussed.[26]

[22] Act of March 4, 1909, sec. 328, 35 Stat. 1088, 1151; Act of June 28, 1932, 47 Stat. 336, 337.

[23] See Chapter 7, fn. 225.

[24] *United States* v. *Whaley*, 37 Fed. 145 (C. C. S. D. Cal. 1888); and see Chapter 7, fn. 227.

[25] 3 Stat. 383. See sec. 4, *infra*.

[26] See Chapter 8, sec. 3D and E.

SECTION 4. CRIMES IN INDIAN COUNTRY BY INDIAN AGAINST NON-INDIAN

An Indian committing offenses in the Indian country against a non-Indian is subject to the Act of March 3, 1885, section 9,[27] which, with an amendment, became section 328 of the United States Criminal Code of 1910 and now is section 548 of title 18 of the United States Code,[28] providing for the prosecution in the federal courts of Indians committing, within Indian reservations, any of 10 (formerly 7, then 8) specially mentioned offenses whether against Indians or against non-Indians.[29] Apart from these "ten major crimes" an Indian committing offenses in the Indian country against a non-Indian is subject to the code of federal territorial offenses,[30] except in two situations: (*a*) Where he "has been punished by the local law of the tribe," and (*b*) "where, by treaty stipulations, the exclusive jurisdiction over such offenses is or may be secured to the Indian tribes respectively." The substance of the present law on this subject goes back to early treaties, some of which antedated the Federal Constitution, stipulating that Indians committing offenses against citizens of the United States should be delivered up by their tribes to the nearest post, to be punished according to the ordinances of the United States.[31]

The first federal enactment dealing generally with crimes by Indians against non-Indians in Indian country was the Act of March 3, 1817.[32] This provision was subsequently incorporated in section 25 of the Trade and Intercourse Act of 1834,[33]

[27] 23 Stat. 362, 385, 18 U. S. C. 548. Interpreted *Gon-Shay-Ee, Petitioner*, 130 U. S. 343 (1889).

[28] Under this section, as originally enacted, the enumerated crimes were within the jurisdiction of territorial courts when sitting as such, and not when sitting as federal district or circuit courts. *Gon-Shay-Ee, Petitioner*, 130 U. S. 343 (1889). This was true regardless of whether the offense was committed within an Indian reservation. *Captain Jack, Petitioner*, 130 U. S. 353 (1889). For a complete history of this act see *United States* v. *Kagama*, 118 U. S. 375 (1886).

[29] Murder committed by an Indian against a non-Indian on a United States Indian reservation is a crime against the authority of the United States and within the cognizance of federal courts without reference to the citizenship of the accused. *Apapas* v. *United States*, 233 U. S. 587 (1914). For the purposes of enforcement of 18 U. S. C. 548, the son of an Indian mother and a half-breed father, both of whom were recognized as Indians and maintained tribal relations, and who himself lived on a reservation and maintained tribal relations and was recognized as an Indian, was an "Indian" within the meaning of the federal statute. *Ex Parte Pero*, 99 F. 2d 28 (C. C. A. 7, 1938), cert. den. 306 U. S. 643. Also see *Alberty* v. *United States*, 162 U. S. 499 (1896).

It is not clear whether or how far the Act of 1885 applied to the so-called "Indian Territory." By Art. 13 of the Cherokee Treaty of July 19, 1866, 14 Stat. 799, 803 (see Chapter 1, sec. 2), the establishment of a court of the United States in the Cherokee territory was provided for

> * * * with such jurisdiction and organized in such manner as may be prescribed by law. *Provided:* That the judicial tribunals of the nation shall be allowed to retain exclusive jurisdiction in all civil and criminal cases arising within their country in which members of the nation, by nativity or adoption, shall be the *only parties*, [italics added] or where the cause of action shall arise in the Cherokee nation, except as otherwise provided in this treaty.

Further, sec. 30 of the Act of May 2, 1890, 26 Stat. 81, 94, providing a temporary government for the Territory of Oklahoma and enlarging the jurisdiction of the United States court in the Indian Territory, provided

> * * * That the judicial tribunals of the Indian nations shall retain exclusive jurisdiction in all civil and criminal cases arising in the country in which members of the nation by nativity or by adoption shall be the *only parties* [italics added]; * * *

and sec. 31 declared that

> * * * nothing in this act shall be so construed as to deprive any of the courts of the civilized nations of exclusive jurisdiction over all cases arising wherein members of said nations, whether by treaty, blood, or adoption, are the *sole parties*, [italics added] nor so as to interfere with the right and power of said civilized nations to punish said members for violation of the statutes and laws enacted by their national councils where such laws are not contrary to the treaties and laws of the United States.

It will be noted that this act omits that portion of the thirteenth article of the treaty, wherein is reserved to the judicial tribunals of the nation exclusive jurisdiction "where the cause of the action shall arise in the Cherokee Nation," and to that extent apparently supersedes the treaty. Construing the word "parties" as meaning parties to the crime and not simply to the prosecution of the crime, it would appear that the Act of 1885 would apply to the "Indian Territory" only in cases where the offense was one of an Indian against a non-Indian. So construed in *Alberty* v. *United States*, 162 U. S. 499 (1896). Followed in *Nofire* v. *United States*, 164 U. S. 657 (1897). In an indictment for murder in the Chickasaw Nation, Indian Territory, averring both deceased and accused were white men, proof that the deceased was a white man establishes the jurisdiction, and the averment as to the citizenship of the accused is surplusage. *Stevenson* v. *United States*, 86 Fed. 106 (C. C. A. 5, 1898), s. c. 162 U. S. 313 (1896). In a case where the Indian defendant is treated as the sole party, the Indian courts would have jurisdiction whether the victim of the crime was Indian or non-Indian. This was done in a case of adultery, in which the name of the prosecuting witness did not appear and since there was no adverse party, the woman being a consenting party, the Indian defendant was regarded as the sole party to the proceeding. *In re Mayfield, Petitioner*, 141 U. S. 107 (1891).

[30] 25 U. S. C. 217–218. See sec. 7, *infra*.

[31] See *e. g.*, Art. IX of Treaty of January 21, 1785, with the Wiandots and others, 7 Stat. 16, 17; Art. VI of Treaty of November 28, 1785, with the Cherokee, 7 Stat. 18. And see Chapter 1, sec. 3, fn. 48.

[32] 3 Stat. 383, designating as a crime any act committed by any person in the Indian country which, under the laws of the United States, would be a crime if committed in a place over which the United States had sole and exclusive jurisdiction. That this act comprehended crimes by Indians is indicated by the fact that the general language was qualified by a proviso excepting crimes by Indians against other Indians. The proviso further declared that existing treaties were to remain unaffected.

[33] Act of June 30, 1834, 4 Stat. 729, 733. Section 29 of this act contained a repealer of the 1817 act. Murder committed by an Indian

and became part of section 3 of the Act of March 27, 1854,[34] from which section 2145 of the Revised Statutes, now 25 U. S. C. 217, was derived.

The first of the two exceptions noted—that relating to Indians punished by the local law of the tribe—first appears in the 1854 act.

The second of the exceptions noted—involving cases where treaties have provided for exclusive tribal jurisdiction—has its origin in the 1817 act.

against a non-Indian without the limits of the state and district of Arkansas and within Indian country, in the absence of a statute attaching the Indian country west of Arkansas thereto, was held not to fall within the jurisdiction of the circuit court, which had no jurisdiction over such country. *United States* v. *Alberty*, 24 Fed. Cas. No. 14426 (C. C. Ark. 1844). The child of an Indian mother and white father was considered to partake of the condition of the mother for the purposes of the criminal provisions of the 1834 Intercourse Act. *United States* v. *Sanders*, 27 Fed. Cas. No. 16220 (C. C. Ark. 1847).

[34] 10 Stat. 269, 270. An offender is amenable for the crime of adultery only to the laws of the nation in accord with Art. 13 of Treaty of July 19, 1866, with the Cherokees, 14 Stat. 799. *In re Mayfield, Petitioner*, 141 U. S. 107 (1891). Also see *Alberty* v. *United States*, 162 U. S. 499 (1896); *Nofire* v. *United States*, 164 U. S. 657 (1897); *Famous Smith* v. *United States*, 151 U. S. 50 (1894) (discussing Indian citizenship in reference to applicability of treaty). A white man incorporated with an Indian tribe at a mature age, by adoption, does not thereby become an Indian, so as to cease to be amenable to the laws of the United States but he may become entitled to certain privileges in the tribe and also make himself amenable to their laws and usages. Therefore, an article of a treaty pardoning all offenses committed by citizens of the Cherokee Nation against the nation had the effect of pardoning an Indian who had previously committed murder in Cherokee country against a white man who had been adopted by that tribe. *United States* v. *Ragsdale*, 27 Fed. Cas. No. 16113 (C. C. Ark. 1847). Murder committed by an Indian against a non-Indian in the Indian country, within the boundaries of the territory, not coming within any of the exceptions, is within the exclusive jurisdiction of the United States branch of the territorial district court. *United States* v. *Monte*, 3 N. M. 173, 3 Pac. 45 (1884). But *cf. United States* v. *Terrel*, 28 Fed. Cas. No. 16452 (C. C. Ark. 1840).

SECTION 5. CRIMES IN INDIAN COUNTRY BY NON-INDIAN AGAINST INDIAN

Generally speaking, offenses by non-Indians against Indians are punishable in federal courts where the offense is one specified in the federal code of territorial offenses.[35]

This was not always the rule. Early treaties frequently provided that non-Indians committing offenses in the Indian country against Indians should be subject to punishment by tribal authorities.[36] This rule, which followed the usual practice in international treaties, was abandoned after a few years of treaty-making, and many of the later treaties expressly provide that white offenders shall be delivered up to the federal authorities for prosecution.[37]

The exercise of federal jurisdiction over non-Indian offenders against Indians in the Indian country was first put on a statutory basis by the original Trade and Intercourse Act, the Act of July 22, 1790.[38] The relevant sections declared:

> SEC. 5. That if any citizen or inhabitant of the United States, or of either of the territorial districts of the United States, shall go into any town, settlement or territory belonging to any nation or tribe of Indians, and shall there commit any crime upon, or trespass against, the person or property of any peaceable and friendly Indian or Indians, which, if committed within the jurisdiction of any state, or within the jurisdiction of either of the said districts, against a citizen or white inhabitant thereof, would be punishable by the laws of such state or district, such offender or offenders shall be subject to the same punishment, and shall be proceeded against in the same manner as if the offence had been committed within the jurisdiction of the state or district to which he or they may belong, against a citizen or white inhabitant thereof.
>
> SEC. 6. That for any of the crimes or offences aforesaid, the like proceedings shall be had for apprehending, imprisoning or bailing the offender, as the case may be, and for recognizing the witnesses for their appearance to testify in the case, and where the offender shall be committed, or the witnesses shall be in a district other than that in which the offence is to be tried, for the removal of the offender and the witnesses or either of them, as the case may be, to the district in which the trial is to be had as by the act to establish the judicial courts of the United States, are directed for any crimes or offenses against the United States.

These provisions were reenacted with minor modifications in the later temporary Trade and Intercourse Acts of 1793, 1796, and 1799,[39] and were embodied in the first permanent Trade and Intercourse Act of 1802[40] as sections 2 to 10, inclusive. The general rule established by these statutes was confirmed in the Act of March 3, 1817,[41] which provided:

> That if any Indian, or other person or persons, shall, within the United States, and within any town, district, or territory, belonging to any nation or nations, tribe or tribes, of Indians, commit any crime, offence, or misdemeanor, which, if committed in any place or district of country under the sole and exclusive jurisdiction of the United States, would, by the laws of the United States, be punished with death, or any other punishment, every such offender, on being thereof convicted, shall suffer the like punishment as is provided by the laws of the United States for the like offences, if committed within any place or district of country under the sole and exclusive jurisdiction of the United States.
>
> SEC. 2. That the superior courts in each of the territorial districts, and the circuit courts and other courts of the United States, of similar jurisdiction in criminal causes, in each district of the United States, in which any offender against this act shall be first apprehended or brought for trial, shall have, and are hereby invested with, full power and authority to hear, try, and punish, all crimes, offences, and misdemeanors, against this act; such courts proceeding therein, in the same manner as if such crimes, offences, and misdemeanors, had been committed within the bounds of their respective districts; *Provided*, That nothing in this act shall be so construed as to affect any treaty now in force between the United States and any Indian nation, or to extend to any offence committed by one Indian against another, within any Indian boundary.
>
> SEC. 3. That the President of the United States, and the governor of each of the territorial districts, where any offender against this act shall be apprehended or brought for trial, shall have, and exercise, the same powers, for the punishment of offences against this act, as they can severally have and exercise by virtue of the fourteenth and fifteenth sections of an act, entitled "An act to regulate trade and intercourse with the Indian tribes, and to preserve peace on the frontiers," passed thirtieth March, one thousand eight hundred and two, for the punishment of offences therein described.

The Trade and Intercourse Act of June 30, 1834,[42] reenacted the rule developed in the earlier statutes. This rule was subsequently

[35] See sec. 7, *infra*.

[36] See Chapter 7, sec. 9, fn. 212; Chapter 3, sec. 3D(1).

[37] *Ibid.*

[38] Secs. 5 and 6, 1 Stat. 137, 138. See Chapter 4, sec. 2; Chapter 15, sec. 10A.

[39] Acts of March 1, 1793, 1 Stat. 329; May 19, 1796, 1 Stat. 469; March 3, 1799, 1 Stat. 743. See Chapter 4, sec. 2; Chapter 15, sec. 10A.

[40] Act of March 30, 1802, 2 Stat. 139. See Chapter 4, sec. 3; Chapter 15, sec. 10A.

[41] 3 Stat. 383.

[42] 4 Stat. 729. See Chapter 4, sec. 6; Chapter 15, sec. 10A.

incorporated in the Revised Statutes as section 2145 and in title 25 of the United States Code as section 217. The exceptions contained in title 25 of the United States Code, section 218, relating to offenses by Indians against Indians and to offenders punished by tribal law have no application to offenses committed by non-Indians against Indians. The third exception in section 218, dealing with the case of a treaty where the exclusive jurisdiction over such offenses is secured to the Indian tribes might have current application, but no such treaty provisions appear to be now in force.

Apart from the foregoing general statutes, Congress has, from time to time, enacted various laws to punish particular offenses committed by non-Indians against Indians within the Indian country.[43]

[43] See Chapter 7, sec. 9, fn. 225.

SECTION 6. CRIMES IN INDIAN COUNTRY BY NON-INDIAN AGAINST NON-INDIAN

Ordinarily offenses committed by a non-Indian against a non-Indian in the Indian country are of no concern to the Federal Goverment and are punishable by the state.[44] For purposes of criminal jurisdiction, where Indians are not involved, an Indian reservation is generally considered to be a portion of the state within which it is located.[45] Exceptions to this rule exist where Congress has specifically provided for exclusive federal jurisdiction over certain areas.[46]

[44] *United States* v. *McBratney*, 104 U. S. 621 (1881). And see Chapter 6.

[45] The provision of the enabling act of Montana, that all Indian lands within the state "shall remain under the absolute jurisdiction and control of the Congress of the United States," does not amount to a reservation by the United States of jurisdiction over crimes committed on such lands by non-Indians against non-Indians and does not deprive the state of its power to try such offenses. *Draper* v. *United States*, 164 U. S. 240 (1896).

[46] 18 U. S. C. 549 (Act of February 2, 1903, 32 Stat. 793; Act of March 4, 1909, sec. 329, 35 Stat. 1088, 1151; Act of March 3, 1911, sec. 291, 36 Stat. 1087, 1167). In this connection also see H. Rept. No. 2704, vol. IX, 57th Cong., 1st sess.

SECTION 7. CRIMES IN AREAS WITHIN EXCLUSIVE FEDERAL JURISDICTION

Section 217, title 25,[47] extends to Indian reservations, with exceptions already noted, "the general laws of the United States as to the punishment of crimes committed in any place within the sole and exclusive jurisdiction of the United States, except the District of Columbia * * *." A list of such offenses will be found in chapters 11 and 13 of title 18, United States Code.[48] This list is meager and inadequate in comparison with most state codes. It is supplemented by section 468 of title 18, United States Code,[49] which makes acts, not made penal by any other laws of Congress, committed upon land within the exclusive jurisdiction of the United States subject to federal prosecution whenever made criminal by state law.

[47] Act of June 30, 1834, sec. 25, 4 Stat. 733 as amended by the Act of March 27, 1854, sec. 3, 10 Stat. 269, 270; R. S. § 2145.

[48] The first of the statutes embodied in this list appears to be the Act of April 30, 1790, 1 Stat. 112.

[49] R. S. § 5391; Act of July 7, 1898, sec. 2, 30 Stat. 717; Act of March 4, 1909, sec. 289, 35 Stat. 1089, 1145 as amended by the Act of June 15, 1933, 48 Stat. 152. See Chapter 6, sec. 2A.

SECTION 8. CRIMES IN WHICH LOCUS IS IRRELEVANT

There are certain offenses covered by federal statutes regarding Indian affairs which are subject to federal jurisdiction regardless of the locus of the offense. Several such offenses are: purchasing I. D. cattle without permission;[50] selling liquor to Indians;[51] making prohibited contracts with Indian tribes.[52]

The power of Congress to punish such crimes outside the Indian country is well established.[53]

[50] Act of March 3, 1865, sec. 8, 13 Stat. 541, 563, R. S. § 2138, as amended by the Act of June 30, 1919, sec. 1, 41 Stat. 3, 9, 25 U. S. C. 214.

[51] See Chapter 17, sec. 3.

[52] Act of March 3, 1871, sec. 3, 16 Stat. 544, 570, R. S. § 2105, 25 U. S. C. 83.

[53] See Chapter 5, sec. 3.

CHAPTER 19

CIVIL JURISDICTION

TABLE OF CONTENTS

SECTION 1. INTRODUCTION

As applied to the courts, jurisdiction may be defined as the power of a court to hear and determine matters or controversies of a justiciable nature arising within the limits to which the judicial power of those courts extends. We may consider the subject of civil jurisdiction [1] from the standpoint of the federal courts, including constitutional and legislative courts, such as the Court of Claims, and federal administrative tribunals, and also from the standpoint of the state courts, and the tribal courts.

[1] On criminal jurisdiction, see Chapter 18. On the constitutional power of federal, state, and tribal governments, see Chapters 5, 6, and 7.

SECTION 2. FEDERAL COURTS

Speaking generally, it may be said that the judicial power of the United States is vested by the Constitution in the Supreme Court and such other courts as Congress shall from time to time ordain and establish.[2]

In considering the jurisdiction of the federal courts, it may be observed that under the Constitution [3] and laws [4] of the United States the federal courts exercise jurisdiction in two different classes of cases: cases where the jurisdiction depends upon the character of the parties, and cases where the jurisdiction depends upon the subject matter of the suit. The distinction between these two classes of cases has been recognized from the beginning. Thus, in *Cohens* v. *Virginia* [5] the Supreme Court of the United States, speaking through Mr. Justice Marshall, said:

> In one description of cases, the jurisdiction of the court is founded entirely on the character of the parties; and the nature of the controversy is not contemplated by the constitution—the character of the parties is everything, the nature of the case nothing. In the other description of cases, the jurisdiction is founded entirely on the character of the case, and the parties are not contemplated by the constitution—in these, the nature of the case is everything, the character of the parties nothing. * * * (P. 393.)

[2] U. S. Const., Art. III, sec. 1.

[3] Art. III, sec. 2.

[4] 28 U. S. C. A. 41.

[5] 6 Wheat. 264 (1821).

Taking this proposition as a point of departure, we shall consider the subject briefly, in so far as the Indians are concerned, under the following headings:

A. Cases where the jurisdiction of the court depends on the character of the parties, including the United States as plaintiff, defendant or intervener; cases where an Indian tribe is plaintiff, defendant or intervener; cases where individual Indians are plaintiffs, defendants or interveners.

B. Cases where the jurisdiction of the court depends on the character of the subject matter.

A. JURISDICTION DEPENDENT UPON PARTIES

(1) United States as plaintiff.

(*a*) *Generally.*—It may be stated as a general proposition that under subdivision 1 of section 41 of title 28 of the United States Code, the district courts of the United States have jurisdiction of all suits of a civil nature, at common law or in equity, in which the United States is the plaintiff. Ordinarily the general jurisdiction of the district court is established by the mere fact that the United States is plaintiff. Thus, in *United States* v. *Board of County Commissioners of Grady County, Oklahoma,*[6] wherein the United States sought to enjoin the defendants from

[6] 54 F. 2d 593 (C. C. A. 10, 1931).

diverting surface drainage water from a state public highway over an Indian allotment, the Circuit Court of Appeals for the Eighth Circuit, notwithstanding the claim of the defendants and the decision of the court that the suit was virtually one against the State of Oklahoma and could not be maintained, upheld the jurisdiction of the district court, saying:

> There was no tenable objection to the general jurisdiction of the District Court. It was expressly conferred by title 28, § 41, subd. 1, of the U. S. Code, 28 U. S. C. A. § 41 (1), in providing that the District Courts shall have jurisdiction, "first, of all suits of a civil nature, at common law or in equity, brought by the United States * * *." (P. 595.)

Nevertheless, as suggested above, in order for the United States to maintain a suit so that the court may pass upon the merits of the case and enter a valid judgment therein, it must be a suit which the United States is authorized to maintain.[7] In cases where the United States is seeking to enforce a measure of government enacted in the exercise of its constitutional powers, there is or can be no question as to the authority of the United States to apply to its own courts for relief.[8] In cases where the United States sues for the benefit of a third party, it may be stated that as a general rule it must have an interest in the subject matter or purpose of the suit and the relief sought. This interest does not necessarily have to be a pecuniary one; it is sufficient if it is a governmental one.[9]

(b) *Indian cases.*—A pecuniary interest of the United States itself need not exist in cases involving restricted Indian lands[10] or land in which the United States is trustee.[11] It is well settled that the United States, by virtue of its peculiar relations with the Indians—often called "guardianship"[12]—or as trustee of their property, has the capacity and the duty to effectuate Government policies by protecting and enforcing their rights in property held by it as trustee,[13] or by the Indians themselves in fee simple, subject to restrictions on alienation.[14]

The United States acts in behalf of itself and as trustee or guardian for the Indians.[15] When proceeding on its own behalf the United States is (a) protecting its guardianship over the Indian, and (b) removing unlawful obstacles to the fulfillment of its obligations.[16] In *United States* v. *Fitzgerald*[17] the court said:

> The United States may lawfully maintain suits in its own courts to prevent interference with the means it adopts to exercise its powers of government and to carry into effect its policies. It may maintain such suits, although it has no pecuniary interest in the subject-matter thereof, for the purpose of protecting and enforcing its governmental rights and to aid in the execution of its governmental policies. (P. 296-297.)

The right of maintaining a suit arises pursuant to provisions in treaties with Indian tribes,[18] or congressional laws, or by virtue of the fact that legal title to land is vested in the United States, subject to the Indian right of occupancy or by reason of the fact that the Indian enjoys a vested right, granted by the Government, to hold land tax-exempt for a specified period.[19] Usually the property involved is restricted land held by an Indian under a trust or other patent from the United States, or purchased for an Indian out of funds derived from the sale of allotted lands and restricted by the Secretary of the Interior;[20] or by a mere right of occupancy, title being in the United States. Sometimes the case involves personal property furnished by the Government to the Indian, to be used by him in connection with an allotment, without the right of disposal except to other Indians, or held in trust by the United States for him, or affected by such trusts.

(c) *Suits involving land.*—It has often been held that the United States lacks the capacity to sue regarding lands held by Indians which have been freed from restrictions,[21] because it is under no duty to the Indians and has no interest in the matter.[22] However, the Government has a duty and an interest to protect the right of the Indian to hold his land free from taxation for the trust period of 25 years, and the relationship between the United States and the Indian with respect to this vested right is regarded as the legal relationship of trusteeship which gives the United States the capacity to sue on behalf of the Indians,

[7] See cases cited in note 181 of sec. 41 (1) of 28 U. S. C. A.

[8] See *Heckman* v. *United States*, 224 U. S. 413 (1912), and cases cited therein.

[9] On the general question of the right of the United States to institute suit for the benefit of a third party, see *United States* v. *San Jacinto Tin Co.*, 125 U. S. 273, 286 (1888); *Curtner* v. *United States*, 149 U. S. 662, 671-673 (1893). On the general subject of the right of the Government to sue, see *In re Debs*, 158 U. S. 564, 584 (1895).

[10] *Heckman* v. *United States*, 224 U. S. 413 (1912); also see 25 Harv. L. Rev. 733, 740 (1912).

[11] *Morrow* v. *United States*, 243 Fed. 854 (C. C. A. 8, 1917).

[12] See Chapter 8, sec. 9.

[13] *United States* v. *Candelaria*, 271 U. S. 432 (1926).

[14] *Goat* v. *United States*, 224 U. S. 458 (1912); *Deming Investment Co.* v. *United States*, 224 U. S. 471 (1912); *Heckman* v. *United States*, 224 U. S. 413 (1912). The United States represents its own interest in enforcing laws for the protection of Indians for whose benefit the suit was brought. *Heckman* v. *United States*, 224 U. S. 413, 444-446 (1912). Also see *United States* v. *Minnesota*, 270 U. S. 181 (1926).

[15] By virtue of its own interest and the interest of the tribe, see *Brewer Elliott Oil & Gas Co.* v. *United States*, 260 U. S. 77 (1922); by virtue of its interest in maintaining restrictions and Indians in possession, *Privett* v. *United States*, 256 U. S. 201 (1921). Also see *Heckman* v. *United States*, 224 U. S. 413 (1912); *United States* v. *Title Insurance Co.*, 265 U. S. 472 (1924); *Osage County Motor Co.* v. *United States*, 33 F. 2d 21 (C. C. A. 8, 1929), cert. den. 280 U. S. 577.

[16] The Supreme Court of the United States, in *United States* v. *Minnesota*, 270 U. S. 181, 194 (1926) said:

> * * * the United States has a real and direct interest in the matter presented for examination and adjudication. Its interest arises out of its guardianship over the Indians and out of its right to invoke the aid of a court of equity in removing unlawful obstacles to the fulfillment of its obligations; and in both aspects the interest is one which is vested in it as a sovereign. *Heckman* v. *United States*, 224 U. S. 413, 437-444; *United States* v. *Osage County*, 251 U. S. 128, 132-133; *LaMotte* v. *United States*, 254 U. S. 570, 575; *Cramer* v. *United States*, 261 U. S. 219, 232; *United States* v. *Beebe*, 127 U. S. 338, 342-343; *United States* v. *New Orleans Pacific Ry. Co.*, 248 U. S. 507, 518.

And see *United States* v. *Nashville, Chattanooga & St. Louis Ry. Co.*, 118 U. S. 120, 126 (1886).

[17] 201 Fed. 295 (C. C. A. 8, 1912). This case was quoted with approval in *Cramer* v. *United States*, 261 U. S. 219, 232-233 (1923).

[18] See *United States* v. *Winans*, 198 U. S. 371 (1905); *Seufert Bros. Co.* v. *United States*, 249 U. S. 194 (1919) (suits brought to prevent interference with Indian fishing rights secured by treaty).

[19] The Circuit Court of Appeals in the case of *United States* v. *Colvard*, 89 F. 2d 312 (C. C. A. 4, 1937) said:

> * * * even if the title were not in the United States, there can be no question as to the right of the United States to institute suit for the protection of the rights of these wards of the nation in and to their property. (P. 314.)

But *cf. Hy-yu-tse-mil-kin* v. *Smith*, 194 U. S. 401 (1904).

[20] *United States* v. *Brown*, 8 F. 2d 564 (C. C. A. 8, 1925), cert. den. 270 U. S. 644 (1926); but *cf. McCurdy* v. *United States*, 246 U. S. 263 (1918).

[21] *Deming Investment Co.* v. *United States*, 224 U. S. 471 (1912); *Mullen* v. *United States*, 224 U. S. 448 (1912); *Goat* v. *United States*, 224 U. S. 458 (1912); *United States* v. *Waller*, 243 U. S. 452 (1917). Accord: *United States* v. *Bartlett*, 235 U. S. 72 (1914); *United States* v. *Chase*, 245 U. S. 89 (1917). Also see *United States* v. *Hemmer*, 241 U. S. 379 (1916). Contra: *United States* v. *Apple*, 262 Fed. 200 (D. C. Kan. 1919).

[22] When an Indian is granted full title, including the right of alienation, and when he conveys such property, the United States cannot maintain suit for his benefit to annul the deed on the ground that it was procured by fraud. *United States* v. *Waller*, 243 U. S. 452 (1917). Also see *United States* v. *Hemmer*, 241 U. S. 379 (1916), and *Larkin* v *Paugh*, 276 U. S. 431 (1928).

to recover illegal taxes or restrain collection of taxes levied on land freed from restrictions.[23]

The United States may sue to enjoin the imposition of local or state taxes on allotted lands or permanent improvements thereon, or personal property obtained from the United States and used by the Indians on the allotted lands. The leading case in which the United States obtained an injunction against county officials attempting to tax allotted lands during the trust period is the case of *United States* v. *Rickert.*[24] The Supreme Court said:

> We do not perceive that the Government has any remedy at law that could be at all efficacious for the protection of its rights in the property in question and for the attainment of its purposes in reference to these Indians. If the personal property and the structures on the land were sold for taxes and possession taken by the purchaser, then the Indians could not be maintained on the allotted lands and the Government, unless it abandoned its policy to maintain these Indians on the allotted lands, would be compelled to appropriate more money and apply it in the erection of other necessary structures on the land and in the purchase of other stock required for purposes of cultivation. And so on, every year. It is manifest that no proceedings at law can be prompt and efficacious for the protection of the rights of the Government, and that adequate relief can only be had in a court of equity, which, by a comprehensive decree, can finally determine once for all the question of validity of the assessment and taxation in question, and thus give security against any action upon the part of the local authorities tending to interfere with the complete control, not only of the Indians by the Government, but of the property supplied to them by the Government and in use on the allotted lands. *Railway Co.* v. *McShane,* 22 Wall. 444; *Coosaw Mining Co.* v. *South Carolina,* 144 U. S. 550, 564–66.
>
> Some observations may be made that are applicable to the whole case. It is said that the State has conferred upon these Indians the right of suffrage and other rights that ordinarily belong only to citizens, and that they ought, therefore, to share the burdens of government like other people who enjoy such rights. These are considerations to be addressed to Congress. It is for the legislative branch of the Government to say when these Indians shall cease to be dependent and assume the responsibilities attaching to citizenship. That is a political question, which the courts may not determine. We can only deal with the case as it exists under the legislation of Congress.

The Supreme Court,[25] in holding that the United States may sue to enjoin discriminatory state taxes levied on allotments of noncompetent Osage Indians, said:

> Certain is it that as the United States as guardian of the Indians had the duty to protect them from spoliation and, therefore, the right to prevent their being illegally deprived of the property rights conferred under the Act of Congress of 1906, the power existed in the officers of the United States to invoke relief for the accomplishment of the purpose stated. Indeed the Act of Congress of 1917, providing for the appraisement of the lands in question, by necessary implication, if not in express terms, treated the power of the officers of the United States to resist the illegal assessments as undoubted.
>
> And the existence of power in the United States to sue which is thus established disposes of the proposition that because of remedies afforded to individuals under the state law the authority of a court of equity could not be invoked by the United States. This necessarily follows because, in the first place, as the authority of the United States extended to all the non-competent members of the tribe it obviously resulted that the interposition of a court of equity to prevent the wrong complained of was essential in order to avoid a multiplicity of suits (see *Union Pacific Ry. Co.* v. *Cheyenne,* 113 U. S. 516; *Smyth* v. *Ames,* 169 U. S. 466, 517; *Cruickshank* v. *Bidwell,* 176 U. S. 73, 81; *Boise Artesian Water Co.* v. *Boise City,* 213 U. S. 276, 283; *Greene* v. *Louisville & Interurban R. R. Co.,* 244 U. S. 499, 506); in the second place because, as the wrong relied upon was not a mere mistake or error committed in the enforcement of the state tax laws, but a systematic and intentional disregard of such laws by the state officers for the purpose of destroying the rights of the whole class of non-competent Indians, who were subject to the protection of the United States, it follows that such class wrong and disregard of the state statute gave rise to the right to invoke the interposition of a court of equity in order that an adequate remedy might be afforded. *Cummings* v. *National Bank,* 101 U. S. 153; *Reagan* v. *Farmers' Loan & Trust Co.,* 154 U. S. 362, 390; *Pittsburgh, etc., Ry. Co.* v. *Backus,* 154 U. S. 421; *Coulter* v. *Louisville & Nashville R. R. Co.,* 196 U. S. 599; *Raymond* v. *Chicago Union Traction Co.,* 207 U. S. 20; *Greene* v. *Louisville & Interurban R. R. Co.,* 244 U. S. 499, 507. In fact the subject is fully covered by the ruling in *Union Pacific R. R. Co.* v. *Weld County,* 247 U. S. 282 (pp. 133, 134).

Where restrictions on land are transgressed, the Government can choose such legal remedies as are necessary to protect the Indian. It may maintain an action to quiet the title to land;[26] set aside conveyances made prior to the expiration of the trust period, restore possession to the Indian even though the allottee is a citizen,[27] or where title has been vested in the allottee but the right of alienation is restricted.[28] The Government may bring suit to cancel deeds and mortgages;[29] to set aside conveyances;[30] to annul a patent issued by the United States in order to establish possessory rights of individual Indians;[31] to set aside inequitable contracts;[32] to sue for a cancellation of a mining lease and assignment of rents and royalties issuing therefrom;[33] to cancel oil and gas leases.[34] The Government may sue a lessee and a surety company which signed a faithful performance bond, for a breach of a lease, involving trust lands, made

---

[23] *Morrow* v. *United States,* 243 Fed. 854 (C. C. A. 8, 1917); *McCurdy* v. *United States,* 264 U. S. 484 (1924). Also see *Board of County Commissioners of Tulsa County, Oklahoma* v. *United States,* 94 F. 2d 450 (C. C. A. 10, 1938); and *United States* v. *Moore,* 284 Fed. 86 (C. C. A. 8, 1922), in which the United States brought suit to recover royalties paid under an assignment illegally made during the period of restrictions, after the period had expired. The court said, in *United States* v. *Southern Surety Co.,* 9 F. 2d 664 (D. C. E. D. Okla. 1925):

> * * * removal of restrictions against the alienation of allotted land does not preclude the United States from maintaining an action to remove a cloud illegally placed on such title during the restricted period. This action is properly brought in the name of the United States. (P. 665.)

United States v. *Gray,* 201 Fed. 291 (C. C. A. 8, 1912); and *United States* v. *Sherburne Mercantile Co.,* 68 F. 2d 155 (C. C. A. 9, 1933).

The Federal Government may sue to recover taxes illegally levied upon personal property such as livestock and farm implements which it issued to members or to a tribe, *United States* v. *Dewey County, S. D.,* 14 F. 2d 784 (D. C. S. Dak. 1926).

[24] 188 U. S. 432, 444, 445 (C. C. A. 8, 1903).

[25] *United States* v. *Osage County,* 251 U. S. 128 (1919).

[26] Title to distributed land claimed by, or thought to be the property of, an Indian, may be determined by suit brought by the United States to quiet Indian title. *United States* v. *Wildcat,* 244 U. S. 111 (1917); *United States* v. *Atkins,* 260 U. S. 220 (1922); *United States* v. *Title Insurance Co.,* 265 U. S. 472 (1924); *United States* v. *Jackson,* 280 U. S. 183 (1930).

[27] *Bowling* v. *United States,* 233 U. S. 528 (1914); and *Tiger* v. *Western Investment Co.,* 221 U. S. 286 (1911). Knoepfler, Legal Status of the American Indian and His Property (1922), 7 Ia. L. B., pp. 232, 246. The Act of June 25, 1910, 36 Stat. 703, 744, and the Act of July 1, 1916, 39 Stat. 262, 312, and subsequent appropriation acts provided for the expenses of such suits.

[28] All conveyances of such land made prior to the expiration of the restriction on alienation are void. *United States* v. *Noble,* 237 U. S. 74 (1915).

[29] *Deming Investment Co.* v. *United States,* 224 U. S. 471 (1912).

[30] *United States* v. *First National Bank,* 234 U. S. 245 (1914).

[31] *Cramer* v. *United States,* 261 U. S. 219, 232–233 (1923).

[32] *United States* v. *Boyd,* 68 Fed. 577 (C. C. W. D. N. C. 1895).

[33] *United States* v. *Noble,* 237 U. S. 74 (1915).

[34] *Brewer Elliott Oil and Gas Co.* v. *United States,* 260 U. S. 77 (1922).

by an allottee and approved by the Secretary.[35] The United States may sue to enjoin trespassing on tribal lands and on restricted allotments.[36] It may enjoin the assertion of rights under leases of restricted allotments or of land held by the United States in trust for a tribe obtained from an Indian without conforming to the statutory and administrative requirements, and may enjoin the negotiation of such unlawful leases in the future.[37]

Even where unrestricted Indians are involved, the federal court has jurisdiction over cases based on statutory tax-exemptions.[38] The right of the United States to bring suits in behalf of Indians involving their lands after the period of trust or restrictions has expired, and to which the United States has no title, is upheld in many cases, among them *United States* v. *Moore*,[39] in which the United States brought suit to recover royalties paid under an assignment illegally made during the period of restrictions; the suit being brought after the period had expired.[40]

(*d*) *Suits involving personal property*.—The United States may maintain an action for trover;[40a] an action to replevy timber cut by a few members of a tribe from a part of a reservation not occupied in severalty, and made into saw logs and sold to a third party;[41] and to replevy a team of horses bought by the superintendent of an Indian agency with the trust money of an incompetent Indian, where the bill of sale recited the source of the purchase money, even though the defendant had incurred expenses for veterinary services and for care of the team while it was in the control of the Indian.[42]

The United States may recover damages for the wrongful taking of wool sheared from sheep furnished to an Indian by the Government to be used on his allotment,[43] and for the recovery of funds disbursed after a certificate of competency was issued,[44] and may bring action for rent on behalf of an individual Indian[45] or a tribe.[46] It may recover restricted funds deposited in a local bank, such indebtedness of the bank being an indebtedness to the United States and entitled to priority over other deposits.[47]

(*e*) *Other suits*.—The right of the United States to bring suit on behalf of Indians has been upheld in a variety of cases not involving restricted property. Thus it has been held that the Government may recover in a suit filed in connection with a contract of employment of Indians in a wild-west show. The damages would include breach of contract and expenses incurred returning the Indians to the agency, as well as the amount due the Indians.[48]

(*f*) *Effect of judgment*.—The Government is not bound unless it is a party to the litigation.[49] No judgment of any court, state or federal, rendered in a suit between an Indian and a private party, involving property under the control of the Government, to which the Government is a stranger, can bind the Government or its administrative officers.[50] Where the Government has employed and paid a special attorney to represent the Indians, or the United States Attorney has joined as associate counsel with the attorneys representing the Indians in the litigation and filed a motion to vacate the judgment, the United States is bound as effectively as if it were a party, by the judgment in a suit instituted and prosecuted to final judgment by this special attorney.[51]

---

[35] *United States* v. *Gray*, 201 Fed. 291 (C. C. A. 8, 1912).

[36] *Ash Sheep Co.* v. *United States*, 252 U. S. 159 (1920). Also see *Taylor* v. *United States*, 44 F. (2d) 531 (C. C. A. 9, 1930).

[37] *United States* v. *Flournoy Live-Stock and Real-Estate Co.*, 71 Fed. 576 (C. C. Nebr. 1896). Also see *Brewer Elliott Oil and Gas Co.* v. *United States*, 260 U. S. 77 (1922).

[38] In *United States* v. *Morrow*, 243 Fed. 854 (C. C. A. 8, 1917), suit was brought by the United States not as guardian but as trustee of lands for a mixed-blood Indian against Becker County, Minn., officials to restrain collection of taxes levied upon certain allotted lands. In this case the Government had terminated the guardianship over the Indian owner with respect to his land by the Acts of June 21, 1906, 34 Stat. 325, 353, and March 1, 1907, 34 Stat. 1015, 1034. The court held that the right of the Indian to hold his land free from taxation for the trust period of 25 years was a vested right which the Government could not alter and that hence where the Indian was claiming no rights under the Acts of June 21, 1906, and March 1, 1907, but was insisting upon holding his land under the trust patent his land could not be taxed by the state. The relationship between the United States and the Indian with respect to this vested right was looked upon by the court as the legal relationship of trusteeship, giving the United States capacity to sue in behalf of the Indian.

[39] 284 Fed. 86 (C. C. A. 8, 1922).

[40] See also *United States* v. *Gray*, 201 Fed. 291 (C. C. A. 8, 1912), and *United States* v. *Southern Surety Co.*, 9 F. 2d, 664 (D. C. E. D. Okla. 1925), in which it was said,

> * * * removal of restrictions against the alienation of allotted land does not preclude the United States from maintaining an action to remove a cloud illegally placed on such title during the restricted period. This action is properly brought in the name of the United States. (P. 665.)

And see *United States* v. *Sherburne Mercantile Co.*, 68 F. 2d 155 (C. C. A. 9, 1933).

[40a] *Pine River Logging & Improvement Co.* v. *United States*, 186 U. S. 279 (1902).

[41] *United States* v. *Cook*, 19 Wall. (86 U. S.) 591 (1873).

[42] *United States* v. *O'Gorman*, 287 Fed. 135 (C. C. A. 8, 1923).

[43] *United States* v. *Fitzgerald*, 201 Fed. 295 (C. C. A. 8, 1912).

[44] In the case of *United States* v. *Mashunkashey*, 72 F. 2d. 847 (C. C. A. 10, 1934), the court said:

> But we entertain no doubt that a court of equity has the power to cancel it (certificate of competency) effective from the date of its issuance as to persons participating in the acts evoking the cancellation or having knowledge of the facts and acquiring rights with that knowledge. (P. 850.)

[45] *United States* v. *Chase*, 245 U. S. 89 (1917).

[46] *Kirby* v. *United States*, 260 U. S. 423 (1922).

[47] *Bramwell* v. *U. S. Fidelity Co.*, 269 U. S. 483 (1926).

[48] *United States* v. *Pumphrey*, 11 App. D. C. 44 (1897).

[49] *Sunderland* v. *United States*, 266 U. S. 226 (1924); *Privett* v. *United States*, 256 U. S. 201 (1921). The United States is an indispensable party to condemnation proceedings brought by the state to acquire a right-of-way over lands which the United States holds in trust for Indian allottees. *Minnesota* v. *United States*, 305 U. S. 382 (C. C. A. 8, 1939).

[50] *Bowling* v. *United States*, 233 U. S. 528 (1914); *United States* v. *Board of Nat. Missions of Presbyterian Church*, 37 F. 2d 272 (C. C. A. 10, 1929).

[51] *United States* v. *Candelaria*, 271 U. S. 432 (1926). Also see Op. Sol. I. D., M.27788, August 6, 1934. For other examples of a special attorney employed to assist in the conduct of legal proceedings pertaining to claims in behalf of Osage Indians for the recovery of royalties on oil produced from tribal lands, see Act of August 25, 1937, 50 Stat. 805; Act of March 2, 1895, 28 Stat. 848, 859–860; Act of June 4, 1897, 30 Stat. 11, 56; Act of July 1, 1898, 30 Stat. 597, 641; Act of March 3, 1899, 30 Stat. 1074, 1113; Act of June 25, 1910, 36 Stat. 703, 744; Act of August 24, 1912, 37 Stat. 417, 464; Act of August 1, 1914, 38 Stat. 609, 653; Act of March 3, 1915, 38 Stat. 822, 866; Act of July 1, 1916, 39 Stat. 262, 312; Act of June 12, 1917, 40 Stat. 105, 156; Act of July 19, 1919, 41 Stat. 163, 208; Act of March 4, 1921, 41 Stat. 1367, 1411.

Mr. Justice Van Devanter, in the case of *United States* v. *Candelaria*, said:

> The Indians of the pueblo are wards of the United States and hold their lands subject to the restriction that the same cannot be alienated in any-wise without its consent. A judgment or decree which operates directly or indirectly to transfer the lands from the Indians, where the United States has not authorized or appeared in the suit, infringes that restriction. The United States has an interest in maintaining and enforcing the restriction which cannot be affected by such a judgment or decree. This Court has said in dealing with a like situation: "It necessarily follows that, as a transfer of the allotted lands contrary to the inhibition of Congress would be a violation of the governmental rights of the United States arising from its obligation to a dependent people, no stipulations, contracts, or judgments rendered in suits to which the Government is a stranger, can affect its interest. The authority of the United States to enforce the restraint lawfully created cannot be impaired by any action without its consent." *Bowling and Miami Improvement Co.* v. *United States*, 233 U. S. 528, 534. And that ruling has been recognized and given effect in other cases. *Privett* v. *United States*, 256 U. S. 201, 204; *Sunderland* v. *United States*, 266 U. S. 226, 232, (Pp. 443–434.)
>
> But, as it appears that for many years the United States has employed and paid a special attorney to represent the Pueblo

In *United States* v. *Candelaria*[52] two judgments had been obtained against a Pueblo in New Mexico in suits brought by it to clear title to its land—one in a territory court, concluded in the state courts after statehood, and the other in the federal court—in neither of which the United States was a party. Ordinarily, judgments rendered in a suit to which the United States is not a party are not binding upon the United States. The court, after adverting to the fact that under territorial laws, sanctioned by Congress, the Pueblo was a juristic person, with capacity to sue and defend with respect to its land, citing *Lane* v. *Pueblo of Santa Rosa*,[53] held that the state court of New Mexico had jurisdiction to enter a judgment in an action by an Indian Pueblo against opposing claimants concerning title to land, which would be conclusive on the United States if the latter authorized the bringing or prosecution of the suit, or if an attorney employed by the United States appeared on behalf of the Pueblo in the case.

The United States is not bound by a judgment in which a tribal attorney, employed by the tribe under a contract approved by the Secretary of the Interior and paid from tribal funds, had appeared and represented individual Indians. In *Logan* v. *United States*,[54] the Circuit Court of Appeals, said:

> * * * To sustain the plea, appellant's counsel relies upon United States v. Candelaria, 271 U. S. 432, 46 S. Ct. 561, 70 L. Ed. 1023. The distinction, as we see it, between that case and this is that it appears therein that the attorney who represented prior litigation in a case of the same character and between the same parties in the state court was employed and paid by the United States, whereas in this case the superintendent and his attorney, in making the interplea in the probate court, were not paid as such officers by the United States; but annual appropriations have been made by Congress and were being made at that time, and it was provided that they should be paid out of the funds held by the Secretary of the Interior for the Osage Indians. The tribal attorney was selected by the tribe. They were not, therefore, the representatives of the United States in making the interplea. There is no showing that the Secretary of the Interior advised that the interplea be made. We, therefore, conclude that the United States, as plaintiff in this suit, was not bound by the action of the county court in denying the interplea. * * * (P. 698.)

If the United States is entitled to institute an action on its own behalf and on behalf of the Indians, the Indians cannot determine the course of the suit or settle it contrary to the position of the Government.[55] The Indians, being represented by the Government, are not necessary parties.[56]

The 6-year statute of limitations which runs against the United States in relation to annulling land patents is inapplicable when the suit is to protect the rights of Indians,[57] and does not run against members of Indian tribes for claims on federal income taxes wrongfully deducted by the Indian superintendent from funds due to them.[58] It is also settled that said statutes of limitation or other state statutes neither bind nor have any application to the United States when suing to enforce a public right or to protect the interests of its wards.[59]

If Congress provides a statutory method for determining Indian land claims, and the claim is held invalid, the United States cannot later reopen the question.[60]

Some statutes instruct the Attorney General to bring suit in the name of the United States to quiet title to Indian land;[61] or authorize the Attorney General, upon the request of the Secretary of the Interior, to appear in suits involving Indian tribal lands,[62] without requiring Indians to be made parties; or, authorize the Secretary to instruct the Attorney General to bring suit in the name of the United States to quiet and settle title to distributed tribal[63] or allotted lands.[64]

(2) United States as defendant.—The general rule is that the United States cannot be sued in any court, whether state or federal, without its consent.[65]

The immunity of the United States to suit without its consent

---

> Indians and look after their interests, our answer is made with the qualification that, if the decree was rendered in a suit begun and prosecuted by the special attorney so employed and paid, we think the United States is as effectually concluded as if it were a party to the suit. *Souffront* v. *Compagnie des Sucreries*, 217 U. S. 475, 486; *Lovejoy* v. *Murray*, 3 Wall. 1, 18; *Claflin* v. *Fletcher*, 7 Fed. 851, 852; *Maloy* v. *Duden*, 86 Fed. 402, 404; *James* v. *Germania Iron Co.*, 107 Fed. 597, 618. (Pp. 443–444.)

[52] 271 U. S. 432 (1926). See sec. 2A(1)(f), *supra*. See Chapter 20, sec. 7.

[53] 249 U. S. 110 (1919).

[54] 58 F. 2d 697 (C. C. A. 10, 1932).

[55] *Heckman* v. *United States*, 224 U. S. 413 (1912); also see *Pueblo of Picuris in State of New Mexico* v. *Abeyta*, 50 F. 2d 12 (C. C. A. 10, 1931).

[56] *Minnesota* v. *Hitchcock*, 185 U. S. 373, 387 (1902). In the case of *Heckman* v. *United States*, the Supreme Court said:

> The argument necessarily proceeds upon the assumption that the representation of these Indians by the United States is of an incomplete or inadequate character; that although the United States, by virtue of the guardianship it has retained, is prosecuting this suit for the purpose of enforcing the restrictions Congress has imposed, and of thus securing possession to the Indians, their presence as parties to the suit is essential to their protection. This position is wholly untenable. There can be no more complete representation than that on the part of the United States in acting on behalf of these dependents—whom Congress, with respect to the restricted lands, has not yet released from tutelage. Its efficacy does not depend upon the Indian's acquiescence. It does not rest upon convention, nor is it circumscribed by rules which govern private relations. It is a representation which traces its source to the plenary control of Congress in legislating for the protection of the Indians under its care, and it recognizes no limitations that are inconsistent with the discharge of the national duty.
>
> When the United States instituted this suit, it undertook to represent, and did represent, the Indian grantors whose conveyances it sought to cancel. It was not necessary to make these grantors parties, for the Government was in court on their behalf. Their presence as parties could not add to, or detract from, the effect of the proceedings to determine the violation of the restrictions and the consequent invalidity of the conveyances. As by the act of Congress they were precluded from alienating their lands, they were likewise precluded from taking any position in the legal proceedings instituted by the Government to enforce the restrictions which would render such proceedings ineffectual or give support to the prohibited acts. The cause colud not be dismissed upon their consent; they could not compromise it; nor could they asume any attitude with respect to their interest which would derogate from its complete representation by the United States. This is involved necessarily in the conclusion that the United States is entitled to sue, and in the nature and purpose of the suit. (Pp. 444–445.)

[57] *Cramer* v. *United States*, 261 U. S. 219 (1923). See also *United States* v. *Minnesota*, 270 U. S. 181, 196 (1926).

[58] 34 Op. A. G. 302 (1924).

[59] *United States* v. *Thompson*, 98 U. S. 486 (1878); *Ches. & Del. Canal Co.* v. *United States*, 250 U. S. 123, 125 (1919). *United States* v. *Minnesota*, 270 U. S. 181, 196 (1926).

The same rule is applicable to the principle of laches. See *United States* v. *Nashville, etc., R'y Co.*, 118 U. S. 120 (1886). The Government retains such an interest in restricted lands as would render applicable the well-settled rule that the statute of limitations does not run against the sovereign. *Schrimpscher* v. *Stockton*, 183 U. S. 290 (1902).

When the United States sues on behalf of an Indian tribe to recover compensation from a railroad, it stands in the shoes of the tribe and is bound by estoppel. *United States* v. *Ft. Smith & W. R. Co.*, 195 Fed. 211 (C. C. A. 8, 1912).

[60] *United States* v. *Atkins*, 260 U. S. 220 (1922); *United States* v. *Title Insurance Co.*, 265 U. S. 472 (1924). Also see *United States* v. *Wildcat*, 244 U. S. 111 (1917).

[61] Joint Resolution of March 3, 1879, 20 Stat. 488 (Shawnee).

[62] Act of March 2, 1901, 31 Stat. 950, 43 U. S. C. 868. The Attorney General is sometimes authorized to employ a special attorney, upon the recommendation of the Secretary. Act of March 3, 1901, 31 Stat. 1133, 1181; Act of April 28, 1904, 33 Stat. 452, 506.

[63] Joint Resolution of March 3, 1879, 20 Stat. 488 (Shawnee); Act of March 1, 1889, 25 Stat. 768 (Shawnee).

[64] Act of March 3, 1915, 38 Stat. 822, 866.

[65]
> * * * the decisions that no suit or action can be maintained against the Nation in any of its courts without its consent * * * only recognize the obvious truth that a nation is not without its consent subject to the controlling action of any of its instrumentalities or agencies. The creature cannot rule the creator. *Kawananakoa* v. *Polyblank, Trustee, &c.* 205 U. S. 349. * * * (*Kansas* v. *Colorado*, 206 U. S. 46, 83 (1907).)

See also *Minnesota* v. *United States*, 305 U. S. 382 (1939), and cases cited therein, and sec. 3, *infra*.

extends to cases in which a state of the Union is the plaintiff. Thus in *Minnesota* v. *United States*[66] the Supreme Court held that the United States could not be made a party defendant in proceedings instituted by the State of Minnesota to condemn allotted Indian lands held in trust by the United States for the allottee. The court said:

> * * * A proceeding against property in which the United States has an interest is a suit against the United States. *The Siren*, 7 Wall. 152, 154; *Carr* v. *United States*, 98 U. S. 433, 437; *Stanley* v. *Schwalby*, 162 U. S. 255. Compare *Utah Power & Light Co.* v. *United States*, 243 U. S. 389. It is confessedly the owner of the fee of the Indian allotted lands and holds the same in trust for the allottees. As the United States owns the fee of these parcels, the right of way cannot be condemned without making it a party. (P. 386.)

But the United States cannot be made a party in such a suit without its consent. The court further said:

> The exemption of the United States from being sued without its consent extends to a suit by a State. Compare *Kansas* v. *United States*, 204 U. S. 331, 342; *Arizona* v. *California*, 298 U. S. 558, 568, 571, 572. Compare *Minnesota* v. *Hitchcock*, 185 U. S. 373, 382–387; *Oregon* v. *Hitchcock*, 202 U. S. 60. Hence Minnesota cannot maintain this suit against the United States unless authorized by some act of Congress. (P. 387.)

If the required consent is given, the objection being removed, the court may settle the controversy involved.[67]

The United States is improperly joined as a party defendant in a suit against an Indian tribe under a special act authorizing the Court of Claims to consider and adjudicate such claim where neither the special act nor any general statute authorized suit against the United States, although the United States is joined in the suit in the capacity of trustee for an Indian tribe.[68]

Terms and conditions on which consent is given may be prescribed and must be met.[69] Not only may the sovereign prescribe the terms and conditions on which it consents to be sued, but it may also determine the manner in which the suit shall be conducted and may withdraw its consent whenever it supposes that justice to the public requires such withdrawal.[70]

The cases in which the United States has expressly given its consent to be sued in Indian matters either in the Court of Claims or in the district courts are numerous.[71]

Cases in which consent to be sued seem to have been attributed to the United States without express authority from Congress are not so numerous. An instance is the case of *United States* v. *Equitable Trust Co.*[72] In that case a suit was instituted by a next friend in behalf of an incompetent full-blood Creek Indian under guardianship to recover accumulated royalties which had come into the hands of the Secretary of the Interior in trust for the Indian and were subsequently distributed upon a written request in the name of the Indian procured by fraud. The United States intervened in the litigation. By this act, the Supreme Court held, it impliedly consented to reasonable allowances for services and expenses, even if the fund was subject to statutory restrictions. This decision, however, may be explained by the fact that the United States had intervened in the suit in the character of a party plaintiff.

(3) **United States as intervener.**—In view of the established doctrine that the United States cannot be sued without its consent, the question arises whether the United States can become a party to a pending suit by intervention, and, if so, under what circumstances. It appears that where an intervention places the Government in the position of a plaintiff, as in *New York* v. *New Jersey*[73] and *Oklahoma* v. *Texas*,[74] the Government may properly become an intervener. It is clear, however, that if by such intervention the Government would become virtually a defendant in the suit, its appearance as an intervener would come in direct conflict with the ruling that the United States cannot be sued. The consent of the United States cannot be given by any officer of the United States unless authority to do so has been conferred upon him by some act of Congress. This proposition is illustrated in the case of *Stanley* v. *Schwalby*,[75] in which the Supreme Court said:

> * * * The United States, by various acts of Congress, have consented to be sued in their own courts in certain classes of cases; but they have never consented to be sued in the courts of a State in any case. Neither the Secretary of War nor the Attorney General, nor any subordinate of either, has been authorized to waive the exemption of the United States from judicial process, or to submit the United States, or their property, to the jurisdiction of the court in a suit brought against their officers. *Case* v. *Terrell*, 11 Wall. 199, 202; *Carr* v. *United States*, 98 U. S. 433, 438; *United States* v. *Lee*, 106 U. S. 196, 205. * * * (P. 270.)

In other words, in the absence of congressional authority no officer of the United States can bind the United States as a party defendant, whether in an original suit or by way of intervention. Instances in which the United States has given such consent are to be found in the Act of February 6, 1901,[76] permitting suits for allotment in the district courts of the United States, providing for service of process upon the Attorney General and requiring the District Attorney, upon whom service is also to be made, to appear and defend the interests of the United States in the suit; and in the Act of April 10, 1926,[77] providing a process whereby the United States may be compelled to appear and defend its interests in any suit pending in the federal or state courts of Oklahoma in which restricted members of the Five Civilized Tribes are parties. The practice adopted under this statute is for the United States Attorney to appear for and in behalf of the United States, within the statutory period, upon service of the notice upon the superintendent as provided by the statute.

(4) **Indian tribe as party litigant.**—As already seen,[78] the Indian tribes within the territory of the United States, while

[66] 305 U. S. 382 (1939).

[67] *National Casket Co.* v. *United States*, 263 Fed. 246 (D. C. S. D. N. Y., 1920); *Keokuk & Hamilton Bridge Co.* v. *United States*, 260 U. S. 125 (1922). See sec. 3, *infra*.

[68] *Turner* v. *United States*, 248 U. S. 354 (1919). Cf. *Green* v. *Menominee Tribe*, 233 U. S. 558 (1914). Also see *Winton* v. *Amos*, 255 U. S. 373 (1921).

[69] *Trest* v. *Farmers' Loan & Trust Co.*, 185 Fed. 760 (C. C. A. 2, 1911); *Reid Wrecking Co.* v. *United States*, 202 Fed. 314 (D. C. N. D. Ohio 1913).

[70] *United States* v. *Clarke*, 8 Pet. 436 (1834); *Murray's Lessee* v. *Hoboken Land and Improvement Co.*, 18 How. 272 (1855); *Beers* v. *Arkansas*, 20 How. 527 (1857); *Ball* v. *Halsell*, 161 U. S. 72 (1896).

[71] See *infra*. sec. 3, Court of Claims. See also Act of December 21, 1911, 37 Stat. 46, amendatory of Act of August 15, 1894, 28 Stat. 286, 305, as amended by Act of February 6, 1901, 31 Stat. 760, and Act of March 3, 1911, 36 Stat. 1004, 25 U. S. C. 345, conferring jurisdiction upon the district courts of the United States of

> * * * all actions, suits, or proceedings involving the right of any person, in whole or in part of Indian blood or descent, to any allotment of land under any law or treaty.

and authorizing and directing that the United States be made a party to such suit. This act followed the decisions of the Supreme Court in the cases of *Hy-yu-tse-mil-kin* v. *Smith*, 194 U. S. 401 (1904) and *McKay* v. *Kalyton*, 204 U. S. 458 (1907), in which the Supreme Court had held that the United States was not a necessary party to such suit for allotment. And see fn. 184, *infra*.

[72] 283 U. S. 738 (1931).

[73] 256 U. S. 296 (1921).

[74] 258 U. S. 574 (1922).

[75] 162 U. S. 255 (1896).

[76] 31 Stat. 760, 25 U. S. C. 345.

[77] 44 Stat. 239.

[78] See Chapter 14, sec. 3.

having some of the attributes of sovereignty usually possessed by independent communities, have been declared by the Supreme Court not to be either states of the Union or foreign nations within the meaning of Article III, section 2 of the United States Constitution giving original jurisdiction to the Supreme Court in controversies in which a state of the Union or a citizen thereof, and a foreign state or subjects and citizens thereof are parties.[79] Consequently an Indian tribe as such cannot sue, be sued, or intervene in any case where the original jurisdiction of the Supreme Court is invoked.[80]

Whether a tribe can sue or be sued under the diversity of citizenship clause of section 41 (1) of title 28 of the United States Code in the federal courts is a moot question. An Indian tribe as such is not a citizen within the meaning of that clause. If it were incorporated under the laws of the United States it could not sue or be sued under the diversity of citizenship clause unless there were an act of Congress providing that a tribe should be considered as possessing a state citizenship for jurisdictional purposes.[81]

The statutes which confer upon tribes capacity to sue or to be sued, and the question of whether, in the absence of such a statute such suits may be maintained, are elsewhere treated.[82]

(5) **Individual Indian as party litigant.**—As a general rule, an Indian irrespective of his citizenship or tribal relations, may sue in any state court of competent jurisdiction to redress any wrong committed against his person or property outside the limits of the reservation.[83] But the mere fact that the plaintiff is an Indian does not vest jurisdiction in the federal courts.[84]

This being true, the only grounds upon which a federal court could take jurisdiction of a suit by an Indian would be either because of diversity of citizenship between the plaintiff and defendant or because the cause of action arose under the Constitution, treaties, or laws of the United States. In *Deere* v. *St. Lawrence River Power Company*,[85] the rule as to the first branch of this proposition is succinctly stated:

> Diversity of citizenship is not relied upon to grant jurisdiction. Nor may this action be maintained merely because the appellant is an Indian. * * * (P. 551.)

Originally the members of an Indian tribe were not regarded as citizens unless naturalized, either collectively or individually, under some treaty or law of the United States, and, consequently, they could not sue in the federal courts on the ground of diversity of citizenship.[86] In cases, however, where an individual Indian, although a member of a tribe, was a citizen of the United States by virtue of some treaty or law of Congress, if all other elements of federal jurisdiction were present, he could sue under this clause.[87]

B. JURISDICTION DEPENDENT UPON CHARACTER OF SUBJECT MATTER

As to the character of the subject matter as an element of federal jurisdiction, it is to be observed that the cases are considerably in conflict in determining whether an action arises under the Constitution, treaties, or laws of the United States. It is quite clear, however, that the federal question must appear by specific allegations in the bill of complaint, and not from facts developed either in the answer or in the course of the trial.[88]

A number of general statutes contain jurisdictional provisions conferring jurisdiction over defined subjects of Indian concern upon the federal courts.[89]

---

[79] *Cherokee Nation* v. *Georgia*, 5 Pet. 1 (1831).

[80] Congress cannot refer directly to the Supreme Court for adjudication of the claim of an Indian tribe, for that would be equivalent to invoking an original jurisdiction which that court cannot exercise under the Constitution, but the matter may be referred to an inferior court and brought to the Supreme Court by appeal if the necessary legislation to that end is provided. *Yankton Sioux Tribe* v. *United States*, 272 U. S. 351 (1926).

[81] See *Banker's Trust Co.* v. *Tex. & Pac. Ry.*, 241 U. S. 295 (1916). The words "citizens" and "aliens," as used in the judiciary acts, have been considered as including corporations. *Barrow S. S. Co.* v. *Kane*, 170 U. S. 100 (1898).

[82] See Chapter 14, sec. 6.

[83] *Wiley* v. *Keokuk*, 6 Kan. 94, 110 (1870); *Ain-Dus-Oke-Shig* v. *Beaulieu*, 98 Minn. 98, 100, 107 N. W. 820 (1906); *Brown* v. *Anderson*, 61 Okla. 136, 160 Pac. 724, 726 (1916); *Y-ta-tah-wah* v. *Rebock et al.* 105 Fed. 257 (C. C. N. D. Iowa 1900); *Felix* v. *Patrick*, 145 U. S. 317, 330 (1892). See Chapter 8, sec. 6.

[84] *United States* v. *Seneca Nation of New York Indians*, 274 Fed. 946, 950 (D. C. W. D. N. Y. 1921).

[85] 32 F. 2d 550 (C. C. A. 2, 1929).

[86] *Elk* v. *Wilkins*, 112 U. S. 94 (1884). See Chapter 8, sec. 2.

[87] See *Felix* v. *Patrick*, 145 U. S. 317 (1892) wherein the Supreme Court said:

> It is scarcely necessary to say in this connection that, while until this time [the granting of citizenship under Art. VI, Treaty of April 29, 1868, 15 Stat. 635] they were not citizens of the United States, capable of suing as such in the Federal courts, the courts of Nebraska were open to them as they are to all persons irrespective of race or color. *Swartsel* v. *Rogers*, 3 Kansas, 374; *Blue Jacket* v. *Johnson County*, 3 Kansas 299; *Wiley* v. *Keokuk*, 6 Kansas 94. (P. 332.)

And see Chapter 8, sec. 6.

[88] *Schulthis* v. *McDougal*, 225 U. S. 561 (C. C. A. 8, 1912):

> To sustain the contention that the suit was one arising under the laws of the United States, counsel for the appellants point out the statutes (Acts March 1, 1901, 31 Stat. 861, c. 676; June 30, 1902, 32 Stat. 500, c. 1323; April 26, 1906, 34 Stat. 137, c. 1876, § 22) relating to the allotment in severalty of the lands of the Creek Nation, the leasing and alienation thereof after allotment, the making of allotments to the heirs of deceased children, and the rights of the heirs, collectively and severally, under such allotments; but the bill makes no mention of those statutes or of any controversy respecting their validity, construction or effect. Neither does it by necessary implication point to such a controversy. True, it contains enough to indicate that those statutes constitute the source of the complainant's title or right, and also shows that the defendants are in some way claiming the land, and particularly the oil and gas, adversely to him; but beyond this the nature of the controversy is left unstated and uncertain. Of course, it could have arisen in different ways wholly independent of the source from which his title or right was derived. So, looking only to the bill, as we have seen that we must, it cannot be held that the case as therein stated was one arising under the statutes mentioned. As was said in *Blackburn* v. *Portland Gold Mining Co.*, *supra*, a controversy in respect of lands has never been regarded as presenting a Federal question merely because one of the parties to it has derived his title under an act of Congress. (P. 570.)
>
> * * * * *
>
> 3. A suit to enforce a right which takes its origin in the laws of the United States is not necessarily, or for that reason alone, one arising under those laws, for a suit does not so arise unless it really and substantially involves a dispute or controversy respecting the validity, construction or effect of such a law, upon the determination of which the result depends. This is especially so of a suit involving rights to land acquired under a law of the United States. If it were not, every suit to establish title to land in the central and western States would so arise, as all titles in these States are traceable back to those laws. *Little York Gold-Washing and Water Co.* v. *Keyes*, 96 U. S. 199; *Colorado Central Mining Co.* v. *Turck*, *supra*; *Blackburn* v. *Portland Gold Mining Co.*, 175 U. S. 571; *Florida Central & P. Railroad Co.* v. *Bell*, 176 U. S. 321; *Shoshone Mining Co.* v. *Rutter*, 177 U. S. 505; *De Lamar's Nevada Co.* v. *Nesbitt*, *Id.* 523. (P. 569–570.)

Where a bill involving the right to a lease of Indian land fails to show that the right depended upon construction of an act of Congress, but the parties and courts below proceeded upon the theory that it did so, the Supreme Court of the United States may permit amendment of the bill so as to allege that fact, and so establish jurisdiction. *Smith* v. *McCullough*, 270 U. S. 456 (1926). See also *Woodhouse* v. *Budwesky*, 70 F. 2d 61 (C. C. A. 4, 1934).

[89] Act of June 30, 1834, 4 Stat. 729, 733, 734 (trade and intercourse); Act of March 30, 1802, 2 Stat. 139, 145 (trade and intercourse).

Civil rights: Act of March 1, 1875, 18 Stat. 335.

Naturalization and citizenship: Act of June 29, 1906, 34 Stat. 596.

Bankruptcy: Act of July 1, 1898, 30 Stat. 544, 11 U. S. C. 1, 11, 110.

Statutes of limitation: Act of May 31, 1902, 32 Stat. 284, 25 U. S. C. 347.

Right to allotment: Act of February 6, 1901, 31 Stat. 760, 25 U. S. C. 345; Act of December 21, 1911, 37 Stat. 46:

> "And the judgment or decree of any such court in favor of any claimant to an allotment of land shall have the same effect, when

Other statutes contain provisions conferring jurisdiction over various matters upon territorial courts or courts of the United States in the territories.[90]

Finally, numerous special statutes contain jurisdictional provisions, relating to specific subjects.[91]

---

properly certified to the Secretary of the Interior, as if such allotment had been allowed and approved by him; but this provision shall not apply to any lands now or heretofore held by either of the Five Civilized Tribes, the Osage Nation of Indians, nor to any of the lands within the Quapaw Indian Agency: *Provided*, That the right of appeal shall be allowed to either party as in other cases."

And see Chapter 11, sec. 2; Chapter 4, sec. 12. In *Hy-Yu-tse-mil-kin* v. *Smith*, 194 U. S. 401 (1904), the Supreme Court held that the United States was not a necessary party to a suit brought under this statute.

Approval of expenditures made by guardians and trustees of Indian minors of pensions and bounties money: Joint Resolution of July 14, 1870, 16 Stat. 390.

[90] Idaho Territory: Act of July 3, 1882, 22 Stat. 148.

Montana Territory—damages from construction of railroad: Act of July 10, 1882, 22 Stat. 157.

Indian Territory: Act of March 1, 1889, 25 Stat. 783, 784 (extent of court's jurisdiction); Act of October 1, 1890, 26 Stat. 655, 656; Act of March 3, 1891, 26 Stat. 826; Act of March 1, 1895, 28 Stat. 693, 694; Joint Resolution of March 2, 1895, 28 Stat. 974; Act of May 7, 1900, 31 Stat. 170; Act of February 18, 1901, 31 Stat. 794; Act of February 8, 1896, 29 Stat. 6; Act of June 7, 1897, 30 Stat. 62, 83; Act of June 28, 1898, 30 Stat. 495, 496, 497; Act of July 1, 1898, 30 Stat. 567, 569; Act of March 1, 1901, 31 Stat. 861, 869; Act of March 24, 1902, 32 Stat. 90; Act of June 30, 1902, 32 Stat. 500, 501; Act of March 7, 1904, 33 Stat. 60; Act of April 28, 1904, 33 Stat. 573; Act of June 21, 1906, 34 Stat. 325, 342; Act of March 3, 1909, 35 Stat. 838.

Territory of Oklahoma: Act of May 2, 1890, 26 Stat. 81, 86; Act of June 7, 1897, 30 Stat. 62, 70–71; Act of June 16, 1906, 34 Stat. 267, 277.

Michigan Territory: Act of January 30, 1823, 3 Stat. 722.

[91] Accounting disputes concerning Iowa Indian trust lands: Act of June 9, 1892, 27 Stat. 768.

Prohibiting ejectment suits by Pueblo Indians in certain cases: Act of May 31, 1933, 48 Stat. 108, 111.

Cancellation of leases on lands upon Shoshone Indian Reservation: Act of August 21, 1916, 39 Stat. 519.

To quiet and finally settle the titles to the lands claimed by or under the Black Bob Band of Shawnee Indians in Kansas: Joint Resolution of March 3, 1879, 20 Stat. 488.

Controversies between the Fort Smith and Chocktaw Bridge Co. and the Chocktaw Tribe of Indians: Act of March 2, 1889, 25 Stat. 884.

Private land claims: Act of March 3, 1891, 26 Stat. 854.

Condemnation of Pueblo lands in the State of New Mexico: Act of May 10, 1926, 44 Stat. 498.

Condemnation of Indian lands in the Colville Reservation in the State of Washington: Act of July 1, 1892, 27 Stat. 62, 64; and see Act of April 5, 1890, 26 Stat. 45.

Accountings under any trust created under the act involved, Indians of the Five Civilized Tribes: Act of January 27, 1933, 47 Stat. 777, 778.

Cancellations of trust created under the act involving Indians of the Five Civilized Tribes: Act of January 27, 1933, 47 Stat. 777, 778–779.

Appeals to district courts from approval by county courts of conveyances of inherited lands by full-blood Indians of the Five Civilized Tribes: Act of January 27, 1933, 47 Stat. 777, 779.

Partition of Kickapoo Indian lands: Act of June 29, 1936, 49 Stat. 2368.

Ownership of Pipestone Reservation: Act of August 15, 1894, 28 Stat. 286, 317–318.

Enforcement of certain awards in State of Kansas: Act of March 3, 1873, 17 Stat. 623, 625.

Removal of restrictions upon lands of members of the Eastern Band of Cherokee Indians of North Carolina not to affect jurisdictions of United States courts to entertain suit by United States to protect such lands: Act of June 4, 1924, 43 Stat. 376, 381.

Quieting title of lands of Seneca Indian: Act of May 29, 1908, 35 Stat. 444, 445.

To quiet title to lands of Pueblo Indians of New Mexico under certain conditions: Act of June 7, 1924, 43 Stat. 636, 637.

Process for making United States party in certain suits involving Indians of the Five Civilized Tribes: Act of April 10, 1926, 44 Stat. 239, 240.

SECTION 3. COURT OF CLAIMS

While the United States cannot be sued without its consent,[92] yet it may be sued with its consent in any court or tribunal which Congress shall create or designate for the purpose, upon such terms or conditions and regulations as Congress shall see fit to prescribe; and the jurisdiction thus conferred must be held to be subject to whatever limitations are prescribed in the act or resolution of Congress conferring such jurisdiction.

So far as the Court of Claims is concerned its jurisdiction rests upon these general propositions, and therefore the extent of that jurisdiction is to be measured by the provisions of the jurisdictional act of Congress by which it is conferred in particular instances where such jurisdiction is invoked.[93] In other words, the Court of Claims has no general jurisdiction over claims against the United States, and can take cognizance only of those which by the terms of some act of Congress are committed to it.[94] Statutes which extend the jurisdictions of the Court of Claims and permit the Government to be sued are usually strictly construed, and the grant of jurisdiction therein contained must be shown clearly to cover the case and if it does not it will not be applied.[95]

With reference to claims by Indians against the United States the rule is not different from that stated above, since "the moral obligations of the Government toward the Indians, whatever they may be, are for Congress alone to recognize, and the courts can exercise only such jurisdiction over the subject as Congress may confer upon them."[96] In *Klamath Indians* v. *United States*,[97] the Supreme Court, in construing the Act of May 26, 1920,[98] conferring jurisdiction upon the Court of Claims to adjudicate "all claims of whatsoever nature" of the Klamath Indians against the United States "which had not theretofore been determined by that Court," declared that jurisdictional acts conferring upon an Indian tribe the privilege of suing the United States in the Court of Claims are to be strictly construed and held, accordingly, that the Act of 1920 did not embrace a claim which the Indians had settled with the Government before and for which they had given a valid release, even though the consideration for this release was grossly inadequate. In this connection the Supreme Court said:

> If the release stands, no money or property is due plaintiffs, for the settlement and release wiped out the claim.

---

[92] See Section 2A(2), *supra*.

[93] See *De Groot* v. *United States*, 5 Wall. 419 (1866); *Ex parte Russell*, 13 Wall. 664 (1871); *McElrath* v. *United States*, 102 U. S. 426 (1880); *United States* v. *Gleeson*, 124 U. S. 255 (1888); *Johnson* v. *United States*, 160 U. S. 546 (1896); *Thurston* v. *United States*, 232 U. S. 469 (1914); *Harley* v. *United States*, 198 U. S. 229 (1905); *Kendall* v. *United States*, 107 U. S. 123 (1882); *Hussey* v. *United States*, 222 U. S. 88 (1911).

[94] *Thurston* v. *United States*, 232 U. S. 469, 476 (1914); citing *Johnson* v. *United States*, 160 U. S. 546, 549 (1896). Note, however, that under 28 U. S. C. 257 (Judicial Code, sec. 151), either house of Congress may refer a pending bill to the Court of Claims for a report on the law and the facts. See *Creek Nation* v. *United States*, 74 C. Cls. 663 (1932) for a discussion of the conditions under which such report will be made.

[95] *Blackfeather* v. *United States*, 190 U. S. 368 (1903). *Cf. Shillinger* v. *United States*, 155 U. S. 163 (1894).

[96] *Blackfeather* v. *United States*, 190 U. S. 368, 373 (1903); *Klamath Indians* v. *United States*, 296 U. S. 244 (1935). *Cf. Johnson* v. *United States*, 160 U. S. 546 (1896); *Yerke* v. *United States*, 173 U. S. 439 (1899).

[97] 296 U. S. 244 (1935).

[98] 41 Stat. 623, amended by Act of May 15, 1936, 49 Stat. 1276; and see *United States* v. *Klamath Indians*, 304 U. S. 119 (1938).

> If the Act is sufficient to give jurisdiction of this claim, then it permits plaintiffs to bring into the Court of Claims for determination *de novo* all claims, whether released or not, that they ever had against the United States, excepting only those already there determined. It goes without saying that, if Congress intended to grant so sweeping and unique a privilege, it would have made that purpose unmistakably plain. As shown in the opinion below, Acts intended to waive settlements employ terms quite different from the provisions under consideration. (Pp. 250–251.)

The jurisdiction of the Court of Claims under the several acts of Congress concerning claims by Indian tribes or members thereof against the United States, varies considerably as to particular tribes. In some cases the jurisdiction is conferred as to "the claims of" [99] or "all claims" [100] or "all claims of whatsoever nature" [101] or "all legal and equitable claims" [102] or "all legal and equitable claims of whatsoever nature" [103] or "all questions of difference arising out of treaty stipulations" [104] or "claims to some right, title and interest or to lands ceded by treaty" [105] or "just rights in law or in equity" [106] or "as justice and equity shall require" [107] or "any claim arising under treaty stipulations or otherwise" [108] or "all claims according to principles of justice and equity, and as upon a full and fair arbitration.[109]

In some instances, the court is also to consider any right of set-off or counter-claim by the United States as against the tribe,[110] sometimes to exclude gratuities,[111] and sometimes to include gratuities.[112]

In some of these cases the jurisdiction is limited to claims arising under the provisions of treaties or acts of Congress, or both.[113] In some other cases the jurisdiction is limited to a

[99] Act of February 25, 1889, 25 Stat. 694 (Western Cherokees); Act of January 28, 1893, 27 Stat. 426 (New York Indians); Act of March 3, 1919, 40 Stat. 1316 (Cherokee Nation); Act of April 28, 1920, 41 Stat. 585 (Iowa tribe), amended by Act of January 11, 1929, 45 Stat. 1073; Act of February 6, 1921, 41 Stat. 1097 (Osage Nation); Act of March 3, 1931, 46 Stat. 1487 (Pillager Bands of Chippewas).

[100] Act of March 1, 1907, 34 Stat. 1055 (Sac and Fox); Act of July 3, 1926, 44 Stat. 807 (Crow tribe), amended by Joint Resolution of August 15, 1935, 49 Stat. 655; Act of March 2, 1927, 44 Stat. 1263 (Assiniboine Indians), amended by Joint Resolution of June 9, 1930, 46 Stat. 531; Act of June 28, 1938, 52 Stat. 1212 (Red Lake Band of Chippewas).

[101] Act of June 22, 1910, 36 Stat. 580 (Omaha tribe), see *United States v. Omaha Tribe of Indians*, 253 U. S. 275 (1920); Act of April 11, 1916, 39 Stat. 47 (Sisseton and Wahpeton Sioux), see *Sioux Indians v. United States*, 58 C. Cls. 302 (1923), cert. den. 275 U. S. 528 (1927), and *Sioux Indians v. United States*, 277 U. S. 424 (1928); Act of February 11, 1920, 41 Stat. 404 (Fort Berthold Indians); Act of May 26, 1920, 41 Stat. 623 (Klamath, etc.), amended by Act of May 15, 1936, 49 Stat. 1276, see *Klamath Indians v. United States*, 296 U. S. 244 (1935), and *United States v. Klamath Indians*, 304 U. S. 119 (1938); Act of June 3, 1920, 41 Stat. 738 (Sioux), amended by Act of June 24, 1926, 44 Stat. 764; Act of February 7, 1925, 43 Stat. 812 (Delaware Indians); Act of May 18, 1928, 45 Stat. 602 (Indians of California); Act of August 30, 1935, 49 Stat. 1049 (Chippewa).

[102] Act of February 11, 1920, 41 Stat. 404 (Fort Berthold Indians); Act of March 13, 1924, 43 Stat. 21 (Indians in Montana, Idaho, and Washington), amended by Act of February 3, 1931, c. 101, 46 Stat. 1060; Act of March 19, 1924, 43 Stat. 27 (Cherokee), amended by Joint Resolution of May 19, 1926, 44 Stat. 568, Joint Resolution of February 19, 1929, 45 Stat. 1229, Act of June 16, 1934, 48 Stat. 972, and Act of August 16, 1937, 50 Stat. 650; Act of May 20, 1924, 43 Stat. 133 (Seminole), amended by Joint Resolution of May 19, 1926, 44 Stat. 568, Joint Resolution of February 19, 1929, 45 Stat. 1229, and Act of August 16, 1937, 50 Stat. 650; Act of May 24, 1924, c. 181, 43 Stat. 139 (Creek), amended by Joint Resolution of May 19, 1926, 44 Stat. 568, Joint Resolution of February 19, 1929, 45 Stat. 1229, and Act of August 16, 1937, 50 Stat. 650, see *United States v. Creek Nation*, 295 U. S. 103 (1935); Act of June 7, 1924, 43 Stat. 537 (Choctaw and Chickasaw), amended by Joint Resolution of May 19, 1926, 44 Stat. 568, Joint Resolution of February 19, 1929, 45 Stat. 1229, and Act of August 16, 1937, 50 Stat. 650; Act of June 7, 1924, 43 Stat. 644 (Stockbridge); Act of March 3, 1925, 43 Stat. 1133 (Kansas or Kaw), amended by Act of February 23, 1929, 45 Stat. 1258; Act of May 14, 1926, 44 Stat. 555 (Chippewa), amended by Act of April 11, 1928, 45 Stat. 423, Act of May 18, 1928, 45 Stat. 601, Act of June 18, 1934, 48 Stat. 979, Act of May 15, 1936, 49 Stat. 1272, and Joint Resolution of June 22, 1936, 49 Stat. 1826; Act of July 2, 1926, 44 Stat. 801 (Pottawatomie); Act of March 3, 1927, 44 Stat. 1349 (Shoshone of Wind River Reservation); Act of December 17, 1928, 45 Stat. 1027 (Winnebago tribe); Act of February 23, 1929, 45 Stat. 1256 (Indians of Oregon), amended by Act of June 14, 1932, 47 Stat. 307; Act of April 25, 1932, 47 Stat. 137 (Eastern Cherokee and Western or Old Settler Cherokee), amended by Act of June 16, 1934, 48 Stat. 972; Act of August 26, 1935, 49 Stat. 801 (Indians of Oregon).

[103] Act of January 9, 1925, 43 Stat. 729 (Ponca tribe); Act of February 12, 1925, 43 Stat. 886 (Indians in State of Washington); Act of February 20, 1929, 45 Stat. 1249 (Nez Perce); Act of December 23, 1930, 46 Stat. 1033 (Oregon or Warm Springs tribe); Act of June 19, 1935, 49 Stat. 388 (Tlingit and Haida Indians); Act of September 3, 1935, 49 Stat. 1085 (Menominee), amended by Act of April 8, 1938, 52 Stat. 208; Act of June 28, 1938, 52 Stat. 1209 (Ute).

[104] Act of March 3, 1881, 21 Stat. 504 (Choctaw Nation). See *Choctaw Nation v. United States*, 119 U. S. 1 (1886); Act of March 19, 1890, 26 Stat. 24 (Pottawatomie).

[105] Act of June 6, 1900, 31 Stat. 672 (Fort Hall Indian Reservation).

[106] Act of October 1, 1890, 26 Stat. 636 (Shawnee, Delaware, and freedmen of Cherokee Nation), amended by Act of July 6, 1892, 27 Stat. 86. See *Blackfeather v. United States*, 190 U. S. 368 (1903).

[107] Act of March 1, 1907, 34 Stat. 1055 (Sac and Fox).

[108] Act of June 25, 1910, 36 Stat. 829 (Chippewa).

[109] Act of April 28, 1920, 41 Stat. 585 (Iowa tribe), amended by Joint Resolution of January 11, 1929, 45 Stat. 1073; Act of February 6, 1921, 41 Stat. 1097 (Osage Nation); Act of March 3, 1931, 46 Stat. 1487 (Pillager Bands of Chippewa); Act of June 28, 1938, 52 Stat. 1212 (Red Lake Band of Chippewa).

[110] Act of February 25, 1889, 25 Stat. 694 (Old Settlers or Western Cherokees); Act of June 22, 1910, 36 Stat. 580 (Omaha tribe), see *United States v. Omaha Tribe of Indians*, 253 U. S. 275 (1920); Act of April 11, 1916, 39 Stat. 47 (Sisseton and Wahpeton Sioux). See *Sioux Indians v. United States*, 58 C. Cls. 302 (1923), cert. den. 275 U. S. 528, and *Sioux Indians v. United States*, 277 U. S. 424 (1928); Act of February 11, 1920, 41 Stat. 404 (Fort Berthold Indians); Act of April 28, 1920, 41 Stat. 585 (Iowa tribe), amended by Act of January 11, 1929, 45 Stat. 1073; Act of March 13, 1924, 43 Stat. 21 (Indians in Montana, Idaho, and Washington), amended by Act of February 3, 1931, c. 101, 46 Stat. 1060.

[111] Act of April 11, 1916, 39 Stat. 47 (Sisseton and Wahpeton Sioux). See *Sioux Indians v. United States*, 58 C. Cls. 302 (1923), cert. den. 275 U. S. 528 and *Sioux Indians v. United States*, 277 U. S. 424 (1928).

[112] Act of February 11, 1920, 41 Stat. 404 (Fort Berthold Indians); Act of May 26, 1920, 41 Stat. 623 (Klamath, etc.), amended by Act of May 15, 1936, 49 Stat. 1276. See *Klamath Indians v. United States*, 296 U. S. 244 (1935) and *United States v. Klamath Indians*, 304 U. S. 119 (1938); Act of June 3, 1920, 41 Stat. 738 (Sioux), amended by Act of June 24, 1926, 44 Stat. 764; Act of February 6, 1921, 41 Stat. 1097 (Osage Nation); Act of March 13, 1924, 43 Stat. 21 (Indians in Montana, Idaho, and Washington), amended by Act of February 3, 1931, c. 101, 46 Stat. 1060; Act of February 12, 1925, 43 Stat. 886 (Indians in State of Washington); Act of March 3, 1925, 43 Stat. 1133 (Kansas or Kaw tribe), amended by Act of February 23, 1929, 45 Stat. 1258; Act of May 14, 1926, 44 Stat. 555 (Chippewa), amended by Act of April 11, 1928, 45 Stat. 423, Act of May 18, 1928, 45 Stat. 601, Act of June 18, 1934, 48 Stat. 979, Act of May 15, 1936, 49 Stat. 1272, and Joint Resolution of June 22, 1936, 49 Stat. 1826; Act of July 2, 1926, 44 Stat. 801 (Pottawatomie); Act of August 12, 1935, 49 Stat. 571, 596.

[113] Act of February 25, 1889, 25 Stat. 694 (Old Settlers or Western Cherokee Indians); Act of October 1, 1890, 26 Stat. 636 (Shawnee, Delaware Indians, and freedmen of Cherokee Nation), amended by Act of July 6, 1892, 27 Stat. 86; Act of April 21, 1904, 33 Stat. 189, 208. See *Blackfeather v. United States*, 190 U. S. 368 (1903); Act of January 28, 1893, 27 Stat. 426 (New York Indians); Act of March 3, 1919, 40 Stat. 1316 (Cherokee); Act of April 28, 1920, 41 Stat. 585 (Iowa tribe), amended by Joint Resolution of January 11, 1929, 45 Stat. 1073; Act of March 13, 1924, 43 Stat. 21 (Indians in Montana, Idaho, and Washington), amended by Act of February 3, 1931, c. 101, 46 Stat. 1060; Act of March 19, 1924, 43 Stat. 27 (Cherokee), amended by Joint Resolution of May 19, 1926, 44 Stat. 568, Joint Resolution of February 19, 1929, 45 Stat. 1229, Act of June 16, 1934, 48 Stat. 972, and Act of August 16, 1937, 50 Stat. 650; Act of May 20, 1924, 43 Stat. 133 (Seminole Indians), amended by Joint Resolution of May 19, 1926, 44 Stat. 568, Joint Resolution of February 19, 1929, 45 Stat. 1229, and Act of August 16, 1937, 50 Stat. 650; Act of May 24, 1924, 43 Stat. 139 (Creek), amended by Joint Resolution of May 19, 1926, 44 Stat. 568, Joint Resolution of February 19, 1929, 45 Stat. 1229, and Act of August 16, 1937, 50 Stat. 650. See *United States v. Creek Nation*, 295 U. S. 103 (1935); Act of June 7, 1924, 43 Stat. 537 (Choctaw and Chickasaw),

determination of the amounts of sums due or claimed to be due the Indians from the United States under any treaty or law of Congress.[114]

In most instances, the jurisdiction is conferred to hear, determine, and render judgment,[115] or "to hear and determine and to render final judgment" [116] or "to hear, examine, and adjudicate, and render judgment," [117] or "to hear, adjudicate, and render judgment" [118] or "to hear, determine, adjudicate, and render final judgment" [119] or "to consider and determine" [120] or "to hear, examine, adjudicate, and render final judgment" [121] or "to consider and adjudicate" [122] or "to hear and determine" [123] or "to try and determine" [124] or "to try and render judgment" [125] or "to determine and report from findings of fact reported before" [126] or "to proceed upon findings of fact already made" [127] or "to hear and enter up judgment" [128] or "to hear and report a finding of fact" [129] or "to hear, consider, and determine" [130] or "to hear, ascertain, and report" to Congress.[131]

In many of the cases, the court is to take jurisdiction "notwithstanding the lapse of time or statutes of limitations" [132] and

amended by Joint Resolution of May 19, 1926, 44 Stat. 568, Joint Resolution of February 19, 1929, 45 Stat. 1229, and Act of August 16, 1937, 50 Stat. 650; Act of June 7 1924, 43 Stat. 644 (Stockbridge); Act of February 12, 1925, 43 Stat. 886 (Indians in State of Washington); Act of March 3, 1925, 43 Stat. 1133 (Kansas or Kaw), amended by Act of February 23, 1929, 45 Stat. 1258; Act of May 14, 1926, 44 Stat. 555 (Chippewa), amended by Act of April 11, 1928, 45 Stat. 423, Act of May 18, 1928, 45 Stat. 601, Act of June 18, 1934, 48 Stat. 979, Act of May 15, 1936, 49 Stat. 1272, and Joint Resolution of June 22, 1936, 49 Stat. 1826; Act of July 2, 1926, 44 Stat. 801 (Pottawatomie); Act of July 3, 1926, 44 Stat. 807 (Crow tribe), amended by Joint Resolution of August 15, 1935, 49 Stat. 655; Act of March 2, 1927, 44 Stat. 1263 (Assiniboine), amended by Joint Resolution of June 9, 1930, 46 Stat 531; Act of March 3, 1927, 44 Stat. 1349 (Shoshone tribe of Wind River Reservation). See *Shoshone Tribe* v. *United States*, 299 U. S. 476 (1937); Act of December 17, 1928, 45 Stat. 1027 (Winnebago); Act of February 28, 1929, 45 Stat. 1407 (Shoshone); Act of March 3, 1931, 46 Stat. 1487 (Pillager Band of Chippewa); Act of April 25, 1932, 47 Stat. 137 (Eastern Cherokee and Western Cherokee or Old Settler), amended by Act of June 16, 1934, 48 Stat. 972; Act of August 26, 1935, 49 Stat. 801 (Indians in Oregon).

[114] Act of April 11, 1916, 39 Stat. 47 (Sisseton and Wahpeton Sioux). See *Sioux Indians* v. *United States*, 58 C. Cls. 302 (1923), cert. den. 275 U. S. 528, and *Sioux Indians* v. *United States*, 277 U. S. 424 (1928); Act of March 4, 1917, 39 Stat. 1195 (Medawakanton and Wahpakoota Sioux); Act of February 11, 1920, 41 Stat. 404 (Fort Berthold Indians); Act of May 26, 1920, 41 Stat. 623 (Klamath, etc.), amended by Act of May 15, 1936, 49 Stat. 1276. See *Klamath Indians* v. *United States*, 296 U. S. 244 (1935) and *United States* v. *Klamath Indians*, 304 U. S. 119 (1938); Act of June 3, 1920, 41 Stat. 738 (Sioux), amended by Act of June 24, 1926, 44 Stat. 764; Act of February 6, 1921, 41 Stat. 1097 (Osage Nation); Act of March 3, 1931, 46 Stat. 1487 (Pillager Band of Chippewa); Act of June 19, 1935, 49 Stat. 388 (Tlingit and Haida Indians); Act of August 30, 1935, 49 Stat. 1049 (Chippewa); Act of June 28, 1938, 52 Stat. 1212 (Red Lake Band of Chippewa).

[115] Act of March 2, 1895, 28 Stat. 876, 898 (Choctaw and Chickasaw). See *United States* v. *Choctaw Nation and Chickasaw Nation*, 179 U. S. 494 (1900); Act of June 6, 1900, 31 Stat. 672, 680 (Choctaw and Chickasaw); Act of March 3, 1903, 32 Stat. 982, 1010, 1011. See *United States* v. *Cherokee Nation*, 202 U. S. 101 (1906); Act of June 22, 1910, 36 Stat. 580 (Omaha tribe). See *United States* v. *Omaha Tribe of Indians*, 253 U. S. 275 (1920); Act of April 11, 1916, 39 Stat. 47 (Sisseton and Wahpeton Sioux). See *Sioux Indians* v. *United States*, 58 C. Cls. 302 (1923), cert. den. 275 U. S. 528, and *Sioux Indians* v. *United States*, 277 U. S. 424 (1928); Act of April 28, 1920, 41 Stat. 585 (Iowa tribe), amended by Act of January 11, 1929, 45 Stat. 1073; Act of May 26, 1920, 41 Stat. 623 (Klamath, etc.), amended by Act of May 15, 1936, 49 Stat. 1276. See *Klamath Indians* v. *United States*, 296 U. S. 244 (1935), and *United States* v. *Klamath Indians*, 304 U. S. 119 (1938); Act of June 3, 1920, 41 Stat. 738 (Sioux), amended by Act of June 24, 1926, 44 Stat. 764; Act of February 6, 1921, 41 Stat. 1097 (Osage Nation); Act of February 7, 1925, 43 Stat. 812 (Delaware Indians); Act of March 3, 1931, 46 Stat. 1487 (Pillager Bands of Chippewa); Act of June 19, 1935, 49 Stat. 388 (Tlingit and Haida Indians).

[116] Act of March 4, 1917, 39 Stat. 1195 (Medawakanton and Wahpakoota Sioux); Act of January 9, 1925, 43 Stat. 729 (Ponca tribe); Act of February 12, 1925, 43 Stat. 886 (Indians in State of Washington); Act of May 18, 1928, 45 Stat. 602 (Indians of California); Act of June 28, 1938, 52 Stat. 1209 (Ute); Act of June 28, 1938, 52 Stat. 1212 (Red Lake Band of Chippewa).

[117] Act of March 19, 1924, 43 Stat. 27 (Cherokee), amended by Joint Resolution of May 19, 1926, 44 Stat. 568, Joint Resolution of February 19, 1929, 45 Stat. 1229, Act of June 16, 1934, 48 Stat. 972, and Act of August 16, 1937, 50 Stat. 650; Act of May 20, 1924, 43 Stat. 133 (Seminole), amended by Joint Resolution of May 19, 1926, 44 Stat. 568, Joint Resolution of February 19, 1929, 45 Stat. 1229, and Act of August 16, 1937, 50 Stat. 650; Act of May 24, 1924, c. 181, 43 Stat. 139 (Creek), amended by Joint Resolution of May 19, 1926, 44 Stat. 568, Joint Resolution of February 19, 1929, 45 Stat. 1229, and Act of August 16, 1937, 50 Stat. 650, see *United States* v. *Creek Nation*, 295 U. S. 103 (1935); Act of June 7, 1924, 43 Stat. 537 (Choctaw and Chickasaw), amended by Joint Resolution of May 19, 1926, 44 Stat. 568, Joint Resolution of February 19, 1929, 45 Stat. 1229, and Act of August 16, 1937, 50 Stat. 650; Act of June 7, 1924, 43 Stat. 644 (Stockbridge); Act of March 3, 1925, 43 Stat. 1133 (Kansas or Kaw), amended by Act of February 23, 1929, 45 Stat. 1258; Concurrent Resolution No. 21 of June 5, 1924, 43 Stat. 1612 (Choctaw and Chickasaw); Act of May 14, 1926, 44 Stat. 555 (Chippewa), amended by Act of April 11, 1928, 45 Stat. 423, Act of May 18, 1928, 45 Stat. 601, Act of June 18, 1934, 48 Stat. 979, Act of May 15, 1936, 49 Stat. 1272, and Joint Resolution of June 22, 1936, 49 Stat. 1826; Act of March 2, 1927, 44 Stat. 1263 (Assiniboine), amended by Joint Resolution of June 9, 1930, 46 Stat. 531; Act of March 3, 1927, 44 Stat. 1349 (Shoshone tribe of Wind River Reservation). See *Shoshone Tribe* v. *United States*, 299 U. S. 476 (1937); Act of December 17, 1928, 45 Stat. 1027 (Winnebago tribe); Act of April 25, 1932, 47 Stat. 137 (Eastern Cherokee and Western or Old Settler Cherokee), amended by Act of June 16, 1934, 48 Stat. 972; Act of August 30, 1935, 49 Stat. 1049 (Chippewa).

[118] Act of July 3, 1926, 44 Stat. 807 (Crow), amended by Joint Resolution of August 15, 1935, 49 Stat. 655; Act of February 28, 1929, 45 Stat. 1407 (Shoshone).

[119] Act of March 1, 1907, 34 Stat. 1055 (Sac and Fox); Act of February 20, 1929, 45 Stat. 1249 (Nez Perce).

[120] Act of March 3, 1909, 35 Stat. 781, 789 (Ute); Act of March 13, 1924, 43 Stat. 21 (Indians in Montana, Idaho, and Washington), amended by Act of February 3, 1931, c. 101, 46 Stat. 1060.

[121] Act of February 23, 1929, 45 Stat. 1256 (Indians of State of Oregon), amended by Act of June 14, 1932, 47 Stat. 307; Act of December 23, 1930, 46 Stat. 1033 (Middle Oregon or Warm Springs Tribe); Act of August 26, 1935, 49 Stat. 801 (Indians in Oregon); Act of September 3, 1935, 49 Stat. 1085 (Menominee), amended by Act of April 8, 1938, 52 Stat. 208.

[122] Act of June 25, 1910, 36 Stat. 829 (Chippewa).

[123] Act of October 1, 1890, 26 Stat. 636 (Shawnee, Delaware, and freedmen of Cherokee Nation), amended by Act of July 6, 1892, 27 Stat. 86. See *Blackfeather* v *United States*, 190 U. S. 368 (1903); Act of March 3, 1891, 26 Stat. 989, 1021 (Pottawatomie).

[124] Act of February 25, 1889, 25 Stat. 694 (Old Settlers or Western Cherokee); Act of June 6, 1900, 31 Stat. 672 (Fort Hall Indian Reservation).

[125] Act of March 3, 1881, 21 Stat. 504 (Choctaw Nation). See *Choctaw Nation* v. *United States*, 119 U. S. 1 (1886); Act of March 19, 1890, 26 Stat. 24 (Pottawatomie).

[126] Act of January 9, 1925, 43 Stat. 730 (Yankton Sioux).

[127] Act of January 28, 1893, 27 Stat. 426 (New York Indians).

[128] Act of January 28, 1893, 27 Stat. 426 (New York Indians).

[129] Act of April 4, 1910, 36 Stat. 269, 284 (Sioux).

[130] Act of March 3, 1919, 40 Stat. 1316 (Cherokee Nation).

[131] Act of March 3, 1901, 31 Stat. 1058, 1078.

[132] Act of March 3, 1891, 26 Stat. 989, 1021 (Pottawatomie); Act of June 22, 1910, 36 Stat. 580 (Omaha); Act of February 11, 1920, 41 Stat. 404 (Fort Berthold Indians); Act of May 26, 1920, 41 Stat. 623 (Klamath, etc.), amended by Act of May 15, 1936, 49 Stat. 1276. See *Klamath Indians* v. *United States*, 296 U. S. 244 (1935) and *United States* v. *Klamath Indians*, 304 U. S. 119 (1938); Act of June 3, 1920, 41 Stat. 738 (Sioux) amended by Act of June 24, 1926, 44 Stat. 764; Act of February 6, 1921, 41 Stat. 1097 (Osage Nation); Act of March 13, 1924, 43 Stat. 21 (Indians in Montana, Idaho, and Washington), amended by Act of February 3, 1931, 46 Stat. 1060; Act of May 20, 1924, 43 Stat. 133 (Seminole), amended by Joint Resolution of May 19, 1926, 44 Stat. 568, Joint Resolution of February 19, 1929, 45 Stat. 1229, and Act of August 16, 1937, 50 Stat. 650; Act of May 24, 1924, 43 Stat. 139 (Creek), amended by Joint Resolution of May 19, 1926, 44 Stat. 568, Joint Resolution of February 19, 1929, 45 Stat. 1229, and Act of August 16, 1937, 50 Stat. 650. See *United States* v. *Creek Nation*, 295 U. S. 103 (1935); Act of June 7, 1924, 43 Stat. 537 (Choctaw and Chickasaw), amended by Joint Resolution of May 19, 1926, 44 Stat. 568, Joint Resolution of February 19, 1929, 45 Stat. 1229 and Act of August 16, 1937,

in most, the right is granted to both parties to appeal to the Supreme Court.[133]

In many instances the jurisdiction of the court is limited to matters in which the claim has not heretofore been determined by the Court of Claims or the Supreme Court.[134]

In some instances Congress has authorized submission to the Court of Claims of Indian claims theretofore settled and adjusted.[135]

So far as claims of individuals against Indian tribes or members thereof are concerned, it is unquestionable that Congress may refer such claims to the Court of Claims or any other tribunal and vest in that court such general or limited jurisdiction as it shall see fit, and may authorize the United States to be made a party defendant to the proceedings.[136] Jurisdictional statutes of this nature are not infrequent,[137] and the jurisdiction conferred by such statutes upon the Court of Claims is usually expressed

---

50 Stat. 650; Act of June 7, 1924, 43 Stat. 644 (Stockbridge); Act of February 7, 1925, 43 Stat. 812 (Delaware Indians); Act of February 12, 1925, 43 Stat. 886 (Indians in State of Washington); Act of March 3, 1925, 43 Stat. 1133 (Kansas or Kaw) amended by Act of February 23, 1929, 45 Stat. 1258; Act of May 14, 1926, 44 Stat. 555 (Chippewa), amended by Act of April 11, 1928, 45 Stat. 423, Act of May 18, 1928, 45 Stat. 601, Act of June 18, 1934, 48 Stat. 979, Act of May 15, 1936, 49 Stat. 1272, and Joint Resolution of June 22, 1936, 49 Stat. 1826; Act of July 2, 1926, 44 Stat. 801 (Pottawatomie); Act of July 3, 1926 44 Stat. 807 (Crow), amended by Joint Resolution of August 15, 1935, 49 Stat. 655; Act of March 2, 1927, 44 Stat. 1263 (Assiniboine), amended by Joint Resolution of June 9, 1930, 46 Stat. 531; Act of March 3, 1927, 44 Stat. 1349 (Shoshone Tribe of Wind River Reservation). See *Shoshone Tribe* v. *United States*, 299 U. S. 476 (1937); Act of February 20, 1929, 45 Stat. 1249 (Nez Perce); Act of February 28, 1929, 45 Stat. 1407 (Shoshone); Act of December 23, 1930, 46 Stat. 1033 (Middle Oregon or Warm Springs); Act of April 25, 1932, 47 Stat. 137 (Cherokee), amended by Act of June 16, 1934, 48 Stat. 972.

[133] Act of March 3, 1881, 21 Stat. 504 (Choctaw). See *Choctaw Nation* v. *United States*, 119 U. S. 1 (1886); Act of March 19, 1890, 26 Stat. 24 (Pottawatomie); Act of October 1, 1890, 26 Stat. 636 (Shawnee, Delaware, and freedmen of Cherokee Nation), amended by Act of July 6, 1892, 27 Stat. 86. See *Blackfeather* v. *United States*, 190 U. S. 368 (1903); Act of March 3, 1891, 26 Stat. 989, 1021 (Pottawatomie); Act of March 2, 1895, 28 Stat. 876, 898 (Choctaw and Chickasaw). See *United States* v. *Choctaw and Chickasaw Nation*, 179 U. S. 494 (1900); Act of June 6, 1900, 31 Stat. 672, 680 (Fort Hall Indian Reservation); Act of March 3, 1903, 32 Stat. 982, 1010, 1011. See *United States* v. *Cherokee Nation*, 202 U. S. 101 (1906); Act of March 1, 1907, 34 Stat. 1055 (Sac and Fox); Act of February 15, 1909, 35 Stat. 619. See *United States* v. *Mille Lac Chippewas*, 229 U. S. 498 (1913); Act of June 22, 1910, 36 Stat. 580 (Omaha tribe). See *United States* v. *Omaha Tribe of Indians*, 253 U. S. 275 (1920); Act of June 25, 1910, 36 Stat. 829 (Chippewa); Act of April 11, 1916, 39 Stat. 47 (Sisseton and Wahpeton Sioux). See *Sioux Indians* v. *United States* 58 C. Cls. 302 (1923), cert. den. 275 U. S. 528 and *Sioux Indians* v. *United States*, 277 U. S. 424 (1928); Act of March 3, 1919, 40 Stat. 1316 (Cherokee Nation); Act of February 11, 1920, 41 Stat. 404 (Fort Berthold Indians); Act of April 28, 1920, 41 Stat. 585 (Iowa tribe), amended by Act of January 11, 1929, 45 Stat. 1073; Act of May 26, 1920, 41 Stat. 623 (Klamath, etc.), amended by Act of May 15, 1936, 49 Stat. 1276. See *Klamath Indians* v. *United States*, 296 U. S. 244 (1935) and *United States* v. *Klamath Indians*, 304 U. S. 119 (1938); Act of June 3, 1920, 41 Stat. 738 (Sioux), amended by Act of June 24, 1926, 44 Stat. 764; Act of February 6, 1921, 41 Stat. 1097 (Osage Nation); Act of March 19, 1924, 43 Stat. 27 (Cherokee), amended by Joint Resolution of May 19, 1926, 44 Stat. 568, Joint Resolution of February 19, 1929, 45 Stat. 1229, Act of June 16, 1934, 48 Stat. 972, and Act of August 16, 1937, 50 Stat. 650; Act of May 20, 1924, 43 Stat. 133 (Seminole), amended by Joint Resolution of May 19, 1926, 44 Stat. 568, Joint Resolution of February 19, 1929, 45 Stat. 1229, and Act of August 16, 1937, 50 Stat. 650; Act of May 24, 1924, 43 Stat. 139 (Creek), amended by Joint Resolution of May 19, 1926, 44 Stat. 568, Joint Resolution of February 19, 1929, 45 Stat. 1229, and Act of August 16, 1937, 50 Stat. 650. See *United States* v. *Creek Nation*, 295 U. S. 103 (1935); Act of June 7, 1924, 43 Stat. 537 (Choctaw and Chickasaw), amended by Joint Resolution of May 19, 1926, 44 Stat. 568, Joint Resolution of February 19, 1929, 45 Stat. 1229, and Act of August 16, 1937, 50 Stat. 650; Act of June 7, 1924, 43 Stat. 644 (Stockbridge); Act of January 9, 1925, 43 Stat. 729 (Ponca); Act of February 7, 1925, 43 Stat. 812 (Delaware Indians); Act of March 3, 1925, 43 Stat. 1133 (Kansas or Kaw), amended by Act of February 23, 1929, 45 Stat. 1258; Act of May 14, 1926, 44 Stat. 555 (Chippewa), amended by Act of April 11, 1928, 45 Stat. 423, Act of May 18, 1928, 45 Stat. 601, Act of June 18, 1934, 48 Stat. 979, Act of May 15, 1936, 49 Stat. 1272, and Joint Resolution of June 22, 1936, 49 Stat. 1826; Act of July 2, 1926, 44 Stat. 801 (Pottawatomie); Act of July 3, 1926, 44 Stat. 807 (Crow), amended by Joint Resolution of August 15, 1935, 49 Stat. 655; Act of March 2, 1927, 44 Stat. 1263 (Assiniboine), amended by Joint Resolution of June 9, 1930, 46 Stat. 531; Act of March 3, 1927, 44 Stat. 1349 (Shoshone tribe of Wind River Reservation). See *Shoshone Tribe* v. *United States*, 299 U. S. 476 (1937); Act of May 18, 1928, 45 Stat. 602 (Indians of California); Act of December 17, 1928, 45 Stat. 1027 (Winnebago); Act of February 20, 1929, 45 Stat. 1249 (Nez Perce); Act of December 23, 1930, 46 Stat. 1033 (Middle Oregon or Warm Springs tribe); Act of March 3, 1931, 46 Stat. 1487 (Pillager Bands of Chippewa); Act of August 26, 1935, 49 Stat. 801 (Indians in State of Oregon); Act of August 30, 1935, 49 Stat. 1049 (Chippewa); Act of June 28, 1938, 52 Stat. 1212 (Chippewa).

[134] Act of February 11, 1920, 41 Stat. 404 (Fort Berthold Indians); Act of May 26, 1920, 41 Stat. 623 (Klamath, etc.), amended by Act of May 15, 1936, 49 Stat. 1276. See *Klamath Indians* v. *United States*, 296 U. S. 244 (1935) and *United States* v. *Klamath Indians*, 304 U. S. 119 (1938); Act of June 3, 1920, 41 Stat. 738 (Sioux) amended by Act of June 24, 1926, 44 Stat. 764; Act of March 19, 1924, 43 Stat. 27 (Cherokee), amended by Joint Resolution of May 19, 1926, 44 Stat. 568, Joint Resolution of February 19, 1929, 45 Stat. 1229, Act of June 16, 1934, 48 Stat. 972, and Act of August 16, 1937, 50 Stat. 650; Act of May 20, 1924, 43 Stat. 133 (Seminole), amended by Joint Resolution of May 19, 1926, 44 Stat. 568, Joint Resolution of February 19, 1929, 45 Stat. 1229, and Act of August 16, 1937, 50 Stat. 650; Act of May 24, 1924, 43 Stat. 139 (Creek), amended by Joint Resolution of May 19, 1926, 44 Stat. 568, Joint Resolution of February 19, 1929, 45 Stat. 1229, and Act of August 16, 1937, 50 Stat. 650. See *United States* v. *Creek Nation*, 295 U. S. 103 (1935); Act of June 7, 1924, 43 Stat. 537 (Choctaw and Chickasaw), amended by Joint Resolution of May 19, 1926, 44 Stat. 568, Joint Resolution of February 19, 1929, 45 Stat. 1229, and Act of August 16, 1937, 50 Stat. 650; Act of June 7, 1924, 43 Stat. 644 (Stockbridge); Act of May 14, 1926; 44 Stat. 555 (Chippewa), amended by Act of April 11, 1928, 45 Stat. 423, Act of May 18, 1928, 45 Stat. 601, Act of June 18, 1934, 48 Stat. 979, Act of May 15, 1936, 49 Stat. 1272, and Joint Resolution of June 22, 1936, 49 Stat. 1826; Act of July 2, 1926, 44 Stat. 801 (Pottawatomie); Act of July 3, 1926, 44 Stat. 807 (Crow), amended by Joint Resolution of August 15, 1935, 49 Stat 655; Act of March 2, 1927, 44 Stat. 1263 (Assiniboine), amended by Joint Resolution of June 9, 1930, 46 Stat. 531; Act of March 3, 1927, 44 Stat. 1349 (Shoshone tribe of Wind River Reservation). See *Shoshone Tribe* v. *United States*, 299 U. S. 476 (1937); Act of December 17, 1928, 45 Stat. 1027 (Winnebago); Act of April 25, 1932, 47 Stat. 137 (Cherokee), amended by Act of June 16, 1934, 48 Stat. 972; Act of February 28, 1929, 45 Stat. 1407 (Shoshone); Act of August 30, 1935, 49 Stat. 1049 (Chippewa).

[135] Act of February 7, 1925, 43 Stat. 812, as amended March 3, 1927, 44 Stat. 1358: "The said courts shall consider all such claims de novo * * * and without regard to any decision, finding, or settlement heretofore had in respect of any such claims:" construed in *Delaware Tribe* v. *United States*, 72 C. Cls. 483 (1931); *id.* 525; 74 C. Cls. 368. Act of March 3, 1881, 21 Stat. 504. Under a treaty of 1855, 11 Stat. 611, a determination had been made by the Senate and account was stated by the Secretary of the Interior. The act authorized the court "to review the entire question of differences de novo" and declared that the court "shall not be estopped by any action had or award made by the Senate." Construed in *Choctaw Nation* v. *United States*, 19 C. Cls. 243 (1884) and 119 U. S. 1, 29 (1886).

Cf. statutes authorizing submission of claims not theretofore finally settled and released: Acts of February 11, 1920, 41 Stat. 404; June 3, 1920, 41 Stat. 738; March 19, 1924, 43 Stat. 27; May 20, 1924, 43 Stat. 133; May 24, 1924, 43 Stat. 139. See *United States* v. *Creek Nation*, 295 U. S. 103 (1935); June 4, 1924, 43 Stat. 366; June 7, 1924, 43 Stat. 537; June 7, 1924, 43 Stat. 644; February 7, 1925, 43 Stat. 812; March 3, 1925, 43 Stat. 1133; May 14, 1926, 44 Stat. 555; July 2, 1926, 44 Stat. 801; July 3, 1926, 44 Stat. 807; March 2, 1927, 44 Stat. 1263; March 3, 1927, 44 Stat. 1349. See *Shoshone Tribe* v. *United States*, 299 U. S. 476 (1937).

[136] In *United States* v. *Gorham*, 165 U. S. 316 (1897), the Supreme Court held that under the Indian Depredation Act of March 3, 1891, c. 538, 26 Stat. 851, the Court of Claims could render a judgment against the United States alone, when the tribe could not be identified, and the inability to identify the tribe was stated in the petition.

[137] See Chapter 14, sec. 1, fns. 14–20.

in such language as to "inquire into and finally adjudicate" [138] to "hear, adjudicate, and render judgment" [139] to "hear, consider, and adjudicate" [140] to "hear, determine, and render final judgment," [141] to "rehear, retry, determine, and finally adjudicate," [142] to "rehear and reconsider and determine the motion filed" therein by the claimants,[143] or to "reinstate" causes so far as the same pertain to the claim of the claimant, upon facts as previously found and returned by the court, and is authorized to enter judgment in said cause in favor of the plaintiff,[144] or a claim is referred to the court together with the record or papers in a previous cause formerly heard in said court and the court is authorized and directed "to order proof to be taken" with respect to the claim.[145]

In some instances the court has been authorized and directed to entertain jurisdiction in Indian depredation claims[146] or a private claimant has been authorized to prosecute an Indian's depredation claim pending in that court and to receive judgment therein,[147] or the claimant is authorized to bring suit in the Court of Claims against the United States.[148]

By section 182 of the Judicial Code,[149] in any case brought in the Court of Claims under any act of Congress by which that court is authorized to render a judgment or decree against the United States, or against any Indian tribe or any Indians, or against any fund held in trust by the United States for any Indian tribe or for any Indians, the claimant, or the United States, or the tribe of Indians, or other party in interest shall have the same right of appeal as is conferred by the other sections of the code; and such a right is to be exercised only within the time and in the manner that is prescribed.

In individual claims with respect to Indian lands alleged by the claimant to have been appropriated by the United States Government without right or title thereto, and without authority either in law or in equity, the jurisdiction is conferred on the Court of Claims "to proceed, according to the principles and rules of both law and equity, to find the facts" embracing the amount that is to be paid to the claimants.[150]

While Congress may refer to the Court of Claims or any other tribunal which it may create or designate any Indian claim for adjudication, it cannot refer such claim directly to the Supreme Court for that purpose. The reason is that under the Constitution the original jurisdiction of the Supreme Court extends only to cases "affecting Ambassadors, other public Ministers and Consuls, and those in which a State shall be party," [151] and Congress can neither enlarge nor restrict that jurisdiction.[152] Thus, it having been early decided in *Cherokee Nation* v. *Georgia*,[153] that an Indian tribe is not a state in the sense that this word is used in the Constitution, the Supreme Court has held that Congress cannot refer directly to it, for adjudication, the claim of an Indian tribe, for that would be to invoke a jurisdiction which that Court cannot exercise under the Constitution, although the matter might be referred to the Court of Claims in the first instance, and brought to the Supreme Court by way of appeal if the necessary congressional legislation to that end was provided.[154]

Nor has Congress constitutional authority to enlarge the appellate jurisdiction of the Supreme Court by allowing appeals from judgments of the Court of Claims in cases not of a judicial nature, for conceding that Congress may confer upon the Court of Claims extra-judicial power as it has in numerous instances, yet the appellate jurisdiction of the Supreme Court under the Constitution is strictly judicial, and any attempt on the part of Congress either to enlarge or to diminish that jurisdiction would be unconstitutional and void, as an encroachment on the judicial power vested by the Constitution in that tribunal.[155]

With respect to so-called moral claims, or claims based on a supposed moral obligation of the United States toward the Indians, whatever the circumstances under which they may arise, if they exist at all, it is for Congress to consider whether they shall be recognized, and being political in nature they would seem to fall outside the jurisdiction of the courts.[156] It is believed, however, that Congress may properly refer such claims to the Court of Claims for adjudication.[157] Whether it may also allow an appeal from the decision of the Court of Claims to the Supreme Court is a question upon which the Supreme Court has not passed. But if Congress should provide by appropriate legislation a definite standard upon which the validity of the claim could be determined and proper relief afforded to the parties to the suit as a matter of law, there would seem to be no objection to the allowance of the appeal, for then the judicial power of the United States would be called into play in any case or controversy arising under such legislation and submitted to the Court of Claims in the first instance, and the Supreme Court on appeal for adjudication. In other words, the claim under such legislation would be justiciable in nature, and therefore cognizable by the Court.[158]

[138] Act of March 3, 1891, 26 Stat. 851, amended by Act of January 11, 1915, 38 Stat. 791. See *Johnson* v. *United States*, 160 U. S. 546 (1896); *Leighton* v. *United States*. 161 U. S. 291 (1895); *Marks* v. *United States*, 161 U. S. 297 (1896); *Collier* v. *United States*, 173 U. S. 79 (1899); *Corralitos Co.* v. *United States*, 178 U. S. 280 (1900); *Montoya* v. *United States*, 180 U. S. 261 (1901); Act of February 9, 1907, 34 Stat. 2411.

[139] Act of May 29, 1908, 35 Stat. 444, 445. See *Garland's Heirs* v. *Choctaw Nation*, 256 U. S. 439 (1921); *Green* v. *Menominee Tribe*, 233 U. S. 558 (1914).

[140] Act of June 28, 1934, 48 Stat. 1467.

[141] Act of May 29, 1908, 35 Stat. 444, 445; Act of February 6, 1923, 42 Stat. 1768; Act of April 4, 1910, 36 Stat. 269, 287.

[142] Act of April 28, 1916, 39 Stat. 1262.

[143] Act of June 30, 1902, 32 Stat. 1492, c. 1348.

[144] Act of June 30, 1902, 32 Stat. 1492, c. 1349.

[145] Act of February 9, 1863, 12 Stat. 915.

[146] Act of February 9, 1907, 34 Stat. 2411. See Chapter 14, sec. 1.

[147] Act of June 6, 1900, 31 Stat. 1617.

[148] Act of June 4, 1880, 21 Stat. 544.

[149] Act of March 3, 1911, 36 Stat. 1087, 1142, 25 U. S. C. 288.

[150] Act of February 24, 1905, 33 Stat. 743, 808.

[151] U. S. Const., Art. III, sec. 2, cl. 2.

[152] *Muskrat* v. *United States*, 219 U. S. 346 (1911). And see sec. 2A (4), *supra*.

[153] 5 Pet. 1 (1831).

[154] *Yankton Sioux Tribe* v. *United States*, 272 U. S. 351, 356 (1926). By the Act of March 3, 1883, the claims of the New York Indians for the value of certain lands in Kansas set apart for them under the Treaty of January 15, 1838, 7 Stat. 550, were referred to the Court of Claims with direction to report its proceedings to the Senate. The court reported the findings to the Senate on January 16, 1892, and thereupon, on January 28, 1893, Congress passed an act authorizing the Court of Claims "to hear and determine these claims and to enter up judgment as if it had original jurisdiction of this case without regard to the statute of limitations", with the right of appeal by either party to the Supreme Court. *New York Indians* v. *United States*, 170 U. S. 1 (1898). See also sec. 2A(2), *supra*.

[155] *Muskrat* v. *United States*, 219 U. S. 346 (1911); *Gordon* v. *United States*, 117 U. S. 697 (1864). See *United States* v. *Old Settlers*, 148 U. S. 427, 466 (1893); *Pam-to-pee* v. *United States*, 187 U. S. 371, 383 (1902); sec. 2A(2), *supra*.

[156] See cases cited in fn. 155.

[157] See *Duwamish Indians* v. *United States*, 79 C. Cls. 530 (1934), cert. den. 295 U. S. 755; *Blackfeet Indians* v. *United States*, 81 C. Cls. 101 (1935). These cases would seem to hold, in effect, that in the absence of congressional legislation the Court of Claims has no power to award a judgment based upon a moral claim by an Indian tribe or tribes against the United States.

[158] The judicial power of the United States, vested by the Consituation in the federal courts, embraces all controversies of a justiciable nature, except so far as there are limitations expressed in that instrument on the general grant of judicial power. *Kansas* v. *Colorado*, 206 U. S. 46 (1907). A case or controversy, in order that the judicial power of the United States may be exercised thereon, implies the exist-

Ordinarily the Supreme Court will not review findings of facts of the Court of Claims [159] and the opinion of the Court of Claims will not be referred to for the purpose of eking out, controlling, or modifying the scope of the findings.[160] The Supreme Court has repeatedly held that the findings of the Court of Claims in an action at law determine all matters of fact, like the verdict

ence of present or possible adverse parties whose contentions are submitted to the court for adjudication. *Chisholm* v. *Georgia*, 2 Dall. 419, 431 (1792). A case arises under the Constitution or laws of the United States, whenever its decision depends upon the correct construction of either. *Cohens* v. *Virginia*, 6 Wheat. 264, 379 (1821); *Osborn* v. *Bank of the United States*, 9 Wheat. 738 (1824).

[159] *The Sisseton & Wahpeton Indians* v. *United States*, 208 U. S. 561, 566 (1908), citing *McClure* v. *United States*, 116 U. S. 145 (1885); *District of Columbia* v. *Barnes*, 197 U. S. 146, 150 (1905).

[160] *United States* v. *Shoshone Tribe*, 304 U. S. 111, 115 (1938), citing *Stone* v. *United States*, 164 U. S. 380, 383 (1896); *Luckenbach S. S. Co.* v. *United States*, 272 U. S. 533, 539–540 (1926). *Cf. American Propeller Co.* v. *United States*, 300 U. S. 475, 479–480 (1937).

of a jury, and that where there is any evidence of a fact which they find, and no exception is taken, their finding is final.[161] Nor will findings of mixed fact and law be reviewed by the Supreme Court on appeal from the Court of Claims.[162]

It may be added that after the Supreme Court has received a judgment of the Court of Claims and affirmed it, the Court of Claims, like any other court whose judgment has been reviewed by the Supreme Court, must give effect to it and carry it into effect according to the mandate, without variation or other further relief.[163]

[161] *Collier* v. *United States*, 173 U. S. 79 (1899); *United States* v. *New York Indians*, 173 U. S. 464 (1899); s. c. 170 U. S. 1, 170 U. S. 614; *Stone* v. *United States*, 164 U. S. 380 (1896); *Desmare* v. *United States*, 93 U. S. 605 (1876); *Talbert* v. *United States*, 155 U. S. 45 (1894).

[162] *United States* v. *Omaha Indians*, 253 U. S. 275, 281 (1920), citing *Ross* v. *Day*, 232 U. S. 110, 116–117 (1914).

[163] *Eastern Cherokee* v. *United States*, 225 U. S. 572, 582 (1912), citing, *In re Sanford Fork & Tool Co.*, 160 U. S. 247 (1895).

SECTION 4. FEDERAL ADMINISTRATIVE TRIBUNALS

While the judicial power of the Federal Government is vested by Article III of the Constitution in the Supreme Court, and in such inferior courts as the Congress may from time to time ordain and establish with respect to cases therein enumerated, yet there are many matters relating to the execution of powers delegated to Congress by other provisions of the Constitution which are susceptible of judicial determination, and these Congress may or may not bring within the cognizance of the federal courts, as it may deem proper.[164] That Congress may refer such matters to special tribunals and clothe them with functions deemed essential or helpful in carrying into execution other powers delegated to it by other articles of the Constitution, would seem to be beyond question.

With reference to the Choctaw and Chickasaw Citizenship Court, otherwise known as the Dawes Commission, which was originally created by the Act of March 3, 1893,[165] the Supreme Court said in the case of *Ex parte Bakelite Corp.*:[166]

> * * * It was created to hear and determine controverted claims to membership in two Indian tribes. The tribes were under the guardianship of the United States, which in virtue of that relation was proceeding to distribute the lands and funds of the tribes among their members. How the membership should be determined rested in the discretion of Congress. It could commit the task to officers of the department in charge of Indian Affairs, to a commission or to a judicial tribunal. As the controversies were difficult of solution and large properties were to be distributed, Congress chose to create a special court and to authorize it to determine the controversies. In *Wallace* v. *Adams*, 204 U. S. 415, this was held to be a valid exertion of authority belonging to Congress by reason of its control over the Indian tribes. (P. 457.)

When a matter has been entrusted by an act of Congress to the exclusive cognizance of a special tribunal or administrative officer, and the decision of that tribunal or officer made exclusive, the federal courts have no jurisdiction to reexamine it for alleged errors of law. Thus in *Hallowell* v. *Commons*,[167] in which the question involved was as to the jurisdiction of the federal courts under the Acts of August 15, 1894,[168] and

[164] *Murray's Lessee* v. *Hoboken Land and Improvement Co.*, 18 How. 272 (1856).

[165] Sec. 16, 27 Stat. 612, 645, as amended by Act of June 10, 1896, 29 Stat. 321, 339, 340. And see Chapter 5, sec. 6.

[166] 279 U. S. 438 (1929).

[167] 239 U. S. 506 (1916).

[168] 28 Stat. 286.

February 6, 1901,[169] to review a decision of the Secretary of the Interior determining the heirs of a deceased allottee under the Act of June 25, 1910,[170] the Supreme Court, in affirming the decree of the court below dismissing the bill for want of jurisdiction, said:

> It is unnecessary to consider whether there was jurisdiction when the suit was begun. By the act of June 25, 1910, c. 431, 36 Stat. 855, it was provided that in a case like this of the death of the allottee intestate during the trust period the Secretary of the Interior should ascertain the legal heirs of the decedent and his decision should be final and conclusive; with considerable discretion as to details. This act restored to the Secretary the power that had been taken from him by acts of 1894 and February 6, 1901, c. 217, 31 Stat. 760. *McKay* v. *Kalyton*, 204 U. S. 458, 468 [1907]. It made his jurisdiction exclusive in terms, it made no exception for pending litigation, but purported to be universal and so to take away the jurisdiction that for a time had been conferred upon the courts of the United States.[171]

The judgment of a special tribunal empowered to pass upon judicial questions cannot be attacked for fraud or mistake unless the fraud alleged and proved is such as to prevent a full hearing. Thus in *United States* v. *Atkins*[172] the Supreme Court held that the Dawes Commission in enrolling a name as that of a Creek Indian alive on April 1, 1899, when duly approved by the Secretary of the Interior as provided by the Act of June 10, 1896,[173] amounted to a judgment in an adversary proceeding, establishing the existence of the individual and his right to membership; that such judgment was not subject to attack and could not be annulled for fraud unless the fraud alleged and proved was such as to have prevented a full hearing within the doctrine approved in former decisions of the Court.[174]

[169] 31 Stat. 760.

[170] 36 Stat. 855, 25 U. S. C. 372, 373.

[171] See to the same effect *Lane* v. *United States ex. rel. Mickadiet and Tiebault*, 241 U. S. 201 (1916); *First Moon* v. *White Tail*, 270 U. S. 243 (1926); *United States* v. *Bowling*, 256 U. S. 484 (1921).

The power to determine heirs given to the Secretary of the Interior by the Act of 1910 terminates when the trust patent is terminated and a patent in fee issued. *Larkin* v. *Paugh*, 276 U. S. 431 (1928). See also *Brown* v. *Hitchcock*, 173 U. S. 473 (1899); *Lane* v. *United States ex rel. Mickadiet and Tiebault*, 241 U. S. 201, 207 *et seq.* (1916). Also see Chapter 5. sec. 11C.

[172] 260 U. S. 220 (1922). See also Chapter 5, sec. 13.

[173] 29 Stat. 321, 339, amending Act of March 3, 1893, 27 Stat. 612, 645.

[174] See *United States* v. *Throckmorton*, 98 U. S. 61 (1878); *Vance* v. *Burbank*, 101 U. S. 514 (1879); *Hilton* v. *Guyot*, 159 U. S. 113 (1895).

Congress has enacted a considerable number of general statutes[175] and a much larger number of special statutes relating to particular cases or areas,[176] which confer upon administrative authorities power to determine controversies arising out of Indian relations.

[175] On control of traders, see Act of May 6, 1822, 3 Stat. 682; Act of February 13, 1862, 12 Stat. 338.

On settlement of claims for property loss see Act of March 30, 1802, 2 Stat. 139; Act of June 30, 1834, 4 Stat. 729.

On control over agricultural entries on surplus coal lands in Indian reservations, see Act of February 27, 1917, 39 Stat. 944.

On duties and powers of "inspectors," see Act of February 14, 1873, 17 Stat. 437, 463.

On jurisdiction over inheritance cases, see Chapter 5, sec. 11C; Chapter 10, sec. 10; Chapter 11, sec. 6.

[176] Relief of persons sustaining damages from Sioux Indian depredations: Act of February 16, 1863, 12 Stat. 652; Act of March 3, 1863, 12 Stat. 803.

Assessment of damages for railroad right of way: Act of August 2, 1882, 22 Stat. 181; Act of July 4, 1884, 23 Stat. 73, construed in *Cherokee Nation v. Kansas Railway Co.*, 135 U. S. 641 (1890); Act of July 1, 1886, 24 Stat. 117; Act of July 6, 1886, 24 Stat. 124; Act of February 24, 1887, 24 Stat. 419; Act of March 2, 1887, 24 Stat. 446; Act of February 18, 1888, 25 Stat. 35; Act of May 14, 1888, 25 Stat. 140; Act of May 30, 1888, 25 Stat. 162; Act of June 26, 1888, 25 Stat. 205; Act of January 16, 1889, 25 Stat. 647; Act of February 26, 1889, 25 Stat. 745; Act of May 8, 1890, 26 Stat. 102; Act of September 26, 1890, 26 Stat. 485; Act of October 1, 1890, 26 Stat. 632; Act of February 24, 1891, 26 Stat. 783; Act of March 3, 1891, 26 Stat. 844; Act of July 6, 1892, 27 Stat. 83; Act of July 30, 1892, 27 Stat. 336; Act of February 20, 1893, 27 Stat. 465; Act of December 21, 1893, 28 Stat. 22; Act of August 4, 1894, 28 Stat. 229; Act of March 2, 1896, 29 Stat. 40; Act of March 18, 1896, 29 Stat. 69; Act of March 30, 1896, 29 Stat. 80; Act of April 6, 1896, 29 Stat. 87; Act of January 29, 1897, 29 Stat. 502; Act of February 14, 1898, 30 Stat. 241; Act of March 30, 1898, 30 Stat. 347; Act of February 28, 1899, 30 Stat. 906; Act of March 2, 1899, 30 Stat. 990. In nearly all the foregoing cases assessment of damages is to be made by assessors appointed for the purpose. In the last statute cited the Secretary of the Interior is given power to assess damages to the tribe.

Awards for the relief of certain Indians: Act of March 3, 1873, 17 Stat. 623.

Determination of attorneys' fees and expenses in connection with prosecution of suits brought in the Court of Claims in behalf of Creek Nation: Act of May 29, 1928, 45 Stat. 944.

Individual claims of Indians based on depredations by citizens of the United States on Cherokee Indian lands: Act of July 13, 1832, 4 Stat. 576.

Appointment of guardians and trustees for Indian minors entitled to pensions and bounties: Joint Resolution of July 14, 1870, 16 Stat. 390.

Citizenship in Five Civilized Tribes: Act of June 10, 1896, 29 Stat. 321.

Appraisement and sale of Winnebago Indian lands: Act of February 21, 1863, 12 Stat. 658.

Settlement of disputes concerning allotments, Kansas or Kaw tribe of Indians: Act of July 1, 1902, 32 Stat. 636, 638, 640.

Determination of fairness of assessment of lands of Indians subject to drainage taxations: Act of March 27, 1914, 38 Stat. 310 (Five Civilized Tribes).

Determination of membership of the Eastern Band of Cherokee Indians of North Carolina: Act of June 4, 1924, 43 Stat. 376.

Determination of contests relating to selection of allotments by members of the Eastern Band of Cherokee Indians of North Carolina: Act of June 4, 1924, 43 Stat. 376, 378.

Determination of contests over ownership of so-called private lands claims against tribal lands of the Eastern Band of Cherokee Indians of North Carolina: Act of June 4, 1924, 43 Stat. 376, 379.

Cancellation of allotments of land to members of the Eastern Band of Cherokee Indians of North Carolina: Act of June 4, 1924, 43 Stat. 376, 379.

Determination of heirs of deceased members of the Eastern Band of Cherokee Indians of North Carolina: Act of June 4, 1924, 43 Stat. 376, 380.

Determination of competency of members of the Eastern Band of Cherokees of North Carolina for the purpose of making leases of their allotted lands: Act of June 4, 1924, 43 Stat. 376, 380.

Settlement of all questions relating to enrollment and other matters involving dispositions of land and moneys of the Eastern Band of Cherokees of North Carolina: Act of June 4, 1924, 43 Stat. 376, 381.

Determination of lands granted or confirmed to Pueblo Indians of New Mexico, title to which had not been extinguished excluding claims of non-Indians occupying those lands by adverse possession: Act of June 7, 1924, 43 Stat. 636.

Townsites: Act of May 29, 1908, 35 Stat. 444, 446 (Choctaw and Chickasaw).

Distribution of funds: Acts of May 29, 1908, 35 Stat. 444, 446, 447 (Cherokee).

Sale of unallotted lands for school purposes: Act of May 29, 1908, 35 Stat. 444, 447 (Five Civilized Tribes).

Appraisal and sale of tribal lands: Act of May 29, 1908, 35 Stat. 444, 447, 448 (Oklahoma).

Cancellation of patents upon determinations of nonexistence of allottee: Act of May 29, 1908, 35 Stat. 444, 451 (Yankton Sioux allottee).

Determination of land allotment to heirs of deceased Sioux Indians: Act of May 29, 1908, 35 Stat. 444, 451, 452.

Return of forfeited money in cases of error under previous acts: Act of May 29, 1908, 35 Stat. 444, 458 (Kiowa-Comanche and Apache).

Private claims against Chickasaw tribe of Indians: Act of August 15, 1894, 28 Stat. 286, 312.

Determination of wastefulness and squandering of income by Osage Indians: Act of February 27, 1925, 43 Stat. 1008, 1009.

Sale of lands and disposal of funds by Osage Indians: Act of February 27, 1925, 43 Stat. 1008, 1009–1010.

Cancellation of certificates of competency of Osage Indians: Act of February 27, 1925, 43 Stat. 1008, 1010.

SECTION 5. STATE COURTS

In matters not affecting either the Federal Government or the tribal relations, an Indian has the same status to sue and be sued in state courts as any other citizen.[177]

It may be stated however, as a general proposition, that the state courts have no jurisdiction in civil matters affecting the restricted property or tribal relations of the Indians, unless otherwise provided by Congress,[178] so long at least as the United States retains governmental control over them. This is particularly so with respect to allotted lands and the transfer of any

[177] See *Felix v. Patrick*, 145 U. S. 317, 332 (1892). *Ke-tuc-e-Mun-guah v. McClure*, 122 Ind. 541, 23 N. E. 1080 (1890) (suit against Indian on promissory note); *Stacy v. La Belle*, 99 Wis. 520, 75 N. W. 60 (1898) (suit against Indian on contract); *Missouri Pac. Ry. Co. v. Cullers*, 81 Tex. 382, 17 S. W. 19 (1891) (cause of action against railroad assigned by Indian) commented on in note, 13 L. R. A. 542; and see cases therein cited. With respect to the jurisdiction of state courts over Indians, a leading student of the subject declares: "* * * Indians are not extraterritorial but only subject to a special rule of substantive law." (P. 93.) The same writer comments:

> In civil matters the lacunae of federal legislation are so enormous that the general law, though theoretically inapplicable, practically fills the gaps, subject to proof of a positive Indian custom that varies the law. Thus federal legislation and, in default thereof, Indian custom rule; but state law practically covers much of the ground. (W. G. Rice, The Position of the American Indian in the Law of the United States (1934) 16 J. Comp. Leg. 78, 92.)

And see sec. 2A(5), *supra*; Chapter 8, sec. 6.

[178] Some special statutes containing provisions conferring jurisdiction on state courts arranged by subject matter are:

> Partitions of lands of Five Civilized Tribes: Act of June 14, 1918, 40 Stat. 606.
>
> Determination of heirs of Five Civilized Tribes: Act of June 14, 1918, 40 Stat. 606.
>
> Approval of conveyances of inherited lands by full-blood Indians of the Five Civilized Tribes: Act of April 10, 1926, 44 Stat. 239.
>
> Process for making United States party defendant in certain suits pending in the state courts of Oklahoma, and for their removal to the federal courts: Act of April 10, 1926, 44 Stat. 239, 240.
>
> Subjecting person and property of minor allottees of Five Civilized Tribes to state courts in probate matters: Act of May 27, 1908, 35 Stat. 312.
>
> Appointment of representative of Secretary of the Interior in probate matters: Act of May 27, 1908, 35 Stat. 312, 314.
>
> United States right to institute suit in federal courts not affected by jurisdiction of state court in probate matters: Act of May 27, 1908, 35 Stat. 312, 314–315.

Compare the following special statutes conferring concurrent jurisdiction on state and federal courts:

> Act of February 27, 1925, 43 Stat. 1008, 1010 (Suits against guardians of Osage Indians).
>
> Act of February 19, 1875, 18 Stat. 330 (Recovery of rents and possession of lands—Seneca Nation).

right, title, or interest thereto whether by way of purchase or descent, including wills, partition, condemnation, or judicial decree.[179] As stated by the Supreme Court in *McKay* v. *Kalyton:*[180]

> The *Rickert case* [188 U. S. 432, 435 (1903)] settled that, as the necessary result of the legislation of Congress, the United States retained such control over allotments as was essential to cause the allotted land to enure during the period in which the land was to be held in trust "for the sole use and benefit of the allottees." As observed in the *Smith* case, 194 U. S. 408 [*Hy-yu-tse-mil-kin* v. *Smith*, 194 U. S. 401, 408 (1904)], prior to the passage of the act of 1894 [Act of August 15, 1894, 28 Stat. 286, amended by the Act of February 6, 1901, 31 Stat. 760], "the sole authority for settling disputes concerning allotments resided in the Secretary of the Interior." This being settled, it follows that prior to the act of Congress of 1894 controversies necessarily involving a determination of the title and incidentally of the right to the possession of Indian allotments while the same were held in trust by the United States were not primarily cognizable by any court, either state or Federal. (P. 468.)

As to the question of jurisdiction to determine heirs and effectuate a distribution or partition of allotted lands, a distinction must be noted as between lands held under a trust patent and lands held under a patent in fee. As to the latter it is sufficient to notice that after a fee patent has been issued all question relating to the transfer of title to the allotted lands must be determined by the laws of the state where the land is located.[181] The reason for this is simply that the allottee holds the land in his individual capacity, and as to that land he has become emancipated, and since the land is located within the limits of the state, the tribal laws, as opposed to the state laws, cannot reach that land.[182]

As to lands held by the allottee under a trust patent, it will be observed that the provisions of section 5 of the General Allotment Act are silent as to the question of jurisdiction to determine heirs or to effectuate a partition of lands. Since Congress has conferred upon the Secretary of the Interior final authority to determine heirs and to effectuate partition of such lands[183] it is clear that no court, state or federal, has jurisdiction to determine heirs with respect to allotted Indian lands while the title thereto remains in the United States.[184] Nor has any court, whether state or federal, any jurisdiction to partition or distribute such lands.[185] And the same is true as to lands allotted to Indians under fee simple patents subject to restrictions upon alienation without the approval of the Secretary of the Interior or some other federal agency selected by Congress for the purpose.[186]

---

[179] "Although the federal right was first claimed in the state court in the petition for rehearing, if the question was raised, was necessarily involved, and was considered and decided adversely by the state court, this court has jurisdiction under Rev. Stat., § 709.

"The United States has retained such control over the allotments to Indians that, except as provided by acts of Congress, controversies involving the determination of title to, and right to possession of, Indian allotments while the same are held in trust by the United States are not primarily cognizable by any court, state or Federal.

"The act of August 15, 1894, 28 Stat. 286, delegating to Federal courts the power to determine questions involving the rights of Indians to allotments did not confer upon state courts authority to pass upon any questions over which they did not have jurisdiction prior to the passage of such act, either as to title to the allotment, or the mere possession thereof which is of necessity dependent upon the title." (*McKay* v. *Kalyton*, 204 U. S. 458 (1907).)

[180] 204 U. S. 458 (1907).

[181] See *Dickson* v. *Luck Land Co.*, 242 U. S. 371 (1917); *United States* v. *Waller*, 243 U. S. 452 (1917). As to wills see *La Motte* v. *United States*, 254 U. S. 570 (1921).

[182] The judicial determination of controversies concerning lands allotted to Indians in severalty and held by the United States in trust for the allottee has been commonly committed exclusively to federal courts, and not to the state courts. *Minnesota* v. *United States*, 305 U. S. 382 (1939); *McKay* v. *Kalyton*, 204 U. S. 458 (1907), yet after the issuance of a fee patent in the name of a deceased allottee under the General Allotment Act of February 8, 1887, 24 Stat. 388, as amended by the Act of March 8, 1906, 34 Stat. 182, all questions pertaining to the title to the allotted land are subject to examination and determination by the courts—appropriately those in the state where the land is situated. And see *United States* v. *Waller*, 243 U. S. 452, 460 (1917), wherein the doctrine of partial emancipation is clearly recognized. See also and compare *Larkin* v. *Paugh*, 276 U. S. 431 (1928).

[183] Act of June 25, 1910, 36 Stat. 855. See Chapter 5, sec. 11 and Chapter 11, sec. 6.

[184] *McKay* v. *Kalyton*, 204 U. S. 458 (1907); *Little Bill* v. *Swanson*, 64 Wash. 650, 117 Pac. 481 (1911); *Gray* v. *McKnight*, 75 Okla. 268, 183 Pac. 489 (1919).

The federal courts first assumed jurisdiction in matters involving inheritance of Indian lands after the passage of the Act of August 15, 1894, 28 Stat. 286, as amended by the Act of February 6, 1901, 31 Stat. 760, 25 U. S. C. 345, providing that one who claimed to have been unlawfully denied or excluded from any allotment to which he claimed lawfully to be entitled under any treaty or act of Congress, might commence and prosecute or defend any action, suit, or proceeding in relation to his right thereto in the proper circuit court (district court) of the United States, and that the judgment or decree of any such court in favor of any claimant should have the same effect, when properly certified to the Secretary of the Interior, as if such allotment had been allowed and approved by him. This act, however, did not apply to the Five Civilized Tribes, nor to any lands within the Quapaw Indian Agency. But clearly the purpose of this act was not to confer jurisdiction upon the federal courts in matters of inheritance or descent as such; its purpose had reference merely to the right of an Indian to sue in those courts for an original allotment. *McKay* v. *Kalyton*, 204 U. S. 458 (1907); and *cf. Sloan* v. *United States*, 193 U. S. 614 (1904). As to the determination of heirs the Act of 1901, with its 1901 amendments, if applicable at all, was repealed by the Act of June 25, 1910, 36 Stat. 853, conferring jurisdiction in such matters upon the Secretary of the Interior, *Bond* v. *United States*, 181 Fed. 613 (C. C. Ore. 1910); *Pel-Ata-Yakot* v. *United States*, 188 Fed. 387 (C. C. Idaho N. D. 1911); *Parr* v. *Colfax*, 197 Fed. 302 (C. C. A. 9, 1912). The Act of 1910 did not repeal, however, the Act of 1894, nor the amendatory act of 1901 with respect to the right of Indians to sue in the federal courts for an allotment. *United States* v. *Payne*, 264 U. S. 446 (1924); *First Moon* v. *White Tail*, 270 U. S. 243 (1926). Nor did the Act of 1910 make new law respecting the jurisdiction of the Secretary to determine heirs, since it was merely declaratory of the previously existing law. See *Hallowell* v. *Commons*, 239 U. S. 506 (1916). And neither the Act of 1894, nor the Act of 1901 affected the authority of the Secretary of the Interior, but only gave to the federal courts concurrent jurisdiction in such matters. *Daugherty* v. *McFarland*, 40 S. D. 1, 166 N. W. 143 (1918). The method and procedure adopted by the Secretary of the Interior in exercising his authority under the Act of 1910 is thus stated in his decision in the *Grace Cox* case, 42 L. D. 493, 495-6 (1913):

> The Secretary of the Interior is, as it were, counsel for both plaintiff and defendant as well as judge upon the bench. He does not wait for a case to be brought before him, but on the contrary, institutes the necessary proceedings through his representatives in the field, collects the necessary evidence which may be in the form of decrees of the State courts, *ex parte* or interrogatory affidavits, etc., and renders his decision on legal and equitable grounds. The act of [of June 25, 1910] defining the scope of his duties specifically provides that his decisions shall be under *"such rules and regulations as he may prescribe."* It is evident, therefore, that the Secretary is *not* "bound" by the decisions or decrees of *any court* in inheritance matters affecting Indian trust lands, and that it rests entirely in his discretion, from the evidence submitted, as to the determination of Indian heirs.

[185] *Daugherty* v. *McFarland*, 40 S. D. 1, 166 N. W. 143 (1918); *United States* v. *Bellm*, 182 Fed. 161 (C. C. E. D. Okla. 1910). And see *McKay* v. *Kalyton*, 204 U. S. 458 (1907). In the *Bellm* case, *supra*, it was held that the proviso in the General Allotment Act adopting the laws of descent of the state was merely for the purpose of providing a rule by which the heirs should be determined, and the partition statutes were adopted only so far as they provided for a division of the land in case the heirs could not agree to hold it in common, and there was no intention of abrogating the trust in any case, and the clause "except as herein otherwise provided" excluded the application of a provision of a state partition statute authorizing a sale of the land where it could not be advantageously divided; and such a sale of land in the Indian Territory, although under an order of court based on the Kansas statute, was null and void.

[186] Partition of Indian lands constitute an "alienation" within the meaning of federal laws imposing restrictions thereon. *Coleman* v. *Battiest*, 65 Okla. 71, 162 Pac. 786 (1917); *Lewis* v. *Gillard*, 70 Okla. 231, 173 Pac. 1136 (1918). In *Eysenbach* v. *Naharkey*, 114 Okla. 217,

A suit for the possession of allotted Indian lands instituted under state laws is not within the jurisdiction of the state courts regardless of the merits of the controversy so long as the title to those lands is in the United States.[187] That state courts have no jurisdiction to entertain a suit for the condemnation of allotted Indian lands held by the United States in trust for the allottee unless such jurisdiction is specifically conferred by an act of Congress has been settled by the Supreme Court in *Minnesota v. United States*, decided in 1939,[188] and the same rule applies in cases involving tribal lands.[189] With respect to lands allotted in severalty to Indians while the title remains in the United States it is to be observed that under the second paragraph of section 3 of the Act of March 3, 1901,[190] such lands may be condemned for any public purpose under the laws of the state or territory where they are located "in the same manner as land owned in fee may be condemned," and the money awarded as damages is to be paid to the allottee. But this provision does not authorize a suit in the courts of a state to condemn such land; it merely authorizes condemnation for "any public purpose under the laws of the State or Territory where located."[191]

The fact that such a suit may have been removed to a federal court on petition of the United States and that a stipulation may have been entered into by its attorney in relation thereto is without legal significance, for where jurisdiction has not been conferred by Congress no officer of the United States has power to give to any court jurisdiction of a suit against the United States.[192]

As Congress has not given its consent to the institution of a condemnation suit of this sort in the state courts, the federal courts are therefore without jurisdiction upon its removal for the jurisdiction of the federal court upon such removal is, in a limited sense, a derivative jurisdiction and where the state court lacks jurisdiction of the subject matter or of the parties, the federal court acquires none, although in a like suit originally brought in a federal court it would have had jurisdiction.[193]

The controlling principle which prevents a court, whether state or federal, from exercising any power or jurisdiction to adjudicate any matter involving the transfer of any right, title, or interest in or to restricted allotted Indian lands is that the United States in the exercise of its plenary and exclusive power over the Indians and their property may adopt such measures as it may deem necessary and proper for their welfare and protection[194] and the state courts without legislative authority have no power or jurisdiction to interfere with or circumvent those measures.[195] Consequently the mere fact that the lands involved in a suit brought in a state court may have been allotted to an Indian is not sufficient to oust the state court jurisdiction. It must also appear that such lands are either held by the United States in trust for the allottee or his heirs, or that they are subject to restrictions against alienation under some act of Congress or treaty of the United States with the Indians. It is to be observed, also in this connection, that the mechanics of a suit in court require that the facts showing the existence or nonexistence of jurisdiction shall appear. Thus if the bill makes out a case within the jurisdiction of the court that jurisdiction is not ousted or defeated merely because the defendant may allege in its answer that the land or other property is restricted, for that only puts in issue the determination of a fact upon which the court necessarily must pass in order to determine whether it can proceed; and if the court's decision on that issue is in favor of the defendant the suit, of course, must be dismissed for want of jurisdiction; otherwise the court may proceed to judgment, and that judgment, unless appealed from and reversed by the appellate court, will be binding on the parties, whether the decision is right or wrong.[196]

The United States, however, would not be concluded by such judgment if it were not a party to the suit or did not give its consent thereto.[197]

---

246 Pac. 608 (1926), modifying opinion 110 Okla. 207, 236 Pac. 619 (1925), a decree in partition, rendered by the United States Court for the Western District of the Indian Territory, of inherited land between full-blood citizens of the Creek Nation was held to be void for want of jurisdiction of the subject matter since section 22 of the act of Congress of April 26, 1906, 34 Stat. 137, restricted the inherited land of full-blood citizens of Creek tribe against alienation and the decree in attempting to partition the land was, in effect "an alienation" of certain portions of the land away from certain heirs and vesting the title in other heirs.

[187] See *McKay v. Kalyton*, 204 U. S. 458 (1907). In that case the Supreme Court said:

> The suggestion made in argument that the controversy here presented involved the mere possession and not the title to the allotted land is without merit, since the right of possession asserted of necessity is dependent upon the existence of an equitable title in the claimant under the legislation of Congress to the ownership of the allotted lands. Indeed, that such was the case plainly appears from the excerpt which we have made from the concluding portion of the opinion of the Supreme Court of Oregon.
>
> Because from the considerations previously stated we are constrained from the conclusion that the court below was without jurisdiction to entertain the controversy, we must not be considered as intimating an opinion that we deem that the principles applied by the court in disposing of the merit of the case were erroneous. (P. 469.)

[188] 305 U. S. 382.

[189] See *United States v. Colvard*, 89 F. 2d 312 (C. C. A. 4, 1937).

[190] 31 Stat. 1058, 1083–1084.

[191] *Minnesota v. United States*, 305 U. S. 382, 389 (1939).

[192] *Minnesota v. United States*, 305 U. S. 382, 389 (1939), citing "*Case v. Terrell*, 11 Wall. 199, 202; *Carr v. United States*, 98 U. S. 433, 435–439; *Finn v. United States*, 123 U. S. 227, 232–233; *Stanley v. Schwalby*, 162 U. S. 255, 270; *United States v. Garbutt Oil Co.*, 302 U. S. 528, 533–535." (P. 389.)

[193] *Minnesota v. United States*, 305 U. S. 382, 389 (1939), citing: "*Lambert Run Coal Co. v. Baltimore & Ohio R. Co.*, 258 U. S. 377, 388; *General Investment Co. v. Lake Shore & M. S. Ry. Co.*, 260 U. S. 261, 288." (P. 389.)

[194] See *United States v. Rickert*, 188 U. S. 432 (1903); *Heckman v. United States*, 224 U. S. 413 (1912).

[195] *Tidal Oil Co. v. Flanagan*, 87 Okla. 231, 209 Pac. 729 (1922), writ of error dismissed, 263 U. S. 444 (1924); *Cotton v. McClendon*, 128 Okla. 48, 261 Pac. 150 (1927); *Bilby v. Malone*, 130 Okla. 217, 266 Pac. 760 (1928); *Brink v. Canfield*, 78 Okla. 189, 187 Pac. 223 (1919), cert. den. 253 U. S. 493 (1920); *Miller v. Tidal Oil Co.*, 106 Okla. 212, 233 Pac. 696 (1925); *Southwestern Surety Ins. Co. v. Farriss*, 118 Okla. 188, 247 Pac. 392 (1926).

[196] Jurisdiction, after all, is a matter of power and covers right and wrong decisions. *Fauntleroy v. Lum*, 210 U. S. 230, 234–235 (1908); *Burnet v. Desmornes Y. Alvarez*, 226 U. S. 145, 147 (1912). Even in cases where the jurisdiction of the court depends upon the subject matter it has repeatedly been held by the Supreme Court that if the allegations of the bill or declaration make a claim that if well founded is within the jurisdiction of the court, it is within that jurisdiction whether well founded or not. *Hart v. Keith Vaudeville Exchange*, 262 U. S. 271, 273 (1923); *Louisville & Nashville R. R. Co. v. Rice*, 247 U. S. 201, 203 (1918); *Geneva Furniture Manufacturing Co. v. S. Karpen & Bros.*, 238 U. S. 254, 258 (1915); *The Fair v. Kohler Die & Specialty Co.*, 228 U. S. 22, 25 (1913). In *Geneva Furniture Manufacturing Co. v. S. Karpen & Bros., supra*, the Supreme Court said that jurisdiction is

> * * * the power to consider and decide one way or the other as the law may require, and is not to be declined merely because it is not foreseen with certainty that the outcome will help the plaintiff. (P. 259.)

And in *Hart v. Keith Vaudeville Exchange, supra*, the Supreme Court said:

> The jurisdiction of the District Court is the only matter to be considered on this appeal. That is determined by the allegations of the bill, and usually if the bill or declaration makes a claim that if well founded is within the jurisdiction of the Court it is within that jurisdiction whether well founded or not. (P. 273.)

[197] *Bowling v. United States*, 233 U. S. 528 (1914); *Privett v. United States*, 256 U. S. 201 (1921); *Sunderland v. United States*, 266 U. S. 226 (1924). See and *cf. United States v. Logan*, 105 Fed. 240 (C. C. Ore. 1900); *United States v. Candelaria*, 271 U. S. 432 (1926); *United States v. Mashunkashey*, 72 F. 2d 847 (C. C. A. 10, 1934), rehear'g. den. 73 F. 2d 487 (C. C. A. 10, 1934), cert. den. 294 U. S. 724 (1935).

Of course, if it appears from the record that the court had no jurisdiction, the judgment must be regarded as absolutely void,[198] and may be attacked either directly or collaterally.[199]

Where Indian territory within the physical boundaries of a state has been excluded from the state by treaty and statute, the state courts have no jurisdiction even over non-Indians thereon.[200]

[198] *Elliott* v. *Piersol*, 1 Pet. 328 (1828); *Williamson* v. *Berry*, 49 U. S. 495 (1850); *In re Sawyer*, 124 U. S. 200 (1888); *Roth* v. *Union Nat. Bank*, 58 Okla. 604, 160 Pac. 505 (1916); *Morgan* v. *Karcher*, 81 Okla. 210, 197 Pac. 433 (1921); *Winona Oil Co.* v. *Barnes*, 83 Okla. 248, 200 Pac. 981 (1921); *Carlile* v. *Nat. Oil & Development Co.*, 83 Okla. 217, 201 Pac. 377 (1921).

[199] *United States* v. *Bellm*, 182 Fed. 161 (C. C. E. D. Okla., 1910); *Lewis* v. *Gillard*, 70 Okla. 231, 173 Pac. 1136 (1918); *Winona Oil Co.* v. *Barnes*, 83 Okla. 248, 200 Pac. 981 (1921); *Eysenbach* v. *Naharkey*, 114 Okla. 127, 246 Pac. 603 (1926).

A court having jurisdiction over the subject matter and the parties, is competent to decide questions arising as to its own jurisdiction, and its decisions on such questions are not open to collateral attack. *Ex parte Harding*, 219 U. S. 363, 367, 369 (1911), citing *Dowell* v. *Applegate*, 152 U. S. 327, 337 (1894), and *Hine* v. *Morse*, 218 U. S. 493 (1910).

[200] *Harkness* v. *Hyde*, 98 U. S. 476 (1878), qualified in *Langford* v. *Monteith*, 102 U. S. 145 (1880).

SECTION 6. TRIBAL COURTS

That an Indian tribe has power to confer upon its own courts jurisdiction over controversies involving Indians is a proposition supported by authorities which have been already analyzed.[201] That "full faith and credit" are due to decisions rendered by tribal courts in cases properly within their jurisdiction, is a second basic principle in the field of civil jurisdiction which is supported by authorities elsewhere analyzed.[202] There remains the question how far the power to confer upon tribal courts such jurisdiction has been actually exercised.

This is a matter on which there are few federal statutes, the question having been left primarily to the action of the tribes themselves. One of the few federal statutes which refer to tribal jurisdiction over civil cases is section 229 of title 25 of the United States Code.[203] This statute provides that where injuries to property are committed by an Indian, application for redress shall be made by the appropriate federal authorities "to the nation or tribe to which such Indian shall belong, for satisfaction." It has been noted by the Solicitor for the Interior Department[204] that this provision assumes that the Indian tribe has the means of compelling return of stolen property or other forms of satisfaction where its members have violated the rights of non-Indians.

Apart from this general statute, special provision has been made by federal law with respect to the tribal courts in the Indian Territory. The jurisdiction of these courts, both in civil and in criminal matters, over Indians belonging to the same tribe, was specifically recognized by the Act of May 2, 1890,[205] which provided for a temporary government for the Territory of Oklahoma and enlarged the jurisdiction of the United States court in the Indian Territory.

Under sections 30 and 31 of this act, the exclusive jurisdiction preserved to the judicial tribunals of the Indian nations in all civil and criminal cases is limited to those cases in which "members of said Nations" are the sole parties, which creates an ambiguity as to the meaning of the words "only parties" or "sole parties." This ambiguity, however, was dispelled by the Supreme Court in the case of *Alberty* v. *United States*.[206] In this connection the court said:

> The real question as respects the jurisdiction in this case is as to the meaning of the words "sole" or only "parties." These words are obviously susceptible of two interpretations. They may mean a class of actions as to which there is but one party; but as these actions, if they exist at all, are very rare, it can hardly be supposed that Congress intended to legislate with respect to them to the exclusion of the much more numerous actions to which there are two parties. They may mean actions to which members of the Nations are the sole or only parties, to the exclusion of white men, or persons other than members of the Nation; and as respects civil cases at least, this seems the more probable construction. (P. 503.)

Under section 6 of the Act of March 1, 1889,[207] creating the United States court in the Indian Territory, that court had jurisdiction of a suit brought by a citizen of the United States who had become a member and citizen of the Chickasaw Nation against another citizen of that nation.[208]

The termination of the authority of the tribal courts of the Five Civilized Tribes is elsewhere discussed.[209]

A typical provision of a contemporary Indian code relating to civil jurisdiction is the following provision from the tribal code of the Rosebud tribe:[210]

> The Superior Courts of the Rosebud Sioux Tribe shall have jurisdiction of all suits wherein the defendant is a member of the tribe or tribes within their jurisdiction, and of all other suits between members and non-members which are brought before the Courts by stipulation of both parties. * * *

In general, tribes which have not adopted ordinances of their own on the subject and which have Courts of Indian Offenses, are governed by the following regulation of the Department of the Interior:[211]

> The Courts of Indian Offenses shall have jurisdiction of all suits wherein the defendant is a member of the tribe or tribes within their jurisdiction, and of all other suits between members and nonmembers which are brought before the Courts by stipulation of both parties. * * *

Judgments in civil cases rendered by Courts of Indian Offenses may be satisfied out of restricted Indian moneys at the order of the Secretary of the Interior, and such judgments are considered lawful debts in probate proceedings held by the Interior Department or by Courts of Indian Offenses.[212]

[201] See Chapter 7, sec. 9.

[202] See Chapter 7, sec. 9; Chapter 14, sec. 3.

[203] R. S. § 2156, derived from Act of June 30, 1834, sec. 17, 4 Stat. 729, 731, amended Act of February 28, 1859, sec. 8, 11 Stat. 388, 401.

[204] 55 I. D. 14, 63 (1934).

[205] 26 Stat. 81. The relevant provisions, secs. 30 and 31, are quoted in Chapter 18, sec. 4.

[206] 162 U. S. 499 (1896).

[207] 25 Stat. 783, 784.

[208] *Roff* v. *Burney*, 168 U. S. 218 (1897).

[209] See Chapter 23, sec. 6.

[210] Ordinance No. 4, adopted April 8, 1937, approved by superintendent April 13, 1937, approved by Secretary of the Interior, July 7, 1937, Rosebud Tribal Court and Code of Offenses, Chapter 2, sec. 1.

[211] 25 C. F. R. 161.22.

[212] 25 C. F. R. 161.26.

CHAPTER 20

PUEBLOS OF NEW MEXICO[1]

TABLE OF CONTENTS

The peculiarities of federal Indian law with respect to the Pueblos of New Mexico arise primarily from the peculiar status which was accorded to the Pueblos under Spanish and Mexican law. It is necessary, therefore, in order to understand the present legal status of these Pueblos to allude to certain basic principles developed prior to the acquisition of New Mexico by the United States.

SECTION 1. STATUS OF PUEBLOS UNDER SPANISH LAW

When the Spaniards entered the Rio Grande Valley in the sixteenth century they found certain Indian groups or communities living in villages and these Indians they designated "Indios Naturales" or "Indios de los Pueblos" to distinguish them from the "Indios Barbaros," by which term the nomadic and warlike Indians of the region were designated. The Indians who were called Pueblo Indians were not of a single tribe and they had no common organization or language. Each village maintained its own government, its own irrigation system, and its own closely integrated community life.

From an early date the Spanish Government enacted legislation to protect the lands of the Pueblos from trespass. Grants were made to the individual Pueblos for the purpose of defining and protecting the boundaries of pueblo lands. The general practice developed of fixing Pueblo boundaries at one league in each of the cardinal directions from the central church. Thus each grant normally comprised 4 square leagues or 17,712 acres. The policy of the Spanish Government towards the Pueblo Indians of New Mexico is set forth and documented in a recent study of "Pueblo Indian Land Grants of the 'Rio Abajo,' New Mexico" (1939) by Herbert O. Brayer of the University of New Mexico,[2] from which the following summary of the status of the Pueblos is excerpted:

> 1. The Pueblo Indians of New Mexico were considered wards of the Spanish crown.
>
> 2. The fundamental legal basis for the Pueblo land grants lies in the royal ordinances. The 1689 grants, purporting to convey land to the Indians, are spurious.
>
> 3. Only the viceroy, governors, and captains-general could make grants to the Indians, and only these officials had the authority to validate sales of land by the Indians.
>
> 4. All non-Indians were expressly forbidden to reside upon Pueblo lands.
>
> 5. The Spanish Government provided legal advice, protection, and defense for the Indians. Provincial officials had the authority to appeal cases directly to the audiencias in Mexico.
>
> 6. The Indians had prior water rights to all streams, rivers, and other waters which crossed or bordered their lands.
>
> 7. The Pueblo Indians held their lands in common, the land being granted to the Indians in the name of their pueblo.

The most important of the Spanish laws governing the Pueblo Indians are: the Act of March 21, 1551,[3] providing that the Indians should not live separated in the mountains, deprived of spiritual and temporal benefits, but should all be brought to

[1] The phrase "Pueblos of New Mexico" is commonly used to designate the Rio Grande Pueblos, which at the present time, comprise:

> Acoma, Cochiti, Isleta, Jemes, Laguna, Nambe, Pojoaque, Picuris, Sandia, San Felipe, San Ildefonso, San Juan, Santa Ana, Santa Clara, Santo Domingo, Taos, Tesuque, Zia.

The Zuni Indians of New Mexico and the Hopi Indians of Arizona are classed as Pueblo Indians, anthropologically, but administratively and politically they have frequently been excluded from rules and laws applicable to the Rio Grande Pueblos. For this reason they are not considered within the scope of this chapter except as particularly noted.

The Pueblo of Pecos, nearly extinct in fact, was merged with the Pueblo of Jemes by the Act of June 19, 1936, 49 Stat. 1528. A similar legislative merger of the Pueblos of Pojoaque and Nambe was recommended in a report on the "Status of Pueblo of Pojoaque" submitted on November 3, 1932, by George A. H. Fraser, Special Attorney.

[2] The University of New Mexico Bulletin No. 334, p. 16.

[3] Recopilacion de las Indias, law 1, title 2, book 6.

live in villages (Pueblos); the Acts of December 1, 1573, and October 10, 1618,[4] defining the areas and rights of the Pueblos; the royal cedula of June 4, 1687, authorizing the viceroy and president of the royal audiencia to define the areas of land granted to the Indians and increasing the amounts hitherto granted; which is in turn amended so as to reduce the areas in question, by the royal cedula of July 12, 1695; the statute[5] requiring sales of land and of personal property by Indians to be made before a judge with prescribed formalities; the decree of February 23, 1781, prohibiting unlicensed sales of real property by Indians; the decree of January 5, 1811, for the protection of Indians in their person and property; and Decree 31 of February 9, 1811, guaranteeing to the Indian and Spanish residents of New Spain full political equality with the European Spaniards.[6]

Through this course of legislation one finds the same problems that are dealt with by Congress in the Pueblo Lands Act of June 7, 1924.[7] The Indians complain that the areas of land granted them by the central government are infringed upon by their non-Indian neighbors. The non-Indian neighbors claim that lands which they have acquired and improved in good faith are subsequently claimed by the Indians. The central government is grieved to find that white ranch owners "are encroaching upon the lands of the latter (Indians), taking the same away from them, either by fraud or violence, by reason of the poor Indians abandoning their houses and settlements, this being what the Spaniards long for and aim at."[8] Through the language of all the laws and decrees enacted for the protection of the Indians there runs an implicit recognition that past laws to achieve this protection have not been adequately enforced, and the implicit hope that more adequate enforcement will attend the new legislation.

[4] Recopilacion, law 8, title 3, book 6.

[5] Recopilacion, law 27, title 1, book 6.

[6] These laws are translated and discussed in chaps. 7 and 8 of Hall's Laws of Mexico (1885).

[7] 43 Stat. 636. See sec. 4c.

[8] Royal cedula June 4, 1687, translated in Hall, Laws of Mexico (1885) p. 64.

SECTION 2. THE PUEBLOS UNDER MEXICAN RULE

The status of the Indian under Mexican rule is well summarized in the opinion of the Supreme Court of the Territory of New Mexico, in *Territory* v. *Delinquent Taxpayers.*[9] In that case the court, after noting that the Pueblo Indians "seem to have been considered by the Spanish as wards of the government, and entitled to special privileges and protection," went on to declare, *per* Parker, *J.*:

> But a complete change took place in the status of these people when Mexico threw off the Spanish yoke. Among those engaged in that struggle for independence, this Aztec race far outnumbered the Mexicans and its success was due in a large measure to their efforts. It was but natural and fitting that in the formation of the new government they should take a prominent, if not a leading, part, and that they should be placed upon an equal footing as to all civil and political rights. And so we find that the revolutionary government of Mexico, February 24, 1821, a short time before the subversion of Spanish power, adopted what is known as "The Plan of Iguala" (Iguala was the place of the revolutionary army headquarters), in which it is declared that: "All the inhabitants of New Spain, without distinction, whether Europeans, Africans or Indians, are citizens of this monarchy, with the right to be employed in any post according to their merit and virtues;" and that: "The person and property of every citizen will be respected and protected by the government." I Ordenes y Decretos, by Galvan, page 3; *U. S.* v. *Ritchie*, 17 How. (U. S.) 524, 538; *U. S.* v. *Lucero, supra* [1 N. M. 422 (1869)].
>
> The same principles were reaffirmed in the Treaty of Cordova, of August 24, 1821. 1 Ordenes y Decretos, by Galvan, page 6, and in the Declaration of Independence, of October 6, 1821. Id., page 8.
>
> The Mexican congress thereafter followed with at least four acts in each of which "The Plan of Iguala" was uniformly considered as a fixed principle of Mexican law. *U. S.* v. *Ritchie, supra;* 2 Ordenes y Decretos, pages 1 and 92, and 3 Id. page 65.
>
> This latter act was passed August 18, 1824, only twenty-four years before the Treaty of Guadalupe Hidalgo, whereby we acquired this Territory and these people. (Pp. 142–143.)

The United States Supreme Court in *United States* v. *Ritchie,*[10] in 1854, commented on the foregoing Mexican statutes in the following terms, *per* Nelson, *J.:*

> The Indian race having participated largely in the struggle resulting in the overthrow of the Spanish power, and in the erection of an independent government, it was natural that in laying the foundations of the new government, the previous political and social distinctions in favor of the European or Spanish blood should be abolished, and equality of rights and privileges established. Hence the article to this effect in the plan of Iguala, and the decree of the first Congress declaring the equality of civil rights, whatever may be their race or country. These solemn declarations of the political power of the government had the effect, necessarily, to invest the Indians with the privileges of citizenship as effectually as had the declaration of independence of the United States, of 1776, to invest all those persons with these privileges residing in the country at the time, and who adhered to the interests of the colonies. 3 Pet., 99, 121.[11]

The historian Brayer presents persuasive evidence[12] that the grant of citizenship to the Pueblo Indians, under Mexican rule, did not dissolve the status of wardship or the limitations upon land alienation established under Spanish sovereignty. It would be beyond the scope of this work to enter into this controversial field of historical research, but the conclusions of the historian cited are worthy of notice:

> 1. That the Pueblo Indians of New Mexico were still considered wards of the government even though they were given the title "citizens."
>
> 2. Only the most important of the government officials could authorize the sale of Indian lands. That the local officials in New Mexico continued to exercise the same powers as they had during the Spanish regime throughout the entire period of Mexican sovereignty.
>
> 3. That the Spanish laws in force previous to 1821, relative to the Pueblo Indian and to land policy, remained in full force.
>
> 4. That because of the laxity on the part of local officials during the Mexican period a great many non-Indians were able to obtain holdings on Indian lands. The legality of such holdings needs little consideration, but the failure of the Mexican government to take action left the problem up to the United States after 1846.
>
> 5. That the title to the Pueblo lands remained in the name of the individual Pueblos, and that no individual Indian held the title to any portion thereof.[13]

[9] 12 N. M. 139, 76 Pac. 307 (1904).

[10] 17 How. 525, 539–540 (1854).

[11] See also *United States* v. *Lucero*, 1 N. M. 422, 428–435 (1869).

[12] Pueblo Indian Land Grants of the "Rio Abajo," New Mexico (1939), pp. 18–19.

[13] Pueblo Indian Land Grants of the "Rio Abajo," New Mexico (1939), pp. 19–20.

SECTION 3. THE PUEBLOS UNDER THE NEW MEXICAN TERRITORIAL GOVERNMENT

By Article 8 of the Treaty of Guadalupe Hidalgo,[14] the residents of the territory ceded by Mexico were given the option of retaining their Mexican citizenship by declaring such intention within a year from the date of exchange of ratifications,

> * * * and those who shall remain in the said territories after the expiration of that year, without having declared their intention to retain the character of Mexicans, shall be considered to have elected to become citizens of the United States.

None of the Pueblo Indians elected to retain Mexican citizenship, according to the opinion in the *Lucero* case:

> Colonel Washington made proclamation requiring the people to elect by signing a declaration before the clerk of the courts in the different districts, if they wished to retain the title and rights of Mexican citizens. In that test, which is a public printed document, the name is not found of a single Pueblo Indian; and hence, by the express terms of the eighth article of the treaty, they became citizens of the United States, as they were previously citizens of the Mexican republic. (P. 440.)

While the conclusion that the Pueblo Indians thus became citizens of the United States cannot be considered free from doubt, in view of the comment[15] of the Supreme Court in *United States* v. *Sandoval*, "it remains an open question whether they have become citizens," it would appear that the historical evidence supports the claim that the Pueblo Indians did enjoy citizenship, both under Mexican and under United States rule.[16] It seems clear, in any event, that, as Mexicans, they were protected by section 9 of the Treaty of Guadalupe Hidalgo which promised, eventually, "all the rights of citizens of the United States" and, immediately, "free enjoyment of their liberty and property."[17]

A. HISTORY OF PUEBLO LEGISLATION

For several years following the Treaty of Guadalupe Hidalgo, Congress apparently took little notice of the Pueblo Indians. Until 1854, at least, the local authorities appear to have legislated in pueblo matters with such congressional approval as was given by silence. The course of this local legislation was thus summarized by the Chief Justice of the territorial supreme court, in *United States* v. *Lucero*:[18]

> * * * General Kearny, after taking possession of New Mexico, eighteenth of August, 1846, established a system of civil government in New Mexico, organized courts, appointed judges, and convened a legislative body, and in December, 1847, that legislative assembly passed the following act:
>
> "INDIANS.
>
> "SECTION 1. That the inhabitants within the territory of New Mexico, known by the name of pueblo Indians, and living in towns or villages built on lands granted to such Indians by the laws of Spain and Mexico, and conceding to such inhabitants certain lands and privileges to be used for the common benefit, are severally hereby created and constituted bodies politic and corporate, and shall be known in the law by the name of the pueblo de ——— (naming it) and by that name they and their successors shall have perpetual succession, sue and be sued, plead and be impleaded, bring and defend in any court of law or equity all such actions, pleas, and matters whatsoever proper to recover, protect, reclaim, demand, or assert the right of such inhabitants, or any individual thereof, to any lands, tenements, or hereditaments possessed, occupied, or claimed, contrary to law, by any person whatever, and to bring and defend all such actions, and to resist any encroachment, claim or trespass made upon such lands, tenements, or hereditaments belonging to said inhabitants, or any individual:" See Compiled Laws of New Mexico, 470.
>
> On the tenth of January, 1853, a law was passed, prohibiting the sale of liquor to Indians, with a proviso, "that the pueblo Indians that live among us are not included in the word Indian:" See Compiled Laws, p. 472, sec. 5. January 21, 1861, an act was passed, requiring the pueblos of Indians to work *acequias* (ditches) and highways, and extending the act of January 13, 1860, over the pueblo Indians as to trespasses of their stock on the fields of their neighbors: See Id. 470, 471. On the sixteenth of February, 1854, the legislative assembly of New Mexico passed the following act, section 70: "That the pueblo Indians of this territory for the present, and until they shall be declared by the congress of the United States to have the right, are excluded from the privilege of voting at the popular elections of the territory, except in the elections for overseers of ditches to which they belong, and in the elections proper to their own pueblos to elect their officers according to their ancient customs." The seventh section of the organic act of September 9, 1850, invests the legislative assembly of New Mexico with the power to legislate upon all rightful subjects of legislation consistent with the constitution of the United States and the provisions of that act, and further provided that "all laws passed by the legislative assembly and governor, shall be submitted to the congress of the United States, and if disapproved, shall be null and of no effect."
>
> As this act of the sixteenth of February, 1854, passed by the legislative assembly of New Mexico, has never been disapproved by congress, it must be regarded as in force in New Mexico, and deprives the pueblo Indians of one of the dearest and most valued rights, the right to be heard by their ballots in the selection of agents to make laws for their government. (Pp. 438–440.)

By the Act of July 22, 1854,[19] Congress provided for the appointment of a Surveyor-General for New Mexico who was, "under such instructions as may be given by the Secretary of the Interior, to ascertain the origin, nature, character, and extent of all claims to lands under the laws, usages, and customs of Spain and Mexico; * * * shall also make a report in regard to all pueblos existing in the Territory, showing the extent and locality of each, stating the number of inhabitants in the said pueblos, respectively, and the nature of their titles to the land." (P. 309.) This reference to "Pueblos" made no distinction between Indian Pueblos and non-Indian Pueblos.

The Pueblo Indians are mentioned in the annual Indian Department Appropriation Acts of August 30, 1852,[20] and July 31, 1854.[21] The former of these acts contains this item:

> For defraying expenses incident to the visit of the Pueblo Indians and their attendants from New Mexico to Washington, and to defray their expenses to their homes, the sum of seven thousand five hundred dollars. (P. 55.)

The second of the acts cited contains a provision:

> For the expenses of making presents of agricultural implements and farming utensils to the bands of Pueblo Indians in the territory of New Mexico, ten thousand dollars: * * *. (P. 330.)

[14] Signed February 2, 1848, ratification exchanged May 30, 1848, proclaimed July 4, 1848, 9 Stat. 922.

[15] 231 U. S. 28, 39 (1913). See also *United States* v. *Joseph*, 94 U. S. 614, 618 (1876); *Jaeger* v. *United States*, 29 C. Cls. 172, 173 (1894).

[16] Brayer, *op. cit.* 17–18, 23–24.

[17] See fn. 14, *supra*.

[18] 1 N. M. 422 (1869).

[19] 10 Stat. 308.

[20] 10 Stat. 41.

[21] 10 Stat. 315

The Pueblo Indians are next mentioned by Congress in the Indian Department Appropriation Act of March 3, 1857,[22] which contains this provision:

> For expenses of surveying and marking the external boundaries of Indian pueblos, in the Territory of New Mexico, three thousand seven hundred and fifty dollars. (P. 184.)

On December 22, 1858, Congress acted favorably upon the report of the Surveyor-General for the territory of New Mexico, confirming pueblo land claims of the following Pueblos: Jemez, Acoma, San Juan, Picuris, San Felipe, Pecos, Cochiti, Santo Domingo, Taos, Santa Clara, Tesuque, San Ildefonso, Pojuaque, Zia, Sandia, Isleta, and Nambe.[23]

This congressional confirmation of pueblo titles is subject to the usual proviso "That this confirmation shall only be construed as a relinquishment of all title and claim of the United States to any of said lands, and shall not affect any adverse valid rights, should such exist."

To the foregoing list of confirmed pueblo claims there was added, in 1869, the claim of the Pueblo of Santa Ana.[24] Many years later, a similar patent was issued to the Zuni Pueblo Indians.[25]

> All that the United States could give was a quit-claim deed, transferring to the Pueblo Indians its own share; it could not transfer property from one private owner to another.
>
> The courts of the United States would always have the right, on due consideration of all the facts involved, to determine the actual ownership of any given piece of land. But it has never been within the power of either the legislative or the executive to change private land titles. The judicial power alone could settle the question of the encroachments upon the lands of the Pueblo Indians—encroachments dating back for centuries, arising partly from greed, partly from interrelationship, partly from the need of a common defense against "Indios barbaros." Some of these settlers outside the pueblo walls claimed title from Mexican and Spanish grants, as did the Pueblos themselves; some had obtained their land by purchase from the Indian communities; some were intruders pure and simple, no doubt; some, beginning with a valid title, had skillfully enlarged their holdings by less defensible means. All these problems came as an unhappy heritage to the new government of the land.[26]

In the Appropriation Act of July 15, 1870,[27] a sum is appropriated "to be expended in establishing schools among the Pueblo Indians," and similar provisions reappear in later acts.

In the Act of May 29, 1872,[28] the Indian Department Appropriation Act for 1873, and regularly in succeeding appropriation acts,[29] provision is made for pay of an Indian agent at the Pueblo Agency. Thereafter congressional appropriations for the work of the Indian Department among the Pueblo Indians of New Mexico are gradually elaborated.

In the Indian Department Appropriation Act for 1875,[30] and in subsequent appropriation acts, provision is made for pay of interpreters at the Pueblo agency.

The Appropriation Act for 1883 [31] contains the following provision embodying the first assumption of federal responsibility for "civilizing" the Pueblo Indians:

> For civilization and instruction of the Pueblo Indians of New Mexico, including pay of teachers and purchase of seeds and agricultural implements, seven thousand five hundred dollars; and of this sum not exceeding one thousand five hundred dollars may, in the discretion of the Commissioner of Indian Affairs, be used in constructing irrigating ditches at Zuni and Jemez Pueblos. (P. 83.)

The foregoing provision is substantially repeated in subsequent Indian Department appropriation acts.[32]

The next addition to the scope of congressional responsibility for the Pueblo Indians appears in the appropriation act for 1899,[33] which establishes the post of "special attorney for the Pueblo Indians of New Mexico" by virtue of the following provision:

> To enable the Secretary of the Interior to employ a special attorney for the Pueblo Indians of New Mexico, one thousand five hundred dollars.

This provision is reenacted, in substance, in succeeding appropriation acts.[34]

The Appropriation Act of March 3, 1905, for the fiscal year 1906 contains the following item of permanent legislation, called forth, apparently, by the decision of the New Mexico Territorial Court rendered on March 3, 1904, in the case of *Territory* v. *Delinquent Taxpayers*.[35]

> That the lands now held by the various villages or pueblos of Pueblo Indians, or by individual members thereof, within Pueblo reservations or lands, in the Territory of New Mexico, and all personal property furnished said Indians by the United States, or used in cultivating said lands, and any cattle and sheep now possessed or that may hereafter be acquired by said Indians shall be free and exempt from taxation of any sort whatsoever, including taxes heretofore levied, if any, until Congress shall otherwise provide. (P. 1069.)[36]

Up to the admission of New Mexico to statehood, there is no further federal legislation for the Pueblo Indians of that state except in the Indian Department appropriation acts (redesignated, beginning with the Act of April 4, 1910,[37] as the Bureau of Indian Affairs appropriation acts). These acts include special appropriations for irrigation for the Zuni Pueblo,[38] and for the building of two bridges across the Rio Grande at or near Isleta and San Felipe Indian Pueblos, with preference given to Indian labor.[39]

---

[22] 11 Stat. 169.

[23] 11 Stat. 374.

[24] Act of February 9, 1869, c. 26, 15 Stat. 438.

[25] Act of March 3, 1931, c. 438, 46 Stat. 1509.

[26] Seymour, Land Titles in the Pueblo Indian Country (1924), 10 A. B. A. Jour. 36, 38.

[27] 16 Stat. 335, 357.

[28] 17 Stat. 165.

[29] See *Romero* v. *United States*, 24 C. Cls. 331 (1889).

[30] Act of June 22, 1874, 18 Stat. 146.

[31] Act of May 17, 1882, 22 Stat. 68.

[32] Act of March 1, 1883, 22 Stat. 433; Act of July 4, 1884, 23 Stat. 76; Act of March 3, 1885, 23 Stat. 362; Act of May 15, 1886, 24 Stat. 29; Act of March 2, 1887, 24 Stat. 449; Act of June 29, 1888, 25 Stat. 217; Act of March 2, 1889, 25 Stat. 980; Act of August 19, 1890, 26 Stat. 336; Act of March 3, 1891, 26 Stat. 989; Act of July 13, 1892, 27 Stat. 120; Act of March 3, 1893, 27 Stat. 612; Act of March 2, 1895, 28 Stat. 876; Act of June 10, 1896, 29 Stat. 321; Act of June 7, 1897, 30 Stat. 62; Act of July 1, 1898, 30 Stat. 571; Act of March 1, 1899, 30 Stat. 924.

[33] Act of July 1, 1898, 30 Stat. 571, 594.

[34] Act of March 1, 1899, 30 Stat. 924; Act of March 3, 1901, 31 Stat. 1058; Act of May 27, 1902, 32 Stat. 245; Act of March 3, 1903, 32 Stat. 982; Act of April 21, 1904, 33 Stat. 189; Act of March 3, 1905, 33 Stat. 1048; Act of June 21, 1906, 34 Stat. 325; Act of March 1, 1907, 34 Stat. 1015; Act of April 30, 1908, 35 Stat. 70; Act of March 3, 1909, 35 Stat. 781; Act of April 4, 1910, 36 Stat. 269; Act of March 3, 1911, 36 Stat. 1058; Act of August 24, 1912, 37 Stat. 518; Act of June 30, 1913, 38 Stat. 77; Act of August 1, 1914, 38 Stat. 582; Act of May 18, 1916, 39 Stat. 123; Act of March 2, 1917, 39 Stat. 969; Act of May 25, 1918, 40 Stat. 561; Act of June 30, 1919, 41 Stat. 3; Act of February 14, 1920, 41 Stat. 408; Act of March 3, 1921, 41 Stat. 1225; Act of May 24, 1922, 42 Stat. 552; Act of January 24, 1923, 42 Stat. 1174; Act of June 5, 1924, 43 Stat. 390; Act of December 6, 1924, 43 Stat. 704; Act of March 3, 1925, 43 Stat. 1141; Act of May 10, 1926, 44 Stat. 453; Act of January 12, 1927, 44 Stat. 934; Act of March 7, 1928, 45 Stat. 200; Act of March 4, 1929, 45 Stat. 1562; Act of May 14, 1930, 46 Stat. 279; Act of February 14, 1931, 46 Stat. 1115; Act of April 22, 1932, 47 Stat. 91; Act of February 17, 1933, 47 Stat. 820.

[35] 12 N. M. 139, 76 Pac. 307 (1904). See p. 384, *supra*.

[36] 33 Stat. 1048. *Cf.* Chapter 13, sec. 2.

[37] 36 Stat. 269.

[38] Acts of April 30, 1908, 35 Stat. 70; March 3, 1909, 35 Stat. 781.

[39] Act of March 3, 1911, 36 Stat. 1058.

B. HISTORY OF JUDICIAL AND EXECUTIVE ATTITUDES TOWARDS PUEBLOS

During the period which the foregoing history of federal legislation covers, judicial and executives attitudes towards the Pueblos were undergoing a gradual change parallel to the gradual increase in the activities of the Indian Bureau among the Pueblo Indians.

For many years after the accession of New Mexico the Pueblos were not considered Indian tribes within the meaning of existing statutes. During the 23 years that elapsed between the Treaty of Guadalupe Hidalgo and the Act of March 3, 1871,[40] which terminated the practice of making treaties with Indian tribes, no treaty was ever negotiated with any of the Pueblos. The reasons for distinguishing between the Pueblo Indians and other aborigines are set forth at length and in colorful terms by the Supreme Court of New Mexico Territory, in the case of *United States* v. *Lucero*,[41] decided in January 1869. That case involved an attempt by the United States to invoke section 11 of the Indian Intercourse Act[42] of June 30, 1834, which made unauthorized settlement of tribal lands a federal offense, as extended by section 7 of the Appropriation Act of February 27, 1851,[43] "over the Indian tribes in the Territories of New Mexico and Utah."

The territorial court dismissed the suit on demurrer, declaring, *per* Watts, *C. J.*:

> * * * If these pueblos, twenty-one in number, were really included in the provisions of the intercourse act, intended for a different class of Indians, the Indian department, during the last twenty years that they have been under their pretended control, would have had spread upon our statutes at large certainly not less than eighty treaties with these twenty-one *quasi* nations. (P. 437.)
>
> * * * It will thus be seen by a reference to the acts of congress above cited, that no person has ever been authorized by congress to be appointed agent for the pueblo Indians, nor has any one ever been commissioned as agent for them, and the designation of an agent for the pueblos by the Indian department is without any authority of congress or the decision of any judicial tribunal authorized to pass upon the question, and the transfer of eight thousand of the most honest, industrious, and law-abiding citizens of New Mexico to the provisions of a code of laws made for savages, by the simple stroke of the pen of an Indian commissioner, will never be assented to by congress or the judicial tribunals of the country so long as solemn treaties and human laws afford any protection to the liberty and property of the citizens. (P. 438.)

After reviewing the history of territorial legislation with regard to the pueblo Indians of New Mexico, the court continued:

> * * * it is the right and duty of the courts to see that every citizen of the territory of New Mexico, in conformity with the ninth article of the treaty of Guadalupe Hidalgo, "shall be maintained and protected in the free enjoyment of their liberty and property, and secured in the free exercise of their religion without restriction."
>
> This court, under this section of the treaty of Guadalupe Hidalgo, does not consider it proper to assent to the withdrawal of eight thousand citizens of New Mexico from the operation of the laws, made to secure and maintain them in their liberty and property, and consign their liberty and property to a system of laws and trade made for wandering savages and administered by the agents of the Indian department. If such a destiny is in store for a large number of the most law-abiding, sober, and industrious people of New Mexico, it must be the result of the direct legislation of congress or the mandate of the supreme court. This court feels itself incompetent to construe them into any such condition. This court has known the conduct and habits of these Indians for eighteen or twenty years, and we say, without the fear of successful contradiction, that you may pick out one thousand of the best Americans in New Mexico, and one thousand of the best Mexicans in New Mexico, and one thousand of the worst pueblo Indians, and there will be found less, vastly less, murder, robbery, theft, or other crimes among the thousand of the worst pueblo Indians than among the thousand of the best Mexicans or Americans in New Mexico. The associate justice now beside me, Hon. Joab Houghton, has been judge and lawyer in this territory for over twenty years, and the chief justice for over seventeen years, and during all that time not twenty pueblo Indians have been brought before the courts in all New Mexico, accused of violation of the criminal laws of this territory. For the Indian department to insist, as they have done for the last fifteen years, upon the reduction of these citizens to a state of vassalage, under the Indian intercourse act, is passing strange. A law made for wild, wandering savages, to be extended over a people living for three centuries in fenced abodes and cultivating the soil for the maintenance of themselves and families, and giving an example of virtue, honesty, and industry to their more civilized neighbors, in this enlightened age of progress and proper understanding of the civil rights of man, is considered by this court as wholly inapplicable to the pueblo Indians of New Mexico. (Pp. 441–442.)
>
> It has already been shown that the people of Cochiti are a corporate body, and that a full and ample remedy is given them to protect and defend their title to their individual and common lands, and that they do not need any assistance from the penal statutes of the United States to accomplish that purpose. * * * let the Indian department have placed under their control the twenty-one pueblos of New Mexico, and get the laws of trade and intercourse, designed to regulate the commerce of the country with savages, extended over these peaceful and industrious citizens, and in less than six months they will have fifty lawsuits on hand about questions settled by a former government fifty years ago. (Pp. 444–445.)

One of the grounds of the *Lucero* decision was demolished when the Appropriation Act of May 29, 1872,[44] made provision for an agent for "the Pueblo agency," thus treating the Pueblos on a parity with other tribes. The United States thereupon renewed the effort that had been defeated by the *Lucero* decision, to invoke the Act of June 30, 1834, for the protection of pueblo lands against trespass. Again the territorial court denied the applicability of the statute to the Pueblos,[45] and this time the United States took an appeal to the Supreme Court. The Supreme Court, in *United States* v. *Joseph*,[46] affirmed the decision of the territorial court, offering these reasons for its holding:

> The character and history of these people are not obscure, but occupy a well-known page in the story of Mexico, from the conquest of the country by Cortez to the cession of this part of it to the United States by the treaty of Guadaloupe Hidalgo. The subject is tempting and full of interest, but we have only space for a few well-considered sentences of the opinion of the chief justice of the court whose judgment we are reviewing.
>
> "For centuries," he says, "the pueblo Indians have lived in villages, in fixed communities, each having its own municipal or local government. As far as their history can be traced, they have been a pastoral and agricultural people, raising flocks and cultivating the soil. Since the introduction of the Spanish Catholic missionary into the country, they have adopted mainly not only the Spanish language, but the religion of a Christian church. In every

[40] 16 Stat. 544, 566.

[41] 1 N. M. 422 (1869).

[42] Act of June 30, 1834, sec. 11, 4 Stat. 729, 730.

[43] 9 Stat. 574.

[44] 17 Stat. 165.

[45] *United States* v. *Santistevan*, 1 N. M. 583 (1874); *United States* v. *Varela*, 1 N. M. 593 (1874); *United States* v. *Koslowski*, *ibid.*, *United States* v. *Joseph*, *ibid.*

[46] 94 U. S. 614 (1876).

pueblo is erected a church, dedicated to the worship of God, according to the form of the Roman Catholic religion, and in nearly all is to be found a priest of this church, who is recognized as their spiritual guide and adviser. They manufacture nearly all of their blankets, clothing, agricultural and culinary implements, &c. Integrity and virtue among them is fostered and encouraged. They are as intelligent as most nations or people deprived of means or facilities for education. Their names, their customs, their habits, all similar to those of the people in whose midst they reside, or in the midst of whom their pueblos are situated. The criminal records of the courts of the Territory scarcely contain the name of a pueblo Indian. In short, they are a peaceable, industrious, intelligent, honest, and virtuous people. They are Indians only in feature, complexion, and a few of their habits; in all other respects superior to all but a few of the civilized Indian tribes of the country, and the equal of the most civilized thereof. This description of the pueblo Indians, I think, will be deemed by all who know them as faithful and true in all respects. Such was their character at the time of the acquisition of New Mexico by the United States; such is their character now."

At the time the act of 1834 was passed there were no such Indians as these in the United States, unless it be one or two reservations or tribes, such as the Senecas or Oneidas of New York, to whom, it is clear, the eleventh section of the statute could have no application. (Pp. 616–617.)

The tribes for whom the act of 1834 was made were those semi-independent tribes whom our government has always recognized as exempt from our laws, whether within or without the limits of an organized State or Territory, and, in regard to their domestic government, left to their own rules and traditions; in whom we have recognized the capacity to make treaties, and with whom the governments, state and national, deal, with a few exceptions only, in their national or tribal character, and not as individuals.

If the pueblo Indians differ from the other inhabitants of New Mexico in holding lands in common, and in a certain patriarchal form of domestic life, they only resemble in this regard the Shakers and other communistic societies in this country, and cannot for that reason be classed with the Indian tribes of whom we have been speaking.

We have been urged by counsel, in view of these considerations, to declare that they are citizens of the United States and of New Mexico. But abiding by the rule which we think ought always to govern this court, to decide nothing beyond what is necessary to the judgment we are to render, we leave that question until it shall be made in some case where the rights of citizenship are necessarily involved. But we have no hesitation in saying that their *status* is not, in the face of the facts we have stated, to be determined solely by the circumstance that some officer of the government has appointed for them an agent, even if we could take judicial notice of the existence of that fact, suggested to us in argument.

Turning our attention to the tenure by which these communities hold the land on which the settlement of defendant was made, we find that it is wholly different from that of the Indian tribes to whom the act of Congress applies. The United States have not recognized in these latter any other than a passing title with right of use, until by treaty or otherwise that right is extinguished. And the ultimate title has been always held to be in the United States, with no right in the Indians to transfer it, or even their possession, without consent of the government.

It is this fixed claim of dominion which lies at the foundation of the act forbidding the white man to make a settlement on the lands occupied by an Indian tribe.

The pueblo Indians, on the contrary, hold their lands by a right superior to that of the United States. Their title dates back to grants made by the government of Spain before the Mexican revolution,—a title which was fully recognized by the Mexican government, and protected by it in the treaty of Guadaloupe Hidalgo, by which this country and the allegiance of its inhabitants were transferred to the United States. (Pp. 617–618.)

If the defendant is on the lands of the pueblo, without the consent of the inhabitants, he may be ejected, or punished civilly by a suit for trespass, according to the laws regulating such matters in the Territory. If he is there with their consent or license, we know of no injury which the United States suffers by his presence, nor any statute which he violates in that regard. (P. 619.)

Some years later, the Supreme Court would ascribe the views expressed in 1876 in the *Joseph* case to inaccurate information,[47] but for nearly four decades the *Joseph* case fixed the law governing the New Mexico Pueblos.[48]

In 1891, the Attorney General ruled[49] that federal statutes authorizing the Commissioner of Indian Affairs to license and regulate Indian traders[50] had no application to the Pueblos.

In 1894, the Assistant Attorney General for the Department of the Interior ruled that laws relating to the approval of leases of Indian tribal land had no application to the Pueblos.[51]

In 1900, in the case of *Pueblo of Nambe* v. *Romero*,[52] the territorial court, in a suit to quiet title brought by an alleged conveyee of pueblo lands, issued a decree against the Pueblo, basing such decree upon a finding that the Pueblo had validly granted away the land in question and upon a holding that the territorial statute of limitations[53] ran against the Pueblo.

In 1904, in the case of *Territory of New Mexico* v. *Delinquent Taxpayers*,[54] the attempt to collect taxes on pueblo lands was upheld by the territorial court on the basis of the reasoning in the *Lucero* and *Joseph* cases. This ruling, however, as we have seen, was reversed by congressional enactment.[55]

In 1907, in *United States* v. *Mares*,[56] the territorial court held that the Pueblo Indians were not covered by Indian liquor laws[57] making it an offense to sell or give intoxicants to "any Indian to whom allotment of land has been made while the title to the same shall be held in trust by the government, or to any Indian a ward of the government under charge of any Indian superintendent or agent, or any Indian, including mixed bloods, over whom the government, through its departments, exercises guardianship."

This ruling, again, was reversed by Congress, in the New Mexico Enabling Act, which will be treated in the following section.

By way of summary, it may be said that during the period from the accession of New Mexico to the granting of statehood, the Pueblos had a legal status sharply distinguished from that of most other Indian tribes and comprehended under Indian legislation only where Congress had expressly so provided, as in the matter of agency maintenance, "civilization" appropriations, and tax exemption. In all other respects, each Pueblo had a status substantially similar to that of any other municipal corporation of the territory.[58]

---

[47] See *United States* v. *Sandoval*, 231 U. S. 28, 48 (1913). See *infra*, sec. 4.

[48] The effect of this decision was to confirm the opinions and judgment that had before that time been rendered with respect to the Pueblo Indians. As they were further advanced in civilization than the nomadic tribes, better versed in the arts and industries of ordinary life, so they were recognized as deserving the treatment accorded to civilized and industrious people. But with the greater freedom and privilege of their status went a greater responsibility. If their land was their own they must use their own judgment in the disposition of it. The Supreme Court had decided that the United States had no right to interfere.

Our highest tribunal had spoken. Through many years the decision went unchallenged. The Pueblo governors managed the lands of their people as they had always done, and back of every sale was the assurance of the Supreme Court that they had a perfect and complete right to make it. (Seymour, Land Titles in the Pueblo Indian Country [1924] 10 A. B. A. Jour. 36, 39.)

[49] 20 Op. A. G. 215 (1891).

[50] Acts of August 15, 1876, sec. 5, 19 Stat. 176, 200; July 31, 1882, 22 Stat. 179.

[51] 19 L. D. 326 (1894).

[52] 10 N. M. 58, 61 Pac. 122 (1900).

[53] N. M. Compiled Laws (1897) sec. 2938.

[54] 12 N. M. 139, 76 Pac. 316 (1904).

[55] *Supra*, p. 386.

[56] 14 N. M. 1, 88 Pac. 1128 (1907).

[57] Act of January 30, 1897, 29 Stat. 506

[58] See, however, fn. 187, *infra*.

SECTION 4. THE PUEBLOS IN THE STATE OF NEW MEXICO

While New Mexico was a territory and thus an agency of the Federal Government there was a tendency to leave to the territorial government control of the Pueblos, and the territorial authorities sought generally to assimilate the Pueblos to the status of other municipal corporations of the territory. This tendency, as we have seen, was checked in the matter of taxation, but in all other respects the relation of the Pueblos to the federal executive was extremely tenuous.

With the admission of New Mexico to statehood, however, a sharp reversal occurred in these tendencies. The termination of the territorial government created a clear distinction between state and federal authority and the center of control over the Pueblos shifted from Santa Fe to Washington. Thus the Pueblos came to be treated more and more as other Indian tribes.

The first important step in this direction was taken in the New Mexico Enabling Act, which contained a specific provision that "the terms 'Indian' and 'Indian country' shall include the Pueblo Indians of New Mexico and the lands now owned or occupied by them." [59]

A. THE SANDOVAL DECISION

The constitutionality of this extension of federal control over the Pueblos was upheld in 1913 in the case of *United States* v. *Sandoval*.[60] That case involved a prosecution for the offense of introducing liquor into the Indian country. The Supreme Court held that Congress had expressed a clear intent to reverse the rule laid down by the territorial court in *United States* v. *Mares*.[61] On the question of the constitutionality of this extension of federal control, the court pointed out that neither the outright ownership of land by the Pueblos nor the claim of the Pueblo Indians to citizenship (the validity of which was not here passed upon) stood as an obstacle to the exercise of federal guardianship by Congress. The court declared, *per* Van Devanter, *J.*:

> Of course, it is not meant by this that Congress may bring a community or body of people within the range of this power by arbitrarily calling them an Indian tribe, but only that in respect of distinctly Indian communities the questions whether, to what extent, and for what time they shall be recognized and dealt with as dependent tribes requiring the guardianship and protection of the United States are to be determined by Congress, and not by the courts. (P. 46.)
>
> We are not unmindful that in *United States* v. *Joseph*, 94 U. S. 614, there are some observations not in accord with what is here said of these Indians, but as that case did not turn upon the power of Congress over them or their property, but upon the interpretation and purpose of a statute not nearly so comprehensive as the legislation now before us, and as the observation there made respecting the Pueblos were evidently based upon statements in the opinion of the territorial court, then under review, which are at variance with other recognized sources of information, now available, and with the long-continued action of the legislative and executive departments, that case cannot be regarded as holding that these Indians or their lands are beyond the range of Congressional power under the Constitution. (Pp. 48–49.)

B. EFFECT OF THE SANDOVAL DECISION

The effect of the *Sandoval* decision was to spread consternation among the people of New Mexico who held lands to which the Pueblos laid claim. The situation is thus described in a letter to the Attorney General, dated June 11, 1929, from George A. H. Fraser, who served for some years as special assistant to the Attorney General:

> The great majority of the claimants had bought and possessed their lands in good faith and in reliance on a series of decisions of the Territorial Supreme Court of New Mexico, beginning in 1859 and extending to about 1908, to the general effect that the Pueblo Indians were emancipated, that they had the right to sell their lands and the liability of losing them by adverse possession, and that the Nonintercourse Act of 1834 did not apply to them. The last-mentioned idea was supported by the Joseph case in 94 U. S., decided in 1877, in which the United States was defeated in an attempt to remove settlers from the Pueblo of Taos under the provisions of said Act. Up to 1913, therefore, when the Sandoval case was decided (231 U. S. 28), all the law there was, including that announced by the highest tribunal, was to the effect aforesaid. The Sandoval decision came as a great surprise, and it was natural that any proceedings interfering with titles so long supposed to be valid should be resisted in every possible way.[62]

Herbert O. Brayer, author of the leading history of pueblo land grants,[63] comments on the *Sandoval* decision in these terms:

> From the Sandoval decision, in 1913, to the passage of the Pueblo lands act of 1924, every possible means to evade the consequences of the supreme court decision was utilized by those non-Indians who were in possession of Pueblo lands.[44]
>
> [44] Leo Crane, *Desert Drums* (Boston, 1928), 275–311.

The constant friction between the non-Indian claimants and the Pueblo Indians finally culminated in an investigation by the sixty-seventh congress. This investigation disclosed that there were approximately three thousand non-Indian claimants to lands within the exterior boundaries of the Pueblo grants. It was estimated that these three thousand claimants represented families aggregating twelve thousand persons. With the seriousness of the situation impressed upon them by these figures, congress began to seek a remedy for the situation. Senator Holm O. Bursum of New Mexico introduced into the senate of the sixty-seventh congress a bill entitled, "An act to quiet title to lands within Pueblo Indian land

---

[59] Act of June 20, 1910, 36 Stat. 557. The pertinent portions of the act provide:

> SEC. 2. * * * that * * * the said convention shall be, and is hereby, authorized to form a constitution and provide for a state government for said proposed State, all in the manner and under the conditions contained in this Act. * * *
>
> And said convention shall provide, by an ordinance irrevocable without the consent of the United States and the people of said State—
>
> First. That * * * the sale, barter, or giving of intoxicating liquors to Indians and the introduction of liquors into Indian country, which term shall also include all lands now owned or occupied by the Pueblo Indians of New Mexico, are forever prohibited.
>
> Second. That the people inhabiting said proposed State do agree and declare that they forever disclaim all right and title * * * to all lands lying within said boundaries owned or held by any Indian or Indian tribes the right or title to which shall have been acquired through or from the United States or any prior sovereignty, and that until the title of such Indian or Indian tribes shall have been extinguished the same shall be and remain subject to the disposition and under the absolute jurisdiction and control of the Congress of the United States; * * * but nothing herein, or in the ordinance herein provided for, shall preclude the said State from taxing, as other lands and other property are taxed, any lands and other property outside of an Indian reservation owned or held by any Indian, save and except such lands as have been granted or acquired as aforesaid or as may be granted or confirmed to any Indian or Indians under any Act of Congress, but said ordinance shall provide that all such lands shall be exempt from taxation by said State so long and to such extent as Congress has prescribed or may hereafter prescribe.
>
> * * * * *
>
> Eighth. That whenever hereafter any of the lands contained within Indian reservations or allotments in said proposed State shall be allotted, sold, reserved, or otherwise disposed of, they shall be subject for a period of twenty-five years after such allotment, sale, reservation, or other disposal to all the laws of the United States prohibiting the introduction of liquor into the Indian country; and the terms "Indian" and "Indian country" shall include the Pueblo Indians of New Mexico and the lands now owned or occupied by them.

[60] 231 U. S. 28 (1913).

[61] 14 N. M. 1, 88 Pac. 1128 (1907). See sec. 3B, *supra*.

[62] D. J. File No. 232544.

[63] Pueblo Indian Land Grants of the "Rio Abajo," New Mexico (The Univ. of New Mexico Bulletin No. 334, 1939), pp. 26–28.

grants and for other purposes." On the surface the bill seemed to be just what was needed. A close study of the Bursum bill disclosed, however, that it would have served to place the non-Indian holders of Indian land in a favorable position to obtain a clear title to holdings within the Pueblo grants, and to have put the burden of disproving the right of these private land holders upon the government. This would have entirely reversed the usual procedure with regard to land claims. [The burden of proof in such cases is always upon the claimant.] One authority, notably biased in favor of the Indians, distinctly charges an attempt on the part of Senator Bursum and the secretary of the interior, at that time, Albert B. Fall of New Mexico, to provide an easy means by which the non-Indians could make certain of obtaining a title to their lands which would be forever secure.[62]

The Bursum bill received the backing of the Harding administration and seemed slated for enactment. To the defense of the Indians, and to the attack on the Bursum proposal, a strong opposition developed, led by two groups, the small New Mexico association on Indian affairs and the general federation of women's clubs. The latter organization, in 1921, had formed a committee on Indian welfare. Under the leadership of Mrs. Stella M. Atwood, this organization employed Mr. John Collier, a student of Indian affairs, as field representative. As legal counsel the services of Francis C. Wilson of Santa Fe were obtained. Two congressional committees heard the case against the Bursum bill. The arguments presented by Mr. Wilson were strong and conclusive, and, together with the testimony of many who opposed the enactment of the proposed law, succeeded in "killing" the bill.

A counter-proposal known as the Jones-Leatherwood bill was suggested by the adversaries of the Bursum act, but this measure also failed to obtain the approval of the congress. Pressed by constituents from New Mexico, Senator Bursum introduced a new measure on December 10, 1923, which called for the appointment of a commission to investigate Pueblo land titles. Congress failed to pass the measure during the 1923 session. In 1924, however, the act was revived and approved by congress on June 7. Known as the *Pueblo Lands Act*, this measure provided the means by which a final solution was made of the thousands of non-Indian claims within the lands of the Pueblo Indians.[63]

C. THE PUEBLO LANDS ACT

The Pueblo Lands Act established a "Pueblo Lands Board" consisting of the Secretary of the Interior, the Attorney General, and a third member appointed by the President. This board was, by section 2 of the act, given the duty of determining "the exterior boundaries of any land granted or confirmed to the Pueblo Indians of New Mexico by any authority of the United States of America, or any prior sovereignty, or acquired by said Indians as a community by purchase or otherwise," and to determine the status of all lands within such boundaries, subject to the requirement that a finding that Indian title had been extinguished required a unanimous vote of the board.

The Attorney General was directed, in section 3 of the Pueblo Lands Act, to bring suit to quiet title to all lands listed as pueblo lands by the Lands Board.

Section 4 of the act provided that non-Indian claimants, in order to substantiate their claims, must demonstrate either (*a*) continuous adverse possession under color of title since January 6, 1902, supported by payment of taxes on the land, or (*b*) continuous adverse possession since March 16, 1889, supported by payment of taxes, but without color of title.

With respect to all lands and water rights found to have been lost by the Pueblos which might have been recovered by seasonable prosecution on the part of the United States, the United States was to reimburse the Pueblos the fair market value of the lands and water rights. (Sec. 6.) On the other hand, the board was to report back to Congress the value of all improvements lost by non-Indian claimants whose claims were rejected. (Secs. 7, 15.)

Other provisions of the Pueblo Lands Act provided for the filing of suit by the United States "in its sovereign capacity as guardian of said Pueblo Indians" in the nature of a bill of discovery (sec. 1); the investigation of lands and improvements of successful non-Indian claimants which might be purchased for the benefit of the Pueblos (sec. 8), the patenting of lands to successful non-Indian claimants (sec. 13); the adjudication of non-Indian claims superior to the original Pueblo grants and the filing of recommendations by the Secretary of the Interior respecting such adjudications (sec. 14); and various other matters of procedure (secs. 6, 9, 10, 11, 12, 18, 19).

Where lands for which the pueblo title was confirmed were inconveniently located, the Secretary of the Interior "with the consent of the governing authorities of the pueblo" might order them to be sold and the proceeds, after deducting the value of improvements of a losing claimant, were to "be paid over to the proper officer, or officers, of the Indian community." (Sec. 16.)

Section 17 of the Pueblo Lands Act is a measure of substantive law directed to the prevention of future disputes rather than to the settlement of past disputes.

Inasmuch as past disputes had arisen generally out of controversies concerning the validity of purported transfers of land or interests in land by pueblo authorities or individual Pueblo Indians, this section laid down an absolute rule that no such transfer should be of any validity in the future, unless approved in advance by the Secretary of the Interior. Thus the final step was taken in assimilating pueblo lands to the status of other tribal lands.[64] The section in question declares:

> No right, title, or interest in or to the lands of the Pueblo Indians of New Mexico to which their title has not been extinguished as hereinbefore determined shall hereafter be acquired or initiated by virtue of the laws of the State of New Mexico, or in any other manner except as may hereafter be provided by Congress, and no sale, grant, lease of any character, or other conveyance of lands, or any title or claim thereto, made by any pueblo as a community, or any Pueblo Indian living in a community of Pueblo Indians, in the State of New Mexico, shall be of any validity in law or in equity unless the same be first approved by the Secretary of the Interior.[65]

The constitutionality of the Pueblo Lands Act was upheld in a series of cases in the federal courts in which its provisions were applied.[66] The end results of the Pueblo Lands Act are thus described in the study of Herbert O. Brayer:[67]

> Following the final adjudication of the pueblo titles, the special attorney for the Pueblo Indians was faced with

[62] Crane, *loc. cit.* Leo Crane was connected with the Indian service for many years, serving as agent to the Hopi and Navajo Indians in Arizona and later becoming Indian agents for the Pueblo Indians of New Mexico.

[63] *An Act to Quiet Title to Lands within Pueblo Indian Land Grants, and for other Purposes*, 43 Statutes 636.

[64] See Chapter 15, sec. 18, for a discussion of the restrictions upon alienation of tribal lands generally.

[65] The possible application of this statute to internal pueblo affairs is discussed in sec. 5 of this chapter.

[66] *United States* v. *Wooten*, 40 F. 2d 882 (1930), holding that tax payments, within the statutory requirement, need not have been made prior to delinquency; *Garcia* v. *United States*, 43 F. 2d 873 (1930), discussed at p. 398, *infra*; *Pueblo de San Juan* v. *United States*, 47 F. 2d 446 (1931), holding burden is upon Pueblo to show error in finding of Pueblo Lands Board that lands lost by Pueblo could not have been recovered by seasonable prosecution on the part of the United States; *Pueblo of Picuris in State of New Mexico* v. *Abeyta*, 50 F. 2d 12 (1931), discussed at p. 397, *infra*; *Pueblo de Taos* v. *Gusdorf*, 50 F. 2d 721 (1931), holding that redemption of land by claimant after tax sale is not payment of taxes within the requirements of the statute; *United States* v. *Algodones Land Co.*, 52 F. 2d 359 (1931), holding claimant's adverse possession under color of title presumably extends to entire area covered by such title; *Pueblo de Taos* v. *Archuleta*, 64 F. 2d 807; *Same* v. *Anaya* (1933), dismissing pueblo suits for want of seasonable prosecution where pendency constituted cloud on settlers' titles. See also Op. Sol., I. D., M. 28850, December 16, 1936, interpreting sec. 13.

[67] Pueblo Indian Land Grants of the "Rio Abajo," New Mexico (The Univ. of New Mexico Bulletin No. 334, 1939), pp. 30–31.

the tremendous task of ejecting those claimants whose titles had been declared invalid. This official and the superintendent of the United Pueblos agency withheld any action in this regard until the awards made by the Pueblo lands board had been provided for by the congress of the United States and paid to the holders of the rejected claims. Following this settlement the special attorney began the tedious process of clearing the Indian lands of all persons having no right to be upon them. At this writing, August 10, 1938, the special attorney for the Pueblo Indians, Mr. William Brophy of Albuquerque, states that all such non-Indian claimants have been removed. For the first time, therefore, since late in the seventeenth century, the Pueblo Indians of New Mexico are free from land controversy.

Under a special acquisition program the Indian service is proceeding rapidly to purchase such lands as were confirmed to non-Indians by the Pueblo lands board and the courts, and which were deemed desirable for the needs of the Indians. With the conclusion of this program the Pueblo Indians will have no grounds for further disputes over lands granted them by the Spanish authorities and confirmed by the United States.

The Pueblo Lands Act was implemented by a series of enactments carrying into effect the purposes of that act. Sums of money were appropriated for the expenses of the board [68] and for payments to the Pueblos and to non-Indian claimants, in the cases covered by the Pueblo Lands Act and in other cases which Congress deemed worthy of special consideration because of inadequacy of awards or special hardships.[69]

The Pueblo Lands Act was further implemented and amended by the Act of May 31, 1933,[70] a comprehensive measure directed primarily to the execution of awards under the original act. Section 1 of the Act of May 31, 1933, provides that appropriations for awards to the Pueblos

> * * * shall be expended by the Secretary of the Interior, subject to approval of the governing authorities of each pueblo in question, at such times and in such amounts as he may deem wise and proper; for the purchase of lands and water rights to replace those which have been divested from said pueblos under the Act of June 7, 1924, or for the purchase or construction of reservoirs, irrigation works, or other permanent improvements upon or for the benefit of the lands of said pueblos.

Section 2 of the act authorizes awards in addition to those made by the Pueblo Lands Board to the following Pueblos: Jemez, Nambe, Taos, Santa Ana, Santo Domingo, Sandia, San Felipe, Isleta, Picuris, San Ildefonso, San Juan, Santa Clara, Cochiti, and Pojoaque. The Secretary of the Interior is directed to report back to Congress errors or omissions in the authorizations contained in this section "measured by the present fair market value of the lands involved" (p. 108–109).

Section 3 of the act authorizes money awards to white settlers and non-Indian claimants whose claims have been rejected by the Pueblo Lands Board (p. 109). Again the Secretary of the Interior is directed to report back to Congress errors in the amount specified measured by the present fair market value of the lands involved (p. 109).

Section 4 of the act directs the Secretary of Agriculture to issue a permit to the Pueblo of Taos "upon application of the governor and council thereof," such permit to grant to the Pueblo the right to use certain designated lands "upon which lands said Indians depend for water supply, forage for their domestic livestock, wood and timber for their personal use and as the scene of certain of their religious ceremonials" (p. 109).[71]

Section 5 of this act regulates the manner in which the Secretary of the Interior may disburse funds awarded to the Pueblo in purchasing lands, water rights, options, etc. (p. 110). This section contains the following provisos establishing the policy of pueblo control, subject to departmental consent, in the utilization of pueblo funds:

> That the Secretary of the Interior shall not make any expenditures out of the pueblo funds resulting from the appropriations set forth herein, or prior appropriations for the same purpose, without first obtaining the approval of the governing authorities of the pueblo affected: *And provided further*, That the governing authorities of any pueblo may initiate matters pertaining to the purchase of lands in behalf of their respective pueblos, which matters, or contracts relative thereto, will not be binding or concluded until approved by the Secretary of the Interior. (P. 110.)

Section 6 of this act safeguards the right of the Pueblos to prosecute independent suits for the recovery of lands claimed by third parties. This section also provides that the Pueblos may enter into agreement with the Secretary of the Interior to abandon such suit and to accept instead awards provided by this act.

Section 7 of the act amends section 16 of the Act of June 7, 1924, the original Pueblo Lands Act, providing that the Secretary of the Interior may, "with the consent of the governing authorities of the pueblo," order the sale of land to the highest bidder where such land although awarded to the Pueblo is not wanted (p. 111).

Section 8 of the act regulates the fees of attorneys employed by the Pueblos (p. 111).

Section 9 safeguards existing water rights (p. 111).

Section 10 provides that the awards authorized to be appropriated under section 2 of this act to the Pueblos shall be appropriated in three annual installments beginning with the fiscal year 1937 (p. 111).

D. THE DEVELOPMENT OF FEDERAL CONTROL

The development of plenary federal control over the Pueblos of New Mexico, inaugurated in the Enabling Act, confirmed in the *Sandoval* case, and carried into effect by the Pueblo Lands Act and supplementary statutes, characterizes congressional legislation, judicial decisions, and administrative policies in the period from 1910 to the present. This period in the legal history of the Pueblos is characterized by several legislative developments which parallel the solution of pueblo land problems:

(1) A marked increase in the federal services provided for the New Mexico Pueblos by the Bureau of Indian Affairs, under authority of the regular appropriation acts.

(2) As a correlative of this extension of federal services, the imposition of various debts and liens against the Pueblos.

(3) A prohibition against the alienation of pueblo lands.

(4) A number of lesser statutes further defining the status of the Pueblo Indians.

[68] Act of January 20, 1925, 43 Stat. 753; Act of February 27, 1925, 43 Stat. 1014; Act of March 8, 1926, 44 Stat. 161; Act of April 29, 1926, 44 Stat. 330; Act of February 24, 1927, 44 Stat. 1178; Act of February 15, 1928, 45 Stat. 64; Act of May 29, 1928, 45 Stat. 883; Act of January 25, 1929, 45 Stat. 1094; Act of April 18, 1930, 46 Stat. 173.

[69] Act of December 22, 1927, 45 Stat. 2; Act of March 4, 1929, 45 Stat. 1562; Act of May 14, 1930, 46 Stat. 279; Act of February 14, 1931, 46 Stat. 1115; Act of March 4, 1931, 46 Stat. 1552; Act of April 22, 1932, 47 Stat. 91; Act of July 1, 1932, 47 Stat. 525; Act of February 17, 1933, 47 Stat. 820; Act of June 16, 1933, 48 Stat. 274; Act of June 16, 1933, 48 Stat. 254; Act of May 9, 1935, 49 Stat. 176; Act of August 26, 1935, 49 Stat. 800; Act of June 4, 1936, 49 Stat. 1459; Act of June 22, 1936, 49 Stat. 1757; Act of May 15, 1936, 49 Stat. 2294; Act of August 9, 1937, 50 Stat. 564; Pub., No. 15, 76th Cong., 1st sess. (March 28, 1939); Pub., No. 68, 76th Cong., 1st sess. (May 10, 1939).

[70] 48 Stat. 108. An exhaustive analysis of the reasons for this legislation will be found in pt. 20 of the Survey of Conditions of the Indians in the United States (71st Cong., 2d sess., Hearings, Sen. Subcomm. of Comm. on Ind. Aff.) pp. 11081–11317. And see American Indian Life, Bulletin No. 19 (January 1932), pp. 1–7.

[71] *Cf.* Act of March 27, 1928, c. 255, 45 Stat. 372, protecting the watershed of Taos Pueblo within the Carson National Forest.

A brief commentary on these developments in the law governing the Pueblos is in order.

(1) The increase of federal services administered for the benefit of the Pueblos through the Department of the Interior is evident upon a reading of the appropriation acts for the Bureau of Indian Affairs and, beginning with the Act of May 24, 1922,[72] for the Department of the Interior. The most important of the federal appropriations for the Pueblos, since 1910, are for irrigation,[73] drainage of pueblo lands,[74] increased educational facilities for the Pueblo Indians,[75] construction of bridges and roads,[76] and the establishment of a sanatorium for the Pueblo Indians.[77]

A number of difficult questions have arisen in connection with the reclamation of pueblo lands through the Middle Rio Grande Conservancy District. This is a political subdivision of the State of New Mexico. Within the area of its operations lie the lands of several Pueblos. The Act of February 14, 1927,[78] authorized an appropriation of federal funds for reconnaissance work on the lands of Cochiti, Santo Domingo, San Felipe, Santa Ana, Sandia, and Isleta Pueblos. Upon the completion of the survey thus authorized[79] there was enacted the Act of March 13, 1928,[80] which authorized the Secretary of the Interior to enter into a contract with the Middle Rio Grande Conservancy District for conservation, irrigation, drainage, and flood-control work covering pueblo lands. The statute fixed a maximum construction cost of $1,593,311, payable in not less than five annual installments. Such payments were to be made by the United States, subject to reimbursement "under such rules and regulations as may be prescribed by the Secretary of the Interior." To ensure such payments, the statute imposed a lien upon newly reclaimed pueblo lands and declared that reimbursement should be made out of rentals of newly reclaimed lands, or, if such lands were ever sold, out of the proceeds of the sale. No lien for construction costs was imposed on those lands already irrigated by the Pueblo Indians, and it was provided that "such irrigated area of approximately 8,346 acres shall not be subject by the district or otherwise to any pro rata share of the cost of future operation and maintenance or betterment work performed by the district." Further protection of Indian rights is contained in provisions assuring the priority of Indian water rights, preference to Indian lessees in the leasing of newly reclaimed lands, and free leasing of 4,000 acres of such lands to Indians cultivating the same.

Under the foregoing statute a contract was executed between the Secretary of the Interior and the Middle Rio Grande Conservancy District on December 14, 1928.

As construed by the Solicitor of the Interior Department, the statute and the contract permitted the district to charge operation and maintenance costs on pueblo lands outside of the 8,346 acres already irrigated but did not authorize the payment of such charges either by the United States or by the Pueblos.[81] This omission was remedied by the Act of August 27, 1935,[82] which authorized the Secretary of the Interior to contract for the payment of operation and maintenance costs on the newly reclaimed lands for 5 years[83] on a reimbursable basis.

Appropriations have been made from time to time by Congress to meet the obligations to the Middle Rio Grande Conservancy District assumed under the 1928 and 1935 acts.[84]

(2) A number of the appropriations above discussed are, by the express language of the appropriation acts, reimbursable in accordance with rules and regulations which the Secretary of the Interior shall prescribe.[85]

(3) While section 17 of the Pueblo Lands Act, as we have noted, bars transfers of pueblo land not approved in advance by the Secretary of the Interior, section 4 of the Act of June 18, 1934,[86] goes further and bars all transfers of tribal land except such as are made in exchange for lands of equal value.[87]

The Act of June 18, 1934, applies to all the Pueblos of New Mexico except the Pueblo of Jemez, as a result of referendum elections held in each Pueblo pursuant to section 18 of the act. The present situation, therefore, is that the Pueblo of Jemez, with the approval of the Secretary of the Interior, may alienate pueblo lands or interests therein, but that the other Pueblos can alienate lands or interests in land only where two conditions are met: Land of equal value must be received in exchange; and the approval of the Secretary of the Interior must be obtained in advance.

(4) The admission of New Mexico to statehood was promptly followed by a series of legislative measures designed to prevent the further expansion of Indian lands within the state. The Appropriation Act of June 30, 1913,[88] attached the following proviso to the regular appropriation for the survey and allotment of lands in severalty:

> *Provided*, That no part of said sum shall be used for survey, resurvey, classification, appraisement, or allotment of any land in severalty upon the public domain to any Indian, whether of the Navajo or other tribes, within the State of New Mexico and the State of Arizona. (P. 78.)

---

[72] 42 Stat. 552.

[73] Practically all regular appropriation acts from statehood to date.

[74] Act of February 14, 1920, 41 Stat. 408, 423; Act of March 3, 1921, 41 Stat. 1225, 1239; Act of May 24, 1922, 42 Stat. 552; Act of January 24, 1923, 42 Stat. 1174, 1193; Act of June 5, 1924, 43 Stat. 390, 403.

[75] See Act of May 10, 1926, 44 Stat. 453, 468. See Act of January 12, 1927, 44 Stat. 934, 948.

[76] Legislation governing appropriations for a road through the Santa Clara Pueblo establishes a special control over the admission to the Puye Cliff Ruins for the benefit of the Pueblo. Act of March 4, 1929, 45 Stat. 1562, 1586–1587.

[77] Act of March 26, 1930, 46 Stat. 90, 104.

[78] 44 Stat. 1098.

[79] The report in question, transmitted by the Secretary of the Interior on January 12, 1928 (House Doc. No. 141, 70th Cong., 1st sess.), estimated that the project would benefit approximately 132,000 acres, of which approximately 23,000 acres were Pueblo Indian lands. Of the latter, approximately 8,346 were found to be under cultivation.

[80] 45 Stat. 312. For regulations adopted pursuant to this law, see 25 C. F. R. 129.1.

[81] Op. Sol. I. D., M.27512, February 20, 1935.

[82] C. 745, 49 Stat. 887.

[83] This authorization was extended to 1945 by sec. 5 of the Act of June 20, 1938, 52 Stat. 778, 779. This act also authorized outright (nonreimbursable) federal appropriations for construction costs and past and future operation and maintenance charges on lands of the Albuquerque School, authorized payment, on a reimbursable basis, for extra construction work not contemplated in the original plan, and authorized reimbursable payments on lands newly acquired. *Cf.* Op. Sol. I. D., M.28108, March 18, 1936, holding that the Secretary may contract for payment of construction costs on newly acquired lands.

[84] Act of May 29, 1928, 45 Stat. 883, 900; Act of March 4, 1929, 45 Stat. 1623, 1640; Act of March 26, 1930, 46 Stat. 90, 104; Act of May 14, 1930, 46 Stat. 279, 292; Act of February 14, 1931, 46 Stat. 1115, 1128; Act of March 4, 1931, 46 Stat. 1552, 1567; Act of April 22, 1932, 47 Stat. 91, 102; Act of February 17, 1933, 47 Stat. 820, 831; Act of March 2, 1934, 48 Stat. 362, 371; Act of June 19, 1934, 48 Stat. 1021, 1033; Act of May 9, 1935, 49 Stat. 176, 188 ("final payment"); Act of June 22, 1936, 49 Stat. 1757, 1770; Act of August 9, 1937, 50 Stat. 564, 579; Act of August 25, 1937, 50 Stat. 755, 764; Act of May 9, 1938, 52 Stat. 291, 306 ("final payment").

[85] See, for example, Act of February 14, 1920, 41 Stat. 408, 423, and acts cited in preceding footnote. And see Chapter 12, sec. 7.

[86] 48 Stat. 984, 25 U. S. C. 464. See Chapter 15, sec. 18C.

[87] On the effect of the restraints on alienation contained in sec. 17 of the Act of June 18, 1934, 25 U. S. C. 477, in the event that any of the Pueblos should be chartered thereunder, see Chapter 15, sec. 18.

[88] 38 Stat. 77.

This proviso is repeated in every regular Indian Bureau and Interior Department appropriation act up to and including the appropriation act of February 17, 1933.[89]

In the Appropriation Act of May 25, 1918,[90] the following item of permanent substantive law appears:

> That hereafter no Indian reservation shall be created, nor shall any additions be made to one heretofore created, within the limits of the States of New Mexico and Arizona, except by Act of Congress. (P. 570.)

The Appropriation Act of June 22, 1936,[91] contained a third limitation on the expansion of Indian lands in New Mexico, in the form of a proviso attached to the appropriation for land purchases pursuant to section 5 of the Act of June 18, 1934. This proviso, which has been substantially reenacted in each succeeding appropriation act,[92] declared:

> *Provided*, That within the States of Arizona, New Mexico, and Wyoming no part of said sum shall be used for the acquisition of land outside of the boundaries of existing Indian reservations. (P. 1765.)

While these legislative barriers were being erected against acquisition of non-Indian lands for Indian use, the acquisition of Indian lands for non-Indian use was facilitated by the Act of May 10, 1926,[93] entitled "An Act To provide for the condemnation of the lands of Pueblo Indians in New Mexico for public purposes, and making the laws of the State of New Mexico applicable to such proceedings." Under this act pueblo lands "may be condemned for any public purpose and for any purpose for which lands may be condemned under the laws of the State of New Mexico." Condemnation proceedings under this act must be brought in the federal courts, and notice of suit must be "served upon the superintendent or other officer in charge of the particular pueblo where the land is situated."

This act is substantially similar to the general statute governing condemnation of allotted lands, but there is no parallel statute governing tribal lands generally, so that the Pueblos are subjected to a type of action from which other tribes are immune.

[89] Act of August 1, 1914, 38 Stat. 582; Act of May 18, 1916, 39 Stat. 123; Act of March 2, 1917, 39 Stat. 969; Act of May 25, 1918, 40 Stat. 561; Act of June 30, 1919, 41 Stat. 3; Act of February 14, 1920, 41 Stat. 408; Act of March 3, 1921, 41 Stat. 1225; Act of May 24, 1922, 42 Stat. 552; Act of June 5, 1924, 43 Stat. 390; Act of March 3, 1925, 43 Stat. 1141; Act of May 10, 1926, 44 Stat. 453; Act of January 12, 1927, 44 Stat. 934; Act of March 7, 1928, 45 Stat. 200; Act of March 4, 1929, 45 Stat. 1562; Act of May 14, 1930, 46 Stat. 279; Act of February 14, 1931, 46 Stat. 1115; Act of April 22, 1932, 47 Stat. 91; Act of Feb. 17, 1933, 47 Stat. 820.

[90] 40 Stat. 561. A year later a general prohibition against the creation of Indian reservations except by act of Congress, was included in the Appropriation Act of June 30, 1919, sec. 27, 41 Stat. 3, 34, which was later supplemented by the Act of March 3, 1927, sec. 4, 44 Stat. 1347, prohibiting the alteration of reservation boundaries except by act of Congress. See Chapter 15, sec. 7.

[91] 49 Stat. 1757.

[92] Act of August 9, 1937, 50 Stat. 564; Pub. No. 68, 76th Cong., 1st sess. (May 10, 1939).

[93] C. 282, 44 Stat. 498.

By the Act of April 21, 1928,[94] general laws governing the acquisition of rights-of-way through Indian lands[95] were made applicable to the Pueblos of New Mexico.

The extension of Indian liquor laws to the Pueblos, effected by the Enabling Act of 1910,[96] called forth a special reference to the Pueblos in a provision of the Appropriation Act of August 24, 1912,[97] exempting sacramental wine from such laws.[98]

A further piece of special legislation for the Pueblo Indians is found in the Appropriation Act of March 2, 1917,[99] which contains a proviso to the effect that no part of the sum appropriated for pay of judges of Indian courts "shall be used to pay any judge for the Pueblo Indians of New Mexico, and that no such judge shall be appointed for such Indians by any United States official or employee."

This account of legislation peculiarly affecting the Pueblo Indians, during the period of statehood, would not be complete without a reference to the course of legislation affecting the expenditure of tribal funds. At first, the funds awarded to the Pueblos under the Pueblo Lands Act were expendible by the Secretary of the Interior for the purchase of land and water rights for such Indians.[100] The purposes for which such funds might be expended were broadened in subsequent appropriation acts to cover fencing, irrigation, improvement, and the repayment of federal loans to Pueblos for "industry and self-support,"[101] and purchase of agricultural machinery.[102] Until the Act of May 31, 1933, however, discretion in the expenditure of pueblo funds was vested in the Secretary of the Interior. The act of that date made the consent of the governing authorities of the Pueblo concerned a condition precedent to the expenditure of pueblo funds. The principle thus established was generalized a year later in section 16 of the Act of June 18, 1934.[103]

For eight decades the Pueblos had faced the choice of being treated like other Indian tribes and subjected to federal control of their internal affairs or being treated like non-Indians and finding themselves cut loose from federal services and their lands cut loose from federal protection. Recent legislation and administration have overcome this dilemma by recognizing the right of self-government to be an inherent right of the Pueblos and of other tribes, and by revising the scope of federal supervision in the field of Indian affairs so that the Pueblos, like other tribes, may enjoy federal services and federal protection without surrendering control over their internal municipal life.

[94] C. 400, 45 Stat. 442. The reasons for this enactment are set forth in H. Rept. No. 816, 70th Cong., 1st sess.

[95] 25 U. S. C. 311, 312, 313, 314, 315, 317, 318, 319, 321; 43 U. S. C. 934–935.

[96] Act of June 20, 1910, 36 Stat. 557. See p. 389, *supra*.

[97] 37 Stat. 518.

[98] See Chapter 17, sec. 4.

[99] 39 Stat. 969, 972.

[100] See Act of December 22, 1927, 45 Stat. 2, at pp. 17–18.

[101] Acts of March 4, 1929, 45 Stat. 1562; May 14, 1930, 46 Stat. 279.

[102] Acts of February 14, 1931, 46 Stat. 1115; July 1, 1932, 47 Stat. 525; February 17, 1933, 47 Stat. 820.

[103] 48 Stat. 984, 986, 25 U. S. C. 476. See Chapter 5, sec. 10.

SECTION 5. PUEBLO SELF-GOVERNMENT[104]

At least since the *Sandoval* decision, in 1913, there has been no room for doubt that the Pueblos of New Mexico are Indian tribes entitled to the same rights of self-government, under the Constitution and laws of the United States, as other Indian tribes. The scope of these rights of self-government has been outlined in Chapter 7 of this volume and need not be discussed further at this point. The actual exercise of these rights, however, by the Pueblos has given rise to at least three legal problems which deserve special mention, namely: (1) The legal au-

[104] Although in matters of self-government each pueblo is autonomous, mention should be made of the all-Pueblo Council, which has functioned as a consultative body in matters of common concern to the New Mexico Pueblos since 1922. On the operation of this body, see American Indian Life, Bulletin No. 10 (October-November 1927), pp. 7–13.

thority of pueblo officers; (2) the status of religious liberties of pueblo members, in view of the intimate connection between religious and political affairs in the pueblo system of government; and (3) the right of the Pueblo to control occupancy rights of individual members in pueblo lands.

(1) The question of the authority of pueblo officers has generally arisen in connection with the validity of agreements purportedly executed on behalf of a Pueblo. The case of *Pueblo of Santa Rosa* v. *Fall*,[105] turned on the issue of whether the "captain" of an alleged Pueblo in the State of Arizona had authority to act for the Pueblo in executing a contract affecting tribal claims to land. The Supreme Court held that according to the custom of the Pueblo the "captain" would have no authority to act on behalf of the Pueblo in a matter of this importance, declaring:

> That Luis was without power to execute the papers in question, for lack of authority from the Indian council, in our opinion is well established. (Pp. 319–320.)

The suit based upon the alleged agreement with the pueblo "captain," was ordered dismissed "without prejudice to the bringing of any other suit hereafter by and with the authority of the alleged Pueblo of Santa Rosa." (P. 321.)

The rule announced in the case of the Pueblo of Santa Rosa has been applied to the Pueblos of New Mexico. The Solicitor of the Department of the Interior held, in a memorandum of March 11, 1935, that a grant of a right-of-way executed by the Governor of Pojoaque Pueblo was invalid for the reason that "According to the custom of the pueblo, a grant of lands cannot be made by the governor, but only by the governor and council, or by an assembly of the entire pueblo."

In matters of lesser importance than the disposition of pueblo lands and claims, pueblo authority will generally be exercised by the civil officers or the civil council of the Pueblo. Among the Rio Grande Pueblos, the roster of officers generally includes a governor, the chief executive of the Pueblo; a lieutenant governor, and one or more war captains (who in addition to their religious duties generally act as police officers), fiscales (who are charged with care of graveyards and church property), and sheriffs (messengers of the Governor and council), all elected for 1-year terms. The civil council will generally include the officers and a number of "principales." The status of "principales" is a more or less permanent status generally conferred upon those who have held the post of governor and sometimes upon those who have held other elective offices in the Pueblo.

Within this general framework of pueblo government there are, of course, many variations of structure and except in the Pueblos of Laguna and Santa Clara, which operate under written constitutions,[106] questions of governmental structure and authority would require specific inquiry into the custom of the particular Pueblo.

(2) Questions involving religious aspects of pueblo social life are fraught with such difficulty and complexity that it would be rash to attempt to formulate the law governing this field of pueblo life except in terms of very specific fact situations. It may be worth while, however, to note several caveats against hasty and tempting conclusions in this field.

In the first place, it must be recognized that while the Spaniards insisted upon a separation of religious and lay authority within each Pueblo, and the regular civil officers and civil council were set up in response to this insistence, this separation has probably nowhere been completely carried through, except at the Pueblo of Laguna. Thus one may find that nominations to civil office are made by the caciques, the native religious leaders of the Pueblo, and in some Pueblos, always elected unanimously thereafter by the pueblo assembly.

In the second place, it should be noted that the distinction between religious and civil services required of pueblo members is a distinction on which two experts will seldom agree.

Finally, it should be remembered that the doctrine of separation of church and state, although fundamental in the government of the United States, has never been imposed by Congress as a formula to which the Pueblos must adhere.

In view of these difficulties, efforts to apply to the Pueblos canons of religious liberty which would apply to federal or state governments must be viewed with extreme reserve.

The memorandum submitted to Assistant Attorney General Blair by Special Assistant to the Attorney General G. A. Iverson, on October 3, 1936, dealing with suppression of the use of peyote in the Pueblo of Taos, illustrates the difficulties of the subject and provides a useful guide for further inquiries of this nature. In this case certain Indians using peyote in violation of a tribal custom or ordinance had been tried by the pueblo council and punished by having their land assignments taken away from them. The Iverson memorandum deals with the question of whether the Federal Government might intervene to correct an apparent injustice done to the peyote users of the Pueblo.

The memorandum reaches the conclusion that the Pueblo Indians are entitled to the protection of the First Amendment guaranteeing religious liberty, but that this amendment is inapplicable to the action of the Pueblo authorities themselves as distinguished from the action of federal authorities;[107] that the authority of the tribal court of the Pueblo was clear; that the executive officers of the United States would have no authority to interfere with the administration of justice by the pueblo court in matters affecting relations between members of the Pueblo;[108] that the revocation of an assignment by the Pueblo council, which had been imposed as a penalty, was in violation of the Act of June 7, 1924,[109] so that the Secretary of the Interior would be justified in taking the position "that the attempted coercion is invalid and without force and effect";[110] and finally, that the Federal Government would not be able by any judicial proceeding to interfere with the action of the tribal council in these cases.[111]

The Iverson opinion apparently assumed that the occupancy interest of the Indians concerned was an interest in land within the meaning of the Act of June 7, 1924, which governs the transfer of interests in land of the Pueblo Indians. The factual correctness of this assumption with respect to the land of the Pueblo Indians of Taos is perhaps open to question.[112] This does not affect the validity of the argument presented in the Iverson memorandum that the officials of a Pueblo would not be authorized to transfer interests in land from one individual to another. If, however, no such action is attempted, that is to say, if what the individual pueblo member has is not an interest in land but a privilege of use terminable at the will of the Pueblo itself, it would appear that the limitation referred to in the Iverson memorandum is of no practical importance in the situation dealt with. If in point of fact the individual member has only a privilege of occupancy terminable at the will of the Pueblo, then the Pueblo

[105] 273 U. S. 315 (1927).

[106] That of Laguna was adopted by the Laguna Indians on January 1, 1908, without any specific congressional authorization or departmental supervision. That of Santa Clara Pueblo was adopted by the Indians on December 14, 1935, and approved by the Secretary of the Interior on December 20, 1935, pursuant to the Act of June 18, 1934, 48 Stat. 984, 25 U. S. C. 461 *et seq.*

[107] 8 Memoranda, Lands Division D. J. [1936], 220, 221–223.

[108] *Ibid.*, pp. 231–236.

[109] 43 Stat. 636.

[110] 8 Memoranda, Lands Division D. J. [1936], p. 230.

[111] *Ibid.*, p. 240.

[112] See pp. 395–396, *infra*.

would clearly be justified in terminating that occupancy without the approval of the Secretary of the Interior.

The Iverson opinion contains an illuminating analysis of the judicial authority of the Pueblo council:

> The Indian officials who assumed to dispose of the controversy in the instant case obtained their authority, whatever it was, from the Indian tribe under this governmental policy of self-development or self-determination. They constituted a determining body as a part of a local government which in its principal aspects contained the elements of representative government as that term is understood in our system. It appears to have been created upon deliberate action on the part of the tribe, and while its exercise of authority was necessarily limited by various and sundry acts of Congress, it rested upon what appears to have been a custom of long duration. True, it is not a court with such dignity as that for example of the Seneca Indians of New York who had adopted a constitutional charter relating to various domestic subjects connected with domestic relations and even property rights (*Rice* v. *Maybee*, 2 Fed. Supp. 669), but patently the absence of formality or regularity of procedure is not a requirement going to or affecting the validity or binding force and effect of conclusions reached or judgments announced within the scope of the limited authority of such an institution.
>
> * * * * *
>
> In what has been said above it is assumed that worship by the Indians and the practice of religious ceremonies are internal affairs of the Indians. * * * Accordingly, if the use of peyote was outlawed as pernicious to the welfare of the Indians, the right of the Indian Council to regulate its use or prevent it altogether cannot be questioned because forsooth it was used as a part of a religious ceremony. It seems to me that the question in either event presents a tribal matter and must under the authorities be left to tribal determination. True, the present Council may be wrong. It may be actuated by bias or prejudice against the members of the Native American Church. It may be that their actions were influenced by ulterior motives and that a wrong should be corrected, but as before stated, the Indians themselves created the tribunal and custom and usage support the validity of its judgments. Next year another election will probably be held and a different tribunal inducted into office. The government of the Indians in this case being in a measure at least representative, they should be left in matters of this character to their own devices. There being no appeal from the judgment of the court, the right of appeal being purely statutory, the judgment cannot be reviewed, but this fact does not affect either the jurisdiction or the power.[113]

(3) The right of the Pueblo to control occupancy rights of individual members in pueblo lands is essentially similar to the right of other tribes with respect to tribal lands, discussed in Chapter 9 of this volume. Although, as noted, the Iverson memorandum held that the council of the Pueblo could not, without the approval of the Secretary of the Interior, revoke or transfer an interest in land possessed by a member of the Pueblo, the assumption that individual Taos Indians held such interests in land is not supported by any facts set forth in the Iverson memorandum. A recent memorandum of the Solicitor of the Interior Department on this point[114] declares, after setting forth the language of section 17 of the Act of June 7, 1924:[115]

> Under the foregoing language, it must be held that if an assignment in the Santa Clara Pueblo amounts to a transfer of right, title, or interest in real property, any purported assignment, whether to an Indian or to a non-Indian, made by the pueblo without the prior approval of the Secretary of the Interior is without validity in law or equity. On the other hand, if an assignment does not convey an interest in the land itself, it does not fall within the scope of the statute cited. It becomes important, therefore, to distinguish between those transactions which convey an interest in real property and those transactions which, while relating to the use of real property, do not create an interest therein.
>
> This distinction has been considered by the courts in a great variety of cases which seek to distinguish an interest in land from a mere license. A recent decision in the Circuit Court of Appeals for the Eighth Circuit holds:
>
> "A mere permission to use land, dominion over it remaining in the owner and no interest or exclusive possession of it being given, is but a license. (Citing authorities.)" (*Tips* v. *United States*, 70 F. (2d) 525, 526.) [C. C. A. 5, 1934.]
>
> The essential characteristic of a license to use real property, as distinguished from an interest in real property, is that in the former case the licensee has no vested right as against the licensor or third parties. He has only a privilege, which the licensor may terminate.
>
> As Justice Holmes pointed out, in *Marrone* v. *Washington Jockey Club*, 227 U. S. 633, "A contract binds the person of the maker but does not create an interest in the property that it may concern, unless it also operates as a conveyance. * * * But if it did not create such an interest, that is to say, a right in rem valid against the landowner and third persons, the holder had no right to enforce specific performance by self-help. His only right was to sue upon the contract for the breach." (At p. 636.)
>
> Put in its simplest terms, the rule is that a landowner does not transfer an interest in his land by allowing another to use the land. Thus, for instance, a member of the landowner's family, inasmuch as he is "a bare licensee of the owner, who has no legal interest in the land," cannot derive from his legal privilege to use the land a right against the landowner or against third parties. *Elliott* v. *Town of Mason*, 81 Atl. 701 (N. H. 1911). See also *Keystone Lumber Co.* v. *Kolman*, 69 N. W. 165 (Wis. 1896).
>
> The distinction established by the cases between a license and an interest in land is entirely consistent with the purpose of the Pueblo Land Act of June 7, 1924.
>
> A reading of the legislative history of that act shows that it was designed to stop the loss of pueblo lands by stopping transactions from which a claim against the pueblo might ultimately be derived. Thus if a pueblo, under the guise of making assignments, should in effect grant a life estate or even a leasehold interest to an individual member of the pueblo, there would be a transaction upon which a claim adverse to the pueblo might be founded either by the individual or by a third party to whom he might convey his rights. On the other hand, the action or inaction of the pueblo authorities in permitting a pueblo member to use a designated area of pueblo land would not of itself create any interest in land adverse to the title of the pueblo itself, any more than the decision of a family council to allot certain rooms or buildings to certain members of the family would constitute a transfer of an interest in land.
>
> In between these two extremes difficult "twilight zone" cases may appear. In these cases the courts have looked to the intention of the parties to determine whether the transaction was intended to create a right against the landowner and against third parties. If it was so intended, the transaction must be regarded as a conveyance of an interest in real property. If not, a mere license relationship is established.
>
> Even the language of leasing will not suffice to create a lease relationship if the transaction leaves complete power over the land in the hands of the landowner. Thus, in the case of *Tips* v. *United States*, 70 F. (2d) 525 [C. C. A. 5, 1934], the court found that an instrument which used the terms "landlord," "tenant," "lease," etc., was nevertheless a mere license, because the so-called lessor, the War Department, had no power to lease the property or to grant more than a revocable permit to use the property.
>
> * * * * *
>
> It would be entirely improper for me to attempt to apply the general principles, above set forth, to an imaginary assignment that may be made to an imaginary Indian under an imaginary ordinance that has not yet been passed. When an actual assignment is made or pro-

[113] 8 Memoranda, Lands Division D. J. [1936], 220, 226, 227–228.

[114] Memo. Acting Sol. I. D., April 14, 1939.

[115] 43 Stat. 636; discussed at p. 390, *supra*.

posed and the bylaws, ordinances, unwritten customs or expressed intentions of the parties which bear upon the issues above presented are laid before me, I shall be glad to render an opinion on the question of whether such assignment involves a conveyance of an interest in land and is therefore invalid without prior Secretarial approval.

The foregoing discussion however should make clear the right of the pueblo to grant a mere license for the use of lands to the members of the pueblo. It should be equally clear, under the principles above set forth, that the pueblo lacks power to grant more than a mere license and that any oral transaction or written instrument purporting to grant an interest in land valid against the pueblo itself or against third parties would be void at law and in equity.

SECTION 6. PUEBLO LAND TITLES

Without further reference to the history of pueblo land titles, dealt with in the earlier sections of this chapter, we may attempt a statement of the incidents of pueblo land ownership today. At the present time the land ownership of the Pueblos is of two types. There is, in the first place, land to which the Pueblos hold fee title, under grants of the Spanish, the Mexican, or the United States Governments, or by reason of purchases made by the Pueblo. In the second place, there is land to which legal title is held by the United States, the equitable ownership of which is vested in the Pueblo. Such lands include statutory reservations[116] and Executive order reservations of lands formerly part of the public domain.[117] Likewise, lands purchased by the United States for the benefit of the Pueblo, whether through the use of pueblo funds or through the use of gratuity appropriations, may fall under this category. In its relations to third parties, however, the rights of the Pueblo are not substantially affected by the distinction between the two forms of title.[118] As a legal owner or as an equitable owner the Pueblo has all the ordinary rights of a landowner with respect to third parties except the right of alienation. The Pueblo has the right to exclude third parties from its land,[119] and it has the right to qualify this exclusion by specific conditions under which third parties will be permitted to enter upon pueblo lands. As a landowner the Pueblo may insist that its licensees pay a sum of money for the privilege of entering the pueblo lands, and that while they are within the pueblo boundaries they refrain from certain types of conduct which the pueblo authorities classify as offensive. As a landowner the Pueblo may grant revocable rights of occupancy, grazing permits, or other licenses to nonmembers, provided that no property interest is thereby alienated, and subject to the approval of the Interior Department where such approval is required by existing law. Likewise, the Pueblo may lease pueblo lands to members or to outsiders subject to the approval of the Secretary of the Interior. The necessity of obtaining the consent of the United States to any transaction involving alienation of a property interest, whether by sale, mortgage, exchange, gift, or lease is a matter to which we have already given consideration at pages 390 and 395.

The legal authority of the Pueblo to exercise the rights of a landowner does not depend upon the peculiar facts with respect to the legal title of pueblo grant lands. Its rights are cognate with the rights of other tribes, which have been analyzed in Chapter 15 of this volume.

The limitations upon those rights, while generally similar to the limitations placed upon land ownership by other tribes, are made specific by the terms of the Pueblo Lands Act of June 7, 1924, which has been discussed on page 390. Briefly summarized, it may be said that in its relations with the states, the Federal Government, the members of the Pueblo, and third parties generally, the Pueblo is the owner of lands granted or reserved to it, except that it does not have the right to dispose of the land or any interest therein without the approval of the United States.

[116] Act of April 12, 1924, c. 90, 43 Stat. 92 (Zia Pueblo); Act of May 23, 1928, 45 Stat. 717 (Acoma); Act of February 11, 1929, 45 Stat. 1161 (San Ildefonso).

[117] See Chapter 15, sec. 7.

[118] The conclusion of the process of assimilating pueblo grant lands to the status of other tribal lands is found in *United States* v. *Chavez*, 290 U. S. 357 (1933), holding that pueblo lands are "Indian country" for purposes of federal criminal jurisdiction. The opinion of Mr. Justice Van Devanter contains a brief but informative resumé of the legal history of the New Mexico Pueblos.

[119] *Pueblo de San Juan* v. *United States*, 47 F. 2d 446 (C. C. A. 10, 1931). See Chapter 15, sec. 20.

SECTION 7. THE RELATION OF THE PUEBLOS TO THE FEDERAL GOVERNMENT

That the Pueblos are wards of the United States in the sense in which that phrase was first used, i. e., that Congress possesses plenary power to govern the Pueblos, is a proposition that has not been cast in doubt since the *Sandoval* case.[120] There remains the question how far Congress has exercised this power and, in particular, how far Congress has conferred upon the Executive branch of the Federal Government authority over the Pueblos. The question of the scope of Executive power with respect to the Pueblos is dealt with in a recent opinion of the Solicitor of the Interior Department[121] from which the following passage is quoted:

> One of the points on which administrative control is clearly established relates to the disposition of real property. Here the cases hold that the Pueblos have no power to dispose of real property except with the consent of the United States. Such consent may be given expressly by the Secretary of the Interior, or implicitly through a legal action involving pueblo lands. In the latter case the United States must be a party to the action, or else the Pueblos must be represented by an attorney appointed by the United States, if the decree against the Pueblos is to have validity.

The chief authority cited for this statement is the case of *United States* v. *Candelaria*,[122] in which the following question was certified to the Supreme Court:

> 1. Are Pueblo Indians in New Mexico in such status of tutelage as to their lands in that State that the United States, as such guardian, is not barred either by a judgment in a suit involving title to such lands begun in the territorial court and passing to judgment after statehood or by a judgment in a similar action in the United States District Court for the District of New Mexico, where, in each of said actions, the United States was not a party nor was the attorney representing such Indians therein authorized so to do by the United States? (P. 438.)

This question the Supreme Court answered in the following terms, *per* Van Devanter, *J.*:

> Many provisions have been enacted by Congress—some general and other special—to prevent the Government's

[120] 231 U. S. 28 (1913), discussed at pp. 389–390, *supra*.

[121] Op. Sol. I. D., M.29566, August 9, 1939.

[122] 271 U. S. 432 (1926).

Indian wards from improvidently disposing of their lands and becoming homeless public charges. One of these provisions, now embodied in section 2116 of the Revised Statutes, declares: "No purchase, grant, lease, or other conveyance of lands, or of any title or claim thereto from any Indian nation or tribe of Indians, shall be of any validity in law or equity, unless the same be made by treaty or convention entered into pursuant to the Constitution." This provision was originally adopted in 1834, c. 161, sec. 12, 4 Stat. 730, and, with others "regulating trade and intercourse with the Indian tribes," was extended over "the Indian tribes" of New Mexico in 1851, c. 14, sec. 7, 9 Stat. 587.

While there is no express reference in the provision to Pueblo Indians, we think it must be taken as including them. They are plainly within its spirit and, in our opinion, fairly within its words, "any tribe of Indians." Although sedentary, industrious and disposed to peace, they are Indians in race, customs and domestic government, always have lived in isolated communities, and are a simple, uninformed people, ill-prepared to cope with the intelligence and greed of other races. It therefore is difficult to believe that Congress in 1851 was not intending to protect them, but only the nomadic and savage Indians then living in New Mexico. A more reasonable view is that the term "Indian tribe" was used in the acts of 1834 and 1851 in the sense of "a body of Indians of the same or a similar race, united in a community under one leadership or government, and inhabiting a particular though sometimes ill-defined territory." *Montoya* v. *United States*, 180 U. S. 261, 266. In that sense the term easily includes Pueblo Indians.

Under the Spanish law Pueblo Indians, although having full title to their lands, were regarded as in a state of tutelage and could alienate their lands only under governmental supervision. See *Chouteau* v. *Molony*, 16 How. 203, 237. Text writers have differed about the situation under the Mexican law; but in *United States* v. *Pico*, 5 Wall. 536, 540, this Court, speaking through Mr. Justice Field, who was specially informed on the subject, expressly recognized that under the laws of Mexico the government "extended a special guardianship" over Indian pueblos and that a conveyance of pueblo lands to be effective must be "under the supervision and with the approval" of designated authorities. And this was the ruling in *Sunol* v. *Hepburn*, 1 Cal. 254, 273, *et seq.* Thus it appears that Congress in imposing a restriction on the alienation of these lands, as we think it did, was but continuing a policy which prior governments had deemed essential to the protection of such Indians.

* * * * *

With this explanation of the status of the Pueblo Indians and their lands, and of the relation of the United States to both, we come to answer the questions propounded in the certificate.

To the first question we answer that the United States is not barred. Our reasons will be stated. The Indians of the pueblo are wards of the United States and hold their lands subject to the restriction that the same cannot be alienated in any-wise without its consent. A judgment or decree which operates directly or indirectly to transfer the lands from the Indians, where the United States has not authorized or appeared in the suit, infringes that restriction. The United States has an interest in maintaining and enforcing the restriction which cannot be affected by such a judgment or decree. This Court has said in dealing with a like situation: "It necessarily follows that, as a transfer of the allotted lands contrary to the inhibition of Congress would be a violation of the governmental rights of the United States arising from its obligation to a dependent people, no stipulations, contracts, or judgments rendered in suits to which the Government is a stranger, can affect its interest. The authority of the United States to enforce the restraint lawfully created cannot be impaired by any action without its consent." *Bowling and Miami Improvement Co.* v. *United States*, 233 U. S. 528, 534. And that ruling has been recognized and given effect in other cases. *Privett* v. *United States*, 256 U. S. 201, 204; *Sunderland* v. *United States*, 266 U. S. 226, 232.

But, as it appears that for many years the United States has employed and paid a special attorney to represent the Pueblo Indians and look after their interests, our answer is made with the qualification that, if the decree was rendered in a suit begun and prosecuted by the special attorney so employed and paid, we think the United States is as effectually concluded as if it were a party to the suit. *Souffront* v. *Compagnie des Sucreries*, 217 U. S. 475, 486; *Lovejoy* v. *Murray*, 3 Wall. 1, 18; *Claflin* v. *Fletcher*, 7 Fed. 851, 852; *Maloy* v. *Duden*, 86 Fed. 402, 404; *James* v. *Germania Iron Co.*, 107 Fed. 597, 613. (Pp. 441 to 444.)

The decision reached in the *Candelaria* case has been followed in a number of cases arising on appeals from decrees of the Pueblo Lands Board.[138]

The opinion of the Solicitor of the Interior Department quoted above goes on to analyze the scope of Federal executive power over the Pueblos in the following terms:

> The power of the Executive extends to the bringing of suits on behalf of a pueblo in matters affecting pueblo lands and controlling the conduct of such litigation. The basis of such power is set forth in the passage above quoted from *United States* v. *Candelaria*, in which Mr. Justice Van Devanter said: "The suit was brought on the theory that these Indians are wards of the United States and that it therefore has authority and is under a duty to protect them in the ownership and enjoyment of their lands." (271 U. S., at 437.) Under section 1 of the Pueblo Lands Act which provides that "the United States of America, in its sovereign capacity as guardian of said pueblo Indians" shall institute certain actions to quiet title of pueblo lands, a number of suits have been brought on behalf of Indian pueblos.
>
> See for example *United States* v. *Board of National Missions of Presbyterian Church, supra; Garcia* v. *United States, supra; Pueblo of Picuris* v. *Abeyta, supra.*
>
> In the last cited case the question was raised whether the pueblo itself was precluded from appealing an adverse decision sustained in an action instituted by the United States on behalf of the pueblo. The court declared:
>
> * * * * *
>
> "It thus appears that at any time prior to the filing of the field notes and plats by the Secretary of the Interior in the office of the Surveyor General of New Mexico (Pueblo Lands Act, sec. 13, 43 Stat. 640 [25 U. S. C. A. sec. 331 note]) either the United States or the pueblo may maintain an action involving the title and right to lands of the pueblo; but a decree rendered in a suit brought by the pueblo does not bind the United States, while a decree rendered in a suit brought by the United States does bind the pueblo.
>
> * * * * *
>
> "The statutory power of the United States to initiate actions for the Pueblo Indians necessarily involves the power to control such litigation. If the private attorneys of the pueblo could dictate the averments of the bill, or could prevail in questions of judgment in the introduction of evidence, there would be no substance to the guardianship of the United States over the Indians. There cannot be a divided authority in the conduct of litigation; divided authority results in hopeless confusion. If the United States has power to dismiss with prejudice prior to trial, as has been held, it certainly has power to decline to appeal after trial, if it believes the decision of the trial court is without error." (At pp. 13 to 14.)
>
> In view of the foregoing authorities it is clear that the United States is empowered by virtue of its relation to the pueblo and pursuant to special legislation based on that relationship to conduct and control litigation on behalf of the pueblos concerned for the protection of pueblo lands.
>
> No attempt will be made in this opinion to analyze exhaustively the realm in which the Executive arm of the

[138] *United States* v. *Board of National Missions of the Presbyterian Church*, 37 F. 2d 272 (C. C. A. 10, 1929); *Garcia* v. *United States*, 43 F. 2d 873 (C. C. A. 10, 1930); *Pueblo of Picuris* v. *Abeyta*, 50 F. 2d 12 (C. C. A. 10, 1931).

Federal Government is empowered to supervise acts of the pueblo government. It is enough for the present to point on the one hand to the foregoing cases upholding such supervision in matters affecting the disposition of pueblo lands and litigation with reference to such lands and to note, on the other hand, that pueblo rights of self-government in matters internal to the pueblo have been constantly recognized in all the decided cases. In the Constitution of the Santa Clara Pueblo, approved by the Secretary of the Interior on December 20, 1935, an attempt was made to distinguish between matters over which the pueblo has sovereign power, under existing Federal law, and matters over which the Interior Department has final control. This attempt is embodied in the fifth numbered paragraph of Article IV, section 1 of the Pueblo Constitution. This paragraph, dealing with powers which are not specifically enumerated in section 16 of the act of June 18, 1934, but which are comprehended under the general phrase "all powers vested in any Indian tribe or tribal council by existing law," reads as follows:

> "5. To enact ordinances, not inconsistent with the constitution and bylaws of the pueblo, for the maintenance of law and order within the pueblo and for the punishment of members, and the exclusion of nonmembers violating any such ordinances, for the raising of revenue and the appropriation of available funds for pueblo purposes, for the regulation of trade, inheritance, landholding, and private dealings in land within the pueblo, for the guidance of the officers of the pueblo in all their duties, and generally for the protection of the welfare of the pueblo and for the execution of all other powers vested in the pueblo by existing law: *Provided*, That any ordinance which affects persons who are not members of the pueblo shall not take effect until it has been approved by the Secretary of the Interior or some officer designated by him."

A third point in the relation of the pueblo to the Federal Government is raised by the question whether the pueblos may resort to legal proceedings against the United States or its officers. While this question is essentially a question of legal procedure, the substantive rights of the pueblos must depend in a very large degree upon the answer given to this question. The question is distinctly and unmistakably answered in the opinion of the Supreme Court read by Mr. Justice Van Devanter in *Lane* v. *Pueblo of Santa Rosa* [249 U. S. 110 (1919)], *supra*. In that case the pueblo of Santa Rosa was recognized as entitled to bring suit against the Secretary of the Interior to enjoin that official from offering, listing, or disposing of, as public lands of the United States, certain lands claimed by the Indian pueblo.

Again, in the case of *Pueblo de San Juan* v. *United States* [47 F. 2d 446 (C. C. A. 10, 1931)], *supra*, the right of a pueblo to bring suit against the United States, under the Pueblo Lands Act (43 Stat. 637), was upheld.

In accordance with the familiar rule a suit against the United States must be based upon legislation through which the United States permits itself to be sued. Suits against officers of the United States based on alleged illegal acts require no such statutory authority.

A final question which the relation of the pueblo to the Federal Government has raised is the question whether the pueblos are entitled to the protection of the Federal Constitution with respect to acts done under Federal authority.

The opinion of the Supreme Court in the above-cited case of *Lane* v. *Pueblo of Santa Rosa* answers this question in the following terms:

> "The defendants assert with much earnestness that the Indians of this pueblo are wards of the United States—recognized as such by the legislative and executive departments—and that in consequence the disposal of their lands is not within their own control, but subject to such regulations as Congress may prescribe for their benefit and protection. Assuming, without so deciding, that this is all true, we think it has no real bearing on the point we are considering. Certainly it would not justify the defendants in treating the lands of these Indians—to which, according to the bill, they have a complete and perfect title—as public lands of the United States and disposing of the same under the public land laws. That would not be an exercise of guardianship, but an act of confiscation. Besides, the Indians are not here seeking to establish any power or capacity in themselves to dispose of the lands, but only to prevent a threatened disposal by administrative officers in disregard of their full ownership. Of their capacity to maintain such a suit we entertain no doubt. The existing wardship is not an obstacle, as is shown by repeated decisions of this court, of which *Lone Wolf* v. *Hitchcock*, 187 U. S. 553, is an illustration." (At pp. 113 to 114.)

Again, it was held in the case of *Garcia* v. *United States*, *supra*, that Congress could not constitutionally deprive a pueblo of the right to plead a New Mexico statute of limitations. The court declared:

> "We conclude that such Indian pueblos were entitled to the benefits of the New Mexico statutes of limitation and that the United States, as their guardian, may plead such statutes in their behalf.
>
> "If this be true, then the Pueblo of Taos, having acquired fee simple title to the Tenorio tract under section 3364, *supra*, prior to the adoption of the Pueblo Lands Act, could not be deprived of that title by legislative fiat." (At p. 878.)

In accordance with the foregoing decisions it is plain that while the Indian pueblos have been considered for certain purposes as wards of the Federal Government they are entitled not only to bring suit against that Government and its officers but to claim as against such Government and officers the protections guaranteed by the Federal Constitution.

SECTION 8. THE RELATION OF THE PUEBLOS TO THE STATE

We have already noted that the terms upon which New Mexico was admitted to statehood left no room for a claim by the state to governmental power over the Pueblos. The general rule that the Pueblos are not subject to state control must, however, be qualified in several respects.

In the first place, as noted in Chapter 6 of this volume, pueblo lands, like other Indian reservations, are part of the state in which they are situated for purposes of state jurisdiction over non-Indians.

In the second place, Congress has made various state laws, such as laws respecting health and education,[124] applicable on Indian reservations, and these laws are as applicable to the Pueblos as to other Indian tribes.[125]

In the third place, the judgments and decrees of the Pueblo in matters properly within its jurisdiction would appear to merit the same faith and credit that is owing to other recognized agencies of tribal government under the decisions discussed elsewhere in this volume.[126]

A significant problem of the relation of the Pueblos to the State of New Mexico is raised by the possibility of suit by a Pueblo in a state court.[127] On this question an opinion of the Solicitor of the Interior Department[128] declares:

> It has occasionally been assumed that where a State has no jurisdiction over the land of an Indian pueblo, the

[124] 25 U. S. C. 231.

[125] See Chapter 6, sec. 2.

[126] See Chapter 14, sec. 3.

[127] Examples of such suits in state or territorial courts are: *Pueblo of Laguna* v. *Pueblo of Acoma*, 1 N. M. 220 (1857), dispute over possession of sacred picture; *Victor de la O* v. *The Pueblo of Acoma*, 1 N. M. 226 (1857), dispute over possession of document of title; *Pueblo of Isleta* v. *Tondre and Picard*, 18 N. M. 388, 137 Pac. 86 (1913), condemnation of right-of-way.

[128] Op. Sol. I. D., M.29566, August 9, 1939.

pueblo has no standing in the courts of the State. This assumption is entirely erroneous. Despite the lack of State jurisdiction over pueblo lands, the pueblo may, nevertheless, bring suit in State courts, so far as State law permits, and demand, in other respects, recognition as a public corporation. The judgments and ordinances of a pueblo are entitled to the same sort of recognition that State courts give to the acts of another State or nation. The pueblo as a sovereign body is not subject to suit in State courts, except with its own consent. The pueblo is not for that reason a pariah. It is entitled at the very least to all the rights which a foreigner may assert in the courts of a State.

The foregoing views are based upon the judgment of the Supreme Court in *United States* v. *Candelaria*.[129] In this case the United States, as guardian of the Pueblo of Laguna, brought a suit to quiet title. The objection was made that prior decisions in the state courts barred the action. The Court commented on the validity of the earlier decrees, in the following terms:

> In their answer the defendants denied the wardship of the United States and also set up in bar two decrees rendered in prior suits brought against them by the pueblo to quiet the title to the same lands. One suit was described as begun in 1910 in the territorial court and transferred when New Mexico became a State to the succeeding state court, where on final hearing a decree was given for the defendants on the merits. * * * In the replication the United States alleged that it was not a party to either of the prior suits; that it neither authorized the bringing of them nor was represented by the attorney who appeared for the pueblo; and therefore that it was not bound by the decrees.
>
> On the case thus presented the court held that the decrees operated to bar the prosecution of the present suit by the United States, and on that ground the bill was dismissed. An appeal was taken to the Circuit Court of Appeals, which after outlining the case as just stated, has certified to this Court the following questions:
>
> * * * * *
>
> 2. Did the state court of New Mexico have jurisdiction to enter a judgment which would be *res judicata* as to the United States, in an action between Pueblo Indians and opposed claimants concerning title to land, where the result of that judgment would be to disregard a survey made by the United States of a Spanish or Mexican grant pursuant to an act of Congress confirming such grant to said Pueblo Indians? (Pp. 438 to 439.)
>
> Coming to the second question, we eliminate so much of it as refers to a possible disregard of a survey made by the United States, for that would have no bearing on the court's jurisdiction or the binding effect of the judgment or decree, but would present only a question of whether error was committed in the course of exercising jurisdiction. With that eliminated, our answer to the question is that the state court had jurisdiction to entertain the suit and proceed to judgment or decree. (P. 444.)

The case of *Trujillo* v. *Prince*,[130] establishing the proposition that an Indian, outside of his Pueblo, is within the scope of the state wrongful death statute, so that his administrator may be entitled to recover damages in a state court against a non-Indian, demonstrates that where state law does not interfere with congressional or tribal power it may be invoked in certain cases between Indians and non-Indians. This case does not involve any peculiarities of pueblo law, and the general issues which it raises are dealt with elsewhere in this volume.[131]

[129] 271 U. S. 432 (1926). That portion of the opinion in this case which relates to the first question certified is set forth and discussed above at pp. 396–397.

[130] 42 N. M. 337, 78 P. 2d 145 (1938).

[131] See Chapter 8, sec. 6; Chapter 19, sec. 5.

SECTION 9. THE PUEBLO AS A CORPORATE ENTITY

We have already noted that the Pueblos of New Mexico were given the status of corporations by one of the first acts of the New Mexican Territorial Government.[132] This legislative chartering may be viewed as a translation into Anglo-Saxon terms of the corporate recognition which the Pueblos had long enjoyed under Spanish and Mexican law. In the case of *Lane* v. *Pueblo of Santa Rosa*,[133] the Supreme Court declared, *per* Van Devanter, *J.*:

> During the Spanish, as also the Mexican, dominion it enjoyed a large measure of local self-government and was recognized as having capacity to acquire and hold lands and other property. With much reason this might be regarded as enabling and entitling it to become a suitor for the purpose of enforcing or defending its property interests. See *School District* v. *Wood*, 13 Massachusetts, 193, 198; Cooley's Const. Lim., 7th ed., p. 276; 1 Dillon Munic. Corp., 5th ed., secs. 50, 64, 65. But our decision need not be put on that ground, for there is another which arises out of our own laws and is in itself sufficient. After the Gadsden Treaty Congress made that region part of the Territory of New Mexico and subjected it to "all the laws" of that Territory. Act August 4, 1854, c. 245, 10 Stat. 575. One of those laws provided that the inhabitants of any Indian pueblo having a grant or concession of lands from Spain or Mexico, such as is here claimed, should be a body corporate and as such capable of suing or defending in respect of such lands. Laws New Mex. 1851–2, pp. 176 and 418. If the plaintiff was not a legal entity and juristic person before, it became such under that law; and it retained that status after Congress included it in the Territory of Arizona, for the act by which this was done extended to that Territory all legislative enactments of the Territory of New Mexico. Act February 24, 1863, c. 56, 12 Stat. 664. The fact that Arizona has since become a State does not affect the plaintiff's corporate status or its power to sue. See *Kansas Pacific R. R. Co.* v. *Atchison, Topeka & Santa Fe R. R. Co.*, 112 U. S. 414. (P. 112.)

The corporate status of the Pueblos has been recognized in many cases.[134]

In *United States* v. *Candelaria*, the Supreme Court, *per* Van Devanter, *J.*, commented on the *Lane* case in these terms:

> It was settled in *Lane* v. *Pueblo of Santa Rosa*, 249 U. S. 110, that under territorial laws enacted with congressional sanction each pueblo in New Mexico—meaning the Indians comprising the community—became a juristic person and enabled to sue and defend in respect of its lands. * * * That was a suit brought by the Pueblo of Santa Rosa to enjoin the Secretary of the Interior and the Commissioner of the General Land Office from carrying out what was alleged to be an unauthorized purpose and attempt to dispose of the Pueblo's lands as public lands of the United States. Arizona was formed from part of New Mexico and when in that way the pueblo came to be in the new territory it retained its juristic status. * * * (Pp. 442–443.)

The incidents of corporate status[135] attaching to the Pueblos are analyzed in a recent opinion of the Solicitor of the Interior Department[136] in the following passage:

> It is clear that the decided cases leave no room for doubt on the proposition that the pueblos of New Mexico

[132] Laws, New Mexico, 1851–1852, p. 418. See sec. 2, *supra*.

[133] 249 U. S. 110 (1919).

[134] *United States* v. *Candelaria*, 271 U. S. 432, 442–443 (1926); *Pueblo of Zia* v. *United States*, 168 U. S. 198 (1897); *Garcia* v. *United States*, 43 F. 2d 873, 878 (C. C. A. 10, 1930); *Pueblo de San Juan* v. *United States*, 47 F. 2d 446 (C. C. A. 10, 1931), cert. den. 284 U. S. 626.

[135] The right of the Pueblos, as corporations, to receive grazing permits under the Taylor Grazing Act (Act of June 28, 1934, 48 Stat.

are corporations, with power to bring suits against third parties, and liability to suits brought by third parties.[137]

It is not so clear what manner of corporation the pueblos are. The most explicit characterization found in any of the Federal cases heretofore decided is found in the case of *Garcia* v. *United States, supra*, where the Pueblo of Taos is classified under the category of "municipal or public corporations":

> "* * * By the Act of December, 1847, Rev. St. N. M. 1855, p. 420, section 69–101, N. M. Stat. Ann. Comp. 1929, the Indian Pueblos were given the status of bodies politic and corporate and, as such, empowered to sue in respect of their lands. *Lane* v. *Pueblo of Santa Rosa*, 249 U. S. 110, 39 S. Ct. 185, 63 L. Ed. 504. A statute of limitation, in the absence of provision therein to the contrary, runs not only for, but against municipal or public corporations. *Metropolitan R. Co.* v. *Dist. of Columbia*, 132 U. S. 1, 11–12, 10 S. Ct. 19, 33 L. Ed. 231; *Little* v. *Emmett Irr. Dist.*, 45 Idaho 485, 263 P. 40, 56 A. L. R. 822; *Rosedale S. D. No. 5* v. *Towner County*, 56 N. D. 41, 216 N. W. 212, 215. We conclude that such Indian Pueblos were entitled to the benefits of the New Mexico statutes of limitation and that the United States, as their guardian, may plead such statutes in their behalf." (P. 878.)

While the Pueblos of New Mexico fall within certain definitions of "municipal corporations,"[138] it is not intended to suggest that they are municipal corporations of the State of New Mexico within the meaning of state statutes on the rights and powers of such corporations. Such an inference would run counter to the basic doctrines of tribal self-government and congressional sovereignty in Indian affairs. The term "public corporation" is therefore perhaps more appropriate as a characterization of the legal status of the Pueblos. The content of any term of characterization, however, must depend largely upon judicial decisions which have not yet been rendered.

1269, as amended by the Act of June 26, 1936, 49 Stat. 1976) is affirmed in two of the opinions of the Solicitor of the Interior Department which contain an exhaustive analysis of Pueblo corporate status. Op. Sol. I. D., M.28869, February 13, 1937; Op. Sol. I. D., M.29797, May 14, 1938. On the general problem of the corporate status of Indian tribes, see Chapter 14, sec. 4.

[136] Op. Sol. I. D. M.29566, August 9, 1939.

[137] Insofar as the quoted statement indicates that a Pueblo has legal capacity to defend an action, the statement is amply supported by the language of the Supreme Court in the *Lane* and *Candelaria* cases, above quoted, and by certain decisions of the Territorial court. (See fn. 127 *supra*.) The inference, however, at a Pueblo may be sued without its consent would find no support in these opinions of the Supreme Court, and would run contrary to the rule that a sovereign body is immune from suits to which it has not consented. The application of this rule in Five Civilized Tribe cases has been upheld. *Turner* v. *United States*, 248 U. S. 354 (1919); *Adams* v. *Murphy*, 165 Fed. 304 (C. C. A. 8, 1908); *Thebo* v. *Choctaw Tribe of Indians*, 66 Fed. 372 (C. C. A. 8, 1895); and see *United States* v. *United States Fidelity Co.*, 106 F. 2d 804, 809 (C. C. A. 10, 1939). That a similar holding would be reached in the case of the New Mexicon Pueblos is indicated by *United States* v. *Sandoval*, 231 U. S. 28, 48 (1913).

[138] "A *municipal corporation*, in its strict and proper sense, is the body politic and corporate constituted by the incorporation of the inhabitants of a city or town for the purposes of local government thereof. * * * *We may, therefore, define a municipal corporation* in its historical and strict sense to be the incorporation, by the authority of the government, of the inhabitants of a particular place or district, and authorizing them in their corporate capacity to exercise subordinate specified powers of legislation and regulation with respect to their local and internal concerns. This power of local government is the distinctive purpose and the distinguishing feature of a municipal corporation proper." 1 Dillon on Municipal Corporations (5th ed. 1911) secs. 31–32. The essential feature of local self-government has been discussed under an earlier heading. The fact that the Pueblo is a membership corporation rather than a stock corporation is too obvious to call for discussion. The relation of the corporation to a particular area of land and the inhabitants thereof is made clear in the territorial statute establishing the corporate status of the Pueblos which has been quoted above.

CHAPTER 21

ALASKAN NATIVES

TABLE OF CONTENTS

SECTION 1. CLASSIFICATION OF ALASKAN NATIVES

The term "Natives of Alaska" has been defined to include members of the aboriginal races inhabiting Alaska at the time of its annexation to the United States, and their descendants of the whole or mixed blood.[1] Important native groups comprise the Eskimos, which are distinct from, although related to, the American Indian,[2] the kindred Aleuts, and the Indians. Among the Indian groups[3] are the Athapascans, Tlingits,[4] Haidas, and Tsimshians, which include the Metlakahtlans.[5] According to many reputable anthropologists, all these strains migrated to the New World by way of Bering Strait.[6]

The Eskimos (including the Aleuts) constitute almost two-thirds of the natives.[7] They inhabit the shores of the Arctic

[1] The following are some of the statutory provisions defining this term:

The Act of June 25, 1938, 52 Stat. 1169, amending the Alaska game law, defines "Indian" to include "Natives of one-half or more Indian blood," and "Eskimo" to include "Natives of one-half or more Eskimo blood."

Sec. 2 of the Act of April 16, 1934, 48 Stat. 594, 596, which grants special fishing privileges to "native Indians," defines "native Indians" to mean "members of the aboriginal races inhabiting Alaska when annexed to the United States, and their descendants of the whole or half blood;" the term "Indian" is defined similarly in section 142 of the Act of March 3, 1899, 30 Stat. 1253, 1274.

Sec. 15 of the Reindeer Act of September 1, 1937, 50 Stat. 900, 902, defines the term "natives of Alaska" as meaning—

> the native Indians, Eskimos, and Aleuts of whole or part blood inhabiting Alaska at the time of the Treaty of Cession of Alaska to the United States and their descendants of whole or part blood, together with the Indians and Eskimos who, since the year 1867 and prior to the enactment hereof, have migrated into Alaska from the Dominion of Canada, and their descendants of the whole or part blood.

Sec. 19 of the Act of June 18, 1934, 48 Stat. 984, 988, provides: "For the purposes of this Act, Eskimos and other aboriginal peoples of Alaska shall be considered Indians."

C. 80, section 142 of the Penal Code of Alaska, Act of February 6, 1909, 35 Stat. 600, 603, which makes the sale of liquor to Indians a crime, provides:

> That the term "Indian" * * * shall be construed to include the aboriginal races inhabiting Alaska when annexed to the United States, and their descendants of the whole or half blood, who have not become citizens of the United States.

The Indians of Alaska and Eskimos equally fall within the category of Natives of Alaska. *In re Minook*, 2 Alaska 200 (1904); 49 L. D. 592 (1923); 52 L. D. 597 (1929); 53 I. D. 593 (1932).

[2] Dr. Aleš Hrdlička, Curator of Physical Anthropology, Smithsonian Institution, in The Coming of Man from Asia in the Light of Recent Discoveries, Annual Report, Smithsonian Inst. for 1935, H. Doc. No. 324, pt. 1, 74th Cong., 2d sess. (1936), p. 469, expresses the opinion that the Eskimo, though a later comer to Alaska, is a blood relation of the Indian:

> The Eskimo appears to be a later offshoot from the same old stock that gave us the Indian. He came later and in two subtypes, one nearer to, the other farther from, the Indian. The relation of the Indian and the Eskimo may best perhaps be represented by a hand with outstretched fingers. The diverging fingers are the different types of the Indian: the thumb, which should be double, represents the Eskimo. The thumb is farther apart but originates from the same hand, which is the old or paleo-Asiatic yellow-brown strain, a strain that gave us the ancestry of all the aboriginal Americans.

"Later studies by ethnologists have resulted in classifying all the natives except the Eskimos as remote offshoots of the North American Indian stock." I Encyclopaedia Britannica (14th ed. 1936), p. 502.

[3] The 1940 census reports native Indians and Eskimos under six linguistic groups—Aleutian, Eskimauan, Athapascan, Haidan, Tlingit, and Tsimshian. All other Indians come under United States or Canadian stocks.

[4] See Jones, A Study of the Thlingets of Alaska (1914).

[5] See Survey of the Conditions of Indians in the United States, pt. 35 (Metlakahtla Indians), 74th Cong., 2d sess., Hearings Sen. Subcomm. on Ind. Affairs (1936). For an account of the conversion and civilization of these people through the indefatigable efforts of the missionary, William Duncan, see Arctander, The Apostle of Alaska (1909), and Wellcome, The Story of Metlakahtla (2d ed. 1909). Also see The Metlakahtlan, vol. 1, Nos. 1–8 (1888–91), a magazine published at Metlakahtla. The more recent history of these people is discussed in *Alaska Pacific Fisheries* v. *United States*, 248 U. S. 78 (1918), affg. 240 Fed. 274 (C. C. A. 9, 1917), and *Territory of Alaska* v. *Annette Island Packing Co.*, 289 Fed. 671 (C. C. A. 9, 1923), cert. den. 263 U. S. 708 (1923).

[6] The chief deduction of American anthropology, in the substance of which all serious students concur, is that this continent was peopled essentially from northeastern Asia. The deduction is based on the facts that man could not have originated in the New World, and hence must have come from the Old; that the American aborigines are throughout of one fundamental race, the nearest relatives of which exist to this day over wide parts of northern and eastern Asia; and that the only practicable route for man in such a cultural stage as he must have been in at the time of his first coming to America was that between northeastern Asia and Alaska.

Hrdlička, *op. cit.*, Annual Report, Smithsonian Inst. for 1935, H. Doc. No. 324, 74th Cong., 2d sess. (1936), p. 463. See also Wissler, The American Indian (1922), pp. 389–400; Jenness, Anthropology—Prehistoric Culture Waves from Asia to America, 30 Jour. Washington Academy of Sciences No. 1 (1940), pp. 1–15.

Senator Charles Sumner alluded to this theory on April 9, 1867, in a speech before the Senate of the United States urging the ratification of the treaty between the United States and Russia for the purchase of Alaska. XI The Works of Charles Sumner (1875), p. 264. This speech (pp. 186–349) is an excellent summary of the contemporary knowledge of Alaska.

[7] Fifteenth Census of the United States, Outlying Territories and Possessions (1932), pp. 19, 20. On October 1, 1929, there were 19,028 Eskimos (including the Aleuts) and 10,955 natives of other linguistic stock. The total population was 59,278, of which the natives total slightly over half, or 29,983. For a discussion of the composition and distribution of the population, see Alaska, Its Resources and Development, H. Doc. No. 485, 75th Cong., 3d sess. (1938), pp. 35–38, 183. The unreliability of much of the contemporary writings on Alaska at the time of its purchase is evidenced by the fact that its population was then variously estimated at from 54,000 to 400,000. Probably the former figure was more nearly accurate, for it was adopted by the "Almanach de Gotha" for 1867 and the "Les Peuples de la Russie," the best authority at that time. It was estimated that there were not more than 2,500

Ocean, the islands of Bering Sea, and the Aleutian chain, and one-third of them live north of the Arctic circle.[8]

The Aleuts inhabit the Aleutian Islands and the adjacent mainland, while the Athapascan Indians, perhaps the most primitive, occupy the interior, reaching the coast only at Cook's Inlet.[9] The coastal Indians, which include the Tlingits,[10] a race of maritime nomads, the related Haidas, and the Tsimshians have their homes along the coastal area of Cook's Inlet, the Gulf of Alaska, and the shores of southeast Alaska.[11]

The natives reside in small, widely separated villages,[12] communities, or fishing camps, scattered along the 25,000 miles of coast and on the great rivers, principally along the southern and far northwestern coast. For the most part they do not fall into well-defined tribal groups occupying a fixed geographical area.[13] Most of them are engaged in hunting and fishing, sometimes supplementing these occupations by agriculture. The raising of reindeer provides subsistence for some and is expected to become more important in their economy.[14] An increasing number of natives are finding wage employment.[15]

Russians and Creoles, and 8,000 aborigines under the direct government of the Russian American Co., and between 40,000 and 50,000 other aborigines who had only a temporary or casual contact with the company for purposes of trade. XI The Works of Charles Sumner (1875), pp. 261–263.

Sec. 236 of Art. 3, Charter of the Russian-American Company defines Creoles as follows:

> Children born of a European or Siberian father and a native American mother, or of a native American father and a European or Siberian mother, shall be regarded as creoles, equally with the children of these latter, of whom a special record is preserved.

See *In re Minook*, 2 Alaska 200, 214 (1904).

Dall, Alaska and Its Resources (1870), p. 537, estimates that the population of Alaska around 1867 was 29,097, of which 26,843 were natives and 1,421 Creoles or half bloods. At present the mixed-blood population is increasing. XI Encyclopaedia of the Social Sciences (1935), p. 269.

[8] Spicer, The Constitutional Status and Government of Alaska (1927), p. 98; Jenness, The Eskimos of Northern Alaska: A Study in the Effect of Civilization, V Geographical Review (1918), pp. 89–101.

[9] Osgood, The Distribution of the Northern Athapaskan Indians, Yale University Publications in Anthropology, No. 7 (1936); Ethnography of the Tanaina, *ibid.*, No. 16 (1937).

[10] Knapp and Childe, The Thlinkets of Southeastern Alaska (1896).

[11] Anderson and Eells, Alaska Natives (1935), p. 6, *et seq.*; Krieger Indian Villages of Southeast Alaska, Annual Report, Smithsonian Inst. for 1927, H. Doc. No. 58, pt. 1, 70th Cong., 1st sess. (1928), pp. 467–494; also see Clark, History of Alaska (1930), pp. 22–31.

[12] A discussion of an Eskimo village is contained in Anderson and Eells, *op. cit.*, pp. 31–37. Also see Stefansson, My Life with the Eskimo (1913).

[13] Report of the Commissioner of Indian Affairs in Annual Report of the Secretary of the Interior (1937), pp. 200–201.

[14] See sec. 8. See also Alaska—Its Resources and Development, *op. cit.*, 41, 198.

[15] Alaska—Its Resources and Development, *op. cit.*, p. 41; for a table of the number of natives gainfully employed in all industries see Fifteenth Census of the United States, Outlying Territories and Possessions (1932), p. 27. Also see hearings before the subcommittee of the House Committee on Appropriations on the Interior Department Appropriations Bill for 1941, pt. I, pp. 875–876.

SECTION 2. CLASSIFICATION OF NATIVES UNDER RUSSIAN RULE

In determining the status of the natives with respect to civilization and citizenship, the courts have given considerable weight to their ethnology, the state of their civilization and their relationship to the antecedent Russian Government.[16] During the 67 years prior to acquisition by the United States of Alaska,[17] the Russian American Company, exercised practically absolute dominion over this country.[18] The imperial law of Russia recognized the settled natives, including the Aleuts, Kodiaks, Eskimos, and Tlingits, who embraced the Christian faith, as Russian citizens, on the same footing as white subjects.

> * * * the independent tribes of pagan faith who acknowledged no restraint from the Russians, and practised their ancient customs—were classed as uncivilized native tribes by the Russian laws.[19]

The interest of the Russian Government in trade with the natives[20] is indicated by the treaty made with the United States on April 17, 1824,[21] which deals incidentally with the natives of Alaska. Article I permitted the citizens of both contracting powers to navigate and fish in the Pacific Ocean and Article IV permitted trading with the natives. Article V excepted from this commerce the sale of "spirituous liquors, fire-arms, other arms, powder, and munitions of war of every kind * * *."[22] Several years later, Congress implemented this treaty by the Act of May 19, 1828,[23] which provided for the punishment of violators of Article V.

[16] *In re Minook*, 2 Alaska 200 (1904); *United States* v. *Berrigan*, 2 Alaska 442 (1905).

[17] Before its cession, this territory was called Russian America.

[18] Organized in 1799 under a charter from the Russian Emperor. XI The Works of Charles Sumner (1875), p. 247. The company failed to renew its charter in 1863. Clark, History of Alaska (1930), pp. 50–59. See Andrews, Alaska Under the Russians, VII Washington Historical Quarterly (1916), pp. 278–295.

[19] *In re Minook*, 2 Alaska 200, 218 (1904).

[20] See Sumner, *op. cit.*, pp. 262–263.

[21] 8 Stat. 302. Ratified January 11, 1825, proclaimed January 12, 1825.

[22] Art. IV limited to 10 years the navigation of ships in the interior seas for the purpose of fishing and trading with the natives.

[23] C. 57, 4 Stat. 276.

SECTION 3. TREATY OF CESSION

Alaska was ceded to the United States by Russia for $7,200,000 in gold by the treaty concluded March 30, 1867.[24] Article III, which deals with the inhabitants makes no distinction based on color or racial origin. It provides:

> The Inhabitants of the ceded territory, according to their choice, reserving their natural allegiance, may return to Russia within three years; but if they should prefer to remain in the ceded territory, they, with the exception of uncivilized native tribes, shall be admitted to the enjoyment of all the rights, advantages, and immunities of citizens of the United States, and shall be maintained and protected in the free enjoyment of their liberty, property, and religion. The uncivilized tribes will be subject to such laws and regulations as the United States may, from time to time, adopt in regard to aboriginal tribes of that country.

The Treaty thus divided the Alaskan inhabitants into the following three classes:

(1) Those who returned to Russia within 3 years, and thereby reserved their natural allegiance;

(2) Those who remained in the territory, except "uncivilized native tribes"; and

(3) "Uncivilized native tribes."

[24] 15 Stat. 539. Ratified by the United States May 28, 1867, exchanged June 20, 1867, proclaimed by the United States June 20, 1867. For further details concerning the history of the purchase, see the bibliography cited, pp. 116, 117, in Spicer, *op. cit.* Also see Clark, *op cit.*, pp. 60–80.

SECTION 4. SOURCES OF FEDERAL POWER

The primary sources of federal power over the Alaskan natives are three.[25] First, since Alaska is a recognized territory,[26] it is subject to the paramount and plenary authority of Congress to enact laws for the government of the territory and its inhabitants.[27] Section 3 of the Organic Act of August 24, 1912,[28] provides:

> That the Constitution of the United States, and all the laws thereof which are not locally inapplicable, shall have the same force and effect within the said Territory as elsewhere in the United States * * *.[29]

Second, the vacant, unoccupied and unappropriated land at the date of the cession became a part of the public domain of the United States.[30] Since 99 percent of Alaska consists of public lands,[31] the federal control over its property is a vital source of power.

Third, it is said that Congress may enact any legislation it deems proper for the benefit and protection of the natives of Alaska, because they are wards of the United States[32] in the sense that they are subject to the plenary power of Congress over Indian affairs.

It has been said that from the viewpoint of congressional power the question of the Indian or non-Indian origin of the natives is unimportant.[33] In view of the broad powers over territories and wards, this statement is accurate. However, where the congressional power is derived from a source wholly applicable to Indians such as the power to regulate commerce with Indian tribes,[34] the distinction between Indians and non-Indians must be borne in mind.[35]

This exercise of federal power over territories, public property, and wards has been judicially sustained in two cases. The first, the *Alaska Pacific Fisheries* case,[36] involved the right of the President to issue a proclamation without express statutory authority withdrawing from the public domain the waters adjacent to the Annette Islands and reserving the waters within 3,000 feet from the shore at mean low tide. The purpose of this reservation was to develop an Indian fishing industry.[37]

The Supreme Court of the United States enjoined the defendant corporation from maintaining a fish trap in the navigable waters within the territorial limit, holding that the creation of the reservation was a valid exercise of federal power, and that the reservation included the adjacent submerged land and deep waters supplying fisheries essential to the welfare of the Indians who might otherwise become a public charge.

The decision was based on the judicial conclusion that Congress intended to assist the Indians in their effort to become self-sustaining and civilized, and that Congress undoubtedly had the power to reserve waters, which were the property of the United States, since it protected the food supply of the Indians. In reaching this decision, the Court stated that it was influenced by the following considerations:

> * * * the circumstances in which the reservation was created, the power of Congress in the premises, the location and character of the islands, the situation and needs of the Indians and the object to be attained.[38] (P. 87.)

The Circuit Court of Appeals in a later case[39] involving the attempt of the Territory of Alaska to encroach upon the federal control of the Indians by levying an occupation tax on the output of a private salmon cannery on the Annette Island Reservation, operating under a lease executed by the Secretary of the Interior, held that the Territory of Alaska was not authorized to levy such a tax, on the ground that the lessee was an instrumentality of the Government to assist the Metlakahtla Indians to become self-supporting. The power of the Secretary of the Interior to execute the lease was also sustained.[40]

The exercise of federal power over other natives of Alaska has been similarly upheld. Thus, by virtue of his power to supervise the public business relating to Indians, the Secretary of the Interior may supervise a reservation created to enable the Department through the Bureau of Education to maintain a school, and may enter into a lease with a third party for the operation of a salmon cannery.[41]

Furthermore, even prior to the extension of the Wheeler-Howard Act[42] to Alaska, it was recognized that Congress possessed the power to create Indian reservations in Alaska.[43]

[25] Op. Sol., I. D. M.29147, May 6, 1937. See Chapter 5, sec. 1.

[26] *Steamer Coquitlam* v. *United States*, 163 U. S. 346, 352 (1896).

[27] See Chapter 5, sec. 5.

[28] C. 387, 37 Stat. 512.

[29] 54 I. D. 39, 46 (1932).

[30] *United States* v. *Berrigan*, 2 Alaska 442, 448 (1905).

[31] Alaska, Its Resources and Development, *op. cit.*, p. 143.

[32] *Alaska Pacific Fisheries* v. *United States*, 248 U. S. 78 (1918), affg. 240 Fed. 274 (C. C. A. 9, 1917); *Territory of Alaska* v. *Annette Island Packing Co.*, 289 Fed. 671 (C. C. A. 9, 1923); *United States* v. *Berrigan*, 2 Alaska 442 (1905); *United States* v. *Cadzow*, 5 Alaska 125 (1914); *Nagle* v. *United States*, 191 Fed. 141, 142 (C. C. A. 9, 1911); 49 L. D. 592 (1923); 50 L. D. 315 (1924); 51 L. D. 155 (1925); 52 L. D. 597 (1929); 53 I. D. 593 (1932); 54 I. D. 15 (1932); Op. Sol., I. D. M.29147, May 6, 1937. Sec. 6 discusses this subject.

[33] 54 I. D. 39 (1932); 53 I. D. 593, 595 (1932).

[34] U. S. Const., Art. I, sec. 8, cl. 3. See Chapter 5, sec. 3.

[35] For an example of the exercise of this power see Chapter 16.

[36] 240 Fed. 274 (C. C. A. 9, 1917), aff'd. 248 U. S. 78 (1918).

[37] The Proclamation of April 28, 1916, 39 Stat. 1777, creating the Annette Island Fishery Reserve provides:

> * * * the waters within three thousand feet from the shore lines at mean low tide of Annette Island, Ham Island, Walker Island, Lewis Island, Spire Island, Hemlock Island, and adjacent rocks and islets, * * * also the bays of said islands, rocks, and islets, are hereby reserved for the benefit of the Metlakahtlans and such other Alaskan natives as have joined them or may join them in residence on these islands, to be used by them under the general fisheries laws and regulations of the United States as administered by the Secretary of Commerce.

[38] The Court also approved the portion of the regulations, prescribed by the Secretary of the Interior in 1915, recognizing the Indians as the only persons to whom permits may be issued for erecting salmon traps at these islands. See 25 C. F. R. § 1.1–1.68.

[39] *Territory of Alaska* v. *Annette Island Packing Co.*, 289 Fed. 671 (C. C. A. 9, 1923), cert. den. 263 U. S. 708 (1923).

[40] Accord: 49 L. D. 592 (1923). See Op. Sol., I. D. M.28978, April 19, 1937, which discusses the Alaska Fisheries case. Also see *Sutter* v. *Heckman*, 1 Alaska 188, 192 (1901), aff'd. *Heckman* v. *Sutter*, 119 Fed. 83 (C. C. A. 9, 1902). The court said "* * * no one, other perhaps than the natives, can acquire any exclusive right, either in navigating said waters or fishing therein."

[41] *Alaska Pacific Fisheries* v. *United States*, 248 U. S. 78 (1918), aff'g. 240 Fed. 274 (C. C. A. 9, 1917); *Territory of Alaska* v. *Annette Island Packing Co.*, 289 Fed. 671 (C. C. A. 9, 1923); 49 L. D. 592 (1923), cited in 53 I. D. 593 (1932).

[42] For a discussion of the Wheeler-Howard Act and Alaska see sec. 9 *infra*.

[43] 18 Op. A. G. 557 (1887); 53 I. D. 593, 602 (1932); *Alaska Pacific Fisheries* v. *United States*, 248 U. S. 78 (1918), affg. 240 Fed. 274 (C. C. A. 9, 1917).

SECTION 5. CITIZENSHIP

The Treaty of Cession provided for the collective naturalization of the members of the civilized native tribes of Alaska. Congress impliedly consented to this contract which obligated it to incorporate the inhabitants, except uncivilized tribes, as citizens of the United States, by extending certain laws to the Territory and by passing the Organic Acts of 1884 and 1912.[44]

The difficulty of defining civilization made the legal status

[44] Act of May 17, 1884, 23 Stat. 24, providing for a partial civil government. Act of August 24, 1912, c. 387, 37 Stat. 512, providing for a civil government. See Spicer, *op. cit.*, pp. 24–36.

of the natives of Alaska a matter of much doubt and uncertainty. The Minook case [45] throws some light on the distinction between civilized and uncivilized tribes. In denying the application for citizenship of the son of a Russian father and an Eskimo mother, and the husband of a native woman, Judge Wickersham held that the applicant was not a Russian citizen, though he was born in Alaska in 1849, and, together with his parents, was a member of the Greek Church and a subject of Russia at the time of the cession. The court held that Minook was a citizen of the United States by virtue of the third article of the treaty with Russia, either as one of those inhabitants who accepted the benefits of the proffered naturalization, or as a member of an uncivilized native tribe who has voluntarily taken up his residence separate from any tribe of Indians and has adopted the habits of civilized life.[46]

In order to discover the intentions of the signatory nations, Judge Wickersham quoted and discussed portions of the charter of the Russian American Co. He also drew upon the science of ethnology to determine whether the tribe was civilized and quoted Prof. W. H. Dall [47] of the Smithsonian Institution, as to which natives were civilized. The next year he quoted with approval portions from this opinion and again used the same technique to prove that natives belonging to the Athapascan stock were uncivilized at the time of the cession and hence, as wards of the Government, were entitled to an injunction against the trespass of white men on their property.[48]

The General Allotment Act gave to two additional classes of Alaskan natives the status of citizenship: (1) Allottees, and (2) nonallottees who severed tribal relationship and adopted the habits of civilization.[49]

The Territorial Act of April 27, 1915,[50] provided a method whereby a nonallottee could secure a certificate of citizenship.[51] This procedure included proof of his general qualifications as a voter, his total abandonment of tribal customs, and his adoption of the culture of civilization.

This statute became obsolete with the passage of the Citizenship Act,[52] which included the Alaskan natives,[53] and was finally repealed in 1933.[54]

In the case of *United States* v. *Lynch*,[55] the court held that though the members of the Tlingit tribe would undoubtedly have been classed as uncivilized, under the provisions of Article III of the Treaty of Cession, they, together with other native Indian tribes of the United States, were collectively naturalized by the Citizenship Act. Consequently, proof of civilization is no longer a condition precedent to citizenship.

[45] *In re Minook*, 2 Alaska 200 (1904).

[46] *Ibid.*, pp. 219, 220.

[47] See fn. 7 *supra*.

[48] *United States* v. *Berrigan*, 2 Alaska 442 (1905).

[49] The case of *Nagle* v. *United States*, 191 Fed. 141 (C. C. A. 9, 1911), held that sec. 6 of the Act of February 8, 1887, 24 Stat. 388, 390, known as the General Allotment Act, in conferring citizenship on Indians who severed their tribal relation and adopted the habits and customs of civilized life, applied to the Territory of Alaska. Contra: *In re Incorporation of Haines Mission*, 3 Alaska, 588 (1908).

[50] C. 24, Laws of Alaska, 1915, p. 52, repealed by c. 34, Laws of Alaska, 1933, p. 73.

[51] For the effect of citizenship on land rights of the Alaskan natives, see sec. 8C, *infra*.

[52] Act of June 2, 1924, c. 233, 43 Stat. 253. For a discussion of citizenship see Chapter 8, sec. 2.

[53] 53 I. D. 593 (1932).

[54] C. 34, Laws of Alaska, 1933, p. 73.

[55] 7 Alaska 568 (1927).

SECTION 6. STATUS OF NATIVES

The legal position of the individual Alaskan natives has been generally assimilated to that of the Indians in the United States.[56] It is now substantially established that they occupy the same relation to the Federal Government as do the Indians residing in the United States; that they, their property, and their affairs are under the protection of the Federal Government; that Congress may enact such legislation as it deems fit for their benefit and protection; and that the laws of the United States with respect to the Indians resident within the boundaries of the United States proper are generally applicable to the Alaskan natives.[57]

For example, it has been administratively held that the general laws enacted by Congress empowering the Secretary of the Interior to probate the estates of deceased Indians are applicable to Alaskan natives.[58]

The placing of the Alaskan natives on the same footing as other American Indians was the culmination of a shifting policy which has been well described in an opinion of the Solicitor for the Department of the Interior:[59]

> In the beginning, and for a long time after the cession of this Territory Congress took no particular notice of these natives; has never undertaken to hamper their individual movements; confine them to a locality or reservation, or to place them under the immediate control of its officers, as has been the case with the American Indians; and no special provision was made for their support and education until comparatively recently. And in the earlier days it was repeatedly held by the courts and the Attorney General that these natives did not bear the same relation to our Government, in many respects, that was borne by the American Indians. (16 Ops. Atty. Gen., 141; 18 id., 139); *United States* v. *Ferueta Seveloff* (2 Sawyer U. S., 311); *Hugh Waters* v. *James B. Campbell* (4 Sawyer U. S., 121); *John Brady et al.* (19 L. D., 323).
>
> With the exception of the act of March 3, 1891 (26 Stat., 1095, 1101), which set apart the Annette Islands as a reservation for the use of the Metlakahtlans, a band of British Columbian natives who immigrated into Alaska in a body, and also except the authorization given to the Secretary of the Interior to make reservations for landing places for the canoes and boats of the natives, Congress has not created or directly authorized the creation of reservations of any other character for them.

[56] 49 L. D. 592 (1923); 53 I. D. 593 (1932).

Delegate A. J. Dimond, of Alaska, has said (83 Cong. Rec., pt. 9, pp. 179–180, 75th Cong., 3d sess. 1938):

> * * * special appropriations for the education and medical welfare of the natives of Alaska * * * can be based only upon the theory that the Government, and therefore Congress, does owe a special duty to the natives of Alaska. (P. 180.) * * * analogous to that owed by a guardian to his ward, a trustee to the beneficiary of the trust, or a father to his children. (P. 182.) * * * the Government * * * is bound in honor and good morals to enact suitable measures for their benefit and their economic welfare. (P. 180.)

[57] 52 L. D. 597 (1929); 53 I. D. 593 (1932); *Alaska Pacific Fisheries Case, supra*; *United States* v. *Berrigan*, 2 Alaska 442 (1905); *United States* v. *Cadzow*, 5 Alaska 125 (1914); *Territory of Alaska* v. *Annette Island Packing Co.*, 289 Fed. 671 (C. C. A. 9, 1923), cert. den. 263 U. S. 708 (1923).

[58] Op. Sol. I. D., M.27127, July 26, 1932, and *cf.* sec. 1919, Compiled Laws of Alaska, 1933, referring to ward Indians. Also see 54 I. D. 15 (1932), in which the Solicitor of the Department of the Interior ruled that although the provisions of the Act of June 25, 1910, 36 Stat. 855, as amended, which relates to the administration of the restricted property of deceased Indians, are applicable to Alaskan natives, a subordinate officer, such as an employee of the Reindeer Service, lacks the power to settle such estates.

[59] 49 L. D. 592, 594–595 (1923). This portion of the opinion was quoted with approval in 53 I. D. 593 (1932). Also see 54 I. D. 39 (1932). But *cf.* 19 L. D. 323, 324–325 (1894).

Later, however, Congress began to directly recognize these natives as being, to a very considerable extent at least, under our Government's guardianship and enacted laws which protected them in the possession of the lands they occupied; made provision for the allotment of lands to them in severalty, similar to those made to the American Indians; gave them special hunting, fishing and other particular privileges to enable them to support themselves, and supplied them with reindeer and instrutions as to their propagation. Congress has also supplied funds to give these natives medical and hospital treatment and finally made and is still making extensive appropriations to defray the expenses of both their education and *their support*.

Not only has Congress in this manner treated these natives as being wards of the Government but they have been repeatedly so recognized by the courts. See *Alaska Pacific Fisheries* v. *United States* (248 U. S., 78); *United States* v. *Berrigan et al.* (2 Alaska Reports, 442); *United States* v. *Cadzow et al.* (5 id., 125), and the unpublished decision of the District Court of Alaska, Division No. 1, in the case of *Territory of Alaska* v. *Annette Islands Packing Company et al.*, rendered June 15, 1922.

From this it will be seen that these natives are now unquestionably considered and treated as being under the guardianship and protection of the Federal Government, at least to such an extent as to bring them within the spirit, if not within the exact letter, of the laws relative to American Indians; and this conclusion is supported by the fact that in creating the territorial government of Alaska and vesting that territory with the powers of legislation and control over its internal affairs, including public schools, Congress expressly excluded from that legislation and control the schools maintained for the natives and declared that such schools should continue to remain under the control of the Secretary of the Interior.

An explanation of the reasons for this changing policy will be helpful in understanding the legal position of the Alaskan natives. The United States at first followed the example of Russia. From 1867 to 1884, when the Organic Act of 1884[60] made Alaska a civil and judicial district, this vast land had hardly the shadow of a civil government and was little more than a geographical subdivision of the United States.[61] Save for the occasional activity of the military authorities, the natives shifted for themselves.[62] This neglect is indicated by the failure of the United States to provide a regular agent for them, as in the case of Indians generally. The responsible duties of such an official were delegated to a military commandant.[63]

One of the few exceptions to the failure to enact legislation was the extension of prohibitory liquor laws to Alaska.[64] However, these laws were flagrantly violated and little attempt to enforce them was made during the first two decades of American rule.[65]

Although the purchase of Alaska on June 20, 1867, occurred while the United States still was making treaties with Indian tribes,[66] no attempt was made to enter into treaties with the natives. This was primarily because the reasons which were responsible for treaty making by the Federal Government with the American Indians[67] were not present in Alaska, where there was plenty of land and little danger of serious hostilities. Alaska was not considered Indian country[68] until 1873 when sections 20 and 21 of the Trade and Intercourse Act,[69] prohibiting liquor traffic in Indian country and with the Indians, were extended to include this territory. There was therefore no necessity for statutes and treaties extinguishing Indian title. The legal theory was adopted of considering these Indians subjects and not dependent or domestic nations having titles to be extinguished. Reservations were not established with the exception of the Annette Island Reservation and those for educational purposes.[70]

There was an absence of federal laws in most fields[71] and even the few which were considered applicable to Alaska were not enforced. Questions concerning the effect of tribal laws and customs were rarely raised. *In re Sah Quah*[72] was one of the few cases in which this issue was directly involved. In granting a writ of habeas corpus to the petitioner, a slave of a Tlingit Indian, the court said:

> What, then, is the legal *status* of Alaska Indians? Many of them have connected themselves with the mission churches, manifest a great interest in the education of their youth, and have adopted civilized habits of life. Their condition has been gradually changing until the attributes of their original sovereignty have been lost, and they are becoming more and more dependent upon and subject to the laws of the United States, and yet they are not citizens within the full meaning of that term. (P. 328–329.)
>
> * * * * *
>
> The United States has at no time recognized any tribal independence or relations among these Indians, has never treated with them in any capacity, but from every act of congress in relation to the people of this territory it is clearly inferable that they have been and now are regarded as dependent subjects, amenable to the penal laws of the United States, and subject to the jurisdiction of its courts. Upon a careful examination of the habits of these natives, of their modes of living, and their traditions, I am inclined to the opinion that their system is essentially patriarchal, and not tribal, as we understand that term in its application to other Indians. They are practically in a state of pupilage, and sustain a relation to the United States similar to that of a ward to a guardian, and have no such independence or supremacy as will permit them to sustain and enforce a system of forced servitude at variance with the fundamental laws of the United States. (P. 329.)

Nevertheless, tribal custom and law is recognized in some cases.[73] In the absence of federal legislation, a marriage between the natives belonging to the uncivilized tribes, such as the Athapascans, when entered into according to long-established

[60] Act of May 17, 1884, 23 Stat. 24. For a discussion of the history and interpretation of this act, see Nichols, Alaska (1924), pp. 71–113.

[61] Clark, *op. cit.*, pp. 81–97.

[62] They (the Alaska Indians) are too little known, and their relations to other inhabitants of that country and to our own government too little ascertained, to make it practicable to consider them.

Thayer, A People Without Law (1891), 68 Atlantic Monthly 540, 541. See also Hellenthal, The Alaskan Melodrama (1936), pp. 284, *et seq.*

[63] The Attorney General upheld the validity of such delegation by the President. 14 Op. A. G. 573 (1875). See also *In re Carr*, 5 Fed. Cas. No. 2432 (D. C. Ore. 1875), involving a false imprisonment by a military officer.

[64] For a discussion of these laws see Chapter 17, sec. 4.

[65] Wickersham, Old Yukon (1938), p. 123.

[66] Act of March 3, 1871, 16 Stat. 544, 566, declared it to be the policy of the United States not to treat further with the Indians as tribes. See Chapter 3, sec. 5.

[67] See Chapter 3, sec. 4.

[68] See Chapter 1, sec. 3, and Chapter 17, fn. 85.

[69] Act of June 30, 1834, 4 Stat. 729, 732–733; Act of March 3, 1873, 17 Stat. 510, 530.

[70] Because of the restriction of native activities which accompanied the reservation policy among the Indians of the continental United States, the natives of Alaska, with the exception of the transplanted colony of Metlakahtla, have steadfastly opposed the development of reservations in Alaska. This opposition was part of an insistent resistance to racial discrimination.

Alaska, Its Resources and Development, *op. cit.*, p. 10.

[71] A license to trade in Alaska is not required. See *Waters* v. *Campbell*, 29 Fed. Cas. No. 17264 (C. C. Ore. 1876); and see Chapter 16, sec. 2.

[72] 31 Fed. 327 (D. C. Alaska 1886); for a discussion of the power of the Federal Government over tribes see *Kie* v. *United States*, 27 Fed. 351 (C. C. Ore. 1886), modify'g *United States* v. *Kie*, 26 Fed. Cas. No. 15528a (D. C. Alaska 1885); *United States* v. *Seveloff*, 27 Fed. Cas. No. 16252 (D. C. Ore. 1872); *United States* v. *Lynch*, 7 Alaska 568 (1927).

[73] 54 I. D. 39 (1932).

customs, is valid, irrespective of the territorial laws regulating marriage among the inhabitants.[74]

The extension of the Wheeler-Howard Act[75] to Alaska has removed almost the last significant difference between the position of the American Indian and that of the Alaskan native.[76] The report of the Director of the Division of Territories and Island Possessions, Department of the Interior, for 1936 lists the "protection of the welfare of the native population," as the first of the "immediate considerations for the attainment of major ends." The director, Dr. Ernest Gruening, later Governor of Alaska, also wrote:

> The extension of the economic and social benefits of the Indian reorganization act to Alaska has paved the way for the security of approximately one-half of the present population of the Territory, whose stabilized future is not only an essential act of humanitarianism but also an important item of wholesome advance.[77]

[74] This is in accordance with the general rule. R. A. Brown, The Indian Problem and The Law (1930), 39 Yale L. J. 307, 315. Also see Chapter 7, sec. 5.

[75] Act of June 18, 1934, 48 Stat. 984; Act of May 1, 1936, c. 254, 49 Stat. 1250. These statutes are discussed in sec. 9 *infra*.

[76] In holding that sec. 23 of the Act of June 25, 1910, 36 Stat. 855, 861, regarding preference to purchase of Indian products applies to Alaskan natives, the Solicitor said:

> In considering the application to Alaskan natives of laws relating to Indians it is well to bear in mind the following point: The laws which relate specifically to Alaska normally define the terms "natives" or "Indians" and define them as including Indians, Eskimos, Aleuts and other aboriginal tribes. Illustrations of such laws are the Alaska Reorganization Act, the act penalizing the sale of liquor or firearms to Indians in Alaska (sec. 142, chap. 8, act of March 3, 1899, 30 Stat. 1253), and various acts appropriating funds for the education of the natives. However, in the case of the application to the natives of laws drafted to cover the Indians in the United States, it is apparent that the law itself will refer only to "Indians," and the general rule must be followed that the laws relating to Indians in the United States are applicable to the natives in Alaska in so far as they are suitable to the circumstances of the case. The outstanding example of such a law is the Indian Citizenship Act of June 2, 1924 (43 Stat. 253). Memo. Sol. I. D., June 5, 1940.

[77] Annual Report of the Secretary of Interior (1936), p. 30.

SECTION 7. EDUCATION [78]

From 1884 to March 16, 1931, the Bureau of Education,[79] rather than the Office of Indian Affairs, controlled native education and welfare work. Such service presents peculiarly difficult and important administrative problems.

The area of Alaska is about one-fifth the size of the United States. Many settlements are beyond the limits of transportation and regular mail service, and one-third of the natives live north of the Arctic Circle.[80] Villages are usually far apart and transportation is largely limited to boats for coastal travel, dog teams for interior travel, and aeroplanes. Even on the coast and rivers, boats are infrequent, and in the winter can be used only in the south.

Neither the federal control over education on reservations, nor the system of annuities for educational purposes, nor the boarding school program was carried into this Territory. The importation of reindeer, and instruction in herd management were integrated with the educational system for northern and western Alaska.[81] Vocational training was also established.[82]

Reservations have been created which are devoted to educational purposes,[83] and such diverse activities as native assistance on road building[84] and the leasing of canneries[85] have been justified as incidental to education.

Originally no differentiation was made between the education of the natives and the whites.[86] As a result of the Act of January 27, 1905,[87] a dual system of education was instituted; one part was mainly devoted to white children and the other to the children of the Natives.[88]

The interpretation of the term "civilization" as used in this statute was an issue in the case of *Davis* v. *Sitka School Board*.[89] In denying the petition for a writ of mandamus to require the school board to admit the plaintiff's children who were of mixed blood, the court took the view that civilization is achieved only when the natives have adopted the white man's way of life and associated with white men and women.[90]

[78] See Chapter 12, sec. 2. For a discussion of native education see 53 I. D. 593 (1932); also see Spicer, *op. cit.*, pp. 97–101; Alaska, Its Resources and Development, *op. cit.*, pp. 43–44; Anderson and Eells, *op. cit.*, pt. 2.

[79] Now known as the United States Office of Education. See Cook, Public Education in Alaska, Bull. No. 12 (1936), Office of Education, Department of Interior, pp. 20–54.

Commissioner of Indian Affairs Rhoads, in his annual report for 1931, wrote:

> The administrative change whereby responsibility for education in Alaska was transferred to the Office of Indian Affairs in March, 1931, is particularly important as an indication of a national unified policy for the education of various indigenous groups. More important than this, however, is the fact that the Alaskan education enterprise has been carried out in the past with a different philosophy and different practice. In contrast to the Indian Service, with its boarding schools, the Office of Education in Alaska until very recently confined its efforts to local community schools and a program of education that took into account in an amazing way the health and social and economic life of the native group. The Alaska program, therefore, represented the other extreme from the Indian policy in the States. * * * (P. 12.)

[80] Spicer, *op. cit.*, p. 98.

[81] Spicer, *op. cit.*, p. 98.

[82] Act of February 25, 1925, c. 320, 43 Stat. 978, authorizes the Secretary of the Interior to establish a system of vocational training for aboriginal native people of the Territory of Alaska, and to construct and maintain suitable school buildings. See U. S. Bureau of Education, Department of Interior, A Course of Study for United States Schools for Natives of Alaska (1926), particularly pp. 2–3.

[83] 53 I. D. 111 (1930).

[84] *United States* v. *Sitarangok*, 4 Alaska 667 (1913).

[85] *Alaska Pacific Fisheries* v. *United States*, 248 U. S. 78 (1918), aff'g, 240 Fed. 274 (C. C. A. 9, 1917); 49 L. D. 592 (1923).

[86] The Organic Act of 1884 (Act of May 17, 1884, sec. 13, 23 Stat. 24, 27), authorizes the Secretary of the Interior to provide for "the education of the children of school age in the Territory of Alaska, without reference to race * * *." This phrase was repeated in other appropriation acts, such as the Act of March 3, 1899, 30 Stat. 1074, 1101.

[87] 33 Stat. 616, 619, sec. 7:

> * * * schools for and among the Eskimos and Indians of Alaska shall be provided for by an annual appropriation, and the Eskimo and Indian children of Alaska shall have the same right to be admitted to any Indian boarding school as the Indian children in the States or Territories of the United States.

For a discussion of this statute see *Sing* v. *Sitka School Board*, 7 Alaska 616 (1927). The Act of August 24, 1912, c. 387, sec. 3, 37 Stat. 512, creating the Territory of Alaska, expressly reserves from the legislature any power to amend this statute and acts amendatory thereof.

[88] See Alaska, Its Resources and Development, *op. cit.*, pp. 43–44, and Anderson and Eells, *op. cit.*, pp. 202–204 for a discussion of segregation.

[89] 3 Alaska 481 (1908). The court laid down the following test of civilization:

> * * * as to whether or not the persons in question have turned aside from old associations, former habits of life, and easier modes of existence; in other words, have exchanged the old barbaric, uncivilized environment for one changed, new, and so different as to indicate an advanced and improved condition of mind, which desires and reaches out for something altogether distinct and unlike the old life. (P. 488.)
>
> Civilization * * * includes * * * more than a prosperous business, a trade, a house, white man's clothes, and membership in a church. (P. 491.)

The attitude of another court toward the native culture is brought out in the case of *In re Can-Ah-Couqua*, 29 Fed. 687 (D. C. Alaska 1887), involving the rights of a mother of a child attending a mission school. This case is discussed in Chapter 12, fn. 62.

[90] Considerable stress was placed on the fact that the playmates of the children were native and that the children joined in the hunting

The territorial legislature was first granted power over schools by the Act of March 3, 1917,[91] which empowered it "to establish and maintain schools for white and colored children and children of mixed blood who lead a civilized life * * *.[92] Pursuant to this act a writ of mandamus was granted[93] compelling the city of Ketchikan, Alaska, to admit to its schools attended by the whites a resident child of mixed blood who led a civilized life, although she could attend an Indian school in the city, and thereby make room for the attendance of nonresident white children. The court said:

> The legislative power of the territory of Alaska with regard to schools derived from this section makes no provision as to the segregation of races, nor does it refer to the race or color of the children to be provided for in the municipal schools, and such act must necessarily be construed in the light of the section quoted limiting the authority of the Legislature to provide schools for white and colored children and children of mixed blood. (P. 147.)

Only mission schools existed between 1867, the date of the purchase of Alaska, and 1884.[94] Thereafter, until 1900, annual federal appropriations, ranging from a few thousand dollars to $50,000 were made for the education of native and white children.[95] For the next 5 years education was supported by a license tax. Schools in incorporated towns were under local control, while the Secretary of the Interior continued to direct rural schools. Beginning with 1905, annual appropriations in increasing amounts were made enabling the Secretary of the Interior, in his discretion, to provide for the education and support of the natives of Alaska.[96] The territorial schools established in 1905 were supported by territorial and federal funds and served white children and "children of mixed blood who lead a civilized life."[97]

The Indian Service maintains schools in approximately 100 villages.[98] During the fiscal year 1933–1934, 4,338 native children were enrolled in the federal schools, 1,874 in the territorial schools, and approximately 1,000 in mission schools.[99]

By the Act of May 14, 1930,[100] the Secretary of the Interior was authorized to contract with school boards which maintained schools in certain cities and towns to educate children of nontaxpaying natives, including those of mixed native and white blood, to lease school buildings owned by the United States Government to such boards, and to pay such boards for services rendered an amount not in excess of the cost of operating a school for natives under present appropriations in such town.

Chapter 85, Laws of Alaska, 1935, authorized the Territorial Board of Administration of the Territory of Alaska to enter into a contract or contracts with the Secretary of the Interior for educational and welfare work among the Alaskan natives.[101]

The Act of May 31, 1938,[102] authorized the Secretary of the Interior to withdraw and permanently reserve small tracts of land not exceeding 640 acres each, of the public domain in Alaska for schools, hospitals, and other necessary purposes in administering the affairs of the natives.[103]

Congress has recognized that in many places the Alaska school service is the only federal agency in daily contact with the natives. The Act of March 3, 1909,[104] authorized the Attorney General to appoint as special peace officers employees of the educational service designated by the Secretary of the Interior. These officers were endowed with the ordinary authority of a policeman to arrest natives charged with the violation of any provision of the Criminal Code of Alaska or white men charged with the violation of any of its provisions to the detriment of any native of the Territory.[105]

and fishing expeditions of the native bands. Apparently the court did not recognise that hunting and fishing were recreations of social significance among the whites and a source of livelihood for some whites and many natives.

[91] C. 167, 39 Stat. 1131.

[92] The schools were under the general supervision of the Territorial Board of Education authorized by the Legislature of Alaska, Spicer, *op. cit.*, p. 99.

[93] *Jones* v. *Ellis*, 8 Alaska 146 (1929).

[94] Beatty, The Federal Government and the Education of Indians and Eskimos, Journal of Negro Education, vol. 7, No. 3 (July 1938), p. 271.

[95] The first statute, the Act of July 4, 1884, 23 Stat. 76, 91, appropriated $15,000. Some appropriation acts, during this period, authorized the Secretary of the Interior to use a specified sum from the general education appropriation "for the education of Indians in Alaska," e. g., Act of March 2, 1895, 28 Stat. 876, 904.

[96] Act of March 3, 1905, 33 Stat. 1156, 1188. See also Act of June 30, 1906, 34 Stat. 697, 729; Act of May 24, 1922, c. 199, 42 Stat. 552, 583. From 1884 to 1934 the United States has spent almost nine million dollars for native education and welfare. Anderson and Eells, *op. cit.* p. 227.

[97] Act of January 27, 1905, sec. 7, 33 Stat. 616, 619.

[98] Report of the Commissioner of Indian Affairs in Annual Report, Interior Department (1939), p. 25; Annual Report of the Governor of Alaska (1939), pp. 47–49.

[99] Information supplied by Alaska Section, Office of Indian Affairs, Department of the Interior. The present appropriation for native education exceeds $900,000 annually. Hearings before Subcommittee of House Committee on Appropriations, 76th Cong., 3d sess., on Interior Department Appropriation Bill for 1941, Pt. II, pp. 377 *et seq.*

[100] C. 273, 46 Stat. 279, 321.

[101] This statute was passed to secure the benefits of the Johnson-O'Malley Act of April 16, 1934, 48 Stat. 596. See Chapter 12, sec. 2A.

[102] C. 304, 52 Stat. 593.

[103] "This authority is proving of material assistance in the development of the Alaska program." Report of Commissioner of Indian Affairs in Annual Report, Interior Department (1938), p. 213.

[104] 35 Stat. 837.

[105] Then described as the District of Alaska.

SECTION 8. PROPERTY RIGHTS

Problems relating to the property rights of Alaskan natives arise out of their activities in hunting and fishing, their use and ownership of land and their ownership of reindeer. Land, except mineral land, is comparatively unimportant in the Alaskan economy.[106] This is due to the fact that the population is sparse (averaging one person per 10 square miles)[107] and that most of the land is unsuitable for agriculture.[108] Therefore, much greater attention must be paid to other forms of property.

A. FISHING AND HUNTING RIGHTS[109]

Fishing is the most important industry of Alaska[110] and from time immemorial has been the principal source of food for the

[106] Clark, *op. cit.* pp. 156–180; Anderson and Eells, *op cit.* pp. 195–202; Thomas, Economic Rehabilitation of the Indians of Alaska with Special Reference to Fishing, Trapping, and Reindeer, Indians of the United States (Indians at Work, April 1940, Supp.), p. 53; Brooks, The Future of Alaska, Annals of the Association of American Geographers (December 1925), p. 178; Department of the Interior, The Problem of Alaskan Development (April 1940).

[107] Fifteenth Census of the United States, Outlying Territories and Possessions (1932), p. 7.

[108] Although the gross area of the land and water of Alaska is 586,400 square miles, only about 65,000 square miles are suitable for agriculture, *ibid.*, p. 7, and see Alaska, Its Resources and Development, *op. cit.*, p. 114.

[109] Sec. 3 of the Organic Act of Alaska, Act of August 24, 1912, c. 387, 37 Stat. 512, provides that the authority granted to the legislature of the Territory shall not extend to general laws of the United States or to the "game, fish, and fur-seal laws and laws relating to fur-bearing animals of the United States applicable to Alaska * * *."

[110] Alaska, Its Resources and Development, *op. cit.*, pp. 17, 41, 55–74. See Pacific Fisherman Yearbook (1939). There were 30,331 persons

natives.[111] "Fur production is third in rating of all commodities in Alaska as to total value." [112] Fur trading was the primary occupation of the Russians who came to Alaska during the latter half of the eighteenth century.[113] Since that time the natives have depended on fur trading for a substantial part of their livelihood.[114]

The Bureau of Fisheries, formerly with the approval of the Secretary of Commerce, and now with that of the Secretary of the Interior, drafts fishing regulations specifying the areas in which traps may be operated, and their number.[115] A license for a trap must be obtained from the territorial treasurer, and to prevent obstructions to navigation, the Secretary of War must authorize the plans. In 1927 the number of traps in operation reached almost 800, but there has subsequently been a steady decline in this figure.

Judicial and legislative cognizance has been taken of the importance of fishing and hunting in the native economy. The Supreme Court of the United States in the *Alaska Pacific Fisheries* case [116] said:

> They (the Metlakatlans) were largely fishermen and hunters, accustomed to live from the returns of those vocations, and looked upon the islands as a suitable location for their colony, because the fishery adjacent to the shore would afford a primary means of subsistence and a promising opportunity for industrial and commercial development. (P. 88.)

In many conservation statutes the natives are given special privileges. The Act of July 1, 1870, [117] makes unlawful the killing of fur seals upon the Pribilof Islands except during the months of June, July, September, and October in each year, and the killing of such seals at any time by firearms. The privilege of killing young seals necessary for food and clothing and old seals necessary for clothing and boats by the natives for their own use was permitted, subject to regulations of the Secretary of the Treasury.[118]

The validity of section 6 of the Act of July 27, 1868,[119] which prohibits the killing of fur-bearing animals within the limits of the Territory, or in the waters thereof, and empowers the court, in its discretion, to confiscate vessels violating this statute, was upheld in *The James G. Swan* [120] case. The court sustained the libel for the forfeiture of a boat owned by an Indian of the Makah Tribe, despite the contention that such forfeiture violated a treaty with this tribe.[121]

The Act of April 6, 1894,[122] prohibits the killing of fur seals by United States citizens in waters of the Pacific Ocean surrounding the Pribilof Islands. It also prohibits the killing of fur seals from May 1 to July 31 in a circumscribed part of the Pacific Ocean, including Bering Sea.[123]

Section 6 permits Indians dwelling on the coasts of the United States to take fur-bearing seals in open, unpowered boats not manned by more than five persons using primitive methods, excluding firearms. Such fishing may not be done pursuant to a contract of employment.[124] The Act of December 29, 1897,[125] prohibiting the slaying of fur seals in the North Pacific Ocean contained a similar exemption.

Section 3 of the Act of April 21, 1910,[126] provides that whenever seals are taken, the natives of the Pribilof Islands shall be employed in such killing and shall receive fair compensation. Section 6 permits the natives of these islands to kill such young seals as may be necessary for their own clothing and the manufacture of boats for their own use, subject to regulations prescribed by the Secretary of Commerce. Section 9 authorizes this official to furnish food, clothing, shelter, and other necessities to the native inhabitants and to provide for their education.[127]

The Act of August 24, 1912,[128] gave effect to the Convention of July 7, 1911,[129] between the United States, Great Britain, Japan,

---

engaged in the fishing industry in Alaska in 1937. Salmon, which is the backbone of the Territory's economic structure, accounted for 75 percent of the total weight and 90 percent of the total value of its fisheries products in 1937, Annual Report of Secretary of Commerce (1938), p. 104. Also see reports on Alaska fishing and fur-seal industry, collected in Bulletin of the Bureau of Fisheries, vol. XLVII, No. 13 (1933).

[111] The salmon formed one of the important food supplies for the natives from prehistoric times. Bulletin of Bureau of Fisheries, vol. XLIV, Doc. No. 1041 (1928), p. 41. *Alaska Pacific Fisheries* v. *United States*, 248 U. S. 78 (1918), affg. 240 Fed. 274 (C. C. A. 9, 1917); *Territory of Alaska* v. *Annette Island Packing Co.*, 289 Fed. 671 (C. C. A. 9, 1923), cert. den. 263 U. S. 708 (1923). Also see *Heckman* v. *Sutter*, 119 Fed. 83 (C. C. A. 9, 1902), affg. *Sutter* v. *Heckman*, 1 Alaska 188 (1901), in which the court said: "The fact that at that time the Indians and other occupants of the country largely made their living by fishing was no doubt well known to the legislative branch of the government * * *." (P. 88.) See also *United States* v. *Lynch*, 8 Alaska 135 (1929), and *Johnson* v. *Pacific Coast S. S. Co.*, 2 Alaska 224 (1904).

The Commissioner of Indian Affairs in his Annual Report for 1937, p. 232, notes the destruction of the balanced primitive economy of the natives; instead of fishing and hunting for their own needs, they fish for, or work in the canneries. See also Hearings on Alaskan Fisheries, held pursuant to H. Res. 162, 76th Cong., 1st sess. (1939), pp. 118, 152, 444–449, 596. On employment of natives in canneries, see *ibid.*, p. 347.

[112] Alaska, Its Resources and Development, *op. cit.*, p. 107. Also see pp. 84–90, 108.

[113] XI, The Works of Charles Sumner (1875), p. 263; Alaska, Its Resources and Development, *op. cit.*, p. 84.

The fur-bearing aquatic mammals had been ruthlessly exploited during the period of Russian occupancy and were facing extinction at the time of the cession. Alaska, Its Resources and Development, pp. 55, 56.

Until the development of the gold industry, the fur resources were considered the most valuable by the Americans. It is, therefore, not surprising that, prior to 1884, legislation for the new territory was mainly confined to the protection of the seal fisheries and other fur interests of the District. Sen. Doc. No. 142, 59th Cong., 1st sess. (1905–1906), p. 7.

[114] Annual Report, Chief of Bureau of Biological Survey, Department of Agriculture (1937), p. 55.

[115] Act of June 6, 1924, 43 Stat. 464, c. 272, sec. 1, amended by Act of June 18, 1926, 44 Stat. 752. The preparation and enforcement of these regulations are difficult tasks, especially since the Bureau lacks sufficient funds for biological research and enforcement. See Hearings on Alaskan Fisheries, held pursuant to H. Res. 162, 76th Cong., 1st sess. (1939), pp. 46–47, 135–150, 394, 510.

[116] *Alaska Pacific Fisheries* v. *United States*, 248 U. S. 78 (1918), affg. 240 Fed. 274 (C. C. A. 9, 1917); also see *Johnson* v. *Pacific Coast S. S. Co.*, 2 Alaska 224 (1904); Act of May 14, 1898, sec. 10, 30 Stat. 409, 413.

[117] C. 189, 16 Stat. 180.

[118] The Act of April 22, 1874, 18 Stat. 33, authorized the Secretary of the Treasury to study the fur trade in Alaska and "the condition of the people or natives, especially those upon whom the successful prosecution of the fisheries and fur trade is dependent * * *." By Act of April 5, 1890, 26 Stat. 46, the Secretary was authorized to study the condition of the seal fisheries of Alaska. See Alaska, Its Resources and Development, *op. cit.*, p. 90.

[119] 15 Stat. 240, 241, R. S. § 1956.

[120] *United States* v. *James G. Swan*, 50 Fed. 108 (D. C. Wash. 1892).

[121] Treaty of January 31, 1855, 12 Stat. 939.

[122] Art. 1, 28 Stat. 52.

[123] *Ibid.*, Art. 2.

[124] The Makah Indians are subject to the prohibitions of this act save for the exception of sec. 6. 21 Op. A. G. 466 (1897).

[125] Sec. 6, 30 Stat. 226.

[126] C. 183, 36 Stat. 326.

[127] In this and subsequent acts, Congress has made appropriations for this purpose. More than 400 natives of these islands are largely dependent upon the United States for subsistence. Alaska, Its Resources and Development, *op. cit.*, p. 66.

[128] C. 373, 37 Stat. 499.

[129] 37 Stat. 1542. To terminate the gross economic waste which threatened to destroy all the herds of fur seals, the United States arranged a conference of interested nations known as the International Fur Seal Conference which convened from May 11 to July 7, 1911. This meeting adopted the Convention of July 7, 1911, 37 Stat. 1542, between the United States, Great Britain, Japan, and Russia. Ratification advised July 24, 1911. Ratified by the President November 24, 1911. Ratified by Great Britain August 25, 1911. Ratified by Japan November

and Russia by prohibiting citizens and subjects of the United States from killing fur seals, but by sections 3 and 11 natives of the islands were permitted to kill annually a sufficient number of male seals to provide food and clothing.

As early as 1902 Congress passed conservation legislation containing special exceptions for the natives of Alaska and the white residents. The Act of June 7, 1902,[130] as amended by the Act of May 11, 1908,[131] prohibits the wanton destruction of wild game animals or wild birds for the purpose of shipment from Alaska. It also provides that—

> Nothing in this Act shall * * * prevent the killing of any game animal or bird for food or clothing at any time by natives, or by miners or explorers, when in need of food; but the game animals or birds so killed during closed season shall not be shipped or sold.

Section 1 of the Act of June 14, 1906,[132] as amended by the Act of June 25, 1938,[133] without changing the provisions respecting natives, prohibits all companies, corporations, or associations not authorized to transact business under federal, state, or territorial laws and aliens without first papers, from catching or killing, except with rod, spear, or gaff, any fish of any kind or species in any of the waters of Alaska under the jurisdiction of the United States. By amendments to section 4 of the act for the protection and regulation of the fisheries of Alaska,[134] commercial fishing of any species of salmon except by hand, rod, spear, or gaff in any streams of Alaska or near their mouth, is unlawful excepting in the Karluk, Ugashik, Yukon, and Kuskokwim Rivers. The exception of the two last-named rivers is applicable only to native Indians and permanent white inhabitants taking king salmon under conditions prescribed by the Secretary of Commerce (now by the Secretary of the Interior).[135]

Article II, clause 3, of the treaty between the United States and Great Britain for the protection of migratory birds in the United States and Canada provides:[136]

> The close season on other migratory nongame birds shall continue throughout the year, except that Eskimos and Indians may take at any season auks, auklets, guillemots, murres, and puffins, and their eggs, for food and their skins for clothing, but the birds and eggs so taken shall not be sold or offered for sale.

Regulations prohibiting the killing of whales, walruses, and sea lions have special provisions regarding natives.[137] Many other rules regarding refuges and hunting of migratory birds grant special privileges to the natives.[138]

The Alaska Game Law[139] regulates the taking of food game during the regular season, but exempts the natives from the necessity of securing hunting and trapping or fur dealers licenses. Native cooperative or mission stores are also exempt.[140] And, subject to regulations of the Secretary of the Interior regarding animals whose extinction is imminent, the law permits them to take game during the closed season when in absolute need of food and other game is not available.[141] Section 3 empowers the Secretary of Agriculture, now Secretary of the Interior, to safeguard the livelihood of the natives and conserve the fur animals requiring nonresident trappers to reside 3 years in the territory instead of one, before becoming eligible for resident trapping license.

B. REINDEER OWNERSHIP

Reindeer constitute one of the most valuable assets of the natives, supplying them with food and clothing and acting as

6, 1911. Ratified by Russia October 22, 1911. Ratifications exchanged December 12, 1911. Proclaimed December 14, 1911. A treaty between the United States and Great Britain, concluded February 7, 1911, 37 Stat. 1538, providing for the preservation and protection of fur seals, became effective on December 14, 1911, the date of the proclamation of the treaty between the United States, Great Britain, Japan, and Russia.

[130] 32 Stat. 327.

[131] 35 Stat. 102. Sec. 10 of the Alaska Game Law, Act of January 13, 1925, 43 Stat. 739, amended Act of February 14, 1931, 46 Stat. 1111, and Act of June 25, 1938, 52 Stat. 1169, empowers the Secretary of Agriculture to make regulations for taking game animals, etc., upon consultation with the Alaska Game Commission, but except as provided such regulations shall not prohibit

> * * * any Indian or Eskimo, prospector, or traveler to take animals or birds during the closed season when he is in absolute need of food and other food is not available, but the shipment or sale of any animals or birds or parts thereof so taken shall not be permitted, except that the hides of animals so taken may be sold within the Territory * * *.

[132] 34 Stat. 263.

[133] 52 Stat. 1174.

[134] Act of June 26, 1906, 34 Stat. 478, amended by Act of June 6, 1924, c. 272, 43 Stat. 464, and Act of April 16, 1934, 48 Stat. 594.

[135] Pursuant to the Reorganization Act of April 3, 1939, 53 Stat. 561, Reorganization Plan No. 2 transmitted May 9, 1939, 53 Stat. 1431, and Public Resolution No. 20, 76th Cong., 1st sess., approved June 7, 1939, the Bureau of Fisheries was transferred from the Department of Commerce to the Department of the Interior, effective July 1, 1939. On the same date, the Bureau of Biological Survey was transferred to the Interior Department from the Department of Agriculture. By Plan No. 3, April 2, 1940, the two Bureaus were consolidated under the name Fish and Wildlife Service, H. Doc. No. 681, 76th Cong., 3d sess.

[136] 39 Stat. 1702, signed August 16, 1916; ratification advised by the Senate August 29, ratified by the President September 1, and by Great Britain October 20; ratifications exchanged December 7 and proclaimed December 8, 1926.

[137] Alaska, Its Resources and Development, *op. cit.*, p. 67; Department of Commerce Circular No. 286, Ninth Edition, June 29, 1939, pp. 1 and 3; amended Act of February 14, 1931, 46 Stat. 1111, and Act of June 25, 1938, 52 Stat. 1169.

[138] 50 C. F. R. 92.4. See Act of January 13, 1925, 43 Stat. 739, sec. 11, which provides for exemption for natives attesting that they possess one-half or more of Indian or Eskimo blood, from the resident hunting and trapping license. Bureau of Biological Survey, Regulations for the Aleutian Islands Reservation, Alaska (1939), Regulation 7, provides—

> * * * in reassigning islands for fur and fox farming and other uses, primary consideration shall be given to the welfare of native villages and communities of the Aleutian Chain. Permits involving a native or native interest shall be issued or reissued only for the benefit of the community or village of which he is a member.

For exemption of native residents from requirement of permit to capture certain game, see Bureau of Biological Survey Regulations for the Administration of the Aleutian Islands Reservation, Alaska (1939), Regulation 8. Bureau of Biological Survey, Department of the Interior Wildlife Circular 1 (1939), Regulations Relating to Migratory Birds and Certain Game Mammals, Regulation 7 provides:

> In Alaska, Eskimos and Indians may take, in any manner and at any time, and may possess and transport, auks, auklets, guillemots, murres, and puffins and their eggs and skins for use of themselves and their immediate families for food and clothing.

And see 50 C. F. R. 91.3.

Also see Cameron, The Bureau of Biological Survey (1929), p. 103.

[139] Act of January 13, 1925, 43 Stat. 739, amended by Act of February 14, 1931, 46 Stat. 1111, and Act of June 25, 1938, 52 Stat. 1169. For a list of the laws protecting wildlife in Alaska and regulations of the Alaska Game Commission, Juneau, Alaska, see circulars issued by this Commission. For history of Alaskan game legislation, see Cameron, The Bureau of Biological Survey (1929), pp. 110–124. On work of Alaska Game Commission see Annual Report of Governor of Alaska (1939), pp. 29–30.

[140] Act of January 13, 1925, c. 75, sec. 11H, 43 Stat. 739, 745, amended Act of February 14, 1931, c. 185, sec. 10, 46 Stat. 1111, 1113, and Act of June 25, 1938, sec. 5, 52 Stat. 1169, 1171–1172. The Consolidated Purchasing and Shipping Unit, Division of Territories and Island Possessions, Department of the Interior, acts as agent for the native cooperative stores, buying their supplies, and selling, for their benefit, such items as reindeer meat and hides, furs, and ivories. The purchasing procedure is similar to that used by it in procuring supplies for governmental agencies.

[141] A resident citizen or Alaskan native must obtain a registered guide license when acting as guide for a nonresident in any section of the Territory where the regulations of the Alaska Game Law and Game Commission require nonresidents to employ guides. Compiled Laws of Alaska, 1933, sec. 51D. See Act of January 13, 1925, sec. 11D, 43 Stat. 739, 744, 745.

633058—45——28

beasts of burden[142] The animals were first introduced into Alaska from Siberia from 1891 to 1902 by Dr Sheldon Jackson, the United States General Agent in Alaska[143] The original purpose of importation was to augment the dwindling source of native food supply consisting of game and fish, which had been seriously depleted by the whites The total importation by 1902, when shipments ceased, was about 1,280 head, and by 1938 the original stock expanded into a reindeer population estimated at 600,000 head[144]

The Federal Government, in recent years, has conducted numerous experiments on the cross-breeding of reindeer and native caribou,[145] on the control of predatory enemies, and on reindeer grazing[146]

The Federal Government has passed many statutes to protect the natives against food shortage due to periodic depletion of game or sea food and to encourage the raising of reindeer for their own subsistence and eventually for sale on the market[147]

The Bureau of Indian Affairs[148] gives instructions to the natives and distributes reindeer on terms which enable them eventually to acquire a qualified ownership The Government, however, retains a reversionary ownership so that an act of the territorial legislature imposing a tax upon each reindeer killed for market was held inapplicable to reindeer killed for market by natives of Alaska[149]

It has been administratively held[150] that Congress had conferred upon the Secretary of the Interior the power to make regulations and impose restrictions upon the disposition of reindeer transferred to the natives by the Government, and these regulations may be enforced by suit to recover the animal illegally transferred or its value

Despite the safeguards created by statute and administrative rules, by 1920 about a quarter of all the reindeer in Alaska was owned by whites[151]

The most important law relating to reindeer is the Act of September 1, 1937,[152] which is designed to establish for the natives of Alaska a self-sustaining economy by acquiring for them the whole reindeer business, and to develop native activity in all branches of the industry The Secretary of the Interior is empowered to acquire by purchase or other lawful means, including condemnation, "reindeer, reindeer-range equipment, abattoirs, cold-storage plants, warehouses, and other property, real or personal, the acquisition of which he determines to be necessary to the effectuation of the purposes of this Act" (sec 2), and to make distribution thereof to the natives or to their organizations[153] under such conditions as he may prescribe (sec 8) He is also

---

[142] Supplement No 9 to the Public Health Reports, December 12, 1913, p. 3 Alaska, Its Resources and Development, *op cit*, p 124 "The importance of the reindeer industry to the social and economic welfare of these native people can scarcely be overemphasized" Also see *ibid* p 41, Spicer, *op cit*, pp 98–99

The District Court considered the importance of the reindeer to the natives in the construction of the Act of April 27, 1904, 33 Stat 391, 392, 393, which provided that each road overseer in Alaska shall require all male persons between the ages of 18 and 50 to work on the public roads for 2 days or to be subject to a road tax In the discretion of the overseer, the tax could be performed by the man with a team of dogs, horses, or "a reindeer team of not less than two reindeer and sleigh or cart" In holding that an Eskimo was subject to this duty the court said that the legislative intent to include the Eskimo was shown by the provision concerning reindeer *United States* v *Sitarangok*, 4 Alaska 667 (1913) Also see Annual Report of the Secretary of Interior (1937), p 311, Annual Report of the Governor of Alaska (1939), p 51

[143] "The wild reindeer were an important part of the Eskimo food supply before the coming of whites but * * * the introduction of firearms quickly decimated them, rendering the Eskimos almost destitute" Anderson and Eells, Alaska Natives, *op cit*, p 195. Also see Cameron, The Bureau of Biological Survey (1929), pp 117–118 and the annual reports of the United States Bureau of Education, 1891–1931

[144] Alaska, Its Resources and Development, *op cit*, p 122 The Fifteenth Census of the United States, Outlying Territories and Possessions (1932), p 30, contains an estimate of 712,500 reindeer as of 1930 No longer, as in the past, in danger of starvation, some of the Eskimos have gained a livelihood by raising reindeer. Alaska, Its Resources and Development, *op cit*, p 41 Although it has been estimated that the Territory was capable of grazing between three and four million animals (Estimate of Bureau of Biological Survey The Bureau of Education estimated ten million Cameron, *op cit*, p 117), the predatory animals like wolves and coyotes have in recent years killed many reindeer, especially on the Arctic Coast This menace increased because the reindeer, formerly herded by attendants, have been allowed in recent years to roam, and are corralled only at certain seasons By this change in herd management the reindeer scatter widely over the ranges, and increasing numbers of wolves and coyotes have seriously menaced the industry The territorial legislature, by special bounty appropriations, has cooperated with the Reindeer Service, the Forest Service, Office of Indian Affairs, the Alaska Game Commission, and the Bureau of Biological Survey, which, since 1937, has resumed its work in investigating and reducing depredations of predatory animals (Report of the Chief of the Bureau of Biological Survey (1937), pp 56, 59–60 *Ibid* (1938), p 68) Despite those efforts toward predatory control, a recent survey indicated that coyotes and wolves are increasing, and that their depredations on reindeer herds are becoming more serious (*Ibid* (1939), p 67)

[145] Report of Chief of the Bureau of Biological Survey (1937), p 51

[146] Reindeer in Alaska, Department of Agriculture Bull, No 1089 (1922), and Progress of Reindeer Grazing Investigations in Alaska, Bull, No 1423 (1926) Also see Cameron, *op cit* (1929), pp 118–119, 133, 134, 156–157

[147] 51 L D 155, 157 (1925), see Act of March 4, 1907, 34 Stat. 1295, 1338; Act of May 24, 1922, 42 Stat 552, 584; Act of January 24, 1923, 42 Stat. 1174, 1205; Act of June 5, 1924, 43 Stat. 390, 427; Act of March 3, 1925, c 462, 43 Stat 1141, 1181; Act of January 12, 1927, 44 Stat 934, 968 Also see *United States* v *Sitarangok*, 4 Alaska 667 (1913); 53 I D 71 (1930); 54 I D 13 (1932) Outside capital gradually established a commercial reindeer business Alaska, Its Resources and Development, *op cit*, p 123 In the Report of the Governor of Alaska for 1925, p 65, it was estimated that of the 200,000 reindeer in Alaska, two-thirds belonged to the natives In the 1938 Report, p 46, it was estimated that of the 544,000 reindeer, 67 percent were owned by the natives

The Act of March 4, 1921, 41 Stat 1367, 1400, authorizes the Commissioner of Education to sell male reindeer and invest the proceeds in the purchase of female reindeer for distribution by him among the natives who had not been supplied with them.

[148] In 1929 the supervision of the reindeer was turned over to the Governor, but on July 1, 1937, the reindeer service was transferred from his supervision to the Office of Indian Affairs, Governor's Report for 1938, p 46 Direct supervision of herds and the business of the native cooperative stores had been handled by federal teachers, and hence full responsibility for the reindeer service was placed under the Education Division of the Indian Office Annual Report of the Secretary of the Interior, 1937, p 232

[149] 51 L D 156, 157–158 (1925)

The following discussion by the Solicitor of the regulations gives an idea of the administrative system:

> As has already been intimated, the absolute ownership of all reindeer in Alaska was in the Government originally, and such interests in them as are held by the natives grow out of contractual relations between the individual natives and the United States based on regulations issued for that purpose By these regulations the natives who hold reindeer are divided into two classes, one known as "apprentices," to whom a stated number of reindeer are issued by the Government from its herds, and the other as "herders" The regulations provided that the reindeer issued to these natives shall revert to the Government in the case of the death of either an apprentice or a herder without heirs, or with heirs who are not competent or do not manifest a desire to take charge of the herd, or in case of an apprentice who abandons his herd, or where a herder becomes intemperate and fails to reform within one year, or continuously neglects his herd, and the members of his family are not competent to control the herd and fail to provide a competent herder
>
> Each apprentice and herder is required to enter into a contract with the Government, of which the regulations mentioned are made a part, and in which there are other stipulations calling for the reversion of the herd to the Government under certain contingencies

[150] Op Sol I D, M 20690, September 16, 1931.

[151] Cameron *op. cit*, pp. 117–118

[152] 50 Stat 900 See Annual Report of Secretary of Interior (1937) pp 256–7

[153] Alaska, Its Resources and Development, *op. cit*, p. 123:

> A survey by that Department (Department of the Interior) in 1933 showed 78 native reindeer associations with 5,878 members, owning herds varying in size from a few hundred to many thousand head. Less than 20 of these herds were owned by other than natives.

authorized to issue rules and regulations to prevent the transfer or devise of reindeer to non-natives (sec 10), and regulate the ranging of reindeer on public lands (sec 14) [154] Criminal sanctions are provided for violations of this statute (secs 10 and 14), and $2,000,000 is authorized to be appropriated for expenditure by the Secretary of the Interior in carrying out the provisions of this act (sec 16) [155] By the Acts of May 9, 1938,[156] and June 25, 1938,[157] a total of $50,000 was appropriated for a survey and appraisal of the property and reindeer authorized to be acquired for the natives This study has been made under the supervision of a congressional committee authorized by the Act of May 9, 1938, which recommended to Congress that funds be made available to carry out the purposes of the Reindeer Act [158] By the Third Deficiency Appropriation Act, fiscal year 1939,[159] $720,000 was appropriated for the purchase of reindeer, equipment, abattoirs, corrals, etc, owned by non-natives and $75,000 was appropriated for administrative expenses Payments for reindeer are limited to an average of $4 per head [160]

C LANDS

Congress and administrative authorities have consistently recognized and respected the rights of the natives of Alaska in the land occupied by them [161] The rights of the natives are in many respects the same as those generally enjoyed by the Indians residing in the United States, viz the right of use and occupancy, with the fee in the United States [162]

Article III of the Treaty of Cession [163] provides that the members of the civilized native tribes shall be protected in the free enjoyment of their property

Section 8 [164] of the Act of May 17, 1884,[165] establishing a civil government in Alaska and extending to it the laws of the United States relating to mining claims is the first legislation which recognizes the rights of Alaska Indians to the possession of lands in their actual use and occupancy [166] In interpreting this provision, the court in *Heckman* v *Sutter*, said:

> The prohibition contained in the act of 1884 against the disturbance of the use or possession of any Indian or other person of any land in Alaska claimed by them is sufficiently general and comprehensive to include tide lands as well as lands above high-water mark Nor is it surprising that congress, in first dealing with the then sparsely settled country, was disposed to protect its few inhabitants in the possession of lands, of whatever character, by means of which they eked out their hard and precarious existence The fact that at that time the Indians and other occupants of the country largely made their living by fishing was no doubt well known to the legislative branch of the government, as well as the fact that that business, if conducted on any substantial scale, necessitated the use of parts of the tide flats in the putting out and hauling in of the necessary seines Congress saw proper to protect by its act of 1884 the possession and use by these Indians and other persons of any and all land in Alaska against intrusion by third persons, and so far has never deemed it wise to otherwise provide (Pp 88–89)

A subsequent judicial decision [167] also stresses the importance of interpreting the statute in the light of the communal habits of the natives

> It is well known that the native Indians of this country by their peculiar habits live in villages here and there, in some of which they remain most of the year and in others during certain summer months, that while their habits are somewhat migratory, they have well-settled places of abode, and these usually are not abandoned, though they may vacate them for a few months at a time The history of the habits of these people is well understood (P 239)
>
> * * * * *
>
> It is believed that the language of this act does not refer to lands held by Indians in severalty, but as to holdings by them collectively in their villages and such places as were occupied by them, that their methods of life were well understood by the lawmaking power, and that they were understood to occupy lands in common either in villages where they lived, or for fishing, hunting, and like purposes
>
> No doubt I think exists as to the rights of those Indians who had occupied some particular tract of land solely and exclusively by himself, and had actually occupied the same continuously before and at the time and since the passage of the act of May 17, 1884 He could maintain his possessory right to this property by virtue of this act, and the rights of the native might and should have protection under such circumstances But it is evident to the court that the native Indians who occupied the land in dispute, if they occupied it exclusively and continuously, if they were in the actual undisputed possession thereof at the time the act of 1884 went into effect, were occupying it as a village, where a number had settled, and were there as common occupants, and not as individual claimants to any particular portion of the same If they occupied the same exclusively as a village or otherwise, their right to the same must be protected, if protected at all, under section 8, above referred to If the Congress of the United States have made no provision for this class of residents acquiring title to lands since the act of 1884, then they may not obtain title [168] (Pp. 239–240)

---

[154] Of the estimated 115,000 square miles of grazing land in Alaska, 200,000 square miles are considered suitable only for reindeer grazing Alaska, Its Resources and Development, *op cit*, pp 123, 126

[155] *Ibid*

[156] 52 Stat 291, 313

[157] 52 Stat 1114, 1132

[158] Hearings before the Subcommittee of the House Committee on Appropriations, 76th *Cong*, 1st session on the Interior Department Appropriation bill for 1940, pt II, pp 537 *et seq* Also see hearings before same committee on the bill for 1941, pt II, pp 463, *et seq*

[159] Act of August 9, 1939, 53 Stat 1301, 1315 Act of May 10 1939, 53 Stat 685, 708, segregated $3,000 out of the $75,000 appropriation for reindeer service, for the purchase and distribution of reindeer

[160] This limitation does not apply to the purchase of reindeer located on Nunivak Island *Act of August 9, 1939*, 53 Stat 1301, 1315

[161] *United States* v *Berrigan* 2 Alaska 442, 448 (1905), 13 L D 120 (1891), 23 L D 335 (1896), 26 L D 517 (1898), 28 L D 427 (1899), 37 L D 334 (1908), 50 L D 315 (1924), 52 L D 397 (1928), 53 I D 194 (1930), 53 I D 593 (1932)

The following acts of Congress contain provisions protecting the Alaskan natives in the use and occupancy of land occupied by them at the time

> Act of May 17 1884, 23 Stat 24 26, Act of March 3, 1891, 26 Stat 1095, 1100, Act of June 6, 1900 31 Stat 321, 330 The Act of June 19, 1935, 49 Stat 388 authorizes the Tlinget and Haida Indians of Alaska to sue the United States to determine property claims

For a discussion of the power of Congress over land, see sec 1, *supra* and Chapter 5, sec 5

[162] 50 L D 315 (1924)

[163] 15 Stat 539, 542 (1867) The full text of this provision is set forth in section 8 of this chapter

[164] This section provides in part

> That the Indians or other persons in said district shall not be disturbed in the possession of any lands actually in their use or occupation or now claimed by them but the terms under which such persons may acquire title to such lands is reserved for future legislation by Congress * * *

Section 12 empowers the Secretary of the Interior to select two officers, who together with the Governor shall constitute a Commission to examine and report on the condition of the Indians, "what lands, if any, should be reserved for their use," etc

[165] 23 Stat 24

[166] *Heckman* v *Sutter*, 119 Fed 83 (C C A 9, 1902), aff'g *Sutter* v *Heckman*, 1 Alaska 188 (1901), *United States* v *Berrigan*, 2 Alaska 442 (1905), 37 L D 334 (1908), 49 L D 592 (1923)

[167] *Johnson* v *Pacific Coast S S Co*, 2 Alaska 224 (1904)

[168] *Cf* the following excerpt from an administrative holding, 37 L D 334, 336–337 (1908)

> Congress had a purpose in withholding from these Indians the title to their possessions, especially without restraint upon alienation It protects them in their possessions under the legal title held by the United States by declaring in the act of May 17, 1884 that they shall not be disturbed in the possession of any lands

This act protects land held by Indians and other persons in Alaska at the time of its passage and not lands subsequently acquired,[169] nor land occupied within a public reservation.[170]

The Act of March 3, 1891,[171] which extends the Homestead Law to Alaska and provides for the acquisition by an individual group or association of 160 acres of land for trade or manufacturing purposes, expressly excepts "any lands * * * to which the natives of Alaska have prior rights by virtue of actual occupation * * *." The possessory rights of the natives cannot be infringed by the granting of townsites.[172]

Section 1 of the Act of May 25, 1926,[173] authorizes the townsite trustee to issue a restricted deed to an Alaskan native for a tract in a townsite occupied and set apart for him. Section 3 provides that whenever the Secretary of the Interior shall find nonmineral public lands to be claimed and occupied by natives, as a town or village, he may issue a patent therefor to a trustee who shall convey by restricted deed such land to the individual native, exclusive of that embraced in streets or alleys.

The determination of persons eligible to receive patents under this act was delegated to the Department of the Interior, which has frequently changed its interpretation of the natives eligible to acquire title to the public domain. Regulations[174] were promulgated providing that the act applied only to natives who had not secured certificates of citizenship under the Territorial Law.[175] Although the wisdom of permitting the issuance of unrestricted deeds to natives, solely because of their citizenship was questioned,[176] such regulations were authorized by law.[177]

Though the statute provided that all of the deeds should contain restrictions on alienation, levy, sale, and encumbrance, the townsite trustees exercised discretion as to whether natives should receive restricted or unrestricted deeds, and they reached an understanding with the General Land Office that natives leading a civilized life should be treated in all respects as white citizens, but that the lands possessed by other Indians or natives should not be assessed nor conveyed but should be set apart for them as Indian possessions.[178]

Section 10 of the Act of May 14, 1898,[179] extending the homestead laws of the United States to Alaska, authorizes the Secretary of the Interior to reserve for the use of the natives of Alaska,

> suitable tracts of land along the water front of any stream, inlet, bay, or sea shore for landing places for canoes and other craft used by such natives * * *.

Title to such reserved land cannot be acquired by any individual or group of individuals, even with Indian consent.[180]

In the case of *United States* v. *Lynch*,[181] it was held that an order of the Secretary of the Interior reserving certain tidelands for a landing place for the boats of the natives did not reserve any land for any particular native and that the United States was the proper party to sue in an action of trespass. The court stressed the communal nature of the life and occupation of the Indians as a guide to congressional intention:

> There has been no legislation by Congress particularly appertaining to the lands occupied by the Indians of Alaska on May 7, 1884. It is true that there is a provision for the Indians of the United States to enter lands under the Homestead Act. 23 Stat. 96 (43 U. S. C. A. § 190). This act is also applicable to the Indians of Alaska who may enter lands under the Homestead Act, but the entry of lands under the Homestead Act is necessarily restricted to lands above the line of ordinary high-water mark. There is no specific provision of legislation relative to the acquisition of title to public lands by Indians occupying them on May 17, 1884, that I am aware of.[182] (P. 573.)

Section 27 of the Act of June 6, 1900,[183] establishing a civil government for Alaska, provides that—

> The Indians * * * shall not be disturbed in the possession of any lands now actually in their use or occupation, * * *.

The case of *United States* v. *Berrigan*[184] held that this statute not only prohibits an entry, under the land laws, upon land occupied by the natives but also forbids any other action which will disturb their possession and renders void any attempt to dispossess them by contract. The court also held that the United States, and not an individual Indian, was the proper party to sue out a mandatory injunction against trespass on Indian land.[185]

Under the Act of May 17, 1906,[186] the Secretary of the Interior may allot nonmineral land not exceeding 160 acres to any native who is the head of a family or who is 21 years of age. It also provides that such allotment shall be deemed the homestead of the allottee and his heirs forever and shall be inalienable and nontaxable until Congress provides otherwise.

Title remains in the United States,[187] and moneys received from trespass on timber on such allotted land is not paid to the allottee, but must be deposited in the public funds of the United States.[188]

After the approval of an allotment, the allottee's rights are

---

> actually in their actual use or occupation, or claimed by them at the date of that act.
>
> Such recognition by Congress of a right of occupancy and possession prevents the acquisition of title to such lands without legislative authority, and while the title remains in the Government the Indians' right to occupancy cannot be impaired nor can the land be assessed for taxes or charged or burdened with any obligation or incumbrance that could not be lawfully imposed upon public lands of the United States or other lands to which it holds the title. It was evidently contemplated by the act that these Indians should enjoy every right and privilege of a land owner except the right to encumber the land or to convey title thereto.

[169] *Heckman* v. *Sutter*, 119 Fed. 83 (C. C. A. 9, 1902), affg. *Sutter* v. *Heckman*, 1 Alaska 188 (1901); *Columbia Canning Co.* v. *Hampton*, 161 Fed. 60 (C. C. A. 9, 1908); 13 L. D. 120 (1891); 37 L. D. 334 (1908).

[170] 26 L. D. 104 (1898).

[171] 26 Stat. 1095, 1100. Discussed in Memo. Acting Sol. I. D., February 17, 1939.

[172] 28 L. D. 427 (1899); 28 L. D. 535 (1899). The Department of the Interior has refused to approve townsites which would interfere with the native use of water for domestic purposes, 24 L. D. 312 (1897); or which would interfere with the native use of a right-of-way, 26 L. D. 512 (1898).

[173] 44 Stat. 629.

[174] 50 L. D. 27, 46 (1923).

[175] Memo. Acting Sol. I. D., February 17, 1939.

[176] *Ibid.* For a discussion of citizenship, see sec. 5, *supra.*

[177] 50 L. D. 27, 46 (1923); 51 L. D. 501 (1926).

[178] Memo. Acting Sol. I. D., February 17, 1939.

[179] 30 Stat. 409, 413.

[180] 50 L. D. 315 (1924); 48 L. D. 362 (1921); 52 L. D. 597 (1929), modified by 53 I. D. 194 (1930).

[181] 7 Alaska 568 (1927).

[182] An administrative holding, 50 L. D. 315, 317–318 (1924), interpreting this provision, states:

> * * * there is no authority under existing law by which these lands can be sold. * * * As previously shown, until Congress grants some greater title, the right of the natives in Alaska is simply one of use and occupancy. Nor does the reservation of a particular area for their benefit result in placing actual title in the Indians. * * * the tide or other lands occupied by or reserved for the Indians at Ketchikan, Alaska, cannot be disposed of under existing law but that the power rests with Congress, by statute, with or without the consent of the Indians, to provide for the ultimate disposal of those lands.

See 44 L. D. 441 (1915), for a discussion of the riparian rights of the natives.

[183] 31 Stat. 321, 330.

[184] 2 Alaska 442 (1905). Accord: *United States* v. *Cadzow*, 5 Alaska 125 (1914).

[185] Also see *United States* v. *Cadzow*, 5 Alaska 125 (1914).

[186] C. 2469, 34 Stat. 197. Only a small area is held by beneficiaries under this act. Land Use in Alaska, Preliminary Report, Advisory Committee on Land Use and Subcommittees to Alaska Planning Council (1938), p. 50.

[187] See 50 L. D. 315 (1924).

[188] 44 L. D. 113 (1915). The trespass occurred prior to the approval of the allotment.

not defeated by a subsequent reservation by Executive order of a tract of land, which includes the allotment.[189]

In the words of a recent administrative holding:[190]

> That Congress did not intend that an allottee's right should be less than a "vested right," or be subject to extinction at the pleasure of the Executive branch of the Government, is very clearly shown by the fact that it went further in the act conferring that right than it has done in other kindred statutes by declaring in emphatic words that "the land so allotted shall be deemed the homestead of the allottee and his heirs in perpetuity."

Actual occupancy and continuous use of a tract of land by a native, prior to its inclusion within a national forest, confers upon the occupant a preference right to an allotment, even though the application for an allotment was filed subsequent to the creation of a reservation.[191]

The Allotment Act[192] does not limit the use of the land by the allottee nor the duration of his occupancy, nor the character of his improvements.[193]

The Secretary of the Interior was empowered by section 2 of the Act of May 1, 1936:[194]

> * * * to designate as an Indian reservation any area of land which has been reserved for the use and occupancy of Indians or Eskimos by section 8 of the Act of May 17, 1884 (23 Stat. 26), or by section 14 or section 15 of the Act of March 3, 1891 (26 Stat. 1101), or which has been heretofore reserved under any executive order and placed under the jurisdiction of the Department of the Interior or any bureau thereof, together with additional public lands adjacent thereto, within the Territory of Alaska, or any other public lands which are actually occupied by Indians or Eskimos within said Territory: *Provided*, That the designation by the Secretary of the Interior of any such area of land as a reservation shall be effective only upon its approval by the vote, by secret ballot, of a majority of the Indian or Eskimo residents thereof who vote at a special election duly called by the Secretary of the Interior upon thirty days' notice: *Provided, however*, That in each instance the total vote cast shall not be less than 30 per centum of those entitled to vote.

A provision is also made that this act shall not affect existing rights.

There have already been a number of administrative interpretations of this act. It has been held that a reservation may include sufficient water frontage to protect and provide for the fishing occupations of the Indians.[195] Although water in connection with the reservation of the uplands cannot be independently reserved under section 2, waters adjacent to any lands already reserved or being reserved may be reserved for the natives occupying the rest of the reservation.[196] Waters may not be withdrawn as far from the shore as the territorial limits of Alaska.

Adopting the test formulated by the Supreme Court in the *Alaska Pacific Fisheries* case,[197] it was held to be the intent of Congress that under section 2 only those adjacent waters may be reserved which are essential for the effective use and are an integral part of the reserved land. A recent opinion[198] on this question advised:

> It appears that for all practical purposes the extent of water designated by the President in connection with the Annette Islands Reservation, namely, 3,000 feet from the shore at mean low tide, should be used as the standard and even as the maximum unless it is shown that the natives have been using and actually need a further area. (Pp. 9–10.)

The principal part of each reservation must be land upon which the natives are actually residing.[199]

[189] 48 L. D. 435 (1922). Memo. Sol. I. D., March 28, 1939; also see *Worthen Lumber Mills* v. *Alaska Juneau Gold Mining Co.*, 229 Fed. 966 (C. C. A. 9, 1916).

[190] 48 L. D. 435, 437 (1922).

[191] 48 L. D. 362 (1921).

[192] Act of May 17, 1906, c. 2469, 34 Stat. 197. Also see 48 L. D. 70 (1921), and 50 L. D. 27, 48 (1923), as modified by 51 L. D. 145 (1925).

[193] 52 L. D. 597 (1929).

[194] C. 254, 49 Stat. 1250.

[195] Op. Sol. I. D., M.28978, April 19, 1937.

[196] *Ibid.*

[197] *Alaska Pacific Fisheries* v. *United States*, 248 U. S. 78 (1918), aff'g 240 Fed. 274 (C. C. A. 9, 1917). This case is more fully discussed in sec. 4, *supra*.

[198] Op. Sol. I. D., M.28978, April 19, 1937.

[199] Memo. Sol. I. D., September 14, 1937. Op. Sol. I. D., M.28978, April 19, 1937.

SECTION 9. TRIBES AND ASSOCIATIONS

Indian villages have been organized under the Municipal Incorporation Law of Alaska[200] and the Indian Village Act.[201] It is reported that some Indian villages not organized under either of these laws have an informal organization with a council, usually elected annually.[202]

Section 19 of the Act of June 18, 1934,[203] provides that Eskimos and other aboriginal peoples of Alaska shall be considered Indians for the purpose of the act, and section 13 provides that sections 9, 10, 11, 12, and 16 shall apply to the Territory of Alaska. These provisions relate to tribal organization, loans for economic development and for tuition in vocational schools, and preference to Indians for positions in the Indian Service. The Act of May 1, 1936,[204] extends to Alaska all the remaining sections except sections 2, 3, 4, and 18, relating to tribal lands and reservations, which are largely inapplicable to this territory. This act offered a new source of federal protection to the natives "who in the past," according to Commissioner of Indian Affairs Collier, "have seen their land rights almost universally disregarded, their fishing rights increasingly invaded, and their economic situation grow each year more desperate."[205]

The Act of May 1, 1936, was passed to remedy the failure of the Act of June 18, 1934 to extend the incorporation and credit privileges of that act to the organizations in Alaska, and, what was equally important, to authorize a type of organization more suited to the existing native groupings and activities than the organizations authorized for Indians in the States.

By an oversight, apparently, of the congressional conference committee considering the Act of June 18, 1934, section 17 of that act providing for incorporation of tribes, was omitted from the list of sections made applicable to Alaska, and this resulted in the ruling that the credit funds made available by section 10 to incorporated organizations could not be made available in Alaska in the absence of the privilege of incorporation.[206] The

[200] Compiled Laws of Alaska for 1933, ch. 44. Pursuant to this act Klawock was organized as a city of the first class and Hydaburg and Saxman, as cities of the second class.

[201] Session Laws of Alaska for 1915, ch. 11; amended Session Laws of Alaska for 1917, ch. 25; repealed Session Laws of Alaska for 1929, ch. 23; villages like Angoon and Hoonah, organized before the repeal of this law, continue to function, although their status is doubtful.

[202] Most, if not all, of these villages are within the area of the Tongass National Forest Reservation.

[203] 48 Stat. 984.

[204] C. 254, 49 Stat. 1250.

[205] Annual Report of Secretary of Interior (1936) p. 163.

[206] Op. Sol. I. D., M.28978, April 19, 1937.

omission was remedied in the Act of 1936 by the express extension of section 17 to Alaska organizations and by the provision that the groups of Indians authorized to organize may receive charters of incorporation and credit loans in accordance with the Act of June 18, 1934.[207]

The type of organization authorized by the latter act was the organization of Indian bands or tribes, or the Indians residing on a reservation. However, since most of the natives in Alaska do not live on reservations and are not grouped as bands or tribes, as in the States,[208] and since most of the natives live in native villages or communities and many groups of natives work in particular kinds of occupations or have other ties that bind their interests together, it was provided in section 1 of the Act of May 1, 1936, that

> groups of Indians in Alaska not heretofore recognized as bands or tribes, but having a common bond of occupation, or association, or residence within a well-defined neighborhood, community, or rural district, may organize to adopt constitutions and bylaws and to receive charters of incorporation and Federal loans under sections 16, 17, and 10 of the Act of June 18, 1934 (48 Stat. 984).

The criterion of organization was adopted from section 9 of the Federal Credit Union Act,[209] and the interpretation of this language by the authorities administering that act is looked to for guidance in determining the eligibility of native groups seeking to organize.

Under the interpretation and application of the Act of May 1, 1936, the Interior Department has held, as a matter of law and policy, that, like a band or tribe, a group which may organize under the act must be a previously existing group, bound by common interests or economic ties, and not a newly formed group established solely for the purpose of receiving benefits under the Indian Reorganization Act. The Interior Department has also held that, as in the organization of a band or tribe, the group organizing acts as a unit and includes at the outset all those natives who belong to the group, although individuals may withdraw later from the organization.

The instructions on organization in Alaska, approved by the Secretary of the Interior on December 22, 1937, set forth the kinds of organization possible under the act:

(1) A group consisting of all the native residents of a locality may organize to carry on municipal and public activities as well as economic enterprises. This type of organization would be suitable for exclusively native villages. Authority for municipal activities is based on the provision of section 16 of the Act of June 18, 1934, providing that the constitutions may contain all powers of an Indian group recognized under existing law. The best example of this type of organization is the organization of the Eskimo villages.[210]

(2) Groups comprising all the native residents of a locality may organize solely for business purposes without contemplating municipal activities. This type of organization is specially suitable in the case of Indian groups residing in white communities, which communities already provide for municipal activities. Examples of such an organization are the organizations at Craig [211] and Sitka.[212]

(3) A group not comprising all the residents of a locality but comprising persons having a common bond of occupation or association may organize to carry on economic activities. In the case of such organizations, cooperative and democratic features in the method of organization are encouraged and as wide a base among the natives is sought as is possible in the circumstances of the case. An example of such an organization is the Hydaburg Cooperative Association, composed of resident Native fishermen of Hydaburg who have a "common bond of occupation in the fish industry, including the catching, processing and selling of fish and the building of fishing boats and equipment.[213]

As of February 1, 1941, 38 native groups had organized and received charters under the Alaska act.[214]

Although the Alaskan Native Brotherhood, is neither a tribe nor a group organized under the Act of May 1, 1936, it must be considered in any survey of native organizations. The Brotherhood was organized in the fall of 1913 with the announced objective of preparing the natives of Alaska to exercise the rights and duties of citizenship. The Brotherhood is governed by an annual convention composed of delegates from its "local camps."

---

[207] From the standpoint of the Alaskan economy, this means that credit funds may be loaned to finance such enterprises as fishing, trading, cannery operations, and reindeer development. Report of Governor of Alaska for 1938, p. 45.

[208] Annual Report of the Commissioner of Indian Affairs (1937), pp. 200–201.

The native villages vary "from 30 or 40 to 300 or 400 persons. Except in southeastern Alaska, these villages are widely separated and have little or no communication with each other. The village and not the ethnological tribe is the unit." Letter by R. L. Wilbur, in Hearings before the Senate Committee on Indian Affairs on March 23, 1932, on S. 1196, 72nd Cong., 1st sess., p. 16.

> * * * It was established that the villages in Alaska were the natural form of Indian organization and that no tribal organizations existed as they are known in the United States. It was found that the word "tribe" was used in Alaska to denote ethnic or language groups and did not signify "domestic dependent nations" as the tribes were recognized to be in the United States. (Memo. Sol. I. D., May 25, 1940)
>
> * * * While the native organizations and associations in Alaska do not have the character or status of tribes, they may equally be considered instrumentalities of the United States where they are operating under a loan agreement from the United States or are organized and chartered as Federal corporations under the Indian Reorganization Act. (Memo. Sol. I. D., June 10, 1940)

[209] Act of June 26, 1934, c. 750, 48 Stat. 1216, 1219, 12 U. S. C. 1759.

[210] See, for example, Constitution of the Native Village of Shishmaref, ratified August 2, 1939, and charter ratified on the same date.

[211] Constitution of the Craig Community Association, ratified October 8, 1938, and charter ratified on the same date. This association, composed of about 200 members of the Haida and Tlingit tribes residing in the neighborhood of Craig, granted loans to many members with which they bought new boats, made repairs, and renovated their old boats. See Alaskan Fisheries Hearings, H. Res. 162, 76th Cong., 1st sess., pt. II (1939), p. 628.

[212] Constitution of the Sitka Community Association, ratified October 11, 1938, and charter ratified on the same date.

[213] Constitution of the Hydaburg Cooperative Association ratified April 14, 1938, and charter ratified on the same date. Also see Annual Report, Governor of Alaska (1939), pp. 50–51.

[214] Act of May 1, 1936, sec. 1, 49 Stat. 1250, 48 U. S. C. 362.

Hydaburg Cooperative Association of Alaska, constitution and charter ratified April 14, 1938; Klawock Cooperative Association of Alaska, October 4, 1938; Craig Community Association of Craig, Alaska, October 8, 1938; Sitka Community Association of Alaska, October 11, 1938; Organized Village of Kasaan, October 15, 1938; King Island Native Community, January 31, 1939; Native Village of Atka, May 23, 1939; Native Village of Nikolski, June 12, 1939; Native Village of Wales, July 29, 1939; Native Village of Shishmaref, August 2, 1939; Native Village of Karluk, August 23, 1939; Hoonah Indian Association, October 23, 1939; Angoon Community Association, November 15, 1939; Nome Eskimo Community, November 23, 1939; Native Village of Elim, November 24, 1939; Native Village of White Mountain, November 25, 1939; Native Village of Tyonek, November 27, 1939; Stebbins Community Association, December 5, 1939; Native Village of Noatak, December 28, 1939; Native Village of Unalakleet, December 30, 1939; Native Village of Minto, December 30, 1939; Native Village of Stevens, December 30, 1939; Native Village of Gambell, December 31, 1939; Native Village of Fort Yukon, January 2, 1940; Native Village of Nunapitchuk, January 2, 1940; Native Village of Kwethluk, January 11, 1940; Native Village of Venetie, January 25, 1940; Ketchikan Indian Corporation, January 27, 1940; Native Village of Shaktoolik, January 27, 1940; Native Village of Diomede, January 31, 1940; Native Village of Chanega, February 8, 1940; Native Village of Kivalina, February 7, 1940; Native Village of Point Hope, February 29, 1940; Native Village of Selawik, March 15, 1940; Native Village of Barrow, March 21, 1940; Native Village of Tetlin, March 26, 1940; Native Village of Mekoryuk, August 24, 1940; Native Village of Saxman, January 14, 1941.

Executive officers, including the Grand Secretary, who is the administrative head, are elected annually.[215]

The Grand President becomes a member of a permanent "Executive Committee" which exercises the powers of the convention between sessions.

This society takes an active interest in legislation and other matters which affect the natives.[216]

Unique among native communities is that of the Metlakahtla Indians. Encouraged by federal officials about 800 of these Indians migrated in 1887 to the Annette Islands in southeast Alaska from their homes in Metlakahtla, British Columbia.[217] A ruling of the Attorney General[218] held that the President of the United States lacked authority to establish a reservation for these Indians on the public domain without congressional sanction, because they were aliens, born outside of the boundaries of the United States proper. By the Act of March 3, 1891,[219] Congress created a reservation for the use of these immigrants and such other Alaskan natives as might join them, to be used in common under rules and regulations prescribed by the Secretary of the Interior.[220] By the Act of March 4, 1907,[221] Congress permitted these Indians to be licensed as masters, pilots, and engineers of steamboats and as operators of motor boats, as if citizens of the United States. Congress granted collective naturalization by the Act of May 7, 1934,[222] to the Metlakahtlans and the Indians who emigrated from British Columbia not later than January 1, 1900, and resided continuously in Annette Island.

The community has flourished; it owns a salmon cannery[223] which is operated under a lease from the Department of the Interior. Out of their receipts they have built up a large trust fund[224] in the Treasury of the United States, bearing 4 percent interest.

The community income is used by the directors of the town council for civic improvements, care of dependents, etc. From the profits, the community has built and equipped a hydro-electric plant which furnishes each house with electricity free of charge.

The privilege of joining the Metlakahtlan community and occupying any part of the Island is subject to vote of the Metlakahtlan council. To obtain membership, except by birth, requires the approval of three-fourths of the members of the town council. The land and resources of the reservation are held in common; individuals occupy land by permits from the council. Local self-government is recognized in rules and regulations of the Secretary of the Interior.[225]

[215] For a brief discussion of this organization, see testimony by Judge Wickersham before the Senate Committee on Indian Affairs on March 23, 1932, on S. 1196, 72nd Cong., 1st sess., pp. 10–11.

[216] The significance of the Brotherhood as the representatives of an important portion of the natives is shown by the fact that the Delegate from Alaska declined to sponsor legislation extending the Wheeler-Howard Act to Alaska until learning its views. 83 Cong. Rec. pt. 9, p. 180 (1938).

At the outset a number of "local camps" and many officers had vigorously opposed the provisions of the Wheeler-Howard Act referring to "Indian reservations" because they thought that these provisions would deprive them of some of their rights of citizenship. When it was demonstrated that this fear was groundless, the Executive Committee approved the measure. *Ibid.* 180.

[217] For a brief account of the development of this colony, see Department of the Interior, The Problem of the Alaskan Development (April 1940), pp. 44–47. See also fn. 5, *supra.*

[218] 18 Op. A. G. 557 (1877).

[219] 26 Stat. 1095, 1101.

[220] Secretary of the Interior Lane issued such rules and regulations on January 28, 1915. 25 C. F. R. 1.1–1.68.

[221] C. 2929, 34 Stat. 1411.

[222] C. 221, 48 Stat. 667. The Alaska legislature had urged Congress to grant citizenship to these Indians. H. Joint Memorial, No. 10, Laws of Alaska (1929), pp. 341–342. For a private act naturalizing a single Metlakahtlan, see Act of April 15, 1938, 52 Stat. 1299.

[223] See Survey of Conditions of the Indians of the United States, pt. 35 (Metlakahtla Indians, Alaska), 74th Cong., 2d sess., Hearings, S. Subcomm. on Ind. Aff. The success of this community is discussed in Hearings on Alaskan Fisheries held pursuant to H. Res. 162, 76th Cong., 1st sess. (1939), pp. 158–159, 638, 652–659, 719–725, 995–999.

[224] Act of August 28, 1937, 50 Stat. 873.

[225] 25 C. F. R. pt. 1 (Rules and Regulations for Annette Islands Reserve, Alaska (1915)).

CHAPTER 22

NEW YORK INDIANS

TABLE OF CONTENTS

There are more Indians in the State of New York than there are in Wyoming, Colorado, and Utah combined.[1] Because of the persistence of traditional forms of tribal organization,[2] and because of treaty arrangements with New York which preceded the Federal Constitution and special dealings with the state since that time, the various New York tribes have a peculiar status, which has been the subject of a series of cases, federal[3] and state,[4] and at least two excellent legal studies.[5] While the complexity of the subject and limitations of space and time preclude an exhaustive analysis of the status of the New York tribes in this work, two aspects of the subject may be briefly treated: the history of federal and state relations; and the present status of these tribes with respect to local government.

[1] As of January 1, 1938, the Indian population of these states was, according to the Indian Office: New York, 6,610; Wyoming, 2,328; Colorado, 856; Utah, 2,184.

[2] See American Assn. of Indian Affairs, Inc., News-Letter Supplement, May 15, 1939.

[3] *Fellows* v. *Blacksmith*, 19 How. 366 (1856) (denying right of assignee of ultimate fee to Seneca lands to dispossess Indians); *New York ex rel. Cutler* v. *Dibble*, 21 How. 366 (1858) (A statute of the State of New York making it unlawful for any other than Indians to settle upon tribal lands in New York is not contrary to the Constitution or a usurpation of federal power. It is exercise of state power to make police regulations); *New York Indians*, 5 Wall. 761 (1866) (denying power of New York to tax land of New York Indians); *Seneca Nation* v. *Christy*, 162 U. S. 283 (1896) (Seneca Indians barred by statute of limitation in the suit, under New York statutes, to invalidate conveyances of land to private individuals); *New York Indians* v. *United States*, 170 U. S. 1 (1898) (Under Treaty of Buffalo Creek, January 15, 1838, 7 Stat. 550, the New York Indians were held entitled to value of certain lands in Kansas, set apart for these Indians and later sold by the United States, as well as for amounts of money agreed to be paid upon their removal); *Oneida Indians of Canada* v. *United States*, 39 C. Cls. 116 (1903) (Oneida Indians of Canada claim to share in fund under decision of Supreme Court in 170 U. S. 1); *New York Indians* v. *United States*, 40 C. Cls. 448 (1905) (claims arising out of alleged unexecuted stipulations of the Treaty of Buffalo Creek of January 15, 1838, 7 Stat. 550); *New York Indians* v. *United States*, 41 C. Cls. 462 (1906) (claims of New York Indians excluded from the membership rolls to share in judgment rendered in suit reported in 40 C. Cls. 448); *Kennedy* v. *Becker*, 241 U. S. 556 (1916) (hunting and fishing rights of Seneca Indians on ceded lands); *United States ex rel. Kennedy* v. *Tyler*, 269 U. S. 13 (1925) (State court jurisdiction over lands and members of the Seneca Tribe); *Spears* v. *United States*, 64 C. Cls. 684 (1928) (claim of New York Indians not considered in the absence of jurisdictional act). See also, on power of state and federal government over New York Indians, note, Ann. Cas. 1914B, 652, 653–654; note, Ann. Cas. 1915D, 371, 373.

[4] See *Patterson* v. *Council of Seneca Nation*, 245 N. Y. 433, 157 N. E. 734 (1927), and cases cited.

[5] Rice, The Position of the American Indian in the Law of the United States (1934), 16 J. Comp. Leg. 78; Pound, Nationals without a Nation (1922), 22 Colum. L. Rev. 97.

SECTION 1. HISTORICAL BACKGROUND[6]

The Iroquois Indian Confederacy, sometimes called the Five Nations or the Six Nations, consisted of the Seneca, Cayuga, Onondaga, Oneida and Mohawk tribes of Indians and, during the latter period of its existence, the Tuscarora tribe. They occupied all of what is now northern and western New York, and their league is acknowledged by historians as being the triumph of

[6] Material on the historical background of the New York Indians and their relations with various colonial governments and the United States is taken, almost in its entirety, from the brief in the case of *United States* v. *Charles*, 23 F. Supp. 346 (D. C. W. D. N. Y. 1938), filed by the

Indian legislation. Not only did the Iroquois outstrip all other Indians north of Mexico in their political institutions, but they were likewise the most powerful. Their territory at one time extended from the hills of New England to the Mississippi River and from upper Canada into North Carolina. Other tribes occupying this expanse were either annihilated, expelled, subjugated, aligned with, or absorbed by the Iroquois. The Iroquois' possession of the strategic water routes (the natural gateway to the interior), along with their power and control over the important western fur trade, gave to these Indians a position in history which has profoundly influenced the present day status of all American Indians.

The controlling object and interest of the Dutch who settled New York, was to trade with the Indians. Their meager needs for land did not affect the Iroquois who were situated to the north and west of Albany (Fort Orange) and in their desire for trade they took particular pains to cultivate the friendship of the Iroquois and accordingly afforded them the status of independent nations which they demanded.

When the English took over the Dutch colony in 1664, they were careful to continue a trade which was to make Albany the fur capital of North America during the latter part of the seventeenth and the early part of the eighteenth centuries.

A. RESISTANCE BY IROQUOIS TO FRENCH

The French fully appreciated the importance of the Iroquois. The Iroquois and Dutch (later the English) possession of New York made necessary for the French a chain of forts some 2,000 miles in length, and it was ever the purpose of the French to reduce the length of forts to about 300 miles by taking possession of New York.

Diversion of fur trade to the English was effected by the Iroquois from as far as what is now Illinois and Wisconsin, and this along with the Iroquois occupation of northern and western New York was an obstacle to the trade and territorial interests and ambitions of France.

The official French attitude toward these Indians might well be considered as summed up in a letter written by Du Chesneau in 1681:[7]

> There is no doubt, and it is the universal opinion, that if the Iroquois are allowed to proceed they will subdue the Illinois, and in a short time render themselves masters of all the Outawa tribes, and divert the trade to the English, so that it is absolutely necessary to make them our friends or to destroy them.

Failing to cultivate a friendship which was detrimental to the Iroquois' independence and trading interests, the French spent about a hundred years in trying to destroy the Iroquois. In this they failed.

The Iroquois resisted every attempt upon their territories and independence with unparalleled ferocity and with very little or no aid from their allies, the English, until quite late in the struggle, when the English, at the request of the Iroquois, established one or two under-manned forts in their territory.

New York was cognizant of the importance of the Iroquois, both from the standpoint of trade and colonial defense.[8]

The friendship of these Indians was a highly important, if not a decisive, factor in the struggle of France and England for this Continent. The history of this struggle, as enacted in America, is largely the history of these Indians, who in defending their own lands, played an international role which brought them recognition in treaties between France and England. It is no wonder that the Iroquois were "courted and concilliated" by England and that their national character was scrupulously observed and recognized.[9]

Department of Justice on behalf of the United States. The statements therein contained are corroborated by statements found in *New York Indians* v. *United States*, 170 U. S. 1 (1898).

An interesting account of the tribes inhabiting western New York during the early colonial period, some of whom no longer reside in the state, is contained in a memorandum of John R. T. Reeves, Chief Counsel, Office of Indian Affairs, which appears in H. Doc. No. 1590, 63d Cong., 3d sess. (1915), and reads as follows:

> Early colonists in what is now western New York found the country more or less densely populated by aborigines of various tribes, principally the Senecas, Cayugas, Onondagas, Oneidas, and Mohawks. These five tribes or nations were united in a common league, known among themselves as Ho-de-no-sau-nee, but generally designated by the whites as "Iroquois," and were much feared during the early days. In the Iroquois council the Onondagas, as the founders of the league, kept the central fire; the Mohawks guarded the eastern portal, and the Senecas the western. The Oneidas were stationed between the central fire and the east, while the Cayugas occupied a similar position in the west. * * *
>
> About 1710 the Tuscaroras, then living in North Carolina, became involved in quarrels with white settlers and adjoining Indian tribes there. Having been severely defeated in battle they migrated to New York and were formally united with the five tribes just mentioned, thus making the Six Nations of New York, by which name these Indians are now most commonly known. At the period of its greatest strength—the latter part of the seventeenth century—the Iroquois league numbered 15,000 souls, and even to this day the union still continues to some extent, although its component membership as to tribes has materially changed.
>
> With the exception of the Oneidas and a part of the Tuscaroras, these Indians sided with the mother country in the Revolution and were left unmentioned and unprovided for in the treaty of peace between Great Britain and the confederated Colonies. Naturally considerable unrest existed among them at the close of the Revolution, due to the fact that in the main they had sided with the losing party in that great struggle. The Mohawks moved to Canada and settled on lands provided for them by the British Government, where a remnant of this tribe still lives. By treaty the Mohawks ceded to the State whatever title they had to any land in New York, and subsequently the St. Regis Indians were formally adopted by the Six Nations in place of the Mohawks.
>
> The Cayugas also sold their land to the State and gradually migrated westward, locating first in the Ohio Valley, but finally removing to the Indian Territory and becoming affiliated with other tribes there. A few Cayugas still remain in New York, residing principally with the Senecas and Tonawandas—the latter an offspring of the Seneca Tribe—being frequently designated "The Tonawanda Band of Seneca Indians." The State paid the Cayugas at the rate of 4 shillings per acre and thereafter sold the land for 16 shillings per acre. About 1853 representatives of the tribe began to petition the State for the difference in price between the one paid to them and that received by the State. Finally, in 1909, the legislative assembly authorized the land commissioner to adjust and settle the claim of the Cayuga Indians against the State for a sum not exceeding $297,131.20, with an additional allowance of $27,131.20 for legal expenses incurred.
>
> The Oneidas also, by various treaties, sold all of their land, except about 850 acres, to the State, and removed to the reservation in Wisconsin procured from the Menominees by treaty with the Federal Government. The 350 acres in New York belonging to the Oneidas have long since been divided in severalty under State laws, and as a tribe these Indians are known no more in that State. Six tribes still remain in New York, to be regarded as of any importance at this time, viz. the Senecas, Tonawandas Tuscaroras, Onondagas, St. Regis, and Shinnecocks, the latter, however, never having formed a unit in the Six Nations, although at one time they did pay tribute to the Mohawks. * * * (P. 11.)

See appendix of H. Doc. No. 1590, 63d Cong., 3d sess., *supra*, for a list of treaties, statutes, documents, and cases relating to the New York Indians. For a discussion of treaties between New York State and the New York Indians, see *Seneca Nation of Indians* v. *Christy*, 126 N. Y. 122, 27 N. E. 275 (1891).

[7] Brodhead, Documents Relative to the Colonial History of the State of New York (1855) (Edited by E. B. O'Callaghan), vol. 9, p. 165.

[8] Lieutenant Governor Clark, in an address to the Assembly on April 15, 1741, said:

> The house at Oswego being of highest Importance to the furr-trade, ought by all means to be preserved from falling into the hands of the french * * *. If you suffer Oswego to fall into the hands of the french, I much fear you will loose the Six Nations, an event which will expose the whole country to the merciless spoil and barbarous cruelty of a savage enemy, * * *; wherefore at any expense Oswego ought to be maintaind that the fidelity of the Six Nations may be Preserved * * *. (New York Assembly Journal 1691–1743 (1861 ed.), 22d Assembly, 6th session, p. 769)

[9] This is illustrated by the following excerpt from a memorandum of the Lands Division of the Department of Justice:

> In 1768, acting under a Commission of the British Crown, Sir William Johnson entered into a treaty with the Six Nations by the terms of which the boundaries of the Iroquois Confederacy were defined and located, and the territory of these Nations definitely set apart from the lands of the Colony of New York. By this treaty the Indians sold and granted to the King "all that Tract of Land situate in North America at the Back of the

B. AFFAIRS OF IROQUOIS AS AFFECTING ALL COLONIES

With their territory, dominance, and influence extending into many of the colonies, intercourse with these Indians invariably affected the interests of the colonies as well as the Crown.

The intercolonial aspect of the Iroquois resulting from the extent of their territory and influence, made relations with them of serious concern to all of the northern and central colonies, and more than one treaty with these Indians was negotiated by several of the colonies acting together. Such was the Treaty of 1745 between the Iroquois and New York, Massachusetts, Connecticut, and Pennsylvania. Franklin's famous Plan of Union of the colonies was proposed at one of the joint congresses held in June 1754, at Albany, by the states of New York, Massachusetts, Connecticut, Pennsylvania, New Hampshire, Rhode Island, and Maryland "for the purpose of treating with the Six Nations and concerting a scheme of general union of the British American Colonies." [10]

Another factor favoring control by the central authority of the Crown was the conflict of land settlements and trade. More than one self-seeking colony would act in such a manner (or sanction the actions of its settlers or traders) as to embroil the entire frontier in an Indian war—the consequences of which often would be borne by all of the colonies.

C. SHIFT OF CONTROL OF IROQUOIS AFFAIRS FROM ALBANY TO COLONY TO CROWN

Relations with the Iroquois were in the beginning for the most part a matter of trade and nominally conducted in the name of the King of England. In fact, the actual management of affairs with the Iroquois was with the city of Albany. The charter of this city of 1686 gave to Albany the

> Sole & only Managmt of the Trade with the Indians as well within this whole County as without the same to the Eastward Northward and Westward thereof so farr as his Maties Dominion here does or may extend * * *.[11]

Though Albany was the fur capital of North America during colonial days, the regulation of affairs with these Indians was not a municipal matter as is readily seen from the foregoing, and accordingly the colony assumed an ever increasing control until the charter was finally revoked. But regulation of the relations with the Iroquois was no more a colonial matter than it was a municipal proposition and therefore the Crown of England abandoned its nominal control in favor of an active and actual supervision.

D. NATIONAL AND INTERNATIONAL ASPECT OF IROQUOIS AS AFFECTING FEDERAL CONSTITUTION

1. *Iroquois in Revolutionary War.*—At the beginning of the Revolutionary War the Confederated Government took immediate steps to secure the neutrality of the Iroquois, and though the League remained neutral, the several tribes took sides, some with the colonies, some with their traditional ally, the Crown, and some fought on both sides.[12] The Senecas participated throughout the war with England.

Sullivan's campaign against the hostile tribes of the Iroquois was one of the major military operations of the Revolutionary War against Indians. The long years of incessant warfare with the French and the havoc wrought by Sullivan's expedition had broken the power of the Iroquois, and they were left by England at the end of the war to make their separate peace with the newly created Union.

2. *Importance to union of peace negotiations with Iroquois.*—The treaty of peace between the United States and the Iroquois was considered of considerable importance to the Central Government. Washington, in 1783, made a personal trip to the lands of the Iroquois to familiarize himself with conditions. The negotiations of peace in 1784 were closely followed by Washington in Virginia and Jefferson in Paris, and such personalities as James Madison, James Monroe, Lafayette, and General Butler were present as negotiators or observers.

The Iroquois insisted on acting in their collective capacity and, though they had been harried by Sullivan's expedition, any effort to expel the hostile tribes of the Iroquois from their ancient lands or any attempt to break up the League into its several tribes, would have been attended by a prolonged frontier war which the new Union was not prepared to prosecute.

The controlling purpose of the Central Government was to make peace with the Iroquois and to drive a wedge between them and the western tribes—to separate the Iroquois from the subjugated western tribes and to undermine the influence of the League over them.

New York on the other hand was more than anxious to rid the state of the hostile Senecas, Cayugas, Onondagas, and Mohawks and to move the friendly Oneidas and Tuscaroras to a small part of the lands of the Senecas in western New York. She considered herself as supreme (under the Articles of Confederation) in dealing with the New York Indians and intended to separate the different tribes of the Iroquois. In her futile attempt to carry out these purposes she stopped at nothing, even arresting agents of the Confederated Government who were trying to negotiate the treaty of peace.[13]

Had New York's attempts in obstructing the peace treaty prevailed over the efforts of the Central Government in this respect, New York would have probably consolidated the Iroquois instead of dividing them, and this might well have resulted in a united League serving as the spear head of a cruel, prolonged, and costly Indian war of all of the western Indians (more than 35 tribes) under the influence and leadership of the Iroquois.

Though under the Articles of Confederation there was a question of whether the Confederated Government was invading the rights of the State of New York relative to the Iroquois, the necessity of the times and the importance of these Indians in relation to all of the states made it imperative that the Central Government take definite action.

British Settlements bounded by a line which we have now agreed upon and do hereby establish as the Boundary between us and the British colonies in America." This is followed by a description of the boundaries, with its beginning and ending. (New York Colonial Documents, Vol. 8, p. 136; Ethnology Bureau Report, Pt. 2, 1897, p. 584). (1 L. D. Memo. 35 (1925).)

[10] Massachusetts Historical Society Collections (1836), series III, vol. 5, p. 5.

[11] N. Y. Colonial Laws, vol. 1, pp. 195, 211.

[12] "When the Revolution came, the Six Nations as a whole determined on neutrality, but left the constituent tribes to side with either party, which they did." *McCandless v. United States*, 25 F. 2d 71, 72 (C. C. A. 3, 1928).

[13] Richard Henry Lee, later President of the Continental Congress, in writing to George Washington concerning the efforts of New York to obstruct the treaty, said:

> * * * I understand, from Mr. Wolcott, that the commissioners of the United States met many difficulties, thrown in their way by New York, which they overcame, at last, by much firmness and perseverance. It is unfortunate when private views obstruct public measures, and more especially when a state becomes opposed to the States; because, it seems to confirm the predictions of those who wish us not well, and who cherish hopes from a discord arising from different interests." (Ballagh, James Curtis, The Letters of Richard Henry Lee (1911), vol. 2, p. 298.)

The ensuing treaty was in effect three treaties:[14] (*a*) A treaty of peace and general amnesty between the Iroquois and the United States with provisions for prisoners of war and a relinquishment of their claim to roughly all lands west and south of what is now New York; (*b*) a treaty with Pennsylvania relinquishing all lands in that state; and (*c*) a treaty between New York and the Oneidas and Tuscaroras, relinquishing certain of their lands.

In the drafting of the Federal Constitution, Madison, who had attended the Treaty of 1784 and realized the importance of placing the management of affairs of the Iroquois Indians in the hands of the proposed United States Government, introduced a resolution on August 18, 1787, intending to give Congress the power:

> To regulate affairs with the Indians, as well within as without the limits of the United States.[15]

The principles of this resolution are embodied in the Constitution of the United States.

E. EFFECT OF TREATIES OF 1789 AND 1794

The United States entered into the treaties of 1789[16] and 1794[17] with the Iroquois (Six Nations) Indians, recognizing the Indians as distinct and separate political communities capable of managing their internal affairs as they had always done. These treaties were entered into for the purpose of meeting a serious situation confronting the United States. Great Britain still retained possession of certain forts in New York and the Northwest Territory in violation of the treaty of peace, and was apparently encouraging and provoking the western Indians and the Iroquois to hostilities against the United States—even providing them with arms with which to resist encroachments upon their lands.

The settlement of the Northwest Territory brought the usual friction between the Indians and the settlers which broke out into frontier wars. The Iroquois felt a responsibility toward these western tribes since they believed that part of the difficulties of these tribes, which were once dependent on the Iroquois, was due to the sale by the Iroquois of all of their western lands. The problem confronting the Federal Government was to make peace with the Iroquois, and particularly the Senecas, before the almost inevitable strife began and thus prevent the Iroquois from acting as a spear head in a united general offensive by the scores of western Indian tribes (once subjects of the Iroquois) under their leadership and directing influence.

The Treaty of 1789[18] granted to the Iroquois a substantial annuity and they in turn agreed to continue at peace. Thereafter certain of the influential Seneca chiefs were induced to go to the West on behalf of the peace efforts of the United States. These western Indian wars, nevertheless, created a decided unrest, particularly among the Senecas, and the United States prudently entered into a third treaty with the Iroquois (Six Nations) in 1794,[19] of mutual peace, and restoring certain of the Seneca's lands to them within the State of New York west of a line drawn due south from Buffalo to the Pennsylvania line.

These several treaties[20] guaranteed to the Iroquois (Six Nations) the right of occupancy of their well-defined territories and had the effect of placing the tribes and their reservations beyond the operation and effect of general state laws.

F. FEDERAL MANAGEMENT OF NEW YORK INDIAN AFFAIRS

1. *Education and civilization.*[21]—Some of the first efforts and experiments of the United States Government in educating Indians were with the New York Indians. For a number of years the only effort to educate these Indians was by the aid rendered by the Federal Government and private philanthropy. By about 1860, the state had been making slight efforts to educate the Indians in the state but such efforts were admitted by the state to have done probably as much harm as good.

Aside from the sporadic aid the state gave to the Indians mainly in the way of education,[22] the state left the Indians to manage their own internal affairs as they saw fit, as had been implicitly guaranteed by federal treaty. Such activities merely confer a privilege on the Indians and are not an attempt to regulate their internal affairs or tribal matters.

2. *Restrictions on alienation of lands.*[23]—Pursuant to the specific delegation of authority by the Constitution to regulate Indian commerce, Congress immediately imposed restrictions upon the alienation of Indian lands. Where the states claimed the fee title subject to Indian occupancy as claimed by Georgia, or the "preemption right" as claimed by New York, all purchases were prohibited except at treaties under supervision of the United States.

Many, but not all, purchases from the Seneca Nation of Indians (with the exception of one very small tract of a few acres), whether by the State of New York or its grantee of the "preemption right," were made by treaties under the supervision of United States agents appointed for that purpose pursuant to the restrictive act of Congress. Approximately four million acres

---

[14] Treaty October 22, 1784, with the Six Nations, 7 Stat. 15.

[15] Elliot, Jonathan, The Debates in the Several State Conventions on the Adoption of the Federal Constitution, vol. 5, (1937 ed.), p. 439.

[16] Treaty of January 9, 1789, 7 Stat. 33.

[17] Treaty of November 11, 1794, 7 Stat. 44.

[18] Treaty of January 9, 1789, 7 Stat. 33.

[19] Treaty of November 11, 1794, 7 Stat. 44, interpreted in 1 Op. A. G. 465 (1821).

[20] Treaties of October 22, 1784, January 9, 1789, and November 11, 1794, *supra*.

[21] For a further discussion see Chapter 12, sec. 2.

[22] "* * * From time to time New York has enacted sundry laws pertaining to the Indians within her borders, has provided schools for their youth, appointed attorneys to protect their interests, and has delegated jurisdiction in some instances to her courts to entertain their complaints." (H. Doc. No. 1590, 63d Cong., 3d sess., 1915, p. 14.)

The State of New York has for 100 years or more legislated for and dealt with the Indians within its borders. The Revised Statutes of the State of New York of 1882, pp. 272–336, show the extent and purport of this legislation. Beginning with chapter 29 of the Laws of 1813 (N. Y.), prohibiting the purchase or occupancy of any Indian lands in New York by any person without the consent of the legislature, these statutes contain provisions for the improvement of the reservations, to prevent the destruction of timber on the same, for the appointment of peacemakers on certain reservations and giving them jurisdiction of actions for divorce, and to hear actions to determine title to real estate between Indians, to authorize certain Indians to hold land in severalty and to sell and buy the same, provisions for the appointment of attorneys to represent the Indians, and for the support of schools, ministers and churches on the reservations, to authorize the construction of railroads upon Indian lands, to prohibit the sale of liquor to the Indians, to establish laws of descent among them, and to provide the manner of conveying their lands and restricting conveyance of the same, police regulations, and for the purchase of lands of Indians by the state. 1 L. D. Memo. 35 D. J. (1929).

See also *United States ex rel. Kennedy* v. *Tyler*, 269 U. S. 13 (1925); *United States* v. *Waldow*, 294 Fed. 111 (D. C. W. D., N. Y., 1923), and *Benson* v. *United States*, 44 Fed. 178 (C. C. N. D., N. Y., 1890).

[23] See Chapter 15, sec. 18.

of land from time to time were thus purchased from the Seneca Indians under federal authority.[24]

3. *Removal to the West—Treaties of 1838 and 1842.*—In 1815, and perhaps before, Governor Tompkins of New York was agitating for the removal of the New York Indians by the United States to the West.[25] The question of removal was obviously a function which could be executed only by the Federal Government. Whether the Indians were to be removed at all, and if so, where to, could only be determined by the Federal Government.

On February 12, 1816, the Secretary of War, by authority of the President, gave the New York Indians permission to negotiate with the western tribes, at their own expense, for the purchase of lands. In 1820 and 1821, the Government aided some 10 Indians, representing certain New York Indian tribes, in exploring Wisconsin with a view of selecting lands and making arrangements with the Indians residing there for a portion of their country.[26]

On August 18, 1821, the Menomonee Indians ceded to the Stockbridge, Oneida, Tuscarora, St. Regis, and Munsee Nations lands in Wisconsin for a consideration paid by these tribes. All but the last named of these tribes were New York Indians. The settlement of members of these tribes on the lands was one of the first removals in the Federal Government's policy of removal of Indian tribes to the West. The uncertain right of the New York Indians in these western lands was in dispute. On February 8, 1831, the United States, to settle conflicting claims, negotiated a treaty with the Menomonees[27] and Winnebagos for the benefit of the New York Indians. The lands in which they were previously entitled to share with the other tribes were reduced to exclusive possession and two parcels, one of 500,000 acres and one of 89,120 acres, were purchased for a consideration of $20,000 paid by the United States, and set aside for the New York Indians.

These lands were set apart in Wisconsin for the future home of the New York Indians provided they removed thereto within 3 years. However, most of the New York Indians caring to migrate had already moved to the West.

In the meantime, Wisconsin was being settled by whites and this Indian reserve was needed for expansion. Accordingly, a treaty was negotiated with the New York Indians to exchange these lands in Wisconsin for lands in Kansas and by treaty of January 15, 1838,[28] this exchange was made. Those of the New York Indians who had already migrated to Wisconsin were secured in the possession of their lands. The first allotment of lands in severalty in the United States was to these Indians, an action which anticipated by almost 40 years the general policy of the Federal Government as embodied in the general allotment act of 1887.[29]

The treaty negotiated by the Federal Government with the New York Indians made an exchange of 1,824,000 acres of land in fee simple in Kansas for 435,000 acres at Green Bay, Wisconsin. In addition, Congress was to appropriate the sum of $400,000 for the use of the Indians in emigrating from New York to Kansas and in establishing themselves after arriving in Kansas.

All of the New York tribes of Indians assented to this treaty. However, the St. Regis Indians, with their reservation lying in New York and Canada, entered into a supplemental article to the effect that they would not be compelled to remove unless they chose to do so.[30] No difficulties were encountered in the negotiation of the treaty except with the Seneca Indians. With these Indians, there was also a deed to the Ogden Land Co., so called (grantee of New York's preemption right), of all of the Senecas' lands, consisting of the valuable Buffalo Creek Reservation of 49,920 acres, some of which land comprises the site of the city of Buffalo, as well as the Tonawanda Reservation of 12,800 as it existed at that time, and the Cattaraugus (21,680 acres) and Allegany (30,469 acres) as they now exist.

This deed to the Ogden Land Co., so called, was denounced by the Indians on the ground that it had not been signed by a majority of the chiefs of the Seneca Nation, and that bribes, liquor, and fraud had been used and practiced by the Ogden Land Co. in securing many of the signatures of the chiefs to the deed. The treaty was nevertheless recognized as binding by the Federal Government.

The Seneca Nation refused to move to the West or leave its reservations and the Federal Government was not inclined to repeat in respect to the New York Indians any such forced removal as was experienced by the southern Indians a decade before. The Ogden Land Co. accordingly negotiated the compromise Treaty of May 20, 1842,[31] whereby the company released to the Senecas the Allegany and Cattaraugus Reservations and the Senecas released the Buffalo Creek and Tonawanda Reservations. The original consideration was proportionately reduced. The value of the improvements of the individual Indians was to be determined by appraisers appointed by the Secretary of War and the Ogden Land Co.

The Senecas on the Buffalo Creek Reservation gradually withdrew to the Cattaraugus and Allegany Reservations.

In 1845, the United States appointed a special agent for the removal of such of the New York Indians as desired to move to their western lands. He enrolled 271 Indians, of whom 73 did not leave New York with the party. He arrived in Kansas on June 15, 1846, with 191 and 17 arrived later. Of this number, 17 returned to New York. Only 32 received patents or certificates of allotment in accordance with the terms of the treaty, and of those, none settled permanently in Kansas.[32] A council was called by the Indian Commissioner June 2, 1846, to determine the final disposition of the Indians on emigration. Only 7 persons requested to be enrolled.[33]

4. *State encroachment on ceded reservations.*—The Legislature of the State of New York, expecting the Indians to remove from the ceded reservations, in 1840 and 1841, enacted laws for the assessment and collection of taxes and for the surveying of the lands, laying out roads and the construction of bridges on the ceded reservations. The Act of May 9, 1840, was declared void by the state courts on the theory that the state could not tax the lands of the Indians, and the Supreme Court of the United States, in *The New York Indians*,[34] in considering the "saving clause" of the Act of May 4, 1841, said:

> * * * "But no sale for the purpose of collecting said taxes shall in any manner affect the right of the Indians to occupy said lands." It is true that this clause undertakes

[24] The State of New York acquired from the Indians all the western one-half of that state by nearly 200 treaties not participated in by the United States Government. (See brief of Plaintiff in Error in *Boylan* v. *United States*, No. 111, vol. 20, p. 3, answering motion to dismiss, Records and Briefs in United States cases, United States Supreme Court.) 1 L. D. Memo. D. J. 35 (1929). This memorandum analyzes many of the decisions of the New York courts concerning the New York Indians.

[25] Indian Office Letter Book C, p. 271.

[26] *New York Indians* v. *United States*, 30 C. Cls. 413, 414, 415 (1895).

[27] 7 Stat. 342.

[28] 7 Stat. 550, interpreted in *New York Indians* v. *United States*, 170 U. S. 1 (1898); *United States* v. *New York Indians*, 173 U. S. 464 (1899); *New York Indians* v. *The United States*, 40 C. Cls. 448 (1905); and 3 Op. A. G. 624 (1841).

[29] Act of February 8, 1887, 24 Stat. 388, 25 U. S. C. 331, *et seq.*

[30] Supplemental articles of February 13, 1838, 7 Stat. 561.

[31] 7 Stat. 586.

[32] Sen. Rep. No. 910, 52d Cong., 1st sess., pp. 5–6.

[33] *New York Indians* v. *United States*, 30 C. Cls. 413, 427 (1895).

[34] 5 Wall. 761 (1866).

> to save this right, which the act of 1840 did not; but the rights of the Indians do not depend on this or any other statutes of the State, but upon treaties, which are the supreme law of the land; it is to these treaties we must look to ascertain the nature of these rights, and the extent of them. (P. 768.)

5. *Federal recognition of Seneca constitution.*—In 1848 a convention of the Seneca Nation was called which promulgated a complete constitution, which provided for the abolition of the chiefs, the establishment of an elective council and courts, and in general altered and modified the entire tribal form of government, though not abolishing it.

There was some question of whether this constitution represented the wishes of the majority of the Indians, and the United States investigated the matter and decided to recognize the new form of government as it might apply to the Indians on the Allegany and Cattaraugus Reservations. William Medill, Commissioner of Indian Affairs, by letter of February 2, 1849, directed the United States Indian agent for New York as follows:

> The new form of Government of the Indians on the *Cattaraugus* and *Allegany* Reservation having been adopted by a majority, will be recognized by the Government, and so far as may be necessary, the relations of the Government with those Indians will be made to conform thereto.

6. *Separation from Seneca Nation of Tonawanda band.*—As to the Tonawanda Reservation, the compromise Treaty of 1842 [35] did not assist the Ogden Land Co. in gaining possession. The Indians on that reservation protested that they had not been a party to the treaty of either 1838 [36] or 1842 and refused to move. In fact none of the chiefs of this band of the Seneca Nation had signed either treaty and the other bands of the Seneca Nation (Cattaraugus, Allegany, and Buffalo Creek), by "selling out" the Tonawanda Reservation, had caused the latter band to split off from the Seneca Nation, an action which was recognized by the Federal Government when the Seneca Nation (Allegany and Cattaraugus) adopted their constitution.

The appraisers appointed by the Government and the Ogden Land Co. had attempted to appraise the lands and improvements of the Tonawanda Reservation pursuant to the treaty stipulations:

> * * * but had been prevented from so doing by the Indians in possession, and had been removed and led off the land, the Indians not even delaying to procure legal process.[37]

The Ogden Land Co., however, paid into the United States Treasury the whole amount awarded by the arbitrators, and "by force attempted to eject some of the Indians from possession." The Indians brought the matter into the courts by the action of *Blacksmith* v. *Fellows*,[38] which reached the United States Supreme Court in 1856 as *Fellows* v. *Blacksmith*.[39] The Supreme Court decided that even though the Indians had sold their lands they were to be considered as on the land under their original right of possession and entitled to the protection of treaties and that they could be removed only by the United States Government.

The formal recognition by the United States of the Tonawanda tribe of Indians, by the Treaty of 1857,[40] as a separate and distinct tribe of Indians and independent of the Seneca Nation on the Allegany and Cattaraugus Reservations, is significant in view of the history of the bands of the Seneca Indians. The Tonawandas were satisfied with their chiefs who had refused to participate in the sale of their lands, and this tribe has continued to regulate its internal affairs under its original tribal form of government and has continued to enforce its ancient laws, usages, and customs as modified by practice.

7. *Indian leases.*—Prior to 1875, the village of Salamanca on the Allegany Reservation grew up through numerous alleged leases of Indian lands, ostensibly under state laws and authority, but contrary to federal laws. A careful consideration of the validity of these leases under state authority led state courts to the conclusion that such leases were void as being in violation of federal restrictions on Indian lands against leasing or alienation. To place these illegal leases on a legal basis, the state legislature passed a concurrent resolution as follows:

> Whereas, The Legislature of the State of New York has, at different times, ratified and confirmed leases between Indian and white settlers on the Allegany Indian reservation in said State; and
>
> Whereas, The courts of this State have decided that said ratification is null and void, the Congress of the United States alone possessing power to deal with and for the Indians * * *; now therefore,
>
> Resolved (if the Senate concur), That our Senators and Representatives in Congress are requested to lay the matter before Congress, at an early day, and procure the passage of a law, or take some action for the relief of said white settlers.
>
> Resolved (if the Senate concur), That a copy of this resolution be furnished to each of the members of the Senate and Congress from this State.[41]

Congress legalized part of these leases for 5 years and provided for the establishment of certain villages on the Cattaraugus and Allegany Indian Reservations, and further provided for new and renewal leases.[42] Provision was also made for the extension of the highway laws of the State of New York over the Allegany and Cattaraugus Reservations of the Seneca Nation "with the consent of said Seneca Nation in council." By this act, as amended by Act of September 30, 1890,[43] and Act of February 28, 1901,[44] the Federal Government has regulated leases on the Allegany and Cattaraugus Indian Reservations and continues to do so.

[35] 7 Stat. 586, *supra*.
[36] 7 Stat. 550, *supra*.
[37] N. Y. State Assembly, Doc. 51, vol. 8, 1889, p. 30.
[38] 7 N. Y. 401 (1852).
[39] 19 How. 366 (1856).
[40] Treaty of November 5, 1857, 11 Stat. 735.
[41] N. Y. Session Laws, 1875, 98th sess., p. 819.
[42] Act of February 19, 1875, 18 Stat. 330 (Seneca), discussed in *Benson* v. *United States*, 44 Fed. 178 (C. C. N. D. N. Y. 1890).
[43] 26 Stat. 558 (Seneca Nation).
[44] 31 Stat. 819 (Seneca Nation). Also applicable to Oil Springs Reservation.

SECTION 2. THE PRESENT STATUS OF TRIBAL GOVERNMENT [45]

The Indian reservations now occupied by the New York Indians are the Allegany, Cattaraugus, Oil Springs, Cornplanter,[46] Tonawanda, St. Regis, Tuscarora, Onondaga,[47] Shinnecock, and Poosepatuck. All save the Shinnecock and Poosepatuck, which are on Long Island, are inhabited by descendants of the famous Iroquois League of Six Nations (originally Five Nations, the sixth, the Tuscarora, joining the League in 1722). The Tuscarora and Onondaga Reservations are held by the Tuscarora and Onondaga Nations. The St. Regis Reser-

[45] Material in this section is based, except where otherwise noted, on a report of Paul Gordon on New York Indians (Indian Office Files, 1935).
[46] The Cornplanter Reservation is actually in Pennsylvania, but residents are recognized by Senecas of the Allegany and Cattaraugus Reservations.
[47] For a discussion of the Onondaga Reservation, see Memo. by C. E. Collett, 5 L. D. Memo. D. J. 179, April 29, 1935.

vation is held by the St. Regis Mohawks; the Tonawanda by the Tonawanda Band of Senecas; and the Allegany, Cattaraugus, and Oil Springs Reservations by "The Seneca Nation of Indians," a corporate body under the laws of New York. The Cornplanter Reservation of Pennsylvania is held by the descendants of Cornplanter, who unite with the Seneca Nation in affairs affecting that nation.[48] The Indians of this reservation are grouped with those of the Allegany Reservation for purposes of local government and voting.

A. SENECA NATION

The government of the Seneca Indians is covered by Articles 4 and 5 of the New York Indian Code.[49] The constitution now in force among these Indians provides for three departments of government: executive, legislative, and judiciary. The legislative power is vested in a council of 16 members elected biennially, 8 from the Cattaraugus Reservation and 8 from the Allegany Reservation.[50]

The executive power is vested in a president who presides, fills vacancies, and has a casting vote.[51]

The judiciary power is vested in peacemakers' and surrogate's courts. The peacemakers' courts are composed of three members each from the respective reservations.[52] Peacemakers' courts are given powers to enforce the attendance of witnesses in the same manner as provided for courts of justices of the peace of the state.[53] Peacemakers have, by statute, jurisdiction to grant divorces between Indians residing on the reservations, and to determine all questions between individual Indians involving title or possession of lands.[54] Appeal may be taken to the council.[55]

The surrogate court is composed of one person from the Allegany and one from the Cattaraugus Reservation, elected by voters of each reservation for a term of 2 years. The procedure is the same as in the surrogate court of the state, and appeal may be taken to the council.[56]

Treaty making is declared to be a prerogative of the council, subject to approval by three-fourths of the legal voters and consent of three-fourths of the mothers of the reservation.[57] The constitution provides for a clerk and a treasurer,[58] and permits the council to provide for highway commissioners, overseers of the poor, assessors and policemen.[59] Officers may be removed for cause.[60]

Male Indians of 21 or over who shall not have been convicted of a felony are eligible to vote and hold office.[61]

---

[48] Members of the several nations have intermarried and have taken up residence "abroad," with the result that members of every nation are found on every reservation.

[49] McKinney's Con. Laws of New York Annotated, Bk. 25, New York Indian Code.

> The Allegany Reservation, claimed by the Senecas, contains 30,469 acres, and is located on both sides of the Allegany River in Cattaraugus County, N. Y. It is about 40 miles long and averages from 1 to 3 miles in width. It is a part of the area specifically reserved to the Seneca Indians in the treaty with Robert Morris at "Big Tree" September 17, 1797. This entire reservation is subject to the "preemption right" or "claim" of the Ogden Land Co., to which reference is hereinafter more fully made.
>
> The Cattaraugus Reservation contains 21,680 acres, located principally in Erie County, a small part lying in each of the counties of Cattaraugus and Chautauqua. This reservation was conveyed to the Seneca Indians by Wilhelm Willnick, et al., predecessors of the Ogden Land Co., by agreement dated June 30, 1802 (7 Stat., 70), in return for which the Seneca Indians surrendered to the company certain other lands which had been reserved to them by the treaty at Big Tree. This reservation is also subject to the preemption right of the Ogden Land Co., such right being specifically retained in the agreement referred to.
>
> The Oil Spring Reservation, located partly in Allegany and partly in Cattaraugus Counties, contains only 640 acres. Its name is derived from a muddy pool, about 20 feet in diameter, located near the center of the tract, from which the Indians formerly gathered a sort of crude petroleum locally known as "Seneca oil," and which was used quite extensively by them in early days for medicinal purposes. The Senecas fully understood that this tract was reserved to them in the sale to Robert Morris at Big Tree, but this fact does not appear from an examination of the treaty itself. At any rate, this reserve was included in a sale by Robert Morris to the Holland Land Co., so-called, and several mesne conveyances transpired until by deed dated February 28, 1855, one Philoneus Pattison became the ostensible owner of a part thereof. On taking possession, the Seneca Indians promptly began an action in ejectment against Pattison. A verdict in favor of the Indians was rendered by the lower court; the case was appealed to the supreme court of the State and finally to the court of appeals, both of which affirmed the decision of the trial court, and the Indians have since remained in undisturbed possession. A written opinion of the case does not appear to have been handed down, but the pleadings, transcript of evidence, judgment, and decree of the court are still on file in Little Valley, the county seat of Cattaraugus County. (H. Doc. No. 1590, 63d Cong., 3d sess., 1915, pp. 11–12.)

[50] *Ibid.*, sec. 41, 42. See amended constitution of the Seneca Nation, 1893, which provides for annual election of councilors (sec. 2).

[51] Constitution, *supra*, sec. 3. See, too, New York Indian Code, *supra*, sec. 72.

[52] New York Indian Code, *supra*, sec. 41.

[53] *Ibid.*, sec. 46. Although the New York Indian Code expressly provides for similarity in proceedings only insofar as compelling attendance of witnesses is concerned, the 1893 constitution provides for such similarity also in jurisdiction and proceedings. (sec. 4).

[54] On the power of the peacemakers' courts of the Seneca Indians of the Cattaraugus Reservation, see *Washburn* v. *Parker*, 7 F. Supp. 120 (D. C. W. D. N. Y. 1934). In the absence of congressional legislation, the federal courts lack jurisdiction over internal questions relating to property rights of individual Indians of the Cattaraugus Reservation, *United States* v. *Seneca Nation*, 274 Fed. 946 (D. C. W. D. N. Y., 1921); *Rice* v. *Maybee*, 2 F. Supp. 669 (D. C. W. D. N. Y. 1933).

The court in *Rice* v. *Maybee*, 2 F. Supp. 669 (D. C. W. D. N. Y., 1933), described the Seneca government as follows:

> In 1848 the Seneca Indians adopted a so-called "Constitutional Charter," abolishing the ancient form of government by chiefs, and setting up a new form of government composed of legislative, executive, and judiciary departments. In the judiciary department it provided for Peacemakers' Courts in which the jurisdiction would be "the same as in courts of justices of the peace of the state of New York, except in proof of wills, and the settlement of deceased persons' estates, in which cases the Peacemakers shall have such power as shall be conferred by law." It also provided that "all cases of which the Peacemakers have not jurisdiction may be heard before the Council, or such courts of the state of New York as the Legislature thereof shall permit." The council is the lawmaking body. This charter also provided that all laws of the state of New York, not inconsistent with the provisions of the charter, were to continue in full force. This charter was amended in 1898 to provide that these courts have "exclusive jurisdiction in all civil cases arising between Indians residing on said reservation except those of which the Surrogate's Court has jurisdiction." Since the organization of New York state, that state has written upon its statute books many laws relative to the management of the affairs of the Indians in these reservations. The Indian charter contemplates a measure of control by the state. The general Indian Law of New York state is included in chapter 26 of the Consolidated Laws, and among its many provisions with reference to the Seneca Indians we find that it provides for a Peacemakers' Court, with "authority to hear and determine all matters, disputes and controversies between any Indians residing upon such reservation, whether arising upon contracts or for wrongs, and particularly for any encroachments or trespass on any land cultivated or occupied by any one of them, and which shall have been entered and described in the clerk's books of records" (section 46), and, further, "jurisdiction * * * to hear and determine all questions and actions between individual Indians residing thereon involving the title to real estate on such reservations." It is clear that the provisions of the Indian charter and this section of the Indian Law include actions such as the one at bar and the action brought before the Peacemakers' Court. Section 50 of the Indian Law, New York, provides for an appeal from the decision of the Peacemakers' Court to the council, which was the lawmaking body in the Indian reservation. Here we have both the tribal law and the state law purporting to confer jurisdiction.
>
> The Peacemakers' Court did not originate with the state. It was the creation of the Indians themselves. As the court in *Mulkins* v. *Snow*, *supra*, said: "It is an Indian court which has been recognized and given strength and authority by statute. It does not owe its existence to the state statute and is only in a qualified sense a state court." Matter of *Patterson* v. *Council of Seneca Nation*, 245 N. Y. 433, 157 N. E. 734. (P. 671.)

[55] New York Indian Code, *supra*, sec. 50.

[56] Amended Constitution, *supra*, sec. 4.

[57] *Ibid.*, sec. 5.

[58] *Ibid.*, sec. 6.

[59] *Ibid.*, sec. 8.

[60] *Ibid.*, sec. 9.

[61] *Ibid.*, sec. 10. The statute (New York Indian Code, *supra*, Art. 4, secs. 42, 43) contains no requirement that voters shall not have been convicted of felonies.

The council is given power to make laws not inconsistent with the Constitution of the United States, the State of New York, or the Seneca Nation.[61]

The constitution may be altered or amended at any time by a prescribed process.[62]

B. TONAWANDA BAND OF SENECAS

The government of the Tonawanda band is separate and distinct from that of the rest of the Seneca Nation.[64]

The legislative branch of the government of this band is placed in a council of the chiefs,[65] who are apparently chosen as in the days of the Confederate League of the Iroquois. The power and jurisdiction of this council is recognized and supported by the Indian code of the New York State law.[66] The council is given power to pass bylaws not inconsistent with this law and is given jurisdiction over animal trespasses, lands, and fences.[67]

The judiciary appears to be in the hands of three peacemakers elected annually by Tonawanda Senecas; males over 21 years of age may vote. Peacemakers try cases involving local ordinances and differences among Indians, and hear suits for divorce.

Additional officers are a president, clerk, treasurer, and marshal.

C. ST. REGIS MOHAWKS[68]

The local government of the St. Regis Mohawks[69] is covered by a separate article of the Indian code of the State of New York.[70] This permits and supports a local governmental unit of three elected chiefs, and three subchiefs, who serve when the chiefs are unable to do so.[71] One chief and one subchief are elected each year, to serve for a period of 3 years,[72] by male Indians 21 or over residing on the American side of the international boundary, and entitled to draw yearly annuity money.[73]

The three chiefs have power to pass by-laws not inconsistent with law, relating to common land, fences and animal trespasses,[74] have jurisdiction over allotment of lands,[75] their consent is necessary for sales of timber,[76] and they may hear differences arising among Indians regarding trespass and titles to land.[77] The only other elective office provided for is that of clerk.[78]

D. TUSCARORA NATION

The Tuscarora Reservation is governed by chiefs of the Tuscarora Nation[79] tacitly recognized by the New York code,[80] who have been given power to allot lands[81] and control timber sales.[82] The statute does not provide for a peacemakers' court on the Tuscarora Reservation. The statute provides no mechanism for election of chiefs and they appear to be chosen by ancient methods.

---

[61] Amended Constitution, *supra*, sec. 13. The statute (*supra*, fn. 61, sec. 73) limits the legislative power of the council to the passing of by-laws and ordinances relative to common land, fences, trespass of animals.

[62] *Ibid.*, sec. 16.

[63] *Cf.* New York Indian Code, *supra*, fn. 49, which deals with the Tonawanda Senecas separately in Art. 6.

[64] "The Tonawanda Reservation now comprises but 7,549 acres lying partly in Erie, Genesee, and Niagara Counties. Originally it comprised upward of 45,000 acres, being a part of the lands reserved to the Seneca Indians in the sale to Robert Morris at Big Tree. This reservation was conveyed to Thomas Ludlow Ogden and Joseph Fellows by agreement with the Six Nations, dated January 15, 1838 (7 Stats., 550), and the subsequent treaty with the Senecas of May 20, 1842 (7 Stats., 586). The lands embraced within the present reserve were repurchased from Ogden and Fellows for the sum of $100,000, in accordance with article 3 of the treaty with the Tonawanda Indians, dated November 5, 1857 (11 Stats., 735). Title was first taken in the Secretary of the Interior, who held the lands until February 14, 1862, on which date, by deed, they were conveyed to the comptroller of the State of New York 'in trust and in fee for the Tonawanda Indians.' This settlement effectually extinguished whatever preemption right the Ogden Land Co. ever had in and to the lands within this reservation." (H. Doc. No. 1590, 63d Cong., 3d sess., 1915 p. 12.)

[65] *Ibid.*, sec. 82. Although this section provides for the filling of vacancies in elective offices by the chiefs it does not specifically provide that only a chief may be elected.

[66] *Ibid.*, sec. 80.

[67] See Memo. of C. E. Collett, 5 L. D. Memo. D. J. 236, May 13, 1935.

[68] *Ibid.*

[69] Subsequent to an act of the New York legislature in 1791 authorizing the sale of waste lands in New York, Alexander McComb attempted to purchase all lands between Lake Champlain and the St. Lawrence, proposing to exclude a tract 6 miles square for the St. Regis Indians. His offer was rejected. In 1792, 1793, and 1794, the Seven Nations of Canada, Iroquois who had sided with the British in the Revolution, waited upon the Governor of New York asserting their rights to a greater area, but without favorable results. In 1796 the New York legislature authorized the Governor to appoint a commission to extinguish the Indian titles to lands in the northern part of the state. On May 31, 1796, 7 Stat. 55, a treaty was made before Ogden as Commissioner for the United States by which the St. Regis Indians ceded all lands to the United States except an area 6 miles square at St. Regis, a mile square on the Salmon River, receiving $3,200 and an annuity of $535.

[70] New York Indian Code, *supra*, Art. 8.

[71] *Ibid.*, sec. 109, 110.

[72] *Ibid.*, sec. 110.

[73] *Ibid.*, sec. 108.

[74] *Ibid.*, sec. 107.

[75] *Ibid.*, sec. 102.

[76] *Ibid.*, secs. 103, 104.

[77] *Ibid.*, sec. 106.

[78] An attorney is appointed by the Governor who acts as treasurer and prosecutor for the band.

[79] "The Tuscarora Reservation lies in Niagara County about 9 miles northeast of Niagara Falls, and contains 6,249 acres. The Tuscarora Indians having been adopted by the Iroquois League as one of the Six Nations, by deed dated March 30, 1808, the Seneca Nation granted 1 square mile (640 acres) to the Tuscarora Indians. (Liber 1, folio 56, Land Records of Niagara County.) It is reported that subsequently the Holland Land Co., assignee of Robert Morris, "ratified" this grant, and gave to the Tuscaroras 1,280 acres more, but no record of any paper title to this effect can be found. At any rate, the Tuscaroras occupy and claim these lands as a part of their present reserve, which are subject to the preemption right of the Ogden Land Co. (7 Stat., 560), although the Indians deny this, basing their claim on a decree of the State court in Buffalo, handed down in 1850. This suit resulted from an agreement with the Federal Government, January 15, 1838, under which the Six Nations were to remove west of the Mississippi River, and in anticipation of their removal the chiefs of the Tuscarora Tribe executed a deed to Thomas Ludlow Ogden and Joseph Fellows, predecessors of the Ogden Land Co., conveying to said Ogden and Fellows, as owners of the preemptive right, the 1,920 acres last referred to. The deed was placed in the hands of Herman B. Potter, in escrow, pending the performance of certain conditions precedent to delivery. The expected removal failed to materialize and in 1849 Wm. B. Chew et al., chiefs of the tribe, instituted suit against Herman B. Potter and Joseph Fellows (Thomas L. Ogden then being deceased), looking to a surrender and cancelation of the deed. A verdict in favor of the Indians was rendered and the deed canceled by the decree of the court, which resulted only in placing the matter in statu quo, as far as the preemptive right of Ogden and Fellows was concerned. The execution of the deed was an admission of the existence of the preemptive right, and the contention of the Indians that the decree of the court canceling the deed also effectually extinguished the right of preemption in the Ogden people does not appear well founded. The records in the case are still on file in the county clerk's office at Buffalo.

About the year 1800 a delegation of Tuscarora Indians visited the governor of North Carolina and negotiated a sale of their lands in that State for approximately $15,000, which money was deposited with the United States in trust. In 1804 Congress authorized the Secretary of War to purchase with this money additional land for these Indians. With these funds 4,329 acres, lying to the south and east of the 1,920 acres already occupied by them, were purchased for the Tuscarora Indians. Title to these lands was taken by the Secretary of War in trust for the Indians, but subsequently (January 2, 1809) the lands were conveyed directly to the Tuscarora Tribe, who now own the fee. (Book "A" p. 5, Niagara County clerk's office.)" (H. Doc. No. 1590, 63rd Cong., 3d sess., 1915, pp. 12–13.)

[80] New York Indian Code, *supra*, Art. 7.

[81] *Ibid.*, sec. 95.

[82] *Ibid.*, secs. 96, 98.

E. ONONDAGA NATION

The governing body of the Onondaga Nation appears to be a council of chiefs chosen and installed according to dictates of ancient tradition. This body is recognized by inference by the Indian code of the New York State law.[82] It has jurisdiction to lease lands with the consent of the agent,[84] and its consent is necessary before timber may be removed.[85] It also settles disputes among Indians.

F. CAYUGA NATION

The Cayuga Nation[86] has no reservation of its own,[87] but maintains a tribal organization of chieftains, four chiefs forming the governing body, with headquarters on the Cattaraugus Reservation.[88]

G. SHINNECOCK INDIANS

The Shinnecock Indians,[89] occupying the 450-acre Shinnecock Reservation on Long Island, have always been distinct and separate from the Iroquois League, although at one time it is said they paid tribute to the Mohawks.

The New York Indian code[90] provides for the election of three trustees by the adult males who have lived on the Shinnecock Reservation for 6 months prior to the election date.[91] These trustees have authority over tribal land and timber matters.[92] Authority, however, is vested in the justices of the peace in the town of Southampton to pass on leases of tribal lands proposed by the trustees.[93]

H. POOSEPATUCK INDIANS

About a dozen families were reported in 1936 to occupy the 50-acre Poosepatuck Reservation on Long Island.[94] There appear to be no extant statutes specifically relating to this reservation, which had its origin in a grant by Governor William Smith in 1700.[95] Land matters are managed by a board of trustees, elected annually in April,[96] under authority of the "General Provisions" of the New York State Indian law.[97]

---

82 *Ibid.*, Art. 3, sec. 22, 23, and 24.

83 "The Onondaga Reservation contains 6,100 acres and is located in Onondaga County about 5 miles south of the city of Syracuse. Prior to 1793 this reservation embraced something over 65,000 acres. March 11 of that year, however, the Indians sold over three-fourths of their reservation to the State, and by subsequent treaties in 1795, 1817, and 1822 the reservation was reduced to its present area. Under State laws these Indians are authorized to lease land owned or possessed by individuals, and small areas within the reservation are so leased. The lands within this reservation are not covered by the claim of the Ogden Land Co." (H. Doc. No. 1590, 63d Cong., 3d sess., 1915, p. 12.)

84 *Ibid.*, sec. 24.

85 *Ibid.*, sec. 22.

86 By the Treaty of February 27, 1789, the Cayuga Nation sold certain lands to the State of New York, reserving only 100 square miles around Cayuga Lake, a small parcel on Seneca River, and a square mile at Cayuga Ferry. These reservations were later sold to the state, on July 27, 1795. The larger portion of the Cayugas has removed to the west of the Mississippi, but approximately 200 remain in New York. They live for the most part with the Senecas, but a few are with the Tonawandas.

87 For reference to the reservation of the Cayuga and Seneca who removed to Indian Territory, see Chapter 23.

88 The Cayugas are not treated by the New York Indian Code.

89 There are about 100 persons belonging to this tribe.

"The Shinnecock Reservation, containing some 450 acres, is located on a neck of land running into Shinnecock Bay, Long Island. Southampton was an early colonial town, established in the seventeenth century, and the town trustees negotiated with "Shinnecock," chief of the tribe, for a sale of the lands. Tribal tradition has it that the chief sold out to the whites and skipped with the money. While this does not comport with accepted ideas of the honesty and integrity of aboriginal chiefs, yet it is a matter of record that the town trustees of Southampton in the early days gave a lease for a thousand years to the Shinnecock Indians covering some 3,600 acres, known as the Shinnecock Hills and Shinnecock Neck. Matters stood thus until about the middle of the nineteenth century, when the town had developed to such an extent that a more satisfactory arrangement was desired. Accordingly, in 1859 the state authorized the town trustees to negotiate with the Indians for a cession of their leasehold estate. An agreement was reached, under which the Indians surrendered the hills, in exchange for which they received in fee Shinnecock Neck." (H. Doc. No. 1590, 63d Cong., 3d sess., 1915, p. 13.)

90 New York Indian Code, *supra*, Art. 9.

91 *Ibid.*, sec. 120.

92 *Ibid.*, secs. 121, 122.

93 *Ibid.*, sec. 121.

94 Report on the Shinnecock and Poosepatuck Indian Reservations in Relation to the Reorganization Act, by Allan G. Harper, January, 1936 (Indian Office files).

95 *Ibid.*

96 *Ibid.*

97 New York Indian Code, *supra*, Art. 2.

Chapter 23

SPECIAL LAWS RELATING TO OKLAHOMA

TABLE OF CONTENTS

The laws governing the Indians of Oklahoma are so voluminous that analysis of them would require a treatise in itself. In fact, two treatises have already been written on the subject,[1] and at least two more are in the course of preparation. No attempt, therefore, will be made in this volume to deal *in extenso* with this mass of legislation or with the thousands of state and federal cases in which that legislation is applied and construed. It must be recognized, however, that in many respects the statutes and legal principles discussed in other chapters of this work as generally applicable to Indians of the United States, also apply to Oklahoma Indians, while in other respects Oklahoma Indians, or certain groups thereof, are excluded from the scope of such statutes and legal principles. In order to clarify the scope of the laws, decisions, and rulings discussed in other chapters of this work, it is therefore deemed appropriate to survey the most important fields in which Oklahoma Indians have received distinctive treatment and which present distinctive legal problems.

These fields include enrollment, property laws affecting the Five Civilized Tribes, taxation, and, among the Osages, questions of head-rights, competency, wills, and leasing. In each field our effort will be to note how far principles generally applicable to Indians are applicable or inapplicable in Oklahoma, rather than to explore the distinctive problems of the various Oklahoma tribes, many of which are still unsettled by the courts.

Before proceeding to this survey, however, it is useful to pass over, in brief review, the historical background out of which the peculiarities of Oklahoma Indian law emerge.

[1] Mills, Oklahoma Indian Land Laws (2d ed. 1924); Bledsoe, Indian Land Laws (2d ed. 1913).

SECTION 1. OKLAHOMA TRIBES

Reference is sometimes made to the Five Civilized Tribes (the Cherokees, Choctaws, Chickasaws, Creeks and Seminoles), and the Osages, as if they were the only tribes resident in the State of Oklahoma.[2] In fact, the Indian tribes residing in the state include also the Cheyenne, Arapaho, Apache, Comanche, Kiowa, Caddo, Delaware, Wichita, Kaw, Otoe, Tonkawa, Pawnee, Ponca, Shawnee, Ottawa, Quapaw, Seneca, Wyandotte, Iowa, Sac and Fox, Kickapoo and Pottawatomi.[3]

Many general statutes are expressly made inapplicable to the Five Civilized Tribes[4] or the Osages[5] or to these nations and the Osages[6] or to all tribes in Oklahoma.[7] Congress has passed many special laws for Oklahoma tribes, especially for the Five Civilized Tribes and the Osages.[8]

[2] Former Commissioner of Indian Affairs Leupp cites a blunder by a Congressman who drafted an amendment which excepted from its operation "the Indians of the Indian Territory" out of which the State of Oklahoma was later carved, and of its passage by the House of Representatives in the belief that the Five Civilized Tribes were the only Indians in the Territory. Leupp, The Indian and His Problem (1910), p. 206.

[3] See Act of June 18, 1934, sec. 13, 48 Stat. 984, 986, which excluded from its provisions these tribes in the State of Oklahoma. The tribes in Oklahoma number not less than 100,000 members. (Hearings before the Comm. on Ind. Aff. on H. R. 6234, 74th Cong., 1st sess., 1935, p. 9.) There are 72,000 members of the Five Civilized Tribes, of whom about 28,000 are half to full-blood (*ibid.* p. 90). The Osages number over 3,300, of which about 650 are full-bloods (*ibid.* p. 113). The remaining Indians of Oklahoma number about 19,000, of which about 70 percent are of half or more Indian blood. (Hearings before the Comm. on Ind. Aff. on S. 2047, 74th Cong. 1st sess., 1935, p. 23.)

[4] Act of July 31, 1882, 22 Stat. 179, R. S. 2133, 25 U. S. C. 264; Act of January 6, 1883, 22 Stat. 400; Act of August 9, 1888, 25 Stat. 392, 25 U. S. C. 181.

[5] Act of June 24, 1938, sec. 1, 52 Stat 1037, 25 U. S. C. 162a.

[6] Act of June 25, 1910, sec. 33, 36 Stat. 855, 863. 25 U. S. C. 353; similarly, amendment by the Act of February 14, 1913, 37 Stat. 678, 679. Also see Act of June 30, 1919, sec. 1, 41 Stat. 3, 9, 25 U. S. C. 163, which is also inapplicable to the Chippewas of Minnesota and the Menominees of Wisconsin.

[7] Act of June 18, 1934, sec. 13, 48 Stat. 984, 988, 25 U. S. C. 478.

[8] See other sections of this chapter. On Five Civilized Tribes also see Act of March 1, 1907, 34 Stat. 1015, 1027, 25 U. S. C. 199; Act of May 24, 1922, 42 Stat. 552, 575, 25 U. S. C. 124. For an example of a special law applying to lesser known Oklahoma tribes see Act of June 30, 1919, sc. 17, 41 Stat. 3, 20, 25 U. S. C. 125 (Quapaw Agency).

SECTION 2. REMOVAL

Few of these tribes were indigenous to this part of the country. It was to Oklahoma, originally "Indian Territory," that Indians residing on lands desired for other purposes migrated or were moved by the United States Government.[9] Attorney General Daugherty[10] described the conditions under which the Five Civilized Tribes migrated to Oklahoma in the 1830's:

> When the southern portion of the United States, east of the Mississippi, was settled, the above-mentioned tribes [Cherokees, Choctaws, Chickasaws, Creeks, and Seminoles] were occupying and claiming ownership of all that territory.
>
> By treaty and the use of a degree of force in instances, the tribes agreed to take up their abode farther west, out of the way of the white man, on the land that was afterward designated as Indian Territory. It was a part of the consideration for the removal that they should possess the said land unmolested forever as an independent people with their own forms of government and should not in all future time be embarrassed by having extended around them the lines of, or by having placed over them the jurisdiction of a Territory or State, or by being encroached upon by the extension in any way of the limits of an existing Territory or State.

The westward migration of these and other tribes has been considered elsewhere.[11]

[9] See Chapter 3, sec. 4. Tribes were moved to Oklahoma from the Atlantic seaboard, many portions of the Middle West, and even as far north as western New York. (Hearings before the Comm. on Ind. Aff., on H. R. 6234, 74th Cong., 1st sess., 1935, p. 9.) The Attorney General said:

> The Cherokees were among the most powerful of the aboriginal nations, and occupied the principal part of the country now comprising the States of North and South Carolina, Georgia, Alabama, and Tennessee. It was as the result of several treaties that they relinquished that great domain and were finally seated in comparatively limited territory now occupied by them, and which was accepted by them as an exchange for the territory they had abandoned and ceded to the United States.
>
> The territory thus accepted, the United States, by repeated treaties, pledges its faith shall be a "permanent home" (treaty 28 May, 1828, preamble, 7 Stat., 311) to the Cherokees, and "be and remain theirs forever" (*ibid*), and guaranties them "the quiet and peaceable possession of their country," and that it shall be conveyed to them by patent subject to the single condition that the lands ceded shall "revert to the United States" in case the Indian grantees shall become extinct or shall abandon them. (Treaty 12th April, 1834, 7 Stat. 414; act 28 May, 1830, sec. 3, 4 Stat., 411.) (Cited in 19 Op. A. G. 42, 43–44 (1887).)

[10] 34 Op. A. G. 275 (1924). On the history of the Cherokee removal see 5 Op. A. G. 320 (1851); *Holden* v. *Joy*, 17 Wall. 211 (1872). Kinney, A Continent Lost—A Civilization Won (1937), pp. 27–80, discusses the agitation for the removal of Indians. Schmeckebier, The Office of Indian Affairs, Its History, Activities and Organization (1927), pp. 99–142, discusses the history of the Five Civilized Tribes, Indian Territory and Oklahoma. On removal of Indians to Oklahoma, see also *ibid.*, pp. 29–38. And see Foreman, Indian Removal, The Emigration of the Five Civilized Tribes of Indians (1932); Lumpkin, Removal of the Cherokee Indians from Georgia (1907).

[11] Chapter 3, sec. 4E, and Chapter 15, sec. 6.

SECTION 3. SELF-GOVERNMENT[12]

Various guarantees of tribal self-government and of territorial integrity were made to induce the Indians to sign "removal" treaties. The Supreme Court in the case of *Atlantic and Pacific Railroad Company* v. *Mingus*[13] described some of the guarantees:

> * * * a reference to some of the treaties, under which it [the Indian Territory] is held by the Indians, indicates that it stands in an entirely different relation to the United States from other Territories, and that for most purposes it is to be considered as an independent country. Thus in the treaty of December 29, 1835, 7 Stat. 478, with the Cherokees, whereby the United States granted and conveyed by patent to the Cherokees a portion of this territory, the United States, in article 5, convenanted and agreed that the land ceded to the Cherokees should "in no future time, without their consent, be included within the territorial limits or jurisdiction of any State or Territory"; and by further treaty of August 16, 1846, 9 Stat. 871, provided (Art. 1) "that the lands now occupied by the Cherokee Nation shall be secured to the whole Cherokee people for their common use and benefit, and a patent shall be issued for the same." So, too, by treaty with the Choctaws of September 27, 1830, 7 Stat. 333, granting a portion of the Indian Territory to them, the United States (Art. 4) secured to the "Choctaw Nation of Red People the jurisdiction and government of all the persons and property that may be within their limits west, so that no Territory or State shall ever have the right to pass laws for the government of the Choctaw Nation of Red People and their descendants, and that no part of the land granted shall ever be embraced in any Territory or State; but the United States shall forever secure said Choctaw Nation from, and against, all laws except such as from time to time may be enacted in their own national councils, not inconsistent," etc. And in a treaty of March 24, 1832, 7 Stat. 366, with the Creeks (Art. 14), the Creek country west of the Mississippi was solemnly guaranteed to these Indians, "nor shall any State or Territory ever have a right to pass laws for the government of such Indians, but they shall be allowed to govern themselves, so far as may be compatible with the general jurisdiction which Congress may think proper to exercise over them."
>
> Under the guaranties of these and other similar treaties the Indians have proceeded to establish and carry on independent governments of their own, enacting and executing their own laws, punishing their own criminals, appointing their own officers, raising and expending their own revenues. Their position, as early as 1855, is indicated by the following extract from the opinion of this court in *Mackey* v. *Coxe*, 18 How. 100, 103:
>
> > "A question has been suggested whether the Cherokee people should be considered or treated as a foreign state or territory. The fact that they are under the Constitution of the Union, and subject to acts of Congress regulating trade, is a sufficient answer to the suggestion. They are not only within our jurisdiction, but the faith of the nation is pledged for their protection. In some respects they bear the same relation to the Federal Government as a Territory did in its second grade of Government under the ordinance of 1787. Such Territory passed its own laws, subject to the approval of Congress, and its inhabitants were subject to the Constitution and acts of Congress. The principal difference consists in the fact that the Cherokees enact their own laws, under the restriction stated, appoint their own officers, and pay their own expenses. This, however, is no reason why the laws and proceedings of the Cherokee territory, so far as relates to rights claimed under them, should not be placed upon the same footing as other Territories in the Union. It is not a foreign, but a domestic territory—a Territory which orignated under our Constitution and laws."
>
> Similar language is used with reference to these Indians in *Holden* v. *Joy*, 17 Wall. 211, 242. * * * (Pp. 435–437)

[12] See Chapter 7, and Chapter 9, sec. 5A and B.

[13] 165 U. S. 413 (1897).

Practically all of the Oklahoma tribes were well organized when they moved to the Indian Territory, and in the new land. * * * They maintained complete governments; particularly in the East, five tribe areas; they had their own schools, their own legislative assemblies, their own courts. And they did the job well. Under all the conditions they made a record which would have been creditable to any municipality or State in this country.[14]

Certain of the Five Civilized Tribes adopted the political forms of the white world,[15] and administrative rulings and opinions have frequently upheld their power of self-government.[16]

[14] Hearings before the Comm. on Ind. Aff., on S. 2047, 74th Cong., 1st sess., 1935, p. 10. With the exception of the Seminoles, all the Five Civilized Tribes had written and printed constitutions and laws. Schmeckebier, The Office of Indian Affairs, Its History, Activities and Organization (1927), p. 127. But see Leupp, The Indian and His Problem (1910), p. 332.

[15] J. Collier, 4 Indians at Work No. 21 (June 15, 1937), p. 1.

[16] A few opinions exemplify this view.

The Attorney General in advising the Secretary of the Treasury that a national bank cannot lawfully be established at Muscogee, a town in the territory of the Creek Nations, said:

> The right of the Creek Nation to govern itself, so carefully guarded and protected by these treaties, is a right founded on a consideration of great value, moving directly from the Creek Nation to the United States, and the faith of the latter is pledged for the protection of the Creeks in all the rights secured to them by the treaties mentioned. (19 Op. A. G. 342, 344 (1889).)

The Supreme Court in *Turner* v. *United States*, 248 U. S. 354 (1919), said:

> The Creek or Muskogee Nation or Tribe of Indians had, in 1890, a population of 15,000. Subject to the control of Congress, they then exercised within a defined territory the powers of a sovereign people; having a tribal organization, their own system of laws, and a government with the usual branches, executive, legislative, and judicial. The territory was divided into six districts; and each district was provided with a judge. (Pp. 354–355.)

The Supreme Court in the case of *Marlin* v. *Lewallen*, 276 U. S. 58, 60–61 (1928), said:

> For many years the Creeks maintained a government of their own, with executive legislative and judicial branches. They were located in the Indian Territory and occupied a large district which belonged to the tribe as a community, not to the members severally or as tenants in common. The situation was the same with the Cherokees, Choctaws, Chickashaws and Seminoles, who with the Creeks were known as the five civilized tribes. All were under the guardianship of the United States and within territory over which it had plenary jurisdiction, thus enabling it to exercise full control over them and their districts whenever it perceived a need therefor. [*Stephens* v. *Cherokee Nation*, 174 U. S. 445, 483, et seq.; *Cherokee Nation* v. *Hitchcock*, 187 U. S. 294, 305, et seq.] In the beginning and for a long period, during which the districts were widely separated from white communities, the United States refrained in the main from exerting its power of control and left much to the tribal governments. Accordingly the tribes framed and put in force various laws which they regarded as adapted to their situations, including laws purporting to regulate descent and distribution [Bledsoe's Indian Land Laws, 2d ed., pp. 640–643] and to exclude persons who were not members from sharing in tribal lands or funds. [Perryman's Creek Laws 1890, c. 7; McKellop's Creek Laws 1893, c. 22; Cherokee Intermarriage Cases, 203 U. S. 76.]

The Supreme Court in the case of *Morris* v. *Hitchcock*, 194 U. S. 384, 388–389 (1904), per Mr. Justice White, said:

> While it is unquestioned that by the Constitution of the United States Congress is vested with paramount power to regulate commerce with the Indian tribes, yet it is also undoubted that in treaties entered into with the Chickasaw Nation, the right of that tribe to control the presence within the territory assigned to it of persons who might otherwise be regarded as intruders has been sanctioned, and the duty of the United States to protect the Indians "from aggression by other Indians and white persons, not subject to their jurisdiction and laws," has also been recognized. Arts. 7 and 14, Treaty June 22, 1855, 11 Stat. 611; Art. 8, Treaty April 28, 1866, 14 Stat. 769. And it is not disputed that under the authority of these treaties the Chickasaw Nation has exercised the power to attach conditions to the presence within its borders of persons who might otherwise not be entitled to remain within the tribal territory.

Also see brief submitted by Commissioner of Indian Affairs relating to power of Congress over Indians—Hearings before the Comm. on Ind. Aff., United States Senate, 73d Congress, 2d sess., on S. 2755 and S. 3645, pt. 2 (1934), pp. 268, 269–270; 18 Op. A. G. 34 (1884); Treaty of June 14, 1866, Art. X, 14 Stat. 785, 788; Reports of the Comm. of Ind. Aff. (1888), pp. 116, 114; (1889), p. 202; (1890), pp. 89, 90; (1891), vol. I, pp. 240–241.

Excerpts from the constitution of the Cherokees, are contained in *Cherokee Nation* v. *Journeycake*, 155 U. S. 196 (1894). For a decision holding that certain lands were "occupied" by the Cherokee Nation for the purpose of criminal and taxing jurisdiction see *United States* v. *Rogers*, 23 Fed. 658 (D. C. W. D. Ark., 1885). In executing treaties, the view of the United States, and not of the Cherokee council governs federal action. 16 Op. A. G. 404 (1879).

SECTION 4. GOVERNMENT OF INDIAN TERRITORY

As a result of the adherence of the Five Civilized Tribes to the Confederacy during the Civil War, the President of the United States was empowered to abrogate existing treaties with these Indians.[17] Accordingly during 1866 new treaties were negotiated with each of the tribes.[18] For the purpose of forming a federated Indian government of the tribes, certain identical provisions were inserted in each treaty.[19] Though the plan failed to materialize,[20] the territory intended to be thus organized became known as the Indian Territory.[21]

Soon it was apparent that the seclusion and isolation which the Indians sought was to be disturbed. Land-hungry whites overflowed into the Indian Territory and reached about a quarter of a million at the beginning of the last decade of the nineteenth century.[22] Despite treaty obligations, many whites strongly desired to substitute their own methods of government for those of the tribes. In part this was due to the fact that Indian laws and courts had no jurisdiction over the white settlers[23] and the Indian Territory became the refuge for criminals from neighboring states. By the Act of May 2, 1890,[24] a portion of the Indian Territory was created into the Territory of Oklahoma. This act provided that until after the adjournment of the first territorial assembly the provisions of the compiled laws of Nebraska with respect to probate courts and decedents, so far as locally applicable and consistent with the laws of the United States and that act, should be in force in the Territory of Oklahoma. The act also provided that as to the portion of the former Indian Territory comprising the lands of the Five Civilized Tribes, and lands occupied by other tribes and certain other lands described in the act, the laws of Arkansas, as published in Mansfield's Digest for 1884, including descent and distribution, should be operative therein until Congress should otherwise provide, insofar as those laws were not locally in

[17] Act of July 5, 1862, 12 Stat. 512, 528.

[18] For further details, see Chapter 3, sec. 4; Chapter 8, sec. 11; provisions in some of the treaties for the removal by the United States Government of freedmen from the Indian Territory were not fulfilled (The Chickasaw Freedmen, 193 U. S. 115, 126 (1904)); and provisions for the granting of tribal membership and other rights to freedmen were often not complied with by the tribe or completed after a long delay. See Wardwell, A Political History of the Cherokee Nation (1938), p. 331. The history of the litigation and legislation regarding the freedmen of the Cherokee Nation is discussed in *Choctaw and Chickasaw Nations* v. *United States*, 81 C. Cls. 63 (1935), which cites many leading cases. Also see *Keetoowah Society* v. *Lane*, 41 App. D. C. 319 (1914).

[19] See Mills, *op. cit.*, pp. 2–3.

[20] *Ibid.*, p. 3.

[21] *Ibid.* The reduced Indian Territory after the separation of Oklahoma Territory was described by metes and bounds in the Act of May 2, 1890, sec. 29, 26 Stat. 81, 93. Also see Chapter 1, sec. 3.

[22] 34 Op. A. G. 275 (1924).

[23] See *Leak Glove Manuf'g. Co.* v. *Needles* 69 Fed. 68 (C. C. A. 8, 1895).

[24] 26 Stat. 81. For a discussion of the provisions of this law relating to courts, see Chapter 18, sec. 4 and Chapter 19, secs. 2B and 6.

applicable nor in conflict with any law of Congress or the provisions of the act.

Under the provisions of this act, the legislature of the Territory of Oklahoma during its first session, which expired on December 24, 1890, passed laws of descent or succession, which became effective on that date. Concerning the laws of that portion of the Indian Territory which continued to be so designated, Assistant Attorney General for the Interior Department, later Associate Justice of the Supreme Court of the United States, Van Devanter, in an opinion dated October 15, 1898, after pointing out that the laws of descent and distribution of Arkansas were in conflict with the provisions of the General Allotment Act referred to above, held that such laws, under the 1890 Act were "inapplicable" to the estates of Indian allottees in the Indian Territory and therefore that the laws of Kansas, as provided in the General Allotment Act did not apply to the Quapaw tribe. The Arkansas law, under the Act of 1890 applied to the Indians of that tribe. After this preliminary legislation, in 1893 Congress inaugurated a policy of terminating the tribal existence and government of the Five Civilized Tribes and allotting their lands in severalty.[25] Agreements were negotiated by the Dawes Commission with each of the tribes in order to carry out these objectives.[26] The Supreme Court has described this condition and the resulting legislation in the case of *Marlin* v. *Lewallen:*[27]

> In time the tribes came, through advancing settlements, to be surrounded by a large and increasing white population, many of the whites entering their districts and living there—some as tenant farmers, stock growers and merchants, and others as mere adventurers. The United States then perceived a need for making a larger use of its powers. [*Heckman* v. *United States*, 224 U. S. 413, 431–435; *Sizemore* v. *Brady*, 235 U. S. 441, 446.] What it did in that regard has a bearing on the questions before stated. (P. 61)
>
> By an act of March 1, 1889, c. 333, 25 Stat. 783, a special court was established for the Indian Territory and given jurisdiction of many offenses against the United States and of certain civil cases where not wholly between persons of Indian blood. By an act of May 2, 1890, c. 182, §§ 29–31, 26 Stat. 93, that jurisdiction was enlarged and several general statutes of the State of Arkansas, published in Mansfield's Digest, were put in force in the Territory so far as not locally inapplicable or in conflict with laws of Congress; but these provisions were restricted by others to the effect that the courts of each tribe should retain exclusive jurisdiction of all cases wholly between members of the tribe, and that the adopted Arkansas statutes should not apply to such cases. By an act of March 3, 1893, c. 209, § 16, 27 Stat. 645, a commission to the five civilized tribes was created and specially authorized to conduct negotiations with each of the tribes looking to the allotment of a part of its lands among its members, to some appropriate disposal of the remaining lands and to further adjustments preparatory to the dissolution of the tribe. By an act of June 7, 1897, c. 3, 30 Stat. 83–84, the special court was given exclusive jurisdiction of all future cases, civil and criminal, and the laws of the United States and the State of Arkansas in force in the Territory were made applicable to "all persons therein, irrespective of race," but with the qualification that any agreement negotiated by the commission with any of the five civilized tribes, when ratified, should supersede as to such tribe any conflicting provision in the act. By an act of June 28, 1898, c. 517, §§ 26 and 28, 30 Stat. 495, the enforcement of tribal laws in the special court was forbidden and the tribal courts were abolished.
>
> Thus the congressional enactments gradually came to the point where they displaced the tribal laws and put in force in the Territory a body of laws adopted from the statutes of Arkansas and intended to reach Indians as well as white persons, except as they might be inapplicable in particular situations or might be superseded as to any of the five civilized tribes by future agreements. (Pp. 61–62.)

By the Act of April 28, 1904,[28] it was provided that:

> All the laws of Arkansas heretofore put in force in the Indian Territory are hereby continued and extended in their operation, so as to embrace all persons and estates in said Territory, whether Indian, freedmen, or otherwise, and full and complete jurisdiction is hereby conferred upon the district courts in said Territory in the settlements of all estates of decedents, the guardianships of minors and incompetents, whether Indians, freedmen, or otherwise. * * *

[25] Act of March 3, 1893, sec. 16, 27 Stat. 612, 645.

[26] See *Ex parte Webb*, 225 U. S. 663. (1912).

[27] 276 U. S. 58 (1928). The court established in 1889 had jurisdiction of all offenses committed in the Indian Territory against any of the laws of the United States, not punishable with death or imprisonment at hard labor. On the offenses covered, see *In re Mills*, 135 U. S. 263 (1890); *In re Mayfield, Petitioner*, 141 U. S. 107, 114 (1891). The court also possessed jurisdiction over all civil controversies where the amount involved was $100 or more, except where both parties were members of Indian tribes.

As to what constitutes a marriage under the laws or tribal customs of any Indian nation within the meaning of the Act of May 2, 1890, c. 182, sec. 38, 26 Stat. 81, 98, see *Carney* v. *Chapman*, 247 U. S. 102 (1918). In *Leak Glove Manufacturing Co.* v. *Needles*, 69 Fed. 68 (C. C. A. 8, 1895), the Circuit Court of Appeals, in interpreting the Act of May 2, 1890, sec. 29, 26 Stat. 81, 93, said:

> * * * Section 3061 of Mansfield's Digest is the law of the Indian Territory, just as much as if it had been enacted by congress in haec verba. It is a mistake to suppose that chapter 60, containing the section in question, is to be treated in the Indian Territory as an Arkansas statute, as would be the case if a question should arise under it in the circuit court of the United States for the district of Arkansas. * * * The act of congress adopting an entire code of laws for the Indian Territory is not to receive the limited and restricted construction placed upon the process acts (section 914, Rev. St.), which merely required the circuit courts to conform the practice and pleadings in those courts to the practice and pleadings in the state courts "as near as may be." * * * (Pp. 69-70.)

Also see *Adkins* v. *Arnold*, 235 U. S. 417 (1914); *Joines* v. *Patterson*, 274 U. S. 544 (1927); *Sanger* v. *Flow*, 48 Fed. 152 (C. C. A. 8, 1891); *Blaylock* v. *Incorporated Town of Muskogee*, 117 Fed. 125 (C. C. A. 8, 1902).

For a detailed account of the history of the courts see *Ansley* v. *Ainsworth*, 180 U. S. 253 (1901).

For other cases interpreting this law see *United States* v. *Pridgeon*, 153 U. S. 48 (1894); *Alberty* v. *United States*, 162 U. S. 499 (1896); *Raymond* v. *Raymond*, 83 Fed. 721 (C. C. A. 8, 1897); *McCullough* v. *Smith*, 243 Fed. 823 (C. C. A. 8, 1917). The statute did not empower the court to entertain an action against the Choctaw Nation. *Thebo* v. *Choctaw Tribe of Indians*, 66 Fed. 372 (C. C. A. 8, 1895); nor repeal the Act of February 18, 1888 (25 Stat. 35), *Gowen* v. *Harley*, 56 Fed. 973 (C. C. A. 8, 1899). For an analysis of what cases might be considered in exclusive jurisdiction of the tribal court, see *Crabtree* v. *Madden*, 54 Fed. 426 (C. C. A. 8, 1893).

[28] 33 Stat. 573, sec. 2.

SECTION 5. STATEHOOD

The virtual dissolution of the tribal governments in the Indian Territory cleared the way for the creation of another state. Accordingly on June 16, 1906,[29] an act was passed making possible the admission into the Union of both Indian Territory and Oklahoma Territory as the State of Oklahoma. This so-called enabling act has been well summarized by the Supreme Court in *Jefferson* v. *Fink:*[30]

> By the enabling act of June 16, 1906, c. 3335, 34 Stat. 267, provision was made for admitting into the Union

[29] Act of June 16, 1906, 34 Stat. 267.

[30] 247 U. S. 288, 292 (1918).

At the time of the enabling act there was a large population of Indians in the Indian Territory, but a much larger population of whites.

both the Territory of Oklahoma and the Indian Territory as the State of Oklahoma. Each Territory had a distinct body of local laws. Those in the Indian Territory, as we have seen, had been put in force there by Congress. Those in the Territory of Oklahoma had been enacted by the territorial legislature. Deeming it better that the new State should come into the Union with a body of laws applying with practical uniformity throughout the State, Congress provided in the enabling act (§ 13) that "the laws in force in the *Territory of Oklahoma*, as far as applicable, shall *extend over and apply to said State* until changed by the legislature thereof," and also (§ 21) that "all laws in force in the *Territory of Oklahoma* at the time of the admission of said State into the Union shall be in force *throughout said State*, except as modified or changed by this act or by the constitution of the State." The people of the State, taking the same view, provided in their constitution (Art. 25, § 2) that "all laws in force in the *Territory of Oklahoma* at the time of the admission of the State into the Union, which are not repugnant to this Constitution, and which are not locally inapplicable, shall be *extended to and remain in force in the State of Oklahoma* until they expire by their own limitation or are altered or repealed by law." (Pp. 292–293.)

It should be noted that the act expressly provides that federal authority over the Indians should in no way be impaired; nor should the property rights of the Indians be limited.[31]

On November 16, 1907, the Territory of Oklahoma and the Indian Territory were admitted into the Union as the State of Oklahoma under the enabling act passed by Congress on June 16, 1906,[32] as amended by the Act of March 4, 1907.[33] The enabling act and the constitution of the new state united in declaring that, with certain exceptions, not material here, "the laws in force in the Territory of Oklahoma" at the time of the state's admission should be in force throughout the state and that the "courts of original jurisdiction of such State" should be the successors of "all courts of original jurisdiction of said Territories." The laws of the Territory of Oklahoma which were thus put in force "throughout" the new state included comprehensive provisions for the administration of estates of decedents, the appointment of guardians of minors and incompetents, and the management and sale of their property. In the territory of Oklahoma this jurisdiction was vested in probate courts and by the constitution of the new state that jurisdiction was committed to the county courts.[34]

The general condition existing in the State of Oklahoma at the time of its admission to the Union has been described as follows:[35]

> Oklahoma, with 1,500,000 population, became a State on November 16, 1907, upon a pledge contained in her constitution that she would never question the jurisdiction of the Federal Government over the Indians and their lands or its power to legislate by law or regulation concerning their rights or property. Immediately she had a delegation in Congress and at once began a determined campaign for further repeal of the laws enacted for the protection of the Indians. The main argument employed was that the Indians were competent to care for their property and needed no legislative protection against improvidence; that the State could be trusted to afford them all the protection they required and that Federal guardianship and supervision should cease, as an interference with the personal privileges and rights of citizens of Oklahoma. * * *
>
> This fight * * * resulted in the enactment of a law on May 27, 1908, effective July 27, 1908, repealing the restrictions on the sale of a large class of land, including all homesteads of freedmen and of mixed bloods of less than half blood, freeing from restrictions all told over 9,720,000 acres. It provided also that all homesteads, as well as all lands from which restrictions against sale were removed, should become taxable the same as lands of white people, whether sold by the allottee or not. This late act violated the terms of the agreement made with the Indians under which the homesteads of the Creeks and the allotments, or parts thereof, of the Choctaw and other tribes were exempted from taxation for a given period. (The American Indian, by Warren K. Moorehead, the Andover Press, Andover, Mass., p. 142.)

Joplin Mercantile Co. v. *United States*, 236 U. S. 531, 544–545 (1915). Under section 14 of the Curtis Act of June 28, 1898, 30 Stat. 495, 499, towns had been organized and were growing rapidly, and much of the land had been allotted.

> The requirement by Congress and the acceptance by the State that "every member of any Indian nation or tribe located within the State should be permitted to participate in the organization and conduct of the government of the state" conferred upon all such Indians citizenship in the state and in the United States.
>
> Allotments to the members of the various Indian tribes in Oklahoma had been substantially completed at the time of the admission of Oklahoma to statehood. * * * (Bledsoe, Indian Land Laws, (2d ed., 1913), p. 37.)

[31] Under secs. 16 and 20 of the Oklahoma Enabling Act the state took the place of the United States in regard to a prosecution for adultery, commenced in Indian Territory in one of the temporary courts of the United States, and all essential parts of the prosecution passed to the state. *Southern Surety Co.* v. *Okla.*, 241 U. S. 582 (1916).

[32] 34 Stat. 267.

[33] 34 Stat. 1286.

[34] See *Stewart* v. *Keyes*, 295 U. S. 403 (1935), pet. for rehearing den., 296 U. S. 661 (1935).

[35] Quoted from Hearings before the Comm. on Ind. Aff., House of Representatives, 74th Cong., 1st sess., on H. R. 6234 (1935), pp. 71–72.

SECTION 6. TERMINATION OF TRIBAL GOVERNMENT—FIVE CIVILIZED TRIBES

The Commission to the Five Civilized Tribes, first known as the Dawes Commission, prepared the groundwork for the termination of the tribes by procuring agreements with the several nations relative to the allotment of their lands.[36] Commissioner Collier has said:[37]

> * * * the time came when the pressure of white population made inevitable a break-up of the Indian territory, a break-up of the Indian ownership of that vast domain. That break-up was sought through allotting the land in severalty. In addition the tribal governments were practically abolished by statute. And the tribal treasures were amalgamated with the United States Treasury, but the fundamental technique was allotting the lands in severalty and that was done and at various times restrictions were lifted and methods were applied in various parts of the State different from those applied to the tribes in the West. And there grew up roughly two bodies of Indian law, one affecting the five tribes and largely the Osages, the other affecting the tribes of the West, and who had mostly come from the plains area.

The termination of the tribal governments is described by Ex-Commissioner of Indian Affairs Leupp:[38]

> * * * by successive acts of Congress the Five Civilized Tribes were shorn of their governmental functions: their courts were abolished and United States courts established; their chief executive officers were made subject to removal by the President, who was authorized to fill

[36] See sec. 8. The work of this commission is described in 34 Op. A. G. 275 (1924), and in *Woodward* v. *DeGraffenried*, 238 U. S. 284 (1915).

[37] Hearings before the Sen. Comm. on Ind. Aff., United States Senate, 74th Cong., 1st sess., on S. 2047, 1935, pp. 10–11. Also see secs. 4–5.

[38] The Indian and His Problem (1910). It should be noted that the termination of tribal government was finally effectuated by agreements with the interested tribes. See secs. 8A–8D.

by appointment the vacancies thus created; provision was made for the supersession of their tribal schools by a public school system maintained by general taxation; their tribal taxes were abolished; the sale of their public buildings and lands was ordered; their legislatures were forbidden to remain in session more than thirty days in any one year; and every legislative act, ordinance and resolution was declared invalid unless it received the approval of the President. The only present shadow or fiction of the survival of the tribes as tribes is their grudging recognition till all their property, or the proceeds thereof, can be distributed among the individual members. As one of the federal judges has summed it up, this is "a continuance of the tribes in mere legal effect, just as in many States corporations are continued as legal entities after they have ceased to do business and are practically dissolved, for the purpose of winding up their affairs." (Pp. 336–337.)

The Act of June 28, 1898,[39] commonly known as the Curtis Act, abolished tribal courts[40] and declared Indian law unenforceable in federal courts.[41] The Supreme Court in the case of *Morris v. Hitchcock*[42] explained the purpose of the Curtis Act in regard to one of the Five Civilized Tribes:

> Viewing the Curtis Act in the light of the previous decisions of this court and the dealings between the Chickasaws and the United States, we are of opinion that one of the objects occasioning the adoption of that act by Congress, having in view the peace and welfare of the Chickasaws, was to permit the continued exercise, by the legislative body of the tribe, of such a power as is here complained of, subject to a veto power in the President over such legislation as a preventive of arbitrary and injudicious action. (P. 393.)

By agreement,[43] or statute,[44] provisions were made for the termination of the tribal governments by March 4, 1906, at the latest. It was thought that by that time the tribal land would be allotted. However, the necessity for the continuance of the tribes became apparent before the date set for their demise and the Joint Resolution of March 2, 1906,[45] provided for the continuance of tribal existence and government of these tribes until the distribution of the tribal property "unless hereafter otherwise provided by law." The next month a comprehensive law was passed covering all the tribes.

The Act of April 26, 1906,[46] provided for the final disposition of the affairs of the Five Civilized Tribes. It provided for the completion by the Secretary of the Interior of the enrollments of the tribal members, one set comprising the freedmen and the second the remaining members. It empowered the President of the United States to remove the principal chief of the Choctaw, Cherokee, Creek, or Seminole tribe, or the governor of the Chickasaw tribe for failure to perform his duties, and to "fill any vacancy arising from removal, disability or death of the incumbent, by appointment of a citizen by blood of the tribe." The Secretary of the Interior was granted considerable power in regard to tribal affairs including control of tribal schools,[47] the collection of tribal revenues,[48] and funds,[49] sale of certain tribal lands, buildings and other property of the tribes,[50] and the per capita distribution of tribal funds.[51] Section 27 provided that the lands of the Five Civilized Tribes upon their dissolution "shall be held in trust by the United States for the use and benefit of the Indians" of each of the tribes "and their heirs" as shown by the final rolls.

Section 28 provided for the continuance of tribal existence and the present tribal governments with limited powers. Their actions were made subject to the approval of the President of the United States.[52]

Mr. Justice Van Devanter in the case of *Southern Surety Company v. Oklahoma*[53] described the formation of the State of Oklahoma and contrasted it with the previous government of the Territory by Congress:

> By reason of the conditions arising out of the presence of the Five Civilized Tribes no organized territorial government was ever established in the Indian Territory. Up to the time it became a part of the State of Oklahoma it was governed under the immediate direction of Congress, which legislated for it in respect of many matters of local or domestic concern which in a State are regulated by the state legislature, and also applied to it many laws dealing with subjects which under the Constitution are within Federal rather than state control. In what was done Congress did not contemplate that this situation should be of long duration, but on the contrary that the Territory should be prepared for early inclusion in a State. Courts designated as "United States courts" were temporarily established and invested with a considerable measure of civil and criminal jurisdiction, and there was also provision for beginning public prosecutions before subordinate magistrates. There being no organized local government, such prosecutions, regardless of their nature, were commenced and conducted in the name of the United States, and in taking bail bonds it was named as the obligee.
>
> The Enabling Act, June 16, 1906, c. 3335, 34 Stat. 267; March 4, 1907, c. 2911, *ibid.* 1286, provided that the new State should embrace the Indian Territory as well as the Territory of Oklahoma. It contemplated that the State, by its constitution, would establish a system of courts of its own, and provided for dividing the State into two districts and creating therein United States courts like those in other States. The temporary courts were to go out of existence and this made it necessary to provide for the disposition of the business pending before them in various stages. (Pp. 584–585.)

[39] 30 Stat. 495. The constitutionality of this act was upheld in *Stephens v. Cherokee Nation*, 174 U. S. 445 (1899); *Cherokee Nation v. Hitchcock*, 187 U. S. 294 (1902).

[40] Sec. 28.

[41] Sec. 26.

[42] 194 U. S. 384 (1904).

[43] Choctaw-Chickasaw Agreement in the Act of June 28, 1898, 30 Stat. 495, 512; Creek Agreement of March 1, 1901, par. 46, 31 Stat. 861, 872; Cherokee Agreement in the Act of July 1, 1902, sec. 63, 32 Stat. 716, 725.

[44] Act of March 3, 1903, sec. 8 (Seminole), 32 Stat. 982, 1008.

[45] 34 Stat. 822.

[46] 34 Stat. 137.

[47] Sec. 10.

[48] Sec. 11.

[49] Sec. 18.

[50] Secs. 12 and 15.

[51] Sec. 17.

[52] For examples see statement of D. H. Johnston, Governor of the Chickasaw Nation, relating to tribal affairs, Pt. 14, Survey of Indians in the United States (1931), pp. 5352–5365, and of Ben Dwight, Chief of the Choctaws, *ibid.*, pp. 5371–5389.

[53] 241 U. S. 582 (1916).

SECTION 7. ENROLLMENT—FIVE CIVILIZED TRIBES

The general policy of the Federal Government for a number of years had been to bring about the allotment in severalty of tribal property with certain restrictions upon alienation, and to confer citizenship, state and national, upon allottees.[54] The Dawes Commission, appointed by virtue of the Act of March 3, 1893,[55] had undertaken to negotiate with the Five Civilized Tribes for just such a purpose. However, after three years of attempt-

[54] See Chapter 3, sec. 4G; Chapter 4, sec. 11; Chapter 11, sec. 1.

[55] Act of March 3, 1893, 27 Stat. 612, 645, supplemented by Act of March 2, 1895, 28 Stat. 910, 939.

ing to reach agreements with the Indians which would provide for allotment in severalty, Congress despaired of receiving voluntary action and directed the Commission, in the following paragraphs of the Act of June 10, 1896,[66] to prepare rolls of the tribes:

> That said commission is further authorized and directed to proceed at once to hear and determine the application of all persons who may apply to them for citizenship in any of said nations, and after such hearing they shall determine the right of such applicant to be so admitted and enrolled: *Provided, however*, That such application shall be made to such Commissioners within three months after the passage of this Act. The said commission shall decide all such applications within ninety days after the same shall be made. That in determining all such applications said commission shall respect all laws of the several nations or tribes, not inconsistent with the laws of the United States, and all treaties with either of said nations or tribes, and shall give due force and effect to the rolls, usages, and customs of each of said nations or tribes: *And provided further*, That the rolls of citizenship of the several tribes as now existing are hereby confirmed, and any person who shall claim to be entitled to be added to said rolls as a citizen of either of said tribes and whose right thereto has either been denied or not acted upon, or any citizen who may within three months from and after the passage of this Act desire such citizenship, may apply to the legally constituted court or committee designated by the several tribes for such citizenship, and such court or committee shall determine such application within thirty days from the date thereof.
>
> In the performance of such duties said commission shall have power and authority to administer oaths, to issue process for and compel the attendance of witnesses, and to send for persons and papers, and all depositions and affidavits and other evidence in any form whatsoever heretofore taken where the witnesses giving said testimony are dead or now residing beyond the limits of said Territory, and to use every fair and reasonable means within their reach for the purpose of determining the rights of persons claiming such citizenship, or to protect any of said nations from fraud or wrong, and the rolls so prepared by them shall be hereafter held and considered to be the true and correct rolls of persons entitled to the rights of citizenship in said several tribes: *Provided*, That if the tribe, or any person, be aggrieved with the decision of the tribal authorities or the commission provided for in this Act, it or he may appeal from such decision to the United States district court: *Provided, however*, That the appeal shall be taken within sixty days, and the judgment of the court shall be final.
>
> That the said commission, after the expiration of six months, shall cause a complete roll of citizenship of each of said nations to be made up from their records, and add thereto the names of citizens whose right may be conferred under this Act, and said rolls shall be, and are hereby, made rolls of citizenship of said nations or tribe, subject, however, to the determination of the United States courts, as provided herein.
>
> The commission is hereby required to file the lists of members as they finally approve them with the Commissioner of Indian Affairs to remain there for use as the final judgment of the duly constituted authorities. And said commission shall also make a roll of freedmen entitled to citizenship in said tribes and shall include their names in the lists of members to be filed with the Commissioner of Indian Affairs. And said commission is further authorized and directed to make a full report to Congress of leases, tribal and individual, with the area, amount and value of the property leased and the amount received therefor, and by whom and from whom said property is leased, and is further directed to make a full and detailed report as to the excessive holdings of members of said tribes and others.
>
> It is hereby declared to be the duty of the United States to establish a government in the Indian Territory which will rectify the many inequalities and discriminations now existing in said Territory and afford needful protection to the lives and property of all citizens and residents thereof.

The following further provisions regarding enrollment were made the next year in the Act of June 7, 1897:[67]

> That said commission shall continue to exercise all authority heretofore conferred on it by law to negotiate with the Five Tribes, and any agreement made by it with any one of said tribes, when ratified, shall operate to suspend any provisions of this Act if in conflict therewith as to said nation: *Provided*, That the words "rolls of citizenship," as used in the Act of June tenth, eighteen hundred and ninety-six, making appropriations for current and contingent expenses of the Indian Department and fulfilling treaty stipulations with various Indian tribes for the fiscal year ending June thirtieth, eighteen hundred and ninety-seven, shall be construed to mean the last authenticated rolls of each tribe which have been approved by the council of the nation, and the descendants of those appearing on such rolls, and such additional names and their descendants as have been subsequently added, either by the council of such nation, the duly authorized courts thereof, or the commission under the Act of June tenth, eighteen hundred and ninety-six. And all other names appearing upon such rolls shall be open to investigation by such commission for a period of six months after the passage of this Act. And any name appearing on such rolls and not confirmed by the Act of June tenth, eighteen hundred and ninety-six, as herein construed, may be stricken therefrom by such commission where the party affected shall have ten days previous notice that said commission will investigate and determine the right of such party to remain upon such roll as a citizen of such nation: *Provided, also*, That any one whose name shall be stricken from the roll by such commission shall have the right of appeal, as provided in the Act of June tenth, eighteen hundred and ninety-six.

The determination of Congress to proceed with allotment without the consent of the tribes found expression in the Act of June 28, 1898,[68] commonly called the Curtis Act.[69] This act contained elaborate stipulations regarding enrollment, providing for two rolls for each of the Civilized Tribes, one tracing rights through former slaves, called the Freedmen roll; the other tracing such rights through Indian blood, called the Indian roll,[70] for making the rolls descriptive of the persons thereon[71] and for making them "alone constitute the several tribes which they represent."[72]

[66] 29 Stat. 321, 339–340. Also see Act of July 1, 1898, 30 Stat. 571, 591; Act of March 3, 1901, 31 Stat. 1058, 1077.

[67] Act of June 7, 1897, 30 Stat. 62, 84.

[68] 30 Stat. 495.

[69] The tribes bitterly opposed this act, which was strongly advocated by the Commission to the Five Civilized Tribes. Mills, *op. cit.* p. 8.

[70] Act of April 21, 1904, sec. 1, 33 Stat. 189, 204. On status of freedmen, see Schmeckebier, The Office of Indian Affairs (1927), p. 134; *Tiger* v. *Fewell*, 22 F. 2d 786 (C. C. A. 8, 1927). Act of May 27, 1908, sec. 3, 35 Stat. 312, provided that the rolls of Freedmen of the Five Civilized Tribes approved by the Secretary of the Interior shall be conclusive evidence of the quantum of Indian blood of any enrolled freedmen of said tribe and the enrollment records of the Commissioner, conclusive evidence of their age. After being entered on rolls made and approved by the Secretary of the Interior, in accordance with a statute, a freedman acquired rights, which could not be divested without notice of hearing essential to due process of law. *Garfield* v. *Goldsby*, 211 U. S. 249 (1908). Notice to an attorney of such freedman is insufficient if given a few hours before a hearing of a motion to strike out his name on the ground that his enrollment was procured by perjury. *United States* v. *Fisher*, 222 U. S. 204 (1911).

[71] Sec. 21. See *United States* v. *Mid-Continent Petroleum Corp.*, 67 F. 2d 37, 43–44 (C. C. A. 10, 1933). Also see Chapter 5, sec. 13.

[72] Sec. 21. See *Kemohah* v. *Shaffer Oil & Refining Co.*, 38 F. 2d 665 (D. C. N. D. Okla., 1930).

The effect of the enrollment statutes has been considered from time to time. In the case of *United States* v. *Atkins*,[63] the Supreme Court said:

> In *United States* v. *Wildcat*, 244 U. S. 111, 118, 119, it was insisted that the Indian died prior to April 1, 1899, and that his enrollment as of that date was beyond the jurisdiction of the Dawes Commission and void within the doctrine of *Scott* v. *McNeal*, 154 U. S. 34. Much consideration was given to the statutes creating and defining the powers of the Commission and the effect of an enrollment. This Court said:
>
> > "There was thus constituted a *quasi*-judicial tribunal whose judgments within the limits of its jurisdiction were only subject to attack for fraud or such mistake of law or fact as would justify the holding that its judgments were voidable. Congress by this legislation evidenced an intention to put an end to controversy by providing a tribunal before which those interested could be heard and the rolls authoritatively made up of those who were entitled to participate in the partition of the tribal lands. It was to the interest of all concerned that the beneficiaries of this division should be ascertained. To this end the Commission was established and endowed with authority to hear and determine the matter * * *.
> >
> > "When the Commission proceeded in good faith to determine the matter and to act upon information before it, not arbitrarily, but according to its best judgment, we think it was the intention of the act that the matter, upon the approval of the Secretary, should be finally concluded and the rights of the parties forever settled, subject to such attacks as could successfully be made upon judgments of this character for fraud or mistake.
> >
> > "We cannot agree that the case is within the principles decided in *Scott* v. *McNeal*, 154 U. S. 34, and kindred cases, in which it has been held that in the absence of a subject-matter of jurisdiction an adjudication that there was such is not conclusive, and that a judgment based upon action without its proper subject being in existence is void * * *. We think the decision of such tribunal, when not impeached for fraud or mistake, conclusive of the question of membership in the tribe, when followed, as was the case here, by the action of the Interior Department confirming the allotment and ordering the patents conveying the lands, which were in fact issued."
>
> It must be accepted now as finally settled that the enrollment of a member of an Indian tribe by the Dawes Commission, when duly approved, amounts to a judgment in an adversary proceeding determining the existence of the individual and his right to membership subject, of course, to impeachment under the well established rules where such judgments are involved. (Pp. 224–226.)

Shortly after the passage of the Curtis Act, Congress, by Act of July 1, 1898,[64] adopted the agreement concluded with the Seminoles on December 16, 1897. Convinced now of the futility of resistance, other tribes followed suit, until by the end of 1902 all of the Five Civilized Tribes had become parties to agreements with the United States providing for allotment to land in severalty.[65] Most of these agreements[66] contained provisions concerning enrollment. Sections 25 to 31 of the Cherokee Agreement[67] are perhaps typical:

> SEC. 25. The roll of citizens of the Cherokee Nation shall be made as of September first, nineteen hundred and two, and the names of all persons then living and entitled to enrollment on that date shall be placed on said roll by the Commission to the Five Civilized Tribes.
>
> SEC. 26. The names of all persons living on the first day of September, nineteen hundred and two, entitled to be enrolled as provided in section twenty-five hereof, shall be placed upon the roll made by said Commission, and no child born thereafter to a citizen, and no white person who has intermarried with a Cherokee citizen since the sixteenth day of December, eighteen hundred and ninety-five, shall be entitled to enrollment or to participate in the distribution of the tribal property of the Cherokee Nation.
>
> SEC. 27. Such rolls shall in all other respects be made in strict compliance with the provisions of section twenty-one of the Act of Congress approved June twenty-eighth, eighteen hundred and ninety-eight (Thirtieth Statutes, page four hundred and ninety-five), and the Act of Congress approved May thirty-first, nineteen hundred (Thirty-first Statutes, page two hundred and twenty-one).
>
> SEC. 28. No person whose name appears upon the roll made by the Dawes Commission as a citizen or freedman of any other tribe shall be enrolled as a citizen of the Cherokee Nation.
>
> SEC. 29. For the purpose of expediting the enrollment of the Cherokee citizens and the allotment of lands as herein provided, the said Commission shall, from time to time, and as soon as practicable, forward to the Secretary of the Interior lists upon which shall be placed the names of those persons found by the Commission to be entitled to enrollment. The lists thus prepared, when approved by the Secretary of the Interior, shall constitute a part and parcel of the final roll of citizens of the Cherokee tribe, upon which allotment of land and distribution of other tribal property shall be made. When there shall have been submitted to and approved by the Secretary of the Interior lists embracing the names of all those lawfully entitled to enrollment, the roll shall be deemed complete. The roll so prepared shall be made in quadruplicate, one to be deposited with the Secretary of the Interior, one with the Commissioner of Indian Affairs, one with the principal chief of the Cherokee Nation, and one to remain with the Commission to the Five Civilized Tribes.
>
> SEC. 30. During the months of September and October, in the year nineteen hundred and two, the Commission to the Five Civilized Tribes may receive applications for enrollment of such infant children as may have been born to recognized and enrolled citizens of the Cherokee Nation on or before the first day of September, nineteen hundred and two, but the application of no person whomsoever for enrollment shall be received after the thirty-first day of October, nineteen hundred and two.
>
> SEC. 31. No person whose name does not appear upon the roll prepared as herein provided shall be entitled to in any manner participate in the distribution of the common property of the Cherokee tribe, and those whose names appear thereon shall participate in the manner set forth in this Act: *Provided*, That no allotment of land or other tribal property shall be made to any person, or to the heirs of any person, whose name is on said roll and who died prior to the first day of September, nineteen hundred and two. The right of such person to any interest in the lands or other tribal property shall be deemed to have become extinguished and to have passed to the tribe in general upon his death before said date, and any person or persons who may conceal the death of anyone on said roll as aforesaid for the purpose of profiting by said concealment, and who shall knowingly receive any portion of any land or other tribal property or of the proceeds so arising from any allotment prohibited by this section, shall

[63] 260 U. S. 220 (1922).

[64] 30 Stat. 567, supp. by Act of June 2, 1900, 31 Stat. 250.

[65] Act of June 28, 1898, 30 Stat. 495 (Choctaw-Chickasaw); Act of March 1, 1901, 31 Stat. 861, supp. by Act of June 30, 1902, 32 Stat. 500 (Creek); Act of July 1, 1902, 32 Stat. 716 (Cherokee).

[66] Act of June 2, 1900, 31 Stat. 250 (Seminole); Act of March 1, 1901, 31 Stat. 861 (Creek); Act of June 30, 1902, 32 Stat. 500 (Creek); Act of July 1, 1902, 32 Stat. 641 (Choctaw-Chickasaw); Act of July 1, 1902, 32 Stat. 716 (Cherokee).

Sec. 30 of the Act of July 1, 1902, 32 Stat. 641, was considered by the court in *Garfield* v. *Goldsby*, 211 U. S. 249 (1908).

[67] Act of July 1, 1902, 32 Stat. 716.

be deemed guilty of a felony, and shall be proceeded against as may be provided in other cases of felony, and the penalty for this offense shall be confinement at hard labor for a period of not less than one year nor more than five years, and in addition thereto a forefeiture to the Cherokee Nation of the lands, other tribal property, and proceeds so obtained.

The Choctaw-Chickasaw Agreement[68] contained an unusual enrollment device. A quasi-judicial body was established in sections 31-33, which has been described as follows:[69]

It appears that the agreement in these paragraphs provides for the establishment of the Choctaw and Chickasaw Citizenship Court, and gives it jurisdiction of a test suit to annul and vacate the decisions of the United States courts in the Indian Territory admitting persons to citizenship and enrollment as citizens of the Choctaw and Chickasaw nations, respectively, on the ground of want of notice to both of said nations and because the United States courts tried such cases *de novo*, with a right, in the event such judgments should be annulled because of either or both of the irregularities mentioned on the part of any party thus deprived of a favorable judgment to remove his case to the Citizenship court, where such further proceedings were to be had therein "as ought to have been had in the court to which the same was taken on appeal from the Commission to the Five Civilized Tribes, and if no judgment or decision had been rendered therein;" and also "appellate jurisdiction over all judgments of the courts in Indian Territory, rendered under said act of Congress of June tenth, eighteen hundred and ninety-six, admitting persons to citizenship or to enrollment in either of said nations." In the exercise of such appellate jurisdiction the citizenship court was "authorized to consider, review, and revise all such judgments, both as to findings of fact and conclusions of law, and may, whenever in its judgment substantial justice will thereby be subserved, permit either party to any such appeal to take and present such further evidence as may be necessary to enable said court to determine the very right of the controversy."

It will be noted that the agreement further provides (paragraph 33) that "the judgment of the citizenship court in *any or all* of the suits or proceedings so committed to its jurisdiction *shall be final*." (P. 141.)

Congress was now anxious to bring to a close the work of enrollment, and in 1904, 1905, and 1906 legislative steps were taken to bring this about. These have been summarized by the Attorney General:[70]

By the act of April 21, 1904 (33 Stat. 189, 204), it was provided that the Commisison to the Five Civilized Tribes should conclude its work and terminate on or before July 1, 1905, and cease to exist on that date, the powers theretofore conferred upon it being continued.

By the act of March 3, 1905 (33 Stat. 1048, 1060), it was provided "that the work of completing the unfinished business, if any, of the Commission to the Five Civilized Tribes shall devolve upon the Secretary of the Interior, and that all the powers heretofore granted to the said Commission to the Five Civilized Tribes are hereby conferred upon the said Secretary on and after the first of July, nineteen hundred and five."

By the act of April 26, 1906 (34 Stat. 137), it was provided:

"That after the approval of this act no person shall be enrolled as a citizen or freedman of the Choctaw, Chickasaw, Cherokee, Creek, or Seminole tribes of Indians in the Indian Territory, except as herein otherwise provided, unless application for enrollment was made prior to December first, nineteen hundred and five, and the records in charge of the Commissioner to the Five Civilized Tribes shall be conclusive evidence as to the fact of such application; and no motion to reopen or reconsider any citizenship case, in any of said tribes, shall be entertained unless filed with the Commissioner to the Five Civilized Tribes within sixty days after the date of the order or decision sought to be reconsidered except as to decisions made prior to the passage of this act, in which cases such motion shall be made within sixty days after the passage of this act."

By that act the rolls of citizenship of the several tribes were required to be completed by March 4, 1907. (Pp. 142-143.)

The Act of May 27, 1908,[71] made conclusive the enrollment records[72] of the Commissioner to the Five Civilized Tribes as to the age of the citizens and freedmen. At the request of Mr. Bledsoe,[73] the Commissioner prepared the following statement of what constituted the enrollment records in his office:

The enrollment records, in the matter of the enrollment of any person as a citizen or freedman of the Five Civilized Tribes, consist of the application made for their enrollment, together with all of the records, evidence and other papers filed in connection therewith prior to the rendition of the decision granting the application.

In the early days of enrollment in the Five Civilized Tribes appointments were made by the Commission at various places in the different nations at which the Indians and freedmen appeared to make application for enrollment. At that time the applicants were duly sworn before a notary public, but their testimony was only taken orally and placed upon a card, with the exception of Cherokees. Written testimony was taken in all Cherokee cases. In a great majority of the early enrollments, except Cherokee cases, the only records shown are the statements that were thus taken from the applicants personally and placed on the cards, which constitute the enrollment record, together with any other evidence that may have been obtained. In a great many instances, at that time, where there was doubt as to the rights of the applicants to enrollment, and they could not then be identified from the tribal rolls, the written testimony of the applicants was taken and made a part of the record. Additional testimony was also taken at later dates.

As the work proceeded, and the enrollment of all citizens by blood or intermarriage, and freedmen, who were clearly identified upon the tribal rolls was completed, written testimony was taken in all doubtful cases. Written testimony was also taken in all applications made for the identification of Mississippi Choctaws and in practically all other cases as the work neared completion.

The tribal rolls of the various nations came into the possession of the Commissioner to the Five Civilized Tribes, and were used for identification and as a basis for enrollment.

As enrollments were completed, the names of all persons whom the Commission had decided were entitled to enrollment were placed on the rolls. These rolls show the name, age, sex, degree of blood and the number of the census card, which is generally known as the "enrollment card," on which each citizen was enrolled, and a number was placed opposite each name appearing on this roll, beginning at 1 and running down until the final number was completed. This roll was made out in quintuplicate and forwarded to the Secretary of the Interior for his approval, who approved same if he found no objections thereto and returned three copies for the files of this office. The roll thus approved is known as the "approval roll," and is the basis on which allotments were made, except in the cases of a large number of Creeks, to whom allotments were made before the approval of their enrollment, which allotments were subsequently confirmed by Congress.

The Secretary of the Interior holds, for the purposes of the government, that the date of the application for enrollment shall be construed as the date of the anni-

[68] Act of July 1, 1902, 32 Stat. 641 (Choctaw-Chickasaw).

[69] 26 Op. A. G. 128 (1907).

[70] 26 Op. A. G. 127 (1907).

[71] 35 Stat. 312, sec. 3.

[72] Of the applicants, 101,228 were enrolled. Of these, 2,506 were intermarried persons; 23,382, freedmen; 50,671, mixed bloods, and 24,669, full bloods. Rept. Comm. Ind. Aff., 1907, p. 112.

[73] Bledsoe, *op. cit.*, p. 160.

versary of the birth of the applicant, unless the records show otherwise.

The Act of Congress makes the *enrollment records* of the Commissioner to the Five Civilized Tribes conclusive evidence in determining the ages of allottees of the Five Civilized Tribes. The enrollment records consist of:

First, what is known as the "census card"; that is, the card on which the applicant was listed for enrollment. Sometimes in the early enrollment some persons were listed on what is known as a "doubtful card," and later on the names appearing on the doubtful cards were transferred to a regular census card, when the Commission rendered its decision holding that they were entitled to enrollment. It has been discovered, in looking over the enrollment records in many cases, that sometimes the date shown on the lower right-hand corner is the date on which they were transferred from the doubtful card, and not the date on which application was made for their enrollment. In such cases, in the absence of any other testimony or evidence, the date shown on the doubtful card is the date on which application was made for enrollment;

Second, all testimony taken in the matter of the application at various times prior to rendition of the decision granting the application;

Third, birth affidavits, affidavits of death, and other evidence and papers filed in connection with the application made for enrollment; and

Fourth, the enrollment as shown on the approved roll.

Persons seeking information as to the ages of allottees should ask to be furnished with a certified copy of the *enrollment records* pertaining thereto. Scarcely any testimony was taken in the enrollment of Seminoles, save orally, which is shown on the census cards. No date was placed on these cards at the time of enrollment; consequently they are not of much value in determining the ages of the persons whose names appear thereon. A certificate appears on the approved Seminole roll, showing the dates the enrollments were made, which dates will probably govern in determining their ages, in the absence of any other testimony or evidence in the enrollment records to the contrary. (Pp. 160–163.)

SECTION 8. ALIENATION AND TAXATION OF ALLOTTED LANDS OF FIVE TRIBES

Basic statutes controlling the alienability and taxability of the lands of individual members of the Five Civilized Tribes may be divided into two groups: Those dealing with specific tribes and those applicable to all of the Five Civilized Tribes.[74] The first group is earliest in point of time, including treaties or agreements entered into with the various tribes providing

[74] A few statutes applied in part to the Five Civilized Tribes and in part to one of the tribes. The most notable example of this type of statute is the Curtis Act of June 28, 1898, 30 Stat. 495. The latter part (pp. 505–515) comprised the Atoka Agreement with the Choctaws and Chickasaws, which is discussed in sec. 8B of this chapter. The early portion of the Curtis Act supplemented the Act of March 1, 1889, 25 Stat. 783, sec. 15; Act of May 2, 1890, 26 Stat. 81, 95; Act of March 3, 1893, 27 Stat. 612, 641; Act of June 10, 1896, 29 Stat. 321, 329. It was supplemented by the Act of March 3, 1899, 30 Stat. 1074; Act of March 3, 1899, 30 Stat. 1214; Act of June 2, 1900, 31 Stat. 250; Act of March 1, 1901, 31 Stat. 848; Act of March 1, 1901, 31 Stat. 861; Act of July 1, 1902, 32 Stat. 716; Act of January 21, 1903, 32 Stat. 774; and was cited in Cabell, J. V., Descent and Distribution of Indian Lands (1932) 3 Okla. S. B. J. 208; Krieger, Heinrich, Principles of the Indian Law and the Act of June 18, 1934 (1935), 3 Geo. Wash. L. Rev. 279; 23 Op. A. G. 528 (1901); 25 Op. A. G. 163 (1904); 25 Op. A. G. 168 (1904); 26 Op. A. G. 171 (1907); 26 Op. A. G. 340 (1907); Memo. Sol. I. D., December 11, 1918; Op. Sol. I. D., M.7316, April 5, 1922; Op. Sol. I. D., M.7316, May 28, 1924; Op. Sol. I. D., M.18772, December 24, 1926; Op. Sol. I. D., M.27759, January 22, 1935; Memo. Sol. I. D., March 18, 1936; 54 I. D. 109 (1932); 54 I. D. 207 (1933); *Adams* v. *Murphy*, 165 Fed. 304 (C. C. A. 8, 1908); *Armstrong* v. *Wood*, 195 Fed. 137 (C. C. E. D. Okla., 1911); *Bartlett* v. *Okla. Oil Co.*, 218 Fed. 380 (D. C. E. D. Okla., 1914); *Boudinot* v. *Boudinot*, 2 Ind. T. 107, 48 S. W. 1019 (1899); *Brought* v. *Cherokee Nation*, 129 Fed. 192 (C. C. A. 8, 1904); *Brown* v. *United States*, 44 C. Cls. 283 (1907), revd. sub nom. *Brown and Gritts* v. *United States*, 219 U. S. 346 (1911); *Browning* v. *United States*, 6 F. 2d 801 (C. C. A. 8, 1925), cert. den. 269 U. S. 568 (1925); *Buster* v. *Wright*, 135 Fed. 947 (C. C. A. 8, 1905), app. dism. 203 U. S. 599; *Campbell* v. *Wadsworth*, 248 U. S. 169 (1918); *Cherokee Intermarriage Cases*, 203 U. S. 76 (1906); *Cherokee Nation* v. *Hitchcock*, 187 U. S. 294 (1902); *Cherokee Nation* v. *United States*, 85 C. Cls. 76 (1937); *Cherokee Nation* v. *Whitmire*, 223 U. S. 108 (1912); *Choate* v. *Trapp*, 224 U. S. 665 (1912); *Creek Nation* v. *United States*, 78 C. Cls. 474 (1933); *Daniels* v. *Miller*, 4 Ind. T. 426, 69 S. W. 925 (1902); *Delaware Indians* v. *Cherokee Nation*, 193 U. S. 127 (1904); *Denton* v. *Capital Townsite Co.*, 5 Ind. T. 396, 82 S. W. 852 (1904); *Dick* v. *Ross*, 6 Ind. T. 85, 89 S. W. 664 (1905); *Donohoo* v. *Howard*, 4 Ind. T. 433, 69 S. W. 927 (1902); *English* v. *Richardson, Treasurer of Tulsa County, Okla.*, 224 U. S. 680 (1912); *Evans* v. *Victor*, 204 Fed. 361 (C. C. A. 8, 1913); *Ex parte Webb*, 225 U. S. 663 (1912); *Fink* v. *County Commissioners*, 248 U. S. 399 (1919); *Fish* v. *Wise*, 52 F. 2d 544 (C. C. A. 10, 1931), cert. den. 282 U. S. 903 (1931), 284 U. S. 688 (1932); *Ford* v. *United States*, 260 Fed. 657 (C. C. A. 8, 1919); *Garfield* v. *United States ex rel. Allison*, 211 U. S. 264 (1908); *George* v. *Robb*, 4 Ind. T. 61, 64 S. W. 615 (1901); *German-American Ins. Co.* v. *Paul*, 5 Ind. T. 703 (1904), 53 S. W. 442 (1899); *Hargrove* v. *Cherokee Nation*, 3 Ind. T. 478, 58 S. W. 667 (1900); *Hargrove* v. *Cherokee Nation*, 129 Fed. 186 (C. C. A. 8, 1904); *Harnage* v. *Martin*, 242 U. S. 386 (1917); *Harris* v. *Hardridge*, 7 Ind. T. 532, 104 S. W. 826 (1907); *Harris* v. *Hardridge*, 166 Fed. 109 (C. C. A. 8, 1908); *Heckman* v. *United States*, 224 U. S. 413 (1912); *Henny Gas Co.* v. *United States*, 191 Fed. 132 (C. C. A. 8, 1911); *Hockett* v. *Alston*, 110 Fed. 910 (C. C. A. 6, 1901); *Hubbard* v. *Chism*, 5 Ind. T. 95, 82 S. W. 686 (1904); *In re Grayson*, 3 Ind. T. 497, 61 S. W. 984 (1901); *In re Lands of Five Civilized Tribes*, 199 Fed. 811 (D. C. E. D. Okla., 1912); *Iowa Land & Trust Co.* v. *United States*, 217 Fed. 11 (C. C. A. 8, 1914); *Jefferson* v. *Fink*, 247 U. S. 288 (1918); *Jonah* v. *Armstrong*, 52 F. 2d 343 (C. C. A. 10, 1931); *Joplin Mercantile Co.* v. *United States*, 236 U. S. 531 (1915); *Kansas or Kaw Indians* v. *United States*, 80 C. Cls. 264 (1934), cert. den. 296 U. S. 577; *Kemohah* v. *Shaffer Oil & Refining Co.*, 38 F. 2d 665 (D. C. N. D. Okla., 1930); *Lowe* v. *Fisher*, 223 U. S. 95 (1912); *McAllaster* v. *Edgerton*, 3 Ind. T. 704, 64 S. W. 583 (1901); *McCullough* v. *Smith*, 243 Fed. 823 (C. C. A. 8, 1917); *Malone* v. *Alderdice*, 212 Fed. 668 (C. C. A. 8, 1914); *Mandler* v. *United States*, 49 F. 2d 201 (C. C. A. 10, 1931), rehearing den. 52 F. 2d 713 (C. C. A. 10, 1931); *Marlin* v. *Lewallen*, 276 U. S. 58 (1928); *Matter of Heff*, 197 U. S. 488 (1905), overruled, 241 U. S. 591; *Maxey* v. *Wright*, 3 Ind. T. 243, 54 S. W. 807 (1900); *Moore* v. *Carter Oil Co.*, 43 F. 2d 322 (C. C. A. 10, 1930), cert. den. 282 U. S. 903; *Morris* v. *Hitchcock*, 194 U. S. 384 (1904); *Morrison* v. *United States*, 6 F. 2d 811 (C. C. A. 8, 1925); *Mullen* v. *United States*, 224 U. S. 448 (1912); *Nivens* v. *Nivens*, 4 Ind. T. 574, 76 S. W. 114 (1903); *Nunn* v. *Hazelrigg*, 216 Fed. 330 (C. C. A. 8, 1914); *Owens* v. *Eaton*, 5 Ind. T. 275, 82 S. W. 746 (1904); *Persons Claiming Rights in Cherokee Nation*, 40 C. Cls. 411 (1905); *Price* v. *Cherokee Nation*, 5 Ind. T. 518, 82 S. W. 893 (1904); *Quigley* v. *Stephens*, 3 Ind. T. 265, 54 S. W. 814 (1900); *Ross* v. *Stewart*, 227 U. S. 530 (1913); *St. Louis & S. F. Ry. Co.* v. *Pfennighausen*, 7 Ind. T. 685, 104 S. W. 880 (1907); *Sayer* v. *Brown*, 7 Ind. T. 675, 104 S. W. 877 (1907); *Schellenbarger* v. *Fewell*, 236 U. S. 68 (1915); *Seminole Nation* v. *United States*, 78 C. Cls. 455 (1933); *Stephens* v. *Cherokee Nation*, 174 U. S. 445 (1899); *Thomason* v. *McLaughlin*, 7 Ind. T. 1, 103 S. W. 595 (1907); *Tiger* v. *Slinker*, 4 F. 2d 714 (D. C. E. D. Okla., 1925); *Tuttle* v. *Moore*, 3 Ind. T. 712, 64 S. W. 585 (1901); *United States* v. *Atkins*, 260 U. S. 220 (1922); *United States* v. *Board of Comrs. of McIntosh Cty.*, 284 Fed. 103 (C. C. A. 8, 1922), app. dism. 263 U. S. 691; *United States* v. *Ferguson*, 247 U. S. 175 (1918); *United States* v. *Hayes*, 20 F. 2d 873 (C. C. A. 8, 1927), cert. den. 275 U. S. 555; *United States* v. *Lewis*, 5 Ind. T. 1, 76 S. W. 299 (1903); *United States* v. *Mid Continent Pet. Corp.*, 67 F. 2d 37 (C. C. A. 10, 1933), cert. den. 290 U. S. 702; *United States* v. *Rea-Read Mill & Elevator Co.*, 171 Fed. 501 (C. C. E. D. Okla., 1909); *United States* v. *Seminole Nation*, 299 U. S. 417 (1937); *United States* v. *Smith*, 266 Fed. 740 (D. C. E. D. Okla., 1920); *United States* v. *Western Inv. Co.*, 226 Fed. 726 (C. C. A. 8, 1915); *United States* v. *Wildcat*, 244 U. S. 111 (1917); *United States* v. *Wright*, 53 F. 2d 300 (C. C. A. 4, 1931), cert. den. 285 U. S. 539; *Vinson* v. *Graham*, 44 F. 2d 772 (C. C. A. 10, 1930), cert. den. 283 U. S. 819; *W. O. Whitney Lumber & Grain Co.* v. *Crabtree*, 166 Fed. 738 (C. C. A. 8, 1908); *Washington* v. *Miller*, 235 U. S. 422 (1914); *Welty* v. *Reed*, 231 Fed. 930 (C. C. A. 8, 1916); *Woodward* v. *De Graffenried*, 238 U. S. 284 (1915).

for the allotment of the tribal land in severalty.[75] In contrast to the General Allotment Act,[76] the legal title to the lands so allotted vested in each instance in the allottee. Exemption from taxation was provided either expressly or by restricting the allotment against alienation. The extent of the exemption or the duration of the restriction varied with each agreement.[77]

A. CHEROKEES

The Cherokee Allotment Act[78] provided for the selection of a homestead of value equal to 40 acres, inalienable during the lifetime of the allottee, not exceeding 21 years from the date of the allotment certificate. During the time the homestead is held by the allottee it is made nontaxable by the act.[79]

The grant of land expressly declared nontaxable by the Cherokee Agreement extended only to the homestead. Whatever exemption from taxation the surplus enjoyed was by reason of general restrictions upon alienation.[80]

B. CHOCTAWS AND CHICKASAWS

The Atoka Agreement, embodied in the Curtis Act,[81] provided for the allotment of surface rights to lands of the Choctaws and Chickasaws in Indian Territory and stated that:

---

[75] On the relations of the United States and the Choctaw and Chickasaw Indians in regard to the allotment of lands and the restrictions on alienation, see *Mullen* v. *United States*, 224 U. S. 448 (1912); on history of allotments of Creeks and other nations, see *Tiger* v. *Western Investment Co.*, 221 U. S. 286 (1911).

[76] Act of February 8, 1887, 24 Stat. 388, 25 U. S. C. 331, 334, 348, 349, 381, 339, 341, and 342.

[77] *Ledbetter* v. *Wesley*, 23 F. 2d 81 (C. C. A. 8, 1927). Also see *Glenn* v. *Lewis*, 105 F. 2d 398 (C. C. A. 10, 1939), cert. den. 60 Sup. Ct. 130. For a discussion of some allotment problems of the Five Civilized Tribes see 27 Op. A. G. 530 (1909). On restrictions on alienation see Bledsoe, Oklahoma Indian Land Laws, 2d ed. 1913, pp. 52–157. The Attorney General in 34 Op. A. G. 275 (1924) gave the following description of the background of the allotment agreements:

> Finally, by the Act of March 3, 1893 (27 Stat. 612, 645, secs. 15 and 16), the Commission of Five Civilized Tribes, commonly referred to as the Dawes Commission, was created to enter into negotiations with the Five Indian Nations for the purpose of extinguishing the national or tribal title to any lands in that Territory held by such tribes by allotment of the lands in severalty to the individual Indian or such other just and equitable method as might be agreed upon between the Indians and the United States. After three years of negotiation, the commissioner was unable to effect an agreement.
>
> By Act of June 10, 1896 (29 Stat. 321, 339–340), the commission was directed to prepare rolls of the tribes as preliminary to allotment. Various statutory enactments were made, gradually asserting the authority of the United States over the Indian Territory. Congress announced: "It is hereby declared to be the duty of the United States to establish a government in the Indian Territory which will rectify the many inequalities and discriminations now existing in said Territory and afford needful protection to the lives and property of all citizens and residents thereof." and by mandatory direction to the committee made clear its intention to proceed with the allotment, whether the Indians agreed or not. All of the tribes assented finally but the Cherokees.
>
> Under these conditions, Congress passed the Act of June 28, 1898 (30 Stat. 495), known as the Curtis Act, which provided preliminary measures for allotment. The Government plan was so obnoxious to the Indians and so contradictory to the arrangement under which the tribes moved on to these lands long before and under which they had continued their tribal relations that it was necessary for the Government to make concessions to the allottees to obtain their consent to a relinquishment of the individual interest in the tribal property for a division in severalty. (Pp. 276–279.)

[78] Act of July 1, 1902, 32 Stat. 716. Amending Act of June 28, 1898, 30 Stat. 495; Act of May 31, 1900, 31 Stat. 221. Supplemented by Act of March 3, 1903, 32 Stat. 982; Act of June 21, 1906, 34 Stat. 325; Act of June 30, 1906, 34 Stat. 634; Act of March 1, 1907, 34 Stat. 1015; Act of August 1, 1914, 38 Stat. 582.

Cited in 26 Op. A. G. 171 (1907); 26 Op. A. G. 330 (1907); 26 Op. A. G. 351 (1907); 34 Op. A. G. 275 (1924); Op. Sol. I. D., D.40462, October 31, 1917; *Anicker* v. *Gunsburg*, 246 U. S. 110 (1918); *Barnsdall* v. *Delaware Indian Oil Co.*, 200 Fed. 522 (C. C. A. 8, 1912); *Barnsdall* v. *Owen*, 200 Fed. 519 (C. C. A. 8, 1912); *Bartlett* v. *Okla. Oil Co.*, 218 Fed. 380 (D. C. E. D. Okla., 1914); *Board of Commissioners of Tulsa County, Okla.* v. *United States*, 94 F. 2d 450 (C. C. A. 10, 1938); *Brown* v. *United States*, 44 C. Cls. 283 (1907), rev'd sub nom. *Brown & Gritts* v. *United States*, 219 U. S. 346 (1911); *Bunch* v. *Cole*, 263 U. S. 250 (1923); *Cherokee Intermarriage Cases*, 203 U. S. 76 (1906); *Cherokee Nation* v. *United States*, 85 C. Cls. 76 (1937); *Cherokee Nation* v. *United States*, 270 U. S. 476 (1926); *Cherokee Nation* v. *Whitmire*, 223 U. S. 108 (1912); *Chisholm* v. *Creek & Ind. Dev. Co.*, 273 Fed. 589 (D. C. E. D. Okla., 1921), aff'd in part and rev'd in part sub nom. *Sperry Oil Co.* v. *Chisholm*, 264 U. S. 488 (1924); *Delaware Indians* v. *Cherokee Nation*, 193 U. S. 127 (1904); *Delaware Tribe* v. *United States*, 74 C. Cls. 368 (1932); *Dick* v. *Ross*, 6 Ind. T. 85, 89 S. W. 664 (1905); *Eastern Cherokees* v. *United States*, 225 U. S. 572 (1912); *Eastern Cherokees* v. *United States*, 45 C. Cls. 104 (1910); *Eastern or Emigrant Cherokees* v. *United States*, 82 C. Cls. 180 (1935), cert. den. 299 U. S. 551; *Ex parte Webb*, 225 U. S. 663 (1912); *Fish* v. *Wise*, 52 F. 2d 544 (C. C. A. 10, 1931), cert. den. 282 U. S. 903 (1931), 284 U. S. 688 (1932); *Garfield* v. *United States ex rel. Lowe*, 34 App. D. C. 70 (1909); *Gritts* v. *Fisher*, 224 U. S. 640 (1912); *Harnage* v. *Martin*, 242 U. S. 368 (1917); *Heckman* v. *United States*, 224 U. S. 413 (1912); *Henny Gas Co.* v. *United States*, 191 Fed. 132 (C. C. A. 8, 1911); *Holmes* v. *United States*, 33 F. 2d 688 (C. C. A. 8, 1929); *In re Lands of Five Civilized Tribes*, 199 Fed. 811 (D. C. E. D. Okla., 1912); *Jennings* v. *Wood*, 192 Fed. 507 (C. C. A. 8, 1911); *Knight* v. *Lane*, 228 U. S. 6 (1913); *Lowe* v. *Fisher*, 223 U. S. 95 (1912); *Missouri, Kansas, & Texas Ry. Co.* v. *United States*, 47 C. Cls. 59 (1911); *Muskrat* v. *United States*, 219 U. S. 346 (1911); *Persons Claiming Rights in Cherokee Nation* v. *United States*, 40 C. Cls. 411 (1905); *Robinson* v. *Long Gas Co.*, 221 Fed. 398 (C. C. A. 8, 1915); *Ross* v. *Day*, 232 U. S. 110 (1914); *Ross* v. *Stewart*, 227 U. S. 530 (1913); *Sperry Oil & Gas Co.* v. *Chisholm*, 264 U. S. 488 (1924); *Sunday* v. *Mallory*, 248 U. S. 545 (1919); *Talley* v. *Burgess*, 246 U. S. 104 (1918); *Tiger* v. *Western Investment Co.*, 221 U. S. 286 (1911); *Truskett* v. *Closser*, 236 U. S. 223 (1915); *United States* v. *Board of Commissioners of McIntosh County*, 284 Fed. 103 (C. C. A. 8, 1922); *United States* v. *Cherokee Nation*, 202 U. S. 101 (1906); *United States* v. *Halsell*, 247 Fed. 390 (C. C. A. 8, 1918); *United States* v. *Reynolds*, 250 U. S. 104 (1919); *United States* v. *Smith*, 266 Fed. 740 (D. C. E. D. Okla., 1920); *United States* v. *Whitmire*, 236 Fed. 474 (C. C. A. 8, 1916); *Welch* v. *First Trust & Savings Bank*, 15 F. 2d 184 (C. C. A. 8, 1926).

The Attorney General said in 34 Op. A. G. 275, 279 (1924):

> The tribal lands of the Cherokees were allotted in severalty pursuant to an agreement with them as set forth in the Act of July 1, 1902 (32 Stat. 716), under which (Sec. 11), the members each received an allotment of land equal in value to 110 acres of the average allottable land of the tribe.

An agreement for the allotment of lands of the Cherokees ratified by Congress by Act of March 1, 1901, 31 Stat. 848, failed of ratification by the tribe. A previous agreement concluded between the Cherokee Commissioners and the Commission to the Five Civilized Tribes on January 14, 1899, and ratified by the tribe January 31, 1899, was not ratified by Congress. Mills, Oklahoma Indian Land Laws, 2d ed. (1924), p. 10.

[79] This provision also has been held to create a vested right to a homestead tax exemption which is protected by the Fifth Amendment. *Board of Com'rs of Tulsa County, Okla.* v. *United States*, 94 F. 2d 450 (C. C. A. 10, 1938); *Grotkop* v. *Stuckey*, 140 Okla. 178, 282 Pac. 611 (1929); *Weilep* v. *Audrain*, 36 Okla. 288, 128 Pac. 254 (1912); *Whitmire* v. *Trapp*, 33 Okla. 429, 126 Pac. 578 (1912). *Cf. United States* v. *Board of County Com'rs (Tulsa County)*, 19 F. Supp. 635 (D. C. N. D. Okla., 1937), aff'd sub nom. *Board of Com'rs of Tulsa County, Okla.* v. *United States*, 94 F. 2d 450 (C. C. A. 10, 1938).

[80] See *Rider* v. *Helms*, 48 Okla. 610, 150 Pac. 154 (1915). For cases dealing with taxability of surplus lands see *Kidd* v. *Robert*, 43 Okla 603, 143 Pac. 862 (1914); *Brown* v. *Denny*, 52 Okla. 380, 152 Pac. 1103 (1915).

[81] Act of June 28, 1898, 30 Stat. 495, 505–518. Supplementing Treaty of September 27, 1830, with Choctaw Nation, 7 Stat. 333; Treaty of June 22, 1852, with the Chickasaws, 10 Stat. 974; Treaty of April 28, 1866, with the Choctaws and Chickasaws, 14 Stat. 769. Supplemented by Act of December 21, 1898, 30 Stat. 770; Act of February 9, 1900, 31 Stat. 7; Act of May 31, 1900, 31 Stat. 221; Act of March 3, 1901, 31 Stat. 1058; Act of April 29, 1902, 32 Stat. 177; Act of May 27, 1902, 32 Stat. 245; Act of July 1, 1902, 32 Stat. 641; Act of April 21, 1904, 33 Stat. 189; Act of April 28, 1904, 33 Stat. 571; Act of March 3, 1905, 33 Stat. 1048; Act of March 29, 1906, 34 Stat. 91; Act of June 21, 1906, 34 Stat. 325; Act of March 1, 1907, 34 Stat. 1015; Act of May 29, 1908, 35 Stat. 444.

Cited: 23 Op. A. G. 214 (1900); 24 Op. A. G. 689 (1903); 25 Op. A. G. 460 (1905); 26 Op. A. G. 127 (1907); 27 Op. A. G. 530 (1909); 29 Op. A. G. 131 (1911); 29 Op. A. G. 231 (1911); 34 Op. A. G. 275 (1924); Op. Sol. I. D. 22121, April 12, 1927; Op. Sol. I. D., M.25260, August 1, 1929; 53 I. D. 502 (1931); *Atoka Coal & Mining Co.* v. *Adams*, 3 Ind. T. 189, 53 S. W. 539 (1899); *Atoka Coal & Mining Co.* v. *Adams*, 104 Fed. 471 (C. C. A. 8, 1900); *Ballinger* v. *United States ex rel. Frost*, 216 U. S. 240 (1910); *Barton* v. *Hulsey*, 4 Ind. T. 260, 69 S. W. 868 (1902); *Bruner* v. *United States*, 4 Ind. T. 580, 76 S. W.

> * * * the lands allotted shall be nontransferable until after full title is acquired and shall be liable for no obligations contracted prior thereto by the allottee, and shall be nontaxable while so held. * * * (Sec. 11.)

---

244 (1903); *Campbell* v. *Scott*, 3 Ind. T. 462, 58 S. W. 719 (1900); *Carpenter* v. *Shaw*, 280 U. S. 363 (1930); *Casteel* v. *McNeely*, 4 Ind. T. 1, 64 S. W. 594 (1901); *Chickasaw Nation* v. *United States*, 87 C. Cls. 91 (1938), cert. den. 307 U. S. 646; *Chickasaw Freedmen* v. *Choctaw Nation & Chickasaw Nation*, 193 U. S. 115 (1904); *Choctaw & Chickasaw Nations* v. *United States*, 81 C. Cls. 63 (1935); *Choctaw Nation* v. *United States*, 81 C. Cls. 1 (1935), cert. den. 296 U. S. 644; *Choctaw Nation* v. *United States*, 83 C. Cls. 140 (1936), cert. den. 287 U. S. 643; *Choctaw O. & G. R. Co.* v. *Bond*, 6 Ind. T. 515, 98 S. W. 335 (1906); *Choctaw & Gulf R. R.* v. *Harrison*, 235 U. S. 292 (1914); *Crowell* v. *Young*, 4 Ind. T. 36, 64 S. W. 607 (1901); *Ellis* v. *Fitzpatrick*, 3 Ind. T. 656, 64 S. W. 567 (1901); *Ellis* v. *Fitzpatrick*, 118 Fed. 430 (C. C. A. 8, 1902); *Engleman* v. *Cable*, 4 Ind. T. 336, 69 S. W. 894 (1902); *Fleming* v. *McCurtain*, 215 U. S. 56 (1909); *Fraer* v. *Washington*, 125 Fed. 280 (C. C. A. 8, 1903); *Frame* v. *Bivens*, 189 Fed. 785 (C. C. E. D. Okla. 1909); *Garfield* v. *United States ex rel. Goldsby*, 211 U. S. 249 (1908); *Gleason* v. *Wood*, 224 U. S. 679 (1912); *Glenn* v. *Lewis*, 105 F. 2d 398 (C. C. A. 10, 1939), cert. den. 60 Sup. Ct. 130; *Hayes* v. *Barringer*, 168 Fed. 221 (C. C. A. 8, 1909); *Hill* v. *Reynolds*, 242 U. S. 361 (1917); *Ikard* v. *Minter*, 4 Ind. T. 314, 69 S. W. 852 (1902); *In re Poff's Guardianship*, 7 Ind. T. 59, 103 S. W. 765 (1907); *Joines* v. *Robinson*, 4 Ind. T. 556, 76 S. W. 107 (1903); *Kelly* v. *Harper*, 7 Ind. T. 541, 104 S. W. 829 (1907); *Kimberlin* v. *Comm. to Five Civilized Tribes*, 104 Fed. 653 (C. C. A. 8, 1900); *Longest* v. *Langford*, 276 U. S. 69 (1928); *McBride* v. *Farrington*, 149 Fed. 114 (C. C. A. 2, 1906); *McCalib, Admr.*, v. *United States*, 83 C. Cls. 79 (1936); *McMurray* v. *Choctaw Nation*, 62 C. Cls. 458 (1926), cert. den. 275 U. S. 524; *McNee* v. *Whitehead*, 253 Fed. 546 (C. C. A. 8, 1918); *Sharrock* v. *Krieger*, 6 Ind. T. 466, 98 S. W. 161 (1906); *Southwestern Coal & Improvement Co.* v. *McBride*, 185 U. S. 499 (1902); *Swinney* v. *Kelley*, 5 Ind. T. 12, 76 S. W. 303 (1903); *Thompson* v. *Morgan*, 4 Ind. T. 412, 69 S. W. 920 (1902); *Turner* v. *Gilliland*, 4 Ind. T. 606, 76 S. W. 253 (1903); *Tynon* v. *Crowell*, 3 Ind. T. 346, 58 S. W. 565 (1900); *United States* v. *Choctaw Nation*, 38 C. Cls. 558 (1903); *United States* v. *Dowden*, 220 Fed. 277 (C. C. A. 8, 1915), app. dism. 242 U. S. 661; *United States* v. *Eastern Coal & Mining Co.*, 66 F. 2d 923 (C. C. A. 10, 1933); *United States* v. *McMurray*, 181 Fed. 723 (C. C. E. D. Okla., 1910); *United States* v. *Missouri-Kansas-Texas R. Co.*, 66 F. 2d. 919 (C. C. A. 10, 1933); *United States* v. *Richards*, 27 F. 2d 284 (C. C. A. 8, 1928); *United States ex rel. McAlester Edwards Coal Co.* v. *Fall*, 277 Fed. 573 (App. D. C., 1922); *Wallace* v. *Adams*, 204 U. S. 415 (1907); *Ward* v. *Love County*, 253 U. S. 17 (1920); *Williams* v. *First Nat. Bank*, 216 U. S. 582 (1910); *Williams* v. *Johnson*, 239 U. S. 414 (1915); *Williams* v. *Works*, 4 Ind. T. 587, 76 S. W. 147 (1903); *Winton* v. *Amos*, 255 U. S. 373 (1921).

The following statutes relate to the coal and asphalt deposits of the Choctaw and Chickasaw Nations:

Act of June 28, 1898, 30 Stat. 495, 510.

Act of July 1, 1902, 32 Stat. 641, 653–655. Cited in 24 Op. A. G. 689 (1903); 25 Op. A. G. 152 (1904); 25 Op. A. G. 320 (1905); 25 Op. A. G. 460 (1905); 26 Op. A. G. 127 (1907); 27 Op. A. G. 530 (1909); 29 Op. A. G. 131 (1911); 34 Op. A. G. 275 (1924); 35 Op. A. G. 259 (1927); Op. Sol. I. D., M.7316, May 28, 1924; Op. Sol. I. D., M.18772, December 24, 1926; 53 I. D. 502 (1931); *Alfrey* v. *Colbert*, 168 Fed. 231 (C. C. A. 8, 1909); *Arnold* v. *Ardmore Chamber of Commerce Ind. Corp.*, 4 F. 2d 838 (C. C. A. 8, 1925); *Ballinger* v. *United States ex rel. Frost*, 216 U. S. 240 (1910); *Bartlett* v. *Okla. Oil Co.*, 218 Fed. 380 (D. C. E. D. Okla., 1914); *Blundell* v. *Wallace*, 267 U. S. 373 (1925); *Brader* v. *James*, 246 U. S. 88 (1918); *Chickasaw Freedmen* v. *Choctaw Nation & Chickasaw Nation*, 193 U. S. 115 (1904); *Chickasaw Nation* v. *United States*, 87 C. Cls. 91 (1938) cert. den. 307 U. S. 646; *Choate* v. *Trapp*, 224 U. S. 665 (1912); *Choctaw and Chickasaw Nations* v. *United States*, 75 C. Cls. 494 (1932); *Choctaw Nation* v. *United States*, 81 C. Cls. 1 (1935), cert. den. 296 U. S. 643; *Choctaw Nation* v. *United States*, 83 C. Cls. 140 (1936), cert. den. 287 U. S. 643; *Choctaw, O. & G. R. Co.* v. *Bond*, 6 Ind. T. 515 (1906); *Davis* v. *Cundiff*, 5 Ind. T. 47 (1904); *Dawes* v. *Benson*, 5 Ind. T. 50 (1904); *Dawes* v. *Harris*, 5 Ind. T. 53 (1904); *Duncan Townsite Co.* v. *Lane*, 245 U. S. 308 (1912); *English* v. *Richardson, Treasurer of Tulsa County, Oklahoma*, 224 U. S. 680 (1912); *Ex parte Webb*, 225 U. S. 663 (1912); *Fink* v. *County Commissioners*, 248 U. S. 399 (1919); *Fish* v. *Wise*, 52 F. 2d 544 (C. C. A. 10, 1931), cert. den. 282 U. S. 903 (1931), 284 U. S. 688 (1932); *Fleming* v. *McCurtain*, 215 U. S. 56 (1909); *Frame* v. *Bivens*, 189 Fed. 785 (C. C. E. D. Okla. 1909); *Gannon* v. *Johnston*, 243 U. S. 108 (1917); *Garfield* v. *United States ex rel. Allison*, 211 U. S. 264 (1908); *Garfield* v. *United States ex rel. Goldsby*, 211 U. S. 249 (1908); *Gleason* v. *Wood*, 224 U. S. 679 (1912); *Gooding* v. *Watkins*, 5 Ind. T 578 (1904), rev'd by 142 Fed. 112 (C. C. A. 8, 1905); *Harris* v. *Hardridge*, 7 Ind. T. 532 (1907); *Hayes* v. *Barringer*, 168 Fed. 221 (C. C. A. 8, 1909); *Hill* v. *Reynolds*, 242 U. S. 361 (1917); *In re Jessie's Heirs*, 259 Fed. 694 (D. C. E. D. Okla., 1919); *In re Lands of Five Civilized Tribes*, 199 Fed. 811 (D. C. E. D. Okla., 1912); *Joines* v. *Patterson*, 274 U. S. 544 (1927); *Kelly* v. *Harper*, 7 Ind. T. 541 (1907); *Longest* v. *Langford*, 276 U. S. 69 (1928); *McCalib, Adm'r.* v. *United States*, 83 C. Cls. 79 (1936); *McMurray* v. *Choctaw Nation*, 62 C. Cls. 458 (1926), cert. den. 275 U. S. 524; *Missouri, Kansas, and Texas R'y Co.* v. *United States*, 47 C. Cls. 59 (1911); *Mullen* v. *Simmons*, 234 U. S. 192 (1914); *Mullen* v. *Pickens*, 250 U. S. 590 (1919); *Mullen* v. *United States*, 224 U. S. 448 (1912); *Ne-Kah-Wah-She-Tun-Kah* v. *Fall*, 290 Fed. 303 (App. D. C. 1923), app. dism. 266 U. S. 595 (1925); *Sayer* v. *Brown*, 7 Ind. T. 675, 104 S. W. 877 (1907); *Sharrock* v. *Krieger*, 6 Ind. T. 466 (1906); *Taylor* v. *Parker*, 235 U. S. 42 (1914); *Thomason* v. *Willman & Rhoades*, 206 Fed. 895 (C. C. A. 8, 1913); *Tiger* v. *Western Inv. Co.*, 221 U. S. 286 (1911); *United States* v. *Dowden*, 220 Fed. 277 (C. C. A. 8, 1915), app. dism. 242 U. S. 661; *United States* v. *Marshall*, 210 Fed. 595 (C. C. A. 8, 1914); *United States* v. *One Cadillac Eight Automobile*, 255 Fed. 173 (D. C. M. D. Tenn., 1918); *United States* v. *Reynolds*, 250 U. S. 104 (1919); *United States* v. *Richards*, 27 F. 2d 284 (C. C. A. 8, 1928), cert. den. 278 U. S. 630; *United States* v. *Smith*, 266 Fed. 740 (D. C. E. D. Okla., 1920); *United States* v. *Wright*, 53 F. 2d 300 (C. C. A. 4, 1931), cert. den. 285 U. S. 539; *Wallace* v. *Adams*, 6 Ind. T. 32 (1905); *Wallace* v. *Adams*, 204 U. S. 415 (1907); *Whitchurch* v. *Crawford*, 92 F. 2d 249 (C. C. A. 10, 1937); *Williams* v. *Johnson*, 239 U. S. 414 (1915); *Williams* v. *White*, 218 Fed. 797 (C. C. A. 8, 1914); *Winton* v. *Amos*, 255 U. S. 373 (1921).

Act of April 28, 1904, 33 Stat. 544.

Act of April 26, 1906, 34 Stat. 137, 141, 142, *infra*, fn. 101.

Joint Resolution of December 8, 1913, 38 Stat. 767.

Joint Resolution of January 11, 1917, 39 Stat. 866.

Act of January 25, 1917, 39 Stat. 870.

Act of February 8, 1918, 40 Stat. 433. Cited in 35 Op. A. G. 259 (1927); 36 Op. A. G. 473 (1931); Memo. Sol. I. D., December 11, 1918; Op. Sol. I. D., M.7316, April 5, 1922; Op. Sol. I. D., M.7316, May 28, 1924; *United States ex rel. McAlester Edwards Coal Co.* v. *Fall*, 277 Fed. 573 (App. D. C. 1922).

Act of February 22, 1921, 41 Stat. 1107.

Act of May 25, 1928, 45 Stat. 737.

Act of June 19, 1930, 46 Stat. 788.

Act of April 21, 1932, 47 Stat. 88.

Act of June 26, 1934, 48 Stat. 1240.

Act of May 11, 1938, 52 Stat. 347, 25 U. S. C. 396a–396e. Cited in *United States* v. *Watashe*, 102 F. 2d 428 (C. C. A. 10, 1939). This act excepted these coal and asphalt lands from the general statutory provision for the leasing of lands for mining purposes.

The following appropriation acts appropriate money to advertise for the disposition of Chickasaw and Choctaw coal and asphalt deposits:

Act of August 24, 1912, sec. 18, 37 Stat. 518; Act of June 30, 1913, sec. 18, 38 Stat. 77; Act of August 1, 1914, sec. 17, 38 Stat. 582; Act of May 18, 1916, sec. 19, 39 Stat. 123; Act of March 2, 1917, sec. 18, 39 Stat. 969; Act of May 25, 1918, sec. 18, 40 Stat. 561; Act of June 30, 1919, sec. 18, 41 Stat. 3; Act of February 14, 1920, sec. 18, 41 Stat. 408; Act of March 3, 1921, sec. 18, 41 Stat. 1225; Act of May 24, 1922, 42 Stat. 552, 575; Act of January 24, 1923, 42 Stat. 1174, 1196; Act of March 3, 1925, 43 Stat. 1141, 1148; Act of May 10, 1926, 44 Stat. 453, 460; Act of January 12, 1927, 44 Stat. 934, 941; Act of March 7, 1928, 45 Stat. 200, 206; Act of March 4, 1929, 45 Stat. 1562, 1568; Act of May 14, 1930, 46 Stat. 279, 286.

For regulations regarding the leasing of segregated coal and asphalt deposits, see 25 C. F. R. 207.1–207.12; regarding mining operations on segregated coal and asphalt lands, see *ibid.*, 210.1–210.2; regarding sale of coal and asphalt deposits in segregated mineral area, see *ibid.*, 213.1–213.17.

Many other special statutes have been passed dealing with tribal property of the Choctaw and Chickasaw Nations, such as:

Act of March 4, 1913, c. 152, 37 Stat. 1007; Act of June 25, 1910, 36 Stat. 832. Amended by Act of January 25, 1917, 39 Stat. 870. These acts all related to certain coal leases.

Act of May 26, 1930, 46 Stat. 385. Supplementing Act of May 25, 1928, 45 Stat. 737. Relating to tribal lands for oil, gas, and other purposes.

Act of April 28, 1904, 33 Stat. 571. Supplementing Act of June 28, 1898, 30 Stat. 495. Amended by Act of May 24, 1924, 43 Stat. 138, relating to townsite lands.

25 U. S. C. A. 414, Act of August 25, 1937, 50 Stat. 810 provides:

> That hereafter, in all sales of tribal lands of the Choctaw and Chickasaw Indians in Oklahoma provided for by existing law, the Secretary of the Interior is hereby authorized to offer such lands for sale subject to a reservation of the mineral rights therein, including oil and gas, for the benefit of said Indians, whenever in his judgment the interests of the Indians will best be served thereby.

The act further directed the issuance of patents and stated that:

> All the lands allotted shall be nontaxable while the title remains in the original allottee, but not to exceed twenty-one years from date of patent, and each allottee shall select from his allotment a homestead of one hundred and sixty acres, for which he shall have a separate patent, and which shall be inalienable for twenty-one years from date of patent. * * *[82]

The leading case of *Choate* v. *Trapp*[83] held that under this statute allottees acquired a vested property right to exemption from state taxation which was binding on Oklahoma and could not be impaired by subsequent congressional action without violation of the Fifth Amendment of the Federal Constitution. The exemption extends to prevent the state from imposing a tax on oil and gas royalties accruing to the Indian owner under a lease of the allotment.[84] The exemption does not, however, run with the land, and therefore does not attach in favor of the heirs or grantees.[85]

The Choctaw and Chickasaw freedmen, unlike the freedmen of the other tribes, were not members of the tribes, and their right of participation in the lands of the nations extended only to 40 acres each. The claim of the Choctaw freedmen was based upon the action of the Choctaw Nation in bestowing such right in pursuance of the treaty with the United States of 1866.[86] The Chickasaws took no action to secure the rights of their freedmen under said treaty and allotments of 40 acres each were made to them by virtue of section 29 of the Atoka Agreement, which exempted the lands of the members of the tribes from taxation, and specified that:

> * * * This provision shall also apply to the Choctaw and Chickasaw freedmen to the extent of his allotment. * * *

It has been held that the allotments of Chickasaw freedmen under the Atoka Agreement and 1902 supplemental agreement became taxable when the Act of May 27, 1908, removed the tax exemption.[87] In distinguishing the case of *Choate* v. *Trapp*, the court declared that the exemption enjoyed by members of the tribes could not be abrogated by Congress because it had been granted in consideration of this relinquishment of some of their rights and therefore vested in the Indians a property right of which they could not be deprived under the Fifth Amendment of the Constitution; but that the freedmen had relinquished nothing and were therefore in a different position, and that by the terms of the Atoka Agreement, the rights of the freedmen remained subject to subsequent acts of Congress, and therefore the tax exemption could be removed.

The same reasoning would seem equally applicable to the Choctaw freedmen.

[82] Act of June 28, 1898, 30 Stat. 495, 507, sec. 29. See fn. 81 *supra*.

[83] 224 U. S. 665 (1912); followed in *Gleason* v. *Wood*, 224 U. S. 679 (1912). See Chapter 13, secs. 1B. 7A.

[84] *Carpenter* v. *Shaw*, 280 U. S. 363 (1930). The court reasoned that since the royalty interest was a right attached to the reversionary interest in the land, the royalty was not taxable.

[85] *McNee* v. *Whitehead*, 253 Fed. 546 (C. C. A. 8, 1918).

[86] Treaty of April 28, 1866, Art. 3, 14 Stat. 769.

[87] *Allen* v. *Trimmer*, 45 Okla. 83, 144 Pac. 795 (1914), writ of error 248 U. S. 590 (1918).

C. CREEKS[87a]

Under the Creek Agreements[88] allotments were made inalienable for 5 years from June 30, 1902, and each citizen was allowed to:

> * * * select from his allotment forty acres of land, or a quarter of a quarter section, as a homestead, which

[87a] While the Creeks are most commonly referred to as a tribe, they are also referred to in various treaties, acts of Congress, judicial opinions and administrative rulings as a confederacy consisting of tribes, bands, or "towns". Thus in *Mitchel* v. *United States*, 9 Pet. 711 (1835), the Supreme Court upheld land titles based upon "deeds from various tribes of Indians belonging to the great Creek Confederacy" (at p. 725). And see Memo. Sol. I. D. July 15, 1937, cited in Chapter 14, sec. 1. Creek "towns" which have adopted tribal constitutions are Thlopthlocco Tribal Town (constitution ratified, December 27, 1938; charter ratified, April 13, 1939) and Alabama-Quassarte Tribal Town (constitution ratified, January 10, 1939, charter ratified, May 24, 1939).

[88] Original agreement: Act of March 1, 1901, 31 Stat. 861. Supplementing Act of March 24, 1832, 7 Stat. 366, 367; Act of June 14, 1866, 14 Stat. 785, 787; Act of June 28, 1898, 30 Stat. 495, 498, 500, 520. Amended by Act of June 30, 1902, 32 Stat. 500. Repealed in part, Act of June 30, 1902, 32 Stat. 500. Supplemented by Act of June 30, 1902, 32 Stat. 500; Act of March 3, 1903, 32 Stat. 982; Act of March 3, 1905, 33 Stat. 1048; Act of August 1, 1914, 38 Stat. 582; Act of August 24, 1922, 42 Stat. 831. Cited: 24 Op. A. G. 623 (1903); 25 Op. A. G. 163 (1904); 34 Op. A. G. 275 (1924); Op. Sol. I. D. D.40462, October 31, 1917; Op. Sol. I. D. M.10526, December 13, 1923; Memo. Sol. I. D., September 17, 1936; 53 I. D. 502 (1931); *Armstrong* v. *Wood*, 195 Fed. 137 (C. C. E. D. Okla., 1911); *Bagby* v. *United States*, 60 F. 2d 80 (C. C. A. 10, 1932); *Bartlett* v. *Okla. Oil Co.*, 218 Fed. 380 (D. C. E. D. Okla., 1914); *Brann* v. *Bell*, 192 Fed. 427 (C. C. E. D. Okla., 1911); *Brown* v. *United States*, 27 F. 2d 274 (C. C. A. 8, 1928); *Browning* v. *United States*, 6 F. 2d 801 (C. C. A. 8, 1925), cert. den. 269 U. S. 568 (1925); *Buster* v. *Wright*, 135 Fed. 947 (C. C. A. 8, 1905), app. dism. 203 U. S. 599; *Campbell* v. *Wadsworth*, 248 U. S. 169 (1918); *Capital Townsite Co.* v. *Fox*, 6 Ind. T. 223 (1906); *Carter Oil Co.* v. *Scott*, 12 F. 2d 780 (D. C. N. D. Okla., 1926), rev'd. sub nom. *Knight* v. *Carter Oil Co.*, 23 F. 2d 481 (C. C. A. 8, 1927); *Choctaw O. & G. R. R. Co.* v. *Mackey*, 256 U. S. 531 (1921); *City of Tulsa* v. *Southwestern Bell Tel. Co.*, 75 F. 2d 343 (1935), cert. den. 295 U. S. 744; *Creek Nation* v. *United States*, 78 C. Cls. 474 (1933); *Evans* v. *Victor*, 204 Fed. 361 (C. C. A. 8, 1913); *Ex parte Webb*, 225 U. S. 663 (1912); *Fink* v. *County Commissioners*, 248 U. S. 399 (1919); *Fish* v. *Wise*, 52 F. 2d 544 (C. C. A. 10, 1931), cert. den. 282 U. S. 903 (1931), 284 U. S. 688 (1932); *Folk* v. *United States*, 233 Fed. 177 (C. C. A. 8, 1916); *Fulsom* v. *Quaker Oil & Gas Co.*, 35 F. 2d 84 (C. C. A. 8, 1929); *Gilcrease* v. *McCullough*, 249 U. S. 178 (1919); *Grayson* v. *Harris*, 267 U. S. 352 (1925); *Harris* v. *Bell*, 254 U. S. 103 (1920); *Harris* v. *Hardridge*, 7 Ind. T. 532 (1907); *Harris* v. *Hardridge*, 166 Fed. 109 (C. C. A. 8, 1908); *Hawkins* v. *Okla. Oil Co.*, 195 Fed. 345 (C. C. E. D. Okla. 1911); *Hopkins* v. *United States*, 235 Fed. 95 (C. C. A. 8, 1916); *In re Lands of Five Civilized Tribes*, 199 Fed. 811 (D. C. E. D. Okla. 1912); *Indian L. & T. Co.* v. *Shoenfelt*, 5 Ind. T. 41 (1904) rev'd by 135 Fed. 484 (1905); *Iowa Land & Trust Co.* v. *United States*, 217 Fed. 11 (C. C. A. 8, 1914); *Jefferson* v. *Fink*, 247 U. S. 288 (1918); *Janus* v. *United States, ex rel. Humphrey*, 38 F. 2d 431 (C. C. A. 9, 1930); *Joplin Mercantile Co.* v. *United States*, 236 U. S. 531 (1915); *Kemohah* v. *Shaffer Oil & Refining Co.*, 38 F. 2d 665 (D. C. N. D. Okla., 1930); *King* v. *Ickes*, 64 F. 2d 979 (App. D. C. 1933); *Knight* v. *Carter Oil Co.*, 23 F. 2d 481 (C. C. A. 8, 1927); *Locke* v. *M'Murry*, 287 Fed. 276 (C. C. A. 8, 1923); *Missouri, Kansas & Texas Ry. Co.* v. *United States*, 47 C. Cls. 59 (1911); *McDougal* v. *McKay*, 237 U. S. 372 (1915); *McKee* v. *Henry*, 201 Fed. 74 (C. C. A. 8, 1912); *Malone* v. *Alderdice*, 212 Fed. 668 (C. C. A. 8, 1914); *Mandler* v. *United States*, 49 F. 2d 201 (C. C. A. 10, 1931); *Mandler* v. *United States*, 52 F. 2d 713 (C. C. A. 10, 1931); *Marlin* v. *Lewallen*, 276 U. S. 58 (1928); *Morrison* v. *United States*, 6 F. 2d 811 (C. C. A. 8,

> shall be and remain nontaxable, inalienable, and free from any incumbrance whatever for twenty-one years from the date of the deed therefor, and a separate deed shall be issued to each allottee for his homestead, in which this condition shall appear.[89]

These provisions conferred a right to hold the homestead exempt from taxation,[90] which was vested and protected by the Fifth Amendment of the Federal Constitution.[91] The Creek Agreements did not expressly confer upon Creek Indians any general exemption from taxation; only the homesteads were expressly exempted.[92]

In the hands of a purchaser from an allottee, the homestead lands have been held taxable and the Supreme Court, in distinguishing *Choate* v. *Trapp*,[93] has limited its doctrine to cases where the land is still in the possession of the allottee.[94]

D. SEMINOLES

The Act of July 1, 1898,[95] ratifying the Seminole Agreement, provides for allotment in severalty of lands of the Seminole Nation and states that

> * * * Each allottee shall designate one tract of forty acres, which shall, by the terms of the deed, be made inalienable and nontaxable as a homestead in perpetuity.

Section 8 of the Act of March 3, 1903,[96] provided that these homesteads

> * * * shall be inalienable during the lifetime of the allottee, not exceeding twenty-one years from the date of the deed for the allotment. * * *

Although no specific restrictions are imposed by these statutes on lands other than homestead, it has been said that since the lands were nontaxable at the time of the agreement, and since it was the settled policy of the United States to protect the lands from taxation until the Indians were given full power of disposition, an exemption may be implied.[97] Thus, when restrictions on alienation were expressly imposed on surplus lands of full bloods by later acts,[98] these lands were held nontaxable.[99]

1925); *Mullen* v. *United States*, 224 U. S. 448 (1912); *Norton* v. *Larney*, 226 U. S. 511 (1925); *Parker* v. *Richard*, 250 U. S. 235 (1919); *Parker* v. *Riley*, 250 U. S. 66 (1919); *Pigeon* v. *Buck*, 237 U. S. 386 (1915); *Porter* v. *Murphy*, 7 Ind. T. 395, 104 S. W. 658 (1907), rev'd sub nom. *Adams* v. *Murphy*, 165 Fed. 304 (C. C. A. 8, 1908); *Priddy* v. *Thompson*, 204 Fed. 955 (C. C. A. 8, 1913); *Reed* v. *Welty*, 197 Fed. 419 (D. C. E. D. Okla., 1912), rev'd, 219 Fed. 864, aff'd on rehearing, 231 Fed. 930; *Roubedeaux* v. *Quaker Oil & Gas Co. of Okla.*, 23 F. 2d 277 (C. C. A. 8, 1927), cert. den. 276 U. S. 636; *St. Louis & S. F. R. Co.* v. *Pfennighausen*, 7 Ind. T. 685, 104 S. W. 880 (1907); *Schellenbarger* v. *Fewell*, 236 U. S. 68 (1915); *Shulthis* v. *McDougal*, 225 U. S. 561 (1912); *Sizemore* v. *Brady*, 235 U. S. 441 (1914); *Skelton* v. *Dill*, 235 U. S. 206 (1914); *Stancliff* v. *Fox*, 152 Fed. 697 (C. C. A. 8, 1907), app. dism. 215 U. S. 619; *Stewart* v. *Keyes*, 295 U. S. 403 (1935), rehearing den. 296 U. S. 661 (1935); *Sunday* v. *Mallory*, 248 U. S. 545 (1919); *Sweet* v. *Schock*, 245 U. S. 192 (1917); *Tiger* v. *Slinker*, 4 F. 2d 714 (D. C. E. D. Okla., 1925); *Tiger* v. *Twin State Oil Co.*, 48 F. 2d 509 (C. C. A. 10, 1931); *Tiger* v. *Western Inv. Co.*, 221 U. S. 286 (1911); *Turner* v. *United States*, 51 C. Cls. 125 (1916); *Turner* v. *United States*, 248 U. S. 354 (1919); *United States* v. *Atkins*, 260 U. S. 220 (1922); *United States* v. *Equitable Tr. Co.*, 283 U. S. 738 (1931); *United States* v. *Ferguson*, 247 U. S. 175 (1918); *United States* v. *Ft. Smith & W. R. Co.*, 195 Fed. 211 (C. C. A. 8, 1912); *United States* v. *Gypsy Oil Co.*, 10 F. 2d 487 (C. C. A. 8, 1925); *United States* v. *Hayes*, 20 F. 2d 873 (C. C. A. 8, 1927), cert. den. 275 U. S. 555; *United States* v. *Jacobs*, 195 Fed. 707 (C. C. A. 8, 1912); *United States* v. *Lena*, 261 Fed. 144 (C. C. A. 8, 1919); *United States* v. *Martin*, 45 F. 2d 836 (D. C. E. D. Okla., 1930); *United States* v. *Mid Continent Pet. Corp.*, 67 F. 2d 37 (C. C. A. 10, 1933), cert. den. 290 U. S. 702 (1933); *United States* v. *Rea-Read Mills & Elev. Co.*, 171 Fed. 501 (C. C. E. D. Okla., 1909); *United States* v. *Shock*, 187 Fed. 862, (C. C. E. D. Okla., 1911); *United States* v. *Smith*, 279 Fed. 136 (D. C. E. D. Okla., 1922); *United States* v. *Smith*, 288 Fed. 356 (C. C. A. 8, 1923) *United States* v. *Southern Surety Co.*, 9 F. 2d 664 (D. C. E. D. Okla., 1925); *United States* v. *Tiger*, 19 F. 2d 35 (C. C. A. 8, 1927); *United States* v. *Western Inv. Co.*, 226 Fed. 726 (C. C. A. 8, 1915); *United States* v. *Wildcat*, 244 U. S. 111 (1917); *United States Express Co.* v. *Friedman*, 191 Fed. 673 (C. C. A. 8, 1911); *W. O. Whitney Lumber & Grain Co.* v. *Crabtree*, 166 Fed. 738 (C. C. A. 8, 1908); *Wade* v. *Fisher*, 39 App. D. C. 245 (1912); *Washington* v. *Miller*, 235 U. S. 422 (1914); *Welty* v. *Reed*, 231 Fed. 930 (C. C. A. 8, 1916); *Willmott* v. *United States*, 27 F. 2d 277 (C. C. A. 8, 1928); *Woodward* v. *De Graffenried*, 238 U. S. 284 (1915). For annotations to Act of June 30, 1902, 32 Stat. 500, supplementing the Original Creek Agreement, see fn. 89, *infra*.

[89] Act of June 30, 1902, sec. 16, 32 Stat. 500, 503. This act supplemented the Act of June 30, 1834, 4 Stat. 729; Act of May 31, 1900, 31 Stat. 221, 231; Act of March 1, 1901, 31 Stat. 861, 869, secs. 7 and 8; amended Act of March 1, 1901, 31 Stat. 861, 862, sec. 3, par. 2, 864, sec. 8, 871, sec. 37; repealed Act of March 1, 1901, 31 Stat. 861, 864, 868, sec. 24; and was supplemented by Act of April 21, 1904, 33 Stat. 189; Act of June 21, 1906, 34 Stat. 325; Act of August 1, 1914, 38 Stat. 582; Act of August 24, 1922, 42 Stat. 831. It was cited in 26 Op. A. G. 317 (1907); Op. Sol. I. D., M.13807, January 23, 1925; *Adkins* v. *Arnold*, 235 U. S. 417 (1914); *Alfrey* v. *Colbert*, 168 Fed. 231 (C. C. A. 8, 1909); *Blackburn* v. *Muskogee Land Co.*, 6 Ind. T. 232, 91 S. W. 31 (1906); *Brader* v. *James*, 246 U. S. 88 (1918); *Heckman* v. *United States*, 224 U. S. 413 (1912); *Hill* v. *Rankin*, 289 Fed. 511 (D. C. E. D. Okla., 1923); *Lanham* v. *McKeel*, 244 U. S. 582 (1917); *Moore* v. *Sawyer*, 167 Fed. 826 (C. C. E. D. Okla., 1909); *Morrison* v. *Burnette*, 154 Fed. 617 (C. C. A. 8, 1907), app. dism. 212 U. S. 291 (1909); *Muskogee Land Co.* v. *Mullins*, 165 Fed. 179 (C. C. A. 8, 1908); *Nunn* v. *Hazelrigg*, 216 Fed. 330 (C. C. A. 8, 1914); *Pitman* v. *Commissioner of Internal Revenue*, 64 F. 2d 740 (C. C. A. 10, 1933); *Reynolds* v. *Fewell*, 236 U. S. 58 (1915); *Self* v. *Prairie Oil & Gas Co.*, 28 F. 2d 590 (C. C. A. 8, 1928); *Taylor* v. *United States*, 230 Fed. 580 (C. C. A. 8, 1916); *United States* v. *Bartlett*, 235 U. S. 72 (1914); *United States* v. *Black*, 247 Fed. 942 (C. C. A. 8, 1917); *United States* v. *Board of Commissioners of McIntosh County*, 284 Fed. 103 (C. C. A. 8, 1922), app. dism. 263 U. S. 691; *United States* v. *Cook*, 225 Fed. 756 (C. C. A. 8, 1915); *United States* v. *Knight*, 206 Fed. 145 (C. C. A. 8, 1913); *United States* v. *Shock*, 187 Fed. 870 (C. C. E. D. Okla., 1911); *United States* v. *Smith*, 266 Fed. 740 (D. C. E. D. Okla., 1920); *United States* v. *Woods*, 223 Fed. 316 (C. C. A. 8, 1915). For annotations on the Original Creek Agreement, see fn. 88 *supra*.

[90] *United States* v. *Southern Surety Co.*, 9 F. 2d 664 (D. C. E. D. Okla., 1925).

[91] *English* v. *Richardson*, 224 U. S. 680 (1912). *Cf. Choate* v. *Trapp*, 224 U. S. 665 (1912), discussed in Chapter 13, secs. 1, 3, 7.

[92] As in the case of the Cherokees, the grant of nontaxable land by the agreement extended only to the homestead, and such exemption, as attached to the surplus, was by reason of the general restrictions against alienation.

[93] 224 U. S. 665 (1912).

[94] *Fink* v. *County Commissioners*, 248 U. S. 399 (1919); *Sweet* v. *Schock*, 245 U. S. 192 (1917).

[95] 30 Stat. 567, 568. Repealing in part Act of June 7, 1897, 30 Stat. 62. Supplemented by Act of March 3, 1903, 32 Stat. 982. Cited in 26 Op. A. G. 340 (1907); 34 Op. A. G. 275 (1924); 35 Op. A. G. 421 (1928); 53 I. D. 502 (1931); *Ex parte Webb*, 225 U. S. 663 (1912); *Fish* v. *Wise*, 52 F. 2d 544 (C. C. A. 10, 1931); *Goat* v. *United States*, 224 U. S. 458 (1912); *In re Grayson*, 3 Ind. T. 497 (1901); *In re Lands of Five Civilized Tribes*, 199 Fed. 811 (D. C. E. D. Okla., 1912); *Moore* v. *Carter Oil Co.*, 43 F. 2d 322 (C. C. A. 10, 1930); *Seminole Nation* v. *United States*, 78 C. Cls. 455 (1933); *Tiger* v. *Western Inv. Co.*, 221 U. S. 286 (1911); *United States* v. *Bean*, 253 Fed. 1 (C. C. A. 8, 1918); *United States* v. *Board of Com'rs of McIntosh Cty.*, 284 Fed. 103 (C. C. A. 8, 1922); *United States* v. *Seminole Nation*, 299 U. S. 417 (1937); *United States* v. *Smith*, 266 Fed. 740 (D. C. E. D. Okla., 1920; *United States* v. *Stigall*, 226 Fed. 190 (C. C. A. 8, 1915); *United States Express Co.* v. *Friedman*, 191 Fed. 673 (C. C. A. 8, 1911); *Vinson* v. *Graham*, 44 F. 2d 772 (C. C. A. 10, 1930); *Woodward* v. *DeGraffenried*, 238 U. S. 284 (1915).

The Act of June 15, 1933, 48 Stat. 146, provided for per capita payment to the Seminole Indians from funds standing to their credit in the Treasury.

The Act of April 27, 1932, 47 Stat. 140, required the General Council of the Seminole Tribe or Nation to approve the disposal of any tribal land.

[96] 32 Stat. 982, 1008.

[97] See *United States* v. *Bean*, 253 Fed. 1 (C. C. A. 8, 1918).

[98] Act of April 26, 1906, 34 Stat. 137, see fn. 101, *infra*; Act of May 27, 1908, 35 Stat. 312, 315, discussed *infra*, fn. 102.

[99] See *United States* v. *Bean*, 253 Fed. 1 (C. C. A. 8, 1918).

E. FIVE CIVILIZED TRIBES AS A GROUP

Shortly after the passage of these special allotment acts, Congress began to legislate for the Five Civilized Tribes as a group.[100]

The link between restrictions and tax exemptions is clearly demonstrated by the Act of April 26, 1906,[101] providing for the final disposition of the affairs of the Five Civilized Tribes. This statute imposes restrictions against alienation on allotments of full bloods for 25 years unless removed sooner by Congress, and provides that:

> * * * all lands upon which restrictions are removed shall be subject to taxation, and the other lands shall be exempt from taxation as long as title remains in the original allottee.

---

[100] For many years there was a congressional committee on the Five Civilized Tribes in addition to the Committee on Indian Affairs. See, for example, Act of April 17, 1900, 31 Stat. 86, 88; Act of March 3, 1901, 31 Stat. 960, 961.

Also see 49 L. D. 348 (1922); and 53 I. D. 48 (1930), which stated among other things:

> By later legislation as found in the acts of April 26, 1906 (34 Stat. 137), and May 27, 1908 (35 Stat. 312), Congress set up a new and uniform set of restrictions applicable alike to all of the Five Civilized Tribes. Without discussing the provisions of this later legislation in detail, it is sufficient for present purposes to point out that the restrictions against alienation of lands allotted to certain members of these tribes, including full-bloods and three-fourths bloods, not theretofore removed by or under any prior law, were continued to April 26, 1931, and the restrictions as to certain other lands were removed with the provision that such lands should thereupon become subject to taxation by the State. (P. 50.)

Other statutes dealing with allotments of the Five Civilized Tribes include:

Act of August 24, 1912, c. 562, 37 Stat. 497. Amending Act of April 26, 1906, 34 Stat. 137. Cited in Memo. Sol. I. D., May 19, 1936; *Bowling* v. *United States*, 299 Fed. 438 (C. C. A. 8, 1924). This act authorized the Secretary of the Interior to sell land and timber reserved from allotment under sec. 7 of the Act of April 26, 1906, 34 Stat. 137, *infra*, fn. 101.

The Act of June 28, 1898, 30 Stat. 495, see fn. 78, *supra*.

The disposition of timber belonging to these tribes was also dealt with in the Act of January 21, 1903, 32 Stat. 774. Supplementing Act of February 8, 1887, 24 Stat. 388; Act of May 27, 1902, 32 Stat. 245. Repealed in part by the Act of March 3, 1905, 33 Stat. 1048. Supplemented by Act of March 3, 1903, 32 Stat. 982; Act of June 21, 1926, 34 Stat. 325. Cited: Op. Sol. I. D., M.22121, April 12, 1927; *Gibson* v. *Anderson*, 131 Fed. 39 (C. C. A. 9, 1904); *United States* v. *Gray*, 201 Fed. 291 (C. C. A. 8, 1912), app. dism. 263 U. S. 689; *Ute Indians* v. *United States*, 45 C. Cls. 440 (1910).

Act of March 27, 1914, 38 Stat. 310, as amended by the Act of March 2, 1921, 41 Stat. 1204, which provided for the drainage of Indian allotments of the Five Civilized Tribes. For other statutes dealing with the Five Civilized Tribes, see the Act of August 24, 1922, 42 Stat. 831, supplementing Act of March 1, 1901, 31 Stat. 861, 863; Act of June 30, 1902, 32 Stat. 500, 503; Act of March 3, 1903, 32 Stat. 982, 996; Act of April 21, 1904, 33 Stat. 189, 204; Act of April 26, 1906, 34 Stat. 137, 145; Act of June 21, 1906, 34 Stat. 325, 373; Act of May 27, 1908, 35 Stat. 312, which validated certain deeds executed by members of the Five Civilized Tribes; and sec. 409a of title 25 of the U. S. Code, derived from the Act of March 2, 1931, 46 Stat. 1471, which relieved restricted Indians in the Five Civilized Tribes, whose nontaxable lands are required for state, county, or municipal improvements, or sold to other persons, from taxation of land purchased with money received. By the amendment of the Act of June 30, 1932, 47 Stat. 474, this statute was made applicable to all tribes.

The Act of May 26, 1920, 41 Stat. 625, as amended by Act of January 7, 1925, 43 Stat. 728, empowered the Secretary of the Interior to pay out of any funds of the Creek, Cherokee, Choctaw, Chickasaw, and Seminole Nations, part of the cost of town improvements. The 1920 act amended the Act of June 30, 1913, 38 Stat. 77, 96.

For an example of a provision found in many appropriation statutes, see Act of February 14, 1920, sec. 18, 41 Stat. 408, 426.

Some provisions applied to all the Five Civilized Tribes, but the Seminoles. See, for example, the Appropriation Act of May 31, 1900, 31 Stat. 221, 236–238. For regulations relating to removal of restrictions and sale of lands of members of the Five Civilized Tribes and reinvestment of funds in nontaxable lands, see 25 C. F. R. 241.34–241.48.

[101] Sec. 19, 34 Stat. 137, 144. This act also contained many other important provisions dealing with the leasing of allotments (secs. 19 and 20; also see sec. 9 of this chapter); authorizing adult heirs to alienate inherited allotments (sec. 22), and providing for descent (sec. 5), reversion to tribe in default of heirs (sec. 21), and devise of allotments (sec. 23).

The Act of April 26, 1906, supplemented the Act of May 31, 1900, 31 Stat. 221; Act of February 28, 1902, 32 Stat. 43; Act of February 19, 1903, 32 Stat. 841; Act of March 3, 1905, 33 Stat. 1048. Amended by Act of June 21, 1906, 34 Stat. 325; Act of May 27, 1908, 35 Stat. 312; Act of August 24, 1912, 37 Stat. 497; Act of April 10, 1926, 44 Stat. 239; Act of May 10, 1928, 45 Stat. 495. Supplemented by Act of March 1, 1907, 34 Stat. 1015; Concurrent Resolution of April 19, 1906, 34 Stat. 2832; Act of April 30, 1908, 35 Stat. 70; Act of May 29, 1908, 35 Stat. 444; Act of March 3, 1909, 35 Stat. 781; Act of April 4, 1910, 36 Stat. 269; Act of February 19, 1912, 37 Stat. 67; Act of August 24, 1912, c. 562, 37 Stat. 497; Act of August 24, 1922, 42 Stat. 831; Act of June 28, 1934, 48 Stat. 1467. Cited in Cabell, J. V., Descent and Distribution of Indian Lands (1932), 3 Okla. S. B. J. 208; 26 Op. A. G. 127 (1907); 26 Op. A. G. 340 (1907); 26 Op. A. G. 351 (1907); 27 Op. A. G. 530 (1909); 29 Op. A. G. 131 (1911); 29 Op. A. G. 231 (1911); 34 Op. A. G. 275 (1924); 34 Op. A. G. 302 (1924); Op. Sol. I. D., M.7996, August 2, 1922; Op. Sol. I. D., D.46987, November 13, 1922; Op. Sol. I. D., M.10526, December 13, 1923; Op. Sol. I. D., M.7316, May 28, 1924; Op. Sol. I. D., October 4, 1926; Report of Status of Pueblo of Pojoaque, November 3, 1932; Op. Sol. I. D., M.27843, January 22, 1935; Op. Sol. I. D., M.27759, January 22, 1935; Op. Sol. I. D., M.27814, January 30, 1935; Memo. Sol. I. D., September 20, 1935; Op. Sol. I. D., M.27814, April 23, 1936; Memo. Sol. I. D., May 19, 1936; Memo. Sol. I. D., September 17, 1936; Memo. Sol. I. D., August 25, 1937; 53 I. D. 48 (1930); 53 I. D. 471 (1931); 53 I. D. 502 (1931); 53 I. D. 637 (1932); 54 I. D. 109 (1932); *Anchor Oil Co.* v. *Gray*, 256 U. S. 519 (1921); *Anicker* v. *Gunsburg*, 246 U. S. 110 (1918); *Barnett* v. *Kunkel*, 259 Fed. 394 (C. C. A. 8, 1919); *Bartlett* v. *Okla. Oil Co.*, 218 Fed. 380 (D. C. E. D. Okla., 1914); *Bilby* v. *Stewart*, 246 U. S. 255 (1918); *Blundell* v. *Wallace*, 267 U. S. 373 (1925); *Brader* v. *James*, 246 U. S. 88 (1918); *Brown* v. *United States*, 44 C. Cls. 283 (1907), revd. sub nom. *Brown & Gritts* v. *United States*, 219 U. S. 346 (1911); *Bunch* v. *Cole*, 263 U. S. 250 (1923); *Caesar* v. *Burgess*, 103 F. 2d 503 (C. C. A. 10, 1939); *Cherokee Nation* v. *United States*, 85 C. Cls. 76 (1937); *Choctaw Nation* v. *United States*, 81 C. Cls. 1 (1935), cert. den. 296 U. S. 643; *Choctaw Nation* v. *United States*, 83 C. Cls. 49 (1936); *City of Tulsa* v. *Southwestern Bell Tel. Co.*, 75 F. 2d 343 (C. C. A. 10, 1935), cert. den. 295 U. S. 744; *Cochran* v. *United States*, 276 Fed. 701 (C. C. A. 8, 1921); *Cully* v. *Mitchell*, 37 F. 2d 493 (C. C. A. 10, 1930), cert. den. 281 U. S. 740; *Darks* v. *Ickes*, 69 F. 2d 230 (App. D. C., 1934); *David* v. *Younken*, 250 Fed. 208 (C. C. A. 8, 1918); *Derrisaw* v. *Schaffer*, 8 F. Supp. 876 (D. C. E. D. Okla., 1934); *Duncan Townsite Co.* v. *Lane*, 245 U. S. 308 (1912); *Eslick* v. *United States*, 51 C. Cls. 266 (1916); *Fleming* v. *McCurtain*, 215 U. S. 56 (1909); *Frame* v. *Bivins*, 189 Fed. 785 (C. C. E. D. Okla., 1909); *Fulsom* v. *Quaker Oil & Gas Co.*, 35 F. 2d 84 (C. C. A. 8, 1929); *Gannon* v. *Johnston*, 243 U. S. 108 (1917); *Garfield* v. *United States ex rel. Allison*, 211 U. S. 264 (1908); *Garfield* v. *United States ex rel. Goldsby*, 211 U. S. 249 (1908); *Garfield* v. *United States ex rel. Lowe*, 34 App. D. C. 70 (1909); *Glenn* v. *Lewis*, 105 F. 2d 398 (C. C. A. 10, 1939), cert. den. 60 Sup. Ct. 130; *Goat* v. *United States*, 224 U. S. 458 (1912); *Gritts* v. *Fisher*, 224 U. S. 640 (1912); *Hallam* v. *Commerce Mining & Royalty Co.*, 49 F. 2d 103 (C. C. A. 10, 1931), cert. den. 284 U. S. 643 (1931); *Harris* v. *Bell*, 254 U. S. 103 (1920); *Harris* v. *Gale*, 188 Fed. 712 (C. C. E. D. Okla., 1911); *Heckman* v. *United States*, 224 U. S. 413 (1912); *Henny Gas Co.* v. *United States*, 191 Fed. 132 (C. C. A. 8, 1911); *In re Jessie's Heirs*, 259 Fed. 694 (D. C. E. D. Okla., 1919); *In re Lands of Five Civilized Tribes*, 199 Fed. 811 (D. C. E. D. Okla., 1912); *In re Palmer's Will*, 11 F. Supp. 301 (D. C. E. D. Okla., 1935); *Iowa Land & Trust Co.* v. *United States*, 217 Fed. 11 (C. C. A. 8, 1914); *Jack* v. *Hood*, 39 F. 2d 594 (C. C. A. 10, 1935); *Jennings* v. *Wood*, 192 Fed. 507 (C. C. A. 8, 1911); *King* v. *Ickes*, 64 F. 2d 979 (App. D. C., 1933); *Knight* v. *Lane*, 228 U. S. 6 (1913); *Ledbetter* v. *Wesley*, 23 F. 2d 81 (C. C. A. 8, 1927), cert. den. 276 U. S. 631 (1928), 276 U. S. 636 (1928); *Ligon* v. *Johnston*, 164 Fed. 670 (C. C. A. 8, 1908), app. dism. 223 U. S. 741; *Locke* v. *McMurry*, 287 Fed. 276 (C. C. A. 8, 1923); *M. K. & T. Ry. Co.* v. *United States*, 47 C. Cls. 59 (1911); *Moore* v. *Carter Oil Co.*, 43 F. 2d 322 (C. C. A. 10, 1930), cert. den. 282 U. S. 903; *Morrison* v. *Burnette*, 154 Fed. 617 (C. C. A. 8, 1907), app. dism. sub nom. *Laurel Oil & Gas Co.* v. *Morrison*, 212 U. S. 291 (1909); *Mullen* v. *Pickens*, 250 U. S. 590 (1919); *Mullen* v. *United States*, 224 U. S. 448 (1912); *Muskrat* v. *United States*, 219 U. S. 346 (1911); *Ne-Kah-Wah-She-Tun-Kah* v. *Fall*, 290 Fed. 303 (App. D. C., 1923), app. dism. 266 U. S. 595 (1925); *Nunn* v. *Haselrigg*, 216 Fed. 330 (C. C. A. 8, 1914); *Parker* v. *Riley*,

This provision was made more emphatic in the Act of May 27, 1908,[108] the next major act relating to the Five Tribes. Section 4 provides:

> * * * all land from which restrictions have been or shall be removed shall be subject to taxation and all other civil burdens as though it were the property of other persons than allottees of the Five Civilized Tribes * * *.

250 U. S. 66 (1919); *Reed* v. *Welty*, 197 Fed. 419 (D. C. E. D. Okla., 1912), revd. sub nom. *Welty* v. *Reed*, 219 Fed. 864 (C. C. A. 8, 1915); affd. on rehearing sub nom. *Welty* v. *Reed*, 231 Fed. 930 (C. C. A. 8. 1916); *Rogers* v. *Rogers*, 263 Fed. 160 (D. C. E. D. Okla., 1919); *Roubedeaux* v. *Quaker Oil & Gas Co. of Okla.*, 23 F. 2d 277 (C. C. A. 8, 1927), cert. den. 276 U. S. 636; *Seminole Nation* v. *United States*, 78 C. Cls. 455 (1933); *Shulthis* v. *McDougal*, 225 U. S. 561 (1912); *Stewart* v. *Keyes*, 295 U. S. 403 (1935), rehearing den. 296 U. S. 661 (1935); *Sunday* v. *Mallory*, 248 U. S. 545 (1919); *Superintendent* v. *Commissioner*, 295 U. S. 418 (1935); *Sweet* v. *Schock*, 245 U. S. 192 (1917); *Talley* v. *Burgess*, 246 U. S. 104 (1918); *Taylor* v. *Parker*, 235 U. S. 42 (1914); *Tiger* v. *Western Investment Co.*, 221 U. S. 286 (1911); *United States* v. *Bartlett*, 235 U. S. 72 (1914); *United States* v. *Bean*, 253 Fed. 1 (C. C. A. 8, 1918); *United States* v. *Board of Commissioners of McIntosh County*, 284 Fed. 103 (C. C. A. 8, 1922), app. dism. 263 U. S. 691; *United States* v. *Comet Oil and Gas Co.*, 202 Fed. 849 (C. C. A. 8, 1913); *United States ex rel. Johnson* v. *Payne*, 253 U. S. 209 (1920); *United States* v. *Ferguson*, 247 U. S. 175 (1918); *United States* v. *First National Bank*, 234 U. S. 245 (1914); *United States* v. *Fooshee*, 225 Fed. 521 (C. C. A. 8, 1915); *United States* v. *Gypsy Oil Co.*, 10 F. 2d 487 (C. C. A. 8, 1925); *United States* v. *Halsell*, 247 Fed. 390 (C. C. A. 8, 1918); *United States* v. *Hayes*, 20 F. 2d 873 (C. C. A. 8, 1927), cert. den. 275 U. S. 555; *United States* v. *Hinkle*, 261 Fed. 518 (C. C. A. 8, 1919); *United States* v. *Knight*, 206 Fed. 145 (C. C. A. 8, 1913); *United States* v. *Rea-Read Mill & Elevator Co.*, 171 Fed. 501 (C. C. E. D. Okla., 1909); *United States* v. *Seminole Nation*, 299 U. S. 417 (1937); *United States* v. *Shock*, 187 Fed. 862 (C. C. E. D. Okla., 1911); *United States* v. *Shock*, 187 Fed. 870 (C. C. E. D. Okla., 1911); *United States* v. *Smith*, 266 Fed. 740 (D. C. E. D. Okla., 1920); *United States* v. *Smith*, 279 Fed. 136 (D. C. E. D. Okla., 1922), revd. by 288 Fed. 356 (C. C. A. 8, 1923); *United States* v. *Stigall*, 226 Fed. 190 (C. C. A. 8, 1915); *United States* v. *Tiger*, 19 F. 2d 35 (C. C. A. 8, 1927); *United States* v. *Western Inv. Co.*, 226 Fed. 726 (C. C. A. 8, 1915); *United States* v. *Whitmire*, 236 Fed. 474 (C. C. A. 8, 1916); *U. S. Express Co.* v. *Friedman*, 191 Fed. 673 (C. C. A. 8, 1911); *Vinson* v. *Graham*, 44 F. 2d 772 (C. C. A. 10, 1930), cert. den. 283 U. S. 819; *Wade* v. *Fisher*, 39 (App. D. C. 245, 1912); *Williams* v. *White*, 218 Fed. 797 (C. C. A. 8, 1914); *Winton* v. *Amos*, 255 U. S. 373 (1921).

[108] 35 Stat. 312.[9] Other provisions in this statute included the removal of restrictions upon alienation on all lands of allottees enrolled as intermarried whites, as freedmen, and as mixed-blood Indians having less than half Indian blood, including minors; and all lands except homesteads of allottees enrolled as mixed-blood Indians having half or more than half and less than three-quarters Indian blood. The homesteads of such Indians shall be restricted until April 26, 1931, except that the Secretary of the Interior may remove such restrictions (sec. 1). It also contained provisions relating to the leasing of allotted lands (secs. 2, 3, and 6; also see sec. 9 of this chapter) and the alienation of inherited lands (sec. 9; also see sec. 11 of this chapter).

This act supplemented Act of February 28, 1902, 32 Stat. 43; Act of April 26, 1906, 34 Stat. 137. Amending Act of April 26, 1906, 34 Stat. 137. Amended by Act of April 10, 1926, 44 Stat. 239. Supplemented by Act of March 3, 1909, 35 Stat. 781; Act of April 4, 1910, 36 Stat. 269; Act of August 24, 1922, 42 Stat. 831; Act of March 7, 1928, 45 Stat. 200; Act of May 10, 1928, 45 Stat. 495; Act of March 4, 1929, 45 Stat. 1562; Act of March 4, 1929, 45 Stat. 1623; Act of March 26, 1930, 46 Stat. 90; Act of May 14, 1930, 46 Stat. 279; Act of February 14, 1931, 46 Stat. 1115; Act of April 22, 1932, 47 Stat. 91; Act of February 17, 1933, 47 Stat. 820; Act of January 27, 1933, 47 Stat. 777; Act of March 2, 1934, 48 Stat. 362; Act of May 9, 1935, 49 Stat. 176; Act of June 22, 1936, 49 Stat. 1757; Act of August 9, 1937, 50 Stat. 564; Act of May 9, 1938, 52 Stat. 291.

Cited in J. V. Cabell, Descent and Distribution of Indian Lands (1932), 3 Okla. S. B. J. 208; J. K. Dixon, The Indian (1917), 23 Case and Com. 712; H. Krieger, Principles of the Indian Law and the Act of June 18, 1934 (1935), 3 Geo. Wash. L. Rev. 279; J. R. T. Reeves, Probating Indian Estates (1917), 23 Case and Com. 727; I. F. Russell, The Indian Before the Law (1909), 18 Yale L. J. 328; J. H. Wigmore, The Federal Senate as a Fifth Wheel (1929), 24 Ill. L. Rev. 89; 27 Op. A. G. 530 (1909); 34 Op. A. G. 275 (1924); 35 Op. A. G. 421 (1928); Op. Sol. I. D., D.40462, October 31, 1917; Op. Sol. I. D., M.26067, April 29, 1922; Op. Sol. I. D., M.7996, August 2, 1922; Op. Sol. I. D., D.46987, November 13, 1922; Op. Sol. I. D., October 4, 1926; Op. Sol. I. D., M.18320, December 21, 1926; Op. Sol. I. D., 22121, April 12, 1927; Memo. Sol. I. D., September 20, 1935; Ass't. Secy's. Letter to A. G., February 1, 1935; Memo. Sol. I. D., June 4, 1935; Memo. Sol. I. D., September 21, 1935; Memo. of Commr., August 11, 1936; Memo. Sol. I. D., September 17, 1936; Memo. Sol. I. D., January 13, 1937; Memo. Sol. I. D., January 23, 1937; Memo. Sol. I. D., February 5, 1937; Memo. Sol. I. D., April 8, 1937; Memo. Sol. I. D., May 14, 1938; 49 L. D. 348 (1922); 50 L. D. 691 (1924); 53 I. D. 48 (1930); 53 I. D. 471 (1931); 53 I. D. 412 (1931); 53 I. D. 502 (1931); 54 I. D. 382 (1934); *Anchor Oil Co.* v. *Gray*, 256 U. S. 519 (1921); *Anicker* v. *Gunsburg*, 246 U. S. 110 (1918); *Bagby* v. *United States*, 60 F. 2d 80 (C. C. A. 10, 1932); *Barbre* v. *Hood*, 228 Fed. 658 (C. C. A. 8, 1916); *Bartlett* v. *Oklahoma Oil Co.*, 218 Fed. 380 (D. C. E. D. Okla., 1914); *Baze* v. *Scott*, 24 F. Supp. 806 (D. C. E. D. Okla., 1938); *Bell* v. *Cook*, 192 Fed. 597 (C. C. E. D. Okla., 1911); *Bilby* v. *Stewart*, 246 U. S. 255 (1918); *Board of Comm'rs. of Tulsa County, Okla.* v. *United States*, 94 F. 2d 450 (C. C. A. 10, 1938); *Bond* v. *Tom*, 25 F. Supp. 157 (D. C. N. D. Okla., 1938); *Brown* v. *United States*, 27 F. 2d 274 (C. C. A. 8, 1928); *Bunch* v. *Cole*, 263 U. S. 250 (1923); *Burgess* v. *Nail*, 103 F. 2d 37 (C. C. A. 10, 1939); *Caesar* v. *Burgess*, 103 F. 2d 503 (C. C. A. 10, 1939); *Carpenter* v. *Shaw*, 280 U. S. 363 (1930); *Chisholm* v. *Creek & Ind. Dev. Co.*, 273 Fed. 589 (D. C. E. D. Okla., 1921); aff'd. in part and rev'd. in part sub nom. *Sperry Oil Co.* v. *Chisholm*, 264 U. S. 488 (1924); *Choate* v. *Trapp*, 224 U. S. 665 (1912); *Commr. of Internal Revenue* v. *Owens*, 78 F. 2d 768 (C. C. A. 10, 1935); *Conner* v. *Cornell*, 32 F. 2d 581 (C. C. A. 8, 1929), cert. den. 280 U. S. 583; *Cully* v. *Mitchell*, 37 F. 2d 493 (C. C. A. 10, 1930), cert. den. 281 U. S. 740; *Derrisaw* v. *Schaffer*, 8 F. Supp. 876 (D. C. E. D. Okla., 1934); *English* v. *Richardson, Treasurer of Tulsa County, Oklahoma*, 224 U. S. 680 (1912); *Etchen* v. *Cheney*, 235 Fed. 104 (C. C. A. 8, 1916); *Ex parte Pero*, 99 F. 2d 28 (C. C. A. 7, 1938), cert. den. 306 U. S. 643; *Fink* v. *County Comm'rs.*, 248 U. S. 399 (1919); *Fulsom* v. *Quaker Oil & Gas Co.*, 35 F. 2d 84 (C. C. A. 8, 1929); *Gilcrease* v. *McCullough*, 249 U. S. 178 (1919); *Gleason* v. *Wood*, 224 U. S. 679 (1912); *Glenn* v. *Lewis*, 105 F. 2d 398 (C. C. A. 10, 1939), cert. den. 60 Sup. Ct. 130; *Goat* v. *United States*, 224 U. S. 458 (1912); *Hallam* v. *Commerce Mining & Royalty Co.*, 49 F. 2d 103 (C. C. A. 10, 1931), cert. den. 284 U. S. 643 (1931); *Hampton* v. *Ewart*, 22 F. 2d 81 (C. C. A. 8, 1927), cert. den. 276 U. S. 623 (1928); *Harjo* v. *Empire Gas & Fuel Co.*, 28 F. 2d 596 (C. C. A. 8, 1928); *Harris* v. *Bell*, 254 U. S. 103 (1920); *Harris* v. *Gale*, 188 Fed. 712 (C. C. E. D. Okla., 1911); *Heckman* v. *United States*, 224 U. S. 413 (1912); *Hill* v. *Rankin*, 289 Fed. 511 (D. C. E. D. Okla., 1923); *Holmes* v. *United States*, 33 F. 2d 688 (C. C. A. 8, 1929); *Holmes* v. *United States*, 53 F. 2d 960 (C. C. A. 10, 1931); *Hopkins* v. *United States*, 235 Fed. 95 (C. C. A. 8, 1916); *Ickes* v. *United States, ex rel. Perry*, 64 F. 2d 982 (App. D. C. 1933); *In re Jessie's Heirs*, 259 Fed. 694 (D. C. E. D. Okla., 1919); *In Re Palmer's Will*, 11 F. Supp. 301 (D. C. E. D. Okla., 1935); *Indian Territory Oil Co.* v. *Board*, 288 U. S. 325 (1933), app. dism. 287 U. S. 573; *Jack* v. *Hood*, 39 F. 2d 594 (C. C. A. 10, 1935); *Jackson* v. *Gates Oil Co.*, 297 Fed. 549 (C. C. A. 8, 1924); *Jackson* v. *Harris*, 43 F. 2d 513 (C. C. A. 10, 1930); *Jefferson* v. *Fink*, 247 U. S. 288 (1918); *Johnson* v. *United States*, 64 F. 2d 674 (C. C. A. 10, 1933), cert. den. 290 U. S. 651 (1933); *Jones* v. *Prairie Oil Co.*, 273 U. S. 195 (1927); *Kemmerer* v. *Midland Oil & Drilling Co.*, 229 Fed. 872 (C. C. A. 8, 1915); *Kiker* v. *United States*, 63 F. 2d 957 (C. C. A. 10, 1933); *King* v. *Ickes*, 64 F. 2d 979 (App. D. C. 1933); *Ledbetter* v. *Wesley*, 23 F. 2d 81 (C. C. A. 8, 1927), cert. den. 276 U. S. 631, 636 (1928); *Locke* v. *M'Murry*, 287 Fed. 276 (C. C. A. 8, 1923); *McDaniel* v. *Holland*, 230 Fed. 945 (C. C. A. 8, 1916); *McNee* v. *Whitehead*, 253 Fed. 546 (C. C. A. 8, 1918); *Malone* v. *Alderdice*, 212 Fed. 668 (C. C. A. 8, 1914); *Mars* v. *McDougal*, 40 F. 2d 247 (C. C. A. 10, 1930); *Moore* v. *Carter Oil Co.*, 43 F. 2d 322 (C. C. A. 10, 1930), cert. den. 282 U. S. 903; *Moore* v. *Sawyer*, 167 Fed. 826 (C. C. E. D. Okla., 1909); *Mudd* v. *Perry*, 14 F. 2d 430 (D. C. N. D. Okla., 1926), aff'd 25 F. 2d 85 (C. C. A. 8, 1928), cert. den. 278 U. S. 601; *Mullen* v. *Pickens*, 250 U. S. 590 (1919); *Nunn* v. *Hazelrigg*, 216 Fed. 330 (C. C. A. 8, 1914); *Okla., K. & M. I. Ry. Co.* v. *Bowling*, 249 Fed. 592 (C. C. A. 8, 1918); *Parker* v. *Richard*, 250 U. S. 235 (1919); *Parker* v. *Riley*, 250 U. S. 66 (1919); *Pitman* v. *Comm'r. of Internal Revenue*, 64 F. 2d 740 (C. C. A. 10, 1933); *Powell* v. *City of Ada*, 61 F. 2d 283 (C. C. A. 10, 1932); *Priddy* v. *Thompson*, 204 Fed. 955 (C. C. A. 8, 1913); *Privett* v. *United States*, 256 U. S. 201 (1921); *Roberts* v. *Anderson*, 66 F. 2d 874 (C. C. A. 10, 1933); *Rogers* v. *Rogers*, 263 Fed. 160 (D. C. E. D. Okla., 1919); *Self* v. *Prairie Oil & Gas Co.*, 28 F. 2d 590 (C. C. A. 8, 1928), cert. den. 278 U. S. 659; *Seminole Nation* v. *United States*, 78 C. Cls. 455 (1933); *Shaw* v. *Gibson-Zahniser Oil Corp.*, 276 U. S. 575 (1928); *Stewart* v. *Keyes*, 295 U. S. 403 (1935), rehearing den. 296 U. S. 661 (1935); *Sunderland* v. *United States*, 266 U. S. 226 (1924); *Superintendent* v.

The Act of May 27, 1908,[103] together with the 1906 Act,[104] and the Acts of April 12, 1926,[105] May 10, 1928,[106] May 24, 1928,[107] and January 27, 1933,[108] are the principal statutes defining restrictions, and the corresponding tax exemptions, with reference to the property of the Five Civilized Tribes. Without detailed discussion, the only general statement that can be made is that Congress has sought to protect from taxation and alienation, homesteads in the hands of Indians who have high percentages of Indian blood, at the same time subjecting excess land holdings, lands in the hands of mixed-blood heirs of original allottees (up to 1933),[109] and lands in the hands of Indians of lesser degrees of Indian blood, to state taxation.

The Act of May 27, 1908[110] provided that no homesteads of mixed bloods of half or more than half Indian blood and no allotted lands of enrolled full bloods and enrolled mixed bloods of three-quarters or more Indian blood should be subject to alienation or any other encumbrance prior to April 26, 1931, except that the Secretary of the Interior might remove such restrictions for the benefit of the Indian.

Section 9 of this act also provided that:

> * * * the death of any allottee of the Five Civilized Tribes shall operate to remove all restrictions upon the alienation of said allottee's land * * *.

but required that the conveyance of any interest of a full-blood heir be approved by the court having jurisdiction over the estate of the decedent.[111]

Commissioner, 295 U. S. 418 (1935); *Sweet* v. *Schock*, 245 U. S. 192 (1917); *Taylor* v. *Parker*, 235 U. S. 42 (1914); *Taylor* v. *United States*, 230 Fed. 580 (C. C. A. 8, 1916); *Tiger* v. *Fewell*, 22 F. 2d 786 (C. C. A. 8, 1927), cert. den. 269 U. S. 572 (1925), writ of error dism. 271 U. S. 649 (1926), cert. den. 276 U. S. 620; *Tiger* v. *Slinker*, 4 F. 2d 714 (D. C. E. D. Okla., 1925); *Tiger* v. *Western Investment Co.*, 221 U. S. 286 (1911); *Truskett* v. *Closser*, 236 U. S. 223 (1915); *United States* v. *Allen*, 179 Fed. 13 (C. C. A. 8, 1910); *United States* v. *Bartlett*, 235 U. S. 72 (1914); *United States* v. *Bean*, 253 Fed. 1 (C. C. A. 8, 1918); *United States* v. *Black*, 247 Fed. 942 (C. C. A. 8, 1917); *United States* v. *Board of Comm'rs. of McIntosh County*, 284 Fed. 103 (C. C. A. 8, 1922), app. dism. 263 U. S. 691; *United States* v. *Brown*, 8 F. 2d 564 (C. C. A. 8, 1925), cert. den. 270 U. S. 644 (1926); *United States* v. *Cook*, 225 Fed. 756 (C. C. A. 8, 1915); *United States* v. *Equitable Trust Co.*, 283 U. S. 738 (1931); *United States* v. *Ferguson*, 247 U. S. 175 (1918); *United States* v. *Gray*, 284 Fed. 103 (C. C. A. 8, 1922), app. dism. 263 U. S. 689; *United States* v. *Gypsy Oil Co.*, 10 F. 2d 487 (C. C. A. 8, 1925); *United States* v. *Haddock*, 21 F. 2d 165 (C. C. A. 8, 1927); *United States* v. *Halsell*, 247 Fed. 390 (C. C. A. 8, 1918); *United States* v. *Knight*, 206 Fed. 145 (C. C. A. 8, 1913); *United States* v. *Law*, 250 Fed. 218 (C. C. A. 8, 1918); *United States* v. *Lee*, 24 F. Supp. 814 (D. C. E. D. Okla., 1938); *United States* v. *Martin*, 45 F. 2d 836 (D. C. E. D. Okla., 1930); *United States* v. *Mid Continent Petroleum Corp.*, 67 F. 2d 37 (C. C. A. 10, 1933), cert. den. 290 U. S. 702 (1933); *United States* v. *Mott*, 37 F. 2d 860 (C. C. A. 10, 1930), aff'd sub nom. *Mott* v. *United States*, 283 U. S. 747 (1931); *United States* v. *Ransom*, 284 Fed. 108 (C. C. A. 8, 1922); *United States* v. *Richards*, 27 F. 2d 284 (C. C. A. 8, 1928), cert. den. 278 U. S. 630; *United States* v. *Shock* 187 Fed. 862 (C. C. E. D. Okla., 1911); *United States* v. *Shock*, 187 Fed. 870 (C. C. E. D. Okla., 1911); *United States* v. *Smith*, 266 Fed. 740 (D. C. E. D. Okla., 1920); *United States* v. *Smith*, 288 Fed. 356 (C. C. A. 8, 1923), rev'g 279 Fed. 136 (D. C. E. D. Okla., 1922); *United States* v. *Tiger*, 19 F. 2d 35 (C. C. A. 8, 1927); *United States* v. *Watashe*, 102 F. 2d 428 (C. C. A. 10, 1939); *United States* v. *Western Inv. Co.*, 226 Fed. 726 (C. C. A. 8, 1915); *United States* v. *Woods*, 223 Fed. 316 (C. C. A. 8, 1915); *United States ex rel. Warren* v. *Ickes*, 73 F. 2d 844 (App. D. C. 1934); *Vinson* v. *Graham*, 44 F. 2d 772 (C. C. A. 10, 1930), cert. den. 283 U. S. 819; *Ward* v. *Love County*, 253 U. S. 17 (1920); *Welch* v. *First Trust & Savings Bank*, 15 F. 2d 184 (C. C. A. 8, 1926); *Whitebird* v. *Eagle-Picher Lead Co.*, 40 F. 2d 479 (C. C. A. 10, 1930), aff'g 28 F. 2d 200 (D. C. N. D. Okla., 1928), cert. den. 282 U. S. 844; *Williams* v. *White*, 218 Fed. 797 (C. C. A. 8, 1914); *Willmott* v. *United States*, 27 F. 2d 277 (C. C. A. 8, 1928); *Winton* v. *Amos*, 255 U. S. 373 (1921).

This exemption related to land and not to income derived from the investment of surplus income from land. *Superintendent* v. *Commissioner*, 295 U. S. 418, 421 (1935).

Section 1 of the Act of May 27, 1908, 35 Stat. 312, declared that:

> * * * all allotted lands of * * * enrolled mixed-bloods of three-quarters or more Indian blood, * * * shall not be subject to alienation, contract to sell, power of attorney, or any other incumbrance prior to April twenty-sixth, nineteen hundred and thirty-one * * *.

In *Johnson* v. *United States*, 64 F. 2d 674 (C. C. A. 10, 1933), the Circuit Court defined the purpose of this statute as follows:

> The purpose of the statute was to release restrictions from much of the empire occupied by the Five Civilized Tribes, and put it on the tax rolls. (P. 677.)

In *United States* v. *Bartlett*, 235 U. S. 72 (1914), it was held that this extension upon the restriction on alienation was not intended to reimpose restrictions of lands on which the original restriction upon alienation had expired before its passage.

[103] 35 Stat. 312, *supra*, fn. 102.

[104] Act of April 26, 1906, 34 Stat. 137, *supra*, fn. 101.

[105] 44 Stat. 239. Supplementing Act of April 26, 1906, 34 Stat. 137, 145. Amending Act of May 27, 1908, 35 Stat. 312, 315. Supplemented by Act of May 10, 1928, 45 Stat. 495. Cited in Memo. Sol. I. D., September 15, 1934; Memo. Sol. I. D., January 14, 1935; Memo. Sol. I. D., June 4, 1935; Memo. Sol. I. D., September 21, 1935; Letter of Asst. Secy. to A. G., October 15, 1936; 53 I. D. 637 (1932); *Anderson* v. *Peck*, 53 F. 2d 257 (D. C. N. D. Okla., 1931); *Baze* v. *Scott*, 24 F. Supp. 806 (D. C. E. D. Okla., 1938); *Board of Comm'rs of Tulsa County, Okla.* v. *United States*, 94 F. 2d 450 (C. C. A. 10, 1938); *Brown* v. *United States*, 27 F. 2d 274 (C. C. A. 8, 1928); *Burgess* v. *Nail*, 103 F. 2d 37 (C. C. A. 10, 1939); *Caesar* v. *Burgess*, 103 F. 2d 503 (C. C. A. 10, 1939); *Derrisau* v. *Schaffer*, 8 F. Supp. 876 (D. C. E. D. Okla., 1934); *In re Palmer's Will*, 11 F. Supp. 301 (D. C. E. D. Okla., 1935); *Kiker* v. *United States*, 63 F. 2d 957 (C. C. A. 10, 1933); *King* v. *Ickes*, 64 F. 2d 979 (App. D. C. 1933); *Stewart* v. *Keyes*, 295 U. S. 403 (1935), rehearing den. 296 U. S. 661 (1935); *United States ex rel. Warren* v. *Ickes*, 73 F. 2d 844 (App. D. C. 1934); *United States* v. *Mid Continent Petroleum Corp.*, 67 F. 2d 67 (C. C. A. 10, 1933), cert. den. 290 U. S. 702 (1933); *United States* v. *Watashe*, 102 F. 2d 428 (C. C. A. 10, 1939); *Whitchurch* v. *Crawford*, 92 F. 2d 249 (C. C. A. 10, 1937).

[106] 45 Stat. 495. Supplementing Act of April 26, 1906, 34 Stat. 137; Act of May 27, 1908, 35 Stat. 312; Act of April 10, 1926, 44 Stat. 239. Repealing in part, Act of April 10, 1926, 44 Stat. 239. Amended by Act of May 24, 1928, 45 Stat. 733; Act of February 14, 1931, c. 179, 46 Stat. 1108; Act of March 12, 1936, 49 Stat. 1160. Supplemented by Act of January 27, 1933, 47 Stat. 777. Cited in Op. Sol. I. D., M.25258, June 26, 1929; Op. Sol. I. D., M.27158, August 5, 1932; Memo. Sol. I. D., June 4, 1935; Letter of Asst. Secy. to A. G., October 15, 1936; Memo. Sol. I. D., January 18, 1937; Memo. Sol. I. D., January 28, 1937; Memo. Sol. I. D., May 14, 1938; 53 I. D. 48 (1930); 53 I. D. 471 (1931); 53 I. D. 502 (1931); 53 I. D. 637 (1932); 54 I. D. 382 (1934); *Bond* v. *Tom*, 25 F. Supp. 157 (D. C. N. D. Okla., 1938); *Burgess* v. *Nail*, 103 F. 2d 37 (C. C. A. 10, 1939), rehearing den. May 1, 1939; *Caesar* v. *Burgess*, 103 F. 2d 503 (C. C. A. 10, 1939); *Carpenter* v. *Shaw*, 280 U. S. 363 (1930); *Glenn* v. *Lewis*, 105 F. 2d 398 (C. C. A. 10, 1939), cert. den. 60 Sup. Ct. 130; *King* v. *Ickes*, 64 F. 2d 979 (App. D. C. 1933); *United States* v. *Equitable Trust Co.*, 283 U. S. 738 (1931); *United States* v. *Watashe*, 102 F. 2d 428 (C. C. A. 10, 1939); *Whitchurch* v. *Crawford*, 92 F. 2d 249 (C. C. A. 10, 1937).

[107] 45 Stat. 733. Amending Act of May 10, 1928, 45 Stat. 495, 496. Cited in 53 I. D. 48 (1930); 53 I. D. 471 (1931); 53 I. D. 502 (1931); 53 I. D. 637 (1932); *King* v. *Ickes*, 64 F. 2d 979 (App. D. C. 1933).

[108] 47 Stat. 777. Supplementing Act of May 27, 1908, 35 Stat. 312; Act of May 10, 1928, 45 Stat. 495. Cited in Hearings, Sen. Comm. on Ind. Aff., 72d Cong., 1st sess., S. 1839; 37 Op. A. G. 193 (1933); Memo. Sol. I. D., October 25, 1934; Memo. Sol. I. D., June 4, 1935; Op. Sol. I. D., M.28125, August 12, 1935; Memo. Sol. I. D., October 22, 1935; Memo. Sol. I. D., May 1, 1936; Memo. of Comm'r, August 11, 1936; Letter of Asst. Secy. to A. G., October 15, 1936; Memo. Sol. I. D., January 13, 1937; Memo. Sol. I. D., January 23, 1937; Memo. Sol. I. D., February 5, 1937; Memo. Sol. I. D., April 8, 1937; Memo. Acting Sol. I. D., May 11, 1937; Memo. Sol. I. D., May 14, 1938; Memo. Sol. I. D., November 28, 1938; 54 I. D. 310 (1933); 54 I. D. 382 (1934); *Bond* v. *Tom*, 25 F. Supp. 157 (D. C. N. D. Okla., 1938); *Burgess* v. *Nail*, 103 F. 2d 37 (C. C. A. 10, 1939) rehearing den. May 1, 1939, 103 F. 2d 37; *Darks* v. *Ickes*, 69 F. 2d 231 (App. D. C. 1934); *Glenn* v. *Lewis*, 105 F. 2d 398 (C. C. A. 10, 1939), cert. den. 60 Sup. Ct. 130; *Ickes* v. *United States ex rel. Perry*, 64 F. 2d 982 (App. D. C. 1933); *In re Palmer's Will*, 11 F. Supp. 301 (D. C. E. D. Okla., 1935); *King* v. *Ickes*, 64 F. 2d 979 (App. D. C. 1933); *United States ex rel. Warren* v. *Ickes*, 73 F. 2d 844 (App D. C. 1934); *Whitchurch* v. *Crawford*, 92 F. 2d 249 (C. C. A. 10, 1937)

[109] Act of January 27, 1933, 47 Stat. 777, *supra*, fn. 108.

[110] 35 Stat. 312, *supra*, fn. 102.

[111] Act of May 27, 1908, 35 Stat. 312, 315. It has been held under this section that lands allotted to a half-blood Choctaw Indian, and therefore exempt from taxation while held by him, become taxable

This section contained a proviso that as to allotments of Indians of one-half or more Indian blood who died leaving issue born since March 4, 1906, the homestead should remain inalienable for the life of the issue or until April 26, 1931, unless removal of restrictions should be sooner authorized by the Secretary of the Interior.[112] By the Act of May 10, 1928,[113] restrictions on alienation of allotments of allottees of half blood or more were extended until April 26, 1956. The Act of May 24, 1928,[114] amending section 4 of the Act of May 10, 1928, limited the tax exemption to 160 acres of land to be selected by the Indian, who shall receive a certificate designating it.[115] The exemption was to continue so long as the title remained in the Indian designated or in any full-blood heir or devisee of the land. The May 10, 1928 Act also contained a provision that nothing in the act should be construed to exempt from taxation any lands subject to taxation under existing law.[116]

The first indication of the swing in policy toward expansion of exemptions is found in the Act of March 2, 1931,[117] providing that where nontaxable land of a restricted Indian of the Five Civilized Tribes is sold under existing law, the Secretary of the Interior may reinvest the proceeds in other land, which will be nontaxable and restricted from alienation. Under the Act of June 30, 1932,[118] it was provided that the restrictions should appear in the deed.

The Act of January 27, 1933,[119] provided that

> * * * where the entire interest in any tract of restricted and tax-exempt land belonging to members of the Five Civilized Tribes is acquired by inheritance, devise, gift, or purchase, with restricted funds, by or for restricted Indians, such lands shall remain restricted and tax-exempt during the life of and as long as held by such restricted Indians, but not longer than April 26, 1956, unless restrictions are removed in the meantime in the manner provided by law.

The act also provided:

> That such restricted and tax-exempt land held by anyone, acquired as herein provided, shall not exceed one hundred and sixty acres: *And provided further*, That all minerals including oil and gas, produced from said land so acquired shall be subject to all State and Federal taxes as provided in section 3 of the Act approved May 10, 1928 (45 Stat. L. 495).

upon his death and the descent of the title to his minor heirs of less than half Indian blood. The fact of minority of the heir does not seem to continue the restriction and therefore the tax exemption is removed by this section. *McNee v. Whitehead*, 253 Fed. 546 (C. C. A. 8, 1918). *Cf. Wynn v. Fugate, Okla.*, 299 Pac. 890 (1931).

[112] This section was amended in minor particulars by the Act of April 10, 1926, 44 Stat. 239, fn. 105 *supra*. The court in *United States v. Lee*, 24 F. Supp. 814 (D. C. E. D. Okla., 1938), aff'd 108 F. 2d 936 (C. C. A. 10, 1939), held that if allottee's surviving issue born since March 4, 1906, died before April 26, 1931, the homestead allotment descends free from restrictions, because of the language of the proviso in the 1908 Act, even in the hands of full-blood heirs.

[113] Sec. 1, 45 Stat. 495, *supra*, fn. 106. It was provided that the Secretary of the Interior may remove the restrictions upon applications of the Indian owners, in whole or in part, under such rules and regulations as he shall prescribe. Prior to April 26, 1931, allotted lands held by the original allottees and allotted lands acquired by full-blood Indians through devise or inheritance from an allottee and held by the heir or devisee were nontaxable. See sec. 4, Act of May 27, 1908, 35 Stat. 312, 313, *supra*, fn. 102; *Powell v. City of Ada*, 61 F. 2d 283, 285 (C. C. A. 10, 1932). Contra: *Wynn v. Fugate*, *supra*. On the death of the allottee, allotted lands, except those passing by devise or inheritance to full-blood Indian heirs, became subject to taxation. *United States v. Shock*, 187 Fed. 870, 872, 873 (C. C. E. D. Okla., 1911).

[114] 45 Stat. 733, *supra*, fn. 107.

[115] 45 Stat. 495, *supra*, fn. 106. Sec. 3 of the May 10, 1928 Act, as amended by the Act of February 14, 1931, 46 Stat. 1108, and the Act of March 12, 1936, 49 Stat. 1160, provides:

> * * * That all minerals, including oil and gas, produced on or after April 26, 1931, from restricted allotted lands of members of the Five Civilized Tribes in Oklahoma, or from inherited restricted lands of full-blood Indian heirs or devisees of such lands, shall be subject to all State and Federal taxes of every kind and character the same as those produced from lands owned by other citizens of the State of Oklahoma; and the Secretary of the Interior is hereby authorized and directed to cause to be paid, from the individual Indian funds held under his supervision and control and belonging to the Indian owners of the lands, the tax or taxes so assessed against the royalty interest of the respective Indian owners in such oil, gas, and other mineral production: *Provided*, That nothing in this Act shall be construed to impose or provide for double taxation and, in those cases where the machinery or equipment used in producing oil or other minerals on restricted Indian lands are subject to the ad valorem tax of the State of Oklahoma for the fiscal year ending June 30, 1931, the gross production tax which is in lieu thereof shall not be imposed prior to July 1, 1931: *Provided further*, That in the discretion of the Secretary of the Interior, the tax or taxes due the State of Oklahoma may be paid in the manner provided by the Statutes of the State of Oklahoma.

[116] Sec. 5. 45 Stat. 495, *supra*, fn. 106.

[117] 46 Stat. 1471, *supra*, fn. 100.

[118] 47 Stat. 474, 25 U. S. C. 409a. amending Act of March 2, 1931, 46 Stat. 1471. Cited in Memo. Sol. I. D., December 21, 1936; Memo. Sol. I. D., November 29, 1937; *Minnesota v. United States*, 305 U. S. 382 (1939).

[119] 47 Stat. 777, *supra*, fn. 108. In *Glenn v. Lewis*, 105 F. 2d 398 (C. C. A. 10, 1939), cert. den. 60 Sup. Ct. 130, the court held that this act was intended to restrict lands of half bloods or more acquired by inheritance, and hence the one-third interest in an Indian homestead allotment which a seven-eighth blood Choctaw Indian inherited was restricted, and mortgage and deeds executed by a Choctaw Indian without approval of the Secretary of the Interior or the Oklahoma County court were invalid.

SECTION 9. LEASING OF ALLOTTED LANDS OF FIVE CIVILIZED TRIBES

Some of the allotment agreements permitted allottees to lease their allotments for specified purposes and periods.[120] Section 19 of the Act of April 26, 1906,[121] in extending for 25 years the restrictions upon alienation by full-blooded allottees, provided that such allottees might lease any lands other than homesteads for more than one year under rules and regulations prescribed by the Secretary of the Interior, "and in case of the inability of any full-blood owner of a homestead, on account of infirmity or age, to work or farm his homestead, the Secretary of the Interior, upon proof of such inability, may authorize the leasing of such homestead under such rules and regulations." Section 20 required all leases and rental contracts of full-blood allottees to be in writing and approved by the Secretary of the Interior, except (1) if for not exceeding a year for agricultural purposes, for lands other than homesteads; (2) the proper court might rent or lease allotments of minors or incompetents. All leases for a period exceeding a year were required to be recorded in conformity to the law of the Indian Territory.

Section 2 of the Act of May 27, 1908,[122] provided:

> * * * That all lands other than homesteads allotted to members of the Five Civilized Tribes from which restrictions have not been removed may be leased by the allottee if an adult, or by guardian or curator under order of the proper probate court if a minor or incompetent, for a period not to exceed five years, without the privilege of

[120] For example, the Original Creek Agreement of March 1, 1901. sec. 37, 31 Stat. 861, 871; Cherokee Allotment Agreement, of July 1, 1902, sec. 72, 32 Stat. 716, 726–727.

[121] 34 Stat. 137, 144, *supra*, fn. 101.

[122] 35 Stat. 312, 313, fn. 102 *supra*. For a criticism of this provision see Meriam, The Problem of Indian Administration (1928) pp. 801–802. For a discussion of its interpretation see Bledsoe, *op. cit.*, pp. 241–245.

By sec. 5, leases of restricted lands in violation of the law before or after the approval of this act were made null and void. For regulations relating to leasing of restricted lands for mining, see 25 C. F. R. 183.1–183.49.

renewal: *Provided*, That leases of restricted lands for oil, gas, or other mining purposes, leases of restricted homesteads for more than one year, and leases of restricted lands for periods of more than five years, may be made, with the approval of the Secretary of the Interior, under rules and regulations provided by the Secretary of the Interior, and not otherwise: *And provided further*, That the jurisdiction of the probate courts of the State of Oklahoma over lands of minors and incompetents shall be subject to the foregoing provisions, and the term minor or minors, as used in this Act, shall include all males under the age of twenty-one years and all females under the age of eighteen years.

Section 18 of the Act of February 14, 1920,[133] authorized the Superintendent for the Five Civilized Tribes to approve, reject, or disapprove all uncontested leases (except oil and gas leases), but permitted an aggrieved party the right to appeal from the decision of the Superintendent to the Secretary of the Interior within 30 days from the date of the decision.

Changes in laws relating to alienation have created many problems in the field of leasing. For example section 1 of the Act of January 27, 1933,[134] quoted at the end of the preceding section, affects leases as well as sales.

The effect of this provision on leases was thus analyzed by the Solicitor of the Department of the Interior:[135]

> In my opinion of March 14, 1934 (54 I. D. 382), it was held that the foregoing provision was not retroactive and applied only to acquisitions after the date of the enactment. Accordingly, the status of lands acquired by inheritance, devise, etc., prior to that enactment is determined by the laws then in force. Under those laws, which it is unnecessary to cite here, the death of an allottee terminated all restrictions if the heirs or devisees were less than the full-blood, but if the lands passed to full-bloods the restrictions were relaxed to permit conveyances by them with the approval of the county court having jurisdiction of the settlement of the deceased allottee's estate. Accordingly, lands acquired prior to January 27, 1933, by Indians of less than full-blood, whether such lands were restricted and tax exempt or restricted and taxable, passed to them free from all restrictions. Such lands, therefore, are subject to sale or lease without the approval of the Secretary of the Interior or the county court, unless, of course, some disability rested upon the owner under the State law. If, however, the heirs or devisees are of the full-blood, any conveyance of their interests or an oil and gas lease thereof must not only receive the approval of the county court having jurisdiction of the settlement of the deceased allottee's estate (section 9 of the act of May 27, 1908, 35 Stat. 312, as amended by the act of April 12, 1926, 44 Stat. 239; *United States* v. *Gypsy Oil case*, 10 Fed. (2d) 487), but such approval must be given in open court after notice in accordance with the rules of procedure in probate matters adopted by the Supreme Court of Oklahoma in June 1914 (section 8, act of January 27, 1933). The rules just stated apply also to lands acquired after January 27, 1933, unless such lands are both restricted and tax exempt and the entire interest therein is acquired by a restricted Indian or restricted Indians.
>
> The first proviso of section 1 of the act of January 27, 1933, is without application unless the lands involved are both restricted and tax exempt and unless the entire interest therein is acquired by restricted Indians. The language immediately preceding the first proviso shows that the term "restricted Indians" was intended to embrace Indians of the Five Civilized Tribes of one-half or more Indian blood. In my opinion of March 14, 1934, it was pointed out that the lands to which the first proviso of the act of 1933 applied fall into two classes, first, restricted allotments of living allottees which have been designated by them as tax exempt under the act of May 10, 1928 (45 Stat. 495), which lands were under the jurisdiction of the Secretary of the Interior and could be leased for oil and gas mining purposes only with his approval and not otherwise under section 2 of the act of May 27, 1908, *supra*. Second, lands inherited by or devised to full-blood Indians prior to January 27, 1933, and designated by them as tax exempt under the act of 1928, which lands were subject to the restriction that no conveyance by the full-blood should be valid unless approved by the county court having jurisdiction of the settlement of the deceased allottee's estate, and which lands could be leased by the full-blood for oil and gas mining purposes with the approval of the said court and without the approval of the Secretary of the Interior.
>
> It was further pointed out in my opinion of March 14 that the first proviso of the act of 1933 was designed to preserve the existing restrictions and not to reimpose restrictions once removed or to change the form of existing restrictions. Accordingly, where the entire interest in lands of the first class is acquired by Indians of the Five Civilized Tribes of one-half or more Indian blood, they take the same subject to the same restrictions which rested upon the lands of the allottee. Such lands, therefore, continue to be subject to lease for oil and gas mining purposes only with the approval of the Secretary of the Interior and not otherwise. The county court having jurisdiction of the settlement of the deceased allottee's estate has no authority to approve a conveyance or lease of such lands. The only jurisdiction which the probate courts may exercise in this class of cases is confined to conveyances and leases made by guardians of minors and incompetents and in such cases the conveyance or lease must be made under order of the proper probate court. See sections 2 and 6 of the act of May 27, 1908, *supra*.
>
> Where the entire interest in lands of the second class—that is, tax-exempt lands acquired by full-blood heirs or devisees prior to January 27. 1933—passes into the hands of Indians of one-half or more Indian blood after that date, such Indians take the lands subject to the restriction resting upon the previous owner, namely, they cannot convey without the approval of the county court having jurisdiction of the settlement of the deceased allottee's estate. With such approval they may convey or lease, but such approval as to the interest of any full-blood must be given in open court after notice, as provided by section 8 of the act of January 27, 1933.

The Act of February 11, 1936,[136] provided that leases of restricted lands on behalf of minors and Indians *non compos mentis* of the Five Civilized Tribes may be made, for periods not exceeding 5 years for farming and grazing purposes, by the superintendent or other official in charge of the Five Civilized Tribes Agency; and empowered other Indians to make such leases, subject to the approval of such official.[137]

Several questions arising under this act have been recently discussed by the Solicitor of the Department of the Interior:[138]

> A. Do farming and grazing leases require approval by this office—
> (1) Where the allottee died prior to January 27, 1933?
> (2) Where any heir is less than half blood and the other heirs are one-half blood or more?
> (3) Where the land is not tax exempt?
>
> B. Do farming and grazing leases by full-blood adult heirs require approval by the County Court or by this office?
>
> * * * * *
>
> * * * the foregoing act applies to restricted lands belonging to Indians of the Five Civilized Tribes of one-half or more Indian blood. Ownership by an Indian of one-half or more Indian blood is not sufficient to bring the case within the statute. The lands must also be restricted.

[133] 41 Stat. 408, 25 U. S. C. 356.

[134] 47 Stat. 777. See fn. 108, *supra*.

[135] Memo. Sol. I. D., June 4, 1935; also see 54 I. D. 382 (1934).

[136] 49 Stat. 1135, 25 U. S. C. 393a. Cited in Memo. Sol. I. D., August 7, 1936; Memo. Sol. I. D., January 13, 1937; Memo. Sol. I. D., May 14, 1938; *Glenn* v. *Lewis*, 105 F. 2d 398 (C. C. A. 10, 1939), cert. den. 60 Sup. Ct. 130. For regulations see 25 C. F. R. 174.1–174.24.

[137] Memo. Sol. I. D., August 7, 1936.

[138] Memo. Sol. I. D., January 13, 1937.

Save for the requirement that the Superintendent must approve all leases of restricted lands belonging to Indians of the degree of blood mentioned, the act makes no change in the prior laws dealing with the restrictions on lands of Indians of the Five Civilized Tribes and we must look to those laws for the purpose of ascertaining whether the lands in any particular are or are not restricted.

The act of January 27, 1933 (47 Stat. 777), will be first considered. That act is confined to the restrictions on restricted and tax-exempt lands inherited by restricted Indians; that is, Indians of one-half or more Indian blood. That act has no application to lands or interests therein inherited prior to the date of the enactment. Solicitor's Opinion of March 14, 1934 (54 I. D. 382). It is further without application unless (a) the lands are both restricted and tax exempt, and (b) the entire interest is inherited by Indians of one-half or more Indian blood. Questions A (1), (2), and (3) all deal with cases to which the act of January 27, 1933, has no application and the question of whether the inherited interests be determined by the laws in force prior to January 27, 1933. Under section 9 of the act of May 27, 1908 (35 Stat. 312), as amended April 12, 1926 (45 Stat. 495), the death of an allottee of the Five Civilized Tribes removed all restrictions against alienation except where the heirs are of the full-blood and as to such full-blood heirs the restrictions are not removed but relaxed to the extent of sanctioning conveyances made with the approval of the proper county court. As the county court in approving such conveyances acts as a Federal agency, the inherited interest of the full-blood heir remained restricted. *Parker* v. *Richard* (250 U. S. 235). Accordingly, questions A (1), (2), and (3) may be answered by stating that where the heir is a full-blood, a lease of his inherited interest under the act of February 11, 1936, requires the approval of the Superintendent. Interests inherited by heirs of less than the full-blood are unrestricted and may be leased without approval.

Answering question B it may be said that lands inherited by a full-blood heir prior to January 27, 1933, or in any case to which the act of January 27, 1933, has no application, are restricted in the sense that a Federal agent, the county court, must approve the conveyance. If the entire interest in a tract of restricted and tax-exempt land is inherited by an Indian or Indians of one-half or more Indian blood after January 27, 1933, the existing restrictions are preserved by the act of that date. Solicitor's Opinion of March 14, 1934, *supra*. It is immaterial whether the approving agency is the county court or the Secretary of the Interior, as in either case the inherited interest is restricted and a farming and grazing lease thereon to be valid must, under the act of February 11, 1936, *supra*, receive the approval of the Superintendent.

SECTION 10. TRUSTS OF RESTRICTED FUNDS OF MEMBERS OF FIVE TRIBES

The Act of January 27, 1933,[129] provided that all funds and other securities held under the supervision of the Secretary of the Interior belonging to Indians of the Five Civilized Tribes in Oklahoma of one-half or more Indian blood, enrolled or unenrolled, shall be restricted and shall remain under the jurisdiction of the Secretary until April 26, 1956, "subject to expenditure in the meantime for the use and benefit of the individual Indians" who own them, under rules and regulations prescribed by the Secretary.

The Secretary was empowered[130] to permit any adult Indian of the Five Civilized Tribes to create and establish out of restricted funds or other property under the Secretary's supervision, trusts for a maximum period of 21 years after the death of the last survivor of the named beneficiaries in the respective trust period, for the benefit of such Indian, his heirs or other designated beneficiaries, by contracts or agreements between the Indian and incorporated trust companies or banks.

No trust company or bank may act as a trustee in any trust created under this act "which has paid or promised to pay to any person other than an officer or employee on the regular pay roll thereof any charge, fee, commission, or remuneration for any service or influence in securing or attempting to secure for it the trusteeship in any trust." Trust agreements or contracts made prior to January 27, 1933, the day of this law's approval, and not approved prior to such enactment by the Secretary of the Interior, are declared void.[131]

The Secretary is authorized to transfer the funds or property required by the terms of an approved trust agreement to the trustee,[132] which must keep these assets segregated from all other assets.

None of the restrictions upon the corpus under the terms of the trust agreement may be released during the restrictive period, except as provided by such agreement, and neither the corpus of said trust nor the income derived therefrom, during the restrictive period, provided by law, is alienable.[133]

The trustee is to render an annual accounting to the Secretary and the beneficiary.[134]

Such trust agreements are irrevocable except with the Secretary's consent.[135] If a trust agreement is annulled, the corpus of the trust estate with all accrued and unpaid interest must be returned to the Secretary as restricted individual Indian property.

Illegally procured trusts are to be cancelled by proceedings instituted by the Attorney General in the federal courts.[136]

[129] 47 Stat. 777, *supra*, fn. 108. For a discussion of this act, see 54 I. D. 382 (1934); *Darks* v. *Ickes*, 69 F. 2d 231 (App. D. C. 1934); *United States ex rel. Warren* v. *Ickes*, 73 F. 2d 844 (App. D. C. 1934); *Burgess* v. *Noll*, 103 F. 2d 37 (C. C. A. 10, 1939), rehearing den. 103 F. 2d 37.

For regulations regarding creation of trusts for restricted property, see 25 C. F. R. 227.1–227.12.

[130] Act of January 27, 1933, sec. 2 and 7, 47 Stat. 777, *supra*, fn. 108.

[131] *Ibid.*, sec. 2.

[132] *Ibid.*, sec. 3.

[133] *Ibid.*, sec. 4.

[134] *Ibid.*

[135] *Ibid.*, sec. 5.

[136] *Ibid.*, sec. 6.

SECTION 11. INHERITANCE AMONG FIVE CIVILIZED TRIBES[137]

A. INTESTATE SUCCESSION

Among the Five Civilized Tribes, as among all other tribes, tribal law governs descent in the absence of congressional legislation.[138] The General Allotment Act[139] did not apply to the Five Civilized Tribes, and so its provisions on inheritance have no application to these tribes.

[137] The Act of June 25, 1910, 36 Stat. 855, 863, which provides, among other things, for the determination of heirs of deceased Indians, excludes the Five Civilized Tribes (sec. 33) except for the following provision:

> SEC. 32. Where deeds to tribal lands in the Five Civilized Tribes have been or may be issued, in pursuance of any tribal agreement or Act of Congress, to a person who had died, or who hereafter dies before the approval of such deed, the title to the land designated therein shall inure to and become vested in the heirs, devisees, or assigns of such deceased grantee as if the deed had issued to the deceased grantee during life.

[138] See Chapter 7, sec. 6.

[139] Act of February 8, 1887, 24 Stat. 388.

The Supreme Court in the case of *Jefferson* v. *Fink*,[140] summarized the early congressional legislation regarding descent and distribution as follows:

> By acts passed in 1890, 1896, 1897 and 1898, Congress manifested its purpose to allot or divide in severalty the lands of the Five Civilized Tribes with a view to the ultimate creation of a State embracing the Indian Territory; put in force in the Territory several statutes of Arkansas, including Chapter 49 of Mansfield's Digest relating to descent and distribution; provided that those statutes should apply to all persons in the Territory, irrespective of race; and substantially abrogated the laws of the several tribes, including those relating to descent and distribution. Acts May 2, 1890, c. 182, 26 Stat. 81, § 31; March 3, 1893, c. 209, 27 Stat. 645, § 16; June 7, 1897, c. 3, 30 Stat. 83; June 28, 1898, c. 517, 30 Stat. 495, §§ 11 and 26. This was the situation when the Act of 1901, known as the Original Creek Agreement, was adopted. That act in the course of providing for the allotment in severalty of the lands of the Creeks revived their tribal law of descent and distribution by making it applicable to their allotments, §§ 7 and 28. But the revival was only temporary, for the Act of 1902, known as the Supplemental Creek Agreement, not only repealed so much of the Act of 1901 as gave effect to the tribal law but reinstated the Arkansas law with the qualification that Creek heirs, if there were such, should take to the exclusion of others.[1] *Washington* v. *Miller*, 235 U. S. 422, 425–426. The allotment in question was made and the tribal deeds issued shortly after the Act of 1902 became effective. And this was followed by the Act of April 28, 1904, c. 1824, 33 Stat. 573, § 2, declaring that all statutes of Arkansas theretofore put in force in the Indian Territory should be taken "to embrace all persons and estates in said Territory, whether Indian, freedmen, or otherwise." (Pp. 291–292.)
>
> [1] The repealing and reinstating portion of the act was as follows:
>
> "6. The provisions of the act of Congress approved March 1, 1901 (31 Stat. L., 861), in so far as they provide for descent and distribution according to the laws of the Creek Nation, are hereby repealed and the descent and distribution of land and money provided for by said act shall be in accordance with chapter 49 of Mansfield's Digest of the Statutes of Arkansas now in force in Indian Territory: *Provided*, That only citizens of the Creek Nation, male and female, and their Creek descendants shall inherit lands of the Creek Nation: *And provided further*, That if there be no person of Creek citizenship to take the descent and distribution of said estate, then the inheritance shall go to noncitizen heirs in the order named in said chapter 49."
>
> There was a like provision, but without the provisos, in the Act of May 27, 1902, c. 888, 32 Stat. 258.
>
> Referring to the purpose with which the Arkansas statutes were put in force in that Territory and to their statutes there, this court said in *Shulthis* v. *McDougal*, 225 U. S. 561, 571: "Congress was then contemplating the early inclusion of that Territory in a new State, and the purpose of those acts was to provide, for the time being, a body of laws adapted to the needs of the locality and its people in respect of matters of local or domestic concern. There being no local legislature, Congress alone could act. Plainly, its action was intended to be merely provisional. . . ."
>
> By the enabling act of June 16, 1906, c. 3335, 34 Stat. 267, provision was made for admitting into the Union both the Territory of Oklahoma and the Indian Territory as the State of Oklahoma. Each Territory had a distinct body of local laws. Those in the Indian Territory, as we have seen, had been put in force there by Congress. Those in the Territory of Oklahoma had been enacted by the territorial legislature. Deeming it better that the new State should come into the Union with a body of laws applying with practical uniformity throughout the State, Congress provided in the enabling act (§ 13) that "the laws in force in the *Territory of Oklahoma*, as far as applicable, shall *extend over and apply to said State* until changed by the legislature thereof," and also (§ 21) that "all laws in force in the *Territory of Oklahoma* at the time of the admission of said State into the Union shall be in force *throughout said State*, except as modified or changed by this act or by the constitution of the State." The people of the State, taking the same view, provided in their constitution (Art. 25, § 2) that "all laws in force in the *Territory of Oklahoma* at the time of the admission of the State into the Union, which are not repugnant to this Constitution, and which are not locally inapplicable, shall be *extended to and remain in force in the State of Oklahoma* until they expire by their own limitation or are altered or repealed by law."
>
> The State was admitted into the Union November 16, 1907; and thereupon the laws of the Territory of Oklahoma relating to descent and distribution (Rev. Stats. Okla. 1903, c. 86, art. 4) became laws of the State. Thereafter Congress, by the Act of May 27, 1908, c. 199, 35 Stat. 312, § 9, recognized and treated "the laws of descent and distribution of the State of Oklahoma" as applicable to the lands allotted to members of the Five Civilized Tribes. (Pp. 292–293.)

[140] 247 U. S. 288 (1918).

B. WILLS

Section 23 of the Act of April 26, 1906,[141] provided for the making of wills, but invalidated a will of a full-blood Indian which disinherits the parent, wife, spouse, or children, unless acknowledged before and approved by a judge of the United States Court for the Indian Territory or a United States Commissioner.[142] In *Blundell* v. *Wallace*,[143] the Supreme Court said in interpreting this section:

> * * * The general policy of Congress prior to the adoption of § 23, plainly had been to consider the local law of descents and wills applicable to the persons and estates of Indians except in so far as it was otherwise provided. Thus, by § 2 of the Act of April 28, 1904, c. 1824, 33 Stat. 573, the laws of Arkansas, theretofore put in force in the Indian Territory, were expressly "continued and extended in their operation, so as to embrace all persons and estates in said Territory, whether Indian, freedmen, or otherwise," and jurisdiction was conferred upon the courts of the Territory in the settlement of the estates of decedents, etc., whether Indian, freedmen, or otherwise.
>
> Section 23 must be read in the light of this policy; and, so reading it, we agree with the ruling of the state supreme court that Congress intended thereby to enable "the Indian to dispose of his estate on the same footing as any other citizen, with the limitation contained in the proviso thereto." The effect of § 23 was to remove a restriction theretofore existing upon the testamentary power of the Indians, leaving the regulatory local law free to operate as in the case of other persons and property. (P. 376.)

C. PROBATE JURISDICTION

The Act of May 27, 1908,[144] was enacted at the request of the Oklahoma delegation, as part of the plan for removal of restrictions from Indian lands of the Five Civilized Tribes.[145] Section 6 conferred jurisdiction upon the probate (county) courts of the State of Oklahoma over the estates of Indian minors and incompetents of the Five Civilized Tribes.[146] The probate court was

[141] 34 Stat. 137, *supra*. fn. 101.

[142] Amended by Act of May 27, 1908, sec. 8, 35 Stat. 312, 315, to include "or a judge of a county court of the State of Oklahoma."

[143] 267 U. S. 373 (1925).

[144] 35 Stat. 312, *supra*., fn. 102. The Act of April 28, 1904, sec. 2, 33 Stat. 573, conferred jurisdiction upon the district court to settle estates of decedents and the guardianship of minors and incompetents, whether Indians, freedmen, or otherwise. See *Taylor* v. *Parker*, 235 U. S. 42 (1914).

By sec. 22 of the Act of April 26, 1906, 34 Stat. 137, 145, adult heirs of a deceased allottee of the Five Civilized Tribes were permitted to sell and convey lands inherited from the decedent, and minor heirs were permitted to join in the sale of such inherited lands by a guardian appointed by the appropriate court for the Indian Territory.

[145] See Meriam, The Problem of Indian Administration (1928) pp. 799–801, which criticizes this law.

[146] Interpreted in *Harris* v. *Bell*, 254 U. S. 108 (1920). On the jurisdiction of the county courts see Oklahoma constitution, Art. 7, secs. 12–14, and *United States* v. *Bond*, 108 F. 2d 504 (C. C. A. 10, 1939).

also given, by section 9, authority to approve conveyances by full-blood heirs.[147]

Provisions were also made for the appointment of probate attorneys by the Secretary of the Interior, with prescribed duties relating to restricted lands.

Section 8 of the Act of January 27, 1933,[148] makes it the duty of these probate attorneys to appear and represent any restricted member of the Five Civilized Tribes before the county courts or in the appellate courts.[149]

Section 1 of the act of June 14, 1918,[150] vested in the state courts jurisdiction to probate wills and determine heirs in accordance with state laws of any deceased citizen allottee of the Five Civilized Tribes who died leaving restricted heirs. However, to the extent that creditors, attorneys, and personal representatives must depend on restricted property and funds for payment of fees and claims, the Secretary of the Interior retained sole jurisdiction to pass upon the reasonableness of their claims.

D. PARTITION

Section 2 of this law[151] also made the "lands of full-blood members of any of the Five Civilized Tribes" subject to the laws of the State of Oklahoma providing for the partition of real estate.

If the court finds that an equitable partition is impossible, it may order the sale of the land and the division of the proceeds among the heirs.[152]

This provision has been interpreted as follows:[153]

> * * * The wide sweep of the language contained in the statute [sec. 2, Act of June 14, 1918, *supra*] expressly subjecting the lands of full-blood Indians to the laws of the state for partition fails to indicate a legislative purpose to limit the grant or consent of jurisdiction to district courts in proceedings affecting lands of living Indians, to the exclusion of proceedings in the county court in the administration and settlement of estates of deceased full-bloods. (P. 507.)
> * * * it [sec. 1, Act of January 27, 1933, 47 Stat. 777] does not narrow that part of the Act of 1918, *supra*, which consents to the making of the lands of full-blood members of the Five Civilized Tribes subject to the laws of the State of Oklahoma relating to the partition of real estate. Instead, it provides that the restrictions there imposed upon restricted and tax-exempt land belonging to a member of such tribes which is acquired by or for restricted Indians by inheritance, gift, or purchase with restricted funds, shall remain restricted during the period fixed therein, unless the restrictions are removed in the meantime in the manner provided by law. At least two separate and distinct methods existed at that time for the removal of restrictions against alienation. One was by the Secretary of the Interior, and the other was by partition and sale in the county court in the course of the administration and settlement of the estate of a deceased full-blood Indian. The concluding language in the proviso is plainly broad enough to include both. (P. 508.)

[147] Amended by Act of April 12, 1926, 44 Stat. 239, fn. 105 *supra*; and Act of May 10, 1928, sec. 2, 45 Stat. 495, fn. 106 *supra*.

[148] 47 Stat. 777, fn. 108, *supra*.

[149] Seven attorneys, including a supervising attorney, handle Five Tribes matters. Most of their work involves appearances and intervention in court proceedings in which the title to restricted land or the taxability of the Indians is being investigated. *Anderson* v. *Peck*, 53 F. 2d 257 (D. C. N. D. Okla., 1931); Annual Report of the Comm. of Ind. Aff. (1931) p. 28.

For a discussion of the work of the probate Division of the Bureau of Indian Affairs of the Department of the Interior, especially in regard to the Five Civilized Tribes and the Osages, see Hearings H. Comm. on Ind. Aff., H. R. 6234, 74th Cong., 1st sess., 1935, pp. 121–131. On the work of the probate attorneys of the Five Civilized Tribes see pt. XIV, Survey of Conditions of Indians in the United States (1931) pp. 5457–5497, 5676–5682; Meriam, The Problem of Indian Administration (1928) pp. 798–800.

An adjudication in a proceeding to determine the heirs of restricted members of the Five Civilized Tribes does not bind the United States in the absence of the service of notice upon the superintendent of the Five Civilized Tribes pursuant to sec. 3 of the Act of April 12, 1926, 44 Stat. 239, fn. 105, *supra*. Under the provision of sec. 3 of the April 12, 1926 act, the United States can intervene in cases to quiet title to a restricted allotment inherited by a member of the Five Civilized Tribes and can have the case removed to a federal court. *Anderson* v. *Peck*, 53 F. 2d 257 (D. C. N. D. Okla., 1931).

[150] 40 Stat. 606, 25 U. S. C. 375. This statute is cited in Memo. Sol. I. D., September 15, 1934; Memo. Sol. I. D., September 21, 1935; *Anderson* v. *Peck*, 53 F. 2d 257 (D. C. N. D. Okla., 1931); *Bond* v. *Tom*, 25 F. Supp. 157 (D. C. N. D. Okla., 1938); *In re Jessie's Heirs*, 259 Fed. 694 (D. C. E. D. Okla., 1919); *Knight* v. *Carter Oil Co.*, 23 F. 2d 481 (C. C. A. 8, 1927); *McDougal* v. *Black Panther Oil & Gas Co.*, 273 Fed. 113 (C. C. A. 8, 1921); *Pitman* v. *Com'r of Internal Revenue*, 64 F. 2d 740 (C. C. A. 10, 1933); *Roberts* v. *Anderson*, 66 F. 2d 874 (C. C. A. 10, 1933).

[151] 25 U. S. C. 355. It also provided that any land allotted in partition proceedings to a full-blood Indian, or conveyed to him upon his election to take the same at the appraisement, shall remain subject to all restrictions upon alienation and taxation obtaining prior to such partition, but "In case of a sale under any decree, or partition, the conveyance thereunder shall operate to relieve the lands described of all restrictions of every character."

[152] For discussion of restricted status of proceeds from a partition sale, see Chapter 10, sec. 3.

[153] *United States* v. *Bond*, 108 F. 2d 504 (C. C. A. 10, 1939), aff'g. *Bond* v. *Tom*, 25 F. Supp. 157 (D. C. N. D. Okla., 1938). Accord: Memo. Sol. I. D., September 21, 1935.

SECTION 12. SPECIAL LAWS GOVERNING OSAGE TRIBE[154]

The special laws governing the Osage Tribe and the decisions applying and construing them are of a complexity and volume that preclude any detailed treatment in this work.

There may be some value, however, in a bird's-eye view of the special legislation beginning in 1906 which was designed to secure the individualization of Osage lands and funds while maintaining tribal ownership of the very valuable minerals that were found to underlie the Osage Reservation.

A good introduction to the subject is found in the opinion of Justice Brandeis in the case of *McCurdy* v. *United States*:[155]

> The Osage Tribe of Indians consisted in 1906 of two thousand persons. Their reservation, located in Oklahoma Territory between the Arkansas River and the Kansas state line, contained about a million and a half acres of

[154] For a history of the Osages see *United States* v. *Aaron*, 183 Fed. 347 (C. C. W. D. Okla., 1910); *Labadie* v. *United States*, 6 Okla. 400, 51 Pac. 666 (1897). The Osage lands were purchased by the United States pursuant to Art. 16 of the Treaty of July 19, 1866, 14 Stat. 799, 804, in which the Cherokee Indians in the Indian Territory agreed that the United States might purchase part of their lands for the purpose of settling friendly Indians thereon.

Many special statutes were enacted concerning the lands of the Osage Nation in Kansas. The following statutes concern the sale of Osage Indian lands in that state; Act of May 9, 1872, 17 Stat. 90, R. S. §§ 2283, 2284, 2285, superseded by Act of June 23, 1874, 18 Stat. 283; Act of May 28, 1880, 21 Stat. 143; Act of June 16, 1880, 21 Stat. 291; Act of March 3, 1881, 21 Stat. 509; Act of March 3, 1891, sec. 23, 26 Stat. 1095, 1102; Act of June 6, 1900, 31 Stat. 659. The following acts dealt with the sale of land of the Great and Little Osage Tribe in Kansas; Joint Resolution of April 10, 1869, 16 Stat. 55; Act of August 11, 1876, 19 Stat. 127. The following laws dealt with rights-of-way through the Osage Reservation: Act of February 15, 1897, 29 Stat. 529; Act of February 28, 1902, sec. 23, 32 Stat. 43, 50, 51, 25 U. S. C. 312; Act of April 21, 1904, 33 Stat. 240, cited in *Moore* v. *Sawyer*, 167 Fed. 826 (C. C. E. D. Okla., 1909).

[155] 246 U. S. 263 (1918). Also see *Work* v. *United States ex rel. Mosier*, 261 U. S. 352 (1923).

fertile well-watered prairie land and a heavily timbered hill lands, largely underlaid with petroleum, natural gas, coal and other minerals. At that time the United States held for the tribe a trust fund of $8,373,658.54, received under various treaties as compensation for relinquishing other lands. The annual income of the tribe from interest on this trust fund and from rentals of grazing, oil, and gas lands was nearly $1,000,000; that is $500 for every man, woman and child, in addition to the earnings of individuals.[1] Congress, concluding apparently that the enjoyment of wealth without responsibility was demoralizing to the Osages, decided upon the policy of gradual emancipation. By Act of June 28, 1906, 34 Stat. 539, it provided for an equal division among them of the trust fund and the lands. The trust fund was to be divided by placing to the credit of each member of the tribe his pro rata share which should thereafter be held for the benefit of himself and his heirs for the period of twenty-five years and then paid over to them respectively (§§ 4 and 5).[2]

[1] Annual Reports, Dept. Interior (1905), pp. 306–312; (1906), pp. 448, 451.

[2] Footnote omitted.

* * * * *

The lands were to be divided by giving to each member the right to make, from the tribal lands, three selections of 160 acres each and to designate which of these should constitute his homestead. A commission was appointed to divide among the members also the remaining lands, after setting aside enough for county use, school-sites and other small reservations. The oil, gas, coal and other mineral rights were reserved to the tribe for the period of twenty-five years with provision for leasing the same. The homesteads were made inalienable and non-taxable for twenty-five years or until otherwise provided by Congress. All other allotted lands—which were known as "surplus lands," were made inalienable for twenty-five years and non-taxable for three years, except that power was vested with the Secretary of the Interior to issue to any adult member, upon his petition, a certificate of competency, authorizing him to sell all of his surplus land; and upon its issue all his surplus lands became immediately taxable. (Pp. 265–266.)

A. ALLOTMENTS

The Osage Allotment Act of June 28, 1906,[156] providing for the distribution of Osage lands[157] in severalty, allowed each member of the tribe to make three selections of 160 acres each, one of which was to be designated as a homestead to be "inalienable and nontaxable until otherwise provided by act of Congress."[158] After each member had made the three selections, the remaining lands of the tribe, except as otherwise provided in the act, were to be divided as equally as practicable among the tribal members by a commission to be appointed. Under the latter provision each Indian received an additional tract averaging between 175 and 200 acres.

[156] 34 Stat. 539. This statute is discussed at length in *Levindale Lead & Zinc Mining Co.* v. *Coleman*, 241 U. S. 432 (1916), which held that the restrictions on alienation imposed by law do not apply to land owned by white men who are not members of the tribe.

The General Allotment Act was inapplicable to territory occupied by the Osages. Sec. 8 of the Act of April 23, 1904, 33 Stat. 299, refers to "the Osage Nation or allottees therein." The Act of March 3, 1905, 33 Stat. 1049, reserved from selection and allotment certain lands, including selections for townsites.

The Act of June 28, 1906, repealed in part the Act of August 15, 1894, 28 Stat. 286, 305 and supplemented the Act of March 3, 1905, 33 Stat. 1048, 1061. It was amended by the Acts of April 18, 1912, 37 Stat. 86; January 18, 1917, 39 Stat. 867; May 25, 1918, 40 Stat. 561; March 3, 1921, 41 Stat. 1249; April 12, 1924, 43 Stat. 94; February 27, 1925, 43 Stat. 1008; March 2, 1929, 45 Stat. 1478; supplemented also by the Joint Resolution No. 19 of February 27, 1909, 35 Stat. 1167; Act of April 8, 1912, 37 Stat. 86; Act of May 25, 1918, 40 Stat. 561; Act of March 2, 1929, 45 Stat. 1478; and is cited in Reeves, Probating Indian Estates (1917) 23 Case and Com. 727; 33 Op. A. G. 60 (1921); 34 Op. A. G. 26 (1922); Op. Sol. I. D., M.5805, November 22, 1921; Op. Sol. I. D., M.4017, January 4, 1922; Op. Sol. I. D., M.8370, August 15, 1922; Op. Sol I. D., M. 27963, January 26, 1937; 48 L. D. 470 (1921); 53 I. D. 169 1926; Op. Sol. I. D., M.18320, December 21, 1926; Op. Sol. I. D., M.21642, March 26, 1927; Op. Sol. I. D., M.24293, June 19, 1928; Op. Sol. I. D., M.25107, May 4, 1929; Memo. Sol. I. D., December 17, 1935; Op. Sol I. D., M.27963, January 26, 1937; 48 L. D. 470 (1921); 53 I. D. 169 (1930); 54 I. D. 105 (1932); 54 I. D. 341 (1933); 55 I. D. 456 (1936); *Adams* v. *Osage Tribe of Indians*, 59 F. 2d 653 (C. C. A. 10, 1932), aff'g 50 F. 2d 918 (D. C. N. D. Okla., 1931), cert. den. 287 U. S. 652; *Bartlett* v. *Okla. Oil Co.*, 218 Fed. 380 (D. C. E. D. Okla., 1914); *Brewer Elliott Oil & Gas Co.* v. *United States*, 260 U. S. 77 (1922); *Browning* v. *United States*, 6 F. 2d 801 (C. C. A. 8, 1925), cert. den. 269 U. S. 568 (1925); *Choteau* v. *Burnet*, 283 U. S. 691 (1931); *Choteau* v. *Comm'r of Internal Revenue*, 38 F. 2d 976 (C. C. A. 10, 1930); *Comm'rs* v. *United States*, 270 Fed. 110 (C. C. A. 8, 1920), aff'g. *United States* v. *Hutchings*, 252 Fed. 841 (D. C. W. D. Okla., 1918), writ of error dism. 260 U. S. 753 (1922); *Continental Oil Co.* v. *Osage Oil & Refining Co.*, 69 F. 2d 19 (C. C. A. 10, 1934), cert. den. 287 U. S. 616; *Drummond* v. *United States*, 34 F. 2d 755 (C. C. A. 8, 1929); *Fish* v. *Wise*, 52 F. 2d 544 (C. C. A. 10, 1931), cert. den. 282 U. S. 908 (1931), 284 U. S. 688 (1932); *Globe Indemnity Co.* v. *Bruce*, 81 F. 2d 143 (C. C. A. 10, 1935), cert. den. 297 U. S. 716; *Harrison* v. *Moncravie*, 264 Fed. 776 (C. C. A. 8, 1920), app. dism. 255 U. S. 562 (1921); *Hickey* v. *United States*, 64 F. 2d 628 (C. C. A. 10, 1933); *Iokes* v. *Pattison*, 80 F. 2d 708 (App. D. C. 1935), cert. den. 297 U. S. 713; *In re Dennison*, 38 F. 2d 662 (D. C. W. D. Okla. 1930), app. dism. 45 F. 2d 585, *In re Irwin*, 60 F. 2d 495 (C. C. A. 10, 1932); *In re Penn*, 41 F. 2d 257 (D. C. W. D. Okla., 1929); *Johnson* v. *United States*, 64 F. 2d 674 (C. C. A. 10, 1933), cert. den. 290 U. S. 651 (1933); *Jump* v. *Ellis*, 100 F. 2d 130 (C. C. A. 10, 1938), aff'g 22 F. Supp. 380 (D. C. N. D. Okla., 1938), cert. den. 306 U. S. 645 (1938); *Kenny* v. *Miles*, 250 U. S. 58 (1919), *La Motte* v. *United States*, 254 U. S. 570 (1921); *McCurdy* v. *United States*, 246 U. S. 263 (1918); *Morrison* v. *United States*, 6 F. 2d 811 (C. C. A. 8, 1925); *Mosier* v. *United States*, 198 Fed. 54 (C. C. A. 8, 1912), cert. den. 229 U. S. 619 (1913); *Ne-Kah-Wah-She-Tun-Kah* v. *Fall*, 290 Fed. 303 (App. D. C. 1923), app. dism. 266 U. S. 595 (1925); *Osage County Motor Co.* v. *United States*, 33 F. 2d 21 (C. C. A. 8, 1929), cert. den. 280 U. S. 577; *Quarles* v. *Denison*, 45 F. 2d 585 (C. C. A. 10, 1930); *Tapp* v. *Stuart*, 6 F. Supp. 577 (D. C. N. D. Okla, 1934); *Taylor* v. *Tayrien*, 51 F. 2d 884 (C. C. A. 10, 1931), cert. den. 284 U. S. 672 (1931); *United States* v. *Aaron*, 183 Fed. 347 (C. C. W. D. Okla., 1910); *United States* v. *Bd. of Comm'rs*, 26 F. Supp. 270 (D. C. N. D. Okla., 1939); *United States* v. *Bd. of Comm'rs of Osage Co., Okla.*, 193 Fed. 485 (C. C. W. D. Okla., 1911); *United States* v. *Board of Comm'rs of Osage Co., Okla.*, 216 Fed. 883 (C. C. A. 8, 1914; *United States* v. *Bd. of Comm'rs of McIntosh County*, 284 Fed. 103 (C. C. A. 8, 1922), app. dism. 263 U. S. 689, 263 U. S. 691; *United States* v. *Hale*, 51 F. 2d 629 (C. C. A. 10, 1931); *United States* v. *Harris*, 293 Fed. 389 (C. C. A. 8, 1923), aff'g 265 Fed. 261 (C. C. A. 8, 1920), app. dism. 257 U. S. 623 (1922); *United States* v. *Hughes*, 6 F. Supp. 972 (D. C. N. D. Okla., 1934); *United States* v. *Hutchings*, 252 Fed. 841 (D. C. W. D. Okla., 1918), aff'd sub nom. *Commissioners* v. *United States*, 270 Fed. 110 (C. C. A. 18, 1920), app. dism. 260 U. S. 753; *United States* v. *Johnson*, 87 F. 2d 155 (C. C. A. 10, 1936); *United States* v. *La Motte*, 67 F. 2d 788 (C. C. A. 10, 1933); *United States* v. *Mashunkashey*, 72 Fed. 847 (C. C. A. 10, 1934), rehear'g den. 73 F. 2d 487 (C. C. A. 10, 1934), cert. den. 294 U. S. 724 (1935); *United States* v. *Mummert*, 15 F. 2d 926 (C. C. A. 8, 1926); *United States* v. *Osage County*, 251 U. S. 128 (1919); *United States* v. *Ramsey*, 271 U. S. 467 (1926); *United States* v. *Sands*, 94 F. 2d 156 (C. C. A. 10, 1938); *United States* v. *Sandstrom*, 22 F. Supp. 190 (D. C. N. D. Okla., 1938); *United States ex rel. Brown* v. *Lane*, 232 U. S. 598 (1914); *Utilities Production Corp.* v. *Carter Oil Co.*, 2 F. Supp. 81 (D. C. N. D. Okla., 1933); *Work* v. *United States ex rel. Mosier*, 261 U. S. 352 (1923).

[157] This included only surface rights; all oil, gas, and other minerals being reserved to the tribe for 25 years. The Act of March 3, 1909, 35 Stat. 778, *infra* fn. 162, authorized the Secretary of the Interior to sell part or all of the surplus lands of members of the Osage Tribe, "*Provided*, That the sale of the Osage lands shall be subject to the reserved rights of the tribe in oil, gas, and other minerals."

[158] Act of June 28, 1906, sec. 2, 34 Stat. 539, 541 see fn. 156 *supra*, sec. 3 of this act was amended by Act of March 3, 1921, 41 Stat. 1249. The Joint Resolution of February 27, 1909, 35 Stat. 1167, designated lands which might constitute homesteads. The Appropriation Act of May 25, 1918, 40 Stat. 561, 579, provided:

> That the allottees of the Osage Nation may change the present designation of homesteads to an equal area of their unencumbered surplus lands, upon application to, and under such rules and regulations as the Secretary of the Interior may prescribe: *Provided*, That each tract after the change and designation shall take the status of the other as it existed prior to the change in designation as to alienation, taxation, or otherwise, and that any order of change of designation shall be recorded in the proper office of

The lands other than homestead were made inalienable[159] for 25 years, except that in his discretion the Secretary of the Interior, at the request of an adult member, might issue a certificate of competency authorizing him to sell any of the lands except the homestead, which was to remain inalienable and nontaxable for a period of 25 years, or during the life of the homestead allottee. Upon the issuance of the certificate of competency the surplus lands became alienable and subject to state taxation.[160] Subdivision 7 of section 2 of this statute also provided:

> That the surplus lands shall be nontaxable for the period of three years from the approval of this Act, except where certificates of competency are issued or in case of the death of the allottee * * *[161]

The Act of March 3, 1909,[162] authorized and empowered the Secretary of the Interior, upon application, to sell, under rules and regulations to be prescribed by him, part or all of the surplus lands of any member of the Osage Tribe. This Act provided that such sales should be subject to the reserved rights of the tribe in oil, gas, and other minerals.

The Act of April 18, 1912,[163] section 3, conferred jurisdiction on the county courts of the State of Oklahoma in probate matters affecting the property of deceased and of orphan minor, insane, or other incompetent allottees of the Osage Tribe, with the provision that no land should be sold or alienated under that section without the approval of the Secretary of the Interior. Section 6 conferred jurisdiction on the courts of Oklahoma to partition Osage allotted lands but provided that no partition or sale of the restricted lands of a deceased Osage allottee should be valid until approved by the Secretary of the Interior. It also removed the restrictions from lands held by heirs having certificates of competency or who were nonmembers of the tribe. Section 7 secured the lands allotted to members of the tribe against any lien for any debt or obligation contracted or incurred prior to the issuance of a certificate of competency, or removal of restrictions on alienation. It also provided that no lands or moneys inherited from Osage allottees shall be subject to, or be taken or sold to secure the payment of, any indebtedness incurred by such heir prior to the time such lands and moneys are turned over to them. Section 8 of the act authorized the disposition by will by any adult member of the Osage Tribe of his estate, real, personal, or mixed, including trust funds, from which restrictions on alienation had not been removed, in accordance with the laws of the State of Oklahoma, except that no such will should be admitted to probate or have any validity unless approved before or after the death of the testator by the Secretary of the Interior.

The Appropriation Act of May 25, 1918,[164] authorized Osage allottees in accordance with regulations of the Secretary of the Interior, to change the present designation of homesteads to an equal area of their unencumbered surplus lands, each tract, after the change of designation, to take the status of the other as it existed prior to such change as to alienation, taxation, or otherwise. This act also authorized the Secretary of the Interior, where it would be for the best interest of the Osage allottee, to permit the sale of homestead and surplus allotments, wholly or in part, under regulations to be prescribed by him.

The Act of March 3, 1921,[165] amending the 1906 act,[166] declared the Osages citizens of the United States and removed

---

Osage County: *Provided further*, That the Secretary of the Interior be, and he is hereby, authorized where the same would be for the best interest of Osage allottees, to permit the sale of surplus and homestead allotments, wholly or in part, of Osage allottees under such rules and regulations as he may prescribe and upon such terms as he shall approve.

[159] A distinction is drawn here between alienability and taxability. It is to be noted that although the surplus lands were made inalienable for 25 years, they were exempted from taxability for only 3 years. The homesteads, however, were made both inalienable and nontaxable for 25 years. *United States* v. *Board of Com'rs. of Osage County*, 216 Fed. 883 (C. C. A. 8, 1914).

[160] *United States* v. *Board of Com'rs. of Osage County*, 216 Fed. 883 (C. C. A. 8, 1914).

[161] The death of the allottee does not subject the homestead to taxation under this section. *United States* v. *Board of Com'rs. of Osage County, Okla.*, 193 Fed. 485 (C. C. W. D. Okla., 1911).

[162] 35 Stat. 778. This act is cited in *Adams* v. *Osage Tribe of Indians*, 59 F. 2d 653 (C. C. A. 10. 1932), cert. den. 287 U. S. 652; *Browning* v. *United States*, 6 F. 2d 801 (C. C. A. 8, 1925), cert. den. 269 U. S. 568 (1925); *Drummond* v. *United States*, 34 F. 2d 755 (C. C. A. 8, 1929); *Kansas or Kaw Indians* v. *United States*, 80 C. Cls. 264 (1934), cert. den. 296 U. S. 577; *Levindale Lead & Zinc Mining Co.* v. *Coleman*, 241 U. S. 432 (1916); *Morrison* v. *United States*, 6 F. 2d 811 (C. C. A. 8, 1925); *United States* v. *Aaron*, 183 Fed. 347 (C. C. W. D. Okla., 1910); *Work* v. *United States ex rel. Lynn*, 266 U. S. 161 (1924).

[163] 37 Stat. 86. The Act of April 18, 1912, supplemented Act of June 7, 1897, 30 Stat. 62, 90; Act of June 28, 1906, 34 Stat. 539, 543; amended Act of June 28, 1906, 34 Stat. 539, 544; and amended by Act of May 25, 1918, 40 Stat. 561; and was cited in Reeves, Probating Indian Estates (1917), 23 Case and Com. 727; Op. Sol. I. D., M.4017, January 4, 1922; Op. Sol. I. D., M.8370, August 15, 1922; Op. Sol. I. D., M.18320, December 21, 1926; Op. Sol. I. D., M.24293, June 19, 1928; Op. Sol. I. D., M.26731, October 14, 1931; Op. Comp. Gen. A. 40178, February 4, 1932; Op. Sol. I. D., M.27833, November 28, 1934; Op. Sol. I. D., M.27963, January 26, 1937; 54 I. D. 555 (1934); 55 I. D. 456 (1936); *Browning* v. *United States*, 6 F. 2d 801 (C. C. A. 8, 1925), cert. den. 269 U. S. 568 (1925); *Drummond* v. *United States*, 34 F. 2d 755 (C. C. A. 8, 1929); *Globe Indemnity Co.* v. *Bruce*, 81 F. 2d 143 (C. C. A. 10, 1935), cert. den. 297 U. S. 716; *Harrison* v. *Moncravie*, 264 Fed. 776 (C. C. A. 8, 1920), app. dism. 255 U. S. 562 (1921); *In re Dennison*, 38 F. 2d 662 (D. C. W. D. Okla., 1930), app. dism. 45 F. 2d 585; *In re Irwin*, 60 F. 2d 495 (C. C. A. 10, 1932); *Kenny* v. *Miles*, 250 U. S. 58 (1919); *La Motte* v. *United States*, 254 U. S. 570 (1921); *Levindale Lead & Zinc Mining Co.* v. *Coleman*, 241 U. S. 432 (1916); *McCurdy* v. *United States*, 246 U. S. 263 (1918); *Morrison* v. *United States*, 6 F. 2d 811 (C. C. A. 8, 1925); *Mudd* v. *Perry*, 14 F. 2d 430 (D. C. N. D. Okla., 1926), cert. den. 278 U. S. 601; *Ne-Kah-Wah-She-Tun-Kah* v. *Fall*, 290 Fed. 308 (App. D. C. 1923), app. dism. 266 U. S. 595 (1925); *Shaw* v. *Gibson-Zahniser Oil Corp.*, 276 U. S. 575 (1928); *Tapp* v. *Stuart*, 6 F. Supp. 577 (D. C. N. D. Okla. 1934); *Taylor* v. *Jones*, 51 F. 2d 892 (C. C. A. 10, 1931), cert. den. 284 U. S. 663 (1931); *Taylor* v. *Tayrien*, 51 F. 2d 884 (C. C. A. 10. 1931), cert. den. 284 U. S. 672 (1931); *United States* v. *Board of Commrs.*, 26 F. Supp. 270 (D. C. N. D. Okla., 1939); *United States* v. *Carson*, 19 F. Supp. 616 (D. C. N. D. Okla., 1937), app. dism. 98 F. 2d 1023; *United States* v. *Gray*, 284 Fed. 103 (C. C. A. 8, 1922), aff'g. 271 Fed. 747 (D. C. E. D. Okla., 1921), app. dism. 263 U. S. 689; *United States* v. *Hale*, 51 F. 2d 629 (C. C. A. 10, 1931); *United States* v. *Harris*, 293 Fed. 389 (C. C. A. 8, 1923), aff'g. 265 Fed. 261 (C. C. A. 8, 1920), app. dism. 257 U. S. 623 (1922); *United States* v. *Howard*, 8 F. Supp. 617 (D. C. N. D. Okla., 1934); *United States* v. *Hughes*, 6 F. Supp. 972 (D. C. N. D. Okla., 1934); *United States* v. *Johnson*, 87 F. 2d 155 (C. C. A. 10, 1936); *United States* v. *La Motte*, 67 F. 2d 788 (C. C. A. 10, 1933); *United States* v. *Law*, 250 Fed. 218 (C. C. A. 8, 1918); *United States* v. *Mummert*, 15 F. 2d 926 (C. C. A. 8, 1926); *United States* v. *Ransom*, 284 Fed. 108 (C. C. A. 8, 1922); *United States* v. *Sands*, 94 F. 2d 156 (C. C. A. 10, 1938); *United States* v. *Yakima County*, 274 Fed. 115 (D. C. E. D. Wash., 1921); *Work* v. *United States ex rel. Lynn*, 266 U. S. 161 (1924).

[164] 40 Stat. 561, 579.

[165] Sec. 3, 41 Stat. 1249. This act amended the Act of June 28, 1906, 34 Stat. 539; was amended by Act of February 27, 1925, 43 Stat. 1008; Act of March 2, 1929, 45 Stat. 1478; supplemented by Act of January 31, 1931, 46 Stat. 1047; and cited in 33 Op. A. G. 60 (1921); 36 Op. A. G. 98 (1929); Op. Sol. I. D., M.4017, January 4, 1922; Op. Sol. I. D., M.8370, August 15, 1922; Op. Sol. I. D., D.46929, September 30, 1922; Op. Sol. I. D., 17687, December 19, 1925; Op. Sol. I. D., March 16, 1926; Op. Sol. I. D., M.19190, June 2, 1926; Op. Sol. I. D., M.21642, March 26, 1927; Op. Sol. I. D., M.24293, June 19, 1928; Op. Sol. I. D., M.25107, May 4, 1929; Op. Sol. I. D., M.25280, August 21, 1929; Op. Sol. I. D., M.26731, October 14, 1931; Op. Sol. I. D., M.27963, January 26, 1937; 49 L. D. 420 (1922); 50 L. D. 672 (1924); 53 I. D. 169 (1930); 54 I. D. 260 (1933); 54 I. D. 341 (1933); 55 I. D. 456 (1936); *Adams* v. *Osage Tribe of Indians*, 59 F. 2d 653 (C. C. A. 10, 1932), aff'g 50 F. 2d 918 (D. C. N. D. Okla., 1931), cert. den. 287 U. S. 652; *Browning* v. *United States*, 6 F. 2d 801 (C. C. A. 8, 1925), cert. den. 269 U. S. 568 (1925); *Globe Indemnity Co.* v. *Bruce*, 81 F. 2d 143 (C. C. A. 10, 1935); cert. den. 297 U. S. 716; *Hickey* v. *United States*,

> * * * all restrictions against alienation of their allotment selections, both surplus and homestead, of all adult Osage Indians of less than one-half Indian blood * * *.[167]

The act also provided that:

> The homestead allotments of the members of the Osage Tribe shall not be subject to taxation if held by the original allottee prior to April 8, 1931.

The Supreme Court of the United States in *La Motte* v. *United States*[168] held that approval of an Osage will by the Secretary of the Interior removed restrictions theretofore existing on the lands of the allottee. Congress under section 3 of the Act of February 27, 1925,[169] continued restrictions on such lands, and on lands inherited by certain classes of Osage Indians, as follows:

> Lands devised to members of the Osage Tribe of one-half or more Indian blood or who do not have certificates of competency, under wills approved by the Secretary of the Interior, and lands inherited by such Indians, shall be inalienable unless such lands be conveyed with the approval of the Secretary of the Interior.

As oil production of the Osage Reservation increased and Osage headrights became more valuable, Osage Indians became increasingly attractive to individuals seeking wealthy husbands or wives, and the Osage tribe became gravely concerned at the passing of Osage wealth out of the tribe by the process of inheritance. Congress attempted to meet this problem in section 7 of the 1925 act[170] as follows:

> Hereafter none but heirs of Indian blood shall inherit from those who are of one-half or more Indian blood of the Osage Tribe of Indians any right, title, or interest to any restricted lands, moneys, or mineral interests of the Osage Tribe: *Provided*, That this section shall not apply to spouses under existing marriages.

By the provisions of the Act of March 2, 1929,[171] the lands, moneys, and other properties now or hereafter held in trust or under the supervision of the United States for the Osage tribe

---

64 F. 2d 628 (C. C. A. 10, 1933); *In re Dennison*, 38 F. 2d 662 (D. C. W. D. Okla., 1930), app. dism. 45 F. 2d 585; *In re Penn*, 41 F. 2d 257 (D. C. W. D. Okla., 1929); *Jump* v. *Ellis*, 100 F. 2d 130 (C. C. A. 10, 1938), aff'g 22 F. Supp. 380 (D. C. N. D. Okla., 1938), cert. den. 306 U. S. 645 (1938); *Morrison* v. *United States*, 6 F. 2d 811 (C. C. A. 8, 1925); *Ne-Kah-Wah-She-Tun-Kah* v. *Fall*, 290 Fed. 303 (App. D. C. 1923), app. dism. 266 U. S. 595 (1925); *Osage County Motor Co.* v. *United States*, 33 F. 2d 21 (C. C. A. 8, 1929), cert. den. 280 U. S. 577; *Silurian Oil Co.* v. *Essley*, 54 F. 2d 43 (C. C. A. 10, 1931); *Tapp* v. *Stuart*, 6 F. Supp. 577 (D. C. N. D. Okla., 1934); *Taylor* v. *Tayrien*, 51 F. 2d 884 (C. C. A. 10, 1931), cert. den. 284 U. S. 672 (1931); *United States* v. *Barnett*, 7 F. Supp. 573 (D. C. N. D. Okla., 1934); *United States* v. *Hughes*, 6 F. Supp. 972 (D. C. N. D. Okla., 1934); *United States* v. *Johnson*, 87 F. 2d 155 (C. C. A. 10, 1936); *United States* v. *Lynch*, 7 Alaska 568 (1 Div. 1927); *United States* v. *Mullendore*, 74 F. 2d 286 (C. C. A. 10, 1934); *United States* v. *Sands*, 94 F. 2d 156 (C. C. A. 10, 1938); *Webster* v. *Fall*, 266 U. S. 507 (1925); *Williams* v. *Clinton*, 83 F. 2d 143 (C. C. A. 10, 1936); *Work* v. *United States ex rel. Lynn*, 266 U. S. 161 (1924); *Work* v. *United States ex rel. Mosier*, 261 U. S. 352 (1923).

[166] Act of June 28, 1906, 34 Stat. 539, fn. 156, *supra*.

[167] It has been said that while this act removes restrictions from and makes taxable lands of Osages of less than half blood, it does not affect the lands of Indians of half or more Indian blood. These lands remained nontaxable. *United States* v. *Mullendore*, 74 F. 2d 286 (C. C. A. 10, 1934). The Fourth Circuit Court of Appeals concurred in *Board of County Commissioners* v. *United States*, 64 F. 2d 775 (C. C. A. 10, 1933).

[168] 254 U. S. 570 (1921), mod'g and aff'g 256 Fed. 5 (C. C. A. 8, 1919).

[169] 43 Stat. 1008. Amending Act of March 3, 1921, 41 Stat. 1249, 1250. Amended by Act of March 2, 1929, 45 Stat. 1478. Cited in 36 Op. A. G. 98 (1929); 38 Op. A. G. 577 (1937); Op. Sol. I. D., M.17687, December 19, 1925; Op. Sol. I. D., M.18423, March 16, 1926; Op. Sol. I. D., M.19190, June 2, 1926; Op. Sol. I. D., M.19225, June 7, 1926; Op. Sol. I. D., M.21642, March 26, 1927; Op. Sol. I. D., M.25107, May 4, 1929; Letter to Commr. Ind. Aff. from Sec'y. Interior. September 1930; Op. Sol. I. D., M.26731, October 14, 1931; Op. Comp. Gen. to Sec'y, February 4, 1932; Op. Sol. I. D., M.27788, August 6, 1934; Memo. Sol. I. D., May 1, 1936; Op. Sol. I. D., M.27963, January 26, 1937; Letter from A. G. to Secy. of Int., February 13, 1937; Letter from Asst. Secy. to A. G., October 27, 1937; 53 I. D. 169 (1930); 54 I. D. 105 (1932); 54 I. D. 260 (1933); 54 I. D. 341 (1933); 55 I. D. 456 (1936); 56 I. D. 48 (1937); *Browning* v. *United States*, 6 F. 2d 801 (C. C. A. 8, 1925), cert. den. 269 U. S. 568 (1925); *Choteau* v. *Burnet*, 283 U. S. 691 (1931); *Globe Indemnity Co.* v. *Bruce*, 81 F. 2d 143 (C. C. A. 10, 1935), cert. den. 297 U. S. 716; *Hickey* v. *United States*, 64 F. 2d 628 (C. C. A. 10, 1933); *Logan* v. *United States*, 58 F. 2d 697 (C. C. A. 10, 1932), cert. den. 287 U. S. 630; *Morrison* v. *United States*, 6 F. 2d 811 (C. C. A. 8, 1925); *Osage County Motor Co.* v. *United States*, 33 F. 2d 21 (C. C. A. 8, 1929), cert. den. 280 U. S. 577; *Tapp* v. *Stuart*, 6 F. Supp. 577 (D. C. N. D. Okla., 1934); *Taylor* v. *Tayrien*, 51 F. 2d 884 (C. C. A. 10, 1931), cert. den. 284 U. S. 672 (1931); *United States* v. *Board of Commissioners*, 26 F. Supp. 270 (D. C. N. D. Okla., 1939); *United States* v. *Carson*, 19 F. Supp. 616 (D. C. N. D. Okla., 1937), app. dism. 98 F. 2d 1023; *United States* v. *Howard*, 8 F. Supp. 617 (D. C. N. D. Okla., 1934); *United States* v. *Hughes*, 6 F. Supp. 972 (D. C. N. D. Okla., 1934); *United States* v. *Johnson*, 87 F. 2d 155 (C. C. A. 10, 1936); *United States* v. *Mashunkashey*, 72 F. 2d 847 (C. C. A. 10, 1934), rehearing den. 73 F. 2d 487 (C. C. A. 10, 1934), cert. den. 294 U. S. 724 (1935); *United States* v. *Mullendore*, 74 F. 2d 286 (C. C. A. 10, 1934); *Williams* v. *Clinton*, 83 F. 2d 143 (C. C. A. 10, 1936).

By the Act of February 27, 1925, the loose wording of the 1921 act regarding the payment to guardians of incompetent Osages was clarified. It was provided that the moneys in excess of the $1,000 quarterly that had been paid to the guardians since 1921 through an administrative interpretation of the 1921 act prior to the decision in *Work* v. *United States ex rel. Lynn*, 266 U. S. 161 (1924) which were still in the control or possession of the guardian were to be returned by them to the Secretary of the Interior, together with all property purchased or investments made by the guardian out of such excess funds. See *United States* v. *Barnett*, 7 F. Supp. 573 (D. C. N. D. Okla., 1934). The Secretary was to hold these funds or dispose of them as be deemed for the best interest of the Indians to whom the money belonged. Under section 1 of the act, the control of the Secretary was reimposed over all funds in the possession of the guardian which in their inception had been under the supervision and control of the Secretary. See *Hickey* v. *United States*, 64 F. 2d 628 (C. C. A. 10, 1933); *United States* v. *Hughes*, 6 F. Supp. 972 (D. C. N. D. Okla., 1934). Though the 1925 act reimposes restrictions on certain funds, it broadened the authority of the Secretary of the Interior over Indian funds and permitted the investment of such funds in

> * * * first mortgage real estate loans not to exceed 50 per centum of the appraised value of such real estate, and where the member is a resident of Oklahoma such investment shall be in loans on Oklahoma real estate, stock in Oklahoma building and loan associations, livestock * * *: *Provided*, That the Secretary of the Interior shall not make any investment for an adult member without first securing the approval of such member of such investment * * *.

This provision was interpreted in Op. Sol. I. D., M.27636, December 8, 1933. It also provided:

> All bonds, securities, stocks, and property purchased and other investments made by legal guardians shall not be subject to alienation, sale, disposal, or assignment without the approval of the Secretary of the Interior.

[170] 43 Stat. 1008, 1011. See fn. 169, *supra*.

[171] 45 Stat. 1478. Supplementing Act of June 28, 1906, 34 Stat. 539, 545. Amending Act of March 3, 1921, 41 Stat. 1249; Act of February 27, 1925, 43 Stat. 1008, 1010, 1011. Amended by Act of June 24, 1938, sec. 3, 52 Stat. 1034. Supplemented by Act of January 31, 1931, 46 Stat. 1047. Discussed in 38 Op. A. G. 577 (1937) and 56 I. D. 48 (1937). Also cited in Op. Sol. I. D., M.25258, June 26, 1929; Op. Sol. I. D., M.27788, August 6, 1934; Op. Sol. I. D., M.27963, January 26, 1937; 53 I. D. 169 (1930); 54 I. D. 105 (1932); 55 I. D. 456 (1936); *Adams* v. *Osage Tribe of Indians*, 59 F. 2d 653 (C. C. A. 10, 1932), aff'g 50 F. 2d 918 (D. C. N. D. Okla., 1931), cert. den. 287 U. S. 652; *Choteau* v. *Burnet*, 283 U. S. 691 (1931); *Choteau* v. *Comm'r of Int. Rev.*, 38 F. 2d 976 (C. C. A. 10, 1930), aff'd sub. nom. *Choteau* v. *Burnet*, 283 U. S. 691 (1931), cert. den. 281 U. S. 714, 281 U. S. 759; *Continental Oil Co.* v. *Osage Oil & Refining Co.*, 69 F. 2d 19 (C. C. A. 10, 1934), cert. den. 287 U. S. 616; *Globe Indemnity Co.* v. *Bruce*, 81 F. 2d 143 (C. C. A. 10, 1935), cert. den. 297 U. S. 716; *In re Dennison*, 38 F. 2d 662 (D. C. W. D. Okla., 1930), app. dism., 45 F. 2d 585; *Silurian Oil Co.* v. *Essley*, 54 F. 2d 43 (C. C. A. 10, 1931); *Stuart* v. *Tapp*, 81 F. 2d 155 (C. C. A. 10, 1935); *Tapp* v. *Stuart*, 6 F. Supp. 577 (D. C. N. D. Okla., 1934); *Taylor* v. *Tayrien*, 51 F. 2d 884 (C. C. A. 10, 1931), cert. den. 284 U. S. 672 (1931);

of Indians, the members thereof, or their heirs and assigns, were continued subject to such trust and supervision until January 1, 1959, unless otherwise provided by act of Congress. This act also provided that homestead allotments of Osage Indians not having a certificate of competency shall remain exempt from taxation while the title remains in the original allottee of one-half or more of Osage Indian blood and in his unallotted heirs or devisees of one-half or more of Osage Indian blood until January 1, 1959, with the proviso that the tax-exempt land of any such Indian allottee, heir, or devisee shall not at any time exceed 160 acres.

Section 5 of this Act provides:

> The restrictions concerning lands and funds of allotted Osage Indians, as provided in this Act and all prior Acts now in force, shall apply to unallotted Osage Indians born since July 1, 1907, or after the passage of this Act, and to their heirs of Osage Indian blood, except that the provisions of section 6 of the Act of Congress approved February 27, 1925, with reference to the validity of contracts for debt, shall not apply to any allotted or unallotted Osage Indian of less than one-half degree Indian blood: *Provided*, That the Osage lands and funds and other property which has heretofore or which may hereafter be held in trust or under supervision of the United States for such Osage Indians of less than one-half degree Indian blood not having a certificate of competency shall not be subject to forced sale to satisfy any debt or obligation contracted or incurred prior to the issuance of a certificate of competency: *Provided further*, That the Secretary of the Interior is hereby authorized in his discretion to grant a certificate of competency to any unallotted Osage Indian when in the judgment of the said Secretary such member is fully competent and capable of transacting his or her own affairs.

The Act of June 24, 1938,[172] continued the restrictions on the lands, moneys, and other properties now or hereafter held in trust or under the supervision of the United States for Osage Indians, until January 1, 1984, unless otherwise provided by act of Congress. This act also continued the tax exemption on homestead allotments of Osage Indians not having a certificate of competency, while the title remains in the original allottee of one-half or more of Osage Indian blood or in his unallotted heirs or devisees of one-half or more Osage Indian blood, until January 1, 1984.

No general exemption of Osage Indians as such from the payment of taxes can be implied from these statutes. On the contrary, the plan has been to teach the Indians, by partial taxation, to assume the responsibilities of citizenship.[172a]

B. HEADRIGHTS AND COMPETENCY

Section 4 of the Act of June 28, 1906 provides, in part:

> That all funds belonging to the Osage tribe, and all moneys due, and all moneys that may become due, or may hereafter be found to be due the said Osage tribe of Indians, shall be held in trust by the United States for the period of twenty-five years from and after the first day of January, nineteen hundred and seven, except as herein provided:

> FIRST. That all the funds of the Osage tribe of Indians, and all the moneys now due or that may hereafter be found to be due to the said Osage tribe of Indians, and all moneys that may be received from the sale of their lands in Kansas under existing laws, and all moneys found to be due to said Osage tribe of Indians on claims against the United States, after all proper expenses are paid, shall be segregated as soon after January first, nineteen hundred and seven, as is practicable and placed to the credit of the individual members of the said Osage tribe on a basis of a pro rata division among the members of said tribe, as shown by the authorized roll of membership as herein provided for, or to their heirs as hereinafter provided, said credit to draw interest as now authorized by law; and the interest that may accrue thereon shall be paid quarterly to the members entitled thereto, except in the case of minors, in which case the interest shall be paid quarterly to the parents until said minor arrives at the age of twenty-one years: *Provided*, That if the Commissioner of Indian Affairs becomes satisfied that the said interest of any minor is being misused or squandered he may withhold the payment of such interest: *And provided further*, That said interest of minors whose parents are deceased shall be paid to their legal guardians, as above provided.

> SECOND. That the royalty received from oil, gas, coal, and other mineral leases upon the lands for which selection and division are herein provided, and all moneys received from the sale of town lots, together with the buildings thereon, and all moneys received from the sale of the three reservations of one hundred and sixty acres each heretofore reserved for dwelling purposes, and all moneys received from grazing lands, shall be placed in the Treasury of the United States to the credit of the members of the Osage Tribe of Indians as other moneys of said tribe are to be deposited under the provisions of this Act, and the same shall be distributed to the individual members of said Osage tribe according to the roll provided for herein, in the manner and at the same time that payments are made of interest on other moneys held in trust for the Osages by the United States, except as herein provided.

Under the provisions of the foregoing act, the pro rata share of each Indian allottee aggregating $3,819.76 was placed to his credit in the Treasury of the United States. The royalty received from oil, gas, coal, and other minerals, together with the interest on the pro rata shares were disbursed to the Indians quarterly as they accrued.[173]

Section 5 of the Act of 1906 provides:

> That at the expiration of the period of twenty-five years from and after the first day of January, nineteen

United States v. *Board of Comm'rs*, 26 F. Supp. 270 (D. C. N. D. Okla., 1939); *United States* v. *Johnson*, 87 F. 2d 155 (C. C. A. 10, 1936); *United States* v. *La Motte*, 67 F. 2d 788 (C. C. A. 10, 1933); *United States* v. *Sands*, 94 F. 2d 156 (C. C. A. 10, 1938); *Utilities Production Corp.* v. *Carter Oil Co.*, 2 F. Supp. 81 (D. C. N. D. Okla., 1933); *Williams* v. *Clinton*, 83 F. 2d 148 (C. C. A. 10, 1936).

[172] 52 Stat. 1034, 1036.

[172a] See *Choteau* v. *Burnet*, 283 U. S. 691 (1931). Section 510 of title 25 of the U. S. Code (Act of August 25, 1937, 50 Stat. 806) provides:

> Whenever restricted Indian lands in the State of Oklahoma are subject to gross production tax on minerals, including oil and gas, the Secretary of the Interior, in his discretion, may cause such tax or taxes due the State of Oklahoma to be paid in the manner provided for by the statutes of the State of Oklahoma.

[173] See Hearings, H. Comm. on Ind. Aff., H. R. 6234, 74th Cong., 1st sess., 1935, p. 115, and Act of June 24, 1938, 52 Stat. 1034, 1037. The District Court, in *In re Dennison*, 38 F. 2d 662 (D. C. W. D. Okla., 1930), app. dism. 45 F. 2d 585, defined a headright;

> What is an Osage "head-right?" This is thoroughly defined by the Act of 1906, and is nothing more than the interest that a member of the tribe has in the Osage tribal trust estate, and the trust consists of the oil, gas, and mineral rights, and the funds which were placed to the credit of the Osage tribe, all fully set out in the above act. (P. 664.)

Another court has defined a headright as follows: "The right to receive the trust funds and the mineral interests at the end of the trust period, and during that period to participate in the distribution of the bonuses and royalties arising from the mineral estates and the interest on the trust funds, is an Osage headright." *Globe Indemnity Co.* v. *Bruce*, 81 F. 2d 143, 148–149 (C. C. A. 10, 1935). The tribal income derived from oil and gas sources up to June 1939 aggregated $267,606,990.93, which entire sum, less the amounts authorized by Congress to be expended for the expenses of the Osage Agency, were distributed under various acts of Congress, to which reference will hereinafter be made, to the Indians per capita, the shares of deceased Indians being paid to their heirs or devisees. Also see *In re Irwin*, 60 F. 2d 495 (C. C. A. 10, 1932). Headrights are not transferable and do not pass to a trustee in bankruptcy. *Taylor* v. *Tayrien*, 51 F. 2d 884 (C. C. A. 10, 1931), cert. den. 284 U. S. 672 (1931); *Taylor* v. *Jones*, 51 F. 2d. 892 (C. C. A. 10, 1931), cert. den. 284 U. S. 663 (1931).

> hundred and seven, the lands, mineral interests, and moneys, herein provided for and held in trust by the United States shall be the absolute property of the individual members of the Osage tribe, according to the roll herein provided for, or their heirs, as herein provided, and deeds to said lands shall be issued to said members, or to their heirs, as herein provided, and said moneys shall be distributed to said members, or to their heirs, as herein provided, and said members shall have full control of said lands, moneys, and mineral interest, except as hereinbefore provided.

Section 6 provides that the lands, moneys, and mineral interests, provided for in the act, of any deceased member of the Osage tribe shall descend to his or her legal heirs, according to the laws of the Territory of Oklahoma, or of the State in which said reservation may be hereinafter incorporated, except where the decedent leaves no issue, nor husband, nor wife, in which case the lands, moneys, and mineral interests must go to the mother and father equally.

When the Secretary of the Interior is satisfied that an individual Indian is able to manage his own property, the Secretary is permitted to issue to that Indian a certificate of competency.[174] So long as the Indian has not received a certificate of competency, the income derived as his share of the tribal royalty is exempt from the application of federal income tax laws.[175] The exemption, however, does not apply in favor of a white woman who receives income from land inherited from her children, members of the Osage tribe.[176]

Under section 3 of the Act of April 18, 1912,[177] jurisdiction of the property of deceased and of orphan minor, insane, or other incompetent allottees of the Osage tribe was conferred on the county courts of the State of Oklahoma. The act provided that a copy of all papers filed in the county court shall be served on the Superintendent of the Osage Agency at the time of filing, and authorized the superintendent, whenever the interests of the allottee require, to appear in court for the protection of the interests of the allottee. The act further authorized the superintendent or the Secretary of the Interior, to investigate the conduct of executors, administrators, and guardians and to prosecute any remedy, civil or criminal, as the exigencies of the case and the preservation and protection of the allottee or his estate may require.

Section 5 of the Act of April 18, 1912, authorizes the Secretary of the Interior, in his discretion, under rules and regulations to be prescribed by him and upon application therefor, to pay to Osage allottees, including the blind, insane, crippled, aged, or helpless, all or part of the funds in the Treasury of the United States to their individual credit, with the proviso that he shall first be satisfied of the competency of the allottee or that the release of said individual trust funds would be to the manifest best interests and welfare of the allottee, and further, that no trust funds of a minor or of an allottee who is incompetent shall be released and paid over except to a guardian of such person duly appointed by the proper court and after the filing by such guardian and approval by the court of a sufficient bond satisfactorily to administer the funds released.

Section 6 of this act provides that the proceeds of partition sales due minor heirs, including such minor Indian heirs as may not be tribal members and those Indian heirs not having certificates of competency, shall be paid into the Treasury of the United States and placed to the credit of the Indians upon the same condition as attached to segregated shares of the Osage tribal fund, or with the approval of the Secretary of the Interior paid to the duly appointed guardian. The same disposition as provided in the act with reference to the proceeds of inherited lands sold is to be made of the money in the Treasury of the United States to the credit of deceased Osage allottees.

Section 7 of the act protected the funds of Osage Indians against any claim arising prior to the grant of a certificate of competency. It provided further that no lands or moneys inherited from Osage allottees shall be subject to or taken or sold to secure the payment of any indebtedness incurred by such heir prior to the time such lands and moneys are turned over to such heirs.

Section 8 authorized the disposition by will of all of the estate of an Osage Indian, including trust funds, with the provision that no such will should be admitted to probate or have any validity unless approved before or after the death of the testator by the Secretary of the Interior.

As stated by the United States Supreme Court in *Work* v. *Lynn*,[178] it was believed when the 1906 Act was passed:

> * * * that the income to be paid quarterly would not be in excess of the current needs of the members. For about ten years that proved to be true. Thereafter increased production of oil and gas under the leases that were given resulted in royalties which swelled the income to a point where the quarterly payments were greatly in excess of current needs and were leading to gross extravagance and waste. Administrative measures restricting the payments were adopted, but their validity was questioned (see *Work* v. *Mosier*, 261 U. S. 352) and the matter was called to the attention of Congress by the Secretary of the Interior. (P. 167.)

Because of the conditions outlined above, Congress in section 4 of the Act of March 3, 1921,[179] amended the Act of June 28, 1906, as follows:

> That from and after the passage of this Act the Secretary of the Interior shall cause to be paid at the end of each fiscal quarter to each adult member of the Osage Tribe having a certificate of competency his or her pro rata share, either as a member of the tribe or heir of a deceased member, of the interest on trust funds, the bonus received from the sale of leases, and the royalties received during the previous fiscal quarter, and so long as the income is sufficient to pay to the adult members of said tribe not having a certificate of competency $1,000 quarterly except where incompetent adult members have legal guardians, in which case the income of such incompetents shall be paid to their legal guardians, and to pay for maintenance and education to the parents or natural guardians or legal guardians actually having minor members under twenty-one years of age personally in charge $500 quarterly out of the income of said minors all of said quarterly payments to legal guardians and adults, not having certificates of competency to be paid under the supervision of the Superintendent of the Osage Agency, and to invest the remainder after paying all the taxes of such members either in United States bonds or in Oklahoma State, county, or school bonds, or place the same on time deposits at interest in banks in the State of Oklahoma for the benefit of each individual member under such rules and regulations as the Secretary of the

---

[174] For rules regarding certificates of competency to Osage adults, see 25 C. F. R. 241.5.

[175] *Blackbird* v. *Commissioner of Internal Revenue*, 38 F. 2d 976 (C. C. A. 10, 1930).

[176] *Pettit* v. *Commissioner of Internal Revenue*, 38 F. 2d 976 (C. C. A. 10, 1930), cert. den. 281 U. S. 759 (1930); aff'd sub nom. *Choteau* v. *Burnet*, 283 U. S. 691 (1931).

[177] 37 Stat. 86, amending Act of June 28, 1906, 34 Stat. 539; see fn. 168 *supra*. In *Work* v. *United States ex rel. Mosier*, 261 U. S. 352 (1923), the Supreme Court said:

> * * * Until he has had a full opportunity to exercise this discretion, neither he [Assistant Secretary] nor the Secretary can be compelled by mandamus to make the payment, and if in its exercise, he does not act capriciously, arbitrarily or beyond the scope of his authority, the writ will not issue at all. (P. 362.)

[178] 266 U. S. 161 (1924).

[179] 41 Stat. 1249. See fn. 165, *supra*.

Interior may prescribe: *Provided*, That at the beginning of each fiscal year there shall first be reserved and set aside out of the Osage tribal funds available for that purpose a sufficient amount of money for the expenditures authorized by Congress out of the Osage funds for that fiscal year: *Provided further*, That all just existing individual obligations of adults not having certificates of competency outstanding upon the passage of this Act, when approved by the Superintendent of the Osage Agency, shall be paid out of the money of such individual as the same may be placed to his credit in addition to the quarterly allowance provided for herein.

Prior to the decision of the United States Supreme Court in *Work* v. *Lynn* the foregoing provision was administratively interpreted as requiring payment to the legal guardians of adult restricted Osage Indians of the entire income of such Indians. As a result of the decision in the *Lynn* case, Congress in the Act of February 27, 1925,[180] provided for the return by legal guardians to the Secretary of the Interior of all moneys in their possession or control, theretofore paid them in excess of $4,000 per annum for adults and $2,000 for minors under the Act of March 3, 1921. The act also provided for delivery by the guardians to the Secretary of the Interior of all property, bonds, securities, and stock purchased, or investments made by such guardians out of the moneys paid them, to be held by the Secretary of the Interior or disposed of by him, as he shall deem to be for the best interests of the members to whom the same belongs. The act further provided that all funds other than as above mentioned, and other property theretofore or thereafter received by a guardian of a member of the Osage tribe of Indians, which was theretofore under the supervision and control of the Secretary of the Interior or the title to which was held in trust for such Indians by the United States, shall not thereby become divested of the supervision and control of the Secretary of the Interior or the United States be relieved of its trust; and that the guardians should not dispose of or otherwise encumber such fund or property without the approval of the Secretary of the Interior, and in accordance with the orders of the county court of Osage County, Oklahoma. The act also provided that in case of the death, resignation, or removal from office of such a guardian, the funds and property in his possession subject to supervision and control of the Secretary of the Interior or to which the United States held the title in trust should be immediately delivered to the Superintendent of the Osage Agency, to be held by him and supervised and invested as provided by the terms of the act.

Congress also modified the payments to be made in behalf of enrolled or unenrolled minor members above 18 years of age so as to permit the parents or legal guardians of such minors to receive $1,000 quarterly. The provision with regard to the payment under the 1925 act reads as follows:

> That the Secretary of the Interior shall cause to be paid at the end of each fiscal quarter to each adult member of the Osage Tribe of Indians in Oklahoma having a certificate of competency his or her pro rata share, either as a member of the tribe or heir or devisee of a deceased member, of the interest on trust funds, the bonus received from the sale of oil or gas leases, the royalties therefrom, and any other moneys due such Indian received during each fiscal quarter, including all moneys received prior to the passage of this Act and remaining unpaid; and so long as the accumulated income is sufficient the Secretary of the Interior shall cause to be paid to the adult members of said tribe not having a certificate of competency $1,000 quarterly, except where such adult members have legal guardians, in which case the amounts provided for herein may be paid to the legal guardian or direct to such Indian in the discretion of the Secretary of the Interior the total amounts of such payments, however, shall not exceed $1,000 quarterly except as hereinafter provided; and shall cause to be paid for the maintenance and education, to either one of the parents or legal guardians actually having personally in charge, enrolled or unenrolled, minor member under twenty-one years of age, and above eighteen years of age, $1,000 quarterly out of the income of each said minors, and out of the income of minors under eighteen years of age, $500 quarterly, and so long as the accumulated income of the parent or parents of a minor who has no income or whose income is less than $500 per quarter is sufficient, shall cause to be paid to either of said parents having the care and custody of such minor $500 quarterly, or such proportion thereof as the income of such minor may be less than $500, in addition to the allowances above provided for such parents. Rentals due such adult members from their lands and their minor children's lands and all income from such adults' investments shall be paid to them in addition to the allowance above provided. All payments to legal guardians of Osage Indians shall be expended subject to the joint approval in writing of the court and the superintendent of the Osage Agency. All payments to adults not having certificates of competency, including amounts paid for each minor, shall, in case the Secretary of the Interior finds that such adults are wasting or squandering said income, be subject to the supervisions of the superintendent of the Osage Agency: *Provided*, That if an adult member, not having a certificate of competency so desires, his entire income accumulating in the future from the sources herein specified may be paid to him without supervision, unless the Secretary of the Interior shall find, after notice and hearing, that such member is wasting or squandering his income, in which event the Secretary of the Interior shall pay to such member only the amounts hereinbefore specified to be paid to adult members not having certificates of competency. The Secretary of the Interior shall invest the remainder, after paying the taxes of such members, in United States bonds, Oklahoma State bonds, real estate, first-mortgage real-estate loans not to exceed 50 per centum of the appraised value of such real estate, and where the member is a resident of Oklahoma such investment shall be in loans on Oklahoma real estate, stock in Oklahoma building and loan associations, livestock, or deposit the same in banks in Oklahoma, or expend the same for the benefit of such member, such expenditures, investments, and deposits to be made under such restrictions, rules, and regulations as he may prescribe: *Provided*, That the Secretary of the Interior shall not make any investment for an adult member without first securing the approval of such member of such investment. * * * (Pp. 1008–1009.)

Under the same section Congress provided that no guardian shall be appointed, except on the written application or approval of the Secretary of the Interior, for the estate of a member of the Osage tribe of Indians who does not have a certificate of competency or who is of one-half or more Indian blood.

Section 3 of this act provides in part:

> Property of Osage Indians not having certificates of competency purchased as hereinbefore set forth shall not be subject to the lien of any debt, claim, or judgment except taxes, or be subject to alienation, without the approval of the Secretary of the Interior.

Section 4 of the Act of February 27, 1925,[181] newly vested in the Secretary of the Interior power to revoke certificates of competency issued to an Osage Indian of more than one-half Indian blood, whom he finds, after notice and hearing, to be squandering or misusing his funds.[182]

---

[180] 43 Stat. 1008. See fn. 169, *supra*.

[181] 43 Stat. 1008. See fn. 169 *supra*. On the general subject of revocation of certificate of competency of Osage Indian, see 53 I. D. 169 (1930).

[182] Even if an Osage Indian were manifestly incompetent, and his business interests would be safeguarded thereby, his certificate could not be revoked unless he squandered or misused his income. On limitation on the amount of credit which may be granted on Osage Indian, see Act of March 3, 1901, 31 Stat. 1058, 1065–1066.

In section 6 of the act it was provided:

> No contract for debt hereafter made with a member of the Osage Tribe of Indians not having a certificate of competency, shall have any validity, unless approved by the Secretary of the Interior. * * *

In section 1 of the Act of March 2, 1929,[133] Congress provides:

> The lands, moneys, and other properties now or hereafter held in trust or under the supervision of the United States for the Osage Tribe of Indians, the members thereof, or their heirs and assigns, shall continue subject to such trust and supervision until January 1, 1959, unless otherwise provided by Act of Congress.

Section 3 of this act provides:

> That section 1 of the Act of Congress of February 27, 1925 (Forty-third Statutes at Large, page 1008), is hereby amended by adding thereto the following:
>
> "The Secretary of the Interior be, and is hereby, authorized, in his discretion, under such rules and regulations as he may prescribe, upon application of any member of the Osage Tribe of Indians not having a certificate of competency, to pay all or any part of the funds held in trust for such Indians: *Provided*, That the Secretary of the Interior shall, within one year after this Act is approved, pay to each enrolled Indian of less than half Osage blood, one-fifth part of his or her proportionate share of accumulated funds. And such Secretary shall on or before the expiration of ten years from the date of the approval of this Act, advance and pay over to such Osage Indians of less than one-half Osage Indian blood, all of the balance appearing to his credit of accumulated funds, and shall issue to such Indian a certificate of competency: *And provided further*, That nothing herein contained shall be construed to interfere in any way with the removal by the Secretary of the Interior of restrictions from and against any Osage Indian at any time."

Section 4 of this act provides:

> That section 2 of the Act of Congress approved February 27, 1925 (Forty-third Statutes at Large, page 1011), being an Act to amend the Act of Congress of March 3, 1921 (Forty-first Statutes at Large, page 1249), be, and the same is hereby, amended to read as follows:
>
> "Upon the death of an Osage Indian of one-half or more Indian blood who does not have a certificate of competency, his or her moneys and funds and other property accrued and accruing to his or her credit and which have heretofore been subject to supervision as provided by law may be paid to the administrator or executor of the estate of such deceased Indian or direct to his heirs or devisees, or may be retained by the Secretary of the Interior in the discretion of the Secretary of the Interior, under regulations to be promulgated by him: *Provided*, That the Secretary of the Interior shall pay to administrators and executors of the estates of such deceased Osage Indians a sufficient amount of money out of such estates to pay all lawful indebtedness and costs and expenses of administration when approved by him; and, out of the shares belonging to heirs or devisees, above referred to, he shall pay the costs and expenses of such heirs or devisees, including attorney fees, when approved by him, in the determination of heirs or contests of wills. Upon the death of any Osage Indian of less than one-half of Osage Indian blood or upon the death of an Osage Indian who has a certificate of competency, his moneys and funds and other property accrued and accruing to his credit shall be paid and delivered to the administrator or executor of his estate to be administered upon according to the laws of the State of Oklahoma: *Provided*, That upon the settlement of such estate any funds or property subject to the control or supervision of the Secretary of the Interior on the date of the approval of this Act, which have been inherited by or devised to any adult or minor heir or devisee of one-half or more Osage Indian blood who does not have a certificate of competency, and which have been paid or delivered by the Secretary of the Interior to the administrator or executor shall be paid or delivered by such administrator or executor to the Secretary of the Interior for the benefit of such Indian and shall be subject to the supervision of the Secretary as provided by law."

Under section 5 of the act, the restrictions concerning lands and funds of allotted Osage Indians, as provided in that act and all prior acts then in force, shall apply to unallotted Osage Indians born since July 1, 1907, or thereafter, and to their heirs of Osage Indian blood, except that the provision of section 6 of the Act of February 27, 1925, with reference to the validity of contracts for debt, shall not apply to any allotted or unallotted Osage Indian of less than one-half degree Indian blood, and subject to the further proviso that the Osage lands and funds and any other property which had theretofore or which may thereafter be held in trust or under supervision of the United States for Osage Indians of less than one-half degree Indian blood not having a certificate of competency shall not be subject to forced sale to satisfy any debt or obligation contracted or incurred prior to the issuance of a certificate of competency, and with the further provision that the Secretary of the Interior was authorized in his discretion to grant a certificate of competency to any unallotted Osage Indian when in the judgment of the said Secretary such member is fully competent and capable of transacting his or her own affairs.

The Act of June 24, 1938,[134] further modified Osage payments as follows:

> That hereafter the Secretary of the Interior shall cause to be paid to each adult member of the Osage Tribe of Indians not having a certificate of competency his or her pro rata share, either as a member of the tribe or heir or devisee of a deceased member, of the interest on trust funds, the bonus received from the sale of oil or gas leases, and the royalties therefrom received during each fiscal quarter, not to exceed $1,000 per quarter; and if such adult member has a legal guardian, his current income not to exceed $1,000 per quarter may be paid to such legal guardian in the discretion of the Secretary of the Interior: *Provided*, That when an adult restricted Indian has surplus funds in excess of $10,000 there shall be paid such Indian sufficient funds from his accumulated surplus in addition to his current income to aggregate $1,000 quarterly; but in the event of any adult restricted Indian has surplus funds of less than $10,000, such Indian shall receive quarterly only his current income not to exceed $1,000 per quarter: *Provided further*, That the Secretary of the Interior is hereby authorized to and may in his discretion pay out of any money heretofore accrued or hereafter accruing to the credit of any person of Osage Indian blood who does not have a certificate of competency or who is one-half or more Osage Indian blood, all of said person's taxes of every kind and character, for which said person is now or hereafter may be liable, before paying to or for such person any funds as required by law: *And provided further*, That upon application and consent of any restricted Osage Indian the Secretary of the Interior may cause payment to be made of additional funds from the accumulated surplus to the credit of any Osage Indian under such rules and regulations as he may prescribe. Rentals due such adult members from their lands and their minor children's lands and all income from such adults' investments, including interest on deposits to their credit, shall be paid to them in addition to the current allowances above provided.
>
> Whenever minor members of the Osage Tribe of Indians have funds or property subject to the control or supervision of the Secretary of the Interior, the said Secretary may in his discretion pay or cause to be paid to the parents, legal guardian, or any person, school, or institution having actual custody of such minors,

[133] 45 Stat. 1478. See fn. 171 *supra*.

[134] 52 Stat. 1034. See fn. 172, *supra*.

> such amounts out of the income or funds of the said minors as he deems necessary, and when such a minor is eighteen years of age or over, the Secretary of the Interior may in his discretion cause disbursement of funds for support and maintenance or other specific purposes to be made direct to such minor. (Pp. 1034–1035.)

C. INHERITANCE

Exclusive jurisdiction of the probate of wills and the determination of heirs of the Osages is vested in the state courts.[185]

If an Osage dies testate, the Secretary of the Interior is authorized to approve or disapprove the will prior to institution of probate proceedings in the local court.[186] In the event that the will is disapproved, it may not be offered for probate, but if the will is approved, the state court is not bound by the Secretary's determination as to validity and it may permit the issue to be relitigated before it.

The power of an Osage Indian to make a will has been discussed by the Solicitor for the Department of the Interior:[187]

> There is no provision in the act of 1906, authorizing an Osage Indian to make a will. That authority is contained in Section 8 of the act of April 18, 1912 (37 Stat. 86, 88), entitled "An Act supplementary to and amendatory of the act" of June 28, 1906, which section provides:
>
> > "That any *adult* member of the Osage Tribe of Indians not mentally incompetent may dispose of any or all of his estate, real, personal, or mixed, including trust funds, from which restrictions as to alienation have not been removed, by will, in accordance with the laws of the State of Oklahoma: *Provided*, That no such will shall be admitted to probate or have any validity unless approved before or after the death of the testator by the Secretary of the Interior."
>
> The act in section 3 thereof, subjects the property of deceased and incompetent Osage allottees in probate matters to the jurisdiction of the County Courts of the State of Oklahoma. The land of such persons, however, cannot be sold or alienated and no will can be admitted to probate without the prior approval of the Secretary of the Interior. The word "minor" or "minors" is used throughout the act of 1912, in connection with provisions similar to those found in the act of 1906. The clear indications are that the word as used in the later act means the same thing that it was declared to mean in the former act, that is, a person under 21 years of age. As stated the word "adult" in the act of 1906, as applied to both males and females refers to a person 21 years of age or over. In view of the fact that the act of 1912 is "supplemental to and amendatory of the act" of 1906, section 8 thereof which authorizes any "adult" member of the Osage tribe of Indians to dispose of his property by will must be read into the act of 1906. The section thus becomes a part of and must be construed in connection with said act of 1906. In this view there is no escape from the conclusion that the word "adult" in said section 8 means a person 21 years of age or over. It was the exclusive right of Congress to determine at what age an Osage Indian becomes capable of making a will. It declared that age to be 21 or majority. A law of Oklahoma declaring a person to be competent to make a will at 18 years of age is directly in conflict with the Federal statute and the latter is controlling. *Truskett* v. *Closser* (198 Fed. 835; 236 U. S. 223); *Priddy* v. *Thompson* (204 Fed. 955); *Letts* v. *Letts* (176 Pac. 234). It follows that testatrix not having reached the age of 21 years was for that reason incapable of making a valid will.

D. LEASING

1. *Tribal oil and gas and mineral leases.*—The greater part of the income from leases of the Osage Indians is derived from oil and gas lands. During the fiscal year 1924 the oil rights to 70,737 acres in the Osage Reservation were sold by means of bids for $17,530,800.[188] In the introduction to the discussion of the Osages, it has been shown that the title to the oil and gas in the Osage Reservation is held for the benefit of the tribe even though the surface has been allotted in severalty to individuals.

Section 3 of the Osage Allotment Act of June 28, 1906,[189] directed that the oil, gas, coal, or other minerals covered by the allotted lands should be reserved to the Osage tribe for 25 years from and after April 8, 1906, and provided that mineral leases for such lands might be made by the tribal council with the approval of the Secretary of the Interior under such rules and regulations as he might prescribe.[190] Under the seventh paragraph of section 2 it was provided that oil, gas, and other minerals should become the property of the owner of the land at the expiration of 25 years, unless otherwise provided by Congress.

Section 3 of the 1906 act was amended by the Act of March 3, 1921,[191] so as to extend the reservation of minerals to the tribe to April 7, 1946. All valid existing oil and gas leases on April 7, 1931, were renewed upon the same terms, and extended, until April 8, 1946, and so long thereafter as oil or gas was found in paying quantities. The 1921 act also directed the Secretary of the Interior and the Osage Council "to offer for lease for oil and gas purposes all of the remaining portions of the unleased Osage land prior to April 8, 1931, offering the same annually at a rate of not less than one-tenth of the unleased area."

This provision was again amended by the Act of March 2, 1929,[192] which extended the period of reservation to the Osage tribe of the minerals covered by such lands until April 8, 1958, unless otherwise provided by act of Congress. The 1929 act also amended the provision requiring the leasing of lands by the Secretary of the Interior and the Osage Council by providing:[193]

> * * * That not less than twenty-five thousand acres shall be offered for lease for oil and gas mining purposes during any one year: *Provided further*, That as to all lands hereafter leased, the regulations governing same and the leases issued thereon shall contain appropriate provisions for the conservation of the natural gas for its economic use, to the end that the highest percentage of ultimate recovery of both oil and gas may be secured: *Provided, however*, That nothing herein contained shall be construed as affecting any valid existing lease for oil or gas or other minerals, but all such leases shall continue as long as gas, oil, or other minerals are found in paying quantities.

Section 3 of the Act of June 24, 1938,[194] amended the 1929 act to provide that the minerals covered by such reserved lands shall be reserved:

> * * * until the 8th day of April, 1983, unless otherwise provided by Act of Congress, and all royalties and bonuses arising therefrom shall belong to the Osage Tribe of Indians, and shall be disbursed to members of the Osage Tribe or their heirs or assigns as now provided by law, after reserving such amounts as are now or may hereafter be authorized by Congress for specific purposes.
>
> The lands, moneys, and other properties now or hereafter held in trust or under the supervision of the United States for the Osage Tribe of Indians, the members

[185] Act of April 18, 1912, sec. 3, 37 Stat. 86. See fn. 163, *supra*. Also see subsection A, *supra*.

[186] *Ibid.*, sec. 8, 37 Stat. 86, 88.

[187] Op. Sol. I. D., D.47112, April 16, 1920.

[188] Schmeckebier, The Office of Indian Affairs, Its History, Activities and Organization (1927), p. 183.

[189] 34 Stat. 539, fn. 156, *supra*.

[190] See *Work* v. *United States ex rel. Mosier*, 261 U. S. 352 (1923).

[191] 41 Stat. 1249, fn. 165 *supra*.

[192] Sec. 1, 45 Stat. 1478. See fn. 171, *supra*.

[193] *Ibid.*, 1479.

[194] 52 Stat. 1034, 1035. For regulations regarding the leasing of Osage Reservation lands for oil and gas mining, see 25 C. F. R. 180.1–180.94. For regulations regarding the leasing of such lands for mining except oil and gas, see *ibid.* 204.1–204.30.

thereof, or their heirs and assigns, shall continue subject to such trusts and supervision until January 1, 1984, unless otherwise provided by Act of Congress.

2. *Agricultural leases of restricted lands.*—Section 7 of the Osage Allotment Agreement of June 28, 1906,[195] authorizes the allottees of the Osage tribe and their heirs to lease their lands for farming, grazing, or other purposes, but requires all leases for the benefit of the individual allottees of the tribe or their heirs to be approved by the Secretary of the Interior before becoming effective.[196]

[195] 34 Stat. 539.

[196] It was held under this section and sec. 12 that the Secretary of the Interior had authority to adopt rules and regulations for the leasing of such lands and all such leases, unless approved by the Secretary of the Interior, were void. See *La Motte* v. *United States*, 254 U. S. 570 (1921). For regulations regarding such leases, see 25 C. F. R. 177.1–177.18.

SECTION 13. THE OKLAHOMA INDIAN WELFARE ACT[197]

The Wheeler-Howard bill as originally introduced applied to the State of Oklahoma.[198] The bill was amended at the suggestion of Senator Thomas of Oklahoma, chairman of the Senate Indian Affairs Committee, so as to make inapplicable to the tribes in Oklahoma[199] those sections which extended existing trust periods, limited alienation of restricted land, authorized the establishment of new reservations, and authorized tribal organization.

Two years later these provisions of the Wheeler-Howard Act were extended to Oklahoma, with some modifications to fit the peculiarities of the local legal situation. Under the Thomas-Rogers Oklahoma Indian Welfare Act, the Indians of Oklahoma became eligible to share in the program of self-government, corporate organization, credit and land purchase. This act also provided for the organization of Indians into voluntary cooperative associations for the purposes of credit administration, production, marketing, consumers' protection or land management, and authorized an appropriation of $2,000,000 for loans to such associations and to individual Indians of the state.[200]

Under this act a considerable number of the Oklahoma tribes have adopted tribal constitutions and obtained corporate charters.[201]

These constitutions and charters differ in several respects from those adopted by tribes of other states.[202] For one thing, the substantive powers of the tribe are set forth in the charters, rather than in constitutions. The constitutions are restricted to such topics as membership and tribal organization. Another important characteristic of the Oklahoma tribal constitutions and charters is that none of them contain the broad police and judicial powers found in many other tribal documents. This lack may be ascribed to legislation already discussed,[203] depriving tribal courts in the Indian Territory of all power, and to the practical assumption by the State of Oklahoma of responsibilities which are elsewhere divided between federal and tribal authorities.

[197] Act of June 26, 1936, 49 Stat. 1967, 25 U. S. C. 501, *et seq.* Supplementing Act of June 18, 1934, 48 Stat. 984. Supplemented by Act of August 9, 1937, 50 Stat. 564; Act of May 9, 1938, 52 Stat. 291. Cited: Circular of Commr., No. 3170, July 28, 1936; Memo. Sol. I. D., July 31, 1936; Statement by Commr. on S. 1736, to repeal Wheeler-Howard Act, March 3, 1937; Memo. Sol. I. D., March 4, 1937; Memo. Acting Sol. I. D., July 14, 1937; Memo. Sol. I. D., November 29, 1937; Memo. Sol. I. D., April 22, 1938; Memo. Sol. I. D., May 24, 1938; Letter of Asst. Commr. to Five Civilized Tribes Agency, June 29, 1938; Memo. Sol. I. D., September 13, 1938; Ind. Off. Letter from Supt. Quapaw Agency, October 17, 1938; Memo. Sol. I. D., December 13, 1938; Memo. Sol. I. D., April 3, 1939.

[198] See Hearings, H. Comm. on Ind. Aff., H. R. 6234, 74th Cong., 1st sess., 1935, pp. 11–12.

[199] Hearings, Sen. Comm. on Ind. Aff., S. 2047, 74th Cong., 1st sess., 1935, p. 9.

[200] For regulations regarding this law, see 25 C. F. R. 22.1–23.27 (organization and loans to Indian cooperative associations); 24.1–25.26 (loans to and by Indian credit associations); 26.1–26.26 (loans by United States to individual Indians).

[201] Seneca-Cayuga Tribe of Oklahoma, constitution ratified May 15, 1937, charter ratified June 26, 1937; Wyandotte Tribe of Oklahoma, July, 24, 1937, charter, October 30, 1937; Cheyenne-Arapaho Tribes of Oklahoma, September 18, 1937; Kickapoo Tribe of Oklahoma, September 18, 1937, charter January 18, 1938; Iowa Tribe of Oklahoma, October 23, 1937, charter February 5, 1938; Sac and Fox Tribe of Indians of Oklahoma, December 7, 1937; Pawnee Indians of Oklahoma, January 6, 1938, charter April 28, 1938; Caddo Indian Tribe of Oklahoma, January 17, 1938, charter November 15, 1938; Tonkawa Tribe of Indians of Oklahoma, April 21, 1938; Ottawa Tribe of Oklahoma, November 30, 1938, charter June 2, 1939; Absentee Shawnee Tribe of Indians of Oklahoma, December 5, 1938; Citizen Band of Potawatomi Indians of Oklahoma, December 12, 1938; Thlopthlocco Tribal town, December 27, 1938, charter April 13, 1939; Alabama Quassarte Tribal Town, January 10, 1939, charter May 24, 1939; Miami Tribe of Oklahoma, October 10, 1939, charter June 1, 1940; Peoria Tribe of Indians of Oklahoma, October 10, 1939, charter June 1, 1940; Eastern Shawnee Tribe of Oklahoma, December 22, 1939, charter December 12, 1940.

[202] See Chapter 7, sec. 3.

[203] See sec. 4, *supra*.

REFERENCE TABLES AND INDEX

633058—45——31

EXPLANATION OF REFERENCE TABLES AND INDEX

The various tables that comprise this supplement constitute the first comprehensive attempt to collect and systematize the basic materials of Federal Indian law. These materials include the statutes and treaties of the United States, the decisions of federal courts, including territorial courts, the administrative rulings of the Attorney General and of the Department of the Interior, legal texts and periodicals and congressional and other public documents. An attempt has been made to make these compilations complete with respect to published statutes, treaties (published and unpublished), reported federal cases, published opinions of the Attorney General and published rulings of the Interior Department. Such completeness, however, extends only to the date on which this compilation was begun, April 14, 1939. A few later items of special importance, appearing between this date and the completion of the compilation and handbook on July 1, 1940, have been inserted in the various tables. With respect to unpublished administrative rulings, legal texts and periodicals, and congressional and other public documents, a complete coverage has not been attempted but an effort has been made to include in this compilation the most important materials in the field. The analysis of unpublished memoranda of the Lands Division of the Department of Justice goes back as far as the year 1929, and the search for unpublished decisions and memoranda in the files of the Interior Department was carried back as far as October 31, 1917. The published decisions of the Interior Department go back to July, 1881. Statutes, court decisions, and other official materials have been compiled as far back as the adoption of the Constitution in 1789, except that treaties of the United States preceding the Constitution, and recognized therein, have been included.

A count of the number of items of each category collected and utilized in the preparation of this supplement gives the following approximate figures:

Statutes	4,264
Treaties	389
Reported Cases	1,725
Opinions of the Attorney General, etc.	523
Interior Department Rulings	838
Legal Texts and Articles	629
Tribal Constitutions	141
Tribal Charters	112
Congressional Reports and Miscellaneous	301
Total Number of Items	8,922

This supplement to the Handbook of Federal Indian Law is composed of seven parts: (*1*) the tribal index of materials on Indian law, (*2*) the annotated table of statutes and treaties, (*3*) the table of federal cases, (*4*) the table of Interior Department rulings, (*5*) the table of Attorney General's opinions, (*6*) the bibliography, and (*7*) the index. A few words concerning each of these parts may be of assistance to those who make use of this supplement.

Tribal Index of Materials on Indian Law.—The tribal index attempts to show, for each tribe, the special statutes, treaties, decisions and other legal materials that concern that tribe.

The importance of a tribe-by-tribe index of materials on Indian law arises from the fact that during the greater part of our national existence we have dealt with Indian tribes through treaty or agreement, through special legislation, and, most recently, through tribal constitutions approved by the Federal Government and federal charters approved by the Indian tribes. Thus there has developed, for each tribe and reservation, a special body of law which supplements or modifies general legislation on Indian affairs. Thus any general analysis of problems of federal Indian law, such as is attempted in the Handbook itself, necessarily contains an element of incompleteness. To help in the filling of that gap this guide to special legal materials affecting each tribe and reservation has been prepared.

An attempt has been made to reflect faithfully legislative and administrative usage in the designation of Indian groups covered by federal legislation. In many instances the groups thus designated are not "tribes" in the anthropological sense, but portions or groupings of such "tribes." Political existence rather than racial unity has been the chief criterion of group existence in the history of Indian treaties and Indian legislation. This index is primarily a roster of such political entities. Where ethnological designations vary from political usage, such ethnological designations have been noted parenthetically following the primary listing.

Since a single tribe is frequently referred to in several different groupings, cross-references have been included to show other designations for a given tribe and to show the designations of other groups that include the tribe in question or are included therein.

Annotated Table of Statutes and Treaties.—In the statutory index an effort has been made to annotate each act of Congress, treaty, and joint or concurrent resolution with pertinent legal materials, statutory and non-statutory. The effect of this statutory index is to show for each provision of federal law relating to Indians, the legal background against which the law was enacted and the functioning of the law since its enactment.

The annotations include under each statutory item the following materials: (*1*) Reference to earlier and later statutes and treaties, which supplement, amend, or repeal, or are supplemented, amended, or repealed by, the annotated item; (*2*) Reference to federal cases in which the statutory item is cited; (*3*) Similar references to Attorney General's opinions in which the statutory item is cited; (*4*) Parallel citations to Revised Statutes; (*5*) Parallel citations to the United States Code; (*6*) Historical annotations taken from the United States Code Annotated; (*7*) Published and unpublished decisions and memoranda of the Interior Department; (*8*) Unpublished memoranda of the Lands Division of the Department of Justice; (*9*) Legal texts; (*10*) Legal periodicals; (*11*) Congressional and other government documents.

Table of Federal Cases.—The table of federal cases on Indian law covers reported cases in the federal (including the territorial) courts during the period from 1790 to 1939 in which issues of federal Indian law are considered. In this table the various cases are annotated for appeals, overrulings, and related decisions.

Table of Interior Department Rulings.—The table of Interior Department rulings on Indian matters from 1881 to 1939, contains volume and page reference to published rulings and file number reference to unpublished materials, together with the date and indication of subject matter for each ruling. Included in this table are a number of rulings of other agencies which are available in Interior Department files.

Table of Attorney General's Opinions.—The table of published Attorney General's Opinions from 1789 to 1939 on matters of Indian law contains volume, page, date and title for each opinion. Unpublished memoranda of the Lands Division of the Department of Justice collected by that Department from 1929 to 1939 are cited in the tribal and statutory indices, but are not listed as a separate table.

Bibliography.—The bibliography is composed of four parts: the major compilations of federal Indian laws, treaties and regulations; important legal literature—periodicals and texts; background materials, including works on Indian policy and administration; and congressional documents (including American Archives, American State Papers, and Journals of the Continental Congress) pertaining to Indian affairs, either cited in the various indices or the Handbook or of prime importance to an understanding of the development of Indian legislation and policy in the United States.

Index.—The index covers the principal topics treated in the Handbook of Federal Indian Law. It may be supplemented by reference to the Analysis of Chapters, at pages XIX to XXIV of the Handbook.

In order to conserve space, references to case materials, statutory materials and other materials cited in this supplement are given in the most concise form possible. These citations, however, may be elaborated by reference to the appropriate table. Thus, a case cited by the first word or phrase, e. g., Adams, 59 F. 2d 653, may be identified in the table of federal cases more fully described as **ADAMS v. OSAGE TRIBE OF INDIANS, 59 F. 2d 653 (C. C. A. 10, 1932), aff'g** 50 F. 2d 918 (D. C. N. D. Okla. 1931), cert. den. 287 U. S. 652. Where the first party named in the title of the case is the United States, the citation includes in addition the first word or phrase identifying the adverse party. Likewise a citation to a legal text, law review article or congressional document can be amplified by a reference to the bibliography. Thus, for example, the citation: "Black, IL" will be found by reference to *Part II, Literature on Indian Law, Section 2, Texts,* to designate a volume of Henry Campbell Black entitled Intoxicating Liquors, published in 1892.

The following abbreviations have been generally used:

A.	Amended
Aff'd	Affirmed
Aff'g	Affirming
Ag.	Amending
App. dism.	Appeal dismissed
Approp. St.	Appropriation Statutes
Archives 1	National Archives, Unpublished Treaty No. 1
C.	Congress
C:1	Congress, First Session
Cert. den.	Certiorari denied
Comm.	Committee
Comm'r.	Commissioner
Compt. Gen'ls Rulings	Comptroller General's Rulings
Const.	Constitution
Den.	Denied
Dism.	Dismissed
Gov. Pub.	Government Publications
H.	House of Representatives
I. D. Regs.	Interior Department Regulations
I. D. Rulings	Interior Department Rulings
L. D.	Land Decisions, Interior Department
L. D. Memo. (D. J.)	Memorandum of Lands Division, Department of Justice
Memo. Sol.	Memorandum, Solicitor, Interior Department
Memo. Sol. Off.	Memorandum, Solicitor's Office Interior Department
Mod.	Modified
Mod'g	Modifying
Op. A. G.	Opinion of the Attorney General
Op. Sol.	Opinion, Solicitor, Interior Department
Per.	Periodicals
Priv. St.	Private Statutes
R.	Repealed
Rev.	Reversed

Rev'g.	Reversing
Rg.	Repealing
Rp.	Repealed in part
Rpg.	Repealing in part
S.	Senate
S.	Supplemented
S. c.	Same case
Sg.	Supplementing
Spec. St.	Special Statutes
St.	Statutes

The publication of this supplement affords a welcome opportunity to acknowledge the contributions of those who have labored in the collection and systematization of the thousands of items comprised in these various tables. The collection and analysis of legal materials was in the hands of attorneys Fred V. Folsom, Jr., Abraham Glasser, Theodore H. Haas, Samuel Miller, Mrs. Mima Pollitt, Miss Bettie Renner, and Miss Doris Williamson, all of the Department of Justice. The collection of subsidiary historical, anthropological, and administrative materials was accomplished by Miss Lucy Kramer and Dr. David Rodnick, ethnologists in the Office of Indian Affairs, Fred A. Baker, Field Agent of the Office of Indian Affairs, and Miss Mary K. Morris, of the Department of Justice. The compiling of the annotated table of statutes was the work of Miss Renner; the index of tribal materials and the table of Interior Department rulings were compiled by Mrs. Pollitt; the table of federal cases was prepared by Samuel Miller; the bibliography is the work of Miss Morris and Miss Kramer; and the index was prepared by Miss Irene R. Shriber, an attorney in the Office of Indian Affairs.

The arduous task of putting all these materials into form for publication was assumed by Mrs. Griselda G. Lobell and Miss Marie J. Turinsky. To John H. Ady, Chief of the Publications Section of the Department of the Interior, went the task of seeing this supplement through the press.

F. S. C.

JULY 1, 1941.

TRIBAL INDEX OF MATERIALS ON INDIAN LAW

ABSENTEE SHAWNEE TRIBE OF INDIANS. See also KANSAS; OKLAHOMA; SHAWNEE. *Const.* Dec. 5, 1938.

ACOMA RESERVATION. See also NEW MEXICO; PUEBLO. *Approp. St.* 44:453. *I. D. Rulings* Memo. Sol. May 12, 1936, May 25, 1936.

AGUA CALIENTE (DIEGUENO). See also CALIFORNIA; MISSION; PALA; PALM SPRINGS. *Approp. St.* 40:561; 41:3; 42:832.

AK CHIN RESERVATION (ACACHIN; PAPAGO). See also ARIZONA; PAPAGO. *Approp. St.* 40:561; 41:1225; 42:552, 1174; 43:390, 1141; 44:453, 934; 45:200, 1562; 46:1115; 47:91, 820; 48:362; 49:176, 1757; 50:564; 52:291.

ALABAMA (ALIBAMA). See also OKLAHOMA; ALABAMA-COUSHATTA TRIBES OF TEXAS; ALABAMA-QUASSARTE TRIBAL TOWN; FIVE CIVILIZED TRIBES. *Spec. St.* 2:527; 45:1186. *Approp. St.* 36:269; 42:437; 45:383. *Treaties* 7:180. *I. D. Rulings* Memo. Sol. Nov. 11, 1937.

ALABAMA-COUSHATTA TRIBES OF TEXAS. See also ALABAMA; TEXAS. *Spec. St.* 45:1186. *Approp. St.* 40:561; 41:1225; 43:390, 1141; 44:453, 934; 45:200, 1562; 46:279; 47:91, 820; 48:362; 49:176, 1757. *I. D. Rulings* Memo. Sol. Nov. 11, 1937. *Const.* August 19, 1938. *Charter* Oct. 17, 1939.

ALABAMA-QUASSARTE TRIBAL TOWN. See also ALABAMA; OKLAHOMA. *Const.* Jan. 10, 1939. *Charter* May 24, 1939.

ALASKA. See also ALEUTS; ANGOON COMMUNITY ASSOCIATION; ANNETTE ISLAND RESERVATION; CRAIG COMMUNITY ASSOCIATION OF CRAIG; ESKIMO; HAIDA; HOONAH INDIAN ASSOCIATION; HYDABURG COOPERATIVE ASSOCIATION; KETCHIKAN INDIAN CORPORATION; KING ISLAND NATIVE COMMUNITY; KLAWOCK COOPERATIVE ASSOCIATION; METLAKAHTLA; NATIVE VILLAGE OF ATKA; NATIVE VILLAGE OF BARROW; NATIVE VILLAGE OF CHANEGA; NATIVE VILLAGE OF DIOMEDE; NATIVE VILLAGE OF ELIM; NATIVE VILLAGE OF FORT YUKON; NATIVE VILLAGE OF GAMBELL; NATIVE VILLAGE OF KARLUK; NATIVE VILLAGE OF KIVALINA; NATIVE VILLAGE OF KWETHLUK; NATIVE VILLAGE OF MEKORYUK; NATIVE VILLAGE OF MINTO; NATIVE VILLAGE OF NIKOLSKI; NATIVE VILLAGE OF NOATAK; NATIVE VILLAGE OF MUNAPITCHUK; NATIVE VILLAGE OF POINT HOPE; NATIVE VILLAGE OF SAXMAN; NATIVE VILLAGE OF SELAWIK; NATIVE VILLAGE OF SHAKTOOLIK; NATIVE VILLAGE OF SHIRSHMAREF; NATIVE VILLAGE OF STEVENS; NATIVE VILLAGE OF TETLIN; NATIVE VILLAGE OF UNALAKLEET; NATIVE VILLAGE OF VENETIE; NATIVE VILLAGE OF WALES; NATIVE VILLAGE OF WHITE MOUNTAIN; NOME ESKIMO COMMUNITY; ORGANIZED VILLAGE OF KASAAN; SITKA COMMUNITY ASSOCIATION; STEBBINS COMMUNITY ASSOCIATION; STIKEEN COMMUNITY ASSOCIATION; THLINGIT; TSIMSHIAN; TYONEK. *Gov. Pub.* 72 Cong., 1 sess., Hearings, S. Comm. Ind. Aff., S. 1196; 74 Cong., 2 sess., Hearings, S. Comm. Ind. Aff., Part 35—Metlakahtla Indians, Alaska, May 19, 1934, July 12, 1936; Part 36—Alaska (Including Reindeer), July 1936. *Spec. St.* 26:46; 30:1253; 31:321; 32:327; 33:616; 34:197, 263; 35:102, 600, 837; 36:326; 37:499; 38:240, 1222; 39:1131; 43:739, 978; 44:629, 1452; 48:984; 52:593, 1169, 1174. *Approp. St.* 23:362, 446; 24:449; 26:336, 989; 27:282, 349, 572, 612; 28:286, 372, 876, 910; 29:267, 321, 413; 30:11, 62, 105, 226, 571, 597, 924, 1074, 1214; 31:588, 1133; 32:245, 419, 552, 982, 1031, 1083; 33:189, 394, 452; 34:325, 697, 1015, 1295; 35:70, 317, 781, 945; 36:269, 703, 1363; 37:417, 518, 912; 38:4, 77, 379, 559, 582, 609, 822; 39:14, 123, 262, 969; 40:2, 105, 634, 821; 41:3, 35, 163, 408, 874, 1015, 1156, 1225, 1367; 42:29, 470, 552, 1110, 1174, 1527; 43:33, 205, 390, 704, 1014, 1141, 1313; 44:161, 330, 453, 841, 934, 1178; 45:2, 64, 200, 883, 1562, 1607, 1623; 46:173, 279, 392, 1064, 1115, 1309, 1552; 47:15, 91, 475, 525, 820, 1371, 1602; 48:362; 49:49, 67, 176, 1309, 1421, 1757; 50:213, 564; 52:291, 1114. *Priv. St.* 44:1746; 46:1857; 49:2063. *Treaties* 8:302, 15:539; 37:1538, 1542. *Cases* Campbell, 221 Fed. 186; Columbia, 161 Fed. 60; Hickman, 119 Fed. 83; In re Carr, 5 Fed. Cas. No. 2432; In re Incorporation, 3 Alaska 588; In re Minook, 2 Alaska 200; Kie, 27 Fed. 351; Jones, 8 Alaska 146; U. S. v. Cadzow, 5 Alaska 125; U. S. v. Berrigan, 2 Alaska 442; U. S. v. Nelson, 29 Fed. 202; U. S. v. Provoe, 283 U. S. 753; U. S. v. Seveloff, 27 Fed. Cas. No. 16252; U. S. v. Sitarangok, 4 Alaska 667; U. S. v. Stephens, 12 Fed. 52; U. S. v. Warwick, 51 Fed. 280; Waters, 29 Fed. Cas. No. 17264; Waters, 29 Fed. Cas. No. 17265; Northern, 229 Fed. 966. *Op. A. G.* 18:557. *I. D. Rulings* 50 L. D. 315, Mar. 12, 1924; Op. Sol. Feb. 24, 1932, April 19, 1937, May 6, 1937; Memo. Sol. Sept. 14, 1937, Feb. 17, 1939, Mar. 28, 1939. *I. D. Regs.* 25 CFR 1.1–1.68.

ALEUTS. See ALASKA; NATIVE VILLAGE OF ATKA; NATIVE VILLAGE OF CHANEGA; NATIVE VILLAGE OF KARLUK; NATIVE VILLAGE OF NIKOLSKI.

ALGIC (Term referring to Algonquian tribes). *Per.* 9 J. H. Univ. Studies 541.

ALGONQUIN (ALGONKIN). *Per.* James, 12 J. H. Univ. Studies 467.

ALLEGANY RESERVATION. See also NEW YORK: CATTARAUGUS; ONONDAGA; SENECA; TONAWANDA. *Gov. Pub.* 72 Cong., 2 sess., Hearings, S. Comm. Ind. Aff., S. 5302. *Spec. St.* 22:432; 26:558; 27:470; 31:819. *Cases* Fellows, 19 How. 366; New York, 5 Wall. 761; U. S. v. Seneca, 274 Fed. 947. *I. D. Rulings* Memo. Sol. May 24, 1937.

ALSEA AND SILETZ RESERVATION. See also OREGON; SILETZ RESERVATION. *Approp. St.* 18:420; 28:286; 31:221.

ANA-DA-CA (ANADARKO). See also OKLAHOMA; CADDO. *Treaties* 9:844.

ANGOON COMMUNITY ASSOCIATION (TLINGIT). See also ALASKA; THLINGIT. *Const.* Nov. 15, 1939. *Charter* Nov. 15, 1939.

ANNETTE ISLAND RESERVATION (TSIMSHIAN). See also ALASKA; METLAKAHTLA. *Approp. St.* 49:1597; 50:213. *I. D. Rulings* Op. Sol., April 19, 1937. *I. D. Regs.* 25 C. F. R. Part 1.

APACHE. See also ARIZONA; NEW MEXICO; APACHE, KIOWA, COMANCHE; APACHE, KIOWA, COMANCHE, WICHITA; APACHE TRIBE OF THE MESCALERO RESERVATION; ARAPAHOE, CHEYENNE, APACHE, KIOWA, COMANCHE, WICHITA; COMANCHE, KIOWA, APACHE; COMANCHE, KIOWA, APACHE OF THE ARKANSAS RIVER; APACHE, FORT APACHE; FORT McDOWELL MOJAVE COMMUNITY; JICARILLA APACHE TRIBE OF THE JICARILLA RESERVATION; KIOWA, APACHE, COMANCHE; MESCALERO; SAN CARLOS; TONTO; WHITE MOUNTAIN; YAVAPAI; YUMA. *Texts* Manypenny, OIW. *Per.* Brown, 39 Yale L. J. 307; Gates, 21 Am. J. Soc. Sci. 112. *Spec. St.* 13:323; 22:47; 27:469; 29:529; 31:672, 1093; 39:1199; 40:1318; 42:991; 45:492, 986; 47:39; 48:501. *Approp. St.* 10:315; 14:255, 492; 15:198; 16:544; 17:5, 122, 165, 437, 530; 18:133, 146, 402, 420; 19:41, 53, 176, 271, 363; 20:63, 295, 410; 21:67, 114, 414, 485; 22:7, 68, 257; 23:76, 362, 446; 24:449; 25:47, 217, 980; 26:336, 504, 989; 27:120, 612; 28:286, 654; 29:60, 321; 30:62, 105, 571, 652, 924; 31:221, 727, 1058, 1133; 32:245, 419, 982; 33:1048; 34:325, 1015; 35:70, 781; 37:518; 38:77, 582; 39:123; 42:1154; 43:1573; 45:2; 46:279, 1115; 47:91, 820; 48:362, 984, 176, 1757; 50:564; 52:291. *Priv. St.* 15:356; 17:661. *Treaties* 10:979, 1013; 14:703, 713; 15:589. *Cases* Abrew, 37 C. Cls. 510; Brown, 32 C. Cls. 432; Buchanan, 28 C. Cls. 127; Captain, 180 U. S. 353; Collier, 173 U. S. 79; Coaralitos, 178 U. S. 380; Coaralitos, 33 C. Cls. 342; Coutzen, 33 C. Cls. 474; Dobbs, 33 C. Cls. 308; Duran, 31 C. Cls. 353; French, 49 C. Cls. 337; Garcia, 37 C. Cls. 243; Gon-Shay-Ee, 130 U. S. 343; Hernandez, 31 C. Cls. 455; Light, 10 Okla. 732; Lone, 187 U. S. 553; Luke, 35 C. Cls. 15; Mares, 29 C. Cls. 197; Montoya, 180 U. S. 261; Oklahoma, 258 U. S. 574; Otero's, 48 C. Cls. 219; Rhine, 33 C. Cls. 481; Sanchez, 48 C. Cls. 224; Scott, 33 C. Cls. 486; Tully, 32 C. Cls. 1; U. S. v. Myers, 206 Fed. 387; U. S. v. Rowell, 243 U. S. 464;

U. S. v. Wightman, 230 Fed. 277; Valencia, 31 C. Cls. 388; Yerke, 173 U. S. 439. *Op. A. G.* 29:239. *I. D. Rulings* Op. Sol. Mar. 10, 1922, Aug. 14, 1926; Memo. Sol. Oct. 23, 1936.

APACHE, FORT APACHE. See also ARIZONA; APACHE; WHITE MOUNTAIN APACHE. *Spec. St.* 42:1288, 1769; 43:93; 45:962, 1344; 46:1517. *Approp. St.* 38:582; 41:3; 42:552, 1174; 43:1313; 46:1115; 47:91, 820; 49:176; 52:1114. *Priv. St.* 46:1943; 48:1411.

APACHE, JICARILLA. See also ARIZONA; APACHE; JICARILLA. *Spec. St.* 34:91, 1413; 44:1089; 49:1544. *Approp. St.* 22:68; 302; 28:286; 45:200, 1562; 47:91, 525. *Priv. St.* 49:2064. *Cases* Mares, 29 C. Cls. 197. *I. D. Rulings* Memo. Sol. Feb. 8, 1935, May 19, 1936, Oct. 7, 1937.

APACHE, KIOWA, COMANCHE. See also ARIZONA; OKLAHOMA; APACHE; COMANCHE; KIOWA. *Approp. St.* 16:13, 335, 544; 17:165, 437; 18:146, 420; 19:176, 271; 20:63, 295; 21:114, 485; 22:68, 433; 23:76; 24:449; 25:217, 980; 26:336, 989; 27:120, 612; 28:286, 876; 29:321; 30:62; 31:1058; 32:245; 33:189; 34:80; 35:49; 37:33; 43:1367; 45:2045.

APACHE, KIOWA, COMANCHE AND WICHITA. See also APACHE; KIOWA; COMANCHE; WICHITA. *Approp. St.* 23:362; 27:120, 612; 28:286, 876; 29:321; 30:62, 571, 924; 31:221, 1058; 32:982; 33:1048; 34:325, 1015; 35:70, 781.

APACHE TRIBE OF THE MESCALERO RESERVATION. See also NEW MEXICO; APACHE. *Spec. St.* 21:81; 42:1222; 45:1716. *Approp. St.* 20:206; 21:485; 22:302; 40:561; 42:1527; 45:200; 47:91, 820; 49:1757; 50:213; 52:291. *Priv. St.* 45:2012. *I. D. Rulings* Memo. Sol. Off. Aug. 8, 1933, Nov. 9, 1937; Memo. Sol. Dec. 20, 1937. *Const.* Mar. 25, 1936. *Charter* Aug. 1, 1936.

APACHE, WHITE MOUNTAIN. See WHITE MOUNTAIN APACHE.

APALACHICOLA (LOWER CREEK). See also FLORIDA; CREEK. *Approp. St.* 4:636, 682, 705. *Treaties* 7:377, 427.

ARAPAHOE. See also OKLAHOMA; WYOMING; ARAPAHOE AND CHEYENNE; ARAPAHOE, CHEYENNE, APACHE, KIOWA, COMANCHE AND WICHITA; ARAPAHOE AND CHEYENNE INDIANS OF THE UPPER ARKANSAS RIVER; ARAPAHOE AND SHOSHONE; CANTONMENT; KIOWA; NORTHERN CHEYENNE; SEGER; SHOSHONE AND ARAPAHOE; SOUTHERN ARAPAHOE; WIND RIVER RESERVATION. *Texts* Manypenny, OIW. *Approp. St.* 30:924; 35:907; 45:2, 1607; 48:984. *Priv. St.* 25:1306. *Treaties* 14:713. *Cases* Brice, 32 C. Cls. 23; Brown, 32 C. Cls. 432; Campbell, 44 C. Cls. 488; Clarke, 39 F. 2d 800; Connors, 180 U. S. 271; Crow, 32 C. Cls. 16; Fenlow, 17 C. Cls. 138; Keith, 8 Okla. 446; Litchfield, 33 C. Cls. 203; Mascarinas, 33 C. Cls. 94; Pike, 4 Mackey 531; Ryan, 8 C. Cls. 265; Shoshone, 85 C. Cls. 331; Shoshone, 82 C. Cls. 23; Stone, 29 C. Cls. 111; Sully, 195 Fed. 113; U. S. v. Cherokee, 202 U. S. 101; U. S. v. Rogers, 23 Fed. 658; U. S. v. Shoshone, 304 U. S. 111; Wadsworth, 148 Fed. 771. *Op. A. G.* 14:451; 18:235.

ARAPAHOE AND CHEYENNE. See also ARAPAHOE; CHEYENNE. *Gov. Pub.* 76 Cong., 1 sess., Hearings, H. Comm. Ind. Aff., H. R. 2775. *Spec. St.* 28:3; 37:131; 39:937; 43:253; 44:764; 45:380; 48:501. *Approp. St.* 12:44, 12:774; 23:478; 27:120, 612; 28:286, 876; 29:321; 30:62, 571, 924; 31:221, 1058; 32:245, 982; 33:1048; 34:325, 1015; 35:70, 781; 36:269; 37:518; 38:77; 39:14. *Priv. St.* 18:535; 21:588; 32:1606. *Treaties* 14:703; 15:593. *I. D. Rulings* Memo. Sol. Off. Aug. 3, 1937; Memo. Sol. June 30, 1938.

ARAPAHOE, CHEYENNE, APACHE, KIOWA, COMANCHE AND WICHITA. See also ARAPAHOE; CHEYENNE; APACHE; KIOWA; COMANCHE; WICHITA. *Approp. St.* 17:5, 165, 437; 18:146, 420; 19:176, 271; 20:63, 295, 410; 21:67, 114, 414, 485; 22:7, 47, 68, 257, 433; 23:76, 362; 24:449; 25:217, 980; 26:336, 504, 989.

ARAPAHOE AND CHEYENNE INDIANS OF THE UPPER ARKANSAS RIVER. See also COLORADO; KANSAS; ARAPAHOE; CHEYENNE. *Approp. St.* 12:512, 774; 13:161, 541; 14:255, 492.

ARAPAHOE AND SHOSHONE. See also OKLAHOMA; WYOMING; ARAPAHOE; SHOSHONE. *Spec. St.* 34:78. *Approp. St.* 27:120.

ARIKARA (ARICKAREE). See NORTH DAKOTA; FORT BERTHOLD; THREE AFFILIATED TRIBES OF FORT BERTHOLD RESERVATION.

ARIZONA. See also APACHE; COLORADO RIVER INDIAN TRIBES OF THE COLORADO RIVER RESERVATION; COSNEJO RESERVATION; APACHE, FORT APACHE; FORT McDOWELL MOHAVE-APACHE COMMUNITY; FORT MOJAVE; GILA RIVER; HAVASUPAI TRIBE OF THE HAVASUPAI RESERVATION; HOPI TRIBE; HUALAPAI TRIBE OF THE HAVASUPAI RESERVATION; LEUPP EXTENSION RESERVATION; MARICOPA; MOJAVE; MOQUI; NAVAJO; PAPAGO; PIMA; PIMA MARICOPA; SALT RIVER RESERVATION; SAN CARLOS APACHE TRIBE; SAN XAVIER; TRUXTON CANYON; WALAPAI; WHITE MOUNTAIN APACHE TRIBE; YAVAPAI APACHE INDIAN COMMUNITY; YUMA. *Gov. Pub.* 71 Cong. 1 sess. S. Doc. 16. *Approp. St.* 16:13, 544; 17:165, 437; 18:146, 420; 19:176, 271; 20:63, 295; 21:114, 485; 26:504, 862; 33:189; 35:478; 38:77, 582; 40:561; 42:1174, 1527.

ARIZONA AND NEW MEXICO. See also ARIZONA; NEW MEXICO. *Approp. St.* 20:63, 295; 28:876; 33:1214; 36:269; 37:518; 38:582; 40:561.

ARKANSAS. See CADDO; CHEROKEE; DELAWARE; OSAGE; QUAPAW.

ASSINIBOINE (ASSINABOINE). See also MONTANA; FORT BELKNAP INDIAN COMMUNITY. *Per.* MacLeod, 28 J. Crim. L. 181; Oskison, 23 Case & Com. 722. *Gov. Pub.* 68 Cong., 2 sess., S. Rep. 1116; 68 Cong., 2 sess., H. Rep. 1214. *Spec. St.* 17:787; 44:1263; 46:531. *Approp. St.* 14:492; 15:198; 16:13, 335, 544; 17:165, 437; 18:146, 420; 19:271; 20:63, 410; 21:114, 485; 22:68, 433; 23:76, 362; 24:449. *Treaties* 11:657. *Cases* Albright, 53 C. Cls. 247; Assiniboine, 77 C. Cls. 347; Winters, 207 U. S. 564. *I. D. Rulings* Op. Sol. M. 7599, June 9, 1922.

ASSINIBOINE AND GROS VENTRE AT FORT BELKNAP, MONTANA. See also ASSINIBOINE; GROS VENTRE; FORT BELKNAP. *Approp. St.* 18:146, 420.

ATKA, NATIVE VILLAGE OF (ALEUT). See also ALASKA; ALEUTS. *Const.* May 23, 1939. *Charter* May 23, 1939.

BAD RIVER BAND OF THE LAKE SUPERIOR TRIBE OF CHIPPEWA INDIANS OF THE STATE OF WISCONSIN. See also WISCONSIN; CHIPPEWA; LA POINTE. *Spec. St.* 31:766. *Approp. St.* 41:3. *Priv. St.* 42:1594. *Cases* Ex p. Pero, 99 F. 2d 28; In re Blackbird, 109 Fed. 139; U. S. v. Auger, 153 Fed. 671; U. S. v. Raiche, 31 F. 2d 624; Wisconsin, 201 U. S. 202. *I. D. Rulings* Op. Sol. Aug. 3, 1934; Memo. Sol. Feb. 18, 1938. *Const.* June 20, 1936. *Charter* May 21, 1938.

BALANTSE-ETOA (HIDATSA). See also NORTH DAKOTA; FORT BERTHOLD; GROS VENTRE (HIDATSA). *Treaties* 7:261.

BANNOCK. See also IDAHO; OREGON; LEMHI; SHOSHONE AND BANNOCK; SHOSHONE; BANNOCK AND OTHER BANDS IN IDAHO AND SOUTHEASTERN OREGON; SHOSHONE-BANNOCK TRIBES OF THE FORT HALL RESERVATION. *Spec. St.* 18:291; 22:148; 25:452, 687; 31:672; 39:1199. *Approp. St.* 15:198; 16:335, 544; 17:165, 437; 18:146, 420; 19:176, 271; 20:63, 295, 410; 21:114, 485; 22:433; 23:76; 24:449; 25:217, 980; 26:336; 28:876; 29:321; 31:221, 1058; 32:245, 982; 33:189, 1048; 34:325, 1015; 35:70, 781; 36:269; 37:518; 38:77, 582; 39:123, 969; 40:561; 41:3, 408, 1225; 42:552, 1174; 43:390, 704, 1141; 44:453, 934; 45:200, 1562, 1623; 46:279. *Priv. St.* 27:810; 31:1493; 35:1437; 38:1446; 41:1547; 43:1557; 45:1833, 1088, 2379; 46:1886. *Treaties* 15:673. *Cases* Brown, 32 C. Cls. 432; Cox, 29 C. Cls. 349; Marks, 161 U. S. 297; U. S. v. Portneuf-Marsh, 213 Fed. 601; Utah, 116 U. S. 28; Ward, 163 U. S. 504.

BARONA RANCH. See CALIFORNIA; CAPITAN GRANDE; MISSION.

BARROW, NATIVE VILLAGE OF. See also ALASKA; ESKIMO. *Const.* Mar. 21, 1940. *Charter* Mar. 21, 1940.

BAY MILLS INDIAN COMMUNITY. See also MICHIGAN; CHIPPEWA. *Const.* Nov. 4, 1936. *Charter* Nov. 27, 1937.

BEAR ISLAND. See also CHIPPEWA; MINNESOTA. *Priv. St.* 39:1594.

BIG PINE RESERVATION (PAIUTE). See also PAHUTE (PAIUTE); SHOSHONE, CALIFORNIA. *Approp. St.* 41:3.

BIG VALLEY BAND OF POMO INDIANS OF THE BIG VALLEY RANCHERIA. See also CALIFORNIA. *Const.* Jan. 15, 1936.

BILOXI (MISSISSIPPI). *Cases* U. S. v. Heirs, 14 How. 189.

BLACK BOB BAND (Shawnee Band in Kansas, 1854–68). *Approp. St.* 16:291.

BLACKFEET TRIBE OF BLACKFEET INDIAN RESERVATION. See also MONTANA; BLACKFEET, BLOOD AND PIEGAN; GROS VENTRE, PIEGAN, BLOOD, BLACKFEET, RIVER CROW. *Per.* Dixon, 23 Case & Com. 712

Mac Leod, 28 J. Crim. L. 181. *Gov. Pub.* 67 Cong., 3 sess., H. Rep. 1596, S. Rep. 1073; 71 Cong., 2 sess., H. Rep. 113. *Spec. St.* 18:28; 19:254; 24:402; 25:113; 33:816; 36:1080; 37:64; 41:549; 42:857, 1289; 43:21, 252; 44:303, 1263; 46:276, 334, 1495; 47:144; 50–864. *Approp. St.* 10:315; 11:65, 169, 273, 388; 12:44, 221, 512, 774; 13:161, 541; 14:191; 22:7; 23:267, 516; 25:217, 980; 26:336, 989; 27:612; 28:286, 876; 29:321; 30:62, 571, 924; 31:221, 280, 1058; 32:245, 982; 33:189, 1048; 34:325, 1015; 35:781; 36:269; 37:518; 38:77, 321, 582, 822; 39:123, 262, 969; 40:105, 561, 634; 41:3, 408, 1156, 1224; 42:552, 1048, 1174, 1527; 43:390, 704, 1141; 44:161, 453, 934; 45:200, 1562, 1623; 46:279, 860, 1115; 47:91, 820; 48:362; 49:176, 1757; 50:564; 52:291, 1114. *Priv. St.* 17:703; 42:1710, chap. 355; 47:1699. *Treaties* 11:657. *Cases* Albright, 53 C. Cls. 247; Blackfeet, 81 C. Cls. 100; British, 299 U. S. 159; Henkel, 237 U. S. 45; McKnight, 130 Fed. 659; Montana, 95 F. 2d 897; U. S. v. Conrad, 161 Fed. 829; U. S. v. Glacier, 17 F. Supp. 411; U. S. v. 29 Gallons, 45 Fed. 847; Winters, 207 U. S. 564. *I. D. Rulings*, Op. Sol. May 12, 1925; Memo. Sol. Off. Jan. 23, 1932, Feb. 15, 1932, Aug. 22, 1932; Op. Sol. Oct. 1, 1936; Memo. Sol., May 22, 1937, March 14, 1938; Memo. Sol. Off. July 7, 1938, July 16, 1938; Memo. Sol. Aug. 26, 1938, Feb. 17, 1939, Mar. 16, 1939. *Const.* Dec. 13, 1935. *Charter* Aug. 15, 1936.

BLACKFEET, BLOOD AND PIEGAN. See also BLACKFEET; BLOOD; PIEGAN. *Spec. St.* 49:1568. *Approp. St.* 16:335, 544; 17:165, 437; 18:133, 146, 420; 19:176, 271; 20:63, 295; 21:114, 485; 22:68, 257, 433; 23:76, 362; 24:449; 27:120.

BLOOD. See also MONTANA; BLACKFEET, BLOOD, AND PIEGAN; GROS VENTRE; PIEGAN, BLOOD, BLACKFEET, RIVER CROW. *Spec. St.* 18:28; 25:113; 33:816; 36:1080; 43:21. *Approp. St.* 22:7.

BOIS FORT. See also MINNESOTA; CHIPPEWA. *Approp. St.* 36:1289. *Priv. St.* 36:1698.

BOKOWTONDAN RESERVATION (CHIPPEWA). See also MICHIGAN; CHIPPEWA. *Cases* Francis, 203 U. S. 233.

BROTHERTOWN, WISCONSIN (Eastern Algonquin Indians from Mass. and Conn. settled here in 1833). See also WISCONSIN; STOCKBRIDGE INDIANS. *Spec. St.* 5:349; 20:513. *Approp. St.* 4:682; 5:766; 10:315. *Priv. St.* 6:813. *Treaties* 7:342, 405, 550. *Cases* Elk, 112 U. S. 94; New York, 170 U. S. 1; New York, 40 C. Cls. 448. *Op. A. G.* 3:322.

BRULE. See LOWER BRULE.

BUFFALO CREEK RESERVATION. See also NEW YORK; TONAWANDA. *Treaties* 11:735. *Cases* Fellows, 19 How. 366; New York, 5 Wall. 761.

CADDO INDIAN TRIBE OF OKLAHOMA. See also OKLAHOMA; ANA-DA-CA; CADDO AND COMANCHE. *Spec. St.* 9:762; 48:501. *Approp. St.* 4:780; 5:36, 158, 298, 323, 402, 584, 704; 32:245; 33:189; 38:77; 48:984. *Treaties* 7:232, 424, 470; 9:844. *Cases* Johnson 283 Fed. 954; U. S. v. Belt, 128 Fed. 68; U. S. v. Brooks, 10 How. 442; U. S. v. Choctaw, 179 U. S. 494; Young, 176 Fed. 612. *Const.* Jan. 17, 1938. *Charter* Nov. 15, 1938.

CAGHANAWAGA (CHRISTIAN IROQUOIS). See also SIX NATIONS; NEW YORK. *Treaties* 7:55.

CAHOKIA (PEORIA). See also ILLINOIS; KASKASKIA. *Treaties* 7:78, 181. *Approp. St.* 8:517.

CAHUILLA. See also CALIFORNIA; MISSION. *Spec. St.* 44:252; 46:1522. *Approp. St.* 44:841; 47:91. *Cases* Apapas, 233 U. S. 587.

CALAPOOIA, MOLALA, CLAKAMAS. See also OREGON; MOLALA; MOLEL; UMPQUA. *Approp. St.* 10:643; 11:65, 169, 273, 329, 388; 12:44, 221, 512; 13:161, 541; 14:255, 492; 15:198; 16:13, 335, 544; 17:165, 437; 18:146. *Treaties* 10:1125.

CALESPEL. See also KALISPEL; WASHINGTON. *Approp. St.* 26:989.

CALIFORNIA. See also AGUA CALIENTE; BIG PINE RESERVATION; BIG VALLEY BAND OF POMO INDIANS; CAHUILLA; CAPITAN GRANDE; COLORADO RIVER INDIANS OF THE COLORADO RIVER RESERVATION; CUYAPAIPE; DIEGUENOS; DIGGER; FORT YUMA; FRESNO AND KINGS RIVER RESERVATION; GRINDSTONE CREEK RESERVATION; HOOPA VALLEY; INDIAN RANCH; KASHIA BAND OF POMO INDIANS OF THE STEWART'S POINT RANCHERIA; KLAMATH RIVER; LAGUNA; LA JOLLA RESERVATION; LA POSTA; MALKI; MANCHESTER BAND OF POMO INDIANS; MENDOCINO RESERVATION; MERCED RESERVATION; MESA GRANDE; ME-WUK INDIAN COMMUNITY OF THE WILTON RANCHERIA; MISSION; MORONGO; PALA MISSION; PALM SPRINGS; PECHANGA; QUARTZ VALLEY INDIAN COMMUNITY; QUECHAN; REDWOOD; RINCON; ROUND VALLEY RESERVATION; RUSSIAN RIVER; SACRAMENTO; SANTA YSABEL; SHASTA; SMITH RIVER RESERVATION; SOBOBA; SYCUAN; TEMECULA; TORRES-MARTINEZ; TULE RIVER INDIAN TRIBE; TUOLUMNE BAND OF ME-WUK INDIANS OF THE TUOLUMNE RANCHERIA; UPPER LAKE BAND OF POMO INDIANS OF THE UPPER LAKE RANCHERIA; VOLCAN INDIAN RESERVATION; WASHOE; YUMA. *Texts* Hoopes IAA. *Per.* Goodrich, 14 Calif. L. Rev. 83, 157. *Gov. Pub.* 74 Cong., 1 sess., Hearings, S. Comm. Ind. Aff. S. 1793, S. Rep. 1164; 75 Cong., 1 sess., Hearings, S. Comm. Ind. Aff., S. 1651, Hearings, S. Comm. Ind. Aff., S. 1651 & S. 1779, Hearings, H. Comm. Ind. Aff., S. 1651, Hearings, H. Comm. Ind. Aff., H. R. 5243 & H. R. 1908; 76 Cong., 1 sess., Hearings, H. Comm. Ind. Aff., H. R. 3765. *Spec. St.* 9:519; 13:39, 538; 21:510; 32:399; 39:1199; 42:994; 43:1101; 46:259. *Approp. St.* 9:544, 570; 10:41, 226, 315, 686; 11:65, 169, 329, 388; 12:44, 221; 13:161, 541; 14:255, 492; 15:198; 16:13, 544; 17:165, 437, 530; 18:146, 420; 19:176, 271; 33:1048; 34:325, 1015; 35:70, 781; 36:269; 37:518, 912; 38:77, 312, 582, 1138; 39:14, 123, 969; 40:2, 561, 1020; 41:3, 408, 1156, 1225; 42:437, 552, 1174; 43:33, 390, 704, 1141; 44:453, 934; 45:200, 1562; 46:90, 279, 1115; 50:564. *Priv. St.* 12:841, 847; 16:667; 34:2188, 2207; 35:1219, 1389; 36:1815; 38:1278, 1447; 40:1489; 45:2002. *Cases* Belt, 15 C. Cls. 92; Fremont, 2 C. Cls. 461. *I. D. Rulings* Op. Sol. July 8, 1930, April 19, 1933, April 21, 1933.

CAMP McDOWELL. See FORT McDOWELL MOJAVE-APACHE COMMUNITY.

CAMP VERDE. See YAVAPAI-APACHE; ARIZONA.

CAMPO RESERVATION. See also CALIFORNIA; MISSION. *Approp. St.* 41:408.

CAMP McDERMITT (PAVIOTSO). See also NEVADA. *Spec. St.* 17:623.

CANTONMENT AGENCY. See also OKLAHOMA; SOUTHERN ARAPAHO; SOUTHERN CHEYENNE. *Approp. St.* 41:3, 408.

CAPITAN GRANDE. See also CALIFORNIA; BARONA RANCH; MISSION. *Spec. St.* 44:1061; 50:72; 47:146. *Approp. St.* 41:1225; 42:552. *I. D. Rulings* Op. Sol., July 14, 1934.

CAPOTE. See also COLORADO; UTAH; TABEGUACHE, MAUCHE, CAPOTE, WEEMINUCHE, YAMPA, GRAND RIVER, UINTAH BANDS OF UTES. *Spec. St.* 28:677. *Treaties* 15:619.

CARRO. See also CADDO. *Treaties* 9:844.

CASS LAKE. See also MINNESOTA; CHIPPEWA. *Op. A. G.* 25:416.

CATAWBA. See also NORTH CAROLINA; SOUTH CAROLINA. *Approp. St.* 9:252; 10:315. *I. D. Rulings* Memo. Sol., June 9, 1937.

CATTARAUGUS. See also NEW YORK; ALLEGHENY; SENECA. *Per.* 31 Yale L. J. 330. *Gov. Pub.* 72 Cong., 2 sess., Hearings, S. Comm. Ind. Aff., S. 5302. *Spec. St.* 20:535; 26:558; 27:470; 31:819. *Cases* Button, 7 F. Supp. 597; Fellows, 19 How. 360; New York, 5 Wall. 761; Seneca, 162 U. S. 283; U. S. v. Seneca, 274 Fed. 947; U. S. ex rel. Kennedy, 269 U. S. 13; Washburn, 7 F. Supp. 120. *I. D. Rulings* Memo. Sol., May 24, 1937.

CAYUGA. See also NEW YORK; OKLAHOMA; SENECA-CAYUGA TRIBE OF OKLAHOMA. *Approp. St.* 5:612. *Treaties* Archives 19; 7:550. *Cases* New York, 41 C. Cls. 462; New York, 40 C. Cls. 448; U. S. v. New York, 173 U. S. 464.

CAYUSE. See also OREGON; UMATILLA; WALLA WALLA. *Spec. St.* 9:566; 10:30, 180; 32:399. *Approp. St.* 10:311; 11:206; 25:47; 36:1289. *Priv. St.* 34:2380; 35:1389, 1406, 1432, 1616; 36:1753; 38:1447; 40:1486. *Cases* Bonifer, 166 Fed. 846; Hy-Tu-Tse-Mil-Kin, 194 U. S. 401; Langford, 12 C. Cls. 338; McKay, 204 U. S. 458; U. S. v. Brookfield, 24 F. Supp. 712; U. S. v. Matlock, 26 Fed. Cas. No. 15744.

CEDAR BAND. See PAHUTE (PAIUTE).

CHANEGA, NATIVE VILLAGE OF (ALEUT). See also ALASKA; ALEUTS. *Const.* Feb. 3, 1940. *Charter* Feb. 3, 1940.

CHASTA (SHASTA), SCOTON, UMPQUA. See also OREGON; SHASTA. *Approp. St.* 10:643; 11:65, 169, 273, 329, 388; 12:44, 221, 512, 774; 13:161, 541; 14:255, 492; 15:198; 16:13. *Treaties* 10:1122.

CHEHALIS. See also WASHINGTON; COWLITZ; LOWER CHEHALIS; UPPER CHEHALIS. *Spec. St.* 43:886. *Approp. St.* 34:325. *Cases* Duwamish, 79 C. Cls. 530; Halbert, 283 U. S. 753; U. S. v. Chehalis, 217 Fed. 281; U. S. v. Provoe, 283 U. S. 753; U. S. v. Walkawsky, 283 U. S. 753; U. S. ex rel. Charley, 62 Fed. 955.

CHEMEHUEVI. See CALIFORNIA.

CHEROKEE. See also NORTH CAROLINA; OKLAHOMA; CHEROKEE, EASTERN BAND; CHEROKEE, NORTH CAROLINA; CHEROKEE, WESTERN BAND; CHEROKEE, OLD SETTLERS; FIVE CIVILIZED TRIBES. *Texts* Andrews, AL; Baker, ACU; Baldwin, GVO; Bledsoe, ILL; Duer, CLC; Kent, CAL; McLaughlin, CHU; Manypenny, OIW; Willoughby, CLU. *Per.* Cohen, 3 Ind. at W. No. 19; James, 12 J. H. Univ. Studies 467; Meserve, 5 Okla. S. B. J. 130; Oskison, 23 Case & Com. 722; Shinn, 23 Case & Com. 842. *Spec. St.* 2:381, 649, 649, c. 25; 3:461, 702; 4:39, 305, 576, 735; 5:470, 473, 504, 603, 719; 9:339; 10:121; 12:834; 17:98, 228; 18:41, 476; 19:28, 265; 22:349, 755; 23:552; 24:121; 25:608, 694; 26:636, 794, 844; 27:86, 281; 28:693; 29:529; 30:407, 495; 31:848; 32:399, 716; 34:267, 1220; 35:553; 39:1199; 40:561, 1316; 43:27; 45:2034; 46:431; 52:636. *Approp. St.* 1:563; 2:66, 108, 407, 440, 443, 548; 3:326, 393, 463, 749; 4:92, 181, 267, 300, 352, 361, 397, 463, 470, 505, 528, 532, 616, 631, 636, 682, 705, 780; 5:36, 73, 158, 241, 402, 417, 435, 493, 523, 681, 704, 766; 9:598; 10:181, 214; 11:200; 14:324; 17:530; 19:102; 21:236; 22:302, 582, 603; 23:236; 28:58, 286; 29:267; 34:634; 38:77; 41:3, 408, 1225; 45:2; 46:1115; 47:820; 48:984. *Priv. St.* 4:491; 6:34, 98, 349, 387, 432, 441, 480, 483, 507, 519, 572, 641, 685, 710, 775, 797, 835, 858, 878, 879, 920, 930; 9:651, 673, 704, 716, 746, 748, 799, 806, 807; 10:771, 794, 842; 11:460; 12:835, 850; 21:544; 24:835; 25:1180; 26:1359, 1385; 27:831; 30:1416, 1517; 31:1668, 1723, 1770, 1770 c. 723; 32:1241, 1279, 1314, 1365, 1377, 1386, 1400, 1577, 1578; 33:1362, 1496, 1523, 1547, 1548, 1582, 1619, 1848, 2052, 2058; 34:1513, 1529, 1618, 1687, 1756, 1787, 1813, 1877, 1939, 1982 2012, 2043, 2099, 2269, 2274, 2382, 2386, 2482, 2535, 2592, 2593, 2594, 2753; 35:1219, 1375, 1389, 1406, 1462; 36:1760, 1816; 38:1326, 1439, 1446; 49:2326. *Treaties* 7:18, 39, 42, 43, 56, 62, 93, 95, 101, 138, 139, 148, 156, 183, 195, 289, 311, 348, 414, 474, 478, 533, 550; 9:871; 14:799; 16:727. *Cases* Adams, 59 F. 2d 653; Alberty, 162 U. S. 499; Anicker, 246 U. S. 110; Armsworthy, 1 Fed. Cas. No. 550; Barbé, 228 Fed. 658; Barnsdall, 200 Fed. 522; Barnsdall, 200 Fed. 519; Bell, 63 Fed. 417; Blackfeather, 190 U. S. 368; Board, 94 F. 2d 450; Brewer, 260 U. S. 77; Boudinot, 2 Ind. T. 107; Brown, 44 C. Cls. 283; Bunch, 263 U. S. 250; Campbell, 3 Ind. T. 462; Case, 2 Ind. T. 8; Cherokee, 155 U. S. 218; Cherokee, 5 Pet. 1; Cherokee, 135 U. S. 641; Cherokee, 270 U. S. 476; Cherokee, 223 U. S. 108; Cherokee, 80 C. Cls. 1; Cherokee, 85 C. Cls. 76; Cherokee, 11 Wall. 616; Chisholm, 273 Fed. 589; Commissioners, 270 Fed. 110; Crawford, 3 Ind. T. 10; Crowell, 4 Int. T. 36; Danforth, 1 Wheat. 155; Daniels, 4 Ind. T. 426; Davenport, 1 Ind. T. 424; Delaware, 38 C. Cls. 234; Delaware, 74 C. Cls. 368; Dick, 6 Ind. T. 85; Donohoo, 4 Ind. T. 433; Duvall, 4 Ind. T. 94; Eastern, 19 C. Cls. 35; Eastern, 117 U. S. 288; Eastern, 20 C. Cls. 449; Eastern, 225 U. S. 572; Eastern, 45 C. Cls. 104; Eastern, 45 C. Cls. 229; Eastern, 82 C. Cls. 180; Etchen, 235 Fed. 104; Ex p. Kenyon, 14 Fed. Cas. No. 7720; Ex p. Kyle, 67 Fed. 306; Ex p. Morgan, 20 Fed. 298; Famous, 151 U. S. 50; German-American, 5 Ind. T. 703; Garfield, 211 U. S. 264; Garfield, 34 App. D. C. 70; Gritts, 224 U. S. 640; Guthrie, 1 Okla. 454; Hanks, 3 Ind. T. 415; Hargrove, 129 Fed. 186; Hargrove, 3 Ind. T. 478; Hargrove, 4 Ind. T. 129; Harnage, 242 U. S. 386; Heckman, 224 U. S. 413; Henny, 191 Fed. 132; Hockett, 110 Fed. 910; Holden, 17 Wall. 211; Hubbard, 5 Ind. T. 95; Hunt, 3 Ind. T. 275; In re Delks, 2 Ind. T. 572; In re Mayfield, 141 U. S. 107; In re Wolf, 27 Fed. 606; Jackson, 34 C. Cls. 441; James, 3 Ind. T. 447; Jennings, 192 Fed. 507; Journeycake, 28 C. Cls. 281; Journeycake, 31 C. Cls. 140; Keetoowah, 41 App. D. C. 319; Kelly, 4 Ind. T. 110; Knight, 228 U. S. 6; Labadie, 6 Okla. 400; Langdon, 14 Fed. Cas. No. 8062; Lattimer, 14 Pet. 4; Lowe, 223 U. S. 95; McAlester, 3 Ind. T. 704; McDaniel, 230 Fed. 945; Mackay, 18 How. 100; Mehlin, 56 Fed. 12; Meigs, 9 Cranch, 11; Midland, 179 Fed. 74; Minis, 15 Pet. 423; Moore, 2 Wyo. 8; Muskrat, 219 U. S. 346; Mivens, 4 Ind. T. 30; Nofire, 164 U. S. 657; Owens, 5 Ind. T. 275; Park, 11 How. 362; Patterson, 2 Pet. 216; Persons, 40 C. Cls. 411; Porterfield, 2 How. 76; Preston, 1 Wheat. 115; Price, 5 Ind. T. 518; Raymond, 83 Fed. 721; Robinson, 221 Fed. 398; Rogers, 263 Fed. 160; Ross, 232 U. S. 110; Ross, 227 U. S. 530; Rush, 2 Ind. T. 557; Sanders, 97 Fed. 863; Seep, 179 Fed. 77; Smythe, 41 Fed. 705; Sperry, 264 U. S. 488; St. Louis, 49 Fed. 440; Stroud, 23 Fed. Cas. No. 13547; Sunday, 248 U. S. 545; Talley, 246 U. S. 104; Talton, 163 U. S. 376; Thomas, 169 U. S. 264; Thomason, 7 Ind. T. 1; Truskett, 236 U. S. 223; Turner, 167 Fed. 646; Tynon, 3 Ind. T. 346; U. S. v. Bailey, 24 Fed. Cas. No. 14495; U. S. v. Blackfeather, 155 U. S. 180; U. S. v. Boyd, 68 Fed. 577; U. S. v. Cherokee, 202 U. S. 101; U. S. v. Duval, 25 Fed. Cas. No. 15015; U. S. v. Halsell, 247 Fed. 390; U. S. v. Hunter, 21 Fed. 615; U. S. v. Knight, 206 Fed. 145; U. S. v. Law, 250 Fed. 218; U. S. v. Payne, 22 Fed. 426; U. S. v. Pridgeon, 153 U. S. 48; U. S. v. Ragsdale, 27 Fed. Cas. No. 16113; U. S. v. Reese, 27 Fed. Cas. No. 16137; U. S. v. Rogers, 4 How. 567; U. S. v. Rogers, 23 Fed. 658; U. S. v. Sanders, 27 Fed. Cas. No. 16220; U. S. v. Smith, 266 Fed. 740; U. S. v. Smith, 279 Fed. 136; U. S. v. Smith, 288 Fed. 356; U. S. v. Soule, 30 Fed. 918; U. S. v. Terrell, 28 Fed. Cas. No. 16452; U. S. v. Terrell, 28 Fed. Cas. No. 16453; U. S. v. Whitmore, 236 Fed. 474; Wallace, 204 U. S. 415; Welch, 15 F. 2d 184; Welch, 32 C. Cls. 106; Wellsville, 243 U. S. 6; Western, 82 C. Cls. 566; Western, 27 C. Cls. 1; Wilson, 38 C. Cls. 6; Worcester, 6 Pet. 515. *Op. A. G.* 1:645; 2:321, 360, 402; 3:207, 297, 304, 326, 367, 431, 504; 4:73, 116, 175, 500, 504, 560, 580, 597, 613, 621; 5:36, 268, 320; 7:54; 9:48; 12:57; 16:404, 470; 18:235, 555; 19:42, 173, 229; 20:749; 23:528; 25:168; 26:123, 171, 351; 30:284. *L. D. Memo.* (*D. J.*) 7:249. *I. D. Rulings* 25 L. D. 297, Aug. 1, 1897; Op. Sol., Mar. 3, 1930, Sept. 4, 1931, Oct. 14, 1931, Sept. 21, 1933; Memo. Sol., Feb. 13, 1934, Mar. 18, 1936, April 23, 1936, July 29, 1937.

CHEROKEE, EASTERN BAND. See also NORTH CAROLINA; CHEROKEE; CHEROKEE, NORTH CAROLINA. *Spec. St.* 15:228; 19:139; 27:348; 45:1094; 46:1518; 47:137; 49:1513. *Approp. St.* 11:81; 19:176, 363; 22:68, 257, 433, 582; 23:76, 362; 24:449; 25:565; 26:989; 27:120, 612; 28:16, 286, 424; 30:62, 571, 1214; 31:280, 1058; 32:245, 982; 34:634, 1371; 35:781; 41:3, 408, 1225; 42:552; 43:390, 1141; 44:934; 45:200, 1623. *Priv. St.* 52:1347. *Treaties* 9:871. *Cases* Eastern, 19 C. Cls. 35; Eastern, 117 U. S. 288; Eastern, 20 C. Cls. 449; Eastern, 45 C. Cls. 104; Eastern, 45 C. Cls. 229; Eastern, 225 U. S. 572; Eastern, 82 C. Cls. 180; Old, 148 U. S. 427; Owen, 217 U. S. 488; Rollins, 23 C. Cls. 106; U. S. v. Boyd, 68 Fed. 577; U. S. v. Boyd, 83 Fed. 547; U. S. v. Cherokee, 202 U. S. 101; U. S. v. Colvard, 89 F. 2d 312; U. S. v. Rose, 20 F. Supp. 350; U. S. v. 7,405.3 Acres, 97 F. 2d 417; U. S. v. Swain, 46 F. 2d 99; U. S. v. Wright, 53 F. 2d 300; Western, 82 C. Cls. 566; Western, 27 C. Cls. 1. *Op. A. G.* 16:225, 300; 17:72; 26:330. *L. D. Memo.* (*D. J.*) 7:249, 517; 11:579; 12:206. *I. D. Rulings* Memo. Sol., Mar. 14, 1939.

CHEROKEE, NORTH CAROLINA. See also CHEROKEE; CHEROKEE, EASTERN BAND. *Spec. St.* 43:376; 46:787; 50:699. *Approp. St.* 9:252, 342; 10:290, 546, 686; 16:13; 18:133, 204, 402; 19:271; 21:114; 25:217, 980; 26:336; 28:876; 31:221; 33:1048; 34:325, 1015; 35:70, 781; 36:269; 37:518; 39:123, 969; 41:3, 408, 1248; 42:29, 437, 1174; 43:704; 44:453; 45:200, 1562; 46:279, 1115; 48:362; 49:176, 1757; 50:564; 52:291. *L. D. Memo.* (*D. J.*) 8:196.

CHEROKEE, WESTERN BAND. See also OKLAHOMA; CHEROKEE; FIVE CIVILIZED TRIBES. *Spec. St.* 47:137. *Approp. St.* 39:321. *Priv. St.* 28:1009. *Cases* Kendall, 1 C. Cls. 261; Old, 148 U. S. 427. *I. D. Rulings* Op. Sol., Oct. 4, 1938; Memo Sol., Mar. 14, 1939.

CHETTIMANCHI (CHITIMACHA). *Approp. St.* 41:3, 408.

CHEYENNE. See also OKLAHOMA; SOUTH DAKOTA; ARAPAHOE, CHEYENNE, APACHE, KIOWA, COMANCHE AND WICHITA; CHEYENNE, APACHE, KIOWA AND COMANCHE; CHEYENNE, ARAPAHOE, KIOWA AND COMANCHE; CHEYENNE OF THE UPPER PLATTE RIVER; CHEYENNE RIVER RESERVATION; NORTHERN CHEYENNE; SEGAR; SIOUX CHEYENNE; TWO KETTLE SIOUX. *Texts* Manypenny, OIW. *Per.* Mac Leod, 28 J. Crim. L. 181. *Spec. St.* 19:254; 22:47; 24:3; 26:14; 28:3; 37:131; 39:937, 1199; 43:253; 44:764; 45:380; 48:501, 972. *Approp. St.* 10:686; 16:335; 17:5; 20:377, 410; 21:67, 259, 414; 22:7, 257; 23:478; 26:504; 32:1031; 33:189; 34:1015; 38:208; 39:14, 123; 45:492; 48:984; 49:176; 50:564. *Priv. St.* 17:766; 20:603; 21:549; 25:1223; 32:1606. *Treaties* 7:255; 14:703, 713; 15:593. *Cases* Brown, 32 C. Cls. 432; Campbell, 44 C. Cls. 488; Coffield, 52 C. Cls. 17; Conners 33 C. Cls. 317; Connors, 180 U. S. 271; Fenlon, 7 C. Cls 138; Gagnon, 38 C. Cls. 10; Hegimer, 30 C. Cls. 405; Hosford 29 C. Cls. 42; Labadi, 31 C. Cls. 205; Labadie, 33 C. Cls. 476 Litchfield, 33 C. Cls. 203; Mascarinos, 33 C. Cls. 94; Montoya, 32 C. Cls. 71; Moore, 32 C. Cls. 596; Pike, 4 Mackey 531; Salois, 32 C. Cls. 68; Salois, 33 C. Cls. 326; Stone, 29 C. Cls. 111; U. S. v. Cherokee, 202 U. S. 101; U. S. v. Dewey, 14 F. 2d 784; U. S. v. Hoyt, 167 Fed. 301; U. S. v. Pearson, 231 Fed. 270; U. S. v. Rogers, 23 Fed. 658. *Op. A. G.* 14:451; 18:235. *I. D. Rulings* Memo. Sol., July 18, 1937; Memo. Sol. Off., Aug. 3, 1937; Memo. Sol., June 30, 1938.

CHEYENNE OF THE UPPER PLATTE RIVER. See also CHEYENNE; UPPER PLATTE. *Approp. St.* 14:492.

CHEYENNE-ARAPAHOE TRIBES OF OKLAHOMA. See also CHEYENNE; ARAPAHOE. *Spec. St.* 27:1, 753; 30:495; 35:444. *Approp. St.* 15:198; 16:13, 335, 544, 704; 17:165, 437; 18:133, 146, 420; 19:176, 271; 20:63, 295; 21:114, 485; 22:68, 433; 23:76, 362; 24:449; 25:217, 980; 26:336, 989; 27:120, 612; 28:286, 876; 29:321; 30:62; 31:221; 32:245, 982; 33:189, 1048; 34:325; 35:70, 781; 37:518; 38:582; 39:123, 969, 40:561; 41:3, 408, 1225; 42:1174; 43:390, 704, 1313; 44:453, 934; 45:883, 1562, 1607, 1623; 46:279, 1115; 47:91; 48:362; 50:213. *Priv. St.* 22:804; 49:2155. *Treaties* 12:1163. *I. D. Rulings* 13 L. D. 185, Aug. 20, 1891; 20 L. D. 46, Jan. 21 1895. *Const.* Sept. 18, 1937.

CHEYENNE, ARAPAHOE, KIOWA AND COMANCHE INDIANS. See also CHEYENNE; CHEYENNE-ARAPAHOE KIOWA; COMANCHE. *Spec. St.* 39:1199. *Approp. St.* 18:420; 38:77.

CHEYENNE RIVER SIOUX TRIBE. See also CHEYENNE. *Spec. St.* 25:888; 26:720; 35:460; 36:196, 265, 602; 37:84, 653; 41:1446; 42:499; 43:1184; 44:1389; 45:400, 1487, 1488; 46:1107; 47:300; 49:2191. *Approp. St.* 29:321; 30:62, 571; 31:221; 34:1015; 36:269; 37:518; 41:3, 408, 1248; 49:1757; 52:291. *Priv. St.* 34:2408; 42:1768. *Cases* Rousseau, 45 C. Cls. 1; Ryan, 8 C. Cls. 265; U. S. v. La Plant, 200 Fed. 92. *I. D. Rulings* Memo. Sol., Feb. 27, 1935, Mar. 22, 1935; Memo. Sol. Off., Oct. 27, 1938. *Const.* Dec. 27, 1935.

CHICKASAW. See also OKLAHOMA; CHOCTAW AND CHICKASAW; FIVE CIVILIZED TRIBES. *Texts* Manypenny, OIW. *Per.* James, 12 J. H. Univ. Studies 467. *Spec. St.* 2:649, 649, c. 25; 3:461, 702; 4:188, 653, 735; 5:10, 116, 490, 727; 9:202; 10:630; 11:200; 18:7; 24:28, 76; 27:492, 495; 28:693; 33:743; 39:870; 40:3; 41:1364; 45:737; 48:791; 50:537, 810; 52:347. *Approp. St.* 1:563; 2:66, 108, 440, 548; 3:393, 517; 4:181, 315, 397, 470, 526, 616, 636, 682, 705, 780; 5:36, 158, 402, 417, 435, 493, 704, 766; 9:598; 10:76, 290, 686; 11:410; 12:104; 28:286; 31:1010; 32:552, 1031; 33:394; 38:559; 40:2, 579; 45:1607; 48:984. *Priv. St.* 6:98, 473, 779, 861; 9:735; 11:514; 38:1547; 43:1367; 49:2246. *Treaties* 7:24, 65, 66, 89, 101, 150, 192, 381, 450; 10:974; 11:611; 14:769. *Cases* Atoka, 3 Ind. T. 189; Ayres, 44 C. Cls. 48; Ayres, 44 C. Cls. 110; Ayres, 42 C. Cls. 385; Ballinger, 216 U. S. 240; Best, 18 Wall. 112; Blocker, 6 Ind. T. 482; Brader, 246 U. S. 88; Brown, 2 Ind. T. 329; Bruner, 4 Ind. T. 580; Buttz, 119 U. S. 55; Byrd, 44 C. Cls. 498; Campbell, 44 C. Cls. 488; Carney, 247 U. S. 102; Carter, 1 Ind. T. 342; Chickasaw, 193 U. S. 115; Chickasaw, 19 C. Cls. 133; Chickasaw, 22 C. Cls. 222; Chickasaw, 75 C. Cls. 426; Chickasaw, 87 C. Cls. 91; Choctaw, 75 C. Cls. 494; Choctaw, 81 C. Cls. 63; Choctaw, 235 U. S. 292; Choctaw, 83 C. Cls. 140; Choctaw, 119 U. S. 1; Clark, 13 Pet. 195; Crowell, 4 Ind. T. 36; Davis, 271 U. S. 484; Dukes, 5 Ind. T. 145; Elliot, 7 Ind. T. 679; Ellis, 118 Fed. 430; Ex p. Carter, 4 Ind. T. 539; Fleming, 215 U. S. 56; Fraer, 125 Fed. 280; Frame, 189 Fed. 785; Gannon, 243 U. S. 108; Glonn, 105 F. 2d 398; Gooding, 142 Fed. 112; Hass, 17 F. 2d 894; Hamilton, 42 C. Cls. 282; Harrington, 3 Ind. T. 65; Hampton, 4 Ind. T. 503; Hayes, 168 Fed. 221; Hayes, 44 C. Cls. 493; Hill, 242 U. S. 361; Holford, 136 Fed. 553; Howell, 5 Ind. T. 718; In re Poff's, 7 Ind. T. 59; Ickes, 64 F. 2d 982; Jackson, 34 C. Cls. 441; Johnson, 64 F. 2d 674; Joines, 4 Ind. T. 556; Kelly, 7 Ind. T. 541; Kimberlin, 104 Fed. 653; Kimberlin, 3 Ind. T. 16; Ligon, 164 Fed. 670; Longest, 276 U. S. 69; Love, 21 Fed. 755; McBride, 149 Fed. 114; McLish, 141 U. S. 661; McMurray, 62 C. Cls. 458; Mullen, 250 U. S. 590; Myers, 2 Ind. T. 3; Porter, 7 Ind. T. 616; Porterfield, 2 How. 76; Powell, 61 F. 2d. 283; Reynolds, 4 Ind. T. 679; Roff, 168 U. S. 218; Roberts, 237 U. S. 386; Rogers, 3 Ind. T. 562; Rowe, 4 Ind. T. 597; Sass, 3 Ind. T. 536; Southwestern, 3 Ind. T. 223; Stevenson, 86 Fed. 106; Swinney, 5 Ind. T. 12; Taylor, 235 U. S. 42; Thomas, 3 Ind. T. 545; Thomason, 206 Fed. 895; Thompson, 4 Ind. T. 412; Turner, 4 Ind. T. 606; Tye, 2 Ind. T. 113; U. S. v. Baker, 4 Ind. T. 544; U. S. v. Choctaw, 38 C. Cls. 558; U. S. v. Choctaw, 179 U. S. 494; U. S. v. Dowden, 220 Fed. 277; U. S. v. Lewis, 5 Ind. T. 1; U. S. v. McMurray, 181 Fed. 723; U. S. v. Missouri, 66 F. 2d 919; U. S. ex rel. McAlester, 277 Fed. 573; Wallace, 6 Ind. T. 32; Westmoreland, 155 U. S. 545; Whitchwich, 92 F. 2d 249; White, 1 Ind. T. 98; Wilcoxen, 1 Ind. T. 138; Williams, 216 U. S. 582; Williams, 4 Ind. T. 587; Wilson, 86 Fed. 573; Wilson, 38 C. Cls. 6. *Op. A. G.* 3:34, 41, 170; 17:134, 265. *L. D. Memo.* (*D. J.*) 1:99, 227; 3:64; 12:289. *I. D. Rulings.* Memo. Sol. Off., Dec. 11, 1918; Op. Sol., Mar. 10, 1922, May 28, 1924, Nov. 11, 1924, Dec. 24, 1926, April 12, 1927, Aug. 1, 1929; Memo. Sol., Jan. 2, 1934, Mar. 9, 1936.

CHINOOK. See also OREGON; CHINOOK AND SAN JUAN. *Spec. St.* 43:886. *Approp. St.* 34:325; 37:518. *Cases* Halbert, 283 U. S. 753; McKay, 16 Fed. Cas. No. 8840; U. S. v. Provoe, 283 U. S. 753; U. S. v. Walkowsky, *id.*; U. S. ex rel. Charley, 62 F. 2d 955.

CHINOOK & SAN JUAN. See also CHINOOK. *Approp. St.* 33:1048. *Cases* Duwamish, 79 C. Cls. 530.

CHIPPEWA (CHIPPEWAY). See also MICHIGAN; MINNESOTA; WISCONSIN; BAD RIVER RESERVATION; BAY MILLS COMMUNITY; BEAR ISLAND; BOIS FORT; CASS LAKE; CHIPPEWA INDIAN COOPERATIVE MARKETING ASSOCIATION; CHIPPEWA OF MICHIGAN; CHIPPEWA OF MINNESOTA; CHIPPEWA OF MISSISSIPPI AND LAKE SUPERIOR; CHIPPEWA OF SAGINAW; CHIPPEWA OF WISCONSIN; CHIPPEWAS, MENOMONEES, CHIPPEWA-CREE TRIBE OF THE ROCKY BOY'S RESERVATION; CHIPPEWAYS, OTTAWAYS AND POTTAWATAMIE; FOND DU LAC; GRAND PORTAGE RESERVATION; KEWEENAW BAY INDIAN COMMUNITY OF THE L'ANSE RESERVATION; LA POINTE; LAC COURT D'OREILLE; LAKE SUPERIOR CHIPPEWA; LEECH LAKE; MILLE LAC; MOLE LAKE BAND; RED CLIFF; RED LAKE BAND; ROCKY BOY RESERVATION; ST. CROIX; TURTLE MOUNTAIN; WHITE EARTH RESERVATION; WILD RICE INDIAN RESERVATION; WINNEBAGOSHISH. *Texts* Manypenny, OIW; Moorehead, AI. *Per.* Brosius, 23 Case & Com. 739; Cain, 2 Minn. L. Rev. 177; Dixon, 23 Case & Com. 712; Harsha, 134 N. A. Rev. 272; Tydings, 23 Case & Com. 743; 9 J. H. Univ. Studies 541. *Gov. Pub.* 63 Cong., 3 sess., H. Doc. 1253, H. Doc. 1663; 70 Cong., 1 sess., S. Rep. 330, H. Rep. 746; 71 Cong., 3 sess., Hearings, H. Comm. Ind. Aff., H. R. 13527; 73 Cong., 2 sess., S. Doc. 179; 74 Cong., 1 sess., H. Rep. 336. *Spec. St.* 3:308, 319; 4:302; 5:680; 10:598; 12:207; 14:370; 19:55, 212; 25:642; 26:24, 669; 28:112, 489; 29:12, 17, 92; 31:801; 32:400; 35:169, 268, 444, 465, 1167; 36:330, 829, 855; 39:739; 43:1, 819; 45:314, 423, 601, 684; 46:1045, 1107, 1108; 47:306, 337; 48:254, 668, 927; 49:312, 321, 496, 1272; 52:215, 688, 697, 1212. *Approp. St.* 1:460; 2:467; 3:393, 517, 608; 4:92, 232, 267, 300, 361, 390, 394, 403, 432, 463, 505, 526, 616, 631, 636, 682, 705, 780; 5:36, 73, 158, 298, 323, 402, 493, 612, 704, 766; 9:252, 342, 544, 570; 10:315, 643; 11:65, 169, 273, 388, 431; 12:44, 221, 512, 774; 13:161, 541; 14:492, 255; 15:7, 198; 16:13, 335, 544; 17:165, 437, 580; 18:146, 420; 19:176, 271; 20:63, 295; 21:114, 414, 485; 22:257, 433; 23:76, 362, 446; 24:449; 25:217, 980; 26:34, 336, 504, 989; 27:120, 612; 28:286, 876; 29:17, 321; 30:62, 571, 652, 924, 1214; 31:221, 1058; 32:245, 982; 33:189, 1048; 34:325, 634, 1015; 35:8, 781; 36:269, 1289; 37:518, 595; 38:77, 208, 582; 39:123, 801, 969; 41:3, 35, 327, 408, 1015, 1156, 1225; 42:29, 192, 327, 437, 552, 1174, 1527; 43:390, 704, 753, 1141, 1313; 44:453, 934; 45:2, 200, 1562, 1623; 46:90, 279, 1115; 47:91, 525, 820; 48:362; 49:176, 1757; 50:213, 564; 52:291. *Priv. St.* 6:639, 913, 919; 9:741, 777, 791; 11:556; 12:883; 35:1620; 36:2064; 43:1597; 45:2024; 46:1933, 1979; 48:1420; 49:2106, 2210. *Treaties* Archives No. 44; 7:16, 28, 49, 87, 105, 112, 131, 160, 203, 206, 207, 218, 272, 290, 303, 315, 320, 323, 326, 491, 503, 506, 536, 565, 591; 8:116; 9:904, 952; 10:1064, 1109, 1172; 11:621, 631, 633; 12:1105; 13:667, 689, 693; 15:657, 765; 16:719. *Cases* Beaulieu, 32 App. D. C. 398; Bisek, 5 F. 2d 994; Brown, 265 Fed. 623; Chippewa, 301 U. S. 358; Chippewa, 305 U. S. 479; Chippewa, 80 C. Cls. 410; Dickson, 242 U. S. 371; Ex p. Pero, 99 F. 2d 28; Fairbanks, 223 U. S. 215; Fee, 162 U. S. 602; Francis, 203 U. S. 233; Godfrey, 10 Fed. Cas. No. 5497; Gravelle, 253 Fed. 549; Harris, 249 Fed. 41; Hyne, 27 C. Cls. 113; In re Blackbird, 109 Fed. 139; Johnson, 234 U. S. 422; Jones, 175 U. S. 1; Lane, 246 U. S. 110; La Roque, 239 U. S. 62; Minnesota, 185 U. S. 373; Morrow, 243 Fed. 854; Ottawa, 42 C. Cls. 240; Ottawa, 42 C. Cls. 518; Pam-To-Pee, 187 U. S. 371; Pine, 186 U. S. 279; Prentice, 50 Fed.

437; Shepard, 46 Fed. 341; Spalding, 160 U. S. 394; Thayer, 20 C. Cls. 737; U. S. v. Auger, 153 Fed. 671; U. S. v. Bonness, 125 Fed. 485; U. S. v. Cass, 240 Fed. 617; U. S. v. Flynn, 25 Fed. Cas. No. 15124; U. S. v. 43 Gallons, 93 U. S. 188; U. S. v. 43 Gallons, 106 U. S. 491; U. S. v. 4,450.72 Acres, 27 F. Supp. 167; U. S. v. Holliday, 3 Wall. 407; U. S. v. Holt, 270 U. S. 49; U. S. v. Joyce, 240 Fed. 610; U. S. v. La Roque, 198 Fed. 645; U. S. v. Law, 250 Fed. 218; U. S. v. Mille, 229 U. S. 498; U. S. v. Minnesota, 270 U. S. 181; U. S. v. Raiche, 31 F. 2d 624; U. S. v. Spaeth, 24 F. Supp. 465; U. S. v. Thomas, 47 Fed. 488; U. S. v. Waller, 243 U. S. 452; U. S. v. Walters, 17 F. 2d 116; U. S. v. Wirt, 28 Fed. Cas. No. 16745; U. S. ex rel. Coburn, 18 F. 2d 822; U. S. ex rel. Detling, 18 Fed. 822; U. S. ex rel. Kadrie, 30 F. 2d 989; Westling, 60 F. 2d 398; Wisconsin, 201 U. S. 202; Woodbury, 170 Fed. 302. *Op. A. G.* 3:206; 7:746; 19:710; 25:416; 29:455; 31:95. *L. D. Memo.* (*D. J.*) 12:1. *I. D. Rulings* 9 L. D. 392, Sept. 23, 1889; 15 L. D. 104, July 25, 1892; 26 L. D. 44, Jan. 17, 1898; 29 L. D. 132, Aug. 25, 1899; 29 L. D. 408, Jan. 18, 1900; 35 L. D. 143, Sept. 7, 1906; 44 L. D. 524, Jan. 15, 1916; 44 L. D. 531, Jan. 29, 1916; Op. Sol., Oct. 29, 1921, April 19, 1924; Memo. Sol. Off., Feb. 15, 1932, Oct. 18, 1932; Memo. Sol. Jan., 1935, April 8, 1933; Op. Sol., July 19, 1934, Aug. 3, 1934; Memo. Sol., Aug. 8, 1934, Dec. 18, 1934, Mar. 24, 1936; Op. Sol., June 30, 1936; Memo. Sol., Dec. 19, 1936, Jan. 26, 1937, Mar. 15, 1937, May 1, 1937; Memo. Sol. Off., June 6, 1938, June 25, 1938.

CHIPPEWA, BOIS FORTE. See also CHIPPEWA; BOIS FORTE. *Spec. St.* 36:582. *Approp. St.* 10:686; 18:146, 420; 22:68. *Treaties* 10:1109. *Cases* Pond, 58 Fed. 448.

CHIPPEWA-CREE TRIBE OF THE ROCKY BOY'S RESERVATION. See also CHIPPEWA; CREE; ROCKY BOY'S RESERVATION. *I. D. Rulings* Memo. Sol., July 16, 1937. *Const.* Nov. 23, 1935. *Charter* July 27, 1936.

CHIPPEWA, FOND DU LAC. See also CHIPPEWA; FOND DU LAC. *Approp. St.* 27:120; 30:62. *I. D. Rulings* Op. Sol., Oct. 27, 1924, Dec. 13, 1934.

CHIPPEWA, LAC DU FLAMBEAU. See also CHIPPEWA; LAC DU FLAMBEAU. *Spec. St.* 43:132. *I. D. Rulings* Memo. Sol. Off., June 6, 1938; Memo. Sol., Nov. 18, 1938.

CHIPPEWA, LAKE. See also CHIPPEWA OF LAKE SUPERIOR. *Approp. St.* 10:181.

CHIPPEWA OF LAKE SUPERIOR, WISCONSIN. See also CHIPPEWA; CHIPPEWA, LAKE; CHIPPEWA OF MISSISSIPPI AND LAKE SUPERIOR. *Spec. St.* 28:970; 32:795; 47:169. *Approp. St.* 9:382; 10:686; 12:44, 221, 512, 774; 13:161, 541; 18:133, 146, 420; 22:68; 23:362; 26:989; 27:120, 612; 28:286; 30:62, 571, 924; 40:561. *Cases* Hartman, 76 Fed. 157; Prentice, 43 Fed. 270; Prentice, 113 U. S. 435; Starr, 208 U. S. 527; U. S. v. First, 234 U. S. 245; U. S. v. Stearns, 245 U. S. 436; Vezina, 245 Fed. 411.

CHIPPEWA OF MICHIGAN. See also MICHIGAN; CHIPPEWA. *Spec. St.* 18:516; 43:137.

CHIPPEWA, MILLE LAC. See also CHIPPEWA; MILLE LAC. *Spec. St.* 35:619. *Cases* Mille, 46 C. Cls. 424. *I. D. Rulings* 5 L. D. 541, April 4, 1887.

CHIPPEWA, MINNESOTA. See also MINNESOTA; CHIPPEWA. *Spec. St.* 29:17, 245, 592, 702; 39:846; 40:1055, 1321; 42:221; 43:95, 798, 816, 818, 819, 1052; 44:77, 555, 763, 888; 45:986; 46:54; 47:49, 773; 48:979, 980; 49:1826. *Approp. St.* 12:512; 20:115; 29:17; 30:62; 43:33, 1141; 46:1552; 47:820. *Priv. St.* 17:739. *Treaties* 12:1249. *Cases* Chippewa, 80 C. Cls. 410; Chippewa, 305 U. S. 479; Chippewa, 307 U. S. 1; Morrison, 266 U. S. 481; Naganab, 202 U. S. 473; Work, 18 F. 2d 820. *I. D. Rulings* Op. Sol., May 31, 1924, June 17, 1924, Nov. 6, 1924, Dec. 13, 1934; Memo. Sol., Aug. 27, 1935; Memo. Sol. Off., Oct. 28, 1935; Op. Sol., Feb. 19, 1938. *Const.* July 24, 1936. *Charter* Nov. 13, 1937.

CHIPPEWA OF MISSISSIPPI. See also MISSISSIPPI; CHIPPEWA; CHIPPEWA OF MISSISSIPPI AND LAKE SUPERIOR. *Spec. St.* 18:31; 47:808. *Approp. St.* 5:298, 402, 417; 9:382, 544, 574; 10:41; 12:44, 221, 512, 774; 13:161, 541; 18:146, 420; 22:68; 30:62, 571; 40:561. *Treaties* 10:1165; 12:1249. *Cases* Mille, 46 C. Cls. 424; Naganab, 202 U. S. 473; Oakes, 172 Fed. 305; Prentice, 43 Fed. 270; Prentice, 113 U. S. 435; U. S. v. First, 234 U. S. 245; U. S. v. Heyfron, 138 Fed. 968. *I. D. Rulings* 16 L. D. 427, April 1, 1893.

CHIPPEWA OF MISSISSIPPI AND LAKE SUPERIOR. See also MISSISSIPPI; CHIPPEWA. *Spec. St.* 34:1217. *Approp. St.* 9:20, 132, 252, 382, 544, 574; 10:41, 226, 315, 686; 30:62. *Cases* Fond, 34 C. Cls. 426; Hitchcock, 22 App. D. C. 275; Minnesota, 305 U. S. 382.

CHIPPEWA, PEMBINA BAND. See also CHIPPEWA; RED LAKE; MINNESOTA. *Approp. St.* 22:257; 23:362; 26:989; 27:612; 28:286; 30:62, 571, 924. *Treaties* 13:667. *Cases* U. S. v. Le Bris, 121 U. S. 278. *I. D. Rulings* Op. Sol., June 30, 1936.

CHIPPEWA, PILLAGER BAND. See also CHIPPEWA; MINNESOTA. *Gov. Pub.* 71 Cong., 2 sess., H. R. 1669. *Spec. St.* 46:1487. *Approp. St.* 9:252, 544; 18:146, 420; 22:257.

CHIPPEWA, RED CLIFF. See also CHIPPEWA; RED CLIFF. *I. D. Rulings* Memo. Sol., Oct. 5, 1936.

CHIPPEWA-RED LAKE. See also CHIPPEWA; RED LAKE. *Spec. St.* 31:134; 49:444. *Approp. St.* 22:257; 23:362; 26:989; 27:612; 28:286; 30:62, 571, 924. *Treaties* 13:667. *I. D. Rulings* Memo. Sol., Dec. 26, 1935; Op. Sol., June 30, 1936, Feb. 19, 1938, Aug. 1, 1938.

CHIPPEWA OF SAGINAW. See also CHIPPEWA; SAGINAW. *Approp. St.* 5:298, 402, 417; 9:20, 132, 252, 382, 544, 574; 10:41, 226, 315, 686. *Priv. St.* 9:777; 12:843. *Treaties* 7:528, 578.

CHIPPEWA OF WISCONSIN. See also WISCONSIN; CHIPPEWA. *Spec. St.* 49:1049.

CHIPPEWA INDIAN COOPERATIVE MARKETING ASSOCIATION. See CHIPPEWA. *Spec. St.* 49:654.

CHIPPEWA, MENOMINEES, WINNEBAGOES. See also CHIPPEWA; MENOMINEE; WINNEBAGO; WISCONSIN. *Approp. St.* 4:780; 5:36, 158, 298, 323, 402, 417, 493, 704, 766; 9:20, 132, 252, 382, 544, 574; 10:15, 41, 226, 315, 686; 11:273; 12:44, 221, 512, 774; 13:161, 541; 14:492.

CHIPPEWAYS, OTTAWAYS & PATTAWATAMIE. See also CHIPPEWA; OTTAWA; POTAWATOMIE. *Approp. St.* 4:616, 682, 770; 5:36, 158, 298, 323, 402, 417, 493, 704, 766; 9:20, 132; 12:44. *Treaties* 7:431.

CHITIMACHA. See LOUISIANA; CHETTIMANCHI.

CHO-BAH-AH-BISH (CHOBAABISH). See WASHINGTON.

CHOCTAW. See also OKLAHOMA; CHOCTAW OF MISSISSIPPI; CHOCTAW AND CHICKASAW; FIVE CIVILIZED TRIBES. *Texts* Manypenny, OIW. *Per.* James, 12 J. H. Univ. Studies 467. *Gov. Pub.* 71 Cong., 3 sess., H. Doc. 819; 75 Cong., 3 sess., H. Rep. 2233. *Spec. St.* 2:83, 229, 479; 3:461, 680, 690; 4:40, 95, 188, 302, 464, 653; 5:180, 211, 251, 513; 9:114, 473; 10:121, 349, 630, 704; 11:200, 248, 314; 18:476; 21:504; 24:76; 25:184, 884; 26:640; 27:747; 28:502; 29:13, 40; 30:495; 31:657; 33:240; 35:444; 37:189; 39:870; 40:433; 45:737; 50:810; 52:347. *Approp. St.* 2:108, 467; 3:315, 393, 633, 749; 4:92, 181, 214, 470, 528, 616, 619, 631, 636, 682, 705, 780; 5:36, 73, 158, 402, 417, 493, 612, 681, 704, 766; 9:342; 18:402; 30:1074; 40:561; 41:3, 408; 42:552, 1174; 43:672, 753, 1141; 44:841, 934; 45:1562; 48:791, 984; 52:667. *Priv. St.* 6:143, 267, 521, 581, 596, 607, 614, 633, 671, 769, 856; 9:735, 742, 799; 10:752; 11:538; 33:1664; 34:2415; 49:2105, 2246. *Treaties* 7:21, 66, 80, 95, 98, 234, 311, 417, 333, 474, 533; 11:611; 14:769. *Cases* Ansley, 5 Ind. T. 563; Atoka, 3 Ind. T. 189; Arnold, 4 F. 2d 838; Atoka, 104 Fed. 471; Ayres, 44 C. Cls. 48; Ayres, 42 C. Cls. 385; Ballinger, 216 U. S. 240; Barton, 4 Ind. T. 260; Baze, 24 F. Supp. 806; Blocker, 6 Ind. T. 482; Blundell, 267 U. S. 373; Brader, 246 U. S. 88; Brown, 2 Ind. T. 329; Bruner, 4 Ind. T. 580; Carpenter, 280 U. S. 363; Castell, 4 Ind. T. 1; Central, 283 Fed. 368; Cherokee, 135 U. S. 641; Chickasaw, 193 U. S. 115; Chickasaw, 75 C. Cls. 426; Choctaw, 75 C. Cls. 494; Choctaw, 81 C. Cls. 63; Choctaw, 235 U. S. 292; Choctaw, 119 U. S. 1; Choctaw, 19 C. Cls. 243; Choctaw, 21 C. Cls. 59; Choctaw, 81 C. Cls. 1; Choctaw, 83 C. Cls. 49; Choctaw, 83 C. Cls. 140; Choctaw, 6 Ind. T. 515; Choctaw, 4 Ind. T. 36; Dukes, 5 Ind. T. 145; Ellis, 118 Fed. 430; Ex p. Reynolds, 20 Fed. Cas. No. 11719; Fisk, 166 Fed. 744; Fleming, 215 U. S. 56; Fraer, 125 Fed. 280; Franklin, 233 U. S. 269; Gaines, 9 How. 356; Garland's, 256 U. S. 439; Garland's, 272 U. S. 728; Gleason, 224 U. S. 679; Glonn, 105 F. 2d 398; Gowen, 56 Fed. 973; Hampton, 4 Ind. T. 503; Harris, 181 Fed. 712; Hayes, 168 Fed. 221; Hill, 242 U. S. 361; Holmes, 33 F. 2d 688; Holmes, 53 F. 2d 960; Howell, 5 Ind. T. 718; Ikard, 4 Ind. T. 314; In re Poff's, 7 Ind. T. 59; Jackson, 297 Fed. 549; Joines, 4 Ind. T. 556; Kelly, 1 Ind. T. 184; Leftridge, 6 Ind. T. 305; Lucas, 163 U. S. 612; Lanham, 244 U. S. 582; Ledbetter, 23 F. 2d 81; Ligon, 164 Fed. 670; Longest, 276 U. S. 69; McCalib, 83 C. Cls. 79; McCurtain, 1 Ind. T. 107; McMurray, 62 C. Cls. 458; McNee, 253 Fed. 546; Mullen, 250 U. S. 590; Mullen, 234 U. S. 192; Pell, 45 C. Cls. 154; Porter, 7 Ind. T. 616; Reynolds, 4 Ind. T. 679; Riddle,

58 Fed. 490; Robinson, 2 Ind. T. 509; St. Louis, 49 Fed. 440; Schaap, 210 Fed. 853; Southwestern, 185 U. S. 499; Standley, 59 Fed. 836; Swinney, 5 Ind. T. 12; Taylor, 7 How. 572; Taylor, 7 Ind. T. 666; Thebo, 66 Fed. 372; Thompson, 4 Ind. T. 412; Turner, 4 Ind. T. 606; Tye, 2 Ind. T. 113; U. S. v. Choctaw, 179 U. S. 494; U. S. v. Choctaw, 38 C. Cls. 558; U. S. v. Dowden, 220 Fed. 277; U. S. v. Dunn, 288 Fed. 158; U. S. v. Eastern, 66 F. 2d 923; U. S. v. Fooshe, 225 Fed. 521; U. S. v. Haddock, 21 F. 2d 165; U. S. v. Lee, 24 F. Supp. 814; U. S. v. McMurray, 181 Fed. 723; U. S. v. Marshall, 210 Fed. 595; U. S. v. Martin, 45 F. 2d 836; U. S. v. Missouri, 66 F. 2d 919; U. S. v. Richards, 27 F. 2d 284; U. S. v. Tiger, 19 F. 2d 35; U. S. ex rel. McAlester, 77 Fed. 573; U. S. ex rel. Sykes, 258 Fed. 520; Walker, 204 U. S. 302; Walker, 1 Ind. T. 191; Wallace, 204 U. S. 415; Ward, 253 U. S. 17; Whitchurch, 92 F. 2d 249; Williams, 239 U. S. 414; Williams, 218 Fed. 797; Williams, 4 Ind. T. 587; Wilson, 6 Wall. 83; Winton, 255 U. S. 373; Wright, 158 U. S. 232. *Op. A. G.* 2:462, 465, 693; 3:48, 106, 107, 113, 365, 408, 467, 517; 4:45, 107, 344, 346, 452, 513; 5:251; 12:208, 516; 13:354, 546; 17:134, 265; 18:242, 486; 19:109, 179; 24:689; 26:127; 28:568; 35:251. *L. D. Memo. (D. J.)* 1:99, 227; 10:364. *I. D. Rulings* Memo. Sol., Dec. 11, 1918; Op. Sol., May 28, 1924, Dec. 24, 1926, April 12, 1927, Aug. 1, 1929; Memo. Sol. Off., Jan. 2, 1934; Memo. Sol., Aug. 31, 1936, May 14, 1938.

CHOCTAW OF MISSISSIPPI. See also CHOCTAW; CHOCTAW AND CHICKASAW. *Per.* Houghton, 19 Calif. L. Rev. 507. *Gov. Pub.* 71 Cong., 3 sess., Hearings, H. Commn. Ind. Aff., S. 2134. *Approp. St.* 30:62; 41:3, 1225; 42:1048; 43:390, 704, 1141, 1313; 44:453; 46:279, 1115. *Priv. St.* 48:1467. *Cases* Ikard, 4 Ind. T. 314. *L. D. Memo. (D. J.)* 12:73. *I. D. Rulings* Op. Sol., Jan. 14, 1938.

CHOCTAW AND CHICKASAW. See also CHOCTAW; CHICKASAW; CHOCTAW OF MISSISSIPPI; OKLAHOMA. *Texts* Bledsoe, ILL. *Gov. Pub.* 60 Cong., 1 sess., S. Doc. 483; 65 Cong., 1 sess., H. Rep. 192; 65 Cong., 2 sess., S. Rep. 207; 72 Cong., 1 sess., Hearings, S. Comm. Ind. Aff., S. 2268, Hearings, S. Comm. Ind. Aff., H. R. 6803, Hearings, H. Comm. Ind. Aff., H. R. 6852. *Spec. St.* 15:177; 22:181; 25:162; 27:753; 30:816; 32:90, 177; 33:544, 571; 36:832; 37:67, 78, 1007; 38:767; 39:866; 40:1585; 41:1105, 1107; 43:138, 537, 1612; 44:1370; 46:385, 788. *Approp. St.* 4:682; 18:204; 32:1031; 47:525. *Priv. St.* 39:1470; 42:1569; 48:1467. *Treaties* 7:56; 10:1116; 11:573, 611. *Cases* Davis, 5 Ind. T. 47; Davies, 5 Ind. T. 50; Dawes, 5 Ind. T. 53; Dukes, 4 Ind. T. 156. *Op. A. G.* 3:591; 7:142, 174; 8:300; 18:34; 19:389; 25:152, 320, 460; 29:131; 35:259; 36:473. *L. D. Memo. (D. J.)* 3:499; 7:87; 12:10. *I. D. Rulings* Op. Sol., April 5, 1922, Nov. 19, 1928.

CHRISTIAN INDIANS. *Spec. St.* 11:312. *Approp. St.* 4:181, 526, 616, 682, 780; 5:36, 158, 298, 323, 402, 493, 704, 766; 9:20, 132, 252, 382, 544, 574; 10:41, 226, 315, 686; 11:65; 12:774; 15:198; 16:544; 30:62.

CITIZEN BAND OF POTAWATOMI INDIANS OF OKLAHOMA. See also OKLAHOMA; POTAWATOMIE. *Const.* Dec. 12, 1938.

CLALLAM. See also WASHINGTON; S'KLALLAM. *Approp. St.* 43:1102; 44:161; 45:1623; 46:90. *I. D. Rulings* Memo. Sol. Off., June 25, 1938.

CLEAR LAKE. See CALIFORNIA.

CLATSOP (CHINOOK). See also OREGON *Approp. St.* 33:1048. *Cases* U. S. v. Wirt, 28 Fed. Cas. No. 16745; U. S. v. ex rel. Charley, 62 F. 2d 955.

COAST RANGE RESERVATION. See also OREGON. *Spec. St.* 49:801.

COCHITI PUEBLO. See NEW MEXICO; PUEBLO.

COEUR D'ALENE. See also IDAHO; PEND D'OREILLE; SALISH. *Spec. St.* 25:160; 34:1229; 35:50, 626; 37:85, 1025. *Approp. St.* 20:63; 24:449; 25:980; 26:336, 989; 27:120, 612; 28:286, 876; 29:321; 30:62, 571, 924; 31:221, 1058; 32:245, 982; 33:189, 1048; 34:325, 1015; 35:70, 781; 36:202, 269, 774; 37:518; 38:559; 39:123, 969; 40:561; 41:3, 408, 1225; 42:552, 1174; 43:390, 704, 1141, 1313; 44:453, 934; 45:200, 1562, 1623; 46:279, 1115; 47:91. *Cases* Eugene, 274 Fed. 47; Gibson, 131 Fed. 39; Louie, 254 U. S. 548; Swendig, 265 U. S. 322; U. S. v. Benewah, 290 Fed. 628; U. S. v. Saunders, 96 Fed. 268. *I. D. Rulings* Op. Sol., Aug. 18, 1932.

COLORADO. See also GRAND RIVER; GRAND RIVER AND UINTAH; MUACHE; MOACHES; SOUTHERN UTE TRIBE OF THE SOUTHERN UTE RESERVATION; TABEGUACHE, MUACHE, CAPOTE, WEEMINUCHE, YAMPA, GRAND RIVER AND UINTAH BANDS OF UTES; UNCOMPAHGRE; UTE; WEEMINUCHES. *Approp. St.* 17:165, 437; 18:146, 402, 420; 19:176, 271; 20:63, 295; 21:114, 485.

COLORADO RIVER INDIAN TRIBES OF THE COLORADO RIVER RESERVATION. See also ARIZONA; CALIFORNIA; MOJAVE; MOJARIS; YUMA. *Spec. St.* 35:43; 36:879; 47:335. *Approp. St.* 14:492; 17:165; 19:363; 20:63; 21:114; 23:76; 24:449; 25:217, 980; 26:336, 989; 35:70; 36:269; 37:518; 38:77, 582; 39:123, 969; 40:561; 41:3, 35, 408, 1225; 42:552, 1154, 1174; 43:390, 704, 1141; 44:453, 934; 45:200, 1562; 46:90, 279, 1115; 47:15, 91, 820; 48:362; 49:176, 1757; 50:213; 52:291. *I. D. Rulings* Irrigation Memo. April 21, 1927; Memo. Sol., Sept. 13, 1935. *Const.* Aug. 13, 1937.

COLUMBIA RESERVATION. See also WASHINGTON; COLUMBIA AND COLVILLE; COLVILLE. *Spec. St.* 34:55, 934, 2833; 43:133, 357. *Approp. St.* 33:1048. *Cases* Starr, 227 U. S. 613; U. S. v. Moore, 161 Fed. 513. *I. D. Rulings* 16 L. D. 151, Jan. 6, 1893; 32 L. D. 568, April 25, 1904; 40 L. D. 212, May 23, 1911.

COLUMBIA & COLVILLE. See also WASHINGTON; COLUMBIA. *Approp. St.* 23:76, 362; 24:449; 25:217, 980; 26:336, 989; 27:120, 612; 28:286, 876; 29:321; 30:62, 571, 924.

COLVILLE. See also WASHINGTON; COLUMBIA RESERVATION; SPOKANE. *Spec. St.* 26:102; 29:44; 30:430; 32:803; 33:567; 34:55, 80, 2829; 36:855; 37:197, 594, 634; 38:111; 39:672; 40:449; 41:535; 42:507; 43:133; 44:558; 47:334. *Approp. St.* 20:63; 21:114, 485; 23:76; 24:449; 25:217, 980; 26:336; 28:286, 876; 29:267; 29:321; 30:571; 31:221, 280, 1058; 32:245, 982; 33:189, 1048; 34:325, 1015; 35:781; 36:269; 37:518, 595, 912; 38:77; 39:14, 123, 696; 40:2, 821; 41:3, 408, 1156, 1225; 42:192, 552, 1174; 43:390, 704, 1141, 1313; 44:161, 453, 934, 1250; 45:2, 200, 883, 1562, 1623; 46:279, 1115; 47:91, 820; 48:362; 49:176, 1757; 50:564; 52:291. *Priv. St.* 43:1362, 1563. *Cases* Blackfeet, 81 C. Cls. 101; Butler, 43 C. Cls. 497; Collins, 73 Fed. 735; Dull, 222 Fed. 471; Gordon, 34 App. D. C. 508; La Chapelle, 62 Fed. 545; McFadden, 87 Fed. 154; Mason, 302 U. S. 186; Starr, 227 U. S. 613; U. S. v. Ferry, 24 F. Supp. 399; U. S. v. Four Sour-Mash, 90 Fed. 720; U. S. v. Gardner, 133 Fed. 285; U. S. v. Harris, 100 F. 2d 268; U. S. v. Heyfron, 138 Fed. 964; U. S. v. Moore, 161 Fed. 513; U. S. v. Pelican, 232 U. S. 442. *I. D. Rulings* 32 L. D. 568, April 25, 1904; 35 L. D. 220, Oct. 6, 1906; 39 L. D. 44, June 24, 1910; 40 L. D. 212, May 23, 1911; 45 L. D. 63, Nov. 24, 1916; 50 L. D., Dec. 24, 1924; Op. Sol., Dec. 24. 1924; Memo. Sol., July 8, 1933; Op. Sol., Dec. 13, 1935; Memo. Sol. Off., Jan. 17, 1936.

COMANCHE. See also OKLAHOMA; APACHE, KIOWA, COMANCHE; APACHE, KIOWA, COMANCHE, WICHITA; ARAPAHOE, CHEYENNE, APACHE, KIOWA, COMANCHE AND WICHITA; CADDO; CHEYENNE, ARAPAHOE, KIOWA AND COMANCHE; COMANCHE, APACHE; COMANCHE AND KIOWA; COMANCHE, KIOWA AND APACHE; COMANCHE, KIOWA, AND APACHE OF THE ARKANSAS RIVER. *Texts* Manypenny, OIW. *Per.* Brown, 39 Yale L. J. 307. *Spec. St.* 9:203; 13:323; 22:47; 29:529; 31:672; 1093; 39:1199; 40:1318; 43:1573; 44:762; 45:492, 986; 47:39; 48:501. *Approp. St.* 4:780; 5:298, 493, 612, 704; 10:315; 11:169; 16:291; 17:5; 20:410; 21:67, 414; 22:7; 23:362; 26:504; 30:105, 652; 31:280, 727; 32:552, 1031; 33:394, 1048, 1214; 34:325; 35:478; 45:2, 200; 48:984. *Priv. St.* 6:466; 17:732; 21:549, 640; 30:1563. *Treaties* 7:474, 533; 9:844; 10:1013; 14:717; 15:581. *Cases* Abrew, 37 C. Cls. 510; Ball, 161 U. S. 72; Brown, 32 C. Cls. 432; Byrd, 44 C. Cls. 498; Friend, 29 C. Cls. 425; Gamel, 31 C. Cls. 321; Gorham, 29 C. Cls. 97; Gossett, 31 C. Cls. 325; Hayes, 44 C. Cls. 493; Light, 10 Okla. 732; Lone, 187 U. S. 553; McKee, 33 C. Cls. 99; Morten, 46 C. Cls. 372; Murray, 46 C. Cls. 101; Oklahoma, 258 U. S. 574; Price, 28 C. Cls. 422; U. S. v. Andrews, 179 U. S. 96; U. S. v. Board, 6 F. Supp. 401; U. S. v. Gorham, 165 U. S. 316; U. S. v. Loving, 34 Fed. 715; U. S. v. Myers, 206 Fed. 387; U. S. v. Rowell, 243 U. S. 464; Weston, 29 C. Cls. 420; Wynn, 29 C. Cls. 15. *Op. A. G.* 18:235. *I. D. Rulings* Op. Sol., Mar. 10, 1922, Aug. 14, 1926.

COMANCHE (TEXAS) AND APACHE. See also APACHE; COMANCHE; TEXAS. *Approp. St.* 10:686.

COMANCHE & KIOWAY (KIOWA). See also COMANCHE; KIOWA; OKLAHOMA. *Approp. St.* 14:255, 492.

COMANCHE, KIOWA, AND APACHE OF THE ARKANSAS RIVER. See also APACHE; COMANCHE; KIOWA; OKLAHOMA. *Approp. St.* 10:41, 315, 686; 11:65, 169, 273,

388; 12:44, 221, 512, 774; 13:161, 541; 14:492; 31:1010.

COMANCHE, KIOWA AND APACHE. See also APACHE; COMANCHE; COMANCHE, KIOWA, APACHE OF THE ARKANSAS RIVER; KIOWA; OKLAHOMA. *Spec. St.* 32:63; 44:1369. *Approp. St.* 31:1010.

CONFEDERATED PEORIA. See PEORIA; KASKASKIA; PIANKESHAW; QUAPAW; SENECA; WEA.

CONFEDERATED SALISH AND KOOTENAI TRIBES OF THE FLATHEAD RESERVATION. See also MONTANA; FLATHEAD; KOOTENAI; SALISH. *Approp. St.* 52:291. *Const.* Oct. 26, 1935. *Charter* April 21, 1936.

CONFEDERATED TRIBES OF THE GRANDE RONDE COMMUNITY. See OREGON; GRANDE RONDE COMMUNITY.

CONFEDERATED TRIBES OF THE WARM SPRINGS RESERVATION. See OREGON; WARM SPRINGS.

CONNECTICUT. See also NARRAGANSETT; PEQUOT. *Per.* Varney, 13 Green Bag 399.

COOS BAY. See also OREGON; KALAWATSET; UMPQUA. *Spec. St.* 45:1256; 47:307; 49:801.

CORNPLANTER RESERVATION. See also NEW YORK; PENNSYLVANIA; SENECA. *I. D. Rulings* Memo. Sol., May 24, 1937.

COSNEJO. See ARIZONA; MOJAVE; NAVAJO. *Cases* Barrow, 30 C. Cls. 54.

COVELO INDIAN COMMUNITY OF THE ROUND VALLEY INDIAN RESERVATION. See also ROUND VALLEY RESERVATION. *Const.* Dec. 16, 1936. *Charter* Nov. 6, 1937.

COW CREEK. See also OREGON; GALEESE CREEK; UMPQUA. *Priv. St.* 27:773. *Treaties* 10:1125.

COWLITZ. See also WASHINGTON; CHEHALIS. *Cases* Halbert, 283 U. S. 753; U. S. v. Provoe, 283 U. S. 753; U. S. v. Seufert, 252 Fed. 51; U. S. ex rel. Charley, 62 F. 2d 955.

CRAIG COMMUNITY ASSOCIATION OF CRAIG, ALASKA (THLINGIT). See also ALASKA; THLINGIT. *Const.* Oct. 8, 1938. *Charter* Oct. 8, 1938.

CREE. See also MONTANA; CHIPPEWA; TURTLE MOUNTAIN. *Spec. St.* 29:117. *Treaties* 11:657.

CREEK. See also OKLAHOMA; APPALACHICOLA; FIVE CIVILIZED TRIBES; KIALIGEE; MUSCOGEE; SEMINOLE. *Texts* Bledsoe, ILL; Kent, CAL; McLaughlin, CHU; Manypenny, OIW. *Per.* Gates, 21 Am. J. Soc. Sci. 112; Hagan, 23 Case & Com. 735; James, 12 J. H. Univ. Studies 467. *Spec. St.* 3:228, 374, 380, 461, 484, 485, 517; 4:187, 433, 721; 729; 5:186, 256, 397, 504, 506; 6:441; 9:344; 10:349, 630; 17:626; 18:29; 22:301; 25:757; 26:14, 659, 749; 27:281; 28:693; 29:502; 30:495, 567; 31:861; 32:399, 500; 35:553; 37:122; 39:1199; 43:139; 45:944; 52:752. *Approp. St.* 1:568; 2:66, 108, 407; 3:378, 418, 480, 633, 748; 4:36, 37, 92, 181, 191, 257, 267, 300, 315, 348, 397, 470, 526, 528, 532, 616, 636, 682, 705, 780; 5:17, 33, 36, 73, 148, 158, 402, 417, 493, 612, 704, 766; 9:284; 10:214, 576; 11:409; 15:311; 17:122; 18:402; 23:194, 446; 25:565; 48:984, 1021. *Priv. St.* 6:103, 171, 191, 213, 278, 297, 322, 323, 342, 428, 465, 472, 530, 583, 592, 597, 622, 640, 677, 678, 689, 759, 788, 792, 813, 822, 849, 855, 913, 928; 9:659, 678, 708, 765; 10:734, 793, 810, 842; 11:483, 538, 547; 12:840; 22:755; 25:1131; 26:1173, 1205, 1231, 1232, 1249, 1332, 1333, 1336, 1358, 1359, 1377, 1378, 1379, 1398, 1401, 1420, 1423; 27:769, 817; 28:1025; 30:1416, 1437, 1457, 1501, 1586; 31:1606, 1686, 1708; 32:1294, 1352, 1395, 1493, 1497, 1514, 1526, 1600, 1607, 1696, 1730; 33:1353, 1398, 1402, 1407, 1496, 1497, 1504, 1531, 1637, 1640, 1662, 1942, 2001; 34:1514, 1627, 1693, 1697, 1841, 2015, 2037, 2050, 2246, 2747, 2783, 2809; 35:1389, 1406; 45:2035, 2036. *Treaties* Archives No. 17; 7:35, 56, 68, 95, 96, 120, 171, 192, 215, 217, 237, 286, 289, 307, 311, 366, 368, 414, 417, 423, 427, 574; 9:821; 11:599, 699; 14:785. *Cases* Adkins, 235 U. S. 414; Anchor, 256 U. S. 519; Anderson, 53 F. 2d 257; Arbor, 45 F. 2d 746; Armstrong, 195 Fed. 137; Bagby, 60 F. 2d 80; Barbee, 1 Ind. T. 199; Barnett, 84 F. 2d 916; Barnett, 21 F. 2d 325; Barnett, 259 Fed. 394; Barnett, 19 F. 2d 504; Bell, 192 Fed. 597; Bilby, 246 U. S. 947; Caesar, 103 F. 2d 503; Capital, 6 Ind. T. 223; Cate, 299 U. S. 30; City of Tulsa, 75 F. 2d 343; Clark, 51 F. 2d 42; Coffee, 123 U. S. 1; Commissioner, 78 F. 2d 763; Conner, 19 C. Cls. 695; Conner, 32 F. 2d 581; Crabtree, 54 Fed. 432; Crabtree, 54 Fed. 426; Creek, 63 C. Cls. 270; Creek, 74 C. Cls. 663; Creek, 77 C. Cls. 159; Creek, 78 C. Cls. 474; Creek, 77 C. Cls. 226; Creek, 84 C. Cls. 12; Creek, 302 U. S. 620; Darks, 69 F. 2d 231; Daugherty, 3 Ind. T. 197; Davis, 40 F. 2d 264; Davidson, 56 Fed. 443; Denton, 5 Ind. T. 396; Derrisaw, 8 F. 255; Blackburn, 6 Ind. T. 232; Bond, 25 F. Supp. 157; Brown, 27 F. 2d 374; Burgess, 103 F. 2d 37; Buster, 135 Fed. Supp. 876; Eddy, 163 U. S. 456; English, 224 U. S. 680; Ex p. Tiger, 2 Ind. T. 41; Ex p. Dickson, 4 Ind. T. 481; Fink, 248 U. S. 392; Forsythe, 3 Ind. T. 599; Fulson, 35 F. 2d 84; Garrison, 30 C. Cls. 272; George, 4 Ind. T. 61; Gilcrease, 249 U. S. 178; Gillespie, 257 U. S. 501; Goat, 224 U. S. 458; Grayson, 267 U. S. 352; Harris, 7 Ind. T. 532; Harris, 254 U. S. 103; Harris, 166 Fed. 109; Hawkins, 195 Fed. 345; Hopkins, 235 Fed. 95; In re Grayson, 3 Ind. T. 497; Indian, 5 Ind. T. 41; Ingram, 47 F. 2d 135; Iowa, 217 Fed. 11; Jack, 39 F. 2d 594; Jackson, 34 C. Cls. 441; Jefferson, 247 U. S. 288; Jones, 273 U. S. 195; Ladiga, 2 How. 581; Kemohah, 38 Fed. 665; Kunkel, 10 F. 2d 804; Locke, 287 Fed. 276; Lucas, 15 F. 2d 32; McDougal, 273 Fed. 113; McDougal, 237 U. S. 372; McFadden, 2 Ind. T. 260; McKee, 201 Fed. 74; Malone, 212 Fed. 668; Mandler, 49 F. 2d 201; Mandler, 52 F. 2d 713; Marlin, 276 U. S. 58; Mars, 40 F. 2d 247; Maxey, 3 Ind. T. 243; Mitchell, 9 Pet. 711; Moore, 167 Fed. 826; Morrison, 154 Fed. 617; Muskogee, 4 Ind. T. 18; Muskogee, 165 Fed. 179; Muskogee, 118 Fed. 382; Norton, 266 U. S. 511; Nunn, 216 Fed. 330; Parker, 250 U. S. 235; Parker, 250 U. S. 66; Patterson, 2 Pet. 216; Pigeon, 237 U. S. 386; Pitman, 64 F. 2d 740; Porter, 7 Ind. T. 395; Porter, 260 Fed. 1; Priddy, 204 Fed. 955; Quigley, 3 Ind. T. 265; Reed, 197 Fed. 419; Reynolds, 236 U. S. 58; Roberts, 66 F. 2d 874; Roubedeaux, 23 F. 2d 277; Schellenbarger, 236 U. S. 68; Self, 28 F. 2d 590; Shaw, 276 U. S. 575; Shulthis, 225 U. S. 561; Sizemore, 255 U. S. 441; Skelton, 235 U. S. 206; Stanclift, 152 Fed. 697; Stephens, 126 Fed. 148; Stewart, 295 U. S. 403; Sunderland, 266 U. S. 226; Sweet, 245 U. S. 192; Taylor, 230 Fed. 580; Tiger, 22 F. 2d 786; Tiger, 4 F. 2d 714; Tiger, 48 F. 2d 509; Tiger, 221 U. S. 286; Turner, 51 C. Cls. 125; Turner, 248 U. S. 354; Tuttle, 3 Ind. T. 712; U. S. v. Atkins, 260 U. S. 220; U. S. v. Bartlett, 235 U. S. 72; U. S. v. Black, 247 Fed. 942; U. S. v. Board, 284 Fed. 103; U. S. v. Brown, 8 F. 2d 564; U. S. v. Brown, 15 F. 2d 565; U. S. v. Comet, 202 Fed. 849; U. S. v. Cook, 225 Fed. 756; U. S. v. Crawford, 47 Fed. 561; U. S. v. Creek, 295 U. S. 103; U. S. v. Equitable, 283 U. S. 738; U. S. v. Ferguson, 247 U. S. 175; U. S. v. Fort, 195 Fed. 211; U. S. v. Gray, 284 Fed. 103; U. S. v. Gypsy, 10 Fed. 2d 487; U. S. v. Hayes, 20 F. 2d 873; U. S. v. Jacobs, 195 Fed. 707; U. S. v. Lena, 261 Fed. 144; U. S. v. McGugin, 28 F. 2d 76; U. S. v. Mackay, 216 Fed. 126; U. S. v. Mid, 67 F. 2d 37; U. S. v. Mott, 37 F. 2d 860; U. S. v. Ranson, 284 Fed. 108; U. S. v. Rea-Read, 171 Fed. 501; U. S. v. Shock, 187 Fed. 870; U. S. v. Southern, 9 F. 2d 644; U. S. v. Stigall, 226 Fed. 190; U. S. v. Tiger, 19 F. 2d 35; U. S. v. Watashe, 102 F. 2d 428; U. S. v. Western, 226 Fed. 726; U. S. v. Wildcat, 244 U. S. 111; U. S. v. Woods, 223 Fed. 316; U. S. ex rel. Johnson, 253 U. S. 738; U. S. ex rel. McIntosh, 47 Fed. 561; U. S. ex rel. Warren, 73 F. 2d 844; U. S. ex rel. West, 205 U. S. 80; U. S. Express Co., 191 Fed. 673; W. O. Whitney, 166 Fed. 738; Wade, 39 App. D. C. 245; Washington, 235 U. S. 422; Wassom, 3 Ind. T. 365; Welty, 231 Fed. 930; Wilmott, 27 F. 2d 277; Wilson, 38 C. Cls. 6; Woodward, 238 U. S. 284. *Op. A. G.* 2:110, 575; 3:40, 230, 238, 259, 288, 389, 423, 578, 585, 596, 644; 4:75, 77, 85, 96, 491; 5:46, 98; 16:31; 19:342; 24:623; 25:163; 26:317. *L. D. Memo.* (*D. J.*) 2:307; 8:384. *I. D. Rulings* Op. Sol., Dec. 18, 1923, Nov. 8, 1924, Jan. 23, 1925, July 20, 1931; Memo. Sol., Jan. 20, 1932, Sept. 12, 1935, Oct. 22, 1935, July 29, 1937, Aug. 7, 1937, April 8, 1937, July 15, 1937; Memo. Sol. Off., May 24, 1933.

CROW. See also MONTANA; RIVER CROW. *Texts* Copp, USM. *Per.* Gates, 21 Am. J. Soc. Sci. 112; Mac Leod, 28 J. Crim. L. 181. *Spec. St.* 17:626; 22:42, 157; 25:167, 660; 26:14, 468, 659; 27:529; 33:352; 40:958; 42:625, 994; 43:1301; 44:251, 566, 658, 807, 922, 1365; 45:429, 482, 1496; 46:168, 1105, 1494, 1495; 47:420; 49:244, 336, 655, 1543; 50:884; 52:347. *Approp. St.* 14:492; 15:198; 16:13, 335, 544; 17:165, 437; 18:146, 420; 19:176, 271; 20:63, 295, 410; 21:114, 414, 485; 22:68, 257, 302, 433; 23:76, 267, 362, 516; 24:449; 25:4, 217, 980; 26:336, 989; 27:120, 612; 28:286, 876; 29:321; 30:62, 571, 652, 924, 1214; 31:221, 280, 1010, 1058; 32:245, 982; 33:189, 1048; 34:205, 325, 1015; 35:781; 36:269; 37:518; 38:77, 582; 39:123, 969; 40:561; 41:3, 163, 408, 1225; 42:552, 1174; 43:390, 704, 1141; 44:453, 841, 934; 45:200, 883, 1562, 1623; 46:279, 860, 1115; 47:91, 525, 820; 49:176, 1757; 50:564; 52:85, 291. *Priv. St.* 17:787; 34:2215, 2220; 44:1485; 45:2035; 46:1633, 1634, 1634, c. 145, 2135, 2148; 47:1657, 1657, c. 67; 48:1437; 49:2121. *Treaties* 7:266; 11:657; 15:649. *Cases* Bean, 159 Fed. 651; Brown, 32 C. Cls. 432; Crow, 81 C. Cls. 238; Davis, 27 C. Cls. 181; Draper, 164 U. S. 240; Kirby, 260 U. S. 423; Truscott, 73

Fed. 60; U. S. v. Fidelity, 121 Fed. 766; U. S. v. Heinrich, 16 F. 2d 112; U. S. v. Hoyt, 167 Fed. 301; U. S. v. Powers, 305 U. S. 527; U. S. v. Soldana, 246 U. S. 530; U. S. v. Stocking, 87 Fed. 857; U. S. v. 12 Bottles, 201 Fed. 191; Winters, 207 U. S. 564. *Op. A. G.* 20:517; 35:438. *L. D. Memo. (D. J.)* 18:118. *I. D. Rulings* 5 L. D. 138, Sept. 8, 1886; 27 L. D. 305, Aug. 5, 1898; 48 L. D. 479, Nov. 22, 1921; Op. Sol., Nov. 22, 1921; 49 L. D. 376, Dec. 28, 1922; Op. Sol., Sept. 21, 1927; Memo Sol. Off., Oct. 17, 1938; Memo. Sol., Feb. 10, 1939, May 5, 1939.

CROW CREEK. See also LOWER BRULE SIOUX TRIBE; MINNECONJOU; SIOUX; TWO KETTLE. *Spec. St.* 25:888; 36:1087; 47:300. *Approp. St.* 27:5, 612; 28:286; 32:245; 35:781. *Priv. St.* 49:2222, 2319. *Treaties* 12:981. *Cases* King, 111 Fed. 860; Redfield, 27 C. Cls. 473; Schewson, 31 C. Cls. 192; Sioux, 277 U. S. 424; U. S. v. Partello, 48 Fed. 670. *Op. A. G.* 18:141. *I. D. Rulings* Op. Sol., Nov. 21, 1924; Memo. Sol. Off., Oct. 12, 1934.

CUYAPAIPE. See CALIFORNIA; MISSION.

DAKOTAS. See also SIOUX. *Per.* Cain, 2 Minn. L. Rev. 177; Mac Leod, 28 J. Crim. L. 181; 9 J. H. Univ. Studies 541. *Gov. Pub.* 66 Cong., 1 sess., S. Rep. 185. *Spec. St.* 39:1199. *Approp. St.* 17:165, 437; 18:146, 420; 19:176, 271; 20:63, 295; 21:114, 485. *Treaties* 14:695, 699, 723, 727, 731, 735, 739, 743, 747.

DELAWARE. See also OKLAHOMA; DELAWARE AND SHAWNEE; MUNSEE AND DELAWARE. *Texts* Jackson, CD; Manypenny, OIW. *Gov. Pub.* 75 Cong., 3 sess., Hearings, S. Comm. Ind. Aff., S. 2326, Hearings, H. Comm. Ind. Aff., S. 2326. *Spec. St.* 2:448; 3:308, 319, 517, 575; 4:464, 594; 9:55, 337; 11:312; 12:539; 25:608; 27:86; 28:580; 30:495; 31:848; 32:716; 43:812; 44:1358; 49:1459. *Approp. St.* 1:460; 2:338, 407, 607; 4:181, 267, 526, 532, 616, 636, 682, 780, 5:36, 158, 298, 323, 402, 417, 493, 704, 766; 9:20, 252, 382, 544, 574; 10:41, 181, 226, 315, 576, 686; 11:65, 169, 273; 12:44, 221, 512, 774; 13:161, 541; 14:255, 492; 15:198; 16:13, 335, 544; 17:165, 437; 18:146, 420; 19:176, 271; 20:63, 295; 21:485, 114; 22:68, 433; 23:76, 362; 24:449; 25:217; 26:336, 989; 27:120, 612; 28:286, 424; 33:189; 45:2; 48:984. *Priv. St.* 6:270; 17:787. *Treaties* 7:13, 16, 28, 49, 74, 81, 91, 113, 115, 116, 118, 131, 160, 188, 284, 326, 327, 391, 397; 8:116; 9:987; 12:1129, 1177, 1191; 14:793. *Cases* Blackfeather, 190 U. S. 368; Blackfeather, 28 C. Cls. 447; Cherokee, 155 U. S. 196; Delaware, 193 U. S. 127; Delaware, 38 C. Cls. 234; Delaware, 72 C. Cls. 483; Delaware, 74 C. Cls. 368; Delaware, 84 C. Cls. 535; Elk, 112 U. S. 94; Harnage, 242 U. S. 386; Hicks, 12 Fed. Cas. No. 6458; Johnson, 283 Fed. 954; Journeycake, 28 C. Cls. 281; Journeycake, 31 C. Cls. 140; Kindred, 225 U. S. 582; New Jersey, 7 Cranch 164; Ross, 232 U. S. 110; Shawnee, 47 C. Cls. 321; U. S. v. Brindle, 110 U. S. 688; U. S. v. Choctaw, 179 U. S. 494; Wilson, 38 C. Cls. 6. *Op. A. G.* 6:658; 9:25, 45; 25:308. *I. D. Rulings* Memo. Sol., Mar. 18, 1936.

DELAWARE AND SHAWNEE. See also DELAWARE; SHAWNEE. *Approp. St.* 28:876.

DEVIL LAKE RESERVATION (FORT TOTTEN). See also FORT TOTTEN; SIOUX. *Spec. St.* 31:1436, 1447; 33:319. *Approp.* St. 19:363; 32:245; 34:325; 41:408. *Cases* Buttz, 119 U. S. 55; Sioux, 277 U. S. 424; U. S. v. Kiya, 126 Fed. 879.

DIEGUENOS. See also CALIFORNIA; MISSION. *Cases* Bell, 39 C. Cls. 350.

DIGGER INDIANS. See also CALIFORNIA. *Approp. St.* 27:612; 28:286; 30:62, 924, 1214; 31:221, 1058; 32:245, 982.

DIOMEDE, NATIVE VILLAGE OF. See also ALASKA; ESKIMO. *Const.* Jan. 31, 1940. *Charter* Jan. 31, 1940.

DRESSLERVILLE INDIAN COLONY (WASHOE). See also NEVADA; WASHOE. *Spec. St.* 44:560. *Approp. St.* 44:841.

DUCK VALLEY RESERVATION. See also IDAHO; NEVADA; PAH-UTE (PAIUTE); SHOSHONE-PAIUTE TRIBES OF THE DUCK VALLEY RESERVATION. *Spec. St.* 23:677; 52:193. *Approp. St.* 47:91.

DUCKWATER SHOSHONE TRIBE OF INDIANS OF THE DUCKWATER RESERVATION. See also NEVADA; SHOSHONE. *Const.* Nov. 28, 1940. *Charter* Nov. 30, 1940.

DWAMISH. See also WASHINGTON; SKAGIT; SNOHOMISH; SQUAXON; STELLA-QUAMISH. *Approp. St.* 12:4, 221, 512, 774; 13:161, 541; 14:255; 15:198; 16:13, 335, 544; 17:165, 437; 18:146, 420; 19:176, 271; 20:63, 295; 21:114, 485; 22:68, 433; 23:76, 362; 24:449; 25:217, 980; 26:336, 989; 27:120, 612; 28:286, 876; 29:321; 30:62, 571, 924; 31:221, 1058; 32:245, 982; 33:189, 1048; 34:325, 1015; 35:70, 781; 36:269; 37:518; 38:77; 39:123, 969; 40:561; 41:3, 408, 1225; 42:552, 1174; 43:704. *Treaties* 12:933. *Cases Corrigan*, 169 Fed. 477; Dwamish, 79 C. Cls. 530; Jackson, 34 C. Cls. 441.

EASTERN BAND OF CHEROKEE. See NORTH CAROLINA; CHEROKEE; CHEROKEE, NORTH CAROLINA; CHEROKEE, EASTERN BAND.

EASTERN SHAWNEE TRIBE OF INDIANS. See also OKLAHOMA; SHAWNEE. *Const.* Dec. 22, 1939.

EEL RIVER (MIAMI). See also INDIANA; EEL RIVER AND WEA; MIAMI. *Approp. St.* 1:460; 2:607; 3:308, 319; 4:181, 526, 616, 682, 780; 5:36, 158, 298, 323, 402, 417, 493, 704, 766; 9:20, 132, 252, 382, 544, 574; 10:41, 226, 315. *Treaties* 7:49, 74, 77, 91, 113, 115, 116; 8:116. *Cases* Painter, 33 C. Cls. 114.

EEL RIVER AND WEA. See also EEL RIVER; WEA. *Approp. St.* 2:407.

ELIM, NATIVE VILLAGE OF (ESKIMO). See also ALASKA; ESKIMO. *Const.* Nov. 24, 1939. *Charter* Nov. 24, 1939.

ELKO INDIAN VILLAGE. See also NEVADA; SHOSHONE. *Approp. St.* 46:1552; 47:525.

ELY, NEVADA INDIAN COLONY. See also NEVADA. *Spec. St.* 46:820.

ESKIMO. See ALASKA; KING ISLAND NATIVE COMMUNITY; NATIVE VILLAGE OF BARROW; NATIVE VILLAGE OF DIOMEDE; NATIVE VILLAGE OF ELIM; NATIVE VILLAGE OF GAMBELL; NATIVE VILLAGE OF KIVALINA; NATIVE VILLAGE OF KWETHLUK; NATIVE VILLAGE OF MEKORYUK; NATIVE VILLAGE OF NOATAK; NATIVE VILLAGE OF NUNAPITCHUK; NATIVE VILLAGE OF POINT HOPE; NATIVE VILLAGE OF SELAWIK; NATIVE VILLAGE OF SHISHMAREF; NATIVE VILLAGE OF SHAKTOOLIK; STEBBINS COMMUNITY ASSOCIATION; NATIVE VILLAGE OF TETLIN; NATIVE VILLAGE OF UNALAKLEET; NATIVE VILLAGE OF WALES; NOME ESKIMO COMMUNITY.

FIVE CIVILIZED TRIBES. See also OKLAHOMA; INDIAN TERRITORY; CHEROKEE; CHICKASAW; CHOCTAW; CREEK; SEMINOLE; ALABAMA-QUASSARTE TRIBAL TOWN. *Texts* Bennet, LTI; Butt, LSA; Cheadle, ADI; Foster, FPC; Meriam, IA; Bledsoe, ILL; Mills, LFC. *Per.* Brosius, 23 Case & Com. 739; Brown, 39 Yale L. J. 307; Brown, 15 Minn. L. Rev. 182; Cabell, 3 Okla. S. B. J. 208; Dixon, 23 Case & Com. 712; Flynn, 62 Cent. L. J. 399; Knoepfler, 7 Ia. L. B. 232; Platt, 160 N. A. Rev. 195; Reeves, 23 Case & Com. 727; Rice, 16 J. Comp. Leg. 78; Rosser, 3 Okla. B. A. 159; Thayer, 68 Atl. Month. 540, 676; Weeden, 2 J. H. Univ. Studies 385. *Gov. Pub.* 65 Cong., 2 sess., S. Rep. 330; 67 Cong., 1 sess., H. Rep. 264; 67 Cong., 2 sess., H. Rep. 545; 72 Cong., 1 sess., Hearings S. Comm. Ind. Aff., H. R. 8750; 73 Cong., 2 sess., H. Rep. 624; 76 Cong., 1 sess., Hearings S. Comm. Ind. Aff., S. J. Res. 101. *Spec. St.* 10:121; 12:116, 614; 16:390; 22:179, 400; 24:388; 25:392, 757, 783; 26:81; 29:80; 30:493, 495, 844, 1368; 31:182, 250, 660, 672, 760, 848; 32:500, 641, 774, 841, 1769; 33:299, 583; 34:137, 267, 822; 35:312; 36:855; 37:44, 46, 497, 678; 38:310, 780; 39:944; 40:606; 41:529, 625; 42:831, 994; 43:244, 722, 728; 44:239; 45:495, 733, 737, 1229; 46:1108, 1471; 47:88, 474, 777; 48:105, 501; 49:1135, 1160; 50:650. *Approp. St.* 5:298, 323; 9:20, 87, 132, 252, 382, 544, 570, 574; 10:15, 41, 226, 315, 643, 686; 11:65, 169, 273, 320, 362, 388; 12:44, 221, 774; 13:161, 541; 14:255, 310, 492; 15:198; 16:13, 335, 544; 17:165, 437; 18:133, 146, 420; 19:176, 271; 20:63, 206, 295, 377; 21:114, 485; 22:68, 433, 582; 23:362; 25:4, 217, 980; 26:336, 989; 27:120, 612; 28:286, 876; 29:321; 30:62, 571, 652, 924, 1214; 31:7, 86, 221, 861, 960, 1058; 32:245, 854, 982; 33:15, 85, 1048, 1214; 34:325, 389, 841, 935, 1015, 2832; 35:70, 781; 36:202, 269, 468, 774, 1058, 1170, 1289, 1363; 37:360, 417, 595, 912; 38:77, 312, 454, 582, 609, 997, 1138; 39:14, 123, 262, 801, 969, 1070; 40:105, 561, 634; 41:3, 35, 163, 408, 631, 1156, 1225, 1252; 42:29, 552, 767, 1174, 1527; 43:33, 390, 704, 753, 1141; 44:453, 841, 934; 45:200, 883, 1562, 1623; 46:279, 860, 1115, 1552; 47:91, 820, 1602; 48:362; 49:1757; 50:564; 52:35, 1114. *Priv. St.* 34:2833; 45:2029, 2265; 49:2325. *Cases* Adams, 165 Fed. 304; Alfrey, 168 Fed. 231; Anchor, 256 U. S. 519; Anderson, 53 F. 2d 257; Ansley, 180 U. S. 253; Atlantic, 165 U. S. 413; Barbre, 228 Fed. 658; Bartlett, 218 Fed. 380; Baze, 24 F. Supp. 806; Bell, 192 Fed. 597; Blundell, 267 U. S. 373; Board, 94 F. 2d 450; Bond, 181 Fed. 613; Brader, 246 U. S. 88; Brann, 192 Fed. 427; Brought, 129 Fed. 192; Caesar, 103 F. 2d 503;

Campbell, 248 U. S. 169; Carter, 12 F. 2d 780; Cherokee, 187 U. S. 294; Cherokee, 155 U. S. 196; Choate, 224 U. S. 665; Cochran, 276 Fed. 701; Cully, 37 F. 2d 493; David, 250 Fed. 208; Delaware, 193 U. S. 127; Derrisaw, 8 F. Supp. 876; Duncan, 245 U. S. 308; Elk, 112 U. S. 94; Engleman, 4 Ind. T. 336; Eslick, 51 C. Cls. 266; Ex p. Webb, 225 U. S. 663; Fink, 248 U. S. 399; Folk, 233 Fed. 177; Frame, 189 Fed. 785; Fulsom, 35 F. 2d 84; Gannon, 243 U. S. 108; Gilcrease, 249 U. S. 178; Glenn-Tucker, 4 Ind. T. 511; Goat, 224 U. S. 458; Hampton, 22 F. 2d 81; Harris, 188 Fed. 712; Harris, 254 U. S. 103; Heckman, 224 U. S. 413; Hill, 289 Fed. 511; Holmes, 53 F. 2d 960; Hopkins, 235 Fed. 95; Ickes, 64 F. 2d 982; Indian, 288 U. S. 325; In re Lands, 199 Fed. 811; In re Palmer's, 11 F. Supp. 301; Jackson, 43 F. 2d 513; Jefferson, 247 U. S. 288; Jennings, 192 Fed. 507; Johnson, 64 F. 2d 674; Jonah, 52 F. 2d 343; Joplin, 236 U. S. 531; Kemmerer, 229 Fed. 872; Keokuk, 4 Okla. 5; Kiker, 63 F. 2d 957; Knight, 23 F. 2d 481; Kunkel, 10 F. 2d 804; Ledbetter, 23 F. 2d 81; McNee, 253 Fed. 546; Marlin, 276 U. S. 58; Martin, 7 Ind. T. 451; Missouri, 46 C. Cls. 50; Moore, 167 Fed. 826; Morris, 194 U. S. 384; Mullen, 224 U. S. 448; Perryman, 238 U. S. 148; Privett, 256 U. S. 201; Rogers, 263 Fed. 160; Seminole, 78 C. Cls. 455; Southern, 241 U. S. 582; Stephens, 174 U. S. 445; Sunday, 248 U. S. 545; Superintendent, 295 U. S. 418; Texas, 194 Fed. 1; Thebo, 66 Fed. 372; Tiger, 22 F. 2d 786; Tiger, 4 F. 2d 714; Tiger, 221 U. S. 286; Truskett, 236 U. S. 223; U. S. v. Allen, 179 Fed. 13; U. S. v. Bartlett, 235 U. S. 72; U. S. v. Bowling, 256 U. S. 484; U. S. v. Ferguson, 247 U. S. 175; U. S. v. Hayes, 20 F. 2d 873; U. S. v. Jacobs, 195 Fed. 707; U. S. v. Knight, 206 Fed. 145; U. S. v. Lee, 24 F. Supp. 814; U. S. v. Oklahoma, 261 U. S. 252; U. S. v. Rea-Read, 171 Fed. 501; U. S. v. Shock, 187 Fed. 862; U. S. v. Smith, 35 Fed. 49; U. S. v. Soule, 30 Fed. 918; U. S. v. Tiger, 19 F. 2d 35; U. S. v. Watashe, 102 F. 2d 428; U. S. ex rel. Reynolds, 45 App. D. C. 50; Whitebird, 40 F. 2d 479; Whitechurch, 92 F. 2d 249; Woodward, 238 U. S. 284. *Op. A. G.* 19:342; 20:724; 23:214; 26:340, 351; 27:530; 29:231; 34:275, 302; 37:193. *L. D. Memo (D. J.)* 4:63, 396, 552; 5:113; 12:289. *I. D. Rulings.* Op. Sol., April 29, 1922, Dec. 13, 1923, Nov. 8, 1924, Oct. 4, 1926, Mar. 3, 1930, Sept. 22, 1931; Memo. Sol. Off., Dec. 21, 1931; Op. Sol., Mar. 30, 1932, Aug. 5, 1932; Memo. Sol. Off., Nov. 3, 1932; Op. Sol., Dec. 9, 1932; Memo. Sol. Off., June 14, 1933, Aug. 2, 1933, Sept. 19, 1933, Feb. 5, 1934; Op. Sol., Mar. 14, 1934; Memo. Sol. Off., July 9, 1934; Memo. Sol., Sept. 15, 1934; Memo. Sol. Off., Jan. 14, 1935; Op. Sol., Jan. 22, 1935, Jan. 22, 1935, Jan. 30, 1935; Memo. Sol. Off., Mar. 8, 1935; Op. Sol., June 4, 1935; Memo. Sol., June 4, 1935; Op. Sol., Aug. 12, 1935; Memo. Sol., Sept. 20, 1935, Sept. 21, 1935; Op. Sol., Oct. 14, 1935, April 16, 1936; Memo. Sol., May 1, 1936, May 19, 1936, Aug. 7, 1936; Memo. Sol. Off., Aug. 11, 1936; Memo. Sol., Sept. 17, 1936, Dec. 21, 1936, Jan. 13, 1937, Jan. 23, 1937, Feb. 5, 1937, July 15, 1937, Aug. 25, 1937; Memo. Sol. Off., Oct. 9, 1937; Memo. Sol., Nov. 29, 1937; Memo. Sol. Off., June 29, 1938; Memo. Sol., Nov. 28, 1938, Feb. 10, 1939, Mar. 24, 1939.

FLANDREAU INDIANS (SANTEE SIOUX). See also SOUTH DAKOTA; SIOUX. *Priv. St.* 43:1561.

FLANDREAU SANTEE SIOUX TRIBE. See also SOUTH DAKOTA; FLANDREAU; SANTEE; SIOUX. *Const.* April 24, 1936. *Charter* Oct. 31, 1936.

FLATHEAD. See also MONTANA; CONFEDERATED SALISH AND KOOTENAI TRIBES OF THE FLATHEAD RESERVATION; FLATHEAD AND OTHER CONFEDERATED TRIBES; FLATHEAD, KOOTENAI AND PEND D'OREILLE; KOOTENAI; PEND D'OREILLE. *Gov. Pub.* 71 Cong., 2 sess., S. Doc. 153, H. Doc. 595. *Spec. St.* 18:15; 25:47; 26:1091; 31:267; 33:302; 35:444; 36:296, 855; 37:192; 38:510; 40:616, 1053, 1203; 41:452; 43:21, 246; 49:328; 52:193. *Approp. St.* 12:4, 44, 221; 14:255, 492; 17:165; 18:133, 146, 420; 19:176, 271; 20:63, 295; 21:114, 485; 22:68, 257; 23:76, 362; 24:449; 25:217, 980; 26:336, 989; 27:120, 612; 28:286, 876; 29:267, 321; 30:62, 571, 652, 924; 1214; 31:221, 280, 1010, 1058; 32:245, 982, 1031; 33:1048; 34:205, 325, 1015; 35:8, 70, 251, 781, 1039; 36:269, 703; 37:518; 38:77, 312, 582; 39:123, 969; 40:561; 41:3, 408, 1225; 42:552, 1174; 43:390, 704, 1141, 1313; 44:453, 934; 45:200, 1562, 1623; 46:90, 279, 1115, 1552; 47:91, 820, 1602; 48:362; 49:176, 1757; 50:564; 52:291. *Priv. St.* 46:1634; 47:1753; 48:1296, 1380, 1391; 49:2078. *Cases* Catholic, 200 U. S. 118; Clairmont, 225 U. S. 551; Pronovost, 232 U. S. 487; Scheer, 48 F. 2d 327; Territory of Montana, 9 Mont. 46; U. S. v. Barnaby, 51 Fed. 20; U. S. v. Heyfron, 138 Fed. 964; U. S. v. Heyfron, 138 Fed. 968; U. S. v. Higgins, 103 Fed. 348; U. S. v. Higgins, 110 Fed. 609; U. S. v. Hoyt, 167 Fed. 301; U. S. v. McIntire, 101 F. 2d 650; U. S. v. Partello, 48 Fed. 670. *I. D. Rulings* 22 L. D. 37, Jan. 22, 1896; Op. Sol., Nov. 16, 1921, Jan. 28, 1924, June 6, 1924, Oct. 9, 1924, April 24, 1925; Memo. Sol. Off., June 20, 1929; Op. Sol., Aug. 5, 1930; Memo. Sol., Dec. 18, 1937.

FLATHEAD AND OTHER CONFEDERATED TRIBES. See also FLATHEAD. *Approp. St.* 12:512, 774; 13:161, 541; 14:255, 492; 15:198; 16:13, 335, 554; 17:437; 18:133, 146, 420; 19:176, 271; 20:63; 21:114, 485; 22:433.

FLATHEAD, KOOTENAI & PEND D'OREILLE. See also FLATHEAD; KOOTENAI; PEND D'OREILLE; MONTANA. *Spec. St.* 17:226. *Approp. St.* 23:76. *Treaties* 12:975.

FLORIDA. See also APPALACHICOLA; CREEK; SEMINOLE. *Spec. St.* 4:735; 5:7. *Approp. St.* 4:37, 194, 214, 217, 532, 526, 616, 682, 780; 5:36, 158, 298, 323, 402, 417, 493, 704, 766; 9:20, 132, 252, 382, 544, 574; 10:41, 226, 315, 686; 11:65, 169, 273, 409. *Priv. St.* 6:341, 354, 527; 22:797; 23:699; 24:803, 926; 25:1142, 1206, 1209, 1214, 1332; 26:1132, 1132 c. 130, 1144, 1227, 1227 c. 734, 1233, 1275, 1359, 1378, 1397, 1407, 1411, 1417; 27:779, 788, 788 c. 290, 797, 802, 804, 817; 30:1401, 1406, 1420, 1499, 1512, 1518; 31:1488, 1783; 32:1261, 1287, 1294, 1316, 1355, 1357, 1411, 1555, 1569, 1644, 1648, 1677, 1703, 1729, 1751; 33:1326, 1363, 1376, 1472, 1498, 1560, 1580, c. 1425, 1637, 1713, 1769, 1876, 1937, 2018, 2058; 34:1513, 1526, 1568, 1569, 1570, 1704, 1740 c. 1492, 1803, 1987, 2027, 2036, 2051, 2057, 2093, 2095, 2096, 2108, 2134, 2143, 2147, 2194, 2198, 2202, 2204, 2205, 2210, 2222, 2248, 2249, 2249 c. 123, 2250, 2250 c. 126, 2251, 2276, 2303, 2314, 2377, 2378, 2379, 2383, 2384, 2499, 2522, 2544, 2559, 2567, 2577, 2583, 2590, 2593, 2763; 35:1179, 1179 c. 49, 1179 c. 50, 1204, 1219, 1375, 1389, 1406, 1462, 1536, 1573, 1616, 1616 c. 291; 36:1762, 1805, 1807, 1813, 1818, 1860, 1982, 2000, 2099; 37:1030; 38:1337, 1439, 1443; 39:1382, 1588; 43:1381. *Treaties* 7:224. *Cases* U. S. v. Fernandez, 10 Pet. 303.

FOND DU LAC (CHIPPEWA). See also MINNESOTA; CHIPPEWA. *Spec. St.* 25:558; 28:112. *Approp. St.* 29:321; 32:245; 33:189; 38:582. *I. D. Rulings* 42 L. D. 446, Oct. 1, 1913.

FOREST COUNTY POTAWATOMI COMMUNITY, WISCONSIN. See also WISCONSIN; POTAWATOMI. *Const.* Feb. 6, 1937. *Charter* Oct. 30, 1937.

FORT BELKNAP INDIAN COMMUNITY. See also MONTANA; ASSINIBOINE; GROS VENTRE (ATSINA). *Spec. St.* 44:902. *Approp. St.* 23:267, 516; 25:980; 26:336, 989; 27:120, 612; 28:286, 876; 29:321; 30:62, 571; 33:1048; 34:325, 1015; 35:70, 781; 36:269; 37:518, 595; 38:77, 208, 312, 582; 39:123, 969; 40:561; 41:3, 408, 1225; 42:29, 437, 552, 1174; 43:390, 704, 1313, 1141; 44:453, 934; 45:200, 883, 1562; 46:90, 279, 1115; 47:91, 820; 48:362; 49:176, 1757; 50:564; 52:291. *Cases* Blackfeet, 81 C. Cls. 101; Bridgemen, 140 Fed. 577; Power, 18 C. Cls. 263; Stookey, 58 F. 2d 522; Utah, 116 U. S. 28; Winters, 207 U. S. 564. *I. D. Rulings* Memo. Sol. Off., Jan. 23, 1932, Feb. 15, 1932, April 9, 1935; Op. Sol., July 17, 1935; Memo. Sol. Off., Oct. 15, 1935; Memo. Sol., July 12, 1937. *Const.* Dec. 13, 1935. *Charter* Aug. 25, 1937.

FORT BERTHOLD. See also GROS VENTRE (HIDATSA); MANDAN; THREE AFFILIATED TRIBES OF THE FORT BERTHOLD RESERVATION. *Spec. St.* 24:402; 34:894; 36:455; 37:631; 38:383, 681; 39:1131; 41:404, 595; 43:139, 817; 46:88. *Approp. St.* 26:989; 27:5, 120, 612; 28:286, 876; 29:321; 30:62, 571, 924; 31:221; 32:245, 982; 33:189, 1048; 34:325, 1015; 35:70, 781; 36:269; 37:518; 38:77, 582; 39:123, 969; 40:2, 561; 41:3, 408, 1225; 42:29, 552; 43:390, 704, 1141, 1313; 44:453, 934; 45:200, 1562, 1623; 46:279, 1115. *Priv. St.* 45:2036. *Cases* Fort Berthold, 71 C. Cls. 308. *I. D. Rulings* 49 L. D. 354, Nov. 16, 1922; Memo. Sol., Dec. 26, 1935; Op. Sol., Mar. 31, 1936; Memo. Sol., Jan. 11, 1937, Oct. 16, 1938; Memo. Asst. Sec'y, Dec. 5, 1938. *Const.* June 29, 1936. *Charter* April 24, 1937.

FORT BIDWELL INDIAN COMMUNITY. See also CALIFORNIA; PAH-UTE (PAIUTE). *Spec. St.* 37:652; 38:1374; 45:375. *Approp. St.* 40:561; 41:408; 46:1115. *I. D. Rulings* Memo. Sol., Nov. 12, 1935; Memo. Sol. Off., Nov. 23, 1935. *Const.* Jan. 28, 1936.

FORT DUCHESNE. See UTAH; GRAND RIVER; UINTAH.

FORT HALL. See also IDAHO; BANNOCK; SHOSHONE; SHOSHONE-BANNOCK TRIBES OF THE FORT HALL RESERVATION. *Gov. Pub.* 71 Cong., 2 sess., Hearings,

S. Comm. Ind. Aff., S. 3938; 75 Cong., 3 sess., Hearings, H. Comm. Ind. Aff., H. R. 6559; Hearings, H. Comm. Ind. Aff., S. 2253. *Spec. St.* 31:672; 33:153, 2078, 2079; 34:213; 40:592; 43:117; 44:566, 1397, 1398; 46:1061; 47:146, 1755; 52:198. *Approp. St.* 15:198; 16:13, 544; 19:363; 20:410; 21:114; 22:68, 433; 23:76, 362; 24:449; 26:336, 989; 27:120, 612; 28:286, 424, 876; 29:267, 321; 30:62, 571, 924; 31:221, 1058; 32:245, 982, 1031; 33:189, 1048; 34:325, 697, 1015; 35:781; 36:269, 703; 37:518; 38:77, 582; 39:123, 801, 969; 40:561; 41:3, 408, 1156, 1225; 42:552, 1174; 43:390, 672, 704, 1141; 44:453, 934, 1250; 45:377, 883, 1562, 1623; 46:279, 1115; 47:91, 820; 48:362; 49:176, 1757; 50:564; 52:291, 1114. *Priv. St.* 49:2222. *Cases* Skeem, 273 Fed. 93; U. S. v. Hoyt, 167 Fed. 301; U. S. v. Portneuf-Marsh, 213 Fed. 601; U. S. ex rel. Ray, 27 F. 2d 909; Ward, 163 U. S. 504. *I. D. Rulings* Op. Sol., Sept. 21, 1921; 48 L. D. 455, Sept. 29, 1921; Op. Sol., June 19, 1923, July 10, 1931; Memo. Sol. Off., May 28, 1936; Memo. Sol., Nov. 17, 1936.

FORT LAPWAI (NEZ PERCE). See also IDAHO; NEZ PERCE. *Spec. St.* 43:533. *Approp. St.* 35:781; 41:3, 408, 1225; 42:552, 1174; 43:390, 1141, 1313; 44:453, 934; 45:1562; 46:1115; 47:820. *Priv. St.* 35:1407. *Cases* Blackfeet, 81 C. Cls. 101; Dick, 208 U. S. 340. *I. D. Rulings* Memo. Sol., June 15, 1937; Memo Sol. Off., Oct. 7, 1938.

FORT McDERMITT PAIUTE AND SHOSHONE TRIBE OF THE FORT McDERMITT INDIAN RESERVATION. See also NEVADA; PAIUTE; SHOSHONE. *Gov. Pub.* 74 Cong., 1 sess., H. Rep. 337. *Spec. St.* 49:1094. *Approp. St.* 41:408, 1225; 42:552, 1174; 43:390, 1141; 44:453, 934; 46:1115. *I. D. Rulings* Memo. Sol. Off., Nov. 14, 1935. *Const.* July 2, 1936. *Charter* Nov. 21, 1936.

FORT McDOWELL MOJAVE-APACHE COMMUNITY. See also ARIZONA; APACHE; MOJAVE. *Const.* Nov. 24, 1936. *Charter* June 6, 1938.

FORT MOJAVE INDIAN RESERVATION. See also ARIZONA; MOJAVE; MOJARIS. *Spec. St.* 48:795. *Approp. St.* 26:989; 27:612; 30:571, 924; 38:582; 40:561; 41:1225; 42:1174; 43:1141; 44:453, 934.

FORT PECK. See also MONTANA; SIOUX. *Spec. St.* 25:114, 35:558; 39:994; 41:365, 549; 42:857; 43:667, 1267; 44:303, 498, 746, 1401; 45:774; 46:1106, 1108; 47:420; 49:327, 328, 329. *Approp. St.* 20:63, 295, 410; 21:114; 22:68, 433; 23:76, 267, 362, 446, 516; 24:449; 25:980; 26:336, 504, 989; 27:120, 612; 28:286, 876; 29:321; 30:62; 31:1058; 32:245, 982; 33:189, 1048; 34:325, 1015; 35:70, 781; 36:269; 37:518; 38:77, 582; 39:123, 969; 40:561; 41:3, 408, 1156, 1225; 42:552, 1174; 43:390, 1141, 1313; 44:453, 934, 1250; 45:200, 1562; 46:90, 279, 1115; 47:91; 49:176, 1757; 50:564, 755; 52:291. *Priv. St.* 44:1706; 46:1986; 47:1680; 48:1385. *Op. A. G.* 36:506. *I. D. Rulings* Memo. Sol., July 17, 1935.

FORT ROBINSON RESERVATION. See NEBRASKA; OGLALA; SIOUX.

FORT TOTTEN. See also DEVIL'S LAKE RESERVATION; SIOUX. *Approp. St.* 26:989; 27:612; 28:286; 30:571, 924; 35:781; 40:561; 44:161. *I. D. Rulings* Memo. Sol., July 20, 1934.

FORT YUKON, NATIVE VILLAGE OF, (ATHAPASCAN). See also ALASKA. *Const.* Jan. 2, 1940. *Charter* Jan. 2, 1940.

FORT YUMA. See also ARIZONA; CALIFORNIA; APACHE; YUMA. *Spec. St.* 43:94. *Approp. St.* 41:408; 46:1115; 47:91, 820. *I. D. Rulings* Asst. Secy's Letter to U. S. Atty., Feb. 26, 1932; Memo. Sol., Mar. 29, 1935.

FOX. See also IOWA; OKLAHOMA; SAC, FOX AND IOWAY; SAC AND FOX; SAUK & FOX. *Texts* Blanchard, MMM; Manypenny, OIW. *Spec. St.* 2:343; 4:302, 394, 464, 665, 740; 5:48, 522, 622, 666. *Approp. St.* 2:338; 4:92, 181, 470, 526, 616, 682, 780; 5:36, 158, 612, 681. *Treaties* 7:135, 378. *Cases* Choteau, 16 How. 203.

FRESNO AND KINGS RIVER RESERVATION. See also CALIFORNIA. *Approp. St.* 20:115.

GALEESE CREEK. See also OREGON; COW CREEK; SILETZ RESERVATION. *Treaties* 10:1125.

GAMBELL, NATIVE VILLAGE OF. See also ALASKA; ESKIMO. *Const.* Dec. 31, 1939. *Charter* Dec. 31, 1939.

GEORGETOWN. See WASHINGTON; SHOALWATER OR GEORGETOWN RESERVATION.

GILA RIVER. (GILA RIVER PIMA-MARICOPA INDIAN COMMUNITY). See also ARIZONA; MARICOPA; PIMA. *Spec. St.* 29:527; 46:1519. *Approp. St.* 33:1048; 34:325; 36:269; 37:518; 38:582; 39:123, 969; 40:561; 41:3, 408, 1225; 42:552, 1174; 43:33, 390, 704, 1141; 44:453, 934; 45:2, 200, 883, 1562, 1607; 46:279, 1115; 47:91, 820; 48:362; 49:176, 1757; 50:564; 52:291. *Cases* Ter. of Ariz., 8 Ariz. 302. *I. D. Rulings* Letter Comm. Nov. 5, 1934; Sec'ys Letter to Atty. Gen., Mar. 20, 1935; Memo. Sol., Mar. 29, 1935, Mar. 30, 1935. *Compt. Gen'ls Rulings* A. 86599. *Const.* May 14, 1936. *Charter* Feb. 28, 1938.

GOSHUTE. See also UTAH; SHOSHONE-GOSHIP; SKULL VALLEY RESERVATION. *Spec. St.* 52:216. *Cases* U. S. v. Leathers, 26 Fed. Cas. No. 15, 581.

GRAND PORTAGE RESERVATION (PIGEON RIVER). See also MINNESOTA; CHIPPEWA. *Spec. St.* 31:785, 1455. *Approp. St.* 29:267. *Cases* Minnesota, 305 U. S. 382; U. S. v. Minnesota, 95 F. 2d 468. *I. D. Rulings* Letter from Ass't Com'r Ind. Aff., Feb. 19, 1935.

GRAND RIVER. See also GRAND RIVER AND UINTAH BANDS; TABEGUACHE, MUACHE, CAPOTE, WEEMINUCHE, YAMPA, GRAND RIVER AND UINTAH BANDS OF UTES; UTAH; COLORADO; UTE INDIANS. *Treaties* 15:619.

GRAND RIVER AND UINTAH BANDS. See also GRAND RIVER; UINTAH. *Spec. St.* 12:498. *Approp. St.* 15:198.

GRANDE RONDE COMMUNITY, CONFEDERATED TRIBES OF. See also OREGON. *Spec. St.* 33:567; 49:801. *Approp. St.* 16:544; 17:165; 20:63, 295; 21:114, 485; 23:76; 24:449; 25:217, 980; 26:336; 29:321; 31:221, 1058; 32:245, 982; 33:189, 1048; 34:325, 1015; 35:70, 781; 36:269; 37:518; 38:77, 582; 39:123, 969; 41:3, 408, 1225; 42:552, 1174; 43:390, 704, 1141. *Cases* Bond, 181 Fed. 813; Ex p. Savage, 158 Fed. 205; U. S. v. Earl, 17 Fed. 75; U. S. v. McClane, 74 Fed. 153; U. S. v. Sinnott, 26 Fed. 89; U. S. v. Sinnott, 26 Fed. 84; Wheeler, 153 Fed. 471. *Const.* May 13, 1936. *Charter* Aug. 22, 1936.

GRASS VALLEY BAND. See PAH-UTE (PAIUTE).

GREAT OSAGE NATION. See also OKLAHOMA; OSAGE. *Spec. St.* 5:209; 16:55; 19:127. *Approp. St.* 5:323. *Treaties* 7:133, 222, 240, 268, 576.

GREEN RIVER (DWAMISH). See also WASHINGTON. *Cases* D'wamish, 79 C. Cls. 530.

GRINDSTONE CREEK RESERVATION. See also CALIFORNIA. *Approp. St.* 41:3.

GROS VENTRE (ATSINA, OF MONTANA). See also MONTANA; FORT BELKNAP INDIAN COMMUNITY; GROS VENTRE, PIEGAN, BLOOD, BLACKFEET, RIVER CROW. *Spec. St.* 17:787; 18:28; 25:113; 33:816; 36:1080; 43:21; 49:1569. *Approp. St.* 10:315; 16:335, 544; 17:122, 165, 437, 530; 18:146, 420; 19:271; 20:63, 295; 21:114, 485; 22:68, 433; 23:76, 362; 24:449; 26:504; 28:843. *Cases* Albright, 53 C. Cls. 247; Stookey, 58 F. 2d 522; Winters, 207 U. S. 564. *I. D. Rulings* Memo. Sol. M. 7599, June 9, 1922; Memo. Sol., Dec. 2, 1936.

GROS VENTRE (HIDATSA, OF NORTH DAKOTA). See also NORTH DAKOTA; THREE AFFILIATED TRIBES OF THE FORT BERTHOLD RESERVATION. *Spec. St.* 46:1481.

GROS VENTRE, PIEGAN, BLOOD, BLACKFEET, AND RIVER CROW INDIANS. See also BLACKFEET; BLOOD; GROS VENTRE (ATSINA); PIEGAN; RIVER CROW. *Spec. St.* 40:1204. *Approp. St.* 26:336.

HAIDA. See also ALASKA. *Spec. St.* 49:388.

HANNAHVILLE INDIAN COMMUNITY (CHIPPEWA). See also MICHIGAN. *Const.* July 23, 1936. *Charter* Aug. 21, 1937.

HAVASUPAI TRIBE OF THE HAVASUPAI RESERVATION. See also ARIZONA; APACHE; TRUXTON CANYON. *Spec. St.* 40:1175. *Approp. St.* 49:1757. *Priv. St.* 49:2296. *Const.* Mar. 27, 1939.

HOH (QUILEUTE). See also WASHINGTON; QUILEUTE. *Spec. St.* 36:1345. *Cases* Mitchell, 22 F. 2d 771; U. S. v. Provoe, 283 U. S. 753.

HOONAH INDIAN ASSOCIATION (TLINGIT). See also ALASKA; THLINGIT. *Const.* Oct. 23, 1939. *Charter* Oct. 23, 1939.

HOOPA (HUPA) VALLEY. See also CALIFORNIA; SMITH RIVER RESERVATION. *Spec. St.* 13:538; 45:589. *Approp. St.*, 15:198; 16:13; 20:63, 295; 21:114; 23:76; 24:449; 25:217, 980; 26:336, 989; 28:286, 876; 31:221, 1058; 32:245, 982; 33:189, 1048; 34:325, 1015; 35:70, 781; 38:77; 40:561; 41:3, 408, 1225; 42:552, 1174; 43:390, 1141; 44:453; 45:883; 46:279, 1115; 47:15; 50:564. *Priv. St.* 19:508. *Cases* Donnelly, 228 U. S. 243; Osborn, 33 C. Cls. 304; U. S. v. 48 Lbs. of Rising Star Tea, 35 Fed. 403; U. S. v. Kagama, 118 U. S. 375.

HOPI. See also ARIZONA; MOQUI. *Per.* Beaglehole, 20 Ia. L Rev. 304. *Gov. Pub.* 72d Cong., 2d Sess., Hearings, Ind. Aff. Comm., Senate. *Approp. St.* 40:561; 41:3, 327, 408, 503; 1015, 1156, 1225; 42:552, 1174, 1527; 43:1141; 44:453, 934; 45:200, 1562, 1607, 1623; 46:279, 1115; 47:91, 820, 1602; 48:362; 49:176, 1757; 50:564; 52:291. *Op. A. G.* 35:107. *I. D. Rulings* Colton, Museum Notes (Survey Hopi Common Law); Op. Sol., 17187, Jan. 20, 1926; Memo. Sol., Dec. 14, 1937. *Constr.* Dec. 19, 1936.

HUALAPAI (WALAPAI) TRIBE OF THE HUALAPAI RESERVATION. See also ARIZONA; TRUXTON CANYON. *Approp. St.* 23:76, 362; 24:449; 25:217, 980; 26:336, 989; 27:120, 612; 28:286, 876; 29:321; 30:62, 571, 924; 31:221, 1058; 32:245, 982. *Priv. St.* 39:1243. *Cases* Luke, 35 C. Cls. 15. *Const.* Dec. 17, 1938.

HUMPTULIP. See also WASHINGTON. *Spec. St.* 43:886.

HUPA VALLEY. See HOOPA (HUPA) VALLEY.

HURON CEMETERY (KANSAS, 1842–67). See also KANSAS. *Priv. St.* 42:1785

HYDABURG COOPERATIVE ASSOCIATION (HAIDA). See also ALASKA; HAIDA. *Const.* April 14, 1938. *Charter* April 14, 1938.

IDAHO. See also COEUR D'ALENE; CONFEDERATED SALISH; DUCK VALLEY RESERVATION; FLATHEAD; FLATHEAD, KOOTENAI AND PEND D'OREILLE; FORT HALL; FORT LAPWAI; KOOTENAI; LEMHI; NEZ PERCE; PEND D'OREILLE; SALISH; SHOSHONE; SHOSHONE-BANNOCK TRIBES OF THE FORT HALL RESERVATION. *Approp. St.* 17:165, 437; 18:146, 420; 19:176, 271; 20:63, 295; 21:114, 485.

ILLINOIS. See also IOWA; KASKASKIA AND PEORIA; KASKASKIA, PEORIA, WEA AND PIANKESHAW; KICKAPOO; MIAMI; OMAHA; OTTAWA; PIANKESHAW AND WEAS; TAMAROA; WABASH; WEA. *Treaties* 7:78, 181, 200, 208, 403.

INDIAN RANCH, INYO COUNTY. See also CALIFORNIA. *Spec. St.* 45:162.

INDIAN TERRITORY. See also OKLAHOMA; APACHE; ARAPAHOE; CAYUGA; COMANCHE; FIVE CIVILIZED TRIBES; IOWA; KANSAS; KAW; KICKAPOO; KIOWA; MISSOURI; MODOC; OSAGE; OTTOE; OTTAWA; PAWNEE; PEORIA AND MIAMI; PONCA; POTAWATOMIE; QUAPAW; SENECA; SHAWNEE; WICHITA; WYANDOTTE. *Spec. St.* 13:62; 27:465, 487, 492, 524; 28:974; 29:13; 30:715, 544; 32:43, 641; 34:267, 596. *Approp. St* 17:165, 437; 18:146, 420; 19:176, 271; 20:63, 295; 21:114, 485; 22:433; 30:1121; 31:1058; 32:1031; 33:1117; 34:325 634, 1015, 1073; 35:478, 907. *Priv. St.* 35:1404; 38:1305. *Cases* Binyon, 4 Ind. T. 642; Bohart, 2 Ind. T. 45; Boyt, 4 Ind. T. 47; Brown, 2 Ind. T. 582; Burch, 7 Ind. T. 284; Choctaw, 6 Ind. T. 432; Denison, 3 Ind. T. 104; Dennee, 4 Ind. T. 233; Ellis, 6 Ind. T. 292; Foreman, 7 Ind. T. 478; Glover, 6 Ind. T. 262; Incorp. Town, 5 Ind. T. 497; In re Terrell's, 6 Ind. T. 412; Luce, 4 Ind. T. 54; Martin, 1 Ind. T. 495; Mays, 3 Ind. T. 774; Moore, 5 Ind. T. 384; Murray, 1 Ind. T. 28; Oats, 1 Ind. T. 152; Parris, 1 Ind. T. 43; Pilgrim, 7 Ind. T. 623; Poplin, 1 Ind. T. 157; Purcell, 6 Ind. T. 78; Sayer, 7 Ind. T. 675; Simon, 4 Ind. T. 688; Tally, 6 Ind. T. 331; Taylor, 6 Ind. T. 351; U. S. v. Buckles, 6 Ind. T. 319; U. S. v. Cohn, 2 Ind. T. 474; U. S. v. Fidelity, 7 Ind. T. 83; Watkins, 3 Ind. T. 281; Williams, 4 Ind. T. 204; Willis, 6 Ind. T. 424.

INDIANA. See EEL RIVER; MIAMI; WABASH; WEA.

INK-PA-DU-TAH (INKPA, WAHPETON SIOUX). See also SIOUX, INK-PA-DU-TAH BAND. *Spec. St.* 11:362.

I-ON-I (HASINAI CADDOANS). See also TEXAS. *Treaties* 9:844.

IOWA (STATE). See POTAWATOMIE; SAC; SAC AND FOX; SAC AND FOX TRIBE OF MISSISSIPPI IN IOWA; WINNEBAGO.

IOWA (IOWAY) INDIANS. See also KANSAS; OKLAHOMA; IOWA TRIBE IN NEBRASKA AND KANSAS; IOWA TRIBE OF OKLAHOMA; OMAHA; SAC, FOX, IOWA, SIOUX, OMAHA, OTTOES, MISSOURIAS; SAC, FOX AND IOWAY. *Per.* Mac Leod, 28 J. Crim. L. 181. *Spec. St.* 4:464; 23:351; 24:367; 26:749; 28:580; 29:95; 34:262; 36:368; 41:585; 45:1073; 46:260; 48:501. *Approp. St.* 4:92, 526, 616, 636, 682, 780; 5:36, 158, 298, 323, 402, 417, 493, 704, 766; 9:20, 132, 252, 382, 544, 574; 10:41, 226, 315, 686; 11:65, 169, 273, 388; 12:44, 221, 512, 539, 774; 13:161, 541; 14:255, 492; 15:198; 16:13, 335, 544; 17:165, 437; 18:146, 420; 19:176, 271; 20:63, 295; 21:114, 485; 22:68, 433; 23:76, 362; 24:449; 25:217, 980; 26:336, 989; 27:120, 612; 28:286, 424, 876; 29:321; 30:62, 571, 924; 31:221, 1058; 32:245, 982; 33:189, 1048; 34:325, 1015; 35:70; 48:984. *Priv. St.* 6:913. *Treaties* 7:136, 231, 272, 328, 511, 517, 547; 10:1069; 12:1171. *Cases* Iowa, 68 C. Cls. 585; State of Missouri, 7 How. 660; U. S. v. Choctaw, 179 U. S. 494. *Op. A. G.* 6:658. *I. D. Rulings* 30 L. D. 532, Mar. 13, 1901.

IOWA TRIBE IN NEBRASKA AND KANSAS. See also IOWA (IOWAY) INDIANS. *Const.* Feb. 26, 1937. *Charter* June 19, 1937.

IOWA TRIBE OF OKLAHOMA. See also IOWA (IOWAY) INDIANS. *Const.* Oct. 23, 1937. *Charter* Feb. 5, 1938.

IROQUOIS. See also NEW YORK; CAYUGA; MOHAWK; ONEIDA; ONONDAGA; ST. REGIS, SENECA; SIX NATIONS; TONAWANDA. *Per.* Hagan, 23 Case & Com. 735; James, 12 J. H. Univ. Studies 467; Parker, 23 Case & Com. 717; Pound, 22 Colum. L. Rev. 97; Weeden, 2 J. H. Univ. Studies 385. *Cases* Bonifer, 166 Fed. 846; McCandless, 25 F. 2d 71; New York, 40 C. Cls. 448.

ISABELLA RESERVATION. See MICHIGAN; CHIPPEWA.

ISLETA PUEBLO. See NEW MEXICO; PUEBLO.

JEMEZ PUEBLO. See NEW MEXICO; PUEBLO.

JICARILLA APACHE TRIBE. See also NEW MEXICO; APACHE, JICARILLA. *Const.* Aug. 4, 1937. *Charter* Sept. 4, 1937.

JOCKO. See also MONTANA; KOOTENAI; FLATHEAD. *Spec. St.* 25:871. *Approp. St.* 22:68; 25:217, 980; 26:989; 27:120; 28:286; 49:176.

KAIBAB (PAIUTE). See also ARIZONA; UTAH; PAIUTE; SHIVWITS. *Spec. St.* 45:401. *Approp. St.* 30:571, 924; 32:245, 982; 35:317; 39:123; 40:561; 41:3, 408, 1225; 42:1174; 43:390, 1141; 44:453, 934; 45:200.

KALAPUYA. See OREGON; CALAPOOIA, CLAKAMAS; MOLALA.

KALAWATSET. (LOWER UMPQUA). See OREGON; UMPQUA.

KALISPEL INDIAN COMMUNITY OF KALISPEL RESERVATION. See also CALESPEL; WASHINGTON. *Cases* U. S. v. Heyfron, 138 Fed. 964. *Const.* Mar. 24, 1938. *Charter* May 28, 1938.

KANOSH. See also UTAH; UTE; PAH-UTE (PAIUTE). *Spec. St.* 45:1161; 49:393.

KANSAS. See also BLACK BOB; CHIPPEWA; DELAWARE; FOX; IOWA TRIBE IN NEBRASKA AND KANSAS; KAW; KICKAPOO; MIAMI; MUNSEE; NEOSHO; PIANKESHAW; POTAWATOMI; SAC AND FOX TRIBE OF MISSOURI OF THE SAC AND FOX RESERVATION IN KANSAS AND NEBRASKA; SHAWNEE; WEA; WYANDOTTE. *Spec. St.* 9:570; 12:630; 17:85, 228; 19:74; 32:636; 42:1561, 1589; 43:176, 1133; 44:134; 45:1258. *Approp. St.* 4:217, 361, 526, 616, 682, 705, 780; 5:36, 158, 298, 323, 402, 417, 612, 704, 766; 9:20, 40, 123, 252, 382, 544, 574; 10:41, 226, 315, 686; 11:65, 169, 273, 388; 12:44, 221, 512, 774; 13:161, 541; 14:255, 492; 15:7, 198; 16:13, 335, 544; 17:165, 437; 18:133, 146, 272, 420; 19:176, 271; 20:63, 295; 21:114, 485; 22:68, 257, 433; 23:76, 362; 24:449; 25:217, 980; 26:336, 989; 27:120, 612; 28:286, 876; 29:321; 30:62, 571, 924; 31:221, 1058; 32:245, 982; 33:189, 1048; 34:325, 1015; 35:70, 781; 36:269; 37:518; 38:77, 582; 39:123, 969; 40:561; 41:3, 408, 1225; 42:552, 1174; 43:390, 704, 1141. *Priv. St.* 6:852; 22:728. *Treaties* 7:137, 244, 270; 9:842; 12:1111, 1129, 1221, 14:769. *Cases* Drummond, 34 F. 2d 755; Goodson, 7 Okla. 117; Kansas, 80 C. Cls. 264; Shore, 60 F. 2d 1; Smith, 10 Wall. 321; State of Missouri, 7 How. 660; Swope, 23 Fed. Cas. No. 13704; U. S. v. Ward, 28 Fed. Cas. No. 16639. *Op. A. G.* 9:110; 13:531; 17:200.

KANSAS SHAWNEE. See KANSAS; BLACK BOB; SHAWNEE.

KARLUK, NATIVE VILLAGE OF (ALEUT). See also ALASKA; ALEUTS. *Const.* Aug. 23, 1939. *Charter* Aug. 23, 1939.

KASAAN, ORGANIZED VILLAGE OF (TSIMSHIAN). See also ALASKA. *Const.* Oct. 15, 1938. *Charter* Oct. 15, 1938.

KASHIA BAND OF POMO INDIANS OF THE STEWART'S POINT RANCHERIA. See also CALIFORNIA; SACRAMENTO. *Const.* Mar. 11, 1936.

KASKASKIA. See also ILLINOIS; CAHOKIA; KASKASKIA, PEORIA, WEA AND PIANKESHAW; KASKASKIA AND PEORIA; PEORIA AND KASKASKIA; PIANKESHAW; PIANKESHAW AND WEA; QUAPAW; WEA. *Texts* Manypenny, OIW. *Spec. St.* 2:277; 3:308, 319, 690; 4:594; 12:539; 17:631. *Approp. St.* 1:460; 3:517; 4:526,

616, 636; 5:298; 10:576; 17:122; 18:420; 21:435; 25:505, 565; 28:424. *Treaties* 7:49, 74, 77, 78, 83, 100, 403; 8:116; 10:1062; 15:513. *Cases* Bowling, 233 U. S. 528; Lykins, 184 U. S. 169; U. S. v. Bowling, 256 U. S. 484; U. S. v. Brindle, 110 U. S. 688; U. S. v. Rundell, 181 Fed. 887. *Op. A. G.* 19:115.

KASKASKIA AND PEORIA. See also **ILLINOIS; KASKASKIA; PEORIA; PEORIA AND KASKASKIA.** *Approp. St.* 4:636, 682, 780; 5:36, 158, 323, 402, 417, 493; 10:686.

KASKASKIA, PEORIA, WEA AND PIANKESHAW. See also **KASKASKIA; ILLINOIS.** *Spec. St.* 25:1013. *Approp. St.* 4:780; 5:36, 158; 10:686; 11:65, 169, 273, 388; 13:161; 16:335, 544; 17:165, 437; 18:146, 420; 19:176, 271; 20:63, 295; 21:114, 485; 22:68, 257, 433; 23:76, 362; 24:449; 25:217, 980; 26:336, 989; 31:321.

KA-TA-KA (KIOWA APACHE). See also **KIOWA.** *Treaties* 7:533.

KAW. See also **KANSAS; OKLAHOMA.** *Spec. St.* 17:228; 32:636; 35:778; 43:111, 722; 48:501. *Approp. St.* 15:311; 17:122; 18:133; 33:189; 48:984. *Treaties* 12:1129; 14:793. *Cases* Drummond, 34 F. 2d 755; Gay, 5 Okla. 1; Taylor, 51 F. 2d 892; Thomas, 169 U. S. 264. *Op. A. G.* 35:1. *I. D. Rulings* Op. Sol., Dec. 23, 1934, May 14. 1935.

KETCHIKAN INDIAN CORPORATION (TSIMSHIAN). See also **ALASKA.** *Const.* Jan. 27, 1940. *Charter* Jan. 27, 1940.

KEWEENAW BAY INDIAN COMMUNITY (OF THE L'ANSE RESERVATION). See also **MICHIGAN; CHIPPEWA; L'ANSE AND VIEUX DESERT INDIAN RESERVATION.** *Const.* Dec. 17, 1936. *Charter* July 17, 1937.

KIALIGEE (KIALADSHI). See also **CREEK.** *Case* U. S. v. Mid Continent, 67 F. 2d 37.

KICKAPOO. See also **KANSAS; OKLAHOMA; ILLINOIS.** *Texts* Manypenny, OIW. *Per.* Brosius, 23 Case & Com. 739; 9 J. H. Univ. Studies 541. *Spec. St.* 3:308, 319, 690; 4:594; 22:177; 24:219; 30:909; 47:819; 48:501. *Approp. St.* 1:460; 2:607; 3:698; 4:526, 636, 682, 705, 780; 5:36, 158, 298, 323, 402, 417, 435, 493, 704, 766; 9:20, 132, 252, 382, 544, 574; 10:41, 315, 686; 11:65, 169, 273, 388; 12:44, 221, 512, 774; 13:161, 541; 14:255, 492; 15:198; 16:13, 335, 544; 17:165, 437; 18:27, 133, 146, 402, 420; 19:176, 271; 20:63, 295, 410; 21:114, 414, 485; 22:68; 23:76, 362; 24:449; 25:217, 980; 26:336, 989; 27:120, 612; 28:286, 876; 29:321; 30:62, 571, 652, 924, 1214; 31:221, 280, 1010, 1058; 32:245, 552, 982; 33:189, 1048, 1214; 34:325, 1015; 35:70, 781, 945; 36:269, 703, 1363; 37:518, 38:77, 582; 39:14, 123, 969; 40:561; 41:3, 35, 408, 503, 1015, 1156, 1225; 42:29, 552, 1174; 43:390, 704, 1141; 44:453, 984; 45:200; 48:984. *Treaties* 7:49, 74, 77, 91, 116, 117, 118, 130, 145, 185, 200, 208, 202, 391; 8:116; 10:1069, 1078; 13:623. *Cases* Briggs, 43 Fed. 102; Briggs, 37 Fed. 135; Elk, 112 U. S. 94; Johnson, 283 Fed. 954; Lowe, 37 C. Cls. 413; Matter, 197 U. S. 488; U. S. v. Belt, 128 Fed. 68; U. S. v. Estill, 62 F. 2d 620; U. S. v. Kilgore, 27 F. Supp. 1; U. S. v. Reilly, 290 U. S. 33. *Op. A. G.* 19:255. *Const.* Feb. 26, 1937. *Charter* June 19, 1937.

KIKIALLAS. See also **WASHINGTON.** *Cases* D'wamish, 79 C. Cls. 530.

KING ISLAND NATIVE COMMUNITY (ESKIMO). See also **ALASKA; ESKIMO.** *Const.* Jan. 31, 1939. *Charter* Jan. 31, 1939.

KIOWA. See also **OKLAHOMA; TEXAS; APACHE; APACHE, KIOWA, COMANCHE; APACHE, KIOWA, COMANCHE AND WICHITA; ARAPAHOE, CHEYENNE, APACHE, KIOWA, COMANCHE AND WICHITA; ARAPAHOE AND KIOWA; CADDO; CHEYENNE, ARAPAHOE, KIOWA AND COMANCHE; COMANCHE; KIOWA AND COMANCHE; WICHITA.** *Texts* Manypenny, IOW. *Per.* Brown, 39 Yale L. J. 307. *Spec. St.* 13:323; 16:337; 22:47; 29:529; 31:672, 1093; 39:445, 1199; 40:1318; 43:1573; 45:986; 47:39; 48:501. *Approp. St.* 11:169; 16:291; 20:377, 410; 21:67, 414; 22:7; 26:504; 30:105, 652; 33:189, 1048; 34:325; 36:269; 39:123; 41:408, 1225; 42:552, 1174; 43:390, 1313; 45:2, 492, 1623; 48:984. *Priv. St.* 21:549, 640; 25:1306; 44:1609; 45:2021; 49:2197, 2296. *Treaties* 7:533; 10:1013; 14:717; 15:581, 589. *Cases* Ball, 161 U. S. 72; Brown, 32 C. Cls. 432; Crow, 32 C. Cls. 16; Gamel, 31 C. Cls. 321; Gorham, 29 C. Cls. 97; Gossett, 31 C. Cls. 304; King, 31 C. Cls. 304; Light, 10 Okla. 732; Lone, 187 U. S. 553; McCoy, 38 C. Cls. 163; Montoya, 32 C. Cls. 71; Oklahoma, 258 U. S. 574; Price, 28 C. Cls. 422; Swope, 33 C. Cls. 223; U. S. v. Andrews, 179 U. S. 96; U. S. v. Gorham, 165 U. S. 316; U. S. v. Loving, 34 Fed. 715; U. S. v. Martinez, 195 U. S. 469; U. S. v. Myers, 206 Fed. 387; U. S. v. Rowell, 243 U. S. 464. *Op. A. G.* 18:235. *I. D. Rulings* 31 L. D. 439, Dec. 15, 1902; Op. Sol., Mar. 10, 1922, Aug. 14, 1926; Memo. Sol., Aug. 28, 1934, Mar. 25, 1936; Memo. Sol. Off., Oct. 9, 1937.

KIOWA, COMANCHE; See also **APACHE, KIOWA, COMANCHE; ARAPAHOE, CHEYENNE, KIOWA, COMANCHE, APACHE; KIOWA, APACHE, COMANCHE; OKLAHOMA.** *Spec. St.* 29:69; 34:550. *Approp. St.* 18:133; 30:924; 32:982, 1031; 38:77; 44:453; 46:279. *Priv. St.* 21:640.

KIOWA, APACHE AND COMANCHE. See also **KIOWA; APACHE; COMANCHE; OKLAHOMA.** *Gov. Pub.* 76 Cong. 1 sess., Hearings, S. Comm. Ind. Aff., S. J. Res. 130. *Spec. St.* 34:213, 2830; 35:41, 444, 636; 36:265, 533, 855; 37:91; 38:1219; 43:795, 1003; 44:740; 48:972. *Approp. St.* 13:161; 15:198; 16:544; 33:189; 34:1015; 35:781; 36:269; 37:518; 38:582, 1086; 39:969; 40:561; 41:3, 408, 1225; 42:552, 1174; 43:390, 1141; 44:453, 934; 45:200, 883, 1562, 1623; 46:1115, 1552; 47:91, 820; 48:362.

KIVALINA, NATIVE VILLAGE OF. See also **ALASKA; ESKIMO.** *Const.* Feb. 7, 1940. *Charter* Feb. 7, 1940.

KLAMATH. See also **OREGON; KLAMATH, MODOC, AND YAHOOSKIN BAND OF SNAKE INDIANS; MODOC; MOLALA; PAIUTE; PITT RIVER; SNAKE; YAHOOSKIN.** *Gov. Pub.* 71 Cong., 2 sess., Hearings, S. Comm. Ind. Aff., S. 3156. 71 Cong., 2 sess., Hearings, H. Comm. Ind. Aff., S. 3156. 71 Cong., 2 sess., Hearings, S. Comm. Ind. Aff., S. 4156. 71 Cong., 1 sess., Hearings, H. Comm. Ind. Aff., S. 2671. 72 Cong., 1 sess., Hearings, S. Comm. Ind. Aff., S. 3588. 75 Cong., 1 sess., Hearings, H. Comm. Ind. Aff., H. R. 6071. 75 Cong., 3 sess., S. Rep. 1774. 75 Cong., 3 sess., S. Rep. 1785. *Approp. St.* 33:189; 39:123, 969; 40:561; 43:1141, 1313; 45:200, 883, 1562; 46:279, 1115; 47:820; 49:176, 1757; 50:564; 52:291, 1114. *Priv. St.* 48:1380.

KLAMATH, MODOC AND YAHOOSKIN BAND OF SNAKE INDIANS. See also **KLAMATH; MODOC; YAHOOSKIN BAND OF SNAKE INDIANS; OREGON.** *Spec. St.* 12:199; 13:37; 29:84; 33:1033; 41:623; 44:741; 45:1439; 46:1105; 47:1568; 48:311; 50:872; 52:605, 1207. *Approp. St.* 14:255, 492; 15:198; 16:13, 335, 544; 17:165, 437; 18:146, 420; 19:176, 271; 20:63, 295; 21:114, 485; 22:68, 433; 23:76, 362; 24:449; 25:4, 217, 980; 26:336, 989; 27:120, 612; 28:286, 876; 29:321; 30:62, 571, 924; 31:221, 280, 1058; 32:245, 982, 1031; 33:1048; 34:325, 1015; 35:781; 36:269; 37:518, 595; 38:77, 582; 39:123, 801, 969; 40:2, 345; 41:3, 35, 408, 1225; 42:327, 552, 1174; 43:390; 44:453, 934, 1250; 45:1562, 1623; 46:1115; 47:91; 48:362, 984; 49:1109. *Priv. St.* 26:1465. *Cases* Bramwell, 269 U. S. 483; California, 87 Fed. 532; Davis, 32 F. 2d 860; Donnelly, 228 U. S. 243; Klamath, 296 U. S. 244; Klamath, 86 C. Cls. 614; Klamath, 81 C. Cls. 79; Knapp, 53 C. Cls. 18; Oregon, 202 U. S. 60; Painter, 33 C. Cls. 114; Thompson, 44 C. Cls. 359; U. S. v. Algoma, 305 U. S. 415; U. S. v. Anderson, 228 U. S. 52; U. S. v. 48 Lbs., 35 Fed. 403; U. S. v. Klamath, 304 U. S. 119; U. S. v. Oregon, 103 Fed. 549. *Op. A. G.* 19:35, 56. *L. D. Memo. (D. J.)* 11:497; 12:510, 578, 703. *I. D. Rulings* 32 L. D. 664, May 26, 1904; 33 L. D. 205, Aug. 30, 1904; 38 L. D. 559, Feb. 16, 1910; Op. Sol., May 9, 1928; Memo. Sol. Off., April 10, 1933; Op. Sol., July 26, 1933; Memo. Sol., Jan. 30, 1934; Letter by Sp. Agent to Comm'r, Sept. 29, 1934; Memo. Sol., Mar. 9, 1935.

KLAMATH RIVER. See also **CALIFORNIA.** *Spec. St.* 27:52. *Cases* Thompson, 44 C. Cls. 359.

KLAWOCK COOPERATIVE ASSOCIATION (TLINGIT). See also **ALASKA; THLINGIT.** *Const.* Oct. 4, 1938. *Charter* Oct. 4, 1938.

KOOSHAREM. See also **UTAH; PAIUTE.** *Spec. St.* 45:162; 50:241.

KOOTENAI (KOOTENAY). See also **IDAHO; MONTANA; CONFEDERATED SALISH AND KOOTENAI TRIBES OF THE FLATHEAD RESERVATION; FLATHEAD, KOOTENAI AND PEND D'OREILLE; JOCKO; SALISH.** *Spec. St.* 43:21; 44:202; 45:938. *Approp. St.* 12:44, 221, 774; 13:161, 541; 14:492; 15:198; 17:437; 18:146; 45:1562; 46:279; 47:91, 820. *Cases* Clairmont, 225 U. S. 551; U. S. v. Heyfron, 138 Fed. 964; U. S. v. Ladley, 51 F. 2d 756; U. S. v. Ladley, 4 F. Supp. 580. *I. D. Rulings* 20 L. D. 462, May 19, 1895; Memo. Sol. I. D., Mar. 17, 1937.

KOWES. See **OREGON; COOS BAY.**

KWETHLUK, NATIVE VILLAGE OF. See also **ALASKA; ESKIMO.** *Const.* Jan. 11, 1940. *Charter* Jan. 11, 1940.

L'ANSE AND VIEUX DESERT INDIAN RESERVATION (CHIPPEWA). See also **MICHIGAN; KEWEENAW BAY INDIAN COMMUNITY; LAKE SUPERIOR.** *Approp. St.* 44:161. *Priv. St.* 43:1486.

LA JOLLA RESERVATION. See also **CALIFORNIA; MISSION.** *Approp. St.* 41:3, 408.

LA POINTE (CHIPPEWA). See also **WISCONSIN; BAD RIVER RESERVATION.** *Spec. St.* 34:1217. *Approp. St.* 34:325; 36:118, 774; 41:3, 408. *Priv. St.* 36:1700. *Cases* Ex. p. Pero, 99 F. 2d 28; Hitchcock, 22 App. D. C. 275; Wisconsin, 201 U. S. 202.

LAC COURT D'OREILLE (CHIPPEWA). See also **WISCONSIN; CHIPPEWA.** *Spec. St.* 43:92. *Approp. St.* 39:123. *Cases* Quagon, 5 F. 2d 608; Thayer, 20 C. Cls. 137; U. S. v. Thomas, 47 Fed. 488. *I. D. Rulings* Op. Sol., Oct. 27, 1924; Memo. Sol., Feb. 25, 1938.

LAC DU FLAMBEAU BAND OF LAKE SUPERIOR CHIPPEWA INDIANS OF WISCONSIN. See also **WISCONSIN; CHIPPEWA.** *Spec. St.* 25:169; 46:149; 47:153. *Approp. St.* 31:221; 39:123; 41:408, 1225; 42:552, 1174; 43:390, 1141, 1313; 44:453, 934; 45:200, 1562; 46:279, 1115; 47:91, 820; 49:1757; 52:1114. *Priv. St.* 43:1597; 49:2317. *Cases* U. S. v. Amo, 261 Fed. 106; Wisconsin, 201 U. S. 202. *I. D. Rulings* Mem. Sol., Nov. 11, 1937. *Const.* Aug. 15, 1936. *Charter* May 8, 1937.

LAGUNA PUEBLO. See **NEW MEXICO; PUEBLO.**

LAKE SUPERIOR (CHIPPEWA). See also **MICHIGAN; CHIPPEWA; L'ANSE AND VIEUX DESERT INDIAN RESERVATION.** *Spec. St.* 47:169.

LAKE TRAVERSE RESERVATION (SISSETON SIOUX). See also **SIOUX.** *Cases* Buttz, 119 U. S. 55; Farrell, 110 Fed. 942; Sioux, 277 U. S. 424.

LEECH LAKE. See also **CHIPPEWA; MINNESOTA.** *Spec. St.* 25:1010; 28:112, 489; 29:12. *Approp. St.* 38:582.

LEMHI. See also **IDAHO; SHOSHONE; SHEEPEATERS.** *Spec. St.* 37:195. *Approp. St.* 22:68; 23:76; 34:325, 697; 35:70, 781; 36:269.

LEPAN (LIPAN APACHE). See also **TEXAS.** *Treaties* 9:844.

LEUPP EXTENSION RESERVATION (NAVAJO). See also **ARIZONA; NAVAJO.** *Spec. St.* 48:960. *Approp. St.* 42:1527; 47:820.

LEWIS & SCOUTASH TOWNS (SHAWNEE SETTLEMENTS IN OHIO, 1817–31). See also **SHAWNEE.** *Approp. St.* 3:518.

LITTLE OSAGE NATION. See also **OKLAHOMA; OSAGE.** *Spec. St.* 5:209; 10:704; 16:55; 19:127. *Approp. St.* 2:660; 5:323. *Treaties* 7:133, 222, 240, 268, 576.

LOAFER SIOUX (OGLALA SIOUX). See **SIOUX.**

LONG-WHA (TONKAWA). See also **TEXAS.** *Treaties* 9:844.

LOUISIANA. See **CHETTIMANCHI.**

LOWER BRULE SIOUX TRIBE. See also **SIOUX; CROW CREEK.** *Spec. St.* 19:254; 26:14; 30:1362; 31:790; 34:124; 47:300. *Approp. St.* 26:989; 27:612; 28:286; 29:321; 30:62; 35:781. *I. D. Rulings* Memo. Sol. Off., Oct. 12, 1934. *Const.* Nov. 27, 1935. *Charter* July 11, 1936.

LOWER SIOUX INDIAN COMMUNITY. See also **MINNESOTA; PIPESTONE INDIAN SCHOOL.** *Const.* June 11, 1936. *Charter* July 17, 1937.

LUMMI. See also **WASHINGTON.** *Spec. St.* 44:211; 45:366. *Approp. St.* 41:3; 44:841; 45:200, 883; 47:1602; 49:176, 1597, 1757; 52:291. *Cases* Duwamish, 79 C. Cls. 530; U. S. v. Alaska, 79 Fed. 152; U. S. v. Boynton, 53 F. 2d 297; U. S. v. Romaine, 255 Fed. 253.

MACKINAC (CHIPPEWA). See also **MICHIGAN.** *Approp. St.* 41:3, 408, 1225; 43:1141; 44:453, 934; 45:1562; 46:1115.

MAIDU. See **CALIFORNIA.**

MAINE (PENOBSCOT; PENNACOOK). *Per.* Varney, 13 Green Bag 399.

MAKAH INDIAN TRIBE. See also **WASHINGTON; NEAH BAY; QUILEUTE; QUINAIELT.** *Spec. St.* 44:614. *Approp. St.* 12:4, 221, 512, 774; 13:161, 541; 14:255, 492; 15:198; 16:13, 335, 544; 17:165, 437; 18:146, 420; 19:176, 271; 20:63, 295; 21:114, 485; 22:68, 433; 23:76, 362; 24:449; 25:217, 980; 26:336, 989; 27:120, 612; 28:286, 876; 29:321; 30:62, 571, 924; 31:221, 280, 1058; 32:245, 982; 33:189, 1048; 34:325, 1015; 35:70, 781; 36:269; 37:518; 38:77, 582; 39:123, 969; 40:561; 41:3, 408, 1225; 42:552, 1174, 1527; 43:704; 49:1757. *Priv. St.* 18:555. *Treaties* 12:933, 939, 971. *Cases* Jackson, 34 C. Cls. 441; Swan, 50 Fed. 108; Taylor, 44 F. 2d 53. *Op. A. G.* 21:466. *I. D. Rulings* Memo Sec'y, Feb. 20, 1937; Memo. Sol., May 13, 1937; Memo. Sol. Off., May 18, 1937; Memo. Sol., Jan. 18, 1936. *Const.* May. 16, 1936. *Charter* Feb. 27, 1937.

MALHEUR. See also **OREGON.** *Approp. St.* 17:437; 18:146, 402, 420; 19:176, 271, 363; 20:63, 295; 21:114; 22:433. *Priv. St.* 20:543.

MALKI. See also **CALIFORNIA; MISSION INDIANS.** *Approp. St.* 41:1225; 42:552.

MANCHESTER BAND OF POMO INDIANS. See also **CALIFORNIA.** *Const.* Mar. 11, 1936. *Charter* Feb. 27, 1937.

MANDAN TRIBE. See also **FORT BERTHOLD; THREE AFFILIATED TRIBES OF FORT BERTHOLD RESERVATION; ARICKAREE; GROS VENTRE (HIDATSA).** *Treaties* 7:264.

MARICOPA. See also **ARIZONA; GILA RIVER PIMA-MARICOPA INDIAN COMMUNITY.** *Approp. St.* 23:76; 24:449; 25:217, 980; 26:336, 989; 41:408. *Cases* Lake, 35 C. Cls. 15; Maricopa, 156 U. S. 347. *I. D. Rulings* Memo. Sol., June 11, 1936.

MASSACHUSETTS. See also **STOCKBRIDGE INDIANS.** *Per.* Varney, 13 Green Bag 399. Weeden, 2 J. H. Univ. Studies 385.

MDEWAKANTON. See **SIOUX, MDEWAKANTON.**

MEKORYUK, NATIVE VILLAGE OF. See also **ALASKA; ESKIMO.** *Const.* Aug. 24, 1940. *Charter* Aug. 24, 1940.

MENDOCINO INDIAN RESERVATION (POMO AND WAPPO). See also **CALIFORNIA.** *Approp. St.* 11:221; 15:198.

MENOMINEE. See also **WISCONSIN; CHIPPEWA, WINNEBAGO.** *Per.* Mac. Leod, 28 J. Crim. L. 181. *Spec. St.* 4:464, 594, 682; 5:349, 645; 9:55; 10:7; 16:410; 18:46; 19:37, 89; 22:30; 26:146; 27:83; 32:207; 34:547; 35:51, 444; 43:793; 46:1102, 1468; 47:307; 48:112, 964, 965; 49:1085; 52:208. *Approp. St.* 4:92, 403, 636, 682, 780; 5:36, 158, 298, 323, 402, 417, 493, 704, 766; 9:20, 132, 252, 382, 544, 574, 598; 10:15, 41, 226, 315, 576, 645, 686; 11:65, 169, 273, 388; 12:44, 221, 512, 774; 13:161, 541; 14:255, 492; 15:198; 16:13, 335, 544; 17:165, 437, 530; 18:146, 420; 19:176, 271; 20:63, 295; 21:114, 485; 22:68, 433; 23:76, 362; 24:449; 25:217, 980; 26:336, 989; 27:120, 612; 33:189; 34:325; 35:781; 36:269; 37:518; 38:582; 39:123, 969; 40:561; 41:3, 408, 1225; 42:552, 1174; 43:390, 1141, 1313; 44:934; 45:200, 883, 1562, 1623; 46:90, 279, 1064, 1115; 47:91, 820, 1602; 48:97, 362; 49:176, 571, 1597, 1757; 50:564; 52:291. *Priv. St.* 10:792; 20:513; 36:1866; 49:2246. *Treaties* 7:153, 272, 290, 303, 342, 403, 405, 506, 550, 566, 591; 9:952, 955; 10:1064; 11:577, 679. *Cases* Beecher, 95 U. S. 517; Green, 233 U. S. 558; Green, 46 C. Cls. 68; Green, 47 C. Cls. 281; New York, 170 U. S. 1; U. S. v. Cardish, 143 Fed. 640; U. S. v. Cardish, 145 Fed. 242; U. S. v. Cook, 19 Wall. 591; U. S. v. Kempf, 171 Fed. 1021; U. S. v. Paine, 206 U. S. 467; U. S. ex rel. Besau, 6 F. 2d 694; Wisconsin, 245 U. S. 427. *Op. A. G.* 3:322; 5:31; 8:256. *I. D. Rulings* 25 L. D. 17, July 12, 1897; 54 I. D. 218, June 5, 1933; Op. Sol., June 16, 1924; Memo. Sol., May 15, 1933; Memo. Sol. Off., Sept. 3, 1935; Memo. Sol., Jan. 10, 1935, Oct. 20, 1936, Nov. 9, 1937; Op. Sol., Nov. 28, 1938.

MERCED RESERVATION. See also **CALIFORNIA.** *Cases* Belt, 15 C. Cls. 92.

MERCED RIVER INDIANS. See also **CALIFORNIA.** *Priv. St.* 16:667.

MESA GRANDE. See also **CALIFORNIA; MISSION; SANTA YSABEL RESERVATION.** *Spec. St.* 44:496.

MESCALERO. See **APACHE TRIBE OF THE MESCALERO RESERVATION.**

METLAKAHTLA (TSIMSHIAN). See also **ALASKA; ANNETTE ISLAND RESERVATION; TSIMSHIAN.** *Spec. St.* 26:1095; 34:1411; 48:667; 50:873; 52:1299. *Approp. St.* 50:564. *Cases* Alaska, 248 U. S. 78; Territory of Alaska, 289 Fed. 671. *I. D. Rulings* Op. Sol. June 30, 1936.

MEWUK (MIWOK). See **TUOLUMNE BAND OF THE MEWUK INDIANS OF THE TUOLUMNE RANCHERIA, CALIFORNIA; SACRAMENTO AGENCY; MEWUK INDIAN COMMUNITY OF THE WILTON RANCHERIA.** See also **CALIFORNIA.**

MEXICAN KICKAPOO. See **KICKAPOO; SHAWNEE AGENCY, OKLAHOMA.**

MIAMI TRIBE OF OKLAHOMA. See also **INDIANA; OHIO; OKLAHOMA; EEL RIVER; PEORIA AND MIAMI.** *Texts* Hilliard, LT; Manypenny, OIW. *Per.* Canfield, 15 Am. L. Rev. 21; 9 J. H. Univ. Studies 541. *Gov. Pub.* 76 Cong., 1 sess., Hearings, H. Comm. Ind. Aff., H. R. 2306. *Spec. St.* 3:308, 319; 4:185; 5:251, 453, 542; 9:50; 10:704; 17:213, 417, 631; 18:273; 22:63, 116; 24:388; 25:1013; 48:501. *Approp. St.* 1:460; 2:407, 607; 3:517; 4:232, 300, 361, 432, 463, 470, 526, 616, 682, 780; 5:36, 158, 298, 323, 402, 417, 493, 704, 766; 9:20, 132, 252, 382, 544, 574; 10:41, 226, 315, 576, 643, 686; 11:65, 169, 273, 388; 12:44, 221, 512, 774; 13:161, 541; 14:492; 15:198; 16:13, 335, 544;

17:165, 437; 18:146, 420; 19:176, 271; 20:63, 206, 295; 21:114, 414, 435; 22:68, 433; 23:76, 362; 24:222, 449; 25:217, 565, 980; 26:336, 989; 28:876; 30:62; 32:245; 44:453. *Priv. St.* 6:343, 519, 601, 942; 9:801, 806; 13:584; 45:2046. *Treaties* 7:49, 74, 81, 91, 113, 115, 118, 131, 189, 300, 309, 458, 569, 582; 8:116; 15:513. *Cases* Bowling, 232 U. S. 528; Elk, 112 U. S. 94; Finley, 4 Ind. T. 386; Kansas, 5 Wall. 737; Mungosah, 17 Fed. Cas. No. 9924; Peck, 19 Fed. Cas. No. 10891; Wau-pe-man-qua, 28 Fed. 489. *Op. A. G.* 2:563, 631; 6:440; 11:384; 12:236; 17:381, 410. *I. D. Rulings* Memo. Sol., Dec. 13, 1938. *Const.* Oct. 10, 1939.

MICHIGAN. See also BAY MILLS INDIAN COMMUNITY; CHIPPEWA; HANNAHVILLE INDIAN COMMUNITY; ISABELLA RESERVATION; KEWEENAW BAY INDIAN COMMUNITY OF THE L'ANSE RESERVATION; L'ANSE RESERVATION; MACKINAC; ONTONAGON; POTAWATOMIE; SAGINAW CHIPPEWA INDIAN TRIBE OF THE ISABELLA RESERVATION. *Approp. St.* 8:517; 10:315; 11:65, 169, 388; 17:165, 437; 18:146, 420; 19:176, 271; 20:63, 295; 21:114, 485. *Treaties* 7:78, 181.

MIDDLE OREGON. See also WARM SPRINGS AGENCY *Spec. St.* 46:1033.

MILLE LAC (CHIPPEWA). See also MINNESOTA; CHIPPEWA. *Spec. St.* 26:290; 28:576; 30:745; 32:245; 33:1048; 41:408.

MINNECONJOU (SIOUX). See also SOUTH DAKOTA; ROSEBUD; SIOUX. *Spec. St.* 19:254.

MINNESOTA. See also MICHIGAN; MINNESOTA AND MICHIGAN; WISCONSIN; BOIS FORT; CHIPPEWA; FOND DU LAC; GRAND PORTAGE; LOWER SIOUX INDIAN COMMUNITY; MILLE LAC; MINNESOTA CHIPPEWA TRIBE; NETT LAKE; PEMBINA; PIPESTONE; PRAIRIE ISLAND INDIAN COMMUNITY; RED LAKE; RED PIPESTONE; SIOUX; TEETON; VERMILLION LAKE; WHITE EARTH; WILD RICE LAKE INDIAN RESERVATION. *Approp. St.* 11:65, 388; 17:165, 437; 18:146, 420; 19:176, 271; 20:63, 295; 21:114, 485; 30:62. *Priv. St.* 31:1566; 44:1813. *Cases* Chippewa, 301 U. S. 358.

MINNESOTA CHIPPEWA TRIBE. See also CHIPPEWA; MINNESOTA. *Const.* July 24, 1936. *Charter* Nov. 13, 1937.

MINNESOTA AND MICHIGAN. See also MINNESOTA; MICHIGAN. *Approp. St.* 12:44; 221, 512, 774; 13:161, 541; 14:255, 492; 15:198; 16:13, 335, 544; 17:165, 437; 18:146.

MINTO, NATIVE VILLAGE OF (ATHAPASCAN). See also ALASKA. *Const.* Dec. 30, 1939. *Charter* Dec. 30, 1939.

MISSION. See also CALIFORNIA; AGUA CALIENTE; CAHUILLA; CAPITAN GRANDE; DIEGUENOS; LA JOLLA; MALKI; MESA GRANDE; MORONGO; PALM SPRINGS; RINCON; SANTA YSABEL; SOBOBA; TEMECULA; TORRES MARTINEZ; VOLCAN. *Spec. St.* 26:712; 27:61; 32:822; 40:1206; 47:146; 49:1106; 50:69. *Approp. St.* 16:13; 18:146, 420; 21:114; 23:76; 24:449; 25:980; 26:336, 989; 27:612; 28:286; 29:321; 30:11, 62, 105, 597, 924, 1074; 31:221, 280, 1010, 1058, 1133; 32:245, 419, 982, 1031, 1083; 33:189, 452, 1048; 34:325, 1015; 35:70, 781; 39:912; 38:208; 39:969; 40:561; 45:1562; 46:1115, 1552; 47:91, 820; 48:362; 49:1757; 50:564, 755; 52:291. *Priv. St.* 49:2093. *Cases* Andreas, 71 F. 2d 908; Barker, 181 U. S. 481; Bell, 39 C. Cls. 350; Donnelly, 228 U. S. 243; St. Marie, 24 F. Supp. 237; U. S. v. Title, 265 U. S. 472. *I. D. Rulings* Op. Sol., April 8, 1937.

MISSISSIPPI. See BILOXI; CHOCTAW; CHOCTAW OF MISSISSIPPI.

MISSOURI. See also SAC, FOXES, IOWAS, SIOUX, OMAHAS, OTTOES AND MISSOURIAS. *Spec. St.* 4:464; 19:208; 21:380; 26:81. *Approp. St.* 4:526, 705; 17:510; 20:115; 22:302, 603; 33:189. *Treaties* 7:277, 328, 429, 511, 524; 11:605. *Cases* Maust, 283 Fed. 912; Otoe, 52 C. Cls. 424; Stevens, 34 C. Cls. 244; U. S. v. Homeratha, 40 F. 2d 305.

MOACHE (UTE). See also COLORADO; UTAH; UTE. *Spec. St.* 28:677.

MOAPA RIVER (PAIUTE). See also NEVADA; PAIUTE. *Approp. St.* 36:269; 40:561; 41:1225; 42:552. *Cases* Ex p. Sloan, 22 Fed. Cas. No. 12994. *I. D. Rulings* Letter to Col. J. C. Scrugham by John F. Truesdell, April 1, 1921.

MODOC. See also OKLAHOMA; OREGON; INDIAN TERRITORY; KLAMATH; MODOC; KLAMATH, MODOC AND YAHOOSKIN BAND OF SNAKES. *Spec. St.* 12:199; 13:37; 22:7, 111, 399; 35:751; 41:623; 48:501. *Approp. St.* 18:133, 146, 420; 19:176, 271; 20:63, 295; 21:114, 485; 22:68, 433; 23:76, 362; 24:449; 25:4, 217, 980; 26:336, 504, 989; 27:120, 612; 28:286, 876; 29:321; 30:62, 571, 924; 31:221, 1058; 41:3. *Priv. St.* 23:525, 672; 38:1598; 45:1968. *Cases* Klamath, 81 C. Cls. 79; Oregon, 202 U. S. 60; U. S. v. Klamath, 304 U. S. 119; U. S. v. Miller, 105 Fed. 944; U. S. v. Oregon, 103 Fed. 549. *L. D. Memo (D. J.)* 11:497; 12:510, 703. *I. D. Rulings* Op. Sol., May 9, 1928.

MOHAWK. See also NEW YORK; SIX NATIONS. *Treaty* 7:61. *Cases* New York, 170, U. S. 1.

MOHICAN. See STOCKBRIDGE-MUNSEE COMMUNITY.

MOJAVE. See also ARIZONA; COSNEJO; FORT McDOWELL MOJAVE-APACHE COMMUNITY; FORT MOJAVE INDIAN RESERVATION. *Approp. St.* 22:257; 41:408. *Cases* Barrow, 30 C. Cls. 54; Luke, 35 C. Cls. 15.

MOJARIS (MOHAVE). See also CALIFORNIA. *Cases* Luke, 35 C. Cls. 15.

MOLALA. See also OREGON; CALAPOOIA, MOLALA, CLAKAMAS; KLAMATH; SILETZ. *Cases* U. S. v. Sinnott, 26 Fed. 84.

MOLE LAKE INDIANS (CHIPPEWA). See also WISCONSIN; CHIPPEWA. *I. D. Rulings* Memo. Sol., Feb. 8, 1937.

MOLEL INDIANS (MOLALA). See also OREGON; MOLALA; SILETZ. *Approp. St.* 12:4, 221, 512, 774; 13:161, 541; 14:255, 492; 15:198; 16:13, 335, 544; 17:165, 437; 18:146, 420; 19:176, 271; 20:63, 295; 21:114, 485; 22:68, 433; 23:76, 362; 24:449; 25:217, 980; 26:336, 989; 27:120, 612; 28:286, 876; 29:321; 30:62, 571, 924; 31:221, 1058; 32:245, 982; 33:189, 1048; 34:325, 1015; 35:70, 781; 36:269. *Treaties* 12:981.

MONTANA. See also ASSINIBOINE; BLACKFEET TRIBE OF THE BLACKFEET RESERVATION; CHIPPEWA-CREE TRIBE OF THE ROCKY BOY'S RESERVATION; CONFEDERATED SALISH AND KOOTENAI TRIBES OF THE FLATHEAD RESERVATION; CROW; FLATHEAD, KOOTENAI AND PEND D'OREILLE; FORT BELKNAP INDIAN COMMUNITY; FORT PECK; GROS VENTRE; ASSINIBOINE AND GROS VENTRE; JOCKO; KOOTENAI; NORTHERN CHEYENNE; PEND D'OREILLE; PIEGAN; RIVER CROW; ROCKY BOY; SALISH; SALISH AND KOOTENAI; SIOUX; SIOUX AT FORT PECK AGENCY; TONGUE RIVER RESERVATION. *Gov. Pub.* 73 Cong., Hearings, S. Comm. Ind. Aff., July 2, 1934. *Approp. St.* 16:13, 544; 17:165, 437; 18:146, 420; 19:176, 271; 20:63, 295; 21:114, 485. *Priv. St.* 17:787.

MONTAUK TRIBE. See NEW YORK. *Per.* 9 Yale L. J. 378. *I. D. Rulings* Memo. Sol. Off., Oct. 25, 1936.

MOQUI. See also ARIZONA; HOPI. *Spec. St.* 39:504; 48:960. *Approp. St.* 26:989; 27:120, 612; 28:286; 34:1015; 41:1225; 42:1174.

MORONGO (SERRANO). See also CALIFORNIA; MISSION. *Spec. St.* 44:679. *Approp. St.* 41:3, 408, 1225; 42:552, 1174; 43:390; 44:453, 934; 45:200, 1562; 46:1115; 47:91, 820; 48:362; 49:176.

MOUNTAIN CROW. See CROW.

MUACHE. See COLORADO; UTAH; MOACHE; TABEGUACHE, MUACHE, CAPOTE, WEEMINUCHE, YAMPA, GRAND RIVER AND UINTAH BANDS OF UTES; UTES.

MUCKLESHOOT INDIAN TRIBE OF THE MUCKLESHOOT RESERVATION. See also WASHINGTON. *Spec. St.* 43:886. *Cases* Duwamish, 79 C. Cls. 530. *Const.* May 13, 1936. *Charter* Oct. 31, 1936.

MUNSEE. See also WISCONSIN; DELAWARE; STOCKBRIDGE AND MUNSEE; MUNSEE AND DELAWARE; WYANDOTS, MUNSEE AND DELAWARE. *Spec. St.* 16:404; 27:744. *Approp. St.* 5:323; 28:286; 30:62; 39:123. *Treaties* 7:405, 550; 11:577; 12:1105. *I. D. Rulings* Op. Sol., Dec. 29, 1921.

MUNSEE AND DELAWARE. See also DELAWARE; MUNSEE; WYANDOTTE, MUNSEE AND DELAWARE. *Approp. St.* 2:407; 4:526. *Treaties* Archives No. 44; 7:87.

MUSCOGEE (CREEK). See also OKLAHOMA; CREEK. *Approp. St.* 28:876. *Treaties* 7:474.

NAMBE PUEBLO. See also NEW MEXICO; PUEBLO. *Priv. St.* 52:1353. *L. D. Memo.* (*D. J.*) 12:298.

NARRAGANSETT. See also CONNECTICUT; RHODE ISLAND. *Per.* 2 J. H. Univ. Studies 385.

NATCHEZ. *Per.* Mac Leod, 28 J. Crim. L. 181.

NAVAJO. See also ARIZONA; NEW MEXICO; UTAH; COSNEJO; LEUPP EXTENSION RESERVATION. *Per.* 39 Yale L. J. 307; Gates, 21 Am. J. Soc. Sci. 112. *Gov. Pub.* 71 Cong., 2 sess., Hearings, S. Comm. Ind. Aff., S. 3782; 72 Cong., 2 sess., Hearings, S. Comm. Ind. Aff., Dec. 7, 1932; 74 Cong., 1 sess., H. Rep. 473. *Spec. St.* 9:570; 13:328; 15:264; 32:657; 39:926; 42:1288; 43:91, 606, 800, 994, 1114; 45:1080;

OIL SPRINGS RESERVATION. See also NEW YORK. *Gov. Pub.* 72 Cong., 2 sess., Hearings, S. Comm. Ind. Aff., S. 5302. *Spec. St.* 31:819.

OJIBWAY. See also CHIPPEWA; MINNESOTA; WISCONSIN; MICHIGAN. *Per. Cain*, 2 Minn. L. Rev. 177; Mac Leod, 28 J. Crim. L. 181.

OKANAGAN. See OAKINAKANE.

OKLAHOMA. See also ABSENTEE SHAWNEE TRIBE OF INDIANS OF OKLAHOMA; ALABAMA-QUASSARTE TRIBAL TOWN; APACHE; CADDO INDIAN TRIBE OF OKLAHOMA; CHEROKEE; CHEYENNE-ARAPAHOE TRIBES OF OKLAHOMA; CHICKASAW; CHOCTAW; CITIZEN BAND OF POTAWATOMI INDIANS OF OKLAHOMA; CREEK; DELAWARE; EASTERN SHAWNEE TRIBE OF INDIANS; FIVE CIVILIZED TRIBES; IOWA TRIBE OF OKLAHOMA; KAW; KICKAPOO TRIBE OF OKLAHOMA; MIAMI TRIBE OF OKLAHOMA; MODOC; MUSCOGEE; OSAGE; OTTAWA TRIBE OF OKLAHOMA; OTTOE; PAWNEE INDIAN TRIBE OF OKLAHOMA; PEORIA TRIBE OF INDIANS OF OKLAHOMA; PONCA; OTTOE AND MISSOURIAS; POTAWATOMIE; QUAPAW: SAC AND FOX TRIBE OF INDIANS; SHAWNEE; SEGER; SEMINOLE; SENECA-CAYUGA TRIBE OF OKLAHOMA; SIOUX; THLOPTHLOCO TRIBAL TOWN; TONKAWA TRIBE OF INDIANS; WICHITA; WYANDOTTE TRIBE OF OKLAHOMA. *Texts* Abel, SI; Stewart, GDO. *Gov. Pub.* 60 Cong., 1 sess., H. Rep. 1454; 74 Cong., 1 sess., Hearings, S. Comm. Ind. Aff., S. 2047; 74 Cong., 2 sess., Hearings, H. Comm. Ind. Aff., S. 2047. *I. D. Rulings*, Memo. Sol., April 22, 1938, May 24, 1938.

OMAHA TRIBE OF NEBRASKA. See also NEBRASKA; OMAHA AND WINNEBAGOE; OTTOE; SACS, FOXES, IOWAS, SIOUX, OMAHAS, OTTOES AND MISSOURIAS; SANTEE SIOUX, WINNEBAGO; YANCTON. *Per.* Gates, 21 A. J. Soc. Sci. 112; Mac Leod, 28 J. Crim. L. 181; Thayer, 68 Atl. Month. 540, 676. *Spec. St.* 4:464; 11:385; 17:391; 22:341; 24:214; 25:150; 26:329; 28:276, 507; 30:344, 912; 32:183; 36:348, 580; 37:111; 38:1188; 39:865; 43:726, 820. *Approp. St.* 4:526, 616, 682, 780; 5:36, 158, 298, 323, 402, 417, 493, 704, 766; 9:20, 132, 382, 544, 574, 252; 10:41, 226 315, 686; 11:65, 169, 273, 319, 329, 388; 12:44, 221, 512 774; 13:161, 541; 14:255, 492; 15:198; 16:13, 335, 544; 17:165, 437, 510; 18:146, 420; 19:176, 271; 20:63, 295; 21:114, 485; 22:68, 433; 23:76, 362, 446; 24:449; 27:612; 32:235; 36:269; 39:123; 41:3, 408, 1225; 42:327, 552, 1174; 43:33, 390, 1141, 1313; 44:161, 453, 934; 45:200; 46:1115; 47:91, 820; 49:1757. *Treaties* 7:129, 282, 328, 511, 524; 10:1043, 1132; 12:927, 933, 939, 951, 957, 975; 14:667. *Cases* Beck, 65 Fed. 30; Chase, 256 U. S. 1; Chase, 238 Fed. 887; Clay, 282 Fed. 268; Dixon, 268 Fed. 285; First, 59 F. 2d 367; Gilpin, 256 U. S. 10; Hallowell, 239 U. S. 506; Hallowell. 221 U. S. 317; Jacobs, 223 U. S. 200; Meeker, 173 Fed. 216; Omaha, 53 C. Cls. 549; Ross, 56 Fed. 855; Sloan. 118 Fed. 283; Sloan, 95 Fed. 193; U. S. v. Celestine, 215 U. S. 278; U. S. v. Chase, 245 U. S. 89; U. S. v First, 56 F. 2d 634; U. S. v. Flournoy, 69 Fed. 886; U. S. v. Flournoy. 71 Fed. 576; U. S. v. Kopp, 110 Fed. 160; U. S. v. Mathewson, 32 F. 2d 745; U. S. v. Mummert, 15 F. 2d 926; U. S. v. Omaha, 253 U. S. 275; U. S. v. Phillips, 56 F. 2d 477; U. S. v. Sutton, 215 U. S. 291; U. S. ex rel. Standing, 25 Fed. Cas. No. 14891. *I. D. Rulings* 27 L. D. 299, Sept. 14, 1898; Memo. Sol., Jan. 22, 1936; April 14, 1938; Memo. Sol. Off., Dec. 30, 1938. *Const.* Mar. 30, 1936. *Charter* Aug. 22, 1936.

OMAHA AND WINNEBAGOE. See also OMAHA TRIBE OF NEBRASKA. *Spec. St.* 29:512; 33:311; 35:628. *Approp St.* 15:110.

ONEIDA TRIBE OF INDIANS OF WISCONSIN. See also NEW YORK; WISCONSIN; IROQUOIS; SIX NATIONS. *Spec. St.* 16:588. *Approp. St.* 5:158, 298; 9:20, 574; 25:217; 32:245; 33:1048; 34:325; 35:781; 39:123, 969. *Priv. St.* 6:895. *Treaties* Archives No. 19; No. 28. 7:47, 550, 566. *Cases* New York, 170 U. S. 1; New York, 40 C. Cls. 448; Oneida, 89 C. Cls. 116; U. S. v. Boylan, 265 Fed. 165; U. S. v. Cook, 19 Wall. 591; U. S. v. Elm, 25 Fed. Cas. No. 15048; U. S. v. Foster, 25 Fed. Cas. No. 15141; U. S. v. Hall, 171 Fed. 214; U. S. v. King, 81 Fed. 625; U. S. v. N. Y., 173 U. S. 464. *I. D. Rulings* Memo. Sol., Jan. 16, 1934. *Const.* Dec. 21, 1936. *Charter* May 1, 1937.

ONONDAGA. See also NEW YORK; ALLEGANY; IROQUOIS; SIX NATIONS. *Per.* Harsha, 134 N. A. Rev 272. *Approp. St.* 5:612. *Priv. St.* 6:609, 835. *Treaties* Archives No. 19; 7:550. *Cases* New York, 41 C. Cls. 462; New York, 40 C. Cls. 448; U. S. v. New York, 173 U. S. 464. *L. D. Memo. (D. J.)* 5:179, *I. D. Rulings* Memo Sol., May 24, 1937.

ONTONAGON (CHIPPEWA). See also MICHIGAN; CHIPPEWA. *Approp. St.* 47:91.

OREGON. See also ALSEA AND SILETZ RESERVATION; CAYUSE; CALAPOOIA, MOLALA, CLAKAMAS; CLATSOP; COAST RANGE; CONFEDERATED TRIBES OF THE GRANDE RONDE COMMUNITY; COOS BAY; COW CREEK; GALEESE; GRANDE RONDE RESERVATION; KLAMATH; KLAMATH, MODOC, YAHOOSKIN BAND OF SNAKES; MALHEUR; MOLALA; MODOC; MOLEL; OREGON AND WASHINGTON TERRITORY; PAHUTE; PITT RIVER; ROGUE RIVER; SCOTONS; SHASTA; SILETZ; SNAKE; SIUSLAW; TILLAMOOK; UMATILLA; UMPQUA; WALLA WALLA; WARM SPRINGS. *Spec. St.* 11:362; 13:324; 28:86; 49:801. *Approp. St.* 9:544; 10:15, 315, 686; 11:169, 329, 388; 12:4, 44, 221, 512, 774; 13:161, 541; 14:255, 492; 15:198; 16:13, 335, 544; 17:165, 437; 18:146, 420; 19:176, 271; 20:63, 295; 21:114, 485; 22:68, 433; 23.76, 362; 24:449; 25:217, 980; 26:336, 989; 27:120, 612; 28:286; 29:321; 30:62, 571, 924; 31:221, 280, 1058; 32:245, 982; 33:189, 1048; 36:1289; 37:518; 38:1443; 40:561. *Priv. St.* 12:908; 25:1332; 26:1164; 28:1013, 1041; 33:1415, 1423, 1521, 1678, 1965, 2024, 2048; 34:1456, 2820; 35:1204, 1219, 1375, 1389, 1406, 1431, 1446, 1573, 1606; 36:1609, 1751, 1752, 1753, 1760, 1762, 1806, 1807, 1815, 1843, 1859, 1984, 2000, 2099; 37:1030; 39:1588; 40:1484, 1486, 1536; 41:1596; 42:1718. *Treaties* 12:963; 14:751.

OREGON AND WASHINGTON TERRITORY. See also OREGON; WASHINGTON. *Texts* Hoopes, IAA. *Approp St.* 12:512, 774; 13:161, 541; 14:255, 492; 15:198. *Priv. St.* 34:1456, 1559, 1642, 1741, 1910, 2047, 2108, 2483, 2587, 2668, 2752, 2757; 35:1462; 36:1609; 40:1489.

OSAGE. See also OKLAHOMA; FIVE CIVILIZED TRIBES; GREAT OSAGE NATION; LITTLE OSAGE NATION. *Texts* Cheadle, ADI; Manypenny, OIW. *Per.* Dixon, 23 Case & Com. 712; Harsha, 134 N. A. Rev. 272; Reeves, 23 Case & Com. 727; 3 Okla. S. B. J. 146. *Gov. Pub.* 68 Cong., 1 sess., H. Rep. 165; 68 Cong., 1 sess., H. Rep. 243; 74 Cong., 1 sess., H. Rep. 740; 75 Cong., 3 sess., Hearings, S. Comm. Ind. Aff., S. 3980 & S. 4036; 75 Cong., 3 sess., S. Rep. 1798; H. Rep. 2700; Hearings, H. Comm. Ind. Aff., H. R. 8701. *Spec. St.* 4:25, 729; 12:28, 834; 17:90; 18:283; 19:221; 21:143, 291, 509; 24:388; 26:1095; 29:529; 31:659; 32:43; 33:240, 299; 34:208, 267, 539; 35:778, 1167; 36:855; 37:46, 86; 39:867; 41:1097, 1249; 43:94, 244, 722, 1008; 46:1047; 48:501; 50:805; 52:347, 1037. *Approp. St.* 3:277; 4:92, 217, 361, 470, 526, 616, 682, 705, 780; 5:36, 73, 158, 298, 323, 402, 417, 493, 704, 766; 9:20, 132, 252, 382, 544, 574, 570; 10:41, 226, 315, 686; 11:65, 169, 273, 388; 12:44, 221, 512, 774; 13:161, 541; 14:255, 492; 15:110, 198; 16:13, 335, 544; 17:165, 437, 530; 18:146, 420; 19:176, 271; 20:63, 295, 410; 21:40, 114, 485; 22:68, 257, 433, 603; 23:76, 362; 24:449; 25:217, 980; 26:336, 989; 27:120, 612; 28:286, 876; 29:321; 30:62, 571, 924; 31:221, 1058; 32:245, 982; 33:189, 1048; 34:325, 1015, 1371; 35:614; 37:518; 38:582; 39:123, 969; 40:561; 41:3, 408, 1225; 42:552, 1174; 43:390, 1141; 44:453, 934; 45:200, 883, 1562, 1623; 46:279, 1115, 1552; 47:91, 820; 48:362, 984; 49:176, 1757; 50:564; 52:291, 1114. *Priv. St.* 6:408, 929; 17:730; 21:652; 24:851; 26:1414. *Treaties* 7:107, 183, 474, 533, 550; 14:687. *Cases* Adams, 59 F. 2d 653; Ammerman, 267 Fed. 136; Bailey, 43 C. Cls. 353; Board, 64 F. 2d 775; Brewer, 260 U. S. 77; Brown, 146 Fed. 975; Browning, 6 F. 2d 801; Butterfield, 241 Fed. 556; Choteau, 283 U. S. 691; Chouteau, 38 F. 2d 976; Continental, 69 F. 2d 19; Drummond, 34 F. 2d 755; Gay, 5 Okla. 1; Gillespie, 257 U. S. 501; Globe, 81 F. 2d 143; Gordon, 7 Okla. 117; Haeff, 10 Okla. 338; Harrison, 264 Fed. 776; Heiner, 275 U. S. 232; Herd, 13 Okla. 512; Hickey, 64 F. 2d 628; Hot, 92 U. S. 698; Ickes, 80 F. 2d 708. In re Dennison, 38 F. 2d 662; In re Ingram, 12 Okla. 54; In re Irwin, 60 F. 2d 495; In re Penn. 41 F. 2d 257; Indian, 240 U. S. 522; Jump, 100 F. 2d 130; Kansas, 80 C. Cls. 264; Kenny, 250 U. S. 58; Labadie, 6 Okla. 400; La Motte, 254 U. S. 570; Lasater, 10 Okla. 335; Leavenworth, 92 U. S. 733; Levindale, 241 U. S. 432; Logan, 58 F. 2d 697; McCurdy, 246 U. S. 263; McCurdy, 264 U. S. 484; Merchant, 35 C. Cls. 403; Missouri, 152 U. S. 114; Morgan, 224 Fed. 698; Morrison, 6 F. 2d 811; Mosier, 198 Fed. 54; Modd, 14 F. 2d 430; Ne-Kan-Wah-She-Tun-Kah, 290 Fed. 303; Oklahoma, 220 U. S. 290; Osage, 35 F. 2d 21; Osage,

66 C. Cls. 64; Price, 174 U. S. 373; Price, 33 C. Cls. 106; Quarles, 45 F. 2d 585; Rogers, 45 C. Cls. 388; Russell, 10 Okla. 340; Scheff, 33 F. 2d 263; Shore, 60 F. 2d 1; Silurian, 54 F. 2d 43; State of Missouri, 7 How. 660; Stewart, 39 C. Cls. 321; Tapp. 6 F. Supp. 577; Taylor, 51 F. 2d 884; Thomas, 169 U. S. 264; Thomison, 35 C. Cls. 395; Tinker, 231 U. S. 681; Townsend, 265 Fed. 519; U. S. v. Aaron, 183 Fed. 347; U. S. v. Barnett, 7 F. Supp. 573; U. S. v. Bowling, 256 U. S. 484; U. S. v. Carson, 19 F. Supp. 616; U. S. v. Cha-to-ka-na-pe-pha, 25 Fed. Cas. No. 14789a; U. S. v. Hale, 51 F. 2d 629; U. S. v. Harris, 293 Fed. 389; U. S. v. Howard, 8 F. Supp. 617; U. S. v. Hughes, 6 F. Supp. 972; U. S. v. Hutchings, 252 Fed. 841; U. S. v. Johnson, 87 F. 2d 155; U. S. v. La Motte, 67 F. 2d 788; U. S. v. Law, 250 Fed. 218; U. S. v. Luther, 260 Fed. 579; U. S. v. Mashunkashey, 72 F. 2d 847; U. S. v. Mullendore, 74 F. 2d 286; U. S. v. Ramsey, 271 U. S. 467; U. S. v. Sands, 94 F. 2d 156; U. S. v. Sandstorm, 22 F. Supp. 190; U. S. v. Ta-wan-ga-ca, 28 Fed. Cas. No. 16435; U. S. ex rel. Bown, 232 U. S. 598; United Express, 191 Fed. 673; Utilities, 2 F. Supp. 81; Watson, 263 Fed. 700; Webster, 266 U. S. 507; Williams, 83 F. 2d 143; Wilhite, 5 Ind. T. 621; Work, 266 U. S. 161; Work, 261 U. S. 352. *Op. A. G.* 18:5; 19:117; 21:131; 33:60; 34:26; 38:577. *L. D. Memo. (D. J.)* 3:187; 6:641; 10:32; 11:620, 665; 12:642. *I. D. Rulings.* 34 L. D. 419, Jan. 25, 1906; Op. Sol., Jan. 4, 1922, Aug. 16, 1922, Sept. 30, 1922, Nov. 1, 1922, Dec. 23, 1924; Memo. Sol., Dec. 18, 1925; Op. Sol. Dec. 19, 1925, Mar. 16, 1926; Memo. Sol. Off., July 23, 1926; Memo. Sol., Sept. 3, 1926; Memo. Sol. Off., Sept. 14, 1926; Memo. Sol., Sept. 29, 1926; Memo. Sol. Off., Oct. 27, 1926, Mar. 3, 1927; Op. Sol., Mar. 26, 1927; Memo. Sol. Off., Sept. 12, 1927, Sept. 13, 1927, May 14, 1928; Op. Sol., June 19, 1928; Memo. Sol. Off., July 31, 1928, Oct. 31, 1928, Feb. 21, 1929, April 18, 1929; Op. Sol., May 4, 1929; Memo. Sol. Off., May 31, 1929; Op. Sol., June 26, 1929; Memo. Sol. Off., Sept. 18, 1929, Feb. 3, 1930, Mar. 4, 1930, July 8, 1930; Op. Sol., Aug. 13, 1930; Memo. Sol. Off., Nov. 5, 1930, Dec. 30, 1930, Mar. 10, 1931, April 9, 1931, May 29, 1931; Op. Sol., Oct. 14, 1931, Feb. 4, 1932; Memo. Sol. Off., Dec. 15, 1932, April 8, 1933, May 27, 1933, May 27, 1933, June 29, 1933, July 13, 1933; Op. Sol., July 22, 1933; Memo. Sol., Oct. 22, 1933. Op. Sol., Dec. 8, 1933. Memo. Sol. Off., Dec. 21, 1933; Op. Sol., Aug. 6, 1934; Memo. Sol. Off., Sept. 26, 1934; Memo. Sol., Oct. 3, 1934; Memo. Sol. Off., Oct. 17, 1934; Memo. Sol., Nov. 14, 1934; Op. Sol., Nov. 28, 1934, Dec. 16, 1935; Memo. Sol., Dec. 17, 1935; Op. Sol., April 23, 1936; Memo. Sol., May 8, 1936; Op. Sol., Jan. 4, 1937, Jan. 26, 1937; Memo. Sol. Off., Feb. 13, 1937, Oct. 27, 1937; Memo. Sol., Nov. 5, 1937; Memo. Sol. Off., Jan. 30, 1938.

OTTAWA TRIBE OF OKLAHOMA. See also **OKLAHOMA; CHIPPEWA, OTTAWA AND POTTAWATOMIE; OTTAWA AND CHIPPEWA; OTTAWA, POTTAWATOMIE, CHIPPEWA AND OTHER TRIBES OF INDIANS.** *Texts* Manypenny, OIW. *Spec. St.* 3:308, 319, 690; 4:302; 9:342; 12:207; 14:370; 17:388, 623; 18:516; 19:55; 21:511; 26:24. *Approp. St.* 1:460; 2:407, 467; 3:393, 517; 4:390, 394, 505, 526, 528, 616, 631, 636, 682, 705, 780; 5:36, 73, 158, 298, 323, 402, 417, 493, 704, 766; 9:20, 132, 252, 382, 544, 574; 10:41, 226, 315, 686; 11:65, 169, 273, 388; 12:44, 221, 512, 774; 13:161, 541; 14:255; 15:198; 16:13, 544; 17:122, 437; 26:989; 29:321; 33:1048; 34:325; 48:984. *Priv. St.* 6:887, 919, 920, 924, 741; 11:556; 12:883. *Treaties* Archives No. 44; 7:16, 28, 49, 87, 112, 118, 131, 146, 160, 178, 207, 218, 272, 315, 320, 323, 326, 420, 491; 8:116; 11:621; 12:1237; 14:657; 15:513. *Cases* Dubuque, 109 U. S. 329; Elk, 112 U. S. 94; Godfrey, 10 Fed. Cas. No. 5497; Libby, 118 U. S. 250; Ottawa, 42 C. Cls. 240; Ottawa, 42 C. Cls. 518; Pam-to-pee, 187 U. S. 371; Spalding, 160 U. S. 394; Wiggan, 163 U. S. 56. *Op. A. G.* 2:562; 3:206, 209; 13:336. *I. D. Rulings* Memo. Sol., May 1, 1937. *Const.* Nov. 30, 1938. *Charter* June 2, 1939.

OTTAWA AND CHIPPEWA. See also **OTTAWA; WISCONSIN; CHIPPEWAYS, OTTAWAYS AND POTTAWATOMIE.** *Spec. St.* 17:381. *Approp. St.* 5:158, 298, 323, 402, 417, 493, 704, 766; 9:20, 132, 252, 382, 544, 574; 10:15, 41, 226, 315, 686; 11:65, 169, 273, 388; 12:44, 221, 512, 774; 13:161, 541, 14:255, 492; 15:198; 16:13, 335, 544; 17:165, 437; 18:146, 420; 19:176, 271; 20:63, 295; 21:114, 485; 22:68, 433; 23:76, 362; 33:1048; 35:70.

OTTAWA, POTTAWATOMIE, CHIPPEWA, AND OTHER TRIBES OF INDIANS. See also **OTTAWA; OTTAWA AND CHIPPEWA; WISCONSIN; CHIPPEWAYS, OTTAWAYS AND POTTAWATOMIES.** *Priv. St.* 9:741.

OTTOE. See also **OKLAHOMA; OMAHA; SAC, FOXES, IOWAS, SIOUX, OMAHAS, OTTOES AND MISSOURIAS; PONCA.** *Per.* MacLeod, 28 J. Crim. L. 181. *Spec. St.* 4:464; 19:208; 21:380; 26:81; 48:501. *Approp. St.* 4:705; 5:158; 17:510; 19:102, 363; 20:115; 22:608; 41:408, 1225; 42:552; 43:390; 44:934; 45:1623; 47:91; 48:984. *Treaties* 7:154, 277, 328, 429, 511, 524; 11:605. *Cases* Foster, 189 U. S. 325; Maust, 283 Fed. 912; Otoe, 52 C. Cls. 424; Reeves, 16 Okla. 342; Sharp, 138 Fed. 878; Sloan, 118 Fed. 283; Stevens, 34 C. Cls. 244; U. S. v. Homeratha, 40 F. 2d 305.

OTTOE AND MISSOURIAS. See also **OKLAHOMA; PONCA; OTTOE; MISSOURI.** *Gov. Pub.* 72 Cong., 1 sess., Hearings, H. Comm. Ind. Aff., H. R. 10927. *Spec. St.* 17:391; 20:471; 27:568; 28:84; 30:834; 31:59; 36:855. *Approp. St.* 4:616, 682, 705, 780; 5:36, 158, 298, 323, 402, 417, 493, 704, 766; 9:20, 132, 252, 382, 544, 574; 10:41, 226, 315, 686; 11:65, 169, 273, 329, 388; 12:44, 221, 512, 774; 13:161, 541; 14:255, 492; 15:198; 16:13, 335, 544; 17:165, 437; 18:146, 420; 19:176, 271; 20:63, 115, 295; 21:114, 485; 22:68, 433; 23:76, 362; 24:449; 25:217, 980; 26:336, 989; 27:120, 612; 28:286, 876; 32:245; 33:189, 1048; 34:325. *Priv. St.* 24:969. *Treaties* 10:1038, 1130. *Cases* Axhelm, 9 Okla. 321; Dubuque, 109 U. S. 329.

OURAY. See **TABEGUACHE, MUACHE, CAPOTE, WEEMINUCHE, YAMPA, GRAND RIVER AND UINTAH BANDS OF UTES; UINTAH.**

OZETTE. See also **NEAH BAY; WASHINGTON.** *Spec. St.* 36:1345. *Cases* Mitchell, 22 F. 2d 771.

PAH-UTE (PAIUTE). See also **ARIZONA; CALIFORNIA; NEVADA; OREGON; BIG PINE RESERVATION; FORT BIDWELL; FORT McDERMITT, PAIUTE, SHOSHONE TRIBE OF THE FORT McDERMITT INDIAN RESERVATION; KAIBAB; KANOSH; MOAPA RIVER; PYRAMID LAKE PAIUTE TRIBE OF THE PYRAMID LAKE RESERVATION; RENO-SPARKS INDIAN COLONY; SAN JUAN; SHEBIT; SHEWITS; SHOSHONE-PAIUTE TRIBE OF DUCK VALLEY RESERVATION; SNAKES; WALKER RIVER PAIUTE TRIBE OF THE WALKER RIVER RESERVATION; WARM SPRINGS; WINNEMUCCA INDIAN COLONY; YERINGTON PAIUTE TRIBE.** *Spec. St.* 36:855; 42:1246; 43:246, 595, 1096; 44:761, 771; 45:160; 46:820; 50:239, 241. *Approp. St.* 16:544; 20:63, 295; 21:114, 485; 22:582; 23:76; 24:449; 25:217, 980; 26:336, 989; 27:120, 612; 28:286, 876; 29:321; 30:62, 571, 924; 31:1058; 32:245, 982; 33:189, 1048; 34:325; 41:1225; 42:552; 44:161, 453; 45:2, 200, 1562; 46:279, 1115; 47:91, 525, 820; 48:362; 49:176, 1757; 50:564. *Priv. St.* 26:1164; 46:1832; 48:1389. *Cases* Marks, 161 U. S. 297; Marks, 28 C. Cls. 147; U. S. v. Lewis, 253 Fed. 469; U. S. v. Miller, 105 Fed. 944; U. S. v. Sturgeon, 27 Fed. Cas. No. 16413; U. S. v. Walker, 104 F. 2d 334. *I. D. Rulings* Memo. Sol., July 25, 1934, Aug. 22, 1936, Oct. 19, 1938.

PALA MISSION. See **CALIFORNIA; MISSION.** *Approp. St.* 39:123; 41:3, 408; 42:1174; 43:390, 1141; 44:453, 934; 45:200, 1562; 46:1115; 47:91; 48:362; 49:176, 1757. *I. D. Rulings* Op. Sol., April 9, 1935.

PALM SPRINGS. See also **CALIFORNIA; AGUA CALIENTE, MISSION.** *Gov. Pub.* 75 Cong., 1 sess., Hearings, S. Comm. Ind. Aff., S. 1424; 75 Cong., 3 sess., Hearings, H. Comm. Ind. Aff., H. R. 7450. *Spec. St.* 50:811. *I. D. Rulings* Memo. Sol. Off. I. D., June 7, 1937. Memo. Sol. I. D., Oct. 21, 1938.

PAPAGO. See also **ARIZONA; AK CHIN; SAN XAVIER.** *Per.* Brown, 39 Yale L. J. 307. *Gov. Pub.* 73 Cong., 2 sess., Hearings, S. Comm. Ind. Aff., S. J. Res. 95. *Spec. St.* 22:299; 25:639; 44:762, 775; 45:617; 46:1202; 48:984; 50:536; 52:347. *Approp. St.* 16:544; 37:518; 38:77, 208, 312, 582; 39:123; 40:561, 821; 41:3, 35, 327, 408, 1156, 1225; 42:29, 552, 1174; 43:390, 1141; 44:453, 1250; 45:2, 200, 883, 1562; 46:279, 1115, 1552; 47:820; 48:362; 49:1757; 50:564; 52:291. *Cases* Bailey, 47 F. 2d 702. *Op. A. G.* 38:121. *I. D. Rulings* Op. Sol., May 7, 1934; Op. Atty. Gen., Nov. 1, 1934; Op. Sol., Oct 16, 1935, Dec. 28, 1937; Memo. Sol. Off., Nov. 29, 1938; Memo. Sol., Feb. 23, 1939. *Const.* Jan. 6, 1937.

PAWNEE INDIAN TRIBE OF OKLAHOMA. See also **OKLAHOMA; GRAND RIVER; PONCA; YANCTON; SIOUX; TONKAWA TRIBE OF INDIANS OF OKLAHOMA.** *Per.* Mac Leod, 28 J. Crim. L. 181. *Spec. St.* 19:28; 20:541; 34:267; 26:60, 81; 28:71; 29:529; 35:465; 45:939; 48:501. *Approp. St.* 4:705, 780; 5:36, 158, 298, 323, 402, 493, 704.

766; 9:20, 252, 382, 544, 574; 10:41, 226, 315, 686; 11:65, 169, 273, 329, 388; 12:44, 113, 221, 512, 774; 13:161, 541; 14:255, 492; 15:198; 16:13, 335, 544; 17:165, 437, 510; 18:146, 420; 19:102, 176, 271; 20:63, 295; 21:67, 114, 485; 22:68, 257, 302, 433, 608; 23:76, 362; 25:217, 980; 26:336, 989; 27:120, 612; 28:286, 424, 876; 29:321; 30:62, 105, 924; 31:221, 1058; 32:245, 982; 33:189, 1048, 1214; 34:325, 1015, 1371; 35:70, 781; 36:202, 269, 774; 37:518; 38:77, 582; 39:123, 969; 40:561; 41:3, 408, 503, 1015, 1125, 1156; 42:29, 552, 1174; 43:390, 704, 1141; 44:453, 934; 45:200, 1562, 1623; 46:279, 1115; 47:91, 820; 48:362, 984; 49:176, 1757; 50:564; 52:291. *Priv. St.* 9:688, 789. *Treaties* 7:172, 173, 279, 448; 9:949; 11:729. *Cases* Pawnee, 56 C. Cls. 1; U. S. v. Board, 13 F. Supp. 641; U. S. v. Sa-coo-da-cot, 27 Fed. Cas. No. 16212. *I. D. Rulings* Memo. Sol. Off., May 15, 1935. *Const.* Jan. 6, 1938. *Charter* April 28, 1938.

PAWNEE, PONCA & YANCTON SIOUX. See also PAWNEE; PONCA; YANCTON; SIOUX; OKLAHOMA. *Approp. St.* 12:44, 512, 774; 13:161, 541; 14:255, 492; 15:198; 16:13; 46:90.

PAW PAW (QUAPAW). See also OKLAHOMA; QUAPAW. *Cases* Wilson, 38 C. Cls. 6.

PECHANGA RESERVATION. See CALIFORNIA. *Texts* Manypenny, OIW.

PEMBINA BAND. See MINNESOTA; CHIPPEWA; CHIPPEWA, PEMBINA BAND; RED LAKE.

PEND D'OREILLE. See also MONTANA; COEUR D'ALENE; FLATHEAD, KOOTENAI AND PEND D'OREILLE; SALISH. *Spec. St.* 43:21. *Approp. St.* 12:44, 221, 774; 13:161, 541; 14:492; 15:198; 17:437; 18:146. *Cases* Clairmont, 225 U. S. 551; U. S. v. Heyfron, 138 Fed. 964; U. S. v. Heyfron, 138 Fed. 968.

PENNSYLVANIA. See CORNPLANTER RESERVATION.

PEORIA TRIBE OF INDIANS OF OKLAHOMA. See also OKLAHOMA; ILLINOIS INDIANS; INDIAN TERRITORY; KASKASKIAS AND PEORIA; PEORIA AND MIAMI; MIAMI; PEORIA, KASKASKIAS, PIANKESHAW AND WEAS; PIANKESHAW; PIANKESHAWS AND WEAS; WEAS. *Texts* Manypenny, OIW. *Per.* Flynn, 62 Cent. L. J. 399. *Spec. St.* 4:594; 12:539; 17:631; 24:388. *Approp. St.* 3:517; 4:636; 10:576; 17:122; 21:435; 25:505, 565; 28:424; 29:321; 30:62. *Treaties* 7:181, 403; 10:1082; 15:513. *Cases* Bowling, 233 U. S. 528; Bowling, 299 Fed. 438; Elk, 112 U. S. 94; Finley, 4 Ind. T. 386; Lykins, 184 U. S. 169; Oklahoma, 258 U. S. 574; Richardville, 28 Fed. 52; U. S. v. Bowling, 256 U. S. 484; U. S. v. Brindle, 110 U. S. 688; U. S. v. Rundell, 181 Fed. 887. *Op. A. G.* 19:115. *I. D. Rulings* Memo. Sol., Dec. 13, 1938. *Const.* Oct. 10, 1939.

PEORIA AND KASKASKIA. See also KASKASKIA; PEORIA; PEORIA, KASKASKIA, WEA AND PIANKESHAW; PEORIA AND MIAMI; ILLINOIS. *Treaties* 7:410.

PEORIA, KASKASKIA, WEA AND PIANKESHAW. See also KASKASKIA; PEORIA; PEORIA AND KASKASKIA; PEORIA AND MIAMI; WEA; ILLINOIS. *Approp. St.* 16:13; 17:165; 25:980.

PEORIA AND MIAMI. See also MIAMI; PEORIA; PEORIA AND KASKASKIA; PEORIA, KASKASKIA, WEA AND PIANKESHAW; ILLINOIS. *Approp. St.* 31:221; 32:245. *I. D. Rulings* 12 L. D. 168, June 25, 1890.

PEQUOT (PEQUODS). See also CONNECTICUT; RHODE ISLAND. *Per.* Thayer, 68 Atl. Month. 540, 676. Weeden, 2 J. H. Univ. Studies 385.

PIANKESHAW. See also ILLINOIS; MISSOURI; PEORIAS, KASKASKIAS, WEAS, PIANKESHAWS; PIANKESHAWS AND WEAS; QUAPAW. *Spec. St.* 3:308, 319; 4:594; 12:539; 17:631. *Approp. St.* 1:460; 2:338, 448; 4:526, 616, 636, 682, 780; 5:36, 158, 298, 323, 402, 417, 493, 704, 766; 9:20, 252, 382, 544; 574; 10:41, 226, 315, 576; 17:122; 21:435; 25:505, 565; 28:424. *Treaties* 7:49, 74, 77, 81, 83, 91, 100, 124; 8:116; 10:1082; 15:513. *Cases* Bowling, 233 U. S. 528; Johnson, 8 Wheat. 543; Richardville, 28 Fed. 52; U. S. v. Bowling, 256 U. S. 484; U. S. v. Brindle, 110 U. S. 688; U. S. v. Rundell, 181 Fed. 887. *Op. A. G.* 19:115.

PIANKESHAW AND WEAS. See also ILLINOIS; MISSOURI; PIANKESHAW; WEA. *Texts* Manypenny, OIW. *Approp. St.* 4:636; 10:686. *Treaties* 7:410.

PICURIS PUEBLO. See NEW MEXICO; PUEBLO.

PIEGAN. See also MONTANA; BLACKFEET; BLACKFEET, BLOODS AND PIEGANS; BLOOD; GROS VENTRE. *Texts* Manypenny, OIW. *Spec. St.* 18:28; 22:7; 25:113; 33:816; 36:1080; 43:21. *Cases* Albright, 58 C. Cls. 247; Henkel, 237 U. S. 45; U. S. v. Higgins, 103 Fed. 348; Winters, 207 U. S. 564.

PIMA. See also ARIZONA; FORT McDOWELL MOJAVE APACHE COMMUNITY; GILA RIVER; GILA RIVER PIMA MARICOPA INDIAN COMMUNITY; MARICOPA COMMUNITY; PIMA AND MARICOPA; SALT RIVER RESERVATION. *Per.* Brown, 39 Yale L. J. 307. *Spec. St.* 41:786. *Approp. St.* 23:76; 24:449; 25:217, 980; 26:336, 989; 27:120; 31:221; 32:245, 982; 33:189; 1048; 34:325, 1015; 35:781; 36:269; 37:518; 38:582, 1138; 39:14, 123, 969; 40:561; 41:3, 408, 1225; 42:552, 1174; 43:390, 704, 1141; 44:453, 934; 45:200, 883, 1562; 46:90, 279, 860, 1115; 47:91; 48:362; 49:176; 50:564; 52:291. *Cases* Estate of Walker, 5 Ariz. 70; Luke, 35 C. Cls. 15; Maricopa, 156 U. S. 347. *I. D. Rulings* Memo. Sol., Feb. 19, 1933; Memo. Sol. Off., Dec. 27, 1934.

PIMA AND MARICOPA. See also ARIZONA; GILA RIVER PIMA-MARICOPA INDIAN COMMUNITY; MARICOPA; PIMA. *Approp. St.* 18:146; 20:63; 21:114; 27:120.

PINE RIDGE. See also SOUTH DAKOTA; OGLALA; SIOUX. *Spec. St.* 25:88; 36:440, 448, 1087; 41:1193; 45:747; 46:169; 47:300. *Approp. St.* 26:989; 31:221; 32:245, 982, 1031; 33:1048; 34:325, 1015; 35:478, 781; 38:77; 46:90; 47:525; 50:755. *Priv. St.* 38:1471. *Cases* Fisher, 226 Fed. 156; John, 177 U. S. 529; Reynolds, 174 Fed. 212; Reynolds, 205 Fed. 685. *I. D. Rulings* Memo. Sol., Aug. 23, 1937, Mar. 12, 1938.

PIPESTONE. See also MINNESOTA; LOWER SIOUX INDIAN COMMUNITY IN MINNESOTA; PRAIRIE ISLAND INDIAN COMMUNITY IN MINNESOTA; RED PIPESTONE; SIOUX; YANKTON. *Spec. St.* 26:764. *Approp. St.* 28:286. *Priv. St.* 49:2342.

PITT RIVER. See also CALIFORNIA; OREGON; SACRAMENTO. *Spec. St.* 12:199. *Priv. St.* 38:1350. *Cases* Butler v. U. S., 38 C. Cls. 167.

POINT HOPE, NATIVE VILLAGE OF. See also ALASKA; ESKIMO. *Const.* Feb. 29, 1940. *Charter* Feb. 29, 1940.

POJOAQUE (TEWA). See NEW MEXICO; PUEBLO.

POMO. See CALIFORNIA; BIG VALLEY BAND; KASHIA BAND; MANCHESTER BAND; ROUND VALLEY RESERVATION.

PONCA. (PONCA TRIBE OF NATIVE AMERICANS.) See also NEBRASKA; OKLAHOMA; OTTOE; OTTOE AND MISSOURIA; PAWNEE. *Per.* Canfield, 15, Am. L. Rev. 21; Harsha, 134 N. A. Rev. 272; Mac Leod, 28 J. Crim. L. 181. *Spec. St.* 12:113; 25:94, 888; 26:81; 28:72; 30:834; 38:1188; 39:237; 43:729; 48:501. *Approp. St.* 12:4, 44, 221, 512, 774; 13:161, 541; 14:255, 492; 15:198; 16:13, 335, 515, 544; 17:165, 437; 18:146, 420; 19:176, 271; 20:63, 295, 877; 21:114, 414, 485; 22:68, 257, 433, 603; 23:76, 362; 24:449; 25:217, 980; 26:336, 989; 27:120, 612, 646; 28:286, 876; 29:267, 321; 30:62, 571, 924; 31:221, 1058; 32:245, 982; 33:189, 1048; 34:325, 1015; 35:70, 781; 36:269; 37:518; 38:77, 582; 39:123, 969; 40:561; 41:3, 408, 1225; 42:552, 767, 1174; 43:390, 704, 1141; 44:453, 934; 45:200, 1562, 1623; 46:1115; 47:91; 48:984. *Treaties* 7:155, 247; 12:997; 14:675. *Cases* Conway, 149 Fed. 261; Davidson, 34 C. Cls. 169; First, 270 U. S. 243; Foerster, 116 Fed. 860; Foster, 189 U. S. 325; Megreedy, 12 Okla. 666; Miller, 57 F. 2d 987; Pam-to-pee, 187 U. S. 371; Sharp, 138 Fed. 878; U. S. v. Hutto, No. 1, 256 U. S. 524; U. S. ex. rel. Standing, 25 Fed. Cas. No. 14891; Wilson, 38 C. Cls. 6. *I. D. Rulings* 34 L. D. 252, Nov. 7, 1905; Memo. Sol., Oct. 17, 1934, April 9, 1936, Mar. 12, 1938, April 14, 1938. *Const.* April 3, 1936. *Charter* Aug. 15, 1936.

PORT GAMBLE INDIAN COMMUNITY. See also WASHINGTON. *Const.* Sept. 7, 1939.

PORT MADISON. See also WASHINGTON; SNOHOMISH; TULALIP. *Approp. St.* 33:1048. *I. D. Rulings* Memo. Sol., July 2, 1935.

POTAWATOMIE. See also KANSAS; WISCONSIN; CITIZEN BAND OF POTAWATOMI INDIANS OF OKLAHOMA; FOREST COUNTY POTAWATOMIE COMMUNITY; HURON; OTTOWA AND POTAWATOMIE. *Texts* Manypenny, OIW. *Per.* 9 J. H. Univ. Studies 541: *Gov. Pub.* 75 Cong., 3 sess., Hearings, S. Comm. Ind. Aff., S. 2854, S. Rep 1919. *Spec. St.* 3:308, 319, 690; 4:185, 234, 302, 564; 9:213; 14:370; 17:159; 20:282, 542; 25:79; 26:24; 27:394; 28:3; 30:909; 37:194; 43:819; 44:801; 45:159; 48:501. *Approp. St.* 1:460; 2:407, 467, 607; 3.393, 517; 4:232, 361, 390, 394, 432, 463, 470, 505, 526, 532, 616, 631, 636, 669,

682, 705, 780; 5:36, 73, 158, 298, 323, 402, 493, 517, 704, 766; 9:20, 132, 252, 382, 544, 574; 10:15, 41, 226, 315, 686; 11:65, 169, 273, 388; 12:44, 207, 221, 512, 774; 13:161, 541; 14:255, 492; 15:198; 16:13, 335, 544; 17:165, 437; 18:146, 402, 420; 19:176, 271; 20:63, 295; 21:114, 485; 22:68, 433; 23:76, 362; 24:449; 25:217, 980; 26:336, 989; 27:120, 612; 28:286, 424, 876; 29:321; 30:62, 924; 31:221, 1058; 32:245, 982; 33:189, 1048; 34:325, 1015; 35:70, 781; 36:269; 37:518, 595; 38:77; 39:123, 969; 40:561; 41:3, 408, 1225; 42:552, 1174; 43:390, 704, 1141; 44:453, 934; 45:200, 883, 1562; 46:279, 1115; 47:91; 48:984. *Priv. St.* 6:409, 473, 676, 749, 816, 818, 834, 896, 915, 919, 920, 922, 927; 9:710, 741; 11:556; 12:883, 915; 29:804; 31:1469, 1572; 39:1477; 44:1475. *Treaties* Archives No. 44; 7:28, 49, 74, 87, 91, 105, 112, 113, 115, 118, 123, 131, 146, 160, 185, 200, 208, 218, 272, 295, 305, 315, 317, 320, 323, 326, 342, 378, 394, 399, 467, 468, 469, 490, 496, 499, 500, 505, 513, 514, 515, 528, 532; 8:116; 9:853; 12:1191; 14:657, 763; 15:531. *Cases* Bertrand, 36 F. 2d 351; Board, 100 F. 2d 929; Briggs, 37 Fed. 135; Crews, 1 Black 352; Doe, 23 How. 457; Elk, 112 U. S. 94; Elwood, 104 U. S. 562; Godfrey 10 Fed. Cas. No. 5497; Goodfellow, 10 Fed. Cas. No. 5537; Gray, 10 Fed. Cas. No. 5714; Laughton, 75 Fed. 789; Lowry, 15 Fed. Cas. No. 8584; Miller, 249 U. S. 308; Mulligan, 120 Fed. 98; Nadeau, 253 U. S. 442; Pam-to-Pee, 187 U. S. 371; Pka-O-Wah-Ash-Kum, 8 Fed. 740; Potawatomie, 27 C. Cls. 403; Renfrow, 3 Okla. 161; Sage, 235 U. S. 99; U. S. v. Downing, 25 Fed. Cas. No. 14991; U. S. v. Getzelman, 89 F. 2d. 531; U. S. v. Navarre, 173 U. S. 77; U. S. v. Parkhurst-Davis 176 U. S. 317; U. S. v. Payne, 27 Fed. Cas. No. 16014; U. S. v. Patrick, 73 Fed. 800; Williams, 242 U. S. 434. *Op. A. G.* 3:33; 5:284; 6:49, 711; 16:310, 325; 18:447, 497, 517; 19:134, 242. *I. D. Rulings* 11 L. D. 103, July 14, 1890; 13 L. D. 318, May 14, 1891; 13 L. D. 310, Aug. 28, 1891; 13 L. D. 314, Sept. 3, 1891; 24 L. D. 511, June 8, 1897; 28 L. D. 71, Jan. 30, 1899; Memo. Sol. April 4, 1933; Memo. Sol. Off. Sept. 21, 1937; Memo. Sol. Dec. 18, 1937; Op. Sol., Feb. 7, 1938; Memo. Sol., Dec. 22, 1938.

PRAIRIE ISLAND INDIAN COMMUNITY. See also MINNESOTA; SIOUX, MDEWAKANTON. *I. D. Rulings* Memo. Sol., April 15, 1936. *Const.* June 20, 1936. *Charter* July 23, 1937.

PUEBLO. See also NEW MEXICO; ACOMA; NAMBE; ZUNI. *Texts* Brayer, PIL. *Per.* Brown, 15 Minn. L. Rev. 182; Brown, 39 Yale L. J. 307; Quail, 6 J. B. A. Kan. 158; Renehan, 33 N. M. S. B. A. 72; Russell, 18 Yale L. J. 328; Seymour, 10 A. B. A. Jour. 36; Thayer, 68 Atl. Month. 540, 676. *Gov. Pub.* 69 Cong., 1 sess., S. Rep. 716, H. Rep. 955; 70 Cong., 1 sess., H. Doc. 141; 71 Cong., 3 sess., S. 5828; 72 Cong., 1 sess., H. R. 9071; 75 Cong., 3 sess., S. Rep. 1986. *Spec. St.* 9:631; 11:374; 36:557; 43:92, 636; 44:498, 1098; 45:312, 442, 717, 1161; 46:1509; 48:108; 49:800, 1459, 1528; 52:778. *Approp. St.* 9:974; 10:41, 315; 11:169; 16:335, 544; 17:165; 18:146; 20:63, 295; 21:485; 22:68, 433; 23:76, 362; 24:449; 25:217, 980; 26:336, 989; 27:120, 612; 28:286, 876; 29:321; 30:62, 571, 924; 31:1058; 32:245, 982; 33:189, 1048; 34:325, 1015; 35:70, 781; 36:269, 1058; 37:518; 38:77, 582; 39:123, 969; 40:561; 41:3, 408, 1156, 1225; 42:29, 487, 552, 1174; 43:390, 704, 753, 1014, 1141, 1313; 44:161, 330, 453, 934, 1178; 45:2, 64, 200, 883, 1094, 1562, 1623; 46:90, 173, 279, 1115, 1552; 47:91, 820; 48:274, 362; 49:176, 1757; 50:564; 52:291. *Priv. St.* 43:1597. *Cases* De La O, 1 N. M. 226; Garcia, 43 F. 2d 873; Jaeger, 29 C. Cls. 172; Lane, 249 U. S. 110; Luke, 35 C. Cls. 15; Pueblo of Laguna, 1 N. M. 220; Pueblo Picuris, 50 F. 2d 12; Pueblo de San Juan, 47 F. 2d 446; Pueblo of Santa Rosa, 273 U. S. 315; Pueblo de Taos, 64 F. 2d 807; Pueblo de Taos, 50 F. 2d 721; Romero, 24 C. Cls. 331; Territory, 12 N. M. 139; U. S. v. Algondones, 52 F. 2d 359; U. S. v. Board, 37 F. 2d 272; U. S. v. Candelaria, 271 U. S. 432; U. S. v. Chavez, 175 U. S. 509; U. S. v. Chaves, 175 U. S. 357; U. S. v. Conway, 175 U. S. 60; U. S. v. Joseph, 94 U. S. 614; U. S. v. Pico, 5 Wall. 536; U. S. v. Ritchie, 17 How. 525; U. S. v. Sandoval, 231 U. S. 28; U. S. v. Wooten, 40 F. 2d 882; Zia, 168 U. S. 198. *Op. A. G.* 20:215. *L. D. Memo. (D. J.)* 8:220. *I. D Rulings* 19 L D. 326, June 30, 1894; Op. Sol., Aug. 7, 1929, Aug. 4, 1932; Report on Status of Pueblo of Pojoaque, Nov. 3, 1932; Memo. Sol., June 23, 1933, Aug. 17, 1933; Op. Sol., Sept. 1, 1933; Memo. Sol. Off., Sept. 29, 1933; Memo. Sol. Mar. 14, 1934; Memo. Sol. Off., July 21, 1934, Oct. 9, 1934; Memo. Sol., Oct. 23, 1934; Op. Sol., Feb. 20, 1935; Memo. Sol., Mar. 11, 1935; Op. Sol., Mar. 18, 1936; Memo. Sol., Aug. 21, 1936; Memo. Sol. Off., Sept. 12, 1936, Oct. 25, 1936; Op. Sol., Dec. 16, 1936. Feb. 13, 1937; Memo. Sol., Sept. 21, 1937; Memo. Commr., April 1, 1938; Letter Sol., April 23, 1938; Op. Sol., May 14, 1938; Memo. Sol., April 14, 1939.

PUEBLO OF SANTA CLARA. See also PUEBLO. *Const.* Dec. 20, 1935.

PUGET SOUND. See also WASHINGTON. *Approp. St.* 10:643.

PUYALLUP. See also WASHINGTON; NISQUALLY; NISQUALLY, PUYALLUP AND OTHER TRIBES AND BANDS OF INDIANS. *Spec. St.* 25:350; 27:468; 33:565; 45:378; 46:1526. *Approp. St.* 21:238; 26:336; 27:612; 28:876; 29:71, 321; 30:62, 571, 924; 31:221, 1058; 32:245, 982, 1048, 1015; 35:781; 36:269; 37:518, 595, 912; 38:77; 39:14, 123, 969; 40:2; 41:408, 1225; 42:552, 1174; 43:390, 1141; 44:453, 934; 45:200; 46:279, 1115; 47:91, 820; 48:362; 49:1757; 50:564; 52:291. *Treaties* 12:927. *Cases* Bird, 129 Fed. 472; Duwamish, 79 C. Cls. 530; Fowler, 4 F. Supp. 565; Goudy, 203 U. S. 146; Jacobs, 223 U. S. 200; LaClair, 184 Fed. 128; Meeker, 173 Fed. 216; Mitchell, 22 F. 2d 771; National, 147 Fed. 87; Ross, 56 Fed. 855; U. S. v. Ashton, 110 Fed. 160; U. S. v. Kopp, 110 Fed. 160; U. S. v. Law, 250 Fed. 218. *Op. A. G.* 20:245. *I. D. Rulings* 20 L. D. 157; 29:628; Memo Sol., Jan. 9, 1936; Memo. Sol. Off., Nov. 9, 1937; Memo. Sol., Mar. 25, 1939. *Const.* May 13, 1936.

PYRAMID LAKE PAIUTE TRIBE. See also NEVADA; PAH-UTE (PAIUTE). *Spec. St.* 43:596. *Approp. St.* 20:63, 295; 21:114, 485; 23:76; 24:449; 25:217, 980; 26:336, 989; 28:876; 29:321; 31:1058; 32:245, 982; 33:189, 1048; 34:325; 35:781; 36:269; 39:123, 969; 40:561; 41:3, 408, 1225; 42:552, 1174; 43:390, 1141; 44:453, 934; 45:200, 1562; 46:279, 1115; 47:91, 820; 48:362; 49:176, 1757; 50:564; 52:291. *Cases* U. S. v. Leathers, 26 Fed. Cas. No. 15,581; U. S. v. Miller, 105 Fed. 944; U. S. v. Sturgeon, 27 Fed. Cas. No. 16,413. *Const.* Jan. 15, 1936. *Charter* Nov. 21, 1936.

QUAPAW. See also OKLAHOMA; PAW-PAW. *Texts* Devlin, LRP; Foster, FPC. *Gov. Pub.* 64 Cong., 1 sess., S. Rep. 193; 75 Cong., 1 sess., Hearings, H. Comm. Ind. Aff., H. R. 559. *Spec. St.* 17:228; 26:81; 27:24; 28:693; 31:658, 760; 32:841; 35:444, 751; 37:46; 41:355, 529; 42:1570; 43:722, 723; 48:501; 50:68. *Approp. St.* 3:517; 4:41, 92, 267, 348, 526, 616, 705, 705, 780; 5:36, 158, 298, 323, 402, 417, 493, 704, 766; 9:20, 132, 252, 382, 544, 574; 10:41, 226, 315, 686; 11:65, 169, 273, 388; 12:44, 221, 512, 774; 13:161, 541; 14:255, 492; 15:198; 16:13, 335, 544; 17:122, 165, 437; 18:146, 420; 19:176, 271; 20:63, 295; 21:114, 485; 22:68, 433; 23:76, 362; 24:449; 25:217, 980; 26:336, 989; 27:120, 612; 28:286, 876; 29:321; 30:62, 571, 924; 31:221, 760, 1058; 32:245, 982; 33:189, 1048; 34:325, 1015; 35:70, 781; 36:269; 37:518; 38:77, 582; 39:123, 969; 40:561; 41:3, 408, 1225; 42:552, 1174; 43:390, 704, 1141; 44:453, 934; 45:200, 1562, 1623; 46:279, 1115, 1552; 47:91, 820, 1602; 48:362, 984; 49:176, 1757; 50:564; 52:291. *Treaties* 7:176, 232, 424, 474, 533; 15:513. *Cases* Blanset, 256 U. S. 319; Bond, 181 Fed. 613; Childers, 270 U. S. 555; Dyer, 20 C. Cls. 166; Eagle-Picher, 28 F. 2d 472; Ewert, 259 U. S. 129; Goodrum, 162 Fed. 817; Hallam, 49 F. 2d 103; Hampton, 22 F. 2d 81; Hot, 92 U. S. 698; Jaybird, 271 U. S. 609; Kendall, 259 U. S. 139; McCullough, 243 Fed. 823; Moore, 5 Ind. T. 384; Ricknor, 4 Ind. T. 660; Robinson, 291 Fed. 9; Smith, 270 U. S. 456; Unkle, 281 Fed. 29; U. S. v. Abrams, 194 Fed. 82; U. S. v. Choctaw, 179 U. S. 494; U. S. v. Moore, 284 Fed. 86; U. S. v. Noble, 237 U. S. 74; U. S. v. Wright, 197 Fed. 297; Whitebird, 40 F. 2d 479. *Op. A. G.* 3:106; 25:532; 27:588; 34:439. *L. D. Memo. (D. J.)* 3:388, 435, 477. *I. D. Rulings* 40 L. D. 211, May 3, 1911; Op. Sol., Dec. 4, 1923, Oct. 6, 1927, Aug. 21, 1929; Memo. Sol Off., May 6, 1932, July 22, 1932; Memo. Sol., Aug. 18, 1934; Op. Sol., Oct. 28, 1937, Oct. 28, 1937.

QUARTZ VALLEY INDIAN COMMUNITY. See CALIFORNIA. *Const.* June 15, 1939. *Charter* Mar. 12, 1940.

QUECHAN TRIBE (YUMA). See ARIZONA; YUMA. *Const.* Dec. 18, 1936.

QUILEUTE INDIAN TRIBE OF THE QUILEUTE INDIAN RESERVATION. See also WASHINGTON; MAKAH; NEAH BAY; QUINAIELT AND QUILLEHUTE. *Spec. St.* 36:1345; 44:614. *Approp. St.* 33:189; 39:969; 40:561; 41:408; 49:176, 1757. *Treaties*, 12:939. *Cases* Fowler, 4 F. Supp. 565; Mitchell, 22 F. 2d 771; Taylor, 44 F. 2d 53; U. S. ex rel. Charley, 62 F. 2d 955; U. S. v. Payne, 264 U. S. 446. *I. D. Rulings* Op. Sol., May 14, 1928. *Const.* Nov. 11, 1936. *Charter* Aug. 21, 1937.

QUINAIELT. See also WASHINGTON; QUILEUTE; QUINAIELT AND QUILLEHUTE. *Spec. St.* 36:1345; 38:704; 39:353; 43:247; 44:135, 303; 47:37; 48:811, 910. *Approp. St.*

33:189; 40:561; 41:408, 1225; 42:29, 1174, 1527; 43:1141; 44:453; 45:1562; 46:279, 1115; 47:91, 820, 362; 49:176, 1757; 50:564; 52:1114. *Cases* Fowler, 4 F. Supp. 565; Halbert, 283 U. S. 753; Mason, 5 F. 2d 255; Mitchell, 22 F. 2d 1771; Pape, 19 F. 2d 219; U. S. ex rel. Charley, 62 F. 2d; U. S. v. Provoe, 283 U. S. 753; U. S. v. Rolfson, 38 F. 2d 806; U. S. v. Walkowsky, 283 U. S. 753. *I. D. Rulings* Op Sol., May 14, 1928; Memo. Sol., July 5, 1932; Op. Sol., Sept. 23, 1932, May 22, 1935.

QUINAIELT & QUILLEHUTE. See also WASHINGTON; QUILEUTE; QUINAIELT. *Approp. St.* 12:4, 221, 512, 774; 13:161, 541; 14:255, 492; 15:198; 16:13, 335, 544; 17:165, 437; 18:146, 420; 19:176, 271; 20:63, 295; 21:114, 485; 22:68, 433; 23:76, 362; 24:449; 25:217, 980; 26:336, 989; 27:120, 612; 28:286, 876; 29:321; 30:62, 571, 924; 31:221, 1058; 32:245, 982; 33:1048; 34:325, 1015; 35:70, 781; 36:269; 37:518; 38:77, 582; 41:3, 1225; 42:552, 1174. *Treaties* 12:971.

RED CLIFF BAND OF LAKE SUPERIOR CHIPPEWA INDIANS. See also WISCONSIN; CHIPPEWA. *Spec. St.* 28:970. *Approp. St.* 38:77; 39:123. *Const.* June 1, 1936. *Charter* Oct. 24, 1936.

RED CLOUD. See also NEBRASKA; FORT ROBINSON; OGLALA; SIOUX. *Spec. St.* 26:14; 28:5. *Approp. St.* 19:102; 20:206. *Cases* Connors, 180 U. S. 271.

RED LAKE. See also MINNESOTA; CHIPPEWA; PEMBINA RESERVATION. *Spec. St.* 26:660; 33:46, 708, 989; 35:169. 465; 36:265, 292, 913; 41:1105; 43:357; 46:1102. *Approp. St.* 32:982; 36:269; 38:582; 39:123; 46:1552; 47:91. *Cases* 43 Cases, 14 Fed. 539; Palcher, 11 Fed. 47; U. S. v. LeBris, 121 U. S. 278. *I. D. Rulings* Sol. Letter, July 19, 1934; Memo. Sol., Nov. 20, 1934, May 14, 1935; Op. Sol., Aug. 1, 1938, Nov. 28, 1938.

RED PIPESTONE. See also MINNESOTA; SIOUX. *Spec. St.* 25:1012.

RENO. See also NEVADA; PAHUTE (PAIUTE); RENO-SPARKS INDIAN COLONY; SHOSHONE; WASHOE. *Spec. St.* 44:496. *Approp. St.* 42:1174; 43:1313; 44:841. *Cases* U. S. v. McGowan, 89 F. 2d 201; 302 U. S. 535. *I. D. Rulings* Memo. Sol., June 9, 1937.

RENO-SPARKS INDIAN COLONY. See also NEVADA; RENO. *Spec. St.* 44:1369. *Approp. St.* 45:200. *Const.* Jan. 15, 1936. *Charter* Jan. 7, 1938.

RHODE ISLAND. See also NARRAGANSET; PEQUOT. *Per.* Varney, 13 Green Bag 399.

RINCON. See also CALIFORNIA; MISSION. *Approp. St.* 41:3, 408, 1225; 42:1174; 43:390, 1141; 44:453; 46:1115; 48:362.

RIVER CROW. See also MONTANA; CROW; GROS VENTRE (ATSINA). *Spec. St.* 18:28; 25:113; 33:816; 36:1080. *Approp. St.* 16:335, 544; 17:165, 437; 18:146, 420. *Cases* Albright, 53 C. Cls. 247.

ROCHE DE BOEUF (OTTAWAS). See also KANSAS; SENECAS, MIXED SENECAS, SHAWNEES, QUAPAWS, CONFEDERATED PEORIAS, KASKASKIAS, WEAS, PIANKESKAW. *Treaties* 15:513.

ROCKY BOYS RESERVATION. See also MONTANA; CHIPPEWA; CHIPPEWA CREE TRIBE OF THE ROCKY BOYS RESERVATION; CREE. *Spec. St.* 49:217. *Approp. St.* 40:561; 42:552; 47:91; 52:291. *I. D. Rulings* Memo. Sol., Aug. 26, 1938; Feb. 17, 1939.

ROGUE RIVER INDIANS. See also OREGON. *Spec. St.* 10:307; 16:401; 25:47. *Approp. St.* 10:226, 315, 643, 686; 11:65, 169, 273, 388; 12:44, 221, 512, 774; 13:161, 541; 14:255, 492; 15:198; 16:13, 335, 544; 17:165, 437; 18:146; 22:582; 23:446; 25:4, 905; 26:504; 30:105; 36:202. *Priv. St.* 27:778. *Treaties* 10:1018, 1119; 12:981. *Cases* Falk, 27 C. Cls. 321; Love, 29 C. Cls. 332; McCallum, 33 C. Cls. 469; Redfield, 27 C. Cls. 473; Ross, 29 C. Cls. 176; Valk, 22 C. Cls. 241; Valk, 29 C. Cls. 62.

ROSEBUD SIOUX TRIBE. See also SOUTH DAKOTA; MINNECONJOU; SIOUX; TEETON. *Spec. St.* 26:14; 30:1362; 33:254, 700; 34:1230; 36:265, 448, 1087; 38:792; 40:1320; 41:1460; 45:380; 47:300. *Approp. St.* 26:989; 29:321; 30:62; 31:221; 33:1048; 35:781; 38:77. *Priv. St.* 46:1858. *Cases* Estes, 225 Fed. 980; Hollister, 145 Fed. 773; U. S. v. Frank, 282 Fed. 349; U. S. v. Nice, 241 U. S. 591; U. S. v. Pumphrey, 11 App. D. C. 44. *I. D. Rulings* Memo. Sol. Off., Oct. 12, 1934. *Const.* Dec. 20, 1935. *Charter* March 23, 1937.

ROUND VALLEY RESERVATION (POMO, YUKI). See also CALIFORNIA; COVELO. *Spec. St.* 17:633; 26:658; 33:706; 43:138; 49:331. *Approp. St.* 14:492; 15:198; 16:13; 20:63, 295; 21:114; 23:76; 24:449; 25:217, 980; 26:336, 989; 28:876; 31:221, 1058; 32:245, 982; 33:189, 1048; 34:325, 1015; 35:70, 781; 41:3, 408, 1225; 42:552, 1174; 43:390, 1141; 44:453, 934; 45:1562; 46:1115; 47:91, 820. *Priv. St.* 23:533. *Cases* Donnelly, 228 U. S. 243; In re Lincoln, 129 Fed. 247; U. S. v. 48 Lbs., 35 Fed. 403. *I. D. Rulings* Letter from Comp. Gen., July 24, 1937.

SACRAMENTO. See CALIFORNIA; COVELO INDIAN COMMUNITY OF THE ROUND VALLEY INDIAN RESERVATION; GRINDSTONE CREEK RESERVATION; MANCHESTER BAND OF POMO INDIANS OF THE MANCHESTER RANCHERIA; ROUND VALLEY; SHASTA; TULE RIVER; TUOLUMNE BAND OF MEWUK INDIANS OF THE TUOLMNE RANCHERIA.

SAC. See also IOWA INDIANS; KANSAS; MISSOURI; NEBRASKA; OKLAHOMA; FOX; FOX AND IOWA; IOWA AND SAC; SAC AND FOX; SAC, FOX AND IOWAY; SAC AND FOX OF MISSISSIPPI; SAC AND FOX OF MISSOURI; SAC AND FOX RESERVATION, IOWA; SAC, FOX, IOWA, SIOUX, OMAHA, OTOE AND MISSOURIA; SAC, FOX, WINNEBAGO AND SIOUX. *Spec. St.* 2:343; 4:302, 464, 665, 740; 5:48, 522, 622, 666. *Approp. St.* 2:338, 4:92, 394, 470, 526, 616, 682, 780; 5:36, 158, 612, 681. *Priv. St.* 29:736. *Treaties* 7:28, 134, 141, 378.

SAC AND FOX. See also IOWA; KANSAS; MISSOURI; NEBRASKA; OKLAHOMA; FOX; FOX AND IOWA; IOWA SAC; SAC; SAC, FOX AND IOWAY; SAC AND FOX OF MISSISSIPPI; SAC AND FOX OF MISSOURI; SAC AND FOX RESERVATIONS, IOWA; SAC, FOX, IOWA, SIOUX, OMAHA, OTTOE AND MISSOURIA; SAC, FOX, WINNEBAGO AND SIOUX. *Per.* Knoepfler, 7 Iowa L. B. 232; Thayer, 68 Atl. Month, 540, 676; Thompson, 6 Ill. L. Q. 204, 9 J. H. Univ. Studies 541. *Spec. St.* 10:704; 11:122; 12:630; 17:391, 626; 19:208; 20:471; 23:351; 24:367, 388; 26:749, 794; 27:557; 29:95; 32:399; 34:1055; 36:368; 39:673; 44:561; 47:906; 48:501. *Approp. St.* 4:616, 636, 682, 705, 780; 5:36, 158, 298, 323, 402, 417, 493, 704, 766; 9:20, 132, 544; 10:315, 686; 11:65, 169, 273, 388; 12:221, 512, 774; 13:161, 541; 14:255, 492; 15:198; 16:13, 335, 544; 17:165, 437, 510; 18:146; 420; 19:176, 271; 20:63, 295; 21:114, 485; 22:68, 433; 23:76, 362; 24:449; 25:217, 980; 26:336, 989; 27:120, 612; 28:286, 876; 29:321; 30:62, 571, 924; 31:221, 1010, 1058; 32:5, 245, 982; 33:189, 1048; 34:325; 35:781; 36:269; 37:518; 38:77, 582; 41:3, 408, 1225; 42:552, 1174; 43:390, 1141, 1313; 44:453, 934; 45:200, 1562; 46:279, 1115; 47:91, 820; 48:362, 984; 49:176, 1757; 50:564; 52:291. *Priv. St.* 6:659, 913; 9:812; 10:750, 781; 24:876; 28:996, 1030; 29:736; 30:1416; 47:1755. *Treaties* 7:84, 146, 223, 229, 272, 315, 328, 374, 511, 516, 517, 540, 543, 568, 596; 10:1074; 12:1105, 1171; 15:467, 495. *Cases* Creek, 302 U. S. 620; Creek, 77, C. Cls. 159; Creek, 84 C. Cls. 12; In re Lelan-Puc-Ka-Chee, 98 Fed. 429; Keokuk, 4 Okla. 5; Marsh, 8 How. 223; Mixon, 265 Fed. 603; Pennock, 103 U. S. 44; Peters, 111 Fed. 244; Renfrow, 3 Okla. 161; Sac, 220 U. S. 481; State of Missouri, 7 How. 660; U. S. v. Creek, 295 U. S. 103. *Op. A. G.* 20:494. *I. D. Rulings* 15 L. D. 287, Sept. 9, 1892; Op. Sol., Oct. 8, 1930.

SAC AND FOX TRIBE OF THE MISSISSIPPI IN IOWA. See also SAC; SAC AND FOX; SAC, FOX AND IOWAY; SAC AND FOX RESERVATION, IOWA; SAC AND FOX OF MISSOURI; SAC, FOX, IOWA, SIOUX, OTTOE AND MISSOURIA; SAC, FOX, WINNEBAGO AND SIOUX. *Approp. St.* 5:298; 9:252, 382, 544, 574; 10:15, 41, 226, 315; 12:44; 33:1048; 34:1015. *Cases* Sac, 45 C Cls. 287. *Const.* Dec. 20, 1937.

SAC AND FOX TRIBE OF MISSOURI. See also SAC; SAC AND FOX OF MISSISSIPPI; SAC AND FOX RESERVATION, IOWA; SAC, FOX, IOWA SIOUX, OTTOE AND MISSOURIA; SAC, FOX, WINNEBAGO AND SIOUX. *Spec. St.* 34:262. *Approp. St.* 5:298; 9:252, 382, 544, 574; 10:41, 226, 315; 34:1015; 39:969. *Treaties* 10:1069. *Const.* Mar. 2, 1937. *Charter* June 19, 1937.

SAC, FOX AND IOWAY. See also SAC; SAC AND FOX; SAC AND FOX, IOWA; SAC, FOX, IOWA, SIOUX, OTTOE AND MISSOURIA; SAC, FOX, WINNEBAGO AND SIOUX. *Approp. St.* 4:616, 682, 780; 5:36, 158; 15:198.

SACS, FOXES, IOWAS, SIOUX, OMAHAS, OTTOES AND MISSOURIAS. See also SAC; SAC AND FOX; SAC AND FOX, IOWA; SAC, FOX AND IOWAY; SAC, FOX, WINNEBAGO AND SIOUX. *Approp. St.* 5:298, 323, 402.

SAC AND FOX RESERVATION, IOWA. See also **SAC; SAC AND FOX; SAC, FOX AND IOWAY; SAC, FOX, IOWA, SIOUX, OTTOE AND MISSOURIA; SAC, FOX, WINNEBAGO AND SIOUX.** *Approp. St.* 32:982; 34:1015; 42:1174. *I. D. Rulings* Memo. Sol., June 9, 1937; Memo. Sol. Off., Nov. 9, 1937.

SAC, FOX, WINNEBAGO AND SIOUX. See also **SAC; SAC AND FOX; SAC AND FOX RESERVATION, IOWA; SAC, FOX AND IOWAY; SAC, FOX, IOWA, SIOUX, OTTOE AND MISSOURIA.** *Approp. St.* 5:417.

SAGINAW CHIPPEWA INDIAN TRIBE OF THE ISABELLA RESERVATION OF MICHIGAN. See also **MICHIGAN; CHIPPEWA.** *Const.* May 6, 1937. *Charter* Aug. 28, 1937.

ST. CROIX. See also **CHIPPEWA; MINNESOTA.** *Approp. St.* 41:3, 408, 1225. *Cases* Ex p. Pero, 99 F. 2d 28. *I. D. Rulings* Memo. Sol., Feb. 8, 1937, Mar. 15, 1937; Memo. Sol. Off., June 25, 1938.

ST. REGIS (IROQUOIS). See also **NEW YORK.** *Spec. St.* 10:15. *Approp. St.* 9:20. *Treaties* 7:55, 342, 550. *Cases* Deere, 32 F. 2d 550; Deere, 22 F. 2d 851; New York, 170 U. S. 1; New York, 40 C. Cls. 448; U. S. v. New York, 173 U. S. 464. *L. D. Memo. (D. J.)* 5:236.

SALISH. See **IDAHO; MONTANA; COEUR D'ALENE; CONFEDERATED SALISH AND KOOTENAI TRIBES OF THE FLATHEAD RESERVATION; KOOTENAI; PEND D'OREILLE; SAMISH; SNOQUALMIE.**

SALT RIVER RESERVATION (PIMA). See also **ARIZONA; PIMA.** *Approp. St.* 40:561; 41:3, 408, 408, 1225; 43:390, 1141; 44:453, 934; 49:1757; 50:564; 52:291. *I. D. Rulings* Memo. Sol. Off., April 4, 1933; Contract, June 3, 1935.

SALT RIVER PIMA-MARICOPA INDIAN COMMUNITY. See also **ARIZONA; MARICOPA; PIMA; PIMA AND MARICOPA.** *Const.* June 11, 1940.

SAMISH. See also **WASHINGTON.** *Cases* Dwamish, 79 C. Cls. 530.

SAN CARLOS APACHE TRIBE. See also **ARIZONA; APACHE.** *Spec. St.* 30:227; 45:973, 1344; 52:193. *Approp. St.* 19:58; 22:68; 23:446; 29:321; 31:1010; 37:518; 38:77, 312, 582; 40:561; 42:552, 1174; 45:883; 46:90, 1552; 47:820; 49:176. *Cases* Dobbs, 33 C. Cls. 308; Tully, 32 C. Cls. 1; U. S. v. Wightman, 230 Fed. 277. *I. D. Rulings* Memo. Sol. Off., Feb. 7, 1934; Memo. Sol., Mar. 29, 1935; Op. Sol., May 29, 1936; Memo. Sol., Oct. 23, 1936, July 19, 1937, Aug. 9, 1937. *Const.* Jan. 17, 1936.

SAN FELIPE. See **NEW MEXICO; PUEBLO.**

SAN ILDEFONSO. See **NEW MEXICO; PUEBLO.**

SAN JUAN. See also **NEW MEXICO; PUEBLO.** *Spec. St.* 43:886. *Approp. St.* 35:317; 40:561, 408, 1225.

SAN MANUEL. See **CALIFORNIA.**

SAN PASQUAL. See **CALIFORNIA.**

SAN XAVIER. See also **ARIZONA; PAPAGO; AK CHIN RESERVATION.** *Approp. St.* 40:561; 41:3, 408, 1156, 1225; 42:552, 1174; 43:390, 704, 1141; 44:453, 934, 1250; 45:200, 1562; 49:1757; 50:213, 564; 52:291, 291.

SANDIA. See **NEW MEXICO; PUEBLO.**

SANS ARC. See **SIOUX; CHEYENNE RIVER SIOUX TRIBE.**

SANTA ANA. See **NEW MEXICO; PUEBLO.**

SANTA CLARA. See also **NEW MEXICO; PUEBLO.** *I. D. Rulings* Memo. Sol. Off., April 14, 1939.

SANTA YSABEL. See also **CALIFORNIA; MESA GRANDE.** *Spec. St.* 44:690. *Approp. St.* 44:841.

SANTIAM. See **OREGON.**

SANTEE SIOUX TRIBE OF NEBRASKA. See also **NEBRASKA; SIOUX, SANTEE.** *Spec. St.* 4:464; 35:53. *Approp. St.* 4:526; 5:158. *Treaties* 7:524. *Cases* Sloan, 118 Fed. 283; U. S. v. Hammer, 241 U. S. 379; U. S. v. Mitchell, 109 U. S. 146. *I. D. Rulings* Memo. Commr., Jan. 6, 1937. Memo. Sol., April 14, 1938. *Const.* April 3, 1936. *Charter* Aug. 22, 1936.

SANTO DOMINGO. See **NEW MEXICO; PUEBLO.**

SAUK AND FOX. See **IOWA; OKLAHOMA; FOX; SAC, SAC AND FOX.**

SAXMAN, NATIVE VILLAGE OF. See also **ALASKA.** *Const.* Jan. 14, 1941. *Charter* Jan. 14, 1941.

SCOTON. See **OREGON; CHASTA; MOLALA; SCOTONS, CHESTAS AND GRAVE CREEK; SHASTA; UMPQUA.**

SCOTONS, CHESTAS AND GRAVE CREEKS. See also **OREGON; CHASTAS.** *Treaties* 12:981.

SEGER AGENCY. See also **OKLAHOMA; ARAPAHOE, CHEYENNE.** *Approp. St.* 41:3, 408, 1225; 42:552.

SELAWIK, NATIVE VILLAGE OF. See also **ALASKA; ESKIMO.** *Const.* Mar. 15, 1940. *Charter* Mar. 15, 1940.

SEMINOLE. See also **FLORIDA; OKLAHOMA; FIVE CIVILIZED TRIBES.** *Texts* Bledsoe, ILL. *Gov. Pub.* 71 Cong., 2 sess., Hearings, S. Comm. Ind. Aff., S. 3041; 71 Cong., 3 sess., S. Doc. 314. *Spec. St.* 3:459, 676; 4:70; 5:316, 504, 506; 17:159, 626; 18:29; 27:281; 28:693; 30:567; 31:170; 32:399; 39:1199; 41:1364; 43:133; 47:140; 48:146; 49:339. *Approp. St.* 4:519, 580, 705, 780; 5:1, 1, c. 3, 36, 73, 158, 357, 414, 704; 9:20, 544; 10:105, 181, 214; 15:311; 22:68; 23:362; 25:905; 26:989; 27:120, 612; 28:286; 30:62, 571, 597, 924; 31:1010; 35:70; 36:269, 703; 38:559, 582; 39:123, 969; 40:105, 561; 41:3, 408, 1225; 43:390, 704, 1141; 48:984; 50:564. *Priv. St.* 6:252, 272, 282, 296, 322, 328, 336, 472, 703, 771, 819; 9:678, 718, 738; 10:734, 791, 796, 842, 871, 871, J. Res. no. 20; 24:926; 25:1124; 26:1163, 1173, 1231, 1371, 1389; 27:791, 797, 804; 28:1034; 29:788; 30:1416; 31:1488, 1517, 1565, 1587, 1629, 1634; 32:1355, 1468, 1491, 1580, 1580, c. 392, 1581; 33:1374, 1393, 1393, c. 482, 1452, 1535, 1535, c. 1179; 1180; 1181; 1538, 1633, 1656, 1656, c. 1881, 1769, 1860, 1861, 1802, 1981, 2048; 34:1400, 1505, 1508, 1548, 1549, 1557, 1676, 1691, 1812, 1828, 1836, 1842, 1843, 1958, 1958, c, 2563, 2121, 2133, 2138, 2263, 2265, 2274, 2386, 2442, 2455, 2456, 2486, 2522, 2554, 2556, 2583, 2593, 2724, 2726; 35:1178, 1178, 1179, 1179, C. 48, 1204, 1219, 1375, 1389, 1462, 1573, 1606; 36:1609, 1752, 1753, 1766, 1806, 1807, 1810, 1816, 1843, 1859, 1982, 1984, 2099; 38:1569, 1594; 40:1478, 1484; 41:1472, 1533; 42:1718. *Treaties* Archives No. 17; 7:366, 368, 423, 427; 9:821; 11:699; 14:755, 785. *Cases* Cate, 299 U. S. 30; Cherokee, 155 U. S. 196; Deming, 224 U. S. 471; Fish, 52 F. 2d 544; Goat, 224 U. S. 458; Harjo, 28 F. 2d 596; Jackson, 43 F. 2d 513; Jackson, 67 F. 2d 719; Jackson, 34 C. Cls. 441; Kiker, 63 F. 2d 957; Mars, 40 F. 2d 247; Mitchell, 9 Pet. 711; Moore, 43 F. 2d 322; Seminole, 78 C. Cls. 455; U. S. v. Bean, 253 Fed. 1; U. S. v. Ferguson, 247 U. S. 175; U. S. v. Payne, 8 Fed. 883; U. S. v. Seminole, 299 U. S. 417; U. S. v. Stigall, 226 Fed. 190; U. S. Express, 191 Fed. 673; Vinson, 44 F. 2d 772; Washington, 235 U. S. 422; Wilson, 38 C. Cls. 6. *Op. A. G.* 26:340; 35:421. *I. D. Rulings* 26 L. D. 117, Jan. 31, 1898; Memo. Sol. Off., Aug. 17, 1931, Mar. 13, 1935; Memo. Sol., Sept. 12, 1935.

SENECA. See also **NEW YORK; OKLAHOMA; ALLEGHANY RESERVATION; BUFFALO CREEK RESERVATION; CATTARAUGUS RESERVATION; CAYUGA; SENECA AND SHAWNEE; SENECA, MIXED SENECAS AND SHAWNEES, QUAPAWS, CONFEDERATED PEORIA, KASKASKIAS, WEAS, AND PIANKESHAWS.** *Per.* L. M. G., 9 N. Y. U. L. Q. Rev. 498; 31 Yale L. J. 330. *Gov. Pub.* 71 Cong., 3 sess., Hearings, H. Comm. Ind. Aff., H. R. 10515 and H. R. 11203. *Spec. St.* 4:442, 578; 11:362; 17:388; 18:330; 20:535; 21:511; 22:432; 26:558; 27:470; 31:316; 35:444; 36:927; 44:252, 932; 45:1857; 48:501. *Approp. St.* 3:517; 4:526, 528, 616, 636, 682, 780; 5:36, 158, 298, 323, 402, 417, 493, 612, 704, 766; 9:20, 132, 252, 382, 544, 574; 10:15, 41, 226, 315, 686; 11:65, 169, 388; 12:44, 221, 512, 774; 13:161, 541; 14:255, 492; 15:198; 16:13, 335, 544; 17:122, 165, 437; 18:146, 420; 19:102, 176, 271; 20:63, 295; 21:114, 485; 22:68, 433; 23:76, 362; 25:217, 980; 26:336, 989; 27:120, 612; 28:286, 876; 29:321; 30:62, 571, 924; 31:221, 1058; 32:245, 982; 33:1048; 34:325, 1015; 35:781; 36:269; 37:518; 38:77, 582; 39:123, 969; 40:561; 41:3, 408, 1225; 42:552, 1174; 43:390, 1141; 44:453, 841, 934; 45:200, 1562; 46:279, 1115; 47:91, 820, 48:362, 984; 49:176, 1757; 50:564; 52:291. *Priv. St.* 4:491; 6:167, 416, 609; 31:1809; 37:1027; 43:1367. *Treaties* Archives No. 19; 7:61, 70, 72, 118, 131, 160, 178, 348, 351, 355, 411, 474, 533, 550, 586, 601; 12:991; 15:513. *Cases* Benson, 44 Fed. 178; Button, 7 F. Supp. 597; Conley, 210 U. S. 84; Deere, 22 F. 2d 851; Jackson, 13 Fed. Cas. No. 7143; Kennedy, 241 U. S. 556; Kennedy, 23 F. Supp. 771; New York, 21 How. 366; New York, 5 Wall. 761; New York, 170 U. S. 1; New York, 40 C. Cls. 448; New York, 41 C. Cls. 462; People, 8 F. Supp. 295; Rice, 2 F. Supp. 669; Seneca, 162 U. S. 283; Spears, 64 C. Cls. 684; U. S. v. Charles, 23 F. Supp. 346; U. S. v. New York, 173 U. S. 464; U. S. v. Seneca, 274 Fed. 947; U. S. ex rel. Kennedy, 269 U. S. 13; U. S. ex rel. Lynn, 173 U. S. 464; Washburn, 7 F. Supp. 120. *Op. A. G.* 1:465; 3:624. *I. D. Rulings* 6 L. D. 159, Sept. 28, 1887; Memo. Sol. Off., Oct. 25, 1936; Memo. Sol., May 24, 1937.

SENECA CAYUGA TRIBE OF OKLAHOMA. See also **OKLAHOMA; CAYUGA; SENECA.** *Const.* Apr. 26, 1937. *Charter* June 26, 1937.

**SENECAS, MIXED SENECAS AND SHAWNEES, QUAPAWS, CONFEDERATED PEORIAS, KASKASKIAS, WEAS AND PIANKESHAWS, OTTAWAS OF BLANCHARDS FORK AND ROCHE DE BOEUF AND CERTAIN WYAN-

DOTTS. See also KASKASKIA; OTTAWA; PEORIA; PIANKESHAW; QUAPAW; ROCHE DE BOEUF; SENECA; SHAWNEE; WYANDOTTE. *Approp. St.* 16:13, 335, 544; 17:165, 437.

SENECAS, SHAWNEES, QUAPAWS, PEORIAS, KASKASKIAS, OTTAWAS, WYANDOTS, AND OTHERS. See also KASKASKIAS; OTTAWAS; PEORIAS; QUAPAW; SENECAS; SHAWNEES; WYANDOTTE. *Approp. St.* 18:146.

SENECA AND SHAWNEE. See also SENECA; SHAWNEE; ILLINOIS. *Spec. St.* 10:181. *Approp. St.* 4:705; 5:36, 158, 298, 323, 402, 417, 493, 704, 766; 9:20, 252, 382, 544, 574; 10:41, 226, 315, 686; 11:65, 169, 273, 388; 12:44, 221, 512, 774; 13:161, 541; 14:255, 492; 15:198; 16:13, 335, 544; 17:165, 437; 18:146, 420; 19:176, 271; 20:63. *Priv. St.* 14:616. *Treaties* 7:326.

SHASTA. See also CALIFORNIA; OREGON; CHASTA; SACRAMENTO INDIAN AGENCY; SCOTONS, CHESTAS, AND GRAVE CREEK. *Spec. St.* 12:199.

SHAKTOOLIK, NATIVE VILLAGE OF. See also ALASKA; ESKIMO. *Const.* Jan 27, 1940. *Charter* Jan. 27, 1940.

SHAWNEE. See also OKLAHOMA; ABSENTEE SHAWNEE TRIBE OF INDIANS OF OKLAHOMA; BLACK BOB; CITIZEN BAND OF POTAWATOMI INDIANS OF OKLAHOMA; DELAWARE; LEWIS AND SCOUTASH TOWNS; IOWA TRIBE OF OKLAHOMA; KICKAPOO; KICKAPOO TRIBE OF OKLAHOMA; SENECA AND SHAWNEE. *Texts* Hilliard, LT; Manypenny, OIW. *Per.* Canfield, 15 Am. L. Rev. 21; Thompson, 6 Ill. L. Rev. 204. *Spec. St.* 3:308, 319; 4:594; 5:800; 17:228, 388; 21:377, 511; 22:7; 25:608, 768; 26:652; 27:86; 28:3; 37:194; 45:1550. *Approp. St.* 1:460; 2:407; 3:517; 4:526, 528, 616, 636, 682, 780; 5:36, 158, 298, 323, 402, 417, 493, 704, 766; 9:20, 132, 252, 382, 544, 574; 10:41, 226, 315, 576, 686; 11:65, 169, 273, 329, 388; 12:15, 44, 221, 512, 774; 13:161, 541; 14:255, 492; 15:198; 16:13, 53, 335, 544; 17:122, 165, 437; 18:146, 420; 19:176, 271; 20:63, 295; 21:114, 414, 485; 22:68, 433; 23:76, 236, 362; 24:449; 25:217, 980; 26:336, 989; 27:120, 612; 28:286; 29:267, 321; 30:62, 105, 571, 652, 924; 31:221, 1010, 1058; 32:245, 982; 33:189, 1048; 34:325; 44:453, 841; 45:2; 46:90, 115; 47:91; 48:362, 984; 49:176, 1757. *Priv. St.* 6:639, 901; 9:777; 11:514; 39:1477. *Treaties* Archives No. 44; 7:28, 49, 74, 87, 118, 178, 284, 351, 355, 397, 411; 8:116; 10:1053; 15:513. *Cases* Blackfeather, 190 U. S. 368; 28 C. Cls. 447, 37 C. Cls. 233; Cherokee, 155 U. S. 218; Dunbar, 198 U. S. 166; Ex p. Forbes, 9 Fed. Cas. No. 4921; Johnson, 283 Fed. 954; Journeycake, 28 C. Cls. 281, 31 C. Cls. 140; Kansas, 5 Wall. 737; Mandler, 49 F. 2d 201; Shawnee, 47 C. Cls. 321; U. S. v. Bellm, 182 Fed. 161; U. S. v. Blackfeather, 155 U. S. 180; U. S. v. Reynolds, 250 U. S. 104; U. S. v. Ward, 28 Fed. Cas. No. 16639. *Op. A. G.* 11:145. *I. D. Rulings* 10 L. D. 606, May 24, 1890; 13 L. D. 316, Sept. 9, 1891; Op. Sol., Sept. 21, 1933; Memo. Sol., Aug. 8, 1934.

SHEBIT. See UTAH; SHIVWITS.

SHEEPEATERS. See also IDAHO; LEMHI; SHOSHONES, BANNOCKS AND SHEEPEATERS. *Spec. St.* 25:687.

SHINNECOCKS (LONG ISLAND INDIANS). See NEW YORK.

SHISHMAREF, NATIVE VILLAGE OF. See also ALASKA; ESKIMO. *Const.* Aug. 2, 1939. *Charter* Aug. 2, 1939.

SHIVWITS (SHEBIT, SHEWITS) BAND OF PAIUTE INDIANS OF THE SHIVWITS RESERVATION. See also UTAH; KAIBAB PAIUTE. *Approp. St.* 26:989; 27:120, 612; 30:924; 31:1058; 32:245, 982; 34:325; 40:561; 41:3, 163; 42:1174; 43:1313. *Const.* Mar. 21, 1940.

SHOALWATER OR GEORGETOWN RESERVATION. See also WASHINGTON; GEORGETOWN RESERVATION; WILLAPAH. *Gov. Pub.* 74 Cong., 1 sess., H. Rep. 471. *Spec. St.* 50:289. *I. D. Rulings* Op. Sol., Sept. 23, 1932.

SHOSHONE. See also CALIFORNIA; IDAHO; NEVADA; WYOMING; ARAPAHOE; ARAPAHOE AND SHOSHONE; BANNOCKS; BIG PINE RESERVATION; DUCK VALLEY RESERVATION; DUCKWATER SHOSHONE TRIBE OF INDIANS OF THE DUCKWATER RESERVATION; ELKO INDIAN VILLAGE; FORT McDERMITT PAIUTE SHOSHONE TRIBE OF THE FORT McDERMITT INDIAN RESERVATION; GOSHUTE; LEMHI; MIXED SHOSHONES; PAIUTE; RENO-SPARKS INDIAN COLONY; SHOSHONE-BANNOCK TRIBES OF THE FORT HALL RESERVATION; SHOSHONE-PAIUTE TRIBES OF THE DUCK VALLEY RESERVATION, IDAHO AND NEVADA; SHOSHONE AND ARAPAHOE; SHOSHONE AND BANNOCK; SHOSHONE-GOSHIP; SHOSHONE OF NEVADA; SHOSHONE, BANNOCKS AND OTHER BANDS OF INDIANS IN IDAHO AND SOUTHEASTERN OREGON; SNAKES; TEMOAK; WIND RIVER RESERVATION; WINNEMUCCA INDIAN COLONY; YOMBA SHOSHONE. *Per.* Canfield, 15 Am. L. Rev. 21. *Gov. Pub.* 76 Cong., 1 sess. Hearings, S. Comm. Ind. Aff., S. 1878. *Spec. St.* 18:291; 22:148; 25:452, 687; 31:672; 33:1016; 34:825, 849; 36:855; 39:519; 45:160, 371, 1407; 50:700; 52:347, 778. *Approp. St.* 12:512, 629; 13:161, 541; 14:255, 492; 15:198; 16:13, 335, 544; 17:165, 437; 18:146, 420; 19:176, 271; 20:63, 295; 21:67, 114, 485; 22:67, 114, 485; 22:68, 433; 23:76, 362, 446; 24:449; 25:217, 980; 26:336, 504, 989; 27:120, 612; 28:286, 876; 29:321; 30:62, 571, 924; 31:221, 280, 1058; 32:245, 982; 33:189, 1048; 34:205, 325, 1015; 35:70, 781; 36:269, 1289; 37:518; 38:77, 559, 582; 39:123, 969; 40:561; 41:3, 35, 408, 1015, 1156, 1225; 42:29, 552, 1174, 1527; 43:390, 704, 1141, 1313; 44:453, 934; 45:200, 883, 1562, 1623; 46:90, 279, 1115; 47:91, 820; 48:362; 49:176, 1757; 50:564; 52:291. *Priv. St.* 49:2343. *Treaties* 12:945; 13:663; 15:673; 18:685, 689. *Cases* Brown, 32 C. Cls. 432; Clarke, 39 F. 2d 800; Fremont, 3 Wyo. 200; Harkness, 98 U. S. 476; Janus, 38 F. 2d 431; Marks, 161 U. S. 297; Moore, 2 Wyo. 8; Shoshone, 82 C. Cls. 23; Shoshone, 85 C. Cls. 331; Skeem, 273 Fed. 93; U. S. v. Corporation, 101 F. 2d 156; U. S. v. Leathers, 26 Fed. Cas. No. 15581; U. S. v. Parkins, 18 F. 2d 642; U. S. v. Parkins, 18 F. 2d 643; U. S. v. Portneuf-Marsh, 213 Fed. 601; U. S. v. Shoshone, 304 U. S. 111; Utah, 116 U. S. 28; Wadsworth, 148 Fed. 771; Ward, 163 U. S. 504. *Op. A. G.* 25:524; 33:25. *I. D. Rulings* 49 L. D. 370, Dec. 15, 1922; Op. Sol., Jan. 25, 1930; Memo. Sol., Nov. 12, 1934, Nov. 5, 1937, June 3, 1938.

SHOSHONE OF NEVADA. See also NEVADA; SHOSHONE. *Approp. St.* 45:1623. *I. D. Rulings* Memo. Sol., Jan. 4, 1937.

SHOSHONE AND ARAPAHOE. See also ARAPAHOE; ARAPAHOE AND SHOSHONE; SHOSHONE; WIND RIVER. *Spec. St.* 45:467; 46:88, 1060; 50:700. *Approp. St.* 28:286; 30:62, 571, 924; 31:221, 1058; 32:245.

SHOSHONE-BANNOCK TRIBES OF THE FORT HALL RESERVATION. See also BANNOCK; SHOSHONE. *Spec. St.* 17:214. *Approp. St.* 16:13, 335, 544; 17:437; 18:146; 19:176, 271; 20:63, 295; 21:114, 114, 485; 22:68, 433; 23:76, 362; 24:449; 25:217, 980; 26:336, 989; 27:120, 612; 28:286, 876; 29:321; 30:62, 571, 924; 31:221, 1058; 32:245, 982; 33:1048. *Cases* Moore, 2 Wyo. 8. *I. D. Rulings* Op. Sol. June 19, 1923; Memo. Sol. Off., May 28, 1935; Memo. Sol., May 24, 1937. *Const.* Apr. 20, 1936. *Charter* Apr. 17, 1937.

SHOSHONE-GOSHIP. See also UTAH; GOSHIP; GOSHUTE; SHOSHONE. *Treaties* 13:681.

SHOSHONE (WIND RIVER) RESERVATION. See also WYOMING; SHOSHONE; SHOSHONE AND ARAPAHOE; WIND RIVER. *Spec. St.* 34:825, 849; 35:650; 41:1466; 45:617; 46:218; 47:88. *Approp. St.* 40:821; 52:291. *Priv. St.* 49:2343. *I. D. Rulings* Memo. Sol. Off., May 25, 1933.

SHOSHONES, BANNOCKS, AND OTHER BANDS OF INDIANS IN IDAHO AND SOUTHEASTERN OREGON. See also IDAHO; OREGON; WYOMING; BANNOCKS; SHOSHONES. *Approp. St.* 18:146, 420; 19:271; 21:485.

SHOSHONES (MIXED), BANNOCKS & SHEEPEATERS. See also IDAHO; BANNOCKS; SHEEPEATERS; SHOSHONE. *Approp. St.* 16:335, 544; 17:165, 437; 18:133, 146, 420; 19:176, 271; 20:63, 295; 21:114, 485; 22:257, 433; 23:76, 362; 24:449; 25:217, 980; 26:336, 989; 27:120, 612; 28:286, 876; 29:321; 30:62, 571, 924; 31:221, 1058; 32:245, 982; 33:189, 1048; 34:325, 1015; 35:781; 36:269. *Priv. St.* 27:810.

SHOSHONE-PAIUTE TRIBE OF DUCK VALLEY RESERVATION. See also NEVADA; PAIUTE; SHOSHONE. *Const.* Apr. 20, 1936. *Charter* Aug. 22, 1936.

SILETZ RESERVATION. See also OREGON; ALSEA AND SILETZ RESERVATION; CHASTA; CONFEDERATED TRIBES OF THE GRANDE RONDE COMMUNITY; COW CREEK; GALEESE CREEK; GRANDE RONDE; MOLEL; MOLALA; ROGUE RIVER; SIUSLAW; TILLAMOOK. *Spec. St.* 35:444; 36:367, 582, 1356; 49:801. *Approp. St.* 16:13; 19:271; 20:63, 295; 21:114, 485; 23:76; 24:449; 25:980; 26:336; 29:321; 31:221, 1058; 32:245, 982; 33:1048; 34:325, 1015; 35:781; 36:269; 37:518; 38:77; 39:969; 41:3, 408, 1225; 42:552; 43:390, 704, 1141. *Priv. St.* 41:1459. *Cases* Coos, 87 C. Cls. 143; U. S. *v.* Howard, 17 Fed. 638; U. S. v. Logan, 105 Fed. 240.

SIOUX. See also MONTANA; NEBRASKA; CHEYENNE RIVER; DAKOTAS; DEVILS LAKE RESERVATION; FLANDREAU INDIANS; FLANDREAU SANTEE SIOUX

TRIBE; FORT TOTTEN; LAKE TRAVERSE; LOWER BRULE SIOUX TRIBE; OGLALA; PIPESTONE; PINE RIDGE; PRAIRIE ISLAND INDIAN COMMUNITY; RED PIPESTONE; ROSEBUD SIOUX TRIBE; SIOUX, ST. PETER; SANTEE SIOUX TRIBE OF NEBRASKA; SIOUX, INKPADUTAH; SIOUX, MDEWAKANTON (MED-AY-WA-KANTOAN); SIOUX OF MINNESOTA; SIOUX OF MISSISSIPPI; SIOUX OF MISSOURI; SPOTTED TAIL; STANDING ROCK RESERVATION; TEETON; TWO KETTLE; WAHPETON; YANKTON. *Texts* Manypenny, OIW. *Per.* Cain, 2 Minn. L. Rev. 177; Harsha, 134 N. A. Rev. 272; Mac Leod, 27 J. Crim. L. 181. *Gov. Pub.* 71 Cong., 2 sess., Hearings, H. Comm. Ind. Aff., H. R. 8921; 72 Cong., 1 sess., Hearings, H. Comm. Ind. Aff., H. R. 8089; 75 Cong., 1 sess., Hearings, H. Comm. Ind. Aff., H. R. 5753. *Spec. St.* 4:464; 10:290, 304; 11:292, 362; 12:652, 803, 819, 1042; 13:427; 15:39; 16:370; 17:281, 340, 475; 18:47, 52; 19:28, 252; 21:11; 22:7, 582; 23:344; 25:94, 852, 611, 888; 26:14, 15, 34, 720; 28:4, 653; 29:10; 30:748, 1362; 31:805; 32:203; 33:154, 254, 319, 700; 34:78; 35:444; 38:383, 1188, 1189; 39:47, 1195, 1199, 1606; 41:738; 43:477, 730; 44:135, 251; 45:484, 684, 747, 939, 966; 47:300, 818; 49:340; 50:441. *Approp. St.* 4:92, 526, 682, 780; 5:36, 158, 323, 493, 612, 704, 766; 9:544; 10:41, 315, 686; 11:65, 169, 273, 388, 409; 12:44, 221; 13:92, 161, 541; 14:255, 492; 15:7, 198; 16:13, 291, 335, 544; 17:122, 165, 437, 530; 18:133, 146, 204, 402, 420; 19:41, 102, 176, 271, 344; 20:63, 295, 377; 21:114, 238. *Approp. St.* 414, 485; 22:68, 257, 433, 582, 603; 23:76, 362, 446; 24:449; 25:217, 980; 26:336, 504, 862, 989; 27:5, 120, 612; 28:286, 424, 843, 876; 29:267, 321; 30:62, 105, 571, 652, 924, 1214; 31:221, 1010, 1058; 32:5, 245, 552, 982, 1031; 33:189, 394, 1048, 1214; 34:325, 634, 1015; 35:8, 70, 478, 781, 907; 36:202, 269, 774, 1289; 37:518, 595, 912; 38:77, 208, 312, 559, 582, 1138; 39:14, 123, 801, 969; 40:2, 345, 561, 821; 41:3, 35, 327, 408, 503, 1015, 1156, 1225; 42:29, 192, 327, 437, 552, 767, 1048, 1154, 1174; 43:33, 390, 672, 704, 753, 1141, 1313; 44:453, 841, 934, 1250; 45:2, 200, 1562, 1607, 1623; 46:90, 279, 1115, 1552; 47:15, 91, 820, 1602; 48:362; 49:49, 176, 571, 1109, 1597, 1757; 50:564, 564, 755; 52:85, 291, 1114. *Priv. St.* 9:672; 10:843; 13:595; 16:684, 17:675, 730, 730 c. 145; 18:543; 19:549; 21:640; 24:736, 736 c. 276; 25:1315, 1327; 26:1197; 30:1432; 31:1484, 1670; 32:1492, 1492, c. 1349; 33:1411; 34:2469; 35:1623; 36:1687; 42:1718; 45:1833; 46:1986, 1986, c. 199. *Treaties* 7:126, 127, 143, 250, 252, 257, 272, 328, 374, 429, 510, 511, 527, 538, 568; 9:908; 10:949, 954, 1172; 11:657; 12:1031; 14:695, 699, 723, 727, 731, 735, 739, 743, 747; 15:635. *Cases* Ashbough, 35 C. Cls. 554; Baker, 38 C. Cls. 370; Beam, 43 C. Cls. 61; Bruce, 17 How. 437; Carter, 31 C. Cls. 441; Church, 48 C. Cls. 262; Coffield, 52 C. Cls. 17; Drapeau, 195 Fed. 130; Dubuque, 109 U. S. 329; Egan, 246 U. S. 227; Elk, 112 U. S. 94; Estes, 225 Fed. 980; Ex p. Crow, 109 U. S. 556; Ex p. Van, 221 Fed. 954; Farrell, 110 Fed. 942; Felix, 145 U. S. 317; Fish, 52 F. 2d 544; French, 2 Dak. 346; Gagnon, 38 C. Cls. 10; Gerrard, 43 C. Cls. 67; Golden, 2 Dak. 378; Hatton, 99 F. 2d 501; Hollister, 145 Fed. 773; Hosford, 29 C. Cls. 42; In re Sanborn, 148 U. S. 222; Janis, 32 C. Cls. 407; John, 177 U. S. 529; King, 111 Fed. 860; Leighton, 161 U. S. 291; Leighton, 29 C. Cls. 288; Litchfield, 32 C. Cls. 585; McCall, 1 Dak. 320; McKinzie, 34 C. Cls. 278; Midway, 183 U. S. 619; Mitchell, 27 C. Cls. 316; Monson, 231 U. S. 341; Moore, 32 C. Cls. 593; Myrick, 99 U. S. 291; Nesbitt, 86 U. S. 153; Reynolds, 174 Fed. 212; Reynolds, 205 Fed. 685; Rousseau, 45 C. Cls. 1; Roy, 45 C. Cls. 1; Roy, 45 C. Cls. 177; Sioux, 277 U. S. 424; Sioux, 85 C. Cls. 181; Sioux, 85 C. Cls. 16; Sioux, 86 C. Cls. 299; Sioux, 86 C. Cls. 299; Sloan, 118 Fed. 283; Sully, 195 Fed. 113; Taylor, 147 U. S. 640; U. S. v. Debell, 227 Fed. 760; U. S. v. Debell, 227 Fed. 771; U. S. v. Debell, 227 Fed. 775; U. S. v. Douglas, 190 Fed. 482; U. S. v. Nice, 241 U. S. 591; U. S. v. Omaha, 253 U. S. 275; U. S. v. Pearson, 231 Fed. 270; U. S. v. Pumphrey, 11 App. D. C. 44; U. S. v. Quiver, 241 U. S. 602; U. S. v. Rickert, 188 U. S. 432; U. S. v. Shoshone, 304 U. S. 111; U. S. ex rel. Gordon, 179 Fed. 391; Vincent, 39 C. Cls. 456; Waldron, 143 Fed. 413; Yankton, 61 C. Cls. 40. *Op. A. G.* 6:462; 18:141, 230; 19:467; 20:711. *I. D. Rulings* 12 L. D. 292, Mar. 5, 1891; 13 L. D. 307, July 22, 1891; 13 L. D. 683, Dec. 14, 1891; 14 L. D. 156, Feb. 8, 1892; 17 L. D. 142, Aug. 2, 1893; 17 L. D. 457, Aug. 18, 1893; 18 L. D. 188, Feb. 14, 1894; 19 L. D. 311, Oct. 20, 1894; 20 L. D. 562, June 17, 1895; 24 L. D. 330, Apr. 19, 1897; 29 L. D. 331, Nov. 29, 1899; 34 L. D. 702, June 21, 1906; 40 L. D. 4, Apr. 7, 1911; 40 L. D. 9, Apr. 7, 1911; 42 L. D. 192, June 21, 1931; Op. Sol., Dec. 28, 1926, Mar. 1, 1934; Memo. Sol., Aug. 8, 1934; Memo. Sol. Off., Oct. 12, 1934; Memo. Sol., Nov. 20, 1934; Letter from Acting Sec'y of Int. to Compt. Gen., Apr. 16, 1935; Memo. Sol., Apr. 15, 1936; Memo. Sol. Off., June 25, 1938; Memo. Sol., Aug. 8, 1938.

SIOUX AT FORT PECK AGENCY. See also MONTANA; FORT PECK; SIOUX; YANKTONAIS. *Cases* Baker, 28 C. Cls. 370.

SIOUX, INK-PA-DU-TAH BAND (WAHPETON). *Approp. St.* 12:200.

SIOUX, MDEWAKANTON (MED-AY-WA-KANTOAN). See also MINNESOTA; SIOUX. *Approp. St.* 30:62, 571, 924. *Priv. St.* 28:1007. *I. D. Rulings* Memo. Sol., Oct. 20, 1937.

SIOUX OF MINNESOTA. See also MINNESOTA; SIOUX; ST. PETER. *Approp. St.* 10:315. *Priv. St.* 14:640.

SIOUX OF MISSISSIPPI. See also MINNESOTA; SIOUX. *Approp. St.* 4:616, 682; 5:158, 298, 402, 417; 9:20, 132, 252, 382, 544, 574; 10:15, 41, 226, 315, 686; 12:44, 221, 512, 774. *Cases* Sisseton, 58 C. Cls. 302.

SIOUX OF MISSOURI. See also MISSOURI; SIOUX. *Cases* Sisseton, 58 C. Cls. 302.

SIOUX, OGLALA (TETON). See OGLALA; PINE RIDGE; SIOUX; TEETON. *Per.* Gates, 21 Am. J. Soc. Sci. 112. *Cases* Carter, 31 C. Cls. 441; Leighton, 29 C. Cls. 288; McKinzie, 34 C. Cls. 278; Reynolds, 205 Fed. 685; Ray, 45 C. Cls. 177; Salois, 32 C. Cls. 68; Salois, 33 C. Cls. 326. *I. D. Rulings* Memo. Sol., Dec. 11, 1937, May 14, 1938; Memo. Asst. Sec'y., Aug. 25, 1938; Memo. Sol., Mar. 25, 1939.

SIOUX, ROSEBUD TRIBE. See also ROSEBUD SIOUX; TEETON. *Gov. Pub.* 71 Cong., 2 sess., Hearings, S. Comm. Ind. Aff., Feb. 26, 1930. *Spec. St.* 39:509; 42:994; 45:497. *I. D. Rulings* Memo. Sol., Aug. 23, 1937, Apr. 12, 1938; Memo. Sol. Off., Apr. 13, 1938; Memo. Sol., July 12, 1938.

SIOUX, ST. PETER. See also SIOUX; MINNESOTA; SIOUX OF MINNESOTA. *Approp. St.* 9:544; 10:15.

SIOUX, SANTEE. See also NEBRASKA; SIOUX; SANTEE SIOUX. *Spec. St.* 25:888. *Approp. St.* 22:68, 257; 23:362; 26:989; 27:120, 612; 28:286; 30:62, 571, 924; 49:49; 50:755. *Priv. St.* 48:1805. *Cases* Mdewakantan 57 C. Cls. 357.

SIOUX, SISSETON. See SIOUX; LAKE TRAVERSE RESERVATION.

SITKA (TLINGIT). See also ALASKA; THLINGIT. *Cases* U. S. v. Seveloef, 27 Fed. Cas. No. 16252.

SIUSLAW. See also OREGON. *Spec. St.* 45:1256; 47:307; 49:801.

SIX NATIONS. See also NEW YORK; CAYUGA; IROQUOIS; MOHAWK; ONEIDA; ONONDAGA; SENECA; TUSCARORAS. *Texts* Kent, CAL; Manypenny, OIW. *Per.* Rice, 16 J. Comp. Leg. 78. *Approp. St.* 1:563; 2:66, 108; 4:526, 616, 682, 780; 5:36, 323, 402, 417, 493, 612, 704, 766; 9:20, 132, 252, 382, 544, 574; 10:15, 41, 226, 315, 686; 11:65, 169, 273, 388; 12:44, 221, 512, 774; 13:161, 541; 14:255, 492; 15:198; 16:13, 335, 544; 17:165, 437; 18:146, 420; 19:176, 271; 20:63, 295; 21:114, 485; 22:68, 433; 23:76, 362; 24:449; 25:217, 980; 26:336, 989; 27:120, 612; 28:286, 876; 29:321; 30:62, 571, 924; 31:221, 1058; 32:245, 982; 33:189, 1048; 34:325, 1015; 35:70, 781; 36:269; 37:518; 38:77; 39:123, 969; 40:561; 41:3, 408, 1225; 42:552, 1174; 43:390, 1141; 44:453, 934; 45:200, 1562; 46:279, 1115; 47:91, 820; 48:362; 49:176, 1757; 50:564; 52:291. *Priv. St.* 6:416. *Treaties* 7:15, 33, 44, 342, 405, 550; 11:735; 12:991. *Cases* U. S. v. Boylon, 265 Fed. 165; U. S. v. Seneca, 274 Fed. 947. *L. D. Memo. (D. J.)* 5:179, 236.

SKAGIT. See also WASHINGTON; DWAMISH. *Cases* Dwamish, 79 C. Cls. 530.

SKOKOMISH INDIAN TRIBE OF THE SKOKOMISH INDIAN RESERVATION. See WASHINGTON; S'KLALLAM. *Cases* Dwamish, 79 C. Cls. 530; U. S. ex rel. Charley, 62 F. 2d 955. *Const.* May 3, 1938. *Charter* July 22, 1939.

S'KLALLAM. See also WASHINGTON; CLALLAM; SKOKOMISH. *Spec. St.* 43:886. *Approp. St.* 12:4, 221, 512, 774; 13:161, 541; 14:255, 492; 15:198; 16:13, 335, 544; 17:165, 437; 18:146, 420; 19:176, 271; 20:63, 295; 21:114, 485; 22:68, 433; 23:76, 362; 24:449; 25:217, 980; 26:336, 989; 27:120, 612; 28:286, 876; 29:321; 30:62. *Treaties* 12:933, 939. *Cases* Jackson, 34 C. Cls. 441.

SKOTON. See OREGON; SCOTONS, CHESTAS AND GRAVE CREEKS.

SKULL VALLEY RESERVATION. See also UTAH; GOSHUTE TRIBE. *Spec. St.* 47:50.

SMITH RIVER RESERVATION. See also CALIFORNIA; HOOPA VALLEY. *Approp. St.* 15:198. *Cases* Donnelly, 228 U. S. 243; U. S. v. 48 Lbs., 35 Fed. 403.

SNAKE. See also OREGON; WYOMING; KLAMATH; MODOC AND YAHOOSKIN; PAHUTE (PAIUTE); YAHOOSKIN; SHOSHONE. *Spec. St.* 13:37; 41:623; 49:1276; 52:605. *Approp. St.* 14:492; 15:198; 16:13, 335, 544; 17:165, 437; 18:146, 420; 19:176, 271; 20:63, 295; 21:114, 485; 34:325. *Priv. St.* 25:1306. *Treaties* 11:657; 14:683; 16:707. *Cases* Oregon, 202 U. S. 860; U. S. v. Klamath, 304 U. S. 119; U. S. v. Oregon, 103 Fed. 549. *L. D. Memo. (D. J.)* 12:703.

SNOHOMISH. See also WASHINGTON; DWAMISH; PORT MADISON. *Cases* Dwamish, 79 C. Cls. 530; Gho, 1 Wash. T. 325.

SNOQUALMIE. See also WASHINGTON SALISH. Dwamish, 79 C. Cls. 530.

SOBOBA. See also CALIFORNIA; MISSION. *Spec. St.* 45:1229. *Approp. St.* 41:1225; 42:552. *Priv. St.* 38:1452. *I. D. Rulings* Memo. Sol., Aug. 11, 1937.

SOKAOGAN CHIPPEWA COMMUNITY. See MINNESOTA; CHIPPEWA; MOLE LAKE. *Const.* Nov. 9, 1938. *Charter* Oct. 7, 1939.

SOUTH CAROLINA. See CATAWBA.

SOUTH DAKOTA. See CHEYENNE RIVER SIOUX; FLANDREAU SANTEE SIOUX TRIBE; LAKE TRAVERSE; LOWER BRULE SIOUX TRIBE; MINNECONJOU; OGLALA SIOUX; PINE RIDGE; ROSEBUD SIOUX TRIBE; SIOUX; TETON; TWO KETTLE; UNCPAPAS; YANKTON; WAHPETON.

SOUTHERN NAVAJO RESERVATION. See ARIZONA; NEW MEXICO; NAVAJO.

SOUTHERN UTE TRIBE OF THE SOUTHERN UTE RESERVATION. See COLORADO; CONSOLIDATED UTE TRIBE; UTE. *Const.* Nov. 4, 1936. *Charter* Nov. 1, 1938.

SPOKANE RESERVATION. See also WASHINGTON; COLVILLE. *Spec. St.* 32:744; 33:1006; 35:458; 37:23; 49:1273. *Approp. St.* 26:989; 27:120, 612; 28:286, 876; 29:321; 30:62, 571, 924; 31:221, 1058; 32:245, 982; 33:189, 1048; 34:325, 634, 1015; 35:8, 70, 781; 36:269; 37:518; 38:77, 582; 39:123, 521, 969; 40:561; 41:3, 408, 1225; 42:552, 1174; 43:390, 704, 1141; 44:453, 934; 45:200, 1562; 46:279, 1115; 49:1757. *Priv. St.* 47:1656. *Treaties* 12:951, 957. *Cases* Eugene, 274 Fed. 47; Gibson, 131 Fed. 39; Northern, 208 Fed. 469; Northern, 246 U. S. 283; Taylor, 193 Fed. 968; U. S. v. Higgins, 110 Fed. 609. *I. D. Rulings* Memo. Sol., July 8, 1933.

SPOTTED TAIL (SIOUX). See also NEBRASKA; RED CLOUD; SIOUX. *Approp. St.* 19:102; 20:232.

SQUAXON (SQUAXIN). See also WASHINGTON; DWAMISH. *Cases* Dwamish, 79 C. Cls. 530; Mitchell, 22 F. 2d 771; U. S. v. O'Brien, 170 Fed. 508.

SQUINAHMISH. See WASHINGTON.

STALUCK-WHAMISH (STAILACOOMAMISH). See WASHINGTON.

STANDING ROCK RESERVATION. See also SIOUX; TEETON; UNCPAPAS; YANKTONAIS. *Spec. St.* 26:14, 720; 35:460; 36:196, 265; 37:84, 653, 675; 41:1446; 42:499; 43:1184; 45:400; 46:1107; 47:300. *Approp. St.* 31:221; 32:245, 982, 1031; 34:325, 1015; 35:478; 36:269; 37:518; 38:77, 582; 40:561; 44:453. *Priv. St.* 49:2064. *I. D. Rulings* Memo. Sol. Off., Nov. 10, 1934.

STEBBINS, COMMUNITY ASSOCIATION. See also ALASKA; ESKIMO. *Const.* Dec. 5, 1939. *Charter* Dec. 5, 1939.

STELLAQUAMISH (STILLAQUAMISH). See also WASHINGTON. *Cases* Dawamish, 79 C. Cls. 530.

STEVENS. THE NATIVE VILLAGE OF (ATHAPASCAN) See also ALASKA. *Const.* Dec. 30, 1939. *Charter* Dec. 30, 1939.

STIKEEN (TLINGIT). See also ALASKA; WASHINGTON THLINGIT. *Cases* U. S. v. Kie., 26 Fed. Cas. No. 15528a; Halbert v. U. S., 283 U. S. 753.

STOCKBRIDGE INDIANS. See also WISCONSIN; MENOMINEE; STOCKBRIDGE MUNSEE COMMUNITY OF WISCONSIN; BROTHERTON. *Spec. St.* 5:645; 9:55; 16:404; 27:744; 43:644. *Approp. St.* 1:563; 5:158, 323, 766; 9:20, 370, 544, 574; 10:41, 226, 315, 686; 28:286, 876; 34:325; 39:123. *Priv. St.* 6:244; 10:746; 14:604. *Treaties* Archives 19; 7:47, 405, 550; 11:577. *I. D. Rulings* Op. Sol., Dec. 29, 1921.

STOCKBRIDGE MUNSEE COMMUNITY. See also WISCONSIN; MUNSEE AND DELAWARE. *Per.* Thayer, 68 Atl. Month. 540, 676. *Gov. Pub.* 74 Cong., 1 sess., H. Reps. 288, 289. *Spec. St.* 13:530; 27:744. *Approp. St.* 4:682; 5:402; 10:226, 686; 11:65; 13:541; 17:530; 18:146; 33:189. *Treaties* 9:955. *Cases* Beecher, 95 U. S. 517; Elk, 112 U. S. 94; New York, 170 U. S. 1; New York, 40 C. Cls. 448; Oakes, 172 Fed. 305; Stockbridge, 61 C. Cls. 472; Stockbridge, 68 C. Cls. 268; U. S. v. Anderson, 225 Fed. 825; U. S. v. Gardner, 189 Fed. 690; U. S. v. New York, 173 U. S. 464; U. S. v. Paine, 206 U. S. 467. *I. D. Rulings* 25 L. D. 17, July 12, 1897. *Const.* Oct. 30, 1937. *Charter* May 21, 1938.

SUATTLE INDIANS. See also WASHINGTON. *Spec. St.* 48:886.

SUMMIT LAKE (PAIUTE). See also NEVADA; PAH-UTE (PAIUTE). *Approp. St.* 44:934; 47:91, 820; 49:1757; 50:564; 52:291.

SUQUAMISH. See also WASHINGTON; PORT MADISON. *Treaties* 12:933. *Cases* Duwamish, 79 C. Clas. 530.

SWINOMISH INDIAN TRIBAL COMMUNITY (SWINAMISH). See also WASHINGTON. *Approp. St.* 34:325; 50:564. *Cases* Corrigan, 169 Fed. 477; Duwamish, 79 C. Cls. 530. *I. D. Rulings* Memo. Sol., June 15, 1934, July 9, 1936, Sept. 13, 1938. *Const.* Jan. 27, 1936. *Charter* July 25, 1936.

SYCUAN. See CALIFORNIA; MISSION.

TABEGUACHE. See also TABEGUACHE, MUACHE, CAPOTE, WEEMINUCHE, YAMPA, GRAND RIVER AND UINTAH BANDS OF UTES. *Treaties* 13:673; 15:619.

TABEGUACHE, MUACHE, CAPOTE, WEEMINUCHE, YAMPA, GRAND RIVER AND UINTAH BANDS OF UTES. See also CAPOTE; GRAND RIVER; MUACHE, TABEGUACHE, UINTAH; UTAH; UTE; YAMPA. *Approp. St.* 16:13; 18:146, 420.

TAH-WA-CARRO (TAWAKONI). See also TAH-WAH; TEXAS; CARRO; CADDO; TOWAKONI; WICHITA AND AFFILIATED BANDS. *Treaties* 7:533.

TAH WAH (TAWAKONI). See also CARRO; TAH-WA-CARRO; TAWAKONI; WICHITA AND AFFILIATED BANDS. *Treaties* 9:844.

TAHOLAH. See also WASHINGTON; MAKAH; QUILEUTE; S'KLALLAM; SKOKOMISH; SQUAXON. *Approp. St.* 39:123, 969; 41:3, 1225; 42:552, 1174; 43:390; 44:453, 934; 45:200, 1562, 1623. *I. D. Rulings* Memo. Sol., July 8, 1933.

TAMAROIS (TOMAROA). See also ILLINOIS. *Approp. St.* 3:517. *Treaties* 7:78.

TAOS PUEBLO. See NEW MEXICO; PUEBLO.

TEETON TRIBE (TETON). See also MINNESOTA; SOUTH DAKOTA; SIOUX. *Treaties* 7:125.

TEMECULA (LUISENO). See also CALIFORNIA; MISSION; PECHANGA RESERVATION. *Spec. St.* 46:1201.

TEMOAK BANDS OF WESTERN SHOSHONE INDIANS. See also NEVADA; SHOSHONE. *Approp. St.* 43:596, 1141; 45:200. *Const.* Aug. 24, 1938. *Charter* Dec. 12, 1938.

TENINO. See OREGON; WARM SPRINGS.

TESUQUE PUEBLO. See NEW MEXICO; PUEBLO.

TETLIN, NATIVE VILLAGE OF. See also ALASKA; ESKIMO. *Const.* Mar. 26, 1940. *Charter* Mar. 26, 1940.

TEXAS. See also ALABAMA-COUSHATTA TRIBE OF TEXAS; CADDO; KIOWA; TOWAKANI; WICHITA; WICHITA AND AFFILIATED BANDS; LEPAN. *Approp. St.* 9:382, 544, 598; 10:15, 41, 226, 315, 686; 11:65, 329, 388; 12:44, 221, 512, 774; 13:161, 541; 14:255, 492; 15:198; 16:13. *Priv. St.* 9:769; 34:1719, 1814, 1993, 2243, 2650; 35:1375, 1389, 1431, 1606; 36:1758, 1760, 1762, 1805, 1813, 1815, 1816, 1848, 1880, 2000, 2099; 38:1278; 39:1858; 41:1472.

THLINGIT. See also ALASKA; HAIDA. *Spec. St.* 49:388. *Cases* In re Sah Quah, 31 Fed. 327; Nagle, 191 Fed. 141; Terr. of Alaska, 289 Fed. 671; U. S. v. Lynch, 7 Alaska 568.

THLOPTHLOCCO TRIBAL TOWN. See also OKLAHOMA; CREEK. *Const.* Dec. 27, 1938. *Charter* Apr. 13, 1939.

THREE AFFILIATED TRIBES OF THE FORT BERTHOLD RESERVATION. See also FORT BERTHOLD, MANDAN; GROS VENTRE (HIDATSA). *Spec. St.* 46:1481. *Approp. St.* 14:492; 15:198; 16:13, 335, 544; 17:122, 165, 437, 530; 18:133, 146, 420; 19:176, 271; 20:63, 295; 21:114, 485; 22:68, 433; 23:76, 362; 24:449; 25:217, 980; 26:336, 504, 989; 28:843. *Treaties* 7:259. *Const.* June 29, 1936. *Charter* Apr. 24, 1937.

TILLAMOOK. See also OREGON, GRAND RONDE. *Approp. St.* 30:62; 33:1048.;

TITUTNI. See OREGON, SILETZ RESERVATION.

TLINGIT. See ALASKA; THLINGIT.

TONAWANDA. See also NEW YORK; ALLEGANY; BUFFALO CREEK RESERVATION; SENECA. *Approp. St.* 11:409. *Treaties* 11:735; 12:1031. *Cases* Fellows, 19 How. 366; N. Y. ex rel. Cutler, 21 How. 366; N. Y. Indians, 5 Wall.

Martinez, 195 U. S. 469; U. S. v. Morrison, 203 Fed. 364; U. S. v. Pierson, 145 Fed. 814; Ute, 45 C. Cls. 440; Ute, 46 C. Cls. 225; White, 43 C. Cls. 260. *Op. A. G.* 17:262; 21:131. *I. D. Rulings* Memo. Sol., Sept. 12, 1934, July 13, 1936; Memo. Sol. Off., Sept. 22, 1936; Memo. Sol., Sept. 11, 1937, Sept. 29, 1937; Memo. Sol. Off., Nov. 23, 1937; Op. Sol., June 15, 1938; Memo. Sol., Aug. 27, 1938, Mar. 28, 1939.

UTE INDIAN TRIBE OF THE UINTAH AND OURAY RESERVATION. See also UTAH; UINTAH. *Const.* Jan. 19, 1937. *Charter* Aug. 10, 1938.

VENETIE, NATIVE VILLAGE OF (ATHAPASCAN). See also ALASKA. *Const.* Jan. 25, 1940. *Charter* Jan. 25, 1940.

VERDE RIVER VALLEY (MOHAVE APACHE). See also ARIZONA; CAMP McDOWELL. *Approp. St.* 33:189.

VERMILLION LAKE. See MINNESOTA; CHIPPEWA.

VOLCAN INDIAN RESERVATION. See also CALIFORNIA; MISSION. *Approp. St.* 41:408.

WABASH. See also ILLINOIS; INDIANA. *Spec. St.* 2:277, 343.

WALAPAI RESERVATION. See also ARIZONA; HUALAPAI. *Spec. St.* 43:954. *Priv. St.* 47:1753.

WALES, NATIVE VILLAGE OF (ESKIMO). See also ALASKA. *Const.* July 29, 1939. *Charter* July 29, 1939.

WALKER RIVER PAIUTE TRIBE. See also NEVADA; PAH UTES (PAIUTE). *Spec. St.* 32:744; 45:160. *Approp. St.* 20:63, 295; 21:114, 485; 23:76; 24:449; 25:217, 980; 26:336, 989; 28:876; 29:321; 30:652, 924, 1214; 31:1058; 32:552, 245, 982; 33:189, 1048; 34:325; 35:8, 781; 36:269; 40:561; 41:3, 408, 1225; 42:552, 1174; 43:390, 1141; 44:453, 934; 45:200, 1562; 46:279, 1115; 47:91; 48:362; 49:176, 1757; 50:564; 52:291. *Cases* U. S. v. Walker, 104 F. 2d 334. *I. D. Rulings* Op. Sol., Feb. 5, 1935. *Const.* Mar. 26, 1937. *Charter* May 8, 1937.

WALLA WALLA. See also OREGON; CAYUSE; UMATILLA. *Spec. St.* 25:47. *Approp. St.* 12:4, 221, 512, 774; 13:161, 541; 14:255, 492; 15:198; 16:13, 335, 544; 17:165, 437; 18:146, 420; 19:176; 20:63, 295; 21:114, 271, 485; 22:68, 433; 23:76, 362; 24:449; 25:217, 980; 26:336, 989; 27:120, 612; 28:286, 876; 29:321; 30:62, 571, 924; 31:221, 280, 1058; 32:245, 982; 33:189, 1048; 34:325, 1015; 35:70, 781; 36:269; 37:518; 38:77. *Treaties* 12:945, 951, 957. *Cases* Bonifer, 166 Fed. 846; Hy-Tu-Tse-Mil-Kin, 194 U. S. 401; Morrisett, 132 Fed. 891; Seufert, 249 U. S. 194; Smith, 132 Fed. 889; U. S. v. Barnhart, 17 Fed. 579; U. S. v. Bridleman, 7 Fed. 894; U. S. v. Brookfield, 24 F. Supp. 712; U. S. v. Motlock, 26 Fed. Cas. No. 15744; Ya-koot-sa, 262 Fed. 398.

WAPAGHKONETTA RESERVATION (SHAWNEE VILLAGE IN OHIO, 1795–1831). See also OHIO; SHAWNEES. *Priv. St.* 6:639.

WARM SPRINGS. See also OREGON; CONFEDERATED TRIBES OF THE WARM SPRINGS RESERVATION; PAIUTE; MIDDLE OREGON. *Gov. Pub.* 64 Cong., 1 sess., S. Rep. 702. *Spec. St.* 28:86. *Approp. St.* 26:336; 35:70; 37:518, 595; 38:582; 39:123, 801, 969; 41:3, 408, 1225; 42:1174; 43:390, 704, 1141, 1313; 44:934; 45:1562; 46:279, 1115; 49:1757; 52:291. *Priv. St.* 35:1404. *Cases* U. S. v. Earl, 17 Fed. 75; U. S. v. Osborne, 2 Fed. 58. *I. D. Rulings* Memo. of Counsel, Ind. Off., Dec. 4, 1931; Memo. Sol. Off., Jan. 23, 1932, Feb. 15, 1932. *Const.* Feb. 14, 1938. *Charter* Mar. 31, 1938.

WASHINGTON. See also CHEHALIS RESERVATION; CHINOOK; CHO-BAH-AH-BISH; CLALLAM; COLUMBIA; COLVILLE; COWLITZ; D'WAMISH; GREEN RIVER; HOH; HUMPTULIPS; KALISPEL; KALISPEL INDIAN COMMUNITY OF THE KALISPEL RESERVATION; KIKIALLUS; LUMMI; MAKAH TRIBE OF THE MAKAH INDIAN RESERVATION; MUCKLESHOOT INDIAN TRIBE OF THE MUCKLESHOOT RESERVATION; NEAH BAY; NISQUALLY RESERVATION; NOOKSACK; OAKINAKANE; OKANAGAN; OZETTE RESERVATION; PORT GAMBLE INDIAN COMMUNITY; PORT MADISON RESERVATION; PUGET SOUND; PUYALLUP TRIBE; QUILEHUTE TRIBE; QUINAIELT AND QUILLEHUTE; SAMISH; SHOALWATER OR GEORGETOWN RESERVATION; SKAGIT; S'KLALLAM; SKOKOMISH INDIAN TRIBE OF THE SKOKOMISH INDIAN RESERVATION; SNOHOMISH; SNOQUALMIE; SPOKANE RESERVATION; SQUAXIN ISLAND RESERVATION; SQUAXON; STELLAQUAMISH; SUATTLE; SUQUAMISH; SWINOMISH TRIBAL COMMUNITY; TAHOLAH; TULALIP TRIBE; WALLA WALLA; WENATCHEE; WENATSHAPAMA; WHITLEY ISLAND; WILLAPAH; YAKIMA. *Approp. St.* 10:315; 11:169, 329, 388; 12:221; 15:198; 16:13, 544; 17:165, 437; 18:146, 420; 19:176, 271; 20:63, 295; 21:114, 485; 22:433; 28:876. *Priv. St.* 35:1204, 1219, 1375, 1389, 1406, 1431, 1446, 1573, 1606; 36:1751, 1752, 1753, 1760, 1762, 1806, 1807, 1815, 1816, 1843, 1859, 1984, 2000, 2099; 37:1030; 38:1337; 39:1588; 40:1484, 1486, 1489, 1536; 41:1596; 42:1718. *Treaties* 12:927, 933, 957, 975.

WASHOE TRIBE. See also NEVADA; CALIFORNIA. *Const.* Jan. 24, 1936. *Charter* Feb. 27, 1937.

WEA (MIAMI-PEORIA). See also ILLINOIS; INDIANA; KANSAS; CONFEDERATED PEORIA; KASKASKIAS; PEORIAS; PIANKESHAWS; QUAPAWS. *Texts* Hilliard, LT; Manypenny, OIW. *Per.* Canfield, 15 Am. L. Rev. 21. *Spec. St.* 3:308, 319, 783; 4:594; 10:704; 12:539; 17:631; 28:580. *Approp. St.* 1:460; 2:607; 3:517; 4:526, 616, 636, 682, 780; 5:36, 158, 298, 323, 402, 417, 493, 704, 766; 9:20, 252, 382, 544, 574; 10:41, 226, 315, 576; 12:774; 13:161; 17:122; 21:435; 25:505, 565; 26:989; 28:424. *Treaties* 7:49, 74, 91, 116, 145, 186, 209; 8:116; 10:1082; 15:513. *Cases* Bowling v. U. S. 233 U. S. 528; Citizen v. U. S., 26 C. Cls. 323 Kansas, 5 Wall. 737; Okla. K. & M., 249 Fed. 592; Richardville, 28 Fed. 52; U. S. v. Bowling, 256 U. S. 484; U. S. v. Brindle, 110 U. S. 688; U. S. v. Rundell, 181 Fed. 887. *Op. A. G.* 6:658; 10:253; 19:115.

WEEMINUCHE (WIMINUCHE UTES). See also TABEGUACHE, MUACHE, CAPOTE, WEEMINUCHE, YAMPA, GRAND RIVER AND UINTAH BANDS OF UTES. *Spec. St.* 28:677. *Treaties* 15:619.

WENATSHAPAMA. See also COLVILLE; WASHINGTON; WENATCHEE. *Approp. St.* 23:286.

WENATCHEE. See also WENATSHAPAMA; COLVILLE; WASHINGTON. *Approp. St.* 33:189.

WHITE EARTH RESERVATION. See also MINNESOTA; CHIPPEWA. *Spec. St.* 25:647, 606, 1010; 28:112; 33:539; 35:1620; 36:330; 46:785. *Approp. St.* 17:165; 19:271; 20:63, 295; 21:114, 485; 22:433; 23:362; 24:449; 25:980; 26:336, 989; 27:612; 28:286, 876; 30:62, 571, 924; 32:982; 34:1015; 36:269; 37:518; 38:77; 40:561. *Priv. St.* 38:1308. *Cases* Chippewa, 301 U. S. 358; Fairbanks, 223 U. S. 215; Gravelle, 253 Fed. 549; U. S. v. Park Land Co., 188 Fed. 383; U. S. v. Stone, 19 Fed. 807. *L. D. Memo. (D. J.)* 5:492. *I. D. Rulings* Sol. Letter, July 19, 1934.

WHITE MOUNTAIN, NATIVE VILLAGE OF. See also ALASKA; ESKIMO. *Const.* Nov. 25, 1939. *Charter* Nov. 25, 1939.

WHITE MOUNTAIN APACHE TRIBE. See also ARIZONA; APACHE; FORT APACHE. *Spec. St.* 31:952; 45:1344. *Approp. St.* 23:76. *Cases* U. S. v. Tadish, 211 Fed. 490; U. S. v. Wightman, 230 Fed. 277. *Const.* Aug. 26, 1938.

WHITE OAK POINT. See MINNESOTA; CHIPPEWA.

WHITE RIVER INDIANS. See also UTAH; COLORADO INDIANS; UINTAH; UTAH INDIANS IN TERRITORY OF NEW MEXICO; UTE. *Approp. St.* 23:76; 47:15; 48:1021. *Cases* Dwamish Inds. v. U. S., 79 C. Cls. 530.

WHITLEY (WHIDBY) ISLAND. See also WASHINGTON; DWAMISH. *Cases* Dwamish Inds. v. U. S., 79 C. Cls. 530.

WICHITA. See also CADDO; WICHITA AND OTHER AFFILIATED BANDS; TEXAS; TAH-WAH-CARRO. *Spec. St.* 22:7, 47; 29:529; 32:63; 43:366; 47:74, 87; 48:501. *Approp. St.* 11:169; 12:44, 221, 512, 774; 13:161; 15:198; 16:13, 544; 20:410; 21:67, 414; 22:68; 26:504; 28:876; 30:105, 652; 31:1010; 32:245; 33:180; 34:325; 36:269; 38:77, 582; 39:123, 969; 40:561; 41:3, 408, 1225; 42:552, 1174; 43:390, 704, 1141, 1313; 45:1623; 48:984; 49:1597. *Treaties* 7:474, 533, 844; 11:611. *Cases* Board, 87 F. 2d 55; Campbell, 44 C. Cls. 488; Johnson, 283 Fed. 954; U. S. v. Choctaw Nation, 179 U. S. 494; U. S. v. Loving, 34 Fed. 715; U. S. ex rel. West, 205 U. S. 80. *L. D. Memo. (D. J.)* 4:641.

WICHITAS AND OTHER AFFILIATED BANDS. See also OKLAHOMA; TEXAS; APACHE, ARAPAHOE, CHEYENNE, KIOWA, COMANCHE, WICHITA; ARAPAHOE, CHEYENNE, KIOWA, COMANCHE, WICHITA; KIOWA; KIOWA, APACHE, COMANCHE, WICHITA. *Spec. St.* 31:1093. *Approp. St.* 12:512, 774; 13:161, 541; 14:255, 492; 15:198; 16:335, 544; 17:165, 437; 18:133, 146, 420; 19:176, 271; 20:63, 295; 21:114; 41:485.

WILD INDIANS OF THE PRAIRIE. See also COLORADO; KANSAS; MONTANA; NEBRASKA; OKLAHOMA; TEXAS. *Approp. St.* 9:20, 40, 570.

WILD RICE LAKE INDIAN RESERVATION (CHIPPEWA). See also MINNESOTA; CHIPPEWA. *Spec. St.* 49:496.

WILLAMETTE VALLEY INDIANS. See also OREGON; GRAND RONDE. *Treaties* 10:1143.

WILLAPAH. See also WASHINGTON; GEORGETOWN;

SHOALWATER OR GEORGETOWN. *Cases* U. S. ex rel. Charley, 62 F. 2d 955.

WIND RIVER RESERVATION. See also WYOMING; ARAPAHOE; ARAPAHOE AND SHOSHONE; SHOSHONE; SHOSHONE (WIND RIVER) RESERVATION; SHOSHONE AND ARAPAHOE. *Spec. St.* 34:849; 37:91; 39:341, 519; 46:430. *Approp. St.* 25:217; 34:325; 35:70; 36:269; 42:192; 43:33; 45:200; 46:1064. *Priv. St.* 39:1301; 42:1591. *Cases* Wadsworth, 148 Fed. 771. *Op. A. G.* 25:524; 33:25. *I. D. Rulings* 49 L. D. 370, Dec. 15, 1922.

WINNEBAGO TRIBE OF NEBRASKA. See also NEBRASKA; WISCONSIN; OMAHA; CHIPPEWAS; FOX; MENOMINEE; POTAWATOMIE; SAC; WINNEBAGO AND POTAWATOMIE. *Texts* Manypenny, OIW. *Per.* Gates, 21 Am. J. Soc. Sci. 112; James, 12 J. H. Univ. Studies 467. *Spec. St.* 4:302, 445, 464, 729; 9:55, 439, 570; 11:122; 12:628, 658; 21:315; 25:240; 26:659; 28:95, 679; 30:344, 912; 32:183; 36:873, 877; 37:187; 38:1188; 39:865; 43:138, 1114; 45:1027. *Approp. St.* 4:352, 361, 390, 394, 403, 505, 532, 526, 616, 636, 682, 705, 780; 5:36, 73, 158, 298, 323, 402, 417, 493, 704, 766; 9:20, 132, 252, 382, 544, 574; 10:15, 41, 150, 226, 306, 315, 643, 686; 11:65, 169, 273, 329, 388, 450; 12:44, 221, 512, 774; 13:161, 541; 14:255, 492; 15:198; 16:13, 335, 544; 17:165, 437; 18:27, 146, 420; 19:176, 271; 20:63, 195; 21:114, 485; 22:68, 433, 603; 23:76, 362; 24:449, 25:217, 980; 26:336, 989; 27:5, 120, 612; 28:286, 876; 29:321; 30:62, 105, 571, 924; 31:221, 1058; 32:245, 982; 33:189, 1048; 34:325, 1015; 35:70, 781; 36:118, 269; 39:123; 41:3, 408, 1225; 42:327, 552; 43:390; 44:453. *Priv. St.* 6:790, 792; 11:536; 12:873, 883; 28:1013. *Treaties* 7:144, 272, 303, 315, 323, 342, 370, 544, 550, 591; 9:878, 952, 955; 10:1172; 12:1101; 14:667, 671. *Cases* Beck, 65 Fed. 30; Chase, 238 Fed. 887; Clay, 282 Fed. 268; Elk, 112 U. S. 94; In re Lincoln, 202 U. S. 178; King, 111 Fed. 860; Lane, 241 U. S. 201; Larkin, 276 U. S. 431; Lemmon, 106 Fed. 650; McClure, 19 C. Cls. 193; Mickadiet, 258 U. S. 609; N. Y., 170 U. S. 1; Pilgrim, 69 Fed. 895; Rainbow, 161 Fed. 835; Schwesau, 31 C. Cls. 192; U. S. v. Ashford, 99 F. 2d 946; U. S. v. Corp., 101 F. 2d 156; U S. v Flournoy, 69 Fed. 886; U. S. v. Flournoy, 71 Fed. 576; U. S v Hemmer, 241 U. S. 379; U. S. v. Holliday, 3 Wall. 407; U. S. v. Mullin, 71 Fed 682; U. S. v. Saunders, 96 Fed. 268 *Op. A. G.* 3:471, 584; 18:141; 19:161. *L. D. Memo (D. J.)* 2:368. *I. D. Rulings* 3 L. D. 580, June 4, 1885; 27 L. D. 399, Sept. 14, 1898; Memo. Sol., Apr. 14, 1938, Mar. 11, 1939.

WINNEBAGO AND POTAWATOMIE. See also POTAWATOMIE; WINNEBAGO; WISCONSIN; NEBRASKA. *Approp. St.* 13:541; 14:255; 17:165.

WINNEBAGOSHISH (CHIPPEWA). See also MINNESOTA; CHIPPEWA. *Spec. St.* 28:489.

WINNEMUCCA INDIAN COLONY. See also NEVADA; PAIUTE; SHOSHONE. *Spec. St.* 45:618.

WISCONSIN. See also MICHIGAN; MINNESOTA; BAD RIVER BAND OF CHIPPEWA INDIANS; BROTHERTOWN RESERVATION; CHIPPEWA; FLAMBEAU; FOREST COUNTY POTAWATOMIE COMMUNITY, WISCONSIN; LA POINTE; LAC COURT D'OREILLE RESERVATION; LAC DU FLAMBEAU BAND OF LAKE SUPERIOR CHIPPEWA INDIANS; MENOMINEE; MOLE LAKE; MUNSEE; MUNSEE AND DELAWARE; ONEIDA TRIBE OF INDIANS; RED CLIFF BAND OF LAKE SUPERIOR CHIPPEWA INDIANS; SOKAOGON CHIPPEWA COMMUNITY; STOCKBRIDGE AND MUNSEE; ST. CROIX WINNEBAGO. *Approp. St.* 11:65, 388; 17:165, 437; 18:146, 420; 19:176, 271; 20:63, 295; 21:114, 485.

WYANDOTTE. See also KANSAS; OKLAHOMA; DELAWARE; QUAPAW; MUNSEE; WYANDOTTE, MUNSEE AND DELEWARE; WYANDOTTE TRIBE OF OKLAHOMA. *Texts* Manypenny, OIW. *Spec. St.* 2:527; 3:308, 319; 4:75; 5:624; 9:337, 570; 10:15; 14:309; 21:511; 33:519; 37:668; 48:501, 1184; 49:894. *Approp. St.* 1:460; 2:407, 467; 4:526, 528, 532, 616, 677, 682, 780; 5:36, 158, 298, 323, 402, 417, 453, 493, 576, 704, 766; 9:20, 132, 252, 382, 544, 574; 10:41, 226, 315, 643, 686; 11:65, 169; 16:13; 17:122, 165; 21:414; 26:286, 989; 28:876; 29:321; 30:62; 34:325; 39:844; 41:3; 48:984; 49:176. *Priv. St.* 6:936; 9:674, 675, 708; 10:831; 30:1573; 44:1609; 47:1692. *Treaties* Archives No. 44; 7:16, 28, 49, 77, 105, 112, 118, 131, 160, 178, 326, 355, 364, 502; 8:116; 9:987; 10:1159; 11:581; 12:1129; 15:513. *Cases* Conley, 216 U. S. 84; Elk, 112 U. S. 94; Hicks, 12 Fed. Cas. No. 6458; Gray, 10 Fed. Cas. No. 5714; Karraho, 14 Fed. Cas. No. 7614; Schrimpscher, 183 U. S. 290; Staley, 36 F. 2d 91; U. S. v. Cisna, 25 Fed. Cas. No. 14795; U. S. v. Osborn, 2 Fed. 58. *Op. A. G.* 3:458; 6:2; 9:45; 11:197.

WYANDOTTE TRIBE OF OKLAHOMA. See also OKLAHOMA; WYANDOTTE. *Const.* July 24, 1937. *Charter* Oct. 30, 1937.

WYANDOTTE, MUNSEE AND DELEWARE. See also MUNSEE AND DELAWARE. *Approp. St.* 4:616, 682, 780; 5:36, 158, 298, 323, 402, 417, 493.

WYOMING. See also ARAPAHOE; SHOSHONES, BANNOCKS AND OTHER BANDS IN IDAHO AND SOUTHEASTERN OREGON; SHOSHONE; WIND RIVER. *Approp. St.* 17:165, 437; 18:146, 420; 19:176, 271; 20:63, 295; 21:114, 485.

YAGA CREEK (YAGER CREEK). See also CALIFORNIA; HOOPA (HUPA) VALLEY. *Cases* Painter, 33 C. Cls. 114.

YAHOOSKIN (YAHUSKIN). See also OREGON; KLAMATH, MODOC AND YAHOOSKIN; SNAKE. *Cases* Oregon, 202 U. S. 60.

YAKIMA. See also WASHINGTON. *Per.* Dixon, 23 Case & Com. 712; Gates, 21 Am. J. Soc. Sci. 112. *Gov. Pub.* 76 Cong., 1 sess., Hearings, S. Comm. Ind. Aff., S. 773; 76 Cong., 1 sess., H. Rep. 749. *Spec. St.* 26:661; 28:118; 33:595; 34:53; 35:49; 36:348; 42:595; 44:768; 49:330; 50:210; 52:80. *Approp. St.* 12:4, 44, 221, 512, 774; 13:161, 541; 14:255, 492; 15:198; 16:13, 335, 544; 17:165, 437; 18:146, 420; 19:176, 271; 20:63, 195; 21:114, 485; 22:68, 257, 433; 23:76, 362; 24:449; 25:217, 980; 26:336, 989; 27:120, 612; 28:286, 876; 29:321; 30:62, 105, 571, 924; 31:221, 280, 1058; 32:245, 982; 33:1048; 34:205, 325, 1015; 35:70, 478, 781; 36:202, 269; 37:518, 595; 38:77, 582; 39:14, 123, 801, 969; 40:105, 561; 41:3, 163, 408, 874, 1015, 1156, 1225, 1367; 42:29, 552, 1154, 1174, 1527; 43:390, 704, 1141, 1313; 44:161, 453, 934, 1250; 45:200, 1562; 46:279, 860, 1115; 47:91, 820, 1602; 48:362; 49:176, 1757; 50:564; 52:291. *Priv. St.* 35:1406. *Treaties* 12:951. *Cases* La Clair, 184 Fed. 128; Mitchell, 22 F. 2d 771; National, 147 Fed. 87; Northern, 227 U. S. 355; Seufert, 249 U. S. 194; Seufert, 193 Fed. 200; U. S. v. Brookfield, 24 F. Supp. 712; U. S. v. Dooley, 151 Fed. 697; U. S. v. First, 282 Fed. 330; U. S. v. Hadley, 99 Fed. 437; U. S. v. Hoyt, 167 Fed. 301; U. S. v. Inaba, 291 Fed. 416; U. S. v. Seufert, 252 Fed. 51; U. S. v. Sulton, 215 U. S. 291; U. S. v. Winans, 198 U. S. 371; U. S. v. Yakima, 274 Fed. 115; Yohowan, 291 Fed. 425. *L. D. Memo (D. J.)* 13:472, 481, 492. *I. D. Rulings* Letter of Comm'r to Sen. Seldon P. Spencer, Sept. 5, 1922; Op. Sol., June 7, 1929, May 23, 1930; Memo. Ind. Off., June 12, 1933; Op., Sol. Apr. 5, 1934; Memo. Sol., June 15, 1937, Oct. 7, 1938.

YAMPA (UTE). See also UTAH; TABEGUACHE, MUACHE, CAPOTE, WEEMINUCHE, YAMPA, GRAND RIVER AND UINTAH BANDS OF UTES; UINTAH; UTE. *Treaties* 15:619.

YANCTON (YANKTON SIOUX). See also OMAHA; PAWNEE; ROSEBUD; SIOUX; YANCTON SANTEE; YANCTONAIS. *Spec. St.* 47:300. *Approp. St.* 5:158; 30:62; 32:982; 35:781; 42:552. *Priv. St.* 34:1768.

YANCTON AND SANTEE. See also YANCTON; SANTEE-SIOUX; SIOUX. *Approp. St.* 4:616, 682, 780; 5:36, 158, 298, 402, 417, 493, 704, 766; 9:20, 132, 252.

YANCTONAIS (YANKTONAI). See also YANCTON; SIOUX. *Spec. St.* 19:254.

YAVAPAI. See also ARIZONA; TRUXTON CANYON. *Spec. St.* 49:332. *Cases* Luke, 35 C. Cls. 15.

YAVAPAI-APACHE INDIAN COMMUNITY. See ARIZONA; TRUXTON CANYON. *Const.* Feb. 12, 1937.

YERINGTON PAIUTE TRIBE OF THE STATE OF NEVADA. See also NEVADA; PAIUTE. *Const.* Jan. 4, 1937. *Charter* Apr. 10, 1937.

YOMBA SHOSHONE TRIBE. See also NEVADA; SHOSHONE. *Const.* Dec. 20, 1939. *Charter* Dec. 23, 1939.

YUMA. See also ARIZONA; CALIFORNIA; APACHE; FORT YUMA; QUECHAN. *Spec. St.* 26:764; 27:420, 456; 36:829, 879; 44:776; 45:1321. *Approp. St.* 28:286; 33:189; 35:70; 37:518; 38:77, 582; 39:123, 969; 40:561; 41:408, 1225; 42:552, 1174; 43:390, 1141; 44:453, 934; 45:200, 1562; 47:820; 48:362; 49:176, 1757; 50:564; 52:291. *Cases* Jaeger, 27 C. Cls. 278; Jaeger, 29 C. Cls. 172; Jaeger, 33 C. Cls. 214; Luke, 35 C. Cls. 15. *I. D. Rulings* Op. Sol., Nov. 25, 1932; Memo. by Imperial Irrigation District Attorney, Oct. 11, 1935; Op. Sol., Jan. 8, 1936.

ZIA PUEBLO. See NEW MEXICO; PUEBLO.

ZUNI. See also NEW MEXICO; PUEBLO. *Spec. St.* 45:501; 49:393. *Approp. St.* 22:68; 35:781; 41:408, 1225; 42:552, 1174; 43:1141; 44:453, 934; 45:200, 883, 1562; 46:1115; 47:91, 525, 820; 48:362; 49:176. *Priv. St.* 48:1465.

ANNOTATED TABLE OF STATUTES AND TREATIES

1 STAT.

1 St. 49; Aug. 7, 1789; C. 7—An Act to establish an Executive Department, to be denominated the Department of War.[1] Sec. 1—R. S. 161, 214, 216; Sec. 2—R. S. 217; Sec. 4—R. S. 217.

1 St. 50; Aug. 7, 1789; C. 8—An Act to provide for the Government of the Territory Northwest of the river Ohio.[2]

1 St. 54; Aug. 20, 1789; C. 10—An Act providing for the Expenses which may attend Negotiations or Treaties with the Indian Tribes, and the appointment of Commissioners for managing the same.[3]

1 St. 67; Sept. 11, 1789; C. 13—An Act for establishing the Salaries of the Executive Officers of Government, with their Assistants and Clerks.

1 St. 95; Sept. 29, 1789; C. 25—An Act to recognize and adapt to the Constitution of the United States the establishment of the Troops raised under the Resolves of the United States in Congress assembled, and for other purposes therein mentioned.

1 St. 101; Mar. 1, 1790; C. 2—An Act providing for the enumeration of the Inhabitants of the United States.

1 St. 106; Apr. 2, 1790; C. 6—An Act to accept a cession of the claims of the state of North Carolina to a certain district of Western territory.[4]

1 St. 112; Apr. 30, 1790; C. 9—An Act for the Punishment of certain crimes against the United States.[5] Sec. 3—R.S. 5339, Sec. 6—R. S. 5390; Sec. 7—R. S. 5341, 5343; Sec. 13—R. S. 5348; Sec. 16—R. S. 5356; Sec. 17—R. S. 5357.

1 St. 123; May 26, 1790; C. 14—An Act for the Government of the Territory of the United States, south of the river Ohio.[6]

1 St. 136; July 22, 1790; C. 31—An Act providing for holding a Treaty or Treaties to establish Peace with certain Indian tribes.[7]

1 St. 137; July 22, 1790; C. 33—An Act to regulate trade and intercourse with the Indian tribes.[8]

1 St. 190; Feb. 11, 1791; C. 6—An Act making Appropriations for the support of Government during the year 1791, and for other purposes.

1 St. 225; Mar. 3, 1791, J. Res. IV.[9]

1 St. 226; Dec. 23, 1791; C. 3—An Act making Appropriations for the Support of Government for the year 1792.

1 St. 241; Mar. 5, 1792; C. 9—An Act for making further and more effectual Provision for the Protection of the Frontiers of the United States.[10]

1 St. 264; May 2, 1792; C. 28—An Act to provide for calling forth the Militia to execute the laws of the Union, suppress insurrections and repel invasions.[11]

1 St. 279; May 18, 1792; C. 37—An Act making alterations in the Treasury and War Departments.

1 St. 325; Feb. 28, 1793; C. 18—An Act making Appropriations for the support of Government for the year 1793.

1 St. 329; Mar. 1, 1793; C. 19—An Act to regulate Trade and Intercourse with the Indian Tribes.[12]

1 St. 333; Mar. 2, 1793; C. 21—An Act making an Appropriation to defray the expense of a Treaty with the Indians northwest of the Ohio.[13]

1 St. 346; Mar. 21, 1794; C. 10—An Act making Appropriations for the support of the Military establishment of the United States, for the year 1794.

1 St. 419; Feb. 23, 1795; C. 27—An Act to establish the Office of Purveyor of Public Supplies.

1 St. 424; Feb. 28, 1795; C. 36—An Act to provide for calling forth the Militia to execute the laws of the Union, suppress insurrections, and repel invasions; and to repeal the Act now in force for those purposes.[14] Sec. 1—R. S. 1642, 1654, 5297.

1 St. 430; Mar. 3, 1795; C. 44—An Act for continuing and regulating the military establishment of the United States, and for repealing sundry acts heretofore passed on that subject.[15]

1 St. 438; Mar. 3, 1795; C. 46—An Act making further Appropriations for the Military and Naval establishments and for the support of Government.

1 St. 443; Mar. 3, 1795; C. 51—An Act making provision for the purposes of Trade with the Indians.

1 St. 452; Apr. 18, 1796; C. 13—An Act for establishing Trading Houses with the Indian Tribes.[16]

1 St. 460; May 6, 1796; C. 20—An Act making Appropriations for defraying the Expenses which may arise in carrying into effect a Treaty made between the United States and certain Indian Tribes, northwest of the river Ohio.[17]

1 St. 464; May 18, 1796; C. 29—An Act providing for the Sale of the Lands of the United States, in the territory northwest of the river Ohio, and above the mouth of the Kentucky river.[18] Sec. 1—R. S. 2228; sec. 2—R. S. 2395.

1 St. 469; May 19, 1796; C. 30—An Act to regulate Trade and Intercourse with the Indian Tribes, and to preserve Peace on the Frontiers.[19]

1 St. 490; June 1, 1796; C. 46—An Act regulating the grants of land appropriated for Military services, and for the Society of the United Brethren, for propagating the Gospel among the Heathen.[20]

1 St. 493; June 1, 1796; C. 51—An Act making Appropriations for the support of the Military and Naval Establishments for the year 1796.

1 St. 498; Mar. 3, 1797; C. 8—An Act making Appropriations for the support of Government, for the year 1797.[21]

1 St. 508; Mar. 3, 1797; C. 17—An Act making Appropriations for the Military and Naval establishments for the year 1797.

1 St. 527; July 5, 1797; C. 10—An Act to continue in force to the end of the next session, certain acts, and parts of acts, of limited duration.

1 St. 536; Jan. 15, 1798; C. 2—An Act making certain partial appropriations for the year 1798.

1 St. 539; Feb. 27, 1798; C. 14—An Act appropriating a certain sum of money to defray the expense of holding a Treaty or Treaties with the Indians.

---

1 *Cited*: Memo. Sol. Feb. 28, 1935.

2 *Sg.* N. W. Ord. 1787, U. S. C. (1934 ed.) p. XXIII. *S.* 1 St. 123; 2 St. 309; 2 St. 514. *Cited*: In re Sah Quah, 31 Fed. 327; U. S. v. Douglas, 190 Fed. 482; Waw-Pe-Man-Qua, 28 Fed. 489.

3 *S.* 1 St. 136. *Cited*: Leighton, 29 C. Cls. 288.

4 *Sg.* N. W. Ord. 1787, U. S. C. (1934 ed.) p. XXIII. S. 1 St. 123.

5 S. 3 St. 654. *Cited*: Anonymous, 1 Fed. Cas. No. 447.

6 *Sg.* N. W. Ord. 1787, U. S. C. (1934 ed.) p. XXIII; 1 St. 50; 1 St. 106.

7 *Sg.* 1 St. 54. *Cited*: Leighton, 29 C. Cls. 288.

8 *R.* 1 St. 329, 469. *S.* 9 St. 984; 10 St. 974, 1165, 1172; 11 St. 699, 743; 12 St. 957, 963, 997, 1031, 1037, 1101, 1105, 1163; 14 St. 647, 667, 769, 799; 15 St. 467; 19 St. 102; 22 St. 131, 302, 603; 23 St. 69, 73, 194, 478; 24 St. 78, 117, 124, 222, 419, 446, 509; 25 St. 35, 162, 205, 350, 452, 505, 647, 684, 745, 939; 26 St. 102, 170, 184, 371, 485, 632, 765, 783, 844; 27 St. 2, 83, 336, 465, 487, 492, 524, 747; 28 St. 22, 27, 86, 229, 372, 505; 29 St. 13; 30 St. 241, 327, 341, 345, 347, 806, 816, 844, 914, 1368, 31 St. 588; 33 St. 66, 567; 35 St. 184. *Cited*: 18 Op. A. G. 235; Jaeger, 27 C. Cls. 278; Jones, 175 U. S. 1; Price, 33 C. Cls. 106; U. S. v. Bichard, 1 Ariz. 81; U. S. v. Douglas, 190 Fed. 482; U. S. v. Hunter, 21 Fed. 615; U. S. v. Leathers, 26 Fed. Cas. No. 15581; U. S. v. McGowan, 302 U. S. 535, rev'g 89 F. 2d 201.

9 *S.* 7 St. 78.

10 *R.* 1 St. 430.

11 *R.* 1 St. 424.

12 *Rg.* 1 St. 137. *Rp.* 1 St. 469. *S.* 1 St. 743. *Cited*: 18 Op. A. G. 235; Chinn, 5 Fed. Cas. No. 2684; Jones, 175 U. S. 1; Leighton, 29 C. Cls. 288; Price, 33 C. Cls. 106; U. S. v. Bichard, 1 Ariz. 81.

13 *S.* 1 St. 498.

14 *Rg.* 1 St. 264.

15 *Rg.* 1 St. 119, 222, 241.

16 *S.* 2 St. 173, 207, 283; 3 St. 654. *Cited*: U. S. v. Douglas, 190 Fed. 482; U. S. v. Hutto, No. 1, 256 U. S. 524; U. S. v. Hutto, No. 2, 256 U. S. 530; 6 Cong., 1 sess., Ex. Doc., Apr. 22, 1800.

17 *Sg.* 7 St. 47, Art. 4.

18 *Sg.* 28 Jour. Cont. Cong. 375. *S.* 1 St. 490; 2 St. 179, 277. *Cited*: Reynolds, 2 Pet. 417.

19 *Rg.* 1 St. 137, 329. *S.* 2 St. 39. *Cited*: 1 Op. A. G. 65; Reynolds, 2 Pet. 417.

20 *Sg.* N. W. Ord. 1787, U. S. C. (1934 ed.) p. XXIII; 1 St. 464. *A.* 1 St. 724. *S.* 3 St. 749.

21 *Sg.* 1 St. 333.

1 St. 549; Apr. 7, 1798; C. 28—An Act for an amicable settlement of limits with the state of Georgia, and authorizing the establishment of a government in the Mississippi territory.[22]

1 St. 563; June 12, 1798; C. 52—An Act making appropriations for the Military establishment, for the year 1798; and for other purposes.[23]

1 St. 618; Feb. 19, 1799; C. 9—An Act appropriating a certain sum of money to defray the expense of holding a Treaty or Treaties with the Indians.

1 St. 618; Feb. 25, 1799; C. 11—An Act making appropriations for defraying the expenses which may arise, in carrying into effect certain Treaties between the United States and several tribes or nations of Indians.[24]

1 St. 627; Mar. 2, 1799; C. 22—An Act to regulate the collection of duties on imports and tonnage.[25]

1 St. 717; Mar. 2, 1799; C. 25—An Act making appropriations for the support of Government for the year 1799.

1 St. 724; Mar. 2, 1799; C. 29—An Act to amend the act intituled "An Act regulating the grants of land appropriated for military services, and for the Society of the United Brethren, for propagating the Gospel among the Heathen."[26]

1 St. 741; Mar. 2, 1799; C. 44—An Act making appropriations for the support of the Military Establishment, for the year 1799.

1 St. 743; Mar. 3, 1799; C. 46—An Act to regulate trade and intercourse with the Indian tribes, and to preserve peace on the frontiers.[27]

2 STAT.

2 St. 6; Jan. 17, 1800; C. 5—An Act for the preservation of peace with the Indian tribes.[28]

2 St. 11; Feb. 28, 1800; C. 12—An Act providing for the Second Census or enumeration of the Inhabitants of the United States.

2 St. 39; Apr. 22, 1800; C. 30—An Act supplementary to the Act to regulate trade and intercourse with the Indian Tribes, and to preserve peace on the Frontiers.[29]

2 St. 58; May 7, 1800; C. 41—An Act to divide the territory of the United States northwest of the Ohio, into two separate governments.[30]

2 St. 66; May 10, 1800; C. 48—An Act making appropriations for the Military Establishment of the United States, in the year 1800.

2 St. 82; May 13, 1800; C. 62—An Act to appropriate a certain sum of money to defray the expense of holding a treaty or treaties with the Indians.[31]

2 St. 82; May 13, 1800; C. 63—An Act directing the payment of a detachment of the militia under the command of Major Thomas Johnson, in the year 1794.[32]

2 St. 83; May 13, 1800; C. 65—An Act to authorize certain expenditures, and to make certain appropriations for the year 1800.

2 St. 85; May 13, 1800; C. 68—An Act to make provision relative to rations for Indians, and to their visits to the seat of Government.[33]

2 St. 87; Apr. 16, 1800; J. Res. V. respecting the Copper Mines on the south side of Lake Superior.

2 St. 108; Mar. 2, 1801; C. 18—An Act making appropriations for the Military establishment of the United States, for the year 1801.

2 St. 139; Mar. 30, 1802; C. 13—An Act to regulate trade and intercourse with the Indian tribes, and to preserve peace on the frontiers.[34]

2 St. 173; Apr. 30, 1802; C. 39—An Act to revive and continue in force, an act intituled "An Act for establishing trading houses with the Indian tribes."[35]

2 St. 173; Apr. 30, 1802; C. 40—An Act to enable the people of the Eastern division of the territory northwest of the river Ohio to form a constitution and state government, and for the admission of such state into the Union, on an equal footing with the original States, and for other purposes.[36]

2 St. 179; May 1, 1802; C. 44—An Act to extend and continue in force the provisions of an act entituled "An act giving a right of pre-emption to certain persons who have contracted with John Cleves Symmes or his associates, for lands lying between the Miami rivers, in the territory northwest of the Ohio, and for other purposes."[37]

2 St. 183; May 1, 1802; C. 46—An Act making appropriations for the Military Establishment of the United States in the year 1802.[38]

2 St. 189; May 3, 1802; C. 48—An Act further to alter and establish certain Post Roads; and for the more secure carriage of the Mail of the United States.

2 St. 207; Feb. 28, 1803; C. 14—An Act for continuing in force a law, entituled "An act for establishing trading houses with the Indian tribes."[39]

2 St. 210; Mar. 2, 1803; C. 19—An Act making appropriations for the support of Government for the year 1803.

2 St. 225; Mar. 3, 1803; C. 21—An Act in addition to, and in modification of, the propositions contained in the act entituled "An act to enable the people of the Eastern division of the territory northwest of the river Ohio, to form a Constitution and state government, and for the admission of such state into the Union, on an equal footing with the original States, and for other purposes."[40]

2 St. 227; Mar. 3, 1803; C. 24—An Act making appropriations for the Military establishment of the United States, in the year 1803.

2 St. 229; Mar. 3, 1803; C. 27—An Act regulating the grants of land, and providing for the disposal of the lands of the United States, south of the state of Tennessee.[41]

2 St. 235; Mar. 3, 1803; C. 28—An Act concerning the Salt Springs on the waters of the Wabash river.

2 St. 245; Oct. 31, 1803; C. 1—An Act to enable the President of the United States to take possession of the territories ceded by France to the United States, by the treaty concluded at Paris, on the thirtieth of April last; and for the temporary government thereof.[42]

2 St. 249; Feb. 10, 1804; C. 11—An Act making appropriations for the support of the Military establishment of the United States, in the year 1804.

2 St. 264; Mar. 14, 1804; C. 21—An Act making appropriations for the support of government, for the year 1804.[43]

2 St. 274; Mar. 23, 1804; C. 33—An Act to ascertain the boundary of the lands reserved by the state of Virginia, northwest of the river Ohio, for the satisfaction of her officers and soldiers on continental establishment, and to limit the period for locating the said lands.[44]

2 St. 277; Mar. 26, 1804; C. 35—An Act making provision for the disposal of the public lands in the Indiana territory, and for other purposes.[45]

---

[22] *Sg.* N. W. Ord. 1787, U. S. C. (1934 ed.) p. XXIII.

[23] *Sg.* 7 St. 47.

[24] *Sg.* 7 St. 24, 35, 44, 56, 62. *S.* 4 St. 780; 5 St. 36, 704, 766; 9 St. 20, 132, 252, 382, 544, 574; 10 St. 41, 226, 315, 686; 11 St. 65, 273, 388; 12 St. 44, 160, 221, 512, 774; 13 St. 161, 511; 14 St. 255, 492, 769; 16 St. 13; 24 St. 29, 449; 25 St. 217, 980; 26 St. 336, 989; 27 St. 612; 28 St. 286, 876; 29 St. 321; 30 St. 571; 31 St. 221, 1058.

[25] *Cited:* 18 Op. A. G. 544.

[26] *Ag.* 1 St. 490.

[27] *Sg.* 1 St. 329. *S.* 2 St. 6, 39. *Cited:* 18 Op. A. G. 235; Johnson, 29 C. Cls. 1; Leighton, 29 C. Cls. 288; Marks, 161 U. S. 297; Pino, 38 C. Cls. 64; Price, 33 C. Cls. 106; Rex, 53 C. Cls. 320; Douglas, 190 Fed. 482; Valk, 22 C. Cls. 241; Valk, 29 C. Cls. 62.

[28] *Sg.* 1 St. 743. *S.* 2 St. 139, 332; 3 *St.* 383, 682. *R.* 4 St. 729; 48 St. 787. *Cited:* Leighton, 29 C. Cls. 288.

[29] *Sg.* 1 St. 469, 743. Cited: Leighton, 29 C. Cls. 288.

[30] *Sg.* N. W. Ord. 1787, U. S. C. (1934 ed.) p. XXIII.

[31] *S.* 2 St. 183.

[32] *S.* 2 St. 264.

[33] *S.* 2 St. 283; 3 St. 654. *R.* 4 St. 729.

[34] *Rg.* 1 St. 496, 617. *A.* 3 St. 682. *R.* 4 St. 729. *Sg.* 2 St. 6. *S.* 3 St. 332, 383; 4 St. 150, 217, 428, 267, 352, 373, 470, 576; 5 St. 147; 6 St. 480, 581; 7 St. 68, 195, 215, 217, 601. *Cited:* Thayer, 68 Atl. Month. 540, 676; 14 Op. A. G. 290; 18 Op. A. G. 235; 5 L. D. Memo. 286; American Fur., 2 Pet. 358; Ash, 252 U. S. 159; Bates, 95 U. S. 204; Browning, 6 F. 2d 801; Cherokee, 5 Pet. 1; Chinn, 5 Fed. Cas. No. 2684; Corralitos, 178 U. S. 280; Deere, 22 F. 2d 851; Ex P. Crow Dog, 109 U. S. 556; Holden, 17 Wall. 211; Hot Springs, 92 U. S. 698; Janus, 38 F. 2d 431; Johnson, 29 C. Cls. 1; Jones, 175 U. S. 1; Leighton, 29 C. Cls. 288; Marks, 161 U. S. 297; Moore, 2 Wyo. 8, overruled 3 Wyo. 432; Morrison, 6 F. 2d 811; New York ex rel. Cutler, 21 How. 366; Pino, 38 C. Cls. 64; Price, 33 C. Cls. 106; Rex, 53 C. Cls. 320; Seneca Nation, 162 U. S. 283; U. S. v. Alberty, 24 Fed. Cas. No. 14426; U. S. v. Bailey, 24 Fed. Cas. No. 14495; U. S. v. Bichard, 1 Ariz. 31; U. S. v. Boyland, 265 Fed. 165; U. S. v. Cisna, 25 Fed. Cas. No. 14795; U. S. v. Kie, 26 Fed. Cas. No. 15528a; U. S. v. Leathers, 26 Fed. Cas. No. 15581; U. S. v. Quiver, 241 U. S. 602; U. S. v. Sa-Coo-Da-Cot, 27 Fed. Cas. No. 16212; U. S. v. Soveloff, 27 Fed. Cas. No. 16252; U. S. Exp., 191 Fed. 673; Valk, 22 C. Cls. 241; Valk, 29 C. Cls. 62; Ward, 17 Wall. 253; Worcester, 6 Pet. 515.

[35] *Sg.* 1 St. 452. *S.* 2 St. 207, 225, 274, 283.

[36] *Sg.* N. W. Ord. 1787, U. S. C. (1934 ed.) p. XXIII.

[37] *Sg.* 1 St. 464; 2 St. 73, 112.

[38] *Sg.* 2 St. 82.

[39] *Sg.* 1 St. 452; 2 St. 173.

[40] *Sg.* N. W. Ord. 1787, U. S. C. (1934 ed.) p. XXIII; 2 St. 173. *S.* 2 St. 274.

[41] *Sg.* 7 St. 73. *Rp.* 2 St. 303. *S.* 2 St. 324.

[42] *Sg.* 2 St. 241; 8 St. 200. *S.* 2 St. 283.

[43] *Ag.* 2 St. 82.

[44] *Sg.* N. W. Ord. 1787, U. S. C. (1934 ed.) p. XXIII; 2 St. 173, 225. *Cited:* Reynolds, 2 Pet. 417.

[45] *Sg.* 1 St. 464; 2 St. 73; 7 St. 74, 78. *S.* 2 St. 343; 4 St. 180. *Cited:* Reynolds, 2 Pet. 417.

2 St. 283; Mar. 26, 1804; C. 38—An Act erecting Louisiana into two territories, and providing for the temporary government thereof.[46]

2 St. 291; Mar. 26, 1804; C. 43—An Act to make further appropriations for the purpose of extinguishing the Indian claims.

2 St. 303; Mar. 27, 1804; C. 61—An Act supplementary to the act intituled, "An act regulating the grants of land, and providing for the disposal of the lands of the United States, south of the state of Tennessee."[47]

2 St. 309; Jan. 11, 1805; C. 5—An Act to divide the Indiana Territory into two separate governments.[48]

2 St. 315; Feb. 14, 1805; C. 17—An Act making appropriations for the support of the Military establishment of the United States, for the year 1805.

2 St. 324; Mar. 2, 1805; C. 26—An Act for ascertaining and adjusting the titles and claims to land, within the territory of Orleans, and the district of Louisiana.[49]

2 St. 331; Mar. 3, 1805; C. 31—An Act further providing for the government of the district of Louisiana.[50]

2 St. 338; Mar. 3, 1805; C. 36—An Act making appropriations for carrying into effect certain Indian treaties, and for other purposes of Indian trade and intercourse.

2 St. 343; Mar. 3, 1805; C. 43—An Act supplementary to the act intituled "An act making provision for the disposal of the public lands in the Indiana territory, and for other purposes."[51]

2 St. 352; February 28, 1806; C. 11—An Act extending the powers of the Surveyor-general to the territory of Louisiana; and for other purposes.

2 St. 381; Apr. 18, 1806; C. 31—An Act to authorize the state of Tennessee to issue grants and perfect titles to certain lands therein described, and to settle the claims to the vacant and unappropriated lands within the same.[52]

2 St. 396; Apr. 21, 1806; C. 41—An Act to regulate and fix the compensation of clerks, and to authorize the laying out certain public roads; and for other purposes.[53]

2 St. 402; Apr. 21, 1806; C. 48.—An Act for establishing trading houses with the Indian tribes.[54]

2 St. 407; Apr. 21, 1806; C. 53—An Act making appropriations for carrying into effect certain Indian treaties.[55]

2 St. 408; Apr. 18, 1806; C 54—An Act making appropriations for the support of the Military establishment of the United States, for the year 1806.

2 St. 412; Jan. 10, 1807; C. 3—An Act making appropriations for the support of the Military establishment of the United States, for the year 1807.

2 St. 424; Mar. 2, 1807; C. 21—An Act to extend the time for locating Virginia military [land] warrants, for returning surveys thereon to the office of the Secretary of the department of War, and appropriating lands for the use of schools, in the Virginia military reservation, in lieu of those heretofore appropriated.

2 St. 432; Mar. 3, 1807; C. 29—An Act making appropriations for the support of Government during the year 1807.

2 St. 437; Mar. 3, 1807; C. 34—An Act regulating the grants of land in the territory of Michigan.[56]

2 St. 440; Mar. 3, 1807; C. 35—An Act making appropriations for carrying into effect a treaty between the United States and the Chickasaw tribe of Indians; and to establish a land-office in the Mississippi territory.[57]

2 St. 443; Mar. 3, 1807; C. 41—An Act making appropriations for carrying into effect certain treaties with the Cherokee and Piankeshaw tribes of Indians.[58]

2 St. 448; Mar. 3, 1807; C. 49—An Act making provision for the disposal of the Public lands, situated between the United States military tract and the Connecticut reserve, and for other purposes.[59]

2 St. 455; Jan. 9, 1808; C. 9—An Act extending the right of suffrage in the Mississippi territory; and for other purposes.

2 St. 462; Feb. 10, 1808; C. 17—An Act making appropriations for the support of Government during the year 1808.

2 St. 467; Feb. 19, 1808; C. 20—An Act making appropriations for carrying into effect certain Indian Treaties.[60]

2 St. 469; Feb. 26, 1808; C. 24—An Act extending the right of suffrage in the Indiana territory.

2 St. 470; Mar. 3, 1808; C. 27—An Act making appropriations for the support of the Military establishment of the United States, for the year 1808.

2 St. 479; Mar. 31, 1808; C. 40—An Act concerning the sale of the Lands of the United States, and for other purposes.[61]

2 St. 502; Apr. 25, 1808; C. 67—An Act supplemental to "An act regulating the grants of land in the territory of Michigan."[62]

2 St. 514; Feb. 3, 1809; C. 13—An Act for dividing the Indiana Territory into two separate governments.[63]

2 St. 525; Feb. 27, 1809; C. 19—An Act extending the right of suffrage in the Indiana territory, and for other purposes.

2 St. 527; Feb. 28, 1809; C. 23—An Act for the relief of certain Alibama and Wyandott Indians.[64]

2 St. 544; Mar. 3, 1809; C. 34—An Act supplemental to the act intituled "An act for establishing trading houses with the Indian tribes."[65]

2 St. 545; Mar. 3, 1809; C. 36—An Act making appropriations for the support of the Military establishment, and of the Navy of the United States, for the year 1809.

2 St. 548; June 15, 1809; C. 4—An Act supplementary to an act, intitled "An Act making appropriations for carrying into effect a treaty between the United States and the Chickasaw tribe of Indians; and to establish a land-office in the Mississippi Territory."[66]

2 St. 563; Mar. 2, 1810; C. 15—An Act making appropriations for the support of the Military establishment of the United States, for the year 1810.

2 St. 564; Mar. 2, 1810; C. 17—An Act providing for the third census or enumeration of the inhabitants of the United States.

2 St. 590; Apr. 30, 1810; C. 35—An Act providing for the sale of certain lands in the Indiana territory, and for other purposes.[67]

2 St. 592; Apr. 30, 1810; C. 37—An Act regulating the Post-office Establishment.

2 St. 607; May 1, 1810; C. 43—An Act making appropriations for carrying into effect certain Indian treaties.[68]

2 St. 615; Feb. 6, 1811; C. 9—An Act making appropriations for the support of the Military establishment of the United States, for the year 1811.

2 St. 641; Feb. 20, 1811; C. 21—An Act to enable the people of the Territory of Orleans to form a constitution and state government, and for the admission of such state into the Union, on an equal footing with the original states, and for other purposes.[69]

2 St. 643; Feb. 20, 1811; C. 22—An Act making appropriations for the support of Government for the year 1811.

2 St. 649; Feb. 25, 1811; C. 24—An Act providing for the sale of a tract of land lying in the state of Tennessee, and a tract in the Indiana territory.

2 St. 649; Feb. 25, 1811; C. 25—An Act providing for the removal of the land office established at Nashville, in the state of Tennessee, and Canton in the state of Ohio; and to authorize the register and receiver of public monies to superintend the public sales of land in the district east of Pearl river.

2 St. 652; Mar. 2, 1811; C. 30—An Act for establishing trading houses with the Indian tribes.[70]

2 St. 659; Mar. 3, 1811; C. 38—An Act to extend the right of suffrage in the Indiana territory, and for other purposes.

2 St. 660; Mar. 3, 1811; C. 41—An Act making appropriations for carrying into effect a treaty between the United States and the Great and Little Osage nations of Indians, concluded at

---

[46] *Sg.* 1 St. 452; 2 St. 85, 173, 245. *Rp.* 2 St. 331, 743. *Cited:* Leighton, 29 C. Cls. 288; Hot Springs, 92 U. S. 698.

[47] *Rg.* 2 St. 2?0, sec. 8.

[48] *Sg.* N. W. Ord. 1787, U. S. C. (1934 ed.) p. XXIII; 1 St. 50.

[49] *Sg.* 2 St. 229, sec. 10.

[50] *Rpg.* 2 St. 283. *Rp.* 2 St. 743.

[51] *Sg.* 2 St. 277; 7 St. 49.

[52] *Cited:* 30. Op. A. G. 284.

[53] *Sg.* 7 St. 49.

[54] *S.* 2 St. 544. *R.* 2 St. 652. *Cited:* U. S. v. Hutto, No. 1, 256 U. S. 524; U. S v. Hutto, No. 2, 256 U. S. 530.

[55] *Sg.* 7 St. 87, 91, 93, 95, 96.

[56] *S.* 2 St. 502; 3 St. 4?3; 10 St. 1082. *Cited:* 2 Op. A. G. 674.

[57] *Sg.* 7 St. 89. *S.* 2 St. 548.

[58] *Sg.* 7 St. 100.

[59] *S.* 3 St. 575; 10 St. 1048.

[60] *Sg.* 7 St. 98, 104.

[61] *Sg.* 7 St. 98.

[62] *Sg.* Treaty of Paris, Feb. 10, 1763; Treaty of Peace, Sept. 3, 1783; 2 St. 437; 7 St. 105.

[63] *Sg.* N. W. Ord. 1787, U. S. C. (1934 ed.) p. XXIII; 1 St. 50. *S.* 2 St. 741.

[64] *S.* 7 St. 180.

[65] *Rg.* 2 St. 402, sec. 12. *Sg.* 2 St. 402. *R.* 2 St. 652.

[66] *Sg.* 7 St. 89; 2 St. 440.

[67] *Sg.* 7 St. 113.

[68] *Sg.* 7 St. 49, 113, 115, 116, 117.

[69] *Sg.* 8 St. 200.

[70] *Rg.* 2 St. 402, 544; *S.* 2 St. 686; 3 St. 239, 363, 428, 514, 544, 641. *R.* 3 St. 679. *Cited:* U. S. v. Hutto, No. 1, 256 U. S. 524; U. S. v. Hutto, No. 2, 256 U. S. 530; 11 Cong. 2 sess., Ex. Doc., Apr. 14, 1810.

Fort Clarke, on the tenth day of November, 1808, and for other purposes.[71]

2 St. 666; Jan. 15, 1811; J. Res. relative to the occupation of the Floridas by the United States of America.[72]

2 St. 666: Mar. 3. 1811: C. 47—An Act concerning an act to enable the President of the United States, under certain contingencies, to take possession of the country lying east of the river Perdido, and south of the state of Georgia and the Mississippi territory, and for other purposes, and the declaration accompanying the same.[73]

2 St. 668; Dec. 12, 1811; C. 8—An Act to authorize the surveying and marking of certain roads, in the state of Ohio, as contemplated by the treaty of Brownstown in the territory of Michigan.[74]

2 St. 670; Jan. 2, 1812; C. 11—An Act authorizing the President of the United States to raise certain companies of Rangers for the protection of the frontier of the United States.

2 St. 682; Feb. 21, 1812; C. 26—An Act making appropriations for the support of the Military Establishment of the United States, for the year 1812.

2 St. 686; Feb. 26, 1812; C. 33—An Act making appropriations for the support of Government for the year 1812.[75]

2 St. 704; Apr. 10, 1812; C. 54—An Act for the relief of the officers and soldiers who served in the late campaign on the Wabash.

2 St. 716; Apr. 25, 1812; C. 68—An Act for the establishment of a General Land-Office in the Department of the Treasury.[76]
Sec. 1–R. S. 440, 453.

2 St. 728; May 6, 1812; C. 77—An Act to provide for designating, surveying and granting the Military Bounty Lands.[76a]

2 St. 741; May 20, 1812; C. 90—An Act to extend the right of suffrage in the Illinois territory, and for other purposes.[77]

2 St. 743; June 4, 1812; C. 95—An Act providing for the government of the territory of Missouri.[78]

2 St. 748; June 13, 1812; C. 99—An Act making further provision for settling the claims to land in the territory of Missouri.

2 St. 781; July 6, 1812; C. 131—An Act making additional appropriations for the Military Establishment and for the Indian Department for the year 1812.[79]

2 St. 822; Mar. 3, 1813; C. 57—An Act making appropriations for the support of the military establishment and of the volunteer militia in the actual service of the United States, for the year 1813.[80]

2 St. 829; Mar. 3, 1813; C. 61—An Act vesting in the President of the United States the power of retaliation.

3 STAT.

3 St. 104; Mar. 19, 1814; C. 25—An Act making appropriations for the support of the military establishment of the United States, for one year 1814.[81]

3 St. 143; Oct. 25, 1814; C. 1—An Act further to extend the right of suffrage, and to increase the number of members of the legislative council in the Mississippi territory.

3 St. 201; Feb. 4, 1815; C. 33—An Act attaching to the Canton district, in the state of Ohio, the tract of land lying between the foot of the rapids of the Miami of Lake Erie, and the Connecticut western reserve.[82]

3 St. 222; Mar. 3, 1815; C. 72—An Act making appropriations for the support of the military establishment, for the year 1815

3 St. 228; Mar. 3, 1815; C. 88—An Act to provide for ascertaining and surveying of the boundary lines fixed by the treaty with the Creek Indians, and for other purposes.[83]

3 St. 230; Mar. 3, 1815; C. 99—An Act to continue in force, for a limited time, the act entitled "An act for establishing trading-houses with the Indian tribes.[84]

3 St. 277; Apr. 16. 1816; C. 45—An Act making appropriations for the support of government for the year 1816.[85]

3 St. 285; Apr. 16, 1816; C. 53—An Act to authorize the President of the United States to alter the road laid out from the foot of the rapids of the river Miami of Lake Erie, to the western line of the Connecticut reserve.[86]

3 St. 289; Apr. 19, 1816; C. 57—An Act to enable the people of the Indiana Territory to form a constitution and state government, and for the admission of such state into the Union on an equal footing with the original states.[87]

3 St. 308; Apr. 26, 1816; C. 102—An Act providing for the sale of the tract of land at the lower rapids of Sandusky river.[88]

3 St. 315; Apr. 27, 1816; C. 112—An Act making appropriations for repairing certain roads therein described.

3 St. 319; Apr. 27, 1816; C. 132—An Act providing for the sale of the tract of land, at the British fort at the Miami of the Lake, at the foot of the Rapids, and for other purposes.[89]

3 St. 325; Apr. 29, 1816; C. 151—An Act to provide for the appointment of a surveyor of the public lands in the territories of Illinois and Missouri.
Sec. 1–R. S. 2223.

3 St. 326; Apr. 29, 1816; C. 152—An Act making appropriations for carrying into effect a treaty between the United States and the Cherokee tribe of Indians, concluded at Washington, on the twenty-second day of March, 1816.[90]

3 St. 330; Apr. 29, 1816; C. 160—An Act making appropriations for the support of the military establishment of the United States, for the year 1816.

3 St. 332; Apr. 29, 1816; C. 164—An Act to authorize the survey of two millions of acres of the public lands, in lieu of that quantity heretofore authorized to be surveyed, in the territory of Michigan, as military bounty lands.[91]

3 St. 332; Apr. 29, 1816; C. 165—An Act supplementary to the act passed the thirtieth of March, 1802, to regulate trade and intercourse with the Indian tribes, and to preserve peace on the frontiers.[92]

3 St. 348; Mar. 1, 1817; C. 23—An Act to enable the people of the western part of the Mississippi territory to form a constitution and state government, and for the admission of such state into the Union, on an equal footing with the original states.[93]

3 St. 359; Mar. 3, 1817; C. 35—An Act making provision for the support of the military establishment for the year 1817.

3 St. 363; Mar. 3, 1817; C. 43—An Act to continue in force an act, entitled "An act for establishing trading houses with the Indian tribes."[94]

3 St. 374; Mar. 3, 1817; C. 61—An Act to set apart and dispose of certain public lands, for the encouragement of the cultivation of the vine and olive.[95]

3 St. 375; Mar. 3, 1817; C. 62—An Act to authorize the appointment of a surveyor for the lands in the northern part of the Mississippi territory, and the sale of certain lands therein described.

3 St. 378; Mar. 3, 1817; C. 86—An Act making additional appropriations to defray the expenses of the army and militia during the late war with Great Britain.[96]

3 St. 380; Mar. 3, 1817; C. 88—An Act making provision for the location of the lands reserved by the first article of the treaty of the ninth of August, 1814, between the United States and the Creek nation, to certain chiefs and warriors of that nation, and for other purposes.[97]

3 St. 383; Mar. 3, 1817; C. 92—An Act to provide for the punishment of crimes and offences committed within the Indian boundaries.[98]

3 St. 393; Mar. 3, 1817; C. 106—An Act making appropriations for carrying into effect certain Indian treaties, and for other purposes.[99]

3 St. 397; Mar. 3, 1817; C. 110—An Act to amend the act "authorizing the payment for property lost, captured, or destroyed by the enemy, while in the military service of the United States.

---

[71] *Sg.* 2 St. 617; 7 St. 107. *S.* 3 St. 277.
[72] *See:* 3 St. 471.
[73] Not published until 3 St. 471.
[74] *Sg.* 7 St. 49, 112. *S.* 3 St. 285.
[75] *Sg.* 2 St. 652.
[76] *Cited:* Op. Sol., M. 11094, Nov. 5, 1928.
[76a] *Rp.* 3 St. 332.
[77] *Sg.* 2 St. 514.
[78] *Rpg.* 2 St. 283, 331. *S.* 3 St. 493.
[79] *Sg.* 2 St. 696, 720, 735, 742.
[80] *Sg.* 2 St. 791, sec. 1.
[81] *Sg.* 3 St. 93.
[82] *Sg.* 7 St. 112.
[83] *Sg.* 7 St. 120. *S.* 3 St. 374, 378, 485.
[84] *Sg.* 2 St. 652.
[85] *Sg.* 2 St. 660. *S.* 6 St. 215.
[86] *Sg.* 2 St. 668; 7 St. 112.
[87] *Sg.* N. W. Ord. 1787, U. S. C. (1934 ed.) p. XXIII. *S.* 3 St. 339.
[88] *Sg.* 7 St. 49.
[89] *Sg.* 7 St. 49.
[90] *Sg.* 7 St. 138.
[91] *Rpg.* 2 St. 728.
[92] *Sg.* 2 St. 139. *R.* 4 St. 729. *Cited:* Leighton 29 C. Cls. 288.
[93] *Sg.* N. W. Ord. 1787, U. S. C. (1934 ed.) p. XXIII. *S.* 3 St. 348, 472; 5 St. 116. *A.* 5 St. 727; 9 St. 202.
[94] *Sg.* 2 St. 652. *R.* 4 St. 729.
[95] *Sg.* 7 St. 120; 3 St. 228.
[96] *Sg.* 7 St. 120; 3 St. 228.
[97] *Sg.* 7 St. 120; Art. 9. *S.* 3 St. 484. *Cited:* Thayer, 68 Atl. Monthly. 540, 676; 3 Op. A. G. 280.
[98] *Sg.* 2 St. 6, 139, secs. 14 & 15. *R.* 4 St. 729. *Cited:* Leighton 29 C. Cls. 288; U. S. v. Bailey, 24 Fed. Cas. No. 14495; U. S. v. Sa-Coo-Da-Cot. 27 Fed. Cas. No. 16212.
[99] *Sg.* 7 St. 146; 148, 150, 152.

and for other purposes." passed the ninth of April, 1816.[1]

3 St. 399; Dec. 11, 1816; J. Res. I—Resolution for admitting the state of Indiana into the Union.[2]

3 St. 407; Feb. 19, 1818; C. 13—An Act making appropriations for the military service of the United States for the year 1818.

3 St. 418; Apr. 9, 1818; C. 45—An Act making appropriation for the support of government for the year 1818.[3]

3 St. 423; April 11, 1818; C. 47—An Act to extend the time for locating Virginia military land warrants, and returning surveys thereon to the General Land Office; and for designating the western boundary line of the Virginia military tract.[4]

3 St. 428; Apr. 16, 1818; C. 66—An Act directing the manner of appointing Indian Agents, and continuing the "Act for establishing trading houses with the Indian tribes."[5]

3 St. 428; Apr. 18, 1818; C. 67—An Act to enable the people of the Illinois territory to form a constitution and state government, and for the admission of such state into the Union on an equal footing with the original states.[6]

3 St. 445; Apr. 20, 1818; C. 87—An Act to regulate and fix the compensation of the clerks in the different offices.[7]

3 St. 459; Apr. 20, 1818; C. 101—An Act to increase the pay of the militia while in actual service, and for other purposes.

3 St. 461; Apr. 20, 1818; C. 104—An Act fixing the compensation of Indian agents and factors.[8]

3 St. 463; Apr. 20, 1818; C. 109—An Act supplementary to the several acts making appropriations for the year 1818.[9]

3 St. 466; Apr. 20, 1818; C. 126—An Act respecting the surveying and sale of the public lands in the Alabama territory.

3 St. 471; Jan. 15, 1811; J. Res.—Relative to the Occupation of the Floridas by the United States of America.

3 St. 471; Jan. 15, 1811; An Act to enable the President of the United States, under certain contingencies, to take possession of the country lying east of the river Perdido, and south of the state of Georgia and the Mississippi territory, and for other purposes.[10]

3 St. 472; Feb. 12, 1812; An Act authorizing the President of the United States to take possession of a tract of country lying south of the Mississippi territory and west of the river Perdido.

3 St. 472; Mar. 3, 1811; An Act concerning an act to enable the President of the United States, under certain contingencies, to take possession of the country lying east of the river Perdido, and south of the state of Georgia and the Mississippi territory, and for other purposes, and the declaration accompanying the same.[11]

3 St. 472; Dec. 10, 1817; J. Res. I—Resolution for the admission of the State of Mississippi into the Union.[12]

3 St. 478; Dec. 16, 1818; C. 3—An Act making a partial appropriation for the military service of the United States, for the year 1819, and to make good a deficit in the appropriation for holding treaties with the Indians.

3 St. 480; Feb. 15, 1819; C. 18—An Act making appropriations for the military service of the United States for the year 1819.[13]

3 St. 482; Feb. 16, 1819; C. 22—An Act authorizing the election of a delegate from the Michigan territory to the Congress of the United States, and extending the right of suffrage to the citizens of said territory.

3 St. 484; Feb. 20, 1819; C. 28—An Act authorizing the President of the United States to purchase the lands reserved by the act of the third of March, 1817, to certain chiefs, warriors, or other Indians, of the Creek nation.[14]

3 St. 485; Feb. 20, 1819; C. 31—An Act providing for a grant of land for the seat of government in the State of Mississippi, and for the support of a seminary of learning within the said state.[15]

3 St. 489; Mar. 2, 1819; C. 47—An Act to enable the people of the Alabama territory to form a constitution and state government, and for the admission of such state into the Union on an equal footing with the original states.[16]

3 St. 493; Mar. 2, 1819; C. 49—An Act establishing a separate territorial government in the southern part of the territory of Missouri."

3 St. 496; Mar. 3, 1819; C. 54—An Act making appropriations for the support of government for the year 1819.

3 St. 514; Mar. 3, 1819; C. 80—An Act to continue in force, for a further term, the act entitled "An act for establishing trading houses with the Indian tribes," and for other purposes.[18]

3 St. 516; Mar. 3, 1819; C. 85—An Act making provision for the civilization of the Indian tribes adjoining the frontier settlements.[19] R. S. 2071, 25 U. S. C. 271.[20]

3 St. 517; Mar. 3, 1819; C. 87—An Act making appropriations to carry into effect treaties concluded with several Indian tribes therein mentioned.[21]

3 St. 521; Mar. 3, 1819; C. 92—An Act to designate the boundaries of districts, and establish land offices for the disposal of the public lands not heretofore offered for sale in the states of Ohio and Indiana.[22]

3 St. 523; Mar. 3, 1819; C. 93—An Act to authorize the President of the United States to take possession of East and West Florida, and establish a temporary government therein.[23]

3 St. 526; Mar. 3, 1819; C. 99—An Act concerning invalid pensions.

3 St. 536; Dec. 3, 1818; J. Res. I—Resolution declaring the admission of the state of Illinois into the Union.[24]

3 St. 544; Mar. 4, 1820; C. 20—An Act to continue in force for a further time, the act entitled "An act for establishing trading-houses with the Indian tribes."[25]

3 St. 545; Mar. 6, 1820; C. 22—An Act to authorize the people of the Missouri territory to form a constitution and state government, and for the admission of such state into the Union on an equal footing with the original states, and to prohibit slavery in certain territories.[26]

3 St. 548; Mar. 14, 1820; C. 24—An Act to provide for taking the fourth census, or enumeration of the inhabitants of the United States, and for other purposes.

3 St. 555; Apr. 11, 1820; C. 40—An Act making appropriations for the support of government, for the year 1820.[27]

3 St. 562; Apr. 14, 1820; C. 45—An act making appropriations for the military service of the United States, for the year 1820.

3 St. 575; May 11, 1820; C. 89—An Act authorizing the sale of thirteen sections of land, lying within the land district of Canton, in the state of Ohio.[28]

3 St. 576; May 11, 1820; C. 92—An Act to amend the act, entitled "An act to provide for the publication of the laws of the United States, and for other purposes."[29]

3 St. 577; May 11, 1820; C. 94—An Act to annex certain lands within the territory of Michigan to the district of Detroit.[30]

3 St. 607; May 15, 1820; C. 135—An Act granting to the state of Ohio the right of preemption to certain quarter sections of land.[31]

3 St. 608; Dec. 14, 1819; J. Res. I—Resolution declaring the admission of the state of Alabama into the Union.[32]

3 St. 608; May 15, 1820; C. 137—An Act making appropriations for carrying into effect the treaties concluded with the Chippewa and Kickapoo nations of Indians.[33]

---

1 *Ag.* 3 St. 261; sec. 9. *S.* 4 St. 618.
2 *Sg.* N. W. Ord. 1787, U. S. C. (1934 ed.) p. XXIII; 3 St. 289.
3 *Sg.* 7 St. 171.
4 *Sg.* 7 St. 49; 2 St. 487. *Cited:* Reynolds, 2 Pet. 417.
5 *Sg.* 2 St. 652. *R.* 4 St. 729.
6 *Sg.* N. W. Ord. 1787, U. S. C. (1934 ed.) p. XXIII. *S.* 3 St. 536.
7 *S.* 3 St. 628; 4 St. 233.
8 *S.* 3 St. 514. *R.* 4 St. 729. *Cited:* U. S., 25 Fed. Cas. No. 15015.
9 *Sg.* 7 St. 138.
10 *Sg.* 2 St. 666; *S.* 3 St. 472.
11 *Sg.* 3 St. 471.
12 *Sg.* N. W. Ord. 1787, U. S. C. (1934 ed.) p. XXIII; 3 St. 348.
13 *Sg.* 7 St. 68, 192.
14 *Sg.* 3 St. 380.
15 *Sg.* 3 St. 228, sec. 5.
16 *Sg.* N. W. Ord. 1787, U. S. C. (1934 ed.) p. XXIII; Vol. I, Am. St. Papers, Public Lands, p. 125. *S.* 5 St. 116; 10 St. 630.
17 *Sg.* 2 St. 743.
18 *Sg.* 2 St. 652; 3 St. 461. *Rp.* 4 St. 729.
19 *S.* 11 St. 65, 169, 273. *Rp.* 17 St. 437, 461. *Cited:* U. S. ex rel. Young, 4 Mont. 38.
20 *See:* 25 U. S. C. 452 (48 St. 596, sec. 1 as amended 49 St. 1458); 25 U. S. C. 453 (48 St. 596, sec. 2 as amended 49 St. 1458); 25 U. S. C. 455 (48 St. 596, sec. 3 as amended 49 St. 1458); 25 U. S. C. 455 (48 St. 596, sec. 4 as amended 49 St. 1458); 25 U. S. C. 471 (48 St. 986, sec. 11).
21 *Sg.* 7 St. 68, 160, 171, 176, 181, 183, 185, 186, 188, 189, 192. *Rp.* 4 St. 729; 17 St. 437.
22 *Sg.* 7 St. 49.
23 *Sg.* 8 St. 252.
24 *Sg.* N. W. Ord. 1787, U. S. C. (1934 ed.) p. XXIII; 3 St. 428.
25 *Sg.* 2 St. 652.
26 *S.* 10 St. 277; 22 St. 35.
27 *Sg.* Vol. I, Am. St. Papers, Public Lands, p. 125.
28 *Sg.* 2 St. 448; 7 St. 160, Art. 18.
29 *Rg.* 3 St. 439, sec. 1. *Cited:* 6 Op. A. G. 627.
30 *Sg.* 7 St. 203.
31 *Sg.* 7 St. 176.
32 *Sg.* N. W. Ord. 1787, U. S. C. (1934 ed.) p. XXIII; Vol. I, Am. St. Papers, Public Lands, p. 125.
33 *Sg.* 7 St. 202, 203. *S.* 4 St. 780; 5 St. 36; 7 St. 528.

3 St. 628; Mar. 3, 1821; C. 34—An Act making appropriations for the support of government, for the year 1821.[34]

3 St. 633; Mar. 3, 1821; C. 35—An Act making appropriations for the military service of the United States, for the year 1821.[35]

3 St. 637; Mar. 3, 1821; C. 39—An Act for carrying into execution the treaty between the United States and Spain, concluded at Washington on the twenty-second day of February, 1819.[36]

3 St. 641; Mar. 3, 1821; C. 45—An Act to continue in force, for a further time, the act, entitled "An act for establishing trading-houses with the Indian tribes."[37]

3 St. 654; Mar. 30, 1822; C. 13—An Act for the establishment of a territorial government in Florida.[38]

3 St. 676; May 4, 1822; C. 48—An Act for the relief of the officers, volunteers, and other persons, engaged in the late campaign against the Seminole Indians.[39]

3 St. 679; May 6, 1822; C. 54—An Act to abolish the United States' trading establishment with the Indian tribes.[40]

3 St. 680; May 6, 1822; C. 55—An Act providing for the disposal of the public lands in the state of Mississippi, and for the better organization of the land districts in the states of Alabama and Mississippi.[41]

3 St. 682; May 6, 1822; C. 58—An Act to amend an act, entitled "An act to regulate trade and intercourse with the Indian tribes, and to preserve peace on the frontiers," approved thirtieth March, 1802.[42]

3 St. 686; May 7, 1822; C. 80—An Act making further appropriations for the military service of the United States for the year 1822, and for other purposes.[43]

3 St. 690; May 7, 1822; C. 93—An Act to provide for annuities to the Ottawas, Pattawatimas, Kickapoos, Choctaws, Kaskaskias, to Mushalatubbee, and to carry into effect the treaty of Saginaw.[44]

3 St. 701; May 8· 1822; C. 126—An Act to designate the boundaries of a land district and for the establishment of a land office, in the state of Indiana.

3 St. 702; May 8, 1822; C. 127—An Act to establish certain post-roads, and to discontinue others, and for other purposes.

3 St‡ 722; Jan. 30, 1823; C. 8—An Act to provide for the appointment of an additional judge for the Michigan territory, and for other purposes.

3 St. 748; Mar. 3, 1823; C. 26—An Act making appropriations for the military service of the United States, for the year 1823.[45]

3 St. 749; Mar. 3, 1823; C. 27—An Act making further appropriations for the military service of the United States, for the year 1823, and for other purposes.[46]

3 St. 750; Mar. 3, 1823; C. 28—An Act to amend "An act for the establishment of a territorial government in Florida," and for other purposes.[47]

3 St. 769; Mar. 3, 1823; C. 36—An Act to amend the ordinance and acts of Congress for the government of the territory of Michigan, and for other purposes.[48]

3 St. 783; Mar. 3, 1823; C. 60—An Act supplementary to the act, entitled "An act to designate the boundaries of districts, and establish land offices for the disposal of the public lands, not heretofore offered for sale, in the states of Ohio and Indiana."[49]

4 STAT.

4 St. 25; May 18, 1824; C. 89—An Act providing for the appointment of an agent for the Osage Indians, west of the state of Missouri, and territory of Arkansas, and for other purposes.[50]

4 St. 35; May 25, 1824; C. 146—An act to enable the President to hold treaties with certain Indian tribes, and for other purposes.[51]

4 St. 36; May 26, 1824; C. 149—An Act making further appropriations for the military service of the United States, for the year 1824, and for other purposes.[52]

4 St. 37; May 26, 1824; C. 150—An Act appropriating a sum of money to Benjamin Huffman, of the state of Indiana.[53]

4 St. 37; May 26, 1824; C. 151—An Act making appropriations to carry into effect certain Indian treaties.[54]

4 St. 39; May 26, 1824; C. 154—An Act concerning pre-emption rights in the territory of Arkansas.[55]

4 St. 40; May 26, 1824; C. 155—An Act to fix the western boundary line of the territory of Arkansas, and for other purposes.[56]

4 St. 41; May 26, 1824; C. 156—An Act making an appropriation towards the extinguishment of the Quapau title to lands in the territory of Arkansas.[57]

4 St. 56; May 26, 1824; C. 174—An Act providing for the disposition of three several tracts of land in Tuscarawas county, in the state of Ohio, and for other purposes.[58]

4 St. 70; May 26, 1824; C. 187—An Act explanatory of an act, entitled "An act for the relief of the officers, volunteers, and other persons, engaged in the late campaign against the Seminole Indians, passed the fourth of May, 1822."[59]

4 St. 75; May 26, 1824; C. 194—An Act reserving to the Wyandot tribe of Indians a certain tract of land, in lieu of a reservation made to them by treaty.[60]

4 St. 92; Mar. 3, 1825; C. 16—An Act making further appropriations for the military service for the year 1825.[61]

4 St. 95; Mar. 3, 1825; C. 46—An Act to establish certain post-roads, and to discontinue others.

4 St. 100; Mar. 3, 1825; C. 50—An Act to authorize the President of the United States to cause a road to be marked out from the western frontier of Missouri, to the confines of New Mexico.[62]

4 St. 102; Mar. 3, 1825; C. 64—An Act to reduce into one the several acts establishing and regulating the Post-office Department.

4 St. 150; Mar. 25, 1826; C. 16—An Act making appropriations for the Indian department, for the year 1826.[63]

4 St. 154; Apr. 20, 1826; C. 27—An Act appropriating a sum of money for the repair of the post-roads between Jackson and Columbus in the state of Mississippi.

4 St. 180; May 20, 1826; C. 90—An Act concerning a seminary of learning in the territory of Michigan.[64]

4 St. 181; May 20, 1826; C. 110—An Act making appropriation to defray the expenses of negotiating and carrying into effect certain Indian treaties.[65]

4 St. 185; May 20, 1826; C. 126—An Act to enable the President to hold treaties with certain Indian tribes.

4 St. 187; May 20, 1826; C. 133—An Act to aid certain Indians of the Creek Nation in their removal to the west of the Mississippi.[66]

4 St. 188; May 20, 1826; C. 135—An Act to enable the President of the United States to hold a treaty with the Choctaw and Chicasaw nations of Indians.

4 St. 191; May 22, 1826; C. 148—An Act making appropriations to carry into effect the treaty concluded between the United States and the Creek nation, ratified the twenty-second of April, 1826.[67]

---

[34] *Sg.* 3 St. 445. *Cited:* Moore, 2 Wyo. 8

[35] *Sg.* 7 St. 215. *S.* 4 St. 40.

[36] *Sg.* 8 St. 252.

[37] *Sg.* 2 St. 652.

[38] *Sg.* 1 St. 112. 452; 2 St. 85. *R.* 3 St. 750.

[39] *S.* 4 St. 70; 6 St. 328. 336.

[40] *Sg.* 2 St. 652. *Cited:* Leighton, 29 C. Cls. 288.

[41] *Sg.* 7 St. 210.

[42] *Rg.* 2 St. 139, sec. 7. *R.* 4 St. 729. *Sg.* 2 St. 6. *S.* 10 St. 2. *Cited:* American Fur. 2 Pet. 358; U. S. v. Leathers, 26 Fed. Cas. No. 15581; U. S. Exp., 101 Fed. 673; 17 Cong., 2 sess., Rep. of Comm. 104; 18 Cong., 1 sess., Rep. of Comm. 129.

[43] *Sg.* Vol. 1. Am. State Papers, Public Lands, p. 125; 3 St. 652; 7 St. 215, 218. *S.* 4 St. 36.

[44] *Sg.* 7 St. 78, 203, 210, Art. 13; 7 St. 218.

[45] *Sg.* 7 St. 215. *S.* 4 St. 470.

[46] *S.* 1 St. 490; *Sg.* 7 St. 120, 156, 195, 210, 215; *S.* 4 St. 397.

[47] *Ag.* 8 St. 252. Art. 15. *Rg.* 3 St. 654.

[48] *Rpg.* N. W. Ord. 1787, U. S. C. (1934 ed.) p. XXIII.

[49] *Sg.* 7 St. 176, Art. 2; 209.

[50] *R.* 4 St. 729. *Cited:* Jump, 100 F. 2d 130.

[51] *Rp.* 4 St. 729. *S.* 10 St. 2. *Cited:* 5 Op. A. G. 572.

[52] *Sg.* 3 St. 686.

[53] Identical with 6 St. 314.

[54] *Sg.* 7 St. 215. Art. 4; 224, Art. 3, 5, 6, 7. *S.* 4 St. 532, 470; 5 St. 704; 766; 9 St. 544.

[55] *Sg.* 3 St. 121; 7 St. 156.

[56] *Sg.* 3 St. 633; 7 St. 210.

[57] *S.* 36 St. 1058.

[58] *S.* 4 St. 181, 9 St. 20, 132, 382, 544, 570, 10 St. 41, 226, 315, 686 11 St. 65.

[59] *Sg.* 3 St. 676.

[60] *Sg.* 7 St. 178.

[61] *Sg.* 7 St. 215, Art. 4, 228, 231, Art. 2, 232, Art. 2, 234. *S.* 4 St. 191. 348.

[62] *S.* 5 St. 36; 7 St. 268, 270. *Cited:* Kansas, 80 C. Cls. 264.

[63] *Sg.* 2 St. 139, Sec. 13.

[64] *Sg.* 2 St. 277.

[65] *Sg.* 4 St. 56; 4 St. 74, 189, 215, Art. 4. 228. 229, Art. 3, 4, 5. 231. Art. 2, 4, 5. 232. Art. 2, 234. Art. 2, 3, 10, 240, 244, 272, 284. *S.* 4 St. 348, 470, 780; 5 St. 36, 704, 766; 9 St. 20, 132, 252, 382, 544, 574; 10 St. 41, 226, 315, 686; 11 St. 65.

[66] *Sg.* 7 St. 286, Jan. 24, 1826, (correct date). *S.* 4 St. 267. *Rp.* 4 St. 729.

[67] *Sg.* 4 St. 92; 7 St. 286. *S.* 4 St. 348, 532.

4 St. 194; May 22, 1826; C. 155—An Act for the relief of the Florida Indians.

4 St. 200; Jan. 29, 1827; C. 6—An Act to allow the citizens of the territory of Michigan to elect the members of their legislative council, and for other purposes.

4 St. 202; Feb. 8, 1827; C. 9—An Act to provide for the confirmation and settlement of private land claims in East Florida, and for other purposes.[68]

4 St. 214; Mar. 2, 1827; C. 29—An Act making appropriations for the military service of the United States, for the year 1827.[69]

4 St. 217; Mar. 2, 1827; C. 32—An Act making appropriations for the Indian department, for the year 1827.[70]

4 St. 232; Mar. 2, 1827; C. 49—An Act making appropriations to carry into effect certain Indian treaties.[71]

4 St. 233; Mar. 2, 1827; C. 50—An Act in addition to "An act to regulate and fix the compensation of the clerks in the different offices," passed April, 1818.[72]

4 St. 234; Mar. 2, 1827; C. 52—An Act to authorize the state of Indiana to locate and make a road therein named.[73]

4 St. 235; Mar. 2, 1827; C. 53—An Act concerning a seminary of learning in the territory of Arkansas.

4 St. 247; Feb. 12, 1828; C. 6—An Act making appropriations for the support of government for the year 1828.[74]

4 St. 257; Mar. 21, 1828; C. 21—An Act making appropriations for the military service of the United States, for the year 1828.[75]

4 St. 264; Apr. 28, 1828; C. 40—An Act extending the limits of certain land offices in Indiana, and for other purposes.

4 St. 267; May 9, 1828; C. 47—An Act making appropriations for the Indian department, for the year 1828.[76]

4 St. 276; May 19, 1828; C. 57—An Act for the punishment of contraventions of the fifth article of the treaty between the United States and Russia.[77]

4 St. 300; May 24, 1828; C. 94—An Act making appropriations to carry into effect certain Indian treaties.[78]

4 St. 302; May 24, 1828; C. 97—An Act to enable the President of the United States to hold a treaty with the Chippewas, Ottawas, Pattawattimas, Winnebagoes, Fox and Sacs nations of Indians.

4 St. 305; May 24, 1828; C. 108—An Act to aid the state of Ohio in extending the Miami canal from Dayton to Lake Erie, and to grant a quantity of land to said state to aid in the construction of the canals authorized by law; and for making donations of land to certain persons in Arkansas territory.[79]

4 St. 315; May 24, 1828; C. 124—An Act making appropriations to enable the President of the United States to defray the expenses of delegations of the Choctaw, Creek, Cherokee, and Chickasaw, and other tribes of Indians, to explore the country west of the Mississippi.

4 St. 323; Jan. 6, 1829; C. 1—An Act making appropriations for the support of government, for the first quarter of the year 1829.[80]

4 St. 336; Mar. 2, 1829; C. 24—An Act making additional appropriations for the support of government for the year 1829.[81]

4 St. 348; Mar. 2, 1829; C. 26—An Act making additional appropriations for the military service of the United States, for the year 1829.[82]

4 St. 352; Mar. 2, 1829; C. 32—An Act making appropriations for the Indian department, for the year 1829.[83]

4 St. 361; Mar. 2, 1829; C. 50—An Act making appropriations for carrying into effect certain treaties with the Indian tribes, and for holding a treaty with the Pattawatimas.[84]

4 St. 373; Feb. 27, 1830; C. 26—An Act making appropriations for the Indian department, for the year 1830.[85]

4 St. 383; Mar. 23, 1830; C. 40—An Act to provide for taking the fifth census or enumeration of the inhabitants of the United States.

4 St. 390; March 25, 1830; C. 41—An Act making appropriations to carry into effect certain Indian treaties.[86]

4 St. 394; Apr. 7, 1830; C. 60—An Act making appropriations to pay the expenses incurred in holding certain Indian treaties.

4 St. 397; Apr. 30, 1830; C. 84—An Act for the re-appropriation of certain unexpended balances for former appropriations.[87]

4 St. 403; May 20, 1830; C. 90—An Act making appropriations to carry into effect the treaty of Butte des Mortes.[88]

4 St. 411; May 28, 1830; C. 148—An Act to provide for an exchange of lands with the Indians residing in any of the states or territories, and for their removal west of the river Mississippi.[89]
Secs. 7–8—R. S. 2114, 25 U. S. C. 174.

4 St. 428; May 31, 1830; C. 235—An Act for the relief of sundry citizens of the United States, who have lost property by the depredations of certain Indian tribes.[90]

4 St. 432; Jan. 13, 1831; C. 3—An Act making appropriations for carrying into effect certain Indian treaties.[91]

4 St. 433; Jan. 27, 1831; C. 8—An Act for closing certain accounts, and making appropriations for arrearages in the Indian department.

4 St. 442; Feb. 19, 1831; C. 26—An Act to provide hereafter for the payment of $6,000 annually to the Seneca Indians, and for other purposes.[92]

4 St. 442; Feb. 19, 1831; C. 27—An Act to establish a land office in the territory of Michigan, and for other purposes.

4 St. 445; Feb. 25, 1831; C. 32—An Act to authorize the appointment of a subsequent agent to the Winnebago Indians, on Rock River.[93]

4 St. 463; Mar. 2, 1831; C. 59—An Act making appropriation for carrying into effect certain Indian treaties.[94]

4 St. 464; Mar. 2, 1831; C. 60—An Act to carry into effect certain Indian treaties.[95]

4 St. 465; Mar. 2, 1831; C. 61—An Act making appropriations for the military service for the year 1831.[96]

4 St. 470; Mar. 2, 1831; C. 64—An Act making appropriations for the Indian department for the year 1831.[97]

4 St. 491; Mar. 3, 1831; C. 104—An Act for the benefit of Percis Lovely, and for other purposes.[98]

4 St. 492; Mar. 3, 1831; C. 116—An Act to create the office of surveyor of the public lands for the state of Louisiana.[99]

4 St. 501; Mar. 31, 1832; C. 58—An Act to add a part of the southern to the northern district of Alabama.[1]

4 St. 505; Apr. 20, 1832; C. 71—An Act making appropriations in conformity with the stipulations of certain Indian treaties.[2]

4 St. 514; May 5, 1832; C. 75—An Act to provide the means of extending the benefits of vaccination, as a preventive of the small-pox, to the Indian tribes, and thereby, as far as pos-

---

[68] *Sg.* 7 St. 224.
[69] *Sg.* 7 St. 210, Oct. 18, 1820. *S.* 4 St. 397, 631.
[70] *Sg.* 2 St. 139, Sec. 13; 7 St. 224, 240, Art. 3, 244, Art. 3.
[71] *Sg.* 7 St. 290, 295, 300.
[72] *Sg.* 3 St. 445. *S.* 4 St. 247, 328.
[73] *Sg.* 7 St. 295.
[74] *Sg.* 4 St. 233, Sec. 7.
[75] *Sg.* 1 St. 408.
[76] *Sg.* 2 St. 139, Sec. 13; 4 St. 187, Sec. 2; 7 St. 156, 195, 282, Art. 5, 286, Art. 7 & 8. *S.* 4 St. 532.
[77] *Sg.* 8 St. 302, Art. 5.
[78] *Sg.* 7 St. 290, 295, 300, 307, 309, 311. *S.* 4 St. 348, 470, 682.
[79] *Sg.* 7 St. 311, Art. 1.
[80] *Sg.* 4 St. 233. *S.* 4 St. 336.
[81] *Sg.* 4 St. 328. *S.* 4 St. 463.
[82] *Sg.* 4 St. 92, 181, 191, 300.
[83] *Sg.* 2 St. 139; 3 St. 195; 7 St. 18, 39, 42, 48, 62, 98, 95, 138, 148, 156, 188, 195, 228, 311.
[84] *Sg.* 7 St. 240, Art. 4, 244, Art. 4, 290, Art. 6, 295, Art. 3, 300, Art. 4, 6, 311, 315, Art. 2, 317, Art. 2, 3 & 5. *S.* 4 St. 532.
[85] *Sg.* 2 St. 139.
[86] *Sg.* 7 St. 320. *S.* 4 St. 631.
[87] *Sg.* 3 St. 749; 4 St. 214; 7 St. 195, 210. *S.* 4 St. 631.
[88] *Sg.* 7 St. 303. *S.* 4 St. 631.
[89] *S.* 4 St. 595, 631; 7 St. 351, 355, 359, 366, 478, 550; *Rp.* 5 St. 323. *Cited:* Mannypenny, OIW; 19 Op. A. G. 42; 27 Op. A. G. 530; 35 Op. A. G. 251; Op. Sol. M. 18772 Dec. 24, 1926; Brown, 44 C. Cls. 283; Brown & Gritts, 219 U. S. 346; Buster, 135 Fed. 947; Cherokee, 187 U. S. 294; Choctaw, 83 C. Cls. 140; Gray, 10 Fed. Cas. No. 5714; Heckman, 224 U. S. 413; Jordan, 1 Okla. 406; Kansas, 5 Wall. 737; Maxey, 3 Ind. T. 243; New York Indians, 170 U. S. 1; Renfrow, 3 Okla. 161; Tuttle, 8 Ind. T. 712; U. S. v. Choctaw, 179 U. S. 494; U. S. v. Payne, 8 Fed. 883; U. S. v. Rea-Read, 171 Fed. 501; U. S. v. Reese, 27 Fed. Cas., No. 16137; Walker, 16 Wall. 436.
[90] *Sg.* 2 St. 139, Sec. 14. *S.* 6 St. 581; 7 St. 550. *Cited:* Hayt, 38 C. Cls. 455.
[91] *Sg.* 7 St. 290, Art. 6; 295, Art. 3; 300, Art. 4, 6; 317, Art. 2.
[92] *S.* 4 St. 682, 780; 5 St. 36, 704, 766; 9 St. 252, 382, 544, 574; 10 St. 41, 226, 315, 686; 11 St. 65, 169, 273, 388; 12 St. 221, 512, 774; 13 St. 161, 541; 14 St. 255, 492; 15 St. 198; 16 St. 13, 335, 544; 17 St. 165, 437; 18 St. 146, 420; 19 St. 176, 271; 20 St. 63, 295; 21 St. 114, 485; 22 St. 68, 433; 23 St. 76, 362; 24 St. 29, 449; 25 St. 217, 980; 26 St. 336, 989; 27 St. 120, 612; 28 St. 286, 876; 29 St. 321; 30 St. 62, 571, 924; 31 St. 221, 1058; 32 St. 245, 982; 33 St. 1048, 189; 34 St. 325, 1015; 35 St. 70, 781; 36 St. 269, 1058; 37 St. 518; 38 St. 77, 582; 39 St. 123, 969; 40 St. 561; 41 St. 3, 408, 1225; 42 St. 552, 1174; 43 St. 390, 1141; 44 St. 453, 934; 45 St. 200, 1562; 46 St. 279, 1115; 47 St. 91, 820; 48 St. 362; 49 St. 176, 1757; 50 St. 564; 52 St. 291.
[93] *R.* 4 St. 729.
[94] *Sg.* 4 St. 336; 7 St. 290, 295, Art. 3; 300, Art. 4, 6; 311, Art. 5. *S.* 10 St. 15.
[95] *Sg.* 7 St. 188, 327, 333.
[96] *Sg.* U. S. Const., Art. I, Sec. 10.
[97] *Sg.* 2 St. 139; 3 St. 748; 4 St. 37, 181, 300; 7 St. 295, 300, 307.
[98] *Sg.* 7 St. 158, Art. 5; 311, 348.
[99] *S.* 7 St. 491.
[1] *S.* 5 St. 1, 33, 65.
[2] *Sg.* 7 St. 156, 195, 317.

sible, to save them from the destructive ravages of that disease.

4 St. 519; May 31, 1832; C. 109—An Act making appropriations for the Indian department for the year 1832.[3] Sec. 2—R. S. 2063, 25 U. S. C. 39.

4 St. 526; May 31, 1832; C. 115—An Act defining the qualifications of voters in the territory of Arkansas.

4 St. 526; June 4, 1832; C. 123—An Act making appropriations for Indian annuities, and other similar objects, for the year 1832.[4]

4 St. 528; June 4, 1832; C. 124—An Act making appropriations in conformity with the stipulations of certain treaties with the Creeks, Shawnees, Ottoways, Senecas, Wyandots, Cherokees, and Choctaws.[5]

4 St. 532; June 15, 1832; C. 130—An Act for the re-appropriation of certain unexpended balances of former appropriations; and for other purposes.[6]

4 St. 564; July 9, 1832; C. 174—An Act to provide for the appointment of a commissioner of Indian Affairs, and for other purposes.[7] Sec. 1—R. S. 462–463, 25 U. S. C. 1 & 2 (42 St. 1180). See Historical Note 25 U. S. C. A. 1 & 2. Sec. 3—R. S. 464, 25 U. S. C. 8 (42 St. 24). See Historical Note 25 U. S. C. A. 8. Sec. 4—R. S. 2139, 25 U. S. C. 241[8] (19 St. 244, sec. 1; 27 St. 260; 29 St. 506, sec. 1).[9] See Historical Note 25 U. S. C. A. 241. Sec. 5—R. S. 2073, 25 U. S. C. 65 (19 St. 244, sec. 1). USCA Historical Note: R. S. 2073 was derived from sec. 5 re above Act which, with the exception of the use of the words "Secretary of War" in place of the words "Secretary of Interior," is identical with the Code section. R. S. 2073 did not contain the word "agents," and had, after the words "in consequence of the," the word "immigration." The word "agents" was inserted and "immigration" was changed to "emigration," by amendment by Act Feb. 27, 1877, c. 69, sec. 1, 19 St. 244.

4 St. 564; July 9, 1832, C. 175—An Act to enable the President to extinguish Indian title within the state of Indiana, Illinois, and territory of Michigan.

4 St. 571; July 10, 1832; C. 193—An Act to establish additional land districts in the state of Alabama, and for other purposes.

4 St. 576; July 13, 1832; C. 200—An Act to carry into effect certain Indian treaties.[10]

4 St. 578; July 13, 1832; C. 206—An Act authorizing the Secretary of War to pay to the Seneca tribe of Indians, the balance of an annuity, of $6,000, usually paid to said Indians, and remaining unpaid for the year 1829.

4 St. 580; July 14, 1832; C. 224—An Act supplementary to the several acts making appropriations for the civil and military service during the year 1832.[11]

4 St. 594; July 14, 1832; C. 228—An Act to provide for the extinguishment of the Indian title to lands lying in the states of Missouri and Illinois, and for other purposes.[12]

4 St. 595; July 14, 1832; C. 231—An Act to provide for the appointment of three commissioners to treat with the Indians, and for other purposes.[13]

4 St. 601; July 14, 1832; C. 240—An Act to authorize the sale of certain public lands in the state of Ohio.[14]

4 St. 613; Feb. 19, 1833; C. 33—An Act for the payment of horses and arms lost in the military service of the United States against the Indians on the frontiers of Illinois and the Michigan territory.[15]

4 St. 616; Feb. 20, 1833; C. 40—An Act making appropriations for Indian annuities, and other similar objects, for the year 1833.[16]

4 St. 619; Mar. 2, 1833; C. 54—An Act making appropriations for the civil and diplomatic expenses of government for the year 1833.[17] R. S. 470–471.

4 St. 631; Mar. 2, 1833; C. 56—An Act making appropriations for the Indian Department for the year 1833.[18]

4 St. 636; Mar. 2, 1833; C. 59—An Act making appropriations to carry into effect certain Indian treaties, and for other purposes, for the year 1833.[19]

4 St. 652; Mar. 2, 1833; C. 76—An Act for the more perfect defence of the frontiers.[20]

4 St. 653; Mar. 2, 1833; C. 77—An Act to create sundry new land offices, and to alter the boundaries of other land offices of the United States.[21]

4 St. 665; Mar. 2, 1833; C. 95—An Act to extend the provisions of the act of the third March, 1807, entitled "An Act to prevent settlements being made on lands ceded to the United States, until authorized by law."[22]

4 St. 669; Mar. 2, 1833; J. Res. IV—A Resolution authorizing the Secretary of War to correct certain mistakes.[23]

4 St. 673; May 14, 1834; C. 41—An Act making appropriations for the support of the army for the year 1834.

4 St. 677; June 18, 1834; C. 47—An Act making appropriations for the Indian Department for the year 1834.[24]

4 St. 682; June 26, 1834; C. 74—An Act making appropriations for Indian annuities, and other similar objects, for the year 1834.[25]

4 St. 686; June 26, 1834; C. 76—An Act to create additional land districts in the states of Illinois and Missouri, and in the territory north of the state of Illinois.

4 St. 705; June 28, 1834; C. 105—An Act making appropriations to carry into effect certain Indian treaties, and for other purposes.[26]

4 St. 716; June 30, 1834; C. 137—An Act authorizing the selection of certain Wabash and Erie Canal lands in the state of Ohio.[27]

4 St. 721; June 30, 1834; C. 145—An Act to carry into full eect the fourth article of the treaty of the eighth of January, 1821, with the Creek nation of Indians, so far as relates to the claims of citizens of Georgia against said Indians, prior to 1802.[28]

4 St. 726; June 30, 1834; C. 153—An Act to provide for the payment of claims, for property lost, captured, or destroyed, by the enemy, while in the military service of the United States, during the late war with the Indians on the frontiers of Illinois and Michigan territory.[29]

4 St. 729; June 30, 1834; C. 161—An Act to regulate trade and intercourse with the Indian tribes, and to preserve peace on the frontiers.[30] Sec. 2—R. S. 2129, 2131;[31] Sec. 3—R. S.

---

[3] *Sg.* 7 St. 244. *S.* 4 St. 580.

[4] *Sg.* 7 St. 178, 828. *Cited:* 6 Op. A. G. 627.

[5] *Sg.* 7 St. 311, 333, 351, 355, 364, 366. *S.* 10 St. 15, 11 St. 65.

[6] *Sg.* 4 St. 87, 101, 267, 361, 452, 501.

[7] *A.* 29 St. 506. *R.* 30 St. 105. *Cited:* 17 Op. A. G. 258; Op. Sol. M 27487, July 26, 1933; Memo. Sol., July 25, 1935; Ayres, 44 C. Cls. 48; Ayres, 42 C. Cls. 385; Belt, 15 C. Cls. 92; Brugier, 1 Dak. 5; Fremont, 2 C. Cls. 461; Jump, 100 F. 2d 130; Sarlis, 152 U. S. 570; U. S. v. Belt, 128 Fed. 68; U. S. v. Cohn, 2 Ind. T. 474; U. S. v. Sutton 215 U. S. 291; U. S. ex rel. Scott, 1 Dak. 142; U. S. Exp., 191 Fed. 673

[8] *See* 25 U. S. C. 241a (28 St. 697, sec. 8).

[9] *A.* 52 St. 696, sec. 1.

[10] *Sg* 2 St. 139.

[11] *Sg.* 4 St. 519.

[12] *Sg.* 7 St. 319, 346. *S.* 5 St. 36, 704, 766; 6 St. 901.

[13] *Sg.* 4 St. 411, Sec 6.

[14] *Sg.* 7 St. 327, 359.

[15] *Sg.* 8 St. 261, 397. *S.* 4 St. 619. *R.* 5 St. 142.

[16] *Sg.* 7 St. 303, 328, 338, 359, Art. 5, 7; 367, Art. 3, 5.

[17] *Sg.* 4 St. 618.

[18] *Sg.* 4 St. 214, 286, 390, 397, 403, 411; 7 St. 210, 303, 320.

[19] *Sg.* 7 St. 203, 283, 286, 303, 333, 370, 374, 376, 377, 378, 391, 393, 394, 397, 399, 403, 410, 420.

[20] *Sg.* 4 St. 533.

[21] *Sg.* 7 St. 210, 333.

[22] *Sg.* 2 St. 445.

[23] *Sg.* 7 St. 378.

[24] *S.* 5 St. 704, 766.

[25] *Sg.* 4 St. 300, 442; 7 St. 272, 286, 328, 366, 374, 377, 378, 394, 397, 405.

[26] *Sg.* 7 St. 156, 203, 229, 240, 244, 286, 289, 311, 323, 328, 329, 333, 351, 368, 370, 374, 391, 414, 417, 424, 427, 429, 449.

[27] *Sg.* 4 St. 236. *Cited:* 2 Op. A. G. 698.

[28] *Sg.* 7 St. 215. *Cited:* 4 Op. A. G. 72.

[29] *R.* 5 St. 142.

[30] *Rg.* 2 St. 6, 85, 139; 3 St. 332, 363, 388, 461, 487, 682; 4 St. 25, 145. *Rpg.* 3 St. 428, sec. 1, 2; 514, sec. 2; 517, sec 8; 4 St 35 secs. 3, 4 5; 187, sec. 2. *S* 5 St. 680; 10 St. 269 315 598; 11 St 65; 12 St 15 44. *A.* 9 St. 203; 12 St. 338; 18 St. 29; 22 St. 179; 32 St. 500, 792. *Rp.* 9 St. 252; 11 St. 388; 12 St. 120; 48 St 787. *Cited:* Brown 39 Yale L. J. 307; Thayer, 68 Atl. Month. 540 676; Kent, CAL; 19 L. D 326; 9 Op. A. G. 24; 9 Op A. G. 110; 13 Op A. G. 470; 14 Op. A. G. 290; 18 Op. A G. 235; 18 Op A. G. 555; 22 Op. A G. 232; Memo. Sol. Off. Apr. 26 1933; Op Sol. M 27487, July 26, 1933; Memo. Sol., Dec. 17, 1935; Nov. 17, 1936; Memo. Sol. Off., Nov 29, 1938; Memo. Sol., Apr. 14 1930; Anonymous, 1 Fed. Cas. No. 447; Ash, 252 U S. 159; Ayres, 35 C. Cls. 26; Bailey, 47 F. 2d 702; Bates, 95 U S 204; Blackfeather, 190 U. S. 368; Brown, 32 C. Cls. 432; Brown, 265 Fed. 623; Browning, 6 F. 2d 801; Brugier, 1 Dak. 5; Caldwell, 67 Fed 391; Campbell, 44 C. Cls. 488; Cherokee, 203 U. S. 76; Clairmont, 225 U. S. 551; Corralitos, 178 U. S. 280; Corralitos, 33 C. Cls. 342; Crow, 32 C. Cls. 16; De Baca 37 C. Cls. 482; Evans, 204 Fed. 361; Ex P. Crow Dog, 109 U S. 556; Ex P. Hart, 157 Fed. 130; Fowler, 1 Wash. Ter. 3; French, 49 C. Cls. 337; Garcia, 43 F. 2d 873; Garrison, 30 C Cls. 272; Hegmer, 30 C. Cls. 405; Holden, 17 Wall. 211; In re Sah Quah, 31 Fed. 327; Jaeger, 27 C. Cls. 278; Jaeger, 33 C. Cls. 214; Janus, 38 F. 2d 431; Johnson, 234 U. S. 422; Johnson, 29 C. Cls. 1; Jones, 175 U. S 1; Kie 27 Fed. 351; Leavenworth, 92 U. S. 733; Leighton, 29 C. Cls. 288; Leighton, 161 U. S. 291; Lowe, 37 C. Cls., 413; Marks, 161 U. S. 297; Merchant, 35 C. Cls. 403; Minis, 15 Pet. 423; Mitchell, 27 C. Cls. 316; M. K., & T. Ry., 92 U S. 760; Moore, 2 Wyo. 8; Morrison, 6 F. 2d 811; McCoy, 33 C. Cls. 163; McKinzie, 34 C. Cls. 278; New

2180, 2132, 25 U. S. C. 263;[31] Sec. 4—R. S. 2133, 25 U. S. C. 264 (22 St. 179);[32] USCA Historical Note: R. S. 2133 as originally enacted contained only the provision set forth in the Code section preceding the provisos, without the words, "of the full blood," and the words "or on any Indian reservation." R. S. 2133 was amended by inserting said words and adding the two provisos, to read as set forth here, by Act July 31, 1882. 22 St. 179. Sec. 6—R. S. 2134, 25 U. S. C. 219;[33] Sec. 7—R. S. 2135, 25 U. S. C. 265;[34] Sec. 8—R. S. 2137, 25 U. S. C. 216; Sec. 9—R. S. 2117, 25 U. S. C. 179 (31 St. 871, sec. 37; 32 St. 504, sec. 17);[35] USCA Historical Note: The last sentence of the Code section was derived from sec. 37, 31 St. 871, which was entitled "An Act to ratify and confirm an agreement with the Muskogee or Creek tribe of Indians and for other purposes." Sec. 10—R. S. 2147, 25 U. S. C. 220;[36] Sec. 11—R. S. 2118, 25 U. S. C. 180;[37] Sec. 12—R. S. 2116, 25 U. S. C. 177;[38] Sec. 13—R. S. 2111, 25 U. S. C. 171;[39] Sec. 14—R. S. 2112, 25 U. S. C. 172;[40] Sec. 15—R. S. 2113, 25 U. S. C. 173;[41] Sec. 16—R. S. 2154, 2155, 25 U. S. C. 227, 228;[42] Sec. 17—R. S. 2156, 25 U. S. C. 229; USCA Historical Note: R. S. 2156 was derived from the above. Sec. 17, contained a provision that pending satisfaction by the nation or tribe to which the offending Indian or Indians belonged of the injuries caused by him or them, the United States guaranteed to the party injured an eventual indemnification. This provision was repealed by sec. 8 of Act Feb. 28, 1859, c. 66, 11 St. 401, being the Indian appropriation act for the fiscal year 1864. Sec. 18—R. S. 2157, 25 U. S. C. 230;[43] Sec. 19—R. S. 2152, 25 U. S. C. 225;[44] Sec. 21—R. S. 2141, 25 U. S. C. 251;[45] R. S. 2150, 25 U. S. C. 223;[46] Sec. 22—R. S. 2126, 25 U. S. C. 194;[47] Sec. 23—R. S. 2150, 25 U. S. C. 223;[48] R. S. 2151, 25 U. S. C. 224;[49] Sec. 24—R. S. 533; Sec. 25—R. S. 2145, 25 U. S. C. 217. USCA Historical Note: R. S. 2145 was derived from above sec. 25 and sec. 3 of Act Mar. 27, 1854, c. 26, 10 St. 270; said sec. 3 containing the exception as to the laws enacted for the District of Columbia. Also see annotations under 18 U. S. C. A. 451, 548. Sec. 27—R. S. 2124, 25 U. S. C. 201;[51] Sec. 28—R. S. 2125, 25 U. S. C. 193;[52] Sec. 30—R. S. 2139, 25 U. S. C. 241[53] (19 St. 244, sec. 1; 27 St. 260; 29 St. 506, sec. 1).[54] See Historical Note 25 U. S. C. A. 241.

4 St. 735; June 30, 1834; C. 162—An Act to provide for the organization of the department of Indian Affairs.[55] Sec. 3—R. S. 2050; Sec. 4—R. S. 2060, 25 U. S. C. 30; R. S. 2059, 25 U. S. C. 62; R. S. 2062, 25 U. S. C. 27;[56] Sec. 5—R. S. 2065; Sec. 7—R. S. 2058, 25 U. S. C. 31; R. S. 2066, 25 U. S. C. 40; USCA Historical Note: The derivative sections for R. S. 2058 were re above sec. 7, sec. 4 of Act of June 5, 1850, c. 16, 9 St. 437, and sec. 5 of Act Feb. 27, 1851, c. 14, 9 St. 587. No appropriation for any superintendent of Indian affairs has been made since Act Mar. 3, 1877, c. 101, sec. 1, 19 St. 271. USCA Historical Note: The derivative sections for R. S. 2066 were re above sec. 7 and sec. 1 of Act Mar. 3, 1847, c. 66, 9 St. 203, amendatory of re above 1834 Act. Sec. 8—R. S. 2075, 25 U. S. C. 51;[57] Sec. 9—R. S. 2068, 25 U. S. C. 42;[58] R. S. 2069, 25 U. S. C. 45;[59] R. S. 2072, 25 U. S. C. 48; USCA Historical Note for 25 U. S. C. 45; R. S. 2069 was derived from re above sec. 9

R. S. 2070 provided as follows: "The salaries of interpreters lawfully employed in the service of the United States, in Oregon, Utah, and New Mexico, shall be $500 a year each, and of all so employed elsewhere, $400 a year each." Act Feb. 27, 1851, sec. 8, 9 St. 587; Act Feb. 14, 1873, sec. 1, 17 St. 437. It was repealed by sec. 1 of an Act of May 17, 1882, 22 St. 70. The number and compensation of the interpreters depends on the various annual Appropriation Acts. Sec. 10—R. S. 2074, 25 U. S. C. 50;[60] R. S. 2076, 25

York Indians, 5 Wall. 761; New York ex rel. Cutler, 21 How. 366; Palcher, 11 Fed. 47; Pickett, 1 Idaho 523; Pino, 38 C. Cls. 64; Price, 33 C. Cls. 106; Rex, 58 C. Cls. 820; Roy, 45 C. Cls. 177; Schaap, 210 Fed. 853; Shoshone, 82 C. Cls. 23; Stevens, 34 C. Cls. 244; Stone, 29 C. Cls. 111; Territory of Oregon, 1 Oreg. 101; Thomison, 35 Ct Cls. 395; Thurston, 232 U. S. 469; Uhlig, 2 Dak. 71; U. S. Exp., 101 Fed. 673; U. S. v. Alberty, 24 Fed. Cas. No. 14426; U. S. v. Andrews, 179 U. S. 96; U. S. v. Berry, 4 Fed. 779; U. S. v. Belt, 128 Fed. 68; U. S. v. Bichard, 1 Ariz. 31; U. S. v. Birdsall, 233 U. S. 223; U. S. v. Board, 37 F. 2d 272; U. S. v. Bridleman, 7 Fed. 894; U. S. v. Candelaria, 271 U. S. 432; U. S. v. Carr, 2 Mont. 234; U. S. v. Celestine, 215 U. S. 278; U. S. v. Chavez, 290 U. S. 357; U. S. v. Dawson, 15 How. 467; U. S. v. Douglas, 190 Fed. 482; U. S. v. Downing, 25 Fed. Cas. No. 14991; U. S. v. Ewing, 47 Fed. 809; U. S. v. 43 Gallons, 93 U. S. 188; U. S. v. 43 Gallons, 108 U. S. 491; U. S. v. Holliday, 3 Wall. 407 U. S. v. Howard, 17 Fed. 638; U. S. v. Kie, 26 Fed. Cas. No. 15528a; U. S. v. Knowlton, 8 Dak. 58; U. S. v. Leathers, 26 Fed. Cas. No. 15581; U. S. v. Lucero, 1 N. M. 422; U. S. v. LeBris, 121 U. S. 278; U. S. v. McGowan, 89 F. 2d 201; U. S. v. McGowan, 302 U. S. 535; U. S. v. Matlock, 26 Fed. Cas. No. 15744; U. S. v. Myers, 206 Fed. 387; U. S. v. Nelson, 29 Fed. 202; U. S. v. Buffalo, 1 Mont. 489; U. S. v. Quiver, 241 U. S. 602; U. S. v. Rogers, 4 How. 567; U. S. v. Sa-coo-da-cat, 27 Fed. Cas. No. 16212; U. S. v. Sanders, 27 Fed. Cas. No. 16220; U. S. v. Santistevan, 1 N. M. 583; U. S. v. Seveloff, 27 Fed. Cas. No. 16252; U. S. v. Shaw-Mux, 27 Fed. Cas. No. 16268; U. S. v. Starr, 27 Fed. Cas. No. 16379; U. S. v. Stephens, 12 Fed. 52; U. S. v. Stocking, 87 Fed. 857; U. S. v. Tadish, 211 Fed. 490; U. S. v. Tom, 1 Ore. 26; U. S. v. Varela, 1 N. M. 593; U. S. v. Ward, 28 Fed. Cas. No. 16639; U. S. v. Warwick, 51 Fed. 280; U. S. v. Wirt, 28 Fed. Cas. No. 16745; U. S. v. Wright, 53 F. 2d 300; U. S. ex rel. Scott, 1 Dak. 142; Valk, 22 C. Cls. 241; Valk, 29 C. Cls. 62; Walker, 16 Wall. 436; Waters, 29 Fed. Cas. No. 17264; Waters, 29 Fed. Cas. No. 17265; Welch, 32 C. Cls. 106; Westmoreland, 155 U. S. 545; Woolverton, 29 C. Cls. 107.

[31] *Cited:* 27 Op. A. G. 588; 43 Cases, 14 Fed. 539; Palcher, 11 Fed. 47; U. S. v. Celestine, 215 U. S. 278; U. S. v. Leathers, 26 Fed. Cas. No. 15581; U. S. v. Sturgeon, 27 Fed. Cas. No. 16413; Waters, 29 Fed. Cas. No. 17264; Waters, 29 Fed. Cas. No. 17265

[32] *Cited:* 43 Cases, 14 Fed. 539; Palcher, 11 Fed. 47; U. S. v. Celestine, 215 U. S. 278; U. S. v. Leathers, 26 Fed. Cas. No. 15581.

[33] *Cited:* 27 Op. A. G. 588; Benson, 44 Fed. 178; 43 Cases, 14 Fed. 539; Palcher v. U. S., 11 Fed. 47; U. S. v. Bridleman, 7 Fed. 894; U. S. v. Celestine, 215 U. S. 278; U. S. v. 48 Lbs., 35 Fed. 403; U. S. v. Leathers, 26 Fed. Cas. No. 15581; U. S. v. Martin, 14 Fed. 817.

[34] *R.* 48 St. 787. *Cited:* 18 Op. A. G. 555; Benson, 44 Fed. 178; Cherokee, 203 U. S. 76; 43 Cases, 14 Fed. 539; Palcher, 11 Fed. 47; U. S. v. Celestine, 215 U. S. 278; U. S. v. Leathers, 26 Fed. Cas. No. 15581

[35] *Cited:* Cherokee, 203 U. S. 76; 43 Cases, 14 Fed. 539; Palcher, 11 Fed. 47; U. S. v. Celestine, 215 U. S. 278; U. S. v. Leathers, 26 Fed. Cas. No. 15581.

[36] *Cited:* 16 Op. A. G. 568; 18 Op. A. G. 91; Ash, 252 U. S. 159; Forsythe, 8 Ind. T. 590; Kirby, 260 U. S. 423; Pike, 4 Mackey (15 D. C.) 581; U. S. v. Boylan, 265 Fed. 165; U. S. v. Loving, 34 Fed. 715.

[37] *R.* 48 St. 787. *Cited:* Sol. Op. M. 25358, May 14, 1928; 20 Op. A. G. 245; 23 Op. A. G. 214; Cherokee, 203 U. S. 76; 43 Cases, 14 Fed. 539; In re Blackbird, 109 Fed. 139; Morris, 194 U. S. 384; Palcher, 11 Fed. 47; Quigley, 3 Ind. T. 265; Stephens, 126 Fed. 148; U. S. v. Celestine, 215 U. S. 278; U. S. v. Martin, 14 Fed. 817; U. S. v. Payne, 8 Fed. 883; U. S. v. Payne, 22 Fed. 426; U. S. v. Sturgeon, 27 Fed. Cas. No. 16413; U. S. ex rel. Gordon, 179 Fed. 391.

[38] *Cited:* 20 Op. A. G. 245; Ansley, 5 Ind. T. 563; Denton, 5 Ind. T. 396; German-American 5 Ind. T. 703; Jaeger, 29 C. Cls. 172; Langforth, 1 Idaho 612; Pike, 4 Mackey (15 D. C.) 531; Uhlig, 2 Dak. 71; U. S. v. Berry, 4 Fed. 779; U. S. v. Boylan, 264 Fed. 165; U. S. v. Joseph, 94 U. S. 614; U. S. v. Mullin, 71 Fed. 682; U. S. v. Payne, 22 Fed. 426; Walker, 204 U. S. 302.

[39] *Cited:* 18 Op. A. G. 235; 18 Op. A. G. 486; German-American, 5 Ind. T. 703; Franklin, 283 U. S. 269; Light, 10 Okla. 732; McBride, 149 Fed. 114; Pike, 4 Mackey (15 D. C.) 531; Pueblo of Santa Rosa, 273 U. S. 315; U. S. v. Berry, 4 Fed. 779; U. S. v. Boylan, 265 Fed. 165; U. S. v. Hunter, 21 Fed. 615; U. S. v. 7405.3 Acres, 99 F. 2d 417.

[40] *R.* 48 St. 787; *Cited:* U. S. v. Boylan, 265 Fed. 165.

[41] *R.* 48 St. 787; *Cited:* U. S. v. Boylan, 265 Fed. 165.

[42] *R.* 48 St. 787; *Cited:* In re Lelah-puc-ka-chee, 98 Fed. 429; U. S. v. Boylan, 265 Fed. 165.

[43] *Cited:* Blackfeather, 190 U. S. 368; 43 Cases, 14 Fed. 539; Janis v. U. S., 32 C. Cls. 407; Leighton v. U. S., 29 C. Cls. 288; Palcher v. U. S., 11 Fed. 47; U. S. v. Celestine, 215 U. S. 278.

[44] *Cited:* Quigley, 3 Ind. T. 265; Thurston, 232 U. S. 469; U. S. v. Celestine, 215 U. S. 278.

[45] *R.* 48 St. 787. *Cited:* 21 Op. A. G. 72; 43 Cases, 14 Fed. 539; Palcher, 11 Fed. 47; U. S. v. Celestine, 215 U. S. 278.

[46] *See* 25 U. S. C. 241a. *Cited:* 22 Op. A. G. 232; 43 Cases, 14 Fed. 539; Johnson, 234 U. S. 422; Palcher, 11 Fed. 47; Townsend, 265 Fed. 519; U. S. v. Birdsall, 233 U. S. 223; U. S. v. Celestine, 215 U. S. 278; U. S. v. Luther, 260 Fed. 579; U. S. Exp., 191 Fed. 673.

[47] *R.* 48 St. 787. *Cited:* 18 Op. A. G. 544; 23 Op. A. G. 214; Janus, 38 F. 2d 431; Morris, 194 U. S. 384; Stephens, 126 Fed. 148; U. S. v. Baker, 4 Ind. T. 514; U. S. v. Celestine, 215 U. S. 278; U. S. ex rel. Gordon, 179 Fed. 391; U. S. ex rel. Standing Bear, 25 Fed. Cas. No. 14891; U. S. Exp., 191 Fed. 673.

[48] *Cited:* U. S. v. Boylan, 265 Fed. 165.

[49] See footnote "47" above.

[50] *R.* 48 St. 787. *Cited:* Janus, 38 F. 2d 431; U. S. v. Celestine, 215 U. S., 278; U. S. ex rel. Gordon, 179 Fed. 391.

[51] *Cited:* U. S. v. Boylan, 265 Fed. 165; U. S. ex rel. Gordon, 179 Fed. 391; U. S. v. Howard, 17 Fed. 638; U. S. v. Payne, 22 Fed. 426; U. S. v. Stocking, 87 Fed. 857.

[52] *Cited:* 18 Op. A. G. 544; U. S. v. Boylan, 265 Fed. 165; U. S. ex rel. Gordon, 179 Fed. 391.

[53] *See:* 25 U. S. C. 241a (28 St. 697, sec. 8).

[54] *A.* 52 St. 696, sec. 1.

[55] *S.* 4 St. 746; 5 St. 36, 158, 298, 402, 417, 498, 704, 766; 6 St. 685; 9 St. 20, 132, 252, 382, 544, 574; 10 St. 41, 266, 315, 686; 11 St. 169; 12 St. 44, 221, 512, 774. *A.* 9 St. 203. *Rp.* 9 St. 252. *Cited:* 6 Op. A. G. 49; 17 Op. A. G. 258; Memo. Ind. Off., Aug. 27, 1928; Op. Sol. M. 27487, July 26, 1933; Memo. Sol., July 25, 1935, June 14, 1938; Memo. Sol. Off., July 7, 1938, July 16, 1938, Oct. 28, 1938; Memo. Sol., Feb. 17, 1939; Belt, 15 C. Cls. 92; Fremont, 2 C. Cls. 461; Jump, 100 F. 2d 130; Leighton, 29 C. Cls. 288; U. S. v. Douglas, 190 Fed. 482; U. S. v. Humason, 26 Fed. Cas. No. 15420; U. S. v. Hutto, No. 1, 256 U. S. 524; U. S. v. Hutto, No. 2, 256 U. S. 530; U. S. v. McDougall's Adm'r, 121 U. S. 89; U. S. v. Mitchell, 109 U. S. 146; U. S. v. Watashe, 102 F. 2d 428; U. S. Fidelity, 214 U. S. 507.

[56] *Cited:* 14 Op. A. G. 573; 15 Op. A. G. 405; Renfrow, 8 Okla. 161; U. S. v. Mullin, 71 Fed. 682.

[57] *Cited:* U. S. v. Humason, 26 Fed. Cas. No. 15420.

[58] *Cited:* U. S. v. Mitchell, 109 U. S. 146.

[59] *See:* 25 U. S. C. 472.

[60] *See:* 5 U. S. C. 30a. *Cited:* 20 Op. A. G. 494.

U. S. C. 60; R. S. 2077, 25 U. S. C. 54;[61] USCA Historical Note: R. S. 2077 was derived re sec. 10 above. Appropriations for traveling and incidental expenses of special agents and others, in accord with provisions of this section, are made in the annual Indian appropriation Acts. The provision of the fiscal year 1917 was by Act of May 18, 1916, sec. 1, 39 St. 127, which limits the subsistence allowance of special agents and inspectors to $3 per day. Sec. 11—R. S. 2086, 25 U. S. C. 111;[62] USCA Historical Note: R. S. 2086 was derived sec. 11 re above; sec. 3 of Act Mar. 3, 1847, 9 St. 203; sec. 3 of Act Aug. 30, 1852, 10 St. 56, being the Indian appropriation act for the fiscal year of 1853, and secs. 2 and 3 of Act July 15, 1870, 16 St. 360, being the Indian appropriation act for the fiscal year 1871. Sec. 12—R. S. 2062, 25 U. S. C. 27; R. S. 2082, 25 U. S. C. 115; Sec. 13—R. S. 2083, 25 U. S. C. 91;[63] R. S. 2088, 25 U. S. C. 112; R. S. 2091; Sec. 14—R. S. 2078, 25 U. S. C. 68;[64] Sec. 16—R. S. 2110, 25 U. S. C. 141; USCA Historical Note: The Interior Department, commenting on this section says: "The practice of issuing army rations to Indians is no longer in use, and this section should therefore be repealed." Sec. 17—R. S. 465, 25 U. S. C. 9.[65]

4 St. 740; June 30, 1834; C. 167—An Act to relinquish the reversionary interest of the United States in a certain Indian reservation lying between the rivers Mississippi and Desmoins.[66]

4 St. 746; Jan. 27, 1835; C. 2—An Act making appropriations for the current expenses of the Indian department for the year 1835.[67]

4 St. 760; Mar. 3, 1835; C. 30—An Act making appropriations for the civil and diplomatic expenses of government for the year 1835.[68]

4 St. 780; Mar. 3, 1835; C. 50—An Act making appropriations for Indian annuities and other similar objects, for the year 1835.[69]

5 STAT.

5 St. 1; Jan. 14, 1836; C. 1—An Act making an appropriation for repressing hostilities commenced by the Seminole Indians.

5 St. 1; Jan. 29, 1836; C. 3—An Act making an additional appropriation for repressing hostilities commenced by the Seminole Indians.[70]

5 St. 6; Mar. 19, 1836; C. 43—An Act authorizing the Secretary of War to transfer a part of the appropriation for the suppression of Indian hostilities in Florida, to the credit of subsistence.

5 St. 7; Mar. 19, 1836; C. 44—An Act to provide for the payment of volunteers and militia corps, in the service of the United States.[71]
R. S. 1657.

5 St. 8; Apr. 1, 1836; C. 46—An Act making a further appropriation for the suppression of Indian hostilities in Florida.

5 St. 10; Apr. 20, 1836; C. 53—An Act to carry into effect the treaties concluded by the Chickasaw tribe of Indians on the twentieth October, 1832, and the twenty-fourth May, 1834.[72]

5 St. 10; Apr. 20, 1836; C. 54—An Act establishing the Territorial Government of Wisconsin.[73]

5 St. 17; Apr. 29, 1836; C. 57—An Act making a further appropriation for suppressing Indian hostilities in Florida.[74]

5 St. 17; May 9, 1836; C. 59—An Act making appropriations for the civil and diplomatic expenses of Government for the year 1836.

5 St. 26; May 9, 1836; C. 60—An Act providing for the salaries of certain officers therein named, and for other purposes.[75]

5 St. 32; May 23, 1836; C. 80—An Act authorizing the President of the United States to accept the service of volunteers, and to raise an additional regiment of dragoons or mounted riflemen.

5 St. 33; May 23, 1836; C. 81—An Act making appropriations for the suppression of hostilities by the Creek Indians.[76]

5 St. 34; June 7, 1836; C. 86—An Act to extend the western boundary of the State of Missouri to the Missouri river.[77]

5 St. 36; June 14, 1836; C. 88—An Act making appropriations for the current expenses of the Indian Department, for Indian annuities, and other similar objects, for the year 1836.[78]

5 St. 48; June 15, 1836; C. 98—An Act to divide the Green Bay land district in Michigan, and for other purposes.[79]

5 St. 65; July 2, 1836; C. 254—An Act making appropriations for the suppression of Indian hostilities and for other purposes.[80]

5 St. 67; July 2, 1836; C. 258—An Act to provide for the better protection of the western frontier.

5 St. 71; July 2, 1836; C. 263—An Act for the payment of certain companies of the militia of Missouri and Indiana, for services rendered against the Indians in 1832.

5 St. 73; July 2, 1836; C. 267—An Act making further appropriations for carrying into effect certain Indian treaties.[81]

5 St. 116; July 4, 1836; C. 355—An Act to carry into effect, in the States of Alabama, and Mississippi, the existing compacts with those States in regard to the five per cent. fund, and the school reservations.[82]

5 St. 131; Feb. 1, 1836; J. Res. No. I—Resolution authorizing the President to furnish rations to certain inhabitants of Florida.

5 St. 131; May 9, 1836; J. Res. No. III—Resolution to suspend the sale of a part of the public lands acquired by the treaty of Dancing Rabbit Creek.[83]

5 St. 135; Jan. 9, 1837; C. 1—An Act to regulate, in certain cases, the disposition of the proceeds of lands ceded by Indian tribes to the United States.[84] Sec. 1–R. S. 2093, 25 U. S. C. 152;[85] Sec. 2–R. S. 2094, 25 U. S. C. 153; Sec. 3–R. S. 2095, 25 U. S. C. 157; Sec. 4–R. S. 2096, 25 U. S. C. 158.[86]

5 St. 135; Jan. 9, 1837; C. 2—An Act making an appropriation for the suppression of Indian hostilities.[87]

5 St. 142; Jan. 18, 1837; C. 5—An Act to provide for the payment of horses and other property lost or destroyed in the military service of the United States.[88]

5 St. 147; Mar. 1, 1837; C. 16—An Act to extend the jurisdiction of the District Court of the United States, for the district of Arkansas.[89]

5 St. 148; Mar. 1, 1837; C. 17—An Act making appropriations for the support of the army for the year 1837, and for other purposes.

5 St. 152; Mar. 2, 1837; C. 20—An Act making an additional appropriation for the suppression of Indian hostilities, for the year 1837.[90]

5 St. 158; Mar. 3, 1837; C. 31—An Act making appropriations for the current expenses of the Indian Department, and for fulfilling treaty stipulations with the various Indian tribes, for the year 1837.[91]

---

[61] *See:* 5 U. S. C. 73, 73a, 73b and c. 16 of Tit. 5. *Cited:* U. S. v. Smith 35 Fed. 490.

[62] *See:* 25 U. S. C. 474 (48 St. 987, sec. 14).

[63] Superseded by 36 St. 861, sec. 28. *See:* 25 U. S. C. 93.

[64] *Cited:* Memo. Ind. Off., Mar. 18, 1927; Ewert, 259 U. S. 129; Kendall, 259 U. S. 139; U. S. v. Douglas, 190 Fed. 482; U. S. v. Hutto, No. 1, 256 U. S. 524; U. S. v. Hutto, No. 2, 256 U. S. 530.

[65] *Cited:* 5 L. D. 520; Chippewa, 301 U. S. 358; In re Bya-Lil-Le, 12 Ariz. 150; Romero, 24 C. Cls., 331; U. S. v. Birdsall, 233 U. S. 223; U. S. v. Leathers, 26 Fed. Cas. No. 15581; U. S. v. Thurston, 143 Fed. 287; U. S. Fidelity, 214 U. S. 507.

[66] *Sg.* 7 St. 229. *Cited:* March, 8 How. 223; U. S. v. Higgins, 103 Fed. 348; Webster, 11 How. 437.

[67] *Sg.* 4 St. 735.

[68] *Cited:* Minis, 15 Pet. 423.

[69] *Sg.* 1 St. 618; 3 St. 608; 4 St. 181, 442; 7 St. 16, 35 43, 44, 49, 62, 66, 68, 74, 84, 87, 91, 100, 105, 107, 113, 152, 178, 185, 186, 188, 189, 203, 210, 224, 228, 231, 234 240, 244, 284, 286, 290, 295, 300, 303, 311, 317, 320, 323, 327, 328, 333, 348, 355, 366, 368, 370, 374, 378, 393, 394, 397, 399, 403, 410, 414, 417, 424, 429, 449, 450. *S.* 5 St. 704.

[70] *Sg.* 4 St. 501.

[71] *S.* 5 St. 33, 65, 135, 152, 205, 209, 241, 357, 458.

[72] *Sg.* 7 St. 388, 450. *S.* 5 St. 36. *Cited:* Ayres, 42 C. Cls. 385.

[73] *Sg.* N. W. Ord. 1787, U. S. C. (1934 ed.) p. XXIII.

[74] 5 St. 678.

[75] *Rpg.* 2 St. 698, 742. *S.* 5 St. 26, 409, 528.

[76] *Sg.* 1 St. 408; 4 St. 501; 5 St. 7.

[77] *Cited:* State of Missouri, 7 How. 660.

[78] *Sg.* 1 St. 618; 3 St. 608; 4 St. 100, 181, 442, 504, 735; 5 St. 10; 7 St. 43, 44, 49, 66, 74, 84, 87, 93, 98, 100, 105, 107, 113, 137, 152, 160, 178, 185, 186, 188, 203, 210, 218, 228, 234, 284, 290, 295, 300, 303, 311, 317, 320, 323, 327, 328, 338, 342, 348, 351, 355, 366, 370, 374, 378, 393, 391, 397, 399, 403, 410, 414, 424, 429, 431, 449, 450, 467, 470. *S.* 5 St. 73, 135.

[79] *Sg.* 7 St. 374. *S.* 5 St. 678.

[80] *Sg.* 1 St. 408; 4 St. 501; 5 St. 7. *S.* 5 St. 135, 152, 205, 209, 241, 357.

[81] *Sg.* 5 St. 36; 7 St. 478; 488, 490, 491, 496, 498, 499, 500, 501, 503. *S.* 9 St. 746; 10 St. 15, 41. *Cited:* Eastern Band, 20 C. Cls. 449; Holden, 17 Wall. 211; Ward, 17 Wall. 253; 4 Op. A. G. 621.

[82] *Sg.* 7 St. 388; 3 St. 348, 489, Sec. 6. *A.* 5 St. 490, 727; 9 St. 202.

[83] *Sg.* 7 St. 333. *S.* 5 St. 180.

[84] *Sg.* 5 Stat. 36. *Cited:* Holden, 17 Wall. 211; Kansas, 80 C. Cls. 261; Leavenworth, 92 U. S. 733; M. K. & T. Ry., 92 U. S. 760; Ward, 17 Wall. 253.

[85] *See:* 25 U. S. C. 154 (23 St. 98, sec. 10). *Cited:* U. S. v. Berry, 4 Fed. 779.

[86] *Cited:* U. S. v. Berry, 4 Fed. 779; U. S. v. Blackfeather, 155 U. S. 180; U. S. v. Omaha, 253 U. S. 275.

[87] *Sg.* 1 St. 408; 4 St. 500; 5 St. 7, 65.

[88] *Rg.* 4 St. 613, 726. *S.* 5 St. 204.

[89] *Sg.* 2 St. 139.

[90] *Sg.* 1 St. 408; 4 St. 500; 5 St. 7, 65.

[91] *Sg.* 3 St. 261; 4 St. 735; 7 St. 229, 240, 244, 320, 323, 327, 328, 333, 366, 420, 431, 505, 506, 510, 511, 514, 515, 516, 517, 524, 527, 532. *S.* 5 St. 131, 298, 402, 417, 493, 704, 766; 9 St. 20, 182, 252, 382, 544, 574.

5 St. 163; Mar. 3, 1837; C. 33—An Act making appropriations for the civil and diplomatic expenses of Government for the year 1837. R. S. 447.

5 St. 180; Mar. 3, 1837; C. 39—An Act for the appointment of commissioners to adjust the claims to reservations of land under the fourteenth article of the treaty of 1830 with the Choctaw Indians.[92]

5 St. 186; Mar. 3, 1837; C. 41—An Act to authorize and sanction the sales of reserves, provided for Creek Indians in the treaty of March 24, 1832, in certain cases, and for other purposes.[93]

5 St. 195; Mar 3, 1837; C. 46—An Act to provide for continuing the construction, and for the repair of certain roads, and for other purposes, during the year 1837.[94]

5 St. 204; Oct. 12, 1837; C. 4—An Act to continue in force certain laws to the close of the next session of Congress.[95]

5 St. 205; Oct. 16, 1837; C. 7—An Act making an additional appropriation for the suppression of Indian hostilities, for the year 1837.[96]

5 St. 209; Jan. 16, 1838; C. 3—An Act to provide for the payment of the annuities which will become due and payable to the Great and Little Osages, in the year 1838, and for other purposes.

5 St. 209; Jan. 30, 1838; C. 4—An Act making a partial appropriation for the suppression of Indian hostilities for the year 1838.[97]

5 St. 211; Feb. 22, 1838; C. 13—An Act to amend an act entitled "An act for the appointment of commissioners to adjust the claims to reservations of land under the fourteenth article of the treaty of 1830 with the Choctaw Indians."[98]

5 St. 216; Apr. 6, 1838; C. 54—An Act making appropriations for the civil and diplomatic expenses of Government for the year 1838.

5 St. 235; June 12, 1838; C. 96—An Act to divide the Territory of Wisconsin and to establish the Territorial Government of Iowa.[99]

5 St. 241; June 12, 1838; C. 97—An Act making appropriations for preventing and suppressing Indian hostilities for the year 1838 and for arrearages for the year 1837.[1]

5 St. 244; June 12, 1838; C. 110—An Act concerning a seminary of learning in the Territory of Wisconsin.

5 St. 251; June 22, 1838; C. 119—An Act to grant pre-emption rights to settlers on the public lands.[2]

5 St. 256; July 5, 1838; C. 161—An Act to authorize the issuing of patents to the last bona fide transferee of reservations under the treaty between the United States and the Creek tribe of Indians which was concluded on the twenty-fourth of March, 1832.[3]

5 St. 256; July 5, 1838; C. 162—An Act to increase the present military establishment of the United States, and for other purposes.
Sec. 31—R. S. 1224.

5 St. 264; July 7, 1838; C. 169—An Act to provide for the support of the Military Academy of the United States for the year 1838, and for other purposes.

5 St. 296; July 7, 1838; C. 183—An Act ceding to the State of Ohio the interest of the United States in a certain road within that State.[4]

5 St. 298; July 7, 1838; C. 186—An Act making appropriations for the current and contingent expenses of the Indian department, and for fulfilling treaty stipulations with the various Indian tribes, for the year 1838.[5]

5 St. 316; Feb. 13, 1839; C. 24—An Act to provide for the location and temporary support of the Seminole Indians removed from Florida.

5 St. 323; Mar. 3, 1839; C. 71—An Act making appropriations for the current and contingent expenses of the Indian Department, and for fulfilling treaty stipulations with the various Indian tribes, for the year 1839.[6]

5 St. 331; Mar. 3, 1839; C. 80—An Act to provide for taking the sixth census or enumeration of the inhabitants of the United States.

5 St. 339; Mar. 3, 1839; C. 82—An Act making appropriations for the civil and diplomatic expenses of Government for the year 1839.[7]

5 St. 349; Mar. 3, 1839; C. 83—An Act for the relief of the Brothertown Indians in the Territory of Wisconsin.[8]
R. S. 1765–1779.

5 St. 352; Mar. 3, 1839; C. 86—An Act to authorize the construction of a road from Dubuque, in the Territory of Iowa, to the northern boundary of the State of Missouri, and for other purposes.[9]

5 St. 357; Mar. 3, 1839; C. 93—An Act making appropriations for preventing and suppressing Indian hostilities, for the year 1839.[10]

5 St. 371; May 8, 1840; C. 22—An Act making appropriations for the civil and diplomatic expenses of the Government for the year 1840.

5 St. 397; July 20, 1840; C. 49—An Act to annex a certain tract of land to the Coosa land district, and for other purposes.[11]

5 St. 402; July 20, 1840; C. 53—An Act making appropriations for the current and contingent expenses of the Indian Department, and for fulfilling treaty stipulations with the various Indian tribes, for the year 1840.[12]

5 St. 409; May 2, 1840; J. Res. No. I—Joint Resolution authorizing the Secretary of War to continue certain clerks employed in the office of the Commissioner of Indian Affairs.[13]

5 St. 412; Feb. 18, 1841; C. 6—An Act making appropriations for the payment of revolutionary and other pensioners of the United States, for the year 1841, and for other purposes.

5 St. 414; Mar. 2, 1841; C. 21—An Act making an appropriation to defray the expense of a delegation of the Seminole Indians west of the Mississippi to Florida, and for other purposes.[14]

5 St. 417; Mar. 3, 1841; C. 33—An Act making appropriations for the current and contingent expenses of the Indian Department, and for fulfilling treaty stipulations with the various Indian tribes, for the year 1841.[15]

5 St. 421; Mar. 3, 1841; C. 35—An Act making appropriations for the civil and diplomatic expenses of the Government for the year 1841.

5 St. 435; Mar. 3, 1841; C. 37—An Act making an appropriation for the temporary support of certain destitute Kickapoo Indians, and to defray the expense of removing and subsisting the Swan Creek and Black River Indians of Michigan.

5 St. 453; Sep. 4, 1841; C. 16—An Act to appropriate the proceeds of the sales of the public lands, and to grant pre-emption rights.[16]
R. S. 2258, 2259, 2260, 2261.

5 St. 458; Sep. 9, 1841; C. 17—An Act making appropriations for various fortification, for ordnance, and for preventing and suppressing Indian hostilities.[17]

5 St. 470; Mar. 4, 1842; C. 5—An Act to provide for the early disposition of the lands lying in the State of Alabama, acquired from the Cherokee Indians by the treaty of twenty-ninth of December, 1835.[18]

5 St. 473; Apr. 14, 1842; C. 24—An Act to provide for the allowance of invalid pensions to certain Cherokee warriors, under the provisions of the fourteenth article of the treaty of 1835.[19]

---

[92] *Sg.* 5 St. 131; 7 St. 333. *A.* 5 St. 211. *S.* 5 St. 513. *Cited:* 3 Op. A. G. 408; 26 Op. A. G. 127; Choctaw, 21 C. Cls. 59, rev'd 119 U. S. 1; Wilson, 6 Wall. 83.

[93] *Sg.* 7 St. 366. *S.* 11 St. 169, 699. *Cited:* 3 Op. A. G. 596; 4 Op. A. G. Op. A. G. 75; 4 Op. A. G. 77; 16 Op. A. G. 31; Creek, 77 C. Cls. 226; Creek, 77 C. Cls. 159, rev'd 295 U. S. 103, same case 302 U. S. 620.

[94] *Sg.* 4 St. 22.

[95] *Sg.* 5 St. 142.

[96] *Sg.* 5 St. 7, 65.

[97] *Sg.* 5 St. 7, 65.

[98] *Ag.* 5 St. 180. *Rp.* 5 St. 513.

[99] *Sg.* N. W. Ord. 1787, U. S. C. (1934 ed.) p. XXIII. *S.* 5 St. 522. *Cited:* State of Missouri, 7 How. 660; Western Cherokee, 27 C. Cls. 1, mod. 28 C. Cls. 557.

[1] *Sg.* 5 St. 7, 65, 488. *S.* 5 St. 612, 678; 9 St. 544. *Cited:* 4 Op. A. G. 621; Old Settlers, 148 U. S. 427.

[2] *Sg.* 4 St. 420; 7 St. 333. *Rp.* 5 St. 453. *S.* 9 St. 50. *Cited:* 3 Op. A. G. 408.

[3] *Sg.* 7 St. 366. *Cited:* 3 Op. A. G. 423.

[4] *Sg.* 7 St. 112.

[5] *Sg.* 4 St. 735; 5 St. 158; 7 St. 240, 397, 528, 536, 540, 542, 543, 544, 547, 550, 565, 566.

[6] *Rg.* 4 St. 411, sec. 2; *Sg.* 7 St. 321, 378, 478, 491, 511, 534, 538, 540, 550, 569, 574, 578. *S.* 5 St. 612; 10 St. 15.

[7] *Cited:* 3 Op. A. G. 431; Minis, 15 Pet. 423.

[8] *Sg.* 7 St. 346, 405. *S.* 5 St. 766; 813; 19 St. 41. *Cited:* Elk, 112 U. S. 94

[9] *Cited:* King, 111 Fed. 860.

[10] *Sg.* 5 St. 7, 65. *S.* 5 St. 612, 673, 678.

[11] *Sg.* 7 St. 120.

[12] *Sg.* 4 St. 735; 5 St. 158; 7 St. 189, 536, 544, 565, 569, 576, 580.

[13] *Sg.* 5 St. 26, Sec. 1, Cl. 16. *S.* 5 St. 583.

[14] *S.* 9 St. 544.

[15] *Sg.* 4 St. 735; 5 St. 158.

[16] *Sg.* 7 St. 333, 532, 569. *Rpg.* 5 St. 251. *S.* 5 St. 619; 10 St. 7, 308; 12 St. 413; 15 St. 186. *Cited:* 6 Op. A. G. 658; 7 Op. A. G. 742; Hartman, 76 Fed. 157; King, 111 Fed. 860; Spalding, 160 U. S. 394.

[17] *Sg.* 5 St. 7.

[18] *Sg.* 7 St. 478.

[19] *Sg.* 7 St. 478, Art. 16.

5 St. 475; May 18, 1842; C. 29—An Act making appropriations for the civil and diplomatic expenses of Government for the year 1842.
R. S. 1888.

5 St. 490; June 13, 1842; C. 40—An Act to amend an act entitled "An act to carry into effect, in the States of Alabama and Mississippi, the existing compacts with those States with regard to the five per cent. fund and the school reservations."[20]

5 St. 493; July 17, 1842; C. 64—An Act making appropriations for the current and contingent expenses of the Indian Department, and for fulfilling treaty stipulations with the various Indian tribes, for the year 1842.[21]

5 St. 504; Aug. 11, 1842; C. 127—An Act to provide for the settlement of the claims of the State of Georgia for the services of her militia.

5 St. 506; Aug. 16, 1842; C. 178—An Act authorizing the settlement and payment of certain claims of the State of Alabama.[22]

5 St. 513; Aug. 23, 1842; C. 187—An Act to provide for the satisfaction of claims arising under the fourteenth and nineteenth articles of the treaty of Dancing Rabbit creek, concluded in September, 1830.[23]

5 St. 522; Aug. 23, 1842; C. 194—An Act to authorize the selection of school lands in lieu of those granted to the half-breeds of the Sac and Fox Indians.[24]

5 St. 523; Aug. 26, 1842; C. 202—An Act legalizing and making appropriations for such necessary objects as have been usually included in the general appropriation bills without authority of law, and to fix and provide for certain incidental expenses of the Departments and offices of the Government, and for other purposes.[25]

5 St. 542; Aug. 29, 1842; C. 262—An Act to authorize the States of Indiana and Illinois to select certain quantities of land, in lieu of like quantities heretofore granted to the said States, for the construction of the Wabash and Erie and the Illinois and Michigan canals.[26]

5 St. 545; Aug. 29, 1842; C. 264—An Act to provide for the reports of the decisions of the Supreme Court of the United States.
R. S. 677, 681, 682, 683.

5 St. 576; Aug. 31, 1842; C. 275—An Act making appropriations to carry into effect a treaty with the Wyandott Indians, and for other purposes.[27]

5 St. 583; May 18, 1842; J. Res. No. IV—Joint Resolution to continue two clerks in the business of reservations and grants under Indian treaties.[28]

5 St. 584; Aug. 30, 1842; J. Res. No. X—Joint Resolution to institute proceedings to ascertain the title to Rush Island, ceded in the Caddo Treaty.[29]

5 St. 586; Dec. 24, 1842; C. 2—An Act making appropriations for the civil and diplomatic expenses of Government for the half calendar year ending the thirtieth day of June 1843.

5 St. 603; Mar. 1, 1843; C. 50—An Act to perfect the titles to lands south of the Arkansas river, held under New Madrid locations, and pre-emption rights under the act of 1814[15].[30]

5 St. 611; Mar. 3, 1843; C. 78—An Act authorizing the sale of lands, with the improvements thereon erected by the United States, for the use of their agents, teachers, farmers, mechanics, and other persons employed amongst the Indians.[31] Sec. 1—R. S. 2122, 25 U. S. C. 188; Sec. 2—R. S. 2123, 25 U. S. C. 189.

5 St. 612; Mar. 3, 1843; C. 80—An Act making appropriations for fulfilling treaty stipulations with the various Indian tribes, and for the current and contingent expenses of the Indian department, for the half calendar year beginning the first day of January and ending the thirtieth day of June, 1843; and for the fiscal year beginning the first day of July, 1843, and ending the thirtieth day of June, 1844, and for other purposes.[32]

5 St. 619, Mar. 3, 1843; C. 86—An Act to authorize the investigation of alleged frauds under the pre-emption laws, and for other purposes.[33] R. S. 2272.

5 St. 622; Mar. 3, 1843; C. 88—An Act directing the survey of the northern line of the reservation for the half-breeds of the Sochs [Sacs] and Fox tribes of Indians by the treaty of August 1824.[34]

5 St. 624; Mar. 3, 1843; C. 91—An Act providing for the sale of certain lands in the States of Ohio and Michigan, ceded by the Wyandot tribe of Indians, and for other purposes.[35]

5 St. 630; Mar. 3, 1843; C. 100—An Act making appropriations for the civil and diplomatic expenses of Government for the fiscal year ending the thirtieth day of June, 1844.

5 St. 645; Mar. 3, 1843; C. 101—An Act for the relief of the Stockbridge tribe of Indian, in the Territory of Wisconsin.[36]

5 St. 666; June 15, 1844; C. 54—An Act to repeal an act entitled "An act directing the survey of the northern line of the reservation for the half-breeds of the Sac and Fox tribes of Indians, by the treaty of August, 1824," approved March 3, 1843.[37]

5 St. 673; June 15, 1844; C. 73—An Act making an appropriation for the payment of horses lost by the Missouri volunteers in the Florida war.[38]

5 St. 678; June 17, 1844; C. 99—An Act to enable the War Department to supply certain balances of appropriation, and for other purposes.[39]

5 St. 680; June 17, 1844; C. 103—An Act supplementary to the act entitled "An act to regulate trade and intercourse with the Indian tribes, and to preserve peace on the frontiers," passed thirtieth June, 1834.[40]

5 St. 680; June 17, 1844; C. 104—An Act explanatory of the Treaty made with the Chippewa Indians at Saganaw, the twenty-third of January, 1838.[41]

5 St. 681; June 17, 1844; C. 105—An Act making appropriations for the civil and diplomatic expenses of Government for the fiscal year ending the thirtieth day of June 1845, and for other purposes.[42]

5 St. 704; June 17, 1844; C. 108—An Act making appropriations for the current and contingent expenses of the Indian Department, and for fulfilling treaty stipulations with the various Indian tribes, for the fiscal year commencing on the first day of July, 1844, and ending on the thirtieth day of June, 1845.[43]

5 St. 718; June 12, 1844; J. Res. No. XII—A Resolution to continue two clerks in the business of reservations and grants under Indian treaties.[44]

5 St. 719; June 15, 1844; J. Res. No. XV—A Resolution for the relief of certain claimants under the Cherokee treaty of 1836.[45]

5 St. 727; Feb. 26, 1845; C. 25—An Act to amend an act entitled "An act to carry into effect, in the States of Alabama and Mississippi, the existing compacts with those States with regard to the 5 per cent. fund and the school reservations.[46]

5 St. 752; Mar. 3. 1845; C. 71—An Act making appropriations for the civil and diplomatic expenses of the Government for the year ending the thirtieth June, 1846, and for other purposes.[47]

5 St. 766; Mar. 3, 1845; C. 72—An Act making appropriations for the current and contingent expenses of the Indian Department, and for fulfilling treaty stipulations with the

---

[20] *Ag.* 5 St. 116.
[21] *Sg.* 4 St. 785; 5 St. 158; 7 St. 582. *S.* 9 St. 40, 544.
[22] *S.* 10 St. 214.
[23] *Sg.* 5 St. 180, 211; 7 St. 333, 340. *S.* 5 St. 612, 704; 9 St. 114, 132, 544; 10 St. 15, 41. *Cited:* 4 Op. A. G. 107; 4 Op. A. G. 344; 4 Op. A. G. 346; 4 Op. A. G. 452; 4 Op. A. G. 513; Choctaw, 119 U. S. 1, rev'g 21 C. Cls. 59; Wilson, 6 Wall. 83.
[24] *Sg.* 5 St. 235.
[25] *Rpg.* 5 St. 26. *Sg.* 5 St. 583, May 18, 1842; 7 St. 478. *S.* 5 St. 704. *Cited:* Pawnee, 56 C. Cls. 1.
[26] *Sg.* 7 St. 569, 582.
[27] *Sg.* 11 St. 581.
[28] *Sg.* 5 St. 409. *S.* 5 St. 523, 718.
[29] *Sg.* 7 St. 470.
[30] *Sg.* 3 St. 211; 3 St. 668; 4 St. 52.
[31] *Cited:* 8 L. D. 425.

[32] *Sg.* 5 St. 241, 323, 357, 513; 7 St. 333, 591, 596. *S.* 5 St. 681; 9 St. 544. *Cited:* Pawnee, 56 C. Cls. 1.
[33] *Sg.* 5 St. 453, sec. 10. *S.* 9 St. 50.
[34] *Sg.* 7 St. 229. *R.* 5 St. 666.
[35] *Sg.* 11 St. 581. *S.* 6 St. 936; 43 St. 1141. *A.* 10 St. 15.
[36] *Sg.* 7 St. 342, 405. *R.* 9 St. 55. *S.* 9 St. 955; 10 St. 686; 11 St. 65, 663. *Cited:* Elk, 112 U. S. 94.
[37] *Rg.* 5 St. 622.
[38] *Sg.* 5 St. 357, 359.
[39] *Sg.* 5 St. 17, 48, 241, 357.
[40] *Sg.* 4 St. 729. *Cited:* U. S. v. Dawson, 15 How. 467; U. S. v. Starr, 27 Fed. Cas. No. 16379.
[41] *Sg.* 7 St. 565, Art. 1. 2.
[42] *Sg.* 5 St. 612; 7 St. 833, 478, 596.
[43] *Sg.* 1 St. 618; 4 St. 37, 181, 442, 594, 677, 735, 780; 5 St. 158, 523, 766; 7 St. 35, 44, 49, 68, 74, 84, 91, 98, 100, 105, 113, 115, 160, 178, 185, 186, 188, 189, 203, 206, 210, 218, 224, 229, 234, 240, 244, 284, 286, 289, 290, 295, 300, 303, 317, 320, 323, 327, 328, 333, 348, 351, 353, 355, 366, 368, 370, 374, 391, 394, 397, 399, 414, 417, 424, 429, 431, 442, 450, 458, 491, 506, 517, 536, 538, 540, 543, 544, 568, 569, 574, 576, 581, 582, 591, 596; 11 St. 581.
[44] *Sg.* 5 St. 583.
[45] *Sg.* 7 St. 488. *S.* 9 St. 746.
[46] *Rg.* 5 St. 116, sec. 4. *Sg.* 3 St. 348; 7 St. 450. *A.* 9. St. 202.
[47] *S.* 9 St. 659, 698.

various Indian tribes, for the fiscal year commencing on the first day of July, 1845, and ending on the thirtieth day of June, 1846.[48]

5 St. 797; Mar. 1, 1845; J. Res. No. VII—A Resolution amendatory of the resolution passed April 30, 1844, "respecting the application of certain appropriations heretofore made."[49]

5 St. 800; Mar. 3, 1845; J. Res. No. XI—A Joint Resolution authorizing the Secretary of War to pay any balance that may be due the Shawnee Indians who served in the Florida war.

6 STAT.

6 St. 3; Aug. 11, 1790; C. 44—An Act for the relief of disabled soldiers and seamen lately in the service of the United States, and of certain other persons.

6 St. 7; Apr. 12, 1792; C. 19—An Act for ascertaining the bounds of a tract of land purchased by John Cleves Symmes.[50]

6 St. 12; Feb. 27, 1793; C. 14—An Act making provision for the persons therein mentioned.

6 St. 16; May 31, 1794; C. 38—An Act to compensate Arthur St. Clair.

6 St. 32; Jan. 20, 1798; C. 7—An Act for the relief of John Frank.

6 St. 34; May 8, 1798; C. 41—An Act directing the payment of a detachment of militia, for services performed in the year 1794, under Major James Ore.

6 St. 46; Mar. 16, 1802; C. 10—An Act for the relief of Francis Duchouquet.

6 St. 46; Apr. 3, 1802; C. 18—An Act for the relief of Isaac Zane.

6 St. 57; Mar. 2, 1805; C. 25—An Act for the relief of the widow and orphan children of Robert Elliot.

6 St. 57; Mar. 3, 1805; C. 37—An Act making provision for the widow and orphan children of Thomas Flinn.

6 St. 58; Mar. 3, 1805; C. 45—An Act for the relief of Richard Taylor.

6 St. 67; Mar. 3, 1807; C. 48—An Act concerning invalid pensioners.

6 St. 98; Feb. 25, 1811; C. 24—An Act providing for the sale of a tract of land lying in the state of Tennessee, and a tract in the Indiana territory.

6 St. 103; Dec. 12, 1811; C. 7—An Act for the relief of Josiah H. Webb.

6 St. 125; Aug. 2, 1813; C. 52—An Act for the relief of David Henley.

6 St. 143; Apr. 18, 1814; C. 86—An Act for the relief of John Pitchlyn.

6 St. 149; Feb. 24, 1815; C. 52—An Act for granting and securing to Anthony Shane, the right of the United States to a tract of land in the State of Ohio.

6 St. 167; Apr. 26, 1816; C. 97—An Act for the relief of Young King, a chief of the Seneca tribe of Indians.

6 Sts. 171; Apr. 27, 1816; C. 122—An Act for the relief of Samuel Manác.[51]

6 St. 191; Mar. 3, 1817; C. 68—An Act for the relief of certain Creek Indians.

6 St. 196; Mar. 3, 1817; C. 98—An Act for the relief of Alexander Holmes and Benjamin Hough.

6 St. 213; Apr. 20, 1818; C. 119—An Act for the relief of Peggy Bailey.

6 St. 215; Apr. 20, 1818; C. 130—An Act for the relief of Cornelia Mason.[52]

6 St. 229; Mar. 3, 1819; C. 57—An Act in behalf of the Connecticut Asylum for teaching the Deaf and Dumb.

6 St. 244; May 4, 1820; C. 65—An Act for the relief of Jacob Konkopot, and others, of the Nation of Stockbridge Indians, residing in the State of New York.

6 St. 252; May 15, 1820; C. 129—An Act for the relief of Joshua Newsom, Peter Crook, and James Rabb.

6 St. 267; May 6, 1822; C. 60—An Act confirming the title to a tract of land to Alzira Dibrel and Sophia Hancock.[53]

6 St. 270; May 7, 1822; C. 76—An Act granting a tract of land to William Conner and wife and to their children.

6 St. 272; May 7, 1822; C. 84—An Act for the relief of William Dooly.

6 St. 278; May 7, 1822; C. 120—An Act for the relief of John Holmes.

6 St. 282; Mar. 3, 1823; C. 76—An Act for the relief of John B. Hogan.

6 St. 296; May 5, 1824; C. 55—An Act for the benefit of Alfred Moore and Sterling Orgain, assignees of Morris Linsey.

6 St. 297; May 5, 1824; C. 60—An Act to authorize the settlement of the accounts of Benjamin Lincoln, and others.

6 St. 300; May 17, 1824; C. 73—An Act for the relief of the representatives of Samuel Mims, deceased.

6 St. 314; May 26, 1824; C. 150—An Act appropriating a sum of money to Benjamin Huffman, of the State of Indiana.[54]

6 St. 316; May 26, 1824; C. 201—An Act for the relief of John Holliday.

6 St. 322; Mar. 3, 1825; C. 30—An Act for the relief of Samuel Dale, of Alabama.

6 St. 323; Mar. 3, 1825; C. 33—An Act granting certain rights to David Tate, Josiah Fletcher, and John Weatherford.[55]

6 St. 328; Mar. 3, 1825; C. 59—An Act for the relief of the Companies of Mounted Rangers commanded by Captains Boyle and M'Girth.[56]

6 St. 336; Mar. 3, 1825; C. 118—An Act for the relief of William Little, administrator of Minor Reeves.[57]

6 St. 339; Apr. 5, 1826; C. 24—An Act for the benefit of the incorporated Kentucky Asylum, for teaching the deaf and dumb.

6 St. 341; May 16, 1826; C. 52—An Act for the relief of James Gibson, of Vincennes, Indiana, and James Kay, of Kentucky.

6 St. 341; May 16, 1826; C. 53—An Act for the relief of William Hambly and Edmund Doyle.[58]

6 St. 342; May 16, 1826; C. 57—An Act relinquishing the right of the United States in a certain tract of land, to Samuel Brashiers.[59]

6 St. 342; May 16, 1826; C. 60—An Act relinquishing the right of the United States in a certain tract of land, to William Hollinger.[60]

6 St. 343; May 18, 1826; C. 68—An Act for the relief of James Wolcott, and Mary his wife, of the State of Ohio.[61]

6 St. 349; May 20, 1826; C. 104—An Act to make compensation to Hugh McClung, for a tract of land situate in the state of Tennessee.[62]

6 St. 354; May 22, 1826; C. 155—An Act for the relief of the Florida Indians.

6 St. 360; Mar. 2, 1827; C. 53—An Act concerning a Seminary of Learning in the Territory of Arkansas.

6 St. 361; Mar. 2, 1827; C. 65—An Act for the relief of William Morrison.

6 St. 378; May 19, 1828; C. 65—An Act for the relief of Thomas Brown and Aaron Stanton, of the state of Indiana.[63]

6 St. 379; May 23, 1828; C. 74—An Act making an appropriation to extinguish the Indian title to a reserve allowed to Peter Lynch, of the Cherokee tribe of Indians, within the limits of the state of Georgia, by the treaty of 1819, between the United States and said tribe of Indians.[64]

6 St. 387; May 24, 1828; C. 138—An Act for the benefit of John Winton, of the state of Tennessee.[65]

6 St. 408; Mar. 25, 1830; C. 42—An Act to provide for the payment of sundry citizens of the territory of Arkansas, for trespasses committed on their property by the Osage Indians, in the years 1816, 1817, and 1823.

6 St. 409; Mar. 25, 1830; C. 46—An Act for the relief of Francis Comparet.[66]

6 St. 411; Apr. 7, 1830; C. 61—An Act for the relief of the legal representatives of Jean Baptiste Couture.

6 St. 412; Apr. 7, 1830; C. 66—An Act for the relief of Hubert La Croix.

6 St. 416; May 20, 1830; C. 97—An Act for the relief of sundry revolutionary and other officers and soldiers, and for other purposes.

---

[48] *Sg.* 1 St. 618; 4 St. 37, 181, 442, 594, 677, 735; 5 St. 158, 349, 513, 523, 704; 7 St. 35, 44, 49, 68, 74, 84, 91, 98, 100, 105, 113, 115, 160, 178, 186, 188, 189, 203, 210, 218, 224, 229, 234, 240, 284, 286, 289, 290, 300, 303, 317, 320, 323, 327, 328, 333, 348, 351, 353, 355, 370, 374, 391, 394, 397, 399, 414, 417, 424, 429, 431, 442, 449, 450, 458, 491, 517, 528, 536, 538, 540, 543, 544, 568, 569, 574, 576, 581, 582, 591, 596; Sen. Res., Jan. 19, 1838, Cong., Globe, Vol. 6, p. 121. *S.* 9 St. 132, 544; 10 St. 15, 41. *Cited*: Choctaw, 119 U. S. 1, rev'g 21 C. Cls. 59.

[49] *Sg.* 5 St. 716.

[50] *Sg.* 7 St. 33.

[51] *Cited*: U. S. v. Higgins, 103 Fed. 848.

[52] *Sg.* 3 St. 277.

[53] *Sg.* 7 St. 98, Art. 1.

[54] Identical with 4 St. 37.

[55] *Sg.* 7 St. 120, Art. 1.

[56] *Sg.* 3 St. 676.

[57] *Sg.* 3 St. 676.

[58] *Sg.* 7 St. 224.

[59] *Sg.* 7 St. 120.

[60] *Sg.* 7 St. 120.

[61] *Sg.* 7 St. 189.

[62] *Sg.* 7 St. 195.

[63] *Sg.* 7 St. 295.

[64] *Sg.* 7 St. 195.

[65] *Sg.* 7 St. 195.

[66] *Sg.* 7 St. 317.

6 St. 428; May 28, 1830; C. 118—An Act for the relief of Henry Williams.

6 St. 432; May 28, 1830; C. 133—An Act for the relief of Captain John Woods.

6 St. 438; May 29, 1830; C. 167—An Act for the relief of Thomas W. Newton, assignee of Robert Crittenden.

6 St. 441; May 29, 1830; C. 184—An Act to relinquish the reversionary interest of the United States in certain Indian reservations in the State of Alabama.[67]

6 St. 448; May 31, 1830; C. 221—An Act authorizing the county of Allan to purchase a portion of the reservation including Fort Wayne.[68]

6 St. 448; May 31, 1830; C. 223—An Act for the relief of John Baptiste Jerome.

6 St. 450; May 31, 1830; C. 226—An Act for the relief of Gabriel Godfroy.

6 St. 465; Mar. 3, 1831; C. 106—An Act for the relief of John Nicks.

6 St. 466; Mar. 3, 1831; C. 107—An Act for the relief of Brevet Major Riley, and Lieutenants Brook and Seawright.

6 St. 472; Jan. 19, 1832; C. 5—An Act for the relief of Lewis Anderson.

6 St. 472; Jan. 19, 1832; C. 7—An Act for the relief of Charles Cassedy.

6 St. 473; Jan. 23, 1832; C. 11—An Act for the relief of Robert A. Forsythe.

6 St. 473; Jan. 23, 1832; C. 12—An Act for the relief of William D. King, James Daviess, and Garland Lincicum.

6 St. 480; Mar. 15, 1832; C. 45—An Act for the relief of Anthony Foreman, John G. Ross, Cherokee delegation.[69]

6 St. 483; Mar. 31, 1832; C. 59—An Act for the relief of John Rodgers.[70]

6 St. 494; May 31, 1832; C. 122—An Act for the relief of Joseph W. Torrey.

6 St. 503; July 4, 1832; C. 168—An Act for the relief of Samuel Dale.

6 St. 507; July 13, 1832; C. 211—An Act for the relief of Joseph Elliot.[71]

6 St. 519; July 14, 1832; C. 272—An Act for the relief of William D. Gaines and William M. King.[72]

6 St. 519; July 14, 1832; C. 274—An Act for the relief of William Wayne Wells, of the state of Indiana.[73]

6 St. 521; July 14, 1832; C. 280—An Act granting to Middleton McKay, a section of land in lieu of the reservation given him by the treaty of Dancing Rabbit Creek.[74]

6 St. 527; July 14, 1832; C. 300—An Act for the relief of Mary Daws, Robert Bond, James Patridge, and John G. Smith.[75]

6 St. 530; Jan. 30, 1833; C. 15—An Act for the relief of George Mayfield.[76]

6 St. 534; Feb. 9, 1833; C. 28—An Act for the relief of Gabriel Godfroy and Jean Baptiste Beaugraud.

6 St. 572; June 28, 1834; C. 111—An Act for the relief of George Elliott.

6 St. 581; June 30, 1834; C. 180—An Act for the relief of sundry citizens of the United States, who have lost property by the depredations of certain Indian tribes.[77]

6 St. 583; June 30, 1834; C. 190—An Act for the relief of Alexander J. Robinson.

6 St. 592; June 30, 1834; C. 224—An Act for the relief of James Fife, a Creek Indian.

6 St. 596; June 30, 1834; C. 242—An Act for the relief of Charles J. Hand.

6 St. 596; June 30, 1834; C. 243—An Act for the relief of Hishe Homa, otherwise called Captain Red Pepper, an Indian of the Choctaw tribe.[78]

6 St. 597; June 30, 1834; C. 245—An Act for the relief of the legal representatives of Thomas H. Boyles, deceased.[79]

6 St. 601; June 30, 1834; C. 261—An Act to confirm the selection and survey of two sections of land to Francis Lafontain and son, and their assignees.[80]

6 St. 607; Feb. 13, 1835; C. 20—An Act for the relief of Silas D. Fisher.[81]

6 St. 609; Mar. 3, 1835; C. 59—An Act placing Captain Cole, a Seneca Indian chief, on the pension roll.

6 St. 613; Mar. 3, 1835; C. 83—An Act for the relief of John Dougherty, an Indian agent.

6 St. 614; Mar. 3, 1835; C. 87—An Act for the relief of Richard T. Archer.

6 St. 622; Feb. 17, 1836; C. 12—An Act for the relief of Joseph Cooper.

6 St. 625; Feb. 17, 1836; C. 26—An Act for the relief of Benjamin Franklin Stickney.

6 St. 627; Feb. 17, 1836; C. 35—An Act for the relief of Abner Stilson.

6 St. 633; May 28, 1836; C. 83—An Act for the relief of Silas Fisher, a Choctaw Indian.[82]

6 St. 639; June 23, 1836; C. 122—An Act to authorize the President of the United States to cause to be issued to Albert J. Smith, and others, patents for certain reservations of land in Michigan Territory.[83]

6 St. 639; June 23, 1836; C. 123—An Act for the relief of Henry Stoddard.[84]

6 St. 640; June 23, 1836; C. 128—An Act for the relief of James Caulfield.[85]

6 St. 641; June 23, 1836; C. 132—An Act for the relief of Benjamin and Nancy Merrill.[86]

6 St. 659; July 1, 1836; C. 240—An Act for the relief of James Alexander, and Ira Nash.

6 St. 660; July 1, 1836; C. 245—An Act for the relief of Scioto Evans.

6 St. 661; July 1, 1836; C. 247—An Act for the relief of Joshua Pitcher.

6 St. 661; July 1, 1836; C. 250—An Act confirming to the legal representatives of Thomas F. Reddick, a tract of six hundred and forty acres of land.

6 St. 671; July 2, 1836; C. 306—An Act for the relief of Joseph Bogy.

6 St. 676; July 2, 1836; C. 327—An Act for the relief of Josette Beaubien and her children.[87]

6 St. 677; July 2, 1836; C. 333—An Act for the relief of Samuel Smith, Lynn MacGhee, and Semoice, friendly Creek Indians.[88]

6 St. 678; July 2, 1836; C. 334—An Act for the relief of Susan Marlow.[89]

6 St. 685; Feb. 9, 1837; C. 11—An Act for the relief of John E. Wool.[90]

6 St. 689; Mar. 2, 1837; C. 29—An Act to amend an act approved the second of July, 1836, for the relief of Samuel Smith, Linn McGhee, and Semoice, Creek Indians; and, also, an act passed the second July, 1836, for the relief of Susan Marlow.[91]

6 St. 703; Feb. 22, 1838; C. 10—An Act for the relief of John B. Perkins.

6 St. 707; Mar. 19, 1838; C. 36—An Act for the relief of James Baker.

6 St. 707; Mar. 19, 1838; C. 37—An Act for the relief of Jonathan Davis.

6 St. 710; Apr. 6, 1838; C. 50—An Act for the relief of Isaac Wellborn, junior, and William Wellborn.[92]

6 St. 729; July 7, 1838; C. 203—An Act for the relief of William A. Whitehead.

6 St. 747; Feb. 6, 1839; C. 11—An Act for the relief of Jean B Valle.[93]

6 St. 749; Feb. 6, 1839; C. 19—An Act to confirm the sale of certain reservations.[94]

6 St. 759; Mar. 2, 1839; C. 68—An Act for the relief of the legal representatives of Thomas T. Triplett.[95]

6 St. 769; Mar. 3, 1839; C. 138—An Act for the relief of Milley Yates.[96]

---

[67] *Sg.* 7 St. 120, 156.
[68] *Sg.* 4 St. 236.
[69] *Sg.* 2 St. 139, Sec. 4.
[70] *Sg.* 7 St. 156, Art. 6.
[71] *Sg.* 7 St. 156 (Dec. 26, 1817, correct date).
[72] *Sg.* 7 St. 156, 195.
[73] *Sg.* 7 St. 189.
[74] *Sg.* 7 St. 338.
[75] *Sg.* 7 St. 154, 224.
[76] *Sg.* 7 St. 120.
[77] *Sg.* 2 St. 139, Sec. 14; 4 St. 428 (May *31*, 1830, correct date).
[78] *Sg.* 7 St. 333.
[79] *Sg.* 6 St. 169.
[80] *Sg.* 7 St. 189, Art. 3.
[81] *Sg.* 7 St. 340, Art. 2. *S.* 6 St. 633.
[82] *Sg.* 7 St. 340; 6 St. 607.
[83] *Sg.* 7 St. 203, Art. 3.
[84] *Sg.* 7 St. 355, Art. II.
[85] *Sg.* 7 St. 120.
[86] *Sg.* 7 St. 156, 195.
[87] *Sg.* 7 St. 378.
[88] *Sg.* 7 St. 120. *S.* 10 St. 735. *A.* 6 St. 689.
[89] *Sg.* 7 St. 120. *A.* 6 St. 689.
[90] *Sg.* 4 St. 735, sec. 13; 7 St. 478, Art. 18.
[91] *Rpg.* 6 St. 677, 678; *Sg.* 7 St. 120.
[92] *Sg.* 7 St. 156, 195.
[93] *Sg.* 7 St. 188, Art. 7.
[94] *Sg.* 7 St. 378, Art. 2.
[95] *Sg.* 7 St. 286.
[96] *Sg.* 7 St. 333, Art. 14.

6 St. 771; Mar. 3, 1839; C. 148—An Act for the relief of Winslow Lewis.

6 St. 775; Mar. 3, 1839; C. 166—An Act for the relief of Henry Grady, of Macon county, North Carolina.

6 St. 776; Mar. 3, 1839; C. 169—An Act for the relief of A. J. Picket and George W. Gayle.

6 St. 779; Mar. 3, 1839; C. 179—An Act for the relief of certain settlers, living on what is called the Salt Lick reservation, in the western district of Tennessee.[97]

6 St. 787; Mar. 3, 1839; C. 210—An Act for the relief of Cornelius Taylor.

6 St. 788; Mar. 3, 1839; C. 215—An Act to authorize the President of the United States to cause to be issued to Michael Ambrister, assignee of Us-se-yoholo, a Creek Indian, a patent for a certain reservation of land in the State of Alabama.[98]

6 St. 789; Mar. 3, 1839; C. 221—An Act providing for paying three companies of militia in the State of Indiana, called into the service of the United States.

6 St. 790; Mar. 3, 1839; C. 223—An Act for the relief of John Dougherty, of Wisconsin.[99]

6 St. 792; Mar. 3, 1839; C. 232—An Act for the relief of Jamison and Williamson.

6 St. 792; Mar. 3, 1839; C. 235—An Act for the relief of Susan Gratiot, administratrix, and Charles H. Gratiot, administrator, of Henry Gratiot, deceased.

6 St. 792; Mar. 3, 1839; C. 236—An Act for the relief of John L. McCarty.

6 St. 797; Apr. 27, 1840; C. 9—An Act for the relief of Sutten Stephens.[1]

6 St. 810; July 20, 1840; C. 90—An Act granting two townships of land for the use of a University in the Territory of Iowa.

6 St. 813; July 21, 1840; C. 99—An Act for the relief of Chastelain and Ponvert, and for other purposes.[2]

6 St. 816; July 21, 1840; C. 100—An Act for the relief of Hyacinth Lassel.[3]

6 St. 818; Feb. 18, 1841; C. 8—An Act for the relief of Gurdon S. Hubbard, Robert A. Kinzie, and others.[4]

6 St. 819; Feb. 18, 1841; C. 9—An Act supplementary to an act entitled "An Act to encourage the introduction, and promote the cultivation of tropical plants," approved seventh July, eighteeen hundred and thirty-eight.[5]

6 St. 822; Mar. 3, 1841; C. 27—An Act for the relief of Avery, Saltmarsh, and Company.

6 St. 834; July 9, 1842; C. 52—An Act for the relief of Obed P. Lacoy.[6]

6 St. 835; July 9, 1842; C. 59—An Act for the relief of Peter Sky, an Onondaga Indian.

6 St. 835; July 9, 1842; C. 60—An Act for the relief of Lieutenant John L. Kline.[7]

6 St. 849; Aug. 9, 1842; C. 125—An Act for the relief of David M. Hughes, Charles Shipman, and John Henderson.

6 St. 852; Aug. 11, 1842; C. 139—An Act for the relief of John C. Reynolds, late disbursing agent of the Indian Department.

6 St. 852; Aug. 11, 1842; C. 140—An Act for the relief of Marston C. Clark.

6 St. 855; Aug. 11, 1842; C. 152—An Act for the relief of the legal representatives of John Scott.

6 St. 856; Aug. 11, 1842; C. 154—An Act for the relief of Jubal B. Hancock.[8]

6 St. 858; Aug. 11, 1842; C. 162—An Act for the relief of George W. Paschal.

6 St. 859; Aug. 11, 1842; C. 165—An Act for the relief of Hezekiah L. Thistle.

6 St. 859; Aug. 11, 1842; C. 167—An Act for the relief of the legal representatives of Richard T. Banks, of the state of Arkansas.

6 St. 861; Aug. 16, 1842; C. 174—An Act for the relief of the president, directors, and company of the Agricultural Bank of Mississippi.[9]

6 St. 878; Jan. 20, 1843; C. 5—An Act for the relief of Cornelius Wilson and James Canter.

6 St. 879; Jan. 20, 1843; C. 7—An Act for the relief of Elisha Moreland, William M. Kennedy, Robert J. Kennedy, and Mason E. Lewis.[10]

6 St. 887; Mar. 1, 1843; C. 61—An Act for the relief of John E. Hunt and others.

6 St. 888; Mar. 1, 1843; C. 63—An Act for the relief of William G. Sanders.

6 St. 895; Mar. 3, 1843; C. 132—An Act granting a pension to David Welch.

6 St. 896; Mar. 3, 1843; C. 138—An Act for the relief of Johnson Patrick.

6 St. 901; Mar. 3, 1843; C. 161—An Act for the relief of George C. Johnston.[11]

6 St. 913; June 10, 1844; C. 43—An Act for the relief of Daniel G. Skinner, of Alabama.

6 St. 913; June 12, 1844; C. 48—An Act for the relief of Joseph Bryan, Harrison Young and Benjamin Young.[12]

6 St. 913; June 15, 1844; C. 76—An Act for the relief of George Wallis.

6 St. 913; June 15, 1844; C. 77—An Act authorizing a patent to be issued to Joseph Campau for a certain tract of land in the state of Michigan.[13]

6 St. 915; June 15, 1844; C. 84—An Act for the relief of George W. Allen and Reuben Allen.[14]

6 St. 919; June 17, 1844; C. 114—An Act for the relief of Isaac S. Ketchum.

6 St. 920; June 17, 1844; C. 115—An Act for the relief of Isaac S. Ketchum, late special Indian agent.

6 St. 920; June 17, 1844; C. 119—An Act for the relief of William Henson.

6 St. 922; June 17, 1844; C. 128—An Act for the relief of Harvey Heth.

6 St. 924; June 17, 1844; C. 135—An Act for the relief of Henry S. Commager.[15]

6 St. 925; June 17, 1844; C. 141—An Act for the relief of William P. Duval.

6 St. 927; June 17, 1844; C. 151—An Act for the relief of William R. Davis.

6 St. 928; June 17, 1844; C. 154—An Act granting a pension to "Milly," an Indian woman of the Creek nation.

6 St. 929; June 17, 1844; C. 157—An Act for the relief of F. A. Kerr.

6 St. 930; June 17, 1844; C. 160—An Act for the relief of Benjamin Murphy.

6 St. 936; Feb. 26, 1845; C. 23—An Act vesting in the county commissioners of the county of Wyandot the right to certain town lots and out lots in the town of Upper Sandusky, in the state of Ohio.[16]

6 St. 942; Mar. 3, 1845; J. Res. No. 12—A Joint Resolution for the benefit of Frances Slocum and her children and grandchildren of the Miami tribe of Indians.[17]

7 STAT.

7 St. 13; Sept. 17, 1778—Treaty (articles of agreement and confederation) with Delaware Nation.[18]

7 St. 15; Oct. 22, 1784—Treaty with Six Nations.[19]

7 St. 16; Jan. 21, 1785—Treaty with Wiandot, Delaware, Chippawa and Ottawa Nations.[20]

7 St. 18; Nov. 28, 1785—Treaty (articles) with Cherokees.[21]

7 St. 21; Jan. 3, 1786—Treaty with Choctaw Nation.[22]

7 St. 24; Jan. 10, 1786—Treaty with Chickasaws.[23]

---

[97] *Sg.* 7 St. 192, Art. 4.
[98] *Sg.* 7 St. 366.
[99] *Sg.* 7 St. 323; Art. 5.
[1] *Sg.* 7 St. 156.
[2] *Sg.* 5 St. 349.
[3] *Sg.* 7 St. 205.
[4] *Sg.* 7 St. 378.
[5] *Sg.* 5 St. 302.
[6] *Sg.* 7 St. 317, Art. 8.
[7] *Sg.* 7 St. 478, Art. 16.
[8] *Sg.* 7 St. 333, Art. 14.
[9] *Sg.* 7 St. 450, Art. 11.

[10] *Sg.* 7 St. 195.
[11] *Sg.* 4 St. 594.
[12] *Sg.* 7 St. 366.
[13] *Sg.* 7 St. 203.
[14] *Sg.* 7 St. 394.
[15] *Sg.* 7 St. 49, 105, 178, 218, 320, 431, 442, 491.
[16] *Sg.* 5 St. 624.
[17] *Sg.* 9 St. 806. *Cited:* 6 Op. A. G. 440.
[18] *Cited:* Labadie, 6 Okla. 400; U. S. v. Boylan, 265 Fed. 165; Worcester, 6 Pet. 515.
[19] *S.* 7 St. 28, 33. *Cited:* 1 L. D. Memo 85; Commonwealth, 4 Dall. 170; Deere, 32 F. 2d 550; New York Indians, 5 Wall. 761; U. S. v. Boylan, 265 Fed. 165; U. S. v. Douglas, 190 Fed. 482; U. S. ex rel. Kennedy, 269 U. S. 13; U. S. v. Seneca, 274 Fed. 946.
[20] *S.* 4 St. 980. *Cited:* Commonwealth, 4 Dall. 170; Hicks, 12 Fed. Cas. No. 6458; Jones, 175 U. S. 1.
[21] *S.* 4 St. 352; 7 St. 43, 56. *Cited:* 1 Op. A. G. 645; 2 Op. A. G. 321; Cherokee, 5 Pet. 1; Cherokee, 135 U. S. 641; Eastern Band, 117 U. S. 288; Eastern Band, 20 C. Cls. 449; Ex P. Crow Dog, 109 U. S. 556; Heckman, 224 U. S. 413; Labadie, 6 Okla. 400; Lattimer, 14 Pet. 4; Maxey, 3 Ind. T. 243; Muskrat, 219 U. S. 346; Old Settlers, 148 U. S. 427; Porterfield, 2 How. 76; U. S. v. Swain, 46 F. 2d 99; U. S. v. Wright, 53 F. 2d 300; Worcester, 6 Pet. 515.
[22] *S.* 12 St. 221. *Cited:* Mullen, 224 U. S. 448.
[23] *S.* 1 St. 618; 7 St. 56, 65, 66, 89. *Cited:* Porterfield v. Clark, 2 How. 76.

7 St. 26; Jan 31, 1786—Treaty with Shawanoe Nation[24]

7 St. 28, Jan 9, 1789—Treaty with Wiandot, Delaware, Ottowa, Chippewa, Pattawatima and Sac Nations (2 separate articles)[25]

7 St. 33; Jan. 9, 1789—Treaty with Six Nations (separate article)[26]

7 St 35, Aug 7, 1790—Treaty with Creek Nation[27]

Archives No 17, Aug 7, 1790—Unpublished Treaty with Creek Nation

7 St 39; July 2, 1791—Treaty with Cherokee Nation[28]

7 St 42; Feb 17, 1792—Treaty (additional article) with Cherokees[29]

Archives No 19, Apr 23, 1792—Unpublished Treaty with Five Nations

7 St 43; June 26, 1794—Treaty with Cherokee Nation[30]

7 St 44, Nov 11, 1794—Treaty with Six Nations[31]

7 St 47, Dec. 2, 1794—Treaty with Oneida, Tuscorora, and Stockbridge Indians[32]

7 St. 49, Aug 3, 1795—Treaty with Wyandots, Delawares, Shawanoes, Ottawas, Chipewas, Putawatimes, Miamis, Eel-river, Weea's, Kickapoos, Piankashaws, and Kaskaskias[33]

7 St 55, May 31, 1796—Treaty with Seven Nations of Canada[34]

7 St. 56, June 29, 1796—Treaty with Creek Nation[35]

7 St 61, Mar 29, 1797—Treaty (relinquishment) with Mohawk Nation

Archives No. 28; June 1, 1798—Unpublished Treaty with Oneida Nation.

7 St 62, Oct. 2, 1798—Treaty with Cherokee Indians[36]

7 St 65; Oct 24, 1801—Treaty with Chickasaws[37]

7 St 66; Dec 17, 1801—Treaty with Choctaw Nation[38]

7 St 68, June 16, 1802—Treaty with Creek Nation[39]

7 St 70, June 30, 1802—Treaty (indenture) with Seneca Nation[40]

7 St 72, June 30, 1802—Treaty with Seneca Nation[41]

7 St 73 Oct 17, 1802—Treaty (provisional convention) with Choctaw Nation[42]

7 St 74 June 7, 1803—Treaty with Delawares, Shawanoes, Putawatimies, Miamies, Eel River, Weeas, Kickapoos, Piankashaws, and Kaskaskias Nations[43]

7 St 77, Aug 7, 1803—Treaty (at a council) with any Indian nations north west of the River Ohio (Eel River, Wyandot, Piankashaw, and Kaskaskia Nations, and also Kikapoos, by their representatives, the Eel River Nation).[44]

7 St 78, Aug 13 1803—Treaty with Kaskaskia Tribe[45]

7 St 80, Aug. 31, 1803—Treaty with Choctaw Nation[46]

Archives No 14, July 4, 1805—Unpublished Treaty with Wyandot, Ottawa, Chippawa, Munsee and Delaware, Shawnee and Pottawatima Nations

7 St 81, Aug 18, 1804—Treaty with Delaware Tribe[47]

7 St 83, Aug 27, 1804—Treaty with Piankeshaw Tribe[48]

7 St 84; Nov 3, 1804—Treaty with Sac and Fox Indians[49]

7 St 87, July 4, 1805—Treaty with Wyandot, Ottawa, Chippewa, Munsee and Delaware, Shawnee, and Pottawatima Nations[50]

7 St 89, July 23, 1805—Treaty with Chickasaw Nation[51]

7 St 91, Aug 21, 1805—Treaty with Delawares, Pottawatimies, Miamies, Eel River, and Weas Tribes[52]

7 St 93; Oct 25, 1805—Treaty with Cherokee Indians[53]

7 St 95; Oct 27, 1805—Treaty with Cherokee Indians[54]

7 St. 96, Nov 14, 1805—Treaty (convention) with Creek Nation[55]

7 St 98, Nov 16, 1805—Treaty with Chaktaw Nation[56]

7 St 100; Dec 30, 1805—Treaty with Piankishaw Tribe[57]

7 St 101, Jan 7, 1806—Treaty (convention) with Cherokee Nation.[58]

---

[24] *Sg* Treaty with Great Britain and Shawanoe Nation, Jan 14, 1784. *S* 7 St 28 62

[25] *Sg* 7 St 16, 26. *Cited* Jones, 175 U S 1, Sac and Fox, 45 C Cls 287, U S v Cisna, 25 Fed Cas No 14795

[26] *Sg* 7 St 16, 6 St 33 *Cited* N Y Ind, 5 Wall 761; U S v Boylan, 265 Fed 165, U S v Seneca Nation of N Y Ind, 274 Fed 947, 1 L D Memo 37

[27] *S* 1 St 618, 4 St 780, 5 St 704, 766, 7 St 56, 120; 9 St 20, 132, 252, 382, 514, 574, 10 St 41, 226 315 686, 11 St 65, 169, 273, 388, 699; 12 St 44, 221, 612, 774, 13 St 161, 541, 14 St 255, 492; 15 St 198, 16 St 13, 335, 514; 17 St 165, 437; 18 St 146 420, 19 St 176 271, 20 St 63 205, 21 St 114, 485, 22 St 68 433, 23 St 76 362, 24 St 29 449; 25 St 217, 980, 26 St 336, 989, 27 St 120, 612; 28 St 286, 876, 29 St 321, 30 St 62, 571 924, 31 St 221, 1058; 32 St 245 *Cited* 2 Op A G 110; Creek, 63 C Cls 270; Patterson, 2 Pet 216

[28] *Sg* 4 St. 852 *A* 7 St 42, 43, 62 *Cited:* New York Indians, 5 Wall 761

[29] *Ag* 7 St 39 *S* 4 St. 552 *Cited* Eastern Band, 20 C. Cls 449; Labadie, 6 Okla 400

[30] *Sg* 7 St 15 *Ag* 7 St 39 *A* 7 St. 62 *S* 4 St 352, 780, 5 St 36, 7 St 56 *Cited:* Cherokee, 5 Pet 1; Eastern Band, 117 U S 288, Eastern Band, 20 C Cls 449; Lattimer, 14 Pet. 4, Jones, 175 U. S 1; Leighton, 29 C Cls 288, Worcester, 6 Pet 515

[31] *Sg* Archives No 19 *S*, 4 St 618, 780 5 St 36, 704 766, 9 St 20, 132, 252, 382, 514, 574, 10 St 41 226, 315 686; 11 St 65 169 273, 388, 664 12 St 44, 221, 612, 774, 13 St 161, 541, 14 St 255, 15 St 198, 16 St 13, 335 544; 17 St 165; 18 St 146 420 19 St 176 271; 20 St 63, 205 21 St 117, 485, 22 St, 68, 433; 23 St 76, 362 24 St 29 449, 25 St 217, 980; 26 St 336, 989; 27 St 120, 612; 28 St 286, 876, 29 St 321, 30 St 62, 571, 924; 31 St 221, 1058; 32 St 245, 982; 33 St 189, 1048, 34 St 325, 1015, 35 St 70 781; 36 St 269, 37 St 518 38 St 77, 592, 39 St 123, 969; 40 St 561, 41 St 3 408 1225, 42 St 552 1174, 43 St 890 1141, 44 St 453, 45 St 200, 1562, 46 St 279, 47 St 820, 48 St 362, 49 St 1757, 50 St 564, 52 St 291 *Cited:* 1 Op. A G 465, 1 L D Memo 35; Burton 7 F Supp 597, New York Indians, 40 C Cls 448; New York ex rel Cutler, 21 How 366; Massachusetts, 273 U S 65; People ex rel Charles, 8 F Supp 295, Seneca, 162 U. S 283, U S v Boylan, 265 Fed 165; U S. v. Seneca, 274 Fed 947

[32] *S* 1 St 460 563, 7 St 80; 11 St 699. *Cited:* U S v Boylan, 265 Fed 165, 1 L D Memo. 35.

[33] *S* 2 St 343 390 607 668; 3 St 308, 319, 428, 521, 4 St 780, 5 St 36, 704, 766; 6 St 924; 7 St 74, 81, 87, 100 112, 113, 117, 131 145 160 189 208 351, 359; 8 St 116, 9 St 20 132 252 382 544, 574 735, 10 St 41 226, 315, 576, 686, 1058; 11 St 65 169 273, 298, 388; 12 St. 44, 221, 512, 774 13 St. 161, 541; 14 St 255, 492, 15 St. 198; 16 St 13, 335, 541; 17 St 165, 437, 18 St 146, 420; 19 St 176, 271; 20 St 63 205; 21 St 114, 485, 22 St 68 433, 23 St 76, 362; 24 St. 29, 449, 25 St 217, 980, 26 St 336, 989; 27 St 120 612; 28 St 286, 876, 29 St 321, 30 St 62, 571, 924; 31 St 221, 1058; 32 St 245, 982; 33 St 189, 1048, 34 St 325, 1015; 35 St. 70 781. *Cited:* 1 L D Memo 35 Balfour, 4 Dall 803, Chippewa, 301 U S 358, Commonwealth 4 Dall 120, Johnson, 8 Wheat 543, Jones, 175 U S 1; Morris's, 4 Dall 200; Patterson, 2 Pet. 216; Potawatomie, 27 C Cls 403, Renfrow 3 Okla 161; Reynolds, 2 Pet. 417; Williams, 242 U S 434

[34] *Cited:* 1 L. D. Memo 35; Deere, 32 F 2d 550; Deere 22 F. 2d 851

[35] *Ag* 7 St 35; *Sg* 7 St 19, 24, 43 *S*. 1 St, 618, 7 St 68. *Cited* 2 Op A G 110.

[36] *Sg* 7 St 22, 26 *Ag*. 7 St. 39, 43 *S*. 1 St 618 4 St, 852, 780 *Cited* Cherokee, 5 Pet 1; Eastern Band, 20 C. Cls 449; Eastern Band, 117 U S 288, Labadie, 6 Okla 400; Lattimer, 14 Pet 4; Preston, 1 Wheat 115; Worcester, 6 Pet 515

[37] *Sg* 7 St. 24

[38] *Sg*. 7 St 24. *S* 4 St 780; 5 St. 36, 7 St 89

[39] *Sg* 2 St 139 7 St 36 *S* 3 St 480 517, 4 St 780, 5 St 704 766; 9 St 20, 132, 252, 382, 514, 574, 10 St 41, 226, 315 686 11 St 65 169 169, 273, 388, 699, 12 St 44, 221, 512, 774, 13 St 161, 541, 14 St 255 492, 15 St 198, 16 St 13 335 544, 17 St 165 437 18 St 146 420 19 St 176, 271 20 St 63 205; 21 St 114, 485 22 St 68 433; 23 St 76, 362, 24 St 29, 449, 25 St 217, 980, 26 St 989, 27 St 120, 612, 28 St 286, 876; 29 St 321, 30 St 62, 571 924, 31 St 221, 1058, 32 St 245 *Cited* 2 Op A G 110 Coffee, 123 U S 1

[40] *Sg* 7 St 601 *S* 12 St 512, *Cited* New York Indians, 5 Wall 761.

[41] *Cited* 1 L D Memo 35

[42] *S* 2 St 229

[43] *Sg* 7 St 49 *S* 2 St 277; 4 St 181, 780, 5 St 36, 701, 766; 7 St 81, 83, 113, 403, 9 St 20, 132, 252, 544, 571, 10 St 41, 226 *Cited* Johnson, 8 Wheat 543

[44] *S* 7 St 403 *Cited* Johnson 8 Wheat 543

[45] *Sg* 1 St 225 *S* 2 St 277, 3 St 690; 7 St 181, 403

[46] *Sg* 7 St 47

[47] *Sg*. 7 St 19, 74, *S* 7 St 91

[48] *Sg* 7 St. 74 *Cited* Johnson, 8 Wheat 543

[49] *S* 4 St 780, 5 St 36 704, 766, 7 St 134, 135 141, 146 223, 543; 9 St 20 132 252, 382, 544, 774, 10 St 41 226, 315, 686, 11 St 65 169, 273 388, 12 St 44 221 512 774; 13 St 161 541; 14 St 492, 15 St, 198, 16 St 13 335 544, 17 St 165 437, 18 St 146, 420; 19 St 176 271, 20 St 63 205; 21 St 114 485, 22 St 68 433, 23 St 76, 362; 24 St 29, 449; 25 St 217, 980; 26 St 336, 989, 27 St 120 612, 28 St 286, 876, 29 St 321, 30 St 62, 571, 924; 31 St 221, 1058, 32 St, 245 982, 33 St 189 1048; 34 St 325 1015, 35 St 70, 781 *Cited* Sac & Fox 220 U S 481 Sac & Fox 45 C Cls 287

[50] *Sg* 7 St 49 *S* 2 St. 407; 4 St. 780; 5 St 36 *Cited* Chippewa, 301 U S 358

[51] *Sg* 7 St 24 66 *S* 2 St 410, 518

[52] *Ag* 7 St 81 *S* 2 St. 407; 4 St 780; 5 St 704 766, 7 St 115, 9 St 20, 132, 252, 382, 544, 571, 10 St 41, 226, 315, 686, 11 St 65, 169, 273 388, 12 St 44 221 512 774, 13 St 161 541; 14 St 255, 492; 15 St 198; 16 St 13, 335, 514, 17 St 165, 437, 18 St, 146 420; 19 St 176 271; 20 St 63 205, 21 St 114, 485, 22 St 68, 433; 23 St 76 362; 24 St 29, 449, 25 St 217

[53] *S* 2 St 407 4 St 372, 5 St 36; 9 St 382 *Cited* Cherokee 5 Pet 1; Eastern Band, 20 C Cls 449; Eastern Band, 117 U S. 288; Meigs, 9 Cranch 11, Worcester, 6 Pet 515

[54] *S* 2 St 407; 4 St. 852 *Cited*. Cherokee, 5 Pet 1; Worcester, 6 Pet 515

[55] *S*, 2 St. 407 *Cited:* Coffee, 123 U S, 1; Labadie, 6 Okla 400

[56] *S* 2 St 467, 470; 5 St 36, 704 766, 6 St 287; 9 St 20 132 252, 382, 541, 574; 10 St 41, 226, 315 686, 11 St 65 169, 273 388, 12 St 44, 221, 512, 774; 13 St 161, 541, 14 St 255, 492, 15 St 198, 16 St 13 335 544, 17 St 165, 437; 18 St 146, 420; 19 St. 176, 271, 20 St 205, 21 St 114, 485; 22 St 68 433, 23 St 76 362, 24 St 29, 449; 25 St 217, 980; 26 St 336, 989; 27 St 120, 612; 28 St. 286, 876, 29 St 321; 30 St 62, 571, 924, 31 St 221, 1058, 32 St. 245, 982, 33 St 189, 1048, 34 St. 325, 1015; 35 St, 70 781, 36 St 269, 1078; 37 St, 518, 38 St 77, 582; 39 St 123 969, 40 St 561, 41 St, 509, 1225; 42 St 552, 1174; 43 St. 890, 1111, 44 St 453, 934; 45 St 200, 1562; 46 St 279, 47 St 820; 48 St 362; 49 St 1757; 50 St. 564, 52 St 291.

[57] *Sg* 7 St 49 *S* 2 St 448, 4 St, 780, 5 St 36, 704, 766; 7 St 202; 9 St 20, 132 252, 382, 544, 574, 10 St 41, 226, 315. *Cited* Johnson, 8 Wheat, 543

[58] *S* 2 St 467; 7 St, 139 *Cited* Cherokee, 5 Pet 1; Eastern Band, 20 C. Cls 449, Labadie, 6 Okla. 400; Worcester, 6 Pet. 515.

7 St 105, Nov 17, 1807—Treaty with Ottoway, Chippeway, Wyandotte, and Pottawatamie Nations[59]

7 St 107, Nov 10, 1808—Treaty with Great and Little Osage Nations[60]

7 St 112, Nov 25, 1808—Treaty with Chippewa, Ottawa, Pottawatamie, Wyandot, and Shawanoese Nations[61]

7 St 113, Sept 30, 1809—Treaty with Delawares, Potawatimies, Miamies, and Eel River Miamies Tribes[62]

7 St 115, Sept 30, 1809—Treaty (separate article) with Miami, Eel River, Delawares and Putawatimies Tribes[63]

7 St 116, Oct 26, 1809—Treaty (convention) with Indian tribes north-west of the Ohio and the Wea tribe[64]

7 St 117 Dec 9, 1809—Treaty with Kickapoo Tribe[65]

7 St 118, July 22 1814—Treaty with Wyandots, Delawares, Shawanoese, Senecas, and Miamies

7 St 120, Aug 9, 1814—Treaty (articles of agreement and capitulation) with Creek Nation[66]

7 St 123 July 18, 1815—Treaty with Poutawatamie Tribe

7 St 124 July 18, 1815—Treaty with Piankishaw Tribe

7 St 125, July 19, 1815—Treaty with Teeton Tribe

7 St 126, July 19, 1815—Treaty with Siouxs of the Lakes[67]

7 St 127, July 19, 1815—Treaty with Siouxs of the river St Peter's[68]

7 St 128, July 19, 1815—Treaty with Yankton Tribe

7 St 129, July 20, 1815—Treaty with Mahas Tribe

7 St 130 Sept 2, 1815—Treaty with Kickapoo Tribe

7 St 131, Sept 8 1815—Treaty with Wyandot, Delaware, Seneca, Shawanoe, Miami, Chippewa, Ottawa, and Potawatimie Tribes[69]

7 St 133, Sept 12, 1815—Treaty with Great and Little Osage Nations[70]

7 St 134 Sept 13, 1815—Treaty with Sac Nation[71]

7 St 135, Sept 14, 1815—Treaty with Fox Nation[72]

7 St 136 Sept 16, 1815—Treaty with Ioway Nation

7 St 137, Oct 28 1815—Treaty with Kansas Tribe[73]

7 St 138, Mar 22, 1816—Treaty with Cherokee Nation[74]

7 St 139, Mar 22, 1816—Treaty with Cherokee Nation (convention)[75]

7 St 141, May 13 1816—Treaty with Sacs of Rock River[76]

7 St 143, June 1, 1816—Treaty with Sioux of the Leaf, Siouxs of the Broad Leaf, and the Siouxs who shoot in the Pine Tops[77]

7 St 144, June 3, 1816—Treaty with Winnebago tribe

7 St 145, June 4, 1816—Treaty with Weas and Kickapoos[79]

7 St 146, Aug 24, 1816—Treaty with united tribes of Ottawas, and Chipawas, and Pottowotomees[80]

7 St 148, Sept 14, 1816—Treaty with Cherokees[81]

7 St 150, Sept 20 1816—Treaty with Chickasaws[82]

7 St 152, Oct 24, 1816—Treaty with Choctaw Nation[83]

7 St 153, Mar 30, 1817—Treaty with Menomenee Nation

7 St 154, June 24, 1817—Treaty with Ottoes Tribe

7 St 155, June 25, 1817—Treaty with Poncarar Tribe[84]

7 St 156, July 8, 1817—Treaty with Cherokee Nation[84a]

7 St 160, Sept 29, 1817—Treaty with Wyandot, Seneca, Delaware, Shawanese, Potawatomees, Ottawas, and Chippeway Tribe[84b]

7 St 171, Jan 22, 1818—Treaty with Creek Nation[84c]

7 St 172, June 18, 1818—Treaty with Grand Pawnee Tribe

7 St 173, June 19, 1818—Treaty with Pitavirate Noisy Pawnee Tribe

7 St 174, June 20, 1818—Treaty with Pawnee Republic

7 St 175, June 22, 1818—Treaty with Pawnee Marhar Tribe

7 St 176, Aug 24, 1818—Treaty with Quapaw Nation[84d]

7 St 178, Sept 17, 1818—Treaty with Wyandot, Seneca, Shawnee, and Ottawas Tribes[84e]

7 St 180, Sept 20, 1818—Treaty with Wyandot Tribe[84f]

7 St 181, Sept 25, 1818—Treaty with Peoria, Kaskaskia, Mitchigamia, Cahokia, and Tamarois Tribes[84g]

7 St 183, Sept 25, 1818—Treaty with Great and Little Osage Nation[84h]

7 St 185, Oct 2, 1818—Treaty with Potawatamie Nation[84i]

7 St 186, Oct 2, 1818—Treaty with Wea Tribe[85]

7 St 188, Oct 3, 1818—Treaty with Delaware Nation[86]

7 St 189, Oct 6, 1818—Treaty with Miamie Nation[87]

7 St 192, Oct 19, 1818—Treaty with Chickasaw[88]

---

[59] S 2 St 502, 4 St 780, 5 St 36 704 766, 6 St 924, 7 St 112 119, 379, 120 703 729, 9 St 20 132 272 382, 541, 574, 10 St 41, 226 313 650, 11 St 65, 169, 273 388, 638, 12 St 44, 221, 512, 774 1105, 13 St 161, 14 St 255, 492, 15 St 198, 16 St 13, 335, 544, 17 St 165, 437, 18 St 146 420, 19 St 176, 271, 20 St 63, 295, 21 St 114 485, 22 St 68, 437 23 St 76, 362, 24 St 29, 449, 25 St 217 *Cited* Chippewa, 301 U S 358

[60] S 2 St 660, 4 St 780, 5 St 36, 7 St 183, 222, 240, 12 St 1105 *Cited* Hot Springs 92 U S 698, Labadie, 6 Okla 400, Osage Tribe, 68 C Cls 64, State of Missouri, 7 How 660

[61] Sg 7 St 49, 105 S 2 St 608, 3 St 201, 285, 5 St 298

[62] Sg 7 St 49, 74 S 2 St 590, 607, 4 St 780, 5 St 36, 704, 766, 7 St 117, 189 9 St 20, 182 272 382 544 574 10 St 41 226 315, 576, 686, 11 St 65 169 273 398, 12 St 41 221 512 774, 13 St 161, 541, 14 St 255 492, 15 St 198, 16 St 13, 335, 544, 17 St 165, 437, 18 St 146, 420, 19 St 271 20 St 63, 295 21 St 114, 495 22 St 68 433, 23 St 70, 362, 24 St 29, 449, 25 St 217, 980, 26 St 336, 27 St 120 612, 28 St 286 876, 29 St 321 30 St 62, 571, 924, 31 St 221 1058, 32 St 245 982, 33 St 189, 1048, 34 St 325, 1015, 35 St 70, 781 *Cited* Potawatomie, 27 C Cls 403

[63] Sg 7 St 91 S 2 St 607, 5 St 704, 766, 7 St 116, 17 St 187, 18 St 146 420

[64] Sg 7 St 115 S 2 St 607, 15 St 198, 16 St 335

[65] Sg 7 St 19 113 S 2 St 607, 7 St 145

[66] Sg 7 St 85 S 3 St 228, 374, 378, 350 749, 5 St 307, 6 St 328 342, c 57 342, c 60 441 530 640, 677, 678, 680, 7 St 139, 9 St 346, 10 St 910, 11 St 169 487, 37 St 122 *Cited* 8 Op A G 230, 8 Op A G 860, Coffee, 128 U S 1; Creek, 63 C Cls 270, Creek, 74 C Cls 668

[67] *Cited* Graham, 30 C Cls 318

[68] *Cited*, Graham, 30 C Cls 318

[69] Sg 7 St 40

[70] *Cited* Labadie, 6 Okla 400, State of Missouri, 7 How 660

[71] Sg 7 St 84

[72] Sg 7 St 84 S 7 St 141, 171

[73] S 5 St 36 *Cited* Kansas 80 C Cls 264

[74] S 3 St. 326, 163, 4 St 852 *Cited*. Cherokee, 5 Pet 1, Labadie, 6 Okla 400, Worcester, 6 Pet 515

[75] Sg 7 St, 101, 120 *Cited* Cherokee, 5 Pet 1, Eastern Band, 20 C. Cls, 449; Labadie, 6 Okla 400

[76] Sg 7 St 84, 135, 8 St 218

[77] *Cited* Graham, 30 C Cls 318.

[78] Sg 7 St 49, 117

[80] Sg 7 St 84. S 3 St 393, 7 St 272, 378

[81] S 1 St 393, 4 St 353 *Cited* Eastern Band, 20 C Cls 449, Worcester, 6 Pet 515

[82] S 3 St 301

[83] S 3 St 393, 4 St 780, 5 St 36

[84] S 6 St 527

[84a] S 3 St 740 4 St 39, 267, 352, 491, 506, 705, 6 St 441, 483, 507, 519 641, 710, 197, 7 St 195 311 10 St 771 *Cited* 2 Op A G 321, 2 Op A G 300, 3 Op A G 297, 3 Op A G 326, 3 Op A G 367 4 Op A G 116 4 Op A G 500, 4 Op A G 504, 4 Op A G 580, 4 Op A G 613, Cherokee 5 Pet 1, Eastern Band, 117 U S 288, Eastern Band, 20 C Cls 449, Eastern or Emigrant, 82 C Cls 180, Elk 112 U S 94, Heckman, 234 U S 418, Holden, 17 Wall 211 Labadie, 6 Okla 400, Marsh, 8 How 223, Old Settlers, 148 U S 427, Ward, 17 Wall 253 Western Cherokees, 82 C Cl 506, Western Cherokees, 27 C Cls 1 Worcester 6 Pet 515

[84b] Sg 7 St 49 S 3 St 517, 575, 5 St 30, 704, 766, 7 St 178, 218 326, 331, 355, 359, 420 502, 9 St 20, 182 252 382 544 574, 10 St 41, 226, 315 686, 11 St 65, 169 278, 388, 12 St 14, 221, 512 774, 13 St 161, 541, 14 St 255 492 15 St 199 613, 16 St 13, 335 544, 17 St 165, 437, 18 St 146, 420, 19 St 176, 271, 20 St 63, 295, 21 St 114, 485, 511, 22 St 68, 434, 23 St 76, 362, 24 St 29, 449, 25 St 217, 980, 26 St 336 989, 27 St 120, 612, 28 St 286, 876, 29 St 321, 30 St 62 571 924, 31 St 221 1058 *Cited* 6 L D 150, 3 Op A G 458, Chinn, 5 Fed Cas No 2684, Kansas, 5 Wall 737, U S v Higgins, 108 Fed 318

[84c] Sg 7 St 135 S 3 St 418, 517 *Cited* 4 Op A G 580, 4 Op A G 613

[84d] S 3 St 607, 517, 521 763, 7 St 232 *Cited* 3 L D Memo, 435, 7 Op A G 106, Hot Springs, 92 U S 698, U S v Choctaw, 179 U S 494

[84e] Sg 7 St 160 S 4 St 76, 528, 780, 5 St 36, 104 766, 6 St 924, 7 St 502, 9 St 20 182 272 382, 544 574, 10 St 41 226, 315, 656, 11 St 65 169, 273, 848, 12 St 41, 221 512 774, 13 St 161, 14 St 255 492, 15 St 198, 16 St 13 335 544, 17 St 165, 437, 18 St 146, 420, 19 St 176 271 20 St 63, 295, 21 St 114, 485 511, 22 St 68, 433, 23 St 76 362 24 St 29 449, 25 St 217 938, 26 St 330 989, 27 St 120, 612, 28 St 286, 876, 29 St 321 30 St 62, 571, 924, 31 St 221, 1058 *Cited* 6 L D 150, 3 Op A G 458

[84f] Sg 2 St 627

[84g] Sg 7 St 78 S 3 St 517 7 St 403

[84h] Sg 7 St 107 S 3 St 517, 33 St 189 *Cited* Labadie, 6 Okla 400, Osage Tribe 68 C Cls 64

[84i] S 3 St 517, 4 St 780, 5 St 36, 704 766, 7 St 200 208, 9 St 182, 252 382 544 574, 10 St 41, 226, 315 686, 11 St 65 169, 273, 355, 12 St 44, 221, 512, 774, 13 St 161 541, 14 St 255 492, 15 St 198, 591, 16 St 13, 335 544, 17 St 105, 437, 18 St 146, 420, 19 St 176, 271, 20 St 63, 295; 21 St 114, 485, 22 St 68 488, 23 St 76, 362, 24 St 29 449, 25 St 217, 980, 26 St 336, 989, 27 St 120, 612, 28 St 286, 876, 30 St 62, 571 924, 31 St 221, 1058, 32 St 245 982; 33 St 1048, 34 St 325 1015, 35 St 70 781 *Cited* Lowry, 15 Fed Cas No 8584, Potawatomie, 27 C Cls 408

[85] S 3 St 517, 4 St 780 5 St 36 704, 766, 7 St 209, 9 St 20 132, 252, 382, 544, 574, 10 St 41, 226, 315 *Cited* U S v Stone, 2 Wall 525

[86] S 3 St 517, 4 St 852, 464, 780; 5 St 36, 704 766, 6 St 747, 7 St 327, 9 St 20 182 252 382 544 574, 10 St 41 226, 315, 576, 11 St 273, 398, 12 St 44 221, 512, 774, 13 St 161, 541, 14 St 255, 492, 15 St 198, 16 St 13, 335, 544, 17 St 165 *Cited* Wau-pe-man-qua, 28 Fed 489

[87] Sg 7 St 49, 114 S 3 St 517, 4 St 181, 780, 5 St 402, 704, 766, 6 St 848, 519, 801, 7 St 295 300 309, 343, 351, 355, 364, 394, 458, 569; 9 St 20 182 252 382. 544, 574, 10 St 41, 226, 315 686, 1093, 11 St 65, 169, 273, 388, 12 St 44, 221, 512, 774, 13 St 161, 14 St 255, 492, 15 St 198, 16 St 13, 335 544, 17 St 165, 18 St 146, 19 St 176, 271, 20 St 63, 295, 21 St 114 485, 22 St 68 483, 23 St 76, 362, 24 St 29, 449, 25 St 217, 980, 26 St 336 *Cited* Wau-pe-man-qua, 28 Fed 489

[88] S 3 St 480, 517, 6 St 770, 7 St 450; 10 St 974, 13 St 541, 584. *Cited*, Clark, 13 Pet 195, Porterfield, 2 How 76.

7 St. 195; Feb. 27, 1819—Treaty (articles of a convention) with Cherokee Nation.[89]
7 St. 200; July 30, 1819—Treaty with Kickapoo Tribe.[90]
7 St. 202; Aug. 30, 1819—Treaty with Kickapoos of Vermilion.[91]
7 St. 203; Sept. 24, 1819—Treaty with Chippewa Nation.[92]
7 St. 206; June 16, 1820—Treaty with Chippeway Tribe.[93]
7 St. 207; July 6, 1820—Treaty with Ottawa and Chippewa Nations.[94]
7 St. 208; July 19, 1820—Treaty with Kickapoo Nation.[95]
7 St. 209; Aug. 11, 1820—Treaty with Wea Tribe.[96]
7 St. 210; Sept. 5, 1820—Treaty (articles of a convention) with Tribe of Kickapoos of the Vermilion.[97]
7 St. 210; Oct. 18, 1820—Treaty with Choctaw Nation.[98]
7 St. 215; Jan. 8, 1821—Treaty with Creek Nation.[99]
7 St. 217; Jan. 8, 1821—Treaty (articles of agreement) with Creek Nation. Also Discharge for all Claims on the Creeks.[1]
7 St. 218; Aug. 29, 1821—Treaty with Ottawa, Chippewa, and Pottawatomie Nations.[2]
7 St. 222; Aug. 31, 1822—Treaty with Great and Little Osage Indians.[3]
7 St. 223; Sept. 3, 1822—Treaty with United Sac and Fox Tribes.[4]
7 St. 224; Sept. 18, 1823—Treaty with Florida Tribes.[5]
7 St. 228; Oct. 24, 1804—Treaty with Cherokee Indians.[6]
7 St. 229; Aug. 4, 1824—Treaty with Sock and Fox Indians.[7]
7 St. 231; Aug. 4, 1824—Treaty with Ioway Nation.[8]
7 St. 232; Nov. 15, 1824—Treaty with Quapaw Nation.[9]
7 St. 234; Jan. 20, 1825—Treaty (articles of a convention) with Choctaw Nation.[10]
7 St. 237; Feb. 12, 1825—Treaty (articles of a convention) with Creek Nation.[11]
7 St. 240; June 2, 1825—Treaty with Great and Little Osage Tribes.[12]
7 St. 244; June 3, 1825—Treaty with Kansas Nation.[13]
7 St. 247; June 9, 1825—Treaty with Poncar Tribe.
7 St. 250; June 22, 1825—Treaty with Teton, Yancton, and Yanctonies bands of Sioux Tribes.[14]
7 St. 252; July 5, 1825—Treaty with Sioune and Ogallala Tribes.[15]
7 St. 255; July 6, 1825—Treaty with Chayenne Tribe.[16]
7 St. 257; July 16, 1825—Treaty with Hunkpapa Band of the Sioux.[17]
7 St. 259; July 18, 1825—Treaty with Ricara Tribe.
7 St. 261; July 30, 1825—Treaty with Belantse-etoa or Minnetsaree Tribe.
7 St. 264; July 30, 1825—Treaty with Mandan Tribe.[18]
7 St. 266; Aug. 4, 1825—Treaty with Crow Tribe.
7 St. 268; Aug. 10, 1825—Treaty with Great and Little Osage Nations.[19]
7 St. 270; Aug. 16, 1825—Treaty with Kansas Indians.[20]
7 St. 272; Aug. 19, 1825—Treaty with Sioux and Chippewa, Sacs and Fox, Menominie, Ioway, Sioux, Winnebago, and a portion of the Ottawa, Chippewa, and Potawattomie Tribes.[21]
7 St. 277; Sept. 26, 1825—Treaty with Ottoe and Missouri Tribe.
7 St. 279; Sept. 30, 1825—Treaty with Pawnee Tribe.
7 St. 282; Oct. 6, 1825—Treaty with Maha Tribe.
7 St. 284; Nov. 7, 1825—Treaty (articles of a convention) with Shawonee Nation.[23]
7 St. 286; Jan. 24, 1826—Treaty with Creek Nation.[24]
7. St. 289; Mar. 31, 1826—Supplementary Article to Creek Treaty, Jan. 24, 1826.[25]
7 St. 290; Aug. 5, 1826—Treaty with Chippewa Tribe.[26]
7 St. 295; Oct. 16, 1826—Treaty with Potawatamie Tribe.[27]
7 St. 300; Oct. 23, 1826—Treaty with Miami Tribe.[28]

---

[89] *Sg.* 2 St. 139; 7 St. 156. *S.* 3 St. 749; 4 St. 267, 352, 397, 505; 6 St. 349, 379, 387, 519, 641, 710, 879; 7 St. 195, 311. *Cited:* 2 Op. A. G. 321; 2 Op. A. G. 360; 3 Op. A. G. 297; 3 Op. A. G. 326; Cherokee, 5 Pet. 1; Cherokee, 270 U. S. 476; Eastern Band, 117 U. S. 288; Eastern Band, 20 C. Cls. 449; Eastern or Emigrant, 82 C. Cls. 180; Heckman, 224 U. S. 413; Holden, 17 Wall. 211; Marsh, 8 How. 223; Old Settlers, 148 U. S. 427; Ward, 17 Wall. 253; Western Cherokees, 82 C. Cls. 566; Western Cherokees, 27 C. Cls. 1; Worcester, 6 Pet. 515.

[90] *Sg.* 7 St. 185. *S.* 7 St. 208.

[91] *Sg.* 7 St. 100. *S.* 3 St. 608; 7 St. 210.

[92] *Sg.* 7 St. 49. *S.* 3 St. 577, 608, 690; 4 St. 636, 705, 780; 5 St. 36, 704, 766; 6 St. 639, 913; 7 St. 528; 9 St. 20, 132, 252, 382, 544, 574; 10 St. 41, 226, 315, 686. *Cited:* Chippewa, 301 U. S. 358; Francis, 203 U. S. 233; Shepard, 40 Fed. 341.

[93] *S.* 5 St. 704; 11 St. 169, 621, 631. *Cited:* Chippewa, 301 U. S. 358; Spalding, 160 U. S. 394.

[94] *Cited:* Chippewa, 301 U. S. 358.

[95] *Sg.* 7 St. 185, 200. *S.* 7 St. 391.

[96] *Sg.* 7 St. 186. *S.* 8 St. 783.

[97] *Ag.* 7 St. 202.

[98] *S.* 3 St. 680, 690, 749; 4 St. 40, 214, 397, 631, 653, 780; 5 St. 36, 704, 766; 9 St. 20, 132, 252, 382, 544, 574; 10 St. 41, 226, 315, 686; 11 St. 65, 169, 273; 12 St. 44, 512, 774; 13 St. 161, 541; 14 St. 255, 492; 15 St. 198; 16 St. 13, 335, 544; 17 St. 165, 437; 18 St. 146, 420; 19 St. 176, 271; 20 St. 63, 295; 21 St. 114, 485; 22 St. 68, 433; 23 St. 76, 362; 24 St. 29, 449; 25 St. 217, 980; 26 St. 336, 989; 27 St. 120, 612; 28 St. 286, 876; 29 St. 321; 30 St. 62, 571, 924; 31 St. 221, 1058; 32 St. 245; 33 St. 189, 1048; 34 St. 325, 1015; 35 St. 70, 781; 36 St. 269, 1058; 37 St. 518; 38 St. 77, 582; 39 St. 123, 909; 40 St. 561; 41 St. 408, 1225; 42 St. 552, 1174; 43 St. 390, 1141; 44 St. 453, 934; 45 St. 200, 1562; 46 St. 279; 47 St. 820; 48 St. 362; 49 St. 1757; 50 St. 564; 52 St. 291. *Cited:* Op. Sol. M. 18772, Dec. 24, 1926; 25 Op. A. G. 251; Chickasaw, 75 C. Cls. 426; Choctaw, 119 U. S. 1; Elk, 112 U. S. 94; Fleming, 215 U. S. 56; Mullen, 224 U. S. 448; U. S. v. Choctaw, 179 U. S. 404.

[99] *Sg.* 2 St. 139. *S.* 3 St. 633, 686, 748, 749; 4 St. 37, 92, 181, 721; 7 St. 237; 9 St. 284. *Cited:* 2 Op. A. G. 110.

[1] *Sg.* 2 St. 139.

[2] *Sg.* 7 St. 105, 160. *S.* 3 St. 686, 690; 5 St. 36, 704, 766; 6 St. 924; 7 St. 141, 491; 9 St. 20, 132, 252, 382, 544, 574; 10 St. 41, 226, 315, 686; 11 St. 65, 169, 273, 388; 12 St. 44, 221, 512, 774. *Cited:* 13 L. D. 511; 3 Op. A. G. 209; Chippewa, 301 U. S. 358; Godfrey, 10 Fed. Cas. No. 5497; Potawatomie, 27 C. Cls. 403.

[3] *Ag.* 7 St. 107. *Cited:* Labadie, 6 Okla. 400.

[4] *Ag.* 7 St. 84.

[5] *S.* 4 St. 37, 202, 217, 780; 5 St. 704, 766; 6 St. 341, 527; 7 St. 368, 377, 427; 9 St. 20, 132, 252, 382, 544, 574; 10 St. 41. *Cited:* Memo. Ind. Off., Mar. 13, 1935; Cherokee, 5 Pet. 1; Worcester, 6 Pet. 515.

[6] *S.* 4 St. 92, 181, 352, 780; 5 St. 36.

[7] *S.* 4 St. 181, 705, 740; 5 St. 158, 622, 704, 766; 7 St. 272, 543, 596; 9 St. 20, 132, 252, 544. *Cited:* Marsh, 8 How. 223; State of Missouri, 7 How. 660; Taylor, 44 F. 2d 58; U. S. v. Higgins, 103 Fed, 348; Webster, 11 How. 437.

[8] *S.* 4 St. 92, 181, 780; 7 St. 568; 20 St. 63.

[9] *Sg.* 7 St. 176. *S.* 4 St. 92, 181, 267; 7 St. 424. *Cited:* 34 Op. A. G. 429; 3 L. D. Memo. 435; Moore, 5 Ind. 384; U. S. v. Higgins, 103 Fed. 348.

[10] *Ag.* 7 St. 210. *Sg.* 7 St. 210. *S.* 4 St. 92, 181, 780; 5 St. 36, 704, 766; 9 St. 20, 132, 252, 382, 544, 574; 10 St. 41, 226, 315, 686; 11 St. 65, 169, 273, 388; 12 St. 44, 221, 512, 774; 13 St. 161; 14 St. 255, 492; 15 St. 198; 16 St. 13, 335, 544; 17 St. 165, 437; 18 St. 146, 420; 19 St. 176, 271; 20 St. 63, 295; 21 St. 114, 485; 22 St. 68, 433; 23 St. 76, 362; 24 St. 29, 449; 25 St. 217, 980; 26 St. 336, 989; 27 St. 120, 612; 28 St. 286, 876; 29 St. 321; 30 St. 62, 571, 924; 31 St. 221, 1058; 32 St. 245, 982; 33 St. 189, 1048; 34 St. 325, 1015; 35 St. 70, 781; 36 St. 269, 1058; 37 St. 518; 38 St. 77, 582; 39 St. 123, 969; 40 St. 561, 924; 41 St. 3, 408, 1225; 42 St. 552, 1174; 43 St. 390, 1141; 45 St. 200, 1562; 46 St. 279; 47 St. 820; 48 St. 362; 49 St. 1757; 50 St. 564; 52 St. 291. *Cited:* Op. Sol. M. 18772, Dec. 24, 1926; 2 Op. A. G. 465; 35 Op. A. G. 251; Choctaw, 119 U. S. 1; Elk, 112 U. S. 94.

[11] *Sg.* 7 St. 215; 28 Am. St. Papers (Public Lands, Cl. VIII, Vol. 1) p. 125. S. 7 St. 286, 303, 828.

[12] *Ag.* 7 St. 107. *S.* 4 St. 181, 217, 361, 705, 780; 5 St. 158, 298, 704, 766; 7 St. 478, 576; 9 St. 20, 132, 252, 382, 544, 574; 10 St. 41, 226, 315; 14 St. 492; 16 St. 13, 544; 17 St. 165, 237; 18 St. 146, 420; 19 St. 176, 271; 20 St. 63, 295; 21 St. 114, 485; 22 St. 68, 433; 23 St. 76, 362; 24 St. 29, 449; 25 St. 217, 980; 26 St. 336, 989; 27 St. 120, 612; 28 St. 286, 876; 29 St. 321; 30 St. 62, 571, 924; 31 St. 221, 1058; 32 St. 245, 982; 33 St. 189, 1048; 34 St. 325, 1015. *Cited:* Holden, 17 Wall. 211; Kansas, 80 C. Cls. 264; Labadie, 6 Okla. 400; Leavenworth, 92 U. S. 733; M. K. & T. Ry., 152 U. S. 114; M. K. & T. Ry., 92 U. S. 760; Osage Tribe, 66 C. Cls. 64; Quick Bear, 210 U. S. 50; Shore, 60 F. 2d 1; Shoshone, 85 C. Cls. 331; U. S. v. Higgins, 103 Fed. 348; Ward, 17 Wall. 253.

[13] *S.* 4 St. 181, 217, 361, 519, 705, 780; 5 St. 158, 704, 9 St. 20, 132, 842; 12 St. 21. *Cited:* 9 Op. A. G. 110; Jones, 175 U. S. 1; Kansas, 80 C. Cls. 264; Smith, 10 Wall. 321; State of Missouri, 7 How. 660; Swope, 23 Fed. Cas. No. 13704.

[14] *Cited:* Graham, 30 C. Cls. 318.

[15] *Cited:* Graham, 30 C. Cls. 318.

[16] *Cited:* Labadi, 31 C. Cls. 205.

[17] *Cited:* Graham, 30 C. Cls. 318.

[18] *Cited:* 25 L. D. 252.

[19] *Sg.* 4 St. 100. *Cited:* Labadie, 6 Okla. 400.

[20] *Sg.* 4 St. 100. *Cited:* Kansas, 80 C. Cls. 264.

[21] *Sg.* 7 St. 146, 229; *S.* 4 St. 181, 682; 7 St. 290, 328, 429, 431, 510, 511, 516, 548, 568; *Cited:* Cain, 2 Minn. L. Rev. 177; 25 L. D. 17; 5 Op. A. G. 31; Beecher, 95 U. S. 517; Chippewa, 301 U. S. 358; Chippewa, 80 C. Cls. 410; Graham, 30 C. Cls. 318

[23] *S.* 4 St. 780; 5 St. 36, 704, 766; 7 St. 355, 359; 9 St. 20, 132, 252. *Cited:* Blackfeather, 28 C. Cls. 447; Kansas, 5 Wall. 737; U. S. v. Blackfeather, 155 U. S. 180; Walker, 16 Wall. 436.

[24] *Rg.* 7 St. 237. *S.* 4 St. 187, 191, 267, 636, 682, 705, 780; 5 St. 704, 766; 6 St. 759; 7 St. 307, 366, 414, 417; 9 St. 20, 132, 252, 284, 382, 544, 574; 10 St. 41, 226, 315, 686; 11 St. 65, 169, 273, 388; 12 St. 44, 221, 774; 13 St. 541; 14 St. 255, 492; 15 St. 198; 16 St. 13, 335, 544; 17 St. 165, 437; 18 St. 146, 420; 19 St. 176, 271; 20 St. 63, 295; 21 St. 114, 485; 22 St. 68, 433; 23 St. 76, 362; 24 St. 29, 449; 25 St. 217, 980; 26 St. 336, 989; 27 St. 120, 612; 28 St. 286, 876; 29 St. 321; 30 St. 62, 571, 924; 31 St. 221, 1058; 32 St. 245. *Cited:* 5 Op. A. G. 98; Creek, 77 C. Cls. 226; U. S. v. Hayes, 20 F. 2d 873; U. S. v. Ben-Read, 171 Fed. 501; Woodward, 238 U. S. 284.

[25] *S.* 4 St. 705; 5 St. 704, 766.

[26] *Sg.* 7 St. 272. *S.* 4 St. 232, 300, 361, 432, 463, 780; 5 St. 36, 704, 766; 9 St. 20, 132, 252, 382, 544, 574; 10 St. 41, 226, 315, 686. *Cited:* Chippewa, 301 U. S. 358; U. S. v. Higgins, 103 Fed. 348.

[27] *Sg.* 7 St. 189. *S.* 4 St. 232, 234, 300, 361, 432, 463, 470, 780; 5 St. 36, 704, 766; 6 St. 378, 816; 7 St. 394, 458; 9 St. 132, 252, 382, 544, 574; 10 St. 41, 315, 686; 11 St. 65, 169, 273, 388; 12 St. 44, 221, 512, 774, 915; 13 St. 161, 541; 14 St. 255, 492; 15 St. 198; 16 St. 13, 335, 544; 17 St. 165, 437; 18 St. 146, 420; 19 St. 176, 271; 20 St. 63, 295; 21 St. 114, 485; 22 St. 68, 433; 23 St. 76, 362; 24 St. 29, 449; 25 St. 217, 980; 26 St. 336, 989; 27 St. 120, 612; 28 St. 286, 876; 29 St. 321; 30 St. 62, 571, 924; 31 St. 221, 1058; 32 St. 245, 982; 34 St. 325, 1015; 35 St. 70, 781. *Cited:* 6 Op. A. G. 711; Op. Sol. M. 28619. Potawatomie, 27 C. Cls. 403; U. S. v. Higgins, 103 Fed. 348.

[28] *Sg.* 7 St. 189. *S.* 4 St. 282, 300, 361, 432, 463, 470, 780; 5 St. 36, 704, 766; 7 St. 458, 569, 582; 9 St. 20, 132, 252, 382, 544, 574; 10 St. 41, 226, 315, 1093. *Cited:* 13 L. D. 511; 2 Op. A. G. 563; 2 Op. A. G. 631; 6 Op. A. G. 440; 12 Op. A. G. 236; Wau-pe-man-qua, 28 Fed. 489.

7 St. 303; Aug. 11, 1827—Treaty with Chippewa, Menomonie, and Winebago Tribes.[29]
7 St. 305; Sept. 19, 1827—Treaty with Potawatamie Tribe.[30]
7 St. 307; Nov. 15, 1827—Treaty (articles of agreement) with Creek Nation.[31]
7 St. 309; Feb. 11, 1828—Treaty with Eel River, or, Thorntown party of Miami Indians.[32]
7 St. 311; May 6, 1828—Treaty (articles of a convention) with Cherokee Nation.[33]
7 St. 315; Aug. 25, 1828—Treaty (articles of agreement) with United Tribes of Potawatamie, Chippewa and Ottawa Indians, and Winnebago Tribe.[34]
7 St. 317; Sept. 20, 1828—Treaty with Potowatami Tribe.[35]
7 St. 320; July 29, 1829—Treaty with United Nations of Chippewa, Ottawa, and Potawatamie Indians.[36]
7 St. 323; Aug. 1, 1829—Treaty with Winnebaygo Indians.[37]
7 St. 326; Aug. 3, 1829—Treaty (articles of agreement) with Delaware Indians.[38]
7 St. 327; Sept. 24, 1829—Supplementary Article to Delaware Treaty, Oct. 3, 1818.[39]
7 St. 328; July 15, 1830—Treaty with Confederated Tribes of the Sacs and Foxes; the Medawah-Kanton, Wahpacoota, Wahpeton and Sissetong Bands or Tribes of Sioux, the Omahas, Ioways, Ottoes and Missourias.[40]
7 St. 333; Sept. 27, 1830—Treaty with Choctaw Nation.[41]
7 St. 342; Feb. 8, 1831—Treaty (articles of agreement with Menomonee Nation.[42]
7 St. 348; Feb. 28, 1831—Treaty (articles of agreement and convention) with Seneca Tribe.[43]
7 St. 351; July 20, 1831—Treaty (articles of agreement and convention) with Wyandots, Senecas and Shawnees.[44]
7 St. 355; Aug. 8, 1831—Treaty (articles of agreement and convention) with Wyandots, Senecas and Shawnees.[45]
7 St. 359; Aug. 30, 1831—Treaty (articles of agreement and convention) with Ottoway Indians.[46]
7 St. 364; Jan. 19, 1832—Treaty (articles of agreement and convention) with Wyandots.[47]
7 St. 366; Mar. 24, 1832—Treaty with Creek Tribe.[48]
7 St. 368; May 9, 1832—Treaty with Seminoles.[49]
7 St. 370; Sept. 15, 1832—Treaty with Winnebago Nation.[50]
7 St. 374; Sept. 21, 1832—Treaty with Sac and Fox Indians.[51]
7 St. 377; Oct. 11, 1832—Treaty with Appalachicola Band.[52]
7 St. 378; Oct. 20, 1832—Treaty with Potawatamie Tribe.[53]
7 St. 381; Oct. 20, 1832—Treaty with Chickasaw Nation.[54]
7 St. 391; Oct. 24, 1832—Treaty with Kickapoo Tribe.[55]

---

[29] *Sg.* 7 St. 237. *S.* 4 St. 408, 616, 631, 636, 780; 5 St. 36, 704, 766; 7 St. 342, 506, 591; 9 St. 20, 132, 252, 382, 544, 574; 10 St. 41, 226 315, 686; 11 St. 65, 169, 273, 388, 663; 12 St. 44, 221, 512; 13 St. 161, 541; 14 St. 255, 492: *Cited:* 5 Op. A. G. 31; Chippewa, 301 U. S 358; New York Indians, 170 U. S. 1.

[30] *S.* 7 St. 399, 431, 528.

[31] *Sg.* 7 St. 286; *S.* 4 St. 300, 470.

[32] *Sg.* 7 St. 189; *S.* 4 St. 300; 7 St. 469.

[33] *Sg.* 7 St. 156, 195. *S.* 4 St. 300, 305, 352, 361, 463, 491, 528, 705, 780; 5 St. 36; 7 St. 414, 417, 478; 9 St. 132, 871; 30 St. 62, 571, 924; 31 St. 221, 1058. *Cited:* 2 Op. A. G. 402; 5 Op. A. G. 320; 19 Op A. G. 42; 34 Op. A. G. 275; Brewer-Elliott, 260 U. S. 77; Cherokee, 155 U. S. 218; Cherokee, 5 Pet. 1; Cherokee, 187 U. S. 294; Cherokee, 155 U. S. 196; Cherokee Nation, 80 C. Cls. 1; Corralitos, 33 C. Cls. 342; Eastern Band, 20 C. Cls. 449; Eastern Band, 117 U. S. 288; Eastern or Emigrant, 82 C. Cls. 180; Guthrie, 1 Okla. T. 458; Hanks, 3 Ind. T. 415; Heckman, 224 U. S. 413; Holden, 17 Wall. 211; Jordan, 1 Okla. T. 406; Labadie, 6 Okla. 400; M. K. & T. Ry., 46 C. Cls. 59; Old Settlers, 148 U. S. 427; St. Louis, 49 Fed. 440; Thomas, 169 U. S. 264; U. S. v. Cherokee, 202 U. S. 101; U. S. v. Duval, 25 Fed. Cas. No. 15,015; U. S. v. Reese, 27 Fed. Cas. No. 16,137; U. S. v. Soule, 30 Fed. 918; Ward, 17 Wall. 253; Western Cherokees, 82 C. Cls. 566; Western Cherokees, 27 C. Cls. 1.

[34] *S.* 4 St. 361.

[35] *S.* 4 St. 361, 432, 505, 594, 780; 5 St. 36, 704, 766; 6 St. 409, 834; 7 St. 394, 390; 9 St. 132, 252, 382, 544, 574; 10 St. 41, 226, 315, 686; 11 St. 65, 169, 273, 388; 12 St. 44, 221, 512, 774; 13 St. 161, 541; 14 St. 255, 492; 15 St. 198; 16 St. 13, 335, 544; 17 St. 165 437; 18 St. 146, 420; 19 St. 176, 271; 20 St. 63, 295; 21 St. 114, 485; 22 St. 68, 433; 23 St. 76, 362; 24 St. 29, 449; 25 St. 980; 26 St. 336, 989; 27 St. 120, 612; 28 St. 286, 876; 29 St. 321; 30 St. 62, 924; 32 St. 245, 982; 33 St. 189, 1048; 34 St. 325, 1015; 35 St. 70, 781. *Cited:* Potawatomie, 27 C. Cls. 403.

[36] *S.* 4 St. 390, 631, 780; 5 St. 36, 158, 323, 704, 766; 6 St. 924; 7 St. 568; 9 St. 20, 132, 252, 382, 544, 574; 10 St. 41, 226, 315 686; 11 St. 65 169, 273, 388; 12 St. 44, 221, 512, 774; 13 St. 161, 541; 14 St. 255, 492; 15 St. 198, 531; 16 St. 13, 335, 544; 17 St. 165, 437; 18 St. 146, 420; 19 St. 176, 271; 20 St. 63, 295; 21 St. 114, 485; 22 St. 68, 433; 23 St. 76, 362; 24 St. 29, 449; 25 St. 217, 980; 26 St. 336, 989; 27 St. 120, 612; 28 St. 286 876; 29 St. 321; 30 St. 62, 571, 924; 31 St. 221, 1058; 32 St. 245, 982; 33 St. 189, 1048; 34 St. 325, 1015; 35 St. 70, 781; *Cited:* 16 Op. A. G. 310; Jones, 175 U. S. 1; Pickering, 145 U S 310; Potawatomie, 27 C. Cls. 403.

[37] *Sg.* 7 St. 272. *S.* 4 St. 705, 780; 5 St. 36, 158 704, 766; 6 St. 790; 9 St. 20, 132, 252, 382, 544, 574; 10 St. 15 (Ch. 66), 41, 226, 315, 686; 11 St. 65, 169, 273. *Cited:* 3 Op. A. G. 584; U. S. v. Higgins, 103 Fed. 348.

[38] *Sg.* 7 St. 160.

[39] *Sg.* 7 St. 188. *S.* 4 St. 464, 601, 780; 5 St. 36, 158, 704, 766; 9 St 132, 252, 382, 544, 574; 10 St. 41, 226 315, 686, 1048; 11 St. 65, 169, 273, 388; 12 St. 44, 221, 512, 774, 1129; 14 St. 255, 492, 793; 15 St. 198; 16 St. 13, 335, 544; 17 St. 165; 18 St. 146, 420. *Cited:* Delaware, 74 C. Cls. 368; Hicks, 12 Fed. Cas. No. 6458; Kindred, 225 U. S. 582; U. S. v. Stone, 2 Wall. 525.

[40] *Sg.* 7 St 237. *S* 4 St. 526, 616, 682, 705, 780; 5 St. 36, 158, 704 766; 7 St. 370, 524, 527, 540, 542, 543; 9 St. 20, 132, 252, 382, 544, 574; 10 St. 41, 226, 304, 315, 576; 11 St. 169, 319, 388, 611; 12 St. 207; 14 St. 492; 34 St. 325. *Cited:* 20 Op. A. G. 742; 17 L. D. 457; Op. Sol., M. 18772 Dec. 24, 1926; Dubuque, 109 U. S. 329; Graham, 30 C. Cls. 318; Kansas, 80 C. Cls. 264; Myrick, 99 U. S. 291; Sloan, 95 Fed. 193; Sloan, 118 Fed. 283; State of Missouri, 7 How. 660; U. S. v. Higgins 103 Fed. 348.

[41] *S.* 4 St. 464, 528, 616, 636, 653, 705, 780; 5 St. 36, 131, 158 180, 251, 453 513, 612, 681, 704 766; 6 St. 521, 596 607, 633, 769, 856; 9 St. 20, 132, 252, 382, 544, 574 955; 10 St. 15 (Ch. 66), 41, 226; 11 St. 65; 30 St. 495; 32 St. 641; 37 St. 189; 38 St. 1375. *Cited:* Houghton 19 Calif. L. Rev. 507; 2 Op. A. G. 465 (7 St. 340); 2 Op. A. G. 693; 3 Op. A. G. 48; 3 Op. A. G. 106; 3 Op. A. G. 107; 3 Op. A. G. 113; 3 Op. A. G. 365; 3 Op. A. G 408; 3 Op. A. G. 517; 4 Op. A. G. 45; 4 Op. A. G. 107; 4 Op. A. G. 344; 4 Op. A. G. 346; 4 Op. A. G. 452; 4 Op. A. G. 513; 5 Op. A. G. 251; 7 Op. A. G. 142; 7 Op. A. G. 174; 15 Op. A. G. 601; 19 Op. A. G. 109; 24 Op. A. G. 689; 26 Op. A. G. 127; 34 Op. A. G. 275; 35 Op. A. G. 251; 1 L. D. Memo. 99; Op. Sol., M. 7316; Memo. Sol., Aug. 31, 1936; Anonymous, 1 Fed. Cas. No. 447; Atlantic, 165 U. S. 413; Ayres, 42 C. Cls. 385; Ballinger, 216 U. S. 240; Chickasaw, 75 C. Cls. 426; Choctaw & Chickasaw, 75 C. Cls. 494; Choctaw, 21 C. Cls. 59; Choctaw, 81 C. Cls. 1; Choctaw, 83 C. Cls. 49; Choctaw, 83 C. Cls. 140; Choctaw, 119 U. S. 1; Elk, 112 U. S. 94; Fleming, 215 U. S. 56; Gaines, 9 How. 356; In re Lands, 199 Fed. 811; Jones, 175 U. S. 1; Ligon, 164 Fed. 670; McBride, 149 Fed. 114; McCalib, 83 C. Cls. 79; M. K. & T. Ry., 46 C. Cls. 59; Mullen, 224 U. S. 448; St. Louis, 49 Fed. 440; Taylor, 7 How. 572; Thebo, 66 Fed. 372; U. S. v. Choctaw, 179 U. S. 494; Wallace, 204 U. S. 415; Wilson, 6 Wall. 83; Winton, 255 U. S. 373.

[42] *Ag.* 7 St. 303. *S.* 4 St. 594; 5 St. 36, 349, 645; 7 St. 405, 506, 550, 566; 11 St. 663; 20 St. 513. *Cited:* 3 Op. A. G. 322; 5 Op. A. G. 31; 25 L. D. 17; Memo. Sol. Off., Jan. 16, 1934; Beecher, 95 U. S. 517; Goodfellow, 10 Fed Cas. No. 5537; New York Indians, 170 U. S. 1; U. S. v. Cook, 19 Wall. 591; U. S. v. Foster, 25 Fed Cas. No. 15141.

[43] *Sg.* 7 St. 189. *S.* 4 St. 491, 780; 5 St. 36, 704, 766; 7 St. 351, 411; 9 St. 20, 252, 382, 544, 574; 10 St. 41, 226, 315, 686; 11 St. 65, 169, 273, 388; 12 St. 44, 221, 512, 774; 13 St. 161, 541; 16 St. 13, 335, 544; 17 St. 165, 437; 18 St. 146, 420; 20 St. 63, 295; 21 St. 114, 485; 22 St. 68, 433; 23 St. 76, 362; 24 St. 449; 25 St. 217, 980; 26 St. 336, 989; 27 St. 120, 612; 28 St. 286, 876; 29 St. 321. *Cited:* 6 L. D. 159; Goodfellow, 10 Fed. Cas. No. 5537; Libby, 118 U. S. 250.

[44] *Sg.* 4 St. 411; 7 St. 49 160, 189, 348. *S.* 4 St. 528, 705, 780; 5 St. 36, 704, 766; 7 St. 411; 9 St. 20, 132, 252, 574, 544; 10 St. 41, 226, 315, 686; 11 St. 65, 169, 273, 388; 12 St. 44, 221, 512, 774; 13 St. 161, 541; 14 St. 255, 492; 15 St. 198; 16 St. 13; 18 St. 146, 420; 19 St. 176, 271; 20 St. 63, 295; 21 St. 114, 485; 22 St. 68, 433; 24 St. 29, 449; 25 St. 217, 980; 26 St. 989; 27 St. 120, 612; 28 St. 286, 876; 29 St. 321; 30 St. 62, 571, 924; 31 St. 221, 1058.

[45] *Sg.* 4 St. 411; 7 St. 160, 189, 284; *S.* 4 St. 528, 780; 5 St. 36, 704, 766; 6 St. 639; 7 St. 420; 9 St. 20, 132, 252, 382, 544, 574; 10 St. 41, 226, 315, 1053. *Cited:* Blackfeather, 28 C. Cls. 447; Kansas, 5 Wall. 737; U. S. v. Blackfeather, 155 U. S. 180; U. S. v. Ward, 28 Fed Cas. No. 16639; Walker, 16 Wall. 436.

[46] *Sg.* 4 St. 411; 7 St. 49, 105, 160, 284. *S.* 4 St. 601, 616. *Cited:* 2 Op. A. G. 575; U. S. v. Higgins, 103 Fed 348.

[47] *Sg.* 7 St. 189. *S.* 4 St. 528; 12 St. 840. *Cited:* Woodward, 238 U. S. 284.

[48] *Sg.* 4 St. 411; 7 St. 286. *S.* 4 St. 528, 616, 682, 780; 5 St. 36, 158, 186, 256, 704, 766; 6 St. 788, 913; 9 St. 20, 132, 252, 382, 544, 574; 10 St. 41, 226, 315, 686; 11 St. 65, 538, 699; 22 St. 301; 26 St. 989; 31 St. 861; 32 St. 245; 37 St. 122. *Cited:* 3 Op. A. G. 40; 3 Op. A. G. 238; 3 Op. A. G. 288; 3 Op. A. G. 423; 3 Op. A. G. 578; 3 Op. A. G. 585; 3 Op. A. G. 596; 3 Op. A. G. 614; 4 Op. A. G. 491; 16 Op. A. G. 31; 34 Op. A. G. 275; Anonymous, 1 Fed. Cas. No. 447; Atlantic, 165 U. S. 413; Buster, 135 Fed. 947; Creek, 77 C. Cls. 159; Creek, 77 C. Cls. 226; McKee, 201 Fed. 74; U. S. v. Hayes, 20 F. 2d 873; U. S. ex rel. Search, 3 Okla. 404.

[49] *Sg.* 7 St. 224. *S.* 4 St. 705, 780; 5 St. 704, 766; 7 St. 417, 423, 427; 9 St. 20, 132, 252, 382, 544, 574, 821; 10 St. 41, 315, 686; 11 St. 65, 169, 273, 388, 699; 12 St. 44, 221, 512, 774; 25 St. 565. *Cited:* Memo. Ind. Off., Mar. 13, 1935; Buster, 135 Fed. 947; Crabtree, 54 Fed. 432; Crabtree, 54 Fed. 426; Creek, 78 C. Cls. 474; Goat, 224 U. S. 458; U. S. ex rel. Search, 3 Okla. 404.

[50] *Sg.* 7 St. 328. *S.* 4 St. 636, 705, 780; 5 St. 36, 704, 766; 7 St. 431; 9 St. 20, 132, 252, 382, 544, 574; 10 St. 15 (Ch. 66), 41, 226, 315, 686; 11 St. 65, 169, 273. *Cited:* U. S. v. Higgins, 103 Fed. 348.

[51] *S.* 4 St. 636, 682, 705, 780; 5 St. 36, 48, 704, 766; 7 St. 517, 540, 544, 596; 9 St. 20 132, 252, 382, 544, 574; 10 St. 15 (Ch. 66), 41, 226, 315, 686; 11 St. 65, 169, 273, 388; 12 St. 44, 221; 29 St. 736. *Cited:* U. S. v. Higgins, 103 Fed. 348; Webster, 11 How. 437.

[52] *Sg.* 7 St. 224. *S.* 4 St. 636, 682. *Cited:* Memo. Ind. Off., Mar. 13, 1935.

[53] *Sg.* 7 St. 146. *S.* 4 St. 636, 669, 682, 780; 5 St. 36, 323; 6 St. 676, 740, 818; 7 St. 450, 490, 500, 501; 9 St. 20, 132, 213, 252, 382, 544, 574; 10 St. 15 (Ch. 66), 41, 226, 315, 686; 11 St. 65, 169, 273, 388; 12 St. 44, 221, 512, 774; 13 St. 161, 541; 14 St. 255, 492; 15 St. 198; 16 St. 13, 544. *Cited:* 3 Op. A. G. 33; Jones, 175 U. S. 1; Potawatomie, 27 C. Cls. 403.

[54] *S.* 5 St. 10, 116; 10 St. 613, 974, 1078; 15 St. 228; 33 St. 743. *Cited:* 11 L. D. Memo. 400; 3 Op. A. G. 591; 7 Op. A. G. 142; Ayres, 44 C. Cls. 48; Ayres, 42 C. Cls. 385; Best, 18 Wall. 112; Chickasaw, 193 U. S. 115; Chickasaw, 22 C. Cls. 222; Choctaw, 83 C. Cls. 140; Lane, 21 Fed. 755; M. K. & T. Ry., 46 C. Cls. 59.

[55] *Sg.* 7 St. 208. *S.* 4 St. 636, 705, 780; 5 St. 36, 704, 766; 9 St. 20, 132, 252, 382, 544, 574; 10 St. 41, 1078. *Cited:* U. S. v. Reily, 290 U. S. 33.

7 St. 394; Oct. 26, 1832—Treaty with Pottawatimie Indians.[56]
7 St. 397; Oct. 26, 1832—Treaty with Shawnoes and Delawares.[57]
7 St. 399; Oct. 27, 1832—Treaty with Potowatomies.[58]
7 St. 403; Oct. 27, 1832—Treaty with Kaskaskia and Peoria tribes, and Michigamia, Cahokia and Tamarois bands, now united with two first named tribes, formerly composed Illinois Nation.[59]
7 St. 405; Oct. 27, 1832—Treaty with Menominee Nation.[60]
7 St. 410; Oct. 29, 1832—Treaty with Piankeshaw and Wea Tribes.[61]
7 St. 411; Dec. 29, 1832—Treaty with "United Nation" of Senecas and Shawnee Indians (articles of agreement).[62]
7 St. 414; Feb. 14, 1833—Treaty (articles of agreement and convention) with Cherokee Nation.[63]
7 St. 417; Feb. 14, 1833—Treaty (articles of agreement and convention) with Muskogee or Creek Nation.[64]
7 St. 420; Feb. 18, 1833—Treaty with Ottawa Indians.[65]
7 St. 423; Mar. 28, 1833—Treaty with Seminole Indians.[66]
7 St. 424; May 13, 1833—Treaty (articles of agreement) with Quapaw Indians.[67]
7 St. 427; June 18, 1833—Treaty with Appalachicola Band.[68]
7 St. 428; June 18, 1833—Relinquishment by certain chiefs, of land reserved by treaty of Sept. 18, 1823.
7 St. 429; Sept. 21, 1833—Treaty (articles of agreement and convention) with united bands of Otoes and Missourias.[69]
7 St. 431; Sept. 26, 1833—Treaty with United Nation of Chippewa, Ottowa and Potawatamie Indians.[70]
7 St. 448; Oct. 9, 1833—Treaty (articles of agreement and convention) with confederated bands of Pawnees—Grand Pawnees, Pawnee Loups, Pawnee Republicans, Pawnee Tappaye.[71]
7 St. 450; May 24, 1834—Treaty (articles of convention and agreement) with Chickasaw Nation.[72]
7 St. 458; Oct. 23, 1834—Treaty with Miami Tribe.[73]
7 St. 467; Dec. 4, 1834—Treaty with Potawattimie Tribe.[74]
7 St. 467; Dec. 10, 1834—Treaty with Potawattamie Tribe.[75]
7 St. 468; Dec. 16, 1834—Treaty with Potawattamis Indians.[76]
7 St. 469; Dec. 17, 1834—Treaty with Potawattimie Tribe.[77]
7 St. 470; July 1, 1835—Treaty with Caddo Nation.[78]
7 St. 474; Aug. 24, 1835—Treaty with Comanche and Witchetaw Indians.[79]
7 St. 478; Dec. 29, 1835—Treaty with Cherokee Tribe.[80]
7 St. 490; Mar. 26, 1836—Treaty with Pottawatamy Tribe.[81]
7 St. 491; Mar. 28, 1836—Treaty with Ottawa and Chippewa Nations (supplemental article).[82]
7 St. 498; Mar. 29, 1836—Treaty with Pottawatamy Band.[83]
7 St. 499; Apr. 11, 1836—Treaty with Aub-ba-naub-ba's band of Potawattimie Indians.[84]
7 St. 500; Apr. 22, 1836—Treaty with Patawattimie Tribe.[85]
7 St. 501; Apr. 22, 1836—Treaty with Patawattimie Tribe.[86]
7 St. 502; Apr. 23, 1836—Treaty with Wyandot Tribe.[87]
7 St. 503; May 9, 1836—Treaty with Chippewa Nation.[88]
7 St. 505; Aug. 5, 1836—Treaty with Potawattimie Tribe.[89]
7 St. 506 Sept. 3, 1836—Treaty (articles of agreement) with Menomonies.[90]
7 St. 510; Sept. 10, 1836—Convention with Sioux of Wa-Ha-Shaw's Tribe.[91]
7 St. 511; Sept. 17, 1836—Treaty with Ioway Tribe and Band of Sacks and Foxes of the Missouri.[92]
7 St. 513; Sept. 20, 1836—Treaty with Patawattimie Tribe.[93]

---

[56] *Sg.* 7 St. 185, 189, 295, 317. *S.* 4 St. 686, 682, 780; 5 St. 36, 704, 766; 6 St. 915; 7 St. 467, 468, 469, 505, 582; 7 St. 20, 132, 152, 282, 544, 574; 10 St. 41; 12 St. 207. *Cited:* 3 Op. A. G. 33; Doe, 23 How. 457; Pka-o-wah-ash-kum, 8 Fed. 740.

[57] *S.* 4 St. 636, 682, 780; 5 St. 36, 298, 704, 766; 9 St. 20, 132, 252, 382, 544, 574; 10 St. 41, 226, 315, 686; 11 St. 65, 169.

[58] *Sg.* 7 St. 305, 317. *S.* 4 St. 636, 780; 5 St. 36, 704, 766; 7 St. 490, 582; 9 St. 132, 252, 382, 544, 574; 10 St. 41, 226, 315, 686; 11 St. 65, 169, 273, 388; 12 St. 512, 774; 16 St. 18, 335; 26 St. 989. *Cited:* 3 Op. A. G. 33; Crows, 1 Black 352; Jones, 175 U. S. 1; Mullen, 250 U. S. 590; U. S. v. Higgins, 103 Fed. 348.

[59] *Sg.* 7 St. 74, 77, 78, 181. *S.* 4 St. 636, 780; 5 St. 36; 10 St. 1082. *Cited:* Bowling, 233 U. S. 528.

[60] *Ag.* 7 St. 342. *S.* 4 St. 682; 5 St. 349, 645; 7 St. 506, 566; 10 St. 1082; 20 St. 513.

[61] *S.* 4 St. 636, 780; 5 St. 36. *Cited:* Bowling, 233 U. S. 528.

[62] *Sg.* 7 St. 348, 351. *S.* 7 St. 550; 9 St. 20. *Cited:* Eastern Band, 117 U. S. 288; Holden, 17 Wall. 211; M. K. & T. Ry., 46 C. Cls. 59; Ward 17 Wall. 253; Woodward, 238 U. S. 284.

[63] *Rpg.* 7 St. 311; *Sg.* 7 St. 286. *S.* 4 St. 705, 780; 5 St. 36, 704, 766; 7 St. 423, 478; 9 St. 20, 132, 252, 544. *Cited:* Brewer-Elliott, 260 U. S. 77; Brown, 44 C. Cls. 283; Cherokee, 155 U. S. 218; Cherokee, 187 U. S. 294; Cherokee, 155 U. S. 196; Cherokee, 135 U. S. 641; Cherokee, 80 C. Cls. 1; Eastern Band, 20 C. Cls. 449; Eastern or Emigrant, 82 C. Cls. 180; Guthrie, 1 Okla. T. 414; Heckman, 224 U. S. 413; Holden, 17 Wall. 211; Jordan, 1 Okla. T. 406; Labadie, 6 Okla. 400; Mehlin, 56 Fed. 12; M. K. & T. Ry., 46 C. Cls. 59; Persons, 40 C. Cls. 411; U. S. v. Reese, 27 Fed. Cas. No. 16137; U. S. v. Soule, 30 Fed. 918; Ward, 17 Wall. 253; Western Cherokees, 82 C. Cls. 566; Western Cherokees, 27 C. Cls. 1.

[64] *Sg.* 7 St. 286, 311, 368. *S.* 4 St. 705, 780; 5 St. 704, 766; 9 St. 20, 132, 252, 574, 821; 10 St. 41, 226, 315, 686; 11 St. 65, 169, 273, 388, 699; 12 St. 44, 221, 512, 774; 13 St. 161, 541; 14 St. 255; 15 St. 198; 16 St. 13; 18 St. 146; 19 St. 176, 271. *Cited:* Corralitos, 33 C. Cls. 342; Creek, 77 C. Cls. 159; Creek, 302 U. S. 620; Eastern Band, 117 U. S. 288; Goat, 224 U. S. 458; Hanks, 3 Ind. T. 415; McKee, 201 Fed. 74; M. K. & T. Ry., 46 C. Cls. 59; Tiger, 221 U. S. 286; U. S. v. Creek, 295 U. S. 103; U. S. Hayes, 20 F. 2d 873; U. S. v. Payne, 8 Fed. 888; U. S. v. Rea-Read, 171 Fed. 501; U. S. ex rel. Search, 3 Okla. 404.

[65] *Sg.* 7 St. 105, 160, 358. *S.* 4 St. 636. *Cited:* 2 Op. A. G. 562.

[66] *Sg.* 7 St. 368, 414. *Cited:* Memo. Ind. Off., March 13, 1935; Goat, 224 U. S. 458; U. S. ex rel. Search, 3 Okla. 404.

[67] *Sg.* 7 St. 232. *S.* 4 St. 705, 780; 5 St. 36, 704, 766; 9 St. 20, 132, 252, 382, 544, 574; 10 St. 41, 226, 315, 686; 11 St. 65, 169, 273; 12 St. 44, 221, 512, 774; 13 St. 161, 541; 14 St. 255; 15 St. 198, 513; 16 St. 13, 335, 544; 17 St. 165, 437; 18 St. 146, 420; 19 St. 176, 271; 20 St. 63, 295; 21 St. 485; 22 St. 68, 433; 23 St. 76, 362; 24 St. 29, 449; 25 St. 217, 980; 26 St. 336, 989; 27 St. 612; 28 St. 286, 876; 29 St. 321; 30 St. 62, 571, 924; 31 St. 221, 1058; 32 St. 245, 982; 33 St. 189, 1048; 34 St. 325, 1015; 35 St. 70, 781; 36 St. 269, 1058; 37 St. 518; 38 St. 77, 582; 39 St. 123, 969; 40 St. 561, 934; 41 St. 3, 408, 1225; 42 St. 552, 1174; 43 St. 390, 1141; 44 St. 453; 45 St. 200, 1562; 46 St. 279. *Cited:* 34 Op. A. G. 439; 3 L. D. Memo. 435; Moore, 5 Ind. T. 384; U. S. v. Noble, 237 U. S. 74; Whitebird, 40 F. 2d 479.

[68] *Sg.* 7 St. 224, 368. *S.* 4 St. 705. *Cited:* Memo. Ind. Off., Mar. 13, 1935.

[69] *Sg.* 7 St. 272. *S.* 4 St. 705, 780; 5 St. 36, 158, 704, 766; 9 St. 20, 132, 252, 382, 574; 10 St. 41, 226.

[70] *Sg.* 7 St. 272, 305, 370. *S.* 5 St. 36, 158, 704, 766; 6 St. 924; 9 St. 20, 132, 252, 382, 544, 574; 10 St. 41, 226, 252, 315, 686; 11 St. 65, 169, 273, 388; 12 St. 44, 207, 221, 512, 774; 13 St. 161, 541; 14 St. 255, 492; 15 St. 198; 16 St. 335, 544; 33 St. 189; 44 St. 934; 45 St. 159, 883. *Cited:* 7 Op. A. G. 142; Pam-to-pee, 187 U. S. 371; Potowatomie, 27 C. Cls. 403.

[71] *S.* 4 St. 705, 780; 5 St. 36; 9 St. 20, 132, 252, 382, 544, 574; 10 St. 41, 226, 315, 686; 11 St. 65, 169, 273. *Cited:* Pawnee, 56 C. Cls. 1.

[72] *Sg.* 7 St. 192. *Ag.* 7 St. 378. *S.* 4 St. 780; 5 St. 10, 36, 704, 766, 727; 6 St. 861; 9 St. 20, 37, 132, 252; 10 St. 41, 974; 15 St. 228; 38 St. 743. *Cited:* 3 Op. A. G. 34; 3 Op. A. G. 41; 3 Op. A. G. 170; 3 Op. A. G. 591; 7 Op. A. G. 174; 34 Op. A. G. 275; 11 L. D. Memo. 400; Ayres, 44 C. Cls. 48; Ayres, 42 C. Cls. 385; Best, 18 Wall. 112; Chickasaw, 22 C. Cls. 222; Jones, 175 U. S. 1; Love, 21 Fed. 755; M. K. & T. Ry., 46 C. Cls. 59.

[73] *Sg.* 7 St. 189, 295, 300. *S.* 5 St. 704, 766; 9 St. 20, 252, 544, 574; 10 St. 41, 226, 315, 576, 686, 1093; 11 St. 65, 169, 273, 388; 12 St. 44, 774; 13 St. 161; 14 St. 255, 492; 15 St. 198; 16 St. 13, 335, 544; 17 St. 165, 437; 18 St. 146; 19 St. 176, 271; 20 St. 63, 295; 21 St. 114, 485; 22 St. 68, 433; 23 St. 76, 362; 24 St. 29, 449; 25 St. 217, 980; 26 St. 336. *Cited:* Old Settlers, 148 U. S. 427; Wau-pe-man-qua, 28 Fed. 489.

[74] *Sg.* 7 St. 394. *S.* 5 St. 36.

[75] *Sg.* 7 St. 394.

[76] *Sg.* 7 St. 396.

[77] *Sg.* 7 St. 309, 394.

[78] *S.* 5 St. 36, 584. *Cited:* Jones, 175 U. S. 1; U. S. v. Brooks, 10 How. 442.

[79] *Cited:* 4 Op. A. G. 560; 4 Op. A. G. 597; 4 Op. A. G. 621; 5 Op. A. G. 36.

[80] *Sg.* 4 St. 411; 7 St. 240, 311, 414. *S.* 5 St. 73, 241, 323, 470, 473, 523, 681, 719; 6 St. 685, 835; 9 St. 20, 203, 252, 570, 746, 785, 871; 10 St. 41, 181, 643, 686, 771; 11 St. 65; 12 St. 44, 834, 850; 14 St. 799. *Cited.* Cohen, 3 Ind. at W., No. 19; 3 Op. A. G. 207; 3 Op. A. G. 297; 3 Op. A. G. 326; 3 Op. A. G. 431; 3 Op. A. G. 504; 4 Op. A. G. 73; 4 Op. A. G. 175; 4 Op. A. G. 500; 4 Op. A. G. 504; 4 Op. A. G. 560; 4 Op. A. G. 580; 4 Op. A. G. 597; 4 Op. A. G. 613; 5 Op. A. G. 36; 5 Op. A. G. 268; 5 Op. 320; 7 Op. A. G. 54; 16 Op. A. G. 225; 16 Op. A. G. 300; 17 Op. A. G. 72; 30 Op. A. G. 284; 34 Op. A. G. 275; 7 L. D. Memo. 517; 8 L. D. Memo. 196; Memo. Sol., Feb. 28, 1935, Apr. 23, 1936, Aug. 14, 1937. Atlantic 165 U. S. 413; Brewer-Elliott, 260 U. S. 77; Cherokee, 155 U. S. 218; Cherokee, 187 U. S. 294; Cherokee, 155 U. S. 196; Cherokee, 135 U. S. 641; Cherokee, 270 U. S. 476; Cherokee, 80 C. Cls. 1; Corralitos, 33 C. Cls. 342; Delaware, 38 C. Cls. 234; Eastern Band, 20 C. Cls. 449; Eastern Cherokees, 45 C. Cls. 229; Eastern or Emigrant, 82 C. Cls. 180; Elk, 112 U. S. 94; Glenn-Tucker, 4 Ind. T. 511; Guthrie, 1 Okla. 454; Heckman, 224 U. S. 413; Holden, 17 Wall. 211; Jordan, 1 Okla. T. 406; Labadie, 6 Okla. 478; Langdon, 14 Fed. Cas. No. 8062; Mackey, 18 How. 100; Mehlin, 56 Fed. 12; Moore, 2 Wyo. 8; M. K. & T. Ry., 46 C. Cls. 59; Old Settlers, 148 U. S. 427; Persons, 40 C. Cls. 411; Raymond, 83 Fed. 721; Stephens, 174 U. S. 455; Talton, 163 U. S. 376; Thomas, 169 U. S. 264; U. S. v. Boyd, 68 Fed. 577; U. S. v. Boyd, 83 Fed. 547; U. S. v. Cherokee, 202 U. S. 101; U. S. v. Hayes, 20 F. 2d 378; U. S. v. Reese, 27 Fed. Cas. No. 16137; U. S. v. Rogers, 23 Fed. 658; U. S. v. Swain, 46 F. 2d 99; U. S. v. Wright, 53 F. 2d 300; Ward, 17 Wall. 253; Western Cherokees, 82 C. Cls. 566; Western Cherokees, 27 C. Cls. 1.

[81] *Sg.* 7 St. 399. *S.* 5 St. 78.

[82] *Sg.* 4 St. 492; 7 St. 218. *S.* 5 St. 73, 328, 704, 766; 6 St. 924; 9 St. 20, 132, 252, 342, 382, 544, 574; 10 St. 15 (C. 66), 41, 226, 315, 686; 11 St. 169, 621; 12 St. 221, 512; 33 St. 1048. *Cited:* 3 Op. A. G. 206; Ottawa, 42 C. Cls. 240; Spalding, 160 U. S. 394; U. S. v. Higgins, 103 Fed. 348.

[83] *S.* 5 St. 73.

[84] *Sg.* 7 St. 378. *S.* 5 St. 73.

[85] *Sg.* 7 St. 378. *S.* 5 St. 73.

[86] *Sg.* 7 St. 378. *S.* 5 St. 73.

[87] *Sg.* 7 St. 160; 7 St. 178.

[88] *Sg.* 7 St. 105. *S.* 5 St. 73; 11 St. 633; 12 St. 1105. *Cited:* Chippewa, 80 C. Cls. 410; Chippewa, 301 U. S. 358.

[89] *Sg.* 7 St. 394. *S.* 5 St. 158; 7 St. 532.

[90] *Sg.* 7 St. 303, 342, 405. *S.* 5 St. 158, 704; 9 St. 132, 252, 382, 544, 574, 952; 10 St. 15 (C. 66), 41, 226, 315, 686, 792. *Cited:* 5 Op. A. G. 31.

[91] *Ag.* 7 St. 272. *S.* 5 St. 158. *Cited:* Graham, 30 C. Cls. 318.

[92] *Ag.* 7 St. 272. *S.* 5 St. 158, 328; 7 St. 548, 568. *Cited:* State of Missouri, 7 How. 660.

[93] *S.* 9 St. 20.

7 St. 514; Sept. 22, 1836—Treaty with Potawattimie Tribe.[94]
7 St. 515; Sept. 23, 1836—Treaty with Potawattamie Indians.[95]
7 St. 516; Sept. 27, 1836—Convention with Sac and Fox Tribe.[96]
7 St. 517; Sept. 28, 1836—Treaty with Sac and Fox Tribe.[97]
7 St. 524; Oct. 15, 1836—Treaty (articles of a convention) with Otoes, Missouries, Omahaws and Yankton and Santee bands of Sioux.[98]
7 St. 527; Nov. 30, 1836—Convention with Wahpaakootah, Susseton, and Upper Medawakanton tribes of Sioux Indians.[99]
7 St. 528; Jan. 14, 1837[1]—Treaty with Saganaw tribe of Chippewa Nation.[2]
7 St. 532; Feb. 11, 1837—Treaty with Potawatomie Tribe.[3]
7 St. 533; May 26, 1837—Treaty with Kioway, Ka-ta-ka and Ta-wa-ka-ro Nations.[4]
7. St. 536; July 29, 1837—Treaty with Chippewa Nation.[5]
7 St. 538; Sept. 29, 1837—Treaty with Sioux Nation.[6]
7 St. 540; Oct. 21, 1837—Treaty with confederated tribes of Sacs and Foxes.[7]
7 St. 542; Oct. 21, 1837—Treaty with Yankton tribe of Sioux Indians.[8]
7 St. 543; Oct. 21, 1837—Treaty with Sacs and Foxes of Missouri.[9]
7 St. 544; Nov. 1, 1837—Treaty with Winnebago Nation.[10]
7 St. 547; Nov. 23, 1837—Treaty with Ioway Indians.[11]
7 St. 547; Dec. 20, 1837[12]—Treaty with Saganaw tribe of Chippewas.[13]
7 St. 550; Jan. 15, 1838—Treaty with New York Indians.[14]
7 St. 565; Jan. 23, 1838—Treaty with Chippewa Nation.[15]
7 St. 566; Feb. 3, 1838—Treaty with Oneida Indians. (First Christian and Orchard parties).[16]
7 St. 568; Oct. 19, 1838—Treaty with Ioway Tribe.[17]
7 St. 569; Nov. 6, 1838—Treaty with Miami Tribe.[18]

[94] *S.* 5 St. 158.
[95] *S.* 5 St. 158; 7 St. 532.
[96] *Ag.* 7 St. 272. *S.* 5 St. 158. *Cited:* State of Missouri, 7 How. 660.
[97] *Sg.* 7 St. 374. *S.* 5 St. 158, 704, 766; 10 St. 750; 11 St. 65.
[98] *Ag.* 7 St. 328. *S.* 5 St. 158.
[99] *Sg.* 7. St. 328. *S.* 5 St. 158; 11 St. 169.
[1] Included with this Treaty as an amendment is the Treaty of Dec. 20, 1837, 7 St. 547.
[2] *Sg.* 3 St. 608; 5 St. 766; 7 St. 105, 203, 305; 8 St. 218. *S.* 5 St. 298, 565, 578; 9 St. 20, 132, 252, 382, 544, 574, 777; 10 St. 41, 226, 315, 686; 12 St. 512, 843. *Cited:* Chippewa, 301 U. S. 358; New York Indians, 5 Wall. 761; Shepard, 40 Fed. 341; U. S. v. Kie, 26 Fed. Cas. No. 15528a.
[3] *Sg.* 7 St. 394, 399, 505, 515. *S.* 5 St. 158, 453.
[4] *S.* 5 St. 323.
[5] *S.* 5 St. 298, 402, 704, 766; 7 St. 591; 9 St. 20, 132, 252, 382, 544, 574; 10 St. 41, 226, 315, 686; 11 St. 65. *Cited:* Cain, 2 Minn. L. Rev. 177; Op. Sol. M. 11380, June 17, 1924, M. 27381, Dec. 13, 1934, M. 28107, June 30, 1936; Chippewa, 80 C. Cls. 410; U. S. v. First, 234 U. S. 245; U. S. v. Higgins, 103 Fed. 348; U. S. v. Minnesota, 270 U. S. 181.
[6] *S.* 5 St. 323, 704, 766; 9 St. 20, 132, 252, 382, 544; 10 St. 41, 226, 315, 686, 954; 11 St. 65, 169, 273, 388; 12 St. 41; 39 St. 1195. *Cited:* Cain, 2 Minn. L. Rev. 177; Graham, 80 C. Cls. 318; Medawakanton, 57 C. Cls. 357; U. S. v. Higgins, 103 Fed. 348.
[7] *Sg.* 7 St. 328, 374. *S.* 5 St. 298, 323, 704, 766; 7 St. 596; 9 St. 20, 132, 252, 382, 544, 574; 10 St. 41, 226, 315, 686; 11 St. 65, 169, 273, 388; 12 St. 41, 221, 512, 774; 13 St. 161, 541; 14 St. 255, 492; 15 St. 198; 16 St. 13, 335, 544; 17 St. 165, 437; 18 St. 146, 420; 19 St. 176, 271; 20 St. 295; 21 St. 114, 485; 22 St. 68, 433; 23 St. 76, 362; 24 St. 29, 449; 25 St. 217, 980; 26 St. 336, 989; 27 St. 120, 612; 28 St. 286, 876; 29 St. 321; 30 St. 62, 571, 924; 31 St. 221, 1058; 32 St. 245, 982; 33 St. 189, 1048; 34 St. 325, 1015; 35 St. 70, 781; 36 St. 368. *Cited:* Sac & Fox, 220 U. S. 481.
[8] *Sg.* 7 St. 328. *S.* 5 St. 298 *Cited:* Graham, 80 C. Cls. 318.
[9] *Sg.* 7 St. 84, 229, 272, 328, 511. *S.* 5 St. 298, 402, 704; 11 St. 273; 19 St. 176, 271; 20 St. 295; 21 St. 114, 485; 22 St. 68, 438; 24 St. 29, 449; 25 St. 217.
[10] *Sg.* 7 St. 374. *S.* 5 St. 298, 402, 704, 766; 9 St. 20, 132, 252, 382, 544, 570, 574, 878; 10 St. 41, 226, 315, 686; 11 St. 65, 169, 273, 329, 388; 12 St. 44, 774; 13 St. 161, 541; 14 St. 255, 492; 15 St. 198; 16 St. 13, 335, 544; 17 St. 165, 437; 18 St. 146, 420; 19 St. 176, 271; 20 St. 295; 21 St. 114, 485; 22 St. 68, 433; 23 St. 76, 362; 24 St. 29, 449; 25 St. 217, 980; 26 St. 336, 989; 27 St. 120, 612; 28 St. 286, 876; 29 St. 321; 30 St. 62, 571, 924; 31 St. 221, 1058; 32 St. 245; 33 St. 189, 1048; 34 St. 325, 1015; 35 St. 70, 781. *Cited:* 3 Op. A. G. 471; U. S. v. Higgins, 103 Fed. 348.
[11] *Sg.* 7 St. 528.
[12] See Treaty of Jan. 14, 1837, 7 St. 528.
[13] *S.* 5 St. 298. *Cited:* Chippewa, 301 U. S. 358; Shepard, 40 Fed. 341.
[14] *Sg.* 4 St. 411, 428; 7 St. 342, 411. *S.* 5 St. 298, 323; 7 St. 586; 9 St. 20, 252; 10 St. 15 (Ch. 66); 11 St. 425, 735; 12 St. 991. *Cited:* 3 Op. A. G. 624; 1 L. D. Memo. 35; Fellows, 19 How. 366; New York Indians, 170 U. S. 1; U. S. v. Boylan, 265 Fed. 165; U. S. v. New York Indians, 173 U. S. 464.
[15] *Sg.* 7 St. 528. *S.* 5 St. 298, 402, 680. *Cited:* Shepard, 40 Fed. 341.
[16] *Sg.* 7 St. 342, 405. *S.* 5 St. 298. *Cited:* Memo. Sol. Off., Jan. 16, 1934; U. S. v. Boylan, 265 Fed. 165; U. S. v. Foster, 25 Fed. Cas. No. 15141; U. S. v. Paine, 206 U. S. 467.
[17] *Sg.* 7 St. 231, 272, 320, 511. *S.* 5 St. 704, 766; 9 St. 132, 252, 382, 544, 574; 10 St. 41, 226, 315, 686; 11 St. 65, 169, 273, 388; 12 St. 44, 221, 512, 774; 14 St. 255.
[18] Sg. 7 St. 189, 300. S. 5 St. 323, 402, 453, 542, 704, 766; 9 St. 20, 132, 252, 801; 10 St. 576, 1093. *Cited:* 6 Op. A. G. 440; 12 Op. A. G. 236; 17 Op. A. G. 410; Wau-pe-man-qua, 28 Fed. 489.

7 St. 574; Nov. 23, 1838—Treaty with Creek Nation.[19]
7 St. 576; Jan. 11, 1839—Treaty with Great and Little Osage Indians.[20]
7 St. 578; Feb. 7, 1839—Articles Supplementary to certain treaties with Saganaw tribe of Chippewas.[21]
7 St. 580; Sept. 3, 1839—Treaty with the Stockbridges and Munsee Tribes.[22]
7 St. 582; Nov. 28, 1840—Treaty with Miami Tribe.[23]
7 St. 586; May 20, 1842—Treaty with Seneca Nation.[24]
7 St. 591; Oct. 4, 1842—Treaty with Chippewa Indians.[25]
7 St. 596; Oct. 11, 1842—Treaty with confederated tribes of Sac and Fox Indians.[26]
7 St. 601; Sept. 15, 1797—Contract with the Seneca nation of Indians.[27]

8 STAT.

8 St. 116; Nov. 19, 1794—Treaty with Great Britain.[28]
8 St. 188; Oct. 27, 1795—Treaty with Spain.[29]
8 St. 200; Apr. 30, 1803—Treaty with France.[30]
8 St. 218; Dec. 24, 1814—Treaty with Great Britain.[31]
8 St. 252; Feb. 22, 1819; Oct. 29, 1820—Treaty with Spain.[32]
8 St. 302; Apr. 5, 17, 1824—Convention with Russia.[33]
8 St. 410; Apr. 5, 1831—Treaty with Mexico.

9 STAT.

9 St. 13; May 19, 1846; C. 22—An Act to provide for raising a Regiment of mounted Riflemen, and for establishing military Stations on the Route to Oregon.
9 St. 20; June 27, 1846; C. 34—An Act making appropriations for the current and contingent expenses of the Indian Department, and for fulfilling treaty stipulations with the various Indian Tribes, for the year ending June 30, 1847.[34] R. S. 2092, 25 U. S. C. 131. U. S. C. A. Historical Note: R. S. 2093 was derived from sec. 1 instant Act. No appro-

[19] *S.* 5 St. 323, 704, 766; 9 St. 20, 132, 252, 382, 544, 574; 10 St. 41, 226, 315, 576; 11 St. 599.
[20] *Sg.* 7. St. 240, 241. *S.* 5 St. 402, 704, 766; 9 St. 20, 132, 252, 382, 544, 574; 10 St. 41, 226, 315, 686; 11 St. 65, 169; 16 St. 335. *Cited:* Labadie, 6 Okla. 400; Osage Tribe, 66 C. Cls. 64.
[21] *Sg.* 7 St. 528. *S.* 5 St. 328.
[22] *S.* 5 St. 402.
[23] *Sg.* 7 St. 300. *S.* 5 St. 493, 542, 704, 766; 9 St. 20, 132, 252, 382, 544, 574; 10 St. 41, 226, 315, 686, 1093; 11 St. 65, 169, 273, 388; 12 St. 44, 221, 512, 774; 13 St. 161, 541; 17 St. 213. *Cited:* 6 Op. A. G. 440; 12 Op. A. G. 236; 17 Op. A. G. 410; Wau-pe-man-qua, 28 Fed. 489.
[24] *Ag.* 7 St. 550. *S.* 9 St. 20; 11 St. 735; 12 St. 991. *Cited:* Fellows, 19 How. 366; New York Indians, 5 Wall. 761; New York ex rel. Cutler, 21 How. 366; U. S. v. Seneca, 274 Fed. 947.
[25] *Sg.* 7 St. 303, 536. *S.* 5 St. 612, 704, 766; 9 St. 20, 132, 252, 382, 544, 574; 10 St. 41, 226, 315, 686; 11 St. 65, 169, 273, 388; 12 St. 44, 221, 512, 774; 13 St. 161, 541; 14 St. 255, 492; 16 St. 13, 335, 544; 17 St. 165, 437; 18 St. 146, 420; 19 St. 176. *Cited:* Cain, 2 Minn. L. Rev. 177; 19 L. D. 518; Op. Sol., M. 27381, Dec. 13, 1934, M. 28107, June 30, 1936; Chippewa, 80 C. Cls. 410; Chippewa, 301 U. S. 358; U. S. v. First, 234 U. S. 245; U. S. v. Higgins, 103 Fed. 348; U. S. v. Stearns, 245 U. S. 436; U. S. v. Thomas, 47 Fed. 488; Wisconsin, 201 U. S. 202.
[26] *Sg.* 7 St. 220, 374, 540. *S.* 5 St. 612, 681, 704, 766; 7 St. 70, 596, 601; 9 St. 20, 132, 252, 382, 544, 574; 10 St. 41, 226, 315, 686; 11 St. 65, 169, 273, 388; 12 St. 44, 221, 512, 774; 13 St. 161, 541; 14 St. 255, 492; 15 St. 198; 16 St. 13, 335, 544; 17 St. 165, 437; 18 St. 146, 420; 19 St. 176, 271; 20 St. 295; 21 St. 114, 485; 22 St. 68, 433; 23 St. 76, 362; 24 St. 29, 449; 25 St. 217, 980; 26 St. 336, 989; 27 St. 120, 612; 28 St. 286; 29 St. 321; 30 St. 571; 31 St. 221; 32 St. 245, 982; 33 St. 189; 34 St. 325; 35 St. 781. *Cited:* 53 I. D. 187; In re Lelah-Puc-Pa-Chee, 98 Fed. 429; Kennedy, 241 U. S. 556; New York Indians, 5 Wall. 761; Pennock, 103 U. S. 44; Peters, 111 Fed. 244; Sac & Fox, 45 C. Cls. 287; Sac & Fox, 220 U. S. 481.
[27] *Sg.* 2 St. 139; 7 St. 70.
[28] *Sg.* 7 St. 49. *Cited:* McCandless, 25 F. 2d 71.
[29] *S.* 8 St. 200.
[30] *S.* 2 St. 245, 641. *Sg.* 8 St. 138.
[31] *S.* 7 St. 141, 528. *Cited:* Kansas, 80 C. Cls. 264; McCandless, 25 F. 2d 71.
[32] *S.* 3 St. 523, 687, 750; 23 St. 296. *Cited:* Chickasaw, 75 C. Cls. 426.
[33] *S.* 4 St. 276.
[34] *Sg.* 1 St. 618; 4 St. 56, 181, 735; 5 St. 158; 7 St. 35, 44, 49, Art. 4, 68, 74, 84, 91, 98, 100, 105, 118 (Sept. 30, 1809, correct date); 7 St. 160, 178, 186, 188, 189, 203, 210, 218, 224, 229, 234, 240, 244, 284, 286, 290, 300, 303, 320, 323, 328, 333, 348, 351, 355, 366, 368, 370, 374, 378, 391, 394, 397, 411, 414, 417, 424, 429, 431, 449, 450, 458 (Oct. 23, 1834, correct date); 7 St. 463 (Oct. 23, 1834, correct date); 7 St. 463 (Oct. 23, 1834, correct date); 7 St. 478, 487, 491, 492, 513, 528, 536, 538, 540, 544, 550, 569, 574, 576, 582, 586, 591, 596, 766; 9 St. 821; 11 St. 581. *S.* 9 St. 132, 252, 382, 544, 574; 10 St. 15, 41, 226, 686; 11 St. 65, 169, 273, 362, 388; 12 St. 44, 221, 512, 774; 13 St. 161, 541; 14 St. 255, 492; 15 St. 198; 16 St. 13, 335, 544; 17 St. 165, 437; 18 St. 420; 19 St. 176, 271; 20 St. 63, 295; 21 St. 114, 485; 22 St. 68, 433; 23 St. 76, 362; 24 St. 29, 449; 25 St. 217, 980; 26 St. 336, 989; 27 St. 120, 612; 28 St. 286, 876; 29 St. 321; 30 St. 62, 571, 924; 31 St. 221, 1058; 32 St. 245, 982; 33 St. 189, 1048; 34 St. 325, 1015; 35 St. 70, 781. *Cited:* 16 Op. A. G. 225; 16 Op. A. G. 300; Seneca, 162 U. S. 283; U. S. v. Humason, 26 Fed. Cas. No. 15420.

priation for any superintendent of Indian Affairs has been made since the Act Mar. 3, 1877, sec. 1, 19 St. 271.

9 St. 37; July 15, 1846; C. 37—An Act to legalize certain land sales made at Chocchuma and Columbus, in the State of Mississippi, and to indemnify the Chickasaws therefor.[35]

9 St. 40; July 23, 1846; C 65—An Act making Appropriations for certain Objects of Expenditure therein specified.[36]

9 St. 50; Aug. 3, 1846; C. 77—An Act to grant the right of preemption to actual settlers on the lands acquired by treaty from the Miami Indians in Indiana.[37]

9 St. 55; Aug. 6, 1846; C. 85—An Act to repeal an Act entitled "An Act for the relief of the Stockbridge Tribe of Indians in the territory of Wisconsin," approved March 3, 1843, and for other purposes.[38]

9 St. 85; Aug. 10, 1846; C. 175—An Act making Appropriations for the civil and diplomatic expenses of Government, for the year ending the thirtieth day of June, 1847, and for other purposes.

9 St. 114; Aug. 3, 1846; J. Res. No. XVII—Joint Resolution to authorize the Secretary of War to adjudicate the claims of the Su-quah-natch-ah, and other clans of Choctaw Indians, whose cases were left undetermined by the Commissioners for the want of the Township Maps.[39]

9 St. 132; Mar. 1, 1847; C. 31—An Act making Appropriations for the current and contingent expenses of the Indian Department, and for fulfilling treaty stipulations with the various Indian Tribes, for the year ending June 30, 1848.[40]

9 St. 155; Mar. 3, 1847; C. 47—An Act making appropriations for the civil and diplomatic expenses of Government for the year ending the thirtieth day of June, 1848, and for other purposes.

9 St. 202; Mar. 3, 1847; C. 64—An Act to amend an Act entitled "An Act to amend 'An Act to carry into effect in the States of Alabama and Mississippi the existing compacts with those States with regard to the five per cent. fund and the school reservations.'"[41]

9 St. 203; Mar. 3, 1847; C. 66—An Act to amend an Act entitled "An Act to provide for the better organization of the Department of Indian affairs," and an Act entitled "An Act to regulate Trade and Intercourse with the Indian Tribes, and to preserve peace on the Frontiers," approved June 30, 1834, and for other purposes.[42] Sec. 1—R. S. sec. 2066, 25 U. S. C. 40. USCA Historical Note: R. S. 2066 was derived from sec. 7 of Act June 30, 1834, 4 St. 736, entitled "An act to provide for the organization of the department of Indian affairs," and from sec. 1 re above Act, amendatory of the said act of 1834. Sec. 3—R. S. 2086, 2087, 25 U. S. C. 111.[43] USCA Historical Note: R. S. 2086 was derived from sec. 11 of act June 30, 1834, 4 St. 737, entitled "An act to provide for the organization of the department of Indian Affairs"; sec. 3 of Act March 3, 1847, 9 St. 203; sec. 3 of Act Aug. 30, 1852, 10 St. 56, being the Indian appropriation act for the fiscal year 1853, and secs. 2 and 3 of act July 15, 1870, 16 St. 360 being the Indian appropriation act for the fiscal year 1871.

9 St. 213; Mar. 9, 1848; C. 15—An Act authorizing persons, to whom Reservations of Land have been made under certain Indian Treaties, to alienate the same in Fee.[44]

9 St. 252; July 29, 1848; C. 118—An Act making appropriations for the current and contingent expenses of the Indian Department, and for fulfilling treaty stipulations with the various Indian tribes, for the year ending June 30, 1849, and for other purposes.[45] Sec. 2—R. S. 2099;[46] Sec. 4—R. S. 3689.

9 St. 265; July 29, 1848; C. 120—An Act for the relief of certain surviving widows of officers and soldiers of the Revolutionary Army.[47]

9 St. 284; Aug. 12, 1848; C. 166—An Act making appropriations for the civil and diplomatic expenses of Government for the year ending the thirtieth day of June, 1849, and for other purposes.[48]

9 St. 323; Aug. 14, 1848; C. 177—An Act to establish the territorial government of Oregon.[49]

9 St. 337; July 25, 1848; J. Res. No. XIX—A Resolution to sanction an agreement made between the Wyandotts and Delawares for the purchase of certain lands by the former, of the latter tribe of Indians.[50]

9 St. 339; Aug. 7, 1848; J. Res. No. XXI—A Resolution authorizing the proper accounting officers of the Treasury to make a just and fair statement of the claims of the Cherokee Nation of Indians, according to the principles established by the treaty of August, 1846.[51]

9 St. 342; Jan. 26, 1849; C. 24—An Act to supply deficiencies in the appropriations for the service of the fiscal year ending the thirtieth of June, 1849.[52]

9 St. 344; Jan. 26, 1849; C. 25—An Act authorizing the payment of interest upon the advances made by the State of Alabama for the use of the United States Government, in the suppression of the Creek Indian hostilities of 1836 and 1837, in Alabama.[53]

9 St. 346; Feb. 19, 1849; C. 55—An Act to relinquish the reversionary interest of the United States in a certain Indian Reservation in the State of Alabama.[54]

9 St. 354; Mar. 3, 1849; C. 100—An Act making appropriations for the civil and diplomatic expenses of government for the year ending the thirtieth of June, 1850, and for other purposes.

9 St. 370; Mar. 3, 1849; C. 101—An Act making appropriations for the support of the Army for the year ending the thirtieth of June, 1850.[55]

9 St. 382; Mar. 3, 1849; C. 106—An Act making appropriations for the current and contingent expenses of the Indian Department; and for fulfilling treaty stipulations with the various Indian tribes, for the year ending June 30, 1850.[56]

9 St. 395; Mar. 3, 1849; C. 108—An Act to establish the Home Department, and to provide for the Treasury Department an Assistant Secretary of the Treasury, and a Commissioner of the Customs.[57] Sec. 1–R. S. 161, 277, 437, 440; Sec. 2–R. S. 444; Sec. 3–R. S. 248, 441; Sec. 5–R. S. 441; 5 U. S. C. 485; Sec. 6–R. S. 441; Sec. 7–R. S. 441, 443; Sec. 8–R. S. 441; Sec. 9–R. S. 441; Sec. 12–R. S. 269, 316, 317, 318, 2639; Sec 13–R. S. 234, 246, 2204.

9 St. 403; Mar. 3, 1849; C. 121—An Act to establish the Territorial Government of Minnesota.[58]

---

[35] *Sg.* 7 St. 450.

[36] *Sg.* 5 St. 493; 9 St. 842 (*Jan.* 14, 1846, correct date).

[37] *Sg.* 5 St. 251; 5 St. 382, 619.

[38] *Rg.* 5 St. 645; *S.* 9 St. 955; 10 St. 686; 11 St. 663.

[39] *Rg.* 5 St. 513. *S* 9 St. 544.

[40] *Sg.* 1 St. 618; 4 St. 20, 56, 181, 735; 5 St. 158 513, 766; 7 St. 35 44, 49, Art. 4; 68, 74, 84, 91, 98, 100, 105, 113 (Sept. *30*, 1809, correct date), 160 178, 185 186, 188 189, 203, 210, 218 224, 229, 234 240, 244, 284, 286, 290 295, 300 303 311, 317, 320, 323, 327, 328, 333 351, 355, 366, 368, 370, 374, 378, 391, 394, 397, 399, 414, 417, 424 429, 431, 449, 450, 491, 492, 506, 528, 536 538, 540, 544, 568, 569, 574, 576, 582, 591, 596; 9 St. 20, 821, 842, 858, 871, 878; 10 St. 701; 11 St. 581.

[41] *Ag.* 5 116, 727. *Sg.* 3 St. 348, sec. 5.

[42] *Ag* 4 St. 729 sec. 20; 4 St. 735, sec. 11. *Sg.* 7 St. 478, 488. *S.* 9 St. 252, 544, 570; 10 St. 15, 226, 315. *Cited:* 6 Op. A. G. 49; 14 Op. A. G 290; 16 Op. A. G. 225; 16 Op. A. G. 300; Memo. Sol., July 3, 1936; Fowler, 1 Wash. T. 3; Gho, 1 Wash. T. 325; Hicks, 12 Fed. Cas. No. 6458; U. S. Exp., v., 191 Fed. 673; Kent, CAL.

[43] *See:* 25 U. S. C. 474 (48 St. 987, sec. 14). *Cited:* U. S Exp., 191 Fed. 673; Webster, 266 U. S. 507.

[44] *Sg.* 7 St. 378, Art. 2.

[45] *Sg.* 1 St. 618; 4 St. 20, 56 181, 442 729, 735; 5 St. 158; 7 St. 35, 44, 49, Art. 4; 68, 74, 84 91, 98, 100, 105, 113, 160, 178, 185, 186 188, 189 203, 210, 218 224, 229 234, 240, 284, 286 290, 295, 300, 303, 317, 320 323, 327, 328, 333, 348, 351, 355, 366, 368, 370, 374, 378, 391 394, 397, 399, 414, 417, 424, (May *13*, 1833 correct date), 429, 431, 449 450 458, 463, 478, 491, 506, 528, 536, 538, 540 544, 550, 568, 569, 574, 576 581, 582 591 596; 9 St. 20, 203, 821, 842, 853, 878, 904, 908 (Aug. *21*, 1847, correct date). *S.* 9 St. 342 544; 10 St. 290 686; 11 St. 362 581; 18 St. 402, 420; 27 St. 612. *Cited:* 17 Op. A. G. 72; Memo. Sol. Off., Feb 13, 1934; Eastern Band, 20 C. Cls. 449; Jump, 100 F. 2d 180; U. S. v. Boyd, 68 Fed. 577; U. S. v. Boyd, 83 Fed. 547; U. S. v. Wright, 58 F. 2d 800; Western Cherokees, 27 C. Cls. 1.

[46] *Cited:* U. S v. Berry, 4 Fed. 779.

[47] *S.* 27 St. 612.

[48] *Sg.* 7 St. 215, Art. 4; 286, Art. 9. *Cited:* 5 Op. A. G. 46; 5 Op. A. G. 98

[49] *Sg.* N. W. Ord. 1787, U. S. C. (1934 ed.) p. XXIII. *S.* 9 St 342, 423, 437; 33 St. 2006. *Cited:* 7 Op. A. G. 293; 14 Op. A. G. 568; 20 Op. A. G. 42; Memo. Ind. Off., Dec. 4, 1931; Pickett, 1 Ind. T. 528.

[50] *S.* 10 St. 1048, 1159.

[51] *Sg.* 9 St. 871. *Cited:* Eastern Band, 20 C. Cls. 449; Old Settlers 148 U. S. 427; Western Cherokees, 82 C. Cls. 566.

[52] *Sg.* 7 St. 491; 9 St. 252, 323.

[53] *S.* 10 St. 214.

[54] *Sg.* 7 St. 120.

[55] *Sg.* 9 St. 955.

[56] *Sg.* 1 St. 618; 4 St. 20, 56, 181, 442, 735; 5 St. 158; 7 St. 35, 44, 49, Art. 4; 68, 84, 91, 94, 98, 100, 105, 113, 160, 178, 185, 186, 188, 189, 203, 210, 218, 224, 234, 240, 286, 290, 296, 300, 303, 317, 320, 323, 327, 328, 333, 348, 355, 366, 368, 370, 374, 378, 391, 394, 397, 399, 431, 424 (May 13, 1823, correct date), 429, 449, 491, 506, 528, 536, 540, 544, 568, 574, 576, 582, 591, 596; 9 St. 20, 821, 842, 853, 878, 952; 11 St. 581. *S.* 10 St. 576. *Cited:* Memo. Sol., Nov. 11, 1935.

[57] *Sg.* 9 St. 59. *Cited:* 36 Op. A. G. 98; 1 L. D. Memo. 103; 3 L. D. 425; Op. Sol., M. 25258, June 26, 1929; Op. A. G. to Sec. Int., Oct. 5, 1929; Memo. Sol., Feb. 28, 1935; Belt, 15 C. Cls. 92; Bowling, 299 Fed. 438; King, 111 Fed. 860; U. S. v. McDougall's, 121 U. S. 89.

[58] *Cited:* Minnesota, 155 U. S. 373.

9 St. 423; May 15, 1850; C. 10—An Act to supply deficiences in the appropriations for the service of the fiscal year ending the thirtieth of June, 1850.[59]

9 St. 428; May 23, 1850; C. 11—An Act providing for the taking of the seventh and subsequent censuses of the United States, and to fix the number of members of the House of Representatives, and provide for their future apportionment among the several states. Sec. 1–R. S. 2176; Sec. 25–R. S. 21.

9 St. 437; June 5, 1850; C. 16—An Act authorizing the negotiation of treaties with the Indian Tribes in the Territory of Oregon, for the extinguishment of their claims to lands lying west of the Cascade Mountains, and for other purposes.[60] Sec. 2—R. S. 2046; Sec. 4—R. S. 2058, 25 U. S. C. 31. U. S. C. A. Historical Note: The derivative sections for R. S. 2058 were sec. 7 of Act June 30, 1834, 4 St. 736; sec. 4 of Act June 5, 1850, 9 St. 437; and sec. 5 of Act Feb. 27, 1851, 9 St. 587. No appropriation for any superintendent of Indian Affairs has been made since Act Mar. 3, 1877, c. 101, sec. 1, 19 St. 271.

9 St. 439; July 18, 1850; C. 23—An Act for the construction of certain roads in the Territory of Minnesota, and for other purposes.[61]

9 St. 446; Sept. 9, 1850; C. 49—An Act proposing to the State of Texas the establishment of her Northern and Western Boundaries, the relinquishment by the said State of all territory claimed by her exterior to said boundaries, and of all her claims upon the United States, and to establish a territorial government for New Mexico.[62] Sec. 2—R. S. 1839, 1840, 1896; Sec. 3—R. S. 1841, 1842; Sec. 5—R. S. 1847, 1848, 1849, 1922; Sec. 6—R. S. 1846, 1859, 1860; Sec. 7—R. S. 1850, 1851; Sec. 17—R. S. 1891.

9 St. 453; Sept. 9, 1850; C. 51—An Act to establish a territorial government for Utah.[63] Sec. 1—R. S. 1839, 1840, 1897; Sec. 2—R. S. 1841, 1842; Sec. 4—R. S. 1846, 1847, 1848, 1849, 1922; Sec. 5—R. S. 1859, 1860; Sec. 6—R. S. 1850, 1851; Sec. 17—R. S. 1891.

9 St. 473; Sept. 27, 1850; C. 75—An Act to establish certain Post Roads in the United States.

9 St. 496; Sept. 27, 1850; C. 76—An Act to create the Office of Surveyor General of the Public Lands in Oregon, and to provide for the survey, and to make donations to settlers of the said Public Lands.[64]

9 St. 519; Sept. 28, 1850; C. 82—An Act to authorize the appointment of Indian Agents in California.[65]

9 St. 519; Sept. 28. 1850; C. 83—An Act for the payment of a company of Indian volunteers.

9 St. 520; Sept. 28. 1850; C. 85—An Act granting Bounty Land to certain Officers and Soldiers who have been engaged in the Military Service of the United States.[66] Sec. 1—R. S Secs. 2418, 2421, 2438; 43 U. S. C. 791.

9 St. 523; Sept. 30, 1850; C. 90—An Act making appropriations for the civil and diplomatic expenses of Government for the year ending the thirtieth of June, 1851, and for other purposes.

9. St. 544; Sept. 30, 1850; C. 91—An Act making appropriations for the current and contingent expenses of the Indian Department, and for fulfilling treaty stipulations with various Indian tribes, for the year ending June 30, 1851.[67]

9 St. 566; Feb. 14, 1851; C. 7—An Act to settle and adjust the expenses of the people of Oregon in defending themselves from the attacks and hostilities of Cayuse Indians, in the years 1847 and 1848.[68]

9 St. 568; Feb. 19, 1851; C. 10—An Act to authorize the Legislative Assemblies of the territories of Oregon and Minnesota to take charge of the school lands in said Territories, and for other purposes.

9 St. 570; Feb. 27, 1851; C. 12—An Act to supply deficiencies in the Appropriations for the service of the fiscal year ending the thirtieth of June, 1851.[69]

9 St. 574; Feb. 27, 1851; C. 14—An Act making appropriations for the current and contingent expenses of the Indian Department, and for fulfilling treaty stipulations with various Indian Tribes, for the year ending June the thirtieth, 1852.[70] Sec. 2—R. S. 2046, 2050; Sec. 5—R. S. 2058, 25 U. S. C. 31. U. S. C. A. Historical Note: The derivative sections for R. S. 2058 were Sec. 7 of Act June 30, 1834, 4 St. 736; Sec. 4 of Act June 5, 1850, 9 St. 437, and Sec. 5 re above Act. No appropriation for any superintendent of Indian Affairs has been made since Act Mar. 3, 1877, c. 101, Sec. 1, 19 St. 271. Sec. 6—R. S. 2048, 2049; R. S. 2056, 25 U. S. C. 28 (22 St. 87, Sec. 1). U. S. C. A. Historical Note: R. S. 2056 as originally enacted was based on Sec. 6, re above Act and Act Apr. 8, 1864, Sec. 4, 13 St. 40, and did not contain the words at the end thereof "and until his successor is duly appointed and qualified." That clause was added by amendment by Act May 17, 1882, above cited. R. S. 2057, 25 U. S. C. 29. See Historical Note 25 U. S. C. A. 29. Sec. 8—R. S. 2069-2070, 25 U. S. C. A. 45.[71] U. S. C. A. Historical Note: R. S. 2069 was derived from Sec. 9 of Act of June 30, 1834, 4 St. 737. See Historical Note 25 U. S. C. A. 9. R. S. 2070 provided as follows: "The salaries of interpreters lawfully employed in the service of the United States, in Oregon, Utah, and New Mexico, shall be $500 a year each, and of all so employed elsewhere, $400 a year each." Act Feb. 27, 1851, Sec. 8, 9 St. 587; Act Feb. 14, 1873, Sec. 1, 17 St. 437. It was repealed by Sec. 1 of an Act of May 17, 1882, 22 St. 70. The number and compensation of the interpreters depends on the various annual Appropriation Acts.

9 St. 594; Mar. 3, 1851; C. 24—An Act to divide the District of Arkansas into two Judicial Districts.[72] Sec. 1—R. S. 533, 608; Sec. 2—R. S. 572, 581; Sec. 3—R. S. 5571, 608, 1002; Sec. 4—R. S. 556, 767, 770, 776, 781.

9 St. 598; Mar. 3, 1851; C. 32—An Act making Appropriations for the Civil and Diplomatic expenses of Government, for the year ending the thirtieth of June,[73] 1852, and for other purposes.

9 St. 626; March 3, 1851;[74] C. 35—An Act to authorize the Secretary of War to allow the Payment of Interest to the State of Georgia for Advances made for the Use of the United States, in the Suppression of the Hostilities of the Creek, Seminole, and Cherokee Indians, in the Years 1836, 1837 and 1838.

9 St. 631; Mar. 3, 1851; C. 41—An Act to ascertain and settle the private Land Claims in the State of California.[75]

9 St. 651; June 6, 1846; C. 27—An Act for the Relief of the legal Representatives of George Duval, a Cherokee Indian.[76]

---

[59] *Sg.* 9 St. 378.

[60] *Rng.* 9 St. 323. *S.* 9 St. 544. 574; 10 St. 41. 226. 315. 686; 11 St. 65. 169. 273. 388; 12 St. 44. 221. 512. 774. *Cited:* 7 Op. A. G. 293; Fowler, 1 Wash. T. 3; Pickett, 1 Ind. T. 523; U. S. v. Barnhart, 17 Fed. 579; U. S. v. Bridleman, 7 Fed. 894; U. S. v. Humason, 26 Fed. Cas. No. 15420; U. S. v. Seveloff, 27 Fed. Cas. No. 16252; U. S. v. Tom, 1 Ore. 26; U. S. v. Wirt, 28 Fed. Cas. No. 16745.

[61] *S.* 10 St. 150, 10 St. 306.

[62] *Sg.* 9 St. 922. *S.* 20 St. 178. *Cited:* De Baca, 37 C. Cls. 482; In re Wilson, 140 U. S. 575.

[63] *Sg.* 9 St. 922. *S.* 20 St. 178. *Cited:* U. S. v. Berry, 4 Fed. 779; Ute, 45 C. Cls. 440.

[64] *S.* 17 St. 226. *Cited:* Duwamish, 79 C. Cls. 530; U. S. v. Ashton, 170 Fed. 509.

[65] *S.* 9 St. 574; 10 St. 41. 226. 643; 11 St. 65. 169. 273. 388; 12 St. 44. *Cited:* Belt, 15 C. Cls. 92; Fremont, 2 C. Cls. 461; U. S. v. McDougall's, 121 U. S. 89.

[66] *S.* 10 St. 701. *Cited:* Alire, 1 C. Cls. 233.

[67] *Sg.* 1 St. 618; 4 St. 20. 37. 56. 181. 442. 785; 5 St. 158. 241. 414. 493. 513 (Aug. 23. 1842, correct date). 612; 7 St. 35. 44. 49. Art. 4. 68. 74. 84, 91. 98 (Nov. 16. 1805. correct date); 7 St. 100. 105. 113. 160. 178. 185. 186. 188. 189. 203. 210. 218. 224. 229. 234. 240. 286. 290. 295. 300. 303. 317. 320. 323. 327. 328. 333. 348. 351. 355. 366. 368. 370. 374. 378. 391. 394. 397. 399. 414. 424. 431. 449. 458. 463. 491. 506. 528. 536. 538. 540. 544. 568. 574. 576. 582. 591. 596 (Oct. 11. 1842. correct date); 9 St. 114. 203. 252. 437. 570. 821. 842. 853. 871. 878. 904. 908. 952. 955; 11 St. 581. *S.* 9 St. 570. 598; 10 St. 15; 23 St. 362. *Cited:* 25 L. D. 17; 5 Op. A. G. 320; Belt. 15 C. Cls. 92; Eastern Band, 20 C. Cls. 449; Eastern Cherokees, 45 C. Cls. 229; Eastern or Emigrant, 82 C. Cls. 180; Elk, 112 U. S. 94; Fremont, 2 C. Cls. 461; Hanks, 3 Ind. T. 415; Kendall, 1 C. Cls. 261; Old Settlers, 148 U. S. 427; U. S. v. Cherokee, 202 U. S. 101; Western Cherokees, 82 C. Cls. 566; Western Cherokees, 27 C. Cls. 1.

[68] *A.* 10 St. 30.

[69] *Sg.* 7 St. 478. 544; 9 St. 203. 544. 871. *S.* 10 St. 15. 214. *Cited:* 5 Op. A. G. 320; Cherokee, 270 U. S. 476; Eastern Band, 20 C. Cls. 449; Eastern Cherokees, 45 C. Cls. 229; Eastern or Emigrant, 82 C. Cls. 180.

[70] *Sg.* 1 St. 618; 4 St. 20. 56. 158. 181. 442. 785; 5 St. 158; 7 St. 35. 44. 49. 68. 74. 84. 91. 98. 100. 105. 113. 160. 178. 185. 186. 188. 189. 203. 210. 218. 224. 234. 240. 286. 290. 295. 300. 303. 317. 320. 323. 327. 328. 333. 348. 351. 355. 366. 368. 370. 374. 378. 391. 394. 397. 399. 417. 424. 429. 431. 449. 458. 491. 506. 528. 536. 540. 544. 568. 574. 576. 582. 591. 596; 9 St. 20. 49. 437. 519. 821. 842. 853. 878. 904. 955; 11 St. 581. *S.* 9 St. 598; 10 St. 41. 226. 315. 686; 11 St. 65. 169. 273. 388; 12 St. 44. 221. 512. 774; 13 St. 161; 18 St. 420. *Cited:* 5 Op. A. G. 305; 13 Op. A. G. 470; 20 Op. A. G. 215; 19 L. D. 326; Belt. 15 C. Cls. 92; Fremont. 2 C. Cls. 461; Garcia, 43 F. 2d 878; Hoyt. 38 C. Cls. 455; Pino, 38 C. Cls. 64; U. S. v. Berry, 4 Fed. 779; U. S. v. Bichard, 1 Ariz. 31; U. S. v. Board, 37 F. 2d 272; U. S. v. Candelaria, 271 U. S. 432; U. S. v. Chavez, 290 U. S. 357; U. S. v. Joseph, 94 U. S. 614; U. S. v. Lucero, 1 N. M. 422; U. S. v. McDougall's, 121 U. S. 89; U. S. v. Leathers, 26 Fed. Cas. No. 15581; U. S. v. Mitchell, 109 U. S. 146.

[71] *Cited:* U. S. v. Mitchell, 109 U. S. 146.

[72] *A.* 10 St. 269.

[73] *Sg.* 9 St. 544, 574. *Cited:* Eastern Band, 20 C. Cls. 449.

[74] *S.* 10 St. 214.

[75] *S.* 12 St. 44; 45 St. 602. *Cited:* Goodrich, 14 Calif. L. Rev. 83–157; Barker, 181 U. S. 481; Super, 271 U. S. 643; U. S. v. Ritchie, 17 How. 525; U. S. v. Title, 265 U. S. 472.

[76] *S.* 9 St. 680.

9 St. 658; Aug. 8, 1846; C. 79—An Act for the Relief of the legal Representatives of Pierre Menard, Josiah T. Betts, Jacob Feaman, and Edmund Roberts, of the State of Illinois, Sureties of Felix St. Vrain, late Indian Agent, deceased.

9 St. 659; Aug. 6, 1846; C. 86—An Act to provide for the final Settlement of the Accounts of John Crowell, late Agent for the Creek Indians.[77]

9 St. 672; Aug. 8, 1846; C. 159—An Act for the Relief of the Heirs and legal Representatives of Cyrus Turner, deceased.

9 St. 673; Aug. 8, 1846; C. 162—An Act for the Relief of Langtry and Jenkins.

9 St. 674; Aug. 8, 1846; C. 172—An Act authorizing the Inhabitants of Township one, of Range thirteen east, Seneca County, Ohio, to relinquish certain Lands selected for Schools, and to obtain others in Lieu of them.[78]

9 St. 675; Aug. 8, 1846; C. 173—An Act authorizing the Trustees of Tymochtee Township, Wyandott County, Ohio, to select Lands for Schools within the Wyandott Cession.

9 St. 677; Aug. 10, 1846; C. 182—An Act to allow Elijah White Reimbursement of Expenses incurred by him as acting Sub-Agent of Indian Affairs west of the Rocky Mountains.

9 St. 678; Aug. 10, 1846; C. 186—An Act for the Relief of James Erwin, of Arkansas, and others.

9 St. 680; June 19, 1846; J. Res. No. 8—A Resolution to correct a clerical Error in the Act approved June 6, 1846, "for the Relief of the legal Representatives of George Duval, a Cherokee Indian."[79]

9 St. 688; Mar. 2, 1847; C. 42—An Act for the Relief of Elijah White, and others.

9 St. 698; Mar. 3, 1847; C. 92—An Act for the Relief of Doctor Clark Lillybridge.[80]

9 St. 703; Mar. 3, 1847; C. 114—An Act for the Relief of the legal Representatives of the late Joseph E. Primeau and Thomas J. Chapman.

9 St. 704; Mar. 3, 1847; C. 117—An Act for the Relief of George B. Russel and others.

9 St. 708; Mar. 3, 1847; J. Res. No. 13—Joint Resolution for the Relief of the Children of Stephen Johnson, deceased.[81]

9 St. 708; Mar. 3, 1847; J. Res. No. 14—Joint Resolution for the Relief of William B. Stokes, surviving Partner of John N. C. Stockton and Company.

9 St. 710; Feb. 15, 1848; C. 11—An Act for the Relief of Joseph and Lindley Ward.

9 St. 712; Apr. 12, 1848; C. 30—An Act for the Relief of the legal Representatives of George Fisher, deceased.

9 St. 716; May 31, 1848; C. 58—An Act for the Relief of Samuel W. Bell, a Native of the Cherokee Nation.

9 St. 718; June 13, 1848; C. 66—An Act for the Relief of Charles L. Dell.

9 St. 735; Aug. 11, 1848; C. 162—An Act for the Relief of Joseph Perry, a Choctaw Indian, or his Assignees.[82]

9 St. 738; Aug. 14, 1848; C. 184—An Act for the Relief of Charles M. Gibson.

9 St. 739; Aug. 14, 1848; C. 188—An Act for the Relief of Milledge Galphin, Executor of the last Will and Testament of George Galphin, deceased.

9 St. 740; Aug. 14, 1848; C. 192—An Act for the Relief of the legal Representatives of Thomas J. V. Owen, deceased.

9 St. 741; Aug. 14, 1848; C. 197—An Act for the Relief of John P. B. Gratiot and the Legal Representatives of Henry Gratiot.

9 St. 742; Aug. 14, 1848; C. 200—An Act to compensate R. M. Johnson, for the Erection of certain Buildings for the Use of the Choctaw Academy.

9 St. 746; Mar. 14, 1848; J. Res. No. 3—A Resolution for the Relief of Betsey McIntosh.[83]

9 St. 748; Aug. 14, 1848; J. Res. No. 28—A Resolution for the Relief of H. B. Gaither.

9 St. 762; February 19, 1849; C. 54—An Act to authorize the Secretary of War to make Reparation for the killing of a Caddo Boy by Volunteer Troops in Texas.

9 St. 765; Feb. 22, 1849; C. 67—An Act for the Relief of Thomas T. Gammage.

9 St. 769; Mar. 2, 1849; C. 92—An Act for the Relief of E. B. Cogswell.

9 St. 777; Mar. 3, 1849; C. 134—An Act for the relief of Henry D. Garrison.[84]

9 St. 777; Mar. 3, 1849; C. 136—An Act for the Relief of P. Chouteau, Junior, and Company.

9 St. 777; Mar. 3, 1849; C. 137—An Act for the Relief of George Center.

9 St. 785; Mar. 3, 1849; C. 169—An Act for the Relief of Lowry Williams.[85]

9 St. 789; Mar. 3, 1849; C. 183—An Act for the Relief of Thomas Talbot and others.

9 St. 791; Feb. 22, 1849; J. Res. No. 3—A Resolution to defray the Expenses of certain Chippewa Indians and their interpreter.

9 St. 799; July 29, 1850; C. 35—An Act for the Relief of Joseph P. Williams.

9 St. 801; Aug. 30, 1850; C. 46—An Act for the Relief of Al-lo-lah and his legal Representatives and their Grantees.[86]

9 St. 804; Sept. 28, 1850; C. 83—An Act for the Payment of a Company of Indian Volunteers.

9 St. 806; May 1, 1850; J. Res. No. 6—A Resolution to extend the Provisions of a "Joint Resolution for the Benefit of Frances Slocum and her Children and Grandchildren, of the Miami Tribe of Indians," approved Mar. 3, 1845, to certain other individuals of the same tribe.[87]

9 St. 806; Aug. 10, 1850; J. Res. No. 12—A Resolution for the Settlement of Accounts with the Heirs and Representatives of Colonel Pierce M. Butler, late Agent for the Cherokee Indians.

9 St. 807; Sept. 16, 1850; J. Res. No. 14—A Resolution for the Settlement of Accounts with the Heirs and Representatives of Colonel Pierce M. Butler, late Agent for the Cherokee Indians.

9 St. 812; Mar. 3, 1851; C. 31—An Act for the Relief of H. J. McClintock, Harrison Gill, and Mansfield Carter.

9 St. 821; Jan. 4, 1845—Treaty with Creeks and Seminoles.[88]

9 St. 842; Jan. 14, 1846—Treaty with Kansas Indians.[89]

9 St. 844; May 15, 1846—Treaty with Comanches and other tribes (I-on-i, Ana-da-ca, Cadoe, Lepan, Long-wha, Keechy, Tah-wa-carro Wi-chita, and Wacoe Tribes).[90]

9 St. 853; June 5 & 17, 1846—Treaty with Pottowautomie Nation.[91]

9 St. 871; Aug. 6, 1846—Treaty with the Cherokees.[92]

9 St. 878; Oct. 13, 1846—Treaty with Winnebago Indians.[93]

9 St. 904; Aug. 2, 1847—Treaty with Chippewas.[94]

---

[77] *Sg.* 5 St. 752. *S.* 12 St. 544.

[78] *Ag.* 4 St. 179.

[79] *Sg.* 9 St. 651.

[80] *Sg.* 5 St. 752.

[81] *Sg.* 6 St. 812.

[82] *Sg.* 7 St. 50.

[83] *Sg.* 5 St. 73, 719; 7 St. 478.

[84] *Sg.* 7 St. 528.

[85] *Sg.* 7 St. 478.

[86] *Sg.* 7 St. 569.

[87] *Sg.* 6 St. 942. *Cited:* 6 Op. A. G. 440.

[88] *Sg.* 7 St. 368, 417. *S.* 9 St. 20, 132, 252, 382, 544, 574; 10 St. 41, 226, 315, 686; 11 St. 65, 169, 273, 388, 699; 12 St. 44, 221, 512, 774. *Cited:* Memo. Ind. Off., Mar. 13, 1935; 3 Op. A. G. 644; Goat, 224 U. S. 458.

[89] *Sg.* 7 St. 244. *S.* 9 St. 40, 132, 252, 382, 544, 574, 853; 10 St. 41, 226, 315, 686; 11 St. 65, 169, 273, 388; 12 St. 44, 221, 512, 774; 14 St. 255, 492; 15 St. 198; 16 St. 13, 335, 544; 17 St. 165, 437; 18 St. 146, 420; 19 St. 176, 271; 20 St. 63, 295; 21 St. 114, 485; 22 St. 68, 433; 23 St. 76, 362; 24 St. 29, 449; 25 St. 217, 980; 26 St. 336, 989; 27 St. 120, 612; 28 St. 286, 876; 29 St. 321; 30 St. 62, 571, 924; 31 St. 221, 1058; 32 St. 245, 636, 982. *Cited:* 9 Op. A. G. 110; Kansas, 80 C. Cls. 264.

[90] *Cited:* McKee, 33 C. Cls. 99.

[91] *Sg.* 9 St. 842. *S.* 9 St. 132, 252, 382, 544, 574; 10 St. 15, 41, 226, 315, 686; 11 St. 65, 169, 273, 388; 12 St. 44, 207, 221, 512, 774, 1191; 13 St. 161, 541; 14 St. 255, 492; 15 St. 198; 16 St. 13, 335, 544; 17 St. 165, 437; 18 St. 420; 19 St. 176, 271; 20 St. 63, 295; 21 St. 114, 485; 22 St. 68, 433; 23 St. 76, 362; 24 St. 29, 449; 25 St. 217, 980; 26 St. 336, 989; 27 St. 120, 612; 28 St. 286, 876; 29 St. 321; 30 St. 62, 571, 924; 31 St. 221, 1058; 32 St. 245, 982; 33 St. 189, 1048; 34 St. 325, 1015; 35 St. 70, 781. *Cited:* Goodfellow, 10 Fed. Cas. No. 5537; Nadeau, 253 U. S. 442.

[92] *Sg.* 7 St. 311, 478. *S.* 9 St. 132, 339, 544, 570; 10 St. 315; 16 St. 544. *Cited:* 5 Op. A. G. 320; 16 Op. A. G. 225; 16 Op. A. G. 300; Op. Sol. M. 27540, Sept. 21, 1933; Atlantic, 165 U. S. 413; Ayres, 42 C. Cls. 385; Cherokee, 135 U. S. 641; Cherokee, 80 C. Cls. 1; Cherokee, 270 U. S. 476; Eastern Band, 20 C. Cls. 449; Eastern Band, 117 U. S. 288; Eastern Cherokees, 45 C. Cls. 220; Eastern or Emigrant, 82 C. Cls. 180; Guthrie, 1 Okla. T. 454; Hanks, 3 Ind. T. 415; Heckman, 224 U. S. 413; Kendall, 1 C. Cls. 261; Old Settlers, 148 U. S. 427; Stephens, 174 U. S. 445; U. S. v. Cherokee, 202 U. S. 101; U. S. v. Ragsdale, 27 Fed. Case No. 16113; Western Cherokees, 82 C. Cls. 566; Western Cherokees, 27 C. Cls. 1.

[93] *Sg.* 7 St. 544. *S.* 9 St. 132, 252, 382, 544, 574, 952; 10 St. 41, 226, 315, 686, 1172; 11 St. 65, 169, 273, 388; 12 St. 44, 221, 512, 774, 878; 13 St. 541; 14 St. 255, 492; 15 St. 198; 16 St. 13, 335, 544; 17 St. 165, 437; 18 St. 146; 19 St. 176.

[94] *S.* 9 St. 252, 252, 544, 574, 952; 10 St. 41; 14 St. 492; 15 St. 198; 16 St. 335, 544, 719; 17 St. 165; 18 St. 146, 420; 19 St. 176, 271; 20 St. 63, 295; 21 St. 114, 485; 22 St. 433; 23 St. 76, 362; 24 St. 29, 449; 25 St. 217, 980; 26 St. 336, 989; 27 St. 120; 28 St. 876; 29 St. 321; 30 St. 62, 571, 924; 31 St. 221, 1058; 32 St. 245. *Cited:* Cain, 2 Minn. L. Rev. 177; Op. Sol. M. 27881, Dec. 18, 1934; Chippewa, 80 C. Cls. 410; Chippewa, 310 U. S. 358; U. S. v. First, 234 U. S. 245; Westling 60 F. 2d 398.

9 St. 908; Aug. 21, 1847—Treaty with Pillager Band of Chippewa.[95]

9 St. 922; Feb. 2, 1848—Treaty with Republic of Mexico.[96]

9 St. 949; Aug. 6, 1848—Treaty with Pawnees.[97]

9 St. 952; Oct. 18, 1848—Treaty with Menomonee Tribe.[98]

9 St. 955; Nov. 24, 1848—Treaty with Stockbridge Tribe.[99]

9 St. 974; Sept. 9, 1849—Treaty with Navajo Tribe.[1]

9 St. 984; Dec. 30, 1849—Treaty with Utah Indians.[2]

9 St. 987; Apr. 1, 1850—Treaty with Wyandot Indians.[3]

10 STAT.

10 St. 2; Mar. 3, 1852; C. 11—An Act to provide for the Appointment of a Superintendent of Indian Affairs in Calif.[4]

10 St. 7; May 27, 1852; C. 43—An Act to grant to certain Settlers on the Menomonee Purchase, north of Fox River, in the State of Wisconsin, the right of Preemption.[5]

10 St. 15; July 12, 1852; C. 60—An Act to amend an Act entitled "An act providing for the Sale of certain Lands in the States of Ohio and Michigan, ceded by the Wyandott Tribe of Indians, and for other purposes," approved on the third day of March, 1843.[6]

10 St. 15; July 21, 1852; C. 66—An Act to supply Deficiencies in the Appropriations for the Service of the fiscal Year ending the thirtieth of June 1852.[7]

10 St. 30; Aug. 21, 1852, C. 85—An Act to amend an act entitled "An Act to settle and adjust the Expenses of the People of Oregon in defending themselves from Attacks and Hostilities of Cayuse Indians, in the Years 1847 and 1848," approved February 14, 1851.[8]

10 St. 41; Aug. 30, 1852; C. 103—An Act making Appropriation for the current and contingent Expenses of the Indian Department, and for fulfilling Treaty Stipulations with various Indian Tribes, for the Year ending June 30, 1853.[9] Sec. 3—R. S. 2086, 25 U. S. C. 111.[10] USCA Historical Note: R. S. 2086 was derived from sec. 11 of Act June 30, 1834, 4 St. 737, entitled "An Act to provide for the organization of the department of Indian Affairs"; sec. 3 of Act Mar. 3, 1847, 9 St. 203; and secs. 2 and 3 of Act July 15, 1870, 16 St. 360, being the Indian appropriation act for the fiscal year 1871.

10 St. 76; Aug. 31, 1852; C. 108—An Act making Appropriations for the Civil and Diplomatic Expenses of the Government for the Year ending the thirtieth of June, 1853, and for other purposes.[11]

10 St. 105; Aug. 31, 1852; C. 110—An Act making Appropriations for the Support of the Army, for the Year ending the thirtieth of June, 1853.

10 St. 121; Aug. 31, 1852; C. 113—An Act to establish certain Post-roads, and for other purposes.

10 St. 150; Jan. 7, 1853; C. 7—An Act making further Appropriations for the Construction of Roads in the Territory of Minnesota.[12]

10 St. 172; Mar. 2, 1853; C. 90—An Act to establish the Territorial Government of Washington.[13] Sec. 1—R. S. 1839, 1840, 1898. Sec. 2—R. S. 1841. Sec. 5—R. S. 1859, 1860. Sec. 6—R. S. 1850, 1851, 1924. Sec. 12—R. S. 1952.[14]

10 St. 180; Mar. 2, 1853; C. 94—An Act to amend an Act, entitled "An Act to amend an Act to settle and adjust the Expenses of the People of Oregon, from Attacks and Hostilities of Cayuse Indians, in the years 1847 and 1848," approved August 21, 1852.[15]

10 St. 181; Mar. 3, 1853; C. 96—An Act to Supply Deficiencies in the Appropriations for the Service of the Fiscal Year ending the thirtieth of June, 1853.[16]

10 St. 189; Mar. 3, 1853; C. 97—An Act making Appropriations for the Civil and Diplomatic Expenses of Government for the year ending the thirtieth of June, 1854.

10 St. 214; Mar. 3, 1853; C. 98—An Act making Appropriations for the support of the Army for the year ending the thirtieth of June, 1854.[17]

10 St. 226; Mar. 3, 1853; C. 104—An Act making Appropriations for the current and contingent Expenses of the Indian Department, and for fulfilling Treaty Stipulations with various Indian Tribes, for the year ending June 30, 1854.[18] Sec. 4—R. S. 5483.

10 St. 244; Mar. 3, 1853; C. 145—An Act to provide for the Survey of the Public Lands in California, the granting of Preemption Rights therein, and for other purposes.

10 St. 269; Mar. 27, 1854; C. 26—An Act to amend an Act, entitled "An Act to Divide the State of Arkansas into Two Judicial Districts," approved March the third, 1851.[19] Sec. 1—R. S. 533; sec. 3—R. S. 2145, 25 USC 217. USCA Historical Note—R. S. 2145 was derived from section 25 of Act June 30, 1834, 4 St. 733, and section 3 instant act; said section 3 containing the exception as to the laws enacted for the District of Columbia. R. S. 2146; 25 USC 218 (18 St. 318, Sec. 1). USCA Historical Note—R. S. 2146 was derived from section 3 instant act with the exception of the words "crimes committed by one Indian against the person or property of another Indian, nor to." Said words were inserted by amendment, making the section read as set forth in 25 USC 218. Indians committing any of seven crimes specified, if committed within a Territory, were made subject to the laws of the Territory, and if committed within an Indian reservation in any State were made subject to the same laws as persons committing any of said crimes within the exclusive jurisdiction of the United States, by the Seven Crimes Act, Act Mar. 3, 1885, Sec. 9, 23 St. 385, sec. 548 of Tit. 18, Criminal Code and Criminal Procedure. Sec. 4—R. S. 2143.[20] 25 USC 212. USCA Historical Note—Arson was one of the crimes specified in sec. 9 of Act Mar. 3, 1885, 23 St. 385, known as the Seven Crimes Act, making Indians committing any of said crimes if within a Territory, subject to the laws of the Territory, and if within an Indian reservation in any

---

[95] *S.* 9 St. 252, 544, 952; 10 St. 1064; 46 St. 1487. *Cited:* Cain, 2 Minn. L. Rev. 177; Chippewa, 80 C. Cls. 410; Chippewa, 301 U. S. 358.

[96] *S.* 9 St. 446, 453, 974; 10 St. 1031; 26 St. 854; 31 St. 796. *Cited:* Russell, 18 Yale L. J. 328; Op. Sol. M. 25278, Apapas v. U. S., 233 U. S. 587; Barker, 181 U. S. 481; De Baca, 36 C. Cls. 407; De Baca, 37 C. Cls. 482; Donnelly, 228 U. S. 243; Fremont, 2 C. Cls. 461; French, 49 C. Cls. 337; Hoyt, 38 C. Cls. 455; Jaeger, 29 C. Cls. 172; Quick Bear, 210 U. S. 50; Super, 271 U. S. 613; U. S. v. Kagama, 118 U. S. 375; U. S. v. McGowan, 89 F. 2d 201; U. S. v. Sandoval, 231 U. S. 28; U. S. v. Santistevan, 1 N. M. 583; U. S. v. Varela, 1 N. M. 593; U. S. v. Walker River, 104 F. 2d 334; Vallejos, 35 C. Cls. 489; Zia, 168 U. S. 198.

[97] *Cited:* Dubuque, 109 U. S. 329; Memo. Sol., Oct. 20, 1936.

[98] *Sg.* 7 St. 506; 9 St. 878, 904, 908, 974. *S.* 9 St. 892, 544; 10 St. 7, 15, 226, 315, 576, 643, 686, 1064; 11 St. 65, 169, 273, 388, 679; 12 St. 44, 221, 512, 774; 13 St. 161, 541; 14 St. 255, 492; 49 St. 1085. *Cited:* 8 Op. A. G. 256; Beecher, 95 U. S. 517; Dubuque, 109 U. S. 329; U. S. v. Higgins, 103 Fed. 348; U. S. ex rel. Besaw, 6 F. 2d 694; Wisconsin, 245 U. S. 427.

[99] *Sg.* 5 St. 645; 7 St. 341; 9 St. 55. *S.* 9 St. 370, 544, 574; 10 St. 41, 226, 315, 686; 11 St. 65, 663; 22 St. 68. *Cited:* Elk, 112 U. S. 94.

[1] *Sg.* 9 St. 922. *S.* 10 St. 315, 686; 11 St. 65, 169, 273. *Cited:* De Baca, 37 C. Cls. 482; Pino, 38 C. Cls. 64; U. S. v. Lucero, 1 N. M. 422.

[2] *Sg.* 1 St. 187. *S.* 10 St. 315, 686; 11 St. 65, 169, 273. *Cited:* 25 L. D. 408; Op. Sol. M. 29798, June 15, 1938; Hoyt, 38 C. Cls. 455; Ute, 45 C. Cls. 440.

[3] *Sg.* 11 St. 581. *Cited:* 6 Op. A. G. 2; 9 Op. A. G. 45; U. S. v. Ritchie, 17 How. 525.

[4] *Sg.* 3 St. 682, sec. 6; 4 St. 35, sec. 5. *S.* 10 St. 15, 226, 315, 686, 701; 11 St. 65, 169, 273, 388; 12 St. 44. *Cited:* 5 Op. A. G. 572.

[5] *Sg.* 5 St. 458; 9 St. 952.

[6] *Ag.* 5 St. 624, sec. 5.

[7] *Sg.* 4 St. 463, 528, June 4, 1832; 5 St. 73, 323, 513, 766; 7 St. 328, 333, 370, 374, 378, 491, 506, 550; 9 St. 20, 203, 544, 570, 853, 952; 10 St. 2, 748. *Cited:* Choctaw, 21 C. Cls. 59; Choctaw, 119 U. S. 1.

[8] *Ag.* 9 St. 566. *A.* 10 St. 180.

[9] *Sg.* 1 St. 618; 4 St. 20, 56, 181, 442, 735; 5 St. 73, 513, 766; 7 St. 35, 44, 49, 68, 74, 84, 91, 98, 100, 105, 113, 160, 178, 185, 186, 188, 189, 203, 210, 218, 224, 234, 240, 286, 290, 295, 300, 303, 317, 320, 323, 327, 328, 333, 348, 351, 355, 366, 368, 370, 374, 378, 391, 394, 397, 399, 417, 424, 429, 431, 449, 450, 458 (Oct. 23, 1834, correct date); 7 St. 478, 491, 506, 528, 536, 538, 540, 544, 568, 574, 576, 582, 591, 596; 9 St. 20, 437, 519, 574, 821, 842, 853, 878, 904, 955; 10 St. 949, 954, 11 St. 581. *S.* 10 St. 315, 1093. *Cited:* 6 Op. A. G. 462; Fremont, 2 C. Cls. 461; Jackson, 1 C. Cls. 260; Sac & Fox, 220 U. S. 481; Wisconsin, 170 Fed. 302.

[10] *See:* 25 U. S. C. 474 (48 St. 987, sec. 14).

[11] *S.* 10 St. 181, 226.

[12] *Sg.* 9 St. 439. *S.* 10 St. 306, 701.

[13] *S.* 20 St. 178.

[14] *S.* 33 St. 2006. *Cited:* 14 Op. A. G. 568; 20 Op. A. G. 42; Duwamish, 79 C. Cls. 530; Langford, 12 C. Cls. 338.

[15] *Ag.* 10 St. 30.

[16] *Sg.* 7 St. 478; 10 St. 76; 11 St. 743.

[17] *Sg.* 5 St. 506; 9 St. 344, 570, 626.

[18] *Sg.* 1 St. 618; 4 St. 20, 56, 181, 442, 735; 7 St. 35, 44, 49, 68, 74, 84, 91, 98, 100, 105, 113, 160, 178, 185, 186, 188, 189, 203, 210, 218, 234, 240, 286, 290, 300, 303, 317, 320, 323, 327, 328, 333, 348, 351, 355, 366, 370, 374, 378, 397, 399, 417, 424, 429, 431, 449, 458, 491, 506, 528, 536, 538, 540, 544, 568, 574, 576, 580, 581, 582, 591, 596; 9 St. 20, 203, 437, 519, 574, 821, 842, 853, 878, 952, 955; 10 St. 2, 76, 949, 954; 11 St. 581, 743. *S.* 10 St. 315; 12 St. 44. *Cited:* 33 L. D. 205; 6 Op. A. G. 462; Blackfeather, 28 C. Cls. 447; Fremont, 2 C. Cls. 461; Jackson, 1 C. Cls. 260; Kansas, 80 C. Cls. 264; Leighton, 29 C. Cls. 288; Moore, 32 C. Cls. 593; Roy, 45 C. Cls. 177; U. S. v. Leathers, 26 Fed. Cas. No. 15581.

[19] *Ag.* 9 St. 594. *Sg.* 4 St. 729, Sec. 25. *A.* 18 St. 316. *Cited:* Op. Sol., M. 27487, July 26, 1933; Memo. Sol., Dec. 17, 1935; Bailey, 47 F. 2d 702; Ex p. Crow Dog, 109 U. S. 556; Ex p. Hart, 157 Fed. 130; U. S. v. Kie, 26 Fed. Cas. No. 15528a; U. S. v. Miller, 105 Fed. 944; U. S. v. Shaw-Mux, 27 Fed. Cas. No. 16268; U. S. v. Williams, 2 Fed. 61; U. S. v. Winslow, 28 Fed. Cas. No. 16742; U. S. ex rel. Scott, 1 Dak. 142.

[20] *Cited:* 43 Cases, 14 Fed. 539; In re Blackbird, 109 Fed. 139; Palcher, 11 Fed. 47; U. S. v. Cardish, 145 Fed. 242; U. S. v. Celestine, 215 U. S. 278; U. S. v. Kie, 26 Fed. Cas. No. 15528a.

State, subject to the laws of the United States. Sec. 5—R. S. 2142,[21] 25 USC 213—See Historical Note re Sec. 4.

10 St. 277; May 30, 1854; C. 59—An Act to Organize the Territories of Nebraska and Kansas.[22]

10 St. 290; May 31, 1854; C. 60—An Act to supply Deficiencies in the Appropriations for the service of the fiscal year ending the thirtieth of June, 1854, and for other purposes.[23]

10 St. 304; July 17, 1854; C. 83—An Act to authorize the President of the United States to cause to be surveyed the tract of land in the Territory of Minnesota, belonging to the half-breeds or mixed-bloods of the Dacotah or Sioux nation of Indians, and for other purposes.[24]

10 St. 306; July 17, 1854; C. 85—An Act making further Appropriations for continuing the Construction of Roads in the Territory of Minnesota, in accordance with the Estimates made by the War Department.[25]

10 St. 307; July 17, 1854; C. 86—An Act to Refund to the Territory of Utah the Expenses incurred by said Territory in suppressing Indian Hostilities.

10 St. 307; July 17, 1854; C. 87—An Act to authorize the Secretary of War to settle and adjust the Expenses of the Rogue River Indian War.[26]

10 St. 308; July 22, 1854; C. 103—An Act to establish the offices of Surveyor-General of New Mexico, Kansas, and Nebraska, to grant Donation to actual Settlers therein, and for other purposes.[27]

10 St. 311; July 27, 1854; C. 106—An Act making Appropriations to Defray the Expenses of the Cayuse War.

10 St. 315; July 31, 1854; C. 167—An Act making Appropriations for the current and contingent Expenses of the Indian Department, and for fulfilling Treaty Stipulations with various Indian Tribes, for the year ending June 30, 1855, and for other purposes.[28]

10 St. 349; Aug. 3, 1854; C. 230—An Act to establish certain Post-Roads.[29]

10 St. 546; Aug. 4, 1854; C. 242—An Act making Appropriations for the Civil and Diplomatic Expenses of Government for the year ending the thirtieth of June, 1855, and for other purposes.[30]

10 St. 576— Aug. 5, 1854; C. 267—An Act making Appropriations for the Support of the Army for the year ending the thirtieth of June, 1855.[31]

10 St. 598; Dec. 19, 1854; C. 7—An Act to provide for the extinguishment of the title of the Chippewa Indians to the Lands owned and claimed by them in the Territory of Minnesota, and State of Wisconsin, and for their Domestication and Civilization.[32]

10 St. 630; Mar. 2. 1855; C. 139—An Act to settle certain Accounts between the United States and the State of Alabama.[33]

10 St. 635; Mar. 3, 1855; C. 169—An Act making Appropriations for the Support of the Army, for the year ending the thirtieth of June, 1856, and for other Purposes.[34]

10 St. 643; Mar. 3, 1855; C. 175—An Act making Appropriations for the Civil and Diplomatic Expenses of Government, for the year ending the thirtieth of June, 1856, and for other Purposes.[35] Sec. 22—R. S. 2051.

10 St. 686; March 3, 1855; C. 204—An Act making Appropriations for the Current and Contingent Expenses of the Indian Department, and for fulfilling Treaty Stipulations with various Indian Tribes, for the year ending June 30, 1856, and for other Purposes.[36] Sec. 8—R. S. 2144; 25 USC 215.[37] Sec. 10—R. S. 2064; 25 USC 35.[38]

10 St. 701; Mar. 3, 1855; C. 207—An Act in Addition to certain Acts granting Bounty Land to certain Officers and Soldiers who have been engaged in the Military Service of the United States.[39] Sec. 1—R. S. 2425, 2426, 2438. Sec. 2—R. S. 2428, 2429, 2430. Sec. 3—R. S. 2425, 2427, 2431. Sec. 7—R. S. 2434; 43 U. S. C. 806.

10 St. 704; Mar. 3, 1855; C. 211—An Act to Establish certain Post-roads.

10 St. 734; July 30, 1852; C. 76—An Act for the Relief of the legal Representatives of James C. Watson, of Georgia.

10 St. 735; Aug. 16, 1852; C. 84—An Act for the Relief of the Heirs of Semoice, a friendly Creek Indian.[40]

10 St. 746; Jan. 27, 1853; C. 37—An Act for the Relief of John W. Quinney, a Stockbridge Indian.

10 St. 750; Feb. 3, 1853; C. 54—An Act for the Relief of Margaret Farrar.[41]

10 St. 752; Feb. 9, 1853; C. 61—An Act for the Relief of C. L. Swayze, in relation to the Location of certain Choctaw Scrip.

10 St. 771; Mar. 3. 1853; J. Res. No. 20—A Resolution for the Relief of the Heirs of David Corderey.[42]

10 St. 781; June 22, 1854; C. 65—An Act for the Relief of the Widow and Heirs of Elijah Beebe.

10 St. 790; July 27, 1854; C. 112—An Act for the Relief of the Representatives of Joseph Watson, deceased.

10 St. 790; July 27, 1854; C. 113—An Act for the Relief of the Executrix of the late Brevet-Colonel A. C. W. Fanning of the United States Army.

10 St. 791; July 27, 1854; C. 115—An Act for the Relief of William Senna Factor.

10 St. 792; July 27, 1854; C. 120—An Act for the Relief of Robert Grignon.[43]

10 St. 793; July 27, 1854; C. 124—An Act for the Relief of the Legal Representative of Joshua Kennedy, deceased.

10 St. 794; July 27, 1854; C. 129—An Act for the Relief of Thomas Snodgrass.

10 St. 796; July 27, 1854; C. 136—An Act for the Relief of John Phagan.

10 St. 801; July 27, 1854; C. 155—An Act for the Relief of James Edwards and others.

10 St. 804; July 29, 1854; C. 165—An Act authorizing the Secretary of the Treasury to pay John Charles Fremont for beef furnished the California Indians.[44]

10 St. 810; Aug. 2, 1854; C. 190—An Act to Relinquish the Reversionary Interest of the United States to a certain Res-

---

[21] *Cited:* 43 Cases, 14 Fed. 539; In re Blackbird, 109 Fed. 139; Palcher, 11 Fed. 47; U. S. v. Celestine, 215 U. S. 278; U. S. v. Kie, 26 Fed. Cas. No. 15528a.

[22] *Sg.* 3 St. 545. *Cited:* New York Indians, 170 U. S. 1; U. S. v. Sa-coo-da-cot, 27 Fed. Cas. No. 16212; Utah, 3 Pac. 3.

[23] *Sg.* 9 St. 252; 10 St. 949, 954. *Cited:* Eastern Band, 20 C. Cls. 449; U. S. v. Boyd, 68 Fed. 577; U. S. v. Boyd, 83 Fed. 547.

[24] *Sg.* 7 St. 328, Art. 9. *S.* 10 St. 686; 17 St. 226. *A.* 11 St. 292. *Cited:* 20 Op. A. G. 742; 17 L. D. 457; 44 L. D. 188; Felix, 145 U. S. 317; Midway, 183 U. S. 602; Midway, 183 U. S. 619; Myrick, 99 U. S. 291.

[25] *Sg.* 9 St. 439; 10 St. 150.

[26] *S.* 16 St. 401.

[27] *Sg.* 5 St. 453. *S.* 46 St. 1509. *Cited:* 6 Op. A. G. 658; U. S. v. Conway, 175 U. S. 60; U. S. v. Lucero, 1 N. M. 422; U. S. v. Sandoval, 231 U. S. 28; Walker, 16 Wall. 436.

[28] *Sg.* 1 St. 618; 4 St. 20, 56, 181, 442, 729, 735; 7 St. 35, 44, 49, 68, 84, 91, 98, 100, 105, 113, 160, 178, 185, 186, 188, 189, 203, 210, 218, 234, 240, 286, 290, 295, 300, 303, 317, 320, 323, 327, 328, 348, 351, 355, 366, 386, 370, 374, 378, 397, 399, 417, 424, 431, 449, 458, 491, 506, 528, 536, 538, 540, 544, 568, 574, 576, 582, 591, 596; 9 St. 20, 203, 437, 574, 821, 842, 853, 871, 878, 952, 955, 974, 984; 10 St. 2, 41, 226, sec. 8, 686, 919, 951, 974, 1013, 1018, 1027, 1038, 1043, 1048, 1069; 11 St. 581, 743. *S.* 10 St. 576, 643, 686; 11 St. 65, 81, 169, 273, 388; 12 St. 44, 221, 512, 774, 1037, 1042. *Cited:* 7 Op. A. G. 54; Delaware, 74 C. Cls. 368; Duwamish, 79 C. Cls. 530; Eastern Cherokees, 45 C. Cls. 229; Medawakanton, 57 C. Cls. 357; Ross, 29 C. Cls. 176; Sisseton, 58 C. Cls. 302; U. S. v. Barnhart, 17 Fed. 579; U. S. v. Lucero, 1 N. M. 422; U. S. v. Sandoval, 231 U. S. 28.

[29] *Cited:* U. S. v. Lucero, 1 N. M. 422.

[30] *S.* 11 St. 102. *Cited:* Eastern Band, 20 C. Cls. 449; U. S. v. 43 Gallons, 93 U. S. 188.

[31] *Sg.* 7 St. 49, 113, 188, 327, 463, 570, 574; 9 St. 382, 952; 10 St. 315, 1053, 1064, 1082, 1093; 11 St. 599. *S.* 10 St. 701; 11 St. 81, 410; 12 St. 91, 221, 512, 774; 13 St. 161, 541; 15 St. 171; 28 St. 843. *Cited:* Belt v. U. S., 15 C. Cls. 92.

[32] *Sg.* 4 St. 729. *S.* 31 St. 801. *Cited:* Op. Sol. M. 27381, Dec. 13, 1934; Fee, 162 U. S. 602.

[33] *Sg.* 8 St. 489. *S.* 11 St. 200.

[34] *Sg.* 10 St. 303.

[35] *Sg.* 7 St. 381, 478; 9 St. 519, 952; 10 St. 315, 686 (correct date, Mar. 3, 1855), 1064, 1093, 1119, 1122, 1125, 1132, 1143 (correct date, Jan. 22, 1855), 1159, 1165. *S.* 11 St. 65, 388; 12 St. 44, 221, 512, 774; 13 St. 161, 541. *Cited:* Holden, 17 Wall. 211; Ward, 17 Wall. 253.

[36] *Sg.* 1 St. 618; 4 St. 56, 181, 442, 735; 5 St. 365, 645; 7 St. 35, 44, 49, 68, 84, 91, 98, 105, 113, 160, 178, 185, 189, 203, 210, 218, 234, 286, 290, 295, 303, 317, 320, 323, 327, 348, 351, 366, 368, 370, 374, 378, 397, 399, 417, 424, 431, 442, 449, 458, 478, 491, 506, 528, 536, 538, 540, 544, 568, 576, 582, 591, 596; 9 St. 20, 55, 252, 437, 574, 821, 842, 853, 878, 952, 955, 974, 984; 10 St. 2, 304, 315, 949, 1013, 1018, 1027, 1038, 1043, 1048, 1053, 1069, 1074, 1078, 1082, 1093, 1109; 11 St. 581, 743. *S.* 10 St. 643; 11 St. 65, 81, 169, 273, 388, 410, 663; 12 St. 44, 91, 221, 512, 774. *Cited:* 33 L. D. 205; Eastern Band, 20 C. Cls. 449; Eastern Cherokees, 45 C. Cls. 229; Holden, 17 Wall. 211; U. S. v. Boyd, 68 Fed. 577; U. S. v. Boyd, 83 Fed. 547; U. S. v. Brindle, 110 U. S. 688; U. S. v. 48 Lbs., 35 Fed. 403; U. S. v. Leathers, 26 Fed. Cas. No. 15581; Ward, 17 Wall. 253.

[37] *Cited:* 43 Cases, 14 Fed. 539; In re Blackbird, 109 Fed. 139; Palcher, 11 Fed. 47; U. S. v. Cardish, 145 Fed. 242; U. S. v. Celestine, 215 U. S. 278; U. S. v. Kie, 26 Fed. Cas. No. 15528a.

[38] *Cited:* 20 Op. A. G. 494; 43 Cases, 14 Fed. 539; Quigley, 3 Ind. T. 265; Palcher, 11 Fed. 47.

[39] *Sg.* 9 St. 132, 232, 520; 10 St. 3, 150, 267, 576, sec. 3. *S.* 11 St. 249, 362, 410; 12 St. 91, 221, 774; 13 St. 541. *Cited:* Alire, 1 C. Cls. 233.

[40] *Sg.* 6 St. 677.

[41] *Sg.* 7 St. 517.

[42] *Sg.* 7 St. 156, 478.

[43] *Sg.* 7 St. 506.

[44] *Cited:* Belt, 15 C. Cls. 92; Fremont, 2 C. Cls. 461; Jackson, 1 C. Cls. 260; U. S. v. McDougall's, 121 U. S. 89.

ervation therein mentioned, and to confirm the title of Charles G. Gunter thereto.[45]

10 St. 831; Aug. 1, 1854; J. Res. No. 21—Joint Resolution for the Relief of John A. Bryan.

10 St. 842; Jan. 12, 1855; C. 38—An Act for the Relief of the Legal Representatives of James Erwin, of Arkansas, and others.

10 St. 842; Jan. 12, 1855; C. 39—An Act for the Relief of Susan Coody, and others.

10 St. 843; Jan. 18, 1855; C. 42—An Act for Indemnifying Moses D. Hogan, for Cattle destroyed by the Indians in eighteen hundred and forty-two.

10 St. 849; Feb. 10, 1855; C. 68—An Act for the Relief of the Heirs of Joseph Gerard.

10 St. 871; Mar. 3, 1855; J. Res. No. 19—Joint Resolution for the Relief of James Hughes.

10 St. 871; Mar. 3, 1855; J. Res. No. 20—Joint Resolution for the Relief of Joel Henry Dyer.

10 St. 949; July 23, 1851—Treaty with Sioux.[46]

10 St. 954; Aug. 5, 1851—Treaty with Sioux.[47]

10 St. 974; June 22, 1852—Treaty with Chickasaws.[48]

10 St. 979; July 1, 1852—Treaty with Apaches.[49]

10 St. 1013; July 27, 1853—Treaty with Camanches.[50]

10 St. 1018; Sept. 10, 1853—Treaty with Rogue River Indians.[51]

10 St. 1027; Sept. 19, 1853—Treaty with Cow Creek Indians.[52]

10 St. 1031; Dec. 30, 1853—Treaty with Mexico.[53]

10 St. 1038; Mar. 15, 1854—Treaty with Ottoes and Missourias.[54]

10 St. 1043; Mar. 16, 1854—Treaty with Omahas.[55]

10 St. 1048; May 6, 1854—Treaty with Delawares.[56]

10 St. 1053; May 10, 1854—Treaty with Shawnees.[57]

10 St. 1064; May 12, 1854—Treaty with Menomonees.[58]

10 St. 1069; May 17, 1854—Treaty with Ioways.[59]

10 St. 1074; May 18, 1854—Treaty with Sacs and Foxes.[60]

10 St. 1078; May 18, 1854—Treaty with Kickapoos.[61]

10 St. 1082; May 30, 1854—Treaty with Kaskaskias, Peoria, Piankeshaw, and Wea Tribes.[62]

10 St. 1093; June 5, 1854—Treaty with Miami Indians.[63]

10 St. 1109; Sept. 30, 1854—Treaty with Chippewas.[64]

10 St. 1116; Nov. 4, 1854—Treaty with Choctaws and Chickasaws.[65]

10 St. 1119; Nov. 15, 1854—Treaty with Rogue Rivers.[66]

10 St. 1122; Nov. 18, 1854—Treaty with Chastas, and other tribes.[67]

10 St. 1125; Nov. 29, 1854—Treaty with Umpquas and Calapoolas.[68]

10 St. 1130—Dec. 9, 1854—Treaty with Ottoes and Missourias

10 St. 1132; Dec. 26, 1854—Treaty with Nisquallys.[69]

10 St. 1143; Jan. 22, 1855—Treaty with Willamette Indians.[70]

10 St. 1159; Jan. 31, 1855—Treaty with Wyandotts.[71]

10 St. 1165; Feb. 22, 1855—Treaty with Chippewas.[72]

---

[45] *Sg.* 7 St. 120.

[46] *S.* 10 St. 41, 226, 290, 315, 686; 11 St. 65, 169, 273, 388; 12 St. 44, 221, 512, 1037, 1042; 27 St. 612; 28 St. 876; 31 St. 1058; 34 St. 325. *Cited:* Cain, 2 Minn. L. Rev. 177; 44 L. D. 188; Graham, 30 C. Cls. 318; Medawakanton, 57 C. Cls. 357; Sioux, 277 U. S. 424; Sisseton, 42 C. Cls. 416; Sisseton, 58 C. Cls. 302, and (952); U. S. v. Sisseton, 208 U. S. 561.

[47] *Sg.* 7 St. 538; *S.* 10 St. 41, 226, 290, 315, 954; 11 St. 65, 169, 273, 388; 12 St. 44, 221, 512, 1031, 1042; 39 St. 1195. *Cited:* Cain, 2 Minn. L. Rev. 177; 20 Op. A. G. 742; Graham, 30 C. Cls. 318; Medawakanton, 57 C. Cls. 357; Sioux, 277 U. S. 424; Sisseton, 58 C. Cls. 302.

[48] *Sg.* 1 St. 137; 7 St. 192, 381, 450. *S.* 10 St. 315; 25 St. 980; 26 St. 989; 30 St. 495. *Cited:* 7 Op. A. G. 142; Ayres, 44 C. Cls. 48; Chickasaw, 19 C. Cls. 133; Chickasaw, 22 C. Cls. 222.

[49] *Cited:* Mares, 29 C. Cls. 197; Tully, 32 C. Cls. 1; U. S. v. Monte, 3 N. M. 173.

[50] *S.* 10 St. 315, 686; 11 St. 65, 169, 273, 388; 12 St. 44, 221, 512, 774; 13 St. 161, 541; 14 St. 255, 492. *Cited:* Crow, 32 C. Cls. 16; McKee, 33 C. Cls. 99; Price, 28 C. Cls. 422; Tully, 32 C. Cls. 1.

[51] *S.* 10 St. 315, 686, 1119; 11 St. 65, 169, 273, 388; 12 St. 44, 221, 512, 774, 981; 13 St. 161; 14 St. 255, 492; 15 St. 198; 16 St. 13, 335, 544; 17 St. 165, 437; 18 St. 146; 49 St. 801. *Cited:* Falk, 27 C. Cls. 321; Lane, 29 C. Cls. 332; Ross, 29 C. Cls. 176; Valk, 22 C. Cls. 241; Valk, 29 C. Cls. 62.

[52] *S.* 10 St. 315, 686; 11 St. 65, 169, 273, 388; 12 St. 44, 221, 512, 774; 13 St. 161, 541; 14 St. 255, 492; 15 St. 198; 16 St. 13, 335, 544; 17 St. 165, 437; 49 St. 801.

[53] *Ag.* 9 St. 922. *Cited:* Lane, 249 U. S. 110; Sisseton, 58 C. Cls. 302.

[54] *S.* 10, 315, 686; 11 St. 65, 169, 273, 329, 388; 12 St. 44, 221, 512, 774; 13 St. 161, 541; 14 St. 255, 492; 15 St. 198; 16 St. 13, 335, 544; 17 St. 165, 437; 18 St. 146, 420; 19 St. 176, 271; 20 St. 63, 295; 21 St. 114, 485; 22 St. 68, 433; 23 St. 76, 362; 24 St. 29, 449; 25 St. 217, 980; 26 St. 336, 989; 27 St. 120, 612; 28 St. 286.

[55] *S.* 10. St. 315, 686, 1132; 11 St. 65, 169, 273, 329, 388; 12 St. 44, 221, 512, 774, 927, 933, 939, 951, 957, 971, 975; 13 St. 161, 541; 14 St. 255, 492, 667; 15 St. 198; 16 St. 13, 335, 544; 17 St. 165, 437; 18 St. 146, 420; 19 St. 176, 271; 20 St. 63, 295; 21 St. 114, 485; 22 St. 68, 433; 23 St. 76, 362; 24 St. 29, 449; 25 St. 150; 36 St. 580; 43 St. 820. *Cited:* 20 L. D. 157; 29 L. D. 628; Memo. Sol. Off., Jan. 22, 1936; Bird, 129 Fed. 472; Duwamish, 79 C. Cls. 530; First, 59 F. 2d 367; Gilpin, 256 U. S. 10; Goudy, 203 U. S. 146; Halbert, 283 U. S. 753; Jacobs, 223 U. S. 200; Meeker, 173 Fed. 216; Omaha Tribe, 53 C. Cls. 549; Ross, 56 Fed. 855; U. S. v. Celestine, 215 U. S. 278; U. S. v. Higgins, 108 Fed. 348; U. S. v. Omaha Tribe, 253 U. S. 275; U. S. v. Payne, 264 U. S. 446; U. S. v. Sutton, 215 U. S. 291.

[56] *Sg.* 2 St. 448; 7 St. 327; 9 St. 337. S. Res. Jan. 19, 1838. *S.* 10 St. 315, 686; 11 St. 65, 169, 273, 312, 388; 12 St. 44, 221, 512, 774, 1129; 14 St. 255, 492, 793; 15 St. 198; 16 St. 13, 335, 544; 17 St. 165, 437; 18 St. 146, 420; 28 St. 580. *Cited:* 6 Op. A. G. 658; 9 Op. A. G. 25; 18 Op. A. G. 167; 18 Op. A. G. 223; Delaware, 72 C. Cls. 483; Delaware, 74 C. Cls. 368; Kindred, 225 U. S. 582; U. S. v. Brindle, 110 U. S. 688; U. S. v. Stone, 2 Wall. 525.

[57] *Sg.* 7 St. 49, 355. *S.* 10 St. 576, 686; 11 St. 65, 169, 273, 329, 388; 12 St. 44, 221, 774; 13 St. 161, 541; 14 St. 255, 492; 15 St. 198; 16 St. 13, 53, 335, 544; 17 St. 165, 437; 18 St. 146, 420; 19 St. 176, 271; 20 St. 63, 295; 21 St. 114, 377, 485; 22 St. 68, 433; 23 St. 76, 236, 256, 362; 24 St. 29, 449; 25 St. 217, 980; 26 St. 336, 989; 27 St. 120, 612; 28 St. 286. *Cited:* 11 Op. A. G. 145; 10 L. D. 606; 13 L. D. 511; 25 L. D. 252; Blackfeather, 28 C. Cls. 447; Blackfeather, 37 C. Cls. 233; Blackfeather, 190 U. S. 368; Dunbar, 198 U. S. 166; Ex p. Forbes, 9 Fed. Cas No. 4921; Jones, 175 U. S. 1; Kansas, 5 Wall. 737; Moore, 2 Wyo. 8; U. S. v. Blackfeather, 155 U. S. 180; Walker, 16 Wall. 436.

[58] *Sg.* 9 St. 908, 952. *S.* 10 St. 576, 643; 11 St. 65, 169, 273, 679; 12 St. 44, 221, 512, 774; 13 St. 161, 541; 14 St. 255, 492; 15 St. 198; 16 St. 13, 335, 544; 17 St. 165, 437; 18 St. 146, 420; 19 St. 176, 271; 20 St. 63, 295; 21 St. 114; 49 St. 1085. *Cited:* Cain, 2 Minn. L. Rev. 177; 25 L. D. 17; Sol. Memo., Oct. 20, 1936; Beecher, 95 U. S. 517; U. S. ex rel. Besaw, 6 F. 2d 694; Wisconsin, 245 U. S. 427.

[59] *S.* 10 St. 315, 686; 11 St. 65, 169, 273, 388; 12 St. 44, 221, 512, 774, 1171; 14 St. 255, 492; 15 St. 198; 16 St. 13, 335, 544; 17 St. 165, 437; 18 St. 146, 420; 19 St. 176, 271; 20 St. 63, 295; 21 St. 114, 485; 22 St. 68, 433; 23 St. 76, 362; 24 St. 29, 449; 25 St. 217, 980; 26 St. 336, 989; 27 St. 120, 612; 28 St. 286, 580, 876; 29 St. 321; 30 St. 62, 571, 924; 31 St. 221, 1058; 32 St. 245, 982; 33 St. 189, 1048; 34 St. 325, 1015. *Cited:* Iowa Tribe, 68 C. Cls. 585.

[60] *S.* 10 St. 686; 11 St. 65, 169; 12 St. 1171.

[61] *Sg.* 7 St. 388, 393. *S.* 10 St. 686; 11 St. 65, 169, 273, 388; 12 St. 44, 221, 512, 774; 13 St. 161, 541, 623; 14 St. 255, 492; 15 St. 198; 16 St. 13, 335, 544; 17 St. 165, 437; 18 St. 146, 402, 420; 19 St. 176, 271; 20 St. 63, 205; 21 St. 114, 485; 22 St. 68, 433; 23 St. 76, 362; 24 St. 29, 449; 25 St. 217, 980; 26 St. 336, 989; 27 St. 120, 612; 28 St. 286, 876; 29 St. 321; 30 St. 62, 571, 924; 31 St. 221, 1058; 32 St. 245, 982; 33 St. 189, 1048; 34 St. 325, 1015. *Cited:* 6 Op. A. G. 658; U. S. v. Reilly, 290 U. S. 33.

[62] *Sg.* 2 St. 437; 7 St. 403, 409. *S.* 10 St. 576, 686; 11 St. 65, 169, 273, 388; 28 St. 580. *Cited:* 10 Op. A. G. 253; 18 Op. A. G. 107; 19 Op. A. G. 115; 2 L. D. Memo. 263; Bowling, 233 U. S. 528; Kansas, 5 Wall. 737; Lykins, 184 U. S. 169; U. S. v. Brindle, 110 U. S. 688.

[63] *Sg.* 7 St. 190, 300, 464, 569, 571, 583; 10 St. 41. *S.* 10 St. 576, 648, 686; 11 St. 65, 169, 273, 329, 388; 12 St. 44, 221, 512, 774; 13 St. 161, 541; 14 St. 255, 492; 15 St. 198; 16 St. 13, 335, 544; 17 St. 165, 417, 437, 631; 18 St. 146, 420; 19 St. 176, 271; 20 St. 63, 206, 295; 21 St. 114, 414, 485; 22 St. 63, 68, 433; 23 St. 76, 362; 24 St. 29, 449; 25 St. 217, 980; 26 St. 336, 989. *Cited:* 11 Op. A. G. 384; 12 Op. A. G. 236; 17 Op. A. G. 410; Mungosah, 17 Fed. Cas. No. 9924; Wan-pe-man-qua, 28 Fed. 489.

[64] *S.* 10 St. 686; 11 St. 65, 169, 273, 388; 12 St. 44, 221, 512, 774, 1249; 13 St. 161, 541; 14 St. 255, 492, 765; 15 St. 198; 16 St. 13, 335, 544; 17 St. 165, 437; 18 St. 133, 146, 420; 19 St. 176, 271; 20 St. 63, 295; 21 St. 114; 28 St. 970; 30 St. 62; 31 St. 766; 32 St. 795; 34 St. 1217; 38 St. 582; 41 St. 408, 1225; 42 St. 552, 1174; 43 St. 92, 390, 1141; 44 St. 453, 934; 45 St. 200, 1562; 46 St. 279, 1115; 47 St. 91, 820; 48 St. 362, 927. *Cited:* Cain, 2 Minn. L. Rev. 177; 19 Op. A. G. 710; 9 L. D. 392; 11 L. D. 103; 19 L. D. 518; 26 L. D. 44; 42 L. D. 446; Op. Sol. M. 6088, Oct. 29, 1921, A. 2592, Feb. 12, 1924; Memo. Sol. Off., July 21, 1933; Op. Sol. M. 27700, Aug. 3, 1934, M. 11380, June 17, 1924; Sol. Letter, July 19, 1934; Op. Sol., M. 27381, Dec. 13, 1934; Memo. Sol., Jan. 1935; Op. Sol. M. 28107, June 30, 1936; Memo. Sol., Feb. 8, 1937; 54 I. D. 555; Chippewa, 80 C. Cl. 410; Chippewa, 301 U. S. 358; Ex p. Pero, 99 F. 2d 28; Fee, 162 U. S. 602; Fond Du Lac, 34 C. Cls. 426; Hartman, 76 Fed. 157; Hitchcock, 22 App. D. C. 275; In re Blackbird, 109 Fed. 139; Lemieux, 15 F. 2d 518; Minnesota, 305 U. S. 382; Prentice, 50 Fed. 437; Prentice, 43 Fed. 270; Prentice, 113 U. S. 435; Starr, 208 U. S. 527; Thayer, 20 C. Cls. 137; U. S. v. Auger, 153 Fed. 671; U. S. v. First, 234 U. S. 245; U. S. v. Holt, 270 U. S. 49; U. S. v. Law, 250 Fed. 218; U. S. v. Raiche, 31 F. 2d 624; U. S. v. Stearns, 245 U. S. 436; U. S. v. Thomas, 47 Fed. 488; Vezina, 245 Fed. 411; Wisconsin, 201 U. S. 202.

[65] *Cited:* Choctaw, 81 C. Cls. 1; Choctaw, 83 C. Cls. 140; McBride, 149 Fed. 114.

[66] *Sg.* 10 St. 1018. *S.* 10 St. 643. *Cited:* Leighton, 29 C. Cls. 288.

[67] *S.* 10 St. 643; 11 St. 65, 169, 273, 329, 388; 12 St. 44, 221, 512, 774, 981; 13 St. 161, 541; 14 St. 255, 492; 15 St. 198; 16 St. 13; 49 St. 801.

[68] *S.* 10 St. 643; 11 St. 65, 169, 273, 329, 388; 12 St. 44, 221, 512, 981; 13 St. 161, 541; 14 St. 255, 492; 15 St. 198; 16 St. 13, 335; 16 St. 544; 17 St. 165, 437; 18 St. 146; 49 St. 801. *Cited:* U. S. v. Sinnott, 26 Fed. 84.

[69] *Sg.* 10 St. 1044. *S.* 10 St. 643; 11 St. 65, 169, 273, 329, 388; 12 St. 44, 221, 512, 774, 927, 933; 13 St. 161, 541; 14 St. 255, 492; 15 St. 198; 16 St. 13, 335, 544; 17 St. 165, 437; 18 St. 146; 43 St. 886. *Cited:* 29 L. D. 628; Bird, 129 Fed. 472; Duwamish, 79 C. Cls. 530; Goudy, 203 U. S. 146; LaClair, 184 Fed. 128; Meeker, 173 Fed. 216; Ross, 56 Fed. 855; U. S. v. Ashton, 170 Fed. 509; U. S. v. Kopp, 110 Fed. 160.

[70] *S.* 10 St. 643; 11 St. 65, 169, 273, 329, 388; 12 St. 44, 221, 512, 774; 13 St. 541; 14 St. 255, 492; 15 St. 198; 16 St. 13; 18 St. 146; 49 St. 801. *Cited:* 54 I. D. 517.

[71] *Sg.* 9 St. 337. *S.* 10 St. 643; 11 St. 65, 169; 15 St. 513; 16 St. 335; 26 St. 989; 34 St. 325; 37 St. 668. *Cited:* 11 Op. A. G. 197; Conley, 216 U. S. 84; Elk, 112 U. S. 94; Goudy, 203 U. S. 146; Gray, 10 Fed. Cas. No. 5714; Hicks, 12 Fed. Cas. No. 6458; Karrahoo, 14 Fed. Cas. No. 7614; Schrimpscher, 183 U. S. 290; Staley, 36 F. 2d 91; Walker, 16 Wall. 436.

[72] *Sg.* 1 St. 137. *S.* 10 St. 643; 11 St. 65, 169, 273, 388; 12 St. 44, 221, 512, 774, 1249; 13 St. 161, 541, 693; 14 St. 255, 492; 15 St. 198; 16 St. 13, 335, 544; 17 St. 165, 437; 18 St. 146, 420; 19 St. 176, 271; 20 St. 63, 295; 21 St. 114, 485; 22 St. 68, 433; 23 St

10 St. 1172; Feb. 27, 1855—Treaty with Winnebagoes.[73]

11 STAT.

11 St. 3; Apr. 5, 1856; C. 13—An Act making Appropriations for restoring and maintaining the peaceable Disposition of the Indian Tribes on the Pacific, and for other purposes.[74]

11 St. 65; Aug. 18, 1856; C. 128—An Act making Appropriations for the Current and Contingent Expenses of the Indian Department, and for fulfilling Treaty Stipulations with various Indian Tribes, for the Year ending June 30, 1857.[75] Sec. 2—R. S. 2148, 25 USC 221.[76]

11 St. 81; Aug. 18, 1856; C. 129—An Act making Appropriations for certain Civil Expenses of the Government for the Year ending the thirtieth of June, 1857.[77]

11 St. 102; Aug. 18, 1856; C. 162—An Act making Appropriations for the Legislative, Executive, and Judicial Expenses of Government for the Year ending the thirtieth of June, 1857.[78]

11 St. 122; Aug. 18, 1856; C. 168—An Act to establish certain Post-Roads.

11 St. 169; Mar. 3, 1857; C. 90—An Act making Appropriations for the Current and Contingent Expenses of the Indian Department and for fulfilling Treaty Stipulations with various Indian Tribes, for the Year ending June 30, 1858.[79] Sec. 1—R. S. 2089,[80] 25 USC 113. Sec. 3—R. S. 2046.

11 St. 195; Mar. 3, 1857; C. 99—An Act making a grant of Land to the Territory of Minnesota, in alternate Sections, to aid in the Construction of certain Railroads in said Territory, and granting Public Lands in alternate Sections to the State of Alabama, to aid in the Construction of a certain Railroad in said State.[81]

11 St. 200; Mar. 3, 1857; C. 104—An Act to settle certain Accounts between the United States and the State of Mississippi and other States.[82]

11 St. 200; Mar. 3, 1857; C. 106—An Act making Appropriations for the Support of the Army for the Year ending the thirtieth June, 1858.

11 St. 206; Mar. 3, 1857; C. 107—An Act making Appropriations for the Legislative, Executive, and Judicial Expenses of Government for the Year ending the thirtieth of June, 1858. Sec. 1, page 212—R. S. 2207, 2213.

11 St. 221; Mar. 3, 1857; C. 108—An Act making Appropriations for certain Civil Expenses of the Government for the Year ending the thirtieth of June, 1858.

11 St. 248; Mar. 3, 1857; C. 112—An Act for the Relief of certain actual Settlers and Cultivators who purchased Lands subject to Graduation, within the Limits of the Choctaw Cession of 1830, at a less Rate than the true graduated Price, under the "Act to graduate and reduce the Price of the Public Land to actual Settlers and Cultivators," approved the fourth of August 1854, and for other purposes.[83]

11 St. 249; Mar. 3, 1857; C. 115—An Act to extend the Provisions of the Act entitled "An Act in Addition to certain Acts granting Bounty Land to certain Officers and Soldiers who have been engaged in the Military Services of the United States," to the Officers and Soldiers of Major David Bailey's Battalion of Cook County (Illinois) Volunteers.[84]

11 St. 262; Apr. 7, 1858; C. 13—An Act to provide for the Organization of a Regiment of Mounted Volunteers for the Defence of the Frontier of Texas, and to authorize the President to call into the Service of the United States two additional Regiments of Volunteers.

11 St. 269; May 4, 1858; C. 26—An Act for the Admission of the State of Kansas into the Union.

11 St. 273; May 5, 1858; C. 29—An Act making Appropriations for the current and contingent Expenses of the Indian Department, and for fulfilling Treaty Stipulations with various Indian Tribes, for the year ending June 30, 1859.[85]

11 St. 292; May 19, 1858; C. 43—An Act to amend an Act entitled "An Act to authorize the President of the United States to cause to be surveyed the Tract of Land, in the Territory of Minnesota, belonging to the Half-breeds or mixed Bloods of the Dacotah or Sioux Nation of Indians, and for other Purposes," approved seventeenth July, 1854.[86]

11 St. 292; May 24, 1858; C. 44—An Act to create a Land District in the Territory of New Mexico.

11 St. 295; June 2, 1858; C. 82—An Act making Appropriations for the Legislative, Executive, and Judicial Expenses of Government for the Year ending the thirtieth of June 1859.[87]

11 St. 312; June 8, 1858; C. 122—An Act to confirm the Sale of the Reservation held by the Christian Indians, and to provide a permanent Home for said Indians.[88]

11 St. 314; June 11, 1858; C. 148—An Act for the Relief of certain Purchasers of Lands within the Limits of the Choctaw Cession of 1830.

11 St. 319; June 12, 1858; C. 154—An Act making Appropriations for sundry Civil Expenses of the Government for the Year ending the thirtieth of June, 1859.[89]

11 St. 329; June 12, 1858; C. 155—An Act making supplemental Appropriations for the Current and Contingent Expenses of the Indian Department, and for fulfilling Treaty Stipulations with the various Indian Tribes, for the Year ending June 30, 1859.[90] Sec. 2—R. S. 2149, 25 USC 222.[91]

11 St. 332; June 12, 1858; C. 156—An Act making Appropriations for the Support of the Army for the Year ending the thirtieth June, 1859.

11 St. 337; June 14, 1858; C. 162—An Act to establish certain Post-Roads.

11 St. 362; June 14, 1858; C. 163—An Act to supply Deficiencies in the Appropriations for the Current and Contingent Expenses of the Indian Department, and for fulfilling Treaty

---

76, 362; 24 St. 29, 449; 25 St. 217, 980; 26 St. 336, 989; 27 St. 120, 612; 28 St. 286; 38 St. 77; 47 St. 808; 48 St. 927. *Cited:* 25 Op. A. G. 416; 5 L. D. 541; 12 L. D. 52; 32 L. D. 664; Sol. Letter, July 19, 1934; Beaulieu, 32 App. D. C. 398; Brown, 265 Fed. 623; Chippewa, 301 U. S. 358; Harris, 249 Fed. 41; Johnson, 234 U. S. 422; Mille Lac, 46 C. Cls. 424; U. S. v. First, 234 U. S. 245; U. S. v. Higgins, 103 Fed. 348; U. S. v. Holt, 270 U. S. 49; U. S. v. Mille Lac, 229 U. S. 498; U. S. v. Minnesota, 270 U. S. 181; Westling, 60 F. 2d 398.

[73] *Sg.* 1 St. 137; 9 St. 878. *S.* 45 St. 1027. *Cited:* Johnson, 234 U. S. 422; U. S. v. Higgins, 103 Fed. 348.

[74] *Cited:* Allire, 1 C. Cls. 233.

[75] *Sg.* 1 St. 618; 3 St. 311, 516; 4 St. 56, 181, 442, 528, 729; 5 St. 645; 7 St. 35, 44, 49, 51, 68, 84, 91, 99, 105, 113, 114, 160, 178, 179, 185, 189, 212, 220, 235, 286, 296, 304, 317, 320, 323, 327, 336, 337, 348, 351, 366, 368, 371, 374, 379, 397, 401, 417, 425, 432, 448, 458, 478, 520, 536, 538, 540, 545, 568, 576, 582, 592, 596; 9 St. 20, 372, 437, 519, 574, 587, 821, 842, 854, 878, 952, 955, 974, 984; 10 St. 2, 315, 643, 673, 686, 949, 954, 1013, 1018, 1027, 1038, 1043, 1048, 1053, 1064, 1069, 1074, 1078, 1082, 1093, 1109, 1122, 1125, 1132, 1143, 1159, 1165; 11 St. 611, 613, 615, 623, 633; 657, 663, 749. *S.* 11 St. 169, 273, 388; 12 St. 44, 221, 512, 744. *Cited:* Letter Col. J. G. Scrugham from Sp. Asst. to A. G., Apr. 1, 1921; Op. Sol., M. 27487, July 26, 1933; Holden, 17 Wall. 211; Karrahoo, 14 Fed. Cas. No. 7614; U. S. v. Howard, 17 Fed. 638; U. S. v. Lucero, 1 N. M. 422; U. S. v. Myers, 206 Fed. 387; U. S. v. Stocking, 87 Fed. 857; Ward, 17 Wall. 253.

[76] *R.* 48 St. 787. *Cited:* Cherokee, 203 U. S. 76; 43 Cases, 14 Fed. 539; In re Blackbird, 109 Fed. 139; Morris, 194 U. S. 384; Palcher, 11 Fed. 47; Stephens, 126 Fed. 148; U. S. v. Bridleman, 7 Fed. 894; U. S. v. Celestine, 215 U. S. 278; U. S. ex rel. Gordon, 179 Fed. 391; U. S. v. Howard, 17 Fed. 638; U. S. v. Leathers, 26 Fed. Cas. No. 15581; U. S. v. Martin, 14 Fed. 817; U. S. v. Myers, 206 Fed. 887; U. S. v. Payne, 8 Fed. 883; U. S. v. Payne, 22 Fed. 426; U. S. v. Stocking, 87 Fed. 857; U. S. v. Sturgeon, 26 Fed. Cas. No. 16413.

[77] *Sg.* 10 St. 315, 576, 686. *S.* 28 St. 843. *Cited:* Eastern Band, 20 C. Cls. 449; Eastern Cherokees, 45 C. Cls. 229.

[78] *Sg.* 10 St. 546.

[79] *Sg.* 1 St. 618; 3 St. 516; 4 St. 442, 735; 5 St. 186; 7 St. 35, 44, 49, 51, 68, 84, 91, 99, 105, 113, 114, 120, 160, 178, 179, 185, 189, 206, 212, 220, 235, 286, 296, 304, 317, 320, 323, 327, 328, 348, 351, 368, 371, 374, 379, 397, 401, 419, 425, 432, 448, 458, 484, 527, 538, 540, 545, 568, 576, 582, 583, 592, 596; 9 St. 20, 437, 519, 574, 587, 821, 822, 842, 855, 878, 952, 974, 984; 10 St. 2, 315, 330, 686, 949, 954, 1013, 1018, 1027, 1038, 1043, 1048, 1053, 1064, 1069, 1074, 1078, 1082, 1093, 1109, 1122, 1125, 1132, 1143, 1159, 1165; 11 St. 65, 611, 613, 623, 631, 633, 657, 679, 700, 749. *S.* 11 St. 273, 362, 388; 12 St. 44, 221, 512, 774. *Cited:* Allire, 1 C. Cls. 233; U. S. v. Lucero, 1 N. M. 422; U. S. v. Humason, 26 Fed. Cas. No. 15420.

[80] *Cited:* 15 Op. A. G. 66; Hanks, 3 Ind. T. 415.

[81] *Cited:* M. K. & T. Ry., 46 C. Cls. 59.

[82] *Sg.* 10 St. 630.

[83] *Sg.* 10 St. 6, 574.

[84] *Sg.* 10 St. 701.

[85] *Sg.* 1 St. 618; 3 St. 516; 4 St. 442; 7 St. 36, 46, 51, 69, 85, 91, 99, 105, 114, 161, 179, 185, 188, 189, 213, 220, 235, 287, 296, 304, 317, 320, 323, 327, 349, 352, 368, 369, 371, 375, 379, 401, 419, 425, 432, 448, 458, 464, 538, 540, 543, 545, 568, 582, 592, 596; 9 St. 20, 35, 437, 519, 574, 822, 842, 855, 878, 952, 974, 984; 10 St. 2, 315, 686, 949, 954, 1014, 1018, 1027, 1039, 1044, 1049, 1056, 1064, 1071, 1078, 1082, 1093, 1109, 1122, 1125, 1132, 1144, 1165; 11 St. 65, 169, 611, 623, 633, 657, 699, 749. *S.* 11 St. 329. *Cited:* McKee, 33 C. Cls. 99.

[86] *Ag.* 10 St. 304.

[87] *S.* 28 St. 594.

[88] *Sg.* 10 St. 1051. *S.* 12 St. 1105.

[89] *Sg.* 7 St. 328. *S.* 11 St. 388; 12 St. 44.

[90] *Sg.* 7 St. 545; 10 St. 1039, 1044, 1056, 1093, 1122, 1125, 1132, 1143; 11 St. 273, 729. *S.* 11 St. 388; 17 St. 631. *Cited:* 11 Op. A. G. 384; 17 Op. A. G. 410; Janus, 38 Fed. 431; Letter Col. J. G. Scrugham from Sp. Asst. to A. G., Apr. 1, 1921; Op. Sol. M. 27487, July 26, 1933.

[91] *R.* 48 St. 787. *Cited:* 14 Op. A. G. 451; 20 Op. A. G. 245; 8 L. D. Memo. 220; Buster, 135 Fed. 947; Ex p. Carter, 4 Ind. T. 539; 43 Cases, 14 Fed. 539; In re Blackbird, 109 Fed. 139; In re Byn-Lil-Le, 12 Ariz. 150; Janus, 38 F. 2d 431; Morris, 194 U. S. 384; Northern Pac., 246 U. S. 283; Palcher, 11 Fed. 47; Rainbow, 161 Fed. 835; Stephens, 126 Fed. 148; U. S. v. Celestine, 215 U. S. 278; U. S. ex rel. Gordon, 179 Fed. 391; U. S. ex rel. Standing Bear, 25 Fed. Cas. No. 14891; U. S. v. Mullin, 71 Fed. 682; U. S. v. Myers, 206 Fed. 887; U. S. v. Sturgeon, 27 Fed. Cas. No. 16413.

Stipulations with various Indian Tribes, for the Year ending June 30, 1858.[92] Sec. 3—R. S. 2153,[93] 25 USC 226.[94]

USCA Historical Note: The Act of June 4, 1888, 25 Stat. 167, provided: "That after the passage of this act any U. S. marshal is hereby authorized and required, when necessary to execute any process connected with any criminal proceedings issued out of the Circuit or District Court of the United States for the district of which he is marshal, or by any commissioner of either of said courts, to enter the Indian Territory, and to execute the same therein in the same manner that he is now required by law to execute like processes in his own district." This Act was expressly repealed by a provision in 30 St. 1237.

11 St. 374; Dec. 22, 1858; C. 5—An Act to conform the Land Claim of certain Pueblos and Towns in the Territory of New Mexico.[95]

11 St. 385; Feb. 26, 1859; C. 59—An Act to protect the Land Fund for School Purposes in Sarpy County, Nebraska Territory.

11 St. 388; Feb. 28, 1859; C. 66—An Act making Appropriations for the current and contingent Expenses of the Indian Department, and for fulfilling Treaty Stipulations with various Indian Tribes, for the Year ending June 30, 1860.[96] Sec. 8—R. S. 2156.[97]

11 St. 409; Mar. 3, 1859; C. 79—An Act making appropriations for fulfilling Treaty Stipulations with the Yancton and Tonawanda Indians for the Year ending June 30, 1860, and for other Purposes.[98]

11 St. 410; Mar. 3, 1859; C. 80—An Act making Appropriations for the Legislative, Executive, and Judicial Expenses of Government for the Year ending the thirtieth of June, 1860.[99]

11 St. 425; Mar. 3, 1859; C. 82—An Act making Appropriations for sundry Civil Expenses of the Government for the Year ending the thirtieth of June, 1860.[1]

11 St. 431; Mar. 3, 1859; C. 83—An Act making Appropriations for the Support of the Army for the Year ending the thirtieth of June, 1860.

11 St. 448; May 29, 1856; C. 34—An Act for the Relief of William M. F. Magraw.

11 St. 450; June 14, 1856; C. 46—An Act making Appropriation[s] for the Payment of certain Claims.

11 St. 451; July 3, 1856; C. 52—An Act authorizing a Settlement of the Accounts of Charles P. Babcock, late Indian Agent at Detroit, in the State of Michigan.

11 St. 460; Aug. 11, 1856; C. 90—An Act for the Relief of Bridget Maher.

11 St. 465; Aug. 16, 1856; C. 110—An Act for the Relief of Dempsey Pittman.

11 St. 469; Aug. 18, 1856; C. 141—An Act for the Relief of Brevet Brigadier-General John B. Walbach, of the United States Army.

11 St. 475; July 3, 1856; J. Res. No. 11—Joint Resolution authorizing the Secretary of the Interior to settle the Accounts of Oliver M. Wozencraft.

11 St. 483; Aug. 23, 1856; C. 23—An Act for the Relief of James M. Lindsay.[2]

11 St. 488; Jan. 21, 1857; C. 17—An Act for the Relief of the Heirs of Major-General Arthur St. Clair.

11 St. 503; Mar. 2, 1857; C. 71—An Act for the Relief of Jesse Morrison, of Illinois.

11 St. 514; Mar. 3, 1857; C. 145—An Act for the Relief of John Ryley, an Indian, of the State of Michigan.

11 St. 514; Mar. 3, 1857; C. 146—An Act for the Relief of Mrs. Mary Gay.

11 St. 514; Mar. 3, 1857; C. 147—An Act for the Relief of Jefferson Wilson, Administrator, with the Will annexed, of John F. Wray, deceased.

11 St. 538; June 1, 1858; C. 79—An Act for the Relief of William B. Trotter.[3]

11 St. 538; June 3, 1858; C. 87—An Act for the Relief of the Heirs or Legal Representatives of Richard D. Rowland, deceased, and others.

11 St. 547; June 8, 1858; C. 130—An Act for the Relief of the Heirs of Richard Tarvin.

11 St. 556; Jan. 12, 1859; C. 7—An Act for the Relief of Joseph Hardy and Alton Long.

11 St. 573; Jan. 17, 1837—Treaty with Choctaws and Chickasaws.[4]

11 St. 577; Sept. 3, 1839—Treaty with Stockbridges and Munsees.

11 St. 581; Mar. 17, 1842—Treaty with Wyandott Indians.[5]

11 St. 599; June 13, 1854—Treaty (supplementary article) with Creeks.[6]

11 St. 605; Dec. 9, 1854—Treaty with Ottoes and Missourias.

11 St. 611; June 22, 1855—Treaty with Choctaws and Chickasaws.[7]

11 St. 621; July 31, 1855—Treaty with Ottowas and Chippewas.[8]

11 St. 631; Aug. 2, 1855—Treaty with Chippewas of Sault Ste. Marie.[9]

11 St. 633; Aug. 2, 1855—Treaty with Chippewas.[10]

11 St. 657; Oct. 17, 1855—Treaty with Blackfoot Indians.[11]

11 St. 663; Feb. 5, 1856—Treaty with Stockbridges and Munsees.[12]

11 St. 679; Feb. 11, 1856—Treaty with Menomonees.[13]

11 St. 699; Aug. 7, 1856—Treaty with Creeks and Seminoles.[14]

---

[92] *Sg.* 9 St. 20, Sec. 2; 9 St. 252, Sec. 4; 10 St. 701, Sec. 7; 11 St. 169. *Rp.* 48 St. 787. *Cited:* Eastern Band, 20 C. Cls. 449; U. S. v. Bichard, 1 Ariz. 31.

[93] *Cited:* 43 Cases, 14 Fed. 539; Palcher, 11 Fed. 47; U. S. v. Celestine, 215 U. S. 278.

[94] *R.* 48 St. 787.

[95] *Cited:* 19 L. D. 826; Territory, 12 N. M. 189; U. S. v. Algodones, 52 F. 2d 359; U. S. v. Conway, 175 U. S. 60; U. S. v. Joseph, 94 U. S. 614; U. S. v. Lucero, 1 N. M. 422; U. S. v. Sandoval, 231 U. S. 28; U. S. v. Varela, 1 N. M. 598.

[96] *Rg.* 4 St. 442, 729, sec. 17. *S.* 12 St. 120. *Sg.* 1 St. 618; 4 St. 442; 7 St. 36, 46, 51, 69, 85, 91, 99, 105, 114, 160, 161, 179, 185, 188, 189, 220, 235, 287, 296, 304, 317, 320, 327, 330, 349, 352, 368, 375, 379, 401, 419, 432, 458, 464, 538, 540, 545, 568, 582, 592, 596; 9 St. 20, 35, 437, 519, 574, 822, 842, 855, 878, 952; 10 St. 2, 315, 643, 673, 686, 949, 954, 1014, 1018, 1027, 1038, 1049, 1056, 1071, 1078, 1082, 1093, 1109, 1122, 1125, 1132, 1144, 1165; 11 St. 65, 169, 319, 329, 611, 621, 633, 657, 699, 729, 749. *S.* 12 St. 774; 19 St. 553. *Cited:* Ayres, 35 C. Cls. 26; Brown, 32 C. Cls. 432; Corralitos, 178 U. S. 280; French, 49 C. Cls. 337; Garrison, 30 C. Cls. 272; Leighton, 29 C. Cls. 288; Love, 29 C. Cls. 332; McKee, 33 C. Cls. 99; Maricopa, 156 U. S. 347; Merchant, 35 C. Cls. 403; Thomison, 35 C. Cls. 395; Thurston, 232 U. S. 469; Vincent, 39 C. Cls. 456; Welch, 32 C. Cls. 106; Woolverton, 29 C. Cls. 107.

[97] *R.* 32 St. 792.

[98] *Sg.* 11 St. 699, 735, 743.

[99] *Sg.* 10 St. 576, 686, 701; *S.* 12 St. 221. *Cited:* 10 L. D. 606.

[1] *Sg.* 7 St. 550. *Cited:* 10 Op. A. G. 253; 2 L. D. Memo. 263; 13 L. D. 511; 25 L. D. 252; Kansas, 5 Wall. 737; Lykins, 184 U. S. 169; New York Indians, 170 U. S. 1.

[2] *Sg.* 7 St. 120.

[3] *Sg.* 7 St. 366.

[4] *Cited:* 7 Op. A. G. 142; 35 Op. A. G. 251; Op. Sol. M. 7816, May 28, 1924, M. 18772, Dec. 24, 1926; Chickasaw, 75 C. Cls. 426; Choctaw, 81 C. Cls. 1; Choctaw, 83 C. Cls. 140; Fleming, 215 U. S. 56; Ligon, 164 Fed. 670; M. K. & T. Ry., 46 C. Cls. 59; Mullen, 224 U. S. 448.

[5] *S.* 5 St. 576, 624, 704; 9 St. 20, 132, 252, 382, 544, 574, 987; 10 St. 41, 226, 315, 686. *Cited:* Gray, 10 Fed. Cas. No. 5714; Staley, 36 F. 2d 91; Walker, 16 Wall. 436.

[6] *Sg.* 7 St. 574. *S.* 10 St. 576.

[7] *Sg.* 7 St. 330; 8 St. 333. *S.* 11 St. 65, 169, 273, 388; 12 St. 44, 221, 512, 774; 13 St. 161, 541; 14 St. 255, 492, 769; 15 St. 198; 16 St. 13, 335, 544; 17 St. 165, 437; 18 St. 146, 204, 420; 19 St. 176, 271; 20 St. 63, 295; 21 St. 114, 485, 504; 22 St. 68, 433; 23 St. 76, 362; 24 St. 29, 449; 25 St. 217, 980; 26 St. 336, 989; 27 St. 120, 612; 28 St. 286, 876; 29 St. 321; 30 St. 62, 571, 924; 31 St. 221, 280, 1058; 32 St. 245, 982; 33 St. 189, 1048; 34 St. 325, 1015; 35 St. 70, 781; 36 St. 202, 269, 1058, 1289; 37 St. 518, 595, 912; 38 St. 77, 812, 559, 582, 1138; 39 St. 123, 969; 40 St. 2, 561; 41 St. 3, 408, 1225; 42 St. 552, 1174; 43 St. 390, 1141; 44 St. 453, 934; 45 St. 200, 1562; 46 St. 279, 1115; 47 St. 91, 820; 48 St. 362; 49 St. 176, 1757; 50 St. 564; 52 St. 291. *Cited:* 8 Op. A. G. 300; 12 Op. A. G. 516; 13 Op. A. G. 354; 15 Op. A. G. 601; 17 Op. A. G. 134; 17 Op. A. G. 265; 18 Op. A. G. 34; 19 Op. A. G. 109; 25 Op. A. G. 460; 29 Op. A. G. 131; 35 Op. A. G. 251; Op. Sol., M. 18772, Dec. 24, 1926; Ansley, 5 Ind. T. 563; Byrd, 44 C. Cls. 498; Campbell, 44 C. Cls. 488; Chickasaw, 193 U. S. 115; Chickasaw, 75 C. Cls. 426; Choctaw, 19 C. Cls. 243; Choctaw, 21 C. Cls. 59; Choctaw, 81 C. Cls. 1; Choctaw, 83 C. Cls. 140; Choctaw, 119 U. S. 1; Corralitos, 33 C. Cls. 342; Dukes, 4 Ind. T. 156; Fleming, 215 U. S. 56; Gillfillan, 159 U. S. 303; Glenn-Tucker, 4 Ind. T. 511; Hayes, 44 C. Cls. 493; Klamath, 296 U. S. 244; McKee, 33 C. Cls. 99; Maxey, 3 Ind. T. 243; M. K. & T. Ry., 46 C. Cls. 59; Morris, 194 U. S. 384; Mullen, 224 U. S. 448; Roff, 168 U. S. 218; U. S. v. Choctaw, 179 U. S. 494; Wallace, 204 U. S. 415.

[8] *Sg.* 7 St. 206, 491. *S.* 11 St. 65, 169, 273, 388; 12 St. 44, 221, 512, 774; 13 St. 161, 541; 14 St. 255, 492; 15 St. 198; 16 St. 13, 544; 17 St. 381; 18 St. 516; 33 St. 1048. *Cited:* 15 L. D. 104; Memo. Sol., May 1, 1937; Ottawa, 42 C. Cls. 240.

[9] *Sg.* 7 St. 206 *S.* 11 St. 169; 14 St. 657. *Cited:* Shepard, 40 Fed. 341; Spalding, 160 U. S. 394.

[10] *Sg.* 7 St. 105, 503. *S.* 11 St. 65; 11 St. 273, 388; 12 St. 221, 512, 774, 1105; 13 St. 161, 541; 14 St. 255, 492, 657; 15 St. 462; 38 St. 582. *Cited:* U. S. v. Holliday, 3 Wall. 407.

[11] *Sg.* 15 St. 635. *S.* 11 St. 65, 169, 273, 388; 12 St. 44, 221, 774; 13 St. 161, 541; 43 St. 21; 44 St. 1263; 46 St. 531. *Cited:* Assiniboine, 77 C. Cls. 347; Blackfeet, 81 C. Cls. 101; British-American, 299 U. S. 159; U. S. v. 196 Buffalo, 1 Mont. 489.

[12] *Sg.* 5 St. 645; 7 St. 44, 303, 342, 580; 9 St. 55, 657, 955; 10 St. 686, 699. *S.* 11 St. 65, 679. *Cited:* Elk, 112 U. S. 94; McKee, 201 Fed. 74; New York Indians, 40 C. Cls. 448; U. S. v. Paine, 206 U. S. 467.

[13] *Sg.* 9 St. 952; 10 St. 1064; 11 St. 663. *S.* 11 St. 169. *Cited:* 25 L. D. 17.

[14] *Sg.* 1 St. 137; 5 St. 155, 186; 7 St. 35, 47, 68, 366, 368, 417; 9 St. 822. *S.* 11 St. 169, 273, 388, 409; 12 St. 44, 221, 512, 774; 13 St. 161, 541; 14 St. 255, 492, 755; 15 St. 198; 16 St. 13, 335, 544; 17 St. 165, 437; 18 St. 29, 146, 420; 19 St. 176, 271; 20 St. 63, 295; 21 St. 114, 485; 22 St. 68, 433; 23 St. 76, 362; 24 St. 29, 449; 25 St. 217, 980; 26 St. 336, 989; 27 St. 120, 612; 28 St. 286, 876; 29 St. 321; 30 St. 62,

11 St. 729; Sept. 24, 1857—Treaty with Pawnees.[15]

11 St. 735; Nov. 5, 1857—Treaty with Seneca Indians.[16]

11 St. 743; Apr. 19, 1858—Treaty with Yancton tribe of Sioux.[17]

12 STAT.

12 St. 4; Mar. 29, 1860; C. 10—An Act making Appropriations for fulfilling Treaty Stipulations with the Ponca Indians, and with certain Bands of Indians in the State of Oregon and Territory of Washington, for the Year ending June 30, 1860.[18]

12 St. 15; May 9, 1860; C. 40—An Act to provide Payment for Depredations committed by the Whites upon the Shawnee Indians in Kansas Territory.[19]

12 St. 16; May 16, 1860; C. 50—An Act to create an additional Land District in Washington Territory.

12 St. 17; May 24, 1860; C. 56—An Act to supply Deficiencies in the Appropriations for the Service of the fiscal Year ending the thirtieth of June, 1860.[20]

12 St. 21; May 26, 1860; C. 61—An Act to settle the Titles to certain Lands set apart for the Use of certain Half-Breed Kansas Indians, in Kansas Territory.[21]

12 St. 28; June 7, 1860; C. 79—An Act for the Relief of certain Settlers in the State of Iowa.

12 St. 28; June 9, 1860; C. 84—An Act to pay to the State of Missouri the Amount expended by said State in repelling the Invasion of the Osage Indians.

12 St. 44; June 19, 1860; C. 157—An Act making Appropriations for the current and contingent Expenses of the Indian Department, and for fulfilling Treaty Stipulations with various Indian Tribes, for the Year ending June 30, 1861.[22]

12 St. 64; June 21, 1860; C. 163—An Act making Appropriations for the Support of the Army for the Year ending the thirtieth of June, 1861.

12 St. 91; June 23, 1860; C. 205—An Act making Appropriations for the Legislative, Executive, and Judicial Expenses of Government for the Year ending the thirtieth of June, 1861.[23]

12 St. 104; June 25, 1860; C. 211—An Act making Appropriations for sundry Civil Expenses of the Government for the Year ending the thirtieth of June, 1861.[24]

12 St. 113; June 25, 1860; C. 213—An Act to establish two Indian Agencies in Nebraska Territory, and one in the Territory of New Mexico.[25]

12 St. 116; June 15, 1860; J. Res. No. 18—A Resolution for Supplying the Choctaw, Cherokee, and Chickasaw Nations with such Copies of the Laws, Journals, and public printed Documents as are furnished to the States and Territories.

12 St. 120; June 25, 1860; J. Res. No. 26—A Resolution explanatory of the eighth Section of the Act of Congress approved February 28, 1859.[26]

12 St. 126; Jan. 29, 1861; C. 20—An Act for the Admission of Kansas into the Union.[27] Sec. 4—R. S. 531, 551, 767, 770, 776, 781.

12 St. 130; Feb. 8, 1861; C. 30—An Act to provide for a Superintendent of Indian Affairs for Washington Territory and additional Agents.[28] R. S. 2046.

12 St. 133; Feb. 20, 1861; C. 44—An Act making Appropriations for the Legislative, Executive, and Judicial Expenses of the Government for the Year ending the thirtieth of June, 1862.

12 St. 151; Feb. 27, 1861; C. 56—An Act to refund to the Territory of Utah the Expenses incurred in suppressing Indian Hostilities in the Year 1853.

12 St. 151; Feb. 27, 1861; C. 57—An Act establishing certain Post Routes.

12 St. 172; Feb. 28, 1861; C. 59—An Act to provide a temporary Government for the Territory of Colorado.[29] Sec. 1—R. S. 1839, 1840, 1847,[30] 1848, 1849,[31] 1899; Sec. 2—R. S. 1841; Sec. 4—R. S. 1846, 1922;[32] Sec. 5—R. S. 1859, 1860; Sec 6—R. S. 1851, 1925, 1857; Sec. 11—R. S. 1877, 1878, 1935, 1939.

12 St. 198; Mar. 2, 1861; C. 70—An Act to provide for the Payment of Expenses incurred by the Territories of Washington and Oregon in the Suppression of Indian Hostilities therein, in the Years 1855 and 1856.[33]

12 St. 199; Mar. 2, 1861; C. 71—An Act for the Payment of Expenses incurred in the Suppression of Indian Hostilities in the State of California.[34]

12 St. 200; Mar. 2, 1861; C. 72—An Act making Appropriations for the Support of the Army for the Year ending thirtieth of June, 1862.

12 St. 207; Mar. 2, 1861; C. 74—An Act for the Relief of certain Chippewa, Ottawa, and Pottawatomie Indians.[35]

12 St. 209; Mar. 2, 1861; C. 83—An Act to organize the Territory of Nevada.

12 St. 214; Mar. 2, 1861; C. 84—An Act making Appropriations for sundry Civil Expenses of the Government for the Year ending June 30, 1862.[36]

12 St. 221; Mar. 2, 1861; C. 85—An Act making Appropriations for the current and contingent Expenses of the Indian Department, and for fulfilling Treaty Stipulations with various Indian Tribes, for the Year ending June 30, 1862.[37]

12 St. 239; Mar. 2, 1861; C. 86—An Act to provide a temporary Government for the Territory of Dakota, and to create the Office of Surveyor General therein.[38] Sec. 1—R. S. 1839, 1840, 1900; Sec. 2—R. S. 1841; Sec. 3—R. S. 1846, 1847,[39]

571, 597, 924; 31 St. 221, 1058; 32 St. 245, 982; 33 St. 189, 1048; 34 St. 325 1015; 35 St. 70, 781. *Cited:* 16 Op. A. G. 31; 19 Op. A. G. 342; Memo. Ind. Off., Mar. 18, 1935; Buster, 135 Fed. 947; Conner, 19 C Cls. 675; Crabtree, 54 Fed. 432; Crabtree, 54 Fed. 426; Creek, 63 C. Cls 270; Creek, 77 C. Cls. 226; Creek, 78 C. Cls. 474; Garrison, 30 C. Cls. 272; Goat, 224 U. S. 458; Maxey, 3 Ind. T. 243; Muskogee, 4 Ind. T. 18; U. S. v. Payne, 8 Fed. 883; U. S. v. Seminole, 299 U. S. 417; Woodward 238 U. S. 284.

[15] *S.* 11 St. 829, 888; 12 St. 44, 221, 512, 774; 13 St. 161, 541; 14 St. 255 492; 15 St. 198; 16 St. 13, 335, 544; 17 St. 165, 437; 18 St 146, 420; 19 St. 176, 271; 20 St. 63, 295; 21 St. 114, 485; 22 St. 68, 433; 23 St. 76, 362; 24 St. 29, 449; 25 St. 217, 980; 26 St. 336, 989; 27 St. 120, 612; 28 St. 286, 876; 29 St. 321; 30 St. 62, 571, 924; 31 St. 221, 1058; 32 St. 245, 982; 33 St. 189, 1048; 34 St. 325, 1015; 35 St. 70 781; 36 St. 269, 1085; 37 St. 518; 38 St. 77, 582; 39 St. 123 969; 40 St. 561; 41 St. 3, 408, 1225; 42 St. 552, 1174; 43 St. 390, 1141; 44 St. 453, 934; 45 St. 200, 1562; 46 St. 279, 1115; 47 St. 91, 820; 48 St. 362; 49 St. 176 1757; 50 St. 564; 52 St. 291. *Cited:* Pawnee, 56 C. Cls. 1; U. S. v. Higgins, 103 Fed. 348; U. S. v. Sa-coo-da-cot, 27 Fed Cas. No. 16212.

[16] *Ag.* 7 St. 550, 586. *S.* 11 St. 409. *Cited:* 1 L. D. Memo. 35; New York Indians, 170 U. S. 1.

[17] *Sg.* 1 St. 137. *S.* 10 St. 15, 181, 226, 315, 686; 11 St. 169, 273, 388 409; 12 St. 44, 221, 512, 648, 774; 13 St. 161, 541; 14 St. 191, 255, 492 15 St. 198; 16 St. 13, 335, 544; 17 St. 165 437; 18 St. 146, 420; 19 St. 176 271; 20 St. 63, 295; 21 St. 114, 485; 22 St. 68, 433; 23 St 76, 362; 24 St. 29, 449; 25 St. 217, 980; 26 St. 336, 989; 27 St. 120 612; 28 St. 286, 876; 29 St. 321; 30 St. 62, 571, 924; 31 St. 221, 1058; 32 St. 245, 982; 33 St. 189, 1048; 34 St. 325 1015; 46 St. 531. *Cited:* Op Sol. M. 27671, Mar. 1, 1934; Graham, 80 C. Cls. 318; Perrin, 232 U. S 478; U. S. v. Carpenter, 111 U. S. 347; U. S. v. Ewing, 47 Fed 809; Yankton, 61 C. Cls. 40.

[18] *Sg.* 12 St. 927, 934, 940, 947, 953, 964, 972, 976, 981, 997. *Cited.* Duwamish, 79 C. Cls. 530.

[19] *Sg.* 4 St. 729. *Cited:* Blackfeather, 190 U. S. 368.

[20] *S.* 12 St. 344; 14 St. 570.

[21] *Sg.* 7 St. 244. *Rp.* 12 St. 628. *Cited:* Jones, 175 U. S. 1; Smith, 10 Wall. 321; Swope, 23 Fed. Cas. No. 18704.

[22] *Sg.* 1 St. 618; 4 St. 729, 735; 7 St. 36, 46, 51, 69, 85, 91, 99, 105, 114, 160, 179, 185, 188, 191, 213, 220, 235, 287, 296, 304, 317 320, 327, 349, 352, 368, 375, 379, 419, 425, 432, 459, 478, 538, 540, 545, 568, 582, 592, 596; 9 St. 20, 35, 437, 442, 519, 574, 634, 659, 822, 842, 855, 878, 952; 10 St. 226, 315, 643, 673, 686, 949, 955, 1014, 1018, 1027, 1039, 1044, 1049, 1053, 1064, 1071, 1078, 1095, 1100, 1122, 1127, 1134, 1144, 1165; 11 St. 65, 169, 319, 628, 700, 702, 729, 744, 749; 12 St. 577, 953, 958, 965, 997. *S.* 12 St. 221, 512. *Cited:* Chippewa, 80 C. Cls. 410; Lemmon, 106 Fed. 650; McKee, 33 C. Cls. 99.

[23] *Sg.* 10 St. 576; 10 St. 686, 700, 701. *Cited:* U. S. v. Provoe, 38 F. 2d 799.

[24] *S.* 28 St. 843.

[25] *S.* 12 St. 221, 512, 774. *Cited:* U. S. v. Lucero, 1 N. M. 422.

[26] *S.* 4 St. 729; 11 St. 401, sec. 8. *Cited:* Corralitos, 178 U. S. 280; French, 49 C. Cls. 337; Leighton, 29 C. Cls. 288; Merchant, 35 C. Cls. 403; Thomison, 35 C. Cls. 395; Thurston, 232 U. S. 469.

[27] *S.* 21 St. 291. *Cited:* Canfield, 15 Am. L. Rev. 21; 19 Op. A. G. 117; Kansas, 5 Wall. 737; M. K. & T. Ry., 152 U. S. 114; New York Indians, 170 U. S. 1; U. S. v. Parkhurst-Davis, 176 U. S. 317; U. S. v. Ward, 28 Fed. Cas. No. 16639.

[28] *S.* 12 St. 512, 774.

[29] *A* 12 St. 700. *Cited:* U. S. v. McBrathey, 104 U. S. 621; Ute, 45 C. Cls. 440.

[30] Rp 20 S. 178.

[31] R. P. 20 S. 178.

[32] *Rp.* 20 St. 178.

[33] *Sg.* 9 St. 414. *S.* 18 St. 371.

[34] *S.* 15 St. 24.

[35] *Sg.* 7 St. 329, 394, 431, 442; 9 St. 853. *S.* 15 St. 531.

[36] *S.* 39 St. 123; 43 St. 793

[37] *Sg.* 1 St. 618; 4 St. 442, 735; 7 St. 21, 36, 46, 51, 69, 85, 91, 99, 105, 114, 160, 161, 179, 185, 188, 191, 220, 235, 287, 296, 304, 317, 320, 327, 349, 352, 368, 375, 379, 419, 425, 432, 495, 540, 568, 582, 592, 596; 8 St. 545; 9 St. 20, 35, 437, 574, 822, 842, 855, 878, 952; 10 St. 315, 576, 643, 686, 702, 949, 951, 955, 1014, 1018, 1027, 1039, 1044, 1048, 1056, 1063, 1071, 1078, 1093, 1109, 1122, 1127, 1134, 1144, 1165; 11 St. 65, 165, 169, 419, 613, 614, 623, 634, 659, 700, 702, 709, 729, 743, 744, 747, 749; 12 St. 44, 57, 113, 927, 934, 940, 947, 953, 958, 964, 972, 976, 981, 997. *S.* 16 St. 544; 17 St. 437; 35 St. 478. *Cited:* 13 Op. A. G. 354; Choctaw, 19 C. Cls. 243; Choctaw, 21 C. Cls. 59; Choctaw, 119 U. S. 1; Delaware, 74 C. Cls. 368; McKee, 38 C. Cls. 99; Sioux, 227 U. S. 424; Sisseton, 58 C. Cls. 302.

[38] *A.* 12 St. 700. *Cited:* Canfield, 15 Am. L. Rev. 21; Nadeau, 253 U. S. 442; U. S. v. Ewing, 47 Fed. 809.

[39] *Rp.* 20 St. 178.

1848, 1849,[40] 1922;[41] Sec. 5—R. S. 1859, 1860; Sec. 6—R. S. 1851, 1925; Sec. 11—R. S. 1877, 1878, 1935, 1939, 1942; Sec. 16—R. S. 1891.

12 St. 338; February 13, 1862; C. 24—An Act to amend an Act entitled "An Act to regulate Trade and Intercourse with the Indian Tribes, and to preserve Peace on the Frontiers," approved June 30, 1834.[42]

12 St. 344; Feb. 22, 1862; C. 30—An Act to authorize a Change of Appropriations for the Payment of necessary Expenditures in the Service of the United States for Indian Affairs.[43]

12 St. 348; Mar. 1, 1862; C. 34—An Act making Appropriations for sundry Civil Expenses of the Government for the Year ending the thirtieth of June, 1863, and additional Appropriations for the Year ending the thirtieth of June, 1862.

12 St. 355; Mar. 14, 1862; C. 41—An Act making Appropriations for the Legislative, Executive, and Judicial Expenses of the Government for the Year ending thirtieth of June, 1863, and additional Appropriations for the Year ending thirtieth of June, 1862.[44]

12 St. 413; June 2, 1862; C. 94—An Act to establish a Land Office in Colorado Territory, and for other Purposes.[45] R. S. 2257.[46]

12 St. 413; June 2, 1862; C. 95—An Act to establish certain Post-Routes, and for other Purposes.

12 St. 427; June 14, 1862; C. 101—An Act to protect the Property of Indians who have adopted the Habits of civilized Life.[47] Sec. 1—R. S. 2119,[48] 25 USC 185; Sec. 2—R. S. 2120, 25 USC 186;[49] Sec. 3—R. S. 2121, 25 USC 187.

12 St. 489; July 1, 1862; C. 120—An Act to aid in the Construction of a Railroad and Telegraph Line from the Missouri River to the Pacific Ocean, and to secure to the Government the Use of the same for Postal, Military, and Other Purposes.[50]

12 St. 498; July 1, 1862; C. 123—An Act to provide for the Appointment of an Indian Agent in Colorado Territory.

12 St. 512; July 5, 1862; C. 135—An Act making Appropriations for the current and contingent Expenses of the Indian Department, and for fulfilling Treaty Stipulations with various Indian Tribes, for the Year ending June 30, 1863.[51] Sec. 1, p. 528—R. S. 2080, 25 USC 72; Sec. 5—R. S. 2084; Sec. 6—R. S. 2108,[52] 25 USC 159.

12 St. 539; July 12, 1862; C. 156—An Act relating to Trust Funds of several Indian Tribes invested by the Government in certain State Bonds abstracted from the Custody of the late Secretary of the Interior.[53]

12 St. 566; July 14, 1862; C. 165—An Act for the Relief of Preemptors on the Home Reservation of the Winnebagoes, in the Blue-earth Region, in the State of Minnesota.[54]

12 St. 614; Feb. 22, 1862; J. Res. No. 13—A Resolution for the Relief of the loyal Portion of the Creek, Seminole, Chickasaw, and Choctaw Indians.[55]

12 St. 628; July 17, 1862; J. Res. No. 67—A Resolution to repeal and modify Secs. 2 and 3 of an Act entitled "An Act to settle the Titles to certain Lands set apart for the Use of certain Half-breed Kansas Indians in Kansas Territory," approved May 26, 1860, and to repeal part of sec. 1 of said Act.[56]

12 St. 628; July 17, 1862; J. Res. No. 69—Joint Resolution authorizing the Secretary of the Interior to expend, from a Fund in the United States Treasury belonging to the Winnebago Indians, the sum of $50,000, or so much thereof as may be necessary, for the Benefit of said Indians.[57]

12 St. 629; July 17, 1862; J. Res. No. 71—A Resolution making further Appropriations for the current and contingent Expenses of the Indian Department, and for fulfilling Treaty Stipulations with the various Indian Tribes, for the Year ending June 30, 1863.

12 St. 630; July 17, 1862; J. Res. No. 72—A Resolution suspending the Sale by sealed Bids, of the Lands of the Kansas and Sac and Fox Indians.

12 St. 648; Feb. 12, 1863; C. 32—An Act to supply Deficiencies in the Appropriations for the Service of the Fiscal Year ending June 30, 1863.[58]

12 St. 652; Feb. 16, 1863; C. 37—An Act for the Relief of Persons for Damages sustained by Reason of Depredations and Injuries by certain Bands of Sioux Indians.[59]

12 St. 658; Feb. 21, 1863; C. 53—An Act for the Removal of Winnebago Indians, and for the sale of their Reservation in Minnesota for their Benefit.[60]

12 St. 664; Feb. 24, 1863; C. 56—An Act to provide a temporary Government for the Territory of Arizona, and for other Purposes.[61] Sec. 1—R. S. 1839, 1840, 1901. Sec. 2—R. S. 702, 1841, 1842, 1843, 1844, 1846, 1847,[62] 1848, 1849,[63] 1850, 1851, 1854, 1857, 1859, 1860, 1862, 1863, 1864, 1865, 1866, 1867, 1868, 1869, 1870, 1871, 1872, 1873, 1875, 1876, 1877, 1878, 1881, 1882, 1883, 1885, 1891, 1908, 1909, 1910, 1913, 1918, 1922,[64] 1935, 1939, 1942, 1944, 1946.

12 St. 682; Feb. 25, 1863; C. 59—An Act making Appropriations for the Legislative, Executive, and Judicial Expenses of the Government for the Year ending thirtieth June, 1864, and for the Year 1863, and for other Purposes.

12 St. 700; Mar. 2, 1863; C. 70—An Act to amend an Act entitled "An Act to provide a Temporary Government for the Territory of Colorado."[65] Sec. 4—R. S. 1842.

12 St. 744; Mar. 3, 1863; C. 79—An Act making Appropriations for sundry Civil Expenses of the Government for the Year ending June 30, 1864, and for the Year ending the 30th of June, 1863, and for other Purposes.[66]

12 St. 774; Mar. 3, 1863; C. 99—An Act making Appropriations for the current and contingent Expenses of the Indian Department, and for fulfilling Treaty Stipulations with various Indian Tribes, for the Year ending June 30, 1864.[67] Sec. 1, p. 792—R. S. 2067, 25 U. S. C. 41.

12 St. 803; Mar. 3, 1863; C. 107—An Act supplementary to an Act entitled "An Act for the Relief of Persons for Damages sustained by Reason of Depredations and Injuries by certain Bands of Sioux Indians," approved February 16, 1863.[68]

---

[40] *Rp.* 20 St. 178.

[41] *Rp.* 20 St. 178.

[42] *Ag.* 4 St. 732, sec. 30. *Cited:* 14 Op. A. G. 290; U. S. v. Bridleman, 7 Fed. 894; U. S. v. Downing, 25 Fed. Cas. No. 14991; U. S. v. 43 Gallons, 93 U. S. 188; U. S. v. Holliday, 3 Wall. 407; U. S. v. Kie, 26 Fed. Cas. No. 15528a; U. S. v. Miller, 105 Fed. 944; U. S. v. Sevcloff, 27 Fed. Cas. No. 16252; U. S. v. Shaw-Mux, 27 Fed. Cas. No. 16268; U. S. v. Winslow, 28 Fed. Cas. No. 16742; U. S. Exp., 191 Fed. 673.

[43] *Sg.* 12 St. 17. *S.* 14 St. 570.

[44] *Cited:* Bowling, 299 Fed. 438.

[45] *Sg.* 5 St. 453. *Cited:* Holden, 17 Wall. 211; Osborn, 33 C. Cls. 304; Ward, 17 Wall. 253.

[46] *Cited:* Buttz, 119 U. S. 55.

[47] *Cited:* Letter to Col. J. G. Scrugham from Sp. Asst. to the A. G., April 1, 1921; Report on Status of Pueblo of Pojoaque, Nov. 3, 1932.

[48] *Cited:* Hatch, 66 Fed. 668; U. S. v. Boylan, 265 Fed. 165; U. S. v. Kopp, 110 Fed. 160; U. S. v. Mullin, 71 Fed. 682.

[49] *R.* 48 St. 787.

[50] Kindred, 225 U. S. 582; M. K. & T. Ry., 47 C. Cls. 59; Nadeau, 253 U. S. 442.

[51] *Sg.* 1 St. 618; 4 St. 442, 735; 7 St. 36, 46, 51, 69, 71, 85, 91, 98, 105, 114, 160, 161, 179, 185, 188, 191, 213, 220, 235, 296, 304, 317, 320, 327, 349, 352, 368, 379, 401, 419, 425, 432, 495, 530, 540, 568, 582, 592, 596; 8 St. 179, 545; 9 St. 20, 35, 437, 574, 822, 842, 855, 878, 952; 10 St. 315, 576, 634, 643, 686, 949, 951, 955, 1014, 1018, 1027, 1039, 1044, 1049, 1065, 1071, 1078, 1095, 1109, 1122, 1127, 1134, 1144, 1165; 11 St. 65, 169, 287, 614, 623, 633, 700, 702, 729, 743, 744, 747, 749, 759; 12 St. 44, 57, 113, 130, 927, 934, 940, 947, 953, 958, 964, 972, 976, 981, 997, 1163. *S.* 13 St. 541. *Cited:* Memo. Sol. Off., Aug. 17, 1933; Memo. Sol., Oct. 7, 1937; Holden, 17 Wall. 211; McKee, 33 C. Cls. 99; U. S. v. Choctaw, 179 U. S. 494; Ward, 17 Wall. 253.

[52] *Cited:* U. S. v. Blackfeather, 155 U. S. 180.

[53] *S.* 16 St. 13; 18 St. 420. *Cited:* Delaware, 72 C. Cls. 483.

[54] *S.* 13 St. 541.

[55] *Cited:* 16 Op. A. G. 31.

[56] *Rg.* 12 St. 21, secs. 2 & 3. *Cited:* Smith, 10 Wall. 321; Swope, 23 Fed. Cas. No. 13704.

[57] *S.* 15 St. 198; 16 St. 13, 335, 544; 17 St. 165, 437; 18 St. 146, 420; 19 St. 176, 271; 20 St. 63, 295; 21 St. 114, 485; 22 St. 68, 433; 23 St. 76, 362; 24 St. 29, 449; 25 St. 217, 980; 26 St. 336, 989; 27 St. 120, 612; 28 St. 286, 876; 29 St. 321; 30 St. 62, 571, 924; 31 St. 221, 1058; 32 St. 245; 33 St. 189, 1048.

[58] *Sg.* 11 St. 749.

[59] *S.* 12 St. 803; 13 St. 22, 92; 23 St. 344; 27 St. 612; 30 St. 62; 31 St. 1058; 34 St. 325; 35 St. 1623; 39 St. 1195. *Cited:* 44 L. D. 188; Love, 29 C. Cls. 332; Medawakanton, 57 C. Cls. 357; Sisseton, 39 C. Cls. 172; Sisseton, 42 C. Cls. 416; Sisseton, 58 C. Cls. 302; U. S. v. Sisseton, 208 U. S. 561.

[60] *Sg.* 12 St. 1101. *S.* 16 St. 335; 21 St. 315; 43 St. 1114; 45 St. 1027. *A.* 28 St. 679. *Cited:* 3 L. D. 580; Sol. Op. M. 12509, Aug. 27, 1924; Beck, 65 Fed. 30; U. S. v. Flournoy, 69 Fed. 886.

[61] *Cited:* Goodson, 7 Okla. 117; In re Wilson, 140 U. S. 575; Lane, 249 U. S. 110; U. S. v. Bichard, 1 Ariz. 31; Memo. Sol. Off., Feb. 7, 1934.

[62] *Rp.* 20 St. 178.

[63] *Rp.* 20 St. 178.

[64] *Rp.* 20 St. 178.

[65] *Ag.* 12 St. 172, 239.

[66] *Sg.* 12 St. 276. *S.* 13 St. 344; 16 St. 13; 34 St. 634.

[67] *Sg.* 1 St. 618; 4 St. 442, 735; 7 St. 36, 46, 51, 69, 85, 91, 99, 105, 114, 160, 161, 178, 179, 185, 188, 191, 213, 220, 235, 287, 296, 304, 317, 320, 327, 349, 352, 368, 379, 401, 419, 425, 432, 459, 540, 545, 568, 582, 592, 596; 8 St. 592; 9 St. 20, 35, 437, 574, 822, 842, 855, 878, 952; 10 St. 315, 576, 643, 686, 702, 1014, 1018, 1027, 1039, 1044, 1049, 1056, 1065, 1071, 1078, 1093, 1095, 1109, 1122, 1134, 1144, 1165; 11 St. 65, 169, 401, 614, 628, 634, 657, 700, 702, 729, 743, 744, 749; 12 St. 44, 113, 130, 927, 934, 940, 947, 953, 958, 964, 972, 976, 981, 997, 1165, 1238. *Cited:* Holden, 17 Wall. 211; Medawakanton, 57 C. Cls. 357; U. S. v. Leathers, 26 Fed. Cas. No. 15581; U. S. v. Walker River, 104 F. 2d 234; Ward, 17 Wall. 253.

[68] *Sg.* 12 St. 652.

12 St. 808; Mar. 3, 1863; C. 117—An Act to provide a temporary Government for the Territory of Idaho.[69] **Sec. 1—R. S. 1839, 1840, 1902; Sec. 2—R. S. 1841; Sec. 5—R. S. 1859, 1860; Sec. 6—R. S. 1842, 1851; Sec. 13—R. S. 1862, 1863, 1891, 1906; Sec. 17—R. S. 1949.**

12 St. 819; Mar. 3, 1863; C. 119—An Act for the Removal of the Sisseton, Wahpaton, Medawakanton, and Wahpakoota Bands of Sioux or Dakota Indians, and for the Disposition of their Lands in Minnesota and Dakota.[70]

12 St. 834; Apr. 11, 1860; C. 16—An Act for the Relief of the American Board of Commissioners for Foreign Missions.[71]

12 St. 834; Apr. 11, 1860; C. 19—An Act for the Relief of William Geiger.

12 St. 840; May 9, 1860; C. 42—An Act for the Relief of Madison Sweetzer.

12 St. 840; May 9, 1860; C. 44—An Act for the Relief of Tilman Leak.[72]

12 St. 841; May 9, 1860; C. 46—An Act for the Relief of George Stealey.

12 St. 843; June 1, 1860; C. 70—An Act for the Relief of the legal Representatives of Wetonsaw, Son of James Conner.[73]

12 St. 845; June 1, 1860; C. 75—An Act for the Relief of Wendell Trout.

12 St. 847; June 9, 1860; C. 86—An Act for the Relief of Samuel J. Hensley.[74]

12 St. 848; June 9, 1860; C. 91—An Act for the Relief of John Dixon.

12 St. 850; June 9, 1860; C. 104—An Act for the Relief of W. Y. Hansell, the Heirs of W. H. Underwood, and the Representatives of Samuel Rockwell.[75]

12 St. 860; June 16, 1860; C. 144—An Act for the Relief of the Missionary Society of the Methodist Episcopal Church.

12 St. 860; June 16, 1860; C. 145—An Act for the Relief of Anson Dart.

12 St. 873; May 25, 1860; J. Res. No. 13—A Resolution for the Relief of A. M. Fridley, late Agent for the Winnebago Indians.[76]

12 St. 878; Jan. 15, 1861; C. 10—An Act for the Relief of Richard C. Martin.

12 St. 879; Jan. 23, 1861; C. 14—An Act for the Relief of O. F. D. Fairbanks, Frederick Dodge, and the Pacific Mail Steamship Company.

12 St. 883; Feb. 8, 1861; C. 32—An Act for the Relief of Moses Meeker.

12 St. 886; Feb. 23, 1861; C. 55—An Act for the Relief of Samuel Perry.

12 St. 889; Mar. 2, 1861; C. 93—An Act for the Relief of John Y. Sewell.

12 St. 908; July 14, 1862; C. 176—An Act granting an Invalid Pension to Hugh H. Howard, of Hockingport, State of Ohio.

12 St. 915; Feb. 9, 1863; C. 30—An Act to authorize the Court of Claims of the United States to hear and determine the Claim of the Heirs of Stephen Johnston, deceased.[77]

12 St. 918; Feb. 24, 1863; C. 57—An Act for the Relief of Colonel Joseph Paddock.

12 St. 927; Jan. 22, 1855—Treaty with Dwamish, Suquamish, and other allied and subordinate Tribes.[78]

12 St. 933; Jan. 26, 1855—Treaty with S'Klallams.[79]

12 St. 939; Jan. 31, 1855—Treaty with Makah Tribe.[80]

12 St. 945; June 9, 1855—Treaty with Walla-Wallas, Cayuses, and Umatilla Tribes.[81]

12 St. 951; June 9, 1855—Treaty with Yakamas.[82]

12 St. 957; June 11, 1855—Treaty with Nez Perces.[83]

12 St. 963; June 25, 1855—Treaty with Indians in Middle Oregon.[84]

12 St. 971; July 1, 1855 and Jan. 25, 1856—Treaty with Qui-nai-elts, and Quil-leh-ute Indians.[85]

12 St. 975; July 16, 1855—Treaty with Flatheads, Kootenay, and Upper Pend d' Oreilles Indians.[86]

12 St. 981; Dec. 21, 1855—Treaty with Molels.[87]

12 St. 991; Nov. 5, 1857—Treaty with Tonawanda Band of Seneca Indians.[88]

12 St. 997; Mar. 12, 1858—Treaty with Poncas.[89]

12 St. 1031; June 19, 1858—Treaty with Mendawakanton and Wahpakoota Bands of Dakota or Sioux Indians.[90]

12 St. 1037; June 19, 1858—Treaty with Sisseeton and Wahpaton Bands of Dakota or Sioux Tribes.[91]

12 St. 1042; June 27, 1860—Resolution of the Senate of the United States—Right and Title of certain bands of Sioux Indians.[92]

12 St. 1101; Apr. 15, 1859—Treaty with Winnebago Indians.[93]

12 St. 1105; July 16, 1859—Treaty with Swan Creek and Black River Chippewas, and the Munsee or Christian Indians.[94]

12 St. 1111; Oct. 5, 1859—Treaty with Kansas Tribe.[95]

12 St. 1129; May 30, 1860—Treaty with Delaware Indians.[96]

---

[69] *S.* 13 St. 85. *Cited:* 20 Op. A. G. 42; Harkness, 98 U. S. 476; Langford, 102 U. S. 145; Pickett, 1 Idaho 523; Utah, 3 Pac. 3; Utah, 116 U. S. 28.

[70] *S.* 15 St. 39; 30 St. 571. *A.* 16 St. 335; 36 St. 855. *Cited:* 18 Op. A. G. 141; 42 L. D. 192; Farrell, 110 Fed. 942; Medawakanton, 57 C. Cls. 357; Sioux, 277 U. S. 424; Sisseton, 58 C. Cls. 302.

[71] *Ag.* 7 St. 478.

[72] *Sg.* 7 St. 364.

[73] *Sg.* 7 St. 528.

[74] *Cited:* Belt, 15 C. Cls. 92; Fremont, 2 C. Cls. 461—also Jackson, 1 C. Cls. 260; U. S. v. McDougall's, 121 U. S. 89.

[75] *Sg.* 7 St. 478.

[76] *Sg.* 9 St. 878.

[77] *Sg.* 6 St. 812; 7 St. 295.

[78] *Sg.* 10 St. 1043, 1132. *S.* 12 St. 4, 221, 512, 774, 933; 13 St. 161, 541; 14 St. 255, 492; 15 St. 198; 16 St. 13, 335, 544; 17 St. 165, 437; 18 St. 146, 420; 19 St. 176, 271; 20 St. 63, 295; 34 St. 325; 43 St. 886. *Cited:* Op. Sol., A. 2592, Feb. 12, 1924; Corrigan, 169 Fed. 477; Duwamish, 79 C. Cls. 530; Jackson, 34 C. Cls. 441; U. S. v. Alaska, 79 Fed. 152; U. S. v. Boynton, 53 F. 2d 297; U. S. v. Celestine, 215 U. S. 278; U. S. v. Romaine, 255 Fed. 253; U. S. v. Snohomish, 246 Fed. 112; U. S. v. Stotts, 49 F. 2d 619.

[79] *Sg.* 10 St. 1043, 1132; 12 St. 927. *S.* 12 St. 4, 221, 512, 774; 13 St. 161, 541; 14 St. 255, 492; 15 St. 198; 16 St. 13, 335, 544; 17 St. 165, 437; 18 St. 146, 420; 19 St. 176, 271; 20 St. 63, 295; 43 St. 886. *Cited:* Duwamish, 79 C. Cls. 530; Jackson, 34 C. Cls. 441.

[80] *Sg.* 10 St. 1043. *S.* 12 St. 4, 221, 512, 774, 971; 13 St. 161, 541; 14 St. 255, 492; 15 St. 198; 16 St. 13, 335, 544; 17 St. 165, 437; 18 St. 146, 420; 19 St. 176, 271; 20 St. 63, 295. *Cited:* Jackson, 34 C. Cls. 441; Swan, 50 Fed. 108.

[81] *S.* 12 St. 4, 221, 512, 774; 13 St. 161, 541; 14 St. 255, 492; 15 St. 198; 16 St. 13, 335, 544; 17 St. 165, 437; 18 St. 146, 429; 19 St. 176, 271; 20 St. 63, 295; 21 St. 271. *Cited:* Bonifer, 166 Fed. 846; Hy-tu-tse-mil-kin, 194 U. S. 401; Parr, 153 Fed. 462; U. S. v. Barnhart, 17 Fed. 579; U. S. v. Bridleman, 7 Fed. 894; U. S. v. Brookfield, 24 F. Supp. 712; U. S. v. Clapox, 35 Fed. 575; U. S. v. Martin, 14 Fed. 817.

[82] *Sg.* 10 St. 1043. *S.* 12 St. 4, 44, 221, 512, 774; 13 St. 161, 541; 14 St. 255, 492; 15 St. 198; 16 St. 13, 335, 544; 17 St. 165, 437; 18 St. 146, 420; 19 St. 176, 271; 20 St. 63, 295; 28 St. 286. *Cited:* 20 Op. A. G. 814; 13 L. D. Memo. 472, Aug. 25, 1938; Op. Sol., M. 252114, June 7, 1929; Memo. Sol. Off., Aug. 11, 1933; La Clair, 184 Fed. 128; Northern, 227 U. S. 355; Seufert, 193 Fed. 200; U. S. v. Brookfield, 24 F. Supp. 712; U. S. v. Sutton, 215 U. S. 291; U. S. v. Taylor, 3 Wash. T. 88; U. S. v. Winnans, 198 U. S. 371.

[83] *Sg.* 1 St. 137; 10 St. 1043. *S.* 12 St. 44, 221, 512, 744; 13 St. 161, 541; 14 St. 255, 492, 647; 15 St. 198; 16 St. 13, 335, 544; 17 St. 165, 437, 627; 18 St. 146, 420; 19 St. 176, 271; 20 St. 63, 295; 45 St. 1249. *Cited:* 14 Op. A. G. 568; 17 Op. A. G. 306; 20 Op. A. G. 42; Caldwell, 67 Fed. 391; Langford, 12 C. Cls. 338; Pickett, 1 Idaho 523; U. S. v. Lewis, 95 F. 2d 236; U. S. v. Nez Perce, 95 F. 2d 232; Woolverton, 29 C. Cls. 107.

[84] *Sg.* 1 St. 137; 10 St. 1043. *S.* 12 St. 4, 44, 221, 512, 774; 13 St. 161, 324, 541; 14 St. 255, 492, 751; 15 St. 198; 16 St. 13, 335, 544; 17 St. 165, 437; 18 St. 146; 19 St. 176, 271; 20 St. 63, 295; 26 St. 336; 28 St. 86; 39 St. 969; 46 St. 1033. *Cited:* Memo. Ind. Off., Dec. 4, 1931; Memo. Sol. Off., Feb. 15, 1932; U. S. v. Barnhart, 22 Fed. 285; U. S. v. Brookfield, 24 F. Supp. 712; U. S. v. Earl, 17 Fed. 75.

[85] *Sg.* 10 St. 1043; 12 St. 939. *S.* 12 St. 4, 221, 512, 774; 13 St. 161, 541; 14 St. 255, 492; 15 St. 198; 16 St. 13, 335, 544; 17 St. 165, 437; 18 St. 146, 420; 19 St. 176, 271; 20 St. 63, 295; 36 St. 1345; 43 St. 886. *Cited:* Op. Sol., M. 24358, May 14, 1928, M. 24173, Sept. 23, 1932; Fowler, 4 F. Supp. 565; Halbert, 283 U. S. 753; Mason, 5 F. 2d 255; Taylor, 44 F. 2d 53; U. S. v. Payne, 264 U. S. 446; U. S. v. Powers, 305 U. S. 527; U. S. ex rel. Charley, 62 F. 2d 955.

[86] *Sg.* 9 St. 870; 10 St. 1043. *S.* 12 St. 4, 221, 512, 774; 13 St. 161, 541; 14 St. 255, 492; 15 St. 198; 16 St. 13, 335, 544; 17 St. 165, 226, 437; 18 St. 146, 420; 19 St. 176, 271; 20 St. 63, 295; 21 St. 114; 33 St. 302; 43 St. 21. *Cited:* 20 L. D. 462; Op. Sol., M. 11410, Jan. 28, 1924; Op. Sol., M. 12498, June 6, 1924, M. 26075, Aug. 5, 1930; Blackfeet, 81 C. Cls. 101; Clairmont, 225 U. S. 551; Pronovost, 232 U. S. 487; Scheer, 48 F. 2d 327; U. S. v. Heyfron, 138 Fed. 964; U. S. v. Higgins, 103 Fed. 348; U. S. v. McIntire, 101 F. 2d 650.

[87] *Sg.* 10 St. 1018, 1122, 1125. *S.* 12 St. 4, 221, 512, 774; 13 St. 161, 541; 14 St. 255, 492; 15 St. 198; 16 St. 13; 18 St. 146, 420; 19 St. 176, 271; 20 St. 63, 295; 21 St. 114, 485; 22 St. 68, 433; 23 St. 76, 362; 24 St. 29, 449; 25 St. 217, 980; 26 St. 336, 989; 27 St. 120, 612; 28 St. 286, 876; 29 St. 321; 30 St. 62, 571, 924; 31 St. 221, 1058; 32 St. 245, 982; 33 St. 189, 1048; 34 St. 325, 1015; 35 St. 70, 781; 36 St. 269; 49 St. 801. *Cited:* U. S. v. Sinnott, 26 Fed. 84.

[88] *Sg.* 7 St. 550, 586.

[89] *Sg.* 1 St. 137. *S.* 12 St. 4, 44, 221, 512, 774; 13 St. 161, 541; 14 St. 255, 492, 675; 15 St. 198; 16 St. 13, 335, 544; 17 St. 165, 437; 18 St. 146, 420; 19 St. 176, 271; 20 St. 63, 295; 21 St. 114, 485; 22 St. 68, 433; 23 St. 76, 362; 24 St. 29, 449; 25 St. 217. *Cited:* U. S. v. Higgins, 103 Fed. 348; U. S. ex rel. Standing Bear, 25 Fed. Cas. No. 14891.

[90] *Sg.* 1 St. 137; 10 St. 954. *S.* 12 St. 1042. *Cited:* Graham, 30 C. Cls. 318; Medawakanton, 57 C. Cls. 357; Sioux, 277 U. S. 424; Sisseton, 58 C. Cls. 302.

[91] *Sg.* 1 St. 137; 10 St. 315, 949. *S.* 15 St. 505; 18 St. 47; 29 St. 321; 31 St. 1058. *Cited:* Graham, 30 C. Cls. 318; Medawakanton, 57 C. Cls. 357; Roy, 45 C. Cls. 177; Sisseton, 42 C. Cls. 416; U. S. v. Sisseton, 208 U. S. 561.

[92] *Sg.* 10 St. 326, 949, 954, 957; 12 St. 1031. *Cited:* Sioux, 277 U. S. 424; Sisseton, 58 C. Cls. 302.

[93] *Sg.* 1 St. 137. *S.* 12 St. 658; 16 St. 335; 17 St. 165.

[94] *Sg.* 1 St. 137; 7 St. 105, 107, 503; 11 St. 312, 683. *S.* 30 St. 62.

[95] *Sg.* 15 St. 137. *S.* 17 St. 85; 18 St. 272; 19 St. 74; 22 St. 257. *Cited:* 13 Op. A. G. 531; Kansas, 80 C. Cls. 264.

[96] *Sg.* 7 St. 327; 10 St. 1048. *S.* 12 St. 1177; 14 St. 793; 26 St. 989; 27 St. 120. *Cited:* Delaware, 74 C. Cls. 368; Kindred, 225 U. S. 582; U. S. v. Stone, 2 Wall. 525.

12 St. 1163; Feb. 18, 1861—Treaty with Araphoes and Cheyenne Indians.[97]

12 St. 1171; Mar. 6, 1861—Treaty with Sacs, Foxes, and Iowas.[98]

12 St. 1177; July 2, 1861—Treaty with Delawares.[99]

12 St. 1191; Nov. 15, 1861—Treaty with Pottawatomies.[1]

12 St. 1221; Mar. 13, 1862—Treaty with Kansas Indians.[2]

12 St. 1237; June 24, 1862—Treaty with Ottawa Indians.[3]

12 St. 1249; Mar. 11, 1863—Treaty with Chippewa Indians of Mississippi, and the Pillager and Lake Winibigoshish bands of Chippewa Indians of Minnesota.[4]

13 STAT.

13 St. 22; Mar. 14, 1864; C. 30—An Act to supply Deficiencies in the Appropriations for the Service of the Fiscal Year ending the thirtieth of June, 1864, and for other Purposes.[5]

13 St. 29; Mar. 15, 1864; C. 33.—An Act to amend an Act entitled "An Act to regulate Trade and Intercourse with the Indian Tribes, and to preserve Peace on the Frontiers," approved June 30, 1834.[6] R. S. 2139,[7] 2140.[8]

13 St. 37; Mar. 25, 1864; C. 41—An Act to authorize the President to negotiate a Treaty with the Klamath, Modoc, and other Indian tribes in Southeastern Oregon.[9]

13 St. 39; Apr. 8, 1864; C. 48—An Act to provide for the better Organization of Indian Affairs in California.[10] Sec. 1—R. S. 2046; Sec. 4—R. S. 2056; Sec. 6—R. S. 2115;[11] Sec. 7—R. S. 2061.[12]

13 St. 62; May 3, 1864; C. 74—An Act to aid the Indian Refugees to return to their Homes in the Indian Territory.

13 St. 63; May 5, 1864; C. 77.—An Act to vacate and sell the present Indian Reservations in Utah Territory, and to settle the Indians of said Territory in the Uinta Valley.[13]

13 St. 85; May 26, 1864; C. 95—An Act to provide a temporary Government for the Territory of Montana.[14] Sec. 1—R. S. 1839, 1840, 1903; Sec. 2—R. S. 1841; Sec. 5—R. S. 1859, 1860; Sec. 6—R. S. 1842, 1851; Sec. 13—R. S. 1891; Sec. 17—R. S. 1949.

13 St. 92; May 28, 1864; C. 97—An Act making Appropriations for the Payment of the Awards made by the Commissioners appointed under and by virtue of an Act of Congress entitled "An Act for the Relief of Persons for Damages sustained by Reason of the Depredations and Injuries by certain Bands of Sioux Indians." Approved, February 16, 1863.[15]

13 St. 145; June 25, 1864; C. 147—An Act making Appropriations for the Legislative, Executive, and Judicial Expenses of the Government for the Year ending June 30, 1865, and for other Purposes.

13 St. 161; June 25, 1864; C. 148—An Act making Appropriations for the current and contingent Expenses of the Indian Department, and for fulfilling Treaty Stipulations with various Indian Tribes, for the Year ending June 30, 1865, and for other Purposes.[16]

13 St. 316; June 30, 1864; C. 175—An Act to establish certain Post-Roads.

13 St. 323; June 30, 1864; C. 177—An Act to aid in the Settlement, Subsistence, and Support of the Navajoe Indian Captives upon a Reservation in the Territory of New Mexico.[17]

13 St. 324; June 30, 1864; C. 181—An Act to authorize the President of the United States to negotiate with certain Indians of Middle Oregon for a Relinquishment of certain Rights secured to them by treaty.[18]

13 St. 344; July 2, 1864; C. 210—An Act making Appropriations for sundry Civil Expenses of the Government for the Year ending the Thirtieth of June, 1865, and for other Purposes.[19]

13 St. 356; July 2, 1864; C. 216—An Act to amend an Act entitled "An Act to aid in the Construction of a Railroad and Telegraph Line from the Missouri River to the Pacific Ocean, and to secure to the Government the Use of the same for Postal, Military, and other Purposes," approved July 1, 1862.[20]

13 St. 365; July 2, 1864; C. 217—An Act granting Lands to aid in the Construction of a Railroad and Telegraph Line from Lake Superior to Puget's Sound, on the Pacific Coast, by the Northern Route.[21]

13 St. 413; June 30, 1864; J. Res. No. 57—Joint Resolution for the Relief of the Officers of the Fourth and Fifth Indian Regiments.

13 St. 427; Feb. 9, 1865; C. 29—An Act for the Relief of certain friendly Indians of the Sioux Nation, in Minnesota.

13 St. 432; Feb. 23, 1865; C. 45—An Act to extinguish the Indian Title to Lands in the Territory of Utah suitable for agricultural and mineral Purposes.[22]

13 St. 432; Feb. 23, 1865; C. 46—An Act to provide for the Payment of the Value of certain Lands and Improvements of private Citizens, appropriated by the United States for Indian Reservations, in the Territory of Washington.

13 St. 445; Mar. 2, 1865; C. 73—An Act making Appropriations for the legislative, executive, and judicial Expenses of the Government for the Year ending June 30, 1866, and additional Appropriations for the current fiscal Year.

13 St. 522; Mar. 3, 1865; C. 104—An Act to establish certain Post-Roads.

13 St. 530; Mar. 3, 1865; C. 109—An Act to authorize the Issuing of Patents for certain Lands in the Town of Stockbridge, State of Wisconsin, and for other Purposes.[23]

13 St. 538; Mar. 3, 1865; C. 122—An Act to amend an Act entitled "An Act to provide for the better Organization of Indian Affairs in California."[24]

---

[97] *Sg.* 1 St. 137. *S.* 12 St. 512, 774; 14 St. 255; 18 St. 535. *Cited:* Hesmer, 30 C. Cls. 405; Moore, 32 C. Cls. 593.

[98] *Sg.* 10 St. 1069, 1074. *S.* 15 St. 198; 18 St. 146, 420; 19 St. 271; 20 St. 63, 295; 21 St. 114, 485; 22 St. 68, 433; 23 St. 76, 362; 24 St. 29, 449; 25 St. 217, 980; 26 St. 336, 989; 27 St. 120, 612; 28 St. 286, 876; 29 St. 321; 30 St. 62, 571, 924; 31 St. 221, 1058; 32 St. 245, 982; 33 St. 189, 1048; 34 St. 325, 1015; 35 St. 70, 781; 36 St. 269, 1085; 37 St. 518; 38 St. 77, 582.

[99] *Sg.* 12 St. 1129. *Cited:* Delaware, 74 C. Cls. 368.

[1] *Sg.* 9 St. 853. *S.* 14 St. 763; 15 St. 198, 531; 16 St. 13, 335, 544; 17 St. 165, 437; 20 St. 542; 34 St. 325; 35 St. 781; 38 St. 77. *Cited:* Bd. of C. Com'rs of the City of Jackson, 100 F. 2d 929; Elk, 112 U. S. 94; Goodfellow, 10 Fed. Cas. No. 5537; Laughton, 75 Fed. 789; Matter of Heff, 197 U. S. 488.

[2] *Cited:* 17 Op. A. G. 200; Kansas, 80 C. Cls. 264.

[3] *S.* 12 St. 774; 13 St. 161, 541; 14 St. 255; 15 St. 513; 17 St. 388. *Cited:* 13 Op. A. G. 336; Elk, 112 U. S. 94; Libby, 118 U. S. 250; Wiggan, 163 U. S. 56.

[4] *Sg.* 10 St. 1109, 1165. *S.* 49 St. 321, 1757. *Cited:* Cain, 2 Minn. L. Rev. 177; 5 L. D. 541; 12 L. D. 52; Beaulieu, 32 App. D. C. 398; Chippewa, 80 C. Cls. 410; Johnson, 234 U. S. 422; Mille Lac, 46 C. Cls. 424; U. S. v. 43 Gallons, 93 U. S. 188; U. S. v. Mille Lac, 229 U. S. 498; U. S. v. Minnesota, 270 U. S. 181

[5] *Sg.* 12 St. 653.

[6] *Ag.* 4 St. 732, sec. 20. *A.* 52 St. 696. *S.* 30 St. 105. *Cited:* 14 Op. A. G. 290; Bates, 95 U. S. 204; Browning, 6 F. 2d 801; Bruguier, 1 Dak. 5; Moore v. County Com'rs, 2 Wyo. 8; Morrison, 6 F. 2d. 811; Sarlis, 152 U. S. 570; Shawnee, 249 Fed. 583; U. S. v. Belt, 128 Fed. 68; U. S. v. Bichard, 1 Ariz. 31; U. S. v. Bridleman, 7 Fed. 894; U. S. v. Flynn, 25 Fed. Cas. No. 15124; U. S. v. 43 Gallons, 93 U. S. 188; U. S. v. 43 Gallons, 108 U. S. 491; U. S. v. LeBris, 121 U. S. 278; U. S. v. Miller, 105 Fed. 944; U. S. v. One Cadillac, 255 Fed. 173; U. S. v. One Chevrolet, 58 F. 2d. 235; U. S. v. Seveloff, 27 Fed. Cas. No. 16252; U. S. v. Shaw-Mux, 27 Fed. Cas. No. 16268; U. S. v. Steam Boat Cora, 1 Dak. 1; U. S. v. Winslow, 28 Fed. Cas. No. 16742; U. S. v. Wright, 229 U. S. 226; U. S. Exp., 191 Fed. 673; Waters, 29 Fed. Cas. No. 17265.

[7] *S.* 29 St. 506.

[8] *S.* 34 St. 1015; 39 St. 969. *Cited:* 19 Op. A. G. 306; 25 Op. A. G. 416; Browning, 6 F. 2d 801; Commercial, 261 Fed. 330; Evans, 204 Fed. 361; Ford, 260 Fed. 657; 43 Cases, 14 Fed. 539; Hawley, 15 F. 2d 621; Johnson, 234 U. S. 422; Morrison, 6 F. 2d 811; One Buick, 275 Fed. 809; Palcher, 11 Fed. 47; Shawnee, 249 Fed. 583; U. S. v. Celestine, 215 U. S. 278; U. S. v. Luther, 260 Fed. 579; U. S. v. One Automobile, 237 Fed. 891; U. S. v. One Buick, 255 Fed. 793; U. S. v. One Buick, 244 Fed. 961; U. S. v. One Cadillac, 255 Fed. 173; U. S. v. One Chevrolet, 58 F. 2d 235; U. S. v. One Ford, 259 Fed. 645; U. S. v. One Seven-Passenger, 259 Fed. 641; U. S. v. Tadish, 211 Fed. 490; U. S. v. 29 Gallons, 45 Fed. 847; U. S. v. 2 Gallons, 213 Fed. 986; U. S. Exp., 191 Fed. 673.

[9] *Cited:* California, 87 Fed. 532; Klamath, 81 C. Cls. 79; Klamath, 296 U. S. 244; Klamath, 86 C. Cls. 614; U. S. v. Klamath, 304 U. S. 119; U. S. v. Oregon, 103 Fed. 549.

[10] *S.* 13 St. 538. *Cited:* 33 L. D. 205; Op. Sol., A. 2592, Feb. 12, 1924, M. 29232, June 2, 1937; Donnelly, 228 U. S. 243; M. K. & T. Ry., 46 C. Cls. 59; U. S. v. 48 Pounds, 35 Fed. 403; U. S. v. Leathers, 26 Fed. Cas. No. 15581.

[11] *Cited:* French, 4 C. Cls. 252; U. S. v. Boylan, 265 Fed. 165.

[12] *R.* 46 St. 1028.

[13] *S.* 14 St. 492; 15 St. 110, 198; 16 St. 13, 335, 544; 20 St. 165. *Cited:* 25 L. D. 408; Sol. Op., June 14, 1930; Hayt, 38 C. Cls. 455.

[14] *Sg.* 12 St. 808. *S.* 20 St. 178. *Cited:* Draper, 164 U. S. 240; Truscott, 73 Fed. 60.

[15] *Sg.* 12 St. 652. *Cited:* Medawakanton, 57 C. Cls. 357.

[16] *Sg.* 1 St. 61; 4 St. 442; 7 St. 36, 46, 51, 69, 85, 91, 99, 105, 114, 161, 179, 185, 188, 191, 213, 235, 296, 304, 317, 320, 349, 352, 379, 419, 425, 432, 450, 540, 545, 582, 592, 596; 8 St. 287; 9 St. 35, 578, 855, 952; 10 St. 576, 643, 1014, 1018, 1027, 1039, 1044, 1056, 1065, 1078, 1095, 1109, 1122, 1127, 1134, 1165; 11 St. 614, 621, 634, 659, 700, 702, 729, 744, 749; 12 St. 927, 934, 940, 947, 953, 958, 964, 972, 976, 981, 997, 1238; 13 St. 668, 689. *S.* 21 St. 315; 34 St. 325; 45 St. 159, 883. *Cited:* Medawakanton, 57 C. Cls. 357.

[17] *Cited:* U. S. v. Lucero, 1 N. M. 422.

[18] *Sg.* 12 St. 963.

[19] *Sg.* 12 St. 754. *S.* 16 St. 13; 43 St. 596. *Cited:* Bruguier, 1 Dak. 5.

[20] *S.* 18 St. 482. *Cited:* M. K. & T. Ry., 46 C. Cls. 59.

[21] *S.* 22 St. 157. *Cited:* 5 L. D. 188; Buttz, 119 U. S. 55; Clairmont, 225 U. S. 551; Fort Berthold, 71 C. Cls. 308; M. K. & T. Ry., 46 C. Cls. 59; Northern, 3 Dak. 217; Northern, 227 U. S. 355; Northern, 246 U. S. 283; U. S. v. La Plant, 200 Fed. 92.

[22] *Cited:* Hayt, 38 C. Cls. 455.

[23] *S.* 14 St. 604.

[24] *Ag.* 13 St. 40.

13 St. 541; Mar. 3, 1865; C. 127—An Act making Appropriations for the current and contingent Expenses of the Indian Department, and for fulfilling Treaty Stipulations with various Indian Tribes for the Year ending thirtieth June, 1866, and for other Purposes.[25] Sec. 3—R. S. 2081, 25 USC 114;[26] Sec. 4—R. S. 2310, 2311, 2312,[27] 43 USC 101; Sec. 8—R. S. 2138,[28] 25 USC 214 (41 St. 9, sec. 1). USCA Historical Note: R. S. 2138 was amended by 41 Stat. 9, sec. 1, so as to read as set forth in 25 USC 214. Sec. 9—R. S. 2127,[29] 25 USC 192.

13 St. 572; Mar. 3, 1865; J. Res. No. 33—A Resolution directing Inquiry into the Condition of the Indian Tribes, and their Treatment by the Civil and Military Authorities.

13 St. 582; June 30, 1864; C. 188—An Act for the Relief of the Estate of B. F. Kendall.

13 St. 583; July 2, 1864; C. 227—An Act for the Relief of Richard C. Murphy.

13 St. 584; July 2, 1864; C. 231—An Act for the Relief of William Sawyer and Others, of the State of Ohio.[30]

13 St. 586; July 4, 1864; C. 256—An Act for the Relief of Richard G. Murphy.

13 St. 591; July 2, 1864; J. Res. No. 71—Joint Resolution for the Relief of Thomas J. Galbraith.

13 St. 595; Feb. 9, 1865; C. 31—An Act for the Relief of Louis Roberts.

13 St. 623; June 28, 1862—Treaty with Kickapoo Indians.[31]

13 St. 663; July 30, 1863—Treaty with Shoshonee Indians.[32]

13 St. 667; Oct. 2, 1863—Treaty with Chippewa Indians. (Red Lake and Pembina Bands.)[33]

13 St. 673; Oct. 7, 1863—Treaty with Tabeguache Band of Utah Indians.[34]

13 St. 681; Oct. 12, 1863—Treaty with Shoshone-Goship Bands of Indians.[35]

13 St. 689; Apr. 12, 1864—Treaty with Red Lake and Pembina Bands of Chippewa Indians.[36]

13 St. 693; May 7, 1864—Treaty with Chippewas of Mississippi, and Pillager and Lake Winnebagoshish Bands of Chippewas.[37]

---

[25] *Sg.* 1 St. 618; 4 St. 442; 7 St. 36, 46, 51, 69, 85, 91, 99, 114, 161, 185, 188, 192, 213, 287, 296, 304, 317, 320, 349, 352, 379, 419, 425, 432, 540, 545, 582, 592, 596; 9 St. 35, 855, 878, 952; 10 St. 576, 613, 702, 1014, 1027, 1039, 1044, 1056, 1065, 1078, 1095, 1109, 1122, 1127, 1134, 1144, 1165; 11 St. 614, 623, 634, 700, 702, 729, 744, 749; 12 St. 39, 328, 528, 566, 927, 934, 940, 947, 953, 958, 964, 972, 976, 981, 997, 1238; 13 St. 668, 675, 693, 694. *S.* 14 St. 492; 41 St. 3. *Cited:* 13 Op. A. G. 354; Memo. Ind. Off., Apr. 21, 1927; Op. Sol., M. 15954, Jan. 8, 1927; Memo. Sol., July 25, 1935, Dec. 26, 1935, Sept. 15, 1936; Blackfeet, 81 C. Cls. 101; Cherokee, 11 Wall. 616; Elk, 112 U. S. 94; Fisher, 226 Fed. 156; Leighton, 29 C. Cls. 288; Medawakanton, 57 C. Cls. 357; Moore, 32 C. Cls. 593; Oakes, 172 Fed. 305; Pape, 19 F. 2d 219; Roy, 45 C. Cls. 177; U. S. v. Cass, 240 Fed. 617; U. S. v. Joyce, 240 Fed. 610; U. S. v. Leathers, 26 Fed. Cas. No. 15581; U. S. v. Paine, 206 U. S. 467; Ute, 45 C. Cls. 440.

[26] *See:* 31 U. S. C. 315b (48 St. 340, sec. 5).

[27] *Cited:* Snyder, 7 F. Supp. 597; U. S. v. Lynch, 7 Alaska 568.

[28] *Cited:* Fisher, 226 Fed. 156; 43 Cases, 14 Fed. 539; Palcher, 11 Fed. 47; U. S. v. Celestine, 215 U. S. 278; U. S. v. Leathers, 26 Fed. Cas. No. 15581.

[29] *Cited:* Fisher, 226 Fed. 156; 43 Cases, 14 Fed. 539; McKnight, 130 Fed. 659; Palcher, 11 Fed. 47; U. S. v. Celestine, 215 U. S. 278; U. S. v. Leathers, 26 Fed. Cas. No. 15581; U. S. v. Pumphrey, 11 App. D. C. 44.

[30] *Sg.* 7 St. 192.

[31] *Sg.* 10 St. 1078. *S.* 17 St. 165, 437; 18 St. 402; 22 St. 177; 23 St. 76; 24 St. 29, 219; 25 St. 217; 26 St. 336; 27 St. 120; 28 St. 286; 30 St. 571; 35 St. 70. *Cited:* 19 Op. A. G. 255; Briggs, 43 Fed. 102; Briggs, 37 Fed. 135; Elk, 112 U. S. 94; U. S. v. Reily, 290 U. S. 33.

[32] *Sg.* 18 St. 685. *S.* 14 St. 255, 492; 15 St. 198; 16 St. 13, 335, 544; 17 St. 165, 437; 18 St. 146, 420; 19 St. 176, 271; 20 St. 63, 295; 21 St. 114, 485; 22 St. 68, 433.

[33] *S.* 13 St. 161, 541, 689; 14 St. 255, 492; 15 St. 198; 16 St. 13, 335 544; 17 St. 165, 437; 18 St. 146, 420; 19 St. 176, 271; 52 St. 1212 *Cited:* Cain, 2 Minn. L. Rev. 177; Browning, 6 F. 2d 801; Chippewa, 80 C. Cls. 410; Chippewa, 301 U. S. 358; Jones, 175 U. S. 1; Minnesota, 185 U. S. 373; Morrison, 6 F. 2d 811; Perrin, 232 U. S. 478; U. S. v. 43 Gallons, 93 U. S. 188; U. S. v. 43 Gallons, 108 U. S. 491; U. S. v. Holt, 270 U. S. 49; U. S. Exp. Co., 191 Fed. 673.

[34] *S.* 13 St. 541; 14 St. 255, 492; 15 St. 198, 619; 16 St. 13, 335, 544; 17 St. 165, 437; 18 St. 146, 420; 19 St. 176, 271; 20 St. 63, 295; 21 St. 114, 485; 22 St. 68, 433; 23 St. 76, 362; 24 St. 29, 449; 25 St. 217, 980; 26 St. 336, 989; 27 St. 120, 612; 28 St. 286, 876; 29 St. 321; 30 St. 62, 571, 924; 31 St. 221, 1058; 32 St. 245, 982; 33 St. 189, 1048; 34 St. 325, 1015; 35 St. 70, 781. *Cited:* Op. Sol., M. 29798, June 15, 1938; Hayt, 38 C. Cls. 455; Thurston, 232 U. S. 469; Ute, 45 C. Cls. 440.

[35] *S.* 14 St. 255; 15 St. 198; 16 St. 13, 335, 544; 17 St. 165; 18 St. 146, 420; 19 St. 176, 271; 20 St. 63, 295; 21 St. 114, 485; 22 St. 68, 433. *Cited:* 25 L. D. 408; Blanchard, MMM.

[36] *Sg.* 13 St. 683. *S.* 13 St. 161; 14 St. 255; 15 St. 198; 16 St. 13, 335, 544, 719; 17 St. 165, 437; 18 St. 146, 420; 19 St. 176, 271; 20 St. 63. *Cited:* Chippewa, 301 U. S. 358; Chippewa, 80 C. Cls. 410.

[37] *Sg.* 10 St. 1165. *S.* 14 St. 492; 13 St. 541; 14 St. 255; 15 St. 198; 16 St. 13, 335, 544, 719; 17 St. 165, 437; 18 St. 146, 420; 19 St. 176, 271; 20 St. 63, 295; 21 St. 114, 485; 22 St. 68, 433; 23 St. 76, 362; 24 St. 29, 449; 25 St. 217, 980; 26 St. 336, 989; 27 St. 120, 612; 28 St. 286; 49 St. 321, 1757. *Cited:* Cain, 2 Minn. L. Rev. 177; 5 L. D. 541; 32 L. D. 664; Chippewa, 80 C. Cls. 410; Chippewa, 301 U. S. 358; Johnson, 234 U. S. 422; Mille Lac, 46 C. Cls. 424; U. S. v. Mille Lac, 229 U. S. 498; U. S. v. Minnesota, 270 U. S. 181.

14 STAT.

14 St. 5; Mar. 14, 1866; C. 16—An Act to establish certain Post Roads.

14 St. 14; Apr. 7, 1866; C. 28—An Act making additional Appropriations, and to supply the Deficiencies in the Appropriations for sundry civil Expenses of the Government for the fiscal Year ending the thirtieth of June, 1866, and for other Purposes.[38]

14 St. 26; Apr. 7, 1866; C. 29—An Act to provide Arms and Ammunition for the Defence of the Inhabitants of Dakota Territory.

14 St. 27; Apr. 9, 1866; C. 31—An Act to protect all persons in the United States in their Civil Rights, and furnish the Means of their Vindication.[39] Sec. 1—R. S. 690, 1978, 1992;[40] Sec. 3—R. S. 563, 629, 641, 642, 646, 699, 722; Sec. 4—R. S. 1982, 1983; Sec. 5—R. S. 1984, 1985; Sec. 7—R. S. 1986, 1987; Sec. 8—R. S. 1988; Sec. 9—R. S. 1989; Sec. 10—R. S. 699.

14 St. 191; July 23, 1866; C. 208—An Act making Appropriations for the Legislative, Executive, and Judicial Expenses of the Government for the Year ending the thirtieth of June, 1867, and for other Purposes.[41]

14 St. 218; July 23, 1866; C. 219—An Act to quiet Land Titles in California.

14 St. 236; July 25, 1866; C. 241—An Act granting Lands to the State of Kansas to aid in the Construction of the Kansas and Neosho Valley Railroad and its Extension to Red River.[42]

14 St. 247; July 25, 1866; C. 248—An Act providing for the Appointment of a Commission to examine and report upon certain Claims of the State of Iowa.

14 St. 255; July 26, 1866; C. 266—An Act making Appropriations for the Current and Contingent Expenses of the Indian Department, and for fulfilling Treaty Stipulations with various Indian Tribes for the Year ending thirtieth June, 1867, and for other purposes.[43] Sec. 2—R. S. 2097, 25 USC 122;[44] Sec. 4—R. S. 2128.[45]

14 St. 280; July 26, 1866; C. 267—An Act to establish certain Post-Roads.

14 St. 289; July 26, 1866; C. 270—An Act granting Lands to the State of Kansas to aid in the Construction of a Southern Branch of the Union Pacific Railway and Telegraph, from Fort Riley, Kansas, to Fort Smith, Arkansas.[46]

14 St. 292; July 27, 1866; C. 278—An Act granting Lands to aid in the Construction of a Railroad and Telegraph Line from the States of Missouri and Arkansas to the Pacific Coast.[47]

14 St. 307; July 27, 1866; C. 289—An Act authorizing the Reimbursement to the Territory of Nebraska of certain Expenses incurred in repelling Indian Hostilities.[48]

14 St. 309; July 28, 1866; C. 295—An Act for the Relief of the Trustees and Stewards of the Mission Church of the Wyandotte Indians.

14 St. 310; July 28, 1866; C. 296—An Act making Appropriations for sundry Civil Expenses of the Government for the Year ending June 30, 1867, and for other Purposes.[49]

14 St. 324; July 28, 1866; C. 297—An Act to supply Deficiencies

---

[38] *Cited:* Lemmon, 106 Fed. 650.

[39] *Sg.* U. S. Const. Art. 14. *S.* 16 St. 140. *Cited:* Elk, 112 U. S. 94; In re Sah Quah, 31 Fed. 327; Karrahoo, 14 Fed. Cas. No. 7614; U. S. v. Elm, 25 Fed. Cas. No. 15048.

[40] *Cited:* Farrell, 110 Fed. 942; U. S. v. Hadley, 99 Fed. 437.

[41] *Sg.* 11 St. 749.

[42] *Cited:* 13 Op. A. G. 285.

[43] *Sg.* 1 St. 618; 4 St. 442; 7 St. 36, 46, 51, 69, 91, 99, 105, 114, 161, 179, 185, 188, 191, 213, 235, 287, 296, 304, 317, 320, 327, 352, 379, 419, 425, 432, 459, 540, 545, 568, 592, 596; 9 St. 85, 842, 855, 878, 952; 10 St. 1014, 1018, 1027, 1039, 1044, 1045, 1048, 1056, 1065, 1071, 1078, 1095, 1109, 1111, 1122, 1126, 1134, 1144, 1165, 1169; 11 St. 614, 623, 634, 700, 702, 729, 744; 12 St. 927, 934, 940, 947, 953, 958, 964, 972, 976, 981, 997, 1165, 1238; 13 St. 663, 668, 675, 682, 689, 694; 14 St. 649, 667, 668, 671, 686, 695, 699, 703, 717, 723, 727, 731, 743, 747, 764, 768, 779. *Cited:* Carter, 31 C. Cls. 441; Leighton, 29 C. Cls. 288; Medawakanton, 57 C. Cls. 357; Potawatomie, 27 C. Cls. 403; U. S. v. Oregon, 103 Fed. 549; U. S. v. Seminole, 299 U. S. 417; Memo. Sol., Nov. 20, 1934.

[44] *Cited:* U. S. v. Berry, 4 Fed. 779; Eastern Band, 20 C. Cls. 449; Hauks, 3 Ind. T. 415.

[45] *Cited:* 27 Op. A. G. 588; Crabtree, 54 Fed. 432; Crabtree, 54 Fed. 426; McKnight, 130 Fed. 659; U. S. v. Celestine, 215 U. S. 278; U. S. v. Leathers, 26 Fed. Cas. No. 15581.

[46] *Cited:* 13 Op. A. G. 285; M. K. & T. Ry., 46 C. Cls. 59; M. K. & T. Ry., 92 U. S. 760.

[47] *Cited:* Atlantic, 165 U. S. 413; Bell, 63 Fed. 417.

[48] *Cited:* Litchfield, 32 C. Cls. 585.

[49] *Sg.* 14 St. 72. *S.* 17 St. 122.

in the Appropriations for the Service of the Fiscal Year ending June 30, 1866, and for other Purposes.[50]

14 St. 332; July 28, 1866; C. 299—An Act to increase and fix the Military Peace Establishment of the United States.[51] Sec. 6—R. S. 1112, 1276; 10 U. S. C. 786.

14 St. 347; Dec. 21, 1865; J. Res. No. 1—A Resolution authorizing the President to divert certain Funds heretofore, appropriated, and cause the same to be used for immediate subsistence and clothing, & c., for destitute Indians and Indian Tribes.[52]

14 St. 358; June 15, 1866; J. Res. No. 47—A Resolution making an Appropriation to enable the President to negotiate Treaties with certain Indian Tribes.

14 St. 358; June 16, 1866; J. Res. No. 48—Joint Resolution proposing an Amendment to the Constitution of the United States.[53]

14 St. 360; June 18, 1866; J. Res. No. 52—A Resolution to provide for the payment of Bounty to certain Indian Regiments.

14 St. 370; July 28, 1866; J. Res. No. 97—Joint Resolution for the Relief of certain Chippewa, Ottawa, and Pottawatomie Indians.[54]

14 St. 379; Jan. 25, 1867; C. 15—An Act to regulate the elective Franchise in the Territories of the United States. R. S. 1860.

14 St. 391; Feb. 9, 1867; C. 36—An Act for the Admission of the State of Nebraska into the Union.

14 St. 426; Mar. 2, 1867; C. 150—An Act amendatory of "An Act to provide a temporary Government for the Territory of Montana," approved May 26, 1864.[55]

14 St. 428; Mar. 2, 1867; C. 153—An Act to provide for the more efficient Government of the Rebel States.[56]

14 St. 440; Mar. 2, 1867; C. 166—An Act making Appropriations for the legislative, executive, and judicial Expenses of the Government for the Year ending the thirtieth of June, 1868, and for other Purposes.

14 St. 457; Mar. 2, 1867; C. 167—An Act making Appropriations for sundry Civil Expenses of the Government for the Year ending June 30, 1868, and for other Purposes.

14 St. 468; Mar. 2, 1867; C. 168—An Act making Appropriations and to supply Deficiencies in the Appropriations for the Service of the Government for the fiscal year ending June 30, 1867, and for other Purposes.

14 St. 492; Mar. 2, 1867; C. 173—An Act making Appropriations for the current and contingent Expenses of the Indian Department, and for fulfilling Treaty Stipulations with various Indian Tribes for the Year ending June 30, 1868.[57] Sec. 2—R. S. 2100,[58] 25 U. S. C. 127;[59] Sec. 3—R. S. 468.

14 St. 542; Mar. 2, 1867; C. 179—An Act to create the Office of Surveyor-General in the Territory of Montana, and establish a Land Office in the Territories of Montana and Arizona.

14 St. 570; Mar. 1, 1867; J. Res. No. 42—Joint Resolution authorizing the Secretary of the Interior to pay certain Claims out of the Balance of an Appropriation for the Payment of necessary Expenditures in the Service of the United States for Indian Affairs in the Territory of Utah.[60]

14 St. 581; Apr. 17, 1866; C. 49—An Act for the Relief of the Administrators and Securities of Almon W. Babbitt, late Secretary of Utah.

14 St. 604; July 27, 1866; C. 291—An Act to authorize Samuel Stevens, a Stockbridge Indian, to enter and purchase a certain Tract of Land in the Stockbridge Reservation, Wisconsin.[61]

14 St. 608; June 22, 1866; J. Res. No. 56—A Resolution for the Relief of Samuel Norris.[62]

14 St. 609; June 29, 1866; J. Res. No. 60—Joint Resolution for the Relief of Elizabeth Woodward and George Chorpenning, of Pennsylvania.

14 St. 616; Jan. 22, 1867; C. 14—An Act for the Relief of James Pool.

14 St. 618; Feb. 5, 1867; C. 33—An Act for the Relief of Captain James Starkey.

14 St. 633; Mar. 2, 1867; C. 198—An Act for the Relief of Richard Chenery.

14 St. 640; Feb. 8, 1867; J. Res. No. 13—Joint Resolution for the Relief of certain Settlers on the Sioux Reservation, in the State of Minnesota.

14 St. 647; June 9, 1863—Treaty with Nez Perce Tribe.[63]

14 St. 657; Oct. 18, 1864—Treaty with Chippewa Indians of Saginaw, Swan Creek, and Black River, Michigan.[64]

14 St. 667; Mar. 6, 1865—Treaty with Omaha Tribe.[65]

14 St. 671; Mar. 8, 1865—Treaty with Winnebago Tribe.[66]

14 St. 675; Mar. 10, 1865—Treaty (supplemental) with Ponca Tribe.[67]

14 St. 683; Aug. 12, 1865—Treaty with Woll-pah-pe Tribe of Snake Indians.[68]

14 St. 687; Sept. 29, 1865—Treaty with Great and Little Osage Indians.[69]

14 St. 695; Oct. 10, 1865—Treaty with Minneconjon Band of Dakota or Sioux Indians.[70]

14 St. 699; Oct. 14, 1865—Treaty with Lower Brule Band of Dakota or Sioux Indians.[71]

14 St. 703; Oct. 14, 1865—Treaty with Cheyenne and Arrapahoe Tribes of Indians.[72]

14 St. 713; Oct. 17, 1865—Treaty with Apache, Cheyenne, and Arrapahoe Tribes.[73]

14 St. 717; Oct. 18, 1865—Treaty with Camache and Kiowa Tribes of Indians.[74]

14 St. 723; Oct. 19, 1865—Treaty with The Two Kettles Band of Dakota or Sioux Indians.[75]

14 St. 727; Oct. 19, 1865—Treaty with the Blackfeet Band of Dakota or Sioux Indians.[76]

14 St. 731; Oct. 20, 1865—Treaty with the Sans Arcs Band of Dakota or Sioux Indians.[77]

---

[50] *Cited:* Holden, 17 Wall. 211; Ward, 17 Wall. 253.

[51] *A.* 19 St. 181.

[52] *Sg.* 3 St. 532.

[53] *Sg.* U. S. Const. Art. 14.

[54] *S.* 26 St. 24. *Cited:* Pam-to-pee, 187 U. S. 371.

[55] *Cited:* Pickett, 1 Idaho 523.

[56] *Sg.* U. S. Const., 14th Amend.

[57] *Sg.* 1 St. 618; 4 St. 442; 7 St. 36, 51, 69, 85, 99, 105, 114, 161, 179, 185, 188, 191, 212, 235, 240, 287, 296, 304, 317, 320, 327, 330, 352, 379, 432, 459, 540, 545, 592, 596; 9 St. 35, 855, 878, 904; 10 St. 1014, 1018, 1027, 1039, 1044, 1048, 1056, 1065, 1071, 1078, 1095, 1109, 1122, 1126, 1134, 1144, 1165; 11 St. 614, 623, 634, 700, 702, 729, 744; 12 St. 927, 934, 940, 947, 953, 958, 964, 972, 976, 981, 997; 13 St. 68, 558, 559, 663, 668, 673, 694; 14 St. 509, 649, 668, 683, 694, 695, 699, 704, 713, 718, 723, 727, 731, 734, 735, 738, 743, 747, 748, 764, 765, 773, 785, 793; 15 St. 797, 801. *Cited:* 12 Op. A. G. 236; Op. Sol., 26163, Oct. 8, 1930; Memo. Ind. Off., Apr. 21, 1927; Holden, 17 Wall. 211; Leighton 29 C. Cls. 288; Medawakanton, 57 C. Cls. 357; Sac & Fox, 45 C. Cls. 287; Sac & Fox, 220 U. S. 481; U. S. v. Oregon, 103 Fed. 549; Ward, 17 Wall. 253.

[58] *Cited:* Leighton, 29 C. Cls. 288; U. S. v. Berry, 4 Fed. 779.

[59] Rp. 45 St. 992, sec. 1 (81).

[60] *Sg.* 12 St. 17, 844.

[61] *Sg.* 13 St. 580.

[62] *Cited:* Belt, 15 C. Cls. 92; U. S. v. McDongall's, 121 U. S. 89.

[63] *Sg.* 1 St. 137; 12 St. 958. *S.* 14 St. 255, 492; 15 St. 198, 693; 16 St. 13, 335, 544; 17 St. 165, 437; 18 St. 146, 420; 19 St. 176; 20 St. 63; 21 St. 114, 485; 22 St. 68, 433; 23 St. 76, 362; 24 St. 29, 449; 25 St. 217, 980; 26 St. 336, 989; 27 St. 120, 612; 28 St. 286, 876; 29 St. 321; 30 St. 62, 571, 924; 45 St. 1249. *Cited:* 14 Op. A. G. 568; 17 Op. A. G. 306; Caldwell, 67 Fed. 391; Langford, 12 C. Cls. 338; Langford, 1 Idaho 612; Pickett, 1 Idaho 523; U. S. v. Lewis, 95 F. 2d 236; U. S. v. Nez Perce, 95 F. 2d 232; Woolverton, 29 C. Cls. 107.

[64] *Sg.* 11 St. 631, 633. *S.* 15 St. 198; 16 St. 13; 18 St. 420. *Cited:* 28 L. D. 310.

[65] *Sg.* 1 St. 137; 10 St. 1043. *S.* 14 St. 255, 492; 15 St. 198; 16 St. 13, 544; 17 St. 165, 437; 18 St. 146, 420; 19 St. 176, 271; 22 St. 341. *Cited:* Memo. Sol. Off., Jan. 22, 1936; Chase, 256 U. S. 1; Chase, 238 Fed. 887; Gilpin, 256 U. S. 10; Sloan, 118 Fed. 283; U. S. v. Chase, 245 U. S. 89; U. S. v. Flournoy, 69 Fed. 886; U. S. v. Omaha, 253 U. S. 275; U. S. v. Phillips, 56 F. 2d 447.

[66] *S.* 14 St. 255; 18 St. 146. *Cited:* Beck, 65 Fed. 30; U. S. v. Flournoy, 69 Fed. 886; U. S. v. Mullin, 71 Fed. 682.

[67] *Sg.* 12 St. 997. *S.* 15 St. 198. *Cited:* U. S. ex rel. Standing Bear, 25 Fed. Cas. No. 14891.

[68] *Sg.* 16 St. 707 (Oct. 14, 1864, correct date). *S.* 255, 14 St. 492; 15 St. 198; 16 St. 13, 335, 544; 17 St. 165, 437; 18 St. 146, 420; 19 St. 176, 271; 20 St. 63, 295; 21 St. 114, 485.

[69] *S.* 15 St. 110, 198; 16 St. 13, 55; 16 St. 544; 17 St. 122, 165, 437; 18 St. 146, 420; 19 St. 127, 176, 271; 20 St. 63, 295; 21 St. 114, 291, 485; 22 St. 68, 433; 32 St. 982; 36 St. 1058; 41 St. 1097. *Cited:* 19 Op. A. G. 117; Memo. Sol. Off., June 7, 1930; 6 L. D. 175; Adams, 59 F. 2d 653; Brewer-Elliott, 260 U. S. 77; Leavenworth, 92 U. S. 733; Labadie, 6 Okla. 400; M. K. & T. Ry., 152 U. S. 114; Osage, 66 C. Cls. 64; Quick Bear, 210 U. S. 50; Rogers, 45 C. Cls. 388; Stewart, 39 C. Cls. 321; Shore, 60 F. 2d 1; Thomas, 169 U. S. 264; U. S. v. Higgins, 103 Fed. 348.

[70] *S.* 14 St. 255, 492; 15 St. 198. *Cited:* Ashbaugh, 35 C. Cls. 554; Graham, 30 C. Cls. 318; Litchfield, 32 C. Cls. 585; Litchfield, 33 C. Cls. 203; Mitchell, 27 C. Cls. 316.

[71] *S.* 14 St. 255, 492; 15 St. 198. *Cited:* Graham, 30 C. Cls. 318; Journeycake, 28 C. Cls. 781; Litchfield, 32 C. Cls. 585; Litchfield, 33 C. Cls. 203; Pawnee, 56 C. Cls. 1.

[72] *S.* 14 St. 255, 492, 713. *Cited:* Litchfield, 32 C. Cls. 585; U. S. v. Higgins, 103 Fed. 348.

[73] *Sg.* 14 St. 703. *S.* 14 St. 492; 15 St. 198. *Cited:* Litchfield, 32 C. Cls. 585; Tully, 32 C. Cls. 1; U. S. v. Rogers, 23 Fed. 658.

[74] *S.* 14 St. 255, 492; 15 St. 198, 581. *Cited:* Litchfield, 32 C. Cls. 585; McKee, 33 C. Cls. 99; Swope, 33 C. Cls. 223.

[75] *S.* 14 St. 255, 492; 15 St. 198. *Cited:* Graham, 30 C. Cls. 318; Litchfield, 32 C. Cls. 585; Litchfield, 33 C. Cls. 203.

[76] *S.* 14 St. 255, 492; 15 St. 198. *Cited:* Graham, 30 C. Cls. 318; Litchfield, 32 C. Cls. 585; Litchfield, 33 C. Cls. 203.

[77] *S.* 14 St. 255, 492; 15 St. 198. *Cited:* Graham, 30 C. Cls. 318; Litchfield, 32 C. Cls. 585; Litchfield, 33 C. Cls. 203.

14 St. 735; Oct. 20, 1865—Treaty with the Yanktonai Band of Dakota or Sioux Indians.[78]

14 St. 739; Oct. 20, 1865—Treaty with Onkpahpah Band of Dakota or Sioux Indians.[79]

14 St. 743; Oct. 28, 1865—Treaty with Upper Yanktonais Band of Dakota or Sioux Indians.[80]

14 St. 747; Oct. 28, 1865—Treaty with O'Gallala Band of Dakota or Sioux Indians.[81]

14 St. 751; Nov. 15, 1865—Treaty with Confederated Tribes and Bands of Indians of Middle Oregon.[82]

14 St. 755; Mar. 21, 1866—Treaty with Seminole Nation.[83]

14 St. 763; Mar. 29, 1866—Treaty (supplemental article) with Pottawatomie Tribe.[84]

14 St. 765; Apr. 7, 1866—Treaty with Bois Forte Band of Chippewa Indians.[85]

14 St. 769; Apr. 28, 1866—Treaty with Choctaw and Chickasaw Indians.[86]

14 St. 785; June 14, 1866—Treaty with Creek Nation of Indians.[87]

14 St. 793; July 4, 1866—Treaty with Delaware Tribe.[88]

14 St. 799; July 19, 1866—Treaty with Cherokee Nation.[89]

---

[78] *S.* 14 St. 492; 15 St. 198. *Cited:* Graham, 30 C. Cls. 318; Litchfield, 32 C. Cls. 585; Litchfield, 33 C. Cls. 203.

[79] *S.* 15 St. 198. *Cited:* Graham, 30 C. Cls. 318; Litchfield, 32 C. Cls. 585; Litchfield, 33 C. Cls. 203.

[80] *S.* 14 St. 255. 492; 15 St. 198. *Cited:* Graham, 30 C. Cls. 318; Litchfield, 32 C. Cls. 585; Litchfield, 33 C. Cls. 203.

[81] *S.* 14 St. 255. 492; 15 St. 198; 22 St. 68. *Cited:* Carter, 31 C. Cls. 441; Graham, 30 C. Cls. 318; Leighton, 161 U. S. 291; Leighton, 29 C. Cls. 288; Litchfield, 32 C. Cls. 585; Litchfield, 33 C. Cls. 203.

[82] *Ag.* 12 St. 964. *S.* 46 St. 1003. *Cited:* Memo. Sol., June 15, 1937.

[83] *Sg.* 11 St. 699. *S.* 15 St. 198, 311; 16 St. 13, 335, 544; 17 St. 122, 165, 437, 626; 18 St. 146, 402, 420; 19 St. 176, 271; 20 St. 63, 295; 21 St. 114, 485; 22 St. 433; 23 St. 76, 362; 24 St. 29, 440; 25 St. 217, 757, 980; 26 St. 336, 989; 27 St. 120, 612; 28 St. 286, 876; 29 St. 321; 30 St. 62, 571, 924; 31 St. 221, 1058; 32 St. 245, 982; 33 St. 189, 1048; 34 St. 325; 35 St. 70, 781. *Cited:* 26 Op. A. G. 340; 27 Op. A. G. 530; 11 L. D. 103; Atlantic, 165 U. S. 413; Cherokee, 155 U. S. 218; Cherokee, 155 U. S. 196; Goat, 224 U. S. 458; Jackson, 34 C. Cls. 441; Seminole, 78 C. Cls. 455; U. S. v. Choctaw, 179 U. S. 494; U. S. v. Higgins, 103 Fed. 348; U. S. v. Payne, 8 Fed. 883; U. S. v. Seminole, 299 U. S. 417; U. S. ex rel. Scott, 1 Dak. 142; Woodward, 238 U. S. 284.

[84] *Ag.* 12 St. 1191. *S.* 14 St. 255, 492; 15 St. 198; 16 St. 13, 544; 17 St. 165, 437. *Cited:* Bd. of Co. Com'rs of Co. of Jackson, 100 F. 2d 929.

[85] *Sg.* 10 St. 1109. *S.* 14 St. 255, 492; 15 St. 198; 16 St. 13, 335, 544; 17 St. 165, 437; 18 St. 146, 420; 19 St. 176, 271; 20 St. 63, 295; 21 St. 114; 22 St. 68. *Cited:* Chippewa, 80 C. Cls. 410; Chippewa, 301 U. S. 358; Mullen, 224 U. S. 448; Pond, 58 Fed. 448.

[86] *Sg.* 1 St. 137, 618; 11 St. 614. *S.* 14 St. 255, 492; 15 St. 177, 531; 16 St. 13, 335, 544; 17 St. 165, 437; 18 St. 146, 420; 19 St. 176, 271; 20 St. 63; 21 St. 114, 485; 22 St. 68, 433; 23 St. 76, 362; 29 St. 321; 30 St. 495; 32 St. 641. *Cited:* Op. Sol., M. 18772, Dec. 24, 1926; 12 Op. A. G. 516; 13 Op. A. G. 354; 17 Op. A. G. 134; 17 Op. A. G. 265; 18 Op. A. G. 84; 18 Op. A. G. 141; 19 Op. A. G. 109; 19 Op. A. G. 389; 35 Op. A. G. 251; Byrd, 44 C. Cls. 498; Campbell, 44 C. Cls. 488; Cherokee, 155 U. S. 218; Cherokee, 155 U. S. 196; Chickasaw, 75 C. Cls. 426; Chickasaw, 193 U. S. 115; Choctaw, 75 C. Cls. 494; Choctaw, 81 C. Cls. 63; Choctaw, 81 C. Cls. 1; Choctaw, 83 C. Cls. 140; Ex p. Reynolds, 20 Fed. Cas. No. 11719; Fleming, 215 U. S. 56; Gilfillan, 159 U. S. 303; Glenn-Tucker, 4 Ind. T. 511; Hamilton, 42 C. Cls. 282; Hayes, 44 C. Cls. 493; Jackson, 34 C. Cls. 441; Kimberlin, 104 Fed. 653; Ligon, 164 Fed. 670; Lucas, 163 U. S. 612; M. K. & T. Ry., 46 C. Cls. 59; Morris, 194 U. S. 384; Mullen, 224 U. S. 448; Roff, 168 U. S. 218; Seminole, 78 C. Cls. 455; U. S. v. Choctaw, 38 C. Cls. 558; U. S. v. Choctaw, 179 U. S. 494; U. S. v. Payne, 8 Fed. 883; Westmoreland, 155 U. S. 545.

[87] *S.* 14 St. 492; 15 St. 198, 311; 16 St. 13, 335, 544; 17 St. 122, 165, 437, 626; 18 St. 146, 402, 420; 19 St. 176, 271; 20 St. 295; 21 St. 114 485; 22 St. 68, 433; 23 St. 76, 194, 362; 24 St. 29, 449; 25 St. 217, 757, 980; 26 St. 336; 27 St. 120, 612; 28 St. 286, 876; 29 St. 321; 30 St. 62 571, 924; 31 St. 221, 861, 1058; 32 St. 245. *Cited:* 16 Op. A. G. 31; 19 Op. A. G. 342; 25 Op. A. G. 163; 11 L. D. 103; Buster, 135 Fed. 947; Cannon, 30 C. Cls. 272; Cherokee, 155 U. S. 196; Cherokee, 203 U. S. 76; Cherokee, 155 U. S. 218; Chickasaw, 193 U. S. 115; Crabtree, 54 Fed. 432; Crabtree, 54 Fed. 426; Creek, 77 C. Cls. 159; Creek, 78 C. Cls. 474; Creek, 302 U. S. 620; Davison, 56 Fed. 443; Garrison, 30 C. Cls. 272; Jackson, 34 C. Cls. 441; M. K. & T. Ry., 46 C. Cls. 59; Muskogee, 4 Ind. T. 18; Nunn, 216 Fed. 330; Pawnee, 56 C. Cls. 1; Seminole, 78 C. Cls. 455; Turner, 51 C. Cls. 125; Turner, 248 U. S. 354; Turtle, 3 Ind. T. 712; U. S. v. Creek, 295 U. S. 103; U. S. v. Hayes, 20 F. 2d 873; U. S. v. Payne, 8 Fed. 883; U. S. ex rel Search, 3 Okla. 404.

[88] *Sg.* 7 St. 327; 10 St. 1048; 12 St. 1129. *S.* 14 St. 492; 16 St. 335; 18 St. 146; 26 St. 989. *Cited:* Delaware, 38 C. Cls. 483; Delaware, 74 C. Cls. 368; Elk, 112 U. S. 94; Kindred, 225 U. S. 582; Persons, 40 C. Cls. 411.

[89] *Sg.* 1 St. 137; 7 St. 478. *S.* 14 St. 492; 16 St. 335, 544, 727; 17 St. 98, 165, 228, 437; 18 St. 41, 146, 420; 19 St. 176; 21 St. 544; 22 St. 349; 23 St. 362; 25 St. 608, 757; 26 St. 636; 28 St. 286. *Cited:* 12 Op. A. G. 57; 16 Op. A. G. 470; 18 Op. A. G. 555; 19 Op. A. G. 173; Op. Sol., M. 27540, Sept 21, 1933; 25 L. D. 297; Adams, 59 F. 2d 653; Alberty, 162 U. S. 499; Armsworthy, 1 Fed. Cas. No. 550; Bell, 63 Fed. 417; Brewer-Elliott, 260 U. S. 77; Brown, 44 C. Cls. 283; Cherokee, 80 C. Cls. 1; Cherokee, 85 C. Cls. 76; Cherokee, 155 U. S. 218; Cherokee, 155 U. S. 196; Cherokee, 135 U. S. 641; Cherokee, 117 U. S. 294; Cherokee, 270 U. S. 476; Cherokee, 223 U. S. 108; Cherokee, 11 Wall. 616; Corralitos, 33 C. Cls. 342; Delaware, 38 C. Cls. 234; Eastern Band, 20 C. Cls. 449; Eastern Band, 117 U. S. 288; Garfield, 34 App. D. C. 70; Glenn-Tucker, 4 Ind. T. 511; Heckman, 224 U. S. 413; Holden, 17 Wall. 211; In re Mayfield, 141 U. S. 107; In re Wolf, 27 Fed. 606; Jackson, 34 C. Cls. 441; Jordan, 1 Okla. T. 406; Journeycake, 31 C. Cls. 140; Keetoowah, 41 App. D. C. 319; Labadie, 6 Okla. 400; Langdon, 14 Fed. Cas. No 8062; Lowe, 233 U. S. 95; M. K. & T. Ry., 46 C. Cls. 59; Mehlin, 56 Fed. 12; Persons, 40 C. Cls. 411; Raymond, 83 Fed. 721; Roff, 168 U. S. 218; Seminole, 78 C. Cls. 455; Stephens, 174 U. S. 445; Stroud, 23 Fed. Cas. No. 13547; Talton, 163 U. S. 376; Thomas, 169 U. S. 264; U. S. v. Aaron, 183 Fed. 347; U. S. v. Payne, 8 Fed. 883; U. S. v. Rogers, 28 Fed. 658; Ward, 17 Wall. 253.

15 STAT.

15 St. 1; Mar. 14, 1867; C. 2—An Act making Appropriations for the Expenses of Commissioners sent by the President to the Indian Country.

15 St. 7; Mar. 29, 1867; C. 13—An Act making Appropriations to supply Deficiencies in Appropriations for contingent Expenses of the Senate of the United States for the fiscal Year ending June 30, 1867, and for other Purposes.[90]

15 St. 17; July 20, 1867; C. 32—An Act to establish Peace with certain Hostile Indian Tribes.[91]

15 St. 18; July 20, 1867; C. 34—An Act amendatory of "An Act making Appropriations to supply Deficiencies in the Appropriations for contingent Expenses of the Senate of the United States for the fiscal Year ending June 30, 1867, and for other Purposes."[92]

15 St. 24; Mar. 28, 1867; J. Res. No. 16—A Resolution declaring the Meaning of the second Section of the Act of the second of March 1861, relative to Property lost in the military Service.[93]

15 St. 39; Mar. 6, 1868; C. 21—An Act for the Relief of Settlers on the late Sioux Indian Reservation in the State of Minnesota.[94]

15 St. 72; June 22, 1868; C. 69—An Act to admit the State of Arkansas to Representation in Congress.[95]

15 St. 80; June 25, 1868; C. 78—An Act appropriating Money to sustain the Indian Commission and carry out Treaties made thereby.[96]

15 St. 92; July 20, 1868; C. 176—An Act making Appropriations for the legislative, executive, and judicial Expenses of the Government, for the Year ending the thirtieth of June, 1869.

15 St. 110; July 20, 1868; C. 177—An Act making Appropriations for sundry civil Expenses of the Government for the year ending June 30, 1869, and for other Purposes.[97]

15 St. 171; July 25, 1868; C. 233—An Act making Appropriations and to supply Deficiencies in the Appropriations for the Service of the Government for the fiscal Year ending June 30, 1868, and for other Purposes.[98]

15 St. 177; July 25, 1868; C. 234—An Act for the Relief of the loyal Choctaw and Chickasaw Indians.[99]

15 St. 178; July 25, 1868; C. 235—An Act to provide a temporary Government for the Territory of Wyoming.[1] Sec. 1—R. S. 1839, 1840, 1904; Sec. 2—R. S. 1841; Sec. 4—R. S. 1846, 1847,[2] 1848, 1849,[3] 1922[4]; Sec. 6—R. S. 1842, 1857, 1925; Sec. 16—R. S. 1891; Sec. 17—R. S. 1948.

15 St. 186; July 25, 1868; C. 240—An Act to confirm the Title to certain Lands in the State of Nebraska.[5]

15 St. 198; July 27, 1868; C. 248—An Act making Appropriations for the current and contingent Expenses of the Indian Department, and for fulfilling Treaty Stipulations with various Indian Tribes for the Year ending thirtieth of June, 1869, and for other Purposes.[6]

15 St. 228; July 27, 1868; Ch. 259—An Act to transfer to the Department of the Interior, certain Powers and Duties now exercised by the Secretary of the Treasury in connection

---

[90] *Rp.* 15 St. 18.

[91] *S.* 15 St. 80; 15 St. 171. *Cited:* U. S. ex rel. Gordon, 179 Fed. 891.

[92] *Rp.* 15 St. 7, sec. 6.

[93] *Sg.* 9 St. 414; 12 St. 199.

[94] *Sg.* 12 St. 819. *S.* 16 St. 370; 17 St. 840.

[95] *Sg.* U. S. Const., Art. 14.

[96] *Sg.* 15 St. 17.

[97] *Sg.* 13 St. 63; 14 St. 688. *S.* 34 St. 325, 1015.

[98] *Sg.* 10 St. 582; 15 St. 17. *S.* 28 St. 843.

[99] *Sg.* 14 St. 780, Art. 49. *Cited:* Memo. Sol., Nov. 9, 1937.

[1] *Cited:* Fremont Co., 3 Wyo. 200; Moore, 2 Wyo. 8; Ward, 163 U. S. 504.

[2] *Rp.* 20 St. 178.

[3] *Rp.* 20 St. 178.

[4] *Rp.* 20 St. 178.

[5] *Sg.* 5 St. 453.

[6] *Sg.* 4 St. 442; 7 St. 36, 46, 51, 69, 85, 91, 99, 105, 114, 116, 161, 179, 185, 188, 191, 212, 236, 287, 296, 317, 320, 327, 352, 379, 419, 425, 432, 459, 540, 545, 596; 8 St. 592; 9 St. 35, 842, 855, 878, 904; 10 St. 1018, 1027, 1039, 1044, 1049, 1056, 1065, 1071, 1078, 1095, 1109, 1111, 1122, 1126, 1133, 1144, 1167; 11 St. 614, 623, 700, 702, 729, 744; 12 St. 628, 928, 934, 940, 946, 953, 958, 965, 972, 976, 981, 997, 1174, 1192; 13 St. 63, 663, 668, 675, 682, 689, 693; 14 St. 596, 649, 658, 668, 676, 683, 687, 696, 700, 713, 717, 724, 728, 732, 735, 739, 744, 748, 756, 763, 765, 786; 15 St. 507, 584, 590, 651, 670. *S.* 16 St. 544; 22 St. 202. *Cited:* 33 L. D. 205; Memo. Ind. Off., Apr. 21, 1927; Carter, 31 C. Cls. 441; Donnelly, 228 U. S. 243; Elk, 112 U. S. 94; Holden, 17 Wall. 211; Leighton, 29 C. Cls. 288; U. S. v. 48 Pounds, 85 Fed. 403; U. S. v. Oregon, 103 Fed. 549; Ward, 17 Wall. 253.

with Indian Affairs.[7] Sec. 1—R. S. 463, 25 U. S. C. 2. U. S. C. A. Historical Note: The derivative sections for sec. 463 of the Rev. Stat. were section 1 of Act July 9, 1832, 4 St. 564, providing for the appointment by the President of a Commissioner of Indian Affairs to act under the direction of the Secretary of War and sec. 1 of Act July 27, 1868, 15 St. 228, providing that all supervisory and appellate powers and duties in regard to Indian Affairs theretofore vested in the Secretary of the Treasury shall thereafter be exercised and performed by the Secretary of the Department of the Interior.

15 St. 234; July 27, 1868; C. 263—An Act making Appropriations for certain executive Expenses of the Government for the fiscal Year ending June 30, 1869.

15 St. 264; July 27, 1868; J. Res. No. 83—Joint Resolution to aid in relieving from Peonage Women and Children of the Navajo Indians.

15 St. 275; Feb. 25, 1869; C. 46—An Act making Appropriations (in part) for the Expenses of the Indian Department, and for fulfilling Treaty Stipulations.

15 St. 283; Mar. 3, 1869; C. 121—An Act making Appropriations for the Legislative, Executive, and Judicial Expenses of the Government for the Year ending the thirtieth of June, 1870.[8]

15 St. 301; Mar. 3, 1869; C. 122—An Act making Appropriations for sundry Civil Expenses of the Government for the Year ending June 30, 1870, and for other Purposes.

15 St. 311; Mar. 3, 1869; C. 123—An Act making Appropriations to supply Deficiencies in the Appropriations for the Service of the Government for the fiscal Year ending June 30, 1869, and for other Purposes.[9]

15 St. 327; Mar. 3, 1869; C. 131—An Act to establish certain Post-Roads.

15 St. 356; Mar. 2, 1868; C. 18—An Act for the Relief of the Heirs of the late Major-General I. B. Richardson, deceased.

15 St. 462; Mar. 3, 1869; C. 178—An Act confirming certain Purchases of Lands in the Ionia District, Michigan, made by Charles H. Rodd and Andrew J. Campeau.[10]

15 St. 467; Oct. 1, 1859—Treaty with Confederated Tribes of Sacs and Foxes of the Mississippi.[11]

15 St. 495; Feb. 18, 1867—Treaty with Tribe of Sac and Fox Indians of the Mississippi.[12]

15 St. 505; Feb. 19, 1867—Treaty with Sissiton and Warpeton Bands of Dakota or Sioux Indians.[13]

15 St. 513; Feb. 23, 1867—Treaty with Senecas, Mixed Senecas and Shawnees, Quapaws, Confederated Peorias, Kaskaskias, Weas, and Piankeshaws, Ottawas of Blanchard's Fork and Roche de Boeuf, and certain Wyandottes.[14]

15 St. 531; Feb. 27, 1867—Treaty with Pottawatomie Tribe.[15]

15 St. 539; Mar. 30, 1867—Treaty with Russia.[16]

15 St. 581; Oct. 21, 1867—Treaty with Kiowa and Comanche Tribes.[17]

15 St. 589; Oct. 21, 1867—Treaty with Kiowa, Comanche and Apache Tribes.[18]

15 St. 593; Oct. 28, 1867—Treaty with Cheyenne and Arapahoe Tribes.[19]

15 St. 619; Mar. 2, 1868—Treaty with Tabeguache, Muache, Capote, Weeinuche, Yampa, Grand River, and Uintah Bands of Ute Indians.[20]

15 St. 635; Apr. 29, et seq., 1868—Treaty with different Tribes of Sioux Indians.[21]

15 St. 649; May 7, 1868—Treaty with Crow Tribe.[22]

15 St. 655; May 10, 1868—Treaty with Northern Cheyenne and Northern Arapahoe Tribes.[23]

15 St. 667; June 1, 1868—Treaty with Navajo Tribe.[24]

15 St. 673; July 3, 1868—Treaty with Eastern Band of Shoshones and the Bannock Tribe of Indians.[25]

---

[7] *Rg.* 7 St. 385, 454. *Cited:* Op. Sol., M. 27487, July 26, 1933; Memo. Sol., July 25, 1935, June 9, 1936; Eastern Band, 20 C. Cls. 449; Jump, 100 F. 2d. 130; U. S. v. Boyd, 83 Fed. 547; U. S. v. Wright, 53 F. 2d 300.

[8] *Cited:* 8 L. D. 196; Eastern Band, 20 C. Cls. 449.

[9] *Sg.* 14 St. 756, 787. *Cited:* U. S. v. Kie, 26 Fed. Cas. No. 15528a.

[10] *Sg.* 11 St. 633.

[11] *Sg.* 1 St. 137. *S.* 15 St. 495. *Cited:* 53 I. D. 187; Brown, 32 C. Cls. 432; Pennock, 103 U. S. 44; Sac & Fox, 45 C. Cls. 287; Sac & Fox, 220 U. S. 481.

[12] *Sg.* 15 St. 467. *S.* 16 St. 13; 17 St. 626. *Cited:* Creek, 77 C. Cls. 159; Creek, 84 C. Cls. 12; Creek, 302 U. S. 620; Keokuk, 4 Okla. 5; Pennock, 103 U. S. 44; Sac & Fox, 45 C. Cls. 287; Sac & Fox, 220 U. S. 481; U. S. v. Creek, 295 U. S. 103.

[13] *Sg.* 12 St. 1037. *S.* 15 St. 198; 16 St. 13; 17 St. 281, 437; 18 St. 146, 420; 19 St. 176, 271; 20 St. 63, 295; 21 St. 114, 485; 22 St. 68; 25 St. 611; 26 St. 989. *Cited:* 18 Op. A. G. 141; Op. Sol., M. 12509, Aug. 27, 1924; Buttz, 119 U. S. 55; Farrell, 10 Fed. 942; Graham, 30 C. Cls. 318; Medawakanton, 57 C. Cls. 357; Sisseton, 42 C. Cls. 416; Sisseton, 58 C. Cls. 302; U. S. v. Sisseton, 208 U. S. 561; Northern, 8 Dak. 217.

[14] *Sg.* 7 St. 160, 424, 1159; 12 St. 1237. *S.* 16 St. 13, 335, 544; 17 St. 122, 165, 228, 388, 437; 18 St. 146, 420; 19 St. 176, 271; 20 St. 63, 295; 21 St. 114, 414, 485; 22 St. 68, 433; 23 St. 76, 362; 24 St. 29, 449; 25 St. 217, 980, 1013; 26 St. 336, 989; 27 St. 120, 612; 28 St. 286, 876; 29 St. 321; 30 St. 62, 571, 924; 31 St. 221, 1058; 45 St. 1550; 46 St. 90, 1115; 47 St. 91, 820; 48 St. 362; 49 St. 176. *Cited:* 13 Op. A. G. 336; Bowling, 223 U. S. 528; Citizen, 26 C. Cls. 323.

[15] *Sg.* 7 St. 185, 320; 12 St. 207, 1191; 14 St. 769. *S.* 16 St. 13; 20 St. 542; 23 St. 362; 24 St. 256; 25 St. 980; 26 St. 989; 44 St. 801. *Cited:* Elk, 112 U. S. 94; Goodfellow, 10 Fed. Cas. No. 5537; Laughton, 75 Fed. 789; Renfrow, 3 Okla. 161; U. S. v. Navarre, 173 U. S. 77; U. S. v. Payne, 8 Fed. 883; U. S. v. Payne, 27 Fed. Cas. No. 16014.

[16] *Cited:* 50 L. D. 315; 53 I. D. 593; 54 I. D. 39; Davis, 3 Alaska 481; In re Sah Quah, 31 Fed. 327; Kie, 27 Fed. 351; U. S. v. Berrigan, 2 Alaska 442.

[17] *Sg.* 14 St. 717. *S.* 15 St. 198, 589; 16 St. 13, 335, 544; 17 St. 5, 165, 437; 18 St. 146, 420; 19 St. 176, 271; 20 St. 63, 295; 21 St. 114, 485; 22 St. 68, 433; 23 St. 76, 362; 24 St. 29, 449; 25 St. 217, 980; 26 St. 336, 989; 27 St. 120, 612; 28 St. 286, 876; 29 St. 321; 30 St. 62, 924. *Cited:* Op. Sol., M.7002, Mar. 10, 1922; Brown, 32 C. Cls. 432; Friend, 29 C. Cls. 425; Lone Wolf, 187 U. S. 553; Okla., 258 U. S. 574; Swope, 33 C. Cls. 223; U. S. v. Andrews, 179 U. S. 96; U. S. v. Myers, 206 Fed. 387; U. S. v. Rowell, 243 U. S. 464.

[18] *Sg.* 15 St. 581. *S.* 15 St. 198; 16 St. 13, 335; 17 St. 5, 165, 437; 18 St. 146, 420; 19 St. 176, 271; 20 St. 63, 295; 21 St. 114, 485; 22 St. 68, 433; 23 St. 76, 362; 24 St. 29, 449; 25 St. 217, 980; 26 St. 336, 989; 27 St. 120, 612; 28 St. 286, 876; 29 St. 321; 30 St. 62, 924. *Cited:* Op. Sol., M.7002, Mar. 10, 1922; Brown, 32 C. Cls. 432; Lone Wolf, 187 U. S. 553; Okla., 258 U. S. 574; Tully, 32 C. Cls. 1; U. S. v. Rowell, 243 U. S. 464.

[19] *S.* 15 St. 655; 16 St. 13, 335, 544; 17 St. 5, 165, 437; 18 St. 146, 420; 19 St. 176, 271; 20 St. 63, 295; 21 St. 485, 593; 22 St. 68, 433; 23 St. 76, 362, 478; 24 St. 449; 25 St. 217, 980; 26 St. 336, 989; 27 St. 120, 612; 28 St. 286, 876; 29 St. 321; 30 St. 62, 924. *Cited:* 14 Op. A. G. 451; Memo. Sol. Off., Aug. 3, 1937; Brown, 32 C. Cls. 432; Mascarinas, 33 C. Cls. 94; U. S. v. Rogers, 23 Fed. 658.

[20] *Sg.* 13 St. 673. *S.* 16 St. 13, 335, 544; 17 St. 55, 165, 437; 18 St. 36, 146, 420; 19 St. 176, 271; 20 St. 63, 295; 21 St. 114, 199, 485; 22 St. 68, 433; 23 St. 76, 362; 24 St. 29, 449; 25 St. 217, 980; 26 St. 336, 989; 27 St. 120, 612; 28 St. 286, 876; 29 St. 321; 30 St. 62, 571, 924; 31 St. 221, 1058; 32 St. 245, 982; 33 St. 189, 1048; 34 St. 325, 1015; 35 St. 70, 781; 36 St. 269, 1058; 37 St. 518; 38 St. 77, 582; 39 St. 123, 969; 40 St. 561; 41 St. 3, 408, 1225; 42 St. 552, 1174; 43 St. 390, 1141; 44 St. 453, 934; 45 St. 200, 1562; 46 St. 279, 1115. *Cited:* 56 I. D. 330; Brown, 32 C. Cls. 432; Hayt, 38 C. Cls. 455; Thurston, 232 U. S. 469; U. S. v. Berry, 4 Fed. 779; U. S. v. McBratney, 104 U. S. 621.

[21] *Sg.* 11 St. 657. *S.* 15 St. 655; 16 St. 335, 544; 17 St. 165, 437; 18 St. 146, 402, 420; 19 St. 176, 271; 20 St. 63, 295; 21 St. 114, 485; 22 St. 68, 433, 603; 23 St. 76, 362; 24 St. 29, 449; 25 St. 94, 217, 888, 980; 26 St. 336, 989; 27 St. 120, 612; 28 St. 286, 876; 29 St. 321; 30 St. 62, 571, 924; 31 St. 221, 1058; 32 St. 245, 982; 33 St. 189 1048; 34 St. 325, 1015; 35 St. 70, 781; 36 St. 269, 1058; 37 St. 518; 38 St. 77, 582; 39 St. 123, 969, 1195; 40 St. 561; 41 St. 3, 408, 1225; 42 St. 552, 1174; 43 St. 390, 1141; 44 St. 453, 934; 45 St. 200, 1562; 46 St. 279, 1115; 47 St. 91, 820; 48 St. 362. *Cited:* 18 Op. A. G. 141; 18 Op. A. G. 230; 13 L. D. 307; 17 L. D. 457; 34 L. D. 702; 42 L. D. 192; Assiniboine, 77 C. Cls. 347; Beam, 43 C. Cls. 61; Brown, 32 C. Cls. 432; Carter, 31 C. Cls. 441; Conway, 149 Fed. 261; Ex p. Crow Dog, 109 U. S. 556; Ex p. Van Moore, 221 Fed. 954; Graham, 30 C. Cls. 318; Hatten, 99 F. 2d 501; King, 111 Fed. 860; Janis, 32 C. Cls. 407; Leighton, 29 C. Cls. 288; Medawakanton, 57 C. Cls. 357; Quick Bear, 210 U. S. 50; Reynolds, 205 Fed. 685; Roy, 45 C. Cls. 177; Sioux, 85 C. Cls. 181; Sioux, 84 C. Cls. 16; Sioux, 86 C. Cls. 299; Sully, 195 Fed. 113; Tully, 32 C. Cls. 1; Uhlig, 2 Dak. 71; U. S. v. Beebe, 2 Dak. 292; U. S. v. Knowlton, 3 Dak. 58; U. S. ex rel. Gordon, 179 Fed. 391; U. S. ex rel. Standing Bear, 25 Fed. Cas. No. 14891; U. S. ex rel. Young, 4 Mont. 38; Waldron, 143 Fed. 413.

[22] *S.* 15 St. 198, 655; 16 St. 13, 335, 544; 17 St. 165, 437; 18 St. 146, 420; 19 St. 176, 271; 20 St. 63, 295; 21 St. 114, 485; 22 St. 42, 68, 433; 23 St. 76, 362; 24 St. 29, 449; 25 St. 217, 980; 26 St. 336, 989; 27 St. 120, 612; 28 St. 286, 876; 29 St. 321; 30 St. 62, 571, 924; 31 St. 221, 1058; 34 St. 325, 1015; 35 St. 70, 781; 36 St. 269, 1058; 37 St. 518; 38 St. 77, 582; 39 St. 123, 969; 40 St. 561; 41 St. 3, 408, 1225; 42 St. 552, 1174; 43 St. 390, 1141; 44 St. 453, 807, 934; 45 St. 200, 1562; 46 St. 168, 279, 1115. *Cited:* 13 L. D. Memo. 118; Op. Sol. M. 5805, Nov. 22, 1921; Memo. Sol. Off., May 5, 1938; 5 L. D. 138; 19 L. D. 24; 48 L. D. 479; Brown, 32 C. Cls. 432; Crow, 81 C. Cls. 238; Draper, 164 U. S. 240; Truscott, 73 Fed. 60; U. S. v. Partello, 48 Fed. 670; U. S. v. Powers, 305 U. S. 527; U. S. v. 12 Bottles, 201 Fed. 191.

[23] *Sg.* 15 St. 593, 635, 649. *S.* 16 St. 13, 335, 544; 17 St. 165, 437; 18 St. 146, 420; 19 St. 176, 271; 20 St. 63, 295; 21 St. 114, 485; 22 St. 68, 433; 23 St. 76, 362; 24 St. 29, 449; 25 St. 217, 980; 26 St. 336, 989; 27 St. 120, 612; 28 St. 286, 876; 29 St. 321; 30 St. 62, 924; 31 St. 1058; 32 St. 245; 33 St. 189, 1048; 34 St. 325; 35 St. 70, 781, 907; 36 St. 269; 37 St. 518; 38 St. 77, 582; 39 St. 123, 969; 40 St. 561; 41 St. 3, 408, 1225; 42 St. 552, 1174; 43 St. 390. *Cited:* Brown, 32 C. Cls. 432.

[24] *S.* 15 St. 198; 16 St. 13, 335, 544; 17 St. 165, 437; 18 St. 146, 420; 19 St. 176, 271; 20 St. 63, 295; 21 St. 114; 35 St. 70; 38 St. 77, 582; 39 St. 123, 969; 40 St. 561; 41 St. 3 408, 1225; 42 St. 552, 1174; 43 St. 390, 1141; 44 St. 453, 934; 45 St. 200; 48 St. 960. *Cited:* 32 Op. A. G. 586; 49 L. D. 189; Brown, 32 C. Cls. 432; In re Rya-Lil-Le, 12 Ariz. 150; U. S. v. Lucero, 1 N. M. 422; U. S. v. Monte, 3 N. M. 173.

[25] *S.* 16 St. 335, 544; 17 St. 165, 437; 18 St. 146, 420; 19 St. 176, 271; 20 St. 63, 295; 21 St. 114, 485; 22 St. 68, 148, 433; 23 St. 76, 362; 24 St. 29, 449; 25 St. 217, 452, 980; 26 St. 336, 989; 27 St. 120, 612; 28 St. 286, 876; 29 St. 321; 30 St. 62, 571, 924; 31 St. 221, 672, 1058; 32 St. 245, 982; 33 St. 189, 1048; 34 St. 325, 1015; 35 St. 70, 181; 36 St. 269, 1058; 37 St. 518; 38 St. 77, 582; 39 St. 123, 969; 40 St. 561; 41 St. 3, 408, 1225; 42 St. 552, 1174;

15 St. 693; Aug. 13, 1868—Treaty (amendatory) with the Nez Perce Tribe.[26]

16 STAT.

16 St. 9; Apr. 10, 1869; C. 15—An Act making Appropriations to supply Deficiencies in the Appropriations for the Service of Government for the fiscal Year ending June 30, 1869, and additional Appropriations for the Year ending June 30, 1870, and for other Purposes.

16 St. 13; Apr. 10, 1869; C. 16—An Act making Appropriations for the current and contingent Expenses of the Indian Department, and for fulfilling Treaty Stipulations with various Indian Tribes for the Year ending June 30, 1870.[27] Sec. 2—R. S. 2090, 25 U. S. C. 132; R. S. 2101, 25 U. S. C. 138[28]; Sec. 4—R. S. 2039, 25 U. S. C. 21.[29]

16 St. 53; Apr. 7, 1869; J. Res. No. 9—A Resolution for the Relief of Settlers upon the Absentee Shawnee Lands in Kansas.[30]

16 St. 55; Apr. 10, 1869; J. Res. No. 18—A Resolution enabling bona fide Settlers to purchase certain Lands acquired from the Great and Little Osage Tribe of Indians.[31]

16 St. 59; Dec. 22, 1869; C. 3—An Act to promote the Reconstruction of the State of Georgia.

16 St. 62; Jan. 26, 1870; C. 10—An Act to admit the State of Virginia to Representation in the Congress of the United States.

16 St. 67; Feb. 23, 1870; C. 19—An Act to admit the State of Mississippi to Representation in the Congress of the United States.

16 St. 69; Mar. 5, 1870; C. 22—An Act to establish certain Post-Roads.

16 St. 80; Mar. 30, 1870; C. 39—An Act to admit the State of Texas to Representation in the Congress of the United States.

16 St. 83; Apr. 20, 1870; C. 56—An Act making Appropriations to supply Deficiencies in the Appropriations for the Service of the Government for the fiscal Year ending June 30, 1870, and for other Purposes.

16 St. 140; May 31, 1870; C. 114—An Act to enforce the Right of Citizens of the United States to vote in the several States of this Union, and for other Purposes.[32] Sec. 1—R. S. 629, 28 U. S. C. 41; R. S. 2004, 8 U. S. C. 31; Sec. 2—R. S. 629, 28 U. S. C. 41; R. S. 2005, 2006; Sec. 3—R. S. 629, 28 U. S. C. 41; R. S. 2007, 2008; Sec. 4—R. S. 629, 28 U. S. C. 41; R. S. 2009, 5506; Sec. 5—R. S. 5507; Sec. 6—R. S. 5508, 18 U. S. C. 51; Sec. 7—R. S. 5509; Sec. 8—R. S. 629, 28 U. S. C. 41; R S. 1022, 18 U. S. C. 555; Sec. 9—R. S. 1982, 8 U. S. C. 49; R. S. 1983, 8 U. S. C. 50; Sec. 10—R. S. 1984, 8 U. S. C. 50; R. S. 1985, 8 U. S. C. 51; R. S. 5517, 8 U. S. C. 51; Sec. 11—R. S. 5516, 18 U. S. C. 246; Sec. 12—R. S. 1986, 8 U. S. C. 52; R. S. 1987, 8 U. S. C. 53; Sec. 13—R. S. 1989, 8 U. S. C. 55; Sec. 14—R. S. 563, 28 U. S. C. 41; R. S. 629, 28 U. S. C. 41; R. S. 1786, 5 U. S. C. 14a; Sec. 15—R. S. 1787; Sec. 16—R. S. 563, 28 U. S. C. 41; R. S. 629, 28 U. S. C. 41; R. S. 641, 28 U. S. C. 74; R. S. 699; R. S. 1977, 8 U. S. C. 41; R. S. 2164, 8 U. S. C. 135; Sec. 17—R. S. 5510, 18 U. S. C. 52; Sec. 18—R. S. 563, 28 U. S. C. 41; R. S. 629, 28 U. S. C. 41; R. S. 699; R. S. 722, 28 U. S. C. 729; Sec. 23—R. S. 563, 28 U. S. C. 41; R. S. 629, 28 U. S. C. 41; R. S. 2010.

16 St 180; July 1, 1870; C. 189—An Act to prevent the Extermination of Fur-bearing Animals in Alaska. Sec. 1—R. S. 1960, 16 U. S. C. 647; Sec. 2—R. S. 1961, 16 U. S. C. 649; Sec. 4—R. S. 1963, 1964, 1971; Sec. 5—R. S. 1963, 1965, 1966, 1967, 1968; Sec. 6—R. S. 1963, 1969, 1970; Sec. 8—R. S. 1972.

16 St. 230; July 12, 1870; C. 251—An Act making Appropriations for the legislative, executive, and judicial Expenses of the Government for the Year ending the thirtieth of June, 1871.

16 St. 291; July 15, 1870; C. 292—An Act making Appropriations for sundry civil Expenses of the Government for the Year ending June 30, 1871, and for other Purposes.[33]

16 St. 335; July 15, 1870; C. 296—An Act making Appropriations for the current and contingent Expenses of the Indian Department and for fulfilling Treaty Stipulations with various Indian Tribes for the Year ending June 30, 1871, and for other Purposes.[34] Sec. 2—R. S. 2085, 25 U. S. C. 98; R. S. 2086, 25 U. S. C. 111.[35] USCA Historical Note: R. S. sec. 2086 was derived from sec. 11 of Act June 30, 1834, 4 St. 737, entitled "An Act to provide for the organization of the department of Indian Affairs"; sec. 3 of Act Mar. 3, 1847, 9 St. 203; sec. 3 of Act Aug. 30, 1852, 10 St. 56, being the Indian appropriation act for the fiscal year 1853, and secs. 2 and 3 instant Act. Sec. 3—R. S. 2039, 25 U. S. C. 21.[36] USCA Historical Note: The derivative sections for R. S. 2039 were sec. 4 of Act of Apr. 10, 1869, 16 St. 40, and sec. 3 of Act July 15, 1870, 16 St. 360. R. S. 2040; R. S. 2041; R. S. 2086, 25 U. S. C. 111.[37] USCA Historical Note: See sec. 2 above. Sec. 4—R. S. 2098,[38] 25 U. S. C. 126. USCA Historical Note: The Secretary of the Interior recommends that this section be repealed as present day conditions make it unnecessary. Sec. 6—R. S. 2054.

16 St. 370; Mar. 14, 1870; J. Res. No. 21—A Resolution in Relation to Settlers on the late Sioux Indian Reservation in the State of Minnesota.[39]

16 St. 377; May 15, 1870; J. Res. No. 62—Joint Resolution for the Relief of Helen Lincoln and Heloise Lincoln, and for the Withholding of Moneys from Tribes of Indians holding American Captives.[40]

16 St. 384; July 1, 1870; J. Res. No. 98—A Resolution instructing the President to negotiate with the Indians upon the Umatilla Reservation, in Oregon.

16 St. 387; July 13, 1870; J. Res. No. 110—A Resolution to pay Expenses of Delegations of Indians visiting the City of Washington.[41]

16 St. 390; July 14, 1870; J. Res. No. 118—A Resolution authorizing the Commissioner of Indian Affairs to appoint Guardians or Trustees for minor Indian Children who may be entitled to Pensions or Bounties under the existing Laws.

16 St. 401; Feb. 2, 1871; C. 32—An Act to pay two Companies of Oregon Volunteers.[42]

16 St. 404; Feb. 6, 1871; C. 38—An Act for the Relief of the

---

43 St. 390, 1141; 44 St. 453, 934, 1349; 45 St. 200, 1562; 46 St. 279, 1115. *Cited:* 49 L. D. 370; Op. Sol., M. 5386, June 19, 1923; Brown, 32 C. Cls. 432; Fremont, 3 Wyo. 200; Harkness, 98 U. S. 476; James, 88 F. 2d 431; Marks, 28 C. Cls. 147; Marks, 161 U. S. 297; Moore, 2 Wyo. 8; Shoshone, 85 C. Cls. 331; Shoshone, 82 C. Cls. 23; Skeem, 278 Fed. 93; U. S. v. Parkins, 18 F. 2d 642; U. S. v. Portneuf-Marsh 213 Fed. 601; U. S. v. Powers, 305 U. S. 527; U. S. v. Shoshone, 304 U. S. 111; U. S. ex rel. Ray, 27 F. 2d 909; Utah, Idaho, 3 Pac. 3; Ward, 163 U. S. 504.

[26] *Sg.* 14 St. 647. *Cited:* 20 Op. A. G. 42; Memo. Sol. Off., June 7, 1930; 53 I. D. 133; Langford, 12 C. Cls. 338.

[27] *Sg.* 1 St. 618; 4 St. 422; 7 St. 36, 46, 51, 69, 85, 91, 99, 105, 114, 161, 179, 185, 188, 191, 212, 236, 240, 287, 296, 317, 320, 327, 349 352, 370, 401, 419, 425, 433, 459, 540, 541, 545, 592, 596; 9 St. 35, 842, 855, 878; 10 St. 1018, 1027, 1039, 1044, 1049, 1056, 1065, 1071, 1079, 1095, 1109, 1111, 1122, 1126, 1133, 1144, 1167; 11 St. 614, 623 700, 702, 729, 744; 12 St. 539, 628, 744, 754, 928, 934, 940, 946, 953, 958, 965, 972, 976, 981, 997, 1192; 13 St. 63, 351, 663, 668, 675, 682, 689, 694; 14 St. 649, 658, 668, 683, 687, 756, 763, 765, 780, 786, 787; 15 St. 495, 506, 514, 515, 533, 581, 589, 596, 620, 622, 655, 669; 16 St 568, 708. *S.* 16 St. 635, 544; 17 St. 165, 437; 18 St. 146, 420; 19 St. 271; 20 St. 63; 21 St. 114, 259; 22 St. 433; 24 St. 29, 449; 25 St. 217, 980; 26 St. 336, 989; 27 St. 120, 612; 28 St. 286, 876; 29 St. 321; 30 St. 62, 571, 924; 31 St. 221, 1058; 32 St. 245, 982; 33 St. 189, 1048; 34 St. 325, 1015; 35 St. 70, 781. *Cited:* 33 L. D. 205; Lobenstein, 91 U. S. 324; Medawakanton, 57 C. Cls. 357; Ryan, 8 C. Cls. 265; Sac & Fox, 220 U. S. 481; Uhlig, 2 Dak. 71; U. S. v. Oregon, 103 Fed. 549.

[28] *Cited:* U. S. v. Berry, 4 Fed. 779.

[29] Superseded by Ex. Or. 6145 May 25, 1933.

[30] *Sg.* 10 St. 1053. *S.* 21 St. 377; 26 St. 652.

[31] *Sg.* 14 St. 687. *Cited:* Leavenworth, 92 U. S. 733; M. K. & T. Ry., 92 U. S. 760.

[32] *Sg.* 14 St. 27.

[33] *S.* 17 St. 530; 18 St. 402.

[34] *Sg.* 4 St. 442; 7 St. 36, 46, 51, 69, 85, 91, 99, 105, 114, 116, 161, 179, 185, 188, 191, 212, 236, 287, 296, 317, 320, 327, 349, 401, 425, 433, 459, 540, 541, 545, 576, 592, 596; 9 St. 35, 842, 855, 878, 904; 10 St. 1018, 1027, 1039, 1044, 1049, 1056, 1065, 1071, 1079, 1095, 1109, 1111, 1126, 1133, 1159, 1167; 11 St. 614, 700, 702, 729, 744; 12 St. 628, 658, 819, 928, 934, 940, 947, 953, 958, 965, 972, 976, 997, 1101, 1192; 13 St. 63, 663, 668, 675, 682, 689, 694; 14 St. 650, 683, 756, 758, 765, 772, 774, 786, 788, 796, 802; 15 St. 515, 516, 518, 584, 590, 596, 622, 636, 651, 655, 669, 674; 16 St. 40, 708, 720. *Rpg.* 16 St. 20. *S.* 16 St. 544; 17 St. 122, 165, 228, 288, 530; 18 St. 27, 146, 402, 420; 19 St. 176, 221, 271; 20 St. 63, 295; 21 St. 40, 114, 199, 485; 22 St. 68, 257, 302; 23 St. 76, 362; 24 St. 449; 25 St. 217, 980; 27 St. 120; 28 St. 286, 679, 876; 29 St. 321; 30 St. 62, 924; 31 St. 221, 1058; 32 St. 245; 33 St. 189, 1048; 35 St. 781. *A.* 16 St 544; 17 St. 90. *Cited:* 21 Op. A. G. 131; Adams, 59 F. 2d 653; Brewer Elliott, 260 U. S. 77; Delaware, 74 C. Cls. 368; Elk, 112 U. S. 94; Holden, 17 Wall. 211; Kansas, 80 C. Cls. 264; Medawakanton, 57 C. Cls. 357; Quick Bear, 210 U. S. 50; Shore, 60 F. 2d 1; Thomas, 169 U. S. 264; Thurston, 232 U. S. 469; Sioux, 86 C. Cls. 299; Sisseton, 58 C. Cls. 302; Uhlig, 2 Dak. 71; U. S. v. Boyd, 68 Fed. 577; U. S. v. Boyd, 83 Fed. 547; U. S. v. 7,405.3 Acres, 97 F. 2d 417; U. S. v. Wright, 58 F. 2d 300; Ward, 17 Wall. 253.

[35] *See:* 25 U. S. C. 474 (48 St. 987, Sec. 14).

[36] Superseded by Ex. Or. 6145, May 25, 1933, which provided that the Board of Indian Commissioners created by this section be abolished, that its affairs be wound up by the Secretary of the Interior, and that its records, property, and personnel be transferred and/or remain under the supervision of the Secretary of the Interior.

[37] *See:* 25 U. S. C. 474 (48 St. 987).

[38] *Cited:* 21 Op. A. G. 131; Ayres, 35 C. Cls. 26; Leighton, 29 C. Cls. 288; Thurston, 232 U. S. 469; U. S. v. Berry, 4 Fed. 779.

[39] *Aq.* 15 St. 39.

[40] *Cited:* Fort Berthold, 71 C. Cls. 308.

[41] *S.* 16 St. 544.

[42] *Sg.* 10 St. 807.

Stockbridge and Munsee Tribe of Indians, in the State of Wisconsin.[43]

16 St. 410; Feb. 18, 1871; C. 48—An Act to authorize the Sale of Certain Lands reserved for the Use of the Menomonee Tribe of Indians, in the State of Wisconsin.

16 St. 460; Feb. 28, 1871; C. 101—An Act to establish certain Post-Roads.

16 St. 475; Mar. 3, 1871; C. 113—An Act making Appropriations for the legislative, executive, and judicial Expenses of the Government for the Year ending June 30, 1872.

16 St. 495; Mar. 3, 1871; C. 114—An Act making Appropriations for sundry civil Expenses of the Government for the fiscal Year ending June 30, 1872, and for other Purposes.

16 St. 515; Mar. 3, 1871; C. 115—An Act making Appropriations to supply Deficiencies in the Appropriations for the Service of the Government for the fiscal Years ending June 30, 1870, and June 30, 1871, and for former Years, and for other Purposes.[44]

16 St. 521; Mar. 3, 1871; C. 116—An Act making Appropriations for the Support of the Army for the Year ending June 30, 1872, and for other Purposes.

16 St. 544; Mar. 3, 1871; C. 120—An Act making Appropriations for the current and contingent Expenses of the Indian Department, and for fulfilling Treaty Stipulations with various Indian Tribes, for the Year ending June 30, 1872, and for other Purposes.[45] Sec. 1—R. S. 2079, 25 U. S. C. 71;[46] R. S. 2107;[47] Sec. 3—R. S. 2103, 25 U. S. C. 81;[48] R. S. 2105, 25 U. S. C. 83. USCA Historical Note: R. S. 2103 was derived from a provision of sec. 3 instant Act, and from provisions of secs. 1, 2 and 3 of Act May 21, 1872, 17 St. 136, 137, which was entitled "An Act regulating the Mode of making private Contracts with Indians." Provisions of the same nature as those of this section, relating to private contracts or agreements with Indian tribes or Indians, made prior to the date of said Act May 21, 1872, were made by Act Apr. 29, 1874, 18 St. 35. That act is omitted, as temporary merely. Sec. 4 of Act Mar. 1, 1889, 25 St. 757, authorized the Secretary of the Treasury to make certain payments to the Creek Nation as directed and required by the national council of the nation, and this provision has been held (U. S. v. Crawford [C. C. Ark. 1891] 47 F. 561) to have been intended as a substitute for this sec. and sec. 82 of this title in the particular cases embraced in said sec. 4. This provision has been omitted from the Code as having been executed.

16 St. 588; Mar. 3, 1871; C. 142—An Act granting the Right of Way to the Green Bay and Lake Pepin Ry. Co. for its Road across the Oneida Reservation, in the State of Wisconsin.

16 St. 634; Apr. 12, 1870; C. 53—An Act to compensate Mrs. Fannie Kelly for important Services.

16 St. 667; June 23, 1870; Res. No. 81—A Resolution to provide for the Payment of the Claim of Martha A. Estill, Administratrix of the Estate of James M. Estill, deceased, Redick McKee, and Pablo de la Toba.

16 St. 696; Mar. 3, 1871; C. 178—An Act granting a Pension to Julia Traynor.

16 St. 704; Feb. 27, 1871; J. Res. No. 44—Joint Resolution for the Relief of Lucy A. Smith, Widow and Admin'x of James Smith, deceased.

16 St. 707; Oct. 14, 1864; Treaty with Klamath and Moadoc Tribes and Yahooskin Band of Snake Indians.[49]

16 St. 719; Mar. 19, 1867; Treaty with Chippewa Indians of Mississippi.[50]

16 St. 727; Apr. 27, 1868; Treaty (supplemental article) with Cherokee Nation.[51]

17 STAT.

17 St. 5; Apr. 20, 1871; C. 21—An Act making Appropriations to supply Deficiencies in the appropriations for the Service of the Year ending June 30, 1871, and for additional Appropriations for the Service of the Year ending June 30, 1872, and for other Purposes.[52]

17 St. 55; Apr. 23, 1872; C. 115—An Act authorizing the Secretary of the Interior to make certain Negotiations with the Ute Indians in Colorado.[53]

17 St. 61; May 8, 1872; C. 140—An Act making Appropriations for the legislative, executive, and judicial Expenses of the Government for the Year ending June 30, 1873, and for other Purposes.

17 St. 85; May 8, 1872; C. 141—An Act to provide for the Removal of the Kansas Tribe of Indians to the Indian Territory, and to dispose of their Lands in Kansas to actual Settlers.[54]

17 St. 90; May 9, 1872; C. 149—An Act for the Relief of Settlers on the Osage Lands in the State of Kansas.[55] Sec. 1—R. S. 2283; Sec. 3—R. S. 2284, 2285.

17 St. 98; May 11, 1872; C. 157—An Act to carry out certain Provisions of the Cherokee Treaty of 1866, and for the Relief of Settlers on the Cherokee Lands in the State of Kansas.[56]

17 St. 100; May 14, 1872; C. 159—An Act to Establish certain Post-roads.

17 St. 122; May 18, 1872; C. 172—An Act making Appropriations to supply Deficiencies in the Appropriations for the Service of the Government for the fiscal Year ending June 30, 1872, and for former Years, and for other Purposes.[57]

17 St. 136; May 21, 1872; C. 177—An Act regulating the Mode of making private Contracts with Indians.[58] Sec. 1—R. S. 2103, 25 U. S. C. 81;[59] USCA Historical Note: See 16 St. 544, sec. 3. Sec. 2—R. S. 2106, 25 U. S. C. 84 (See sec. 1 instant Act); Sec. 3—R. S. 2104, 25 U. S. C. 82.

17 St. 138; May 21, 1872; C. 181—An Act to authorize the Issue of a Supply of Arms to the Authorities of the Territory of Montana.

17 St. 159; May 23, 1872; C. 206—An Act to provide Homes for the Pottawatomie and Absentee Shawnee Indians in the Indian Territory.[60]

17 St. 165; May 29, 1872; C. 233—An Act making Appropriations

---

[43] *S.* 18 St. 146; 27 St. 744. *Cited:* Beecher, 95 U. S. 517; Elk, 112 U. S. 94; Shoshone, 85 C. Cls. 381; Stockbridge, 61 C. Cls. 472; Stockbridge, 68 C. Cls. 268; U. S. v. Gardner, 189 Fed. 690; U. S. v. Paine, 206 U. S. 467.

[44] *Cited:* 19 Op. A. G. 115.

[45] *Sg.* 4 St. 442; 7 St. 36, 46, 51, 69, 85, 91, 99, 105, 114, 161, 179, 185, 188, 191, 212, 236, 240, 287, 296, 317, 320, 321, 327, 349, 379, 425, 433, 459, 540, 541, 545, 592, 596; 9 St. 35, 842, 855, 875, 878, 904; 10 St. 1018, 1027, 1039, 1044, 1049, 1056, 1065, 1071, 1078, 1094, 1095, 1109, 1111, 1126, 1138, 1167, 11 St. 614, 623, 700, 702, 729, 744; 12 St. 239, 628, 928, 934, 940, 947, 953, 958, 965, 972, 976, 997, 1192; 13 St. 63, 663, 668, 675, 682, 689, 694; 14 St. 650, 668, 683, 687, 756, 758, 763, 765, 772, 786, 788, 802; 15 St. 213, 513, 515, 581, 596, 622, 636, 651, 655, 669, 676; 16 St. 40, 321, 346, 360, 361, 363, 387, 708, 720. *S.* 17 St. 226, 437; 18 St. 27, 146; 32 St. 641; 43 St. 812, 1133; 49 St. 1984. *Cited:* Brown, 39 Yale L. J. 307; Goodrich, 14 Calif. L. Rev. 83, 157; Houghton, 19 Calif. L. Rev. 507; Krieger, 3 Geo. Wash. L. Rev. 279; 58 I. D. 593; Memo. Sol., July 25, 1934; Memo. Ind. Off., Mar. 13, 1935; Op. Sol., M. 28033, June 4, 1935; Memo. Sol., Dec. 26, 1935, Jan. 23, 1937, Aug. 6, 1938; Memo. Sol. Off., Oct. 7, 1938; Op. Sol., M. 30146, Feb. 8, 1939; Blackfeet, 81 C. Cls. 101; Brown, 32 C. Cls. 432; Cherokee, 187 U. S. 294; Choctaw, 75 C. Cls. 494; Choctaw, 21 C. Cls. 59; Conway, 149 Fed. 261; Crow, 81 C. Cls. 238; Elk, 112 U. S. 94; Ex p. Crow Dog, 109 U. S. 556; Holden, 17 Wall. 211; Marks, 161 U. S. 297; Matter of Heff, 197 U. S. 488; Medawakanton, 57 C. Cls. 357; Nagle, 191 Fed. 141; New York Indians, 170 U. S. 1; Nunn, 216 Fed. 330; Scheer, 48 F. 2d 327; Uhlig, 2 Dak. 71; U. S. v. Osborn, 2 Fed. 58; U. S. v. Seneca, 274 Fed. 947; Ward, 17 Wall. 253.

[46] *See:* 25 U. S. C. 476 (48 St. 987, sec. 16); 25 U. S. C. 477 (48 St. 988, sec. 17).

[47] *Cited:* Power, 18 C. Cls. 263.

[48] *See:* 25 U. S. C. 81a (49 St. 1984, sec. 1); 25 U. S. C. 81b (49 St. 1984, sec. 2).

[49] *S.* 14 St. 683; 16 St. 13, 335, 544; 17 St. 165, 437; 18 St. 146, 420; 19 St. 176, 271; 20 St. 63, 295; 21 St. 114, 485; 22 St. 68, 433; 23 St. 76, 362; 24 St. 29; 30 St. 571; 41 St. 623. *Cited:* 12 L. D. Memo. 510, 578; 12 L. D. Memo. 703; 32 L. D. 664; California, 87 Fed. 532; Klamath, 81 C. Cls. 79; Klamath, 86 C. Cls. 614; Oregon, 202 U. S. 60; U. S. v. Klamath, 304 U. S. 119; U. S. v. Oregon, 103 Fed. 549.

[50] *Sg.* 9 St. 904; 13 St. 689, 693, 694. *S.* 16 St. 335, 544; 17 St. 165, 437; 18 St. 146, 420; 19 St. 176, 271; 20 St. 63, 295; 21 St. 114, 485; 22 St. 68, 433; 23 St. 76, 362; 24 St. 29, 449; 25 St. 217, 647, 980; 26 St. 336, 989; 27 St. 120, 612; 28 St. 286, 876; 29 St. 321; 30 St. 62, 571, 924; 31 St. 221, 1058; 32 St. 245, 982; 33 St. 189, 539, 1048; 34 St. 325, 1015; 35 St. 70, 781; 36 St. 269, 1058; 37 St. 518; 38 St. 77, 582; 39 St. 123, 969; 40 St. 561; 41 St. 3, 408, 1225; 42 St. 552, 1174; 43 St. 390, 1141; 44 St. 453, 934; 45 St. 200, 1562; 46 St. 279, 1115; 49 St. 321, 1757. *Cited:* Cain, 2 Minn. L. Rev. 177; 16 L. D. 427; 29 L. D. 408; Chippewa, 80 C. Cls. 410; Chippewa, 301 U. S. 358; Fairbanks, 223 U. S. 215; Gravelle, 253 Fed. 549; Johnson, 234 U. S. 422; Mille Lac, 46 C. Cls. 424; Morrow, 243 Fed. 854; Oakes, 172 Fed. 305; U. S. v. First, 234 U. S. 245; U. S. v. Mille Lac, 229 U. S. 498; U. S. v. Waller, 243 U. S. 452; U. S. v. Walters, 17 F. 2d 116; Woodbury, 170 Fed. 302.

[51] *Sg.* 14 St. 799. *Cited:* Eastern Band, 20 C. Cls. 449.

[52] *Sg.* 15 St. 581, 589, 593.

[53] *Sg.* 15 St. 619. *S.* 18 St. 36, 402. *Cited:* Ute, 45 C. Cls. 440.

[54] *Sg.* 12 St. 1111. *S.* 18 St. 272; 19 St. 74.

[55] *Ag.* 16 St. 362. *S.* 21 St. 40, 114. *Cited:* Hartman, 76 Fed. 157.

[56] *Sg.* 14 St. 799. *S.* 18 St. 41; 19 St. 265; 26 St. 989. *Cited:* Eastern Band, 20 C. Cls. 449.

[57] *Sg.* 14 St. 319, 688, 758, 788; 15 St. 513, 515; 16 St. 362.

[58] *S.* 18 St. 35; 30 St. 924; 32 St. 641; 37 St. 518; 43 St. 812, 1133. *Cited:* Memo. Sol., July 25, 1934; Op. Sol., M. 28033, June 4, 1935; Memo. Sol., Jan. 23, 1937, Aug. 6, 1938; Memo. Off. Sol., Oct. 7, 1938; Op. Sol., M. 30146, Feb. 8, 1939; Rollins, 23 C. Cls. 106.

[59] *S.* 31 St. 848; 33 St. 189. *See:* 25 U. S. C. 81a (49 St. 1984, sec. 1); 25 U. S. C. 81b (49 St. 1984, sec. 2).

[60] *S.* 31 St. 221, 1469; 32 St. 245. *Cited:* 11 L. D. 103; 13 L. D. 185; 13 L. D. 314; 13 L. D. 318; 20 L. D. 46; U. S. v. Payne, 8 Fed. 883.

for the current and contingent Expenses of the Indian Department, and for fulfilling Treaty Stipulations with various Indian Tribes, for the Year ending June 30, 1873, and for other Purposes.[61] Sec. 1—R. S. 2042, 25 U. S. C. 24;[62] Sec. 7—R. S. 445, 446.

17 St. 213; June 1, 1872; C. 262—An Act to authorize the Secretary of the Interior to make Partition of the Reservation of Me-shin-go-me-sia, a Miami Indian.[63]

17 St. 214; June 1, 1872; C. 263—An Act to authorize the President of the United States to negotiate with the Chiefs and Head-men of the Shoshone and Bannock Tribes of Indians for the Relinquishment of a Portion of their Reservation in Wyoming Territory.[64]

17 St. 226; June 5, 1872; C. 308—An Act to provide for the Removal of the Flathead and other Indians from the Bitter Root Valley, in the Territory of Montana.[65]

17 St. 228; June 5, 1872; C. 309—An Act to carry into Effect the fourth Article of the Treaty of February 23, 1867, with the Seneca, Shawnee, Quapaw, and other Indians.[66]

17 St. 228; June 5, 1872; C. 310—An Act to confirm to the Great and Little Osage Indians a Reservation in the Indian Territory.[67]

17 St. 258; June 6, 1872; C. 316—An Act making Appropriations for the Support of the Army for the Year ending June 30, 1873, and for other Purposes.

17 St. 281; June 7, 1872; C. 325—An Act to quiet the Title to certain Lands in Dakota Territory.[68]

17 St. 283; June 8, 1872; C. 335—An Act to revise, consolidate, and amend the Statutes relating to the Postoffice Department.[69]

17 St. 340; June 8, 1872; C. 358—An Act in Relation to Settlers on certain Indian Reservations in the State of Minnesota.[70]

17 St. 347; June 10, 1872; C. 415—An Act making Appropriations for sundry civil Expenses of the Government for the fiscal Year ending June 30, 1873, and for other Purposes.

17 St. 381; June 10, 1872; C. 424—An Act for the Restoration to Market of certain Lands in Michigan.[71] Sec. 2—R. S. 2313, 2314; Sec. 3—R. S. 2315; Sec. 4—R. S. 2316.

17 St. 382; June 10, 1872; C. 427—An Act to establish certain Post-roads.

17 St. 388; June 10, 1872; C. 430—An Act for the Relief of certain Indians in the Central Superintendency.[72]

17 St. 391; June 10, 1872; C. 436—An Act for the Relief of certain Tribes of Indians in the northern Superintendency.[73]

17 St. 395; May 7, 1872; J. Res. No. 4—Joint Resolution appointing Commissioners to inquire into Depredations on the Frontiers of the State of Texas.[74]

17 St. 397; Dec. 13, 1872; C. 2—An Act to authorize the Issuance of College Scrip to the State of Arkansas, and for other Purposes.[75]

17 St. 406; Jan. 8, 1873; C. 20—An Act to provide for the Expenses of the Commission to enquire into Depredations on the Frontiers of the State of Texas.[76]

17 St. 417; Jan. 23, 1873; C. 52—An Act authorizing the Removal of Restrictions upon the Alienation of certain Miami Indian Lands in the State of Kansas.[77]

17 St. 437; Feb. 14, 1873; C. 138—An Act making Appropriations for the current and contingent Expenses of the Indian Department, and for fulfilling Treaty Stipulations with various Indian Tribes, for the Year ending June 30, 1874, and for other Purposes.[78] Sec. 1—R. S. 467, 25 U. S. C. 266; R. S. 2046; R. S. 2052, 25 U. S. C. 26. USCA Historical Note: Instead of the words "certain Indian agents" in the Code section, R. S. 2052 contained the words "following Indian agents," enumerating the agents authorized to be appointed for specified tribes, and fixing their salaries. This provision was practically superseded by the appropriations for subsequent years, which provided for such agents in numbers and at salaries different from those authorized by R. S. 2052 varying from year to year, and the number diminishing greatly in the recent appropriation acts; the duties of the office, in many cases, having been devolved upon other offices, pursuant to a provision of Act Mar. 1, 1907, incorporated in the Code under 25 U. S. C. 66. Sec. 1 (cont.) R. S. 2053, 25 U. S. C. 64 (sec. 1, 18 St. 147; 18 St. 421). R. S. 2055; R. S. 2070;[79] R. S. 2136, 25 U. S. C. 266. Sec. 6—R. S. 2043; R. S. 2044; R. S. 2045; R. S. 2047. Sec. 7—R. S. 469; R. S. 2109, 25 U. S. C. 146.

17 St. 466; Feb. 19, 1873; C. 167—An Act to provide for the Sale of certain New York Indian Lands in Kansas.[80]

17 St. 475; Feb. 24, 1873; C. 188—An Act for the Relief of Settlers on the late Sioux Indian Reservation, in the State of Minnesota.

17 St. 484; Mar. 1, 1873; C. 217—An Act to transfer the Control of certain Powers and Duties in Relation to the Territories to the Department of the Interior. R. S. 442, 5 U. S. C. 486.

17 St. 485; Mar. 3, 1873; C. 226—An Act making Appropriations for the legislative, executive and judicial Expenses of the Government for the Year ending June 30, 1874, and for other Purposes.

17 St. 510; Mar. 3, 1873; C. 227—An Act making Appropriations for sundry civil Expenses of the Government for the fiscal Year ending June 30, 1874, and for other Purposes.[81]

17 St. 530; Mar. 3, 1873; C. 228—An Act making Appropriations to supply Deficiencies in the Appropriations for the Service of the Government for the fiscal Year ending June 30, 1873, and for other Purposes.[82]

17 St. 543; Mar. 3, 1873; C. 229—An Act making Appropriations for the Support of the Army for the Year ending June 30, 1874.

17 St. 566; Mar. 3, 1873; C. 234—An Act to revise, consolidate, and amend the Laws relating to Pensions.[83] Sec. 1—R. S. 4692, 38 U. S. C. 151; R. S. 4693, 38 U. S. C. 152; R. S. 4694, 38 U. S. C. 155; Sec. 11—R. S. 4705, 38 U. S. C. 198; Sec. 15—R. S. 4709; Sec. 16—R. S. 4710; Sec. 23—R. S. 4716; Sec. 28—R. S. 4721.

17 St. 579; Mar. 3, 1873; C. 241—An Act to provide for the Preparation and Presentation to Congress of the Revision of the Laws of the United States, consolidating the Laws relating to the Post-Roads, and a Code relating to military Offenses,

---

[61] *Sg.* 4 St. 442; 7 St. 36, 46, 51, 69, 85, 91, 99, 105, 114, 161, 179, 185, 188, 191, 212, 236, 240, 287, 296, 317, 320, 327, 349, 425, 459, 540, 541, 545, 592, 596; 9 St. 35, 842, 855, 878, 904; 10 St. 1018, 1027, 1039, 1044, 1049, 1056, 1065, 1071, 1078, 1095, 1109, 1110, 1111, 1126, 1133, 1167; 11 St. 614, 700, 702, 729, 744; 12 St. 628, 928, 934, 940, 947, 953, 958, 965, 972, 976, 997, 1101, 1192; 13 St. 624, 663, 668, 675, 682, 689, 694; 14 St. 650, 668, 683, 687, 755, 756, 758, 763, 765, 772, 785, 786, 788, 799, 802; 15 St. 515, 516, 584, 590, 594, 596, 622, 638, 651, 655, 669, 676; 16 St. 40, 359, 361, 708, 720. *S.* 17 St. 437; 18 St. 31, 146; 19 St. 102; 28 St. 679. *Cited:* Memo. Ind. Off., Apr. 21, 1927; Ayres, 35 C. Cls. 26; Brown, 32 C. Cls. 432; Butler, 38 C. Cls. 167; Campbell, 44 C. Cls. 488; Cherokee, 155 U. S. 218; Cherokee, 155 U. S. 196; Chippewa, 80 C. Cls. 410; Chippewa, 80 C. Cls. 410; Corralitos, 178 U. S. 280; In re Wolf, 27 Fed. 606; Leighton, 161 U. S. 291; Leighton, 29 C. Cls. 288; Love, 29 C. Cls. 332; Medawakanton, 57 C. Cls. 357; Nesbitt, 186 U. S. 153; Pino, 38 C. Cls. 64; Stone, 29 C. Cls. 111; Thurston, 232 U. S. 469; U. S. v. Ashton, 170 Fed. 509; U. S. v. Sandoval, 231 U. S. 28.

[62] Superseded by Ex. Or. 6145, May 23, 1933. (See Historical Note 25 U. S. C. A. 21).

[63] *Sg.* 7 St. 583.

[64] *S.* 18 St. 146, 420; 19 St. 176, 271; 20 St. 63.

[65] *Sg.* 9 St. 496; 10 St. 158, 305; 12 St. 975; 13 St. 184; 16 St. 583. *A.* 18 St. 15. *S.* 18 St. 133, 146, 420; 25 St. 871. *Cited:* U. S. v. Heyfron, 138 Fed. 964; U. S. v. Higgins, 103 Fed. 348.

[66] *Sg.* 15 St. 514, 526. *S.* 17 St. 530. *Cited:* 35 Op. A. G. 1; Op. Sol., M. 27996, May 14, 1935; Adams, 59 F. 2d 653; Brewer Elliott, 260 U. S. 77; Commissioners, 270 Fed. 110; Eastern Band, 20 C. Cls. 449; Kansas, 80 C. Cls. 264; Levindale, 241 U. S. 432; U. S. v. Aaron, 183 Fed. 347; U. S. v. Hutchings, 252 Fed. 841; Work, 266 U. S. 161.

[67] *Sg.* 14 St. 799; 16 St. 362.

[68] *Sg.* 15 St. 506. *S.* 17 St. 437; 18 St. 146, 420; 19 St. 176, 271; 20 St. 63, 295; 21 St. 114, 485; 22 St. 68. *Cited:* Butts, 119 U. S. 55; Sioux, 277 U. S. 424; Sisseton, 42 C. Cls. 416; Sisseton, 58 C. Cls. 302.

[69] *Cited:* Memo. Sol., Feb. 28, 1935.

[70] *Sg.* 15 St. 39. *Cited:* Fee, 162 U. S. 602.

[71] *Sg.* 11 St. 621. *A.* 18 St. 516.

[72] *Sg.* 12 St. 1238; 15 St. 518. *Rp.* 17 St. 628.

[73] *S.* 17 St. 510; 18 St. 146. *Rp.* 19 St. 28.

[74] *S.* 17 St. 406.

[75] *Sg.* 12 St. 503; 14 St. 208; 15 St. 227; 16 St. 116.

[76] *Sg.* 17 St. 395.

[77] *Sg.* 10 St. 1098.

[78] *Rpg.* 3 St. 517. *Sg.* 4 St. 442; 7 St. 36, 51, 69, 85, 91, 99, 105, 114, 115, 161, 179, 185, 212, 236, 240, 287, 296, 317, 320, 349, 425, 459, 540, 541, 545, 592, 596; 9 St. 35, 842, 855, 878; 10 St. 1018, 1027, 1039, 1044, 1049, 1056, 1065, 1071, 1078, 1095, 1109, 1111, 1126, 1133, 1167; 11 St. 614, 700, 702, 729, 744; 12 St. 239, 628, 928, 934, 940, 947, 953, 958, 965, 972, 976, 997, 1192; 13 St. 623, 624, 663, 668, 675, 689, 694; 14 St. 647, 668, 683, 687, 756, 758, 763, 765, 772, 786, 788, 802; 15 St. 505, 515, 520, 584, 590, 596, 622, 638, 651, 655, 669, 676; 16 St. 40, 544, 570, 708, 720; 17 St. 179, 188, 281; 18 St. 685, 689. *Rp.* 18 St. 420; 36 St. 855. *S.* 17 St. 530; 18 St. 133, 146, 420; 19 St. 176, 271; 20 St. 295; 21 St. 114, 485. *Cited:* Memo. Sol., Feb 4, 1938; Belknap, 150 U. S. 588; Buttz, 119 U. S. 55; Choctaw, 21 C. Cls. 59; Eastern Band, 20 C. Cls. 449; Jump, 100 F. 2d 130; Kansas, 80 C. Cls. 264; Medawakanton, 57 C. Cls. 357; Sioux, 277 U. S. 424; U. S. v. Wirt, 28 Fed. Cas. No. 16745; Ute, 45 C. Cls. 440.

[79] *Cited:* U. S. v. Mitchell, 109 U. S. 146.

[80] *S.* 18 St. 273. *A.* 20 St. 36.

[81] *Sg.* 17 St. 391. *Cited:* U. S. v. Warwick, 51 Fed. 280.

[82] *Sg.* 16 St. 310, 362; 17 St. 228, 462. *S.* 18 St. 146. *Cited:* Adams, 59 F. 2d 653; Brewer Elliott, 260 U. S. 77; Chippewa, 80 C. Cls. 410; In re Carr, 5 Fed. Cas. No. 2432; In re Sah Quah, 31 Fed. 327; Kansas, 80 C. Cls. 264; Medawakanton, 57 C. Cls. 357; Kie, 27 Fed. 351; U. S. v. Aaron, 183 Fed. 347; U. S. v. Stephens, 12 Fed. 52; Waters, 29 Fed. Cas. No. 17264; Waters, 29 Fed. Cas. No. 17265.

[83] *R.* 27 St. 281. *Cited:* Elk, 112 U. S. 94.

and the Revision of Treaties with the Indian Tribes now in Force.

17 St. 586; Mar. 3, 1873; C. 255—An Act to establish certain Post-Roads.[84]

17 St. 613; Mar. 3, 1873; C. 294—An Act to enable the Secretary of War to pay the Expenses incurred in suppressing the Indian Hostilities in the Territory of Montana, in the Year 1867.

17 St. 623; Mar. 3, 1873; C. 317—An Act for the temporary Relief of the Indians at Camp McDermit, in Humboldt County, Nevada.

17 St. 623; Mar. 3, 1873; C. 319—An Act repealing an Act entitled "An Act for the Relief of certain Indians in the Central Superintendency" approved June 10, 1872.[85] An Act supplemental to an Act entitled "An Act for the Relief of certain Indians in the Central Superintendency" approved June 10, 1872, and to settle by Commission all Rights and Equities respecting the Property to which said Act refers.

17 St. 626; Mar. 3, 1873; C. 321—An Act to authorize the Secretary of the Interior to negotiate with the Chiefs and Headmen of the Crow Tribe of Indians, for the Surrender of their Reservation or a Part thereof in the Territory of Montana.

17 St. 626; Mar. 3, 1873; C. 322—To authorize the Secretary of the Interior to negotiate with the Creek Indians for the Cession of a Portion of their Reservation, occupied by friendly Indians.[86]

17 St. 627; Mar. 3, 1873; C. 324—An Act to enable the Commissioner of Indian Affairs to purchase and pay for certain Improvements within the Nez Perce Indian Reservation in the Territory of Idaho.[87]

17 St. 631; Mar. 3, 1873; C. 332—An Act to abolish the tribal Relations of the Miami Indians, and for other Purposes.[88]

17 St. 633; Mar. 3, 1873; C. 333—An Act to restore a Part of the Round Valley Indian Reservation, in California, to the public Lands and for other Purposes.[89]

17 St. 661; May 21, 1872; C. 190—An Act for the Relief of Charles F. Tracy.

17 St. 675; June 5, 1872; C. 314—An Act for the Relief of Mrs. Fanny Kelly.

17 St. 680; June 8, 1872; C. 380—An Act for the Relief of Albert D. Pierce, Postmaster at Sumnerville, Ottawa County, Kansas.

17 St. 690; June 10, 1872; C. 442—An Act for the Relief of Jane Allen Birckhead and Virginia Campbell, sole Heirs at Law of Alexander Watson, deceased.

17 St. 701; June 10, 1872; C. 457—An Act for the Relief of Elbridge Gerry.

17 St. 703; June 10, 1872; C. 468—An Act for the Relief of William J. Clark, Adm'r of Gad E. Upson, deceased.

17 St. 703; June 10, 1872; C. 469—An Act for the Relief of Dwight J. McCann.

17 St. 730; Feb. 14, 1873; C. 143—An Act for the Relief of J. and C. M. Dailey.

17 St. 730; Feb. 14, 1873; C. 144—An Act relating to the Claim of John B. Chapman.

17 St. 730; Feb. 14, 1873; C. 145—An Act for the Relief of S. E. Ward.

17 St. 732; Feb. 17, 1873; C. 158—An Act for the Relief of R. H. Pratt.

17 St. 739; Mar. 1, 1873; C. 221—An Act to authorize the accounting Officers of the Treasury to settle the Accounts of Charles T. Brown and J. J. S. Hassler, late Agents for the Chippewa Indians of Minnesota, on the Grounds of Equity and Justice.

17 St. 766; Mar. 3, 1873; C. 348—An Act for the Relief of Mrs. Ann Marble, (now Strong,) Adm'x.

17 St. 787; Mar. 3, 1873; C. 449—An Act to authorize the Secretary of the Interior to settle the Claims of Messrs. Durfee and Peck and E. H. Durfee for Supplies furnished the Indians in Montana in the Winter of 1869.

17 St. 787; Mar. 3, 1873; C. 450—An Act for the Relief of John L. Pendery, surviving Partner of Pendery and Gamble, Attorneys.

---

[84] *Cited:* Op. Sol., M. 11880, June 17, 1924.

[85] *Rpg.* 17 St. 388.

[86] *Sg.* 14 St. 756, 786; 15 St. 496. *S.* 22 St. 257. *Cited:* Goat, 224 U. S. 458.

[87] *Sg.* 12 St. 960. *Cited:* Caldwell, 67 Fed. 391.

[88] *Sg.* 10 St. 1093; 11 St. 332. *S.* 18 St. 278; 19 St. 271; 22 St. 63, 68. *Cited:* Bowling, 233 U. S. 528; Elk, 112 U. S. 94.

[89] *S.* 26 St. 658.

18 STAT.

18 St. 7; Feb. 4, 1874; C. 21—An Act to establish certain post-routes.

18 St. 15; Feb. 11, 1874; C. 25—An act to amend the act entitled "An act to provide for the removal of the Flathead and other Indians from the Bitterroot Valley, in the Territory of Montana," approved June 5, 1872.[90]

18 St. 17; Feb. 20, 1874; C. 32—An act to authorize the Secretary of War to ascertain the amount of expense incurred by the territorial authorities of Dakota for arms, equipments, military stores, supplies, and all other expenses of the volunteer forces of the Indian war of 1862.

18 St. 27; Apr. 3, 1874; C. 77—An act appropriating certain unexpended balances of appropriations for removal of Indians.[91]

18 St. 28; Apr. 15, 1874; C. 96—An act to establish a reservation for certain Indians in the Territory of Montana.[92]

18 St. 29; Apr. 15, 1874; C. 97—An act authorizing the payment of annuities into the treasury of the Seminole tribe of Indians.[93]

18 St. 31; Apr. 18, 1874; C. 111—An act to secure to the Domestic and Foreign Missionary Society of the Protestant Episcopal Church in the United States the land in the White Earth Indian reservation in Minnesota, on which is situated their church and other buildings.

18 St. 31; Apr. 18, 1874; C. 112—An act to authorize the use of certain unexpended balance for payment of expenses of Board of Indian Commissioners.[94]

18 St. 33; Apr. 22, 1874; C. 122—An act to enable the Secretary of the Treasury to gather authentic information as to the condition and importance of the fur-trade in the Territory of Alaska.

18 St. 35; Apr. 29, 1874; C. 135—An act relative to private contracts or agreements made with Indians prior to May 21, 1872.[95]

18 St. 36; Apr. 29, 1874; C. 136—An act to ratify an agreement with certain Ute Indians in Colorado, and to make an appropriation for carrying out the same.[96]

18 St. 41; Apr. 29, 1874; C. 137—An act for the relief of settlers on the Cherokee strip in Kansas.[97]

18 St. 46; May 15, 1874; C. 176—An act giving the assent of Congress for the improvement of the Wolf River across the Menomonee Indian reservation, in the State of Wisconsin.

18 St. 47; May 16, 1874; C. 181—An act to authorize the Secretary of the Interior to discharge certain obligations of the United States to the creditors of the Upper and Lower Bands of Sioux Indions.[98]

18 St. 51; June 3, 1874; C. 205—An act to provide for the better protection of the frontier settlements of Texas against Indian and Mexican depredations.[99]

18 St. 52; June 3, 1874; C. 206—An act to extend the time to pre-emptors on the public lands in the State of Minnesota, to make final payment.

18 St. 72; June 16, 1874; C. 285—An Act making appropriations for the support of the Army for the fiscal year ending June 30, 1875, and for other purposes.[1]

18 St. 83; June 18, 1874; C. 313—An act to authorize the Secretary of War to ascertain the amount of expenses incurred by the States of Oregon and California in the suppression of Indian hostilities in the years 1872 and 1873.

18 St. 85; June 20, 1874; C. 328—An act making appropriations for the legislative, executive, and judicial expenses of the Government for the year ending June 30, 1875, and for other purposes.

18 St. 113; June 20, 1874; C. 333—An act providing for publication of the revised statutes and the laws of the United States.[2]

18 St. 133; June 22, 1874; C. 388—An act making appropriations to supply deficiencies in the appropriations for the service

---

[90] *Sg.* 17 St. 226. *R.* 26 St. 1095.

[91] *Sg.* 16 St. 190, 359, 569.

[92] *S.* 24 St. 402; 25 St. 113; 44 St. 807; 46 St. 531. *Cited:* Assiniboine, 77 C. Cls. 347; British-American, 299 U. S. 159; Crow, 81 C. Cls. 238; Winters, 207 U. S. 564.

[93] *Sg.* 11 St. 702, art. 8.

[94] *Sg.* 17 St. 186.

[95] *Sg.* 17 St. 136. *Rn.* 21 St. 109. *S.* 30 St. 924; 31 St. 848; 32 St. 641; 33 St. 189; 37 St. 518; 43 St. 812, 1138; 49 St. 1984.

[96] *Sg.* 15 St. 619; 17 St. 55. *S.* 18 St. 420; 19 St. 271; 41 St. 408. *Cited:* 56 I. D. 330; Ute, 45 C. Cls. 440.

[97] *Sg.* 14 St. 799; 17 St. 98.

[98] *Sg.* 12 St. 1038. *Cited:* Medawakanton, 57 C. Cls. 357.

[99] *S.* 19 St. 102; 19 St. 344.

[1] *Cited:* Hanks, 3 Ind. T. 415.

[2] *S.* 19 St. 268.

of the Government for the fiscal years ending June 30, 1873 and 1874, and for other purposes.[3]

18 St. 146; June 22, 1874; C. 389—An act making appropriations for the current and contingent expenses of the Indian Department, and for fulfilling treaty stipulations with various Indian tribes, for the year ending June 30, 1875, and for other purposes.[4] Sec. 1—p. 147, R. S. 2053; 25 U. S. C. 64 (17 St. 437, Sec. 1; 18 St. 421); Sec. 10—25 U. S. C., 87.[5]

18 St. 204; June 23, 1874; C. 455—An act making appropriations for sundry civil expenses of the Government for the fiscal year ending June 30, 1875, and for other purposes.[6]

18 St. 256; June 23, 1874; C. 470—An act to establish certain post-routes.

18 St. 272; June 23, 1874; C. 471—An act providing for the sale of the Kansas Indian lands in Kansas to actual settlers, and for the disposition of the proceeds of the sale.[7]

18 St. 273; June 23, 1874; C. 472—An act to further provide for the sale of certain Indian lands in Kansas.[8]

18 St. 283; June 23, 1874; C. 488—An act to extend the time for completing entries of Osage Indian lands in Kansas.

18 St. 291; Dec. 15, 1874; C. 2—An act to confirm an agreement made with the Shoshone Indians (eastern band) for the purchase of the south part of their reservation in Wyoming Territory.[9]

18 St. 295; Jan. 11, 1875; C. 14—An act explanatory of the resolution entitled "A resolution for the relief of settlers upon the Absentee Shawnee lands in Kansas," approved April 7, 1869.[10]

18 St. 316; Feb. 18, 1875; C. 80—An act to correct errors and to supply omissions in the Revised Statutes of the United States.[11] Sec. 1—R. S. 2146, 25 U. S. C. 218. USCA Historical Note: R. S. 2146 was derived from sec. 3 of Act Mar. 27, 1854, 10 St. 270, with the exception of the words "crimes committed by one Indian against the person or property of another Indian, nor to." Said words were inserted by amendment, making the section read as set forth here, by Act Feb. 18, 1875, sec. 1, 18 St. 316. Indians committing any of seven crimes specified, if committed within a Territory, were made subject to the laws of the Territory, and if committed within an Indian reservation in any State were made subject to the same laws as persons committing any of said crimes within the exclusive jurisdiction of the United States, by the Seven Crimes Act, Act Mar. 3, 1885, s. 9, 23 St. 385, sec. 548 of Tit. 18, Criminal Code and Criminal Procedure. See historical note under section 212 of this title.

18 St. 330; Feb. 19, 1875; C. 90—An act to authorize the Seneca Nation of New York Indians to lease lands within the Cattaraugus and Allegany reservations, and to confirm existing leases.[12]

18 St. 335; Mar. 1, 1875; C. 114—An act to protect all citizens in their civil and legal rights.[13]

18 St. 343; Mar. 3, 1875; C. 129—An act making appropriations for the legislative, executive, and judicial expenses of the Government for the year ending June 30, 1876, and for other purposes.

18 St. 371; Mar. 3, 1875; C. 130—An Act making appropriations for sundry civil expenses of the Government for the fiscal year ending June 30, 1876, and for other purposes.[15]

18 St. 402; Mar. 3, 1875; C. 131—An act making appropriations to supply deficiencies in the appropriations for fiscal years ending June 30, 1875, and prior years, and for other purposes.[16] Sec. 5—43 U. S. C. 938.

18 St. 420; Mar. 3, 1875; C. 132—An act making appropriations for the current and contingent expenses of the Indian Department, and for fulfilling treaty-stipulations with various Indian tribes, for the year ending June 30, 1876, and for other purposes.[17] Sec. 1—p. 421, R. S. 2053, 25 U. S. C. 64 (17 St. 437, Sec. 1, 18 St. 147, sec. 1); p. 424, 25 U. S. C. 129; Sec. 2—25 U. S. C. 128; Sec. 3—25 U. S. C. 137; Sec. 4—25 U. S. C. 133. USCA Historical Note: A provision similar to this section, but only "for the purpose of properly distributing the supplies appropriated for" in the similar appropriation act for the fiscal year 1878, was made by Sec. 2 of said act, Act Mar. 3, 1877, 19 St. 293. Sec. 5—See Historical Note 25 U. S. C. A. 37. Sec. 6—25 U. S. C. 135. USCA Historical Note: A provision made by Act June 7, 1897, Sec. 11, 30 St. 93, "That hereafter, where funds appropriated in specific terms for particular object are not sufficient for the object named, any other appropriation, general in its terms, which otherwise would be available may, in the discretion of the Secretary of the Interior, be used to accomplish the object for which the specific appropriation was made," was repealed by Act Mar. 3, 1911, sec. 1, 36 St. 1062. Sec. 7—25 U. S. C. 96 (28 St. 205, 206, secs. 3, 7; 42 St. 24, sec. 304). See USCA Historical Note for 39 St. 129. Sec. 9—25 U. S. C. 95 (39 St. 129, sec. 1).[18] USCA Historical Note: By a provision of sec. 1 of 39 St. 129, sec. 9, 18 St. 450 was amended to read as set forth in the Code section. A provision similar to the original sec. 9, except in the use of the words "or solvent national bank" in place of the words "or some one of such solvent national banks as the Secretary of the Interior may designate," was contained in the Indian Appropriation Act of June 22, 1874, sec. 6, 18 St. 176, for the fiscal year 1875. Sec. 10—25 U. S. C. 37 (35 St. 784). See U. S. C. A. Historical Note secs. 29 and 37.

18 St. 452; Mar. 3, 1875; C. 133—An act making appropriations for the support of the Army for the fiscal year ending June 30, 1876, and for other purposes.

18 St. 474; Mar. 3, 1875; C. 139—An act to enable the people of Colorado to form a constitution and State government, and for the admission of the said State into the Union on an equal footing with the original States.[19]

18 St. 476; Mar. 3, 1875; C. 140—An act to establish the boundary-line between the State of Arkansas and the Indian country.[20]

18 St. 482; Mar. 3, 1875; C. 152—An act granting to railroads the

---

[3] *Sg.* 10 St. 1109; 17 St. 227, 440, 463. *S.* 21 St. 114. *Cited:* Medawakanton, 57 C. Cls. 357.

[4] *Sg.* 4 St. 442; 6 St. 904; 7 St. 36, 44, 51, 69, 85, 91, 99, 105, 114, 115, 161, 179, 185, 191, 213, 236, 240, 287, 296, 317, 320, 327, 349, 352, 419, 425, 459, 540, 541, 545, 592, 596; 9 St. 842, 878, 904; 10 St. 1019, 1039, 1044, 1049, 1056, 1065, 1071, 1078, 1095, 1098, 1110, 1111, 1126, 1133, 1144, 1167; 11 St. 35, 614, 700, 702, 729, 744; 12 St. 628, 928, 940, 947, 953, 958, 965, 972, 976, 977, 981, 982, 997, 1172, 1173; 13 St. 663, 668, 681, 682, 684, 689, 694; 14 St. 650, 668, 671, 675, 683, 687, 756, 758, 765, 766, 772, 774, 786, 788, 796, 802; 15 St. 506, 514, 515, 584, 590, 596, 622, 635, 638, 651, 657, 669, 675, 676; 16 St. 40, 359, 362, 404, 568, 673, 678, 708, 720; 17 St. 165, 189, 214, 227, 281, 391, 392, 405, 456, 473, 539; Sen. Res. Jan. 9, 1938. *S.* 18 St. 420; 19 St. 176, 271; 20 St. 63, 295; 21 St. 114, 315, 485; 22 St. 68; 43 St. 793; 46 St. 793. *Cited:* Belknap, 150 U. S. 588; Delaware, 74 C. Cls. 368; Medawakanton, 57 C. Cls. 357; Sioux, 277 U. S. 424; Sisseton, 42 C. Cls. 416; Sisseton, 58 C. Cls. 302; Stockbridge, 61 C. Cls. 472; U. S. v. Sandoval, 231 U. S. 28.

[5] *See:* 25 U. S. C. 87a (53 St. 840).

[6] *Sg.* 11 St. 614. *S.* 19 St. 271. *Cited:* Choctaw, 119 U. S. 1; Sioux, 85 C. Cls. 181; U. S. v. Boyd, 68 Fed. 577; U. S. v. Boyd, 83 Fed. 547.

[7] *Sg.* 12 St. 1111; 17 St. 85. *S.* 21 St. 68. *Cited:* Kansas, 80 C. Cls. 264.

[8] *Sg.* 17 St. 466, 631.

[9] *S.* 45 St. 1407. *Cited:* 49 L. D. 370; Shoshone, 82 C. Cls. 23.

[10] *S.* 26 St. 652, c. 1265; 30 St. 234.

[11] *Ag.* 10 St. 270. *Cited:* Rice, 16 J. Comp. Leg. 78; Memo. Sol., Nov. 17, 1936. Bailey, 47 F. 2d 702; Ex p. Crow Dog, 109 U. S. 556; Ex p. Hart, 157 Fed. 130; In re Camille, 6 Fed. 256; In re Mayfield, 141 U. S. 104; U. S. v. Seneca, 274 Fed. 947; U. S. ex rel. Scott, 1 Dak. 142.

[12] *S.* 19 St. 102; 22 St. 432. *A.* 26 St. 558. *Cited:* 18 Op. A. G. 235; Benson, 44 Fed. 178.

[13] *S.* 21 St. 199.

[15] *Sg.* 12 St. 198. *S.* 19 St. 102, 344; 20 St. 206; 22 St. 302.

[16] *Sg.* 9 St. 264; 10 St. 1078; 12 St. 392; 13 St. 628; 14 St. 755, 785; 15 St. 635; 16 St. 310, 362; 17 St. 55. *Cited:* 26 L. D. 71; 31 L. D. 417; 35 L. D. 80; 48 L. D. 567; Lanham, 244 U. S. 582; Taylor, 147 U. S. 640; U. S. v. Boyd, 83 Fed. 547; U. S. v. Cass, 240 Fed. 617; U. S. v. Corporation, 101 F. 2d 156; U. S. v. Hemmer, 241 U. S. 379; U. S. v. Joyce, 240 Fed. 610; U. S. ex rel. Besaw, 6 F. 2d 694.

[17] *Sg.* 4 St. 442; 7 St. 36, 44, 51, 69, 85, 91, 99, 105, 114, 115, 161, 179, 185, 213, 236, 240, 287, 296, 317, 320, 327, 349, 352, 425, 540, 541, 545, 591, 592, 596; 9 St. 35, 264, 587, 842, 853, 855, 904; 10 St. 1039, 1040, 1043, 1049, 1056, 1065, 1071, 1078, 1093, 1095, 1110, 1111, 1167; 11 St. 614; 700, 702, 729, 744; 12 St. 540, 628, 928, 934, 940, 947, 953, 958, 972, 977, 981, 997, 1172, 1173; 13 St. 663, 668, 675, 682, 689, 694; 14 St. 650, 658, 668, 683, 687, 756, 758, 765, 766, 772, 774, 786, 788, 802; 15 St. 506, 514, 515, 584, 590, 596, 622, 635, 638, 651, 657, 669, 675, 676; 16 St. 34, 40, 362, 708, 720; 17 St. 214, 227, 281, 456; 18 St. 36, 146, 158, 167, 686, 690; Unpub'd. treaty with Chickasaws, Feb. 25, 1799; Agreement with Shawnees, June 23, 1874; Ex. Or., Nov. 9, 1855; Ex. Or., Dec. 21, 1865. *Rg.* 17 St. 437, sec. 6. *Rpg.* 18 St. 160. *S.* 19 St. 176; 20 St. 63, 295; 21 St. 114, 315; 22 St. 68; 31 St. 848; 32 St. 641; 33 St. 189; 35 St. 781; 39 St. 123; 43 St. 812, 1133; 49 St. 1984. *Rp.* 36 St. 855. *Cited:* 18 Op. A. G. 41; 18 Op. A. G. 557; 19 Op. A. G. 161; 19 Op. A. G. 559; 48 L. D. 567; 11 L. D. Memo. 296; Sol. Op. M. 15954, Jan. 8, 1927; Memo. of Comm'r., Jan. 6, 1937; Memo. Sol., Mar. 6, 1937, Mar. 19, 1938; Belknap, 150 U. S. 588; Coos, 87 C. Cls. 143; Eastern Band, 20 C. Cls. 449; Elk, 112 U. S. 94; Halbert, 283 U. S. 753; Jump, 100 F. 2d 130; Lanham, 244 U. S. 582; Medawakanton, 57 C. Cls. 357; Oakes, 172 Fed. 305; Pape, 19 F. 2d 219; Seaples, 246 Fed. 501; Sioux, 277 U. S. 424; Sisseton, 58 C. Cls. 302; Smith, 87 C. Cls. 119; U. S. v. Cain-Benness, 215 Fed. 212; U. S. v. Cass, 240 Fed. 617; U. S. v. Corporation, 101 F. 2d 156; U. S. v. Hemmer, 241 U. S. 379; U. S. v. Johnson, 53 F. 2d 267; U. S. v. Joyce, 240 Fed. 610; U. S. v. Patrick, 73 Fed. 800; U. S. v. Smith, 35 Fed. 490; U. S. v. Stowe, 19 Fed. 807; U. S. v. Swain, 46 F. 2d 99; U. S. v. Wright, 53 F. 2d 300; U. S. ex rel. Kadrie, 30 F. 2d 989.

[18] *R.* 53 St. 551.

[19] *Cited:* Canfield, 15 Am. L. Rev. 21; Goodson v. U. S., 7 Okla. 117; U. S. v. Berry, 4 Fed. 779; U. S. v. McBratney, 104 U. S. 621.

[20] *S.* 19 St. 344.

right of way through the public lands of the United States.[21]

18 St. 486; Mar. 3, 1875; C. 158—An act to establish certain post-roads.

18 St. 516; Mar. 3, 1875; C. 188—An act to amend the act entitled "An act for the restoration to homestead-entry and to market of certain lands in Michigan," approved June 10, 1872, and for other purposes.[22]

18 St. 535; Apr. 11, 1874; C. 84—An act for the relief of Robert Bent and Jack Smith.[23]

18 St. 543; Apr. 28, 1874; C. 133—An act for the relief of Siloma Deck.

18 St. 555; June 3, 1874; C. 212—An act for the relief of Henry A. Webster, V. B. McCollum, and A. Colby, of Washington Territory, pre-emptors on the Makah Indian Reservation.

18 St. 568; June 17, 1874; C. 296—An act for the relief of John M. McPike.

18 St. 685; July 2, 1863—Treaty with Eastern Bands of Shoshonee Indians.[24]

18 St. 689; Oct. 1, 1863—Treaty with Western Bands of Shoshonee Indians.[25]

19 STAT.

19 St. 12; Apr. 3, 1876; C. 42—An act establishing postroads.

19 St. 28; Apr. 6, 1876; C. 47—An act to supply a deficiency in the appropriations for certain Indians.

19 St. 28; Apr. 10, 1876; C. 51—An act to authorize the sale of the Pawnee Reservation.[26]

19 St. 37; Apr. 25, 1876; C. 79—An act authorizing the sale of logs cut by the Indians of the Menomonee reservation in Wisconsin under the direction of the Interior Department.

19 St. 41; May 1, 1876; C. 88—An act making appropriations to supply deficiencies in the appropriations for the fiscal years ending June 30, 1876, and for prior years, and for other purposes.[27]

19 St. 53; May 9, 1876; C. 94—An act appropriating $50,000 for subsistence supplies for Apache Indians in Arizona Territory, and for the removal of the Indians of the Chiricahau Agency to San Carlos Agency.

19 St. 55; May 23, 1876; C. 104—An act to extend the time to pre-emptors on the public lands.[28]

19 St. 55; May 23, 1876; C. 105—An act extending the time within which homestead entries upon certain lands in Michigan may be made.[29]

19 St. 58; June 10, 1876; C. 122—An act transferring the custody of certain Indian trust-funds.[30] 25 U. S. C. 160.

19 St. 74; July 5, 1876; C. 168—An act providing for the sale of the Kansas Indian lands in Kansas to actual settlers, and for the disposition of the proceeds of the sale.[31]

19 St. 88; July 12, 1876; C. 182—An act to authorize the Commissioner of Indian Affairs to purchase supplies for the Indian Bureau in open market.

19 St. 89; July 12, 1876; C. 184—An act to authorize the Northwestern Improvement Company, a corporation organized under the laws of the State of Wisconsin, to enter upon the Menomonee Indian reservation, and improve the Oconto River, its branches and tributaries.

19 St. 97; July 24, 1876; C. 226—An act making appropriations for the support of the Army for the fiscal year ending June 30, 1877, and for other purposes.[32]

19 St. 102; July 31, 1876; C. 246—An act making appropriations for sundry civil expenses of the Government for the fiscal year ending June 30, 1877, and for other purposes.[33]

19 St. 123; Aug. 3, 1876; C. 253—An act to further authorize the Commissioner of Indian Affairs to purchase supplies for the Indian Bureau in open market.

19 St. 127; Aug. 11, 1876; C. 259—An act providing for the sale of the Osage ceded lands in Kansas to actual settlers.[34]

19 St. 131; Aug. 12, 1876; C. 263—An act concerning the employment of Indian Scouts.[35] 10 U. S. C. 915; 10 U. S. C. 611.

19 St. 139; Aug. 14, 1876; C. 268—An act to authorize the Commissioner of Indian Affairs to receive lands in payment of judgments to Eastern Band of Cherokee Indians.[36]

19 St. 143; Aug. 15, 1876; C. 287—An act making appropriations for the legislative, executive, and judicial expenses of the Government for the year ending June 30, 1877, and for other purposes.

19 St. 176; Aug. 15, 1876; C. 289—An act making appropriations for the current and contingent expenses of the Indian Department, and for fulfilling treaty-stipulations with various Indian tribes, for the year ending June 30, 1877, and for other purposes.[37] Sec. 3—25 U. S. C. 97 (sec. 4, 28 St. 205; 34 St. 328; sec. 304, 42 St. 24. USCA Historical Note: Sec. 97 was derived from sec. 3 instant act, with the exception of the words "General Accounting Office," the derivative section using instead the words "the Second Comptroller of the Treasury." By sec. 4, 28 St. 205, the offices of Commissioner of Customs and of Second Comptroller of the Treasury were abolished and the First Comptroller of the Treasury was thereafter to be known as Comptroller of the Treasury with the powers and duties theretofore pertaining to the First and Second Comptrollers of the Treasury and the Commissioner of Customs, and the phrase "General Accounting Office" was substituted in the Code section by reason of 42 Stat. 24, creating the General Accounting Office and transferring thereto powers and duties theretofore exercised and discharged by the Comptroller of the Treasury as explained in historical notes under sections 8 and 96 of tit. 25. Sec. 5—25 U. S. C. 261. USCA Historical Note: Sec. 261, together with the provisions of section 262 of title 25, supersede those of R. S. secs. 2128–2131.

19 Stat. 204; Aug. 15, 1876; C. 301—An act to increase the cavalry force of the United States, to aid in suppressing Indian hostilities.[38]

19 St. 208; Aug. 15, 1876; C. 308—An act to provide for the sale of a portion of the reservation of the confederated Otoe and Missouria and the Sac and Fox of the Missouri Tribes of Indians in the States of Kansas and Nebraska.[39]

19 St. 212; Apr. 6, 1876; J. Res. No. 6—Joint resolution for the relief of Turtle Mountain band of Chippewa Indians.

19 St. 214; July 3, 1876; J. Res. No. 13—Joint resolution authorizing the Secretary of War to issue arms.

19 St. 216; Aug. 5, 1876; J. Res. No. 20—Joint resolution prohibiting supply of special metallic cartridges to hostile Indians. See note re 25 U. S. C. A. 266.

19 St. 221; Jan. 12, 1877; C. 19—An act authorizing the use of certain funds now in the Treasury, belonging to the Osage Indians.[40]

19 St. 240; Feb. 27, 1877; C. 69—An act to perfect the revision of the statutes of the United States, and of the statutes relating to the District of Columbia.[41] Sec. 1—R. S. 2073, 25 U. S. C. 65. USCA Historical Note: R. S. 2073 was derived from sec. 5 of Act July 9, 1832, 4 St. 564, said sec. 5, with the exception of the use of the words, "Secretary of War" in place of the words "Secretary of Interior," being identical with the Code section. R. S. sec. 2073 did not contain the word "agents," and had, after the words "in consequence of the," the word "immigration." The word "agents" was inserted, and "immigration" was changed to

---

[21] *Sg.* 13 St. 357. *S.* 28 St. 653; 29 St. 44; 30 St. 430, 475, 906, 918, 990; 31 St. 134; 37 St. 634; 45 St. 442.

[22] *Ag.* 17 St. 381. *Sg.* 11 St. 621. *Cited:* 15 L. D. 104.

[23] *Sg.* 12 St. 1168.

[24] *S.* 13 St. 663; 17 St. 437; 18 St. 420; 45 St. 1407. *Cited:* Shoshone, 85 C. Cls. 331; Shoshone, 82 C. Cls. 23.

[25] *S.* 17 St. 437; 18 St. 420; 19 St. 176, 271; 20 St. 63, 295; 21 St. 114, 485; 22 St. 68, 433. *Cited:* U. S. v. Leathers, 26 Fed. Cas. No. 15581.

[26] *Sg.* 17 St. 391. *S.* 26 St. 60. *Cited:* Medawakanton, 57 C. Cls. 357; Pawnee, 56 C. Cls. 1.

[27] *Sg.* 5 St. 349, 510. *Cited:* Uhlig, 2 Dak. 71.

[28] *S.* 19 St. 405.

[29] *Ag.* 17 St. 469.

[30] *Cited:* 18 Op. A. G. 581.

[31] *Sg.* 12 St. 1111; 17 St. 85. *S.* 21 St. 68. *Cited:* Kansas, 80 C. Cls. 264; Labadie, 6 Okla. 400.

[32] *Rp.* 19 St. 131. *S.* 19 St. 204.

[33] *Sg.* 1 St. 137; 17 St. 190; 18 St. 51, 330, 388.

[34] *Sg.* 14 St. 687.

[35] *Ag.* 14 St. 28, 333; 16 St. 142; 18 St. 72. *Rpg.* 19 St. 97.

[36] *Cited:* U. S. v. Boyd, 83 Fed. 547.

[37] *Sg.* 4 St. 442; 7 St. 36, 46, 51, 69, 85, 91, 99, 106, 161, 179, 185, 191, 213, 236, 242, 287, 296, 317, 318, 320, 352, 419, 425, 464, 540, 543, 545, 592, 596; 9 St. 35, 842, 854, 855, 878, 904; 10 St. 1039, 1044, 1056, 1065, 1071, 1078, 1094, 1095, 1099, 1110, 1167; 11 St. 614, 700, 701, 702, 729, 744; 12 St. 628, 928, 934, 940, 946, 953, 958, 964, 972, 977, 981, 997; 13 St. 663, 668, 675, 681, 689, 694; 14 St. 650, 656, 668, 684, 687, 758, 766, 772, 774, 786, 788, 802; 15 St. 506, 515, 584, 590, 596, 597, 621, 638, 651, 657, 669, 673, 675, 676; 16 St. 355, 362, 708, 720; 17 St. 214, 281, 456; 18 St. 166, 167, 447, 690. *Rn.* 34 St. 325. *S.* 19 St. 271; 21 St. 315, 380; 23 St. 194. *Cited:* 20 Op. A. G. 215; Memo. Sol., Nov. 20, 1934; Belknap, 150 U. S. 588; Eastern Band, 20 C. Cls. 449; Ex p. Crow Dog, 109 U. S. 556; Medawakanton, 57 C. Cls. 357; Sioux, 277 U. S. 424; Sisseton, 58 C. Cls. 302; Uhlig, 2 Dak. 71; U. S. v. Boyd, 68 Fed. 577; U. S. v. Boyd, 83 Fed. 547; U. S. ex rel. Standing Bear, 25 Fed. Cas. No. 14891.

[38] *Sg.* 19 St. 97.

[39] *A.* 20 St. 471. *S.* 19 St. 271; 20 St. 63, 295; 28 St. 286.

[40] *Sg.* 16 St. 362.

[41] *A.* 29 St. 506. *Cited:* Op. Sol., M. 29147, May 6, 1937; Harris, 249 Fed. 41; In re Mills, 135 U. S. 263; Sarlls, 152 U. S. 570; U. S. v. Belt, 128 Fed. 68.

"emigration," by amendment instant Act. Sec. 1—R. S. sec. 2139, 25 U. S. C. 241 (27 St. 260; sec. 1, 29 St. 506).[42] See Historical Note 25 U. S. C. A. 241.

19 St. 254; Feb. 28, 1877; C. 72—An act to ratify an agreement with certain bands of the Sioux Nation of Indians and also with the Northern Arapaho and Cheyenne Indians.[43]

19 St. 265; Feb. 28, 1877; C. 75—An act to provide for the sale of certain lands in Kansas.[44]

19 St. 268; Mar. 2, 1877; C. 82—An act to provide for the preparation and publication of a new edition of the Revised Statutes of the United States.[45]

19 St. 271; Mar. 3, 1877; C. 101—An act making appropriations for the current and contingent expenses of the Indian Department, and for fulfilling treaty-stipulations with various Indian tribes, for the year ending June 30, 1878, and for other purposes.[46] 25 U. S. C. 100 (30 St. 676, sec. 1). USCA Historical Note: Provisions similar to these, to some extent, were made by previous Indian appropriation acts.

19 St. 294; Mar. 3, 1877; C. 102—An act making appropriations for the legislative, executive, and judicial expenses of the Government for the year ending June 30, 1878, and for other purposes.

19 St. 319; Mar. 3, 1877; C. 103—An act establishing post-roads and for other purposes.

19 St. 344; Mar. 3, 1877; C. 105—An act making appropriations for sundry civil expenses of the Government for the fiscal year ending June 30, 1878, and for other purposes.[47]

19 St. 363; Mar. 3, 1877; C. 106—An act making appropriations to supply deficiencies in the appropriations for the fiscal year ending June 30, 1877, and prior years, and for other purposes.

19 St. 405; Mar. 3, 1877; C. 127—An act for the relief of certain settlers on the public lands.[48]

19 St. 447; July 12, 1876; C. 188—An act for the relief of the sureties of J. W. P. Huntington, deceased, late superintendent of Indian Affairs in Oregon.

19 St. 494; Aug. 15, 1876; C. 314—An act for the relief of Floyd C. Babcock.

19 St. 496; Aug. 15, 1876; C. 326—An act for the relief of the heirs of William Stevens.

19 St. 503; Jan. 16, 1877; C. 26—An act for the relief of Assistant Surgeon Thomas F. Aspell, United States Army.

19 St. 541; Mar. 3, 1877; C. 161—An act for the relief of Redick McKee.

19 St. 549; Mar. 3, 1877; C. 200—An act for the relief of Hans C. Peterson.[49]

19 St. 553; Mar. 3, 1877; C. 214—An act for the relief of Rosetta Hert, (late Rosetta Scoville) Charles C. Benoist, Emily Benoist, and Logan Fanfan, half-breed Indians.[50]

[42] *A.* 52 St. 696. Also see 25 U. S. C. 421a (28 St. 697); 25 U. S. C. 244a (48 St. 396).

[43] *S.* 20 St. 63, 295; 21 St. 114, 485; 22 St. 68, 433, 582; 23 St. 76, 362; 24 St. 29, 449; 25 St. 217, 980; 26 St. 336, 989; 27 St. 5, 120, 612; 28 St. 286, 876; 29 St. 321; 30 St. 62, 571, 924; 31 St. 221, 1058; 32 St. 245, 982; 33 St. 189, 1048; 34 St. 325, 1015; 35 St. 70, 781, 907; 36 St. 269, 1058; 37 St. 518; 38 St. 77, 582; 39 St. 123, 969; 40 St. 561; 41 St. 2, 3, 408, 1225; 42 St. 552, 1174; 43 St. 390, 1141; 44 St. 453, 934; 45 St. 200, 1562; 46 St. 279, 1115; 47 St. 91, 820; 48 St. 362. *Cited:* Op. Sol., M. 27514, Aug. 1, 1933; Beam, 43 C. Cls. 61; Ex p. Crow Dog, 109 U. S. 556; French, 2 Dak. 346; Golden, 2 Dak. 378; Quick Bear, 210 U. S. 50; Salois, 33 C. Cls. 326; Sioux, 85 C. Cls. 181; Sioux, 86 C. Cls. 299; Sioux, 86 C. Cls. 299; Uhlig, 2 Dak. 71.

[44] *Sg.* 17 St. 98. *S.* 26 St. 989. *Cited:* Eastern Band, 20 C. Cls. 449.

[45] *Sg.* 14 St. 74; 18 St. 113. *A.* 20 St. 27.

[46] *Sg.* 4 St. 442; 7 St. 36, 46, 51, 69, 85, 91, 99, 106, 114, 161, 179, 185, 191, 212, 213, 236, 242, 287, 296, 317, 318, 320, 352, 419, 425, 464, 540, 543, 545, 596; 9 St. 35, 842, 854, 855, 904; 10 St. 1039, 1044, 1056, 1065, 1071, 1079, 1095, 1099, 1111, 1167, 1168; 11 St. 614, 700, 702, 729, 744; 12 St. 628, 928, 934, 940, 946, 947, 953, 958, 964, 972, 976, 977, 981, 997, 1172; 13 St. 663, 668, 669, 675, 681, 689, 694; 14 St. 668, 684, 687, 694, 756, 766, 774, 786, 950; 15 St. 505, 515, 584, 590, 596, 622, 638, 640, 651, 657, 673, 676; 16 St. 40, sec. 4; 16 St. 355, 362, sec. 12, 708, 720; 17 St. 214, 281, 456, 631; 18 St. 36, 166, 167, 213, 690; 19 St. 187, 197, 208. *Ag.* 19 St. 197. *S.* 20 St. 63, 206, 295; 21 St. 114, 315, 485; 22 St. 68, 433; 23 St. 76, 362; 24 St. 29, 449; 25 St. 217, 980; 26 St. 989; 27 St. 120, 612; 28 St. 286, 876; 30 St. 62, 571, 652, 924; 31 St. 221, 1058; 32 St. 245, 982; 33 St. 189, 1048; 34 St. 325, 1015; 35 St. 70, 781. *Cited:* 18 Op. A. G. 41; Belknap, 150 U. S. 588; Chippewa, 80 C. Cls. 410; Eastern Band, 20 C. Cls. 449; Medawakanton, 57 C. Cls. 357; Osage, 66 C. Cls. 64; Sioux, 277 U. S. 424; Sisseton, 58 C. Cls. 302; U. S. v. Mitchell, 109 U. S. 146; Wilder, 16 C. Cls. 528.

[47] *Sg.* 1 St. 137; 18 St. 51, 388, 476.

[48] *Sg.* 18 St. 21; 19 St. 54, c. 102; 19 St. 55, c. 104; 19 St. 59, c. 184.

[49] *Cited:* Medawakanton, 57 C. Cls. 357.

[50] *Sg.* 11 St. 388.

20 STAT.

20 St. 1; Nov. 21, 1877; C. 1—An act making appropriations for the support of the Army for the fiscal year ending June 30, 1878, and for other purposes.[51]

20 St. 14; Jan. 14, 1878; C. 7—An act establishing postroads.

20 St. 27; Mar. 9, 1878; C. 26—An act to amend an act entitled "An act to provide for the preparation and publication of a new edition of the Revised Statutes of the United States", approved March 2, 1877.[52]

20 St. 27; Mar. 9, 1878; C. 28—An act amending the laws granting pensions to the soldiers and sailors of the war of 1812, and their widows, and for other purposes.[53]

20 St. 36; Apr. 17, 1878; C. 59—An act to amend an act entitled "An act to provide for the sale of certain New York Indian lands in Kansas," approved February 19, 1873.[54]

20 St. 48; May 3, 1878; C. 87—An act authorizing the President of the United States to make certain negotiations with the Ute Indians in the State of Colorado.

20 St. 63; May 27, 1878; C. 142—An act making appropriations for the current and contingent expenses of the Indian Department, and for fulfilling treaty stipulations with various Indian tribes, for the year ending June 30, 1879, and for other purposes.[55]

20 St. 89; June 5, 1878; C. 151—An act for the sale of timber lands in the States of California, Oregon, Nevada, and in Washington Territory.[56]

20 St. 115; June 14, 1878; C. 191—An act making appropriations to supply deficiencies in the appropriations for the fiscal year ending June 30, 1878, and prior years, and for those heretofore treated as permanent, for reappropriations, and for other purposes.[57]

20 St. 145; June 18, 1878; C. 263—An act making appropriations for the support of the Army for the fiscal year ending June 30, 1879, and for other purposes.

20 St. 165; June 18, 1878; C. 266—An act for the restoration to market of certain lands in the Territory of Utah.[58]

20 St. 178; June 19, 1878; C. 329—An act making appropriations for the legislative, executive, and judicial expenses of the government for the fiscal year ending June 30, 1879, and for other purposes.[59]

20 St. 206; June 20, 1878; C. 359—An act making appropriations for sundry civil expenses of the government for the fiscal year ending June 30, 1879, and for other purposes.[60]

20 St. 252; June 7, 1878; J. Res. No. 26—Joint resolution providing for issue of arms to Territories.

20 St. 275; Jan. 29, 1879; C. 33—An act making appropriations to enable the Secretary of the Treasury to carry out the provisions of sec. 254 of the Rev. Stat., and to appropriate $40,000 for the miscellaneous expenses of the House of Representatives, and for other purposes.

20 St. 282; Feb. 4, 1879; C. 47—An act for the relief of the Domestic and Indian Missions and Sunday School Board of the Southern Baptist Convention.

20 St. 292; Feb. 15, 1879; C. 82—An act to provide for holding term of the circuit and district courts in the district of Colorado.[61]

20 St. 295; Feb. 17, 1879; C. 87—An act making appropriations for the current and contingent expenses of the Indian Department, and for fulfilling treaty stipulations with various

[51] *S.* 20 St. 115.

[52] *Ag.* 19 St. 268.

[53] *Ag.* 12 St. 387; 14 St. 571; 17 St. 500, 569, sec. 28.

[54] *Ag.* 17 St. 466.

[55] *Sg.* 4 St. 442; 7 St. 36, 46, 51, 60, 85, 91, 106, 114, 161, 179, 185, 191, 212, 231, 236, 242, 287, 296, 317, 318, 320, 349, 352, 425, 464; 9 St. 35, 842, 854, 855, 904; 10 St. 1039, 1044, 1056, 1064, 1071, 1079, 1094, 1095, 1099, 1111 1167, 1168; 11 St. 614, 700, 701, 702, 729, 730, 744; 12 St. 628, 928, 929, 934, 935, 940, 941, 946, 947, 953, 958, 959, 964, 965, 972, 973, 976, 977, 981, 997, 1172; 13 St. 663, 675, 682, 689, 690, 694; 14 St. 69, 649, 650, 684, 687, 756, 766, 774; 15 St. 505, 515, 581, 590, 596, 597, 621, 622, 638, 640, 651, 652, 657, 658, 669, 673, 675, 676; 16 St. 40, 355, 362, 708, 720; 17 St. 214, 281; 18 St. 166, 167, 449, 690; 19 St. 208, 254, 256, 287. *S.* 20 St. 206, 21 St. 315. *Rp.* 20 St. 115. *Cited:* Baker, 28 C. Cls. 370; Belknap, 150 U. S. 588; Medawakanton, 57 C. Cls. 357; Sioux, 277 U. S. 424; Sisseton, 58 C. Cls. 302; U. S. v. Leathers, 26 Fed. Cas. No. 15581.

[56] *S.* 28 St. 594. *Cited:* Leecy, 190 Fed. 289.

[57] *Sg.* 20 St. 1, 63.

[58] *Rpg.* 13 St. 68. *Cited:* 25 L. D. 408; 53 I. D. 128; Hayt, 38 C. Cls. 455.

[59] *Rpg.* 5 St. 670; 9 St. 448, 454; 10 St. 173; 12 St. 172, 178, 240, 665, 808, 809; 13 St. 87; 15 St. 179; 17 St. 416. *S.* 21 St. 23.

[60] *Sg.* 10 St. 1094; 18 St. 388; 19 St. 292; 20 St. 80. *Rp.* 20 St. 377; 21 St. 81. *S.* 22 St. 302.

[61] *Sg.* 19 St. 61.

Indian tribes, for the year ending June 30, 1880, and for other purposes.[62]

20 St. 377; Mar. 3, 1879; C. 182—An act making appropriations for sundry civil expenses of the government for the fiscal year ending June 30, 1880, and for other purposes.[63]

20 St. 410; Mar. 3, 1879; C. 183—An act making appropriations to supply deficiencies in the appropriations for the fiscal year ending June 30, 1879, and for prior years, and for those heretofore treated as permanent, and for other purposes.

20 St. 427; Mar. 3, 1879; C. 184—An act to establish post-routes.

20 St. 471; Mar. 3, 1879; C. 190—An act to amend an act to provide for the sale of a portion of the reservation of the Confederated Otoe and Missouria and the Sac and Fox of the Missouri tribes of Indians in the States of Kansas and Nebraska.[64]

20 St. 473; Mar. 3, 1879; C. 195—An act to provide for the taking the tenth and subsequent censuses.[65]

20 St. 487; Dec. 21, 1878; J. Res. No. 3—Joint resolution extending time for Joint Committee on transfer of Indian Bureau to report.

20 St. 488; Mar. 3, 1879; J. Res. No. 12—Joint resolution instructing the Attorney-General of the United States to bring suit in the name of the United States to quiet and settle the titles to lands of the Black Bob band of Shawnee Indians.[66]

20 St. 513; Apr. 20, 1878; C. 63—An act to authorize the issue of a patent of certain lands in the Brothertown reservation, in the State of Wisconsin, to the persons selected by the Brothertown Indians.[67]

20 St. 535; May 25, 1878; C. 139—An act to authorize the survey of the Cattaraugus Indian reservation in the State of New York.

20 St. 541; June 10, 1878; C. 179—An act to pay for clerical services and extraordinary expenses, under the seventh section of the act of August 18, 1856, in the Pawnee land-district in Kansas.[68]

20 St. 542; June 14, 1878; C. 200—An act to legalize certain patents issued to members of the Pottawatomie tribe of Indians.[69]

20 St. 543; June 14, 1878; C. 201—An act for the relief of James McGregor.

20 St. 590; Jan. 13, 1879; C. 13—An act for the relief of James W. Richard and J. S. Brown and Brother, of Denver, Colorado.

20 St. 593; Feb. 7, 1879; C. 51—An act for the relief of Jesse Turner and others, sureties upon the officio bond of George W. Clarke, formerly Indian agent.

20 St. 603; Mar. 1, 1879; C. 128—An act for the relief of Catharine and Sophia Germain.

20 St. 668; Mar. 3, 1879; C. 306—An act for the relief of Henry T. Fuller and others, sureties upon the official bond of William H. Waterman.

20 St. 669; Jan. 31, 1879; J. Res. No. 4—Joint resolution providing for transportation by the military authorities of John J. Manuel and two infant daughters from Camp Howard, Idaho Territory, to St. Charles, Missouri.

21 STAT.

21 St. 11; June 12, 1879; C. 19—An act to extend the time for the payment of pre-emptors on certain public lands in the State of Minnesota and Territory of Dakota.

21 St. 11; June 12, 1879; C. 21—An act to establish post routes.

21 St. 23; June 21, 1879; C. 34—An act making appropriations for the legislative, executive, and judicial expenses of the government for the fiscal year ending June 30, 1880, and for other purposes.[70]

21 St. 30; June 23, 1879; C. 35—An act making appropriations for the support of the Army for the fiscal year ending June 30, 1880, and for other purposes. Sec. 7—25 U. S. C. 273 (see 25 U. S. C. 276).

21 St. 40; June 28, 1879; C. 45—An act making additional appropriations for the service of the Post Office Department for the fiscal years ending June 30, 1879, and June 30, 1880, and for other purposes.[71]

21 St. 67; Mar. 10, 1880; C. 36—An act making additional appropriations for the support of certain Indian tribes, for the year ending June 30, 1880.

21 St. 68; Mar. 16, 1880; C. 39—An act for the relief of certain actual settlers on the Kansas trust and diminished reserve lands in the State of Kansas.[72]

21 St. 70; Apr. 1, 1880; C. 41—An act to authorize the Secretary of the Interior to deposit certain funds in the United States Treasurer in lieu of investment.[73] Sec. 1—25 U. S. C. 161[74] USCA Historical Note: Effective July 1, 1935, the permanent appropriation provided for in the last clause of this section was repealed by Act June 26, 1934, s. 2, 48 St. 1225, such act authorizing, in lieu thereof, an annual appropriation from the general fund of the Treasury. See sec. 725a (b) of Tit. 31.

21 St. 81; Apr. 23, 1880; C. 61—An act to amend an act entitled "An act for the removal of certain Indians in New Mexico", approved June 20, 1878.[75]

21 St. 81; Apr. 30, 1880; C. 71—An act for the establishment of a land-office in the Territory of Montana.

21 St. 90; May 3, 1880; C. 74—An act to establish post-routes.

21 St. 110; May 4, 1880; C. 81—An act making appropriations for the support of the Army for the fiscal year ending June 30, 1881, and for other purposes.

21 St. 114; May 8, 1880; C. 84—An act to authorize the sale of Fort Logan, Montana Territory, and to establish a new post on the frontier.

21 St. 114; May 11, 1880; C. 85—An act making appropriations for the current and contingent expenses of the Indian Department, and for fulfilling treaty stipulations with various Indian tribes, for the year ending June 30, 1881, and for other purposes.[76] Sec. 1—25 U. S. C. 104; Sec. 4—See Historical Note 25 U. S. C. A. 174.

21 St. 143; May 28, 1880; C. 107—An act for the relief of settlers upon the Osage trust and diminished reserve lands in Kansas, and for other purposes.

21 St. 154; June 3, 1880; C. 119—An act providing for the reapportionment of the members of the legislatures in the Territories of Montana, Idaho, and Wyoming.

21 St. 199; June 15, 1880; C. 223—An act to accept and ratify the agreement submitted by the confederated bands of Ute Indians in Colorado, for the sale of their reservation in said State, and for other purposes, and to make the necessary appropriations for carrying out the same.[77]

21 St. 205; June 15, 1880; C. 224—An act to establish Post Roads.

21 St. 210; June 15, 1880; C. 225—An act making appropriations for the legislative, executive, and judicial expenses of the government for the fiscal year ending June 30, 1881, and for other purposes.

21 St. 238; June 16, 1880; C. 234—An act making appropriations to supply deficiencies in the appropriations for the fiscal year ending June 30, 1880, and for prior years, and for those cer-

---

[62] *Sg.* 4 St. 442; 7 St. 36, 46, 51, 69, 85, 91, 99, 106, 114, 161, 179, 185, 191, 212, 213, 236, 242, 287, 296, 317, 318, 320, 349, 352, 425, 464, 540, 543, 545, 596; 9 St. 35, 842, 854, 904; 10 St. 1039, 1044, 1056, 1065, 1071, 1079, 1095, 1099, 1111, 1167, 1168; 11 St. 614, 700, 702, 729, 744; 12 St. 628, 928, 934, 940, 946, 953, 958, 964, 972, 977, 981, 997, 1172; 13 St. 663, 675, 682, 694; 14 St. 684, 687, 756, 766, 786; 15 St. 505, 515, 584, 590, 596, 597, 622, 638, 651, 657, 669, 676; 16 St. 355, 708, 719, 720; 17 St. 281, 456; 18 St. 167, 448, 689; 19 St. 208, 254, 287. *S.* 21 St. 315. *Cited:* Belknap, 150 U. S. 588; Medawakanton, 57 C. Cls. 357; Sioux, 277 U. S. 424; Sisseton, 58 C. Cls. 302; U. S. v. Leathers, 26 Fed. Cas. No. 15581.

[63] *Rpg.* 20 St. 206. *Sg.* 20 St. 279.

[64] *Ag.* 19 St. 208.

[65] *R.* 25 St. 760.

[66] *R.* 25 St. 768.

[67] *Sg.* 7 St. 342, 405.

[68] *Cited:* 18 Op. A. G. 223.

[69] *Sg.* 12 St. 1191; 15 St. 531.

[70] *Sg.* 20 St. 178.

[71] *Sg.* 16 St. 362, sec. 12; 17 St. 90, sec. 2.

[72] *Sg.* 18 St. 272; 19 St. 74, sec. 1, 2, 3. *Cited:* Kansas, 80 C. Cls. 264.

[73] *S.* 21 St. 114; 28 St. 286; 32 St. 636; 49 St. 1085. *Cited:* 17 Op. A. G. 104; 20 Op. A. G. 517; Blackfeather, 28 C. Cls. 447; Iowa, 68 C. Cls. 585; Kansas, 80 C. Cls. 264; Quick Bear, 210 U. S. 50.

[74] *See:* 25 U. S. C. 161a (45 St. 1164, sec. 1, as amended 46 St. 584). See sec. 725s of Tit. 31; 25 U. S. C. 161b (43 St. 1164, sec. 2, as amended 46 St. 584). See sec. 725s of Tit. 31; 25 U. S. C. 161c (45 St. 1164, sec. 3, as amended 46 St. 584). See sec. 725s of Tit. 31; 25 U. S. C. 161d (45 St. 1164, sec. 4, as amended 46 St. 584). See sec. 725s of Tit. 31.

[75] *Rg.* 20 St. 232.

[76] *Sg.* 4 St. 442; 7 St. 36, 46, 51, 69, 85, 91, 99, 106, 114, 161, 179, 185, 191, 212, 213, 236, 242, 287, 296, 317, 318, 320, 349, 352, 425, 464, 540, 543, 545, 596; 9 St. 35, 842, 854, 855, 904; 10 St. 1039, 1044, 1056, 1065, 1071, 1079, 1094, 1095, 1099, 1109, 1167, 1168; 11 Stat. 614, 700, 701, 702, 729, 730, 744; 12 St. 628, 975, 981, 997, 1171; 13 St. 663, 675, 682, 694; 14 St. 649, 684, 687, 756, 765, 766, 774, 786; 15 St. 505, 514, 515, 584, 590, 593, 622, 638, 640, 651, 652, 655, 669, 676; 16 St. 40, 355, 360, 362, 708, 720; 17 St. 90, 281, 456; 18 St. 140, 167, 449, 689; 19 St. 254, 287; 21 St. 70. *S.* 21 St. 259, 315. *Rp.* 39 St. 123. *Cited:* 17 Op. A. G. 531; Belknap, 150 U. S. 588; Dyer, 20 C. Cls. 166; Medawakanton, 57 C. Cls. 357; Sioux, 277 U. S. 424; Sisseton, 58 C. Cls. 302; Smith, 37 C. Cls. 119; U. S. v. Pumphrey, 11 App. D. C. 44; U. S. v. Sandoval 231 U. S. 28.

[77] *Sg.* 15 St. 619; 16 St. 335; 17 St. 32; 18 St. 35, 336. *S.* 21 St. 435; 22 St. 178, 302, 433; 23 St. 76; 28 St. 286, 677; 30 St. 234; 34 St. 1056; 35 St. 781; 45 St. 711; 49 St. 1272. *Rp.* 23 St. 22. *Cited:* 17 Op. A. G. 262; 17 Op. A. G. 366; 21 Op. A. G. 131; Memo. Sol., Sept. 29, 1937, Aug. 27, 1938; 25 L. D. 408; 56 L. D. 330; U. S. v. Morrison, 203 Fed. 364; Ute, 45 C. Cls. 440.

tified as due by the accounting-officers of the Treasury in accordance with section four of the act of June 14, 1878, heretofore paid from permanent appropriations, and for other purposes.

21 St. 259; June 16, 1880; C. 235—An act making appropriations for the sundry civil expenses of the government for the fiscal year ending June 30, 1881, and for other purposes.[78]

21 St. 291; June 16, 1880; C. 251—An act to carry into effect the second and sixteenth articles of the treaty between the United States and the Great and Little Osage Indians, proclaimed January 21, 1867.[79]

21 St. 308; June 7, 1880; J. Res. No. 44—Joint resolution to provide for the publication and distributing of a supplement to the Revised Statutes.

21 St. 310; June 16, 1880; J. Res. No. 57—Joint resolution authorizing the Secretary of the Interior to certify school lands to the State of Kansas.

21 St. 315; January 18, 1881; C. 23—An act for the relief of the Winnebago Indians in Wisconsin, and to aid them to obtain subsistence by agricultural pursuits, and to promote their civilization.[80]

21 St. 346; February 24, 1881; C. 79—An act making appropriations for the support of the Army for the fiscal year ending June 30, 1882, and for other purposes.

21 St. 352; February 28, 1881; C. 90—An act to establish post-routes.

21 St. 377; March 1, 1881; C. 97—An act for the relief of settlers upon the Absentee Shawnee lands in Kansas, and for other purposes.[81]

21 St. 380; March 3, 1881; C. 128—An act to provide for the sale of the remainder of the reservation of the Confederated Otoe and Missouria Tribes of Indians, in the States of Nebraska and Kansas, and for other purposes.[82]

21 St. 385; March 3, 1881; C. 130—An act making appropriations for the legislative, executive, and judicial expenses of the government for the fiscal year ending June 30, 1882, and for other purposes.

21 St. 414; Mar. 3, 1881; C. 132—An act making appropriations to supply deficiencies in the appropriations for the fiscal year ending June 30, 1881, and for prior years, and for those certified as due by the accounting officers of the Treasury in accordance with sec. 4 of the act of June 14, 1878, heretofore paid from permanent appropriations, and for other purposes.[83]

21 St. 435; Mar. 3, 1881; C. 133—An act making appropriations for sundry civil expenses of the government for the fiscal year ending June 30, 1882, and for other purposes.[84]

21 St. 468; Mar. 3, 1881; C. 136—An act making appropriations for the construction, completion, repair, and preservation of certain works on rivers and harbors, and for other purposes.

21 St. 485; Mar. 3, 1881; C. 137—An act making appropriations for the current and contingent expenses of the Indian Department, and for fulfilling treaty stipulations with various Indian tribes, for the year ending June 30, 1882, and for other purposes.[85]

21 St. 504; Mar. 3, 1881; C. 139—An act for the ascertainment of the amount due the Choctaw Nation.[86]

21 St. 509; Mar. 3, 1881; C. 149—An act to graduate the price and dispose of the residue of the Osage Indian trust and diminished-reserve lands, lying east of the sixth principal meridian, in Kansas.

21 St. 510; Mar. 3, 1881; C. 152—An act for the payment of certain Indian war bonds of the State of California.[87]

21 St. 511; Mar. 3, 1881; C. 155—An act to confirm the title to certain lands in the State of Ohio.[88]

21 St. 520; Mar. 3, 1881; J. Res. No. 25—Joint resolution directing the Secretary of War to investigate the claim of the State of Florida against the United States for expenditures made in suppressing Indian hostilities in said State between the years 1855 and 1860, and to report the result of such investigation to Congress.

21 St. 543; June 4, 1880; C. 122—An act for the relief of certain homestead and pre-emption settlers in Kansas and Nebraska.

21 St. 544; June 4, 1880; C. 123—An act to permit Elias C. Boudinot, of the Cherokee Nation, to sue in the Court of Claims.[89]

21 St. 549; June 8, 1880; C. 158—An act for the relief of Henry Warren.

21 St. 588; June 16, 1880; C. 259—An act for the relief of Amanda M. Cook.

21 St. 640; Mar. 3, 1881; C. 161—An act for the relief of Dodd, Brown and Company of St. Louis, Missouri.

21 St. 641; Mar. 3, 1881; C. 162—An act for the relief of citizens of Montana who served with the United States troops in the war with the Nez Perces, and for the relief of the heirs of such as were killed in such service.

21 St. 652; Mar. 3, 1881; C. 196—An act for the relief of William Redus.

22 STAT.

22 St. 7; Mar. 4, 1882; C. 21—An act for the relief of the Eastern Shawnee Indians at the Quapaw Agency, Indian Territory.

22 St. 7; Mar. 6, 1882; C. 24—An act to provide for certain of the most urgent deficiencies in the appropriations for the fiscal year ending June 30, 1882, and for other purposes.[90]

22 St. 13; Mar. 6, 1882; C. 27—An act to establish post-routes.

22 St. 30; Mar. 22, 1882; C. 46—An act authorizing the sale of certain logs cut by the Indians of the Menomonee Reservation in Wisconsin.[91]

22 St. 30; Mar. 22, 1882; C. 47—An act to amend sec. 5352 of the Revised Statutes of the United States, in reference to bigamy, and for other purposes.[92] Sec. 8—48 U. S. C. 1461.

22 St. 35; Mar. 28, 1882; C. 52—An act to extend the northern boundary of the State of Nebraska.[93]

22 St. 36; Mar. 31, 1882; C. 55—An act to confirm certain instructions given by the Department of the Interior to the Indian agent at Green Bay Agency, in the State of Wisconsin, and to legalize the acts done and permitted by said Indian agent pursuant thereto.

22 St. 42; Apr. 11, 1882; C. 74—An act to accept and ratify the agreement submitted by the Crow Indians of Montana for the sale of a portion of their reservation in said Territory, and for other purposes, and to make the necessary appropriations for carrying out the same.[94]

22 St. 47; Apr. 21, 1882; C. 85—An act to provide a deficiency for the subsistence of the Arapahoe, Cheyenne, Kiowa, Comanche, Apache and Wichita Indians.

22 St. 63; May 15, 1882; C. 144—An act to provide for the sale of the lands of the Miami Indians in Kansas.[95]

22 St. 68; May 17, 1882; C. 163—An act making appropriations for the current and contingent expenses of the Indian Department, and for fulfilling treaty stipulations with various Indian tribes, for the year ending June 30, 1883, and for other purposes.[96] Sec. 1—p. 70, 25 U. S. C. 23.[97] USCA

---

[78] *Sg.* 16 St. 13, sec. 4; 21 St. 117.

[79] *Sg.* 12 St. 126; 14 St. 687. *S.* 24 St. 851; 26 St. 1414. *Cited:* Kansas, 80 C. Cls. 264; Quick Bear, 210 U. S. 50.

[80] *Sg.* 12 St. 658; 13 St. 172; 18 St. 170, 420, sec. 15, 444; 19 St. 194, 288; 20 St. 82, 312; 21 St. 128. *S.* 22 St. 603. *Cited:* 19 Op. A. G. 161; 19 Op. A. G. 559; 11 L. D. Memo. 296; Op. Sol. Off., May 15, 1933; Memo. Sol., Mar. 6, 1937; U. S. v. Cain-Bonness, 215 Fed. 212; U. S. v. Cass, 240 Fed. 617; U. S. v. Corporation, 101 F. 2d 156; U. S. v. Joyce, 240 Fed. 610; U. S. v. Saunders, 96 Fed. 268.

[81] *Sg.* 10 St. 1053; 16 St. 53.

[82] *Sg.* 19 St. 176. *S.* 22 St. 302; 24 St. 214; 27 St. 568. *A.* 28 St. 84.

[83] *Sg.* 10 St. 1095; 15 St. 513. *S.* 25 St. 980. *Cited:* Eastern Band, 20 C. Cls. 449.

[84] *Sg.* 21 St. 202, sec. 2; Sen. Res. Oct. 16, 1877; Sen. Res. Jan. 16, 1879. *Cited:* Ute, 45 C. Cls. 440.

[85] *Sg.* 4 St. 442; 7 St. 36, 46, 51, 69, 85, 91, 99, 106, 114, 161, 179, 185, 191, 212, 213, 236, 242, 287, 296, 317, 318, 320, 349, 352, 425, 464, 540, 543, 545, 596; 9 St. 35, 842, 854, 855, 904; 10 St. 1039, 1044, 1056, 1071, 1079, 1095, 1099, 1167, 1168; 11 St. 614, 700, 701, 702, 729, 744; 12 St. 628, 981, 997, 1172; 13 St. 633, 675, 682, 694; 14 St. 649, 650, 684, 687, 756, 776, 786; 15 St. 505, 514, 515, 584, 590, 596, 621, 622, 638, 640, 651, 655, 676; 16 St. 355, 708, 720; 17 St. 281, 456; 18 St. 167, 689; 19 St. 254, 287. *S.* 33 St. 724. *Cited:* 17 Op. A. G. 381; Belknap, 150 U. S. 588; Dyer, 20 C. Cls. 166; Medawakanton, 57 C. Cls. 357; Sioux, 277 U. S. 424; Sisseton, 58 C. Cls. 302.

[86] *Sg.* 11 St. 611. *Cited:* Choctaw, 119 U. S. 1; Choctaw, 19 C. Cls. 243; Choctaw, 21 C. Cls. 59; Gilfillan, 159 U. S. 303; Thebo, 66 Fed. 372.

[87] *Sg.* 10 St. 582. *S.* 28 St. 843.

[88] *Sg.* 7 St. 160, 178.

[89] *Sg.* 14 St. 799; 15 St. 125. *Cited:* 18 Op. A. G. 66.

[90] *Cited:* Medawakanton, 57 C. Cls. 357.

[91] *S.* 40 St. 1085. *Cited:* Quick Bear, 210 U. S. 50.

[92] *Cited:* Ute, 45 C. Cls. 440.

[93] *Sg.* 3 St. 545. *S.* 25 St. 94, 888.

[94] *Sg.* 15 St. 649. *S.* 22 St. 302, 433; 23 St. 76, 362; 24 St. 29, 449; 25 St. 217, 980; 26 St. 336, 989; 27 St. 120, 612; 28 St. 286, 876; 29 St. 321; 30 St. 62, 571, 924; 31 St. 221, 1058; 32 St. 245, 982; 33 St. 189, 1048; 34 St. 325. *Cited:* 19 L. D. 24; 48 L. D. 479; 49 L. D. 376; Op. Sol., M. 5805, Nov. 22, 1921; 13 L. D. Memo. 118; Crow, 81 C. Cls. 238; Draper, 164 U. S. 240; Truscott, 73 Fed. 60; U. S. v. Powers, 305 U. S. 527; U. S. v. 12 Bottles, 201 Fed. 191.

[95] *Sg.* 10 St. 1093; 17 St. 631. *A.* 22 St. 116.

[96] *Sg.* 7 St. 36, 46, 51, 69, 85, 91, 99, 106, 114, 161, 179, 185, 191, 212, 236, 242, 287, 296, 317, 320, 349, 352, 425, 464, 540, 543, 544, 596; 9 St. 35, 842, 854, 855; 10 St. 1039, 1044, 1056, 1071, 1079, 1094, 1165; 11 St. 614, 699, 729, 744; 12 St. 628, 981, 997, 1172; 13 St. 663, 673, 682, 693; 14 St. 650, 687, 750, 766, 769, 786; 15 St. 505, 514, 584, 590, 596, 638, 651, 657; 16 St. 355, 708, 720; 17 St. 281, 631; 18 St. 167, 437, 689; 19 St. 254, 287. *S.* 22 St. 302, 433; 23 St. 76, 268. *Cited:* 17 Op. A. G. 647; 19 Op. A. G. 252;

Historical Note: This provision superseded R. S. 2041, prescribing the duties of the commissioners, and authorizing them to supervise all expenditures of money appropriated for the benefit of Indians, as well as to inspect goods purchased, etc. An inquiry into conditions in the Indian service, with a view to ascertaining any and all facts relating to the conduct and management of the Bureau of Indian Affairs, and of recommending such changes in the administration of Indian affairs as would promote the betterment of the service and the well-being of Indians, by commission to be known as the Joint Commission to Investigate Indian Affairs, to be composed of 3 Members of the Senate, and 3 Members of the House of Representatives, which was authorized to examine into the conduct and management of the Bureau of Indian Affairs and all its branches and agencies, their organization and administration, the findings, conclusions, and recommendations of such commission to be reported to Congress during the 63d Congress, was provided for by Act June 30, 1913, s. 1, 38 St. 81. Sec. 1—p. 86, 25 U. S. C. 55[98]; sec. 1—p. 87, R. S. 2056, 25 U. S. C. 28. USCA Historical Note: R. S. 2056 as originally enacted in the Rev. Stat. was based on Act of Feb. 27, 1851, sec. 6, 9 St. 587; and Act Apr. 8, 1864, sec. 4, 13 St. 40, and did not contain the words at the end thereof "and until his successor is duly appointed and qualified." This clause was added by amendment by instant Act. Sec. 6—25 U. S. C. 46 (23 St. 97, sec. 6.)[99] USCA Historical Note: 23 St. 97, sec. 6 also contains a provision substantially in the same terms as those of the Code section. 25 U. S. C. 63 (23 St. 97, sec. 6). Sec. 7—25 U. S. C. 3.

22 St. 111; June 27, 1882; C. 241—An act to authorize the Secretary of the Treasury to examine and report to Congress the amount of all claims of the States of Texas, Colorado, Oregon, Nebraska, California, Kansas, and Nevada, and the Territories of Washington and Idaho, for money expended and indebtedness assumed by said States and Territories in repelling invasions and suppressing Indian hostilities, and for other purposes.

22 St. 116; June 27, 1882; C. 246—An act to amend section two of an act entitled "An act to provide for the sale of the lands of the Miami Indians in Kansas," approved May 15, 1882.[1]

22 St. 117; June 30, 1882; C. 254—An act making appropriations for the support of the Army for the fiscal year ending June 30, 1883, and for other purposes.

22 St. 148; July 3, 1882; C. 268—An act to accept and ratify an agreement with the Shoshone and Bannock Indians for the sale of a portion of their reservation in Idaho Territory required for the use of the Utah and Northern Railroad, and to make the necessary appropriation for carrying out the same.[2]

22 St. 157; July 10, 1882; C. 284—An act to accept and ratify an agreement with the Crow Indians for the sale of a portion of their reservation in the Territory of Montana required for the use of the Northern Pacific Railroad, and to make the necessary appropriations for carrying out the same.[3]

22 St. 177; July 28, 1882; C. 356—An act to provide for the sale of certain Kickapoo Indian lands in Kansas.[4]

22 St. 178; July 28, 1882; C. 357—An act relating to lands in Colorado lately occupied by the Uncompahgre and White River Ute Indians.[5]

22 St. 179; July 31, 1882; C. 360—An act to amend sec. 2133 of the Revised Statutes in relation to Indian traders.[6] Sec. 1—R. S. 2133, 25 U. S. C. 264.

22 St. 181; July 31, 1882; C. 363—An act to provide additional industrial training-schools for Indian youth, and authorizing the use of unoccupied military barracks for such purpose.[7] Sec. 1—25 U. S. C. 276. (Superseded R. S. 2099.)[8]

22 St. 181; Aug. 2, 1882; C. 371—An act to grant a right of way for a railroad and telegraph line through the lands of the Choctaw and Chickasaw Nations of Indians to the St. Louis and San Francisco Ry. Co., and for other purposes.[9]

22 St. 191; Aug. 2, 1882; C. 375—An act making appropriations for the construction, repair, and preservation of certain works on rivers and harbors, and for other purposes.

22 St. 219; Aug. 5, 1882; C. 389—An act making appropriations for the legislative, executive, and judicial expenses of the government for the fiscal year ending June 30, 1883, and for other purposes.

22 St. 257; Aug. 5, 1882; C. 390—An act making appropriations to supply deficiencies in the appropriations for the fiscal year ending June 30, 1882, and for prior years, and for those certified as due by the accounting officers of the Treasury in accordance with sec. 4 of the act of June 14, 1878, heretofore paid from permanent appropriations, and for other purposes.[10]

22 St. 297; Aug. 5, 1882; C. 392—An act authorizing the Secretary of the Interior to dispose of certain lands adjacent to the town of Pendleton, in the State of Oregon, belonging to the Umatilla Indian Reservation, and for other purposes.

22 St. 299; Aug. 5, 1882; C. 394—An act granting the right of way to the Arizona Southern R. Co. through the Papago Indian Reservation, in Arizona.

22 St. 301; Aug. 7, 1882; C. 432—An act to reimburse the Creek orphan fund.[11]

22 St. 302; Aug. 7, 1882; C. 433—An act making appropriations for sundry civil expenses of the government for the fiscal year ending June 30, 1883, and for other purposes.[12]

22 St. 341; Aug. 7, 1882; C. 434—An act to provide for the sale of a part of the reservation of the Omaha tribe of Indians in the State of Nebraska, and for other purposes.[13]

22 St. 345; Aug. 7, 1882; C. 439—An act to authorize the auditing of certain unpaid claims against the Indian Bureau by the accounting officers of the Treasury.[14]

22 St. 349; Aug. 7, 1882; C. 446—An act for the manufacture of salt in the Indian Territory.[15]

22 St. 350; Aug. 7, 1882; C. 448—An act to establish post-routes.

22 St. 373; Aug. 8, 1882; C. 469—An act to amend sec. 4766, tit. 57, of the Rev. Stat. of the U. S.[16]

22 St. 399; Jan. 6, 1883; C. 12—An Act to reimburse the State of Oregon and State of California and the citizens thereof for moneys paid by said States in the suppression of Indian hostilities during the Modoc war in the years 1872 and 1873.

22 St. 400; Jan. 6, 1883; C. 13—An act to provide for holding a term of the District Court of the United States at Wichita, Kansas, and for other purposes.[17]

22 St. 432; Mar. 1, 1883; C. 59—An act to authorize the Seneca Nation of Indians, of the State of New York, to grant title to lands for cemetery purposes.[18]

22 St. 433; Mar. 1, 1883; C. 61—An act making appropriations for the current and contingent expenses of the Indian Department, and for fulfilling treaty stipulations with various Indian tribes, for the year ending June 30, 1884, and for other purposes.[19]

---

8 L. D. 580; Belknap, 150 U. S. 588; Choctaw, 81 C. Cls. 63; Conners, 33 C. Cls. 317; Lucas, 163 U. S. 612; Mdawakanton, 57 C. Cls. 357; Pawnee, 56 C. Cls. 1; Romero, 24 C. Cls. 331; Sac & Fox, 220 U. S. 481; Sac & Fox, 45 C. Cls. 287; Shoshone, 82 C. Cls. 23; Sioux, 277 U. S. 424; Sisseton, 58 C. Cls. 302; U. S. v. Mitchell, 109 U. S. 146; U. S. v. Sandoval, 231 U. S. 28.

[97] This section has been superseded by Ex. Or. 6145, May 25, 1933. See note to 25 U. S. C. 21.

[98] *See:* 5 U. S. C. 821, et seq.

[99] *See:* 25 U. S. C. 472.

[1] *Ag.* 22 St. 63.

[2] *Sg.* 15 St. 673. *Cited:* Op. Sol., M. 5386, June 19, 1923.

[3] *Sg.* 13 St. 365; 15 St. 49. *Cited:* Crow, 81 C. Cls. 238.

[4] *Sg.* 13 St. 629.

[5] *Sg.* 21 St. 203. *Cited:* Ute, 45 C. Cls. 440.

[6] *Ag.* 4 St. 729. *Cited:* 20 Op. A. G. 215; 27 Op. A. G. 558; Memo. Sol., Nov. 20, 1934; U. S. v. 48 Pounds, 35 Fed. 408.

[7] *Sg.* 1 St. 137.

[8] *See:* 25 U. S. C. 273.

[9] *A.* 24 St. 76. *Cited:* Choctaw, 83 C. Cls. 140.

[10] *Sg.* 12 St. 1112; 16 St. 362; 17 St. 626. *Cited:* Goat, 224 U. S. 458; Kansas, 80 C. Cls. 264; Ute, 45 C. Cls. 440.

[11] *Sg.* 7 St. 366. *S.* 25 St. 565. *Cited:* Creek, 77 C. Cls. 159.

[12] *Sg.* 1 St. 137; 15 St. 223; 16 St. 360; 18 St. 388; 20 St. 219; 21 St. 202, 380; 22 St. 42, 85. *S.* 22 St. 433; 25 St. 694. *Cited:* Thayer, 68 Atl. Month, 540, 676; Eastern Band, 20 C. Cls. 449; Old Settlers, 148 U. S. 427; U. S. v. Boyd, 68 Fed. 577; U. S. v. Boyd, 83 Fed. 547.

[13] *Sg.* 14 St. 668. *A.* 27 St. 612. *S.* 23 St. 362; 24 St. 214; 25 St. 150; 26 St. 329; 28 St. 276; 32 St. 245; 37 St. 111; 43 St. 726. *Cited:* Memo. Sol. Off., Jan. 22, 1936; 27 L. D. 399; 38 L. D. 559; 42 L. D. 493; 48 L. D. 222; Chase, 256 U. S. 1; Chase, 238 Fed. 887; Clay, 282 Fed. 268; Dixon, 268 Fed. 285; First, 59 F. 2d 367; Gilpin, 256 U. S. 10; Hallowell, 239 U. S. 506; Hallowell, 221 U. S. 317; Sloan, 995 Fed. 193; Sloan, 118 Fed. 283; U. S. v. Chase, 245 U. S. 89; U. S. v. Flourney, 69 Fed. 886; U. S. v. Law, 250 Fed. 218; U. S. v. Pelican, 232 U. S. 442; U. S. v. Thurston, 143 Fed. 287; Work, 29 F. 2d 393.

[14] *Cited:* Byrd, 44 C. Cls. 498.

[15] *Sg.* 14 St. 799.

[16] *Ag.* 16 St. 194.

[17] *Cited:* Ex p. Crow Dog, 109 U. S. 556; Lucas, 163 U. S. 612; U. S. v. Rogers, 23 Fed. 658; U. S. v. Soule, 30 Fed. 918.

[18] *Sg.* 18 St. 330.

[19] *Sg.* 4 St. 442; 7 St. 36, 46, 51, 69, 85, 91, 99, 106, 114, 161, 179, 185, 191, 212, 213, 236, 242, 287, 296, 317, 320, 349, 352, 425, 464, 540, 543, 545, 596; 9 St. 35, 842, 854, 855, 904; 10 St. 1039, 1044, 1056, 1071, 1079, 1094, 1095, 1167, 1168; 11 St. 614, 700, 702, 729, 744; 12 St. 628, 981, 997, 1172; 13 St. 638, 675, 682, 694; 14 St. 650, 687, 756, 774, 772.

22 St. 456; Mar. 3, 1883; C. 93—An act making appropriations for the support of the Army for the fiscal year ending June 30, 1884, and for other purposes.

22 St. 462; Mar. 3, 1883; C. 95—An act making appropriations to provide for the expenses of the Government of the District of Columbia for the fiscal year ending June 30, 1884, and for other purposes.

22 St. 488; Mar. 3, 1883; C. 121—An act to reduce internal-revenue taxation, and for other purposes.[20]

22 St. 531; Mar. 3, 1883; C. 128—An act making appropriations for the legislative, executive, and judicial expenses of the government for the fiscal year ending June 30, 1884 and for other purposes.

22 St. 572; Mar. 3, 1883; C. 139—An act to establish certain post-routes.

22 St. 582; Mar. 3, 1883; C. 120—An act to create three additional land districts in the Territory of Dakota.

22 St. 582; Mar. 3, 1883; C. 141—An act making appropriations to supply deficiencies in the appropriations for the fiscal year ending June 30, 1883, and for prior years, and for those certified as due by the accounting officers of the Treasury in accordance with section four of the act of June 14, 1878, heretofore paid from permanent appropriations, and for other purposes.[21] Sec. 1—p. 590, 25 U. S. C. 155 (24 St. 463; 44 St. 560, sec. 1; 45 St. 991, sec. 1).[22]

22 St. 603; Mar. 3, 1883; C. 143—An act making appropriations for sundry civil expenses of the government for the fiscal year ending June 30, 1884, and for other purposes.[23]

22 St. 716; July 15, 1882; C. 305—An act granting a pension to George C. Quick.

22 St. 717; July 22, 1882; C. 319—An act granting a pension to Jacob Nix.

22 St. 725; Aug. 1, 1882; C. 369—An act granting a pension to Amanda J. McFadden.

22 St. 727; Aug. 5, 1882; C. 409—An act for the relief of Eugene B. Allen.

22 St. 728; Aug. 5, 1882; C. 406—An act for the relief of Joab Spencer and James R. Mead.

22 St. 733; Aug. 7, 1882; C. 450—An act for the relief of Joseph Hertford.

22 St. 755; Feb. 22, 1883; C. 54—An act for the relief of E. P. Smith.

22 St. 755; Mar. 1, 1883; C. 63—An act for the allowance of certain claims reported by the accounting officers of the United States Treasury Department.

22 St. 797; Mar. 2, 1883; C. 70—An act granting a pension to Thomas Allcock.

22 St. 804; Mar. 3, 1883; C. 113—An act for the relief of Powers and Newman and D. and B. Powers.

22 St. 934; July 29, 1882—Agreement—Mexico.[24]

22 St. 939; Sept. 21, 1882—Agreement—Mexico.[25]

23 STAT.

23 St. 15; May 1, 1884; C. 37—An act to provide for certain of the most urgent deficiencies in the appropriations for the service of the Government for the fiscal year ending June 30, 1884, and for other purposes.[26]

23 St. 22; May 14, 1884; C. 50—An act to repeal section eight of an act entitled "An act to accept and ratify the agreement submitted by the confederated bands of Ute Indians in Colorado for the sale of their reservation in said State, and for other purposes, and to make the necessary appropriations for carrying out the same," approved June 15, 1880.[27]

23 St. 24; May 17, 1884; C. 53—An act providing a civil government for Alaska.[28]

23 St. 69; July 4, 1884; C. 177—An act to Grant to the Gulf, Colorado and Santa Fe Ry. Co. a right of way through the Indian Territory, and for other purposes.[29]

23 St. 73; July 4, 1884; C. 179—An act to grant the right of way through the Indian Territory to the Southern Kansas Ry. Co. and for other purposes.[30]

23 St. 76; July 4, 1884; C. 180—An act making appropriations for the current and contingent expenses of the Indian Department, and for fulfilling treaty stipulations with various Indian tribes, for the year ending June 30, 1885, and for other purposes.[31] Sec. 1—25 U. S. C. 195, 25 U. S. C. 249; 43 U. S. C. 190; Sec. 6—25 U. S. C. 46 (22 St. 88, sec. 6),[32] 25 U. S. C. 63 (22 St. 88, sec. 6); Sec. 8—25 U. S. C. 88; Sec. 9—25 U. S. C. 298; Sec. 10—25 U. S. C. 154.

23 St. 107; July 5, 1884; C. 217—An act making appropriations for the support of the Army for the fiscal year ending June 30, 1885, and for other purposes.

23 St. 159; July 7, 1884; C. 331—An act making appropriations for the legislative, executive, and judicial expenses of the Government for the fiscal year ending June 30, 1885, and for other purposes.

23 St. 194; July 7, 1884; C. 332—An act making appropriations for sundry civil expenses of the Government for the fiscal year ending June 30, 1885, and for other purposes.[33]

23 St. 256; July 7, 1884; C. 334—An act making appropriations to supply deficiencies in the appropriations for the fiscal year ending June 30, 1884, and for prior years, and for those certified as due by the accounting officers of the Treasury in accordance with section four of the act of June 14, 1878, heretofore paid from permanent appropriations, and for other purposes.[34]

23 St. 267; Feb. 8, 1884; J. Res. No. 8—Joint resolution appropriating $100 000 for the support of certain destitute Indians.

23 St. 268; Feb. 25, 1884; J. Res. No. 14—Joint resolution authorizing an expenditure of money for Indian educational purposes.[35]

23 St. 296; Jan. 31, 1885; C. 47—An act to authorize the appointment of a commission by the President of the United States to run and mark the boundary lines between a portion of the Indian Territory and the State of Texas, in connection with a similar commission to be appointed by the State of Texas.[36]

23 St. 340; Mar. 3, 1885; C. 319—An act providing for allotment of lands in severalty to the Indians residing upon the Uma-

---

786; 15 St. 514, 515, 584, 590, 596, 622, 635, 638, 651, 652, 655, 657, 676; 16 St. 13, 355, 708, 709, 720; 18 St. 689; 19 St. 254, 287; 21 St. 200; 22 St. 42, 68, 328. *S.* 23 St. 76. *Cited:* 34 L. D. 702; 42 L. D. 192; Medawakanton, 57 C. Cls. 357; U. S. v. Mitchell, 109 U. S. 146; U. S. v. Pierson, 145 Fed. 814.

[20] *Ag.* 17 St. 35.

[21] *Sg.* 19 St. 254. *S.* 24 St. 449; 39 St. 123; 46 St. 584. *A.* 44 St. 560. *Rp.* 45 St. 986. *Cited:* Memo. Ind. Off., Jan. 17, 1936; Eastern Band, 117 U. S. 288; Creek, 78 C. Cls. 474; Eastern Band, 19 C. Cls. 35; Eastern Band, 20 C. Cls. 449; Medawakanton, 57 C. Cls. 357; Shoshone, 85 C. Cls. 331; Shoshone, 82 C. Cls. 23; U. S. v. Algoma, 305 U. S. 415.

[22] *See:* 25 U. S. C. 161b; 31 U. S. C. 725s.

[23] *Sg.* 1 St. 137; 15 St. 635; 21 St. 316; 22 St. 217. *S.* 25 St. 608; 28 St. 876. *Cited:* Brewer-Elliott, 260 U. S. 77; Eastern Band, 20 C. Cls. 449; Ex p. Crow, 109 U. S. 556; Labadie, 6 Okla. 400; Kansas, 80 C. Cls. 264; Pawnee, 56 C. Cls. 1; U. S. v. Hutchings, 252 Fed. 841.

[24] *A.* 22 St. 939.

[25] *Ag.* 22 St. 934.

[26] *Cited:* Glavey, 35 C. Cls. 242.

[27] *Rpg.* 21 St. 199, sec. 8.

[28] *Sg.* 17 St. 424. *S.* 49 St. 1250. *Rp.* 80 St. 600, 1253. *Cited:* 18 Op. A. G. 557; 50 L. D. 815; 53 I. D. 593; Memo. Sol., Feb. 17, 1939; Columbia, 161 Fed. 60; Endleman, 86 Fed. 456; Heckman, 119 Fed. 83; In re Minook, 2 Alaska 200; Johnson, 2 Alaska 224; Kie, 27 Fed. 351; McGrath, 167 Fed. 473; Nagle, 191 Fed. 141; Nelson, 30 Fed. 112; Worthen, 229 Fed. 966; U. S. v. Berrigan, 2 Alaska 442; U. S. v. Cadzow, 5 Alaska 125; U. S. v. Lynch, 7 Alaska 568; U. S. v. Nelson, 29 Fed. 202; U. S. v. Warwick, 51 Fed. 280.

[29] *Sg.* 1 St. 137.

[30] *Sg.* 1 St. 137. *Cited:* Cherokee, 135 U. S. 611; Oklahoma, 220 U. S. 277; Thebo, 66 Fed. 372.

[31] *Sg.* 4 St. 442; 7 St. 36, 44, 51, 69, 85, 91, 99, 106, 113, 114, 161, 179, 185, 191, 210, 234, 242, 287, 296, 317, 320, 349, 425, 464, 540, 545, 596; 9 St. 35, 842, 853, 904; 10 St. 1039, 1044, 1056, 1069, 1078, 1093, 1095, 1167; 11 St. 611, 699, 702, 743; 12 St. 628, 981, 997, 1172; 13 St. 619, 623, 675, 694; 14 St. 650, 756, 776, 786; 15 St. 515, 584, 590, 596, 619, 635, 649, 657, 673, 675; 16 St. 355, 708, 720; 19 St. 254, 287; 21 St. 199; 22 St. 42, 86. *Rg.* 22 St. 449. *S.* 23 St. 362; 24 St. 29, 449; 25 St. 217, 980; 26 St. 336, 989; 27 St. 120, 612; 28 St. 286, 876; 29 St. 321; 30 St. 62, 571, 924; 33 St. 1048; 34 St. 55, 325; 38 St. 77; 43 St. 133, 357; 47 St. 1418; 48 St. 960. *A.* 23 St. 362. *Cited:* 19 Op. A. G. 161; 19 Op. A. G. 559; 20 Op. A. G. 561; 11 L. D. Memo. 296; Op. Sol. Off., May 15, 1933; Memo. Sol., July 25, 1935; Memo. Sol. Off., Aug. 20 1935; 5 L. D. 541; 6 L. D. 43; 12 L. D. 52; 16 L. D. 15; 24 L. D. 214; 31 L. D. 417; 32 L. D. 568; 35 L. D. 80; 40 L. D. 212; 48 L. D. 567; 54 I. D. 90; Conners, 33 C. Cls. 317; Elk, 112 U. S. 94; Fisher, 226 Fed. 156; Gordon, 34 App. D. C. 508; In re Can-Ah Couqua, 29 Fed. 687; In re McDonough, 49 Fed. 360; McKnight, 130 Fed. 659; Maryland, 37 F. 2d 318; M. K. & T. Ry. Co., 46 C. Cls. 59; Medawakanton, 57 C. Cls. 357; Mille Lac, 46 C. Cls. 424; Sac & Fox, 45 Cls. 287; Sac & Fox, 220 U. S. 481; Seaples, 246 Fed. 501; Starr, 227 U. S. 613; U. S. v. Anderson, 228 U. S. 52; U. S. v. Cass, 240 Fed. 617; U. S. v. Corporation, 101 F. 2d 156; U. S. v. Douglas, 190 Fed. 482; U. S. v. Ferry, 24 F. Supp. 399; U. S. v. Hemmer, 241 U. S. 379; U. S. v. Jackson, 280 U. S. 183; U. S. v. Johnson, 53 F. 2d 267; U. S. v. Joyce, 240 Fed. 610; U. S. v. Lewis, 253 Fed. 469; U. S. v. Lynch, 7 Alaska 568; U. S. v. Mille Lac, 229 U. S. 498; U. S. v. Moore, 161 Fed. 513; U. S. v. Pearson, 231 Fed. 270; U. S. v. Pelican, 232 U. S. 442; U. S. v. Pierson, 145 Fed. 817; U. S. v. Saunders, 96 Fed. 268; U. S. Exp., 191 Fed. 673; U. S. Fidelity, 214 U. S. 507.

[32] *See:* 25 U. S. C. 472.

[33] *Sg.* 1 St. 137; 14 St. 786; 19 St. 197. *S.* 27 St. 282.

[34] *Sg.* 10 St. 1053. *Cited:* Blackfeather, 28 C. Cls. 447; Blackfeather, 190 U. S. 368; U. S. v. Blackfeather, 155 U. S. 180.

[35] *Sg.* 22 St. 86.

[36] *Sg.* 8 St. 252. *S.* 23 St. 296.

tilla Reservation, in the State of Oregon, and granting patents therefor, and for other purposes.[37]

23 St. 344; Mar. 3, 1885; C. 320—An act to authorize the Secretary of the Interior to ascertain the amounts due to citizens of the United States for supplies furnished to the Sioux or Dakota Indians of Minnesota subsequent to June 1, 1861, and prior to the massacre of August 1862, and providing for the payment thereof.[38]

23 St. 350; Mar. 3, 1885; C. 335—An act to provide for the settlement of the claims of officers and enlisted men of the Army for loss of private property destroyed in the military service of the United States. See 31 U. S. C. 218–222.

23 St. 351; Mar. 3, 1885; C. 337—An act to provide for the sale of the Sac and Fox and Iowa Indian Reservations, in the States of Nebraska and Kansas, and for other purposes.[39]

23 St. 356; Mar. 3, 1885; C. 339—An act making appropriations for the support of the Army for the fiscal year ending June 30, 1886, and for other purposes.

23 St. 362; Mar. 3, 1885; C. 341—An act making appropriations for the current and contingent expenses of the Indian Department, and for fulfilling treaty stipulations with various Indian tribes, for the year ending June 30, 1886, and for other purposes.[40] Sec. 9—18 U. S. C. 548.

23 St. 388; Mar. 3, 1885; C. 343—An act making appropriations for the legislative, executive, and judicial expenses of the Government for the fiscal year ending June 30, 1886, and for other purposes.

23 St. 446; Mar. 3, 1885; C. 359—An act making appropriations to supply deficiencies in the appropriations for the fiscal year ending June 30, 1885, and for prior years, and for other purposes.

23 St. 478; Mar. 3, 1885; C. 360—An act making appropriations for sundry civil expenses of the Government for the fiscal year ending June 30, 1886, and for other purposes.[41]

23 St. 516; Jan. 12, 1885; J. Res. No. 6—Joint resolution appropriating $50,000 for the support of certain destitute Indians.

23 St. 525; Mar. 20, 1884; C. 13—An act for the relief of Louisa Boddy.

23 St. 528; May 7, 1884; C. 42—An act to adjust the accounts of John B. Monteith, deceased.

[37] *S.* 26 St. 745, 989; 27 St. 120, 417, 612; 28 St. 37; 32 St. 730; 33 St. 1048; 37 St. 665; 39 St. 923. *A.* 25 St. 217, 558; 45 St. 1008. *Cited:* Colya, 14–17 Tenn. Bar Assoc. 144; Memo. Sol. Off., Dec. 30, 1938; 24 L. D. 323; 27 L. D. 312; 40 L. D. 9; 43 L. D. 101; 55 I. D. 295; Beam, 162 Fed. 260; Bonifer, 166 Fed. 846; Brown, 146 Fed. 975; Guyett, 154 Fed. 784; Hy-Yu-Tse-Mil-Kin, 194 U. S. 401; In re Russie, 96 Fed. 609; Lemieux, 15 F. 2d 518; McKay, 204 U. S. 458; Parr, 197 Fed. 302; Parr, 153 Fed. 462; Patawa, 132 Fed. 893; Smith, 132 Fed. 889; Toy Toy, 212 U. S. 223; U. S. v. Kagama 118 U. S. 375; U. S. v. Raley, 173 Fed. 159; Yakima Joe, 191 Fed. 516.

[38] *Sg.* 12 St. 652. *Cited:* Medawakanton, 57 C. Cls. 357; U. S. v. Sisseton, 208 U. S. 561; Sisseton, 42 C. Cls. 416.

[39] *A.* 24 St. 367.

[40] *Sg.* 4 St. 442; 7 St. 36, 44, 51, 69, 85, 91, 99, 106, 113, 114, 161, 179, 185, 191, 210, 234, 242, 287, 296, 317, 320, 349, 425, 464, 540, 545, 596, 699; 9 St. 35, 556, 842, 853, 904; 10 St. 1039, 1044, 1056, 1069, 1078, 1093, 1167; 11 St. 611, 699, 702, 720, 743; 12 St. 628, 981, 997, 1172; 13 St. 675, 694; 14 St. 650, 755, 756, 769, 776, 780, 786, 799; 15 St. 515, 521, 533, 584, 590, 596, 619, 635, 649, 657, 678; 16 St. 355, 707, 720; 19 St. 254, 287; 22 St. 42, 341; 23 St. 87, 91; Pamphlet Laws, 48 Cong., 1 sess., p 70. *Rg.* 23 St. 92. *S.* 24 St. 3, 449; 25 St. 217, 757, 980; 26 St. 336, 851, 989; 28 St. 589; 34 St. 1371. *Rp.* 29 St. 487; 35 St. 1088. *Cited:* Brown, 39 Yale L. J. 307; Goodrich, 14 Calif. L. Rev. 83, 157; Houghton, 19 Calif. L. Rev. 507; Pound, 22 Colum. L. Rev. 97; Russell, 18 Yale L. J. 328; 1 L. D. Memo. 35; Memo. Sol. Off., Jan. 19, 1937; Andreas, 71 F. 2d 908; Apapas, 233 U. S. 587; Ayres, 35 C. Cls. 26; Bailey, 47 F. 2d 703; Buchanan, 28 C. Cls. 127; Campbell, 44 C. Cls. 488; Corralitos, 178 U. S. 280; Cox, 20 C. Cls. 349; Creek, 77 C. Cls. 159; Crow, 32 C. Cls. 16; Donnelly, 228 U. S. 243; Draper, 164 U. S. 240; Eugene Sol Louie, 274 Fed. 47; Ex p. Hart, 157 Fed. 130; Ex p. Pero, 99 F. 2d 28; Ex p. Savage, 158 Fed. 205; Falk, 27 C. Cls. 321; Friend, 29 C. Cls. 425; Gon-Shay-Ee, 130 U. S. 343; Good Shot, 104 Fed. 257; Goodson, 7 Okla. 117; Graham, 30 C. Cls. 318; Hegner, 30 C. Cls. 405; Herd, 13 Okla. 512; Hollister, 145 Fed. 773; Hyne, 27 C. Cls. 118; In re Blackbird, 109 Fed. 139; In re Can-Ah-Couqua, 29 Fed. 687; In re Minook, 2 Alaska 200; In re Sah Quah, 31 Fed. 327; Johnson, 160 U. S. 546; Johnson, 29 C. Cls. 1; Labadi, 31 C. Cls. 205; Leighton, 29 C. Cls. 288; Litchfield, 33 C. Cls. 203; Louie, 254 U. S. 548; Love, 29 C. Cls. 332; Lucas, 163 U. S. 612; McKee, 33 C. Cls. 99; Mares, 29 C. Cls. 197; Marks, 28 C. Cls. 147; Medawakanton, 57 C. Cls. 357; Mitchell, 27 C. Cls. 316; Moore, 32 C. Cls. 593; Pino, 38 C. Cls. 64; Price, 28 C. Cls. 422; Quagon, 5 F. 2d 608; Shoshone, 82 C. Cls. 23; Swope, 33 C. Cls. 223; Thurston, 232 U. S. 469; U. S. v. Barnaby, 51 Fed. 20; U. S. v. Boylan, 265 Fed. 165; U. S. v. Cardish 143 Fed. 640; U. S. v. Cardish, 145 Fed. 242; U. S. v. Celestine, 215 U. S. 278; U. S. v. Hadley, 90 Fed. 437; U. S. v. Hall, 171 Fed. 214; U. S. v. Kagama, 118 U. S. 375; U. S. v. Kie, 26 Fed. Cas. No. 15528a; U. S. v. King, 81 Fed. 625; U. S. v. La Plant, 200 Fed. 92; U. S. v. Logan, 105 Fed. 240; U. S. v. Navarre, 173 U. S. 77; U. S. v. Quiver, 241 U. S. 602; U. S. v. Seneca, 274 Fed. 947; U. S. v. Thomas, 47 Fed. 488; U. S. v. Ward, 42 Fed. 320; U. S. v. Whaley, 37 Fed. 145; Valk, 22 C. Cls. 241; Valk, 29 C. Cls. 62; Wisconsin, 201 U. S. 202; Yerke, 173 U. S. 439; Yohyowan, 291 Fed. 425.

[41] *Sg.* 1 St. 137; 15 St. 593.

23 St. 533; June 12, 1884; C. 90—An act for the relief of I. L. Burchard.

23 St. 552; July 5, 1884; C. 237—An act for the allowance of certain claims reported by the accounting officers of the United States Treasury Department, and for other purposes.[42]

23 St. 658; Feb. 28, 1885; C. 266—An act granting a pension to William Lockhart.

23 St. 660; Feb. 28, 1885; C. 279—An act granting an increase of pension to Colonel Samuel M. Thompson.

23 St. 672; Mar. 3, 1885; C. 378—An act granting a pension to Mrs. Cordelia Brainerd Thomas.

23 St. 674; Mar. 3, 1885; C. 389—An act for the relief of John M. Dorsey and William F. Shepard.

23 St. 677; Mar. 3, 1885; C. 399—An act for the relief of certain settlers on the Duck Valley Indian Reservation in Nevada.

23 St. 699; Mar. 3, 1885; C. 502—An act granting a pension to Sylvester Greenough.

23 St. 734; June 29, 1883; Memorandum of an Agreement—Mexico.[43]

23 St. 806; Oct. 31, 1884; Protocol—Mexico.[44]

24 STAT.

24 St. 3; Feb. 9, 1886; C. 7—An act authorizing the Secretary of the Interior to use certain unexpended balances for the relief of the Northern Cheyennes in Montana.[45]

24 St. 28; May 15, 1886; C. 332—An act to authorize the Red River Bridge Company of Texas to maintain a bridge across Red River.

24 St. 29; May 15, 1886; C. 333—An act making appropriations for the current and contingent expenses of the Indian Department, and for fulfilling treaty stipulations with various Indian tribes, for the year ending June 30, 1887, and for other purposes.[46]

24 St. 73; June 1, 1886; C. 395—An act to authorize the Kansas and Arkansas Valley Railway to construct and operate a railway through the Indian Territory, and for other purposes.[46a]

24 St. 76; June 1, 1886; C. 397—An act to amend an act entitled "An act to grant a right of way for a railroad and telegraph line through the lands of the Choctaw and Chickasaw Nations of Indians to the St. Louis and San Francisco Ry. Co., and for other purposes."[47]

24 St. 93; June 30, 1886; C. 574—An act making appropriations for the support of the Army for the fiscal year ending June 30, 1887, and for other purposes.

24 St. 117; July 1, 1886; C. 601—An act to authorize the Denison and Washita Valley Ry. Co. to construct and operate a railway through the Indian Territory, and for other purposes.[48]

24 St. 121; July 2, 1886; C. 608—An act to provide for the sale of the Cherokee Reservation in the State of Arkansas.

24 St. 124; July 6, 1886; C. 744—An act to authorize the Kansas City, Fort Scott and Gulf Ry. Co. to construct and operate a railway through the Indian Territory, and for other purposes.[49]

24 St. 159; July 28, 1886; C. 799—An act to authorize the Secretary of War to credit the State of Kansas with certain sums of money on its ordnance account with the General Government.

24 St. 172; July 31, 1886; C. 827—An act making appropriations for the legislative, executive, and judicial expenses of the Government for the fiscal year ending June 30, 1887, and for other purposes.[50]

[42] *Sg.* 13 St. 387.

[43] *Rp.* 23 St. 806.

[44] *Rpg.* 23 St. 734.

[45] *Sg.* 23 St. 379.

[46] *Sg.* 1 St. 619; 4 St. 442; 7 St. 36, 46, 51, 69, 85, 91, 99, 106, 114, 161, 179, 185, 191, 212, 236, 242, 287, 296, 317, 320, 352, 425, 464, 540, 543, 545, 596; 9 Stat. 35, 842, 853, 904; 10 St. 1039, 1044, 1056, 1071, 1079, 1093, 1168; 11 St. 614, 700, 701, 702, 729, 744; 12 Stat. 628, 981, 997, 1173; 13 St. 624, 675, 694; 14 St. 650, 757, 787; 15 St. 514, 515, 581, 589, 593, 622, 638, 651, 655, 676; 16 St. 13, 708, 720; 19 St. 254, 287; 22 St. 43; 23 St. 79, 87. *S.* 25 St. 113; 33 St. 189. *Cited:* 18 Op. A. G. 440; Blackfeet, 81 C. Cls. 101; Chippewa, 80 C. Cls. 410; Crow, 81 C. Cls. 238; Johnson, 160 U. S. 546; Leighton, 29 C. Cls. 288; Medawakanton, 57 C. Cls. 357; Mille Lac, 46 C. Cls. 424; Mitchell, 27 C. Cls. 316; Moore, 32 C. Cls. 593; Pino, 38 C. Cls. 64; Stone, 29 C. Cls. 111; Tiger, 221 U. S. 286.

[46a] *Sg.* 1 St. 137. *S.* 26 St. 21, 783. *Cited:* 19 Op. A. G. 42; Thebo, 66 Fed. 372.

[47] *Sg.* 22 St. 181.

[48] *Sg.* 1 St. 137. *A.* 26 St. 147.

[49] *Sg.* 1 St. 137. *Cited:* Thebo, 66 Fed. 372.

[50] *Cited:* Thebo, 66 Fed. 372

24 St. 214; Aug. 2, 1886; C. 844—An act authorizing the Secretary of the Interior to extend the time of payment to purchasers of lands of the Otoe and Missouria and of the Omaha Indians.[51]

24 St. 219; Aug. 4, 1886; C. 897—An act to provide for the settlement of the estates of deceased Kickapoo Indians in the State of Kansas, and for other purposes.[52]

24 St. 222; Aug. 4, 1886; C. 902—An act making appropriations for sundry civil expenses of the Government for the fiscal year ending June 30, 1887, and for other purposes.[53]

24 St. 256; Aug. 4, 1886; C. 903—An act making appropriations to supply deficiencies in the appropriations for the fiscal year ending June 30, 1886, and for prior years, and for other purposes.[54]

24 St. 349; Aug. 5, 1886; J. Res. No. 37—Joint resolution to print the annual bulletins of the Bureau of Ethnology.

24 St. 361; Jan. 17, 1887; C. 26—An act to grant the Maricopa and Phoenix Ry. Co. of Arizona the right of way through the Gila River Indian Reservation.

24 St. 367; Jan. 26, 1887; C. 47—An act to amend the third section of an act entitled "An act to provide for the sale of the Sac and Fox and Iowa Indian Reservations, in the States of Nebraska and Kansas, and for other purposes," approved March 3, 1885.[55]

24 St. 388; Feb. 8, 1887; C. 119—An act to provide for the allotment of lands in severalty to Indians on the various reservations, and to extend the protection of the laws of the United States and the Territories over the Indians, and for other purposes.[56] Sec. 1—25 U. S. C. 331 (26 St. 794, sec. 1, 36 St. 859, sec. 17). See Historical Note 25 U. S. C. A. 331. Sec. 2—25 U. S. C. 332. Sec. 3—25 U. S. C. 333 (36 Stat. 858, sec. 9). Sec. 4—25 U. S. C. 334.[57] Sec. 5—25 U. S. C. 348 (31 St. 1085, sec. 9). Sec. 6—25 U. S. C. 349 (34 St. 182). Sec. 7—25 U. S. C. 381. Sec. 8—25 U. S. C. 339. Sec. 10—25 U. S. C. 341. Sec. 11—25 U. S. C. 342.

24 St. 394; Feb. 9, 1887; C. 127—An act making appropriations for the support of the Army for the fiscal year ending June 30, 1888, and for other purposes.

24 St. 402; Feb. 15, 1887; C. 130—An act granting to the Saint Paul, Minneapolis and Manitoba Ry. Co. the right of way through the Indian reservations in Northern Montana and Northwestern Dakota.[58]

24 St. 419; Feb. 24, 1887; C. 254—An act to authorize the Fort Worth and Denver City Ry. Co. to construct and operate a railway through the Indian Territory, and for other purposes.[59]

24 St. 432; Feb. 28, 1887; C. 282—An act to authorize the Secretary of War to credit the Territory of Dakota with certain sums for ordnance and ordnance stores issued to said Territory, and for other purposes.

24 St. 446; Mar. 2, 1887; C. 319—An act to grant the right of way through the Indian Territory to the Chicago, Kansas and Nebraska Railway, and for other purposes.[60]

24 St. 449; Mar. 2, 1887; C. 320—An act making appropriations for the current and contingent expenses of the Indian Department, and for fulfilling treaty stipulations with the various Indian tribes, for the year ending June 30, 1888, and

---

[51] *Sg.* 21 St. 380; 22 St. 341.

[52] *Sg.* 13 St 624. *S.* 25 St. 217; 26 St. 336; 28 St. 286; 30 St. 62, 924; 32 St. 982; 33 St. 189, 1048. *Cited:* 19 Op. A. G. 255; Briggs, 37 Fed. 135.

[53] *Sg.* 1 St. 137.

[54] *Sg.* 15 St. 533. *S.* 25 St. 79.

[55] *Ag.* 23 St. 352.

[56] *S.* 24 St. 449; 25 St. 217, 611, 642, 980, 1013; 26 St. 336, 658, 989; 27 St. 52, 62, 120, 557, 612; 28 St. 286, 876; 29 St. 321; 30 St. 62, 571, 924; 31 St. 221, 672, 1058; 32 St. 245, 744, 982, 1606; 33 St. 189, 989, 1048; 34 St. 325, 1015, 1413; 35 St. 8, 70, 781; 36 St. 269, 855, 1058, 2064; 37 St. 518; 38 St. 77, 582; 39 St. 128, 739, 969; 40 St. 561; 41 St. 3, 408, 751, 1225; 42 St. 552, 1174, 1246; 43 St. 132, 390, 1114, 1141, 1313; 44 St. 453, 566, 658, 690, 934; 45 St. 200, 482, 617, 1562; 46 St. 279, 1115, 1205; 47 St. 91, 820; 50 St. 210. *A.* 26 St. 794; 31 Stat. 1058, 1447; 34 St. 182, 325. *Rp.* 48 St. 1224. *Cited:* Abbot, 2 How. L. Rev. 167; Brosius, 23 Case & Com. 739; Brown, 39 Yale L. J. 307; Cain, 2 Minn. L. Rev. 177; Colya, 14–17 Tenn. Bar Assoc. 144; Goodrich, 14 Calif. L. Rev. 83, 157; Houghton, 19 Calif. L. Rev. 507; Knoepfler, 7 Ia. L. B. 232; Krieger, 3 Geo. Wash. L. Rev. 279; Platt, 160 N. A. Rev. 195; Reeves, 23 Case & Com. 727; Rice, 16 J. Comp. Leg. 78; Russell, 18 Yale L. J. 328; Leupp, IP; Stewart, GDO; 46 Cong., 2d sess., H. Rept. No. 1319; 46 Cong., 2d sess., H. Rept. No. 1576; 18 Op. A. G. 593; 19 Op. A. G. 14; 19 Op. A. G. 161; 19 Op. A. G. 183; 19 Op. A. G. 232; 19 Op. A. G. 255; 19 Op. A. G. 559; 20 Op. A. G. 42; 22 Op. A. G. 232; 25 Op. A. G. 416; 25 Op. A. G. 483; 29 Op. A. G. 239; 34 Op. A. G. 181; 1 L. D. Memo. 103; 2 L. D. Memo. 284; 3 L. D. Memo. 388; 3 L. D Memo 435; 4 L. D. Memo. 72; 5 L. D. Memo. 168; 8 L. D. Memo. 764; 11 L. D. Memo. 296; 12 L. D. Memo. 652; 14 L. D. Memo. 493; 5 L. D. 520; 6 L. D. 43; 8 L. D. 647; 9 L. D. 392; 11 L. D. 103; 12 L. D. 162; 12 L. D. 168; 12 L. D. 181; 12 L. D. 205; 13 L. D. 185; 13 L. D. 310; 13 L. D. 316; 13 L. D. 318; 15 L. D. 287; 18 L. D. 209; 18 L. D. 497; 19 L. D. 326; 19 L. D. 329; 20 L. D. 319; 20 L. D. 46; 20 L. D. 157; 20 L. D. 167; 20 L. D. 462; 22 L. D. 709; 24 L. D. 311; 24 L. D. 511; 26 L. D. 71; 26 L. D. 44; 28 L. D. 71; 28 L. D. 564; 29 L. D. 251; 29 L. D. 331; 29 L. D. 680; 30 L. D. 258; 30 L. D. 532; 31 L. D. 417; 32 L. D. 17; 33 L. D. 205; 33 L. D. 454; 34 L. D. 252; 34 L. D. 702; 35 L. D. 80; 35 L. D. 549; 35 L. D. 648; 38 L. D. 422; 38 L. D. 553; 38 L. D. 558; 38 L. D. 559; 40 L. D. 9; 40 L. D. 148; 41 L. D. 626; 42 L. D. 446; 42 L. D. 489; 43 L. D. 125; 43 L. D. 504; 44 L. D. 188; 44 L. D. 391; 44 L. D. 520; 48 L. D. 455; 48 L. D. 479; 48 L. D. 567; 50 L. D. 676; 50 L. D. 691; 53 I. D. 507; 53 I. D. 133; 53 I. D. 593; 54 I. D. 71; 54 I. D. 160; 54 I. D. 297; 55 I. D. 295; Op. Sol., M. 5379, July 14, 1921; M. 4018, July 29, 1921, M. 5805 Nov. 22, 1921, M. 6882, Mar. 29, 1922, M. 5379, Apr. 27, 1922, M. 5702, Apr. 27, 1922, A. 2592, Feb. 12, 1924, M. 11665, Apr. 19, 1924, M. 12498, June 6, 1924, M. 11380, June 17, 1924, M. 12509, Aug. 27, 1924, M. 13270, Nov. 6, 1924, M. 18604, Mar. 6, 1926, M. 20612, Dec. 28, 1926, M. 15954, Jan. 8, 1927; Memo. Ind. Off., Apr. 21, 1927; Op. Sol., M. 24358, May 14, 1928, M. 25214, June 7, 1929, M. 25258, June 26, 1929; Op. A. G., Oct. 5, 1929; Op. Sol., M. 25347, Jan. 25, 1930; Report on Status of Pueblo of Pojoaque, Nov. 3, 1932; Memo. Sol. Off., Apr. 4, 1933; Jan. 16, 1934; Memo. Ind. Off., Jan. 31, 1934; Memo. Sol., Aug. 8, 1934; Op. Sol., M. 27381, Dec. 13, 1934; Memo. Sol. Off., Aug. 20, 1935, Nov. 14, 1935; Op. Sol., M. 27878, May 20, 1936; Memo. of Comm'r, Jan. 8, 1937; Memo. of Ass't Sec'y to Comm'r, Feb. 17, 1937; Memo. Sol. Off., June 3, 1937; Memo. Sol., Sept. 23, 1937, Mar. 19, 1938; Bartlett v. Okla. Oil Co., 218 Fed. 380; Beam, 162 Fed. 260; Beam, 159 Fed. 651; Beck, 85 Fed. 30; Bird, 129 Fed. 472; Bd. of Co. Com'rs of Jackson City, 100 F. 2d 929; Board of Com'rs of Caddo County, 87 F. 2d 55; Bond, 181 Fed. 613; Bowling, 233 U. S. 529; Browning, 6 F. 2d 801; Button, 7 F. Supp. 597; Chippewa, 80 C. Cls. 410; Coos Bay Ind. Tr., 87 C. Cls. 143; Dick, 208 U. S. 340; Dickson, 242 U. S. 371; Draper, 164 U. S. 240; Dupuis, 5 F. 2d 281; Eugene Sol Louie, 274 Fed. 47; Ex p. Dick, 141 Fed. 5; Ex p. Pero, 99 F. 2d 28; Ex p. Savage, 158 Fed. 205; Ex p. Van Moore, 221 Fed. 954; Ex p. Viles, 189 Fed. 68; Fairbanks, 223 U. S. 215; Farrell, 110 Fed. 942; Finley, 4 Ind. T. 386; Fond du Lac Band, 34 C. Cls. 426; Finley, 129 Fed. 734; First Moon, 270 U. S. 243; Fish, 52 F. 2d 544; Goodson, 7 Okla. 117; Goodrum, 162 Fed. 817; Goudy, 203 U. S. 146; Gravelle, 253 Fed. 549; Hallowell, 221 U. S. 317; Heckman, 224 U. S. 413; Hitchcock, 22 App. D. C. 275; Hollister, 145 Fed. 773; In re Incorporation, 3 Alaska 588; In re Jessie's Heirs, 259 Fed. 94; In re Minook, 2 Alaska 200; In re Penn, 41 F. 2d 257; In re Wilson, 140 U. S. 575; Jefferson, 247 U. S. 288; Johnson, 234 U. S. 422; Johnson, 283 Fed. 954; Jones, 175 U. S. 1; La Clair, 184 Fed. 128; Lane, 241 U. S. 201; Larkin, 276 U. S. 431; La Roque, 239 U. S. 62; Laughton, 75 Fed. 789; Leecy, 190 Fed. 289; Lemieux, 15 F. 2d 518; Lemmon, 106 Fed. 650; M. K. & T. Ry., 46 C. Cls. 59; McKay, 204 U. S. 458; McKnight, 130 Fed. 659; Mandler, 49 F. 2d 201; Mandler, 52 F. 2d 713; Matter of Heff, 197 U. S. 488; Meeker, 173 Fed. 216; Miller, 57 F. 2d 987; Minnesota, 305 U. S. 382; Minnesota, 185 U. S. 373; Monson, 231 U. S. 341; Morrison, 266 U. S. 481; Morrison, 6 F. 2d 811; Morrow, 243 Fed. 854; Mosier, 198 Fed. 94; Mulligan, 120 Fed. 98; Muskrat, 219 U. S. 346; Nagle, 191 Fed. 141; Nimrod, 24 F. 2d 613; Oakes, 172 Fed. 305; Oregon, 202 U. S. 60; Pape, 19 F. 2d 219; Pel-Ata-Yakot, 188 Fed. 387; People, 8 F. Supp. 295; Perrin, 232 U. S. 478; Porter, 239 U. S. 170; Rainbow, 161 Fed. 835; Red Hawk, 39 F. 2d 293; Renfrow, 3 Okla. 161; Reynolds, 205 Fed. 685; Ross, 56 Fed. 855; Sage, 235 U. S. 99; Scheer, 48 F. 2d 327; Seaples, 246 Fed. 501; Shoshone, 85 C. Cls. 331; Sisseton, 58 C. Cls. 302; Smith, 142 Fed. 225; St. Marie, 24 F. Supp. 237; Taylor, 51 F. 2d 884; Toy-Toy, 212 U. S. 542; U. S. v. Aaron, 183 Fed. 347; U. S. v. Abrams, 194 Fed. 82; U. S. v. Allen, 179 Fed. 13; U. S. v. Ashton, 170 Fed. 509; U. S. v. Barnett, 7 F. Supp. 573; U. S. v. Bellm, 182 Fed. 161; U. S. v. Benewah Co., 290 Fed. 628; U. S. v. Bd. of Com'rs of Comanche Co., 6 F. Supp. 401; U. S. v. Bd. of Co. Com'rs, 13 F. Supp. 641; U. S. v. Boss, 160 Fed. 132; U. S. v. Boyd, 83 Fed. 547; U. S. v. Cain-Bonness, 215 Fed. 212; U. S. v. Cardish, 145 Fed. 242; U. S. v. Caster, 271 Fed. 615; U. S. v. Celestine, 215 U. S. 278; U. S. v. Chehalis, 217 Fed. 281; U. S. v. Choctaw, 179 U. S. 494; U. S. v. Conrad, 161 Fed. 829; U. S. v. Dewey, 14 F. 2d 784; U. S. v. Dooley, 151 Fed. 697; U. S. v. Estill, 62 F. 2d 620; U. S. v. Ferry, 24 F. Supp. 399; U. S. v. First, 234 U. S. 245; U. S. v. First, 282 Fed. 330; U. S. v. Fitzgerald, 201 Fed. 295; U. S. v. Flournoy, 69 Fed. 886; U. S. v. Gardner, 183 Fed. 285; U. S. v. Gardner, 189 Fed. 690; U. S. v. Getzelman, 89 F. 2d 531; U. S. v. Glacier, 17 F. Supp. 411; U. S. v. Gray, 201 Fed. 291; U. S. v. Hall, 171 Fed. 214; U. S. v. Heinrich, 16 F. 2d 112; U. S. v. Homeratha, 40 F. 2d 305; U. S. v. Howard, 8 F. Supp. 617; U. S. v. Inaba, 291 Fed. 416; U. S. v. Jackson, 280 U. S. 183; U. S. v. Johnson, 53 F. 2d 267; U. S. v. Kiya, 126 Fed. 879; U. S. v. Ladley, 4 F. Supp. 580; U. S. v. La Roque, 198 Fed. 645; U. S. v. Law, 250 Fed. 218; U. S. v Leslie, 167 Fed. 670; U. S. v. Lewis, 253 Fed. 469; U. S. v. Lewis, 95 F. 2d 236; U. S. v. Lynch, 7 Alaska 568; U. S. v. McIntire, 101 F. 2d 650; U. S. v. Nez Perce, 95 F. 2d 232; U. S. v. Nice, 241 U. S. 591; U. S. v. Paine, 206 U. S. 467; U. S. v. Park, 188 Fed. 383; U. S. v. Parkhurst-Davis, 176 U. S. 317; U. S. v. Payne, 264 U. S. 446; U. S. v. Pearson, 231 Fed. 270; U. S. v. Pelican, 232 U. S. 442; U. S. v. Powers, 305 U. S. 527; U. S. v. Pumphrey, 11 App. D. C. 44; U. S. v. Reily, 290 U. S. 33; U. S. v. Reynolds, 250 U. S. 104; U. S. v Rundell, 181 Fed 887; U. S. v. Saunders, 96 Fed. 268; U. S. v. Seufert, 252 Fed. 51; U. S. v. Sherburne, 68 F. 2d 155; U. S. v. Smith, 279 Fed. 136; U. S. v. Spaeth, 24 F. Supp. 465; U. S. v. Sutton, 215 U. S. 291; U. S. v. Swain, N. C., 46 F. 2d 99; U. S. v. Thurston, 143 Fed. 287; U. S. v. Walker River, 104 F. 2d 334; U. S. v. Waller, 243 U. S. 452; U. S. v. Wright, 229 U. S. 226; U. S. v. Wright, 53 F. 2d 300; U. S. v. Yakima, 274 Fed. 115; U. S. ex rel. Besaw, 6 F. 2d 694; U. S. ex rel. Kadrie, 30 F. 2d 989; U. S. ex rel. Zane, 4 Ind. T. 185; U. S. Ex., 191 Fed. 673; Westling, 60 F. 2d 398; Wheeler, 153 Fed. 471; Whitebird, 40 F. 2d 479; Williams, 16 Okla. 104; Woodward, 238 U. S 284; Work, 29 F. 2d 393; Work, 18 F. 2d 820; Yakima Joe, 191 Fed. 516.

[57] R. 48 St. 1225, sec. 1.

[58] *Sg.* 18 St. 28. *Cited:* U. S. v. Lindahl, 221 Fed. 143.

[59] *Sg.* 1 St. 137. *A.* 26 St. 661. *Cited:* Thebo, 66 Fed. 372.

[60] *Sg* 1 St. 187. *S.* 27 St. 495. *Rp.* 26 St. 181. *Cited:* Thebo, 66 Fed. 372.

for other purposes.[61] Sec. 1—p. 463, See Historical Note 25 U. S. C. A. 155; p. 465, 25 U. S. C. 299.[62]

24 St. 509; Mar. 3, 1887; C. 362—An act making appropriations for sundry civil expenses of the Government for the fiscal year ending June 30, 1888, and for other purposes.[63]

24 St. 545; Mar. 3, 1887; C. 366—An act granting to the Rocky Fork and Cooke City Ry. Co. the right of way through a part of the Crow Indian Reservation, in Montana Territory.[64]

24 St. 548; Mar. 3, 1887; C. 368—An act granting the Utah Midland Railway Company the right of way through the Uncompahgre and Uintah Reservations, in the Territory of Utah, and for other purposes.

24 St. 594; Mar. 3, 1887; C. 392—An act making appropriations for the legislative, executive, and judicial expenses of the Government for the fiscal year ending June 30, 1888, and for other purposes.

24 St. 635; Mar. 3, 1887; C. 397—An act to amend an act entitled "An act to amend sec. 5352 of the Revised Statutes of the United States, in reference to bigamy, and for other purposes," approved March 22, 1882.[65] Sec. 1—28 U. S. C. 633; Sec. 2—28 U. S. C. 660; Sec. 3—18 U. S. C. 516; Sec. 26—48 U. S. C. 1480a.

24 St. 694; May 7, 1886; C. 104—An act granting a pension to David McKinney.

24 St. 736; May 8, 1886; C. 275—An act for the relief of George A. Roberts.

24 St. 736; May 8, 1886; C. 276—An act granting a pension to Frederick North.

24 St. 803; June 24, 1886; C. 477—An act granting an increase of pension to Thomas Allcock.

24 St. 828; July 3, 1886; C. 630—An act for the relief of James M. Bacon.

24 St. 835; July 6, 1886; C. 664—An act granting a pension to Solomon Messer.

24 St. 851; July 14, 1886; C. 766—An act for the relief of J. M. Hiatt, only surviving partner of Hiatt and Company.[66]

24 St. 868; Aug. 3, 1886; C. 882—An act for the relief of Jacob Nix.

24 St. 876; Aug. 4, 1886; C. 923—An act for the relief of Mary E. Casey.[67]

24 St. 926; Mar. 2, 1887; C. 321—An act for the relief of Alpheus R. French.

24 St. 929; Mar. 3, 1887; C. 400—An act for the relief of J. M. Hobbs.

24 St. 969; Mar. 3, 1887; C. 446—An act for the relief of William M. Morrison.

25 STAT.

25 St. 4; Feb. 1, 1888; C. 4—An act making appropriations to supply deficiencies in the appropriations for the fiscal year ending June 30, 1887, and for prior years, and for other purposes.[68]

25 St. 33; Feb. 15, 1888; C. 10—An act to punish robbery, burglary, and larceny, in the Indian Territory.[69]

25 St. 35; Feb. 18, 1888; C. 13—An act to authorize the Choctaw Coal and Ry. Co. to construct and operate a railway through the Indian Territory, and for other purposes.[70]

25 St. 47; Mar. 30, 1888; C. 47—An act to provide for certain of the most urgent deficiencies in the appropriations for the service of the Government for the fiscal year ending June 30, 1888, and for other purposes.

25 St. 79; Apr. 4, 1888; C. 59—An act to enable the Secretary of the Interior to pay certain creditors of the Pottawattomie Indians out of the funds of said Indians.[71]

25 St. 90; Apr. 24, 1888; C. 192—An act granting the right of way to the Duluth, Rainy Lake River and Southwestern Ry. Co. through certain Indian lands in the State of Minnesota.

25 St. 94; Apr. 30, 1888; C. 206—An act to divide a portion of the reservation of the Sioux Nation of Indians in Dakota into separate reservations and to secure the relinquishment of the Indian title to the remainder.[72]

25 St. 113; May 1, 1888; C. 213—An act to ratify and confirm an agreement with the Gros Ventre, Piegan, Blood, Blackfeet, and River Crow Indians in Montana, and for other purposes.[73]

25 Stat. 140; May 14, 1888; C. 248—An act to grant a right of way to the Kansas City and Pacific R. Co. through the Indian Territory, and for other purposes.[74]

25 St. 150; May 15, 1888; C. 255—An act for the relief of the Omaha tribe of Indians in Nebraska, to extend time of payment to purchasers of land of said Indians, and for other purposes.[75]

25 St. 157; May 24, 1888; C. 310—An act to restore to the public domain a part of the Uintah Valley Indian Reservation, in the Territory of Utah, and for other purposes.[76]

25 St. 160; May 30, 1888; C. 336—An act granting to the Washington and Idaho R. Co. the right of way through the Coeur d'Alene Indian Reservation.[77]

25 St. 162; May 30, 1888; C. 337—An act to grant to the Fort Smith and El Paso Ry. Co. a right of way through the Indian Territory, and for other purposes.[78]

25 St. 166; June 4, 1888; C. 340—An act to amend sec. 5388 of the Revised Statutes of the United States, in relation to timber depredations.[79] 18 U. S. C. 104.

25 St. 167; June 4, 1888; C. 343—An act to authorize the United States marshals to arrest offenders and fugitives from justice in Indian Territory.[80] Sec. 1—See Historical Note 25 U. S. C. A. 226.

25 St. 167; June 4, 1888; C. 344—An act granting to the Billings, Clark's Fork and Cooke City R. Co. the right of way through the Crow Indian Reservation.

25 St. 169; June 4, 1888; C. 345—An act granting to the Milwaukee, Lake Shore and Western Ry. Co. the right of way through the Lac de Flambeau Indian Reservation, in the State of Wisconsin.

25 St. 178; June 9, 1888; C. 382—An act for the protection of the officials of the United States in the Indian Territory.

25 St. 184; June 18, 1888; C. 390—An act to authorize the Fort Smith and Choctaw Bridge Co. to construct a bridge across the Poteau River in the Choctaw Nation, near Fort Smith, Arkansas.[81]

25 St. 205; June 26, 1888; C. 494—An act to authorize the Paris, Choctaw and Little Rock Ry. Co. to construct and operate a railway, telegraph and telephone line through the Indian Territory, and for other purposes.[82]

25 St. 217; June 29, 1888; C. 503—An act making appropriations for the current and contingent expenses of the Indian Department, and for fulfilling treaty stipulations with various Indian tribes, for the year ending June 30, 1889, and for other purposes.[83] Sec. 8—See Historical Note 25 U. S. C. A. 272.

---

[61] *Sg.* 1 St. 619; 4 St. 442; 7 St. 36, 46, 51, 69, 85, 91, 99, 106, 114, 161, 179, 185, 191, 212, 236, 242, 287, 296, 317, 320, 349, 352, 425, 464, 541, 543, 545, 596; 9 St. 35, 842, 854, 855, 904; 10 St. 1039, 1044, 1056, 1071, 1079, 1095, 1168; 11 St. 614, 700, 702, 729, 730, 744; 12 St. 628, 981, 997, 1173; 13 St. 675, 694; 14 St. 650, 757, 787; 15 St. 515, 584, 590, 596, 622, 638, 651, 657, 676; 16 St. 40, 355, 720; 19 St. 254, 287; 22 St. 42, 590; 23 St. 79, 376; 24 St. 388. *A.* 44 St. 560. *Rp.* 45 St. 986. *S.* 25 St. 217, 980; 26 St. 336, 989; 39 St. 123. *Cited:* Creek, 78 C. Cls. 474; Medawakanton, 57 C. Cls. 357; Osage, 66 C. Cls. 64; Price, 28 C. Cls. 422; Shoshone, 82 C. Cls. 28; Stone, 20 C. Cls. 111.

[62] *R.* 45 St. 986, 990, sec. 1.

[63] *Sg.* 1 St. 137.

[64] *Cited:* Crow, 81 C. Cls. 238.

[65] *Ag.* 12 St. 501, sec. 1. *Cited:* Ex p. Hart, 157 Fed. 130; In re Mayfield, 141 U. S. 107; U. S. v. Quiver, 241 U. S. 602.

[66] *Sg.* 21 St. 291.

[67] *Sg.* 4 St. 80; 11 St. 387, sec. 1.

[68] *Sg.* 12 St. 740, sec. 10.

[69] *Cited:* Herd, 13 Okla. 512; U. S. v. Pridgeon, 153 U. S. 48.

[70] *Sg.* 1 St. 137. *A.* 25 St. 668; 26 St. 765; 28 St. 27. *Cited:* Memo. Sol., Aug. 25, 1937; Ansley, 5 Ind. T. 563; Choctaw, 256 U. S. 531; Gowen, 56 Fed. 973; Thebo, 66 Fed. 372; U. S. ex rel. Scott, 1 Dak. 142; Walker, 204 U. S. 302.

[71] *Sg.* 24 St. 272. *Cited:* 19 Op. A. G. 134; 19 Op. A. G. 242.

[72] *Sg.* 12 St. 637; 14 St. 67, sec. 1; 15 St. 635, 638; 17 St. 333, sec. 1; 19 St. 73, 377; 22 St. 36; 25 St. 96. *S.* 25 St. 888; 28 St. 286; 34 St. 1015. *Cited:* U. S. v. Jackson, 280 U. S. 183.

[73] *Ag.* 18 St. 28. *Sg.* 12 St. 393, sec. 8; 24 St. 44. *S.* 25 St. 217, 980; 26 St. 336, 989; 27 St. 120, 612; 28 St. 286, 677, 876; 29 St. 321; 30 St. 62; 33 St. 816; 46 St. 531. *A.* 36 St. 1080. *Cited:* Op. Sol. M. 15849, May 12, 1925; Memo. Sol. Off. Feb. 15, 1932; Assinboine, 77 C. Cls. 347; Blackfeet, 81 C. Cls. 101; British-American, 299 U. S. 159; McKnight, 130 Fed. 659; U. S. v. Anderson, 228 U. S. 52; U. S. v. Conrad, 161 Fed. 829; U. S. v. Powers, 305 U. S. 527; U. S. v. Soldona, 246 U. S. 530; U. S. v. Walker River, 104 F. 2d 334; Winters, 207 U. S. 564.

[74] *A.* 26 St. 32. *Cited:* Thebo, 66 Fed. 372.

[75] *Sg.* 10 St. 1044; 22 St. 341.

[76] *Cited:* 25 L. D. 408.

[77] *Cited:* 19 Op. A. G. 199.

[78] *Sg.* 1 St. 137. *Cited:* Thebo, 66 Fed. 372.

[79] *Ag.* 3 St. 513, sec. 5. *Rp.* 35 St. 1088. *Cited:* 19 Op. A. G. 183; Sol. Op. 22121, Apr. 12, 1927; Labadie, 6 Okla. 400; U. S. v. Konkapot, 43 Fed. 64.

[80] *R.* 30 St. 1214.

[81] *A.* 25 St. 884.

[82] *Sg.* 1 St. 137. *Cited:* Thebo, 66 Fed. 372.

[83] *Sg.* 1 St. 619; 4 St. 442; 7 St. 36, 46, 51, 69, 85, 91, 99, 106, 114, 161, 179, 185, 191, 212, 236, 242, 287, 296, 320, 349, 352, 425, 464, 541, 543, 545, 596; 9 St. 35, 842, 855, 904; 10 St. 1039, 1056, 1069, 1078, 1095, 1168, 11 St. 614, 700, 702, 729, 744; 12 St. 628, 766, sec. 7, 981, 997, 1173; 13 St. 624, 675, 694; 14 St. 650, 757, 787; 15 St. 515, 500, 596, 622, 638, 651, 657, 676; 16 St. 40, 355, 720; 19 St. 254, 287; 22 St. 42;

25 St. 240; July 4, 1888; C. 510—An act authorizing the sale of a portion of the Winnebago Reservation in Nebraska.

25 St. 256; July 11, 1888; C. 615—An act making appropriations for the legislative, executive, and judicial expenses of the Government for the fiscal year ending June 30, 1889, and for other purposes.

25 St. 347; July 26, 1888; C. 716—An act granting to the Newport and King's Valley R. Co. the right of way through the Siletz Indian Reservation.

25 St. 349; July 26, 1888; C. 717—An act granting to the Oregon Railway and Navigation Co. the right of way through the Nez Perce Indian Reservation.

25 St. 350; July 26, 1888; C. 718—An act to grant to the Puyallup Valley Ry. Co. a right of way through the Puyallup Indian Reservation in Washington Territory, and for other purposes.[84]

25 St. 392; Aug. 9, 1888; C. 818—An act in relation to marriage between white men and Indian women.[85] Sec. 1—25 U. S. C. 181; Sec. 2—25 U. S. C. 182; Sec. 3—25 U. S. C. 183.

25 St. 452; Sept. 1, 1888; C. 936—An act to accept and ratify an agreement made with the Shoshone and Bannack Indians, for the surrender and relinquishment to the United States of a portion of the Fort Hall Reservation, in the Territory of Idaho, for the purposes of a town-site, and for the grant of a right of way through said reservation to the Utah and Northern Ry. Co., and for other purposes.[86]

25 St. 481; Sept. 22, 1888; C. 1027—An act making appropriations for the support of the Army for the fiscal year ending June 30, 1889, and for other purposes.

25 St. 505; Oct. 2, 1888; C. 1069—An act making appropriations for sundry civil expenses of the Government for the fiscal year ending June 30, 1889, and for other purposes.[87]

25 St. 558; Oct. 17, 1888; C. 1186—An act granting to the Duluth and Winnipeg Ry. Co. the right of way through the Fond du Lac Indian Reservation in the State of Minnesota, and for other purposes.[88]

25 St. 565; Oct. 19, 1888; C. 1210—An act making appropriations to supply deficiencies in the appropriations for the fiscal year ending June 30, 1888, and for prior years, and for other purposes.[89] Sec. 3—5 U. S. C. 417.

25 St. 608; Oct. 19, 1888; C. 1211—An act to secure to the Cherokee freedmen and others their proportion of certain proceeds of lands, under the act of March 3, 1883.[90]

25 St. 611; Oct. 19, 1888; C. 1214—An act authorizing the Secretary of the Interior to accept the surrender of and cancel land patents to Indians in certain cases.[91] Sec. 2—25 U. S. C. 350.

25 St. 639; Jan. 1, 1889; C. 18—An act granting to Citrous Water Co. right of way across Papago Indian Reservation in Maricopa County, Arizona.

25 St. 642; Jan. 14, 1889; C. 24—An act for the relief and civilization of the Chippewa Indians in the State of Minnesota.[92]

25 St. 646; Jan. 16, 1889; C. 48—An act to provide certain arms, ammunition, and equipage to the State of Oregon for the militia thereof.

25 St. 647; Jan. 16, 1889; C. 49—An act granting the right of way through certain lands in the State of Minnesota to the Moorhead, Leech Lake and Northern Ry. Co.[93]

25 St. 658; Feb. 9, 1889; C. 120—An act to punish, as a felony, the carnal and unlawful knowing of any female under the age of 16 years. 18 U. S. C. 458.

25 St. 660; Feb. 12, 1889; C. 134—An act granting to the Big Horn Southern Railroad Company a right of way through a part of the Crow Indian Reservation in Montana Territory.[94]

25 St. 668; Feb. 13, 1889; C. 152—An act to amend an act entitled "An act to authorize the Choctaw Coal and Ry. Co. to construct and operate a railway through the Indian Territory, and for other purposes," approved February 18, 1888.[95]

25 St. 673; Feb. 16, 1889; C. 172—An act in relation to dead and fallen timber on Indian Lands.[96] 25 U. S. C. 196.

25 St. 676; Feb. 22, 1889; C. 180—An act to provide for the division of Dakota into two States and to enable the people of North Dakota, South Dakota, Montana, and Washington to form constitutions and State governments and to be admitted into the Union on an equal footing with the original States, and to make donations of public lands to such States.[97] 48 U. S. C. 1460a.

25 St. 684; Feb. 23, 1889; C. 202—An act granting the right of way to the Yankton and Missouri Valley Ry. Co. through the Yankton Indian Reservation in Dakota.[98]

25 St. 687; Feb. 23, 1889; C. 203—An act to accept and ratify the agreement submitted by the Shoshones, Bannocks, and Sheepeaters of the Fort Hall and Lemhi Reservation in Idaho May 14, 1880, and for other purposes.[99]

25 St. 694; Feb. 25, 1889; C. 238—An act to authorize Court of Claims to hear, determine, and render final judgment upon the claim of the Old Settlers or Western Cherokee Indians.[1]

25 St. 696; Feb. 25, 1889; C. 241—An act granting to the Saint Paul, Minneapolis and Manitoba Ry. Co. the right of way through the White Earth Indian Reservation in the State of Minnesota.

25 St. 705; Feb. 26, 1889; C. 279—An act making appropriations for the legislative, executive, and judicial expenses of the Government for the fiscal year ending June 30, 1890, and for other purposes.[2]

25 St. 745; Feb. 26, 1889; C. 280—An act granting the right of way to the Fort Smith, Paris and Dardanelle Ry. Co. to construct and operate a railroad, telegraph, and telephone line from Fort Smith, Arkansas, through the Indian Territory, to or near Baxter Springs, in the State of Kansas.[3]

25 St. 757; Mar. 1, 1889; C. 317—An act to ratify and confirm an agreement with the Muscogee (or Creek) Nation of Indians in the Indian Territory, and for other purposes.[4]

---

23 St. 79, 368, 376; 24 St. 219, 389, 464; 25 St. 133. *Ag.* 23 St. 342. *S.* 25 St. 980; 26 St. 652; 33 St. 1048. *Cited:* 19 Op. A. G. 252; Garland's 256 U. S. 439; Gilfallen, 159 U. S. 303; Johnson, 160 U. S. 546; Medawakanton, 57 C. Cls. 357.

[84] *Sg.* 1 St. 137.

[85] *Cited:* Krieger, 3 Geo. Wash. L. Rev. 279; Report on Status of Pueblo of Pojoaque, Nov. 3, 1932; Memo. of Comm'r, Jan. 6, 1937; 20 L. D. 157; 31 L. D. 417; Carney, 247 U. S. 102; Cherokee, 203 U. S. 76; McKnight, 130 Fed. 659; Oakes, 172 Fed. 305; Pape, 19 F. 2d 219; U. S. ex rel. Kadrie, 30 F. 2d 989.

[86] *Sg.* 1 St. 137; 15 St. 673. *S.* 26 St. 989. *Cited:* Op. Sol., M. 5386, June 19, 1923.

[87] *Sg.* 1 St. 137. *Cited:* Memo. Ind. Off., Jan. 7, 1937.

[88] *Rpg.* 23 St. 340.

[89] *Sg.* 7 St. 368; 22 St. 301; 25 St. 580.

[90] *Sg.* 14 St. 799; 22 St. 624. *S.* 25 St. 980. *Cited:* Eastern Cherokees, 45 C. Cls. 229; U. S. ex rel. Scott, 1 Dak. 142.

[91] *Sg.* 15 St. 505; 24 St. 388. *Cited:* 43 L. D. 84; Op. Sol., M. 12408, June 6, 1924, M. 12409, Aug. 27, 1924; U. S. v. Getzelman, 89 F. 2d 531.

[92] *Sg.* 24 St. 388. *A.* 29 St. 17, c. 32; 32 St. 400; 34 St. 325. *S.* 26 St. 336, 989; 27 St. 120, 612; 28 St. 286, 576, 876; 29 St. 17, c. 33, 245, 321; 30 St. 62, 571, 652, 924, 1214; 31 St. 221, 1058; 32 St. 245, 982; 33 St. 189, 539, 1005, 1048; 34 St. 325, 1015; 35 St. 70, 781, 1167, 1620; 36 St. 269, 330, 855, 1058; 37 St. 518; 38 St. 77, 582; 39 St. 128, 801, 969; 40 St. 561, 1821; 41 St. 3, 408, 1225; 42 St. 221, 552, 1174; 43 St. 1, 33, 95, 390, 798, 816, 1052, 1141; 44 St. 7, 161, 453, 555, 888, 934; 45 St. 200, 314, 1562, 1623; 46 St. 54, 90, 279, 1107, 1108, 1115, 1487; 47 St. 91, 525, 773, 820; 48 St. 362, 979; 49 Stat. 176, 321, 1757; 50 St. 213, 564; 52 St. 215, 291, 688, 697, 1212. *Cited:* Cain, 2 Minn. L. Rev. 177; 29 Op. A. G. 455; 31 Op. A. G. 95; Op. Sol. M. 11665, Apr. 19, 1924, M. 11879, May 31, 1924, M. 11380, June 17, 1924, M. 13270, Nov. 6, 1924, M. 16954, Jan. 8, 1927; Memo. Sol. Off., Feb. 15, 1932; Op. Sol., Aug. 18, 1932; Memo. Sol. Off., Apr. 8, 1933, May 25, 1933; Memo. Sol., Aug. 8, 1934; Op. Sol. M. 27381, Dec. 13, 1934; Memo. Sol., Aug. 27, 1935; Memo. Sol. Off., Oct. 28, 1935; Jan. 22, 1936; Op. Sol., M. 29616, Feb. 19, 1938, M. 29791, Aug. 1, 1938; 12 L. D. 52; 24 L. D. 413; 29 L. D. 132; 29 L. D. 408; 42 L. D. 446; Bisek, 5 F. 2d 994; Chippewa, 80 C. Cls. 410; Chippewa, 305 U. S. 479; Chippewa, 307 U. S. 1; Chippewa, 301 U. S. 358; Dickson, 242 U. S. 371; Fairbanks, 223 U. S. 215; Fond du Lac, 34 C. Cls. 426; Gravelle, 253 Fed. 549; Johnson, 234 U. S. 422; Lane, 246 U. S. 214, La Roque, 239 U. S. 62; Leecy, 190 Fed. 289; Lemieux, 15 F. 2d 518; Minnesota, 305 U. S. 382; Minnesota, 185 U. S. 373; Morrison, 266 U. S. 481; Morrow, 243 Fed. 854; Oakes, 172 Fed. 305; U. S. v. First, 234 U. S. 245; U. S. v. Holt, 270 U. S. 49; U. S. v. La Roque, 198 Fed. 645; U. S. v. Mille Lac, 229 U. S. 498; U. S. v. Minnesota, 270 U. S. 181; U. S. v. Park, 188 Fed. 383; U. S. v. Spaeth, 24 F. Supp. 465; U. S. v. Waller, 243 U. S. 452; U. S. ex rel. Coburn, 18 F. 2d 822; U. S. ex rel. Detling, 18 F. 2d 822; U. S. ex rel. Kadrie, 30 F. 2d 989; Vezina, 245 Fed. 411; Westling, 60 F. 2d 398; Woodbury, 170 Fed. 302; Work, 18 F. 2d 820.

[93] *Sg.* 1 St. 137; 16 St. 720.

[94] *A.* 27 St. 529. *Cited:* Crow, 81 C. Cls. 238; U. S. v. Soldana, 246 U. S. 530.

[95] *Ag.* 25 St. 35. *A.* 26 St. 765; 28 St. 27. *Cited:* Choctaw, 256 U. S. 531; Choctaw, 6 Ind. T. 515.

[96] *Cited:* U. S. v. Algoma, 305 U. S. 415; U. S. v. Bonness, 125 Fed. 485; U. S. v. Paine, 206 U. S. 467; U. S. v. Pine River, 89 Fed. 907; Memo. Sol. Off., Oct. 22, 1936.

[97] *Cited:* 20 Op. A. G. 245; Sol. Op. M. 24358, May 14, 1928; 55 I. D. 475; Browning, 6 F. 2d 801; Clairmont, 225 U. S. 551; Corrigan, 169 Fed. 477; Cramer, 261 U. S. 219; Draper, 164 U. S. 240; Fowler, 4 F. Supp. 565; Morrison, 6 F. 2d 811; Pronovost, 232 U. S. 487; Taylor, 44 F. 2d 53; Truscott, 73 Fed. 60; U. S. v. Ferry, 24 F. Supp. 399; U. S. v. Glacier, 17 F. Supp. 411; U. S. v. McIntire, 101 F. 2d 650; U. S. v. Pearson, 231 Fed. 270; U. S. v. Sutton, 215 U. S. 291; U. S. v. Yakima, 274 Fed. 115; Winters, 207 U. S. 564.

[98] *Sg.* 1 St. 137.

[99] *S.* 26 St. 336; 26 St. 989; 27 St. 120, 612; 28 St. 286, 876; 29 St. 321; 30 St. 62, 571, 924; 31 St. 221, 1058; 32 St. 245, 982; 33 St. 189, 1048; 34 St. 325, 697, 1015; 35 St. 70, 781; 36 St. 269; 47 St. 146. *Cited:* Letter to W. P. Havenor, Pocatello, Idaho, from the A. G., Jan. 22, 1920; 48 L. D. 455; Skeem, 273 Fed. 93.

[1] *Sg.* 22 St. 328. *Cited:* Old Settlers, 148 U. S. 427; Western Cherokees, 82 C. Cls. 566; Western Cherokees, 27 C. Cls. 1.

[2] *Cited:* Op. Sol., M. 11380, June 17, 1924.

[3] *Sg.* 1 St. 137. *Cited:* Thebo, 66 Fed. 372.

[4] *Sg.* 12 St. 893, sec. 8; 14 St. 755, 785, 799; 23 St. 384. *S.* 25 St.

25 St. 760; Mar. 1, 1889; C. 319—An act to provide for taking the eleventh and subsequent censuses.[5]

25 St. 768; Mar. 1, 1889; C. 321—An act to provide for the settlement of the titles to the lands claimed by or under the Black Bob band of Shawnee Indians in Kansas, or adversely thereto, and for other purposes.[6]

25 St. 783; Mar. 1, 1889; C. 333—An act to establish a United States court in the Indian Territory, and for other purposes.[7]

25 St. 825; Mar. 2, 1889; C. 372—An act making appropriations for the support of the Army for the fiscal year ending June 30, 1890, and for other purposes.

25 St. 852; Mar. 2, 1889; C. 378—An act granting right of way to the Forest City and Watertown R. Co. through the Sioux Indian Reservation.

25 St. 871; Mar. 2, 1889; C. 391—An act to provide for the sale of lands patented to certain members of the Flathead band of Indians in Montana Territory, and for other purposes.[8]

25 St. 884; Mar. 2, 1889; C. 402—An act to amend an act entitled "An act to authorize the Fort Smith and Choctaw Bridge Co. to construct a bridge across the Poteau River, in the Choctaw Nation, near Fort Smith, Arkansas."[9]

25 St. 888; Mar. 2, 1889; C. 405—An act to divide a portion of the reservation of the Sioux Nation of Indians in Dakota into separate reservations and to secure the relinquishment of the Indian title to the remainder, and for other purposes.[10]

25 St. 905; Mar. 2, 1889; C. 410—An act making appropriations to supply deficiencies in the appropriations for the fiscal year ending June 30, 1889, and for prior years and for other purposes.

25 St. 939; Mar. 2, 1889; C. 411—An act making appropriations for sundry civil expenses of the Government for the fiscal year ending June 30, 1890, and for other purposes.[11]

25 St. 980; Mar. 2, 1889; C. 412—An act making appropriations for the current and contingent expenses of the Indian Department, and for fulfilling treaty stipulations with various Indian tribes, for the year ending June 30, 1890, and for other purposes.[12] Sec. 10—p. 1003, 25 U. S. C. 272.[13]

25 St. 1010; Mar. 2, 1889; C. 416—An act granting to the Duluth and Winnipeg Ry. Co. the right of way through the Leech Lake and White Earth Indian Reservations in the State of Minnesota.

25 St. 1012; Mar. 2, 1889; C. 421—An act for the disposition of the agricultural lands embraced within the limits of the Pipestone Indian Reservation in Minnesota.[14]

25 St. 1013; Mar. 2, 1889; C. 422—An act to provide for allotment of land in severalty to United Peorias and Miamies in Indian Territory, and for other purposes.[15] Sec. 1—25 U. S. C. 340.

25 St. 1027; Mar. 14, 1888; C. 32—An act for the relief of S. D. Barclay, G. D. Adams, and William H. Kimbrew.

25 St. 1087; June 20, 1888; C. 437—An act increasing the pension of Jesse Dickey.

25 St. 1119; July 9, 1888; C. 603—An act granting a pension to Peter Thompson.

25 St. 1124; July 16, 1888; C. 635—An act granting a pension to John C. Wagoner.

25 St. 1124; July 16, 1888; C. 636—An act granting a pension to John F. O. Mittag.

25 St. 1131; July 17, 1888; C. 669—An act granting a pension to Elisha Wilkins.

25 St. 1142; Aug. 6, 1888; C. 766—An act granting a pension to Frederick W. Travis.

25 St. 1171; Sept. 3, 1888; C. 943—An act granting a pension to Jacob Copes.

25 St. 1172; Sept. 3, 1888; C. 946—An act to grant a pension to Joseph F. Garrett.

25 St. 1180; Sept. 6, 1888; C. 988—An act for the relief of Nathan Cook.

25 St. 1190; Sept. 26, 1888; C. 1042—An act for the relief of Patrick H. Winston, junior.

25 St. 1201; Oct. 12, 1888; C. 1112—An act granting a pension to Lieutenant Starkey R. Powell, of Black Hawk war.

25 St. 1206; Oct. 15, 1888; C. 1138—An act granting a pension to Washington Ryan.

25 St. 1207; Oct. 15, 1888; C. 1141—An act granting a pension to Henry Mitchell Youngblood.

25 St. 1208; Oct. 15, 1888; C. 1146—An act to increase the pension of George C. Quick.

25 St. 1209; Oct. 15, 1888; C. 1153—An act for the relief of Mary Vanbuskirk.

25 St. 1211; Oct. 16, 1888; C. 1161—An act to compensate Mrs. Sarah L. Larimer for important services rendered the military authorities in 1864 at Deer Creek Station, Wyoming.

25 St. 1214; Oct. 16, 1888; C. 1173—An act granting a pension to Charles Junot.

25 St. 1222; Oct. 19, 1888; C. 1230—An act for the relief of S. T. Marshall.

25 St. 1223; Oct. 19, 1888; C. 1231—An act for the relief of Eliza A. Cutler Jones.

25 St. 1260; Jan. 16, 1889; C. 60—An act granting a pension to John W. Ellis.

25 St. 1286; Feb. 23, 1889; C. 220—An act granting a pension to Elisha C. Paschal.

25 St. 1286; Feb. 23, 1889; C. 221—An act granting a pension to Isham T. Howse.

25 St. 1294; Feb. 25, 1889; C. 263—An act granting a pension to John H. Starr.

25 St. 1306; Mar. 1, 1889; C. 348—An act for the relief of H. L. Newman.

25 St. 1306; Mar. 1, 1889; C. 350—An act for the relief of J. M. Hogan.

25 St. 1315; Mar. 2, 1889; C. 451—An act granting a pension to Lucy, widow of Muck-apecwak-ken-zah, or "John", an Indian who served the United States and saved the lives of many white persons in the Indian outbreak or war of 1862, and died from effects of wounds received therein.

25 St. 1316; Mar. 2, 1889; C. 452—An act granting a pension to George Hunter.

25 St. 1327; Mar. 2, 1889; C. 484—An act for the relief of James Devine.

25 St. 1331; Mar. 2, 1889; C. 503—An act granting a pension to Littleberry W. Baker.

980; 26 St. 81; 28 St. 876. *Cited:* 19 Op. A. G. 306; 11 L. D. 103; Cherokee, 155 U. S. 218; Cherokee, 155 U. S. 196; Creek, 77 C. Cls. 159; Creek, 78 C. Cls. 474; Creek, 302 U. S. 620; Smith, 1 Okla. T. 117; U. S. v. Choctaw, 179 U. S. 491; U. S. v. Crawford, 47 Fed. 561; U. S. v. Creek, 295 U. S. 103; U. S. ex rel. McIntosh, 47 Fed. 561; U. S. ex rel. Scott, 1 Dak. 142.

[5] *Rg.* 20 St. 473.

[6] *Rg.* 20 St. 488. *S.* 29 St. 267. *Cited:* Axhelm, 9 Okla. 321.

[7] *S.* 26 St. 81; 30 St. 495. *Cited:* 19 Op. A. G. 293; Ansley, 180 U. S. 253; Bohart, 2 Ind. T. 45; Carter, 1 Ind. T. 342; Crabtree, 54 Fed. 432; Crabtree, 54 Fed. 426; Crowell, 4 Ind. T. 36; Denison, 3 Ind. T. 104; Goodson, 7 Okla. 117; Gowen, 56 Fed. 973; In re Mayfield, 141 U. S. 107; In re Mills, 135 U. S. 263; Leak Glove, 69 Fed. 68; Lucas, 163 U. S. 612; M. K. & T. Ry., 46 C. Cls. 59; McBride, 149 Fed. 114; Marlin, 276 U. S. 58; Martin Browne, 1 Ind. T. 495; Morrison, 154 Fed. 617; Roff, 168 U. S. 218; St. Louis, 49 Fed. 440; Standley, 59 Fed. 836; Stephens, 174 U. S. 445; Thebo, 66 Fed. 372; U. S. v. Pridgeon, 153 U. S. 48; Westmoreland, 155 U. S. 545; Wilson, 86 Fed. 573; Wilson, 1 Ind. T. 163.

[8] *Sg.* 17 St. 227. *S.* 30 St. 571; 31 St. 267; 41 St. 1225. *Cited:* 22 L. D. 37.

[9] *Ag.* 25 St. 184.

[10] *Sg.* 12 St. 637; 15 St. 635; 17 St. 333, sec. 1; 22 St. 36; 25 St. 99. *A.* 29 St. 10; 35 St. 444. *Rp.* 45 St. 986; 48 St. 1224. *S.* 26 St. 336, 720, 1095; 27 St. 120, 612; 28 St. 286, 876; 29 St. 321; 30 St. 62, 571, 924, 1074; 31 St. 1058; 32 St. 245, 982; 33 St. 189, 1048; 34 St. 325, 1015; 35 St. 70, 781; 36 St. 269, 1058, 1687; 37 St. 518; 38 St. 77, 582, 1189; 42 St. 994; 45 St. 200, 684; 48 St. 1224; 49 St. 176 1757; 50 St. 213, 564; 52 St. 291, 1114. *Cited:* 19 Op. A. G. 467; 20 Op. A. G. 711; 20 Op. A. G. 742; 14 L. D. Memo. 493; Op. Sol., M. 6882, Mar. 20, 1922, M. 20612, Dec. 28, 1926; Memo. Sol. Off., July 10, 1933; Op. Sol., M. 27514, Aug. 1, 1933; Memo. Sol., Aug. 8, 1934; 12 L. D. 162; 12 L. D. 292; 13 L. D. 307; 13 L. D. 683; 17 L. D. 142; 17 L. D. 457; 18 L. D. 188; 18 L. D. 209; 20 L. D. 562; 24 L. D. 330; 29 L. D. 331; 30 L. D. 532; 34 L. D. 252; 40 L. D. 4; 40 L. D. 192; 42 L. D. 582; 50 L. D. 676; Conway, 149 Fed. 261; Dewey, 26 F. 2d 434; Drapeau, 195 Fed. 130; Egan, 246 U. S. 227; Ex p. Van Moore, 221 Fed. 954; Fisher, 226 Fed. 156; Hatten, 99 F. 2d 501; King, 111 Fed. 860; Mulligan, 120 Fed. 98; Quick Bear, 210 U. S. 50; Reynolds, 174 Fed. 212; Sully, 195 Fed. 113; U. S. v. Nice, 241 U. S. 591; U. S. v. Pearson, 231 Fed. 270; U. S. v. Pumphrey, 11 App. D. C. 44; Waldron, 143 Fed. 413.

[11] *Sg.* 1 St. 137.

[12] *Sg.* 1 St. 619; 4 St. 442; 7 St. 36, 46, 51, 69, 85, 99, 114, 161, 179, 185, 191, 212, 236, 242, 287, 296, 317, 320, 349, 352, 425, 464, 541, 543, 545, 596; 9 St. 35, 842, 855, 904; 10 St. 974, 1039, 1056, 1071, 1079, 1095, 1168; 11 St. 614, 700, 701, 702, 729, 744; 12 St. 393, sec. 8, 628, 981, 1173; 13 St. 675, 694; 14 St. 541, 650, 756, 757, 787; 15 St. 515, 536, 584, 590, 596, 622, 638, 651, 657, 676; 16 St. 40, 855, 720; 17 St. 333, sec. 1; 18 St. 254, sec. 3; 19 St. 254, 287; 21 St. 434; 22 St. 42; 23 St. 79, 376, 385; 24 St. 388, 464; 25 St. 133, 229, 238, 528, 609, 757, 759. *S.* 26 St. 81, 836, 989; 27 St. 120, 612; 28 St. 589; 29 St. 321; 34 St. 1371; 39 St. 969. *Cited:* 19 Op. A. G. 306; 19 Op. A. G. 511; 11 L. D. 103; 13 L. D. 185; 15 L. D. 287; 20 L. D. 46; Cherokee, 270 U. S. 476; Eastern, 45 C. Cls. 229; Johnson, 160 U. S 546; Medawakanton, 57 C. Cls. 357; Smith, 1 Okla. T. 117; Swan, 50 Fed. 108; U. S. v. Cherokee, 202 U. S. 101; U. S. v. Choctaw, 179 U. S 494; Yankton, 272 U. S. 351.

[13] Also see 25 U. S. C. 272a (33 St. 1049, sec. 1).

[14] *Cited:* 55 I. D. 295.

[15] *Sg.* 15 St. 520; 24 St. 388. *S.* 26 St. 989. *Rp.* 32 St. 245. *Cited:* 22 Op. A. G 232; 12 L. D 16; 19 L. D. 329; 44 L. D. 524; Bowling, 233 U. S. 528; Bowling, 209 Fed. 438; Finley, 4 Ind. T. 386; U. S. v Bowling, 256 U. S. 484; U. S. v. Boylan, 265 Fed. 165; U. S. v. Reynolds, 250 U. S. 104; U. S. v. Rundell, 181 Fed. 887.

25 St. 1331; Mar. 2, 1889; C. 504—An act granting a pension to Robert W. Andrews.

25 St. 1332; Mar. 2, 1889; C. 505—An act granting a pension to Bennett Cooper.

25 St. 1332; Mar. 2, 1889; C. 506—An act to pension William J. Martin.

26 STAT.

26 St. 13; Feb. 27, 1890; C. 20—An act to authorize the President to confer brevet rank on officers of the United States army for gallant services in Indian campaigns. Sec. 2—10 U. S. C. 526.

26 St. 14; Feb. 27, 1890; C. 21—An act to provide for the time and place of holding the terms of the United States circuit and district courts in the State of South Dakota.

26 St. 15; Feb. 27, 1890; C. 22—An act for the relief of the Sioux Indians at Devil's Lake Agency, North Dakota.[16]

26 St. 21; Mar. 15, 1890; C. 35—An act to authorize the construction of a bridge over the Arkansas River, in the Indian Territory.[17]

26 St. 24; Mar. 19, 1890; C. 39—An act to ascertain the amount due the Pottawatomie Indians of Michigan and Indiana.[18]

26 St. 32; Mar. 28, 1890; C. 55—An act to extend "An act to grant the right of way to the Kansas City and Pacific Railroad Company through the Indian Territory, and for other purposes."[19]

26 St. 34; Apr. 4, 1890; C. 63—An act to provide for certain of the most urgent deficiencies in the appropriations for the service of the Government for the fiscal year ending June 30, 1890, and for other purposes.[20]

26 St. 45; Apr. 5, 1890; C. 65—An act to provide for the times and places to hold terms of the United States courts in the State of Washington.

26 St. 46; Apr. 5, 1890; C. 66—An act to enable the Secretary of the Treasury to gather full and authentic information as to the present condition and preservation of the fur-seal interests of the Government in the region of Alaska, as compared with its condition in 1870; also full information as to the impending extinction of the sea-otter industry, and kindred lines of inquiry, and so forth.

26 St. 50; Apr. 9, 1890; C. 73—An act to continue the publication of the Supplement to the Revised Statutes.

26 St. 60; Apr. 22, 1890; C. 150—An act requiring purchasers of lands in the Pawnee Reservation, in the State of Nebraska, to make payment, and for other purposes.[21]

26 St. 81; May 2, 1890; C. 182—An act to provide a temporary government for the Territory of Oklahoma, to enlarge the jurisdiction of the United States Court in the Indian Territory, and for other purposes.[22] Sec. 18—43 U. S. C. 1091: Sec. 27—43 U. S. C. 1097.

26 St. 102; May 8, 1890; C. 198—An act granting the Spokane Falls and Northern Ry. Co. the right of way through the Colville Indian Reservation.[23]

26 St. 104; May 8, 1890; C. 199—An act granting to the Palouse and Spokane Ry. a right of way through the Nez Perce Indian Reservation in Idaho.[24]

26 St. 126; June 2, 1890; C. 391—An act granting to the Duluth and Winnipeg R. Co. a right of way through certain Indian reservations in Minnesota.[25]

26 St. 130; June 10, 1890; C. 405—An act to authorize the Secretary of War to issue ordnance and ordnance stores to the State of Washington in payment for ordnance and ordnance stores borrowed by the State of Oregon and said State whilst a Territory during the Nez Perce Indian war of 1877 and 1878, and for other purposes.

26 St. 146; June 12, 1890; C. 418—An act to authorize the sale of timber on certain lands reserved for the use of the Menomonee tribe of Indians, in the State of Wisconsin.[26]

26 St. 147; June 12, 1890; C. 419—An act to amend section one and sec. 9 of an act entitled, "An act to authorize the Denison and Washita Valley Ry. Co. to construct and operate a railway through the Indian Territory, and for other purposes," approved July 1, 1886.[27]

26 St. 148; June 13, 1890; C. 423—An act making appropriations for the support of the Army for the fiscal year ending June 30, 1891, and for other purposes.[28]

26 St. 170; June 21, 1890; C. 479—An act to grant the right of way to the Galena, Guthrie and Western Ry. Co. through the Indian Territory, and for other purposes.[29]

26 St. 181; June 27, 1890; C. 633—An act granting to The Chicago, Kansas and Nebraska Ry. Co. power to sell and convey to the Chicago, Rock Island and Pacific Ry. Co. all the railway, property, rights, and franchises of The Chicago, Kansas and Nebraska Ry. Co. in the Territory of Oklahoma and in the Indian Territory.[30]

26 St. 184; June 30, 1890; C. 638—An act to grant the right of way to the Pittsburgh, Columbus and Fort Smith Ry. Co. through the Indian Territory, and for other purposes.[31]

26 St. 228; July 11, 1890; C. 667—An act making appropriations for the legislative, executive, and judicial expenses of the Government for the fiscal year ending June 30, 1891, and for other purposes.

26 St. 290; July 22, 1890; C. 714—An act granting right of way to Little Falls, Mille Lac, and Lake Superior Railroad across Mille Lac Indian Reservation.[32]

26 St. 329; Aug. 19, 1890; C. 803—An act extending the time of payment to purchasers of land of the Omaha tribe of Indians in Nebraska, and for other purposes.[33]

26 St. 336; Aug. 19, 1890; C. 807—An act making appropriations for the current and contingent expenses of the Indian Department, and for fulfilling treaty stipulations with various Indian tribes, for the year ending June 30, 1891, and for other purposes.[34]

26 St. 371; Aug. 30, 1890; C. 837—An act making appropriations for sundry civil expenses of the Government for the fiscal year ending June 30, 1891, and for other purposes.[35]

26 St. 417; Aug. 30, 1890; C. 841—An act to apply a portion of

---

[16] *S.* 26 St. 34.

[17] *Sg.* 24 St. 73.

[18] *Sg.* 14 St. 370. *Cited:* Pam-to-pee, 187 U. S. 371; Potawatomie, 27 C. Cls. 403.

[19] *Sg.* 25 St. 140.

[20] *Sg.* 26 St. 15.

[21] *Sg.* 19 St. 28.

[22] *Sg.* 10 St. 167, sec. 3; 12 St. 761, sec. 1; 13 St. 197, sec 1; 17 St. 333; 23 St. 206; 25 St. 757, 783, 1004. *S.* 26 St. 371, 948; 27 St. 282; 28 St. 843; 29 St. 267; 30 St. 495; 38 St. 1192. *Cited:* Cavell, 3 Okla. S. B. J. 208; Krieger, 3 Geo. Wash. L. Rev. 279; 18 Yale L. J. 250; 20 Op. A. G. 742; 22 Op. A. G. 232; 25 Op. A. G. 163; Adkins, 235 U. S. 417; Alberty, 162 U. S. 499; Ansley, 180 U. S. 253; Armstrong, 195 Fed. 137; Arnold, 4 F. 2d 838; Arnold, 3 Ind. T. 550; Bartlett, 218 Fed. 380; Blanset, 256 U. S. 319; Blaylock, 117 Fed. 125; Bohart, 2 Ind. T. 45; Bowling, 233 U. S. 528; Brown, 2 Ind. T. 329; Buster, 135 Fed. 947; Carney, 247 U. S. 102; Carter, 1 Ind. T. 342; Carter, 12 F. 2d 780; Cherokee, 203 U. S. 76; Choctaw, 6 Ind. T. 432; Crabtree, 54 Fed. 432; Crabtree, 54 Fed. 426; Creek, 77 C. Cls. 159; Crowell, 4 Ind. T. 36; Daugherty, 3 Ind. T. 197; Davison, 56 Fed. 443; Denison, 3 Ind. T. 104; Eddy, 163 U. S. 456; Engleman, 4 Ind. T. 336; Ex p. Dickson, 4 Ind. T. 481; Ex p. Kyle, 67 Fed. 306; Ex p. Webb, 225 U. S. 663; Foreman, 7 Ind. T. 478; Faster, 189 U. S. 325; Gay, 5 Okla. 1; Glenn-Tucker, J., 4 Ind. T. 511; Glover 6 Ind. T. 262; Goodson, 7 Okla. 117; Gowen, 56 Fed. 973; Grayson, 267 U. S. 352; Gulf, 157 U. S. 348; Hampton, 4 Ind. T. 503; Incorporated, 5 Ind. T. 497; In re Delks Est., 2 Ind. T. 572; Herd, 13 Okla. 512; In re Grayson, 8 Ind. T. 497; In re Ingram, 12 Okla. 54; In re Mayfield, 141 U. S. 107; Jefferson, 247 U. S. 288; Joines, 274 U. S. 544; Keokuk, 4 Okla. 5; Kimberlin, 3 Ind. T. 16; Leak Glove, 69 Fed. 68; Lucas, 163 U. S. 612; Luce, 4 Ind. T. 54; McBride, 149 Fed. 114; McClellan, 50 Fed. 686; McCullough, 243 Fed. 823; McFadden, 3 Ind. T. 224; Marlin, 276 U. S. 58; Mays, 3 Ind. T. 774; Morrison, 154 Fed. 617; Murray, 1 Ind. T. 28; Noyes, 100 Fed. 555; Perryman, 238 U. S. 148; Porter, 239 U. S. 170; Priddy, 204 Fed. 955; Pyeatt, 51 Fed. 551; Quigley, 3 Ind. T. 265; Raymond, 1 Ind. T. 334; Raymond, 83 Fed. 721; Reagan, 35 C. Cls. 90; Reynolds, 236 U. S. 58; Robinson, 2 Ind. T. 509; Robinson, 221 Fed. 398; Robinson, 187 U. S. 41; Roff, 168 U. S. 218; St. Louis, 49 Fed. 440; Sanger, 48 Fed. 152; Shellenbarger, 236 U. S. 68; Simon, 4 Ind. T. 688; Smith, 1 Okla. T. 117; Springston, 3 Ind. T. 388; Standley, 59 Fed. 836; Stephens, 174 U. S. 445; Thebo, 66 Fed. 372; Thomas, 169 U. S. 264; Tootle, 7 Ind. T. 64; U. S. v. Pridgeon, 153 U. S. 48; U. S. v. Sherburne, 38 F. 2d 155; U. S. ex rel. Search, 8 Okla. 404; Washington, 285 U. S. 422; Weeks, 2 Ind. T. 162; Wesamoreland, 155 U. S. 545; Williams, 4 Ind. T. 201; Wilson, 1 Ind. T. 163; Wilson, 86 Fed. 573.

[23] *Sg.* 1 St. 137.

[24] *Cited:* Ex p. Tilden, 218 Fed. 920.

[25] *Cited:* Minnesota, 185 U. S. 373.

[26] *S.* 34 St. 547; 39 St. 123, 969; 40 St. 561; 41 St. 1225; 42 St. 1174; 44 St. 453; 49 St. 1085. *Cited:* Quick Bear, 210 U. S. 50; U. S. ex rel. Besaw, 6 F. 2d 694.

[27] *Ag.* 24 St. 117.

[28] *Cited:* Sisseton, 42 C. Cls. 416.

[29] *Sg.* 1 St. 137.

[30] *Sg.* 24 St. 446. *Cited:* Arnold, 4 F. 2d 838; Brown, 146 Fed. 975.

[31] *Sg.* 1 St. 137.

[32] *Cited:* Mille Lac, 46 C. Cls. 424; U. S. v. Mille Lac, 229 U. S. 498.

[33] *Ag.* 22 St. 341.

[34] *Sg.* 1 St. 619; 4 St. 442; 7 St. 36, 46, 51, 85, 99, 114, 161, 179 185, 191, 212, 236, 242, 287, 296, 317, 320, 349, 425, 464, 541, 545, 596; 9 St. 35, 842, 855, 904; 10 St. 1039, 1056, 1071, 1079, 1095, 1168; 11 St. 614, 700, 702, 729, 744; 12 St. 628, 963, 981, 1173; 13 St. 624, 675, 694; 14 St. 650, 757, 787; 15 St. 515, 584, 590, 596, 622, 638, 651, 657, 676; 16 St. 40, 720; 19 St. 254, 256; 22 St. 42, 43; 23 St. 79, 376; 24 St. 219, 389, 464; 25 St. 114, 642, 688, 895, 1002, 1005. *S.* 28 St. 86, 876; 34 St. 325. *Cited:* 12 L. D. 292; Butler, 43 C. Cls. 497; Chippewa, 307 U. S. 1; Chippewa, 301 U. S. 358; Collins, 73 Fed. 735; Ickes, 80 F. 2d 708; Johnson, 160 U. S. 546; Jump, 100 F. 2d 130; McFadden, 87 Fed. 154; Medawakanton, 57 C. Cls. 357; Quick Bear, 210 U. S. 50; Shoshone, 82 C. Cls. 23; U. S. v. Ashton, 170 Fed. 509; U. S. v. Sandoval, 231 U. S. 28; U. S. v. Wright, 53 F. 2d 300.

[35] *Sg.* 1 St. 137; 26 St. 92. *Cited:* Op. Sol., M. 26489, July 10, 1931; Memo. Ind. Off., Jan. 7, 1937; Op. Sol., M. 29908, Aug. 25, 1938.

the proceeds of the public lands to the more complete endowment and support of the colleges for the benefit of agriculture and the mechanic arts established under the provisions of an act of Congress approved July 2, 1862."[36] Sec. 1—7 U. S. C. 322, 323; Sec. 6—7 U. S. C. 328.

26 St. 468; Sept. 25, 1890; C. 913—An act to authorize the Secretary of the Interior to procure and submit to Congress a proposal for the sale to the United States of the western part of the Crow Indian Reservation, in Montana.

26 St. 485; Sept. 26, 1890; C. 947—An act granting the right of way to the Hutchinson and Southern R. Co. to construct and operate a railroad, telegraph, and telephone line from the city of Anthony, in the State of Kansas, through the Indian Territory, to some point in the county of Grayson, in the State of Texas.[37]

26 St. 504; Sept. 30, 1890; C. 1126—An act making appropriations to supply deficiencies in the appropriations for the fiscal year ending June 30, 1890, and for prior years, and for other purposes.[38]

26 St. 552; Sept. 30, 1890; C. 1127—An act to provide for the sale of certain New York Indian lands in Kansas.

26 St. 558; Sept. 30, 1890; C. 1132—An act to authorize the Seneca Nation of New York Indians to lease lands within the Cattaraugus and Allegany Reservations, and to confirm existing leases.[39]

26 St. 567; Oct. 1, 1890; C. 1244—An act to reduce the revenue and equalize duties on imports, and for other purposes.

26 St. 632; Oct. 1, 1890; C. 1248—An act granting the right of way to the Sherman and Northwestern Ry. Co. through the Indian Territory, and for other purposes.[40]

26 St. 636; Oct. 1, 1890; C. 1249—An act to refer to the Court of Claims certain claims of the Shawnee and Delaware Indians and the freedmen of the Cherokee Nation, and for other purposes.[41]

26 St. 640; Oct. 1, 1890; C. 1252—An act giving, upon conditions and limitations therein contained, the assent of the United States to certain leases of rights to mine coal in the Choctaw Nation.[42]

26 St. 652; Oct. 1, 1890; C. 1264—An act to reconvey certain lands to the county of Ormsby, State of Nevada.[43]

26 St. 652; Oct. 1, 1890; C. 1265—An act to authorize the conveyance of certain Absentee Shawnee Indian lands in Kansas.[44]

26 St. 655; Oct. 1, 1890; C. 1268—An act to provide for railroad crossings in the Indian Territory.[45]

26 St. 658; Oct. 1, 1890; C. 1271—An act to provide for the reduction of the Round Valley Indian Reservation in the State of California, and for other purposes.[46]

26 St. 659; Oct. 1, 1890; C. 1272—An act authorizing the Secretary of the Interior to ascertain damages resulting to any person who had settled upon the Crow Creek and Winnebago Reservations in South Dakota between February 27, 1885, and April 17, 1885.[47]

26 St. 660; Oct. 1, 1890; C. 1273—An act granting right of way to the Red Lake and Western Railway and Navigation Co. across Red Lake Reservation, in Minnesota, and granting said company the right to take lands for terminal railroad and warehouse purposes.

26 St. 661; Oct. 1, 1890; C. 1274—An act to extend and amend "An act to authorize the Fort Worth and Denver City Ry. Co. to construct and operate a railway through the Indian Territory, and for other purposes."[48]

26 St. 661; Oct. 1, 1890; C. 1275—An act granting to the Northern Pacific and Yakima Irrigation Co. a right of way through the Yakima Indian Reservation in Washington.

26 St. 663; Oct. 1, 1890; C. 1277—An act granting to the Newport and King's Valley R. Co. the right of way through the Siletz Indian Reservation.

26 St. 664; Oct. 1, 1890; C. 1278—An act to authorize the Secretary of the Interior to convey to the Rio Grande Junction Ry. Co. certain lands in the State of Colorado in lieu of certain other lands in said State conveyed by the said company to the United States.

26 St. 668; Feb. 11, 1890; J. Res. No. 9—Joint resolution for the relief of certain Chippewa Indians of the La Pointe Agency, Wisconsin.

26 St. 682; Sept. 26, 1890; J. Res. No. 52—Joint resolution authorizing the transfer of certain appropriations for the Indian Service, on the books of the Treasury.

26 St. 712; Jan. 12, 1891; C. 65—An act for the relief of the Mission Indians in the State of California.[49]

26 St. 720; Jan. 19, 1891; C. 77—An act to enable the Secretary of the Interior to carry out, in part, the provisions of "An act to divide a portion of the reservation of the Sioux Nation of Indians in Dakota into separate reservations and to secure the relinquishment of the Indian title to the remainder, and for other purposes," approved March 2, 1889, and making appropriations for the same and for other purposes.[50]

26 St. 745; Feb. 10, 1891; C. 129—An act granting to the Umatilla Irrigation Co. a right of way through the Umatilla Indian Reservation in the State of Oregon.[51]

26 St. 749; Feb. 13, 1891; C. 165—An act to ratify and confirm agreements with the Sac and Fox Nation of Indians, and the Iowa tribe of Indians, of Oklahoma Territory, and to make appropriations for carrying out the same.[52]

26 St. 764; Feb. 16, 1891; C. 240—An act for the construction and completion of suitable school buildings for Indian industrial schools in Wisconsin and other States.[53]

26 St. 765; Feb. 21, 1891; C. 249—An act to amend act authorizing Choctaw Coal and Ry. Co. to construct road through Indian Territory.[54]

26 St. 770; Feb. 24, 1891; C. 284—An act making appropriations for the support of the Army for the fiscal year ending June 30, 1892, and for other purposes.

26 St. 783; Feb. 24, 1891; C. 288—An act to authorize the Kansas and Arkansas Valley Railway to construct and operate additional lines of railway through the Indian Territory, and for other purposes.[55]

26 St. 794; Feb. 28, 1891; C. 383—An act to amend and further extend the benefits of the act approved February 8, 1887, entitled "An act to provide for the allotment of land in severalty to Indians on the various reservations, and to extend the protection of the laws of the United States over the Indians, and for other purposes."[56] Sec. 3—25 U. S. C. 397; Sec. 4—25 U. S. C. 336 (36 St. 860, sec. 17);[57] Sec. 5—

---

[36] *Sg.* 12 St. 503. *S.* 32 St. 803.

[37] *Sg.* 1 St. 137. *A.* 27 St. 2.

[38] *Sg.* 2 St. 111; 12 St. 274. *Cited:* Medawakanton, 57 C. Cls. 357; 26 Op. A. G. 330.

[39] *Sg.* 18 St. 330.

[40] *Sg.* 1 St. 137.

[41] *Sg.* 14 St. 799. *S.* 27 St. 86. *A.* 27 St. 86; 33 St. 189. *Cited:* Blackfeather, 190 U. S. 368; Blackfeather, 28 C. Cls. 447; Blackfeather, 37 C. Cls. 233; Cherokee, 155 U. S. 218; Cherokee, 155 U. S. 196; Cherokee, 223 U. S. 108; Cherokee, 85 C. Cls. 76; Journeycake, 28 C. Cls. 28; Keetoowah, 41 App. D. C. 319; Lowe, 223 U. S. 95; U. S. v. Algoma, 305 U. S. 415; U. S. v. Blackfeather, 155 U. S. 180.

[42] *S.* 28 St. 502. *Cited:* Choctaw, 256 U. S. 531.

[43] *Sg.* 25 St. 236.

[44] *Sg.* 16 St. 53; 18 St. 295.

[45] *Cited:* Dick v. U. S., 208 U. S. 340.

[46] *Sg.* 17 St. 634; 24 St. 388. *S.* 33 St. 706. *Cited:* Letter of Comp. Gen. to Sec'y., July 24, 1937; In re Lincoln, 129 Fed. 247.

[47] *S.* 27 St. 5; 28 St. 876.

[48] *Ag.* 24 St. 419.

[49] *S.* 27 St. 61; 32 St. 822; 46 St. 1201; 44 St. 1061; 46 St. 1522; 49 St. 1106. *A.* 34 St. 1015; 39 St. 969. *Cited:* Op. Sol., M. 27939, Apr. 9, 1935; 56 I. D. 102; St. Marie, 24 F. Supp. 237.

[50] *Sg.* 25 St. 888. *Cited:* Medawakanton, 57 C. Cls. 357.

[51] *Sg.* 23 St. 340. *S.* 28 St. 37.

[52] *S.* 27 St. 120, 282, 612; 28 St. 286, 876; 29 St. 321; 30 St. 62, 571, 924; 31 St. 221; 34 St. 325. *Cited:* 30 L. D. 532; Creek, 77 C. Cls. 159; Creek, 84 C. Cls. 12; Creek, 302 U. S. 620; Iowa, 68 C. Cls. 585; Keokuk, 4 Okla. 5; Mixon, 265 Fed. 603; U. S. v. Creek, 295 U. S. 103.

[53] *Cited:* Yankton, 272 U. S. 351.

[54] *Sg.* 1 St. 137; 25 St. 35, 668. *S.* 28 St. 27. *Cited:* Choctaw, 256 U. S. 531; U. S. ex rel. Search, 3 Okla. 404.

[55] *Sg.* 1 St. 137; 24 St. 73. *A.* 28 St. 86. *Cited:* Thebo, 66 Fed. 372.

[56] *Ag.* 24 St. 388. *A.* 36 St. 855. *Rp.* 28 St. 876; 48 St. 1224. *S.* 27 St. 62; 28 St. 286, 876; 31 St. 672; 32 St. 245, 1606; 33 St. 189, 319, 539, 1048; 34 St. 1015; 36 St. 2064; 38 St. 582; 40 St. 958; 43 St. 132, 244; 45 St. 200, 1562, 1623; 46 St. 90, 279, 1115; 47 St. 91, 820; 48 St. 362; 49 St. 176, 1757; 50 St. 564; 52 St. 291. *Cited:* Prosius, 23 Case & Com. 739; Brown, 39 Yale L. J. 307; Rice, 16 J. Comp. Leg. 78; Russell, 18 Yale L. J. 328; Op. Sol., A. 2592, Feb. 12, 1924, M. 11665, Apr. 19, 1924; Memo. Sol., Off., May 11, 1934; Memo. Sol., Dec. 14, 1934; Feb. 6, 1935; Op. Sol. M. 27996, May 14, 1935, Memo., Sol., July 25, 1935, Nov. 11, 1935; Memo. Sol. Off., Nov. 23, 1935, May 28, 1936, Oct. 22, 1936; Memo. Sol., Jan. 12, 1937, Feb. 17, 1937, Dec. 17, 1937, Oct. 21, 1938, Mar. 25, 1939; 5 L. D. 520; 13 L. D. 310; 18 L. D. 497; 20 L. D. 46; 24 L. D. 311; 25 L. D. 364; 25 L. D. 408; 28 L. D. 564; 29 L. D. 628; 30 L. D. 258; 32 L. D. 17; 33 L. D. 205; 35 L. D. 549; 40 L. D. 148; 43 L. D. 125; 44 L. D. 188; 44 L. D. 520; 49 L. D. 139; 53 I. D. 107; Adams, 59 F. 2d 653; Beck, 65 Fed. 30; Bird, 129 Fed. 472; British-American, 299 U. S. 159; Button, 7 F. Supp. 597; Ex p. Van Moore, 221 Fed. 954; Fairbanks, 223 U. S. 215; First Moon, 270 U. S. 243; Hampton, 22 F. 2d 81; Henkel, 237 U. S. 45; Indian Oil, 240 U. S. 522; Kirby, 260 U. S. 423; Lemmon, 106 Fed. 650; Miller, 249 U. S. 308; Miller, 57 F. 2d 987; Minnesota, 185 U. S. 373; People, 8 F. Supp. 295; Perrin, 232 U. S. 478; Porter 239 U. S. 170; Reeves, 16 Okla. 342; Sharp, 138 Fed. 878; Smith, 142 Fed. 225; Thomas, 169 U. S. 264; U. S. v. Barnett, 7 F. Supp. 573; U. S. v. Belin, 182 Fed. 161; U. S. v. Dooley, 151 Fed. 697; U. S. v. Ferry, 24 F. Supp. 399; U. S. v. First, 234 U. S. 245; U. S. v. Flournoy, 69 Fed. 886; U. S. v. Glacier, 17 F. Supp. 411; U. S. v. Gray, 201 Fed. 291; U. S. v. Howard, 8 F. Supp.

25 U. S. C. 371. USCA Historical Note: A further provision annexed to the derivative section, "that no allotment of lands shall be made or annuities of money paid to any of the Sac and Fox of the Missouri Indians who were not enrolled as members of said tribe on Jan. 1, 1890, but this shall not be held to impair or otherwise affect the rights or equities of any person whose claim to membership in said tribe is now pending and being investigated," was repealed by a provision of the Indian Appropriation Act of March 2, 1895, s. 1, 28 St. 902. Also see Historical Notes under secs. 331 and 348 of Tit. 25.

26 St. 796; Feb. 28, 1891; C. 384—An act to amend secs. 2275 and 2276 of the Revised Statutes of the United States providing for the selection of lands for educational purposes in lieu of those appropriated for other purposes.[58]

26 St. 826; Mar. 3, 1891; C. 517—An act to establish circuit courts of appeals and to define and regulate in certain cases the jurisdiction of the courts of the United States, and for other purposes.[59] Sec. 2—See 28 U. S. C. 212, 219, 221, 543, 544. Sec. 3—See 28 U. S. C. 216, 223.

26 St. 844; Mar. 3, 1891; C. 535—An act to authorize the Fort Gibson, Tahlequah and Great Northeastern Ry. Co. to construct and operate a railway through the Indian Territory, and for other purposes.[60]

26 St. 851; Mar. 3, 1891; C. 538—An act to provide for the adjudication and payment of claims arising from Indian depredations.[61]

26 St. 854; Mar. 3, 1891; C. 539—An act to establish a court of private land claims, and to provide for the settlement of private land claims in certain States and Territories.[62]

26 St. 862; Mar. 3, 1891; C. 540—An act making appropriations to supply deficiencies in the appropriations for the fiscal year ending June 30, 1891, and for prior years, and for other purposes.[63]

26 St. 908; Mar. 3, 1891; C. 541—An act making appropriations for the legislative, executive, and judicial expenses of the Government for the fiscal year ending June 30, 1892, and for other purposes.[64]

26 St. 948; Mar. 3, 1891; C. 542—An act making appropriations for sundry civil expenses of the Government for the fiscal year ending June 30, 1892, and for other purposes.[65]

26 St. 989; Mar. 3, 1891; C. 543—An act making appropriations for the current and contingent expenses of the Indian Department, and for fulfilling treaty stipulations with various Indian tribes, for the year ending June 30, 1892, and for other purposes.[66] Sec. 16—43 U. S. C. 1098. Sec. 37—43 U. S. C. 1099.

26 St. 1091; Mar. 3, 1891; C. 556—An act granting to the Missoula and Northern R. Co. the right of way through the Flathead Indian Reservation, in the State of Montana.[67]

26 St. 1095; Mar. 3, 1891; C. 561—An act to repeal timber-culture laws, and for other purposes.[68] Sec. 6—43 U. S. C. 173; Sec. 10—25 U. S. C. 426; Sec. 15—48 U. S. C. 358.

26 St. 1111; Dec. 9, 1890; J. Res. No. 3—Joint resolution to authorize the Secretary of War to issue one thousand stands of arms to each of the States of North and South Dakota, Wyoming, Montana, and Nebraska.[69]

26 St. 1114; Mar. 2, 1891; J. Res. No. 12—Joint resolution amendatory of and supplementary to joint resolution number 3, approved Dec. 9, 1890.[70]

26 St. 1124; Apr. 16, 1890; C. 87—An act to correct the patent to John-Sechler to certain lands in Bent County, Colorado.

26 St. 1132; Apr. 21, 1890; C. 129—An act granting a pension to Robert Hill.

26 St. 1132; Apr. 21 1890; C. 130—An act granting a pension to William R. Scurlock.

26 St. 1134; Apr. 21, 1890; C. 142—An act to pension John D. Prator for service in the Indian war.

26 St. 1135; Apr. 21, 1890; C. 143—An act to pension Joel B. Tribble for service in the Indian War.

26 St. 1135; Apr. 21, 1890; C. 144—An act to pension Henry S. Morgan.

26 St. 1135; Apr. 21, 1890; C. 145—An act to pension Green B. Lee.

26 St. 1144; May 19, 1890; C. 225—An act granting a pension to Washington F. Short.

26 St. 1144; May 19, 1890; C. 228—An act granting a pension to Johnson Reddick.

617; U. S. v. LaRoque, 198 Fed. 645; U. S. v. Payne, 264 U. S. 446; U. S. v. Pelican, 232 U. S. 442; U. S. v. Powers, 305 U. S. 527; U. S. v. Seufert, 252 Fed. 51; U. S. v. Waller, 243 U. S. 452; Wadsworth, 148 Fed. 771; Williams, 16 Okla. 104.

[57] Effective July 1, 1935, the permanent appropriation provided for in the last sentence of this section was repealed by Act June 26, 1934, sec. 1, 48 St. 1225. Also see 31 U. S. C. 725 (b).

[58] *Ag.* 4 St. 179, sec. 1; 11 St. 385; 18 St. 202.

[59] *Cited:* 53 I. D. 593; Ansley, 180 U. S. 253; Crabtree, 54 Fed. 432; Crabtree, 54 Fed. 426; Goodshot, 104 Fed. 257; McLish, 141 U. S. 661; Morrison, 154 Fed. 617; Pickett, 216 U. S. 456; Sloan, 118 Fed. 283; Stephens, 174 U. S. 445; Ward, 163 U. S. 504.

[60] *Sg.* 1 St. 137.

[61] *Sg.* 23 St. 376. *A.* 38 St. 791. *Rp.* 45 St. 986. *S.* 27 St. 557; 28 St. 286, 424, 843; 29 St. 267; 30 St. 105, 571, 652, 924, 1214; 31 St. 7, 221, 260, 672, 1010, 1058; 32 St. 5, 245, 1031; 33 St. 15, 394; 34 St. 634, 1371; 35 St. 478, 907; 36 St. 202, 774, 1289; 37 St. 595, 912; 38 St. 208, 312, 559, 1138; 39 St. 14, 801; 40 St. 2, 345, 821; 41 St. 35, 503, 1015. *Cited:* Abrew, 37 C. Cls. 510; Albright, 53 C. Cls. 247; Ayres, 35 C. Cls. 26; Ball, 161 U. S. 72; Barrow, 30 C. Cls. 54; Beam, 43 C. Cls. 61; Beddo, 28 C. Cls. 69; Bell, 39 C. Cls. 350; Brice, 32 C. Cls. 23; Buchanan, 28 C. Cls. 127; Butler, 38 C. Cls. 167; Byrd, 44 C. Cls. 498; Campbell, 44 C. Cls. 488; Carter, 31 C. Cls. 441; Church, 48 C. Cls 262; Collier, 173 U. S. 79; Conners, 33 C. Cls. 317; Corralitos, 178 U. S. 280; Corralitos, 33 C. Cls. 342; Cox, 29 C. Cls. 349; Davenport, 31 C. Cls. 430; Davidson, 34 C. Cls. 169; De Baca, 37 C. Cls. 482; Dobbs, 33 C. Cls. 308; Duran, 31 C. Cls. 353; Duran, 32 C. Cls. 273; Duwamish, 79 C. Cls. 530; Falk, 27 C. Cls. 321; French, 49 C. Cls. 337; Friend, 29 C. Cls. 425; Gagnon, 38 C. Cls. 10; Gallegos, 39 C. Cls. 86; Gamel, 31 C. Cls. 321; Garcia, 37 C. Cls. 243; Garrison, 30 C. Cls. 272; Gerrard, 43 C. Cls. 67; Giddings, 29 C. Cls. 12; Gorhan, 29 C. Cls. 97; Graham, 30 C. Cls. 318; Hamilton, 42 C. Cls. 282; Hayes, 44 C. Cls. 493; Hayt, 38 C. Cls. 455; Hegmer, 30 C. Cls. 405; Hernandez, 34 C. Cls. 455; Herring, 32 C. Cls. 536; Hosford, 29 C. Cls. 42; Hyne, 27 C. Cls. 113; Jackson, 34 C. Cls. 441; Jaeger, 27 C. Cls. 278; Jaeger, 33 C. Cls. 214; Jaramillo, 37 C. Cls. 208; Johnson, 160 U. S. 546; Johnson, 29 C. Cls. 1; Jones, 35 C. Cls. 36; King, 31 C. Cls. 304; Labadi, 31 C. Cls. 205; Labadie, 33 C. Cls. 476; Labadie, 31 C. Cls. 436; Labadie, 32 C. Cls. 368; Leighton, 161 U. S. 291; Leighton, 29 C. Cls. 288; Litchfield, 32 C. Cls. 585; Litchfield, 33 C. Cls. 203; Love, 29 C. Cls. 332; Lowe, 37 C. Cls. 413; Luke, 35 C. Cls. 15; McCollum, 33 C. Cls. 469; McCoy, 38 C. Cls. 163; McKee, 33 C. Cls. 99; McKenzie, 34 C. Cls. 278; Mares, 29 C. Cls. 197; Marks, 28 C. Cls. 147; Martin, 46 C. Cls. 199; Martin, 46 C. Cls. 373; Mascarinas, 33 C. Cls. 94; Mayer, 38 C. Cls. 553; Merchant, 35 C. Cls. 403; Mitchell, 27 C. Cls. 316; Montana, 32 C. Cls. 71; Montoya, 180 U. S. 261; Moore, 32 C. Cls. 593; Murray, 46 C. Cls. 101; Nesbitt, 186 U. S. 153; Osborn, 33 C. Cls. 304; Otero, 48 C. Cls. 216; Otero's, 48 C. Cls. 219; Painter, 33 C. Cls. 114; Pino, 38 C. Cls. 64; Price, 28 C. Cls. 422; Price, 174 U. S. 373; Price, 33 C. Cls. 106; Redfield, 27 C. Cls. 473; Rex, 53 C. Cls. 320; Rhine, 33 C. Cls. 481; Roy, 45 C. Cls. 177; Salois, 32 C. Cls. 68; Salois, 33 C. Cls. 326; Sanchez, 48 C. Cls. 224; Scott, 33 C. Cls. 486; Stevens, 34 C. Cls. 244; Stone, 29 C. Cls. 111; Swope, 33 C. Cls. 223; Tanner, 32 C. Cls. 192; Terrill, 35 C. Cls. 218; Thompson, 35 C. Cls. 395; Thompson, 44 C. Cls. 359; Thurston, 232 U. S. 469; Tully, 32 C. Cls. 1; U. S. v. Andrews, 179 U. S. 96; U. S. v. Conway, 175 U. S. 60; U. S. v. Gorham, 165 U. S. 316; U. S. v. Martinez, 195 U. S. 469; U. S. v. Northwestern, 164 U. S. 686; Valencia, 31 C. Cls. 388; Valk, 22 C. Cls. 241; Valk, 29 C. Cls. 62; Vallejos, 35 C. Cls. 489; Vincent, 39 C. Cls. 356; Welch, 32 C. Cls. 106; Weston, 29 C. Cls. 420; Wilson, 38 C. Cls. 6; Woolverton, 29 C. Cls. 107; Wynn, 29 C. Cls. 15; Yerke, 173 U. S. 439.

[62] *Sg.* 9 St. 922. *Cited:* 54 I. D. 71.

[63] *Cited:* 21 Op. A. G. 131.

[64] *S.* 27 St. 282.

[65] *Sg.* 1 St. 437; 26 St. 92. *Cited:* 13 L. D. 310; 13 L. D. 318.

[66] *Sg.* 1 St. 619; 4 St. 442; 7 St. 36, 46, 51, 69, 85, 99, 160, 161, 179, 185, 213, 236, 242, 287, 296, 317, 321, 349, 352, 367, 401, 425, 541, 545, 596; 9 St. 35, 842, 855, 904; 10 St. 973, 1039, 1056, 1071, 1079, 1093, 1159, 1168; 11 St. 614, 700, 701, 702, 729, 744; 12 St. 393, Sec. 8, 628, 981, 1131, 1173; 13 St. 675, 694; 14 St. 650, 757, 797, 894; 15 St. 505, 515, 517, 533, 536, 584, 590, 622, 638, 651, 657, 676; 16 St. 40, 720; 17 St. 98, 333, sec. 1; 19 St. 256, 265, 287; 22 St. 42, 48; 23 St. 79, 342, 372, 376; 24 St. 388, 464; 25 St. 114, 455, 642, 645, 688, 983, 1002, 1005, 1015. *S.* 27 St. 1, 5, 120, 282, 612; 28 St. 3, 286, 876, 987; 29 St. 321; 30 St. 62, 571, 924; 31 St. 221, 1058; 32 St. 245, 982; 33 St. 189, 1048; 34 St. 325, 894, 1015; 35 St. 70, 781; 36 St. 269, 1058; 37 St. 518; 38 St. 77, 582; 39 St. 123, 969; 40 St. 561; 41 St. 3, 408, 1225; 42 St. 552, 1174; 43 St. 390, 1141; 44 St. 453, 934; 45 St. 200, 1532; 46 St. 279, 1105, 1115. *Cited:* 20 Op. A. G. 517; 8 L. D. Memo. 764; 13 L. D. Memo. 118; 13 L. D. 185; 13 L. D. 316; 25 L. D. 364; Op. Sol., M. 5805, Nov. 22, 1921, Aug. 18, 1932; Memo. Sol., Nov. 11, 1935, Dec. 26, 1935; Memo. Sol. Off., May 5, 1938; Choctaw, 83 C. Cls. 140; Citizen, 26 C. Cls. 323; Creek, 78 C. Cls. 474; Crow, 81 C. Cls. 238; Eugene Sol. Louie, 274 Fed. 47; Farrell, 110 Fed. 942; Fort Berthold, 71 C. Cls. 308; In re Sanborn, 148 U. S. 222; Johnson, 283 Fed. 954; McMurray, 62 C. Cls 458; Medawakanton, 57 C. Cls. 357; Renfrow, 3 Okla. 161; Sisseton, 58 C. Cls. 302; Sisseton, 42 C. Cls. 416; U. S. v. Choctaw, 179 U. S. 494; U. S. v. Getzelman, 89 F. 2d 531; U. S. v. Jackson, 280 U. S. 183; U. S. v. Navarre, 173 U. S. 77; U. S. v. Powers, 305 U. S. 527; U. S. v. Reynolds, 250 U. S. 104; U. S. v. Sisseton, 208 U. S. 561; U. S. v. 12 Bottles, 201 Fed. 191.

[67] *Cited:* Renfrow, 3 Okla. 161.

[68] *Sg.* 12 St. 392, sec. 1; 18 St. 15, 22; 25 St. 888, 893. *Ag.* 12 St. 393, sec. 8. *S.* 28 St. 594; 30 St. 745; 44 St. 629; 48 St. 667; 49 St. 1250; 50 St. 873. *A.* 28 St. 4. *Cited:* 25 L. D. 17; 45 L. D. 563; 50 L. D. 315; 53 I. D. 593; 56 I. D. 110; Memo. Ind. Off., Jan. 7, 1937; Memo. Sol., June 30, 1938, July 1, 1938, Feb. 17, 1939; Alaska, 248 U. S. 78; Cramer, 261 U. S. 219; Heckman, 119 Fed. 83; Johnson, 2 Alaska 224; King, 111 Fed. 860; LaClair, 184 Fed. 128; LaRoque, 239 U. S. 62; McGrath, 167 Fed. 473; Northern, 227 U. S. 355; Territory, 289 Fed. 671; U. S. v. Berrigan, 2 Alaska 442; U. S. v. Cadzow, 5 Alaska 125; U. S. v. Conrad, 161 Fed. 829; U. S. v. LaRoque, 198 Fed. 645; U. S. v. Minnesota, 270 U. S. 181; U. S. v. Portneuf-Marsh, 218 Fed. 601; U. S. v. Powers, 305 U. S. 527; Ute, 45 C. Cls. 440; Winters, 207 U. S. 564.

[69] *Sg.* 24 St. 401. *A.* 26 St. 1114.

[70] *Ag.* 26 St. 1111.

26 St. 1163; May 24, 1890; C. 330—An act to pension Samuel Wyrick for service in the Indian War.

26 St. 1163; May 24, 1890; C. 331—An act to pension William J. Dunn for service in the Indian War.

26 St. 1163; May 24, 1890; C. 332—An act to pension William B. Carter for service in the Indian War.

26 St. 1163; May 24, 1890; C. 333—An act to pension Mary J. Mann, widow of John W. Mann, who served in the Indian War.

26 St. 1164; May 24, 1890; C. 336—An act to pension Christina Edson for meritorious services rendered the Government during the Indian wars in the Oregon Territory, now the State of Oregon.

26 St. 1164; May 24, 1890; C. 337—An act to pension William G. Hill.

26 St. 1165; May 24, 1890; C. 342—An act to pension Thomas K. Edwards for service in the Indian War.

26 St. 1166; May 24, 1890; C. 343—An act to grant a pension to Huldah Burton.

26 St. 1166; May 24, 1890; C. 344—An act to grant a pension to Samuel L. Dark.

26 St. 1166; May 24, 1890; C. 345—An act to grant a pension to John Green Reed.

26 St. 1166; May 24, 1890; C. 347—An act to increase the pension of Stephen Cooper.

26 St. 1171; May 27, 1890; C. 373—An act granting a pension to Jonathan Hayes.

26 St. 1173; May 27, 1890; C. 379—An act to pension Bartola Thebant, a soldier in the Florida Seminole Indian war of 1849 and 1850.

26 St. 1181; June 20, 1890; C. 456—An act granting a pension to William Crowford.

26 St. 1182; June 20, 1890; C. 458—An act granting a pension to William H. Chapman.

26 St. 1184; June 20, 1890; C. 468—An act to increase the pension of George C. Quick.

26 St. 1197; June 21, 1890; C. 536—An act for the relief of Isabel Hensley.

26 St. 1198; June 21, 1890; C. 539—An act to grant a pension to Elizabeth T. Garrett.

26 St. 1205; June 24, 1890; C. 577—An act granting a pension to Joseph Morris.

26 St. 1211; June 24, 1890; C. 608—An act to pension James T. Furlow for service in the Indian war.

26 St. 1227; Aug. 13, 1890; C. 733—An act granting a pension to Thompson N. Statham.

26 St. 1227; Aug. 13, 1890; C. 734—An act to pension George W. Scott for service in the Florida war.

26 St. 1228; Aug. 15, 1890; C. 741—An act granting a pension to Mrs. Christiana Frederika Zeutmeyer, of Fairfield, Minnesota.

26 St. 1231; Aug. 15, 1890; C. 754—An act granting a pension to A. B. Reeves.

26 St. 1231; Aug. 15, 1890; C. 758—An act granting a pension to Mrs. M. M. Boyle.

26 St. 1232; Aug. 15, 1890; C. 759—An act granting a pension to Mrs. Martha E. Grant.

26 St. 1233; Aug. 15, 1890; C. 767—An act granting a pension to Oran M. Collinsworth.

26 St. 1243; Aug. 29, 1890; C. 833—An act granting a pension to G. L. Pease.

26 St. 1248; Sept. 2, 1890; C. 859—An act granting a pension to John L. Russell.

26 St. 1249; Sept. 2, 1890; C. 865—An act granting a pension to Mary E. Greening, widow of Orlando A. Greening, who served in the Indian war.

26 St. 1275; Sept. 27, 1890; C. 1028—An act to pension Stacey Keener, widow of Tillman B. Keener, deceased, who served in the Indian war.

26 St. 1275; Sept. 27, 1890; C. 1029—An act to pension Mathew Lambert for service in the Indian war.

26 St. 1276; Sept. 27, 1890; C. 1032—An Act to grant a pension to James Knetsar.

26 St. 1286; Sept. 29, 1890; C. 1093—An act to pension Gabriel Stephens.

26 St. 1297; Sept. 30, 1890; C. 1163—An act granting a pension to Calvin Gunn.

26 St. 1298; Sept. 30, 1890; C. 1168—An act granting a pension to Thompson Riley.

26 St. 1311; Sept. 30, 1890; C. 1231—An act to increase of pension to Mrs. Mary B. Cushing.

26 St. 1319; Oct. 1, 1890; C. 1304—An act granting a pension to Samuel S. Humphreys.

26 St. 1320; Oct. 1, 1890; C. 1305—An act granting a pension to Asa Joiner.

26 St. 1330; Dec. 15, 1890; C. 21—An act to pension John D. Bagby.

26 St. 1332; Jan. 6, 1891; C. 55—An act granting a pension to B. S. Roan.

26 St. 1333; Jan. 6, 1891; C. 56—An act granting a pension to Robert A. England.

26 St. 1333; Jan. 6, 1891; C. 57—An act to pension Carroll Renfro.

26 St. 1333; Jan. 6, 1891; C. 58—An act to pension Willis Brooks.

26 St. 1336; Jan. 21, 1891; C. 90—An act granting a pension to Mrs. E. J. Baldy, widow of W. H. Baldy.

26 St. 1342; Feb. 12, 1891; C. 142—An act granting a pension to Nancy Hartley.

26 St. 1358; Feb. 14, 1891; C. 222—An act to pension Walker H. Fomby for service in the Indian war.

26 St. 1359; Feb. 14, 1891; C. 225—An act to pension Thomas Gorham.

26 St. 1359; Feb. 14, 1891; C. 226—An act to pension William A. Todd.

26 St. 1359; Feb. 14, 1891; C. 227—An act to pension Sarah Thomasson.

26 St. 1369; Feb. 23, 1891; C. 267—An act granting a pension to Levi Danley.

26 St. 1371; Feb. 23, 1891; C. 277—An act granting a pension to Nathan C. Moore.

26 St. 1377; Feb. 25, 1891; C. 314—An act granting a pension to Mrs. G. W. Griffith.

26 St. 1378; Feb. 25, 1891; C. 318—An act granting a pension to Mrs. Lydia N. Atkinson.

26 St. 1378; Feb. 25, 1891; C. 320—An act granting a pension to Mrs. Matilda Kent.

26 St. 1379; Feb. 25, 1891; C. 322—An act granting a pension to Mrs. Mary B. Floyd.

26 St. 1379; Feb. 25, 1891; C. 323—An act granting a pension to Mary Williams.

26 St. 1385; Feb. 27, 1891; C. 351—An act granting a pension to William C. Young.

26 St. 1387; Feb. 27, 1891; C. 357—An act granting a pension to Joel Hendricks.

26 St. 1387; Feb. 27, 1891; C. 358—An act granting a pension to Elizabeth P. Satterfield.

26 St. 1389; Feb. 27, 1891; C. 368—An act granting a pension to Marcellus A. Stovall.

26 St. 1391; Feb. 27, 1891; C. 380—An act to grant a pension to Margaret Hawkins.

26 St. 1397; Feb. 28, 1891; C. 412—An act granting a pension to Andrew J. Wallace.

26 St. 1398; Feb. 28, 1891; C. 416—An act granting a pension to Doctor Francis Lambert.

26 St. 1400; Feb. 28, 1891; C. 426—An act granting a pension to Catherine McRoberts.

26 St. 1401; Feb. 28, 1891; C. 429—An act granting a pension to Walter Scott.

26 St. 1401; Feb. 28, 1891; C. 430—An act granting a pension to Mrs. Nancy Springer.

26 St. 1407; Feb. 28, 1891; C. 461—An act to grant a pension to Mary E. Dubridge.

26 St. 1408; Feb. 28, 1891; C. 462—An act to grant a pension to Martha Tennery, widow of James H. Tennery, of Captain Griffin's company, First Illinois, Black Hawk war.

26 St. 1409; Feb. 28, 1891; C. 467—An act to grant a pension to Nancy F. Glenn.

26 St. 1411; Feb. 28, 1891; C. 480—An act granting a pension to Henry Allhorn.

26 St. 1414; Feb. 28, 1891; C. 489—An act for the relief of A. J. McCreary, administrator of the estate of J. M. Hiatt, deceased, and for other purposes.[n]

26 St. 1415; Mar. 2, 1891; C. 504—An act granting a pension to Cynthia M. West.

26 St. 1417; Mar. 2, 1891; C. 514—An act to grant a pension to Mary C. Hoffman, widow of General William Hoffman.

26 St. 1417; Mar. 2, 1891; C. 515—An act to grant a pension to Nancy Jane Knetsar, of Moline, Illinois.

26 St. 1420; Mar. 3, 1891; C. 576—An act granting a pension to Nancy E. Ellis.

---

[n] *Sg.* 21 St. 291.

26 St. 1423; Mar. 3, 1891; C. 592—An act granting a pension to Mrs. Martha A. Brooks.

26 St. 1429; Mar. 3, 1891; C. 619—An act to pension David S. Sanders.

26 St. 1430; Mar. 3, 1891; C. 626—An act granting a pension to Susan A. Malone.

26 St. 1465; Mar. 3, 1891; C. 729—An act granting a pension to William Hale.

26 St. 1465; Mar. 3, 1891; C. 732—An act granting a pension to Robert A. Ware.

27 STAT.

27 St. 1; Jan. 28, 1892; C. 2—An act providing for the completion of the allotment of lands to the Cheyenne and Arapahoe Indians.[72]

27 St. 2; Feb. 3, 1892; C. 3—An act to amend an act entitled "An act granting the right of way to the Hutchison and Southern R. Co. through the Indian Territory."[73]

27 St. 5; Mar. 8, 1892; C. 12—An act making appropriations to supply a deficiency in the appropriation for the expenses of the Eleventh Census, and for other purposes.[74]

27 St. 8; Mar. 18, 1892; C. 18—An act to provide for certain of the most urgent deficiencies in the appropriations for the service of the Government for the fiscal year ending June 30, 1892.

27 St. 24; May 3, 1892; C. 59—An act to create a third division of the district of Kansas for judicial purposes, and to fix the time for holding court therein.

27 St. 52; June 17, 1892; C. 120—An act to provide for the disposition and sale of lands known as the Klamath River Indian Reservation.[75]

27 St. 61; July 1, 1892; C. 139—An act to authorize the Secretary of the Interior to carry into effect certain recommendations of the Mission Indian commission, and to issue patents for certain lands.[76]

27 St. 62; July 1, 1892; C. 140—An act to provide for the opening of a part of the Colville Reservation, in the State of Washington, and for other purposes.[77]

27 St. 72; July 5, 1892; C. 145—An act to provide the times and places for holding terms of the United States courts in the States of Idaho and Wyoming.[78] 28 U. S. C. 151.

27 St. 83; July 6, 1892; C. 150—An act to authorize the Marinette and Western R. Co. to construct a railroad through the Menominee Reservation, in the State of Wisconsin.[79]

27 St. 86; July 6, 1892; C. 151—An act supplementary and amendatory to an act entitled "An act to refer to the Court of Claims certain claims of the Shawnee and Delaware Indians and the freedmen of the Cherokee Nation and for other purposes," approved October 1, 1890.[80]

27 St. 88; July 13, 1892; C. 158—An act making appropriations for the construction, repair and preservation of certain public works or rivers and harbors, and for other purposes.

27 St. 120; July 13, 1892; C. 164—An act making appropriations for the current and contingent expenses of the Indian Department, and for fulfilling treaty stipulations with various Indian tribes, for the fiscal year ending June 30, 1893, and for other purposes.[81] Sec. 1—p. 120, R. S. 2062, 25 U. S. C. 27 (4 St. 735, 737, secs. 4, 12; 30 St. 573, sec. 1); p. 143, 25 U. S. C. 284.

27 St. 174; July 16, 1892; C. 195—An act making appropriations for the support of the Army for the fiscal year ending June 30, 1893, and for other purposes. 10 U. S. C. 877.

27 St. 183; July 16, 1892; C. 196—An act making appropriations for the legislative, executive, and judicial expenses of the Government for the fiscal year ending June 30, 1893, and for other purposes.[82]

27 St. 260; July 23, 1892; C. 234—An act to amend secs. 2139, 2140, and 2141 of the Revised Statutes touching the sale of intoxicants in the Indian country; and for other purposes.[83] Sec. 1—25 U. S. C. 241 (R. S. sec. 2139, 19 St. 244, sec. 1; 29 St. 506, sec. 1).[84] See Historical Note 25 U. S. C. A. 241. 25 U. S. C. 243.[85] USCA Historical Note: Instant section was derived from provisions added to R. S. sec. 2139 as part of the amendments of that section made by instant Act. Said provisions contained a clause relating to arrests in the Indian Territory which was omitted from the Code section as having been superseded by the admission of that Territory and the Territory of Oklahoma into the Union as the State of Oklahoma, pursuant to Act June 16, 1906, 34 St. 267.

27 St. 272; July 26, 1892; C. 256—An act to legalize the deed and other records of the Office of Indian Affairs, and to provide and authorize the use of a seal by said office.[86] Sec. 1—25 U. S. C. 4. USCA Historical Note: The deed records legalized by this act begin in 1825. These deeds show the transfer of lands granted to individual Indians under the several treaties since 1817 whenever a restriction was made that the lands should not be sold without the consent of the President; also the transfer of those lands allotted to individual Indians, the patent for which contained a similar restrictive clause upon the sale of the land. The other records referred to are those of the current correspondence of the office, of treaties before ratification, of contracts made with special attorneys, and of similar papers. Some of those records run back to 1800, and a few even prior to that date, when the office was under the War Department, but it was not until the year 1824 that a regular record of all the correspondence of the office was inaugurated and kept up. Sec. 2—25 U. S. C. 5. (See Historical Note sec. 1); 38 U. S. C. 43. Sec. 3—25 U. S. C. 6. (See Historical Note sec. 1.) Sec. 4—25 U. S. C. 7. (See Historical Note sec 1.)

27 St. 281; July 27, 1892; C. 277—An act granting pensions to the survivors of the Indian wars of 1832 to 1842, inclusive, known as the Black Hawk war, Creek war, Cherokee disturbances, and the Seminole war.[87] Secs. 1, 2—38 U. S. C. 371; Sec. 3—38 U. S. C. 379; Sec. 5—38 U. S. C. 378.

27 St. 282; July 23, 1892; C. 311—An act making appropriations to supply deficiencies in the appropriations for the fiscal year ending June 30, 1892, and for prior years, and for other purposes.[88]

27 St. 336; July 30, 1892; C. 329—An act to authorize the Denison and Northern Ry. Co. to construct and operate a railway through the Indian Territory, and for other purposes.[89]

27 St. 348; Aug. 4, 1892; C. 376—An act for the relief of the Eastern Band of Cherokee Indians.[90]

27 St. 349; Aug. 5, 1892; C. 380—An act making appropriations

---

[72] *Sg.* 26 St. 1023.

[73] *Sg.* 1 St. 137. *Ag.* 26 St. 485. *A.* 28 St. 505.

[74] *Sg.* 19 St. 254; 26 St. 659, 1002. *Rp.* 34 St. 325.

[75] *Sg.* 24 St. 388. *A.* 39 St. 969. *Cited:* 33 L. D. 205; Donnelly 228 U. S. 243.

[76] *Sg.* 26 St. 712.

[77] *Sg.* 17 St. 333, sec. 1; 24 St. 388; 26 St. 794. *S.* 29 St. 9, 267; 30 St. 571; 34 St. 325, 1015; 35 St. 70, 781; 36 St. 269, 1058; 43 St. 599. *Cited:* 35 L. D. 220; 45 L. D. 563; 50 L. D. 691; Collins, 73 Fed. 735; McFadden, 87 Fed. 154; U. S. v. Ferry, 24 F. Supp. 399; U. S. v. Gardner, 133 Fed. 285; U. S. v. Pelican, 232 U. S. 442.

[78] *A.* 30 St. 423.

[79] *Sg.* 1 St. 137.

[80] *Sg.* 26 St. 636. *Cited:* Blackfeather, 190 U. S. 368; Blackfeather, 28 C. Cls. 447; Blackfeather, 37 C. Cls. 233; Journeycake, 28 C. Cls. 281; U. S. v. Algoma, 305 U. S. 415.

[81] *Sg.* 4 St. 442; 7 St. 36, 46, 51, 69, 85, 99, 114, 161, 179, 185, 213, 236, 242, 287, 296, 317, 320, 349, 352, 425, 541, 545, 596; 9 St. 35, 842, 854, 855, 904; 10 St. 1039, 1056, 1071, 1079, 1168; 11 St. 614, 700, 702, 729, 744; 12 St. 628, 981, 1130, 1173; 13 St. 624, 675, 694; 14 St. 650, 757, 787; 15 St. 515, 584, 590, 596, 622, 638, 651, 657, 676; 16 St. 40, 355, 720; 19 St. 254, 256, 287; 22 St. 43; 23 St. 79, 341; 24 St. 388; 25 St. 114, 643, 645, 688, 894, 1005; 26 St. 756, 1028, 1033, 1037, 1040, 1048. *S.* 27 St. 612; 28 St. 286, 876; 29 St. 321; 30 St. 62, 571, 924; 31 St. 221, 1058; 32 St. 245, 982; 33 St. 189, 1048; 34 St. 325, 1015; 35 St. 70, 781; 36 St. 269; 37 St. 518; 38 St. 77, 582; 39 St. 123, 969; 40 St. 561; 41 St. 3, 408, 1225; 42 St. 552, 1174; 43 St. 390, 1141; 44 St. 453, 934; 45 St. 200, 1562; 46 St. 279, 1115. *Cited:* 20 Op. A. G. 517; 44 L. D. 524; Beck, 65 Fed. 30; Farrell, 110 Fed. 942; Kindred, 225 U. S. 582; Medawakanton, 57 C. Cls. 357; U. S. v. Boyd, 68 Fed. 577; U. S. v. Boyd, 83 Fed. 547.

[82] *Cited:* Op. Sol., M. 8860, Nov. 1, 1922.

[83] *Sg.* 1 St. 91, sec. 33; 1 St. 384, sec. 4; 5 St. 516, sec. 1. *Ag.* 4 St. 564, sec. 4; 13 St. 29; 19 St. 244. *S.* 28 St. 876; 40 St. 561; 41 St. 3. *Rp.* 29 St. 506; 48 St. 396. *Cited:* Russell, 18 Yale L. J. 328; 25 Op. A. G. 416; Browning, 6 F. 2d 801; Buchanan, 15 F. 2d 496; Buffo, 213 Fed. 222; Cecil, 225 Fed. 368; Chambliss, 218 Fed. 154; Clairmont, 225 U. S. 551; Dick, 208 U. S. 340; Edwards, 5 F. 2d 17; Elom, 7 F. 2d 887; Ex p. Webb, 225 U. S. 663; Harris, 249 Fed. 41; Johnson, 234 U. S. 422; Joplin, 236 U. S. 531; Kennedy, 265 U. S. 344; Lucas, 15 F. 2d 32; McClintic, 283 Fed. 781; Morgan, 224 Fed. 698; Morrison, 6 F. 2d 809; Morrison, 6 F. 2d 811; Nelson, 18 F. 2d 522; Parks, 225 Fed. 369; Parris, 1 Ind. T. 43; Renfro, 15 F. 2d 991; Renfrow, 3 Okla. 161; Salazar, 236 Fed. 541; Sarlls, 152 U. S. 570; Schaap, 210 Fed. 853; Sharpe, 16 F. 2d 876; Swafford, 25 F. 2d 581; U. S. v. Belt, 128 Fed. 68; U. S. v. Birdsall, 233 U. S. 223; U. S. v. Luther, 260 Fed. 579; U. S. v. Miller, 105 Fed. 944; U. S. v. 12 Bottles, 201 Fed. 191; U. S. v. Wright, 229 U. S. 226; U. S. Exp., 191 Fed. 678; Memo. Sol., Oct. 13, 1933; Op. Sol., M. 29147, May 6, 1937.

[84] *A.* 52 St. 696, sec. 1. Also see 25 U. S. C. 241a (28 St. 697, sec. 8) and 25 U. S. C. 244a (48 St. 396).

[85] *R.* as to former "Ind. Territory", Okla., by 25 U. S. C. 244a.

[86] *Cited:* 25 Op. A. G. 460; Bowling 299 Fed. 438.

[87] *Rpg.* 17 St. 573, sec. 25. *S.* 27 St. 429; 30 St. 1416. *A.* 32 St. 399; 35 St. 553; 37 St. 679; 39 St. 1199; 44 St. 1361; 50 St. 786. *Cited:* Duwamish, 79 C. Cls. 530

[88] *Sg.* 23 St. 194; 26 St. 81, 749, 938, 1009.

[89] *Sg.* 1 St. 137. *A.* 29 St. 128; 30 St. 345.

[90] *S.* 28 St. 594. *Cited:* U. S. v. Boyd, 68 Fed. 577; U. S. v. Swain Co., N. C., 46 F. 2d 99; U. S. v. Wright, 58 F. 2d 800.

for sundry civil expenses of the Government for the fiscal year ending June 30, 1893, and for other purposes.

27 St. 394; Apr. 6, 1892; J. Res. No. 6—Joint resolution construing article four of the agreement with the Citizen Band of Pottawatomie Indians in Oklahoma Territory and elsewhere.

27 St. 417; Jan. 12, 1893; C. 32—An act granting to the Blue Mountain Irrigation and Improvement Co. a right of way for reservoir and canals through the Umatilla Indian Reservation in the State of Oregon.[91]

27 St. 420; Jan. 20, 1893; C. 39—An act granting to the Yuma Pumping Irrigation Co. the right of way for two ditches across that part of the Yuma Indian Reservation lying in Arizona.

27 St. 426; Jan. 28, 1893; C. 52—An act to authorize the Court of Claims to hear and determine the claims of certain New York Indians against the United States.[92]

27 St. 429; Feb. 3, 1893; C. 58—An act relating to proof of citizenship of applicants for Indian-war pensions under the act of Congress approved July 27, 1892.[93] 38 U. S. C. 377.

27 St. 456; Feb. 15, 1893; C. 120—An act granting right of way to the Colorado River Irrigation Co. through the Yuma Indian Reservation in California.[94]

27 St. 465; Feb. 20, 1893; C. 144—An act to grant to the Gainesville, Oklahoma and Gulf Ry. Co. a right of way through the Indian Territory, and for other purposes.[95]

27 St. 468; Feb. 20, 1893; C. 145—An act to ratify and confirm agreement between the Puyallup Indians and the Northern Pacific R. Co. for right of way through the Puyallup Indian Reservation.

27 St. 469; Feb. 20, 1893; C. 147—An act to restore to the public domain a portion of the White Mountain Apache Indian Reservation, in the Territory of Arizona, and for other purposes.[96]

27 St. 470; Feb. 20, 1893; C. 148—An act to ratify and confirm an agreement made between the Seneca Nation of Indians and William B. Barker.[97]

27 St. 473; Feb. 23, 1893; C. 154—An act to provide for the publication of the Eleventh Census.

27 St. 478; Feb. 27, 1893; C. 168—An act making appropriations for the support of the Army for the fiscal year ending June 30, 1894, and for other purposes.

27 St. 487; Feb. 27, 1893; C. 169—An act to authorize the Kansas City, Pittsburg and Gulf R. Co. to construct and operate a railroad, telegraph, and telephone line through the Indian Territory, and for other purposes.[98]

27 St. 492; Feb. 27, 1893; C. 171—An act to grant to the Chicago, Rock Island and Pacific Ry. Co. a right of way through the Indian Territory, and for other purposes.[99]

27 St. 495; Feb. 28, 1893; C. 175—An act granting to the Chicago, Rock Island and Pacific Ry. Co. the use of certain lands at Chickasha Station, and for a "Y" in the Chickasaw Nation, Indian Territory.[1]

27 St. 523; Mar. 1, 1893; C. 187—An act making appropriations for the payment of invalid and other pensions of the United States for the fiscal year ending June 30, 1894, and for other purposes.

27 St. 524; Mar. 1, 1893; C. 188—An act to grant to the Gainesville, McCallister and St. Louis Ry. Co. a right of way through the Indian Territory, and for other purposes.[2]

27 St. 529; Mar. 1, 1893; C. 192—An act extending the time for the construction of the Big Horn Southern Railroad through the Crow Indian Reservation.[3]

27 St. 557; Mar. 3, 1893; C. 203—An act to ratify and confirm an agreement with the Kickapoo Indians in Oklahoma Territory, and to make appropriations for carrying the same into effect.[4]

27 St. 568; Mar. 3, 1893; C. 205—An act to provide for the adjustment of certain sales of lands in the late reservation of the confederated Otoe and Missouria tribes of Indians in the States of Nebraska and Kansas.[5]

27 St. 572; Mar. 3, 1893; C. 208—An act making appropriations for sundry civil expenses of the Government for the fiscal year ending June 30, 1894, and for other purposes.

27 St. 612; Mar. 3, 1893; C. 209—An act making appropriations for current and contingent expenses, and fulfilling treaty stipulations with Indian tribes, for fiscal year ending June 30, 1894.[6] Sec. 1—p. 614, 25 U. S. C. 67; p. 628, 25 U. S. C. 283; p. 631, 25 U. S. C. 175, 178; p. 635, 25 U. S. C. 283.

27 St. 646; Mar. 3, 1893; C. 210—An act making appropriations to supply deficiencies in the appropriations for the fiscal year ending June 30, 1893, and for prior years, and for other purposes.[7]

27 St. 675; Mar. 3, 1893; C. 211—An act making appropriations for the legislative, executive, and judicial expenses of the Government for the fiscal year ending June 30, 1894, and for other purposes.

27 St. 744; Mar. 3, 1893; C. 219—An act for the relief of the Stockbridge and Munsee tribe of Indians, in the State of Wisconsin.[8]

27 St. 747; Mar. 3, 1893; C. 224—An act to authorize the Interoceanic Ry. Co. to construct and operate railway, telegraph, and telephone lines through the Indian Terirtory.[9]

27 St. 753; Jan. 18, 1893; J. Res. No. 7—Joint resolution to authorize the Secretary of the Treasury to cover back into the Treasury $48,000 of the appropriation to Choctaw and Chickasaw Indians.

27 St. 768; June 9, 1892; C. 111—An act for the relief of the estate of John W. Whitfield, late register of the land office in the Delaware land district of Kansas.

27 St. 769; June 17, 1892; C. 121—An act to pension Elizabeth R. Crawford, widow of C. A. Crawford, soldier in Creek war of 1836.

27 St. 772; July 13, 1892; C. 167—An act granting a pension to Eliza M. Boatright, the surviving widow of Alexander M. Boatright, who was a soldier in the Black Hawk war.

27 St. 773; July 14, 1892; C. 178—An act to pension Andrew J. Jones, for services in the Indian wars.

27 St. 773; July 14, 1892; C. 180—An act granting a pension to William S. Woodward.

27 St. 774; July 14, 1892; C. 182—An act granting a pension to Noah Staley.

---

[91] *Sg.* 23 St. 341.

[92] *Cited:* New York Indians, 41 C. Cls. 462; New York Indians, 40 C. Cls. 448; New York Indians, 170 U. S. 1; U. S. v. New York Indians, 173 U. S. 464.

[93] *Sg.* 27 St. 281.

[94] *S.* 28 St. 286.

[95] *Sg.* 1 St. 137.

[96] *S.* 31 St. 952. *Cited:* 29 Op. A. G. 289; Op. Sol., M. 27878, May 20, 1936.

[97] *S.* 30 St. 62.

[98] *Sg.* 1 St. 137. *A.* 28 St. 744; 29 St. 6.

[99] *Sg.* 1 St. 137. *S.* 30 St. 327.

[1] *Sg.* 24 St. 446.

[2] *Sg.* 1 St. 137. *A.* 29 St. 44; 30 St. 891.

[3] *Ag.* 25 St. 660, sec. 4. *Cited:* U. S. v. Soldana, 246 U. S. 530.

[4] *Sg.* 12 St. 893, sec. 8; 17 St. 333, sec. 1; 24 St. 388; 26 St. 851. *S.* 30 St. 354; 32 St. 982; 34 St. 325. *Cited:* U. S. v. Reily, 29 U. S. 33; U. S. ex rel. Search, 3 Okla. 404.

[5] *Sg.* 21 St. 380. *S.* 31 St. 59.

[6] *Sg.* 1 St. 619; 4 St. 442; 7 St. 36, 46, 51, 69, 85, 99, 114, 161, 179, 185, 213, 236, 242, 287, 296, 317, 320, 348, 352, 425, 541, 545, 596; 9 St. 35, 265, 842, 854, 855; 10 St. 949, 1039, 1056, 1071, 1079, 1168; 11 St. 614, 700, 702, 729, 744; 12 St. 628, 652, 981, 1173; 13 St. 675, 694; 14 St. 541, 650, 757, 787; 15 St. 515, 584, 590, 596, 622, 637, 638, 651, 657, 676; 16 St. 40, 355, 720; 18 St. 254, sec. 8; 19 St. 254, 256, 287; 22 St. 43, 341; 23 St. 79; 24 St. 388; 25 St. 114, 642, 643, 645, 688, 894, 1005; 26 St. 81, 340, 756, 894, 1026, 1028, 1033, 1035, 1037, 1038; 27 St. 139. *Ag.* 23 St. 342. *S.* 28 St. 286, 579, 764, 876, 910; 29 St. 17, 267, 321; 30 St. 62, 495, 571, 924; 31 St. 221, 1058; 32 St. 245, 982; 33 St. 565; 34 St. 325, 1015; 35 St. 70, 781; 36 St. 269; 37 St. 518, 1058; 38 St. 77, 582; 39 St. 123, 696, 969; 40 St. 561; 40 St. 1316; 41 St. 3, 408, 1156, 1225; 42 St. 552, 1174; 43 St. 390, 1141; 44 St. 453, 934; 45 St. 200, 378, 1562; 46 St. 279, 1115; 47 St. 91, 820; 48 St. 362; 49 St. 176, 1757; 50 St. 564; 52 St. 291. *Cited:* 20 Op. A. G. 620; 20 Op. A. G. 724; 20 Op. A. G. 749; 27 Op. A. G. 580; 16 L. D. 431; 20 L. D. 157; 38 L. D. 559; 53 I. D. 48; 53 I. D. 502; Memo. Sol. Off., Jan. 22, 1936; 1 L. D. Memo. 85; 1 L. D. Memo. 502; 2 L. D. Memo. 386; Bird, 129 Fed. 472; Chase, 256 U. S. 1; Chase, 238 Fed. 887; Cherokee, 85 C. Cls. 76; Cherokee, 187 U. S. 294; Cherokee, 270 U. S. 476; Cherokee, 223 U. S. 108; Choate, 224 U. S. 665; Choctaw, 81 C. Cls. 1; Choctaw, 83 C. Cls. 140; Clay, 282 Fed. 268; Crawford, 3 Ind. T. 10; Dick, 6 Ind. T. 85; Duwamish, 79 C. Cls. 530; Eastern Cherokees, 45 C. Cls. 104; Eastern or Emigrant, 82 C. Cls. 180; English, 224 U. S. 680; First, 59 F. 2d 367; Fish, 52 F. 2d 544; Gilpin, 256 U. S. 10; Gleason, 224 U. S. 679; Goat, 224 U. S. 458; Goudy, 203 U. S. 146; Heckman, 224 U. S. 413; In re Lands of Five, 199 Fed. 811; In re Lelah-Puc-Ka-Chee, 98 Fed. 429; Jacobs, 223 U. S. 200; Jefferson, 247 U. S. 288; Kimberlin, 104 Fed. 653; Lowe, 223 U. S. 95; M. K. & T. Ry., 46 C. Cls. 59; Malone, 212 Fed. 668; Marlin, 276 U. S. 58; Matter of Heff, 197 U. S. 488; Medawakanton, 57 C. Cls. 357; Meeker, 178 Fed. 216; Mullen, 224 U. S. 448; Nunn, 216 Fed. 330; Pawnee, 56 C. Cls. 1; Seminole, 78 C. Cls. 455; Sisseton, 42 C. Cls. 416; Sloan, 118 Fed. 283; Stephens, 174 U. S. 445; Tiger, 221 U. S. 286; U. S. v. Allen, 179 Fed. 13; U. S. v. Ashton, 170 Fed. 509; U. S. v. Chase, 245 U. S. 89; U. S. v. Cherokee, 202 U. S. 101; U. S. v. Hayes, 20 F. 2d 873; U. S. v. Kopp, 110 Fed. 160; U. S. v. Mathewson, 32 F. 2d 745; U. S. v. Shock, 187 Fed. 862; U. S. v. Sisseton, 208 U. S. 561; U. S. v. Watashe, 102 F. 2d 428; Wallace, 204 U. S. 415; Winton, 255 U. S. 373; Woodward, 238 U. S. 284.

[7] *S.* 30 St. 62.

[8] *Sg.* 16 St. 404. *S.* 28 St. 876; 34 St. 325; 39 St. 123. *Cited:* 25 L. D. 17; Op. Sol., D. 42071, Dec. 29, 1921; Memo. Sol. Off., Jan. 2, 1934; Stockbridge, 61 C. Cls. 472; U. S. v. Paine, 206 U. S. 467.

[9] *Sg.* 1 St. 137. *A.* 29 St. 93.

27 St. 774; July 14, 1892; C. 183—An act granting a pension to James A. Davis.

27 St. 774; July 14, 1892; C. 184—An act granting a pension to Harmon H. McElvery.

27 St. 775; July 14, 1892; C. 185—An act granting a pension to David C. Barrow.

27 St. 775; July 14, 1892; C. 186—An act granting a pension to Mary Catlin.

27 St. 776; July 14, 1892; C. 191—An act for the relief of Frederick Meredith, late a soldier in the Indian war of 1832.

27 St. 779; July 20, 1892; C. 211—An act for the relief of Mrs. Sarah J. Waggoner.

27 St. 783; July 23, 1892; C. 245—An act granting a pension to Joseph J. Cranberry.

27 St. 788; July 27, 1892; C. 287—An act to increase the pension of John D. Prator.

27 St. 788; July 27, 1892; C. 288—An act to pension Reuben Riggs.

27 St. 788; July 27, 1892; C. 290—An act to pension Nancy Campbell.

27 St. 789; July 27, 1892; C. 292—An act granting relief to Jeremiah White, of Osage City, Kansas.

27 St. 791; July 27, 1892; C. 301—An act granting a pension to James Smith.

27 St. 795; July 30, 1892; C. 335—An act granting a pension to John Mercer.

27 St. 795; July 30, 1892; C. 337—An act granting a pension to Stark Frazier.

27 St. 796; July 30, 1892; C. 342—An act granting a pension to James W. Kirtley.

27 St. 797; July 30, 1892; C. 346—An act granting a pension to Susanna Davis.

27 St. 797; July 30, 1892; C. 347—An act granting a pension to Henry J. Alvis.

27 St. 802; Aug. 4, 1892; C. 377—An act granting a pension to Ellen Carpenter.

27 St. 804; Aug. 5, 1892; C. 393—An act granting a pension to W. W. Harllee.

27 St. 804; Aug. 5, 1892; C. 394—An act granting a pension to John A. Dean.

27 St. 810; Dec. 19, 1892; C. 5—An act granting a pension to Tendoy, chief of the Bannocks, Shoshones, and Sheepeaters tribe of Indians.

27 St. 817; Feb. 11, 1893; C. 87—An act granting a pension to Abraham B. Simmons, of Captain Thomas Tripp's company, in Colonel Brisbane's regiment, South Carolina Volunteers, in the Florida Indian war.

27 St. 817; Feb. 11, 1893; C. 88—An act to pension Susan S. Murphy.

27 St. 824; Feb. 15, 1893; C. 134—An act granting a pension to Jesse Cleaveland.

27 St. 831; Mar. 3, 1893; C. 233—An act for the relief of Louis G. Sanderson, of Craighead County, Arkansas.

27 St. 952; Apr. 18, 1892—Convention—Great Britain.

28 STAT.

28 St. 3; Oct. 20, 1893; C. 5—An Act Granting settlers on certain lands in Oklahoma Territory the right to commute their homestead entries, and for other purposes.[10]

28 St. 4; Nov. 1, 1893; C. 7—An Act To amend section six of the act approved March 3, 1891, entitled "An act to repeal timber culture laws, and for other purposes."[11]

28 St. 5; Nov. 3, 1893; C. 10—An Act To provide for the time and place of holding the terms of the United States circuit and district courts in the State of South Dakota.

28 St. 9; Nov. 3, 1893; C. 16—An Act To regulate the fees of the clerk of the United States Court for the Indian Territory.

28 St. 12; Oct. 14, 1893; J. Res. No. 9—Joint Resolution Authorizing the State of Wisconsin to place in Statuary Hall at the Capitol the statue of Pere Marquette.

28 St. 16; Dec. 21, 1893; C. 3—An Act Making appropriations to supply further urgent deficiencies in the appropriations for the fiscal year ending June 30, 1894, and for prior years, and for other purposes.

28 St. 22; Dec. 21, 1893; C. 9—An Act To grant the right of way to the Kansas, Oklahoma Central and Southwestern Ry. Co. through the Indian Territory and Oklahoma Territory, and for other purposes.[12]

[10] *Sg.* 26 St. 989. *S.* 28 St. 876.
[11] *Ag.* 26 St. 1095.
[12] *Sg.* 1 St. 137. *A.* 29 St. 529; 30 St. 844.

28 St. 27; Jan. 22, 1894; C. 14—An Act To extend the time for the construction of the railway of the Choctaw Coal and Ry. Co.[13]

28 St. 37; Feb. 9, 1894; C. 26—An Act Extending the time allowed the Umatilla Irrigation Co. for the construction of its ditch across the Umatilla Indian Reservation, in the State of Oregon.[14]

28 St. 41; Mar. 12, 1894; C. 37—An Act Making appropriations to supply further urgent deficiencies in the appropriations for the fiscal year ending June 30, 1894, and for prior years, and for other purposes.

28 Stat. 47; Mar. 29, 1894; C. 49—An Act To regulate the making of property returns by officers of the Government. Sec. 1–31 U. S. C. 89; Sec. 2–31 U. S. C. 90; Sec. 3–31 U. S. C. 91; Sec. 4–31 U. S. C. 92.

28 St. 58; Apr. 21, 1894; C. 61—An Act To provide for further urgent deficiencies in the appropriations for the service of the Government for the fiscal year ending June 30, 1894, and for other purposes.

28 St. 71; May 4, 1894; C. 68—An Act To ratify the reservation of certain lands made for the benefit of Oklahoma Territory, and for other purposes.

28 St. 72; May 7, 1894; C. 69—An Act To authorize the reconstruction of a bridge across the Niobrara River near the village of Niobrara, Nebraska, and making an appropriation therefor.

28 St. 84; May 30, 1894; C. 86—An Act To amend an Act entitled "An Act to provide for the sale of the remainder of the reservation of the Confederated Otoe and Missouria Indians in the States of Nebraska and Kansas, and for other purposes," approved March 3, 1881.[15]

28 St. 86; June 6, 1894; C. 93—An Act Defining and permanently fixing the northern boundary line of the Warm Spring Indian Reservation, in the State of Oregon.[16]

28 St. 86; June 6, 1894; C. 94—An Act To extend and amend an Act entitled "An Act to authorize the Kansas and Arkansas Valley Railway to construct and operate additional lines of railway through the Indian Territory, and for other purposes," approved February 24, 1891.[17]

28 St. 87; June 6, 1894; C. 95—An Act Granting the right of way to the Albany and Astoria R. Co. through the Grand Ronde Indian Reservation, in the State of Oregon.

28 St. 95; June 27, 1894; C. 117—An Act Granting to the Eastern Nebraska and Gulf Ry. Co. right of way through the Omaha and Winnebago Indian reservations, in the State of Nebraska.[18]

28 St. 99; July 6, 1894; C. 125—An Act Granting to the Brainerd and Northern Minnesota Ry. Co. a right of way through the Leech Lake Indian Reservation in the State of Minnesota.

28 St. 103; July 16, 1894; C. 136—An Act To authorize the construction of a wagon and foot bridge across the South, or Main, Canadian River at or near the town of Noble, in Oklahoma Territory.

28 St. 107; July 16, 1894; C. 138—An Act To enable the people of Utah to form a constitution and State government, and to be admitted into the Union on an equal footing with the original States.[19]

28 St. 112; July 18, 1894; C. 140—An Act Granting to the Saint Paul, Minneapolis and Manitoba Ry. Co. the right of way through the White Earth, Leech Lake, Chippewa, and Fond du Lac Indian reservations in the State of Minnesota.[20]

28 St. 113; July 18, 1894; C. 141—An Act Making appropriations for the payment of invalid and other pensions of the United States for the fiscal year ending June 30, 1895, and for other purposes.

28 St. 118; July 23, 1894; C. 152—An Act Granting to the Columbia Irrigation Company a right of way through the Yakima Indian Reservation, in Washington.[21]

28 St. 162; July 31, 1894; C. 174—An Act Making appropriations for the legislative, executive, and judicial expenses of the Government for the fiscal year ending June 30, 1895, and for other purposes. Sec. 3, p. 205—25 U. S. C. 96 (18 St. 450,

[13] *Sg.* 1 St. 137; 25 St. 38; 25 St. 668. *Ag.* 26 St. 765. *Cited:* Choctaw. 6 Ind. T. 515; Choctaw, O. & G. R. R., 256 U. S. 531; U. S. ex rel. Search, 3 Okla. 404.
[14] *Sg.* 23 St. 340. *Ag.* 26 St. 745.
[15] *Ag.* 21 St. 380.
[16] *Sg.* 12 St. 963; 26 St. 355. *S.* 46 St. 1033.
[17] *Sg.* 1 St. 137. *Ag.* 26 St. 783.
[18] *A.* 29 St. 512.
[19] *S.* 47 St. 1418. *Cited:* Cramer, 261 U. S. 219.
[20] *S.* 29 St. 592.
[21] *S.* 29 St. 321; 30 St. 571.

sec. 7; 42 St. 24, sec. 304) See Historical Note 25 U. S. C. A. 96; Sec. 4, p. 206—25 U. S. C. 97 (19 St. 199, sec. 3; 34 St. 328; 42 St. 24, sec. 304); Sec. 7, p. 206—25 U. S. C. 96 (See sec. 3 re above).

28 St. 215; Aug. 1, 1894; C. 179—An Act to regulate enlistments in the Army of the United States.[22]

28 St. 229; Aug. 4, 1894; C. 215—An Act To grant to the Arkansas, Texas and Mexican Central Ry. Co. a right of way through the Indian Territory, and for other purposes.[23]

28 St. 233; Aug. 6, 1894; C. 228—An Act Making appropriations for the support of the Army for the fiscal year ending June 30, 1895, and for other purposes.[24]

28 St. 263; Aug. 8, 1894; C. 236—An Act To require railroad companies operating railroads in the Territories over a right of way granted by the Government to establish stations and depots at all town sites on the lines of said roads established by the Interior Department.

28 St. 276; Aug. 11, 1894; C. 255—An Act Extending the time of payment to purchasers of lands of the Omaha tribe of Indians in Nebraska, and for other purposes.[25]

28 St. 286; Aug. 15, 1894; C. 290—An Act Making appropriations for current and contingent expenses of the Indian Department and fulfilling treaty stipulations with various Indian tribes for the fiscal year ending June 30, 1895, and for other purposes.[26] Sec. 1, p. 305—25 U. S. C. 345 (31 St. 760, sec. 1; 36 St. 1167, sec. 291). USCA Historical Note: This section (345) was derived from sec. instant act, as amended by 31 St. 760, sec. 1, entitled, "An Act Amending the Act of August 15, 1894, entitled 'An Act'" etc. The derivative section, as originally enacted, did not contain the provision in parenthesis, now found in the code section, the amendment consisting in inserting this provision. In the Code section the word "district" was substituted wherever the word "circuit" was found in the original derivative section because of the abolition of the circuit courts and the transfer of their jurisdiction to the district courts by 36 St. 1167, and the words in the code section "held Aug. 15, 1894" just before the words "by either of the Five Civilized Tribes" were substituted for the words "now held" in the original derivative section. Sec. 1, p. 305—25 U. S. C. 402;[27] Sec. 1, p. 311—25 U. S. C. 281; Sec. 4—25 U. S. C. 99; Sec. 10—25 U. S. C. 44 (See 25 U. S. C. 472); Sec. 11—25 U. S. C. 286 (28 St. 906, sec. 1).

28 St. 372; Aug. 18, 1894; C. 301—An Act Making appropriations for sundry civil expenses of the Government for the fiscal year ending June 30, 1895, and for other purposes.[28]

28 St. 424; Aug. 23, 1894; C. 307—An Act Making appropriations to supply deficiencies in the appropriations for the fiscal year ending June 30, 1894, and for prior years, and for other pruposes.[29]

28 St. 489; Aug. 23, 1894; C. 311—An Act Granting to the Northern Mississippi Ry. Co. right of way through certain Indian reservations in Minnesota.

28 St. 502; Aug. 24, 1894; C. 330—An Act To authorize purchasers of the property and franchises of the Choctaw Coal and Ry. Co. to organize a corporation and to confer upon the same all the powers, privileges, and franchises vested in that company.[30]

28 St. 504; Aug. 27, 1894; C. 342—An Act Granting to the Duluth and Winnipeg R. Co. a right of way through the Chippewa and White Earth Indian reservations in the State of Minnesota.

28 St. 505; Aug. 27, 1894; C. 343—An Act To amend an Act entitled "An Act to amend an Act entitled 'An Act granting the right of way to the Hutchison and Southern R. Co. through the Indian Territory.'"[31]

28 St. 507; Aug. 27, 1894; C. 346—An Act Authorizing the issue of a patent to the Presbyterian Board of Home Missions for certain lands on the Omaha Indian reservation for school purposes.

28 St. 509; Aug. 27, 1894; C. 349—An Act To reduce taxation, to provide revenue for the Government, and for other purposes.

28 St. 576; Dec. 19, 1893; J. Res. No. 5—Joint Resolution For the protection of those parties who have heretofore been allowed to make entries for lands within the former Mille Lac Indian Reservation in Minnesota.[32]

28 St. 579; Mar. 31, 1894; J. Res. No. 16—Joint Resolution Authorizing and directing the Secretary of the Treasury to receive at the sub-treasury in the city of New York from R. T. Wilson and Company, or assigns, the money amounting to $6,740,000, to be paid to the Cherokee Nation, and to place the same to the credit of the Cherokee Nation.[33]

28 St. 580; Apr. 2, 1894; J. Res. No. 17—Joint Resolution Authorizing the Secretary of the Interior to cause the settlement of the accounts of Special Agents Moore and Woodson, under the treaty of 1854, with the Delaware Indians, and so forth.[34]

28 St. 589; Aug. 6, 1894; J. Res. No. 42—Joint Resolution Authorizing proper officers of the Treasury Department to examine and certify claims in favor of certain counties in Arizona.[35]

28 St. 592; Aug. 28, 1894; J. Res. No. 53—Joint Resolution To change the initials of a name in the Indian appropriation bill.

28 St. 594; Dec. 13, 1894; C. 3—An Act To provide for the location and satisfaction of outstanding military bounty land warrants and certificates of location under section three of the Act approved June 2, 1858.[36]

28 St. 635; Jan. 21, 1895; C. 37—An Act To permit the use of the right of way through the public lands for tramroads, canals, and reservoirs, and for other purposes.[37] 43 U. S. C. 956.

28 St. 641; Jan. 26, 1895; C. 50—An Act Authorizing the Secretary of the Interior to correct errors where double allotments of land have erroneously been made to an Indian, to correct errors in patents, and for other purposes.[38] 25 U. S. C. 343 (33 St. 297). U. S. C. A. Historical Note: The derivative act originally contained the provisions set forth in the Code section down to and including the words "ought to be canceled for error in the issue thereof," followed by a clause, "or for the best interests of the Indian," and the further clause set forth here, "and, if possession of the original patent cannot be obtained, such cancellation shall be effective if made upon the records of the General Land

---

[22] *Rp.* 41 St. 1077.

[23] *Sg.* 1 St. 137. *A.* 30 St. 399.

[24] *S.* 34 St. 1371. *Cited:* 53 I. D. 133.

[25] *Sg.* 22 St. 341.

[26] *Sg.* 1 St. 619; 4 St. 442; 7 St. 36, 46, 51, 69, 85, 99, 114, 161, 179, 185, 218, 236, 242, 287, 296, 317, 320, 321, 349, 352, 425, 541, 545, 596; 9 St. 35, 842, 855; 10 St. 1039, 1053, 1071, 1079, 1168; 11 St. 318, 614, 700, 702, 729, 744; 12 St. 628, 981, 1173; 13 St. 624, 675, 694; 14 St. 650, 757, 787, 804; 15 St. 515, 584, 590, 596, 622, 638, 651, 657, 676; 16 St. 40, 355, 579, 720; 19 St. 208, 254, 256, 287; 21 St. 70, 200; 22 St. 43; 23 St. 79; 24 St. 219, 388; 25 St. 94, 114, 645, 688, 894; 26 St. 659, 756, 794, 851, 1016, 1028, 1033, 1037; 27 St. 139, 456, 616, 631, 640, 645. *Rpg.* 12 St. 954, 618. *A.* 28 St. 876; 31 St. 221, 760. *Rp.* 34 St. 539. *S.* 28 St. 876; 29 St. 267, 321; 30 St. 62; 31 St. 221, 280; 33 St. 519; 36 St. 367; 41 St. 3; 45 St. 1167, 1249. *Cited:* Cain, 2 Minn. L. Rev. 177; Brown, 39 Yale L. J. 307; 36 Op. A. G. 98; Op. Sol., M. 25258, June 26, 1929; Op. A. G., Oct. 5, 1929; Ass't Sec'y Letter to Sec'y of War, Feb. 26, 1932; Memo. Sol. Off., Apr. 4, 1933, Aug. 11, 1933; Op. Sol., M. 27671, Mar. 1, 1934; Memo. Sol. Off., May 11, 1934; Memo. Sol., Nov. 11, 1935; Op. Sol., M. 28198, Jan. 8, 1936; Memo. Sol. Off., Jan. 22, 1936; Memo. Sol., May 15, 1936; Memo. of Ass't Sec'y to Comm'r, Feb. 17, 1937; Memo. Sol., Oct. 21, 1938; 24 L. D. 511; 25 L. D. 364; 25 L. D. 408; 29 L. D. 251; 53 I. D. 133; Bird, 129 Fed. 472; Browning, 6 F. 2d 801; Chickasaw, 193 U. S. 115; Clay, 282 Fed. 268; Coos Bay, 87 C. Cls. 143; Dick, 208 U. S. 340; Egan, 246 U. S. 227; Ex p. Dick, 141 Fed. 5; Ex p. Tilden, 218 Fed. 920; Ex p. Viles, 139 Fed. 68; First Moon, 270 U. S. 243; Halbert, 283 U. S. 752; Hallowell, 239 U. S. 506; Hampton, 22 F. 2d 81; Hy-Yu Tse-Mil-Kin, 194 U. S. 401; Heckman, 224 U. S. 413; Ickes, 80 F. 2d 708; In re Jessie's Heirs, 259 Fed. 94; Jackson, 84 C. Cls. 441; Johnson, 234 U. S. 422; Kennedy, 23 F. Supp. 771; Kirby, 260 U. S. 423; Lemieux, 15 F. 2d 518; Lucas, 15 F. 2d 32; McKay, 204 U. S. 458; Medawakanton, 57 C. Cls. 357; Miller, 249 U. S. 308; Mitchell, 22 F. 2d 771; Morrison, 6 F. 2d 811; Pape, 19 F. 2d 219; Patawa, 132 Fed. 893; Pel-Ata-Yakot, 188 Fed. 387; Perrin, 232 U. S. 478; Reynolds, 174 Fed. 212; Sage, 235 U. S. 99; Sloan, 118 Fed. 283; Sloan, 95 Fed. 193; Smith, 142 Fed. 225; U. S. v. Choctaw, 38 C. Cls. 558; U. S. v. Getzelman, 89 F. 2d 531; U. S. v. Gray, 201 Fed. 291; U. S. v. Hayes, 20 F. 2d 873; U. S. v. Heyfron, 138 Fed. 964; U. S. v. One Cadillac, 255 Fed. 173; U. S. v. Paine, 206 U. S. 467; U. S. v. Payne, 264 U. S. 446; U. S. v. Zumwalt, 186 Fed. 596; Ute, 45 C. Cls. 440; Vezina, 245 Fed. 411; Wadsworth, 148 Fed. 771; Ya-Koot-Sa, 262 Fed. 398; Yancton, 272 U. S. 351; Yankton, 61 C. Cls. 40; Young, 176 Fed. 612.

[27] Also see 25 U. S. C. 402a (44 St. 894).

[28] *Sg.* 1 St. 137. *S.* 34 St. 1056; 35 St. 644; 36 St. 269.

[29] *Sg.* 26 St. 851. *S.* 28 St. 876; 30 St. 62; 43 St. 390; 52 St. 291. *Rp.* 45 St. 986. *Cited:* 21 Op. A. G. 131; Hanks, 3 Ind. T. 415; McCollum, 33 C. Cls. 469; Pam-To-Pee, 187 U. S. 371; U. S. v. Wright, 53 F. 2d 300.

[30] *Sg.* 26 St. 640. *A.* 29 St. 98. *Rp.* 31 St. 52. *Cited:* Choctaw, O. & G. R. R., 256 U. S. 531; Choctaw, 6 Ind. T. 515; U. S. ex rel. Search, 8 Okla. 404.

[31] *Sg.* 1 St. 137. *Ag.* 27 St. 2. *A.* 29 St. 702.

[32] *Sg.* 25 St. 642. *Cited:* Mille Lac, 46 C. Cls. 424.

[33] *Sg.* 27 St. 640.

[34] *Sg.* 10 St. 1048, 1069, 1082.

[35] *Sg.* 23 St. 385; 25 St. 1004. *S.* St. 843; 30 St. 105.

[36] *Sg.* 11 St. 295; 17 St. 605; 19 St. 377; 20 St. 89, 118; 26 St. 1097; 27 St. 348.

[37] *Cited:* U. S. v. Portneuf-Marsh, 213 Fed. 601.

[38] *A.* 33 St. 297. *Cited:* LaClair, 184 Fed. 128; Mandler, 52 F. 2d 713; U. S. v. LaRoque, 198 Fed. 645; 24 L. D. 214; 29 L. D. 251; 30 L. D. 258; 38 L. D. 556; 43 L. D. 84; Op. Sol. M. 12498, June 6, 1924, M. 12509, Aug. 27, 1924.

Office," ending with a provision, "and no proclamation shall be necessary to open the lands so allotted to settlement." The amendment by said act of 1904 consisted in omitting said clause, "or for the best interests of the Indian," in changing said last clause to read, "and no proclamation shall be necessary to open to settlement the lands to which such an erroneous allotment patent has been canceled, provided such lands would otherwise be subject to entry," and in adding the two provisos, to read substantially as set forth here.

28 St. 653; Feb. 12, 1895; C. 81—An Act Granting right of way to the Forest City and Sioux City R. Co. through the Sioux Indian Reservation.[39]

28 St. 654; Feb. 12, 1895; C. 83—An Act Making appropriations for the support of the Army for the fiscal year ending June 30, 1896, and for other purposes.

28 St. 665, Feb. 18, 1895; C. 95—An Act Granting to the Gila Valley, Globe and Northern R. Co. a right of way through the San Carlos Indian Reservation in the Territory of Arizona.[40]

28 St. 677; Feb. 20, 1895; C. 113—An Act To disapprove the treaty heretofore made with the Southern Ute Indians to be removed to the Territory of Utah, and providing for settling them down in severalty where they may so elect and are qualified, and to settle all those not electing to take lands in severalty on the west forty miles of present reservation and in portions of New Mexico, and for other purposes, and to carry out the provisions of the treaty with said Indians June 15, 1880.[41]

28 St. 679; Feb. 20, 1895; C. 114—An Act For the relief of certain Winnebago Indians in Minnesota.[42]

28 St. 693; Mar. 1, 1895; C. 145—An Act To provide for the appointment of additional judges of the United States court in the Indian Territory, and for other purposes.[43] Sec. 8—25 U. S. C. 241a.

28 St. 703; Mar. 2, 1895; C. 161—An Act Making appropriations for the payment of invalid and other pensions of the United States for the fiscal year ending June 30, 1896, and for other purposes.

28 St. 744; Mar. 2, 1895; C. 175—An Act To amend sec. 9 of an Act entitled "An Act to authorize the Kansas City, Pittsburg and Gulf R. Co. to construct and operate a railroad, telegraph, and telephone line through the Indian Territory, and for other purposes."[44]

28 St. 764; Mar. 2, 1895; C. 177—An Act Making appropriations for the legislative, executive, and judicial expenses of the Government for the fiscal year ending June 30, 1896, and for other purposes.[45]

28 St. 843; Mar. 2, 1895; C. 187—An Act Making appropriations to supply deficiencies in the appropriations for the fiscal year ending June 30, 1895, and for prior years, and for other purposes.[46]

28 St. 876; Mar. 2, 1895; C. 188—An Act Making appropriations for current and contingent expenses of the Indian Department and fulfilling treaty stipulations with various Indian tribes for the fiscal year ending June 30, 1896, and for other purposes.[47] Sec. 1, p. 906—25 U. S. C. 286 (28 St. 313, sec. 11); 43 U. S. C. 856. Also see Historical Note 25 U. S. C. A. 395, 28 St. 910; Mar. 2, 1895; C. 189—An Act Making appropriations for sundry civil expenses of the Government for the fiscal year ending June 30, 1896, and for other purposes.[48]

28 St. 966; Mar. 2, 1895; C. 195—An Act To provide for the salaries of the judges and other officers of the United States court in the Indian Territory.

28 St. 970; Feb. 20, 1895; J. Res. No. 16—Joint Resolution To confirm the enlargement of the Red Cliff Indian Reservation in the State of Wisconsin, made in 1863, and for the allotment of same.[49]

28 St. 974; Mar. 2, 1895; J. Res. No. 27—Joint Resolution Continuing the present officers of the courts in the Indian Territory until the bill for the reorganization of the judiciary of that Territory which has passed both Houses of Congress and awaits the signature of the President of the United States becomes a law.

28 St. 987; June 20, 1894; C. 112—An Act For the relief of the heirs of Edward Morrison and Nellie Morrison, now deceased.[50]

28 St. 998; Aug. 4, 1894; C. 223—An Act For the relief of Benjamin F. Poteet.

28 St. 1007; Aug. 11, 1894; C. 276—An Act For the relief of Walter S. McLeod.

28 St. 1009; Aug. 15, 1894; C. 297—An Act To enable the Secretary of the Interior to pay John T. Heard for professional services rendered the "Old Settlers" or Western Cherokee Indians out of the funds of said Indians.

28 St. 1013; Aug. 23, 1894; C. 326—An Act For the relief of Henry W. Lee.

28 St. 1013; Aug. 24, 1894; C. 331—An Act Granting a pension to Jesse Davenport, of Company A, Second Regiment Oregon Mounted Volunteers, in Oregon Indian wars of 1855 and 1856.

28 St. 1015; Aug. 24, 1894; C. 337—An Act Granting a pension to Adaline J. Props.

28 St. 1018; Aug. 4, 1894; J. Res. No. 41—Joint Resolution Authorizing the Secretary of the Interior to approve a certain lease made in Polk County, Minnesota.[51]

28 St. 1025; Jan. 22, 1895; C. 41—An Act To pension Willis Manasco.

28 St. 1029; Feb. 8, 1895; C. 69—An Act For the relief of John J. Patman.

28 St. 1030; Feb. 8, 1895; C. 72—An Act To increase the pension of Pickens T. Reynolds, of Hall County, Georgia.

28 St. 1030; Feb. 8, 1895; C. 74—An Act Granting a pension to Rosanna Cobb, widow of Edmond Cobb, deceased, late of Sac and Fox war.

28 St. 1031; Feb. 12, 1895; C. 85—An Act For the relief of William T. Holman.

28 St. 1034; Feb. 21, 1895; C. 122—An Act To pension Mary R. Williams.

---

[39] *Sg.* 18 St. 482.

[40] *A.* 30 Stat. 227.

[41] *Sg.* 21 St. 199; 25 St. 183. *S.* 29 St. 321; 30 St. 105; 45 St. 200. *Cited:* Ute, 45 C. Cls. 440.

[42] *Sg.* 12 St. 659; 16 St. 361; 17 St. 185.

[43] *S.* 29 St. 6; 30 St. 105; 31 St. 657; 32 St. 90; 33 St. 189; 34 St. 697; 35 St. 8. *Cited:* 22 Op. A. G. 232; Memo. Sol., Oct. 13, 1933; Ammerman, 267 Fed. 136; Ansley, 180 U. S. 253; Archard, 212 Fed. 146; Binyon, 4 Ind. T. 642; Bise, 5 Ind. T. 602; Boyt, 4 Ind. T. 47; Blackwell, 236 Fed 912; Brown, 2 Ind. T. 582; Browning, 6 F. 2d 801; Buchanan, 15 F. 2d 496; Burch, 7 Ind. T. 284; Burton, 31 F. 2d 966; Butterfield, 241 Fed. 556; Chambliss, 218 Fed. 154; Chancellor, 237 Fed. 193; Choctaw, 6 Ind. T. 432; Collier, 221 Fed. 64; Collins, 243 Fed. 495; Commercial, 261 Fed. 330; DeMoss, 250 Fed. 87; Dennee, 4 Ind. T. 233; Edwards, 5 F. 2d 17; Evans, 204 Fed. 361; Ex p. Webb, 225 U. S. 663; Fiedler, 227 Fed. 832; Flack, 272 Fed. 680; Ford, 260 Fed. 657; Glenn-Tucker 4 Ind. T. 511; Greer, 245 U. S. 559; Hawley, 15 F. 2d 621; Isbell, 227 Fed. 788; Johnson, 234 U. S. 422; Jones, 274 U. S. 544; Joplin, 236 U. S. 531; Lucas, 15 F. 2d 32; Luce, 4 Ind. T. 54; McSpadden, 224 Fed. 935; Morrison, 6 F. 2d 811; Oats, 1 Ind. T. 152; Oklahoma, 249 Fed. 592; One Buick, 275 Fed. 809; Parmenter, 6 Ind. T. 530; Parris, 1 Ind. T. 43; Prosser, 265 Fed. 252; Purcell, 6 Ind. T. 78; Renfro, 15 F. 2d 991; Robinson, 221 Fed. 398; Royal, 217 Fed. 146; Schaap, 210 Fed. 853; Segna, 218 Fed. 791; Sharpe, 16 F. 2d 876; Simon, 4 Ind. T. 688; Stephens, 174 U. S. 445; Swofford, 25 F. 2d 581; Tally, 6 Ind. T. 331; Taylor, 6 Ind. T. 351; Tucker, 236 Fed. 542; U. S. v. Buckles, 6 Ind. T. 319; U. S. v. Cohn, 2 Ind. T. 474; U. S. v. Luther, 260 Fed. 597; U. S. v. One Buick, 244 Fed. 961; U. S. v. One Cadillac, 225 Fed. 173; U. S. v. One Ford, 259 Fed. 645; U. S. v. Wright, 229 U. S. 226; Warren, 250 Fed. 89; Watkins, 3 Ind. T. 281; Wilson, 1 Ind. T. 163; Willis, 6 Ind. T. 424; Williams, 4 Ind. T. 204; Wilson, 260 Fed. 840; Wright, 227 Fed. 855.

[44] *Ag.* 27 St. 487, sec. 9.

[45] *Sg.* 27 St. 643. *Cited:* 22 L. D. 709; Cherokee, 270 U. S. 476.

[46] *Sg.* 10 St. 582; 11 St. 91; 12 St. 104; 15 St. 175; 21 St. 510; 26 St. 92, 853; 28 St. 589. *Cited:* Medawakanton, 57 C. Cls. 357.

[47] *Sg.* 1 St. 619; 4 St. 442; 7 St. 36, 46, 51, 69, 85, 99, 114, 161, 179, 185, 213, 236, 242, 287, 296, 317, 320, 349, 352, 425, 541, 545, 752; 9 St. 35, 842, 855, 904; 10 St. 950, 1071, 1079; 11 St. 614, 700, 702, 729, 744; 12 St. 628, 981, 1173; 13 St. 675; 14 St. 650, 757, 787; 15 St. 515, 584, 590, 596, 622, 637, 638, 651, 657, 676; 16 St. 40, 355, 720; 17 St. 333 sec. 1; 19 St. 254, 256, 287; 22 St. 43, 603; 23 St. 79; 24 St. 388, 389; 25 St. 114, 645, 688, 759, 894; 26 St. 352, 659, 756, 794, 1026, 1028, 1033, 1036, 1037; 27 St. 137, 139, 260, 624, 630, 641, 745; 28 St. 3, 301, 307, 308, 450. *S.* 29 St. 321; 30 St. 62, 1362; 31 St. 1010, 1093; 32 St. 245, 982; 33 St. 519; 34 St. 325; 43 St. 390, 1313. *Rp.* 36 St. 855. *A.* 41 St. 1225. *Cited:* 29 Op. A. G. 239; 34 Op. A. G. 439; 3 L. D. Memo. 388; 3 L. D. Memo. 435; Op. Sol., M. 12746, Oct. 8, 1924; Memo. Sol. Off., Feb. 7, 1934; 25 L. D. 364; Cherokee, 85 C. Cls. 76; Childers, 270 U. S. 555; Creek, 63 C. Cls. 270; Eagle-Picher, 28 F. 2d 472; Ewert, 259 U. S. 129; Goodrum, 162 Fed. 817; Hallam, 49 F. 2d 103; In re Land of Five, 199 Fed. 811; In re Lelah-Puc-Ka-Chee, 98 Fed. 429; Jaybird 271 U. S. 609; Kendall, 259 U. S. 139; McCullough, 243 Fed. 823; Medawakanton, 57 C. Cls. 357; Moore, 5 Ind. T. 384; Pam-To-Pee, 187 U. S. 371; Peel, 45 C. Cls. 154; Sac & Fox, 45 C. Cls. 287; Sac & Fox, 220 U. S. 481; Schewson, 31 C. Cls. 192; Sisseton, 42 C. Cls. 416; Smith, 270 U. S. 456; Smith, 37 C. Cls. 119; U. S. v. Abrams, 194 Fed. 82; U. S. v. Choctaw, 179 U. S. 494; U. S. v. Moore, 284 Fed. 86; U. S. v. Noble, 237 U. S. 74; U. S. v. Reynolds, 250 U. S. 104; U. S. v. Rundell, 181 Fed. 887; U. S. v. Sisseton, 208 U. S. 561; U. S. ex rel. West, 205 U. S. 80; Williams, 16 Okla. 104; Whitebird, 40 F. 2d 479.

[48] *Rpg.* 27 St. 645. *S.* 29 St. 321; 30 St. 62, 571, 924; 31 St. 221, 1058; 32 St. 245, 982; 43 St. 1313. *Cited:* Cherokee, 187 U. S. 294; Cherokee, 223; U. S. 108; Dick, 6 Ind. T. 85; Journeycake, 31 C. Cls. 140; Kimberlin, 104 Fed. 653; Lowe, 223 U. S. 95; Nunn, 216 Fed. 330.

[49] *Sg.* 10 St. 1109.

[50] *Sg.* 26 St. 989, 1022.

[51] *Cited:* Jones, 175 U. S. 1.

28 St. 1041; Mar. 2, 1895; C. 209—An Act To pension David H. Sexton for services in Oregon Indian wars.

28 St. 1042; Mar. 2, 1895; C. 211—An Act to pension Mary E. Hamilton, widow of David Hamilton, soldier in Indian war of 1818.

28 St. 1044; Mar. 2, 1895; C. 220—An Act Granting a pension to James Jones.

28 St. 1044; Mar. 2, 1895; C. 221—An Act Granting a pension to Alexander M. Laughlin.

28 St. 1045; Mar. 2, 1895; C. 227—An Act To grant a pension to Mrs. Mary Button, of Arkansas, widow of Asa Button, deceased.

28 St. 1047; Mar. 2, 1895; C. 234—An Act Granting an increase of pension to Thomas M. Chill.

29 STAT.

29 St. 6; Feb. 8, 1896; C. 14—An Act To extend the jurisdiction of the United States circuit court of appeals, eighth circuit, over certain suits now pending therein on appeal and writ of error from the United States court in the Indian Territory.[52]

29 St. 6; Feb. 13, 1896; C. 19—An Act To amend an Act entitled "An Act to authorize the Kansas City, Pittsburg and Gulf Railroad Company to construct and operate a railroad, telegraph, and telephone line through the Indian Territory, and for other purposes," approved February 27, 1893.[53]

29 St. 9; Feb. 20, 1896; C. 24—An Act To extend the mineral-land laws of the United States to lands embraced in the north half of the Colville Indian Reservation.[54]

29 St. 10; Feb. 20, 1896; C. 26—An Act To amend section twenty-one of an Act entitled "An Act to divide a portion of the reservation of the Sioux Nation of Indians in Dakota into separate reservations, and to secure the relinquishment of the Indian title to the remainder, and for other purposes," approved March 2, 1889.[55]

29 St. 12; Feb. 24, 1896; C. 29—An Act Granting to the Brainerd and Northern Minnesota Ry. Co. a right of way through the Leech Lake Indian Reservation and Chippewa Indian Reservation, in Minnesota.

29 St. 13; Feb. 24, 1896; C. 30—An Act To authorize the Arkansas and Choctaw Ry. Co. to construct and operate a railway through the Choctaw Nation, in the Indian Territory, and for other purposes.[56]

29 St. 16; Feb. 26, 1896; C. 31—An Act Granting leave of absence for one year to homestead settlers upon the Yankton Indian Reservation, in the State of South Dakota, and for other purposes.

29 St. 17; Feb. 26, 1896; C. 32—An Act To amend an Act entitled "An Act for the relief and civilization of the Chippewa Indians in the State of Minnesota."[57]

29 St. 17; Feb. 26, 1896; C. 33—An Act Making appropriations to supply urgent deficiencies in the appropriations for the fiscal year ending June 30, 1896, and for prior years, and for other purposes.[58]

29 St. 40; Mar. 2, 1896; C. 38—An Act To grant the Fort Smith and Western Coal R. Co. a right of way through the Indian Territory, and for other purposes.[59]

29 St. 44; Mar. 4, 1896; C. 41—An Act To amend an Act entitled "An Act to grant to the Gainesville, McAlester and St. Louis R. Co. a right of way through the Indian Territory."[60]

29 St. 44; Mar. 6, 1896; C. 42—An Act Granting to the Columbia and Red Mountain Ry. Co. a right of way through the Colville Indian Reservation, in the State of Washington, and for other purposes.[61]

29 St. 45; Mar. 6, 1896; C. 46—An Act Making appropriations for the payment of invalid and other pensions of the United States for the fiscal year ending June 30, 1897, and for other purposes. 38 U. S. C. 323.

29 St. 60; Mar. 16, 1896; C. 59—An Act Making appropriations for the support of the Army for the fiscal year ending June 30, 1897.

29 St. 69; Mar. 18, 1896; C. 60—An Act To authorize the St. Louis and Oklahoma City R. Co. to construct and operate a railway through the Indian and Oklahoma Territories, and for other purposes.

29 St. 77; Mar. 28, 1896; C. 76—An Act To authorize the Kansas City, Fort Scott and Memphis R. Co. to extend its line of railroad into the Indian Territory, and for other purposes.

29 St. 80; Mar. 30, 1896; C. 82—An Act Authorizing the St. Louis, Oklahoma and Southern Ry. Co. to construct and operate a railway through the Indian Territory and Oklahoma Territory, and for other purposes.[62]

29 St. 84; Mar. 31, 1896; C. 85—An Act Providing for disposal of lands lying within the Fort Klamath Hay Reservation, not included in the Klamath Indian Reservation, in Oregon.

29 St. 87; Apr. 6, 1896; C. 93—An Act Authorizing the Arkansas Northwestern Ry. Co. to construct and operate a railway through the Indian Territory, and for other purposes.[63]

29 St. 92; Apr. 14, 1896; C. 100—An Act Granting to the Duluth and North Dakota R. Co. right of way through certain Indian reservations in the State of Minnesota.[64]

29 St. 93; Apr. 14, 1896; C. 101—An Act To amend an Act to authorize the Interoceanic Ry. Co. to construct and operate railway, telegraph, and telephone lines through the Indian Territory.[65]

29 St. 95; Apr. 18, 1896; C. 108—An Act Granting to the Atchison and Nebraska R. Co. and the Chicago, Burlington and Quincy R. Co., its lessee in perpetuity, the right of way over a part of the Sac and Fox and Iowa Indian Reservation in the States of Kansas and Nebraska.

29 St. 98; Apr. 24, 1896; C. 122—An Act To amend an Act approved August 24, 1894, entitled "An Act to authorize purchasers of the property and franchises of the Choctaw Coal and Ry. Co. to organize a corporation and to confer upon the same all the powers, privileges, and franchises vested in that company."[66]

29 St. 109; Apr. 25, 1896; C. 141—An Act To grant to railroad companies in Indian Territory additional powers to secure depot grounds.

29 St. 117; May 13, 1896; C. 175—An Act Making provision for the deportation of refugee Canadian Cree Indians from the State of Montana and their delivery to the Canadian authorities.

29 St. 128; May 21, 1896; C. 213—An Act To amend an Act entitled "An Act to authorize the Denison and Northern Ry. Co. to construct and operate a railway through the Indian Territory, and for other purposes."[67]

29 St. 136; May 25, 1896; C. 242—An Act Making it unlawful to shoot at or into any railway locomotive or car, or at any person thereon, or to throw any rock or other missile at or into any locomotive or car in the Indian Territory, and for other purposes.

29 St. 140; May 28, 1896; C. 252—An Act Making appropriations for the legislative, executive, and judicial expenses of the Government for the fiscal year ending June 30, 1897, and for other purposes.[68]

29 St. 202; June 3, 1896; C. 314—An Act Making appropriations for the construction, repair, and preservation of certain public works on rivers and harbors, and for other purposes.

29 St. 245; June 3, 1896; C. 316—An Act For the relief of settlers on the Northern Pacific Railroad indemnity lands.[69]

29 St. 267; June 8, 1896; C. 373—An Act Making appropriations to supply deficiencies in the appropriations for the fiscal year ending June 30, 1896, and for prior years, and for other purposes.[70]

---

[52] *Sg.* 28 St. 698.
[53] *Ag.* 27 St. 487, sec. 1.
[54] *Sg.* 27 St. 64, sec. 6. *Cited:* McFadden, 87 Fed. 154; U. S. v. Pelican, 232 U. S. 442.
[55] *Ag.* 25 St. 897, sec. 21.
[56] *Sg.* 1 St. 137.
[57] *Ag.* 25 St. 644, sec. 5.
[58] *Sg.* 25 St. 644; 26 St. 612; 27 St. 633; 29 St. 17, c. 32. *S.* 29 St. 321.
[59] *A.* 30 St. 433, c. 391. *Cited:* Northern, 227 U. S. 355.
[60] *Ag.* 27 St. 524, sec. 1, 2, 6. *Sg.* 27 St. 524, sec. 9. *A.* 30 St. 715.
[61] *Sg.* 18 St. 482. *Cited:* U. S. v. Ferry Co., 24 F. Supp. 399.
[62] *A.* 30 St. 886.
[63] *A.* 30 St. 995.
[64] *Cited:* Chippewa, 80 C. Cls. 410.
[65] *Ag.* 27 St. 747, sec. 1, 2, 6. *Sg.* 27 St. 750.
[66] *Ag.* 28 St. 502, sec. 4. *Rp.* 31 St. 52. *Cited:* Choctaw, O. & G. R. Co., 6 Ind. T. 515; Choctaw, 256 U. S. 581.
[67] *Ag.* 27 St. 339, sec. 2, 6, 8.
[68] *A.* 29 St. 538.
[69] *Sg.* 25 St. 644.
[70] *Sg.* 25 St. 768; 26 St. 92, sec. 25, 853; 27 St. 64, 641; 28 St. 306, sec. 7. *Cited:* Memo. Ind. Off., Mar. 13, 1935.
[71] *Sg.* 1 St. 619; 4 St. 442; 7 St. 36, 46, 51, 69, 84, 85, 99, 114, 161, 179, 185, 212, 213, 236, 242, 287, 296, 317, 318, 320, 321, 349, 352, 425, 540, 541, 545, 596; 9 St. 35, 842, 854, 855, 904; 10 St. 1071, 1079; 11 St. 614, 700, 701, 702, 729, 744; 12 St. 628, 981, 1040, 1173; 13 St. 675; 14 St. 650, 757, 777, 787; 15 St. 515, 584, 590, 596, 621, 622, 637, 638, 651, 657, 676; 16 St. 40, 355, 720; 19 St. 254, 256; 22 St. 43; 23 St. 79; 24 St. 388; 25 St. 114, 133, 642, 645, 688, 890, 894, 1005; 26 St. 756, 1028, 1033, 1037; 27 St. 139, 633, 645; 28 St. 118, 301, 677, 876, 894, 908, 939; 29 St. 23. *A.* 40 St. 561; 48 St. 984. *Rp.* 35 St. 1088. *S.* 30 St. 62, 495, 571, 924; 31 St. 221, 280, 672, 1010, 1058; 32 St. 245, 641, 982; 33 St. 189, 352, 1048; 34 St. 325;

29 St. 321; June 10, 1896; C. 398—An Act Making appropriations for current and contingent expenses of the Indian Department and fulfilling treaty stipulations with various Indian tribes for the fiscal year ending June 30, 1897, and for other purposes.[71] Sec. 1, p. 336—25 U. S. C. 117. USCA Historical Note: By the Act of Mar. 2, 1895, s. 11, 28 St. 188, the Secretary of the Interior was authorized to detail an officer from his department or appoint a special agent to superintend and inspect payments or disbursements of moneys to Indians individually. This was repealed by Act of Apr. 21, 1904, s. 9, 35 St. 218. The Act of June 28, 1898, s. 19, 30 St. 502, contained the following provision: "Sec. 19. That no payment of any moneys on any account whatever shall hereafter be made by the United States to any of the tribal governments or to any officer thereof for disbursement, but payments of all sums to members of said tribes shall be made under direction of the Secretary of the Interior by an officer appointed by him; and per capita payments shall be made direct to each individual in lawful money of the United States, and the same shall not be liable to the payment of any previously contracted obligation." Sec. 1, p. 343—18 U. S. C. 111; Sec. 1, p. 348—25 U. S. C. 287.

29 St. 413; June 11, 1896; C. 420—An Act Making appropriations for sundry civil expenses of the Government for the fiscal year ending June 30, 1897, and for other purposes.[72]

29 St. 487; Jan. 15, 1897; C. 29—An Act To reduce the cases in which the penalty of death may be inflicted.[73] 18 U. S. C. 548.

29 St. 493; Jan. 20, 1897; C. 70—An Act To validate the appointments, acts, and services of certain deputy United States marshals in the Indian Territory, and for other purposes.

29 St. 502; Jan. 29, 1897; C. 108—An Act To authorize the Muskogee, Oklahoma and Western R. Co. to construct and operate a line of railway through Oklahoma and the Indian Territory, and for other purposes.

29 St. 506; Jan. 30, 1897; C. 109—An Act To prohibit the sale of intoxicating drinks to Indians, providing penalties therefor, and for other purposes.[74] Sec. 1—25 U. S. C. 241 (R. S. sec. 2139; Sec. 1, 19 St. 244; 27 St. 260).[75] See Historical Note 25 U. S. C. A. 241.

29 St. 510; Feb. 3, 1897; C. 136—An Act Relating to mortgages in the Indian Territory.[76]

29 St. 512; Feb. 6, 1897; C. 170—An Act To amend an Act entitled "An Act granting to the Eastern Nebraska and Gulf Ry. Co. right of way through the Omaha and Winnebago Indian reservations, in the State of Nebraska," by extending the time for the construction of said railway.[77]

29 St. 527; Feb. 15, 1897; C. 228—An Act To grant to the Hudson Reservoir and Canal Co. the right of way through the Gila River Indian Reservation.

29 St. 529; Feb. 15, 1897; C. 230—An Act To extend and amend an Act entitled "An Act to grant the right of way to the Kansas, Oklahoma Central and Southwestern Ry. Co., through the Indian Territory and Oklahoma Territory, and for other purposes," approved December 21, 1893.[78]

29 St. 538; Feb. 19, 1897; C. 265—An Act Making appropriations for the legislative, executive, and judicial expenses of the Government for the fiscal year ending June 30, 1898, and for other purposes.[79]

29 St. 592; Feb. 23, 1897; C. 308—An Act To extend the time for the completion of the Saint Paul, Minneapolis and Manitoba Ry. Co. through the White Earth, Leech Lake, Chippewa, and Fond du Lac Indian reservations in the State of Minnesota.[80]

29 St. 609; Mar. 2, 1897; C. 362—An Act Making appropriations for the support of the Army for the fiscal year ending June 30, 1898.[81]

29 St. 698; Jan. 30, 1897; J. Res. No. 7—Joint Resolution To authorize the Secretary of the Interior to use Fort Bidwell for an Indian training school.

29 St. 702; Feb. 23, 1897; J. Res. No. 17—Joint Resolution To amend an Act granting to the Duluth and Winnipeg R. Co. a right of way through the Chippewa and White Earth Indian reservations in the State of Minnesota.[82]

29 St. 715; Apr. 24, 1896; C. 124—An Act To authorize the Secretary of the Interior to settle the claims of the legal representatives of S. W. Marston, late United States Indian agent of Union Agency, Indian Territory, for services and expenses.

29 St. 736; May 30, 1896; C. 288—An Act For the Relief of Kate Eberle, an Indian woman.[83]

29 St. 748; June 6, 1896; C. 360—An Act Granting a pension to Carrie H. Greene.

29 St. 762; Jan. 13, 1897; C. 15—An Act To grant a pension to Armstead M. Rawlings, of Arkansas.

29 St. 768; Jan. 16, 1897; C. 48—An Act Granting a pension to Mary Prince, widow of Ellis Prince.

29 St. 769; Jan. 16, 1897; C. 49—An Act Granting a pension to Nancy B. Prince, widow of Elbert Prince.

29 St. 788; Feb. 4, 1897; C. 157—An Act Granting a pension to Silas S. White.

29 St. 801; Feb. 10, 1897; C. 215—An Act For the relief of Hiram T. Gorum and Silas W. Davis, of Oregon.

29 St. 804; Feb. 17, 1897; C. 245—An Act For the relief of Silas P. Keller.

29 St. 821; Feb. 25, 1897; C. 321—An Act For the relief of Daniel T. Tollett.

30 STAT.

30 St. 11; June 4, 1897; C. 2—An Act Making appropriations for sundry civil expenses of the Government for the fiscal year ending June 30, 1898, and for other purposes.[84]

30 St. 62; June 7, 1897; C. 3—An Act Making appropriations for the current and contingent expenses of the Indian Department and for fulfilling treaty stipulations with various Indian tribes for the fiscal year ending June 30, 1898, and

---

39 St. 969; 45 St. 684. *Cited:* Cavell, 3 Okla. S. B. J. 208; 25 Op. A. G. 152; 25 Op. A. G. 163; 26 Op. A. G. 127; 26 Op. A. G. 171; 3 L. D. Memo. 435; Sol. Op. M. 11108, Dec. 4, 1928; Sol. Op. M. 20612, Dec. 28, 1926; Rep. on Status of Pueblo of Pojoaque, Nov. 3, 1932; Op. Sol., Aug. 1, 1933; Memo. Sol. Off., Feb. 7, 1934; Memo. Sol., Aug 8, 1934; Memo. Ind. Off., Mar. 13, 1935; Letter from Act. Sec'y of Int. to Compt. Gen., Apr. 16, 1935; Sol. Op. 26163, Oct. 8, 1930; 44 L. D. 531; Ansley, 180 U. S. 253; Blackfeet, 81 C. Cls. 101; British-American, 299 U. S. 159; Cherokee, 85 C. Cls. 76; Cherokee, 187 U. S. 294; Choctaw, 81 C. Cls. 1; Choctaw, 83 C. Cls. 140; Crawford, 3 Ind T. 10; Dick, 6 Ind. T. 85; Dukes, 5 Ind. T. 145; Eagle-Picher, 28 F. 2d 472; Folk, 233 Fed. 177; Garfield, 211 U. S. 264; Garfield, 211 U. S. 249; Henkel, 237 U. S. 45; In re Lelah-Puc-Ka-Chee, 98 Fed. 429; Keimohah, 38 F. 2d 665; Kimberlin, 3 Ind. T. 16; Klamath, 86 C. Cls. 614; McMurray, 62 C. Cls. 458; McKnight, 130 Fed. 659; Malone, 212 Fed. 668; Medawakanton, 57 C. Cls. 357; Mullen, 224 U. S. 448; Nunn, 216 Fed. 330; Peters, 111 Fed. 244; Quick Bear, 210 U. S. 50; Sac & Fox, 220 U. S. 481; Seminole, 78 C. Cls. 455; Smith, 142 Fed. 225; Stephens, 174 U. S. 445; U. S. v. Anderson, 228 U. S. 52; U. S. v. Atkins, 260 U. S. 220; U. S. v Hayes, 20 F. 2d 873; U. S. v. Hoyt, 167 Fed. 301; U. S. v. Noble, 237 U S. 74; U. S. v. Pearson, 231 Fed. 270; U. S. v. Watashe, 102 F. 2d 428; U. S. v. Wildcat, 244 U. S. 111; Wallace, 204 U. S. 415; Winters, 207 U. S. 564; Winton, 255 U. S. 373.

[72] *S.* 35 St. 644; 36 St. 269.

[73] *Rg.* 23 St. 385, sec. 9. *Cited:* Memo. Sol. Off., Jan. 19, 1937; Apapas, 233 U. S. 587; Bailey, 47 F. 2d 702; Eugene Sol Louie, 274 Fed. 47; Ex p. Pero, 99 F. 2d 28; Good Shot, 104 Fed. 254; Louie, 254 U. S. 548; Pickett, 216 U. S. 456; Quagon, 5 F. 2d 608; U. S. v. Celestine, 215 U. S. 278; U. S. v. Kiya, 126 Fed. 879; U. S. v. Seneca, 274 Fed. 947; Yohowan, 291 Fed. 425.

[74] *Ag.* 4 St. 564; 13 St. 29; 19 St. 244. *Rng.* 27 St. 260. *S.* 39 St. 123; 40 St. 561; 41 St. 3; 48 St. 927, 1245; 50 St. 884; 52 St. 696. *Rp.* 48 St. 396. *Cited:* Russell, 18 Yale L. J. 328; 25 Op A. G. 416; Op. Sol., M. 8860, Nov. 1, 1922; Sol. Letter, July 19, 1934; Op. Sol., M. 29147, May 6, 1937; Browning, 6 F. 2d 801; Buchanan, 15 F. 2d 496; Butterfield, 241 Fed. 556; Chambliss, 218 Fed. 154; Clairmont, 225 U. S. 551; Collins, 243 Fed. 495; Edwards, 5 F. 2d 17; Elam, 7 F. 2d 887; Evans, 204 Fed. 361; Ex p. Dick, 141 Fed. 5; Ex p. Margrave, 275 Fed. 200; Ex p. Viles, 139 Fed. 68; Ex p. Webb, 225 U. S. 663; Farrell, 110 Fed. 942; Feeley, 236 Fed. 903; Hallowell 221 U. S. 317; In re Lincoln, 202 U. S. 178; Johnson, 234 U. S. 422; Joplin, 236 U. S. 531; Katzenmeyer, 225 Fed. 523; Kennedy, 265 U. S. 344; McClintic, 283 Fed 781; McSpadden, 224 Fed. 935; Matter of Heff, 197 U. S. 488; Morris, 19 F. 2d 131; Morgan, 224 Fed. 698; Morrison, 6 F. 2d 809; Morrison, 6 F. 2d 811; Mosier, 198 Fed. 54; Mulligan, 120 Fed. 98; Nelson, 18 F. 2d 522; Renfro, 15 F. 2d 991; Royal, 217 Fed 146; Salazar, 236 Fed. 541; Schaap, 210 Fed. 853; Sharpe, 16 F. 2d 876; Shecil, 226 Fed. 184; Swafford, 25 F. 2d 581; Townsend, 265 Fed. 519; U. S. v. Belt, 128 Fed. 68; U. S. v. Birdsall, 233 U. S. 223; U. S. v. Boss, 160 Fed. 132; U. S. v. Buckles, 6 Ind. T. 319; U. S. v. Cohn, 2 Ind. T. 474; U. S. v. 4 Bottles, 90 Fed. 720; U. S v. Hall, 171 Fed. 214; U. S. v. Healy, 202 Fed. 349; U. S. v. Kiya, 126 Fed. 879; U. S. v. Kopp, 110 Fed. 160; U. S. v. Luther, 260 Fed. 579; U. S. v. Mares, 14 N. M. 1; U. S. v. Miller, 105 Fed. 944; U. S. v. Nice, 241 U. S. 591; U. S. v. Paine, 206 U. S. 467; U. S. v. Pelican, 232 U. S. 442; U. S. v. Ramsey, 271 U. S. 467; U. S v. Sandoval, 231 U. S. 28; U. S. v Soldana, 246 U S. 530; U. S. v. Stoffelo, 8 Ariz. 461; U. S. v. Sutton, 215 U. S. 291; U. S. v. 12 Bottles, 201 Fed. 263; U. S. v. Wright, 229 U. S. 226; U. S. Exp., 191 Fed 673; Voves, 249 Fed. 191; Wright, 227 Fed. 855.

[75] *A.* Sec. 1, 52 St. 696. Also see 25 U. S. C. 241a (sec. 8, 28 St. 697) and 25 U. S. C. 244a (48 St. 396).

[76] *Ag.* 26 St. 95. *Cited:* McFadden, 2 Ind. T. 260.

[77] *Sg.* 28 St. 96.

[78] *Ag.* 28 St. 22, sec. 1. *Sg.* 28 St. 22. *A.* 30 St. 844. *S.* 30 St. 844.

[79] *Sg.* 29 St. 186, sec. 19, 21, 22, 24.

[80] *Sg.* 28 St. 113, sec. 3.

[81] *Cited:* Memo. Sol., Nov. 12, 1935.

[82] *Ag.* 28 St. 505, sec. 5.

[83] *Sg.* 7 St. 374.

[84] *Cited:* 26 L. D. 71.

for other purposes.[85] Sec. 1, p. 79—25 U. S. C. 278, (39 St. 988, sec. 21). USCA Historical Note. A proviso following the derivative provision in sec. 1, 30 St. 62, which authorized the Secretary of the Interior to make contracts with schools of various denominations for the education of Indian pupils during the fiscal year 1898, but only at places where nonsectarian schools could not be provided, was omitted as temporary merely. A provision of Act June 29, 1888, s. 10, 25 Stat. 239, that at certain schools, at which "church organizations are assisting in the educational work, the Christian Bible may be taught in the native language of the Indians," etc., may be regarded as superseded by a provision that the Government should, as early as practi cable, make provision for the education of Indian children in Government schools, made by Act Mar. 2, 1895, s. 1, 28 St. 904, and by said derivative provisions. Similar provisions to the Code section were made by the Indian appropriation act of June 10, 1896, sec. 1, 29 Stat. 345. Sec. 1, p. 83—25 U. S. C. 274. (See 25 U. S. C. 472) Sec. 1, p. 90—25 U. S. C. 58 (sec. 10, 37 St. 88; sec. 1, 37 St. 521: sec. 17, 40 St. 578; 45 St. 1307). See Historical Note 25 U. S. C. A. 58. Sec. 1, p. 90—25 U. S. C. 184. USCA Historical Note: The derivative section used the word "heretofore" instead of the words of the Code section "prior to June 7, 1897." Sec. 1, p. 90—25 U. S. C. 197 (32 St. 404, sec. 4). USCA Historical Note: Sec. 1, 30 St. 90 originally provided with reference to the Chippewa Indians of Minnesota, that the Secretary of the Interior might authorize them to "fell, cut, remove, sell or otherwise dispose of the dead timber, etc., and the amendment by said sec. 4 of 32 St. 404, consisted in repealing so much of the quoted phrase as authorized the sale of dead timber, standing or fallen under regulations prescribed by the Secretary of the Interior. USCA Pocket Supplement: 25 U. S. C. 197 was repealed except as to then existing contracts by 32 St. 404. Sec. 11—25 USCA 135 Historical Note: A provision made by Act June 7, 1897, sec. 11, 30 St. 93, "That hereafter, where funds appropriated in specific terms for particular object are not sufficient for the object named, any other appropriation, general in its terms, which otherwise would be available may, in the discretion of the Secretary of the Interior, be used to accomplish the object for which the specific appropriation was made," was repealed by Act Mar. 3, 1911, sec. 1, 36 St. 1062.

30 St. 105; July 19, 1897; C. 9—An Act Making appropriations to supply deficiencies in the appropriations for the fiscal year ending June 30, 1897, and for prior years, and for other purposes.[86]

30 St. 226; Dec. 29, 1897; C. 3—An Act Prohibiting the killing of fur seals in the waters of the North Pacific Ocean.[87]

30 St. 227; Jan. 13, 1898; C. 4—An Act To amend an Act granting to the Gila Valley, Globe and Northern Ry. Co. a right of way through the San Carlos Indian Reservation, in Arizona.[88]

30 St. 234; Jan. 27, 1898; C. 10—An Act To amend sec. 2234 of the Revised Statutes.[89] 43 U. S. C. 72.

30 St. 234; Jan. 28, 1898; C. 11—An Act Making appropriations to supply urgent deficiencies in the appropriations for the fiscal year ending June 30, 1898, and for prior years, and for other purposes.[90]

30 St. 241; Feb. 14, 1898; C. 18—An Act Authorizing the Muscogee Coal and Ry. Co. to construct and operate a railway through the Indian Territory and Oklahoma Territory, and for other purposes.[91]

30 St. 277; Mar. 15, 1898; C. 68—An Act Making appropriations for the legislative, executive, and judicial expenses of the Government for the fiscal year ending June 30, 1899, and for other purposes.

30 St. 318; Mar. 15, 1898; C. 69—An Act Making appropriations for the support of the Army for the fiscal year ending June 30, 1899.[92]

30 St. 327; Mar. 17, 1898; C. 71—An Act To extend the time for the construction of the railway of the Chicago, Rock Island and Pacific Ry. Co. through the Indian Territory.[93]

30 St. 341; Mar. 23, 1898; C. 87—An Act To grant the right of way through the Indian Territory to the Denison, Bonham and New Orleans Ry. Co. for the purpose of constructing a railway, and for other purposes.[94]

30 St. 344; Mar. 26, 1898; C. 100—An Act Granting the right to the Omaha Northern Ry. Co. to construct a railway across, and establish stations on, the Omaha and Winnebago reservations, in the State of Nebraska, and for other purposes.[95]

30 St. 345; Mar. 29, 1898; C. 102—An Act To amend an Act entitled "An Act to authorize the Denison and Northern Ry. Co. to construct and operate a railway through the Indian Territory, and for other purposes."[96]

30 St. 347; Mar. 30, 1898; C. 104—An Act Authorizing the Nebraska, Kansas and Gulf Ry. Co. to construct and operate a railway through the Indian Territory, and for other purposes.[97]

30 St. 354; Apr. 11, 1898; C. 120—An Act Extending the right of commutation to certain homestead settlers on lands in Oklahoma Territory, opened to settlement under the provisions of the Act entitled "An Act to ratify and confirm the agreement with the Kickapoo Indians in Oklahoma Territory, and to make appropriations for carrying the same into effect."[98]

30 St. 361; Apr. 22, 1898; C. 187—An Act To provide for temporarily increasing the military establishment of the United States in time of war, and for other purposes.[99]

30 St. 364; Apr. 26, 1898; C. 191—An Act For the better organization of the line of the Army of the United States.

30 St. 390; May 4, 1898; C. 235—An Act Making appropriations to supply deficiencies in the appropriations for support of the Army for the fiscal year 1898, and for other purposes.[1]

30 St. 399; May 7, 1898; C. 246—An Act To amend section nine of an Act entitled "An Act to grant to the Arkansas, Texas and Mexican Central Ry. Co. a right of way through the Indian Territory, and for other purposes."[2]

30 St. 407; May 14, 1898; C. 298—An Act Authorizing the Campbell-Lynch Bridge Company to construct a bridge across

---

[85] *Ag.* 29 St. 358. *Sg.* 4 St. 442; 7 St. 36, 46, 51, 69, 85, 99, 114, 161, 179, 185, 213, 236, 242, 287, 296, 314, 318, 320, 321, 352, 425, 541, 545; 9 St. 35, 842, 855, 904; 10 St. 1071, 1079, 1109; 11 St. 614, 700, 702, 729, 744; 12 St. 628, 652, 981, 1106, 1173; 13 St. 675; 14 St. 650, 757, 787; 15 St. 515, 584, 590, 596, 622, 637, 638, 653, 657; 676; 16 St. 40, 355, 720; 19 St. 254, 256, 287; 22 St. 43; 23 St. 79; 24 St. 219, 388; 25 St. 114, 642, 645, 688, 894; 26 St. 756, 1028, 1037; 27 St. 139, 470, 633, 645; 28 St. 301, 330, 451, 908, 939; 29 St. 339, 341, 344, 355. *A.* 37 St. 518. *Rp.* 30 St. 567; 32 St. 245, 400. *S.* 30 St. 105, 571, 652, 924; 31 St. 7, 221, 1058; 32 St. 245, 982; 33 St. 189, 1048; 34 St. 78, 325, 1015; 35 St. 70, 781; 36 St. 269, 1058; 37 St. 86, 518; 38 St. 77; 40 St. 561. *Cited:* Cavell, 3 Okla. S. B. J. 208; Dixon, 23 Case & Com. 712; Reeves, 23 Case & Com. 727; 26 Op. A. G. 127; 26 Op. A. G. 171; 27 Op. A. G. 588; 3 L. D. Memo. 435; Op. Sol., M. 11108, Dec. 4, 1923, M. 11880, June 17, 1924, M. 12874, Oct. 27, 1924, M. 13270, Nov. 6, 1924, M. 15954, Jan. 8, 1927; Rept. on Status of Pueblo of Pojonque, Nov. 3, 1932; Memo. Sol. Off., May 11, 1934; Op. Sol., M. 27381, Dec. 13, 1934; Memo. Sol., Dec. 18, 1934; Memo. Sol. Off., Mar. 13, 1935; Memo. Sol., May 14, 1935, Nov. 11, 1935; Op. Sol., May 20, 1936; Memo. Sol. Off., Oct. 22, 1936; Memo. to Comm'r, Jan. 6, 1937; Memo. Sol. Off., Nov. 9, 1937, May 29, 1938; 25 L. D. 364; 26 L. D. 44; 29 L. D. 239; 29 L. D. 408; 50 L. D. 551; Ansley, 180 U. S. 253; Armstrong, 195 Fed. 137; Bartlett, 218 Fed. 380; Bird, 129 Fed. 472; Bowling, 233 U. S. 528; Cherokee, 208 U. S. 76; Cherokee, 187 U. S. 294; Cherokee, 85 C. Cls. 76; Choctaw, 81 C. Cls. 1; Dick, 6 Ind. T. 85; Duwamish, 79 C. Cls. 530; Eagle-Picher, 28 F. 2d 472; Ex p. Pero, 99 F. 2d 28; Farrell, 110 Fed. 942; Folk, 233 Fed. 177; Fond du Lac, 34 C. Cls. 426; Goodson, 7 Okla. 117; Halbert, 283 U. S. 753; Hallam, 49 F. 2d 103; Hampton, 22 F. 2d 81; Hanks, 3 Ind. T. 415; Hayes, 168 Fed. 221; Heckman, 224 U. S. 413; Jacobs, 223 U. S. 200; Jaybird, 271 U. S. 609; Jefferson, 247 U. S. 288; Kimberlin, 104 Fed. 653; McCullough, 243 Fed. 823; McKnight, 130 Fed. 659; McMurray, 62 C. Cls. 458; Maxey, 3 Ind. T. 243; Martin, 276 U. S. 58; Medawakanton, 57 C. Cls. 357; Miller, 249 U. S. 308; Mullen, 224 U. S. 448; Myers, 2 Ind. T. 3; Oakes, 172 Fed. 305; Pape, 19 F. 2d 219; Quick Bear, 210 U. S. 50; Schellenbarger, 236 U. S. 68; Shoshone, 85 C. Cls. 331; Shoshone, 82 C. Cls. 23; Sloan, 118 Fed. 283; Smith, 270 U. S. 456; Stephens, 174 U. S. 445; Steward, 295 U. S. 403; Stoakey, 58 F. 2d 522; U. S. v. Abrams, 194 Fed. 82; U. S. v. Atkins, 260 U. S. 220; U. S. v. Haddock, 21 F. 2d 165; U. S. v. Hayes, 20 F. 2d 873; U. S. v. Heyfron, 138 Fed. 964; U. S. v. Moore, 284 Fed. 86; U. S. v. Noble, 237 U. S. 74; U. S. v. Rolfson, 38 F. 2d 806; U. S. v. Shoshone, 304 U. S. 111; U. S. v. Walkowsky, 283 U. S. 753; U. S. v. Watashe, 102 F. 2d 428; U. S. v. Wildcat, 244 U. S. 111; U. S. ex rel. Besaw, 6 F. 2d 694; Ute, 45 C. Cls. 440; Vezina, 245 Fed. 411; Waldron, 143 Fed. 413; Washington, 285 U. S. 422; Whitebird, 40 F. 2d 479; Winton, 255 U. S. 373; Yankton, 272 U. S. 351.

[86] *Sg.* 4 St. 564, sec. 4; 13 St. 29; 19 St. 244; 26 St. 853; 28 St. 589, 677, 695, 697; 30 St. 84. *R.* 48 St. 583. *Cited:* Medawakanton, 57 C. Cls. 357.

[87] *Sg.* 28 St. 54.

[88] *Ag.* 28 St. 665, 666, sec. 5.

[89] *Ag.* 18 St. 34, sec. 2, 122, cs. 340, 341, 123 c. 342, 295, sec. 2.

[90] *Sg.* 21 St. 199. *Cited:* Ute, 45 C. Cls. 440.

[91] *Sg.* 1 St. 137.

[92] *A.* 30 St. 1350; 31 St. 32. *S.* 30 St. 433.

[93] *Sg.* 1 St. 137; 27 St. 492.

[94] *Sg.* 1 St. 137. *A.* 30 St. 914.

[95] *A.* 32 St. 183; 33 St. 311.

[96] *Sg.* 1 St. 137; 27 St. 336.

[97] *Sg.* 1 St. 137.

[98] *Sg.* 27 St. 562; 29 St. 868.

[99] *A.* 30 St. 421.

[1] *S.* 30 St. 772.

[2] *Ag.* 26 St. 229, sec. 9.

the Arkansas River at or near Webbers Falls, Indian Territory.

30 St. 409; May 14, 1898; C. 299—An Act Extending the homestead laws and providing for right of way for railroads in the District of Alaska, and for other purposes.[3]

30 St. 417; May 17, 1898; C. 340—An Act Declaring the Federal jail at the city of Fort Smith, Arkansas, a national prison for certain purposes.

30 St. 421; May 28, 1898; C. 367—An Act To amend sections ten and thirteen of an Act entitled "An Act to provide for temporarily increasing the military establishment of the United States in time of war, and for other purposes," approved April 22, 1898.[4]

30 St. 423; June 1, 1898; C. 369—An Act To amend "An Act to provide the times and places for holding terms of the United States courts in the States of Idaho and Wyoming," approved July 5, 1892, as amended by the amendatory Act approved November 3, 1893.[5]

30 St. 429; June 4, 1898; C. 376—An Act For the appointment of a commission to make allotments of lands in severalty to Indians upon the Uintah Indian Reservation in Utah, and to obtain the cession to the United States of all lands within said reservation not so allotted.

30 St. 430; June 4, 1898; C. 377—An Act Granting to the Washington Improvement and Development Company a right of way through the Colville Indian Reservation, in the State of Washington.[6]

30 St. 431; June 4, 1898; C. 578—An Act Granting additional powers to railroad companies operating lines in the Indian Territory.

30 St. 433; June 7, 1898; C. 391—An Act To amend section eight of the Act of Congress approved March 2, 1896, granting a right of way to the Fort Smith and Western Coal R. Co. through the Indian Territory, and for other purposes.[7]

30 St. 433; June 7, 1898; C. 392—An Act To suspend the operation of certain provisions of law relating to the War Department, and for other purposes.[8]

30 St. 437; June 8, 1898; C. 395—An Act Making appropriations to supply urgent deficiencies in the appropriations for the support of the Military and Naval establishments for the fiscal year 1898, and for other purposes.[9]

30 St. 475; June 18, 1898; C. 465—An Act Granting to the Kettle River Valley Ry. Co. a right of way through the north half of the Colville Indian Reservation in the State of Washington.[10]

30 St. 484; June 21, 1898; C. 489—An Act To make certain grants of land to the Territory of New Mexico, and for other purposes.

30 St. 492; June 27, 1898; C. 500—An Act To authorize the Kansas, Oklahoma and Gulf Ry. Co. to construct and operate a railway through the Chilocco Indian Reservation, Territory of Oklahoma, and for other purposes.

30 St. 493; June 27, 1898; C. 502—An Act To authorize the Missouri, Kansas and Texas Ry. Co. to straighten and restore the channel of the South Canadian River, in the Indian Territory, at the crossing of said railroad.

30 St. 495; June 28, 1898; C. 517—An Act For the protection of the people of the Indian Territory, and for other purposes.[11] Sec. 19, p. 502—See 25 USCA 117 Historical Note.

30 St. 544; July 1, 1898; C. 541—An Act To establish a uniform system of bankruptcy throughout the United States. Sec. 1, 11 U. S. C. 1; Sec. 2, 11 U. S. C. 11; Sec. 70, 11 U. S. C. 110.

30 St. 567; July 1, 1898; C. 542—An Act To ratify the agreement between the Dawes Commission and the Seminole Nation of Indians.[12]

30 St. 571; July 1, 1898; C. 545—An Act Making appropriations for the current and contingent expenses of the Indian Department and for fulfilling treaty stipulations with various Indian tribes for the fiscal year ending June 30, 1899, and for other purposes.[13] Sec. 1, p. 573—25 U. S. C. 27 (secs. 4 & 12, 4 St. 734, 737; R. S. sec. 2062; sec. 1, 27 St. 120). Sec. 1, p. 595—25 U. S. C. 32. Sec. 6, p. 596—25 U. S. C. 191 (36 St. 861, sec. 22). Sec. 7, p. 596—25 U. S. C. 136.

30 St. 597; July 1, 1898; C. 546—An Act Making appropriations for sundry civil expenses of the Government for the fiscal year ending June 30, 1899, and for other purposes.[14]

30 St. 652; July 7, 1898; C. 571—An Act Making appropriations to supply deficiencies in the appropriations for the fiscal year ending June 30, 1898, and for prior years, and for other purposes.[15] Sec. 1—25 U. S. C. 100 (19 St. 291, sec. 1).

30 St. 715; July 7, 1898; C. 574—An Act To amend an Act entitled "An Act to amend an Act to grant to the Gaines-

---

[3] *Cited:* 53 I. D. 593; Columbia, 161 Fed. 60; Heckman, 119 Fed. 83; U. S. v. Berrigan, 2 Alaska 442; U. S. v. Cadzow, 5 Alaska 125; U. S. v. Lynch, 7 Alaska 568.

[4] *Ag.* 30 St. 361, sec. 10, 13.

[5] *Ag.* 27 St. 72.

[6] *Sg.* 18 St. 482. *S.* 37 St. 634.

[7] *Ag.* 29 St. 40, sec. 8.

[8] *Ag* 30 St. 322. *A.* 30 St. 1350.

[9] *S.* 30 St. 722.

[10] *Sg.* 18 St. 482. *Cited:* Cabell, 3 Okla. S. B. J. 208; U. S. v. Ferry, 24 F. Supp. 399; U. S. v. Pelican, 232 U. S. 442.

[11] *Sg.* 7 St. 333; 10 St. 974; 14 St. 769; 25 St. 783, sec. 15; 26 St. 95; 27 St. 641; 29 St. 329. *S.* 30 St. 770, 1074, 1214; 31 St. 7, 221, 250, 848, 861, 1058; 32 St. 177, 245, 641, 716, 774; 33 St. 189, 571, 1048; 34 St. 91, 325, 1015; 35 St. 444. *Cited:* Cabell, 3 Okla. S. B. J. 208; Krieger, 3 Geo. Wash. L. Rev. 279; 23 Op. A. G. 214; 23 Op. A. G. 214; 23 Op. A. G. 528; 24 Op. A. G. 689; 25 Op. A. G. 168; 25 Op. A. G. 168; 25 Op. A. G. 460; 26 Op. A. G. 127; 26 Op. A. G. 171; 26 Op. A. G. 340; 27 Op. A. G. 530; 29 Op. A. G. 131; 29 Op. A. G. 231; 34 Op. A. G. 275; 1 L. D. Memo. 99; 3 L. D. Memo. 499; Memo. Sol., Dec. 11, 1918; Op. Sol., M. 7316, Apr. 5, 1922; M. 7316, May 28, 1924; M. 18772, Dec. 24, 1926; M. 22121, Apr. 12, 1927; M. 25260, Aug. 1, 1929; Report of Status of Pueblo of Pojoaque Nov. 8, 1932; Sol. Op. M. 27759, Jan. 22, 1935; Sol. Memo., Mar. 18, 1936; 53 I. D. 502; 54 I. D. 109; 54 I. D. 297; Adams, 165 Fed. 304; Armstrong, 195 Fed. 137; Atoka, 3 Ind. T. 189; Atoka, 104 Fed. 471; Ballinger, 216 U. S. 240; Bartlett, 218 Fed. 380; Barton, 4 Ind. T. 260; Boudinot, 2 Ind. T. 107; Brought, 129 Fed. 192; Brown, 44 C. Cls. 288; Browning, 6 F. 2d 801; Bruner, 4 Ind. T. 580; Buster, 135 Fed. 947; Campbell, 3 Ind. T. 462; Campbell, 248 U. S. 169; Carpenter, 280 U. S. 363; Casteel, 4 Ind. T. 1; Cherokee, 203 U. S. 76; Cherokee, 187 U. S. 294; Cherokee, 85 C. Cls. 76; Cherokee, 223 U. S. 108; Chickasaw, 87 C. Cls. 91; Chickasaw, 193 U. S. 115; Choate, 224 U. S. 665; Choctaw, 81 C. Cls. 63; Choctaw, 81 C. Cls. 1; Choctaw, 83 C. Cls. 140; Choctaw, 6 Ind. T. 515; Choctaw, 235 U. S. 292; Creek, 78 C. Cls. 474; Crowell, 4 Ind. T. 36; Daniels, 4 Ind. T. 426; Delaware, 193 U. S. 127; Denton, 5 Ind. T. 396; Dick, 6 Ind. T. 85; Donohoo, 4 Ind. T. 433; Ellis, 3 Ind. T. 656; Ellis, 118 Fed. 430; Engleman, 4 Ind. T. 336; English, 224 U. S. 680; Evans, 204 Fed. 361; Ex p. Webb, 225 U. S. 663; Fink, 248 U. S. 399; Fish, 52 F. 2d 544; Fleming, 215 U. S. 56; Ford, 260 Fed. 657; Fraer, 125 Fed. 280; Frame, 189 Fed. 785; Garfield, 211 U. S. 264; Garfield, 211 U. S. 249; George, 4 Ind. T. 61; German-American, 5 Ind. T. 703; Gleason, 224 U. S. 679; Glenn, 105 F. 2d 398; Hargrove, 3 Ind. T. 478; Hargrove, 4 Ind. T. 129; Hargrove, 129 Fed. 186; Harnage, 242 U. S. 386; Harris, 7 Ind. T. 532; Harris, 166 Fed. 109; Hayes, 168 Fed. 221; Heckman, 224 U. S. 413; Henny, 191 Fed. 132; Hill, 242 U. S. 361; Hockett, 110 Fed. 910; Hubbard, 5 Ind. T. 95; Ikard, 4 Int. T. 314; In re Grayson, 3 Ind. T. 497; In re Lands of Five, 199 Fed. 811; In re Poff's Guardianship, 7 Ind. T. 59; Iowa, 217 Fed. 11; Jefferson, 247 U. S. 288; Joines, 4 Ind. T. 556; Jonah, 52 F. 2d 343; Joplin, 236 U. S. 531; Kansas, 80 C. Cls. 264; Kelly, 7 Ind. T. 541; Kemohah, 38 F. 2d 665; Kimberlin, 104 Fed. 653; Longest, 276 U. S. 69; Lowe, 223 U. S. 95; McAlester, 3 Ind. T. 704; McBride, 149 Fed. 114; McCalib, 83 C. Cls. 79; McCullough, 243 Fed. 823; McMurray, 62 C. Cls. 458; McNee, 253 Fed. 546; Malone, 212 Fed. 668; Mandler, 49 F. 2d 201; Mandler, 52 F. 2d 713; Marlin, 276 U. S. 58; Matter of Heff, 197 U. S. 488; Maxey, 3 Ind. T. 243; Moore, 43 F. 2d 322; Morris, 194 U. S. 384; Morrison, 6 F. 2d 811; Mullen, 224 U. S. 448; Nivens, 4 Ind. T. 30; Nunn, 216 Fed. 330; Owens, 5 Ind. T. 275; Persons, 40 C. Cls. 411; Price, 5 Ind. T. 518; Quigley, 3 Ind. T. 265; Ross, 227 U. S. 530; St. Louis, 7 Ind. T. 685; Sayer, 7 Ind. T. 675; Schellenbarger, 236 U. S. 68; Seminole, 78 C. Cls. 455; Sharrock, 6 Ind. T. 466; Southwestern, 3 Ind. T. 223; Southwestern, 185 U. S. 499; Stephens, 174 U. S. 445; Swinney, 5 Ind. T. 12; Thomason, 7 Ind. T. 1; Thompson, 4 Ind. T. 412; Tiger, 4 F. 2d 714; Turner, 4 Ind. T. 606; Tuttle, 3 Ind. T. 712; Tynon, 8 Ind. T. 346; U. S. v. Atkins, 260 U. S. 220; U. S. v. Bd. of Com'rs of McIntosh Cty., 284 Fed. 103; U. S. v. Choctaw, 38 C. Cls. 558; U. S. v. Dowden, 220 Fed. 277; U. S. v. Eastern, 66 F. 2d 923; U. S. v. Ferguson, 247 U. S. 175; U. S. v. Hayes, 20 F. 2d 873; U. S. v. Lewis, 5 Ind. T. 1; U. S. v. McMurray, 181 Fed. 723; U. S. v. Mid-Continent, 67 F. 2d 37; U. S. v. M. K. & T. Ry., 66 F. 2d 919; U. S. v. Rea-Read, 171 Fed. 501; U. S. v. Richards, 27 F. 2d 284; U. S. v. Seminole, 299 U. S. 417; U. S. v. Smith, 266 Fed. 740; U. S. v. Western, 226 Fed. 726; U. S. v. Wildcat, 244 U. S. 111; U. S. v. Wright, 53 F. 2d 300; U. S. ex rel. McAlester, 277 Fed. 573; Vinson, 44 F. 2d 772; W. C. Whitney, 166 Fed. 738; Wallace, 204 U. S. 415; Ward, 253 U. S. 17; Washington, 235 U. S. 422; Welty, 231 Fed. 930; Williams, 216 U. S. 582; Williams, 239 U. S. 414; Williams, 4 Ind. T. 587; Winton, 255 U. S. 373; Woodward, 238 U. S. 284.

[12] *Rpg.* 30 St. 62. *S.* 32 St. 982. *Cited:* 26 Op. A. G. 340; 34 Op. A. G. 275; 35 Op. A. G. 421; 53 I. D. 502; Deming, 224 U. S. 471; Ex p. Webb, 225 U. S. 663; Fish, 52 F. 2d 544; Goat, 224 U. S. 458; In re Grayson, 3 Ind. T. 497; In re Lands, 199 Fed. 811; Moore, 43 F. 2d 322; Seminole, 78 C. Cls. 455; Tiger, 221 U. S. 286; U. S. v. Bean, 253 Fed. 1; U. S. v. Bd. of Com'rs of McIntosh Cty., 284 Fed. 103; U. S. v. Seminole, 299 U. S. 417; U. S. v. Smith, 266 Fed. 740; U. S. v. Stigall, 226 Fed. 190; U. S. Exp., 101 Fed. 678; Vinson, 44 F. 2d 772; Woodward, 238 U. S. 284.

[13] *Sg.* 1 St. 619; 4 St. 442; 7 St. 36, 46, 51, 69, 85, 99, 114, 161, 179, 185, 213, 236, 242, 287, 296, 314, 320, 352, 425, 541, 545, 596; 9 St. 35, 842, 854, 855, 904; 10 St. 1071, 1079; 11 St. 614, 700, 702, 729, 744, 628, 810, 981, 1173; 13 St. 343, sec. 2, 623, 675; 14 St. 650, 757, 787; 15 St. 515, 622, 638, 651, 676; 16 St. 40, 657, 707, 720; 19 St. 254, 256, 287; 22 St. 43; 23 St. 79; 24 St. 388, 389; 25 St. 645, 688, 871, 894; 26 St. 756, 851, 1028, 1033, 1037; 27 St. 62, 139, 645; 28 St. 110, 939; 29 St. 341, 354, 382; 30 St. 68, 86, 94. *A.* 30 St. 924; 36 St. 855. *S.* 30 St. 924, 1214; 31 St. 221; 32 St. 982; 34 St. 325. *Cited:* Ansley, 180 U. S. 253; Farrell, 110 Fed. 942; Medawakanton, 57 C. Cls. 357; Quick Bear, 210 U. S. 50; Stephens, 174 U. S. 445; U. S. v. Algoma, 305 U. S. 415; U. S. v. Candelaria, 271 U. S. 432; U. S. v. Ferry, 24 F. Supp. 399; U. S. v. 4 Bottles, 90 Fed. 720; U. S. v. Hoyt, 167 Fed. 301; U. S. v. Pelican, 232 U. S. 442; U. S. v. Sandoval, 231 U. S. 28; U. S. v. Watashe, 102 F. 2d 428; Wallace, 204 U. S. 415; Woodward, 238 U. S. 284.

[14] *Sg.* 11 St. 704. *Rpg.* 23 St. 24.

[15] *Sg.* 19 St. 291; 25 St. 648; 26 St. 853; 30 St. 86. *S.* 30 St. 772; 32 St. 245, 1081.

ville, McAlester and St. Louis Ry. Co. a right of way through the Indian Territory."[16]

30 St. 745; May 27, 1898; J. Res. No. 40—Joint Resolution Declaring the lands within the former Mille Lac Indian Reservation, in Minnesota, to be subject to entry under the land laws of the United States.[17]

30 St. 748; June 25, 1898; J. Res. No. 51—Joint Resolution To authorize and direct the Secretary of the Treasury to refund and return to the Chicago, Milwaukee and St. Paul Ry. Co. $15,335.76, in accordance with the decision of the Secretary of the Interior dated March 3, 1898.

30 St. 770; Dec. 21, 1898; C. 35—An Act Making an appropriation to execute certain provisions of the Act of Congress for the protection of the people of the Indian Territory.[18]

30 St. 772; Jan. 5, 1899; C. 41—An Act Making appropriations to supply urgent deficiencies in the appropriations for the support of the military and naval establishments for the last six months of the fiscal year ending June 30, 1899, and for other purposes.[19]

30 St. 806; Jan. 28, 1899; C. 65—An Act To authorize the Arkansas and Choctaw Ry. Co. to construct and operate a railway through the Choctaw and Chickasaw nations, in the Indian Territory, and for other purposes.

30 St. 816; Feb. 4, 1899; C. 88—An Act To authorize the Little River Valley Ry. Co. to construct and operate a railway through the Choctaw and Chickasaw nations, in the Indian Territory, and branches thereof, and for other purposes.[20]

30 St. 834; Feb. 9, 1899; C. 129—An Act To authorize the Missouri and Kansas Telephone Co. to construct and maintain lines and offices for general business purposes in the Ponca, Otoe, and Missouria Reservation, in the Territory of Oklahoma.

30 St. 836; Feb. 13, 1899; C. 153—An Act To amend an Act granting to the St. Louis, Oklahoma and Southern Ry. Co. a right of way through the Indian Territory and Oklahoma Territory, and for other purposes.[21]

30 St. 844; Feb. 21, 1899; C. 178—An Act To extend and amend the provisions of an Act entitled "An Act to grant the right of way to the Kansas, Oklahoma Central and Southwestern Ry. Co. through the Indian Territory and Oklahoma Territory, and for other purposes," approved December 21, 1893, and also to extend and amend the provisions of a supplemental Act approved Feb. 15, 1897, entitled "An Act to extend and amend an Act entitled 'An Act to grant the right of way to the Kansas, Oklahoma Central and Southwestern Ry. Co. through the Indian Territory and Oklahoma Territory, and for other purposes.' "[22]

30 St. 846; Feb. 24, 1899; C. 187—An Act Making appropriations for the legislative, executive, and judicial expenses of the Government for the fiscal year ending June 30, 1900, and for other purposes.

30 St. 891; Feb. 25, 1899; C. 193—An Act To amend an Act to grant to the Gainesville, McAlester and St. Louis Ry. Co. a right of way through the Indian Territory."[23]

30 St. 906; Feb. 28, 1899; C. 219—An Act Granting to the Clearwater Valley R. Co. a right of way through the Nez Perces Indian lands in Idaho.[24]

30 St. 909; Feb. 28, 1899; C. 222—An Act Providing for the sale of the surplus lands on the Pottawatomie and Kickapoo Indian reservations in Kansas, and for other purposes.[25]

30 St. 912; Feb. 28, 1899; C. 225—An Act Authorizing the Sioux City and Omaha Ry. Co. to construct and operate a railway through the Omaha and Winnebago Reservation, in Thurston County, Nebraska, and for other purposes.

30 St. 914; Feb. 28, 1899; C. 226—An Act To amend an Act entitled "An Act to grant the right of way through the Indian Territory to the Denison, Bonham and New Orleans Ry. Co. for the purpose of constructing a railway, and for other purposes," approved March 28, 1898, and to vest in The Denison, Bonham and Gulf Ry. Co. all the rights, privileges, and franchises therein granted to said first-named company.[26]

[16] *Sg.* 29 St. 44.

[17] *Sg.* 26 St. 1097. *S.* 33 St. 1048. *Cited:* Mille Lac, 46 C. Cls. 424; U. S. v. Mille Lac, 229 U. S. 498.

[18] *Sg.* 30 St. 495.

[19] *Sg.* 30 St. 390; 30 St. 437, 696.

[20] *Sg.* 1 St. 137.

[21] *Ag.* 29 St. 80.

[22] *Sg.* 1 St. 137; 28 St. 22; 29 St. 520.

[23] *Sg.* 27 St. 524, sec. 9.

[24] *Sg.* 18 St. 482. *A.* 32 St. 198.

[25] *A.* 32 St. 982.

[26] *Sg.* 1 St. 137. *Ag.* 30 St. 341.

30 St. 918; Mar. 1, 1899; C. 316—An Act Granting to the Clearwater Short Line Ry. Co. a right of way through the Nez Perces Indian lands in Idaho.[27]

30 St. 924; Mar. 1, 1899; C. 324—An Act Making appropriations for the current and contingent expenses of the Indian Department and for fulfilling treaty stipulations with various Indian tribes for the fiscal year ending June 30, 1900, and for other purposes.[28] Sec. 1—25 U. S. C. 36; Sec. 8—25 U. S. C. 116.

30 St. 990; Mar. 2, 1899; C. 374—An Act To provide for the acquiring of rights of way by railroad companies through Indian reservations, Indian lands, and Indian allotments, and for other purposes.[29] Sec. 1—25 U. S. C. 312 (sec. 22, 32 St. 50; sec. 16, 36 St. 859). See Historical Note 25 USCA 312. Sec. 2—25 U. S. C. 313 (34 St. 330). See Historical Note 25 USCA 313. Sec. 3—25 U. S. C. 314 (sec. 23, 32 St. 50). USCA Historical Note: Sec. 3, 30 St. 991, as originally enacted contained a clause giving the right of appeal, in case the land in question was the Indian Territory, by original petition to the United States court in the Indian Territory sitting at the place nearest and, most convenient to the property sought to be condemned. This clause was omitted in the Code section because of 32 St. 50, sec. 23 which repealed 30 St. 991, sec. 3 so far as it applied to the Indian Territory and Oklahoma Territory. In the Code section the word "Oklahoma" was substituted for the words "Indian Territory" used in said derivative section because of the admission to the Union of Indian Territory and the Territory of Oklahoma as the state of Oklahoma. See Historical Note under sec. 312 of title 25. Sec. 4—25 U. S. C. 315. See Historical Note 25. USCA 312. Sec. 6-25 U. S. C. 316. See Historical Note 25 USCA 312. Sec. 7—25 U. S. C. 317. See Historical Note 25 USCA 312. Sec. 8—25 U. S. C. 318. USCA Historical Note: The above cited derivative section (318) used after the word repeal, the words "this act or any portion thereof." See Historical Note 25 USCA 312.

30 St. 995; Mar. 2, 1899; C. 380—An Act To amend an Act entitled "An Act authorizing the Arkansas Northwestern Ry. Co. to construct and operate a railway through the Indian Territory, and for other purposes," and extending the time for constructing and operating the said railway for two years from the fifth day of April, 1899.[30]

30 St. 1064; Mar. 3, 1899; C. 423—An Act Making appropriation for the support of the Regular and Volunteer Army for the fiscal year ending June 30, 1900.

30 St. 1074; Mar. 3, 1899; C. 424—An Act Making appropriations for sundry civil expenses of the Government for the fiscal year ending June 30, 1900, and for other purposes.[31]

30 St. 1121; Mar. 3, 1899; C. 425—An Act Making appropriations for the construction, repair, and preservation of certain public works on rivers and harbors, and for other purposes.[32]

30 St. 1161; Mar. 3, 1899; C. 426—An Act For the allowance of certain claims for stores and supplies reported by the Court of Claims under the provisions of the Act approved Mar. 3, 1883, and commonly known as the Bowman Act, and for other purposes.

30 St. 1214; Mar. 3, 1899; C. 427—An Act Making appropriations to supply deficiencies in the appropriations for the fiscal year ending June 30, 1899, and for prior years, and for other purposes.[33]

30 St. 1253; Mar. 3, 1899; C. 429—An Act To define and punish

[27] *Sg.* 18 St. 482.

[28] *Sg.* 4 St. 442; 7 St. 36, 46, 51, 69, 85, 99, 114, 161, 179, 185, 218, 236, 242, 287, 296, 314, 318, 320, 321, 352, 425, 541, 545; 9 St. 35, 842, 855, 904; 10 St. 1071, 1079; 11 St. 614, 700, 702, 729, 744; 12 St. 628, 981, 1173; 13 St. 675; 14 St. 650, 757, 787; 15 St. 515, 584, 590, 595, 622, 637, 638, 652, 658, 676; 16 St. 40, 355, 570, sec. 3, 720; 17 St. 136, secs. 1, 2; 18 St. 35, 450, sec. 9; 19 St. 254, 256, 287; 22 St. 43; 23 St. 79; 24 St. 219, 388; 25 Stat. 645, 688, 890, 894, 753, 851, 1028, 1033, 1037, 1038, 1039; 27 St. 139, 645; 28 St. 939; 29 St. 354; 30 St. 87, 94, 589, 590, 593. *S.* 31 St. 221. *Cited:* Farrell, 110 Fed. 942; Medawakanton, 57 C. Cls. 357; Quick Bear, 210 U. S. 50; Sisseton, 58 C. Cls. 302; U. S. v. Powers, 305 U. S. 527; Ute, 45 C. Cls. 440.

[29] *Sg.* 18 St. 482. *A.* 34 St. 325; 36 St. 855. *Rp.* 32 St. 43; 48 St. 1224. *S.* 33 St. 708, 1006; 35 St. 43, 70; 37 St. 634; 38 St. 111; 45 St. 442. *Cited:* Memo. Sol. Off., May 25, 1933; 39 L. D. 44; Clarke, 39 F. 2d 800; U. S. v. Ft. Smith, 195 Fed. 211.

[30] *Ag.* 29 St. 87, sec. 8.

[31] *Sg.* 25 St. 888, 896; 30 St. 495.

[32] *S.* 41 St. 3.

[33] *Rg.* 25 St. 167. *Sg.* 25 St. 642; 26 St. 853; 30 St. 495, 576, 592. *Cited:* Western Cherokee, 82 C. Cls. 566.

crimes in the District of Alaska and to provide a code of criminal procedure for said district.[34]

30 St. 1350; Mar. 3, 1899; C. 436—An Act To amend an Act entitled "An Act to suspend the operation of certain provisions of law relating to the War Department, and for other purposes."[35]

30 St. 1362; Mar. 3, 1899; C. 450—An Act To ratify agreements with the Indians of the Lower Brule and Rosebud reservations in South Dakota, and making an appropriation to carry the same into effect.[36]

30 St. 1368; Mar. 3, 1899; C. 453—An Act To authorize the Fort Smith and Western R. Co. to construct and operate a railway through the Choctaw and Creek nations, in the Indian Territory, and for other purposes.[37]

30 St. 1398; Mar. 5, 1898; C. 43—An Act Granting a pension to Mrs. Martha Frank.

30 St. 1398; Mar. 5, 1898; Ch. 44—An Act Granting a pension to John F. Hathaway.

30 St. 1400; Mar. 5, 1898; C. 50—An Act Directing the issue of a duplicate of lost check, drawn by Charles E. McChesney, United States Indian agent, in favor of C. J. Holman and Brother.[38]

30 St. 1401; Mar. 14, 1898; C. 64—An Act Granting an increase of pension to Esther Williams.

30 St. 1406; Mar. 23, 1898; C. 96—An Act To increase the pension of Martha S. Harllee, widow of W. W. Harllee, a soldier in the Florida war.

30 St. 1410; Apr. 11, 1898; C. 124—An Act Granting a pension to Sarah M. Spyker.

30 St. 1416; Apr. 11, 1898; C. 153—An Act Granting a pension to Thomas Lane.[39]

30 St. 1416; Apr. 11, 1898; C. 155—An Act Granting pension to R. G. English.

30 St. 1420; Apr. 15, 1898; C. 176—An Act Granting an increase of pension to Daniel J. Smith.

30 St. 1427; Apr. 27, 1898; C. 214—An Act To increase the pension of John C. Wagoner.

30 St. 1427; Apr. 27, 1898; C. 216—An Act Granting a pension to Matthew B. Nale.

30 St. 1432; May 7, 1898; C. 254—An Act Granting a pension to Francis Shetais, alias Frank Stay.

30 St. 1433; May 7, 1898; C. 262—An Act To grant a pension to Sarah A. Blazer.

30 St. 1437; May 7, 1898; C. 281—An Act Granting a pension to Daniel J. Melvin.

30 St. 1438; May 7, 1898; C. 285—An Act Granting an increase of pension to Elizabeth Rogers.

30 St. 1441; May 14, 1898; C. 309—An Act Granting a pension to "Itawayaka," or "One-armed Jim."

30 St. 1455; June 8, 1898; C. 412—An Act Granting a pension to Bettie Gresham.

30 St. 1457; June 8, 1898; C. 422—An Act Granting a pension to Mary E. Taylor.

30 St. 1459; June 10, 1898; C. 434—An Act Granting a pension to Philip F. Castleman, of Oregon.

30 St. 1475; July 1, 1898; C. 555—An Act Granting an increase of pension to William Christenberry.

30 St. 1484; July 7, 1898; C. 611—An Act Granting a pension to Henrietta Fowler.

30 St. 1486; July 7, 1898; C. 622—An Act Granting an increase of pension to Warren W. Morgan.

30 St. 1499; Dec. 20, 1898; C. 12—An Act Granting an increase of pension to Theodore W. Cobin.

30 St. 1501; Dec. 20, 1898; C. 20—An Act Granting a pension to A. A. Pinkston.

30 St. 1512; Feb. 4, 1899; C. 100—An Act Granting an increase of pension to Alexander Keen.

30 St. 1517; Feb. 9, 1899; C. 131—An Act Granting a pension to Henry Farmer.

30 St. 1518; Feb. 9, 1899; C. 132—An Act Granting an increase of pension to William W. Tumblin, of Bradford County, Florida.

30 St. 1519; Feb. 9, 1899; C. 140—An Act Granting a pension to Martha E. Huddleston.

30 St. 1519; Feb. 9, 1899; C. 141—An Act To pension William Russell for services in Oregon Indian wars.

30 St. 1521; Feb. 14, 1899; C. 156—An Act For the relief of Joseph Tousaint, alias Tousin.

30 St. 1525; Feb. 25, 1899; C. 197—An Act Granting a pension to Isom Gibson.

30 St. 1546; Feb. 28, 1899; C. 311—An Act Granting a pension to Emily McLain.

30 St. 1546; Feb. 28, 1899; C. 312—An Act Granting a pension to Judith Doherty.

30 St. 1563; Mar. 3, 1899; C. 520—An Act Granting a pension to James H. Preston.

30 St. 1573; Mar. 3, 1899; C. 569—An Act For the relief of Eudora Hill.

30 St. 1586; Mar. 3, 1899; C. 626—An Act Granting an increase of pension to John E. Gullett.

30 St. 1587; Mar. 3, 1899; C. 632—An Act Granting an increase of pension to Andrew J. Taylor.

30 St. 1805; Feb. 9, 1899—Con. Res. Report Superintendent of Indian Schools.

31 STAT.

31 St. 7; Feb. 9, 1900; C. 14—An Act Making appropriations to supply urgent deficiencies in the appropriations for the fiscal year ending June 30, 1900, and for prior years, and for other purposes.[40]

31 St. 32; Feb. 24, 1900; C. 24—An Act To amend an Act entitled "An Act to amend an Act to suspend the operation of certain provisions of law relating to the War Department, and for other purposes."[41]

31 St. 52; Mar. 28, 1900; C. 111—An Act Enlarging the powers of the Choctaw, Oklahoma and Gulf R. Co.[42]

31 St. 59; Apr. 4, 1900; C. 156—An Act Approving a revision and adjustment of certain sales of Otoe and Missouria lands in the States of Nebraska and Kansas.[43]

31 St. 72; Apr. 9, 1900; C. 182—An Act To settle the title to real estate in the city of Sante Fe, New Mexico.

31 St. 86; Apr. 17, 1900; C. 192—An Act Making appropriations for the legislative, executive, and judicial expenses of the Government for the fiscal year ending June 30, 1901, and for other purposes.[44]

31 St. 134; Apr. 17, 1900; C. 193—An Act Granting the right of way to the Minnesota and Manitoba R. Co. across the ceded portion of the Chippewa (Red Lake) Indian Reservation in Minnesota.[45]

31 St. 170; May 7, 1900; C. 384—An Act For the appointment of an additional United States commissioner of the northern judicial district of the Indian Territory.

31 St. 179; May 17, 1900; C. 479—An Act Providing for free homesteads on the public lands for actual and bona fide settlers, and reserving the public lands for that purpose.[46] Sec. 1—25 U. S. C. 421. (See USCA Historical Note).

31 St. 182; May 24, 1900; C. 546—An Act To amend section eight of the Act of Congress entitled "An Act to authorize the Fort Smith and Western R. Co. to construct and operate a railway through the Choctaw and Creek nations, in the Indian Territory, and for other purposes."[47]

31 St. 205; May 26, 1900; C. 586—An Act Making appropriation for the support of the Regular and Volunteer Army for the fiscal year ending June 30, 1901.

31 St. 221; May 31, 1900; C. 598—An Act Making appropriations for the current and contingent expenses of the Indian Department and for fulfilling treaty stipulations with various Indian tribes for the fiscal year ending June 30, 1901, and for other purposes.[48] Sec. 1—25 U. S. C. 395. (See USCA Historical Note) (Also see 25 U. S. C. 394)

---

[34] *Rpg.* 23 St. 24, sec. 14. *A.* 35 St. 600. *S.* 35 St. 837. *Cited:* Op. Sol., M. 29147, May 6, 1937; 53 I. D. 593; Lott, 205 Fed. 28; U. S. v. Lynch, 7 Alaska 568.

[35] *Ag.* 30 St. 318, 433. *A.* 31 St. 32.

[36] *Sg.* 25 St. 882, sec. 8; 28 St. 882, sec. 8. *Cited:* 42 L. D. 582; Drapeau, 195 Fed. 130; Sully, 195 Fed. 113; U. S. v. Nice, 241 U. S. 591.

[37] *Sg.* 1 St. 137. *A.* 31 St. 182. *Cited:* U. S. v. Ft. Smith, 195 Fed. 211.

[38] *Sg.* 17 St. 29, sec. 1; 28 St. 306.

[39] *Sg.* 27 St. 281.

[40] *Sg.* 26 St. 853; 30 St. 92, 500. *S.* 31 St. 1058; 38 St. 189. *Cited:* Oneida, 39 C. Cls. 116.

[41] *Ag.* 30 St. 328, 1350.

[42] *Rg.* 28 St. 503, sec. 4. *Ag.* 29 St. 98. *Cited:* Choctaw, 256 U. S. 581.

[43] *Sg.* 27 St. 568.

[44] *Cited:* U. S. v. Wildcat, 244 U. S. 111.

[45] *Sg.* 18 St. 482. *S.* 35 St. 465.

[46] *S.* 44 St. 161.

[47] *Ag.* 30 St. 1371.

[48] *Sg.* 1 St. 619; 4 St. 442; 7 St. 36, 46, 51, 69, 85, 99, 114, 161, 179, 185, 213, 236, 242, 287, 296, 314, 320, 352, 425, 541, 545, 596; 9 St. 35, 842, 855, 904; 10 St. 1071, 1079; 11 St. 614, 700, 702, 729, 744; 12 St. 628, 981, 1173; 13 St. 675; 14 St. 756, 757, 787; 15 St. 515, 519, 622, 637, 652, 655, 676; 16 St. 40, 355, 720; 17 St. 159; 19 St. 254, 256, 287; 22 St. 43; 24 St. 388; 25 St. 645, 688; 26 St. 753, 851, 1028, 1033, 1037; 27 St. 139, 645; 28 St. 286, 295, 323, 939; 29 St. 341, 354; 30 St. 72, 75, 87, 94, 500, 505, 513, 596, 941.

31 St. 250; June 2, 1900; C. 610—An Act To ratify an agreement between the Commission to the Five Civilized Tribes and the Seminole tribe of Indians.[49]

31 St. 267; June 5, 1900; C. 716—An Act For the relief of the Colorado Cooperative Colony, to permit second homesteads in certain cases, and for other purposes.[50]

31 St. 280; June 6, 1900; C. 785—An Act Making appropriations to supply deficiencies in the appropriations for the fiscal year ending June 30, 1900, and for prior years, and for other purposes.[51]

31 St. 321; June 6, 1900; C. 786—An Act Making further provision for a civil government for Alaska, and for other purposes.[52] Sec. 27—48 U. S. C. 356.

31 St. 588; June 6, 1900; C. 791—An Act Making appropriations for sundry civil expenses of the Government for the fiscal year ending June 30, 1901, and for other purposes.[53]

31 St. 657; June 6, 1900; C. 795—An Act Changing place for holding court in the central division of the Indian Territory from Cameron to Poteau, and for other purposes.[54]

31 St. 658; June 6, 1900; C. 798—An Act To authorize the Seneca Telephone Co. to construct and maintain lines in the Indian Territory.

31 St. 659; June 6, 1900; C. 799—An Act To provide for the sale of isolated and disconnected tracts or parcels of the Osage trust and diminished reserve lands in the State of Kansas.[55]

31 St. 660; June 6, 1900; C. 802—An Act To provide for the use of timber and stone for domestic and industrial purposes in the Indian Territory.[56]

31 St. 672; June 6, 1900; C. 813—An Act To ratify an agreement with the Indians of the Ft. Hall Indian Reservation in Idaho, and making appropriations to carry the same into effect.[57]

31 St. 727; Jan. 4, 1901; C. 8—An Act Making appropriations to supply urgent deficiencies in the appropriations for the fiscal year ending June 30, 1901, and for other purposes.[58]

31 St. 740; Jan. 26, 1901; C. 180—An Act To allow the commutation of homestead entries in certain cases.[59] 25 U. S. C. 422. USCA Historical Note: R. S. sec. 2301, as amended by Act Mar. 3, 1891, s. 6, 26 St. 1098, sec. 173 of Tit. 43, Public Lands, provided that all persons entitled to avail themselves of the provisions of R. S. sec. 2289, sec. 161 of said title 43, might pay the minimum price for the quantity of land entered by them at any time after the expiration of fourteen calendar months from the date of their entry, and obtain a patent therefor, upon making proof of settlement and of residence and cultivation for such period of fourteen months. The above-cited act made section 173 applicable to all settlers on Indian lands ceded and opened to settlement prior to May 17, 1900, although the acts under which the original entries were made forbade the commutation. The laws authorizing the commutation of homesteads in the Territory of Oklahoma generally are applicable to the commutation of homesteads in Greer county, Okl., by Act Jan. 18, 1897, s. 7, sec. 1134 of Tit. 43, Public Lands. Homestead settlers on certain ceded Indian lands in South Dakota were to be entitled to the provisions of the above-cited act, by Act May 22, 1902, s. 1, 32 St. 203.

31 St. 760; Feb. 6, 1901; C. 217—An Act Amending the Act of August 15, 1894, entitled "An Act making appropriations for current and contingent expenses of the Indian Department and fulfilling treaties and stipulations with various Indian tribes for the fiscal year ending June 30, 1895," and for other purposes.[60] Sec. 1—25 U. S. C. 345 (Sec. 1, 28 St. 305)[61] See Historical Note 25 U. S. C. A. 345. Sec. 2—25 U. S. C. 346.

31 St. 766; Feb. 11, 1901; C. 350—An Act Providing for allotments of lands in severalty to the Indians of the LaPointe or Bad River Reservation, in the State of Wisconsin.[62]

31 St. 785; Feb. 12, 1901; C. 360—An Act Granting permission to the Indians on the Grand Portage Indian Reservation, in the State of Minnesota, to cut and dispose of the timber on their several allotments on said reservation.

31 St. 786; Feb. 12, 1901; C. 361—An Act To authorize Arizona Water Company to construct power plant on Pima Indian Reservation in Maricopa County, Arizona.

31 St. 790; Feb. 13, 1901; C. 370—An Act To provide for the entry of lands formerly in the Lower Brule Indian Reservation, South Dakota.[63]

31 St. 790; Feb. 15, 1901; C. 372—An Act Relating to rights of way through certain parks, reservations, and other public lands.[64] 43 U. S. C. 959.

31 St. 794; Feb. 18, 1901; C. 379—An Act To put in force in the Indian Territory certain provisions of the laws of Arkansas relating to corporations, and to make said provisions applicable to said Territory.[65]

31 St. 796; Feb. 18, 1901; C. 380—An Act To confirm in trust to the city of Albuquerque, in the Territory of New Mexico, the town of Albuquerque Grant, and for other purposes.[66]

31 St. 801; Feb. 23, 1901; C. 467—An Act Confirming two locations of Chippewa half-breed scrip in the State (than Territory) of Utah.[67]

31 St. 805; Feb. 25, 1901; C. 474—An Act For the relief of the Medawakanton band of Sioux Indians, residing in Redwood County, Minnesota.

31 St. 816; Feb. 27, 1901; C. 616—An Act To confirm a lease with the Seneca Nation of Indians.

31 St. 819; Feb. 28, 1901; C. 622—An Act To regulate the collection and disbursement of moneys arising from leases made by the Seneca Nation, of New York Indians, and for other purposes.

31 St. 848; Mar. 1, 1901; C. 675—An Act To ratify and confirm an agreement with the Cherokee tribe of Indians, and for other purposes.[69]

31 St. 861; Mar. 1, 1901; C. 676—An Act To ratify and confirm an agreement with the Muscogee or Creek tribe of Indians, and for other purposes.[70] Sec. 37—25 U. S. C. 179 (R. S.

---

943. *S.* 31 St. 848. 1994; 32 St. 245, 500, 641, 716, 982; 34 St. 137. *Cited:* Brown, 39 Yale L. J. 307; Cavell, 3 Okla. S. B. J. 208; 26 Op. A. G. 127; 51 L. D. 618; Memo. Sol. Off., May 11, 1934; Memo. Sol., Nov. 11, 1935, June 14, 1938; Ballinger, 216 U. S. 240; Bird. 129 Fed. 472; Bowling, 233 U. S. 528; Brown, 44 C. Cls. 283; Cherokee. 203 U. S. 76; Cherokee, 85 C. Cls. 76; Cherokee, 223 U. S. 108; Choctaw, 81 C. Cls. 1; Coos, 87 C. Cls. 143; Farrell, 110 Fed. 942; Ikard, 4 Ind. T. 314; McMurray, 62 C. Cls. 458; Medawakanton, 57 C. Cls. 357; Miller, 249 U. S. 308; Persons, 40 C. Cls. 411; Ross, 227 U. S. 530; Sac & Fox, 220 U. S. 481; Sage, 235 U. S. 99; Stanclift, 152 Fed. 697; U. S. v. Dowden, 220 Fed. 227; U. S. v. Powers, 305 U. S. 527; U. S. v. Watashe, 102 F. 2d 428; Winton, 255 U. S. 373.

[49] *Sg.* 30 St. 502. *Cited:* 26 Op. A. G. 340; Memo. Ind. Off., Mar. 13, 1935; Bartlett, 218 Fed. 380; Campbell, 248 U. S. 169; Fish, 52 F. 2d 544; Jonah, 52 F. 2d 343; Seminole, 78 C. Cls. 455; U. S. v. Bd. of Comm'rs of McIntosh Co., 284 Fed. 103; U. S. v. Ferguson, 247 U. S. 175.

[50] *Sg.* 25 St. 871.

[51] *Sg.* 5 St. 621, sec. 9; 11 St. 611; 26 St. 853; 28 St. 831; 29 St. 341. *Cited:* 53 I. D. 593; U. S. v. Hoyt, 167 Fed. 301.

[52] R. 48 St. 583. *Cited:* 53 I. D. 593; Chisolm, 273 Fed. 589; Nagle, 191 Fed. 141; Tiger, 221 U. S. 286; U. S. v. Berrigan, 2 Alaska 442; U. S. v. Cadzow, 5 Alaska 125.

[53] *Sg.* 1 St. 137.

[54] *Ag.* 28 St. 694.

[55] *Sg.* 9 St. 51, sec. 5; 28 St. 687.

[56] *A.* 32 St. 774 *S.* 33 St. 299. *Cited:* Op. Sol. M. 2121, Apr. 12, 1927.

[57] *Sg.* 15 St. 673; 17 St. 333, sec. 1; 24 St. 388; 26 St. 794, 851; 29 St. 341. *Rp.* 34 St. 213. *S.* 31 St. 727, 1010, 1058, 1093; 33 St. 153; 34 St. 325; 35 St. 444; 47 St. 146. *Cited:* Op. Sol., M. 7002, Mar. 10, 1922, M. 5386, June 19, 1923; Letter from Asst. Sec'y to Comm'r. M. 17096, Aug. 14, 1926; Op. Sol., M. 18772, Dec. 24, 1926; Letter of Comm. to Ind. Agents, Oct. 9, 1937; Lone Wolf, 187 U. S. 553; Oklahoma, 258 U. S. 574; Skeem, 273 Fed. 93; U. S. v. Myers, 206 Fed. 387; U. S. ex rel. Ray, 27 F. 2d 909

[58] *Sg.* 31 St. 676. *S.* 31 St. 1010, 1058. *Cited:* Lone Wolf, 187 U. S. 553.

[59] *Ag.* 12 St. 393, sec. 8. *S.* 32 St. 203.

[60] *Ag.* 28 Stat. 305. *Cited:* Brown, 39 Yale L. J. 307; 56 I. D. 102; Bond, 181 Fed. 613; Chase, 238 Fed. 887; Drapeau, 195 Fed. 130; First Moon, 270 U. S. 243; Halbert, 283 U. S. 753; Heckman, 224 U. S. 413; Hy-Yu-Tse-Mil-Kin, 194 U. S. 401; In re Jessie's, 259 Fed. 94; Kennedy, 23 F. Supp. 771; La Clair, 184 Fed. 128; Leecy, 190 Fed. 289; Lemieux, 15 F. 2d 518; McKay, 204 U. S. 458; Mickadiet, 258 U. S. 609; Mitchell, 9 Pet. 711; Morrison, 266 U. S. 481; Oakes, 172 Fed. 305; Pape, 19 F. 2d 219; Parr, 197 Fed. 302; Parr, 132 Fed. 1004; Patawa, 132 Fed. 893; Pel-Ata-Yakot, 188 Fed. 387; Reynolds, 174 Fed. 212; St. Marie, 24 F. Supp. 237; Sloan, 118 Fed. 283; Smith, 142 Fed. 225; Sully, 195 Fed. 113; U. S. v. Heyfron, 138 Fed. 964; U. S. v. Paine, 206 U. S. 467; U. S. v. Payne, 264 U. S. 446; Vezina, 245 Fed. 411; Waldron, 143 Fed. 413; Woodbury, 170 Fed. 302; Ya-Koot-Sa, 262 Fed. 398; Young, 176 Fed. 612.

[61] *S.* 36 St. 1167, sec. 291.

[62] *Sg.* 10 St. 1109, Art. 3. *A.* 34 St. 1217.

[63] *Sg.* 30 St. 1362. *Cited:* Op. Sol. M. 10068, Feb. 16, 1927; Swendig, 265 U. S. 322; U. S. v. Portneuf-Marsh, 213 Fed. 601; Ute, 45 C. Cls. 440.

[64] *Sg.* 14 St. 221, sec. 1; 19 St. 232.

[65] *Cited:* Dukes, 4 Ind. T. 156; Shulthis, 225 U. S. 561.

[66] *Sg.* 9 St. 922.

[67] *Sg.* 10 St. 598.

[69] *Sg.* 16 St. 570, sec. 3; 17 St. 136, sec. 1, 2; 18 St. 35; 450, sec. 9; 30 St. 498, 499, 504, 500, 502, 505; 31 St. 237. *Ag.* 4 St. 730, sec. 9. *Cited:* Ballinger, 216 U. S. 240.

[70] *Sg.* 7 St. 367; 14 St. 787; 30 St. 498, 500; 30 St. 520. *A.* 32 St. 500. *Rp.* 32 St. 500. *S.* 32 St. 245, 500, 982; 33 St. 1048; 38 St. 582; 42 St. 831. *Cited:* 24 Op. A. G. 623; 25 Op. A. G. 163; 34 Op. A. G. 275; Op. Sol. D. 40462, Oct. 31, 1917; M. 10526, Dec. 13, 1923; Memo. Sol Off., Apr. 26, 1933; 53 I. D. 502; Armstrong, 195 Fed. 137; Bagby, 60 F. 2d 80; Bartlett, 218 Fed. 380; Brann, 192 Fed. 427; Brown, 27 F. 2d 274; Browning, 6 F. 2d 801; Buster, 135 Fed. 947; Campbell, 248 U. S. 169; Capital, 6 Ind. T. 223; Carter, 12 F. 2d 780; Choctaw, 256 U. S. 531; City of Tulsa, 75 F. 2d 343; Creek, 78 C. Cls. 474; Evans, 204 Fed. 361; Ex p. Webb, 225 U. S. 663; Fink, 248 U. S. 392; Fish, 52 F. 2d 544; Folk, 233 Fed. 177; Fulsom, 85 F. 2d 84; Gilcrease,

sec. 2117)[71] USCA Historical Note: With the exception of the last sentence, this section was derived from the above-cited section of the Revised Statutes, which was derived from section 9 of Act June 30, 1834, 4 St. 730. The last sentence of the Code section was derived from section 37 instant Act.

31 St. 895; Mar. 2, 1901; C. 803—An Act Making appropriation for the support of the Army for the fiscal year ending June 30, 1902.

31 St. 950; Mar. 2, 1901; C. 808—An Act Authorizing the Attorney-General, upon the request of the Secretary of the Interior, to appear in suits brought by States relative to school lands.[72] 43 U. S. C. 868.

31 St. 952; Mar. 2, 1901; C. 810—An Act To restore to the public domain a small tract of the White Mountain Apache Indian Reservation, in the Territory of Arizona.[73]

31 St. 960; Mar. 3, 1901; C. 830—An Act Making appropriations for the legislative, executive, and judicial expenses of the Government for the fiscal year ending June 30, 1902, and for other purposes.

31 St. 1010; Mar. 3, 1901; C. 831—An Act Making appropriations to supply deficiencies in the appropriations for the fiscal year ending June 30, 1901, and for prior years, and for other purposes.[74]

31 St. 1058; Mar. 3, 1901; C. 832—An Act Making appropriations for the current and contingent expenses of the Indian Department and for fulfilling treaty stipulations with various Indian tribes for the fiscal year ending June 30, 1902, and for other purposes.[75] Sec. 1—25 U. S. C. 262;[76] 25 U. S. C. 424. Sec. 3—25 U. S. C. 319; 25 U. S. C. 357. Sec. 4—25 U. S. C. 311. Sec. 9—25 U. S. C. 348 (sec. 5, 24 St. 389). USCA Historical Note: Another proviso, authorizing the Secretary of the Interior, whenever any Indian of the Siletz Indian reservation, in the State of Oregon, fully capable of managing his own affairs, etc., should become the owner of more than 80 acres of land upon said reservation, to cause patent to be issued to him for all such land over 80 acres was added to the derivative section by section 9, 31 St. 1085. Said proviso is omitted, as special only. A provision in said derivative section as to the application of the laws of Kansas regulating descent and partition to lands in Indian Territory, which might be allotted in severalty under the provisions of the General Allotment Act, is also omitted because of the admission of the Indian Territory into the Union as a part of the State of Oklahoma. Also see Historical Note 25 USCA 331.

31 St. 1093; Mar. 3, 1901; C. 846—An Act to supplement existing laws relating to the disposition of lands, and so forth.[77]

31 St. 1133; Mar. 3, 1901; C. 853—An Act Making appropriations for sundry civil expenses of the Government for the fiscal year ending June 30, 1902, and for other purposes.[78]

31 St. 1436; Mar. 3, 1901; C. 856—An Act Authorizing and directing the Secretary of the Interior to issue a patent to the heir or heirs of one Tawamnoha, or Martha Crayon, conveying to them certain lands in the State of North Dakota, confirming certain conveyances thereof, and for other purposes.

31 St. 1439; Mar. 3, 1901; C. 862—An Act To amend chapter 559 of the Revised Statutes of the United States, approved March 3, 1891. 16 U. S. C. 607, 613.

31 St. 1447; Mar. 3, 1901; C. 868—An Act To amend sec. 6, chapter 119, United States Statutes at Large numbered 24.[79] 8 U. S. C. 3.

31 St. 1447; Mar. 3, 1901; C. 869—An Act Granting a right of way to the Jamestown and Northern Railway through the Devils Lake Indian Reservation, in the State of North Dakota.

31 St. 1455; Mar. 3, 1901; C. 878—An Act To authorize the Pigeon River Improvement, Slide, and Boom Co., of Minnesota, to enter upon the Grand Portage Indian Reservation, and improve the Pigeon River in said State at what is known as the cascades of said river.

31 St. 1462; Feb. 28, 1901; J. Res. No. 10—Joint Resolution Authorizing the Secretary of the Interior to remove from the files of the Department of the Interior certain letters to be donated to the State of Iowa.

31 St. 1469; Mar. 10, 1900; C. 40—An Act For the relief of John Anderson, a Pottawatomie Indian, and his adult children.[80]

31 St. 1484; Mar. 31, 1900; C. 122—An Act For the relief of Hattie A. Phillips.

31 St. 1488; Apr. 2, 1900; C. 137—An Act Granting a pension to James L. Whidden.

31 St. 1493; Apr. 4, 1900; C. 167—An Act Granting a pension to James J. Wheeler.

31 St. 1517; Apr. 23, 1900; C. 292—An Act Granting an increase of pension to William Padgett.

31 St. 1565; May 24, 1900; C. 548—An Act Granting an increase of pension to Sarah E. Tradewell.

31 St. 1566; May 25, 1900; C. 560—An Act Granting a pension to Edward Harris.

31 St. 1572; May 26, 1900; C. 592—An Act for the relief of Northrup and Chick, and also of Thomas N. Stinson.

31 St. 1587; June 4, 1900; C. 677—An Act Granting an increase of pension to Robert Gamble, junior.

31 St. 1606; June 5, 1900; C. 767—An Act Granting a pension to Sophia A. Lane.

31 St. 1611; June 6, 1900; C. 836—An Act For the relief of John D. Hale, of Tilford, Meade County, South Dakota.

31 St. 1617; June 6, 1900; C. 858—An Act For the relief of Fred Weddle.

31 St. 1629; June 7, 1900; C. 917—An Act Granting a pension to James M. Ellett.

31 St. 1630; June 7, 1900; C. 923—An Act Granting an increase of pension to Samuel S. White.

31 St. 1634; Dec. 20, 1900; C. 5—An Act Granting an increase of pension to Michael Dempsey.

31 St. 1653; Jan. 17, 1901; C. 98—An Act Granting a pension to Maria H. Hixson.

31 St. 1668; Jan. 25, 1901; C. 171—An Act Granting a pension to Erie E. Farmer.

31 St. 1670; Jan. 31, 1901; C. 187—An Act Granting a pension to B. H. Randall.

---

249 U. S. 178; Grayson, 267 U. S. 352; Harris, 254 U. S. 103; Harris, 7 Ind. T. 532; Harris, 166 Fed. 109; Hawkins, 195 Fed. 345; Hopkins, 285 Fed. 95; In re Lands of Five, 199 Fed. 811; Indian, 5 Ind. T. 41; Iowa, 217 Fed. 11; Jefferson, 247 U. S. 288; James, 88 F. 2d 431; Joplin, 236 U. S. 531; Kemohah, 38 Fed. 2d 665; King, 64 F. 2d 979; Knight, 28 F. 2d 481; Locke, 287 Fed. 276; M. K. & T. Ry., 47 C. Cls. 59; McDougal, 237 U. S. 372; McKee, 201 Fed. 74; Malone, 212 Fed. 668; Mandler, 49 F. 2d 201; Mandler, 52 F. 2d 713; Marlin, 276 U. S. 58; Morrison, 6 F. 2d 811; Mullen, 224 U. S. 448; Norton, 266 U. S. 511; Parker, 250 U. S. 235; Parker, 250 U. S. 66; Pigeon, 237 U. S. 386; Porter, 7 Ind. T. 395; Priddy, 204 Fed. 955; Reed, 197 Fed. 419; Roubedeaux, 28 F. 2d 277; St. Louis, 7 Ind. T. 685; Schellenbarger, 286 U. S. 68; Shulthis, 225 U. S. 561; Sizemore, 285 U. S. 441; Skelton, 235 U. S. 206; Stancliff, 152 Fed. 697; Stewart, 295 U. S. 403; Sunday, 248 U. S. 545; Sweet, 245 U. S. 192; Tiger, 4 F. 2d 714; Tiger, 48 F. 2d 509; Tiger, 221 U. S. 286; Turner, 51 C. Cls. 125; Turner, 248 U. S. 354; U. S. v. Atkins, 260 U. S. 220; U. S. v Equitable, 288 U. S. 738; U. S. v. Ferguson, 247 U. S. 175; U. S. v. Ft. Smith, 195 Fed. 211; U. S. v. Gypsy, 10 F. 2d 487; U. S. v. Hayes, 20 F. 2d 873; U. S. v. Jacobs, 195 Fed. 707; U. S. v. Lena, 261 Fed. 144; U. S. v. Martin, 45 F. 2d 836; U. S. v. Mid Continent, 67 F. 2d 37; U. S. v. Rea-Read, 171 Fed. 501; U. S. v. Shock, 187 Fed. 862; U. S. v. Smith, 279 Fed. 136; U. S. v. Smith, 288 Fed. 356; U. S. v. Southern, 9 F. 2d 664; U. S. v. Tiger, 19 F. 2d 35; U. S. v. Western, 226 Fed. 726; U. S. v. Wildcat, 244 U. S. 111; U. S. Exp., 191 Fed. 673; W. O Whitney, 166 Fed. 738; Wade, 30 App. D. C. 245; Washington, 235 U. S. 422; Welty, 231 Fed. 930; Willmott, 27 F. 2d 277; Woodward, 238 U. S. 284.

[71] *S.* 32 St. 504, sec. 17.

[72] *Cited:* Minnesota, 185 U. S. 373; Oregon, 202 U. S. 60.

[73] *Sg.* 27 St. 469. *Cited:* 29 Op. A. G. 239.

[74] *Sg.* 26 St. 853; 28 St. 895; 29 St. 341; 31 St. 676; 31 St. 727. *Cited:* Garfield, 211 U. S. 249; U. S. v. Hoyt, 167 Fed. 301.

[75] *Sg.* 1 St. 619; 4 St. 442; 7 St. 36, 46, 51, 69, 85, 99, 114, 161, 179 185, 213, 236, 242, 287, 296, 314, 320, 352, 425, 541, 5'5; 9 St. 35, 842 855, 904; 10 St. 949, 1071, 1079; 11 St. 614, 700, 702, 729, 744; 12 St. 628, 652, 981, 1038, 1173; 13 St. 675; 14 St. 757, 787; 15 St. 515, 622 637, 652, 655, 676; 16 St. 40, 355, 720; 19 St. 254, 256, 287; 22 St. 43; 24 St. 388; 25 St. 645, 688, 888, 894; 26 St. 851, 1028; 27 St. 120, 139 645; 28 St. 939; 29 St. 354; 30 St. 75, 87, 94, 500, 505; 31 St. 7, 672 678, 727. *Ag.* 24 St. 389. *A.* 32 St. 982; 34 St. 325. *Rp.* 36 St. 855 *S.* 32 St. 177, 245, 982, 1031; 33 St. 189, 394; 34 St. 325; 41 St. 599; 45 St. 442. *Cited:* Rice, 16 J. Comp. Leg. 78; 26 Op. A. G. 127; 27 Op. A. G. 588; 12 L. D. Memo. 289; Op. Sol., D. 40462, Oct. 31, 1917; M. 13344, Oct. 9, 1924; Memo. Sol. Off., Oct. 31, 1928; Letter of Ass't Comm'r to Collier Buffington Sept. 8 1932; Memo. Sol., Sept. 17, 1936 July 1, 1938; Op. Sol. M. 29961, Oct. 4, 1938, 53 I. D. 637; Brown, 44 C. Cls. 283; Cherokee, 85 C. Cls. 76; Cherokee, 223 U. S. 108; Chippewa 80 C. Cls. 410; City of Tulsa, 75 F. 2d 343; Ex p. Pero, 99 F. 2d 28; Fleming, 215 U. S. 56; Garfield, 211 U. S. 204; Green, 46 C. Cls. 68; Lone Wolf, 187 U. S. 553; Lowe, 223 U. S. 95; Medawakanton, 57 C. Cls 357; Minnesota, 305 U. S. 382; Muskogee, 4 Ind. T. 18; Muskogee, 118 Fed. 382; Muskrat, 219 U. S. 346; New York Indians, 41 C. Cls. 462; New York Indians, 40 C. Cls. 448; Oneida, 39 C. Cls. 116; Sisseton, 39 C. Cls. 172; Sisseton, 42 C. Cls. 416; Swendig, 265 U. S. 322; Tinker, 231 U. S 681; U. S. v. Colvard, 89 F. 2d 312; U. S. v. Ferry, 24 F. Supp. 399; U. S. v. Minn., 95 F. 2d 468; U. S. v. Sisseton, 208 U. S. 561; U. S. v. Spaeth, 24 F. Supp. 465; U. S. v. Watashe, 102 F. 2d 428.

[76] *S.* 32 St. 1009, sec. 10.

[77] *Sg.* 28 St. 894; 31 St. 676. *S.* 35 St. 444; 35 St. 781. *Cited:* Lone Wolf, 187 U. S. 553.

[78] *S.* 32 St. 1031; 35 St. 644.

[79] *Ag.* 24 St. 390. *Cited:* Houghton, 19 Calif. L. Rev. 507; Krieger, 3 Geo. Wash. L. Rev. 279; Muskrat, 219 U. S. 346; Owen, 217 U. S. 488; Tiger, 4 F. 2d 714; U. S. v. Abrams, 191 Fed. 82; U. S. v. Hayes, 20 F. 2d 873; U. S. v. Richards, 27 F. 2d 284; Williams, 239 U. S. 414.

[80] *Sg.* 17 St. 159.

31 St. 1686; Feb. 7, 1901; C. 270—An Act Granting a pension to Mary Black.

31 St. 1703; Feb. 12, 1901; C. 367—An Act Granting a pension to Eliza L. Reese.

31 St. 1723; Feb. 25, 1901; C. 488—An Act Granting an increase of pension to William C. Griffin.

31 St. 1731; Feb. 25, 1901; C. 525—An Act Granting an increase of pension to Robert P. Currin.

31 St. 1731; Feb. 25, 1901; C. 526—An Act Granting a pension to Sampson D. Bridgman.

31 St. 1737; Feb. 25, 1901; C. 551—An Act Granting an increase of pension to John T. Knox.

31 St. 1770; Mar. 1, 1901; C. 722—An Act Granting an increase of pension to Elias M. Lynch.

31 St. 1770; Mar. 1, 1901; C. 723—An Act Granting an increase of pension to Jeremiah Jackson.

31 St. 1783; Mar. 1, 1901; C. 780—An Act Granting an increase of pension to Warren Damon.

31 St. 1809; Mar. 3, 1901; C. 954—An Act Confirming a lease between J. A. Peglow and the Seneca Nation of New York Indians.

31 St. 1992; Apr. 27, 1900—Conc. Res. Researches, etc., American aborigines.

31 St. 1994; May 26, 1900—Conc. Res. Indian Appropriation Bill.[81]

32 STAT.

32 St. 5; Feb. 14, 1902; C. 17—An Act Making appropriations to supply urgent deficiencies in the appropriations for the fiscal year ending June 30, 1902, and for prior years, and for other purposes.[82]

32 St. 43; Feb. 28, 1902; C. 134—An Act To grant the right of way through the Oklahoma Territory and the Indian Territory to the Enid and Anadarko Ry. Co., and for other purposes.[83] Sec. 23—25 U. S. C. 312 (sec. 1, 30 St. 990).[84] See USCA Historical Note. 25 U. S. C. 314 (sec. 3, 30 St. 991). See USCA Historical Note.

32 St. 63; Mar. 11, 1902; C. 180—An Act Providing for the commutation for townsite purposes of homestead entries in certain portions of Oklahoma.[85]

32 St. 90; Mar. 24, 1902; C. 276—An Act To change the boundaries between the southern and central judicial districts of the Indian Territory.[86]

32 St. 120; Apr. 28, 1902; C. 594—An Act Making appropriations for the legislative, executive, and judicial expenses of the Government for the fiscal year ending June 30, 1903, and for other purposes.[87]

32 St. 175; Apr. 29, 1902; C. 639—An Act Providing for a monument to mark the site of the Fort Phil Kearny massacre.

32 St. 177; Apr. 29, 1902; C. 642—An Act For the relief of certain indigent Choctaw and Chickasaw Indians in the Indian Territory, and for other purposes.[88]

32 St. 183; Apr. 30, 1902; C. 673—An Act To amend an Act entitled "An Act granting the right to the Omaha Northern Ry. Co. to construct a railway across, and establish stations on, the Omaha and Winnebago Reservation, in the State of Nebraska, and for other purposes," by extending the time for the construction of said railway.[89]

32 St. 198; May 14, 1902; C. 788—An Act To amend an Act entitled "An Act granting to the Clearwater Valley R. Co. a right of way through the Nez Perces Indian land in Idaho."[90]

32 St. 200; May 19, 1902; C. 816—An Act For the protection of cities and towns in the Indian Territory, and for other purposes.[91]

32 St. 203; May 22, 1902; C. 821—An Act To allow the commutation of and second homestead entries in certain cases.[92] Sec. 2—25 U. S. C. 423.

32 St. 207; May 27, 1902; C. 887—An Act For the allowance of certain claims for stores and supplies reported by the Court of Claims under the provisions of the Act approved March 3, 1883, and commonly known as the Bowman Act, and for other purposes.[93]

32 St. 245; May 27, 1902; C. 888—An Act Making appropriations for the current and contingent expenses of the Indian Department and for fulfilling treaty stipulations with various Indian tribes for the fiscal year ending June 30, 1903, and for other purposes.[94] Sec. 7—25 U. S. C. 379.

32 St. 284; May 31, 1902; C. 946—An Act Providing that the statute of limitations of the several States shall apply as a defense to actions brought in the United States courts for the recovery of lands patented in severalty to members of any tribe of Indians under any treaty between it and the United States of America. Sec. 1—25 U. S. C. 347.

32 St. 327; June 7, 1902; C. 1037—An Act For the protection of game in Alaska, and for other purposes.[95]

32 St. 384; June 13, 1902; C. 1080—An Act Providing for free homesteads in the Ute Indian Reservation in Colorado. 43 U. S. C. 203.

32 St. 395; June 21, 1902; C. 1137—An Act To fix the fees of United States marshals in the Indian Territory, and for other purposes.[96]

32 St. 399; June 27, 1902; C. 1156—An Act To extend the provisions, limitations, and benefits of an Act entitled "An Act granting pensions to the survivors of the Indian wars of 1832 to 1842, inclusive, known as the Black Hawk war, Creek war, Cherokee disturbances, and the Seminole war," approved July 27, 1892.[97] 38 U. S. C. 372.

32 St. 400; June 27, 1902; C. 1157—An Act To amend an Act entitled "An Act for the relief and civilization of the Chippewa Indians in the State of Minnesota," approved January 14, 1889.[98] Sec. 4—25 U. S. C. 197 (sec. 1, 30 St. 90) (Sec. 197 repealed except as to then existing contracts by instant Act). See Historical Note 25 USCA 197.

32 St. 419; June 28, 1902; C. 1301—An Act Making appropriations for sundry civil expenses of the Government for the fiscal year ending June 30, 1903, and for other purposes.[99]

32 St. 500; June 30, 1902; C. 1323—An Act To ratify and confirm a supplemental agreement with the Creek tribe of Indians, and for other purposes.[1] Sec. 17—25 U. S. C. 179 (R. S. sec. 2117; sec. 37, 31 St. 871).

---

[81] *Ag.* 31 St. 221.

[82] *Sg.* 26 St. 853. *Cited:* Creek, 78 C. Cls. 474.

[83] *Rg.* 30 St. 990. *S.* 34 St. 187; 35 St. 312. *Cited:* Op. Sol., M. 27814 Jan. 30, 1935; 55 I. D. 456; Choctaw, 6 Ind. T. 515; Oklahoma, 241 Fed. 592; St. Louis, 6 Ind. T. 515; St. Louis, 7 Ind. T. 685.

[84] *S.* 36 St. 859, sec. 16; 45 St. 442.

[85] *Sg.* 26 St. 91, sec. 22; 28 St. 894; 31 St. 676. *S.* 38 St. 1192.

[86] *Sg.* 28 St. 694.

[87] *Cited:* Whitchurch, 92 F. 2d 249.

[88] *Sg.* 30 St. 495, 509; 31 St. 1062. *S.* 32 St. 245.

[89] *Ag.* 30 St. 345. *A.* 33 St. 311.

[90] *Ag.* 30 St. 908, sec. 5.

[91] *Cited:* Incorporated, 5 Ind. T. 497.

[92] *Sg.* 31 St. 740.

[93] Sg. 22 St. 485.

[94] *Ag.* 25 St. 1014; 31 St. 864. *Sg.* 4 St. 442; 7 St. 35, 46, 51, 68, 85, 99, 114, 185, 213, 236, 242, 286, 296, 317, 320, 367, 425, 541, 545, 596; 9 St. 35, 842, 855, 904; 10 St. 1071, 1079; 11 St. 614, 699, 702, 729, 744; 12 St. 628, 981, 1178; 13 St. 675; 14 St. 757, 785; 15 St. 622, 640, 658, 676; 16 St. 40, 355, 720; 17 St. 159; 19 St. 254, 256, 287; 22 St. 43, 341; 24 St. 388; 25 St. 642, 645, 688, 894, 1013; 26 St. 794, 851, 1028, 1041; 27 St. 139, 645; 28 St. 898, 939; 29 St. 354; 30 St. 75, 84, 87, 90, 94, 497, 500, 505, 679; 31 St. 237, 861, 1062, 1068, 1077; 32 St. 178. *Rp.* 36 St. 855. *S.* 32 St. 742, 744, 982, 1031; 33 St. 189, 989, 1048; 34 St. 9; 35 St. 8, 70, 268; 36 St. 269, 1058; 37 St. 196. *Cited:* Brosius, 23 Case & Com. 739; Cain, 2 Minn. L. Rev. 177; Reeves, 23 Case & Com. 727; 25 Op. A. G. 582; 34 Op. A. G. 439; 36 Op. A. G. 98; Op. Sol., M. 6083, Oct. 29, 1921; M. 25258, June 26, 1929; Op. A. G. to Sec'y of Int., Oct. 5, 1929; Memo. Sol., Aug. 28, 1934, Dec. 26, 1935; 38 L. D. 422; 40 L. D. 179; 48 L. D. 455; 48 L. D. 472; Bowling, 233 U. S. 528; Buster, 135 Fed. 947; Creek, 78 C. Cls. 474; Egan, 246 U. S. 227; Ewert, 259 U. S. 129; Gibson, 131 Fed. 39; Hallowell, 221 U. S. 317; Jefferson, 247 U. S. 288; Leecy, 190 Fed. 289; Locke, 287 Fed. 276; Medawakanton, 57 C. Cls. 357; Mille Lac, 46 C. Cls. 424; Minnesota, 305 U. S. 382; Morris, 194 U. S. 384; National, 147 Fed. 87; N. Y. Inds., 40 C. Cls. 448; Oneida, 89 C. Cls. 116; Reynolds, 236 U. S. 58; Schellenbarger, 236 U. S. 68; Sizemore, 235 U. S. 441; U. S. v. Boss, 160 Fed. 132; U. S. v. Comet, 202 Fed. 849; U. S. v. Gray, 201 Fed. 291; U. S. v. Hall, 171 Fed. 214; U. S. v. Jackson, 280 U. S. 183; U. S. v. Law, 250 Fed. 218; U. S. v. Leslie, 167 Fed. 670; U. S. v. Park, 188 Fed. 383; U. S. v. Thurston, 143 Fed. 287; U. S. v. Walker, 104 Fed. 334; U. S. v. Watashe, 102 F. 2d 428; U. S. Exp. 191 Fed. 673; Ute, 45 C. Cls. 440; Washington, 235 U. S. 422; Woodward, 238 U. S. 284.

[95] *A.* 35 St. 102.

[96] *Sg.* 10 St. 163, 167, 168; 18 St. 333, 334; 19 St. 62.

[97] *Sg.* 27 St. 281. *S.* 37 St. 679.

[98] *Ag.* 25 St. 642. *Rpg.* 30 St. 90. *A.* 34 St. 325; 35 St. 268. *S.* 32 St. 982; 33 St. 1048; 34 St. 325; 36 St. 855. *Cited:* 31 Op. A. G. 95; Memo. Sol. Off., Oct. 22, 1936; 44 L. D. 531; Chippewa, 305 U. S. 479; Mille Lac, 46 C. Cls. 424; Morrison, 266 U. S. 481; Westling, 60 F. 2d 398.

[99] *Sg.* 1 St. 437. *Cited:* Ex p. Carter, 4 Ind. T. 539.

[1] *Sg.* 4 St. 730; 31 St. 231, 861, 869, secs. 7 & 8. *Ag.* 31 St. 861, 862, sec. 3, par. 2; 31 St. 864, sec. 8; 31 St. 871, sec. 37. *Rg.* 31 St. 864, 868, sec. 24. *S.* 33 St. 189; 34 St. 325; 38 St. 582; 42 St. 831. *Cited:* 25 Op. A. G. 163; 26 Op. A. G. 317; 34 Op. A. G. 275; Op. Sol., D. 40462, Oct. 31, 1917, M. 13807, Jan. 23, 1925; Memo. Sol., Sept. 17, 1936; 53 I. D. 502; Adkins, 235 U. S. 417; Alfrey, 168 Fed. 231; Armstrong, 195 Fed. 137; Bagby, 60 F. 2d 80; Bartlett, 218 Fed. 380; Blackburn, 6 Ind. T. 232; Brader, 246 U. S. 88; Brann, 192 Fed. 427; Campbell, 248 U. S. 169; Carter, 12 F. 2d 780; Creek, 78 C. Cls. 474; Ex p. Webb, 225 U. S. 663; Fink, 248 U. S. 399; Fish, 52 F. 2d 544; Fulsom, 85 F. 2d 84; Gilcrease, 249 U. S. 178; Grayson, 267 U. S. 352; Harris, 264 U. S. 103; Harris, 166 Fed. 109; Heckman, 224 U. S. 413; Hill, 289 Fed. 511; Hopkins, 285 Fed. 95; In re Lands, 199 Fed. 811; Iowa, 217 Fed. 11; Jefferson, 247 U. S. 288; King, 64 F. 2d 979; Knight, 28 F. 2d 481; Lanham, 244 U. S. 582; McDougal,

32 St. 507; June 30, 1902; C. 1328—An Act Making appropriation for the support of the Army for the fiscal year ending June 30, 1903.

32 St. 552; July 1, 1902; C. 1351—An Act Making appropriations to supply deficiencies in the appropriations for the fiscal year ending June 30, 1902, and for prior years, and for other purposes.[2]

32 St. 630; July 1, 1902; C. 1355—An Act For the further distribution of the reports of the Supreme Court, and for other purposes.

32 St. 631; July 1, 1902; C. 1356—An Act To amend an Act entitled "An Act for the protection of the lives of miners in the Territories."[3]

32 St. 636; July 1, 1902; C. 1361—An Act To accept, ratify, and confirm a proposed agreement submitted by the Kansas or Kaw Indians of Oklahoma, and for other purposes.[4]

32 St. 641; July 1, 1902; C. 1362—An Act to ratify and confirm an agreement with the Choctaw and Chickasaw tribes of Indians, and for other purposes.[5]

32 St. 657; July 1, 1902; C. 1363—An Act Authorizing the adjustment of rights of settlers on the Navajo Indian Reservation, Territory of Arizona.[6]

32 St. 716; July 1, 1902; C. 1375—An Act To provide for the allotment of the lands of the Cherokee Nation, for the disposition of town sites therein, and for other purposes.[7]

32 St. 730; July 1, 1902; C. 1380—An Act To provide for the sale of the unsold portion of the Umatilla Indian Reservation.[8]

32 St. 742; J. Res. May 27, 1902; No. 24—Joint Resolution Fixing the time when certain provisions of the Indian appropriation Act for the year ending June 30, 1903, shall take effect.[9]

32 St. 742; J. Res. May 27, 1902; No. 25—Joint Resolution Fixing the time when a certain provision of the Indian appropriation Act for the year ending June 30, 1903, shall take effect.[10]

32 St. 744; June 19, 1902; J. Res. No. 31—Joint Resolution Supplementing and modifying certain provisions of the Indian appropriation Act for the year ending June 30, 1903.[11]

32 St. 774; Jan. 21, 1903; C. 195—An Act To amend an Act entitled "An Act to provide for the use of timber and stone for domestic and industrial purposes in the Indian Territory," approved June 6, 1900.[12]

32 St. 791; Feb. 2, 1903; C. 349—An Act To enable the Secretary of Agriculture to more effectually suppress and prevent the spread of contagious and infectious diseases of live stock, and for other purposes.[13]

32 St. 792; Feb. 2, 1903; C. 350—An Act Fixing the punishment for the larceny of horses, cattle, and other live stock in the Indian Territory, and for other purposes.[14]

32 St. 793; Feb. 2, 1903; C. 351—An Act Conferring jurisdiction upon the circuit and district courts for the district of South Dakota in certain cases, and for other purposes.[15] 18 U. S. C. 549; 28 U. S. C. 51.

32 St. 795; Feb. 3, 1905; C. 399—An Act Providing for allotments of lands in severalty to the Indians of the Lac Courte Oreille and Lac du Flambeau reservations in the State of Wisconsin.[16]

32 St. 803; Feb. 7, 1903; C. 514—An Act Providing for free homesteads on the public lands for actual and bona fide settlers in the north one-half of the Colville Indian Reservation, State of Washington, and reserving the public lands for that purpose.[17]

32 St. 820; Feb. 9, 1903; C. 531—An Act To extend the provisions of chapter 8, title 32 of the Revised Statutes of the United States, entitled "Reservation and sale of town sites on the public lands" to the ceded Indian lands in the State of Minnesota.[18] 25 U. S. C. 427. (See USCA Historical Note).

32 St. 822; Feb. 11, 1903; C. 542—An Act Granting to the State of California 640 acres of land in lieu of section 16, township 7 south, range 8 east, San Bernardino meridian, State of California, now occupied by the Torros band or village of Mission Indians.[19]

32 St. 841; Feb. 19, 1903; C. 707—An Act Providing for record of deeds and other conveyances and instruments of writing in Indian Territory, and for other purposes.[20]

32 St. 854; Feb. 25, 1903; C. 755—An Act Making appropriations

---

237 U. S. 372; McKee, 201 Fed. 74; Marlin, 276 U. S. 58; Moore, 167 Fed. 826; Morrison, 154 Fed. 617; Muskogee, 165 Fed. 179; Nunn, 216 Fed. 330; Parker, 250 U. S. 235; Parker, 250 U. S. 66; Pigeon, 237 U. S. 386; Pitman, 64 F. 2d 740; Priddy, 204 Fed. 955; Reed, 197 Fed. 419; Reynolds, 236 U. S. 58; Roubedeaux, 23 F. 2d 277; Schellenbarger, 236 U. S. 68; Self, 28 F. 2d 590; Shulthis, 225 U. S. 561; Sizemore, 235 U. S. 441; Skelton, 235 U. S. 206; Stewart, 295 U. S. 403; Sunday, 248 U. S. 545; Sweet, 245 U. S. 192; Taylor, 230 Fed. 580; Tiger, 4 F. 2d 714; Tiger, 221 U. S. 286; U. S. v. Bartlett, 235 U. S. 72; U. S. v. Black, 247 Fed. 942; U. S. v. Board, 284 Fed. 103; U. S. v. Cook, 225 Fed. 756; U. S. v. Equitable, 283 U. S. 738; U. S. v. Ferguson, 247 U. S. 175; U. S. v. Gypsy, 10 F. 2d 487; U. S. v. Hayes, 20 F. 2d 873; U. S. v. Jacobs, 195 Fed. 707; U. S. v. Knight, 206 Fed. 145; U. S. v. Shock, 187 Fed. 862; U. S. v. Shock, 187 Fed. 870; U. S. v. Smith, 266 Fed. 740; U. S. v. Southern, 9 F. 2d 664; U. S. v. Tiger, 19 F. 2d 35; U. S. v. Woods, 223 Fed. 316; Washington, 235 U. S. 422; Welty, 231 Fed. 930; Woodward, 238 U. S. 284.

[2] *S.* 32 St. 982.

[3] *Ag.* 26 St. 1105, sec. 6.

[4] *Sg.* 9 St. 842; 21 St. 70. *A.* 42 St. 1589. *S.* 33 St. 1048, 1561; 43 St. 176, 1133; 44 St. 134. *Cited:* Cabell, 3 Okla. S. B. J. 208; 35 Op. A. G. 1; Op. Sol., M. 14237, Dec. 23, 1924; M. 27996, May 14, 1935; Kansas, 80 C. Cls. 264.

[5] *Sg.* 7 St. 335; 14 St. 769; 16 St. 570; 17 St. 136; 18 St. 35, 450; 29 St. 321, 339; 30 St. 495, 503, 508, 513; 31 St. 221. *S.* 32 St. 982, 1031; 33 St. 189, 544; 34 St. 325, 1015; 36 St. 269; 37 St. 67, 518; 40 St. 433, 561; 48 St. 1467. *Cited:* 24 Op. A. G. 689; 25 Op. A. G. 152; 25 Op. A. G. 320; 25 Op. A. G. 460; 26 Op. A. G. 127; 27 Op. A. G. 530; 29 Op. A. G. 131; 34 Op. A. G. 275; 35 Op. A. G. 259; 1 L. D. Memo. 99; Op. Sol., M. 7316, May 28, 1924; M. 18772, Dec 24, 1926; 53 I. D. 502; Alfrey, 168 Fed. 231; Arnold, 4 F. 2d 838; Ballinger, 216 U. S. 240; Bartlett, 218 Fed. 380; Blundell, 267 U. S. 373; Brader, 246 U. S. 88; Chickasaw, 193 U. S. 115; Chickasaw, 87 C. Cls. 91; Choate, 224 U. S. 665; Choctaw, 75 C. Cls. 494; Choctaw, 81 C. Cls. 1; Choctaw, 83 C. Cls. 140; Choctaw, 6 Ind. T. 515; Davis, 5 Ind. T. 47; Dawes, 5 Ind. T. 50; Dawes, 5 Ind. T. 53; Duncan, 245 U. S. 308; English, 224 U. S. 680; Ex p. Webb, 225 U. S. 663; Fink, 248 U. S. 392; Fish, 52 F. 2d 544; Fleming, 215 U. S. 56; Frame, 180 Fed. 785; Gannon, 243 U. S. 108; Garfield, 211 U. S. 264; Garfield, 211 U. S. 249; Gleason, 224 U. S. 679; Gooding, 5 Ind. T. 578; Harris, 7 Ind. T. 532; Hayes, 168 Fed. 221; Hill, 242 U. S. 361; In re Jessie's, 259 Fed. 94; In re Lands, 199 Fed. 811; Joines, 274 U. S. 544; Kelly, 7 Ind. T. 541; Longest, 276 U. S. 69; McCalib, 83 C. Cls. 79; McMurray, 62 C. Cls. 458; M. K. & T. Ry., 47 C. Cls. 59; Mullen, 234 U. S. 192; Mullen, 250 U. S. 590; Mullen, 224 U. S. 448; Ne-Kah-Wah-She-Tun-Kah, 290 Fed. 303; Sayer, 7 Ind. T. 675; Sharrock, 6 Ind. T. 466; Taylor, 235 U. S. 42; Thomason, 206 Fed. 895; Tiger, 221 U. S. 286; U. S. v. Dowden, 220 Fed. 277; U. S. v. Marshall, 210 Fed. 595; U. S. v. One Cadillac, 255 Fed. 173; U. S. v. Reynolds, 250 U. S. 104; U. S. v. Richards, 27 F. 2d 284; U. S. v. Smith, 266 Fed. 740; U. S. v. Wright, 53 F. 2d 300; Wallace, 6 Ind. T. 32; Wallace, 204 U. S. 415; Whitchurch, 92 F. 2d 249; Williams, 239 U. S. 414; Williams, 218 Fed. 797; Winton, 255 U. S. 373.

[6] *Sg.* Ex. Or. Jan. 6, 1880.

[7] *Ag.* 30 St. 495; 31 St. 221. *S.* 32 St. 982; 33 St. 189; 34 St. 325, 634, 1015; 38 St. 582. *Cited:* 25 Op. A. G. 171; 26 Op. A. G. 330; 26 Op. A. G. 351; 34 Op. A. G. 275; Op. Sol., D. 40462, Oct. 31, 1917; Anicker, 246 U. S. 110; Barnsdall, 200 Fed. 522; Barnsdall, 200 Fed. 519; Bartlett, 218 Fed. 380; Bd. of Comm'rs of Tulsa, 94 F. 2d 450; Brown, 44 C. Cls. 283; Bunch, 263 U. S. 250; Cherokee, 203 U. S. 76; Cherokee, 85 C. Cls. 76; Cherokee, 270 U. S. 476; Cherokee, 223 U. S. 108; Chisholm, 273 Fed. 589; Delaware, 193 U. S. 127; Delaware, 74 C. Cls. 368; Dick, 6 Ind. T. 85, 89 S. W. 664; Eastern Cherokees, 225 U. S. 572; Eastern Cherokees, 45 C. Cls. 104; Eastern or Emigrant, 82 C. Cls. 180; Ex p. Webb, 225 U. S. 663; Fish, 52 F. 2d 544; Garfield, 34 App. D. C. 70; Gritts, 224 U. S. 640; Harnage, 242 U. S. 386; Heckman, 224 U. S. 413; Henny, 191 Fed. 132; Holmes, 33 F. 2d 688; In re Lands, 199 Fed. 811; Jennings, 192 Fed. 507; Knight, 228 U. S. 6; Lowe, 223 U. S. 95; M. K. & T. Ry., 47 C. Cls. 59; Muskrat, 219 U. S. 346; Persons, 40 C. Cls. 411; Robinson, 221 Fed. 398; Ross, 232 U. S. 110; Ross, 227 U. S. 530; Sperry, 264 U. S. 488; Sunday, 248 U. S. 545; Talley, 246 U. S. 104; Tiger, 221 U. S. 286; Truskett, 236 U. S. 223; U. S. v. Board, 284 Fed. 103; U. S. v. Cherokee, 202 U. S. 101; U. S. v. Halsell, 247 Fed. 390; U. S. v. Reynolds, 250 U. S. 104; U. S. v. Smith, 266 Fed. 740; U. S. v. Whitmire, 236 Fed. 474; Welch, 15 F. 2d 184.

[8] *Ag.* 23 St. 340. *S.* 33 St. 1048; 37 St. 655; 39 St. 923. *Cited:* U. S. v. Raley, 173 Fed. 159.

[9] *Sg.* 32 St. 245.

[10] *Sg.* 30 St. 266. *Cited:* Gibson, 131 Fed. 39; Reynolds, 236 U. S. 58; Schellenbarger, 236 U. S. 68; Sizemore, 235 U. S. 441. Op. Sol., D. 46987, Nov. 13, 1922; Memo. Sol., Mar. 18, 1936; Sept. 17, 1936; 49 L. D. 348; 53 I. D. 48; 53 I. D. 502; Anicker, 246 U. S. 110; Barnsdall, 200 Fed. 522; Barnsdall, 200 Fed. 519; Bartlett, 218 Fed. 380; Bd. of Com'rs of Tulsa Co., 94 F. 2d 450; Brown, 44 C. Cls. 283; Bunch, 263 U. S. 250; Cherokee, 85 C. Cls. 76; Cherokee, 203 U. S. 76; Cherokee, 270 U. S. 476; Cherokee, 223 U. S. 108; Chisholm, 273 Fed. 589; Delaware, 74 C. Cls. 368; Delaware, 193 U. S. 127; Dick, 6 Ind. T. 85; Eastern Cherokees, 45 C. Cls. 104; Eastern or Emigrant, 82 C. Cls. 180; Eastern Cherokees, 225 U. S. 572; Ex p. Webb, 225 U. S. 663; Fish, 52 F. 2d 544; Garfield, 34 App. D. C. 70; Gritts, 224 U. S. 640; Harnage, 242 U. S. 386; Heckman, 224 U. S. 413; Henny, 191 Fed. 132; Holmes, 33 F. 2d 688; In re Lands, 199 Fed. 811; Jennings, 192 Fed. 507; Knight, 228 U. S. 6; Lowe, 223 U. S. 95; M. K. & T. Ry., 46 C. Cls. 59; Muskrat, 219 U. S. 346; Persons, 40 C. Cls. 411; Robinson, 221 Fed. 398; Ross, 232 U. S. 110; Ross, 227 U. S. 530; Sperry, 264 U. S. 488; Sunday, 248 U. S. 545; Talley, 246 U. S. 104; Tiger, 221 U. S. 286; Truskett, 236 U. S. 223; U. S. v. Board, 284 Fed. 103; U. S. v. Cherokee, 202 U. S. 101; U. S. v. Halsell, 247 Fed. 390; U. S. v. Reynolds, 250 U. S. 104; U. S. v. Smith, 266 Fed. 740; U. S. v. Whitmire, 236 Fed. 474; Welch, 15 F. 2d 184.

[11] *Sg.* 24 St. 388; 32 St. 260, 263, 264, 266. *Rp.* 33 St. 1048. *S.* 32 St. 982; 34 St. 325. *Cited:* Op. Sol. 2.2121, Apr. 12, 1927; Gibson, 131 Fed. 39; U. S. v. Gray, 201 Fed. 291; Ute, 45 C. Cls. 440.

[12] *Sg.* 30 St. 501, sec. 16. *Ag.* 31 St. 660. *S.* 33 St. 299.

[13] *Sg.* 23 St. 31, sec. 4.

[14] *Ag.* 4 St. 731; 11 St. 401.

[15] *A.* 35 St. 1088; 47 St. 336. *Cited:* Hatten, 99 F. 2d 501; Hollister, 145 Fed. 773; U. S. v. Frank Black Spotted Horse, 282 Fed. 349; U. S. v. La Plant, 200 Fed. 92; U. S. v. Quiver, 241 U. S. 602.

[16] *Sg.* 10 St. 1109.

[17] *Sg.* 12 St. 503; 26 St. 417; 31 St. 1965.

[18] *Sg.* 12 St. 754; 13 St. 343, 344, 530; 14 St. 541; 15 St. 67; 16 St. 183; 18 St. 254; 19 St. 264, 392.

[19] *Sg.* 26 St. 712.

[20] *S.* 33 St. 189, 1048; 34 St. 325, 1015. *Cited:* Adkins, 235 U. S. 417.

for the legislative, executive, and judicial expenses of the Government for the fiscal year ending June 30, 1904, and for other purposes.[21]

32 St. 927; Mar. 2, 1903; C. 975—An Act Making appropriation for the support of the Army for the fiscal year ending June 30, 1904.

32 St. 982; Mar. 3, 1903; C. 994—An Act Making appropriations for the current and contingent expenses of the Indian Department and for fulfilling treaty stipulations with various Indian tribes for the fiscal year ending June 30, 1904, and for other purposes.[22] Sec. 10—25 U. S. C. 262.

32 St. 1031; Mar. 3, 1903; C. 1006—An Act Making appropriations to supply deficiencies in the appropriations for the fiscal year ending June 30, 1903, and for prior years, and for other purposes.[23]

32 St. 1083; Mar. 3, 1903; C. 1007—An Act Making appropriations for sundry civil expenses of the Government for the fiscal year ending June 30, 1904, and for other purposes.

32 St. 1241; Feb. 27, 1902; C. 44—An Act Granting a pension to Sarah McCord.

32 St. 1261; Feb. 27, 1902; C. 133—An Act Granting an increase of pension to Virginia Terrill.

32 St. 1279; Mar. 21, 1902; C. 239—An Act Granting a pension to Adella G. Chandler.

32 St. 1287; Mar. 28, 1902; C. 283—An Act Granting a pension to Elizabeth M. Folds.

32 St. 1290; Mar. 28, 1902; C. 297—An Act Granting a pension to Melvina C. Stith.

32 St. 1294; Mar. 28, 1902; C. 314—An Act Granting an increase of pension to John Garner.

32 St. 1314; Apr. 4, 1902; C. 404—An Act Granting a pension to Alice Angel.

32 St. 1316; Apr. 4, 1902; C. 413—An Act Granting an increase of pension to David A. Frier.

32 St. 1352; Apr. 28, 1902; C. 602—An Act Granting an increase of pension to Mary J. Clark.

32 St. 1355; Apr. 28, 1902; C. 614—An Act Granting an increase of pension to Mariah J. Anderson.

32 St. 1355; Apr. 28, 1902; C. 616—An Act Granting a pension to Esther A. C. Hardee.

32 St. 1357; Apr. 28, 1902; C. 626—An Act Granting a pension to James F. P. Johnston.

32 St. 1365; Apr. 29, 1902; C. 665—An Act Granting an increase of pension to William O. Gray.

32 St. 1377; May 5, 1902; C. 730—An Act Granting an increase of pension to Isaac Phipps.

32 St. 1380; May 5, 1902; C. 743—An Act Granting a pension to John R. Homer Scott.

32 St. 1380; May 5, 1902; C. 747—An Act Granting a pension to Amanda C. Bayliss.

32 St. 1386; May 5, 1902; C. 773—An Act Granting an increase of pension to Delania Ferguson.

32 St. 1388; May 15, 1902; C. 791—An Act For the relief of Mrs. Arivella D. Meeker.

32 St. 1389; May 17, 1902; C. 798—An Act Granting a pension to Rebecca Coppinger.

32 St. 1395; May 23, 1902; C. 831—An Act Granting a pension to Frances J. Abercrombie.

32 St. 1400; May 23, 1902; C. 852—An Act Granting a pension to Matthew V. Ellis.

32 St. 1411; May 28, 1902; C. 907—An Act Granting a pension to Hester A. Furr.

32 St. 1468; June 27, 1902; C. 1209—An Act Granting a pension to Martha E. Kendrick.

32 St. 1491; June 30, 1902; C. 1346—An Act Granting an increase of pension to Elizabeth A. Turner.

32 St. 1492; June 30, 1902; C. 1348—An Act For the relief of Joseph H. Penny, John W. Penny, Thomas Penny, and Harvey Penny, surviving partners of Penny and Sons.

32 St. 1492; June 30, 1902; C. 1349—An Act For the relief of John Hornick.

32 St. 1493; July 1, 1902; C. 1388—An Act Granting a pension to William G. Miller.

32 St. 1497; July 1, 1902; C. 1405—An Act Granting an increase of pension to Caroline A. Hammond.

32 St. 1514; Dec. 27, 1902; C. 54—An Act Granting an increase of pension to Mary A. B. Scott.

32 St. 1526; Jan. 12, 1903; C. 120—An Act Granting an increase of pension to Melinda Heard.

32 St. 1555; Jan. 22, 1903; C. 261—An Act Granting an increase of pension to William G. Cantley.

32 St. 1569; Jan. 23, 1903; C. 323—An Act Granting a pension to Dicey Woodall.

32 St. 1577; Feb. 2, 1903; C. 379—An Act Granting an increase of pension to William Flinn.

32 St. 1578; Feb. 2, 1903; C. 384—An Act Granting an increase of pension to Mary Manes.

32 St. 1580; Feb. 2, 1903; C. 391—An Act Granting an increase of pension to Thomas Starrat.

32 St. 1580; Feb. 2, 1903; C. 392—An Act Granting an increase of pension to Stephen J. Houston.

32 St. 1581; Feb. 2, 1903; C. 396—An Act Granting a pension to Mary J. Ivey.

32 St. 1600; Feb. 5, 1903; C. 491—An Act Granting a pension to Susan Kennedy.

32 St. 1606; Feb. 6, 1903; C. 511—An Act For the relief of the heirs of Mary Clark and Francis or Jenny Clark, deceased, and for other purposes.[24]

32 St. 1607; Feb. 7, 1903; C. 520—An Act For the relief of Colonel H. B. Freeman.

32 St. 1607; Feb. 7, 1903; C. 522—An Act Granting an increase of pension to James Hunter.

32 St. 1644; Feb. 19, 1903; C. 711—An Act Granting a pension to Susan Kent.

32 St. 1648; Feb. 19, 1903; C. 732—An Act Granting a pension to Delania Preston.

32 St. 1677; Feb. 28, 1903; C. 882—An Act Granting a pension to Margaret J. McCranie.

32 St. 1696; Feb. 28, 1903; C. 965—An Act Granting an increase of pension to Elbert H. Dagnall.

32 St. 1697; Mar. 2, 1903; C. 984—An Act Granting a pension to Lavinia Cook.

32 St. 1703; Mar. 3, 1903; C. 1043—An Act Granting an increase of pension to Emily Hawkins.

32 St. 1729; Mar. 3, 1903; C. 1159—An Act Granting an increase of pension to Mary Ann Garrison.

32 St. 1730; Mar. 3, 1903; C. 1162—An Act Granting a pension to Nancy McGuire.

32 St. 1751; Mar. 3, 1903; C. 1257—An Act Granting an increase of pension to Fannie T. Fisher.

32 St. 1753; Mar. 3, 1903; C. 1267—An Act Granting an increase of pension to Alexander T. Sullinger, alias Alexander Patillo.

32 St. 1768; May 10, 1902—Concurrent Res. Revised Course of Study for Indian Schools.

32 St. 1769; May 13, 1902—Concurrent Res. Report of Commission to the Five Civilized Tribes.

33 STAT.

33 St. 15; Feb. 18, 1904; C. 160—An Act Making appropriations to supply urgent deficiencies in the appropriations for the fiscal year ending June 30, 1904, and for prior years, and for other purposes.[25]

33 St. 46; Feb. 20, 1904; C. 161—An Act To authorize the sale of a part of what is known as the Red Lake Indian Reservation, in the State of Minnesota.[26]

33 St. 60; Mar. 7, 1904; C. 405—An Act Establishing a United States court at Marietta, Indian Territory.

33 St. 65; Mar. 11, 1904; C. 505—An Act Authorizing the Secre-

[21] *Cited:* 25 Op. A. G. 460; Locke, 287 Fed. 276.

[22] *Sg.* 4 St. 442; 7 St. 46, 51, 85, 99, 114, 185, 212, 236, 242, 296, 317, 320, 321, 425, 541, 596; 9 St. 35, 842, 855; 10 St. 1071, 1079; 11 St. 614, 702, 729, 744; 12 St. 981, 1173; 13 St. 675; 14 St. 687; 15 St. 622, 640, 676; 16 St. 40, 720; 19 St. 256, 287; 22 St. 43; 24 St. 219, 388; 25 St. 644, 645, 688, 888, 894; 26 St. 1028, 1038; 27 St. 139, 558, 624, 645; 28 St. 889, 939; 29 St. 354; 30 St. 87, 568, 596, 909; 31 St. 237, 869, 1066, 1074; 32 St. 257, 260, 263, 264, 401, 575, 646, 726, 744. *A.* 33 St. 189; 34 St. 325. *S.* 33 St. 189, 1048; 34 St. 9, 634; 42 St. 831; 24 Op. A. G. 623; 25 Op. A. G. 163; 25 Op. A. G. 320; 26 Op. A. G. 330; 27 Op. A. G. 588; 35 Op. A. G. 421; Memo. Sol., Nov. 20, 1934; Bailey, 43 C. Cls. 353; Ballinger, 216 U. S. 240; Chippewa, 80 C. Cls. 410; Creek, 78 C. Cls. 474; Eastern Cherokees, 45 C. Cls. 104; Eastern or Emigrant, 82 C. Cls. 180; Eastern Cherokees, 225 U. S. 572; Goat, 224 U. S. 458; In re Lands, 199 Fed. 811; McCalib, 83 C. Cls. 79; McMurray, 62 C. Cls. 458; Medawakanton, 57 C. Cls. 357; Owen, 217 U. S. 488; Rainbow, 161 Fed. 835; Sweet, 245 U. S. 192; U. S. v. Board, 284 Fed. 103; U. S. v. Cherokee, 202 U. S. 101; U. S. v. Seminole, 299 U. S. 417; U. S. v. Watashe, 102 F. 2d 428; Winton, 255 U. S. 373.

[23] *Sg.* 26 St. 853; 30 St. 679; 31 St. 1081, 1155; 32 St. 257, 276, 656.

[24] *Sg.* 24 St. 388; 26 St. 794.

[25] *Sg.* 24 St. 505; 26 St. 853. *S.* 33 St. 583.

[26] *Sg.* 12 St. 393. *S.* 34 St. 325, 1015; 35 St. 70, 465; 36 St. 265; 40 St. 917. *Cited:* Tydings, 23 Case & Com. 743; Sol. Op. M. 29616, Feb. 19, 1938; Chippewa, 80 C. Cls. 410; Chippewa, 301 U. S. 358; Morrison, 266 U. S. 481.

tary of the Interior to grant right of way for pipe lines through Indian lands.[27] Sec. 1 & 2—25 U. S. C. 321.[28]

33 St. 66; Mar. 11, 1904; C. 506—An Act Permitting the Kiowa, Chickasha and Fort Smith Ry. Co. to sell and convey its railroad and other property in the Indian Territory to the Eastern Oklahoma Ry. Co., and the Eastern Oklahoma Ry. Co. to lease all its railroad and other property in the Indian Territory to the Atchison, Topeka and Santa Fe Ry. Co., and thereafter to sell its railroad and other property to the said Atchison, Topeka and Santa Fe Ry. Co.[29]

33 St. 80; Mar. 14, 1904; C. 544—An Act Authorizing bail in criminal cases upon appeal in the courts of Indian Territory.

33 St. 85; Mar. 18, 1904; C. 716—An Act Making appropriations for the legislative, executive, and judicial expenses of the Government for the fiscal year ending June 30, 1905, and for other purposes.

33 St. 153; Mar. 30, 1904; C. 854—An Act Relating to ceded lands on the Fort Hall Indian Reservation.[30]

33 St. 154; Mar. 30, 1904; C. 855—An Act To authorize the State of South Dakota to select school and indemnity lands in the ceded portion of the Great Sioux Reservation, and for other purposes.

33 St. 189; Apr. 21, 1904; C. 1402—An Act Making appropriations for the current and contingent expenses of the Indian Department and for fulfilling treaty stipulations with various Indian tribes for the fiscal year ending June 30, 1905, and for other purposes.[31] Sec. 1, p. 191—25 U. S. C. 52a[32]; p. 211—25 U. S. C. 292[33]; p. 211, 43 U. S. C. 149.

33 St. 240; Apr. 21, 1904; C. 1410—An Act Permitting the Missouri, Kansas and Oklahoma R. Co. to sell its railroads and properties to the Missouri, Kansas and Texas Ry. Co.[34]

33 St. 254; Apr. 23, 1904; C. 1484—An Act To ratify and amend an agreement with the Sioux tribe of Indians of the Rosebud Reservation, in South Dakota, and making appropriation and provision to carry the same into effect.[35]

33 St. 259; Apr. 23, 1904; C. 1485—An Act Making appropriation for the support of the Army for the fiscal year ending June 30, 1905, and for other purposes.

33 St. 297; Apr. 23, 1904; C. 1489—An Act Amending the Act of Congress approved January 26, 1895, entitled "An Act authorizing the Secretary of the Interior to correct errors where double allotments of land have erroneously been made to an Indian, to correct errors in patents, and for other purposes."[36] 25 U. S. C. 343 (28 St. 641).

33 St. 299; Apr. 23, 1904; C. 1492—An Act To extend the provisions of the Act of January 21, 1903, to the Osage Reservation in Oklahoma Territory, and for other purposes.[37]

33 St. 299; Apr. 23, 1904; C. 1493—An Act Regulating the practice of medicine and surgery in the Indian Territory.

33 St. 302; Apr. 23, 1904; C. 1495—An Act For the survey and allotment of lands now embraced within the limits of the Flathead Indian Reservation, in the State of Montana, and the sale and disposal of all surplus lands after allotment.[38]

33 St. 311; Apr. 26, 1904; C. 1606—An Act To amend an Act entitled "An Act to amend an Act entitled 'An Act granting the right to the Omaha Northern Ry. Co. to construct a railway across and establish stations on the Omaha and Winnebago Reservation, in the State of Nebraska, and for other purposes,' by extending the time for the construction of said railway," by a further extension of time for the construction of said railway.[39]

33 St. 314; Apr. 27, 1904; C. 1614—An Act Permitting the Ozark and Cherokee Central R. Co. and the Arkansas Valley and Western Ry. Co., and each or either of them, to sell and convey their railroads and other property in the Indian Territory to the St. Louis and San Francisco R. Co. or to the Chicago, Rock Island and Pacific Ry. Co., and for other purposes.

33 St. 319; Apr. 27, 1904; C. 1620—An Act To modify and amend an agreement with the Indians of the Devils Lake Reservation, in North Dakota, to accept and ratify the same as amended, and making appropriation and provision to carry the same into effect.[40]

33 St. 352; Apr. 27, 1904; C. 1624—An Act To ratify and amend an agreement with the Indians of the Crow Reservation in Montana, and making appropriations to carry the same into effect.[41]

33 St. 394; Apr. 27, 1904; C. 1630—An Act Making appropriations to supply deficiencies in the appropriations for the fiscal year ending June 30, 1904, and for prior years, and for other purposes.[42]

33 St. 452; Apr. 28, 1904; C. 1762—An Act Making appropriations for sundry civil expenses of the Government for the fiscal year ending June 30, 1905, and for other purposes.

33 St. 519; Apr. 28, 1904; C. 1767—An Act To authorize the Absentee Wyandotte Indians to select certain lands, and for other purposes.[43]

33 St. 539; Apr. 28, 1904; C. 1786—An Act To provide allotments to Indians on White Earth Reservation in Minnesota.[44]

33 St. 539; Apr. 28, 1904; C. 1787—An Act To provide for the care and support of insane persons in the Indian Territory.[45]

33 St. 544; Apr. 28, 1904; C. 1794—An Act To authorize the Secretary of the Interior to add to the segregation of coal and asphalt lands in the Choctaw and Chickasaw nations, Indian Territory, and for other purposes.[46]

33 St. 550; Apr. 28, 1904; C. 1806—An Act In relation to pharmacy in the Indian Territory.

33 St. 565; Apr. 28, 1904; C. 1816—An Act Confirming the removal of restrictions upon alienation by the Puyallup Indians of the State of Washington of their allotted lands.[47]

33 St. 567; Apr. 28, 1904; C. 1819—An Act To permit the construction of a smelter on the Colville Indian Reservation, and for other purposes.[48]

33 St. 567; Apr. 28, 1904; C. 1820—An Act To ratify and amend an agreement with the Indians located upon the Grande Ronde Reservation, in the State of Oregon, and to make an appropriation to carry the same into effect.

33 St. 571; Apr. 28, 1904; C. 1822—An Act Authorizing the pay-

---

[27] *A.* 39 St. 969. *S.* 45 St. 442. *Cited:* Brown, 44 C. Cls. 283; Muskrat, 219 U. S. 346.

[28] *S.* 39 St. 973, sec. 1.

[29] *Sg.* 1 St. 137.

[30] *Sg.* 31 St. 672. *S.* 33 St. 2078, 2079.

[31] *Sg.* 4 St. 442; 7 St. 46, 51, 85, 99, 114, 183, 213, 236, 242, 317, 320, 425, 431, 442, 541, 545, 596; 9 St. 35, 855; 10 St. 1071, 1079; 11 St. 614, 702, 714, 729, 730, 757; 12 St. 628, 981, 1173; 13 St. 675; 14 St. 757; 15 St. 622, 637, 640, 658, 676; 16 St. 40, 355, 570, sec. 3; 720; 17 St. 136, sec. 1, 2; 18 St. 35, 450, sec. 9; 19 St. 256, 287; 22 St. 43; 24 St. 34, 219, 388; 25 St. 645, 688, 888, 894, 895; 26 St. 636, 794, 1028; 27 St. 139; 28 St. 695; 29 St. 341, 342, 354; 30 St. 90, 495, 800; 31 St. 27, 1078, 1442; 32 St. 257, 260, 263, 270, 388, 500, 641, 716; 36 St. 1058; 42 St. 831. *A.* 36 St. 1058. 32 St. 502, 648, 655, 722, 842, 992, 998. *Ag.* 26 St. 636; 32 St. 654. *Rpg.* 28 St. 910. *A.* 34 St. 325. *Rp.* 33 St. 1048; 34 St. 325; 48 St. 1224. *S.* 33 St. 1048, 1214; 34 St. 325, 1015; 35 St. 70, 781; 36 St. 269; 38 St. 582; 42 St. 831; 44 St. 453; 45 St. 200. *Cited:* Cavell, 3 Okla. S. B. J. 208; Tydings, 23 Case & Com. 743; 25 Op. A. G. 308; 26 Op. A. G. 127; 26 Op. A. G. 351; 27 Op. A. G. 530; 29 Op. A. G. 131; 1 L. D. Memo. 99; Op. Sol., M. 7996, Aug. 2, 1922; M. 7316, May 28, 1924; Memo. Ind. Off., Apr. 21, 1927; Letter of Asst. Sec'y to Sec'y of War, Feb. 26, 1932; Memo. Sol., July 1, 1938; 44 L. D. 524; 53 I. D. 471; Alfrey, 168 Fed. 231; Chisholm, 273 Fed. 589; Cully, 37 F. 2d 493; Delaware, 74 C. Cls. 368; Deming, 224 U. S. 471; Franklin, 233 U. S. 269; Glonn, 105 F. 2d 398; Goat, 224 U. S. 458; Green, 46 C. Cls. 68; Harris, 7 Ind. T. 532; Hawkins, 195 Fed. 345; In re Lands, 199 Fed. 811; Lanham, 244 U. S. 582; Medawakanton, 57 C. Cls. 357; Moore, 43 F. 2d 822; Mullen, 250 U. S. 590; New York Indians, 41 C. Cls. 462; New York Indians, 40 C. Cls. 448; Rogers, 263 Fed. 160; Sayer, 7 Ind. T. 675; Tiger, 22 F. 2d 786; U. S. v. Benewah, 290 Fed. 628; U. S. v. Board, 284 Fed. 103; U. S. v. Dowden, 220 Fed. 277; U. S. v. Ferry, 24 F. Supp. 399; U. S. v. Jacobs, 195 Fed. 707; U. S. v. Shock, 187 Fed. 862; U. S. v. Smith, 266 Fed. 740; U. S. v. Watashe, 102 F. 2d 428; U. S. v. Whitmire, 236 Fed. 474; Vinson, 44 F. 2d 772; Welch, 15 F. 2d 184; Williams, 239 U. S. 414; Woodward, 238 U. S. 284.

[32] *S.* 36 St. 125.

[33] Effective July 1, 1935, the appropriation provided for by this section was affected by Act June 26, 1934, sec. 4, 48 St. 1227. See Tit. 31, 725c (b).

[34] *Cited:* Moore, 167 Fed. 826.

[35] *S.* 33 St. 700.

[36] *Ag.* 28 St. 641. *Cited:* Op. Sol., M. 12509, Aug. 27, 1924; M. 14233, Apr. 24, 1925; 34 L. D. 252; 35 L. D. 80; 38 L. D. 556; 43 L. D. 84; Bisek, 5 F. 2d 994; La Clair, 184 Fed. 128; La Roque, 239 U. S. 62; Mandler, 52 F. 2d 718; U. S. v. Chehalis, 217 Fed. 281; U. S. v. La Roque, 198 Fed. 645.

[37] *Ag.* 31 St. 660; 32 St. 774. *S.* 34 St. 539.

[38] *Sg.* 12 St. 975; 17 St. 833, sec. 1. *A.* 33 St. 1048; 34 St. 325; 35 St. 444, 781; 36 St. 296; 40 St. 1203. *S.* 34 St. 205; 35 St. 70, 251; 38 St. 510; 39 St. 123. *Cited:* Pronovost, 232 U. S. 487; Op. Sol., M. 11410, Jan. 28, 1924, M. 12498, June 6, 1924; 49 L. D. 376; 53 I. D. 154.

[39] *Sg.* 30 St. 344; 32 St. 183.

[40] *Sg.* 12 St. 393, sec. 8; 17 St. 338, sec. 1; 26 St. 794. *A.* 34 St. 1015. *S.* 33 St. 700; 34 St. 325; 36 St. 269. *Cited:* Sisseton, 58 C. Cls. 302.

[41] *Sg.* 12 St. 393, sec. 8; 17 St. 338, sec. 1; 29 St. 341; 32 St. 388. *S.* 34 St. 205; 35 St. 781; 41 St. 751. *Cited:* Tydings, 28 Case & Com. 743; 48 L. D. 479; U. S. v. Powers, 305 U. S. 527; U. S. v. 12 Bottles, 201 Fed. 191; U. S. v. Powers, 305 U. S. 527.

[42] *Sg.* 26 St. 853; 31 St. 1074.

[43] *Sg.* 28 St. 286; 28 St. 876.

[44] *Sg.* 16 St. 721; 25 St. 643; 26 St. 794.

[45] *Cited:* Op. Sol., M. 15954, Jan. 8, 1927; 35 L. D. 148; 44 L. D. 531; Chippewa, 301 U. S. 358; Fairbanks, 223 U. S. 215; Gravelle, 253 Fed. 549; Leecy, 190 Fed. 289; Lemieux, 15 F. 2d 518; U. S. v. First, 234 U. S. 245; U. S. v. Waller, 243 U. S. 452; Vezina, 245 Fed. 411; Woodbury, 170 Fed. 802.

[46] *Sg.* 32 St. 641.

[47] *Sg.* 27 St. 633.

[48] *Sg.* 1 St. 137. *Cited:* Dull, 222 Fed. 471.

ment of the Choctaw and Chickasaw town-site fund, and for other purposes.[49]

33 St. 578; Apr. 28, 1904; C. 1824—An Act To provide for additional United States judges in the Indian Territory, and for other purposes.[50]

33 St. 583; Mar. 17, 1904; J. Res. No. 10—Joint Resolution Authorizing the Secretary of the Interior to use five thousand dollars of the amount appropriated by the Act approved February 18, 1904, (Public Numbered 22), for clerical work and labor connected with the sale and leasing of Creek lands and the leasing of Cherokee lands in Indian Territory.[51]

33 St. 591; Apr. 28, 1904; J. Res. No. 35—Joint Resolution Providing for the transfer of certain military rolls and records from the Interior and other Departments to the War Department. 5 U. S. C. 194.

33 St. 595; Dec. 21, 1904; C. 22—An Act To authorize the sale and disposition of surplus or unallotted lands of the Yakima Indian Reservation, in the State of Washington.[52]

33 St. 616; Jan. 27, 1905; C. 277—An Act To provide for the construction and maintenance of roads, the establishment and maintenance of schools, and the care and support of insane persons in the district of Alaska, and for other purposes.[53] Sec. 7—48 U. S. C. 169.

33 St. 631; Feb. 3, 1905; C. 297—An Act Making appropriations for the legislative, executive, and judicial expenses of the Government for the fiscal year ending June 30, 1906, and for other purposes.[54]

33 St. 700; Feb. 7, 1905; C. 545—An Act To provide for the extension of time within which homestead settlers may establish their residence upon certain lands which were heretofore a part of the Rosebud Indian Reservation within the limits of Gregory County, South Dakota, and upon certain lands which were heretofore a part of the Devils Lake Indian Reservation, in the State of North Dakota.[55]

33 St. 706; Feb. 8, 1905; C. 553—An Act To open to homestead settlement and entry the relinquished and undisposed of portions of the Round Valley Indian Reservation, in the State of California, and for other purposes.[56]

33 St. 708; Feb. 8, 1905; C. 556—An Act To allow the Minneapolis, Red Lake and Manitoba Ry. Co. to acquire certain lands in the Red Lake Indian Reservation, Minnesota.[57]

33 St. 714; Feb. 10, 1905; C. 571—An Act To extend the western boundary line of the State of Arkansas.

33 St. 724; Feb. 20, 1905; C. 592—An Act To authorize the registration of trade-marks used in commerce with foreign nations or among the several States or with Indian tribes, and to protect the same.[58] Sec. 1—15 U. S. C. 81; Sec. 2—15 U. S. C. 82; Sec. 16—15 U. S. C. 96; Sec. 30—15 U. S. C. 109.

33 St. 743; Feb. 24, 1905; C. 777—An Act For the allowance of certain claims reported by the Court of Claims, and for other purposes.[59]

33 St. 816; Feb. 27, 1905; C. 1159—An Act Confirming the title of the Saint Paul, Minneapolis and Manitoba Ry. Co. to certain lands in the State of Montana, and for other purposes.[60]

33 St. 821; Mar. 1, 1905; C. 1298—An Act Legalizing a certain ordinance of the city of Purcell, Indian Territory.

33 St. 824; Mar. 2, 1905; C. 1305—An Act To divide Washington into two judicial districts. 28 U. S. C. 193.

33 St. 827; Mar. 2, 1905; C. 1307—An Act Making appropriation for the support of the Army for the fiscal year ending June 30, 1906.

33 St. 989; Mar. 3, 1905; C. 1420—An Act To enable independent school district, numbered 12, Roseau County, Minnesota, to purchase certain lands.[61]

33 St. 991; Mar. 3, 1905; C. 1423—An Act Granting to the Choctaw, Oklahoma and Gulf Railroad Company the power to sell and convey to the Chicago, Rock Island and Pacific Ry. Co. all the railway property, rights, franchises, and privileges of the Choctaw, Oklahoma and Gulf R. Co., and for other purposes.

33 St. 1005; Mar. 3, 1905; C. 1439—An Act Extending the provisions of sec. 2321 of the Revised Statutes of the United States to homestead settlers on lands in the State of Minnesota ceded under the Act of Congress entitled "An Act for the relief and civilization of the Chippewa Indians in the State of Minnesota," approved January 14, 1889.[62]

33 St. 1006; Mar. 3, 1905; C. 1440—An Act Providing for the acquirement of water rights in the Spokane River along the southern boundary of the Spokane Indian Reservation, in the State of Washington, for the acquirement of lands on said reservation for sites for power purposes and the beneficial use of said water, and for other purposes.[63]

33 St. 1016; Mar. 3, 1905; C. 1452—An Act To ratify and amend an agreement with the Indians residing on the Shoshone or Wind River Indian Reservation in the State of Wyoming and to make appropriations for carrying the same into effect.[64]

33 St. 1033; Mar. 3, 1905; C. 1460—An Act To aid in quieting title to certain lands within the Klamath Indian Reservation, in the State of Oregon.[65]

33 St. 1048; Mar. 3, 1905; C. 1479—An Act Making appropriations for the current and contingent expenses of the Indian Department and for fulfilling treaty stipulations with various Indian tribes for the fiscal year ending June 30, 1906, and for other purposes.[66] Sec. 1, p. 1049—25 U. S. C. 272a.

33 St. 1117; Mar. 3, 1905; C. 1482—An Act Making appropriations for the construction, repair, and preservation of certain public works on rivers and harbors, and for other purposes.

33 St. 1156; Mar. 3, 1905; C. 1483—An Act Making appropriations for sundry civil expenses of the Government for the fiscal year ending June 30, 1906, and for other purposes.[67] P. 1206—31 U. S. C. 615.

33 St. 1214; Mar. 3, 1905; C. 1484—An Act Making appropriations to supply deficiencies in the appropriations for the fiscal year ending June 30, 1905, and for prior years, and for other purposes.[68]

33 St. 1326; Feb. 20, 1904; C. 162—An Act Granting a pension to Cynthia Thomas.

33 St. 1353; Feb. 26, 1904; C. 294—An Act Granting an increase of pension to Louiza Phillips.

---

[49] *Sg.* 30 St. 495. *A.* 43 St. 138.

[50] *Cited:* Dixon, 23 Case & Com. 712; Reeves, 23 Case & Com. 727; 25 Op. A. G. 532; 12 L. D. Memo. 73; Bartlett, 218 Fed. 380; Blanset, 256 U. S. 319; Blundell, 267 U. S. 373; Elliott, 7 Ind. T. 679; In re Poff's, 7 Ind. T. 59; Jefferson, 247 U. S. 288; Locke, 287 Fed. 278; Marlin, 276 U. S. 58; Morrison, 154 Fed. 617; Pigeon, 287 U. S. 886; Priddy, 204 Fed. 955; Robinson, 221 Fed. 398; Stewart, 295 U. S. 403; Tiger, 4 F. 2d 714; U. S. v. Bellm, 182 Fed. 161; U. S. v. Tiger, 19 F. 2d 35; Washington, 235 U. S. 422; Whitebird, 40 F. 2d 479.

[51] *Sg.* 33 St. 15.

[52] *Sg.* 17 St. 333, sec. 1. *A.* 36 St. 348. *S.* 34 St. 53, 205, 325, 1015, 1420; 35 St. 70, 781; 36 St. 202, 269; 37 St. 518; 38 St. 77, 582; 39 St. 123, 969; 40 St. 561. *Cited:* Tydings, 23 Case & Com. 743; Letter of Comm'r to Sen. Selden P. Spencer, Sept. 5, 1922; Northern, 227 U. S. 355.

[53] *Cited:* 53 I. D. 593; Davis, 3 Alaska 481; Sing, 7 Alaska 616.

[54] *Cited:* 25 Op. A. G. 460.

[55] *Sg.* 33 St. 254, 319.

[56] *Sg.* 12 St. 393, sec. 8; 26 St. 658.

[57] *Sg.* 30 St. 990. *Cited:* Chippewa, 80 C. Cls. 410.

[58] *Sg.* 21 St. 501; 22 St. 298. *A.* 34 St. 1251; 35 St. 627.

[59] *Sg.* 7 St. 381, 456. *Cited:* Ayres, 44 C. Cls. 48; Ayres, 44 C. Cls. 110; Ayres, 42 C. Cls. 385.

[60] *Sg.* 25 St. 118.

[61] *Sg.* 24 St. 388; 32 St. 261.

[62] *Sg.* 12 St. 393, sec. 8; 25 St. 642.

[63] *Sg.* 30 St. 991. *Cited:* Op. Sol., M. 10068, Feb. 16, 1927.

[64] *Sg.* 12 St. 393, sec. 8. *A.* 34 St. 825; 35 St. 650; 45 St. 371. *S.* 34 St. 205, 325, 349, 1015; 35 St. 70, 781; 36 St. 269; 37 St. 518; 39 St. 341, 519; 37 St. 91; 38 St. 77, 582; 39 St. 123, 969, 1301; 40 St. 561; 41 St. 3, 408; 42 St. 1527; 43 St. 33. *Cited:* 25 Op. A. G. 524; 33 Op. A. G. 25; Op. Sol., M. 25347, Jan. 25, 1930; Memo. Sol. Off., Feb. 21, 1933, May 25, 1933; Memo. Ind. Off., May 27, 1935; 49 L. D. 370; 51 L. D. 613; Clarke, 39 F. 2d 800; Shoshone, 82 C. Cls. 23; U. S. v. Shoshone, 304 U. S. 111; Wadsworth, 148 Fed. 771.

[65] *Sg.* 13 St. 355. *Cited:* Klamath, 81 C. Cls. 79; U. S. v. Klamath, 304 U. S. 119.

[66] *Sg.* 4 St. 442; 7 St. 46, 51, 85, 99, 114, 185, 213, 236, 242, 317, 320, 425, 491, 541, 545; 9 St. 35, 855; 10 St. 1071, 1079; 11 St. 614, 624, 702, 729, 744; 12 St. 333, sec. 1, 628, 981, 1173; 13 St. 675; 14 St. 757; 15 St. 622, 637, 640, 658, 676; 16 St. 40, 355, 720; 19 St. 256, 287; 22 St. 43; 23 St. 79, 80, 342; 24 St. 219, 388; 25 St. 223, 644, 645, 688, 888, 894; 26 St. 794, 1028; 27 St. 139; 29 St. 354, 895; 30 St. 90, 500, 504, 745; 31 St. 847, 862; 32 St. 263, 268, 640, 730, 744, 842, 998; 33 St. 207, 208. *Ag.* 33 St. 304. *Rg.* 33 St. 204. *A.* 34 St. 325. *S.* 34 St. 137, 325, 539, 841, 1015, 1371; 35 St. 70; 36 St. 269, 1058; 38 St. 77; 39 St. 123, 969; 40 St. 561; 41 St. 3, 408, 1225; 42 St. 552, 1174; 43 St. 390, 1141; 46 St. 1519. *Cited:* Tydings, 23 Case & Com. 748; 26 Op. A. G. 127; 53 I. D. 128; Browning, 6 F. 2d 801; Cherokee, 203 U. S. 76; Cherokee, 223 U. S. 108; Choctaw, 81 C. Cls. 1; Dull, 222 Fed. 471; Gont, 224 U. S. 458; Harrison, 254 U. S. 103; In re Terrell's, 6 Ind. T. 412; Indian, 240 U. S. 522; Kansas, 80 C. Cls. 264; Lowe, 223 U. S. 95; McCurdy, 246 U. S. 263; Medawakanton, 57 C. Cls. 357; Monson, 231 U. S. 341; Moore, 43 F. 2d 322; Morrison, 154 Fed. 617; Morrison, 6 F. 2d 811; Norton, 266 U. S. 511; Ottawa, 42 C. Cls. 240; Ottawa, 42 C. Cls. 518; Persons, 40 C. Cls. 411; Pronovost, 232 U. S. 50; Quick Bear, 210 U. S. 50; Robinson, 221 Fed. 398; Ross, 227 U. S. 530; Seminole, 78 C. Cls. 455; Starr, 227 U. S. 613; Stewart, 295 U. S. 403; U. S. v. Boss, 160 Fed. 132; U. S. v. Candelaria, 271 U. S. 432; U. S. v. Chavez, 290 U. S. 357; U. S. v. Mid Continent, 67 F. 2d 37; U. S. v. Moore, 161 Fed. 513; U. S. v. Sandoval, 231 U. S. 28; U. S. v. Watashe, 102 F. 2d 428; U. S. v. Wooten, 40 F. 2d 882; U. S. Fidelity, 7 Ind. T. 83; U. S. v. Board, 193 Fed. 485.

[67] *Cited:* 53 I. D. 593.

[68] *Sg.* 33 St. 189. *S.* 35 St. 478.

33 St. 1353; Feb. 26, 1904; C. 295—An Act Granting an increase of pension to Elizabeth A. Jones.

33 St. 1363; February 26, 1904; C. 333—An Act Granting an increase of pension to Adaline Shaw Lovejoy.

33 St. 1363; Feb. 26, 1904; C. 336—An Act Granting an increase of pension to William P. Hereford.

33 St. 1374; Mar. 3, 1904; C. 392—An Act Granting an increase of pension to Jesse J. Finley.

33 St. 1376; Mar. 5, 1904; C. 403—An Act Granting an increase of pension to Thomas Joyce.

33 St. 1393; Mar. 8, 1904; C. 481—An Act Granting an increase of pension to Swepston B. W. Stephens.

33 St. 1393; Mar. 8, 1904; C. 482—An Act Granting an increase of pension to James E. Harrison.

33 St. 1398; Mar. 11, 1904; C. 508—An Act For the relief of Darwin S. Hall.

33 St. 1398; Mar. 11, 1904; C. 510—An Act Granting a pension to Caroline S. Winn.

33 St. 1402; Mar. 11, 1904; C. 530—An Act Granting a pension to Martha E. Nolen.

33 St. 1407; Mar. 16, 1904; C. 557—An Act Granting a pension to Ann M. Driggars.

33 St. 1411; Mar. 16, 1904; C. 578—An Act Granting a pension to Mary Korth.

33 St. 1415; Mar. 16, 1904; C. 596—An Act Granting a pension to Henry H. Barrett.

33 St. 1423; Mar. 16, 1904; C. 630—An Act Granting a pension to Reuben A. Finnell.

33 St. 1442; Mar. 16, 1904; C. 713—An Act Granting a pension to James S. Lauderdale.

33 St. 1452; Mar. 22, 1904; C. 770—An Act Granting a pension to Ann A. Devore.

33 St. 1472; Apr. 6, 1904; C. 880—An Act Granting an increase of pension to James H. Martin.

33 St. 1496; Apr. 8, 1904; C. 994—An Act Granting an increase of pension to Samuel Parmley.

33 St. 1496; Apr. 8, 1904; C. 998—An Act Granting a pension to Mary Shiver.

33 St. 1497; Apr. 8, 1904; C. 1002—An Act Granting a pension to Jane E. Tatum.

33 St. 1498; Apr. 8, 1904; C. 1006—An Act Granting an increase of pension to Margaret F. Harris.

33 St. 1504; Apr. 8, 1904; C. 1033—An Act Granting a pension to Ellender C. Miller.

33 St. 1516; Apr. 8, 1904; C. 1083—An Act Granting a pension to Louis DeWitt.

33 St. 1521; Apr. 8, 1904; C. 1109—An Act Granting a pension to Francis M. Good.

33 St. 1523; Apr. 8, 1904; C. 115—An Act Granting a pension to Julia A. Allison.

33 St. 1525; Apr. 8, 1904; C. 1127—An Act Granting an increase of pension to Kezia Cherry.

33 St. 1531; Apr. 11, 1904; C. 1163—An Act Granting a pension to John McDermid.

33 St. 1535; Apr. 11, 1904; C. 1178—An Act Granting an increase of pension to Amanda M. Hand.

33 St. 1535; Apr. 11, 1904; C. 1179—An Act Granting an increase of pension to Jesse N. Jones.

33 St. 1535; Apr. 11, 1904; C. 1180—An Act Granting an increase of pension to Julia C. Vanzant.

33 St. 1535; Apr. 11, 1904; C. 1181—An Act Granting an increase of pension to William Varnes.

33 St. 1538; Apr. 11, 1904; C. 1193—An Act Granting an increase of pension to William C. Griffin.

33 St. 1547; Apr. 11, 1904; C. 1234—An Act Granting an increase of pension to Esther J. Reynolds.

33 St. 1548; Apr. 11, 1905; C. 1240—An Act Granting an increase of pension to Jane Allen.

33 St. 1560; Apr. 13, 1904; C. 1304—An Act Granting an increase of pension to Sarah N. Maddox.

33 St. 1580; Apr. 22, 1904; C. 1425—An Act Granting a pension to Mary A. V. Cook.

33 St. 1582; Apr. 22, 1904; C. 1435—An Act Granting a pension to Rachel Tyson.

33 St. 1619; Apr. 27, 1904; C. 1640—An Act Granting a pension to Matilda Witt.

33 St. 1633; Apr. 27, 1904; C. 1702—An Act Granting an increase of pension to Silas T. Overstreet.

33 St. 1637; Apr. 27, 1904; C. 1722—An Act Granting an increase of pension to Mary L. Johnson.

33 St. 1640; Apr. 27, 1904; C. 1733—An Act Granting an increase of pension to Micajah Hill, alias Michael C. Hill.

33 St. 1656; Apr. 28, 1904; C. 1879—An Act Granting an increase of pension to William M. Lang.

33 St. 1656; Apr. 28, 1904; C. 1881—An Act Granting an increase of pension to Jeremiah Gill.

33 St. 1662; Apr. 28, 1904; C. 1908—An Act Granting an increase of pension to Loucinda M. Thompson.

33 St. 1664; Apr. 28, 1904; C. 1919—An Act To pay certain Choctaw (Indian) warrants held by James M. Shackelford.

33 St. 1678; Apr. 28, 1904; C. 1982—An Act Granting a pension to Thomas Smith.

33 St. 1713; Apr. 28, 1904; C. 2136—An Act Granting an increase of pension to James R. Fletcher.

33 St. 1769; Jan. 25, 1905; C. 248—An Act Granting an increase of pension to Alafair Chastain.

33 St. 1769; Jan. 25, 1905; C. 249—An Act Granting an increase of pension to Colon Thomas.

33 St. 1848; Feb. 20, 1905; C. 656—An Act Granting an increase of pension to Susan A. Reynolds.

33 St. 1860; Feb. 20, 1905; C. 710—An Act Granting a pension to Jane Johns.

33 St. 1861; Feb. 20, 1905; C. 715—An Act Granting an increase of pension to Stephen Dampier.

33 St. 1864; Feb. 21, 1905; C. 730—An Act Granting a pension to Philip Lawotte.

33 St. 1876; Feb. 25, 1905; C. 806—An Act Granting a pension to Mahala Alexander.

33 St. 1882; Feb. 25, 1905; C. 831—An Act Granting an increase of pension to Henry S. Riggs.

33 St. 1892; Feb. 25, 1905; C. 875—An Act Granting an increase of pension to Joel J. Addison.

33 St. 1897; Feb. 25, 1905; C. 900—An Act Granting an increase of pension to Nahrvista G. Heard.

33 St. 1933; Feb. 25, 1905; C. 1060—An Act Granting an increase of pension to John A. Cairnes.

33 St. 1937; Feb. 25, 1905; C. 1076—An Act Granting an increase of pension to Mary L. Walker.

33 St. 1942; Feb. 25, 1905; C. 1098—An Act Granting an increase of pension to Caroline Jennings.

33 St. 1943; Feb. 25, 1905; C. 1102—An Act Granting a pension to Avery Dalton.

33 St. 1965; Feb. 28, 1905; C. 1207—An Act Granting a pension to Collin A. Wallace.

33 St. 1981; Feb. 28, 1905; C. 1279—An Act Granting an increase of pension to Martha Haddock.

33 St. 2001; Mar. 2, 1905; C. 1387—An Act Granting an increase of pension to William G. Taylor.

33 St. 2006; Mar. 3, 1905; C. 1513—An Act For the relief of the Mission of Saint James, in the State of Washington.[69]

33 St. 2009; Mar. 3, 1905; C. 1525—An Act Granting an honorable discharge to Eugene H. Ely.

33 St. 2018; Mar. 3, 1905; C. 1566—An Act Granting an increase of pension to Sarah Kearney.

33 St. 2024; Mar. 3, 1905; C. 1592—An Act Granting a pension to Cole B. Fugate.

33 St. 2048; Mar. 3, 1905; C. 1699—An Act Granting an increase of pension to Michael Daniel Kernan.

33 St. 2048; Mar. 3, 1905; C. 1700—An Act Granting a pension to James H. Thomas.

33 Sta. 2052; Mar. 3, 1905; C. 1714—An Act Granting an increase of pension to Malinda Peak.

33 St. 2058; Mar. 3, 1905; C. 1743—An Act Granting an increase of pension to Jacob Fulmer.

33 St. 2058; Mar. 3, 1905; C. 1744—An Act Granting an increase of pension to Nancy Ann Smith.

33 St. 2077; Jan. 28, 1904; Concurrent Res.—Indian Treaties.

33 St. 2078; Mar. 1, 1904; Concurrent Res.—Fort Hall Indian Reservation.[70]

33 St. 2078; Mar. 4, 1904; Concurrent Res.—Fort Hall Indian Reservation.[71]

33 St. 2079; Mar. 15, 1904; Concurrent Res.—Fort Hall Indian Reservation.[72]

33 St. 2079; Mar. 22, 1904; Concurrent Res.—Fort Hall Indian Reservation.[73]

34 STAT.

34 St. 9; Jan. 27, 1906; C. 7—An Act To provide for the extension of time within which homestead settlers may estab-

---

[69] *Sg.* 9 St. 323; 10 St. 172.
[70] *Sg.* 33 St. 153.
[71] *Sg.* 33 St. 153.
[72] *Sg.* 33 St. 153.
[73] *Sg.* 33 St. 153.

lish their residence upon certain lands which were heretofore a part of the Uinta Indian Reservation, within the counties of Uinta and Wasatch, in the State of Utah.[74]

34 St. 27; Feb. 27, 1906; C. 510—An Act Making appropriations to supply urgent deficiencies in the appropriations for the fiscal year ending June 30, 1906, and for prior years, and for other purposes.[75]

34 St. 53; Mar. 6, 1906; C. 518—An Act Authorizing the disposition of surplus and allotted lands on the Yakima Indian Reservation, in the State of Washington, which can be irrigated under the Act of Congress approved June 17, 1902, known as the reclamation Act, and for other purposes.[76]

34 St. 55; Mar. 8, 1906; C. 629—An Act Providing for the issuance of patents for lands allotted to Indians under the Moses agreement of July 7, 1883.[77]

34 St. 78; Mar. 19, 1906; C. 961—An Act Extending the public land laws to certain lands in Wyoming.[78]

34 St. 78; Mar. 19, 1906; C. 962—An Act Authorizing and directing the Secretary of the Interior to sell and convey to the State of Minnesota a certain tract of land situated in the county of Dakota, State of Minnesota.

34 St. 80; Mar. 20, 1906; C. 1125—An Act For the establishment of town sites, and for the sale of lots within the common lands of the Kiowa, Comanche, and Apache Indians in Oklahoma.[79]

34 St. 80; Mar. 22, 1906; C. 1126—An Act To authorize the sale and disposition of surplus or unallotted lands of the diminished Colville Indian Reservation, in the State of Washington, and for other purposes.[80]

34 St. 88; Mar. 27, 1906; C. 1348—An Act Leasing and demising certain lands in La Plata County, Colorado, to the P. F. U. Rubber Co.

34 St. 91; Mar. 28, 1906; C. 1350—An Act Authorizing the sale of timber on the Jicarilla Apache Indian Reservation for the benefit of the Indians belonging thereto.

34 St. 91; Mar. 29, 1906; C. 1351—An Act To consolidate the city of South McAlester and the town of McAlester, in the Indian Territory.[81]

34 St. 124; Apr. 21, 1906; C. 1645—An Act To authorize the sale of a portion of the Lower Brule Indian Reservation in South Dakota, and for other purposes.[82]

34 St. 137; Apr. 26, 1906; C. 1876—An Act To provide for the final disposition of the affairs of the Five Civilized Tribes in the Indian Territory, and for other purposes.[83]

34 St. 182; May 8, 1906; C. 2348—An Act To amend section six of an Act approved February 8, 1887, entitled "An Act to provide for the allotment of lands in severalty to Indians on the various reservations, and to extend the protection of the laws of the United States and the Territories over the Indians, and for other purposes." 25 U. S. C. 349 (sec. 6, 24 St. 390). See Historical Note 25 U. S. C. A. 349, 404. 8 U. S. C. 3.[84]

34 St. 197; May 17, 1906; C. 2469—An Act Authorizing the Secretary of the Interior to allot homesteads to the natives of Alaska.[85]

34 St. 205; May 31, 1906; C. 2567—An Act Making appropriations to supply additional urgent deficiencies in appropriations for the fiscal year 1906, and for other purposes.[86]

34 St. 208; June 4, 1906; C. 2573—An Act Providing for a recorder of deeds, and so forth, in the Osage Indian Reservation, in Oklahoma Territory.

34 St. 213; June 5, 1906; C. 2580—An Act To open for settlement 505,000 acres of land in the Kiowa, Comanche, and Apache Indian reservations, in Oklahoma Territory.[87]

34 St. 240; June 12, 1906; C. 3078—An Act Making appropriations for the support of the Army for the fiscal year ending June 30, 1907.

34 St. 262; June 14, 1906; C. 3298—An Act To enable the Indians allotted lands in severalty within the boundaries of drainage district numbered one, in Richardson County, Nebraska, to protect their lands from overflow, and for the segregation of such of said Indians from their tribal relations as may be expedient, and for other purposes.[88]

34 St. 263; June 14, 1906; C. 3299—An Act To prohibit aliens from fishing in the waters of Alaska.[89] Sec. 1—48 U. S. C. 243.

34 St. 267; June 16, 1906; C. 3335—An Act To enable the people of Oklahoma and of the Indian Territory to form a constitution and State government and be admitted into the Union on an equal footing with the original States; and to enable the people of New Mexico and of Arizona to form a constitution and State government and be admitted into the Union on an equal footing with the original States.[90] Sec. 7—16 U. S. C. 153; Sec. 13—16 U. S. C. 151, 28 U. S. C. 182, 481, 490; Sec. 14—16 U. S. C. 151, 28 U. S. C. 182.

---

[74] *Sg.* 32 St. 263, 998.

[75] *Sg.* 26 St. 853; 33 St. 204, 578, 1049, 1060.

[76] *Sg.* 33 St. 595. *Cited:* Op. Sol., M. 25214, June 7, 1929; Tydings, 23 Case and Com. 743.

[77] *Sg.* 23 St. 79. *S.* 36 St. 1358; 38 St. 77. *Cited:* 40 L. D. 212; Starr, 227 U. S. 613; U. S. v. Moore, 161 Fed. 513.

[78] *Sg.* 30 St. 62.

[79] *S.* 39 St. 445.

[80] *Sg.* 17 St. 333, sec. 1; 32 St. 388. *A.* 39 St. 672. *S.* 34 St. 2829; 37 St. 197; 40 St. 449; 41 St. 535; 42 St. 507; 43 St. 1362; 44 St. 558; 47 St. 334. *Cited:* Tydings, 23 Case & Com. 743; Op. Sol., M. 28028, May 24, 1935; 50 L. D. 691; Mason, 302 U. S. 186; U. S. v. Ferry, 24 F. Supp. 399; U. S. v. Pelican, 232 U. S. 442.

[81] *Sp.* 30 St. 500.

[82] *Sg.* 12 St. 393, sec. 8; 17 St. 333, sec. 1. *S.* 35 St. 8.

[83] *Sg.* 31 St. 221; 32 St. 43, 841; 33 St. 1048. *A.* 34 St. 325; 35 St. 312; 37 St. 497; 44 St. 239; 45 St. 495. *S.* 34 St. 1015, 2832; 35 St. 70, 444, 781; 36 St. 269; 37 St. 67, 497; 42 St. 831; 48 St. 1467. *Cited:* Cabell, 3 Okla. S. B. J. 208; 26 Op. A. G. 127; 26 Op. A. G. 340; 26 Op. A. G. 351; 27 Op. A. G. 530; 29 Op. A. G. 131; 29 Op. A. G. 231; 34 Op. A. G. 275; 34 Op. A. G. 302; 1 L. D. Memo. 99; Op. Sol., M. 7996; Aug. 2, 1922, D. 46987, Nov. 13, 1922; M. 10526, Dec. 13, 1923; M. 7316, May 28, 1924, Oct. 4, 1926; Report of Status of Pueblo of Pojoaque, Nov. 3, 1932; Memo. Sol. Off., May 24, 1933, May 24, 1933; Op. Sol., M. 27843, Jan. 22, 1935; M. 27759, Jan. 22, 1935; M. 27814, Jan. 30, 1935; Memo. Sol., Sept. 20, 1935; Op. Sol., M. 27814, Apr. 23, 1936; Memo. Sol., May 19, 1936, Sept. 17, 1936, Aug. 25, 1937; 49 L. D. 348; 53 I. D. 48; 53 I. D. 471; 53 I. D. 502; 53 I. D. 637; 54 I. D. 109; Anchor, 256 U. S. 519; Anicker, 246 U. S. 110; Barnett, 259 Fed. 394; Bartlett, 218 Fed. 380; Bilby, 246 U. S. 255; Blundell, 267 U. S. 373; Brader, 246 U. S. 88; Brown, 44 C. Cls. 283; Bunch, 263 U. S. 250; Caesar, 103 F. 2d 503; Cherokee, 85 C. Cls. 76; Choctaw, 81 C. Cls. 1; Choctaw, 83 C. Cls. 49; City, 75 F. 2d 343; Cochran, 276 Fed. 701; Cully, 37 F. 2d 493; Darks, 69 F. 2d 231; David, 250 Fed. 208; Derrisaw, 8 F. Supp. 876; Duncan, 245 U. S. 308; Eslick, 51 C. Cls. 266; Fleming, 215 U. S. 56; Frame, 189 Fed. 785; Fulsom, 35 F. 2d 84; Gannon, 243 U. S. 108; Garfield, 211 U. S. 264; Garfield, 211 U. S. 249; Garfield, 34 App. D. C. 70; Glenn, 105 F. 2d 398; Goat, 224 U. S. 458; Gritts, 224 U. S. 640; Hallam, 49 F. 2d 103; Harris, 254 U. S. 103; Harris, 188 Fed. 712; Heckman, 224 U. S. 413; Henny, 191 Fed. 132; In re Jessie's, 259 Fed. 594; In re Lands, 199 Fed. 811; In re Palmer's, 11 F. Supp. 301; Iowa, 217 Fed. 11; Jack, 39 F. 2d 594; Jennings, 192 Fed. 507; King, 64 F. 2d 979; Knight, 228 U. S. 6; Ledbetter, 23 F. 2d 81; Ligon, 164 Fed. 670; Locke, 287 Fed. 276; M. K. & T. Ry., 47 C. Cls. 59; Moore, 43 F. 2d 322; Morrison, 154 Fed. 617; Mullen, 250 U. S. 590; Mullen, 224 U. S. 448; Muskrat, 219 U. S. 346; Ne-Kah-Wah-She-Tun-Kah, 290 Fed. 303; Nunn, 216 Fed. 330; Parker, 250 U. S. 66; Reed, 197 Fed. 419; Rogers, 263 Fed. 160; Roubedeaux, 23 F. 2d 277; Seminole, 78 C. Cls. 455; Shulthis, 225 U. S. 561; Stewart, 296 U. S. 403; Sunday, 248 U. S. 545; Sup., 295 U. S. 418; Sweet, 245 U. S. 192; Talley, 246 U. S. 104; Taylor, 235 U. S. 42; Tiger, 221 U. S. 286; U. S. v. Bartlett, 235 U. S. 72; U. S. v. Bean, 253 Fed. 1; U. S. v. Board, 284 Fed. 103; U. S. v. Comet, O. & G., 202 Fed. 849; U. S. ex rel. Johnson, 258 U. S. 209; U. S. v. Ferguson, 247 U. S. 175; U. S. v. First, 234 U. S. 245; U. S. v. Fooshee, 225 Fed. 521; U. S. v. Gypsy, 10 F. 2d 487; U. S. v. Halsell, 247 Fed. 390; U. S. v. Hayes, 20 F. 2d 873; U. S. v. Hinkle, 261 Fed. 518; U. S. v. Knight, 206 Fed. 145; U. S. v. Rea-Read, 171 Fed. 501; U. S. v. Seminole, 299 U. S. 417; U. S. v. Shock, 187 Fed. 862; U. S. v. Shock, 187 Fed. 870; U. S. v. Smith, 266 Fed. 740; U. S. v. Smith, 279 Fed. 136; U. S. v. Smith, 288 Fed. 356; U. S. v. Stigall, 226 Fed. 190; U. S. v. Tiger, 19 F. 2d 35; U. S. v. Western, 226 Fed. 726; U. S. v. Whitmire, 236 Fed. 474; U. S. Exp., 191 Fed. 673; Vinson, 44 F. 2d 772; Wade, 39 App. D. C. 245; Williams, 218 Fed. 797; Winton, 255 U. S. 373.

[84] *Ag.* 24 St. 388, sec. 8. *S.* 39 St. 969. *Cited:* Brosius, 23 Case & Com. 739; Brown, 39 Yale L. J. 307; Cain, 2 Minn. L. Rev. 177; Krieger, 3 Geo. Wash. L. Rev. 279; 2 L. D. Memo. 284; 4 L. D. Memo 72; 12 L. D. Memo. 652; Op. Sol., M. 5379, July 14, 1921; M. 4018, July 29, 1921; M. 6882, Mar. 20, 1922; Memo. Ind. Off., Apr. 21, 1927; Op. Sol., M. 25258, June 26, 1929; Op. A. G., Oct. 5, 1929; Op. Sol., M. 25847, Jan. 25, 1930, Aug. 18, 1932; Memo. Sol. Off., Jan. 16, 1934; Bisek, 5 F. 2d 994; Bond, 181 Fed. 613; Dickson, 242 U. S. 371; Eugene Sol Louie, 274 Fed. 47; Ex p. Pero, 99 F. 2d 28; Ex p. Van Moore, 221 Fed. 954; Halbert, 283 U. S. 753; Johnson, 283 Fed. 954; Lane, 241 U. S. 201; Larkin, 276 U. S. 431; Locke, 287 Fed. 276; Miller, 57 F. 2d 987; Minnesota, 305 U. S. 382; Scheer, 48 F. 2d 327; Seaples, 246 Fed. 501; U. S. v. Benewah, 290 Fed. 628; U. S. v. Board, 13 F. Supp. 641; U. S. v. Celestine, 215 U. S. 278; U. S. v. Debell, 227 Fed. 771; U. S. v. Debell, 227 Fed. 760; U. S. v. Debell, 227 Fed. 775; U. S. v. Dewey, S. D., 14 F. 2d 784; U. S. v. Ferry, 24 F. Supp. 399; U. S. v. Gardner, 189 Fed. 690; U. S. v. Glacier, 17 F. Supp. 411; U. S. v. Heinrich, 16 F. 2d 112; U. S. v. Jackson, 280 U. S. 183; U. S. v. Lewis, 95 F. 2d 236; U. S. v. Nez Perce, 95 F. 2d 232; U. S. v. Nez Perce, 267 Fed. 495; U. S. v. Pearson, 231 Fed. 270; U. S. v. Pelican, 232 U. S. 442; U. S. v. Powers, 305 U. S. 527; U. S. v. Sherburne, 68 F. 2d 155; U. S. v. Smith, 279 Fed. 136; U. S. v. Waller, 243 U. S. 452; U. S. v. Lynch, 7 Alaska 568; U. S. v. Powers, 305 U. S. 527.

[85] *Cited:* 58 I. D. 593; Worthern, 229 Fed. 966; Memo. Sol., Mar. 28, 1939.

[86] *Sg.* 33 St. 304, 352, 394, 595, 1016. *S.* 34 St. 1295; 35 St. 317.

[87] *Ag.* 31 St. 672. *A.* 34 St. 1015. *S.* 34 St. 550, 2830; 35 St. 41, 444, 636; 36 St. 265; 37 St. 33; 40 St. 1318. *Cited:* Op. Sol., M. 7002, Mar. 10, 1922; Letter from Ass't Sec'y, to Comm'r, Aug. 14, 1926; Op. Sol., M. 18772, Dec. 24, 1926; 35 L. D. 145; 38 L. D. 422; Oklahoma, 258 U. S. 574; U. S. v. Rowell, 243 U. S. 464.

[88] *A.* 36 St. 368.

[89] *A.* 52 St. 1174.

[90] *A.* 34 St. 1286; 35 St. 838. *S.* 34 St. 634. *Cited:* Krieger, 3 Geo. Wash. L. Rev. 279; Op. Sol., M. 7996, Aug. 2, 1922; M. 18807, Jan. 28, 1925; Ammerman, 267 Fed. 136; Bartlett, 218 Fed. 380; Bell, 192 Fed. 597; Browning, 6 F. 2d 801; Butterfield, 241 Fed. 556; Chamblin, 218 Fed. 154; Chisholm, 278 Fed. 589; Collins, 243 Fed. 495; Edwards,

34 St. 325; June 21, 1906; C. 3504—An Act Making appropriations for the current and contingent expenses of the Indian Department, for fulfilling treaty stipulations with various Indian tribes, and for other purposes, for the fiscal year ending June 30, 1907.[91] 25 U. S. C. 279, 25 U. S. C. 391, 25 U. S. C. 97 (sec. 3, 19 St. 199; sec. 4, 28 St. 205),[92] 411, 25 U. S. C. 302, 25 U. S. C. 313 (sec. 2, 30 St. 990), 25 U. S. C. 97 (sec. 3, 19 St. 199; sec. 4, 28 St. 205),[93] 25 U. S. C. 391a.

34 St. 389; June 22, 1906; C. 3514—An Act Making appropriations for the legislative, executive, and judicial expenses of the Government for the fiscal year ending June 30, 1907, and for other purposes.[94]

34 St. 539; June 28, 1906; C. 3572—An Act For the division of the lands and funds of the Osage Indians in Oklahoma Territory, and for other purposes.[95]

34 St. 547; June 28, 1906; C. 3578—An Act To authorize the cutting, sawing into lumber, and sale of timber on certain lands reserved for the use of the Menominee tribe of Indians, in the State of Wisconsin.[96]

34 St. 550; June 18, 1906; C. 3581—An Act Giving preference right to actual settlers on pasture reserve numbered three to purchase land leased to them for agricultural purposes in Comanche County, Oklahoma.[97]

34 St. 596; June 29, 1906; C. 3592—An Act To establish a Bureau of Immigration and Naturalization, and to provide for a uniform rule for the naturalization of aliens throughout the United States.

34 St. 611; June 29, 1906; C. 3599—An Act Granting lands in the former Uintah Indian Reservation to the corporation of the Episcopal Church in Utah.

34 St. 634; June 30, 1906; C. 3912—An Act Making appropriations to supply deficiencies in the appropriations for the fiscal year ending June 30, 1906, and for prior years, and for other purposes.[98]

34 St. 697; June 30, 1906; C. 3914—An Act Making appropriations for sundry civil expenses of the Government for the fiscal year ending June 30, 1907, and for other purposes.[99]

34 St. 822; Mar. 2, 1906; J. Res. No. 7—Joint Resolution Extending the tribal existence and government of the Five Civilized Tribes of Indians in the Indian Territory.[1]

34 St. 825; Mar. 28, 1906; J. Res. No. 12—Joint Resolution Extending the time for opening to public entry the unallotted lands on the ceded portion of the Shoshone or Wind River Indian Reservation in Wyoming.[2]

34 St. 837; June 29, 1906; J. Res. No. 42—Joint Resolution Directing that the Sulphur Springs Reservation be named and hereafter called the "Platt National Park." 16 U. S. C. 151, 153.

34 St. 841; Dec. 19, 1906; C. 2—An Act Making appropriations to supply urgent deficiencies in the appropriations for the fiscal year ending June 30, 1907, and for other purposes.[3]

34 St. 849; Jan. 17, 1907; C. 151—An Act Fixing the time for homestead entrymen on lands embraced in the Wind River or Shoshone Indian Reservation to establish residence on same.[4]

34 St. 894; Feb. 18, 1907; C. 934—An Act To define the status of certain patents and pending entries, selections, and filings on lands formerly within the Fort Berthold Indian Reservation in North Dakota.[5]

34 St. 934; Feb. 25, 1907; C. 1203—An Act Confirming entries and applications under sec. 2306 of the Revised Statutes of the United States for lands embraced in what was formerly the Columbia Indian Reservation, in the State of Washington.[6]

34 St. 935; Feb. 26, 1907; C. 1635—An Act Making appropriations for the legislative, executive, and judicial expenses of the Government for the fiscal year ending June 30, 1908, and for other purposes.[7]

34 St. 1015; Mar. 1, 1907; C. 2285—An Act Making appropriations for the current and contingent expenses of the Indian Department, for fulfilling treaty stipulations with various Indian tribes, and for other purposes, for the fiscal year

---

5 F. 2d 17; Ex p. Webb, 225 U. S. 663; Frame, 189 Fed. 785; Greer, 245 U. S. 559; Hawley, 15 F. 2d 621; In re Palmer's, 11 F. Supp. 301; Jackson, 43 F. 2d 513; Jefferson, 247 U. S. 288; Johnson, 234 U. S. 422; Joines, 274 U. S. 544; Joplin, 236 U. S. 531; Locke, 287 Fed. 276; McCurdy, 264 U. S. 484; Maust, 283 Fed. 912; Morrison, 6 F. 2d 811; Mosier, 198 Fed. 54; Oklahoma, 220 U. S. 277; Oklahoma, 220 U. S. 290; Pitman, 64 F. 2d 740; Priddy, 204 Fed. 955; Southern, 241 U. S. 582; Sperry, 264 U. S. 488; Stewart, 295 U. S. 403; Tiger, 4 F. 2d 714; Tiger, 221 U. S. 286; U. S. v. Aaron, 183 Fed. 347; U. S. v. Abrams, 194 Fed. 82; U. S. v. Board, 26 F. Supp. 270; U. S. v. Board, 193 Fed. 485; U. S. v. Board, 284 Fed. 103; U. S. v. Luther, 260 Fed. 579; U. S. v. Smith, 279 Fed. 136; U. S. v. Wright, 53 F. 2d 300; U. S. Exp., 191 Fed. 673; Ward, 253 U. S. 17; Whitebird, 40 F. 2d 479; Young, 176 Fed. 612.

[91] *Sg.* 4 St. 442; 7 St. 46, 51, 85, 99, 114, 185, 213, 236, 242, 296, 317, 320, 335, 425, 541, 545, 596; 9 St. 35, 855; 10 St. 949, 1071, 1079, 1160; 11 St. 614, 702, 729, 744; 12 St. 118, sec. 5, 652, 927, 981, 1173, 1191; 13 St. 172, 675; 14 St. 467, sec. 10, 757; 15 St. 111, sec. 1; 622, 640, 652, 655, 676; 16 St. 40, 720; 19 St. 176, 256, 287; 22 St. 43; 23 St. 103; 24 St. 388; 25 St. 643, 644, 645, 687, 688, 888, 895; 26 St. 756, 1028; 27 St. 62, 139, 563, 644, 745; 28 St. 907; 29 St. 326, 354; 30 St. 62, 504, 571, 990; 31 St. 672, 1067; 32 St. 400, 502, 653, 722, 744, 841; 33 St. 48, 194, 201, 302, 321, 597, 1017, 1060, 1080. *Ag.* 25 St. 644; 30 St. 990; 31 St. 1065; 32 St. 402, 998; 34 St. 138, 143. *Rg.* 19 St. 199; 27 St. 5; 33 St. 217. *A.* 34 St. 1015; 35 St. 781; 40 St. 1203. *Rp.* 37 St. 668; 47 St. 819; 48 St. 1224. *S.* 34 St. 634, 841, 935, 1015, 1229; 35 St. 8, 70, 169, 317, 781; 36 St. 202, 269, 1058; 37 St. 85, 518; 38 St. 77, 111, 582; 39 St. 123, 969; 40 St. 561; 41 St. 3, 408, 1225; 42 St. 552, 831, 1174; 43 St. 390, 1141; 44 St. 453, 984; 45 St. 442, 1562; 46 St. 279, 1115; 47 St. 15, 91, 820; 48 St. 362; 49 St. 176, 1757; 50 St. 210, 564; 52 St. 291. *Cited:* Brosius, 23 Case & Com. 739; Cain, 2 Minn. L. Rev. 177; Dixon, 23 Case & Com. 712; Tydings, 23 Case & Com. 743; 26 Op. A. G. 123; 26 Op. A. G. 127; 29 Op. A. G. 455; 5 L. D. Memo. 168; 11 L. D. Memo. 296; Op. Sol., M. 18423, Mar. 16, 1926, Aug. 18, 1932, M. 28028, May 24, 1935; Memo. Ind. Off., May 27, 1935; Memo. Sol., Jan. 12, 1937, Aug. 13, 1937; 39 L. D. 44; 44 L. D. 188; 51 L. D. 613; Bailey, 48 C. Cls. 353; Bisek, 5 F. 2d 994; Butler, 43 C. Cls. 497; Cherokee, 85 C. Cls. 76; Conley, 216 U. S. 84; Creek, 77 C. Cls. 159; Cully, 37 F. 2d 498; Duwamish, 79 C. Cls. 530; Eugene Sol Louie, 274 Fed 47; Gordon, 34 App. D. C. 508; Gritts, 224 U. S. 640; Henry, 191 Fed 132; Jack, 39 F. 2d 595; Johnson, 283 Fed. 954; Klamath, 81 C. Cls. 79; Klamath, 86 C. Cls. 614; Klamath, 296 U. S. 244; Ledbetter, 23 F. 2d 81; McCullough, 243 Fed. 823; Malone, 212 Fed. 668; Medawakanton, 57 C. Cls. 357; Morrow, 243 Fed. 854; Muskrat, 219 U. S. 346; Pronovost, 232 U. S. 487; Scheer, 48 F. 2d 327; Sisseton, 42 C. Cls. 416; Smith, 270 U. S. 456; Stockbridge, 61 C. Cls. 472; Swendig, 205 U. S. 322; Tinker, 231 U. S. 681; U. S. v. Anderson, 228 U. S. 52; U. S. v. Benewah, 290 Fed. 628; U. S. v. Birdsall, 233 U. S 223; U. S. v. Corporation, 101 F. 2d 156; U. S. v. Estill, 62 F. 2d 620; U. S. v. Ferguson, 247 U. S. 175; U. S. v. Ferry, 24 F. Supp 399; U. S. v. First, 234 U. S. 245; U. S. v. Gardner, 189 Fed. 690; U. S. v. Jackson, 280 U. S. 183; U. S. v. Johnson, 87 F 2d 155; U. S. v. Kilgore, 27 F. Supp. 1; U. S. v. Klamath, 304 U. S. 119; U. S. v. Luther, 260 Fed. 579; U. S. v. McIntire, 101 F. 2d 650; U. S. v Pearson, 231 Fed. 270; U. S. v. Reily, 290 U. S. 33; U. S. v. Sherburne, 68 F. 2d 155; U. S. v. Sisseton, 208 U. S. 561; U. S. v. Spaeth, 24 F. Supp. 465; U. S. v. Waller, 243 U. S. 452; U. S. v. Watashe, 102 F. 2d 428.

[92] Also see 25 U. S. C. 409a (46 St. 1471 as amended 47 St. 474).

[93] *S.* 42 St. 24, sec. 304.

[94] *S.* 34 St. 634. *Cited:* Op. Sol. 17687, Dec. 19, 1925; 48 L. D. 567.

[95] *Sg.* 33 St. 209, 1061. *Rpg.* 28 St. 305. *A.* 37 St. 86; 39 St. 867; 40 St. 561; 41 St. 1249; 43 St. 94, 1008; 45 St. 1478. *S.* 35 St. 1048, 1049, 1167; 37 St. 86; 40 St. 561. *Cited:* Reeves, 23 Case & Com. 727; 33 Op. A. G. 60; 34 Op. A. G. 26; 6 L. D. Memo. 641; 11 L. D. Memo. 620; 12 L. D. Memo. 642; Op. Sol., M. 5805, Nov. 22, 1921; M. 4017, Jan. 4, 1922, M. 8370, Aug. 15, 1922; D. 46929, Sept. 30, 1922; M. 19190, June 2, 1926; Memo. Sol. Off., Sept. 20, 1926; Op. Sol., M. 18320, Dec. 21, 1926; M. 21642, Mar. 26, 1927; Memo. Sol. Off., Sept. 13, 1927, May 14, 1928; Op. Sol., M. 24293, June 19, 1928; Memo. Sol. Off., Apr. 18, 1929; Op. Sol., M. 25107, May 4, 1929; Memo. Sol. Off., May 31, 1929; Sept. 18, 1929; Feb. 3, 1930; Apr. 22, 1930, July 8, 1930, Dec. 30, 1930, May 29, 1931; Op. Comp. Gen. to Sec'y, Feb. 4, 1932; Letter of Comm'r to Supt., Sept. 26, 1934; Letter of Ass't Comm'r to Sec'y of Interior, Dec. 16, 1935; Memo. Sol., Dec. 17, 1935; Op. Sol., M. 27963, Jan. 26, 1937; Letter from Asst. Sec'y to A. G., Oct. 27, 1937; 48 L. D. 479; 53 I. D. 169; 54 I. D. 105; 54 I. D. 341; 55 I. D. 456; Adams, 59 F. 2d 653; Bartlett, 218 Fed. 380; Brewer-Elliott, 260 U. S. 77; Browning, 6 F. 2d 801; Choteau 283 U. S. 691; Coteau, 38 F. 2d 976; Commissioners, 270 Fed. 110; Continental, 69 F. 2d 19; Drummond, 34 F. 2d 755; Fish, 52 F. 2d 544; Globe, 81 F. 2d 143; Harrison, 264 Fed. 776; Hickey, 64 F. 2d 628; Ickes, 80 F. 2d 708; In re Dennison, 38 F. 2d 662; In re Irwin, 60 F. 2d 495; In re Penn, 41 F. 2d 257; Johnson, 64 F. 2d 674; Jump, 100 F. 2d 130; Kenny, 250 U. S. 58; La Motte, 254 U. S. 570; Levindale, 241 U. S. 432; McCurdy, 246 U. S. 263; Morrison, 6 F. 2d 811; Mosier, 198 Fed. 54; Ne-Kah-Wah-She-Tun-Kah, 290 Fed. 303; Osage, 33 F. 2d 21; Quarles, 45 F. 2d 585; Tapp, 6 F. Supp. 577; Taylor, 51 F. 2d 884; U. S. v. Aaron, 183 Fed. 347; U. S. v. Board, 26 F. Supp. 270; U. S. v. Board, 193 Fed. 485; U. S. v. Board, 216 Fed. 883; U. S. v. Board, 284 Fed. 103; U. S. v. Hale, 51 F. 2d 629; U. S. v. Harris, 293 Fed 369; U. S. v. Hughes, 6 F. Supp. 972; U. S. v. Hutchings, 252 Fed. 841; U. S. v. Johnson, 87 F 2d 155; U. S. v. La Motte, 67 F. 2d 788; U. S. v. Mashunkashey, 72 Fed. 847; U. S. v. Mummert, 15 F. 2d 926; U. S. v. Osage, 251 U. S. 128; U. S. v. Ramsey, 271 U. S. 467; U. S. v. Sands, 94 F. 2d 156; U. S. v. Sandstrom, 22 F. Supp 190; U. S. ex rel. Brown, 232 U. S. 598; Utilities, 2 F. Supp. 81; Work, 261 U. S. 352.

[96] *Sg.* 26 St. 146.

[97] *Sg.* 34 St. 213. *S.* 35 St. 41, 636; 37 St. 91; 40 St. 1318.

[98] *Sg.* 12 St. 754; 26 St. 853; 32 St. 726, 997; 34 St. 268, 381, 417. *S.* 34 St. 1371. *Cited:* 26 Op. A. G. 330; Cherokee, 270 U. S. 476; Eastern Cherokees, 45 C. Cls. 104; Eastern Cherokees, 225 U. S. 572; Eastern or Emigrant, 82 C. Cls. 180.

[99] *Sg.* 25 St. 689; 28 St. 695; *Cited:* 53 I. D. 593; Ass't Secy's Letter to Ass't to the Supt. St. Elizabeths, Apr. 15, 1935; Memo. Sol., Nov. 9, 1937; Op. Sol., M. 26915, Feb. 24, 1932.

[1] *Cited:* 29 Op. A. G. 231; 35 Op. A. G. 421; Goat, 224 U. S. 458; Gritts, 224 U. S. 640; U. S. v. Hayes, 20 F. 2d 873; U. S. v. Seminole, 299 U. S. 417; U. S. Exp., 191 Fed 673.

[2] *Ag.* 33 St. 1021. *A.* 45 St. 371.

[3] *Sg.* 33 St. 1060; 34 St. 137, 340. *Cited:* 25 Op. A. G. 460.

[4] *Sg.* 35 St. 1016.

[5] *Sg.* 26 St. 1032; 27 St. 979. *Cited:* 29 Op. A. G. 239.

[6] *Sg.* 17 St. 333, sec. 2; 32 St. 388.

[7] *Sg.* 34 St. 339.

ending June 30, 1908.[8] 25 U. S. C. 59; 25 U. S. C. 66; 25 U. S. C. 134; 25 U. S. C. 139; 25 U. S. C. 140; 25 U. S. C. 199,[9] 25 U. S. C. 248; 25 U. S. C. 288; 25 U. S. C. 291; 25 U. S. C. 405; 25 U. S. C. 412.[10]

34 St. 1055; Mar. 1, 1907; C. 2290—An Act To authorize the Court of Claims to hear, determine, and adjudicate the claims of the Sac and Fox Indians of the Mississippi in Iowa against the Sac and Fox Indians of the Mississippi in Oklahoma, and the United States, and for other purposes.[11]

34 St. 1056; Mar. 1, 1907; C. 2292—An Act Providing for the granting and patenting to the State of Colorado, desert lands formerly in the Southern Ute Indian Reservation in Colorado.[12]

34 St. 1073; Mar. 2, 1907; C. 2509—An Act Making appropriations for the construction, repair, and preservation of certain public works on rivers and harbors, and for other purposes.

34 St. 1158; Mar. 2, 1907; C. 2511—An Act Making appropriation for the support of the Army for the fiscal year ending June 30, 1908.

34 St. 1217; Mar. 2, 1907; C. 2514—An Act To amend the Act of Congress approved February 11, 1901, entitled "An Act providing for allotments of lands in severalty to the Indians of the La Pointe or Bad River Reservation, in the State of Wisconsin."[13]

34 St. 1220; Mar. 2, 1907; C. 2521—An Act For the relief of certain white persons who intermarried with Cherokee citizens.

34 St. 1221; Mar. 2, 1907; C. 2523—An Act Providing for the allotment and distribution of Indian tribal funds.[14] Sec. 1—25 U. S. C. 119; Sec. 2—25 U. S. C. 121.[15]

34 St. 1229; Mar. 2, 1907; C. 2535—An Act To fix the boundaries of lands of certain landowners and entrymen adjoining the Coeur d'Alene Indian Reservation.[16]

34 St. 1230; Mar. 2, 1907; C. 2536—An Act To authorize the sale and disposition of a portion of the surplus or unallotted lands in the Rosebud Indian Reservation, in the State of South Dakota, and making appropriation and provision to carry the same into effect.[17]

34 St. 1251; Mar. 2, 1907; C. 2573—An Act To amend sections five and six of an Act entitled "An Act to authorize the registration of trade-marks used in commerce with foreign nations or among the several States or with Indian tribes, and to protect the same."[18] Sec. 1—15 U. S. C. 85; Sec. 2—15 U. S. C. 86.

34 St. 1286; Mar. 4, 1907; C. 2911—An Act To amend sections 16, 17, and 20 of an Act entitled "An Act to enable the people of Oklahoma and of the Indian Territory to form a constitution and State government and be admitted into the Union on an equal footing with the original States; and to enable the people of New Mexico and of Arizona to form a constitution and State government and be admitted into the Union on an equal footing with the original States," approved June 16, 1906, and for other purposes.[19]

34 St. 1295; Mar. 4, 1907; C. 2918—An Act Making appropriations for sundry civil expenses of the Government for the fiscal year ending June 30, 1908, and for other purposes.[20]

34 St. 1371; Mar. 4, 1907; C. 2919—An Act Making appropriations to supply deficiencies in the appropriations for the fiscal year ending June 30, 1907, and for prior years, and for other purposes.[21]

34 St. 1410; Mar. 4, 1907; C. 2926—An Act To erect a monument on the Tippecanoe battle ground in Tippecanoe County, Indiana.

34 St. 1411; Mar. 4, 1907; C. 2929—An Act To confer certain civic rights on the Metlakahtla Indians of Alaska.[22] Sec. 1—48 U. S. C. 237; Sec. 2—48 U. S. C. 238.

34 St. 1413; Mar. 4, 1907; C. 2933—An Act To quiet title to lands on Jicarilla Reservation, and to authorize the Secretary of the Interior to cause allotments to be made, and to dispose of the merchantable timber, and for other purposes.[23]

34 St. 1420; Jan. 29, 1907; Joint Res. No. 9—Joint Resolution Extending protection of second proviso of section one of the Act of December 21, 1904, to certain entrymen.[24]

34 St. 1456; Feb. 5, 1906; C. 133—An Act Granting an increase of pension to James Sloan.

34 St. 1460; Feb. 5, 1906; C. 154—An Act Granting an increase of pension to Angelina Hernandez.

34 St. 1505; Feb. 19, 1906; C. 362—An Act Granting an increase of pension to Washington Hogans.

34 St. 1508; Feb. 19, 1906; C. 373—An Act Granting an increase of pension to James A. M. Brown.

34 St. 1513; Feb. 19, 1906; C. 397—An Act Granting an increase of pension to John J. Grant.

34 St. 1513; Feb. 19, 1906; C. 398—An Act Granting an increase of pension to Frances Ann Batchelor.

34 St. 1514; Feb. 19, 1906; C. 402—An Act Granting a pension to Mary K. Lewis.

34 St. 1514; Feb. 19, 1906; C. 403—An Act Granting an increase of pension to Epsy Ann Austin.

34 St. 1526; Feb. 19, 1906; C. 455—An Act Granting an increase of pension to John W. Roache.

34 St. 1529; Feb. 19, 1906; C. 467—An Act Granting an increase of pension to James Eiffert.

34 St. 1548; Mar. 7, 1906; C. 575—An Act Granting an increase of pension to William O. Colson.

34 St. 1549; Mar. 7, 1906; C. 577—An Act Granting an increase of pension to Joseph B. Papy.

34 St. 1557; Mar. 7, 1906; C. 614—An Act Granting an increase of pension to Matthew D. Raker, junior.

34 St. 1559; Mar. 7, 1906; C. 621—An Act Granting an increase of pension to Anthony W. Presley.

34 St. 1568; Mar. 12, 1906; C. 671—An Act Granting an increase of pension to Stephen Weeks.

34 St. 1569; Mar. 12, 1906; C. 672—An Act Granting an increase of pension to Julius D. Rogers.

34 St. 1570; Mar. 12, 1906; C. 679—An Act Granting an increase of pension to Sarah Johnson.

34 St. 1618; Mar. 12, 1906; C. 896—An Act Granting an increase of pension to Sion B. Glazner.

34 St. 1627; Mar. 12, 1906; C. 935—An Act Granting an increase of pension to Martha Miller.

34 St. 1642; Mar. 19, 1906; C. 1017—An Act Granting an increase of pension to Eleanora A. Keeler.

34 St. 1676; Mar. 26, 1906; C. 1178—An Act Granting an increase of pension to Henry W. Perkins.

34 St. 1687; Mar. 26, 1906; C. 1227—An Act Granting an increase of pension to William Miller.

---

[8] *Sg.* 4 St. 442; 7 St. 46, 51, 85, 99, 114, 185, 213, 236, 240, 296, 317, 320, 425, 541, 545; 9 St. 35, 854, 855; 10 St. 1071, 1079; 11 St. 613, 614, 702, 729, 744, 757; 12 St. 118, sec. 5; 220, sec. 10; 393, sec. 8; 441, sec. 1; 754, sec. 2; 981, 1173; 13 St. 29, 675; 14 St. 467, sec. 10; 15 St. 111, sec. 1; 15 St. 622, 637, 652, 676; 16 St. 40, 720; 17 St. 333, sec. 1 and 2; 18 St. 177; 19 St. 256, 287; 24 St. 388; 25 St. 97, 645, 688, 888, 890, 894; 26 St. 794, 1029; 27 St. 62, 139, 644; 30 St. 90, 504; 32 St. 388, 653, 716, 842; 33 St. 48, 201, 204, 205, 208, 321, 597, 1017, 1060; 34 St. 144, 145, 352, 376, 377. *Ag.* 26 St. 712; 34 St. 214, 333. *Rp.* 41 St. 3. *S.* 35 St. 8, 70, 317, 444, 478, 781; 36 St. 269; 37 St. 64, 518; 38 St. 77, 582; 39 St. 123, 969; 40 St. 561; 41 St. 3; 46 St. 1201, 1522. *Cited:* Brown, 39 Yale L. J. 307; Tydings, 23 Case & Com. 743; 29 Op. A. G. 455; 36 Op. A. G. 98; 2 L. D. Memo. 368; 4 L. D. Memo. 72; 5 L. D. Memo. 168; 14 L. D. Memo. 493; Op. Sol. M. 6083, Oct. 29, 1921, M. 25258, June 26, 1929; Op. A. G., Oct. 5, 1929; Letter to Sen. Wm. H. King from Comm'r, Jan. 9, 1931; Memo. Sol., Mar. 25, 1936, July 3, 1936; Memo. Ind. Off., Apr. 12, 1938; Letter from Act'g Comm'r to Supt. Ft. Hall Agency, Sept. 19, 1938; 34 L. D. 419; 38 L. D. 422; 40 L. D. 4; 40 L. D. 9; 40 L. D. 179; 40 L. D. 211; 40 L. D. 212; 43 L. D. 101; 48 L. D. 472; 48 L. D. 455; 49 L. D. 376; Anchor, 256 U. S. 519; Amicker, 246 U. S. 110; Bisek, 5 F. 2d 994; Brown, 41 C. Cls. 283; Browning, 6 F. 2d 801; Creek, 78 C. Cls. 474; Dickson, 242 U. S. 371; Drapeau, 195 Fed. 130; Henkel, 237 U. S. 45; Jump, 100 F. 2d 130; Larkin, 276 U. S. 431; Ledbetter, 23 F. 2d 81; Locke, 287 Fed. 276; Medawakanton, 57 C. Cls. 357; Minnesota, 305 U. S. 382; Morrison, 6 F. 2d 811; Muskrat, 219 U. S. 346; Shawnee, 249 Fed. 583; Sully, 195 Fed. 113; U. S. v. Birdsall, 233 U. S. 223; U. S. v. Board, 193 Fed. 485; U. S. v. Boylan, 265 Fed. 165; U. S. v. Debell, 227 Fed. 771; U. S. v. Debell, 227 Fed. 775; U. S. v. First, 234 U. S. 245; U. S. v. Glacier, 17 F. Supp. 411; U. S. v. Hameratha, 40 F. 2d 305; U. S. v. Nez Perce, 267 Fed. 495; U. S. v. One Ford, 259 Fed. 645; U. S. v. One 7-Passenger, 259 Fed. 641; U. S. v. Park Land, 188 Fed. 383; U. S. v. Seufert, 252 Fed. 51; U. S. v. Stevens, 31 F. 2d 520; U. S. v. Waller, 243 U. S. 452; Work, 29 F. 2d 393.

[9] Also see 25 U. S. C. 199a (48 St. 501).

[10] Also see 25 U. S. C. 412a (sec. 2, 49 St. 1542 as amended 50 St. 188).

[11] *Cited:* Sac and Fox, 45 C. Cls. 287.

[12] *Sg.* 21 St. 199; 28 St. 372.

[13] *Sg.* 10 St. 1109. *Ag.* 31 St. 766.

[14] *A.* 39 St. 123. *Cited:* Op. Sol., M. 11879, May 31, 1924, M. 25258, June 26, 1929; Op. A. G., Oct. 5, 1929; U. S. v. Algoma, 305 U. S. 415.

[15] *S.* 39 St. 128, sec. 1.

[16] *Sg.* 34 St. 355.

[17] *Sg.* 12 St. 393, sec. 8; 12 St. 754, sec. 2; 17 St. 333, sec. 1. *S.* 35 St. 70; 36 St. 265; 37 St. 21. *Cited:* 40 L. D. 4; 40 L. D. 9; U. S. v. Nice, 241 U. S. 591.

[18] *Ag.* 33 St. 724, sec. 5. *A.* 37 St. 649.

[19] *Ag.* 34 St. 267, sec. 16, 17, 20. *Cited:* Joines, 274 U. S. 544; Priddy, 204 Fed. 955; Southern, 241 U. S. 582; Williams, 216 U. S. 582; Young, 176 Fed. 612.

[20] *Sg.* 34 St. 205.

[21] *Sg.* 23 St. 385; 25 St. 1004; 26 St. 853; 28 St. 233; 33 St. 1049; 34 St. 637. *S.* 35 St. 907, 478; 36 St. 202, 1289; 37 St. 595. *Cited:* Browning, 6 F. 2d 801.

[22] *Sg.* 34 St. 193.

[23] *Sg.* 24 St. 388. *A.* 40 St. 561. *Cited:* Memo. Sol., Feb. 8, 1935.

[24] *Sg.* 33 St. 595.

34 St. 1691, Mar. 26, 1906, C. 1244—An Act Granting a pension to Henry R. Hill.
34 St. 1693; Mar. 26, 1906, C. 1256—An Act Granting an increase of pension to Arthur Hatre
34 St. 1697, Mar. 26, 1906, C. 1274—An Act Granting an increase of pension to Elizabeth Morgan
34 St. 1704, Mar. 26, 1906, C. 1302—An Act Granting an increase of pension to Thomas Chandler, alias Thomas Cooper
34 St. 1719, Apr. 11, 1906; C. 1397—An Act Granting an increase of pension to Rufus G. Childress
34 St. 1740, Apr. 11, 1906; C. 1492—An Act Granting an increase of pension to Alphens M. Beall
34 St. 1741; Apr. 11, 1906, C. 1496—An Act Granting a pension to Thomas J. Chambers
34 St. 1756; Apr. 11, 1906, C. 1561—An Act Granting an increase of pension to John Cook
34 St. 1768, Apr. 12, 1906; C. 1618—An Act Granting relief to the estate of James Staley, deceased
34 St. 1787; Apr. 23, 1906, C. 1782—An Act Granting an increase of pension to Nathan Coward.
34 St. 1808; Apr. 23, 1906; C. 1801—An Act Granting an increase of pension to William J. Hays
34 St. 1812, Apr. 23, 1906, C. 1845—An Act Granting an increase of pension to Asa Wall
34 St. 1813, Apr. 23, 1906, C. 1847—An Act Granting an increase of pension to Mary C. Moore.
34 St. 1814; Apr. 23, 1906, C. 1850—An Act Granting an increase of pension to Nancy N. Allen
34 St. 1828; Apr. 26, 1906; C. 1923—An Act Granting an increase of pension to Jesse Alderman
34 St. 1836; Apr. 26, 1906, C. 1960—An Act Granting an increase of pension to James H. Gardner
34 St. 1841, Apr. 26, 1906, C. 1984—An Act Granting an increase of pension to Martha E. Wardlaw.
34 St. 1842, Apr. 26, 1906; C. 1990—An Act Granting a pension to Margaret Lewis.
34 St. 1843, Apr. 26, 1906; C. 1991—An Act Granting an increase of pension to William H. Houston
34 St. 1844, Apr. 27, 1906, C. 1998—An Act Granting a pension to Elizabeth B. Bean.
34 St. 1877, May 7, 1906; C. 2165—An Act Granting an increase of pension to William C. Herridge
34 St. 1910; May 7, 1906, C. 2371—An Act Granting an increase of pension to Sheldon B. Fargo
34 St. 1939; May 10, 1906, C. 2445—An Act Granting an increase of pension to William F. M. Rice.
34 St. 1958; May 21, 1906; C. 2531—An Act Granting a pension to William O. Clark
34 St. 1968; May 26, 1906; C. 2562—An Act Granting a pension to Henry Sistrunk.
34 St. 1968; May 26, 1906, C. 2563—An Act Granting an increase of pension to Isaac L. Duggar.
34 St. 1982, June 6, 1906, C. 2684—An Act Granting an increase of pension to Lawyer Sugs.
34 St. 1987; June 6, 1906; C. 2706—An Act Granting an increase of pension to William Wiley
34 St. 1998; June 6, 1906; C. 2783—An Act Granting an increase of pension to Thomas Crowley.
34 St. 2007; June 6, 1906; C. 2789—An Act Granting a pension to Delilah Moore
34 St. 2012; June 6, 1906; C. 2818—An Act Granting an increase of pension to Mahala Jones.
34 St. 2015; June 6, 1906; C. 2833—An Act Granting an increase of pension to Virginia J. D. Holmes.
34 St. 2027; June 6, 1906; C. 2888—An Act Granting an increase of pension to Asenith Woodall
34 St. 2036; June 6, 1906; C. 2926—An Act Granting an increase of pension to Georgia A. Hughs
34 St. 2037, June 6, 1906; C. 2931—An Act Granting an increase of pension to Sherwood F. Culberson.
34 St. 2040; June 6, 1906, C. 2944—An Act Granting an increase of pension to Josephine L. Jordan
34 St. 2043; June 6, 1906; C. 2961—An Act Granting an increase of pension to Rachel Allen
34 St. 2047; June 6, 1906, C. 2978—An Act Granting an increase of pension to Isaiah H. Haslitt
34 St. 2050; June 6, 1906; C. 2991—An Act Granting an increase of pension to Susan E. Nash.
34 St. 2051; June 6, 1906; C. 2997—An Act Granting an increase of pension to Hannah J. K. Thomas.
34 St. 2057; June 6, 1906; C. 3023—An Act Granting an increase of pension to James G. Wall
34 St. 2093; June 11, 1906, C. 3210—An Act Granting an increase of pension to Andrew C. Woodard
34 St. 2095, June 11, 1906, C. 3219—An Act Granting an increase of pension to Mary McFarlane
34 St. 2096, June 11, 1906; C. 3222—An Act Granting an increase of pension to Mary E. Patterson
34 St. 2099; June 11, 1906, C. 3237—An Act Granting an increase of pension to Martha A. Dunlap
34 St. 2108; June 11, 1906, C. 3275—An Act Granting an increase of pension to Eliza Jane Witherspoon
34 St. 2108; June 11, 1906; C. 3276—An Act Granting an increase of pension to Sophie S. Parker
34 St. 2127, June 18, 1906, C. 3334—An Act Granting an increase of pension to David B. Johnson
34 St. 2133; June 18, 1906, C. 3408—An Act Granting an increase of pension to Mary J. Ives
34 St. 2134; June 18, 1906; C. 3410—An Act Granting an increase of pension to Margaret Simpson
34 St. 2138, June 18, 1906; C. 3427—An Act Granting an increase of pension to George Gardener.
34 St. 2143; June 20, 1906; C. 3466—An Act Granting an increase of pension to Martha Jane Bolt
34 St. 2147, June 20, 1906, C. 3487—An Act Granting an increase of pension to David McCredie
34 St. 2188, June 29, 1906, C. 3788—An Act Granting an increase of pension to James D. Taylor.
34 St. 2191; June 29, 1906, C. 3818—An Act Granting an increase of pension to Joel Gay.
34 St. 2198, June 29, 1906; C. 3831—An Act Granting an increase of pension to Eliza Rebecca Sims
34 St. 2202, June 29, 1906; C. 3849—An Act Granting an increase of pension to Julia A. Abney.
34 St. 2204, June 29, 1906, C. 3860—An Act Granting an increase of pension to Mary Navy.
34 St. 2205; June 29, 1906, C. 3864—An Act Granting an increase of pension to Mary E. Mundy
34 St. 2207; June 29, 1906, C. 3872—An Act Granting a pension to Alexander McAlister
34 St. 2210, June 29, 1906, C. 3888—An Act Granting an increase of pension to Ann W. Whitaker
34 St. 2215, June 30, 1906; C. 3950—An Act For the relief of James W. Watson
34 St. 2220; June 30, 1906; C. 3973—An Act For the relief of Thomas H. Kent.
34 St. 2232, June 30, 1906; C. 3982—An Act Granting a pension to Josephine V. Sparks
34 St. 2243, Jan. 12, 1907, C. 96—An Act Granting an increase of pension to Louisa M. Sees
34 St. 2246; Jan. 12, 1907; C. 108—An Act Granting an increase of pension to Susan M. Osborn.
34 St. 2248, Jan. 12, 1907; C. 119—An Act Granting an increase of pension to Louise J. Pratt.
34 St. 2249; Jan. 12, 1907; C. 121—An Act Granting an increase of pension to Mary Isabella Rykard.
34 St. 2249, Jan. 12, 1907; C. 123—An Act Granting an increase of pension to Susan M. Long.
34 St. 2250; Jan. 12, 1907; C. 125—An Act Granting an increase of pension to Margaret R. Vandiver.
34 St. 2250; Jan. 12, 1907; C. 126—An Act Granting an increase of pension to Anna Lamar Walker.
34 St. 2251; Jan. 12, 1907; C. 131—An Act Granting an increase of pension to Emma L. Patterson.
34 St. 2263; Jan. 18, 1907; C. 191—An Act Granting an increase of pension to Aaron Daniels.
34 St. 2265; Jan. 18, 1907, C. 200—An Act Granting a pension to Jane Metts
34 St. 2269; Jan. 18, 1907; C. 220—An Act Granting an increase of pension to Emily Killian.
34 St. 2274; Jan. 18, 1907; C. 240—An Act Granting an increase of pension to Joseph Johnston.
34 St. 2274; Jan. 18, 1907; C. 241—An Act Granting an increase of pension to Sherrod Hamilton.
34 St. 2276; Jan. 18, 1907; C. 250—An Act Granting an increase of pension to Betsey A. Hodges.
34 St. 2303; Jan. 21, 1907; C. 374—An Act Granting an increase of pension to Emily Fox.
34 St. 2311; Jan. 26, 1907; C. 421—An Act For the relief of Augustus Trabing.
34 St. 2314; Feb. 1, 1907; C. 450—An Act Granting an increase of pension to Mary A. Mickler.
34 St. 2377; Feb. 6, 1907; C. 751—An Act Granting an increase of pension to Susan M. Brunson.

34 St. 2378; Feb. 6, 1907; C. 752—An Act Granting an increase of pension to Mary F. Johnson.

34 St. 2379; Feb. 6, 1907; C. 758—An Act Granting an increase of pension to William F. Clinkscales.

34 St. 2380; Feb. 6, 1907; C. 765—An Act Granting an increase of pension to James Butler.

34 St. 2382; Feb. 6, 1907; C. 772—An Act Granting an increase of pension to Eunice Cook.

34 St. 2383; Feb. 6, 1907; C. 778—An Act Granting an increase of pension to Cassia C. Tyler.

34 St. 2384; Feb. 6, 1907; C. 779—An Act Granting an increase of pension to Mary J. Thurmond.

34 St. 2386; Feb. 6, 1907; C. 788—An Act Granting an increase of pension to Ellen Downing.

34 St. 2386; Feb. 6, 1907; C. 792—An Act Granting an increase of pension to Sarah A. Galloway.

34 St. 2408; Feb. 7, 1907; C. 891—An Act For the relief of Esther Rousseau.[25]

34 St. 2411; Feb. 9, 1907; C. 915—An Act For the relief of John C. Lynch.

34 St. 2411; Feb. 9, 1907; C. 916—An Act For the relief of John B. Brown.

34 St. 2415; Feb. 18, 1907; C. 942—An Act Referring the claim of S. W. Peel for legal services rendered the Choctaw Nation of Indians to the Court of Claims for adjudication.

34 St. 2422; Feb. 18, 1907; C. 977—An Act Granting an increase of pension to William H. Kimball.

34 St. 2442; Feb. 19, 1907; C. 1068—An Act Granting an increase of pension to James C. West.

34 St. 2455; Feb. 19, 1907; C. 1127—An Act Granting an increase of pension to Elvina Adams.

34 St. 2456; Feb. 19, 1907; C. 1128—An Act Granting an increase of pension to William W. Jordan.

34 St. 2469; Feb. 25, 1907; C. 1218—An Act Granting a pension to Mary Schoske.

34 St. 2482; Feb. 25, 1907; C. 1278—An Act Granting a pension to Jesse Harral.

34 St. 2483; Feb. 25, 1907; C. 1284—An Act Granting a pension to Rollin S. Belknap.

34 St. 2483; Feb. 25, 1907; C. 1296—An Act Granting a pension to Celestia E. Outlaw.

34 St. 2499; Feb. 25, 1907; C. 1354—An Act Granting an increase of pension to Martin Heller.

34 St. 2522; Feb. 25, 1907; C. 1457—An Act Granting an increase of pension to John Bryant.

34 St. 2522; Feb. 25, 1907; C. 1459—An Act Granting an increase of pension to Andrew Canova.

34 St. 2535; Feb. 25, 1907; C. 1515—An Act Granting an increase of pension to Sibby Barnhill.

34 St. 2544; Feb. 25, 1907; C. 1558—An Act Granting an increase of pension to Charlotte S. O'Neall.

34 St. 2554; Feb. 25, 1907; C. 1601—An Act Granting an increase of pension to Thomas L. Williams.

34 St. 2556; Feb. 25, 1907; C. 1611—An Act Granting an increase of pension to James L. Colding.

34 St. 2559; Feb. 25, 1907; C. 1624—An Act Granting an increase of pension to Mary Loomis.

34 St. 2567; Feb. 26, 1907; C. 1665—An Act Granting an increase of pension to Joseph J. Brannan.

34 St. 2577; Feb. 26, 1907; C. 1712—An Act Granting an increase of pension to Emma F. Buchanan.

34 St. 2583; Feb. 26, 1907; C. 1737—An Act Granting an increase of pension to David C. Jones.

34 St. 2583; Feb. 26, 1907; C. 1738—An Act Granting an increase of pension to Phoebe E. Sparkman.

34 St. 2587; Feb. 26, 1907; C. 1757—An Act Granting an increase of pension to Timothy Hanlon.

34 St. 2590; Feb. 26, 1907; C. 1772—An Act Granting an increase of pension to Elizabeth Hodge.

34 St. 2592; Feb. 26, 1907; C. 1781—An Act Granting an increase of pension to Shadrack H. J. Alley.

34 St. 2593; Feb. 26, 1907; C. 1782—An Act Granting an increase of pension to Laura G. Hight.

34 St. 2593; Feb. 26, 1907; C. 1784—An Act Granting an increase of pension to Simeon D. Pope.

34 St. 2594; Feb. 26, 1907; C. 1787—An Act Granting an increase of pension to Elizabeth Bulew.

34 St. 2650; Feb. 26, 1907; C. 2042—An Act Granting an increase of pension to Joseph E. Knighten.

[25] *Cited:* Rousseau, 45 C. Cls. 1.

34 St. 2668; Feb. 28, 1907; C. 2130—An Act Granting an increase of pension to Relf Bledsoe.

34 St. 2671; Feb. 28, 1907; C. 2141—An Act Granting an increase of pension to Mary O. Foster.

34 St. 2724; Mar. 1, 1907; C. 2398—An Act Granting an increase of pension to Henderson Stanley.

34 St. 2726; Mar. 1, 1907; C. 2407—An Act Granting an increase of pension to William H. Long.

34 St. 2747; Mar. 1, 1907; C. 2501—An Act Granting an increase of pension to Ann Hudson.

34 St. 2752; Mar. 2, 1907; C. 2603—An Act Granting a pension to John P. Walker.

34 St. 2753; Mar. 2, 1907; C. 2610—An Act Granting an increase of pension to Benjamin James.

34 St. 2757; Mar. 2, 1907; C. 2625—An Act Granting a pension to Edward Miller.

34 St. 2763; Mar. 2, 1907; C. 2653—An Act Granting an increase of pension to Samuel Boyd.

34 St. 2783; Mar. 2, 1907; C. 2744—An Act Granting an increase of pension to Mary Ann Foard.

34 St. 2802; Mar. 2, 1907; C. 2830—An Act Granting an increase of pension to Nancy A. Meredith.

34 St. 2809; Mar. 2, 1907; C. 2859—An Act Granting an increase of pension to Polly Ann Bowman.

34 St. 2820; Mar. 2, 1907; C. 2902—An Act authorizing and directing the Secretary of the Treasury to enter on the roll of Captain Orlando Humason's Company B, First Oregon Mounted Volunteers, the name of Hezekiah Davis.

34 St. 2829; Mar. 8, 1906—Concurrent Res. Colville Indian Reservation.[26]

34 St. 2830; Mar. 26, 1906—Concurrent Res. Kiowa, Comanche, and Apache Indian Reservations, Okla.[27]

34 St. 2832; Apr. 19, 1906—Concurrent Res. Five Civilized Tribes.[28]

34 St. 2833; June 25, 1906—Concurrent Res. Columbia Indian Reservation, Wash.

34 St. 2833; June 28, 1906—Concurrent Res. Five Civilized Tribes.

35 STAT.

35 St. 8; Feb. 15, 1908; C. 27—An Act Making appropriations to supply urgent deficiencies in the appropriations for the fiscal year ending June 30, 1908, and for prior years, and for other purposes.[29]

35 St. 41; Mar. 11, 1908; C. 79—An Act To extend the time of payments on certain homestead entries in Oklahoma.[30]

35 St. 43; Mar. 16, 1908; C. 87—An Act To provide additional station grounds and terminal facilities for the Arizona and California Ry. Co. in the Colorado River Indian Reservation, Arizona Territory.[31]

35 St. 49; Mar. 27, 1908; C. 106—An Act Providing for the platting and selling of the south half of section thirty, township two north, range eleven west of the Indian meridian, in the State of Oklahoma, for town-site purposes.[32]

35 St. 49; Mar. 27, 1908; C. 107—An Act Providing for the disposal of the interests of Indian miners in real estate in Yakima Indian Reservation, Washington.

35 St. 50; Mar. 27, 1908; C. 109—An Act Authorizing the Woodlawn Cemetery Association, of Saint Maries, Idaho, to purchase not to exceed 40 acres of land in the Coeur d'Alene Indian Reservation in Idaho.

35 St. 51; Mar. 28, 1908; C. 111—An Act To authorize the cutting of timber, the manufacture and sale of lumber, and the preservation of the forests on the Menominee Indian Reservation in the State of Wisconsin.[33]

35 St. 53; Mar. 31, 1908; C. 114—An Act To authorize the Secretary of the Interior to issue patent in fee simple for certain lands of the Santee Reservation, in Nebraska, to school district numbered 36, in Knox County, Nebraska.

35 St. 70; Apr. 30, 1908; C. 153—An Act Making appropriations

[26] *Ag.* 34 St. 80.
[27] *Sg.* 34 St. 213.
[28] *Ag.* 34 St. 137
[29] *Sg.* 24 St. 388; 28 St. 695; 32 St. 260; 34 St. 125; 34 St. 342. *Ag.* 34 St. 1047.
[30] *Sg.* 31 St. 213, 550.
[31] *Sg.* 30 St. 990
[32] *Sg.* 12 St. 754, sec. 2. *S.* 38 St. 77. *Cited:* U. S. v. Rowell, 243 U. S. 464.
[33] *A.* 43 St. 793; 48 Ct. 964. *S.* 36 St. 1058; 39 St. 128, 969; 40 St. 561; 41 St. 1225; 42 St. 1174; 43 St. 793, 1313; 44 St. 453; 49 St. 1085; 52 St. 208. *Cited:* U. S. ex rel. Besaw, 6 F. 2d, 694; Memo. Sol., Oct. 20, 1936.

for the current and contingent expenses of the Indian Department, for fulfilling treaty stipulations with various Indian tribes, and for other purposes, for the fiscal year ending June 30, 1909.[34] 25 U. S. C. 47 (sec. 23, 36 St. 61); 25 U. S. C. 52;[35] 25 U. S. C. 94;[36] 25 U. S. C. 295. See USCA Historical Note. 25 U. S. C. 12; 25 U. S. C. 103.[37] USCA Historical Note: Recent Indian appropriation acts make appropriations for the purchase of goods, etc., for the Indian Service, with provisos that no part of the sum so appropriated shall be used for the maintenance of not to exceed three permanent warehouses in the Indian Service. The provision for the fiscal year 1917, was by Act May 18, 1916, sec. 1, 39 St. 123, and limited the appropriation there made to the maintenance of not exceeding two permanent warehouses. 25 U. S. C. 151. USCA Historical Note: A provision, identical with the Code Section, except that the banks which may be selected as depositaries are not confined to National Banks, is contained in sec. 1, of Act June 25, 1910, 36 St. 855, and set out in 25 U. S. C. 372. See Historical Note 25 U. S. C. A. 29. 45 U. S. C. 93; 25 U. S. C. 382.[38]

35 St. 102; May 11, 1908; C. 162—An Act To amend an Act entitled "An Act for the protection of game in Alaska, and for other purposes," approved June 7, 1902.[39]

35 St. 106; May 11, 1908; C. 163—An Act Making appropriation for the support of the Army for the fiscal year ending June 30, 1909.[40]

35 St. 166; May 19, 1908; C. 177—An Act Authorizing the Secretary of the Interior to issue patents in fee to the Board of Missions of the Protestant Episcopal Church for certain lands in the State of Idaho.

35 St. 169; May 20, 1908; C. 181—An Act To authorize the drainage of certain lands in the State of Minnesota.[41]

35 St. 184; May 22, 1908; C. 186—An Act Making appropriations for the legislative, executive, and judicial expenses of the Government for the fiscal year ending June 30, 1909, and for other purposes.[42]

35 St. 251; May 23, 1908; C. 192—An Act Making appropriations for the Department of Agriculture for the fiscal year ending June 30, 1909.[43] 16 U. S. C. 671.

35 St. 268; May 23, 1908; C. 193—An Act Amending the Act of January 14, 1889, and Acts amendatory thereof, and for other purposes.[44]

35 St. 312; May 27, 1908; C. 199—An Act For the removal of restrictions from part of the lands of allottees of the Five Civilized Tribes, and for other purposes.[45]

35 St. 317; May 27, 1908; C. 200—An Act Making appropriations for sundry civil expenses of the Government for the fiscal year ending June 30, 1909, and for other purposes.[46]

35 St. 444; May 29, 1908; C. 216—An Act To authorize the Secretary of the Interior to issue patents in fee to purchasers of Indian lands under any law now existing or hereafter enacted, and for other purposes.[47] Sec. 1—25 U. S. C. 404. (See U. S. C. A. Historical Note.)

35 St. 458; May 29, 1908; C. 217—An Act To authorize the Secretary of the Interior to sell and dispose of the surplus unallotted agricultural lands of the Spokane Indian Reservation, Washington, and for other purposes.[48]

35 St. 460; May 29, 1908; C. 218—An Act To authorize the sale and disposition of a portion of the surplus and unallotted lands in the Cheyenne River and Standing Rock Indian reservations in the States of South Dakota and North Dakota, and making appropriation and provision to carry the same into effect.[49]

35 St. 465; May 29, 1908; C. 220—An Act Authorizing a resurvey of certain townships in the State of Wyoming, and for other purposes.[50]

35 St. 478; May 30, 1908; C. 227—An Act Making appropriations

---

[34] *Sg.* 4 St. 442; 7 St. 51, 85, 99, 114, 185, 213, 236, 296, 317, 320, 321, 425, 541, 545; 9 St. 35, 855; 11 St. 614, 702, 744; 12 St. 981, 1173; 13 St. 624, 675; 14 St. 757; 15 St. 622, 637, 640, 652, 658, 676; 16 St. 40, 720; 19 St. 256, 287; 24 St. 388, 389; 25 St. 642, 688, 888, 894; 26 St. 1029; 27 St. 62, 139, 612; 30 St. 90, 990; 32 St. 267, 888; 33 St. 204, 305, 597, 1016, 1060; 34 St. 137, 333, 352, 368, 377, 1022, 1024, 1230. *Rpg.* 33 St. 50. *A.* 35 St. 444. *Rp.* 45 St. 1534; 46 St. 1028. *S.* 35 St. 781; 36 St. 269, 879; 38 St. 77; 40 St. 561; 41 St. 3; 43 St. 94. *Cited:* 29 Op. A. G. 455; 53 I. D. 187; Brown, 44 C. Cls. 283; Klamath, 81 C. Cls. 79; Klamath, 86 C. Cls. 614; Klamath, 296 U. S. 244; Medawakanton, 57 C. Cls. 357; U. S. v. Algoma, 305 U. S. 415; U. S. v. Birdsall, 253 U. S. 223; U. S. v. Klamath, 304 U. S. 119; U. S. v. Seminole, 299 U. S. 417.

[35] Also see 25 U. S. C. 52a (33 St. 191; 36 St. 125).

[36] *R.* sec. 1, 46 St. 1028.

[37] *R.* sec. 1, 46 St. 1028.

[38] *S.* 35 St. 798.

[39] *Ag.* 32 St. 327. *S.* 35 St. 945; 36 St. 703, 1363; 37 St. 417; 38 St. 4, 77, 609, 822; 39 St. 262; 40 St. 105, 634; 41 St. 163, 874, 1367; 42 St. 552, 1174; 43 St. 390. *A.* 43 St. 668, 822.

[40] *S.* 35 St. 478.

[41] *Sg.* 34 St. 325. *S.* 36 St. 292; 40 St. 1321; 41 St. 1105. *Cited:* 29 Op. A. G. 455; Op. Sol., M. 28791, Aug. 1, 1938.

[42] *Sg.* 1 St. 137. *Cited:* Barnett, 259 Fed. 394.

[43] *Sg.* 33 St. 302. *Cited:* Tydings, 23 Case & Com. 743; 29 Op. A. G. 239.

[44] *Ag.* 32 St. 400. *Sg.* 32 St. 245. *Cited:* 31 Op. A. G. 95; Chippewa, 305 U. S. 479; Chippewa, 305 U. S. 479; Morrison, 266 U. S. 481; Westling, 60 F. 2d. 398.

[45] *Sg.* 32 St. 43; 34 St. 137. *Ag.* 34 St. 137. *A.* 44 St. 239. *S.* 35 St. 781; 36 St. 269; 42 St. 831; 45 St. 200, 495, 1562, 1623; 46 St. 90, 279, 1115; 47 St. 91, 820, 777; 48 St. 362; 49 St. 176, 1757; 50 St. 564; 52 St. 201. *Cited:* Cabell, 3 Okla. S. B. J 208; Dixon, 23 Case & Com. 712; Krieger, 3 Geo. Wash. L. Rev. 279; Reeves 23 Case & Com. 727; Russell, 18 Yale L. J. 328; Wigmore, 24 Ill. L. Rev. 89; 27 Op. A. G. 530; 34 Op. A. G. 275; 35 Op. A. G. 421; 1 L. D. Memo. 227; 2 L. D. Memo. 307; 3 L. D. Memo. 64; 4 L. D. Memo. 63; 4 L. D. Memo. 641; 5 L. D. Memo. 10; 10 L. D. Memo. 364; 12 L. D. Memo. 73; 12 L. D. Memo. 289; Op. Sol., D. 40462, Oct. 31, 1917; Memo. Sol. Off., Dec. 28, 1921; Op. Sol., M. 26067, Apr. 29, 1922; M. 7996, Aug. 2, 1922, D. 46987, Nov. 13, 1922, Oct. 4, 1926, M. 18320, Dec. 21, 1926, 2,2121, Apr. 12, 1927; Memo. Sol. Off., Aug. 21, 1931, Sept. 14, 1931, Sept. 19, 1931, Jan. 20, 1932, June 14, 1933; Sol. Letter of Wm. Keel, Stratford, Okla., Aug. 2, 1933; Memo. Sol. Off., Aug. 15, 1933, Jan. 14, 1935; Memo. Sol., Sept. 20, 1935; Ass't Sec'ys Letter to A. G., Feb. 1, 1935; Memo. Sol. Off., Mar. 8, 1935; Memo. Sol. June 4, 1935; Sept. 21, 1935; Memo. of Comm'r Aug. 11, 1936; Memo. Sol., Sept. 17, 1936; Jan. 13, 1937, Jan. 23, 1937, Feb. 5, 1937, Apr. 8, 1937, May 14, 1938; 49 L. D. 348; 50 L. D. 691; 53 I. D. 48; 53 I. D. 471; 53 I. D. 412; 53 I. D. 502; 54 I. D. 382; Anchor, 256 U. S. 519; Anicker, 246 U. S. 110; Bagby, 60 F. 2d 80; Barbre, 228 Fed. 658; Bartlett, 218 Fed. 380; Baze, 24 F. Supp. 806; Bell, 192 Fed. 597; Bilby, 246 U. S. 255; Bd. of Comm'rs of Tulsa, 94 F. 2d 450; Bond, 25 F. Supp. 157; Brown, 27 F. 2d 274; Bunch, 263 U. S. 250; Burgess, 103 F. 2d 37; Caesar, 103 F. 2d 503; Carpenter, 280 U. S. 363; Chisholm, 273 Fed. 589; Choate, 224 U. S. 665; Commissioner, 78 F. 2d 768; Conner, 32 F. 2d 581; Cully, 37 F. 2d 492; Derrisaw, 8 F. Supp. 876; English, 224 U. S. 680; Etchen, 235 Fed. 104; Ex p. Pero, 99 F. 2d 28; Fink, 248 U. S. 392; Fulsom, 35 F. 2d 84; Gilcrease, 249 U. S. 178; Gleason, 224 U. S. 679; Glenn, 105 F. 2d 398; Goat, 224 U. S. 458; Hallam, 49 F. 2d 103; Hampton, 22 F. 2d 81; Harjo, 28 F. 2d 596; Harris, 254 U. S. 103; Harris, 188 Fed. 712; Heckman, 224 U. S. 413; Hill, 289 Fed. 511; Holmes, 33 F. 2d 688; Holmes, 53 F. 2d 960; Hopkins, 235 Fed. 95; Ickes, 64 F. 2d 982; In re Jessie's, 259 Fed. 95; In re Palmer's, 11 F. Supp. 301; Ind. Ter. Oil, 288 U. S. 317; Jack, 39 F. 2d 595; Jackson, 297 Fed. 549; Jackson, 43 F. 2d 513; Jefferson, 247 U. S. 288; Johnson, 64 F. 2d 674; Jones, 273 U. S. 195; Kemmerer, 229 Fed. 872; Kiker, 63 F. 2d 957; King, 64 F. 2d 979; Ledbetter, 23 F. 2d 81; Locke, 287 Fed. 276; McDaniel, 230 Fed. 945; McNee, 253 Fed. 546; Malone, 212 Fed. 668; Mars, 40 F. 2d 247; Moore, 43 F. 2d 322; Moore, 167 Fed. 826; Mudd, 14 F. 2d 430; Mullen, 240 U. S. 590; Nunn, 216 Fed. 330; Okla., K. & M. I. Ry., 249 Fed. 592; Parker, 250 U. S. 235; Parker, 250 U. S. 66; Pitman, 64 F. 2d 740; Powell, 61 F. 2d 283; Priddy, 204 Fed. 955; Privett, 256 U. S. 201; Roberts, 66 F. 2d 874; Rogers, 263 Fed. 160; Self, 28 F. 2d 590; Seminole, 78 C. Cls. 455; Shaw, 276 U. S. 575; Stewart, 295 U. S. 403; Sunderland, 266 U. S. 226; Supt., 295 U. S. 418; Sweet, 245 U. S. 192; Taylor, 235 U. S. 42; Taylor, 230 Fed. 580; Tiger, 22 F. 2d 786; Tiger, 4 F. 2d 714; Tiger, 221 U. S. 286; Truskett, 236 U. S. 223; U. S. v. Allen, 179 Fed. 13; U. S. v. Bartlett, 235 U. S. 72; U. S. v. Bean, 253 Fed. 1; U. S. v. Black, 247 Fed. 942; U. S. v. Board, 284 Fed. 103; U. S. v. Brown, 8 F. 2d 564; U. S. v. Cook, 225 Fed. 756; U. S. v. Equitable, 283 U. S. 738; U. S. v. Ferguson, 247 U. S. 175; U. S. v. Gray, 284 Fed. 103; U. S. v. Gypsy, 10 F. 2d 487; U. S. v. Haddock, 21 F. 2d 165; U. S. v. Halsell, 247 Fed. 390; U. S. v. Knight, 206 Fed. 145; U. S. v. Law, 250 Fed. 218; U. S. v. Lee, 24 F. Supp. 814; U. S. v. Martin, 45 F. 2d 836; U. S. v. Mid Continent, 67 F. 2d 37; U. S. v. Mott, 37 F. 2d 860; U. S. v. Ransom, 284 Fed. 108; U. S. v. Richards, 27 F. 2d 284; U. S. v. Shock, 187 Fed. 862; U. S. v. Shock, 187 Fed. 870; U. S. v. Smith, 266 Fed. 740; U. S. v. Smith, 279 Fed. 136; U. S. v. Smith, 288 Fed. 356; U. S. v. Tiger, 19 F. 2d 35; U. S. v. Watashe, 102 F. 2d 428; U. S. v. Western Inv. Co., 226 Fed. 726; U. S. v. Woods, 223 Fed. 316; U. S. ex rel. Warren, 73 F. 2d 844; Vinson, 44 F. 2d 772; Ward, 253 U. S. 17; Welch, 15 F. 2d 184; Whitebird, 40 F. 2d 479; Whitechurch, 92 F. 2d 249; Williams, 218 Fed. 797; Willmott, 27 F. 2d 277; Winton, 255 U. S. 373.

[46] *Sg.* 34 St. 205, 354, 1049. *S.* 36 St. 774. *Cited:* 53 I. D. 593; 53 I. D. 637.

[47] *Sg.* 12 St. 393, sec. 8; 17 St. 333, sec. 1; 22 St. 645; 25 St. 888; 30 St. 495; 31 St. 677, 1094; 32 St. 506; 34 St. 62, 137, 140, 213, 1015. *Ag.* 33 St. 302, sec. 9; 35 St. 70. *A.* 36 St. 190, 855; 40 St. 1203. *S.* 35 St. 781; 36 St. 269; 38 St. 510; 39 St. 123; 45 St. 684, c. 662, 1562, 1623; 46 St. 90, 279, 1114; 47 St. 91; 47 St. 820; 48 St. 362; 49 St. 176, 1757; 50 St. 564; 52 St. 291. *Cited:* Brown, 39 Yale L. J. 307; Knoepfler, 7 Iowa L. B. 232; Tydings, 23 Case & Com. 743; 36 Op. A. G. 98; Op. Sol., M. 6376, Nov. 15, 1921, M. 18604, Mar. 6, 1926; Letter from Asst. Sec'y to Comm'r of Ind. Affairs, Aug. 14, 1926; Op. Sol., M. 25258, June 26, 1929; Letter from Dept. of Jus. to Secy of Int., Oct. 5, 1929; 38 L. D. 422; 38 L. D. 427; 38 L. D. 559; 40 L. D. 4; 40 L. D. 179; 40 L. D. 212; Choctaw, 88 C. Cls. 49; Garland's, 256 U. S. 439; Garland's, 272 U. S. 728; Green, 46 C. Cls. 68; Green, 47 C. Cls. 281; Green, 233 U. S. 558; Johnson, 283 Fed. 954; Minnesota, 305 U. S. 382; Scheer, 48 F. 2d 327; Turner, 51 C. Cls. 125; Turner, 248 U. S. 354; U. S. v. Algoma, 305 U. S. 415; U. S. v. McIntire, 101 F. 2d 650; U. S. v. Rowell, 243 U. S. 464; U. S. v. Yakima, 274 Fed. 115; Winton, 255 U. S. 373; Work, 29 F. 2d 393.

[48] *Sg.* 12 St. 393, sec. 8; 17 St. 333, sec. 1. *S.* 40 St. 561. *Cited:* Northern, 246 U. S. 283.

[49] *Sg.* 12 St. 393, sec. 8; 754, sec. 2; 17 St. 333, sec. 1. *A.* 36 St. 196; 40 St. 561. *S.* 36 St. 269, 602, 1058; 37 St. 84, 518, 653, 675; 41 St. 1446; 44 St. 1389. *Cited:* Tydings, 23 Case & Com. 743; Hatten v. Hudspeth, 99 F. 2d 501; U. S. v. La Plant, 200 Fed. 92.

[50] *Sg.* 31 St. 134; 33 St. 46.

to supply deficiencies in the appropriations for the fiscal year ending June 30, 1908, and for prior years, and for other purposes.[51]

35 St. 553; May 30, 1908; C. 230—An Act Pensioning the surviving officers and enlisted men of the Texas volunteers employed in the defense of the frontier of that State against Mexican marauders and Indian depredations from 1855 to 1860, inclusive, and for other purposes.[52] 38 U. S. C. 373.

35 St. 558; May 30, 1908; C. 237—An Act For the survey and allotment of lands now embraced within the limits of the Fort Peck Indian Reservation, in the State of Montana, and the sale and disposal of all the surplus lands after allotment.[53]

35 St. 579; May 30, 1908; J. Res. No. 32—Joint Resolution Authorizing the employment of clerical services in the Department of Justice.

35 St. 597; Feb. 6, 1909; C. 77—An Act Authorizing the Secretary of the Interior to sell isolated tracts of land within the Nez Perces Indian Reservation.

35 St. 600; Feb. 6, 1909; C. 80—An Act Relating to affairs in the Territories.[54]

35 St. 614; Feb. 9, 1909, C. 101—An Act Making appropriations to supply urgent deficiencies in the appropriations for the fiscal year ending June 30, 1909.

35 St. 619; Feb. 15, 1909; C. 126—An Act For the relief of the Mille Lac band of Chippewa Indians in the State of Minnesota, and for other purposes.[55]

35 St. 626; Feb. 17, 1909; C. 138—An Act Authorizing sales of land within the Coeur d'Alene Indian Reservation to the Northern Idaho Insane Asylum and to the University of Idaho.

35 St. 627; Feb. 18, 1909; C. 144—An Act To amend the laws of the United States relating to the registration of trademarks.[56]

35 St. 628; Feb. 18, 1909; C. 145—An Act To enable the Omaha and Winnebago Indians to protect from overflow their tribal and allotted lands located within the boundaries of any drainage district in Nebraska.[57]

35 St. 636; Feb. 18, 1909; C. 147—An Act To extend the time of payments on certain homestead entries in Oklahoma.[58]

35 St. 642; Feb. 20, 1909; C. 167—An Act For the investigation, treatment, and prevention of trachoma among the Indians.

35 St. 644; Feb. 24, 1909; C. 178—An Act To provide for the granting and patenting to the State of Colorado desert lands within the former Ute Indian Reservation in said State.[59] Secs. 1 & 2—43 U. S. C. 647.

35 St. 650; Feb. 25, 1909; C. 197—An Act Extending the time for final entry of mineral claims within the Shoshone or Wind River Reservation in Wyoming.[60]

35 St. 732; Mar. 3, 1909; C. 252—An Act Making appropriation for the support of the army for the fiscal year ending June 30, 1910.

35 St. 751; Mar. 3, 1909; C. 253—An Act For the removal of the restrictions on alienation and lands of allottees of the Quapaw Agency, Oklahoma, and the sale of all tribal lands, school, agency, or other buildings on any of the reservations within the jurisdiction of such agency, and for other purposes.[61]

35 St. 778; Mar. 3, 1909; C. 256—An Act Authorizing the Secretary of the Interior to sell part or all of the surplus lands of members of the Kaw or Kansas and Osage tribes of Indians in Oklahoma, and for other purposes.[62]

35 St. 781; Mar. 3, 1909; C. 263—An Act Making appropriations for the current and contingent expenses of the Indian Department, for fulfilling treaty stipulations with various Indian tribes, and for other purposes, for the fiscal year ending June 30, 1910.[63] Sec. 1—25 U. S. C. 320;[64] 25 U. S. C. 10; 25 U. S. C. 289. USCA Historical Note: By Act May 24, 1922, 42 St. 552, all reservation and non-reservation boarding schools with an average attendance of less than forty-five and eighty pupils respectively were to be discontinued on or before the beginning of the fiscal year 1923, the Hope Indian School for girls at Springfield, South Dakota, however, being excepted from this limitation as to attendance. The pupils in the schools, discontinued pursuant to this act were to be transferred first, if possible, to Indian day schools, or state public schools, second to adjacent reservation or non-reservation boarding schools to the limit of the capacity of said schools. This act also provided for the discontinuance prior to fiscal year 1923 of all day schools with an average attendance of less than 8. 25 U. S. C. 290;[65] 25 U. S. C. 396; 25 U. S. C. 37 (sec. 10, 18 St. 450). See Historical Note 25 U. S. C. A. 37. 25 U. S. C. 344; 25 U. S. C. 382 (35 St. 85).

35 St. 837; Mar. 3, 1909; C. 266—An Act Authorizing the Attorney-General to appoint as special peace officers such employees of the Alaska school service as may be named by the Secretary of the Interior.[66] 48 U. S. C. 172.

35 St. 838; Mar. 3, 1909; C. 269—An Act To amend section 86 of an Act to provide a government for the Territory of Hawaii, to provide for additional judges, and for other judicial purposes.[67]

35 St. 845; Mar. 4, 1909; C. 297—An Act Making appropriations for the legislative, executive, and judicial expenses of the Government for the fiscal year ending June 30, 1910, and for other purposes.

35 St. 907; Mar. 4, 1909; C. 298—An Act Making appropriations for the fiscal year ending June 30, 1909, and for prior years, and for other purposes.[68]

35 St. 945; Mar. 4, 1909; C. 299—An Act Making appropriations for sundry civil expenses of the Government for the fiscal year ending June 30, 1910, and for other purposes.[69]

35 St. 1039; Mar. 4, 1909; C. 301—An Act Making appropriations for the Department of Agriculture for the fiscal year ending June 30, 1910.[70]

35 St. 1088; Mar. 4, 1909; C. 321—An Act To codify, revise, and amend the penal laws of the United States.[71] Sec. 50—18 U. S. C. 104; Sec. 329—18 U. S. C. 549; 28 U. S. C. 51.

35 St. 1167; Feb. 27, 1909; J. Res. No. 18—Joint Resolution To provide for an accounting of certain funds held in trust for the Chippewa Indians in Minnesota.[72]

---

[51] *Sg.* 12 St. 221, 276; 26 St. 853; 33 St. 1224; 34 St. 1035, 1376; 35 St. 108. *S.* 35 St. 907. *Cited:* 49 L. D. 376; Worcester, 6 Pet. 515.

[52] *Sg.* 27 St. 281. *S.* 37 St. 679.

[53] *Sg.* 12 St. 393, sec. 8; 12 St. 754, sec. 2; 17 St. 333, sec. 1; 32 St. 388. *A.* 44 St. 1401. *S.* 38 St. 77, 582; 39 St. 123, 994; 41 St. 365, 408, 549; 44 St. 498, 1250; 45 St. 774. *Cited:* Tydings, 23 Case & Com. 743; Op. Sol. M. 12498, June 6, 1924, M. 28028, May 24, 1935; Memo. Sol., July 17, 1930.

[54] *Ag.* 30 St. 1253, sec. 464, 465, 468. *Rpg.* 15 St. 241, sec. 4; 23 St. 28, sec. 14. *R.* 48 St. 583. *Cited:* 29 Op. A. G. 131; Op. Sol. M. 29147, May 6, 1937; 53 I. D. 593; Lott, 205 U. S. 28; U. S. v. First, 234 U. S. 245.

[55] *S.* 39 St. 801. *Cited:* Mille Lac, 46 C. Cls. 424; U. S. v. Minnesota, 270 U. S. 181.

[56] *Ag.* 16 St. 210, sec. 77; 33 St. 724; 34 St. 169.

[57] *Cited:* 29 Op. A. G. 239.

[58] *Ag.* 34 St. 213, 550. *S.* 38 St. 77.

[59] *Sg.* 28 St. 422; 29 St. 434; 31 St. 1188.

[60] *Ag.* 33 St. 1021. *A.* 45 St. 371.

[61] *A.* 43 St. 723. *S.* 43 St. 722. *Cited:* 3 L. D. Memo. 435; Op. Sol., M. 24284, May 9, 1928; 40 L. D. 211; 40 L. D. 212.

[62] *Cited:* Memo. Sol. Off., Nov. 5, 1930; Adams, 59 F. 2d 653; Browning, 6 F. 2d 801; Drummond, 84 F. 2d 755; Kansas, 80 C. Cls. 264; Levindale, 241 U. S. 432; Morrison, 6 F. 2d 811; U. S. v. Aaron, 183 Fed. 347; Work, 266 U. S. 161.

[63] *Sg.* 4 St. 442; 7 St. 46, 51, 85, 99, 114, 185, 218, 236, 296, 317, 320, 425, 541, 544, 596; 9 St. 35, 855; 11 St. 614, 702, 729; 12 St. 981, 1173, 1191; 13 St. 675; 14 St. 756; 15 St. 622, 637, 640, 652, 658, 676; 16 St. 40, 355, 720; 19 St. 256, 287; 21 St. 199, 204; 24 St. 388; 25 St. 645, 688, 888, 894; 26 St. 1029; 27 St. 62, 139, 644; 30 St. 90; 31 St. 1094; 32 St. 388, 506; 33 St. 189, 194, 201, 302, 304, 360, 394, 597, 1016; 34 St. 62, 145, 354, 375, 377, 1024; 35 St. 83, 87, 312, 444, 448. *Ag.* 18 St. 451; 35 St. 564. *A.* 40 St. 1203. *S.* 36 St. 118, 202, 269, 296, 349, 774, 873; 38 St. 77; 40 St. 433; 42 St. 1174; 45 St. 200, 1562, 1623; 46 St. 90, 279, 1114; 47 St. 91, 820; 48 St. 362; 49 St. 176, 1757; 50 St. 564; 52 St. 291. *Cited:* Brown, 39 Yale L. J. 307; Tydings, 23 Case & Com. 743; 3 L. D. Memo. 435; 3 L. D. Memo. 477; Hallom, 49 F. 2d 103; Kansas, 80 C. Cls. 264; Medawakanton, 57 C. Cls. 357; Montana, 95 F. 2d 897; Pronovost, 232 U. S. 487; U. S. v. Birdsall, 233 U. S. 223; U. S. v. 12 Bottles, 201 Fed. 191; Ute, 45 C. Cls. 440; Op. Sol., M. 7002, Mar. 10, 1922; M. 11410, Jan. 28, 1924; M. 12498, June 6, 1924; M. 12509, Aug. 27, 1924; Memo. Sol. Off., Aug. 15, 1933; Memo. Sol., Nov. 12, 1934, July 8, 1936, Mar. 6, 1937; 43 L. D. 84, 43 L. D. 504; 44 L. D. 188; 44 L. D. 505; 48 L. D. 567; 50 L. D. 676.

[64] *S.* 36 St. 349.

[65] Also see 25 U. S. C. 396a (sec. 1, 52 St. 347); 25 U. S. C. 396b (sec. 2, 52 St. 347); 25 U. S. C. 396c (sec. 3, 52 St. 347); 25 U. S. C. 396d (sec. 4, 52 St. 347); 25 U. S. C. 396e (sec. 5, 52 St. 347); 25 U. S. C. 396f (sec. 6, 52 St. 347).

[66] *Sg.* 30 St. 1253.

[67] *Ag.* 34 St. 267. *Cited:* 50 L. D. 676.

[68] *Sg.* 15 St. 655; 19 St. 254; 26 St. 853; 34 St. 1403; 35 St. 480. *Cited:* Cherokee, 270 U. S. 476; Eastern or Emigrant, 82 C. Cls. 180.

[69] *Sg.* 35 St. 102. *Rp.* 36 St. 855. *S.* 36 St. 118, 774. *Cited:* Heckman, 224 U. S. 413; U. S. v. One Ford, 259 Fed. 645.

[70] *Cited:* Ex p. Tilden, 28 Fed. 920.

[71] *Rg.* 23 St. 362, sec. 9; 25 St. 166; 29 St. 821; 32 St. 793. *A.* 36 St. 855; 47 St. 336. *S.* 49 St. 1513; 50 St. 805. *Cited:* Pound, 22 Colum. L. Rev. 97; Sol. Op. 2.2121, Apr. 12, 1927; Sol. Off. Memo., Jan. 19, 1937; Andreas, 71 F. 2d 908; Apapas, 233 U. S. 589; Bailey, 47 F. 2d 702; Brown, 146 Fed. 975; Davis, 32 F. 2d 860; Eugene Sol Louie, 274 Fed. 47; Ex p. Pero, 99 F. 2d 28; Hatten, 99 F. 2d 501; Janus, 38 F. 2d 431; Joplin, 236 U. S. 531; Lott, 205 Fed. 28; Louie, 254 U. S. 548; Quagon, 5 F. 2d 608; U. S. v. Chavez, 290 U. S. 357; U. S. v. Gardner, 189 Fed. 690; U. S. v. Lewis, 253 Fed. 469; U. S. v. Pelican, 232 U. S. 442; U. S. v. Seneca, 274 Fed. 947; U. S. ex rel. Lynn, 233 Fed. 685; Yohyowan, 291 Fed. 425.

[72] *Sg.* 25 St. 642.

35 St. 1167; Feb. 27, 1909; J. Res. No. 19—Joint Resolution Relative to homestead designations, made and to be made, of members of the Osage Tribe of Indians.[73]

35 St. 1170; Mar. 4, 1909; J. Res. No. 28—Joint Resolution Concerning and relating to the treaty between the United States and Russia.

35 St. 1177; Feb. 25, 1908; C. 39—An Act Granting an increase of pension to John S. Hyatt.

35 St. 1177; Feb. 25, 1908; C. 40—An Act Granting an increase of pension to John Lowder.

35 St. 1178; Feb. 25, 1908; C. 44—An Act Granting an increase of pension to Martha Stewart.

35 St. 1178; Feb. 25, 1908; C. 45—An Act Granting an increase of pension to John Lourcey.

35 St. 1179; Feb. 25, 1908; C. 46—An Act Granting an increase of pension to William C. O'Neal.

35 St. 1179; Feb. 25, 1908; C. 47—An Act Granting an increase of pension to Hester Nite.

35 St. 1179; Feb. 25, 1908; C. 48—An Act Granting an increase of pension to Elizabeth Sweat.

35 St. 1179; Feb. 25, 1908; C. 49—An Act Granting an increase of pension to Nancy Motes.

35 St. 1179; Feb. 25, 1908; C. 50—An Act Granting an increase of pension to Jane C. Stingley.

35 St. 1204; Mar. 9, 1908; C. 74—An Act Granting pensions and increase of pensions to certain soldiers and sailors of the Regular Army and Navy, and certain soldiers and sailors of wars other than the civil war, and to widows and dependent relatives of such soldiers and sailors.

35 St. 1219; Mar. 13, 1908; C. 85—An Act Granting pensions and increase of pensions to certain soldiers and sailors of the war with Spain and other wars, and to the widows of such soldiers and sailors.

35 St. 1375; May 25, 1908; C. 197—An Act Granting pensions and increase of pensions to certain soldiers and sailors of the civil war and other wars, and to certain widows and dependent relatives of such soldiers and sailors.

35 St. 1389; May 27, 1908; C. 207—An Act Granting pension and increase of pension to certain soldiers and sailors of the war with Spain and other wars, and to the widows of such soldiers and sailors.

35 St. 1404; Jan. 22, 1909; C. 36—An Act To reimburse Ulysses G. Winn for money erroneously paid into the Treasury of the United States.

35 St. 1404; Jan. 23, 1909; C. 38—An Act For the relief of D. J. Holmes.

35 St. 1406; Jan. 23, 1909; C. 43—An Act Granting pensions and increase of pensions to certain soldiers and sailors of the Regular Army and Navy, and certain soldiers and sailors of wars other than the civil war, and to widows and dependent relatives of such soldiers and sailors.

35 St. 1407; Jan. 25, 1909; C. 44—An Act For the relief of Charles H. Dickson.

35 St. 1431; Jan. 28, 1909; C. 50—An Act Granting pensions and increase of pensions to certain soldiers and sailors of the Regular Army and Navy, and certain soldiers and sailors of wars other than the civil war, and to widows and dependent relatives of such soldiers and sailors.

35 St. 1432; Feb. 1, 1909; C. 57—An Act To provide for the payment of certain volunteers who rendered service in the Territory of Oregon in the Cayuse Indian war of 1847 and 1848.

35 St. 1437; Feb. 6, 1909; C. 95—An Act For the relief of the heirs of Thomas J. Miller.

35 St. 1446; Feb. 17, 1909; C. 141—An Act Granting pensions and increase of pensions to certain soldiers and sailors of the Regular Army and Navy, and certain soldiers and sailors of wars other than the civil war, and to widows and dependent relatives of such soldiers and sailors.

35 St. 1462; Feb. 18, 1909; C. 154—An Act Granting pensions and increase of pensions to certain soldiers and sailors of wars other than the civil war, and to certain widows and dependent relatives of such soldiers and sailors.

35 St. 1536; Feb. 27, 1909; C. 230—An Act Granting pensions and increase of pensions to certain soldiers and sailors of the Regular Army and Navy, and certain soldiers of wars other than the civil war, and to widows and dependent relatives of such soldiers and sailors.

35 St. 1573; Mar. 3, 1909; C. 285—An Act Granting pensions and increase of pensions to certain soldiers and sailors of the Regular Army and Navy, and certain soldiers and sailors of wars other than the civil war, and to widows and dependent relatives of such soldiers and sailors.

35 St. 1606; Mar. 3, 1909; C. 289—An Act Granting pensions and increase of pensions to certain soldiers and sailors of the Regular Army and Navy, and certain soldiers and sailors of wars other than the civil war, and to widows and dependent relatives of such soldiers and sailors.

35 St. 1616; Mar. 3, 1909; C. 291—An Act Granting pensions and increase of pensions to soldiers and sailors of wars other than the civil war and to certain widows and dependent relatives of such soldiers and sailors.

35 St. 1616; Mar. 3, 1909; C. 292—An Act Granting pensions and increase of pensions to certain soldiers and sailors of wars other than the civil war and to certain dependent relatives of such soldiers and sailors.

35 St. 1617; Mar. 3, 1909; C. 293—An Act Granting pensions and increase of pensions to certain soldiers and sailors of wars other than the civil war and to certain widows and dependent and helpless relatives of such soldiers and sailors.

35 St. 1618; Mar. 3, 1909; C. 296—An Act For the relief of the Herman Andrae Electrical Co., of Milwaukee, Wisconsin.

35 St. 1620; Mar. 4, 1909; C. 327—An Act Authorizing the Secretary of the Interior to ascertain the amount due O bah baum, and pay the same out of the fund known as "For the relief and civilization of the Chippewa Indians."[74]

35 St. 1623; Mar. 4, 1909; C. 339—An Act For the relief of Mrs. M. E. West.[75]

36 STAT.

36 St. 1; July 2, 1909; C. 2—An Act To provide for the Thirteenth and subsequent decennial censuses.[76]

36 St. 118; Aug. 5, 1909; C. 7—An Act Making appropriations to supply urgent deficiencies in appropriations for the fiscal year 1909, and for other purposes.[77] Page 125—25 U. S. C. 52a (33 St. 191). Also see Historical Note 25 U. S. C. A. 29.

36 St. 190; Jan. 31, 1910; C. 21—An Act To amend section twelve of an Act entitled "An Act to authorize the Secretary of the Interior to issue patents in fee to purchasers of Indian lands under any law now existing or hereafter enacted, and for other purposes," approved May 29, 1908, and for other purposes.[78]

36 St. 196; Feb. 17, 1910; C. 40—An Act To amend sections 7 and 8 of the Act of May 29, 1908, entitled "An Act to authorize the sale and disposition of a portion of the surplus and unallotted lands in the Cheyenne River and Standing Rock Indian reservations, in the States of South Dakota and North Dakota, and making appropriation and provision to carry the same into effect."[79]

36 St. 202; Feb. 25, 1910; C. 62—An Act Making appropriations to supply urgent deficiencies in appropriations for the fiscal year 1910, and for other purposes.[80]

36 St. 227; Feb. 25, 1910; C. 63—An Act To amend section eight of an Act to provide for the Thirteenth and subsequent decennial censuses, approved July 2, 1909.

36 St. 243; Mar. 23, 1910; C. 115—An Act Making appropriation for the support of the army for the fiscal year ending June 30, 1911.[81] 10 U. S. C. 811.

36 St. 265; Mar. 26, 1910; C. 129—An Act For the relief of homestead settlers under the Acts of February 20, 1904; June 5 and 28, 1906; March 2, 1907; and May 29, 1928.[82]

36 St. 269; Apr. 4, 1910; C. 140—An Act Making appropriations for the current and contingent expenses of the Bureau of Indian Affairs, for fulfilling treaty stipulations with various Indian tribes, and for other purposes, for the fiscal year ending June 30, 1911.[83] Sec. 1—25 U. S. C. 145 (42 St. 24,

---

[73] *Sg.* 34 St. 539. *Cited:* Kenny, 250 U. S. 58; Levindale, 241 U. S. 432; Work, 266 U. S. 161.

[74] *Sg.* 25 St. 642.

[75] *Sg.* 12 St. 652.

[76] *R.* 40 St. 1291.

[77] *Sg.* 35 St. 798, 985. *S.* 41 St. 1225.

[78] *Ag.* 35 St. 444.

[79] *Ag.* 35 St. 460.

[80] *Sg.* 11 St. 611; 26 St. 853; 33 St. 596; 34 St. 336, 1376; 35 St. 804, 809. *S.* 36 St. 774.

[81] *Cited:* 49 L. D. 414.

[82] *Ag.* 33 St. 46; 34 St. 213, 1230. *S.* 37 St. 21, 91. *Cited:* Chippewa, 80 C. Cls. 410.

[83] *Sg.* 4 St. 442; 7 St. 46, 99, 213, 236, 425; 11 St. 614; 12 St. 981, 1172; 15 St. 622, 637, 640, 652, 658, 676; 16 St. 419, 720; 19 St. 256; 24 St. 388; 25 St. 615, 688, 894; 26 St. 1029; 27 St. 62, 64, 139, 644; 28 St. 422; 29 St. 434; 30 St. 90; 32 St. 263, 264, 388, 650; 33 St. 204, 319, 597, 1016, 1018, 1069, 1081, 2370; 34 St. 140, 145, 375, 377, 1024, 1037; 35 St. 73, 83, 312, 444, 464, 795, 803, 814. *A.* 36 St. 855, 1058; *Rp.* 45 St. 986. *S.* 36 St. 703, 1058; 37 St. 518; 38 St. 77, 582; 39 St. 123, 969; 40 St. 561; 41 St. 3, 408, 1225, 1355; 42 St. 552, 1174; 43 St. 390, 795, 1141; 44 St. 453, 934; 45 St. 200,

sec. 304); USCA Historical Note: This section (145), with the exception of the phrase "by the General Accounting Office," was derived from sec. 1, 36 St. 270. The above quoted phrase was substituted in the Code section for the words in the derivative section "by the proper auditor of the Treasury Department" by reason of sec. 304, 42 St. 24, vesting in and imposing upon the General Accounting Office, powers and duties theretofore exercised and discharged by the Comptroller of the Treasury, the Auditors of the Treasury, etc., as explained in the historical note under section 8 of this title. 25 U. S. C. 338,[84] 25 U. S. C. 383; 25 U. S. C. 385 (sec. 1, 38 St. 583); 25 U. S. C. 364. Sec. 2—25 U. S. C. 43; 25 U. S. C. 385 (sec. 1, 38 St. 583).

36 St. 292; Apr. 8, 1910; C. 146—An Act Authorizing the Secretary of the Interior to appraise certain lands in the State of Minnesota for the purpose of granting the same to the Minnesota and Manitoba R. Co. for a ballast pit.[85]

36 St. 296; Apr. 12, 1910; C. 156—An Act To amend the Act of April 23, 1904 (33 St. 302), entitled "An Act for the survey and allotment of lands now embraced within the limits of the Flathead Indian Reservation, in the State of Montana, and the sale and disposal of all surplus lands after allotment," and all amendments thereto.[86]

36 St. 326; Apr. 21, 1910; C. 183—An Act To protect the seal fisheries of Alaska, and for other purposes.[87] Sec. 1—16 U. S. C. 650; Sec. 3—16 U. S. C. 652; Sec. 6—16 U. S. C. 647; Sec. 9—16 U. S. C. 653, 658.

36 St. 330; Apr. 22, 1910; C. 187—An Act Authorizing the Secretary of the Interior to ascertain the amount due Tay-cum-e-ge-shig, otherwise known as William G. Johnson, and pay the same to his heirs out of the fund known as "For the relief and civilization of the Chippewa Indians, in the State of Minnesota (reimbursable)."[88]

36 St. 348; May 6, 1910; C. 202—An Act Providing for the taxation of the lands of the Omaha Indians in Nebraska.[89]

36 St. 348; May 6, 1910; C. 203—An Act To amend the Act approved December 21, 1904, entitled "An Act to authorize the sale and disposition of surplus or unallotted lands of the Yakima Indian Reservation in the State of Washington."[90]

36 St. 349; May 6, 1910; C. 204—An Act Granting lands for reservoirs, and so forth.[91] Sec. 1—25 U. S. C. 320, (35 St. 781, 782).[92]

36 St. 367; May 13, 1910; C. 233—An Act To authorize the sale of certain lands belonging to the Indians on the Siletz Indian Reservation, in the State of Oregon.[93]

36 St. 368; May 13, 1910; C. 234—An Act To amend sections 1, 2, and 3 of chapter 3298, Thirty-fourth United States Statutes at Large, with reference to the drainage of certain Indian lands in Richardson County, Nebraska.[94]

36 St. 440; May 27, 1910; C. 257—An Act To authorize the sale and disposition of the surplus and unallotted lands in Bennett County, in the Pine Ridge Indian Reservation, in the State of South Dakota, and making appropriation to carry the same into effect.[95]

36 St. 448; May 30, 1910; C. 260—An Act To authorize the sale and disposition of a portion of the surplus and unallotted lands in Mellette and Washabaugh counties in the Rosebud Indian Reservation in the State of South Dakota, and making appropriation and provision to carry the same into effect.[96]

36 St. 455; June 1, 1910; C. 264—An Act To authorize the survey and allotment of lands embraced within the limits of the Fort Berthold Indian Reservation, in the State of North Dakota, and the sale and disposition of a portion of the surplus lands after allotment, and making appropriation and provision to carry the same into effect.[97]

36 St. 468; June 17, 1910; C. 297—An Act Making appropriations for the legislative, executive, and judicial expenses of the Government for the fiscal year ending June 30, 1911, and for other purposes.

36 St. 533; June 17, 1910; C. 299—An Act To open to settlement and entry under the general provisions of the homestead laws of the United States certain lands in the State of Oklahoma, and for other purposes.[98]

36 St. 557; June 20, 1910; C. 310—An Act To enable the people of New Mexico to form a constitution and state government and be admitted into the Union on an equal footing with the original States; and to enable the people of Arizona to form a constitution and state government and be admitted into the Union on an equal footing with the original States.[99]

36 St. 580; June 22, 1910; C. 313—An Act Authorizing the Omaha tribe of Indians to submit claims to the Court of Claims.[1]

36 St. 582; June 22, 1910; C. 315—An Act To pay funeral and transportation expenses of certain Bois Fort Indians.

36 St. 582; June 22, 1910; C. 316—An Act Granting to the Siletz Power and Manufacturing Company a right of way for a water ditch or canal through the Siletz Indian Reservation, in Oregon.

36 St. 588; June 22, 1910; C. 327—An Act To authorize the Lawton and Fort Sill Electric Ry. Co. to construct and operate a railway through the public lands reserved for Indian school purposes, of township two north, range eleven west, Indian meridian, Comanche County, Oklahoma, and for other purposes.[2]

36 St. 602; June 23, 1910; C. 369—An Act To authorize the Secretary of the Interior to sell a portion of the unallotted lands in the Cheyenne Indian Reservation, in South Dakota, to the Milwaukee Land Co. for town-site purposes.[3]

36 St. 703; June 25, 1910; C. 384—An Act Making appropriations for sundry civil expenses of the Government for the fiscal year ending June 30, 1911, and for other purposes.[4]

36 St. 774; June 25, 1910; C. 385—An Act Making appropriations to supply deficiencies in appropriations for the fiscal year 1910, and for other purposes.[5]

36 St. 829; June 25, 1910; C. 400—An Act For the relief of the Saginaw, Swan Creek, and Black River band of Chippewa Indians in the State of Michigan, and for other purposes.[6]

36 St. 832; June 25, 1910; C. 403—An Act Granting to Savanna Coal Company right to acquire additional acreage to its existing coal lease in the Choctaw Nation, Pittsburg County, Oklahoma, and for other purposes.[7]

36 St. 833; June 25, 1910; C. 405—An Act To authorize the cancellation of trust patents in certain cases.

36 St. 836; June 25, 1910; C. 408—An Act To authorize the Secretary of the Interior to issue a patent to the city of Anadarko, State of Oklahoma, for a tract of land, and for other purposes.[8]

36 St. 855; June 25, 1910; C. 431—An Act To provide for determining the heirs of deceased Indians, for the disposition and sale of allotments of deceased Indians, for the leasing of allotments, and for other purposes.[9] Sec. 1—25 U. S. C.

1562; 40 St. 279, 1115; 47 St. 15, 91, 820; 48 St. 362; 49 St. 176, 1757; 50 St. 213, 564; 52 St. 291. *Cited:* Op. Sol. M. 5386, June 19, 1923; Memo. Ind. Off., Apr. 21, 1927; Letter to Sen. Wm. H. King from Comm'r., Jan. 9, 1931; 53 I. D. 128; Mdawakanton, 57 C. Cls. 357; U. S. v. Algoma, 305 U. S. 415; U. S. v. Birdsall, 233 U. S. 223; U. S. v. One Ford, 259 Fed. 645; U. S. v. Rowell, 243 U. S. 464; U. S. v. Sandoval, 231 U. S. 28; Yankton, 272 U. S. 351; Yankton, 61 C. Cls. 40.

[84] *R.* Sec. 1, 45 St. 986, 991.

[85] *Sg.* 35 St. 169.

[86] *Ag.* 33 St. 302. *Sg.* 35 St. 796. *A.* 40 St. 1203.

[87] *Ag.* 2 St. 298, 299; sec. 1, 2; 16 St. 419. *S.* 37 St. 417; 38 St. 379, 582, 609, 822; 39 St. 262; 40 St. 105, 634; 41 St. 163, 874, 1015, 1367; 42 St. 470, 1110, 1527; 43 St. 205, 822, 1014; 44 St. 330, 1178; 45 St. 64, 1004; 46 St. 173, 1309; 47 St. 475, 1371; 48 St. 529; 49 St. 67, 1309; 50 St. 261; 52 St. 248.

[88] *Sg.* 25 St. 642.

[89] *Cited:* Knoepfler, 7 Iowa L. B. 232.

[90] *Ag.* 33 St. 595. *Sg.* 12 St. 754, sec. 2.

[91] *Sg.* 35 St. 781.

[92] Also see 25 U. S. C. 465.

[93] *Sg.* 28 St. 325. *A.* 39 St. 123. *Cited:* Tydings, 23 Case & Com. 743; Coos Bay, 87 C. Cls. 143.

[94] *Sg.* 7 St. 540. *Ag.* 34 St. 262. *S.* 38 St. 582.

[95] *Sg.* 12 St. 393, sec. 8; 12 St. 754, sec. 2; 17 St. 333, sec. 1. *S.* 38 St. 383; 46 St. 169. *A.* 36 St. 1058. *Cited:* Tydings, 23 Cas. & Com. 743.

[96] *Sg.* 17 St. 333, sec. 1. *S.* 38 St. 383; 40 St. 561; 41 St. 3, 408. *A.* 36 St. 1058. *Cited:* Tydings, 23 Case & Com. 743.

[97] *Sg.* 12 St. 393, sec. 8. *S.* 37 St. 631; 38 St. 383, 681; 39 St. 123, 1131; 41 St. 595; 43 St. 817. *Cited:* Tydings, 23 Case & Com. 743.

[98] *S.* 37 St. 33, 518; 39 St. 937. *Cited:* U. S. v. Rowell, 243 U. S. 464.

[99] *S.* 37 St. 39; 46 St. 1202, 1204; 48 St. 960; 50 St. 536. *Cited:* Cavell, 3 Okla. S. B. J. 208; U. S. v. Candelaria, 271 U. S. 432; U. S. v. Chavey, 290 U. S. 357; U. S. v. Sandoval, 231 U. S. 28.

[1] *Sg.* 10 St. 1043. *S.* 43 St. 820. *Cited:* U. S. v. Omaha, 253 U. S. 275; Otoe, 52 C. Cls. 424.

[2] *S.* 37 St. 495.

[3] *Sg.* 35 St. 460.

[4] *Sg.* 3 St. 723, sec. 1; 35 St. 102; 36 St. 274. *Cited:* Heckman, 224 U. S. 413.

[5] *Sg.* 26 St. 853; 35 St. 346, 802, 986; 36 St. 213. *Cited:* 28 Op. A. G. 568; McMurray, 62 C. Cls. 458.

[6] *A.* 43 St. 137.

[7] *A.* 39 St. 870.

[8] *Cited:* Mullen v. U. S., 224 U. S. 448.

[9] *Ag.* 4 St. 737, sec. 13; 12 St. 819; 14 St. 515, sec. 8; 17 St. 463, sec. 7; 18 St. 450, sec. 8; 19 St. 199, sec. 3; 24 St. 388; 25 St. 642; 26 St. 794; 28 St. 876; 30 St. 571, 990; 31 St. 1058; 32 St. 43, 245, 400; 35 St. 444, 1016, 1098, sec. 50, 53; 36 St. 280. *A.* 37 St. 678; 39 St. 123; 45 St. 161; 48 St. 647. *S.* 36 St. 1058; 37 St. 518; 38

372.[10] (See USCA Historical Note); Sec. 2—25 U. S. C. 373.[11] (See USCA Historical Note); Sec. 3—25 U. S. C. 408; Sec. 4—25 U. S. C. 403; Sec. 5—18 U. S. C. 115; Sec. 6—18 U. S. C. 107, 104; Sec. 7—25 U. S. C. 407;[12] Sec. 8—25 U. S. C. 406; Sec. 9—25 U. S. C. 333 (sec. 3, 24 St. 389); Sec. 10—25 U. S. C. 351; Sec. 13—43 U. S. C. 148; Sec. 14—25 U. S. C. 352;[13] Sec. 16—25 U. S. C. 312 (sec. 1, 30 St. 990; sec. 23, 32 St. 50). (See USCA Historical Note); Sec. 17—25 U. S. C. 331 (sec. 1, 24 St. 388; sec. 1, 26 St. 794). (See USCA Historical Note); 25 U. S. C. 336 (26 St. 795, sec. 4);[14] Sec. 22—25 U. S. C. 191 (30 St. 596, sec. 6); Sec. 23—25 U. S. C. 47 (35 St. 71); 25 U. S. C. 93;[15] Sec. 31—25 U. S. C. 337; USCA Historical Note: Section 31 instant Act provided for determining the heirs of, and for the disposition of allotments of, deceased Indians. A reference in this section to the amendment of the General Allotment Laws "by section — of this Act" was intended, apparently, for section 17 of 36 St. 863, amending section 1 of Act February 28, 1891, which section amended section 1 of the General Allotment Act of February 8, 1887, set forth, with said amendments incorporated therein, at 25 U. S. C. 331. Sec. 32—25 U. S. C. 353; Sec. 33—25 U. S. C. 353.

36 St. 873; Jun. 20, 1910; J. Res. No. 5—Joint Resolution Authorizing the Secretary of the Interior to pay to the Winnebago tribe of Indians interest accrued since June 30, 1909.[16]

36 St. 877; Apr. 12, 1910; J. Res. No. 20—Joint Resolution Amending a "Joint Resolution authorizing the Secretary of the Interior to pay to the Winnebago tribe of Indians interest accrued since June 30, 1909," approved January 20, 1910 (Senate J. Res. Numbered 58).[17]

36 St. 879; May 11, 1910; J. Res. No. 26—Joint Resolution To supply a deficiency in the appropriation for printing and binding for the Treasury Department for the fiscal year 1910, and for other purposes.[18]

36 St. 909; Feb. 15, 1911; C. 70—An Act To authorize the Chucawalla Development Company to build a dam across the Colorado River at or near the mouth of Pyramid Canyon, Arizona; also a diversion intake dam at or near Black Point, Arizona, and Blythe, California.[19]

36 St. 913; Feb. 16, 1911; C. 91—An Act Authorizing homestead entries on certain lands formerly a part of the Red Lake Indian Reservation, in the State of Minnesota.[20]

36 St. 927; Feb. 21, 1911; C. 143—An Act To ratify a certain lease with the Seneca Nation of Indians.

36 St. 1037; Mar. 3, 1911; C. 209—An Act Making appropriation for the support of the Army for the fiscal year ending June 30, 1912. 10 U. S. C. 642.

36 St. 1058; Mar. 3, 1911; C. 210—An Act Making appropriations for the current and contingent expenses of the Bureau of Indian Affairs, for fulfilling treaty stipulations with various Indian tribes, and for other purposes, for the fiscal year ending June 30, 1912.[21] Sec. 1—25 U. S. C. 300;[22] 25 U. S. C. 301;[23] See USCA Historical Note. Sec. 17—25 U. S. C. 11; 25 U. S. C. 156. Sec. 27—25 U. S. C. 143. Sec. 28—25 U. S. C. 118.

36 St. 1080; Mar. 3, 1911; C. 218—An Act To amend section three of the Act of Congress of May 1, 1888, and extend the provisions of section 2300 and one of the Revised Statutes of the United States to certain lands in the State of Montana embraced within the provisions of said Act, and for other purposes.[24]

36 St. 1081; Mar. 3, 1911; C. 220—An Act To authorize the Greeley-Arizona Irrigation Co. to build a dam across the Colorado River at or near Head Gate Rock, near Parker, in Yuma County, Arizona.[25]

36 St. 1087; Mar. 3, 1911; C. 231—An Act To codify, revise, and amend the laws relating to the judiciary.[26] p. 1167—25 U. S. C. 345 (sec. 1, 28 St. 305; sec. 1, 31 St. 760). See USCA Historical Note. Sec. 27—28 U. S. C. 51; Sec. 24—28 U. S. C. 41, par. 24; Sec. 291—18 U. S. C. 549.

36 St. 1170; Mar. 4, 1911; C. 237—An Act Making appropriations for the legislative, executive, and judicial expenses of the Government for the fiscal year ending June 30, 1912, and for other purposes.[27]

36 St. 1289; Mar. 4, 1911; C. 240—An Act Making appropriations to supply deficiencies in appropriations for the fiscal year 1911 and for prior years, and for other purposes.[28]

36 St. 1345; Mar. 4, 1911; C. 246—An Act To provide for allotments to certain members of the Hoh, Quileute, and Ozette tribes of Indians in the State of Washington.[29]

36 St. 1356; Mar. 4, 1911; C. 272—An Act Relating to homestead entries in the former Siletz Indian Reservation in the State of Oregon.

36 St. 1358; Mar. 4, 1911; C. 276—An Act Authorizing the sale of portions of the allotments of Nek-quel-e-kin, or Wapato John, and Que-til-qua-soon, or Peter, Moses agreement allottees.[30]

36 St. 1363; Mar. 4, 1911; C. 285—An Act Making appropriations

---

St. 77, 111, 284, 582; 39 St. 123, 969; 41 St. 3, 408, 549, 751, 1225; 42 St. 552, 1174; 43 St. 132, 133, 376, 390, 1141; 45 St. 442; 46 St. 1108; 48 St. 811. *Cited:* Brown, 39 Yale L. J. 307; Cain, 2 Minn. L. Rev. 177; Knoepfler, 7 Iowa L. B. 232; Reeves, 23 Case & Com. 727; Tydings, 23 Case & Com. 743; 29 Op. A. G. 239; 33 Op. A. G. 25; 36 Op. A. G. 98; 8 L. D. Memo. 435; 8 L. D. Memo. 347; 8 L. D. Memo. 764; Letter to W. P. Havenor, County Surveyor, Pocatello, Idaho, Jan. 22, 1920; Op. Sol. M. 5379, July 14, 1921, M. 5805, Nov. 22, 1921, M. 5379, Apr. 27, 1922, M. 7599, June 9, 1922; M. 21849, Mar. 19; 1927; M. 2121, Apr. 12, 1927; Memo. Ind. Off., Apr. 21, 1927; Op. Sol., Sept. 21, 1927; M. 24538, May 14, 1928; M. 25258, June 26, 1929; Op. A. G., Oct. 5, 1929; Memo. Sol., July 8, 1933; Op. Sol., M. 27499, Aug. 8, 1933, M. 27645, Dec. 22, 1933; Memo. Ind. Off., Jan. 31, 1934, May 11, 1934; Memo. Sol., Nov. 11, 1935; Memo. Sol. Off., Oct. 22, 1936; Memo. Sol., Aug. 14, 1937, Aug. 20, 1938; Memo. Ind. Off., Nov. 15, 1938; Memo. Sol., Mar. 28, 1939; 40 L. D. 120; 40 L. D. 179; 40 L. D. 212; 42 L. D. 493; 43 L. D. 101; 43 L. D. 125; 43 L. D. 504; 44 L. D. 188; 44 L. D. 520; 48 L. D. 455; 54 I. D. 401; 54 I. D. 555; Bertrand, 36 F. 2d 351; Blanset, 256 U. S. 319; Bond, 181 Fed. 613; Bowling, 290 Fed. 438; Button, 7 F. Supp. 597; Childers, 270 U. S. 555; Dixon, 268 Fed. 285; Egan, 246 U. S. 227; Ex p. Pero, 99 F. 2d 28; Hallam, 49 F. 2d 103; Hallowell, 239 U. S. 506; Hampton, 22 F. 2d 81; In re Jessie's, 259 Fed. 94; Iowa, 217 Fed. 11; Johnson, 283 Fed. 954; Lane, 241 U. S. 201; McDougal, 273 Fed. 113; Mickadiet, 258 U. S. 609; Miller, 249 U. S. 308; Nimrod, 24 F. 2d 613; Parr, 197 Fed. 302; Pel-ata-yakat, 188 Fed. 387; People ex rel. Charles, 8 F. Supp. 295; Perryman, 238 U. S. 148; Red Hawk, 39 F. 2d 293; Skeem, 273 Fed. 93; St. Marie, 24 F. Supp. 237; Stookey, 58 F. 2d 522; U. S. v. Algoma, 305 U. S. 415; U. S. v. Barnett, 7 F. Supp. 573; U. S. v. Bowling, 256 U. S. 484; U. S. v. Dewey, S. D., 14 F. 2d 784; U. S. v. Glacier, 17 F. Supp. 411; U. S. v. Harris, 100 F. 2d 268; U. S. v. Howard 8 F. Supp. 617; U. S. v. Jackson, 280 U. S. 183; U. S. v. Lewis, 95 F. 2d 236; U. S. v. Mathewson, 32 F. 2d 745; U. S. v. Nez Perce, 95 F. 2d 232; U. S. v. Nez. Perce, 267 Fed. 495; U. S. v. Payne, 264 U. S. 446; U. S. v. Powers, 305 U. S. 527; U. S. v. Sherburne, 68 F. 2d 155; U. S. v. 12 Bottles, 201 Fed. 191.

[10] *A.* 45 St. 161; 48 St. 647.

[11] *S.* 37 St. 678.

[12] Also see 25 U. S. C. 407a (the authority granted by this section—Act Mar. 4, 1933, sec. 1, 47 St. 1568, as amended, June 16, 1933, 48 St. 311; Mar. 5, 1934, 48 St. 397; May 6, 1936, 49 St. 1266, by its terms expired Sept. 4, 1936); 25 U. S. C. 407b (Mar. 4, 1933, sec. 2, 47 St. 1569); 25 U. S. C. 407c (Mar. 4, 1933, sec. 3, 47 St. 1569).

[13] Also see 25 U. S. C. 352a (44 St. 1247); 25 U. S. C. 352b (sec. 2, 44 St. 1247, as added 46 St. 1205).

[14] Effective July 1, 1935, the permanent appropriation provided for in the last sentence of 25 U. S. C. 336 was repealed by Act June 26, 1934, s. 1, 48 St. 1225. See sec. 725 (b) of Title 31.

[15] *S.* 39 St. 126, sec. 1; 44 St. 936. Also see 25 U. S. C. 148.

[16] *Sg.* 35 St. 781. *A.* 36 St. 877. *Cited:* Memo. Sol., Mar. 6, 1937.

[17] *Ag.* 36 St. 873.

[18] *Sg.* 35 St. 70.

[19] *Sg.* 34 St. 386; 36 St. 593.

[20] *Sg.* 27 St. 260. *S.* 40 St. 917. *Cited:* Tydings, 23 Case & Com. 743; Chippewa, 80 C. Cls. 410.

[21] *Sg.* 4 St. 46; 4 St. 442; 7 St. 99, 213, 235, 236, 425; 11 St. 614, 730; 12 St. 1172; 14 St. 687; 15 St. 622, 637, 640, 652, 676; 16 St. 720; 19 St. 256; 24 St. 388; 25 St. 645, 894; 26 St. 1029; 27 St. 62, 139, 644; 30 St. 90; 32 St. 263, 998; 33 St. 207, 1069; 34 St. 375, 377; 35 St. 51, 464; 36 St. 272, 288, 384, 858. *Ag.* 33 St. 224; 36 St. 276, 442, 451. *Rg.* 25 St. 688; 36 St. 275. *Rpg.* 30 St. 93. *A.* 37 St. 518. *Rp.* 38 St. 582; 45 St. 986. *S.* 37 St. 67, 518; 38 St. 77, 582, 1219; 39 St. 123, 969; 40 St. 561; 41 St. 3, 408, 1225; 42 St. 437, 552, 1174; 43 St. 390, 1141; 44 St. 453, 934; 45 St. 200, 1562. *Cited:* Tydings, 23 Case & Com. 743; Op. Sol., M. 5386, June 19, 1923; Memo. Ind. Off., Apr. 21, 1927; Letter of Ass't Sec'y to Sec'y of War, Feb. 26, 1932; 51 I. D. 613; 54 I. D. 90; Creek, 78 C. Cls. 474; Medawakanton, 57 C. Cls. 357; Turner, 248 U. S. 354; U. S. v. Birdsall, 233 U. S. 223; U. S. v. One Ford, 259 Fed. 645; U. S. v. Seminole, 299 U. S. 417; Yankton, 61 C. Cls. 40.

[22] *R.* sec. 1, 45 St. 986, 991.

[23] *R.* sec. 1, 45 St. 986, 991.

[24] *Ag.* 25 St. 133. *Cited:* Memo. Ind. Off., Apr. 21, 1927.

[25] *Sg.* 34 St. 386. *Ag.* 36 St. 593.

[26] *Sg.* 10 St. 612, sec. 1; 12 St. 765, sec. 1; 17 St. 85, sec. 13. *Rg.* 12 St. 706, sec. 7; 12 St. 766, sec. 7; 14 St. 537, sec. 42; 15 St. 75, sec. 2; 18 St. 182, sec. 15. *S.* 49 St. 655. *A.* 37 St. 46, 59; 39 St. 386; 42 St. 816; 44 St. 237, 736; 45 St. 1143; 46 St. 495; 47 St. 300. *Cited:* Brown, 39 Yale L. J. 307; 62d Cong., 1st & 2d sess., Sen. Rept. No. 147, Vol. 1; 8 L. D. Memo. 764; 44 L. D. 531; Button, 7 F. Supp. 597; Ex p. Pero, 99 F. 2d 28; Ford, 260 Fed. 657; In re Jessie's Heirs, 259 Fed. 94; Johnson, 234 U. S. 422; Kennedy, 23 F. Supp. 771; McCullough, 243 Fed. 823; Mitchell, 22 F. 2d 771; People ex rel Charles, 8 F. Supp. 295; Rice, 2 F. Supp. 669; U. S. v. Inaba, 291 Fed. 416; U. S. v. Ladley, 51 F. 2d 756; U. S. v. Seminole, 299 U. S. 417; U. S. ex rel. Charley, 62 F. 2d 955; Vinson, 44 F. 2d 772; Washburn, 7 F. Supp. 120.

[27] *S.* 36 St. 1289.

[28] *Sg.* 11 St. 611; 26 St. 853; 34 St. 1403; 36 St. 1215.

[29] *Sg.* 12 St. 971. *Cited:* Op. Sol., M. 24358, May 14, 1928; 54 I. D. 71; Halbert, 283 U. S. 753; Mitchell, 22 F. 2d 771; U. S. v. Provoe, 283 U. S. 753.

[30] *Sg.* 34 St. 55.

for sundry civil expenses of the Government for the fiscal year ending June 30, 1912, and for other purposes.[31]

36 St. 1609; Mar. 23, 1910; C. 121—An Act Granting pensions and increase of pension to certain soldiers and sailors of the Regular Army and Navy, and certain soldiers and sailors of wars other than the civil war, and to widows and dependent relatives of such soldiers and sailors.

36 St. 1687; Apr. 18, 1910; C. 171—An Act For the relief of Horace C. Dale, administrator of the estate of Antoine Janis, senior, deceased, of Pine Ridge, South Dakota.[32]

36 St. 1698; Apr. 22, 1910; C. 190—An Act Authorizing the Secretary of the Interior to make allotment to Frank H. Pequette.

36 St. 1700; May 6, 1910; C. 214—An Act For the relief of Samuel W. Campbell.

36 St. 1751; June 7, 1910; C. 268—An Act Granting pensions to certain soldiers and sailors of wars other than the civil war and to certain widows and dependent relatives of such soldiers and sailors.

36 St. 1752; June 7, 1910; C. 269—An Act Granting pensions and increase of pensions to certain soldiers and sailors of the regular army and navy and wars other than the civil war and to certain widows of such soldiers and sailors.

36 St. 1753; June 7, 1910; C. 270—An Act Granting pensions and increase of pensions to certain soldiers and sailors of the Regular Army and Navy and wars other than the civil war, and to certain widows and dependent relatives of such soldiers and sailors.

36 St. 1758; June 7, 1910; C. 273—An Act Granting pensions and increase of pensions to certain soldiers and sailors of the Regular Army and Navy, and certain soldiers and sailors of wars other than the civil war, and to widows and dependent relatives of such soldiers and sailors.

36 St. 1760; June 7, 1910; C. 274—An Act Granting pensions and increase of pensions to certain soldiers and sailors of the Regular Army and Navy, and certain soldiers and sailors of wars other than the civil war, and to widows and dependent relatives of such soldiers and sailors.

36 St. 1762; June 7, 1910; C. 275—An Act Granting pensions and increase of pensions to certain soldiers and sailors of the Regular Army and Navy, and certain soldiers and sailors of wars other than the civil war, and to widows and dependent relatives of such soldiers and sailors.

36 St. 1766; June 9, 1910; C. 279—An Act Granting pensions and increase of pensions to certain soldiers and sailors of the Regular Army and Navy and wars other than the civil war and certain widows and dependent relatives of such soldiers and sailors.

36 St. 1805; June 17, 1910; C. 303—An Act Granting pensions and increase of pensions to certain soldiers and sailors of the Regular Army and Navy, and certain soldiers and sailors of wars other than the civil war, and to certain widows and dependent relatives of such soldiers and sailors.

36 St. 1806; June 17, 1910; C. 304—An Act Granting pensions and increase of pensions to certain soldiers and sailors of the Regular Army and Navy, and certain soldiers and sailors of wars other than the civil war, and to widows and dependent relatives of such soldiers and sailors.

36 St. 1807; June 17, 1910; C. 305—An Act Granting pensions and increase of pensions to certain soldiers and sailors of the Regular Army and Navy, and certain soldiers and sailors of wars other than the civil war, and to widows and dependent relatives of such soldiers and sailors.

36 St. 1809; June 22, 1910; C. 333—An Act For the relief of Rasmus K. Hafsos.

36 St. 1810; June 22, 1910; C. 335—An Act Granting pensions and increase of pensions to certain soldiers and sailors of the Regular Army and Navy and wars other than the civil war, and certain widows and dependent relatives of such soldiers and sailors.

36 St. 1811; June 22, 1910; C. 336—An Act For the relief of Garland and Bergh.

36 St. 1813; June 22, 1910; C. 344—An Act Granting pensions and increase of pensions to certain soldiers and sailors of the Regular Army and Navy, and certain soldiers and sailors of wars other than the civil war, and to widows and dependent relatives of such soldiers and sailors.

36 St. 1815; June 22, 1910; C. 345—An Act Granting pensions and increase of pensions to certain soldiers and sailors of the Regular Army and Navy, and certain soldiers and sailors of wars other than the civil war, and to the widows and dependent relatives of such soldiers and sailors.

36 St. 1816; June 22, 1910; C. 346—An Act Granting pensions and increase of pensions to certain soldiers and sailors of the Regular Army and Navy, and certain soldiers and sailors of wars other than the civil war, and to widows and dependent relatives of such soldiers and sailors.

36 St. 1818; June 22, 1910; C. 348—An Act Granting pensions and increase of pensions to certain soldiers and sailors of the Regular Army and Navy, and certain soldiers and sailors of wars other than the civil war, and to widows and dependent relatives of such soldiers and sailors.

36 St. 1843; June 22, 1910; C. 352—An Act Granting pensions and increase of pensions to certain soldiers and sailors of the Regular Army and Navy, and certain soldiers and sailors of wars other than the civil war, and to widows and dependent relatives of such soldiers and sailors.

36 St. 1843; June 22, 1910; C. 353—An Act Granting pensions and increase of pensions to certain soldiers and sailors of the Regular Army and Navy, and certain soldiers and sailors of wars other than the civil war, and to widows and dependent relatives of such soldiers and sailors.

36 St. 1859; June 23, 1910; C. 375—An Act Granting pensions and increase of pensions to certain soldiers and sailors of the Regular Army and Navy, and wars other than the civil war, and certain widows and dependent relatives of such soldiers and sailors.

36 St. 1860; June 23, 1910; C. 376—An Act Granting pensions and increase of pensions to certain soldiers and sailors of the Regular Army and Navy, and certain soldiers and sailors of wars other than the civil war, and to widows and dependent relatives of such soldiers and sailors.

36 St. 1866; June 25, 1910; C. 459—An Act To reimburse G. H. Kitson for money advanced to the Menominee tribe of Indians, of Wisconsin.

36 St. 1982; Feb. 17, 1911; C. 107—An Act Granting pensions and increase of pensions to certain soldiers and sailors of the Regular Army and Navy, and certain soldiers and sailors of wars other than the Civil War, and to widows and dependent relatives of such soldiers and sailors.

36 St. 1984; Feb. 17, 1911; C. 108—An Act Granting pensions and increase of pensions to certain soldiers and sailors of the Regular Army and Navy, and soldiers and sailors of wars other than the Civil War, and to widows and dependent relatives of such soldiers and sailors.

36 St. 2000; Feb. 28, 1911; C. 182—An Act Granting pensions and increase of pensions to certain soldiers and sailors of the Regular Army and Navy, and certain soldiers and sailors of wars other than the Civil War, and to widows and dependent relatives of such soldiers and sailors.

36 St. 2064; Mar. 4, 1911; C. 308—An Act For the relief of Frances Coburn, Charles Coburn, and the heirs of Mary Morrisette, deceased.[33]

36 St. 2099; Mar. 4, 1911; C. 311—An Act Granting pensions and increase of pensions to certain soldiers and sailors of the Regular Army and Navy, and certain soldiers and sailors of wars other than the Civil War, and to widows and dependent relatives of such soldiers and sailors.

37 STAT.

37 St. 21; Aug. 17, 1911; C. 22—An Act Extending the time of payment to certain homesteaders in the Rosebud Indian Reservation, in the State of South Dakota.[34]

37 St. 23; Aug. 19, 1911; C. 28—An Act Granting leave of absence of certain homesteaders.

37 St. 33; Aug. 22, 1911; C. 44—An Act To extend time of payment of balance due for lands sold under Act of Congress approved June 17, 1910.[35]

37 St. 33; Aug. 22, 1911; C. 45—An Act To authorize the Secretary of the Interior to withdraw from the Treasury of the United States the funds of the Kiowa, Comanche, and Apache Indians, and for other purposes.[36]

37 St. 39; Aug. 21, 1911; J. Res. No. 8—Joint Resolution To admit the Territories of New Mexico and Arizona as States into the Union upon an equal footing with the original States.[37]

[31] *Sg.* 3 St. 723, sec. 1; 35 St. 102. *Cited:* Heckman, 224 U. S. 413.
[32] *Sg.* 25 St. 888.
[33] *Sg.* 24 St. 388; 26 St. 794.
[34] *Sg.* 34 St. 1230; 36 St. 265.
[35] *Sg.* 36 St. 533.
[36] *Sg.* 34 St. 213.
[37] *Sg.* 36 St. 557.

37 St. 44; Aug. 22, 1911; J. Res. No 11—Joint Resolution To authorize the Secretary of the Interior to make a per capita payment to the enrolled members of the Choctaw, Chickasaw, Cherokee, and Seminole Indians of the Five Civilized Tribes entitled to share in the funds of said tribes[38]

37 St 45; Dec 8, 1911, C 1—An Act To provide a suitable memorial to the memory of the North American Indian.

37 St. 46, Dec 21, 1911; C 3—An Act to Amend and reenact paragraph 24 of section 24 of Chapter 2 of an Act entitled "An Act to codify, revise, and amend the laws relating to the judiciary," approved March 3, 1911.[39] 25 U S C. 345, 28 U. S. C 41, par 24

37 St 50. Feb 6, 1912, C. 28—An Act To amend secs 90, 99, 105, and 186 of an Act entitled "An Act to codify, revise, and amend the laws relating to the judiciary," approved March 3, 1911.[40] 28 U S C 170; 28 U S C. 180, 186.

37 St. 64, Feb 10, 1912, C 37—An Act To authorize the sale of land within or near the town site of Midvale, Montana, for hotel purposes.[41]

37 St. 67, Feb 19, 1912; C 46—An Act To provide for the sale of the surface of the segregated coal and asphalt lands of the Choctaw and Chickasaw Nations, and for other purposes.[42]

37 St. 78. Apr. 5, 1912; C 70—An Act Authorizing the Secretary of the Interior to permit the Missouri, Kansas and Texas Coal Co. and the Eastern Coal and Mining Co. to exchange certain lands embraced within their existing coal leases in the Choctaw and Chickasaw Nations for other lands within said nations.

37 St 84; Apr. 13, 1912; C 77—An Act Extending the time of payment to certain homesteaders on the Cheyenne River Indian Reservation, in the State of South Dakota, and on the Standing Rock Indian Reservation, in the States of South Dakota and North Dakota[43]

37 St. 85; Apr 15, 1912; C 78—An Act To provide for an extension of time of payment of all unpaid payments due from homesteaders on the Coeur d'Alene Indian Reservation, as provided for under an Act of Congress approved June 21, 1906[44]

37 St. 86; Apr. 18, 1912; C. 83—An Act Supplementary to and amendatory of the Act entitled "An Act for the division of the lands and funds of the Osage Nation of Indians in Oklahoma," approved June 28, 1906, and for other purposes[45] Sec. 10—25 U. S C 58 (sec. 1, 30 St. 90)[46]

37 St 91; Apr. 27, 1912; C 91—An Act Providing for patents to homesteads on the ceded portion of the Wind River Reservation in Wyoming[47]

37 St 91; Apr. 27, 1912; C 92—An Act Authorizing the Secretary of the Interior to subdivide and extend the deferred payments of settlers in the Kiowa-Comanche and Apache ceded lands in Oklahoma[48]

37 St. 111; May 11, 1912, C. 121—An Act To provide for the disposal of the unallotted land on the Omaha Indian Reservation, in the State of Nebraska.[49]

37 St 122. June 4, 1912; C. 161—An Act To relinquish, release, remise, and quitclaim all right, title, and interest of the United States of America in and to all the lands held under claim or color of title by individuals or private ownership or municipal ownership situated in the State of Alabama which were reserved, retained, or set apart to or for the Creek Tribe or Nation of Indians under or by virtue of the treaty entered into between the United States of America and the Creek Tribe or Nation of Indians on March 24, 1832, and under and by virtue of the treaty between the United States of America and the Creek Tribe or Nation of Indians of the ninth day of August, 1814[50]

37 St 125, June 6, 1912, C 155—An Act Authorizing the Secretary of the Interior to classify and appraise unallotted Indian lands[51] 25 U. S C 425

37 St. 131; June 10, 1912; C 164—An Act To authorize the Clinton and Oklahoma Western Ry Co to construct and operate a railway through certain public lands, and for other purposes

37 St. 186; July 1, 1912; C. 189—An Act To authorize the sale of certain lands within the Umatilla Indian Reservation to the city of Pendleton, Oregon.

37 St 187; July 1, 1912, C 190—An Act For the relief of the Winnebago Indians of Nebraska and Wisconsin.[52]

37 St 189, July 9, 1912; C 221—An Act To correct an error in the record of the supplemental treaty of September 28, 1830, made with the Choctaw Indians, and for other purposes.[53]

37 St 192; July 10, 1912; C 229—An Act Authorizing the sale of certain lands in the Flathead Indian Reservation to the town of Ronan, State of Montana, for the purposes of a public park and public-school site

37 St. 194; July 19, 1912; C 240—An Act To provide for the payment of drainage assessments on Indian lands in Oklahoma.[54]

37 St 195; July 19, 1912, C 241—An Act Providing for the sale of the Lemhi School and Agency plant and lands on the former Lemhi Reservation in the State of Idaho.

37 St. 196; July 20, 1912; C. 244—An Act To provide an extension of time for submission of proof by homesteaders on the Uintah Indian Reservation[55]

37 St. 197, July 22, 1912; C. 248—An Act Authorizing the sale of certain lands in the Colville Indian Reservation to the town of Okanogan, State of Washington, for public park purposes.[56]

37 St. 360; Aug 23, 1912; C 350—An Act Making appropriations for the legislative, executive, and judicial expenses of the Government for the fiscal year ending June 30, 1913, and for other purposes.[57] Sec. 1—25 U. S C. 61; 31 U. S. C. 583 (26).

37 St. 417; Aug 24, 1912; C 355—An Act Making appropriations for sundry civil expenses of the Government for the fiscal year ending June 30, 1913, and for other purposes.[58] Sec 8—25 U. S. C. 34.[59]

37 St. 495; Aug. 24, 1912; C. 366—An Act Conferring upon the Lawton Railway and Lighting Co. the privileges, rights, and conditions heretofore granted the Lawton and Fort Sill Electric Company to construct a railroad across certain lands in Comanche County, Oklahoma.[60]

37 St. 497; Aug. 24, 1912; C. 362—An Act To amend an Act entitled "An Act to provide for the final disposition of the affairs of the Five Civilized Tribes in the Indian Territory, and for other purposes," approved April 26, 1906 (34 St 137).[61]

37 St. 497; August 24, 1912; C. 370—An Act To make uniform charges for furnishing copies of records of the Department

---

[38] *Cited* U S v. Seminole, 298 U S 417.

[39] *Ag* 36 St. 1094 *Cited:* Button, 7 F Supp 597; Ex p Fein, 99 F 2d 28; First Moon, 270 U S 243; People, 8 F. Supp 295; Rice, 2 F Supp 669; Washburn, 7 F Supp 120

[40] *Ag* 36 St. 1128 *A* 39 St 886; 44 St 297.

[41] *Sg* 34 St. 1039.

[42] *Sg*, 32 St. 654, 34 St 148, 36 St 1070 *A* 37 St 518, 38 St 77, 767, *S.* 38 St 582; 39 St 128, 866, 870 969; 40 St 488, 561; 41 St 2, 3, 408, 1225. *Cited.* 1 L D, Memo 99, Op Sol, M 7816, May 28, 1924; U S ex rel. McAlester, 277 Fed. 573

[43] *Sg.* 35 St. 462. *S* 39 St 888

[44] *Sg* 34 St 836 *S.* 37 St. 1025

[45] *Sg.* 30 St. 90; 34 St 548 *Ag.* 34 St 544. *A.* 40 St 561 *Cited:* Reeves, 23 Case & Com 727; 12 L D Memo 642; Op Sol, M. 4017, Jan. 4 1922; M. 8370, Aug. 15, 1922; Memo. Sol. Off., June 8, 1926, Op. Sol, M 18820, Dec 21, 1926; M 21298, June 19, 1928; Memo Sol. Off, May 31, 1929, Sept 18, 1929, Apr. 22, 1930, July 8, 1930; Letter to Comm'r of Ind Affairs from Sec'y of Int., Sept. 1930; Memo. Sol Off, Nov. 5, 1930, Mar 10, 1931, Op Sol, M, 26781, Oct 14, 1931, Op. Comp Gen to Sec'y, Feb. 4, 1932; Op. Sol, M, 27888, Nov 28, 1934; Letter of Ass't Comm'r to Sec'y of Int., Dec. 16, 1935; Op. Sol, M. 27968, Jan 26, 1937; 54 I D 555; 55 I D 466; Browning, 6 F 2d 801; Drummond, 34 F 2d 755; Globe, 81 F. 2d 143; Harrison, 264 Fed. 776; In re Dennison, 38 F. 2d 662; In re Irwin, 60 F. 2d 495; Kenny, 250 U. S, 58; La Motte 254 U. S, 570; Levindale, 241 U. S 432; McCurdy, 246 U S 263; Morrison, 6 F 2d 811; Mudd, 14 F 2d 430; Ne-Kah-Wah-She-Tun-Kah, 290 Fed. 303, Shaw, 276 U. S. 575; Tapp, 6 F Supp 577; Taylor, 51 F 2d 892; Taylor, 51 F 2d 884; U. S. v. Board, 26 F Supp, 270; U. S v Carson, 19 F. Supp 616; U S v. Gray, 284 Fed, 103; U. S, v Hale, 51 F 2d 629; U S. v. Harris, 293 Fed 389, U. S. v Howard, 8 F. Supp 617; U. S v. Hughes, 6 F. Supp. 972; U. S, v. Johnson, 87 F. 2d 155; U S. v La Motte, 67 F 2d 788; U. S. v. Law, 250 Fed 218; U. S. v. Mummert, 15 F 2d 926, U S v Ransom, 284 Fed 108; U. S v. Sands, 94 F. 2d 156; U S v. Yakima, 274 Fed 115; Work, 260 U S. 161.

[46] *S* 37 St. 521, sec. 1; 40 St. 578, sec. 17; 45 St. 1307.

[47] *Sg* 33 St. 1021; 36 St. 265

[48] *Sg.* 34 St. 550, 36 St. 266. *S.* 38 St. 582.

[49] *Sg* 22 St 341; 28 St. 630 *A.* 48 St. 726 *Cited* Tydings, 28 Case & Com 748; Memo. Sol. Off, Jan 22, 1936, Dec 30, 1938; Chase, 238 Fed 887; Chase, 256 U. S 1; Clay, 282 Fed. 268.

[50] *Sg* 7 St 120, 366

[51] *Cited* 36 Op. A G 506

[52] *Cited:* Memo. Sol, Mar 6, 1937.

[53] *Ag.* 7 St. 340

[54] *A.* 39 St. 673 *S* 45 St. 1628

[55] *Sg* 32 St. 263

[56] *Sg.* 34 St 80. *A.* 37 St 594.

[57] *S* 37 St. 518; 38 St 77

[58] *Sg* 35 St 102, 36 St. 326. *Cited:* Report of Status of Pueblo of Pojoaque, Nov. 8, 1932

[59] *A.* 58 St. 310

[60] *Sg.* 38 St 268 588

[61] *Ag* 34 St. 137 *Cited;* Memo Sol., May 19, 1936; Bowling, 299 Fed, 438.

of the Interior and of its several bureaus.[63] Sec. 1—5 U. S. C. 488; Sec. 5—15 U. S. C. 134; Sec. 5—35 U. S. C. 14, 78.

37 St. 499; Aug. 24, 1912; C. 373—An Act To give effect to the convention between the Governments of the United States, Great Britain, Japan, and Russia for the preservation and protection of the fur seals and sea otter which frequent the waters of the north Pacific Ocean, concluded at Washington July 7, 1911.[64] Sec. 1—16 U. S. C. 632; Sec. 2—16 U. S. C. 633; Sec. 3—16 U. S. C. 634; Sec. 11—16 U. S. C. 642. 650; Sec. 12—16 U. S. C. 643; Sec. 13—16 U. S. C. 643a.

37 St. 518; Aug. 24, 1912; C. 388—An Act Making appropriations for the current and contingent expenses of the Bureau of Indian Affairs, for fulfilling treaty stipulations with various Indian tribes, and for other purposes, for the fiscal year ending June 30, 1913.[65] Sec. 1—25 U. S. C. 250; 25 U. S. C. 253; 25 U. S. C. 275;[66] 25 U. S. C. 22;[66] 25 U. S. C. 58 (sec. 1, 30 St. 90; sec. 10, 37 St. 88).[67]

37 St. 569; Aug. 24, 1912; C. 391—An Act Making appropriations for the support of the Army for the fiscal year ending June 30, 1913, and for other purposes.

37 St. 594; Aug. 26, 1912; C. 407—An Act To amend an Act entitled "An Act authorizing the sale of certain lands in the Colville Indian Reservation to the town of Okanogan, State of Washington, for public park purposes," approved July 22, 1912.[68]

37 St. 595; Aug. 26, 1912; C. 408—An Act Making appropriations to supply deficiencies in appropriations for the fiscal year 1912 and for prior years, and for other purposes.[69] Sec. 1—31 U. S. C. 423, 583.

37 St. 631; Apr. 3, 1912; J. Res. No. 11—Joint Resolution To authorize allotments to Indians of the Fort Berthold Indian Reservation, North Dakota, of land valuable for coal.[70]

37 St. 634; June 4, 1912; J. Res. No. 22—Joint Resolution To authorize and direct the Great Northern Ry. Co. and the Spokane and British Columbia Ry. Co. in the matter of their conflicting claims or rights of way across the Colville Indian Reservation, in the State of Washington, in the San Poil River Valley, to readjust their respective locations of rights of way at points of conflict, in such manner as to allow each company an equal right of way through said valley; and in case of their failure so to do to authorize and direct the Secretary of the Interior to readjust said rights of way.[71]

37 St. 649; Jan. 8, 1913; C. 7—An Act Amending an Act entitled "An Act to authorize the registration of trademarks used in commerce with foreign nations or among the several States or with the Indian tribes, and to protect the same."[72] 15 U. S. C. 85.

37 St. 652; Jan. 27, 1913; C. 15—An Act Granting certain lands for a cemetery to the Fort Bidwell People's Church Association, of the town of Fort Bidwell, State of California, and for other purposes.

37 St. 653; Jan. 28, 1913; C. 17—An Act Affecting the town sites of Timber Lake and Dupree in South Dakota.[73]

37 St. 665; Feb. 11, 1913; C. 37—An Act Providing when patents shall issue to the purchaser or heirs of certain lands in the State of Oregon.[74]

37 St. 668; Feb. 13, 1915; C. 44—An Act Repealing the provision of the Indian appropriation Act for the fiscal year ending June 30, 1907, authorizing the sale of a tract of land reserved for a burial ground for the Wyandotte Tribe of Indians in Kansas City, Kansas.[75]

37 St. 675; Feb. 14, 1913; C. 54—An Act To authorize the sale and disposition of the surplus and unallotted lands in the Standing Rock Indian Reservation, in the States of South Dakota and North Dakota, and making appropriation and provision to carry the same into effect.[76]

37 St. 678; Feb. 14, 1913; C. 55—An Act Regulating Indian allotments disposed of by will.[77] 25 U. S. C. 373, (36 Stat. 856, sec. 2).

37 St. 679; Feb. 19, 1915; C. 59—An Act To increase the pensions of surviving soldiers of Indian wars in certain cases.[78] 38 U. S. C. 374.

37 St. 704; Mar. 2, 1913; C. 93—An Act Making appropriations for the support of the Army for the fiscal year ending June 30, 1914.

37 St. 739; Mar. 4, 1913; C. 142—An Act Making appropriations for the legislative, executive, and judicial expenses of the Government for the fiscal year ending June 30, 1914, and for other purposes.

37 St. 912; Mar. 4, 1913; C. 149—An Act Making appropriations to supply deficiencies in appropriations for the fiscal year 1913 and for prior years, and for other purposes.[79]

37 St. 1007; Mar. 4, 1913; C. 152—An Act Authorizing the Secretary of the Interior to lease to the operators of coal mines in Oklahoma additional acreage from the unleased segregated coal land of the Choctaw and Chickasaw Nations.

37 St. 1007; Mar. 4, 1913; C. 153—An Act For the relief of Indians occupying railroad lands in Arizona, New Mexico, or California.[80]

37 St. 1015; Mar. 4, 1915; C. 165—An Act To authorize the sale of burnt timber on the public domain.[81] Sec. 1—16 U. S. C. 614; Sec. 2—16 U. S. C. 615.

37 St. 1025; Mar. 3, 1913; J. Res. No. 13—Joint Resolution Providing for extending provisions of the Act authorizing extension of payments to homesteaders on the Coeur d'Alene Indian Reservation, Idaho.[82]

37 St. 1538; Feb. 7, 1911—Treaty with the United Kingdom of Great Britain and Ireland.

37 St. 1542; July 7, 1911—Treaty with Great Britain, Japan and Russia.

37 St. 1027; Aug. 17, 1911; C. 21—An Act For the relief of Eliza Choteau Roscamp.

37 St. 1030; Apr. 12, 1912; C. 76—An Act Granting pensions and increase of pensions to certain soldiers and sailors of the Regular Army and Navy, and certain soldiers and sailors of wars other than the Civil War, and to widows of such soldiers and sailors.

37 St. 1246; July 6, 1912; C. 215—An Act Authorizing the Secretary of the Interior to adjust and settle the claims of the attorney of record involving certain Indian allotments, and for other purposes.[83]

38 STAT.

38 St. 4; June 23, 1913; C. 3—An Act Making appropriations for sundry civil expenses of the Government for the fiscal year ending June 30, 1914, and for other purposes.[84]

38 St. 77; June 30, 1913; C. 4—An Act Making appropriations for the current and contingent expenses of the Bureau of Indian Affairs, for fulfilling treaty stipulations with various Indian tribes, and for other purposes, for the fiscal year end-

[63] *Rg.* 33 St. 185. *Sg.* 34 St. 139.

[64] *Sg.* 37 St. 1542. *S.* 38 St. 4. 1222.

[65] *Sg.* 1 St. 425, sec. 9; 4 St. 442; 7 St. 46, 90, 213, 235, 236, 425; 11 St. 614, 730; 12 St. 282, sec. 7; 1172; 15 St. 622, 637; 15 St. 640, 652, 658, 676; 16 St. 570, sec. 3; 720; 17 St. 136, sec. 1, 2; 18 St. 35, 450; 19 St. 256; 24 St. 388; 25 St. 645, 894; 26 St. 1029; 27 St. 130, 644; 30 St. 90; 32 St. 656; 33 St. 597, 1016; 34 St. 875, 1037, 1050; 35 St. 463; 36 St. 270, 273, 287, 533, 858, 1063, 1070, 1074; 37 St. 399. *Ag.* 36 St. 1066; 37 St. 67. *Rp.* 45 St. 1307. *A.* 38 St. 77, 582; 42 St. 820; 45 St. 493. *S.* 38 St. 77, 208, 582, 767; 39 St. 123, 969; 40 St. 561; 41 St. 3, 408, 1225; 42 St. 552, 991, 1174; 43 St. 33, 390, 1141; 44 St. 453, 934; 45 St. 200, 1562; 46 St. 1510. *Cited:* Tydings 23 Case & Com. 743; Memo. Ind. Off. Apr. 21, 1927; 49 L. D. 370; Creek, 78 C. Cls. 474; Duwamish, 79 C. Cls. 530; Medawakanton, 57 C. Cls. 357; U. S. v. Birdsall, 233 U. S. 223; U. S. v. One Ford, 259 Fed. 645; U. S. v. Seminole, 299 U. S. 417.

[66] *S.* 42 St. 829. *A.* 45 St. 493.

[66] Superseded by Ex. Or. 6145, May 25, 1933. See Historical Note 25 U. S. C. A. 21.

[67] *S.* 40 St. 578, sec. 17; 45 St. 1307.

[68] *Ag.* 37 St. 197.

[69] *Sg.* 11 St. 611; 26 St. 853; 34 St. 1376. *S.* 38 St. 240.

[70] *Sg.* 26 St. 455, Sec. 2.

[71] *Ag.* 18 St. 482; 30 St. 430, 990.

[72] *Ag.* 33 St. 725; 34 St. 1251; 36 St. 918.

[73] *Sg.* 35 St. 463.

[74] *Sg.* 23 St. 342; 32 St. 730.

[75] *Sg.* 10 St. 1160. *Rg.* 34 St. 348.

[76] *Sg.* 12 St. 754, sec. 2; 17 St. 333, sec. 1; 31 St. 847; 35 St. 463. *S.* 39 St. 123; 41 St. 1446. *A.* 40 St. 561. *Cited:* Tydings, 23 Case & Com. 743.

[77] *Ag.* 36 St. 856. *S.* 38 St. 582; 43 St. 376. *Cited:* Brown, 39 Yale L. J. 307; Reeves, 23 Case & Com. 727; 36 Op. A. G. 98; 3 L. D. Memo. 435; Op. Sol. M. 6083, Oct. 29, 1921; M. 5805, Nov. 22, 1921; M. 25258, June 26, 1929; Op. A. G., Oct. 5, 1929; 48 L. D. 472, 479; 54 I. D. 555; Blanset, 256 U. S. 319; Johnson, 283 Fed. 954; Lamotte, 254 U. S. 570; Nimrod, 24 F. 2d 613; U. S. v. Mathewson, 32 F. 2d 745.

[78] *Sg.* 27 St. 282; 32 St. 399; 35 St. 553. *S.* 39 St. 1199; 44 St. 1361; 50 St. 786.

[79] *Sg.* 11 St. 611; 26 St. 853. *S.* 38 St. 582; 39 St. 123, 969; 40 St. 561; 41 St. 3, 408, 1225; 42 St. 552, 1174; 43 St. 390, 1141; 44 St. 453, 934; 45 St. 200, 1562; 46 St. 279; 47 St. 91, 820.

[80] *A.* 39 St. 48; 41 St. 3; 42 St. 994; 43 St. 705; 45 St. 299. *Cited:* U. S. ex. rel. McAlester, 277 Fed. 573.

[81] *A.* 44 St. 890. *Cited:* Op. Sol., 17687, Dec. 19, 1925.

[82] *Ag.* 37 St. 85.

[83] *S.* 38 St. 77.

[84] *Sg.* 35 St. 102; 37 St. 499. *S.* 38 St. 822. *Cited:* 44 L. D. 505.

ing June 30, 1914.[85] Sec. 1—25 U. S. C. 101, 25 U. S. C. 33. See Historical Note 25 U. S. C. A. 377. Sec. 18—25 U. S. C. 285, 25 U. S. C. 85.

38 St. 111; Sept. 17, 1913; C. 12—An Act To provide for the acquiring of station grounds by the Great Northern Ry. Co. in the Colville Indian Reservation in the State of Washington.[86]

38 St. 208; Oct. 22, 1913; C. 32—An Act Making appropriations to supply urgent deficiencies in appropriations for the fiscal year 1913, and for other purposes.[87] Sec. 1—5 U. S. C. 639.

38 St. 234; Oct. 24, 1913; C. 34—An Act To enable the Commissioner of Indian Affairs to employ additional clerks on heirship work in the Indian Office.[88]

38 St. 238; Sept. 11, 1913; J. Res. No. 9—Joint Resolution Authorizing the Secretary of the Senate and the Clerk of the House of Representatives to advance to the chairman of the Commission appointed under the Act approved June 30, 1913, such sums of money as may be necessary for the carrying on of the Commission, and so forth.[89]

38 St. 240; Nov. 15, 1913; J. Res. No. 15—Joint Resolution To relieve destitution among the native people and residents of Alaska.[90]

38 St. 310; Mar. 27, 1914; C. 46—An Act To provide for drainage of Indian allotments of the Five Civilized Tribes.[91]

38 St. 312; Apr. 6, 1914; C. 52—An Act Making appropriations to supply urgent deficiencies in appropriations for the fiscal year 1914 and for prior years, and for other purposes.[92] Sec. 5—5 U. S. C. 55.

38 St. 351; Apr. 27, 1914; C. 72—An Act Making appropriations for the support of the Army for the fiscal year ending June 30, 1915. 31 U. S. C. 653.

38 St. 379; May 25, 1914; C. 96—An Act Making appropriations to supply further urgent deficiencies in appropriations for the fiscal year 1914 and for other purposes.[93]

38 St. 383; May 28, 1914; C. 102—An Act For the relief of settlers on the Fort Berthold, Cheyenne River, Standing Rock, Rosebud, and Pine Ridge Indian Reservations, in the States of North and South Dakota.[94]

38 St. 454; July 16, 1914; C. 141—An Act Making appropriations for the legislative, executive, and judicial expenses of the Government for the fiscal year ending June 30, 1915, and for other purposes. Sec. 5—5 U. S. C. 78. Sec. 6—5 U. S. C. 293.

38 St. 510; July 17, 1914; C. 143—An Act To extend the provisions of the Act of June 23, 1910 (36 St. 592), authorizing assignment of reclamation homestead entries, and of the Act of August 9, 1912 (37 St. 265), authorizing the issuance of patents on reclamation homestead entries, to lands in the Flathead irrigation project, Montana.[95] 43 U. S. C. 593.

38 St. 553; July 21, 1914; C. 192—An Act For the approving and payment of the drainage assessments on Indian lands in Salt Creek drainage district numbered 2, in Pottawatomie County, Oklahoma.[96]

38 St. 559; July 29, 1914; C. 215—An Act Making appropriations to supply deficiencies in appropriations for the fiscal year 1914 and for prior years, and for other purposes.[97]

38 St. 582; Aug. 1, 1914; C. 222—An Act Making appropriations for the current and contingent expenses of the Bureau of Indian Affairs, for fulfilling treaty stipulations with various Indian tribes, and for other purposes, for the fiscal year ending June 30, 1915.[98] Sec. 1—25 U. S. C. 385 (secs. 1 & 3, 36 St. 270, 272). 25 U. S. C. 57.[99] 25 U. S. C. 198. USCA Historical Note: A provision in 38 St. 584 preceding instant provision made an appropriation of $300,000 to relieve distress among Indians and to provide for the prevention and treatment of contagious and infectious diseases and limited the amount of such appropriation to be expended for hospitals to $100,000 and the cost of any hospital to $15,000. The Indian appropriation for the fiscal year 1917, Act May 18, sec. 1, 39 St. 124, appropriated money for similar purposes and also for general medical and surgical attention. It also amended the above provision limiting the cost of any hospital to $15,000, so as to allow the expenditure of an additional $200,000. 25 U. S. C. 200. 25 U. S. C. 374. 25 U. S. C. 376. 25 U. S. C. 144.[1] Sec. 17—25 U. S. C. 25. USCA Historical Note: Revised Statute secs. 2046–2051 provided for the appointment, compensation, etc., of Indian superintendents, their terms, duties, and employees. Such provisions were discontinued by the President under authority vested in him by sec. 6 of the Act of Feb. 14, 1873, s. 6, 17 St. 463, incorporated in R. S. sec. 2047. 25 U. S. C. 86.

38 St. 609; Aug. 1, 1914; C. 223—An Act Making appropriations for sundry civil expenses of the Government for the fiscal year ending June 30, 1915, and for other purposes.[2]

38 St. 681; Aug. 3, 1914; C. 224—An Act To provide for the disposal of certain lands in the Fort Berthold Indian Reservation, North Dakota.[3]

38 St. 704; Aug. 22, 1914; C. 269—An Act To authorize the withdrawal of lands on the Quinaielt Reservation, in the State of Washington, for lighthouse purposes.

38 St. 767; Dec. 8, 1913; J. Res. No. 1—Joint Resolution Extending time for completion of classification and appraisement of surface of segregated coal and asphalt lands of the Choctaw and Chickasaw Nations and of the improvements thereon, and making appropriation therefor.[4]

38 St. 777; Aug. 21, 1914; J. Res. No. 35—Joint Resolution For the appointment of George Frederick Kuns as a member of the North American Indian Memorial Commission.

38 St. 780; Oct. 20, 1914; J. Res. No. 50—Joint Resolution To correct an error in the enrollment of certain Indians enumerated in Senate Document Numbered 478, 63d Congress, second session, enacted into law in the Indian appropriation Act approved August 1, 1914.[5]

38 St. 791; Jan. 11, 1915; C. 7—An Act To amend an Act entitled "An Act to provide for the adjudication and payment of claims arising from Indian depredations," approved March 3, 1891.[6]

38 St. 792; Jan. 11, 1915; C. 8—An Act Providing for the purchase and disposal of certain lands containing the minerals kaolin, koalinite, fuller's earth, china clay, and ball clay, in Tripp County, formerly a part of the Rosebud Indian Reservation in South Dakota.

38 St. 822; Mar. 3, 1915; C. 75—An Act Making appropriations for sundry civil expenses of the Government for the fiscal year ending June 30, 1916, and for other purposes.[7] Sec. 1—43 U. S. C. 90.

---

85 *Sg.* 4 St. 442; 7 St. 46, 99, 213, 235, 236, 425; 10 St. 1168; 11 St. 614, 730; 12 St. 1172, 1191; 15 St. 622, 638, 640, 652, 658, 669, 670, 720; 16 St. 719; 19 St. 256; 23 St. 79; 24 St. 388; 25 St. 645, 888, 894; 26 St. 1029; 27 St. 139, 644; 30 St. 90; 33 St. 597, 1016, 1081; 34 St. 55, 84, 375, 616, 1037, 1050; 35 St. 49, 77, 82, 84, 102, 558, 637, 791; 36 St. 270, sec. 1; 273, 277, 855, 858, 1063; 37 St. 396, 518, 521, 522, 529, 534, 539, 1246. *Ag.* 37 St. 67, 534. *Rg.* 34 St. 617. *A.* 39 St. 123, 969; 40 St. 561; 41 St. 625, 1105; 43 St. 728. *Rp.* 38 St. 312, 582; 45 St. 200. *S.* 38 St. 238, 582, 1219; 39 St. 123, 969; 40 St. 561; 41 St. 3, 408; 42 St. 991; 43 St. 728, 1141; 44 St. 934; 45 St. 159, 200, 883, 973. *Cited:* Reeves, 23 Case & Com. 727; Black, 5 F. 2d 091; Medawakanton, 57 C. Cls. 357; U. S. v. Seminole, 299 U. S. 417.

86 *Sg.* 30 St. 990; 34 St. 330; 36 St. 859.

87 *Sg.* 26 St. 853; 37 St. 518, 520.

88 *Sg.* 36 St. 855; 38 St. 80.

89 *Sg.* 38 St. 101, sec. 23.

90 *Sg.* 37 St. 597.

91 *A.* 41 St. 1204.

92 *Sg.* 11 St. 611; 26 St. 853. *Rg.* 38 St. 82. *S.* 40 St. 561.

93 *Sg.* 36 St. 326.

94 *Sg.* 36 St. 442, 450, 458; 37 St. 84.

95 *Sg.* 33 St. 302; 35 St. 448; 36 St. 592; 37 St. 265. *Cited:* Tydings, 23 Case & Com. 743.

96 *S.* 46 St. 2124. *Cited:* Memo. Sol., Sept. 23, 1937.

97 *Sg.* 11 St. 611; 26 St. 853.

98 *Sg.* 4 St. 442; 7 St. 46, 99, 213, 235, 236, 425; 10 St. 1109; 11 St. 614, 633, 730; 12 St. 1172; 15 St. 619, 622, 638, 640, 652, 658, 669, 676; 16 St. 204, secs. 44, 45, 720; 19 St. 256; 24 St. 388; 25 St. 642, 645, 894; 26 St. 794, 1029; 27 St. 139, 644; 31 St. 861; 32 St. 500, 716, 720; 33 St. 201, 597, 1016; 34 St. 84, 375, 1037, 1050; 35 St. 558; 36 St. 273, 277, 326, 368, 855, 858, sec. 13; 1058, 1063; 37 St. 67, 68, 91, 521, 538, 678, 934; 38 St. 90, 94, 100, sec. 23; 102, sec. 24. *Ag.* 37 St. 533. *Rpg.* 36 St. 1075; 38 St. 85. *A.* 39 St. 123; 48 St. 819. *Rp.* 45 St. 200, 986. *S.* 38 St. 780, 1228; 39 St. 123, 969; 40 St. 105, 561, 634; 41 St. 3, 163, 408, 874, 1225, 1367; 42 St. 552, 1174, 1527; 43 St. 94, 390, 672, 1141; 44 St. 453, 934; 45 St. 200, 1562; 46 St. 279, 1115; 47 St. 15, 91, 820; 48 St. 362; 49 St. 176, 1757; 50 St. 564; 52 St. 291. *Cited:* 33 Op. A. G. 25; Op. Sol., M. 6376, Nov. 15, 1921; M. 7599, June 9, 1922; Letter of Comm'r to Sen. Selden P. Spencer, Sept. 5, 1922; Memo. Ind. Off., Apr. 21, 1927; Op. Sol. M. 25214, June 7, 1929, M. 25347, Jan. 25, 1930; Memo. Ind. Off., June 12, 1933; Memo. Sol. Off., June 20, 1933; Memo. Sol., Feb. 28, 1935; Op. Sol. M. 28033, June 4, 1935; Memo. Sol., Sept. 12, 1935, Feb. 8, 1937, Mar. 15, 1937; Op. Sol. M. 29232, June 2, 1937; 54 I. D. 335; Chippewa, 307 U. S. 1; Choctaw, 81 C. Cls. 1; Medawakanton, 57 C. Cls., 357; Scheer, 48 F. 2d 327; Shoshone, 85 C. Cls. 331; U. S. v. Bowling, 256 U. S. 484; U. S. v. Seminole, 299 U. S. 417; U. S. v. Watashe, 102 F. 2d 428; U. S. ex rel. Kadrie, 30 F. 2d 989.

99 *S.* 40 St. 564, sec. 1; 43 St. 1147.

1 *R.* 45 St. 986, 991, sec. 1.

2 *Sg.* 35 St. 102; 36 St. 326. *S.* 38 St. 822.

3 *Sg.* 36 St. 455. *A.* 39 St. 1131. *Cited:* 49 L. D. 354.

4 *Ag.* 37 St. 68. *Sg.* 37 St. 518, sec. 18.

5 *Sg.* 38 St. 600, sec. 17.

6 *Ag.* 26 St. 851. *Cited:* Coffield v. U. S., 52 C. Cls. 17; Indian Depredation Cases, 50 C. Cls. 395.

7 *Ag.* 14 St. 11; 16 St. 599; 17 St. 417. *Sg.* 30 St. 977; 35 St. 102; 36 St. 326; 38 St. 53, 648. *Cited:* First Moon, 270 U. S. 243.

38 St. 997; Mar. 4, 1915; C. 141—An Act Making appropriations for the legislative, executive, and judicial expenses of the Government for the fiscal year ending June 30, 1916, and for other purposes.

38 St. 1062; Mar. 4, 1915; C. 143—An Act Making appropriations for the support of the Army for the fiscal year ending June 30, 1916.

38 St. 1086; Mar. 4, 1915; C. 144—An Act Making appropriations for the Department of Agriculture for the fiscal year ending June 30, 1916.

38 St. 1138; Mar. 4, 1915; C. 147—An Act Making appropriations to supply deficiencies in appropriations for the fiscal year 1915 and for prior years, and for other purposes.[8]

38 St. 1188; Mar. 4, 1915; C. 161—An Act To authorize the laying out and opening of public roads on the Winnebago, Omaha, Ponca, and Santee Sioux Indian Reservations in Nebraska and on Indian reservations in Montana.[9]

38 St. 1189; Mar. 4, 1915; C. 162—An Act Authorizing the sale of lands in Lyman County, South Dakota.[10]

38 St. 1192; Mar. 4, 1915; C. 168—An Act To provide for the payment of certain moneys to school districts in Oklahoma.[11]

38 St. 1219; Mar. 4, 1915; C. 189—An Act To validate certain homestead entries.[12]

38 St. 1222; Feb. 24, 1915; J. Res. No. 7—Joint Resolution Authorizing the Secretary of Commerce to postpone the sale of fur-seal skins now in the possession of the Government until such time as in his discretion he may deem such sale advisable.[13]

38 St. 1228; Mar. 4, 1915; J. Res. No. 16—Joint Resolution Making appropriations for current and contingent expenses of the Bureau of Indian Affairs, for fulfilling treaty stipulations with various Indian tribes, and for other purposes for the fiscal year ending June 30, 1916.[14]

38 St. 1269; June 15, 1914; C. 108—An Act Granting pensions and increase of pensions to certain soldiers and sailors of the Regular Army and Navy, and of other wars than the Civil War, and certain widows and dependent relatives of such soldiers and sailors.

38 St. 1278; June 15, 1914; C. 110—An Act Granting pensions and increase of pensions to certain soldiers and sailors of the Regular Army and Navy and of wars other than the Civil War, and to certain widows and dependent relatives of such soldiers and sailors.

38 St. 1279; June 15, 1914; C. 111—An Act Granting pensions and increase of pensions to certain soldiers and sailors of the Regular Army and Navy and of wars other than the Civil War, and to certain widows and dependent relatives of such soldiers and sailors.

38 St. 1305; July 17, 1914; C. 166—An Act To carry into effect findings of the Court of Claims in the cases of Charles A. Davidson and Charles M. Campbell.

38 St. 1308; July 17, 1914; C. 177—An Act For the relief of Henry La Roque.

38 St. 1311; July 18, 1914; C. 188—An Act For the relief of George W. Cary.

38 St. 1326; July 21, 1914; C. 194—An Act Granting pensions and increase of pensions to certain soldiers and sailors of the Regular Army and Navy, and certain soldiers and sailors of wars other than the Civil War, and to widows of such soldiers and sailors.

38 St. 1337; July 21, 1914; C. 196—An Act Granting pensions and increase of pensions to certain soldiers and sailors of the Regular Army and Navy, and certain soldiers and sailors of wars other than the Civil War, and to widows of such soldiers and sailors.

38 St. 1350; July 21, 1914; C. 198—An Act Granting pensions and increase of pensions to certain soldiers and sailors of the Regular Army and Navy, and certain soldiers and sailors of wars other than the Civil War, and to widows of such soldiers and sailors.

38 St. 1374; July 21, 1914; C. 203—An Act Authorizing the disposal of a portion of the Fort Bidwell Indian School, California.

38 St. 1375; July 28, 1914; C. 214—An Act To relinquish, release, and quitclaim all right, title, and interest of the United States of America in and to certain lands in the State of Mississippi.[15]

38 St. 1433; Aug. 10, 1914; C. 244—An Act Granting pensions and increase of pensions to certain soldiers and sailors of the Regular Army and Navy, and certain soldiers and sailors of wars other than the Civil War, and to widows of such soldiers and sailors.

38 St. 1439; Aug. 10, 1914; C. 246—An Act Granting pensions and increase of pensions to certain soldiers and sailors of the Regular Army and Navy, and certain soldiers and sailors of wars other than the Civil War, and to widows of such soldiers and sailors.

38 St. 1443; Aug. 13, 1914; C. 248—An Act Granting pensions and increase of pensions to certain soldiers and sailors of the Regular Army and Navy, and of wars other than the Civil War, and to certain widows and dependent relatives of such soldiers and sailors.

38 St. 1444; Aug. 13, 1914; C. 249—An Act Granting pensions and increase of pensions to certain soldiers and sailors of the Regular Army and Navy, and of wars other than the Civil War, and to certain widows and dependent relatives of such soldiers and sailors.

38 St. 1446; Aug. 13, 1914; C. 250—An Act Granting pensions and increase of pensions to certain soldiers and sailors of the Regular Army and Navy, and of wars other than the Civil War, and to certain widows and dependent relatives of such soldiers and sailors.

38 St. 1447; Aug. 13, 1914; C. 251—An Act Granting pensions and increase of pensions to certain soldiers and sailors of the Regular Army and Navy and of wars other than the Civil War, and to certain widows and dependent relatives of such soldiers and sailors.

38 St. 1452; Aug. 22, 1914; C. 272—An Act For the relief of May Stanley.

38 St. 1455; Aug. 22, 1914; C. 280—An Act For the relief of E. F. Anderson.

38 St. 1459; Oct. 17, 1914; C. 326—An Act For the relief of Benjamin A. Sanders.

38 St. 1471; Jan. 7, 1915; C. 6—An Act To reimburse Edward B. Kelley for moneys expended while superintendent of the Rosebud Indian Agency in South Dakota.

38 St. 1478; Feb. 25, 1915; C. 61—An Act Confirming patents heretofore issued to certain Indians in the State of Washington.

38 St. 1547; Mar. 3, 1915; C. 129—An Act To provide for the payment of the claim of J. O. Modisette for services performed for the Chickasaw Indians of Oklahoma.

38 St. 1569; Mar. 4, 1915; C. 194—An Act Granting pensions and increase of pensions to certain soldiers and sailors of the Regular Army and Navy and of wars other than the Civil War, and to certain widows and dependent relatives of such soldiers and sailors.

38 St. 1593; Mar. 4, 1915; C. 221—An Act To award the medal of honor to Major John O. Skinner, surgeon, United States Army, retired.

38 St. 1594; Mar. 4, 1915; C. 223—An Act Granting pensions and increase of pensions to certain soldiers and sailors of the Regular Army and Navy and certain soldiers and sailors of wars other than the Civil War, and to widows of such soldiers and sailors.

39 STAT.

39 St. 14; Feb. 28, 1916; C. 37—An Act Making appropriations to supply further urgent deficiencies in appropriations for the fiscal year ending June 30, 1916, and prior years, and for other purposes.[16]

39 St. 47; Apr. 11, 1916; C. 63—An Act Conferring jurisdiction on the Court of Claims to hear, determine, and render judgment in claims of the Sisseton and Wahpeton bands of Sioux Indians against the United States.[17]

39 St. 48; Apr. 11, 1916; C. 65—An Act To amend an Act entitled "An Act for the relief of Indians occupying railroad lands in Arizona, New Mexico, or California," approved March 4, 1913.[18]

39 St. 66; May 10, 1916; C. 117—An Act Making appropriations for the legislative, executive, and judicial expenses of the

[8] *Sg.* 11 St. 611; 26 St. 853.
[9] *Cited:* Op. Sol., M. 13344, Oct. 9, 1924.
[10] *Sg.* 25 St. 896.
[11] *Sg.* 26 St. 91, sec. 22; 32 St. 63.
[12] *Sg.* 36 St. 1069, sec. 16; 38 St. 92.
[13] *Sg.* 37 St. 502.
[14] *Sg.* 38 St. 582. *Cited:* Lane, 246 U. S. 214; Medawakanton, 57 C. Cls. 357; U. S. v. Seminole, 299 U. S. 417.

[15] *Sg.* 7 St. 333.
[16] *Sg.* 26 St. 853.
[17] *Cited:* Sioux, 277 U. S. 424; Sisseton, 58 C. Cls. 302.
[18] *Ag.* 37 St. 1007, c. 153. *A.* 41 St. 3; 42 St. 994; 43 St. 795; 45 St. 299.

Government for the fiscal year ending June 30, 1917, and for other purposes.[19]

39 St. 123; May 18, 1916; C. 125—An Act Making appropriations for the current and contingent expenses of the Bureau of Indian Affairs, for fulfilling treaty stipulations with various Indian tribes, and for other purposes, for the fiscal year ending June 30, 1917.[20] Sec. 1—25 U. S. C. 245, 252; 25 U. S. C. 93; 41 U. S. C. 6; 25 U. S. C. 378; 25 U. S. C. 121 394; 25 U. S. C. 95; 25 U. S. C. 123; Sec. 27—25 U. S. C. 142. See USCA Historical note.

39 St. 237; June 26, 1916; C. 174—An Act To provide for the construction of a bridge across the Salt Fork of the Arkansas River, near White Eagle Agency, in the Ponca Indian Reservation, Oklahoma.

39 St. 262; July 1, 1916; C. 209—An Act Making appropriations for sundry civil expenses of the Government for the fiscal year ending June 30, 1917, and for other purposes.[21] Sec 1—16 U. S. C. 179.

39 St. 341; July 3, 1916; C. 213—An Act Providing for patents to homesteads on the ceded portion of the Wind River Reservation in Wyoming.[22]

39 St. 353; July 8, 1916; C. 230—An Act To reimburse certain Indians for labor done in building a schoolhouse at Queets River, Quinlault Indian Reservation, in the State of Washington.

39 St. 386; July 17, 1916; C. 248—An Act To amend section ninety-nine of the Act to codify, revise, and amend the laws relating to the judiciary.[23] 28 U. S. C. 180.

39 St. 445; Aug. 9, 1916; C. 304—An Act To provide for the sale of certain Indian lands in Oklahoma, and for other purposes.[24]

39 St. 504; Aug. 11, 1916; C. 315—An Act Authorizing the adjustment of rights of settlers on a part of the Navajo Indian Reservation in the State of Arizona.[25]

39 St. 509; Aug. 11, 1916; C. 320—An Act Authorizing the Secretary of the Interior to make payments to certain Indians of the Rosebud Sioux Reservation, in the State of South Dakota, who were enrolled and allotted under decisions of the United States district and circuit courts for the district of South Dakota.

39 St. 519; Aug. 21, 1916; C. 363—An Act To authorize the Secretary of the Interior to lease, for production of oil and gas, ceded lands of the Shoshone or Wind River Indian Reservation in the State of Wyoming.[26]

39 St. 521; Aug. 21, 1916; C. 366—An Act To appropriate money to build and maintain roads on the Spokane Indian Reservation.

39 St. 524; Aug. 21, 1916; C. 369—An Act Authorizing the Secretary of the Interior to transfer on certain conditions the south half of lot 14 of the southeast quarter of section 21, township 107, range 48, Moody County, South Dakota, to the city of Flandreau, to be used as a public park or playgrounds.

39 St. 619; Aug. 29, 1916; C. 418—An Act Making appropriations for the support of the Army for the fiscal year ending June 30, 1917, and for other purposes.

39 St. 672; Aug. 31, 1916; C. 424—An Act To amend the Act of March 22, 1906, entitled "An Act to authorize the sale and disposition of surplus or unallotted lands of the diminished Colville Indian Reservation, in the State of Washington, and for other purposes."[27]

39 St. 673; Aug. 31, 1916; C. 425—An Act To amend an Act entitled "An Act to provide for the payment of drainage assessments on Indian lands in Oklahoma."[28]

39 St. 739; Sept. 7, 1916; C. 452—An Act To amend the Act of February 11, 1915 (38 St. 807), providing for the opening of the Fort Assiniboine Military Reservation.[29]

39 St. 741; Sept. 7, 1916; C. 455—An Act Providing that Indian schools may be maintained without restrictions as to annual rate of expenditure per pupil.[30]

39 St. 801; Sept. 8, 1916; C. 464—An Act Making appropriations to supply deficiencies in appropriations for the fiscal year ending June 30, 1916, and prior fiscal years, and for other purposes.[31]

39 St. 844; Sept. 8, 1916; C. 468—An Act Making appropriations for the preservation, improvements, and perpetual care of Huron Cemetery, a burial place of the Wyandotte Indians, in the city of Kansas City, Kansas.[32]

39 St. 846; Sept. 8, 1916; C. 472—An Act To authorize the Secretary of the Interior to issue a patent in fee simple to the district school board numbered 112, of White Earth Village, Becker County, Minnesota, for a certain tract of land upon payment therefor to the United States in trust for the Chippewa Indians of Minnesota.

39 St. 865; Dec. 30, 1916; C. 10—An Act Providing for the taxation of the lands of the Winnebago Indians and the Omaha Indians in the State of Nebraska.

39 St. 866; Jan. 11, 1917; C. 12—Joint Resolution Authorizing the Secretary of the Interior to extend the time for payment of the deferred installments due on the purchase of tracts of the surface of the segregated coal and asphalt lands of the Choctaw and Chickasaw Tribes in Oklahoma.[33]

39 St. 867; Jan. 18, 1917; C. 16—An Act Providing for the continuance of the Osage Indian School, Oklahoma, for a period of one year from January 1, 1917.[34]

39 St. 870; Jan. 25, 1917; C. 21—An Act To permit the Denison Coal Company to relinquish certain lands embraced in its Choctaw and Chickasaw coal lease and to include within said lease other lands within the segregated coal area.[35]

39 St. 923; Feb. 17, 1917; C. 87—An Act Providing when patents shall issue to the purchaser or heirs on certain lands in the State of Oregon.[36]

39 St. 926; Feb. 20, 1917; C. 100—An Act To construct a bridge in San Juan County, State of New Mexico.[37]

39 St. 937; Feb. 23, 1917; C. 117—An Act Authorizing a further extension of time to purchasers of land in the former Cheyenne and Arapahoe Indian Reservation, Oklahoma, within which to make payment.[38]

39 St. 944; Feb. 27, 1917; C. 133—An Act To authorize agricultural entries on surplus coal lands in Indian reservations. Sec. 1—30 U. S. C. 86; Sec. 2—30 U. S. C. 87; Sec. 3—30 U. S. C. 88; Sec. 4—30 U. S. C. 89.

39 St. 969; Mar. 2, 1917; C. 146—An Act Making appropriations for the current and contingent expenses of the Bureau of Indian Affairs, for fulfilling treaty stipulations with various Indian tribes, and for other purposes, for the fiscal year ending June 30, 1918.[39] Sec. 1, p. 970—25 U. S. C. 247; Sec. 1,

[19] *S.* 39 St. 123. *Cited:* Cain, 2 Minn. L. Rev. 177; Letter of Comm'r to Ind. Agents, Oct. 9, 1937.

[20] *Sg.* 4 St. 442; 4 St. 732; 7 St. 46, 99, 213, 235, 236, 425; 11 St. 614, 730; 12 St. 220; 13 St. 290; 15 St. 622, 640, 652, 658, 669, 676; 16 St. 720; 19 St. 254, 256; 21 St. 114; 22 St. 590; 24 St. 388, 463; 25 St. 642, 645; 26 St. 146, 1029; 27 St. 120, 612, 745; 29 St. 506; 32 St. 388; 33 St. 304, 595, 597, 1016, 1081; 34 St. 375, 1050; 35 St. 51, 444, 448, 558; 36 St. 273, 277, 455, 858, 1063, 1071; 37 St. 67, 521, 522, 534, 672, 675, 934; 38 St. 77, 88, 89, 102, 103, 583, 584, 591, 599, 602, 603, 604, 686; 39 St. 102. *Ag.* 18 St. 450, sec. 9; 34 St 1221; 35 St. 51; 36 St. 367, 861; 38 St. 584. *Rg.* 21 St. 132, sec. 4 *Rp.* 45 St. 986. *S.* 39 St. 969; 40 St. 2, 561; 41 St. 3, 408, 1225; 42 St. 552, 1174, 1527; 43 St. 390, 1141; 44 St. 303, 453, 560, 934; 45 St. 159, 200, 883, 1562; 46 St. 1519. *Cited:* Brown, 39 Yale L. J. 307; 8 L. D. Memo. 761; Op. Sol., M. 6083, Oct. 29, 1921; M. 6376, Nov. 15, 1921; Letter of Comm'r to Sen. Selden P. Spencer, Sept. 5, 1922; Op. Sol., M. 11879, May 31, 1924; M. 10068, Feb. 16, 1927; Memo. Sol. Off., Apr. 4, 1933, June 12, 1933, June 20, 1933; Contract, June 3, 1935; Memo. Sol., Jan. 24, 1936, Sept. 3, 1936; Comp. Gen's Op., June 30, 1937; Memo. Ind. Off., July 8, 1937; Memo. Sol. Off., June 6, 1938; Memo. Sol., Nov. 11, 1939; 48 L. D. 472; 51 L. D. 613; Chippewa, 80 C. Cls. 410; Chippewa, 307 U. S. 1; Coos Bay, 87 C. Cls. 143; Goff, 257 Fed. 294; Harris, 249 Fed. 41; Medawakanton, 57 C. Cls. 357; Minnesota, 305 U. S. 382; Morrison, 266 U. S. 481; Scheer, 48 F. 2d 327; Shoshone, 82 C. Cls. 23; Stockbridge, 61 C. Cls. 472; Townsend, 265 Fed. 519; U. S. v. Algoma, 305 U. S. 415; U. S. v. Bowling, 256 U. S 484; U. S. v. Luther, 260 Fed. 579; U. S. v. McGowan, 89 F. 2d 201; U. S. v. McGowan, 302 U. S. 535; U. S. v. One Ford, 259 Fed. 645; U. S. v. Seminole, 299 U. S. 417; U. S. ex rel. Besaw, 6 F. 2d 694; U. S. ex rel. Kadrie, 30 F. 2d 989; Work, 18 F. 2d 820.

[21] *Sg.* 35 St. 102; 36 St. 326.

[22] *Sg.* 33 St. 1019.

[23] *Ag.* 36 St. 1121; 37 St. 60. *A.* 44 St. 237.

[24] *Sg.* 34 St. 80.

[25] *Sg.* Ex. Or. Jan. 8, 1900.

[26] *Sg.* 33 St. 1020. *S.* 45 St. 467; 46 St. 88, 1060.

[27] *Ag.* 34 St. 80, sec. 7.

[28] *Ag.* 37 St. 194.

[29] *Sg.* 24 St. 388. *Ag.* 38 St. 809.

[30] *S.* 40 St. 459.

[31] *Sg.* 25 St. 645, sec. 7; 26 St. 853; 35 St. 619.

[32] *S.* 41 St. 3.

[33] *Ag.* 37 St. 67, sec. 5.

[34] *Ag.* 34 St. 539, sec. 4.

[35] *Ag.* 36 St. 832, sec. 2. *Sg.* 37 St. 67.

[36] *Sg.* 23 St. 342; 32 St. 730.

[37] *S.* 40 St. 561; 41 St. 1225; 48 St. 1185.

[38] *Sg.* 36 St. 533.

[39] *Sg.* 4 St. 442; 7 St. 46, 99, 213, 235, 236, 425; 10 St. 1076; 11 St. 614, 730; 12 St. 392, 963; 13 St. 29; 15 St. 622, 640, 652, 658, 669, 676; 16 St. 720; 19 St. 254, 256; 24 St. 388; 25 St. 645, 989; 26 St. 146, 1029; 27 St. 139, 644; 29 St. 331; 33 St. 597, 1016, 1081; 34 St. 182, 227, 1025, 1050; 35 St. 51; 36 St. 273, 277, 858, 859, 1058, 1063; 37 St. 67, 518, 521, 522, 934; 38 St. 102, 583, 604; 39 St. 123, 128, 130, 131, 147, 154. *Ag.* 26 St. 712, sec. 34; 27 St. 53; 33 St. 65; 38 St. 88. *S.* 40 St. 561; 41 St. 3, 408, 1225; 42 St. 1288, 1527; 43 St. 819, 1141; 44 St. 453, 934, 1061; 45 St. 442; 46 St. 1106. *A.* 47 St. 302. *Cited:* 73d Cong., 2d sess., S. Rept. No. 417; Op. Sol. M.8860, Nov. 1, 1922; Memo. Sol. Off., Apr. 4, 1933; Op. Sol. M 27939, Apr. 9, 1935; M. 29097, Apr. 8, 1937; Browning, 6 F. 2d 801; Chippewa, 307 U. S. 1;

p. 973—25 U. S. C. 298; 25 U. S. C. 321 (33 St. 65, sec. 1, 2). See 25 U. S. C. 465. Sec. 17, p. 983—25 U. S. C. 242; [40] Sec. 21, p. 988—25 U. S. C. 278 (30 St. 79, sec. 1).

39 St. 994; Mar. 2, 1917; C. 148—An Act Providing additional time for the payment of purchase money under homestead entries of lands within the former Fort Peck Indian Reservation, Montana. [41]

39 St. 1070; Mar. 3, 1917; C. 163—An Act Making appropriations for the legislative, executive, and judicial expenses of the Government for the fiscal year ending June 30, 1918, and for other purposes.

39 St. 1131; Mar. 3, 1917; C. 167—An Act To authorize the Legislature of Alaska to establish and maintain schools, and for other purposes. [42] 48 U. S. C. 170.

39 St. 1131; Mar. 3, 1917; C. 168—An Act To amend an Act entitled "An Act to provide for the disposal of certain lands in the Fort Berthold Indian Reservation, North Dakota," approved August 3, 1914. [43]

39 St. 1195; Mar. 4, 1917; C. 181—An Act For the restoration of annuities to the Medawakanton and Wahpakoota (Santee) Sioux Indians, declared forfeited by the Act of February 16, 1863. [44]

39 St. 1199; Mar. 4, 1917; C. 189—An Act To pension the survivors of certain Indian wars from January 1, 1859, to January, 1891, inclusive, and for other purposes. [45] Sec. 1—38 U. S. C. 375; Sec. 2—38 U. S. C. 376.

39 St. 1243; Apr. 14, 1916; C. 76—An Act For the relief of Warren E. Day.

39 St. 1262; Apr. 28, 1916; C. 100—An Act For the relief of Ellis P. Garton, administrator of the estate of H. B. Garton, deceased.

39 St. 1299; June 22, 1916; C. 172—An Act For the relief of Mrs. George A. Miller.

39 St. 1301; June 28, 1916; C. 190—An Act Validating certain applications for and entries of public lands. [46]

39 St. 1355; Aug. 11, 1916; C. 336—An Act For the relief of Doctor E. E. Johnson.

39 St. 1358; Aug. 16, 1916; C. 347—An Act For the relief of Thomas P. Sorkilmo.

39 St. 1358; Aug. 18, 1916; C. 351—An Act Granting pensions and increase of pensions to certain soldiers and sailors of the Regular Army and Navy and of wars other than the Civil War, and to certain widows and dependent relatives of such soldiers and sailors.

39 St. 1366; Aug. 18, 1916; C. 354—An Act Granting pensions and increase of pensions to certain soldiers and sailors of the Regular Army and Navy, and certain soldiers and sailors of wars other than the Civil War and to widows of such soldiers and sailors.

39 St. 1369; Aug. 18, 1916; C. 355—An Act Granting pensions and increase of pensions to certain soldiers and sailors of the Regular Army and Navy, and certain soldiers and sailors of wars other than the Civil War, and to widows of such soldiers and sailors.

39 St. 1373; Aug. 18, 1916; C. 356—An Act Granting pensions and increase of pensions to certain soldiers and sailors of the Regular Army and Navy and certain soldiers and sailors of wars other than the Civil War, and to widows of such soldiers and sailors.

39 St. 1382; Aug. 19, 1916; C. 358—An Act Granting pensions and increase of pensions to certain soldiers and sailors of the Regular Army and Navy and to certain soldiers and sailors of wars other than the Civil War, and to widows of such soldiers and sailors.

39 St. 1467; Sept. 8, 1916; C. 482—An Act For the relief of Eva M. Bowman.

39 St. 1470; Jan. 18, 1917; C. 17—An Act For the relief of William H. Woods.

39 St. 1476; Feb. 15, 1917; C. 81—An Act Confirming patents heretofore issued to certain Indians in the State of Washington.

39 St. 1477; Feb. 15, 1917; C. 82—An Act For the relief of Ivy L. Merrill.

39 St. 1477; Feb. 15, 1917; C. 83—An Act for the relief of Alma Provost.

39 St. 1573; Mar. 3, 1917; C. 177—An Act Granting pensions and increase of pensions to certain soldiers and sailors of the Regular Army and Navy, and certain soldiers and sailors of wars other than the Civil War, and to widows of such soldiers and sailors.

39 St. 1580; Mar. 3, 1917; C. 178—An Act Granting pensions and increase of pensions to certain soldiers and sailors of the Regular Army and Navy, and certain soldiers and sailors of wars other than the Civil War, and to widows of such soldiers and sailors.

39 St. 1588; Mar. 4, 1917; C. 197—An Act Granting pensions and increase of pensions to certain soldiers and sailors of the Regular Army and Navy and of wars other than the Civil War, and to certain widows and dependent relatives of such soldiers and sailors.

39 St. 1594; Mar. 4, 1917; C. 198—An Act Granting pensions and increase of pensions to certain soldiers and sailors of the Regular Army and Navy and of wars other than the Civil War, and to certain widows and dependent relatives of such soldiers and sailors.

39 St. 1608; Mar. 2, 1917; Concurrent Res.—Medawakanton and Wahpakoota Indian Bill. [47]

40 STAT.

40 St. 2; Apr. 17, 1917; C. 3—An Act Making Appropriations to supply deficiencies in appropriations for the fiscal year ending June 30, 1917, and prior fiscal years, and for other purposes. [48]

40 St. 40; May 12, 1917; C. 12—An Act Making appropriations for the support of the Army for the fiscal year ending June 30, 1918, and for other purposes.

40 St. 105; June 12, 1917; C. 27—An Act Making appropriations for sundry civil expenses of the Government for the fiscal year ending June 30, 1918, and for other purposes. [49] Sec. 1—43 U. S. C. 399, 415; 16 U. S. C. 179; 48 U. S. C. 49.

40 St. 345; Oct. 6, 1917; C. 79—An Act Making appropriations to supply urgent deficiencies in appropriations for the fiscal year ending June 30, 1918, and prior fiscal years, on account of war expenses, and for other purposes. [50] Sec. 1—20 U. S. C. 15.

40 St. 433; Feb. 8, 1918; C. 12—An Act Providing for the sale of the coal and asphalt deposits in the segregated mineral land in the Choctaw and Chickasaw Nations, Oklahoma. [51]

40 St. 449; Mar. 11, 1918; C. 21—Joint Resolution Providing additional time for the payment of purchase money under homestead entries within the former Colville Indian Reservation, Washington. [52]

40 St. 459; Mar. 28, 1918; C. 28—An Act Making appropriations to supply urgent deficiencies in appropriations for the fiscal year ending June 30, 1918, and prior fiscal years, on account of war expenses, and for other purposes. [53]

40 St. 561; May 25, 1918; C. 86—An Act Making appropriations for the current and contingent expenses of the Bureau of Indian Affairs, for fulfilling treaty stipulations with various Indian tribes, and for other purposes, for the fiscal year ending June 30, 1919. [54] Sec. 1, p. 563—25 U. S. C. 244. [55] Sec.

Commercial, 261 Fed. 330; Elam, 7 F. 2d 887; Ford, 260 Fed. 657; Hawley, 15 F. 2d 621; Lucas, 15 F. 2d 32; McClintic, 283 Fed. 781; Medawakanton, 57 C. Cls. 357; Morrison, 6 F. 2d 811; Nelson, 18 F. 2d 522; One Buick, 275 Fed. 809; Prosser, 265 Fed. 252; Shawnee, 249 Fed 583; St. Marie, 24 F. Supp. 237; Townsend, 265 Fed. 519; U. S. v. Bowling, 256 U. S. 484; U. S. v. McGowan, 89 F. 2d 201; U. S. v. McGowan, 302 U. S. 535; U. S. v. One Buick, 255 Fed. 793; U. S. v. One Buick, 244 Fed. 961; U. S. v. One Cadillac, 255 Fed. 173; U. S. v. One Chevrolet, 58 F. 2d 235; U. S. v. One Chevrolet, 41 F. 2d 782; U. S. v. One Ford, 259 Fed. 645; U. S. v. One 7-Passenger, 259 Fed 641; U. S. v. Osage, 251 U. S. 128; U. S. v. Seminole, 299 U. S. 417; U. S. ex rel. Kadrie, 30 F. 2d 989.

[40] *A.* 47 St. 302.

[41] *Sg.* 35 St. 562; 38 St. 1052. *S.* 41 St. 365.

[42] *Cited:* 53 I. D. 593.

[43] *Sg.* 36 St. 455, sec. 1. *Ag.* 38 St. 682, sec. 3.

[44] *Sg.* 7 St. 583; 10 St. 954; 12 St. 652; 15 St. 635. *S.* 39 St. 1608. *Cited:* Medawakanton, 57 C. Cls. 357.

[45] *Sg.* 17 St. 569, sec. 23; 27 St. 281; 37 St. 679. *A.* 42 St. 834; 44 St. 1361; 50 St. 786.

[46] *Sg.* 12 St. 754; sec. 2; 33 St. 1016.

[47] *Ag.* 39 St. 1196.

[48] *Sg.* 11 St. 611; 26 St. 853; 30 St. 159.

[49] *Sg.* 35 St. 102; 36 St. 326; 38 St. 604; 39 St. 903.

[50] *Sg.* 26 St. 853.

[51] *Sg.* 32 St. 653; 35 St. 805; 37 St. 67. *A.* 45 St. 737. *S.* 40 St. 1585; 41 St. 3, 1107; 46 St. 788; 47 St. 88. *Cited:* 33 Op. A. G. 239; 36 Op. A. G. 473; 1 L. D. Memo. 227; Memo. Sol., Dec. 11, 1918; Op. Sol., M. 7316, Apr. 5, 1922, M. 7316, May 28, 1924; U. S. ex rel. McAlester, 277 Fed. 573.

[52] *Sg.* 31 St. 80. *A.* 41 St. 535.

[53] *Sg.* 39 St. 741.

[54] *Sg.* 4 St. 442; 7 St. 46, 99, 213, 235, 236, 425; 11 St. 614, 780; 15 St. 622, 640, 652, 658, 669, 673, 676; 16 St. 720; 19 St. 254, 256; 24 St. 388; 25 St. 615; 26 St. 146, 1029; 27 St. 139, 260, 644; 29 St. 321, 506; 30 St. 90; 32 St. 641, 646, 648; 33 St. 597, 1016, 1081; 34 St. 375, 541, 1027, 1030; 35 St. 51, 77, 458; 36 St. 273, 277, 448, 1063, 1071, 1076; 37 St. 67, 518, 521, 522, 981; 38 St. 88, 102, 318, 583, 604; 39 St. 123, 144, 147, 151, 154, 158, 926, 969, 981, 982, 983, 988. *Ag.* 29 St. 358; 34 St. 539, 1413; 35 St. 460; 37 St. 88, 675; 39 St. 130, 150. *A.* 41 St. 3. *Rp.* 47 St. 421; 48 St. 396; 52 St. 1037. *S.* 41 St. 2, 3, 163, 408,

1, p. 563—25 U. S. C. 57 (38 St. 584. sec. 1).[56] Sec. 1, p. 564—25 U. S. C. 297. Sec. 1, p. 565—25 U. S. C. 49.[57] Sec. 2, p. 570—25 U. S. C. 211. Also see 25 U. S. C. 467. Sec. 17, p. 578—25 U. S. C. 58 (30 St. 90, sec. 1; 37 St. 88, sec. 10; 521, sec. 1).[58] Sec. 28, p. 591—25 U. S. C. 162.[59]

40 St. 592; May 31, 1918; C. 88—An Act To authorize the establishment of a town site on the Fort Hall Indian Reservation, Idaho.

40 St. 594; June 4, 1918; C. 92—An Act Making appropriations to supply additional urgent deficiencies in appropriations for the fiscal year ending June 30, 1918, on account of war expenses and for other purposes.

40 St. 606; June 14, 1918; C. 101—An Act To provide for determination of heirship in cases of deceased members of the Cherokee, Chickasaw, Choctaw, Creek, and Seminole Tribes of Indians in Oklahoma, conferring jurisdiction upon district courts to partition lands belonging to full-blood heirs of allottees of the Five Civilized Tribes, and for other purposes.[60] Sec. 1—25 U. S. C. 375. Sec. 2—25 U. S. C. 355.

40 St. 616; June 27, 1918; C. 106—An Act To authorize the Secretary of the Interior to issue a deed to G. H. Beckwith for certain land within the Flathead Indian Reservation, Montana.

40 St. 634; July 1, 1918; C. 113—An Act Making appropriations for sundry civil expenses of the Government for the fiscal year ending June 30, 1919, and for other purposes.[61] Sec. 1—16 U. S. C. 451; 16 U. S. C. 34; 24 U. S. C. 10; 31 U. S. C. 662.

40 St. 757; July 3, 1918; C. 130—An Act Making appropriations for the legislative, executive, and judicial expenses of the Government for the fiscal year ending June 30, 1919, and for other purposes.

40 St. 821; July 8, 1918; C. 139—An Act Making appropriations to supply deficiencies in appropriations for the fiscal year ending June 30, 1918, and prior fiscal years, on account of war expenses, and for other purposes.[62]

40 St. 845; July 9, 1918; C. 143—An Act Making appropriations for the support of the Army for the fiscal year ending June 30, 1919. 10 U. S. C. 721; 10 U. S. C. 754; 40 U. S. C. 37.

40 St. 917; July 25, 1918; C. 161—An Act To validate certain public-land entries.[63]

40 St. 958; Sept. 13, 1918; C. 171—An Act Authorizing the State of Montana to select other lands in lieu of lands in section 16, township 2 north, range 30 east, within the limits of the Huntley irrigation project and the ceded portion of Crow Indian Reservation in said State.[64]

40 St. 1020; Nov. 4, 1918; C. 201—An Act Making appropriations to supply deficiencies in appropriations for the fiscal year ending June 30, 1919, and prior fiscal years, on account of war expenses, and for other purposes.

40 St. 1053; Jan. 7, 1919; C. 5—An Act To authorize the sale of certain lands to school district numbered 28, of Missoula County, Montana.

40 St. 1055; Feb. 4, 1919; C. 13—An Act For the sale of isolated tracts of the public domain in Minnesota.[65] 43 U. S. C. 1172.

40 St. 1175; Feb. 26, 1919; C. 44—An Act To establish the Grand Canyon National Park in the State of Arizona.[66] Sec. 1—16 U. S. C. 221; Sec. 3—16 U. S. C. 223.

40 St. 1203; Feb. 28, 1919; C. 71—An Act To provide for stock-watering privileges on certain unallotted lands on the Flathead Indian Reservation, Montana.[67]

40 St. 1204; Feb. 28, 1919; C. 72—An Act For the relief of settlers on certain railroad lands in Montana.

40 St. 1206; Feb. 28, 1919; C. 76—An Act Granting to the city of San Diego certain lands in the Cleveland National Forest and the Capitan Grande Indian Reservation for dam and reservoir purposes for the conservation of water, and for other purposes.[68]

40 St. 1213; Mar. 1, 1919; C. 86—An Act Making appropriations for the legislative, executive, and judicial expenses of the Government for the fiscal year ending June 30, 1920, and for other purposes.[69]

40 St. 1291; Mar. 3, 1919; C. 97—An Act To provide for the fourteenth and subsequent decennial censuses.[70]

40 St. 1316; Mar. 3, 1919; C. 103—An Act Conferring jurisdiction upon the Court of Claims to hear, consider, and determine certain claims of the Cherokee Nation against the United States.[71]

40 St. 1318; Mar. 3, 1919; C. 106—An Act To authorize the contesting and cancellation of certain homestead entries, and for other purposes.[72]

40 St. 1320; Mar. 3, 1919; C. 110—An Act Authorizing the sale of certain lands in South Dakota for cemetery purposes.

40 St. 1321; Mar. 3, 1919; C. 113—An Act To validate and confirm certain erroneously allowed entries in the State of Minnesota.[73] 43 U. S. C. 1028.

40 St. 1466; July 3, 1918; C. 132—An Act Granting pensions and increase of pensions to certain soldiers and sailors of the Regular Army and Navy, and certain soldiers and sailors of wars other than the Civil War, and to widows of such soldiers and sailors.

40 St. 1478; July 3, 1918; C. 136—An Act Granting pensions and increase of pensions to certain soldiers and sailors of the Regular Army and Navy, and certain soldiers and sailors of wars other than the Civil War, and to widows of such soldiers and sailors.

40 St. 1484; July 11, 1918; C. 146—An Act Granting pensions and increase of pensions to certain soldiers and sailors of the Regular Army and Navy and of Wars other than the Civil War, and to certain widows and dependent relatives of such soldiers and sailors.

40 St. 1486; July 11, 1918; C. 147—An Act Granting pensions and increase of pensions to certain soldiers and sailors of the Regular Army and Navy and of wars other than the Civil War, and to certain widows and dependent relatives of such soldiers and sailors.

40 St. 1489; July 11, 1918; C. 148—An Act Granting pensions and increase of pensions to certain soldiers and sailors of the Regular Army and Navy and of wars other than the Civil War, and to certain widows and dependent relatives of such soldiers and sailors.

40 St. 1531; Mar. 3, 1919; C. 120—An Act granting pensions and increase of pensions to certain soldiers and sailors of the Regular Army and Navy, and certain soldiers and sailors of wars other than the Civil War, and to widows of such soldiers and sailors.

40 St. 1536; Mar. 3, 1919; C. 121—An Act Granting pensions and increase of pensions to certain soldiers and sailors of the Regular Army and Navy and of wars other than the Civil War, and to certain widows and dependent relatives of such soldiers and sailors.

40 St. 1538; Mar. 4, 1919; C. 126—An Act Validating certain applications for and entries of public lands, and for other purposes.

40 St. 1562; Mar. 4, 1919; C. 130—An Act Granting pensions and increase of pensions to certain soldiers and sailors of the Regular Army and Navy, and certain soldiers and sailors of wars other than the Civil War, and to widows of such soldiers and sailors.

529, 1225; 42 St. 552, 1174, 1288, 1527; 43 St. 246, 390, 1141; 44 St. 453, 934; 45 St. 159, 200, 883, 1562; 46 St. 279, 1115; 47 St. 91, 421, 820, 1753, 1755; 48 St. 302; 49 St. 176, 1757. *Cited:* 36 Op. A. G. 98; Op. Sol. M. 14233, Apr. 24, 1925; Memo. Ind. Off. Apr. 21, 1927; Op. Att'y Gen., Oct. 5, 1929; Memo. Sol. Off., Nov. 5, 1930, Apr. 4, 1933; Memo. Sol., Feb. 8, 1935; Memo. Sol. Off., Aug. 20, 1935; Op. Sol. M. 28231, Mar. 12, 1936, M. 27878, May 20, 1936; Memo. Sol., May 25, 1936; Op. Sol., M. 28519, May 27, 1936; Letter of Comm'r to Ind. Agents, Oct. 9, 1937; Memo. Sol. Off., Nov. 9, 1937; Op. Sol. M. 20620, Jan. 14, 1938; Brown, 265 Fed. 623; Chippewa, 80 C. Cls. 410; Chippewa, 307 U. S. 1; Elam, 7 F. 2d 887; Kennedy, 265 U. S. 344; McClintic, 283 Fed. 781; McMurray, 62 C. Cls. 458; Morrison, 6 F. 2d 809; Morrison, 6 F. 2d 811; U. S. v. Algoma, 305 U. S. 415; U. S. v. Bowling, 256 U. S. 484; U. S. v. Seminole, 299 U. S. 417; U. S. ex rel. Kadrie, 30 F. 2d 989.

[55] *S.* 41 St. 4, sec. 1. 25 U. S. C. 244 was repealed insofar as it applied to and affected State of Oklahoma formerly known as "Indian Territory" by 25 U. S. C. 244a.

[56] *S.* 43 St. 1147.

[57] *R.* 47 St. 421.

[58] *S.* 45 St. 1307.

[59] *R.* 52 St. 1037, sec. 2. Provisions similar to those of former sec. 162 are now contained in sec. 162a of tit. 25.

[60] *Cited:* 4 L. D. Memo. 63; Memo. Sol., Sept. 15, 1934, Sept. 21, 1935; Anderson, 53 F. 2d 257; Bond, 25 F. Supp. 157; In re Jessie's, 259 Fed. 94; Knight, 23 F. 2d 481; McDougal, 278 Fed. 118; Pitman, 64 F. 2d 740; Roberts, 66 F. 2d 874.

[61] *Sg.* 35 St. 102; 36 St. 826; 38 St. 604.

[62] *Sg.* 26 St. 853.

[63] *Sg.* 33 St. 46; 36 St. 913.

[64] *Sg.* 26 St. 796.

[65] *Sg.* 9 St. 51; 37 St. 77.

[66] *Sg.* Ex. Or. Mar. 31, 1882.

[67] *Ag.* 33 St. 302; 34 St. 355; 35 St. 448, 795; 36 St. 297.

[68] *A.* 47 St. 146. *Cited:* Op. Sol., M. 27750, July 14, 1934.

[69] *S.* 41 St. 3. *Cited:* 53 I. D. 502.

[70] *Rg.* 36 St. 1.

[71] *Sg.* 27 St. 640, sec. 10. *Cited:* Cherokee, 270 U. S. 476.

[72] *Sg.* 34 St. 213, 550. *Cited:* Op. Sol., M. 7002, Mar. 10, 1922.

[73] *Sg.* 25 St. 642; 35 St. 169.

40 St. 1581; June 4, 1917; Concurrent Res.—Statute of Sequoyah.

40 St. 1585; Jan. 24, 1918; Concurrent Res.—Choctaw and Chickasaw Lands.[74]

41 STAT.

41 St. 3; June 30, 1919; C. 4—An Act Making appropriations for the current and contingent expenses of the Bureau of Indian Affairs, for fulfilling treaty stipulations with various Indian tribes and for other purposes, for the fiscal year ending June 30, 1920.[75] Sec. 1, p. 4—25 U. S. C. 244 (40 St. 563, sec. 1).[76] Sec. 1, p. 6—25 U. S. C. 296 (43 St. 958).[77] Sec. 1, p. 9—25 U. S. C. 163. Sec. 17, p. 20—25 U. S. C. 125. Sec. 18, p. 21—See Historical Note 25 U. S. C. 375. Sec. 26, p. 31—25 U. S. C. 399 (41 St. 1231 sec. 1).[78] Sec. 27, p. 34—43 U. S. C. 150.

41 St. 35; July 11, 1919; C. 6—An Act Making appropriations to supply deficiencies in appropriations for the fiscal year ending June 30, 1919, and prior fiscal years, and for other purposes.[79]

41 St. 104; July 11, 1919; C. 8—An Act Making appropriations for the support of the Army for the fiscal year ending June 30, 1920, and for other purposes.

41 St. 163; July 19, 1919; C. 24—An Act Making appropriations for sundry civil expenses of the Government for the fiscal year ending June 30, 1920, and for other purposes.[80]

41 St. 327; Nov. 4, 1919; C. 93—An Act Making appropriations to supply deficiencies in appropriations for the fiscal year ending June 30, 1920, and prior fiscal years, and for other purposes.

41 St. 349; Nov. 6, 1919; C. 94—An Act Authorizing the Commissioner of Indian Affairs to transfer fractional block 6, of Naylor's addition, Forest Grove, Oregon, to the United States of America, for the use of the Bureau of Entomology, Department of Agriculture.

41 St. 350; Nov. 6, 1919; C. 95—An Act Granting citizenship to certain Indians.[81] 8 U. S. C. 3.

41 St. 355; Nov. 18, 1919; C. 109—An Act Authorizing the sale of inherited and unpartitioned allotments for town-site purposes in the Quapaw Agency, Oklahoma.

41 St. 365; Dec. 11, 1919; C. 4—An Act Providing additional time for the payment of purchase money under homestead entries of lands within the former Fort Peck Indian Reservation, Montana.[82]

41 St. 404; Feb. 11, 1920; C. 68—An Act To confer on the Court of Claims jurisdiction to determine the respective rights of and differences between the Fort Berthold Indians and the Government of the United States.[83]

41 St. 408; Feb. 14, 1920; C. 75—An Act Making appropriations for the current and contingent expenses of the Bureau of Indian Affairs, for fulfilling treaty stipulations with various Indian tribes, and for other purposes, for the fiscal year ending June 30, 1921.[84] Sec. 1, p. 409—25 U. S. C. 386. Also see 25 U. S. C. 386a (47 St. 564). Sec. 1, p. 410—25 U. S. C. 282. Also see 25 U. S. C. 284. Sec. 1, p. 412—25 U. S. C. 120. Sec. 1, p. 414—25 U. S. C. 53. Sec. 1, p. 415—25 U. S. C. 294. Sec. 1, p. 415—25 U. S. C. 413,[85] (47 St. 1417). Sec. 18, p. 426—25 U. S. C. 356.

41 St. 434; Feb. 14, 1920; C. 76—Joint Resolution Giving to discharged soldiers, sailors, and marines a preferred right of homestead entry.[86] 43 U. S. C. 186, 438.

41 St. 452; Feb. 25, 1920; C. 87—An Act For the relief of certain members of the Flathead Nation of Indians, and for other purposes.[87] Sec. 1, p. 452—16 U. S. C. 392. Sec. 2, p. 452—16 U. S. C. 392.

41 St. 503; Mar. 6, 1920; C. 94—An Act Making appropriations to supply deficiencies in appropriations for the fiscal year ending June 30, 1920, and prior fiscal years, and for other purposes.[88]

41 St. 529; Mar. 12, 1920; C. 99—Joint Resolution To amend a certain paragraph of the Act entitled "An Act making appropriations for the current and contingent expenses of the Bureau of Indian Affairs, for fulfilling treaty stipulations with various Indian tribes, and for other purposes, for the fiscal year ending June 30, 1921." approved February 14, 1920.[89]

41 St. 535; Mar. 19, 1920; C. 105—Joint Resolution Amending joint resolution extending the time for payment of purchase money on homestead entries in the former Colville Indian Reservation, Washington.[90]

41 St. 549; Apr. 1, 1920; C. 119—An Act To authorize the Secretary of the Interior to acquire certain Indian lands necessary for reservoir purposes in connection with the Blackfeet Indian reclamation project.[91]

41 St. 549; Apr. 1, 1920; C. 120—An Act Authorizing the Secretary of the Interior to issue patent to School District Numbered 8, Sheridan County, Montana, for block one, in Wakea town site, Fort Peck Indian Reservation, Montana, and to set aside one block in each town site on said reservation for school purposes.[92]

41 St. 553; Apr. 15, 1920; C. 143—An Act Authorizing and directing the transfer approximately of 10 acres of land to Rural High School District Numbered 1, Lapwai, Idaho.

41 St. 585; Apr. 28, 1920; C. 163—An Act Conferring jurisdiction on the Court of Claims to hear, determine, and render judgment in claims of the Iowa Tribe of Indians against the United States.[93]

41 St. 595; May 10, 1920; C. 178—An Act For the sale of isolated tracts in the former Fort Berthold Indian Reservation, North Dakota.[94] 43 U. S. C. 1173.

41 St. 599; May 14, 1920; C. 187—An Act To authorize the disposition of certain grazing lands in the State of Utah, and for other purposes.[95]

41 St. 623; May 26, 1920; C. 203—An Act Authorizing certain

---

[74] *Ag.* 40 St. 433.

[75] *Sg.* 4 St. 442; 7 St. 46, 99, 213, 235, 236, 425; 11 St. 614, 730; 13 St. 563; 15 St. 622, 640, 652, 658, 669, 673, 676; 16 St. 720; 19 St. 254, 256; 24 St. 388; 25 St. 645; 26 St. 1029; 27 St. 189, 260, 506, 644; 28 St. 286 330; 29 St. 506; 30 St. 1151; 33 St. 1016, 1081; 34 St. 375; 35 St. 77, 1081; 36 St. 273, 277, 448, 858, 1063, 1071, 37 St. 67, 521, 522, 934, 1007; 38 St. 88, 91, 102, 582, 605; 39 St. 48, 130, 137, 154, 844, 980, 975; 40 St. 483, 504, 569, 570, 571, 573, 574, 576, 577, 591, 592, 1213. *Ag.* 40 St. 579. *Rg.* 34 St. 1015, 1035. *A.* 41 St. 1225; 43 St. 958; 44 St. 922. *Rp.* 48 St. 396. *S.* 41 St. 163, 408, 1225, 1631; 42 St. 552, 994, 1174, 1288, 1710; 43 St. 111, 246, 252, 390, 793, 1141; 44 St. 453, 934; 45 St. 159, 200, 299, 380, 883, 1562; 46 St. 276, 279, 1115; 47 St. 91, 1099, 1753, 1755. *Cited:* Brown, 39 Yale L. J. 307; Op. Sol., M. 8860, Nov. 1, 1922, A. 2592, Feb. 12, 1924, M. 12498, June 6, 1924; M. 14233, Apr. 24, 1925; Memo. Ind. Off., April 21, 1927; Memo. Sol. Off., Aug. 22, 1932; Report on Status of Pueblo of Pojoaque, Nov. 8, 1932; Memo. Sol. Off., Apr. 4, 1933, Aug. 20, 1935; Memo. Sol., Mar. 12, 1936; Op. Sol., M. 27878, May 20, 1936; M. 28614, Oct. 1, 1936; Memo. Sol. Off., Oct. 22, 1936; Memo. Sol., Jan. 12, 1937; Op. Sol., M. 28232, June 2, 1937; Memo. Sol. Off., Nov. 9, 1937; Memo. Sol., Mar. 25, 1939; 49 L. D. 376; 49 L. D. 420; 50 L. D. 672; 56 I. D. 110; Aldridge, 67 F. 2d 956; Billingsley, 16 F. 2d 754; British-American, 299 U. S. 159; Browning, 6 F. 2d 801; Buchanan, 15 F. 2d 496; Cherokee, 270 U. S. 476; Chippewa, 80 C. Cls. 410; Chippewa, 307 U. S. 1; Edwards, 5 F. 2d 17; Ex p. Pero, 99 F. 2d 28; Flack 291 Fed. 376; Hodges, 35 F. 2d 594; Hodges, 36 F. 2d 350; Lucus, 15 F. 2d 32; McMillan, 27 F. 2d 94; Morris, 19 F. 2d 131; Morrison, 6 F. 2d 811; Nelson, 18 F. 2d 522; Perry, 18 F. 2d 477; Renfro, 15 F. 2d 991; Reynolds, 48 F. 2d 762; Sharpe, 16 F. 2d 876; Swafford, 25 F. 2d 581; Tiller, 34 F. 2d 398; U. S. v. Bowling, 256 U. S. 484; U. S. v. Seminole, 299 U. S. 417; U. S. ex rel. Kadrie, 30 F. 2d 989.

[76] *Rp.* 25 U. S. C. 244a (48 St. 396)

[77] *R.* 45 St. 1534.

[78] *A.* 44 St. 922.

[79] *Sg.* 26 St. 853, sec. 6.

[80] *Sg.* 35 St. 102; 36 St. 326; 38 St. 604, sec. 22; 40 St. 587; 41 St. 18. *Cited:* McMurray, 62 C. Cls. 458.

[81] *Cited:* 66th Cong., 1st sess., S. Rep. No. 222; Goodrich, 14 Calif. L. Rev. 83, 157; Krieger, 3 Geo. Wash. L. Rev. 279; U. S. v. Lynch, 7 Alaska 568.

[82] *Sg.* 35 St. 558; 38 St. 1952. *Ag.* 39 St. 994. *S.* 43 St. 1267.

[83] *Cited:* Fort Berthold, 71 C. Cls. 308; Klamath, 296 U. S. 244; Memo. Sol., Dec. 26, 1935.

[84] *Sg.* 4 St. 442; 7 St. 46, 99, 212, 213, 235, 236, 425; 10 St. 1109; 11 St. 614, 730; 15 St. 622, 640, 652, 658, 669, 673, 676; 16 St. 720; 18 St. 41; 19 St. 254, 256; 24 St. 388; 25 St. 645; 26 St. 1029, 1032, 1033; 27 St. 139, 644; 33 St. 1016, 1081; 34 St. 375; 35 St. 558; 36 St. 273, 277, 448, 1063, 1071; 37 St. 67, 521, 522, 934; 38 St. 88, 582, 605; 39 St. 130, 136, 156, 975, 976, 991; 40 St. 564, 570, 571, 588, 591; 41 St. 11, 28. *Ag.* 40 St. 569; 41 St. 21. *A.* 41 St. 529, 1225; 42 St. 395; 47 St. 1317; 52 St. 80. *S.* 41 St. 1225, 1637, 1638; 42 St. 364, 552, 767, 1174, 1527; 43 St. 819; 44 St. 453, 934; 45 St. 200, 1562, 1623; 46 St. 90, 279, 1115; 47 St. 91, 564, 820; 48 St. 362; 49 St. 176, 1757; 50 St. 564; 52 St. 291. *Cited:* 33 Op. A. G. 25; 34 Op. A. G. 302; Op. Sol. M. 6083, Oct. 29, 1921; M. 6376, Nov. 15, 1921; Memo. Ind. Off., Apr. 21, 1927; Op. Sol. M.23117, Oct. 6, 1927; Letter to Sen. Wm. H. King from Comm'r, Jan. 9, 1931; Memo. Ind. Off., June 12, 1933, Jan. 31, 1934; Op. Sol. M.27671, Mar. 1, 1934; Memo. Sol., July 17, 1935, Feb. 8, 1937; Memo. Sol. Off., June 25, 1938; 48 L. D. 472; 54 I. D. 90; Chippewa, 80 C. Cls. 410; Chippewa, 307 U. S. 1; Lucas, 15 F. 2d 32; Medawakanton, 57 C. Cls. 357; Shoshone, 85 C. Cls. 331; U. S. v. Bowling, 256 U. S. 484; U. S. v. Haddock, 21 F. 2d 165; U. S. v. Seminole, 299 U. S. 417; U. S. v. Watashe, 102 F. 2d 427; U. S. ex rel. Kadrie, 30 F. 2d 989.

[85] *A.* 47 St. 1417.

[86] *Sg.* 40 St. 76. *A.* 42 St. 358; 46 St. 580.

[87] *S.* 46 St. 1634. *Cited:* Op. Sol. M.11410, Jan. 28, 1924, M.12498, June 6, 1924; 49 L. D. 130.

[88] *Sg.* 26 St. 853, sec. 6.

[89] *Ag.* 41 St. 427.

[90] *Sg.* 34 St. 80. *Ag.* 40 St. 449. *A.* 47 St. 334.

[91] *Sg.* 36 St. 855, 859, sec. 14.

[92] *Sg.* 35 St. 558.

[93] *S.* 45 St. 1073. *Cited:* Iowa, 68 C. Cls. 585.

[94] *Sg.* 9 St. 51; 36 St. 77, 455.

[95] *Ag.* 31 St. 1070.

tribes of Indians to submit claims to the Court of Claims, and for other purposes.[96]

41 St. 625; May 26, 1920; C. 204—An Act To amend an Act entitled "An Act making appropriations for the current and contingent expenses of the Bureau of Indian Affairs, for fulfilling treaty stipulations with various Indian tribes, and for other purposes, for the fiscal year ending June 30, 1914," approved June 30, 1913.[97]

41 St. 631; May 29, 1920; C. 214—An Act Making appropriations for the legislative, executive, and judicial expenses of the Government for the fiscal year ending June 30, 1921, and for other purposes.

41 St. 738; June 3, 1920; C. 222—An Act Authorizing the Sioux Tribe of Indians to submit claims to the Court of Claims.[98]

41 St. 751; June 4, 1920; C. 224—An Act To provide for the allotment of lands of the Crow Tribe, for the distribution of tribal funds, and for other purposes.[99]

41 St. 874; June 5, 1920; C. 235—An Act Making appropriations for sundry civil expenses of the Government for the fiscal year ending June 30, 1921, and for other purposes.[1] p. 917—48 U. S. C. 422.

41 St. 948; June 5, 1920; C. 240—An Act Making appropriations for the support of the Army for the fiscal year ending June 30, 1921, and for other purposes.

41 St. 1015; June 5, 1920; C. 253—An Act Making appropriations to supply deficiencies in appropriations for the fiscal year ending June 30, 1920, and prior fiscal years, and for other purposes.[2]

41 St. 1063; June 10, 1920; C. 285—An Act To create a Federal Power Commission; to provide for the improvement of navigation; the development of water power; the use of the public lands in relation thereto, and to repeal section 18 of the River and Harbor Appropriation Act, approved August 8, 1917, and for other purposes.[3] Sec. 3, p. 1063—16 U. S. C. 796. Sec. 4, p. 1065—16 U. S. C. 797. Sec. 17—16 U. S. C. 810. Sec. 28, p. 1077—16 U. S. C. 822. Sec. 29, p. 1077—16 U. S. C. 823. Sec. 30, p. 1077—16 U. S. C. 791.

41 St. 1077; June 14, 1920; C. 286—An Act Authorizing the enlistment of non-English speaking citizens and aliens.[4]

41 St. 1097; Feb. 6, 1921; C. 36—An Act Conferring jurisdiction on the Court of Claims to hear, determine, and render judgment in the Osage civilization-fund claim of the Osage Nation of Indians against the United States.[5]

41 St. 1105; Feb. 21, 1921; C. 63—An Act to amend Act of Congress approved June 30, 1913.[6]

41 St. 1105; Feb. 21, 1921; C. 64—An Act To authorize the improvement of Red Lake and Red Lake River, in the State of Minnesota, for navigation, drainage, and flood-control purposes.[7]

41 St. 1107; Feb. 22, 1921; C. 66—An Act Authorizing the Secretary of the Interior to offer for sale remainder of the coal and asphalt deposits in segregated mineral land in the Choctaw and Chickasaw Nations, State of Oklahoma.[8]

41 St. 1156; Mar. 1, 1921; C. 89—An Act Making appropriations to supply deficiencies in appropriations for the fiscal year ending June 30, 1921; and prior fiscal years, and for other purposes.[9]

41 St. 1193; Mar. 1, 1921; C. 91—An Act To authorize a lieu selection by the State of South Dakota for 160 acres on Pine Ridge Indian Reservation, and for other purposes. See Historical Note 25 U. S. C. A. 421.

41 St. 1204; Mar. 2, 1921; C. 111—An Act Amending an Act to provide for drainage of Indian allotments of the Five Civilized Tribes, approved March 27, 1914 (38 St. 310, Public, Numbered 77).[10]

41 St. 1225; Mar. 3, 1921; C. 119—An Act Making appropriations for the current and contingent expenses of the Bureau of Indian Affairs, for fulfilling treaty stipulations with various Indian tribes, and for other purposes, for the fiscal year ending June 30, 1922.[11] Sec. 1, p. 1231—25 U. S. C. 399 (41 St. 31, sec. 20);[12] Sec. 1, p. 1232—25 U. S. C. 303.

41 St. 1249; Mar. 3, 1921; C. 120—An Act to amend section 8 of the Act of Congress of June 28, 1906, entitled "An Act for the division of the lands and funds of the Osage Indians in Oklahoma, and for other purposes."[13] Sec. 3, p. 1250—8 U. S. C. 3.

41 St. 1252; Mar. 3, 1921; C. 124—An Act Making appropriations for the legislative, executive, and judicial expenses of the Government for the fiscal year ending June 30, 1922, and for other purposes.

41 St. 1355; Mar. 3, 1921; C. 135—An Act Providing for the allotment of lands within the Fort Belknap Indian Reservation, Montana, and for other purposes.[14]

41 St. 1364; Mar. 4, 1921; C. 155—An Act To perpetuate the memory of the Chickasaw and Seminole Tribes of Indians in Oklahoma.

41 St. 1367; Mar. 4, 1921; C. 161—An Act Making appropriations for sundry civil expenses of the Government for the fiscal year ending June 30, 1922, and for other purposes.[15]

41 St. 1446; Mar. 4, 1921; C. 174—Joint Resolution Extending the time for payment or purchase money on homestead entries in the former Standing Rock Indian Reservation, in the States of North and South Dakota, and for other purposes.[16]

41 St. 1459; Feb. 11, 1920; C. 72—An Act Restoring to Amy E. Hall her homestead rights and providing that on any homestead entry made by her she shall be given credit for all compliance with the law on her original homestead entry and for all payments made on same.[17]

41 St. 1460; Feb. 17, 1920; C. 78—An Act To authorize the payment of certain amounts for damages sustained by prairie fire on the Rosebud Indian Reservation, in South Dakota.

41 St. 1460; Feb. 17, 1920; C. 79—An Act for the relief of William E. Johnson.

---

[96] *Sg.* 16 St. 707. *A.* 49 St. 1276. *S.* 46 St. 1105. *Cited:* Klamath, 81 C. Cls. 79; Klamath, 86 C. Cls. 614; Klamath, 296 U. S. 244; U. S. v. Klamath, 304 U. S. 119.

[97] *Ag.* 38 St. 96. *A.* 43 St. 728.

[98] *A.* 44 St. 764. *Cited:* Klamath, 296 U. S. 244; Sioux, 85 C. Cls. 181; Sioux, 84 C. Cls. 16; Sioux, 86 C. Cls. 299; U. S. v. Powers, 305 U. S. 527; Yankton, 272 U. S. 351; Yankton, 61 C. Cls. 40.

[99] *Sg.* 24 St. 388; 36 St. 850. *Rg.* 33 St. 353. *A.* 42 St. 994; 43 St. 1301; 44 St. 658. *S.* 44 St. 251, 566; 45 St. 2035; 46 St. 1495, 1633, 1634, c. 144; 1634, c. 145; 2135, 2148; 47 St. 1657, c. 66; 1657, c. 67; 49 St. 244, 1543. *Cited:* Op. Sol. M.5805, Nov. 22, 1921, Sept. 21, 1927; Off. Memo. by Asst. Chief Counsel of Ind. Off., Oct. 17, 1938; 48 L. D. 479; U. S. v. Heinrich, 16 F. 2d 112.

[1] *Sg.* 35 St. 102; 36 St. 326; 38 St. 604, sec. 22.

[2] *Sg.* 26 St. 853; 36 St. 326.

[3] *Sg.* 38 St. 242. *Rg.* 40 St. 269, sec. 18. *S.* 42 St. 832; 45 St. 1344; 48 St. 960. *A.* 49 St. 803. *Cited:* Op. Sol. M. 11410, Jan. 28, 1924.

[4] *Ag.* 28 St. 216.

[5] *Sg.* 14 St. 687.

[6] *Ag.* 38 St. 97.

[7] *Sg.* 35 St. 169. *Cited:* Chippewa, 80 C. Cls. 410.

[8] *Sg.* 40 St. 433. *A.* 45 St. 737. *A.* 42 St. 552, 1174; 43 St. 390, 1141; 44 St. 453, 934; 45 St. 200, 1502; 46 St. 279, 788. *Cited:* 1 L. D. Memo. 90.

[9] *Sg.* 27 St. 612, 644. *S.* 42 St. 1174.

[10] *Ag.* 38 St. 310.

[11] *Sg.* 4 St. 442; 7 St. 46, 99, 212, 213, 235, 236, 425; 10 St. 1109; 11 St. 614, 730; 15 St. 622, 640, 652, 658, 669, 673, 676; 16 St. 720; 19 St. 254, 256; 24 St. 388; 25 St. 645, 871; 26 St. 146, 1029; 27 St. 139, 644; 33 St. 1081; 34 St. 375; 35 St. 51; 36 St. 124, 273, 277, 858, 1062, 1074; 37 St. 67, 521, 522, 934; 38 St. 582, 605; 39 St. 130, 926, 983; 40 St. 564, 570, 571, 577, 588; 41 St. 11, 28, 428, 433. *Ag.* 28 St. 907; 41 St. 31, 426. *A.* 42 St. 552, 1570; 50 St. 68. *S.* 42 St. 4, 364, 552, 1527; 45 St. 200. *Cited:* Brown, 39 Yale L. J. 307; Op. Sol., M 7316, Apr. 5, 1922, A. 2592, Feb. 12, 1924, M. 12746, Oct. 8, 1924, Sept. 21, 1927, M. 25280, Aug. 21, 1929; Memo. Sol. Off., Apr. 22, 1930, June 29, 1933, May 11, 1934; Memo. Sol., July 25, 1935; Memo. Sol. Off., Aug. 20, 1935; Memo. Sol., Jan. 29, 1936, Mar. 12, 1936, May 25, 1936, Aug. 10, 1936; Memo. Sol. Off., Oct. 22, 1936; Memo. Sol., Feb. 8, 1937; Memo. of Ass't Sec'y to Comm'r., Feb. 17, 1937; Memo. Acting Sol., July 13, 1937; Memo. Sol. Off., June 25, 1938; Memo. Sol., Nov. 11, 1939; Childers, 270 U. S. 555; Chippewa, 80 C. Cls. 410; Hallam, 49 F. 2d 103; Jaybird, 271 U. S. 609; Lucas, 15 F. 2d 32; Morrison, 266 U. S. 481; Stoltz, 99 F. 2d 283; U. S. v. Seminole, 299 U. S. 417; Whitebird, 40 F. 2d 479.

[12] *A.* 44 St. 922.

[13] *Ag.* 34 St. 539. *A.* 43 St. 1008; 45 St. 1478. *S.* 46 St. 1047. *Cited:* 33 Op. A. G. 60; 36 Op. A. G. 98; Op. Sol., M. 4017, Jan. 4, 1922, M. 8370, Aug. 15, 1922, D. 46029, Sept. 30, 1922, 17687, Dec. 19, 1925, Mar. 16, 1926, M. 19190, June 2, 1926; Memo. Sol. Off., July 23, 1926; Mar. 3, 1927; Op. Sol. M. 21612, Mar. 26, 1927, M. 2420., June 19, 1928; Memo. Sol. Off., July 31, 1928, Oct. 31, 1928, Apr. 5, 1929; Op. Sol., M. 25107, May 4, 1929; Memo. Sol. Off., May 31, 1929; Op. Sol., M. 25280, Aug. 21, 1929; Op. A. G., Oct. 5, 1929; Memo. Sol. Off., Feb. 3, 1930; Letter to Comm'r of Ind. Affrs. from Sec'y of Int., Sept. 1930; Memo. Sol. Off., Mar. 10, 1931, May 29, 1931; Op. Sol., M. 26731, Oct. 14, 1931; Op. Comp. Gen. to Sec'y, Feb. 4, 1932; Memo. Sol. Off., Dec. 22, 1932, June 29, 1933, May 8, 1936; Op. Sol., M. 27963, Jan. 26, 1937; Letter from Asst. Sec'y to A. G., Oct. 27, 1937; Memo. Sol. Off., Jan. 30, 1938; 49 L. D. 420; 50 L. D. 672; 53 I. D. 169; 54 I. D. 260; 54 I. D. 341; 55 I. D. 458; Adams, 59 F. 2d 653; Browning, 6 F. 2d 801; Globe, 81 F. 2d 143; Hickey, 64 F. 2d 628; In re Dennison, 38 F. 2d 662; In re Penn, 41 F. 2d 257; Jump, 100 F. 2d 130; Morrison, 6 F. 2d 811; Ne Kah-Wah-She-Tun-Kah, 290 Fed. 303; Osage, 33 F. 2d 21; Silurian, 54 F. 2d 43; Tapp, 6 F. Supp. 577; Taylor, 51 F. 2d 884; U. S. v. Barnett, 7 F. Supp. 573; U. S. v. Hughes, 6 F. Supp. 972; U. S. v. Johnson, 87 F. 2d 155; U. S. v. Lynch, 7 Alaska 568; U. S. v. Mullendore, 74 F. 2d 286; U. S. v. Sands, 94 F. 2d 156; Webster, 266 U. S. 507; Williams, 83 F. 2d 143; Work, 266 U. S. 161; Work, 261 U. S. 352.

[14] *Sg.* 19 St. 751. *Rg.* 36 St. 277. *S.* 41 St. 453; 45 St. 1708. *Cited:* Op. Sol., M.7399, June 9, 1922; Memo. Sol., Dec. 2, 1936; 55 I. D. 295; Stockey, 58 F. 2d 522.

[15] *Sg.* 35 St. 102; 36 St. 326; 38 St. 604, sec. 22.

[16] *Sg.* 35 St. 460; 37 St. 675. *A.* 42 St. 499.

[17] *Sg.* 37 St. 123.

41 St. 1466; Apr. 15, 1920; C. 145—An Act Authorizing the Secretary of the Interior to sell certain lands to school district numbered 21 of Fremont County, Wyoming.

41 St. 1468; Apr. 29, 1920; C. 164—An Act Authorizing and directing the Secretary of the Interior to convey to the trustees of the Yankton Agency Presbyterian Church, by patent in fee, certain land within the Yankton Indian Reservation.

41 St. 1469; May 10, 1920; C. 180—An Act Authorizing the Secretary of the Interior to correct an error in an Indian allotment.

41 St. 1472; June 5, 1920; C. 279—An Act Granting pensions and increase of pensions to certain soldiers and sailors of the Regular Army and Navy and of wars other than the Civil War, and to certain widows and dependent relatives of such soldiers and sailors.

41 St. 1531; Mar. 1, 1921; C. 106—An Act For the relief of the widow of Joseph C. Akin.

41 St. 1533; Mar. 3, 1921; C. 140—An Act Granting pensions and increase of pensions to certain soldiers and sailors of the Regular Army and Navy, and certain soldiers and sailors of wars other than the Civil War, and to widows of such soldiers and sailors.

41 St. 1536; Mar. 3, 1921; C. 141—An Act Granting pensions and increase of pensions to certain soldiers and sailors of the Regular Army and Navy, and certain soldiers and sailors of wars other than the Civil War, and to widows of such soldiers and sailors.

41 St. 1542; Mar. 3, 1921; C. 142—An Act Granting pensions and increase of pensions to certain soldiers and sailors of the Regular Army and Navy, and certain soldiers and sailors of wars other than the Civil War, and to widows of such soldiers and sailors.

41 St. 1547; Mar. 3, 1921; C. 143—An Act Granting pensions and increase of pensions to certain soldiers and sailors of the Regular Army and Navy, and certain soldiers and sailors of wars other than the Civil War, and to widows of such soldiers and sailors.

41 St. 1596; Mar. 3, 1921; C. 147—An Act Granting pensions and increase of pensions to certain soldiers and sailors of the Regular Army and Navy, and certain soldiers and sailors of wars other than the Civil War, and to widows of such soldiers and sailors.

41 St. 1631; June 11, 1919; Concurrent Res.—Indian Appropriation Bill.[18]

41 St. 1637; Feb. 4, 1920; Concurrent Res.—Indian Appropriation Bill.[19]

41 St. 1638; Feb. 7, 1920; Concurrent Res.—Indian Appropriation Bill.[20]

42 STAT.

42 St. 4; May 6, 1921; C. 6—Joint Resolution Making the sum of $150,000 appropriated for the construction of a diversion dam on the Crow Indian Reservation, Montana, immediately available.[21]

42 St. 29; June 16, 1921; C. 23—An Act Making appropriations to supply deficiencies in appropriations for the fiscal year ending June 30, 1921, and prior fiscal years, and for other purposes.

42 St. 68; June 30, 1921; C. 33—An Act Making appropriations for the support of the Army for the fiscal year ending June 30, 1922, and for other purposes.

42 St. 192; Aug. 24, 1921; C. 89—An Act Making appropriations to supply urgent deficiencies in appropriations for the fiscal year ending June 30, 1922, and for other purposes.

42 St. 208; Nov. 2, 1921; C. 115—An Act Authorizing appropriations and expenditures for the administration of Indian affairs, and for other purposes.[22] 25 U. S. C. 13.

42 St. 212; Nov. 9, 1921; C. 119—An Act To amend the Act entitled "An Act to provide that the United States shall aid the States in the construction of rural post roads, and for other purposes," approved July 11, 1916, as amended and supplemented, and for other purposes.[23] Sec. 3, p. 212—23 U. S. C. 3a. Sec. 25, p. 219—23 U. S. C. 25.

[18] *Ag.* 41 St. 8.
[19] *Ag.* 41 St. 420.
[20] *Ag.* 41 St. 432.
[21] *Sg.* 41 St. 1237.
[22] *S.* 45 St. 1023. *Cited:* U. S. ex rel. Charley, 62 F. 2d 955.
[23] *Ag.* 39 St. 355. *A.* 43 St. 889; 46 St. 805, 1173; 52 St. 633. *S.* 45 St. 750; 47 St. 709

42 St. 221; Nov. 19, 1921; C. 133—An Act Authorizing a per capita payment to the Chippewa Indians of Minnesota from their tribal funds held in trust by the United States.[24]

42 St. 327; Dec. 15, 1921; C. 1—An Act Making appropriations to supply deficiencies in appropriations for the fiscal year ending June 30, 1922, and prior fiscal years, supplemental appropriations for the fiscal year ending June 30, 1922, and subsequent fiscal years, and for other purposes.[25]

42 St. 358; Jan. 21, 1922; C. 32—Joint Resolution To amend a joint resolution entitled "Joint Resolution giving to discharged soldiers, sailors, and marines a preferred right of homestead entry," approved February 14, 1920.[26] 43 U. S. C. 186, 438.

42 St. 364; Feb. 13, 1922; C. 50—Joint Resolution Relative to payment of tuition for Indian children enrolled in Montana State public schools.[27]

42 St. 422; Mar. 20, 1922; C. 103—An Act Making appropriations for the Legislative Branch of the Government for the fiscal year ending June 30, 1923, and for other purposes.

42 St. 437; Mar. 20, 1922; C. 104—An Act Making appropriations to supply deficiencies in appropriations for the fiscal year ending June 30, 1922, and prior fiscal years, and for other purposes.[28]

42 St. 470; Mar. 28, 1922; C. 117—An Act Making appropriations for the Departments of Commerce and Labor for the fiscal year ending June 30, 1923, and for other purposes.[29]

42 St. 499; Apr. 25, 1922; C. 140—An Act Authorizing extensions of time for the payment of purchase money due under certain homestead entries and Government-land purchases within the former Cheyenne River and Standing Rock Indian Reservations, North Dakota and South Dakota.[30]

42 St. 507; May 9, 1922; C. 183—An Act Extending the period for homestead entries on the south half of the Diminished Colville Indian Reservation.[31]

42 St. 552; May 24, 1922; C. 199—An Act Making appropriations for the Department of the Interior for the fiscal year ending June 30, 1923, and for other purposes.[32] p. 560—See Historical Note 25 U. S. C. A. 385; p. 562—See Historical Note 25 U. S. C. A. 295; p. 575—25 U. S. C. 124; p. 576—See Historical Note 25 U. S. C. A. 297; 42 U. S. C. 16.

42 St. 595; May 25, 1922; C. 201—An Act To amend section 22 of an Act approved February 14, 1920, entitled, "An Act making appropriations for the current and contingent expenses of the Bureau of Indian Affairs, for fulfilling treaty stipulations with various Indian tribes, and for other purposes," for the fiscal year ending June 30, 1921.[33]

42 St. 599; June 1, 1922; C. 204—An Act Making appropriations for the Departments of State and Justice and for the Judiciary for the fiscal year ending June 30, 1923, and for other purposes.

42 St. 625; June 10, 1922; C. 211—An Act Providing for the appropriation of funds for acquiring additional water rights for Indians on the Crow Reservation, in Montana, whose lands are irrigable under the Two Leggins Irrigation Canal.

42 St. 635; June 12, 1922; C. 218—An Act Making appropriations for the Executive and for sundry independent bureaus, boards, commissions, and offices, for the fiscal year ending June 30, 1923, and for other purposes.

42 St. 716; June 30, 1922; C. 253—An Act Making appropriations for the military and nonmilitary activities of the War Department for the fiscal year ending June 30, 1923, and for other purposes.

42 St. 767; July 1, 1922; C. 258—An Act Making appropriations to supply deficiencies in appropriations for the fiscal year ending June 30, 1922, and for prior fiscal years, supplemental

[24] *Sg.* 25 St. 642. *Cited:* Chippewa, 307 U. S. 1; Nelson, 18 F. 2d 522; U. S. ex rel. Kadrie, 30 F. 2d 989; Whitebird, 40 F. 2d 479.
[25] *Sg.* 39 St. 218; 42 St. 23.
[26] *Ag.* 41 St. 434.
[27] *Sg.* 41 St. 421, sec. 10, 1237, sec. 10.
[28] *Sg.* 36 St. 1071.
[29] *Sg.* 36 St. 326.
[30] *Sg.* 41 St. 1446. *A.* 43 St. 1184; 45 St. 400.
[31] *Sg.* 34 St. 80. *A.* 44 St. 558.
[32] *Sg.* 4 St. 442; 7 St. 46, 99, 212, 213, 235, 236, 425; 10 St. 1109; 11 St. 614, 730; 15 St. 622, 640, 652, 658, 669, 673; 16 St. 720; 19 St. 254, 256; 24 St. 388; 25 St. 645; 26 St. 1029; 27 St. 139, 644; 33 St. 1081; 34 St. 375; 35 St. 102; 36 St. 273, 277, 858, 1063; 37 St. 521, 522, 934; 38 St. 582, 604; 39 St. 130, 154, 155; 40 St. 297, 564, 570, 571; 41 St. 11, 28, 423, 437, 1107, 1233, 1234, 1236. *S.* 42 St. 1174; 43 St. 390, 672, 1101, 1141; 44 St. 453, 1398. *Cited:* Letter to Sen. Wm. H. King from Comm'r, Jan. 9, 1931; 53 I. D. 593; Chippewa, 80 C. Cls. 410; Creek, 78 C. Cls. 474; Lucas, 15 F. 2d 32.
[33] *Ag.* 41 St. 408, 431, sec. 22. *A.* 52 St. 80. *Cited:* Memo. Ind. Off., June 12, 1933.

appropriations for the fiscal year ending June 30, 1923, and for other purposes.[34]

42 St. 816; July 1, 1922; C. 267—An Act To provide for the printing and distribution of the Supreme Court Reports, and amending sections 225, 226, 227, and 228 of the Judicial Code.[35] Sec. 3, p. 816—28 U. S. C. 334.

42 St. 829; Aug. 24, 1922; C. 286—An Act Amending the proviso of the Act approved August 24, 1912, with reference to educational leave to employees of the Indian Service.[36] 25 U. S. C. 275 (37 St. 519, sec. 1).[37]

42 St. 830; Aug. 24, 1922; C. 288—An Act To rebuild the school building of the Indian school near Tomah, Wisconsin.[38]

42 St. 831; Aug. 24, 1922; C. 289—An Act To validate certain deeds executed by members of the Five Civilized Tribes, and for other purposes.[39]

42 St. 832; Aug. 26, 1922; C. 295—An Act Authorizing the Secretary of the Interior to dedicate and set apart as a national monument certain lands in Riverside County, California. Sec. 2 & 3, p. 832—16 U. S. C. 435.[40]

42 St. 834; Sept. 1, 1922; C. 302—An Act Granting relief to soldiers and sailors of the War with Spain, Philippine insurrection, and Chinese Boxer rebellion campaign; to widows, former widows, and dependent parents of such soldiers and sailors; and to certain Army nurses; and to amend section 2 of an Act entitled "An Act to pension the survivors of certain Indian wars from January 1, 1859, to January, 1891, inclusive, and for other purposes," approved March 4, 1917.[41] Sec. 6, p. 836—38 U. S. C. 376.

42 St. 857; Sept. 20, 1922; C. 347—An Act To authorize the leasing for mining purposes of unallotted lands on the Fort Peck and Blackfeet Indian Reservations in the State of Montana. 25 U. S. C. 400.

42 St. 990; Sept. 21, 1922; C. 358—An Act Providing for the construction of a spillway and drainage ditch to lower and maintain the level of Lake Andes, South Dakota.[42]

42 St. 991; Sept. 21, 1922; C. 361—An Act For the relief of and purchase of lands for certain of the Apache Indians of Oklahoma lately confined as prisoners of war at Fort Sill Military Reservation, and for other purposes.[43]

42 St. 994; Sept. 21, 1922; C. 367—An Act Extending time for allotments on the Crow Reservation; protecting certain members of the Five Civilized Tribes; relief of Indians occupying certain lands in Arizona, New Mexico, and California; issuing patents in certain cases; establishing a revolving fund on the Rosebud Reservation; memorial to Indians of the Rosebud Reservation killed in the World War; conferring authority on the Secretary of the Interior as to alienation in certain Indian allotments, and for other purposes.[44] Sec. 3, p. 995—25 U. S. C. 280; Sec. 6, p. 995—25 U. S. C. 392.

42 St. 1048; Sept. 22, 1922; C. 420—An Act Making appropriations to supply deficiencies in appropriations for the fiscal year ending June 30, 1922, and prior fiscal years, and for other purposes.[45]

42 St. 1068; Jan. 3, 1923; C. 21—An Act Making appropriations for the Departments of State and Justice and for the Judiciary for the fiscal year ending June 30, 1924, and for other purposes.

42 St. 1110; Jan. 5, 1923; C. 24—An Act Making appropriations for the Departments of Commerce and Labor for the fiscal year ending June 30, 1924, and for other purposes.[46]

42 St .1154; Jan. 22, 1923; C. 29—An Act Making appropriations to supply deficiencies in certain appropriations for the fiscal year ending June 30, 1923, and prior fiscal years, to provide supplemental appropriations for the fiscal year ending June 30, 1923, and for other purposes.[47]

42 St. 1174; Jan. 24, 1923; C. 42—An Act Making appropriations for the Department of the Interior for the fiscal year ending June 30, 1924; and for other purposes.[48]

42 St. 1222; Feb. 6, 1923; C. 50—An Act Promoting civilization and self-support among the Indians of the Mescalero Reservation, in New Mexico.[49]

42 St. 1227; Feb. 13, 1923; C. 72—An Act Making appropriations for the Executive office and sundry independent executive bureaus, boards, commissions, and offices, for the fiscal year ending June 30, 1924, and for other purposes.

42 St. 1246; Feb. 14, 1923; C. 76—An Act To extend the provisions of the Act of February 8, 1887, as amended, to lands purchased for Indians.[50]

42 St. 1246; Feb. 14, 1923; C. 77—An Act Authorizing an appropriation to meet proportionate expenses of providing a drainage system for Piute Indian lands in the State of Nevada within the Newlands reclamation project of the Reclamation Service.[51]

42 St. 1264; Feb. 20, 1923; C. 98—An Act Making appropriations for the Legislative Branch of the Government for the fiscal year ending June 30, 1924, and for other purposes.

42 St. 1288; Feb. 26, 1923; C. 114—An Act Authorizing an appropriation for the construction of a road within the Fort Apache Indian Reservation, Arizona.

42 St. 1288; Feb. 26, 1923; C. 116—An Act To provide for the completion of the bridge across the Little Colorado River near Leupp, Arizona.[52]

42 St. 1289; Feb. 26, 1923; C. 117—An Act Authorizing the Secretary of the Interior to enter into an agreement with Toole County irrigation district, of Shelby, Montana, and the Cut Bank irrigation district, of Cut Bank, Montana, for the settlement of the extent of the priority to the waters of Two Medicine, Cut Bank, and Badger Creeks, of the Indians of the Blackfeet Indian Reservation.

42 St. 1377; Mar. 2, 1923; C. 178—An Act Making appropriations for the military and nonmilitary activities of the War Department for the fiscal year ending June 30, 1924, and for other purposes.

42 St. 1527; Mar. 4, 1923; C. 292—An Act Making appropriations to supply deficiences in certain appropriations for the fiscal year ending June 30, 1923, and prior fiscal years, to provide supplemental appropriations for the fiscal year ending June 30, 1924, and for other purposes.[53]

42 St. 1561; Mar. 4, 1923; C. 297—An Act To authorize the extension of the period of restriction against alienation on surplus lands allotted to minor members of the Kansas or Kaw Tribe of Indians in Oklahoma.[54]

42 St. 1569; Nov. 18, 1921; C. 129—An Act Granting a deed of quitclaim and release to J. L. Holmes of certain land in the town of Whitefield, Oklahoma.

42 St. 1570; Nov. 18, 1921; C. 131—An Act To amend section 26 of an Act entitled "An Act making appropriations for the current and contingent expenses of the Bureau of Indian Affairs," and so forth.[55]

42 St. 1582; February 27, 1922; C. 85—An Act For the payment of certain money to Albert H. Raynolds.

42 St. 1589; Apr. 29, 1922; C. 172—An Act To carry out the provisions of an Act approved July 1, 1902, known as the Act entitled "An Act to accept, ratify, and confirm a proposed agreement submitted by the Kansas or Kaw Indians of Oklahoma, and for other purposes," and to provide for a settlement to Addie May Auld and Archie William Auld, who were enrolled as members of the said tribe after the lands and moneys of said tribe had been divided.[56]

42 St. 1591; May 20, 1922; C. 195—An Act Authorizing the Secre-

---

[34] *Sg.* 41 St. 417, sec. 2.
[35] *Ag.* 36 St. 1154. *A.* 44 St. 736.
[36] *Ag.* 37 St. 510. *A.* 45 St. 493.
[37] *A.* 45 St. 493.
[38] *S.* 42 St. 1048.
[39] *Sg.* 31 St. 863; 32 St. 503, 996; 33 St. 204; 34 St. 145, 873; 35 St. 312.
[40] *Sg.* 34 St. 225; 41 St. 1063.
[41] *Ag.* 30 St. 1200. *A.* 44 St. 614.
[42] *S.* 42 St. 1048; 43 St. 133; 45 St. 200.
[43] *Sg.* 37 St. 534; 38 St. 94. *S.* 42 St. 1154.
[44] *Sg.* 25 St. 895; 37 St. 1007; 39 St. 48; 41 St. 9, 751. *A.* 43 St. 705; 45 St. 200.
[45] *Sg.* 42 St. 830, 990. *S.* 43 St. 133; 45 St. 200; 46 St. 279, 1115. *Cited:* Choctaw, 83 C. Cls. 49.
[46] *Sg.* 36 St. 326. *S.* 42 St. 1527.
[47] *Sg.* 42 St. 991. *A.* 43 St. 889.
[48] *Sg.* 4 St. 442; 7 St. 46, 99, 212, 213, 236, 425; 10 St. 1100; 11 St. 614, 730; 15 St. 622, 640, 652, 658, 660, 673, 690; 16 St. 720; 19 St. 254, 256; 24 St. 388; 25 St. 645; 26 St. 146, 1029; 27 St. 130, 644; 33 St. 1081; 34 St. 375; 35 St. 51, 102, 531, 787; 36 St. 273, 277, 858, 1063; 37 St. 521, 522, 934; 38 St. 582, 604, 605; 39 St. 130, 154; 40 St. 297, 564, 570, 571, 588; 41 St. 28, 423, 437, 441, 448, 1107, 150, 1171; 42 St. 568. *Rp.* 45 St. 986. *S.* 44 St. 453. *Cited:* Browning, 6 F. 2d 801; Chippewa, 80 C. Cls. 410; Jump, 100 F. 2d 130; Lucas, 15 F. 2d 32; Morrison, 6 F. 2d 811; U. S. v. Candelaria, 271 U. S. 432; U. S. v. Seminole, 299 U. S. 417; Memo. Sol. Off. Apr. 4, 1933.
[49] *S.* 42 St. 1527.
[50] *Sg.* 24 St. 388. *Cited:* Button, 7 F. Supp. 597; U. S. v. Swain, 46 F. 2d 99; Work, 29 F. 2d 303.
[51] *A.* 43 St. 595.
[52] *Sg.* 39 St. 975; 40 St. 570; 41 St. 11. *S.* 42 St. 1527.
[53] *Sg.* 33 St. 1021; 36 St. 326; 38 St. 604; 39 St. 154, 969; 40 St. 588; 41 St. 422, 1225; 42 St. 23, 1125, 1222, 1288.
[54] *Sg.* 32 St. 636. *Cited:* 35 Op. A. G. 1; Op. Sol., M, 14237, Dec. 23, 1924.
[55] *Ag.* 41 St. 1248. *Cited:* Op. Sol., M. 12746, Oct. 8, 1924.
[56] *Ag.* 32 St. 638.

tary of the Interior to sell certain lands on the Wind River Reservation, Wyoming.

42 St. 1594; June 26, 1922; C. 244—An Act For the relief of Philip S. Everest.

42 St. 1710; Sept. 20, 1922; C. 353—An Act Authorizing the issuance of a patent in fee to Perry H. Kennerly for land allotted to him on the Blackfoot Reservation, Montana.[57]

42 St. 1710; Sept. 20, 1922; C. 355—An Act Authorizing the issuance of a patent in fee to Jerome Kennerly for land allotted to him on the Blackfoot Reservation, Montana.[58]

42 St. 1718; Sept. 22, 1922; C. 433—An Act Granting pensions and increase of pensions to certain soldiers and sailors of the Regular Army and Navy, and certain soldiers and sailors of wars other than the Civil War, and to widows of such soldiers and sailors.

42 St. 1758; Sept. 22, 1922; C. 434—An Act For the relief of Frances Kelly.

42 St. 1768; Feb. 6, 1923; C. 61—An Act For the relief of Lucy Paradis.

42 St. 1769; Feb. 8, 1923; C. 63—An Act For the relief of Elizabeth Marsh Watkins.

42 St. 1769; Feb. 8, 1923; C. 64—An Act To reimburse the Navajo Timber Company, of Delaware, for a deposit made to cover the purchase of timber.

42 St. 1773; Feb. 26, 1923; C. 127—An Act For the relief of Walter Runke.

42 St. 1785; Mar. 2, 1923; C. 197—An Act For the relief of J. W. Glidden and E. F. Hobbs.

43 STAT.

43 St. 1; Jan. 25, 1924; C. 2—An Act Providing for a per capita payment of $100 to each enrolled member of the Chippewa Tribe of Minnesota from the funds standing to their credit in the Treasury of the United States.[59]

43 St. 21; Mar. 13, 1924; C. 54—An Act For the relief of certain nations or tribes of Indians in Montana, Idaho, and Washington.[60]

43 St. 27; Mar. 19, 1924; C. 70—An Act Conferring jurisdiction upon the Court of Claims to hear, examine, adjudicate, and enter judgment in any claims which the Cherokee Indians may have against the United States, and for other purposes.[61]

43 St. 33; Apr. 2, 1924; C. 81—An Act Making appropriations to supply deficiencies in certain appropriations for the fiscal year ending June 30, 1924, and prior fiscal years, to provide supplemental appropriations for the fiscal year ending June 30, 1924, and for other purposes.[62]

43 St. 91; Apr. 12, 1924; C. 88—An Act To authorize the deposit of certain funds in the Treasury of the United States to the credit of Navajo Tribe of Indians and to make same available for appropriation for the benefit of said Indians.

43 St. 92; Apr. 12, 1924; C. 89—An Act To authorize the Secretary of the Interior to sell certain lands not longer needed for the Rapid City Indian School.

43 St. 92; Apr. 12, 1924; C. 90—An Act Providing for the reservation of certain lands in New Mexico for the Indians of the Zia Pueblo.

43 St. 92; Apr. 12, 1924; C. 91—An Act To validate certain allotments of land made to Indians on the Lac Courts Oreille Indian Reservation in Wisconsin.[63]

43 St. 93; Apr. 12, 1924; C. 92—An Act Authorizing an appropriation for the construction of a road within the Fort Apache Indian Reservation, Arizona, and for other purposes.[64]

43 St. 93; Apr. 12, 1924; C. 93—An Act To authorize the sale of lands and plants not longer needed for Indian administrative or allotment purposes. 25 U. S. C. 190.

43 St. 94; Apr. 12, 1924; C. 94—An Act To authorize the allotment of certain lands within the Fort Yuma Indian Reservation, California, and for other purposes.[65]

43 St. 94; Apr. 12, 1924; Ch. 95—An Act Amending an Act entitled "An Act for the Division of the lands and funds of the Osage Indians in Oklahoma, and for other purposes," approved June 28, 1906, and Acts amendatory thereof and supplemental thereto.[66]

43 St. 95; Apr. 14, 1924; C. 101—An Act To provide for the payment of claims of Chippewa Indians of Minnesota for back annuities.[67]

43 St. 111; Apr. 28, 1924; C. 134—An Act For the relief of dispossessed allotted Indians of the Nisqually Reservation, Washington.[68]

43 St. 111; Apr. 28, 1924; C. 135—An Act To authorize the leasing for mining purposes of unallotted lands in the Kaw Reservation in the State of Oklahoma. 25 U. S. C. 401.

43 St. 117; May 9, 1924; C. 151—An Act Authorizing the acquiring of Indian lands on the Fort Hall Indian Reservation, in Idaho, for reservoir purposes in connection with the Minidoka irrigation project.[69]

43 St. 121; May 19, 1924; 157—An Act To provide adjusted compensation for veterans of the World War, and for other purposes.

43 St. 132; May 19, 1924; C. 158—An Act For the enrollment and allotment of members of the Lac du Flambeau Band of Lake Superior Chippewas, in the State of Wisconsin, and for other purposes.[70]

43 St. 133; May 20, 1924; C. 160—An Act To authorize the sale of lands allotted to Indians under the Moses agreement of July 7, 1883.[71]

43 St. 133; May 20, 1924; C. 161—An Act Authorizing the Commissioner of Indian Affairs to acquire necessary rights of way across private lands, by purchase or condemnation proceedings, needed in constructing a spillway and drainage ditch to lower and maintain the level of Lake Andes, in South Dakota.[72]

43 St. 133; May 20, 1924; C. 162—An Act Conferring jurisdiction upon the Court of Claims to hear, examine, adjudicate, and enter judgment in any claims which the Seminole Indians may have against the United States, and for other purposes.[73]

43 St. 137; May 24, 1924; C. 176—An Act To amend an Act entitled "An Act for the relief of the Saginaw, Swan Creek, and Black River Band of Chippewa Indians in the State of Michigan, and for other purposes," approved June 25, 1910.[74]

43 St. 138; May 24, 1924; C. 177—An Act To cancel an allotment of land made to Mary Crane or Ho-tah-kah-win-kaw, a deceased Indian, embracing land within the Winnebago Indian Reservation in Nebraska.

43 St. 138; May 24, 1924; C. 178—An Act To cancel two allotments made to Richard Bell, deceased, embracing land within the Round Valley Indian Reservation in California.

43 St. 138; May 24, 1924; C. 179—An Act To amend an Act entitled "An Act authorizing the payment of the Choctaw and Chickasaw town-site fund, and for other purposes."[75]

43 St. 139; May 24, 1924; C. 180—An Act Authorizing extensions of time for the payment of purchase money due under certain homestead entries and Government land purchases within the Fort Berthold Indian Reservation, North Dakota. See Historical Note 25 U. S. C. A. 421.

43 St. 139; May 24, 1924; C. 181—An Act Conferring jurisdiction upon the Court of Claims to hear, examine, adjudicate, and enter judgment in any claims which the Creek Indians may have against the United States, and for other purposes.[76]

43 St. 146; May 24, 1924; C. 183—An Act To fix the compensation of officers and employees of the Legislative Branch of the Government.[77]

43 St. 176; May 27, 1924; C. 200—An Act To authorize the extension of the period of restriction against alienation on the

---

[57] *Sg.* 41 St. 16.
[58] *Sg.* 41 St. 16.
[59] *Sg.* 25 St. 642
[60] *Sg.* 11 St. 657; 12 St. 975. *A.* 46 St. 1060. *S.* 40. St. 1568, 1569. *Cited:* Blackfeet, 81 C. Cls 101.
[61] *A.* 45 St. 1229. *S.* 44 St. 568; 45 St. 2034; 47 St. 137; 48 St. 972; 50 St. 650. *Cited:* Cherokee, 80 C. Cls 1; Cherokee, 85 C. Cls. 76; Eastern or Emigrant, 82 C. Cls. 180; Klamath, 296 U. S. 244; Western Cherokees, 82 C. Cls 566.
[62] *Sg.* 25 St. 645, sec. 7; 33 St. 1021; 37 St. 522, sec. 2.
[63] *Sg.* 10 St. 1109.
[64] *S.* 45 St. 200.
[65] *Sg.* 35 St. 77; 38 St. 582. *Cited:* Letter of Ass't Sec'y to Sec'y of War, Feb. 26, 1932.
[66] *Ag.* 34 St. 539. *Cited:* Memo. Sol. Off., May 31, 1929, Feb. 3, 1930, Dec. 30, 1930; Globe, 81 F. 2d 143; In re Irwin, 60 F. 2d 495; In re Penn, 41 F. 2d 257; Taylor, 51 F. 2d 884.
[67] *Sg.* 25 St. 642, sec.7. *Cited:* Op. Sol. M. 12874, Oct. 27, 1924; M. 13270, Nov. 6, 1924.
[68] *Sg.* 41 St. 3, 28. *S.* 43 St. 672.
[69] *S.* 43 St. 672; 44 St. 1397.
[70] *Sg.* 24 St. 388; 26 St. 794; 30 St. 859.
[71] *Sg.* 23 St. 79; 30 St. 855.
[72] *Sg.* 42 St. 990; 42 St. 1051.
[73] *A.* 45 St. 1229. S. 44 St. 568; 45 St. 1562; 46 St. 1115; 48 St. 362; 50 St. 650. *Cited:* Op. Sol. M.28033, June 4, 1935; Klamath, 296 U. S. 244; Seminole, 78 C. Cls. 455; U. S. v. Seminole, 299 U. S. 417.
[74] *Ag.* 36 St. 829.
[75] *Ag.* 38 St. 571, sec. 3.
[76] *A.* 45 St. 1229. *S.* 44 St. 568; 45 St. 944; 46 St. 1115; 50 St. 564, 650. *Cited:* Creek, 302 U. S. 620; Creek, 77 C. Cls. 226; Creek, 63 C. Cls. 270; Creek, 74 C. Cls. 663; Creek, 77 C. Cls. 159; Creek, 78 C. Cls. 474; Creek; 84 C. Cls. 12; Klamath, 296 U. S. 244; Lucas, 15 F. 2d 32; U. S. v. Creek, 295 U. S. 103.
[77] *S.* 40 St. 32.

homestead allotment made to members of the Kansas or Kaw Tribe of Indians in Oklahoma.[78]

43 St. 205; May 28, 1924; C. 204—An Act Making appropriations for the Departments of State and Justice and for the Judiciary, and for the Departments of Commerce and Labor, for the fiscal year ending June 30, 1925; and for other purposes.[79]

43 St. 244; May 29, 1924; C. 210—An Act To authorize the leasing for oil and gas mining purposes of unallotted lands on Indian reservations affected by the proviso to section 3 of the Act of February 28, 1891.[80] 25 U. S. C. 398.

43 St. 246; May 31, 1924; C. 215—An Act To provide for the addition of the names of certain persons to the final roll of the Indians of the Flathead Indian Reservation, Montana.[81]

43 St. 246; May 31, 1924; C. 216—An Act To provide for the reservation of certain lands in Utah as a school site for Ute Indians.

43 St. 246; May 31, 1924; C. 217—An Act Providing for the reservation of certain lands in Utah for certain bands of Paiute Indians.

43 St. 247; May 31, 1924; C. 220—An Act To authorize the setting aside of certain tribal lands within the Quinaielt Indian Reservation in Washington, for lighthouse purposes.[82]

43 St. 252; June 2, 1924; C. 231—An Act to provide for the disposal of homestead allotments of deceased allottees within the Blackfeet Indian Reservation, Montana.[83] See Historical Note 25 U. S. C. A. 331.

43 St. 253; June 2, 1924; C. 232—An Act To provide for the addition of the names of Chester Calf and Crooked Nose Woman to the final roll of the Cheyenne and Arapaho Indians, Seger jurisdiction, Oklahoma.

43 St. 253; June 2, 1924; C. 233—An Act To authorize the Secretary of the Interior to issue certificates of citizenship to Indians.[84] 8 U. S. C. 3, 173.

43 St. 357; June 3, 1924; C. 239—An Act Authorizing payment to certain Red Lake Indians, out of the tribal trust funds, for garden plats surrendered for school-farm use.

43 St. 357; June 3, 1924; C. 240—An Act To authorize acquisition of unreserved public lands in the Columbia or Moses Reservation, State of Washington, under Acts of March 28, 1912, and March 3, 1877, and for other purposes.[85] 43 U. S. C. 208.

43 St. 366; June 4, 1924; C. 249—An Act Authorizing the Wichita and affiliated bands of Indians in Oklahoma to submit claims to the Court of Claims.[86]

43 St. 376; June 4, 1924; C. 253—An Act Providing for the final disposition of the affairs of the Eastern Band of Cherokee Indians of North Carolina.[87] See Historical Note 25 U. S. C. A. 331.

43 St. 390; June 5, 1924; C. 264—An Act Making appropriations for the Department of the Interior for the fiscal year ending June 30, 1925, and for other purposes.[88]

43 St. 475; June 7, 1924; C. 288—An Act For the continuance of construction work on the San Carlos Federal irrigation project in Arizona, and for other purposes.[89]

43 St. 477; June 7, 1924; C. 289—An Act Authorizing the Secretary of the Interior to investigate and report to Congress the facts in regard to the claims of certain members of the Sioux Nation of Indians for damages occasioned by the destruction of their horses.[90]

43 St. 477; June 7, 1924; C. 291—An Act Making appropriations for the military and nonmilitary activities of the War Department for the fiscal year ending June 30, 1925, and for other purposes.

43 St. 521; June 7, 1924; C. 292—An Act Making appropriations for the Executive Office and sundry independent executive bureaus, boards, commissions, and offices, for the fiscal year ending June 30, 1925, and for other purposes.

43 St. 533; June 7, 1924; C. 293—An Act To provide for a girls' dormitory at the Fort Lapwai Sanatorium, Lapwai, Idaho.[91]

43 St. 536; June 7, 1924; C. 298—An Act To pay tuition of Indian children in public schools.

43 St. 537; June 7, 1924; C. 300—An Act Conferring jurisdiction upon the Court of Claims to hear, examine, adjudicate, and enter judgment in any claims which the Choctaw and Chickasaw Indians may have against the United States, and for other purposes.[92]

43 St. 578; June 7, 1924; C. 303—An Act Making appropriations for the Legislative Branch of the Government for the fiscal year ending June 30, 1925, and for other purposes.

43 St. 595; June 7, 1924; C. 309—An Act To amend and Act entitled "An Act authorizing an appropriation to meet proportionate expenses of providing a drainage system for Piute Indian lands in the State of Nevada within the Newlands reclamation project of the Reclamation Service," approved February 14, 1923.[93]

43 St. 596; June 7, 1924; C. 310—An Act Authorizing an appropriation to enable the Secretary of the Interior to purchase a tract of land, with sufficient water right attached, for the use and occupancy of the Temoak Band of homeless Indians, located at Ruby Valley, Nevada.[94]

43 St. 596; June 7, 1924; C. 311—An Act For the relief of settlers and town-site occupants of certain lands in the Pyramid Lake Indian Reservation, Nevada.[95] See Historical Note 25 U. S. C. A. 421.

43 St. 599; June 7, 1924; C. 313—An Act To authorize the payment of certain taxes to Stevens and Ferry Counties, in the State of Washington, and for other purposes.[96]

43 St. 606; June 7, 1924; C. 318—An Act Authorizing annual appropriations for the maintenance of that portion of Gallup-Durango Highway across the Navajo Indian Reservation and providing reimbursement therefor.[97]

43 St. 634; June 7, 1924; C. 328—An Act To provide for quarters, fuel, and light for employees of the Indian field service. 25 U. S. C. 56.

43 St. 636; June 7, 1924; C. 331—An Act To quiet the title to lands within Pueblo Indian land grants, and for other purposes.[98] See Historical Note 25 U. S. C. A. 331.

43 St. 644; June 7, 1924; C. 335—An Act Conferring jurisdiction upon the Court of Claims to hear, examine, adjudicate, and enter judgment in any claims which the Stockbridge Indians

---

[78] *Sg.* 32 St. 636. *Cited:* 35 Op. A. G. 1; Op. Sol. M.14237, Dec. 23, 1924.

[79] *Sg.* 36 St. 326.

[80] *Sg.* 26 St. 795, sec. 3. *S.* 44 St. 1347. *Cited:* Brown, 39 Yale L. J. 307; Op. Sol. M.27906, May 14, 1935; Memo. Sol. Off., Oct. 22, 1936; Memo. Sol., Oct. 21, 1938; British-American, 299 U. S. 159.

[81] *Sg.* 40 St. 591; 41 St. 9. *Cited:* Op. Sol. M.14233, Apr. 24, 1925.

[82] *R.* 47 St. 37.

[83] *Sg.* 41 St. 16, sec. 10.

[84] *S.* 45 St. 1094; 49 St. 388. *Cited:* Brown, 15 Minn. L. Rev. 182; Goodrich, 14 Calif. L. Rev. 83, 157; Houghton, 19 Calif. L. Rev. 507; Krieger, 3 Geo. Wash. L. Rev. 279; Wiel, 12 A. B. A. Jour. 37; 68 Cong., 1st sess., Sen. Rept. No. 441; 12 L. D. Memo. 298; Memo. of Comm'r, Jan. 6, 1937; Memo. Sol., Feb. 17, 1939; 51 L. D. 326; 53 I. D. 593; 54 I. D. 39; Davis, 32 F. 2d 860; Deere, 22 F. 2d 851; Halbert, 283 U. S. 753; Mason, 5 F. 2d 255; U. S. v. Lynch, 7 Alaska 568; U. S. v. Richards, 27 F. 2d 284; U. S. v. Wright, 53 F. 2d 300.

[85] *Sg.* 23 St. 76; 37 St. 77.

[86] *A.* 47 St. 87. *S.* 43 St. 1313. *Cited:* Klamath, 296 U. S. 244.

[87] *Sg.* 36 St. 855; 37 St. 678. *A.* 46 St. 1518. *S.* 43 St. 1141; 44 St. 453, 934; 45 St. 200, 1094, 1623; 46 St. 279. *Cited:* Memo. Sol. Off., Mar. 26, 1934; Memo. Ind. Off., Jan. 3, 1935; U. S. v. Colvard, 89 F. 2d 312; U. S. v. 7,405.3 Acres, 97 F. 2d 417; U. S. v. Swain, 46 F. 2d 99; U. S. v. Wright, 53 F. 2d 300.

[88] *Sg.* 4 St. 442; 7 St. 46, 99, 212, 213, 236, 425; 10 St. 1109; 11 St. 614, 730; 12 St. 411; 15 St. 622, 640, 652, 658, 669, 673, 696; 16 St. 720; 19 St. 254, 256; 24 St. 388; 25 St. 645; 26 St. 1029; 27 St. 139, 644; 28 St. 451, 896; 33 St. 1081; 34 St. 375; 35 St. 102; 36 St. 273, 277, 858, sec. 13; 1063; 37 St. 521, 522, 934; 38 St. 582, 604, sec. 22; 606; 39 St. 130, 138, 154; 40 St. 297, 564, 570, 571; 41 St. 11, 28, 437, 441, 448, 1107; 42 St. 568, 1488. *S.* 43 St. 1313; 44 St. 453; 45 St. 200, 1562; 46 St. 279. *Cited:* Memo. Sol. Off., Apr. 4, 1933; Lucas, 15 F. 2d 32.

[89] *Sg.* 43 St. 401. *S.* 43 St. 1141; 44 St. 453, 841, 934; 45 St. 200, 883, 1562, 1623; 46 St. 90, 279, 1115, 1519, 1552; 47 St. 91. *Cited:* Memo. Sol., Feb. 10, 1933; Memo. Sol. Off., Dec. 27, 1934, Feb. 21, 1935; Sec'y's Letter to A. G., Mar. 20, 1935.

[90] *Rp.* 45 St. 986. *S.* 44 St. 135.

[91] *R.* 43 St. 1141.

[92] *A.* 44 St. 568; 45 St. 1229. *S.* 43 St. 1612; 45 St. 1562; 50 St. 650. *Cited:* Chickasaw, 75 C. Cls. 426; Choctaw, 75 C. Cls. 494; Choctaw, 81 C. Cls. 63; Choctaw, 81 C. Cls. 1; Choctaw, 83 C. Cls. 49; Choctaw, 83 C. Cls. 140; Klamath, 296 U. S. 244.

[93] *Ag.* 42 St. 1246. *Cited:* Memo. Sol., Aug. 22, 1936.

[94] *S.* 45 St. 200.

[95] *Sg.* 13 St. 344. *Cited:* Memo. Sol., Dec. 10, 1935.

[96] *Sg.* 27 St. 63. *S.* 44 St. 161. *Cited:* 50 L. D. 691.

[97] *S.* 43 St. 1141; 45 St. 200.

[98] *S.* 44 St. 161, 1178; 45 St. 64, 1562, 1628; 46 St. 90, 173, 279, 1115, 1552; 47 St. 91, 525, 820; 48 St. 108, 274; 49 St. 176, 800, 1459, 1757; 50 St. 564; 52 St. 291, 778. *Cited:* 71 Cong., 3d sess., Hearings, Sen. Comm. on Ind. Aff., S. 5828, Feb. 18, 1931; 8 L. D. Memo. 220; Report of Status of Pueblo of Pojoaque, Nov. 8, 1932; Memo. Sol. Off., June 23, 1933, Aug. 17, 1933, Sept. 29, 1933; Memo. Sol., Oct. 23, 1934; Op. Sol. M. 28108, Mar. 18, 1936; Memo. Sol. Off., Sept. 12, 1936; Op. Sol., M. 28850, Dec. 16, 1936; Memo. Sol. Apr. 14, 1939; Memo. Sol. Off., Apr. 14, 1939; 54 I. D. 882; Garcia, 48 F. 2d 873; Pueblo de San Juan, 47 F. 2d 446; Pueblo of Picuris, 50 F. 2d 12; U. S. v. Algodones, 52 F. 2d 359; U. S. v. Chavez, 290 U. S. 357; U. S. v. Wooten, 40 F. 2d 882.

may have against the United States, and for other purposes.[60]

43 St. 653; June 7, 1924; C. 348—An Act To provide for the protection of forest lands, for the reforestation of denuded areas, for the extension of national forests, and for other purposes, in order to promote the continuous production of timber on lands chiefly suitable therefor. 16 U. S. C. 471, 499, 505.

43 St. 667; June 7, 1924; C. 372—Joint Resolution Authorizing expenditure of the Fort Peck 4 per centum fund now standing to the credit of the Fort Peck Indians of Montana in the Treasury of the United States.

43 St. 668; June 7, 1924; C. 376—Joint Resolution To provide that the powers and duties conferred upon the Governor of Alaska under existing law for the protection of wild game animals and wild birds in Alaska be transferred to and be exercised by the Secretary of Agriculture.[1]

43 St. 672; Dec. 5, 1924; C. 4—An Act Making appropriations to supply deficiencies in certain appropriations for the fiscal year ending June 30, 1924, and prior fiscal years, to provide supplemental appropriations for the fiscal year ending June 30, 1925, and for other purposes.[2]

43 St. 704; Dec. 6, 1924; C. 5—An Act Making additional appropriations for the fiscal year ending June 30, 1925, to enable the heads of the several departments and independent establishments to adjust the rates of compensation of civilian employees in certain of the field services.[3]

43 St. 722; Jan. 6, 1925; C. 28—An Act To perfect the title of purchasers of Indian lands sold under the provisions of the Act of Congress of March 3, 1909 (35 St. 751), and the regulations pursuant thereto as applied to Indians of the Quapaw Agency.[4]

43 St. 723; Jan. 6, 1925; C. 29—An Act To amend an Act approved March 3, 1909, entitled "An Act for the removal of the restrictions on alienation of lands of allottees of the Quapaw Agency, Oklahoma, and the sale of all tribal lands, school, agency, or other buildings on any of the reservations within the jurisdiction of such agency, and for other purposes."[5]

43 St. 726; Jan. 7, 1925; C. 34—An Act To amend an Act entitled "An Act to provide for the disposal of the unallotted lands on the Omaha Indian Reservation, in the State of Nebraska."[6]

43 St. 728; Jan. 7, 1925; C. 36—An Act To amend an Act entitled "An Act to amend an Act entitled 'An Act making appropriations for the current and contingent expenses of the Bureau of Indian Affairs, for fulfilling treaty stipulations with various Indian tribes, and for other purposes, for the fiscal year ending June 30, 1914,' approved June 30, 1913," approved May 26, 1920.[7]

43 St. 729; Jan. 9, 1925; C. 58—An Act Authorizing the Ponca Tribe of Indians residing in the States of Oklahoma and Nebraska to submit claims to the Court of Claims.

43 St. 730; Jan. 9, 1925; C. 59—An Act Conferring jurisdiction on the Court of Claims to determine and report upon the interest, title, ownership, and right of possession of the Yankton Band of Santee Sioux Indians to the Red Pipestone Quarries, Minnesota.[8]

43 St. 739; Jan. 13, 1925; C. 75—An Act To establish an Alaska Game Commission to protect game animals, land fur-bearing animals, and birds, in Alaska, and for other purposes.[9] Sec. 9, p. 743—48 U. S. C. 197; Sec. 10, p. 743—48 U. S. C. 198; Sec. 16, p. 747—48 U. S. C. 202a.

43 St. 753; Jan. 20, 1925; C. 85—An Act Making appropriations to supply urgent deficiencies in certain appropriations for the fiscal year ending June 30, 1925, and prior fiscal years, to provide urgent supplemental appropriations for the fiscal year ending June 30, 1925, and for other purposes.

43 St. 793; Jan. 27, 1925; C. 101—An Act To amend the law relating to timber operations on the Menominee Reservation in Wisconsin.[10]

43 St. 795; Jan. 29, 1925; C. 108—An Act To amend an Act entitled "An Act for the relief of Indians occupying railroad lands in Arizona, New Mexico, or California," approved March 4, 1913.[11]

43 St. 795; Jan. 29, 1925; C. 109—An Act Providing for an allotment of land from the Kiowa, Comanche, and Apache Indian Reservation, Oklahoma, to James F. Rowell, an intermarried and enrolled member of the Kiowa Tribe.[12]

43 St. 798; Jan. 30, 1925; C. 114—An Act Providing for a per capita payment of $50 to each enrolled member of the Chippewa Tribe of Minnesota from the funds standing to their credit in the Treasury of the United States.[13]

43 St. 800; Jan. 30, 1925; C. 117—An Act To provide for the payment of one-half the cost of the construction of a bridge across the San Juan River, New Mexico.[14]

43 St. 812; Feb. 7, 1925; C. 148—An Act To refer the claims of the Delaware Indians to the Court of Claims, with the right of appeal to the Supreme Court of the United States.[15]

43 St. 816; Feb. 9, 1925; C. 161—An Act To compensate the Chippewa Indians of Minnesota for lands disposed of under the provisions of the Free Homestead Act.[16]

43 St. 817; Feb. 9, 1925; C. 163—An Act Authorizing repayment of excess amounts paid by purchasers of certain lots in the townsite of Sanish, formerly Fort Berthold Indian Reservation, North Dakota.[17]

43 St. 818; Feb. 9, 1925; C. 164—An Act To provide for the payment of certain claims against the Chippewa Indians of Minnesota.

43 St. 819; Feb. 9, 1925; C. 166—An Act Authorizing the Secretary of the Interior to pay certain funds to various Wisconsin Pottawatomi Indians.[18]

43 St. 819; Feb. 9, 1925; C. 168—An Act To amend the Act entitled "An Act making appropriations for the current and contingent expenses of the Bureau of Indian Affairs, for fulfilling treaty stipulations with various Indian tribes, and for other purposes, for the fiscal year ending June 30, 1915," approved August 1, 1914.[19]

43 St. 820; Feb. 9, 1925; C. 169—An Act For the relief of the Omaha Indians of Nebraska.[20]

43 St. 822; Feb. 10, 1925; C. 200—An Act Making appropriations for the Department of Agriculture for the fiscal year ending June 30, 1926, and for other purposes.[21]

43 St. 886; Feb. 12, 1925; C. 214—An Act Authorizing certain Indian tribes, or any of them, residing in the State of Washington to submit to the Court of Claims certain claims growing out of treaties or otherwise.[22]

43 St. 889; Feb. 12, 1925; C. 219—An Act To amend the Act entitled "An Act to provide that the United States shall aid the States in the construction of rural post roads, and for other purposes," approved July 11, 1916, as amended and supplemented, and for other purposes.[23] Sec. 4, p. 890—23 U. S. C. 12.

43 St. 892; Feb. 12, 1925; C. 225—An Act Making appropriations for the military and nonmilitary activities of the War Department for the fiscal year ending June 30, 1926, and for other purposes.

43 St. 954; Feb. 20, 1925; C. 273—An Act To provide for exchanges of Government and privately owned lands in the Walapai Indian Reservation, Arizona.

43 St. 958; Feb. 21, 1925; C. 280—An Act To amend the Act of June 30, 1919, relative to per capita cost of Indian schools.[24] 25 U. S. C. 296 (41 St. 6).[25]

43 St. 978; Feb. 25, 1925; C. 320—An Act For the establishment

---

[60] *Cited:* Klamath, 296 U. S. 244; Stockbridge, 93 C. Cls. 208; Stockbridge, 61 C. Cls. 472.

[1] *Sg.* 35 St. 104. *S.* 43 St. 822.

[2] *Sg.* 38 St. 604; 42 St. 552; 43 St. 111, 117, sec. 3, 5. *S.* 45 St. 1562. *Cited:* 50 L. D. 691.

[3] *S.* 43 St. 1313.

[4] *Sg.* 35 St. 751.

[5] *Ag.* 35 St. 751, sec. 1.

[6] *Sg.* 22 St. 341; 23 St. 630. *Ag.* 37 St. 111. *Cited:* Memo. Sol. Off., Jan. 22, 1936.

[7] *Sg.* 38 St. 96. *Ag.* 41 St. 625. *Cited:* Chippewa, 307 U. S. 1.

[8] *Sg.* 38 St. 284, sec. 22. *Cited:* Yankton, 272 U. S. 351.

[9] *A.* 46 St. 1111; 52 St. 1169. *S.* 45 St. 539, 1189; 46 St. 892; 47 St. 609, 1482; 48 St. 467; 49 St. 247, 1421; 50 St. 395; 52 St. 710.

[10] *Sg.* 12 St. 220, 411; 18 St. 177. *Ag.* 35 St. 51, sec. 2. *Cited:* Memo. Sol., Oct. 20, 1936.

[11] *Ag.* 37 St. 1007; 39 St. 48; 41 St. 9; 42 St. 994. *A.* 45 St. 299.

[12] *Sg.* 30 St. 280.

[13] *Sg.* 25 St. 645. *Cited:* U. S. ex rel. Kadrie, 30 F. 2d 989.

[14] *S.* 44 St. 161.

[15] *Sg.* 16 St. 570; 17 St. 136; 18 St. 35, 450. *A.* 44 St. 1358; 49 St. 1459. *Cited:* Delaware, 72 C. Cls. 483; Delaware, 74 C. Cls. 368; Delaware, 84 C. Cls. 535; Klamath, 296 U. S. 244.

[16] *Sg.* 25 St. 645. *S.* 44 St. 161.

[17] *Sg.* 36 St. 458.

[18] *Sg.* 39 St. 991. *Ag.* 41 St. 432.

[19] *Ag.* 38 St. 582, 590. *S.* 44 St. 161.

[20] *Sg.* 10 St. 1043; 36 St. 580.

[21] *Sg.* 15 St. 246; 35 St. 102; 36 St. 327; 43 St. 668.

[22] *Sg.* 10 St. 1132; 12 St. 927, 933, 971. *S.* 52 St. 1114. *Cited:* Duwamish, 79 C. Cls. 530.

[23] *Ag* 42 St. 214, 661, 1157.

[24] *Ag.* 41 St. 6.

[25] *R.* 45 St. 1534.

of industrial schools for Alaskan native children, and for other purposes. Sec. 1—48 U. S. C. 173; Sec. 2—48 U. S. C. 174.

43 St. 981; Feb. 25, 1925; C. 326—An Act To restore homestead rights in certain cases.[26] 43 U. S. C. 187.

43 St. 994; Feb. 26, 1925; C. 343—An Act Authorizing the construction of a bridge across the Colorado River near Lee Ferry, Arizona.[27]

43 St. 1003; Feb. 26, 1925; C. 356—An Act Authorizing the Secretary of the Interior to sell certain land to provide funds to be used in the purchase of a suitable tract of land to be used for cemetery purposes for the use and benefit of members of the Kiowa, Comanche, and Apache Tribes of Indians.[28]

43 St. 1008; Feb. 27, 1925; C. 359—An Act To amend the Act of Congress of March 3, 1921, entitled "An Act to amend section 3 of the Act of Congress of June 28, 1906, entitled 'An Act of Congress for the division of the lands and funds of the Osage Indians in Oklahoma, and for other purposes.' "[29] See Historical Note 25 U. S. C. A. 331.

43 St. 1014; Feb. 27, 1925; C. 364—An Act Making appropriations for the Departments of State and Justice and for the Judiciary, and for the Departments of Commerce and Labor, for the fiscal year ending June 30, 1926, and for other purposes.[30]

43 St. 1052; Feb. 28, 1925; C. 365—An Act To compensate the Chippewa Indians of Minnesota for timber and interest in connection with the settlement for the Minnesota National Forest.[31]

43 St. 1096; Mar. 2, 1925; C. 394—An Act To authorize an appropriation for the purchase of certain lots in the town of Cedar City, Utah, for the use and benefit of a small band of Piute Indians located thereon.[32]

43 St. 1101; Mar. 3, 1925; C. 414—An Act To authorize the Secretary of the Interior to sell to the city of Los Angeles certain lands in California heretofore purchased by the Government for the relief of homeless Indians.[33]

43 St. 1102; Mar. 3, 1925; C. 415—An Act Appropriating money for the relief of the Clallam Tribe of Indians in the State of Washington, and for other purposes.[34]

43 St. 1114; Mar. 3, 1925; C. 431—An Act To authorize the Secretary of the Interior to cancel restricted fee patents covering lands on the Winnebago Indian Reservation and to issue trust patents in lieu thereof.[35] See Historical Note 25 U. S. C. A. 331.

43 St. 1114; Mar. 3, 1925; C. 432—An Act To provide for the permanent withdrawal of a certain 40-acre tract of public land in New Mexico for the use and benefit of the Navajo Indians.[36]

43 St. 1115; Mar. 3, 1925; C. 433—An Act To provide for exchanges of Government and privately owned lands in the additions to the Navajo Indian Reservation, Arizona, by Executive orders of January 8, 1900, and November 14, 1901.[37]

43 St. 1133; Mar. 3, 1925; C. 459—An Act Conferring jurisdiction upon the Court of Claims to hear, examine, adjudicate, and enter judgment in any and all claims, of whatever nature, which the Kansas or Kaw Tribe of Indians may have or claim to have, against the United States, and for other purposes.[38]

43 St. 1141; Mar. 3, 1925; C. 462—An Act Making appropriations for the Department of the Interior for the fiscal year ending June 30, 1926, and for other purposes.[39] p. 1147—25 U. S. C. 57 (38 St. 584, sec. 1; 40 St. 564, sec. 1); p. 1151—See Historical Note 25 U. S. C. A. 385.

43 St. 1184; Mar. 3, 1925; C. 464—An Act To amend an Act entitled "An Act authorizing extensions of time for the payment of purchase money due under certain homestead entries and Government-land purchases within the former Cheyenne River and Standing Rock Indian Reservation, North Dakota and South Dakota.[40]

43 St. 1198; Mar. 3, 1925; C. 468—An Act Making appropriations for the Executive Office and sundry independent executive bureaus, boards, commissions, and offices, for the fiscal year ending June 30, 1926, and for other purposes.

43 St. 1267; Mar. 4, 1925; C. 533—An Act To provide for extension of payment on homestead entries on ceded lands of the Fort Peck Indian Reservation, State of Montana, and for other purposes.[41]

43 St. 1286; Mar. 4, 1925; C. 540—An Act Making appropriations for the Legislative Branch of the Government for the fiscal year ending June 30, 1926, and for other purposes.

43 St. 1301; Mar. 4, 1925; C. 550—An Act Extending the time for repayment of the revolving fund for the benefit of the Crow Indians.[42] Sec. 2, p. 1302—30 U. S. C. 233a.

43 St. 1313; Mar. 4, 1925; C. 556—An Act Making appropriations to supply deficiencies in certain appropriations for the fiscal year ending June 30, 1925; and prior fiscal years, to provide supplemental appropriations for the fiscal years ending June 30, 1925, and June 30, 1926, and for other purposes.[43]

43 St. 1362; Apr. 14, 1924; C. 103—An Act For the relief of J. G. Seupelt.[44]

43 St. 1367; May 24, 1924; C. 186—An Act Authorizing the removal of the restrictions from 40 acres of the allotment of Isaac Jack, a Seneca Indian, and for other purposes.

43 St. 1367; May 24, 1924; C. 187—An Act To compensate three Comanche Indians of the Kiowa Reservation.

43 St. 1381; Dec. 8, 1924; C. 7—An Act Granting pensions and increase of pensions to certain soldiers and sailors of the Regular Army and Navy, and certain soldiers and sailors of wars other than the Civil War, and to widows of such soldiers and sailors.

43 St. 1557; Feb. 9, 1925; C. 176—An Act For the relief of James J. McAllister.[45]

43 St. 1561; Feb. 9, 1925; C. 191—An Act For the relief of Charles F. Peirce, Frank T. Mann, and Mollie V. Gaither.

43 St. 1563; Feb. 16, 1925; C. 236—An Act For the relief of the heirs of Ko-mo-dal-kiah, Moses agreement allottee numbered 33.

43 St. 1573; Feb. 17, 1925; C. 263—An Act Providing for the payment of any unappropriated moneys belonging to the Apache, Kiowa, and Comanche Indians to Jacob Crew.

43 St. 1574; Feb. 19, 1925; C. 270—An Act For the relief of Ellen B. Walker.

43 St. 1586; Mar. 3, 1925; C. 492—An Act For the relief of settlers and claimants to section 16, lands in the L'Anse and Vieux Desert Indian Reservation, in Michigan, and for other purposes.[46]

43 St. 1588; Mar. 3, 1925; C. 501—An Act For the relief of James E. Jenkins.

---

[26] *S.* 48 St. 1165.

[27] *S.* 44 St. 161.

[28] *Cited:* Memo. Sol. Off., Jan. 30, 1938.

[29] *Ag.* 34 St. 539; 41 St. 1250. *A.* 45 St. 1478. *Cited:* 36 Op. A. G. 98; 38 Op. A. G. 577; 10 L. D. Memo. 82; 12 L. D. Memo. 642; Op. Sol., M. 17687, Dec. 19, 1925; M. 18423, Mar. 16, 1926; M. 19190, June 2, 1926, M. 19225, June 7, 1926; Memo. Sol. Off., June 8, 1926, July 15, 1926, July 20, 1926, July 23, 1926, Sept. 3, 1926, Oct. 26, 1926, Oct. 27, 1926, Feb. 2, 1927; Op. Sol., M. 21642, Mar. 26, 1927; Memo. Sol. Off., Sept. 12, 1927, Feb. 21, 1929, Apr. 5, 1929; Op. Sol., M. 25107, May 4, 1929; Memo. Sol. Off., Sept. 18, 1929; Op. A. G., Oct. 5, 1929; Memo. Sol. Off., Feb. 3, 1930, Apr. 22, 1930, July 8, 1930; Letter to Comm'r of Ind. Affairs from Sec'y of Int., Sept. 1930; Memo. Sol. Off., Dec. 17, 1930, Mar. 10, 1931, Apr. 9, 1931; Op. Off., M. 26731, Oct. 14, 1931; Op. Comp. Gen. to Sec'y, Feb. 4, 1932; Memo. Sol. Off., Apr. 8, 1933, May 27, 1933, June 29, 1933, Dec. 21, 1933; Op. Sol., M. 27788, Aug. 6, 1934, Memo. Sol., May 1, 1936; Op. Sol., M. 27963, Jan. 26, 1937; Letter from A. G. to Sec'y. of Int., Feb. 13, 1937; Letter from Asst. Sec'y. to A. G., Oct. 27, 1937; 53 I. D. 169; 54 I. D. 105; 54 I. D. 260; 54 I. D. 341; 55 I. D. 456; 56 I. D. 48; Browning, 6 F. 2d 801; Choteau, 283 U. S. 691; Globe, 81 F. 2d 143; Hickey, 64 F. 2d 628; Logan, 58 F. 2d 697; Morrison, 6 F. 2d 811; Osage, 33 F. 2d 21; Tapp, 6 F. Supp. 577; Taylor, 51 F. 2d 884; U. S. v. Bd. of Comm'rs., 26 F. Supp. 270; U. S. v. Carson, 19 F. Supp. 619; U. S. v. Howard, 8 F. Supp. 617; U. S. v. Hughes, 6 F. Supp. 972; U. S. v. Johnson, 87 F. 2d 153; U. S. v. Mashunkashey, 72 F. 2d 847; U. S. v. Mellendore, 74 F. 2d 286; Williams, 83 F. 2d 143.

[30] *Ag.* 36 St. 326.

[31] *Sg.* 25 St. 645. *S.* 44 St. 161.

[32] *S.* 44 St. 161.

[33] *Sg.* 42 St. 560. *R.* 48 St. 1228. *S.* 50 St. 574.

[34] *S.* 44 St. 161. *Cited:* Memo. Sol. Off., June 25, 1938.

[35] *Sg.* 12 St. 658; 24 St. 388.

[36] *Cited:* 2 L. D. Memo. 123.

[37] *Sg.* Ex. Orders Jan. 8, 1900, & Nov. 4, 1901.

[38] *Sg.* 16 St. 570; 17 St. 186; 18 St. 85, 450; 32 St. 636, sec. 2. *S.* 45 St. 1258. *A.* 45 St. 1258. *Cited:* Kansas, 80 C. Cls. 264; Klamath, 296 U. S. 244.

[39] *Sg.* 4 St. 442; 5 St. 625; 7 St. 46, 99, 212, 213, 286, 425; 10 St. 1109; 11 St. 614, 730; 12 St. 411; 15 St. 622, 640, 652, 669, 673, 696; 16 St. 720; 19 St. 254, 256; 24 St. 388; 25 St. 645, sec. 7; 26 St. 1029; 27 St. 130, 644; 33 St. 1081; 34 St. 325; 36 St. 273, 858, 1063; 37 St. 521, 522, 934; 38 St. 77, 582, 604, sec. 22, 606; 39 St. 123, 154, 969; 40 St. 207, 561, 564; 41 St. 28, 437, 441, 448, 1107; 42 St. 568, 1488; 43 St. 376, 381, 475, 476, 533, 606, 607. *S.* 44 St. 161; 45 St. 200, 883, 1562. *Cited:* Chippewa, 80 C. Cls. 410; Lucas, 15 F. 2d 32; U. S. v. Seminole, 299 U. S. 417.

[40] *Ag.* 42 St. 499. *A.* 45 St. 400.

[41] *Sg.* 41 St. 365. *S.* 44 St. 746.

[42] *Sg.* 41 St. 755; 42 St. 1448. *S.* 49 St. 244.

[43] *Sg.* 24 St. 388; 28 St. 876; 28 St. 910; 35 St. 51; 42 St. 1488; 43 St. 366, 390, 704, 1557.

[44] *Sg.* 34 St. 81.

[45] *S.* 43 St. 1141.

[46] *S.* 44 St. 161.

43 St. 1597; Mar. 4, 1925; C. 572—An Act For the relief of Doctor C. LeRoy Brock.

43 St. 1597; Mar. 4, 1925; C. 574—An Act For the relief of Mrs. Benjamin Gauthier.

43 St. 1612; June 5, 1924; Concurrent Res.—Choctaw and Chickasaw Indian Claims.

43 St. 1612; June 5, 1924; Concurrent Res.—Status of Sequoah.[47]

44 STAT.

44 St. 7; Feb. 19, 1926; C. 22—An Act Providing for a per capita payment of $50 to each enrolled member of the Chippewa Tribe of Minnesota from the funds standing to their credit in the Treasury of the United States.[48]

44 St. 134; Feb. 27, 1926; C. 37—An Act To authorize the Secretary of the Interior to issue certificates of competency removing the restrictions against alienation of the inherited lands of the Kansas or Kaw Indians in Oklahoma.[49]

44 St. 135; Mar. 1, 1926; C. 40—An Act Authorizing an appropriation for the payment of certain claims due certain members of the Sioux Nation of Indians for damages occasioned by the destruction of their horses.[50]

44 St. 135; Mar. 1, 1926; C. 41—An Act Authorizing an expenditure of $50,000 from the tribal funds of the Indians of the Quinaielt Reservation, Washington, for the improvement and completion of the road from Taholah to Moclips on said reservation.

44 St. 161; Mar. 3, 1926; C. 44—An Act Making appropriations to supply urgent deficiencies in certain appropriations for the fiscal year ending June 30, 1926, and prior fiscal years, to provide urgent supplemental appropriations for the fiscal years ending June 30, 1926, and June 30, 1927, and for other purposes.[51]

44 St. 202; Mar. 11, 1926; C. 51—An Act Authorizing the Secretary of the Interior to dispose of certain allotted land in Boundary County, Idaho, and to purchase a compact tract of land to allot in small tracts to the Kootanai Indians as herein provided, and for other purposes.

44 St. 211; Mar. 18, 1926; C. 60—An Act For the purpose of reclaiming certain lands in Indian and private ownership within and immediately adjacent to the Lummi Indian Reservation, in the State of Washington, and for other purposes.[52]

44 St. 214; Mar. 22, 1926; C. 63—An Act To provide for the withdrawal of certain lands as a camp ground for the pupils of the Indian school at Phoenix, Arizona.[53]

44 St. 237; Apr. 10, 1926; C. 112—An Act To amend section 90 of the Act to codify, revise, and amend the laws relating to the judiciary, and the amendment to said Act approved July 17, 1916, 39 St. c. 248.[54] 28 U. S. C. 180.

44 St. 239; Apr. 12, 1926; C. 115—An Act To amend section 9 of the Act of May 27, 1908 (35 St. 312), and for putting in force, in reference to suits involving Indian titles, the statutes of limitations of the State of Oklahoma, and providing for the United States to join in certain actions, and for making judgments binding on all parties, and for other purposes.[55]

44 St. 242; Apr. 13, 1926; C. 118—An Act Authorizing the use of the funds of any tribe of Indians for payments of insurance premiums for protection of the property of the tribe against fire, theft, tornado, and hail. 25 U. S. C. 123a.

44 St. 251; April 14, 1926; C. 138—An Act Authorizing the Secretary of the Interior to acquire land and erect a monument on the site of the battle with the Sioux Indians in which the commands of Major Reno and Major Benteen were engaged.[56] Sec. 1—16 U. S. C. 427; Sec. 2—16 U. S. C. 427a.

44 St. 251; Apr. 14, 1926; C. 139—An Act Authorizing the payment of tuition of Crow Indian children attending Montana State public schools.[57]

44 St. 252; Apr. 14, 1926; C. 141—An Act Providing for repairs, improvements, and new buildings at the Seneca Indian School at Wyandotte, Oklahoma.[58]

44 St. 252; Apr. 14, 1926; C. 142—An Act To authorize the Secretary of the Interior to purchase certain land in California to be added to the Cahuilla Indian Reservation and authorizing an appropriation of funds therefor.

44 St. 254; Apr. 15, 1926; C. 146—An Act Making appropriations for the military and nonmilitary activities of the War Department for the fiscal year ending June 30, 1927, and for other purposes.

44 St. 300; Apr. 17, 1926; C. 156—An Act To authorize the leasing for mining purposes of land reserved for Indian agency and school purposes. 25 U. S. C. 400a.

44 St. 303; Apr. 19, 1926; C. 165—An Act Authorizing an appropriation of not more than $3,000 from the tribal funds of the Indians of the Quinaielt Reservation, Washington, for the construction of a system of water supply at Taholah on said reservation.[59]

44 St. 303; Apr. 19, 1926; C. 166—An Act To appropriate certain tribal funds for the benefit of the Indians of the Fort Peck and Blackfeet Reservations.[60]

44 St. 305; Apr. 22, 1926; C. 171—An Act Making appropriations for the Executive Office and sundry independent executive bureaus, boards, commissions, and offices for the fiscal year ending June 30, 1927, and for other purposes.

44 St. 330; Apr. 29, 1926; C. 195—An Act Making appropriations for the Departments of State and Justice and for the Judiciary, and for the Departments of Commerce and Labor, for the fiscal year ending June 30, 1927, and for other purposes.[61]

44 St. 453; May 10, 1926; C. 277—An Act Making appropriations for the Department of the Interior for the fiscal year ending June 30, 1927, and for other purposes.[62] Sec. 1—43 U. S. C. 47.

44 St. 496; May 10, 1926; C. 278—An Act To authorize the Secretary of the Interior to purchase certain land in Nevada to be added to the present site of the Reno Indian colony, and authorizing the appropriation of funds therefor.[63]

44 St. 496; May 10, 1926; C. 280—An Act To provide for the reservation of certain land in California for the Indians of the Mesa Grande Reservation, known also as Santa Ysabel Reservation Numbered 1.

44 St. 498; May 10, 1926; C. 282—An Act To provide for the condemnation of the lands of the Pueblo Indians in New Mexico for public purposes and making the laws of the State of New Mexico applicable in such proceedings.

44 St. 498; May 10, 1926; C. 283—Joint Resolution Authorizing expenditures from the Fort Peck 4 per centum fund for visits of tribal delegates to Washington.[64]

44 St. 537; May 13, 1926; C. 294—An Act Making appropriations for the Legislative Branch of the Government for the fiscal year ending June 30, 1927, and for other purposes.

44 St. 555; May 14, 1926; C. 300—An Act Authorizing the Chippewa Indians of Minnesota to submit claims to the Court of Claims.[65]

44 St. 558; May 17, 1926; C. 305—An Act Extending the period of time for homestead entries on the south half of the diminished Colville Indian Reservation.[66]

---

[47] *Sg.* 43 St. 537.

[48] *Sg.* 25 St. 642, sec. 7. *Cited:* Chippewa, 307 U. S. 1.

[49] *Sg.* 32 St. 636, sec. 10.

[50] *Sg.* 43 St. 477. *S.* 44 St. 841.

[51] *Sg.* 25 St. 645, sec. 7; 31 St. 179; 43 St. 599, 636, 800, 816, 819, 820, 894, 1052, 1006, 1102, 1157, 1556. *S.* 45 St. 1562.

[52] *S.* 44 St. 841; 45 St. 200; 46 St. 1115.

[53] *Sg.* Ex. Or. Feb. 27, 1925.

[54] *Ag.* 36 St. 1121; 37 St. 60; 39 St. 886. *A.* 46 St. 405.

[55] *Sg.* 34 St. 145. *Ag.* 35 St. 315. *S.* 45 St. 495. *Cited:* 2 L. D. Memo. 307; 4 L. D. Memo. 396; 4 L. D. Memo. 552; 5 L. D. Memo. 10; 12 L. D. Memo. 10; 12 L. D. Memo. 250; 12 L. D. Memo. 280; Memo. Sol. Off., Dec. 28, 1921, Aug. 17, 1931, Aug. 21, 1931, Sept. 14, 1931, Dec. 21, 1931, Feb. 5, 1934, July 9, 1934; Memo. Sol., Sept. 15, 1934, Jan. 14, 1935; Memo. Sol. Off., Mar. 8, 1935; Memo. Sol., June 4, 1935, Sept. 21, 1935; Letter of Ass't Sec'y to A. G., Oct. 15, 1936; 53 I. D. 637; Anderson, 53 F. 2d 257; Baze, 24 F. Supp. 800; Bd. of Comm'rs of Tulsa, 94 F. 2d 450; Brown, 27 F. 2d 274; Burgess, 103 F. 2d 37; Caesar, 103 F. 2d 503; Derrisaw, 8 F. Supp. 876; In re Palmer's Will, 11 F. Supp. 301; Kiker, 63 F. 2d 957; King, 94 F. 2d 979; Stewart, 295 U. S. 403; U. S. ex rel. Warren, 73 F. 2d 844; U. S. v. Mid Continent, 67 F. 2d 37; U. S. v. Watashe, 102 F. 2d 428; Whitchurch, 92 F. 2d 249.

[56] *S.* 45 St. 200.

[57] *Sg.* 41 St. 757.

[58] *S.* 44 St. 841.

[59] *S.* 44 St. 841.

[60] *Sg.* 30 St. 141.

[61] *Sg.* 36 St. 326.

[62] *Sg.* 4 St. 442; 7 St. 46, 99, 212, 218, 425; 10 St. 1109; 11 St. 614, 731; 12 St. 411; 15 St. 622, 640, 652, 669, 673, 696; 16 St. 720; 19 St. 254, 256; 24 St. 388; 25 St. 645; 26 St. 146, 1029; 27 St. 139, 644; 33 St. 189, 211; 34 St. 375; 35 St. 51; 36 St. 269, 276, 1063, 1070; 37 St. 521, 522, 934; 38 St. 604, 606; 39 St. 130, 138, 144, 974, 982, 988; 40 St. 564, 568; 41 St. 28, 415, 1107, 1357; 42 St. 568, 1192; 43 St. 376, 402, 475; 44 St. 212. *S.* 44 St. 841, 934, 1250; 45 St. 200, 1562. *Cited:* Chippewa, 80 C. Cls. 410; Op. Sol. M. 23117, Oct. 6, 1927.

[63] *S.* 44 St. 841. *Cited:* U. S. v. McGowan, 89 F. 2d 201; U. S. v. McGowan, 302 U. S. 535.

[64] *Sg.* 35 St. 563. *S.* 44 St. 1250.

[65] *Sg.* 25 St. 642. *A.* 45 St. 423; 48 St. 979; 49 St. 1272. *S.* 45 St. 601; 47 St. 337; 49 St. 1826; 52 St. 697. *Cited:* Chippewa, 305 U. S. 479; Chippewa, 307 U. S. 1; Chippewa, 301 U. S. 358; Chippewa, 305 U. S. 479; Klamath, 296 U. S. 244.

[66] *Sg.* 34 St. 80; 42 St. 507.

44 St. 560; May 17, 1926; C. 308—An Act To provide for an adequate water-supply system at the Dresslerville Indian Colony.[67]

44 St. 560; May 17, 1926; C. 309—An Act To authorize the deposit and expenditure of various revenues of the Indian Service as Indian moneys, proceeds of labor.[68] Sec. 1—25 U. S. C. 155 (22 St. 590, sec. 1; 24 St. 463).[69] See 25 U. S. C. 161b; 31 U. S. C. 725s. Sec. 2—See Historical Note 25 U. S. C. A. 155.

44 St. 561; May 17, 1926; C. 312—An Act To confirm the title to certain lands in the State of Oklahoma to the Sac and Fox Nation or Tribe of Indians.

44 St. 566; May 19, 1926; C. 337—An Act Extending the provisions of section 2455 of the United States Revised Statutes to ceded lands of the Fort Hall Indian Reservation.[70] 43 U. S. C. 1176.

44 St. 566; May 19, 1926; C. 338—An Act To allot lands to living children on the Crow Reservation, Montana.[71]

44 St. 568; May 19, 1926; C. 341—Joint Resolution Authorizing the Cherokee Indians, the Seminole Indians, the Creek Indians, and the Choctaw and Chickasaw Indians to prosecute claims, jointly or severally, in one or more petitions, as each of said Indian nations or tribes may elect.[72]

44 St. 614; May 21, 1926; C. 356—An Act To amend the second section of the Act entitled "An Act to pension the survivors of certain Indian wars from January 1, 1859, to January, 1891, inclusive, and for other purposes," approved March 4, 1917, as amended.[73] 38 U. S. C. 376.

44 St. 614; May 21, 1926; C. 357—An Act To provide for the permanent withdrawal of certain lands adjoining the Makah Indian Reservation in Washington for the use and occupancy of the Makah and Quileute Indians.

44 St. 627; May 22, 1926; C. 373—Joint Resolution Authorizing the Secretary of War to lend 350 cots, 350 bed sacks, and 700 blankets for the use of the National Custer Memorial Association, at Crow Agency, Montana, at the semi-centennial of the Battle of the Little Big Horn, June 24, 25, and 26, 1926.

44 St. 629; May 25, 1926; C. 379—An Act To authorize the issuance of deeds to certain Indians or Eskimos for tracts set apart to them in surveys of town sites in Alaska, and to provide for the survey and subdivision of such tracts and of Indian or Eskimo towns or villages.[74] Sec. 1, p. 629—48 U. S. C. 355a; Sec. 2, p. 630—48 U. S. C. 355b; Sec. 3, p. 630—48 U. S. C. 355c; Sec. 4, p. 630—48 U. S. C. 355d.

44 St. 658; May 26, 1926; C. 403—An Act To amend sections 1, 5, 6, 8, and 18 of an Act approved June 4, 1920, entitled "An Act to provide for the allotment of lands of the Crow Tribe, for the distribution of tribal funds and for other purposes."[75]

44 St. 679; June 1, 1926; C. 434—An Act To provide for the setting apart of certain lands in the State of California as an addition to the Morongo Indian Reservation.

44 St. 690; June 3, 1926; C. 458—An Act To authorize the Secretary of the Interior to purchase certain lands in California to be added to the Santa Ysabel Indian Reservation and authorizing an appropriation of funds therefor.[76]

44 St. 690; June 3, 1926; C. 459—An Act To provide for allotting in severalty lands within the Northern Cheyenne Indian Reservation in Montana, and for other purposes.[77]

44 St. 736; June 12, 1926; C. 568—An Act To provide for the distribution of the Supreme Court Reports and amending section 227 of the Judicial Code.[78] 44 U. S. C. 736–738.

44 St. 740; June 12, 1926; C. 572—Joint Resolution Authorizing the Secretary of the Interior to establish a trust fund for the Kiowa, Comanche, and Apache Indians in Oklahoma and making provision for the same.[79]

44 St. 741; June 14, 1926; C. 576—An Act To authorize the expenditure of tribal funds of the Klamath Indians to pay actual expenses of delegate to Washington, and for other purposes.

44 St. 746; June 15, 1926; C. 588—An Act For the relief of certain settlers on the Fort Peck Indian Reservation, State of Montana.[80]

44 St. 746; June 15, 1926; C. 589—An Act Authorizing expenditure of tribal funds of Indians of the Tongue River Indian Reservation, Montana, for expenses of delegates to Washington.

44 St. 761; June 23, 1926; C. 657—An Act To provide for the erection at Burns, Oregon, of a school for the use of the Piute Indian children.

44 St. 762; June 23, 1926; C. 658—An Act Authorizing an appropriation for a monument for Quannah Parker, late Chief of the Comanche Indians.[81]

44 St. 762; June 23, 1926; C. 659—An Act For completion of the road from Tucson to Ajo via Indian Oasis, Arizona.

44 St. 763; June 23, 1926; C. 661—An Act Setting aside Rice Lake and contiguous lands in Minnesota for the exclusive use and benefit of the Chippewa Indians of Minnesota.[82]

44 St. 764; June 24, 1926; C. 667—An Act To amend the Act of June 3, 1920 (41 St. 738), so as to permit the Cheyenne and Arapahoe Tribes to file suit in the Court of Claims.[83]

44 St. 768; June 24, 1926; C. 669—An Act To provide for the permanent withdrawal of Memaloose Island in the Columbia River for the use of the Yakima Indians and Confederated Tribes as a burial ground.

44 St. 771; June 26, 1926; C. 694—An Act To authorize the cancellation and remittance of construction assessments against allotted Paiute Indian lands irrigated under the Newlands reclamation project in the State of Nevada and to reimburse the Truckee-Carson irrigation district for certain expenditures for the operation and maintenance of drains for said lands.

44 St. 775; June 28, 1926; C. 701—An Act To purchase lands for addition to the Papago Indian Reservation, Arizona.[84]

44 St. 776; June 28, 1926; C. 702—An Act To authorize credit upon the construction charges of certain water-right applicants and purchasers on the Yuma and Yuma Mesa auxiliary reclamation projects, and for other purposes.[85]

44 St. 777; June 30, 1926; C. 712—An Act To consolidate, codify, and set forth the general and permanent laws of the United States in force December 7, 1925.

44 St. 801; July 2, 1926; C. 724—An Act Authorizing the Citizen Band of Pottawatomie Indians in Oklahoma to submit claims to the Court of Claims.[86]

44 St. 807; July 3, 1926; C. 734—An Act Conferring jurisdiction upon the Court of Claims to hear, examine, adjudicate, and render judgment in claims which the Crow Tribe of Indians may have against the United States, and for other purposes.[87]

44 St. 830; July 3, 1926; C. 763—An Act To authorize the transfer of surplus books from the Navy Department to the Interior Department. 34 U. S. C. 551a.

44 St. 841; July 3, 1926; C. 771—An Act Making appropriations to supply deficiencies in certain appropriations for the fiscal year ending June 30, 1926, and prior fiscal years, to provide supplemental appropriations for the fiscal years ending June 30, 1926, and June 30, 1927, and for other purposes.[88]

44 St. 888; July 3, 1926; C. 773—An Act Authorizing an expenditure of $6 000 from the tribal funds of the Chippewa Indians of Minnesota for the construction of a road on the Leech Lake Reservation.[89]

44 St. 890; July 3, 1926; C. 779—An Act To amend an Act entitled "An Act to authorize the sale of burnt timber on the

---

[67] *S.* 44 St. 841.

[68] *Ag.* 22 St. 590; 24 St. 403. *Sg.* 39 St. 159. *S.* 45 St. 200, 1562; 46 St. 279; 581, 1115; 47 St. 91, 820; 48 St. 362; 49 St. 176, 1757; 50 St. 564; 52 St. 291. *Cited:* Memo. Ind. Off., Jan. 17, 1936; Memo. Sol., Jan. 24, 1936; Comp. Gen. Op., June 30 1937; Letter of Comp. Gen. to Sec'y, July 24, 1937; U. S. v. Algoma, 305 U. S. 415.

[69] *S.* 45 St. 591, sec. 1 (69).

[70] *Sg.* 9 St. 51; 35 St. 517; 37 St. 77.

[71] *Sg.* 24 St. 388; 41 St. 751. *S.* 44 St. 841. *A.* 45 St. 482.

[72] *Sg.* 43 St. 27, 133, 139 537. *A.* 45 St. 1229. *S.* 50 St. 650. *Cited:* Choctaw, 81 C. Cls. 63; Choctaw, 81 C. Cls. 1; Choctaw, 83 C. Cls. 49; Choctaw, 83 C. Cls. 140; Creek, 63 C. Cls. 270; Creek, 77 C. Cls. 159; Creek, 77 C. Cls. 226; Creek, 78 C. Cls. 474; Seminole, 78 C. Cls. 455; U. S. v. Seminole, 299 U. S. 417.

[73] *Ag.* 42 St. 830.

[74] *Sg.* 26 St. 1099, sec. 11. *Cited:* Memo. Sol., Feb. 17, 1939.

[75] *Sg.* 24 St. 388; 41 St. 757. *Ag.* 41 St. 752, 753. *A.* 44 St. 1365. *S.* 46 St. 279, 1115; 47 St. 91. *Cited:* Op. Sol., Sept. 21, 1927; Ind. Off. Letter from Quapaw Agency Supt., Oct. 17, 1938; U. S. v. Heinrich, 16 F. 2d 112.

[76] *S.* 44 St. 841.

[77] *Sg.* 12 St. 754; 24 St. 388. *S.* 45 St. 200, 1623; 46 St. 860.

[78] *Ag.* 36 St. 1154; 42 St. 816. *A.* 45 St. 1143.

[79] *Sg.* 41 St. 437, sec. 35; 42 St. 1448. *S.* 44 St. 934, 1309; 45 St. 200 1562, 1623; 46 St. 279, 1115, 1552; 47 St. 91, 820; 48 St. 362.

[80] *Sg.* 43 St. 1067.

[81] *S.* 45 St. 200.

[82] *A.* 49 St. 496 *Cited:* U. S. v. 4,450.72 Acres, 27 F. Supp. 167.

[83] *Ag.* 41 St. 738. *A.* 45 St. 380.

[84] *S.* 45 St. 200; 46 St. 1202.

[85] *Sg.* 36 St. 895, 930; 38 St. 686 *A.* 45 St. 1321.

[86] *Sg.* 15 St. 531. *Cited:* Klamath, 296 U. S. 244.

[87] *Sg.* 15 St. 649; 18 St. 28; 1 Kappler 855 (Ex. Or. July 2, 1873). *S.* 44 St. 922; 49 St. 635. *Cited:* Klamath, 296 U. S. 244; Crow, 81 C. Cls. 238.

[88] *Sg.* 43 St. 475; 44 St. 135, 211, 252, 303, 453, 496, 560, 566, 690, 779, 1483, 1485. *S.* 45 St. 200, 883.

[89] *Sg.* 25 St. 642, sec. 7.

public domain," approved March 4, 1913."[90] Sec. 1—16 U. S. C. 614; Sec. 2—16 U. S. C. 615.

44 St. 894; July 3, 1926; C. 787—An Act To authorize the leasing of unallotted irrigable land on Indian reservations. 25 U. S. C. 402a.

44 St. 902; July 3, 1926; C. 797—An Act To authorize an industrial appropriation from the tribal funds of the Indians of the Fort Belknap Reservation, Montana, and for other purposes.

44 St. 922; Dec. 15, 1926; C. 9—An Act Authorizing an expenditure of tribal funds of the Crow Indians of Montana to employ counsel to represent them in their claims against the United States.[91]

44 St. 922; Dec. 16, 1926; C. 12—An Act To amend paragraphs 1 and 2 of section 26 of the Act of June 30, 1919, entitled "An Act making appropriations for the current and contingent expenses of the Bureau of Indian Affairs, for fulfilling treaty stipulations with various Indian tribes, and for other purposes, for the fiscal year ending June 30, 1920."[92] 25 U. S. C. 309 (41 St. 31, s. 26; 41 St. 1231, s. 1).

44 St. 932; Jan. 5, 1927; C. 22—An Act To grant to the State of New York and the Seneca Nation of Indians jurisdiction over the taking of fish and game within the Allegany, Cattaraugus, and Oil Spring Indian Reservations.

44 St. 934; Jan. 12, 1927; C. 27—An Act Making appropriations for the Department of the Interior for the fiscal year ending June 30, 1928, and for other purposes.[93] p. 936, s. 1—25 U. S. C. 93 (36 St. 861, sec. 23; 39 St. 126, sec. 1); p. 939, s. 1—25 U. S. C. 147; 25 U. S. C. 148.

44 St. 1061; Feb. 8, 1927; C. 78—An Act To authorize reimposition and extension of the trust period on lands held for the use and benefit of the Capitan Grande Band of Indians in California.[94]

44 St. 1069; Feb. 11, 1927; C. 104—An Act Making appropriations for the Executive Office and sundry independent executive bureaus, boards, commissions, and offices for the fiscal year ending June 30, 1928, and for other purposes

44 St. 1089; Feb. 12, 1927; C. 112—An Act To authorize an appropriation for the purchase of certain privately owned land within the Jicarilla Indian Reservation, New Mexico.[95]

44 St. 1098; Feb. 14, 1927; C. 138—An Act To authorize an appropriation for reconnaissance work in conjunction with the Middle Rio Grande Conservancy District to determine whether certain lands of the Cochiti, Santo Domingo, San Felipe, Santa Ana, Sandia, and Isleta Indians are susceptible of reclamation, drainage, and irrigation.[96]

44 St. 1106; Feb. 23, 1927; C. 167—An Act Making appropriations for the military and nonmilitary activities of the War Department for the fiscal year ending June 30, 1928, and for other purposes.

44 St. 1146; Feb. 23, 1927; C. 168—An Act Making appropriations for the Legislative Branch of the Government for the fiscal year ending June 30, 1928, and for other purposes.

44 St. 1178; Feb. 24, 1927; C. 189—An Act Making appropriations for the Departments of State and Justice and for the Judiciary, and for the Departments of Commerce and Labor, for the fiscal year ending June 30, 1928, and for other purposes.[97]

44 St. 1247; Feb. 26, 1927; C. 215—An Act To authorize the cancellation, under certain conditions, of patents in fee simple to Indians for allotments held in trust by the United States,[98] 25 U. S. C. 352a; 25 U. S. C. 352b.[99]

44 St. 1249; Feb. 28, 1927; C. 225—An Act For the promotion of certain officers of the United States Army now on the retired list.

44 St. 1250; Feb. 28, 1927; C. 226—An Act Making appropriations to supply urgent deficiencies in certain appropriations for the fiscal year ending June 30, 1927, and prior fiscal years, and to provide urgent supplemental appropriations for the fiscal year ending June 30, 1927, and for other purposes.[1]

44 St. 1263; Mar. 2, 1927; C. 259—An Act Conferring jurisdiction upon the Court of Claims to hear, examine, adjudicate, and enter judgment in any claims which the Assiniboine Indians may have against the United States, and for other purposes.[2]

44 St. 1347; Mar. 3, 1927; C. 299—An Act To authorize oil and gas mining leases upon unallotted lands within Executive order Indian reservations.[3] Sec. 1—25 U. S. C. 398a; Sec. 2—25 U. S. C. 398b; Sec. 3—25 U. S. C. 398c; Sec. 4—25 U. S. C. 398d; Sec. 5—25 U. S. C. 298e.

44 St. 1349; Mar. 3, 1927; C. 302—An Act Authorizing the Shoshone Tribe of Indians of the Wind River Reservation in Wyoming to submit claims to the Court of Claims.[4]

44 St. 1358; Mar. 3, 1927; C. 314—An Act To amend the last paragraph of an Act entitled "An Act to refer the claims of the Delaware Indians to the Court of Claims, with the right of appeal to the Supreme Court of the United States."[5]

44 St. 1361; Mar. 3, 1927; C. 320—An Act Granting pensions to certain soldiers who served in the Indian wars from 1817 to 1898, and for other purposes.[6] Sec. 1, p. 1361—38 U. S. C. 381; Sec. 2, p. 1362—38 U. S. C. 381a; Sec. 3, p. 1363—38 U. S. C. 381b; Sec. 4, p. 1363—38 U. S. C. 381c; Sec. 5, p. 1363—38 U. S. C. 381d.

44 St. 1365; Mar. 3, 1927; C. 325—An Act To amend section 1 of the Act approved May 26, 1926, entitled "An Act to amend sections 1, 5, 6, 8, and 18 of an Act approved June 4, 1920, entitled 'An Act to provide for the allotment of lands of the Crow Tribe, for the distribution of tribal funds, and for other purposes.'"[7]

44 St. 1369; Mar. 3, 1927; C. 328—An Act To provide a water system for the Indians of the Reno-Sparks Indian Colony, Nevada.[8]

44 St. 1369; Mar. 3, 1927; C. 329; An Act To authorize a per capita payment from tribal funds to the Kiowa, Comanche, and Apache Indians of Oklahoma.[9]

44 St. 1370; Mar. 3, 1927; C. 334—An Act Granting the consent of Congress to the city of Fort Smith, Sebastian County, Arkansas, to construct, maintain, and operate a dam across the Poteau River

44 St. 1389; Mar. 3, 1927; C. 357—An Act To authorize the purchase of land for an addition to the United States Indian school farm near Phoenix, Arizona.[10]

44 St. 1389; Mar. 3, 1927; C. 358—An Act To authorize per capita payments to the Indians of the Cheyenne River Reservation, South Dakota.[11]

44 St. 1397; Mar. 3, 1927; C. 369—An Act To authorize a per capita payment from tribal funds to the Fort Hall Indians.[12]

44 St. 1398; Mar. 3, 1927; C. 371—An Act For the irrigation of additional lands within the Fort Hall Indian irrigation project in Idaho.[13]

44 St. 1401; Mar. 3, 1927; C. 376—An Act To amend the Act entitled "An Act for the survey and allotment of lands now embraced within the limits of the Fort Peck Indian Reservation, in the State of Montana, and the sale and disposal of all the surplus lands after allotment," approved May 30, 1908, as amended, and for other purposes.[14]

44 St. 1452; Mar. 4, 1927; C. 513—An Act To provide for the protection, development, and utilization of the public lands in Alaska by establishing an adequate system for grazing

---

90 *Ag.* 37 St. 1015.

91 *Sg.* 44 St. 808. *Cited:* Memo. Sol., Mar. 12, 1936.

92 *Ag.* 41 St. 31, sec. 26.

93 *Sg.* 4 St. 442; 7 St. 90, 212, 213, 236, 425, 443; 10 St. 1109; 11 St. 614, 731; 12 St. 411; 15 St. 622, 640, 652, 669, 673, 696; 16 St. 720; 19 St. 254, 256; 24 St. 388; 25 St. 645; 26 St. 1020; 27 St. 139, 644; 34 St. 325; 36 St. 273, 276, 1063; 37 St. 521, 522, sec. 2; 934; 38 St. 80, 582, 604, 606; 39 St. 130, 982; 40 St. 564, sec. 1; 590; 41 St. 28, 415, 1107; 43 St. 376, 475; 44 St. 212, 463, 464, 469, 740. *Rp.* 45 St. 986. *S.* 45 St. 200, 1562; 46 St. 90. *Cited:* Op. Sol., M. 23117, Oct. 6, 1927; Chippewa, 80 C. Cls. 410; U. S. v. Seminole, 299 U. S. 417.

94 *Sg.* 26 St. 712; 30 St. 976.

95 *S.* 45 St. 200.

96 *S.* 45 St. 312. *Cited:* Op. Sol., M. 28108, Mar. 18, 1936.

97 *Sg.* 36 St. 326; 43 St. 636.

98 *A.* 46 St. 1205. *Cited:* 12 L. D. Memo. 652; Op. Sol., Aug. 18, 1932; Memo. Sol. Off., Mar. 8, 1933; 54 I. D. 160; Bd. of Comm'rs of Caddo Co., 87 F. 2d 55; U. S. v. Bd. of Co. Comm'rs, 13 F. Supp. 611; U. S. v. Ferry, 24 F. Supp. 399; U. S. v. Gracier, 17 F. Supp. 411; U. S. v. Lewis, 95 F. 2d 236; U. S. v. Nez Perce, 95 F. 2d 232.

99 *A.* 46 St. 1205.

1 *Sg.* 35 St. 559; 44 St. 453, 475, 498. *Cited:* 52 L. D. 825.

2 *Sg.* 11 St. 637, 749 *S.* 46 St. 531. *A.* 46 St. 531. *Cited:* Assiniboine, 77 C. Cls. 347; Klamath, 296 U. S. 244.

3 *Sg.* 43 St. 244. *S.* 49 St. 217. *Cited:* Brown, 39 Yale L. J. 307; 69th Cong., 1st sess., Sen. Rept. No. 1019; 69th Cong., 1st sess., Sen. Rept. No. 1131; 14 L. D. Memo. 493; Memo. Sol., Sept. 17, 1934; Memo. Sol. Off., Aug. 20, 1935; Op. Sol., M. 27878, May 20, 1936; Memo. Sol. Off., Oct. 22, 1936; Memo. Sol., Jan. 12, 1937; 56 I. D. 110; British-American, 299 U. S. 159.

4 *Sg.* 15 St. 673. *Cited:* Klamath, 296 U. S. 244; Shoshone, 85 C. Cls. 331; Shoshone, 82 C. Cls. 23; U. S. v. Shoshone, 304 U. S. 111.

5 *Ag.* 43 St. 813. *A.* 49 St. 1459. *Cited:* Delaware, 72 C. Cls. 483; Delaware, 74 C. Cls. 368; Delaware, 84 C. Cls. 535.

6 *Sg.* 27 St. 281; 37 St. 679; 39 St. 1199. *A.* 50 St. 786. *S.* 46 St. 144.

7 *Ag.* 44 St. 659, sec. 1. *Cited:* Op. Sol., Sept. 21, 1927.

8 *S.* 45 St. 200.

9 *Sg.* 44 St. 740.

10 *Sg.* 5 St. 468.

11 *Sg.* 35 St. 463.

12 *Sg.* 43 St. 118.

13 *Sg.* 42 St. 568. *S.* 45 St. 200. *Cited:* Memo. Sol. Off., July 10, 1933.

14 *Ag.* 35 St. 558. *Sg.* 35 St. 500, 504. *S.* 45 St. 774.

livestock thereon. Sec. 13, p. 1454—48 U. S. C. 471–1; Sec. 16, p. 1455—48 U. S. C. 471–o.

44 St. 1475; May 17, 1926; C. 325—An Act For the relief of Ivy L. Merrill.

44 St. 1483; May 29, 1926; C. 427—An Act For the relief of O. H. Lipps.

44 St. 1485; May 29, 1926; C. 432—An Act For the relief of Gagnon and Company, Incorporated.[15]

44 St. 1487; June 1, 1926; C. 443—An Act For the relief of R. P. Rueth, of Chamita, New Mexico.

44 St. 1584; June 17, 1926; C. 606—An Act Granting pensions and increase of pensions to certain soldiers and sailors of the Regular Army and Navy, and so forth, and certain soldiers and sailors of wars other than the Civil War, and to widows of such soldiers and sailors.

44 St. 1593; June 17, 1926; C. 607—An Act Granting pensions and increase of pensions to certain soldiers and sailors of the Regular Army and Navy, and certain soldiers and sailors of wars other than the Civil War, and to widows of such soldiers and sailors.

44 St. 1609; June 18, 1926; C. 620—An Act Authorizing the enrollment of Martha E. Brace as a Kiowa Indian, and directing issuance of trust patents to her and two others to certain land of the Kiowa Indian Reservation, Oklahoma.

44 St. 1704; July 3, 1926; C. 824—An Act For the relief of Sam Tilden.

44 St. 1706; July 3, 1926; C. 830—An Act For the relief of Lewis J. Burshia.

44 St. 1746; July 3, 1926; C. 852—An Act For the relief of certain Indian policemen in the Territory of Alaska.

44 St. 1747; July 3, 1926; C. 854—An Act For the relief of Archie Eggleston, an Indian of the former Isabella Reservation, Michigan.[16]

44 St. 1774; Feb. 17, 1927; C. 158—An Act Granting pensions and increase of pensions to certain soldiers and sailors of the Regular Army and Navy, and certain soldiers and sailors of wars other than the Civil War, and to widows of such soldiers and sailors, and so forth.

44 St. 1795; Feb. 28, 1927; C. 234—An Act For the relief of Joseph B. Tanner.

44 St. 1811; Mar. 3, 1927; C. 423—An Act For the relief of John Ferrell.

44 St. 1813; Mar. 3, 1927; C. 428—An Act Granting pensions and increase of pensions to certain soldiers and sailors of the Regular Army and Navy, and certain soldiers and sailors of wars other than the Civil War, and to widows of such soldiers and sailors, and so forth.

45 STAT.

45 St. 2; Dec. 22, 1927; C. 5—An Act Making appropriations to supply deficiencies in certain appropriations for the fiscal year ending June 30, 1928, and prior fiscal years, to provide supplemental appropriations for the fiscal year ending June 30, 1928, and for other purposes.[17]

45 St. 64; Feb. 15, 1928; C. 57—An Act Making appropriations for the Department of State and Justice and for the Judiciary, and for the Departments of Commerce and Labor, for the fiscal year ending June 30, 1929, and for other purposes.[18]

45 St. 159; Feb. 29, 1928; C. 116—An Act To authorize appropriation of treaty funds due the Wisconsin Pottawatomie Indians.[19]

45 St. 160; Mar. 3, 1928; C. 120—An Act To provide for the withdrawal of certain described lands in the State of Nevada for the use and benefit of the Indians of the Walker River Reservation.

45 St. 160; Mar. 3, 1928; C. 121—An Act To provide for the permanent withdrawal of certain lands bordering on and adjacent to Summit Lake, Nevada, for the Paiute, Shoshone, and other Indians.

45 St. 161; Mar. 3, 1928; C. 122—An Act To amend section 1 of the Act of June 25, 1910 (36 St. 855), "An Act to provide for determining the heirs of deceased Indians, for the disposition and sale of allotments of deceased Indians, for the leasing of allotments, and for other purposes."[20] 25 U. S. C. 372 (36 St. 855, sec. 1; 48 St. 647).[21]

45 St. 162; Mar. 3, 1928; C. 123—An Act To reserve 120 acres on the public domain for the use and benefit of the Koosharem Band of Indians residing in the vicinity of Koosharem, Utah.

45 St. 162; Mar. 3, 1928; C. 124—An Act To provide for the permanent withdrawal of certain lands in Inyo County, California, for Indian use.

45 St. 200; Mar. 7, 1928; C. 137—An Act Making appropriations for the Department of the Interior for the fiscal year ending June 30, 1929, and for other purposes.[22] Sec. 1, p. 206—25 U. S. C. 358. Sec. 1, p. 210—25 U. S. C. 387.[23] Sec. 1—p. 215—25 U. S. C. 292a (44 St. 468; 44 St. 947, sec. 1).[24]

45 St. 299; Mar. 10, 1928; C. 186—An Act To amend an Act entitled "An Act for the relief of Indians occupying railroad lands in Arizona, New Mexico, or California," approved March 4, 1913.[25]

45 St. 312; Mar. 13, 1928; C. 219—An Act Authorizing the Secretary of the Interior to execute an agreement with the Middle Rio Grande Conservancy District providing for conservation, irrigation, drainage, and flood control for the Pueblo Indian lands in the Rio Grande Valley, New Mexico, and for other purposes.[26]

45 St. 314; Mar. 15, 1928; C. 222—An Act Providing for a per capita payment of $25 to each enrolled member of the Chippewa Tribe of Minnesota from the funds standing to their credit in the Treasury of the United States.[27]

45 St. 326; Mar. 23, 1928; C. 232—An Act Making appropriations for the military and nonmilitary activities of the War Department for the fiscal year ending June 30, 1929, and for other purposes.

45 St. 366; Mar. 26, 1928; C. 246—An Act To authorize an appropriation for the construction of a road on the Lummi Indian Reservation, Washington.

45 St. 366; Mar. 26, 1928; C. 247—An Act Authorizing the Secretary of the Interior to purchase certain lands in the city of Bismarck, Burleigh County, North Dakota, for Indian school purposes.[28]

45 St. 371; Mar. 27, 1928; C. 253—An Act To amend section 2 of the Act of March 3, 1905, entitled "An Act to ratify and amend an agreement with the Indians residing on the Shoshone or Wind River Indian Reservation, in the State of Wyoming, and to make appropriations to carry the same into effect."[29]

45 St. 372; Mar. 27, 1928; C. 255—An Act To provide for the protection of the watershed within the Carson National Forest from which water is obtained for the Taos Pueblo, New Mexico.

45 St. 375; Mar. 28, 1928; C. 267—An Act To provide for the construction of a hospital at the Fort Bidwell Indian School, California.[30]

45 St. 375; Mar. 28, 1928; C. 268—An Act To provide for the construction of a school building at the Fort Bidwell Indian School, California.[31]

45 St. 377; Mar. 28, 1928; C. 271—An Act Authorizing an appropriation for the survey and investigation of the placing of water on the Michaud division and other lands in the Fort Hall Indian Reservation.[32]

45 St. 378; Mar. 28, 1928; C. 272—An Act To provide funds for the

---

[15] *Sg.* 44 St. 856.
[16] *S.* 45 St. 200.
[17] *S.* 45 St. 200. 1550; 46 St. 90. *Cited:* 54 I. D. 207.
[18] *Sg.* 36 St. 326; 43 St. 636. *S.* 45 St. 883.
[19] *Sg.* 7 St. 442; 13 St. 172; 38 St. 102; 39 St. 156; 40 St. 580; 41 St. 29. *S.* 45 St. 883.
[20] *Ag.* 36 St. 855, sec. 1.
[21] *A.* 48 St. 647.
[22] *Sg.* 4 St. 442; 7 St. 46, 99, 212, 213, 236, 425; 10 St. 1109; 11 St. 614, 731; 12 St. 441, sec. 1; 15 St. 622, 640, 652, 675, 676, 696; 16 St. 720; 19 St. 254, 256; 24 St. 388; 25 St. 645, 895; 26 St. 795, 1029; 27 St. 139, 644; 28 St. 678; 33 St. 214; 35 St. 312, 783, 787; 36 St. 273, 281, 1063; 37 St. 521, 522, 934; 38 St. 85, 102, 582, 588, 589, 606, 609; 39 St. 144; 40 St. 564; 41 St. 28, 415, 1107, 1242; 42 St. 990, 1051; 43 St. 93, 376, 423, 475, 596, 606, 1149, 1156, 1162; 44 St. 211, 464, 560, 660, 740, 762, 775, 836, 938, 942, 945, 946, 1089, 1369, 1398, 1747; 45 St. 2. *Rpg.* 24 St. 388. *Rg.* 30 St. 152. *S.* 45 St. 401, 883, 1562, 1623; 46 St. 90, 279, 1115, 1552; 47 St. 820; 49 St. 176. *Cited:* Op. Sol., M. 25347, Jan. 25, 1930; Letter by Sec. of Int. to Comp. Gen., Sept. 28, 1932; Memo. Sol. Off., June 20, 1933, July 21, 1933, Feb. 21, 1935; Memo. Sol., Sept. 3, 1936; Chippewa, 80 C. Cls. 410; Shoshone, 85 C. Cls. 331; U. S. v. Seminole, 299 U. S. 417.
[23] *S.* 45 St. 1573, sec. 1; 46 St. 290, sec. 1; 46 St. 1126, sec. 1; 47 St. 100, sec. 1; 829, sec. 1; 48 St. 870, sec. 1; 49 St. 186, sec. 1; 1769, sec. 1; 50 St. 577, sec. 1; 52 St. 304, sec. 1; 53 St. 700, sec. 1.
[24] *S.* 45 St. 1576, sec. 1.
[25] *Sg.* 37 St. 1007; 39 St. 48; 41 St. 9; 42 St. 994; 43 St. 795.
[26] *Sg.* 44 St. 1098. *S.* 45 St. 883, 1623; 46 St. 90, 1115, 1552; 47 St. 91; 48 St. 1021; 49 St. 176, 887; 52 St. 291. *Cited:* 70th Cong., 1st sess., H. Doc. No. 141; 75th Cong., 3d sess., Sen. Rept. No. 1986; Op. Sol., M. 27512, Feb. 20, 1935; M. 28108, Mar. 18, 1936.
[27] *Sg.* 25 St. 645.
[28] *S.* 45 St. 883.
[29] *Ag.* 33 St. 1021; 34 St. 825; 35 St. 650.
[30] *S.* 45 St. 883.
[31] *S.* 45 St. 883.
[32] *S.* 45 St. 883.

upkeep of the Puyallup Indian Cemetery at Tacoma. Washington.[33]

45 St. 380; Mar. 29, 1928; C. 278—An Act For the relief of the Arapahoe and Cheyenne Indians, and for other purposes.[34]

45 St. 380; Mar. 29, 1928; C. 279—An Act To authorize the cancellation of the balance due on a reimbursable agreement for the sale of cattle to certain Rosebud Indians.[35]

45 St. 400; Mar. 31, 1928; C. 305—An Act To amend the Act of April 25, 1922, as amended, entitled "An Act authorizing extensions of time for the payment of purchase money due under certain homestead entries and Government-land purchases within the former Cheyenne River and Standing Rock Indian Reservations, North Dakota and South Dakota."[36]

45 St. 401; Apr. 2, 1928; C. 307—An Act To authorize the construction of a dormitory at Riverside Indian School at Anadarko, Oklahoma.[37]

45 St. 401; Apr. 2, 1928; C. 308—An Act To exempt American Indians born in Canada from the operation of the Immigration Act of 1924. 8 U. S. C. 226a.

45 St. 401; Apr. 2, 1928; C. 310—Joint Resolution To make immediately available the appropriation for a road across the Kaibab Indian Reservation.[38]

45 St. 413; Apr. 10, 1928; C. 335—An Act To provide for cooperation by the Smithsonian Institution with State, educational, and scientific organizations in the United States for continuing ethnological researches on the American Indians.[39] Sec. 1, p. 413—20 U. S. C. 69. Sec. 2, p. 413—20 U. S. C. 70.

45 St. 423; Apr. 11, 1928; C. 357—An Act Amending an Act entitled "An Act authorizing the Chippewa Indians of Minnesota to submit claims to the Court of Claims."[40]

45 St. 429; Apr. 14, 1928; C. 374—An Act To authorize an appropriation from tribal funds to pay part of the cost of the construction of a road on the Crow Indian Reservation. Montana.[41]

45 St. 442; Apr. 21, 1928; C. 400—An Act To provide for the acquisition of rights of way through the lands of the Pueblo Indians of New Mexico.[42] 25 U. S. C. 322.

45 St. 467; Apr. 28, 1928; C. 452—An Act To authorize a per capita payment to the Shoshone and Arapahoe Indians of Wyoming from funds held in trust for them by the United States.[43]

45 St. 482; May 2, 1928; C. 481—An Act To amend an Act to allot lands to children on the Crow Reservation. Montana.[44]

45 St. 484; May 3, 1928; C. 487—An Act Authorizing and directing the Secretary of the Interior to investigate, hear, and determine the claims of individual members of the Sioux Tribe of Indians against tribal funds or against the United States.[45]

45 St. 492; May 7, 1928; C. 506—An Act Authorizing the appropriation of $2,500 for the erection of a tablet or marker at Medicine Lodge, Kansas, to commemorate the holding of the Indian peace council, at which treaties were made with the Plains Indians in October, 1867.

45 St. 493; May 8, 1928; C. 510—An Act To amend the proviso of the Act approved August 24, 1912, with reference to educational leave to employees of the Indian Service.[46] 25 U. S. C. 275 (37 St. 519, sec. 1; 42 St. 829).

45 St. 495; May 10, 1928; C. 517—An Act To extend the period of restriction in lands of certain members of the Five Civilized Tribes, and for other purposes.[47]

[33] *Sg.* 27 St. 633. *S.* 45 St. 883.
[34] *Ag.* 44 St. 764.
[35] *Sg.* 41 St. 26.
[36] *Ag.* 42 St. 490; 43 St. 1184. *A.* 46 St. 1107.
[37] *S.* 45 St. 883.
[38] *Sg.* 45 St. 225.
[39] *S.* 45 St. 883.
[40] *Ag.* 44 St. 555. *S.* 47 St. 337; 52 St. 697. *Cited:* Chippewa, 305 U. S. 479; Chippewa, 305 U. S. 479; Chippewa, 307 U. S. 1.
[41] *S.* 45 St. 883.
[42] *Sg.* 18 St. 482; 30 St. 990; 31 St. 1083; 32 St. 50; 33 St. 65; 34 St. 330; 36 St. 850; 39 St. 973.
[43] *Sg.* 39 St. 519.
[44] *Sg.* 24 St. 388. *Ag.* 44 St. 566.
[45] *S.* 46 St. 279, 1115; 47 St. 818, 1602; 49 St. 340; 50 St. 441.
[46] *Ag.* 37 St. 519; 42 St. 829.
[47] *Sg.* 34 St. 137; 35 St. 312; 44 St. 239. *Rpg.* 44 St. 239. *A.* 45 St. 733; 46 St. 1108; 49 St. 1160. *S.* 47 St. 777. *Cited:* 12 L. D. Memo. 280; Memo. Sol. Off. Dec. 28, 1921; Op. Sol. M. 25258, June 26, 1929; Memo. Sol. Off., Sept. 14, 1931, Dec. 21, 1931; Op. Sol., M. 27158, Aug. 5, 1932; Memo. Sol. Off., June 14, 1933, June 29, 1933, Sept. 19, 1933, Jan. 14, 1935; Memo. Sol., June 4, 1935; Letter of Ass't Sec'y to A. G., Oct. 15, 1936; Memo. Sol., Jan. 13, 1937, Jan. 23, 1937, May 14, 1938; 53 I. D. 48; 53 I. D. 471; 53 I. D. 502; 53 I. D. 637; 54 I. D. 382; Bond, 25 F. Supp. 157; Burgess, 103 F. 2d 37; Caesar, 103 F. 2d 503; Carpenter, 280 U. S. 363; Glenn, 105 F. 2d 398; King, 64 F. 2d 979; U. S. v. Equitable, 283 U. S. 938; U. S. v. Watashe, 102 F. 2d 428; Whitchurch, 92 F. 2d 249.

45 St. 497; May 11, 1928; C. 519—An Act Authorizing a per capita payment to the Rosebud Sioux Indians, South Dakota.

45 St. 500; May 12, 1928; C. 528—An Act To provide for the gratuitous issue of service medals and similar devices, for the replacement of the same, and for other purposes.

45 St. 501; May 12, 1928; C. 531—An Act To Authorize an appropriation for a road on the Zuni Indian Reservation, New Mexico.[48]

45 St. 517; May 14, 1928; C. 551—An Act Making appropriations for the Legislative Branch of the Government for the fiscal year ending June 30, 1929, and for other purposes.

45 St. 539; May 16, 1928; C. 572—An Act Making appropriations for the Department of Agriculture for the fiscal year ending June 30, 1929, and for other purposes.[49]

45 St. 573; May 16, 1928; C. 580—An Act Making appropriations for the Executive Office and sundry independent executive bureaus, boards, commissions, and offices, for the fiscal year ending June 30, 1929, and for other purposes.

45 St. 589; May 16, 1928; C. 582—An Act To authorize an appropriation to pay half the cost of a bridge and road on the Hoopa Valley Reservation, California.[50]

45 St. 600; May 17, 1928; C. 614—An Act To change the boundaries of the Tule River Indian Reservation, California.

45 St. 601; May 18, 1928; C. 623—An Act To confer additional jurisdiction upon the Court of Claims under an Act entitled "An Act authorizing the Chippewa Indians of Minnesota to submit claims to the Court of Claims," approved May 14, 1926.[51]

45 St. 602; May 18, 1928; C. 624—An Act Authorizing the attorney general of the State of California to bring suit in the Court of Claims on behalf of the Indians of California.[52]

45 St. 617; May 21, 1928; C 644—An Act to authorize allotments to unallotted Indians on the Shoshone or Wind River Reservation, Wyoming.[53]

45 St. 617; May 21, 1928; C. 645—An Act Authorizing the construction of a fence along the east boundary of the Papago Indian Reservation, Arizona.

45 St. 618; May 21, 1928; C. 646—An Act For the purchase of land in the vicinity of Winnemucca, Nevada, for an Indian colony, and for other purposes.[54]

45 St. 621; May 21, 1928; C. 652—An Act Withdrawing from entry the northwest quarter section 12, township 30 north, range 19 east, Montana Meridian.

45 St. 684; May 21, 1928; C. 662—An Act To continue the allowance of Sioux benefits.[55]

45 St. 684; May 21, 1928; C. 663—An Act To set aside certain lands for the Chippewa Indians in the State of Minnesota.

45 St. 711; May 22, 1928; C. 686—An Act To add certain lands to the Montezuma National Forest, Colorado, and for other purposes.[56]

45 St. 717; May 23, 1928; C. 707—An Act To reserve certain lands on the public domain in Valencia County, New Mexico, for the use and benefit of the Acoma Pueblo Indians.[57]

45 St. 733; May 24, 1928; Ch. 733—An Act To amend section 4 of the Act entitled "An Act to extend the period of restrictions in lands of certain members of the Five Civilized Tribes, and for other purposes," approved May 10, 1928.[58]

45 St. 737; May 25, 1928; C. 741—An Act To provide for the extension of the time of certain mining leases of the coal and asphalt deposits in the segregated mineral land of the Choctaw and Chickasaw Nations, and to permit an extension of time to the purchasers of the coal and asphalt deposits within the segregated mineral lands of the said nations to complete payments of the purchase price, and for other purposes.[59]

45 St. 747; May 26, 1938; C. 753—An Act To authorize a per capita payment to the Pine Ridge Sioux Indians of South Dakota.

45 St. 750; May 26, 1928; C. 756—An Act To authorize an ap-

[48] *S.* 45 St. 883.
[49] *Sg.* 43 St. 739. *Cited:* Memo. Sol., June 9, 1936.
[50] *S.* 45 St. 883.
[51] *Sg.* 44 St. 555. *Cited:* Chippewa, 301 U. S. 358.
[52] *Sg.* 9 St. 631. *A.* 46 St. 259. *S.* 45 St. 1023; 46 St. 90, 279, 1115; 47 St. 15. *Cited:* Op. Sol., M. 25909, July 8, 1930; Memo. Sol., Apr. 19, 1933; Memo. Sol. Off., Apr. 21, 1933.
[53] *Sg.* 24 St. 388. *S.* 45 St. 883, 1023; 46 St. 90.
[54] *S.* 45 St. 883.
[55] *Sg.* 25 St. 894; 29 St. 334; 35 St. 451.
[56] *Sg.* 21 St. 199.
[57] *Cited:* Memo. Sol., May 12, 1936, May 19, 1936, May 25, 1936.
[58] *Ag.* 45 St. 496. *Cited:* 53 I. D. 48; 53 I. D. 471; 53 I. D. 502; 53 I. D. 637; King, 64 F. 2d 979.
[59] *Ag.* 40 St. 433; 41 St. 1107. *S.* 46 St. 885.

propriation for roads on Indian reservations.[60] 25 U. S. C. 318a.

45 St. 774; May 28, 1928; C. 811—An Act To authorize the leasing or sale of lands reserved for agency, schools, and other purposes on the Fort Peck Indian Reservation, Montana.[61]

45 St. 883; May 29, 1928; C. 853—An Act Making appropriations to supply deficiencies in certain appropriations for the fiscal year ending June 30, 1928, and prior fiscal years, to provide supplemental appropriations for the fiscal years ending June 30, 1928, and June 30, 1929, and for other purposes.[62]

45 St. 938; May 29, 1928; C. 854—An Act Authorizing the Secretary of the Interior to execute an agreement or agreements with drainage district or districts providing for drainage, and reclamation of Kootenai Indian allotments in Idaho within the exterior boundaries of such district or districts that may be benefited by the drainage and reclamation work, and for other purposes.[63]

45 St. 939; May 29, 1928; C. 855—An Act Authorizing the Secretary of the Interior to acquire land and erect a monument on the site of the battle between the Sioux and Pawnee Indian Tribes in Hitchcock County, Nebraska, fought in the year 1873.[64]

45 St. 944; May 29, 1928; C. 857—An Act Authorizing an advancement of certain funds standing to the credit of the Creek Nation in the Treasury of the United States to be paid to the attorneys for the Creek Nation, and for other purposes.[65]

45 St. 962; May 29, 1928; C. 873—An Act To authorize an appropriation for the purchase of certain privately owned lands within the Fort Apache Indian Reservation, Arizona.[66]

45 St. 973; May 29, 1928; C. 880—An Act Authorizing the Secretary of the Interior to dispose of two bridges on the San Carlos Indian Reservation, in Arizona, and for other purposes.[67]

45 St. 986; May 29, 1928; C. 901—An Act To discontinue certain reports now required by law to be made to Congress.[68] p. 989—5 U. S. C. 339, p. 989—10 U. S. C. 1287, p. 991, sec. 1 (68)—25 U. S. C. 155 (22 St. 590, sec. 1; 24 St. 463; 44 St. 560, sec. 1), p. 992, sec. 1 (81)—25 U. S. C. 127 (R. S. 2100). USCA Historical Note: R. S. 2100 was derived from sec. 2 of Act Mar. 2, 1867, 14 St. 515.

45 St. 1008; May 29, 1928; C. 912—An Act To amend an Act of March 3, 1885, entitled "An Act providing for allotment of lands in severalty to the Indians residing upon the Umatilla Reservation, in the State of Oregon, and granting patents therefor, and for other purposes."[69]

45 St. 1022; Dec. 15, 1928; C. 28—An Act To provide for issuance of perpetual easement to the department of fish and game, State of Idaho, to certain lands situated within the original boundaries of the Nez Perce Indian Reservation, State of Idaho.

45 St. 1027; Dec. 17, 1928; C. 36—An Act Conferring jurisdiction upon the Court of Claims to hear, examine, adjudicate, and enter judgment thereon in claims which the Winnebago Tribe of Indians may have against the United States, and for other purposes.[70]

45 St. 1073; Jan. 11, 1929; C. 55—Joint Resolution For the relief of the Iowa Tribe of Indians.[71]

45 St. 1080; Jan. 14, 1929; C. 70—An Act To authorize the construction of a telephone line from Flagstaff to Kayenta on the Western Navajo Indian Reservation, Arizona.[72]

45 St. 1091; Jan. 19, 1929; C. 87—An Act To provide for the acquisition by Parker I-See-O Post Numbered 12, All American Indian Legion, Lawton, Oklahoma, of the east half northeast quarter northeast quarter northwest quarter of section 20, township 2 north, range 11 west, Indian meridian, in Comanche County, Oklahoma.

45 St. 1094; Jan. 25, 1929; C. 101—An Act Declaring the purpose of Congress in passing the Act of June 2, 1924 (43 St. 253), to confer full citizenship upon the Eastern Band of Cherokee Indians, and further declaring that it was not the purpose of Congress in passing the Act of June 4, 1924 (43 St. 376), to repeal, abridge, or modify the provisions of the former Act as to the citizenship of said Indians.[73]

45 St. 1094; Jan. 25, 1929; C. 102—An Act Making appropriations for the Departments of State and Justice and for the Judiciary, and for the Departments of Commerce and Labor, for the fiscal year ending June 30, 1930, and for other purposes.[74]

45 St. 1143; Jan. 29, 1929; C. 113—An Act To amend section 227 of the Judicial Code.[75] 28 U. S. C. 334.

45 St. 1155; Feb. 7, 1929; C. 161—An Act To amend section 8 of Public Act numbered 230 (37 St. 194).[76]

45 St. 1161; Feb. 11, 1929; C. 174—An Act To reserve certain lands on the public domain in Santa Fe County, New Mexico, for the use and benefit of the Indians of the San Ildefonso Pueblo.

45 St. 1161; Feb. 11, 1929; C. 175—An Act To reserve 920 acres on the public domain for the use and benefit of the Kanosh Band of Indians residing in the vicinity of Kanosh, Utah.

45 St. 1164; Feb. 12, 1929; C. 178—An Act To authorize the payment of interest on certain funds held in trust by the United States for Indian tribes.[77] 25 U. S. C. 161a, 161b, 161c, 161d.[78]

45 St. 1167; Feb. 13, 1929; C. 183—An Act Reinvesting title to certain lands in the Yankton Sioux Tribe of Indians.[79]

45 St. 1185; Feb. 15, 1929; C. 216—An Act Authorizing representatives of the several States to make certain inspections and to investigate State sanitary and health regulations and school attendance on Indian reservations, Indian tribal lands, and Indian allotments.[80] 25 U. S. C. 231.

45 St. 1186; Feb. 15, 1929; C. 218—An Act To authorize the Secretary of the Interior to purchase land for the Alabama and Coushatta Indians of Texas, subject to certain mineral and timber interests.[81]

45 St. 1189; Feb. 16, 1929; C. 227—An Act Making appropriations for the Department of Agriculture for the fiscal year ending June 30, 1930, and for other purposes.[82]

45 St. 1229; Feb. 19, 1929; C. 267—An Act To authorize an appropriation to pay half the cost of a bridge near the Soboba Indian Reservation, California.[83]

45 St. 1229; Feb. 19, 1929; J. Res. Chap. 268—Joint Resolution Authorizing an extension of time within which suits may be instituted on behalf of the Cherokee Indians, the Seminole Indians, the Creek Indians, and the Choctaw and Chickasaw Indians to June 30, 1930, and for other purposes.[84]

45 St. 1230; Feb. 20, 1929; C. 270—An Act Making appropriations for the Executive Office and sundry independent executive bureaus, boards, commissions, and offices, for the fiscal year ending June 30, 1930, and for other purposes.[85]

45 St. 1249; Feb. 20, 1929; C. 275—Act For the relief of the Nez Perce Tribe of Indians.[86]

45 St. 1252; Feb. 20, 1929; C. 279—An Act Authorizing the Secretary of the Interior to settle claims by agreement arising under operation of Indian irrigation projects.[87] 25 U. S. C. 388.

45 St. 1256; Feb. 23, 1929; C. 300—An Act Authorizing the Coos (Kowes) Bay, Lower Umpqua (Kalawatset), and Siuslaw Tribes of Indians of the State of Oregon to present their claims to the Court of Claims.[88]

45 St. 1258; Feb. 23, 1929; C. 302—An Act To amend and further extend the benefits of the Act approved March 3, 1925, en-

---

[60] *Sg.* 42 St. 212. *S.* 47 St. 709; 48 St. 993, 1021; 49 St. 176, 1519, 1757; 50 St. 564; 52 St. 291, 633.

[61] *Sg.* 35 St. 558; 44 St. 1402.

[62] *Sg.* 7 St. 442; 13 St. 172; 38 St. 102; 39 St. 156; 40 St. 589; 41 St. 20; 43 St. 475, 1141, 1152; 44 St. 856; 45 St. 78, 159, 210, 312, 377, 401, 413, 429, 447, 501, 589, 617, 618. *A.* 46 St. 276. *S.* 45 St. 1186, 1562; 46 St. 90, 279, 1115; 47 St. 91, 820; 48 St. 362.

[63] *S.* 45 St. 1562; 46 St. 279, 1115; 47 St. 91, 820.

[64] *S.* 45 St. 1562.

[65] *Sg.* 43 St. 139. *S.* 46 St. 1115. *Cited:* Creek, 79 C. Cls. 778.

[66] *S.* 45 St. 1562.

[67] *Sg.* 38 St. 85.

[68] *Rpg.* 14 St. 515; 22 St. 590; 24 St. 463, 465; 25 St. 895; 26 St. 854; 28 St. 477; 36 St. 270, 272, 277, 1060, 1061; 38 St. 584, 587, 594; 39 St. 127, 158; 42 St. 1185; 43 St. 477; 44 St. 941, 954, 955.

[69] *Ag.* 23 St. 342. *Cited:* 11 L. D. Memo. 665.

[70] *Sg.* 10 St. 1172; 12 St. 658. *Cited:* Memo. Sol., Mar. 6, 1937.

[71] *Ag.* 41 St. 585.

[72] *S.* 45 St. 1623.

[73] *Sg.* 43 St. 253, 376.

[74] *Sg.* 36 St. 326; 43 St. 636. *S.* 45 St. 1623.

[75] *Ag.* 36 St. 1154; 44 St. 736.

[76] *S.* 45 St. 1623.

[77] *A.* 46 St. 584. *S.* 49 St. 1085; 52 St. 291.

[78] *A.* 46 St. 584.

[79] *Sg.* 28 St. 286.

[80] *Cited:* Memo. Sol., July 25, 1935; 56 I. D. 88.

[81] *Sg.* 45 St. 883.

[82] *Sg.* 43 St. 739.

[83] *S.* 46 St. 279.

[84] *Sg.* 43 St. 27, 133, 139, 537; 44 St. 568. *A.* 50 St. 650. *Cited:* Chickasaw, 87 C. Cls. 91; Creek, 78 C. Cls. 474; U. S. v. Seminole, 299 U. S. 417.

[85] *Cited:* 52 L. D. 325.

[86] *Sg.* 12 St. 959; 14 St. 647; 28 St. 286, 326, 329. *A.* 48 St. 1216.

[87] *Cited:* 53 I. D. 399.

[88] *A.* 47 St. 307. *S.* 49 St. 801. *Cited:* Coos, 87 C. Cls. 143.

titled "An Act conferring jurisdiction upon the Court of Claims to hear, examine, adjudicate, and enter judgment in any and all claims, of whatever nature, which the Kansas or Kaw Tribe of Indians may have or claim to have against the United States, and for other purposes."[89]

45 St. 1307; Feb. 26, 1929; C. 323—An Act To repeal that portion of the Act of August 24, 1912, imposing a limit on agency salaries of the Indian Service.[90] 25 U. S. C. 58 (30 St. 90, sec. 1; 37 St. 88, sec. 10; 37 St. 521, sec. 1; 40 St. 578, sec. 17).

45 St. 1321; Feb. 26, 1929; C. 339—An Act To amend the Act entitled "An Act to authorize credit upon the construction charges of certain water-right applicants and purchasers on the Yuma and Yuma Mesa auxiliary projects, and for other purposes."[91]

45 St. 1344; Feb. 28, 1929; C. 359—An Act Authorizing the Federal Power Commission to issue permits and licenses on Fort Apache and White Mountain Indian Reservations, Arizona.[92]

45 St. 1349; Feb. 28, 1929; C. 366—An Act Making appropriations for the military and nonmilitary activities of the War Department for the fiscal year ending June 30, 1930, and for other purposes.

45 St. 1387; Feb. 28, 1929; C. 367—An Act Making appropriations for the Legislative Branch of the Government for the fiscal year ending June 30, 1930, and for other purposes.

45 St. 1407; Feb. 28, 1929; C. 377—An Act Conferring jurisdiction upon the Court of Claims to hear, adjudicate, and render judgment in claims which the northwestern bands of Shoshone Indians may have against the United States.[93]

45 St. 1439; Mar. 1, 1929; C. 440—An Act Authorizing the appropriation of tribal funds of Indians residing on the Klamath Reservation, Oregon, to pay expenses of the general council and business committee, and for other purposes.

45 St. 1478; Mar. 2, 1929; C. 493—An Act Relating to the tribal and individual affairs of the Osage Indians of Oklahoma.[94] Sec. 3, 4, 5—See Historical Note 25 U. S. C. A. 331.

45 St. 1487; Mar. 2, 1929; C. 502—An Act To authorize an appropriation to pay one-half the cost of a bridge on the Cheyenne River Indian Reservation in South Dakota.[95]

45 St. 1488; Mar. 2, 1929; C. 504—An Act To authorize an appropriation to pay half the cost of a bridge across Cherry Creek on the Cheyenne River Indian Reservation, South Dakota.[96]

45 St. 1496; Mar. 2, 1929; C. 511—An Act Authorizing an appropriation of Crow tribal funds for payment of council and delegate expenses, and for other purposes.[97]

45 St. 1534; Mar. 2, 1929; C. 576—An Act To repeal the provision in the Act of April 30, 1908, and other legislation limiting the annual per capita cost in Indian schools.[98]

45 St. 1550; Mar. 4, 1929; C. 689—An Act To carry into effect the twelfth article of the treaty between the United States and the Loyal Shawnee Indians proclaimed October 14, 1868.[99]

45 St. 1562; Mar. 4, 1929; C. 705—An Act Making appropriations for the Department of the Interior for the fiscal year ending June 30, 1930, and for other purposes.[1] Sec. 1, p. 1573—25 U. S. C. 387 (45 St. 210, sec. 1);[2] Sec. 1, p. 1576—25 U. S. C. 292a (44 St. 468, sec. 1; 44 St. 947, sec. 1; 45 St. 215, sec. 1); Sec. 1, p. 1583—25 U. S. C. 25a.

45 St. 1607; Mar. 4, 1929; C. 706—An Act Making appropriations to supply urgent deficiencies in certain appropriations for the fiscal year ending June 30, 1929, and prior fiscal years, to provide urgent supplemental appropriations for the fiscal year ending June 30, 1929, and for other purposes.

45 St. 1623; Mar. 4, 1929; C. 707—An Act Making appropriations to supply deficiencies in certain appropriations for the fiscal year ending June 30, 1929, and prior fiscal years to provide supplemental appropriations for the fiscal years ending June 30, 1929, and June 30, 1930, and for other purposes.[3]

45 St. 1708; Mar. 5, 1928; C. 130—An Act To reimburse certain Indians of the Fort Belknap Reservation, Montana, for part or full value of an allotment of land to which they were individually entitled.[4]

45 St. 1711; Mar. 23, 1928; C. 236—An Act For the relief of John F. White and Mary L. White.

45 St. 1716; Mar. 29, 1928; C. 299—An Act To authorize the Secretary of the Interior to issue a patent to the Bureau of Catholic Indian Missions for a certain tract of land on the Mescalero Reservation, New Mexico.

45 St. 1833; May 15, 1928; C. 571—An Act Granting pensions and increase of pensions to certain soldiers and sailors of the Regular Army and Navy, and so forth, and certain soldiers and sailors of wars other than the Civil War, and to widows of such soldiers and sailors.

45 St. 1857; May 22, 1928; C. 691—An Act To approve a deed of conveyance of certain land in the Seneca Oil Spring Reservation, New York.

45 St. 1988; May 28, 1928; C. 834—An Act Granting pensions and increase of pensions to certain soldiers and sailors of the Regular Army and Navy, and so forth, and certain soldiers and sailors of wars other than the Civil War, and to widows of such soldiers and sailors.

45 St. 2002; May 29, 1928; C. 921—An Act Granting pensions and increase of pensions to certain soldiers and sailors of the Regular Army and Navy, and so forth, and certain soldiers and sailors of wars other than the Civil War, and to widows of such soldiers and sailors.

45 St. 2011; May 29, 1928; C. 930—An Act For the relief of William R. Thackrey.[5]

45 St. 2012; May 29, 1928; C. 931—An Act For the relief of William A. Light.

45 St. 2012; May 29, 1928; C. 934—An Act For the relief of Omer D. Lewis.

45 St. 2020; May 29, 1928; C. 959—An Act For reimbursement of W. H. Talbert.

45 St. 2021; May 29, 1928; C. 962—An Act Authorizing the allotment of Carl J. Reid Dussome as a Kiowa Indian, and directing issuance of trust patent to him to certain lands of the Kiowa Indian Reservation, Oklahoma.

45 St. 2024; May 29, 1928; C. 973—An Act For the relief of Frank Murray.

45 St. 2029; May 29, 1928; C. 989—An Act For the relief of C. R. Olberg.

45 St. 2034; Dec. 11, 1928; C. 22—An Act Authorizing an expenditure of certain funds standing to the credit of the Cherokee Nation in the Treasury of the United States to be paid to one of the attorneys for the Cherokee Nation, and for other purposes.[6]

45 St. 2035; Dec. 15, 1928; C. 32—An Act For the relief of Russell White Bear.[7]

45 St. 2035; Dec. 15, 1928; C. 33—Joint Resolution For the relief of Leah Frank, Creek Indian, new born, roll numbered 204.

45 St. 2035; Dec. 15, 1928; C. 34—Joint Resolution For the relief

---

[89] *Ag.* 43 St. 1138. *Cited:* Kansas, 80 C. Cls. 264.

[90] *Rpg.* 37 St. 521.

[91] *Ag.* 44 St. 776.

[92] *Sg.* 41 St. 1063.

[93] *Sg.* 13 St. 663; 18 St. 201, 685.

[94] *Sg.* 34 St. 539, 545. *Ag.* 41 St. 1249; 43 St. 1008, 1010, 1011. *A.* 52 St. 1034. *S.* 46 St. 1047. *Cited:* 39 Op. A. G. 577 (1937); 12 L. D. Memo. 642; Op. Sol., M. 25258, June 26, 1929; Memo. Sol. Off., Feb. 3, 1930, Apr. 22, 1930, Apr. 22, 1930, July 8, 1930; Letter to Comm'r of Ind. Affairs from Sec'y of Int., Sept. 1930, Mar. 10, 1931, Dec. 15, 1932, Dec. 22, 1932, May 27, 1933, June 20, 1933, Dec. 21, 1933; Op. Sol., M. 27785, Aug. 6, 1934; Memo. Sol., Sept. 25, 1936; Op. Sol., M. 27963, Jan. 26, 1937; Letter from A. G. to Sec'y of Int., Feb. 13, 1937; Letter from Ass't Sec'y to A. G., Oct. 27, 1937, 53 I. D. 169; 54 I. D. 105; 55 I. D. 456; 56 I. D. 48; Adams, 59 F. 2d 653; Choteau, 283 U. S. 691; Choteau, 38 F. 2d 976; Continental, 69 F. 2d 19; Globe, 81 F. 2d 143; In re Dennison, 38 F. 2d 662; Spurlan, 54 F. 2d 43; Stuart, 81 F. 2d 155; Tapp, 6 F. Supp. 577; Taylor, 51 F. 2d 884; U. S. v. Bd. of Comm'rs, 26 F. Supp. 270; U. S. v. Johnson, 87 F. 2d 155; U. S. v. La Motte, 67 F. 2d 788; U. S. v. Sands, 94 F. 2d 156; Utilities, 2 F. Supp. 81; Williams, 88 F. 2d 143.

[95] *S.* 46 St. 279.

[96] *S.* 46 St. 279.

[97] *S.* 46 St. 279.

[98] *Rpg.* 35 St. 72; 41 St. 8; 43 St. 958.

[99] *Sg.* 15 St. 516; 45 St. 18. *S.* 46 St. 90, 1115; 47 St. 91, 820; 48 St. 862; 49 St. 176. *Cited:* Memo. Sol., Aug. 8, 1934.

[1] *Sg.* 4 St. 443; 7 St. 46, 99, 212, 213, 230, 425; 10 St. 1109; 11 St. 614, 731; 12 St. 411; 15 St. 622, 640, 652, 673, 676, 690; 16 St. 720; 19 St. 254, 256; 24 St. 388; 25 St. 645, 795, 1029; 27 St. 130, 644; 34 St. 375; 35 St. 312, 444, 783; 36 St. 270, 273, 1063; 37 St. 521, 522, 934; 38 St. 582, 604, sec. 22; 606; 39 St. 144; 40 St. 564, 588; 41 St. 28, 415, 1107, 1350; 43 St. 133, 134, 423, 475, 537, 636, 640, 684, 1141, 1157, 1162; 44 St. 174, 464, 466, 560, 740, 942, 945; 45 St. 205, 208, 211, 212, 237, 238, 899, 938, 962. *S.* 46 St. 279, 1115; 47 St. 91, 820; 48 St. 362. *Cited:* 53 I. D. 187; Chippewa, 80 C. Cls. 410; Chippewa, 307 U. S. 1; U. S. ex rel. Kadrie, 30 F. 2d 989.

[2] *S.* 46 St. 290, sec. 1; 1126, sec. 1; 47 St. 100, sec. 1; 820, sec. 1; 48 St. 370, sec. 1; 49 St. 186, sec. 1; 1760, sec. 1; 50 St. 577, sec. 1; 52 St. 304, sec. 1; 53 St. 700, sec. 1.

[3] *Sg.* 25 St. 645; 26 St. 795; 35 St. 312, 444, 783; 37 St. 104; 41 St. 415; 42 St. 208, 1051, 1488; 43 St. 376, 475–476, 636, sec. 2; 44 St. 690, 740; 45 St. 198, 200, 212, 213, 215, 312, 603, 617, 1080, 1109. *A.* 46 St. 9. *S.* 46 St. 90, 279, 860, 1115, 1552; 49 St. 1507.

[4] *Sg.* 41 St. 1355

[5] *Sg.* 4 St. 246; 5 St. 31.

[6] *Sg.* 43 St. 27.

[7] *Sg.* 41 St. 751.

of Eloise Childers, Creek Indian, minor, roll numbered 354.

45 St. 2036; Dec. 15, 1928; C. 35—Joint Resolution For the relief of Effa Cowe, Creek Indian, new born, roll numbered 78.

45 St. 2036; Dec. 17, 1928; C. 37—An Act For the relief of James Hunts Along.

45 St. 2045; Feb. 2, 1929; C. 134—An Act To authorize the payment to Robert Toquothty of royalties arising from an oil and gas well in the bed of the Red River, Oklahoma.

45 St. 2046; Feb. 2, 1929; C. 138—An Act For the relief of Peter Shapp.

45 St. 2205; Feb. 19, 1929; C. 269—An Act For the relief of Charles J. Hunt.

45 St. 2309; Feb. 20, 1929; C. 284—An Act Granting pensions and increase of pensions to certain soldiers and sailors of the Regular Army and Navy, and so forth, and certain soldiers and sailors of wars other than the Civil War, and to widows of such soldiers and sailors.

45 St. 2339; Feb. 28, 1929; C. 411—An Act Authorizing the Secretary of the Treasury to pay the Gallup Undertaking Company for burial of four Navajo Indians.

45 St. 2346; Mar. 1, 1929; C. 472—An Act For the relief of James E. Jenkins.

45 St. 2355; Mar. 2, 1929; C. 621—An Act For the relief of M. T. Nilan.

45 St. 2379; Mar. 4, 1929; C. 726—An Act Granting pensions and increase of pensions to certain soldiers and sailors of the Regular Army and Navy, and so forth, and certain soldiers and sailors of wars other than the Civil War, and to widows of such soldiers and sailors.

46 STAT.

46 St. 9; June 13, 1929; C. 20—Joint Resolution Amending an appropriation for a consolidated school at Belcourt, within the Turtle Mountain Indian Reservation, North Dakota.[8]

46 St. 21; June 18, 1929; C. 28—An Act To provide for the fifteenth and subsequent decennial censuses and to provide for apportionment of Representatives in Congress. 2 U. S. C. 2a.

46 St. 32; June 20, 1929; C. 33—An Act To fix the compensation of officers and employees of the legislative branch of the Government.[9]

46 St. 54; Dec. 23, 1929; C. 16—An Act Providing for a per capita payment of $25 to each enrolled member of the Chippewa Tribe of Minnesota from the funds standing to their credit in the Treasury of the United States.[10]

46 St. 88; Mar. 22, 1930; C. 86—Joint Resolution Authorizing the use of tribal moneys belonging to the Fort Berthold Indians of North Dakota for certain purposes.

46 St. 88; Mar. 24, 1930; C. 87—An Act Authorizing a per capita payment to the Shoshone and Arapahoe Indians.[11]

46 St. 90; Mar. 26, 1930; C. 92—An Act Making appropriations to supply urgent deficiencies in certain appropriations for the fiscal year ending June 30, 1930, and prior fiscal years, to provide urgent supplemental appropriations for the fiscal years ending June 30, 1930, and June 30, 1931, and for other purposes.[12]

46 St. 144; Apr. 7, 1930; C. 108—An Act To allow credit to homestead settlers and entrymen for military service in certain Indian wars.[13] 43 U. S. C. 243.

46 St. 147; Apr. 8, 1930; C. 115—An Act To provide for the recording of the Indian sign language through the instrumentality of Major General Hugh L. Scott, retired, and for other purposes.[14]

46 St. 149; Apr. 8, 1930; C. 122—An Act To authorize the issuance of a fee patent for block 23 within the town of Lac du Flambeau, Wisconsin, in favor of the local public-school authorities.

46 St. 154; Apr. 10, 1930; C. 130—An Act Granting the consent of Congress to agreements or compacts between the States of Oklahoma and Texas for the purchase, construction, and maintenance of highway bridges over the Red River, and for other purposes.

46 St. 168; Apr. 15, 1930; C. 169—An Act Providing compensation to the Crow Indians for Custer Battle Field National Cemetery, and for other purposes.[15]

46 St. 169; Apr. 15, 1930; C. 170—An Act Authorizing the Secretary of the Interior to erect a marker or tablet on the site of the battle between Nez Perces Indians under Chief Joseph and the command of Nelson A. Miles.[16]

46 St. 169; Apr. 15, 1930; C. 171—An Act To authorize per capita payments to the Indians of the Pine Ridge Indian Reservation, South Dakota.[17]

46 St. 173; Apr. 18, 1930; C. 184—An Act Making appropriations for the Departments of State and Justice and for the Judiciary, and for the Departments of Commerce and Labor, for the fiscal year ending June 30, 1931, and for other purposes.[18]

46 St. 218; Apr. 18, 1930; C. 185—An Act To authorize an appropriation for purchasing twenty acres for addition to the Hot Springs Reserve on the Shoshone or Wind River Indian Reservation, Wyoming.

46 St. 229; Apr. 19, 1930; C. 201—An Act Making appropriations for the Executive Office and sundry independent executive bureaus, boards, commissions, and offices, for the fiscal year ending June 30, 1931, and for other purposes.

46 St. 258; Apr. 29, 1930; C. 221—An Act Authorizing the Secretary of the Interior to erect a monument as a memorial to the deceased Indian chiefs and ex-service men of the Cheyenne River Sioux Tribe of Indians.[19]

46 St. 259; Apr. 29, 1930; C. 222—An Act To amend the Act authorizing the attorney general of the State of California to bring suit in the Court of Claims on behalf of the Indians of California.[20]

46 St. 260; Apr. 29, 1930; C. 224—Joint Resolution To pay the judgment rendered by the United States Court of Claims to the Iowa Tribe of Indians, Oklahoma.

46 St. 263; May 9, 1930; C. 229—An Act To declare valid the title to certain Indian lands.

46 St. 268; May 12, 1930; C. 224—Joint Resolution Authorizing the use of tribal funds belonging to the Yankton Sioux Tribe of Indians in South Dakota to pay expenses and compensation of the members of the tribal business committee for services in connection with their pipestone claim.

46 St. 276; May 13, 1930; C. 265—An Act To amend the Act of Congress approved May 29, 1928, authorizing the Secretary of the Treasury to accept title to certain real estate, subject to a reservation of mineral rights in favor of the Blackfeet Tribe of Indians.[21]

46 St. 279; May 14, 1930; C. 273—An Act Making appropriations for the Department of the Interior for the fiscal year ending June 30, 1931, and for other purposes.[22] Sec. 1, p. 290—25 U. S. C. 387 (45 St. 210, sec. 1; 45 St. 1573, sec. 1).[23]

46 St. 334; May 15, 1930; C. 285—An Act To provide funds for cooperation with the school board at Browning, Montana, in the extension of the high-school building to be available to Indian children of the Blackfeet Indian Reservation.[24]

46 St. 370; May 19, 1930; C. 302—Joint Resolution To carry out certain obligations to certain enrolled Indians under tribal agreement.

46 St. 378; May 23, 1930; C. 317—An Act To eliminate certain land from the Tusayan National Forest, Arizona, as an addition to the Western Navajo Indian Reservation.[25]

46 St. 385; May 26, 1930; C. 333—An Act Authorizing the Secretary of the Interior to lease any or all of the remaining

---

[8] *Ag.* 45 St. 1640.
[9] *Rg.* 43 St. 146.
[10] *Sg.* 25 St. 642. *S.* 46 St. 1107.
[11] *Sg.* 39 St. 519.
[12] *Sg.* 15 St. 513; 25 St. 645; 26 St. 705; 35 St. 312, 444, 783; 41 St. 416; 43 St. 475, 686; 44 St. 940; 45 St. 18, 200, 312, 802, 817 883; 900, 1550, 1641. *S.* 46 St. 1115, 1552; 47 St. 820; 48 St. 362, 49 St. 176.
[13] *Sg.* 44 St. 1361. *A.* 47 St. 1424.
[14] *S.* 46 St. 860.
[15] *Sg.* 15 St. 649.
[16] *S.* 46 St. 1115.
[17] *Sg.* 36 St. 442.
[18] *Sg.* 36 St. 320; 43 St. 636.
[19] *S.* 46 St. 1115.
[20] *Ag.* 45 St. 602; sec. 7. *S.* 46 St. 270; 46 St. 1115; 47 St. 15. *Cited:* Op. Sol., M. 25099, July 8, 1930; Memo. Sol., Apr. 19, 1933; Memo. Sol. Off., Apr. 21, 1933.
[21] *Sg.* 41 St. 17. *Ag.* 45 St. 919.
[22] *Sg* 4 St. 442; 7 St. 46, 99, 212, 236, 425; 10 St. 1109; 11 St. 614, 731; 15 St. 622, 640, 652, 675, 696; 16 St. 720; 19 St. 254, 256; 24 St. 88; 25 St. 645; 26 St. 795, 1029; 27 St. 139, 644; 34 St. 375; 35 St. 312, 781; 36 St. 273; 37 St. 912; 38 St. 582, 604; 39 St. 934; 40 St. 564; 41 St. 415, 416, 1107; 42 St. 1051; 43 St. 376, 423, 475, 630; 44 St. 560, 658, 740; 45 St. 215, 484, 602, 899, 938, 944, 1229, 1487, 1488, 1496, 1571, 1573, 1577, 1601, 1641; 46 St. 259. *S.* 46 St. 860, 1115, 1552; 47 St. 91, 525; 48 St. 105. *Cited:* Chippewa, 80 C. Cls. 410; Coos, 87 C. Cls. 143.
[23] *S.* 46 St. 1126, sec. 1; 47 St. 100, sec. 1; 820, sec. 1; 48 St. 370, sec. 1; 49 St. 180, sec. 1; 1769, sec. 1; 50 St. 577, sec. 1; 52 St. 304, sec. 1; 53 St. 700, sec. 1.
[24] *S* 46 St. 860, 1552.
[25] *A* 46 St. 1204.

tribal lands of the Choctaw and Chickasaw Nations for oil and gas purposes, and for other purposes.[26]

46 St. 392; May 27, 1930; C. 341—An Act Making appropriations for the Department of Agriculture for the fiscal year ending June 30, 1931, and for other purposes.[27]

46 St. 430; May 27, 1930; C. 343—An Act Authorizing reconstruction and improvement of a public road in Wind River Indian Reservation, Wyoming.[28]

46 St. 431; May 28, 1930; C. 347—An Act To authorize the erection of a marker upon the site of New Echota, capital of the Cherokee Indians prior to their removal west of the Mississippi River, to commemorate its location, and events connected with its history.

46 St. 432; May 28, 1930; C. 348—An Act Making appropriations for the military and nonmilitary activities of the War Department for the fiscal year ending June 30, 1931, and for other purposes.

46 St. 468; May 29, 1930; C. 349—An Act to amend the Act entitled "An Act to amend the Act entitled 'An Act for the retirement of employees in the classified civil service, and for other purposes,' approved May 22, 1920, and Acts in amendment thereof," approved July 3, 1926, as amended.[29]

46 St. 495; June 3, 1930; C. 394—An Act To amend section 180, title 28, United States Code, as amended.[30] 28 U. S. C. 180.

46 St. 504; June 6, 1930; C. 407—An Act Making appropriations for the Legislative Branch of the Government for the fiscal year ending June 30, 1931, and for other purposes.

46 St. 531; June 9, 1930; C. 423—Joint Resolution To clarify and amend an Act entitled "An Act conferring jurisdiction upon the Court of Claims to hear, examine, adjudicate, and enter judgment in any claims which the Assiniboine Indians may have against the United States, and for other purposes," approved March 2, 1927.[31]

46 St. 580; June 12, 1930; C. 471—Joint Resolution To amend a joint resolution entitled "Joint resolution giving to discharged soldiers, sailors, and marines a preferred right of homestead entry," approved February 14, 1920, as amended January 21, 1922, and as extended December 28, 1922.[32] 43 U. S. C. 186.

46 St. 581; June 13, 1930; C. 477—An Act To amend the Act entitled "An Act to permit taxation of lands of homestead and desert-land entrymen under the Reclamation Act," approved April 21, 1928, so as to include ceded lands under Indian irrigation projects. 43 U. S. C. 455, 455c.

46 St. 584; June 13, 1930; C. 483—An Act To amend the Act approved February 12, 1929, authorizing the payment of interest on certain funds held in trust by the United States for Indian tribes.[33] 25 U. S. C. 161a, 161b, 161c, 161d (45 St. 1164).

46 St. 785; June 19, 1930; C. 540—An Act Ratifying and confirming the title of the State of Minnesota and its grantees to certain lands patented to it by the United States of America.[34]

46 St. 787; June 19, 1930; C. 544—An Act To confer full rights of citizenship upon the Cherokee Indians resident in the State of North Carolina, and for other purposes. 8 U. S. C. 3a.

46 St. 788; June 19, 1930; C. 545—An Act Providing for the sale of the remainder of the coal and asphalt deposits in the segregated mineral land in the Choctaw and Chickasaw Nations, Oklahoma, and for other purposes.[35]

46 St. 793; June 21, 1930; C. 564—An Act Authorizing an appropriation for payment of claims of the Sisseton and Wahpeton Bands of Sioux Indians.[36]

46 St. 805; June 24, 1930; C. 593—An Act To amend the Act entitled "An Act to provide that the United States shall aid the States in the construction of rural post roads, and for other purposes," approved July 11, 1916, as amended and supplemented, and for other purposes.[37] 23 U. S. C. 3.

46 St. 820; June 27, 1930; C. 636—An Act Authorizing an appropriation for the purchase of land for the Indian colony near Ely, Nevada, and for other purposes.[38]

46 St. 820; June 27, 1930; C. 637—An Act To provide for the payment of benefits received by the Paiute Indian Reservation lands within the Newlands irrigation project, Nevada, and for other purposes.[39]

46 St. 860; July 3, 1930; C. 846—An Act Making appropriations to supply deficiencies in certain appropriations for the fiscal year ending June 30, 1930, and prior fiscal years, to provide supplemental appropriations for the fiscal years ending June 30, 1930, and June 30, 1931, and for other purposes.[40]

46 St. 1028; Dec. 16, 1930; C. 14—An Act To repeal obsolete statutes, and to improve the United States Code.[41]

46 St. 1030; Dec. 20, 1930; C. 19—An Act Making supplemental appropriations to provide for emergency construction on certain public works during the remainder of the fiscal year ending June 30, 1931, with a view to increasing employment.[42]

46 St. 1033; Dec. 23, 1930; C. 23—An Act Authorizing the bands or tribes of Indians known and designated as the Middle Oregon or Warm Springs Tribe of Indians of Oregon or either of them, to submit their claims to the Court of Claims.[43]

46 St. 1045; Jan. 31, 1931; C. 64—An Act Authorizing the Secretary of the Interior to acquire land and erect a monument at the site near Crookston, in Polk County, Minnesota, to commemorate the signing of a treaty on October 2, 1863, between the United States of America and the Chippewa Indians.[44]

46 St. 1046; Jan. 31, 1931; C. 68—An Act To provide for an Indian village at Elko, Nevada.[45]

46 St. 1047; Jan. 31, 1931; C. 70—An Act Authorizing the appropriation of Osage funds for attorneys' fees and expenses of litigation.[46]

46 St. 1060; Feb. 3, 1931; C. 101—An Act To amend an Act for the relief of certain tribes of Indians in Montana, Idaho, and Washington.[47]

46 St. 1060; Feb. 3, 1931; C. 102—An Act Authorizing an additional per capita payment to the Shoshone and Arapahoe Indians.[48]

46 St. 1061; Feb. 4, 1931; C. 104—An Act Authorizing the construction of the Michaud division of the Fort Hall Indian irrigation project, Idaho, an appropriation therefor, and the completion of the project, and for other purposes.[49]

46 St. 1064; Feb. 6, 1931; C. 111—An Act Making appropriations to supply urgent deficiencies in certain appropriations for the fiscal year ending June 30, 1931, and for prior fiscal years, to provide urgent supplemental appropriations for the fiscal year ending June 30, 1931, and for other purposes.[50]

46 St. 1084; February 10, 1931; C. 117—An Act To provide for the advance planning and regulated construction of public works, for the stabilization of industry, and for aiding in the prevention of unemployment during periods of business depression. 29 U. S. C. 48f, 48g.

46 St. 1092; Feb. 13, 1931; C. 124—An Act Authorizing an appropriation for payment to the Uintah, White River, and Uncompahgre Bands of Ute Indians in the State of Utah for certain lands, and for other purposes.[51]

46 St. 1093; Feb. 13, 1931; C. 125—An Act To authorize the Secretary of the Interior to adjust payment of charges due on the Blackfeet Indian Irrigation Project, and for other purposes.[52]

46 St. 1102; Feb. 14, 1931; C. 162—An Act Providing for the sale of timberland in four townships in the State of Minnesota.

46 St. 1102; Feb. 14, 1931; C. 164—An Act Authorizing a per capita payment of $50 to the members of the Menominee

---

[26] *Sg.* 45 St. 737.
[27] *Sg.* 43 St. 739.
[28] *S.* 46 St. 1064. *A.* 47 St. 88.
[29] *Sg.* 41 St. 614; 46 St. 258. *Ag.* 44 St. 904. *Cited:* Memo. Sol. Off., Apr. 30, 1934.
[30] *Ag.* 26 St. 67; 36 St. 1126; 44 St. 237. *A.* 47 St. 341.
[31] *Sg.* 11 St. 657, 749; 18 St. 28; 25 St. 114. *Ag.* 44 St. 1263.
[32] *Sg.* 41 St. 434; 42 St. 358, 1067.
[33] *Sg.* 22 St. 590; 44 St. 560. *Ag.* 45 St. 1164.
[34] *Sg.* 12 St. 3.
[35] *Sg.* 40 St. 438; 41 St. 1107. *A.* 48 St. 1240.
[36] *Sg.* 18 St. 167. *S.* 46 St. 860.
[37] *Ag.* 42 St. 212. *S.* 47 St. 709; 48 St. 993, 1021; 49 St. 247; 50 St. 895; 52 St. 633, 710.
[38] *S.* 46 St. 1115; 47 St. 525.
[39] *S.* 47 St. 525.
[40] *Sg.* 44 St. 690; 45 St. 1623, 1640; 46 St. 147, 168, 218, 288, 834, 798. *S.* 46 St. 1115, 1552.
[41] *Rg.* 13 St. 41, sec. 7. *Rrg.* 35 St. 71, 73.
[42] *Sg.* 42 St. 212; 46 St. 605. *S.* 47 St. 609.
[43] *Sg.* 12 St. 963; 14 St. 751; 28 St. 86.
[44] *S.* 46 St. 1552.
[45] *S.* 46 St. 1552.
[46] *Sg.* 41 St. 1249; 45 St. 1478. *S.* 46 St. 1552.
[47] *Ag.* 43 St. 21.
[48] *Sg.* 39 St. 519.
[49] *Sg.* 45 St. 377. *S.* 47 St. 91, 820. *Cited:* Letter by Sec. of Int. to Comp. Gen., Sept. 28, 1932; 53 I. D. 399.
[50] *Sg.* 43 St. 939; 46 St. 430. *S.* 47 St. 91; 49 St. 2195.
[51] *S.* 46 St. 1552; 47 St. 1488.
[52] *Cited:* 54 I. D. 835.

Tribe of Indians of Wisconsin from funds on deposit to their credit in the Treasury of the United States.

46 St. 1105; Feb. 14, 1931; C. 169—An Act Authorizing the use of tribal funds of Indians belonging on the Klamath Reservation, Oregon, to pay expenses connected with suits pending in the Court of Claims, and for other purposes.[53]

46 St. 1105; Feb. 14, 1931; C. 170—An Act Providing for the sale of isolated tracts in the former Crow Indian Reservation, Montana.[54] 43 U. S. C. 1177.

46 St. 1106; Feb. 14, 1931; C. 171—An Act To authorize the Secretary of the Interior to accept donations to or in behalf of institutions conducted for the benefit of Indians.[55] 25 U. S. C. 451.

46 St. 1106; Feb. 14, 1931; C. 173—An Act To provide funds for cooperation with the school board at Frazer, Montana, in the construction of a high-school building to be available to Indian children of the Fort Peck Indian Reservation.

46 St. 1107; Feb. 14, 1931; C. 1931; C. 174—An Act Providing for payment of $25 to each enrolled Chippewa Indian of Minnesota from the funds standing to their credit in the Treasury of the United States.[57]

46 St. 1107; Feb. 14, 1931; C. 175—An Act To amend the Act of April 25, 1922, as amended, entitled "An Act authorizing extensions of time for the payment of purchase money due under certain homestead entries and Government-land purchases within the former Cheyenne River and Standing Rock Indian Reservations, North Dakota and South Dakota."[58]

46 St. 1108; Feb. 14, 1931; C. 177—An Act Providing for the sale of Chippewa Indian land to the State of Minnesota.[59]

46 St. 1108; Feb. 14, 1931; C. 178—An Act To provide funds for cooperation with the school board at Poplar, Montana, in the extension of the high-school building to be available to Indian children of the Fort Peck Indian Reservation.

46 St. 1108; Feb. 14, 1931; C. 179—An Act To amend section 3 of the Act approved May 10, 1928, entitled "An Act to extend the period of restriction in lands of certain members of the Five Civilized Tribes, and for other purposes.[60]

46 St. 1111; Feb. 14, 1931; C. 185—An Act To amend the Alaska game law.[61] Sec. 10—48 U. S. C. 199. Sec. 13—48 U. S. C. 202.

46 St. 1115; Feb. 14, 1931; C. 187—An Act Making appropriations for the Department of the Interior for the fiscal year ending June 30, 1932, and for other purposes.[62] Sec. 1, p. 1126—25 U. S. C. 387 (45 St. 210, sec. 1; 45 St. 1573, sec. 1; 46 St. 290, sec. 1).[63]

46 St. 1161; Feb. 14, 1931; C. 188—An Act To authorize the President of the United States to establish the Canyon De Chelly National Monument within the Navajo Indian Reservation, Arizona.[64] 16 U. S. C. 445, 445a, 445b.

46 St. 1173; Feb. 20, 1931; C. 231—An Act To amend the Federal Highway Act.[65] 23 U. S. C. 3a.

46 St. 1174; Feb. 20, 1931; C. 234—An Act Making appropriations for the Legislative Branch of the Government for the fiscal year ending June 30, 1932, and for other purposes.

46 St. 1201; Feb. 21, 1931; C. 265—An Act To reserve four hundred and forty acres of public-domain land for addition to the Temecula or Pechanga Reservation, California.[66]

46 St. 1202; Feb. 21, 1931; C. 267—An Act To reserve certain lands on the public domain in Arizona for the use and benefit of the Papago Indians, and for other purposes.[67]

46 St. 1201; Feb. 21, 1931; C. 269—An Act To amend the Act of May 23, 1930 (46 St. 378).[68]

46 St. 1205; Feb. 21, 1931; C. 271—An Act To amend an Act entitled "An Act to authorize the cancellation, under certain conditions, of patents in fee simple to Indians for allotments held in trust by the United States."[69] 25 U. S. C. 352b (44 St. 1247, sec. 2).

46 St. 1242; Feb. 23, 1931; C. 278—An Act Making appropriations for the Department of Agriculture for the fiscal year ending June 30, 1932, and for other purposes.[70]

46 St. 1277; Feb. 23, 1931; C. 279—An Act Making appropriations for the military and nonmilitary activities of the War Department for the fiscal year ending June 30, 1932, and for other purposes.

46 St. 1309; Feb. 23, 1931; C. 280—An Act Making appropriations for the Departments of State and Justice and for the Judiciary, and for the Departments of Commerce and Labor, for the fiscal year ending June 30, 1932, and for other purposes.[71]

46 St. 1355; Feb. 23, 1931; C. 281—An Act Making appropriations for the Executive Office and sundry independent executive bureaus, boards, commissions, and offices, for the fiscal year ending June 30, 1932, and for other purposes.

46 St. 1458; Feb. 28, 1931; C. 341—An Act To authorize an investigation with respect to the construction of a dam or dams across the Owyhee River or other streams within or adjacent to the Duck Valley Indian Reservation, Nevada, and for other purposes.[72]

46 St. 1468; Mar. 2, 1931; C. 369—An Act Authorizing the Menominee Tribe of Indians to employ general attorneys.[73]

46 St. 1471; Mar. 2, 1931; C. 374—An Act To relieve restricted Indians in the Five Civilized Tribes whose nontaxable lands are required for State, county, or municipal improvements or sold to other persons or for other purposes.[74] 25 U. S. C. 409a.[75]

46 St. 1481; Mar. 2, 1931; C. 377—Joint Resolution Authorizing the distribution of the judgment rendered by the Court of Claims to the Indians of the Fort Berthold Indian Reservation, North Dakota.

46 St. 1487; Mar. 3, 1931; C. 401—An Act Authorizing the Pillager Bands of Chippewa Indians, residing in the State of Minnesota, to submit claims to the Court of Claims.[76]

46 St. 1494; Mar. 3, 1931; C. 413—An Act Relating to the adoption of minors by the Crow Indians of Montana.

46 St. 1495; Mar. 3, 1931; C. 414—An Act Authorizing the Secretary of the Interior to change the classification of Crow Indians.[77]

46 St. 1495; Mar. 3, 1931; C. 416—An Act For the enrollment of children born after December 30, 1919, whose parents, or either of them, are members of the Blackfeet Tribe of Indians in the State of Montana, and for other purposes.[78]

46 St. 1509; Mar. 3, 1931; C. 438—An Act To authorize a survey of certain lands claimed by the Zuni Pueblo Indians, New Mexico, and the issuance of patent therefor.[79]

46 St. 1517; Mar. 4, 1931; C. 493—An Act To authorize an appropriation of tribal funds to purchase certain privately owned lands within the Fort Apache Indian Reservation, Arizona.[80]

46 St. 1518; Mar. 4, 1931; C. 494—An Act To amend the Act of June 4, 1924, providing for a final disposition of the affairs of the Eastern Band of Cherokee Indians in North Carolina.[81]

46 St. 1519; Mar. 4, 1931; C. 497—An Act To cancel certain reimbursable charges against certain lands within the Gila River Indian Reservation, Arizona.[82]

46 St. 1522; Mar. 4, 1931; C. 503—An Act To authorize the Secretary of the Interior to purchase certain land in California for addition to the Cahuilla Indian Reservation, and issuance of a patent to the band of Indians therefor.[83]

---

[53] *Sg.* 41 St. 623.

[54] *Sg.* 9 St. 51, sec. 5; 26 St. 1040; 45 St. 253.

[55] *S.* 46 St. 1552.

[57] *Sg.* 25 St. 645; 46 St. 54.

[58] *Sg.* 45 St. 400.

[59] *Sg.* 25 St. 642; 36 St. 862.

[60] *Ag.* 45 St. 496. *A.* 49 St. 1160.

[61] *Ag.* 43 St. 739. *A.* 52 St. 1169. *S.* 47 St. 609, 1432; 48 St. 407; 49 St. 247, 1421; 50 St. 395.

[62] *Sg.* 4 St. 443; 7 St. 99, 212, 213, 236, 425; 10 St. 1109; 11 St. 614, 731; 15 St. 513, 622, 652, 675, 696; 16 St. 720; 19 St. 254, 256; 24 St. 388; 25 St. 645; 26 St. 795, 1029; 27 St. 139, 612; 34 St. 375; 35 St. 312; 36 St. 273; 37 St. 934; 38 St. 582, 604; 40 St. 564; 41 St. 28, 413; 42 St. 1051; 43 St. 133, 139, 475, 636; 44 St. 211, 560, 658, 740; 45 St. 200, 215, 312, 484, 602, 899, 938, 1550, 1567, 1569, 1573, 1574, 1641; 46 St. 105, 169, 258, 283, 287, 288, 296, 290, 876, 877. *S.* 46 St. 1552; 47 St. 15, 91, 525, 820; 48 St. 1021; 49 St. 1757. *Cited:* Memo. Sol. Off., Nov. 28, 1935; Chippewa, 80 C. Cls. 410; Creek, 79 C. Cls. 778.

[63] *S.* 47 100, sec. 1; 829, sec. 1; 48 St. 370, sec. 1; 49 St. 180, sec. 1; 1769, sec. 1; 50 St. 577, sec. 1; 52 St. 804, sec. 1; 53 St. 700, sec. 1.

[64] *A.* 47 St. 1419.

[65] *Ag.* 42 St. 212. *S.* 47 St. 709.

[66] *Sg.* 26 St. 712; 34 St. 1015.

[67] *Sg.* 36 St. 558; 44 St. 775. *S.* 46 St. 1552; 48 St. 984; 50 St. 862. *Cited:* 38 Op. A. G. 121; Op. Sol., M. 27656, May 7, 1934; Memo. Sol., Oct. 12, 1934; Op. Sol., M. 28183, Oct. 16, 1935; Memo. Sol., Mar. 12, 1936.

[68] *Sg.* 36 St. 557. *Ag.* 46 St. 378.

[69] *Ag.* 44 St. 1247. *Sg.* 24 St. 388. *Cited:* Op. Sol., Aug. 18, 1932; Memo. Sol. Off., Nov. 16, 1932, Mar. 8, 1933; U. S. v. Board of Co. Comm'rs, 13 F. Supp. 641; U. S. v. Glacier, 17 F. Supp. 411.

[70] *Sg.* 43 St. 739.

[71] *Sg.* 36 St. 3_6.

[72] *S.* 47 St. 91.

[73] *S.* 48 St. 97.

[74] *A.* 47 St. 471. *Cited:* Memo. Sol. Off., Mar. 26, 1934; Memo. Ind. Off., Jan. 3, 1935; Memo Sol., Dec. 21, 1936; 53 I. D. 637.

[75] *A.* 47 St. 474.

[76] *Sg.* 9 St. 908; 25 St. 642.

[77] *Sg.* 41 St. 751.

[78] *Cited:* Memo. Sol. Off., Aug. 22, 1932.

[79] *Sg.* 10 St. 308.

[80] *S.* 47 St. 91.

[81] *Ag.* 43 St. 376. *Cited:* Op. Sol., M. 29961, Oct. 4, 1938; U. S. v. Colvard, 89 F. 2d 312.

[82] *Sg.* 33 St. 1081; 37 St. 522; 39 St. 123; 43 St. 475.

[83] *Sg.* 34 St. 1015. *Ag.* 26 St. 712. *S.* 47 St. 91.

46 St. 1526; Mar. 4, 1931; C. 507—An Act To provide for distribution of tribal funds of the Puyallup Indians of the State of Washington.

46 St. 1552; Mar. 4, 1931; C. 522—An Act Making appropriations to supply deficiencies in certain appropriations for the fiscal year ending June 30, 1931, and prior fiscal years, to provide supplemental appropriations for the fiscal years ending June 30, 1931, and June 30, 1932, and for other purposes.[84]

46 St. 1633; Apr. 8, 1930; C. 124—An Act For the relief of Frank Yarlott.[85]

46 St. 1634; Apr. 12, 1930; C. 144—An Act For the relief of Josephine Laforge (Sage Woman).[86]

46 St. 1634; Apr. 12, 1930; C. 145—An Act For the relief of Clarence L. Stevens.[87]

46 St. 1634; pr. 12, 1930; C. 146—An Act For the relief of Carl Stanley Sloan, minor Flathead allottee.[88]

46 St. 1832; May 23, 1930; C. 319—An Act Granting pensions and increase of pensions to certain soldiers and sailors of the Regular Army and Navy, and so forth, and certain soldiers and sailors of wars other than the Civil War, and to widows of such soldiers and sailors.

46 St. 1854; June 2, 1930; C. 388—An Act Authorizing the Secretary of the Treasury to pay to Eva Broderick for the hire of an automobile by agents of Indian Service.

46 St. 1857; June 4, 1930; C. 397—An Act For the relief of Albert E. Edwards.

46 St. 1858; June 9, 1930; C. 429—An Act Authorizing the payment of grazing fees to E. P. McManigal.

46 St. 1886; June 13, 1930; C. 486—An Act Granting pensions and increase of pensions to certain soldiers and sailors of the Regular Army and Navy, and so forth, and certain soldiers and sailors of wars other than the Civil War, and to widows of such soldiers and sailors.

46 St. 1909; June 19, 1930; C. 548—An Act For the relief of Hannah Odekirk.

46 St. 1917; June 26, 1930; C. 627—An Act For the relief of Vida T. Layman.

46 St. 1933; June 27, 1930; C. 689—An Act For the relief of Clifford J. Turner.[89]

46 St. 1943; June 28, 1930; C. 728—An Act For the relief of F. G. Baum.

46 St. 1974; Jan. 31, 1931; C. 91—An Act For the relief of H. E. Mills.

46 St. 1979; Feb. 9, 1931; C. 116—An Act To provide for discharging certain obligations of Peter R. Wadsworth, former superintendent and special disbursing agent of the Consolidated Chippewa Indian Agency.

46 St. 1986; Feb. 14, 1931; C. 198—An Act To reimburse William Whitright for expenses incurred as an authorized delegate of the Fort Peck Indians.

46 St. 1986; Feb. 14, 1931; C. 199—An Act To reimburse Charles Thompson for expenses incurred as an authorized delegate of the Fort Peck Indians.

46 St. 2094; Feb. 17, 1931; C. 216—An Act Granting pensions and increase of pensions to certain soldiers and sailors of the Regular Army and Navy, and so forth, and certain soldiers and sailors of wars other than the Civil War, and to widows of such soldiers and sailors.

46 St. 2124; Feb. 27, 1931; C. 324—An Act For the relief of R. A. Ogee, senior.[90]

46 St. 2135; Mar. 3, 1931; C. 460—An Act For the relief of John T. Doyle.[91]

46 St. 2148; Mar. 4, 1931; C. 549—An Act For the relief of Mrs. Thomas Doyle.[92]

47 STAT.

47 St. 15; Feb. 2, 1932; C. 12—An Act Making appropriations to supply urgent deficiencies in certain appropriations for the fiscal year ending June 30, 1932, and prior fiscal years, to provide supplemental appropriations for the fiscal year ending June 30, 1932, and for other purposes.[93]

47 St. 37; Feb. 4, 1932; C. 18—An Act To repeal the Act of Congress approved May 31, 1924 (43 St. 247), entitled "An Act to authorize the setting aside of certain tribal land within the Quinaielt Indian Reservation in Washington, for lighthouse purposes."[94]

47 St. 39; Feb. 6, 1932; C. 23—An Act To authorize the sale of parts of a cemetery reserve made for the Kiowa, Comanche, and Apache Indians in Oklahoma.

47 St. 49; Feb. 12, 1932; C. 45—An Act Providing for payment of $25 to each enrolled Chippewa Indian of Minnesota from the funds standing to their credit in the Treasury of the United States.

47 St. 50; Feb. 12, 1932; C. 46—An Act To reserve certain land on the public domain in Utah for addition to the Skull Valley Indian Reservation.

47 St. 74; Mar. 28, 1932; C. 93—An Act Authorizing the Secretary of the Interior to sell certain unused Indian cemetery reserves on the Wichita Indian Reservation in Oklahoma, to provide funds for purchase of other suitable burial sites for the Wichita Indians and affiliated bands.

47 St. 87; Apr. 21, 1932; C. 122—An Act Amending the Act of Congress entitled "An Act authorizing the Wichita and affiliated bands of Indians in Oklahoma to submit claims to the Court of Claims," approved June 4, 1924.[95]

47 St. 88; Apr. 21, 1932; C. 123—An Act To amend the Act of May 27, 1930, authorizing an appropriation for the reconstruction and improvement of a road on the Shoshone Indian Reservation, Wyoming.[96]

47 St. 88; Apr. 21, 1932; C. 124—An Act To provide for the leasing of the segregated coal and asphalt deposits of the Choctaw and Chickasaw Indian Nations, in Oklahoma, and for an extension of time within which purchasers of such deposits may complete payments.[97]

47 St. 91; Apr. 22, 1932; C. 125—An Act Making appropriations for the Department of the Interior for the fiscal year ending June 30, 1933, and for other purposes.[98] Sec. 1, p. 100—25 U. S. C. 387.

47 St. 137; Apr. 25, 1932; C. 136—An Act To confer jurisdiction on the Court of Claims to hear and determine certain claims of the Eastern or Emigrant and the Western or Old Settler Cherokee Indians against the United States, and for other purposes.[99]

47 St. 140; Apr. 27, 1932; C. 149—An Act To require the approval of the General Council of the Seminole Tribe or Nation in case of the disposal of any tribal land.

47 St. 144; May 2, 1932; C. 155—An Act To accept the grant by the State of Montana of concurrent police jurisdiction over the rights of way of the Blackfeet Highway, and over the rights of way of its connections with the Glacier National Park road system on the Blackfeet Indian Reservation in the State of Montana.[1] Sec. 1—16 U. S. C. 181; Sec. 2—16 U. S. C. 181a; Sec. 3—16 U. S. C. 181b.

47 St. 146; May 4, 1932; C. 164—An Act Extending the provisions of the Act entitled "An Act to provide for the sale of desert lands in certain States and Territories," approved March 3, 1877 (19 St. 377), and Acts amendatory thereof, to ceded lands of the Fort Hall Indian Reservation.[2]

47 St. 146; May 4, 1932; C. 165—An Act Amending an Act of Congress approved February 28, 1919 (40 St. 1206), granting the city of San Diego certain lands in the Cleveland National Forest and the Capitan Grande Indian Reservation for dam and reservoir purposes for the conservation of water, and for other purposes, so as to include additional lands.[3]

47 St. 153; May 13, 1932; C. 177—An Act To authorize the sale, on competitive bids, of unallotted lands on the Lac du

---

[84] *Sg.* 13 St. 667; 43 St. 475, 636; 44 St. 740, 793; 45 St. 200, 312, 1623; 46 St. 90, 104, 334, 876, 1030, 1045, 1046, 1047, 1106, 1108, 1205. *S.* 47 St. 91, 525; 48 St. 1021. *Cited:* Chippewa, 80 C. Cls. 410.

[85] *Sg.* 41 St. 751.

[86] *Sg.* 41 St. 751.

[87] *Sg.* 41 St. 751.

[88] *Sg.* 41 St. 452.

[89] *Ag.* 45 St. 1720.

[90] *Sg.* 38 St. 533.

[91] *Sg.* 41 St. 751.

[92] *Sg.* 41 St. 751.

[93] *Sg.* 34 St. 375; 36 St. 273; 38 St. 582; 45 St. 602; 46 St. 259, 1123.

[94] *Rg.* 43 St. 247.

[95] *Ag.* 43 St. 366.

[96] *Ag.* 46 St. 430.

[97] *Sg.* 40 St. 433. *S.* 48 St. 1240.

[98] *Sg.* 4 St. 442; 7 St. 46, 99, 212, 213, 236; 10 St. 1109; 11 St. 614, 731; 12 St. 441, sec. 1; 15 St. 513, 635; 19 St. 254, 256; 24 St. 388; 25 St. 645, 945; 26 St. 795; 27 St. 644; 28 St. 583; 34 St. 375; 35 St. 312, 781; 36 St. 270, 273; 37 St. 934; 38 St. 582, 604, 607; 40 St. 564; 41 St. 28, 415; 43 St. 475, 636; 44 St. 658, 740; 45 St. 312, 809, 938, 1573, 1574; 46 St. 1061, 1155, 1128, 1458, 1522. *S.* 47 St. 820; 48 St. 274, 362; 52 St. 1114. *Cited:* Sol's Letter to Wm. A. Brophy, Apr. 23, 1938; Chippewa, 80 C. Cls. 410.

[99] *Sg.* 43 St. 27, 28. *S.* 48 St. 972. *Cited:* 7 L. D. Memo. 249; Memo. Sol., Apr. 23, 1936; Eastern or Emigrant, 82 C. Cls. 180; Western Cherokees, 82 C. Cls. 566.

[1] *Sg.* 38 St. 699.

[2] *Sg.* 19 St. 377; 25 St. 687; 31 St. 672.

[3] *Ag.* 40 St. 1206. *S.* 50 St. 72. *Cited:* Op. Sol., M. 27750, July 14, 1934.

Flambeau Indian Reservation, in Wisconsin, not needed for allotment, tribal, or administrative purposes.

47 St. 169; June 6, 1932; C. 207—An Act To authorize transfer of the abandoned Indian-school site and building at Zeba, Michigan, to the L'Anse Band of Lake Superior Indians.

47 St. 169; June 6, 1932; C. 208—An Act To authorize the exchange of a part of the Rapid City Indian School land for a part of the Pennington County Poor Farm, South Dakota.

47 St. 169; June 6, 1932; C. 209—An Act To provide revenue, equalize taxation, and for other purposes.[4] Sec. 624—See note at end of 26 U. S. C. 20; Sec. 629—See note at end of 26 U. S. C. 20; Sec. 1112—26 U. S. C. 1699.

47 St. 300; June 11, 1932; C. 242—An Act To amend section 106 of the Act to codify, revise, and amend the laws relating to the judiciary (U. S. C., tit. 28, sec. 187).[5]

47 St. 302; June 13, 1932; C. 245—An Act To amend the Act of March 2, 1917 (39 St. 983; U. S. Code, title 25, sec. 242).[6]

47 St. 306; June 14, 1932; C. 254—An Act Providing for payment of $25 to each enrolled Chippewa Indian of the Red Lake Band of Minnesota from the timber funds standing to their credit in the Treasury of the United States.

47 St. 307; June 14, 1932; C. 255—An Act To amend an Act (ch. 300) entitled "An Act authorizing the Coos (Kowes) Bay, Lower Umpqua (Kalawatset), and Siuslaw Tribes of Indians of the State of Oregon to present their claims to the Court of Claims," approved February 23, 1929 (45 St. 1256).[7]

47 St. 307; June 14, 1932; C. 257—An Act Authorizing a per capita payment of $50 to the members of the Menominee Tribe of Indians of Wisconsin from funds on deposit to their credit in the Treasury of the United States.

47 St. 324; June 18, 1932; C. 270—An Act Granting to the Metropolitan Water District of Southern California certain public and reserved lands of the United States in the counties of Los Angeles, Riverside, and San Bernardino, in the State of California.

47 St. 334; June 27, 1932; C. 278—An Act For the relief of homesteaders on the Diminished Colville Indian Reservation, Washington.[8]

47 St. 335; June 27, 1932; C. 279—An Act Authorizing expenditures from Colorado River tribal funds for reimbursable loans.[9]

47 St. 336; June 28, 1932; C. 284—An Act To amend sections 328 and 329 of the United States Criminal Code of 1910 and sections 548 and 549 of the United States Code of 1926.[10]

47 St. 337; June 28, 1932; C. 285—An Act To authorize the Secretary of the Interior to extend or renew the contracts of employment of the attorneys employed to represent the Chippewa Indians of Minnesota in litigation arising in the Court of Claims under the Act of May 14, 1926 (44 St. 555).[11]

47 St. 341; June 29, 1932; C. 305—An Act To amend section 99 of the Judicial Code (U. S. C., tit. 28, sec. 180), as amended.[12]

47 St. 382; June 30, 1932; C. 314—An Act Making appropriations for the Legislative Branch of the Government for the fiscal year ending June 30, 1933; and for other purposes.[13]

47 St. 420; June 30, 1932; C. 316—An Act To provide for expenses of the Crow and Fort Peck Indian Tribal Councils and authorized delegates of such tribes.

47 St. 421; June 30, 1932; C. 317—An Act Amending the Act of May 25, 1918, with reference to employing farmers in the Indian Service, and for other purposes.[14]

47 St. 452; June 30, 1932; C. 330—An Act Making appropriations for the Executive Office and sundry independent executive bureaus, boards, commissions, and offices, for the fiscal year ending June 30, 1933, and for other purposes.

47 St. 474; June 30, 1932; C. 333—An Act Relating to the acquisition of restricted Indian lands by States, counties, or municipalities.[15] 25 U. S. C. 409a (46 St. 1471).

47 St. 475; July 1, 1932; C. 361—An Act Making appropriations for the Departments of State and Justice and for the Judiciary, and for the Departments of Commerce and Labor, for the fiscal year ending June 30, 1933, and for other purposes.[16]

47 St. 525; July 1, 1932; C. 364—An Act Making appropriations to supply deficiencies in certain appropriations for the fiscal year ending June 30, 1932, and prior fiscal years, to provide supplemental appropriations for the fiscal years ending June 30, 1932, and June 30, 1933, and for other purposes.[17]

47 St. 564; July 1, 1932; C. 369—An Act To authorize the Secretary of the Interior to adjust reimbursable debts of Indians and tribes of Indians.[18] 25 U. S. C 386a.

47 St. 609; July 7, 1932; C. 443—An Act Making appropriations for the Department of Agriculture for the fiscal year ending, June 30, 1933, and for other purposes.[19]

47 St. 664; July 14, 1932; C. 482—An Act Making appropriations for the military and nonmilitary activities of the War Department for the fiscal year ending June 30, 1933, and for other purposes.

47 St. 709; July 21, 1932; C. 520—An Act To relieve destitution, to broaden the lending powers of the Reconstruction Finance Corporation, and to create employment by providing for and expediting a public-works program.[20]

47 St. 773; Jan. 20, 1933; C. 15—An Act Providing for payment of $25 to each enrolled Chippewa Indian of Minnesota from the funds standing to their credit in the Treasury of the United States.[21]

47 St. 776 Jan. 26, 1933; C. 21—An Act Relating to the deferment and adjustment of construction charges for the years 1931 and 1932 on Indian irrigation projects.[22]

47 St. 777; Jan. 27, 1933; C. 23—An Act Relative to restrictions applicable to Indians of the Five Civilized Tribes in Oklahoma.[23]

47 St. 780; Jan. 30, 1933; C. 26—An Act Making appropriations to supply urgent deficiencies in certain appropriations for the fiscal year ending June 30, 1933, and prior fiscal years, to provide supplemental appropriations for the fiscal year ending June 30, 1933, and for other purposes.[24]

47 St. 807; Feb. 14, 1933; C. 65—Joint Resolution To carry out certain obligations to certain enrolled Indians under tribal agreement.

47 St. 808; Feb. 15, 1933; C. 74—An Act To establish the boundary lines of the Chippewa Indian territory in the State of Minnesota.[25]

47 St. 818; Feb. 16, 1933; C. 93—An Act To authorize an appropriation to carry out the provisions of the Act of May 3, 1928 (45 St. 484).[26]

47 St. 819; Feb. 17, 1933; C. 97—An Act Repealing certain provisions of the Act of June 21, 1906, as amended, relating to the sale and encumbrance of lands of Kickapoo and affiliated Indians of Oklahoma.[27]

47 St. 820; Feb. 17, 1933; C. 98—An Act Making appropriations for the Department of the Interior for the fiscal year ending June 30, 1934, and for other purposes.[28] P. 829, sec. 1–25

---

[4] *Cited:* Op. Sol., May 15, 1933.

[5] *Ag.* 36 St. 1123.

[6] *Ag.* 39 St. 983.

[7] *Ag.* 45 St. 1256.

[8] *Sg.* 34 St. 80; 41 St. 535.

[9] *S.* 47 St. 820; 48 St. 362; 49 St. 176, 1757; 50 St. 564; 52 St. 291.

[10] *Ag.* 32 St. 793; 35 St. 1151. *Cited:* Memo. Sol., Dec. 17, 1935; Andreas, 71 F. 2d 908.

[11] *Sg.* 44 St. 555; 45 St. 423. *A.* 48 St. 980.

[12] *Ag.* 46 St. 495.

[13] *S.* 49 St. 571. *Cited:* 10 L. D. Memo. 864; Memo. Sol. Off., July 29, 1933.

[14] *Rg.* 40 St. 565.

[15] *Ag.* 46 St. 1471. *Cited:* Memo. Sol. Off., Oct. 26, 1932, Mar. 26, 1934; Memo. Ind. Off., Jan. 3, 1935; Memo. Sol., Dec. 21, 1936, Nov. 29, 1937; Minnesota, 305 U. S. 382.

[16] *Sg.* 36 St. 826.

[17] *Sg.* 25 St. 645; 43 St. 636; 46 St. 228, 802, 820, 1122, 1563. *S.* 47 St. 820.

[18] *Sg.* 41 St. 409. *Cited:* 72d Cong., 1st sess., Sen. Rept. No. 807; 72d Cong., 1st sess., Sen. Rept. No. 552; 72d Cong., 1st sess., H. Rept. No. 943; 72d Cong., 1st sess., Hearings, H. Comm. on Ind. Aff., H. R. 8898 & H. R. 10884; Letter by Sec'y. of Int. to Comp. Gen., Sept. 28, 1932; Memo. Sol. Off., June 12, 1933, July 10, 1933, July 25, 1933; Op. Sol., M. 29620, Jan. 14, 1938; Memo. Sol., May 19, 1938; 54 I. D. 90; Shoshone, 82 C. Cls. 23.

[19] *Sg.* 43 St. 739; 46 St. 1031, 1111.

[20] *Sg.* 42 St. 212; 45 St. 750; 46 St. 805, 1173. *S.* St. 195, 467; 49 St. 247.

[21] *Ag.* 25 St. 645.

[22] *Sg.* 47 St. 75. *S.* 49 St. 337. *Cited:* Memo. Sol. Off., July 10, 1933.

[23] *Sg.* 35 St. 312; 45 St. 495. *Cited:* 72d Cong., 1st sess., Hearings, Sen. Comm. on Ind. Aff., S. 1839; 37 Op. A. G. 193; 4 L. D. Memo. 63; 5 L. D. Memo. 10; 10 L. D. Memo. 334; 12 L. D. Memo. 289; Memo. Sol. Off., June 29, 1933; Memo. Sol., Oct. 25, 1934; Memo. Sol. Off., Jan. 14, 1935, Mar. 8, 1935; Memo. Sol., June 4, 1935; Op. Sol., M. 28125, Aug. 12, 1935; Memo. Sol., Oct. 22, 1935; Memo. Sol., May 1, 1936; Memo. of Comm'r, Aug. 11, 1936; Letter of Ass't Sec'y to A. G., Oct. 15, 1936; Memo. Sol., Jan. 13, 1937, Jan. 23, 1937, Feb. 5, 1937, Apr. 8, 1937; Memo. Acting Sol., May 11, 1937; Memo. Sol., May 14, 1938, Nov. 28, 1938; 54 I. D. 310; 54 I. D. 382; Bond, 25 F. Supp. 157; Burgess, 103 F. 2d 37; Darks, 69 F. 2d 281; Glenn, 105 F. 2d 398; Ickes, 64 F. 2d 982; In re Palmer's, 11 F. Supp. 801; King, 64 F. 2d 979; U. S. ex rel. Warren, 73 F. 2d 844; Whitchurch, 92 F. 2d 249.

[24] *S.* 49 St. 571.

[25] *Sg.* 10 St. 1165, 1169.

[26] *Sg.* 45 St. 484. *S.* 47 St. 1602; 49 St. 840.

[27] *Rg.* 34 St. 363. *Cited:* Memo. Ind. Off., July 8, 1937; U. S. v. Reily, 200 U. S. 33.

[28] *Sg.* 7 St. 46, 90, 212, 213, 230; 10 St. 1109; 11 St. 614, 731; 12 St. 441, sec. 1; 15 St. 513, 635; 19 St. 254, 256; 24 St. 388; 25 St. 645; 26 St. 795; 27 St. 644; 34 St. 375; 35 St. 312, 781; 36 St. 269; 37 St. 934; 38 St. 604, 607; 40 St. 561; 41 St. 415; 43 St. 636; 44 St. 560,

U. S. C. 387 (45 St. 210, s. 1; 1578, s. 1; 46 St. 290, s. 1; 46 St. 1126, s. 1; 47 St. 100, s. 1).[29]

47 St. 906; Feb. 25, 1933; C. 123—An Act To authorize the Secretary of the Interior to make payment of part of the expenses incurred in securing improvements in drainage projects of drainage district numbered 1, Richardson County, Nebraska, and for other purposes.

47 St. 907; Feb. 25, 1933; C. 124—An Act To authorize the Veterans' Administration or other Federal agencies to turn over to superintendents of the Indian Service amounts due Indians who are under legal disability, or to estates of such deceased Indians.[30] 25 U. S. C. 14.

47 St. 1350; Feb. 28, 1933; C. 134—An Act Making appropriations for the Legislative Branch of the Government for the fiscal year ending June 30, 1934, and for other purposes.

47 St. 1371; Mar. 1, 1933; C. 144—An Act Making appropriations for the Departments of State and Justice and for the Judiciary, and for the Departments of Commerce and Labor, for the fiscal year ending June 30, 1934, and for other purposes.[31]

47 St. 1417; Mar. 1, 1933; C. 158—An Act To amend the Act of February 14, 1920, authorizing and directing the collection of fees for work done for the benefit of Indians.[32] 25 U. S. C. 413 (41 St. 415, sec. 1).

47 St. 1418; Mar. 1, 1933; C. 160—An Act To permanently set aside certain lands in Utah as an addition to the Navajo Indian Reservation, and for other purposes.[33] Sec. 1—43 U. S. C. 190a.

47 St. 1419; Mar. 1, 1933; C. 161—An Act To amend the description of land described in section 1 of the Act approved February 14, 1931, entitled "An Act to authorize the President of the United States to establish the Canyon De Chelly National Monument within the Navajo Indian Reservation, Arizona." 16 U. S. C. 445.[34]

47 St. 1422; Mar. 2, 1933; C. 183—An Act Providing for an alternate budget for the Indian Service, fiscal year 1935.

47 St. 1424; Mar. 3, 1933; C. 198—An Act To allow credit in connection with homestead entries to widows of persons who served in certain Indian wars.[35] 43 U. S. C. 243a.

47 St. 1427; Mar. 3, 1933; C. 201—An Act To extend temporary relief to water users on irrigation projects on Indian reservations, and for other purposes.[36]

47 St. 1428; Mar. 3, 1933; C. 202—An Act To repeal obsolete sections of the Revised Statutes omitted from the United States Code.[37] Sec. 2—1 U. S. C. 60; Sec. 3—1 U. S. C. 29b.

47 St. 1432; Mar. 3, 1933; C. 203—An Act Making appropriations for the Department of Agriculture for the fiscal year ending June 30, 1934, and for other purposes.[38]

47 St. 1488; Mar. 3, 1933; C. 211—An Act For the relief of the Uintah, White River, and Uncompahgre Bands of Ute Indians of Utah, and for other purposes.[39]

47 St. 1568; Mar. 4, 1933; C. 275—An Act To authorize the Secretary of the Interior to modify the terms of existing contracts for the sale of timber on Indian land when it is in the interest of the Indians so to do.[40] Sec. 1—25 U. S. C. 407a.[41] U. S. C. A. Historical Note: The authority granted by this section, as amended, expired by its terms on Sept. 4, 1936. Sec. 2—25 U. S. C. 407b; Sec. 3—25 U. S. C. 407c.

47 St. 1569; Mar. 4, 1933; C. 276—An Act To provide for expenses of the Northern Cheyenne Indian Tribal Council and authorized delegates of the tribe.

47 St. 1571; Mar. 4, 1933; C. 281—An Act Making appropriations for the military and nonmilitary activities of the War Department for the fiscal year ending June 30, 1934, and for other purposes.

47 St. 1602; Mar. 4, 1933; C. 282—An Act Making appropriations to supply deficiencies in certain appropriations for the fiscal year ending June 30, 1933, and prior fiscal years, to provide supplemental appropriations for the fiscal years ending June 30, 1933, and June 30, 1934, and for other purposes.[42]

47 St. 1656; Feb. 10, 1932; C. 37—An Act For the relief of Harvey K. Meyer, and for other purposes.

47 St. 1657; Mar. 1, 1932; C. 66—An Act For the relief of Thomas C. LaForge.[43]

47 St. 1657; Mar. 1, 1932; C. 67—An Act Authorizing issuance of patents in fee to Benjamin Spottedhorse and Horse Spottedhorse for certain lands.[44]

47 St. 1671; June 9, 1932; C. 228—An Act For the relief of the Sherburne Mercantile Company.

47 St. 1674; June 14, 1932; C. 264—An Act For the relief of Florian Ford.

47 St. 1680; June 28, 1932; C. 304—An Act For the relief of Ross E. Adams.

47 St. 1681; June 30, 1932; C. 336—An Act For the relief of Ellingson and Groskopf (Inc.).

47 St. 1682; June 30, 1932; C. 339—An Act For the relief of J. N. Gordon.

47 St. 1690; July 1, 1932; C. 377—An Act For the relief of Viola Wright.

47 St. 1692; July 1, 1932; C. 381—An Act For the relief of R. K. Stiles and Company.

47 St. 1699; July 2, 1932; C. 415—An Act For the relief of Octavia Gulick Stone.[45]

47 St. 1719; Feb. 8, 1933; C. 44—An Act For the relief of S. F. Stracher.

47 St. 1753; Mar. 3, 1933; C. 260—An Act for the relief of Hamilton Grounds.[46]

47 St. 1753; Mar. 3, 1933; C. 261—An Act To provide for the addition of the names of certain persons to the final roll of the Indians of the Flathead Indian Reservation, Montana, and for other purposes.

47 St. 1755; Mar. 3, 1933; C. 264—An Act To authorize exchange of small tribal acreage on the Fort Hall Indian school reserve in Idaho for adjoining land.

47 St. 1755; Mar. 3, 1933; C. 265—An Act To authorize the addition of certain names to the final roll of the Sac and Fox Indians of Oklahoma.[47]

47 St. 1768; Mar. 4, 1933; C. 316—An Act For the relief of Clive Sprouse and Robert F. Moore.

47 St. 1776; Mar. 31, 1932; Concurrent Res.—Jurisdiction in Management of Indian Country.

48 STAT.

48 St. 97; May 29, 1933; C. 42—An Act Making appropriations to supply deficiencies in certain appropriations for the fiscal year ending June 30, 1933, and prior fiscal years, to provide supplemental appropriations for the fiscal years ending June 30, 1933, and June 30, 1934, and for other purposes.[48]

48 St. 105; May 29, 1933; C. 43—An Act To authorize the Comptroller General to allow claim of district numbered 13, Choctaw County, Oklahoma, for payment of tuition for Indian pupils.[49]

48 St. 108; May 31, 1933; C. 45—An Act To authorize appropriations to pay in part the liability of the United States to the Indian pueblos herein named, under the terms of the Act of June 7, 1924, and the liability of the United States to non-Indian claimants on Indian pueblo grants whose claims, extinguished under the Act of June 7, 1924, have been found by the Pueblo Lands Board to have been claims in good faith; to authorize the expenditure by the Secretary of the Interior of the sums herein authorized and of sums heretofore appropriated, in conformity with the Act of June 7, 1924, for the purchase of needed lands and water rights and the creation of other permanent economic improvements as contemplated by said Act; to provide for the protection

616, 740; 45 St. 212, 899, 938, 1550, 1569; 46 St. 90, 1061, 1127; 47 St. 96, 835, 525. *S.* 48 St. 802. *Cited:* Chippewa, 80 C. Cls. 410.

[29] *S.* 48 St. 370, s. 1; 40 St. 186, s. 1; 1769, s. 1; 50 St. 577, s. 1; 52 St. 804, s. 1; 53 St. 700, s. 1.

[30] *Cited:* Ass't Secy's Letter to Ass't to the Supt. St. Elizabeths, Apr. 15 1935; Memo. Sol., Mar. 23, 1936.

[31] *Sg.* 36 St. 826.

[32] *Ag.* 41 St. 415. S. 49 St. 170.

[33] *Sg.* 23 St. 96; 28 St. 107. *S.* 50 St. 564.

[34] *Ag.* 46 St. 1161.

[35] *Sg.* 46 St. 144.

[36] *Sg.* 47 St. 75. *S.* 49 St. 377. *Cited:* Memo. Ind. Off., June 12, 1938; Memo. Sol Off., July 10, 1938.

[37] *Sg.* 1 St. 137.

[38] *Sg.* 43 St. 739; 46 St. 1111.

[39] *Sg.* 46 St. 1092. *Cited:* Memo. Sol., Sept. 12, 1934; Memo. Sol. Off., Nov. 23, 1937; U. S. v. Sandstrom, 22 F. Supp. 190.

[40] *A.* 48 St. 311; 49 St. 1266. *Cited:* 74th Cong., 1st sess., H. Rept. No. 1688; Memo. Sol. Off., Apr. 10, 1938; Op. Sol., M.27499, Aug. 8, 1933; Memo. Sol., Oct. 23, 1933, Jan. 30, 1934; Op. Sol., M27998, Apr. 27, 1935; Memo. Sol. Off., May 18, 1937.

[41] *A.* 48 St. 311, 397; 49 St. 1266.

[42] *Sg.* 45 St. 484; 47 St. 818.

[43] *Sg.* 41 St. 751.

[44] *Sg.* 41 St. 751.

[45] *Sg.* 41 St. 3.

[46] *Sg.* 40 St. 591; 41 St. 9.

[47] *Sg.* 40 St. 591; 41 St. 9.

[48] *Sg.* 46 St. 1468.

[49] *Sg.* 46 St. 293.

of the watershed within the Carson National Forest for the Pueblo de Taos Indians of New Mexico and others interested, and to authorize the Secretary of Agriculture to contract relating thereto and to amend the Act approved June 7, 1924, in certain respects.[50] 25 U. S. C. 331 note (secs. 4–9).

48 St. 112; June 3, 1933; C. 46—An Act Authorizing a per capita payment of $100 to the members of the Menominee Tribe of Indians of Wisconsin from funds on deposit to their credit in the Treasury of the United States.

48 St. 146; June 15, 1933; C. 76—An Act Providing for per capita payments to the Seminole Indians in Oklahoma from funds standing to their credit in the Treasury.

48 St. 195; June 16, 1933; C. 90—An Act To encourage national industrial recovery, to foster fair competition, and to provide for the construction of certain useful public works, and for other purposes.[51] Sec. 201—40 U. S. C. 401; Sec. 205—40 U. S. C. 405; Sec. 220—40 U. S. C. 411; Sec. 304—15 U. S. C. 712, 40 U. S. C. 414.

48 St. 254; June 16, 1933; C. 95—An Act Providing for payment of $50 to each enrolled Chippewa Indian of the Red Lake Band of Minnesota from the timber funds standing to their credit in the Treasury of the United States.

48 St. 274; June 16, 1933; C. 100—An Act Making appropriations to supply deficiencies in certain appropriations for the fiscal year ending June 30, 1933, and prior fiscal years, to provide supplemental appropriations for the fiscal years ending June 30, 1933, and June 30, 1934, and for other purposes.[52]

48 St. 283; June 16, 1933; C. 101—An Act Making appropriations for the Executive Office and sundry independent executive bureaus, boards, commissions, and offices, for the fiscal year ending June 30, 1934, and for other purposes.

48 St. 311; June 16, 1933; C. 104—An Act To amend Public Act Numbered 435 of the Seventy-second Congress, relating to sales of timber on Indian land.[53] 25 U. S. C. 407a (47 St. 1568, sec. 1)[54]

48 St. 353; Feb. 19, 1934; C. 15—An Act Granting certain property in the State of Michigan for institutional purposes.

48 St. 362; Mar. 2, 1934; C. 38—An Act Making appropriations for the Department of the Interior for the fiscal year ending June 30, 1935, and for other purposes.[55] Sec. 1, p. 366—43 U. S. C. 90; Sec. 1, p. 370—25 U. S. C. 387 (45 St. 210, sec. 1; 1573, sec. 1; 46 St. 290, sec. 1; 1126, sec. 1; 47 St. 100, sec. 1; 829, sec. 1).[56]

48 St. 396; Mar. 5, 1934; C. 43—An Act To repeal certain specific Acts of Congress and an amendment thereto enacted to regulate the manufacture, sale, or possession of intoxicating liquors in the Indian Territory, now a part of the State of Oklahoma.[57] 25 U. S. C. 244a.

48 St. 397; Mar. 5, 1934; C. 46—Joint Resolution To amend Public Act Numbered 81 of the 73d Congress, relating to the sale of timber on Indian land.[58] 25 U. S. C. 407a (47 St. 1568, sec. 1; 48 St. 311).[59]

48 St. 401; Mar. 10, 1934; C. 55—An Act To promote the conservation of wildlife, fish, and game, and for other purposes. Sec. 4—16 U. S. C. 664; sec. 6—16 U. S. C. 666.

48 St. 467; Mar. 26, 1934; C. 89—An Act Making appropriations for the Department of Agriculture and for the Farm Credit Administration for the fiscal year ending June 30, 1935, and for other purposes.[60]

48 St. 501; Mar. 27, 1934; C. 93—An Act To authorize the Secretary of the Interior to place with the Oklahoma Historical Society, at Oklahoma City, Oklahoma, as custodian for the United States, certain records of the Five Civilized Tribes, and of other Indian tribes in the State of Oklahoma, under rules and regulations to be prescribed by him. 25 U. S. C. 199a.

48 St. 509; Mar. 28, 1934; C. 102—An Act Making appropriations for the Executive Office and sundry independent executive bureaus, boards, commissions, and offices, for the fiscal year ending June 30, 1935, and for other purposes.

48 St. 529; Apr. 7, 1934; C. 104—An Act Making appropriations for the Departments of State and Justice and for the judiciary, and for the Departments of Commerce and Labor, for the fiscal year ending June 30, 1935, and for other purposes.[61]

48 St. 583; Apr. 13, 1934; C. 119—An Act To repeal an Act of Congress entitled "An Act to prohibit the manufacture or sale of alcoholic liquors in the Territory of Alaska, and for other purposes," approved February 14, 1917, and for other purposes.[62]

48 St. 594; Apr. 16, 1934; C. 146—An Act To amend sections 3 and 4 of an Act of Congress entitled "An Act for the protection and regulation of the fisheries of Alaska", approved June 26, 1906, as amended by the Act of Congress approved June 6, 1924, and for other purposes.[63] Sec. 1—48 U. S. C. 233; Sec. 2—48 U. S. C. 232.

48 St. 596; Apr. 16, 1934; C. 147—An Act Authorizing the Secretary of the Interior to arrange with States or Territories for the education, medical attention, relief of distress, and social welfare of Indians, and for other purposes.[64] Sec. 1—25 U. S. C. 452;[65] Sec. 2—25 U. S. C. 453;[66] Sec. 3—25 U. S. C. 454;[67] Sec. 4—25 U. S. C. 455;[68] Sec. 5—25 U. S. C. 456.

48 St. 614; Apr. 26, 1934; C. 165—An Act Making appropriations for the military and nonmilitary activities of the War Department for the fiscal year ending June 30, 1935, and for other purposes.

48 St. 647; Apr. 30, 1934; C. 169—An Act To amend section 1 of the Act entitled "An Act to provide for determining the heirs of the deceased Indians, for the disposition and sale of allotments of deceased Indians, for the leasing of allotments, and for other purposes", approved June 25, 1910, as amended.[69] 25 U. S. C. 372 (36 St. 855, sec. 1; 45 St. 161).

48 St. 667; May 7, 1934; C. 221—An Act Granting citizenship to the Metlakahtla Indians of Alaska.[70] Sec. 1—8 U. S. C. 3b; Sec. 2—8 U. S. C. 3c.

48 St. 668; May 7, 1934; C. 223—An Act Providing for payment of $25 to each enrolled Chippewa Indian of Minnesota from the funds standing to their credit in the Treasury of the United States.

48 St. 786; May 21, 1934; C. 319—An Act Authorizing the conveyance of certain lands to the State of Nebraska.

48 St. 787; May 21, 1934; C. 321—An Act Repealing certain sections of the Revised Code of Laws of the United States relating to the Indians.[71]

48 St. 791; May 21, 1934; C. 323—An Act To provide for an appropriation of $50,000 with which to make a survey of the Old Indian Trail known as the "Natchez Trace", with a view of constructing a national road on this route to be known as the "Natchez Trace Parkway."

48 St. 795; May 23, 1934; C. 337—An Act To provide for the exchange of Indian and privately owned lands, Fort Mojave Indian Reservation, Arizona.[72]

48 St. 811; May 28, 1934; C. 364—An Act To authorize the Secretary of the Interior to issue patents for lots to Indians

---

[50] *Sg.* 43 St. 636. *S.* 49 St. 176, 800, 1757; 50 St. 564; 52 St. 291 *Cited:* Memo. Sol. Off., June 23, 1933; Aug. 17, 1933; Memo. Sol., Oct. 23, 1934, Mar. 14, 1935; Op. Sol., M.28850, Dec. 10, 1936; Memo. Sol., Apr. 14, 1939.

[51] *Sg.* 47 St. 717. *S.* 49 St. 1013, 1014. *Cited:* 38 Op. A. G. 118; Memo. Sol., Oct. 23, 1933, Nov. 17, 1933, Jan. 17, 1935; Op. Sol., M 27816, Jan. 22, 1935; Memo. Sol., June 15, 1937; Memo. Sol. Off., Oct. 7, 1938.

[52] *Sg.* 43 St. 636; 47 St. 91. *S.* 49 St. 176, 1757; 50 St. 564.

[53] *Ag.* 47 St. 1568. *A.* 48 St. 397; 49 St. 1266. *Cited:* Memo. Sol., Jan. 30, 1934.

[54] *A.* 48 St. 397; 49 St. 1266. The authority granted by sec. 407a by its terms expired Sept. 4, 1936.

[55] *Sg.* 7 St. 46, 99, 212, 213, 236; 10 St. 1109; 11 St. 614, 731; 15 St. 516, 635; 19 St. 254, 256; 25 St. 645; 26 St. 795; 27 St. 644; 34 St. 325; 35 St. 312, 444, 717, 781; 36 St. 273; 38 St. 604, 607, 741; 40 Stat. 297, 564; 41 St. 415, 437, 1363; 43 St. 133; 44 St. 740; 45 St. 899, 1550, 1569; 46 St. 105; 47 St. 91, 335, 825. *S.* 49 St. 176; 52 St. 1114. *Cited:* Ass't Secy's Memo., Dec. 20, 1935.

[56] *S.* 49 St. 186, sec. 1; 1760, sec. 1; 50 St. 577, sec. 1; 52 St. 804, sec. 1; 53 St. 700 sec. 1.

[57] *Rg.* 27 St. 260; 29 St. 506; 28 St. 697; 40 St. 563; 41 St. 4.

[58] *Ag.* 48 St. 311.

[59] *A.* 49 St. 1266. The authority granted by sec. 407a by its terms expired Sept. 4, 1936.

[60] *Sg.* 43 St. 739; 46 St. 1111; 47 St. 717. *Cited:* Memo. Sol., Sept. 2, 1936; Memo. Acting Sol., May 24, 1937, July 21, 1937; Memo. Secy's, June 14, 1938.

[61] *Sg.* 36 St. 826.

[62] *Rg.* 30 St. 137; 31 St. 332; 35 St. 601; 39 St. 903; 41 St. 307; 42 St. 223; 48 St. 16

[63] *Ag.* 34 St. 479; 43 St. 465.

[64] *A.* 49 St. 1458 *Cited:* Memo. Sol., May 21, 1935; Op. Sol., M. 28197, Oct. 31, 1935; Memo. Sol., Apr. 22, 1936.

[65] *A.* 49 St. 1458.

[66] *A.* 49 St. 1458.

[67] *A.* 49 St. 1458.

[68] *A.* 49 St. 1458.

[69] *Ag.* 36 St. 855.

[70] *Sg.* 26 St. 1101. *S.* 52 St. 1290.

[71] *Rg.* 4 St. 730, sec. 6; 730, sec. 10; 731, sec. 13; 731, sec. 14; 731, sec. 15; 732, sec. 19; 732, sec. 21, 23; 732, sec. 23; 11 St. 80, sec. 2; 332, sec. 2; 363, sec. 8; 12 St. 427, sec. 2. *Cited:* Ind. Off. Circ. No. 3005, July 9, 1934; Memo. Sol. Off., Jan. 19, 1937; Memo. Sol., Oct. 15, 1938; Memo. Sol. Off., Nov. 29, 1938.

[72] *Sg.* Ex. Or. No. 1296. *Cited:* Op. Sol., M. 28589, Aug. 24, 1936.

within the Indian village of Taholah, on the Quinaielt Indian Reservation, Washington.[73]

48 St. 817; May 30, 1934; C. 372—An Act Making appropriations for the Legislative Branch of the Government for the fiscal year ending June 30, 1935, and for other purposes.

48 St. 910; June 6, 1934; C. 407—An Act To authorize the Secretary of the Interior to modify the terms of existing contracts for the sale of timber on the Quinault Indian Reservation when it is in the interest of the Indians so to do.

48 St. 927; June 11, 1934; C. 442—An Act To modify the effect of certain Chippewa Indian treaties on areas in Minnesota.[74]

48 St. 958; June 14, 1934; C. 519—An Act To authorize the establishment of the Ocmulgee National Monument in Bibb County, Georgia.[75] Sec. 1—16 U. S. C. 447a; Sec. 2—16 U. S. C. 447b; Sec. 3—16 U. S. C. 447c.

48 St. 960; June 14, 1934; C. 521—An Act To define the exterior boundaries of the Navajo Indian Reservation in Arizona, and for other purposes.[76]

48 St. 964; June 15, 1934; C. 539—An Act To amend the law relating to timber operations on the Menominee Indian Reservation in Wisconsin.[77]

48 St. 965; June 15, 1934; C. 540—An Act To provide for the enrollment of members of the Menominee Indian Tribe of the State of Wisconsin.[78]

48 St. 972; June 16, 1934; C. 548—An Act To authorize payment of expenses of formulating claims of the Kiowa, Comanche, and Apache Indians of Oklahoma against the United States, and for other purposes.

48 St. 972; June 16, 1934; C. 549—An Act Authorizing and directing the Court of Claims, in the event of judgment or judgments in favor of the Cherokee Indians, or any of them, in suits by them against the United States under the Acts of March 19, 1924, and April 25, 1932, to include in its decrees allowances to Frank J. Boudinot, not exceeding 5 per centum of such recoveries, and for other purposes.[79]

48 St. 979; June 18, 1934; C. 568—An Act To amend an Act approved May 14, 1926 (44 St. 555), entitled "An Act authorizing the Chippewa Indians of Minnesota to submit claims to the Court of Claims."[80]

48 St. 980; June 18, 1934; C. 570—An Act To amend the Act approved June 28, 1932 (47 St. 337).[81]

48 St. 982; June 18, 1934; C. 573—An Act To provide for the creation of the Pioneer National Monument in the State of Kentucky, and for other purposes.[82] Sec. 1—16 U. S. C. 448; Sec. 2—16 U. S. C. 449; Sec. 3—16 U. S. C. 450.

48 St. 984; June 18, 1934; C. 576—An Act To conserve and develop Indian lands and resources; to extend to Indians the right to form business and other organizations; to establish a credit system for Indians; to grant certain rights of home rule to Indians; to provide for vocational education for Indians; and for other purposes.[83] Sec. 1—25 U. S. C. 461. Sec. 2—25 U. S. C. 462. Sec. 3—25 U. S. C. 463 (46 St. 1202).[84] Sec. 4—25 U. S. C. 464. Also see 25 U. S. C. 463c. Sec. 5—25 U. S. C. 465. Also see 25 U. S. C. 320, 321. Sec. 6—25 U. S. C. 466. Sec. 7—25 U. S. C. 467. Also see 25 U. S. C. 211. Sec. 8—25 U. S. C. 468. Sec. 9—25 U. S. C. 469. Sec. 10—25 U. S. C. 470. Sec. 11—25 U. S. C. 471. Sec. 12—25 U. S. C. 472. Also see 25 U. S. C. 44, 45, 46, 47. Sec. 13—25 U. S. C. 473. Also see 25 U. S. C. 503. Sec. 14—25 U. S. C. 474. Sec. 15—25 U. S. C. 475. Sec. 16—25 U. S. C. 476. Sec 17—25 U. S. C. 477. Sec. 18—25 U. S. C. 478.[85] USCA Historical Note: As originally enacted this section provided that the election should be called within one year after June 18, 1934. The amendment of 49 St. 378, extended the time to June 18, 1936. Act June 15, 1935, s. 3, 49 St. 378, provided that the periods of trust or the restrictions on alienation of Indian lands should be extended to Dec. 31, 1936, in case of a vote against the application of sections 461 to 479. Sec. 19—25 U. S. C. 479.

48 St. 993; June 18, 1934; C. 586—An Act To increase employment by authorizing an appropriation to provide for emergency construction of public highways and related projects, and to amend the Federal Aid Road Act, approved July 11, 1916, as amended and supplemented, and for other purposes.[86]

48 St. 1021; June 19, 1934; C. 648—An Act Making appropriations to supply deficiencies in certain appropriations for the fiscal year ending June 30, 1934, and prior fiscal years, to provide supplemental general and emergency appropriations for the fiscal years ending June 30, 1934, and June 30, 1935, and for other purposes.[87]

48 St. 1120; June 19, 1934; C. 664—An Act To amend section 99 of the Judicial Code (U. S. C., tit. 28, sec. 180), as amended.[88]

48 St. 1184; June 21, 1934; C. 688—An Act To authorize the acquisition by the United States of the land upon which the Seneca Indian School, Wyandotte, Oklahoma, is located.[89]

48 St. 1185; June 21, 1934; C. 690—An Act To restore homestead rights in certain cases.[90] 43 U. S. C. 187a.

48 St. 1216; June 26, 1934; C. 749—An Act For the relief of the Nez Perce Tribe of Indians.[91]

---

[73] *Ag.* 36 St. 858. *Cited:* Op. Sol., M. 27770, May 22, 1935.

[74] *Sg.* 10 St. 1109, 1165; 20 St. 566.

[75] *Sg.* 39 St. 535.

[76] *Sg.* 15 St. 667; 23 St. 96; 36 St. 558, 575; 41 St. 1063; Ex. Or. Nov. 14, 1901. *S.* 48 St. 984; 49 St. 176, 1757; 50 St. 564; 52 St. 291.

[77] *Ag.* 35 St. 52. *S.* 50 St. 564.

[78] *Cited:* Memo. Sol., Jan. 10, 1935.

[79] *Sg.* 43 St. 27; 47 St. 137.

[80] *Ag.* 44 St. 555. *Sg.* 25 St. 642. *Cited:* Chippewa, 305 U. S. 479; Chippewa, 301 U. S. 358; Chippewa, 305 U. S. 479; Chippewa, 307 U. S. 1.

[81] *Ag.* 47 St. 337.

[82] *Sg.* 39 St. 535.

[83] *Sg.* Ex. Or. Feb. 1, 1917; 23 St. 894, sec. 17; 25 St. 451; 29 St. 334; 46 St. 1202; 48 St. 960. *A.* 49 St. 1250; 50 St. 862. *S.* 49 St. 176, 571, 378, 801, 1757, 1928, 1967; 50 St. 536, 564; 52 St. 193, 216, 291, 347, 1209. *Cited:* 73d Cong. 2d sess., Hearings, H. Comm on Ind. Aff., H. R. 7902; 73d Cong., 2d sess., Hearings, Sen. Comm. on Ind Aff., S. 2755; 74th Cong., 2d sess., H. Rept. No. 2244; Brown, 18 J. Comp. Leg. 129; Cohen, 6 Ind. at W. 10, p. 40; McNickle, 5 Ind at W. 11; Mueller, 3 Ind. at W. 24; Indian at Work—Special Reorganization Number, July, 1936; 38 Op. A. G. 118; 38 Op. A. G. 121; 5 L. D. Memo. 77; 5 L. D. Memo. 166; 8 L. D. Memo. 220; Memo Sol. Off., Mar. 26, 1934; Memo. Sol., May 15, 1934, July 16, 1934 Aug. 8, 1934, Aug. 8, 1934, Aug. 14, 1934; Memo. Sol. Off., Aug 18, 1934; Memo. Sol., Sept. 6 1934, Oct. 2, 1934, Oct. 3, 1934; Memo. Sol. Off., Oct. 9, 1934; Memo Sol., Oct. 12, 1934; Memo. Sol Off., Oct. 17, 1934, Nov. 1, 1934; Op. A. G., Nov. 1, 1934; Memo Sol. Off., Nov. 10, 1934; Memo. Sol., Nov. 20, 1934, Nov. 21, 1934; Op. Sol., Nov. 22, 1934; List of Ind. Constitutions, Dec. 13, 1934; Memo. Sol., Dec. 14, 1934, Dec. 18, 1934, to Ass't. Comm'r. Ind Off. Dec. 22, 1934, Jan. 17, 1935; Op. Sol., M. 27903; Feb. 5, 1935; Memo Sol., Feb. 8, 1935; Letter from Ass't Comm'r Ind. Aff. to Chairman Fed Pow. Com., Feb. 19, 1935; Memo. Sol., Mar. 9, 1935, Mar. 22 1935, Mar. 29, 1935, Mar. 30, 1935, Apr. 4, 1935; Op. Sol., M. 27939 Apr. 9, 1935; Letter from Acting Sec'y of Int. to Comp. Gen., Apr 18 1935; Op. Sol., M. 27770 May 22, 1935; Memo. Sol., May 27 1935, June 11, 1935, July 17, 1935; Op. Sol., M. 28086, July 17, 1935 Memo. Sol., July 24, 1935, Aug. 27, 1935; Op. Sol., M. 28183, Oct. 16, 1935; Memo. Sol. Off., Oct. 28, 1935; Memo. Sol., Nov. 12, 1935; Memo. Sol. Off., Nov. 14, 1935, Nov. 23, 1935; Memo. Sol., Dec. 5, 1935, Dec. 10, 1935, Jan. 9, 1936; Memo. Sol. Off., Jan. 22, 1936; Memo. Sol., Mar. 12, 1936; Op. Sol., M. 28316, Mar. 18, 1936; Memo. Sol., Mar. 20, 1936; Op. Sol., M. 28317, Mar. 31, 1936; Memo. Sol. Off., Apr. 9, 1936; Memo. Sol., Apr. 15, 1936; Memo. Sol., Apr. 22, 1936; May 12, 1936, May 15, 1936; Op. Sol., M. 27678, May 20, 1936; Memo. Sol., May 25, 1936, May 27, 1936; Memo. Sol. Off., May 28, 1936; Memo. Sol., June 23, 1936, June 30, 1936, July 3, 1936, July 8, 1936, July 9, 1936; Comm'r's. Circular No. 3170, July 28, 1936; Memo. Sol., July 31, 1936, Aug. 22, 1936, Aug. 25, 1936, Aug. 31, 1936, Sept. 15, 1936, Sept. 19, 1936; Memo. Sol. Off., Sept. 22, 1936; Memo. Sol., Oct. 5, 1936, Oct. 5, 1936, Oct. 16, 1936, Oct. 23, 1936, Oct. 23, 1936, Oct. 30, 1936; Op. Comp. Gen's, Dec. 2, 1936; Memo. Sol., Dec. 7, 1936, Dec. 21, 1936, Dec. 31, 1936, Jan. 4, 1937; Memo. Comm'r, Jan. 6, 1937; Memo. Sol., Jan. 11, 1937, Jan. 12, 1937, Jan. 23, 1937; Memo. Sol. Off., Jan. 28, 1937; Memo. Sol., Feb. 3, 1937, Feb. 8, 1937; Memo. Secy's, Feb. 20, 1937; Statement by Comm. on S. 1736 repealing Wheeler-Howard Act, Mar. 3, 1937. Memo. Sol., Mar. 6, 1937; Op. Sol., M. 29097, Apr. 8, 1937, M. 28978, Apr. 19, 1937; Memo. Sol., May 1, 1937; Memo. Sol. Off., May 18, 1937; Memo. Sol., May 22, 1937; Memo. Sol. Off., June 3, 1937; Memo. Sol., July 15, 1937, July 19, 1937; Memo. Acting Sol., July 29, 1937; Memo. Sol., Aug. 14, 1937; Memo. for Comm'r. of Ind. Affs., Aug. 23, 1937; Memo. Sol., Sept. 11, 1937, Sept. 29, 1937; Memo. Sol. Off., Oct. 8, 1937; Memo. Sol., Oct. 20, 1937, Oct. 20, 1937; Nov. 11, 1937, Nov. 11, 1937, Dec. 11, 1937, Dec. 14, 1937; Op. Sol., M. 29560, Dec. 28, 1937; Memo. Sol., Jan. 8, 1938; Op. Sol., M. 29620, Jan. 14, 1938; Memo. Sol., Jan. 18, 1938, Feb. 18, 1938; Op. Sol., M. 29616, Feb. 19, 1938; Memo. Sol., Feb. 25, 1938; Mar. 12, 1938, Mar. 14, 1938, Apr. 12, 1938; Memo. Sol. Off., Apr. 13, 1938; Memo. Sol., Apr. 14, 1938, May 14, 1938; Memo. Sol. Off., June 6, 1938; Memo. Sol., M. 29798, June 15, 1938; Memo. Sol. Off., June 25, 1938; Memo. Acting Sol's., July 12, 1938; Letter from Ass't Sec'y to A. G., July 16, 1938; Memo. Sol. Off., July 16, 1938; Op. Sol., M. 29791, Aug. 1, 1938; Memo Sol., Aug. 2, 1938; Memo. Asst. Sec'y, Aug. 17, 1938, Aug. 23, 1938; Memo. Sol., Aug. 26, 1938, Aug. 27, 1938, Sept. 13, 1938; Op. Sol., M. 29961, Oct. 4, 1938; Memo. Sol., Oct. 15, 1938; Memo. Sol. Off., Oct. 27, 1938; Memo. Sol., Nov. 18, 1938; Memo. Sol. Off., Nov. 29, 1938; Memo. Sol., Dec. 22, 1938; Memo Sol. Off., Dec. 30, 1938; Memo. Sol., Feb. 17, 1939, Feb. 17, 1939; Feb. 17, 1939, Feb. 20, 1939, Feb. 23, 1939, Mar. 11, 1939, Mar. 16, 1939, Mar. 28, 1939, Nov. 11, 1939; Memo. of Asst. Sec'y, Dec. 5, 1938; 54 I. D. 584; Bd. of Co. Comm'rs of Jackson, 100 F. 2d 929; Ex p. Pero, 99 F. 2d 28; Minnesota, 305 U. S. 382; U. S. v. Colvard, 89 F. 2d 312; U. S. v. Lewis, 95 F. 2d 236; U. S. v. Nez Perce, 95 F. 2d 232.

[84] *A.* 50 St. 802.

[85] *S.* 49 St. 378, sec. 2.

[86] *Sg.* 45 St. 751; 46 St. 805. *S.* 49 St. 247, 1757.

[87] *Sg.* 23 St. 234; 34 St. 375; 45 St. 312, 750; 46 St. 805, 1128, 1567. *S.* 49 St. 176, 1757; 50 St. 564, 755; 52 St. 85, 201, 1114. *Cited:* Op. Sol., M. 27759, Jan. 22, 1935.

[88] *Ag.* 26 St. 67.

[89] *S.* 49 St. 176, 894.

[90] *Sg.* 39 St. 926; 43 St. 981.

[91] *Ag.* 45 St. 1249.

48 St. 1224; June 26, 1934; C. 756—An Act Providing that permanent appropriations be subject to annual consideration and appropriation by Congress, and for other purposes.[82] Sec. 1—31 U. S. C. 722; Sec. 4—31 U. S. C. 725c.

48 St. 1240; June 26, 1934; C. 758—An Act To amend the Act of June 19, 1930 (46 St. 788), entitled "An Act providing for the sale of the remainder of the coal and asphalt deposits in the segregated mineral land in the Choctaw and Chickasaw Nations, Oklahoma, and for other purposes." [83]

48 St. 1245; June 27, 1934; C. 846—An Act To modify the operation of the Indian liquor laws on lands which were formerly Indian lands.[84] 25 U. S. C. 254.

48 St. 1269; June 28, 1934; C. 865—An Act To stop injury to the public grazing lands by preventing overgrazing and soil deterioration, to provide for their orderly use, improvement, and development, to stabilize the livestock industry dependent upon the public range, and for other purposes.[85] Sec. 1—43 U. S. C. 315; Sec. 11—43 U. S. C. 315j.

48 St. 1296; Mar. 24, 1933; C. 9—An Act For the relief of the Holy Family Hospital, Saint Ignatius, Montana.

48 St. 1305; Mar. 2, 1934; C. 39—An Act For the relief of William C. Campbell.

48 St. 1365; May 25, 1934; C. 352—An Act For the relief of the widow of D. W. Tanner for expense of purchasing an artificial limb.

48 St. 1380; June 11, 1934; C. 450—An Act For the relief of Milburn Knapp.

48 St. 1380; June 11, 1934; C. 451—An Act For the relief of Peter Pierre.

48 St. 1385; June 11, 1934; C. 462—An Act For the relief of certain Indians of the Fort Peck Reservation, Montana.

48 St. 1389; June 13, 1934; C. 507—An Act For the relief of Jose Ramon Cordova.

48 St. 1391; June 14, 1934; C. 525—An Act For relief of M. M. Twichel.

48 St. 1411; June 18, 1934; C. 643—An Act Authorizing the Secretary of the Treasury to pay Doctor A. W. Pearson, of Peever, South Dakota, and the Peabody Hospital, at Webster, South Dakota, for medical services and supplies furnished to Indians.

48 St. 1411; June 18, 1934; C. 645—An Act For the relief of John W. Adair.[86]

48 St. 1420; June 21, 1934; C. 706—An Act For the relief of Doctor Charles T. Grang[illegible].

48 St. 1422; June 22, 1934; C. 723—An Act For the relief of C. V. Mason.

48 St. 1437; June 26, 1934; C. 784—An Act Authorizing the Secretary of the Interior to pay E. C. Sampson, of Billings, Montana, for services rendered the Crow Tribe of Indians.

48 St. 1448; June 26, 1934; C. 811—An Act For the relief of Erik Nylin.[87]

48 St. 1454; June 26, 1934; C. 825—An Act For the relief of the rightful heirs of Wakicunzewin, an Indian.

48 St. 1459; June 26, 1934; C. 837—An Act For the relief of Jerry O'Shea.

48 St. 1463; June 27, 1934; C. 854—An Act For the relief of Lucy B. Hertz and J. W. Hertz.

48 St. 1464; June 27, 1934; C. 858—An Act For the relief of the estate of Jennie Walton.

48 St. 1465; June 27, 1934; C. 861—An Act For the relief of Ransome Cooyate.

48 St. 1467; June 28, 1934; C. 870—An Act Authorizing the Court of Claims to hear, consider, adjudicate, and enter judgment upon the claims against the United States of J. A. Tippit, L. P. Hudson, Chester Howe, J. E. Arnold, Joseph W. Gillette, J. S. Bounds, W. N. Vernon, T. B Sullivan, J. H. Neill, David C. McCallib, J. J. Beckham, and John Toles.[88]

49 STAT.

49 St. 6; Feb. 2, 1935; C. 3—An Act Making appropriations for the Executive Office and sundry independent executive bureaus, boards, commissions, and offices for the fiscal year ending June 30, 1936, and for other purposes.[89]

49 St. 49; Mar. 21, 1935; C. 36—An Act Making appropriations to supply deficiencies in certain appropriations for the fiscal year ending June 30, 1935, and prior fiscal years, to provide supplemental appropriations for the fiscal year ending June 30, 1935, and for other purposes.

49 St. 67; Mar. 22, 1935; C. 39—An Act Making appropriations for the Departments of State and Justice and for the Judiciary, and for the Departments of Commerce and Labor, for the fiscal year ending June 30, 1936, and for other purposes.[1]

49 St. 120; Apr. 9, 1935; C. 54—An Act Making appropriations for the military and nonmilitary activities of the War Department for the fiscal year ending June 30, 1936, and for other purposes.[2]

49 St. 176; May 9, 1935; C. 101—An Act Making appropriations for the Department of the Interior for the fiscal year ending June 30, 1936, and for other purposes.[3] 25 U. S. C. 387.

49 St. 217; May 14, 1935; C. 108—An Act To add certain public-domain land in Montana to the Rocky Boy Indian Reservation.[4]

49 St. 244; May 15, 1935; C. 112—An Act Extending the time for repayment of the revolving fund for the benefit of the Crow Indians.[5]

49 St. 247; May 17, 1935; C. 131—An Act Making appropriations for the Department of Agriculture and for the Farm Credit Administration for the fiscal year ending June 30, 1936, and for other purposes.[6]

49 St. 286; May 22, 1935; C. 135—An Act Granting a leave of absence to settlers of homestead lands during the year 1935. 43 U. S. C. 237c.

49 St. 312; May 29, 1935; C. 157—An Act To set aside certain lands for the Chippewa Indians in the State of Minnesota.

49 St. 321; June 4, 1935; C. 168—An Act To compensate the Chippewa Indians of Minnesota for lands set aside by treaties for their future homes and later patented to the State of Minnesota under the Swamp Land Act.[7]

49 St. 327; June 7, 1935; C. 188—An Act To provide funds for cooperation with public-school districts in Glacier County, Montana, in the improvement and extension of school buildings to be available to both Indian and white children.[8]

49 St. 327; June 7, 1935; C. 189—An Act To provide funds for cooperation with the public-school board at Wolf Point, Montana, in the construction or improvement of a public-school building to be available to Indian children of the Fort Peck Indian Reservation, Montana.[9]

49 St. 328; June 7, 1935; C. 190—An Act To provide funds for cooperation with school district numbered 23, Polson, Montana, in the improvement and extension of school buildings to be available to both Indian and white children.[10]

49 St. 328; June 7, 1935; C. 191—An Act To provide funds for cooperation with Joint School District Numbered 28, Lake and Missoula Counties, Montana, for extension of public-school buildings to be available to Indian children of the Flathead Indian Reservation.[11]

49 St. 328; June 7, 1935; C. 192—An Act To provide funds for cooperation with the school board at Brockton, Montana, in the extension of the public-school building at that place to be available to Indian children of the Fort Peck Indian Reservation.[12]

49 St. 329; June 7, 1935; C. 193—An Act For expenditure of funds for cooperation with the public-school board at Poplar, Montana, in the construction or improvement of public-school building to be available to Indian children of the Fort Peck Indian Reservation, Montana.[13]

---

[82] *Rg.* 24 St. 389; 25 St. 895; 26 St. 795; 29 St. 334; 30 St. 994; 3[illegible] St. 211; 34 St. 326; 37 St. 728; 43 St. 1101; 44 St. 465; 45 St. 686; 4[illegible] St. 446. *S.* 49 St. 176, 1757, 1928; 50 St. 564, 873; 52 St. 291, 1114.

[83] *Ag.* 46 St. 788. *Sg.* 47 St. 88.

[84] *Sg.* 29 St. 506.

[85] *S.* 50 St. 536. *Cited:* Op. Sol., M. 28869, Feb. 13, 1937; 56 I. D 808; U. S. v. Rose, 20 F. Supp. 350.

[86] *Sg.* 39 St. 744.

[87] *Sg.* 39 St. 746.

[88] *Sg.* 32 St. 641; 34 St. 140; 43 St. 989. *Cited:* McCallib, 8[illegible] C. Cls. 79.

[89] *Cited:* Letter of Comm'r to Ind. Agents, Oct. 9, 1937.

[1] *Sg.* 36. St. 326.

[2] *S.* 49 St. 1278.

[3] *Sg.* 11 St. 611, 729; 15 St. 513; 25 St. 645, 895; 26 St. 794; 27 St. 644; 34 St. 375; 35 St. 312, 444, 783; 36 St. 273; 38 St. 604, 741; [illegible]0 St. 108, 297, 504; 41 St. 415, 437, 1363; 43 St. 636; 44 St. 560; [illegible]5 St. 212, 213, 312, 750, 1550; 46 St. 105; 47 St. 335, 1417; 48 St. [illegible]03, 277, 367, 369, 377, 960, 984, 986, 1033, 1058, 1194, 1227. *S.* 49 St. 571, 1757; 50 St. 564, 755; 52 St. 1114. *Cited:* Op. Sol., M. 28317, Mar. 31, 1936.

[4] *Sg.* 30 St. 739; 44 St. 1347.

[5] *Sg.* 41 St. 755; 43 St. 1301.

[6] *Sg.* 43 St. 739; 46 St. 805, 1111; 47 St. 717; 48 St. 994.

[7] *Sg.* 12 St. 3, 1249; 13 St. 693; 16 St. 719; 25 St. 645. *S.* 49 St. 1757.

[8] *S.* 49 St. 571, 1757; 50 St. 564.

[9] *S.* 49 St. 571, 1757; 50 St. 564.

[10] *S.* 49 St. 571, 1757; 50 St. 564.

[11] *S.* 49 St. 571, 1757; 50 St. 564.

[12] *S.* 49 St. 571, 1757; 50 St. 564.

[13] *S.* 49 St. 571, 1757; 50 St. 564.

49 St. 329; June 7, 1935; C. 195—An Act To provide funds for cooperation with Marysville School District, numbered 325, Snohomish County, Washington, for extension of public-school buildings to be available for Indian children.[14]

49 St. 330; June 7, 1935; C. 196—An Act To provide funds for cooperation with the school board at Queets, Washington, in the construction of a public-school building to be available to Indian children of the village of Queets, Jefferson County, Washington.[15]

49 St. 330; June 7, 1935; C. 197—An Act To provide funds for cooperation with White Swan School District, Numbered 88, Yakima County, Washington, for extension of public-school buildings to be available for Indian children of the Yakima Reservation.[16]

49 St. 331; June 7, 1935; C. 198—An Act To provide funds for cooperation with the public-school board at Covelo, California, in the construction of public-school buildings to be available to Indian children of the Round Valley Reservation, California.[17]

49 St. 331; June 7, 1935; C. 199—An Act To provide funds for cooperation with the school board of Shannon County, South Dakota, in the construction of a consolidated high-school building to be available to both white and Indian children.[18]

49 St. 332; June 7, 1935; C. 202—An Act To transfer certain lands from the Veterans' Administration to the Department of the Interior for the benefit of Yavapai Indians, Arizona.

49 St. 333; June 7, 1935; C. 204—An Act To provide funds for cooperation with school district numbered 27, Big Horn County, Montana, for extension of public-school buildings to be available to Indian children.[19]

49 St. 333; June 7, 1935; C. 205—An Act To provide funds for cooperation with Harlem School District Numbered 12, Blaine County, Montana, for extension of public-school buildings and equipment to be available for Indian children.[20]

49 St. 336; June 11, 1935; C. 215—An Act To provide funds for cooperation with school district numbered 17-H, Big Horn County, Montana, for extension of public-school buildings, to be available to Indian children.[21]

49 St. 336; June 11, 1935; C. 216—An Act To provide funds for cooperation with the school board at Medicine Lake, Montana, in construction of a public-school building to be available to Indian children of the village of Medicine Lake, Sheridan County, Montana.[22]

49 St. 337; June 13, 1935; C. 219—An Act To further extend relief to water users on United States reclamation projects and on Indian irrigation projects.[23]

49 St. 339; June 14, 1935; C. 238—An Act Authorizing the exchange of the lands reserved for the Seminole Indians in Florida for other lands.

49 St. 340; June 14, 1935; C. 239—An Act To authorize an appropriation to carry out the provisions of the Act of May 3, 1928 (45 St. 484).[24]

49 St. 376; June 14, 1935; C. 248—Joint Resolution Making immediately available the appropriation for the fiscal year 1936 for the construction, repair, and maintenance of Indian-reservation roads.

49 St. 378; June 15, 1935; C. 260—An Act To define the election procedure under the Act of June 18, 1934, and for other purposes.[25] Sec. 1—25 U. S. C. 478a; Sec. 2—25 U. S. C. 478 (48 St. 988, sec. 18). USCA Historical Note: As originally enacted this section provided that the election should be called within one year after June 18, 1934. The amendment of June 15, 1935, extended the time to June 18, 1936. Act June 15, 1935, s. 3, 49 St. 378, provided that the periods of trust or the restrictions on alienation of Indian lands should be extended to Dec. 31, 1936, in case of a vote against the application of sections 461 to 479. Sec. 3—See above Historical Note. Sec. 4—25 U. S. C. 478b.

49 St. 388; June 19, 1935; C. 275—An Act Authorizing the Tlingit and Haida Indians of Alaska to bring suit in the United States Court of Claims, and conferring jurisdiction upon said court to hear, examine, adjudicate, and enter judgment upon any and all claims which said Indians may have, or claim to have, against the United States, and for other purposes.[26]

49 St. 393; June 20, 1935; C. 281—An Act To reserve eighty acres on the public domain for the use and benefit of the Kanosh Band of Indians in the State of Utah.

49 St. 393; June 20, 1935; C. 282—An Act Transferring certain national-forest lands to the Zuni Indian Reservation, New Mexico.

49 St. 444; July 2, 1935; C. 358—An Act Providing for the payment of $15 to each enrolled Chippewa Indian of the Red Lake Band of Minnesota from the timber funds standing to their credit in the Treasury of the United States.

49 St. 459; July 8, 1935; C. 374—An Act Making appropriations for the Legislative Branch of the Government for the fiscal year ending June 30, 1936, and for other purposes.

49 St. 496; July 24, 1935; C. 414—An Act To amend an Act entitled "An Act setting aside Rice Lake and contiguous lands in Minnesota for the exclusive use and benefit of the Chippewa Indians of Minnesota", approved June 23, 1926, and for other purposes.[27]

49 St. 571; Aug. 12, 1935; C. 508—An Act Making appropriations to supply deficiencies in certain appropriations for the fiscal year ending June 30, 1935, and for prior fiscal years, to provide supplemental appropriations for the fiscal years ending June 30, 1935, and June 30, 1936, and for other purposes.[28] Sec. 2—25 U. S. C. 475a.

49 St. 612; Aug. 13, 1935; C. 518—An Act To provide funds for acquisition of the property of the Haskell Students Activities Association on behalf of the Indian School known as "Haskell Institute", Lawrence, Kansas.[29]

49 St. 654; Aug. 15, 1935; C. 551—An Act Authorizing a capital fund for the Chippewa Indian Cooperative Marketing Association.[30]

49 St. 655; Aug. 15, 1935; C. 553—Joint Resolution To carry out the intention of Congress with reference to the claims of the Crow Tribe of Indians of Montana and any band thereof against the United States.[31]

49 St. 800; Aug. 26, 1935; C. 683—An Act To authorize an appropriation to pay non-Indian claimants whose claims have been extinguished under the Act of June 7, 1924, but who have been found entitled to awards under said Act as supplemented by the Act of May 31, 1933.[32]

49 St. 801; Aug. 26, 1935; C. 686—An Act Conferring jurisdiction upon the Court of Claims to hear and determine claims of certain bands or tribes of Indians residing in the State of Oregon.[33]

49 St. 803; Aug. 26, 1935; C. 687—An Act To provide for control and regulation of public-utility holding companies, and for other purposes.[34] Sec. 208—16 U. S. C. 810; Sec. 319—16 U. S. C. 825r; Sec. 320—16 U. S. C. 791a.

49 St. 887; Aug. 27, 1935; C. 745—An Act To authorize the Secretary of the Interior to provide by agreement with Middle Rio Grande Conservancy District, a subdivision of the State of New Mexico, for maintenance and operation on newly reclaimed Pueblo Indian lands in the Rio Grande Valley, New Mexico, reclaimed under previous Act of Congress, and authorizing an annual appropriation to pay the cost thereof for a period of not to exceed 5 years.[35]

49 St. 891; Aug. 27, 1935; C. 748—An Act To promote the development of Indian arts and crafts and to create a board to assist therein, and for other purposes.[36] Sec. 1—25 U. S. C. 305; Sec. 2—25 U. S. C. 305a; Sec. 3—25 U. S. C. 305b; Sec. 4—25 U. S. C. 305c; Sec. 5—25 U. S. C. 305d; Sec. 6—25 U. S. C. 305e.

49 St. 894; Aug. 27, 1935; C. 750—An Act Authorizing distribution of funds to the credit of the Wyandotte Indians, Oklahoma.[37]

---

[14] *S.* 49 St. 571, 1757; 50 St. 564.
[15] *S.* 49 St. 571, 1757; 50 St. 564.
[16] *S.* 49 St. 571, 1757; 50 St. 564.
[17] *S.* 49 St. 571, 1757; 50 St. 564.
[18] *S.* 49 St. 571, 1757; 50 St. 564.
[19] *S.* 49 St. 571, 1757; 50 St. 564.
[20] *S.* 49 St. 571, 1757; 50 St. 564.
[21] *S.* 49 St. 571, 1757; 50 St. 564.
[22] *S.* 49 St. 571, 1757; 50 St. 564.
[23] *Sg.* 47 St. 776, 1427; 48 St. 500.
[24] *Sg.* 45 St. 484; 47 St. 818. *S.* 49 St. 1757.
[25] *Sg.* 48 St. 984. *S.* 52 St. 291. *Cited:* Memo. Sol., July 17, 1935.

[26] *Sg.* 43 St. 253, 964.
[27] *Ag.* 44 St. 763. *Cited:* U. S. v. 4,450.72 Acres, 27 F. Supp. 167.
[28] *Sg.* 47 St. 412, 783; 48 St. 984; 49 St. 181, 327, 329, 330, 331, 333, 336. *S.* 49 St. 1757; 50 St. 564; 52 St. 1209. *Cited:* Cherokee, 85 C. Cls. 76.
[29] *S.* 49 St. 1109.
[30] *Sg.* 48 St. 986.
[31] *Sg.* 36 St. 1087; 44 St. 807.
[32] *Sg.* 43 St. 636; 48 St. 109. *S.* 49 St. 1757.
[33] *Sg.* 10 St. 1018, 1027, 1122, 1125, 1143; 12 St. 981; 45 St. 1256; 48 St. 984.
[34] *Ag.* 41 St. 1072.
[35] *Sg.* 45 St. 312. *A.* 52 St. 778. *Cited:* Op. Sol., M. 28108, Mar. 18, 1936.
[36] *Sg.* 42 St. 1488. *S.* 49 St. 1757; 50 St. 564; 52 St. 291. *Cited:* Memo. Sol., Nov. 27, 1936.
[37] *Sg.* 48 St. 1184.

49 St. 1013; Aug. 30, 1935; C. 827—An Act To provide funds for cooperation with Cannon Ball School District, Sioux County, North Dakota, for extension of public-school buildings to be available for Indian children.[38]

49 St. 1014; Aug. 30, 1935; C. 828—An Act To provide funds for cooperation with Fort Yates School District, Sioux County, North Dakota, for extension of public-school buildings to be available for Indian children.[39]

49 St. 1049; Aug. 30, 1935; C. 832—An Act Authorizing the Chippewa Indians of Wisconsin to submit claims to the Court of Claims.

49 St. 1085; Sept. 3, 1935; C. 839—An Act To refer the claim of the Menominee Tribe of Indians to the Court of Claims with the absolute right of appeal to the Supreme Court of the United States.[40]

49 St. 1094; Jan. 17, 1936; C. 7—An Act To reserve certain public-domain lands in Nevada and Oregon as a grazing reserve for Indians of Fort McDermitt, Nevada.

49 St. 1106; Feb. 11, 1936; C. 44—An Act To reimpose and extend the trust period on lands reserved for the Pala Band of Mission Indians, California.[41]

49 St. 1109; Feb. 11, 1936; C. 49—An Act Making appropriations to provide urgent supplemental appropriations for the fiscal year ending June 30, 1936, to supply deficiencies in certain appropriations for the fiscal year ending June 30, 1936, and for prior fiscal years, and for other purposes.[42]

49 St. 1135; Feb. 11, 1936; C. 50—An Act To provide for the leasing of restricted Indian lands of Indians of the Five Civilized Tribes in Oklahoma.[43] 25 U. S. C. 393a.

49 St. 1160; Mar. 12, 1936; C. 138—An Act To amend section 3 of the Act approved May 10, 1928, entitled "An Act to extend the period of restriction in lands of certain members of the Five Civilized Tribes, and for other purposes", as amended February 14, 1931.[44]

49 St. 1167; Mar. 19, 1936; C. 156—An Act Making appropriations for the Executive Office and sundry independent executive bureaus, boards, commissions, and offices, for the fiscal year ending June 30, 1937, and for other purposes.

49 St. 1206; Apr. 14, 1936; C. 215—An Act To create a commission and to extend further relief to water users on United States reclamation projects and on Indian irrigation projects.[45]

49 St. 1214; Apr. 17, 1936; C. 233—An Act Making appropriations for the Legislative Branch of the Government for the fiscal year ending June 30, 1937, and for other purposes.

49 St. 1235; Apr. 20, 1936; C. 239—An Act Granting a leave of absence to settlers of homestead lands during the year 1936. 43 U. S. C. 237e.

49 St. 1250; May 1, 1936; C. 254—An Act To extend certain provisions of the Act approved June 18, 1934, commonly known as the Wheeler-Howard Act (Public Law Numbered 383 73d Congress, 48 St. 984), to the Territory of Alaska, to provide for the designation of Indian reservations in Alaska, and for other purposes.[46] Sec. 1—48 U. S. C. 362; Sec. 2—48 U. S. C. 358a.

49 St. 1266; May 6, 1936; C. 840—Joint Resolution To amend Public Act Numbered 435, 72d Congress.[47] 25 U. S. C. 407a

49 St. 1272; May 15, 1936; C. 390—An Act For the relief of the Confederated Bands of Ute Indians located in Utah, Colorado, and New Mexico.[48]

49 St. 1272; May 15, 1936; C. 391—An Act To amend an Act entitled "An Act authorizing the Chippewa Indians of Minnesota to submit claims to the Court of Claims", approved May 14, 1926 (44 St. 555.)[49]

49 St. 1273; May 15, 1936; C. 392—An Act To provide funds for cooperation with Wellpinit School District Numbered 49 Stevens County, Washington, for the construction of a public-school building to be available for Indian children of the Spokane Reservation.[50]

49 St. 1274; May 15, 1936; C. 394—An Act To provide funds for cooperation with the public-school district at Hays, Montana, for construction and improvement of public-school buildings to be available for Indian children.

49 St. 1276; May 15, 1936; C. 398—An Act To amend an Act entitled "An Act authorizing certain tribes of Indians to submit claims to the Court of Claims, and for other purposes", approved May 26, 1920.[51]

49 St. 1278; May 15, 1936; C. 404—An Act Making appropriations for the military and nonmilitary activities of the War Department for the fiscal year ending June 30, 1937, and for other purposes.[52]

49 St. 1309; May 15, 1936; C. 405—An Act Making appropriations for the Departments of State and Justice and for the Judiciary, and for the Departments of Commerce and Labor, for the fiscal year ending June 30, 1937, and for other purposes.[53]

49 St. 1421; June 4, 1936; C. 489—An Act Making appropriations for the Department of Agriculture and for the Farm Credit Administration for the fiscal year ending June 30, 1937, and for other purposes.[54]

49 St. 1458; June 4, 1936; C. 490—An Act To amend an Act entitled "An Act authorizing the Secretary of the Interior to arrange with States or Territories for the education, medical attention, relief of distress, and social welfare of Indians, and for other purposes."[55] Sec. 1—25 U. S. C. 452 (48 St. 596, s. 1) Sec. 2—25 U. S. C. 453 (48 St. 596, s. 2) Sec. 3—25 U. S. C. 454 (48 St. 596, s. 3) Sec. 4—25 U. S. C. 455 (48 St. 596, s. 4).

49 St. 1459; June 4, 1936; C. 491—An Act To amend the last paragraph, as amended, of the Act entitled "An Act to refer the claims of the Delaware Indians to the Court of Claims, with the right of appeal to the Supreme Court of the United States", approved February 7, 1925.[56]

49 St. 1459; June 4, 1936; C. 492—An Act To authorize an appropriation to pay non-Indian claimants whose claims have been extinguished under the Act of June 7, 1924, but who have been found entitled to awards under said Act as supplemented by the Act of May 31, 1933.[57]

49 St. 1513; June 15, 1936; C. 549—An Act Limiting the operation of sections 109 and 113 of the Criminal Code and section 190 of the Revised Statutes of the United States with respect to counsel in certain cases.[58]

49 St. 1519; June 16, 1936; C. 582—An Act To amend the Federal Aid Highway Act, approved July 11, 1916, as amended and supplemented, and for other purposes.[59] Sec. 6—25 U. S. C. 318b.

49 St. 1528; June 19, 1936; C. 593—An Act To consolidate the Indian pueblos of Jemez and Pecos, New Mexico.

49 St. 1542; June 20, 1936; C. 622—An Act To relieve restricted Indians whose lands have been taxed or have been lost by failure to pay taxes, and for other purposes.[60] Sec. 2—25 U. S. C. 412a.[61]

49 St. 1543; June 20, 1936; C. 624—An Act To provide for the disposition of tribal funds now on deposit, or later placed to the credit of the Crow Tribe of Indians, Montana, and for other purposes.[62]

49 St. 1544; June 20, 1936; C. 627—An Act To reserve certain public-domain lands in New Mexico as an addition to the school reserve of the Jicarilla Indian Reservation.

49 St. 1568; June 20, 1936; C. 649—Joint Resolution Authorizing distribution to the Indians of the Blackfeet Indian Reservation, Montana, of the judgment rendered by the Court of Claims in their favor.[63]

49 St. 1569; June 20, 1936; C. 650—Joint Resolution Authorizing distribution to the Gros Ventre Indians of the Fort Belk-

---

[38] *Sg.* 48 St. 200.
[39] *Fg.* 48 St. 200.
[40] *Sg.* 9 St. 952; 10 St. 1064; 21 St. 70; 22 St. 30; 26 St. 146; 35 St. 51; 45 St. 1164. *A.* 52 St. 208.
[41] *Sg.* 26 St. 712; 39 St. 976.
[42] *Sg.* 49 St. 612.
[43] *Cited:* Memo. Sol., Aug. 7, 1936, Jan. 13, 1937, May 14, 1938; Glenn, 105 F. 2d 398.
[44] *Ag.* 46 St. 1108, sec. 3. *Sg.* 45 St. 496. *S.* 49 St. 2385.
[45] *Sg.* 49 St. 337. *Rn.* 50 St. 737.
[46] *Sg.* 23 St. 26; 26 St. 1101; 48 St. 984. *S.* 52 St. 201. *Cited:* Op. Sol., M. 29147, May 6, 1937; Memo. Sol., Sept. 14, 1937; 56 I. D. 110.
[47] *Ag.* 48 St. 311. *Sg.* 47 St. 1568.
[48] *Sg.* 21 St. 199. *S.* 50 St. 564. *Cited:* Ducker, 104 Fed. 236.
[49] *Ag.* 44 St. 555.
[50] *S.* 50 St. 564.
[51] *Ag.* 41 St. 623. *Cited:* 11 L. D. Memo. 497; 12 L. D. Memo. 703, May 15, 1938; U. S. v. Klamath, 304 U. S. 119.
[52] *Sg.* 49 St. 120.
[53] *Sg.* 36 St. 3:6.
[54] *Sg.* 43 St. 739; 46 St. 1111.
[55] *Ag.* 48 St. 596.
[56] *Ag.* 44 St. 1358 *Sg.* 48 St. 812. *Cited:* Delaware, 84 C. Cls. 535.
[57] *Sg.* 43 St. 109, 639. *S.* 50 St. 564.
[58] *Sg.* 17 St. 202, sec. 5; 35 St. 1107.
[59] *Sg.* 45 St. 750. *S.* 50 St. 564; 52 St. 291, 710.
[60] *A.* 50 St. 188. *S.* 50 St. 564; 52 St. 201. *Cited:* 38 Op. A. G. 577; Memo. Sol., Jan. 16, 1937; Letter from Atty. Gen. to Sec'y of Int., Feb. 13, 1937; Memo. Sol., Nov. 29, 1937; Memo. Sol. Off., Apr. 14, 1938; U. S. v. Bd of Comm'rs, 26 F. Supp. 270.
[61] *A.* 50 St. 188.
[62] *Sg.* 41 St. 754.
[63] *Sg.* 43 St. 21.

nap Reservation, Montana, of the judgment rendered by the Court of Claims in their favor.[64]

49 St. 1597; June 22, 1936; C. 689—An Act Making appropriations to supply deficiencies in certain appropriations for the fiscal year ending June 30, 1936, and prior fiscal years, to provide supplemental appropriations for the fiscal years ending June 30, 1936, and June 30, 1937, and for other purposes.[65]

49 St. 1757; June 22, 1936; C. 691—An Act Making appropriations for the Department of the Interior for the fiscal year ending June 30, 1937, and for other purposes.[66] Sec. 1—25 U. S. C. 387 (45 St. 210, s. 1; 1573, s. 1; 46 St. 290, s. 1; 1126, s. 1; 47 St. 160, s. 1; 829, s. 1; 48 St. 370, s. 1; 49 St. 186, s. 1.)[67].

49 St. 1803; June 22, 1936; C. 692—An Act To authorize the Secretary of the Interior to investigate and adjust irrigation charges on irrigation lands within projects on Indian reservations, and for other purposes. Sec. 1—25 U. S. C. 389. Sec. 2—25 U. S. C. 389a. Sec. 3—25 U. S. C. 389b. Sec. 4—25 U. S. C. 389c. Sec. 5—25 U. S. C. 389d. Sec. 6—25 U. S. C. 389e.

49 St. 1806; June 22, 1936; C. 698—An Act To authorize the Secretary of the Interior to reserve certain lands on the public domain in Nevada for addition to the Walker River Indian Reservation.

49 St. 1826; June 22, 1936; C. 714—Joint Resolution to carry out the intention of Congress with reference to the claims of the Chippewa Indians of Minnesota against the United States.[68]

49 St. 1928; June 25, 1936; C. 814—An Act To modify section 20 of the Permanent Appropriations Repeal Act, 1934, with reference to individual Indian money.[69] 31 U. S. C. 725s note.

49 St. 1967; June 26, 1936; C. 831—An Act To promote the general welfare of the Indians of the State of Oklahoma, and for other purposes.[70] Sec. 1—25 U. S. C. 501. Also see 25 U. S. C. 508. Sec. 2—25 U. S. C. 502. Also see 25 U. S. C. 508. Sec. 3—25 U. S. C. 503. Also see 25 U. S. C. 508. Sec. 4—25 U. S. C. 504. Also see 25 U. S. C. 508. Sec. 5—25 U. S. C. 505. Also see 25 U. S. C. 508. Sec. 6—25 U. S. C. 506. Also see 25 U. S. C. 508. Sec. 7—25 U. S. C. 507. Also see 25 U. S. C. 508. Sec. 8—25 U. S. C. 508. Sec. 9—25 U. S. C. 509. Also see 25 U. S. C. 508.

49 St. 1984; June 26, 1936; C. 851—Joint Resolution To define the term of certain contracts with Indian tribes.[71] Sec. 1—25 U. S. C. 81a; Sec. 2—25 U. S. C. 81b.

49 St. 2051; Apr. 11, 1935; C. 65—An Act For the relief of Charles E. Dagonett.

49 St. 2052; Apr. 11, 1935; C. 67—An Act For the relief of C. B. Dickinson.

49 St. 2064; May 15, 1935; C. 126—An Act For the relief of the rightful heir of Joseph Cayton.

49 St. 2064; May 15, 1935; C. 127—An Act For the relief of Charles L. Graves.

49 St. 2078; June 14, 1935; C. 251—An Act For the relief of certain Indians of the Flathead Reservation killed or injured en route to dedication ceremonies of the Going-to-the-Sun Highway, Glacier National Park.

49 St. 2083; June 17, 1935; C. 273—An Act For the relief of John E. Click.

[64] *Sg.* 43 St. 21. *Cited:* Memo. Sol., Dec. 2, 1936.

[65] *Sg.* 12 St. 441, sec. 1; 45 St. 1641; 48 St. 1227; 49 St. 2246. *S.* 49 St. 1757; 50 St. 844. *Cited:* Memo. Sol., July 13, 1936.

[66] *Sg.* 4 St. 442; 7 St. 46, 99, 212, 213, 236; 11 St. 614, 720; 12 St. 3, 441, sec. 1; 1240; 13 St. 693; 16 St. 710; 25 St. 645, 805; 26 St. 794; 27 St. 644; 34 St. 375, 604; 35 St. 312, 444, 783; 36 St. 273; 38 St. 604, 742; 40 St. 297, 564; 41 St. 415, 433, 437, 1363; 43 St. 636; 44 St. 560; 45 St. 750; 46 St. 1136, 1053; 47 St. 335; 48 St. 108, 109, 277, 961, 984, 986, 995, 1033, 1227; 49 St. 176, 321, 327, 328, 329, 330, 331, 333, 336, 340, 571, 800, 891, 1597. *S.* 50 St. 564, 755; 52 St. 1114. *Cited:* Memo. Sol., Feb. 8, 1937, Oct. 8, 1937.

[67] *S.* 50 St. 577, s. 1; 52 St. 304, s. 1; 53 St. 700, s. 1.

[68] *Sg.* 44 St. 555. *Cited:* Chippewa, 305 U. S. 479; Chippewa, 307 U. S. 1; Chippewa, 301 U. S. 358.

[69] *Sg.* 48 St. 984, 1233, sec. 20.

[70] *Sg.* 48 St. 984. *S.* 50 St. 564; 52 St. 291. *Cited:* Circular of Comm'r, No. 3170, July 28, 1936; Memo. Sol., July 31, 1936; Statement by Comm'r on S. 1736 repealing Wheeler-Howard Act, Mar. 8, 1937; Memo. Sol., Mar. 4, 1937; Memo. Actg. Sol., July 14, 1937; Memo. Sol. Off., Aug. 3, 1937; Memo. Sol., Nov. 29, 1937, Apr. 22, 1938, May 24, 1938; Letter of Asst. Comm's. to Five Civilized Tribes Agency, June 20, 1938; Memo. Sol., Sept. 13, 1938; Ind. Off. Letter from Supt. Quapaw Agency, Oct. 17, 1938; Memo. Sol., Dec. 13, 1938, Apr. 3, 1939.

[71] *Sg.* 16 St. 570, sec. 3; 17 St. 186, sec. 1, 2; 18 St. 35, 450, sec. 9. *Cited:* 74th Cong., 2nd sess., Hearings, H. Comm. on Ind. Aff., S. J. Res. 177; Memo. Sol., Aug. 6, 1938.

49 St. 2093; June 25, 1935; C. 314—An Act For the relief of John W. Dady.

49 St. 2105; July 19, 1935; C. 397—An Act For the relief of Robert J. Enochs.

49 St. 2106; July 19, 1935; C. 399—An Act For the relief of Emanuel Wallin.

49 St. 2121; Aug. 7, 1935; C. 480—An Act For the relief of Thomas Enchoff.

49 St. 2149; Aug. 19, 1935; C. 572—An Act Authorizing and directing the Secretary of the Interior to cancel patent in fee issued to Victoria Arconge.

49 St. 2154; Aug. 20, 1935; C. 586—An Act For the relief of Oliver B. Huston, Anne Huston, Jane Huston, and Harriet Huston.

49 St. 2155; Aug. 20, 1935; C. 589—An Act For the relief of Elliott H. Tasso and Emma Tasso.

49 St. 2191; Aug. 26, 1935; C. 735—An Act For the relief of certain Indians on the Cheyenne River Reservation.

49 St. 2195; Aug. 27, 1935; C. 785—An Act For the relief of L. E. Geary.[72]

49 St. 2197; Aug. 27, 1935; C. 790—An Act For the relief of Doctor Ernest B. Dunlap.

49 St. 2210; Jan. 20, 1936; C. 16—An Act For the relief of Constantin Gilia.

49 St. 2222; Feb. 14, 1936; C. 71—An Act For the relief of Lynn Brothers' Benevolent Hospital.

49 St. 2222; Feb. 14, 1936; C. 72—An Act For the relief of E. E. Sullivan.

49 St. 2223; Feb. 14, 1936; C. 73—An Act For the relief of A. E. Taplin.

49 St. 2246; Apr. 10, 1936; C. 201—An Act For the relief of Mrs. Earl H. Smith.[73]

49 St. 2246; Apr. 10, 1936; C. 202—An Act For the relief of the Ward Funeral Home.

49 St. 2246; Apr. 10, 1936; C. 204—An Act For the relief of David Duquaine, Junior.

49 St. 2247; Apr. 10, 1936; C. 205—An Act For the relief of Thomas F. Gardiner.

49 St. 2263; May 4, 1936; C. 287—An Act For the relief of Edith H. Miller.

49 St. 2296; May 15, 1936; C. 415—An Act For the relief of Maizee Hamley.[74]

49 St. 2317; June 15, 1936; C. 564—An Act For the relief of E. W. Jermark.

49 St. 2319; June 15, 1936; C. 569—An Act For the relief of Grant Anderson.

49 St. 2325; June 19, 1936; C. 614—An Act For the relief of Juanita Filmore, a minor.

49 St. 2326; June 19, 1936; C. 616—An Act For the relief of Doctor Harold W. Foght.

49 St. 2342; June 22, 1936; C. 716—An Act For the relief of Joseph Watkins.

49 St. 2343; June 22, 1936; C. 717—An Act Validating certain applications for and entries of public lands, and for other purposes.

49 St. 2368; June 29, 1936; C. 871—An Act Validating certain conveyances by Kickapoo Indians of Oklahoma made prior to February 17, 1933, providing for actions in partition to certain cases.

49 St. 2385; Feb. 25, 1936; Concurrent Res. Five Civilized Tribes of Indians.[75]

49 St. 2385; Mar. 3, 1936; Concurrent Res. Five Civilized Tribes of Indians.[76]

50 STAT.

50 St. 68; Apr. 17, 1937; C. 108—An Act To amend the last two provisos, section 26, Act of Congress approved March 3, 1921 (41 St. 1225-1248).[77]

50 St. 69; Apr. 17, 1937; C. 111—An Act To authorize the acquisition of 640 acres of land for the use and benefit of the Santa Rosa Band of Mission Indians, State of California.[78]

50 St. 70; Apr. 20, 1937; C. 114—An Act To authorize the Secretary of the Interior to exchange certain lands and water rights in Inyo and Mono Counties, California, with the city of Los Angeles, and for other purposes.[79]

[72] *Sg.* 46 St. 1070.

[73] *S.* 49 St. 1597.

[74] *Sg.* 39 St. 532.

[75] *Sg.* 49 St. 1160.

[76] *Sg.* 49 St. 1160.

[77] *Ag.* 41 St. 1225.

[78] *S.* 50 St. 755.

[79] *Cited:* Op. Sol., M. 20232, June 2, 1937.

50 St. 72; Apr. 22, 1937; C. 123—An Act To reserve certain public domain in California for the benefit of the Capitan Grande Band of Mission Indians.[80]

50 St. 169; May 18, 1937; C. 223—An Act Making appropriations for the Legislative Branch of the Government for the fiscal year ending June 30, 1938, and for other purposes.[81]

50 St. 188; May 19, 1937; C. 227—An Act Amending section 2 of Public Law Numbered 716 of the Seventy-fourth Congress, being an Act entitled "An Act to relieve restricted Indians whose lands have been taxed or have been lost by failure to pay taxes, and for other purposes."[82] 25 U. S. C. 412a (49 St. 1542, sec. 2).

50 St. 210; May 27, 1937; C. 270—An Act to reimpose a trust on certain lands allotted on the Yakima Indian Reservation.[83]

50 St. 213; May 28, 1937; C. 277—An Act Making appropriations to supply deficiencies in certain appropriations for the fiscal year ending June 30, 1937, and prior fiscal years to provide supplemental appropriations for the fiscal years ending June 30, 1937, and June 30, 1938, and for other purposes.[84]

50 St. 239; May 28, 1937; C. 280—An Act to reserve certain lands in the State of Utah for the Kanosh Band of Paiute Indians.

50 St. 239; May 28, 1937; C. 281—An Act To reserve certain lands in the State of Utah for the Shivwitz Band of Paiute Indians.

50 St. 241; May 28, 1937; C. 283—An Act To reserve certain lands in the State of Utah for the Koosharem Band of Paiute Indians.

50 St. 261; June 16, 1937; C. 359—An Act Making appropriations for the Departments of State and Justice and for the Judiciary, and for the Departments of Commerce and Labor, for the fiscal year ending June 30, 1938, and for other purposes.[85]

50 St. 319; June 28, 1937; C. 383—An Act To establish a Civilian Conservation Corps, and for other purposes. Sec. 1—16 U. S. C. 584; Sec. 7—16 U. S. C. 584f; Sec. 8—16 U. S. C. 584g; Sec. 9—16 U. S. C. 584h; Sec. 17—16 U. S. C. 584p; Sec. 18—16 U. S. C. 584q.

50 St. 329; June 28, 1937; C. 396—An Act Making appropriations for the Executive Office and sundry independent executive bureaus, boards, commissions, and offices, for the fiscal year ending June 30, 1938, and for other purposes.

50 St. 395; June 29, 1937; C. 404—An Act Making appropriations for the Department of Agriculture and for the Farm Credit Administration for the fiscal year ending June 30, 1938, and for other purposes.[86]

50 St. 441; June 29, 1937; C. 406—An Act To authorize an appropriation to carry out the provisions of the Act of May 3, 1928 (45 St. 484), and for other purposes.[87]

50 St. 442; July 1, 1937; C. 423—An Act Making appropriations for the Military Establishment for the fiscal year ending June 30, 1938, and for other purposes.

50 St. 488; July 9, 1937; C. 473—Joint Resolution Providing for the participation of the United States in the world's fair to be held by the San Francisco Bay Exposition, Incorporated, in the city of San Francisco during the year 1939, and for other purposes.

50 St. 536; July 28, 1937; C. 527—An Act To extend the boundaries of the Papago Indian Reservation in Arizona.[88] Sec. 1—25 U. S. C. 463a. Sec. 2—25 U. S. C. 463b. Sec. 3—25 U. S. C. 463c.

50 St. 537; July 28, 1937; C. 529—An Act Providing for the sale of the two dormitory properties belonging to the Chickasaw Nation or Tribe of Indians, in the vicinity of the Murray State School of Agriculture at Tishomingo, Oklahoma.

50 St. 564; Aug. 9, 1937; C. 570—An Act Making appropriations for the Department of the Interior for the fiscal year ending June 30, 1938, and for other purposes.[89] Sec. 1, p. 577—25 U. S. C. 387.

50 St. 650; Aug. 16, 1937; C. 651—An Act To authorize the Five Civilized Tribes, in suits heretofore filed under their original Jurisdictional Acts, to present claims to the United States Court of Claims by amended petitions to conform to the evidence; and to authorize said court to adjudicate such claims upon their merits as though filed within the time limitation fixed in said original Jurisdictional Acts.[90]

50 St. 699; Aug. 19, 1937; C. 701—An Act To authorize the exchange of certain lands within the Great Smoky Mountains National Park for lands within the Cherokee Indian Reservation, North Carolina, and for other purposes.[91]

50 St. 700; Aug. 19, 1937; C. 702—An Act To authorize the acquisition by the United States of certain tribally owned lands of the Indians of the Shoshone or Wind River Indian Reservation, Wyoming, for the Wind River irrigation project.

50 St. 737; Aug. 21, 1937; C. 725—An Act To create a commission and to extend further relief to water users on United States reclamation projects and on Indian irrigation projects.[92]

50 St. 755; Aug. 25, 1937; C. 757—An Act Making appropriations to supply deficiencies in certain appropriations for the fiscal year ending June 30, 1937, and for prior fiscal years, to provide supplemental appropriations for the fiscal year ending June 30, 1938, and for other purposes.[93]

50 St. 786; Aug. 25, 1937; C. 759—An Act Granting pensions and increases of pensions to certain soldiers who served in the Indian Wars from 1817 to 1898, and for other purposes.[94] Secs. 1 and 2—38 U. S. C. 381-1.

50 St. 805; Aug. 25, 1937; C. 770—An Act Limiting the operation of sections 109 and 113 of the Criminal Code and section 190 of the Revised Statutes of the United States with respect to counsel in certain cases.[95]

50 St. 806; Aug. 25, 1937; C. 772—An Act Providing for the manner of payment of taxes on gross production of minerals, including gas and oil, in Oklahoma. 25 U. S. C. 510.

50 St. 810; Aug. 25, 1937; C. 778—An Act To authorize the reservation of minerals in future sales of lands of the Choctaw-Chickasaw Indians in Oklahoma. 25 U. S. C. 414.

50 St. 811; Aug. 25, 1937; C. 779—An Act To authorize the Secretary of the Interior to lease or sell certain lands of the Agua Caliente or Palm Springs Reservation, California, for public airport use, and for other purposes.

50 St. 844; Aug. 26, 1937; C. 832—An Act Authorizing the construction, repair, and preservation of certain public works on rivers and harbors, and for other purposes.[96]

50 St. 862; Aug. 28, 1937; C. 866—An Act To amend section 3 of the Act of June 18, 1934 (48 St. 984–988), relating to Indian Lands in Arizona.[97] 25 U. S. C. 463 (48 St. 984).

50 St. 864; Aug. 28, 1937; C. 868—An Act To authorize the Secretary of the Interior to relinquish in favor of the Blackfeet Tribe of the Blackfeet Indian Reservation, Montana, the interest in certain land acquired by the United States under the Federal Reclamation Laws.

50 St. 872; Aug. 28, 1937; C. 874—An Act Authorizing the establishment of a revolving loan fund for the Klamath Indians, Oregon, and for other purposes. Sec. 1—25 U. S. C. 530. Sec. 2—25 U. S. C. 531. Sec. 3—25 U. S. C. 532. Sec. 4—25 U. S. C. 533. Sec. 5—25 U. S. C. 534. Sec. 6—25 U. S. C. 535.

50 St. 873; Aug. 28, 1937; C. 875—An Act Making further provision with respect to the funds of the Metlakahtla Indians of Alaska.[98]

50 St. 884; Aug. 31, 1937; C. 890—An Act Relating to certain lands within the boundaries of the Crow Reservation, Montana.[99]

50 St. 900; Sept. 1, 1937; C. 897—An Act To provide subsistence for the Eskimos and other natives of Alaska by establishing for them a permanent and self-sustaining economy; to encourage and develop native activity in all branches of the reindeer industry; and for other purposes.[1] Sec. 1—48

---

[80] *Sg.* 47 St. 146.
[81] *Cited:* Memo. Sol. Off., Apr. 14, 1938.
[82] *Ag.* 49 St. 1542. *Cited:* Memo. Sol., Nov. 29, 1937, Feb. 14, 1939, Feb. 20, 1939.
[83] *Sg.* 24 St. 388; 34 St. 326.
[84] *Sg.* 25 St. 645, 895; 36 St. 273. *S.* 52 St. 1114.
[85] *Sg.* 36 St. 326.
[86] *Sg.* 43 St. 739; 46 St. 805, 1111; 49 St. 1448, 1519. *S.* 52 St. 1169.
[87] *Sg.* 45 St. 484. *S.* 50 St. 755.
[88] *Sg.* 36 St. 558; 48 St. 984, 1269; 49 St. 1976. *Cited:* Op. Sol., M. 29560, Dec. 28, 1937.
[89] *Sg.* 4 St. 442; 7 St. 46, 99, 212, 213, 236; 11 St. 614, 729; 12 St. 441, sec. 1; 25 St. 645, 895; 26 St. 794; 27 St. 644; 34 St. 375; 35 St. 312, 444, 783; 36 St. 273; 38 St. 604, 742; 41 St. 145, 433, 437, 1363; 43 St. 139, 636, 1101; 44 St. 560; 45 St. 750; 46 St. 1053; 47 St. 335, 1418; 48 St. 108, 109, 277, 960, 961, 964, 984, 986, 1033, 1227, 1228; 49 St. 183, 184, 213, 327, 333, 386, 584, 891, 1040, 1272, 1459, 1521, 1542, 1764, 1765, 1767, 1772, 1773, 1775, 1777, 1778, 1779, 1780, 1967. *S.* 52 St. 291, 1114. *Cited:* Memo. Ind. Off., Mar. 13, 1935; Memo. Sol., May 12, 1936, Oct. 8, 1937.
[90] *Sg.* 43 St. 27, 133, 139, 537; 45 St. 568, 1229; 44 St. 568; 45 St. 1229.
[91] *Sg.* 39 St. 535. *Cited:* Op. Sol., M. 29961, Oct. 4, 1938.
[92] *Rpg.* 49 St. 1206.
[93] *Sg.* 24 St. 157; 40 St. 1309; 41 St. 617; 48 St. 1021; 49 St. 181, 1764; 50 St. 69, 441.
[94] *Sg.* 27 St. 281, 679; 39 St. 1199; 44 St. 1361.
[95] *Sg.* 17 St. 212; 31 St. 844; 35 St. 1107.
[96] *Sg.* 49 St. 115, 1028, 1622.
[97] *Ag.* 48 St. 984. *Sg.* 46 St. 1202.
[98] *Sg.* 26 St. 1095; 36 St. 1101; 48 St. 1224.
[99] *Sg.* 29 St. 506.
[1] *S.* 52 St. 291, 1114.

U. S. C. 250. Sec. 2—48 U. S. C. 250a. Sec. 3—48 U. S. C. 250b. Sec. 4—48 U. S. C. 250c. Sec. 5—48 U. S. C. 250d. Sec. 6—48 U. S. C. 250e. Sec. 7—48 U. S. C. 250f. Sec. 8—48 U. S. C. 250g. Sec. 9—48 U. S. C. 250h. Sec. 10—48 U. S. C. 250i. Sec. 11—48 U. S. C. 250j. Sec. 12—48 U. S. C. 250k. Sec. 13—48 U. S. C. 250-l. Sec. 14—48 U. S. C. 250m. Sec. 15—48 U. S. C. 250n. Sec. 16—48 U. S. C. 250o. Sec. 17—48 U. S. C. 250p.

50 St. 955; May 6, 1937; C. 174—An Act For the relief of Edmond C. Warren.[2]

52 STAT.

52 St. 80; Feb. 24, 1938; C. 33—An Act Amending Acts fixing the rate of payment of irrigation construction costs on the Wapato Indian irrigation project, Yakima, Washington, and for other purposes.[3]

52 St. 85; Mar. 5, 1938; C. 42—An Act Making appropriations to supply deficiencies in certain appropriations for the fiscal year ending June 30, 1938, and prior fiscal years, to provide supplemental appropriations for the fiscal year ending June 30, 1938, and for other purposes.[4]

52 St. 193; Apr. 4, 1938; C. 63—An Act To authorize the Secretary of the Interior to grant concessions on reservoir sites and other lands in connection with Federal Indian irrigation projects wholly or partly Indian, and to lease the lands in such reserves for agricultural, grazing, and other purposes.[5]

52 St. 208; Apr. 8, 1938; C. 120—An Act To amend an Act entitled "An Act to refer the claim of the Menominee Tribe of Indians to the Court of Claims with the absolute right of appeal to to the Supreme Court of the United States", approved September 3, 1935.[6] See 28 U. S. C. A. 259 note.

52 St. 213; Apr. 13, 1938; C. 141—An Act To set aside certain lands in Oklahoma for the Cheyenne and Arapahoe Indians.

52 St. 215; Apr. 13, 1938; C. 144—An Act To provide for a flowage easement on certain ceded Chippewa Indian lands bordering Lake of the Woods, Warroad River, and Rainy River, Minnesota, and for other purposes.[7]

52 St. 216; Apr. 13, 1938; C. 145—An Act For the benefit of the Goshute and other Indians, and for other purposes.[8]

52 St. 248; Apr. 27, 1938; C. 180—An Act Making appropriations for the Department of State and Justice and for the Judiciary, and for the Departments of Commerce and Labor, for the fiscal year ending June 30, 1939, and for other purposes.[9]

52 St. 291; May 9, 1938; C. 187—An Act Making appropriations for the Department of the Interior for the fiscal year ending June 30, 1939, and for other purposes.[10] Sec. 1, p. 303—25 U. S. C. 303. Sec. 1, p. 304—25 U. S. C. 387 (45 St. 210, sec. 1; 1573, sec. 1; 46 St. 200, sec. 1; 1126, sec. 1; 47 St. 100, sec. 1; 829, sec. 1; 48 St. 370, sec. 1; 49 St. 186, sec. 1; 1760, sec. 1; 50 St. 577, sec. 1).[11] Sec. 1, p. 311—48 U. S. C. 50d. Sec. 1, p. 312—25 U. S. C. 562.[12] Sec. 1, p. 313—25 U. S. C. 561.[13] Sec. 1, p. 315—25 U. S. C. 123b.

52 St. 347; May 11, 1938; C. 198—An Act To regulate the leasing of certain Indian lands for mining purposes.[14] Sec. 1—25 U. S. C. 396a. Also see 25 U. S. C. 396a–396f. Sec. 2—25 U. S. C. 396b. Also see 25 U. S. C. 461 et seq. Sec. 3—25 U. S. C. 396c. Sec. 4—25 U. S. C. 396d. Also see 25 U. S. C. 396a—396f. Sec. 5—25 U. S. C. 396e. Sec. 6—25 U. S. C. 396f.

52 St. 381; May 17, 1938; C. 236—An Act Making appropriations for the Legislative Branch of the Government for the fiscal year ending June 30, 1939, and for other purposes.

52 St. 410; May 23, 1938; C. 259—An Act Making appropriations for the Executive Office and sundry independent executive bureaus, boards, commissions, and offices, for the fiscal year ending June 30, 1939, and for other purposes.

52 St. 593; May 31, 1938; C. 304—An Act To authorize the withdrawal and reservation of small tracts of the public domain in Alaska for schools, hospitals, and other purposes. 48 U. S. C. 353a.

52 St. 605; June 1, 1938; C. 310—An Act To authorize payments in lieu of allotments to certain Indians of the Klamath Indian Reservation in the State of Oregon, and to regulate inheritance of restricted property within the Klamath Reservation. Sec. 1—25 U. S. C. 551; Sec. 2—25 U. S. C. 552; Sec. 3—25 U. S. C. 553; Sec. 4—25 U. S. C. 554; Sec. 5—25 U. S. C. 555; Sec. 6—25 U. S. C. 556.

52 St. 633; June 8, 1938; C. 328—An Act To amend the Federal Aid Act, approved July 11, 1916, as amended and supplemented, and for other purposes.[15]

52 St. 636; June 10, 1938; C. 330—Joint Resolution To authorize an appropriation to aid in defraying the expenses of the observance of the seventy-fifth anniversary of the Battles of Chickamauga, Georgia, Lookout Mountain, Tennessee, and Missionary Ridge, Tennessee; and commemorate the one-hundredth anniversary of the removal from Tennessee of the Cherokee Indians, at Chattanooga, Tennessee, and at Chickamauga, Georgia, from September 18 to 24, 1938, inclusive; and for other purposes.

52 St. 667; June 11, 1938; C. 348—An Act Making appropriations for the fiscal year ending June 30, 1939, for civil functions administered by the War Department, and for other purposes.

52 St. 685; June 15, 1938; C. 386—An Act To provide funds for cooperation with School District Numbered 2, Mason County, State of Washington, in the construction of a public-school building to be available to both white and Indian children.

52 St. 688; June 15, 1938; C. 390—An Act Authorizing the Secretary of the Treasury to transfer on the books of the Treasury Department to the credit of the Chippewa Indians of Minnesota the proceeds of a certain judgment erroneously deposited in the Treasury of the United States as public money.[16]

52 St. 696; June 15, 1938; C. 435—An Act To amend section 2139 of the Revised Statutes, as amended.[17] Sec. 1—25 U. S. C. 241; Sec. 2 and 3—See Historical Note 25 U. S. C. A. 241.

52 St. 697; June 15, 1938; C. 436—An Act To divide the funds of the Chippewa Indians of Minnesota between the Red Lake Band and the remainder of the Chippewa Indians of Minnesota, organized as the Minnesota Chippewa Tribe.[18]

52 St. 710; June 16, 1938; C. 464—An Act Making appropriations for the Department of Agriculture and for the Farm Credit Administration for the fiscal year ending June 30, 1939, and for other purposes.[19]

52 St. 752; June 16, 1938; C. 466—An Act To authorize a survey of the old Indian trail and the highway known as "Oglethorpe Trail" with a view of constructing a national roadway on this route to be known as "The Oglethorpe National Trail and Parkway."

52 St. 778; June 20, 1938; C. 524—An Act To purchase certain private lands within the Shoshone (Wind River) Indian Reservation.

52 St. 778; June 20, 1938; C. 525—An Act To authorize an appropriation for repayment to the Middle Rio Grande Conservancy District, a subdivision of the State of New Mexico, of the share of the said district's construction and operation and maintenance costs applicable to certain properties owned by the United States, situate in Bernalillo County, New Mexico, within the exterior boundaries of the district; to authorize the Secretary of the Interior to contract with said district for future operation and maintenance charges against said lands; to authorize appropriation for extra construction work performed by said district for the special benefit of certain Pueblo Indian lands and to authorize appropriation for construction expenditures benefiting certain acquired lands of Pueblo Indians of the State of New Mexico.[20]

52 St. 809; June 21, 1938; C. 554—Joint Resolution Making appropriations for work relief, relief, and otherwise to increase employment by providing loans and grants for public works project.[21]

---

[2] *Sg.* 39 St. 742, sec. 15–20.
[3] *Ag.* 41 St. 431; 42 St. 595.
[4] *Sg.* 48 St. 22, 1021.
[5] *Sg.* 48 St. 984; 49 St. 163.
[6] *Sg.* 35 St. 51. *Ag.* 49 St. 1085.
[7] *Sg.* 25 St. 642; 44 St. 617, 2108; 45 St. 481.
[8] *Sg.* 48 St. 984.
[9] *Sg.* 36 St. 326.
[10] *Sg.* 4 St. 442; 7 St. 46, 99, 212, 218, 236; 11 St. 614, 729; 12 St. 220, sec. 10; 441, sec. 1; 18 St. 177; 25 St. 645, 805; 26 St. 794; 27 St. 644; 28 St. 451; 34 St. 375; 35 St. 312, 444, 783; 36 St. 278; 38 St. 604, 742; 41 St. 415, 437, 1363; 43 St. 636; 44 St. 560, 658; 45 St. 312, 750, 1164; 46 St. 391, 1053; 47 St. 333; 48 St. 109, 960, 961, 984, 986, 1033, 1227; 49 St. 378, 891, 1040, 1250, 1521, 1542, 1967; 50 St. 571, 572, 573, 574, 575, 580, 581, 586, 590, 900. *S.* 52 St. 1114. *Cited:* 71st Cong., 2d sess., H. Rept. No. 897; Op. Sol., M. 29669, Aug. 1, 1938; Memo. Acting Sol., Aug. 2, 1938.
[11] *S.* 53 St. 700, sec. 1.
[12] *S.* 53 St. 707, sec. 1.
[13] *S.* 53 St. 708, sec. 1.
[14] *Sg.* 48 St. 984. *Cited:* U. S. v. Watashe, 102 F. 2d 428.
[15] *Sg.* 39 St. 355; 42 St. 212; 45 St. 750; 46 St. 805.
[16] *Sg.* 25 St. 642.
[17] *Ag.* 4 St. 564, sec. 4; 13 St. 29; 19 St. 244. *Rg.* 29 St. 506. *Sg.* 1 St. 9, sec. 33; 334, sec. 4; 5 St. 516, sec. 1; 27 St. 260.
[18] *Sg.* 25 St. 642; 44 St. 555; 45 St. 423.
[19] *Sg.* 43 St. 739; 46 St. 805; 49 St. 1520.
[20] *Sg.* 43 St. 636; 49 St. 887.
[21] *Cited:* Memo. Sol., Dec 13, 1938.

52 St. 1034; June 24, 1938; C. 645—An Act Relating to the tribal and individual affairs of the Osage Indians of Oklahoma.[22]

52 St. 1037; June 24, 1938; C. 648—An Act To authorize the deposit and investment of Indian funds.[23] Sec. 1—25 U. S. C. 162a; Sec. 3—See Historical Note 25 U. S. C. A. 162a. 25 USCA 162a Historical Note: Section 2 of Act of June 24, 1938, cited to the text repealed Act of May 25, 1918, c. 86, sec. 28, 40 St. 591, which was contained in former sec. 162 of this title, and all inconsistent acts.

52 St. 1114; June 25, 1938; C. 681—An Act Making appropriations to supply deficiencies in certain appropriations for the fiscal year ending June 30, 1938, and for prior fiscal years, to provide supplemental appropriations for the fiscal years ending June 30, 1938, and June 30, 1939, and for other purposes.[24]

52 St. 1169; June 25, 1938; C. 686—An Act To amend the Act of Congress entitled "An Act to establish an Alaska Game Commission, to protect game animals, land fur-bearing animals, and birds in Alaska, and for other purposes", approved January 13, 1925, as amended.[25] Sec. 1—48 U. S. C. 206; Sec. 2—48 U. S. C. 207; Sec. 4—48 U. S. C. 198; Sec. 6—48 U. S. C. 199.

52 St. 1173; June 25, 1938 C. 687—An Act To provide for conveying to the State of North Dakota certain lands within Burleigh County within that State for public use.

52 St. 1174; June 25, 1938; C. 689—An Act To amend an Act approved June 14, 1906 (34 St. 263) entitled "An Act to prevent aliens from fishing in the waters of Alaska."[26] 48 U. S. C. 253.

52 St. 1207; June 25, 1938; C. 710—An Act Authorizing the Secretary of the Interior to pay salaries and expenses of the chairman, secretary, and interpreter of the Klamath General Council, members of the Klamath Business Committee and other committees appointed by said Klamath General Council, and official delegates of the Klamath Tribe.

52 St. 1209; June 28, 1938; C. 776—An Act Conferring jurisdiction upon the United States Court of Claims to hear, examine, adjudicate, and render judgment on any and all claims which the Ute Indians or any Tribe or Band thereof may have against the United States, and for other purposes.[27]

52 St. 1212; June 28, 1938; C. 777—An Act Authorizing the Red Lake Band of Chippewa Indians in the State of Minnesota to file suit in the Court of Claims, and for other purposes.[28]

52 St. 1213; June 28, 1938; C. 779—An Act To authorize the sale of certain lands of the Eastern Band of Cherokee Indians, North Carolina.

52 St. 1241; June 29, 1938; C. 812—An Act To establish the Olympic National Park, in the State of Washington, and for other purposes. Sec. 5—16 U. S. 255.

52 St. 1243; June 29, 1938; C. 814—An Act To authorize the Secretary of the Interior to place certain records of Indian tribes of Nebraska with the Nebraska State Historical Society, at Lincoln, Nebraska, under rules and regulations to be prescribed by him.

52 St. 1274; Apr. 6, 1938; C. 89—An Act For the relief of employees of the Indian Service for destruction by fire of personally owned property in Government quarters at the Pierre Indian School, South Dakota.

52 St. 1293; Apr. 13, 1938; C. 154—An Act For the relief of Frank Christy and other disbursing agents in the Indian service of the United States.

52 St. 1298; Apr. 15, 1938; C. 164—An Act For the relief of Nelson W. Apple, George Marsh, and Camille Carmignani.

52 St. 1299; Apr. 15, 1938; C. 166—An Act To extend the Metlakahtla Indians' Citizenship Act.[29]

52 St. 1308; May 16, 1938; C. 221—An Act For the relief of Wilson H. Parks, Elsa Parks, and Jessie M. Parks.

52 St. 1326; June 14, 1938; C. 369—An Act For the relief of Mr. and Mrs. James Crawford.

52 St. 1331; June 15, 1938; C. 408—An Act For the relief of Josephine Russell.

52 St. 1334; June 15, 1938; C. 414—An Act For the relief of the estate of Lillie Liston, and Mr. and Mrs. B. W. Trent.

52 St. 1347; June 15, 1938; C. 451—An Act For the relief of Sibbald Smith.

52 St. 1348; June 15, 1938; C. 452—An Act For the relief of the Long Bell Lumber Company.

52 St. 1353; June 16, 1938; C. 502—An Act For the relief of Filomeno Jiminez and Felicitas Dominguez.

52 St. 1355; June 16, 1938; C. 507—An Act For the relief of C. G. Bretting Manufacturing Company.[30]

52 St. 1363; June 20, 1938; C. 547—An Act For the relief of certain individuals in connection with the construction, operation, and maintenance of the Fort Hall Indian irrigation project, Idaho.

52 St. 1382; June 23, 1938; C. 621—An Act For the relief of Moses Red Bird.

52 St. 1395; June 25, 1938; C. 656—An Act For the relief of William C. Willahan.

52 St. 1408; June 25, 1938; C. 721—An Act For the relief of John Fanning.

52 St. 1412; June 25, 1938; C. 732—An Act For the relief of John Haslam.

52 St. 1418; June 25, 1938; C. 746—An Act For the relief of William F. Bourland.

52 St. 1437; June 29, 1938; C. 833—An Act For the relief of William Monroe.

52 St. 1438; June 29, 1938; C. 834—An Act For the relief of Emons Wolfer.

---

[22] *Ag.* 45 St. 1478.
[23] *Rg.* 40 St. 591, sec. 28.
[24] *Sg.* 25 St. 805; 43 St. 886; 46 St. 1053; 47 St. 110; 48 St. 366, 376, 1021, 1227; 49 St. 181, 1763, 1764, 1780; 50 St. 222, 564, 570, 571, 576, 577, 591, 900; 52 St. 291. *Ag.* 50 St. 504.
[25] *Ag.* 43 St. 739; 46 St. 1111. *Sg.* 50 St. 395.
[26] *Ag.* 34 St. 263.
[27] *Sg.* 48 St. 984; 49 St. 584. *Cited:* Memo. Sol., Aug. 27, 1938.
[28] *Sg.* 13 St. 667; 25 St. 642.
[29] *Sg.* 48 St. 667.
[30] *Sg.* 12 St. 220, sec. 10; 441, sec. 1; 18 St. 177.

TABLE OF FEDERAL CASES

ABREW v. UNITED STATES, 37 C. Cls. 510 (1902).
ADAMS v. MURPHY, 165 Fed. 304 (C. C. A. 8, 1908), rev'g PORTER v. MURPHY, 7 Ind. T. 395, 104 S. W. 658 (1907).
ADAMS v. OSAGE TRIBE OF INDIANS, 59 F. 2d 653 (C. C. A. 10, 1932), aff'g 50 F. 2d 918 (D. C. N. D. Okla. 1931), cert. den. 287 U. S. 652.
ADKINS v. ARNOLD, 235 U. S. 417 (1914).
ALASKA PACIFIC FISHERIES v. UNITED STATES, 248 U. S. 78 (1918), aff'g 240 Fed. 274 (C. C. A. 9, 1917).
ALBERTY v. UNITED STATES, 162 U. S. 499 (1896).
ALBRIGHT v. UNITED STATES, 53 C. Cls. 247 (1918).
ALDRIDGE v. UNITED STATES, 67 F. 2d 956 (C. C. A. 10, 1933).
ALFREY v. COLBERT, 168 Fed. 231 (C. C. A. 8, 1909).
ALIRE v. UNITED STATES, 1 C. Cls. 233 (1865), rev'd sub nom. UNITED STATES v. ALIRE, 73 U. S. 573 (1867).
ALLRED v. UNITED STATES, 36 C. Cls. 280 (1901).
AMERICAN FUR CO. v. UNITED STATES, 2 Pet. 358 (1829).
AMMERMAN v. UNITED STATES, 267 Fed. 136 (C. C. A. 8, 1920), cert. den. 254 U. S. 650 (1920).
ANCHOR OIL CO. v. GRAY, 256 U. S. 519 (1921), aff'g 257 Fed. 277 (C. C. A. 8, 1919).
ANDERSON v. PECK, 53 F. 2d 257 (D. C. N. D. Okla. 1931).
ANDREAS v. CLARK, 71 F. 2d 908 (C. C. A. 9, 1934), cert. den. 293 U. S. 553.
ANICKER v. GUNSBURG, 246 U. S. 110 (1918), aff'g 226 Fed. 176 (C. C. A. 8, 1915).
ANONYMOUS, 1 Fed. Cas. No. 447 (C. C. Mo. 1843).
ANSLEY v. AINSWORTH, 180 U. S. 253 (1901).
ANSLEY v. McLOUD, 5 Ind. T. 563, 82 S. W. 908 (1904), aff'd sub nom. WALKER v. McLOUD. 138 Fed. 394 (C. C. A. 8, 1905).
APAPAS v. UNITED STATES, 233 U. S. 587 (1914).
ARBOR v. BLUE, 45 F. 2d 746 (C. C. A. 10, 1930).
ARCHARD v. UNITED STATES, 212 Fed. 146 (C. C. A. 8, 1914).
ARMSTRONG v. WOOD, 195 Fed. 137 (C. C. E. D. Okla. 1911).
ARMSWORTHY v. MISSOURI RIVER, FT. S. & G. R. Co., 1 Fed. Cas. No. 550 (C. C. Kan. 1879).
ARNOLD v. ARDMORE CHAMBER OF COMMERCE INDUSTRIAL CORP., 4 F. 2d 838 (C. C. A. 8, 1925).
ARNOLD v. CAMPBELL, 3 Ind. T. 550, 64 S. W. 532 (1901).
ASH SHEEP CO. v. UNITED STATES, 252 U. S. 159 (1920), aff'g 250 Fed. 591 (C. C. A. 9, 1918), and 254 Fed. 59 (C. C. A. 9, 1918).
ASHBAUGH v. UNITED STATES, 35 C. Cls. 554 (1900).
ASSINIBOINE INDIAN TRIBE v. UNITED STATES, 77 C. Cls. 347 (1933), app. dism. and cert. den. 292 U. S. 606.
ATLANTIC AND PACIFIC RAILROAD CO. v. MINGUS, 165 U. S. 413 (1897).
ATOKA COAL AND MINING CO. v. ADAMS, 104 Fed. 471 (C. C. A. 8, 1900), aff'g 3 Ind. T. 189, 53 S. W. 539 (1899).
AYRES v. UNITED STATES, 35 C. Cls. 26 (1899).
AYRES v. UNITED STATES, 44 C. Cls. 48 (1908).
AYRES v. UNITED STATES, 44 C. Cls. 110 (1908).
AYRES, EXECUTOR v. UNITED STATES, 42 C. Cls. 385 (1907).
AXHELM v. UNITED STATES, 9 Okla. 321, 60 Pac. 98 (1900).
BAGBY v. UNITED STATES, 60 F. 2d 80 (C. C. A. 10, 1932), aff'g 53 F. 2d 260 (D. C. N. D. Okla. 1931).
BAILEY v. UNITED STATES, 47 F. 2d 702 (C. C. A. 9, 1931).
BAILEY v. UNITED STATES, 43 C. Cls. 353 (1908).
BAKER v. UNITED STATES, 28 C. Cls. 370 (1893).
BALDWIN v. KEITH, 13 Okla. 624, 75 Pac. 1124 (1904).
BALFOUR v. MEADE, 4 Dall. 363 (1803).
BALL v. HALSELL, 161 U. S. 72 (1896).
BALLINGER v. UNITED STATES ex rel. FROST, 216 U. S. 240 (1910).
BARBEE v. SHANNON, 1 Ind. T. 199, 40 S. W. 584 (1897).
BARBRE v. HOOD, 228 Fed. 658 (C. C. A. 8, 1916), aff'g 214 Fed. 473 (D. C. E. D. Okla. 1914).
BARICHIO v. UNITED STATES, 283 U. S. 753 (1931). See HALBERT v. UNITED STATES, 283 U. S. 753 (1931).
BARKER v. HARVEY, 181 U. S. 481 (1901).
BARNETT v. AMERICAN SURETY CO., 77 F. 2d 225 (C. C. A. 10, 1935).
BARNETT v. EQUITABLE TRUST CO., 34 F. 2d 916 (C. C. A. 2, 1929), mod. UNITED STATES v. EQUITABLE TRUST, 283 U. S. 738 (1931).
BARNETT v. EQUITABLE TRUST CO. OF NEW YORK, 21 F. 2d 325 (D. C. S. D. N. Y. 1927), app. dism. 26 F. 2d 350, cert. den. 278 U. S. 626.
BARNETT v. PRAIRIE OIL AND GAS CO., 19 F. 2d 504 (C. C. A. 8, 1927), aff'g KUNKEL v. BARNETT, 10 F. 2d 804 (D. C. N. D. Okla. 1926), cert. den. 275 U. S. 563, s. c. 256 Fed. 644, 259 Fed. 394, 254 U. S. 620, 283 Fed. 24, 260 U. S. 738, 264 U. S. 160.
BARNETT v. UNITED STATES, 82 F. 2d 765 (C. C. A. 9, 1936), cert. den. 299 U. S. 546, rehearing den. 299 U. S. 620.
BARNSDALL v. DELAWARE INDIAN OIL CO., 200 Fed. 522 (C. C. A. 8, 1912).
BARNSDALL v. OWEN, 200 Fed. 519 (C. C. A. 8, 1912).
BARROW, PORTER & CO. v. UNITED STATES, 30 C. Cls. 54 (1895).
BARTLETT v. OKLA. OIL CO., 218 Fed. 380 (D. C. E. D. Okla. 1914), aff'd sub nom. OKLA. OIL CO. v. BARTLETT, 236 Fed. 488 (C. C. A. 8, 1916).
BARTLETT v. UNITED STATES, 203 Fed. 410 (C. C. A. 8, 1913), aff'd sub nom. UNITED STATES v. BARTLETT, 235 U. S. 72 (1914).
BARTON v. HULSEY, 4 Ind. T. 260, 69 S. W. 868 (1902).
BATES v. CLARK, 95 U. S. 204 (1877).
BAZE v. SCOTT, 24 F. Supp. 806 (D. C. E. D. Okla. 1938).
BEAL v. UNITED STATES, 32 F. 2d 1002 (C. C. A. 8, 1929).
BEAM v. UNITED STATES, 162 Fed. 260 (C. C. A. 9, 1908), aff'g 153 Fed. 474 (C. C. Ore. 1907).
BEAM v. UNITED STATES AND SIOUX INDIANS, 43 C. Cls. 61 (1907).
BEAN v. MORRIS, 221 U. S. 485 (1911), aff'g 159 Fed. 651 (C. C. A. 9, 1908), aff'g MORRIS v. BEAN, 146 Fed. 423 (C. C. Mont. 1906).
BEAULIEU v. GARFIELD, 32 App. D. C. 398 (1909).
BECK v. FLOURNOY LIVE-STOCK AND REAL ESTATE CO., 65 Fed. 30 (C. C. A. 8, 1894), app. dism. 163 U. S. 686.
BECKHAM v. AMOS, 255 U. S. 373 (1921). See WINTON v. AMOS, 255 U. S. 373 (1921).
BEDDO v. UNITED STATES, 28 C. Cls. 69 (1893).
BEECHER v. WETHERBY, 95 U. S. 517 (1877).
BELKNAP v. UNITED STATES, 150 U. S. 588 (1893).
BELL v. ATLANTIC AND P. R. CO., 63 Fed. 417 (C. C. A. 8, 1894).
BELL v. COOK, 192 Fed. 597 (C. C. E. D. Okla. 1911).
BELL v. UNITED STATES, 39 C. Cls. 350 (1904).
BELT v. UNITED STATES, 15 C. Cls. 92 (1879).
BENSON v. UNITED STATES, 44 Fed. 178 (C. C. N. D. N. Y. 1890).
BERRYHILL v. SHULTHIS, 225 U. S. 561. See SHULTHIS v. McDOUGAL, 225 U. S. 561 (1912).
BERTRAND v. DOYLE, 36 F. 2d 351 (C. C. A. 10, 1929).
BEST v. POLK, 18 Wall. 112 (1873).
BILBY v. STEWART, 246 U. S. 255 (1918).
BILLINGSLEY v. UNITED STATES, 16 F. 2d 754 (C. C. A. 8, 1926).
BINYON v. UNITED STATES, 4 Ind. T. 642, 76 S. W. 265 (1903), writ of error dism. 195 U. S. 623.
BIRD v. TERRY, 129 Fed. 472 (C. C. Wash. 1903), app. dism. 129 Fed. 592 (C. C. A. 9, 1904).
BISE v. UNITED STATES, 144 Fed. 374 (1906), aff'g 5 Ind. T. 602, 82 S. W. 921 (1906).
BISEK v. BELLANGER, 5 F. 2d 994 (D. C. Minn. 1925).
BLACKBIRD v. COMMISSIONER OF INTERNAL REVENUE, 38 F. 2d 976 (C. C. A. 10, 1930). See CHOUTEAU v. COMMISSIONER OF INTERNAL REVENUE, 38 F. 2d 976 (C. C. A. 10, 1930).

BLACKBURN v. MUSKOGEE LAND CO., 6 Ind. T. 232, 91 S. W. 31 (1906).
BLACKFEATHER v. UNITED STATES, 190 U. S. 368 (1903), aff'g 37 C. Cls. 233 (1902).
BLACKFEATHER v. UNITED STATES, 28 C. Cls. 447, (1893). rev'd sub nom. UNITED STATES v. BLACKFEATHER, 155 U. S. 180 (1894).
BLACKFEET ET AL. NATIONS v. UNITED STATES, 81 C. Cls. 101 (1935).
BLACKWELL v. UNITED STATES, 236 Fed. 912 (C. C. A. 8, 1916).
BLANSET v. CARDIN, 256 U. S. 319 (1921), aff'g 261 Fed. 309 (1919).
BLAYLOCK v. INCORPORATED TOWN OF MUSKOGEE, 117 Fed. 125 (C. C. A. 8, 1902).
BLOCKER v. McCLENDON, 6 Ind. T. 481, 98 S. W. 166 (1906).
BLUEJACKET v. EWERT, 259 U. S. 129 (1922). See EWERT v. BLUEJACKET, 259 U. S. 129 (1922).
BLUNDELL v. WALLACE, 267 U. S. 373 (1925).
BOARD OF COM'RS OF CADDO COUNTY, OKLA. v. UNITED STATES, 87 F. 2d 55 (C. C. A. 10, 1936).
BOARD OF COM'RS OF TULSA COUNTY, OKLA. v. UNITED STATES, 94 F. 2d 450 (C. C. A. 10, 1938), aff'g UNITED STATES v. BOARD OF COM'RS. etc., 19 F. Supp. 635 (D. C. N. D. Okla. 1937).
BOARD OF COUNTY COM'RS v. UNITED STATES, 64 F. 2d 775 (C. C. A. 10, 1933).
BOARD OF COUNTY COM'RS OF THE COUNTY OF JACKSON v. UNITED STATES, 100 F. 2d 929 (C. C. A. 10, 1938). mod. 60 Sup. Ct. 285.
BOHART v. HULL, 2 Ind. T. 45, 47 S. W. 306 (1898).
BOND v. TOM, 25 F. Supp. 157 (D. C. N. D. Okla. 1938) aff'd sub nom. UNITED STATES v. BOND, 108 F. 2d 504, (C. C. A. 10, 1939).
BOND v. UNITED STATES, 181 Fed. 613 (C. C. Ore. 1910).
BONIFER v. SMITH, 166 Fed. 846 (C. C. A. 9, 1909), aff'g SMITH v. BONIFER, 154 Fed. 883 (C. C. Ore. 1907), s. c. 132 Fed. 889.
BOUDINOT v. BOUDINOT, 2 Ind. T. 107, 48 S. W. 1019 (1899).
BOUNDS v. AMOS, 255 U. S. 373 (1921). See WINTON v. AMOS, 255 U. S. 373 (1921).
BOWLING v. UNITED STATES, 233 U. S. 528 (1914), aff'g 191 Fed. 19 (C. C. A. 8, 1911). See UNITED STATES v. RUNDELL, 181 Fed. 887 (C. C. E. D. Okla. 1910).
BOWLING v. UNITED STATES, 299 Fed. 438 (C. C. A. 8, 1924), s. c. 256 U. S. 484 (1921), rev'g 261 Fed. 657 (1919).
BOYT v. MITCHELL, 4 Ind. T. 47, 64 S. W. 610 (1901).
BRADER v. JAMES, 246 U. S. 88 (1918).
BRAMWELL v. UNITED STATES FIDELITY CO., 269 U. S. 483 (1926), aff'g 299 Fed. 705 (C. C. A. 9, 1924).
BRANN v. BELL, 192 Fed. 427 (C. C. E. D. Okla. 1911).
BREWER-ELLIOTT OIL AND GAS CO. v. UNITED STATES, 260 U. S. 77 (1922), aff'g 270 Fed. 100 (C. C. A. 8, 1920) and 249 Fed. 609 (D. C. W. D. Okla. 1918).
BRICE v. UNITED STATES, 32 C. Cls. 23 (1896).
BRIDGEMAN v. UNITED STATES, 140 Fed. 577 (C. C. A. 9, 1905).
BRIGGS v. SAMPLE, 43 Fed. 102 (C. C. Kan. 1890).
BRIGGS v. WASH-PUK-QUA, 37 Fed. 135 (C. C. Kan. 1888).
BRITISH-AMERICAN CO. v. BOARD, 299 U. S. 159 (1936), rehearing den. 299 U. S. 624.
BROUGHT v. CHEROKEE NATION, 129 Fed. 192 (C. C. A. 8, 1904).
BROWN v. DENNY, 52 Okla. 380, 152 Pac. 1103 (1915).
BROWN v. UNITED STATES, 146 Fed. 975 (C. C. A. 8, 1906). aff'g HERD v. UNITED STATES, 13 Okla. 512, 75 Pac. 291 (1904).
BROWN v. UNITED STATES, 265 Fed. 623 (C. C. A. 8, 1920).
BROWN v. UNITED STATES, 27 F. 2d 274 (C. C. A. 8, 1928).
BROWN v. UNITED STATES, 32 C. Cls. 432 (1897).
BROWN v. UNITED STATES, 2 Ind. T. 582, 52 S. W. 56 (1899).
BROWN v. UNITED STATES, 44 C. Cls. 283 (1907), rev'd sub nom. BROWN & GRITTS v. UNITED STATES, 219 U. S. 346 (1911).
BROWN v. WOOLSEY, 2 Ind. T. 329, 51 S. W. 965 (1899).
BROWN & GRITTS v. UNITED STATES, 219 U. S. 346 (1911), rev'g BROWN v. UNITED STATES, 44 C. Cls. 283 (1907). See MUSKRAT v. UNITED STATES, 219 U. S. 346 (1911).
BROWNING v. UNITED STATES, 6 F. 2d 801 (C. C. A. 8, 1925), cert. den. 269 U. S. 568 (1925).
BRUCE v. GLOBE INDEMNITY CO., 81 F. 2d 143 (C. C. A. 10, 1935), cert. den. 297 U. S. 716. See GLOBE INDEMNITY v. BRUCE, 81 F. 2d 143 (C. C. A. 10, 1935).
BRUCE v. UNITED STATES, 17 How. 437 (1854).
BRUGUIER v. UNITED STATES, 1 Dak. 5 (1867).
BRUNER v. UNITED STATES, 4 Ind. T. 580, 76 S. W. 244 (1903).
BUCHANAN v. UNITED STATES, 28 C. Cls. 127 (1893).
BUCHANAN v. UNITED STATES, 15 F. 2d 496 (C. C. A. 8, 1926).
BUFFO v. UNITED STATES, 213 Fed. 222 (C. C. A. 8, 1914).
BUNCH v. COLE, 263 U. S. 250 (1923).
BURCH v. UNITED STATES, 7 Ind. T. 284, 104 S. W. 619 (1907).
BURGESS v. NAIL, 103 F. 2d 37 (C. C. A. 10, 1939), rehearing den., 103 F. 2d 37, NAIL v. AMERICAN NAT. BANK OF BRISTOW, 21 F. Supp. 385 (D. C. N. D. Okla. 1937), rehearing den. 22 F. Supp. 977 (D. C. N. D. OKLA. 1938).
BURTON v. SMITHERS, 31 F. 2d 966 (C. C. A. 4, 1929).
BUSTER v. WRIGHT, 135 Fed. 947 (C. C. A. 8, 1905), aff'g 82 S. W. 855 (1904), app. dism. 203 U. S. 599 (1906).
BUTLER v. UNITED STATES, 38 C. Cls. 167 (1903).
BUTLER AND VALE v. UNITED STATES, 43 C. Cls. 497 (1908).
BUTTERFIELD v. UNITED STATES, 241 Fed. 556 (C. C. A. 8, 1917).
BUTTON v. SNYDER, 7 F. Supp. 597 (D. C. W. D. N. Y. 1934).
BUTTZ v. NORTHERN PAC. RAILROAD, 119 U. S. 55 (1886).
BYRD v. UNITED STATES, 44 C. Cls. 498 (1909).
CAESAR v. BURGESS, 103 F. 2d 503 (C. C. A. 10, 1939).
CALDWELL v. ROBINSON, 67 Fed. 391 (C. C. A. 9, 1895), aff'g 59 Fed. 653 (C. C. Idaho 1894), app. dism. 165 U. S. 359 (1897).
CALIFORNIA AND OREGON LAND CO. v. RANKIN, 87 Fed. 532 (C. C. Ore. 1898), aff'g CALIFORNIA AND OREGON LAND CO. v. WORDEN, 85 Fed. 94 (C. C. Ore. 1898).
CAMPBELL v. SCOTT, 3 Ind. T. 462, 58 S. W. 719 (1900).
CAMPBELL v. WADSWORTH, 248 U. S. 169 (1918).
CAMPBELL v. UNITED STATES, 44 C. Cls. 488 (1909).
CAMPBELL v. UNITED STATES, 221 Fed. 186 (C. C. A. 8, 1915).
CANTWELL v. UNITED STATES, 81 F. 2d 31 (C. C. A. 9, 1935).
CAPITAL TOWNSITE CO. v. FOX, 6 Ind. T. 223, 90 S. W. 614 (1906), aff'd sub nom. STANCLIFT v. FOX, 152 Fed. 697 (C. C. A. 8, 1907), app. dism. 215 U. S. 619 (1907).
CAPTAIN JACK, PETITIONER, 130 U. S. 353 (1889).
CARNEY v. CHAPMAN, 247 U. S. 102 (1918).
CARPENTER v. SHAW, 280 U. S. 363 (1930).
CARSON v. UNITED STATES, 283 Fed. 954 (C. C. A. 8, 1922). See JOHNSON v. UNITED STATES, 283 Fed. 954 (C. C. A. 8, 1922).
CARTER v. UNITED STATES, 1 Ind. T. 342, 37 S. W. 204 (1896).
CARTER v. UNITED STATES, 31 C. Cls. 441 (1896).
CARTER OIL CO. v. SCOTT, 12 F. 2d 780 (D. C. N. D. Okla. 1926), rev'd sub nom. KNIGHT v. CARTER OIL CO., 23 F. 2d 481 (C. C. A. 8, 1927).
CASE v. HALL, 94 Fed. 300 (C. C. A. 8, 1899), aff'g 2 Ind. T. 8 (1898).
CASTEEL v. McNEELY, 4 Ind. T. 1, 64 S. W. 594 (1901).
CATE v. BEASLEY, 299 U. S. 30 (1936).
CATHOLIC MISSIONS v. MISSOULA COUNTY, 200 U. S. 118 (1906).
CECIL v. UNITED STATES, 225 Fed. 368 (C. C. A. 8, 1915).
CENTRAL NAT. BANK OF TULSA, OKLA. v. UNITED STATES, 283 Fed. 368 (C. C. A. 8, 1922), writ of error dism. 264 U. S. 600 (1924).
CHAMBLISS v. UNITED STATES, 218 Fed. 154 (C. C. A. 8, 1914).
CHANCELLOR v. UNITED STATES, 237 Fed. 193 (C. C. A. 8, 1916).
CHASE v. UNITED STATES, 256 U. S. 1 (1921), aff'g 261 Fed. 833 (C. C. A. 8, 1919) and 238 Fed. 887 (C. A. A. 8, 1916).
CHASE v. UNITED STATES, 272 Fed. 684 (C. C. A. 8, 1921).
CHEROKEE INTERMARRIAGE CASES, 203 U. S. 76 (1906).
CHEROKEE NATION v. BLACKFEATHER, 155 U. S. 218 (1894).
CHEROKEE NATION v. GEORGIA, 5 Pet. 1 (1831).
CHEROKEE NATION v. HITCHCOCK, 187 U. S. 294 (1902).
CHEROKEE NATION v. JOURNEYCAKE, 155 U. S. 196 (1894), aff'g JOURNEYCAKE v. CHEROKEE NATION, 28 C. Cls. 281 (1893).

CHEROKEE NATION v. SOUTHERN KANSAS RAILWAY CO., 135 U. S. 641 (1890), rev'g 33 Fed. 900 (D. C. W. D. Ark. 1888).

CHEROKEE NATION v. UNITED STATES, 202 U. S. 101 (1906). See UNITED STATES v. CHEROKEE NATION, 202 U. S. 101 (1906).

CHEROKEE NATION v. UNITED STATES, 270 U. S. 476 (1926).

CHEROKEE NATION v. UNITED STATES, 80 C. Cls. 1 (1932, 1935).

CHEROKEE NATION v. UNITED STATES, 85 C. Cls. 76 (1937).

CHEROKEE NATION v. WHITMIRE, 223 U. S. 108 (1912).

CHEROKEE TOBACCO, 11 Wall. 616 (1870), aff'g UNITED STATES v. TOBACCO FACTORY, 28 Fed. Cas. No. 16528 (D. C. W. D. Ark. 1870).

CHEROKEE TRUST FUNDS, 117 U. S. 288 (1886) aff'g EASTERN BAND OF CHEROKEE INDIANS v. UNITED STATES, 20 C. Cls. 449 (1885). See EASTERN BAND OF CHEROKEE INDIANS v. UNITED STATES, 117 U. S. 288 (1886).

CHICKASAW FREEDMEN v. CHOCTAW NATION AND CHICKASAW NATION, 193 U. S. 115 (1904), aff'g UNITED STATES v. CHOCTAW NATION, 38 C. Cls. 558 (1903); s. c. 179 U. S. 494 (1900).

CHICKASAW NATION v. ROBINSON, 174 U. S. 445 (1899). See STEPHENS v. CHEROKEE NATION, 174 U. S. 445 (1899).

CHICKASAW NATION v. UNITED STATES, 19 C. Cls. 133 (1884).

CHICKASAW NATION v. UNITED STATES, 22 C. Cls. 222 (1887).

CHICKASAW NATION v. UNITED STATES, 75 C. Cls. 426 (1932), cert. den. 287 U. S. 643.

CHICKASAW NATION v. UNITED STATES, 87 C. Cls. 91 (1938), cert. den. 307 U. S. 646.

CHILDERS v. BEAVER, 270 U. S. 555 (1926).

CHINN v. DARNELL, 5 Fed. Cas. No. 2684 (C. C. Ohio 1848).

CHIPPEWA INDIANS OF MINNESOTA v. UNITED STATES, 301 U. S. 358 (1937), aff'g 80 C. Cls. 410 (1935), rehearing den. 302 U. S. 772.

CHIPPEWA INDIANS OF MINNESOTA v. UNITED STATES, 305 U. S. 479 (1939).

CHIPPEWA INDIANS OF MINNESOTA v. UNITED STATES, 307 U. S. 1 (1939).

CHISHOLM v. CREEK AND IND. DEV. CO., 273 Fed. 589 (D. C. E. D. Okla. 1921), aff'd in part and rev'd in part sub nom. SPERRY OIL CO. v. CHISHOLM, 264 U. S. 488 (1924), s. c. 282 Fed. 93 (C. C. A. 8, 1922).

CHOATE v. TRAPP, 224 U. S. 665 (1912).

CHOCTAW AND CHICKASAW NATIONS v. UNITED STATES 75 C. Cls. 494 (1932).

CHOCTAW AND CHICKASAW NATIONS v. UNITED STATES, 81 C. Cls. 63 (1935), cert. den. 296 U. S. 644.

CHOCTAW AND GULF R. R. v. HARRISON, 235 U. S. 292 (1914).

CHOCTAW NATION v. ROBINSON, 174 U. S. 445 (1899). See STEPHENS v. CHEROKEE NATION, 174 U. S. 445 (1899).

CHOCTAW NATION v. UNITED STATES, 19 C. Cls. 243 (1884).

CHOCTAW NATION v. UNITED STATES, 119 U. S. 1 (1886), rev'g 21 C. Cls. 59 (1886).

CHOCTAW NATION v. UNITED STATES, 179 U. S. 494 (1900). See UNITED STATES v. CHOCTAW NATION, 179 U. S. 494 (1900).

CHOCTAW NATION v. UNITED STATES, 81 C. Cls. 1 (1935), cert. den. 296 U. S. 643.

CHOCTAW NATION v. UNITED STATES, 83 C. Cls. 49 (1936)

CHOCTAW NATION v. UNITED STATES, 83 C. Cls. 140 (1936), cert. den. 300 U. S. 668.

CHOCTAW O. & G. R. CO. v. BOND, 160 Fed. 403 (C. C. A. 8, 1908), aff'g 6 Ind. T. 515, 98 S. W. 335 (1906).

CHOCTAW O. & G. R. CO. v. HARRISON, 235 U. S. 292 (1914).

CHOCTAW O. & G. R. R. CO. v. LOPER BROS., 6 Ind. T. 432, 98 S. W. 150 (1906).

CHOCTAW O. & G. R. R. v. MACKEY, 256 U. S. 531 (1921), aff'g 261 Fed. 342 (C. C. A. 8, 1919).

CHOTEAU v. BURNET, 283 U. S. 691 (1931), aff'g CHOUTEAU v. COMMISSIONER OF INTERNAL REVENUE, etc., 38 F. 2d 976 (C. C. A. 10, 1930).

CHOUTEAU v. MOLONY, 16 How. 203 (1853).

CHOUTEAU v. COMMISSIONER OF INTERNAL REVENUE, etc., 38 F. 2d 976 (C. C. A. 10, 1930), aff'd sub nom. CHOTEAU v. BURNET, 283 U. S. 691 (1931), cert. granted 281 U. S. 714, cert. den. sub nom. PETTIT v. LUCAS, COMM'R OF INTERNAL REVENUE, 281 U. S. 759 (1930).

CHURCH ADM'R v. UNITED STATES, 48 C. Cls. 262 (1913).

CITIZEN INDIANS OF THE WEAS v. UNITED STATES, 26 C. Cls. 323 (1891).

CITY OF TULSA v. SOUTHWESTERN BELL TELEPHONE CO., 75 F. 2d 343 (C. C. A. 10, 1935), aff'g 5 F. Supp. 822 (D. C. N. D. Okla. 1934), cert. den. 295 U. S. 744.

CLAIRMONT v. UNITED STATES, 225 U. S. 551 (1912).

CLARK v. ANTHIS, 51 F. 2d 42 (C. C. A. 10, 1931).

CLARK v. SMITH, 13 Pet. 195 (1839).

CLARKE v. BOYSEN, 39 F. 2d 800 (C. C. A. 10, 1930), cert. den. 282 U. S. 869, s. c. 264 Fed. 492, s. c. 268 Fed. 535, s. c. 273 Fed. 923.

CLAY v. UNITED STATES, 282 Fed. 268 (C. C. A. 8, 1922).

COCHRAN v. UNITED STATES, 276 Fed. 701 (C. C. A. 8, 1921).

COFFEE v. GROOVER, 123 U. S. 1 (1887).

COFFIELD v. UNITED STATES, 52 C. Cls. 17 (1916).

COLBAUGH v. UNITED STATES, 15 F. 2d 929 (C. C. A. 8, 1926).

COLLIER v. UNITED STATES, 221 Fed. 64 (C. C. A. 8, 1915).

COLLIER v. UNITED STATES, 173 U. S. 79 (1899).

COLLINS v. BUBB, 73 Fed. 735 (C. C. Wash. 1896).

COLLINS v. MORGAN, 243 Fed. 495 (C. C. A. 8, 1917), s. c. 219 Fed. 670.

COLLINS v. UNITED STATES, 225 Fed. 365 (C. C. A. 8, 1915), cert. den. 238 U. S. 625, s. c. 219 Fed. 670.

COLUMBIA CANNING CO. v. HAMPTON, 161 Fed. 60 (C. C. A. 9, 1908).

COMMERCIAL INVESTMENT TRUST v. UNITED STATES, 261 Fed. 330 (C. C. A. 8, 1919).

COMMISSIONER OF INTERNAL REVENUE v. OWENS, 78 F. 2d 768 (C. C. A. 10, 1935).

COMMISSIONERS v. UNITED STATES, 270 Fed. 110 (C. C. A. 8, 1920), aff'g UNITED STATES v. HUTCHINGS, 252 Fed. 841 (D. C. W. D. Okla. 1918), writ of error dism. 260 U. S. 753 (1922).

COMMONWEALTH v. COXE, 4 Dall. 170 (1800).

CONLEY v. BALLINGER, 216 U. S. 84 (1910).

CONNER v. CORNELL, 32 F. 2d 581 (C. C. A. 8, 1929), cert. den. 280 U. S. 583.

CONNERS v. UNITED STATES, 180 U. S. 271 (1901), aff'g 33 C. Cls. 317 (1898).

CONNOR v. UNITED STATES, 19 C. Cls. 675 (1884).

CONRAD INVESTMENT CO. v. UNITED STATES, 161 Fed. 829 (C. C. A. 9, 1908), aff'g 156 Fed. 123 (C. C. Mont. 1907).

CONTINENTAL OIL CO. v. OSAGE OIL AND REFINING CO., 69 F. 2d 19 (C. C. A. 10, 1934), cert. den. 287 U. S. 616, s. c. 57 F. 2d 527.

CONTZEN v. UNITED STATES, 179 U. S. 191 (1900), aff'g 33 C. Cls. 475 (1898).

CONWAY v. UNITED STATES, 149 Fed. 261 (C. C. Neb. 1907).

COOS BAY INDIAN TRIBE v. UNITED STATES, 87 C. Cls. 143 (1938), cert. den. 306 U. S. 653.

CORRALITOS CO. v. UNITED STATES, 178 U. S. 280 (1900), aff'g CORRALITOS STOCK CO. v. UNITED STATES, 33 C. Cls. 342 (1898).

CORRIGAN v. BROWN, 169 Fed. 477 (C. C. W. D. Wash. 1907).

CORTEZ OIL CO. v. UNITED STATES, 64 C. Cls. 390 (1928), cert. den. 277 U. S. 600.

COX v. UNITED STATES, 14 C. Cls. 512 (1878).

COX v. UNITED STATES, 29 C. Cls. 349 (1894).

CRABTREE v. BYRNE, 54 Fed. 432 (C. C. N. D. Ill. 1892).

CRABTREE v. MADDEN, 54 Fed. 426 (C. C. A. 8, 1893).

CRAMER v. UNITED STATES, 261 U. S. 219 (1923), rev'g 276 Fed. 78 (C. C. A. 9, 1921).

CRAWFORD v. DUCKWORTH, 3 Ind. T. 10, 53 S. W. 465 (1899).

CREEK NATION v. UNITED STATES, 63 C. Cls. 270 (1927), cert. den. 274 U. S. 751.

CREEK NATION v. UNITED STATES, 74 C. Cls. 663 (1932).

CREEK NATION v. UNITED STATES, 77 C. Cls. 226 (1933), s. c. 81 C. Cls. 973.

CREEK NATION v. UNITED STATES, 78 C. Cls. 474 (1933).

CREEK NATION v. UNITED STATES, 79 C. Cls. 778 (1934).

CREEK NATION v. UNITED STATES, 302 U. S. 620 (1938), rev'g 84 C. Cls. 12, s. c. 295 U. S. 103 (1935), rev'g 77 C. Cls. 159 (1933), s. c. 87 C. Cls. 280 (1938).

CREWS v. BURCHAM, 1 Black 352 (1861).

633058—45——41

CROW v. UNITED STATES, 32 C. Cls. 16 (1896).
CROW NATION v. UNITED STATES, 81 C. Cls. 238 (1935).
CROWELL v. YOUNG, 4 Ind. T. 36, 64 S. W. 607 (1901), mod. 4 Ind. T. 148, 69 S. W. 829 (1902).
CULLY v. MITCHELL, 37 F. 2d 493 (C. C. A. 10, 1930), cert. den. 281 U. S. 740.
DANFORTH'S LESSEE v. THOMAS, 1 Wheat. 155 (1816).
DANFORTH v. WEAR, 9 Wheat. 673 (1824).
DANIELS v. MILLER, 4 Ind. T. 426 69 S. W. 925 (1902).
DARKS v. ICKES, 69 F. 2d 231 (App. D. C. 1934), s. c. 61 App. D. C. 266.
DAUGHERTY v. BOGY, 104 Fed. 938 (C. C. A. 8, 1900), rev'g 3 Ind. T. 197, 53 S. W. 542 (1899), app. dism. 184 U. S. 696 (1901).
DAVENPORT v. BUFFINGTON, 97 Fed. 234 (C. C. A. 8, 1899), aff'g I Ind. T. 424, 45 S. W. 128 (1899).
DAVENPORT, ADMR. v. UNITED STATES, 31 C. Cls. 430 (1896).
DAVID v. YOUNKEN, 250 Fed. 208 (C. C. A. 8, 1918), s. c. 235 Fed. 621.
DAVIDSON v. UNITED STATES, 34 C. Cls. 169 (1899).
DAVIS v. SITKA SCHOOL BOARD, 3 Alaska 481 (1908).
DAVIS v. TOLOWA ROYALTIES, 40 F. 2d 264 (C. C. A. 10, 1930), cert. den. 282 U. S. 841.
DAVIS v. UNITED STATES, 27 C. Cls. 181 (1892).
DAVIS v. UNITED STATES, 32 F. 2d 860 (C. C. A. 9, 1929).
DAVISON v. GIBSON, 56 Fed. 443 (C. C. A. 8, 1893), s. c. 76 Fed. 717.
DAWES v. BENSON, 5 Ind. T. 50, 82 S. W. 1141 (1904).
DAWES v. CUNDIFF, 5 Ind. T. 47, 82 S. W. 228 (1904).
DAWES v. HARRIS, 5 Ind. T. 53, 82 S. W. 1142 (1904).
DE BACA v. UNITED STATES, 36 C. Cls. 407 (1901).
DE BACA v. UNITED STATES, 37 C. Cls. 482 (1901).
DE MOSS v. UNITED STATES, 250 Fed. 87 (C. C. A. 8, 1918).
DEERE v. ST. LAWRENCE RIVER POWER CO., 32 F. 2d 550 (C. C. A. 2, 1929, aff'g 22 F. 2d 851.
DE LA O v. ACOMA, 1 N. M. 226 (1857).
DELAWARE INDIANS v. CHEROKEE NATION, 193 U. S. 127 (1904), mod'g and aff'g 38 C. Cls. 234 (1903).
DELAWARE TRIBE v. UNITED STATES, 72 C. Cls. 483 (1931).
DELAWARE TRIBE v. UNITED STATES, 74 C. Cls. 368 (1932).
DELAWARE TRIBE OF INDIANS v. UNITED STATES, 84 C. Cls. 535 (1937).
DEMING INV. CO. v. UNITED STATES, 224 U. S. 471 (1912).
DENISON & N. RY. CO., v. RANNEY-ALTON MERC. CO., 104 Fed. 595 (C. C. A. 8, 1900), rev'g 3 Ind. T. 104, 53 S. W. 496 (1899).
DENNEE v. McCOY, 4 Ind. T. 233, 69 S. W. 858 (1902).
DENTON v. CAPITAL TOWNSITE CO., 5 Ind. T. 396, 82 S. W. 852 (1904).
DERRISAW v. SCHAFFER, 8 F. Supp. 876 (D. C. E. D. Okla. 1934).
DEWEY COUNTY, S. D. v. UNITED STATES, 26 F. 2d 434 (C. C. A. 8, 1928), aff'g UNITED STATES v. DEWEY COUNTY, S. D., 14 F. 2d 784 (D. C. S. Dak. 1926), cert. den. 278 U. S. 649 (1928).
DICK v. ROSS, 6 Ind. T. 85, 89 S. W. 664 (1905).
DICK v. UNITED STATES, 208 U. S. 340 (1908).
DICKSON v. LUCK LAND CO., 242 U. S. 371 (1917).
DIXON v. COX, 268 Fed. 285 (C. C. A. 8, 1920), app. dism., 258 U. S. 634.
DOBBS v. UNITED STATES, 33 C. Cls. 308 (1898).
DOE v. BEARDSLEY, 10 Fed. Cas. No. 5497 (C. C. Ind. 1841).
DOE v. WILSON, 23 How. 457 (1859).
DONNELLY v. UNITED STATES, 228 U. S. 243 (1913).
DONOHOO v. HOWARD, 4 Ind. T. 433, 69 S. W. 927 (1902).
DOSSET v. UNITED STATES, 248 Fed. 902 (C. C. A. 8, 1918).
DRAPEAU v. UNITED STATES, 195 Fed. 130 (C. C. S. D. 1912).
DRAPER v. UNITED STATES, 164 U. S. 240 (1896).
DRUMMOND v. UNITED STATES, 34 F. 2d 755 (C. C. A. 8, 1929).
DUBUQUE ETC. RAILROAD v. D. M. V. RAILROAD, 109 U. S. 329 (1883).
DUCKER v. BUTLER, 104 Fed. 236 (App. D. C. 1939).
DUKES v. GOODALL, 5 Ind. T. 145, 82 S. W. 702 (1904).
DUKES v. McKENNA, 4 Ind. T. 156, 69 S. W. 832 (1902).
DULL v. LE FEBRE, 222 Fed. 471 (D. C. E. D. Wash., 1914).
DUNCAN TOWNSITE CO. v. LANE, 245 U. S. 308 (1912).
DUNBAR v. GREEN, 198 U. S. 166 (1905).
DUPUIS v. UNITED STATES, 5 F. 2d 231 (C. C. A. 9, 1925).
DURAN v. UNITED STATES, 31 C. Cls. 353 (1896).
DURAN, ADMR. v. UNITED STATES, 32 C. Cls. 273 (1897).
DUVAL v. HENDRICKS, 4 Ind. T. 94, 64 S. W. 1089 (1901).
DUWAMISH INDIANS v. UNITED STATES, 79 C. Cls. 530 (1934), cert. den. 295 U. S. 755.
DYER v. UNITED STATES, 20 C. Cls. 166 (1885).
EAGLE-PICHER LEAD CO. v. FULLERTON, 28 F. 2d 472 (C. C. A. 8, 1928), s. c. 279 U. S. 839.
EASTERN BAND OF CHEROKEES v. CHEROKEE NATION WEST, 19 C. Cls. 35 (1883).
EASTERN BAND OF CHEROKEE INDIANS v. UNITED STATES, 117 U. S. 288 (1886), aff'g 20 C. Cls. 449 (1885). See CHEROKEE TRUST FUNDS, 117 U. S. 288 (1886).
EASTERN CHEROKEES v. CHEROKEE NATION AND UNITED STATES, 202 U. S. 101 (1906). See UNITED STATES v. CHEROKEE NATION, 202 U. S. 101 (1906), s. c. 220 U. S. 84, 225 U. S. 576.
EASTERN CHEROKEES v. UNITED STATES, 225 U. S. 572 (1912), aff'g 45 C. Cls. 104 (1910).
EASTERN CHEROKEES v. UNITED STATES, 45 C. Cls. 229 (1910).
EASTERN CHEROKEES v. UNITED STATES, 225 U. S. 572 (1912).
EASTERN OR EMIGRANT CHEROKEES v. UNITED STATES, 82 C. Cls. 180 (1935), cert. den. 299 U. S. 551.
EDDY v. LAFAYETTE, 163 U. S. 456 (1896), aff'g 49 Fed. 798 (C. C. A. 8, 1892).
EDWARDS v. UNITED STATES, 5 F. 2d 17 (C. C. A. 8, 1925).
EGAN v. McDONALD, 246 U. S. 227 (1918).
ELAM v. UNITED STATES, 7 F. 2d 887 (C. C. A. 8, 1925).
ELK v. WILKINS, 112 U. S. 94 (1884).
ELLIOT v. GARVIN, 166 Fed. 278 (1908), aff'g 7 Ind. T. 679, 104 S. W. 878 (1907).
ELLIOTT v. UNITED STATES, 283 U. S. 753 (1931). See HALBERT v. UNITED STATES, 283 U. S. 753 (1931).
ELLIS v. FITZPATRICK, 118 Fed. 430 (C. C. A. 8, 1902), aff'g 3 Ind. T. 656, 64 S. W. 567 (1901).
ELLIS v. UNITED STATES, 6 Ind. T. 201, 97 S. W. 1018 (1906).
ELWOOD v. FLANNIGAN, 104 U. S. 562 (1881).
ENDLEMAN v. UNITED STATES, 86 Fed. 456 (C. C. A. 9, 1898).
ENGLEMAN v. CABLE, 4 Ind. T. 336, 69 S. W. 894 (1902).
ENGLISH v. RICHARDSON, TREASURER OF TULSA COUNTY, OKLAHOMA, 224 U. S. 680 (1912).
EQUITABLE TRUST CO. v. UNITED STATES, 34 F. 2d 916 (C. C. A. 2, 1929). See BARNETT v. EQUITABLE TRUST, 34 F. 2d 916 (C. C. A. 2, 1929).
ESLICK v. UNITED STATES, 51 C. Cls. 266 (1916).
ESTES v. UNITED STATES, 225 Fed. 980 (C. C. A. 8, 1915).
ETCHEN v. CHENEY, 235 Fed. 104 (C. C. A. 8, 1916).
EUGENE SOL LOUIE v. UNITED STATES, 274 Fed. 47 (C. C. A. 9, 1921), rev'd sub nom. LOUIE v. UNITED STATES, 254 U. S. 548, s. c. 264 Fed. 295.
EVANS v. VICTOR, 204 Fed. 361 (C. C. A. 8, 1913), rev'g 199 Fed. 504 (D. C. E. D. Okla., 1912).
EVANS-SNIDER-BUEL CO. v. McFADDEN, 105 Fed. 293 (C. C. A. 8, 1900), rev'g McFADDEN v. BLOCKER, 2 Ind. T. 260, 48 S. W. 1043 (1899) aff'd sub nom. McFADDIN v. EVANS, SNIDER, BUELL CO., 185 U. S. 505 (1902), s. c. 54 S. W. 873 (1900).
EWERT v. BLUEJACKET, 259 U. S. 129 (1922), aff'g in part and rev'g in part 265 Fed. 823 (C. C. A. 8, 1920).
EX PARTE CARTER, 4 Ind. T. 539, 76 S. W. 102 (1903).
EX PARTE CROW DOG, 109 U. S. 556 (1883).
EX PARTE DICK, 141 Fed. 5 (C. C. A. 9, 1905), rev'd WHITNEY v. DICK, 202 U. S. 132 (1906), s. c. 208 U. S. 340 (1907).
EX PARTE DICKSON, 4 Ind. T. 481, 69 S. W. 943 (1902).
EX PARTE FORBES, 9 Fed. Cas. 4921 (C. C. Kan., 1870).
EX PARTE HART, 157 Fed. 130 (D. C. Ore., 1907).
EX PARTE KANG-GI-SHUN-CA, 109 U. S. 556 (1883). See EX PARTE CROW DOG, 109 U. S. 556 (1883).
EX PARTE KENYON, 14 Fed. Cas. No. 7720 (C. C. W. D. Ark., 1878).
EX PARTE KYLE, 67 Fed. 306 (D. C. W. D. Ark., 1895).
EX PARTE MARGRAVE, 275 Fed. 200 (D. C. N. D. Cal., 1921).
EX PARTE MORGAN, 20 Fed. 298 (D. C. W. D. Ark., 1883).
EX PARTE PERO, 99 F. 2d 28 (C. C. A. 7, 1938), cert. den. 306 U. S. 643.
EX PARTE REYNOLDS, 20 Fed. Cas. No. 11719 (D. C. W. D. Ark., 1879).
EX PARTE SAVAGE, 158 Fed. 205 (C. C. Kan. 1908).
EX PARTE SLOAN, 22 Fed. Cas. No. 12944 (D. C. Nev. 1877).

EX PARTE TIGER, 2 Ind. T. 41, 47 S. W. 304 (1898).
EX PARTE TILDEN, 218 Fed. 920 (D. C. Idaho, 1914).
EX PARTE VAN MOORE, 221 Fed. 954 (D. C. S. D. 1915).
EX PARTE VILES, 139 Fed. 68 (D. C. W. D. Wash. 1905).
EX PARTE WEBB, 225 U. S. 663 (1912), s. c. 225 U. S. 696.
FAIRBANKS v. UNITED STATES, 223 U. S. 215 (1912), aff'g UNITED STATES v. FAIRBANKS, 171 Fed. 337 (C. C. A. 8, 1909).
FALK, EX'R v. UNITED STATES, 27 C. Cls. 321 (1892).
FAMOUS SMITH v. UNITED STATES, 151 U. S. 50 (1894).
FARRELL v. UNITED STATES, 110 Fed. 942 (C. C. A. 8, 1901).
FEE v. BROWN, 162 U. S. 602 (1896).
FEELEY v. UNITED STATES, 236 Fed. 903 (C. C. A. 8, 1916).
FELIX v. PATRICK, 145 U. S. 317, (1892).
FELLOWS v. BLACKSMITH, 19 How. 366 (1856).
FENLON v. UNITED STATES, 17 C. Cls. 138 (1881).
FIELDER v. UNITED STATES, 227 Fed. 832 (C. C. A. 8, 1915).
FIELD v. AMOS, 255 U. S. 373 (1921). See WINTON v. AMOS, 255 U. S. 373 (1921).
FINK v. COUNTY COMMISSIONERS, 248 U. S. 399 (1919).
FINLEY v. ABNER, 129 Fed. 734 (C. C. A. 8, 1904).
FIRST MOON v. WHITE TAIL, 270 U. S. 243 (1926).
FIRST NAT. BANK of DECATUR, NEB. v. UNITED STATES, 59 F. 2d 367 (C. C. A. 8, 1932), aff'g UNITED STATES v. FIRST NAT. BANK of DECATUR, NEB., 56 F. 2d 634 D. C. Neb. 1931).
FISH v. WISE, 52 F. 2d 544 (C. C. A. 10, 1931), cert. den. 282 U. S. 903 (1931), 284 U. S. 688 (1932).
FISHER v. UNITED STATES, 226 Fed. 156 (C. C. A. 8, 1915).
FISK v. ARNOLD, 166 Fed. 744 (C. C. A. 8, 1908).
FITE v. UNITED STATES, 203 U. S. 76 (1906). See CHEROKEE INTERMARRIAGE CASES, 203 U. S. 76 (1906).
FLACK v. UNITED STATES, 272 Fed. 680 (C. C. A. 8, 1921).
FLACK v. UNITED STATES, 291 Fed. 376 (C. C. A. 8, 1923).
FLATHEAD IRR. DIST. v. McINTIRE, 101 F. 2d 650 (C. C. A. 9, 1939), rev'g. 22 F. Supp. 316.
FLEMING v. McCURTAIN, 215 U. S. 56 (1909).
FLETCHER v. PECK, 6 Cranch 87 (1810).
FOERSTER v. UNITED STATES, 116 Fed. 860 (C. C. A. 8, 1902), s. c. 187 U. S. 644.
FOLK v. UNITED STATES, 233 Fed. 177 (C. C. A. 8, 1916) s. c. 268 Fed. 923.
FOND DU LAC BAND OF CHIPPEWA INDIANS v. UNITED STATES, 34 C. Cls. 426 (1899).
FORD v. UNITED STATES, 260 Fed. 657 (C. C. A. 8, 1919), s. c. 259 Fed. 552.
FOREMAN v. MIDLAND VALLEY RY. CO., 7 Ind. T. 478, 104 S. W. 806 (1907).
FORSYTHE v. UNITED STATES, 3 Ind. T. 599 (1901), app. dism. 115 Fed. 1019.
FORT BERTHOLD INDIANS v. UNITED STATES, 71 C. Cls. 308 (1930).
FORTY-THREE CASES COGNAC BRANDY, 14 Fed. 539 (C. C. Minn. 1882), aff'g FORTY-THREE GALLONS of COGNAC BRANDY, 11 Fed. 47 (C. C. Minn. 1882).
FOSTER v. PRYOR, 189 U. S. 325 (1903).
FOWLER v. BRIGHT, 4 F. Supp. 565 (D. C. W. D. Wash. 1933).
FOWLER v. UNITED STATES, 1 Wash. Ter. 3 (1854).
FRAER v. WASHINGTON, 125 Fed. 280 (C. C. A. 8, 1903).
FRAME v. BIVENS, 189 Fed. 785 (C. C. E. D. Okla. 1909).
FRANCIS v. FRANCIS, 203 U. S. 233 (1906), app. dism. 199 U. S. 616.
FRANKLIN v. LYNCH, 233 U. S. 269 (1914).
FREMONT v. UNITED STATES, 2 C. Cls. 461 (1866).
FREMONT v. UNITED STATES, 4 C. Cls. 252 (1868).
FREMONT COUNTY v. MOORE, 3 Wyo. 200, 19 Pac. 438 (1888).
FRENCH v. LANCASTER, 2 Dak. 346, 47 N. W. 395 (1880), s. c. 2 Dak. 276, 9 N. W. 716 (1880).
FRENCH v. UNITED STATES, 49 C. Cls. 337 (1914).
FRIEND v. UNITED STATES, 29 C. Cls. 425 (1894), app. dism. 163 U. S. 687.
FULSON v. QUAKER OIL & GAS CO., 35 F. 2d 84 (C. C. A. 8, 1929), s. c. 28 F. 2d 398.
GAGNON v. UNITED STATES, 193 U. S. 451 (1904), aff'g 38 C. Cls. 10 (1902), 39 C. Cls. 548 (1904).
GAINES v. NICHOLSON, 9 How. 356 (1850).
GAINES v. UNITED STATES, 92 U. S. 698 (1875). See HOT SPRINGS CASES, 92 U. S. 698 (1875).
GALLEGOS v. UNITED STATES, 39 C. Cls. 86 (1903).
GAMEL v. UNITED STATES, 31 C. Cls. 321 (1896).
GANNON v. JOHNSTON, 243 U. S. 108 (1917).
GARCIA v. UNITED STATES, 37 C. Cls. 243 (1902).
GARCIA v. UNITED STATES, 43 F. 2d 873 (C. C. A. 10, 1930).
GARFIELD v. UNITED STATES ex rel. ALLISON, 211 U. S. 264 (1908).
GARFIELD v. UNITED STATES ex rel. GOLDSBY, 211 U. S. 249 (1908).
GARFIELD v. UNITED STATES ex rel. LOWE, 34 App. D. C. 70 (1909), aff'd sub nom. UNITED STATES ex rel. LOWE v. FISHER, 223 U. S. 95 (1912), s. c. 35 App. D. C. 524.
GARLAND'S HEIRS v. CHOCTAW NATION, 256 U. S. 439 (1921), s. c. 272 U. S. 728 (1927).
GARRISON v. UNITED STATES, 30 C. Cls. 272 (1895).
GAY v. THOMAS, 169 U. S. 264 (1898), rev'g 5 Okla. 1, 46 Pac. 578 (1896), overruled in part, 7 Okla. 184, 54 Pac. 444 (1898).
GEORGE v. ROBB, 4 Ind. T. 61, 64 S. W. 615 (1901).
GERMAN-AMERICAN INSURANCE CO. v. PAUL, 5 Ind. T. 703, 83 S. W. 60 (1904), s. c. 2 Ind. T. 625, 53 S. W. 442 (1899).
GERRARD v. UNITED STATES, 43 C. Cls. 67 (1907).
GHO v. JULLES, 1 Wash. Terr. 325 (1871).
GIBSON v. ANDERSON, 131 Fed. 39 (C. C. A. 9, 1904).
GIDDINGS v. UNITED STATES, 29 C. Cls. 12 (1893).
GILCREASE v. McCULLOUGH, 249 U. S. 178 (1919), s. c. 243 U. S. 653.
GILFILLAN v. McKEE, 159 U. S. 303 (1895).
GILLESPIE v. OKLAHOMA, 257 U. S. 501 (1922), lm'td BURNETT v. CORONADO OIL & GAS CO., 285 U. S. 393, 398 (1932), overruled HELVERING v. PRODUCERS CORP., 303 U. S. 376, 387 (1938).
GILPIN v. UNITED STATES, 256 U. S. 10 (1921), s. c. 261 Fed. 841.
GLAVEY v. UNITED STATES, 182 U. S. 595 (1901), rev'g 35 C. Cls. 242 (1900).
GLEASON v. WOOD, 224 U. S. 679 (1912).
GLENN v. LEWIS, 105 F. 2d 398 (C. C. A. 10, 1939), cert. den. 60 Sup. Ct. 130.
GLENN-TUCKER v. CLAYTON, JUDGE, 4 Ind. T. 511, 70 S. W. 8 (1903).
GLOBE INDEMNITY CO. v. BRUCE, 81 F. 2d 143 (C. C. A. 10, 1935), cert. den. 297 U. S. 716, rev'g BRUCE v. GLOBE INDEMNITY CO., 9 F. Supp. 761 (D. C. N. D. Okla. 1935).
GLOVER v. UNITED STATES, 147 Fed. 426 (C. C. A. 8, 1906), rev'g 6 Ind. T. 262, 91 S. W. 41 (1906).
GOAT v. UNITED STATES, 224 U. S. 458 (1912), mod'g and aff'g UNITED STATES v. ALLEN, 179 Fed. 13 (C. C. A. 8, 1910).
GODFREY v. BEARDSLEY, 10 Fed. Cas. No. 5497 (C. C. Ind. 1841).
GOFF v. UNITED STATES, 257 Fed. 294 (C. C. A. 8, 1919).
GOLDEN TERRA MINING CO. v. SMITH, 2 Dak. 377, 11 N. W. 98 (1881), s. c. 2 Dak. 374, 11 N. W. 97 (1881).
GON-SHAY-EE, PETITIONER, 130 U. S. 343 (1889).
GOOD SHOT v. UNITED STATES, 104 Fed. 257 (C. C. A. 8, 1900), cert. den. 179 U. S. 87.
GOODFELLOW v. MUCKEY, 10 Fed. Cas. No. 5537 (C. C. Kan. 1881).
GOODING v. WATKINS, 142 Fed. 112 (C. C. A. 8, 1905), rev'g 5 Ind. T. 578, 82 S. W. 913 (1904).
GOODRUM v. BUFFALO, 162 Fed. 817 (C. C. A. 8, 1908).
GOODSON v. UNITED STATES, 7 Okla. 117, 54 Pac. 423 (1898).
GORDON v. GRYDIR, 34 App. D. C. 508 (1910).
GORHAN v. UNITED STATES, 29 C. Cls. 97 (1894), aff'd sub nom. UNITED STATES v. GORHAN.
GOSSET v. UNITED STATES, 31 C. Cls. 325 (1896).
GOUDY v. MEATH, 203 U. S. 146 (1906).
GOWEN v. HARLEY, 56 Fed. 973 (C. C. A. 8, 1899).
GRAHAM v. UNITED STATES, 30 C. Cls. 318 (1895).
GRAVELLE v. UNITED STATES, 253 Fed. 549 (C. C. A. 8, 1918).
GRAY v. COFFMAN, 10 Fed. Cas. No. 5714 (C. C. Kan. 1874).
GRAYSON v. HARRIS, 267 U. S. 352 (1925), s. c. 263 U. S. 696, 278 U. S. 555, 279 U. S. 300.
GREEN v. MENOMINEE TRIBE OF INDIANS IN WISCONSIN, 233 U. S. 558 (1914), aff'g 46 C. Cls. 68 (1911), s. c. 47 C. Cls. 281 (1912).
GREER v. UNITED STATES, 245 U. S. 559 (1918), aff'g 240 Fed. 320 (C. C. A. 8, 1917).
GRITTS v. FISHER, 224 U. S. 640 (1912).
GROW v. UNITED STATES, 32 C. Cls. 599 (1897).
GULF, ETC., RAILWAY CO. v. SHANE, 157 U. S. 348 (1895).
GUTHRIE v. HALL, 1 Okla. Terr. 454, 34 Pac. 380 (1891).

GUYETT v. M'WHIRK, 154 Fed. 784 (C. C. Ore. 1907), s. c. 133 Fed. 1022.

HALBERT v. UNITED STATES, 283 U. S. 753 (1931), rev'g UNITED STATES v. HALBERT, 38 F. 2d 795 (C. C. A. 9, 1930).

HALE v. UNITED STATES, 92 U. S. 698 (1875). See HOT SPRINGS CASES, 92 U. S. 698 (1875).

HALFF & BRO. v. GREEN, 10 Okla. 338, 62 Pac. 816 (1900).

HALLAM v. COMMERCE MINING & ROYALTY CO., 49 F. 2d 103 (C. C. A. 10, 1931), aff'g 32 F. 2d 371 (D. C. N. D. Okla. 1929), cert. den. 284 U. S. 643 (1931).

HALLOWELL v. COMMONS, 239 U. S. 506 (1916), aff'g 210 Fed. 793 (C. C. A. 8, 1914).

HALLOWELL v. UNITED STATES, 221 U. S. 317 (1911), s. c. 209 U. S. 101.

HAMILTON v. UNITED STATES, 42 C. Cls. 282 (1907).

HAMPTON v. EWERT, 22 F. 2d 81 (C. C. A. 8, 1927), cert. den. 276 U. S. 623 (1928).

HAMPTON v. MAYS, 4 Ind. T. 503, 69 S. W. 1115 (1902), s. c. 3 Ind. 65, 53 S. W. 483 (1899).

HANKS v. HENDRICKS, 3 Ind. T. 415, 58 S. W. 669 (1900).

HARGROVE v. CHEROKEE NATION, 3 Ind. T. 478, 58 S. W. 667 (1900), s. c. 4 Ind. T. 129, 69 S. W. 823 (1902), aff'd 129 Fed. 186, app. dism. 20 Sup. Ct. 1024.

HARGROVE v. CHEROKEE NATION, 129 Fed. 186 (C. C. A. 8, 1904).

HARJO v. EMPIRE GAS & FUEL CO., 28 F. 2d 596 (C. C. A. 8, 1928).

HARKNESS v. HYDE, 98 U. S. 476 (1878).

HARNAGE v. MARTIN, 242 U. S. 386 (1917).

HARRIS v. BELL, 254 U. S. 103 (1920), aff'g 250 Fed. 209 (C. C. A. 8, 1918), s. c. 235 Fed. 626.

HARRIS v. GALE, 188 Fed. 712 (C. C. E. D. Okla. 1911).

HARRIS v. HARDRIDGE, 166 Fed. 109 (C. C. A. 8, 1908), aff'g 7 Ind. T. 532, 104 S. W. 826 (1907).

HARRIS v. UNITED STATES, 249 Fed. 41 (C. C. A. 8, 1918), cert. den. 246 U. S. 675 (1918).

HARRISON v. MONCRAVIE, 264 Fed. 776 (C. C. A. 8, 1920), app. dism. 255 U. S. 562 (1921).

HARTMAN v. WARREN, 76 Fed. 157 (C. C. A. 8, 1896).

HASS v. UNITED STATES, 17 F. 2d 894 (C. C. A. 8, 1927).

HATCH v. FERGUSON, 66 Fed. 668 (C. C. A. 9, 1895), aff'g 57 Fed. 559 (C. C. Wash. 1893), s. c. 52 Fed. 833, 57 Fed. 966, 57 Fed. 972.

HATTEN v. HUDSPETH, 99 F. 2d 501 (C. C. A. 10, 1938).

HAWKINS v. OKLA. OIL CO., 195 Fed. 345 (C. C. E. D. Okla. 1911).

HAWLEY v. UNITED STATES, 15 F. 2d 621 (C. C. A. 8, 1926).

HAYES v. BARRINGER, 168 Fed. 221 (C. C. A. 8, 1909).

HAYES v. UNITED STATES, 44 C. Cls. 493 (1909).

HAYT v. UNITED STATES, 38 C. Cls. 455 (1903).

HECKMAN v. SUTTER, 119 Fed. 83 (C. C. A. 9, 1902), aff'g SUTTER v. HECKMAN, 1 Alaska 188 (1901), s. c. 128 Fed. 393, (C. C. A. 9, 1904).

HECKMAN v. UNITED STATES, 224 U. S. 413 (1912), mod'g and aff'g UNITED STATES v. ALLEN, 179 Fed. 13 (C. C. A. 8, 1910).

HEGMER v. UNITED STATES, 30 C. Cls. 405 (1895).

HEINER v. COLONIAL TRUST CO., 275 U. S. 232 (1927), rev'g LEWELLYN v. COLONIAL TRUST CO., 17 F. 2d 36 (C. C. A. 3, 1927).

HELLEN v. MORGAN, 283 Fed. 433 (D. C. E. D. Wash. 1922).

HENKEL v. UNITED STATES, 237 U. S. 43 (1915), aff'g 196 Fed. 345 (C. C. A. 9, 1912).

HENNY GAS CO v. UNITED STATES, 191 Fed. 132 (C. C. A. 8, 1911).

HERD v. UNITED STATES, 13 Okla. 512, 75 Pac. 291 (1904), aff'd sub. nom. BROWN v. UNITED STATES, 146 Fed. 975.

HERNANDEZ v. UNITED STATES, 34 C. Cls. 455 (1899).

HERRING v. UNITED STATES, 32 C. Cls. 536 (1897).

HICKEY v. UNITED STATES, 64 F. 2d 628 (C. C. A. 10, 1933).

HICKS v. BUTRICK, 12 Fed. Cas. No. 6458 (C. C. Kan. 1875).

HILL v. RANKIN, 289 Fed. 511 (D. C. E. D. Okla. 1923).

HILL v. REYNOLDS, 242 U. S. 361 (1917).

HITCHCOCK v. UNITED STATES ex rel. BIGBOY, 22 App. D. C. 275 (1903).

HOCKETT v. ALSTON, 110 Fed. 910 (C. C. A. 6, 1901), rev'g 3 Ind. T. 432, 58 S. W. 675 (1900).

HODGES v. UNITED STATES, 36 F. 2d 356 (C. C. A. 10, 1929), mod'g 35 F. 2d 594 (C. C. A. 10, 1929).

HODSON v. UNITED STATES, 250 Fed. 421 (C. C. A. 8 1918).

HOLDEN v. JOY, 17 Wall. 211 (1872).

HOLFORD v. JAMES, 136 Fed. 553 (C. C. A. 8, 1905).

HOLLAND v. McDANIEL, 230 Fed. 945 (C. C. A. 8, 1916). See McDANIEL v. HOLLAND, 230 Fed. 945 (C. C. A. 8, 1916).

HOLLAND v. UNITED STATES, 268 Fed. 244 (C. C. A. 8, 1920).

HOLLISTER v. UNITED STATES, 145 Fed. 773 (C. C. A. 8, 1906).

HOLMES v. UNITED STATES, 33 F. 2d 688 (C. C. A. 8, 1929).

HOLMES v. UNITED STATES, 53 F. 2d 960 (C. C. A. 10, 1931).

HOPKINS v. UNITED STATES, 235 Fed. 95 (C. C. A. 8, 1916).

HOSFORD v. UNITED STATES, 29 C. Cls. 42 (1894).

HOT SPRINGS CASES, 92 U. S. 698 (1875).

HOWE v. AMOS, 255 U. S. 373 (1921). See WINTON v. AMOS, 255 U. S. 373 (1921).

HOWELL v. BROWN, 5 Ind. T. 718, 83 S. W. 170 (1904).

HUBBARD v. CHISM, 5 Ind. T. 95, 82 S. W. 686 (1904).

HUNT v. HICKS, 3 Ind. T. 275, 54 S. W. 818 (1900).

HYNE v. UNITED STATES, 27 C. Cls. 113 (1892).

HY-YU-TSE-MIL-KIN v. SMITH, 194 U. S. 401 (1904), aff'g SMITH v. HE-YU-TSE-MIL-KIN, 110 Fed. 60 (C. C. Ore. 1901) and 119 Fed. 114 (C. C. A. 9, 1902).

ICKES v. PATTISON, 80 F. 2d 708 (App. D. C. 1935), cert. den. 297 U. S. 713.

ICKES v. UNITED STATES ex rel. PERRY, 64 F. 2d 982 (App. D. C. 1933).

IKARD v. MINTER, 4 Ind. T. 314, 69 S. W. 852 (1902).

IN RE BLACKBIRD, 109 Fed. 139 (D. C. W. D. Wis. 1901).

IN RE BOYD, 49 Fed. 48 (C. C. A. 8, 1892).

IN RE BURTON, 1 Alaska 111 (1900).

IN RE BYA-LIL-LE, 12 Ariz. 150 (1909).

IN RE CAMILLE, 6 Fed. 256 (C. C. Ore. 1880).

IN RE CAN-AH-COUQUA, 29 Fed. 687 (D. C. Alaska, 1887).

IN RE CARR, 5 Fed. Cas. No. 2432 (D. C. Ore. 1875).

IN RE CELESTINE, 114 Fed. 551 (D. C. Wash. 1902).

IN RE DELKS ESTATE, 2 Ind. T. 572, 52 S. W. 52 (1899).

IN RE DENNISON, 38 F. 2d 662 (D. C. W. D. Okla. 1930) app. dism., 45 F. 2d 585.

IN RE INCORPORATION OF HAINES MISSION, 3 Alaska 588 (1 Div., 1908).

IN RE GRAYSON, 3 Ind. T. 497, 61 S. W. 984 (1901).

IN RE INGRAM, 12 Okla. 54, 69 Pac. 868 (1902).

IN RE IRWIN, 60 F. 2d 495 (C. C. A. 10, 1932).

IN RE JESSIE'S HEIRS, 259 Fed. 694 (D. C. E. D. Okla. 1919).

IN RE LANDS OF FIVE CIVILIZED TRIBES, 199 Fed. 811 (D. C. E. D. Okla. 1912).

IN RE LELAH-PUC-KA-CHEE, 98 Fed. 429 (D. C. N. D. Iowa, 1899).

IN RE LINCOLN, 129 Fed. 247 (D. C. N. D. Cal. 1904).

IN RE LINCOLN, 202 U. S. 178 (1906).

IN RE McDONOUGH, 49 Fed. 360 (D. C. Mont. 1892).

IN RE MAYFIELD, PETITIONER, 141 U. S. 107 (1891).

IN RE MILLS, 135 U. S. 263 (1890).

IN RE MINOOK, 2 Alaska 200 (3 Div. 1904).

IN RE PALMER'S WILL, 11 F. Supp. 301 (D. C. E. D. Okla. (1935).

IN RE PENN, 41 F. 2d 257 (D. C. W. D. Okla. 1929).

IN RE POFF'S GUARDIANSHIP, 7 Ind. T. 59, 103 S. W. 765 (1907).

IN RE RUSSIE, 96 Fed. 609 (D. C. Ore. 1899).

IN RE SAH QUAH, 31 Fed. 327 (D. C. Alaska, 1886).

IN RE SANBORN, 148 U. S. 222 (1893).

IN RE TERRELL'S ESTATE, 6 Ind. T. 412, 98 S. W. 143 (1906).

IN RE WALKER'S ESTATE, 5 Ariz. 70, 46 Pac. 67 (1896), app. dism. sub. nom. WALKER v. DORAN, 18 Sup. Ct. 949 (1897).

IN RE WILSON, 140 U. S. 575 (1891).

IN RE WOLF, 27 Fed. 606 (D. C. W. D. Ark. 1886).

INCORPORATED TOWN OF TAHLEQUAH v. GUINN, 5 Ind. T. 497, 82 S. W. 886 (1904).

INDIAN DEPREDATION CASES, 50 C. Cls. 395 (1915).

INDIAN L. & T. CO. v. SHOENFELT, 135 Fed. 484 (C. C. A. 8, 1905), rev'g 5 Ind. T. 41, 79 S. W. 134 (1904).

INDIAN OIL CO. v. OKLAHOMA, 240 U. S. 522 (1916).

INDIAN TERRITORY OIL CO. v. BOARD, 288 U. S. 325 (1933), app. dism. 287 U. S. 573.

INGRAM v. JONES, 47 F. 2d 135 (C. C. A. 10, 1931).

IOWA LAND & TRUST CO. v. UNITED STATES, 217 Fed. 11 (C. C. A. 8, 1914).

IOWA TRIBE OF INDIANS v. UNITED STATES, 68 C. Cls. 585 (1929).

ISBELL v. UNITED STATES, 227 Fed. 788 (C. C. S. 8, 1915).

JACK v. HOOD, 39 F. 2d 594 (C. C. A. 10, 1930), aff'g 28 F. 2d 118 (D. C. N. D. Okla. 1928).

JACKSON v. BLACK PANTHER OIL & GAS CO., 273 Fed. 113 (C. C. A. 8, 1921), s. c. 277 Fed. 701, 280 Fed. 486. See McDOUGAL v. BLACK PANTHER OIL & GAS CO., 273 Fed. 113 (C. C. A. 8, 1921).
JACKSON v. GATES OIL CO., 297 Fed. 549 (C. C. A. 8, 1924).
JACKSON v. HARRIS, 43 F. 2d 513 (C. C. A. 10, 1930).
JACKSON v. JACKSON, 67 F. 2d 719 (C. C. A. 10, 1933).
JACKSON v. PORTER, 13 Fed. Cas. No. 7143 (C. C. N. D. N. Y. 1825).
JACKSON v. UNITED STATES, 34 C. Cls. 441 (1899).
JACOBS v. PRICHARD, 223 U. S. 200 (1912).
JAEGER v. UNITED STATES, 27 C. Cls. 278 (1892).
JAEGER v. UNITED STATES, 29 C. Cls. 172 (1894), s. c. 33 C. Cls. 214 (1898).
JAMES v. SMITH, 3 Ind. T. 447, 58 S. W. 714 (1900).
JANIS v. UNITED STATES, 32 C. Cls. 407 (1897).
JANUS v. UNITED STATES ex rel. HUMPHREY, 38 F. 2d 431 (C. C. A. 9, 1930), rev'g UNITED STATES ex rel. HUMPHREY v. JANUS, 30 F. 2d 530 (D. C. Idaho 1929).
JARAMILLO v. UNITED STATES, 37 C. Cls. 208 (1902).
JAYBIRD MINING CO. v. WEIR, 271 U. S. 609 (1926).
JEFERSON v. FINK, 247 U. S. 288 (1918).
JENNINGS v. WOOD, 192 Fed. 507 (C. C. A. 8, 1911).
JOHN BAD ELK v. UNITED STATES, 177 U. S. 529 (1900).
JOHNSON v. CREEK NATION, 174 U. S. 445 (1889). See STEPHENS v. CHEROKEE NATION, 174 U. S. 445 (1889).
JOHNSON v. GEARLDS, 234 U. S. 422 (1914), rev'g 183 Fed. 611 (C. C. Minn. 1911).
JOHNSON v. McINTOSH, 8 Wheat. 543 (1823).
JOHNSON v. PACIFIC COAST S. S. CO., 2 Alaska 224 (1 Div. 1904).
JOHNSON v. UNITED STATES, 160 U. S. 546 (1896), aff'g 29 C. Cls. 1 (1893).
JOHNSON v. UNITED STATES, 35 C. Cls. 552 (1900).
JOHNSON v. UNITED STATES, 283 Fed. 954 (C. C. A. 8, 1922).
JOHNSON v. UNITED STATES, 64 F. 2d 674 (C. C. A. 10, 1933), cert. den. 290 U. S. 651 (1933).
JOINES v. PATTERSON, 274 U. S. 544 (1927).
JOINES v. ROBINSON, 4 Ind. T. 556, 76 S. W. 107 (1903).
JONAH v. ARMSTRONG, 52 F. 2d 343 (C. C. A. 10, 1931).
JONES v. ELLIS, 8 Alaska 146 (1 Div. 1929).
JONES v. MEEHAN, 175 U. S. 1 (1899).
JONES v. PRAIRIE OIL CO., 273 U. S. 195 (1927).
JONES v. UNITED STATES, 35 C. Cls. 36 (1900).
JOPLIN MERCANTILE CO. v. UNITED STATES, 236 U. S. 531 (1915), aff'g 213 Fed. 926 (C. C. A. 8, 1914), s. c. 235 U. S. 699.
JORDAN v. GOLDMAN, 1 Okla. 406, 34 Pac. 371 (1891).
JOURNEYCAKE v. CHEROKEE NATION, 28 C. Cls. 281 (1893); s. c. 30 C. Cls. 172, aff'd sub nom. CHEROKEE NATION v. JOURNEYCAKE, 155 U. S. 196 (1894).
JOURNEYCAKE v. CHEROKEE NATION, 31 C. Cls. 140 (1896).
JUMP v. ELLIS, 100 F. 2d 130 (C. C. A. 10, 1938), aff'g 22 F. Supp. 380 (D. C. N. D. Okla. 1938), cert. den. 306 U. S. 645 (1938).
KANSAS INDIANS, THE, 5 Wall. 737 (1866).
KANSAS OR KAW INDIANS v. UNITED STATES, 80 C. Cls. 264 (1934), cert. den. 296 U. S. 577.
KARRAHOO v. ADAMS, 14 Fed. Cas. No. 7614 (C. C. Kan. 1870).
KATZENMEYER v. UNITED STATES, 225 Fed. 523 (C. C. A. 7, 1915).
KEETOOWAH SOCIETY v. LANE, 41 App. D. C. 319 (1914).
KEITH v. UNITED STATES, 8 Okla. 446, 58 Pac. 507 (1899).
KELLY v. CHURCHILL, 4 Ind. T. 110, 69, S. W. 817 (1902).
KELLY v. HARPER, 7 Ind. T. 541, 104 S. W. 829 (1907).
KELLY v. JOHNSON, 82 Fed. 1002 (C. C. A. 8, 1897), aff'g 1 Ind. T. 184, 39 S. W. 532 (1897).
KEMMERER v. MIDLAND OIL & DRILLING CO., 229 Fed. 872 (C. C. A. 8, 1915).
KEMOHAH v. SHAFFER OIL & REFINING CO., 38 Fed. 2d 665 (D. C. N. D. Okla. 1930), aff'd sub nom. TIGER v. TWIN STATE OIL CO., 48 F. 2d 509 (1931).
KENDALL v. EWERT, 259 U. S. 139 (1922), rev'g 264 Fed. 1021 (C. C. A. 8, 1920), s. c. 260 U. S. 703.
KENDALL v. SAN JUAN MINING CO., 144 U. S. 658 (1891).
KENDALL v. UNITED STATES, 7 Wall. 113 (1868), aff'g 1 C. Cls. 261 (1865), s. c. 2 C. Cls. 592.
KENNEDY v. BECKER, 241 U. S. 556 (1916).
KENNEDY v. PUBLIC WORKS ADMINISTRATION, 23 F. Supp. 771 (D. C. W. D. N. Y. 1938).
KENNEDY v. UNITED STATES, 265 U. S. 344 (1924). Questions certified from KENNEDY v. UNITED STATES, 2 F. 2d 597 (C. C. A. 8, 1924).
KENNY v. MILES, 250 U. S. 58 (1919).
KEOKUK v. ULAM, 4 Okla. 5, 38 Pac. 1080 (1895).
KEY v. UNITED STATES, 225 Fed. 368 (C. C. A. 8, 1915).
KIE v. UNITED STATES, 27 Fed. 351 (C. C. Ore. 1886), s. c. 26 Fed. Cas. 15528a, 26 Fed. Cas. 15528b.
KIKER v. UNITED STATES, 63 F. 2d 957 (C. C. A. 10, 1933).
KIMBERLIN v. COMMISSION to FIVE CIVILIZED TRIBES, 104 Fed. 653 (C. C. A. 8, 1900), aff'g KIMBERLIN v. COMMISSION, 3 Ind. T. 16 (1899).
KINDRED v. UNION PACIFIC R. R. CO., 225 U. S. 582 (1912), aff'g 168 Fed. 648 (C. C. A. 8, 1909).
KING v. ICKES, 64 F. 2d 979 (App. D. C. 1933).
KING v. McANDREWS, 111 Fed. 860 (C. C. A. 8, 1901), s. c. 104 Fed. 430.
KING v. UNITED STATES, 31 C. Cls. 304 (1896).
KIRBY v. UNITED STATES, 260 U. S. 423 (1922), aff'g 273 Fed. 391 (C. C. A. 9, 1921).
KLAMATH & MOADOC TRIBES v. UNITED STATES, 296 U. S. 244 (1935), aff'g 81 C. Cls. 79 (1935), s. c. 295 U. S. 729, 304 U. S. 119, 85 C. Cls. 451.
KLAMATH INDIAN TRIBES v. UNITED STATES, 86 C. Cls. 614 (1938).
KNAPP v. UNITED STATES, 53 C. Cls. 18 (1917).
KNIGHT v. CARTER OIL CO., 23 F. 2d 481 (C. C. A. 8, 1927), rev'g CARTER OIL v. SCOTT, 12 F. 2d 780 (D. C. N. D. Okla. 1926).
KNIGHT v. LANE, 228 U. S. 6 (1913).
KUNKEL v. BARNETT, 10 F. 2d 804 (D. C. N. D. Okla. 1926), aff'd sub nom. BARNETT v. PRAIRIE OIL & GAS CO., 19 F. 2d 504 (C. C. A. 8, 1927), cert. den. 275 U. S. 563, s. c. 256 Fed. 644, 254 U. S. 620, 283 Fed. 24, 260 U. S. 738, 264 U. S. 16.
LABADIE v. UNITED STATES, 6 Okla. 400, 51 Pac. 666 (1897).
LABADIE, ADM'R. v. UNITED STATES, 31 C. Cls. 205 (1896).
LABADIE, ADM'R. v. UNITED STATES, 33 C. Cls. 476 (1898), s. c. 32 C. Cls. 368 (1897).
LABADIE, ADM'R. v. UNITED STATES, 31 C. Cls. 436 (1896).
LA CHAPELLE v. BUBB, 62 Fed. 545 (C. C. Wash. 1894), s. c. 69 Fed. 481.
LA CLAIR v. UNITED STATES, 184 Fed. 128 (C. C. E. D. Wash. 1910).
LADIGA v. ROLAND, 2 How. 581 (1844).
LA MOTTE v. UNITED STATES, 254 U. S. 570 (1921), mod'g and aff'g 256 Fed. 5 (C. C. A. 8, 1919).
LANE v. MORRISON, 246 U. S. 214 (1918).
LANE v. PUEBLO OF SANTA ROSA, 249 U. S. 110 (1919), s. c. 273 U. S. 315, 12 F. 2d 332.
LANE v. UNITED STATES EX REL. MICKADIET AND TIEBAULT, 241 U. S. 201 (1916).
LANGDON v. JOY, 14 Fed. Cas. No. 8,062 (C. C. Kan. 1877).
LANGFORD v. UNITED STATES, 101 U. S. 341 (1879), aff'g 12 C. Cls. 338 (1876).
LANGFORD v. MONTEITH, 102 U. S. 145 (1880), aff'g 1 Idaho 612 (1876).
LANHAM v. McKEEL, 244 U. S. 582 (1917).
LARKIN v. PAUGH, 276 U. S. 431 (1928).
LA ROQUE v. UNITED STATES, 239 U. S. 62 (1915), aff'g 198 Fed. 645 (C. C. A. 8, 1912).
LASATER & NOBLE v. GREEN, 10 Okla. 335, 62 Pac. 816 (1900).
LATTIMER v. POTEET, 14 Pet. 4 (1840).
LAUGHTON v. NADEAU, 75 Fed. 789 (C. C. Kan. 1896).
LAUREL OIL AND GAS CO. v. MORRISON, 212 U. S. 291 (1909). See MORRISON v. BURNETTE, 154 Fed. 617 (C. C. A. 8, 1907).
LEAK GLOVE MANUF'G CO. v. NEEDLES, 69 Fed. 68 (C. C. A. 8, 1895).
LEAVENWORTH ETC. R. R. CO. v. UNITED STATES, 92 U. S. 733 (1875).
LEDBETTER v. WESLEY, 23 F. 2d 81 (C. C. A. 8, 1927), cert. den. 276 U. S. 631 (1928), 276 U. S. 636 (1928).
LEE v. PERO, 99 F. 2d 28 (C. C. A. 7, 1938), cert. den. 306 U. S. 643 (1939). See EX PARTE PERO, 99 F. 2d 28 (C. C. A. 7, 1938).
LEECY v. UNITED STATES, 190 Fed. 289 (C. C. A. 8, 1911), app. dism. UNITED STATES v. LEECY, 232 U. S. 731 (1914).
LEFTRIDGE v. UNITED STATES, 6 Ind. T. 305, 97 S. W. 1018 (1906).

LEIGHTON v. UNITED STATES, 161 U. S. 291 (1895), aff'g 29 C. Cls. 288 (1894).
LEMIEUX v. UNITED STATES, 15 F. 2d 518 (C. C. A. 8, 1926), cert. den. 273 U. S. 749.
LEMMON v. UNITED STATES, 106 Fed. 650 (C. C. A. 8, 1901).
LEVINDALE LEAD & ZINC MINING CO. v. COLEMAN, 241 U. S. 432 (1916).
LEWELLYN v. COLONIAL TRUST CO., 275 U. S. 232 (1927), rev'g 17 F. 2d 36 (C. C. A. 3, 1927). See HEINER v. COLONIAL TRUST CO., 275 U. S. 232 (1927).
LIBBY v. CLARK, 118 U. S. 250 (1886).
LIGHT v. CONOVER, 10 Okla. 732, 63 Pac. 966 (1901).
LIGON v. JOHNSTON, 164 Fed. 670 (C. C. A. 8, 1908), app. dism. 223 U. S. 741.
LITCHFIELD v. UNITED STATES, 32 C. Cls. 585 (1897).
LITCHFIELD v. UNITED STATES, 33 C. Cls. 203 (1898).
LOBENSTEIN v. UNITED STATES, 91 U. S. 324 (1875), aff'g 9 C. Cls. 135 (1873).
LOCKE v. M'MURRY, 287 Fed. 276 (C. C. A. 8, 1923), mod'g M'MURRY v. PRODUCERS' OIL CO., 284 Fed. 181 (D. C. E. D. Okla. 1922).
LOGAN v. UNITED STATES, 58 F. 2d 697 (C. C. A. 10, 1932) cert. den. 287 U. S. 630.
LONDON v. AMOS, 255 U. S. 373 (1921). See WINTON v. AMOS, 255 U. S. 373 (1921).
LONE WOLF v. HITCHCOCK, 187 U. S. 553 (1903).
LONGEST v. LANGFORD, 276 U. S. 69 (1928), rev'g 114 Okla. 50, 242 Pac. 569.
LOTT v. UNITED STATES, 205 Fed. 28 (C. C. A. 9, 1913).
LOUIE v. UNITED STATES, 254 U. S. 548 (1921), rev'g EUGENE SOL LOUIE v. UNITED STATES, 274 Fed. 47 (C. C. A. 9, 1921). s. c. 264 Fed. 295.
LOVE v. PAMPLIN, 21 Fed. 755 (C. C. W. D. Tenn. 1884).
LOVE, ADM'R v. UNITED STATES, 29 C. Cls. 332 (1894).
LOWE v. FISHER, 223 U. S. 95 (1912).
LOWE v. UNITED STATES, 37 C. Cls. 413 (1902).
LOWRY v. WEAVER, 15 Fed. Cas. No. 8584 (C. C. Ind. 1846).
LUCAS v. UNITED STATES, 163 U. S. 612 (1896).
LUCAS v. UNITED STATES, 15 F. 2d 32 (C. C. A. 8, 1926).
LUCE v. GARRETT, 4 Ind. T. 54, 64 S. W. 613 (1901).
LUKE v. UNITED STATES, 35 C. Cls. 15 (1899).
LYNCH v. UNITED STATES, 10 F. 2d 947 (C. C. A. 8, 1925).
LYKINS v. McGRATH, 184 U. S. 169 (1902).
McALLASTER v. EDGERTON, 3 Ind. T. 704, 64 S. W. 583 (1901).
McBRIDE v. FARRINGTON, 149 Fed. 114 (C. C. A. 2, 1906) aff'g 131 Fed. 797 (C. C. W. D. N. Y. 1904).
McCALIB, ADM'R. v. UNITED STATES, 83 C. Cls. 79 (1936).
McCALL v. UNITED STATES, 1 Dak. 320, 46 N. W. 608 (1876).
McCANDLESS v. UNITED STATES ex rel. DIABO, 25 F. 2d 71 (C. C. A. 3, 1928), aff'g UNITED STATES ex rel. DIABO v. McCANDLESS, 18 F. 2d 282 (D. C. E. D. Pa. 1927).
McCLELLAN v. PYEATT, 50 Fed. 686 (C. C. A. 8, 1892), s. c. 49 Fed. 259.
McCLINTIC v. UNITED STATES, 283 Fed. 781 (C. C. A. 8, 1922).
McCLURE v. UNITED STATES, 19 C. Cls. 173 (1884).
McCOLLUM, ADM'R. v. UNITED STATES, 33 C. Cls. 469 (1898).
McCOY v. UNITED STATES, 38 C. Cls. 163 (1923).
McCULLOUGH v. SMITH, 243 Fed. 823 (C. C. A. 8, 1917), s. c. 270 U. S. 456, rev'g 285 Fed. 698.
McCURDY v. UNITED STATES, 246 U. S. 263 (1918).
McCURDY v. UNITED STATES, 264 U. S. 484 (1924) aff'g UNITED STATES v. McCURDY, 280 Fed. 103 (C. C. A. 8, 1922).
McCURTAIN v. GRADY, 1 Ind. T. 107, 38 S. W. 65 (1896).
McDANIEL v. HOLLAND, 230 Fed. 945 (C. C. A. 8, 1916).
McDOUGAL v. BLACK PANTHER OIL & GAS CO., 273 Fed. 113 (C. C. A. 8, 1921), s. c. 277 Fed. 701 (1921).
McDOUGAL v. McKAY, 237 U. S. 372 (1915).
McFADDEN v. EVANS-SNIDER-BUEL CO., 185 U. S. 505 (1902), aff'g EVANS-SNIDER BUEL CO. v. McFADDEN, 105 Fed. 292 (C. C. A. 8, 1900); rev'g McFADDEN v. BLOCKER, 2 Ind. T. 260 (1899), s. c. 3 Ind. T. 224, 54 S. W. 873.
McFADDEN v. MOUNTAIN VIEW MINING & MILLING CO., 97 Fed. 670 (C. C. A. 9, 1899), rev'g 87 Fed. 154 (C. C. Wash. 1898), s. c. 180 U. S. 533.
McGEE v. LEDBETTER, 23 F. 2d 81 (C. C. A. 8, 1927), cert. den. 276 U. S. 631, 276 U. S. 636. See LEDBETTER v. WESLEY, 23 F. 2d 81 (C. C. A. 8, 1927).
McGRATH v. VALENTINE, 167 Fed. 473 (C. C. A. 9, 1909), s. c. 199 Fed. 392.
McKAY v. CAMPBELL, 16 Fed. Cas. No. 8840 (D. C. Ore. 1871), s. c. 16 Fed. Cas. No. 8839.
McKAY v. KALYTON, 204 U. S. 458 (1907).
McKEE v. HENRY, 201 Fed. 74 (C. C. A. 8, 1912).
McKEE v. UNITED STATES, 33 C. Cls. 99 (1897).
McKINNEY v. BLACK PANTHER OIL & GAS CO., 273 Fed. 113 (C. C. A. 8, 1921), s. c. 261 U. S. 628, 277 Fed. 701, 280 Fed. 486. See McDOUGAL v. BLACK PANTHER OIL & GAS CO., 273 Fed. 113 (C. C. A. 8, 1921).
McKINZIE v. UNITED STATES, 34 C. Cls. 278 (1899).
McKNIGHT v. UNITED STATES, 130 Fed. 659 (C. C. A. 9, 1904).
McLISH v. ROFF, 141 U. S. 661 (1891).
McMILLAN v. UNITED STATES, 27 F. 2d 94 (C. C. A. 8, 1928), s. c. 28 Fed. 1015.
McMURRAY v. CHOCTAW NATION, 62 C. Cls. 458 (1926), cert. den. 275 U. S. 524.
McMURRY v. LOCKE, 287 Fed. 276 (C. C. A. 8, 1923). See LOCKE v. McMURRY, 287 Fed. 276 (C. C. A. 8, 1923).
McNEE v. WHITEHEAD, 253 Fed. 546 (C. C. A. 8, 1918), s. c. 280 Fed. 95.
McSPADDEN v. UNITED STATES, 224 Fed. 935 (C. C. A. 8, 1915).
MACKEY v. COXE, 18 How. 100 (1855).
MACKEY v. MILLER, 126 Fed. 161 (C. C. A. 9, 1903).
MALONE v. ALDERDICE, 212 Fed. 668 (C. C. A. 8, 1914).
MANDLER v. UNITED STATES, 49 F. 2d 201 (C. C. A. 10, 1931), rehearing den. 52 F. 2d 713 (C. C. A. 10, 1931).
MARES, ADM'R v. UNITED STATES, 29 C. Cls. 197 (1894).
MARICOPA AND PHOENIX RAILROAD v. ARIZONA, 156 U. S. 347 (1895), aff'g TERRITORY OF ARIZONA v. DELINQUENT TAX LIST. 3 Ariz. 302 (1891), 26 Pac. 310.
MARKS v. UNITED STATES, 161 U. S. 297 (1896), aff'g 28 C. Cls. 147 (1893).
MARLIN v. LEWALLEN, 276 U. S. 58 (1928).
MARS v. McDOUGAL, 40 F. 2d 247 (C. C. A. 10, 1930), s. c. 282 U. S. 850.
MARSH v. BROOKS, 8 How. 223 (1850), s. c. 55 U. S. 513.
MARTIN v. UNITED STATES, 168 Fed. 198 (C. C. A. 8, 1909), rev'g 7 Ind. T. 451 (1907).
MARTIN v. UNITED STATES, 46 C. Cls. 199 (1911).
MARTIN v. UNITED STATES, 46 C. Cls. 373 (1911).
MARTIN-BROWN CO. v. MORRIS, 1 Ind. T. 495 (1897), 42 S. W. 423 (1897).
MARYLAND CASUALTY CO. v. UNITED STATES, 37 F. 2d 318 (C. C. A. 4, 1930).
MASCARINAS v. UNITED STATES, 33 C. Cls. 94 (1897).
MASHUNKASHEY v. UNITED STATES, 72 F. 2d 847 (C. C. A. 10, 1934). See UNITED STATES v. MASHUNKASHEY, 72 F. 2d 847 (C. C. A. 10, 1934), cert. den. 294 U. S. 724, s. c. 73 F. 2d 487.
MASON v. HARDY GRIFFIN-SHEFF, 45 F. 2d 587 (C. C. A. 10, 1930).
MASON v. SAMS, 5 F. 2d 255 (D. C. W. D. Wash. 1925).
MASON CO. v. TAX COMMISSION, 302 U. S. 186 (1937).
MASSACHUSETTS v. NEW YORK, 271 U. S. 65 (1926), s. c. 271 U. S. 636.
MATTER OF HEFF, 197 U. S. 488 (1905), overruled, UNITED STATES v. NICE, 241 U. S. 591 (1916).
MAUST v. WARDEN OF THE UNITED STATES PENITENTIARY, 283 Fed. 912 (C. C. A. 8, 1922).
MAXEY v. WRIGHT, 105 Fed. 1003 (C. C. A. 8, 1900), aff'g per cur. 3 Ind. T. 243, 54 S. W. 807 (1900).
MAYER v. UNITED STATES, 38 C. Cls. 553 (1903).
MAYS v. FRIEBERG, KLEIN & CO., 3 Ind. T. 774, 49 S. W. 52 (1899).
MEDAWAKANTON INDIANS v. UNITED STATES, 57 C. Cls. 357 (1922).
MEEKER v. KAELIN, 173 Fed. 216 (C. C. W. D. Wash. 1909).
MEGREEDY v. MACKLIN, 12 Okla. 666, 73 Pac. 293 (1903).
MEHLIN v. ICE, 56 Fed. 12 (C. C. A. 8, 1893).
MEIGS v. McCLUNG'S LESSEE, 9 Cranch 11 (1815).
MERCHANT v. UNITED STATES, 35 C. Cls. 403 (1900).
MICKADIET v. FALL, 258 U. S. 609 (1922), aff'g MICKADIET v. PAYNE, 269 Fed. 194 (App. D. C. 1920).
MIDLAND OIL CO. v. TURNER, 179 Fed. 74 (C. C. A. 8, 1910), mod'g and aff'g TURNER v. SEEP, 167 Fed. 646 (C. C. E. D. Okla. 1909).
MIDWAY CO. v. EATON, 183 U. S. 602 (1902).
MIDWAY CO. v. EATON, 183 U. S. 619 (1902).

MIDWAY CO. v. EATON, 127 Fed. 1020 (C. C. A. 8, 1904). Decided on authority of MIDWAY CO. v. EATON, 183 U. S. 602 (1902).

MILLE LAC CHIPPEWAS v. UNITED STATES, 229 U. S. 498 (1913) rev'g 46 C. Cls. 424 (1911) and 47 C. Cls. 415 (1912), see also 51 C. Cls. 400 (1916).

MILLER v. McCLAIN, 249 U. S. 308 (1919).

MILLER v. UNITED STATES, 57 F. 2d 987 (C. C. A. 10, 1932), cert. den. 287 U. S. 625.

MINIS v. UNITED STATES, 15 Pet. 423 (1841).

MINNESOTA v. HITCHCOCK, 185 U. S. 373 (1902).

MINNESOTA v. UNITED STATES, 305 U. S. 382 (1939), aff'g UNITED STATES v. MINNESOTA, 95 F. 2d 468 (C. C. A. 8, 1938).

MISSOURI, KANSAS, AND TEXAS R'Y CO. v. ROBERTS, 152 U. S. 114 (1894).

MISSOURI, KANSAS, AND TEXAS R'Y CO. v. UNITED STATES, 92 U. S. 760 (1875).

MISSOURI, KANSAS, AND TEXAS R'Y CO. v. UNITED STATES, 235 U. S. 37 (1914), aff'g 47 C. Cls. 59 (1911).

MITCHEL v. UNITED STATES, 9 Pet. 711 (1835), s. c. 33 U. S. 307.

MITCHELL v. UNITED STATES, 22 F. 2d 771 (C. C. A. 9, 1927).

MITCHELL, ADM'R. v. UNITED STATES, 27 C. Cls. 316 (1892).

MIXON v. LITTLETON, 265 Fed. 603 (C. C. A. 8, 1920).

MONSON v. SIMONSON, 231 U. S. 341 (1913).

MONTANA EASTERN LIMITED v. UNITED STATES, 95 F. 2d 897 (C. C. A. 9, 1938).

MONTOYA v. UNITED STATES, 180 U. S. 261 (1901).

MONTOYA, ADM'R. v. UNITED STATES, 32 C. Cls. 71 (1896).

MOODY v. JOHNSTON, 66 F. 2d 999 (C. C. A. 9, 1933), rev'g SCHEER v. MOODY, 48 F. 2d 327 (1931), s. c. 70 F. 2d 835.

MOORE v. CARTER OIL CO., 43 F. 2d 322 (C. C. A. 10, 1930), cert. den. 282 U. S. 903.

MOORE v. COUNTY COMMISSIONERS, 2 Wyo. 8 (1878), overruled TORREY v. BALDWIN, 3 Wyo. 432 (1891), BOARD OF COM'RS v. SEARIGHT CATTLE CO., 3 Wyo. 791, (1892), NOBLE v. AMORETTI, 11 Wyo. 248 (1903).

MOORE v. GIRTEN, 5 Ind. T. 384, 82 S. W. 848 (1904).

MOORE v. SAWYER, 167 Fed. 826 (C. C. E. D. Okla. 1909).

MOORE v. UNITED STATES, 32 C. Cls. 593 (1897).

MORGAN v. WARD, 224 Fed. 698 (C. C. A. 8, 1915), cert. den. 239 U. S. 648, s. c. 248 Fed. 691 (1918), cert. den. 247 U. S. 521.

MORRIS v. HITCHCOCK, 194 U. S. 384 (1904).

MORRIS v. UNITED STATES, 19 F. 2d 131 (C. C. A. 8, 1927), cert. den. 275 U. S. 543.

MORRISETT v. UNITED STATES, 132 Fed. 891 (C. C. Ore. 1904).

MORRISON v. BURNETTE, 154 Fed. 617 (C. C. A. 8, 1907), app. dism. sub nom. LAUREL OIL & GAS CO. v. MORRISON, 212 U. S. 291 (1909).

MORRISON v. UNITED STATES, 6 F. 2d 809 (C. C. A. 8, 1925).

MORRISON v. UNITED STATES, 6 F. 2d 811 (C. C. A. 8, 1925).

MORRISON v. WORK, 266 U. S. 481 (1925), aff'g MORRISON v. FALL, 290 Fed. 306 (App. D. C. 1923).

MORRIS'S LESSEE v. NEIGHMAN, 4 Dall. 209 (1800).

MORROW v. UNITED STATES, 243 Fed. 854 (C. C. A. 8, 1917).

MOSIER v. UNITED STATES, 198 Fed. 54 (C. C. A. 8, 1912), cert. den. 229 U. S. 619 (1913).

MOTT v. UNITED STATES, 283 U. S. 747 (1931).

MUDD v. PERRY, 25 F. 2d 85 (C. C. A. 8, 1928), aff'g 14 F. 2d 430 (D. C. N. D. Okla. 1926), cert. den. 278 U. S. 601.

MULLIGAN v. UNITED STATES, 120 Fed. 98 (C. C. A. 8, 1903).

MULLEN v. GARDNER, 250 U. S. 590 (1919). See MULLEN v. PICKENS, 250 U. S. 590 (1919).

MULLEN v. SIMMONS, 234 U. S. 192 (1914).

MULLEN v. UNITED STATES, 224 U. S. 448 (1912), rev'g UNITED STATES v. ALLEN, 179 Fed. 13 (C. C. A. 8, 1910).

MUNGOSAH v. STEINBROOK, 17 Fed. Cas. No. 9924 (C. C. Kan. 1875).

MURRAY v. UNITED STATES, 1 Ind. T. 28, 35 S. W. 240 (1896).

MURRAY v. UNITED STATES, 46 C. Cls. 101 (1911).

MUSKOGEE LAND CO. v. MULLINS, 165 Fed. 179 (C. C. A. 8, 1908).

MUSKOGEE NAT. TEL. CO. v. HALL, 118 Fed. 382 (C. C. A. 8, 1902), rev'g 4 Ind. T. 18 (1901).

MUSKRAT v. UNITED STATES, 219 U. S. 346 (1911), rev'g 44 C. Cls. 137 (1909).

MYERS v. MATHIS, 2 Ind. T. 3, 46 S. W. 178 (1898).

MYRICK v. THOMPSON, 99 U. S. 291 (1878).

NADEAU v. UNION PAC. R. CO., 253 U. S. 442 (1920).

NAGANAB v. HITCHCOCK, 202 U. S. 473 (1906).

NAGLE v. UNITED STATES, 191 Fed. 141 (C. C. A. 9, 1911).

NATIONAL BANK OF COMMERCE v. ANDERSON, 147 Fed. 87 (C. C. A. 9, 1906).

NEAL v. UNITED STATES, 18 C. Cls. 756 (1882), aff'g 14 C. Cls. 280 (1878).

NE-KAH-WAH-SHE-TUN-KAH v. FALL, 290 Fed. 303 (App. D. C. 1923), app. dism. 266 U. S. 595 (1925).

NELSON v. UNITED STATES, 30 Fed. 112 (C. C. D. Ore. 1887), aff'g UNITED STATES v. NELSON, 29 Fed. 202.

NELSON v. UNITED STATES, 18 F. 2d 522 (C. C. A. 8, 1927).

NESBITT v. UNITED STATES, 186 U. S. 153 (1902).

NEW JERSEY v. WILSON, 7 Cranch 164 (1812).

NEW YORK ex rel. CUTLER v. DIBBLE, 21 How. 366 (1858).

NEW YORK INDIANS, 5 Wall. 761 (1866).

NEW YORK INDIANS v. UNITED STATES, 170 U. S. 1 (1898), rev'g 30 C. Cls. 413, amended 170 U. S. 614, app. dism. 173 U. S. 464 (1899).

NEW YORK INDIANS v. UNITED STATES, 40 C. Cls. 448 (1905).

NEW YORK INDIANS v. UNITED STATES, 41 C. Cls. 462 (1906).

NIMROD v. JANDRON, 24 F. 2d 613 (App. D. C. 1928).

NIVENS v. NIVENS, 133 Fed. 39 (C. C. A. 8, 1904), rev'g 4 Ind. T. 574, 76 S. W. 114 (1903), which aff'd 4 Ind. T. 30, 64 S. W. 604 (1901).

NOFIRE v. UNITED STATES, 164 U. S. 657 (1897).

NOONAN v. CALEDONIA MINING CO., 121 U. S. 393 (1887).

NORTHERN PAC. RY. CO. v. MITCHELL, 208 Fed. 469 (D. C. E. D. Wash. 1913), app. dism. sub nom. MITCHELL v. NORTHERN PAC. RY. CO., 213 Fed. 1022 (C. C. A. 9, 1914).

NORTHERN PAC. RY. CO. v. PERONTO, 3 Dak. 217, 14 N. W. 103 (1882), affd. sub nom. BUTTZ v. NORTHERN PAC. R. CO., 119 U. S. 55 (1886).

NORTHERN PACIFIC RY. CO. v. UNITED STATES, 227 U. S. 355 (1913), aff'g 191 Fed. 947 (C. C. A. 9, 1911).

NORTHERN PACIFIC RY. CO. v. WISMER, 246 U. S. 283 (1918), aff'g 230 Fed. 591 (C. C. A. 9, 1916).

NORTON v. LARNEY, 266 U. S. 511 (1925), aff'g 289 Fed. 395 (C. C. A. 8, 1923).

NOYES v. NEEL, 100 Fed. 555 (C. C. A. 8, 1900).

NUNN v. HAZELRIGG, 216 Fed. 330 (C. C. A. 8, 1914).

OAKES v. UNITED STATES, 172 Fed. 305 (C. C. A. 8, 1909).

OATS v. UNITED STATES, 1 Ind. T. 152, 38 S. W. 673 (1897).

OKLAHOMA v. A. T. & SANTA FE RY., 220 U. S. 277 (1911).

OKLAHOMA v. GULF COL. & SANTA FE RY., 220 U. S. 290 (1911).

OKLAHOMA v. TEXAS, 258 U. S. 574 (1922), s. c. 252 U. S. 372, 253 U. S. 465, 254 U. S. 280, 254 U. S. 603, 254 U. S. 609, 254 U. S. 615, 256 U. S. 70, 256 U. S. 602, 257 U. S. 308, 257 U. S. 609, 257 U. S. 611, 257 U. S. 616, 257 U. S. 621, 258 U. S. 606, 259 U. S. 565, 260 U. S. 606, 260 U. S. 705, 260 U. S. 711, 261 U. S. 340, 261 U. S. 345, 261 U. S. 606, 262 U. S. 505, 262 U. S. 724, 263 U. S. 681, 264 U. S. 565, 265 U. S. 76, 265 U. S. 490, 265 U. S. 493, 265 U. S. 500, 265 U. S. 505, 265 U. S. 513, 265 U. S. 573, 266 U. S. 298, 266 U. S. 303, 266 U. S. 546, 266 U. S. 583, 267 U. S. 7, 267 U. S. 452, 267 U. S. 580, 268 U. S. 252, 268 U. S. 472, 268 U. S. 675, 268 U. S. 676, 268 U. S. 678, 268 U. S. 680, 269 U. S. 314, 269 U. S. 536, 269 U. S. 539, 272 U. S. 21, 273 U. S. 93, 274 U. S. 713, 274 U. S. 714, 276 U. S. 596, 281 U. S. 109, 281 U. S. 689, 281 U. S. 694.

OKLAHOMA, K. & M. I. RY. CO. v. BOWLING, 249 Fed. 592 (C. C. A. 8, 1918).

OLD SETTLERS v. UNITED STATES, 148 U. S. 427 (1893).

OMAHA INDIANS v. UNITED STATES, 253 U. S. 275 (1920). See UNITED STATES v. OMAHA INDIANS, 253 U. S. 275 (1920).

OMAHA TRIBE v. UNITED STATES, 53 C. Cls. 549 (1918), mod. 253 U. S. 275.

ONE BUICK AUTOMOBILE v. UNITED STATES, 275 Fed. 809 (C. C. A. 8, 1921).

ONEIDA INDIANS OF CANADA v. UNITED STATES 39 C. Cls. 116 (1903).

OOLAGAH COAL CO. v. McCALEB, 68 Fed. 86 (C. C. A. 8, 1895).
OREGON v. HITCHCOCK, 202 U. S. 60 (1906).
OSAGE COUNTY MOTOR CO. v. UNITED STATES, 33 F. 2d 21 (C. C. A. 8, 1929), cert. den. 280 U. S. 577.
OSAGE TRIBE OF INDIANS v. UNITED STATES, 66 C. Cls. 64 (1928) app. dism. 279 U. S. 811.
OSBORN v. UNITED STATES, 33 C. Cls. 304 (1898).
OSTROM v. UNITED STATES, 26 F. 2d 245 (C. C. A. 18, 1928), s. c. 18 F. 2d 896.
OTERO ADM'R. v. UNITED STATES, 48 C. Cls. 216 (1913).
OTERO'S ADM'R. v. UNITED STATES, 48 C. Cls. 219 (1913).
OTOE AND MISSOURIA INDIANS v. UNITED STATES, 52 C. Cls. 424 (1917).
OTTAWA AND CHIPPEWA INDIANS v. UNITED STATES, 42 C. Cls. 240 (1907).
OTTAWA AND CHIPPEWA INDIANS v. UNITED STATES, 42 C. Cls. 518 (1907).
OWEN v. DUDLEY, 217 U. S. 488 (1910).
OWENS v. EATON, 5 Ind. T. 275, 82 S. W. 746 (1904).
PAINTER v. UNITED STATES, 33 C. Cls. 114 (1897).
PALCHER v. UNITED STATES, 11 Fed. 47 (C. C. Minn. 1882).
PAM-TO-PEE v. UNITED STATES, 187 U. S. 371 (1902). See PHINEAS PAM-TO-PEE v. UNITED STATES, 148 U. S. 691 (1893).
PAPE v. UNITED STATES, 19 F. 2d 219 (C. C. A. 9, 1927).
PARENT v. PICOTTE, 254 Fed. 301 (C. C. A. 8, 1918), app. dism. 254 U. S. 661.
PARKER v. RICHARD, 250 U. S. 235 (1919), rev'g RICHARD v. PARKER, 245 Fed. 330 (C. C. A. 8, 1917), s. c. 257 Fed. 990.
PARKER v. RILEY, 250 U. S. 66 (1919) rev'g 243 Fed. 42 (C. C. A. 8, 1919), s. c. 218 Fed. 391.
PARKS v. ROSS, 11 How. 362 (1850).
PARKS v. UNITED STATES, 225 Fed. 369 (C. C. A. 8, 1915).
PARMENTER v. UNITED STATES, 6 Ind. T. 530, 98 S. W. 340 (1906).
PARR v. COLFAX, 197 Fed. 302 (C. C. A. 9, 1912).
PARR v. UNITED STATES, 132 Fed. 1004 (C. C. Ore. 1904).
PARR v. UNITED STATES, 153 Fed. 462 (C. C. Ore. 1907).
PARRIS v. UNITED STATES, 1 Ind. T. 43, 35 S. W. 243 (1896).
PATAWA v. UNITED STATES, 132 Fed. 893 (C. D. Ore. 1904).
PATTERSON v. JENKS, 2 Pet. 216 (1829).
PAWNEE IND. v. UNITED STATES, 56 C. Cls. 1 (1920).
PECK v. MIAMI COUNTY, 19 Fed. Cas. No. 10891 (C. C. Kan. 1876).
PEEL v. CHOCTAW NATION, 45 C. Cls. 154 (1910).
PEL-ATA-YAKOT v. UNITED STATES, 188 Fed. 387 (C. C. Idaho 1911).
PENNOCK v. COMMISSIONERS, 103 U. S. 44 (1880).
PEOPLE v. SWEETSER, 1 Dak. 308, 46 N. W. 452 (1876).
PEOPLE OF THE STATE OF NEW YORK ex rel. KENNEDY v. BECKER, 241 U. S. 556 (1916). See KENNEDY v. BECKER, 241 U. S. 556 (1916).
PEOPLE ex rel. CHARLES v. BLACKCHIEF, 8 F. Supp. 295 (D. C. W. D. N. Y. 1934).
PERRIN v. UNITED STATES, 232 U. S. 478 (1914).
PERRY v. UNITED STATES, 18 F. 2d 477 (C. C. A. 8, 1927).
PERRYMAN v. WOODWARD, 238 U. S. 148 (1915).
PERSONS CLAIMING RIGHTS IN THE CHEROKEE NATION BY INTERMARRIAGE v. UNITED STATES, 203 U. S. 76 (1906), aff'g 40 C. Cls. 411 (1905). See CHEROKEE INTERMARRIAGE CASES, 203 U. S. 76 (1906).
PETERS v. MALIN, 111 Fed. 244 (C. C. N. D. Iowa 1901).
PETIT v. UNITED STATES, 283 U. S. 753 (1931), rev'g 38 F. 2d 795. See HALBERT v. UNITED STATES, 283 U. S. 753, (1931).
PETTIT v. COMMISSIONER OF INTERNAL REVENUE, 38 F. 2d 976 (C. C. A. 10, 1930), cert. den. 281 U. S. 759. See CHOUTEAU v. COMMISSIONER OF INTERNAL REVENUE, 38 F. 2d 976 (C. C. A. 10, 1930).
PHINEAS PAM-TO-PEE v. UNITED STATES, 148 U. S. 691 (1893), aff'g 27 C. Cls. 403 (1892), s. c. 187 U. S. 371.
PICKERING v. LOMAX, 173 U. S. 26 (1898), s. c. 145 U. S. 310 (1892).
PICKERNOLL v. UNITED STATES, 283 U. S. 753 (1931). See HALBERT v. UNITED STATES, 283 U. S. 753 (1931).
PICKETT v. UNITED STATES, 1 Idaho 523 (1874).
PICKETT v. UNITED STATES, 216 U. S. 456 (1910).
PIGEON v. BUCK, 237 U. S. 386 (1915).
PIKE v. HUNTER, 4 Mackey (15 D. C.) 531 (1885).
PILGRIM v. BECK, 69 Fed. 805 (C. C. Neb. 1895).
PILGRIM v. McINTOSH, 7 Ind. T. 623, 104 S. W. 858 (1907).
PINE RIVER LOGGING & IMPROVEMENT CO. v. UNITED STATES, 186 U. S. 279 (1902).
PINO v. UNITED STATES, 38 C. Cls. 64 (1903).
PITCHLYNN ET AL. v. CHOCTAW NATION, 272 U. S. 728 (1927). See GARLAND'S HEIRS v. CHOCTAW NATION, 272 U. S. 728 (1927).
PITMAN v. COMMISSIONER OF INTERNAL REVENUE, 64 F. 2d 740 (C. C. A. 10, 1933), s. c. 24 B. T. A. 244, 29 B. T. A. 1428.
PKA-O-WAH-ASH-KUM v. SORIN, 8 Fed. 740 (C. C. N. D. Ill. 1881).
POND v. MINNESOTA IRON CO., 58 Fed. 448 (C. C. Minn. 1893).
PORTER v. CLAUSEN, 1 Ind. T. 157, 38 S. W. 974 (1897).
PORTER v. MURPHY, 7 Ind. T. 395, 104 S. W. 658 (1907), rev'd sub nom. ADAMS v. MURPHY, 165 Fed. 304 (C. C. A. 8, 1908).
PORTER v. UNITED STATES, 7 Ind. T. 616, 104 S. W. 855 (1907).
PORTER v. UNITED STATES, 260 Fed. 1 (C. C. A. 8, 1919).
PORTER v. WILSON, 239 U. S. 170 (1915).
PORTERFIELD v. CLARK, 2 How. 76 (1844).
POTTAWATOMIE INDIANS v. UNITED STATES, 148 U. S. 691 (1893) aff'g 27 C. Cls. 403 (1892). See PHINEAS PAM-TO-PEE v. UNITED STATES, 148 U. S. 691 (1893).
POWELL v. CITY OF ADA, 61 F. 2d 283 (C. C. A. 10, 1932).
POWER v. UNITED STATES, 18 C. Cls. 263 (1883), s. c. 18 C. Cls. 493.
PRENTICE v. DULUTH STORAGE AND FORWARDING CO., 50 Fed. 437 (C. C. A. 8, 1893).
PRENTICE v. NORTHERN PAC. R. CO., 154 U. S. 163 (1893), aff'g 43 Fed. 270 (C. C. Minn. 1890).
PRENTICE v. STEARNS, 113 U. S. 435 (1885), aff'g 20 Fed. 819 (C. C. Minn. 1884).
PRESTON v. BROWDER, 1 Wheat. 115 (1816).
PRICE v. CHEROKEE NATION, 5 Ind. T. 518, 82 S. W. 893 (1904).
PRICE v. UNITED STATES, 28 C. Cls. 422 (1893).
PRICE v. UNITED STATES AND OSAGE INDIANS, 174 U. S. 373 (1899), aff'g 33 C. Cls. 106 (1897).
PRIDDY v. THOMPSON, 204 Fed. 955 (C. C. A. 8, 1913).
PRIVETT v. UNITED STATES, 256 U. S. 201 (1921), aff'g 261 Fed. 351 (C. C. A. 8, 1919).
PRONOVOST v. UNITED STATES, 232 U. S. 487 (1914).
PROSSER v. UNITED STATES, 265 Fed. 252 (C. C. A. 8, 1920).
PROVOE v. UNITED STATES, 283 U. S. 753 (1931). See HALBERT v. UNITED STATES, 283 U. S. 753 (1931).
PUEBLO DE SAN JUAN v. UNITED STATES, 47 F. 2d 446 (C. C. A. 10, 1931), cert. den. 284 U. S. 626.
PUEBLO DE TAOS v. ANAYA, 64 F. 2d 807 (C. C. A. 10, 1933). See PUEBLO DE TAOS v. ARCHULETA, 64 F. 2d 807 (C. C. A. 10, 1933).
PUEBLO DE TAOS v. ARCHULETA, 64 F. 2d 807 (C. C. A. 10, 1933).
PUEBLO DE TAOS v. GUSDORF, 50 F. 2d 721 (C. C. A. 10, 1931).
PUEBLO OF LAGUNA v. PUEBLO OF ACOMA, 1 N. M. 220 (1857).
PUEBLO OF NAMBE v. ROMERO, 10 N. M. 58, 61 Pac. 122 (1900).
PUEBLO OF PICURIS IN STATE OF NEW MEXICO v. ABEYTA, 50 F. 2d 12 (C. C. A. 10, 1931).
PUEBLO OF SANTA ROSA v. FALL, 273 U. S. 315 (1927), rev'g 12 F. 2d 332 (App. D. C. 1926), s. c. 249 U. S. 110 (1918).
PURCELL WHOLESALE GROCERY CO. v. BRYANT, 6 Ind. T. 78, 89 S. W. 662 (1906).
PYEATT v. POWELL, 51 Fed. 551 (C. C. A. 8, 1892).
QUAGON v. BIDDLE, 5 F. 2d 608 (C. C. A. 8, 1925).
QUARLES v. DENISON, 45 F. 2d 585 (C. C. A. 10, 1930), aff'g In re DENISON 38 F. 2d 662 (D. C. W. D. Okla. 1930).
QUEVAS v. HARVEY, 181 U. S. 481 (1901). See BARKER v. HARVEY, 181 U. S. 481 (1901).
QUICK BEAR v. LEUPP, 210 U. S. 50 (1908).
QUIGLEY v. STEPHENS, 3 Ind. T. 265, 54 S. W. 814 (1900), aff'd sub nom. STEPHENS v. QUIGLEY, 126 Fed. 148 (C. C. A. 8, 1903).
RAINBOW v. YOUNG, 161 Fed. 835 (C. C. A. 8, 1908), rev'g 154 Fed. 489.
RAYMOND v. RAYMOND, 83 Fed. 721 (C. C. A. 8, 1897), rev'g 1 Ind. T. 334, 37 S. W. 202 (1896).

REAGAN v. UNITED STATES, 182 U. S. 419 (1901), aff'g 35 C. Cls. 90 (1900).
RECTOR v. UNITED STATES, 92 U. S. 698 (1875). See HOT SPRINGS CASES, 92 U. S. 698 (1875).
RED BIRD v. UNITED STATES, 203 U. S. 76 (1906). See CHEROKEE INTERMARRIAGE CASES, 203 U. S. 76 (1906).
REDFIELD v. UNITED STATES, 27 C. Cls. 473 (1892).
RED HAWK v. WILBUR, 39 F. 2d 293 (App. D. C. 1930).
REED v. WELTY, 197 Fed. 419 (D. C. E. D. Okla. 1912), rev'd sub nom. WELTY v. REED, 219 Fed. 864 (C. C. A. 8, 1915); aff'd on rehearing sub nom. WELTY v. REED, 231 Fed. 930 (C. C. A. 8, 1916).
REEVES & CO. v. SHEETS, 16 Okla. 342, 82 Pac. 487 (1905).
RENFRO v. UNITED STATES, 15 F. 2d 991 (C. C. A. 8, 1926).
RENFROW v. UNITED STATES, 3 Okla. 161, 41 Pac. 88 (1895).
REX v. UNITED STATES, 251 U. S. 382 (1920), aff'g 53 C. Cls. 320 (1918).
REYNOLDS v. CLOWDUS, 4 Ind. T. 679, 76 S. W. 277 (1903).
REYNOLDS v. FEWELL, 236 U. S. 58 (1915).
REYNOLDS v. McARTHUR, 2 Pet. 417 (1829).
REYNOLDS v. UNITED STATES, 174 Fed. 212 (C. C. A. 1909).
REYNOLDS v. UNITED STATES, 205 Fed. 685 (D. C. S. D. 1913).
REYNOLDS v. UNITED STATES, 48 F. 2d 762 (C. C. A. 10, 1931).
REYNOLDS v. UNITED STATES, 252 Fed. 65 (C. C. A. 8, 1918), rev'd 250 U. S. 104 (1919).
RHINE, EXR. v. UNITED STATES, 33 C. Cls. 481 (1898).
RICE v. MAYBEE, 2 F. Supp. 669 (D. C. W. D. N. Y. 1933).
RICHARDVILLE v. THORP, 28 Fed. 52 (C. C. Kans. 1886).
RICKNOR v. CLABBER, 4 Ind. T. 660 (1903), 76 S. W. 271.
RIDDLE v. HUDGINS, 58 Fed. 490 (C. C. A. 8, 1893).
RIVERSIDE OIL AND REFINING CO. v. UNITED STATES, 20 F. 2d 873 (C. C. A. 8, 1927), cert. den. 275 U. S. 552, 275 U. S. 555. See UNITED STATES v. HAYNES, 20 F. 2d 873 (C. C. A. 8, 1927).
ROBERTS v. ANDERSON, 66 F. 2d 874 (C. C. A. 10, 1933).
ROBERTS v. UNDERWOOD, 237 U. S. 386 (1915). See PIGEON v. BUCK, 237 U. S. 386 (1915).
ROBINSON v. EWERT, 291 Fed. 9 (C. C. A. 8, 1923).
ROBINSON v. LONG GAS CO., 221 Fed. 398 (C. C. A. 8, 1915).
ROBINSON v. NAIL, 2 Ind. T. 509, 52 S. W. 49 (1899).
ROBINSON & CO. v. BELT, 187 U. S. 41 (1902), aff'g 100 Fed. 718 (C. C. A. 8, 1900).
ROFF v. BURNEY, 168 U. S. 218 (1897).
ROGERS v. HILL, 3 Ind. T. 562, 64 S. W. 536 (1901), writ of error dism. 123 Fed. 1006 (1903).
ROGERS v. ROGERS, 263 Fed. 160 (D. C. E. D. Okla. 1919).
ROGERS v. UNITED STATES, 45 C. Cls. 388 (1910).
ROLFSON v. UNITED STATES, 283 U. S. 753 (1931). See HALBERT v. UNITED STATES, 283 U. S. 753 (1931), rev'g UNITED STATES v. ROLFSON, 38 F. 2d 806 (C. C. A. 9, 1930).
ROLLINS AND PRESBREY v. UNITED STATES, 23 C. Cls. 106 (1888).
ROMERO v. UNITED STATES, 24 C. Cls. 331 (1889).
ROSS v. DAY, 232 U. S. 110 (1914).
ROSS v. EELLS, 56 Fed. 855 (C. C. Wash. 1893), app. dism. 168 U. S. 702 (1896).
ROSS v. STEWART, 227 U. S. 530 (1913).
ROSS, EX'R. v. UNITED STATES, 29 C. Cls. 176 (1894).
ROUBEDEAUX v. QUAKER OIL & GAS CO., OF OKLAHOMA, 23 F. 2d 277 (C. C. A. 8, 1927), cert. den. 276 U. S. 636.
ROUSSEAU v. UNITED STATES, 45 C. Cls. 1 (1909).
ROWE v. HENDERSON, 4 Ind. T. 597, 76 S. W. 250 (1903).
ROY v. UNITED STATES, 45 C. Cls. 177 (1910).
ROYAL BREWING CO. v. MISSOURI, K. & T. RY. CO., 217 Fed. 146 (D. C. Kans. 1914).
RUBENS v. UNITED STATES, 283 U. S. 753 (1931). See HALBERT v. UNITED STATES, 283 U. S. 753 (1931).
RUSH v. THOMPSON, 2 Ind. T. 557, 53 S. W. 333 (1899).
RUSSELL v. GREEN, 10 Okla. 340, 62 Pac. 817 (1900).
RUSSELL v. UNITED STATES, 92 U. S. 698 (1875). See HOT SPRINGS CASES, 92 U. S. 698 (1875).
RYAN v. UNITED STATES, 8 C. Cls. 265 (1872).
RYAN v. WASHINGTON, 302 U. S. 186 (1937). See MASON CO. v. TAX COMMISSION, 302 U. S. 186 (1937).
SAC AND FOX INDIANS OF THE MISSISSIPPI IN IOWA v. SAC AND FOX INDIANS OF THE MISSISSIPPI IN OKLAHOMA, 220 U. S. 481 (1911), aff'g 45 C. Cls. 287 (1910).
SAGE v. HAMPE, 235 U. S. 99 (1914).
ST. LOUIS & S. F. RY. CO. v. O'LOUGHLIN, 49 Fed. 440 (C. C. A. 8, 1892).
ST. LOUIS & S. F. RY. CO. v. PFENNIGHAUSEN, 7 Ind. T. 685, 104 S. W. 880 (1907).
ST. MARIE v. UNITED STATES, 24 F. Supp. 237 (D. C. S. D. Cal. 1938), aff'd 108 F. 2d 876 (C. C. A. 9, 1940); cert. den. 61 Sup. Ct. 35.
SALAZAR v. UNITED STATES, 236 Fed. 541 (C. C. A. 8, 1916).
SALOIS v. UNITED STATES, 32 C. Cls. 68 (1896).
SALOIS v. UNITED STATES, 33 C. Cls. 326 (1898).
SANCHEZ v. UNITED STATES, 48 C. Cls. 224 (1913).
SANDERS v. THORNTON, 97 Fed. 863 (C. C. A. 8, 1899), aff'g 2 Ind. T. 92, 48 S. W. 1015 (1899).
SANGER v. FLOW, 48 Fed. 152 (C. C. A. 8, 1891), writ of error dism. 149 U. S. 785.
SARLLS v. UNITED STATES, 152 U. S. 570 (1894).
SASS v. THOMAS, 4 Ind. T. 331, 69 S. W. 893 (1902), s. c. 3 Ind. T. 536, 64 S. W. 528 (1901).
SAYER v. BROWN, 7 Ind. T. 675, 104 S. W. 877 (1907).
SCHAAP v. UNITED STATES, 210 Fed. 853 (C. C. A. 8, 1914).
SCHEER v. MOODY, 48 F. 2d 327 (D. C. Mont. 1931), rev'd sub nom. MOODY v. JOHNSTON, 66 F. 2d 999 (C. C. A. 9, 1933).
SCHEFF v. UNITED STATES, 33 F. 2d 263 (C. C. A. 8, 1929).
SCHEWSON v. UNITED STATES, 31 C. Cls. 192 (1896).
SCHRIMPSCHER v. STOCKTON, 183 U. S. 290 (1902).
SCOTT v. UNITED STATES, 33 C. Cls. 486 (1898).
SEAPLES v. CARD, 246 Fed. 501 (D. C. E. D. Wash. 1915).
SEEP v. SPADE, 179 Fed. 77 (C. C. A. 8, 1910).
SEGNA v. UNITED STATES, 218 Fed. 791 (C. C. A. 8, 1914).
SELF v. PRAIRIE OIL & GAS CO., 28 F. 2d 590 (C. C. A. 8, 1928), rev'g 19 F. 2d 481 (C. C. A. 8, 1927), cert. den. 278 U. S. 659.
SEMINOLE NATION v. UNITED STATES, 78 C. Cls. 455 (1933).
SENECA NATION v. CHRISTY, 162 U. S. 283 (1896).
SEUFERT v. OLNEY, 193 Fed. 200 (C. C. E. D. Wash. 1911).
SEUFERT BROS. CO. v. UNITED STATES, 249 U. S. 194 (1919) aff'g UNITED STATES ex rel. WILLIAMS v. SEUFERT BROS. CO., 233 Fed. 579 (D. C. Ore. 1916).
SHARP v. UNITED STATES, 138 Fed. 878 (C. C. A. 8, 1905).
SHARP v. UNITED STATES, 16 F. 2d 876 (C. C. A. 8, 1926), aff'g Ex parte SHARP, 13 F. 2d 651 (D. C. N. D. Okla. 1926).
SHARROCK v. KREIGER, 6 Ind. T. 466, 98 S. W. 161 (1906).
SHAW v. GIBSON-ZAHNISER OIL CORP., 276 U. S. 575 (1928).
SHAWNEE AND DELAWARE INDIANS v. UNITED STATES, 47 C. Cls. 321 (1912).
SHAWNEE NAT. BANK v. UNITED STATES, 249 Fed. 583 (C. C. A. 8, 1918).
SHECIL v. UNITED STATES, 226 Fed. 184 (C. C. A. 7, 1915).
SHELLENBARGER v. FEWELL, 236 U. S. 68 (1915).
SHEPARD v. NORTHWESTERN LIFE INS. CO., 40 Fed. 341 (C. C. E. D. Mich. 1889).
SHORE v. SHELL PETROLEUM CORP., 60 F. 2d 1 (C. C. A. 10, 1932), aff'g 55 F. 2d 696, cert. den. 287 U. S. 656.
SHOSHONE TRIBE OF INDIANS v. UNITED STATES, 299 U. S. 476 (1937), rev'g 82 C. Cls. 23 (1935), s. c. UNITED STATES v. SHOSHONE TRIBE, 304 U. S. 111 (1938), 85 C. Cls. 331 (1937).
SHULTHIS v. McDOUGAL, 225 U. S. 561 (1912), aff'g 170 Fed. 529 (C. C. A. 8, 1909).
SILURIAN OIL CO. v. ESSLEY, 54 F. 2d 43 (C. C. A. 10, 1931).
SIMON v. UNITED STATES, 4 Ind. T. 688, 76 S. W. 280 (1903).
SING v. SITKA SCHOOL BOARD, 7 Alaska 616 (1. Div. 1927).
SIOUX INDIANS v. UNITED STATES, 277 U. S. 424 (1928), aff'g 58 C. Cls. 302 (1923), cert. den. 275 U. S. 528 (1927).
SIOUX INDIANS v. UNITED STATES, 85 C. Cls. 181 (1937), cert. den. 302 U. S. 717.
SIOUX TRIBE OF INDIANS v. UNITED STATES, 84 C. Cls. 16 (1936), cert. den. 302 U. S. 740.
SIOUX TRIBE OF INDIANS v. UNITED STATES, 86 C. Cls. 299 (1938), cert. den. 306 U. S. 642.
SISSETON & WAHPETON BANDS v. UNITED STATES, 39 C. Cls. 172 (1904), s. c. 42 C. Cls. 416.
SISSETON AND WAHPETON BANDS OF SIOUX INDIANS v. UNITED STATES, 208 U. S. 561 (1908), aff'g 42 C. Cls. 416 (1907). See UNITED STATES v. SISSETON AND WAHPETON BANDS OF SIOUX INDIANS, 208 U. S. 561 (1908).
SISSETON AND WAHPETON BANDS OF SIOUX INDIANS v. UNITED STATES, 277 U. S. 424 (1928), aff'g 58 C. Cls. 302 (1923). See SIOUX INDIANS v. UNITED STATES, 277 U. S. 424 (1928).
SITTEL v. WRIGHT, 122 Fed. 434 (C. C. A. 8, 1903).

SIZEMORE v. BRADY, 235 U. S. 441 (1914).
SKEEM v. UNITED STATES, 273 Fed. 93 (C. C. A. 9, 1921).
SKELTON v. DILL, 235 U. S. 206 (1914).
SLOAN v. UNITED STATES, 95 Fed. 193 (D. C. Neb. 1902), app. dism. 193 U. S. 614 (1904).
SLOAN v. UNITED STATES, 118 Fed. 283 (C. D. Neb. 1902), app. dism. 193 U. S. 614 (1904).
SMITH v. BONIFER, 154 Fed. 883 (C. C. Ore. 1907), aff'd sub nom. BONIFER v. SMITH, 166 Fed. 846 (C. C. A. 9, 1909), s. c. 132 Fed. 889.
SMITH v. McCULLOUGH, 270 U. S. 456 (1926), rev'g 285 Fed. 698 (C. C. A. 8, 1922).
SMITH v. STEVENS, 10 Wall. 321 (1870).
SMITH v. TOWNSEND, 148 U. S. 490 (1893), aff'g 1 Okla. Terr. 117 (1892).
SMITH v. UNITED STATES, 37 C. Cls. 119 (1902).
SMITH v. UNITED STATES, 142 Fed. 225 (C. C. Ore. 1905).
SMYTHE v. HENRY, 41 Fed. 705 (C. C. W. D. N. C. 1890).
SNYDER v. FANCHER, 7 F. Supp. 597 (D. C. W. D. N. Y. 1932).
SOUTHERN SURETY CO. v. OKLAHOMA, 241 U. S. 582 (1916).
SOUTHWEST PIPE LINE CO. v. EMPIRE NATURAL GAS CO., 33 F. 2d 248 (C. C. A. 8, 1929), aff'g 25 F. 2d 742.
SOUTHWESTERN COAL & IMPROVEMENT CO. v. McBRIDE, 185 U. S. 499 (1902), aff'g 104 Fed. 1007 (C. C. A. 8, 1900), aff'g 3 Ind. T. 223 (1900).
SPALDING v. CHANDLER, 160 U. S. 394 (1896).
SPEARS v. UNITED STATES, 64 C. Cls. 684 (1928).
SPERRY OIL & GAS CO. v. CHISHOLM, 264 U. S. 488 (1924), aff'g in part and rev'g in part 282 Fed. 92 (C. C. A. 8, 1922), s. c. 273 Fed. 589 (1921) and 261 U. S. 611 (1923).
SPRINGSTON v. WHEELER, 3 Ind. T. 388, 58 S. W. 658 (1900).
STAFFORD v. UNITED STATES, 72 F. 2d 847 (C. C. A. 10, 1934), rehearing den. sub nom. UNITED STATES v. MASHUNKASHEY, 73 F. 2d 487 (C. C. A. 10, 1934), cert. den. 294 U. S. 724 (1934). See UNITED STATES v. MASHUNKASHEY, 72 F. 2d 847 (C. C. A. 10, 1934).
STALEY v. ESPENLAUB, 43 F. 2d 98 (C. C. A. 10, 1930), aff'g 36 F. 2d 91 (D. C. Kan. 1929), cert. den. 283 U. S. 842 (1930).
STANCLIFT v. FOX, 152 Fed. 697 (C. C. A. 8, 1907), aff'g CAPITAL TOWNSITE CO. v. FOX, 6 Ind. T. 223, 90 S. W. 614 (1906), app. dism. 215 U. S. 619 (1909).
STANDLEY v. ROBERTS, 59 Fed. 836 (C. C. A. 8, 1894), app. dism. 17 Sup. Ct. 999 (1896).
STARR v. CAMPBELL, 208 U. S. 527 (1908).
STARR v. LONG JIM, 227 U. S. 613 (1913).
STATE OF MISSOURI v. STATE OF IOWA, 7 How. 660 (1849), s. c. 10 How. 1 (1850) and 160 U. S. 688 (1896).
STEPHENS v. CHEROKEE NATION, 174 U. S. 445 (1899).
STEPHENS v. QUIGLEY, 126 Fed. 148 (C. C. A. 8, 1903), aff'g QUIGLEY v. STEPHENS, 3 Ind. T. 265 (1900).
STEVENS ADM'R v. UNITED STATES, 34 C. Cls. 244 (1899).
STEVENSON v. UNITED STATES, 162 U. S. 313 (1896), rev'g 86 Fed. 106 (C. C. A. 5, 1898).
STEWART v. KEYES, 295 U. S. 403 (1935), rehearing den. 296 U. S. 661 (1935).
STEWART v. UNITED STATES, 206 U. S. 185 (1907), aff'g 39 C. Cls. 321 (1904).
STOCKBRIDGE TRIBE OF INDIANS v. UNITED STATES, 61 C. Cls. 472 (1926).
STOCKBRIDGE TRIBE OF INDIANS v. UNITED STATES, 63 C. Cls. 268 (1927).
STOLTZ v. UNITED STATES, 99 F. 2d 283 (C. C. A. 9, 1938).
STONE v. UNITED STATES, 164 U. S. 380 (1896), aff'g 29 C. Cls. 111 (1894).
STOOKEY v. WILBUR, 58 F. 2d 522 (App. D. C. 1932).
STROUD v. MISSOURI R. FT. S. & G. R. CO., 23 Fed. Cas. No. 13547 (C. C. Kan. 1877).
STUART v. TAPP, 81 F. 2d 155 (C. C. A. 10, 1935), rev'g TAPP v. STUART, 9 F. Supp. 23 (D. C. N. D. Okla. 1934), s. c. 6 F. Supp. 577 (1934).
STUART v. UNITED STATES, 18 Wall. 84 (1873), aff'g 6 C. Cls. 111 (1870).
SULLY v. UNITED STATES, 195 Fed. 113 (C. C. S. D. 1912).
SUNDAY v. MALLORY, 248 U. S. 545 (1919), mod'g and aff'g 237 Fed. 526 (C. C. A. 8, 1916).
SUNDERLAND v. UNITED STATES, 266 U. S. 226 (1924), aff'g 287 Fed. 468 (C. C. A. 8, 1923).
SUPER v. WORK, 271 U. S. 643 (1926), aff'g 3 F. 2d 90 (App. D. C. 1925).
SUPERINTENDENT v. COMMISSIONER, 295 U. S. 418 (1935), aff'g 75 F. 2d 183 (C. C. A. 10, 1935).
SURPLUS TRADING CO. v. COOK, 281 U. S. 647 (1930).
SUTTER v. HECKMAN, 1 Alaska 188 (1901), aff'd HECKMAN v. SUTTER, 119 Fed. 83 (C. C. A. 9, 1902).
SWAFFORD v. UNITED STATES, 25 F. 2d. 581 (C. C. A. 8, 1928).
SWAN, THE JAMES G., 50 Fed. 108 (D. C. Wash. 1892).
SWEET v. SCHOCK, 245 U. S. 192 (1917).
SWENDIG v. WASHINGTON WATER POWER CO., 265 U. S. 322 (1924), aff'g 281 Fed. 900 (C. C. A. 9, 1922).
SWINNEY v. KELLEY, 5 Ind. T. 12, 76 S. W. 303 (1903).
SWOPE v. PURDY, 23 Fed. Cas. No. 13704 (App. D. C. 1801).
SWOPE v. UNITED STATES, 33 C. Cls. 223 (1898).
TALKINGTON v. UNITED STATES, 225 Fed. 367 (C. C. A. 8, 1915).
TALLEY v. BURGESS, 246 U. S. 104 (1918).
TALLY v. KIRK, 6 Ind. T. 331, 97 S. W. 1027 (1906).
TALTON v. MAYES, 163 U. S. 376 (1896).
TANNER v. UNITED STATES, 32 C. Cls. 192 (1897).
TAPP v. STUART, 6 F. Supp. 577 (D. C. N. D. Okla. 1934). See STUART v. TAPP.
TAYLOR v. BROWN, 147 U. S. 640 (1893).
TAYLOR v. HAND, 7 How. 572 (1849).
TAYLOR v. JONES, 51 F. 2d 892 (C. C. A. 10, 1931), cert. den. 284 U. S. 663 (1931).
TAYLOR v. PARKER, 235 U. S. 42 (1914).
TAYLOR v. SOUTHERLAND, 7 Ind. T. 666, 104 S. W. 874 (1907).
TAYLOR v. TAYRIEN, 51 F. 2d 884 (C. C. A. 10, 1931), cert. den. 284 U. S. 672 (1931).
TAYLOR v. UNITED STATES, 6 Ind. T. 351, 98 S. W. 123 (1906).
TAYLOR v. UNITED STATES, 193 Fed. 968 (C. C. A. 9, 1912).
TAYLOR v. UNITED STATES, 230 Fed. 580 (C. C. A. 8, 1916).
TAYLOR v. UNITED STATES, 44 F. 2d 531 (C. C. A. 9, 1930).
TERRILL v. UNITED STATES, 35 C. Cls. 218 (1900).
TERRITORY v. DELINQUENT TAX LIST, 12 N. M. 139, 76 Pac. 307 (1904).
TERRITORY OF ALASKA v. ANNETTE ISLAND PACKING CO., 289 Fed. 671 (C. C. A. 9, 1923), cert. den. 263 U. S. 708 (1923).
TERRITORY OF ARIZONA v. DELINQUENT TAX LIST, 3 Ariz. 302 (1891), 26 Pac. 310, aff'd sub nom. MARICOPA & PHOENIX R. R. v. ARIZONA, 156 U. S. 347 (1895).
TERRITORY OF MONTANA v. GUYOTT, 9 Mont. 46, 22 Pac. 134 (1889).
TERRITORY OF OREGON v. COLEMAN, 1 Ore. 191 (1855).
TEXAS CO. v. CENTRAL FUEL OIL CO., 194 Fed. 1 (C. C. A. 8, 1912).
THAYER v. UNITED STATES, 20 C. Cls. 137 (1885).
THEBO v. CHOCTAW TRIBE OF INDIANS, 66 Fed. 372 (C. C. A. 8, 1895).
THOMAS v. GAY, 169 U. S. 264 (1898).
THOMAS v. SASS, 3 Ind. T. 545, 64 S. W. 531 (1901); s. c. 4 Ind. T. 336, 69 S. W. 894 (1902).
THOMASON v. McLAUGHLIN, 7 Ind. T. 1 (1907), 103 S. W. 595.
THOMASON v. WILLIAM & RHOADES, 206 Fed. 895 (C. C. A. 8, 1913).
THOMISON v. UNITED STATES, 35 C. Cls. 395 (1900).
THOMPSON v. MORGAN, 4 Ind. T. 412, 69 S. W. 920 (1902).
THOMPSON v. UNITED STATES, 44 C. Cls. 359 (1909).
THREDGILL v. PINTARD, 12 How. 24 (1851).
THURSTON v. UNITED STATES, 232 U. S. 469 (1914).
TIGER v. FEWELL, 22 F. 2d 786 (C. C. A. 8, 1927), cert. den. 269 U. S. 572 (1925), writ of error dism. 271 U. S. 649 (1926), cert. den. 276 U. S. 629.
TIGER v. SLINKER, 19 F. 2d 35 (C. C. A. 8, 1927), aff'g 4 F. 2d 714 (D. C. E. D. Okla. 1925).
TIGER v. TWIN STATE OIL CO., 48 F. 2d 509 (C. C. A. 10, 1931), aff'g KEMOHAH v. SHAFFER OIL AND REFINING CO., 38 F. 2d 665 (D. C. N. D. Okla. 1930).
TIGER v. WESTERN INVESTMENT CO., 221 U. S. 286 (1911).
TILLER v. UNITED STATES, 34 F. 2d 398 (C. C. A. 10, 1929).
TINKER v. MIDLAND VALLEY CO., 231 U. S. 681 (1914).
TOOTLE v. McCLELLAN, 7 Ind. T. 64, 103 S. W. 766 (1907).
TOWNSEND v. UNITED STATES, 265 Fed. 519 (C. C. A. 8, 1920).
TOY TOY v. HOPKINS, 212 U. S. 542 (1909).

TRUSCOTT v. HURLBUT LAND & CATTLE CO., 73 Fed. 60 (C. C. A. 9, 1896), app. dism. sub nom. HURLBUT LAND & CATTLE CO. v. TRUSCOTT, 165 U. S. 719 (1897).

TRUSKETT v. CLOSSER, 236 U. S. 223 (1915), aff'g 198 Fed. 835 (C. C. A. 8, 1912).

TUCKER v. UNITED STATES, 236 Fed. 542 (C. C. A. 8, 1916), cert. den. 245 U. S. 659.

TULLY v. UNITED STATES, 32 C. Cls. 1 (1896).

TURNER v. AMERICAN BAPTIST MISSIONARY UNION, 24 Fed. Cas. No. 14251 (C. C. Mich. 1852).

TURNER v. GILLILAND, 4 Ind. T. 606, 76 S. W. 253 (1903).

TURNER v. SEEP, 167 Fed. 646 (C. C. E. D. Okla. 1909), mod. 179 Fed. 74.

TURNER v. UNITED STATES, 248 U. S. 354 (1919), aff'g 51 C. Cls. 125 (1916).

TUTTLE v. MOORE, 3 Ind. T. 712, 64 S. W. 565 (1901).

TYE v. CHICKASHA TOWN CO., 2 Ind. T. 113, 48 S. W. 1021 (1899).

TYNON v. CROWELL, 3 Ind. T. 346, 58 S. W. 585 (1900), app. dism. 109 Fed. 1063.

UHLIG v. GARRISON, 2 Dak. 71, 2 N. W. 253 (1878), s. c. 2 N. W. 258.

UNITED STATES v. AARON, 183 Fed. 347 (C. C. W. D. Okla. 1910), s. c. 204 Fed. 943.

UNITED STATES v. ABRAMS, 194 Fed. 82 (C. C. A. 8, 1912), aff'g 181 Fed. 847 (C. C. E. D. Okla. 1910).

UNITED STATES v. ALASKA PACKER'S ASS'N., 79 Fed. 152 (C. C. Wash. 1897), app. dism. 19 Sup. Ct. 881 (1899).

UNITED STATES v. ALBERTY, 24 Fed. Cas. No. 14426 (C. C. Ark. 1844).

UNITED STATES v. ALGODONES LAND CO., 52 F. 2d 359 (C. C. A. 10, 1931).

UNITED STATES v. ALGOMA LUMBER CO., 305 U. S. 415 (1939), rev'g 86 C. Cls. 226, 188, 171.

UNITED STATES v. ALIRE, 73 U. S. 573 (1867), rev'g 1 C. Cls. 233 (1865).

UNITED STATES v. ALLEN, 36 Fed. 174 (C. C. E. D. Mo. 1888).

UNITED STATES v. ALLEN, 179 Fed. 13 (C. C. A. 8, 1910), rev'g 171 Fed. 907 (C. C. E. D. Okla. 1909), mod. 224 U. S. 413, rev'd sub nom. MULLEN v. UNITED STATES, 224 U. S. 448, mod. 224 U. S. 458, mod. 224 U. S. 471.

UNITED STATES v. AMO., 261 Fed. 106 (D. C. W. D. Wis. 1919).

UNITED STATES v. ANDERSON, 228 U. S. 52 (1913), rev'g 189 Fed. 262 (D. C. Ore. 1911).

UNITED STATES v. ANDERSON, 225 Fed. 825 (D. C. E. D. Wis. 1915).

UNITED STATES v. ANDREWS, 179 U. S. 96 (1900).

UNITED STATES v. ASHFORD, 99 F. 2d 946 (C. C. A. 8, 1938).

UNITED STATES v. ASHTON, 170 Fed. 509 (C. C. W. D. Wash. 1909), app. dism. sub nom. BIRD v. ASHTON, 220 U. S. 604, (1911), without opinion.

UNITED STATES v. ATKINS, 260 U. S. 220 (1922), aff'g 268 Fed. 923 (C. C. A. 8, 1920).

UNITED STATES v. AUGER, 153 Fed. 671 (C. C. W. D. Wis. 1907), app. dism. 170 Fed. 1021 (C. C. A. 7, 1908), without opinion.

UNITED STATES v. BAILEY, 24 Fed. Cas. No. 14495 (C. C. Tenn. 1834).

UNITED STATES v. BAKER, 4 Ind. T. 544, 76 S. W. 103 (1903).

UNITED STATES v. BARNABY, 51 Fed. 20 (C. C. Mont. 1892).

UNITED STATES v. BARNETT, 7 F. Supp. 573 (D. C. N. D. Okla. 1934).

UNITED STATES v. BARNHART, 17 Fed. 579 (C. C. Ore. 1883).

UNITED STATES v. BARNHART, 22 Fed. 285 (C. C. Ore. 1884).

UNITED STATES v. BARTLETT, 235 U. S. 72 (1914), aff'g BARTLETT v. UNITED STATES, 203 Fed. 410 (C. C. A. 8, 1913).

UNITED STATES v. BEAN, 253 Fed. 1 (C. C. A. 8, 1918).

UNITED STATES v. BEEBE, 2 Dak. 292, 11 N. W. 505 (1880).

UNITED STATES v. BELLM, 182 Fed. 161 (C. C. E. D. Okla. 1910).

UNITED STATES v. BELT, 128 Fed. 68 (D. C. M. D. Pa. 1904).

UNITED STATES v. BENEWAH COUNTY, 290 Fed. 628 (C. C. A. 9, 1923).

UNITED STATES v. BERRIGAN, 2 Alaska 442 (3 Div. 1905).

UNITED STATES v. BERRY, 4 Fed. 779 (D. C. Colo. 1880).

UNITED STATES v. BICHARD & CO., 1 Ariz. 31, 25 Pac. 517 (1871).

UNITED STATES v. BIRDSALL, 233 U. S. 223 (1914), rev'g 206 Fed. 818 (D. C. N. D. Iowa 1913). See UNITED STATES v. VAN WERT, 233 U. S. 223 (1914).

UNITED STATES v. BLACK, 247 Fed. 942 (C. C. A. 8, 1917).

UNITED STATES v. BLACKFEATHER, 155 U. S. 180 (1894), rev'g BLACKFEATHER v. UNITED STATES, 28 C. Cls. 447 (1893).

UNITED STATES v. BOARD OF COMMISSIONERS, 26 F. Supp. 270 (D. C. N. D. Okla. 1939).

UNITED STATES v. BOARD OF COM'RS OF COMANCHE COUNTY, OKLA., 6 F. Supp. 401 (D. C. W. D. Okla. 1934).

UNITED STATES v. BOARD OF COUNTY COMMISSIONERS OF OSAGE COUNTY, OKLA., 267 U. S. 587 (1925), aff'g per cur. 1 F. 2d 701 (C. C. A. 8, 1924), s. c. 244 U. S. 663 (1917), 216 Fed. 853 (C. C. A. 8, 1914), 193 Fed. 485 (C. C. W. D. Okla. 1911), s. c. 254 Fed. 570 (C. C. A. 8, 1918).

UNITED STATES v. BOARD OF COUNTY COM'RS OF GRADY COUNTY, OKLA, 54 F. 2d 593 (C. C. A. 10, 1931).

UNITED STATES v. BOARD OF COMMISSIONERS OF McINTOSH COUNTY, 284 Fed. 103 (C. C. A. 8, 1922), aff'g UNITED STATES v. STUCKEY, 271 Fed. 747 (D. C. E. D. Okla. 1921), app. dism. 263 U. S. 691.

UNITED STATES v. BOARD OF COUNTY COM'RS, 13 F. Supp. 641 (D. C. N. D. Okla. 1936).

UNITED STATES v. BOARD OF NAT. MISSIONS OF PRESBYTERIAN CHURCH, 37 F. 2d 272 (C. C. A. 10, 1929).

UNITED STATES v. BOND, 108 F. 2d 504 (C. C. A. 10, 1939), aff'g BOND v. TOM, 25 F. Supp. 157 (D. C. N. D. Okla. 1938).

UNITED STATES v. BONNESS, 125 Fed. 485 (C. C. A. 8, 1903).

UNITED STATES v. BOSS, 160 Fed. 132 (D. C. Utah, 1906).

UNITED STATES v. BOWLING, 256 U. S. 484 (1921), rev'g 261 Fed. 657 (D. C. E. D. N. Y. 1919), s. c. 299 Fed. 438 (1924).

UNITED STATES v. BOYD, 68 Fed. 577 (C. C. W. D. N. C. 1895).

UNITED STATES v. BOYD, 83 Fed. 547 (C. C. A. 4, 1897).

UNITED STATES v. BOYLAN 265 Fed. 165 (C. C. A. 2, 1920), aff'g 256 Fed. 468 (D. C. N. D. N. Y. 1919), app. dism. 257 U. S. 614 (1921).

UNITED STATES v. BOYNTON, 53 F. 2d 297 (C. C. A. 9, 1931), rev'g 49 F. 2d 810 (D. C. W. D. Wash. 1931).

UNITED STATES v. BRAVE BEAR, 3 Dak. 34, 13 N. W. 565 (1882).

UNITED STATES v. BRENTS, 233 U. S. 223 (1914). See UNITED STATES v. BIRDSALL, 233 U. S. 223 (1914).

UNITED STATES v. BRIDLEMAN, 7 Fed. 894 (D. C. Ore. 1881).

UNITED STATES v. BRINDLE, 110 U. S. 688 (1884).

UNITED STATES v. BROOKFIELD FISHERIES, 24 F. Supp. 712 (D. C. Ore. 1938).

UNITED STATES v. BROOKS, 10 How. 442 (1850).

UNITED STATES v. BROWN, 8 F. 2d 564 (C. C. A. 8, 1925), cert. den. 270 U. S. 644 (1926).

UNITED STATES v. BROWN, 15 F. 2d 565 (D. C. N. D. Okla. 1926).

UNITED STATES v. BUCKLES, 6 Ind. T. 319, 97 S. W. 1022 (1906).

UNITED STATES v. CADZOW, 5 Alaska 125 (4 Div. 1914).

UNITED STATES v. CAIN-BONNESS LUMBER & TIMBER CO., 215 Fed. 212 (D. C. W. D. Wash. 1914).

UNITED STATES v. CALIFORNIA & OREGON LAND CO., 192 U. S. 355 (1903), rev'g UNITED STATES v. OREGON CENTRAL MILITARY ROAD CO., 103 Fed. 549 (C. C. Ore. 1900).

UNITED STATES v. CANDELARIA, 271 U. S. 432 (1926).

UNITED STATES v. CARDISH, 145 Fed. 242 (D. C. E. D. Wis. 1906), s. c. 143 Fed. 640 (D. C. E. D. Wis. 1906).

UNITED STATES v. CARPENTER, 111 U. S. 347 (1884).

UNITED STATES v. CARR, 2 Mont. 234 (1875).

UNITED STATES v. CARSON, 19 F. Supp. 616 (D. C. N. D. Okla. 1937), app. dism. 98 F. 2d 1023.

UNITED STATES v. CASS, 240 Fed. 617 (C. C. A. 8, 1917).

UNITED STATES v. CASTER, 271 Fed. 615 (C. C. A. 8, 1921), app. dism. 257 U. S. 666 (1921).

UNITED STATES v. CELESTINE, 215 U. S. 278 (1909).

UNITED STATES v. CERTAIN PROPERTY (See UNITED STATES v. BICHARD & CO.).

UNITED STATES v. CHARLES, 23 F. Supp. 346 (D. C. W. D. N. Y. 1938).

UNITED STATES v. CHASE, 245 U. S. 89 (1917), rev'g 222 Fed. 593 (C. C. A. 8, 1915), cert. granted, 241 U. S. 669 (1916).

UNITED STATES v. CHA-TO-KAH-NA-PE-SHA, 25 Fed. Cas. No. 14789a. (Superior Court, Ark. 1824).
UNITED STATES v. CHAVEZ, 175 U. S. 509 (1899), s. c. 175 U. S. 552.
UNITED STATES v. CHAVEZ, 290 U. S. 357 (1933).
UNITED STATES v. CHEHALIS COUNTY, 217 Fed. 281 (D. C. W. D. Wash. 1914).
UNITED STATES v. CHEROKEE NATION, 202 U. S. 101 (1906), s. c. 220 U. S. 84, 225 U. S. 576.
UNITED STATES v. CHOCTAW NATION, 179 U. S. 494 (1900).
UNITED STATES v. CHOCTAW NATION, 38 C. Cls. 558 (1903), aff'd sub nom. CHICKASAW FREEDMEN, 193 U. S. 115 (1904).
UNITED STATES v. CIMARRON RIVER OIL CO., 20 F. 2d 873 (C. C. A. 8, 1927), cert. den. sub nom. RIVERSIDE OIL & REFINING CO. v. CIMARRON RIVER OIL CO. et al., 275 U. S. 552 (1927).
UNITED STATES v. CISNA, 25 Fed. Cas. No. 14795 (C. C. Ohio 1835).
UNITED STATES v. CLAPOX, 35 Fed. 575 (D. C. Ore., 1888).
UNITED STATES v. COHN, 2 Ind. T. 474, 52 S. W. 38 (1899).
UNITED STATES v. COLVARD, 89 F. 2d 312 (C. C. A. 4, 1937).
UNITED STATES v. COMET OIL AND GAS CO., 202 Fed. 849 (C. C. A. 8, 1913), rev'g 187 Fed. 674 (C. C. E. D. Okla. 1911).
UNITED STATES v. CONWAY, 175 U. S. 60 (1899).
UNITED STATES v. COOK, 225 Fed. 756 (C. C. A. 8, 1915).
UNITED STATES v. COOK, 19 Wall. 591 (1873).
UNITED STATES v. CORPORATION OF THE PRESIDENT, etc., 101 F. 2d 156 (C. C. A. 10, 1939).
UNITED STATES v. CRAWFORD, 47 Fed. 561 (C. C. W. D. Ark., 1891).
UNITED STATES v. CREEK NATION, 302 U. S. 620 (1938), rev'g 84 C. Cls. 12, s. c. 295 U. S. 103 (1935), rev'g 77 C. Cls. 159 (1933); rehearing den. 295 U. S. 769 (1935).
UNITED STATES v. DAVIS, 188 Fed. 383 (C. C. Minn. 1911). See UNITED STATES v. PARK LAND CO., 188 Fed. 383 (C. C. Minn. 1911).
UNITED STATES v. DAWSON, 15 How. 467 (1853).
UNITED STATES v. DEBELL, 227 Fed. 760 (C. C. A. 8, 1915).
UNITED STATES v. DEBELL, 227 Fed. 771 (C. C. A. 8, 1915).
UNITED STATES v. DEBELL, 227 Fed. 775 (C. C. A. 8, 1915).
UNITED STATES v. DETROIT FIRST NAT. BANK, 234 U. S. 245 (1914), aff'g 208 Fed. 988 (C. C. A. 8, 1913).
UNITED STATES v. DEWEY COUNTY, S. D. 14 F. 2d 784 (D. C. S. Dak. 1926), aff'd sub nom. DEWEY COUNTY, S. D. v. UNITED STATES, 26 F. 2d 434 (C. C. A. 8, 1928), cert. den. 278 U. S. 649 (1928).
UNITED STATES v. DOOLEY, 151 Fed. 697 (C. C. E. D. Wash. 1906).
UNITED STATES v. DOUGLAS, 190 Fed. 482 (C. C. A. 8, 1911).
UNITED STATES v. DOWDEN, 220 Fed. 277 (C. C. A. 8, 1915), aff'g 194 Fed. 475 (C. C. E. D. Okla. 1911), app. dism. 242 U. S. 661.
UNITED STATES v. DOWNING, 25 Fed. Cas. No. 14991 (D. C. Kan. 1876).
UNITED STATES v. DUNN, 288 Fed. 158 (C. C. A. 8, 1923), mod. 268 U. S. 121 (1925).
UNITED STATES v. DUVAL, 25 Fed. Cas. No. 15015 (D. C. E. D. Penn. 1833).
UNITED STATES v. EARL, 17 Fed. 75 (C. C. Ore. 1883).
UNITED STATES v. EASTERN COAL & MINING CO., 66 F. 2d 923 (C. C. A. 10, 1933).
UNITED STATES v. ELLIS, 51 Fed. 808 (D. C. W. D. Ark. 1892).
UNITED STATES v. ELM, 25 Fed. Cas. No. 15048 (D. C. N. D. N. Y., 1877).
UNITED STATES v. EQUITABLE TRUST CO., 283 U. S. 738 (1931), mod'g 34 F. 2d 916 (C. C. A. 2, 1929), s. c. 280 U. S. 550.
UNITED STATES v. ESTILL, 62 F. 2d 620 (C. C. A. 10, 1932).
UNITED STATES v. EWING, 47 Fed. 809 (D. C. S. D. 1891).
UNITED STATES v. FAIRBANKS, 171 Fed. 337 (C. C. A. 8, 1909), aff'd 223 U. S. 215 (1912).
UNITED STATES v. FERNANDEZ, 10 Pet. 303 (1836).
UNITED STATES v. FERGUSON, 247 U. S. 175 (1918), aff'g 225 Fed. 974 (C. C. A. 8, 1915).
UNITED STATES v. FERRY COUNTY, WASHINGTON, 24 F. Supp. 399 (D. C. E. D. Wash. 1938).
UNITED STATES v. FIDELITY TRUST CO., 121 Fed. 766 (C. C. A. 9, 1903).
UNITED STATES v. FIRST NATIONAL BANK, 234 U. S. 245 (1914), aff'g 208 Fed. 988 (C. C. A. 8, 1913).
UNITED STATES v. FIRST NAT. BANK, 282 Fed. 330 (D. C. E. D. Wash. 1922).
UNITED STATES v. FIRST NAT. BANK OF DECATUR, NEB., 56 F. 2d 634 (D. C. Neb. 1931), aff'd FIRST NAT. BANK OF DECATUR, NEB. v. UNITED STATES, 59 F. 2d 367.
UNITED STATES v. FITZGERALD, 201 Fed. 295 (C. C. A. 8, 1912).
UNITED STATES v. FLOURNOY LIVE-STOCK and REAL ESTATE CO., 69 Fed. 886 (C. C. Neb. 1895), s. c. 71 Fed. 576 (C. C. Neb. 1896).
UNITED STATES v. FLYNN, 25 Fed. Cas. No. 15124 (C. C. Minn. 1870).
UNITED STATES v. FOOSHEE, 225 Fed. 521 (C. C. A. 8, 1915).
UNITED STATES v. FORREST LUMBER CO., 305 U. S. 415 (1939). See UNITED STATES v. ALGOMA LUMBER CO., 305 U. S. 415 (1939).
UNITED STATES v. FT. SMITH & W. R. CO., 195 Fed. 211 (C. C. A. 8, 1912).
UNITED STATES v. FORTY-EIGHT POUNDS OF RISING STAR TEA, 35 Fed. 403 (D. C. N. D. Cal. 1888), aff'd 38 Fed. 400 (C. C. N. D. Cal. 1889).
UNITED STATES v. FORTY THREE GALLONS OF WHISKEY, 93 U. S. 188 (1876), rev'g 25 Fed. Cas. No. 15136 (D. C. Minn. 1874).
UNITED STATES v. FORTY-THREE GALLONS OF WHISKEY, 108 U. S. 491 (1883).
UNITED STATES v. FOSTER, 25 Fed. Cas. No. 15141 (C. C. E. D. Wis. 1870).
UNITED STATES v. 4,450.72 ACRES OF LAND, CLEARWATER COUNTY, MINN., 27 F. Supp. 167 (D. C. Minn. 1939).
UNITED STATES v. FOUR BOTTLES SOUR-MASH WHISKEY, 90 Fed. 720 (D. C. Wash. 1898).
UNITED STATES v. FRANK BLACK SPOTTED HORSE, 282 Fed. 349 (D. C. S. D. 1922).
UNITED STATES v. GARDNER, 133 Fed. 285 (C. C. A. 9, 1904).
UNITED STATES v. GARDNER, 189 Fed. 690 (D. C. E. D. Wis. 1911).
UNITED STATES v. GETZELMAN, 89 F. 2d 531 (C. C. A. 10, 1937), cert. den. 302 U. S. 708.
UNITED STATES v. GLACIER COUNTY, 17 F. Supp. 411 (D. C. Mont. 1936), mod. 99 F. 2d 733 (1938).
UNITED STATES v. GORHAM, 165 U. S. 316 (1897), aff'g GORHAM v. UNITED STATES, 29 C. Cls. 97 (1894).
UNITED STATES v. GRAY, 201 Fed. 291 (C. C. A. 8, 1912).
UNITED STATES v. GRAY, 284 Fed. 103 (C. C. A. 8, 1922), aff'g 271 Fed. 747 (D. C. E. D. Okla. 1921), app. dism. 263 U. S. 689.
UNITED STATES v. GYPSY OIL CO., 10 F. 2d 487 (C. C. A. 8, 1925).
UNITED STATES v. HADDOCK, 21 F. 2d 165 (C. C. A. 8, 1927).
UNITED STATES v. HADLEY, 99 Fed. 437 (C. C. Wash. 1900).
UNITED STATES v. HALE, 51 F. 2d 629 (C. C. A. 10, 1931), rev'g 39 F. 2d 188 (D. C. N. D. Okla. 1930).
UNITED STATES v. HALL, 171 Fed. 214 (D. C. E. D. Wis. 1909).
UNITED STATES v. HALSELL, 247 Fed. 390 (C. C. A. 8, 1918).
UNITED STATES v. HARRIS, 293 Fed. 389 (C. C. A. 8, 1923), aff'g 265 Fed. 261 (C. C. A. 8, 1920), app. dism. 257 U. S. 623 (1922), s. c. 286 Fed. 910 (C. C. A. 8, 1923).
UNITED STATES v. HARRIS, 100 F. 2d 268 (C. C. A. 9, 1938), rehearing den., 103 F. 2d 1020.
UNITED STATES v. HAWKINS, 217 Fed. 11 (C. C. A. 8, 1914). See IOWA LAND & TRUST CO. v. UNITED STATES, 217 Fed. 11 (C. C. A. 8, 1914).
UNITED STATES v. HAYES, 20 F. 2d 873 (C. C. A. 8, 1927), cert. den. 275 U. S. 555.
UNITED STATES v. HEALY, 202 Fed. 349 (D. C. Mont. 1913).
UNITED STATES v. HEINRICH, 16 F. 2d 112 (C. C. A. 9, 1926), aff'g 12 F. 2d 938 (D. C. Mont. 1926).
UNITED STATES v. HEIRS OF RILLIEUX, 14 How. 189 (1852).
UNITED STATES v. HEMMER, 241 U. S. 379 (1916), aff'g 204 Fed. 898 (C. C. A. 8, 1912).

UNITED STATES v. HEYFRON, 138 Fed. 964 (C. C. Mont. 1905).
UNITED STATES v. HEYFRON, 138 Fed. 968 (C. C. Mont. 1905).
UNITED STATES v. HIGGINS, 103 Fed. 348 (C. C. Mont. 1900).
UNITED STATES v. HIGGINS, 110 Fed. 609 (C. C. Mont. 1901).
UNITED STATES v. HINKLE, 261 Fed. 518 (C. C. A. 8, 1919).
UNITED STATES v. HOLLIDAY, 3 Wall. 407 (1865).
UNITED STATES v. HOLT STATE BANK, 270 U. S. 49 (1926), aff'g 294 Fed. 161 (C. C. A. 8, 1923).
UNITED STATES v. HOMERATHA, 40 F. 2d 305 (D. C. W. D. Okla. 1930), app. dism. 49 F. 2d 1086.
UNITED STATES v. HOWARD, 17 Fed. 638 (C. C. Ore. 1883).
UNITED STATES v. HOWARD, 8 F. Supp. 617 (D. C. N. D. Okla. 1934).
UNITED STATES v. HOYT, 167 Fed. 301 (C. C. A. 9, 1909), aff'g 158 Fed. 162 (C. C. E. D. Wash. 1907).
UNITED STATES v. HUGHES, 6 F. Supp. 972 (D. C. N. D. Okla. 1934).
UNITED STATES v. HUMASON, 26 Fed. Cas. No. 15420 (C. C. Ore. 1879), s. c. 26 Fed. Cas. No. 15,421.
UNITED STATES v. HUNTER, 21 Fed. 615 (C. C. E. D. Missouri, 1884).
UNITED STATES v. HURSHMAN, 53 Fed. 543 (D. C. Wash. 1892).
UNITED STATES v. HUTCHINGS, 252 Fed. 841 (D. C. W. D. Okla. 1918), aff'd sub nom. COMMISSIONERS v. UNITED STATES, 270 Fed. 110 (C. C. A. 8, 1920), app. dism. 260 U. S. 753.
UNITED STATES v. HUTTO, No. 1, 256 U. S. 524 (1921).
UNITED STATES v. HUTTO, No. 2, 256 U. S. 530 (1921).
UNITED STATES v. INABA, 291 Fed. 416 (D. C. E. D. Wash. 1923).
UNITED STATES v. IVY, 26 Fed. Cas. No. 15451 (C. C. Ark. 1803).
UNITED STATES v. JACKSON, 280 U. S. 183 (1930), rev'g 27 F. 2d 751 (D. C. N. D. Cal. 1928), s. c. 38 F. 2d 1021.
UNITED STATES v. JACOBS, 195 Fed. 707 (C. C. A. 8, 1912).
UNITED STATES v. JOHNSON, 53 F. 2d 267 (D. C. W. D. Wash. 1931).
UNITED STATES v. JOHNSON, 87 F. 2d 155 (C. C. A. 10, 1936), aff'g 11 F. Supp. 897 (D. C. N. D. Okla. 1935).
UNITED STATES v. JOSEPH, 94 U. S. 614 (1876), aff'g UNITED STATES v. VARELA, 1 N. M. 593 (1874).
UNITED STATES v. JOYCE, 240 Fed. 610 (C. C. A. 8, 1917).
UNITED STATES v. KAGAMA, 118 U. S. 375 (1886).
UNITED STATES v. KEMPF, 171 Fed. 1021 (D. C. E. D. Wis. 1909).
UNITED STATES v. KIE, 26 Fed. Cas. No. 15528a (D. C. Alaska 1885), s. c. 26 Fed. Cas. No. 15528b, 27 Fed. 351.
UNITED STATES v. KILGORE, 111 F. 2d 665 (C. C. A. 10, 1940) rev'g 27 F. Supp. 1 (D. C. W. D. Okla. 1939).
UNITED STATES v. KING, 81 Fed. 625 (D. C. E. D. Wis. 1897).
UNITED STATES v. KIYA, 126 Fed. 879 (D. C. N. D. 1903).
UNITED STATES v. KLAMATH INDIANS, 304 U. S. 119 (1938), s. c. 296 U. S. 244.
UNITED STATES v. KNIGHT, 206 Fed. 145 (C. C. A. 8, 1913).
UNITED STATES v. KNOWLTON, 3 Dak. 58, 13 N. W. 573 (1882).
UNITED STATES v. KONKAPOT, 43 Fed. 64 (C. C. Wis. 1890).
UNITED STATES v. KOPP, 110 Fed. 160 (D. C. Wash. 1901).
UNITED STATES v. LADLEY, 51 F. 2d 756 (D. C. Idaho, 1931), s. c. 42 F. 2d 474, 4 F. Supp. 580 (D. C. Idaho, 1933).
UNITED STATES v. LAMM LUMBER CO., 305 U. S. 415 (1939). See UNITED STATES v. ALGOMA LUMBER CO., 305 U. S. 415 (1939).
UNITED STATES v. LA MOTTE, 67 F. 2d 788 (C. C. A. 10, 1933).
UNITED STATES v. LA PLANT, 200 Fed. 92 (D. C. S. D. 1911).
UNITED STATES v. LA ROQUE, 198 Fed. 645 (C. C. A. 8, 1912), aff'd sub nom. LA ROQUE v. UNITED STATES, 239 U. S. 62 (1915).
UNITED STATES v. LAW, 250 Fed. 218 (C. C. A. 8, 1918), s. c. UNITED STATES v. SMITH, 288 Fed. 356 (C. C. A. 8, 1923), rev'g 279 Fed. 136 (D. C. E. D. Okla. 1922).
UNITED STATES v. LEATHERS, 26 Fed. Cas. No. 15581 (D. C. Nev. 1879).
UNITED STATES v. LE BRIS, 121 U. S. 278 (1887).
UNITED STATES v. LEE, 108 F. 2d 936 (C. C. A. 10, 1939), aff'g 24 F. Supp. 814 (D. C. E. D. Okla. 1938).
UNITED STATES v. LENA, 261 Fed. 144 (C. C. A. 8, 1919).
UNITED STATES v. LESLIE, 167 Fed. 670 (C. C. S. D. 1909).
UNITED STATES v. LEWIS, 5 Ind. T. 1, 76 S. W. 299 (1903).
UNITED STATES v. LEWIS, 253 Fed. 469 (D. C. S. D. Cal. 1918).
UNITED STATES v. LEWIS COUNTY, IDAHO, 95 F. 2d 236 (C. C. A. 9, 1938), mod'g 16 F. Supp. 267 (D. C. Idaho, 1936), rehearing den. 95 F. 2d 238 (C. C. A. 9, 1938).
UNITED STATES v. LINDAHL, 221 Fed. 143 (D. C. Mont. 1915).
UNITED STATES v. LOGAN, 105 Fed. 240 (C. C. Ore. 1900).
UNITED STATES v. LOVING, 34 Fed. 715 (D. C. N. D. Tex. 1888).
UNITED STATES v. LUCERO, 1 N. M. 422 (1869).
UNITED STATES v. LUTHER, 260 Fed. 579 (D. C. E. D. Okla. 1919).
UNITED STATES v. LYNCH, 7 Alaska 568 (1 Div. 1927).
UNITED STATES v. McBRATNEY, 104 U. S. 621 (1881).
UNITED STATES v. McCLANE, 74 Fed. 153 (C. C. Ore. 1896).
UNITED STATES v. McDOUGALL'S ADM'R., 121 U. S. 89 (1887), s. c. 119 U. S. 477.
UNITED STATES v. McGOWAN, 62 F. 2d 955 (C. C. A. 9, 1933), aff'd per cur. 290 U. S. 592 (1933); s. c. 2 F. Supp. 426.
UNITED STATES v. McGOWAN, 302 U. S. 535 (1938), rev'g 89 F. 2d 201 (C. C. A. 9, 1937), aff'g UNITED STATES v. ONE CHEVROLET SEDAN, 16 F. Supp. 453 (D. C. Nev. 1936), s. c. 302 U. S. 666.
UNITED STATES v. McGUGIN, 28 F. 2d 76 (D. C. Kan. 1928).
UNITED STATES v. McINTIRE, 101 F. 2d 650 (C. C. A. 9, 1939), rev'g McINTIRE v. UNITED STATES, 22 F. Supp. 316 (D. C. Mont. 1937).
UNITED STATES v. McMURRAY, 181 Fed. 723 (C. C. E. D. Okla. 1910).
UNITED STATES v. MACKEY, 216 Fed. 126 (C. C. A. 8, 1914), s. c. 214 Fed. 137.
UNITED STATES v. MARES, 14 N. M. 1, 88 Pac. 1128 (1907).
UNITED STATES v. MARSHALL, 210 Fed. 595 (C. C. A. 8, 1914).
UNITED STATES v. MARTIN, 14 Fed. 817 (D. C. Ore. 1883), s. c. 17 Fed. 150.
UNITED STATES v. MARTIN, 45 F. 2d 836 (D. C. E. D. Okla. 1930).
UNITED STATES v. MARTINEZ, 195 U. S. 469 (1904).
UNITED STATES v. MASHUNKASHEY, 72 F. 2d 847 (C. C. A. 10, 1934), rehearing den. 73 F. 2d 487 (C. C. A. 10, 1934), cert. den. 294 U. S. 724 (1935).
UNITED STATES v. MATHEWSON, 32 F. 2d 745 (C. C. A. 8, 1929).
UNITED STATES v. MATLOCK, 26 Fed. Cas. No. 15744 (D. C. Ore. 1872).
UNITED STATES v. MID CONTINENT PETROLEUM CORP., 67 F. 2d 37 (C. C. A. 10, 1933), cert. den. 290 U. S. 702 (1933).
UNITED STATES v. MILLE LAC BAND OF CHIPPEWA INDIANS, 229 U. S. 498 (1913).
UNITED STATES v. MILLER, 105 Fed. 944 (D. C. Nev. 1901).
UNITED STATES v. MINNESOTA, 270 U. S. 181 (1926), s. c. 271 U. S. 648.
UNITED STATES v. MINNESOTA, 95 F. 2d 468 (C. C. A. 8, 1938), aff'd sub nom. MINNESOTA v. UNITED STATES, 305 U. S. 382 (1939).
UNITED STATES v. MISSOURI-KANSAS-TEXAS R. CO., 66 F. 2d 919 (C. C. A. 10, 1933).
UNITED STATES v. MITCHELL, 109 U. S. 146 (1883).
UNITED STATES v. MONTE, 3 N. M. 173, 3 Pac. 45 (1884).
UNITED STATES v. MOORE, 161 Fed. 513 (C. C. A. 9, 1908), s. c. 154 Fed. 712.
UNITED STATES v. MOORE, 284 Fed. 86 (C. C. A. 8, 1922), rev'g 261 Fed. 523 (D. C. E. D. Okla. 1919).
UNITED STATES v. MORRISON, 203 Fed. 364 (C. C. Colo. 1901).
UNITED STATES v. MOTT, 37 F. 860 (C. C. A. 10, 1930), rev'g 33 F. 2d 340 (D. C. N. D. Okla. 1929), aff'd sub nom. MOTT v. UNITED STATES, 283 U. S. 747 (1931).
UNITED STATES v. MULLENDORE, 74 F. 2d 286 (C. C. A. 10, 1934), s. c. 69 F. 2d 1013.
UNITED STATES v. MULLIN, 71 Fed. 682 (D. C. Neb. 1895).
UNITED STATES v. MUMMERT, 15 F. 2d 926 (C. C. A. 8, 1926).

UNITED STATES v. MYERS, 206 Fed. 387 (C. C. A. 8, 1913).
UNITED STATES v. NAVARRE, 173 U. S. 77 (1899).
UNITED STATES v. NELSON, 29 Fed. 202 (D. C. Alaska 1886), aff'd sub nom. NELSON v. UNITED STATES, 30 Fed. 112 (C. C. Ore. 1887).
UNITED STATES v. NEW YORK INDIANS, 173 U. S. 464 (1899), s. c. 170 U. S. 1, 170 U. S. 614.
UNITED STATES v. NEZ PERCE COUNTY, 95 F. 2d 232 (C. C. A. 9, 1938), mod'g 16 F. Supp. 267 (D. C. Idaho 1936), rehearing den. 95 F. 2d 238 (C. C. A. 9, 1938).
UNITED STATES v. NEZ PERCE COUNTY, IDAHO, 267 Fed. 495 (D. C. D. Idaho 1916, 1917).
UNITED STATES v. NICE, 241 U. S. 591 (1916).
UNITED STATES v. NICHOLS-CHISHOLM LUMBER CO., 188 Fed. 383 (C. C. Minn. 1911). See UNITED STATES v. PARK LAND CO., 188 Fed. 383 (C. C. Minn. 1911).
UNITED STATES v. NOBLE, 237 U. S. 74 (1915), rev'g 197 Fed. 292 (C. C. A. 8, 1912), s. c. 181 Fed. 847.
UNITED STATES v. NORTHWESTERN EXPRESS CO., 164 U. S. 686 (1897).
UNITED STATES v. O'BRIEN, 170 Fed. 508 (C. C. Wash. 1903, 1904).
UNITED STATES v. ODENEAL, 10 Fed. 616 (C. C. Ore. 1882).
UNITED STATES v. O'GORMAN, 287 Fed. 135 (C. C. A. 8, 1923).
UNITED STATES v. OKLAHOMA, 261 U. S. 252 (1923), s. c. 262 U. S. 734.
UNITED STATES v. OLD SETTLERS, 148 U. S. 427 (1893). See OLD SETTLERS v. UNITED STATES, 148 U. S. 427 (1893).
UNITED STATES v. OMAHA TRIBE OF INDIANS, 253 U. S. 275 (1920).
UNITED STATES v. ONE AUTOMOBILE, 237 Fed. 891 (D. C. Mont. 1916).
UNITED STATES v. ONE BUICK AUTOMOBILE, 255 Fed. 793 (D. C. Colo. 1919).
UNITED STATES v. ONE BUICK ROADSTER AUTOMOBILE, 244 Fed. 961 (D. C. E. D. Okla. 1917).
UNITED STATES v. ONE CADILLAC EIGHT AUTOMOBILE, 255 Fed. 173 (D. C. M. D. Tenn. 1918).
UNITED STATES v. ONE CHEVROLET COUPE AUTOMOBILE, 58 F. 2d 235 (C. C. A. 9, 1932).
UNITED STATES v. ONE CHEVROLET FOUR-DOOR SEDAN AUTOMOBILE, 41 F. 2d 782 (D. C. N. D. Okla. 1930).
UNITED STATES v. ONE FORD FIVE PASSENGER AUTOMOBILE, 259 Fed. 645 (D. C. E. D. Okla. 1919).
UNITED STATES v. 196 BUFFALO ROBES, 1 Mont. 489 (1872).
UNITED STATES v. ONE SEVEN-PASSENGER PAIGE CAR, 259 Fed. 641 (D. C. E. D. Okla. 1919).
UNITED STATES v. OREGON CENTRAL MILITARY ROAD CO., 103 Fed. 549 (C. C. Ore. 1900), rev'd sub nom. UNITED STATES v. CALIF. & ORE. LD. CO., 192 U. S. 355 (1903).
UNITED STATES v. OSAGE COUNTY, 251 U. S. 128 (1919), rev'g 254 Fed. 570 (C. C. A. 8, 1918), s. c. 1 F. 2d 701, 244 U. S. 663, 267 U. S. 587.
UNITED STATES v. OSBORN, 2 Fed. 58 (D. C. Ore. 1880).
UNITED STATES v. PAINE LUMBER CO., 206 U. S. 467 (1907), aff'g 154 Fed. 263 (C. C. E. D. Wis. 1904).
UNITED STATES v. PARK LAND CO., 188 Fed. 383 (C. C. Minn. 1911).
UNITED STATES v. PARKHURST-DAVIS CO., 176 U. S. 317 (1900).
UNITED STATES v. PARKINS, 18 F. 2d 642 (D. C. Wyo. 1926).
UNITED STATES v. PARKINS, 18 F. 2d 643 (D. C. Wyo. 1926).
UNITED STATES v. PARTELLO, 48 Fed. 670 (C. C. Mont. 1891).
UNITED STATES v. PATRICK, 73 Fed. 800 (C. C. A. 8, 1896).
UNITED STATES v. PATTERSON, 91 Fed. 854 (C. C. S. D. Iowa 1899).
UNITED STATES v. PAYNE, 8 Fed. 883 (D. C. W. D. Ark. 1881).
UNITED STATES v. PAYNE, 22 Fed. 426 (D. C. Kan. 1884).
UNITED STATES v. PAYNE, 27 Fed. Cas. No. 16014 (C. C. Kan. 1877).
UNITED STATES v. PAYNE, 264 U. S. 446 (1924), aff'g 284 Fed. 827 (C. C. A. 9, 1922).
UNITED STATES v. PEARSON, 231 Fed. 270 (D. C. S. D. 1916).
UNITED STATES v. PELICAN, 232 U. S. 442 (1914).
UNITED STATES v. PHILLIPS, 56 F. 2d 447 (D. C. Neb. 1931).
UNITED STATES v. PICO, 5 Wall. 536 (1866).
UNITED STATES v. PIERSON, 145 Fed. 814 (C. C. A. 8, 1906).
UNITED STATES v. PINE RIVER LOGGING & IMPROVEMENT CO., 89 Fed. 907 (C. C. A. 8, 1898), s. c. 186 U. S. 279, 78 Fed. 319.
UNITED STATES v. PORTER, 22 F. 2d 365 (C. C. A. 9, 1927).
UNITED STATES v. PORTNEUF-MARSH VALLEY IRR. CO., 213 Fed. 601 (C. C. A. 9, 1914), aff'g 205 Fed. 416 (D. C. Idaho 1913).
UNITED STATES v. POWERS, 305 U. S. 527 (1939), aff'g 94 F. 2d 783 (C. C. A. 9, 1938), mod'g 16 F. Supp. 155 (D. C. Mont. 1936).
UNITED STATES v. PRIDGEON, 153 U. S. 48 (1894).
UNITED STATES v. PROVOE, 283 U. S. 753 (1931), rev'g 38 F. 2d 799 (C. C. A. 9, 1930), s. c. 282 U. S. 818.
UNITED STATES v. PUMPHREY, 11 App. D. C. 44 (1897).
UNITED STATES v. QUIVER, 241 U. S. 602 (1916).
UNITED STATES v. RAGSDALE, 27 Fed. Cas. No. 16113 (C. C. Ark. 1847).
UNITED STATES v. RAICHE, 31 F. 2d 624 (D. C. W. D. Wis. 1928).
UNITED STATES v. RALEY, 173 Fed. 159 (D. C. Ore. 1909).
UNITED STATES v. RAMSEY, 271 U. S. 467 (1926).
UNITED STATES v. RANSOM, 263 U. S. 691 (1924), aff'g per cur. 284 Fed. 108 (C. C. A. 8, 1922), aff'g 271 Fed. 747 (D. C. E. D. Okla. 1921).
UNITED STATES v. REA-READ MILL & ELEVATOR CO., 171 Fed. 501 (C. C. E. D. Okla. 1909).
UNITED STATES v. REESE, 27 Fed. Cas. No. 16137 (D. C. Mass. 1868).
UNITED STATES v. REILY, 290 U. S. 33 (1933), rev'g 62 F. 2d 621 (C. C. A. 10, 1932).
UNITED STATES v. REYNOLDS, 250 U. S. 104 (1919), rev'g 252 Fed. 65 (C. C. A. 8, 1918).
UNITED STATES v. RICHARDS, 27 F. 2d 284 (C. C. A. 8, 1928), rev'g sub nom. RICHARDS v. UNITED STATES, 21 F. 2d 94 (D. C. N. D. Okla. 1927), cert. den. 278 U. S. 630.
UNITED STATES v. RICKERT, 188 U. S. 432 (1903).
UNITED STATES v. RITCHIE, 17 How. 525 (1854).
UNITED STATES v. ROBERTS, 10 Fed. 540 (C. C. S. D. Ohio 1882).
UNITED STATES v. ROGERS, 4 How. 567 (1846).
UNITED STATES v. ROGERS, 23 Fed. 658 (D. C. W. D. Ark. 1885).
UNITED STATES v. ROLFSON, 38 F. 2d 806 (C. C. A. 9, 1930), rev'd sub nom. ROLFSON v. UNITED STATES, 283 U. S. 753 (1931), s. c. 282 U. S. 818.
UNITED STATES v. ROMAINE, 255 Fed. 253 (C. C. A. 9, 1919).
UNITED STATES v. ROSE, 20 F. Supp. 350 (D. C. W. D. N. C. 1937).
UNITED STATES v. ROWELL, 243 U. S. 464 (1917).
UNITED STATES v. RUNDELL, 181 Fed. 887 (C. C. E. D. Okla. 1910), aff'd sub nom. BOWLING ET AL. v. UNITED STATES, 191 Fed. 19 (C. C. A. 8, 1911), s. c. 233 U. S. 528.
UNITED STATES v. SA-COO-DA-COT, 27 Fed. Cas. No. 16212 (C. C. Neb. 1870).
UNITED STATES v. SANDERS, 27 Fed. Cas. No. 16220 (C. C. Ark. 1847).
UNITED STATES v. SANDOVAL, 231 U. S. 28 (1913), rev'g 198 Fed. 539 (D. C. N. M. 1912).
UNITED STATES v. SANDS, 94 F. 2d 156 (C. C. A. 10, 1938).
UNITED STATES v. SANDSTROM, 22 F. Supp. 190 (D. C. N. D. Okla. 1938).
UNITED STATES v. SANTISTEVAN, 1 N. M. 583 (1874).
UNITED STATES v. SAUNDERS, 96 Fed. 268 (C. C. Wash. 1899).
UNITED STATES v. SEMINOLE NATION, 299 U. S. 417 (1937).
UNITED STATES v. SENECA NATION OF NEW YORK INDIANS, 274 Fed. 946 (D. C. W. D. N. Y. 1921).
UNITED STATES v. SEUFERT BROS. CO., 252 Fed. 51 (C. C. A. 9, 1918, writ of error dism. 251 U. S. 566 (1920).
UNITED STATES v. SEVELOFF, 27 Fed. Cas. No. 16252 (D. C. Ore. 1872).

UNITED STATES v. 7,405.3 ACRES OF LAND IN MACON, CLAY AND SWAIN COUNTIES, 97 F. 2d 417 (C. C. A. 4, 1938).
UNITED STATES v. SHAW-MUX, 27 Fed. Cas. No. 16268 (D. C. Ore. 1873).
UNITED STATES v. SHERBURNE MERCANTILE CO., 68 F. 2d 155 (C. C. A. 9, 1933).
UNITED STATES v. SHOCK, 187 Fed. 862 (C. C. E. D. Okla. 1911).
UNITED STATES v. SHOCK, 187 Fed. 870 (C. C. E. D. Okla. 1911).
UNITED STATES v. SHOSHONE TRIBE, 304 U. S. 111 (1938), aff'g 85 C. Cls. 331 (1937), s. c. SHOSHONE TRIBE v. UNITED STATES, 299 U. S. 476 (1937).
UNITED STATES v. SINNOTT, 26 Fed. 84 (C. C. Ore. 1886).
UNITED STATES v. SINNOTT, 26 Fed. 89 (C. C. Ore. 1886).
UNITED STATES v. SISSETON AND WAHPETON BANDS OF SIOUX INDIANS, 208 U. S. 561 (1908).
UNITED STATES v. SITARANGOK, 4 Alaska 667 (2 Div. 1913).
UNITED STATES v. SMITH, 35 Fed. 490 (C. C. E. D. Mo. 1888).
UNITED STATES v. SMITH, 266 Fed. 740 (D. C. E. D. Okla. 1920).
UNITED STATES v. SMITH, 288 Fed. 356 (C. C. A. 8, 1923), rev'g 279 Fed. 136 (D. C. E. D. Okla. 1922), s. c. UNITED STATES v. LAW, 250 Fed. 218, (C. C. A. 8, 1918).
UNITED STATES v. SNOHOMISH RIVER BOOM CO., 246 Fed. 112 (C. C. A. 9, 1917), s. c. 234 Fed. 95.
UNITED STATES v. SOLDANA, 246 U. S. 530 (1918).
UNITED STATES v. SOULE, 30 Fed. 918 (C. C. Kan. 1887), rev'g UNITED STATES v. ROGERS, 23 Fed. 658 (D. C. Ark. 1885).
UNITED STATES v. SOUTHERN SURETY CO., 9 F. 2d 664 (D. C. E. D. Okla. 1925).
UNITED STATES v. SPAETH, 24 F. Supp. 465 (D. C. Minn. 1938).
UNITED STATES v. STAHL, 27 Fed. Cas. No. 16373 (C. C. Kan. 1868).
UNITED STATES v. STARR, 27 Fed. Cas. No. 16379 (C. C. Ark. 1846).
UNITED STATES v. STEARNS LUMBER CO., 245 U. S. 436 (1918).
UNITED STATES v. STEPHENS, 12 Fed. 52 (D. C. Ore. 1882).
UNITED STATES v. STEVENS, 31 F. 2d 520 (C. C. A. 7, 1929).
UNITED STATES v. STIGALL, 226 Fed. 190 (C. C. A. 8, 1915).
UNITED STATES v. STOCKING, 87 Fed. 857 (D. C. Mont. 1898).
UNITED STATES v. STOFELLO, 8 Ariz. 461, 76 Pac. 611 (1904).
UNITED STATES v. STONE, 2 Wall. 525 (1864).
UNITED STATES v. STOTTS, 49 F. 2d 619 (D. C. W. D. Wash. 1930).
UNITED STATES v. STOWE, 19 Fed. 807 (D. C. Minn. 1884).
UNITED STATES v. STUCKEY, 271 Fed. 747 (D. C. E. D. Okla. 1921). See UNITED STATES v. BOARD OF COMMISSIONERS OF McINTOSH COUNTY, 271 Fed. 747 (D. C. E. D. Okla. 1921).
UNITED STATES v. STURGEON, 27 Fed. Cas. No. 16413 (D. C. Nev. 1879).
UNITED STATES v. SUTTON, 215 U. S. 291 (1909), rev'g 165 Fed. 253 (D. C. E. D. Wash. 1908).
UNITED STATES v. SWAIN COUNTY, N. C., 46 F. 2d 99 (D. C. W. D. N. C. 1930), rev'd sub nom. UNITED STATES v. WRIGHT, et al., 53 F. 2d 300 (C. C. A. 8, 1931), cert. den. 285 U. S. 539.
UNITED STATES v. THE CORA, 1 Dak. 1, 46 N. W. 503 (1867).
UNITED STATES v. THE JAMES G. SWAN, 50 Fed. 108 (D. C. Wash. 1892). See SWAN, THE JAMES G., 50 Fed. 108 (D. C. Wash. 1892).
UNITED STATES v. TADISH, 211 Fed. 490 (D. C. Ariz. 1913).
UNITED STATES v. TA-WAN-GA-CA, 28 Fed. Cas. No. 16435 (D. C. Ark. 1836).
UNITED STATES v. TAYLOR, 3 Wash. Ter. 88, 13 Pac. 333 (1887).
UNITED STATES v. TERRELL, 28 Fed. Cas. No. 16452 (C. C. Ark. 1840).
UNITED STATES v. TERRELL, 28 Fed. Cas. No. 16453 (C. C. Ark. 1840).
UNITED STATES v. THOMAS, 47 Fed. 488 (C. C. W. D. Wis. 1891), questions answered 151 U. S. 577 (1894).
UNITED STATES v. THURSTON COUNTY, 143 Fed. 287 (C. C. A. 8, 1906), rev'g 140 Fed. 456 (C. C. Neb. 1905).
UNITED STATES v. TIGER, 19 F. 2d 35 (C. C. A. 8, 1927), aff'g TIGER v. SLINKER, 4 F. 2d 714 (D. C. E. D. Okla. 1925).
UNITED STATES v. TITLE INS. CO., 265 U. S. 472 (1924), aff'g 288 Fed. 821 (C. C. A. 9, 1923).
UNITED STATES v. TOM, 1 Ore. 26 (1853).
UNITED STATES v. TORREY CEDAR CO., 154 Fed. 263 (D. C. E. D. Wis. 1904). See UNITED STATES v. PAINE LUMBER CO., 206 U. S. 476 (1907).
UNITED STATES v. TWELVE BOTTLES OF WHISKEY, 201 Fed. 191 (D. C. Mont. 1912).
UNITED STATES v. TWENTY NINE GALLONS OF WHISKEY, 45 Fed. 847 (D. C. Mont. 1891).
UNITED STATES v. TWO GALLONS OF WHISKEY, 213 Fed. 986 (D. C. Mont. 1914).
UNITED STATES v. U. S. FIDELITY CO., 309 U. S. 506 (1940); rev'g 106 F. 2d 804 (C. C. A. 10, 1939).
UNITED STATES v. VAN WERT, 233 U. S. 223 (1914). See UNITED STATES v. BIRDSALL, 233 U. S. 223 (1914).
UNITED STATES v. VARELA. See UNITED STATES v. JOSEPH.
UNITED STATES v. WALKER RIVER IRRIGATION DISTRICT, 104 F. 2d 334 (C. C. A. 9, 1939), rev'g, 11 F. Supp. 158, 14 F. Supp. 10.
UNITED STATES v. WALKOWSKY, 38 Fed. 2d 805 (C. C. A. 9, 1930), rev'd sub nom. WALKOWSKY v. UNITED STATES, 283 U. S. 753 (1931), s. c. 282 U. S. 818.
UNITED STATES v. WALLER, 243 U. S. 452 (1917).
UNITED STATES v. WALTERS, 17 F. 2d 116 (D. C. Minn. 1926).
UNITED STATES v. WARD, 28 Fed. Cas. No. 16639 (C. C. Kan. 1863).
UNITED STATES v. WARD, 42 Fed. 320 (C. C. S. D. Cal. 1890).
UNITED STATES v. WARWICK, 51 Fed. 280 (D. C. Alaska 1892).
UNITED STATES v. WATASHE, 102 F. 2d 428 (C. C. A. 10, 1939), aff'g 21 F. Supp. 903 (D. C. W. D. Okla. 1938).
UNITED STATES v. WESTERN INV. CO., 226 Fed. 726 (C. C. A. 8, 1915).
UNITED STATES v. WHALEY, 37 Fed. 145 (C. C. S. D. Cal. 1883).
UNITED STATES v. WHITMIRE, 236 Fed. 474 (C. C. A. 8, 1916).
UNITED STATES v. WIGHTMAN, 230 Fed. 277 (D. C. Ariz. 1916).
UNITED STATES v. WILDCAT, 244 U. S. 111 (1917).
UNITED STATES v. WILLIAMS, 2 Fed. 61 (C. C. Ore. 1880).
UNITED STATES v. WINANS, 198 U. S. 371 (1905), rev'g 73 Fed. 72 (C. C. Wash. 1896).
UNITED STATES v. WINSLOW, 28 Fed. Cas. No. 16742 (D. C. Ore. 1875).
UNITED STATES v. WIRT, 28 Fed. Cas. No. 16745 (D. C. Ore. 1874).
UNITED STATES v. WOODS, 223 Fed. 316, (C. C. A. 8, 1915).
UNITED STATES v. WOOTEN, 40 F. 2d 882 (C. C. A. 10, 1930).
UNITED STATES v. WRIGHT, 197 Fed. 297 (C. C. A. 8, 1912).
UNITED STATES v. WRIGHT, 229 U. S. 226 (1913).
UNITED STATES v. WRIGHT, 53 F. 2d 300 (C. C. A. 4, 1931), rev'g UNITED STATES v. SWAIN COUNTY, 46 F. 2d 99 (D. C. W. D. N. C. 1930), cert. den. 285 U. S. 539.
UNITED STATES v. WURTZBURGER, 276 Fed. 753 (D. C. Ore. 1921).
UNITED STATES v. YAKIMA COUNTY, 274 Fed. 115 (D. C. E. D. Wash. 1921).
UNITED STATES v. YELLOW SUN, 28 Fed. Cas. No. 16780 (D. C. Neb. 1870). See UNITED STATES v. SA-COO-DA-COT, 27 Fed. Cas. No. 16212 (C. C. Neb. 1870).
UNITED STATES v. YOUNG, 44 Fed. 168 (C. C. E. D. N. Y. 1890).
UNITED STATES v. ZUMWALT, 186 Fed. 596 (D. C. Idaho 1910).
UNITED STATES ex rel. BESAW v. WORK, 6 F. 2d 694 (App. D. C. 1925).
UNITED STATES ex rel. BROWN v. LANE, 232 U. S. 598 (1914).
UNITED STATES ex rel. CHARLEY v. BAKERS BAY FISH CO., 2 F. Supp. 426 (D. C. W. D. Wash. 1931). See UNITED STATES ex rel. CHARLEY v. McGOWAN, 62 F. 2d 955 (C. C. A. 9, 1933).

UNITED STATES ex rel. CHARLEY v. McGOWAN, 290 U. S. 592 (1933), aff'g 2 F. Supp. 426 (D. C. W. D. Wash. 1931), aff'g 62 F. 2d 955 (C. C. A. 9, 1933).
UNITED STATES ex rel. COBURN v. WORK, 18 F. 2d 822 (App. D. C. 1927).
UNITED STATES ex rel. DETLING v. WORK, 18 F. 2d 822 (App. D. C. 1927).
UNITED STATES ex rel. DIABO v. McCANDLESS, 18 F. 2d 282 (D. C. E. D. Penn. 1927). See McCANDLESS v. UNITED STATES ex rel. DIABO, 25 F. 2d 71 (C. C. A. 3, 1938).
UNITED STATES ex rel. GORDON v. CROOK, 179 Fed. 391 (D. C. Neb. 1875).
UNITED STATES ex rel. JOHNSON v. PAYNE, 253 U. S. 209 (1920).
UNITED STATES ex rel. KADRIE v. WEST, 30 F. 2d 989 (App. D. C. 1929), rev'd sub nom. WILBUR v. UNITED STATES ex rel. KADRIE, 281 U. S. 206 (1930).
UNITED STATES ex rel. KENNEDY v. TYLER, 269 U. S. 13 (1925), aff'g UNITED STATES ex rel. PIERCE v. WALDOW, 294 Fed. 111 (D. C. W. D. N. Y. 1923).
UNITED STATES ex rel. KNIGHT v. LANE, 228 U. S. 6 (1913). See KNIGHT v. LANE, 228 U. S. 6 (1913).
UNITED STATES ex rel. LOWE v. FISHER, 223 U. S. 95 (1912). See LOWE v. FISHER, 223 U. S. 95 (1912).
UNITED STATES ex rel. LYNN v. HAMILTON, 233 Fed. 685 (D. C. W. D. N. Y. 1915).
UNITED STATES ex rel. McALESTER EDWARDS COAL CO. v. FALL, 277 Fed. 573 (App. D. C. 1922), aff'd sub nom. WORK v. UNITED STATES ex rel. McALESTER EDWARDS CO., 262 U. S. 200 (1923), s. c. 43 Sup. Ct. 433.
UNITED STATES ex rel. McINTOSH v. CRAWFORD, 47 Fed. 561 (C. C. W. D. Ark. 1891).
UNITED STATES ex rel. RAY v. HIBNER, 27 F. 2d 909 (D. C. Idaho 1928).
UNITED STATES ex rel. REYNOLDS v. LANE, 45 App. D. C. 50 (1916).
UNITED STATES ex rel. SCOTT v. BURDICK, 1 Dak. 142, 46 N. W. 571 (1875).
UNITED STATES ex rel. SEARCH v. CHOCTAW, O. & G. R. R. CO., 3 Okla. 404, 41 Pac. 729 (1895).
UNITED STATES ex rel. STANDING BEAR v. CROOK, 25 Fed. Cas. No. 14891 (C. C. Neb. 1879).
UNITED STATES ex rel. SYKES v. LANE, 258 Fed. 520 (App. D. C. 1919), app. dism. 254 U. S. 618, s. c. 40 Sup. Ct. 484.
UNITED STATES ex rel. WARREN v. ICKES, 73 F. 2d 844 (App. D. C. 1934), s. c. 1 S. C. D. C. (N. S.) 1.
UNITED STATES ex rel. WEST v. HITCHCOCK, 205 U. S. 80 (1907).
UNITED STATES ex rel. YOUNG v. IMODA, 4 Mont. 38, 1 Pac. 721 (1881).
UNITED STATES ex rel. ZANE v. ZANE, 4 Ind. T. 185, 69 S. W. 842 (1902).
UNITED STATES EXPRESS CO. v. FRIEDMAN, 191 Fed. 673 (C. C. A. 8, 1911), rev'g 180 Fed. 1006 (D. C. W. D. Ark. 1910).
UNITED STATES FIDELITY & GUARANTY CO. v. SHIRK, 7 Ind. T. 83, 103 S. W. 773 (1907), s. c. 20 Okla. 576, 95 Pac. 218 (1908).
UNITED STATES FIDELITY AND GUARANTY CO. OF BALTIMORE, MD., v. UNITED STATES, 214 U. S. 507 (1909), aff'g 150 Fed. 550 (C. C. A. 9, 1907).
UNKLE v. WILLS, 281 Fed. 29 (C. C. A. 8, 1922).
UTAH AND NORTHERN RAILWAY v. FISHER, 116 U. S. 28 (1885), aff'g 3 Pac. 3 (1884).
UTE INDIANS v. UNITED STATES, 45 C. Cls. 440 (1910), s. c. 46 C. Cls. 225.
UTE INDIANS v. UNITED STATES, 46 C. Cls. 225 (1911).
UTILITIES PRODUCTION CORP. v. CARTER OIL CO., 2 F. Supp. 81 (D. C. N. D. Okla. 1933), aff'd 72 F. 2d 655 (C. C. A. 10, 1934), s. c. 100 F. 2d 1006.
VALENCIA v. UNITED STATES, 31 C. Cls. 388 (1896).
VALK v. UNITED STATES, 27 C. Cls. 241 (1893).
VALK v. UNITED STATES, 168 U. S. 703 (1897), aff'g 33 C. Cls. 501 (1897), 29 C. Cls. 62 (1894).
VALLEJOS, ADM'R v. UNITED STATES, 35 C. Cls. 489 (1900).
VERNON v. AMOS, 255 U. S. 373 (1921). See WINTON v. AMOS, 255 U. S. 373 (1921).
VEZINA v. UNITED STATES, 245 Fed. 411 (C. C. A. 8, 1917).
VINCENT v. UNITED STATES, 39 C. Cls. 456 (1904).
VINSON v. GRAHAM, 44 F. 2d 772 (C. C. A. 10, 1930), cert. den. 283 U. S. 819.
VOVES v. UNITED STATES, 249 Fed. 191 (C. C. A. 7, 1918).
W. O. WHITNEY LUMBER AND GRAIN CO. v. CRABTREE, 166 Fed. 738 (C. C. A. 8, 1908).
WADE v. FISHER, 39 App. D. C. 245 (1912).
WADSWORTH v. BOYSEN, 148 Fed. 771 (C. C. A. 8, 1906).
WAGONER v. EVANS, 170 U. S. 588 (1898).
WALDRON v. UNITED STATES, 143 Fed. 413 (C. C. S. D. 1905).
WALKER v. HENSHAW, 16 Wall. 436 (1872).
WALKER v. M'LOUD, 204 U. S. 302 (1907), aff'g 138 Fed. 394 (C. C. A. 8, 1905).
WALKER TRADING CO. v. GRADY TRADING CO., 1 Ind. T. 191, 39 S. W. 354 (1897), app. dism. 81 Fed. 1003.
WALKOWSKY v. UNITED STATES, 283 U. S. 753 (1931). See HALBERT v. UNITED STATES, 283 U. S. 753 (1931), rev'g 38 F. 2d 805 (C. C. A. 9, 1930).
WALLACE v. ADAMS, 204 U. S. 415 (1907), aff'g 143 Fed. 716 (C. C. A. 8, 1906), s. c. 6 Ind. T. 32 (1905).
WARD v. LOVE COUNTY, 253 U. S. 17 (1920), s. c. 248 U. S. 556.
WARD v. RACE HORSE, 163 U. S. 504 (1896), rev'g IN RE RACE HORSE, 70 Fed. 598 (C. C. Wyo. 1895).
WARREN v. JOY, 17 Wall. 253 (1872).
WARREN v. UNITED STATES, 250 Fed. 89 (C. C. A. 8, 1918).
WASHBURN v. PARKER, 7 F. Supp. 120 (D. C. W. D. N. Y. 1934).
WASHINGTON v. MILLER, 235 U. S. 422 (1914).
WASSOM v. WILLISTON, 3 Ind. T. 365, 58 S. W. 574 (1900).
WATERS v. CAMPBELL, 29 Fed. Cas. No. 17264 (C. C. Ore. 1876), s. c. 29 Fed. Cas. No. 17265 (C. C. Ore. 1877).
WATKINS v. UNITED STATES, 3 Ind. T. 281, 54 S. W. 819, (1900), s. c. 41 S. W. 1044.
WATSON v. UNITED STATES, 263 Fed. 700 (C. C. A. 8, 1920).
WAU-PE-MAN-QUA v. ALDRICH, 28 Fed. 489 (C. C. Ind. 1886).
WEBSTER v. FALL, 266 U. S. 507 (1925).
WEBSTER v. REID, 11 How. 437 (1850).
WEEKS v. UNITED STATES, 2 Ind. T. 162, 48 S. W. 1036 (1899).
WELCH v. FIRST TRUST AND SAVINGS BANK, 15 F. 2d 184 (C. C. A. 8, 1926).
WELCH, ADM'R v. UNITED STATES, 32 C. Cls. 106 (1897).
WELLSVILLE OIL CO. v. MILLER, 243 U. S. 6 (1917).
WELTY v. REED, 231 Fed. 930 (C. C. A. 8, 1916), aff'g on rehearing REED v. WELTY, 197 Fed. 419 (D. C. E. D. Okla. 1912) and rev'g 219 Fed. 864 (C. C. A. 8, 1915).
WELTY v. UNITED STATES, 14 Okla. 7, 76 Pac. 21 (1904).
WESTERN CHEROKEES v. UNITED STATES, 27 C. Cls. 1 (1891), mod. 148 U. S. 427.
WESTERN CHEROKEES v. UNITED STATES, 82 C. Cls. 566 (1936).
WESTLING v. UNITED STATES, 60 F. 2d 398 (C. C. A. 8, 1932), app. dism. 288 U. S. 590.
WESTMORLAND v. UNITED STATES, 135 U. S. 545 (1895).
WESTON v. UNITED STATES, 29 C. Cls. 420 (1894).
WHEELER v. PETITE, 153 Fed. 471 (C. C. Ore. 1907).
WHITCHURCH v. CRAWFORD, 92 F. 2d 249 (C. C. A. 10, 1937) aff'g WHITCHURCH v. BURGE, 17 F. Supp. 234 (D. C. Okla. 1936).
WHITE v. BROWN, 1 Ind. T. 98, 38 S. W. 335 (1896).
WHITEBIRD v. EAGLE-PICHER LEAD CO., 40 F. 2d 479 (C. C. A. 10, 1930), aff'g 28 F. 2d 200 (D. C. N. D. Okla. 1928), cert. den. 282 U. S. 844.
WHITE RIVER UTES v. UNITED STATES, 43 C. Cls. 260 (1908).
WHITNEY v. DICK, 202 U. S. 132 (1906), rev'g in part Ex parte DICK, 141 Fed. 5 (C. C. A. 9, 1905).
WICHITA AND AFFILIATED BANDS v. CHOCTAW NATION, 179 U. S. 494 (1900). See UNITED STATES v. CHOCTAW etc. NATIONS, 179 U. S. 494 (1900).
WIGGAN v. CONOLLY, 163 U. S. 56 (1896).
WILBUR v. UNITED STATES ex rel. KADRIE, 281 U. S. 206 (1930). See UNITED STATES ex rel. KADRIE v. WEST, 30 F. 2d 989 (App. D. C. 1929).
WILCOXEN v. HYBARGER, 1 Ind. T. 138, 38 S. W. 669 (1897).
WILDER v. UNITED STATES, 16 C. Cls. 528 (1880).
WILHITE v. SKELTON, 149 Fed. 67 (C. C. A. 8, 1906), rev'g 5 Ind. T. 621, 82 S. W. 392 (1904).
WILLIAMS v. CITY OF CHICAGO, 242 U. S. 434 (1917).
WILLIAMS v. CLINTON, 83 F. 2d 143 (C. C. A. 10, 1936), s. c. 11 F. Supp. 456.
WILLIAMS v. FIRST NATIONAL BANK, 216 U. S. 582 (1910).
WILLIAMS v. JOHNSON, 239 U. S. 414 (1915).
WILLIAMS v. STEINMETZ, 16 Okla. 104, 82 Pac. 986 (1905).

WILLIAMS v. UNITED STATES, 4 Ind. T. 204, 69 S. W. 849 (1902).
WILLIAMS v. WHITE, 218 Fed. 797 (C. C. A. 8, 1914).
WILLIAMS v. WORKS, 4 Ind. T. 587, 76 S. W. 246 (1903).
WILLIS v. UNITED STATES, 6 Ind. T. 424, 98 S. W. 147 (1906).
WILLMOTT v. UNITED STATES, 27 F. 2d 277 (C. C. A. 8, 1928).
WILSON v. OWENS, 86 Fed. 571 (C. C. A. 8, 1898), aff'g 1 Ind. T. 163, 38 S. W. 976.
WILSON v. UNITED STATES, 260 Fed. 840 (C. C. A. 8, 1919).
WILSON v. UNITED STATES, 38 C. Cls. 6 (1902).
WILSON v. WALL, 6 Wall. 83 (1867).
WINTERS v. UNITED STATES, 207 U. S. 564 (1908), aff'g 143 Fed. 740 (C. C. A. 9, 1906).
WINTON v. AMOS, 255 U. S. 373 (1921). See HOWE v. AMOS, 255 U. S. 373 (1921).
WISCONSIN v. HITCHCOCK, 201 U. S. 202 (1906).
WISCONSIN v. LANE, 245 U. S. 427 (1918).
WOODBURY v. UNITED STATES, 170 Fed. 302 (C. C. A. 8, 1909).
WOODS v. UNITED STATES, 223 Fed. 316 (C. C. A. 8, 1915). See UNITED STATES v. WOODS, 223 Fed. 316 (C. C. A. 8, 1915).
WOODWARD v. DE GRAFFENRIED, 238 U. S. 284 (1915).
WOOLVERTON, ADM'R v. UNITED STATES, 29 C. Cls. 107 (1894).
WORCESTER v. GEORGIA, 6 Pet. 515 (1832).
WORK v. MUMERT, 29 F. 2d 393 (C. C. A. 8, 1928).
WORK v. UNITED STATES ex rel. GOUIN, 18 F. 2d 820 (App. D. C. 1927).
WORK v. UNITED STATES ex rel. LYNN, 266 U. S. 161 (1924), rev'g 285 Fed. 889 (App. D. C. 1922).
WORK v., UNITED STATES ex rel. MOSIER, 261 U. S. 352 (1923), rev'g PAYNE v. UNITED STATES ex rel. MOSIER, 269 Fed. 871 (App. D. C. 1921).
WORTHEN LUMBER MILLS v. ALASKA JUNEAU G. MIN. CO., 229 Fed. 966 (C. C. A. 9, 1916).
WRIGHT v. UNITED STATES, 227 Fed. 885 (C. C. A. 8, 1915).
WRIGHT AND WADE v. UNITED STATES, 158 U. S. 232 (1895).
WYNN, ADM'R v. UNITED STATES, 29 C. Cls. 15 (1894).
YAKIMA JOE v. TO-IS-LAP, 191 Fed. 516 (C. C. Ore. 1910).
YA-KOOT-SA v. UNITED STATES, 262 Fed. 398 (C. C. A. 9, 1920).
YANKTON SIOUX TRIBE v. UNITED STATES, 272 U. S. 351 (1926), rev'g 61 C. Cls. 40 (1925), s. c. 270 U. S. 637, 277 U. S. 607.
YERKE v. UNITED STATES, 173 U. S. 439 (1899).
YOHYOWAN v. LUCE, 291 Fed. 425 (D. C. E. D. Wash. 1923).
YOUNG v. UNITED STATES, 176 Fed. 612 (C. C. W. D. Okla. 1910).
Y-TA-TAH-WAH v. REBOCK, 105 Fed. 257 (C. C. N. D. Iowa 1900).
ZEVELY v. WEIMER, 5 Ind. T. 646; 82 S. W. 941 (1904), aff'd 138 Fed. 1006.
ZIA, PUEBLO OF v. UNITED STATES, 168 U. S. 198 (1897).
ZUFALL v. UNITED STATES, 1 Ind. T. 638, 43 S. W. 760 (1898).

TABLE OF INTERIOR DEPARTMENT RULINGS

3 L. D. 425, Feb. 27, 1885, Malheur Indian Reservation;
580, June 4, 1885, Indian Homesteads.

5 L. D. 138, Sept. 8, 1886, Railroad Grant—Indian Title;
520, Mar. 29, 1887, Allotments;
541, Apr. 4, 1887, Mille Lac Reservation.

6 L. D. 43, July 22, 1887, Allotments—Old Columbia Reservation;
159, Sept. 28, 1887, Seneca Indian Lands;
175, Oct. 4, 1887, Osage Trust Lands—Military Reservation.

8 L. D. 647, June 22, 1889, Allotments.

9 L. D. 392, Sept. 23, 1889, Lac Du Flambeau Indians.

10 L. D. 606, May 26, 1890, Conveyance—Secretary's Approval.

11 L. D. 103, June 11, 1890, Allotments.

12 L. D. 168, June 25, 1890, Allotments;
181, July 12, 1890, Allotment Rights;
162, Nov. 29, 1890, Allotment—Relinquishment;
205, Dec. 27, 1890, Allotment—Reservation;
52, Jan. 9, 1891, Mille Lac Indian Lands;
292, Mar. 5, 1891, Allotment.

13 L. D. 511, July 11, 1891, Conveyance—Departmental Approval;
307, July 22, 1891, Sioux Allotment—Abandonment;
120, Aug. 4, 1891, Alaska—Indian Occupancy;
185, Aug. 21, 1891, Allotment;
310, Aug. 28, 1891, Allotment—Oklahoma Indian Lands;
314, Sept. 3, 1891, Pottawatomie Allotment;
318, Sept. 3, 1891, Pottawatomie Allotment—Selection;
316, Sept. 9, 1891, Allotment—Absentee Shawnees;
683, Dec. 14, 1891, Children of Indian Woman.

14 L. D. 156, Feb. 8, 1892, Allotment—Riparian Rights.

15 L. D. 104, July 28, 1892, Patent—Allotment;
287, Sept. 9, 1892, Allotments—Minors.

16 L. D. 15, Jan. 6, 1893, Occupancy—Settlement Right—Allotment;
427, Apr. 3, 1893, Allotment;
431, May 10, 1893, Cherokee Allotments.

17 L. D. 142, Aug. 2, 1893, Allotment—Patent;
457, Aug. 18, 1893, Sioux Indian Lands—Allotment.

18 L. D. 188, Feb. 14, 1894, Occupation by Religious Society;
209, Mar. 13, 1894, Occupation by Religious Society;
497, Apr. 10, 1894, Lease of Allotted Lands.

19 L. D. 24, June 25, 1894, Eminent Domain;
326, June 30, 1894, Pueblo Indian Lands—Jurisdiction;
329, July 10, 1894, Allotment—Tribal Rights;
311, Oct. 20, 1894, Citizenship—Membership in Indian Tribe;
518, Nov. 19, 1894, Swamp Grant—Occupancy Right.

20 L. D. 19, Jan. 12, 1895, Allotment—Relinquishment;
46, Jan. 21, 1895, Allotment Rights;
157, Jan. 25, 1895, Puyallup Allotments—Descent;
167, Mar. 2, 1895, Allotment—Tribal Membership;
462, May 19, 1895, Occupancy for Mission Purposes;
562, June 17, 1895, Sioux Indian Lands—Allotment.

22 L. D. 37, Jan. 22, 1896, Appraisements—Loss of Improvements;
709, June 15, 1896, Allotments.

24 L. D. 214, Feb. 15, 1897, Allotment—Trust Patent—Cancelation;
264, Feb. 15, 1897, Allotment—Contest;
311, Mar. 30, 1897, Allotment—Citizenship;
323, Apr. 19, 1897, Allotment Rights—Adverse Claims;
330, Apr. 19, 1897, Allotment;
413, May 6, 1897, Contest—Allotment;
511, June 8, 1897, Allotment—Alienation.

25 L. D. 17, July 12, 1897, Stockbridge and Munsee Swamp Grant;
252, Sept. 9, 1897, Approval of Deed;
297, Oct 5, 1897, Delaware Indians in Cherokee Nation;
364, Nov. 11, 1897, Sisseton and Wahpeton Indians—Leases;
408, Nov. 17, 1897, Uintah Lands—Lease.

26 L. D. 25, Jan. 13, 1898, Approval of Conveyance;
44, Jan. 17, 1898, Red Cliff Reservation—Lease;
71, Jan. 22, 1898, Allotment—Tribal Rights;
104, Jan. 29, 1898, Alaska—Possessory Right—Reservation;
117, Jan. 31, 1898, Swamp Land Certification—Jurisdiction.

27 L. D. 305, Aug. 5, 1898, Relinquishment—Application—Approximation;
312, Aug. 12, 1898, Allotment—Estate by Curtesy;
399, Sept. 14, 1898, Allotment—Law of Descent;
603, Sept. 26, 1898, Allotment—Relinquishment.

28 L. D. 37, Jan. 23, 1899, Allotment—Protest;
71, Jan. 30, 1899, Allotment—Law of Descent;
310, Apr. 19, 1899, Approval of Deed—Probate of Will;
564, June 27, 1899, Allotments.

29 L. D. 132, Aug. 25, 1899, Ceded Chippewa Allotments;
239, Oct. 18, 1899, Peoria and Miami Allotments—Conveyance;
251, Oct. 29, 1899, Mistake in Allotment—Occupancy;
331, Nov. 29, 1899, Indian Lands—Religious Society;
408, Jan. 18, 1900, Chippewa Reservation—Allotment;
628, Mar. 28, 1900, Puyallup Allotments;
680, Apr. 19, 1900, Allotment—Relinquishment.

30 L. D. 258, Sept. 25, 1900, Allotment—Trust Patent—Cancellation;
532, Mar. 13, 1901, Allotment—Selection.

31 L. D. 417, June 28, 1902, Homesteads—Allotment;
439, Nov. 15, 1902, Allotments—Ejection of Intruders.

32 L. D. 17, Feb. 21, 1903, Allotments;
568, Apr. 25, 1904, Reservation—Allotment—Patent;
664, May 26, 1904, Swamp Lands—Klamath Reservation.

33 L. D. 205, Aug. 30, 1904, Klamath River Reservation—Allotment;
454, Mar. 7, 1905, School Land—Indian Occupant.

34 L. D. 252, Nov. 7, 1905, Allotment—Married Woman;
419, Jan. 25, 1906, Townsites in Osage Reservation—Sale of Liquors;
702, June 21, 1906, Allotment—Homestead Entry;
80, July 10, 1906, Homestead Entry—Trust Patent.

35 L. D. 56, July 23, 1906, Crow Lands—Improvements—Preference Right;
143, Sept. 7, 1906, Allotment—Residence;
145, Sept. 7, 1906, Allotment;
220, Oct. 6, 1906, Allotment—Colville Reservation;
549, May 3, 1907, Allotment—Tribal Membership;
643, June 29, 1907, Allotment—Condemnation—Patent.

38 L. D. 422, Jan. 4, 1910, Deceased Allottee—Patent to Heirs;
427, Feb. 5, 1910, Deceased Allottee—Patent to Heirs;
559, Feb. 16, 1910, Allotments—Trust Patents—Beginning of Period;
553, Apr. 12, 1910, Allotments—Reinstatement;
556, Apr. 13, 1910, Trust Patents—Authority to Correct;
558, Apr. 13, 1910, Trust Patent—Surrender and Issuance; Period.

39 L. D. 44, June 24, 1910, Railroad Grant—Forfeiture.

40 L. D. 4, Apr. 7, 1911, Sioux Allotment—Rights of Heirs;
9, Apr. 7, 1911, Sioux Allotment—Rights of Heirs;
120, May 3, 1911, Heirs—Partition—Patent;
211, May 3, 1911, Sale of Quapaw Homesteads;
212, May 23, 1911, Heirs of Moses Agreement Allottees—Sale;
148, June 24, 1911, Allotment—Minor Child;
179, July 7, 1911, Allotments—Sales—Minor Allottees and Heirs.

41 L. D. 626, Mar. 8, 1913, Allotment—Minor Children.

42 L. D. 102, June 21, 1913, Santee Sioux Allotment—Homestead Right;
489, Sept. 20, 1913, Allotment;
493, Sept. 26, 1913, Indian Trust Estates—Heirs;
446, Oct. 1, 1913, Allotment—Death of Allottee;
582, Dec. 24, 1913, Sioux Allotment—Rights of Heirs.

43 L. D. 26, Jan. 2, 1914, Taxation of Lands Purchased with Trust Funds;
84, Jan. 29, 1914, Allotment—Trust Patent;
101, Feb. 7, 1914, Trust Patent—Surrender and Reissuance;

125, Feb. 19, 1914, Indian Woman Married to White Man—Allotment;
149, Feb. 19, 1914, Allotments Limited to Tribal Members;
504, Dec. 16, 1914, Allotment—Settlement.
44 L. D. 441, June 29, 1915, Alaska Tide Lands—Riparian Rights;
188, July 14, 1915, Tribal Enrollment—Right to Allotment;
391, Oct. 26, 1915, Additional Allotment;
505, Dec. 27, 1915, Allotment Exchanges—Ceded Lands;
520, Jan. 15, 1916, Allotments on Reservations and Public Domain;
524, Jan. 15, 1916, Turtle Mountain Indians—Public Domain;
531, Jan. 29, 1916, Chippewa Indians—Membership Roll.
45 L. D. 563, Nov. 24, 1916, Colville Allotments—Right-of-Way—Irrigation.
Op. Sol., D. 40462, Oct. 31, 1917, Five Civilized Tribes—Eminent Domain.
Memo. Sol., Dec. 11, 1918, Five Civilized Tribes—Coal Lessees.
Letter to W. P. Havenor, Pocatello, Idaho, from the A. G., Jan. 22, 1920, Ft. Hall—Taxation of Patented Land.
Letter to Col. J. G. Scrugham from Sp. Asst. to the A. G., Apr. 1, 1921, Water Right—Moapa River Reservation.
Op. Sol., M. 3403, Apr. 4, 1921, Fee Title—Expiration Trust Period;
48 L. D. 70, Apr. 16, 1921, Allotments to Indians and Eskimos—Alaska.
Op. Sol., M. 5379, July 14, 1921, Moapa River Reservation—Water Rights.
Op. Sol., M. 4018, July 29, 1921, Right to Citizenship.
48 L. D. 455, Sept. 29, 1921, Fort Hall Lands.
Op. Sol., M. 6083, Oct. 29, 1921, Chippewa Tribe—Wills by Allottees;
M. 6376, Nov. 15, 1921, Flathead—Penalty against Landowners;
M. 5805, Nov. 22, 1921, Crow—Additional Allotments—Disposition;
M. 6383, Nov. 23, 1921, Osage—Payments to Minors.
48 L. D. 362, Dec. 13, 1921, Occupancy—Preference Right—Withdrawal.
Op. Sol., M. 6366, Dec. 27, 1921, Crow—Mineral—Timber—School Land Grants;
D. 42071, Dec. 29, 1921, Stockbridge—Munsee—Back Annuity;
M. 4017, Jan. 4, 1922., Osage—Payments to Minors.
48 L. D. 567, Jan. 31, 1922, Allotment—Coal Lands—Surface Rights;
435, Feb. 8, 1922, Allotment—Alaska—Withdrawal.
Op. Sol., M. 7002, Mar. 10, 1922, Kiowa, Comanche—Patented Allotments;
M. 6882, Mar. 29, 1922, Cancellation of Fee—Deceased Allottee.
48 L. D. 609, Mar. 29, 1922, Indian and Public Lands—Patent—Heirs.
Op. Sol., M. 7316, Apr. 5, 1922, Choctaw and Chickasaw—Coal Lands;
M. 5379, M. 5702, Apr. 27, 1922, Trust Allotment—Expiration;
M. 7193, Apr. 29, 1922, Winnebago—Tribal Funds;
M. 7599, June 9, 1922, Ft. Belknap—Changes in Allotment Roll.
49 L. D. 139, June 9, 1922, Reservation—Mineral Lands—Oil and Gas;
420, July 10, 1922, Mining Claims Within Reservations.
Op. Sol., M. 7996, Aug. 2, 1922, Jurisdiction of State Probate Courts;
M. 8370, Aug. 15, 1922, Oil and Gas Royalties—Assignment.
Letter of Comm'r to Sen. Selden P. Spencer, Sept. 5, 1922, Water Rights;
D. 46929, Sept. 30, 1922, Osage—Restricted Property—Rights;
M. 8860, Nov. 1, 1922, Osage County—Liquor Sales.
49 L. D. 348, Nov. 13, 1922, Taxability and Alienability—Allotted Lands;
354, Nov. 16, 1922, Fort Berthold Coal Lands.
Op. Sol., M. 8971, Nov. 29, 1922, Disbursement of Tribal Funds;
M. 9094, Dec. 2, 1922, Indian Money—Surety Bonds.
49 L. D. 370, Dec. 15, 1922, Wind River Reservation—Repayment—Irr. Costs;
376, Dec. 28, 1922, School Lands Within Crow Reservation;
396, Jan. 2, 1923, Condemnation of Lands Allotted in Severalty;
414, Jan. 24, 1923, Status of Property Purchased with Trust Funds.
Op. Sol., M. 5386, June 19, 1923, Ft. Hall—Lands for Reservoir;
M. 11094, Nov. 5, 1923, Interior Employees—Land Ownership;
M. 11291, Nov. 28, 1923, Indian Custom Marriage;
M. 11108, Dec. 4, 1923, Quapaw—Mining Lease;
M. 10526, Dec. 13, 1923, Creek—Enrollment—Allotment;
M. 11410, Jan. 28, 1924, Flathead—Power Site on Allotted Land;
A. 2592, Feb. 12, 1924, Mineral Leasing Act.
50 L. D. 315, Mar. 12, 1924, Status of Alaskan Natives—Tide Lands.
Op. Sol., M. 11665, Apr. 19, 1924, Chippewa—Enrollment;
M. 7316, May 28, 1924, Choctaw & Chickasaw—Coal Royalties;
M. 11879, May 31, 1924, Distribution of Tribal Funds—Chippewa;
M. 12498, June 6, 1924, Exchange of Allotted Land—Flathead.
50 L. D. 551, June 16, 1924, Intermarriage—Enrollment of Children Born.
Op. Sol., M. 11380, June 17, 1924, Chippewa—Enrollment;
M. 12509, Aug. 27, 1924, Restricted Fee and Trust Patents;
M. 12746, Oct. 8, 1924, Quapaw—Federal Income Tax;
M. 13344, Oct. 9, 1924, Flathead—Highway Right-of-Way;
M. 12874, Oct. 27, 1924, Chippewa—Back Annuities;
M. 13270, Nov. 6, 1924, Chippewa—Back Annuity Payments;
M. 13807, Nov. 8, 1924, Oil Royalties from Allotted Lands;
M. 13861, Nov. 11, 1924, Five Civilized Tribes—Oil Royalties.
50 L. D. 672, Nov. 15, 1924, Ft. Apache Reservation—Mineral Leases;
676, Nov. 21, 1924, Extent of Title to Lands Patented as Mission Claims;
Op. Sol., M. 14017, Dec. 1, 1924, Title to Land;
M. 14237, Dec. 23, 1924, Quapaw Tribe—Heirship.
50 L. D. 691, Dec. 24, 1924, State Right to Tax Patents in Fee.
Op. Sol., M. 13807, Jan. 23, 1925, Creek—Descent of Lands;
M. 14233, April 24, 1925, Flathead—Enrollment;
M. 15849, May 12, 1925, Pala Mission—Lease of Unallotted Land.
51 L. D. 145, May 16, 1925, Allotments to Indians and Eskimos in Alaska;
98, July 8, 1925, Allotment—Settlement—Jurisdiction.
Memo. Sol. Off., Dec. 18, 1925, Osage—Approval of Partition.
Op. Sol., 17687, Dec. 19, 1925, Disposition of Allotment Funds—Osage.
51 L. D. 326, Jan. 20, 1926, Taxation—Reservation.
Op. Sol., M. 18604, March 6, 1926, Title to Lands;
M. 18423, March 16, 1926, Osage—Certificate of Competency.
Op. Sol., M. 19190, June 2, 1926, Certificate of Competency—Osage;
M. 19225, June 7, 1926, Certificate of Competency—Osage.
Memo. Sol Off., June 8, 1926, Osage—Wills—Disbursements by Executor;
July 15, 1926, Osage—Certificate of Competency.
51 L. D. 501, July 20, 1926, Survey and Disposition of Indian Possessions.
Memo. Sol. Off., July 20, 1926, Osage—Certificate of Competency;
July 23, 1926, Osage—Guardian of Incompetent.
Letter from Asst. Sec'y to Comm'r, Aug. 14, 1926, Title to Kiowa Lands.
Memo. Sol. Off., Sept. 3, 1926, Certificate of Competency Revoked—Claim;
Sept. 14, 1926, Surplus Funds Investment—Osage;
Sept. 29, 1926, Osage—Leases to State.
Op. Sol., Oct. 4, 1926, Jurisdiction of State Probate Courts.
Memo. Sol. Off., Oct. 26, 1926, Osage—Certificate of Competency;
Oct. 27, 1926, Restriction of Alienation of Land.
51 L. D. 613, Nov. 6, 1926, Assessment Charges on Irrigation Projects.
Op. Sol., M. 18320, Dec. 21, 1926, State Tax on Allotments—Osage;
M. 18772, Dec. 24, 1926, Red River—Title to Bed;
M. 20612, Dec. 28, 1926, Sioux Benefits;
M. 15954, Jan. 8, 1927, Chippewa—Back Annuity Claims;
M. 20888, Jan. 14, 1927, Reopening Heirship Findings.
Memo. Sol. Off., Feb. 2, 1927, Secretary's Discretion to Pay Claims.
Op. Sol., M. 10068, Feb. 16, 1927, Spokane Reservation—Water Rights.
Memo. Sol. Off., Feb. 23, 1927, Statutory Allowances Mandatory;
March 3, 1927, Secretary's Discretion to Pay Claims.
Memo. Ind. Off., March 18, 1927, Reservations—Land Acquisition—Employees.

Op. Sol., M. 21849, March 19, 1927, Trust Funds—Priority of U. S. Claims;
M. 21642, March 26, 1927, Validity of Mortgage—Claims;
M. 22121, April 12, 1927, Unlawful Timber Cutting—Choctaw.
Memo. Ind. Off., April 21, 1927, Col. River Irrigation Project—History.
Memo. Sol. Off., Sept. 12, 1927, Revocation of Certificate of Competency;
Sept. 13, 1927, State Tax on Allotment—Osage.
Op. Sol., M. 23421, Sept. 21, 1927, Crow—Farming and Grazing Leases;
M. 23117, Oct. 6, 1927, Reimbursement of Appropriations;
M. 23422, Oct. 17, 1927, Seminole—Oil and Mineral Royalties.
Memo. Sol. Off., Jan. 26, 1928, State Statutes Restricting Voting Rights.
52 L. D. 325, Feb. 24, 1928, Erroneously Issued Fee Patents—Cancellation.
Op. Sol., M. 24284, May 9, 1928, Modoc—Rights of Descendants;
M. 24358, May 14, 1928, Navigable Waters—Exclusion—Quileute Res.
Memo. Sol. Off., May 14, 1928, Osage—Liberty Bonds.
Op. Sol., M. 24293, June 19, 1928, Osage Property—Inheritance.
Memo. Sol. Off., July 31, 1928, Osage Gas Royalties—State Production Tax.
Circular of Com., Aug. 27, 1928, Trading with Indians—Ind. Service Employees.
Memo. Sol. Off., Oct. 31, 1928, Debts of Incompetent Osage.
Op. Sol., M. 24735, Nov. 19, 1928, Segregated Coal and Asphalt Lands.
Memo. Sol. Off., Feb. 21, 1929, Interest on Surplus Funds—Osage;
April 5, 1929, Osage—Restricted Funds.
52 L. D. 597, April 13, 1929, Alaskan Natives—Citizenship.
Memo. Sol. Off., April 18, 1929, Payments to Incompetent Osages.
Op. Sol., M. 25107, May 4, 1929, Osage Restricted Funds.
Memo. Sol. Off., May 31, 1929, Osage Headrights.
Op. Sol., M. 25214, June 7, 1929, Confederated Yakimas—Water Rights.
Letter by Chief Irrigation Service to Comm'r of Indian Affairs, June 20, 1929, Flathead Reservation—Water Rights.
Op. Sol., M. 25258, June 26, 1929, Creation of Trusts by Restricted Indians;
M. 25260, Aug. 1, 1929, Coal and Asphalt Lands—Royalties.
52 L. D. 694, Aug. 7, 1929, Claims within Indian Pueblos—New Mexico.
Op. Sol., M. 25280, Aug. 21, 1929, Quapaw—Mining Leases.
Memo. Sol. Off., Sept. 18, 1929, Payment of Debts from Trust Funds—Osage.
Op. Sol., M. 25347, Jan. 25, 1930, Liability for Irrigation Costs.
Memo. Sol. Off., Feb. 3, 1930, Osage Headrights—Creditor's Rights.
53 I. D. 48, March 3, 1930, Taxability of Cherokee Lands.
Memo. Sol. Off., March 4, 1930, Osage Headrights—Bankruptcy—Creditors;
April 22, 1930, Osage Trust Funds—Creditor's Right;
April 22, 1930, Surplus Funds—Creditors' Rights.
53 I. D. 107, May 23, 1930, Non-taxability of Leases of Restricted Lands.
Memo. Sol. Off., June 7, 1930, Nez Perce Tribe—Allotments.
53 I. D. 128, June 14, 1930, Creation of Indian Reservations.
Memo. Sol. Off., June 26, 1930, Osage Headrights—Distribution.
53 I. D. 133, June 30, 1930, Taxation of Allotments—Trust Period—Expiration.
Op. Sol., M. 26034, July 3, 1930, Power of Secretary—Water Charges.
Memo. Sol. Off., July 8, 1930, Osage Headrights—Creditors' Rights.
Op. Sol., M. 25999, July 8, 1930, Calif. Indians—Enrollment.
53 I. D. 154, Aug. 5, 1930, Status of Flathead Surplus Lands;
157, Aug. 11, 1930, Restrictions upon Lands and Funds—Five Tribes;
169, Aug. 13, 1930, Certification of Competency—Revocation—Effect.
Letter to Comm'r of Indian Affairs from Sec'y of Interior, Sept. 1930, Osage—Jurisdiction of County Court over Estates.
53 I. D. 187, Oct. 8, 1930, Taxation of Sac and Fox Lands, Iowa;
194, Oct. 24, 1930, Alaskan Natives—Allotment—Power of Secretary.
Memo. Sol. Off., Nov. 5, 1930, Osage—Mortgage of Restricted Land;
Dec. 6, 1930, Secretary's Power over Personalty;
Dec. 17, 1930; Revocation of Certificate of Competency;
Dec. 30, 1930, Assignment of Mineral Estate.
Letter to Sen. William H. King from Comm'r, Jan. 9, 1931, Irrigation Projects—Reimbursements, Expenditures, Liens.
Memo. Sol. Off., March 10, 1931, Osage—Mineral Estates—Jurisdiction;
April 9, 1931, Osage—Allowances to Minors;
May 29, 1931, Osage—Mineral Estates.
53 I. D. 399, July 10, 1931, Ft. Hall Irrigation Project—Damages;
412, July 20, 1931, Distribution of Royalties—Deceased Creek.
Memo. Sol. Off., Aug. 17, 1931, Secretary's Control of Royalty Funds;
Aug. 21, 1931, Secretary's Control of Homestead Allotment;
Aug. 30, 1931, Indian Titles and Land Acquisition.
53 I. D. 471, Sept. 4, 1931, Tax Exempt Selections—Five Civilized Tribes.
Memo. Sol. Off., Sept. 14, 1931, Restricted Homestead Allotment.
Op. Sol., M. 26690, Sept. 16, 1931, Alaskan Reindeer Acquisition.
Memo. Sol. Off., Sept. 19, 1931, Creek—Private Trust.
53 I. D. 502, Sept. 22, 1931, Taxation of Mineral Production—Five Tribes.
Op. Sol., M. 26731, Oct. 14, 1931, Osage Funds—Federal Supervision.
Memo. Ind. Off., Dec. 4, 1931, Warm Springs—Power License—State Law.
Memo. Sol. Off., Dec. 21, 1931, Restrictions on Inherited Lands.
Op. Comp. Gen. to the Sec'y, Dec. 30, 1931, Wardship—Fee Patent—Membership.
Memo. Sol. Off., Jan. 20, 1932, Restrictions on Inherited Personalty;
Jan. 23, 1932, Warm Springs—Riparian Rights.
Op. Comp. Gen. to Sec'y, Feb. 4, 1932, Osage—Taxes on Personalty.
Memo. Sol. Off., Feb. 15, 1932, Warm Springs—Water Rights.
53 I. D. 593, Feb. 24, 1932, Status of Alaskan Natives.
Letter of Asst. Sec'y to Sec'y of War, Feb. 26, 1932, Ft. Yuma—Squatters.
53 I. D. 637, March 30, 1932, Tax-exempt Lands—Sale of Restricted Lands.
Memo. Sol. Off., May 6, 1932, Choctaw—Restriction on Alienation;
July 5, 1932, Unit Operation of Leased Oil Lands;
July 22, 1932, Quapaw—Restriction on Alienation.
Op. Sol., M. 27127, July 26, 1932, Alaska Reindeer Service;
M. 27145, Aug. 4, 1932, Land Purchase—Pueblo Indians;
M. 27158, Aug. 5, 1932, Five Tribes—Conveyance—Taxation;
M. 27075, Aug. 18, 1932, Coeur d'Alene—State Taxes.
Memo. Sol. Off., Aug. 22, 1932, Blackfeet—Enrollment.
54 I. D. 39, Sept. 3, 1932, Custom Marriage—Validity—Alaska.
Letter of Ass't Comm'r to Collier Buffington, Sept. 8, 1932, Condemnation of Allotted Land—Jurisdiction of State Courts.
54 I. D. 71, Sept. 23, 1932, Sale of Timber—Georgetown Reservation, Wash.
Letter by Sec'y of Int. to Comp. Gen., Sept. 28, 1932, Irrigation Funds.
Memo. Sol. Off., Oct. 18, 1932, Chippewa—Enrollment of Illegitimate;
Oct. 26, 1932, Investment of Funds in Taxable Property.
Report on Status of Pueblo of Pojoaque, Nov. 3, 1932.
Memo. Sol. Off., Nov. 16, 1932, Cancellation of Fee Patents.
54 I. D. 90, Nov. 25, 1932, Indian-owned Land within Irrigation Projects.
Memo. Sol. Off., Nov. 29, 1932, Tax on Electricity—Reservation Employees.
54 I. D. 105, Nov. 30, 1932, Taxability of Allotments—Osage Tribe;
109, Dec. 9, 1932, Retirement—Service Credit—Five Tribes Schools.
Memo. Sol. Off., Dec. 15, 1932, Osage—"Forced Sale";
Dec. 22, 1932, Osage—"Forced Sale";
Feb. 2, 1933, Mortgages.
54 I. D. 160, Feb. 18, 1933, Authority to Cancel Patent—Lien.
Memo. Sol., Feb. 19, 1933, San Carlos—Priority in Water Rights.
Memo. Sol Off., Feb. 21, 1933, Shoshone—Executive Order Withdrawal;
Feb. 28, 1933, Reservation lands—Trespassing Cattle;
March 8, 1933, Pine Ridge Sioux—Cancellation of Patent.
54 I. D. 195, Mar. 27, 1933, Elimination of Nonirrigable Areas in Ind. Rec. Projects.

Memo. Sol. Off., April 4, 1933, Salt River—Water Rights;
April 4, 1933, Pottowatomie—Cancellation of Trust Patent.
Memo. of Comm'r, April 8, 1933, Chippewa—Enrollment.
Memo. Sol. Off., April 8, 1933, Osage—Mortgage;
April 10, 1933, Chiloquin—Timber Prices;
April 11, 1933, Leases of Irrigable Land.
Memo. Sol., April 19, 1933, California—San Miguel—Enrollment.
Memo. Sol. Off., April 21, 1933, Enrollment—Legislative Report;
April 26, 1933, Pine Ridge—Trespassing Livestock;
May 15, 1933, Sale of Homestead—Limit of Alienability.
Memo. Sol., May 15, 1933, Tax on Electricity—Menominee Power Plant.
Memo. Sol. Off., May 24, 1933, Creek—Compromise of Litigated Will;
May 25, 1933, Burlington—Big Horn Ry.—Right-of-Way;
May 27, 1933, Osage—Secretary's Approval of Will;
May 27, 1933, Osage—Restrictions on Personalty.
54 I. D. 218, June 5, 1933, Taxability of Electric Power—Menominee Reservation.
Memo. Ind. Off., June 12, 1933, Irrigation Projects—Rates.
Memo. Sol. Off., June 14, 1933, Removal of Restrictions—Oil Leases;
June 20, 1933, Yakima Irrigation Project—Water Users;
June 23, 1933, Attorneys—Compensation;
June 29, 1933, Distribution of Funds—Capitan Grande Band;
July 8, 1933, Osage—Life Insurance;
July 10, 1933, Irrigation Projects—Charges against Lessees;
July 10, 1933, Pine Ridge Sioux—Use of Trust Land;
July 12, 1933, Licensed Traders—Taxation;
July 13, 1933, Osage—Oil Leases—Rentals;
July 19, 1933, Trust Agreement—Secretary's Approval;
July 21, 1933, Removal from Reservation—Claim.
54 I. D. 260, July 22, 1933, Investment of Osage Funds.
Memo. Sol. Off., July 25, 1933, Drainage Project—Reimbursable Charges.
Op. Sol., M. 27487, July 26, 1933, Klamath Reservation—Criminal Jurisdiction.
Memo. Sol. Off., July 29, 1933, Attorneys—Approval.
Op. Sol., M. 27514, Aug. 1, 1933, Payment of Tuition—Sectarian Schools.
Sol. Letter to Wm. Keel, Stratford, Okla., Aug. 2, 1933, Five Tribes—Removal of Restrictions.
Op. Sol. M. 27499, Aug. 8, 1933, Sale of Timber—Contracts.
Memo. Sol. Off., Aug. 11, 1933, Wenetchee—Fishing Rights;
Aug. 15, 1933, Oil Leases—Right to Control Production.
Memo. Sol. Off., Aug. 17, 1933, Pueblos—Attorneys' Contracts.
Memo. Sol., Aug. 28, 1933, Enrollment—Illegitimate Child.
Memo. Ind. Off., Aug. 29, 1933, Irrigation—Charges.
Memo. Sol. Off., Sept. 1, 1933, Santa Clara—Attorneys' Fees.
Op. Sol., M. 27541, Sept. 12, 1933, Land Purchase—Validity of Title.
Memo. Sol. Off., Sept. 19, 1933, Taxation—Restricted Lands.
54 I. D. 297, Sept. 21, 1933, Inheritance—Right to Benefits.
Memo. Sol. Off., Sept. 22, 1933, Osage—Administrator's Fees;
Sept. 29, 1933, Nambe Pueblo—Land Title.
Memo. Sol., Oct. 2, 1933, Power of Attorney—Revocability;
Oct. 13, 1933, 21st Amendment—Liquors.
54 I. D. 310, Oct. 14, 1933, Life Insurance Policies.
Memo. Sol., Oct. 16, 1933, Condemnation—Value of Tax Exemption;
Oct. 23, 1933, Navajo—Timber Contract;
Nov. 17, 1933, NIRA—Public Works Project.
54 I .D. 335, Dec. 1, 1933, Irrigation Charges—Extended Payments;
341, Dec. 8, 1933, Home Owners' Loan Bonds for Osages.
Memo. Sol. Off., Dec. 21, 1933, Osage—Mortgage.
Op. Sol., M. 27645, Dec. 22, 1933, Rosebud Fee Patent Issuance.
Memo. Sol. Off., Jan. 2, 1934, Choctaw—Enrollment;
Jan. 16, 1934, Jurisdiction of and Taxation by State.
Memo. Sol., Jan. 30, 1934, Klamath—Tribal Timber Contracts.
Memo. Ind. Off., Jan. 31, 1934, Leases—Unauthorized.
Memo. Sol. Off., Feb. 5, 1934, U. S. Intervention in Litigation;
Feb. 7, 1934, San Carlos Apache—Ceded Lands Claim;
Feb. 13, 1934, Cherokee—Heirship Funds.
Letter from Chief Field Counsel to Comm'r, Feb. 26, 1934, Ft. Hall—Distribution of Snake River Waters—Irrigation.
Op. Sol., M. 27671, March 1, 1934, Yankton Sioux School Lands—Disposal:
M. 27656, March 7, 1934, Papago—Mineral Deposits.
54 I. D. 382, March 14, 1934, Restrictions Applicable to Five Tribes.
Memo. Sol. Off., March 26, 1934, State Taxation—Exemption.
54 I. D. 401, March 30, 1934, Indian Timber Sale Contracts;
418, April 5, 1934, Fishing Rights—Yakima Tribes.
Memo. Sol. Off., April 24, 1934, Shoshone—Attorney's Fee;
April 30, 1934, Minors' Funds—Loans to Parent.
Op. Sol., M. 27656, May 7, 1934, Papago—Mineral Rights.
Memo. Sol. Off., May 11, 1934, Minors' Lands—Leases.
Memo. Sol., May 15, 1934, Indian Corporations—Federal Charters.
54 I. D. 517, June 15, 1934, Migratory Bird Treaty Act.
Ind. Off. Circular No. 3005, July 9, 1934, Repeal of certain Secs. of Rev. Code.
Memo. Sol. Off., July 9, 1934, Five Tribes—U. S. Intervention in Suit;
July 10, 1934, Exclusion of Nonmembers from Tribal Land.
Op. Sol., M. 27750, July 14, 1934, Removal of Remains of Indians.
Memo. Sol., July 16, 1934, Ft. Totten—State School Tax.
Sol. Letter, July 19, 1934, Minn.—Liquor Sales.
Memo. Sol., July 20, 1934, Ft. Totten—State School Tax.
Memo. Sol. Off., July 21, 1934, Pueblos—Land Occupancy.
Memo. Sol., July 25, 1934, Snake—Attorney's Contract.
54 I. D. 555, Aug. 3, 1934, Alienation of Chippewa Alotted Land.
Memo. Sol., Aug. 8, 1934, Chippewa Enrollment.
Op. Sol., M. 27788, Aug. 6, 1934, Osage—Attorney's Fee.
Sol. Letter, Aug. 8, 1934, Shawnee—Awards.
Memo. Sol., Aug. 8, 1934, Rosebud Sioux—Cash Allotment Benefits;
Aug. 9, 1934, Creek—State Oil Production Tax;
Aug. 14, 1934, Wheeler-Howard Act—Fee Patent.
54 I. D. 584, Aug. 17, 1934, Devise of Restricted Lands.
Memo. Sol. Off., Aug. 18, 1934, Ft. Belknap—Exchange of Homestead Allotments.
Memo. Sol., Aug. 21, 1934, Quapaw—Mineral Lease;
Aug. 28, 1934, Kiowa—Sale of Land by Minor.
55 I. D. 362, Aug. 28, 1934, Exchanges of Lands in Arizona.
Memo. Sol., Sept. 6, 1934, Restrictions on Alienation—Easements;
Sept. 12, 1934, Disbursement of Funds;
Sept. 15, 1934, Five Tribes—Partition of Inherited Lands;
Sept. 17, 1934, Temporary Withdrawals of Surplus Trust Lands.
Letter of Comm'r to Supt., Sept. 26, 1934, State Juris. over Oil Production.
Letter to Comm'r from C. L. Walker, Sept. 29, 1934, Klamath—Indian Judges and Policemen.
Memo. Sol., Oct. 2, 1934, Standing Rock—Mortgage on Restricted Lands;
Oct. 3, 1934, Osage—Grant of Right-of-Way through Trust Lands.
Memo. Sol. Off., Oct. 9, 1934, Laguna Pueblo—Organization.
Memo. Sol., Oct. 12, 1934, Papago—Wheeler-Howard Act.
Memo. Sol. Off., Oct. 17, 1934, Osage—Authority of Sec'y to Approve Will.
Memo. Sol., Oct. 23, 1934, Pueblo—Non-Indian Claimants to Lands.
55 I. D. 14, Oct. 25, 1934, Powers of Tribes.
Memo. Sol., Oct. 25, 1934, Chickasaw—Lease Approval Procedure.
Memo. Sol. Off., Nov. 1, 1934, Wheeler-Howard Act.
Letter of Comm'r to Sen. Carl Hayden, Nov. 5, 1934, Gila River—State Taxes on Indian Service Employees.
Memo. Sol. Off., Nov. 10, 1934, Exchanges for State School Lands.
Memo. Sol., Nov. 12, 1934, Shoshone—Oil Lease—Operations;
Nov. 14, 1934, Osage—Exchange of Stock;
Nov. 20, 1934, Red Lake—Trader's License;
Nov. 20, 1934, Sioux—Wheeler-Howard Act—Land Outside Reservation;
Nov. 21, 1934, Wheeler Howard Act—Devisees of Restricted Land;
Nov. 22, 1934, Wheeler-Howard Act—Elections.
Op. Sol., M. 27833, Nov. 28, 1934, Disbursement of Osage Funds;
M. 27381, Dec. 13, 1934, Fond du Lac Chippewas—Enrollment;
M. 27810, Dec. 13, 1934, Wheeler-Howard Act—Interpretation.
List of Indian Constitutions, Dec. 13, 1934.
Memo. Sol., Dec. 14, 1934, Crow—Grazing Privileges;
Dec. 18, 1934, Chippewa—Enrollment;
Dec. 18, 1934, Conveyance to the U. S. to Avoid Taxation;
Dec. 22, 1934, Ft. Belknap—Allotment.
Memo. Sol. Off., Dec. 27, 1934, Gila River—Division of Stored Water.
Memo. Sol., Jan. 17, 1935, Chippewa—Approval of Will.
Memo. Ind. Off., Jan. 3, 1935, Taxation of Restricted Lands.
Memo. Sol., Jan. 10, 1935, Menominee—Enrollment—Regulations.

Memo. Sol. Off., Jan. 14, 1935, U. S. Ex Rel. Warren v. Sec'y of Interior.
Memo. Sol., Jan. 17, 1935, Wheeler-Howard Act—Subsistence Homesteads.
Op. Sol., M. 27759, Jan. 22, 1935, Per Capita Payment from Judgment;
M. 27816, Jan. 22, 1935, Homesteads—Development;
M. 27843, Jan. 22, 1935, Settlement of Estate;
M. 27814, Jan. 30, 1935, Land Title Status.
Asst. Secy's Letter to A. G., Feb. 1, 1935, Removal of Restrictions.
Op. Sol., M. 27903, Feb. 5, 1935, Reservation Elections—Wheeler-Howard Act.
Memo. Sol., Feb. 6, 1935, Mining Leases—Tribal Indian Lands;
Feb. 7, 1935, Flathead Power Site;
Feb. 8, 1935, Jicarilla—Timber.
Letter from Asst. Comm'r to Chairman Fed. Pow. Com., Feb. 19, 1935, Grand Portage—Power Project.
Op. Sol., M. 27512, Feb. 20, 1935, Contract—Conservation of Pueblo Lands.
Memo. Sol. Off., Feb. 21, 1935, San Carlos—Irrigation Project.
Memo. Sol., Feb. 27, 1935, Cheyenne—State Highway Tax on Trucking;
Feb. 28, 1935, Secy's Power to Regulate Conduct of Indians.
Memo. Sol. Off., March 8, 1935, Chickasaw—Heirship.
Memo. Sol., March 9, 1935, Officers of Tribe as U. S. Officers;
March 11, 1935, Right-of-Way Application.
Memo. Ind. Off., March 13, 1935, Florida Seminoles.
Memo. Sol., March 14, 1935, Pueblo—Awards to non-Indian Claimants.
Secy's letter to A. G., March 20, 1935, Priority in Impounded Waters.
Memo. Sol., March 22, 1935, Cheyenne and Standing Rock—Exchanges;
March 29, 1935, San Carlos Apache—Constitution;
March 30, 1935, Gila River—Constitution;
April 4, 1935, Taxable Property—Assignment to U. S. in Trust.
Op. Sol., M. 27939, April 9, 1935, Trust Period—Extension—Mission Inds.
Asst. Secy's Letter to Asst. to the Supt. St. Elizabeths, April 15, 1935, Disposition of Funds of Deceased Insane Ind.
Letter from Acting Sec'y of Int. to Comp. Gen., April 16, 1935, Pine Ridge—Sioux Benefits.
Op. Sol., M. 27998, April 27, 1935, Navajo Timber Sale Contract;
M. 27902, Apr. 30, 1935, Royalty Payment on Gasoline—Osage Res.;
M. 27996, May 14, 1935, Bed of Arkansas River—Title.
Memo. Sol., May 14, 1935, Red Lake Chippewa—Enrollment.
Memo. Sol. Off., May 15, 1935, Pawnee—Enrollment.
Memo. Sol., May 21, 1935, Contract with State for Schooling Indians.
Op. Sol., M. 27770, May 22, 1935, Issuance of Patents—Quinaielt Res.;
M. 28028, May 24, 1935, Reappraisement of Land—Fort Peck Res.
Memo. Ind. Off., May 27, 1935, Papago—Water Rights.
Memo. Sol., May 27, 1935, Reservations—Montana Criminal Code.
55 I. D. 263, May 31, 1935, Determination of Heirs—Wills—Approval.
Contract, June 3, 1935, Salt River Valley—Water Users.
Op. Sol., M. 28033, June 4, 1935, Seminole Nation—Attorneys' Contract.
Memo. Sol., June 4, 1935, Five Tribes—Oil Leasing Regulations.
Memo. Sol. Off., June 11, 1935, Legislation—Sale of Restricted Lands.
55 I. D. 282, June 22, 1935, Public Land Allotments—Alaska.
Memo. Sol., July 18, 1935, Cherokee—Claims to Land;
July 17, 1935, Ft. Peck—Allotments.
July 22, 1935, Tulalip—Tide Lands—Title;
55 I. D. 295, July 17, 1935, Allotment Selections—Ft. Belknap.
Memo. Sol., July 24, 1935, Shawnee—Land Purchases;
July 25, 1935, Grazing on Tribal Lands—Dept. Powers.
Letter from Asst. Sec'y to Osage Tr. Attorney, Aug. 5, 1935, Trade with Indians—Rental of Living Quarters.
Memo. Sol. Off., Aug. 6, 1935, California—Land Claims.
Op. Sol., M. 28125, Aug. 12, 1935, Personnel Employment—Indian Trusts.
Memo. Sol. Off., Aug. 20, 1935, Navajo—Addition to Reservation.
Memo. Sol., Aug. 27, 1935, Chippewa—Constitution—Organization.
Memo. Sol. Off., Sept. 3, 1935, Menominee Indian Mills—Legislation.
Memo. Sol., Sept. 12, 1935, Attorney Contracts;
Sept. 20, 1935, Cherokee—Distribution of Oil Royalties;
Sept. 21, 1935, Five Tribes—Land Partition.
Memo. by Imperial Irrigation District Attorney, Oct. 11, 1935, Yuma—Claims on Account of All-American Canal.
Memo. Sol. Off., Oct. 15, 1935, Ft. Belknap—Water Rights.
Op. Sol., M. 28183, Oct. 16, 1935, Papago Reservation—Mining Charges.
Memo. Sol., Oct. 22, 1935, Creek—Trust Agreements.
Memo. Sol. Off., Oct. 28, 1935, Minn. Reservation—Wheeler-Howard Act.
Op. Sol., M. 28197, Oct, 31, 1935, Education and Relief—State Contract.
Secy's Letter to A. G., Nov. 8, 1935, Irrigation District—Water Rights.
Memo. Sol., Nov. 11, 1935, Grazing Regulations;
Nov. 12, 1935, Ft. Bidwell—Adoption of Constitution.
Memo. Sol. Off., Nov. 14, 1935, Ft. McDermitt—Allotments.
Memo. Sol., Nov. 19, 1935, Determination of Heirs by Indian Court.
Memo. Sol. Off., Nov. 23, 1935, Ft. Bidwell—Indian Reorganization Act.
55 I. D. 401, Nov. 27, 1935, Law and Order Regulations.
Memo. Sol., Dec. 5, 1935, Credit Regulations;
Dec. 10, 1935, Reinstatement of Canceled Sale—Pyramid Lake.
Op. Sol., M. 28259, Dec. 13, 1935, Timber Contracts—Colville Reser.
Letter of Ass't Comm'r to Sec'y of Interior, Dec. 16, 1935, Osage—Will—Minor.
Memo. Sol., Dec. 17, 1935, Navajo—Distribution of Unallotted Property;
Dec. 17, 1935, Osage—Jurisdiction—Crimes and Misdemeanors;
Dec. 19, 1935, Legislation—Exchange of Lands.
Asst. Secy's Memo., Dec. 20, 1935, Ft. Berthold—Claim Against U. S.
Memo. Sol., Dec. 26, 1935, Ft. Berthold—Claim Against U. S.;
Dec. 26, 1935, Chippewa—Enrollment.
55 I. D. 435, Dec. 28, 1935, Grazing Regulations—Tribal Lands.
Op. Sol., M. 28198, Jan. 8, 1936, Yuma Reservation—Title to Lands.
Memo. Sol., Jan. 9, 1936, Puyallup—Constitution.
Memo. Ind. Off., Jan. 17, 1936, Colville—Resettlement Loan—Security.
Memo. Sol. Off., Jan. 22, 1936, Omaha—Resettlement Project.
Comp. Gen's Letter to Supt. Rosebud Ind. Agency, Jan. 23, 1936, Rosebud Sioux—Divorce.
Memo. Sol., Jan. 24, 1936, Colville Resettlement Loan;
Jan. 29, 1936, Sisseton Leases—Supt's Authority.
Memo. Ind. Off., Feb. 18, 1936, Wardship.
Memo. Sol., March 9, 1936, Five Tribes—Sale of Allotment;
March 12, 1936, Unallotted Lands—Prospecting and Lease.
Op. Sol., M. 28231, March 12, 1936, Deposit of Indian Moneys.
Memo. Sol., March 18, 1936, Navajo—Determination of Heirs;
March 18, 1936, Delaware—Appropriation for.
Op. Sol., M. 28316, March 18, 1936, Emergency Funds—Stricken Rural Areas;
M. 28108, March 18, 1936, Payment of Water Right Charges—Pueblos.
Memo. Sol., March 20, 1936, Ft. Belknap Land Purchase—Reorganization Act;
March 24, 1936, Chippewa Enrollment;
March 25, 1936, Kiowa Crop Mortgage;
March 25, 1936, Navajo—Authority of Special Disbursing Agent.
Op. Sol., M. 28317, March 31, 1936, Educational Loans to Indians.
55 I. D. 475, March 31, 1936, Ownership of Island within Reservation.
Memo. Sol. Off., April 9, 1936, Wheeler-Howard Act—Tribal Council's Powers.
Memo. Sol., April 15, 1936, Sioux—Elections on Constitutions.
Op. Sol., M. 28309, April 16, 1936, Five Civilized Tribes—Attorneys' Fees.
Memo. Sol., April 22, 1936, Applicability of Social Security Act to Indians.
55 I. D. 456, April 23, 1936, Title to Right-of-Way Lands.
Memo. Sol., April 23, 1936, Jurisdiction of Ct. of Claims over Cherokee Claims.
55 I. D. 489, April 23, 1936, Disposition of Osage Trust Funds;
500, April 28, 1936, Use of Trust Funds—Annuity Policies.
Memo. Sol., May 1, 1936, Five Tribes—Federal Income and State Taxes.

Memo. Sol. Off., May 8, 1936, Osage—Individual Indebtedness.
Memo. Sol., May 12, 1936, Acoma Reservation Boundaries;
May 15, 1936, Tribal Ownership of Non-Irrigable Lands—Yuma;
May 19, 1936, Jicarilla Apache Boundaries;
May 19, 1936, Five Tribes Timber Sales.
Op. Sol., M. 27878, May 20, 1936, San Carlos Lands Restoration.
Memo. Sol., May 25, 1936, Acoma Boundaries;
May 27, 1936, Law and Order Regulations.
Op. Sol., M. 28519, May 27, 1936, San Carlos Boundaries.
Memo. Sol. Off., May 28, 1936, Ft. Hall Mining Leases.
55 I. D. 560, May 29, 1936, Boundary of San Carlos Reservation.
Memo. Sol., June 9, 1936, Menominee—Keshena Hospital;
June 11, 1936, Salt River Valley Water Users Assn.—Maricopa;
June 25, 1936, Loan Agreement—Indian Reorganization Act.
Op. Sol., M. 28107, June 30, 1936, Red Lake Reservation—Title to Lands.
Memo. Sol., June 30, 1936, Incorporated Pueblo—Liability to Suit;
July 1, 1936, Navajo Coal Mining;
July 3, 1936, 1937 Appropriation Act;
July 8, 1936, Flathead—Taking Tribal Lands for Reservoir;
July 9, 1936, Swinomish Law and Order Code;
July 13, 1936, State Statutes Limiting Indian Right to Vote;
July 21, 1936, Ute Attorney's Contract.
Circular of Comm'r, No. 3170, July 28, 1936, Relief of Taxed Indians.
Memo. Sol., July 31, 1936, Okla. Indians—Loans—Wheeler-Howard Act;
Aug. 7, 1936, Five Tribes—Agricultural and Grazing Leases;
Aug. 10, 1936, Osage Oil Lease.
Memo. of Comm'r, Aug. 11, 1936, Sup'ts Authority to Sign Leases for Heirs.
Memo. Sol., Aug. 21, 1936, Nambe Pueblo—Withdrawal of Land;
Aug. 22, 1936, Pyramid Lake—Cancelled Entries.
Op. Sol., M. 28589, Aug. 24, 1936, Occupancy—Right-of-Way—Reclamation.
Memo. Sol., Aug. 25, 1936, San Carlos Irr. Project—O. and M. Charges;
Aug. 31, 1936, Purchases under Wheeler-Howard Act;
Sept. 2, 1936, Isleta and Santo Domingo Pueblos—Rights-of-way;
Sept. 3, 1936, Flathead Irr. Project—O. and M. Charges.
Memo. Sol. Off., Sept. 12, 1936, Restrictions on Religious Practices.
Memo. Sol., Sept. 15, Col. River Tribes—Constitution;
Sept. 17, 1936, Five Tribes—Rights-of-Way;
Sept. 19, 1936, Registration.
Memo. Sol. Off., Sept. 22, 1936, Prospecting Permits.
56 I. D. 7, Sept. 24, 1936, Irrigation Project Assessments—Fort Hall Res.
Memo. Sol., Sept. 25, 1936, Osage—Administrators' Fees.
Op. Sol., M. 28614, Oct. 1, 1936, Patents—Mineral Rights.
Memo. Sol. Off., Oct. 2, 1936, Tribal Gov'ts—Fed. Constitutional Limitations.
Memo. Sol., Oct. 5, 1936, Restricted Land Use—Lake Superior Chippewa;
Oct. 5, 1936, Expenditure of Tribal Funds;
Oct. 7, 1936, Navajo—Probate.
Letter of Ass't Sec'y to A. G., Oct. 15, 1936, Five Tribes—Partition.
Memo. Sol., Oct. 16, 1936, Lower Brule Sioux—Revolving Credit Fund;
Oct. 16, 1936, Assignment of Property—Forms;
Oct. 20, 1936, Menominee—State Workmen's Compensation Act.
Memo. Sol. Off., Oct. 22, 1936, Resettlement Loans—Unorganized Tribes.
Memo. Sol., Oct. 23, 1936, Law and Order Ordinances—San Carlos Apache;
Oct. 23, 1936, Apache—Loan Agreement.
Memo. Sol. Off., Oct. 25, 1936, Corporate Powers of Indian Tribe.
Memo. Sol., Oct. 30, 1936, Restricted Lands—Security for Loans;
Nov. 2, 1936, Pawnee—Back Annuities;
Nov. 17, 1936, U. S. v. Walker River Irrigation District;
Nov. 27, 1936, Arts and Crafts Shop;
Dec. 2, 1936, Gros Ventre—Enrollment;
Dec. 7, 1936, Menominee Mill—Secretarial Power.
56 I. D. 38, Dec. 11, 1936, State and Fed. Jurisdiction over Restricted Land.
Op. Sol., M. 28850, Dec. 16, 1936, Pueblo Land Grants—Purchase.
Memo. Sol., Dec. 19, 1936, Upper Red Lake—Fishing Rights of Indians;
Dec. 21, 1936, Land Bought with Restricted Funds—Tax;
Dec. 31, 1936, Exchange of Lands.
56 I. D. 48, Jan. 4, 1937, Osage Tax Exemptions.
Memo. Sol., Jan. 4, 1937, IRA—Acquisition of Land.
Memo. of Comm'r, Jan. 6, 1937, Membership—Tribal Power.
Memo. Ind. Off., Jan. 7, 1937, Irrigation—Rights-of-way.
Memo. Sol., Jan. 11, 1937, IRA—Exchange of Land—Indian and White;
Jan. 11, 1937, IRA—Sec. 5;
Jan. 12, 1937, Tribal Land—Mining Lease—Power of Council;
Jan. 13, 1937, Five Civilized Tribes—Leases;
Jan. 16, 1937, Oklahoma—Taxes—Lands.
Memo. Sol. Off., Jan. 19, 1937, Law and Order—Picketing.
Memo. Sol., Jan. 23, 1937, IRA—Attorneys' Contract;
Jan. 23, 1937, Five Civilized Tribes—Conveyance by Heirs.
Op. Sol., M. 27963, Jan. 26, 1937, Deceased Osage Allottee—Inheritance.
Memo. Sol., Jan. 26, 1937, IRA—Attorneys' Contracts.
Memo. Sol. Off., Jan. 28, 1937, Lands—Federal Control over Grazing.
Memo. Sol., Feb. 3, 1937, IRA—Exchange of Land;
Feb. 5, 1937, Five Civilized Tribes—Trust Agreement;
Feb. 8, 1937, Status of St. Croix Chippewas;
Feb. 8, 1937, Status of Mole Lake Chippewas.
56 I. D. 79, Feb. 13, 1937, Eligibility for Grazing Privileges.
Letter A. G. to Sec'y, Feb. 13, 1937, Oklahoma Welfare Act—Osage.
Memo. of Ass't Sec'y to Comm'r, Feb. 17, 1937, Soil Conservation Act.
Memo. Sol., Feb. 20, 1937, Makah Tribe—Tribal Assets.
Statement by Comm'r on S. 1736, To repeal Wheeler-Howard Act, March 3, 1937.
Memo. Sol., March 4, 1937, Oklahoma—Deeds and Guardianship Sales;
March 6, 1937, Status of Wisconsin Winnebago;
March 15, 1937, St. Croix Indians—Enrollees of Dr. Wooster;
March 17, 1937, Salish & Kootenai—Law and Order.
56 I. D. 102, April 8, 1937, Power of Congress to Enact Legislation.
Memo. Sol., April 8, 1937, Estate of Jackson Barnett—Claimants;
April 14, 1937, Corporations—Power of Indian Tribe.
56 I. D. 110, April 19, 1937, Reservation of Waters—Alaska.
Memo. Sol., May 1, 1937, Status of Nahma and Beaver Indians.
56 I. D. 137, May 6, 1937, Liquor Traffic—Alaska.
Letter of Acting Comm'r, May 6, 1937, Inheritance—Murderer of Deceased.
Memo. Sol., May 11, 1937, Oklahoma—Approval of Conveyances.
Memo. Sol. Off., May 13, 1937, Makah—Timber Contract—Tribal Power;
May 18, 1937, Makah—Timber Contract—Tribal Power.
Memo. Sol., May 22, 1937, Blackfeet Tribe—Power over Leases;
May 24, 1937, IRA—Election;
May 24, 1937, Chartering of Subordinate Organizations.
Letter from H. R. Tolley to Comm'r, May 24, 1937, AAA Payments—Set-offs.
Memo. Sol., May 25, 1937, Tribal Land—Leases.
Op. Sol., 20232, June 2, 1937, Land and Water Right Exchanges—Calif.
Memo. Sol. Off., June 3, 1937, Taxes;
June 3, 1937, Estates—Claims;
June 7, 1937, Palm Springs—Collection of Fees.
Memo. Sol., June 9, 1937, Catawba Tribe;
June 9, 1937, Catawba Tribe;
June 15, 1937, Umatilla—Hunting and Fishing.
Op. Sol., M. 29156, June 30, 1937.
Comp. Gen's Op., A. 86599, June 30, 1937, Tribal Moneys—Organized Tribes.
Memo. Sol. Off., July 2, 1937, Tribal Power—Inspection Fees.
Memo. Ind. Off., July 8, 1937, Flathead Irrigation—Interest.
Letter from Acting Sec'y to U. S. Employees' Compensation Comm'n, July 9, 1937, U. S. Employees' Compensation—Rehabilitation Work.
Memo. Sol., July 12, 1937, Ft. Belknap—Leasing of Tribal Lands;
July 13, 1937, Heirship Lands—Leased by Supt.
Memo. Sol. Off., July 14, 1937, Leasing of Lands—Incompetents.
Memo. Sol., July 14, 1937, Oklahoma Loans—White Spouse;
July 15, 1937, Creek Tribal Towns—Organization;
July 16, 1937, Loan Agreements—Tribe;
July 19, 1937, Leases on Tribal Land;
July 21, 1937, Reservations—Wilderness Areas.
Letter of Comp. Gen. to Sec'y, July 24, 1937, Tribal Lands—Reduction Rentals.

Ind. Off. Circular No. 3218, July 29, 1937, Keetowah—Organization as Band.
Memo. Sol., July 29, 1937, Federal Loans—Default by Indians;
Aug. 2, 1937, Tribal Lands—Permits;
Aug. 3, 1937, Cheyenne—Arapaho Organization;
Aug. 7, 1937, Tribal Power—Exclusion of Non-Indian Attorneys;
Aug. 11, 1937, Tribal Land—Control;
Aug. 13, 1937, Suffrage—Discrimination against Indians;
Aug. 13, 1937, Inherited Lands—Removal of Restrictions;
Aug. 14, 1937, Sales—Heirship Lands;
Aug. 23, 1937, Rosebud Sioux—Adoption;
Aug. 25, 1937, Choctaw—Chickasaw—Rights-of-way;
Aug. 25, 1937, Soil Conservation Act—Payments to Indians;
Sept. 11, 1937, Tribal Lands—Leases;
Sept. 14, 1937, Alaska—Reservations;
Sept. 21, 1937, Tribal Power—Membership;
Sept. 21, 1937, Tribal Power—Wrongful Death Action;
Sept. 23, 1937, Inherited Lands—Drainage Charges;
Sept. 29, 1937, Reservation—Surplus Lands;
Oct. 7, 1937, Allotted Lands—Timber and Mineral Rights;
Oct. 8, 1937, Tribal Funds—Reimbursable Loans.
Letter of Comm'r to Indian Agents, Oct. 9, 1937, Comanche and Apache—Non-Indian Members.
Memo. Sol. Off., Oct. 12, 1937, Membership—Adoption.
Memo. Sol., Oct. 20, 1937, Tribal Land—Rights to House;
Oct. 20, 1937, Tribal Power—Land Assignments;
Oct. 26, 1937, San Xavier Reservation—Water Rights.
Letter from Ass't Sec'y to A. G., Oct. 27, 1937, Osage—Restricted Funds.
Op. Sol., Oct. 28, 1937, Quapaw—Mining Leases.
Memo. Sol., Nov. 4, 1937, Chartered Corporations—Chattel Mortgages;
Nov. 5, 1937, Oil and Gas Permits;
Nov. 9, 1937, Federal Contracts—Irrigation.
Memo. Sol. Off., Nov. 9, 1937, Membership—Secretarial Power.
Memo. Sol., Nov. 11, 1937, Lac du Flambeau—Permits;
Nov. 11, 1937, Proposed Constitution.
Memo. Sol. Off., Nov. 23, 1937, Tribal Membership.
Memo. Sol., Nov. 29, 1937, Restricted Property—Taxation;
Dec. 2, 1937, Tribal Adoption;
Dec. 11, 1937, Tribal Leases—Approval of Supt.;
Dec. 14, 1937, Hopi—Family Relations;
Dec. 18, 1937, Membership—Tribal Power;
Dec. 18, 1937, Loan—Crop Mortgages;
Dec. 20, 1937, Inheritance of Personalty—Tribal Law.
Op. Sol., M. 29560, Dec. 28, 1937, Land Purchase—Papago Indians.
Memo. Sol., Dec. 28, 1937, Descent of Unrestricted Property—State Law.
Memo. by Ass't Sec'y Burlew, Jan. 3, 1938, Water Purchase by Indians.
Memo. Sol., Jan. 5, 1938, Trust Lands—Crop Mortgages:
Jan. 8, 1938, Devisee under IRA—Tribal Membership.
Op. Sol., M. 29620, Jan. 14, 1938, Assignment of Lands—Choctaws of Miss.
Memo. Sol., Jan. 18, 1938, Attorneys' Contract—Organized Tribe.
Op. Sol., M. 29596, Jan. 26, 1938, Right of Franchise—State Law.
Memo. Sol. Off., Jan. 30, 1938, Osage Headrights—Power of Secretary.
Memo. Sol., Feb. 4, 1938, Reservation—State Sales Tax.
Op. Sol., M. 29619, Feb. 7, 1938, Indian Lands—Conveyance.
Memo. Sol., Feb. 18, 1938, Hunting and Fishing—Tribal Power—Bad River.
Op. Sol., M. 29616, Feb. 19, 1938, Red Lake Band—Ceded Land—Disposition.
Memo. Sol., Feb. 25, 1938, IRA—Exchanges and Sales:
March 12, 1938, IRA—Transfer of Land to Nonmembers;
March 14, 1938, Blackfeet—Tribal Power—Business Organizations;
March 19, 1938, Expatriation—Rights to Tribal Property.
Memo. of Comm'r, April 1, 1938, Taos Pueblo.
Memo. Sol., April 12, 1938, Rosebud Sioux—Adoption of Members.
Memo. Ind. Off., April 12, 1938, Ft. Hall Indians—Water Rights.
Memo. Sol. Off., April 13, 1938, Rosebud Sioux—Regulation of Medicine Men;
April 14, 1938, Taxation—Indian Lands;
April 14, 1938, Leasing of Tribal Lands.
Memo. Sol., April 22, 1938, Okla. Indian Welfare Act—Cooperatives.
Sol. Letter to Wm. A. Brophy, Albuquerque, New Mexico, April 23, 1938, Pueblo Lands—Taxability.
Memo. Sol. Off., May 5, 1938, Water Rights on Reservation.
Memo. Sol., May 14, 1938, Five Civilized Tribes—Leases;
May 14, 1938, Tribal Council—Delegation of Power.
56 I. D. 308, May 14, 1938, Taylor Grazing Act Licenses—Pueblos.
Memo. Sol., May 19, 1938, Reimbursable Loans—Cancellation of Liens;
May 24, 1938, Loans—Preferences—Degree of Indian Blood;
June 3, 1938, Shoshone Reservation—Renewal of Oil Leases.
Memo. Sol. Off., June 6, 1938, Tribal Mill—Gasoline Tax.
Memo. Sol., June 14, 1938, Revolving Credit Loans—Gov't Employees;
June 14, 1938, Lease—Consent of Indian.
56 I. D. 330, June 15, 1938, Restoration to Tribal Ownership—Ute Lands.
Memo. Sol., June 15, 1938, Lease—Consent of Indian.
Memo. Sol. Off., June 25, 1938, Organization—Indian Band.
Letter of Asst. Comm'r to Supt. Five Civilized Tribes Agency, June 29, 1938, Loans—Security.
Memo. Sol., June 30, 1938, Allotment—Right-of-way;
July 1, 1938, Indian School Land—Right-of-way.
Memo. Sol. Off., July 7, 1938, Tribal Court—Nonmember.
Memo. Sol., July 12, 1938, Adoption of Members.
Memo. Sol. Off., July 16, 1938, Tribal Court—Nonmember.
Letter from Asst. Sec'y to A. G., July 16, 1938, Power of Secretary—Navajo Grazing Regulations.
Memo. Sol., July 19, 1938, Loans—Mortgages;
July 21, 1938, Quapaw—Mining Leases—Type of Surety.
Op. Sol., M. 29669, Aug. 1, 1938, Authority of Officers of Indian Service;
M. 29791, Aug. 1, 1938, Land Exchange—Forfeiture—Minnesota.
Memo. Sol., Aug. 2, 1938, Mining Leases—Deduction for Survey;
Aug. 6, 1938, Claims against United States;
Aug. 8, 1938, Tribal Ordinance—Federal Constitution.
Memo. of Asst. Sec'y, Aug. 17, 1938, Loans—Crop Mortgages.
Memo. Sol., Aug. 20, 1938, Timber Contracts.
Memo. of Asst. Sec'y, Aug. 23, 1938, Leases—Consent of Lessees.
Op. Sol., M. 29908, Aug. 25, 1938, Irrigation—Works—Damages.
Memo. Sol., Aug. 26, 1938, Law and Order—Nonmembers;
Aug. 27, 1938, Southern Utes—Tribal Lands;
Aug. 30, 1938, Probate of Restricted Personalty;
Sept. 8, 1938, Transition from Indian to Tribal Court;
Sept. 10, 1938, Restricted Land—Inheritance by Whites;
Sept. 13, 1938, Sales Tax;
Sept. 13, 1938, Sales Tax.
Letter from Acting Comm'r to Supt. Fort Hall Agency, Sept. 19, 1938, Water Rights—Lessees.
Op. Sol., M. 29961, Oct. 4, 1938, Right-of-way—Eastern Cherokee.
Memo. Sol. Off., Oct. 7, 1938, Bonneville Dam Area—Fishing Rights.
Memo. Sol., Oct. 15, 1938, Law and Order.
Ind. Off. Letter from Quapaw Agency Supt., Oct. 17, 1938, Sales Tax.
Memo. by Asst. Chief Counsel of Ind. Off., Oct. 17, 1938, Irrigation Charges—Decedent's Land.
Memo. Sol., Oct. 19, 1938, Rehabilitation Project—Workmen's Comp. Law;
Oct. 21, 1938, Palm Spring—Leases.
Memo. Sol. Off., Oct. 27, 1938, Tribal Power—Leases:
Oct. 28, 1938, Retired Employee—Residence on Reservation.
Memo. Ind. Off., Nov. 15, 1938, Trust Land—Mortgage.
Memo. Sol., Nov. 18, 1938, Tribal Power—Inheritance.
56 I. D. 395, Nov. 28, 1938, Protection of Occupancy—Mineral Lands.
Op. Sol., M. 29999, Nov. 28, 1938, Menominee & Red. Lake Res.—Wages & Hours.
Memo. Sol., Nov. 28, 1938, Trust Agreements.
Memo. Sol. Off., Nov. 29, 1938, Law and Order—Removal of Nonmembers.
Memo. of Comm'r, Dec. 5, 1938, Estate—Claims.
Memo. of Asst. Sec'y, Dec. 5, 1938, Organized Tribe—Grazing Permits.
Memo. Sol., Dec. 13, 1938, Oklahoma—Recognized Tribes;
Dec. 13, 1938, Indian Employment Preference;
Dec. 22, 1938, Tribal Permit for Ranger Station;
Dec. 22, 1938, Chattel Mortgage Forms.
Memo. Sol. Off., Dec. 30, 1938, Alienability of Tribal Lands.
Op. Sol., M. 30146, Feb. 8, 1939, Employment of Counsel—Canadian Indians.
Memo. Sol., Feb. 10, 1939, Membership in Turtle Mountain Tribe;
Feb. 10, 1939, Investigation of Applicants—Mining Leases;
Feb. 11, 1939, Tribal Jurisdiction over Divorce;
Feb. 14, 1939, Tax Exemption of Indian Homestead;

Feb. 17, 1939, Interest of Employee in Land Transaction;
Feb. 17, 1939, Criminal Jurisdiction of Tribes;
Feb. 17, 1939, Rosebud Sioux Tax Ordinance;
Feb. 17, 1939, Issuance of Deeds to Alaskan Natives;
Feb. 20, 1939, Tax Exemption of Purchased Restricted Land;
Feb. 23, 1939, Papago Ordinance on Cattle Sale;
March 11, 1939, Estate of Mary Big Elk;
March 14, 1939, Cherokee Attorney Contract;
March 16, 1939, Indian Preference in Blackfeet Oil and Gas Leases;
March 24, 1939, Investigation of Alleged Conversion of Oklahoma Indian Funds;
March 25, 1939, Leases of Tribal Land;
March 25, 1939, Acquisition of Puyallup Tribal School Property;
March 28, 1939, Delegation of Departmental Power to Collect Fees;
March 28, 1939, Cancellation of Alaskan Native Allotment;
April 3, 1939, Acquisition of Land at Okla. Tax Sales.
Op. Sol., M. 30133, April 13, 1939, Irrigation Projects—Construction Costs.
Memo. Sol., April 14, 1939, Santa Clara Pueblo Land Assignment.

TABLE OF ATTORNEY GENERAL'S OPINIONS

1 Op. A. G. 65, Powers of the Executive (1796). 465, The Seneca Lands (1821). 645, Right of the Cherokees to Impose Taxes on Traders (1824).

2 Op. A. G. 110, Georgia and the Treaty of Indian Spring (1828). 321, The Cherokees and their Lands (1830). 360, Cherokee Reservations (1830). 402, Trade with the Cherokees (1830). 462, Treaty with the Choctaws (1831). 465, Choctaw Reserves under Supplemental Treaty (1831). 562, Treaty with the Ottowas—Payment to Mr. Forsyth (1833). 563, Treaty with the Miamies (1833). 574, Removal of Intruders from Lands Ceded by the Creeks (1833). 631, Transfer of Certain Miami Reservations (1834). 693, Jurisdiction of the Choctaw Courts (1834).

3 Op. A. G. 33, The three Pottawatomie Treaties (1836). 34, Chickasaw Reservations (1836). 40, Patents to issue for the Creek Reservations (1836). 41, Chickasaw Reservations (1836). 48, Right of Choctaw Reservees to Convey their Lands (1836). 106, Grants under Supplement to Choctaw Treaty (1836). 106, Pre-emption to Lands Ceded by the Quapaw Treaty (1836). 107, Right to Grants of Reservees in the Choctaw Treaty (1836). 113, Location of Choctaw Reserves (1836). 170, Investment of the Chickasaw Funds (1837). 206, Right of Occupancy of the Ottawas and Chippewas (1837). 207, Claims under the Treaty with the Cherokees (1837). 209, Consent Requisite to a Sale of Indian Reserves (1837). 230, Rights of Indian Reservees (1837). 238, The Creek Indian Orphan Fund (1837). 259, Frauds upon the Creeks (1837). 288, Patents for Creek Reservations (1837). 297, Compensation to Cherokee Reservees (1837). 304, Compensation, &c., to Cherokee Reservees (1838). 322, Title of The Brothertowns under the Menominie Treaty (1838). 326, Location of the Cherokee Reserves (1838). 365, Rights of the Choctaws under Treaty of 1830 (1838). 367, Duties of Attorney General—Claims under Cherokee Treaty (1838). 389, Abandonment of Creek Reserves (1838). 408, Choctaw Reservees under Dancing Rabbit Creek Treaty (1839). 423, Transfers of Creek Reservations (1839). 431, The Cherokee Fund not Liable for Damages, &c. (1839). 458, The Wyandot Reserve at Upper Sandusky (1839). 467, Certain Misnomers in Choctaw Treaty Unimportant (1839). 471, The President and the Judiciary—Payment to Winnebagoes (1839). 504, Attorneys of the Cherokee Indians (1840). 517, Sales of Choctaw Reservations (1840). 578, Confirmation of Sales of Creek Reservations (1840). 584, Priority of Claim of Winnebago Reservees to that of Certain Polish Exiles (1840). 585, Patents to Creeks who have Removed into Georgia (1840). 591, Transfer of Stocks from the Chickasaw to the Choctaw Fund (1840). 596, Confirmation of Sales of Certain Creek Reservations (1840). 624, Right of the Senecas to Retain Possession of their Lands (1841). 644, Concerning Patents for Creek Reserve Lands (1841).

4 Op. A. G. 45, Patents for Choctaw Reserves (1842). 72, Claims for Indian Depredations (1842). 73, New Commissioners under the Cherokee Treaty (1842). 75, Sales of Creek Reservations by Administrators (1842). 77, Sales of Creek Reservations by Administrators (1842). 85, Assignments of Creek Indian Reservations (1842). 86, Claim of Colonel Thomas and Accounting Officers (1842). 96, Patents to Assignees of Indian Reserves (1842). 107, Patents for Reservations to Choctaw Children (1842). 116, Cherokee Reservations under Treaty of 1817 (1842). 144, Power of the President to Prevent Indian Exhibitions (1843). 175, Powers of Present Commissioners under the Cherokee Treaty (1843). 344, Land Claims under Treaty of Dancing Rabbit Creek (1844). 346, Land Claims under Treaty of Dancing Rabbit Creek (1844). 452, Choctaw Claims under Treaty of Dancing Rabbit Creek (1845). 491, Patents to Assignees of Creek Reserves (1846). 500, Payment of an Uncertified Award under Treaty, &c. (1846). 504, Payment of an Uncertified Award under Treaty, &c. (1846). 513, Claims under the Treaty of Dancing Rabbit Creek (1846). 560, Pre-emption Claims under Treaty with the Cherokees (1847). 580, Claims for Improvements under Treaty with the Cherokees (1847). 597, Certificates of Awards of the Cherokee Commissioners (1847). 613, Claim under the Treaty with the Cherokees (1847). 621, Payment of an Award of the Cherokee Commissioners (1847). 626, Accounts and Accounting Officers (1847).

5 Op. A. G. 31, Claim of the Menominies to Certain Lands (1848). 36, Payment of Awards of the Cherokee Commissioners (1848). 46, Payment of Certain Moneys to the Creeks (1848). 98, Payment of an Appropriation for the Creeks (1849). 251, Right of a Choctaw Reservee to a Patent (1850). 268, Claim of Board of Foreign Missions under Treaty with Cherokees (1850). 284, Claim of W. G. and G. W. Ewing against Pottawatomies, (1851). 305, By Whom Indian Treaties are to be Negotiated (1851). 320, Payment of Certain Moneys to the Cherokees (1851). 502, Payment to the Cherokees (1851). 572, Duties of Superintendent of Indian Affairs (1852).

6 Op. A. G. 2, Wyandot Annuities (1853). 49, Contracts of the Potawatomie Indians (1853). 440, Miami Indians (1854). 462, Contracts of Indians (1854). 627, Promulgation of Indian Treaties (1854). 658, Pre-emptions in Kansas (1854). 711, Power of the President (1854).

7 Op. A. G. 54, Improvements under the Cherokee Treaty (1855). 142, Choctaw and Chickasaw Union (1855). 174, Jurisdiction of the Courts of the Choctaw Nation (1855). 293, Indians in Oregon (1855). 746, Relation of Indians to Citizenship (1856).

8 Op. A. G. 255, Portage City Case (1856). 300, Chickasaw Constitution (1857).

9 Op. A. G. 24, Christian Indians (1857). 44, Investment of Wyandot and Delaware Funds (1857). 48, Donation to Cherokee Indians (1857). 110, Kansas Indians (1857).

10 Op. A. G. 253, Lands of the Wea Indians in Kansas (1862).

11 Op. A. G. 145, Claim of the Missionary Society of the Methodist Church (1865). 197, Sale of Lands of Incompetent Wyandott Indians (1865). 384, Annuities to Miami Indians (1865).

12 Op. A. G. 57, Sale of the Cherokee Neutral Lands (1866). 206, Taxation of Indian Cotton (1867). 236, Appropriations for Miami Indians (1867). 516, The Choctaw Trust Fund (1868).

13 Op. A. G. 27, Eligibility to Office (1869). 285, Railroads in the Indian Territory (1870). 336 Ottawa University, Kansas (1870). 354, Choctaw Indians (1870). 470, Unlawful Traffic with Indians (1871). 531, Lands of the Kansas Indians (1871). 546, Case of Edward Dwight, a Choctaw Indian (1871).

14 Op. A. G. 290, Indian Country (1873). 451, Cheyenne and Arapahoe Reservation (1874). 568, Nez Perce Reservation—Claim of W. G. Langford (1875). 573, Indian Agent in Alaska (1875).

15 Op. A. G. 66, Disbursement of Funds for Indian Agencies (1875). 405, Indian Agents and Agencies (1877). 601, Indian Territory—Fugitives In (1877). 632, Indian Treaties (1877).

16 Op. A. G. 31, Creek Orphan Fund (1878). 225, Cherokee Indians (1878). 300, Cherokee Indians (1879). 310, Indian Deed, Approval of, by the President (1879). 325, Deed of Indian (1879). 403, Post-Traders—Traffic with Indians (1879). 404, Removal of Intruders from Cherokee Lands (1879). 451, Employment of Indians in Co-operation with Troops (1880). 470, Cherokee Lands—Removal of Intruders (1880). 568, Trespass on Indian Lands (1880).

17 Op. A. G. 72, Removal of North Carolina Cherokees (1881). 104, Indian Trust Funds (1881). 134, Intruders on Lands of the Choctaws and Chickasaws (1881). 200, Treaty with the Kansas Indians (1881). 258, Indian Reservations (1882). 262, Ute Indian Reservation (1882). 265, Missouri, Kansas and Texas Railway (1882). 306, Claim of William G. Langford (1882). 366, Ute Reservation (1882).

381, Miami Indians of Indiana (1882). 384, Case of Zadoc Staab (1882). 391, Indian Inspector—Bond (1882). 410, Sale of Miami Lands in Kansas (1882). 445, Contract with the Osage Nation of Indians (1882). 460, Criminal Jurisdiction over Indian Reservations (1882). 531, Indian Manual and Training Schools (1883). 566, Crimes Committed by Indians (1883). 647, Indian Schools (1884).

18 Op. A. G. 5, Claim of Vann and Adair (1884). 34, Choctaw and Chickasaw Permit Laws (1884). 41, Transportation of Indian Supplies (1884). 54, Registry of Official Letters or Packets (1884). 66, Indian Territory—Internal Revenue in (1884). 91, Driving Stock on Indian Lands (1884). 138, Jurisdiction over Tribal Indians (1885). 141, Old Winnebago and Crow Creek Reservation (1885). 167, Sale of Indian Trust Lands (1885). 181, Appointment of an Indian as Postmaster (1885). 223, Claims of Ely Moore and Others (1885). 230, Sheyenne Island, Missouri River (1885). 235, Lease of Indian Lands for Grazing Purposes (1885). 242, Indian Contract (1885). 423, Emigrant Half-Breed Indians (1886). 440, Indian Police (1886). 447, Pottawatomie Indians (1886). 486, Indian Leases (1886). 497, Indian Contract (1886). 517, Indian Contract (1886). 544, Seizures in the Indian Country (1887). 555, Cherokee Strip (1887). 557, Indian Immigration (1887). 563, Lemhi Indian Reservation (1887). 581, Indian Trust Funds (1887). 593, Allotment of Lands to Indians (1887).

19 Op. A. G. 14, Allotments of Land to Indians (1887). 35, Klamath Indians (1887). 42, Kansas and Arkansas Valley Railroad Company (1887). 56, Klamath Indians (1887). 95, Purchase of Indian Supplies (1888). 109, Laws of the Choctaw Nation (1888). 115, Membership of Indian Tribe (1888). 117, Sales of Indian Lands in Kansas (1888). 134, Pottawatomie Indians (1888), 161, Taxation of Indian Lands (1888). 173, Seizure of Cattle in Indian Territory (1888). 179, Choctaw Citizenship (1888). 183. Timber Depredations on Indian Lands (1888). 194, Timber on Indian Reservations (1888). 199, Washington and Idaho Railroad Company (1888). 229, Cherokee Citizenship (1889). 232, Timber on Indian Lands (1889). 242, Contract with Pottawatomie Indians (1889). 252. Indian School Service (1889). 255, Indian Allottees—Citizenship (1889). 296, Marshal of Indian Territory (1889). 306, Oklahoma (1889). 342, National Bank in Indian Territory (1889). 389, Choctaw and Chickasaw Treaty of 1866 (1889). 467, Great Sioux Reservation (1890). 499, Leases of Indian Lands (1890). 511, Indian Allottees (1890). 559, Indian Allottees under the Act of 1887 (1890). 710, Timber Unlawfully Cut on Indian Lands (1890).

20 Op. A. G. 42, Allotment of Land to Individual Indians (1891). 215, Pueblo Indians (1891). 245. Commissioner of Indian Affairs—Injunction of State Court (1891). 314, Attorney-General (1892). 494, Indian Agent—Deputy Marshal—Attorney-General (1892). 517, Crow Indians of Montana—Modification of Agreement (1893). 561, Disbursing Officer—False Voucher (1893). 620, District Attorneys—Attorney-General (1893). 711, Sioux Mixed Blood—Attorney-General (1894). 723, Attorney-General (1894). 742, Sioux Mixed Bloods—Attorney-General (1894). 749, Assignability of Indebtedness—Cherokee Nation (1894).

21 Op. A. G. 25, Tax on Retail Liquor Dealers (1894). 72, Indian Territory—Use of Military (1894). 131, Indian Depredation Judgments (1895). 466, Makah Indians—Seals (1897).

22 Op. A. G. 232, Indian Country—Distillery (1898).

23 Op. A. G. 214, Trespassers on Indian Lands (1900). 528, Cherokee Indians—Export Tax on Hay (1901).

24 Op. A. G. 623, Loyal Creek Claims—Attorneys' Fees (1903). 689, Identification of Part Blood Mississippi Choctaw Indians (1903).

25 Op. A. G. 152, Choctaw and Chickasaw Citizenship Court—Annulment of Judgment of Citizenship (1904). 163, Loyal Creek Claims—Distribution of Fund (1904). 168, Lease of Cherokee Mineral Lands—Secretary of the Interior (1904). 308, Delaware Indian Claims—Attorneys' Fees (1904). 320, Choctaw and Chickasaw Nations—Secretary of the Interior, Warrant for Attorneys' Fees (1905). 416, Cass Lake Indian Reservation—Intoxicating Liquors (1905). 460, Approval of Patents to Choctaw and Chickasaw Lands (1905). 483, President—Extension of Trust Patents to Indian Lands (1905). 524, Shoshone Indian Lands—Boysen's Right of Selection (1905). 532, Approval of Sale of Inherited Indian Allotments by the Secretary of the Interior (1905).

26 Op. A. G. 123, Cherokee Enrollment—Mrs. Alice L. Owen and Children (1907). 127, Choctaw Citizenship Cases—Citizenship Court—Finality of Judgment (1907). 171, Cherokee Enrollment—John W. Gleeson (1907). 317, Creek Allotments—Period of Alienation (1907). 330, Eastern Cherokee Fund—Deposit of in Banking Institutions (1907). 340, Seminole Indians—Modification of Agreement with (1907). 351, Cherokee Indian Lands—Periods of Alienation (1907). 613, Commissioner to Five Civilized Tribes—Free Registration of Official Mail Matter (1908).

27 Op. A. G., 530, Indian Allotment Lands—Alienation (1909). 588, Indian Quaparo Allotments—Lease for Business Purposes—License (1909).

28 Op. A. G. 568, Employment of Mr. Hill as attorney for Choctaw Nation (1911).

29 Op. A. G. 131, Indian Allotment Lands—Alienation (1911). 231, Appointment of Mining Trustee for the Choctaw Nation (1911). 239, Sales of Timber from Unallotted Lands of Indian Reservation (1911). 455, Disposition of Reclaimed Land Formerly Covered by Mud Lake, Minn. (1912).

30 Op. A. G. 284, Tennessee Land Titles (1914).

31 Op. A. G. 95, Minnesota National Forest (1917).

32 Op. A. G. 586, Establishment of Religious Missions on the Navajo Treaty Reservation (1921).

33 Op. A. G. 25, Indian Lands—Irrigation Construction Charges (1921). 60, Osage Indians—Tax on Oil and Gas Royalties for Road Construction (1921).

34 Op. A. G. 26, Taxation—Sale of Oil and Gas Mining Lease (1922). 181, Executive Order Indian Reservations—Leasing Act (1924). 275, Income Tax—Five Civilized Tribes of Indians (1924). 302, Five Civilized Tribes of Indians—Income Tax Refund—Statute of Limitations (1924). 439, Income Tax—Restricted Lands of Quapaw Indians (1925).

35 Op. A. G. 1. Income Tax—Restricted Lands of Kaw Indians (1925). 107, Income Tax—Tom Pavatea, Hopi Indian (1926). 251, Title to Land in Bed of Red River (1927). 259, Indians—Sale of Coal and Asphalt Deposits—Disposition of Advance Royalties Paid by Lessees (1927). 421, Attorney's Contract to Represent the Seminole Nation (1928). 438, Boundary of Custer Battlefield National Cemetery Reservation (1928).

36 Op. A. G. 98, Trust of Restricted Indian Funds (1929). 473, Indian Coal and Asphalt Lands—Disposition of Royalties (1931). 506, Revocation of an Erroneous Reappraisal of Land within Fort Peck Indian Reservation (1931).

37 Op. A. G. 193, Validity of Trusts for Indians (1933).

38 Op. A. G. 118, Applicability of Sec. 208 of the N. I. R. A. with Respect to Providing Subsistence Homesteads for Indians (1934). 121, Construction of the Act of June 18, 1934 Relating to Indian Lands (1934). 577, Applicability of Act of June 20, 1936. Tax Relief for Osage Indians (1937).

39 Op. A. G. No. 24, Effect of Decision in "Superintendent v. Commissioner", 295 U. S. 418 upon opinion of Attorney General (34 Op. A. G. 439) Regarding Taxability of Income from Certain Restricted Indian Lands (1937).

BIBLIOGRAPHY

PART I. COMPILATIONS OF FEDERAL INDIAN LAWS, TREATIES AND REGULATIONS

1. COLLECTIONS OF STATUTES

U. S. Department of Interior, Office of Solicitor, Statutory Compilation of the Indian Law Survey: A Compendium of Federal Laws and Treaties Relating to Indians (1940, 46 vols. mimeo.).

United States Code Annotated (1925; cumulative supplements), esp. Title 25, "Indians."

Mason's United States Code Annotated (1926; supplements), esp. Title 25, "Indians."

United States Code (1934; cumulative supplements), esp. Title 25, "Indians."

Federal Code Annotated (1936; supplements), esp. Title 25, "Indians."

2. COLLECTIONS OF TREATIES

Indian Treaties, Laws, Regulations (1826).

Indian Treaties: 1778–1837 (1837).

Revision of Indian Treaties in Force in 1873 (1873).

Kappler, Indian Laws and Treaties, vol. 1 (2d ed., 1904), (Laws to Dec. 1, 1902); vol. 2 (2d ed., 1904) (Treaties); vol. 3 (1913) (Laws to Dec. 1, 1913); vol. 4 (1929) (Laws to March 4, 1927).

3. DIGESTS OF CASES AND CASE LAW

American Digest System, "Indians."

Murchison, Digest of Decisions Relating to Indian Affairs (1901).

Ruling Case Law, vol. 14 (1916; supplements), "Indians."

Corpus Juris, vol. 31 (1923; supplements), "Indians."

Federal Digest, vol. 8 (1927; supplements), "Indians."

American Jurisprudence, vol. 27 (1940), "Indians."

4. COLLECTIONS OF REGULATIONS

Regulations of the Indian Office (1884).

Regulations of the Indian Office (1894).

Regulations of the Indian Office (1904).

Rules and Regulations governing the Department of Interior, Pt. 4 (1907).

Code of Federal Regulations (1939–), esp. Title 25, "Indians."

U. S. Interior Dept., Indian Field Service—Regulations (1939).

5. MISCELLANEOUS

Colonial and State Laws Relating to Indians: 1633 to 1831 (1832).

Laws, Decisions, and Regulations Affecting the Work of the Commissioner to the Five Civilized Tribes, 1892–1906 (1906).

Laws Relating to the Five Civilized Tribes: 1890–1914 (1915).

Barney, Laws Relating to Osage Tribe of Indians: 1824–1929 (1929).

U. S. Interior Dept., Executive Orders Relating to Indian Reservations: vol. 1: May 14, 1855–July 1, 1912 (1912); vol. 2: July 1, 1912–July 1, 1922 (1922).

U. S. Interior Dept., General Data concerning Indian Reservations (1929).

For list of Indian Tribal Constitutions and Charters, see Chap. 7, p. 129 of text.

PART II. LITERATURE ON INDIAN LAW

1. PERIODICAL LITERATURE

ABBOT, Austin, Indians and the Law (1888) 2 HARV. L. REV. 167.

BEAGLEHOLE, Ernest, Ownership and Inheritance in an Indian Tribe (1935) 20 IA. L. REV. 304.

BLACKMAR, F. W., Indian Education (1892) 2 AM. ACAD. POL. AND SOC. SCI. 813.

BROSIUS, S. M., Turning the Indian Loose (1917) 23 CASE AND COM. 739.

BROWN, Ray A., The Indian Problem and the Law (1930) 39 YALE L. J. 307. United States of America's New Departure in Dealing with its Native Indian Population (1936) 18 J. COMP. LEG. 129.

BROWN, Robert C., The Taxation of Indian Property (1931) 15 MINN. L. REV. 182.

CABELL, J. V., Descent and Distribution of Indian Lands (1932) 3 OKLA. S. B. J. 208.

CAIN, Gordon, Indian Land Titles in Minnesota (1918) 2 MINN. L. REV. 177.

CANFIELD, George F., Legal Position of the Indian (1881) 15 AM. L. REV. 21.

CHASE, Hiram, The Law and The American Indians in America (1911) 9 OHIO L. R. 345.

CHICAGO RECORD, Indians as Witnesses (1900) 61 ALBANY L. J. 143.

COHEN, Felix S., How Long Will Indian Constitutions Last? (1939) 6 INDIANS AT WORK No. 10, p. 40. Indian Rights and the Federal Courts (1940) 24 MINN. L. REV. 145.

COHEN, L. K., Treaty of New Echota, Ratified May 23, 1836 (1936) 3 INDIANS AT WORK No. 19.

COLYA, A. S., Indians (1895) 14–17 TENN. BAR ASSO. 144.

DESTY, Robert, Note on Indian country—Federal jurisdiction (1882) 11 FED. 51. Note on Indian country (1882 to 1883) 14 FED. 541.

DIXON, Dr. Joseph K., The Indian (1917) 23 CASE AND COM. 712.

EVANS, J. J., Adverse possession against the Federal Government does not form basis of title, rule applies in action by full-blood Indian heirs (Tobley v. Dekinder (Okla.) 237 Pac. 617) (1926) 6 B. U. L. REV. 37.
FLICKINGER, Samuel J., A Lawyer Looks at the American Indian, Past and Present (April–May 1939) 6 INDIANS AT WORK Nos. 8 and 9.
FLYNN, Clinton R., The Legal Status of the Indians in U. S. (1906) 62 CENT. L. J. 399.
GATES, Merrill E., Address on Land and Law as Agents in Educating Indians (1886) 21 AM. J. SOC. SCI. 112.
GOODRICH, Chauncey Shafter, The Legal Status of the California Indian (1926) 14 CALIF. L. REV. 83, 157.
HAGAN, Horace H., Tribal Law of the American Indian (1917) 23 CASE AND COM. 735.
HARSHA, William Justin, Law for the Indians (1882) 134 N. A. REV. 272.
HILL, W. W., Notes on Pima Land Law and Tenure (1936) AMER. ANTH., N. S. 38, 586.
HORNBLOWER, William B., Legal Status of Indians (1891) 14 A. B. A. Rept. 261.
HOUGHTON, N. D., The Legal Status of Indian Suffrage in the United States (1931) 19 CALIF. L. REV. 507.
ICKES, Harold L., Federal Senate and Indian Affairs (1930) 24 ILL. L. REV. 570.
JACOB, Harvey D., Uncle Sam, The Great White Father (1917) 23 CASE AND COM. 703.
JAMES, James Alton, English Institutions and the American Indian (1894) 12 J. H. UNIV. STUDIES 467.
KNOEPFLER, Karl J., Legal Status of American Indian and His Property (1922) 7 IA. L. B. 232.
KRIEGER, Heinrich, Principles of the Indian Law and the Act of June 18, 1934 (1935) 3 GEO. WASH. L. REV. 279.
KUSWA, M. W., Criminal Law, Jurisdiction, Indians (State v. Rufus (Wis.) 237 N. W. 67) (1931) 16 MARQ. L. REV. 57.
KYLE, James H., How Shall the Indians be Educated (1894) 159 N. A. REV. 434.
L. M. C., Tax on Income Received from Sales of Mineral Resources (Leahy v. State Treasurer of Oklahoma (Okla.) 49 Pac. 2d 570) (1936) 24 GEO. L. J. 486 and 45 YALE L. J. 726.
L. M. G., Indians, Jurisdiction of State Laws (Woodin v. Seeley, 252 N. Y. Supp. 818) (1932) 9 N. Y. U. L. Q. REV. 498.
LAMBERTSON, G. U., Indian Citizenship (1886) 20 AM. L. REV. 183.
LEE, Francis B., Legal Status of Indians and Negroes (1892) 15 N. J. L. J. 103.
McNICKLE, D'Arcy, Four Years of Indian Reorganization (1938) 5 INDIANS AT WORK No. 11.
MAC KENZIE, N. A. M., Indians and Treaties in Law (Rex v. Syliboy (1929) 1 D. L. R. 307) (1929) 7 CAN. B. R. 561.
MAC LEOD, W. C., Law, Procedure and Punishment in Early Bureaucracies (1934) 25 J. CRIM. L. 225. Police and Punishment Among Native Americans of the Plains (1937) 28 J. CRIM. L. 181.
MESERVE, J. B., Cadmus of the Cherokees (1934) 5 OKLA. S. B. J. 130.
MUELLER, Louis C., Administration of Reservation Law and Order under the Indian Reorganization Act (1936) 3 INDIANS AT WORK No. 24.
OSKISON, John N., In Governing the Indian Use the Indian (1917) 23 CASE AND COM. 722.
PARKER, Arthur C., Civic and Government Ideals of the Iroquois Confederation (1917) 23 CASE AND COM. 717.
PLATT, Orville H., Problems in the Indian Territory (1895) 160 N. A. Rev. 195.
POUND, Cuthbert, Nationals Without a Nation (1922) 22 COL. L. REV. 97.
QUAIL, K. F., Tragic Story of Pueblo Indian Land Titles (1937) 6 J. B. A. KAN. 158.
REEVES, John R. T., Memorandum on Senecas and other Indians of the Five Nations of New York, H. Doc. No. 1590, 63d Cong., 3d sess. 1915. Probating Indian Estates (1917) 23 CASE AND COM. 727.
RENEHAN, A. B., Pueblo Lands Act (1927) 33 N. M. S. B. A. 72.
RICE, W. G., The Position of the American Indian in the Law of the United States (1934) 16 J. COMP. LEG. 78.
ROSSER, Judge E. N., A New Acquisition as Applied to Inherited Lands of the Five Civilized Tribes (1909) 3 OKLA. B. A. 159.
RUSSELL, Isaac Franklin, The Indian Before the Law (1909) 19 YALE L. J. 328.
SEYMOUR, Flora Warren, Land Titles in the Pueblo Indian Country (1924) 10 A. B. A. JOUR. 36.
SHINN, P. A., Chief Justice Marshall and the American Indian (1917) 23 CASE AND COM. 842.
SIBBALD, Andrew T., Indian Jails (1902) 14 GREEN BAG 437.
STEWART, J. M., Land Acquisition for Indian Use, Reorganization Number, INDIANS AT WORK, July 1936.
STONE, J. C., Present Status of Indian Land Law (1919) 9 OKLA. B. A. 72.
SUMMER, W. G., The Indians in 1887 (1895) 3 FORUM 254.
T. I. S., Restrictions upon Disposition (Cornelias v. Frank (Okla.) 48 Pac. 2d 1064) (1936) 24 GEO. L. J. 497.
THAYER, James Bradley, A People Without Law (1891) 68 ATL. MONTH. 540, 676.
THOMPSON, Joseph J., Law Among the Aborigines (1924) 6 ILL. L. Q. 204.
TYDINGS, Thomas J., Rights of Indians on Public Lands (1917) 23 CASE AND COM. 743.
VARNEY, George J., The Indian Remnant in New England (1901) 13 GREEN BAG 399.
WATSON, Editha L., The Indian as a Lawyer (1930) 7 DICTA 10.
WEEDEN, W. B., Indian Money as a Factor in New England Civilization (1884) 2 J. H. UNIV. STUDIES 385.
WESTWOOD, C. T., Indian Colony Held to be "Indian Country" in Supreme Court Decision (1938) 5 INDIANS AT WORK No. 7. Legal Aspects of Land Acquisition, prepared for First Inter-American Conference on Indian Life, Patzcuaro, Mexico, Office of Indian Affairs, April 1940.
WHEAT, T. W., New Land—A Lasting Indian Heritage (1936) 4 INDIANS AT WORK No. 8.
WIGMORE, John H., The Federal Senate as a Fifth Wheel (1929) 24 ILL. L. REV. 89.
WILLIS, John W., Indian Eloquence in a Judicial Forum (1916) 82 CENT. L. J. 64.
WISE, Jennings C., Indian Law and Needed Reforms (1926) 12 A. B. A. JOUR. 37.
14 A. B. A. REPT. 12 (1891) Open Forum on Legal Status of Indians.
15 A. B. A. REPT. 423 (1892) Report of Committee on Law and Courts for Indians submitted to annual meeting of Association.
16 A. B. A. REPT. 351 (1893) Report of Special Committee on Indian Legislation.
39 COL. L. REV. 986 (1939) Discrimination.
25 HARV. L. REV. 733 (1912) Indians and the United States.
39 HARV. L. REV. 780 (1926) Restrictions imposed on land purchased for Indian by Secretary of Interior (United States v. Brown, 8 F. 2d 564).
39 HARV. L. REV. 895 (1926) Conflict of Laws, Legitimation, Effect of Indian Tribal Law (Green v. Wilson (Okla.) 240 Pac. 1051).
51 HARV. L. REV. 707, 712, fn. 36 (1938) Note on exemption from state taxation of profits from leased Indian land (Gillespie v. Oklahoma, 257 U. S. 501 (1922)).
INDIANS AT WORK—Indian Legislation, vol. 1, No. 13 (1934). Special Reorganization Number (July 1936).
9 J. H. UNIV. STUDIES 541 (1891) The Character and Influence of the Indian Trade in Wisconsin.
52 JUST. PEACE 737 (1888) Red, Marrying.
13 L. R. A. 542 (1891) Right of Indians to resort to state courts for redress of wrongs (Missouri Pac. R. Co. v. Cullers, 81 Tex. 482).
24 MICH. L. REV. 865 (1926) Indian allotments exempt from State Inheritance Tax (Childers v. Beaver, Sup. Ct. Adv. Ops. 202).
9 N. Y. U. L. Q. REV. 498 (1932) Indians—Jurisdiction of State Laws—Note on Woodin v. Seeley, 141 Misc. 207, 252 N. Y. Supp. 818 (1931).
3 OKLA. S. B. J. 146 (1932) Some interesting cases on bankruptcy as regarding Osage Indian headrights.
11 VA. L. REG. N. S. 619 (1926) State and Federal Jurisdiction in Indian Affairs—Habeas Corpus.
7 YALE L. J. 193 (1898) Voting precincts—Establishment—Indians—Citizenship. Note on State ex rel. Tompton et al. v. Denoyer et al. Count Commissioners, N. W. Rep. (N. D.) 1014.
9 YALE L. J. 373 (1900) Indians—Capacity to Sue—Ejectment. Note on Johnson v. L. I. R. Co., 56 N. E. 992 (N. Y.).
13 YALE L. J. 250 (1904) Legal Status of the Indians—Validity of Indian Marriages—Comment.

18 YALE L. J. 366 (1909) Indians—Actions—Jurisdiction of State. Note on Deragon v. Sero, 118 N. W. 839.

31 YALE L. J. 331 (1922) Jurisdiction—Indian Courts—Powers of State Courts in Controversies over Indian Reservation Lands. Note on unreported N. Y. Case. Wilkins v. Snow, Oct. 25, 1921.

36 YALE L. J. 142 (1926) Constitutional Law—Ore extracted from Indian land not taxable by State. Note on Jaybird Mining Co. v. Weir, 46 Sup. Ct. 592 (1926).

2. TEXTS

ABEL, Annie Heloise, The Slaveholding Indians (Vol. 1, The American Indian as Slaveholder and Secessionist; Vol. 2, The American Indian as Participant in the Civil War; Vol. 3, The American Indian under Reconstruction) (SI) 1915–1925.

ANDREWS, James De Witt, American Law (AL) 1900, pp. 231, 235, 600, 601.

APPLETON, John, Rules of Evidence (RE) 1860, pp. 271, 272.

BAKER, A. J., Annotated Constitution of the United States (ACU) 1891.

BALDWIN, Henry, A General View of the Origin and Nature of the Constitution and Government of the United States (GVO) 1837, pp. 87, 94, 95.

BARRINGER, Daniel Moreau, and ADAMS, John Stokes, The Laws of Mines and Mining in the United States (LMM) 1911, pp. 258, 568–570.

BENNETT, John E., Law of Titles to Indian Lands (LTI) 1917.

BIKLÉ, Henry Wolf, Constitutional Power of Congress over the Territory of the United States (CPC) 1901 (Amer. Law Reg., vol. 49 supp.) pp. 99–100.

BLACK, Henry Campbell, Intoxicating Liquors (IL) 1892, pp. 35, 395, 427. The Law of Tax Titles (TT) 1893, p. 53.

BLACKSTONE, Sir William, Commentaries on the Laws of England in Four Books with notes by William Draper Lewis (CLE) 1900, Book 2, pp. 1–9.

BLAKEMORE, Arthur W., Prohibition (P) 3d ed. 1927, sec. 1276.

BLANCHARD, G. A., and WEEKS, Edw. P., The Law of Mines, Minerals and Mining Water Rights (MMM) 1877, p. 93.

BLEDSOE, S. T., Indian Land Laws (ILL) 2d ed. 1913.

BOONE, Charles T., Law of Real Property (RP) 1901, sec. 464.

BOUTWELL, George S., The Constitution of the United States at the End of the First Century (CUS) 1895, pp. 190, 288, 342, 390.

BOYD, J. P., The Expanding Treaty Power, Selected Essays on Constitutional Law, vol. 3, The Nation and the States, 1938, pp. 410–414.

BRAYER, Herbert O., Pueblo Indian Land Grants of the Rio Abajo (Univ. of New Mexico Bull., No. 334) (PIL) 1939.

BRIGGS, Herbert W., The Law of Nations; Cases, Documents and Notes (LNC) 1938, pp. 41–45, 55–62.

BRODHEAD, J. R., Documents Relative to the Colonial History of the State of New York (Holland Documents II, No. 27) 1855, O'Callaghan ed.

BROSIUS, S. M., Need of Protecting Indian Allotments (Indian Rights Ass'n, 2d ser., No. 67) (NPI) 1904.

BUMP, Orlando, Notes on Constitutional Decisions (NCD) 1878, pp. 58–66.

BURDICK, Charles K., The Law of the American Constitution, its Origin and Development (AC) 1922, pp. 4–6, 312–317, 325, 326.

BUTTE, George C., Legal Status of the American Indian (LSA) 1912.

BYRNE, John Elliott, A Manual of Federal Evidence (MFE) 1928, pp. 246, 280.

CAMERON, Jenks, Bureau of Biological Survey, 1929.

CHEADLE, John Begg, Alienation and Descent of Indian Lands of the Five Civilized Tribes and the Osage Nation (ADI) 1923.

CHEROKEE Nation, Compiled Laws, 1892.

CHICKASAW Nation, Compiled Laws, Homer ed., 1899.

CHOCTAW Nation, Compiled Laws, 1894.

CLARK, Horace F., HELTMAN, Charles C., and CONSAUL, Charles F., Mineral Law Digest (MLD) 1897, pp. 442, 443, 460.

CONOVER, Milton, The General Land Office, its History, Activities and Organization, 1923.

COOKE, Frederick H., The Commerce Clause of the Federal Constitution (CCF) 1908, pp. 62–64.

COOLEY, T. M., Taxation, 4th ed. 1924, vol. 1.

COPP, Henry N., Public Land Laws (PLL) 1875. United States Mineral Lands (USM) 1881, pp. 142, 253, 406, 410.

COSTIGAN, George P. Jr., Handbook on American Mining Law (AML) 1908, pp. 44, 89–91, 467, 558–562, 618–640.

CRANDALL, Samuel B., Treaties, Their Making and Enforcement (TME) 2d ed. 1916, pp. 133, 134, 200, 245, 399.

DEMBITZ, Lewis N., A Treatise on Land Titles in the United States (LTU) 1895, pp. 201, 492–498.

DE SOTO, Emilio and MORRISON, A. R., Mining Rights on the Public Domain (MRP) 1936, pp. 426, 427.

DEVLIN, Robert T., The Law of Real Property and Deeds (LRP) 1911, vol. 2, p. 1103.

DICKINSON, Edwin De Witt, The Equality of States in International Law, 1920.

DORSEY, J. Owen, The Law among the Omaha Indians, 2d Annual Report, Bur. Amer. Eth., 1884.

DUER, William Alexander, A Course of Lectures on the Constitutional Jurisprudence of the United States (CLC) 2d ed., 1856, pp. 281–286.

ELLIOT, Jonathan, The Debates in the Several State Conventions on the Adoption of the Federal Constitution, 1937 ed., vol. 5, p. 439.

FARRAND, Max, Indian Boundary Line (IBL) (Vol. X, No. 4, p. 782, American Historical Review) 1905.

FOSTER, Roger, A Treatise on Federal Practice Civil and Criminal (FPC) 1909, pp. 85, 86.

FOWLER, Robt. L., Real Property Law of the State of New York (RPL) 1909, pp. 82, 108, 142, 143.

FREUND, Ernst, The Police Power; Public Policy and Constitutional Rights (PPP) 1904, pp. 64, 559, 714.

GOODNOW, Frank J., Administrative Law of the United States, 1905.

GRAY, James M., Limitations of the Taxing Power (LTP) 1906, secs. 763, 764, 920, 930, 996b, 1720, 1720a.

HALL, Frederic, The Laws of Mexico (LM) 1885, pp. 60–70.

HARRIS, Charles L., Public Land Guide (PLG) 1912, pp. 117–137, 598–607.

HILLIARD, Francis, The American Law of Real Property (ALR) 1846, pp. 79, 80. Law of Taxation (LT) 1875, pp. 61, 103, 144.

HOLST, Dr. H. von, The Constitutional Law of the United States of America (CLU) 1887, vols. 1–4.

HOOPES, Alban W., Indian Affairs and their Administration (IAA) 1932.

HUNT, G., The American Passport, 1898, pp. 146–148.

HURD, John C., The Law of Freedom and Bondage in the United States (FB) 1858.

INDIAN RIGHTS ASSOCIATION, Indian Trust Funds for Sectarian Schools (ITF) 1905 (2d ser. No. 71).

JACKSON, Helen Hunt, A Century of Dishonor (CD) 1881.

JONES, Burr W., HORWITZ, L., Commentaries on the Law of Evidence in Civil Cases (ECC) 1914, secs. 125, 712, n. 9, 713 nn. 27, 32.

JONES, William Carey, Land Titles in California (CLT) 1850, pp. 4, 10, 11, 17–19, 21, 26, 33, 41, 56, 57, 59, 61, 87–93, 96–98, 112–114, 135, 136, 163, 175, 176.

JUDSON Frederick N., A Treatise on the Power of Taxation, State and Federal, in the United States (PTS) 1917, secs. 26–29, 596.

KENT, James, Commentaries on American Law (CAL) Gould ed., 1896, vol. 1, pp. 257–8; vol. 2, pp. 64, 72, 73; vol. 3, pp. 379–399.

KERR, James M., A Treatise on the Law of Real Property (LRP) 1895, pp. 18n., 196, 197.

KINNEY, J. P., A Continent Lost—A Civilization Won (CLC) 1937.

KROEBER, A. L., The Yurok: Law and Custom, Handbook of California Indians, Bull. No. 78, Bur. Amer. Eth., 1925.

LAUBER, Almon W., Indian Slavery in Colonial Times (ISC) 1913.

LEUPP, Francis E., The Indian and His Problem (IP) 1910.

LINDLEY, Curtis H., A Treatise on the American Law Relating to Mines and Mineral Lands (MML) 1903, pp. 235n., 384–395.

LONG, Joseph R., A Treatise on the Law of Irrigation (LI) 1901, p. 67.

McLAUGHLIN, Andrew C., A Constitutional History of the United States (CHU) 1936, pp. 426–429.

MacNUTT, F. A., Bartholomew de Las Casas: His Life, His Apostolate, and His Writings, 1909.

MANYPENNY, George W., Our Indian Wards (OIW) 1880.

MARTIN, Theodore, Martin's Mining Law and Land Office Procedure (MLL) 1908, pp. 29, 30, 33, 204, 345.
MASS. Hist. Soc. Coll., 1836, Ser. III, vol. 5, p. 5.
MERIAM, Lewis and Associates, Problem of Indian Administration (IA) 1928.
MILLS, Lawrence, The Lands of the Five Civilized Tribes (LFC) 1919. Oklahoma Indian Land Laws (OIL) 1924.
MOHR, Walter H., Federal Indian Relations (FIR) 1933.
MOORE, John Bassett, American Diplomacy, 1918. A Treatise on Extradition and Interstate Rendition (EIR) 1891, pp. 850, 851. A Digest of International Law, 1906, vol. 3.
MOORHEAD, Warren K., The American Indian (AI) 1914.
MORRISON, R. S., Mining Rights, 16th ed. De Soto and Morrison, 1936, pp. 426–427.
MUSKOGEE NATION (CREEK), Compiled Laws, McKellop ed., 1893.
NASH, J. B. et al., The New Day for the Indians; A Survey of the Working of the Indian Reorganization Act of 1934 (NDI) 1938.
NICHOLS, Philip, The Power of Eminent Domain (PED) 1909, secs. 174, 254.
ORDRONAUX, John, Constitutional Legislation in the United States (CLU) 1891, pp. 475–478.
OSAGE NATION, Compiled Laws, Fitzpatrick ed., 1895.
PANCOAST, Henry S., The Indian before the Law (IL) 1884 (Indian Rights Association, 1st ser.).
PASCHAL, George W., The Constitution of the United States (CUS) 1876, pp. 109–112, 203, 223–224, 372, 492–493.
PRENTICE, Ezra P., and EGAN, John G., The Commerce Clause of the Federal Constitution, 1898, pp. 9, 42, 60, 99, 311, 340–354.
RANDOLPH, Carman, The Law of Eminent Domain (ED) 1894, secs. 30, 93, 301.
RAPALJE, Stewart, A Treatise on the Law of Witnesses (LW) 1887, p. 26.
RICE, Frank S., A Treatise on the Modern Law of Real Property (MLR) 1897, pp. 80–82.
ROCKWELL, John A., A Compilation of Spanish and Mexican Law in Relation to Mines and Titles to Real Estate, in force in California, Texas and New Mexico, 1851.
ROYCE, Charles C., Indian Land Cessions in the United States, Extract, 18th Annual Report, Bureau of American Ethnology, 1900.
SCHMECKEBIER, Laurence F., The Office of Indian Affairs, Its History, Activities and Organization (OIA) 1927.
SCHOULER, James, Marriage, Divorce, Separation and Domestic Relations, 6th ed. 1921, pp. 24, 1365–1366, 2082.
SEDGWICK, Arthur G., and WAIT, F. S., A Treatise on the Principles and Practice Governing the Trial of Title to Land (PPT) 1882, secs. 194, 228.
SMITH, Archilla, Indian Justice—A Cherokee Murder Trial at Talequah (IJC) 1934.
SNYDER, Wilson I., Mines and Mining (MM) 1902, secs. 154, 171–179, 245.
STEWARD, Dora Ann, Government and Development of Oklahoma Territory (GDO), 1933.
STORY, Joseph, and BIGELOW, M. M., Commentaries on the Constitution of the United States (CCU) 1891, vol. 1, pp. 5–18, 19–104, 106, 107; vol. 2, pp. 9–10, 41–44, 683–684.
SULLIVAN, James, History of Land Titles in Massachusetts (HLT) 1801, pp. 21–27.
SWANTON, John R., Crime and Punishment among the Creek Indians, 42d Annual Report Bur. Amer. Eth. 1928.
THOMPSON, Edward, The Constitution and the Courts (CC) 1924.
THORNTON, W. W., The Law Relating to Oil and Gas (OG) 1925, sec. 293; pp. 2614, 2629, 2643, 2671, 2682, 2710, 2727, 2734, 2744, 2781, 2793, 2794, 2797.
U. S. DEPARTMENT OF JUSTICE, Federal Eminent Domain (1939).
USHER, Roland G., Pan-Americanism, 1915.
VAN DOREN, Carl, Indian Treaties Printed by Benjamin Franklin (1736–1762) 1938 (Intro. by J. P. Boyd). Benjamin Franklin, 1938, pp. 103, 200–209, 307–10, 364–5, 649, 705–6, 758–59, 771.
VAN DYNE, Frederick, Citizenship of the United States (CUS) 1904, pp. 7–15, 58, 121, 230, 235–237.
VATTEL, Emmerich de, The Law of Nations (LN) 1758, Chitty ed. 1839, Book I, c. XVIII.
VICTORIA, Francisco de, De Indis et De Jure Belli Relectiones, 1577, (trans. by John P. Bate 1917).
WALKER, Francis A., The Indian Question (IQ) 1874.
WASHBURN, Emory, A Treatise on the American Law of Real Property (ALR) 1902, p. 169.
WATSON, David K., The Constitution of the United States (CU) 1910, pp. 22, 28–29, 516–519, 618.
WEEKS, Edward P., A Commentary on the Mining Legislation of Congress (MLC) 1880, pp. 45, 46.
WHARTON, Francis, Commentaries on Law (CL) 1884, secs. 26, 265, 434, 585. A Treatise on the Conflict of Laws or Private International Law (CLP) Parmele ed. 1905, pp. 40–45, 50, 152, 307, 570.
WHEATON, Henry, and PHILLIPSON, Coleman, Wheaton's Elements of International Law (EIL) 1916, pp. 66–68.
WHITE, Joseph M., New Recopilacion of the Laws of Spain and the Indies (1839).
WIEL, Samuel C., Water Rights in the Western States (WRW) 1911, pp. 234, 237–241, 342, 409, 572, 785.
WILLIS, Hugh E., Constitutional Law of the United States (CLU) 1936, pp. 182–184, 257, 266.
WILLOUGHBY, W. W., The Constitutional Law of the United States (CLU) 1929, pp. 290, 362, 379–402, 1327, 1368.
WILSON, George G., and TUCKER, George F., International Law, 9th ed. 1935, pp. 63, 112.
WISE, Jennings C., The Red Man in the New World Drama (RMN) 1932.

PART III. BACKGROUND MATERIALS

1. INDIAN ADMINISTRATION AND POLICY

ABEL, Annie H., Indian Consolidation, Amer. Hist. Assn. Rep., vol. 1, p. 361, 1906; Proposals for an Indian State 1778–1878, Amer. Hist. Assn. Rep., vol. 1, p. 89, 1907.
ABERLE, Sophie, Some Aspects of the Personnel Problem of the Indian Service, Indians of the United States, Office of Indian Affairs, April, 1940.
ADAMS, Henry, History of the United States During the First Administration of James Madison (1809–1813), 1890, vols. VI, VII.
AMERICAN INDIAN LIFE, American Indian Defense Association, Bull. 10 (1927) to 24 (1934).
BALLAGH, James C., The Letters of Richard Henry Lee, 1911, vol. 2, p. 298.
BARROWS, Wm., The Indian's Side of the Indian Question, 1887.
BEATTY, W. W., The Federal Government and the Education of Indians and Eskimos, 7 Jour. Negro Education, No. 3, July, 1938.
BLAUCH, L. E., Educational Service for Indians, Staff Study No. 18, Advisory Com. on Education, 1939.
BUREAU OF MUNICIPAL RESEARCH, Administration of the Indian Office, Municipal Research No. 65, 1915.
COHEN, Felix S., Anthropology and the Problems of Indian Administration, 18 Southwestern Social Science Quarterly No. 2, 1937.
COLLIER, John, America's Handling of Its Indigenous Indian Minority, 7 Indians at Work No. 5, Dec. 4, 1939. A Birdseye View of Indian Policy, Historic and Contemporary, Office of Indian Affairs, Washington, 1935 (mimeo.). The Indian Bureau, The Indians and President Roosevelt, Bull. No. 21, American Indian Life, 1933.
COOK, Katherine M., Public Education in Alaska, Bull. No. 12, Office of Education, 1936.
DIMOND, A. J., Speech on Alaska Natives, 83 Cong. Rec. pt. 9, pp. 179–180, 75th Cong., 3d sess. 1938.
FOREMAN, Grant, Indian Removal, 1932.
FRASER, George A. H., Status of Pueblo of Pojoaque, 1932 (unpublished, U. S. Dept. of Interior, Sol. Off.)
GESSNER, Robert, Massacre: A Survey of Today's American Indian, 1931.
GREELEY, Horace, The American Conflict, 1864, vol. I, p. 106.
HARPER, Allan G., Report on the Shinnecock and Poosepatuck Indian Reservations in Relation to the Reorganization Act, Office of Indian Affairs, Jan. 1936 (mimeo.).
KING, William H., The Conditions of the Indians in the United States, Gov't Printing Office, Washington, 1933.

LA FARGE, Oliver, As Long as the Grass Shall Grow, 1940.
LATIMER, Joseph W., Our Indian Bureau System (OIB) 1923.
LEUPP, Francis E., Civil Service Reform Essential to a Successful Indian Administration (Indian Rights Ass'n 2d ser. No. 23) (CSR) 1895.
LORD, Russell, To Hold This Soil, Gov't Printing Office, Washington, 1938 (Misc. Pub. No. 321).
LUMPKIN, Wilson, Removal of the Cherokee Indians from Georgia, 1907.
McCASKILL, Joseph C., The Cessation of Monopolistic Control of Indians, by the Indian Office, Indians of the United States, Office of Indian Affairs, April 1940.
MALIN, James C., Indian Policy and Westward Expansion, 1921.
MASSACHUSETTS HIST. COLL., 1st ser., vol. I, 1792 ed., p. 173.
MORGAN, Thos J., The Present Phase of the Indian Question, 1891 (Pub. No. 10 Boston Indian Citizenship Committee).
NATIONAL ADVISORY COMMITTEE ON EDUCATION, Federal Relations to Education, 1931.
NATIONAL CONFERENCE OF SOCIAL WORK, Comm. on Amer. Ind., Cooperation in Indian Administration (IA) 1931.
NATIONAL RESOURCES PLANNING BOARD, Indian Land Tenure, Economic Status, and Population Trends, 1935.
OTIS, D. S., History of the Allotment Policy, Hearings, H. Comm. on Ind. Aff., 73d Cong., 2d sess., on H. R. 7902, 1934, pt. 9, pp. 428 *et seq.*
RICHARDSON, J. D., Messages and Papers of the Presidents, 1897, vol. IX, pp. 3992–3993.
SUMNER, Charles, Works, 1875, vol. XI, pp. 186–349.
THOMAS, David E., Economic Rehabilitation of Alaska, Indians at Work, April 1940 Supp.
U. S. DEPT. OF INTERIOR, OFFICE OF INDIAN AFFAIRS, A Brief Statement on the Background of Present-day Indian Policy, Nov. 21, 1938 (mimeo.). Reports of Conferences leading to Act of June 18, 1934: Minutes of the Plains Congress, Rapid City Indian School, March 2–5, 1934; Minutes of All-Pueblo Council, Santo Domingo Pueblo, March 15, 1934; Report of Southern Arizona Indian Conference, Phoenix Indian School, March 15–16, 1934; Proceedings of the Conference for the Indians of the Five Civilized Tribes of Oklahoma, Muskogeee, Oklahoma, March 22, 1934. Résumé of Proceedings, Conference on Indian Allotted and Heirship Land Problems, Aug. 14–17, 1938, Glacier Park, Montana, 1938 (mimeo.).
WORK, Hon. Hubert, Indian Policies: Comments on Resolutions of the Advisory Council on Indian Affairs, 1924.

2. MISCELLANEOUS

AMERICAN ASS'N OF INDIAN AFFAIRS, News Letter Supp. May 15, 1940.
ANDERSON, H. D. and EELLS, W. C., Alaska Natives, 1935.
ANDREWS, C. L., Alaska Under the Russians, VII Washington Hist. Quart. 1916.
ARCTANDER, John W., The Apostle of Alaska, 1909.
BANDELIER, Adolph F. and HEWETT, Edgar L., Indians of the Rio Grande Valley, 1937.
BEERS, Henry Putney, The Western Military Frontier, 1935.
BRIMLOW, George F., The Bannock Indian War of 1878, 1938.
BROOKS, Alfred H., The Future of Alaska, Annals of the Association of American Geographers, Dec. 1925.
CLARK, H. W., History of Alaska, 1930.
COLLIER, John, The Indian and Religious Freedom; Even as you Do Unto the Least of These, So You Do Unto Me, Amer. Ind. Defense Ass'n 1924.
CURRY, J. E., Principles of Cooperation, 4 Indians at Work No. 16, April 1, 1937.
DALL, W. H., Alaska and its Resources, 1870.
ELLIS, Edward S., The Indian Wars of the United States, 1892.
ENCYCLOPEDIA BRITANNICA, vol. 1, 14th ed. 1936, p. 502.
ENCYCLOPAEDIA OF THE SOCIAL SCIENCES, vol. XI, 1935, p. 269.
FORD, Worthington, Writings of George Washington, vol. X, 1891, pp. 300–312.
FOREMAN, Grant, Advancing the Frontier, 1933.
FRANKLIN, Benj., Remarks Concerning the Savages of North America, in Two Tracts, etc., 2d ed., 1794.
HELLENTHAL, John A., The Alaskan Melodrama, 1936.
HEWETT, Edgar L., Ancient Life in the American Southwest, 1930.
HODGE, Frederick W., Handbook of American Indians, 2 vols., Gov't Printing Office, Washington, 1907.
HRDLICKA, Ales, The Coming of Man from Asia in the Light of Recent Discoveries, Annual Report, Smithsonian Inst., 1935.
JAMES, Marquis, Andrew Jackson, 1933.
JENNESS, Diamond, Anthropology—Prehistoric Culture Waves from Asia to America, 30 Jour. Wash. Acad. of Sc. No. 1, 1940, pp. 1–15. The Eskimos of Northern Alaska, V Geo. Rev. 1918.
JOHNSON, William E., The Federal Government and the Liquor Traffic, 1911.
JONES, Livingston F., A Study of the Thlingets of Alaska, 1914.
JOURNAL OF NEGRO EDUCATION, The Courts and the Negro Separate School, vol. 4, 1935, p. 289.
KNAPP, F. and CHILDE, R. L., The Thlinkets of Southeastern Alaska, 1896.
KRIEGER, H. W., Indian Villages of Southeast Alaska, Smithsonian Inst. 1928.
LOCKWOOD, Frank C., The Apache Indians, 1938.
MACLEOD, Wm. Christie, The American Indian Frontier, 1928.
METLAKAHTLAN, The, vol. 1, Nos. 1–8, 1888–1891.
NICHOLS, Jeanette P., Alaska, 1924.
OSGOOD, C., Distribution of the Northern Athapaskan Indians, Yale Univ. Pub. in Anthro., No. 7, 1936; Ethnography of the Tanaina, Yale Univ. Pub. in Anthro. No. 16, 1937.
OSKISON, John M., Tecumseh and his Times, 1938.
PACIFIC FISHERMAN YEAR BOOK, 1939.
PAXSON, Frederic A., Pacific Railroad and the Disappearance of the Frontier in America, Amer. Hist. Ass'n Rep., vol. 1, p. 107, 1907.
PHELPS-STOKES FUND, The Navajo Problem, 1939.
SEYMOUR, Flora Warren, The Story of the Red Man, 1929.
SPICER, George W., Constitutional Status and Government of Alaska, 1927.
STEFANSSON, V., My Life with the Eskimo, 1913.
TURNER, Frederick Jackson, The Frontier in American History, 1920.
U. S. AGRICULTURE, Department of
  Bull. No. 1089 (1922) Reindeer in Alaska.
  Bull. No. 1423 (1926) Progress of Reindeer Grazing Investigations in Alaska.
U. S. COMMERCE, Department of
  Annual Report, Secretary of Commerce, 1938.
  Bureau of the Census, The Indian Population of the United States and Alaska, 1930, Gov't Printing Office, 1937.
  15th Census of the United States, Outlying Territories and Possessions (1932).
  Bureau of Fisheries:
    Bull., vol. XLVII, No. 13 (1933) Alaska Fishing and Fur-Seal Industry.
    Bull., vol. XLIV, Doc. No. 1041 (1928) Salmon.
  Circular No. 286. 9th ed. June 29, 1939, Regulations re Alaskan Fishing.
U. S. INTERIOR, Department of
  Alaska, Annual Report of Governor, 1939.
  Problem of Alaskan Development, April 1940.
  Bureau of Biological Survey, Annual Reports 1937–1939.
    Regulations for the Aleutian Islands Reservation, Alaska, 1939.
    Wildlife Circular 1, 1939.
  Bureau of Education, Annual Reports 1891–1931.
    A Course of Study for United States Schools for Natives of Alaska, 1926.
  Dawes Commission Reports 1894–1905.
  Land Utilization Division, Forest Conservation on Lands Administered by the Department of the Interior, 1940.
  Office of Indian Affairs, Annual Reports of Commissioners, 1825–1939; Statistical Supplement, 1938.
    Board of Indian Commissioners, Reports, 1869–1933.
    Indian Office Letter Books (beginning in 1800).
    Indians at Work, semi-monthly magazine, 1933–1937; monthly from 1937.
U. S. NATIONAL RESOURCES PLANNING BOARD, Alaska, Its Resources and Development, 1937.
U. S. SMITHSONIAN INSTITUTION, Bureau of American Ethnology:
  2d Annual Report, The Law among the Omaha Indians (Dorsey), 1884.
  18th Annual Report, Indian Land Cessions in the United States (Royce), 1900.

42d Annual Report, Crime and Punishment among the Creek Indians (Swanton), 1928.
Bull. No. 30, Handbook of American Indians (Hodge), 1907.
Bull. No. 78, Handbook of California Indians (Kroeber), 1925.
U. S. TREASURY DEPARTMENT.
Combined Statement of Receipts etc. of the United States for Fiscal Year ended June 30, 1939, pp. 417–427, on tribal funds.
Public Health Reports, Supp. No. 9, Dec. 12, 1913, on reindeer.

WARDWELL, Morris L., A Political History of the Cherokee Nation, 1938.

WEBB, Walter P., The Great Plains, 1926.

WELLCOME, Henry S., The Story of Metlakahtla, 2d ed. 1909.

WHIPPLE, H. B., Lights and Shadows of a Long Episcopate, 1899.

WICKERSHAM, James, Old Yukon, 1938.

WISSLER, Clark, The American Indian, 1938 (3d ed.)

PART IV. CONGRESSIONAL DOCUMENTS

American Archives
4th series, 1774–1775, Vol. I, Col. 174
5th series, 1776, Vol. III, pp. 800–807
American State Papers
7 (Class II, Ind. Aff. Vol. I) 1789–1815
8 (Class II, Ind. Aff. Vol. II) 1815–1827
36 (Class IX, Claims) p. 193, 1797; pp. 309–310, 1805
Journals of the Continental Congress (Library of Congress ed.), Vols. I–XXXIV, 1774–1789.
Nov. 11, 23, 1775, Vol. III, pp. 350, 351, 365–368. Reference to treaty of neutrality with Six Nations at Albany, Aug. 1775.
Apr. 19, 1776, Vol. IV, pp. 294–295. Instructions to Indian agent to cultivate harmony and friendship with western nations.
June 11, 1776, Vol. V, p. 430. Interview with Indians of Six Nations to gain friendship.
Dec. 3, 1777, Vol. IX, pp. 994–999. Instructions to Commissioner for Indian Affairs on appeals to Six Nations for unity and cooperation.
Oct. 15, 1783, Vol. XXV, pp. 680–695. Instructions to Commissioners on negotiating for peace with hostile Indians of northern and middle department.
Mar. 19, 1784, Vol. XXVI, pp. 152–155. Amendments to instructions on peace negotiations with Indians.
June 15, 1785, Vol. XXVIII, pp. 459–462. On peace treaty with western tribes, and other peace negotiations.
April 17, 1786, Vol. XXX, pp. 185–195. Treaties with Shawanese (Jan. 31, 1786), Cherokees (Nov. 28, 1785), Chickasaws (Jan. 10, 1786), Choctaws (Jan. 3, 1786).
Aug. 3, 1787, Vol. XXXIII, pp. 454–463. Recommendations of committee on Ind. Aff., particularly on land disputes between Creek and Cherokee Indians, and states of North Carolina and Georgia.
Oct. 26, 1787, Vol. XXXIII, pp. 707–714. Instructions to Commissioners for negotiating a treaty between southern Indians and states of North Carolina and Georgia.
Sept. 1, 1788, Vol. XXXIV, pp. 476–479. Proclamation against intrusions on Cherokee lands.

1 C:1 Annals of Congress, 1789, pp. 66 et seq., Message on appointment of commissioners to negotiate and make treaties with the Indians—President George Washington.
Annals of Congress, 1789–91, p. 83, Message on nature of Indian treaties—President George Washington.

2 C:1 Ex. Doc., Nov. 10, 1791, Report on public lands; Indian claims—Sec'y T. T. Jefferson.

2 C:2 Annals of Congress, Nov. 6, 1792, pp. 607–608, Continuance of Indian hostilities—Annual message, President George Washington.

3 C:1 Annals of Congress, Dec. 3, 1793, pp. 12–13, Progress of peace negotiations with Indians; complaints of Cherokees—Annual message, President George Washington.

4 C:1 Annals of Congress, 1796–1797, pp. 229–230, Indian trading houses.

4 C:2 Annals of Congress, Dec. 7, 1796, pp. 1592–1593, Measures taken to establish peace with Indians—Annual Message, President George Washington.

5 C:2 Ex. Doc., Jan. 5, 1798, Relations with the Cherokees re Treaty of 1792 (land cessions, boundary line)—Sec'y Jas. McHenry.

6 C:1 Ex. Doc., April 22, 1800, Report on Indian trading houses.

7 C:1 Ex. Doc., Dec. 8, 1801, Report on the Creek Indians—Indian Agent Benjamin Hawkins.
Ex. Doc., Jan. 7, 1802, Memorial of Society of Friends on Indian Affairs on sale of liquor to Indians.
Annals of Congress, Jan. 28, 1802, pp. 150–151, Message on Indian trading houses; its extension; recommendation of prohibition of liquor from Indian territory—President T. Jefferson.

7 C:2 Ex. Doc., Jan. 18, 1803, Report on Indian Affairs—treaties, boundaries, trading houses—Sec'y H. Dearborn.

8 C:1 Annals of Congress, 1803–4, p. 105, Message on Indian land cessions—President T. Jefferson.

9 C:1 Annals of Congress, 1805–7, p. 15, Message on Indian land cessions—President T. Jefferson.

10 C:2 Annals of Congress, 1808–9, p. 13, Message on Indian relations—President T. Jefferson.

11 C:2 Ex. Doc., April 14, 1810, Report on Indian trading houses—Rep. Jos. Anderson.
Ex. Doc., April 27, 1810, Laws and treaties relating to public lands (Printed by J. Gales, Jr., Washington, D. C.).

12 C:1 Ex. Repts., Jan. 16, 1812, On Indian traders—Sec'y W. Eustis.

13 C:2 Annals of Congress, Dec. 7, 1813, vol. I, pp. 540–541, Incitement of Indians by enemy—Annual message, President Jas. Madison.

14 C:1 Ex. Rept., March 14, 1816, Report on Indian Affairs—Sec'y of War W. H. Crawford.

14 C:2 Sen. Doc., Jan. 17, 1817, Report on the Cherokee land claims—Acting Sec'y of War Graham.
H. Doc., Feb. 4, 1817, Report on Indian trade—Comm. on Ind. Aff.

15 C:1 Annals of Congress, 1817–1818, pt. I, pp. 800–801, Report on establishment of trading houses and encouragement of education.

15 C:2 Sen. State papers No. 47, Dec. 23, 1818, Petition for the civilization of the Indian—Society of Friends.
H. Doc. No. 91, vol. 6, Jan. 15, 1819, On the civilization of the Indian tribes.

16 C:1 Sen. Doc. No. 47, vol. I, Feb. 16, 1820, Report on the Indian Trade and Intercourse—Comm. on Indian Affairs.
Sen. Doc. No. 105, vol. II, April 5, 1820, On abolition of the system of Indian trade.
H. Doc. No. 46, vol. 3, Jan. 15, 1820, Report on Indian Affairs—Sec'y J. C. Calhoun.

16 C:2 Sen. Doc. No. 14, vol. I, Dec. 4, 1820, Indian annuities.

17 C:1 Sen. Doc. No. 10, vol. I, Jan. 14, 1822, the Indian trade, etc.
Sen. Doc. No. 50, vol. I, Feb. 23, 1822, Message on the civilization of the Indians—President James Monroe.
H. Doc. No. 60, vol. VI, Feb. 9, 1822, Letter and papers relating to superintendency of Indian Affairs in Territory of Michigan—Sec'y J. C. Calhoun.
H. Doc. No. 110, vol. VIII, April 11, 1822, Report on the Indian Department—Sec'y J. C. Calhoun.
H. Repts. No. 10, vol. I, Jan. 7, 1822, On the treaties with the Creek and Cherokee Indians.

17 C:2 H. Repts. No. 104, vol. II, March 1, 1823, Abolishing Indian trading establishments—Comm. on Indian Affairs.
H. Repts. No. 106, vol. II, Feb. 13, 1823, Extinguishment of Indian title to lands—Comm. on Public Lands.

18 C:1 Sen. Doc. No. 56, vol. III, Feb. 11, 1824, Request for Information from Secretary of War on plan for peace and trade with Indians—Sen. T. H. Benton, Chairman Comm. on Ind. Aff.

Sen. Doc. No. 79, vol. III, May 14, 1824, Report on Indians in Missouri—Comm. on Indian Affairs.

H. Doc. No. 47, vol. II, Jan. 24, 1824, Statement on disbursement for civilization of Indians—Sec'y J. C. Calhoun.

H. Doc. No. 56, vol. IV, Jan. 12, 1824, Report on Indian agencies—Sec'y J. C. Calhoun.

H. Repts. No. 92, vol. II, March 23, 1824, On civilization of the Indian—Comm. on Indian Affairs.

H. Repts. No. 101, vol. II, April 5, 1824, Creek Indian claims—Comm. of Ways and Means.

H. Repts. No. 129, vol. II, May 25, 1824, Abolition of Indian trading establishments.

18 C:2 H. Doc. No. 19, vol. II, Dec. 23, 1824, Instructions for treaty with Cherokee Indians.

H. Doc. No. 72, vol. IV, Feb. 5, 1825, Creek Indian claims.

19 C:1 H. Doc. No. 21, vol. III, Jan. 3, 1826, Message on treaty with Cherokee Indians—President J. Q. Adams.

H. Doc. No. 74, vol. IV, Feb. 1, 1826, Report on treaty negotiations with Florida Indians.

H. Doc. No. 102, vol. V, Feb. 3, 1826, Report on preservation and civilization of Indian tribes—Sec'y James Barbour.

H. Doc. No. 111, vol. VI, March 1, 1826, Message and correspondence on Florida Indians—President J. Q. Adams.

H. Doc. No. 124, vol. VIII, March 1, 1826, Report on preservation and civilization of the Indians—Gen'l Clark, Supt. Ind. Aff.

H. Doc. No. 146, vol. VIII, March 21, 1826, On establishment of a general superintendency of Indian Affairs in Department of War.

H. Repts. No. 226, vol. II, May 20, 1826, Intercourse with the Indians—Comm. on Indian Affairs.

19 C:2 H. Doc. No. 5, vol. II, Dec. 8, 1826, Message on proposed land donations by Indian Tribes—President J. Q. Adams.

H. Doc. No. 9, vol. II, Dec. 11, 1826, Message on Indian Affairs—President J. Q. Adams.

H. Doc. No. 17, vol. II, Dec. 16, 1826, War Department correspondence relating to Florida Indians.

H. Doc. No. 28, vol. II, Jan. 2, 1827, Removal of the Indians westward.

H. Doc. No. 39, vol. III, Jan. 5, 1827, Encroachments on Choctaw lands.

H. Doc. No. 59, vol. IV, Jan. 8, 1827, Report and resolutions of the legislature of Georgia on differences between the General Government and Georgia.

H. Doc. No. 82, vol. V, Jan. 30, 1827, Florida Indians.

H. Repts. No. 51, vol. I, Jan. 23, 1827, Indian depredations in Missouri.

20 C:1 H. Doc. No. 148, vol. IV, Feb. 15, 1829, On selling spirits to the Indian Tribes.

H. Repts. No. 56, vol. I, Jan. 7, 1828, Report for the removal of Indians—Indian Committee.

H. Repts. No. 128, vol. II, Claims against Creek Indians by citizens of Georgia.

20 C:2 H. Doc. No. 11, vol. I, Dec. 8, 1828, On civilization of the Indians.

21 C:1 Sen. Doc. No. 98, vol. II, March 8, 1830, Documents relative to Georgia jurisdiction over Indians.

Sen. Doc. No. 110, vol. II, March 25, 1830, Report on Indians—Sec'y J. H. Eaton.

H. Doc. No. 89, vol. III, April 2, 1830, Message relative to Cherokee lands—President Andrew Jackson and Report of Sec'y of War J. H. Eaton.

H. Rept. No. 227, Feb. 24, 1830, Removal of Indians.

21 C:2 H. Repts. No. 109, March 2, 1831, Report on removal of Creek Indians—Indian Committee.

22 C:1 H. Doc. No. 102, vol. III, 1832, Memorial of Creek Nation of Indians.

H. Doc. No. 127, vol. IV, Feb. 27, 1832, Statement relative to Indian annuities.

H. Doc. No. 242, vol. VI, May 22, 1832, Indian annuities.

H. Repts. No. 488, vol. V, June 6, 1832, Lease of Indian reservation—Chickasaws—Comm. on Public Lands.

22 C:2 Sen. Doc. No. 24, vol. I, Dec. 20, 1832, Indian annuities payable in 1833.

23 C:1 Sen. Doc. No. 386, vol. V, May 19, 1834, Memorial of Cherokee Indians.

H. Doc. No. 133, vol. III, Feb. 27, 1834, Estimates of Indian annuities now payable under treaty stipulations.

H. Repts. No. 140, vol. I, Jan. 7, 1834, Indian depredation claims—Comm. on Indian Affairs.

H. Repts. No. 474, vol. IV, May 20, 1834, Regulating the Indian Department—Comm. on Indian Affairs.

23 C:2 Sen. Doc. No. 1, vol. I, pp. 237 et seq., Nov. 25, 1834, Report from the Office of Indian Affairs.

H. Doc. No. 186, vol. V, Feb. 26, 1835, Indian annuities.

24 C:1 H. Rept. No. 663, vol. III, Report on Choctaw land claims—House Indian Comm.

24 C:2 H. Rept. No. 301, vol. II, Indian depredations in Florida, Georgia and Alabama.

25 C:2 Sen. Doc. No. 106, vol. II, Jan. 16, 1838, Report on payment of Indian annuities—Sec'y of War J. R. Poinsett.

Sen. Doc. No. 120, vol. II, Jan. 12, 1838. Report and documents relative to the Cherokee Treaty of 1835—Sec'y of War J. R. Poinsett.

Sen. Doc. No. 198, vol. III, Feb. 13, 1838, Letter on Indian annuities—Sec'y of War J. R. Poinsett.

25 C:3 H. Rept. No. 244, vol. I (H. R. 1112), Feb. 6, 1839, Petition of Brothertown Indians.

26 C:1 Sen. Doc. No. 347, vol. VI, March 2, 1840, Difficulties between Government and Cherokees.

26 C:2 Sen. Doc. No. 210, vol. IV, Feb. 22, 1841, Petition concerning Seneca Indian Treaty.

27 C:2 Sen. Doc. No. 188, vol. III, March 9, 1842, Claims arising out of the treaty with the Choctaw Indians.

H. Doc. No. 25, vol. I, Dec. 15, 1841, Caddo Indian Treaty.

H. Rept. No. 1035, vol. V, Aug. 20, 1842, Report on Caddo Indian Treaty.

27 C:3 H. Doc. No. 110, vol. IV, Jan. 31, 1843, Message on Cherokee Claims Commissioners—President John Tyler.

H. Rept. No. 271, vol. III, Feb. 25, 1843, Message on frauds on Indians.

28 C:1 Sen. Doc. No. 229, vol. IV, March 14, 1844, Report on Cherokee Indians—Wm. Wilkins, Sec'y of War.

H. Doc. No. 2, vol. I, Nov. 25, 1843, Report of Comm. of Indian Affairs—T. H. Crawford.

H. Doc. No. 82, vol. IV, Jan. 26, 1844, Message on Florida Indians—President John Tyler.

H. Doc. No. 247, vol. V, April 23, 1844, Report on Indian school fund—Sec'y William Wilkins.

H. Doc. No. 253, vol. VI, May 8, 1844, Report on Indians remaining in Florida—Wm. Wilkins, Sec'y of War.

H. Rept. No. 391, vol. II, (H. R. 3) March 29, 1844, Claims under Cherokee Treaty.

H. Rept. No. 519, vol. III, (H. R. 35) May 29, 1844, Removal of Chippewa, Ottawa and Pottawatomie Indians.

28 C:2 Sen. Doc. No. 1, vol. I, pp. 305–307, Nov. 25, 1844, Report on Indian Affairs.

Sen. Doc. No. 160, vol. IX, March 1, 1845, Transfer of Chickasaw and Choctaw orphan funds.

29 C:1 Sen. Doc. No. 461, vol. IX, (S. 242) July 28, 1846, On extending criminal laws of U. S. over Indian territories.

H. Doc. No. 2, vol. I, pp. 448–643, Nov. 24, 1845, On Indian Affairs.

H. Doc. No. 190, vol. VI, April 27, 1846, Message on Chickasaw Indians.

H. Doc. No. 195, vol. VI, May 6, 1846, Message on Chickasaw Indians—President James Polk.

29 C:2 Sen. Doc. No. 113, vol. III, Jan. 13, 1847, Report of Comm. of Indian Affairs—W. Medill, re claims under Cherokee Treaty of 1835.

30 C:1 Sen. Doc. No. 1, vol. I, pp. 734–943, Nov. 30, 1847, Report of Comm. of Indian Affairs—W. Medill.

H. Rept. No. 826, vol. IV (H. R. 643), Aug. 8, 1848, Claim of Creek Indians.

31 C:1 H. Ex. Doc. No. 5, vol. III, pt. 2, pp. 937–1176, Annual report of Comm. of Indian Affairs—Orlando Brown.

Sen. Rept. No. 176, vol. I, Aug. 8, 1850, Memorial of delegates of Cherokee Nation.

31 C:2 H. Ex. Doc. No. 1, vol. I, pp. 35–168, Nov. 27, 1850, Report on Indian Affairs—Comm. L. Lea.

32 C:1 Sen. Rept. No. 181, vol. I, April 12, 1852, Claims of Choctaw Indians.

32 C:2 Sen. Ex. Doc. No. 1, vol. I, pp. 293–466, Nov. 30, 1852, Report on Indian Affairs—Comm. L. Lea.

Sen. Ex. Doc. No. 57, vol. VII, March 3, 1853, Report on Indian Affairs in California—Sec'y A. H. H. Stuart.

33 C:1 Sen. Ex. Doc. No. 34, vol. VIII, Feb. 9, 1854, On Indian treaties.

H. Ex. Doc. No. 84, vol. X, March 25, 1854, Report on Indian lands west of Missouri and Iowa—President Franklin Pierce.

Sen. Repts. No. 226, vol. II (S. 43) April 20, 1854, Indian War Claims (Creek and Seminole War).

Sen. Repts. No. 323, vol. II, June 26, 1854, Case of Muscogee or Creek Indians.

H. Repts. No. 123, vol. II, March 20, 1854, On Cherokee Indians.

H. Repts. No. 133, vol. II, (H. R. 210), April 7, 1854, Terms of treaties with Indians.

H. Repts. No. 138, vol. II (H. R. 338), April 28, 1854, Sioux lands in Minnesota.

H. Repts. No. 267, vol. III, June 30, 1854, Adverse report on establishment of schools for Indians in California.

33 C:2 Sen. Ex. Doc. No. 45, vol. VII, Feb. 9, 1855, Claim of Brotherton Indians.

H. Ex. Doc. No. 57, vol. V, Feb. 4, 1855, Message on Calif. Indians removal—President Franklin Pierce.

34 C:1 Sen. Ex. Doc. No. 1, pt. 1, vol. I, pp. 121 et seq. (1855), Report of the Secretary of the Interior.

H. Ex. Doc. No. 1, pt. 1, vol. I, pp. 321 et seq., Nov. 26, 1855, Report of the Comm. of Ind. Aff.—Comm. Manypenny.

H. Ex. Doc. No. 1, pt. 1, vol. I, pp. 526–528, March 16, 1855, Instructions to Governor of New Mexico regarding treaties with Indians in New Mexico.

H. Ex. Doc. No. 7, vol. II, Feb. 4, 1856, Report on the Chickasaw fund—Sec'y James Guthrie.

H. Ex. Doc. No. 10, vol. IV, pp. 36–44, Nov. 1, 1855, On amounts due Indians.

H. Ex. Doc. No. 113, vol. XII, June 3, 1856, Message on Federal and Cherokee courts—President Franklin Pierce.

34 C:3 H. Ex. Doc. No. 1, pt. 1, vol. I, p. 826, Oct. 16, 1856, Indian annuities.

H. Ex. Doc. No. 64, vol. VI, Feb. 6, 1857, Report on Chickasaw trust fund—Sec'y James Guthrie.

35 C:1 Sen. Doc. No. 73, vol. XIII, June 14, 1858, Claim of St. Regis Indians.

H. Ex. Doc. No. 93, vol. XI, March 26, 1858, Report on Indian service—Sec'y Howell Cobb.

H. Ex. Doc. No. 134, vol. XIII, June 3, 1858, Treaty stipulations with the Pawnees.

H. Ex. Doc. No. 135, vol. XIII, June 7, 1858, Estimates for preservation of peace in northern superintendency.

35 C:2 Sen. Repts. No. 374, vol. I, Feb. 15, 1859, Memorial of Choctaw delegates.

36 C:1 H. Repts. No. 534, vol. IV, May 18, 1860, On treaties with the Cherokees.

36 C:2 Sen. Repts. No. 298 (H. R. 852), Feb. 6, 1861, On bill re annuities due certain Indian tribes under treaties.

37 C:2 Sen. Ex. Doc. No. 58, vol. V, June 5, 1862, Report on "Half Breed" Kaw lands—Sec'y C. B. Smith.

H. Rept. No. 88, vol. IV, April 24, 1862, Claim of the Sac and Fox Indians.

37 C:3 H. Ex. Doc. No. 47, vol. V, Jan. 28, 1863, On Indian accounts.

38 C:1 Sen. Misc. Doc. No. 127, May 16, 1864, Treaty with Indians in Oregon.

Sen. Misc. Doc. No. 136, July 1, 1864, Claims of the Michigan Indians.

H. Ex. Doc. No. 58, vol. IX, March 14, 1864, Sioux Indian depredations.

H. Ex. Doc. No. 81, vol. XV, May 9, 1864, Chippewa Indian Treaty.

38 C:2 Sen. Rept. No. 138, March 1, 1865, On possessory titles of Indian tribes to the public domain of the United States.

39 C:2 Sen. Rept. No. 156, Jan. 27, 1867, Report on condition of Indian tribes—joint special comm.

H. Misc. Doc. No. 41, vol. I, Feb. 1, 1869, Report on the issue of arms to Indians—Sec'y E. M. Stanton.

H. Rept. No. 10, vol. I, Feb. 5, 1867, Report on investigation of frauds in Indian contracts (majority and minority).

40 C:2 Sen. Ex. Doc. No. 72, vol. II, July 6, 1868, Timber cutting by the Oneidas.

Sen. Ex. Doc. No. 83, vol. II, July 23, 1868, Letter recommending removal of certain Indians in California.

H. Ex. Doc. No. 204, vol. XV, March 5, 1868, On the Choctaw and Chickasaw Indians.

40 C:3 H. Ex. Doc. No. 61, vol. IX, Jan. 28, 1869, Pottawatomie claims.

41 C:2 Sen. Ex. Doc. No. 48, vol. II, Feb. 28, 1870, Message on taxes of the Cherokee Indians—President U. S. Grant.

Sen. Ex. Doc. No. 71, vol. II, March 24, 1870, On freedmen of the Choctaw and Chickasaw Nations.

H. Ex. Doc. No. 130, vol. VI, Feb. 8, 1870, On annuities withheld from Indian tribes.

Sen. Repts. No. 131, (S. 679), April 27, 1870, Consolidation of Indian tribes.

Sen. Rept. No. 145, May 3, 1870, Report on a treaty with New York Indians (adverse).

Sen. Rept. No. 225, June 22, 1870, Tax on cattle by Cherokee Indians.

41 C:3 Sen. Ex. Doc. No. 26, vol. I, Jan. 30, 1871, Message on proceedings of council of Indian tribes at Ocmulgee, Dec. 1870—President U. S. Grant.

H. Misc. Doc. No. 49, vol. I, Jan. 24, 1871, Papers relating to Indian Confederacy.

Sen. Rept. No. 268, vol. VI, Dec. 15, 1870, Citizenship of Indians.

Sen. Rept. No. 299, Jan. 19, 1871, Money due the Pottawatomie Indians.

Sen. Rept. No. 336 (S. 679), Feb. 1, 1871, Organization of Indian Territory.

H. Rept. No. 39, vol. I, Feb. 25, 1871, Report on the Indian Department.

42 C:2 Sen. Misc. Doc. No. 44, vol. I, Jan. 25, 1872, Report on education of Indians—Sec'y C. Delano.

Sen. Misc. Doc. No. 53, vol. I, Jan. 31, 1872, Memorial against Territorial government. Choctaw Nation of Indians.

H. Ex. Doc. No. 193, vol. X, March 12, 1872, Letter on issuing of scrip to Chippewa half breeds.

H. Misc. Doc. No. 46, vol. II, Jan. 23, 1872, Petition of freedmen of the Choctaw and Chickasaw Nation.

Sen. Rept. No. 197, vol. I, May 16, 1872, Removal of Flathead and other Indians.

H. Rept. No. 89, vol. IV, May 27, 1872, Minority report against establishing Indian Territory.

42 C:3 Sen. Ex. Doc. No. 29, vol. I, Jan. 16, 1873, Modoc and other Indian tribes in northern California.

H. Ex. Doc. No. 69, vol. VII, Jan. 6, 1873, Report on the Choctaw claims—Sec'y G. S. Boutwell.

H. Ex. Doc. No. 90, vol. VII, Jan. 6, 1873, Negotiations with the Ute Indians in Colorado.

H. Ex. Doc. No. 199, vol. IX, Feb. 8, 1873, Report on the Miami Indians and the rights of settlers on their lands.

H. Rept. No. 80, vol. I, (H. R. 306), Feb. 22, 1873, Treaty stipulations with Choctaw Nation.

H. Rept. No. 98, vol. III, Investigation of Indian frauds.

43 C:1 Sen. Ex. Doc. No. 33, vol. I, Feb. 23, 1874, Treaty with Chippewa Indians.

Sen. Misc. Doc. No. 71, vol. I, Feb. 20, 1874, Letter relating to Indian lands in New York, and memorial protesting against sale without consent.

Sen. Misc. Doc. No. 95, vol. I (S. 652), March 31, 1874, Letter on jurisdiction of U. S. courts on Indian reservations—Sec'y Columbus Delano.

Sen. Misc. Doc. No. 121, vol. I, June 8, 1874, Memorial—Choctaw Indians.

H. Ex. Doc. No. 12, vol. VIII, Dec. 4, 1873, Report on Cheyenne and Arapahoe Reservation.
H. Ex. Doc. No. 61, vol. IX, Jan. 22, 1874, Treaties with Shoshone and Bannock Indians.
H. Ex. Doc. No. 91, vol. IX, Jan. 2, 1874, Report on the Mission Indians—Acting Sec'y B. R. Cowen.
H. Ex. Doc. No. 129, vol. X, Feb. 3, 1874, Agreement with Bannock Indians in Idaho.
H. Ex. Doc. No. 177, vol. XII, March 9, 1874, Letter on sale of liquor to Indians—Sec'y Columbus Delano.
H. Misc. Doc. No. 87, vol. II, Jan. 22, 1874, Protest by Indians of Indian Territory against establishment of a government without their consent.
Sen. Rept. No. 337, vol. II (S. 650), May 8, 1874, Title to the Absentee Shawnee Lands.
Sen. Rept. No. 367, vol. II (S. 52), May 20, 1874, Jurisdiction over Indian reservation.
H. Rept. No. 478, vol. III (H. R. 3080), April 20, 1874, Seneca Indians in New York.

43 C:2 Sen. Misc. Doc. No. 71, vol. I, Jan. 26, 1875, Memorial of citizens of Creek Nation against establishment of a Territorial government.
H. Ex. Doc. No. 47, vol. XII, Dec. 23, 1874, Liabilities of Choctaw Indians to individuals.
H. Ex. Doc. No. 51, vol. XII, Dec. 22, 1874, Lands of Cherokee Indians of North Carolina.
H. Ex. Doc. No. 61, vol. XII, Dec. 17, 1874, Letter on timber on Indian reservation—Sec'y Columbus Delano.
H. Ex. Doc. No. 101, vol. XV, Jan. 13, 1875, Treaty with Indian tribes in Kansas.

44 C:1 Sen. Ex. Doc. No. 34, March 7, 1867, Report on liquor in the Indian Territory—Acting Sec'y of War G. M. Robeson.
Sen. Misc. Doc. No. 91, vol. I, April 17, 1876, Apache Indians in New Mexico.
H. Misc. Doc. No. 167, vol. V, April 18, 1876, On the management of the Indian Department.
H. Rept. No. 183, vol. I. (H. R. 1316), Feb. 25, 1876, Klamath Indian Reservation.
H. Rept. No. 499, vol. III (H. R. 3463), May 15, 1876, Claims of the Choctaw Indians.
H. Rept. No. 647, vol. V (H. R. 3686), June 9, 1876, A claim of the Cherokee Indians, Eastern Band.

44 C:2 H. Rept. No. 186, vol. II (H. R. 3079), March 2, 1877, On the Osage Indians.

45 C:2 Sen. Ex. Doc. No. 74, vol. II, May 9, 1878, Letter on taxes in Indian Territory—Sec'y Carl Schurz. Rights of Indians to impose taxes.
Sen. Misc. Doc. No. 8, vol. I (S. 107), Dec. 10, 1877, Memorial relating to the Indians, Choctaw delegates
Sen. Misc. Doc. No. 18, vol. I (S. 107), Jan. 14, 1877, Memorial against bill to enable Indians to become citizens.
H. Misc. Doc. No. 8, vol. I (H. R. 2283), Jan. 15, 1878, Memorial for payment of annuities.
H. Rept. No. 95, vol. I (H. R. 2687), Jan. 22, 1878, Election of a delegate from Indian Territory.
H. Rept. No. 251, vol. II (H. R. 3550), Feb. 26, 1878, Case of Choctaw Indians.
H. Rept. No. 1002, vol. V (H. R. 4868), June 17, 1878, Election of delegate from Indian Territory.

45 C:3 Sen. Ex. Doc. No. 62, vol. IV, Feb. 8, 1879, Message on the Ute Indians—President R. B. Hayes.
Sen. Misc. Doc. No. 73, vol. I (S. 1802), Feb. 19, 1879, Memorial against a U. S. court in Indian Territory.
Sen. Rept. No. 731, vol. II (S. 1486), Feb. 6, 1879, Lands in Klamath Indian Reservation.
Sen. Rept. No. 744, vol. III, Feb. 11, 1879, Indian Territory.
H. Rept. No. 75, vol. I (H. R. 6247), Jan. 28, 1879, Klamath Indian Reservation.
H. Rept. No. 165, vol. I (H. R. 6268), March 3, 1879, Lands to Indians in severalty.

46 C:1 Sen. Ex. Doc. No. 29, vol. I, June 20, 1879, Report on arrest of Cherokee Indians—Sec'y G. A. McGrary.
H. Rept. No. 4, vol. I (H. R. 440), May 16, 1879, Amount due the Choctaw Nation.
H. Rept. No. 29, vol. I, June 14, 1879, Indian training schools.

46 C:2 Sen. Ex. Doc. No. 124, vol. IV, March 19, 1880, Land patents to Indians.
Sen. Misc. Doc. No. 46, vol. I, March 3, 1880, Resolution on making the Indian Territory a judicial district.
Sen. Rept. No. 332, vol. I (S. 967), March 3, 1880, Jurisdiction of Northern District of Texas.
Sen. Rept. No. 670, vol. VI (S. 1298), May 31, 1880, Removal of Ponca Indians (majority and minority reports).
Sen. Rept. No. 708, vol. VII (S. Res. 120), June 8, 1880, Removal of Northern Cheyenne Indians.
H. Rept. No. 2, vol. I (H. R. 351), Dec. 10, 1879, Lands of Indian tribes—Warm Springs, Umatilla, etc.
H. Rept. No. 431, vol. II (H. R. 418), March 9, 1880, Creek orphan fund.
H. Rept. No. 430, vol. II (H. R. 350), March 9, 1880, Police for Indian reservations.
H. Rept. No. 752, vol. III (H. R. 1735), April 6, 1880, Industrial school for Indians.
H. Rept. No. 755, vol. III (H. R. 5634), April 6, 1880, U. S. courts in Indian Territory.
H. Rept. No. 755, pt. 2, vol. III (H. R. 5634), April 10, 1880, Minority report on U. S. courts in Indian Territory.
H. R. Rept. No. 1319, vol. IV (H. R. 5038), On lands in severalty to Indians.
H. Rept. No. 1576, vol. V (H. R. 5038), May 28, 1880, Minority report on lands in severalty to Indians.

46 C:3 Sen. Ex. Doc. No. 31, vol. III, Feb. 2, 1881, Letter on Ute commission—Sec'y Carl Schurz. Report and correspondence.
S. Rept. No. 849, vol. I, Feb. 9, 1881, Claims of Western Cherokee Indians.

47 C:2 H. Misc. Doc. vol. 19, chap. XVI, June 30, 1880, Indian reservations from the public domain.

48 C:2 Sen. Ex. Doc. No. 17, vol. I, pt. I, 1885, Leasing of Indian lands in the Indian Territory.
Sen. Ex. Doc. No. 95, vol. II, pt. 2, Special report of 1888 on Indian education and civilization.

49 C:1 Sen. Rept. No. 1278, vol. VIII, IX, Condition of Indians in Indian Territory.

52 C:1 H. Misc. Doc. No. 340, pt. 15, 1892, Report on Indians taxed and not taxed at 11th Census: 1890.
Sen. Rept. No. 281, Vol. II (S. 1548), Report on Indian Affairs.
Sen. Rept. No. 910 (S. 3407), New York Indians.
Sen. Rept. No. 1003, vol. V (S. 2068), Taxation of Indian lands.

52 C:2 26 Cong. Rec., p. 2132, 1893, Indian litigation.
H. Rept. No. 2384, vol. II (H. R. 9377), Indian courts in Indian Territory.

53 C:2 H. Misc. Docs. vol. 37, pt. 2, p. 458, First annual message on removal—President Andrew Jackson.
Sen. Rept. No. 377 (1894), Conditions of lands in Five Civilized Tribes.

54 C:1 Sen. Rept. No. 235, vol. I (S. 265), Taxation of allotted lands.
Sen. Rept. No. 969, vol. V (S. 3051), Rights of mixed blood Indians.
H. Rept. No. 2276, vol. IX (H. R. 8584), To confirm title of mixed blood Indians to their lands.

54 C:2 H. Rept. No. 2992, vol. III (H. R. 5375), Grazing on Indian lands.

55 C:1 Sen. Doc. No. 24, vol. II, Indian Territorial courts, appeal of Cherokees.
Sen. Rept. No. 6, vol. I (S. 375), To confirm title of mixed blood Indians to their lands.
Sen. Rept. No. 7, vol. I (S. 374), Taxation of allotted lands.

55 C:2 Sen. Doc. No. 274, vol. XXII, Protests of Choctaws against H. R. 8581.
H. Rept. No. 593, vol. III (H. R. 8581), Protection of people of Indian Territory.

56 C:2 Sen. Rept. No. 2483, vol. V (H. R. 10701), To admit Indians to citizenship.

57 C:1 35 Cong. Rec., Pt. I, p. 90 (1901), Discussion of Allotment Act in message to Congress.
H. Rept. No. 1732, vol. VII (S. 4264), Indian lands, suits for recovery, stats. of limitations to apply.

H. Rept. No. 2704, vol. IX (H. R. 10300), Jurisdiction over certain crimes on South Dakota Reservations.
57 C:2 Sen. Doc. No. 36, vol. V (H. R. 12543), Hearings on statehood for Indian Territory.
Sen. Rept. No. 2206, vol. I (H. R. 12543), Statehood for Indian Territory.
58 C:1&2 Sen. Doc. No. 169, vol. V, To remove restrictions upon sale of allotments.
Sen. Doc. No. 260, vol. VII, Investigation of allotments in Indian Territory.
H. Doc. No. 528, Investigation court officials Indian Territory.
59 C:1 Sen. Doc. 142 (1905–6), Alaska Territory.
H. Doc. No. 926, Handbook of American Indians north of Mexico (Hodge).
60 C:1 Sen. Doc. No. 215, vols. XIV, XV, XVI, Investigation of affairs of Kickapoo Indians.
Sen. Rept. No. 185, vol. I (S. 4889), Dakota Indians, suit in U. S. Court of Claims.
H. Rept. No. 1454, vol. II (H. 15641), Removal of restrictions on Indian lands in Oklahoma.
61 C:1&2 Sen. Rept. No. 868, vol. III (H. R. 24992), To determine heirs of deceased Indians.
H. Rept. No. 1135 (H. 24992), Determination of heirs of deceased Indians—sale, lease of allotments.
62 C:1&2 Sen. Rept. No. 147, vol. I (S. 3842), Jurisdiction in suits relative to allotments of lands.
Sen. Rept. No. 720, (H. R. 1332), Regulation of Indian allotments disposed of by will.
62 C:3 Sen. Rept. No. 1213, vol. I (H. 26874), Report on appropriations for fulfilling treaty stipulations with various Indian tribes.
63 C:2 H. Doc. No. 1030, vol. 158, Treaty items—Indian appropriation bill.
63 C:3 Sen. Doc. No. 984, vol. XVI, Indian conditions.
H. Doc. No. 1253, vol. 103, St. Croix Chippewa Indians—Tribal rights.
H. Doc. No. 1590 (1915), Senecas and other Indians of the Five Nations of New York.
H. Doc. No. 1663, vol. 104, St. Croix Chippewa Indians—Enrollment.
H. Doc. No. 1669, vol. 104, Indian conditions.
64 C:1 Sen. Rept. No. 193, vol. I (S. 1728), Removal of restrictions from lands of Quapaw allottees.
Sen. Rept. No. 792, vol. III (S. 5916), Warm Springs Reservation—Boundaries.
65 C:1 H. Rept. No. 192 (H. R. 195), Coal and asphalt rights of Choctaw and Chickasaw Nations.
65 C:2 Sen. Rept. No. 207 (H. R. 195), Coal and asphalt rights of Choctaw and Chickasaw Nations.
Sen. Rept. No. 330, vol. I (S. 4151), Five Civilized Tribes—Determination of heirs.
66 C:1 Sen. Rept. No. 185, vol. I (S. 1018), Dakota Indians—Suit in U. S. Court of Claims.
Sen. Rept. No. 222 (H. R. 5007), Citizenship to Indians who served in war with Germany.
H. Rept. No. 140 (H. R. 5007), Citizenship to Indians who served in war with Germany.
67 C:1 H. Rept. No. 264 (S. J. Res. 59), Five Civilized Tribes—Income tax.
67 C:2 H. Rept. No. 545, (S. J. Res. 59) Five Civilized Tribes—Income Tax.
67 C:3 Sen. Rept. No. 1073 (S. 4061), Water rights—Blackfeet Reservation.
H. Rept. No. 1596 (S. 4061), Water rights—Blackfeet Reservation.
67 C:4 H. Rept. No. 1351 (H. R. 11474), Condemnation for public purposes of land included in Indian allotment.
68 C:1 65 Cong. Rec., pp. 8621–8622, 9303–9304. Re: departmental discretion in granting citizenship to Indians.
Sen. Rept. No. 441 (H. R. 6355), Granting citizenship to Indians.
H. Rept. Nos. 165, 243 (H. R. 6483), Osage Indian—Division of lands and funds inherited by person not of Indian blood.
H. Rept. No. 222 (H. R. 6355), Granting citizenship to Indians.
68 C:2 Sen. Rept. No. 1116 (H. R. 7867), Assiniboine Indian claims.
H. Rept. No. 1214 (H. R. 7867), Assiniboine Indian claims.
69 C:1 Hearings, H. Comm. on Ind. Aff., H. R. 7826, Reservation Courts of Indian Offences.
Sen. Rept. No. 982 (S. 1616), Chippewa Indian classification.
Sen. Rept. No. 716 (S. 3953), Condemnation—Pueblo lands.
Sen. Rept. No. 1019 (S. 4347), Development of oil and gas mining leases on Indian reservations.
Sen. Rept. No. 1131 (H. R. 12393), Development of oil and gas mining leases on Indian reservations.
H. Rept. No. 897 (H. R. 11171), Indian trust funds—regulating deposit and expenditure.
H. Rept. No. 955 (H. R. 11201), Condemnation—Pueblo lands.
69 C:2 Sen. Rept. No. 1240 (S. 4896), Oil and gas mining leases on Executive Order reservations.
70 C:1 Hearings, Sen. Subcomm. of Comm. on Ind. Aff., Survey of conditions of the Indians in the United States, Part I—Yakima, Wash., and Klamath Falls, Ore., Nov. 1928; Part II—San Francisco and Riverside, Calif., Salt Lake City, Utah, Nov. 1928; Part III—Health and sanitation on reservations, Dec. 1928—Jan. 1929; Part IV—Individual cases including Jackson Barnett, Feb.–Mar. 1929.
H. Doc. No. 141, Rio Grande Conservancy District.
Sen. Rept. No. 918 (S. 4222), Creation of Indian trust estates.
H. Rept. No. 380 (H. R. 70), Rio Grande Conservancy District.
H. Rept. No. 746 (H. R. 10360), Amend Chippewa Indians jurisdictional act.
H. Rept. No. 816 (H. R. 9483), Rights-of-way through Pueblo Indian land.
H. Rept. No. 1358 (H. R. 7204), Creation of Indian trust estates.
H. Rept. No. 1851 (H. R. 12414), Classification of Chippewa Indians.
70 C:2 Sen. Doc. No. 263 (1928–29), Indian funds.
H. Rept. No. 2135 (H. R. 15523), Inspection of Indian reservations.
71 C:1 Hearings, Sen. Subcomm. of Comm. on Ind. Aff., S. Res. 79 and 308, Survey of conditions of the Indians in the United States, Part V—Haywood, Lac du Flambeau, Madison, Wis., Pierre, S. Dak., Winnebago, Nebr., July, 1929.
Sen. Doc. No. 16, Improvement of conditions on Indian reservations in Arizona.
Sen. Doc. No. 203, Information relative to additional land for Indians.
71 C:2 Hearings, Sen. Comm. on Ind. Aff., Sen. Res. 282, Federal aid to states where nontaxable Indian lands are located.
Hearings, Sen. Comm. on Ind. Aff., S. 1372, Jan. 22 and March 19, 1930, Sisseton and Wahpeton Indians—Claims.
Hearings, Sen. Comm. on Ind. Aff., S. 2561, Feb. 21, 1930, Creation of Indian trust estates.
Hearings, Sen. Comm. on Ind. Aff., S. 3156, Feb. 26, 1930, Final enrollment of Indians of Klamath Reservation.
Hearings, Sen. Comm. on Ind. Aff., S. 3782, March 12, 1930, Addition to Western Navajo Indian Reservation.
Hearings, Sen. Comm. on Ind. Aff., S. 3041, April 18, 1930, Seminole Indians jurisdictional act.
Hearings, Sen. Comm. on Ind. Aff., S. 4165, April 25 and 29, 1930, Incorporation of Klamath Indian Tribe.
Hearings, Sen. Comm. on Ind. Aff., S. 3938, April 30, 1930, Fort Hall, Idaho, Indian irrigation project.
Hearings, Sen. Comm. on Ind. Aff., S. 615, May 1, 1930, Ute Indians jurisdictional act.
Hearings, Sen. Subcomm. of Comm. on Ind. Aff., Survey of conditions of the Indians in the United States, Part 6—Hearings on reimbursable features of Indian appropriations, Washington, D. C., Jan. 21, 1930; Part 7—Pine Ridge, Rosebud, Terry, Waggoner, S. D., July 13–15, 17, 19, 1929; Part 8—Hearings on mismanagement of Phoenix School.

Ariz., and boarding schools in general, at Washington, D. C., May 23, 27, 1930; Part 9—North Dakota, July 1929; Part 10—Flathead power development, July 29, 30, 1929, March 24, 25 and April 10, 1930; Part 12—New York Indians, March 1, Nov. 25-26, 1929, Jan. 3, 1930; Part 14—Oklahoma (Five Civilized Tribes) Nov. 1930; Part 19—New Mexico and Colorado, May 1931; Part 20—Pueblo Land Boards, May 2, 8, 9, 1931, Jan. 26-30, 1932; Part 22—Grazing on Indian lands, Jan. 21, 22, Feb. 4, 1932.

Hearings, H. Comm. on Ind. Aff., H. R. 8921, Feb., April 1930, Claims of Sisseton and Wahpeton Bands of Sioux Indians.

Hearings, H. Comm. on Ind. Aff., H. R. 6979, Feb.-April 1930, Creation of Indian trust estates.

Hearings, H. Comm. on Ind. Aff., H. R. 9720, March 19-April 17, 1930, Indians of New York.

Hearings, H. Comm. on Ind. Aff., H. R. 1669, April 3, 1930, Claims of Pillager Band of Chippewa Indians in Minnesota.

Sen. Doc. No. 153, Flathead power development.

Sen. Rept. No. 158 (S. Res. 79, 70th Cong.), Survey of conditions of Indians—Klamath.

Sen. Rept. No. 372 (S. 1372), Claims of Sisseton and Wahpeton Bands of Sioux Indians.

Sen. Rept. No. 540 (S. 4203), Payment of interest on trust funds of Indian tribes.

H. Rept. No. 113 (H. R. 4021), Police jurisdiction over rights-of-way of Blackfeet Reservation.

H. Rept. No. 1272 (H. R. 11782), Payment of interest on trust funds of Indian tribes.

71 C:3 Hearings, Sen. Subcomm. of Comm. on Ind. Aff., Survey of conditions of the Indians, Part 11—Oil leases and operations in S. W., Jan. 30, 31, Feb. 3, 5, 1931; Part 13—Klamath Oregon logging operations, Jan. 30-31, Feb. 3, 5, 1931; Part 15—Oklahoma, Nov. 17-22, 1930; Part 16—Qualla, Catawba, Seminole Reservations and Choctaw Indian Agency, March 26, 28, 31, 1930, Nov. 6, 8, and Dec. 10, 1930; Part 17—Arizona, April-May, 1931; Part 18—Navajos in Arizona and New Mexico, April, May 1931; Part 21—Hearings at California, Nevada, Oregon, Washington, Jan. 1930, April, May, June, 1931; Part 24—Quapaw mining lease, Oklahoma, Nov., Dec. 1930.

Hearings, Sen. Comm. on Ind. Aff., S. 5828, Feb. 18, 1931, To quiet title of Pueblo Indian land.

Hearings, H. Comm. on Ind. Aff., H. R. 13527, Jan. 19 and 21, 1931, Distribution of permanent fund of Chippewas, Minnesota.

Hearings, H. Comm. on Ind. Aff., H. R. 11203, Feb. 18, 1931, Ratification of leases with Seneca Indians.

Hearings, H. Comm. on Ind. Aff., H. R. 10515, Feb. 23, 1931, Ratification of leases with Seneca Indians.

Hearings, H. Comm. on Ind. Aff., H. R. 12576, Feb. 27, 1931, Emancipated citizenship for American Indians.

Sen. Doc. No. 314 (S. Res. 482), Survey of Seminole Indians of Florida.

72 C:1 Hearings, Sen. Comm. on Ind. Aff., S. 1839, Jan. 20, 1932, Creation of Indian trust estates.

Hearings, Sen. Comm. on Ind. Aff., S. 1196, March 23, 1932, Authorizing Tlingit and Haida Indians to bring suit in Court of Claims.

Hearings, Sen. Comm. on Ind. Aff., S. 2268, March 30, 1932, Providing for Choctaw and Chickasaw enrollments.

Hearings, Sen. Comm. on Ind. Aff., S. 2635, April 7, 1932, Revision of timber contracts with Indians.

Hearings, Sen. Comm. on Ind. Aff., S. 3588, April 19, 1932, Organizing Klamath Indian Corporation.

Hearings, Sen. Comm. on Ind. Aff., S. 3998, April 20, 1932, Apportionment of waters of Ahtanum Creek, Wash.

Hearings, Sen. Comm. on Ind. Aff., S. 2671, May 23-26, 1932, To provide for final enrollment of Indians of Klamath Indian Reservation in Oregon.

Hearings, Sen. Subcomm. of Comm. on Ind. Aff., Survey of conditions of the Indians, Part 23—Montana, July 22-24, 1929; Aug. 1-2, 1929; Part 25—Indian claims against Government, Jan., Mar., Nov., Dec. 1930, May, June 1931; Part 26—Hearings on Indian situations in Missouri, Texas, Oklahoma, and Florida, Jan. 31, Dec. 5, 10, 1930, Jan. 22, June 30, 1932; Part 27—Wyoming, Idaho, Utah, Sept. 12-14, 1932; Part 28—Nevada, Dec. 16, 17, 19, 20, 1932; Part 29—California, Sept. 20-24, 27-28, 1932; Part 32—Idaho and Washington, Oct. 23-25, 28, 1933.

Hearings, H. Comm. on Ind. Aff., H. R. 9071, Feb. 17, 1932, Authorization of appropriations to pay in part liability of United States to certain Pueblos.

Hearings, H. Comm. on Ind. Aff., H. R. 10927, April 28, 1932, Conferring jurisdiction on Court of Claims to adjudicate rights of Otoe and Missouria Tribes of Indians.

Hearings, H. Comm. on Ind. Aff., H. R. 8750, May 16-19, 1932, Extension of restriction period applicable to Indians of Five Civilized Tribes in Oklahoma.

Hearings, H. Comm. on Ind. Aff., H. R. 10884, May 25, 26, 1932, Authorizing reimbursable debts of Indians and tribes of Indians.

Sen. Rept. No. 552 (S. 3675), Irrigation construction charges on Indian projects.

H. Rept. No. 943 (H. R. 8898), Irrigation construction charges on Indian projects.

H. Rept. No. 951 (H. R. 10884), Adjustment of reimbursable Indian debts.

H. Rept. No. 1302 (H. R. 6684), Determination of heirs of deceased Indians in relation to contracts for sale of tribal timber.

72 C:2 Hearings, Sen. Comm. on Ind. Aff., S. 5628, Dec. 7, 1932, Boundary, Navajo-Hopi Indian Reservation.

Hearings, Sen. Comm. on Ind. Aff., S. 5302, Jan. 25, 1933, Fish and Game within Allegany, Cattaraugus, and Oil Springs Reservations.

Sen. Rept. No. 25, pt. 4, Indian irrigation projects.

Sen. Rept. No. 25, pt. 5, Administration of Indian trust funds.

Sen. Rept. No. 1281 (H. R. 6684), Revision of timber contracts with Indians.

Sen. Rept. No. 1365, Tax exempt lands.

73 C:1 Hearings, Sen. Subcomm. of Comm. on Ind. Aff., Survey of the conditions of the Indians, Part 31—Montana, Oct., Nov. 1933; Part 33—San Diego and San Francisco, Calif., June 29, July 2, 1934.

Sen. Doc. No. 12, vol. I, pp. 607-632, Report of Forest Service on Indian forests.

73 C:2 Hearings, Sen. Comm. on Ind. Aff., S. J. Res. 95, April 24, 1932, To restore lands of Papago Indian Reservation in Arizona to exploration and location under public land mining laws.

Hearings, Sen. Comm. on Ind. Aff., S. 2755 and S. 3645, 1934, To grant to Indians living under Federal tutelage freedom to organize for purposes of local self-government and economic enterprise, etc.

Hearings, H. Comm. on Ind. Aff., H. R. 7902, 1934, Readjustment of Indian Affairs.

Sen. Doc. No. 179 (S. 326), Claims of Turtle Mountain Band of Chippewa Indians of North Dakota.

Sen. Rept. No. 147, Survey of conditions of Indians—Flathead power sites.

Sen. Rept. No. 381 (S. 1888), Conservation of grazing resources in Indian lands.

Sen. Rept. No. 382 (S. 1889), Administration of tribal forest and grazing lands.

Sen. Rept. No. 511 (S. 2571) Report on Johnson-O'Malley Bill for federal-state cooperation in education, social welfare, etc. of Indians.

Sen. Rept. No. 634 (S. 2671), Repealing obsolete laws relating to Indians.

Sen. Rept. No. 1080 (S. 3645), To conserve and develop Indian lands and resources (Wheeler-Howard Bill).

Sen. Rept. No. 1250 (S. 3665), Collateral requirements as to deposits of Indian funds.

Sen. Rept. No. 1423 (1934), Modification of Indian liquor laws.
H. Rept. No. 624 (H. R. 5595), Payment of tax upon royalty interests of restricted Indians of Five Civilized Tribes.
H. Rept. No. 825 (H. R. 5075) 1934, Determination of Indian heirs and disposition of allotments of deceased Indians.
H. Rept. No. 862 (H. R. 5871), Conservation of grazing resources in Indian lands.
H. Rept. No. 1099 (S. 1888), Conservation of grazing resources in Indian lands.
H. Rept. No. 1100 (S. 1889), Administration of tribal forest and grazing lands.
H. Rept. No. 1804 (H. R. 7902) 1934, Readjustment of Indian Affairs (Wheeler-Howard Bill).

74 C:1 Hearings, Sen. Comm. on Ind. Aff., S. 2047, April 8–11, 1935, To promote general welfare of Indians of Oklahoma.
Hearings, Sen. Comm. on Ind. Aff., S. 1793, May 6–July 1, 1935, California Indians jurisdictional act.
Hearings, Sen. Comm. on Ind. Aff., S. 2731, June 10 and 17, 1935, To create an Indian Claims Commission.
Hearings, Sen. Comm. on Ind. Aff., S. 3293, July 26 and 27, 1935, Old age pensions for Indians.
Hearings, H. Comm. on Ind. Aff. (H. R. 6234) April–May 1935, Promote welfare of Indians of Oklahoma.
Sen. Rept. No. 436 (S. 2213), Defining exterior boundaries, Navajo Indian Reservation.
Sen. Rept. No. 615 (S. 2656), Granting concessions and leasing lands—re reservoir sites and Indian irrigation projects.
Sen. Rept. No. 900 (S. 2203), To promote the development of Indian arts and crafts and create a board to assist therein.
Sen. Rept. No. 1164 (S. 1793) 1935, California Indians jurisdictional act.
Sen. Rept. No. 1167 (S. 3293), Old age pensions for Indians.
Sen. Rept. No. 1232 (S. 2047), Welfare of Indians of Oklahoma.
H. Rept. Nos. 288, 289 (H. R. 5229, 5230), Claims of Stockbridge and Munsee Indians.
H. Rept. No. 336 (H. R. 2049), Chippewa Indians of Minnesota jurisdictional act.
H. Rept. No. 337 (H. R. 4126), Public-domain lands in Nevada and Oregon as grazing reserve for Indians of Fort McDermitt, Nev. (Paiute and Shoshone).
H. Rep. No. 473 (H. R. 6542), Defining exterior boundaries, Navajo Indian Reservation, New Mexico.
H. Rept. No. 740 (H. R. 6625), Conferring jurisdiction on district courts over Osage Indian drug and liquor addicts, April 19, 1935.
H. Rept. No. 1683 (H. J. Res. 215), Authorize the modification of terms of existing contracts for sale of timber on Indian land.
H. Rept. No. 1767 (H. R. 9018), Old age pensions for Indians.

74 C:2 Hearings, Sen. Comm. on Ind. Aff., S. 2047, 1936, To promote general welfare of Indians of Oklahoma.
Hearings, Sen. Subcomm. of Comm. on Ind. Aff., Survey of the conditions of Indians, Part 35—Metlakahtla Indians, Alaska, May 19, 1934, July 12, 1936; Part 36—Alaska (including reindeer), July, 1936.
Hearings, H. Comm. on Ind. Aff., H. R. 8360, 1936, Condition of Indians in United States.
H. Rept. No. 2244 (H. R. 9866), Extension of provisions of Wheeler-Howard Act to Alaska.
H. Rept. 2398 (H. R. 7764), To relieve restricted Indians whose lands have been taxed, etc.

75 C:1 Hearings, Sen. Comm. on Ind. Aff., S. 1424, Oct. 24, 1935—Aug. 16, 1937, Mission Indians, Palm Springs Band—allotments.
Hearings, Sen. Subcom. of Comm. on Ind. Aff., Survey of conditions of Indians, Part 34—Navajo Boundary and Pueblos in New Mexico, March, May, 1936; Aug. 17–19, 21, 30, 1936.
Hearings, Sen. Comm. on Ind. Aff., S. 1651, March 8–22, May 17, 1937, California Indians jurisdictional act.
Hearings, Sen. Comm. on Ind. Aff., S. 1779, Aug. 9, 1937, California Indians jurisdictional act.
Hearings, H. Comm. on Ind. Aff., H. R. 5243, March 10, 1937, California Indians jurisdictional act.
Hearings, H. Comm. on Ind. Aff., H. R. 5559, March 17, 1937, Tax upon lead and zinc on Quapaw Indian lands in Oklahoma.
Hearings, H. Comm. on Ind. Aff., H. R. 5753, April 21, 22 and July 26, 1937, Conditions of Sioux Indians.
Hearings, H. Comm. on Ind. Aff., H. R. 6071, May 13, 1937, Klamath Indians payments.
Hearings, H. Comm. on Ind. Aff., H. R. 1998, June 24, 1937, California Indians jurisdictional act.
Sen. Rept. No. 332 (S. 150) 1937, To relieve restricted Indians whose lands have been taxed, etc.
Sen. Rept. No. 531 (S. 2163) 1937, To authorize the deposit and investment of Indian funds.
Sen. Rept. No. 985 (S. 2689) 1937, Leasing Indian lands for mining purposes.

75 C:3 83 Cong. Rec. pt. 9, pp. 179–180. Speech by Delegate A. J. Dimond on Natives of Alaska.
Hearings, Sen. Comm. on Ind. Aff., S. 2326, March 22, 1938, Delaware Indians jurisdictional act.
Hearings, Sen. Comm. on Ind. Aff., S. 3980, 4036, Relating to restrictions of Osage property acquired by descent or devise.
Hearings, Sen. Comm. on Ind. Aff., S. 2854, May 6, 1938, Prairie Band of Pottawatomie Indians jurisdictional bill.
Hearings, Sen. Comm. on Ind. Aff., S. Res. 168, May 6, 1938, Loss of Revenue by states due to tax-exempt Indian lands.
Hearings, H. Comm. on Ind. Aff., H. R. 7450, March 15–June 1, 1938, Palm Springs Band of Mission Indians—to authorize sale of part of lands belonging to Palm Springs or Agua Caliente Band of Mission Indians.
Hearings, H. Comm. on Ind. Aff., H. R. 6559, April 11, 1938, Fort Hall Indians jurisdictional act.
Hearings, H. Comm. on Ind. Aff., H. R. 8701, May 19, 1938, Osage Indians, tribal and individual affairs.
H. Doc. 485, Alaska, Its Resources and Development, 1937.
Sen. Rept. No. 1466 (S. 3464) 1939, Citizenship to Metlakahtla Indians—Alaska.
Sen. Rept. No. 1552 (H. R. 4544) 1938, Chippewa Indians—division of funds.
Sen. Rept. No. 1774 (H. R. 5974), Klamath Indian irrigation rights and payments.
Sen. Rept. No. 1785 (S. 3346), Klamath Indian irrigation rights and payments.
Sen. Rept. No. 1798 (S. 4036), Tribal and individual affairs of Osage Indians.
Sen. Rept. No. 1919 (S. 2854) 1938, Pottawatomie Indians—suit in Court of Claims.
Sen. Rept. No. 1986 (S. 3426), Middle Rio Grande Conservancy District.
H. Rept. No. 1872 (H. R. 7626), Leasing Indian lands for mining purposes.
H. Rept. No. 2106 (H. R. 8936), Chippewa Indians—division of funds.
H. Rept. No. 2233 (S. 1478), Mississippi Choctaw Indians jurisdictional act.
H. Rept. No. 2341 (H. R. 9442), Chippewa Indians—correction of error in deposit of judgment money.
H. Rept. No. 2700 (S. 4036), Tribal and individual affairs of Osage Indians.

76 C:1 Hearings, Sen. Comm. on Ind. Aff., S. 1222, Feb. 20, 1939, Osage Indian payment for land sold by United States.
Hearings, Sen. Comm. on Ind. Aff., S. J. Res. 130, Claims of Kiowa, Comanche and Apache.
Hearings, Sen. Comm. on Ind. Aff., S. 773, May 2, 1939, Claims of Yakima Tribe.
Hearings, Sen. Comm. on Ind. Aff., S. J. Res. 69, May 6, 1938, Oklahoma's claim against U. S. arising from tax exemption of Indian lands.

Hearings, Sen. Comm. on Ind. Aff., S. 1878, July 10, 1939, Distribution of judgment funds of Shoshone Tribe.

Hearings, Sen. Comm. on Ind. Aff., S. J. Res. 101, July 17, 1939, Gratuity expense of Five Civilized Tribes.

Hearings, H. Comm. on Ind. Aff., H. R. 3765, April, 1939, California jurisdictional act.

Hearings, H. Comm. on Ind. Aff., H. R. 2306, April 11, 1939, Miami jurisdictional act.

Hearings, H. Comm. on Ind. Aff., H. R. 793, May 5, 1939, Sisseton and Wahpeton Bands.

Hearings, H. Comm. on Ind. Aff., H. R. 2775, June 20, 1939, Arapahoe and Cheyenne Indians jurisdictional act.

Hearings, H. Subcomm. of Comm. on Appro., Interior Dept. Appro. Bill for 1940, pt. II.

Hearings, H. Comm. on Merchant Marine & Fisheries, H. Res. 162, vols. I–III, Alaska Fisheries.

Sen. Rept. No. 642 (S. 607), Employees' compensation, re Menominee Reservation.

Sen. Rept. No. 665 (S. 2634), Yakima Reservation—Right-of-way for Bonneville project.

H. Rept. No. 669 (H. R. 952), Relief of Indians from taxes on allotted lands.

H. Rept. No. 749 (H. R. 2390), Yakima Indian claims.

76 C: 3 Hearings, H. Subcom. of Comm. on Appro., Interior Dept. Appro. Bill for 1941, pts. I and II.

H. Doc. No. 681, Third plan on government reorganization.

77 C: 1 87 Cong. Rec. 79, vol. 87, 1941, Federal Taxation of Indians.

INDEX